COMICS VALUES ANNUAL

2009 EDITION

THE COMIC BOOK PRICE GUIDE

by Alex G. Malloy

edited by Stuart W. Wells III

Preface: Robert J. Sodaro

Published by

krause publications

A subsidiary of F+W Media, Inc.

700 East State Street • Iola, WI 54990-0001
715-445-2214 • 888-457-2873
www.krausebooks.com

Our toll-free number to place an order or obtain
a free catalog is (800) 258-0929.

ISSN: 1062-4503

ISBN-13: 978-0-89689-934-6
ISBN-10: 0-89689-934-9

Designed by Stuart W. Wells III
Edited by Paul Kennedy

About the Cover

Artist Mark Sparacio was commissioned to create this original painting of Wolverine for Comics Values Annual 2009. To see more of Mr. Sparacio's work visit www.marksparacio.com. You can contact him at Marksparacio@aol.com.

Wolverine ©Marvel Characters Inc.

Printed in the United States of America

CONTENTS

Editorial, *by Alex G. Malloy and Robert J. Sodaro* 4

John Barber interview. 6

CVA Grading Guide 13

Artist and General Terms: Name–Abbreviation 16

Artist and General Terms: Abbreviation–Name 20

Bibliography 24

DC Comics Listings & Values. 25

Amalgam Comics Listings & Values. 192

Marvel Comics Listings & Values 193

Golden Age Comics Listings & Values 368

Dark Horse Comics Listings & Values 500

Image Comics Listings & Values 532

Other Publishers Listings & Values (Color) 578

Other Publishers Listings & Values (Black & White) 726

Classics Illustrated Comics Listings & Values 812

Underground Comix Listings & Values. 825

Index. 832

CVA Grading/Price Guide. 864

Editorial

By Alex G. Malloy and Robert J. Sodaro

The view outside the "All-in-Color-for-a-Dime" world of super-heroes, Sci-Fi adventures, ghouls, vampires, zombies and other monsters that go bump in the night may be as bleak as Gotham City. And yes, there may be greater questions that need asking in this world where corporate robber-barons who inhabit Wall Street and the Fortune 500 boardrooms prepare to down-size us working-class poor into a state of destitution resembling something out of Jack "King" Kirby's beloved *Kamandi*'s post apocalyptic America. But still, we can't help but wonder aloud, what is to become of collecting?

For truly, how can the unemployed holding a collapsed hedge fund, a devastated 401k and a sub-prime mortgage past due even consider buying old comics?

Well, the truth of the matter is that often times in the past, whenever the stock market goes down significantly, much of the available investment money goes to collectibles. Here at CVA, we can see a sharp advance in prices on the top comic collectibles. Still, the question really is, "Do the owners choose to sell at this time?" Personally, we do think that the new comics in the marketplace will be soft in value for the foreseeable future.

Needless to say (if only to stave off a blind panic of collectors abandoning the field wholesale) even with the imamate collapse of the Wall Street economy, we took the liberty of chatting up a number of collectors, professionals, and comic book retailers in order to find out how all of this was effecting the day-to-day existence of the collectible market. As do the rest of you, we want to try and understand how all of these bailouts that the federal government is handing out impact the folks who collect comics, and will they have enough money to buy their funny books? Will comics — both the older stuff as well as the newer stuff — still retain their value? Will the sales of new comics go permanently soft? Finally, what effect will the expected (and hoped for) turnaround of the economy have on the current market?

Well, to be entirely truthful, there isn't a great deal of pure direction. Most of the changes this past year were to the Golden Age in a very general, sweeping area. Of course the movie relationships that comic book companies have with the film industry are always very powerful and the anticipatory up and coming (75) super-hero movies that are on the books for 2009 are always a tantalizing carrot that hang in the forefront of any collector.

Not that we expect them all to be *Dark Knight*, *Spider-Man* 1 & 2, *X-Men* 1 & 2-level blockbusters, and (quite frankly) some of them will in all probability be *Catwoman*-awful. There are several of them that quite a few of us truly expect to be out-of-the-park grand slams (*Watchmen*). Still, there are some retailers that tell us — other than the first Tim Burton *Batman* movie — no comic book film has ever translated into any significant increase in their overall business. In fact, some go so far as to say that the comic book companies are really not doing anything to actively bring new converts into the industry.

Overall, we've been informed that the attendance has been down at all conventions this year except for Comic-Con International: San Diego, the New York Comic Con, and the Baltimore Comic Con. Sales at five major shows one professional exhibiter attended in 2008 (from May to November) were all — every single one — down between 30–50% from the previous year. With the quality of his inventory as good as or better than previous years, he expected sales to be higher. All the dealers polled at each of those shows likewise reported lower sales from modern comics and toys to vintage. This includes comic shows, toy shows, and Sci-Fi conventions.

Not to panic, however, for that same retailer reported that the one area of comics collecting that is still very strong is the ultra high-end, high-grade or key issues in the Golden and Silver Age markets. Apparently, serious investors are looking for someplace safe to put their money and the high-end market is actually fairly stable. Anything priced below $500 is selling slowly, either at greatly reduced prices or not at all.

The bottom line: common collectibles – merchandise found easily from any retailer with a decent stock – is slow moving, but the really rare stuff is solid. *Superman* #100 sells fast and for full guide, *Superman* #101 not so much. Another retailer suggested that – projecting out 10 or 20 years into the future of comics – the comics that are selling now could well be the next wave of mid to high-end collectibles. The reason: relatively low print runs of most Modern Age, mid-run comics could make them extremely hard to find and thus more valuable on the secondary market.

By way of example, anyone looking to complete their run of the second volume of *The Amazing Spider-Man* (as Features Editor Bob Sodaro will attest) will find it quite difficult to locate the low numbers of Vol. 2 (1–30) because of the low print runs. Hence, as any truly savvy collector might just do well by stocking up on the current runs of oddball titles from the big three or four publishers, as these will potentially be the comics that will fetch the higher prices.

Here on the home front, we continue to strive to bring you the most accurate pricing in the industry and hope to do so for quite some time to come. A special thanks goes out this time around to Marc Patton for his sage wisdom and advice, as well as to our own Bob Sodaro who stepped up at the last moment to lend an extra (and well-appreciated assist) to Stuart Wells with the production and layout aspect of getting this issue to our publisher. Finally, a grateful thanks to our publisher, Krause Publications, who continues to graciously allow us to bring you this price guide – a labor of love for us – year after year.

Interview with John Barber
Associate Editor: Wolverine
By Bob Sodaro for CVA

John Barber grew up near Chicago, Illinois, and Anaheim, California. He then moved to San Diego to study at the University of California. He stayed in San Diego for a couple of years doing graphic design, then moved to London to go back to school, earning a master's degree in typographic studies at The London College of Printing. Eventually he moved to New York to join the Marvel editorial team. As an assistant editor and editor, John has not only worked on the Ultimate *line, he was instrumental in re-launching the yearly* Marvel Holiday Special. *Among his other credits, we can find not only* Wolverine, *but the* Legion of Monsters *one-shots,* Marvel Zombies, *and* Dark Tower: The Gunslinger Born.

RJS: Wolverine is one of those seminal characters that it seems like everyone wants to write or draw, but there also seems to be almost as many interpretations of Wolverine as there have been writers. How do you, as an editor on the title, try to prevent that from happening, and rectifying it when (if) it does?

Pencils for a Wolverine Manifest Destiny page
© Marvel Entertainment Group

JB: Well, one of the really great things about Wolverine as a character is that there are a lot of different aspects to concentrate on. I mean, Logan is a really multi-faceted character, and different stories can bring out different facets. You can put him in a super-hero situation, where it's big-action and supervillains and bright costumes. You can put him in a real dark noir setting, with no costumes. You can put him in an espionage story. You can put him in a comedy situation and his reactions to that, without going out of character, can be really funny.

So I think there are a lot of really valid ways to write the character while still staying true to his essence. As an editor, I definitely don't want to quash any sense of individuality in the creator's story. Everybody has a slightly different point of view, and I think readers accept that even though the way Brian Michael Bendis approaches Wolverine is different from the way Warren Ellis does, it's still the same character. I think if I — or if Marvel, because Wolverine appears in all kinds of different books in different editorial offices — really tried to enforce a totally singular vision of the character, we'd wind up with some really bland writing.

I think its fun to see somebody come in with something that I wasn't expecting, but that stays true to the core of Wolverine.

That said, I definitely do talk to all the writers on the Wolverine books and try to keep big things in line … stuff like his relationships with other characters. Like his relationship with Cyclops is legendarily strained, of course, and that can lead to personal blow-ups between Logan and Cyclops, like we've seen recently in "Original Sin" (that was running in *Wolverine: Origins* and *X-Men: Legacy*), but there's a professional confidence that maintains between them, where Cyclops trusts Logan to lead X-Force. Logan might resent the position Cyclops has put him in with X-Force, but he can put their personal issues aside and understand that when it comes to the X-Men, Cyclops is the general.

That kind of thing I try to make sure all the Wolverine writers understand, even if that doesn't come up in, say, Jason Aaron's script for *Wolverine: Manifest Destiny*.

RJS: We all know that Wolverine is slated for his solo big-screen debut, how does that (if at all) affect the comic book version?

JB: Maybe he'll finally become a big deal in the comics … No, seriously, there will be a lot of eyes on Wolverine and we want to make sure there's something out there for the movie fan

Pencils for a Wolverine Origins #31 page
© Marvel Entertainment Group

Pencils for X-Force #10 page
© Marvel Entertainment Group

to come and see, but Wolverine as a comics character is a real institution.

We did a good job with Iron Man, where if you came out of the movie theatre, there was a comic about that character that was still 100% Marvel Universe, but that felt like it was part of that same world as the movie. They had the same spirit, and the Iron Man comic was something you could pick up without having a huge background, or a huge investment, in the character, and enjoy. Hopefully, if you DID have a background with the character, it was even more rewarding, but it was a great jumping-on point, a great way to forge new relationships with new Iron Man readers.

So we'd like to try to do something like that and we've got some cool ideas in the works.

RJS: Is it safe to assume that Marvel Comics will capitalize on Wolverine's upcoming movie and roll out a number of one-shots and limited series?

JB: There'll be a fair amount of Wolverine comics out there, but there always are ... We're not going to flood the market. We do want to make sure we have different comics out that make sense to different readers.

RJS: If so will these multiple versions of Wolverine confuse the readership or muddle the character's identity?

JB: Like I said, I don't think Wolverine is really a one-note character. I think it's always a problem when you've had a character that's more-or-less been continually published for almost as long as I've been alive, and when a great deal of that publishing history is in print and is available to readers ... well, it's easy to freeze up if you're a movie or cartoon fan going into the comics section of Borders and seeing dozens of different comics facing you and not knowing where to start. It's a different situation than you'll have with, say, the KICK-ASS movie, where there's going to be one collection to go pick up.

So I think the key is getting the right stuff to the appropriate people. The books aimed at younger readers to places younger readers will go; the comics for teenagers or adults out there where they'll see them. It's tricky but we're making an effort.

The Wolverine: First Class and Weapon X: First Class books are going to be attractive to a different set of readers than the "Old Man Logan" story by Mark Millar and Steve McNiven, which tells a really different story than Wolverine Origins or X-Force. Hopefully there'll be something high-lighting a lot of different aspects of Wolverine, like I mentioned earlier.

RJS: Do you think that Wolverine can stand alone as a film away from the rest of the X-Team?

JB: No way. Not at all. No, I'm kidding. Sure I do! Definitely. Wolverine's one of the … you know, I'll go ahead and say it. I think Wolverine is the best fictional character created since 1970. Yeah, yeah, I know. Han Solo and Darth Vader. Harry Potter. What's that, Millar? Dave Lizewski? Dave Lizewski. Maggie and Hopey. My money's still with Logan.

RJS: Do you feel that all of these film adaptations of comics are bringing anyone back into comic shops to read the comics themselves?

JB: The films and cartoons and everything make the character more public. I mean, my wife, she grew up watching the 1990s X-Men cartoon with her little brother. That was the X-Men to her; she never read the comics. She saw the first movie when it came out — she actually saw it before I did, which was funny — and loved it. A little while later — a year I guess, I forget the time-line now — I handed her the first issue of the Grant Morrison X-Men, and she never stopped reading it.

And I think the comics are more ubiquitous than they used to be. I mean, you see references to comics the same way you do any other type of pop culture element. I think you can see with at least one particular DC property, a genuine interest among the reading public in a comic book. There's absolutely no stigma attached to comics anymore.

Pencils for a Wolverine#70 page
© Marvel Entertainment Group

Whether these people are going into comic books stores — I think in big urban centers with a "walking culture" like Manhattan or London, they definitely are. No question. I know from living in San Diego that it's harder to sort of "happen" upon a comic book store there. You tend to have to have a specific destination in mind and travel there. Most of America is like that. So I think it's a little harder there.

What's great about comic book stores — among other things — is that when somebody DOES come in there after having seen the movie and sees 70 different Wolverine books on the stand, the person working at the comic book store will have that knowledge that someone at Borders or a 'bot on Amazon won't. They'll be able to talk to the new fan and help him or her find a great Wolverine story, for that person. Some people are going to want to read the classic Claremont/Miller book, or the Windsor-Smith *Weapon X*, or the Millar/Romita series, or *Get Mystique*. Different people will respond to different stories, and it takes the kind of knowledge you only get at a good comic book store to be able to feel that out. There isn't a "right" book to like, everybody likes different things.

Pencil drawing for Storm Sword (Wolverine Manifest Destiny) © Marvel Entertainment Group

RJS: I have a 14-year-old nephew, Tony-o, who grew up watching the animated cartoons and films, so for him, that is what is "real" while to me it is the comics that are "real." Is there any way, in your opinion, to rectify this discrepancy, or do you feel that there is no discrepancy? And it really doesn't matter?

JB: Whatever introduced it to you when you were 8 years old is what's real. There's no way around that. Part of my vision of Lex Luthor is always going to be informed by that purple-and-green Legion of Doom costume, or Gene Hackman. I don't think there's anything to rectify. If Tony-o likes the movies, maybe we can entice him in with some of the comics, too, you know? If you take an adversarial role, well, people don't respond to that. If you say, Oh, you like the movie? You shouldn't like the movie, that's fake. The real thing is *Days of Future Past*, read that, they're just going to tune out and not like the thing at all.

It's all addictive. You can like one thing AND another. When I was a kid, I didn't get the Lee/Kirby Fantastic Four. I liked the Byrne stuff, you know, when She-Hulk was on the team. Years later, I learned that the Lee/Kirby stuff was absolutely astounding. Just great stuff. But if you came to me when I was 14 and shoved it under my nose, made it an either-or situation, I'd have probably picked "neither."

RJS: Just for something silly: If you were a tree in a forest, and fell, and there was no one there to see you fall, what sort of sound (if any) would you make?

JB: *Snikt*. Come on. That was easy.

Drawing for Soulstriker (Wolverine Manifest Destiny)
© Marvel Entertainment Group

# # #

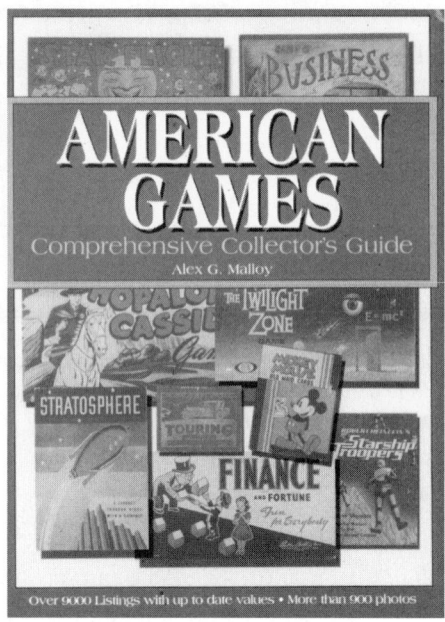

The fearless creators of this book have also written others. Among them are:
Standard Guide to Golden Age Comics by Alex G. Malloy and Stuart W. Wells III
(KP Books, January 2006, ISBN 0-89689-181-X);
American Games by Alex G. Malloy (Krause, May 2000, ISBN 0-930615-60-9);
Kiddy Meal Collectibles by Robert J. Sodaro (Krause, ISBN 0-930625-16-1);
A Universe of Star Wars Collectibles, Identification and Price Guide, 2nd Edition,
by Stuart W. Wells III (Krause, July 2002, ISBN 0-87349-415-6);
See the copyright page for website and catalog information.

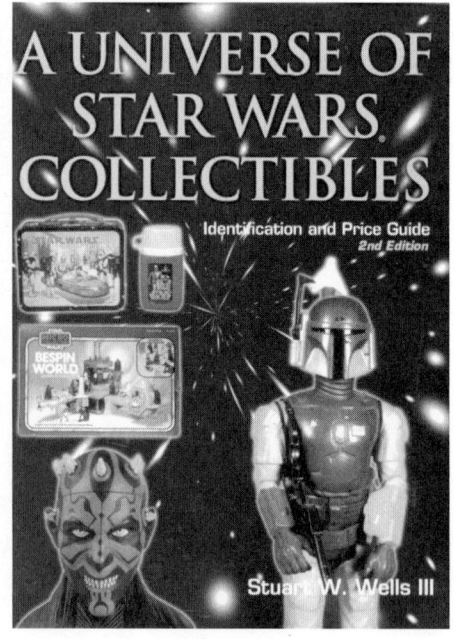

GRADING GUIDE

In David Brin's science fiction–fantasy novel, *The Practice Effect*, things improve with use. You start with a crudely made tool and keep using it until it becomes a fine instrument. If our world worked that way, you could read your Golden Age comics as often as you liked and they would just get better looking each time. Unfortunately, our world does not work that way, and reading your comics (along with just about everything else) causes comics to deteriorate.

Even if you could protect your comics from external light, heat, cold, moisture, pressure and everything else, you couldn't protect them from their own paper. Most comic books were printed on pulp paper, which has a high acid content. This means that the paper slowly turns brittle with age, no matter what you do to it, short of special museum-style preservation.

Very old, well-preserved comics are coveted collector's items. In most cases, people did not save their comic books for future generations. They read them and discarded them. Comic books were considered harmless ephemera for children. When these children outgrew their comics, their parents often threw them away. If everybody kept all of their comics, comics would not be valuable because everybody would have them scattered about the house!

The value of any comic depends on scarcity, popularity and condition. Scarcity increases with age and popularity depends on the whim of the public — only condition automatically decreases with age. Newer comics are generally available in near-mint condition, so newer comics in lesser condition have little collector potential. However, older comics are scarce, so they are still collectible in less than near-mint condition, but the value is obviously less. This is a basic tenet of all collectibles. A car is more valuable with its original paint. A baseball card is more valuable if it has not been marred by bicycle spokes. Coke bottles, stamps, coins, and toys in good condition are all more valuable than their abused counterparts. Comic books are no exception.

New comic book collectors should learn how to assess the prospective value of a comic in order to protect themselves from being fleeced by unscrupulous dealers or hucksters. Yet, a majority of dealers, especially store owners, can be considered reliable judges of comic grade. Because comic retail may be their primary source of income, certain dealers are particularly adept at noticing comic book imperfections, especially in issues they intend to purchase. As such, hobbyists and collectors must understand that dealers need to make a minimum profit on their investments. Buying collectible comics entails certain risks. Therefore, dealers must scrutinize a comic to determine if the particular book will stand a chance of resale. Well-preserved comics are invariably more desirable to dealers because they are more desirable to collectors.

There are eight standard comic grades: mint, near mint, very fine, fine, very good, good, fair, and poor. Clearly, these eight grades could be split into even finer categories when haggling over an exceptionally rare or coveted Golden Age comic. In most cases, however, comic books can be evaluated using these eight standard grades. The values listed in this book are all for comics in "Near Mint" condition. The grading/price chart given at the back of this book should be used to adjust this price for comics in different grades.

For many Golden Age comic issues, there are no known mint condition examples, but most issues have a few near mint copies in the hands of collectors. Many of these come from a few "pedigree" sources like the famous mile-high collection. There are, however, some issues where no known example is in near mint condition. To be consistent, the value listed in this price guide is still for a "near mint" copy, even if no such copy exists. The grading/price chart in the back will still yield a price for the lesser grades that actually exist. And, who knows, maybe there is another treasure trove of old comics somewhere — maybe you'll even be the one who finds it!

Mint (CGC 9.5 or above)

Finding old comics in mint condition is almost impossible because of inferior storage techniques and materials. In the early days of collecting, few people anticipated that the very boxes and bags in which they stored their comics were contributing to decay. Acid from bags, backing boards, and boxes eat away at many comics.. Mint condition comics usually fetch prices higher than price guide listings. Mint comics can sell for 120% or more of the listed price.

Mint comics are perfect comics and allow no room for imperfections. Pages and covers must be free of discoloration, wear, and wrinkles. A mint comic is one that looks like it just rolled off the press. Staples and spine must meet perfectly without cover "rollover." The cover must be crisp, bright, and trimmed perfectly. The staples must not be rusted and the cover should not have any visible creases. The interior pages of a mint comic are equally crisp and new. A mint comic must not show any signs of age or decay. Because of the paper stock used on many older comics, acid and oxygen cause interior pages to yellow and flake.

Near Mint (CGC 9.4)

A near mint comic and a mint comic are close siblings, with their differences slight, even to an experienced eye. Most of the new comics on the shelf of the local comic shop are in near mint condition. These are comics that have been handled gingerly to preserve the original luster of the book. Near mint comics are bright, clean copies with no major or minor defects. Slight stress lines near the staples and perhaps a very minor printing defect are permissible. Corners must still be sharp and devoid of creases. Interior pages of newsprint stock should show almost no discernible yellowing. Near mint comics usually trade for 100% of the listed price, with just a small discount for slightly lower grades.

Very Fine (CGC 8.0)

A very fine comic is one that is routinely found on the shelves and back issue bins of most good direct market comic shops. This grade comic has few defects, none of them major. Stress around the staples of a very fine comic are visible but not yet radical enough to create wrinkles. Both the cover and interior pages should still be crisp and sharp, devoid of flaking and creases. Interior pages may be slightly yellowed from age.

Most high-quality older comics graded as very fine can obtain 80-90% of listed prices. More, if the comic is the highest-graded comic known to exist.

Fine (CGC 6.0)

Fine comics are often issues that may have been stored carefully under a bed or on a shelf by a meticulous collector. This grade of comic is also very desirable because it shows little wear and retains much of its original sharpness. The cover may be slightly off center from rollover. The cover retains less of its original gloss and may even possess a chip or wrinkle. The comers should be sharp but may also have a slight crease. Yellowing begins to creep into the interior pages of a comic graded as fine.

Fine comics are respectable additions to collections and sell for about 40-60% of the listed price.

Very Good (CGC 4.0)

A very good comic may have been an issue passed around or read frequently. This grade is the common condition of older books. Its cover will probably have lost some luster and may have two or three creases around the staples or edges. The corners of the book may begin to show the beginnings of minor rounding and chipping, but it is by no means a damaged or defaced comic. Comics in very good condition sell for about 30-40% of listed price.

Good (CGC 2.0)

A good comic is one that has been well read and is beginning to show its age. Although both front and back covers are still attached, a good grade comic may have a number of serious wrinkles and chips. The corners and edges of this grade comic may show clear signs of rounding and flaking. There should be no major tears in a good comic nor should any pages be clipped out or missing. Interior pages may be fairly yellowed and brittle. Good comics sell for about 15-25% of the listed price.

Fair (CGC 1.0)

A fair comic is one that has definitely seen better days and has considerably limited resale value for most collectors. This comic may be soiled and damaged on the cover and interior. Fair comics should be completely intact and may only be useful as a reading copy, or a comic to lend to friends. Fair comics sell for about 10-20% of the listed price.

Poor

Comics in poor condition are generally unsuitable for collecting or reading because they range from damaged to unrecognizable. Poor comics may have been water damaged, attacked by a small child, or worse, perhaps, gnawed on by the family pet! Interior and exterior pages may be cut apart or missing entirely. A poor comic sells for about 5-15% of the listed price.

Sniffing Out Grades

Despite everything that is mentioned about comic grading, the process remains relative to the situation. A comic that seems to be in very good condition may actually be a restored copy. A restored copy is generally considered to be in between the grade it was previous to restoration and the grade it has become. Many collectors avoid restored comics entirely.

Each collector builds his collection around what he believes is important. Some want every issue of a particular series or company. Others want every issue of a favorite artist or writer. Because of this, many collectors will purchase lower-grade comics to fill out a series or to try out a new series. Mint and near mint comics are usually much more desirable to hardcore collectors. Hobbyists and readers may find the effort and cost of collecting only high-grade comics financially prohibitive.

Getting artists or writers to autograph comics has also become a source of major dispute. Some collectors enjoy signed comics and others consider those very comics defaced! The current trends indicate that most collectors do enjoy signed comics. A signature does not usually change the grade of the comic.

As mentioned, comic grading is a subjective process that must be agreed upon by the buyer and seller. Buyers will often be quick to note minor defects in order to negotiate a better price. Sellers are sometimes selectively blind to their comic's defects.

Name	Abbr.	Name	Abbr.	Name	Abbr.	Name	Abbr.
Abel, Jack	JA	Bernstein, Robert	RbB	Capullo, Greg	GCa	Davis, Guy	GyD
Abell, Dusty	DAb	Bierbaum, Mary	MBm	Cardy, Nick	NC	Davis, Jack	JDa
Abnett, Dan	DAn	Bierbaum, Tom	TBm	Carey, Mike	MCy	Davis, Malcolm	MDa
Abrams, Paul	PlA	Biggs, Geoffrey	GB	Cariello, Sergio	SCi	Davison, Al	ADv
Adams, Art	AAd	Binder, Jack	JaB	Carlin, Mike	MCr	Day, Dan	Day
Adams, Neal	NA	Bingham, Jerry	JBi	Carpenter, Brent D.	BDC	Day, Gene	GD
Addeo, Stephen	StA	Birch, JJ	JJB	Carralero, Ricky	RCl	DeFalco, Tom	TDF
Adkins, Dan	DA	Biro, Charles	CBi	Carrasco, Dario	DoC	Deitch, Kim	KDe
Adlard, Charlie	CAd	Bisley, Simon	SBs	Carter, Joe	JCt	Delano, Jamie	JaD
Albano, John	JAo	Bissette, Stephen	SBi	Case, Richard	RCa	DeLaRosa, Sam	SDR
Albrecht, Jeff.	JAl	Blair, Barry	BaB	Casey, Joe	JoC	Del Bourgo, Maurice	MDb
Alcala, Alfredo	AA	Blaisdell, Tex	TeB	Castellaneta, Dan	DaC	Delgado, Richard	RdD
Alcazar, Vincent	VAz	Blasco, Jesus	JBl	Castellini, Claudio	CCt	Dell, John	JhD
Alexander, Chris	CAx	Blevins, Bret	BBl	Castrillo, Anthony	ACa	DeMatteis, J. M.	JMD
Alibaster, Jo	JoA	Blum, Alex	AB	Chadwick, Paul	PC	DeMulder, Kim	KDM
Allred, Michael	MiA	Bode, Vaughn	VB	Chan, Ernie	ECh	Deodato, Jr., Mike	MD2
Alstaetter, Karl	KlA	Bogdanove, Jon	JBg	Chang, Bernard	BCh	Derenick, Tom	TDr
Althorp, Brian	BAp	Bolland, Brian	BB	Charest, Travis	TC	DeZago, Todd	TDz
Amaro, Gary	GyA	Bolle, Frank	FBe	Chase, Bobbie	BCe	DeZuniga, M.	MDb
Amendola, Sal	Sal	Boller, David	DdB	Chaykin, Howard	HC	DeZuniga, Tony	TD
Ammerman, David	DvA	Bolton, John	JBo	Check, Sid	SC	Diaz, Paco	PaD
Anderson, Bill	BAn	Bond, Philip	PBd	Chen, Mike	MCh	Dillin, Dick.	DD
Anderson, Brent	BA	Booth, Brett	BBh	Chen, Sean	SCh	Dillon, Glyn	GlD
Anderson, Jeff	JAn	Boring, Wayne	WB	Chestney, Lillian	LCh	Dillon, Steve	SDi
Anderson, Murphy	MA	Bossart, William	WmB	Chiarello, Mark	MCo	Dini, Paul	PDi
Andriola, Alfred	AlA	Boxell, Tim	TB	Chichester, D.G.	DGC	Disbrow, Jay	JyD
Andru, Ross	RA	Bradstreet, Tim	TBd	Chiodo, Joe	JCh	Ditko, Steve	SD
Aparo, Jim	JAp	Braithwaite, Doug	DBw	Choi, Brandon	BCi	Dixon, Chuck	CDi
Aragones, Sergio	SA	Brasfield, Craig	CrB	Chriscross	Ccs	Dixon, John	JDx
Arcudi, John	JAr	Braun, Russell	RsB	Christopher, Tom	TmC	Dobbyn, Nigel	ND
Artis, Tom	TAr	Breeding, Brett.	BBr	Chua, Ernie	Chu	Dodson, Terry	TyD
Ashe, Edd	EA	Brereton, Daniel	DlB	Chun, Anthony	ACh	Doherty, Peter	PD
Asamiya	KiA	Brewster, Ann	ABr	Churchhill, Ian	IaC	Dominguez, Luis	LDz
Augustyn, Brian	BAu	Breyfogle, Norm	NBy	Cirocco, Frank	FC	Doran, Colleen	CDo
Austin, Terry	TA	Bridwell, E. Nelson	ENB	Citron, Sam	SmC	Dorey, Mike	MDo
Avison, Al	AAv	Briefer, Dick	DBr	Claremont, Chris	CCl	Dorkin, Evan	EDo
Ayers, Dick	DAy	Bright, Mark	MBr	Clark, Mike	MCl	Dorman, Dave	DvD
Bachalo, Chris	CBa	Brigman, June	JBr	Clark, Scott	ScC	Doucet, Julie	JDo
Badger, Mark	MBg	Broderick, Pat	PB	Cockrum, Dave	DC	Dougherty, H.	HD
Bagley, Mark	MBa	Brodsky, Allyn	AyB	Cohn, Gary	GCh	Drake, Stan	SDr
Baikie, Jim	JBa	Broom, John	JBm	Coker, Tomm	TCk	Dresser, Larry	LDr
Bailey, Bernard	BBa	Broome, Matt	MtB	Colan, Gene	GC	Dringenberg, Mike	MDr
Bailey, M	MBi	Brothers, Hernandez	HB	Colby, Simon	SCy	Drucker, Mort	MD
Bair, Michael	MlB	Brown, Bob	BbB	Cole, Jack	JCo	DuBerkr, Randy	RDB
Baker, Kyle	KB	Browne, Dick	DkB	Cole, Leonard B.	LbC	Duffy, Jo.	JDy
Baker, Matt	MB	Brunner, Frank	FB	Colletta, Vince	ViC	Dumm, Gary	GDu
Balent, Jim.	JBa	Bryant, Rick	RkB	Collins, Max Allan.	MCn	Dunn, Ben	BDn
Banks, Darryl	DBk	Buckingham, Mark	MBu	Collins, Mike	MC	Duranona, Leo	LDu
Barks, Carl	CB	Buckler, Rich.	RB	Collins, Nancy	NyC	Duursema, Jan	JD
Baron, Mike	MBn	Budget, Greg	GBu	Colon, Ernie	EC	Dwyer, Kieron	KD
Barr, Mike	MiB	Bulanadi, Danny	DBl	Conner, Amanda	ACo	Eastman, Kevin	KEa
Barras, John	DBs	Burchett, Rick	RBr	Conway, Gerry	GyC	Eaton, Scott	SEa
Barreiro, Mike	MkB	Burgard, Tim	TmB	Cooper, Dave	DvC	Edginton, Ian	IEd
Barreto, Ed	EB	Burgos, Carl	CBu	Cooper, John	JCp	Edlund, Ben	BEd
Barry, Dan	DBa	Burke, Fred	FBk	Cooper, Sam	SCp	Egeland, Marty	MEg
Batista, Chris	CsB	Burnley, Jack	JBu	Corben, Richard	RCo	Eisner, Will	WE
Battlefield, D.	DB	Burns, John	JBn	Costanza, Peter	PrC	Elder, Bill	BE
Battlefield, Ken	KBa	Burns, Robert	RBu	Cowan, Denys	DCw	Eldred, Tim	TEl
Beatty, John.	JhB	Burroughs, W.	WBu	Cox, Jeromy	JCx	Elias, Lee	LEl
Beatty, Terry	TBe	Buscema, John	JB	Craig, Johnny	JCr	Elliot, D.	DE
Beauvais, Denis	DB	Buscema, Sal	SB	Crandall, Reed	RC	Ellis, Warren	WEl
Beck, C. C.	CCB	Busiek, Kurt.	KBk	Crespo, Steve	SCr	Ellison, Harlan	HaE
Becker, Sam	SaB	Butler, Jeff.	JBt	Crilley, Mark.	MCi	Emberlin, Randy	RyE
Beeston, John	JBe	Butler, Steve.	SBt	Crumb, Robert.	RCr	Englehart, Steve	SEt
Belardinelli, M.	MBe	Buzz	Buzz	Cruz, E. R.	ERC	Ennis, Garth	GEn
Bell, Bob Boze	BBB	Byrd, Mitch	MBy	Cruz, Jerry	JCz	Epting, Steve	SEp
Bell, George	GBl	Byrne, John	JBy	Cruz, Roger	RCz	Erskine, Gary	GEr
Bell, Julie	JuB	Calafiore, Jim	JCf	Cuidera, Chuck	CCu	Erwin, Steve	StE
Bendis, Brian Michael	BMB	Caldes, Charles	CCa	Cullins, Paris	PCu	Esposito, Mike	ME
Benefiel, Scott	ScB	Callahan, Jim	JiC	Currie, Andrew	ACe	Estes, John	JEs
Benes, Ed	EBe	Calnan, John	JCa	Damaggio, Rodolfo	RDm	Estrada, Ric	RE
Benitez, Joe	JBz	Cameron, Don	DCn	Daniel, Tony	TnD	Evans, George	GE
Benjamin, Ryan	RBn	Cameron, Lou	LC	Danner, Paul	PuD	Evans, Ray	REv
Bennett, Joe	JoB	Campbell, Eddie	ECa	Darrow, Geof.	GfD	Everett, Bill	BEv
Bennett, Richard	RiB	Campbell, J. Scott	JSC	David, Peter	PDd	Ewins, Brett	BEw
Benson, Scott	StB	Campbell, Stan	StC	Davis, Alan	AD	Ezquerra, Carlos	CE
Berger, Charles.	ChB	Campenella, Robert	RbC	Davis, Bob	BD	Fabry, Glenn	GF
Bernado, Ramon	RBe	Campos, Marc	MCa	Davis, Dan	DDv	Fago, Al	AFa

Name	Abbr.	Name	Abbr.	Name	Abbr.	Name	Abbr.
Farmer, Mark	MFm	Griffiths, Martin	MGs	Hughes, Adam	AH	Kupperberg, Paul	PuK
Fegredo, Duncan	DFg	Grindberg, Tom	TGb	Hultgren, Ken	KHu	Kurtzman, Harvey	HK
Feldstein, Al	AF	Gross, Daerick	DkG	Hund, Dave	DeH	Kwitney, Alisa	AaK
Ferry, Pascual	PFe	Gross, Peter	PrG	Hunt, Chad	CH	LaBan, Terry	TLa
Fine, Lou	LF	Grossman, R.	RGs	Immonen, Stuart	SI	Lago, Ray	RyL
Fingeroth, Danny	DFr	Gruenwald, Mark	MGu	Infantino, Carmine	CI	Laird, Peter	PLa
Finnocchiaro, Sal	SF	Grummett, Tom	TG	Infantino, Jim	JI	Lamme, Bob	BbL
Fleisher, Michael	MFl	Guardineer, Fred	FGu	Ingles, Graham	GrI	Langridge, Roger	RLg
Fleming, Robert	RFl	Guay, Rebecca	RGu	Iorio, Medio	MI	Lanning, Andy	ALa
Flemming, Homer	HFl	Guice, Jackson	JG	Isherwood, Geoff	GI	Lansdale, Joe	JLd
Flessel, Creig	CF	Guichet, Yvel	YG	Ivie, Larry	LI	Lapham, Dave.	DL
Foreman, Dick	DiF	Guinan, Paul	PGn	Ivy, Chris	CIv	Lark, Michael	MLr
Forte, John	JF	Gulacy, Paul	PG	Jackson, Julius	JJn	Larkin, Bob	BLr
Forton, Gerald	GFo	Gustavson, Paul	PGv	Jaffee, Al	AJ	LaRocque, Greg	GrL
Fosco, Frank	FFo	Gustovich, Mike	MG	Janke, Dennis	DJa	Larroca, Salvador	SvL
Foster, Alan Dean	ADF	Ha, Gene	GeH	Janson, Klaus	KJ	Larsen, Erik	EL
Fox, Gardner	GaF	Haley, Matt	MHy	Javinen, Kirk	KJa	Lash, Batton	BLs
Fox, Gill	GFx	Hall, Bob	BH	Jenkins, Paul	PJe	Lashley, Ken	KeL
Fox, Matt	MF	Halsted, Ted	TeH	Jenney, Robert	RJ	Lavery, Jim	JLv
Fraga, Dan	DaF	Hama, Larry	LHa	Jensen, Dennis	DJ	Lawlis, Dan	DLw
Franchesco	Fso	Hamilton, Tim	TH	Jimenez, Leonardo	LJi	Lawrence, Terral	TLw
Frank, Gary	GFr	Hamner, Cully	CHm	Jimminiz, Phil	PJ	Lawson, Jim	JmL
Frazetta, Frank	FF	Hampton, Bo.	BHa	Johnson, Dave	DvJ	Layton, Bob.	BL
Freeman, John	JFr	Hampton, Scott	SHp	Johnson, Jeff	JJ	Leach, Garry	GL
Freeman, Simon	SFr	Hanna, Scott	SHa	Johnson, Paul	PuJ	Leach, Rick	RkL
Frenz, Ron	RF	Hannigan, Ed	EH	Johnson, Todd	TJn	Lee, Elaine	ELe
Frese, George	GFs	Hanson, Neil	NHa	Johnson, Walter	WJo	Lee, Jae	JaL
Friedman, Michael Jan	MFr	Harmon, Jim	JHa	Jones, Casey	CJ	Lee, Jim	JLe
Friedrich, Mike	MkF	Harras, Bob.	BHs	Jones, Gerard	GJ	Lee, Patrick	PtL
Frolechlich, August	AgF	Harris, N. Steven	NSH	Jones, J.B.	JJo	Lee, Scott	ScL
Fry III, James	JFy	Harris, Tim	THa	Jones, Jeff	JeJ	Lee, Stan	StL
Fujitani(Fuje), Bob	BF	Harris, Tony	TyH	Jones, Kelley	KJo	Leeke, Mike	MLe
Furman, Simon	SFu	Harrison, Lou	LuH	Jones, Malcolm	MJ	Leialoha, Steve	SL
Gaiman, Neil	NGa	Harrison, Simon	SHn	Jones, R.A.	RAJ	Leon, John Paul	JPL
Galan, Manny	MaG	Hart, Ernest	EhH	Jones, Robert	RJn	Leonard, Lank	LLe
Gallant, Shannon	ShG	Hartsoe, Everette	EHr	Jurgens, Dan	DJu	Leonardi, Rick	RL
Gammill, Kerry	KGa	Hathaway, Kurt	KtH	Jusko, Joe	JJu	Levins, Rik	RLe
Garcia, Dave	DaG	Hawkins, Matt	MHw	Kaluta, Mike	MK	Lewis, Brian	BLw
Garner, Alex	AGo	Hayes, Drew	DHa	Kamen, Jack	JKa	Lieber, Larry	LLi
Garney, Ron	RG	Hayes, Rory	RHa	Kaminski, Len	LKa	Liefeld, Rob.	RLd
Garzon, Carlos	CG	Haynes, Hugh	HH	Kane & Romita	K&R	Lightle, Steve	SLi
Gascoine, Phil	PGa	Hazlewood, Douglas	DHz	Kane, Bob	BKa	Lim, Ron.	RLm
Gaudino, Stefano	SGa	Hearnes, David	DvH	Kane, Gil	GK	Linsner, Joseph M.	JLi
Gaughan, Jack	JGa	Hearne, Jack	JH	Kanigher, Bob	BbK	Livingstone, Rolland	RLv
Gecko, Gabe	GG	Heath, Russ	RH	Kaniuga, Trent	TKn	Lloyd, David	DvL
Geggan	Ggn	Hebbard, Robert	RtH	Karounos, Paris T.	PaK	Lobdell, Scott	SLo
Gerard, Ruben	RGd	Heck, Don	DH	Katz, Jack	JKz	Locke, Vince	VcL
Gerber, Steve	SvG	Heisler, Mike.	MHs	Kavanagh, Terry	TKa	Loeb, Jeph	JLb
Giacoia, Frank	FrG	Hempel, Mark	MaH	Kaye, Stan	StK	Lopez, Jose	JL
Giarrano, Vince	VGi	Henry, Flint	FH	Kelly, Walt	WK	Lopresti, Aaron	AaL
Gibbons, Dave	DGb	Herman, Jack	JH	Kennedy, Cam	CK	Louapre, Dave	DLp
Gibson, Ian	IG	Hernandez Brothers	HB	Kennedy, Ian	IK	Lowe, John	Low
Giella, Joe	JoG	Hernandez, Gilbert	GHe	Keown, Dale	DK	Lubbers, Bob.	BLb
Giffen, Keith	KG	Hernandez, Jaime	JHr	Kerschl, Karl.	KlK	Lustbader, Eric Van	ELu
Gilbert, Michael T.	MGi	Herrera,Ben	BHr	Kesel, Babara	BKs	Lyle, Tom	TL
Giordano, Dick	DG	Hester, Phil	PhH	Kesel, Karl	KK	Macchio, Ralph	RMc
Glanzman, Sam	SG	Hewlett, Jamie	JHw	Kiefer, Henry C.	HcK	Mack, David	DMk
Goldberg, Rube	RuG	Hibbard, E.E.	EHi	Kieth, Sam	SK	Mackie, Howard	HMe
Golden, Michael	MGo	Hicklenton, John	JHk	Kihi, H. J.	HjK	Madan, Dev	DeM
Gonzalez, Jorge	JGz	Hicks, Arnold.	AdH	Kildale, Malcolm	MKd	Madureira, Joe	JMd
Goodman, Till	TGo	Higgins, Graham	GHi	King, Hannibal	HbK	Maggin, Elliot S.	ESM
Goodwin, Archie	AGw	Higgins, John	JHi	Kinsler, Everett R.	EK	Maguire, Kevin	KM
Gordon, Al	AG	Higgins, Michael	MHi	Kirby, Jack	JK	Magyar, Rick	RM
Gottfredson, Floyd	FG	Hing, T. F.	TFH	Kirner	Kr	Mahlstedt, Larry	LMa
Gould, Chester	ChG	Hitch, Bryan	BHi	Kisniro, Yukito	YuK	Mahnke, Doug	DoM
Grandmetti, Jerry	JGr	Hobbs, Bill	BlH	Kitchen, Dennis	DKi	Mandrake, Tom	TMd
Grant, Alan.	AlG	Hoberg, Rick	RHo	Kitson, Barry.	BKi	Maneely, Joe.	JMn
Grant, Steve.	StG	Hoffer, Mike	MkH	Klein, George.	GKl	Manley, Graham	GMy
Grau, Peter	PGr	Hogarth, Burne	BHg	Kobasic, Kevin	KoK	Manley, Mike	MM
Gray, Mick	MGy	Holcomb, Art	AHo	Kolins, Scott	ScK	Mann, Roland	RMn
Green, Alfonso	AGn	Holdredge, John	JHo	Krause, Peter	PKr	Mann, Roland	Man
Green, Dan	DGr	Hoover, Dave	DHv	Krenkel, Roy	RKu	Manning, Russ	RsM
Green, Justin	JsG	Hopgood, Kevin	KHd	Krigstein, Bernie	BK	Marais, Raymond	RdM
Green, Randy	RGr	Horie, Richard	RHe	Kristiansen, Teddy H.	TKr	Mariotte, Jeff	JMi
Greene, Sid	SGe	Hotz, Kyle	KHt	Kruse, Brandon	BKr	Maroto, Esteban	EM
Grell, Mike	MGr	Howarth, Matt.	MHo	Kubert, Adam	AKu	Marrinan, Chris	ChM
Griffith, Bill	BG	Howell, Rich	RHo	Kubert, Andy	NKu	Marrs, Lee	LMr
Griffiths, Harley	HyG	Hudnall, James.	JHl	Kubert, Joe	JKu		

Name	Abbr.	Name	Abbr.	Name	Abbr.	Name	Abbr.
Martin, Gary	GyM	Morales, Rags	RgM	Pekar, Harvey	HP	Roach, David	DRo
Martin, Joe	JMt	Moreira, Ruben	RMo	Pelletier, Paul	PaP	Robbins, Frank	FR
Martinbrough, Shawn	SMa	Moretti, Mark	MMo	Peltz, George	GgP	Robbins, Trina	TrR
Martinez, Henry	HMz	Morgan, Tom	TMo	Pence, Eric	ErP	Roberts, Mike	MRo
Martinez, Roy Allan	RMr	Morisi, Pete	PMo	Pennington, Mark	MPn	Robertson, Darrick	DaR
Marz, Ron	RMz	Moritz, Edward	EdM	Pensa, Shea Anton	SAP	Robinson, Cliff	CRb
Marzan, Jose	JMz	Morosco, Vincent	VMo	Perez, George	GP	Robinson, James	JeR
Mason, Tom	TMs	Morrison, Grant	GMo	Perham, James	JPh	Robinson, Jerry	JRo
Massengill, Nathan	NMa	Morrow, Gray	GM	Perlin, Don	DP	Rodier, Denis	DRo
Matsuda, Jeff	JMs	Mortimer, Win	WMo	Perryman, Edmund	EP	Rodriguez, Spain	SRo
Mattsson, Steve	SMt	Moskowitz, Seymour	SMz	Peterson, Brandon	BPe	Roea, Doug	DgR
Maus, Bill	BMs	Motter, Dean	DMt	Peterson, Jonathan	JPe	Rogers, Boody	BRo
Maxwell, Stanley	StM	Moy, Jeffrey	JMy	Petrucha, Stefan	SPr	Rogers, Marshall	MR
Mayer, Sheldon	ShM	Murray, Brian	BrM	Peyer, Tom	TPe	Romita, John	JR
Mayerik, Val	VMk	Musial, Joe	JoM	Phillips, Joe	JoP	Romita, John Jr.	JR2
Mazzucchelli, David	DM	Muth, Jon J.	JMu	Phillips, Scott	SPl	Rosenberger, J.	JRo
McCann, Gerald	GMc	Mychaels, Marat	MMy	Phillips, Sean	SeP	Ross, Alex	AxR
McCarthy, Brendon	BMy	Myers	Mys	Pike, Jay Scott	JsP	Ross, David	DR
McCarthy, Jim	JMy	Naifeh, Ted	TNa	Pini, Richard	RPi	Ross, John	JRs
McCloud, Scott	SMl	Napolitano, Nick	NNa	Pini, Wendy	WP	Ross, Luke	LRs
McCorkindale, B	BMC	Napton, Bob	BNa	Pino, Carlos	CPi	Roth, Werner	WR
McCraw, Tom	TMw	Nauck, Todd	TNu	Platt, Stephen	SPa	Royle, Jim.	JRl
McCrea, John	JMC	Neary, Paul	PNe	Pleece, Warren	WaP	Royle, John	JRe
McDaniel, Scott	SMc	Nebres, Rudy	RN	Ploog, Mike	MP	Rozum, John	JRz
McDaniel, Walter	WMc	Nelson	Nel	Plunkett, Kilian	KPl	Rubano, Aldo	ARu
McDonnell, Luke	LMc	Netzer, Mike	MN	Poch	PcH	Rubi, Melvin	MvR
McDuffie, Dwayne	DMD	Newton, Don	DN	Pollack, Rachel	RaP	Rubinstein, Joe	JRu
McFarlane, Todd	TM	Nguyen, Hoang	HNg	Pollard, Keith	KP	Rude, Steve	SR
McGregor, Don	DMG	Nichols, Art	ANi	Pollina, Adam	AdP	Ruffner, Sean	SRf
McKean, Dave	DMc	Nicieza, Fabian	FaN	Polseno, Jo	JP	Russell, P. Craig	CR
McKeever, Ted	TMK	Nino, Alex	AN	Pope, Paul	PPo	Russell, Vince	VRu
McKenna, Mike	MkK	Nocenti, Ann	ANo	Porch, David	DPo	Ryan, Matt	MRy
McKie, Angus	AMK	Nocon, Cedric	CNn	Portacio, Whilce	WPo	Ryan, Paul	PR
McKone, Mike	MMK	Nodell, Martin	MnN	Porter, Howard	HPo	Ryder, Tom	TmR
McLaughlin, Frank	FMc	Nodel, Norman	NN	Post, Howard	HwP	Sahle, Harry	HSa
McLaughlin, Sean	SML	Nolan, Graham	GN	Potts, Carl	CP	Sakakibara, Mizuki	MiS
McLeod, Bob	BMc	Nord, Cary	CNr	Powell, Bob	BP	Sakai, Stan	SS
McMahon, M.	MMc	Norem, Earl	EN	Power, Dermot	DPw	Sale, Tim	TSe
McManus, Shawn	SwM	Nostrand, Howard	HN	Pratt, George	GgP	Salmons, Tony	TSa
McNeil, Colin	CMc	Novick, Irv	IN	Premaini, Bruno	BPr	Saltares, Javier	JS
McWilliams, Al	AMc	Nowlan, Kevin	KN	Prezio, Victor	VP	Sampson, Steve	SSm
Meagher, Fred	FMe	Nutman, Philip	PNu	Prichard, Pat	PPr	Sanders, Jim III	JS3
Medina, Angel	AMe	O'Barr, James	JOb	Priest, Christopher	CPr	Sasso, Mark	MSo
Medley, Linda	LiM	O'Neil, Denny	DON	Prosser, Jerry	JeP	Saunders, Norm	NS
Mercadoocasio, H.	HMo	O'Neil, Kevin	KON	Pugh, Steve	StP	Saviuk, Alex	AS
Meskin, Mort	MMe	Olbrich, Dave	DO	Pulido, Brian	BnP	Schaffenberger, Kurt	KS
Messmer, Otto	OM	Olivetti, Ariel	AOl	Queen, Randy	RQu	Schane, Tristan	TnS
Messner-Loebs, Bill	BML	Olliffe, Patrick	PO	Quesada, Joe	JQ	Schiller, Fred	FdS
Micale, Albert	AlM	One, Dark	DOe	Quinlan, Charles	CQ	Schmitz, Mark	MaS
Michelinie, David	DvM	Ordway, Jerry	JOy	Quinn, David	DQ	Schomburg, Alex.	ASh
Miehm, Grant	GtM	Orlando, Joe	JO	Quinones, Peter	PQ	Schrotter, Gustav	GS
Mighten, Duke	DMn	Ormston, Dean	DOr	Raab, Ben	BRa	Schultz, Mark	MSh
Mignola, Michael	MMi	Ortiz, Jose	JOt	Raboy, Mac	MRa	Scoffield, Sean	SSc
Miki, Danny	DaM	Oskner, Bob	BO	Ramos, Humberto	HuR	Scott, Jeffery	JSc
Milgrom, Al	AM	Ostrander, John	JOs	Ramos, Rodney	RyR	Scott, Trevor	TvS
Millar, Mark	MMr	Oughton, Thomas	TO	Ramsey, Ray	RR	Seagle, Steven T.	SSe
Miller, Frank	FM	Owen, James	JOn	Randall, Ron	RoR	Sears, Bart	BS
Miller, Mike S.	MsM	Ozkan, Tayyar	TOz	Randon, Arthur	ARn	Sekowsky, Mike	MSy
Miller, Sidney	SyM	Pace, Richard	RPc	Raney, Tom	TR	Semeiks, Val	VS
Miller, Steve	SM	Pacella, Mark	MPa	Rankin, Rich	RRa	Senior, Geoff	GSr
Milligan, Peter	PrM	Pacheco, Carlos	CPa	Rapmund, Norm	NRd	Serpe, Jerry	JyS
Mills, Pat	PMs	Palais, Rudy	RP	Rasmussen, H	HR	Severin, John	JSe
Minor, Jason	JnM	Palais, Walter	WlP	Raymond, Alex	AR	Severin, Marie	MSe
Mitchel, Barry	BM	Palmer, Tom	TP	Raymond, Kim	KR	Shamray, Gerry	GSh
Moder, Lee	LMd	Palmiotti, Jimmy	JP	Redondo, J.	JRd	Shanower, Eric.	EiS
Moe, C. S.	CSM	Pamai, Gene	GPi	Redondo, Nestor	NR	Sharp, Liam	LSh
Moebius	Moe	Panalign, Noly	NPl	Reed, David	DvR	Shaw, Sean	SSh
Moeller, Chris	CsM	Paniccia, Mark	MPc	Reeves-Stevens, Judith	JRv	Shelton, Gilbert	GiS
Moench, Doug	DgM	Panosian, Dan	DPs	Reinhold, Bill	BR	Sheridan, Dave	DSh
Moldoff, Sheldon	SMo	Parkhouse, Annie	APh	Richards, Ted	TR	Sherman, Jim	JSh
Montano, Steve	SeM	Parkhouse, Steve	SvP	Richardson, Mike	MRi	Shoemaker, Terry	TSr
Mooney, Jim	JM	Parobeck, Mike	MeP	Richardson, J	JRi	Shooter, Jim	JiS
Moore, Alan	AMo	Pascoe, James	JmP	Ricketts, Mark	MRc	Shores, Syd	SSh
Moore, Jeff	JMr	Pasko, Martin	MPk	Rico, Don	DRi	Shum, Howard	HSm
Moore, Jerome	JeM	Patterson, Bruce	BrP	Ridgeway, John	JRy	Shuster, Joe	JoS
Moore, John Francis	JFM	Paul, Frank R.	FP	Rieber, John Ney	JNR	Sibal, Jonathan	JSb
Moore, Terry	TMr	Payne, Pop	PP	Riley, John	JnR	Siegel & Shuster	S&S
Morales, Lou	LM	Pearson, Jason	JPn	Riply	Rip	Sienkiewicz, Bill	BSz

Silvestri, Eric . . . . EcS	Straczynski, J.Michael MSz	Valentino, Jim . . . . JV	Wiesenfeld, Aron . . . . AWs
Silvestri, Mark. . . . . MS	Stradley, Randy. . . . . . RSd	Vallejo, Boris. . . . . BV	Wildey, Doug . . . . DW
Sim, Dave . . . . DS	Strazewski, Len . . . . . LeS	Van Buren, Raeburn . . RvB	Wildman, Andrew . . . . Wld
Simon & Kirby . . . . . . S&K	Streeter, Lin . . . . LnS	Van Fleet, John . . . . . JVF	Williams, Anthony . . . . AWi
Simon, Allen. . . . . ASm	Stroman, Larry . . . . . . LSn	Vancata, Brad . . . . BVa	Williams, David . . . . . DdW
Simon, Joe . . . . JSm	Sturgeon, Foolbert	Vance, Steve . . . . SVa	Williams, J.H. . . . . JWi
Simonson, Louise . . . . . LSi	(& Frank Stack) . . . FSt	VanHook, Kevin . . . . . KVH	Williams, Keith . . . . . . KWi
Simonson, Walt . . . . . . WS	Sullivan, Lee . . . . LS	Vargas, Vagner VV	Williams, Kent . . . . . . KW
Simpson, Don . . . . DSs	Sutton, Tom . . . . TS	Veitch, Rick. . . . . RV	Williams, Robert. . . . . RW
Simpson, Howard . . . . HSn	Swan, Curt . . . . CS	Velez, Ivan, Jr. IV	Williams, Scott . . . . . . SW
Simpson, Will . . . . . . WSm	Sweetman, Dan . . . . . DSw	Velluto, Sal . . . . SaV	Williamson, Al. . . . . . . AW
Sinnott, Joe. . . . . JSt	Taggart, Tom . . . . TTg	Vess, Charles CV	Williamson, Skip . . . . . SWi
Siryk. . . . . Syk	Takenaga, Francis . . . . FTa	Vey, Al . . . . AV	Willingham, Bill . . . . . BWg
Skroce, Steve . . . . SSr	Takezaki, Tony . . . . . . ToT	Vigil, Tim . . . . TV	Willis, Damon. . . . . . . DaW
Smith, Andy . . . . ASm	Talbot, Bryan . . . . BT	Vokes, Neil . . . . NV	Wilshire, Mary . . . . . . MW
Smith, Barry W. . . . . . BWS	Tallarico, Tony . . . . . . TyT	Von Eeden, Trevor . . . TVE	Wilson, Colin. . . . . CWi
Smith, Beau . . . . BSt	Tan, Billy . . . . BTn	Vosburg, Mike . . . . . . MV	Wilson, Gahan. . . . . . . GW
Smith, Cam . . . . CaS	Tanaka, Masashi. . . . . MTk	Wagner, Matt. . . . . . . MWg	Wilson, Keith S. . . . . . KSW
Smith, Jeff. . . . . JSi	Tanghal, Romeo . . . . . . RT	Wagner,Ron. . . . . RoW	Wilson, S. Clay . . . . . SCW
Smith, John . . . . JnS	Tappin, Steve . . . . SeT	Waid, Mark . . . . MWa	Woch, Stan. . . . . SnW
Smith, Kevin. . . . . KSm	Tartaglione, John . . . . . JTg	Waldinger, Morris. . . . MsW	Woggin, Bill . . . . BWo
Smith, Malcolm . . . . . . MSt	Taylor, David . . . . DTy	Waldman, Ed . . . . EW	Wojtkiewicz, Chuck . . . Woj
Smith, Paul . . . . PS	Taylor, R.G. . . . . RGT	Walker, Kevin. . . . . . . KeW	Wolf, Chance . . . . CWf
Smith, Robin . . . . RSm	Templeton, Ty . . . . TTn	Waller, Reed . . . . RWa	Wolfe, Joseph . . . . . . JWf
Smith, Ron . . . . RS	Teney, Tom . . . . TmT	Walsh, William . . . . . WmW	Wolfman, Marv . . . . . MWn
Snejbjerg, Peter . . . . . . PSj	Tenney, Mark . . . . MaT	Waltrip, Jason. . . . . . . JWp	Wolverton, Basil. . . . . . BW
Sniegoski, Tom . . . . . . TSg	Texeira, Mark . . . . MT	Waltrip, John . . . . JWt	Wood, Bob. . . . . BoW
Spark . . . . Spk	Thibert, Art . . . . ATi	Ward, Bill . . . . BWa	Wood, Teri Sue. . . . . . TWo
Sparling, Jack . . . . JkS	Thomas, Dann. . . . . . . DTs	Warner, Chris. . . . . CW	Wood, Wally . . . . WW
Spector, Irving . . . . IS	Thomas, Roy . . . . RTs	Warren, Adam . . . . . . AWa	Woodbridge, George . GWb
Spiegelman, Art. . . . . . ASp	Thomason, Derek . . . . DeT	Warren, Jack A. . . . . . . JW	Woodring, Jim. . . . . . . JWo
Spiegle, Dan . . . . DSp	Thompson, Jill. . . . . JIT	Washington 3, Robert 3RW	Wormer, Kirk Van. . . . KWo
Spinks, Frank . . . . FrS	Thorne, Frank . . . . FT	Watkiss, John . . . . JWk	Wright, Greg. . . . . GWt
Springer, Frank . . . . . . FS	Tinker, Ron . . . . RnT	Watson, Jim . . . . JWa	Wrightson, Berni . . . . . BWr
Sprouse, Chris . . . . . . CSp	Todd, Fred . . . . FTd	Webb, Robert. . . . . . . RWb	Wyman, M.C. . . . . . . MCW
St.Pierre, Joe . . . . JPi	Torres, Angelo . . . . AT	Weeks, Lee. . . . . LW	Yaep, Chap. . . . . CYp
Starlin, Jim. . . . . JSn	Toth, Alex. . . . . ATh	Wein, Len . . . . LWn	Yeates, Tom . . . . TY
Starr, Leonard . . . . LSt	Totleben, John . . . . JTo	Weinstein, Howard. . HWe	Yeowell, Steve. . . . . . . SY
Staton, Joe . . . . JSon	Trapain, Sal. . . . . ST	Weiss, M. . . . . MWs	Zabel, Joe . . . . JZe
Steacy, Ken . . . . KSy	Trimpe, Herb. . . . . HT	Welch, Larry . . . . LyW	Zachary, Dean. . . . . . . DZ
Steffan, Dan . . . . DnS	Truman, Timothy . . . . . TT	Welker, Gay . . . . GyW	Zaffino, Jorge. . . . . JZ
Stein, Marvin. . . . . . . MvS	Truog, Chas . . . . ChT	Wendel, Andrew. . . . . AdW	Zansky, Louis. . . . . LZ
Steinberg, Irvin . . . . . . ISb	Tucci, Bill . . . . BiT	Wenzel, David . . . . . . DWe	Zeck, Mike . . . . MZ
Stelfreeze, Brian . . . . . BSf	Tucker, James . . . . JT	Weringo, Mike . . . . . . MeW	Zick, Bruce . . . . BZ
Stephenson, Eric . . . . . ErS	Tukell, George . . . . . . GTk	West, Kevin . . . . KWe	Zulli, Michael . . . . MZi
Steranko, Jim. . . . . . . JSo	Turner, Dwayne. . . . . . DT	Weston, Chris . . . . . . CWn	Zyskowski, Joseph. . . . JZy
Stern, Roger. . . . . RSt	Turner, Ron . . . . RTu	Wheatley, Mark . . . . . MkW	Zyskowski, Steven . . . . SZ
Stern, Steve . . . . SSt	Tuska, George . . . . GT	Whedon, Joss. . . . . . . JoW	
Stevens, Dave . . . . . . DSt	Ulm, Chris. . . . . CU	Whiteman, Ezra . . . . . EzW	
Stiles, Steve . . . . SvS	Ulmer, Al . . . . AU	Whitman, Bill . . . . BWh	
Story, Karl. . . . . KlS	Vachss, Andrew. . . . . . AVs	Whitney, Ogden. . . . . . OW	
Stout, William . . . . WiS	Vado, Dan . . . . DVa	Wiacek, Bob . . . . BWi	

GENERAL ABBREVIATIONS FOR COMICS LISTINGS

Adaptation . . . . Adapt.	Giant Size . . . . G-Size	Prestige Format . . . . PF
Appearance of . . . . A:	Golden Age . . . . G.A.	Preview . . . . Prev.
Anniversary . , ... Anniv.	Graphic Album . . . . GAm	Reprinted issue . . . . rep.
Annual . . . . Ann.#	Graphic Novel . . . . . GN or GNv	Retold . . . . rtd.
Art & Cover . . . . (a&c)	Hardcover . . . . HC	Return/Revival of . . . . R:
Art & Plot . . . . (a&pl)	Identity Revealed . . . . IR:	Scripted/Written by . . . . (s)
Art & Script. . . . . (a&s)	Inks by . . . . (i)	Scripts & inks . . . . (s&i)
Artist . . . . (a)	Introduction of . . . . I:	Silver Age . . . . S.A.
Back-Up Story . . . . BU:	Joins of . . . . J:	Softcover . . . . SC
Beginning of . . . . B:	King Size . . . . K-Size	Special . . . . Spec.
Birth of . . . . b:	Leaving of . . . . L:	Team-up . . . . T.U.
Cameo Appearance . . . . C:	New Costume . . . . N:	Trade Paperback . . . . TPB
Cover . . . . (c)	No Issue Number . . . . N#	Versus . . . . V: or vs.
Cover and Script . . . . (c&s)	Origin of . . . . O:	Wedding of . . . . W:
Crossover with . . . . x-over	Painted Cover . . . . P(c)	With . . . . w/
Death/Destruction of . . . . . . D:	Part . . . . pt. or Pt.	Without . . . . w/o
Edition . . . . Ed.	Pencils by . . . . (p)	
Ending of . . . . E:	Photographic cover . . . . . Ph(c)	
Features . . . . F:	Plotted by . . . . (pl)	

Abbreviation	Name
3RW	Robert Washington 3
AA	Alfredo Alcala
AAd	Art Adams
AaK	Alisa Kwitney
AaL	Aaron Lopresti
AAv	Al Avison
AB	Alex Blum
ABr	Ann Brewster
ACa	Anthony Castrillo
ACe	Andrew Currie
ACh	Anthony Chun
ACo	Amanda Conner
AD	Alan Davis
ADF	Alan Dean Foster
AdH	Arnold Hicks
AdP	Adam Pollina
ADv	Al Davison
AdW	Andrew Wendel
AF	Al Feldstein
AFa	Al Fago
AG	Al Gordon
AgF	A. Frolechlich
AGn	Alfonso Green
AGo	Alex Garner
AGw	Archie Goodwin
AH	Adam Hughes
AHo	Art Holcomb
AIA	Alfred Andriola
AJ	Al Jaffee
AKu	Adam Kubert
ALa	Andy Lanning
AIG	Alan Grant
AIM	Albert Micale
AM	Al Milgrom
AMc	Al McWilliams
AMe	Angel Medina
AMK	Angus McKie
AMo	Alan Moore
AN	Alex Nino
ANi	Art Nichols
ANo	Ann Nocenti
AOl	Ariel Olivetti
APh	Annie Parkhouse
AR	Alex Raymond
ARn	Arthur Randon
ARu	Aldo Rubano
AS	Alex Saviuk
ASh	Alex Schomburg
ASm	Andy Smith
ASm	Allen Simon
ASp	Art Spiegelman
AT	Angelo Torres
ATh	Alex Toth
ATi	Art Thibert
AU	Al Ulmer
AV	Al Vey
AVs	Andrew Vachss
AW	Al Williamson
AWa	Adam Warren
AWi	Anthony Williams
AWs	Aron Wiesenfeld
AxR	Alex Ross
AyB	Allyn Brodsky
BA	Brent Anderson
BaB	Barry Blair
BAn	Bill Anderson
BAp	Brian Althorp
BAu	Brian Augustyn
BB	Brian Bolland
BBa	Bernard Bailey
BbB	Bob Brown
BBB	Bob Boze Bell
BBh	Brett Booth
BbK	Bob Kanigher
BBl	Bret Blevins
BbL	Bob Lamme
BBr	Brett Breeding
BCe	Bobbie Chase
BCh	Bernard Chang
BCi	Brandon Choi
BD	Bob Davis
BDC	Brent D Carpenter
BDn	Ben Dunn
BE	Bill Elder
BEd	Ben Edlund
BEv	Bill Everett
BEw	Brett Ewins
BF	Bob Fujitani(Fuje)
BG	Bill Griffith
BH	Bob Hall
BHa	Do Hampton
BHg	Burne Hogarth
BHi	Bryan Hitch
BHr	Ben Herrera
BHs	Bob Harras
BiT	Bill Tucci
BK	Bernie Krigstein
BKa	Bob Kane
BKi	Barry Kitson
BKr	Brandon Kruse
BKs	Babara Kesel
BL	Bob Layton
BLb	Bob Lubbers
BlH	Bill Hobbs
BLr	Bob Larkin
BLs	Batton Lash
BLw	Brian Lewis
BM	Barry Mitchel
BMB	Brian Michael Bendis
BMc	Bob McLeod
BMC	B. McCorkindale
BML	Bill Messner-Loebs
BMs	Bill Maus
BMy	Brendon McCarthy
BNa	Bob Napton
BnP	Brian Pulido
BO	Bob Oskner
BoW	Bob Wood
BP	Bob Powell
BPe	Brandon Peterson
BPr	Bruno Premaini
BR	Bill Reinhold
BRa	Ben Raab
BrM	Brian Murray
BRo	Boody Rogers
BrP	Bruce Patterson
BS	Bart Sears
BSf	Brian Stelfreeze
BSt	Beau Smith
BSz	Bill Sienkiewicz
BT	Bryan Talbot
BTn	Billy Tan
Buzz	Buzz
BV	Boris Vallejo
BVa	Brad Vancata
BW	Basil Wolverton
BWa	Bill Ward
BWg	Bill Willingham
BWh	Bill Whitman
BWi	Bob Wiacek
BWo	Bill Woggin
BWr	Berni Wrightson
BWS	Barry Windsor-Smith
BZ	Bruce Zick
CAd	Charlie Adlard
CaS	Cam Smith
CAx	Chris Alexander
CB	Carl Barks
CBa	Chris Bachalo
CBi	Charles Biro
CBu	Carl Burgos
CCa	Charles Caldes
CCB	C. C. Beck
CCl	Chris Claremont
Ccs	Chriscross
CCt	Claudio Castellini
CCu	Chuck Cuidera
CDi	Chuck Dixon
CDo	Colleen Doran
CE	Carlos Ezquerra
CF	Creig Flessel
CG	Carlos Garzon
CH	Chad Hunt
ChB	Charles Berger
ChG	Chester Gould
ChM	Chris Marrinan
CHm	Cully Hamner
ChT	Chas Truog
Chu	Ernie Chua
CI	Carmine Infantino
CIv	Chris Ivy
CJ	Casey Jones
CK	Cam Kennedy
CMc	Colin McNeil
CNn	Cedric Nocon
CNr	Cary Nord
CP	Carl Potts
CPa	Carlos Pacheco
CPi	Carlos Pino
CPr	Christopher Priest
CQ	Charles Quinlan
CR	P. Craig Russell
CRb	Cliff Robinson
CrB	Craig Brasfield
CS	Curt Swan
CsB	Chris Batista
CSM	C. S. Moe
CsM	Chris Moeller
CSp	Chris Sprouse
CU	Chris Ulm
CV	Charles Vess
CW	Chris Warner
CWf	Chance Wolf
CWi	Colin Wilson
CWn	Chris Weston
CYp	Chap Yaep
DA	Dan Adkins
DAb	Dusty Abell
DaC	Dan Castellaneta
DaF	Dan Fraga
DaG	Dave Garcia
DaM	Danny Miki
DAn	Dan Abnett
DaR	Darrick Robertson
DaW	Damon Willis
Day	Dan Day
DAy	Dick Ayers
DB	D. Battlefield
DB	Denis Beauvais
DBa	Dan Barry
DBk	Darryl Banks
DBl	Danny Bulanadi
DBr	Dick Briefer
DBs	John Barras
DBw	Doug Braithwaite
DC	Dave Cockrum
DCn	Don Cameron
DCw	Denys Cowan
DD	Dick Dillin
DdB	David Boller
DDv	Dan Davis
DdW	David Williams
DE	D. Elliot
DeH	Dave Hund
DeM	Dev Madan
DeT	Derek Thomason
DFg	Duncan Fegredo
DFr	Danny Fingeroth
DG	Dick Giordano
DGb	Dave Gibbons
DGC	D.G. Chichester
DgM	Doug Moench
DgR	Doug Roea
DGr	Dan Green
DH	Don Heck
DHa	Drew Hayes
DHv	Dave Hoover
DHz	Douglas Hazlewood
DiF	Dick Foreman
DJ	Dennis Jensen
DJa	Dennis Janke
DJu	Dan Jurgens
DK	Dale Keown
DkB	Dick Browne
DkG	Daerick Gross
DKi	Dennis Kitchen
DL	Dave Lapham
DlB	Daniel Brereton
DLp	Dave Louapre
DLw	Dan Lawlis
DM	David Mazzucchelli
DMc	Dave McKean
DMD	Dwayne McDuffie
DMG	Don McGregor
DMk	David Mack
DMn	Duke Mighten
DMt	Dean Motter
DN	Don Newton
DnS	Dan Steffan
DO	Dave Olbrich
DoC	Dario Carrasco
DOe	Dark One
DoM	Doug Mahnke
DON	O'Neil, Denny
DOr	Dean Ormston
DP	Don Perlin
DPo	Porch, David
DPs	Dan Panosian
DPw	Power, Dermot
DQ	David Quinn
DR	Ross, David
Rd	Richard Delgado
DRi	Don Rico
DRo	Denis Rodier
DRo	David Roach
DS	Dave Sim
DSh	Dave Sheridan
DSp	Dan Spiegle
DSs	Don Simpson
DSt	Dave Stevens
DSw	Dan Sweetman
DT	Dwayne Turner
DTs	Dann Thomas
DTy	David Taylor
DvA	David Ammerman
DVa	Dan Vado
DvC	Dave Cooper
DvD	Dave Dorman
DvH	David Hearnes
DvJ	Dave Johnson
DvL	David Lloyd
DvM	David Michelinie
DvR	David Reed
DW	Doug Wildey
DWe	David Wenzel
DZ	Dean Zachary
EA	Edd Ashe
EB	Ed Barreto
EBe	Ed Benes
EC	Ernie Colon
ECa	Eddie Campbell
ECh	Ernie Chan
EcS	Eric Silvestri
EdM	Edward Moritz
EDo	Evan Dorkin
EH	Ed Hannigan
EhH	Ernest Hart
EHi	E.E. Hibbard
EHr	Everette Hartsoe
EiS	Eric Shanower
EK	Everett R. Kinsler
EL	Erik Larsen

Abbr	Name
ELe	Elaine Lee
ELu	Eric Van Lustbader
EM	Esteban Maroto
EN	Earl Norem
ENB	E. Nelson Bridwell
EP	Edmund Perryman
ERC	E.R. Cruz
ErP	Eric Pence
ErS	Eric Stephenson
ESM	Elliot S. Maggin
EW	Ed Waldman
EzW	Ezra Whiteman
FaN	Fabian Nicieza
FB	Frank Brunner
FBe	Frank Bolle
FBk	Fred Burke
FC	Frank Cirocco
FdS	Fred Schiller
FF	Frank Frazetta
FFo	Frank Fosco
FG	Floyd Gottfredson
FGu	Fred Guardineer
FH	Flint Henry
FM	Frank Miller
FMc	Frank McLaughlin
FMe	Fred Meagher
FP	Frank R. Paul
FR	Frank Robbins
FrG	Frank Giacoia
FrS	Frank Spinks
FS	Frank Springer
Fso	Franchesco
FSt	Foolbert Sturgeon
	(& Frank Stack)
FT	Frank Thorne
FTa	Francis Takenaga
FTd	Fred Todd
GaF	Gardner Fox
GB	Geoffrey Biggs
GBl	George Bell
GBu	Greg Budget
GC	Gene Colan
GCa	Greg Capullo
GCh	Gary Cohn
GD	Gene Day
GDu	Gary Dumm
GE	George Evans
GeH	Gene Ha
GEn	Garth Ennis
GEr	Gary Erskine
GF	Glenn Fabry
GfD	Geof Darrow
GFo	Gerald Forton
GFr	Gary Frank
GFs	George Frese
GFx	Gill Fox
GG	Gabe Gecko
Ggn	Geggan
GgP	George Pratt
GHe	Gilbert Hernandez
GHi	Graham Higgins
GI	Geoff Isherwood
GiS	Gilbert Shelton
GJ	Gerard Jones
GK	Gil Kane
GKl	George Klein
GL	Garry Leach
GlD	Glyn Dillon
GLz	Greg Luzniak
GM	Gray Morrow
GMc	Gerald McCann
GMo	Grant Morrison
GMy	Graham Manley
GN	Graham Nolan
GP	George Perez
GPi	Gene Pamai
Grl	Graham Ingles
GrL	Greg LaRocque
GS	Gustav Schrotter
GSh	Gerry Shamray
GSr	Geoff Senior
GT	George Tuska
GTk	George Tukell
GtM	Grant Miehm
GW	Gahan Wilson
GWb	George Woodbridge
GWt	Greg Wright
GyA	Gary Amaro
GyC	Gerry Conway
GyD	Guy Davis
GyM	Gary Martin
GyW	Gay Welker
HaE	Harlan Ellison
HB	Hernandez Brothers
HbK	Hannibal King
HC	Howard Chaykin
HcK	Henry C. Kiefer
HD	H. Dougherty
HFl	Homer Flemming
HH	Hugh Haynes
HjK	H. J. Kihi
HK	Harvey Kurtzman
HMo	H. Mercadoocasio
HMz	Henry Martinez
HN	Howard Nostrand
HNg	Hoang Nguyen
HP	Harvey Pekar
HPo	Howard Porter
HR	H. Rasmussen
HSa	Harry Sahle
HSm	Howard Shum
HSn	Howard Simpson
HT	Herb Trimpe
HuR	Humberto Ramos
HWe	Howard Weinstein
HwP	Howard Post
HyG	Harley Griffiths
IaC	Ian Churchhill
IEd	Ian Edginton
IG	Ian Gibson
IK	Ian Kennedy
IN	Irv Novick
IS	Irving Spector
ISb	Irvin Steinberg
IV	Ivan Velez, Jr.
JA	Jack Abel
JaB	Jack Binder
JaD	Jamie Delano
JaL	Jae Lee
JAl	Jeff Albrecht
JAn	Jeff Anderson
JAo	John Albano
JAp	Jim Aparo
JAr	John Arcudi
JB	John Buscema
JBa	Jim Baikie
JBa	Jim Balent
JBe	John Beeston
JBg	Jon Bogdanove
JBi	Jerry Bingham
JBl	Jesus Blasco
JBm	John Broom
JBn	John Burns
JBo	John Bolton
JBr	June Brigman
JBt	Jeff Butler
JBu	Jack Burnley
JBy	John Byrne
JBz	Joe Benitez
JCa	John Calnan
JCf	Jim Calafiore
JCh	Joe Chiodo
JCo	Jack Cole
JCp	John Cooper
JCr	Johnny Craig
JCt	Joe Carter
JCx	Jeromy Cox
JCz	Jerry Cruz
JD	Jan Duursema
JDa	Jack Davis
JDo	Julie Doucet
JDx	John Dixon
JDy	Jo Duffy
JeJ	Jeff Jones
JeM	Jerome Moore
JeP	Jerry Prosser
JeR	James Robinson
JEs	John Estes
JF	John Forte
JFM	John Francis Moore
JFr	John Freeman
JFy	James Fry III
JG	Jackson Guice
JGa	Jack Gaughan
JGr	Jerry Grandmetti
JGz	Jorge Gonzalez
JH	Jack Herman
JH	Jack Hearne
JHa	Jim Harmon
JhB	John Beatty
JhD	John Dell
JHi	John Higgins
JHk	John Hicklenton
JHl	James Hudnall
JHo	John Holdredge
JHr	Jaime Hernandez
JHw	Jamie Hewlett
JI	Jim Infantino
JiC	Jim Callahan
JiS	Jim Shooter
JJ	Jeff Johnson
JJB	JJ Birch
JJn	Julius Jackson
JJo	J.B. Jones
JJu	Joe Jusko
JK	Jack Kirby
JKa	Jack Kamen
JKs	Jack Sparling
JKu	Joe Kubert
JKz	Jack Katz
JL	Jose Lopez
JLb	Jeph Loeb
JLd	Joe Lansdale
JLe	Jim Lee
JLi	Joseph M. Linsner
JIT	Jill Thompson
JLv	Jim Lavery
JM	Jim Mooney
JMC	John McCrea
JMd	Joe Madureira
JMD	J.M. DeMatteis
JMi	Jeff Mariotte
JmL	Jim Lawson
JMn	Joe Maneely
JmP	James Pascoe
JMr	Jeff Abel
JMs	Jeff Matsuda
JMt	Joe Martin
JMu	Jon J. Muth
JMy	Jeffrey Moy
JMz	Jose Marzan
JnM	Jason Minor
JnR	John Riley
JNR	John Ney Rieber
JnS	John Smith
JO	Joe Orlando
JoA	Jo Alibaster
JoB	Joe Bennett
JoC	Joe Casey
JOb	James O'Barr
JoG	Joe Giella
JoM	Joe Musial
JOn	James Owen
JoP	Joe Phillips
JoS	Joe Shuster
JOs	John Ostrander
JOt	Jose Ortiz
JoW	Joss Whedon
JOy	Jerry Ordway
JP	Jo Polseno
JPl	Jimmy Palmiotti
JPe	Jonathan Peterson
JPh	James Perham
JPi	Joe St.Pierre
JPL	John Paul Leon
JPn	Jason Pearson
JQ	Joe Quesada
JR	John Romita
JR2	John Romita, Jr.
JRd	J. Redondo
JRe	John Royle
JRl	Jim Royle
JRi	J Richardson
JRo	J. Rosenberger
JRo	Jerry Robinson
JRs	John Ross
JRu	Joe Rubinstein
JRv	Judith Reeves-Stevens
JRy	John Ridgeway
JRz	John Rozum
JS	Javier Saltares
JS3	Jim Sanders III
JSb	Jonathan Sibal
JSc	Jeffery Scott
JSC	J. Scott Campbell
JSe	John Severin
JsG	Justin Green
JSh	Jim Sherman
JSi	Jeff Smith
JSm	Joe Simon
JSn	Jim Starlin
JSo	Jim Steranko
JSon	Joe Staton
JsP	Jay Scott Pike
JSt	Joe Sinnott
JT	James Tucker
JTg	John Tartaglione
JTo	John Totleben
JuB	Julie Bell
JV	Jim Valentino
JVF	John Van Fleet
JW	Jack A Warren
JWa	Jim Watson
JWf	Joseph Wolfe
JWi	J.H. Williams
JWk	John Watkiss
JWo	Jim Woodring
JWp	Jason Waltrip
JWt	John Waltrip
JyD	Jay Disbrow
JyS	Jerry Serpe
JZ	Jorge Zaffino
JZe	Joe Zabel
JZy	Joseph Zyskowski
K&R	Kane & Romita
KB	Kyle Baker
KBa	Ken Battlefield
KBk	Kurt Busiek
KD	Kieron Dwyer
KDe	Kim Deitch
KDM	Kim DeMulder
KEa	Kevin Eastman
KeL	Ken Lashley
KeW	Kevin Walker
KG	Keith Giffen
KGa	Kerry Gammill
KHd	Kevin Hopgood
KHt	Kyle Hotz
KHu	Ken Hultgren
KiA	Kia Asamiya

Abbr	Name	Abbr	Name	Abbr	Name	Abbr	Name
KJ	Klaus Janson	MCi	Mark Crilley	MSy	Mike Sekowsky	RA	Ross Andru
KJa	Kirk Javinen	MCl	Mike Clark	MSz	J.Michael Straczynski	RAJ	R.A. Jones
KJo	Kelley Jones	MCn	Max Allan Collins	MT	Mark Texeira	RaP	Rachel Pollack
KK	Karl Kesel	MCo	Mark Chiarello	MtB	Matt Broome	RB	Rich Buckler
KlA	Karl Alstaetter	MCr	Mike Carlin	MTk	Masashi Tanaka	RbB	Robert Bernstein
KlK	Karl Kerschl	MCW	M.C. Wyman	MV	Mike Vosburg	RbC	Robert Campenella
KlS	Karl Story	MCy	Mike Carey	MvR	Melvin Rubi	RBe	Ramon Bernado
KM	Kevin Maguire	MD	Mort Drucker	MvS	Marvin Stein	RBn	Ryan Benjamin
KN	Kevin Nowlan	MD2	Mike Deodato, Jr.	MW	Mary Wilshire	RBr	Rick Burchett
KoK	Kevin Kobasic	MDa	Malcolm Davis	MWa	Mark Waid	RBu	Robert Burns
KON	Kevin O'Neill	MDb	M. DeZuniga	MWg	Matt Wagner	RC	Reed Crandall
KP	Keith Pollard	MDb	Maurice Del Bourgo	MWn	Marv Wolfman	RCa	Richard Case
KPl	Kilian Plunkett	MDo	Mike Dorey	MWs	M. Weiss	RCl	Ricky Carralero
KR	Kim Raymond	MDr	Mike Dringenberg	Mys	Myers	RCo	Richard Corben
Kr	Kirner	ME	Mike Esposito	MZ	Mike Zeck	RCr	Robert Crumb
KS	Kurt Schaffenberger	MEg	Marty Egeland	MZi	Michael Zulli	RCz	Roger Cruz
KSm	Kevin Smith	MeP	Mike Parobeck	NA	Neal Adams	RDB	Randy DuBerkr
KSW	Keith S. Wilson	MeW	Mike Weringo	NBy	Norm Breyfogle	RdM	Raymond Marais
KSy	Ken Steacy	MF	Matt Fox	NC	Nick Cardy	RDm	Rodolfo Damaggio
KtH	Kurt Hathaway	MFl	Michael Fleisher	ND	Nigel Dobbyn	RdD	Richard Delgado
KVH	Kevin VanHook	MFm	Mark Farmer	Nel	Nelson	RE	Ric Estrada
KW	Kent Williams	MFr	Michael Jan Friedman	NGa	Neil Gaiman	REv	Ray Evans
KWe	Kevin West	MG	Mike Gustovich	NHa	Neil Hanson	RF	Ron Frenz
KWi	Keith Williams	MGi	Michael T. Gilbert	NKu	Andy Kubert	RFl	Robert Fleming
KWo	Kirk Van Wormer	MGo	Michael Golden	NMa	Nathan Massengill	RG	Ron Garney
LbC	Leonard B. Cole	MGr	Mike Grell	NN	Norman Nodel	RGd	Ruben Gerard
LC	Lou Cameron	MGs	Martin Griffiths	NNa	Nick Napolitano	RgM	Rags Morales
LCh	Lillian Chestney	MGu	Mark Gruenwald	NPl	Noly Panalign	RGr	Randy Green
LDr	Larry Dresser	MGy	Mick Gray	NR	Nestor Redondo	RGs	R. Grossman
LDu	Leo Duranona	MHi	Michael Higgins	NRd	Norm Rapmund	RGT	R.G. Taylor
LDz	Luis Dominguez	MHo	Matt Howarth	NS	Norm Saunders	RGu	Rebecca Guay
LEl	Lee Elias	MHs	Mike Heisler	NSH	N. Steven Harris	RH	Russ Heath
LeS	Len Strazewski	MHw	Matt Hawkins	NV	Neil Vokes	RHa	Rory Hayes
LF	Lou Fine	MHy	Matt Haley	NyC	Nancy Collins	RHe	Richard Horie
LHa	Larry Hama	MI	Medio Iorio	OM	Otto Messmer	RHo	Rick Hoberg
LI	Larry Ivie	MiA	Michael Allred	OW	Ogden Whitney	RHo	Rich Howell
LiM	Linda Medley	MiB	Mike Barr	PaD	Paco Diaz	RiB	Richard Bennett
LJi	Leonardo Jimenez	MiS	Mizuki Sakakibara	PaK	Paris T. Karounos	Rip	Riply
LKa	Len Kaminski	MJ	Malcolm Jones	PaP	Paul Pelletier	RJ	Robert Jenney
LLe	Lank Leonard	MK	Mike Kaluta	PB	Pat Broderick	RJn	Robert Jones
LLi	Larry Lieber	MkB	Mike Barreiro	PBd	Philip Bond	RkB	Rick Bryant
LM	Lou Morales	MKd	Malcolm Kildale	PC	Paul Chadwick	RkL	Rick Leach
LMa	Larry Mahlstedt	MkF	Mike Friedrich	PcH	Poch	RKu	Roy Krenkel
LMc	Luke McDonnell	MkH	Mike Hoffer	PCu	Paris Cullins	RL	Rick Leonardi
LMd	Lee Moder	MkK	Mike McKenna	PD	Peter Doherty	RLd	Rob Liefeld
LMr	Lee Marrs	MkW	Mark Wheatley	PDd	Peter David	RLe	Rik Levins
LnS	Lin Streeter	MlB	Michael Bair	PDi	Paul Dini	RLg	Roger Langridge
Low	John Lowe	MLe	Mike Leeke	PFe	Pascual Ferry	RLm	Ron Lim
LRs	Luke Ross	MLr	Michael Lark	PG	Paul Gulacy	RLv	R. Livingstone
LS	Lee Sullivan	MM	Mike Manley	PGa	Phil Gascoine	RM	Rick Magyar
LSh	Liam Sharp	MMc	M. McMahon	PGn	Paul Guinan	RMc	Ralph Macchio
LSi	Louise Simonson	MMe	Mort Meskin	PGr	Peter Grau	RMn	Roland Mann
LSn	Larry Stroman	MMi	Michael Mignola	PGv	Paul Gustavson	RMo	Ruben Moreira
LSt	Leonard Starr	MMK	Mike McKone	PhH	Phil Hester	RMr	Roy Allan Martinez
LuH	Lou Harrison	MMo	Mark Moretti	PJ	Phil Jimminiz	RMz	Ron Marz
LW	Lee Weeks	MMr	Mark Millar	PJe	Paul Jenkins	RN	Rudy Nebres
LWn	Len Wein	MMy	Marat Mychaels	PKr	Peter Krause	RnT	Ron Tinker
LyW	Larry Welch	MN	Mike Netzer	PlA	Paul Abrams	RoR	Ron Randall
LZ	Louis Zansky	MnN	Martin Nodell	PLa	Peter Laird	RoW	on Wagner
MA	Murphy Anderson	Moe	Moebius	PMo	Pete Morisi	RP	Rudy Palais
MaG	Manny Galan	MP	Mike Ploog	PMs	Pat Mills	RPc	Richard Pace
MaH	Mark Hempel	MPa	Mark Pacella	PNe	Paul Neary	RPi	Richard Pini
Man	Roland Mann	MPc	Mark Paniccia	PNu	Philip Nutman	RQu	Randy Queen
MaS	Mark Schmitz	MPk	Martin Pasko	PO	Patrick Olliffe	RR	Ray Ramsey
MaT	Mark Tenney	MPn	Mark Pennington	PP	Pop Payne	RRa	Rich Rankin
MB	Matt Baker	MR	Marshall Rogers	PPo	Paul Pope	RS	Ron Smith
MBa	Mark Bagley	MRa	Mac Raboy	PPr	Pat Prichard	RsB	Russell Braun
MBe	M. Belardinelli	MRc	Mark Ricketts	PQ	Peter Quinones	RSd	Randy Stradley
MBg	Mark Badger	MRi	Mike Richardson	PR	Paul Ryan	RsM	Russ Manning
MBi	M. Bailey	MRo	Mike Roberts	PrC	Peter Costanza	RSm	Robin Smith
MBm	Mary Bierbaum	MRy	Matt Ryan	PrG	Peter Gross	RSt	Roger Stern
MBn	Mike Baron	MS	Mark Silvestri	PrM	Peter Milligan	RT	Romeo Tanghal
MBr	Mark Bright	MSe	Marie Severin	PS	Paul Smith	RtH	Robert Hebbard
MBu	Mark Buckingham	MSh	Mark Schultz	PSj	Peter Snejbjerg	RTs	Roy Thomas
MBy	Mitch Byrd	MsM	Mike S. Miller	PtL	Patrick Lee	RTu	Ron Turner
MC	Mike Collins	MSo	Mark Sasso	PuD	Paul Danner	RuG	Rube Goldberg
MCa	Marc Campos	MSt	Malcolm Smith	PuJ	Paul Johnson	RV	Rick Veitch
MCh	Mike Chen	MsW	Morris Waldinger	PuK	Paul Kupperberg	RvB	Raeburn Van Buren

RW . . . . . Robert Williams	SLi . . . . Steve Lightle	TBd . . . . . . Tim Bradstreet	TSr . . . . Terry Shoemaker
RWa . . . . Reed Waller	SLo . . . . Scott Lobdell	TBe . . . . Terry Beatty	TT . . . . . Timothy Truman
RWb . . . . . . Robert Webb	SM. . . . . Steve Miller	TBm . . . . . Tom Bierbaum	TTg. . . . . . . Tom Taggart
RyE . . . . . Randy Emberlin	SMa . Shawn Martinbrough	TC. . . . . . Travis Charest	TTn . . . . . . Ty Templeton
RyL. . . . . Ray Lago	SmC. . . . . . . Sam Citron	TCk . . . . . . Tomm Coker	TV . . . . Tim Vigil
RyR. . . . . Rodney Ramos	SMc . . . . . Scott McDaniel	TD . . . . . Tony DeZuniga	TVE. . . Trevor Von Eeden
S&K. . . . . . Simon & Kirby	SMl . . . . . . Scott McCloud	TDF . . . . . Tom DeFalco	TvS. . . . . . . Trevor Scott
S&S. . . . Siegel & Shuster	SML . . . Sean McLaughlin	TDr. . . . . . Tom Derenick	TWo . . . . . Teri Sue Wood
SA . . . . . Sergio Aragones	SMo . . . . . Sheldon Moldoff	TDz . . . . . Todd DeZago	TY . . . . Tom Yeates
SaB . . . . Sam Becker	SMt . . . . . Steve Mattsson	TeB . . . . . . Tex Blaisdell	TyD. . . . . . Terry Dodson
Sal . . . . Sal Amendola	SMz . . Seymour Moskowitz	TeH . . . . Ted Halsted	TyH . . . . Tony Harris
SAP . . Shea Anton Pensa	SnW . . . . Stan Woch	TEl . . . . Tim Eldred	TyT . . . . . . Tony Tallarico
SaV . . . . Sal Velluto	SPa . . . . . Stephen Platt	TFH. . . . . T. F. Hing	VAz . . . . . Vincent Alcazar
SB. . . . . . . Sal Buscema	Spk . . . . Spark	TG . . . . . . Tom Grummett	VB . . . . Vaughn Bode
SBi . . . . Stephen Bissette	SPl. . . . . . . Scott Phillips	TGb . . . . . Tom Grindberg	VcL. . . . . . . Vince Locke
SBs . . . . . . Simon Bisley	SPr . . . . . Stefan Petrucha	TGo . . . . . Till Goodman	VGi. . . . . . Vince Giarrano
SBt . . . . Steve Butler	SR . . . . Steve Rude	TH. . . . . . . Tim Hamilton	ViC. . . . . . Vince Colletta
SC. . . . . Sid Check	SRf . . . . . . Sean Ruffner	THa . . . . Tim Harris	VMk. . . . . . Val Mayerik
ScB . . . . Scott Benefiel	SRo . . . . Spain Rodriguez	TJn . . . . . . Todd Johnson	VMo. . . Vincent Morosco
ScC . . . . Scott Clark	SS. . . . . Stan Sakai	TKa . . . . Terry Kavanagh	VP . . . . Victor Prezio
SCh . . . . . . Sean Chen	SSc. . . . . Sean Scoffield	TKn . . . . Trent Kaniuga	VRu . . . . . Vince Russell
SCi . . . . Sergio Cariello	SSe. . . . Steven T. Seagle	TKr . Teddy H. Kristiansen	VS . . . . . . Val Semeiks
ScK. . . . . . . Scott Kolins	SSh . . . . . . Sean Shaw	TL . . . . Tom Lyle	VV . . . . . . Vagner Vargas
ScL. . . . . Scott Lee	SSh . . . . Syd Shores	TLa . . . . . . Terry LaBan	WaP . . . . Warren Pleece
SCp . . . . . Sam Cooper	SSm . . . . Steve Sampson	TLw . . . Terral Lawrence	WB . . . . . Wayne Boring
SCr. . . . . . Steve Crespo	SSr . . . . . . Steve Skroce	TM . . . . . Todd McFarlane	WBu . . . . W. Burroughs
SCW. . . . . S. Clay Wilson	SSt. . . . . . . Steve Stern	TmB . . . . . . Tim Burgard	WE . . . . . . Will Eisner
SCy . . . . . Simon Colby	ST . . . . Sal Trapain	TmC . . . Tom Christopher	WEl. . . . . . Warren Ellis
SD . . . . Steve Ditko	StA. . . . . Stephen Addeo	TMd . . . . Tom Mandrake	WiS . . . . . . William Stout
SDi . . . . . . Steve Dillon	StB . . . . . Scott Benson	TMK . . . . Ted McKeever	WJo. . . . Walter Johnson
SDr. . . . . . . Stan Drake	StC . . . . . Stan Campbell	TMo . . . . . Tom Morgan	WK. . . . . . . Walt Kelly
SDR . . . . Sam DeLaRosa	StE . . . . . . Steve Erwin	TmR . . . . . Tom Ryder	Wld . . . . Andrew Wildman
SEa . . . . . . Scott Eaton	StG . . . . . Steve Grant	TMr. . . . . Terry Moore	WIP . . . . . Walter Palais
SeM . . . . Steve Montano	StK. . . . . . Stan Kaye	TMs . . . . Tom Mason	WmB . . . William Bossart
SeP. . . . . . Sean Phillips	StL . . . . Stan Lee	TmT . . . . . Tom Teney	WMc . . Walter McDaniel
SEp . . . . . Steve Epting	StM. . . . Stanley Maxwell	TMw . . . Tom McCraw	WMo. . . . Win Mortimer
SeT . . . . . Steve Tappin	StP. . . . . . . Steve Pugh	TNa. . . . . . Ted Naifeh	WmW . . . William Walsh
SEt . . . . . Steve Englehart	SVa . . . . . . Steve Vance	TnD. . . . . . Tony Daniel	Woj. . . Chuck Wojtkiewicz
SF . . . Sal Finnocchiaro	SvG . . . . . Steve Gerber	TnS . . . Tristan Schane	WP. . . . . . . Wendy Pini
SFr. . . . . . Simon Freeman	SvL. . . . Salvador Larroca	TNu. . . . . Todd Nauck	WPo . . . . Whilce Portacio
SFu . . . . . Simon Furman	SvP. . . . Steve Parkhouse	TO . . . . Thomas Oughton	WR . . . . . Werner Roth
SG. . . . . Sam Glanzman	SvS . . . . . Steve Stiles	ToT . . . . Tony Takezaki	WS. . . . . . Walt Simonson
SGa. . . . Stefano Gaudino	SW . . . . . Scott Williams	TOz . . . . Tayyar Ozkan	WSm . . . . Will Simpson
SGe . . . . . Sid Greene	SWi. . . . . Skip Williamson	TP. . . . . . Tom Palmer	WW . . . . . Wally Wood
SHa . . . . . Scott Hanna	SwM. . . Shawn McManus	TPe. . . . . . Tom Peyer	YG . . . . . Yvel Guichet
ShG. . . Shannon Gallant	SY . . . . . Steve Yeowell	TR . . . . Tom Raney	YuK . . . . . Yukito Kishniro
ShM . . . . . Sheldon Mayer	Syk. . . . . Siryk	TR. . . . . . . Ted Richards	
SHn. . . . . Simon Harrison	SyM. . . . . . Sidney Miller	TrR. . . . . . Trina Robbins	
SHp . . . . . Scott Hampton	SZ . . . . . Steven Zyskowski	TS . . . . Tom Sutton	
SI . . . . . . Stuart Immonen	TA . . . . Terry Austin	TSa . . . . . Tony Salmons	
SK. . . . . Sam Kieth	TAr . . . . Tom Artis	TSe . . . . Tim Sale	
SL. . . . . . . Steve Leialoha	TB . . . . Tim Boxell	TSg. . . . . . Tom Sniegoski	

GENERAL ABBREVIATIONS FOR COMICS LISTINGS

A: . . . . Appearance of	GAm . . . . Graphic Album	pt. or Pt. . . . . Part
(a) . . . . Artist	GN or GNv . . . . . Graphic Novel	rep. . . . . Reprinted issue
Adapt. . . . . Adaptation	G-Size . . . . Giant Size	R: . . . . Return/Revival of
Anniv. . . . . Anniversary	HC . . . . Hardcover	rtd. . . . . Retold
Ann.# . . . . Annual	I: . . . . Introduction of	(s) . . . . Scripted/Written by
(a&c) . . . . Art & Cover	(i) . . . . Inks by	S.A. . . . . Silver Age
(a&pl) . . . . Art & Plot	IR: . . . . Identity Revealed	SC . . . . Softcover
(a&s) . . . . Art & Script	J: . . . . Joins of	(s&i) . . . . Scripts & inks
B: . . . . Beginning of	K-Size . . . . King Size	Spec. . . . . Special
b: . . . . Birth of	L: . . . . Leaving of	TPB . . . . Trade Paperback
BU: . . . . Back-Up Story	N: . . . . New Costume	T.U. . . . . Team-up
C: . . . . Cameo Appearance	N# . . . . No Issue Number	V: or vs. . . . . Versus
(c) . . . . Cover	O: . . . . Origin of	W: . . . . Wedding of
(c&s) . . . . Cover and Script	P(c) . . . . Painted Cover	w/ . . . . With
D: . . . . Death/Destruction of	(p) . . . . Pencils by	w/o . . . . Without
Ed. . . . . Edition	PF . . . . Prestige Format	x-over . . . . Crossover with
E: . . . . Ending of	Ph(c) . . . . . . Photographic cover	
F: . . . . Features	(pl) . . . . Plotted by	
G.A. . . . . Golden Age	Prev. . . . . Preview	

BIBLIOGRAPHY

Daniels, Les. *Comix: A History of Comic Books in America.* New York, NY: Bonanza Books, 1971.

Gerber, Ernst. *The Photo Journal Guide to Comic Books.* Minden, NV: Gerber Publishing, 1989. Vols. 1 & 2.

Gerber, Ernst. *The Photo Journal Guide to Marvel Comics.* Minden, NV: Gerber Publishing, 1991. Vols. 3 & 4.

Goulart, Ron. *The Adventurous Decade.* New Rochelle, NY: Arlington House, 1975.

Goulart, Ron. *Comic Book Culture, An Illustrated History.* Portland, OR: Collectors Press, 2000

Goulart, Ron. *The Encyclopedia of American Comics.* New York, NY. Facts on File Publications, 1990.

Goulart, Ron. *Over 50 Years of American Comic Books.* Lincolnwood, IL: Mallard Press, 1991.

Hegenburger, John. *Collectors Guide to Comic Books.* Radnor, PA: Wallace Homestead Book Company, 1990.

Kennedy, Jay. *The Official Underground and Newave Price Guide.* Cambridge, MA: Boatner Norton Press, 1982.

Malan, Dan. *The Complete Guide to Classics Collectibles.* St. Louis, MO: Malan Classical Enterprises, 1991.

Miller, John Jackson et al. *The Standard Catalog of Comic Books.* Iola, WI: Krause Publications, 2002.

O'Neil, Dennis. *Secret Origins of DC Super Heroes.* New York, NY: Warner Books, 1976.

Overstreet, Robert. *The Overstreet Comic Book Price Guide (35th Edition).* New York, NY. Random House, 2005

Rovin, Jeff. *The Encyclopedia of Super Heroes.* New York, NY: Facts on File Publications, 1985.

Rovin, Jeff. *The Encyclopedia of Super Villians.* New York, NY: Facts on File Publications, 1987.

Thompson, Don & Maggie. *The Golden Age of Comics, Summer 1982.* Tainpa, FL: New Media Publishing, 1982.

DC COMICS

A. BIZARRO
1999
1 (of 4) SvG,MBr,F:Al Bizarro 2.50
2 SvG,MBr,A:Superman 2.50
3 SvG,MBr, ... 2.50
4 SvG,MBr, Viva Bizarro 2.50

ACCELERATE
DC/Vertigo, June, 2000
1 (of 4) Great Escape 3.00
2 Great Escape,pt.2 . . . . 3.00
3 Great Escape,pt.3 . . . . 3.00
4 Great Escape,pt.4,concl. 3.00

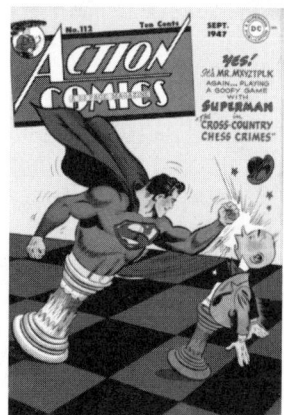

Action Comics #30 © DC Comics, Inc.

ACTION
June, 1938
1 JoS,I&O:Superman;Rescues Evelyn
   Curry from electric chair . 700,000.00
2 JoS,V:Emil Norvell 70,000.00
3 JoS,V:Thorton Blakely 45,000.00
4 JoS,V:Coach Randall 27,000.00
5 JoS,Emergency of
   Vallegho Dam 27,000.00
6 JoS,I:Jimmy Olsen,
   V:Nick Williams 27,000.00
7 JoS,V:Derek Niles 60,000.00
8 JoS,V:Gimpy 18,000.00
9 JoS,A:Det.Captain Reilly . . 18,100.00
10 JoS,Superman fights
   for prison reform 40,000.00
11 JoS,Disguised as
   Homer Ramsey 10,000.00
12 JoS,Crusade against
   reckless drivers 11,000.00
13 JoS,I:Ultra Humanite 20,000.00
14 JoS,BKa,V:Ultra Humanite,
   B:Clip Carson 11,000.00
15 JoS,BKa,Superman in
   Kidtown 15,000.00
16 JoS,BKa,Crusade against
   Gambling 8,000.00
17 JoS,BKa,V:Ultra Humanite. 12,000.00
18 JoS,BKa,V:Mr.Hamilton
   O:Three Aces 8,000.00
19 JoS,BKa,V:Ultra Humanite
   B:Superman (c) 10,000.00
20 JoS,BKa,V:Ultra Humanite. 10,000.00
21 JoS,BKa,V:Ultra Humanite . 7,000.00
22 JoS,BKa,War between Toran
   and Galonia 7,000.00
23 JoS,BKa,SMo,I:Lex Luthor 15,000.00

24 JoS,BKa,BBa,SMo,FGu,Meets
   Peter Carnahan 7,000.00
25 JoS,BKa,BBa,SMo,
   V:Medini 7,000.00
26 JoS,BKa,V:ClarenceCobalt . 7,000.00
27 JoS,BKa,V:Mr & Mrs.Tweed 5,000.00
28 JoS,BKa,JBu,V:Strongarm
   Bandit 5,000.00
29 JoS,BKa,V:Martin 6,000.00
30 JoS,BKa,V:Zolar 5,000.00
31 JoS,BKa,JBu,V:Baron
   Munsdorf 3,000.00
32 JoS,BKa,JBu,I:Krypto Ray Gun
   V:Mr.Preston 3,000.00
33 JoS,BKa,JBu,V:Brett Hall,
   O:Mr. America 3,000.00
34 JoS,BKa,V:Jim Laurg 3,000.00
35 JoS,BKa,V:Brock Walter . . . 3,000.00
36 JoS,BKa,V:StuartPemberton 3,000.00
37 JoS,BKa,V:Commissioner
   Kennedy, O:Congo Bill 3,400.00
38 JoS,BKa,V:Harold Morton . . 3,400.00
39 JoS,BKa,Meets Britt Bryson 3,400.00
40 JoS,BKa,Meets Nancy
   Thorgenson 3,400.00
41 JoS,BKa,V:Ralph Cowan,
   E:Clip Carson 2,900.00
42 V:Lex Luthor,I&O:Vigilante. . 3,800.00
43 V:Dutch O'Leary,Nazi(c) . . . 2,800.00
44 V:Prof. Steffens,Nazi(c) 2,800.00
45 V:Count Von Henzel,
   I:Stuff,Nazi(c) 2,800.00
46 V:The Domino 2,800.00
47 V:Lex Luthor—1st app. w/super
   powers,I:Powerstone 3,800.00
48 V:The Top 2,500.00
49 I:Puzzler 2,500.00
50 Meets Stan Doborak 2,500.00
51 I:Prankster 3,000.00
52 V:Emperor of America 3,200.00
53 JBu,V:Night-Owl 2,500.00
54 JBu,Meets Stanley
   Finchcomb 2,500.00
55 JBu,V:Cartoonist Al Hatt . . . 2,500.00
56 V:Emil Loring 2,500.00
57 V:Prankster 2,500.00
58 JBu,V:Adonis 2,500.00
59 I:Susie Thompkins,Lois
   Lane's niece 2,500.00
60 JBu,Lois Lane-Superwoman 2,500.00
61 JBu,Meets Craig Shaw . . . 2,500.00
62 JBu,V:Admiral Von Storff . . 2,400.00
63 JBu,V:Professor Praline . . . 2,400.00
64 I:Toyman 2,500.00
65 JBu,V:Truman Treadwell . . 2,500.00
66 JBu,V:Mr.Annister 2,500.00
67 JBu,Superman School for
   Officer's Training 2,500.00
68 A:Susie Thompkins 2,500.00
69 V:Prankster 2,500.00
70 JBu,V:Thinker 2,500.00
71 Superman Valentine's
   Day Special 1,800.00
72 V:Mr. Sniggle 1,800.00
73 V:Lucius Spruce 1,800.00
74 Meets Adelbert Dribble 1,800.00
75 V:Johnny Aesop 1,800.00
76 A Voyage with Destiny 1,800.00
77 V:Prankster 1,800.00
78 The Chef of Bohemia 1,800.00
79 JBu,A:J. Wilbur Wolfingham 1,800.00
80 A:Mr. Mxyzptlk (2nd App). . . 2,400.00
81 Meets John Nicholas 1,500.00
82 JBu,V:Water Sprite 1,500.00
83 I:Hocus and Pocus 1,500.00
84 JBu,V:Dapper Gang 1,500.00
85 JBu,V:Toyman 1,500.00

86 JBu,V:Wizard of Wokit 1,500.00
87 V:Truck Hijackers 1,500.00
88 A:Hocus and Pocus 1,500.00
89 V:Slippery Andy 1,500.00
90 JBu,V:Horace Rikker and the
   Amphi-Bandits 1,500.00
91 JBu,V:Davey Jones 1,200.00
92 JBu,V:Nowmie Norman 1,200.00
93 Superman Christmas story . 1,200.00
94 JBu,V:Bullwer 'Bull' Rylie . . . 1,200.00
95 V:Prankster 1,200.00
96 V:Mr. Twister 1,200.00
97 A:Hocus and Pocus 1,200.00
98 V:Mr. Mxyzptlk, A:Susie
   Thompkins 1,400.00
99 V:Keith Langwell 1,200.00
100 I:InspectorErskineHawkins. 1,700.00
101 V:Specs Dour,A-Bomb(c) . . 2,400.00
102 V:Mr. Mxyzptlk 1,300.00
103 V:Emperor Quexo 1,300.00
104 V:Prankster 1,300.00
105 Superman Christmas story 1,300.00
106 Clark Kent becomes Baron
   Edgestream 1,300.00
107 JBu,A:J.Wilbur Wolfingham 1,300.00
108 JBu,V:Vince Vincent 1,300.00
109 V:Prankster 1,300.00
110 A:Susie Thompkins 1,100.00
111 Cameras in the Clouds 1,100.00
112 V:Mr. Mxyzptlk 1,200.00
113 Just an Ordinary Guy 1,200.00
114 V:Mike Chesney 1,200.00
115 Meets Arthur Parrish 1,200.00
116 A:J. Wilbur Wolfingham . . . 1,200.00
117 Superman Christmas story 1,200.00
118 Execution of Clark Kent . . . 1,200.00
119 Meets Jim Banning 1,200.00
120 V:Mike Foss 1,200.00
121 V:William Sharp 1,200.00
122 V:Charley Carson 1,200.00
123 V:Skid Russell 1,200.00
124 Superman becomes
   radioactive 1,000.00
125 V:Lex Luthor 1,000.00
126 V:Chameleon 1,000.00
127 JKu,Superman on Truth or
   Consequences 1,100.00
128 V:'Aces' Deucey 1,000.00
129 Meets Gob-Gob 1,000.00
130 V:Captain Kidder 1,000.00
131 V:Lex Luthor 1,000.00

Action Comics #112 © DC Comics, Inc.

Action Comics #159 © DC Comics, Inc.

132 Superman meets George
   Washington. 1,000.00
133 V:Emma Blotz 1,000.00
134 V:Paul Strong. 1,000.00
135 V:John Morton 1,000.00
136 Superman Show-Off! 1,000.00
137 Meets Percival Winter 1,000.00
138 Meets Herbert Hinkle. . . . 1,000.00
139 Clark Kent...Daredevil!. . . . 1,000.00
140 Superman becomes Hermit 1,000.00
141 V:Lex Luthor. 1,000.00
142 V:Dan the Dip 1,000.00
143 Dates Nikki Larve. 1,000.00
144 O:Clark Kent reporting for
   Daily Planet 1,000.00
145 Meets Merton Gloop 1,000.00
146 V:Luthor. 1,000.00
147 V:'Cheeks' Ross. 1,000.00
148 Superman, Indian Chief. . . 1,000.00
149 The Courtship on Krypton!. 1,000.00
150 V:Morko. 1,000.00
151 V:Mr.Mxyzptlk,Lex Luthor
   and Prankster. 1,000.00
152 I:Metropolis Shutterbug
   Society 1,100.00
153 V:Kingpin 1,000.00
154 V:Harry Reed. 1,000.00
155 V:Andrew Arvin 1,000.00
156 Lois Lane becomes Super-
   woman,V:Lex Luthor 900.00
157 V:Joe Striker 900.00
158 V:Kane Korrell
   O:Superman (retold). 2,000.00
159 Meets Oswald Whimple . . . 900.00
160 I:Minerva Kent. 900.00
161 Meets Antara. 900.00
162 V:'IT!'. 900.00
163 Meets Susan Semple 900.00
164 Meets Stefan Andriessen . . 900.00
165 V:Crime Czar 900.00
166 V:Lex Luthor 900.00
167 V:Prof. Nero 900.00
168 O:Olaf. 900.00
169 Caveman Clark Kent! 900.00
170 V:Mad Artist of Metropolis. . 900.00
171 The Secrets of Superman. . . 900.00
172 Lois Lane..Witch! 900.00
173 V:Dragon Lang 900.00
174 V:Miracle Twine Gang. 900.00
175 V:John Vinden. 900.00
176 V:Billion Dollar Gang. 900.00
177 V:General 900.00
178 V:Prof. Sands 900.00
179 Superman in Mapleville . . . 900.00
180 V:Syndicate of Five. 900.00
181 V:Diamond Dave Delaney . . 800.00

182 Return from Planet Krypton . 800.00
183 V:Lex Luthor 800.00
184 Meets Donald Whitmore 800.00
185 V:Issah Pendleton. 800.00
186 The Haunted Superman 800.00
187 V:Silver 800.00
188 V:Cushions Raymond gang . 800.00
189 Meets Mr.& Mrs. Vandeveir. . 800.00
190 V:Mr. Mxyzptlk. 800.00
191 V:Vic Vordan. 800.00
192 Meets Vic Vordan 800.00
193 V:Beetles Brogan 800.00
194 V:Maln. 800.00
195 V:Tiger Woman 800.00
196 Superman becomes Mental
   Man 800.00
197 V:Stanley Stark 800.00
198 The Six Lives of Lois Lane . . 800.00
199 V:Lex Luthor 800.00
200 V:Morwatha. 800.00
201 'V:Benny the Brute 800.00
202 Lois Lane's X-Ray Vision . . . 700.00
203 Meets Pietro Paresca 700.00
204 Meets Sam Spulby 700.00
205 Sergeant Superman 700.00
206 Imaginary story F:L.Lane . . . 700.00
207 Four Superman Medals! . . . 700.00
208 V:Mr. Mxyzptlk. 700.00
209 V:'Doc' Winters 700.00
210 V:Lex,I:Superman Land 700.00
211 Superman Spectaculars . . . 700.00
212 V:Thorne Varden. 700.00
213 V:Paul Paxton 700.00
214 Superman,Sup.Destroyer! . . 700.00
215 I:Superman of 2956 . . . . . . 700.00
216 A:Jor-El 700.00
217 Meets Mr&Mrs.Roger Bliss . . 700.00
218 I:Super-Ape from Krypton. . . 700.00
219 V:Art Shaler. 700.00
220 Interplanetary Olympics . . . 700.00
221 V:Jay Vorrell 600.00
222 The Duplicate Superman . . . 600.00
223 A:Jor-El 600.00
224 I:Superman Island. 600.00
225 The Death of Superman 600.00
226 V:Lex Luthor 600.00
227 Man with Triple X-Ray Eyes . 600.00
228 A:Superman Museum 600.00
229 V:Dr. John Haley. 600.00
230 V:Bart Wellins 600.00
231 Sir Jimmy Olsen, Knight of
   Metropolis 600.00
232 Meets Johnny Kirk 600.00
233 V:Torm. 600.00
234 Meets Golto 600.00
235 B:Congo Bill,
   B:Tommy Tomorrow. 600.00
236 A:Lex Luthor 600.00
237 V:Nebula Gang 600.00
238 I:King Krypton,the Gorilla . . . 600.00
239 Superman's New Face 600.00
240 V:Superman Sphinx 600.00
241 WB,A:Batman,Fortress of
   Solitude (Fort Superman) . . . 500.00
242 I&O:Brainiac. 4,000.00
243 Lady and the Lion 500.00
244 CS,A:Vul-Kor,Lya-La 500.00
245 WB,V:Kak-Kul 500.00
246 WB,A:Krypton Island. 500.00
247 WB,Superman Lost Parents . 500.00
248 B&I:Congorilla. 500.00
249 A:Lex Luthor 500.00
250 WB,The Eye of Metropolis . . 500.00
251 E:Tommy Tomorrow 500.00
252 I&O:Supergirl 4,000.00
253 B:Supergirl 900.00
254 I:Adult Bizarro 700.00
255 I:Bizarro Lois 600.00
256 Superman of the Future 400.00
257 WB,JM,V:Lex Luthor. 400.00
258 A:Cosmic Man. 400.00
259 A:Lex Luthor,Superboy 400.00

Action Comics #280 © DC Comics, Inc.

260 A:Mighty Maid 400.00
261 I:Streaky,E:Congorilla 400.00
262 A:Bizarro 400.00
263 O:Bizarro World 500.00
264 V:Bizarro 400.00
265 A:Hyper-Man. 400.00
266 A:Streaky,Krypto 400.00
267 JM,3rd A:Legion,I:Invisible
   Kid 800.00
268 WB,A:Hercules 300.00
269 A:Jerro. 300.00
270 CS,JM,A:Batman 400.00
271 A:Lex Luthor 300.00
272 A:Aquaman 300.00
273 A:Mr.Mxyzptlk 300.00
274 A:Superwoman 300.00
275 WB,JM,V:Braimiac 300.00
276 JM,6th A:Legion,I:Brainiac 5,
   Triplicate Girl,Bouncing Boy . 500.00
277 CS,JM,V:Lex Luthor 250.00
278 CS,Perry White Becomes
   Master Man 250.00
279 JM,V:Hercules,Samson 250.00
280 CS,JM,V:Braniac,
   A:Congorilla. 250.00
281 JM,A:Krypto 250.00
282 JM,V:Mxyzptlk. 250.00
283 CS,JM,A:Legion of Super
   Outlaws 300.00
284 A:Krypto,Jerro. 250.00
285 JM,Supergirl Existence Revealed,
   C:Legion (12th app.) 300.00
286 CS,JM,V:Lex Luthor 200.00
287 JM,A:Legion 200.00
288 JM,A:Mon-El 200.00
289 JM,A:Adult Legion. 200.00
290 JM,C:Phantom Girl 200.00
291 JM,V:Mxyzptlk. 200.00
292 JM,I:Superhorse 200.00
293 JM,O:Comet-Superhorse . . . 200.00
294 JM,V:Lex Luthor 200.00
295 CS,JM,O:Lex Luthor 200.00
296 V:Super Ants 200.00
297 CS,JM,A:Mon-El 200.00
298 CS,JM,V:Lex Luthor 200.00
299 O:Superman Robots 200.00
300 JM,A:Mxyzptlk. 250.00
301 CS(c),JM,O:Superhorse 150.00
302 CS(c),JM,O:Superhorse 150.00
303 CS(c),Red Kryptonite story. . 150.00
304 CS,JM,I&O:Black Flame. . . . 175.00
305 CS(c),O:Supergirl 150.00
306 JM,C:Mon-El,Brainiac 5 . . . . 150.00
307 CS,JM,A:Saturn Girl 150.00
308 CS(c),V:Hercules 150.00
309 CS,A:Batman,JFK,Legion. . . 175.00
310 CS,JM,I:Jewel Kryptonite . . . 150.00

311 CS,JM,O:Superhorse	150.00
312 CS,JM,V:Metallo-Superman	150.00
313 JM,A:Supergirl,Lex,Batman	150.00
314 JM,A:Justice League	150.00
315 JM,V:Zigi,Zag	150.00
316 JM,A:Zigi,Zag,Zyra	150.00
317 JM,V:Lex Luthor	150.00
318 CS,JM,A:Brainiac	150.00
319 CS,JM,A:Legion,V:L.Luthor	150.00
320 CS,JM,V:Atlas,Hercules	150.00
321 CS,JM,A:Superhorse	150.00
322 JM,Coward of Steel	150.00
323 JM,A:Superhorse	150.00
324 JM,A:Abdul	150.00
325 CS,JM,SkyscraperSuperman	150.00
326 CS,JM,V:Legion of Super	
Creatures	150.00
327 CS,JM,C:Brainiac	150.00
328 JM,Hands of Doom	150.00
329 JM,V:Drang	150.00
330 CS,JM,Krypto	150.00
331 CS,V:Dr.Supernatural	150.00
332 CS,A:Brainiac	150.00
333 CS(c),A:Lex Luthor	150.00
334 JM(c),A:Lex Luthor,80pgs	150.00
335 CS,V:Lex Luthor	150.00
336 CS,O:Akvar	150.00
337 CS,V:Tiger Gang	150.00
338 CS,JM,V:Muto	150.00
339 CS,V:Muto,Brainiac	150.00
340 JM,I:Parasite	150.00
341 CS,V:Vakox,A:Batman	125.00
342 WB,JM,V:Brainiac	125.00
343 WB,V:Eterno	125.00
344 WB,JM,A:Batman	125.00
345 CS(c),A:Allen Funt	125.00
346 WB,JM	125.00
347 CS(c),A:Supergirl,80pgs	200.00
348 WB,JM,V:Acid Master	100.00
349 WB,JM,V:Dr.Kryptonite	100.00
350 A:JLA	100.00
351 WB,I:Zha-Vam	100.00
352 WB,V:Zha-Vam	100.00
353 WB,JM,V:Zha-Vam	100.00
354 JM,A:Captain Incredible	100.00
355 WB,JM,V:Lex Luthor	100.00
356 WB,JM,V:Jr. Annihilitor	100.00
357 WB,JM,V:Annihilitor	100.00
358 NA(c),CS,JM,A:Superboy	100.00
359 NA(c),CS,KS,C:Batman	100.00
360 CS(c),A:Supergirl,80pgs	150.00
361 NA(c),A:Parasite	75.00
362 RA,KS,V:Lex Luthor	75.00
363 RA,KS,V:Lex Luthor	75.00
364 RA,KS,V:Lex Luthor	75.00
365 A:Legion & J.L.A.	75.00
366 RA,KS,A:J.L.A.	75.00
367 NA(c),CS,KS,A:Supergirl	75.00
368 CS,KS,V:Mxyzptlk	75.00
369 CS,KS,Superman's Greatest	
Blunder	75.00
370 NA(c),CS,KS	75.00
371 NA(c),CS,KS	75.00
372 NA(c),CS,KS	75.00
373 A:Supergirl,(giant size)	150.00
374 NA(c),CS,KS,V:Super Thief	50.00
375 CS,KS,The Big Forget	50.00
376 CS,KS,E:Supergirl	50.00
377 CS,KS,B:Legion	50.00
378 CS,KS,V:Marauder	50.00
379 CS,JA,MA,V:Eliminator	50.00
380 KS,Confessions of Superman	50.00
381 CS,Dictators of Earth	50.00
382 CS,Clark Kent-Magician	40.00
383 CS,The Killer Costume	40.00
384 CS,The Forbidden Costume	40.00
385 CS,The Mortal Superman	40.00
386 CS,Home For Old Supermen	40.00
387 CS,A:Legion,Even	
Supermen Die	40.00
388 CS,A:Legion,Puzzle of	
The Wild Word	40.00

389 A:Legion,The Kid Who	
Struck Out Superman	40.00
390 CS,Self-Destruct Superman	40.00
391 CS,Punishment of	
Superman's Son	40.00
392 CS,E:Legion	40.00
393 CS,MA,RA,A:Super Houdini	40.00
394 CS,MA	40.00
395 CS,MA,A:Althera	40.00
396 CS,MA	40.00
397 CS,MA,Imaginary Story	40.00
398 NA(c),CS,MA,I:Morgan Edge	40.00
399 NA(c),CS,MA,A:Superbaby	40.00
400 NA(c),CS,MA,Kandor Story	60.00
401 CS,MA,V:Indians	40.00
402 NA(c),CS,MA,V:Indians	50.00
403 CS,MA,Vigilante rep	50.00
404 CS,MA,Aquaman rep	50.00
405 CS,MA,Vigilante rep	50.00
406 CS,MA,Atom & Flash rep.	50.00
407 CS,MA,V:Lex Luthor	50.00
408 CS,MA,Atom rep	50.00
409 CS,MA,T.Tommorrow rep.	50.00
410 CS,MA,T.Tommorrow rep.	50.00

Action Comics #423 © DC Comics Inc.

411 CS,MA,O:Eclipso rep	50.00
412 CS,MA,Eclipso rep	50.00
413 CS,MA,V:Brainiac	50.00
414 CS,MA,B:Metamorpho	25.00
415 CS,MA,V:Metroplis Monster	25.00
416 CS,MA	25.00
417 CS,MA,V:Luthor	25.00
418 CS,MA,V:Luthor,	
E:Metamorpho	25.00
419 CS,MA,CI,DG,I:HumanTarget	30.00
420 CS,MA,DG,V:Towbee	25.00
421 CS,MA,B:Green Arrow	25.00
422 CS,DG,O:Human Target	25.00
423 CS,MA,DG,A:Lex Luthor	25.00
424 CS,MA,Green Arrow	25.00
425 CS,DD,NA,DG,B:Atom	50.00
426 CS,MA,Green Arrow	20.00
427 CS,MA,DD,DG,Atom	20.00
428 CS,MA,DG,Luthor	20.00
429 CS,BO,DG,C:JLA	20.00
430 CS,MA,DD,DG,Atom	20.00
431 CS,MA,Green Arrow	20.00
432 CS,MA,DG,Toyman	22.00
433 CS,BO,DD,DG,A:Atom	20.00
434 CS,DD,Green Arrow	20.00
435 FM(c),CS,DD,DG,Atom	20.00
436 CS,DD,Green Arrow	20.00
437 CS,DG,Green Arrow,100-pg	60.00
438 CS,BO,DD,Atom	20.00
439 CS,BO,DD,Atom	20.00

440 1st MGr Green Arrow	30.00
441 CS,BO,MGr,A:Green Arrow,	
Flash,R:Krypto	20.00
442 CS,MS,MGr,Atom	20.00
443 CS,A:JLA(100 pg.giant)	75.00
444 MGr,Green Arrow	20.00
445 MGr,Green Arrow	20.00
446 MGr,Green Arrow	20.00
447 CS,BO,RB,KJ,Atom	20.00
448 CS,BO,DD,JL,Atom	20.00
449 CS,BO,The Super-spy	30.00
450 MGr,Green Arrow	20.00
451 MGr,Green Arrow	15.00
452 CS,MGr,Green Arrow	15.00
453 CS,Atom	15.00
454 CS,E:Atom	15.00
455 CS,Green Arrow	15.00
456 CS,MGr,Green Arrow	15.00
457 CS,MGr,Green Arrow	15.00
458 CS,MGr,I:Black Rock	15.00
459 CS,BO,Blackrock	15.00
460 CS,I:Karb-Brak	15.00
461 CS,V:Karb-Brak	15.00
462 CS,V:Karb-Brak	15.00
463 CS,V:Karb-Brak	15.00
464 CS,KS,V:Pile-Driver	15.00
465 CS,FMc,Luthor	15.00
466 NA(c),CS,V:Luthor	15.00
467 CS,V:Mzyzptlk	15.00
468 NA(c),CS,FMc,V:Terra-Man	15.00
469 CS,TerraMan	15.00
470 CS,Flash Green Lantern	15.00
471 CS,V:Phantom Zone Female	15.00
472 CS,V:Faora Hu-Ul	15.00
473 NA(c),CS,Phantom Zone	
Villians	15.00
474 KS,V:Doctor Light	15.00
475 KS,V:Karb-Brak,A:Vartox	15.00
476 KS,V:Vartox	15.00
477 CS,DD,Land Lords of Earth	15.00
478 CS,Earth's Last	15.00
479 CS,Giant from Golden Atom	15.00
480 CS,A:JLA,V:Amazo	15.00
481 CS,A:JLA,V:Amazo	15.00
482 CS,Amazo	15.00
483 CS,Amazo,JLA	15.00
484 CS,W:Earth 2 Superman	
& Lois Lane	20.00
485 NA(c),CS,rep.Superman#233	18.00
486 GT,KS,V:Lex Luthor	15.00
487 CS,AS,O:Atom	15.00
488 CS,AS,A:Air Wave	15.00
489 CS,AS,A:JLA,Atom	15.00
490 CS,Brainiac	15.00
491 CS,A:Hawkman	15.00
492 CS,Superman's After Life	15.00
493 CS,A:UFO	15.00
494 CS,Secret of the Super-S	15.00
495 CS, Attack of Ultimate Warrior	15.00
496 CS,A:Kandor	15.00
497 CS,Command Performance	15.00
498 CS,Vartox	15.00
499 CS,Vartox	15.00
500 CS,Superman's Life Story	
A:Legion	18.00
501 KS,Mild-Mannered Superman	7.00
502 CS,A:Supergirl,Gal.Golem	7.00
503 CS,A Save in Time	7.00
504 CS,The Power and Choice	7.00
505 CS,Creature that Charmed Kids	7.00
506 CS,V:Jorlan,Jor-El	7.00
507 CS,A:Jonathan Kent	7.00
508 CS,A:Jonathan Kent	7.00
509 CS,JSn,DG	7.00
510 CS,Luthor	7.00
511 CS,AS,V:Terraman,	
A:Air Wave	7.00
512 CS,RT,V:Luthor,A:Air Wave	7.00
513 CS,RT,V:Krell,A:Air Wave	7.00
514 CS,RT,V:Brainiac,A:Atom	7.00
515 CS,AS,A:Atom	7.00
516 CS,AS,V:Luthor,A:Atom	7.00

All comics prices listed are for *Near Mint* condition.

Action Comics #507 © DC Comics, Inc.

Action Comics #677 © DC Comics, Inc.

561 KS,WB,Toyman 7.00
562 KS,Queen Bee 7.00
563 AS,KG,BO,A:Ambush Bug 7.00
564 AS,V:Master Jailer 7.00
565 KG,KS,BO,A:Ambush Bug 7.00
566 BO(i),MR 7.00
567 KS,AS,PB 7.00
568 CS,AW,AN 7.00
569 IN,The Force of Revenge 7.00
570 KS, Jimmy Olsen's Alter-Ego . . 7.00
571 BB(c),AS,A:Thresh 222 . . . . . . 7.00
572 WB,BO 7.00
573 KS,BO,AS 7.00
574 KS 7.00
575 KS,V:Intellax 7.00
576 KS,Earth's Sister Planet 7.00
577 KG,BO,V:Caitiff 7.00
578 KS,Parasite 7.00
579 KG,BO,Asterix Parody 7.00
580 GK(c),KS,Superman's Failure . 7.00
581 DCw(c),KS,Superman
    Requires Legal aid 7.00
582 AS,KS,Superman's Parents
    Alive 7.00
583 CS,KS,AMo(s),Last Pre
    Crisis Superman 15.00
584 JBy,DG,A:NewTeenTitans,
    I:Modern Age Superman. 8.00
585 JBy,DG,Phantom Stranger 7.00
586 JBy,DG,Legends,V:New
    Gods,Darkseid 7.00
587 JBy,DG,Demon 7.00
588 JBy,DG,Hawkman 7.00
589 JBy,DG,Gr.Lant.Corp. 7.00
590 JBy,DG,Metal Men 7.00
591 JBy,V:Superboy,A:Legion 7.00
592 JBy,Big Barda 7.00
593 JBy,Mr. Miracle 7.00
594 JBy,A:Booster Gold 7.00
595 JBy,A:M.Manhunter,
    I:Silver Banshee 8.00
596 JBy,A:Spectre,Millenium 8.00
597 JBy,L.Starr(i),Lois V:Lana 8.00
598 JBy,TyT,I:Checkmate 9.00
599 RA,JBy(i),A:MetalMen,
    Bonus Book 8.00
600 JBy,GP,KS,JOy,DG,CS,MA,
    MMi,A:Wonder Woman;
    Man-Bat,V:Darkseid 10.00

Becomes:

ACTION WEEKLY
1988–89

601 GK,DSp,CS,DJu,TD, B:Superman,
    Gr.Lantern,Blackhawk,Deadman,
    Secret Six,Wilddog 3.50
602 GP(c),GK,DSp,CS,DJu,TD . . . 3.50
603 GK,CS,DsP,DJu,TD 3.50
604 GK,DSp,CS,DJu,TD 3.50
605 NKu/AKu(c),GK,DSp,CS,
    DJu,TD 3.50
606 DSp,CS,DJu,TD 3.50
607 SLi(c),TD,DSp,CS,DJu 3.50
608 DSp,CS,DJu,TD,E:Blackhawk . 3.50
609 BB(c),DSp,DJu,TD,CS,
    E:Wild Dog,B:Black Canary. . . . 3.50
610 KB,DJu,CS,DSp,TD,CS
    A:Phantom Stranger 3.50
611 AN(c),DJu,DSp,CS,BKi,TD,
    BKi,B:Catwoman 3.75
612 PG(c),DSp,CS,BKi,TD,
    E:Secret Six,Deadman 3.50
613 MK(c),BKi,CS,MA,TGr,
    Nightwing,B:Phantom Stranger . 3.50
614 TG,CS,Phantom Stranger
    E:Catwoman 3.50
615 MMi(c),CS,MA,BKi,TGr,
    Blackhawk,B:Wild Dog 3.50
616 ATh(c),CS,MA,E:Bl.Canary . . . 3.50
617 CS,MA,JO,A:Ph.Stranger 3.50
618 JBg(c),CS,MA,JKo,TD,
    B:Deadman,E:Nightwing 3.50

517 CS,DH,A:Aquaman 7.00
518 CS,DH,A:Aquaman 7.00
519 CS,DH,A:Aquaman 7.00
520 CS,DH,A:Aquaman 7.00
521 CS,AS,I:Vixen,A:Atom 7.00
522 CS,AS,A:Atom 7.00
523 CS,AS,A:Atom 7.00
524 CS,AS,A:Atom 7.00
525 JSon,FMc,AS,I:Neutron
    A:Air Wave 7.00
526 JSon,AS,V:Neutron 7.00
527 CS,AS,I:Satanis,A:Aquaman . . 9.00
528 CS,AS,V:Brainiac,A:Aquaman . 7.00
529 GP(c),CS,DA,AS,A:Aquaman,
    V:Brainiac 7.00
530 CS,DA,Brainiac 7.00
531 JSon,FMc,AS,A:Atom 7.00
532 CS,C:New Teen Titans 7.00
533 CS,V:H.I.V.E. 7.00
534 CS,AS,V:Satanis,A:Air Wave . . 7.00
535 GK(c),JSon,AS,
    A:Omega Men 7.00
536 JSon,AS,FMc,A:Omega Men . . 7.00
537 IN,CS,AS,V:Satanis
    A:Aquaman 7.00
538 IN,AS,FMc,V:Satanis,
    A:Aquaman 7.00
539 KG(c),GK,AS,DA,A:Flash,
    Atom,Aquaman 7.00
540 GK,AS,V:Satanis 7.00
541 GK,V:Satanis. 7.00
542 AS,V:Vandal Savage 7.00
543 CS,V:Vandal Savage 7.00
544 CS,MA,GK,GP,45th Anniv.
    D:Ardora,Lexor 10.00
545 GK,Brainiac. 7.00
546 GK,A:JLA,New Teen Titans . . . 7.00
547 GK(c),CS,V:Planeteer 7.00
548 GK(c),AS,Phantom Zone 7.00
549 GK(c),AS,Meets Zod Squad . . 7.00
550 AS(c),GT,Day Earth Exploded . 7.00
551 GK,Starfire becomes
    Red Star 7.00
552 GK,Forgotten Heroes
    (inc.Animal Man) 12.00
553 GK,Forgotten Heroes(inc.
    Animal Man) 12.00
554 GK(a&c) 7.00
555 CS,A:Parasite (X-over
    Supergirl #20) 7.00
556 CS,KS,C:Batman 7.00
557 CS,Terra-man 7.00
558 KS,All-Searing Eyes 7.00
559 KS,AS,Once & Future Peril . . . 7.00
560 AS,KG,BO,A:Ambush Bug 7.00

619 CS,MA,FS,FMc,KJo,TD,FMc,
    B:Sinister Six. 3.50
620 CS,MA,FS,FMc,KJo,TD 3.50
621 JO(c),CS,MA,FS,FMc,KJo,
    TD,MBr,E:Deadman 3.50
622 RF(c),MBr,TL,CS,MA,FS,
    FMc,A:Starman,E:Wild
    Dog,Blackhawk 3.50
623 MBr,TD,CS,MA,FS,FMc,JL,
    JKo,A:Ph.Stranger,
    B:Deadman,Shazam 3.50
624 AD(c),MBr,FS,FMc,CS,MA,
    TD,B:Black Canary 3.50
625 MBr,FS,FMc,CS,MA,
    TD,FMc 3.50
626 MBr,FS,FMc,CS,MA,JKo,TD,
    E:Shazam,Deadman 3.50
627 GK(c),MBr,RT,FS,FMc,CS,
    MA,TMd,B:Nightwing,Speedy . 3.50
628 TY(c),MBr,RT,TMd,CS,MA,
    FS,FMc,B:Blackhawk 3.50
629 CS,MA,MBr,RT,FS,FMc,TMd . 3.50
630 CS,MA,MBr,RT,FS,FMc,TMd,
    E:Secret Six. 3.50
631 JS(c),CS,MA,MBr,RT,TMd,
    B:Phantom Stranger 3.50
632 TGr(c),CS,MA,MBr,RT,TMd . . 3.50
633 CS,MA,MBr,RT,TMd 3.50
634 CS,MA,MBr,RT,TMd,E:Ph.Strangr,
    Nightwing/Speedy,Bl.hawk 3.50
635 CS,MA,MBr,RT,EB,E:Black
    Canary,Green Lantern 3.50
636 DG(c),CS,MA,NKu,MPa,FMc,
    B:Demon,Wild Dog,Ph.Lady,
    Speedy,A:Phantom Stranger . . . 3.50
637 CS,MA,KS,FMc,MPa,
    B:Hero Hotline 3.50
638 JK(c),CS,MA,KS,FMc,MPa . . . 3.50
639 CS,MA,KS,FMc,MPa 3.50
640 CS,KS,MA,FS,FMc,MPa,
    E:Speedy,Hero Hotline 3.50
641 CS,MA,JL,DG,MPa,E:Demon,
    Phant.Lady,Superman,Wild Dog,
    A:Ph.Stranger,Hum.Target. 3.50
642 GK,SD,ATi,CS,JAp,JM,CI,KN,
    Green Lantern,Superman 3.50

Becomes:

ACTION COMICS
1989–2005

643 B:RSt(s),GP,BBr,V:Intergang . . 4.50
644 GP,BBr,V:Matrix 3.50
645 GP,BBr,I:Maxima 3.50
646 KG,V:Alien Creature,
    A:Brainiac 4.00

647 GP,KGa,BBr,V:Brainiac. 3.50	702 JG,DvM,B:DyM(s),R:Bloodsport 3.00	744 SI,JMz,Millennium Giants
648 GP,KGa,BBr,V:Brainiac. 3.50	703 JG,DvM,Zero Hour 3.00	x-over. 3.00
649 GP,KGa,BBr,V:Brainiac. 3.50	704 JG,DvM,Eradicator 3.00	745 SI,JMz,The Prankster 3.00
650 JOy,BBr,CS,BMc,GP,KGa,	705 JG,DvM,Supes real?. 3.00	746 SI,JMz,The Prankster,pt.2 . . 3.00
ATi,DJu,A:JLA,C:Lobo. 5.50	706 JG,DvM,A:Supergirl. 3.00	747 SI,JMz,The Prankster,pt.3 . . . 3.00
651 GP,KGa,BBr,Day of Krypton	707 JG,DvM,V:Shado Dragon 3.00	748 SI,JMz,Dominus Theory 3.00
Man #3,V:Maxima 3.50	708 JG,DvM,R:Deathtrap. 3.00	749 RMz(s),TGb,TP,City of the
652 GP,KGa,BBr,Day of Krypton	709 JG,DvM,A:Guy Gardner,	Future, pt.1 x-over. 3.00
Man #6,V:Eradicator 5.00	Warrior 3.00	750 SI,JMz,I:Crazytop, 48-page . . 3.50
653 BMc,BBr,D:Amanda 3.50	710 JG,DvM,Death of Clark Kent,pt.3	751 SI,JMz,A:Geo-Force 3.00
654 BMc,BBr,A:Batman Pt.3 . . . . . 3.50	[new Miraweb format begins] . . 3.00	752 SI,JMz,Supermen of
655 BMc,BBr,V:Morrisson,Ma	711 JG,DvM,Death of Clark	America x-over 3.00
Kent's Photo Album. 3.50	Kent,pt.7 . . . . 3.00	753 SI,JMz,A:JLA 3.00
656 BMc,BBr,Soul Search #1,	712 Rescue Jimmy Olsen 3.00	754 SI,JMz,R:Dominus,
V:Blaze 3.50	713 Scarlet Salvation. 3.00	A:Wonder Woman. 3.00
657 KGa,BBr,V:Toyman. 3.50	714 R:The Joker 3.00	755 SI&MMr(s),King of the
658 CS,Sinbad Contract #3. . . . . . 3.50	715 DvM,DaR,V:Parasite. 3.00	World aftermath. 3.00
659 BMc,BBr,K.Krimson	716 DvM,DaR,Trial of Superman. . . 3.00	756 VGi,old villain is back 3.00
Kryptonite #3 . . . . 5.00	717 DvM,DaR,Trial of Superman. . . 3.00	757 TPe(s),TGb,Hawkworld,pt.3 . . 3.00
660 BMc,BBr,D:Lex Luthor 4.50	718 DvM,DRo,mystery of Demolitia. 3.00	758 SI,JMz,V:Boss Moxie 3.00
661 BMc,BBr,A:Plastic Man. 3.50	719 DvM,DRo 3.00	759 RF,SB,Strange Visitor,pt.3 . . . 3.00
662 JOy,JM,TG,BMc,V:Silver	720 DvM,DRo,Lois ends	760 JRu,F:Encantadora. 3.00
Banshee,Clark tells	engagement. 3.50	761 JRu 3.00
Lois his identity 5.00	721 DvM,DRo,lottery fever 3.00	762 JRu,V:Demon Etrigan. 3.00
662a 2nd printing 5.00	722 DvM,DaR,Tornados in	763 JRu,V:Brainiac 13 . . . . 3.00
663 BMc,Time & Time Again pt.2,	Smallville 3.00	764 JRu,marital troubles 3.00
A:JSA,Legion. 3.50	723 V:Brainiac 3.00	765 JRu,V:Joker & Harley Quinn. . . 3.00
664 BMc,Time & Time Again,pt.5 . . 3.50	724 V:S.T.A.R.labs monster. 3.00	766 F:Batman 3.00
665 TG,V:Baron Sunday 3.50	725 Tolos 3.00	767 CriticalCondition,pt.4,x-over . . 3.00
666 FH,Red Glass Trilogy,pt.3. . . . 3.50	726 DvM(s),TMo,DRo,Krisis of the	768 F:Marvel Family 3.00
667 JOy,JM,TG,ATi,DJu,Revenge	Krimson Kryptonite follow-up. . . 3.00	769 Superman:Arkham,concl. 4.00
of the Krypton Man,pt.4 . . . . . . 3.75	727 DvM(s),TMo,DRo,brutal weather	770 Superman:Emperor,48-pg. 4.50
668 BMc,Luthor confirmed dead . . . 3.50	in Metropolis, Final Night tie-in . 3.00	771 CDi(s),F:Nightwing 2.50
669 BMc,V:Intergang,A:Thorn 3.50	728 DvM(s),TG,DRo, Some	772 V:Ra's al Ghul,pt.1 . . . . 2.50
670 BMc,A:Waverider,JLA,JLE . . . 3.50	Honeymoon! 3.00	773 V:Ra's al Ghul,pt.2 . . . . 2.50
671 KD,Blackout,pt.2 . . . . 3.50	729 DvM(s),TG,DRo, in Fortress of	774 A:Martian Manhunter 2.50
672 BMc,Superman Meets Lex	Solitude 3.00	775 48-page. 12.00
Luthor II 3.50	730 DvM(s),TG,Ro. 3.00	775a 2nd printing (2004) 4.50
673 BMc,V:Hellgramite 3.50	731 DvM(s),TG,DRo, R:Cauldron . . 3.00	776 Return to Krypton,pt.4. . . . . . . 2.50
674 BMc,Panic in the Sky (Prologue)	732 DvM(s),TG,DRo, Atomic Skull	777 Kancer. 2.50
R:Supergirl(Matrix) 6.00	rampages through Metropolis . . 3.00	778 MWm,Infestation x-over,pt.4 . . 2.50
675 BMc,Panic in the Sky #4,	733 DvM(s),TG,DRo, V:Matallo,	779 V:Killer,pt.1 . . . . 2.50
V:Brainiac 4.00	A:Ray. 3.00	780 V:Killer,pt.2 . . . . 2.50
676 B:KK(s),JG,A:Supergirl,Lex	734 DvM(s),TG,DRo, Superman &	781 Our Worlds at War,All-OutWar . 2.50
Luthor II 3.50	Atom in Kandor 3.00	782 Our Worlds at War,Casualties . 2.50
677 JG,Supergirl V:Superman 3.50	735 DvM(s),TG,DRo, V:Savior. 3.00	783 V:Ocean Master,Scorch 2.50
678 JG,O:Lex Luthor II 3.50	736 DvM(s),TG,DRo. 3.00	784 Joker:Last Laugh tie-in 2.50
679 JG,I:Shellshock 3.50	737 MWa(s),TG,DRo, Luthor gets	785 R:Bizarro. 2.50
680 JG,Blaze/Satanus War,pt.2 . . . 3.50	day in court 3.00	786 PFe,kidnapped by aliens 2.50
681 JG,V:Hellgramite 3.50	738 SI,JMz,Lois sent to Australia . . 3.00	787 PFe,Byakko, Gunshin, Sakki . . 2.50
682 DAb,TA,V:Hi-Tech 3.50	739 SI,JMz,Superman imprisoned. . 3.00	788 PFe,Jikei Ketsuki,pt.1 . . . . 2.50
683 JG,I:Jackal,C:Doomsday. 5.00	740 SI,JMz,Lucy Lane disappears. . 3.00	789 Evil from the Gorge. 2.50
683a 2nd printing 4.00	741 SI,JMz,V:C.O.M.P.U.T.O. 3.00	790 Krypto vs. Kancer 2.50
684 JG,Doomsday Pt.4. . . . . 5.00	742 SI,JMz. 3.00	791 Smallville, flash-back tale 2.50
684a 2nd printing 4.00	743 SI,JMz,F:Slam Bradley 3.00	792 Superman, detective. 2.50
685 JG,Funeral for a Friend#2. . . . 3.50		793 PFe,Return to KryptonII,concl. . 2.50
686 JG,Funeral for a Friend#6. . . . 3.50		794 F:Quintescence. 2.50
687 JG,Reign of Superman #1,Direct		795 Ending Battle,pt.4 . . . . 2.50
Sales,Die-Cut(c),Mini-Poster,		796 Ending Battle,pt.8 . . . . 2.50
F:Last Son of Krypton 3.00		797 New General Zod 2.50
687a newsstand Ed. 3.00		798 Lost Hearts, pt.4 x-over 2.50
688 JG,V:Guy Gardner. 3.00		799 TR,SHa,F:Girl 13 . . . . 2.50
689 JG,V:Man of Steel,A:Superboy,		800 64-page, life re-examined. 4.50
Supergirl,R:Real Superman . . . 3.50		801 metahumans 2.50
690 JG,Cyborg Vs. Superboy 3.00		802 PFe,CaS,The Harvest,pt.1 . . . . 2.50
691 JG,A:All Supermen,V:Cyborg		803 PFe,CaS,The Harvest,pt.2 . . . . 2.50
Superman,Mongul. 3.00		804 PFe,CaS,The Harvest,pt.3 . . . . 2.50
692 JG,A:Superboy,Man of Steel . . 3.00		805 PFe,CaS,The Harvest,pt.4 . . . . 2.50
693 JG,A:Last Son of Krypton 3.00		806 PFe,CaS,The Harvest,pt.5 . . . . 2.50
694 JG,Spilled Blood#2,V:Hi-Tech . 3.00		807 PFe,CaS,Supergirls 2.50
695 JG,Foil(c),I:Cauldron,A:Lobo. . 3.50		808 PFe,CaS,Supergirls 2.50
695a Newsstand Ed. 3.00		809 PFe,CaS,murder suspect 2.50
696 JG,V:Alien,C:Doomsday 3.00		810 PFe,CaS,New Year's 2.25
697 JG,Bizarro's World #3,		811 KlK,Strange New Visitor 3.00
V:Bizarro. 3.00		812 Godfall,pt.1 . . . . 5.00
698 JG,A:Lex Luthor 3.00		812a 2nd printing. 4.50
699 JG,A:Project Cadmus 3.00		813 Godfall,pt.4 . . . . 4.00
700 JG,Fall of Metropolis#1 . . . . . . 4.00		814 MCa,Job in jeopardy. 2.50
700a Platinum Edition 15.00		815 MCa,V:Gog 2.50
700b Gold Edition 17.00		816 MCa,F:Teen Titans 2.50
701 JG,Fall of Metropolis#5,	*Action Comics #739 © DC Comics Inc.*	817 MCa,F:W.Woman & Superboy . 2.50
V:Luthor. 3.00		818 MCa,F:W.Woman & Superboy . 2.50

819 MCa,I:Sodom & Gomorrah 2.50
820 V:Silver Banshee 2.50
821 LRs,MCa,F:Preus 2.50
822 MCa,F:Superboy 2.50
823 MCa,F:Superboy, Krypto 2.50
824 MCa,V:Preus 2.50
825 MCa,Villains unite,40-page 3.00
826 IaC,NRd,F:Captain Marvel 2.50
827 JBy,Nel,F:Dr.Polaris,V:Repulse. 3.00
828 JBy,Nel,V:Repulse 3.00
829 JPfe,Nel,Sacrifice, x-over,pt.2 . . 5.00
829a JBy,Nel,Sacrifice, 2nd editon . 3.00
830 JBy,Nel,Villains United tie-in . . . 2.50
831 JBy,Nel,Villains United tie-in . . . 2.50
832 JBy,Nel,F:Spectre, Satanus . . . 2.50
833 JBy,Nel,F:Queen of Fables. . . . 2.50
834 JBy,Nel,F:Queen of Fables 2.50
835 JBy,Nel,I:Livewire 2.50
836 EBe,DJu,This is your life,
      Superman 2.50
837 KBk,Up,Up & Away,pt.2,x-over. 2.50
838 KBk,Up,Up & Away,pt.4,x-over. 2.50
839 KBk,Up,Up & Away,pt.6,x-over . 3.00
840 KBk,Up,Up & Away,pt.8,x-over . 3.00
841 A:Teen Titans, Nightwing 3.00
842 A:Nightwing, Firestorm 3.00
843 A:Teen Titans 3.00
844 AKu, Last Son, pt.1 . . . . 4.00
844a 2nd printing 5.00
845 AKu, Bizarro returns 3.00
846 AKu,Last Son, pt.3 . . . . 3.00
847 AKu,Last Son, pt.4 . . . . 3.00
847a part in 3-D, inc. glasses 4.00
848 FaN(s) 3.00
849 FaN(s) 3.00
850 KBk(s), F:Supergirl, 48-pgs. . . . 4.50
851 AKu,Last Son, pt.4 . . . . 3.00
851a part in 3-D, inc. glasses 4.00
852 3-2-1 Action, pt.1 . . . . 3.00
853 KBk(s), Countdown tie-in 3.00
854 KBk(s), Countdown tie-in 3.00
855 Escape from Bizarro World,pt.1 3.00
856 Escape from Bizarro World,pt.2 3.00
857 Escape from Bizarro World,pt.3 3.00
858 GFr,Superman, original Legion. 3.50
859 GFr, Return of original Legion . 3.00
859a variant NKu(c) (1:10) 9.00
860 GFr,Return of original Legion . . 3.00
860a variant (c) (1:10) 9.00
861 GFr,Return of original Legion . . 7.00
862 GFr,Return of original Legion . . 7.00
863 GFr,Return of original Legion . . 3.00
863a variant GFr(c) (1:10) 7.00
864 GFr,Life as Clark Kent 3.00
865 F:Toyman 3.00
866 GFr,Brainiac, pt.1 . . . . 3.00
867 GFr,Brainiac, pt.2 . . . . 3.00
868 GFr,Brainiac, pt.3 . . . . 3.00
869 GFr,Brainiac, pt.4 . . . . 3.00
870 GFr,Brainiac, pt.5 . . . . 3.00
871 New Krypton, pt.4, x-over 3.00
870a thru 871a variant (c) (1:10) . @3.00
Ann.#1 AAd,DG,A:Batman 8.00
Ann.#2 MMi,CS,GP,JOy,DJu,BBr,
      V:Mongul 4.00
Ann.#3 TG,Armageddon X-over. . . 3.50
Ann.#4 Eclipso,A:Captain Marvel . 3.50
Ann.#5 MZ(c),Bloodlines, I:Loose
      Cannon 3.50
Ann.#6 Elseworlds,JBy(a&S) 3.50
Ann.#7 Year One Annual 4.50
Ann.#8 DvM,Legends of the Dead
      Earth 3.50
Ann.#9 DvM,VGi,BBr,Pulp Heroes . 4.50
Ann. #10 . . . . 4.00
Ann. #10a variant (c) (1:10). 4.00
Ann. #11 Last Son, concl. (2008) . . 6.00
Ann. #11a variant (c) (1:10) 10.00
Gold.Ann.rep.#1 . . . . 2.50
#0 Peer Pressure,pt.4 (1994) 2.50
Spec.#1,000,000 MSh(s),RLm,JMz. 2.50

ADAM STRANGE
1990
1 NKu,A.Strange on Rann 5.00
2 NKu,Wanted:Adam Strange. 4.00
3 NKu,final issue. 4.00

2nd Series, Sept. 2004
1 (of 8) PFe,R:Adam Strange 3.00
2 PFe 3.00
3 PFe 3.00
4 PFe, F:The Omega Man 3.00
5 PFe,V:L.E.G.I.O.N 3.00
6 PFe,Planet Rann 3.00
7 PFe,Planet Rann, Darkstars 3.00
8 PFe,concl. 3.00

Sept., 2008
Spec. #1 JSn,Holy War tie-in 3.50

Advanced Dungeons & Dragons #1
© DC Comics, Inc.

ADVANCED DUNGEONS & DRAGONS
1988–91
1 JD,I:Onyx,Priam,Timoth,
      Cybriana,Vajra,Luna 5.00
2 JD,V:Imgig Zu,I:Conner 4.00
3 JD,V:Imgig Zu 4.00
4 JD,V:Imgig Zu,I:Kyriani 3.00
5 JD,Spirit of Myrrth I 3.00
6 JD,Spirit of Myrrth II 3.00
7 thru 24 JD . . . . @2.50
25 thru 36 JD . . . . @2.50
Ann.#1 JD,RM,Tmd 4.00

ADVENTURE COMICS
Nov., 1938–83
[Prev: New Adventure Comics]
32 CF(c),S&S 5,000.00
33 CF(c),FGu,S&S,BKa 2,800.00
34 FGu(c),S&S,BKa 2,800.00
35 FGu(c),SMo,S&S,BKa 2,800.00
36 CF,Giant Snake(c),S&S 2,800.00
37 CF,Rampaging Elephant(c) . 2,800.00
38 CF,Tiger(c),S&S 2,800.00
39 CF,Male Bondage(c),S&S . . 2,500.00
40 CF(c),1st app. Sandman . 100,000.00
41 CF,Killer Shark(c),S&S. . . . 14,000.00
42 CF,Sandman(c) 18,000.00
43 CF&FGu(c),WB 6,500.00
44 CF,FGu,Sandman(c) 16,000.00
45 FGu(c),CF,BKa. 6,500.00
46 CF,Sandman(c) 12,000.00
47 CF,Sandman (c). 12,000.00

48 1st app.& B:Hourman 50,000.00
49 SMo(c),BKa,CF 5,000.00
50 BBa,Hourman(c) 5,000.00
51 BBa(c),Sandman(c) 6,500.00
52 BBa(c),Hourman(c) 5,000.00
53 BBa(c),1st app. Minuteman . 5,000.00
54 BBa(c),Hourman(c) 5,000.00
55 BBa(c),Hourman(c) 5,000.00
56 BBa(c),Hourman(c) 5,000.00
57 BBa(c),Hourman(c) 5,000.00
58 BBa(c),Hourman(c) 5,000.00
59 BBa(c),Hourman(c) 5,000.00
60 CF,Sandman(c) 7,000.00
61 CF(c),JBu,Starman(c) 25,000.00
62 JBu(c),JBu,Starman(c). 5,000.00
63 JBu(c),JBu,Starman(c). 4,000.00
64 JBu(c),JBu,Starman(c). 4,000.00
65 JBu(c),JBu,Starman(c). 4,000.00
66 JBu(c),JBu,O:Shining Knight,
      Starman(c) 5,000.00
67 JBu(c),JBu,O:Mist 4,000.00
68 JBu(c),JBu,same 4,000.00
69 JBu(c),JBu,1st app. Sandy,
      Starman(c) 4,000.00
70 JBu(c),JBu,Starman(c). 4,000.00
71 JBu(c),JBu,same 4,000.00
72 JBu(c),S&K,JBu,Sandman. 22,000.00
73 S&K(c),S&K,I:Manhunter . . 28,000.00
74 S&K(c),S&K,You Can't Escape
      Your Fate-The Sandman . . 3,800.00
75 S&K(c),S&K,Sandman and
      Sandy Battle Thor. 3,800.00
76 S&K(c),Sandman(c),S&K. . 3,800.00
77 S&K,(c),S&K,same. 3,800.00
78 S&K(c),S&K,same 3,800.00
79 S&K(c),S&K,Manhunter 5,000.00
80 S&K(c),Sandman(c),S&K. . 3,800.00
81 S&K(c),MMe,S&K,same. . . 2,500.00
82 S&K(c),S&K,Sandman
      X-Mas story 2,500.00
83 S&K(c),S&K,Sandman
      Boxing(c),E:Hourman 2,500.00
84 S&K(c),S&K 2,500.00
85 S&K(c),S&K,Sandman in
      The Amazing Dreams of
      Gentleman Jack 2,500.00
86 S&K(c),Sandman(c). 2,500.00
87 S&K(c),Sandman(c). 2,500.00
88 S&K(c),Sandman(c). 2,500.00
89 S&K(c),Sandman(c). 2,500.00
90 S&K(c),Sandman(c). 2,500.00
91 S&K(c),JK 2,500.00
92 S&K(c) 1,600.00
93 S&K(c),Sandman in Sleep
      for Sale 1,600.00
94 S&K(c),Sandman(c). 1,600.00
95 S&K(c),Sandman(c). 1,600.00
96 S&K(c),Sandman(c). 1,600.00
97 S&K(c),Sandman(c). 1,600.00
98 JK(c),Sandman in Hero
      of Dreams 1,600.00
99 GK,Sandman(c) 1,600.00
100 JK(c&a) 2,000.00
101 S&K(c) 1,600.00
102 S&K(c) 1,600.00
103 B:Superboy stories,(c),BU:
      Johnny Quick,Aquaman,Shining
      Knight,Green Arrow 5,000.00
104 S&S,ToyTown USA 1,900.00
105 S&S,Palace of Fantasy . . . 1,400.00
106 S&S,Weather Hurricane . . 1,400.00
107 S&S,The Sky is the Limit. . 1,400.00
108 S&S,Proof of the Proverbs 1,400.00
109 S&S,You Can't Lose 1,400.00
110 S&S,The Farmer Takes
      it Easy. 1,400.00
111 S&S,The Whiz Quiz Club . 1,400.00
112 S&S,Super Safety First . . . 1,400.00
113 S&S,The 33rd Christmas . . 1,200.00
114 S&S,Superboy Spells
      Danger 1,200.00

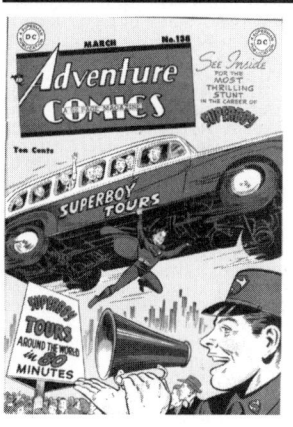

Adventure Comics #138
© *DC Comics, Inc.*

115 S&S,The Adventure of
   Jaguar Boy 1,200.00
116 S&S,JBu,Superboy Toy
   Tester 1,200.00
117 S&S,JBu,Miracle Plane . . . 1,200.00
118 S&S,JBu,The Quiz Biz
   Broadcast 1,200.00
119 WMo,JBu,Superboy
   Meets Girls 1,200.00
120 S&S,JBu,A:Perry White;
   I:Ringmaster 1,300.00
121 S&S,Great Hobby Contest. 1,300.00
122 S&S,Superboy-Super-
   Magician 1,400.00
123 S&S,Lesson For a bully. . . 1,300.00
124 S&S,Barbed Wire Boys
   Town 1,000.00
125 S&S,The Weight Before
   Christmas 1,000.00
126 S&S,Superboy:Crime
   Fighting Poet 1,000.00
127 MMe,O:Shining Knight;
   Super Bellboy 1,000.00
128 WMo,How Clark Kent Met
   Lois Lane 1,000.00
129 WMo,Pupils of the Past . . . 1,000.00
130 WMo,Superboy Super
   Salesman 1,000.00
131 WMo,The Million Dollar
   Athlete 1,000.00
132 WMo,Superboy Super
   Cowboy. 1,000.00
133 WMo,Superboy's Report
   Card 1,000.00
134 WMo,Silver Gloves Sellout 1,000.00
135 WMo,The Most Amazing
   of All Boys 900.00
136 WMo,My Pal Superboy 900.00
137 WMo,Treasure of Tondimo . 900.00
138 WMo,Around the World in
   Eighty Minutes. 900.00
139 WMo,Telegraph Boy 900.00
140 Journey to the Moon. 900.00
141 WMo,When Superboy Lost
   His Powers 900.00
142 WMo,The Man Who Walked
   With Trouble 900.00
143 WMo,Superboy Savings Bank,
   A:Wooden Head Jones 900.00
144 WMo,The Way to Stop
   Superboy. 900.00
145 WMo,Holiday Hijackers. 900.00
146 The Substitute Superboy . . . 900.00
147 Clark Kent,Orphan 900.00
148 Superboy Meets Mummies . . 900.00
149 Fake Superboys 900.00

150 FF,Superboy's Initiation . . . 1,100.00
151 FF,No Hunting(c). 900.00
152 Superboy Hunts For a Job . . 800.00
153 FF,Clark Kent,Boy Hobo. . . . 900.00
154 The Carnival Boat Crimes . . 800.00
155 FF,Superboy-Hollywood
   Actor 900.00
156 The Flying Peril. 800.00
157 FF,The Worst Boy in
   Smallville 900.00
158 The Impossible Task. 800.00
159 FF,Superboy Millionaire? . . . 900.00
160 Superboy's Phoney Father . . 750.00
161 FF. 1,000.00
162 Super-Coach of
   Smallville High! 900.00
163 FF,Superboy's Phoney
   Father 1,000.00
164 Discovers the Secret of
   a Lost Indian Tribe! 900.00
165 Superboy's School for
   Stunt Men! 900.00
166 Town That Stole Superboy . 900.00
167 Lana Lang, Super-Girl! . . . 1,000.00
168 The Boy Who Out Smarted
   Superboy 900.00
169 Clark Kent's Private Butler . . 900.00
170 Lana Lang's Big Crush 750.00
171 Superboy's Toughest Tasks . 750.00
172 Laws that Backfired 750.00
173 Superboy's School of
   Hard Knocks 750.00
174 The New Lana Lang! 750.00
175 Duel of the Superboys 750.00
176 Superboy's New Parents! . . . 750.00
177 Hot-Rod Chariot Race! 750.00
178 Boy in the Lead Mask. 750.00
179 World's Whackiest
   Inventors 750.00
180 Grand Prize o/t Underworld . 750.00
181 Mask for a Hero 750.00
182 Super Hick from Smallville . . 650.00
183 Superboy and Cleopatra. . . . 650.00
184 Shutterbugs of Smallville . . . 650.00
185 The Mythical Monster 650.00
186 Smallville a Ghost Town 650.00
187 25th Century Superboy. 650.00
188 Bull Fighter from Smallville. . 650.00
189 Girl of Steel (Lana Lang) . . . 650.00
190 The Terrible Truant 650.00
191 The Two Clark Kents 650.00
192 Coronation of Queen
   Lana Lang 650.00
193 Superboy's Lost Costume. . . 650.00
194 Super-Charged Superboy. . . 650.00
195 Lana Lang's Romance
   on Mars! 650.00
196 Superboy vs. King Gorilla . . . 650.00
197 V:Juvenile Gangs 650.00
198 Super-Carnival from Space. . 650.00
199 Superboy meets Superlad . . . 650.00
200 Superboy and the Apes! 900.00
201 Safari in Smallville! 600.00
202 Superboy City, U.S.A. 600.00
203 Uncle Superboy! 600.00
204 Super-Brat of Smallville 600.00
205 Journey of the Second
   Superboy! 600.00
206 The Impossible Creatures. . . 600.00
207 Smallville's Worst Athlete . . . 600.00
208 Rip Van Winkle of
   Smallville? 600.00
209 Superboy Week! 600.00
210 I:Krypto,The Superdog
   from Krypton. 7,000.00
211 Superboy's Amazing Dream! 600.00
212 Superboy's Robot Twin. 600.00
213 Junior Jury of Smallville!. . . . 600.00
214 A:Krypto 1,000.00
215 Super-Hobby of Superboy . . 600.00
216 The Wizard City 600.00
217 Farewell to Smallville 600.00

218 Two World's of Superboy . . . 600.00
219 Rip Van Wrinkle of
   Smallville. 600.00
220 Greatest Show on Earth
   A:Krypto. 600.00
221 The Babe of Steel 500.00
222 Superboy's Repeat
   Performance 500.00
223 Hercules Junior. 500.00
224 Pa Kent Superman 500.00
225 Bird with Super-Powers 500.00
226 Superboy's Super Rival! 500.00
227 Good Samaritan of
   Smallville 500.00
228 Clark Kent's Bodyguard 500.00
229 End of the Kent Family 500.00
230 Secret o/t Flying Horse 450.00
231 Super-Feats of Super-Baby . 450.00
232 House where Superboy
   was Born 450.00
233 Joe Smith, Man of Steel 450.00
234 1,001 Rides of Superboy . . . 450.00
235 Confessions of Superboy . . . 450.00
236 Clark Kent's Super-Dad 450.00
237 Robot War of Smallville 450.00
238 Secret Past of
   Superboy's Father. 450.00
239 Super-Tricks of
   the Dog of Steel. 450.00
240 Super Teacher from Krypton. 450.00
241 Super-Outlaw of Smallville . . 450.00
242 The Kid From Krypton 450.00
243 Super Toys from Krypton . . . 450.00
244 Poorest Family in Smallville . 450.00
245 The Mystery of Monster X . . 450.00
246 Girl Who Trapped Superboy . 450.00
247 I&O:Legion 11,000.00
248 Green Arrow 400.00
249 CS,Green Arrow 400.00
250 JK,Green Arrow 400.00
251 JK,Green Arrow 400.00
252 JK,Green Arrow 400.00
253 JK,1st Superboy &
   Robin T.U. 600.00
254 JK,Green Arrow 400.00
255 JK,Green Arrow 400.00
256 JK,O:Green Arrow 1,100.00
257 CS,LEI,A:Hercules,Samson . 350.00
258 LEI,Aquaman,Superboy 350.00
259 I:Crimson Archer 350.00
260 1st S.A. O:Aquaman 1,400.00
261 GA,A:Lois Lane. 300.00
262 O:Speedy 300.00
263 GA,Aquaman,Superboy 300.00
264 GA,A:Robin Hood 300.00

Adventure Comics #260
© *DC Comics Inc.*

DC COMICS

DC COMICS

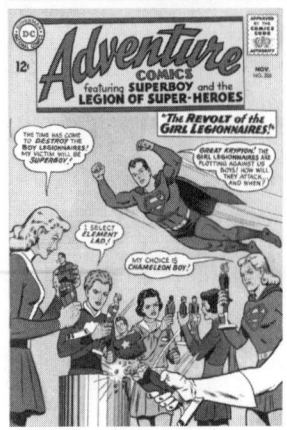

Adventure Comics #326
© DC Comics, Inc.

265 GA,Aquaman,Superboy 300.00
266 GA,I:Aquagirl............. 300.00
267 N:Legion(2nd app.) 1,600.00
268 I:Aquaboy 300.00
269 I:Aqualad,E:Green Arrow . . 450.00
270 2nd A:Aqualad,B:Congorilla . 300.00
271 O:Lex Luthor rtd 450.00
272 I:Human Flying Fish 300.00
273 Aquaman,Superboy 300.00
274 Aquaman,Superboy 300.00
275 O:Superman/Batman
     T.U. rtd............... 400.00
276 Superboy,3rd A:Metallo.... 300.00
277 Aquaman,Superboy 300.00
278 Aquaman,Superboy 300.00
279 CS,Aquaman,Superboy .. 300.00
280 CS,A:Lori Lemaris........ 300.00
281 Aquaman,Superboy
     E:Congorilla........... 300.00
282 5th A:Legion,I:Starboy..... 400.00
283 I:Phantom Zone 400.00
284 CS,JM,Aquaman,Superboy . 250.00
285 WB,B:Bizarro World 350.00
286 I:Bizarro Mxyzptlk 350.00
287 I:Dev-Em,Bizarro Perry White,
     Jimmy Olsen 250.00
288 A:Dev-Em............. 250.00
289 Superboy.............. 250.00
290 8th A:Legion,O&J:Sunboy,
     I:Brainiac 5 .... 400.00
291 A:Lex Luthor 250.00
292 Superboy,I:Bizarro Lucy Lane,
     Lana Lang 250.00
293 CS,O&I:Marv-El,I:Bizarro
     Luthor 350.00
294 I:Bizarro M.Monroe,JFK .. 300.00
295 I:Bizarro Titano 250.00
296 A:Ben Franklin,George
     Washington 250.00
297 Lana Lang Superboy Sister . 250.00
298 The Fat Superboy........ 250.00
299 I:Gold Kryptonite........ 250.00
300 B:Legion,J:Mon-El,
     E:Bizarro World 900.00
301 CS,O:Bouncing Boy 300.00
302 CS,Legion.............. 250.00
303 I:Matter Eater Lad........ 250.00
304 D:Lightning Lad.......... 250.00
305 A:Chameleon Boy........ 250.00
306 I:Legion of Sub.Heroes..... 250.00
307 I:Element Lad 250.00
308 I:Light Lass 250.00
309 I:Legion of Super Monsters . 250.00
310 A:Mxyzptlk............. 250.00
311 CS,V:Legion of Substitue
     Heroes................ 250.00

312 CS&GKl(c),R:Lightning Lad . 250.00
313 CS,J:Supergirl............ 250.00
314 CS&GKl(c),A:Hitler 250.00
315 A:Legion of Substitute
     Heroes............... 250.00
316 CS&GKl(c),O:Legion...... 200.00
317 I&J:Dreamgirl 200.00
318 Mutiny of Legionnaires 200.00
319 Legion's Suicide Squad 200.00
320 CS&GKl(c),A:Dev-Em..... 200.00
321 I:Time Trapper........... 200.00
322 JF,A:Legion of Super Pets .. 150.00
323 JF,BU:Kypto 150.00
324 JF,I:Legion of Super Outlaws 150.00
325 JF,V:Lex Luthor.......... 150.00
326 BU:Superboy............ 150.00
327 I&J:Timber Wolf 150.00
328 Lad who Wrecked Legion .. 150.00
329 I:Legion of Super Bizarros .. 150.00
330 Mystery Legionnaire 150.00
331 Legion of Super-Villains 125.00
332 CS&GKl(c),Legion......... 125.00
333 CS&GKl(c),Legion......... 125.00
334 CS&GKl(c),Legion......... 125.00
335 CS&GKl(c),Legion......... 125.00
336 CS&GKl(c),Legion......... 125.00
337 CS&GKl(c),Legion......... 125.00
338 CS&GKl(c),Legion......... 125.00
339 CS&GKl(c),Legion......... 125.00
340 I:Computo 125.00
341 CS,D:Triplicate Girl (becomes
     Duo Damsel) 110.00
342 CS,Star Boy expelled 100.00
343 CS,V:Lords of Luck........ 100.00
344 CS,Super Stalag,pt.1....... 100.00
345 CS,Super Stalag,pt.2 ...... 100.00
346 CS,I&J:Karate Kid,Princess
     Projectra,I:Nemesis Kid..... 125.00
347 CS,Legion.............. 100.00
348 I:Dr.Regulus 125.00
349 CS,I:Rond Vidar 100.00
350 CS,I:White Witch......... 125.00
351 CS,R:Star Boy........... 150.00
352 CS,I:Fatal Fire........... 150.00
353 CS,D:Ferro Lad.......... 125.00
354 CS,Adult Legion 150.00
355 CS,J:Insect Queen 125.00
356 CS,Five Legion Orphans ... 125.00
357 CS,I:Controller 125.00
358 I:Hunter 125.00
359 CS,Outlawed Legion,pt.1 ... 125.00
360 CS,Outlawed Legion,pt.2 ... 125.00
361 I:Dominators (30th century) . 125.00
362 I:Dr.Mantis Morto 125.00
363 V:Dr.Mantis Morlo 125.00
364 A:Legion of Super Pets..... 125.00
365 CS,I:Shadow Lass,
     V:Fatal Five 125.00
366 CS,J:Shadow Lass 125.00
367 N:Legion H.Q.,I:Dark Circle . 125.00
368 NA,Mutiny of Super-Heroines 125.00
369 CS,JAb,I:Mordru 125.00
370 CS,JAb,V:Mordru 125.00
371 CS,JAb,I:Chemical King 125.00
372 CS,JAb,J:Timber Wolf,
     Chemical King 125.00
373 I:Tornado Twins........... 65.00
374 WM,I:Black Mace 65.00
375 I:Wanderers 65.00
376 Execution of Cham.Boy 65.00
377 Heroes for Hire.......... 65.00
378 Twelve Hours to Live 65.00
379 Burial In Space 65.00
380 The Amazing Space Odyssey
     of the Legion,E:Legion 65.00
381 The Supergirl Gang
     C:Batgirl,B:Supergirl 200.00
382 NA(c),The Superteams Split
     Up,A:Superman.......... 75.00
383 NA(c),Please Stop my Funeral,
     A:Superman,Comet,Streaky . 75.00

384 KS,The Heroine Haters,
     A:Superman............ 75.00
385 Supergirl's Big Sister 75.00
386 The Beast That Loved
     Supergirl 75.00
387 Wolfgirl of Stanhope;
     A:Superman;V:Lex Luthor 75.00
388 Kindergarten Criminal;
     V:Luthor,Brainiac........... 75.00
389 A:Supergirl's Parents,
     V:Brainiac 75.00
390 Linda Danvers Superstar
     (80 page giant) 100.00
391 The Super Cheat;A:Comet ... 50.00
392 Supergirls Lost Costume 50.00
393 KS,Unwanted Supergirl 50.00
394 KS,Heartbreak Prison....... 50.00
395 Heroine in Haunted House ... 50.00
396 Mystery o/t Super Orphan ... 50.00
397 Now Comes Zod,N:Supergirl,
     V:Luthor................ 50.00
398 Maid of Doom,A:Superman,
     Streaky,Krypto,Comet 50.00
399 CI,Johnny Dee,Hero Bum.... 60.00
400 MSy,35th Anniv.,Return of the
     Black Flame............. 40.00
401 MSy,JAb,The Frightened
     Supergirl,V:Lex Luthor....... 40.00
402 MSy,JAb,TD,I:Starfire,
     Dr.Kangle............... 50.00
403 68 page giant 100.00
404 MSy,JAb,V:Starfire 35.00
405 V:Starfire,Dr.Kangle 35.00
406 MSy,JAb,Suspicion 35.00
407 MSy,JAb,Suspicion Confirmed
     N:Supergirl............. 35.00
408 The Face at the Window..... 35.00
409 MSy,DG,Legion rep......... 50.00
410 N:Supergirl 50.00
411 CI,N:Supergirl 50.00
412 rep.Strange Adventures #180
     (I:Animal Man). 55.00
413 GM,JKu,rep.Hawkman 50.00
414 Animal Man rep.......... 50.00
415 BO,GM,CI,Animal Man rep. .. 50.00
416 CI,All women issue,giantsize . 50.00
417 GM,inc.rep.Adventure #161,
     Frazetta art............. 45.00
418 ATh,Black Canary......... 45.00
419 ATh,Black Canary 50.00
420 Animal Man rep.......... 45.00
421 MSy,Supergirl 30.00
422 MSy,Supergirl 30.00
423 MSy,Supergirl 30.00

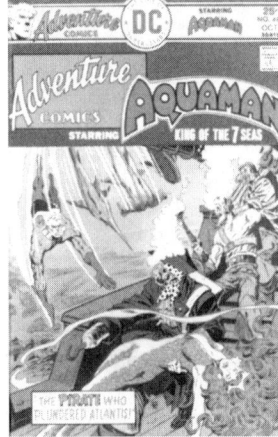

Adventure Comics #441
© DC Comics, Inc.

424 MSy,E:Supergirl,A:JLA 30.00
425 AN,ATh,I:Captain Fear 45.00
426 MSy,DG,JAp,Vigilante 30.00
427 TD, The Voodoo Lizards 38.00
428 TD,I:Black Orchid 100.00
429 TD,AN,Black Orchid 45.00
430 A:Black Orchid 45.00
431 JAp,ATh,B:Spectre 100.00
432 JAp,AN,A:Spectre,Capt.Fear . 45.00
433 JAp,AN, The Swami 45.00
434 JAp, Nightmare Dummies 45.00
435 MGr(1st work),JAp,Aquaman . 45.00
436 JAp,MGr,Aquaman 45.00
437 JAp,MGr,Aquaman 45.00
438 JAp,HC,DD,7 Soldiers 45.00
439 JAp, Voice that Doomed 45.00
440 JAp,O:New Spectre 75.00
441 JAp,B:Aquaman 20.00
442 JAp,A:Aquaman 20.00
443 JAp, The Dolphin Connection . 20.00
444 JAp, Death before Dishonor . . 20.00
445 JAp,RE,JSon,Creeper. 22.00
446 JAp,RE,JSon,Creeper. 22.00
447 JAp,RE,JSon,Creeper. 22.00
448 JAp,Aquaman 20.00
449 JAp,MN,TA,J'onn J'onz. 20.00
450 JAp,MN,TA,Supergirl 20.00
451 JAp,MN,TA,Hawkman 20.00
452 JAp,Aquaman 20.00
453 MA,CP,JRu,B:Superboy
    & Aqualad 20.00
454 CP,DG,A:Kryptonite Kid 20.00
455 CP,DG,A:Kryptonite Kid
    E:Aqualad 15.00
456 JSon,JA. 15.00
457 JSon,JA,JO,B:Eclipso 15.00
458 JSon,JAp,JO,BL,E:Superboy
    & Eclipso 15.00
459 IN,FMc,JAp,JSon,DN,JA,A:Wond.
    Woman,New Gods,Green Lantern,
    Flash,Deadman,(giant size) . . 25.00
460 IN,FMc,JAp,DN,DA,JSon,JA,
    D:Darkseid. 25.00
461 IN,FMc,JAp,JSon,DN,JA,
    B:JSA & Aquaman 50.00
462 IN,FMc,DH,JL,DG,JA,
    D:Earth 2,Batman 50.00
463 DH,JL,JSon,FMc. 20.00
464 DH,JAp,JSon,DN,DA,
    Deadman. 20.00
465 DN,JSon,DG,JL. 20.00
466 MN,JL,JSon,DN,DA 20.00
467 JSon,SD,RT,I:Starman
    B:Plastic Man 25.00
468 SD,JSon 8.00
469 SD,JSon,O:Starman 8.00
470 SD,JSon,O:Starman 8.00
471 SD,JSon,I:Brickface 8.00
472 SD,RT,JSon 8.00
473 SD,RT,JSon 8.00
474 SD,RT,JSon 8.00
475 BB(c),SD,RT,JSon,DG,
    B:Aquaman 8.00
476 SD,RT,JSon,DG 8.00
477 SD,RT,JSon,DG 8.00
478 SD,RT,JSon,DG 8.00
479 CI,DG,JSon,Dial H For Hero,
    E:Starman and Aquaman 8.00
480 CI,DJ,B:Dial H for Hero 8.00
481 CI,DJ. 8.00
482 CI,DJ,DH. 8.00
483 CI,DJ,DH. 8.00
484 GP(c),CI,DJ,DH 8.00
485 GP(c),CI,DJ. 8.00
486 GP(c),DH,RT,TVE 8.00
487 CI,DJ,DH. 8.00
488 CI,DJ,TVE. 8.00
489 CI,FMc,TVE 8.00
490 GP(c),CI,E:Dial H for Hero . . . 8.00
491 KG(c),DigestSize,DN,
    Shazam,rep.other material . . . 20.00
492 KG(c),DN,E:Shazam. 20.00

493 KG(c),GT,B:Challengers of
    the Unknown,reprints 20.00
494 KG(c),GT,Challengers,
    reprints. 20.00
495 ATh,reprints,Challengers. 20.00
496 GK(c),ATh,reprints,
    Challengers 20.00
497 ATh,DA,reps.,E:Challengers . . 20.00
498 GK(c),reprints,Rep.Legion . . . 20.00
499 GK(c),reprints,Rep 20.00
500 KG(c),Legion reprints,Rep . . . 20.00
501 reprints,Rep 20.00
502 reprints,Rep 20.00
503 reprints,final issue. 20.00
Giant #1, 80 page, 7 tales (1998) . 15.00

ADVENTURE COMICS
1999

1 JeR,PSj,F:Starman & The Atom . 2.50

ADVENTURES IN
THE DC UNIVERSE
1997–98

1 F:New JLA 6.00
2 thru 11 . . . . @4.00
12 SVa(s). 4.50
13 thru 17. . . . . @4.00
18 SVa(s),F:JLA. 4.50
19 F:Catwoman, Wonder Woman . . 4.00
Ann.#1 magic amulets,5 stories. . . . 5.00

THE ADVENTURES OF
ALAN LADD
1949–51

1 Ph(c),Damascus Diamond . . 1,500.00
2 Ph(c),inc.Visit to Underworld . . 800.00
3 Ph(c),inc.Stuntman 550.00
4 Ph(c),inc.Hall of Hits 550.00
5 Ph(c),inc.Destination Danger. . 500.00
6 Ph(c),inc.Beautiful Bodyguard . 500.00
7 RMo(c&a),Hollywood Unknown 500.00
8 Grand Duchess takes over . . . 500.00
9 Deadlien in Rapula 500.00

THE ADVENTURES OF
BOB HOPE
1951

1 Ph(c) 3,000.00
2 Ph(c) 1,500.00
3 Ph(c) 1,000.00
4 Ph(c) 1,000.00
5 thru 10 . . . . @750.00

Adventures of Bob Hope #42
© DC Comics Inc.

11 thru 20. . . . . @600.00
21 thru 40. . . . . @400.00
41 thru 60. . . . . @300.00
61 thru 90. . . . . @150.00
91 thru 93. . . . . @125.00
94 C:Aquaman 150.00
95 1st Superhip 150.00
96 thru 105. . . . . @125.00
106 thru 109 NA. . . . . @200.00

ADVENTURES OF
DEAN MARTIN AND
JERRY LEWIS
1952–57

1 . . . . 2,500.00
2 . . . . 1,000.00
3 thru 5 . . . . @750.00
6 thru 10 . . . . @750.00
11 thru 20 . . . . @500.00
21 thru 40. . . . . @300.00
Becomes:

ADVENTURES OF
JERRY LEWIS
1957–71

41 thru 55 . . . . @225.00
56 thru 69. . . . . @200.00
70 thru 87. . . . . @150.00
88 A:Bob Hope. 150.00
89 thru 91. . . . . @100.00
92 C:Superman 90.00
93 Beatles 95.00
94 thru 96. . . . . @90.00
97 A:Batman & Joker. 150.00
98 thru 101. . . . . @75.00
102 NA,Beatles . . . . @150.00
103 and 104 NA. . . . . @120.00
105 A:Superman 100.00
106 thru 111 . . . . @65.00
112 A:Flash 100.00
113 thru 116 . . . . @50.00
117 A:Wonder Woman. 100.00
118 thru 124 . . . . @50.00

ADVENTURES OF
FORD FAIRLANE
1990

1 thru 4 DH . . . . @3.00

ADVENTURES OF
THE OUTSIDERS
**See: BATMAN &
THE OUTSIDERS**

ADVENTURES OF
OZZIE AND HARRIET
1949–50

1 Ph(c) 1,500.00
2 . . . . 900.00
3 thru 5 . . . . @750.00

ADVENTURES OF REX,
THE WONDER DOG
1952–59

1 ATh,Trail of Flower of Evil. . . 2,000.00
2 GK,ATh,Stunt Dog 1,000.00
3 GK,ATh,Circus Detective 900.00
4 GK,CI,Terror Island 800.00
5 GK,Wanted, One P.O.W. 800.00
6 thru 10 . . . . @600.00
11 Atom Bomb 700.00
12 thru 20. . . . . @400.00
21 thru 46. . . . . @300.00

ADVENTURES OF SUPERBOY
See: SUPERBOY

DC COMICS

ADVENTURES OF SUPERMAN
See: SUPERMAN

AIR
Vertigo, Aug., 2008
1 40-pg. 3.00
2 thru 4 . . . . @3.00

ALL-AMERICAN COMICS
1939–48
1 B:Hop Harrigan,Scribbly,Mutt&Jeff,
Red,White&Blue,Bobby Thatcher,
Skippy,Daiseybelle,Mystery Men
of Mars,Toonerville 10,000.00
2 B:Ripley's Believe It or Not . . 4,000.00
3 Hop Harrigan (c) 3,000.00
4 Flag(c) 3,000.00
5 B:The American Way 3,000.00
6 ShM(c),Fredric Marchin in
The American Way 2,500.00
7 E:Bobby Thatcher,C.H.
Claudy's A Thousand Years
in a Minute 2,500.00
8 B:Ultra Man 5,000.00
9 A:Ultra Man 2,500.00
10 ShM(c),E:The American Way,
Santa-X-Mas(c) 2,500.00
11 Ultra Man(c) 2,500.00
12 E:Toonerville Folks. 2,000.00
13 The Infra Red Des'Royers . . 2,000.00
14 Ultra Man 2,000.00
15 E:Tippie and Reg'lar Fellars 2,500.00
16 O&1st App:Green Lantern,
B:Lantern(c) 250,000.00
17 SMo(c) 30,000.00
18 SMo(c) 25,000.00
19 SMo(c),O&I: Atom, E:Ultra
Man. 35,000.00
20 I:Atom's Costume,Hunkle
becomes Red Tornado . . . 10,000.00
21 E:Wiley of West Point
& Skippy 6,000.00
22 SMo(c),F:Green Lantern . . . 5,800.00
23 E:Daieybelle. 6,000.00
24 E:Ripley's Believe It or Not . 7,500.00
25 O&I:Dr. Mid-Nite. 20,000.00
26 O&I:Sargon the Sorcerer . . . 7,000.00
27 I:Doiby Dickles 7,000.00
28 F:Green Lantern 3,000.00
29 ShM(c) 3,000.00
30 ShM(c) 3,000.00
31 Adventures of the Underfed
Orphans 3,000.00
32 F:Green Lantern 2,500.00
33 Green Lantern(c) 2,500.00
34 Green Lantern(c) 2,500.00
35 Doiby discovers Lantern's ID 2,500.00
36 Auto Racing (c) 2,500.00
37 Green Lantern(c) 2,500.00
38 ShM,V:A Modern Napoleon . 2,500.00
39 Green Lantern(c) 2,500.00
40 Doiby Dickles idol(c) 2,500.00
41 Gr.Lantern(c),Doiby Dickles . 2,000.00
42 ShM 2,000.00
43 Gr.Lantern(c),Doiby Dickles . 2,000.00
44 I Accuse the Green Lantern! 2,000.00
45 Gr.Lantern(c),Doiby Dickles . 2,000.00
46 Riddle of Dickles Manor. . . . 2,000.00
47 Hop Harrigan meets the
Enemy,(c) 2,000.00
48 League of Three-Eyed Men . 2,000.00
49 Doiby Dickles Cab 2,000.00
50 E:Sargon 2,000.00
51 Murder Under the Stars 1,500.00
52 Spotlight on Crime 1,500.00
53 Green Lantern delivers
the Mail. 1,500.00
54 Crime is an Art 1,500.00
55 The Riddle of the
Runaway Trolley 1,500.00

All-American Comics #30
© DC Comics, Inc.

56 V:Elegant Esmond 1,500.00
57 V:The Melancholy Men 1,500.00
58 Marvelous Mervyn Mystery . 1,500.00
59 The Story of the Man Who
Couldn't Tell The Truth . . . 1,500.00
60 Desperate Dilemma 1,500.00
61 O:Soloman Grundy,Fighters
Never Quit. 11,000.00
62 Da Distrik Attorney. 1,300.00
63 Garrulous Mr. Gabb 1,300.00
64 A Bag of Assorted Nuts! 1,300.00
65 The Man Who Lost
Wednesday. 1,300.00
66 The Soles of Manhattan! . . . 1,300.00
67 V:King Shark 1,300.00
68 F:Napoleon & Joe Safeen . . 1,300.00
69 Backwards Man! 1,300.00
70 JKu,I:Maximillian O'Leary,
V:Colley, the Leprechaun . . 1,300.00
71 E:Red,White&Blue,The
Human Bomb 1,200.00
72 B:Black Pirate 1,200.00
73 B:Winkey,Blinky&Noddy,
Mountain Music Mayhem . . 1,200.00
74 Slap-Happy Shoes 1,200.00
75 Man Who Heard Too Much . 1,200.00
76 Spring Time for Doiby 1,200.00
77 Hop Harrigan(c) 1,200.00
78 The Giggling Gangsters. . . . 1,200.00
79 Mutt & Jeff 1,200.00
80 Long-Eared Larceny 1,200.00
81 Two Twisted Twerps. 1,200.00
82 The Beloved Bandit 1,200.00
83 Mutt & Jeff 1,200.00
84 The Adventure of the Man
with Two Faces. 1,200.00
85 Rise & Fall of Crusher Crock 1,200.00
86 V:Crime of the Month Club . 1,200.00
87 The Strange Case of
Professor Nobody. 1,200.00
88 Canvas of Crime 1,200.00
89 O:Harlequin 1,700.00
90 O:Icicle 1,700.00
91 Wedding of the Harlequin . . 1,700.00
92 The Icicle goes South 1,700.00
93 Double Crossing Decoy 1,700.00
94 A:Harlequin 1,700.00
95 The Unmasking of the
Harlequin 1,700.00
96 ATh(c),Solve the Mystery
of the Emerald Necklaces! . 1,700.00
97 ATh(c),The Country Fair
Crimes 1,700.00
98 ATh,ATh(c),End of Sports! . . 1,700.00
99 ATh,ATh(c),E:Hop Harrigan . 1,700.00

100 ATh,I:Johnny Thunder 3,000.00
101 ATh,ATh(c),E:Mutt & Jeff . . 2,500.00
102 ATh,ATh(c),E:GrnLantern. . 6,000.00
Becomes:

ALL-AMERICAN WESTERN
1948–52
103 A:Johnny Thunder,The City
Without Guns, All Johnny
Thunder stories 900.00
104 ATh(c),Unseen Allies. 700.00
105 ATh(c),Hidden Guns 600.00
106 ATh(c),Snow Mountain
Ambush 600.00
107 ATh(c),Cheyenne Justice . . 600.00
108 ATh(c),Vengeance of
the Silver Bullet 400.00
109 ATh(c),Secret of
Crazy River 400.00
110 ATh(c),Ambush at
Scarecrow Hills 400.00
111 ATh(c),Gun-Shy Sheriff 400.00
112 ATh(c),Double Danger. 400.00
113 ATh(c),Johnny Thunder
Indian Chief 400.00
114 ATh(c),The End of
Johnny Thunder. 400.00
115 ATh(c),Cheyenne Mystery . . 400.00
116 ATh(c),Buffalo Raiders
of the Mesa 400.00
117 ATh(c),V:Black Lightnin 300.00
118 ATh(c),Challenge of
the Aztecs 300.00
119 GK(c),The Vanishing
Gold Mine 300.00
120 GK(c),Ambush at
Painted Mountain 300.00
121 ATh(c),The Unmasking of
Johnny Thunder. 300.00
122 ATh(c),The Real
Johnny Thunder. 300.00
123 GK(c),Johnny Thunder's
Strange Rival 300.00
124 ATh(c),The Iron Horse's
Last Run 300.00
125 ATh(c),Johnny Thunder's
Last Roundup 300.00
126 ATh(c),Phantoms of the
Desert 300.00
Becomes:

ALL-AMERICAN MEN OF WAR
1952–66
127 (0) JGr(c),Unknown Marine 2,200.00
128 (1) IN, Bridgehead 1,200.00
2 JGr(c),Killer Bait. 900.00
3 Pied Piper of Pyong-Yang . . . 750.00
4 JGr(c),The Hills of Hate 750.00
5 One Second to Zero 750.00
6 IN(c),Jungle Killers. 650.00
7 IN(c),Beach to Hold 650.00
8 IN(c),Sgt. Storm Cloud. 650.00
9 IN(c),Death Mist. 650.00
10 JGr(c),Operation Avalance . . 650.00
11 JGr(c),Dragon's Teeth 650.00
12 JGr(c),Bobsled Bombadier . . 600.00
13 JGr(c),Lost Patrol 600.00
14 IN(c),Pigeon Boss. 600.00
15 JGr(c),Flying Roadblock 600.00
16 JGr(c),The Flying Jeep 600.00
17 JGr(c),Booby Trap Ridge . . . 600.00
18 JKu(c),The Ballad of
Battling Bells 600.00
19 JGr(c),IN,Torpedo Track 500.00
20 JGr(c),JKu,Lifenet to
Beach Road. 500.00
21 JGr(c),IN,RH,The
Coldest War. 500.00
22 JGr(c),IN,JKu,Snipers Nest . . 500.00
23 JGr(c),The Silent War 500.00

DC COMICS

All-American Men of War #88
© DC Comics, Inc.

24 JGr(c),The Thin Line. 500.00
25 JGr(c),IN,For Rent-One
Foxhole 500.00
26 Dial W-A-R 500.00
27 JGr(c),RH,Fighting Pigeon . . . 500.00
28 JGr(c),RA,JKu,Medal
for A Dog 500.00
29 IN(c),JKu,Battle Bridges 500.00
30 JGr(c),RH,Frogman Hunt 500.00
31 JGr(c),Battle Seat 400.00
32 JGr(c),RH,Battle Station 400.00
33 JGr(c),IN,Sky Ambush 400.00
34 JGr(c),JKu,No Man's Alley . . . 400.00
35 JGr(c),IN, Battle Call. 400.00
36 JGr(c),JKu,Battle Window. . . . 400.00
37 JGr(c),RH,The Big Stretch. . . 400.00
38 JGr(c),RH,JKu,The
Floating Sentinel 400.00
39 JGr(c),JKu,The Four Faces
of Sgt. Fay. 400.00
40 JGr(c),IN,Walking Helmet. . . . 400.00
41 JKu(c),RH,JKu,The 50-50 War 300.00
42 JGr(c),JKu,Battle Arm. 300.00
43 JGr(c),JKu,Command Post. . . 300.00
44 JKu(c),The Flying Frogman . . 300.00
45 JGr(c),RH,Combat Waterboy . 300.00
46 JGr(c),IN,RH,Tank Busters . . 300.00
47 JGr(c),RH,MD,Battle Freight . 300.00
48 JGr(c),JKu,MD,Roadblock . . . 300.00
49 JGr(c),Walking Target 300.00
50 IN,RH,Bodyguard For A Sub. . 300.00
51 JGr(c),RH,Bomber's Moon . . . 250.00
52 JKu(c),RH,MD,Back
Seat Driver 250.00
53 JKu(c),JKu,Night Attack 250.00
54 JKu(c),IN,Diary of a
Fighter Pilot 250.00
55 JKu(c),RH,Split-Second Target 250.00
56 JKu,IN,RH,Frogman Jinx 250.00
57 Pick-Up for Easy Co. 250.00
58 JKu(c),RH,MD,A Piece of Sky 250.00
59 JGr(c),JKu,The Hand of War . 250.00
60 JGr(c),The Time Table 250.00
61 JGr(c),IN,MD,Blind Target. . . . 250.00
62 JGr(c),RH,RA,No(c) 250.00
63 JGr(c),JKu,Frogman Carrier . . 250.00
64 JKu(c),JKu,RH,The Other
Man's War 250.00
65 JGr(c),JKu,MD,Same
Old Sarge 250.00
66 JGr(c),The Walking Fort 250.00
67 JGr(c),RH,A:Gunner&Sarge,
The Cover Man 800.00
68 JKu(c),Gunner&Sarge,
The Man & The Gun 300.00

69 JKu(c),A:Tank Killer,
Bazooka Hill 300.00
70 JKu(c),IN,Pigeon
Without Wings. 250.00
71 JGr(c),A:Tank Killer,Target
For An Ammo Boy 200.00
72 JGr(c),A:Tank Killer,T.N.T.
Broom 200.00
73 JGr(c),JKu,No Detour. 200.00
74 The Minute Commandos 200.00
75 JKu(c),Sink That Flattop 200.00
76 JKu(c),A:Tank Killer,
Just One More Tank 200.00
77 JKu(c),IN,MD,Big Fish-
little Fish 200.00
78 JGr(c),Tin Hat for an
Iron Man 200.00
79 JKu(c),RA,Showdown Soldier. 200.00
80 JGr(c),RA,The Medal Men . . . 200.00
81 JGr(c),IN,Ghost Ship of
Two Wars. 150.00
82 IN(c),B:Johnny Cloud,
The Flying Chief 300.00
83 IN(c),Fighting Blind 250.00
84 IN(c),Death Dive 150.00
85 RH(c),Battle Eagle 150.00
86 JGr(c),Top-Gun Ace 150.00
87 JGr(c),Broken Ace 150.00
88 JGr(c),The Ace of Vengeance 150.00
89 JGr(c),The Star Jockey. 150.00
90 JGr(c),Wingmate of Doom . . . 125.00
91 RH(c),Two Missions To Doom 125.00
92 JGr(c),The Battle Hawk 125.00
93 RH(c),The Silent Rider 125.00
94 RH(c),Be Brave-Be Silent. . . . 125.00
95 RH(c),Second Sight
For a Pilot 125.00
96 RH(c),The Last Flight
of Lt. Moon 125.00
97 IN(c),A Target Called Johnny . 125.00
98 The Time-Bomb Ace 125.00
99 IN(c),The Empty Cockpit. 125.00
100 RH(c),Battle o/t Sky Chiefs. . 125.00
101 RH(c),Death Ship of
Three Wars 100.00
102 JKu(c),Blind Eagle-Hungry
Hawk 100.00
103 IN(c),Battle Ship-
Battle Heart 100.00
104 JKu(c),The Last Target 100.00
105 IN(c),Killer Horse-Ship 100.00
106 IN(c),Death Song For
A Battle Hawk 100.00
107 IN(c),Flame in the Sky 100.00
108 IN(c),Death-Dive of the Aces 100.00
109 IN(c),The Killer Slot. 100.00
110 RH(c),The Co-Pilot was
Death 100.00
111 RH(c),E:Johnny Cloud, Tag–
You're Dead. 100.00
112 RH(c),B:Balloon Buster,Lt.
Steve Savage-Balloon Buster 100.00
113 JKu(c),The Ace of
Sudden Death 100.00
114 JKu(c),The Ace Who
Died Twice 100.00
115 IN(c),A:Johnny Cloud,
Deliver One Enemy Ace-
Handle With Care 100.00
116 JKu(c),A:Baloon Buster,
Circle of Death. 100.00
117 Sept.–Oct., 1966 . . . . 100.00

ALL-AMERICAN COMICS
1999
1 RMz(s),F:Green Lantern &
Johnny Thunder. 2.25

ALL-FLASH
1941–47
1 EHi,O:Flash,I:The Monocle. 30,000.00

All-Flash #25
© DC Comics Inc.

2 EHi,The Adventure of Roy
Revenge 7,500.00
3 EHi,The Adventure of
Misplaced Faces 3,500.00
4 EHi,Tale of the Time Capsule 3,500.00
5 EHi,The Case of the Patsy
Colt! Last Quarterly 2,500.00
6 EHi,The Ray that Changed
Men's Souls 2,200.00
7 EHi,Adventures of a Writers
Fantasy, House of Horrors . 2,200.00
8 EHi,Formula to Fairyland!. . . 2,200.00
9 EHi,Adventure of the Stolen
Telescope 2,200.00
10 EHi,Case of the Curious Cat 2,200.00
11 EHi,Troubles Come
in Doubles 1,800.00
12 EHi,Tumble INN to Trouble,
Becomes Quarterly on orders
from War Production Board
O:The Thinker. 1,800.00
13 EHi,I:The King 1,800.00
14 EHi,I:Winky,Blinky & Noddy
Green Lantern (c). 2,200.00
15 EHi,Secrets of a Stranger . 1,800.00
16 EHi,A:The Sinister 1,800.00
17 Tales of the Three Wishes . 1,800.00
18 A:Winky,Blinky&Noddy
B:Mutt & Jeff reprints 1,800.00
19 No Rest at the Rest Home . 1,800.00
20 A:Winky, Blinky & Noddy . . . 1,800.00
21 I:Turtle 1,300.00
22 The Money Doubler, E:Mutt
& Jeff reprints 1,300.00
23 The Bad Men of Bar Nothing 1,300.00
24 I:Worry Wart,3 Court
Clowns Get Caught 1,300.00
25 I:Slapsy Simmons,
Flash Jitterbugs 1,300.00
26 I:The Chef,The Boss,Shrimp
Coogan,A:Winky, Blinky &
Noddy. 1,300.00
27 A:The Thinker, Gangplank
Gus Story 1,300.00
28 A:Shrimp Coogan, Winky,
Blinky & Noddy. 1,300.00
29 The Thousand-Year Old Terror,
A:Winky, Blinky & Noddy . . 2,000.00
30 The Vanishing Snowman . . 1,300.00
31 A:Black Hat,Planet of Sport . 1,300.00
32 I:Fiddler,A:Thinker 2,000.00

ALL FUNNY COMICS
1943–48
1 Genius Jones. 750.00

DC COMICS

2 same 300.00
3 same 200.00
4 same 200.00
5 thru 10 . . . . @200.00
11 Genius Jones 200.00
12 same 200.00
13 same 150.00
14 . . . . 150.00
15 . . . . 150.00
16 A:DC Superheroes 500.00
17 thru 23 . . . . @150.00

ALL-NEW ATOM, THE
July, 2006
1 JBy,TvS,F:Ryan Choi. 3.00
2 thru 25 . . . . @3.00

ALL STAR BATMAN AND ROBIN, THE BOY WONDER
July, 2005
1 FM(s),JLe,SW 3.00
1b Special edition, 48-pg. 20.00
2 FM(s),JLe,SW 3.00
3 FM(s),JLe,SW 3.00
4 FM(s),JLe,SW, F:Black Canary . . 3.00
5 FM,JLe,SW 3.00
6 FM,JLe,SW 3.00
7 FM,JLe,SW 3.00
8 FM,JLe,SW 3.00
9 FM,JLe,SW,yellow-bellied 3.00
10 FM,JLe,F:Batgirl, Catwoman . . . 3.00
11 FM,JLe,SW,War against crime . . 3.00
1a thru 10a variant (c)s . . . . @3.00

ALL-STAR COMICS
1940–51
1 B:Flash,Hawkman,Hourman,
  Sandman,Spectre,Red White
  & Blue 25,000.00
2 B:Green Lantern and Johnny
  Thunder 10,000.00
3 First meeting of Justice Society
  with Flash as Chairman . . 80,000.00
4 First mission of JSA 10,000.00
5 V:Mr. X,I:Hawkgirl 8,000.00
6 Flash Leaves 5,500.00
7 Green Lantern Becomes Chairman,
  L:Hourman, C:Superman,
  Batman & Flash 6,000.00
8 I:Wonder Women;Starman and
  Dr. Mid-Nite Join,Hawkman
  Becomes Chairman 65,000.00

All-Star Comics #29
© DC Comics, Inc.

9 JSA in Latin America. 5,500.00
10 C:Flash & Green Lantern,
  JSA Time Travel story 5,500.00
11 Wonder Women joins;
  I:Justice Battalion 6,000.00
12 V:Black Dragon society 5,000.00
13 V:Hitler 5,000.00
14 JSA in Occupied Europe . . . 5,000.00
15 I:Brain Wave,A:JSA's
  Girl Friends 5,000.00
16 Propaganda/relevance issue 3,000.00
17 V:Brain Wave 3,000.00
18 I:King Bee 3,000.00
19 Hunt for Hawkman 3,000.00
20 I:Monster 3,000.00
21 Time Travel Story 2,500.00
22 Sandman and Dr. Fate Leave,
  I:Conscience, Good Fairy. . 2,500.00
23 I:Psycho-Pirate. 2,500.00
24 Propaganda/relevance issue,
  A:Conscience&Wildcat,Mr.Terrific;
  L:Starman & Spectre; Flash
  & Green Lantern Return . . . 2,500.00
25 JSA whodunit issue 2,800.00
26 V:Metal Men from Jupiter. . . . 2,500.00
27 Handicap issue,A:Wildcat . . 2,500.00
28 Ancient curse comes to life . 2,500.00
29 I:Landor from 25th Century . 2,500.00
30 V:Brain Wave 2,500.00
31 V:Zor 2,500.00
32 V:Psycho-Pirate 2,300.00
33 V:Soloman Grundy,A:Doiby
  Dickles, Last appearance
  Thunderbolt 6,000.00
34 I:Wizard 2,000.00
35 I:Per Degaton. 2,000.00
36 A:Superman and Batman. . . 5,000.00
37 I:Injustice Society of
  the World 2,700.00
38 V:Villians of History,
  A:Black Canary. 3,500.00
39 JSA in Magic World,
  Johnny Thunder leaves . . . 2,500.00
40 A:Black Canary,Junior Justice
  Society of America 2,500.00
41 Black Canary joins,A:Harlequin,
  V:Injustice Society
  of the World 2,500.00
42 I:Alchemist 2,400.00
43 V:Interdimensional gold men 2,400.00
44 I:Evil Star 2,400.00
45 Crooks develop stellar
  JSA powers 2,400.00
46 Comedy issue 2,400.00
47 V:Billy the Kid. 2,400.00
48 Time Travel story 2,400.00
49 V:Comet-Being Invaders . . . 2,400.00
50 V:Flash's Classmate 3,000.00
51 V:Diamond Men from Center
  of the Earth. 2,400.00
52 JSA Disappears from
  Earth for Years 2,400.00
53 Time Travel issue. 2,400.00
54 Circus issue 2,400.00
55 JSA Fly to Jupiter. 2,400.00
56 V:Chameleons from
  31st Century 2,400.00
57 I:Key. 3,100.00
Becomes:

ALL STAR WESTERN
April-May, 1951
58 GK(c),Trigger Twins 800.00
59 GK(c),Trail of Double Decoys . 500.00
60 CI(c),Raiders of Rocky City . . 500.00
61 thru 64 ATh . . . . @400.00
65 CI,Green Bandanna Raiders . 400.00
66 CI,Powderkeg Town 450.00
67 GK,B:Johnny Thunder 500.00
68 thru 81. . . . . @250.00
82 thru 98. . . . . @250.00
99 FF 250.00
100 CI,Sheriff for Hire 250.00

101 thru 104. . . . . @200.00
105 O:JSA, March, 1987 . . . . . . 200.00
106 and 107. . . . . @200.00
108 O:Johnny Thunder 400.00
109 thru 116. . . . . @200.00
117 CI,O:Super-Chief. 250.00
118 Eyes of Johnny Thunder. . . . 200.00
119 Ghost-Town Gunfight 200.00

ALL-STAR COMICS
1976–78
58 RE,WW,R:JSA,I:Power Girl . . . 75.00
59 RE,WW,Brain Wave 40.00
60 KG,WW,I:Vulcan 40.00
61 KG,WW,V:Vulcan 40.00
62 KG,WW,A:E-2 Superman 40.00
63 KG,WW,A:E-2 Superman,
  Solomon Grundy 40.00
64 WW,Shining Knight 40.00
65 KG,WW,E-2 Superman,
  Vandal Savage 40.00
66 JSon,BL,Injustice Society 40.00
67 JSon,BL 40.00
68 JSon,BL 40.00
69 JSon,BL,A:E-2 Superman,
  Starman,Dr.Mid-Nite 60.00
70 JSon,BL,Huntress. 40.00
71 JSon,BL 40.00
72 JSon,A:Golden Age Huntress. . 40.00
73 JSon 40.00
74 JSon 40.00

ALL STAR COMICS
1999
1 JeR(s),F:Justice Society
  of America, V:Stalker's Seven . . 3.00
2 JeR(s) conclusion 3.00
Giant #1 80-page 5.00

ALL STAR SQUADRON
1981–87
1 RB,JOy,JSa,I:Degaton. 8.00
2 RB,JOy,Robotman 5.00
3 RB,JOy,Robotman 5.00
4 RB,JOy,Robotman 5.00
5 RB/JOy,I:Firebrand(Dannette) . . . 5.00
6 JOy,Hawkgirl 5.00
7 JOy,Hawkgirl 5.00
8 DH/JOy,A:Steel 5.00
9 DH/JOy,A:Steel 5.00
10 JOy,V:Binary Brotherhood 5.00
11 JOy,V:Binary Brotherhood. 5.00
12 JOy,R:Dr.Hastor O:Hawkman . . 5.00
13 JOy,photo(c) 5.00
14 JOy,JLA crossover 5.00
15 JOy,JLA crossover 5.00
16 I&D:Nuclear. 5.00
17 Trial of Robotman 5.00
18 V:Thor 5.00
19 V:Brainwave 5.00
20 JOy,V:Brainwave. 5.00
21 JOy,I:Cyclotron (1st JOy
  Superman). 7.00
22 JOy,V:Deathbolt,Cyclotron 5.00
23 JOy,I:Amazing-Man. 5.00
24 JOy,I:Brainwave,Jr.. . . . . 7.00
25 JOy,I:Infinity Inc.. . . . . 7.00
26 JOy,Infinity Inc. 7.00
27 Spectre 5.00
28 JOy,Spectre. 5.00
29 JOy,retold story. 5.00
30 V:Black Dragons 5.00
31 All-Star gathering 5.00
32 O:Freedom Fighters 5.00
33 Freedom Fighters,I:Tsunami . . . 5.00
34 Freedom Fighters 5.00
35 RB,Shazam family 5.00
36 Shazam family 5.00
37 A:Shazam Family 5.00
38 V:The Real American 5.00
39 V:The Real American 5.00

All Star Squadron #29
© *DC Comics Inc.*

40 D:The Real American 5.00
41 O:Starman. 5.00
42 V:Tsunami,Kung 5.00
43 V:Tsunami,Kung 5.00
44 I:Night & Fog. 5.00
45 I:Zyklon 5.00
46 V:Baron Blitzkrieg 5.00
47 TM,O:Dr.Fate 10.00
48 A:Blackhawk 5.00
49 A:Dr.Occult 5.00
50 Crisis 7.00
51 AA,Crisis 5.00
52 Crisis 5.00
53 Crisis,A:The Dummy 5.00
54 Crisis,V:The Dummy 5.00
55 Crisis,V:Anti-Monitor 5.00
56 Crisis 5.00
57 A:Dr.Occult 5.00
58 I:Mekanique 5.00
59 A:Mekanique,Spectre 5.00
60 Crisis 1942, conclusion. 5.00
61 O:Liberty Belle 5.00
62 O:The Shining Knight 5.00
63 O:Robotman 5.00
64 WB/TD,V:Funny Face 5.00
65 DH/TD,O:Johnny Quick 5.00
66 TD,O:Tarantula 5.00
67 TD,Last Issue,O:JSA 5.00
Ann.#1 JOy,O:G.A.,Atom 5.00
Ann.#2 JOy,Infinity Inc. 5.00
Ann.#3 WB,JOy,KG,GP,DN 5.00

ALL STAR SUPERMAN
Nov., 2005
1 GMo(s). 4.00
2 GMo(s), Fortress of Solitude . . . 3.00
3 GMo(s), Lois Lane, Superwoman 3.00
4 GMo(s), F:Jimmy Olsen. 3.00
5 GMo(s),Clark Kent, convict 3.00
6 GMo(s),back to Smallville 3.00
7 GMo(s),V:Bizarro 3.00
8 GMo(s),V:Bizarro 3.00
9 GMo(s). 3.00
10 GMo(s) 3.00
11 GMo(s), Superman dead 3.00
12 GMo(s), Super-challenges 3.00

ALL STAR WESTERN
See: WEIRD WESTERN TALES

AMAZONS ATTACK
Apr., 2007
1 (of 6) 3.00

2 F:JLA, Teen Titans 3.00
3 F:Supergirl and Wonder Girl 3.00
4 Target: Pres. of the US 3.00
5 Final battle begins 3.00
6 Finale 3.00

AMBER:
THE GUNS OF AVALON
Aug., 1996
1 (of 3) adapt. of Roger Zelazny
   classic 7.00
2 and 3 conclusion . . . . @7.00

AMBUSH BUG
1985
1 KG,I:Cheeks. 3.00
2 KG thru 4 . . . . @3.00
Spec.#1 Stocking Stuffer,
   KG,R:Cheeks (1986) 3.00
Spec.#1 Nothing Special
   KG,A:Sandman,Death (1992) . . 3.50

AMBUSH BUG
YEAR NONE
July, 2008
1 (of 6) 3.00
1a variant (c) (1:10) 3.00
2 thru 5 . . . . @3.00

AMERICA VS.
JUSTICE SOCIETY
Jan.–April, 1985
1 AA,R,Thomas Script 10.00
2 AA 7.00
3 AA 7.00
4 AA, ... 7.00

AMERICAN CENTURY
DC/Vertigo, March, 2001
1 HC,vet hijacks plane 5.00
2 HC,Hell hotter for Harry 3.00
3 HC,Guatemalan Revolution 3.00
4 HC,Bananarama 3.00
5 HC,The Protector,pt.1 . . . . 3.00
6 HC,The Protector,pt.2 . . . . 3.00
7 HC,The Protector,pt.3 . . . . 3.00
8 HC,The Protector,pt.4 . . . . 3.00
9 HC,Route 66 . . . . 3.00
10 HC,White Lightning,pt.1 . . . . . . 3.00
11 HC,White Lightning,pt.2 . . . . . . 3.00
12 HC,White Lightning,pt.3 . . . . . . 3.00
13 HC,White Lightning,pt.4 . . . . . . 3.00
14 HC,An American in Paris,pt.1 . . 3.00
15 HC,An American in Paris,pt.2 . . 3.00
16 HC,An American in Paris,pt.3 . . 3.00
17 HC,Coming Home,pt.1 . . . . 3.00
18 HC,Coming Home,pt.2 . . . . 3.00
19 HC,Coming Home,pt.3 . . . . 3.00
20 HC,Coming Home,Pt.4 . . . . 3.00
21 HC,Coming Home,pt.5 . . . . 3.00
22 HC,Tramps,pt.1 . . . . 3.00
23 HC,Tramps,pt.2 . . . . 3.00
24 HC,one-shot 3.00
25 HC,Bite the Big Apple,pt.1 . . . . 3.00
26 HC,Bite the Big Apple,pt.2 . . . . 3.00
27 HC,Bite the Big Apple,pt.3 . . . . 3.00

AMERICAN FREAK: A
TALE OF THE UN-MEN
DC/Vertigo, 1994
1 B:DLp,(s),VcL,R:Un-Men 2.50
2 VcL,A:Crassus 2.50
3 VcL,A:Scylla 2.50
4 VcL,A:Scylla 2.50
5 VcL,Final Issue 2.50

AMERICAN SPLENDOR
DC/Vertigo, Sept., 2006
1 (of 4) HP 3.00
2 HP 3.00
3 HP 3.00
4 HP 3.00

AMERICAN SPLENDOR:
SEASON TWO
Vertigo (B&W), April, 2008
1 (of 4) by Harvey Pekar 3.00
2 thru 3 . . . . @3.00

AMERICAN VIRGIN
DC/Vertigo, March, 2006
1 You Always Remember Your
   First Time. 3.00
2 thru 23 . . . . @3.00

Amethyst Princess of Gemworld #1
© *DC Comics, Inc.*

AMETHYST
[Limited Series], 1983–84
[PRINCESS OF GEMWORLD]
1 Origin 2.50
2 thru 7 EC . . . . @2.50
8 EC,O:Gemworld. 2.50
9 thru 12 EC . . . . @2.50
Spec.#1 KG 2.50
[Regular Series], 1985–86
1 thru 12 EC . . . . @2.50
13 EC,Crisis,A:Dr.Fate. 2.50
14 EC 2.50
15 EC,Castle Amethyst Destroyed . 2.50
16 EC 2.50
Spec.#1 EM 2.50
[Mini-Series], 1987–88
1 EM 2.50
2 EM 2.50
3 EM 2.50
4 EM,O:Mordru 2.50

ANARKY
March, 1997
1 AlG(s),NBy,JRu,Anarky vs.
   Etrigan 4.00
2 AlG(s),NBy,JRu,V:Darkseid 2.50
3 AlG(s),NBy,JRu,A:Batman 2.50
4 AlG(s),NBy,JRu,A:Batman,concl.. . 2.50
2nd Series,1999
1 AlG(s),NBy,JRu,F:JLA 2.50
2 AlG(s),NBy,JRu,F:GreenLantern . 2.50

3 AIG(s),NBy,JRu,F:GreenLantern . 2.50
4 AIG(s),NBy,JRu,V:Ra's al Ghul . 2.50
5 AIG(s),NBy,JRu,V:Ra's
  al Ghul,pt.2 . . . . 2.50
6 AIG(s),NBy,JRu,F:Ra's
  al Ghul,pt.3 . . . . 2.50
7 AIG,NBy,JRu,Day of Judgment . . 2.50
8 AIG(s),NBy,JRu, final issue 2.50

ANGEL & THE APE
1991
1 Apes of Wrath,pt.1 . . . . 3.00
2 Wrath pt.2,A:G.Gardner 3.00
3 Wrath,pt.3,A:InferiorFive 3.00
4 Wrath,pt.4,A:InferiorFive 3.00

ANGEL AND THE APE
DC/Vertigo, Aug., 2001
1 (of 4) HC,F:Angel O'Day 3.00
2 thru 4 HC . . . . @3.00

ANGELTOWN
DC/Vertigo, Nov., 2004
1 (of 5) SMa 3.00
2 thru 4 SMa . . . . @3.00
5 SMa 3.00

Angel and the Ape #2
© DC Comics, Inc.

ANIMA
DC/Vertigo, 1994–95
1 R:Anima 2.50
2 V:Scarecrow. 2.50
3 V:Scarecrow. 2.50
4 A:Nameless one. 2.50
5 CI,V:Arkana 2.50
6 CI,V:Arkana 2.50
7 Zero Hour. 2.50
8 Nameless One 2.50
9 Superboy & Nameless One 2.50
10 A:Superboy 2.50
11 V:Nameless One 2.50
12 A:Hawkman,V:Shrike 2.50
13 A:Hawkman,Shrike 2.50
14 Return to Gotham City 2.50
15 V:Psychic Vampire, final issue . . 3.00

ANIMAL ANTICS
1946–49
1 B:Racoon Kids 650.00
2 . . . . 350.00
3 thru 10 . . . . @200.00
11 thru 23 . . . . @125.00

ANIMAL-MAN
1988–95
1 BB(c),B:GMo(s),ChT,DHz,
  B:Animal Rights,I:Dr.Myers . . . 12.00
2 BB(c),ChT,DHz,A:Superman 6.00
3 BB(c),ChT,DHz,A:B'wana Beast . 5.00
4 BB(c),ChT,DHz,V:B'wana Beast,
  E:Animal Rights 5.00
5 BB(c),ChT,DHz,
  I&D:Crafty Coyote 5.00
6 BB(c),ChT,DHz,A:Hawkman 5.00
7 BB(c),ChT,DHz,D:Red Mask 5.00
8 BB(c),ChT,DHz,V:Mirror Master . . 5.00
9 BB(c),DHz,TG,A:Martian
  Manhunter 5.00
10 BB(c),ChT,DHz,A:Vixen,
  B:O:Animal Man 5.00
11 BB(c),ChT,DHz,I:Hamed Ali,
  Tabu,A:Vixen 3.00
12 BB(c),D:Hamed Ali,A:Vixen,
  B'wanaBeast 3.00
13 BB(c),I:Dominic Mndawe,R:B'wana
  Beast,Apartheid 3.00
14 BB(c),TG,SeM,A:Future Animal
  Man,I:Lennox 3.00
15 BB(c),ChT,DHz,A:Dolphin 3.00
16 BB(c),ChT,DHz,A:JLA. 3.00
17 BB(c),ChT,DHz,A:Mirr.Master . . . 3.00
18 BB(c),ChT,DHz,A:Lennox 3.00
19 BB(c),ChT,DHz,D:Ellen,
  Cliff,Maxine 3.00
20 BB(c),ChT,DHz,I:Bug-Man 3.00
21 BB(c),ChT,DHz,N&V:Bug-Man . . 3.00
22 BB(c),PCu,SeM,A:Rip Hunter . . . 3.00
23 BB(c),A:Phantom Stranger 3.00
24 BB(c),V:Psycho Pirate 3.00
25 BB(c),ChT,MFm,I:Comic
  Book Limbo 3.00
26 BB(c),E:GMo(s),ChT,MFm,
  A:Grant Morrison 3.00
27 BB(c),B:PMi(s),ChT,MFm 3.00
28 BB(c),ChT,MFm,I:Nowhere Man,
  I&D:Front Page 3.00
29 ChT,SDi,V:National Man 3.00
30 BB(c),ChT,MFm,V:Angel Mob . . . 3.00
31 BB(c),ChT,MFm 3.00
32 BB(c),E:PMi(s),ChT,MFm 3.00
33 BB(c),B:TV(s),SDi,A:Travis
  Cody 3.00
34 BB(c),SDi,Requiem. 3.00
35 BB(c),SDi,V:Radioactive Dogs . . 3.00
36 BB(c),SDi,A:Mr.Rainbow. 3.00
37 BB(c),SDi,Animal/Lizard Man . . . 3.00
38 BB(c),SDi,A:Mr.Rainbow. 3.00
39 BB(c),TMd,SDi,Wolfpack in
  San Diego 3.00
40 BB(c),SDi,War of the Gods
  x-over. 3.00
41 BB(c),SDi,V:Star Labs
  Renegades,I:Winky 3.00
42 BB(c),SDi,V:Star Labs
  Renegades 3.00
43 BB(c),SDi,I:Tristess,A:Vixen 3.00
44 BB(c),SDi,A:Vixen. 3.00
45 BB(c),StP,SDi,I:L.Decker. 3.00
46 BB(c),SDi,I:Frank Baker 3.00
47 BB(c),SDi,I:Shining Man,
  (B'wana Beast) 3.00
48 BB(c),SDi,V:Antagon. 3.00
49 BB(c),SDi,V:Antagon. 3.00
50 BB(c),E:TV(s),SDi,I:Metaman . . . 5.00
51 BB(c),B:JaD(s),StP,B:Flesh
  and Blood 3.00
52 BB(c),StP,Homecoming. 3.00
53 BB(c),StP,Flesh and Blood 3.00
54 BB(c),StP,Flesh and Blood 3.00
55 BB(c),StP,Flesh and Blood 3.00
56 BB(c),StP,E:Flesh and Blood,
  Double-sized 6.00

Animal Man #63
© DC Comics, Inc.

DC/Vertigo, 1993
57 BB(c),StP,B:Recreation,
  Ellen in NY. 3.00
58 BB(c),StP,Wild Side 3.00
59 BB(c),RsB,GHi(i),Wild Town 3.00
60 RsB,GHi(i),Wild life. 3.00
61 BB(c),StP,Tooth and Claw#1. . . . 3.00
62 BB(c),StP,Tooth and Claw#2. . . . 3.00
63 BB(c),V:Leviathan 3.00
64 DIB(c),WSm,DnS(i),
  Breath of God 3.00
65 RDB(c),WSm,
  Perfumed Garden 3.00
66 A:Kindred Spirit 3.00
67 StP,Mysterious Ways #1 . . . . 3.00
68 StP,Mysterious Ways #2 . . . . 3.00
69 Animal Man's Family. 3.00
70 GgP(c),StP 3.00
71 GgP(c),StP,Maxine Alive? 3.00
72 StP 3.00
73 StP,Power Life Church 3.00
74 StP,Power Life Church 3.00
75 StP,Power Life Church 3.00
76 StP,Pilgrimage problems. 3.00
77 Cliff shot 3.00
78 StP,Animal Man poisoned. 3.00
79 New Direction 3.00
80 New Direction 3.00
81 Wild Type,pt.1 . . . . 3.00
82 Wild Type,pt.2 . . . . 3.00
83 Wild Type,pt.3 . . . . 3.00
84 F:Maxine,SupernaturalDreams . . 3.00
85 Animal Mundi,pt.1 . . . . 3.00
86 Animal Mundi,pt.2 . . . . 3.00
87 Animal Mundi,pt.3 . . . . 3.00
88 Morphogenetic Fields 3.00
89 final issue 3.00
Ann.#1 BB(c),JaD,TS(i),RIB(i),
  Children Crusade,F:Maxine. . . . 4.25

ANIMANIACS
Warner Bros./DC May, 1995
1 F:Yakko,Wakko,Dot 8.00
2 thru 20 . . . . @4.00
21 thru 59 . . . . @3.00
Christmas Spec. 4.00

ANTHRO
1968–69
1 HwP 120.00
2 HwP 80.00
3 thru 5 HwP . . . . @90.00
6 HwP,WW(c&a) 100.00

AQUAMAN

[1st Regular Series], 1962–78
1 NC,I:Quisp	2,000.00
2 NC,V:Captain Sykes	900.00
3 NC,Aquaman from Atlantis	750.00
4 NC,A:Quisp	500.00
5 NC,The Haunted Sea	500.00
6 NC,A:Quisp	400.00
7 NC,Sea Beasts of Atlantis	400.00
8 NC,Plot to Steal the Seas	400.00
9 NC,V:King Neptune	400.00
10 NC,A:Quisp	400.00
11 I: Mera	325.00
12 NC,The Cosmic Gladiators	325.00
13 NC,Invasion of the Giant Reptiles	325.00
14 NC,AquamanSecretPowers	325.00
15 NC,Menace of the Man-Fish.	325.00
16 NC,Duel of the Sea Queens	325.00
17 NC,Man Who Vanquished Aquaman	325.00
18 W:Aquaman & Mera	325.00
19 NC,Atlanteans for Sale	325.00
20 NC,Sea King's DoubleDoom	325.00
21 NC,I:Fisherman	150.00
22 NC,The Trap of the Sinister Sea Nymphs	150.00
23 NC,I:Aquababy	150.00
24 NC,O:Black Manta	150.00
25 NC,Revolt of Aquaboy	150.00
26 NC,I:O.G.R.E.	150.00
27 NC,Battle of the Rival Aquamen	150.00
28 NC,Hail Aquababy,King of Atlantis	150.00
29 I:Ocean Master	175.00
30 NC,C:JLA	175.00
31 NC,V:O.G.R.E.	175.00
32 NC,V:Tryton	175.00
33 NC,I:Aquagirl	190.00
34 NC,I:Aquabeast.	125.00
35 I:Black Manta	125.00
36 NC,What Seeks the Awesome Threesome?	125.00
37 I:Scavenger	125.00
38 NC,I:Liquidator	125.00
39 NC,How to Kill a Sea King	125.00
40 JAp,Sorcerers from the Sea	125.00
41 JAp,Quest for Mera,pt.1	90.00
42 JAp,Quest for Mera,pt.2	90.00
43 JAp,Quest for Mera,pt.3	90.00
44 JAp,Quest for Mera,pt.4	90.00
45 JAp,Quest for Mera,pt.5	90.00
46 JAp,Quest for Mera concl.	90.00
47 JAp,Revolution in Atlantis #1 rep.Adventure #268	90.00
48 JAp,Revolution in Atlantis #2 rep.Adventure #260	135.00
49 JAp,As the Seas Die.	90.00
50 JAp,NA,A:Deadman	175.00
51 JAp,NA,A:Deadman	175.00
52 JAp,NA,A:Deadman	175.00
53 JAp,Is California Sinking?	35.00
54 JAp,Crime Wave	35.00
55 JAp,Return of the Alien	35.00
56 JAp,I&O:Crusader (1970)	35.00
57 JAp,V:Black Manta (1977)	35.00
58 JAp,O:Aquaman rtd	40.00
59 JAp,V:Scavenger	35.00
60 DN,V:Scavenger	35.00
61 DN,BMc,A:Batman	35.00
62 DN,A:Ocean Master	25.00
63 DN,V:Ocean Master, final issue	25.00

[1st Limited Series], 1986
1 V:Ocean Master	6.00
2 V:Ocean Master	4.00
3 V:Ocean Master	4.00
4 V:Ocean Master	4.00

[2nd Limited Series], 1989
1 CS,Atlantis Under Siege	3.50

2 CS,V:Invaders	3.00
3 CS,Mera turned Psychotic.	3.00
4 CS,Poseidonis Under Siege	3.00
5 CS,Last Stand,final issue.	3.00
Spec#1 MPa,Legend o/Aquaman	3.00

[2nd Regular Series], 1991–92
1 Poseidonis Under Attack, C:J'onn J'onzz,Blue Beetle	4.00
2 V:Oumland	2.50
3 I:Iqula	2.50
4 V:Iqula,A:Queequeg.	2.50
5 A:Aqualad,Titans,M.Manhunter, R:Manta	2.50
6 V: Manta.	2.50
7 R:Mera	2.50
8 A:Batman,V:NKV Demon.	2.50
9 Eco-Wars#1,A:Sea Devils.	2.50
10 Eco-Wars#2,A:Sea Devils.	2.50
11 V:Gigantic Dinosaur	2.50
12 A:Iaula.	2.50
13 V:The Scavenger	2.50
14 V:The Scavenger	2.50

[3rd Regular Series], 1994–2001
0 B:PDd(s),Paternal secret.	7.00
1 PDd(s),R:Aqualad,I:Charybdis.	6.00
2 V:Charybdis	7.00
3 B:PDd(s),Superboy	4.00
4 B:PDd(s),Lobo	4.00
5 New Costume	4.00
6 V:The Deep Six	4.00
7 Kako's Metamorphosis	4.00
8 V:Corona and Naiad	4.00
9 JPi(c&a),V:Deadline,A:Koryak	3.00
10 A:Green Lantern,Koryak	3.00
11 R:Mera	3.00
12 F:Mera.	3.00
13 V:Thanatos	3.00
14 PDd,V:Major Disaster,Underworld Unleashed tie-in	3.00
15 PDd,V:Tiamat	3.00
16 PDd,A:Justice League	3.00
17 PDd,V:underwater gargoyles	3.00
18 PDd,Biblical Sense	3.00
19 PDd,V:Ocean Master	3.00
20 PDd,V:Ocean Master	3.00
21 PDd,JCf,A:Dolphin, V:ThiernaNaOge	3.00
22 PDd(s).	3.00
23 PDd(s),I:Deep Blue (Neptune Perkins)	3.00
24 PDd(s),A:Neptune Perkins	3.00
25 PDd(s),MEg,HSm,Atlantis united, Aquaman king?	3.00
26 PDd(s),MEg,HSm,Oceans threatened, Final Night tie-in	3.00
27 PDd(s),MEg,HSm,V:Demon Gate, dolphin killer.	3.00
28 PDd(s),JCf,JP,A:J'onn J'onzz	3.00
29 PDd(s),MEg,HSm,	3.00
30 PDd(s),MEg,HSm,The Pit.	3.00
31 PDd(s),V:The Shark, mind-controlled aquatic army.	3.00
32 PDd(s),A:Swamp Thing	3.00
33 PDd(s),Aquaman's dark powers affect him physically	3.00
34 PDd(s),V:Triton	3.00
35 PDd(s),JCf,I:Gamesman, A:Animal Man	3.00
36 PDd(s),JCf,R:Poseidonis, Tempest,Vulko	3.00
37 PDd,JCf,Genesis,V:Darkseid	3.00
38 PDd,JCf,capitalism	3.00
39 PDd,JCf,Perkins Family Reunion	3.00
40 PDd,JCf,Dr. Polaris	3.00
41 PDd,JCf,BSf,F:Power Girl.	2.50
42 PDd,JCf.	2.50
43 PDd,JCf,Millennium Giants, pt.2 x-over, A:Superman Red	2.50
44 PDd,JCf,F:Golden Age Flash, Sentinel	2.50
45 PDd,JCf,V:Triton	2.50
46 PDd,JCf,news of Mera	2.50

47 DAn,Shadows on Water,pt.1	2.50
48 DAn,Shadows on Water,pt.2	2.50
49 DAn,ALa,JCf,V:Tempest	2.50
50 EL,NRd,New Costume	2.50
51 EL,NRd,V:King Noble	2.50
52 EL,V:Fire Trolls	2.50
53 EL,A:Superman.	2.50
54 EL,A:Landlovers	2.50
55 EL,wooing Mera	2.50
56 EL,V:Piranha Man,pt.1	2.50
57 EL,V:Piranha Man,pt.2	2.50
58 EL,V:DemonGate & BlackManta.	2.50
59 EL,drugs in Atlantis.	2.50
60 NRd,W:Tempest & Dolphin.	2.50
61 NRd,Day of Judgment x-over	2.50
62 EL(s),NRd.	2.50
63 NRd.	2.50
64 DJu,SEp,NRd	2.50
65 DJu,SEp,NRd.	2.50
66 DJu,PR,NRd,F:JLA.	2.50
67 DJu,SEp,NRd	2.50
68 DJu,SEp,NRd,V:Cerdia.	2.50
69 DJu,SEp,NRd,	2.50
70 DJu,new alliance.	3.00
71 DJu,SEp,NRd,A:Warlord.	3.00
72 DJu,SEp,NRd,V:Ch'Rinn	3.00
73 DJu,SEp,NRd,V:Valgus.	3.00
74 DJu,SEp,NRd,death of friend	3.00
75 DJu,SEp,NRd,final issue	3.00
Ann.#1 Year One Annual, V:Triton, A:Superman,Mera	4.00
Ann.#2 Legends o/t Dead Earth	3.50
Ann.#3 Pulp Heroes (Hard Boiled)	5.00
Ann.#4 PDa, Ghosts	3.50
Ann.#5 JOs(s),MBr,DG, JLApe Gorilla Warfare	3.50
Spec.#1,000,000 DAn&ALa(s),TGb, BAn, King of Waterworld	3.00
Secret Files #1 EL	5.00

[4th Regular Series], Dec. 2002
1 Obsidian Age aftermath	3.00
2 F:Martian Manhunter	3.00
3 New look and costume	3.00
4 F:Tempest	3.00
5 V:The Thirst	3.00
6 V:The Thirst	3.00
7 undead pirates	3.00
8 V:Black Mantra	3.00
9 V:Black Mantra	3.00
10 V:The Thirst	3.00
11 V:The Thirst.	3.00
12 V:The Thirst	3.00
13 Perfect storm	2.50
14 Octo-Man	2.50

Aquaman 3rd Series #51
© DC Comics Inc.

15 American Tidal,pt.1 . . . . 2.50
16 American Tidal,pt.2 . . . . 2.50
17 American Tidal,pt.3 . . . . 2.50
18 American Tidal,pt.4 . . . . 2.50
19 F:Lorena 2.50
20 American Tidal,concl. 2.50
21 With the Fishes,pt.1 . . . . 2.50
22 With the Fishes,pt.2 . . . . 2.50
23 With the Fishes,pt.3 . . . . 2.50
24 JOs(s),CsB, Sharks 2.50
25 JAr(s),in San Diego 2.50
26 JAr(s),I:Aquagirl 2.50
27 JAr(s),V:Ocean Master 2.50
28 JAr(s),V:Malrey 2.50
29 JAr(s),Malrey vs. Conger 2.50
30 JAr(s),Black Manta returns 2.50
31 JAr(s),V:Black Manta 2.50
32 JAr(s),V:Black Manta 2.50
33 JAr(s),V:Black Manta 2.50
34 JAr(s),reunited with Mera 2.50
35 JAr(s),Omac project tie-in 2.50
36 JAr(s),Koryak returns to Atlantis . 2.50
37 JAr(s),V:Spectre 2.50
38 JAr(s),New home in Sub Diego . . 2.50
39 JAr(s),V:Black Manta 2.50
Spec. Secret Files 2003 . . . . 5.00
Becomes:

AQUAMAN:
SWORD OF ATLANTIS
40 KBk,Once and Future, pt.1 . . . . . 3.00
41 KBk,Once and Future, pt.2 . . . . . 3.00
42 KBk,Once and Future, pt.3 . . . . . 3.00
43 KBk,Once and Future, pt.4 . . . . . 3.00
44 KBk,Once and Future, pt.5 . . . . . 3.00
45 KBk,Once and Future, pt.6 . . . . . 3.00
46 KBk,A:King Shark 3.00
47 KBk,A:Mera, Vulko 3.00
48 KBk,Way of the Fisherman 3.00
49 KBk,V:The Fisherman 3.00
50 King of the Sea, 48-pgs. 4.00
51 Black Manta;Trident of Poseidon 3.00
52 V:Black Manta 3.00
53 Control of Sub Diego 3.00
54 SwM,Dweller in the Depths 3.00
55 F:Arthur, Vulko 3.00
56 Aquaman's murky past 3.00
57 New Aquaman 3.00

AQUAMAN: TIME & TIDE
1993–94
1 PDd(s),O:Aquaman 3.00
2 thru 4 PDd(s),O:Aquaman . . . @3.00

ARAK
1981–85
1 EC,O:Ara 3.00
2 thru 12 EC . . . . @2.50
13 thru 23 AA . . . . @2.50
24 Double size 2.50
25 thru 50 . . . . @2.50
Ann.#1 . . . . 2.50

ARCANA: THE BOOKS
OF MAGIC
DC/Vertigo, 1994
Ann.#1 JBo(c),JNR(s),PrG,Children's
   Crusade,R:Tim Hunter,
   A:Free Country 4.00

ARION,
LORD OF ATLANTIS
1982–85
1 JDu,Star Spawn Sun Death 3.00
2 JDu,I:Mara 2.50
3 JDu 2.50
4 JDu,O:Arion 2.50
5 JDu 2.50
6 JDu 2.50

Arion, Lord of Atlantis, Vol. 2 #7
© DC Comics, Inc.

7 thru 12 . . . . @2.50
13 thru 15 JDu . . . . @2.50
16 thru 35 . . . . @2.50
Spec. 2.50

ARION THE IMMORTAL
1992
1 RWi,R:Arion 3.00
2 RWi,V:Garffon 2.50
3 RWi,V:Garn Daanuth 2.50
4 RWi,V:Garn Daanuth 2.50
5 RWi,Darkworlet 2.50
6 RWi,MG,A:Power Girl 2.50

ARKHAM ASYLUM:
LIVING HELL
May 2003
1 (of 6) F:Warren White 3.00
2 Food Fight 3.00
3 Humphry Dumpler 3.00
4 F:Killer Croc 3.00
5 F:Jason Blood 3.00
6 Concl. 3.00

ARMAGEDDON 2001
May, 1991
1 DJu,DG,I&O:Waverider 4.00
1a 2nd printing 2.50
1b 3rd printing (silver) 2.50
2 DJu,ATi,Monarch revealed as Hawk,
   D:Dove,L:Capt Atom(JLE) 3.00
Spec.#1 MR 3.00

ARMAGEDDON 2001
ARMAGEDDON:
THE ALIEN AGENDA
1991–92
1 DJu,JOy,A:Monarch,Capt.Atom . . 2.50
2 V:Ancient Romans 2.50
3 JRu(i),The Old West 2.50
4 DG,GP,V:Nazi's,last issue 2.50

ARMAGEDDON:
INFERNO
1992
1 TMd,LMc,A:Creeper,Batman,
   Firestorm 2.50
2 AAd,LMc,WS,I:Abraxis,A:Lobo . . 2.50

3 AAd,WS,LMc,TMd,MN,R:Justice
   Society 2.50
4 AAd,WS,LMc,TMd,MN,DG,
   V:Abraxis,A:Justice Society 2.50

ARMY@LOVE
Vertigo, Mar., 2007
1 RV,GEr 3.00
2 RV,GEr,Hot Zone Club. 3.00
3 RV,GEr,F:Switzer & Loman 3.00
4 RV,GEr,In Afbaghistan 3.00
5 RV,GEr,In Afbaghistan 3.00
6 RV,GEr, ... 3.00
7 RV,GEr,Circus Elephants 3.00
8 RV,GEr,Allie's inner bigamist 3.00
9 RV,GEr,Allie's inner bigamist 3.00
10 RV,GEr,Mother of Mountain 3.00
11 RV,GEr,Loman & Flabbergast . . . 3.00
12 RV,GEr,season finale 3.00

ARMY@LOVE:
THE ART OF WAR
Vertigo, Aug., 2008
1 (of 6) 3.00
2 thru 4 . . . . @3.00

ARSENAL
Aug., 1998
1 (of 4) F:Black Canary 2.50
2 F:Green Arrow 2.50
3 F:Vandal Savage 2.50
4 conclusion 2.50

ATARI FORCE
1984–85
1 JL,I:TempestDart 5.00
2 JL 3.00
3 JL 3.00
4 RA/JL/JO 3.00
5 RA/JL/JO 3.00
6 thru 12 JL . . . . @3.00
13 KG 3.00
14 thru 21 EB . . . . @3.00

ATLANTIS CHRONICLES
1990
1 EM,Atlantis 50,000 years ago . . . 3.50
2 EM,Atlantis Sunk 3.25
3 EM,Twin Cities of Poseidonis
   & Tritonis 3.25
4 EM,King Orin's Daughter
   Cora Assumes Throne 3.25
5 EM,Orin vs. Shalako 3.25
6 EM,Contact with Surface
   Dwellers 3.25
7 EM,Queen Atlanna gives Birth to
   son(Aquaman)48 pg.final issue. 3.25

ATOM, THE
1962–68
1 MA,GK,I:Plant Master 2,000.00
2 MA,GK,V:Plant Master 750.00
3 MA,GK,I:Chronos 600.00
4 MA,GK,Snapper Carr 500.00
5 MA,GK 500.00
6 MA,GK 500.00
7 MA,GK,1st Atom & Hawkman
   team-up 600.00
8 MA,GK,A:JLA,V:Doctor Light . . 350.00
9 MA,GK 350.00
10 MA,GK 350.00
11 MA,GK 300.00
12 MA,GK 300.00
13 MA,GK 300.00
14 MA,GK 300.00
15 MA,GK 300.00
16 MA,GK 200.00
17 MA,GK 200.00
18 MA,GK 200.00

19 MA,GK,A:Zatanna	200.00
20 MA,GK	200.00
21 MA,GK	135.00
22 MA,GK	135.00
23 MA,GK	135.00
24 MA,GK,V:Jason Woodrue	135.00
25 MA,GK	135.00
26 GK	125.00
27 GK	125.00
28 GK	125.00
29 GK,A:E-2 Atom,Thinker	350.00
30 GK	125.00
31 GK,A:Hawkman	100.00
32 GK	100.00
33 GK	100.00
34 GK,V:Big Head	100.00
35 GK	100.00
36 GK,A:Golden Age Atom	150.00
37 GK,I:Major Mynah	100.00
38 Sinister stopover Earth	100.00

Becomes:

ATOM & HAWKMAN
1968–69

39 MA, V:Tekla	90.00
40 DD,JKu,MA	75.00
41 DD,JKu,MA	75.00
42 MA,V:Brama	75.00
43 MA,I:Gentleman Ghost	75.00
44 DD	75.00
45 DD	75.00

AVATAR
1991

1 A:Midnight & Allies	7.00
2 Search for Tablets	6.00
3 V:Cyric, Myrkul, final issue	6.00

AVENGERS/JLA
DC/Marvel 2003

2 (of 4) KBk,GP(c), 48-pg	6.00
4 KBk,GP,48-pg	6.00

AZRAEL
1994

1 I:New Azrael,Brian Bryan	5.00
2 A:Batman,New Azreal	3.50
3 V:Order of St. Dumas	3.50
4 The System	3.00
5 BKi(c&a),R:Ra's al Ghul,Talia [new Miraweb format begins]	3.00
6 BKi(c&a),Ra's al Ghul,Talia	3.00
7 Sister Lily's Transformation	3.00

Azrael #20
© DC Comics Inc.

8 System Secret	2.50
9 Jean Paul Vanishes	2.50
10 DON,BKi,JmP,F:Neron, Underworld Unleashed tie-in	2.50
11 DON,BKi,JmP,A:Batman	2.50
12 DON,BKi,JmP,Azrael looks for Shondra	2.50
13 DON,BKi,Demon Time,pt.1	2.50
14 DON,BKi,Demon Time,pt.2	2.50
15 DON,BKi,Contagion,pt.5	3.00
16 DON,BKi,Contagion,pt.10	2.50
17 DON,BKi,JmP,A:Dr.Orchid	2.50
18 DON,BKi,JmP,A:Dr.Orchid	2.50
19 DON(s),BKi,Save the Innocents	2.50
20 DON(s),BKi,A Prayer of Fire	2.50
21 DON(s),BKi,Renunciation	2.50
22 DON(s),BKi,JmP,Angel in Hiding, pt.2 (of 3)	2.50
23 DON(s),BKi,JmP,Angel in Hiding, pt.3	2.50
24 DON(s),BKi,JmP,The Order's return	2.50
25 DON(s),BKi,JmP,V:Brother Rollo	2.50
26 DON(s),BKi,Fall of St. Dumas	2.50
27 DON(s),BKi,JmP,Angel Insane, pt.1	2.50
28 DON(s),BKi,JmP,Joker, Riddler & Two-Face escape from Arkham Asylum	2.50
29 DON(s),DBw,JmP, F:Ra's Al Ghul, pt.1	2.50
30 DON(s),DBw,JmP, F:Ra's Al Ghul, pt.2	2.50
31 DON(s),JmP Angel and the Monster Maker, pt.1 (of 3)	2.50
32 DON(s),JmP Angel and the Monster Maker, pt.2	2.50
33 DON(s),JmP Angel and the Monster Maker, pt.3 concl.	2.50
34 DON(s),JmP,Genesis, a parademon	2.50
35 DON(s),JmP,F:Hitman	2.50
36 DON,JmP,Return of Bane,pt.1	2.50
37 DON,JmP,Return of Bane,pt.2	2.50
38 DON,JmP,Return of Bane,pt.3	2.50
39 DON,JmP,Finally to Vanguish	2.50
40 DON,JmP,Cataclysm,pt.4,x-over	4.50
41 DON,JmP,A:Devil Latour	2.50
42 DON,JmP,Madame Kalypso	2.50
43 DON,JmP,Lilhy,Brian Bryan	2.50
44 DON,JmP,Luc & Lilhy disappear	2.50
45 DON,JmP,V:Deathstroke, A:Calibax	2.50
46 DON(s),JmP,V:Calibax	2.50

Becomes:

AZRAEL, AGENT OF THE BAT
1997

47 Road to No Man's Land, flip-book Batman:Shadow of the Bat	5.00
48 DON(s),JmP,No Man's Land	2.50
49 DON(s),JmP,New Costume	2.50
50 DON(s),JmP,New Costume	2.50
51 DON(s),JmP,V:Demonic Trio	2.50
52 DON(s),JmP,No Man's Land	2.50
53 DON(s),JmP,V:Joker	2.50
54 DON(s),JmP,V:Death Dancer	2.50
55 DON(s),JmP,V:Death Dancer	2.50
56 DON(s),JmP,A:Batgirl	2.50
57 DON(s),JmP,No Man's Land	2.50
58 DON(s),JmP,Day of Judgment x-over	2.50
59 DON(s),JmP,F:Catwoman	2.50
60 DON(s),JmP,Evacuation	2.50
61 DON(s),F:Batgirl,V:Joker	2.50
62 DON(s),JmP	2.50
63 DON(s),F:Huntress	2.50
64 DON(s),F:Huntress	2.50
65 DON(s),Nicholas Scratch	2.50
66 DON(s),F:Lilhi	2.50

Azrael Agent of the Bat #47
© DC Comics, Inc.

67 DON(s),JmP,to Africa	2.50
68 DON(s),JmP,Mirage	2.50
69 DON(s),JmP,stranded	2.50
70 DON(s),SCi,JmP,Prophet,pt.1	2.50
71 DON(s),SCi,JmP,Prophet,pt.2	2.50
72 DON(s),SCi,JmP,Prophet,pt.3	2.50
73 DON(s),SCi,JmP,Batman,pt.1	2.50
74 DON(s),SCi,JmP,Batman,pt.2	2.50
75 DON(s),SCi,JmP,N:Azrael, F:Batman	4.50
76 DON(s),SCi,JmP,A:Batman	2.50
77 DON(s),SCi,V:Mr. Prymm	2.50
78 DON(s),SCi,Captain Death	2.50
79 DON(s),SCi,F:Jean Paul	2.50
80 DON(s),SCi,JmP,F:Jean Paul	2.50
81 DON(s),SCi,JmP,imprisoned	2.50
82 DON(s),SCi,JmP,escape	2.50
83 DON(s),SCi,JmP,Jokerized	2.50
84 DON(s),SCi,JmP,madman	2.50
85 DON(s),SCi,JmP,new villain	2.50
86 DON(s),SCi,JmP,Spartan	2.50
87 DON(s),SCi,new foe	2.50
88 DON(s),JmP,SCi,F:Nightwing	2.50
89 DON(s),F:Nightwing	2.50
90 DON(s),F:Nightwing	2.50
91 Bruce Wayne:Fugitive,pt.15	2.50
92 DON(s),SCi,F:Batman	2.50
93 DON(s),SCi,war on crime	3.00
94 DON(s),SCi,Demon Biis	3.00
95 DON(s),SCi,Biis,Two-face	3.00
96 DON(s),SCi,A:Batman, V:Two-Face	3.00
97 DON(s),MZ,JOy,New costume	3.00
98 DON(s),MZ,JOy,on the brink	3.00
99 DON(s),MZ,JOy	3.00
100 DON(s),MZ,JOy,final issue	3.00
Ann.#1 Year One Annual	3.00
Ann.#2 Legends o/t Dead Earth	4.00
Ann.#3 Pulp Heroes (Hard Boiled)	5.00
Spec.#1,000,000 DON(s),VGi,JmP F:Green Arrow,Robin,Hawkman	3.00
GN Azrael/Ash	5.00

AZRAEL/ASH
March, 1997

1 one-shot DON(s),JQ,V:Surtr, A:Batman, x-over	5.00

AZRAEL PLUS
Oct., 1996

1 one-shot, DON(s),VGi,F:Vic Sage, The Question	3.00

THE FINAL RAGE

AZTEK:
THE ULTIMATE MAN
1996–97
1 GMo&MMr(s),NSH,I:Aztek &
 Synth 6.00
2 GMo&MMr(s),NSH,A:Green
 Lantern 4.00
3 GMo&MMr(s),NSH,V:Doll-Face . . 4.00
4 GMo&MMr(s),NSH,I:Lizard King,
 Vanity. 4.00
5 GMo&MMr(s),NSH,O:Aztek,
 V:Lizard King 4.00
6 GMo&MMr(s),NSH,V:Vanity,
 A: Joker 4.00
7 GMo&MMr(s),NSH,A:Batman 4.00
8 GMo&MMr(s),NSH,return to Brotherhood of Zuetzatcoatl,A:Raptor. . 4.00
9 GMo&MMr(s),NSH,V:Parasite,
 A:Superman. 4.00
10 GMo&MMr(s),NSH,A:Justice
 League, final issue 12.00

BABYLON 5
1995
1 From TV series 15.00
2 From TV series 8.00
3 Mysterious Assassin 8.00
4 V:Mysterious Assassin. 8.00
5 Shadows of the Present,pt.1 . . . . 8.00
6 Shadows of the Present,pt.2 . . . . 8.00
7 Shadows of the Present,pt.3 . . . . 7.00
8 Laser-Mirror Starweb,pt.1 . . . . . . 7.00
9 Laser-Mirror Starweb,pt.2 . . . . . . 7.00
10 Laser-Mirror-Starweb,pt.3 . . . . . . 7.00
11 final issue 7.00

BABYLON 5:
IN VALEN'S NAME
Jan., 1998
1 (of 3) PDd, from TV series. 4.00
2 PDd 4.00
3 PDd 4.00

BATGIRL
Feb., 2000
1 No Man's Land follow-up 10.00
1a 2nd printing 2.50
2 saves dying man 7.00
3 A:Batman 4.00
4 A:Batman 4.00
5 V:Ezra 4.00
6 A:Batman 4.00
7 A:Batman, ... 4.00
8 V:Lady Shiva 4.00
9 Batgirl questions her motives . . . 3.50
10 Too slow to stop a killer 3.50
11 This Issue: Batman Dies! 3.50
12 Officer Down tie-in 3.50
13 Government trained killers 3.50
14 A:Batman 3.50
15 RbC,ghastly murders 3.50
16 RbC,young boy's father 3.50
17 RbC,A:Oracle,Cassandra 3.50
18 RbC,A:Robin,V:Deadeye 3.50
19 RbC,Nobody dies tonight 3.50
20 CDi,F:The Spoiler 3.50
21 CDi,Joker:Last Laugh 3.50
22 RbC,F:Cain 3.50
23 RbC,F:Lady Shiva. 3.50
24 RbC,BruceWayne:Murderer,pt.2 . 3.50
25 RbC,V:Lady Shiva,40-pg. 4.00
26 VGi,Spoiler 3.00
27 RbC,Bruce Wayne:Fugitive,pt.4 . 3.00
28 RbC,I:Sensor 3.00
29 RbC,Bruce Wayne:Fugitive,pt.13 3.00
30 CDi,KJ,Roman military cult 3.00
31 CDi,F:Robin, Spoiler 3.00
32 CDi,all-star issue. 3.00
33 RbC,A:Batman,metahunt 3.00

34 RbC,A:Batman,detective skills . . 3.00
35 RbC,V:Alpha,A:Batman 3.00
36 RbC,V:Alpha 3.00
37 RbC,save the child 3.00
38 RbC,F:Spoiler 3.00
39 V:Black Wind. 3.00
40 V:Black Wind. 3.00
41 First date,A:Superboy 3.00
42 I:New Dr. Death 3.00
43 V:Dr. Death 3.00
44 V:Dr. Death 3.00
45 RL,drug Soul 3.00
46 RL,F:Oracle. 3.00
47 RL,V:Doll Man. 2.50
48 missing girl 2.50
49 V:The Lost Girls 2.50
50 RL,V:Batman. 3.25
51 RL,V:Poison Ivy 2.50

Batgirl #41
© DC Comics, Inc.

52 RL,V:Poison Ivy 2.50
53 F:Girl Wonder,V:Penguin 2.50
54 RL,vs. cyborg 2.50
55 War Games,Act 1,pt.6 . . . . 2.50
56 War Games,Act 2,pt.6 . . . . 2.50
57 War Games,Act 3,pt.6 . . . . 2.50
58 Fresh Blood, x-over,pt.2 . . . . 2.50
59 Fresh Blood, x-over,pt.4 . . . . 2.50
60 Bludhaven 2.50
61 Arms deal in Bludhaven 2.50
62 F:Spoiler 2.50
63 F:Deathstroke 2.50
64 V:Deathstroke 2.50
65 CaS,Father's Day 2.50
66 V:Verrraco, The Road Hog 2.50
67 F:Birds of Prey 2.50
68 V:Lady Shiva 2.50
69 Frozen. 2.50
70 Destruction's Daughter 2.50
71 V:Lady Shiva & team 2.50
72 V:Mad Dog, someone dies 2.50
73 End of Cassandra Cain 2.50
Ann.#1 Planet DC,A:Batman 3.50
Spec.#1 V: Cormorant,
 I:Slash (1988) 10.00
Spec. Secret Files #1, 48-pg. 5.00

July, 2008
1 (of 6) F:Cassandra Cain 3.00
2 thru 5 . . . . @3.00

BATGIRL ADVENTURES
Dec., 1997
1-shot RBr,V:Poison Ivy,A:Harley
 Quinn. 4.00

BATGIRL: YEAR ONE
Dec. 2002
1 CDi(s),F:Barbara Gordon. 3.00
2 CDi(s),meets JSA 3.00
3 CDi(s),Dynamic Duo 3.00
4 CDi(s),Dynamic Duo 3.00
5 CDi(s),Killer Moth. 3.00
6 CDi(s),F:Black Canary 3.00
7 CDi(s),A:Robin. 3.00
8 CDi(s),V:Blockbuster 3.00
9 CDi(s),Origin concl. 3.00

BAT LASH
Dec., 2007
1 (of 6) Western 3.00
1a variant (c) (1:10) 3.00
2 thru 6 . . . . @3.00

BATMAN
Spring, 1940
1 I:Joker,Cat (Catwoman),
 V:Hugo Strange 195,000.00
2 V:Joker/Catwoman team . . 30,000.00
3 V:Catwoman 20,000.00
4 V:Joker 15,000.00
5 V:Joker 9,500.00
6 V:Clock Maker 8,000.00
7 V:Joker 8,000.00
8 V:Joker 6,500.00
9 V:Joker 6,500.00
10 V:Catwoman 6,500.00
11 V:Joker,Penguin 15,000.00
12 V:Joker. 5,000.00
13 V:Joker 5,000.00
14 V:Penguin;Propaganda sty . 5,000.00
15 V:Catwoman 5,000.00
16 I:Alfred,V:Joker 9,500.00
17 V:Penguin 4,000.00
18 V:Tweedledum &
 Tweedledee 5,000.00
19 V:Joker. 5,000.00
20 V:Joker. 4,000.00
21 V:Penguin 4,000.00
22 V:Catwoman,Cavalier 4,000.00
23 V:Joker. 5,000.00
24 I:Carter Nichols, V:Tweedledum
 & Tweedledee. 3,000.00
25 V:Joker/Penguin team 4,000.00
26 V:Cavalier 2,700.00
27 V:Penguin 4,000.00
28 V:Joker. 2,500.00
29 V:Scuttler 2,500.00
30 V:Penguin,I:Ally Babble 2,500.00
31 I:Punch and Judy. 2,000.00
32 O:Robin,V:Joker. 2,000.00
33 V:Penguin,Jackall 2,300.00
34 A:Ally Babble 2,000.00
35 V:Catwoman 2,000.00
36 V:Penguin,A:King Arthur . . . 1,700.00
37 V:Joker. 2,500.00
38 V:Penguin 3,000.00
39 V:Catwoman,Xmas Story. . . 1,700.00
40 V:Joker. 2,500.00
41 V:Penguin 2,300.00
42 V:Catwoman 2,400.00
43 V:Penguin 2,000.00
44 V:Joker,A:Carter Nichols,Meets
 ancester Silas Wayne. 2,500.00
45 V:Catwoman 1,300.00
46 V:Joker,A:Carter Nichols,
 Leonardo Da Vinci 1,300.00
47 O:Batman,V:Catwoman 6,000.00
48 V:Penguin, Bat-Cave story . 1,900.00
49 I:Mad Hatter & Vicki Vale. . . 3,000.00
50 V:Two-Face,A:Vicki Vale . . . 1,500.00
51 V:Penguin 1,300.00
52 V:Joker. 1,500.00
53 V:Joker. 1,500.00
54 V:The Treasure Hunter 1,200.00
55 V:Joker. 1,800.00
56 V:Penguin 1,400.00

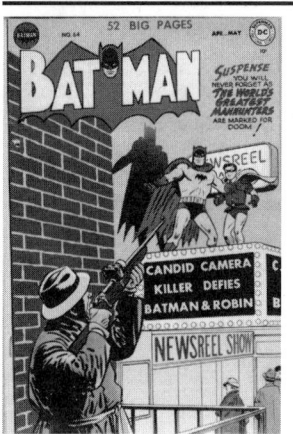

Batman #64
© *DC Comics, Inc.*

57 V:Joker	1,200.00
58 V:Penguin	1,400.00
59 I:Deadshot	1,200.00
60 V:'Shark' Marlin	1,200.00
61 V:Penguin	1,400.00
62 O:Catwoman,I:Knight & Squire	2,000.00
63 V:Joker	1,200.00
64 V:Killer Moth	2,000.00
65 I:Wingman,V:Catwoman	1,500.00
66 V:Joker	1,500.00
67 V:Joker	1,300.00
68 V:Two-Face,Alfred story	1,200.00
69 I:King of the Cats, A:Catwoman	1,500.00
70 V:Penguin	900.00
71 V:Mr. Cipher	900.00
72 The Jungle Batman	900.00
73 V:Joker,A:Vicki Vale	1,500.00
74 V:Joker	1,000.00
75 I:The Gorilla Boss	1,000.00
76 V:Penguin	1,000.00
77 The Crime Predictor	1,000.00
78 The Manhunter from Mars	1,300.00
79 A:Vicki Vale	1,000.00
80 V:Joker	1,200.00
81 V:Two-Face	1,100.00
82 The Flying Batman	1,000.00
83 V:'Fish' Frye	1,000.00
84 V:Catwoman	1,400.00
85 V:Joker	1,000.00
86 V:Joker	1,000.00
87 V:Joker	1,000.00
88 V:Mr. Mystery	1,000.00
89 I:Aunt Agatha	1,000.00
90 I:Batboy	1,000.00
91 V:Blinky Grosset	1,000.00
92 I:Ace, the Bat-Hound	1,400.00
93 The Caveman Batman	800.00
94 Alfred Has Amnesia	800.00
95 The Bat-Train	800.00
96 Batman's College Days	800.00
97 V:Joker	800.00
98 A:Carter Nichols,Jules Verne	800.00
99 V:Penguin,A:Carter Nichols, Bat Masterson	800.00
100 Great Batman Contest	4,500.00
101 The Great Bat-Cape Hunt	900.00
102 V:Mayne Mallok	700.00
103 A:Ace, the Bat-Hound	700.00
104 V:Devoe	700.00
105 A:Batwoman	1,000.00
106 V:Keene Harper Gang	800.00
107 V:Daredevils	700.00
108 Bat-Cave Story	700.00

109 1,000 Inventions of Batman	700.00
110 V:Joker	725.00
111 Gotham City Safari	600.00
112 I:Signalman	600.00
113 I:Fatman	600.00
114 I:Bat Ape	600.00
115 Million-Dollar Clues	600.00
116 City of Ancient Heroes	600.00
117 Mystery of Batman Bus	600.00
118 Battle of Police Island	600.00
119 Arch-Rivals of Gotham City	600.00
120 Curse of the Bat-Ring	600.00
121 I:Mr.Zero (Mr.Freeze)	850.00
122 Prisoners of Sargasso Sea	500.00
123 A:Joker	450.00
124 Mystery Seed from Space	450.00
125 Secret Life of Bat-Hound	450.00
126 Mystery of the 49th Star	450.00
127 A:Superman & Joker	450.00
128 Interplanetary Batman	450.00
129 O:Robin (Retold)	450.00
130 Batman's Deadly Birthday	450.00
131 I:2nd Batman	375.00
132 Lair of the Sea-Fox	375.00
133 Crimes of the Kite-Man	375.00
134 The Rainbow Creature	375.00
135 Crimes of the Wheel	375.00
136 A:Joker, Bat-Mite	375.00
137 V:Mr. Marvel,The Brand	375.00
138 A:Bat-Mite	375.00
139 I:Old Batgirl	375.00
140 A:Joker	375.00
141 V:Clockmaster	375.00
142 Batman Robot Story	375.00
143 A:Bathound	375.00
144 A:Joker,Bat-Mite,Bat-Girl	375.00
145 V:Mr.50,Joker	400.00
146 A:Bat-Mite,Joker	400.00
147 Batman becomes Bat-Baby	300.00
148 A:Joker	350.00
149 V:Maestro	300.00
150 V:Biff Warner,Jack Pine	300.00
151 V:Harris Boys	250.00
152 A:Joker	260.00
153 Other Dimension story	250.00
154 V:Dr. Dorn	200.00
155 1st S.A. Penguin	550.00
156 V:Gorilla Gang	250.00
157 V:Mirror Man	250.00
158 A:Bathound,Bat-Mite	250.00
159 A:Joker,Clayface	250.00
160 V:Bart Cullen	225.00
161 A:Bat-Mite	225.00
162 F:Robin	225.00
163 A:Joker	225.00
164 CI,A:Mystery Analysts,new Batmobile	225.00
165 V:The Mutated Man	225.00
166 Escape story	225.00
167 V:Karabi & Hydra, the Crime Cartel	225.00
168 V:Mr. Mammoth	225.00
169 A:Penguin	225.00
170 V:Getaway Genius	225.00
171 CI,1st S.A. Riddler	800.00
172 V:Flower Gang	225.00
173 V:Elwood Pearson	225.00
174 V:Big Game Hunter	225.00
175 V:Eddie Repp	225.00
176 Giant rep.A:Joker,Catwom.	225.00
177 BK,A:Elongated Man,Atom.	225.00
178 CI	225.00
179 CI,2nd Riddler(Silver)	300.00
180 BK,A:Death-Man	175.00
181 CI,I:Poison Ivy	350.00
182 A:Joker,(giant size rep)	200.00
183 CI,A:Poison Ivy	225.00
184 CI,Mystery of the Missing Manhunters	175.00
185 Giant rep	175.00
186 A:Joker	175.00
187 Giant rep.A:Joker	175.00

188 CI,A:Eraser	125.00
189 CI,A:Scarecrow	200.00
190 CI,A:Penguin	150.00
191 CI,The Day Batman Soldout.	125.00
192 CI,The Crystal ball that betrayed Batman	125.00
193 Giant rep.	150.00
194 MSy,BK,A:Blockbuster,Mystery Analysts of Gotham City	125.00
195 CI	125.00
196 BK,Psychic Super-Sleuth	125.00
197 MSy,A:Bat Girl,Catwoman	200.00
198 A:Joker,Penguin,Catwoman, O:Batman rtd,(G-Size rep)	200.00
199 CI,Peril o/t Poison Rings	125.00
200 NA(c),O:rtd,A:Joker,Pengiun, Scarecrow	300.00
201 A:Batman Villains	150.00
202 BU:Robin	135.00
203 NA(c),(giant size)	200.00
204 FR(s),IN,JG	150.00
205 FR(s),IN,JG	150.00
206 FR(s),IN,JG	150.00
207 FR(s),IN,JG	150.00
208 GK,new O:Batman, A:Catwoman	175.00
209 FR(s),IN,JO	175.00
210 A:Catwoman	175.00
211 FR(s),IN,JG	150.00
212 FR(s),IN,JG	150.00
213 RA,30th Anniv.Batman,new O: Robin,rep.O:Alfred,Joker	125.00
214 IN,A:Batgirl	65.00
215 IN,DG	65.00
216 IN,DG,I:DaphnePennyworth	65.00
217 NA(c)	65.00
218 NA(c),giant	75.00
219 NA,IN,DG,Batman Xmas	75.00
220 NA(c),IN	60.00
221 IN,DG	60.00
222 IN,Rock'n Roll story	65.00
223 NA(c),giant	65.00
224 NA(c)	60.00
225 NA(c),IN,DG	60.00
226 IN,DG I:10-Eyed Man	60.00
227 IN,DG,A:Daphne Pennyworth	60.00
228 giant Deadly Traps rep.	75.00
229 IN	60.00
230 NA(c),Robin	60.00
231 F:Ten-Eyed Man	60.00
232 DON(s),NA,DG, I:Ras al Ghul	275.00
233 giant Bruce Wayne iss	75.00
234 NA,DG,IN,1stS.A.Two-Face	275.00

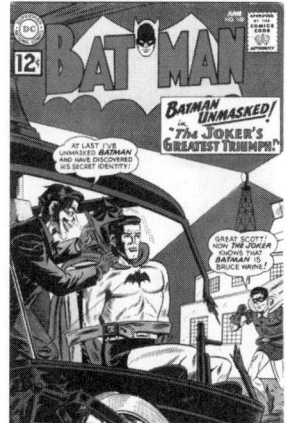

Batman #148
© *DC Comics Inc.*

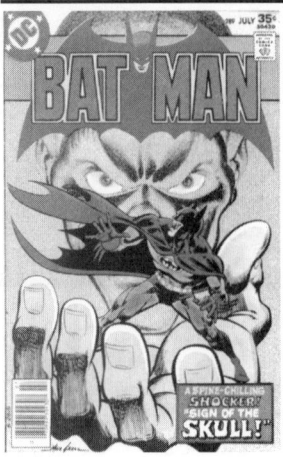

Batman #289 © DC Comics, Inc.

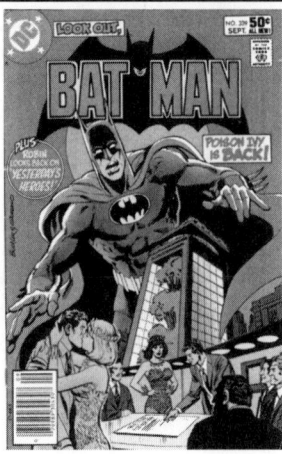

Batman #368 © DC Comics, Inc.

290 MGr,V:Skull Dagger 20.00
291 B:Underworld Olympics #1,
   A:Catwoman 30.00
292 A:Riddler 20.00
293 A:Superman & Luthor 20.00
294 E:DvR(s),E:Underworld
   Olympics,A:Joker. 30.00
295 GyC(s),MGo,JyS,V:Hamton . . 20.00
296 B:DvR(s),V:Scarecrow 20.00
297 RB,Mad Hatter 20.00
298 JCA,DG,V:Baxter Bains 20.00
299 DG. 20.00
300 WS,DG,A:Batman E-2,
   Robin E-2 . . . . 35.00
301 JCa,TeB 15.00
302 JCa,DG,V:Human Dynamo . . . 15.00
303 JCa,DG 15.00
304 E:DvR(s),V:Spook 15.00
305 GyC,JCa,DeH,V:Thanatos . . . 16.00
306 JCa,DeH,DN,V:Black Spider . . 20.00
307 B:LWn(s),JCa,DG,
   I:Limehouse Jack 20.00
308 JCa,DG,V:Mr.Freeze 16.00
309 E:LWn(s),JCa,FMc,
   V:Blockbuster 16.00
310 IN,DG,A:Gentleman Ghost . . . 16.00
311 SEt,FMc,IN,Batgirl,
   V:Dr.Phosphorus 16.00
312 WS,DG,Calenderman 16.00
313 IN,FMc,VTwo-Face 16.00
314 IN,FMc,V:Two-Face 16.00
315 IN,FMc,V:Kiteman 16.00
316 IN,FMc,F:Robin,
   V:Crazy Quilt 16.00
317 IN,FMc,V:Riddler. 17.00
318 IN,I:Fire Bug 16.00
319 JKu(c),IN,DG,A:Gentleman
   Ghost,E:Catwoman 16.00
320 BWr(c). 17.00
321 DG,WS,A:Joker,Catwoman. . . 25.00
322 V:Cap.Boomerang,Catwoman 16.00
323 IN,A:Catwoman. 16.00
324 IN,A:Catwoman. 16.00
325 IN,Death-20 Stories High 16.00
326 A:Catwoman 16.00
327 IN,A:Proffessor.Milo 16.00
328 A:Two-Face. 16.00
329 IN,A:Two-Face 16.00
330 In,Target 16.00
331 DN,FMc,V:Electrocutioner . . . 16.00
332 IN,DN,Ras al Ghul.1st solo
   Catwoman story 20.00
333 IN,DN,A:Catwoman,
   Ras al Ghul 15.00
334 FMc,Ras al Ghul,Catwoman. . 15.00
335 IN,FMc,Catwoman,Ras al
   Ghul 15.00
336 JL,FMc,Loser Villains 15.00
337 DN,V:Snow Man 15.00
338 DN,Deathsport 15.00
339 A:Poison Ivy 15.00
340 GC,A:Mole 15.00
341 A:Man Bat 15.00
342 V:Man Bat 15.00
343 GC,KJ,I:The Dagger 15.00
344 GC,KJ,Poison Ivy 15.00
345 I:New Dr.Death,A:Catwoman . 15.00
346 DN,V:Two Face 15.00
347 A:Alfred 15.00
348 GC,KJ,Man-Bat,A:Catwoman . 15.00
349 GC,AA,A:Catwoman 15.00
350 GC,TD,A:Catwoman 15.00
351 GC,TD,A:Catwoman 15.00
352 Col Blimp 15.00
353 JL,DN,DA,A:Joker. 22.00
354 DN,AA,V:HugoStrange,A:
   Catwoman 15.00
355 DN,AA:A:Catwoman 15.00
356 DG,DN,Hugo Strange 15.00
357 DN,AA,I:Jason Todd 16.00
358 A:King Croc. 15.00
359 DG,O:King Croc,Joker 20.00

235 CI,V:Spook 60.00
236 NA. 60.00
237 NA,I:The Reaper. 200.00
238 NA,JC,JKu,giant 200.00
239 NA,RB. 60.00
240 NA(c),RB,giant,R-Ghul 60.00
241 IN,DG,RB,A:Kid Flash. 60.00
242 RB,MK. 60.00
243 NA,DG,Ras al Ghul 100.00
244 NA,Ras al Ghul. 100.00
245 NA,IN,DG,FMc,Ras al Ghul . 100.00
246 Many Ways Can a Robin Die . 55.00
247 Deadly New Year 55.00
248 Death-Knell for a Traitor 55.00
249 Citidel of Crime. 55.00
250 IN,DG 55.00
251 NA,V:Joker 150.00
252 The Spook's Master Stroke. . . 55.00
253 AN,DG,A:Shadow 55.00
254 NA,GK,B:100 page issues . . 100.00
255 GK,CI,NA,DG,I:CrazyQuilt . . 125.00
256 Catwoman. 100.00
257 IN,DG,V:Penguin. 100.00
258 IN,DG 100.00
259 GK,IN,DG,A:Shadow. 100.00
260 IN,DG,Joker. 125.00
261 CI,GK,E:100 page issues . . . 100.00
262 A:Scarecrow 60.00
263 DG(i),A:Riddler 20.00
264 DON(s),DG,A:Devil Dayre. . . 20.00
265 RB,BWr. 25.00
266 DG,Catwoman(old Costume) . 22.00
267 DG. 20.00
268 DON(s),IN,TeB,V:Sheikh. 20.00
269 A:Riddler 20.00
270 B:DvR(s) 20.00
271 IN,FMc 20.00
272 JLUnderworld Olympics '76 . . 20.00
273 V:Underworld Olympics '76 . . 20.00
274 Gotham City Treasure Hunt . . 20.00
275 Ferry Blows at Midnight 20.00
276 The Haunting of the Spook . . . 20.00
277 Man Who Walked Backwards. 20.00
278 Stop Me Before I Kill Batman . 20.00
279 A:Riddler 22.00
280 The Only Crime in Town 20.00
281 Murder Comes in Black Boxes 20.00
282 Four Doorways to Danger . . . 20.00
283 V:Camouflage 20.00
284 JA,R:Dr.Tzin Tzin 20.00
285 Mystery of Christmas Lost . . . 20.00
286 V:Joker 30.00
287 BWi,MGr,Penguin 25.00
288 BWi,MGr,Penguin 25.00
289 MGr, V:Skull 20.00

360 I:Savage Skull. 15.00
361 DN,Man-Bat,I:Harvey Bullock . 15.00
362 V:Riddler 15.00
363 V:Nocturna 15.00
364 DN,AA,J.Todd 1st full solo
   story (cont'd Detective #531) . 15.00
365 DN,AA,C:Joker 15.00
366 DN,AA,Joker,J.Todd in
   Robin Costume 22.00
367 DN,AA,PoisonIvy 14.00
368 DN,AA,I:2nd Robin
   (Jason Todd) 20.00
369 DN,AA,I:Dr.Fang,V:Deadshot . 12.00
370 DN,AA. 12.00
371 DN,AA,V:Catman 10.00
372 DN,AA,A:Dr.Fang 7.00
373 DN,AA,V:Scarecrow 7.00
374 GC,AA,V:Penguin 8.00
375 GC,AA,V:Dr.Freeze. 7.00
376 DN,Halloween issue 7.00
377 DN,AA,V:Nocturna 7.00
378 V:Mad Hatter. 7.00
379 V:Mad Hatter. 7.00
380 AA,V:Nocturna 7.00
381 V:Batman 7.00
382 A:Catwoman 8.00
383 GC,Night in the Life of Batman. 7.00
384 V:Calender Man 7.00
385 V:Calender Man 7.00
386 I:Black Mask 7.00
387 V:Black Mask 7.00
388 V:Capt.Boomerang & Mirror
   Master 7.00
389 V:Nocturna,Catwoman 7.00
390 V:Nocturna,Catwoman 7.00
391 V:Nocturna,Catwoman 7.00
392 A:Catwoman 7.00
393 PG,V:Cossack 6.00
394 PG,V:Cossack 6.00
395 V:Film Freak 6.00
396 V:Film Freak 6.00
397 V:Two-Face,Catwoman. 7.00
398 V:Two-Face,Catwoman. 7.00
399 HaE(s),Two-Face. 6.00
400 BSz,AAd,GP,BB,A:Joker. 35.00
401 JBy(c),TVE,Legends,
   A:Magpie 6.00
402 JSn,Fake Batman 6.00
403 DCw,Batcave discovered 6.00
404 DM,FM(s),B:Year 1,I:Modern
   Age Catwoman 30.00
405 FM,DM,Year 1. . . . . 16.00
406 FM,DM,Year 1. . . . . 16.00
407 FM,DM,E:Year 1 . . . . 16.00

DC COMICS

408 CW,V:Joker,
 new O:Jason Todd 15.00
408a 2nd printing 3.00
409 DG,RA,V:Crime School 15.00
409a 2nd printing 3.00
410 DC,Jason Todd 15.00
411 DC,DH,V:Two Face 6.00
412 DC,DH,I:Mime 6.00
413 DC,DH 6.00
414 JAp,Slasher 6.00
415 JAp,Millenium Week #2 . . . . . . 6.00
416 JAp,1st Batman/Nightwing
 T.U. 6.00
417 JAp,B:10 Nights,I:KGBeast . . . 12.00
418 JAp,V:KGBeast 12.00
419 JAp,V:KGBeast 12.00
420 JAp,E:10 Nights,D:KGBeast . . 12.00
421 DG 7.00
422 MBr,V:Dumpster Slayer 6.00
423 TM(c),DC,Who is Batman 7.00
424 MBr,Robin 6.00
425 MBr,Gordon Kidnapped 6.00
426 JAp,B:Death in the Family,
 V:Joker 22.00
427 JAp,V:Joker 18.00
428 JAp,D:2nd Robin 18.00
429 JAp,A:Superman,
 E:Death in the Family 15.00
430 JAp,JSn,V:Madman 5.00
431 JAp,Murder Investigation 4.00
432 JAp 4.00
433 JBy,JAp,Many Deaths of the
 Batman #1 . . . . 5.00
434 JBy,JAp,Many Deaths #2 . . . . . 4.50
435 JBy,Many Deaths #3 . . . . 4.50
436 PB,B:Year#3,A:Nightwing,I:Tim
 Drake as child 5.00
436a 2ndPrint(green DC logo) 4.00
437 PB,year#3 . . . . 4.00
438 PB,year#3 . . . . 3.50
439 PB,year#3 . . . . 3.50
440 JAp,Lonely Place of Dying #1,
 A:Tim Drake (face not shown) . . 4.00
441 JAp,Lonely Place Dying 4.00
442 JAp,I:3rd Robin(Tim Drake) . . . 7.00
443 JAp,I:Crimesmith 3.00
444 JAp,V:Crimesmith 3.00
445 JAp,I:K.G.Beast Demon 3.00
446 JAp,V:K.G.Beast Demon 3.00
447 JAp,D:K.G.Beast Demon 3.00
448 JAp,A:Penguin#1 . . . . 3.50
449 MBr,A:Penguin#3 . . . . 3.50
450 JAp,I:Joker II 3.00
451 JAp,V:Joker II 3.00
452 KD,Dark Knight Dark City#1 . . . 3.00
453 KD,Dark Knight Dark City#2 . . . 3.00
454 KD,Dark Knight Dark City#3 . . . 3.00
455 Identity Crisis#1, A:Scarecrow . 3.00
456 IdentityCrisis#2 . . . . 4.00
457 V:Scarecrow,A:Robin,
 New Costume 7.00
457a 2nd printing 3.00
458 R:Sarah Essen 3.00
459 A:Sarah Essen 3.00
460 Sisters in Arms,pt.1
 A:Catwoman 3.50
461 Sisters in Arms,pt.2
 Catwoman V:Sarah.Essen 3.50
462 Batman in San Francisco 3.00
463 Death Valley 3.00
464 V:Two-Hearts 3.00
465 Batman/Robin T.U. 3.50
466 Robin Trapped 3.00
467 Shadowbox #1(sequel to
 Robin Mini-Series) 3.50
468 Shadowbox #2 . . . . 3.00
469 Shadowbox #3 . . . . 3.00
470 War of the Gods x-over 3.00
471 V:Killer Croc 3.00
472 The Idiot Root,pt.1 . . . . 3.00
473 The Idiot Root,pt.3 . . . . 3.00
474 Destroyer,pt.1 (LOTDK#27) . . . 3.50

475 R:Scarface,A:VickiVale 3.00
476 A:Scarface 3.00
477 Ph(c),Gotham Tale,pt.1 . . . . . . 3.00
478 Ph(c),Gotham Tale,pt.2 . . . . . . 3.00
479 TMd,I:Pagan 3.00
480 JAp,To the father I never
 knew 3.00
481 JAp,V:Maxie Zeus 3.00
482 JAp,V:Maxie Zeus 3.00
483 JAp,I:Crash & Burn 3.00
484 JAp,R:Black Mask 3.00
485 TGr,V:Black Mask 3.00
486 JAp,I:Metalhead 3.00
487 JAp,V:Headhunter 3.00
488 JAp,N:Azrael 10.00
489 JAp,Bane vs Killer Croc,
 I:Azrael as Batman 6.00
489a 2nd Printing 3.00
490 JAp,Bane vs.Riddler 7.00
490a 2nd Printing 2.50
490b 3rd Printing 2.00
491 JAp,V:Joker,A:Bane 4.50
491a 2nd Printing 2.00
492 B:DgM(s),NB,Knightfall#1,
 V:Mad Hatter,A:Bane 5.00
492a Platinum Ed. 10.00
492b 2nd Printing 2.00
493 NB,Knightfall,#3,Mr.Zsasz 4.00
494 JAp,TMd,Knightfall #5,A:Bane,
 V:Cornelius,Stirk,Joker 3.50
495 NB,Knightfall#7,V:Poison
 Ivy,A:Bane 3.50
496 JAp,JRu,Knightfall#9,V:Joker,
 Scarecrow,A:Bane 3.50
497 JAp,DG,Knightfall#11,V:Bane,
 Batman gets back broken 7.00
497a 2nd Printing 2.50
498 JAp,JRu,Knightfall#15,A:Bane,
 Catwoman,Azrael Becomes
 Batman 3.00
499 JAp,SHa,Knightfall#17,
 A:Bane,Catwoman 3.00
500 JQ(c),JAp,MM,Die Cut(c),
 Direct Market,Knightfall#19,
 V:Bane,N:Batman 6.00
500a KJo(c),Newstand Ed. 3.50
501 MM,I:Mekros 3.00
502 MM,V:Mekros 3.00
503 MM,V:Catwoman 3.00
504 MM,V:Catwoman 3.00
505 MM,V:Canibal 3.00
506 KJo(c),MM,A:Ballistic 3.00
507 KJo(c),MM,A:Ballistic 3.00
508 KJo(c),MM,V:Abattior 3.00
509 KJo(c),MM,KnightsEnd#1,
 A:Shiva 3.50

Batman #480 © DC Comics Inc.

510 KJo(c),MM,Knights End #7,
 V:Azrael 3.00
511 Zero Hour, A:Batgirl 3.00
512 Killer Croc sewer battles 3.00
513 Two-Face and convicts 3.00
514 Identity Crisis 3.00
515 KJo,Return of Bruce Wayne,
 Troika,pt.1 . . . . 3.00
515 Collector's Edition 3.50
516 V:The Sleeper 3.00
517 V:The Sleeper 3.00
518 V:The Black Spider 3.00
519 KJo,V:The Black Spider
 [new Miraweb format begins] . . 3.00
520 EB,A:James Gordon 3.00
521 R:Killer Croc 3.00
522 R:Scarecrow 3.00
523 V:Scarecrow 3.00
524 DgM,KJo,V:Scarecrow 3.00
525 DgM,KJo,Underworld
 Unleashed tie-in 3.00
526 DgM,A:Alfred,Nightwing,Robin . 3.00
527 DgM,V:Two-Face,I:Schism 3.00
528 DgM,V:Two-Face,pt.2 . . . . 3.00
529 DgM,KJo,Contagion,pt.6 . . . . . 3.50
530 DgM,KJo,The Aztec
 Connection,pt.1 . . . . 3.50
530a collector's edition 3.50
531 DgM,KJo,The Aztec
 Connection,pt.2 . . . . 3.00
531a collectors edition 3.50
532 DgM(s),KJo,The Aztec Connec-
 tion, pt.3, A:Deadman 3.00
532a card stock cover 3.50
533 DgM(s),KJo,Legacy prelude . . . 3.00
534 DgM(s),KJo,Legacy,pt.5 . . . . . 3.00
535 DgM(s),KJo,JhB,I:The Ogre,
 double size 4.00
535a Collector's edition,
 gatefold cover 5.00
536 DgM(s),KJo,JhB,V:Man-Bat,
 Final Night tie-in 3.00
537 DgM(s),KJo,JhB,A:Man-Bat,
 pt.2 . . . . 3.00
538 DgM(s),KJo,JhB,A:Man-Bat,
 pt.3 . . . . 3.00
539 DgM(s),KJo,Boneyard Blues . . 3.00
540 DgM(s),KJo,JhB,Spectre,pt.1 . . 3.00
541 DgM(s),KJo,JhB,Spectre,pt.2 . . 3.00
542 DgM(s),KJo,JhB,V:Faceless,
 pt. 1 . . . . 3.00
543 DgM(s),KJo,JhB,pt. 2 . . . . 3.00
544 DgM(s),KJo,JhB, F:Joker,pt.1 . . 3.00
545 DgM(s),KJo, F:Joker, Demon,
 pt.2 . . . . 3.00
546 DgM(s),KJo,JhB,F:Joker,
 Demon, pt.3 concl. 3.00
547 DgM,KJo,JhB,Genesis tie-in . . . 3.00
548 DgM,KJo,JhB,V:Penguin,pt.1 . 3.00
549 DgM,KJo,JhB,V:Penguin,pt.2 . 3.00
550 DgM,KJo,JhB,I:Chase 3.50
550a deluxe, with file card inserts . . 5.00
551 DgM,KJo,JhB,F:Ragman 2.50
552 DgM, ... 2.50
553 DgM,KJo,SB,Cataclysm
 x-over, pt.3 . . . . 4.50
554 DgM,KJo,SB,Cataclysm, ... 3.00
555 DGm,JhB,SB,BSf,Aftershock . . 2.50
556 DGm,NBy,BSf,Aftershock 2.50
557 DGm,VGi,SB,BSf,F:Ballistic . . . 2.50
558 DGm,JAp,SB,doubts 2.50
559 DgM(s),BH,SB,Aftershock 2.50
560 CDi,SB,A:Nightwing & Robin . . 2.50
561 CDi(s),JAp, No Man's Land . . . 2.50
562 CDi(s),JAp, No Man's Land . . . 2.50
563 No Law and A New Order,pt.3 . 6.00
564 F:Batgirl, Mosaic,pt.1 . . . . 2.50
565 F:Batgirl, Mosaic,pt.3 . . . . 2.50
566 JBg,A:Superman 2.50
567 SCi,F:Batgirl, pt.1,x-over 4.50
568 DJu,BSz,Fruit of the
 Earth, pt.2 . . . . 2.50

Batman #612
© DC Comics, Inc.

569 F:Batgirl. 2.50	
570 MD2,No Man's Land, The	
Code, pt.1 . . . . 2.50	
571 CDi,MtB,Goin'Downtown,pt.1 . . 2.50	
572 Jurisprudence,pt.1 . . . . 2.50	
573 Shellgame,pt.1,A:Lex Luthor . . 2.50	
574 Endgame, pt.2 x-over 2.50	
575 LHa,SMc,KIS. 2.50	
576 LHa,SMc,KIS,kidnapping 2.50	
577 LHa,SMc,KIS,rodents 2.50	
578 LHa,SMc,MPn,serial killer. . . . 2.50	
579 LHa,SMc,KIS,V:Orca,pt.1 . . . . 2.50	
580 LHa,SMc,KIS,V:Orca,pt.2 . . . . 2.50	
581 LHa,SMc,KIS,V:Orca,pt.3 . . . . 2.50	
582 SMc,KIS,Fearless,pt.1 . . . . . . 2.50	
583 SMc,KIs,Fearless,pt.2. . . . . . . 2.50	
584 SMc,KIS,A:Penguin. 2.50	
585 SMc,KIS,V:Penguin. 2.50	
586 SMc,KIS,V:Penguin, This issue:	
Batman Dies!. 2.50	
587 RBr,RyR,Officer Down,pt.1 . . . . 2.50	
588 SMc,KIS,Close Before Striking . 2.50	
589 SMc,KIS,Close Before Striking . 2.50	
590 SMc,KIS,Close Before Striking . 2.50	
591 SMc,KIS,Shot thru the Heart . . 2.50	
592 SMc,KIS,Shot thru the Heart . . 2.50	
593 SMc,KIS,Worlds at War tie-in . . 2.50	
594 SMc,KIS,Worlds at War tie-in . . 2.50	
595 SMc,F:Lew Moxon 2.50	
596 SMc,Joker:Last Laugh 2.50	
597 SMc,V:Zeiss 2.50	
598 SMc,Christmas in Gotham 2.50	
599 Bruce Wayne:Murderer,pt.7 . . . 2.50	
600 Bruce Wayne:Fugitive,pt.1 . . . 6.00	
600a 2nd printing. 4.00	
601 Bruce Wayne:Fugitive,pt.3 . . . . 2.50	
602 SMc,V:Nicodemus 2.50	
603 Bruce Wayne:Fugitive,pt.11 . . . 2.50	
604 SMc,Crime Alley 2.50	
605 Bruce Wayne:Fugitive,concl. . . 3.50	
606 SMc,F:Deadshot 2.50	
607 SMc,F:Deadshot,pt.2 . . . . 2.50	
608 JLb,JLe,SW,Hush,pt.1 . . . . . . 15.00	
608a 2nd printing, new cover 30.00	
609 JLb,JLe,SW,Hush,pt.2 . . . . . . 10.00	
610 JLb,JLe,SW,Hush,pt.3 . . . . 6.00	
611 JLb,JLe,SW,Hush,pt.4. . . . . 6.00	
612 JLb,JLe,SW,Hush,pt.5 . . . . . . 12.00	
612a 2nd printing, B&W(c). 15.00	
613 JLb,JLe,SW,Hush,pt.6 . . . . 7.00	
614 JLb,JLe,SW,Hush,pt.7 . . . . 5.00	
615 JLb,JLe,SW,Hush,pt.8 . . . . . . 18.00	
616 JLb,JLe,SW,Hush,pt.9 . . . . 5.00	
617 JLb,JLe,SW,Hush,pt.10 . . . . . . 4.00	
618 JLb,JLe,SW,Hush,pt.11. . . . . . . 4.00	

619 JLb,JLe,SW,Hush,pt.12 . . . . . . 4.00	
619a newsstand cover. 3.00	
620 Broken City, pt.1 . . . . 2.50	
621 Broken City, pt.2 . . . . 2.50	
622 Broken City, pt.3 . . . . 2.50	
623 Broken City, pt.4 . . . . 2.50	
624 Broken City, pt.5 . . . . 2.50	
625 Broken City, pt.6 . . . . 2.50	
626 As the Crow Flies,pt.1. . . . . . . 2.50	
627 As the Crow Flies,pt.2. . . . . . . 2.50	
628 As the Crow Flies,pt.3. . . . . . . 2.50	
629 As the Crow Flies,pt.4. . . . . . . 2.50	
630 As the Crow Flies,pt.5. . . . . . . 2.50	
631 War Games,Act 1,pt.8 . . . . 2.50	
632 War Games,Act 2,pt.8 . . . . 2.50	
633 War Games,Act 3,pt.8,40-pg . . 2.50	
634 War games epilogue. 2.50	
635 DoM,Under the Hood,pt.1. . . . 10.00	
636 DoM,Under the Hood,pt.2. . . . . 6.00	
637 DoM,Under the Hood,pt.3. . . . . 6.00	
638 DoM,Under the Hood,pt.4. . . . . 6.00	
639 DoM,Family Reunion,pt.1 . . . . . 4.00	
640 DoM,Family Reunion,pt.2 . . . . . 4.00	
641 DoM,Family Reunion,pt.3 . . . . . 3.00	
642 V:Killer Croc 2.50	
643 War Crimes,x-over, pt.2 . . . . . . 2.50	
644 War Crimes,x-over, pt.4 . . . . . . 2.50	
645 Gotham graveyard 2.50	
646 DoM,Infinite Crisis tie-in 2.50	
647 DoM,Infinite Crisis tie-in 2.50	
648 DoM,F:Black Mask 2.50	
649 DoM,Black Mask & Red Houd . . 2.50	
650 DoM,Jason Todd mystery 2.50	
651 Face the Face, pt.2, x-over. . . . 3.00	
652 Face the Face, pt.4, x-over. . . . 3.00	
653 Face the Face, pt.6, x-over. . . . 3.00	
654 Face the Face, pt.8, x-over. . . . 3.00	
655 GMo,NKu, Batman and Son . . . 3.00	
656 GMo,NKu, Batman and Son . . . 4.00	
657 GMo,NKu, Batman and Son . . . 4.00	
658 GMo,NKu, Batman and Son . . . 4.00	
659 GMo,NKu, Joker's revenge . . . 3.00	
660 JOs,TMd,Grotesk, pt.1 . . . . . . 3.00	
661 JOs,TMd,Grotesk, pt.2 . . . . . . 3.00	
662 JOs,TMd,Grotesk, pt.3 . . . . . . 3.00	
663 GMo,JVF,V:Joker 5.00	
664 GMo,NKu,,Police corruption . . . 4.00	
665 GMo,NKu,3 Ghosts of Batman . 4.00	
666 GMo,NKu,Numbers o/t Beast . . 4.00	
667 GMo,NKu,V:Mister Mayhew . . . 4.00	
668 GMo,Club of Heroes. 4.00	
669 GMo,Club of Heroes 4.00	
670 GMo,Resurrection of	
Ra's Al Ghul. 5.00	
670a GMo, variant (c) 15.00	
671 Resurrection of Ra's Al Ghul . 3.00	
672 Imposter Batman, A:Bat-Mite . . 4.00	
673 Young Bruce Wayne 4.00	
674 A:Bat-Mite 4.00	
675 Ra's al Ghul resurrected 4.00	
676 GMo(s),Batman R.I.P., pt.1. . . 7.00	
677 GMo(s),Batman R.I.P., pt.2. . . 3.00	
678 GMo(s),Batman R.I.P., pt.3. . . 3.00	
678a GMo(s),Batman variant (c) . 12.00	
679 GMo(s),Batman R.I.P., pt.4. . . 3.00	
680 GMo(s),Batman R.I.P., pt.5. . . 3.00	
681 Batman R.I.P. concl., 40-pg. . . 4.00	
682 Remembering the Dark Knight . 3.00	
683 Shadows of the Bat 3.00	
678a thru 683a variant (c)s (1:25) @4.00	
Ann.#1 CS,O:Bat Cave. 1,500.00	
Ann.#2 . . . . 800.00	
Ann.#3 A:Joker. 800.00	
Ann.#4 . . . . 500.00	
Ann.#5 . . . . 500.00	
Ann.#6 . . . . 400.00	
Ann.#7 . . . . 300.00	
Ann.#8 TVE,A:Ras al Ghul 10.00	
Ann.#9 JOy,AN,PS. 9.00	
Ann.#10 DCw,DG,V:HugoStrange . . 9.00	
Ann.#11 JBy(c),AMo(s),V:Penguin. 10.00	
Ann.#12 RA,V:Killer 7.00	

Ann.#13 A:Two-Face 8.00	
Ann.#14 O:Two-Face. 6.00	
Ann.#15 Armageddon,pt.3 . . . . 8.00	
Ann.#15a 2nd printing(silver). 4.00	
Ann.#16 SK(c),Eclipso,V:Joker 4.00	
Ann.#17 EB,Bloodline#8,	
I:Decimator 4.00	
Ann.#18 Elseworld Story 5.00	
Ann.#19 Year One, O:Scarecrow. . . 6.00	
Ann.#20 Legends o/t Dead Earth . . 5.00	
Ann.#21 Pulp Heroes (Weird	
Mystery) DgM(s) 6.00	
Ann.#22 BWr(c) Ghosts 5.00	
Ann.#23 CDi(s),GN,MPn, JLApe	
Gorilla Warfare 5.00	
Ann.#24 Planet DC 5.00	
Ann.#25 Jason Todd's Secrets 6.00	
Ann.#26 Head of the Demon 4.00	
Specials & 1-shots	
Giant Ann.#1 Facsimile edition 6.00	
Spec.#0 (1994) 4.00	
Spec.#1 MGo,I:Wrath. 5.00	
Spec.#1,000,000 DgM(s),SB,	
F:Toy Wonder 3.00	
Spec.#1 Our Worlds at War (2001) . 4.00	
Giant #1, 7 tales, 80-page (1998) . . 6.00	
Giant #2, 80-page (1999). 6.00	
Giant #3 CDi(s) 80-page (2000) . . . 7.00	
Batman Allies Secret Files 2005 . . . 5.00	
Batman: Arkham Asylum — Tales	
of Madness, AIG, Cataclysm	
tie-in (1998) 4.00	
Batman: Batgirl, JBa,RBr,	
Girlfrenzy (1998) 3.00	
Batman: Blackgate, CDi(s), JSon,	
in Blackgate prison (1996) 4.50	
Batman: Blackgate — Isle of Men,	
DgM, JAp,BSf,BSz,	
Cataclysm (1998) 3.00	
Batman Dark Knight Gallery (1995). 3.50	
Batman: Day of Judgment. 4.00	
Batman: Death of Innocents, DON(s),	
JSt, BSz, Land mine victims	
(1996) 4.00	
Batman Gallery,collection of past	
(c),posters,pin-ups,JQ(c) (1992) 4.00	
Batman: Gotham By Gaslight,MMi,	
V:Jack the Ripper 6.00	
Gotham City Secret Files #1 . . . . . . 5.00	
Batman: The Hill (2000). 3.00	
Batman: Joker's Apprentice. 4.00	
Batman: The Killing Joke,BB,AMo(s),	
O:Joker,Batgirl paralyzed	
(1988) 15.00	
2nd thru 6th printings. . . . . . . @5.00	

Batman The Killing Joke
© DC Comics, Inc.

Batman: Mitefall, V:Bane
  Mite (1995) 5.00
Batman: Penguin Triumphant
  (1992) 5.00
Batman: Plus (1997) 3.00
Batman Record Comic (1996) 2.00
Batman/Riddler: The Riddle
  Factory (1995) 5.00
Secret Files #1 SMc(c) inc.
  O:Batman (1997) 6.00
Batman: Seduction of the Gun,
  V:Illegal Gun Control (1992) . . . 3.00
Spec. The 10-Cent Adventure 2.00
3-D Batman:Scarecrow 4.00
Spec. Batman vs. Scarecrow, rep... 3.00
Batman 12-cent Adventure #1,
  War Games,pt.1 . . . . 2.00
1-shot Batman/The Spirit (2006) . . . 5.00
Batman/Two-Face: Crime and
  Punishment (1995) 5.00
  2nd printing (1998) 5.00
Two-Face Strikes Twice #1 . . . . . . 5.25
Two-Face Strikes Twice #2 . . . . . . 5.25
Batman: Vengeance of Bane,
  GN,I:Bane (1992) 30.00
  2nd Printing 5.00
Batman: Vengeance of Bane II
  (1995) 4.00
Batman Villains Secret Files,
  AIG,CDi,RMz,BB,F:Greatest Foes
  (1998) 5.00
Batman Villains Secret Files 2005 . . 5.00
Elseworld 1-shots
Batman of Arkham (2000) 6.00
Batman: The Blue, The Grey, and
  The Bat, JL (1992). 6.00
Batman: Brotherhood of the Bat
  (1995) 6.00
Batman: Castle of the Bat 6.00
Batman: Dark Allegiances (1996) . . 6.00
Batman: Holy Terror (1991) 6.50
Batman: I, Joker, BH, in
  2083 (1998) 5.00
Batman: In Darkest Knight
  MiB(s),JBi (1994). 5.50
Batman Knightgallery (1995) 3.50
Batman: Masque, MGr, in turn of
  the century Gotham. 7.00
Batman: Master of the Future,EB,
  Sequel to Goth.by Gaslight
  (1991) 6.00
Batman: Master of the Future(1998) 6.00
Batman: Scar of the Bat (1996). . . . 5.00
Batman: Two Faces (1998) 5.00
Graphic Novels
The Abduction 6.00
Batman A Lonely Place of Dying
  (1990) rep. Batman #440–442
  & New Titans #60–61 . . . . 4.00
Batman: Blind Justice, rep. Detective
  Comics #598–#600 (1992) 7.50
Batman: Bullock's Law. 5.00
The Book of Shadows 6.00
Many Deaths of the Batman;
  rep. #433-#435 (1992). 4.00
Batman: Dreamland (2000) 6.00
Batman: Ego (2000). 7.00
Batman: Full Circle AD,
  A:Reaper (1992) 7.00
Batman/Joker: Switch 7.00
Golden Steets of Gotham 7.00
Gotham Noir, 64-page (2001) 7.00
Batman: Harley Quinn (1998) 6.00
Batman: Man Who Laughs (2005). . . 7.00
Batman: Mr. Freeze 5.00
Batman/Nightwing: Bloodborne
  48-pg. (2002). 6.00
No Man's Land, 48-page No Law
  and a New Order, pt.1 . . . . 3.00
No Man's Land, lenticular (c). 4.00
No Man's Land Gallery 4.00
Nosferatu 6.00

The Order of Beasts (2004). 6.00
Batman: Poison Ivy 5.00
Batman/Poison Ivy:
  Cast Shadows (2004) 7.00
Reign of Terror 6.00
Roomful of Strangers (2004) 6.00
Batman: Scar of the Bat 5.00
Scarface—A Psychodrama (2001) . . 6.00
The Scottish Connection 6.00
Batman: Ten Knights of the Beast,
  rep. #417–#420 (1994) 6.00
Batman: Two Faces 5.00
Batman: The Ultimate Evil:
  1 Novel adaptation (of 2). 6.00
  2 Novel adaptation, finale 6.00
Movies
Batman, JOy, Movie adaptation. . . . 3.00
  Perfect Bound 6.00
Batman Returns, SE,JL Movie
  Adaption, ... 6.00
  Newsstand Format 4.00
Batman: Mask of the Phantasm,
  animated movie adapt. 6.00
  Newstand Ed. 3.50
Batman Forever, Movie Adaptation . 6.00
  Newsstand version 4.00
Batman and Robin, DON(s), Movie
  Adaptation (1997) 4.00
  Collector's edition, ... 6.00
Batman Begins movie adapt (2005) 7.00
GN Batman: Bane, BSz(c) movie
  tie-in (1997) 5.00
GN Batman: Batgirl, BSz(c) movie
  tie-in (1997) 5.00
GN Batman: Mr. Freeze, BSz(c)
  movie tie-in (1997). 5.00
GN Batman: Poison Ivy, BSz(c)
  movie tie-in (1997). 5.00
X-overs
Batman & Superman Adventures:
  World's Finest (1997) adaptation
  of animated adventures, 64pg. . . 7.00
Batman/Captain America (DC/Marvel
  1996) Elseworlds 6.00
Batman/Demon (1996) 5.00
Batman/Demon: A Tragedy (2000) . 6.00
Batman/Green Arrow: The Poison
  Tomorrow,MN,JRu,V:Poison
  Ivy (1992) 6.25
  GN rep. (2000) 6.00
Batman/Houdini: The Devil's
  Workshop (1993). 6.50
Batman: Huntress/Spoiler—Blunt
  Trauma, CDi,Cataclysm (1988). 3.00
Batman/Judge Dredd: Judgement on
  Gotham,SBs,V:Scarecrow, Judge
  Death (1991) 9.00
Batman/Judge Dredd: Vendetta in
  Gotham, AIG(s),V:Ventriliquist
  (1993) 5.25
Batman/Judge Dredd: The Ultimate
  Riddle (1995). 5.00
Batman/Lobo, Elseworlds (2000). . . 6.00
Batman/Phantom Stranger, AIG(s),
  Lemurian artifact (1997) 5.00
Batman/Punisher: Lake of Fire,
  DON(s),BKi,A:Punisher,V:Jigsaw
  (DC/Marvel 1994) 6.00
Batman/Spawn: War Devil, DgM,CDi,
  AIG(s), KJ,V:Croatoan (1994) . . 6.00
Batman/Spawn: War Devil (1999) . . 5.00
Batman/Spider-Man JMD,GN,KK,
  V:Kingpin&Ra's al Ghul(1997). . 5.00
Batman vs. The Incredible Hulk
  (DC/Marvel 1995) 4.00

BATMAN ADVENTURES
1992–95
(Based on cartoon series)
1 MeP,V:Penguin 5.00
2 MeP,V:Catwoman 4.00

Batman Adventures #30
© DC Comics Inc.

3 MeP,V:Joker. 3.00
4 MeP,V:Scarecrow. 3.00
5 MeP,V:Scarecrow. 3.00
6 MeP,A:Robin 3.00
7 MeP,V:Killer Croc,w/card 6.00
8 MeP,Larceny my Sweet. 3.00
9 MeP,V:Two Face 3.00
10 thru 24 MeP . . . . @3.00
25 MeP,dbl.size,Superman 3.50
26 thru 32. . . . . @3.00
33 thru 36 . . . . @2.50
Ann.#1 Roxy Rocket 3.00
Ann.#2 JBa,BBI,DG,TG,SHa,BKi,MM,
  GN,JRu,V:Demon,Ra's al
  Ghul,Etrigan. 3.50
Holiday Special 3.00
Spec. Mad Love. 4.00

BATMAN ADVENTURES:
THE LOST YEARS
Nov., 1997
1 (of 5) BHa,TBe,Batgirl 2.50
2 BHa,TBe,Dick Grayson quits. . . . 2.50
3 . . . . 2.50
4 BHa,TBe,F:Tim Drake 2.50
5 BHa,TBe,Tim Drake new Robin . 2.50
1999
1 (of 6) TBe. 2.50
2 thru 6 . . . . @2.50

BATMAN ADVENTURES
May 2003
1 TTn 2.50
2 thru 17 TTn, ... @2.50

BATMAN/ALIENS II
DC/Dark Horse Dec. 2002
GN #1 (of 3) IEd(s) 6.00
GN #2 IEd(s) 6.00
GN #3 IEd(s) 6.00

BATMAN AND
THE OUTSIDERS
Aug., 1983
1 B:MiB(s),JAp,O:Outsiders,
  O:Geo Force 4.50
2 JAp,V:Baron Bedlam 3.00
3 JAp,V:Agent Orange 2.50
4 JAp,V:Fearsome Five 2.50
5 JAp,A:New Teen Titans 3.00

Batman and the Outsiders #24
© DC Comics Inc.

6 JAp,V:Cryonic Man 2.50
7 JAp,V:Cryonic Man 2.50
8 JAp,A:Phantom Stranger 2.50
9 JAp,I:Master of Disaster 2.50
10 JAp,A:Master of Disaster 2.50
11 JAp,V:Takeo 2.50
12 JAp,DG,O:Katana 2.50
13 JAp,Day,O:Batman 2.50
14 BWg,Olympics,V:Maxi Zeus 2.50
15 TVE,Olympics,V:Maxi Zeus 2.50
16 JAp,L:Halo 2.50
17 JAp,V:Ahk-Ton 2.50
18 JAp,V:Ahk-Ton 2.50
19 JAp,A:Superman. 2.50
20 JAp,V:Syonide,R:Halo 2.50
21 TVE,JeM,Solo Stories. 2.50
22 AD,O:Halo,I:Aurakles 2.50
23 AD,O:Halo,V:Aurakles. 2.50
24 AD,C:Kobra 2.50
25 AD,V:Kobra 2.50
26 AD 2.50
27 AD,V:Kobra 2.50
28 AD,I:Lia Briggs(Looker). 2.50
29 AD,V:Metamorpho. 2.50
30 AD,C:Looker 2.50
31 AD,I&J:Looker. 2.50
32 AD,L:Batman. 2.50
Ann.#1 JA N:Geo-Force,
  I:Force of July 3.00
Ann.#2 V:Tremayne,W:Metamorpho
  & Sapphire Stagg 3.00
Becomes:

ADVENTURES OF
THE OUTSIDERS
May, 1986
33 AD,V:Baron Bedlam 2.50
34 AD,Masters of Disaster. 2.50
35 AD,V:Adolph Hitler 2.50
36 AD,A:Masters of Disaster 2.50
37 thru 38 . . . . @2.50
39 thru 47 JAp,reprints
  Outsiders #1-#9 . . . . @2.50

BATMAN AND
THE OUTSIDERS
Oct., 2007
1 ATi,V:Metahumans. 3.00
1a variant (c) (1:10) 3.00
2 ATi,Assault on London 3.00
3 ATi,Salvation Run tie-in 3.00
4 CDi(s),Green Arrow joins. 3.00
5 CDi(s),Leadership challenge 3.00

6 CDi(s),Search and Rescue 3.00
7 CDi(s),The heart of China 3.00
8 CDi(s),F:Nightwing. 3.00
9 CDi(s),F:Metamorpho 3.00
10 CDi(s),F:The Man-Bat. 3.00
11 Batman R.I.P. tie-in 3.00
12 Batman R.I.P. tie-in 3.00
13 Batman R.I.P. tie-in 3.00

BATMAN AND ROBIN
ADVENTURES, THE
Nov., 1995
1 TTn 3.00
2 TTn,V:Two-Face 3.00
3 TTn,V:The Riddler 3.00
4 TTn,V:The Penguin 3.00
5 TTn 3.00
6 TTn,Robin Fired?. 2.50
7 TTn,V:Scarface 2.50
8 TTn(s) 2.50
9 TTn(s),F:Batgirl & Talia 2.50
10 TTn(s),F:Ra's Al Ghul 2.50
11 TTn(s),Alfred & Robin look
  for monster in Batcave 2.50
12 TTn(s),BKr,RBr, sequel to
  Bane TV episode. 2.50
13 TTn(s),BKr,RBr,V:Scarecrow . . . 2.50
14 TTn(s),BKr,RBr,young criminal
  turns to Batman for help 2.50
15 TTn(s) 2.50
16 TTn(s),V:Catman,A:Catwoman. . 2.50
17 PDi&TTn(s),JSon,RBr,Mad
  Hatter dies in Arkham 2.50
18 TTn(s),BKr,TBe,A:Joker,
  Harley Quinn 2.50
19 TTn(s),BKr,TBe,The Huntress . . 2.50
20 TTn(s),BKr,TBe, office pool 2.50
21 TTn(s),JSon,Riddler kidnaps
  Commissioner Gordon 2.50
22 TTn(s),BKr,TBe,V:Two-Face 2.50
23 TTn(s),TBe,V:Killer Croc. 2.50
24 TTn(c),F:Poison Ivy 2.50
25 TTn,TBe,final issue, 48pg. 3.50
Ann.#1 PDi(s),TTn, sequel to
  Batman: Mask of the Phantasm 3.00
Ann.#2 JSon,TBe,V:Hypnotist 4.00
Sub-Zero one-shot, F:Mr. Freeze,
  Nora, 64pg. 4.00

BATMAN & SUPERMAN:
WORLD'S FINEST
1999
1 (of 10) KK(s),DTy,RbC,48-page. . 7.00
2 KK(s),DTy,RbC. 3.50
3 KK(s),DTy,RbC,Arkham Asylum . 3.00
4 KK(s),DTy,RbC,Metropolis. 3.00
5 KK(s),DTy,RbC,Batgirl 3.00
6 KK(s),DTy,RbC,trade identities . . 3.00
7 KK(s),PD,RbC 3.00
8 KK(s),PD,RbC 3.00
9 KK(s),RbC,split issue. 3.00
10 concl.. . . . . 3.00
GN 7.00

BATMAN: THE ANKH
Nov., 2001
1 (of 2) CDi,JVF,ancient Egypt 6.00
2 CDi,JVF,V:Khatera, concl. 6.00

BATMAN:
BANE OF THE DEMON
Feb., 1998
1 (of 4) CDi,GN,TP, Bane &
  Ra's al Ghul 2.50
2 CDi,GN,TP,Talia. 2.50
3 CDi,GN,TP,the Lazarus Pit 2.50
4 CDi,GN,TP,Bane imprisoned 2.50

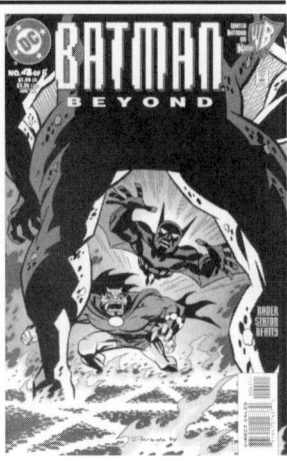

Batman Beyond #4
© DC Comics, Inc.

BATMAN BEYOND
Mini-series 1999
1 (of 6) RBr,TBe,Rebirth 2.50
2 RBr,TBe,Rebirth,pt.2 . . . . 2.50
3 RBr,TBe,V:Blight 2.50
4 JSon,TBe,F:Demon Etrigan. 2.50
5 JSon,TBe,V:Mummy 2.50
6 JSon,TBe,V:Inque 2.50
1999
1 Batman: Classic vs. Future 3.00
2 thru 14 . . . . @2.50
15 thru 20 BSf(c) . . . . @2.50
21 thru 24 . . . . @2.50
Spec. Return of the Joker 3.00

BATMAN BLACK & WHITE
1996
1 JLe(c) numerous artists. 9.00
2 thru 4 . . . . @7.00

BATMAN:
BOOK OF THE DEAD
1999
1 (of 2) DgM(s),BKi,Elseworlds . . . 5.00
2 DgM(s),BKi,Conclusion 5.00

BATMAN: CACOPHONY
Nov., 2008
1 (of 3) NKu(c) 3.00
1a variant NKu(c) (1:25). 3.50
1b variant sketch (c) (1:50). 4.00

BATMAN/CATWOMAN:
TRAIL OF THE GUN
Aug. 2004
1 & 2 48-pg. . . . . @6.00

BATMAN CHRONICLES
1995
1 CDi,LW,BSz, multiple stories. . . . 5.00
2 V:Feedback 4.00
3 All villains issue 4.00
4 F:Hitman 15.00
5 Oracle, Year One story 3.50
6 Ra's Al Ghul. 3.50
7 JOy,LW, woman on death row . . . 3.50
8 Talia goes to Gotham to
  eliminate Batman. 3.50

9 CDi(s),F:Batgirl, Mr. Freeze,
   Poison Ivy 3.50
10 BSn, anthology 3.50
11 CDi,JFM, Elseworlds stories 3.00
12 Cataclysm x-over 3.00
13 F:GCPD 3.00
14 SB(c),F:Alfred,Huntress 3.00
15 Road to No Man's Land 3.00
16 F:Batgirl,No Man's Land tie-in . . 3.00
17 V:Penguin,No Man's Land 3.00
18 No Man's Land 3.00
19 . . . . 3.00
20 SBe(s)&IEd(s),48-pg. 3.00
21 DG,JRu,3 Elsewords tales 3.00
22 F:Lady Shiva,48-pg. 3.00
23 BSf(c) final issue. 3.00
Gallery #1, Pin-ups 3.50
GN The Gauntlet 5.00

BATMAN: CITY OF LIGHT
Oct. 2003
1thru 8 Gotham transformed . . . @3.00

BATMAN: CONFIDENTIAL
Dec., 2006
1 WPo,Rules of Engagement 3.00
2 WPo,Rules of Engagement,pt.2 . 3.00
3 WPo,Rules of Engagement,pt.3 . 3.00
4 WPo,Rules of Engagement,pt.4 . 3.00
5 WPo,Rules of Engagement,pt.5 . 3.00
6 WPo,Rules of Engagement,pt.6 . 3.00
7 Who becomes a Joker?. 3.00
8 Who becomes a Joker?. 3.00
9 Who becomes a Joker?. 3.00
10 Who becomes a Joker? 3.00
11 V:Joker 3.00
12 Lovers and Madmen. 3.00
13 RgM,Wrath Child,pt.1 . . . . 3.00
14 RgM,Wrath Child,pt.2 . . . . 3.00
15 RgM,Wrath Child,pt.3 . . . . 3.00
16 RgM,Wrath Child,pt.4 . . . . 3.00
17 FaN(s),The Bat & the Cat,pt.1 . . 3.00
18 FaN(s),The Bat & the Cat,pt..2. . 3.00
19 FaN(s),The Bat & the Cat,pt.3 . . 3.00
20 FaN(s),The Bat & the Cat,pt.4 . . 3.00
21 FaN(s),The Bat & the Cat,pt.5 . . 3.00
22 Understand These Rights, pt.1 . . 3.00
23 Understand These Rights, pt.2. . 3.00

BATMAN: THE CULT
1988
1 JSn,BWr,V:Deacon Blackfire 8.00
2 thru 4 JSn,BWr. . . . . @6.00

Batman The Cult #3
© DC Comics Inc.

BATMAN: CYBER REVOLUTION
May 2004
1 (of 5) Joker's robot army 3.00
2 thru 5 . . . . @3.00

BATMAN: DARK DETECTIVE
May, 2005
1 (of 6) TA,MR 3.00
2 thru 6 TA,MR . . . . @3.00

BATMAN: DARK KNIGHT OF THE ROUND TABLE
1998
1 (of 2) BL,DG,Elseworlds,48pg . . . 5.00
2 BL,DG, conclusion 5.00

BATMAN: THE DARK KNIGHT RETURNS
1986
1 FM,KJ,V:Two-Face 30.00
1a 2nd printing 5.00
1b 3rd printing 3.00
2 FM,KJ,V:Sons of the Batman . . 20.00
2a 2nd printing 3.00
2b 3rd printing 2.50
3 FM,KJ,D:Joker. 20.00
3a 2nd printing 3.00
4 FM,KJ,Batman vs.Superman,
   A:Green Arrow,D:Alfred 20.00
Paperback book. 20.00
Warner paperback 17.00
   2nd-8th printing 13.00

BATMAN: THE DARK KNIGHT STRIKES AGAIN
Dec., 2001
1 (of 3) FM,80-pg.. . . . . 8.00
2 thru 3 FM, 80-pg. . . . . @8.00

BATMAN: DARK VICTORY
Oct., 1999
1 (of 13) JLb,TSe,48-pg.. . . . . 6.00
2 JLb,TSe 5.00
3 JLb,TSe,V:Scarecrow 4.00
4 JLb,TSe,V:Two-Face 4.00
5 JLb,TSe,F:Catwoman 4.00
6 JLb,TSe,F:Penguin 4.00
7 JLb,TSe,V:Calendar Man 4.00
8 JLb,TSe,V:Hang Man 4.00
9 JLb,TSe,F:Bruce & Dick 4.00
10 JLb,TSe,V:Two-Face 4.00
11 JLb,TSe,V:Poison Ivy 4.00
12 JLb,TSe,Revenge. 4.00
13 JLb,TSe, conclusion 5.00

BATMAN: DEATH AND THE MAIDENS
Aug. 2003
1 (of 9) KJ,V:Ra's al Ghul 4.00
2 KJ,F:Nyssa 3.00
3 KJ,Ra's al Ghul, Nyssa 3.00
4 KJ,Ra's al Ghul 3.00
5 thru 8 KJ. . . . . @3.00
9 KJ 4.00

BATMAN/DEATHBLOW: AFTER THE FIRE
DC/Wildstorm March, 2002
1 (of 3)TBd,x-over,48-pg. 6.00
2 TBd, 48-pg. 6.00
3 TBd, 48-pg., concl. 6.00

BATMAN: DEATH MASK
(B&W) April, 2008
1 thru 4 (of 4) Manga . . . . @6.00

BATMAN: THE DOOM THAT CAME TO GOTHAM
Sept., 2000
1 (of 3) Elseworlds 5.00
2 MMi,DJa, return from the Arctic. . 5.00
3 Elseworlds, concl. 5.00

BATMAN FAMILY
Sept.–Oct., 1975
1 MGr,NA(rep.) Batgirl &
   Robin begins,giant. 42.00
2 V:Clue Master 25.00
3 Batgirl & Robin reveal ID 25.00
4 I:Fatman. 25.00
5 I:Bat Hound 25.00
6 Joker Daughter 28.00
7 CS,A:Sportsmaster,
   G.A.Huntress 20.00
8 First solo Robin story,
   C:Joker's Daughter 20.00
9 Joker's Daughter 28.00
10 R:B'woman,1st solo Batgirl sty . 30.00
11 MR,Man-Bat begins 28.00
12 MR 28.00
13 MR,DN,BWi. 28.00
14 HC/JRu,Man-Bat. 28.00
15 MGo,Man-Bat 28.00
16 MGo,Man-Bat 28.00
17 JA,DH,MG,Batman, B:Huntress
   A:Demon,MK(c),A:Catwoman . 32.00
18 MGo,JSon,BL,Huntress,BM . . . 32.00
19 MGo,JSon,BL,Huntress,BM . . . 32.00
20 MGo,JSon,DH,A:Elongatedman,
   RagMan, Oct.–Nov.,1978 . . . . 32.00

BATMAN: FAMILY
Oct., 2002
1 (of 8) JFM,SFa,RHo,The Tracker 3.50
2 JFM,SFa,RHo,Athena 2.25
3 JFM,SFa,RHo,Bugg & Dr.Excess 2.25
4 JFM,SFa,RHo,Suicide King. 2.25
5 JFM,SFa,RHo,Freeway 2.25
6 JFM,RHo,The Technician 2.25
7 JFM,Mr. Fun. 2.25
8 JFM,RHo,Blackout, 48-pg. 3.50

BATMAN: GCPD
Mini-Series Aug., 1996
1 thru 4 CDi(s),JAp,BSz . . . . . . @2.50

BATMAN: GORDON'S LAW
October, 1996
1 CDi(s),KJ,Gordon looks for
   bad cops 2.50
2 CDi(s),KJ,Gordon vs. corruption . 2.50
3 CDi(s),KJ, ... 2.50
4 (of 4) CDi(s),KJ, concl. 2.50

BATMAN: GORDON OF GOTHAM
April, 1998
1 (of 4) DON,DG,KJ,F:Jim Gordon . 2.50
2 DON,DG,KJ,Cuchulain. 2.50
3 DON,DG,KJ,break-in 2.50
4 DON,DG,KJ,past revealed. 2.50

BATMAN: GOTHAM ADVENTURES
April, 1998
1 TTn,RBr,TBe,F:Joker. 3.50
2 TTn,RBr,TBe,F:Two-Face 2.50

Batman: Gorgon of Gotham #4
© DC Comics, Inc.

3 TTn,RBr,TBe,V:Scarecrow 2.50
4 TTn,RBr,TBe,A:Catwoman 2.50
5 RBr,TBe,TTn,A:Mr.Freeze 2.50
6 TTn,RBr,TBe,O:Deadman 2.50
7 TTn,RBe,TBe,V:Danger Dixon . . . 2.50
8 TTn,RBe,TBe,Batgirl 2.50
9 TTn,RBe,TBe,V:League
    of Assassins 2.50
10 TTn,RBe,TBe,F:Nightwing
    & Robin, A:Harley Quinn 2.50
11 TTn,RBe,TBe,V:Riddler. 2.50
12 TTn,RBe,TBe,V:Two-Face 2.50
13 RBe,TBe,V:Mastermind 2.50
14 TTn(s),TBe,V:Harley Quinn 2.50
15 V:Bane 2.50
16 TBe,Alfred Kidnapped. 2.50
17 TBe 2.50
18 TBe,R:Man-Bat 2.50
19 TBe,Eden's Own,Poison Ivy 2.50
20 TBe, ... 2.50
21 TBe, ... 2.50
22 TBe,F:Comm.Gordon & Batgirl. . 2.50
23 TBe,V:Ra's al Ghul 2.50
24 TBe,F:Killer Croc 2.50
25 TBe,A:Flash 2.50
26 TBe,F:Kristov 2.50
27 TBe, ... 2.50
28 TBe,V:Riddler 2.50
29 CDi(s),TBe,Batman poisoned. . 2.50
30 TBe,F:Clayface 2.50
31 TTn,TBe,Blackout in Gotham . . . 2.50
32 TBe,V:Scarecrow 2.50
33 A:Phantom Stranger 2.50
34 V:Maxie Zeus 2.50
35 TBe,On the jury. 2.50
36 TBe,A:Superman 2.50
37 TBe,V:Joker, Penguin 2.50
38 TBe,F:Robin, Batgirl 2.50
39 TBe,V:Clayface 2.50
40 TBe,V:Mr. Freeze 2.50
41 TBe,The Man called Joe. 2.50
42 Tuesday Night. 2.50
43 TBe,F:Harley Quinn 2.50
44 TBe,F:Two-Face 2.50
45 TBe,Running the Asylum 2.50
46 TBe,Saving Face 2.50
47 TBe,Gotham's Underworld 2.50
48 TBe,RBr,F:Dick Grayson 2.50
49 TBe,Facade 2.50
50 TBe,Catwoman returns. 2.50
51 TA,Mr. Freeze 2.50
52 TBe,Bane 2.50
53 TBe,Poison Ivy superplant 2.50
54 TBe,crime spree 2.50

55 TBe,RBr,mobsters. 2.50
56 TBe,V:Riddler? 2.50
57 TBe,V:Riddler 2.50
58 TTn,V:Ventriloquist 2.50
59 TBe,financial scandal 2.50
60 TBe,final issue 2.50

BATMAN: GOTHAM AFTER MIDNIGHT
May, 2008
1 (of 12) KJo,V:Scarecrow 3.00
2 thru 7 . . . . @3.00

BATMAN: GOTHAM COUNTY LINE
Oct., 2005
1 (of 3) SHp, 48-page 6.00
2 thru 3 SHp, 48-page. . . . . @6.00

BATMAN: GOTHAM KNIGHTS
Feb., 2000
1 WEI,JLe 6.00
2 JBy,BB(c),F:Batgirl. 3.00
3 PPo,PR,BB(c),Samsara,pt.1 . . . . 3.00
4 PR,BB(c),Samsara,pt.2 . . . . 3.00
5 BB(c)V:The Key 3.00
6 WS,PR,JPL,F:Oracle 3.00
7 SD,PR, ... 3.00
8 Transference,pt.1 . . . . 3.00
9 Transference,pt.2 . . . . 3.00
10 Transference,pt.3, ... 3.00
11 BB(c),Transference,pt.4,48-pg. . . 3.50
12 This issue: Batman dies! 3.00
13 Officer Down,x-over,concl. 3.00
14 V:Double Dare 3.00
15 TPe,GC,V:Poison Ivy 3.00
16 Matatoa,pt.1 . . . . 3.00
17 Matatoa,pt.2 . . . . 3.00
18 Cavernous,F:Aquaman 3.00
19 CDi,MSh,DG,F:Titus 3.00
20 A:Superman 3.00
21 TA,Retribution, pt.2 . . . . 3.00
22 TA,Chemical attack 3.00
23 BB(c),F:Scarecrow 3.00
24 TDz,Kls,F:Bruce Wayne 3.00
25 Bruce Wayne:Murderer,pt.4 . . . . 4.00
26 Bruce Wayne:Murderer,pt.10 . . . 4.00
27 DCw,A:Man of Steel 3.00
28 Bruce Wayne:Fugitive,pt.7 . . . . . 3.00
29 Mortician,pt.2 . . . . 3.00
30 Bruce Wayne:Fugitive,pt.14 . . . . 3.00
31 Bruce Wayne:Fugitive,pt.17 . . . . 3.00
32 MK,lives Batman impacts 3.00
33 SBe(s),BSz,F:Bane. 3.00
34 SBe(s),Tabula Rasa,pt.1 . . . . . . 3.00
35 SBe(s),Tabula Rasa,pt.2 . . . . . . 3.50
36 SBe(s),F:Robin,Nightwing. 3.00
37 SBe(s),F:Spoiler 3.00
38 SBe(s),V:Checkmate 3.00
39 SBe(s),V:Checkmate 3.00
40 SBe(s),Knight Moves 3.00
41 SBe(s),V:Elongated Man 3.00
42 SBe(s),Alfred's illness 3.00
43 SBe(s),F:Batgirl,Robin 3.00
44 SBe(s),death of Jason Todd 3.00
45 SBe(s),Knights Passed. 3.00
46 SBe(s),F:Nightwing,Robin. 3.00
47 WPo,F:Bane,Nightwing. 3.00
48 F:Bane,Nightwing 3.00
49 F:Bane 3.00
50 V:Hush 3.00
51 V:Hush,Riddler,Joker 3.00
52 F:Tailor,Hush,40-pg. 3.00
53 F:Hush,Green Arrow,40-pg. 3.00
54 F:Joker,40-pg. 3.00
55 Hush vs. Joker, 48-pg. 4.00
56 War Games,Act 1,pt.4 . . . . 2.50
57 War Games,Act 2,pt.4 . . . . 2.50

58 War Games,Act 3,pt.5 . . . . 2.50
59 CAd,JaL,F:Mr. Freeze. 2.50
60 JaL(c),V:Hush 2.50
61 F:Hush, Ivy 2.50
62 F:Poison Ivy 2.50
63 F:Poison Ivy 2.50
64 F:Poison Ivy, Hush 2.50
65 F:Poison Ivy, conc. 3.00
66 F:Kobra & Prometheus 2.50
67 V:Hush,F:Poison Ivy 2.50
68 F:Alfred 2.50
69 F:Hush, Clayface 2.50
70 F:Clayfaces 2.50
71 Alfred arrested for Murder. 2.50
72 Dead Body, Parents Past 2.50
73 Joker returns. 2.50
74 V:Hush, Joker 2.50

(BATMAN:) GOTHAM NIGHTS
[Mini-Series] 1992
1 Gotham City 2.50
2 thru 4 Gotham Citizens Lives. . @2.50

GOTHAM NIGHTS II
1995
1 Sequel to Gotham Nights 2.50
2 F:Carmine Sansone. 2.50
3 Fire. 2.50
4 JQ(c) Decisions 2.50

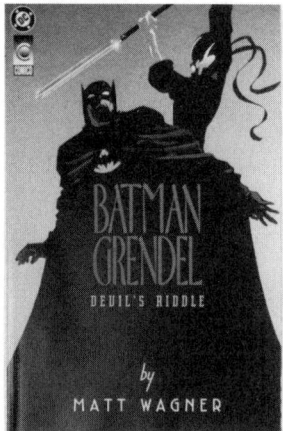

Batman/Grendel 1st Series #1
© DC Comics, Inc.

BATMAN/GRENDEL
[First Series]
DC/Comico, 1993
1 MWg,Devil's Riddle 5.25
2 MWg,Devil's Masque 5.25

[Second Series]
DC/Dark Horse, 1996
1 MWg,Devil's Bones 5.00
2 MWg,Devil's Dance 5.00

BATMAN: HARLEY & IVY
April 2004
1 (of 3) PDi 2.50
2 PDi,Zombie Root 2.50
3 PDi, finale 2.50

BATMAN: HAUNTED GOTHAM
Dec., 1999
1 (of 4) DgM,KJo,JhB,Elseworlds. . 5.00
2 thru 4 DgM,KJo,JhB. . . . . @5.00

BATMAN/HELLBOY/ STARMAN
DC/Dark Horse 1998
1 JeR(s),MMi, x-over 2.50
2 JeR(s),MMi, conclusion 2.50

BATMAN: HOLLYWOOD KNIGHT
Feb., 2001
1 (of 3) DG,Elseworlds 2.50
2 DG,F:Byron Wyatt 2.50
3 DG, concl. 2.50

BATMAN/HUNTRESS: CRY FOR BLOOD
April, 2000
1 (of 6) RBr,O:Huntress 2.50
2 thru 6 RBr. . . . . @2.50

BATMAN: IT'S JOKER TIME
May, 2000
1 thru 3 (of 3) BH . . . . @5.00

BATMAN: JAZZ
Mini-Series 1995
1 I:Blue Byrd 2.50
2 V:Brotherhood of Bop 2.50
3 F:Blue Byrd 2.50

BATMAN: JEKYLL & HYDE
Apr., 2005
1 PJe(s),JaL,SeP(c),F:Two-Face . . 3.00
2 PJe(s),JaL,SeP(c) 3.00
3 PJe(s),JaL,SeP(c) 3.00
4 thru 6 PJe(s),SeP. . . . . @3.00

BATMAN: JOURNEY INTO KNIGHT
Aug., 2005
1 (12) Batman's early years 2.50
2 Plague breaks out 2.50
3 Plague 2.50
4 Plague 2.50
5 V:Carrier. 2.50
6 Double-cross 2.50
7 Crossroads 2.50
8 Mysterious fires 2.50
9 Dangerous revelations. 2.50
10 Batman's early career. 3.00
11 Enter the Joker 3.00
12 V:Joker, finale 3.00

BATMAN/JUDGE DREDD: DIE LAUGHING
1998
1 (of 2) AlG(s),GF 48-pg. 5.00
2 AlG(s),GF conclusion. 5.00

BATMAN: LEAGUE OF BATMEN
April, 2001
1 MBr,RT,48-page, Elseworlds 6.00
2 MBr,RT,48-page, concl. 6.00

BATMAN: LEGENDS OF THE DARK KNIGHT
1989
1 EH,Shaman of Gotham,pt.1,
   Yellow(c) 5.00
1a Blue,Orange or Pink(c) 4.00

2 EH,Shaman of Gotham,pt.2 . . . . 3.00
3 EH,Shaman of Gotham,pt.3 . . . . 3.00
4 EH,Shaman of Gotham,pt.4 . . . . 3.00
5 EH,Shaman of Gotham,pt.5 . . . . 3.00
6 KJ,Gothic,pt.1 . . . . 3.00
7 KJ,Gothic,pt.2 . . . . 3.00
8 KJ,Gothic,pt.3 . . . . 3.00
9 KJ,Gothic,pt.4 . . . . 3.00
10 KJ,Gothic,pt.5 . . . . 3.00
11 PG,TA,Prey,pt.1. . . . . 6.00
12 PG,TA,Prey,pt.2. . . . . 5.00
13 PG,TA,Prey,pt.3. . . . . 5.00
14 PG,TA,Prey,pt.4. . . . . 5.00
15 PG,TA,Prey,pt.5. . . . . 4.00
16 TVE,Venom,pt.1 . . . . 5.00
17 TVE,JL,Venom,pt.2. . . . . 5.00
18 TVE,JL,Venom,pt.3. . . . . 5.00
19 TVE,JL,Venom,pt.4. . . . . 5.00
20 TVE,JL,Venom,pt.5. . . . . 5.00
21 BS,Faith,pt.1 . . . . 3.00
22 BS,Faith,pt.2 . . . . 3.00
23 BS,Faith,pt.3 . . . . 3.00
24 GK,Flyer,pt.1 . . . . 3.00
25 GK,Flyer,pt.2. . . . . 3.00
26 GK,Flyer,pt.3. . . . . 3.00
27 Destroyer,pt.2 (Batman#474) . . . 3.50
28 MWg,Faces,pt.1,V:Two-Face . . . 4.00
29 MWg,Faces,pt.2,V:Two-Face . . . 4.00
30 MWg,Faces,pt.3,V:Two-Face . . . 4.00
31 BA,Family 3.00
32 Blades,pt.1 . . . . 3.00
33 Blades,pt.2 . . . . 3.00
34 Blades,pt.3 . . . . 3.00
35 BHa,Destiny Pt.1 . . . . 3.00
36 BHa,Destiny Pt.2 . . . . 3.00
37 I:Mercy,V:The Cossack. 3.00
38 KON,R:Bat-Mite 3.00
39 BT,Mask#1 . . . . 3.00
40 BT,Mask#2 . . . . 3.00
41 Sunset. 3.00
42 CR,Hothouse #1 . . . . 3.00
43 CR,Hothouse #2,V:Poison Ivy . . 3.00
44 SMc,Turf #1 . . . . 3.00
45 Turf#2 . . . . 3.00
46 RH,A:Catwoman,V:Catman 3.00
47 RH,A:Catwoman,V:Catman 3.00
48 RH,A:Catwoman,V:Catman 3.00
49 RH,A:Catwoman,V:Catman 3.00
50 BBI,JLe,KN,KM,WS,MZ,BB,
   V:Joker 6.00
51 JKu,A:Ragman 3.00
52 Tao #1,V:Dragon 3.00
53 Tao #2,V:Dragon 3.00
54 MMi 3.50
55 B:Watchtower 3.00
56 CDi(s),V:Battle Guards 3.00
57 CDi(s),E:Watchtower 3.00
58 Storm. 3.00
59 DON(s),RoW,B:Qarry 3.00
60 RoW,V:Asp 3.00
61 RoW,V:Asp 3.00
62 RoW,KnightsEnd#4,A:Shiva,
   Nightwing. 4.50
63 Knights End #10,V:Azrael. 3.00
64 CBa 3.00
65 Joker. 3.00
66 Joker 3.00
67 Going Sane,pt.3 . . . . 3.00
68 Going Sane,pt.4 . . . . 3.50
69 Criminals,pt.1 . . . . 3.50
70 Criminals,pt.2 . . . . 3.50
71 Werewolf,pt.1 . . . . 3.00
72 JWk(c&a),Werewolf,pt.2
   [new Miraweb format begins] . . 3.00
73 JWk(c&a),Werewolf,pt.3 . . . . . . 3.00
74 Engins,pt.1 . . . . 3.00
75 Engins,pt.2 . . . . 3.00
76 The Sleeping,pt.1 . . . . 3.00
77 The Sleeping,pt.2 . . . . 3.00
78 The Sleeping,pt.3 . . . . 3.00
79 Favorite Things 3.00
80 Idols,pt.1 . . . . 3.00

81 Idols,pt.2 . . . . 3.00
82 Idols, climax 3.00
83 new villain 3.00
84 WEl(s). 3.00
85 JeR(s) 3.00
86 DgM,JWi,MGy,Conspiracy,pt.1 . . 3.00
87 DgM,JWi,MGy,Conspiracy,pt.2 . . 3.00
88 DgM,JWi,MGy,Conspiracy,pt.3 . . 3.00
89 AlG(s),Clay,pt. 1 . . . . 3.00
90 AlG(s),Clay,pt. 2 . . . . 3.00
91 Freakout, pt.1 . . . . 3.50
92 GEn(s),WSm,Freakout, pt.2 . . . 3.50
93 GEn(s),WSm,Freakout, pt.3 . . . 3.50
94 MGi(s),Saul Fisher's story 3.00
95 DAn&ALa(s),AWi,ALa,Dirty
   Tricks,pt.1 . . . . 3.00
96 DAn&ALa(s),AWi,ALa,Dirty
   Tricks, pt.2 . . . . 3.00
97 DAn&ALa(s),AWi,ALa,,Dirty
   Tricks, concl. 3.00
98 PJe(s),SeP,Steps, pt.1. . . . . 3.00
99 PJe(s),SeP,Steps, pt.2 . . . . 3.00
100 DON,JRo,F:Robin, 64pg. 6.00
101 CE,KN(c)100 years in future. . . 3.00
102 JRo,PuJ,Spook, pt.1 . . . . 3.00
103 JRo,PuJ,Spook, pt.2 . . . . 3.00
104 JRo,PuJ,Spook, pt.3 . . . . 3.00
105 TVE,JRu,Duty, pt.1 . . . . 3.00
106 TVE,JRu,Duty, pt.2 . . . . 3.00
107 LMr,Stalking, pt.1 . . . . 3.00
108 LMr,Stalking, pt.2 . . . . 3.00
109 SEt,DAb,Primal Riddle,pt.1. . . . 3.00
110 SEt,DAb,Primal Riddle,pt.2. . . . 3.00
111 SEt,DAb,Primal Riddle,pt.3 . . . 3.00
112 DVa,FC,V:Lord Demise,pt.1 . . . 3.00
113 DVa,FC,V:Lord Demise,pt.2 . . . 3.00
114 JeR(s),DlB,TBd 3.00
115 LMc,DlB(c) 3.00
116 IEd,Bread and Circuses,pt.1. . . 5.00
117 IEd,Bread and Circuses,pt.2. . . 2.50
118 JPn,Alfred in No Man's Land . . 2.50
119 MD2,Claim Jumping,pt.1. . . . . . 2.50
120 MD2,Assembly. 5.00
121 RBr,V:Mr.Freeze 3.50
122 LHa(s),PG, Low Road to Golden
   Mountain,pt.1. . . . . 3.50
123 PR,ALa,Underground
   Railroad,pt.1 . . . . 3.50
124 CDi(s),MkK,No Man's Land . . . 3.50
125 No Man's Land 3.00
126 Endgame, pt.1 x-over 3.00
127 MRy,F:Green Arrow,pt.1 . . . . . . 2.50
128 MRy,F:Green Arrow,pt.2 . . . . . . 2.50
129 MRy,F:Green Arrow,pt.3 . . . . . . 2.50

Batman Legends of the Dark Knight #136 © DC Comics, Inc.

All comics prices listed are for *Near Mint* condition.

130 MRy,F:Green Arrow,pt.4	2.50
131 MRy,F:Green Arrow,pt.5	2.50
132 AGw,JeR,MR,BWi,Siege,pt.1	2.50
133 AGw,JeR,MR,BWi,Siege,pt.2	2.50
134 AGw,JeR,MR,BWi,Siege,pt.3	2.50
135 AGw,JeR,MR,BWi,Siege,pt.4	2.50
136 AGw,JeR,MR,BWi,Siege,pt.5	2.50
137 DgM,PG,JP,Terror,pt.1	2.50
138 DgM,PG,JP,Terror,pt.2	2.50
139 DgM,PG,JP,Terror,pt.3	2.50
140 DgM,PG,JP,Terror,pt.4	2.50
141 DgM,PG,JP,Terror,pt.5	2.50
142 CDi,JAp,Demon Laughs,pt.1	2.50
143 CDi,JAp,Demon Laughs,pt.2	2.50
144 CDi,JAp,Demon Laughs,pt.3	2.50
145 CDi,JaP,Demon Laughs,pt.4	2.50
146 DgM,BKi,Bad,pt.1	2.50
147 DgM,BKi,Bad,pt.2	2.50
148 DgM,BKi,Bad,pt.3	2.50
149 JMD,TVE, Grimm, pt.1	2.50
150 JMD,TVE, Grimm, pt.2	2.50
151 JMD,TVE, Grimm, pt.3	2.50
152 JMD,TVE, Grimm, pt.4	2.50
153 JMD,TVE, Grimm, pt.5	2.50
154 MBn,BR,Colossus,pt.1	2.50
155 MBn,BR,Colossus,pt.2	2.50
156 DGr,Blink,pt.1	2.50
157 DGr,Blink,pt.2	2.50
158 DGr,Blink,pt.3	2.50
159 JOs,DGr,Loyalties,pt.1	2.50
160 JOs,DGr,Loyalties,pt.2	2.50
161 JOs,DGr,Loyalties,pt.3	2.50
162 JAr(s),Auteurism,pt.1	2.50
163 JAr(s),Auteurism,pt.2	2.50
164 DMD,DGr,Don't Blink,pt.1	2.50
165 DMD,DGr,Don't Blink,pt.2	2.50
166 DMD,DGr,Don't Blink,pt.3	2.50
167 DMD,DGr,Don't Blink,pt.4	2.50
168 Urban Legend	2.50
169 TyH,Irresistible,pt.1	2.50
170 TyH,Irresistible,pt.2	2.50
171 TyH,Irresistible,pt.3	2.50
172 V:Rough Justice	2.50
173 V:Rough Justice	2.50
174 O:Rough Justice	2.50
175 Testament,pt.6	2.50
176 Testament,pt.5	2.50
177 Lost Cargo,pt.1	2.50
178 Lost Cargo,pt.2	2.50
179 O:Fat Man & Little Boy	2.50
180 Virtual Gotham City	2.50
181 Cyber-world	2.50
182 War Games,Act 1,pt.2	2.50
183 War Games,Act 2,pt.2	2.50
184 War Games,Act 3,pt.2	2.50
185 RyR,SeP,Riddle Me That, pt.1	2.50
186 RyR,SeP,Riddle Me That, pt.2	2.50
187 RyR,SeP,Riddle Me That, pt.3	2.50
188 RyR,SeP,Riddle Me That, pt.4	2.50
189 RyR,SeP,Riddle Me That, pt.5	2.50
190 V:Mr. Freeze	2.50
191 V:Mr. Freeze,pt.2	2.50
192 Snow,pt.1,O: Mr. Freeze	2.50
193 Snow,pt.2	2.50
194 Snow,pt.3	2.50
195 Snow,pt.4	2.50
196 Snow,pt.5	2.50
197 Blaze of Glory, pt.1	2.50
198 Blaze of Glory, pt.2	2.50
199 Blaze of Glory, pt.2	2.50
200 ECa,F:Joker in E.R.	5.50
201 Cold Case, pt.1	2.50
202 Cold Case, pt.2	2.50
203 Cold Case, pt. 3	2.50
204 Madmen of Gotham, pt.1	3.00
205 Madmen of Gotham, pt.2	3.00
206 Madmen of Gotham, pt.3	3.00
207 Darker Than Death, pt.1	3.00
208 Darker Than Death, pt.2	3.00
209 Darker Than Death, pt.3	3.00
210 Darker Than Death, pt.4	3.00
211 Darker Than Death, pt.5	3.00

Batman: Legends of the Dark Knight Ann. #7 © DC Comics, Inc.

212 NMa,A cheap date	3.00
213 WS(c),The Otaku	3.00
214	3.00
Ann.#1 JAp,KG,DSp,TL,JRu, MGo,JQ,`Duel',C:Joker	5.50
Ann.#2 MN,LMc,W:Gordn&Essen	5.00
Ann.#3 MM,I:Cardinal Sin	5.00
Ann.#4 JSon(c),Elseworlds Story	5.00
Ann.#5 CDi(s)Year One Annuals, O:Man-Bat	5.00
Ann.#6 Legends o/t Dead Earth	4.00
Ann.#7 Pulp Heroes (War)	7.00
Halloween Spec.I	8.00
Halloween Spec.II	5.00
Ghosts, Halloween Special	5.00

BATMAN/LOBO: DEADLY SERIOUS
Aug., 2007

1 (of 2) SK, 48-pgs.	6.00
2 SK 48-pgs.	6.00

BATMAN: THE LONG HALLOWEEN
Oct., 1996

1 (of 13) JLb,TSe,Who is Holiday? F: usual suspects	11.00
2 JLb(s),TSe,V:Holiday,A:Solomon Grundy	8.00
3 JLb,TSe,	9.00
4 JLb(s),TSe,New Year's Eve	9.00
5 JLb(s),TSe,F:Poison Ivy, Search for Holiday	6.00
6 JLb(s),TSe,F:Poison Ivy, Catwoman	6.00
7 JLb(s),TSe,V:The Riddler	5.00
8 JLb(s),TSe,V:Scarecrow	5.00
9 JLb(s),TSe,A:Holiday,Scarecrow	5.00
10 JLb(s),TSe,V:Scarecrow,Mad Hatter	5.00
11 JLb(s),TSe,V:Holiday	5.00
12 JLb(s),TSe,Harvey Dent	5.00
13 JLb(s),TSe,concl.,48pg.	7.00

BATMAN AND THE MAD MONK
Aug., 2006

1 (of 6) MWg	3.50
2 MWg	3.50
3 MWg	3.50
4 thru 6 MWg	@3.50

BATMAN: MAN-BAT
1995

1 R:Man-Bat, painted series	5.00
2 F:Marilyn Muno	5.00
3 JBo,Elseworlds story, concl.	5.00

BATMAN AND THE MONSTER MEN
Nov., 2005

1 (of 6) MWg, Dark Moon Rising	3.00
2 MWg,V:Super-Villains	3.00
3 MWg,V:Professor Hugo	3.00
4 MWg,Genetic mutants	3.00
5 MWg,Mobsters & Mutants	3.00
6 MWg,concl. 40-pg.	3.50

BATMAN: NEVERMORE
April 2003

1 (of 5) Elseworlds,BWr(c)	2.50
2 GyD,BWr(c),Raven Murders	2.50
3 GyD,BWr(c),Raven Murders	2.50
4 GyD,BWr(c),Raven Murders	2.50
5 GyD,BWr(c),concl.	2.50

BATMAN: NO MAN'S LAND
Sept., 1999

0 F:Huntress	5.00
Secret Files #1	5.00

BATMAN: ORPHEUS RISING
Aug., 2001

1 (of 5) DT,DaM	2.50
2 DT,DaM,caught in cross-fire	2.50
3 DT,DaM,who's behind it	2.50
4 DT,DaM,The Deacons	2.50
5 DT,DaM,concl	2.50

BATMAN: OUTLAWS
July, 2000

1 (of 3) DgM,PG	5.00
2 DgM,PG,V:Bloodhawks	5.00
3 DgM,PG,concl.	5.00

BATMAN: RUN, RIDDLER RUN
1992

1 MBg,Batman V:Riddler	5.50
2 MBg,Batman V:Riddler	5.25
3 MBg,V:Perfect Securities	5.25

BATMAN: SECRETS
March, 2006

1 (of 5) SK, V:The Joker	3.00
2 SK	3.00
3 SK, Toe to toe	3.00
4 SK, Mooley kidnapped.	3.00
5 SK, final battle V:Joker	3.00

BATMAN: SHADOW OF THE BAT
1992–97

1 NB,Last Arkham Pt.1	5.00
1a Collector set,w/posters,pop-up	6.00
2 NB,Last Arkham Pt.2	4.00
3 NB,Last Arkham Pt.3	4.00
4 NB,Last Arkham Pt.4	4.00
5 NB,A:Black Spider	3.00
6 NB,I:Chancer	3.00
7 Misfits Pt.1	3.00
8 Misfits Pt.2	3.00
9 Misfits Pt.3	3.00
10 MC,V:Mad Thane of Gotham	3.00
11 V:Kadaver	2.50

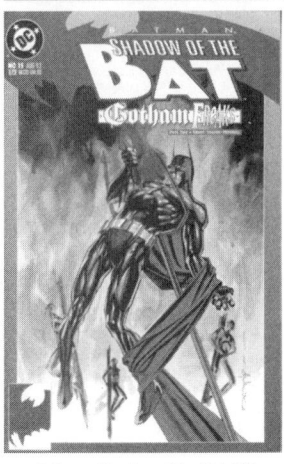

Batman: Shadow of the Bat #15
© DC Comics Inc.

12 V:Kadaver,A:Human Flea 2.50
13 NB,The Nobody 2.50
14 NB,Gotham Freaks#1 . . . . 2.50
15 NB,Gotham Freaks#2 . . . . 2.50
16 BBl,MM,A:Anarchy,Scarecrow . . 2.50
17 BBl,V:Scarecrow 2.50
18 BBl,A:Anarchy,Scarecrow 2.50
19 BBl,Knightquest:The Crusade,pt.2,
　V:Gotham criminals 2.50
20 VGi,Knightquest:The Crusade,
　V:Tally Man 2.50
21 BBl,Knightquest:The Search,
　V:Mr.Asp 2.50
22 BBl,Knightquest:The Search,
　In London 2.50
23 BBl,Knightquest:The Search . . . 2.50
24 BBl,Knightquest:The Crusade . . 2.50
25 BSf(c),BBl,Knightquest: Crusade,
　A:Joe Public,V:Corrosive Man . . 2.50
26 BSf(c),BBl,Knightquest: Crusade,
　V:Clayface 2.50
27 BSf(c),BBl,Knightquest: Crusade,
　I:Clayface Baby 2.50
28 BSf(c),BBl 2.50
29 BBl,KnightsEnd#2,
　A:Nightwing 4.00
30 BSf(c),BBl,KnightsEnd#8,
　V:Azrael 2.50
31 Zero Hour, V:Butler 2.50
32 Ventriloquist,Two-Face 2.50
33 Two-Face 2.50
34 V:Tally Man 2.50
35 BKi,Return of Bruce Wayne,
　Troika,pt.2 . . . . 2.50
35a Collectors Edition 3.50
36 Black Canary 2.50
37 Joker Hunt 2.50
38 V:The Joker 2.50
39 BSf(c),R:Solomon Grundy
　[new Miraweb format begins] . . 2.50
40 BSf(c), F:Anarky 2.50
41 Explosive Dirigible 2.50
42 BSz(c),Day the Music Died. 2.50
43 Secret of the Universe,pt1 . . . . . 2.50
44 AIG,BSz(c) Secret of the
　Universe,pt.3 . . . . 2.50
45 AIG,BSz(c) 100 year old corpse . 2.50
46 AIG,BSz(c) V:Cornelius Stirk . . . 2.50
47 AIG,BSz(c) V:Cornelius Stirk . . . 2.50
48 AIG 2.50
49 AIG,Contagion,pt.7 . . . . 2.50
50 AIG,Nightmare on Gotham,pt.1 . . 2.50
51 AIG,DTy, Nightmare on
　Gotham,pt.2 (of 3) 2.50

52 AIG(s),Nightmare on Gotham,
　pt.3 . . . . 2.50
53 AIG(s),Legacy, prelude 2.50
54 AIG(s),Legacy, pt. 4, x-over . . . 2.50
55 AIG(s),RBr,KJ,Bruce Wayne a
　murderer? A:Nightwing 2.50
56 AIG(s),DTy,SnW,Leaves of
　Grass,pt.1,V:Poison Ivy 2.50
57 AIG(s),DTy,SnW,Grass,pt.2 . . . . 2.50
58 AIG(s),DTy,SnW,Grass,pt.3 . . . . 2.50
59 AIG(s),DTy,SnW,Killer,
　Killer, pt.1 . . . . 2.50
60 AIG(s),DTy,SnW,Killer, pt.2 . . . 2.50
61 AIG(s),JAp,SnW,night of
　second chances 2.50
62 AIG(s),DTy,SnW,Two-Face,pt.1 . 2.50
63 AIG(s),DTy,SnW,Two-Face,pt.2 . 2.50
64 AIG(s),DTy,SnW,A:Jason Blood . 2.50
65 AIG(s),NBy,JRu, A:Oracle, pt.1 . . 2.50
66 AIG(s),NBy,JRu, V:Thinker,
　Cheat, pt.2 . . . . 2.50
67 AIG(s),NBy,SnW,CsM,V:Thinker,
　Cheat, pt.3, concl. 2.50
68 AIG(s),JAp,SnW,annual killer . . 2.50
69 AIG(s),MBu,WF,CsM,
　The Spirit of 2000, pt. 1 . . . . . . 2.50
70 AIG(s),MBu,WF,CsM, pt.2 . . . . . 2.50
71 AIG(s),MBu,WF,CsM,detective . . 2.50
72 AIG(s),MBu,WF 2.50
73 AIG(s),MBu,WF,Cataclysm
　x-over,pt.1 . . . . 3.50
74 AIG(s),MBu,WF,Cataclysm
　cont. 2.50
75 AIG(s),MBu,WF,Aftershock 3.50
76 AIG(s),MBu,WF,Aftershock 2.50
77 AIG(s),MBu,WF,quake-torn 2.50
78 AIG(s),MBu,Aftershock 2.50
79 AIG(s),MBu,V:Mad Hatter,
　Narcosis. 2.50
80 Road to No Man's Land, flip-book
　Azrael:Agent of the Bat #47 . . 5.00
81 AIG(s),MBu,No Man's Land 2.50
82 AIG(s),MBu,No Man's Land 2.50
83 No Law and a New Order, pt.2 . 14.00
84 IEd,Bread and Circuses, pt.2 . . . 5.00
85 IEd(s),Bread & Circuses,concl. . . 5.00
86 GyD,No Man's Land 3.00
87 MD2, Claim Jumping, pt.2 . . . . . 3.00
88 DJu,BSz,Fruit of
　the Earth,pt.1 . . . . 3.00
89 IEd(s),SB,No Man's Land 3.00
90 LHa(s),PG,No Man's Land 3.00
91 PR,ALa,Underground
　Railroad,pt.2 . . . . 3.00
92 No Man's Land,A:Superman. . . . 3.00
93 No Man's Land 3.00
94 final issue 3.00
Ann.#1 TVE,DG,Bloodlines#3,
　I:Joe Public 4.00
Ann.#2 Elseworlds story 4.00
Ann.#3 Year One Annual 4.00
Ann.#4 Legends of the Dead
　Earth 3.00
Ann.#5 AIG(s), Pulp Heroes. 4.00
Spec.#1,000,000 AIG(s),MBu, Origin of
　853rd-century Dark Knight 2.50

BATMAN STRIKES, THE
Sept. 2004
1 thru 50 . . . . @2.50

BATMAN/SUPERMAN/ WONDER WOMAN: TRINITY
June 2003
1 (of 3) MWg, first meeting 7.00
2 MWg,V:Bizarro 7.00
3 MWg,concl. 7.00

BATMAN: SWORD OF AZRAEL
1992–93
1 JQ,KN,I:Azrael 12.00
2 JQ,KN,A:Azrael 9.00
3 JQ,KN,V:Biis,A:Azrael 8.00
4 JQ,KN,V:Biis,A:Azrael 8.00

BATMAN: TENSES
Aug. 2003
1 thru 2 JoC(s) . . . . @7.00

BATMAN: TOYMAN
1998
1 thru 4 LHa(s),AWi,KJ . . . . @2.50

BATMAN: TURNING POINTS
Nov., 2000
1 (of 5) F:Gordon & Batman 2.50
2 TTn(c),Robin arrives 2.50
3 DG,JKu(c),Batgirl dead 2.50
4 CDi,BA HC(c) Azrael 2.50
5 No Man's Land 2.50

BATMAN vs. PREDATOR
DC/Dark Horse 1991–92
1 NKu,AKu,inc.8 trading cards
　bound in (Prestige) 5.00
1a Newsstand 4.00
2 NKu,AKu,Inc. pinups (prestige) . . 4.00
3 NKu,AKu,conclusion,inc.
　8 trading cards (Prestige) 4.00
2a thru 3a Newsstand editions . . @3.00

BATMAN vs. PREDATOR II BLOODMATCH
1994–95
1 R:Predators 3.00
2 A:Huntress 3.00
3 Assassins 3.00
4 V:Head Hunters 3.00

BATMAN/PREDATOR III: BLOOD TIES
DC/Dark Horse 1997
1 thru 4 (of 4) CDi,RDm,RbC, vs.
　pair of Predators . . . . @2.50

Batman Vs Predator II #2
© DC Comics Inc.

BATMAN/WILDCAT
Feb., 1997
1 (of 3) CDi&BSt(s),SCi,ATi,
  Batman and Robin discover
  Secret Ring of combat 2.50
2 CDi&BSt(s),SCi,V:KGBeast,
  Willis Danko 2.50
3 CDi&BSt(s),SCi, Batman vs.
  Wildcat, concl 2.50

BATMAN:
YEAR ONE HUNDRED
Feb., 2006
1 (of 4) PPo,48-pg. 6.00
2 thru 4 PPo, Future Gotham . . . @6.00

BEAST BOY
Nov., 1999
1 (of 4)BRa,Clv 3.00
2 BRa,Clv,A:Nightwing 3.00
3 BRa,Clv,V:Nightwing 3.00
4 BRa,Clv,F:Flamebird 3.00

BATTLE CLASSICS
Sept.–Oct., 1978
1 JKu, reprints 15.00

BEOWOLF
April-May, 1975
1 . . . . 25.00
2 thru 3 . . . . @10.00
4 Dracula 15.00
5 . . . . 10.00
6 Flying Saucer,Feb.–Mar.1976 . . 12.00

BEST OF THE
BRAVE & THE BOLD
1988
1 JL(c),NA,rep.B&B #85. . . . . 5.00
2 thru 6 JL(c),NA,rep.B&B . . . . . @5.00

BEWARE THE CREEPER
1968–69
1 SD,Where Lurks the Menace . 175.00
2 thru 6 SD . . . . @80.00

BEWARE THE CREEPER
DC/Vertigo, April 2003
1 thru 5 . . . . @3.00

Beware the Creeper #2
© DC Comics, Inc.

BIG ALL-AMERICAN
COMIC BOOK
Dec., 1944
1 JKu,132-pages 20,000.00

BIG BOOK OF FUN
COMICS
Spring, 1936
1 . . . . 30,000.00

BIG TOWN
1951–58
1 TV, radio tie-in. 1,100.00
2 . . . . 500.00
3 thru 10 . . . . @350.00
11 thru 20 . . . . @300.00
21 thru 30 . . . . @250.00
31 thru 40 . . . . @150.00
41 thru 50 . . . . @125.00

BILLY BATSON AND
THE MAGIC OF SHAZAM
July, 2008
1 . . . . 2.50
1a variant (c) (1:10) 2.50
2 thru 4 . . . . @2.50

BIRDS OF PREY:
MANHUNT
1996
1 CDi(s),MHy,F:Black Canary,
  Oracle 10.00
2 CDi(s),MHy,V,Archer Braun,
  A:Catwoman 7.00
3 CDi(s),MHy,V:Catwoman,
  Huntress 7.00
4 CDi(s),MHy,V:Lady Shiva 7.00
1-shot Birds of Prey: Batgirl CDi,
  Batgirl & Black Canary (1997). . 3.00
1-shot Birds of Prey: Revolution
  CDi(s),BMc 3.00
1-shot Birds of Prey: The Ravens,
  CDi, Girlfrenzy (1998) 3.00
1-shot Birds of Prey: Wolves
  CDi,DG (1997). 3.00

BIRDS OF PREY
1998
1 CDi(s),Black Canary & Oracle. . 12.00
2 CDi(s),V:Jackie Pajamas 7.00
3 CDi(s),V:Hellbound 7.00
4 CDi(s),V:Ravens 7.00
5 CDi(s),V:Ravens,pt.2 . . . . 3.00
6 CDi(s),V:Ravens,pt.3 . . . . 3.00
7 CDi(s),PKr, ... 3.00
8 CDi(s),F:Nightwing. 42.00
9 CDi(s),V:Iron Brigade. 3.00
10 CDi(s),DG,V:Dr.Pop 3.00
11 CDi(s),DG 3.00
12 CDi(s),DG,F:Catwoman 3.00
13 CDi(s),DG 3.00
14 CDi(s),DG,V:Lashina. 3.00
15 CDi(s),JG 3.00
16 CDi(s),JG,V:maniac. 2.50
17 CDi(s),JG,V:Joker 2.50
18 CDi(s),JG,Transbelvia 2.50
19 CDi(s),JG,A:Nightwing,Robin . . . 2.50
20 CDi(s),Hunt for Oracle,pt.2 . . . . 2.50
21 CDi(s),Hunt for Oracle,concl. . . . 2.50
22 CDi(s),Gorilla City 2.50
23 CDi(s),Gorilla City 2.50
24 CDi,search for heart donor 3.00
25 CDi,Deathstroke,Blue Beetle . . . 2.50
26 CDi,This issue Batman dies! . . . 2.50
27 Officer Down x-over,pt.3 . . . . . . 2.50
28 CDi,History Lession,pt.1 . . . . 2.50
29 CDi,History Lession,pt.2 . . . . 2.50

30 CDi,History Lession,pt.3 . . . . 2.50
31 CDi,star-crossed love 2.50
32 CDi,love, and marriage? 2.50
33 CDi,Black Canary,Ra's Al Ghul. . 2.50
34 CDi,A:Power Girl,Blue Beetle . . . 2.50
35 CDi,rescue Black Canary 2.50
36 CDi,Joker: Last Laugh 2.50
37 CDi,Last Laugh aftermath. 2.50
38 CDi,F:Dinah 2.50
39 CDi,BruceWayne:Murderer,pt.5 . 6.00
40 CDi,BruceWayne:Murderer,pt.12 6.50
41 CDi,BruceWayne:Fugitive,pt.2 . . 6.50
42 CDi,GF,F:Power Girl 5.00
43 CDi,BruceWayne:Fugitive,pt.10 . 2.50
44 CDi,Deathstroke 2.50
45 CDi,Deathstroke, dinosaurs 2.50
46 CDi,Deathstroke 2.50
47 TMr(s),JP,Heartache,pt.1 . . . . . . 2.50
48 TMr(s),JP,Heartache,pt.2 . . . . . . 2.50
49 TMr(s),JP,Heartache,pt.3 . . . . . . 2.50
50 GHe,CJ 2.50
51 GHe,CJ 2.50
52 GHe,CJ 2.50
53 GHe,CJ 2.50
54 GHe,CJ 2.50
55 GHe,CJ 2.50
56 EBe,V:Savant 6.00
57 EBe,V:Savant 5.00
58 EBe,V:Savant 5.00
59 EBe,V:Savant 4.00
60 EBe,R:Huntress 4.00
61 EBe,consequences 3.00
62 EBe,F:Lady Shiva 3.00
63 EBe,F:Lady Shiva 3.00
64 EBe,V:Cheshire 2.50
65 EBe,F:Cheshire. 2.50
66 MGo,MM,ATh(c) 2.50
67 EBe,Sensei and Student. 2.50
68 Date for Huntress 2.50
69 Between Dark and Dawn,pt.1. . . 2.50
70 Between Dark and Dawn,pt.2 . . . 2.50
71 Between Dark and Dawn,pt.3. . . 2.50
72 Between Dark and Dawn,pt.4. . . 2.50
73 Between Dark and Dawn,pt.5. . . 2.50
74 Between Dark and Dawn,pt.6. . . 2.50
75 EBe,40-pg. BU: EB. 3.00
76 EBe,Hero Hunters,pt.1 . . . . 5.00
77 EBe,Hero Hunters,pt.2 . . . . 2.50
78 Hero Hunters,pt.3 . . . . 2.50
79 EBe,Hero Hunters,pt.4 . . . . 2.50
80 EBe,Hero Hunters,pt.5, concl. . . 2.50
81 JoB,The Battle Within 2.50
82 JoB,F:Wildcat 2.50
83 JoB,Omac tie-in 2.50
84 JoB,mission to Singapore 2.50
85 JoB,The Battle Within, concl. . . . 2.50
86 Moving day-to Metropolis 2.50
87 JoB,Oracle, Calculator 2.50
88 JoB,V:Calculator 2.50
89 JoB,V:Calculator 2.50
90 V:Deathstroke 2.50
91 JP,Organ Donar 2.50
92 One Year Later 2.50
93 Vengeance 2.50
94 V:Prometheus 3.00
95 Progeny. 3.00
96 Headhunting,pt.1. . . . . 3.00
97 Headhunting,pt.2. . . . . 3.00
98 A:Batgirl. 3.00
99 New outfits 3.00
100 DHz,New Team, 48-pg. 4.00
101 DHz,F:Oracle, Manhunter 3.00
102 DHz,F:Oracle 3.00
103 DHz,Blood & Circuits finale. . . . 3.00
104 DHz,F:Secret Six 3.00
105 DHz,V:Secret Six 3.00
106 DHz,V:Secret Six 3.00
107 DHz,V:Secret Six 3.00
108 V:Spy Smasher 3.00
109 DHz,Death of a New God. 3.00
110 DHz,F:Oracle 3.00
111 Oracle & Calculator 3.00

112 Lady Blackhawk missing. 3.00
113 DHz,A:Superman 3.00
114 DHz,F:Misfit. 3.00
115 DHz,F:Black Alice 3.00
116 DHz,Platinum Flats 3.00
117 DHz, Misfit & Manhunter 3.00
118 DHz,Misfit & Black Alice 3.00
119 DHz,Back off, Huntress! 3.00
120 DHz,Enigmatic Infinity. 3.00
121 Platinum Flats. 3.00
122 F:Visionary, Scavengers 3.00
123 F:The Joker. 3.00
124 F:Joker, Barbara Gordon 3.00
Spec. Secret Files 2003. . . . . 5.00

BIRDS OF PREY:
Feb. 2003
Catwoman/Batgirl
1 JFM,JP,DaR. 6.00
Catwoman/Oracle
2 JFM,JP,DaR. 6.00

BITE CLUB
DC/Vertigo, April 2004
1 (of 6) HC(s),vampire,mafia 5.00
2 HC(s),Bikinis 4.00
3 HC(s),Leto Del Toro. 3.00
4 HC(s),plot for revenge 3.00
5 HC(s),Leto learns truth 3.00
6 HC(s),concl. 3.00

BITE CLUB:
VAMPIRE CRIME UNIT
DC/Vertigo, April, 2006
1 (of 5) HC, Breathe in, Bleed Out . 3.00
2 thru 5 HC . . . . @3.00

BLACK ADAM:
THE DARK AGE
Aug., 2007
1 (of 8) NRd,DoM 3.00
1a variant AxR (c) (1:10). 3.00
2 DoM,F:Superman,Batman,JSA . . 3.00
3 DoM,V:Hawkman. 3.00
4 thru 6 DoM. . . . . @3.00

BLACK CANARY
[Limited Series], 1991–92
1 TVE/DG,New Wings,pt.1 . . . . 2.50
2 TVE/DG,New Wings,pt.2 . . . . 2.50
3 TVE/DG,New Wings,pt.3 . . . . 2.50

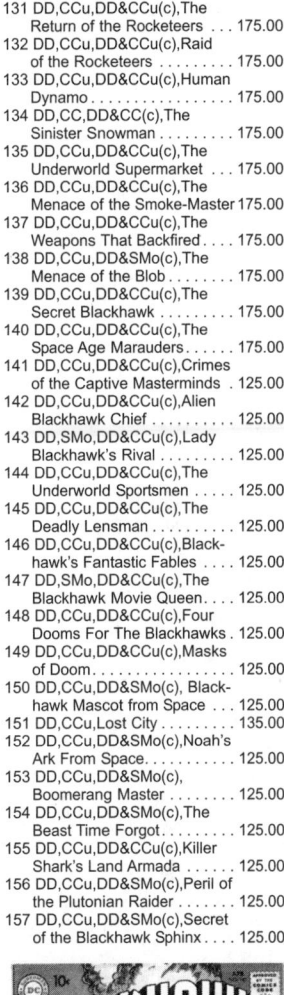

Black Canary #1
© DC Comics Inc.

4 TVE/DG,New Wings,pt.4,Conc . . 2.50
[Regular Series], 1993
1 TVE,Hero Worship,pt.1 . . . . 3.00
2 TVE,Hero Worship,pt.2 . . . . 3.00
3 TVE,Hero Worship,pt.3 . . . . 3.00
4 TVE,V:Whorrsman 3.00
5 TVE,Blynde Woman's Bluff 3.00
6 TVE,Caged Canary 3.00
7 TVE,V:Maniacal Killer 3.00
8 TVE,The Fish. 3.00
9 TVE,A:Huntress. 3.00
10 TVE,A:Nightwing,Huntress 3.00
11 TVE,A:Nightwing. 3.00
12 Canary's Grave, final issue. 3.00

BLACK CANARY
July, 2007
1 (of 4) League of Assassins 3.00
2 thru 4 . . . . @3.00
Spec. Black Canary Wedding
Planer 3.00

BLACK CANARY/ORACLE:
BIRDS OF PREY
1996
1-shot DDi, double size 10.00

BLACK CONDOR
1992–93
1 I&O:Black Condor 3.00
2 thru 11 . . . . @3.00

BLACKHAWK
Prev: Golden Age
1957–1984
108 DD,CCu,DD&CCu(c),The Threat
from the Abyss A:Blaisie 800.00
109 DD,CCu,DD&CCu(c),The
Avalance Kid 275.00
110 DD,CCu,DD&CCu(c),Mystery
of Tigress Island 275.00
111 DD,CCu,DD&CCu(c),Menace
of the Machines. 275.00
112 DD,CCu,DD(c),The Doomed
Dog Fight. 275.00
113 DD,CCu,CCu(c),Volunteers
of Doom. 275.00
114 DD,CCu,DD&CCu(c),Gladiators
of Blackhawk Island. 275.00
115 DD,CCu,DD&CCu(c),The
Tyrant's Return 275.00
116 DD,CCu,DD&CCu(c),Prisoners
of the Black Island. 275.00
117 DD,CCu,DD&CCu(c),Menace
of the Dragon Boat 275.00
118 DD,CCu,DD&SMo(c),FF,The
Bandit With 1,000 Nets 300.00
119 DD,CCu,DD&SMo(c),
V:Chief Blackhawk. 200.00
120 DD,CCu,DD&SMo(c),The
Challenge of the Wizard 200.00
121 DD,CCu,DD&CCu(c),Secret
Weapon of the Archer 200.00
122 DD,CCu,DD&CCu(c),The
Movie That Backfired. 200.00
123 DD,CCu,DD&CCu(c),The
Underseas Gold Fort. 200.00
124 DD,CCu,DD&CCu(c),Thieves
With A Thousand Faces 200.00
125 DD,CCu,DD&CCu(c),Secrets
o/t Blackhawk Time Capsule . 200.00
126 DD,CCu,DD&CCu(c),Secret
of the Glass Fort 200.00
127 DD,CCu,DD&CCu(c),Blackie-
The Winged Sky Fighter 200.00
128 DD,CCu,DD&CCu(c),The
Vengeful Bowman 200.00
129 DD,CCu,DD&CCu(c),The
Cavemen From 3,000 B.C. . . 200.00

130 DD,CCu,DD&SMo(c),The
Mystery Missle From Space . 200.00
131 DD,CCu,DD&CCu(c),The
Return of the Rocketeers . . . 175.00
132 DD,CCu,DD&CCu(c),Raid
of the Rocketeers 175.00
133 DD,CCu,DD&CCu(c),Human
Dynamo 175.00
134 DD,CC,DD&CC(c),The
Sinister Snowman 175.00
135 DD,CCu,DD&CCu(c),The
Underworld Supermarket . . . 175.00
136 DD,CCu,DD&CCu(c),The
Menace of the Smoke-Master 175.00
137 DD,CCu,DD&CCu(c),The
Weapons That Backfired. . . . 175.00
138 DD,CCu,DD&SMo(c),The
Menace of the Blob 175.00
139 DD,CCu,DD&CCu(c),The
Secret Blackhawk 175.00
140 DD,CCu,DD&CCu(c),The
Space Age Marauders. 175.00
141 DD,CCu,DD&CCu(c),Crimes
of the Captive Masterminds . 125.00
142 DD,CCu,DD&CCu(c),Alien
Blackhawk Chief 125.00
143 DD,SMo,DD&CCu(c),Lady
Blackhawk's Rival 125.00
144 DD,CCu,DD&CCu(c),The
Underworld Sportsmen 125.00
145 DD,CCu,DD&CCu(c),The
Deadly Lensman 125.00
146 DD,CCu,DD&CCu(c),Black-
hawk's Fantastic Fables 125.00
147 DD,SMo,DD&CCu(c),The
Blackhawk Movie Queen. . . . 125.00
148 DD,CCu,DD&CCu(c),Four
Dooms For The Blackhawks . 125.00
149 DD,CCu,DD&CCu(c),Masks
of Doom. 125.00
150 DD,CCu,DD&SMo(c),Black-
hawk Mascot from Space . . . 125.00
151 DD,CCu,Lost City 135.00
152 DD,CCu,DD&SMo(c),Noah's
Ark From Space. 125.00
153 DD,CCu,DD&SMo(c),
Boomerang Master 125.00
154 DD,CCu,DD&SMo(c),The
Beast Time Forgot. 125.00
155 DD,CCu,DD&CCu(c),Killer
Shark's Land Armada 125.00
156 DD,CCu,DD&SMo(c),Peril of
the Plutonian Raider 125.00
157 DD,CCu,DD&SMo(c),Secret
of the Blackhawk Sphinx 125.00

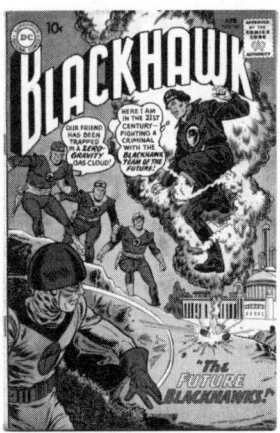

Blackhawk #147
© DC Comics, Inc.

158 DD,CCu,DD&SMo(c),Bandit
Birds From Space 125.00
159 DD,CCu,DD&SMo(c),Master
of the Puppet Men. 125.00
160 DD,CCu,DD&CCu(c),The
Phantom Spy. 125.00
161 DD,SMo,DD&SMo(c),Lady
Blackhawk's Crime Chief. . . . 125.00
162 DD,CCu,DD&CCu(c),The
Invisible Blackhawk 125.00
163 DD,CCu,DD&SMo(c),
Fisherman of Crime. 125.00
164 DD,O:Blackhawk retold. 135.00
165 DD,V:League of Anti
Blackhawks 125.00
166 DD,A:Lady Blackhawk 125.00
167 DD,The Blackhawk Bandits . . 90.00
168 DD,Blackhawk Time
Travelers 80.00
169 DD,Sinister Hunts of Mr.
Safari. 80.00
170 DD,A:Lady Blackhawk,V:Killer
Shark 80.00
171 DD,Secret of Alien Island 80.00
172 DD,Challenge of the
GasMaster. 80.00
173 DD,The Super Jungle Man . . . 80.00
174 DD,Andre's Impossible
World 80.00
175 DD,The Creature with
Blackhawk's Brain 80.00
176 DD,Stone Age Blackhawks . . . 75.00
177 DD,Town that time Forgot. . . . 75.00
178 DD,Return of the Scorpions . . 75.00
179 DD,Invisible Dr.Dunbar 75.00
180 DD,Son of Blackhawk. 75.00
181 DD,I:Tom Thumb Blackhawk . 80.00
182 DD,A:Lady Blackhawk 100.00
183 DD,V:Killer Shark 100.00
184 DD,Island of Super
Monkeys 100.00
185 DD,Last 7 days of the
Blackhawks 100.00
186 DD,A:Lady Blackhawk 100.00
187 DD,V:Porcupine 100.00
188 DD,A:Lady Blackhawk 100.00
189 DD:O:rtd 100.00
190 DD,FantasticHumanStarfish . 100.00
191 DD,A:Lady Blackhawk 100.00
192 DD,V:King Condor 50.00
193 DD,The Jailer's Revenge 50.00
194 DD,The Outlaw Blackhawk . . . 50.00
195 DD,A:Tom Thumb Blackhawk. 50.00
196 DD,Blackhawk WWII Combat
Diary story 50.00

AN OLD BLACKHAWK FOE RETURNS!

BLACKHAWK

KING CONDOR'S WINGED FURIES!

SCATTER, BLACKHAWKS! KING CONDOR IS BACK, IN A FANTASTIC HALF-BIRD HALF-HUMAN FORM!

Blackhawk #209
© DC Comics, Inc.

197 DD:new look 50.00
198 DD:O:rtd 70.00
199 DD,Attack with the Mummy
Insects 70.00
200 DD,A:Lady Blackhawk,
I:Queen Killer Shark 90.00
201 DD,Blackhawk Detached Diary
Story,F:Hendrickson 70.00
202 DD,Combat Diary,F:Andre . . . 70.00
203 DD:O:Chop-Chop. 70.00
204 DD,A:Queen Killer Shark 70.00
205 DD,Combat Diary story. 70.00
206 DD,Combat Diary, F:Olaf 70.00
207 DD,Blackhawk Devil Dolls . . . 70.00
208 DD,Detached service diary
F:Chuck 70.00
209 DD,V:King Condor 70.00
210 DD,Danger..Blackhawk Bait
rep.Blackhawk #139. . . . . 50.00
211 DD,GC,Detached service
diary. 40.00
212 DD,Combat Diary,
F:Chop-Chop. 40.00
213 DD,Blackhawk goes
Hollywood 40.00
214 DD,Team of Traitors 40.00
215 DD,Detached service diary
F:Olaf. 40.00
216 DD,A:Queen Killer Shark 40.00
217 DD,Detached service diary
F:Stanislaus. 40.00
218 DD,7 against Planet Peril 40.00
219 DD,El Blackhawk Peligroso . . 40.00
220 DD,The Revolt of the
Assembled Man. 40.00
221 DD,Detach service diary
F:Hendrickson 40.00
222 DD,The Man from E=MC2 . . . 40.00
223 DD,V:Mr.Quick CHange 40.00
224 DD,Combat Diary,
F:Stanislaus. 40.00
225 DD,A:Queen Killer Shark 40.00
226 DD,Secret Monster of
Blackhawk Island. 40.00
227 DD,Detached Service diary
F:Chop-Chop. 40.00
228 DD (1st art on JLA characters)
Blackhawks become super-heroes,
Junk-Heap heroes #1(C:JLA) . 50.00
229 DD,Junk-Heap Heroes #2
(C:JLA). 40.00
230 DD,Junk-Heap Heroes concl.
(C:JLA) 40.00
231 DD,A:Lady Blackhawk 40.00
232 DD,A:Lady Blackhawk 40.00
233 DD,Too Late,The Leaper 40.00
234 DD,The Terrible Twins 40.00
235 DD,A Coffin for
a Blackhawk 40.00
236 DD,Melt,Mutant, Melt 40.00
237 DD,Magnificent 7 Assassins . . 40.00
238 DD,Walking Booby-Traps 40.00
239 DD,The Killer That Time
Forgot 40.00
240 DD,He Who Must Die 40.00
241 DD,A Blackhawk a Day. 40.00
242 Blackhawks back in blue &
black costumes 40.00
243 Mission Incredible (1968) 40.00

[Series Pause:] 1969–75
244 GE,new costumes,Blackhawks
become mercenaries (1976) . . 25.00
245 GE,Death's Double Deal. 25.00
246 RE,GE,Death's Deadly Dawn. 25.00
247 RE,AM,Operation:Over Kill . . . 25.00
248 JSh,Vengeance is Mine!..
Sayeth the Cyborg. 25.00
249 RE,GE,V:Sky-Skull 25.00
250 RE,GE,FS,D:Chuck (1977). . . 25.00

[Series Pause:] 1978–81
251 DSp,Back to WWII (1982). . . . 20.00
252 thru 258 DSp. . . . . @20.00

259 HC(c),DSp. 20.00
260 HC,ATh. 20.00
261 thru 271 DSp. . . . . @20.00
272 DSp. 20.00
273 DSp. 20.00
274 DSp. 20.00

[2nd Series], 1988
1 HC Mini-series,Blackhawk accused
of communism. 5.00
2 HC,visits Soviet Union 4.00
3 HC,Atom Bomb threat to N.Y. . . . 4.00

[3rd Series], 1989
1 All in color for a Crime,pt.1
I:The Real Lady Blackhawk. . . . 4.00
2 All in color for a Crime,pt.2 . . . . 2.50
3 Agent Rescue Attempt in Rome . 2.50
4 Blackhawk's girlfriend murdered . 2.50
5 I:Circus Organization 2.50
6 Blackhawks on false mission. . . . 2.50
7 V:Circus,A:Suicide Squad, rep.
1st Blackhawk story. 3.00
8 Project: Assimilation. 2.50
9 V:Grundfest 2.50
10 Blackhawks Attacked 2.50
11 Master plan revealed 2.50
12 Raid on BlackhawkAirwaysHQ . . 2.50
13 Team Member Accused of 2.50
14 Blackhawk test pilots 2.50
15 Plans for independence 2.50
16 Independence, final issue. 2.50
Ann.#1 Hawks in Albania. 3.00
Spec.#1 Assassination of JFK
to Saigon,1975 . . . . 3.50

BLACK HOOD
Impact, 1991–92
1 O:Black Hood. 4.00
2 thru 12 . . . . @3.00
Ann#1 Earthquest,w/trading card . . 3.00

BLACK LAMB, THE
DC/Helix, Sept., 1996
1 TT,Vampire saga 2.50
2 thru 6 TT . . . . @2.50

BLACK LIGHTNING
1977–78
1 TVE/FS,I&O:Black Lightning . . . 15.00
2 TVE/FS,A:Talia 7.00
3 TVE,I:Tobias Whale 7.00
4 TVE,A:Jimmy Olsen. 8.00
5 TVE,A:Superman. 8.00
6 TVE,I:Syonide 7.00
7 TVE,V:Syonide. 7.00
8 TVE,V:Tobias Whale 7.00
9 TVE,V:Annihilist 7.00
10 TVE,V:Trickster. 7.00
11 TVE,BU:The Ray. 10.00

[2nd Series], 1995–96
1 He's Back. 3.00
2 V:Painkiller. 3.00
3 V:Painkiller. 3.00
4 V:Painkiller,Royal Family 3.00
5 Flashbacks of Past 3.00
6 V:Gangbuster. 3.00
7 V:Gangbuster. 3.00
8 V:Tobias Whale 3.00
9 I&V:Demolition 3.00
10 Jefferson Pierce becomes Black
Lightning full time 3.00
11 Hunt for Sick Nick 3.00
12 V:Sick Nick's death squad 3.00
13 final issue 3.00

BLACK MASK
1993–94
1 I:Black Mask 5.00
2 V:Underworld 5.00
3 V:Valentine. 5.00

BLACK ORCHID
1993–95
1 DMc,O:Black Orchid,
  A:Batman,Luthor,Poison Ivy . . . 6.00
2 DMc,O:cont,Arkham Asylum 7.00
3 DMc,A:SwampThing,conc. 6.00
DC/Vertigo
1 DMc(c),B:DiF(s),JIT,SnW,I:Sherilyn
  Somers,I:Logos,F:Walt Brody . . 2.50
1a Platinum Ed. 12.00
2 JIT,SnW,Uprooting,V:Logos 2.50
3 JIT,SnW,Tainted Zone,
  V:Fungus 2.50
4 JIT,SnW,I:Nick & Orthia 2.50
5 DMc(c),JIT,SnW,
  A:Swamp Thing 2.50
6 JIT,BMc(i),God in the Cage 2.50
7 JIT,RGu,SnW,
  Upon the Threshold. 2.50
8 DMc(c),RGu,A:Silent People 2.50
9 DMc(c),RGu. 2.50
10 DMc(c),RGu 2.50
11 DMc(c),RGu,In Tennessee 2.50
12 DMc(c),RGu 2.50
13 DMc(c),RGu,F:Walt Brody 2.50
14 DMc(c),RGu,Black Annis 2.50
15 DMc(c),RGu,Kobolds 2.50
16 DMc(c),RGu,Suzy,Junkin 2.50
17 Twisted Season,pt.1 . . . . 2.50
18 Twisted Season,pt.2 . . . . 2.50
19 Twisted Season,pt.3 . . . . 2.50
20 Twisted Season,pt.4 . . . . 2.50
21 Twisted Season,pt.5 . . . . 2.50
22 Twisted Season,pt.6, final iss. . . 2.50
Ann.#1 DMc(c),DiF(s),GyA,JnM,F:Suzy,
  Childrens Crusade,BU:retells
  Adventure Comics#430 . . . . . . 4.25

BLOOD: A TALE
DC/Vertigo, Sept., 1996
[Mini-series,
re-release of Marvel Epic]
1 JMD(s),KW, quest for truth
  begins 3.00
2 JMD(s),KW, Blood falls in love . . 3.00
3 JMD(s),KW, companion dies 3.00
4 JMD(s),KW, finale 3.00

BLOOD & SHADOWS
DC/Vertigo, 1996
1 . . . . 6.00
2 Journal of Justice Jones 6.00
3 Chet Daley flung into
  21st century. 6.00
4 V:God of the Razor, finale 6.00

BLOOD AND WATER
DC/Vertigo March 2003
1 (of 5) F:Adam Heller 3.00
2 vampire 3.00
3 sex for Adam 3.00
4 past, present, future. 3.00
5 concl. 3.00

BLOODBATH
1993
1 A:Superman 4.00
2 A:New Heroes, Hitman 8.00

BLOODHOUND
July 2004
1 F:Travis Clevenger 3.00
2 thru 4 Concl. . . . . @3.00
5 Firestorm x-over. 3.00
6 Return from prison. 3.00
7 Psychic assault 3.00
8 V:Zeiss 3.00
9 V:Zeiss. 3.00
10 V:Zeiss 3.00

BLOODPACK
[Mini-Series], 1995
1 I:Blood Pack, V:Demolition 2.50
2 A:Superboy 2.50
3 Loira's Corpse 2.50
4 Real Heroes Final Issue 2.50

BLOOD OF THE DEMON
March, 2005
1 JBy,F:Jason Blood 2.50
2 JBy,V:Etrigan 2.50
3 JBy,F:Batman & Zatanna. 2.50
4 JBy,F:Morgain Le Fey 2.50
5 JBy,Jason Blood 2.50
6 JBy,F:Batman, Superman 2.50
7 JBy,Day of Vengeance tie-in 2.50
8 JBy,DGr 2.50
9 JBy,DGr 2.50
10 JBy,DGr. 2.50
11 JBy,DGr, Joshua 2.50
12 JBy,DGr. 2.50
13 JBy,DGr, One Year Later 2.50
14 JBy,DGr,Breaking of Etrigan . . . 2.50
15 JBy,V:Lord of the Damned 3.00
16 JBy,DGr, V:Lord of the Damned . 3.00
17 JBy,DGr,final issue 3.00

Blood Syndicate #8
© DC Comics, Inc.

BLOOD SYNDICATE
DC/Milestone, 1993–96
1 I:Blood Syndicate,Rob Chaplick,
  Dir.Mark.Ed.,w/B puzzle piece,
  Skybox card,Poster 3.50
1a Newstand Ed. 2.50
2 thru 9 . . . . @2.50
10 WS(c),Ccs,Shadow War,I:Iota,
  Sideshow,Rainsaw,Slag,Ash,
  Bad Betty,Oro 2.75
11 thru 34 . . . . @2.50
35 final issue 3.50

BLOODY MARY
DC/Helix, Aug., 1996
1 thru 4 GEn(s),CE, near-future
  war, concl. . . . . @3.00

BLOODY MARY:
LADY LIBERTY
DC/Helix, July, 1996
1 (of 4) GEn(s),CE, ... 4.00
2 GEn(s),CE,V:Achilles Seagal . . . 4.00

Bloody Mary Lady Liberty #1
© DC Comics Inc.

3 GEn(s),CE,V:Vatman 4.00
4 GEn(s),CE,V:Vatman, concl. 4.00

BLUE BEETLE
1986–88
1 O:Blue Beetle. 5.00
2 V:Fire Fist 2.50
3 V:Madmen 2.50
4 V:Doctor Alchemy 2.50
5 A:Question 2.50
6 V:Question 2.50
7 A:Question 2.50
8 A:Chronos 2.50
9 A:Chronos 2.50
10 Legends, V:Chronos 2.50
11 A:New Teen Titans 2.50
12 A:New Teen Titans 2.50
13 A:New Teen Titans 2.50
14 Pago Island,I:Catalyst. 2.50
15 RA:V:Carapax 2.50
16 RA,Chicago Murders 2.50
17 R:Dan Garrett/Blue Beetle 2.50
18 D:Dan Garrett 2.50
19 RA,R:Dr. Cyber 2.50
20 RA,Millennium,A:JLI 3.00
21 RA,A:Mr.Miracle,
  Millennium tie in. 2.50
22 RA,Prehistoric Chicago. 2.50
23 DH,V:The Madmen 2.50
24 DH,final issue 2.50

BLUE BEETLE
March, 2006
1 CHm,Who's Under the Mask?. . . 4.00
2 CHm,Totally changed world. 3.00
3 Trouble at 100 m.p.h. 3.00
4 . . . . 3.00
5 Phantom Stranger 3.00
6 Secret of Beetle's armor 3.00
7 CHm, ... 3.00
8 Hits the road 3.00
9 Back in El Paso 3.00
10 CHm,F:Brenda & a Mother Box . 3.00
11 Lost in Space, again 3.00
12 Reach 3.00
13 Alien Scarab owners. 3.00
14 Call for Guy Gardner 3.00
15 Meet Little Blue. 3.00
16 Countdown tie-in. 3.00
17 V:Typhoon. 3.00
18 F:Titans, x-over. 3.00
19 Truce with La Dama 3.00
20 Sinestro Corps War tie-in 3.00

DC COMICS

21 Mind Controlling Earth	3.00
22 Super Villain Assault	3.00
23 Super Villain Assault	3.00
24 Lost in Space	3.00
25 Endgame, concl.	3.00
26 Special Spanish language issue	3.00
27 F:Traci 13	3.00
28 More monsters	3.00
29 Boundaries	3.00
30 Boundaries	3.00
31 F:Dr. Mid-Nite	3.00
32 V:Doctor Polaris	3.00
33 F:Teen Titans	3.00

BLUE DEVIL
1984–86

1 O:Blue Devil	4.00
2 thru 16	@2.50
17 Crisis	3.00
18 Crisis	3.00
19 thru 31	@2.50
Ann.#1	2.50

BOB, THE GALACTIC BUM
[Mini-Series], 1995

1 A:Lobo	2.50
2 Planet Gnulp,A:Lobo	2.50
3 V:Khunds	2.50
4 Rando's Coronation	2.50

BODY DOUBLES
Aug., 1999

1 thru 3) DAn,ALa,JoP	@2.50

Bomba, The Jungle Boy #5
© DC Comics, Inc.

BOMBA,
THE JUNGLE BOY
1967–68

1 CI,MA,I:Bomba	200.00
2 The Phantom City of Death	150.00
3 My Enemy...The Jungle	150.00
4 Deadly Sting of Ana Conda	150.00
5 Tampu Lives–Bombs Dies	150.00
6 Krag	150.00
7 Nightmare	150.00

BOOK OF FATE, THE
1997–98

1 KG(s),RoW,BR,	3.00
2 KG(s),RoW,BR,The Chaos- Order War, pt.1 (of 4)	3.00
3 KG(s),RoW,BR,The Chaos- Order War, pt.2	3.00

4 KG(s),RoW,BR,The Chaos- Order War, pt.3, A:Two-Face	3.00
5 KG(s),RoW,BR,The Chaos- Order War, pt.4	3.00
6 KG(s),RoW,BR,Convergence, pt.1 x-over	3.00
7 KG(s),RoW,BR, Signs, pt.1	3.00
8 KG(s),RoW,BR, Signs, pt.2	3.00
9 KG,AIG,BR,Signs, pt.3	3.00
10 KG,AIG,BR,Signs,pt.4	3.00
11 KG,AIG, in a Swiss Jail	3.00
12 AIG,KG,F:Lobo, final issue	3.00

BOOKS OF FAERIE, THE
DC/Vertigo, Jan., 1997

1 PrG,F:Titania and Auberon	3.00
2 thru 3 PrG,	@3.00

BOOKS OF FAERIE, THE:
AUBERON'S TALE
DC/Vertigo, June, 1998

1 (of 3) PrG,VcL,F:Early life of King Auberon	3.00
2 thru 3 PrG,VcL, early life	@3.00

BOOKS OF FAERIE, THE:
MOLLY'S STORY
DC/Vertigo, 1999

1 (of 4) JNR(s)	3.00
2 thru 4 CV(c)	@3.00

BOOKS OF MAGIC
[Limited Series], 1990–91

1 B:NGa(s),JBo,F:Phantom Stranger, A:J.Constantine,Tim Hunter, Doctor Occult,Mister E.	11.00
2 SHp,F:J.Constantine,A:Spectre, Dr.Fate,Demon,Zatanna	11.00
3 CV,F:Doctor Occult, A:Sandman	8.00
4 E:NGa(s),PuJ,F:Mr.E,A:Death	9.00

[Regular Series]
DC/Vertigo, 1994–97

1 MkB,B:Bindings,R:Tim Hunter	13.00
1a Platinum Edition	25.00
2 CV(c),MkB,V:Manticore	8.00
3 CV(c),MkB,E:Bindings	8.00
4 CV(c),MkB,A:Death	8.00
5 CV(c),I:Khara	4.00
6 Sacrifices,pt.I	4.00
7 Sacrifices,pt.II	4.00
8 Tim vs. evil Tim	4.00
9 Artificial Heart,pt.1	4.00
10 Artificial Heart,pt.2	4.00
11 Artificial Heart,pt.3	4.00
12 Small Glass Worlds,pt.1	4.00
13 Small Glass Worlds,pt.2	4.00
14 CV(c),A:The Wobbly	4.00
15 Hell and Back,pt.1	4.00
16 Hall and Back,pt.2	3.50
17 Playgrounds,pt.1	3.50
18 JNR,PrG,Playgrounds,cont.	3.50
19 JNR,PrG,Playgrounds,concl.	3.50
20 Barabatos gives the orders	3.50
21 JNR,PrG,Molly seeks Mayra	3.50
22	3.50
23 JNR,V:Margraves Strafenkinder	3.50
24 JNR,PrG,F:Molly vs. Amadan	3.50
25 JNR,PrG,Death and the Endless	3.50
26 JNR,PrG,Rites of Passage, pt.1	3.00
27 JNR,PrG,Rites of Passage, pt.2	3.00
28 JNR,PrG,Rites of Passage, pt.3, Cupid & Psyche	3.00
29 JNR,PrG,Rite of Passage	3.00
30 JNR,PrG,Rite of Passage	3.00
31 JNR,PrG,Rite of Passage	3.00
32 JNR(s),PSj,Rites of Passage	3.00
33 JNR(s),PSj,Rites of Passage	3.00

34 JNR(s),PSj,Rites of Passage	3.00
35 JNR(s),PrG,Rites of Passage	3.00
36 JNR,Rites of Passage, cont	3.00
37 JNR,Rites of Passage, cont.	3.00
38 JNR,Rites of Passage, concl.	3.00
39 PrG, at Sphinx casino	3.00
40 JNR(s),F:Tim & Molly	3.00
41 JNR(s),V:Gargoyles	3.00
42 JNR(s),JIT,magical havok	3.00
43 JNR(s),PrG,F:The Wobbly	3.00
44 JNR(s),goodbye to Zatanna	3.00
45 JNR(s) Slave of Heavens,pt.1	3.00
46 JNR(s) Slave of Heavens,pt.2	3.00
47 JNR(s) Slave of Heavens,pt.3	3.00
48 JNR(s) Slave of Heavens,pt.4	3.00
49 JNR(s) Slave of Heavens,pt.5	3.00
50 JNR(s) Slave of Heavens,pt.6	3.00
51 PrG,MK,an Opener	2.50
52 PrG,MK,Homecoming	2.50
54 PrG,MK,V:Thomas	2.50
55 PrG,MK,Coming of the Other	2.50
56 PrG,MK,Last Molly Story	2.50
57 PrG,MK,after car crash	2.50
58 PrG,MK,The Other	2.50
59 PrG,MK,The Other	2.50
60 PrG,MK,The Other	2.50
61 PrG,MK(c),The Other, concl.	2.50
62 PrG,MK(c),crossroads.	2.50
63 GyA,MK(c),	2.50
64 PrG,MK(c),Wild Hunt.	2.50
65 PrG,MK,new life cont.	2.50
66 PrG,A Day,A Night & A Dream,pt.1	2.50
67 PrG,A Day, A Night & A Dream,concl.	2.50
68 PrG	2.50
69 PrG	2.50
70 PrG	2.50
71 PrG,MK(c)	2.50
72 PrG,MK(c),F:Timothy Hunter.	2.50
73 PrG,MK(c),V:Other self	2.50
74 PrG,MK(c),V:Other self	2.50
75 PrG,MK(c), final issue	2.50
Ann.#2 JNR(s) Minotaur	4.00
Ann.#3 PrG	4.00

BOOKS OF MAGICK, THE:
LIFE DURING WARTIME
DC/Vertigo, July 2004

1 NGa(s),F:Timothy Hunter	3.00
2 thru 4 NGa(s)	@3.00
5 DOr	3.00
6 DFg	3.00
7 SeP, pt.1	3.00
8 DOr	3.00
9 Tumbling Dice,pt.1,DOr	3.00
10 Tumbling Dice,pt.2,DOr	3.00
11 DOr	3.00
12 DOr	3.00
13 Losing My Religion,pt.1,DOr.	3.00
14 Losing My Religion,pt.2,DOr.	3.00
15 series finale	3.00

BOOSTER GOLD
1986–88

1 DJ,V:Blackguard	6.00
2 DJ,V:Minddancer	3.00
3 thru 25 DJ	@3.00

Aug., 2007

1 DJu,NRd	3.00
2 DJu,NRd,F:Sinestro.	3.00
3 DJu, NRd,A:Jonah Hex.	3.00
4 DJu,NRo,V:Supernova.	3.00
5 DJu,52 Pick-Up	3.00
6 DJu,Blue and Gold,pt.1	3.00
7 DJu,Blue and Gold, pt.2	3.00
8 DJu,Blue and Gold, pt.3	3.00
9 DJu,Blue and Gold, pt.4	3.00
10 DJu,To save all of time	3.00
11 CDi(s),DJu,F:Batgirl	3.00

12 CDi(s),DJu,Vicious Cycle 3.00
13 JOy,Starro the Conqueror 3.00
14 JOy,Starro the Conqueror 3.00
0 Spec. DJu, Zero Hour x-over 3.00
Spec. #1,000,000 Peter Platinum . . 3.00

Boy Commandos#11
© DC Comics, Inc.

BOY COMMANDOS
Winter, 1942–43
1 S&K,O:Liberty Belle;Sandman
   & Newsboy Legion 13,000.00
2 S&K,Hitler(c) 3,500.00
3 S&K,WWII(c) 2,000.00
4 WWII(c) 1,300.00
5 WWII(c) 1,300.00
6 S&K,WWII(c) 1,300.00
7 S&K,WWII(c) 800.00
8 S&K,WWII(c) 800.00
9 WWII(c) 900.00
10 S&K,WWII(c) 800.00
11 WWII(c) 800.00
12 WWII(c) 800.00
13 WWII(c) 800.00
14 . . . . 800.00
15 1st Crazy Quilt 650.00
16 . . . . 600.00
17 Science Fiction(c) 650.00
18 S&K 500.00
19 S&K 500.00
20 Science Fiction (c) 650.00
21 . . . . 400.00
22 Judy Canova 400.00
23 S&K,S&K,(c) 500.00
24 Superhero 500.00
25 superhero(c) 450.00
26 Science Fiction(c) 450.00
27 . . . . 500.00
28 . . . . 550.00
29 S&K story 500.00
30 Baseball Story 550.00
31 . . . . 500.00
32 A:Dale Evans(c) 550.00
33 . . . . 400.00
34 I:Wolf 400.00
35 . . . . 400.00
36 Sci-Fi(c),Nov.–Dec., 1949 . . . . 500.00

BRAINBANX
DC/Helix, Jan., 1997
1 ELe(s),Down Upon the Darkness 2.50
2 ELe(s),Anna flees to the Sheol . . 2.50
3 ELe(s),Anna stranded 2.50
4 ELe(s),Anna & Logan 2.50
5 ELe(s),To Enter the Kingdom . . . 2.50
6 (of 6) 2.50

BRAVE AND THE BOLD
Aug.–Sept., 1955
1 JKu,RH,IN,I:VikingPrince,Golden
   Gladiator,Silent Knight 7,000.00
2 F:Viking Prince 2,800.00
3 F:Viking Prince 1,500.00
4 F:Viking Prince 1,500.00
5 B:Robin Hood 1,500.00
6 JKu,F:Robin Hood,E:Golden
   Gladiator 1,000.00
7 JKu,F:Robin Hood 1,000.00
8 JKu,F:Robin Hood 1,000.00
9 JKu,F:Robin Hood 1,000.00
10 JKu,F:Robin Hood 1,000.00
11 JKu,F:Viking Prince 750.00
12 JKu,F:Viking Prince 750.00
13 JKu,F:Viking Prince 750.00
14 JKu,F:Viking Prince 750.00
15 JKu,F:Viking Prince 750.00
16 JKu,F:Viking Prince 750.00
17 JKu,F:Viking Prince 750.00
18 JKu,F:Viking Prince 750.00
19 JKu,F:Viking Prince 750.00
20 JKu,F:Viking Prince 750.00
21 JKu,F:Viking Prince 750.00
22 IKu,F:Viking Prince 750.00
23 JKu,O:Viking Prince 1,100.00
24 JKu,E:Viking Prince,Silent
   Knight 750.00
25 RA,I&B:Suicide Squad 950.00
26 F:Suicide Squad 600.00
27 Creature of Ghost Lake 600.00
28 I:Justice League of
   America,O:Snapper Carr . 12,000.00
29 F:Justice League 4,500.00
30 F:Justice League 3,500.00
31 F:Cave Carson 800.00
32 F:Cave Carson 500.00
33 F:Cave Carson 500.00
34 JKu,I&O:S.A. Hawkman 4,500.00
35 JKu:F:Hawkman 1,000.00
36 JKu:F:Hawkman 1,000.00
37 F:Suicide Squad 500.00
38 F:Suicide Squad 400.00
39 F:Suicide Squad 400.00
40 JKu,F:Cave Carson 300.00
41 F:Cave Carson 300.00
42 JKu,F:Hawkman 600.00
43 JKu,O:Hawkman 700.00
44 JKu,F:Hawkman 600.00
45 CI,F:Strange Sports 200.00
46 CI,F:Strange Sports 200.00
47 CI,F:Strange Sports 200.00
48 CI,F:Strange Sports 200.00
49 CI,F:Strange Sports 200.00
50 F:GreenArrow & J'onnJ'onzz . 400.00
51 F:Aquaman & Hawkman 500.00
52 JKu,F:Sgt.Rock 350.00
53 ATh,F:Atom & Flash 275.00
54 I&O:Teen Titans 600.00
55 F:Metal Man & Atom 200.00
56 F:Flash & J'onn J'onzz 200.00
57 I&O:Metamorpho 400.00
58 F:Metamorpho 225.00
59 F:Batman & Green Lantern . 250.00
60 A:Teen Titans,I:Wonder Girl . 250.00
61 MA,O:Starman,BlackCanary . . 300.00
62 MA,O:Starman,BlackCanary . . 300.00
63 F:Supergirl&WonderWoman . . 150.00
64 F:Batman,V:Eclipso 200.00
65 DG,FMc,F:Flash & Doom
   Patrol 150.00
66 F:Metamorpho & Metal Men . . 175.00
67 CI,F:Batman & Flash 150.00
68 F:Batman,Metamorpho,Joker,
   Riddler,Penguin 200.00
69 F:Batman & Green Lantern . . 150.00
70 F:Batman & Hawkman 150.00
71 F:Batman & Green Arrow 150.00
72 CI,F:Spectre & Flash 150.00
73 F:Aquaman & Atom 150.00
74 B:Batman T.U.,A:Metal Men . . 150.00

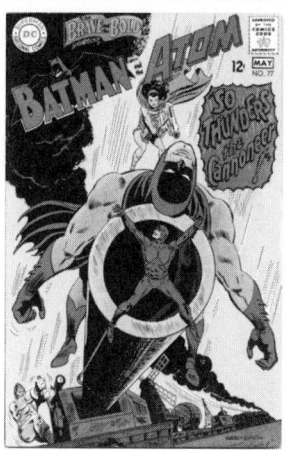

The Brave and the Bold #77
© DC Comics Inc.

75 F:Spectre 150.00
76 F:Plastic Man 150.00
77 F:Atom 150.00
78 F:Wonder Woman 150.00
79 NA,F:Deadman 200.00
80 NA,DG,F:Creeper 150.00
81 NA,F:Flash 150.00
82 NA,F:Aquaman,O:Ocean
   Master 150.00
83 NA,F:Teen Titans 150.00
84 NA,F:Sgt.Rock 150.00
85 NA,F:Green Arrow 150.00
86 NA,F:Deadman 150.00
87 F:Wonder Woman 75.00
88 F:Wildcat 75.00
89 RA,F:Phantom Stranger 75.00
90 F:Adam Strange 75.00
91 F:Black Canary 75.00
92 F:Bat Squad 75.00
93 NA,House of Mystery 100.00
94 NC,F:Teen Titans 90.00
95 F:Plastic Man 90.00
96 F:Sgt.Rock 75.00
97 NC(i),F:Wildcat 75.00
98 JAp,F:Phantom Stranger 75.00
99 NC,F:Flash 75.00
100 NA,F:Green Arrow 100.00
101 JA,F:Metamorpho 50.00
102 NA,JA,F:Teen Titans 50.00
103 FMc,F:Metal Men 35.00
104 JAp,F:Deadman 35.00
105 JAp,F:Wonder Woman 35.00
106 JAp,F:Green Arrow 35.00
107 JAp,F:Black Canary 35.00
108 JAp,F:Sgt.Rock 35.00
109 JAp,F:Demon 35.00
110 JAp,F:Wildcat 35.00
111 JAp,F:Joker 40.00
112 JAp,F:Mr.Miracle 75.00
113 JAp,F:Metal Men 75.00
114 JAp,F:Aquaman 75.00
115 JAp,O:Viking Prince 75.00
116 JAp,F:Spectre 75.00
117 JAp,F:Sgt.Rock 75.00
118 JAp,F:Wildcat,V:Joker 75.00
119 JAp,F:Man-Bat 20.00
120 JAp,F:Kamandi 20.00
121 JAp,F:Metal Men 20.00
122 JAp,F:Swamp Thing 20.00
123 JAp,F:Plastic Man 20.00
124 JAp,F:Sgt.Rock 20.00
125 JAp,F:Flash 20.00
126 JAp,F:Aquaman 20.00
127 JAp,F:Wildcat 20.00

128 JAp,F:Mr.Miracle 20.00
129 F:Green Arrow,V:Joker 25.00
130 F:Green Arrow,V:Joker 25.00
131 JAp,F:WonderWoman,
   A:Catwoman 22.00
132 JAp,F:King Fu Foom 20.00
133 JAp,F:Deadman 20.00
134 JAp,F:Green Lantern 20.00
135 JAp,F:Metal Men 20.00
136 JAp,F:Metal Men,Green Arr. . 20.00
137 F:Demon 20.00
138 JAp,F:Mr.Miracle 20.00
139 JAp,F:Hawkman 20.00
140 JAp,F:Wonder Woman 20.00
141 JAp,F:Bl.Canary,A:Joker 30.00
142 JAp,F:Aquaman 15.00
143 O:Human Target 15.00
144 JAp,F:Green Arrow 15.00
145 JAp,F:Phantom Stranger 15.00
146 JAp,F:E-2 Batman 15.00
147 JAp,A:Supergirl 15.00
148 JSon,JAp,F:Plastic Man 15.00
149 JAp,F:Teen Titans 18.00
150 JAp,F:Superman 15.00
151 JAp,F:Flash 18.00
152 JAp,F:Atom 15.00
153 DN,F:Red Tornado 15.00
154 JAp,F:Metamorpho 15.00
155 JAp,F:Green Lantern 15.00
156 DN,F:Dr.Fate 15.00
157 JAp,F:Kamandi 15.00
158 JAp,F:Wonder Woman 15.00
159 JAp,A:Ras al Ghul 15.00
160 JAp,F:Supergirl 15.00
161 JAp,F:Adam Strange 15.00
162 JAp,F:Sgt.Rock 15.00
163 DGF:Black Lightning 15.00
164 JL,F:Hawkman 15.00
165 DN,F:Man-bat 15.00
166 DG,TA,DSp,F:Black Canary
   A:Penguin,I:Nemesis 15.00
167 DC,DA,F:Blackhawk 15.00
168 JAp,DSp,F:Green Arrow 9.00
169 JAp,DSp,F:Zatanna 9.00
170 JA,F:Nemesis 9.00
171 JL,DSp,V:Scalphunter 9.00
172 CI,F:Firestorm 9.00
173 JAp,F:Guardians 9.00
174 JAp,F:Green Lantern 9.00
175 JAp,A:Lois Lane 9.00
176 JAp,F:Swamp Thing 9.00
177 JAp,F:Elongated Man 9.00
178 JAp,F:Creeper 9.00
179 EC,F:Legion o/Superheroes . . . 9.00
180 JAp,F:Spectre,Nemesis 9.00
181 JAp,F:Hawk & Dove 9.00
182 JAp,F:E-2 Robin 9.00
183 CI,V:Riddler 10.00
184 JAp,A:Catwoman 10.00
185 F:Green Arrow 9.00
186 JAp,F:Hawkman 9.00
187 JAp,F:Metal Men 9.00
188 JAp,F:Rose & Thorn 9.00
189 JAp,A:Thorn 9.00
190 JAp,F:Adam Strange 9.00
191 JAp,V:Joker,Penguin 15.00
192 JAp,F:Superboy 9.00
193 JAp,D:Nemesis 9.00
194 CI,F:Flash 9.00
195 JA,I:Vampire 9.00
196 JAp,F:Ragman 9.00
197 JSon,W:Earth II Batman &
   Catwoman 9.00
198 F:Karate Kid 9.00
199 RA,F:Spectre 9.00
200 DGb,JAp,A:Earth-2 Batman,I:
   Outsiders (GeoForce,Katana,Halo),
   E:Batman T.U.,final issue 15.00
Ann. #1-1969 80-page giant (2001) 10.00

[Limited Series]

1 SAP,Green Arrow/Butcher T.U. . . 2.50
2 SAP,A:Black Canary,Question . . . 2.50

The Brave and the Bold #149
© DC Comics, Inc.

3 SAP,Green Arrow/Butcher 2.50
4 SAP,GA on Trial;A:Black
   Canary 2.50
5 SAP,V:Native Canadians,I.R.A. . . 2.50

Feb., 2007

1 MWa,BWi,GP, Batman (c) 3.00
1 variant Green Lantern (c) 3.00
2 MWa,GP,BWi,F:Supergirl 3.00
3 MWa,GP,BWi,V:Fatal Five 3.00
4 MWa,GP,BWi,F:Lobo 3.00
5 MWa,GP,BWi,Book of Destiny . . . 3.00
6 MWa,GP,BWi,Book of Destiny. . . 3.00
7 MWa,GP,BWi,F:Power Girl 3.00
8 MWa,GP,BWi,F:Doom Patrol . . . 3.00
9 MWa,GP,BWi,Book of Destiny . . . 3.00
10 MWa,GP,BWi,Book of Destiny . . 3.00
11 MWa,JOy,Superman & Ultraman 3.00
12 MWa,JOy,V:Megistus 3.00
13 MWa,JOy,Android Samurai. . . . 3.00
14 MWa,Nanda Parbat threatened . 3.00
15 MWa,Siege of Nanda Parbat . . . 3.00
16 MWa,Superman and Catwoman . 3.00
17 MWa,Supergirl & Raven 3.00
18 F:Supergirl & Raven 3.00
19 Green Lantern oath 3.00

BRAVE OLD WORLD
DC/Vertigo, Dec., 1999

1 (of 4) BML,GyD,PhH,Y2K story . . 2.50
2 thru 4 BML,GyD,PhH . . . . @2.50

BREACH
Jan., 2005

1 F:Major Tim Porter,40-page 3.00
2 Long in the future, in Africa 2.50
3 South Africa 2.50
4 F:JLA 2.50
5 JLA fallout 2.50
6 Fallout continues 2.50
7 Rifter fallout 2.50
8 V:Talia's Kobra forces 2.50
9 F:Heardsman 2.50
10 F:Talia al Ghul. 2.50
11 V:The Smoking Lady. 2.50

BREATHTAKER
1990

1 I:Breathtaker(Chase Darrow) 6.00
2 Chase Darrow captured 6.00
3 O:Breathtaker 6.00
4 V:The Man, final issue 5.00

BROTHER POWER, THE GEEK
Sept.–Oct., 1968

1 . . . . 85.00
2 Nov.–Dec., 1968 . . . . 50.00

BUTCHER, THE
[Limited Series], 1990

1 MB,I:John Butcher 3.50
2 MB,in San Francisco 3.00
3 MB,V:Corporation 3.00
4 MB,A:Green Arrow 2.50
5 MB,A:Corvus,final issue 2.25

BUZZY
1944–58

1 . . . . 500.00
2 . . . . 300.00
3 thru 5 . . . . @250.00
6 thru 15 . . . . @150.00
16 thru 25 . . . . @150.00
26 thru 35 . . . . @125.00
36 thru 45 . . . . @100.00
46 thru 77 . . . . @75.00

CAMELOT 3000
Dec., 1982

1 BB,O:Arthur,Merlin 3.50
2 BB,A:Morgan LeFay 3.00
3 BB,J:New Knights 3.00
4 BB,V:McAllister 3.00
5 BB,O:Morgan Le Fay 3.00
6 BB,TA,W:Arthur 3.00
7 BB,TA,R:Isolde 3.00
8 BB,TA,D:Sir Kay 3.00
9 BB,TA,L:Sir Percival 3.00
10 BB,TA,V:Morgan Le Fay 3.00
11 BB,TA,V:Morgan Le Fay 3.00
12 BB,TA,D:Arthur 3.00

CAPER
Oct. 2003

1 (of 12) organized crime 3.00
2 . . . . 3.00
3 Jewish Mafia hitmen 3.00
4 Jacob & Isadore Weiss 3.00
5 thru 8 JSe . . . . @3.00
9 thru 12 . . . . @3.00

CAPTAIN ACTION
[Based on toy] Oct.–Nov., 1968

1 WW,I:Captain Action,Action
   Boy,A:Superman 150.00
2 GK,WW, V:Krellik. 125.00
3 GK,I:Dr.Evil 125.00
4 GK,A:Dr.Evil 125.00
5 GK,WW,A:Matthew Blackwell . . 75.00

CAPTAIN ATOM
March, 1987

1 PB,O:Captain Atom 4.50
2 PB,C:Batman 2.50
3 PB,O:Captain Atom 2.50
4 PB,A:Firestorm 2.50
5 PB,A:Firestorm 2.50
6 PB,Dr.Spectro 2.50
7 R:Plastique 2.50
8 PB,Capt.Atom/Plastique 2.50
9 V:Bolt 2.50
10 PB,A:JLI 2.50
11 PB,A:Firestorm 2.50
12 PB,I:Major Force 2.50
13 PB,Christmas issue 2.50
14 PB,A:Nightshade. 2.50
15 PB,Dr.Spectro, Major Force 2.50
16 PB,A:JLI,V:Red Tornado 2.50
17 V:Red Tornado;A:Swamp
   Thing,JLI 2.50

18 PB,A:Major Force 2.50
19 PB,Drug War. 2.50
20 FMc,BlueBeetle. 2.50
21 PB,A:Plastique,Nightshade. 2.50
22 PB,A:MaxLord,Nightshade,
     Plastique 2.50
23 PB,V:The Ghost 2.50
24 PB,Invasion X-over. 2.50
25 PB,Invvasion X-over 2.50
26 A:JLA,Top Secret,pt.1 . . . . 2.50
27 A:JLA,Top Secret,pt.2 . . . . 2.50
28 V:Ghost, Top Secret,pt.3 . . . . . . 2.50
29 RT,Captain Atom cleared
     (new direction). 2.50
30 Janus Directive #11,V:Black
     Manta. 2.50
31 RT,Capt.Atom's Powers,
     A:Rocket Red 2.50
32 Loses Powers 2.50
33 A:Batman 3.00
34 C:JLE 2.50
35 RT,Secret o/t Silver Shield,
     A:Major Force 2.50
36 RT,Las Vegas Battle,A:Major
     Force 2.50
37 I:New Atomic Skull 2.50
38 RT,A:Red Tornado,
     Black Racer. 2.50
39 RT,A:Red Tornado. 2.50
40 RT,V:Kobra 2.50
41 RT,A:Black Racer,
     Red Tornado 2.50
42 RT,A:Phantom Stranger,Red
     Tornado,Black Racer,
     Death from Sandman 2.50
43 RT,V:Nekron 2.50
44 RT,V:Plastique. 2.50
45 RT,A:The Ghost,I:Ironfire 2.50
46 RT,A:Superman. 2.50
47 RT,A:SupermanV:Ghost 2.50
48 RT,R:Red Tornado 2.50
49 RT,Plastique on trial 2.50
50 RT,V:The Ghost,DoubleSize. . . 3.00
51 RT 2.50
52 RT,Terror on RTE.91. . . . . 2.50
53 RT,A:Aquaman 2.50
54 RT,A:Rasputin,Shadowstorm . . 2.50
55 RT,Inside Quantum Field 2.50
56 RT,Quantum Field cont. 2.50
57 RT,V:ShadowStorm,
     Quantum.Field. 2.50
Ann.#1 I:Maj.Force. 3.50
Ann.#2 A:RocketRed,Maj.Force. . . . 3.50

CAPTAIN CARROT
1982–83
1 RA,A:Superman,Starro 3.00
2 AA 3.00
3 thru 20 . . . . @3.00

CAPTAIN CARROT AND
THE FINAL ARK
Oct., 2007
1 (of 3) BMo, Countdown tie-in. . . . 3.00
2 BMo,Sandy Eggo Comics Con . . 3.00
3 BMo, Boa's Ark 3.00

CAPTAIN STORM
May-June, 1964
1 IN(c),Killer Hunt 150.00
2 IN(c),First Shot-Last Shot 100.00
3 JKu,Death of a PT Boat. 100.00
4 IN(c),First Command-Last
     Command 100.00
5 IN(c), Killer Torpedo 100.00
6 JKu,IN(c),Medals for an Ocean 100.00
7 IN(c),A Bullet For The General 100.00
8 IN(c),Death of A Sub 125.00
9 IN(c),Sink That Flattop. 100.00
10 IN(c),Only The Last Man Lives 100.00

Captain Carrot #3
© DC Comics Inc.

11 IN(c),Ride a Hot Torpedo 100.00
12 JKu(c),T.N.T. Tea Party Abroad
     PT 47. . . . . 100.00
13 JKu,Yankee Banzai. 100.00
14 RH(c),Sink Capt. Storm 100.00
15 IN(c),My Enemy-My Friend. . . 100.00
16 IN(c),Battle of the Stinging
     Mosquito 100.00
17 IN(c),First Shot for a
     Dead Man 100.00
18 March-April, 1967 . . . . 100.00

CATWOMAN
[Limited Series], 1989
1 O:Catwoman 11.00
2 Catwoman'sSister kidnapped . . 10.00
3 Battle 10.00
4 Final,V:Batman 10.00

[Regular Series], 1993
0 JBa,O:Catwoman. 3.50
1 B:JDy(s),JBa,DG,A:Bane. 5.00
2 JBa,DG,A:Bane 3.50
3 JBa,DG,at Santa Prisca 3.50
4 JBa,DG,Bane's Secret 3.00
5 JBa,V:Ninjas 3.00
6 JBa,A:Batman 3.00
7 JBa,A:Batman 3.00
8 JBa,V:Zephyr 3.00
9 JBa,V:Zephyr 3.00
10 JBa,V:Arms Dealer 3.00
11 JBa 3.00
12 JBa,Knights End #6,A:Batman . . 5.00
13 JBa,Knights End,Aftermath#2. . . 3.00
14 JBa,Zero Hour 3.00
15 JBa,new path 3.00
16 JBa,Island forterss 3.00
17 JBa,Thief of Paris 3.00
18 JBa,Here Comes the Bride. . . . 3.00
19 Amazonia 3.00
20 Hollywood 3.00
21 JBa(c&a)V:Movie Monster
     [new Miraweb format begins] . . 2.50
22 JBa(c&a) Family Ties,pt.1 . . . . . 2.50
23 Family Ties,pt.2. . . . . 2.50
24 JBa,Family Ties,pt.3 . . . . 2.50
25 A:Robin,Psyba-Rats 3.00
26 AIG,JBa,The Secret of the
     Universe,pt.2 (of 3) 2.50
27 CDi,Underworld Unleashed tie-in 2.50
28 CDi,Catwoman enlists help. . . . 2.50
29 CDi,A:Penguin 2.50
30 CDi,JBa,Great Plane Robbery . . 2.50
31 CDi,JBa,Flesh and Fire. 3.00

32 CDi,JBa,Contagion,pt.9 . . . . . . 3.00
33 CDi,JBa,Hellhound,pt.1. . . . . . . 2.50
34 CDi,JBa,Hellbound,pt.2 (of 3). . . 2.50
35 CDi,JBa. 3.00
36 CDi,JBa, Legacy, pt.2 x-over . . . 3.00
37 CDi,JBa, Panara, the Leopard
     Woman 2.50
38 DgM(s),JBa,MPn,Catwoman,
     Year One, pt.1 (of 3) 2.50
39 DgM(s),JBa,MPn,Catwoman,
     Year One, pt. 2 . . . . 2.50
40 DgM(s),JBa,MPn,Catwoman,
     Year One, pt. 3 . . . . 2.50
41 DgM(s),JBa,I:MorelandMcShane 2.50
42 DgM(s),JBa,RedFangClaw,pt.1 . 2.50
43 DgM(s),JBa,RedFangClaw,pt.2 . 2.50
44 DgM(s),JBa,Red FangClaw,pt.3 . 2.50
45 DgM(s),JBa,Nine Deaths of
     the Cat. 2.50
46 DgM(s),JBa,F:Two Face,pt.1 . . 2.50
47 DgM(s),JBa,F:Two Face,pt.2 . . 2.50
48 DgM(s),JBa,V:Morella,pt.1 . . . . 2.50
49 DgM(s),JBa,V:Morella,pt. 2. . . . 2.50
50 DgM(s),JBa,V:Cybercat 3.00
50a metallic cover, collectors ed. . . 3.00
51 DgM(s),JBa,F:Huntress,pt.1 . . . 2.50
52 DgM(s),JBa,F:Huntress,pt.2 . . . 2.50
53 DgM(s),JBa,F:identity learned . . 2.50
54 JBa,improving security 2.50
55 JBa,Shared Mentality 2.50
56 JBa,Cataclysm x-over,pt.6 . . . . 4.00
57 JBa,Cataclysm, V:Poison Ivy . . . 3.00
58 JBa,F:Scarecrow,pt.1. . . . . 2.50
59 JBa,F:Scarecrow, pt.2. . . . . 2.50
60 JBa,F:Scarecrow, pt.3. . . . . 2.50
61 JBa,Bank robbery 2.50
62 JBa,A:Nemesis 2.50
63 JBa,A:Batman & Joker, pt.1 . . . 2.50
64 JBa,A:Batman & Joker, pt.2 . . . 2.50
65 JBa,A:Batman & Joker, pt.3 . . . 2.50
66 JBa,I'll Take Manhattan,pt.1 . . . 2.50
67 JBa,I'll Take Manhattan,pt.2 . . . 2.50
68 JBa,I'll Take Manhattan,pt.3 . . . 2.50
69 JBa,I'll Take Manhattan,pt.4 . . . 2.50
70 JBa,I'll Take Manhattan,pt.5 . . . 2.50
71 JBa,I'll Take Manhattan,pt.6 . . . 2.50
72 JOs(s),JBa,A:Batman 2.50
73 JOs(s),JBa,No Man's Land 2.50
74 JOs(s),JBa,No Man's Land 2.50
75 JOs(s),JBa,No Man's Land 2.50
76 JOs(s),JBa,No Man's Land 2.50
77 JOs(s),JBa,No Man's Land 2.50
78 Plus Ca Change 2.50
79 A:Batman 2.50
80 going to jail 2.50
81 solitary confinement 2.50

Catwoman #9
© DC Comics Inc.

82 payback time. 2.50
83 A:Batman,CommissionerGordon 2.50
84 F:Harley Quinn 2.50
85 anger & revenge 2.50
86 V:Banner. 2.50
87 NSH, from Catwoman's past . . . 2.50
88 V:Banner. 2.50
89 This issue: Batman dies! 2.50
90 Officer Down x-over,pt.4 . . . . . . 2.50
91 Second Catwoman 2.50
92 JFM(s), V:Scarecrow,pt.1 . . . . . 2.50
93 JFM(s), V:Scarecrow,pt.2 . . . . . 2.50
94 JFM(s), final issue. 2.50
Ann.#1 Elseworlds Story,A:Ra's Al
    Ghul. 3.50
Ann.#2 JBa(c&a) Year One Annuals,
    Young Selina Kyle 4.50
Ann.#3 Legends of the Dead Earth. 4.00
Ann.#4 Pulp Heroes (Macabre). . . . 4.50
Spec. Catwoman Defiant,TGr,DG,
    V:Mr.Handsome. 6.00
Spec. Catwoman Plus, LKa,AWi,
    ALa, F:Screamqueen (1997). . . 3.00
Spec.#1,000,000 JBa, on prison
    planet of Pluto 2.00

Nov., 2001

1 MiA,R:Selina Kyle 7.00
2 MiA,serial murders. 4.00
3 MiA,Selina undercover. 3.00
4 MiA,V:Serial killer. 3.00
5 Selina & Holly 2.50
6 F:Holly 2.50
7 Holly in danger. 2.50
8 RBr,East End's Crooked Cops . 2.50
9 RBr,Disguises 2.50
10 RBr,Death's Row killer 2.50
11 F:Slam Bradley 2.50
12 F:Slam Bradley, Bruce Wayne . 2.50
13 F:Slam Bradley, Holly 2.50
14 Holly 2.50
15 V:Black Mask 2.50
16 V:Black Mask 2.50
17 No Easy Way Down,pt.1 . . . . . . 2.50
18 No Easy Way Down,pt.2 . . . . . . 2.50
19 No Easy Way Down,pt.3 . . . . . . 2.50
20 A: Wildcat 2.50
21 V:Captain Cold 2.50
22 V:Captain Cold 2.50
23 Opal City 2.50
24 Wild Ride, concl. 2.50
25 JP,PG,back to Gotham 2.50
26 JP,PG,kidnapping 2.50
27 JP,PG,F:Batman 2.50
28 JP,PG,V:Penguin. 2.50
29 JP,PG 2.50
30 JP,PG,V:Zeiss. 2.50
31 JP,PG,Selina Kyle missing 2.50
32 SeP,East End 2.50
33 PG,JP,V:Galante 2.50
34 War Games,Act 1,pt.7,PG,JP . . 2.50
35 War Games,Act 2,pt.7,PG,JP . . 2.50
36 War Games,Act 3,pt.7,PG,JP . . 2.50
37 JP,PG 2.50
38 JP,PG,I:Wooden Nickel 2.50
39 JP,PG,Wooden Nickel,pt.2 . . . . 2.50
40 JP,PG,Wooden Nickel,pt.3 . . . . 2.50
41 JP,PG,Immigrants from Brazil . . 2.50
42 JP,PG,Dog fights 2.50
43 RBr,V:Killer Croc. 2.50
44 V:Hush 2.50
45 Selina's new apartment 2.50
46 Deal with Hush 2.50
47 V:Hammer and Sickle. 2.50
48 Heart of danger. 2.50
49 V:Black Mask 2.50
50 A:Zatanna 2.50
51 F:Batman 3.50
52 V:Black Mask 3.50
53 Selina Kyle not Catwoman 3.50
54 Holly 2.50
55 New Catwoman in training 3.00
56 A:Wildcat, Angle Man 3.00

57 The Replacements, concl. 3.00
58 F:Zatanna 3.00
59 Baby's Dad, V:Film Freak, ... 3.00
60 Black Mask dead, Holly in Jail . 3.00
61 V:Film Freak 3.00
62 AH(c),Catwoman's baby 3.00
63 AH(c),in Metropolis 3.00
64 AH(c),at LexCorp 3.00
65 AH(c),Escape from LexCorp. . . 3.00
66 AH(c),Hammer and Sickle 3.00
67 AH(c), Body count. 3.00
68 AH(c),Countdown tie-in 3.00
69 AH(c),Catwoman dies, concl. . . 3.00
70 AH(c),Amazons Attack tie-in . . . 3.00
71 AH(c),Amazons Attack tie-in . . . 3.00
72 AH(c),No more Selina Kyle. . . . 3.00
73 AH(c) 3.00
74 AH(c) 3.00
75 AH(c),Salvation Run tie-in. 3.00
76 AH(c),Salvation Run tie-in 3.00
77 AH(c),Salvation Run tie-in 3.00
78 AH(c),V:Cheetah 3.00
79 AH(c),Home Sweet Home?. . . . 3.00
80 AH(c),Battle for the underworld . 3.00
81 . . . . 3.00
82 Final issue. 3.00
GN Catwoman: The Movie 5.00
Spec. Secret Files #1. . . . . 5.00

...GUARDIAN OF GOTHAM
1999

1 (of 2) Elseworlds,V:Bat-Man 6.00
2 DgM,JBa 6.00

...WHEN IN ROME
Sept. 2004

1 (of 6) JLb(s),TSe 3.50
2 JLb(s),TSe 3.50
3 JLb,TSe 3.50
4 JLb,TSe,V:Cheetah 3.50
5 JLb,TSe 3.50
6 JLb,TSe,concl. 3.50

CATWOMAN/WILDCAT
June, 1998

1 (of 4) CDi,TP,SCi,BSf,
    V:Claw Hammer 3.00
2 thru 4 CDi,BSt,TP,SCi,BSf . . . . @3.00

CENTURIONS
June, 1987

1 DH,V:Doc Terror. 2.50
2 DH,O:Centurions 2.50
3 DH,V:Doc Terror. 2.50
4 DH,Sept., 1987 . . . . 2.50

CHAIN GANG WAR
1993–94

1 I:Chain Gang 3.00
2 V:8-Ball 2.50
3 C:Deathstroke 2.50
4 C:Deathstroke 2.50
5 Embossed(c),A:Deathstroke . . . 3.00
6 A:Deathstroke,Batman. 2.50
7 V:Crooked Man 2.50
8 B:Crooked Man 2.50
9 V:Crooked Man 2.50
10 A:Deathstroke,C:Batman 2.50
11 A:Batman. 2.50
12 E:Crooked Man,D:Chain Gang. . 2.50

CHALLENGERS OF
THE UNKNOWN
1958

1 JK&JK(c),The Man Who
    Tampered With Infinity 5,000.00
2 JK&JK(c),The Monster
    Maker. 1,600.00
3 JK&JK(c),The Secret of the
    Sorcerer's Mirror. 1,500.00

Challengers of the Unknown #1
© DC Comics, Inc.

4 JK,WW,JK(c),The Wizard of
    Time. 1,000.00
5 JK,WW&JK(c),The Riddle of
    the Star-Stone. 1,000.00
6 JK,WW,JK(c),Captives of
    the Space Circus 1,000.00
7 JK,WW,JK(c),The Isle of
    No Return 1,000.00
8 JK,WW,JK&WW(c),The
    Prisoners o/t Robot Planet . 1,000.00
9 The Plot To Destroy Earth 600.00
10 The Four Faces of Doom 600.00
11 The Creatures From The
    Forbidden World 500.00
12 The Three Clues To Sorcery . . 500.00
13 The Prisoner of the
    Tiny Space Ball 500.00
14 O: Multi Man 500.00
15 Lady Giant and the Beast. 500.00
16 Prisoners of the Mirage World 350.00
17 The Secret of the
    Space Capsules. 350.00
18 Menace of Mystery Island. . . . 350.00
19 The Alien Who Stole a Planet. 350.00
20 Multi-Man Strikes Back 350.00
21 Weird World That Didn't Exist. 350.00
22 The Thing In
    Challenger Mountain 350.00
23 The Island In The Sky. 150.00
24 The Challengers Die At Dawn 150.00
25 Captives of the Alien Hunter . 150.00
26 Death Crowns The
    Challenge King 150.00
27 Master of the Volcano Men. . . 150.00
28 The Riddle of the
    Faceless Man 150.00
29 Four Roads to Doomsday. . . . 150.00
30 Multi-Man...Villain Turned
    Hero. 150.00
31 O:Challengers. 200.00
32 One Challenger Must Die 100.00
33 Challengers Meet
    Their Master 100.00
34 Beachhead, USA 100.00
35 War Against The Moon Beast. 100.00
36 Giant In Challenger Mountain. 100.00
37 Triple Terror of Mr. Dimension 100.00
38 Menace the Challengers Made100.00
39 Phantom of the Fair 100.00
40 Super-Powers of the
    Challengers 100.00
41 The Challenger Who Quit. 75.00
42 The League of
    Challenger-Haters 75.00
43 New look begins 75.00
44 The Curse of the Evil Eye. 75.00

45 Queen of the
  Challenger-Haters 75.00
46 Strange Schemes of the
  Gargoyle 75.00
47 The Sinister Sponge 75.00
48 A:Doom Patrol. 75.00
49 Tyrant Who Owned the World . . 75.00
50 Final Hours for the
  Challengers 75.00
51 A:Sea Devil 75.00
52 Two Are Dead - Two To Go. . . 75.00
53 Who is the Traitor Among Us? . 75.00
54 War of the Sub-Humans 75.00
55 D:Red Ryan 75.00
56 License To Kill. 75.00
57 Kook And The Kilowatt Killer . . 75.00
58 Live Till Tomorrow. 75.00
59 Seekeenakee - The Petrified
  Giant 75.00
60 R:Red Ryan 75.00
61 Robot Hounds of Chang 75.00
62 Legion of the Weird 75.00
63 None Shall Escape the
  Walking Evil. 75.00
64 JKu(c),Invitation to a Hanging . 75.00
65 The Devil's Circus 50.00
66 JKu(c),Rendezvous With
  Revenge 50.00
67 NA(c),The Dream Killers. 50.00
68 NA(c),One of Us is a Madman . 50.00
69 JKu(c),I:Corinna 50.00
70 NA(c),Scream of Yesterdays. . . 50.00
71 NC(c),When Evil Calls 50.00
72 NA(c),A Plague of Darkness. . . 50.00
73 NC(c),Curse of the Killer
  Time Forgot 50.00
74 GT&NA(c),A:Deadman 125.00
75 JK(c),Ultivac Is Loose. 40.00
76 JKu(c),The Traitorous
  Challenger 40.00
77 JK(c),Menace of the
  Ancient Vials 40.00
78 JK(c),The Island of No Return . 40.00
79 JKu(c),The Monster Maker 40.00
80 NC(c),The Day The Earth
  Blew Up. 40.00
81 MN&NA(c),Multi-Man's
  Master Plan 20.00
82 MN&NA(c),Swamp Thing 20.00
83 Seven Doorways to Destiny . . . 20.00
84 To Save A Monster 20.00
85 The Creature From The End
  Of Time 20.00
86 The War At Time's End 20.00
87 final issue, July, 1978 . . . . 20.00

[Mini-Series], 1991
1 BB(c) In The Spotlight 3.00
2 thru 8 . . . . @2.50

1997
1 StG(s),JPL 3.00
2 StG(s),LKa,JPL,SMa,Zombies. . . 2.50
3 StG(s),JPL,death of Challenger. . 2.50
4 StG&LKa(s),JPL,SMa,
  O:Challengers 2.50
5 StG&LKa(s)JPL,SMa, V:The
  Fearslayer 2.50
6 StG(s),JPL,SMa,Convergence
  pt. 3 x-over 2.50
7 StG(s),JPL,PastPerfect,pt.1 . . . . 2.50
8 StG(s),JPL,PastPerfect,pt.2 . . . . 2.50
9 StG(s),JPL,PastPerfect,pt.3 . . . . 2.50
10 StG(s),JIT,F:Brenda Ruskin . . . 2.50
11 StG(s),JPL,in Gothan, pt.1 . . . . 2.50
12 StG(s),JPL,in Gothan, pt.2 . . . . 2.50
13 StG(s),F:Marlon Corbett 2.50
14 StG(s),Dark Waters. 2.50
15 StG(s),JPL,Millennium Giants
  pt. 3, x-over 2.75
16 StG(s),JPL,MZ, original Chalis . 2.75
17 StG(s),JPL,disappearances . . . 2.75
18 StG(s),DRo,MZ, final issue 2.75

June 2004
1 thru 6 HC . . . . @3.00

CHASE
Dec., 1997
1 JWi,MGy,from Batman #550 . . . 2.50
2 JWi,MGy 2.50
3 JWi,MGy,Rocket Reds. 2.50
4 JWi,MGy,F:Teen Titans 2.50
5 JWi,MGy,flashback story 2.50
6 JWi,MGy,Chase's past. 2.50
7 JWi,Shadowing the Bat,pt.1 . . . . 2.50
8 JWi,Shadowing the Bat,pt.2 . . . . 2.50
9 JWi,MBr,MGy,A:Green Lantern . . 2.50
Spec.#1,000,000 Final Issue 2.50

CHECKMATE
April, 1988
1 From Vigilante & Action Comics . 4.00
2 Chicago Bombings cont. 2.50
3 V:Terrorist Right 2.50
4 V:Crime Lords Abroad,B.U.Story
  `Training of a Knight' begins . . . 2.50
5 Renegade nation of Quarac 2.50
6 Secret Arms Deal. 2.50
7 Checkmate Invades Quarac 2.50
8 Consequences-Quarac Invasion . 2.50
9 Checkmate's security in doubt. . . 2.50
10 V:Counterfeiting Ring 2.50
11 Invasion X-over 2.50
12 Invasion Aftermath extra 2.50
13 CommanderH.Stein's vacation . . 2.50
14 R:Blackthorn 2.50
15 Janus Directive #1 . . . . 2.50
16 Janus Directive #3 . . . . 2.50
17 Janus Directive #6 . . . . 2.50
18 Janus Directive #9 . . . . 2.50
19 Reorganization of Group. 2.50
20 Shadow of Bishop
  A:Peacemaker,pt.1 . . . . 2.50
21 Peacemaker behind Iron
  Curtain,pt.2 . . . . 2.50
22 Mystery of Bishop Cont.,pt.3 . . . 2.50
23 European Lords
  Suicides,pt.4 . . . . 2.50
24 Bishop Mystery cont.,pt.5 . . . . . 2.50
25 Bishop's Identity Revealed 2.50
26 Mazarin kidnaps H.Stein's kids . 2.50
27 Stein rescue attempt,I:Cypher . . 2.50
28 A:Cypher, Bishop-Robots 2.50
29 A:Cypher,Blackthorn 2.50
30 Irish Knight W.O'Donnell/British
  Knight L.Hawkins team-up 2.50
31 Patriotic Knights,pt.1 . . . . 2.50
32 Patriotic Knights,pt.2 . . . . 2.50
33 Patriotic Knights,pt.3 . . . . 2.50
April, 2006
1 Balance of power. 3.00
2 Super-powered nations 3.00
3 F:White Bishop 3.00
4 The Game of Kings 3.00
5 Selection 3.00
6 Suicide Squad returns 3.00
7 Original Suicide Squad member . 3.00
8 Rival agency 3.00
9 Keep the mission alive. 3.00
10 Pawn 502, conclusion. 3.00
11 Corvalho, pt.1 . . . . 3.00
12 Corvalho, pt.2 . . . . 3.00
13 Checkout, pt.1 Outsiders x-over . 3.00
14 Checkout, pt.3 Outsiders x-over . 3.00
15 Checkout, pt.5 Outsiders x-over . 3.00
16 Black Queen vs. White Queen . . 3.00
17 Alpine headquarters 3.00
18 Fall of the Wall, pt.1 . . . . 3.00
19 Fall of the Wall, pt.2 . . . . 3.00
20 Fall of the Wall, concl. 3.00
21 Mademoiselle Marie, pt.1 . . . . . 3.00
22 Mademoiselle Marie, pt.2 . . . . . 3.00
23 Castling, pt.1 . . . . 3.00
24 Castling, pt.2,Kobra's plot. 3.00

25 Castling, concl. 3.00
26 Chimera 3.00
27 Chimera on a mission 3.00
28 Chimera's memories 3.00
29 Chimera, Global Guaridans 3.00
30 F:Chloe 3.00
31 Final issue 3.00

CHILDREN'S CRUSADE
DC/Vertigo, 1993–94
1 NGa(s),CBa,MkB(i),F:Rowland,
  Payne (From Sandman) 4.75
2 NGa(s),AaK(s),JaD(s),PSj,A:Tim
  Hunter,Suzy,Maxine,final issue . 4.50

CHRISTMAS WITH
THE SUPER-HEROES
1988–89
1 JBy(c). 5.00
2 PC,GM,JBy,NKu,DG A:Batman
  Superman,Deadman,(last
  Supergirl appearance). 4.00

CHRONOS
Jan., 1998
1 JFM,PGn,SL,Time Travel 2.50
2 JFM,PGn,SL 2.50
3 JFM,PGn,SL, in 1873 . . . . 2.50
4 JFM,PGn,SL,in Chronopolis 2.50
5 JFM,PGn,DHz,SL,WalkerGabriel. 2.50
6 JFM,PGn,Tattooed man. 2.50
7 JFM,PGn,DRo,SL,Star City 2.50
8 JFM,PGn,DRo,SL,
  V:Metrognomes 2.50
9 JFM(s),PGn,SL, The Man
  Who Chose Not to Exist 2.50
10 JFM(s),PGn,SL,Forever Engin . . 2.50
11 JFM(s),PGn,SL final issue 2.50
Spec.#1,000,000 JFM(s) Steals
  time gauntlets 2.50

CINDER & ASHE
March, 1988
1 JL,I:Cinder & Ashe. 2.50
2 JL,Viet Nam Flashbacks 2.50
3 JL,Truth About Lacey revealed . . 2.50
4 JL,final issue, June, 1988 . . . . . . 2.50

CINNAMON: EL CICLO
Aug. 2003
1 thru 5 RbC,HC(c) . . . . @2.50

Cinnamon: El Ciclo #2
© DC Comics Inc.

CLASH
1991
1 AKu,I:Joe McLash(b/w) 5.00
2 AKu,Panja-Rise to Power 5.00
3 AKu,V:Archons,conclusion. 5.00

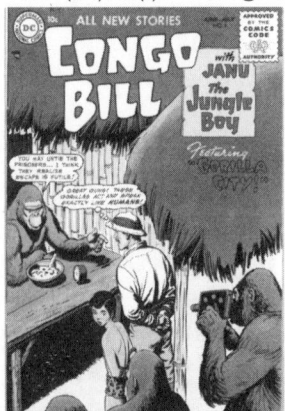

Claw The Unconquered #2
© DC Comics, Inc.

CLAW THE UNCONQUERED
May-June, 1975
1 ECh,I&O:Claw 15.00
2 ECh 8.00
3 ECh,Bloodspear, nudity panel . . 10.00
4 thru 7 ECh . . . . @8.00
8 KG,Master of the Seventh Void . . 8.00
9 KG/BL,Origin 8.00
10 JKu(c),KG,Eater of Souls. 8.00
11 JKu(c),KG,Death at Darkmorn . . 8.00
12 KG/BL,Aug.–Sept., 1978 . . . . . . 8.00

CODENAME: KNOCKOUT
DC/Vertigo, April, 2001
0 sexy spy thriller satire 3.00
1 MFm,JCh,Devil You Say,pt.1 . . . 3.00
1a variant JCh(c) (1:2) 3.00
2 MFm,JCh,Devil You Say,pt.2 . . . . 2.50
3 MFm,Little Orphan Angela. 2.50
4 MFm,St. Grace Under Fire 2.50
5 MFm,Arms & Legs for Hostages . 2.50
6 MFm,Arms & Legs for Hostages . 2.50
7 MFm,Go-Go-A-Go-Go 2.50
8 MFm,A is for Anarchy 2.50
9 JP,ACo,Enigma Variations 2.50
10 Undressed to Kill,pt.1 . . . . 2.50
11 Undressed to Kill,pt.2 . . . . 2.50
12 Undressed to Kill,pt.3 . . . . 2.50
13 Fleshback 1932:Roma 2.50
14a JP,JLe(c) 2.50
14b variant JSC(c). 2.50
15 EBe,F:Whole cast 2.50
16 EBe,Amok in America,pt.1 . . . . . 2.75
17 EBe,Amok in America,pt.2 . . . . . 2.75
18 EBe,Amok in America,pt.3 . . . . . 2.75
19 Fleshback '69 . . . . 2.75
20 Rebel Yell 2.75
21 Secrets & Thighs,pt.1 . . . . 2.75
22 Secrets & Thighs,pt.2 . . . . 2.75
23 final issue 2.75

COMET, THE
Impact, 1991–92
1 TL,I&O:Comet 3.00
2 thru 9 TL. . . . . @2.50

10 thru 18. . . . . @2.50
Ann.#1 Earthquest,w/trading card . . 2.50

COMIC CAVALCADE
1942–43
1 Green Lantern, Flash,
  Wildcat, Wonder Woman,
  Black Pirate 17,000.00
2 ShM,B:Mutt & Jeff. 4,000.00
3 ShM,B:HotHarrigan,Sorcerer 2,700.00
4 Gay Ghost, A:Scribby,
  A:Red Tornado 2,500.00
5 Gr.Lantern,Flash,W.Woman . 2,400.00
6 Flash,W.Woman,Gr.Lantern . 2,000.00
7 A:Red Tornado, E:Scribby . . 2,000.00
8 Flash,W.Woman,Gr.Lantern . 2,000.00
9 Flash,W.Woman,Gr.Lantern . 2,000.00
10 Flash,W.Woman,Gr.Lantern. 2,000.00
11 Flash,W.Woman,Gr.Lantern. 1,500.00
12 E:Red, White & Blue 1,500.00
13 A:Solomon Grundy. 2,500.00
14 Flash,W.Woman,Gr.Lantern. 1,500.00
15 B:Johnny Peril 1,500.00
16 Flash,W.Woman,Gr.Lantern. 1,800.00
17 Flash,W.Woman,Gr.Lantern. 1,500.00
18 Flash,W.Woman,Gr.Lantern. 1,500.00
19 Flash,W.Woman,Gr.Lantern. 1,500.00
20 Flash,W.Woman,Gr.Lantern. 1,500.00
21 Flash,W.Woman,Gr.Lantern. 1,500.00
22 A:Atom 1,500.00
23 A:Atom 1,500.00
24 A:Solomon Grundy. 2,200.00
25 A:Black Canary 2,000.00
26 ATh, E:Mutt & Jeff 2,000.00
27 ATh,ATh(c). 2,000.00
28 ATh E:Flash, Wonder Woman
  Green Lantern 2,000.00
29 E:Johnny Peril 1,500.00
30 RG,B:Fox & Crow 700.00
31 thru 39 RG . . . . @500.00
40 RG,ShM. 300.00
41 thru 49 RG,ShM . . . . @275.00
50 thru 62 RG,ShM . . . . @350.00
63 RG,ShM, July, 1954 . . . . 500.00

CONGO BILL
1954–56
1 NC(c&a),Chota the Chimp . . 2,500.00
2 NC(c&a),Elephants' Grave . . 2,000.00
3 thru 6 NC(c&a) . . . . @1,500.00
7 NC(c&a) 2,000.00

CONGO BILL
DC/Vertigo, 1999
1 thru 4 (of 4) RCo(c) . . . . @3.00

CONGORILLA
1992–93
1 R:Congo Bill. 2.50
2 thru 4 BB(c),V:Congo Bill. . . . @2.50

CONJURORS
1999
1 (of 3) CDi(s),EB, Elseworlds 3.00
2 CDi(s),EB. 3.00
3 CDi(s),EB. 3.00

CONNOR HAWKE: DRAGON'S BLOOD
Nov., 2006
1 (of 6) CDi 3.00
2 thru 6 CDi. . . . . @3.00

CONQUEROR OF THE BARREN EARTH
1985
1 thru 4 RoR, The Ravager. . . . . @3.00

COOL WORLD
1992
1 Prequel to Movie 2.50
2 thru 4 Movie characters . . . . . @2.50
1-shot Movie Adaptation 3.50

COPS
1988–89
1 PB,O:Cops,double-size 3.50
2 PB,V:Big Boss 2.50
3 PB,RT,V:Dr.Bad Vibes 2.50
4 BS,A:Sheriff Sundown 2.50
5 PB,Blitz the Robo-Dog. 2.50
6 PB,A:Ms.Demeaner. 2.50
7 PB,A:Tramplor 2.50
8 PB,V:BigBoss & Ally 2.50
9 PB,Cops Trapped 2.50
10 PB,Dr.Bad Vibes becomes
  Dr.Goodvibes. 2.50
11 PB,V:Big Boss. 2.50
12 PB,V:Dr.Badvibe's T.H.U.G.S . . 2.50
13 Berserko/Ms.Demeanor
  marriage proposal 2.50
14 A:Buttons McBoom-Boom. 2.50
15 Cops vs. Crooks, final issue 2.50

COSMIC BOY
Dec., 1986
1 KG,EC,Legends tie-in 2.50
2 KG,EC,Is History Destiny. 2.50
3 KG,EC,Past,Present,Future. 2.50
4 KG,EC,Legends 2.50

COSMIC ODYSSEY
1988
1 MMi,A:Superman,Batman,John
  Stewart,Starfire,J'onn J'onzz,
  NewGods,Demon,JSn story . . . 6.00
2 MMi,Disaster'(low dist) 6.00
3 MMi,Return to New Genesis 6.00
4 MMi,A:Dr.Fate, final 6.00

COUNTDOWN
May, 2007
51 PDi(s),NKu(c) 3.00
50 JP(s),JCf,NKu(c). 3.00
49 NKu(c). 3.00
48 thru 47. . . . . @3.00
46 JP(s) 3.00
45 thru 44. . . . . @3.00
43 JP(s) 3.00
42 thru 40. . . . . @3.00
39 JCf. 3.00
38 thru 27. . . . . @3.00

Congo Bill #6
© DC Comics, Inc.

Becomes:
COUNTDOWN
(TO FINAL CRISIS)
Nov., 2007
26 ScK,Monitors war council 3.00
25 RLm,JP,Darkseid,Jimmy Olsen . 3.00
24 TDr,Darkseid, Mary Marvel 3.00
23 Superman-Prime, Mr. Myzptlk . . 3.00
22 Fire Pits of Hell 3.00
21 For Goodness' Sake 3.00
20 ATi,Innocence Eclipsed 3.00
19 Carrion Death 3.00
18 ScK,Life & Times of Ray Palmer 3.00
17 RLm,JP,Mary Marvel, Eclipso . . . 3.00
16 TDr,Massacre 3.00
15 TDr,Mission Accomplished? 3.00
14 TDr,Prime Objective 3.00
13 TDr,Obliteration 3.00
12 TDr,JP,Convergence 3.00
11 Eye of the Beholder 3.00
10 ScK,Female Fury 3.00
9 TDr,Revolution 3.00
8 War in Pieces 3.00
7 TDr,Challenge Justice League . . 3.00
6 JP,The Great Disaster 3.00
5 JSn,End Times 3.00
4 The Beginning of the End 3.00
3 Superman vs. Darkseid 3.00
2 ScK,Darkseid, Jimmy Olsen 3.00
1 Great Disaster, Final Crisis 3.00
Spec. Jimmy Olsen 80-pg giant. . 5.00
Spec. The New Gods, 80-pg giant. 5.00
Spce. Omac, 80-pg giant 5.00
Spec. Eclipso 80-pg. giant 5.00
Spec. Kamandi, The Last Boy
   On Earth, 80-pg. giant 5.00

COUNTDOWN: ARENA
Dec, 2007
1 Superheroes vs. themselves 4.00
2 thru 4 . . . . @4.00
1a thru 4a variant (c)s (1:10) . . . . @4.50

COUNTDOWN PRESENTS:
LORD HAVOK AND
THE EXTREMISTS
Oct., 2007
1 (of 6) F:Lord Havok 3.00
2 LSh,V:Challengers of the Beyond 3.00
3 LSh,F:Tracer 3.00
4 LSh,Countdown tie-in 3.00
5 LSh,O:Dr. Diehard 3.00
6 LSh,final issue 3.00

...THE SEARCH FOR
RAY PALMER
Sept., 2007
Spec. #1 RMz(s),AAd(c), Wildstorm 3.00
Spec. #1 Crime Syndicate 3.00
Spec. #1 Gotham by Gaslight 3.00
Spec. #1 Red Rain 3.00
Spec. #1 Red Son 3.00
Spec. #1 Superwoman/Batwoman. . 3.00
Spec. #1 Atom 20-pg Giant 5.00
Spec. #2 Atom-80-pg Giant 5.00

COUNTDOWN
TO ADVENTURE
Aug., 2007
1 (of 8) F:Adam Strange, Starfire . . 4.00
2 F:Champ Hazard, 48-pgs. 4.00
3 F:Starfire, 48-pgs. 4.00
4 F:Healers 4.00
5 F:Forerunner 4.00
6 Starfire, Forerunner 4.00
7 Starfire & Animal Man 4.00
8 Lady Styx virus 4.00

COUNTDOWN
TO MYSTERY
Sept., 2007
1 (of 8) F:Kent Nelson, 48-pgs. . . . 4.00
2 F:Doctor Fate, 48-pgs. 4.00
3 V:Eclipso 4.00
4 F:Doctor Fate 4.00
5 F:Bruce Gordon 4.00
6 F:Bruce Gordon, Eclipso 4.00
7 Crispus Allen 4.00
8 Eclipso, Bruce Gordon. 4.00

CREATURE COMMANDOS
March, 2000
1 (of 8) TT,SEa, ... 2.50
2 TT,SEa,V:Saturna 2.50
3 TT,SEa, ... 2.50
4 TT,SEa, ... 2.50
5 TT,SEa,F:Claw 2.50
6 TT,SEa,V:Saturna 2.50
7 TT,SEa,V:Claw 2.50
8 TT,SEa,War Movie, concl. 2.50

CREEPER, THE
Oct., 1997
1 LKa,SMa,SB,R:Creeper. 3.00
2 LKa,SMa,SB,A:Dr. Skolos 3.00
3 LKa,SMa,SB,V:Proteus 3.00
4 LKa,SMa,SB 3.00
5 LKa,SMa,SB, new job 3.00
6 LKa,SMa,SB, strange meals 3.00
7 LKa,SMa,SB,F:Joker, pt.1 . . . . . . 3.00
8 LKa,SMa,SB,F:Joker, pt.2 . . . . . . 3.00
9 DAn,ALa,All-star issue 3.00
10 LKa,SB,Jack Ryder. 3.00
11 LKa,SB,SMa,Creeper splits
   again 3.00
Spec.#1,000,000 LKa,SB,final issue 3.00
Aug., 2006
1 (of 6) F:Jack Ryder 3.00
2 Axeman 3.00
3 Dr. Katz's serum 3.00
4 A:Batman 3.00
5 V:The Joker 3.00
6 A:Batman 3.00

CRIME BIBLE: THE FIVE
LESSONS OF BLOOD
Oct., 2007
1 (of 5) TMd,Monk o/t Dark Faith . . 3.00
2 A:The Question 3.00
3 The Lesson Greed 3.00
4 Lesson of Murder. 3.00
5 JP,Parable of the Faceless 3.00

CRIMSON AVENGER
1988
1 Mini-series 2.50
2 V:Black Cross 2.50
3 V:Killers of the Dark Cross 2.50
4 V:Dark Cross,final issue 2.50

CRISIS AFTERMATH:
THE BATTLE
FOR BLUDHAVEN
April, 2006
1 (of 6) JP,DJu 3.00
2 thru 6 JP,DJu . . . . @3.00

CRISIS AFTERMATH:
THE SPECTRE
May, 2006
1 (of 3) Spectre has new host 3.00
2 F:Crispus Allen. 3.00
3 Crispus Allen becomes Spectre. . 3.00

CRISIS ON
INFINITE EARTHS
April, 1985
1 B:MWn(s),GP,DG,I:Pariah,I&O:Alex
   Luthor,D:Crime Syndicate 18.00
2 GP,DG,V:Psycho Pirate,
   A:Joker,Batman 12.00
3 GP,DG,D:Losers. 10.00
4 GP,D:Monitor,I:2nd Dr.Light 10.00
5 GP,JOy,I:Anti-Monitor. 10.00
6 GP,JOy,I:2nd Wildcat,A:Fawcett,
   Quality & Charlton heroes 10.00
7 GP,JOy,DG,D:Supergirl 25.00
8 GP,JOy,D:1st Flash 22.00
9 GP,JOy,D:Aquagirl 10.00
10 GP,JOy,D:Psimon,A:Spectre. . . 10.00
11 GP,JOy,D:Angle Man 12.00
12 E:MWn(s),GP,JOy,D:Huntress,Kole,
   Kid Flash becomes 2nd Flash,
   D:Earth 2 . . . . 15.00

CROSSING MIDNIGHT
DC/Vertigo, Nov., 2006
1 . . . . 3.00
2 MCy(s),MPn 3.00
3 MCy(s),MPn 3.00
4 Cut Here, pt.1 . . . . 3.00
5 Cut Here, pt.2 . . . . 3.00
6 A Map of Midnight, pt.1 . . . . 3.00
7 A Map of Midnight, pt.2 . . . . 3.00
8 A Map of Midnight, pt.3 . . . . 3.00
9 A Map of Midnight, pt.4 . . . . 3.00
10 MCy(s),Supernatural slasher . . . 3.00
11 MCy(s),Supernatural slasher . . . 3.00
12 Comb, Mirror, High-heeled shoe. 3.00
13 Kill Kai? 3.00
14 F:Loretta 3.00
15 Toshi & Kai 3.00
16 Memories shared 3.00
17 Blade in the Soul, pt. 1 . . . . 3.00
18 Blade in the Soul, pt. 2 . . . . 3.00
19 Final issue. 3.00

CRUCIBLE
Impact, 1993
1 JQ,F:The Comet 2.50
2 thru 6 JQ . . . . @2.50

CRUEL AND UNUSUAL
DC/Vertigo, 1999
1 (of 4) JaD&TPe(s),JMC,satire . . . 3.00
2 thru 4 JaD&TPe(s),JMC. . . . . . . @3.00

Crucible #4
© *DC Comics Inc.*

CRUSADERS
Impact, May, 1992
1 DJu(c),I:Crusaders,inc Trading
cards 2.50
2 thru 8 . . . . @2.50

CRUSADES, THE
DC/Vertigo, March, 2001
1 KJo,F:Venus 5.00
2 KJo,V:Dark Ages Knight 3.50
3 KJo,MBu,in San Francisco 3.50
4 KJo,MBu,Anton Marx. 3.00
5 KJo,Marx eats crow. 3.00
6 KJo,second Crusade 3.00
7 KJo,V:The Knight. 3.00
8 KJo,Knight's lair. 3.00
9 KJo,Godfrey. 3.00
10 KJo,sex, sin, subjugation 3.00
11 KJo,origin of the Knight?. 3.00
12 KJo,Knight's hidden enclave. . . 3.00
13 KJo,Third Crusade begins 3.00
14 KJo,Ash Wednesday Killer 3.00
15 KJo,Ash Wednesday Killer 3.00
16 KJo,Ash Wednesday Killings . . 3.00
17 KJo,Venus Kostopikas 3.00
18 KJo,Shockjock Anton 3.00
19 KJo,back to Medieval times . . . 3.00
20 KJo,final issue. 3.00
Spec. Urban Decree, KJo,48-page . 4.00

CYBERELLA
DC/Helix, Sept., 1996
1 HC(s),DCn, ... 2.50
2 thru 12 HC(s),DCn, ... @2.50

CYBORG
May, 2008
1 thru 6 (of 6) F:Vic Stone. . . . . . @3.00

DALE EVANS COMICS
1948–52
1 Ph(c),ATh,B:Sierra Smith . . . 1,500.00
2 Ph(c),ATh. 700.00
3 ATh. 500.00
4 thru 11 . . . . @325.00
12 thru 20 . . . . @275.00
21 thru 24 . . . . @250.00

DAMAGE
1994–96
1 I:Damage,V:Metallo 4.00

Dark Mansion of Forbidden Love #3
© DC Comics Inc.

2 Afterschool Special 3.00
3 The Damage Done 3.00
4 Troll's Day,A:Wyldheart 3.00
5 thru 20 . . . . @3.00
Spec. 0 Back Again 3.50

DANGER TRAIL
July–Aug., 1950
1 CI,ATh,I:King For A Day 2,000.00
2 ATh, King Faraday 1,400.00
3 ATh, King Faraday 2,000.00
4 ATh, King Faraday 1,200.00
5 March-April, 1951, John
Pearl. 1,200.00

DANGER TRAIL
[Mini-Series], 1993
1 thru 4 CI,FMc,F:King Faraday
V:Cobra 2.50

DARK MANSION OF FORBIDDEN LOVE, THE
Sept.–Oct., 1971
1 . . . . 350.00
2 NA(c) 150.00
3 and 4 March-April, 1972 . . . @125.00

DARKSEID VS. GALACTUS THE HUNGER
1995
1-shot Orion vs. Silver Surfer 5.00
GN JBy,in Apokolips. 6.00

DARKSTARS
1992–96
0 History 2.50
1 TC(c),LSn,I:Darkstars 3.50
2 TC(c),LSn,F:Ferin Colos 2.50
3 LSn,J:Mo,Flint,V:Evil Star 2.50
4 TC,V:Evilstar 3.00
5 TC,A:Hawkman,Hawkwoman . . 3.00
6 TC,A:Hawkman 2.50
7 TC,V:K'llash 2.50
8 F:Ferris Colos 2.50
9 Colos vs K'lassh 2.50
10 V:Con Artists 2.50
11 TC,Trinity#4,A:Green Lantern,
L.E.G.I.O.N. 2.50
12 TC(c),Trinity#7,A:Green Lantern,
L.E.G.I.O.N. 2.50
13 thru 38. . . . . @2.50

A DATE WITH JUDY
1947
1 Teen-age 500.00
2 . . . . 350.00
3 thru 10 . . . . @300.00
11 thru 20 . . . . @250.00
21 thru 30 . . . . @150.00
31 thru 50 . . . . @125.00
51 thru 78 . . . . @125.00
79 MD 150.00

DAY OF JUDGMENT
Sept., 1999
1 (of 5) Spectre x-over 6.00
2 F:Wonder Woman, Supergirl . . . 5.00
3 F:Superman & Green Lantern . . . 5.00
4 F:Superman's team 5.00
5 conclusion 5.00
Spec. Secret Files #1. . . . . 6.00

DAY OF VENGEANCE
Apr., 2005
1 (of 6) F:Spectre, Enchantress . . . 8.00
1a 2nd printing 5.00
2 WS(c) Shadowpact 3.00

3 WS(c). 2.50
4 WS(c). 2.50
5 WS(c). 2.50
6 WS(c), The Death of Magic 2.50
Spec. Infinite Crisis, 48-pg. 4.00

DC CHALLENGE
Nov., 1985
1 GC,Batman 3.00
2 Superman 2.50
3 CI,Adam Strange 2.50
4 GK/KJ,Aquaman 2.50
5 DGb,Dr.Fate,Capt.Marvel 2.50
6 Dr. 13. 2.50
7 Gorilla Grodd. 2.50
8 DG,Outsiders, New Gods 2.50
9 New Teen Titans,JLA. 2.50
10 CS,New Teen Titans,JLA 2.50
11 KG,Outsiders. 2.50
12 DCw,TMd,DSp,New Teen Titans,
Oct., 1986 . . . . 2.50

DC COMICS PRESENTS
July–Aug., 1978
[all have Superman]
1 JL,DA,F:Flash 35.00
2 JL,DA,F:Flash 20.00
3 JL,F:Adam Strange 20.00
4 JL,F:Metal Men,A:Mr.IQ. 20.00
5 MA,F:Aquaman 8.00
6 CS,F:Green Lantern 8.00
7 DD,F:Red Tornado. 8.00
8 MA,F:Swamp Thing 8.00
9 JSon,JA,RH,F:Wonder Woman . 8.00
10 JSon,JA,F:Sgt.Rock 8.00
11 JSon,F:Hawkman 7.00
12 RB,DG,F:Mr.Miracle 7.00
13 DD,DG,F:Legion 8.00
14 DD,DG,F:Superboy 7.00
15 JSon,F:Atom,C:Batman 7.00
16 JSon,F:Black Lightning 7.00
17 JL,F:Firestorm 7.00
18 DD,F:Zatanna 7.00
19 JSon,F:Batgirl 7.00
20 JL,F:Green Arrow 6.00
21 JSon,JSa,F:Elongated Man . . . 6.00
22 DD,FMc,F:Captain Comet 6.00
23 JSon,F:Dr.Fate 6.00
24 JL,F:Deadman 6.00
25 DD,FMc,F:Phantom Stranger . . 6.00
26 GP,DG,JSn,I:New Teen Titans,
Cyborg,Raven,Starfire
A:Green Lantern 50.00
27 JSn,RT,I:Mongul 7.00
28 JSn,RT,GK,F:Mongul 6.00
29 JSn,RT,AS,F:Spectre 6.00
30 CS,AS,F:Black Canary 6.00
31 JL,DG,AS,F:Robin. 6.00
32 KS,AS,F:Wonder Woman 6.00
33 RB,DG,AS,F:Captain Marvel. . . 6.00
34 RB,DG,F:Marvel Family 6.00
35 CS,GK,F:Man-bat 6.00
36 JSn,F:Starman 7.00
37 JSn,AS,F:Hawkgirl 6.00
38 GP(c),DH,AS,DG,D:Crimson
Avenger,F:Flash 6.00
39 JSon,AS,F:PlasticMan,Toyman . 6.00
40 IN,FMc,AS,F:Metamorpho 6.00
41 JL,FMc,GC,RT,I:New Wonder
Woman,A:Joker. 8.00
42 IN,FMc,F:Unknown Soldier. . . . 6.00
43 BB(c),CS,F:Legion 6.00
44 IN,FMc,F:Dial H for Hero 7.00
45 RB,F:Firestorm 6.00
46 AS,I:Global Guardians 6.00
47 CS,I:Masters of Universe. 20.00
48 GK(c),AA,IN,FMc,F:Aquaman. . 5.00
49 RB,F:Shazam!,V:Black Adam . . 5.00
50 KS,CS,F:Clark Kent 5.00
51 AS,FMc,CS,F:Atom,Masters
of the Universe 9.00

DC Comics Presents #49
© *DC Comics, Inc.*

52 KG,F:Doom Patrol,
   I:Ambush Bug 5.00
53 CS,TD,RA,DG,I:Atari Force 5.00
54 DN,DA,F:Gr.Arrow,Bl.Canary . . . 5.00
55 AS,F:Air Wave,A:Superboy 5.00
56 GK(c),F:Power Girl 5.00
57 AS,FMc,F:Atomic Knights 5.00
58 GK(c),AS,F:Robin,Elongated
   Man 5.00
59 KG,KS,F:Ambush Bug 5.00
60 GK(c),IN,TD,F:Guardians 5.00
61 GP,F:Omac 5.00
62 GK(c),IN,F:Freedom Fighters . . . 5.00
63 AS,EC,F:Amethyst 5.00
64 GK(c),AS,FMc,F:Kamandi 5.00
65 GM,F:Madame Xanadu 5.00
66 JKu,F:Demon 5.00
67 CS,MA,F:Santa Claus 5.00
68 GK(c),CS,MA,F:Vixen 5.00
69 IN,DJ,F:Blackhawk 5.00
70 AS,TD,F:Metal Men 5.00
71 CS,F:Bizarro 5.00
72 AS,DG,F:Phant.Stranger,Joker . . 6.00
73 CI,F:Flash 5.00
74 AS,RT,F:Hawkman 5.00
75 TMd,F:Arion 5.00
76 EB,F:Wonder Woman 5.00
77 CS,F:Forgotten Heroes 5.00
78 CS,F:Forgotten Villains 6.00
79 CS,AW,F:Legion 6.00
80 CS,F:Clark Kent 5.00
81 KG,BO,F:Ambush Bug 5.00
82 KJ,F:Adam Strange 5.00
83 IN,F:Batman/Outsiders 5.00
84 JK,ATh,MA,F:Challengers 7.00
85 RV,AW,AMo(s),
   F:Swamp Thing 7.00
86 Crisis,F:Supergirl 5.00
87 CS,AW,Crisis,I:Earth Prime
   Superboy 5.00
88 KG,Crisis,F:Creeper 5.00
89 MMi(c),AS,F:Omega Men 5.00
90 DCw,F:Firestorm,Capt.Atom . . . 5.00
91 CS,F:Captain Comet 5.00
92 CS,F:Vigilante 5.00
93 JSn(c),AS,KS,F:Elastic Four 5.00
94 GP(c),TMd,DH,Crisis,F:Lady
   Quark,Pariah,Harbinger 5.00
95 MA(i),F:Hawkman 5.00
96 JSon,KS,F:Blue Devil 5.00
97 RV,F:Phantom Zone Villians,
   final issue,double-sized 5.00
Ann.#1,RB,F:Earth 2 Superman . . . 5.00
Ann.#2 GK(c),KP,I:Superwoman . . . 5.00

Ann.#3 GK,F:Captain Marvel 5.00
Ann.#4 EB,JOy,F:Superwoman 5.00

DC COMICS PRESENTS
July 2004
The Atom #1 . . . . 2.50
Batman #1 . . . . 2.50
The Flash #1 . . . . 2.50
Green Lantern #1 . . . . 2.50
Hawkman #1 . . . . 2.50
Justice League of America #1 . . . . . 2.50
Mystery in Space #1 . . . . 2.50
Superman #1 . . . . 2.50

DC COUNTDOWN
March, 2005
1 80-page 3.00

DC/MARVEL:
ALL ACCESS
October 1996
sequel to DC Versus Marvel
1 (of 4) RMzs(s),JG,JRu, crossover
   crisis again, 48pg 4.00
2 RMzs(s),JG,JRu,F:Jubilee,Robin,
   Daredevil,Two-Face 3.00
3 RMzs(s),JG,JRu,F:Doctor
   Strange, X-Men 3.00
4 RMzs(s),JG,JRu,48pg 3.50

DC FIRST
May, 2002
Superman/Lobo, 48-pg. 3.50
The Flash/Superman, 48-pg. 3.50
Batgirl/The Joker, 48-pg. 3.50
Green Lantern/Green Lantern 3.50

DC GRAPHIC NOVEL
Nov., 1983
1 JL,Star Raiders 16.00
2 Warlords 16.00
3 EC,Medusa Chain 16.00
4 JK,Hunger Dogs 70.00
5 Me and Joe Priest 16.00
6 Space Clusters 16.00

DC INFINITE
HALLOWEEN SPECIAL
Oct., 2007
1 13 stories 6.00

DC MILLENNIUM
EDITIONS
Dec., 1999–2000
Action Comics #1 . . . . 4.00
Action Comics #252 . . . . 2.50
Adventure Comics #247 . . . . 2.50
Adventure Comics #761 . . . . 4.00
All-Star Comics #3 . . . . 4.00
All-Star Comics #3, chromium 5.00
All Star Comics #8 . . . . 4.00
All-Star Western #10 . . . . 3.00
Batman #1 . . . . 4.00
Batman #1 chromium 5.00
Batman: Dark Knight Returns #1 . . 6.00
The Brave and the Bold #28 . . . . . . 2.50
The Brave and the Bold #85 . . . . . . 2.50
Crisis on Infinte Earths #1 . . . . 2.50
Detective Comics #27 . . . . 4.00
Detective Comics #38 . . . . 4.00
Detective Comics #327 . . . . 2.50
Detective Comics #359 . . . . 2.50
Detective Comics #395 . . . . 2.50
Flash Comics #1 . . . . 4.00
Flash #123 . . . . 2.50
Gen 13 #1 . . . . 2.50
Green Lantern/Green Arrow #76 . . . 2.50

Hellblazer #1 . . . . 3.00
House of Mystery #1 . . . . 2.50
House of Secrets #92 . . . . 2.50
JLA #1 . . . . 2.50
Justice League #1 . . . . 2.50
Justice League #1, chromium 5.00
Kingdom Come #1 . . . . 6.00
The Man of Steel #1 . . . . 2.50
Military Comics #1 . . . . 4.00
More Fun Comics #101 . . . . 3.00
Mysterious Suspense #1 . . . . 2.50
New Gods #1 . . . . 2.50
New Teen Titans #1 . . . . 2.50
Our Army at War #81 . . . . 2.50
Plop! #1 . . . . 2.50
Police Comics #1 . . . . 4.00
Preacher #1 . . . . 3.00
Saga of the Swamp Thing #21 . . . . 2.50
Sandman #1 . . . . 3.00
Sensation Comics #1 . . . . 4.00
The Shadow #1 . . . . 2.50
Showcase #22 . . . . 2.50
Showcase #4 . . . . 2.50
Spirit #1 . . . . 4.00
Superboy #1 . . . . 3.00
Superman #1 . . . . 4.00
Superman #1 Chromium edition . . . 5.00
Superman #76 . . . . 3.00
Superman #75 Death of Superman . 2.50
Superman's Pal Jimmy Olsen #1 . . 2.50
Watchmen #1 . . . . 2.50
Whiz Comics #2 . . . . 4.00
WildC.A.T.S #1 . . . . 2.50
Wonder Woman 1st.Series #1 . . . . . 4.00
Wonder Woman #1 . . . . 2.50
World's Finest Comics #71 . . . . 2.50
Young Romance #1, JK, JSm 3.00

DC: THE NEW FRONTIER
Jan. 2004
1 (of 6) Silver age universe 8.00
2 thru 6 . . . . @7.00

DC 100-PAGE
SUPERSPECTACULAR
May 2004
Spec. Facsimile edition (2004) . . . 7.00

DC ONE MILLION
1998
1 GMo(s),VS,in 853rd-century 3.00
2 GMo(s),VS,V:Hourman Virus 2.50
3 GMo(s),VS,V:Solaris 2.50
4 GMo(s),VS,finale 2.50

DC REPLICA EDITIONS
1999–2000
DC 100-Page Super-Spectacular:
   Love Stories 7.00
Justice Society of America
   100-page Super Spectacular #1 7.00
Teen Titans Annual #1 (1967) 5.00
Sgt. Rock's Prize Battle Tales
   80-pg. Giant 6.00

DC SCIENCE FICTION
GRAPHIC NOVEL
1985–87
1 KG,Hell on Earth 15.00
2 Nightwings 15.00
3 Frost and Fire 15.00
4 Merchants of Venus 15.00
5 Metalzoic 15.00
6 MR,Demon-Glass Hand 15.00
7 Sandkings 15.00

All comics prices listed are for *Near Mint* condition.

DC SPECIAL
Oct.–Dec., 1968
[All reprint]
1 Cl,F:Flash,Batman,Adam Strange,
 (#1 thru #21 reps) 125.00
2 F:Teen Titans 175.00
3 GA,F:Black Canary 150.00
4 Mystery 75.00
5 JKu,F:Viking Prince/Sgt.Rock . . 75.00
6 Wild Frontier 75.00
7 F:Strangest Sports Stories 75.00
8 Joker-Luthor, Incorporated 75.00
9 F:Strangest Sports Stories 75.00
10 Stop, You Can't Beat the Law . . 75.00
11 NA,BWr,F:Monsters 75.00
12 JKu,F:Viking Prince 75.00
13 F:Strangest Sports Stories 75.00
14 Wanted,F:Penguin/Joker 60.00
15 GA,F:Plastic Man (1971) 60.00
16 F:Super Heroes & Gorillas 30.00
17 F:Green Lantern 30.00
18 Earth Shaking Stories 30.00
19 F:War Against Gianta 30.00
20 Green Lantern. 30.00
21 F:War Against Monsters 30.00
22 Three Musketeers, Robin Hood 30.00
23 Three Musketeers, Robin Hood 30.00
24 Three Musketeers, Robin Hood 30.00
25 Three Musketeers, Robin Hood 30.00
26 F:Enemy Ace 30.00
27 RB,JR,F:Captain Comet 30.00
28 DN,DA,Earth disasters 30.00
29 JSon,BL,O:JSA 50.00

DC SPECIAL SERIES
Sept., 1977
1 MN,DD,IN,FMc,JSon,JA,BMc,
 JRu,F:Batman,Flash,Green
 Lantern,Atom,Aquaman. 45.00
2 BWr(c),BWr,F:Swamp
 Thing rep. 15.00
3 JKu(c),F:Sgt.Rock 18.00
4 AN,RT,Unexpected Annual 18.00
5 CS,F:Superman 24.00
6 BMc(i),Secret Society Vs.JLA . . 20.00
7 AN,F:Ghosts 20.00
8 RE,DG,F:Brave&Bold,Deadman 20.00
9 SD,RH,DAy,F:Wonder Woman . 25.00
10 JSon,MN,DN,TA,Secret Origins,
 O:Dr.Fate 18.00
11 JL,KS,MA,IN,WW,AS,F:Flash . . 18.00
12 MK(c),RT,RH,TS,Secrets of
 Haunted House 20.00
13 JKu(c),RT,SBi,RE,F:Sgt.Rock . . 20.00
14 BWr(c),F:Swamp Thing rep. . . . 18.00
15 MN,JRu,MR,DG,MGo,
 F:Batman. 25.00
16 RH,D:Jonah Hex. 90.00
17 F:Swamp Thing rep. 12.00
18 JK(c),digest,F:Sgt.Rock rep. . . . 18.00
19 digest,Secret Origins
 O:Wonder Woman. 18.00
20 BWr(c),F:Swamp Thing rep. . . . 12.00
21 FM,JL,DG,RT,DA,F:Batman,
 Legion 45.00
22 JKu(c),F:G.I.Combat 18.00
23 digest size,F:Flash 18.00
24 F:Worlds Finest. 18.00
25 F:Superman II,Photo Album . . . 18.00
26 RA,F:Superman's Fortress 22.00
27 JL,DG,F:Batman vs.Hulk. 45.00

DC SPECIAL: THE
RETURN OF DONNA TROY
June, 2005
1 (of 4) GP,PJ 3.00
2 thru 4 GP,PJ . . . . @3.00

DC Super-Star #7
© DC Comics Inc.

DC SUPER-STARS
1976–78
1 F:Teen Titans rep. 35.00
2 F:DC Super-Stars of Space 12.00
3 CS,F:Superman,Legion 12.00
4 DC,MA,F:Super-Stars of Space . 12.00
5 Cl,F:Flash rep. 12.00
6 MA,F:Super-Stars of Space 12.00
7 F:Aquaman rep. 12.00
8 Cl,MA,F:Adam Strange 15.00
9 F:Superman rep. 12.00
10 DD,FMc,F:Superhero Baseball
 Special,A:Joker 15.00
11 GM,Super-Stars of Magic 12.00
12 CS,MA,F:Superboy 12.00
13 SA. 25.00
14 RB,BL,JA,JRu,Secret Origins . . 12.00
15 JKu(c),RB,RT(i),War Heroes . . 12.00
16 DN,BL,I:Star Hunters 12.00
17 JSon,MGr,BL,I&O:Huntress,O:Gr.
 Arrow,D:EarthII Catwoman . . . 65.00
18 RT,DG,BL,F:Deadman,Phantom
 Stranger. 20.00

DC TWO THOUSAND
July, 2000
1 (of 2) TPe,VS. 7.00
2 TPe,VS,JLA & Golden age JSA . 7.00

DC UNIVERSE
1997–2003
Heroes, Secret Files #1 . . . . 5.00
Villains, Secret Files #1 . . . . 5.00
GN Holiday Bash #1 (1997). 4.00
GN Holiday Bash #2 (1998). 4.00
GN Holiday Bash #3 (1999). 5.00
Spec. Infinite X-mas special (2006). 5.00

...AMBUSH BUG
Aug., 2008
Spec. 1 80-pg. rep. 5.00

...BRAVE NEW WORLD
June, 2006
1-shot new projects preview, 80-pg. 3.00

...DECISIONS
Sept., 2008
1 (of 4) Davis Brewster for Pres. . . 3.00
2 thru 4 . . . . @3.00

...HALLOWEEN '08
Oct., 2008
1-shot 80-pg. 3.00

...LAST WILL AND TESTAMENT
Aug., 2008
1-shot 4.00
1-shota variant (c) 4.00

...TRINITY
1993
1 TC,GeH,BKi,F:Darkstars,Green
 Lantern,L.E.G.I.O.N.,V:Triarch . 4.00
2 BKi,SHa,F:Darkstars,Green Lantern,
 L.E.G.I.O.N.,V:Triarch 4.00

...ZERO
April, 2008
1-shot Final Crisis prequel 2.50

DC VS. MARVEL
1996
1 RMz 5.50
1 2nd printing 4.00
2 & 3 see Marvel
4 PDa 5.00

DC/WILDSTORM:
DREAMWAR
April, 2008
1 (of 6) x-over 3.00
1a variant (c) (1:10) 3.00
2 Universes collide 3.00
3 thru 6 . . . . @3.00

DEAD CORPS(E)
DC/Helix, July, 1998
1 StP, C.J.Rataan 2.50
2 StP, CJ becomes an expired . . . 2.50
3 StP,Death is not the end 2.50
4 StP, conclusion. 2.50

DEADENDERS
DC/Vertigo, Jan., 2000
1 WaP,Stealing the Sun,pt.1 . . . . . 2.50
2 WaP,Stealing the Sun,pt.2 . . . . . 2.50
3 WaP,Stealing the Sun,pt.3 . . . . . 2.50
4 WaP,Stealing the Sun,pt.4 . . . . . 2.50
5 WaP,Now and Then,pt.1 . . . . . . 2.50
6 WaP,Now and Then,pt.2 . . . . . . 2.50
7 WaP,Now and Then,pt.3 . . . . . . 2.50
8 WaP,scooter races 2.50
9 More Fun in New World,pt.1 . . . . 2.50
10 More Fun in New World,pt.2 . . . 2.50
11 Sector 9. . . . . 2.50
12 V:Science Corp. 2.50
13 Scooter race 2.50
14 Behind the Wheel, pt.1 . . . . 2.50
15 Behind the Wheel, pt.2 . . . . 2.50
16 Behind the Wheel, pt.3 . . . . 2.50

DEADMAN
May, 1985
1 Cl,NA,rep. 4.00
2 thru 7 NA,rep. . . . . @3.00
[Mini-Series], 1986
1 JL,A:Batman 3.00
2 JL,V:Sensei,A:Batman 3.00
3 JL,D:Sensei 3.00
4 JL,V:Jonah, final issue 3.00
Dec., 2001
1 SVa(s) F:Boston Brand 2.50
2 SVa(s),Sirna. 2.50
3 SVa(s),F:Duroc, drugs 2.50
4 SVa(s),nuclear submarine 2.50
5 SVa(s),Death & the Maiden,pt.1 . 2.50
6 SVa(s),Death & the Maiden,pt.2 . 2.50
7 SVa(s),children of Nanda Parbat . 2.50
8 SVa(s),Nanda Parbat,Onyx 2.50
9 SVa(s),final issue 2.50
DC/Vertigo, Aug., 2006
1 JWk, F:Brandon Caycs 3.00

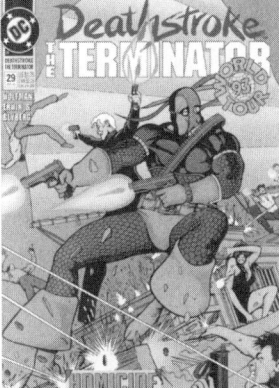

Deadman #3
© *DC Comics, Inc.*

2 thru 4 JWk . . . . @3.00
5 JWk 3.00
6 JWk, Homecoming, pt.1 . . . . . . 3.00
7 JWk, Homecoming, pt.2 . . . . . . 3.00
8 thru 13 JWk . . . . @3.00

...DEAD AGAIN
Aug., 2001
1 SVa,RBr,A:Flash 2.50
2 SVa,RBr,JAp,A:Robin 2.50
3 SVa,RBr,A:Superman,Doomsday 2.50
4 SVa,RBr,MBr,A:Green Lantern . . 2.50
5 SVa,RBr,concl., ... 2.50

...EXORCISM
[Limited-Series], 1992
1 KJo,A:Phantom Stranger 5.25
2 KJo,A:Phantom Stranger 5.25

...LOVEAFTER DEATH
1989–90
1 KJo,Circus of Monsters 4.25
2 KJo,Circus of Monsters 4.25

DEADSHOT
1988–89
1 LMc,From Suicide Squad 2.50
2 LMc,Search for Son. 2.50
3 LMc,V:Pantha 2.50
4 LMc,final issue. 2.50

Dec., 2004
1 (of 5) JP,MZ&JOy(c) 3.00
2 JP,A:Green Arrow 3.00
3 JP,V:Green Arrow. 3.00
4 JP,Star City criminals. 3.00
5 JP,conclusion 3.00

DEATH GALLERY
DC/Vertigo
1 DMc(c),NGa Death Sketch
Various Pinups. 3.50

DEATH: THE HIGH
COST OF LIVING
DC/Vertigo, 1993
1 B:NGa(s),CBa,MBu(i),Death
becomes Human,A:Hettie 6.00
1a Platinum Ed. 40.00
2 CBa,MBu(i),V:Eremite,A:Hettie . 6.00
3 E:NGa(s),CBa,MBu(i),V:Eremite,
A:Hettie 6.00
3a Error Copy 7.00

DEATH OF
THE NEW GODS
Oct., 2007
1 (of 8) JSn. 3.50
1a variant (c) (1:10) 3.50
2 JSn. 3.50
3 JSn,A:Superman 3.50
4 JSn,F:Superman, Mr. Miracle . . . 3.50
5 JSn,Mr. Miracle, Orion 3.50
6 JSn,Orion and death 3.50
7 JSn,Source Wall showdown 3.50
8 JSn, final issue 3.50

DEATH: THE TIME
OF YOUR LIFE
DC/Vertigo, 1995
1 NGa,MBu,four-issue miniseries. . 3.00
2 NGa,MBu,F:Foxglove 3.00
3 NGa,MBu,conclusion 3.00

DEATHSTROKE:
THE TERMINATOR
1991–94
1 MZ(c),(from New Teen Titans)
SE,I:2nd Ravager 4.00
1a Second Printing,Gold. 3.00
2 MZ(c),SE,Quraci Agents 4.00
3 SE,V:Ravager 4.00
4 SE,D:2ndRavager(Jackel) 3.00
5 Winter Green Rescue Attempt. . . 3.00
6 MZ(c),SE,B:City of Assassins,
A:Batman. 3.00
7 MZ(c),SE,A:Batman. 2.50
8 MZ(c),SE,A:Batman. 2.50
9 MZ(c),SE,E:City of Assassins,
A:Batman;I:2nd Vigilante. 2.50
10 MZ(c),ANi,GP,A:2nd Vigilante. . 2.50
11 MZ(c),ANi,GP,A:2nd Vigilante. . 2.50
12 MGo,Short Stories re:Slade . . . 2.50
13 SE,V:Gr.Lant.,Flash,Aquaman . . 2.50
14 ANi,Total Chaos#1,A:New Titans,
Team Titans,V:Nightwing 2.50
15 ANi,Total Chaos#4,A:New Titans,
Team Titans,I:Sweet Lili. 2.50
16 ANi,Total Chaos#7 . . . . 2.50
17 SE,Titans Sell-Out #2
A:Brotherhood of Evil 2.50
18 SE,V:Cheshire,R:Speedy 2.50
19 SE,V:Broth.of Evil,A:Speedy. . . 2.50
20 SE,MZ(c),V:Checkmate 2.50
21 SE,MZ(c),A:Checkmate 2.50
22 MZ(c),Quality of Mercy#1 . . . . . 2.50

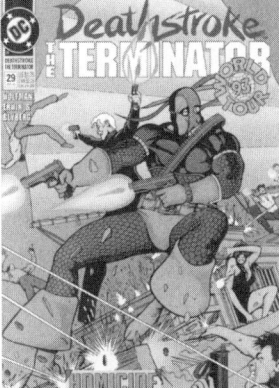

Deathstroke: The Terminator #29
© *DC Comics, Inc.*

23 MZ(c),Quality of Mercy#2 . . . . . 2.50
24 MZ(c),V:The Black Dome 2.50
25 MZ(c),V:The Black Dome 2.50
26 MZ(c),SE,in Kenya 2.50
27 MZ(c),SE,B:World Tour,
in Germany 2.50
28 MZ(c),SE,in France. 2.50
29 KM(c),SE,in Hong Kong 2.50
30 SE,A:Vigilante 2.50
31 SE,in Milwaukie 2.50
32 SE,in Africa 2.50
33 SE,I:Fleur de Lis 2.50
34 SE,E:World Tour 2.50
35 V:Mercenaries 2.50
36 V:British General. 2.50
37 V:Assassin 2.50
38 A:Vigilante 2.50
39 A:Vigilante. 2.50
40 Wedding in Red 2.50
Ann.#1 Eclipso,A:Vigilante. 4.00
Ann.#2 SE,I:Gunfire. 4.00
Ann.#3 Elseworlds Story 4.25
Becomes:

DEATHSTROKE:
THE HUNTED
1994–95
0 Slade 2.50
41 Bronze Tiger 2.50
42 Wounded. 2.50
43 . . . . 2.50
44 . . . . 2.50
45 A:New Titans. 2.50
Becomes:

DEATHSTROKE
1995–96
46 Checkmate,Wintergreen 2.50
47 I:New Vigilante 2.50
48 Crimelord/Syndicate War,pt.1 . . 2.50
49 Crimelord/Syndicate War,pt.4
A:Supergirl, New Titans,
Hawkman, Blood Pack 2.50
50 A:Titans,Outsiders,Steel 3.50
51 No Fate or Future,pt.1 . . . . 2.50
52 No Fate or Future,pt.2 . . . . 2.50
53 The Borgia Plague,pt.1 . . . . 2.50
54 The Borgia Plague,pt.2 . . . . 2.50
55 MWn,Rebirth?. 2.50
56 MWn,Night of the Karrion,pt.2 . . 2.50
57 . . . . 2.50
58 MWn,V:The Joker 2.50
59 MWn,F:Hellriders 2.50
60 MWn,final issue 2.50

DEATHWISH
1994–95
1 New mini-series. 2.50
2 F:Rahme 2.50
3 . . . . 2.50
4 V:Boots 2.50

DEMOLITION MAN
1993–94
1 thru 4 Movie Adapt. 2.50

DEMON
[1st Regular Series], 1972–74
1 JK,I:Demon 90.00
2 JK. 50.00
3 JK. 45.00
4 JK. 45.00
5 JK. 45.00
6 thru 16 JK. . . . . @30.00

[Limited Series], 1987
1 MWg,B:Jason Blood's Case 3.00
2 MWg,Fight to Save Gotham 3.00
3 MWg,Fight to Save Gotham 3.00
4 MWg,final issue 3.00

DC COMICS

DC COMICS

[2nd Regular Series], 1990–95
0 Relationships 2.50
1 VS,A:Etrigan (32 pages) 4.00
2 VS,V:TheCrone 3.00
3 VS,A:Batman 3.00
4 VS,A:Batman 3.00
5 VS,ThePit. 3.00
6 VS,In Hell. 3.00
7 VS,Etrigan-King of Hell 3.00
8 VS,Klarion the Witch Boy 3.00
9 VS,Jason Leaves Gotham. 3.00
10 VS,A:PhantomStranger. 3.00
11 VS,A:Klarion,C:Lobo 3.00
12 VS,Etrigan Vs. Lobo 3.00
13 VS,Etrigan Vs. Lobo 3.00
14 VS,V:Odd Squad,A:Lobo 3.00
15 VS,Etrigan Vs.Lobo 3.00
16 VS,Etrigan & Jason Blood
  switch bodies. 3.00
17 VS, War of the Gods x-over 3.00
18 VS,V:Wotan,A:Scape Goat. 3.00
19 VS,O:Demon,Demon/Lobo
  pin-up. 3.50
20 VS,V:Golden Knight 2.50
21 VS,Etrigan/Jason,
  A:Lobo,Glenda. 2.50
22 MWg,V:Mojo & Hayden 2.50
23 VS,A:Robin 2.50
24 VS,A:Robin 2.50
25 VS,V:Gideon Ryme. 2.50
26 VS,B:America Rules 2.50
27 VS,A:Superman 2.50
28 VS,A:Superman 2.50
29 VS,E:America Rules 2.50
30 R:Asteroth 2.50
31 VS(c),A:Lobo. 2.50
32 VS(c),A:Lobo,W.Woman. 2.50
33 VS(c),A:Lobo,V:Asteroth. 2.50
34 A:Lobo. 2.50
35 A:Lobo,V:Belial 2.50
36 A:Lobo,V:Belial 2.50
37 A:Lobo,Morax 2.50
38 A:Lobo,Morax 2.50
39 A:Lobo. 2.50
40 New Direction,B:GEn(s) 3.50
41 V:Mad Bishop 3.00
42 V:Demons 3.00
43 A:Hitman 10.00
44 V:Gotho-Demon,A:Hitman 15.00
45 V:Gotho-Demon,A:Hitman 15.00
46 R:Haunted Tank 5.00
47 V:Zombie Nazis. 5.00
48 A:Haunted Tank,V:Zombie
  Nazis 5.00
49 b:Demon's Son,A:Joe Gun 2.50
50 GEn(s). 3.00
51 GEn(s),Son & Lovers 2.50
52 Etrigan & son–Hitman. 4.00
53 Glenda & child–Hitman. 4.00
54 Suffer the Children 4.00
55 Rebellion. 2.50
56 F:Etrigan. 2.50
57 Last Stand. 2.50
58 Last issue 2.50
Ann.#1 Eclipso,V:Klarion 3.25
Ann.#2 I:Hitman 15.00

**DEMON, THE:
DRIVEN OUT**
Sept. 2003
1 (of 6) ATi,F:Etrigan. 2.50
2 thru 6 ATi . . . . @2.50

**DESPERADOES:
QUIET OF THE GRAVE**
Homage/DC May, 2001
1 (of 5) JMi,JSe 3.00
2 JMi,JSe 3.00
3 thru 5 JMi,JSe . . . . @3.00

**DESTINY: A CHRONICLE
OF DEATHS FORETOLD**
DC/Vertigo, Sept., 1997
1 (of 3) F:Destiny of the Endless . . 6.00
2 Destiny of the Endless, pt.2. . . . . 6.00
3 Destiny of the Endless, pt.3. . . . . 6.00

DETECTIVE COMICS
March, 1937
1 I:Slam Bradley. 110,000.00
2 JoS, Skyscraper Death. . . . 40,000.00
3 JoS,A Stowaway in Need . . 26,000.00
4 JoS,The Rajah's Ruby 12,000.00
5 JoS,Slam Bradley 10,000.00
6 JoS,Speed Saunders 8,000.00
7 JoS,In Atlantic City 7,500.00
8 JoS,Mr. Chang(c) 12,000.00
9 JoS,Case of the Hobo Hero . 7,500.00
10 CF,Mystery at Oak Gables. . 7,500.00
11 CF,Anarchist Sub Plot 6,000.00
12 CF,Indian Oil Well Mystery . 6,000.00
13 CF,Little Tomm Murder Case 6,000.00
14 CF,Mystery of Hondoku Isle. 6,000.00
15 CF,Mystery of Darby Pearls. 6,000.00
16 CF,Case of Missing Corpse . 6,000.00
17 CF,I:Fu Manchu 6,000.00
18 S&S,Fu Manchu(c) 10,000.00
19 FGu,The Grogan Case 6,000.00
20 I:Crimson Avenger 9,000.00
21 FGu,The Glass of Poison . . 5,000.00
22 S&S,Return of Fui Onyui . . . 6,500.00
23 FGu,The Ski Murder 5,000.00
24 FGu,Persian Jewel Mystery. 5,000.00
25 FGu,The Death Sled 5,000.00
26 FGu,Artists of Death 5,000.00
27 BK,I:Batman. 550,000.00
28 BK,V:Frenchy Blake. 45,000.00
29 BK,I:Doctor Death 70,000.00
30 BK,V:Dr. Death. 15,000.00
31 BK,I:Monk 75,000.00
32 BK,V:Monk 13,000.00
33 O:Batman,V:Scarlet Horde 90,000.00
34 V:Due D'Orterre 10,000.00
35 V:Sheldon Lenox 25,000.00
36 I:Hugo Strange 18,000.00
37 V:Count Grutt, last
  Batman solo 15,000.00
38 I:Robin, the Boy Wonder . 100,000.00
39 V:Green Dragon 14,000.00
40 I:Clayface (Basil Karlo) . . . 15,000.00
41 V:Graves 7,500.00
42 V:Pierre Antal. 5,000.00
43 V:Harliss Greer 5,000.00
44 Robin Dream Story 5,000.00

*Detective Comics #7
© DC Comics, Inc.*

45 V:Joker. 7,500.00
46 V:Hugo Strange 6,500.00
47 Meets Harvey Midas 6,500.00
48 Meets Henry Lewis 6,500.00
49 V:Clayface 6,500.00
50 V:Three Devils 6,500.00
51 V:Mindy Gang 4,000.00
52 V:Loo Chung 4,000.00
53 V:Toothy Hare Gang 4,000.00
54 V:Hook Morgan 4,000.00
55 V:Dr. Death 4,000.00
56 V:Mad Mack 4,000.00
57 Meet Richard Sneed 4,000.00
58 I:Penguin 9,000.00
59 V:Penguin 3,500.00
60 V:Joker,I:Air Wave 3,000.00
61 The Three Racketeers 2,700.00
62 V:Joker. 4,000.00
63 I:Mr. Baffle 2,700.00
64 I:Boy Commandos,V:Joker . 8,000.00
65 Meet Tom Bolton 5,000.00
66 I:Two-Face 8,000.00
67 V:Penguin 4,500.00
68 V:Two-Face 3,200.00
69 V:Joker. 3,200.00
70 Meet the Amazing Carlo . . . 2,200.00
71 V:Joker. 2,600.00
72 V:Larry the Judge 1,900.00
73 V:Scarecrow. 2,300.00
74 I:Tweedledum&Tweedledee. 2,200.00
75 V:Robber Baron 2,200.00
76 V:Joker. 2,800.00
77 V:Dr. Matthew Thorne 2,200.00
78 V:Baron Von Luger 2,200.00
79 Destiny's Auction 2,200.00
80 V:Two-Face 2,500.00
81 I:Cavalier 1,500.00
82 V:Blackee Blondeen. 1,500.00
83 V:Dr. Goodwin 1,600.00
84 V:Ivan Krafft 1,500.00
85 V:Joker. 2,000.00
86 V:Gentleman Jim Jewell . . . 1,500.00
87 V:Penguin 1,600.00
88 V:Big Hearted John 1,500.00
89 V:Cavalier 1,500.00
90 V:Capt. Ben 1,500.00
91 V:Joker. 2,400.00
92 V:Braing Bulow 1,400.00
93 V:Tiger Ragland. 1,400.00
94 V:Lefty Goran. 1,400.00
95 V:The Blaze 1,400.00
96 F:Alfred 1,400.00
97 V:Nick Petri 1,400.00
98 Meets Casper Thurbridge . . 1,400.00
99 V:Penguin 1,400.00
100 V:Digger. 1,400.00
101 V:Joe Bart 1,400.00
102 V:Joker. 1,400.00
103 Meet Dean Gray 1,400.00
104 V:Fat Frank Gang 1,400.00
105 V:Simon Gurlan 1,400.00
106 V:Todd Torrey. 1,400.00
107 V:Bugs Scarpis 1,400.00
108 Meet Ed Gregory 1,400.00
109 V:Joker. 2,500.00
110 V:Prof. Moriarty 1,500.00
111 Coaltown, USA 1,500.00
112 Case Without A Crime 1,500.00
113 V:Blackhand 1,500.00
114 V:Joker. 1,500.00
115 V:Basil Grimes 1,500.00
116 A:Carter Nichols,
  Robin Hood 1,500.00
117 Steeplejack's Slowdown. . . 1,500.00
118 V:Joker. 2,000.00
119 V:Wiley Derek 1,200.00
120 V:Penguin 2,700.00
121 F:Commissioner Gordon . . 1,200.00
122 V:Catwoman 2,500.00
123 V:Shiner 1,100.00
124 V:Joker. 1,600.00
125 V:Thinker 1,000.00

Detective Comics #167
© *DC Comics, Inc.*

126 V:Penguin 1,000.00
127 V:Dr. Agar. 1,000.00
128 V:Joker. 1,600.00
129 V:Diamond Dan Mob 1,200.00
130 BK,V:Briggs Carson 1,200.00
131 V:Trigger Joe 1,200.00
132 V:Human Key. 1,200.00
133 Meets Arthur Loom 1,200.00
134 V:Penguin 1,200.00
135 A:Baron Frankenstein,
    Carter Nichols. 1,200.00
136 A:Carter Nichols. 1,200.00
137 V:Joker. 1,400.00
138 V:Joker,O:Robotman 1,800.00
139 V:Nick Bailey 1,200.00
140 I:Riddler 9,000.00
141 V:Blackie Nason. 1,200.00
142 V:Riddler 2,000.00
143 V:Pied Piper. 1,000.00
144 A:Kay Kyser (radio
    personality). 1,000.00
145 V:Yellow Mask Mob 1,000.00
146 V:J.J. Jason 1,000.00
147 V:Tiger Shark 1,000.00
148 V:Prof. Zero 1,000.00
149 V:Joker. 1,500.00
150 V:Dr. Paul Visio 1,000.00
151 I&O:Pow Wow Smith 1,200.00
152 V:Goblin 1,000.00
153 V:Slits Danton 1,200.00
154 V:Hatch Marlin 1,000.00
155 A:Vicki Vale 1,000.00
156 The Batmobile of 1950 . . . 1,500.00
157 V:Bart Gillis 1,000.00
158 V:Dr. Doom 1,000.00
159 V:T. Worthington Chubb. . . 1,000.00
160 V:Globe-Trotter 1,000.00
161 V:Bill Waters 1,000.00
162 Batman on Railroad. 1,000.00
163 V:Slippery Jim Elgin. 1,000.00
164 Bat-signal story 1,000.00
165 The Strange Costumes
    of Batman. 1,000.00
166 Meets John Gillen 1,000.00
167 A:Carter Nichols, Cleopatra 1,000.00
168 O:Joker 6,500.00
169 V:Squint Tolmar 1,000.00
170 Batman Teams with Navy
    and Coast Guard 1,000.00
171 V:Penguin 1,500.00
172 V:Paul Gregorian 950.00
173 V:Killer Moth 950.00
174 V:Dagger. 950.00
175 V:Kangaroo Kiley 950.00
176 V:Mr. Velvet. 950.00
177 Bat-Cave Story 900.00

178 V:Baron Swane. 900.00
179 Mayor Bruce Wayne 900.00
180 V:Joker. 900.00
181 V:Human Magnet 900.00
182 V:Maestro Dorn. 900.00
183 V:John Cook. 900.00
184 I:Firefly(Garfield Lynns). . . . 900.00
185 Secrets of Batman's
    Utility Belt 900.00
186 The Flying Bat-Cave. 900.00
187 V:Two-Face. 900.00
188 V:William Milden 900.00
189 V:Styx 900.00
190 Meets Dr. Sampson,
    O:Batman. 1,100.00
191 V:Executioner 900.00
192 V: Nails Riley 900.00
193 V:Joker. 900.00
194 V:Sammy Sabre 900.00
195 Meets Hugo Marmon 900.00
196 V:Frank Lumardi 900.00
197 V:Wrecker. 900.00
198 Batman in Scotland. 900.00
199 V:Jack Baker. 900.00
200 V:Brand Keldon 1,100.00
201 Meet Human Target 900.00
202 V:Jolly Roger. 900.00
203 V:Catwoman 1,000.00
204 V:Odo Neral 900.00
205 O:Bat-Cave. 900.00
206 V:Trapper 900.00
207 Meets Merko the Great. 900.00
208 V:Groff. 900.00
209 V:Inventor 900.00
210 V:Brain Hobson. 900.00
211 V:Catwoman 1,000.00
212 Meets Jonathan Bard 900.00
213 O:Mirror-Man 1,000.00
214 The Batman Encyclopedia . . 900.00
215 I:Ranger, Legionary, Gaucho &
    Musketeer,A:Knight & Squire
    (See: World's Finest 89) 750.00
216 A:Brane Taylor 750.00
217 Meets Barney Barrows 750.00
218 V:Dr. Richard Marston 750.00
219 V:Marty Mantee. 750.00
220 A:Roger Bacon, historical
    scientist/philosopher 750.00
221 V:Paul King 750.00
222 V:'Big Jim' Jarrell 750.00
223 V:'Blast' Varner 750.00
224 The Batman Machine 750.00
225 I&O:Martian Manhunter
    (J'onn J'onzz) 10,000.00
226 O:Robin's costume,
    A:J'onn J'onzz 2,500.00
227 A:Roy Raymond, J'onn
    J'onzz. 1,000.00
228 A:Roy Raymond, J'onn
    J'onzz. 1,000.00
229 A:Roy Raymond, J'onn
    J'onzz. 1,000.00
230 A:Martian Manhunter,
    I:Mad Hatter 1,100.00
231 A:Batman,Jr.,Roy Raymond
    J'onn J'onzz. 700.00
232 A:J'onn J'onzz. 700.00
233 SMo(c),I&O:Batwoman . . . 2,400.00
234 SMo(c),V:Jay Caird. 700.00
235 SMo(c),O:Batman's
    Costume 1,100.00
236 SMo(c),V:Wallace Walby . . 1,000.00
237 SMo(c),F:Robin. 700.00
238 SMo(c),V:Checkmate(villain) 700.00
239 SMo(c),Batman robot story. . 700.00
240 SMo(c),V:Burt Weaver 700.00
241 SMo(c),The Rainbow Batman700.00
242 SMo(c),Batcave story 500.00
243 SMo(c),V:Jay Vanney 500.00
244 SMo(c),O:Batarang 500.00
245 SMo(c),F:Comm.Gordon. . . . 500.00
246 SMo(c),. 500.00

247 SMo(c),I:Professor Milo 500.00
248 Around the World in 8 Days . 500.00
249 V:Collector 500.00
250 V:John Stannor. 500.00
251 V:Brand Ballard. 500.00
252 Batman in a movie 500.00
253 I:Terrible Trio 500.00
254 SMo(c),A:Bathound. 500.00
255 V:Fingers Nolan 500.00
256 Batman outer-space story. . 500.00
257 Batman sci-fi story 500.00
258 Batman robot story. 500.00
259 SMo,I:Calendar Man. 500.00
260 Batman outer space story. . 500.00
261 I:Dr. Double X 400.00
262 V:Jackal-Head. 400.00
263 V:The Professor 400.00
264 Peril at Playland Isle. 400.00
265 O:Batman retold 500.00
266 SMo,V:Astro 400.00
267 SMo,I&O:Bat-Mite. 500.00
268 V:'Big Joe' Foster 400.00
269 V:Director 400.00
270 Batman sci-fi story 400.00
271 V:Crimson Knight,O:Martian
    Manhunter(retold) 400.00
272 V:Crystal Creature 400.00
273 A:Dragon Society 300.00
274 V:Nails Lewin 300.00
275 SMo,A:Zebra-Man. 300.00
276 A:Batmite. 300.00
277 Batman Monster story. 300.00
278 A:Professor Simms 300.00
279 Batman robot story 300.00
280 A:Atomic Man 300.00
281 Batman robot story 250.00
282 Batman sci-fi story 250.00
283 V:Phantom of Gotham City . . 250.00
284 V:Hal Durgan 250.00
285 V:Harbin 250.00
286 A:Batwoman 250.00
287 SMo,A:Bathound. 250.00
288 V:Multicreature 250.00
289 SMo,A:Bat-Mite. 250.00
290 SMo,Batman's robot story . . 250.00
291 Batman sci-fi story 250.00
292 Last Roy Raymond 250.00
293 A:Aquaman,J'onn J'onzz . . . 250.00
294 V:Elemental Men,
    A:Aquaman 250.00
295 A:Aquaman 250.00
296 A:Aquaman 250.00
297 SMo,A:Aquaman. 250.00
298 I:Clayface(Matt Hagen). 500.00

Detective Comics #291
© *DC Comics Inc.*

DC COMICS

299 Batman sci-fi stories 250.00
300 SMo,I:Mr.Polka-dot,
    E:Aquaman 250.00
301 A:J'onn J'onzz 200.00
302 A:J'onn J'onzz 150.00
303 A:J'onn J'onzz 150.00
304 A:Clayface,J'onnJ'onz. 150.00
305 Batman sci-fi story 150.00
306 A:J'onn J'onzz 150.00
307 A:J'onn J'onzz 150.00
308 A:J'onn J'onzz 150.00
309 A:J'onn J'onzz 150.00
310 A:Bat-Mite,J'onn J'onzz 150.00
311 I:Cat-Man,Zook 175.00
312 A:Clayface,J'onn J'onzz 150.00
313 A:J'onn J'onzz 150.00
314 A:J'onn J'onzz 150.00
315 I:Jungle Man 150.00
316 A:Dr.Double X,J'onn J'onzz . 150.00
317 A:J'onn J'onzz 150.00
318 A:Cat-Man,J'onn J'onzz 150.00
319 A:J'onn J'onzz 150.00
320 A:Vicki Vale 150.00
321 I:Terrible Trio 150.00
322 A:J'onn J'onzz 150.00
323 I:Zodiac Master,
    A:J'onn J'onzz 150.00
324 A:Mad Hatter,J'onn J'onzz . . 150.00
325 A:Cat-Man,J'onn J'onzz 150.00
326 Batman sci-fi story 150.00
327 CI,25th ann,symbol change . 250.00
328 D:Alfred,I:WayneFoundation. 250.00
329 A:Elongated Man 150.00
330 "Fallen Idol of Gotham". 150.00
331 A:Elongated Man 150.00
332 A:Joker 125.00
333 CK(c),A:Gorla 125.00
334 Man Who Stole from Batman 125.00
335 CI,Trail of the Talking Mask . 125.00
336 CI,V:Outsider. 125.00
337 CI,Deep Freeze Menace. . . . 125.00
338 CI,Power-Packed Punch. . . . 125.00
339 CI,V:Living Beast-Bomb 125.00
340 CI,Outsider Strikes Again . . . 125.00
341 A:Joker 125.00
342 CI,Raid of the Robin Gang . . 125.00
343 BK,CI,Elongated Man 125.00
344 CI,I&V:Johnny Witts 125.00
345 CI,I:Blockbuster. 125.00
346 Inescapable Doom-Trap 125.00
347 CI,Elongated Man 125.00
348 Elongated Man 125.00
349 BK(c),CI,Blockbuster. 125.00
350 Elongated Man 125.00
351 CI,A:Elongated Man,
    I:Cluemaster 125.00
352 BK,Elongated Man 125.00
353 V:Weather Wizard. 125.00
354 BK,Elongated Man,I:Dr.
    Tzin-Tzin 125.00
355 CI,Elongated Man 125.00
356 BK,Outsider,Alfred 125.00
357 CI,Wayne Unmasks Batman. 125.00
358 BK,Elongated Man 125.00
359 CI,I:new Batgirl 275.00
360 Case of Abbreviated Batman 125.00
361 CI,Double-Deathtrap. 125.00
362 CI,Elongated Man 125.00
363 CI,Elongated Man 125.00
364 CI,BK,Elongated Man 125.00
365 CI,A:Joker 125.00
366 CI,Elongated Man 125.00
367 CI,Elongated Man 125.00
368 CI,BK,Elongated Man 125.00
369 CA,Elongated Man,
    Catwoman 175.00
370 NA,BK,Elongated Man 150.00
371 CI,BK,Elongated Man 175.00
372 NA,BK,Elongated Man 100.00
373 BK,Elongated Man 100.00
374 BK,Elongated Man 100.00
375 CI,Elongated Man 100.00

Detective Comics #389
© *DC Comics, Inc.*

376 Batman–Hunted or Haunted. 100.00
377 MA,Elongated Man,
    V:Riddler 100.00
378 Elongated Man 100.00
379 CI,Elongated Man 100.00
380 Elongated Man 100.00
381 GaF,Marital Bliss Miss 100.00
382 FR(s),BbB,JoG,GaF(s),SGe . 100.00
383 FR(s),BbB,JoG,GaF(s),SGe . 100.00
384 FR(s),BbB,JoG,GaF(s),SGe,
    BU:Batgirl 100.00
385 E:FR(s),BbB,JoG,NA(c&a),GK,
    MA,MkF,BU:Batgirl 100.00
386 BbK,MkF,BbB,JoG,
    BU:Batgirl 100.00
387 RA,rep.Detective #27 . . . . . . 150.00
388 JBr(s),BbB,JoG,
    GK,MA,FR(s). 150.00
389 NA,FR(s),BbB,JoG,GK,MA . 100.00
390 FR(s),BbB,JoG,GK,MA,
    A:Masquerader 100.00
391 FR(s),NA(c),BbB,
    JoG,GK,MA 75.00
392 FR(s),BbB,JoG,I:Jason Bard. . 75.00
393 FR(s),BbB,JoG,GK,MA 75.00
394 FR(s),BbB,JoG,GK,MA 75.00
395 FR(s),NA,DG,GK,MA 100.00
396 FR(s),BbB,JoG,GK,MA 75.00
397 DON(s),NA,DG,GK,MA 100.00
398 FR(s),BbB,JoG,GK,ViC 75.00
399 NA(c),DON(s),BbB,JoG,
    GK,ViC,Robin 100.00
400 FR(s),NA,DG,GK,I:Man-Bat . 300.00
401 NA(c),FR(s),JoG,
    BbB,JoG,GK,ViC 60.00
402 FR(s),NA,DG,V:Man-Bat. . . . 100.00
403 FR(s),BbB,JoG,NA(c),GK,ViC,
    BU:Robin 100.00
404 NA,GC,GK,A:Enemy Ace . . . 110.00
405 IN,GK,I:League of Assassins 100.00
406 DON(s),BbB,FrG. 100.00
407 FR(s),NA,DG,V:Man-bat 110.00
408 MWn(s),LWn(s),NA,DG,
    V:DrTzin Tzin 110.00
409 B:FR(s),BbB,FrG,DH,DG 80.00
410 DON(s),FR(s),NA,DG,DH . . . 80.00
411 NA(c),DON(s),BbB,DG,DH . . 70.00
412 NA(c),BbB,DG,DH. 70.00
413 NA(c),BbB,DG,DH. 70.00
414 DON(s),IN,DG,DH. 75.00
415 BbB,DG,DH. 75.00
416 DH. 75.00
417 BbB,DG,DH,BU:Batgirl 75.00
418 DON(s),DH,IN,DG,A:Creeper . 75.00
419 DON(s),DH 75.00

420 DH. 75.00
421 DON(s),BbB,DG,DH,A:Batgirl . 70.00
422 BbB,DG,DH,Batgirl 70.00
423 BbB,DG,DH 70.00
424 BbB,DG,DH,Batgirl 70.00
425 BWr(c),DON(s),IN,DG,DH. . . . 70.00
426 LWn(s),DG,A:Elongated Man . 50.00
427 IN,DG,DH,BU:Batgirl 50.00
428 BbB,DG,ENB(s),DD,JoG,
    BU:Hawkman. 50.00
429 DG,JoG,V:Man-Bat 50.00
430 BbB,NC,ENS(s),DG,
    A:Elongated Man 50.00
431 DON(s),IN,MA. 50.00
432 MA,A:Atom 50.00
433 DD,DG,MA 50.00
434 IN,DG,ENB(s),RB,DG 50.00
435 E:FR(s),DG,IN 50.00
436 MA,(i),DG,A:Elongated Man . 50.00
437 JA,WS,I:Manhunter. 85.00
438 JA,WS,Manhunter. 100.00
439 DG,WS,O:Manhunter,Kid
    Eternity rep. 100.00
440 JAp,WS 100.00
441 HC,WS 100.00
442 ATh,WS 100.00
443 WS,D:Manhunter 100.00
444 JAp,B:Bat-Murderer,
    A:Ra's Al Ghul 100.00
445 JAp,MGr,A:Talia 100.00
446 JAp,last giant 30.00
447 DG(i),A:Creeper 30.00
448 DG(i),E:Bat-Murderer,
    A:Creeper,Ra's Al Ghul 30.00
449 Midnight Rustler in Gotham . . 30.00
450 TA,WS. 30.00
451 TA 30.00
452 ECh,V:The Crime Exchange. . 30.00
453 ECh,V:The Crime Exchange. . 30.00
454 ECh,The Set-Up Caper. 30.00
455 MGr,A:Hawkman,V:Vampire . . 30.00
456 V:Ulysses Vulcan 30.00
457 O:Batman rtd 30.00
458 A:Man Bat 30.00
459 A:Man Bat 30.00
460 I:Capt.Stingaree 30.00
461 V:Capt.Stingaree. 25.00
462 V:Capt.Stingaree,A:Flash . . . 25.00
463 TA,MGr,Atom,I:Calc.,Bl.Spider 25.00
464 MGr,BlackCanary 25.00
465 TA,Elongated Man 25.00
466 MR,TA,V:Signalman 50.00
467 MR,TA,RB 50.00
468 MR,TA,A:JLA 50.00
469 WS,I:Dr.Phosphorus 25.00
470 WS,AM,V:Dr.Phosphorus 25.00
471 MR,TA,A:Hugo Strange 50.00
472 MR,TA,A:Hugo Strange 50.00
473 MR,TA,R:Deadshot 50.00
474 MR,TA,A:Penguin,
    N:Deadshot 50.00
475 MR,TA,A:Joker 100.00
476 MR,TA,A:Joker 100.00
477 MR,DG,rep.NA 50.00
478 MR,DG,TA,I:3rd Clayface 50.00
479 MR,DG,A:3rd Clayface 50.00
480 DN,MA 25.00
481 JSt,CR,DN,DA,MR,
    A:ManBat. 30.00
482 HC,MGo,DG,A:Demon 27.00
483 DN,DA,SD,A:Demon,
    40 Anniv. 25.00
484 DN,DA,Demon,O:1st Robin . . 25.00
485 DN,DA,D:Batwoman,A:Demon
    A:Ras al Ghul 25.00
486 DN,DA,DG,I:Odd Man,
    V:Scarecrow 25.00
487 DN,DA,A:Ras Al Ghul 25.00
488 DN,V:Spook,Catwoman 25.00
489 IN,DH,DN,DA,Ras Al Ghul . . 25.00
490 DN,DA,PB,FMc,A:Black
    Lightning;A:Ras Al Ghul 25.00

491 DN,DA,PB,FMc,A:Black
   Lightning;V:Maxie Zeus 25.00
492 DN,DA,A:Penguin 25.00
493 DN,DA,A:Riddler 25.00
494 DN,DA,V:Crime Doctor 25.00
495 DN,DA,V:Crime Doctor 25.00
496 DN,DA,V:Clayface I 15.00
497 DN,DA 15.00
498 DN,DA,V:Blockbuster 15.00
499 DN,DA,V:Blockbuster 15.00
500 DG,CI,WS,TY,JKu,Deadman,
   Hawkman,Robin 25.00
501 DN,DA 15.00
502 DN,DA 15.00
503 DN,DA,Batgirl,Robin,
   V:Scarecrow 15.00
504 DN,DA,Joker 20.00
505 DN,DA,RB 15.00
506 DN,DA,RB 15.00
507 DN,DA,RB 15.00
508 DN,DA,V:Catwoman 17.00
509 DN,DA,V:Catman,Catwoman . 17.00
510 DN,DA,V:Madhatter 15.00
511 DN,DA,RB,I:Mirage 15.00
512 GC,45th Anniv. 15.00
513 RB,V:Two-Face 17.00
514 RB 15.00
515 RB 15.00
516 RB 15.00
517 The Monster in the Mirror . . . 15.00
518 RB,V:Deadshot 15.00
519 Dreadnought in the Sky 15.00
520 A:Hugo Strange,
   Catwoman 17.00
521 IN,TVE,A:Catwoman,B:
   BU:Green Arrow 20.00
522 D:Snowman 15.00
523 V:Solomon Grundy 15.00
524 2nd A:J.Todd 17.00
525 J.Todd 15.00
526 DN,AA,A:Joker,Catwoman
   500th A:Batman 30.00
527 V:Man Bat 7.00
528 Green Arrow,Ozone 7.00
529 I:Night Slayer,Nocturna 7.00
530 V:Nocturna 7.00
531 GC,AA,Chimera,J.Todd (see
   Batman #364) 7.00
532 GC,Joker 9.00
533 Look to the Mountaintop 7.00
534 GC,A:Gr.Arrow,V:PoisonIvy . . . 7.00
535 GC,A:Gr.Arrow,V:Crazy Quitt
   2nd A:New Robin 9.00
536 GC,A:Gr.Arrow,V:Deadshot . . . 7.00

Detective Comics #574
© *DC Comics, Inc.*

537 GC,A:Gr.Arrow 7.00
538 GC,A:Gr.Arrow,V:Catman 7.00
539 GC,A:Gr.Arrow 7.00
540 GC,A:Gr.Arrow,V:Scarecrow . . 7.00
541 GC,A:Gr.Arrow,V:Penguin 7.00
542 GC,A:Gr.Arrow 9.00
543 GC,A:Gr.Arrow,V:Nightslayer . 7.00
544 GC,A:Gr.Arrow,V:Nightslayer . . 7.00
545 By Darkness Masked 7.00
546 Hill's Descent 7.00
547 PB,KJ 7.00
548 PB,Beasts A-Prowl 7.00
549 PB,KJ,AMo(s),Gr.Arrow 9.00
550 KJ,AMo(s),Gr.Arrow 9.00
551 PB,V:Calendar Man 7.00
552 V:Black Mask 7.00
553 V:Black Mask 7.00
554 KJ,N:Black Canary 7.00
555 GC,DD,GreenArrow 7.00
556 GC,Gr.Arrow,V:Nightslayer . . . 7.00
557 V:Nightslayer 7.00
558 GC,Green Arrow 7.00
559 GC,Green Arrow 7.00
560 GC,A:Green Arrow 7.00
561 GC,Flying Hi 7.00
562 GC,V:Film Freak 7.00
563 V:Two Face 7.00
564 V:Two Face 7.00
565 GC,A:Catwoman 9.00
566 GC,Joker 10.00
567 GC,HarlanEllison 7.00
568 KJ,Legends tie-in,A:Penguin . . 9.00
569 AD,V:Joker 9.00
570 AD,EvilCatwoman,A:Joker 9.00
571 AD,V:Scarecrow 7.00
572 AD,CI,A:Elongated Man,Sherlock
   Holmes,SlamBradley,50thAnn. 10.00
573 AD,V:Mad Hatter 7.00
574 AD,End old J.Todd/Robin sty . . 7.00
575 AD,Year 2,pt.1,I:Reaper 25.00
576 TM,AA,Year 2,pt.2,
   R:Joe Chill 25.00
577 TM,AA,Year 2,pt.3,V:Reaper. . 25.00
578 TM,AA,Year 2,pt.4,
   D:Joe Chill 25.00
579 I:NewCrimeDoctor 6.00
580 V:Two Face 6.00
581 V:Two Face 6.00
582 Millennium X-over 6.00
583 I:Ventriloquist 6.00
584 V:Ventriloquist 6.00
585 I:Rat Catcher 6.00
586 V:Rat Catcher 6.00
587 NB,V:Corrosive Man 6.00
588 NB,V:Corrosive Man 6.00
589 Bonus Book #5 . . . . 6.00
590 NB,V:Hassan 6.00
591 NB,V:Rollo 6.00
592 V:Psychic Vampire 6.00
593 NB,V:Stirh 6.00
594 NB,A:Mr.Potato 6.00
595 IN,bonus book #11 . . . . 6.00
596 V:Sladek 6.00
597 V:Sladek 6.00
598 DCw,BSz,Blind Justice #1 . . 7.00
599 DCw,BSz,Blind Justice #2 . . 7.00
600 DCw,BSz,Blind Justice #3,
   50th Anniv.(double size) 7.00
601 NB,I:Tulpa 4.00
602 NB,A:Jason Blood 3.00
603 NB,A:Demon 3.00
604 NB,MudPack #1,V:Clayface,
   poster insert 3.00
605 NB,MudPack #2,V:Clayface . . 3.00
606 NB,MudPack #3,V:Clayface . . 3.00
607 NB,MudPack #4,V:Clayface,
   poster insert 3.00
608 NB,I:Anarky 3.00
609 NB,V:Anarky 3.00
610 NB,V:Penguin 4.00
611 NB,V:Catwoman,Catman 4.00
612 NB,A:Vicki Vale 3.00

Detective Comics #658
© *DC Comics, Inc.*

613 Search for Poisoner 3.00
614 V:Street Demons 3.00
615 NB,Return Penguin #2 (see
   Batman #448-#449) 3.50
616 NB 3.00
617 A:Joker 3.00
618 NB,DG,A:Tim Drake 3.00
619 NB,V:Moneyspider 3.00
620 NB,V:Obeah,Man 3.00
621 NB,SM,Obeah,Man. 3.00
622 Demon Within,pt.1 . . . . 3.00
623 Demon Within,pt.2 . . . . 3.00
624 Demon Within,pt.3 . . . . 3.00
625 JAp,I:Abattior 3.00
626 JAp,A:Electrocutioner 3.00
627 600th issue w/Batman,rep.
   Detective #27 . . . . 5.00
628 JAp,A:Abattoir 3.00
629 JAp,The Hungry Grass 3.00
630 JAp,I:Stiletto 3.00
631 JAp,V:Neo-Nazi Gangs 3.00
632 JAp,V:Creature 3.00
633 TMd,Fake Batman? 3.00
634 The Third Man 3.00
635 Video Game,pt.1 . . . . 3.00
636 Video Game,pt.2 . . . . 3.00
637 Video Game,pt.3 . . . . 3.00
638 JAp,Walking Time Bomb 3.00
639 JAp,The Idiot Root,pt.2 . . . . . . 3.00
640 JAp,The Idiot Root,pt.4 . . . . . . 3.00
641 JAp,Destroyer,pt.3
   (see LOTDK#27) 3.00
642 JAp,Faces,pt.2 . . . . 3.00
643 JAp,Librarian of Souls. 3.00
644 TL,Electric City,pt.1
   A:Electrocutioner 3.00
645 TL,Electric City,pt.2 . . . . 3.00
646 TL,Electric City,pt.3 . . . . 3.00
647 TL,V:Cluemaster,I:Spoiler 15.00
648 MWg(c),TL,V:Cluemaster 10.00
649 MWg(c),TL,V:Cluemaster 10.00
650 TL,A:Harold,Ace 3.00
651 TL,A Bullet for Bullock 3.00
652 GN,R:Huntress 3.00
653 GN,A:Huntress 3.00
654 MN,The General,pt.1 . . . . 3.00
655 MN,The General,pt.2 . . . . 3.00
656 MN,The General,pt.3,C:Bane . . 4.00
657 MN,A:Azrael,I:Cypher 5.00
658 MN,A:Azrael 3.50
659 MN,Knightfall#2,
   V:Ventriloquist,A:Bane 3.50
660 Knightfall#4,Bane Vs.
   Killer Croc 3.00

All comics prices listed are for *Near Mint* condition.

661 GN,Knightfall#6,V:Firefly,
  Joker,A:Bane 3.00
662 GN,Knightfall#8,V:Firefly,
  Joker,A:Huntress,Bane 3.00
663 GN,Knightfall#10,V:Trogg,
  Zombie,Bird,A:Bane 3.00
664 GN,Knightfall#12,A:Azrael 3.00
665 GN,Knightfall#16,A:Azrael 3.00
666 GN,SHa,A:Azrael,Trogg,
  Zombie,Bird 3.00
667 GN,SHa,Knightquest:Crusade,
  V:Trigger Twins 3.00
668 GN,SHa,Knightquest:Crusade,
  Robin locked out of Batcave . . . 3.00
669 GN,SHa,Knightquest:Crusade,
  V:Trigger Twins 3.00
670 GN,SHa,Knightquest:Crusade,
  F:Rene Montoya 3.00
671 GN,SHa,V:Joker 3.00
672 KJ(c),GN,SHa,Knightquest:
  Crusade,V:Joker 3.00
673 KJ(c),GN,SHa,Knightquest:
  Crusade,V:Joker 3.00
674 KJ(c),GN,SHa,Knightquest:
  Crusade 3.00
675 Foil(c),KJ(c),GN,SHa,Knightquest:
  Crusade,V:Gunhawk,foil(c) 4.00
675a Newsstand ed. 3.00
675b Platinum edition 5.00
676 KJ(c),GN,SHa,Knights End #3,
  A:Nightwing 4.00
677 KJ(c),GN,SHa,Knights End #9
  V:Azrael 3.00
678 GN,SHa,Zero Hour 3.00
679 Ratcatcher 3.00
680 Batman,Two-Face 3.00
681 CDi,GN,KJ,Jean-Paul Valley . . 3.00
682 CDi,GN,SHa,Return of Bruce
  Wayne,Troika,pt.3 . . . . 3.00
682a Collector's Edition 3.50
683 R:Penguin,I:Actuary 3.00
684 Daylight Heist 3.00
685 Chinatown War 3.00
686 V:King Snake,Lynx 3.00
687 CDi,SHa,V:River Pirate 3.00
688 V:Captian Fear 3.00
689 F:Black Mask,Firefly 3.00
690 F:Black Mask,Firefly 3.00
691 V:Spellbinder 3.00
692 CDi,SHa,Underworld
  Unleashed tie-in 3.00
693 CDi,SHa,V:Poison Ivy
  & Agent Orange 3.00
694 CDi,find plant-killer 3.00
695 CDi 3.00
696 CDi,GN,SHa,Contagion,pt.8 . . 3.00
697 CDi,GN,SHa,pt.1 (of 3)
  V:Lock-up 3.00
698 CDi(s),A:Two-Face 3.00
699 CDi(s), ... 3.00
700 double size, Legacy, pt.1
  x-over, R:Bane 3.50
700a cardstock cover 6.00
701 Legacy, pt. 6 x-over, V:Bane . . 3.00
702 CDi(s),GN,SHa,Legacy
  aftermath 3.00
703 CDi(s),GN,SHa, riots in Gotham
  City, Final Night tie-in 3.00
704 CDi(s),GN,TP,V:Al Gabone . . . 3.00
705 CDi(s),GN,Riddler & Cluemaster
  clash 3.00
706 CDi(s),GN 3.00
707 CDi(s),GN,Riddler/Cluemaster
  concl 3.00
708 CDi(s),GN,BSz,F:Deathstroke,
  R:Gunhawk,pt.1 (of 3) 3.00
709 CDi(s),GN,BSz,F:Deathstroke,
  Gunhawk,pt.2 . . . . 3.00
710 CDi(s),GN,BSz,F:Deathstroke,
  Gunhawk,pt.3 . . . . 3.00
711 CDi(s),GN,CaS,Bruce Wayne
  fights crime 3.00

Detective #803
© *DC Comics Inc.*

712 CDi(s),GN,I:Gearhead 3.00
713 CDi(s),GN,V:Gearhead,pt.2 . . . 3.00
714 CDi(s),GN,F:MartianManhunter 3.00
715 CDi(s),GN,F:MartianManhunter 3.00
716 CDi,JAp,SNw,BSf 3.00
717 CDi,GN,BSf,V:Gearhead,pt.1 . . 3.00
718 CDi,GN,BSf,V:Gearhead,pt.2 . . 3.00
719 CDi,JAp,BSz,Sound & Fury . . . 3.00
720 CDi,GN,KJ,Cataclysm
  x-over,pt.5 . . . . 4.00
721 CDi,GN,KJ,Cataclysm 3.00
722 CDi,JAp,BSf,Aftershock 3.00
723 CDi,BSz,Brotherhood of
  the Fist x-over, pt.2 . . . . 3.00
724 CDi,JAp,BSf,F:Nightwing 3.00
725 CDi,TP,BSf,Aftershock 3.00
726 CDi(s),BSf,V:Joker 3.00
727 CDi,SB,Road to No Man's Land 3.00
728 CDi(s),BSf,SB,No Man's Land . 3.00
729 CDi(s),SB,No Man's Land 3.00
730 No Law and a New Order,
  concl 5.00
731 F:Batgirl, Mosaic, pt.2 . . . . 3.00
732 F:Batgirl, Mosaic, pt.4 . . . . 3.00
733 SB,Alfreds advice 3.00
734 F:Batgirl,pt.2 x-over 3.00
735 DJu,BSz,Fruit of
  the Earth,pt.3 . . . . 3.00
736 LHa(s),MD2,V:Bane 3.00
737 TMo, No Man's Land,
  The Code, concl 3.00
738 CDi,MtB,Goin'Downtown,pt.2 . . 3.00
739 Jurisprudence,concl 3.00
740 Shellgame,pt.2 . . . . 3.00
741 Endgame, pt.3,40-pg.x-over . . . 3.00
742 SMa,40-pg 5.00
743 SMa,40-pg,new logo 3.00
744 SMa,40-pg 3.00
745 SMa,V:Whisperer 3.00
746 SMa,B.U.:The Jacobian 3.00
747 JJ,F:Renee Montoya 3.00
748 JJ,Urban Renewal,pt.1 . . . . 3.00
749 JJ,PhH,Urban Renewal,pt.2 . . . 3.00
750 V:Ra's Al Ghul,64-pg 6.00
751 SMa,JJ,DPS,F:Poison Ivy 4.00
752 SMa,JJ,DPs,F:Poison Ivy 3.00
753 SMa,JJ,DPs,This issue:
  Batman dies! 3.00
754 Officer Down x-over,pt.6 . . . . . . 3.00
755 SMa,DPs,V:Two-Face 3.00
756 Lord of the Ring x-over pt.2 . . . 3.00
757 RBr,RyR,DPs,Air Time 3.00
758 SMa,Crooked Cops in Gotham . 3.00
759 SMa,BU:Catwoman,pt.1 . . . . . . 3.00
760 SMa,V:Mad Hatter,BU:pt.2 . . . . 3.00

761 SMa,BU:Catwoman,pt.3 . . . . . . 3.00
762 RBr,BU:Catwoman,concl 3.00
763 SMa,F:Sasha,V:Cucilla 3.00
764 SMa,F:Vesper 3.00
765 RBr,James Gordon 3.00
766 Bruce Wayne:Murderer,pt.1 . . . 3.00
767 Bruce Wayne:Murderer,pt.8 . . . 5.00
768 MGy,shipment of heroin 3.00
769 Bruce Wayne:Fugitive,pt.5 . . . . 3.00
770 Bruce Wayne:Fugitive,pt.8 . . . . 3.00
771 BruceWayne:Fugitive,pt.12 . . . 3.00
772 BruceWayne:Fugitive,pt.16 . . . 2.75
773 F:Sasha Bordeaux in prison . . . 2.75
774 BSz(c),Checkmate 2.75
775 BSz(c),V:Checkmate 48-pg . . . 3.50
776 BWi,A cop's vendetta 3.00
777 Dead Reckoning,pt.1 . . . . 3.00
778 Dead Reckoning,pt.2 . . . . 3.00
779 Dead Reckoning,pt.3 . . . . 3.00
780 Dead Reckoning,pt.4 . . . . 3.00
781 Dead Reckoning,pt.5 . . . . 3.00
782 Dead Reckoning,pt.6 . . . . 3.00
783 SMa,KJ,More Perfect 3.00
784 Made of Wood,pt.1 . . . . 3.00
785 Made of Wood,pt.2 . . . . 3.00
786 Made of Wood,pt.3 . . . . 3.00
787 RBr,Low,Mad Hatter,Man-Bat . . 3.00
788 Randori Stone, pt.1 . . . . 3.00
789 Randori Stone, pt.2 . . . . 3.00
790 CaS,Scarification 3.00
791 CaS,The Surrogate,pt.1 . . . . . . 3.00
792 CaS,The Surrogate,pt.2 . . . . . . 3.00
793 CaS,The Surrogate,pt.3 . . . . . . 3.00
794 CaS,The Rotting,pt.1 . . . . 3.00
795 CaS,The Rotting,pt.2 . . . . 3.00
796 CaS,Mr.Zsasz 3.00
797 War Games,Act 1,pt.1,40-pg . . 3.00
798 War Games,Act 2,pt.1,40-pg . . 3.00
799 War Games,Act 3,pt.1,40-pg . . 3.00
800 DL,CaS,48-page 3.50
801 DL,NMa,City of Crime,pt.1 . . . . 3.00
802 DL,NMa,City of Crime,pt.2 . . . . 3.00
803 DL,NMa,City of Crime,pt.3 . . . . 3.00
804 DL,NMa,City of Crime,pt.4 . . . . 3.00
805 DL,NMa,City of Crime,pt.5 . . . . 3.00
806 DL,NMa,City of Crime,pt.6 . . . . 3.00
807 DL,NMa,City of Crime,pt.7 . . . . 3.00
808 DL,NMa,City of Crime,pt.8 . . . . 3.00
809 War Crimes, x-over, pt.1 . . . . . . 3.00
810 War Crimes, x-over, pt.3 . . . . . . 3.00
811 DL,NMa,City of Crime,pt.9 . . . . 3.00
812 DL,NMa,City of Crime,pt.10 . . . 3.00
813 DL,NMa,City of Crime, pt. 11 . . 3.00
814 DL,NMa,City of Crime,pt. 12 . . 3.00
815 Victims,pt.1 . . . . 3.00
816 Victims,pt.2 . . . . 3.00
817 Face the Face, pt.1, x-over 3.00
818 Face the Face, pt.3, x-over 3.00
819 Face the Face, pt.5, x-over 3.00
820 Face the Face, pt.7, x-over 3.00
821 PDi,JWi, V:Facade 3.00
822 PDi,JWi,F:The Riddler 3.00
823 PDi,F:Poison Ivy 3.00
824 PDi,Night of the Penguin 3.00
825 F:Doctor Phosphorous 3.00
826 PDi,V:Joker,A:Robin 3.00
827 PDi,V:New Ventriloquist 3.00
828 PDi,V:Sea monster 3.00
829 The Siege, pt.1 . . . . 3.00
830 The Siege, pt.2 . . . . 3.00
831 PDi,F:Harley Quinn 3.00
832 V:Terrible Trio 3.00
833 PDi,F:Zatanna, pt.1 . . . . 3.00
834 PDi,F:Zatanna, pt.2 . . . . 3.00
835 TMd,Scarecrow is Back, pt.1 . . 3.00
836 TMd,Scarecrow is Back, pt.2 . . 3.00
837 PDi,F:Harley Quinn & Riddler . . 3.00
838 Resurrection of Ra's Al Ghul . . 4.00
839 Resurrection of Ra's Al Ghul . . 3.00
840 V:The Globe 3.00
841 Scarface, Zatanna 3.00
842 Origins of suit of armor 3.00

843 F:Zatanna 3.00
844 F:Zatanna 3.00
845 Gruesome murders in Gotham . 3.00
846 Heart of Hush, pt.1 . . . . 3.00
847 Heart of Hush, pt.2 . . . . 3.00
848 Heart of Hush, pt.3 . . . . 3.00
849 Heart of Hush, pt.4 . . . . 3.00
850 Heart of Hush, pt.5 . . . . 4.00
Ann.#1 KJ,TD,A:Question,Talia,
   V:Penguin 6.00
Ann.#2 VS,A:Harvey Harris 6.00
Ann.#3 DJu,DG,Batman in Japan . . 3.00
Ann.#4 Armageddon,pt.10 . . . . 3.00
Ann.#5 SK(c),TMd,Eclipso,V:The
   Ventriloquist,Joker 3.00
Ann.#6 JBa,I:Geist 3.00
Ann.#7 CDi,Elseworlds Story 3.25
Ann.#8 CDi,KD(c) Year One Annual
   O:The Riddler 4.00
Ann.#9 Legends o/t Dead Earth . . . 3.00
Ann.#10 Pulp Heroes (War) CDi(s),
   SB,KJ. 4.00
Spec.#1,000,000 CDi(s). 3.00

DETENTION COMICS
Aug., 1996
one-shot DON(s) 64pg, 3 stories. . . 3.50

DEXTER'S LABORATORY
Warner Bros./DC, 1999
1 Kirbytron 6000 . . . . 5.00
2 Let's Save the World, You Jerk . . 4.00
3 thru 10 . . . . @3.00
11 thru 24 . . . . @2.50
25 thru 34 . . . . @2.50

DISAVOWED
Homage/DC Jan., 2000
1 BCi. 2.50
2 thru 6 BCi(s). . . . . @2.50

DMZ
DC/Vertigo, Nov., 2005
1 by Brian Wood 3.00
2 Through War-torn Manhattan . . . 3.00
3 Matty captured by Gov. Army . . . 3.00
4 In Central Park. 3.00
5 Interview with tribal boss 3.00
6 Body of a Journalist, pt.1. . . . . . . 3.00
7 Body of a Journalist, pt.2. . . . . . . 3.00
8 Body of a Journalist, pt.3. . . . . . . 3.00
9 Body of a Journalist, pt.4. . . . . . . 3.00
10 Body of a Journalist, pt.5 . . . . . 3.00
11 Origin of Zee 3.00
12 A Guide to the DMZ 3.00
13 Public Works, pt.1. . . . . 3.00
14 Public Works, pt.2. . . . . 3.00
15 Public Works, pt.3. . . . . 3.00
16 Public Works, pt.4. . . . . 3.00
17 Public Works, pt.5. . . . . 3.00
18 Friendly Fire, pt.1 . . . . 3.00
19 Friendly Fire, pt.2 . . . . 3.00
20 Friendly Fire, pt.3 . . . . 3.00
21 Friendly Fire, pt.4 . . . . 3.00
22 Friendly Fire, pt.5 . . . . 3.00
23 The Hidden War 3.00
24 The Hidden War 3.00
25 The Hidden War 3.00
26 Matty and Zee. 3.00
27 Random Fire 3.00
28 Soames the eco-warrior 3.00
29 Blood in the Game, pt.1 . . . . . . 3.00
30 Blood in the Game, pt.2 . . . . . . 3.00
31 Blood in the Game, pt.3 . . . . . . 3.00
32 Blood in the Game, pt.4 . . . . . . 3.00
33 Blood in the Game, pt.5 . . . . . . 3.00
34 Blood in the Game, pt.6 . . . . . . 3.00
35 The Island, pt.1 . . . . 3.00
36 The Island, pt.2 . . . . 3.50

DOC SAVAGE
1987–88
1 AKu/NKu,D:Orig. Doc Savage . . . 3.00
2 AKu/NKu,V:Nazi's 3.00
3 AKu/NKu,V:Nazi's 3.00
4 AKu/NKu,V:Heinz 3.00

[2nd Series], 1988–90
1 Five in the Sky'(painted cov.) . . . 3.00
2 Chip Lost in Himalayas 3.00
3 Doc declares war on USSR. 3.00
4 Doc Savage/Russian team-up . . . 3.00
5 V:The Erisians 3.00
6 U.S.,USSR,China Alliance
   vs. Erisians 3.00
7 Mind Molder,pt.1, I:Pat Savage . 3.00
8 . . . . 3.00
9 In Hidalgo. 3.00
10 V:Forces of the Golden God. . . . 3.00
11 Sunlight Rising,pt.1 . . . . 3.00
12 Sunlight Rising,pt.2 . . . . 3.00
13 Sunlight Rising,pt.3 . . . . 3.00
14 Sunlight Rising,pt.4 . . . . 3.00
15 SeaBaron #1 . . . . 3.00
16 EB,Shadow & Doc Savage 3.50
17 EB,Shadow & Doc Savage 4.00
18 EB,Shadow/Doc Savage conc . . 4.00
19 All new 1930's story 3.00
20 V:Airlord & his Black Zepplin . . . 3.00
21 Airlord (30's story conc.) 3.00
22 Doc Savages Past,pt.1 . . . . 3.00
23 Doc Savages Past,pt.2 . . . . 3.00
24 Doc Savages Past,pt.3 (final) . . . 3.00
Ann.#1 1956 Olympic Games 4.50

DOCTOR FATE
July, 1987
1 KG,V:Lords of Chaos 3.00
2 KG,New Dr. Fate 3.00
3 KG,A:JLI 3.00
4 KG,V:Lords of Chaos Champion . 3.00

[2nd Series], 1988–92
1 New Dr.Fate,V:Demons 4.00
2 A:Andrew Bennett(I,Vampire) . . . 3.00
3 A:Andrew Bennett(I,Vampire) . . . 3.00
4 V:I,Vampire 3.00
5 Dr.Fate & I,Vampire in Europe. . . 3.00
6 A:Petey 3.00
7 Petey returns home dimension . . 3.00
8 Linda become Dr.Fate again 3.00
9 Eric's Mother's Ghost,
   A:Deadman 3.00
10 Death of Innocence,pt.1 . . . . . . 3.00
11 Return of Darkseid, Death of
   Innocence,pt.2 . . . . 3.00
12 Two Dr.Fates Vs.Darkseid,
   Death of Innocence,pt.3 . . . . . . 3.00
13 Linda in the Astral Realm,
   Death of Innocence,pt.4 . . . . . . 3.00
14 Kent & Petey vs. Wotan 3.00
15 V:Wotan,A:JLI 3.50
16 Flashback-novice Dr.Fate 2.50
17 Eric's Journey thru afterlife 2.50
18 Search for Eric 2.50
19 A:Dr.Benjamine Stoner, Lords of
   Chaos, Phantom Stranger,
   Search for Eric continued 2.50
20 V:Lords of Chaos,Dr.Stoner,
   A:Phantom Stranger 2.50
21 V:Chaos,A:PhantomStranger . . . 2.50
22 A:Chaos and Order. 2.50
23 Spirits of Kent & Inza Nelson . . . 2.50
24 L:Dr.Fate Characters 2.50
25 I:New Dr. Fate 2.50
26 Dr.Fate vs. Orig.Dr.Fate 2.50
27 New York Crime 2.50
28 Diabolism 2.50
29 Kent Nelson 2.50
30 Resurrection 2.50
31 Resurrection' contd. 2.50
32 War of the Gods x-over 2.50

33 War of the Gods x-over 2.50
34 A:T'Gilian. 2.50
35 Kent Nelson in N.Y. 2.50
36 Search For Inza,A:Shat-Ru. 2.50
37 Fate Helmet Powers revealed . . 2.50
38 The Spirit Motor,'Flashback 2.50
39 U.S.Senate Hearing 2.50
40 A:Wonder Woman. 2.50
41 O:Chaos and Order,last issue . . 2.50
Ann.#1 TS,R:Eric's dead mother . . . 3.00

DR. FATE
Aug. 2003
1 (of 5) Hector Hall 2.50
2 Salem mystics 2.50
3 Nabu disappeared 2.50
4 The Curse 2.50
5 Concl. 2.50

DOCTOR FATE
Apr., 2007
1 PG, Helmet of Fate 3.00
1a variant (c) (1:10) 3.00
2 The Accidental Sorcerer 3.00

DOCTOR MID-NITE
1999
1 thru 3 (of 3) MWg,F:Dr. Piter
   Cross . . . . @6.00

DOOM FORCE
1992
Spec.#1 MMi(c),RCa,WS,PCu,KSy,
   I:Doom Force. 3.00

DOOM PATROL
[1st series]
See: MY GREATEST
ADVENTURE

DOOM PATROL
[2nd Regular Series], 1987
1 SLi,R:Doom Patrol,plus Who's Who
   background of team, I:Kalki. . . . 5.00
2 SLi,V:Kalki 3.50
3 SLi,I:Lodestone 3.50
4 SLi,I:Karma 3.50
5 SLi,R:Chief. 3.50
6 B:PuK(s),EL,GyM(i),
   I:Scott Fischer 4.50
7 EL,GyM(i),V:Shrapnel 3.50
8 EL,GyM(i),V:Shrapnel 3.50

Doom Patrol #14 © DC Comics, Inc.

DC COMICS

9 E:PuK(s),EL,GyM(i),V:Garguax,
   & Bonus Book 3.50
10 EL,A:Superman. 3.50
11 EL,R:Garguax 3.00
12 EL,A:Garguax 3.00
13 EL,A:Power Girl 3.00
14 EL,A:Power Girl 3.00
15 EL,Animal-Veg-.Mineral Man . . . 3.00
16 V:GenImmotus,Animal-Veg.-
   Mineral Man. 3.00
17 D:Celsius,A:Aquaman & Sea
   Devils, Invasion tie-in 4.00
18 Invasion. 3.00
19 B:GMo(s),New Direction,
   I:Crazy Jane 8.00
20 I:Rebis(new Negative-Being),
   A:CrazyJane,Scissormen 7.00
21 V:Scissormen 7.00
22 City of Bone,V:Scissormen 7.00
23 A:RedJack,Lodestone kidnap . . . 5.00
24 V:Red Jack 5.00
25 Secrets of New Doom Patrol . . . 5.00
26 I:Brotherhood of Dada 5.00
27 V:Brotherhood of Dada 5.00
28 Trapped in nightmare,V:Dada . . . 5.00
29 Trapped in painting,
   A:Superman. 5.00
30 SBs(s),V:Brotherhood of Dada . . 5.00
31 SBs(c),A:The Pale Police 4.00
32 SBs(c),V:Cult of
   Unwritten Book 4.00
33 SBs(c),V:Cult,A:Anti-God
   the DeCreator 4.00
34 SBs(c),Robotman vs. his brain,
   R:The Brain & Mr.Mallah 4.00
35 SBs(c),A:Men from
   N.O.W.H.E.R.E. 15.00
36 SBs(c),V:Men from
   N.O.W.H.E.R.E. 9.00
37 SBs(c),Rhea Jones Story 4.00
38 SBs(c),V:Aliens 4.00
39 SBs(c),V:Aliens 4.00
40 SBs(c),Aliens 4.00
41 SBS(c),Aliens 4.00
42 O:Flex Mentallo. 6.00
43 SBs(c),V:N.O.W.H.E.R.E. 5.00
44 SBs(c),V:N.O.W.H.E.R.E. 5.00
45 SBs(c),The Beard Hunter 4.00
46 SBs(c),RCa,MkK,A:Crazy Jane,
   Dr.Silence 4.00
47 Scarlet Harlot (Crazy Jane) 4.00
48 V:Mr.Evans 4.00
49 TTg(c),RCa,MGb,I:Mr.Nobody . . 4.00
50 SBs(c),V:Brotherhood of Dada
   & bonus artists portfolio. 4.00
51 SBs(c),Mr.Nobody Runs for
   President 4.00
52 SBs(c),Mr.Nobody saga conc . . . 4.00
53 SBs(c),Parody Issue,A:Phantom
   Stranger,Hellblazer,Mr.E 4.00
54 Rebis Transformation 4.00
55 SBs(c),V:Crazy Jane,
   Candle Maker 4.00
56 SBs(c),RCa,V:Candle Maker . . . 4.00
57 SBs(c),RCa,V:Candle Maker,
   O:Team,Double-sized 4.00
58 SBs(c),V:Candle Maker 4.00
59 TTg(c),RCa,SnW(i),A:Candlemaker
   D:Larry Trainor 4.00
60 JHw(c),RCa,SnW(i),
   V:Candlemaker,A:Magnus 4.00
61 TTg(c),RCa,SnW(i),A:Magnus
   D:Candlemaker 4.00
62 DFg(c),RCa,SnW(i),
   V:Nanomachines 4.00
63 E:GMo(s),RCa,R:Crazy Jane,
   V:Keysmiths,BU:Sliding from the
   Wreckage 4.00

DC/Vertigo, 1993
64 BB(c),B:RaP(s),RCa,SnW(i),
   B:Sliding from the Wreckage,
   R:Niles Caulder 3.00

65 TTg(c),RCa,SnW(i),Nannos 3.00
66 RCa,E:Sliding from the
   Wreckage 3.00
67 TTg(c),LiM,GHi(i),New HQ,I:Charlie,
   George,Marion,V:Wild Girl. 3.00
68 TTg(c),LiM,GHi(i),I:Indentity
   Addict. 3.00
69 TTg(c),LiM,GHi(i),V:Identity
   Addict. 3.00
70 TTg(c),SEa,TS(i),I:Coagula,
   V:Codpiece 3.00
71 TTg(c),LiM,TS(i),Fox & Crow . . . 3.00
72 TTg(c),LiM,TS(i),Fox vs Crow . . . 3.00
73 LiM,GPi(i),Head's Nightmare . . . 3.00
74 LiM,TS(i),Bootleg Steele 3.00
75 BB(c),TMK,Teiresias Wars#1,
   Double size 3.00
76 Teiresias Wars#2 . . . . 3.00
77 BB(c),TMK,N:Cliff 3.00
78 BB(c),V:Tower of Babel. 3.00
79 BB(c),E:Teiresias Wars 3.00
80 V:Yapping Dogs 3.00
81 B:Masquerade. 3.00
82 E:Masquerade. 3.00
83 False Memory 3.00
84 The Healers 3.00
85 Charlie the Doll 3.00
86 Imagine Ari's Friends 3.00
87 KB(c),final issue 3.00
Ann.#1 A:Lex Luthor 3.00
Ann.#2 RaP(s),MkW,Children's
   Crusade,F:Dorothy,A:Maxine . . 4.25
Doom Patrol/Suicide Squad #1 EL,
   D:Mr.104,Thinker,Psi,Weasel . . 3.00

Oct., 2001
1 JAr,R:Doom Patrol. 3.00
2 JAr,F:Robotman, Thayer 3.75
3 JAr,V:Gomz 2.50
4 JAr,new Doom Patrol?. 2.50
5 JAr,Doom Force. 2.50
6 JAr,Robotman gone. 2.50
7 JAr,search for Robotman. 2.50
8 JAr,new Robotman 2.50
9 JAr,Cliff Steele, Robotman. 2.50
10 JAr,Black Vulture,Amazo 2.50
11 JAr,in Hell 2.50
12 JAr,V:Demon Raum 2.50
13 JAr(s),Monsters,pt.1 . . . . 2.50
14 JAr(s),Monsters,pt.2 . . . . 2.50
15 JAr(s),F:Robotman 2.50
16 JAr(s),V:Purple Purposeless. . . . 2.50
17 JAr(s),R:Tycho 2.50
18 JAr(s),ancient China 2.50
19 JAr(s),R:Tycho 2.50
20 television studios 2.50
21 O:Tycho. 2.50
22 final issue 2.50

July 2004
1 JBy,DHz,V:Crucifer 2.50
2 JBy,DHz,escaped specimens . . . 2.50
3 JBy,DHz,Cold Night's Death 2.50
4 JBy,DHz,Waters Under World . . . 2.50
5 JBy,DHz 2.50
6 JBy,DHz,Robot Wars,pt.2 . . . . . . 2.50
7 JBy,DHz,V:Devolutionists,pt.1 . . . 2.50
8 JBy,DHz,V:Devolutionists,pt.2 . . . 2.50
9 JBy,DHz,V:Negative Man. 2.50
10 JBy,DHz,F:Metamorpho 2.50
11 JBy,DHz,F:Metamorpho 2.50
12 JBy,DHz,F:Metamorpho 2.50
13 JBy,DHz,time travel technology . 2.50
14 JBy,TA,alternate realities 2.50
15 JBy,DHz,hospital patients dead . 2.50
16 JBy,DHz,F:Nudge 2.50
17 JBy,DHz,Negative Man. 2.50
18 JBy,DHz,final issue 2.50

DOOMSDAY
1995
Ann.#1 Year One annuals 4.00

DOORWAY TO NIGHTMARE
1978
1 I:Madame Xanadu 20.00
2 thru 5 . . . . @15.00

DOUBLE ACTION COMICS
Jan., 1940
2 Pre-Hero DC. 27,000.00

DRAGONLANCE
1988–91
1 Krynn's Companion's advent. . . . 4.00
2 thru 7 . . . . @3.50
8 thru 34 . . . . @3.00
Ann.#1 Myrella of the Robed
   Wizards 3.00

DREAMING, THE
DC/Vertigo, June, 1996
1 TLa(s),PSj,GoldieFactor,pt.1 . . . . 4.50
2 TLa(s),PSj,GoldieFactor,pt.2 . . . . 4.00
3 TLa(s),PSj,GoldieFactor,pt.3 . . . . 4.00
4 SvP,The Lost Boy,pt.1 . . . . 3.50
5 SvP,The Lost Boy,pt.2 . . . . 2.50
6 SvP,The Lost Boy,pt.3 . . . . 2.50
7 SvP,The Lost Boy,pt.4 . . . . 2.50
8 AaK(s),MZi,visitor from past 2.50
9 BT(s),PD,TOz,Weird Romance,
   pt.1. . . . . 2.50
10 BT(s),PD,TOz,Romance,pt.2 . . . 2.50
11 BT(s),PD,TOz,Romance,pt.3 . . . 2.50
12 BT(s),PD,TOz,Romance,pt.4 . . . 2.50
13 TLa,JIT,Coyote's Kiss,pt.1. . . . . . 2.50
14 TLa,JIT,Coyote's Kiss,pt.2. . . . . . 2.50
15 . . . . 2.50
16 GyA,F:Nuala 2.50
17 PD,DMc,Souvenirs, pt.1 . . . . 2.50
18 PD,DMc,Souvenirs, pt.2 . . . . 2.50
19 PD,DMc,Souvenirs, pt.3 . . . . 2.50
20 ADv, The Dark Rose, pt.1. . . . . . 2.50
21 ADv, The Dark Rose, pt.2. . . . . . 2.50
22 The Unkindness of One,pt.1 . . . 2.50
23 The Unkindness of One, pt.2 . . . 2.50
24 The Unkindness of One, pt.3 . . . 2.50
25 My Life as a Man 2.50
26 Restitution. 2.50
27 Caretaker Cain 2.50
28 Victims of famous fires 2.50
29 PSj,DMc,Abel'sHouse ofSecrets. 2.50

Dreaming #44
© DC Comics, Inc.

30 DMc(c),Lucien's mysteries 2.50
31 House of Secrets, 48-pg. 4.00
32 DG,SvP 2.50
33 The Little Mermaid 2.50
34 MaH, Cave of Nightmares 2.50
35 DMc(c),Kaleidoscope 2.50
36 DMc(c),The Gyres, pt.1 . . . . 2.50
37 DMc(c),The Gyres, pt.2 . . . . 2.50
38 DMc(c),The Gyres, pt.3 . . . . 2.50
39 DMc(c),Lost Language
　of Flowers 2.50
40 DMc(c),Foxes & Hounds,pt.1 . . . 2.50
41 DMc(c),Foxes & Hounds,pt.2 . . . 2.50
42 DMc(c),Foxes & Hounds,pt.3 . . . 2.50
43 DMc(c),Foxes & Hounds,pt.4 . . . 2.50
44 Trinket,pt.1 . . . . 2.50
45 Trinket,pt.2 . . . . 2.50
46 Trinket,pt.3 . . . . 2.50
47 CV,RoR 2.50
48 DMc(c),Scary Monsters 2.50
49 DMc(c),The Dawn Stone 2.50
50 DMc(c),rebuilding 2.50
51 DMc(c),in Manhattan 2.50
52 Exiles,pt.1 . . . . 2.50
53 Exiles,pt.2 . . . . 2.50
54 Exiles,pt.3 . . . . 2.50
55 F:Danny Nod 2.50
56 1stAdventure of CatterinaPoe . . . 2.50
57 Rise,pt.1 . . . . 2.50
58 Rise,pt.2 . . . . 2.50
59 Rise,pt.3 . . . . 2.50
60 Rise,pt.4 . . . . 2.50

DYNAMIC CLASSICS
Sept-Oct., 1978
1 NA,WS,rep.Detective 395&438 . 15.00

ECLIPSO
1992–94
1 BS,MPn,V:South American
　Drug Dealers 2.50
2 BS,MPn,A:Bruce Gordon 2.50
3 BS,MPn,R:Amanda Waller 2.50
4 BS,A:Creeper,Cave Carson 2.50
5 A:Creeper,Cave Carson 2.50
6 LMc,V:Bruce Gordon 2.50
7 London,1891 . . . . 2.50
8 A:Sherlock Holmes 2.50
9 I:Johnny Peril 2.50
10 CDo,V:Darkseid 2.50
11 A:Creeper,Peacemaker,Steel . . . 2.50
12 V:Shadow Fighters 2.50
13 D:Manhunter,Commander Steel,
　Major Victory,Peacemaker,
　Wildcat,Dr.Midnight,Creeper . . . 2.50
14 A:JLA. 2.50
15 A:Amanda Waller 2.50
16 V:US Army 2.50
17 A:Amanda Waller,Martian
　Manhunter,Wonder Woman,Flash,
　Bloodwynd,Booster Gold . . 2.50
18 A:Spectre,JLA,final issue 2.50
Ann.#1 I:Prism 2.50

ECLIPSO: THE DARKNESS WITHIN
1992
1 BS,Direct w/purple diamond,
　A:Superman,Creeper. 4.00
1a BS,Newstand w/out diamond . . 3.00
2 BS,MPn,DC heroes V:Eclipso,
　D:Starman 3.00

EGYPT
1995–96
1 College Experiments 3.50
2 thru 7 . . . . @3.00

80 PAGE GIANTS
Aug., 1964
1 Superman 800.00
2 Jimmy Olsen 450.00
3 Lois Lane 325.00
4 Golden Age-Flash 325.00
5 Batman 325.00
6 Superman 400.00
7 JKu&JKu(c),Sgt. Rock's Prize
　Battle Tales 400.00
8 Secret Origins,O:JLA,Aquaman,
　Robin,Atom, Superman 650.00
9 Flash 300.00
10 Superboy. 600.00
11 Superman,A:Lex Luthor 400.00
12 Batman 350.00
13 Jimmy Olsen 250.00
14 Lois Lane 250.00
15 Superman & Batman 250.00
16 thru 89 in regular series runs

EL DIABLO
1989–91
1 I:El Diablo, double-size 3.00
2 thru 16 . . . . @2.50

DC/Vertigo, Jan., 2001
1 thru 4 Weird Western Tales . . . @2.50

Sept., 2008
1 (of 6) The Haunted Horseman . . . 3.00
2 thru 3 . . . . @3.00

ELECTRIC WARRIOR
1986–87
1 SF series,I:Electric Warriors 2.50
2 thru 18 . . . . @2.50

ELFQUEST
DC 2003
Spec. WP,RPi,25th Anniversary Edition
　rep. Elfquest #1 . . . . 3.00

ELFQUEST: THE DISCOVERY
Jan., 2006
1 thru 4 RPi,WP, F:Sunbeam 24.00

ELONGATED MAN
1992
1 A:Copperhead 2.50
2 Modora,A:Flash,I:Sonar. 2.50
3 A:Flash,V:Wurst Gang 2.50

Elongated Man #1 © DC Comics, Inc.

ELRIC: THE MAKING OF A SORCERER
Sept. 2004
1 (of 4) WS, from M.Moorcock 6.00
2 thru 4 WS . . . . @6.00

ELSEWORLD'S FINEST
DC/Elseworlds 1998
1 (of 2) JFM,KD,F:Bruce Wayne
　and Clark Kent 5.00
2 JFM,KD,concl. 5.00
GN Supergirl & Batgirl 6.00

ELVIRA
1986–87
1 DSp,BB(c) 5.00
2 thru 10 . . . . @4.00
11 DSt(c)Find Cain. 5.00

EMPIRE
June 2003
0 JmP,from Gorilla Comics 5.00
1 thru 6 BKi ,ImP . . . . @2.50

ENEMY ACE: WAR IN HEAVEN
March, 2001
1 (of 2) GEn, 48-page. 6.00
2 GEn,48-page 6.00

ENGINEHEAD
April 2004
1 (of 8) TMK,six heroes in one 2.50
2 thru 6 TMK,why am I here? . . . @2.50

ENIGMA
DC/Vertigo, 1993
1 B:PrM(s),DFg,I:Enigma,Michael
　Smith,V:The Head 3.00
2 DFg,I:The Truth 3.00
3 DFg,V:The Truth,I:Envelope Girl,
　Titus Bird 3.00
4 DFg,D:The Truth,I:Interior
　League. 3.00
5 DFg,I:Enigma's Mother 3.00
6 DFg,V:Envelope Girl 3.00
7 DFg,V:Enigma's Mother,D:Envelope
　Girl,O:Enigma 3.00
8 E:PrM(s),DFg,final issue 3.00

ERADICATOR
1996
1 IV,Low. 2.50
2 IV,Low. 2.50
3 IV,Low,Reign of the Superman
　concl.,A:Superboy 2.50

ESSENTIAL VERTIGO:

SWAMP THING
DC/Vertigo, Sept., 1996
B&W reprints
1 AMo(s), rep. Saga of
　the Swamp Thing #21. . . . . 3.00
2 thru 11 AMo(s), rep. Saga of
　the Swamp Thing #22–#31. . @3.00
12 AMo(s) rep. Saga Ann. #2 . . . . 3.00
13 AMo(s) rep. Saga #32–#42 . . @3.00
24 AMo,Windfall, final issue. 3.00

... THE SANDMAN
DC/Vertigo, 1996
3 NGa(s),SK,MDr,rep. 3.00
4 NGa(s),SK,MDr,rep. F:Etrigan . . 3.00
5 NGa(s),SK,MJ,F:Morpheus,
　John Dee. 3.00

6 NGa(s),SK,MJ,V:Dr. Destiny 3.00
7 . . . . 3.00
8 NGa(s),MDr,MJ,The Sound
   of Her Wings 3.00
9 NGa(s),MDr,MJ,The Doll's
   House, F:Nada 3.00
10 NGa(s),MDr,MJ,Doll's House . . . 3.00
11 NGa(s),MDr,RT 3.00
12 NGa(s),CBa,MJ,Doll'sHouse . . . 3.00
13 NGa,rep.Doll's House,pt.4 . . . . . 3.00
14 NGa,rep.Doll's House,pt.5 . . . . . 3.50
15 NGa,rep.Doll's House,pt.6 . . . . . 3.00
16 NGa,rep.Lost Hearts. 3.00
17 NGa,rep.Dream Country. 3.00
18 NGa,Dream of Thousand Cats . . 3.00
19 NGa,rep.Sandman #19 . . . . 3.00
20 NGa,rep.Sandman #20. . . . . 3.00
21 NGa,rep.Sandman #21. . . . . 3.00
22 NGa,rep.Season of Mists pt.1 . . 3.00
23 NGa,rep.Season of Mists pt.2 . . 3.00
24 NGa,rep.Season of Mists pt.3 . . 3.00
25 NGa,rep.Season of Mists pt.4 . . 3.00
26 NGa,rep.Season of Mists pt.5 . . 3.00
27 NGa,rep.Season of Mists,pt.6. . . 3.00
28 NGa,rep.Season of Mists,epilog. 3.00
29 NGa,rep.Thermidor. 3.00
30 NGa,rep.August 3.00
31 NGa,rep.Three Septembers
   and a January 3.00
32 NGa,rep. Sandman Special #1
   final issue 4.50

EVERYTHING HAPPENS TO HARVEY
1953–54
1 Teen-age humor. 350.00
2 . . . . 175.00
3 thru 7 . . . . @150.00

EXTERMINATORS, THE
DC/Vertigo, Jan., 2006
1 F:Henry James 3.00
2 Bug Brothers, pt.2 . . . . 3.00
3 Bug Brothers, pt.3 . . . . 3.00
4 Bug Brothers, pt.4 . . . . 3.00
5 Bug Brothers, pt.5 . . . . 3.00
6 Insurgency, pt.1 . . . . 3.00
7 Insurgency, pt.2 . . . . 3.00
8 Two Girlfriends. 3.00
9 Insurgency, pt.3 . . . . 3.00
10 Insurgency,pt.4 . . . . 3.00
11 Brother #38, pt.1 . . . . 3.00
12 Brother #38, pt.2 . . . . 3.00
13 Lies of our Fathers, pt.1 . . . . 3.00
14 Lies of our Fathers, pt.2 . . . . 3.00
15 Lies of our Fathers, pt.3 . . . . 3.00
16 Lies of our Fathers, pt.4 . . . . 3.00
17 Showdown at Scatshot, pt.1 . . . 3.00
18 Showdown at Scatshot, pt.2 . . . 3.00
19 Crossfire and Collateral, pt.1 . . . 3.00
20 Crossfire and Collateral, pt.2 . . . 3.00
21 Crossfire and Collateral, pt.3 . . . 3.00
22 Crossfire and Collateral, pt.4 . . . 3.00
23 Crossfire and Collateral,concl. . . 3.00
24 On the Cruise Ship 3.00
25 A.J.s Return 3.00
26 F:Laura 3.00
27 Raising Che 3.00
28 Bug Brothers Forever, pt.1 . . . . 3.00
29 Bug Brothers Forever, pt.2 . . . . . 3.00
30 final issue 3.00

EXTREME JUSTICE
1995–96
O New Group 3.50
1 . . . . 3.00
2 thru 17 . . . . @3.00

EXTREMIST
DC/Vertigo, 1993
1 B:PrM(s),TMK,I:The Order,
   Extremist(Judy Tanner) 2.50
1a Platinum Ed. 5.00
2 TMK,D:Extremist(Jack Tanner) . . 2.25
3 TMK,V:Patrick 2.25
4 E:PrM(s),TMK,D:Tony Murphy. . . 2.25

FABLES
DC/Vertigo, May, 2002
1 SL, Legends in Exile,pt.1. . . . . 20.00
1a variant (c). 20.00
2 SL, Legends in Exile,pt.2. . . . . 15.00
3 SL, Legends in Exile,pt.3. . . . . . 8.00
4 BWg,Legends in Exile,pt.4 . . . . . 7.00
5 SL, Legends in Exile,pt.5. . . . . . 7.00
6 MBu,SL,Animal Farm,pt.1 . . . . . 7.00
7 MBu,SL,Animal Farm,pt.2 . . . . . 4.00
8 MBu,SL,Animal Farm,pt.3 . . . . . 4.00
9 MBu,SL,Animal Farm,pt.4 . . . . . 4.00
10 MBu,SL,Animal Farm,pt.5. . . . . 4.00
11 Jack of the Tales 4.00
12 Fables caper,pt.1 . . . . 4.00
13 Fables caper,pt.2 . . . . 3.00
14 Storybook Love,pt.1 . . . . 3.00
15 Storybook Love,pt.2 . . . . 3.00
16 Storybook Love,pt.3 . . . . 3.00
17 Storybook Love,pt.4 . . . . 3.00
18 The Barley Corn Brides 2.50
19 MBu,SL. 2.50
20 MBu,SL. 2.50
21 MBu,SL. 2.50
22 JP,Ex-wives Club 2.50
23 MBu,SL. 2.50
24 MBu,SL,Boy Blue missing 2.50
25 MBu,SL,Wooden Soldiers. 2.50
26 MBu,SL,Wooden Soldiers. 2.50
27 MBu,SL,Wooden Soldiers. 2.50
28 JP,War Stories,pt.1 . . . . 2.50
29 JP,War Stories,pt.2 . . . . 2.50
30 MBu,SL,The Year After,pt.1 . . . 2.50
31 MBu,SL,The Year After 2.50
32 MBu,SL,The Year After 2.50
33 MBu,SL,The Year After,concl. . . 2.50
34 Jack be Nimble, pt.1 . . . . 2.50
35 Jack be Nimble, pt.2 . . . . 2.50
36 Return to the Homelands,pt.1. . . 2.50
37 Return to the Homelands,pt.2. . . 2.50
38 Return to the Homelands,pt.3. . . 2.50
39 Fabletown 2.50
40 Return to the Homelands,pt.4. . . 3.00
41 Return to the Homelands,pt.5. . . 2.75
42 Arabian Nights & Days 2.75
43 Arabian Nights & Days 2.75
44 Arabian Nights & Days 2.75
45 Arabian Nights & Days 2.75
46 Ballad of Rodney and June 2.75
47 Ballad of Rodney and June 2.75
48 Wolves, pt.1 . . . . 2.75
49 Wolves, pt.2 . . . . 3.00
50 64-pg. 4.00
51 in Smalltown 3.00
52 Sons of the Empire,pt.1 . . . . . . 3.00
53 Sons of the Empire,pt.2 . . . . . . 3.00
54 Sons of the Empire,pt.3 . . . . . . 3.00
55 Sons of the Empire,pt.4 . . . . . . 3.00
56 MBu,X-mas special. 3.50
57 MiA,Father and Son, pt.1 . . . . . 3.00
58 MiA,Father and Son, pt.2 . . . . . 3.00
59 Burning questions answered . . . 3.00
60 The Good Prince, pt.1 . . . . 3.00
61 The Good Prince, pt.2 . . . . 3.00
62 The Good Prince, pt.3 . . . . 3.00
63 The Good Prince, pt.4 . . . . 3.00
64 The Farm 3.00
65 The Magic Mirror. 3.00
66 Homecoming. 3.00
67 The Good Prince. 3.00
68 The Good Prince, pt.8 . . . . 3.00
69 The Good Prince, pt.9 . . . . 3.00

70 Boy Blue, dilemma 3.00
71 Skullduggery, pt.1 . . . . 3.00
72 Skullduggery, pt.2 . . . . 3.00
73 The War begins. 3.00
74 The War Escalates 3.00
75 Someone dies, 64-pg. 5.00
76 . . . . 3.00
77 Life in a Headless Empire. 3.00
78 Life in a Headless Empire. 3.50
Spec. The Last Castle 6.00
Spec. Reprint of #1 (2006). 2.50

FAKER
Vertigo, July, 2007
1 (of 6) MCy 3.00
2 thru 6 MCy . . . . @3.00

FALLEN ANGEL
July 2003
1 PDd(s),Bete Noire 2.50
2 thru 9 PDd(s). . . . . @2.50
10 PDd(s),F:Black Mariah 3.00
11 thru 16 PDd(s). . . . . @2.50
17 thru 20 PDd(s). . . . . @3.00

FAMILY DYNAMIC
Aug., 2008
1 thru 3 (of 3) . . . . @2.50

FAMILY MAN
Paradox 1995
1 I:Family Man 5.50
2 V:Brother Charles 5.50
3 Escape. 5.50

FANBOY
1999
1 (of 6) SA, various artists 2.50
2 A:Hal Jordan 2.50
3 A:JLA 2.50
4 SA, A:Sgt. Rock 2.50
5 SA, A:Batman 2.50
6 SA, A:Wonder Woman, concl. . . . 2.50

FATE
1994–96
0 . . . . 3.00
1 Dr. Fate 2.50
2 Nabu,Astral plane 2.50
3 Bloodstain 2.50
4 Decisions 2.50
5 Judged by Enclave 2.50

Fanboy #2
© DC Comics, Inc.

6 V:Grimoire 2.50
7 V:Dark Agent 2.50
8 V:Dark Agent 2.50
9 Tries to change his destiny 2.50
10 A:Zatanna 2.50
11 . . . . 2.50
12 A:Sentinel 2.50
13 V:Blaze 2.50
14 LKa,ALa,AWi,Underworld
    Unleashed tie-in 2.50
15 LKa,ALa,AWi,V:Charnelle 2.50
16 LKa,ALa,AWi,canibal drug-cult . . 2.50
17 LKa,ALa,AWi. 2.50
18 LKa,ALa,AWi,V:Charnelle 2.50
19 LKa,ALa,AWi,V:men in black . . 2.50

FAULT LINES
DC/Vertigo, March, 1997
Mini-series
1 LMr(s),F:Tracey Farrand 2.50
2 LMr(s) 2.50
3 LMr(s) 2.50
4 LMr(s) 2.50
5 (of 6) LMr(s) 2.50
6 LMrs(s) concl. 2.50

Feature Films #3 © DC Comics Inc.

FEATURE FILMS
1950
1 Captain China 1,200.00
2 Riding High, Bing Crosby . . 1,200.00
3 The Eagle and the Hawk . . . 1,100.00
4 Fancy Pants, Bob Hope 1,400.00

52
May, 2006
1 52 Weeks without Superman,
    Batman & Wonder Woman 2.50
2 Looking Back at Tomorrow 2.50
3 New World Order. 2.50
4 Dances with Monsters 2.50
5 Stars in Their Courses. 2.50
6 F:China's super-hero team 2.50
7 F:Booster Gold. 2.50
8 F:John Henry Irons 2.50
9 New JLA 2.50
10 I:Supernova. 2.50
11 New protector of Gotham 2.50
12 F:Black Adam 2.50
13 F:Sue Dibny 2.50
14 F:Steel and Montoya. 2.50
15 O:Metamorpho 2.50
16 F:Black Adam and Isis 2.50
17 Lobo 2.50
18 Croatoans 2.50
19 Your own superhero identity 2.50

20 O:Adam Strange 2.50
21 Raven 2.50
22 Kon-El didn't die in Crisis 2.50
23 Isis 2.50
24 Join New Justice League 2.50
25 Black Marvel Family 2.50
26 LexCorp 2.50
27 O:Power Girl 2.50
28 Red Tornado 2.50
29 O:Joker 2.50
30 Batman no more 2.50
31 Origin of the Metal Man 2.50
32 Origin of Blue Beetle. 2.50
33 Origin of Two-Face 2.50
34 Cliffhanger. 2.50
35 Origin of Black Canary 2.50
35a variant (c) 2.50
36 Origin of Green Arrow. 2.50
37 Origin of Firestorm 2.50
38 Origin of Red Tornado 2.50
39 Origin of Mr. Terrific 2.50
40 . . . . 2.50
41 . . . . 2.50
42 Dibney dies. 2.50
43 . . . . 2.50
44 Isis dies. 2.50
45 PO. 2.50
46 CsB 2.50
47 JoB 2.50
48 Renee is Question 2.50
49 . . . . 2.50
50 World War III. 2.50
51 Master Mind 2.50
52 World War III 2.50

52 AFTERMATH:
THE FOUR HORSEMEN
Aug., 2007
1 (of 6) KG,PO 3.00
2 KG,PO,The dead walk 3.00
3 KG,PO 3.00
4 thru 6 KG,PO . . . . @3.00

FIGHT FOR TOMORROW
DC/Vertigo, Sept., 2002
1 (of 6) DCw,JLe(c) kung-fu 2.50
2 DCw,KW, more kung-fu 2.50
3 thru 6 DCw. . . . . @2.50

FIGHTING AMERICAN
1994
1 GrL,R:Fighting American 2.50
2 GrL,Media Circus. 2.50

Flighting American #6
© DC Comics, Inc.

3 GrL,I&V:Gross Nation Product,
    Def Iffit. 2.50
4 GrL,V:Gross Nation Product,
    Def Iffit. 2.50
5 GrL,PhorOptor 2.50
6 Final Issue 2.50

FILTH, THE
DC/Vertigo, June, 2002
1 (of 13) GMo 3.00
2 GMo, Perfect Victim. 3.00
3 GMo, unexpected guest 3.00
4 GMo, Otto Von Vermun 3.00
5 GMo, Pornomancer 3.00
6 GMo,World of Anders Klimaaks. . 3.00
7 GMo,Libertania 3.00
8 GMo,Libertania 3.00
9 GMo,Answers 3.00
10 GMo,Mother Dirt 3.00
11 GMo,Greg Feely 3.00
12 GMo,Mother Dirt 3.00
13 GMo,concl. 3.00

FINAL CRISIS
May, 2008
1 (of 7) GMo(s),V:Libra 4.00
1b Director's cut special, 64-pg . . . 5.00
2 GMo(s). 4.00
3 GMo(s),Green Lantern on trial. . . 4.00
4 GMo(s),How to Murder the Earth 4.00
5 GMo(s),V:Darkseid 4.00
6 GMo(s),Dark Monitor 4.00
1a thru 6a variant (c)s. . . . . @4.00
Spec. Final Crisis Sketchbook 3.00
Spec. #1 Final Crisis Requiem 4.00
Spec. #1a Requiem variant (c). . . . 4.00

...LEGION OF THREE WORLDS
Aug., 2008
1 (of 5) F:Time Trapper. 4.00
1a variant (c) 4.00
2 thru 3 . . . . @4.00
2a thru 3a variant (c)s . . . . @4.00

...RAGE OF
THE RED LANTERNS
Oct., 2008
1 Blackest Night prelude, 40-pg. . . 4.00
1a variant (c) 4.00

...RESIST
Oct., 2008
1 F:Cheetah, Snapper Carr 4.00
1a variant (c) 4.00

...REVELATIONS
Aug., 2008
1 (of 5) 4.00
1a variant (c) 4.00
2 thru 4 . . . . @4.00
2a thru 4a variant (c)s. . . . . @4.00

...ROGUES' REVENGE
July, 2008
1 (of 3) Captain Cold & Rogues . . 4.00
2 Libra attacks the Rogues. 4.00
3 F:Secret Society 4.00
1a thru 3a variant (c)s . . . . @4.00

...SUBMIT
Oct., 2008
1 GMo,V:Darkseid. 4.00
1a variant (c) 4.00

...SUPERMAN BEYOND
Aug., 2008
1 (of 2) 40-pg. 4.50
1a variant (c) 4.50
2 . . . . @4.50

DC COMICS

FINAL NIGHT, THE
Sept., 1996
1 KK(s),SI,JMz, Alien crash lands
on Earth. 7.00
2 KK(s),SI,JMz, Earth's sun
extinguished 5.00
3 KK(s),SI,JMz, Attempts to stave
off inevitable 5.00
4 KK(s),SI,JMz, Can they save the
world, and at what price? 10.00

FIREBRAND
1995
1 SaV,Alex Sanchez becomes
Firebrand 2.50
2 SaV 2.50
3 SaV,Generation Prime case
climax 2.50
4 SaV,Young gang member 2.50
5 SaV,V;serial killer(s). 2.50
6 thru 9 . . . . @2.50

FIRESTORM
March, 1978
1 AM,JRu,I&O:Firestorm. 12.00
2 AM,BMc,A:Superman 7.00
3 AM,I:Killer Froat 7.00
4 AM,BMc,I:Hyena 7.00
5 AM,BMc,Hyena 7.00

FIRESTORM
May 2004
1 thru 22 . . . . @2.50
Becomes:

FIRESTORM
THE NUCLEAR MAN
23 One Year Later 2.50
24 Firehawk vs. Killer Frost 2.50
25 V:Killer Frost & Mr. Freeze 3.00
26 F:The Pupil 3.00
27 Firehawk vs. Pupil. 3.00
28 In My Father's House,pt.1 . . . . 3.00
29 In My Father's House,pt.2 . . . . 3.00
30 In My Father's House,pt.3 . . . . 3.00
31 In My Father's House,pt.4 . . . . 3.00
32 In My Father's House, pt.5 . . . . 3.00
33 DMD,DJu,KeL,F:Mr. Miracle . . . 3.00
34 DMD,F:Mr. Miracle 3.00
35 DMD,V:Kalibak, final issue 3.00

FIRESTORM, THE
NUCLEAR MAN
See: FURY OF FIRESTORM

FIRST ISSUE SPECIAL
April, 1975
1 JK,Atlas 20.00
2 Green Team 15.00
3 Metamorpho. 15.00
4 Lady Cop 10.00
5 JK,Manhunter 20.00
6 JK,Dingbats 20.00
7 SD,Creeper 20.00
8 MGr,Warlord. 25.00
9 WS,Dr.Fate 15.00
10 Outsiders(not Batman team). . . 12.00
11 NR,AM Code:Assassin 12.00
12 new Starman. 12.00
13 return of New Gods 30.00

FLASH COMICS
Jan., 1940
1 SMo,SMo(c),O:Flash,Hawkman,The
Whip & Johnny Thunder,B:Cliff
Cornwall,Minute Movies . 150,000.00
2 B:Rod Rain 25,000.00
3 SMo,SMo(c),B:The King. . . 15,000.00
4 SMo,SMo(c),F:The Whip . . 12,000.00

First Issue Special #1
© DC Comics, Inc.

5 SMo,SMo(c),F:The King . . . 10,000.00
6 F:Flash 15,000.00
7 Hawkman(c) 12,000.00
8 Male bondage(c). 6,500.00
9 Hawkman(c) 7,000.00
10 SMo,SMo(c),Flash(c). 7,000.00
11 SMo,SMo(c). 5,000.00
12 SMo,SMo(c),B:Les Watts. . 5,000.00
13 SMo,SMo(c). 5,000.00
14 SMo,SMo(c). 5,500.00
15 SMo,SMo(c). 5,500.00
16 SMo,SMo(c). 5,500.00
17 SMo,SMo(c),E:CliffCornwall 5,500.00
18 SMo,SMo(c). 5,500.00
19 SMo,SMo(c). 5,500.00
20 SMo,SMo(c). 5,500.00
21 SMo(c) 6,000.00
22 SMo,SMo(c). 5,000.00
23 SMo,SMo(c). 5,000.00
24 SMo,SMo(c),Flash V:Spider-
Men of Mars,A:Hawkgirl . . . 5,500.00
25 SMo,SMo(c). 2,700.00
26 SMo,SMo(c). 2,700.00
27 SMo,SMo(c). 2,700.00
28 SMo,SMo(c),Flash goes
to Hollywood. 2,700.00
29 SMo,SMo(c). 2,700.00
30 SMo,SMo(c),Flash inAdventure
of the Curiosity Ray!. 2,700.00
31 SMo,SMo(c),Hawkman(c) . . 2,700.00
32 SMo,SM(c),Flash inAdventure
of the Fictious Villians. 3,000.00
33 SMo,SMo(c). 3,000.00
34 SMo,SMo(c),Flash in The Robbers
of the Round Table 2,700.00
35 SMo,SMo(c). 2,700.00
36 SMo,SMo(c),F:Flash,Mystery of
Doll Who Walks Like a Man 2,700.00
37 SMo,SMo(c). 2,200.00
38 SMo,SMo(c). 2,200.00
39 SMo,SMo(c). 2,200.00
40 SMo,SMo(c),F:Flash, Man Who
Could Read Man's Souls!. . 2,000.00
41 SMo,SMo(c). 2,000.00
42 SMo,SMo(c),Flash V:The
Gangsters Baby!. 2,000.00
43 SMo,SMo(c). 2,000.00
44 SMo,SMo(c),Flash V:The
Liars Club 2,000.00
45 SMo,SMo(c),F:Hawkman,Big
Butch Makes Hall of Fame. 2,000.00
46 SMo,SMo(c). 2,000.00
47 SMo,SMo(c),Hawkman in Crime
Canned for the Duration. . . 1,800.00
48 SMo,SMo(c). 1,800.00
49 SMo,SMo(c). 1,800.00

50 SMo,SMo(c),Hawkman, Tale
of the 1,000 Dollar Bill 1,800.00
51 SMo,SMo(c). 1,800.00
52 SMo,SMo(c),Flash, Machine
that Thinks Like a Man. . . . 1,800.00
53 SMo,SMo(c),Hawkman, Simple
Simon Met the Hawkman . . 1,800.00
54 SMo,SMo(c),Flash, Mysterious
Bottle from the Sea 1,800.00
55 SMo,SMo(c),Hawkman, Riddle of
the Stolen Statuette! 1,800.00
56 SMo,SMo(c). 1,800.00
57 SMo,SMo(c),Hawkman,
Adventure of the Gangster
& the Ghost 1,800.00
58 SMo,SMo(c),Merman meets
the Flash. 1,800.00
59 SMo,SMo(c),Hawkman
V:Pied Piper 1,800.00
60 SMo,SMo(c),Flash
V:The Wind Master. 1,800.00
61 SMo,SMo(c),Hawkman
V:The Beanstalk 1,800.00
62 JKu,Flash in High Jinks
on the Rinks 2,000.00
63 JKu(c),Hawkman in The
Tale of the Mystic Urn. 1,500.00
64 The Fire Bandits 1,500.00
65 JKu(c),Hawkman in Return
of the Simple Simon 1,500.00
66 Flash and the Black Widow . 1,500.00
67 JKu(c). 1,500.00
68 Flash in The Radio that
Ran Wild. 1,500.00
69 Adventure o/t Violent Violin . 1,500.00
70 JKu(c). 1,500.00
71 JKu(c),Hawkman in Battle
of the Birdmen 1,500.00
72 JKu,Wizard o/t Wax Works . 1,500.00
73 JKu(c). 1,500.00
74 JKu(c). 1,500.00
75 JKu(c),Hawkman in Magic
at the Mardi Gras 1,500.00
76 A:Worry Wart 1,500.00
77 Hawkman in The Case of
the Curious Casket. 1,500.00
78 Haunted Halloween 1,500.00
79 Hawkman in The Battle
of the Birds 1,500.00
80 Flash in The Story of
the Boy Genius. 1,500.00
81 JKu(c),Hawkman's Voyage
to Venus 1,500.00
82 A:Walter Jordan 1,500.00
83 JKu,JKu(c),Hawkman in
Destined for Disaster 1,600.00
84 Flash V:The Changeling . . . 1,600.00
85 JKu,JKu(c),Hawkman in
Hollywood. 1,600.00
86 JKu,1st Black Canary,Flash
V:Stone Age Menace 6,000.00
87 Hawkman meets the Foil . . . 2,200.00
88 JKu,Flash in The Case
of the Vanished Year! 2,200.00
89 I:The Thorn 3,500.00
90 Flash in Nine Empty
Uniforms 2,200.00
91 Hawkman V:The Phantom
Menace. 2,500.00
92 1st full-length Black
Canary story. 6,000.00
93 Flash V:Violin of Villainy . . . 2,500.00
94 JKu(c). 2,500.00
95 CI(c),The Golden Flash 2,500.00
96 JKu,Return of the Centaurs . 2,500.00
97 Flash in The Dream
that Didn't Vanish 2,500.00
98 JKu(c),Hawkman in
Crime Costume! 2,500.00
99 Flash in The Star Prize
of the Year 2,500.00

Flash Comics #113
© DC Comics, Inc.

100 Hawkman in The Human
  -Fly Bandits! 5,000.00
101 CI,A Switch in Time 4,500.00
102 Hawkman in The Flying
  Darkness 4,500.00
103 CI,The Sword of Time 4,500.00
104 JKu,Hawkman in Flaming
  Darkness' Feb., 1949 . . . . 15,000.00
Revived as:

FLASH, THE
Feb.–March, 1959
105 CI,O:Flash,I:Mirror
  Master. 14,000.00
106 CI,I&O:Gorilla Grodd,
  O:Pied Piper 5,000.00
107 CI,A:Grodd. 2,500.00
108 CI,A:Grodd. 2,000.00
109 CI,A:Mirror Master 1,500.00
110 CI,MA,I:Kid Flash,
  Weather Wizard 4,000.00
111 CI,A:Kid Flash,The Invasion
  Of the Cloud Creatures . . . 1,500.00
112 CI,I&O:Elongated Man,
  A:Kid Flash 1,500.00
113 CI,I&O:Trickster 1,100.00
114 CI,A:Captain Cold 1,000.00
115 CI,A:Grodd 750.00
116 CI,A:Kid Flash,The Man
  Who Stole Central City 750.00
117 CI,MA,I:Capt.Boomerang . . . 800.00
118 CI,MA 650.00
119 CI,W:Elongated Man 650.00
120 CI,A:Kid Flash,Land of
  Golden Giants 650.00
121 CI,A:Trickster 550.00
122 CI,I&O:The Top 550.00
123 I:Earth 2,R:G.A.Flash 3,200.00
124 CI,A:Capt.Boomerang. 500.00
125 CI,A:Kid Flash,The
  Conquerors of Time. 500.00
126 CI,A:Mirror Master 500.00
127 CI,A:Grodd. 500.00
128 CI,O:Abra Kadabra 500.00
129 CI,A:Capt.Cold,Trickster,A:Gold.
  Age Flash,C:JLA (flashback). 600.00
130 CI,A:Mirror Master,
  Weather Wizard. 450.00
131 CI,A:Green Lantern. 300.00
132 CI,A:Daphne Dean 300.00
133 CI,A:Abra Kadabra 300.00
134 CI,A:Captain Cold 300.00
135 CI,N:Kid Flash. 300.00
136 CI,A:Mirror Master 300.00
137 CI,Vandal Savage,R:JSA,
  A:G.A.Flash 900.00

138 CI,A:Pied Piper 350.00
139 CI,I&O:Prof.Zoom(Reverse
  Flash). 350.00
140 CI,O:Heat Wave 350.00
141 CI,A:Top 250.00
142 CI,A:Trickster 250.00
143 CI,A:Green Lantern. 250.00
144 CI,A:Man Missile,Kid Flash . 250.00
145 CI,A:Weather Wizard 250.00
146 CI,A:Mirror Master 250.00
147 CI,A:Mr.Element,A:Reverse
  Flash 250.00
148 CI,A:Capt.Boomerang. 250.00
149 CI,A:Abra Kadabra 250.00
150 CI,A:Captain Cold 250.00
151 CI,A:Earth II Flash,
  The Shade. 275.00
152 CI,V:Trickster 300.00
153 CI,A:Mr.Element,Rev.Flash. . 300.00
154 CI,The Day Flash Ran Away
  with Himself. 300.00
155 CI,A:MirrorMaster,Capt.Cold,Top
  Capt. Boomerang,Grodd 300.00
156 CI,A:Kid Flash,The Super Hero
  who Betrayed the World 350.00
157 CI,A:Doralla Kon,The Top . . . 300.00
158 CI,V:The Breakaway Bandit
  A:The Justice League 250.00
159 CI,A:Kid Flash. 200.00
160 CI,giant 250.00
161 CI,A:Mirror Master 200.00
162 CI,Who Haunts the Corridor
  of Chills 200.00
163 CI,A:Abra kadabra 200.00
164 CI,V:Pied Piper,A:Kid Flash . 200.00
165 CI,W:Flash,Iris West. 200.00
166 CI,A:Captain Cold 200.00
167 CI,O:Flash,I:Mopee. 200.00
168 CI,A:Green Lantern. 200.00
169 CI,O:Flash rtd,giant. 210.00
170 CI,A:Abra Kadabra,
  G.A.Flash 200.00
171 CI,A:Dexter Myles,Justice
  League,Atom;V:Dr Light 200.00
172 CI,A:Grodd 200.00
173 CI,A:Kid Flash,EarthII Flash
  V:Golden Man 250.00
174 CI,A:Mirror Master,Top
  Captain Cold 200.00
175 2nd Superman/Flash race,
  C:Justice League o/America . 225.00
176 giant-size. 200.00
177 RA,V:The Trickster 200.00
178 CI,(giant size) 225.00
179 RA,Fact or Fiction. 200.00
180 RA,V:Baron Katana. 175.00
181 RA,V:Baron Katana. 150.00
182 A:Abra Kadabra 150.00
183 RA,V:The Frog 150.00
184 RA,V:Dr Yom. 150.00
185 RA,Threat of the High Rise
  Buildings 150.00
186 RA,A:Sargon. 150.00
187 CI,AbraKadabra,giant 125.00
188 A:Mirror Master 100.00
189 JKu(c),RA,A:Kid Flash 100.00
190 JKu(c),RA,A:Dexter Myles . . 100.00
191 JKu(c),RA,A:Green Lantern . 100.00
192 RA;V:Captain Vulcan 100.00
193 A:Captain Cold 100.00
194 NA(c). 100.00
195 GK,MA,NA 100.00
196 CI,giant 125.00
197 GK. 100.00
198 GK. 100.00
199 GK. 100.00
200 IN,MA 100.00
201 IN,MA,A:G.A. Flash. 60.00
202 IN,MA,A:Kid Flash 60.00
203 IN 60.00
204 NA 60.00
205 giant 100.00

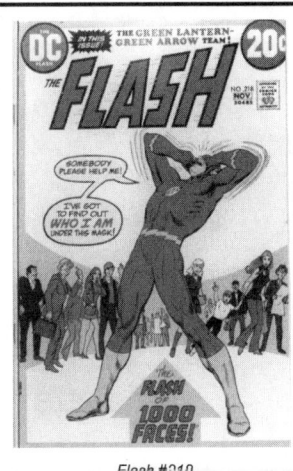

Flash #210
© DC Comics Inc.

206 NA,A:Mirror Master. 60.00
207 NA. 60.00
208 NA. 60.00
209 A:Capt.Boomerang,Grodd
  Trickster. 60.00
210 CI 60.00
211 NA,O:Flash 60.00
212 A:Abra Kadabra 60.00
213 CI,NA 60.00
214 CI,rep.Showcase #37
  (O:Metal Men),giant size. . . . 70.00
215 IN,FMc,NA,rep.Showcase#14. 70.00
216 A:Mr.Element. 70.00
217 NA,A:Gr.Lant,Gr.Arrow 70.00
218 NA,A:Gr.Lant,Gr.Arrow 70.00
219 NA,L:Green Arrow. 70.00
220 IN,DG,A:KidFlash,Gr.Lantern . 60.00
221 IN 30.00
222 IN 30.00
223 DG,Green Lantern. 30.00
224 IN,DG,A:Green Lantern. 30.00
225 IN,DG,A:Gr.Lant,Rev.Flash . . 30.00
226 NA,A:Capt. Cold 35.00
227 IN,FMc,DG,Capt.Boomerang,
  Green Lantern 25.00
228 IN 25.00
229 IN,FMc,A:Green Arrow,
  V:Rag Doll (giant size). 75.00
230 A:VandalSavage,Dr.Alchemy . 25.00
231 FMc. 25.00
232 giant 75.00
233 giant 75.00
234 V:Reverse Flash 20.00
235 DG(c),V:Vandal Savage 18.00
236 MGr. 18.00
237 IN,FMc,MGr,A:Prof Zoom,
  Green Lantern 20.00
238 MGr. 18.00
239 Tailor Made Crimes. 18.00
240 MGr. 18.00
241 A:Mirror Master 18.00
242 MGr,D:Top. 18.00
243 IN,FMc,MGr,TA,O:Top,
  A:Green Lantern 18.00
244 IN,FMc,A:Rogue's Gallery . . . 18.00
245 IN,FMc,DD,TA,I:PlantMaster. . 18.00
246 IN,FMc,DD,TA,I:PlantMaster. . 18.00
247. . . . . 18.00
248 FMc,IN,I:Master 18.00
249 FMc,IN,V:Master 18.00
250 IN,FMc,I:Golden Glider 18.00
251 FMc,IN,V:Golden Glider 15.00
252 FMc,IN,I:Molder 15.00
253 FMc,IN,V:Molder. 15.00
254 FMc. 15.00

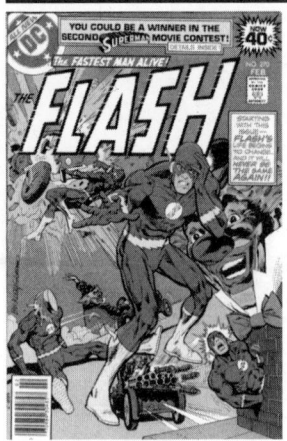

Flash #270
© DC Comics Inc.

255 FMc,A:MirrorMaster 15.00
256 FMc,V:Top. 15.00
257 FMc,A:Green Glider 15.00
258 FMc,A:Black Hand 15.00
259 FMc,IN 15.00
260 FMc,IN 15.00
261 FMc,IN,V:Golden Glider 15.00
262 FMc,IN,V:Golden Glider 15.00
263 FMc,IN,V:Golden Glider 15.00
264 FMc,IN,V:Golden Glider 15.00
265 FMc,IN 15.00
266 FMc,IN,V:Heat Wave 15.00
267 FMc,IN,V:Heat Wave 15.00
268 FMc,IN,A:E2 Flash 15.00
269 FMc,IN,A:Kid Flash. 15.00
270 FMc,IN,V:Clown 15.00
271 RB,V:Clown. 15.00
272 RB,V:Clown. 15.00
273 RB. 15.00
274 RB. 15.00
275 AS,D:Iris West,PCP story 20.00
276 AS,A:JLA. 15.00
277 AS,FMc,A:JLA,
     V:MirrorMaster. 15.00
278 A:Captain.Boomerang
     & Heatwave 15.00
279 A:Captain.Boomerang
     & Heatwave 15.00
280 DH. 15.00
281 DH,V:Reverse Flash 20.00
282 DH,V:Reverse Flash 20.00
283 DH,V:Reverse Flash 20.00
284 DH,Flash's life story
     I:Limbo Lord 15.00
285 DH,V:Trickster. 15.00
286 DH,I:Rainbow Raider 15.00
287 DH,V:Dr.Alchemy 15.00
288 DH,V:Dr.Alchemy 15.00
289 DH,GP,1st GP DC art; V:Dr.
     Alchemy;B:B.U.Firestorm 20.00
290 GP. 10.00
291 GP,DH,V:Sabretooth 10.00
292 GP,DH,V:Mirror Master 10.00
293 GP,DH,V:Pied Piper 10.00
294 GP,DH,V:Grodd. 10.00
295 CI,JSn,V:Grodd. 10.00
296 JSn,A:Elongated Man 10.00
297 CI,A:Captain Cold 10.00
298 CI,V:Shade,Rainbowraider . . . 10.00
299 CI,V:Shade,Rainbowraider . . . 10.00
300 A:New Teen Titans 12.00
301 CI,A:Firestorm. 10.00
302 CI,V:Golden Glider 10.00
303 CI,V:Golden Glider 10.00

304 CI,PB,I:Col.Computron;E:B.U.
     Firestorm 10.00
305 KG,CI,A:G.A.Flash,B:Dr.Fate . 10.00
306 CI,KG,V:Mirror Master. 10.00
307 CI,KG,V:Pied Piper 10.00
308 CI,KG 10.00
309 CI,KG 10.00
310 CI,KG,V:Capt.Boomerang 6.00
311 CI,KG,V:Capt.Boomerang 6.00
312 CI,A:Heatwave 6.00
313 KG,A:Psylon,E:Dr.Fate 6.00
314 CI,I:Eradicator. 6.00
315 CI,V:Gold Face 6.00
316 CI,V:Gold Face 6.00
317 CI,V:Gold Face 6.00
318 CI,DGb,V:Eradicator;B:
     B.U.Creeper. 6.00
319 CI,DGb,V:Eradicator 6.00
320 CI,V:Eradicator 6.00
321 CI,D:Eradicator 5.00
322 CI,V:Reverse Flash. 5.00
323 CI,V:Reverse Flash;E:
     B.U.Creeper 5.00
324 CI,D:Reverse Flash 5.50
325 CI,A:Rogues Gallery 5.00
326 CI,A:Weather Wizard 5.00
327 CI,A:JLA,G.Grodd 5.00
328 CI 5.00
329 CI,A:J.L.A.,G.Grodd 5.00
330 CI,FMc,V:G.Grodd. 5.00
331 CI,FMc,V:G.Grodd. 5.00
332 CI,FMc,V:Rainbow Raider 5.00
333 CI,FMc,V:Pied Piper 5.00
334 CI,FMc,V:Pied Piper 5.00
335 CI,FMc,V:Pied Piper 5.00
336 CI,FMc,V:Pied Piper 5.00
337 CI,FMc,V:Pied Piper 5.00
338 CI,FMc,I:Big Sir. 5.00
339 CI,FMc,A:Big Sir 5.00
340 CI,FMc,Trial,A:Big Sir 5.00
341 CI,FMc,Trial,A:Big Sir 5.00
342 CI,FMc,Trial,V:RogueGallery . . 5.00
343 CI,FMc,Trial,A:GoldFace 5.00
344 CI,O:Kid Flash,Trial. 5.00
345 CI,A:Kid Flash,Trial 5.00
346 CI,FMc,Trial,V:AbraKadabra . . 5.00
347 CI,FMc,Trial,V:AbraKadabra . . 5.00
348 CI,FMc,Trial,V:AbraKadabra . . 5.00
349 CI,FMc,Trial,V:AbraKadabra . . 5.00
350 CI,FMc,Trial,V:AbraKadabra . . 7.00
Ann.#1 O:ElongatedMan,
     G.Grodd 800.00

[2nd Series] June, 1987
1 JG,Legends,C:Vandal Savage . . 12.00
2 JG,V:Vandal Savage 5.00
3 JG,I:Kilgore 5.00
4 JG,A:Cyborg. 4.00
5 JG,V:Speed Demon 4.00
6 JG,V:Speed Demon 4.00
7 JG,V:Red Trinity 4.00
8 JG,V:BlueTrinity,Millennium 4.00
9 JG,I:Chunk,Millennium. 4.00
10 V:Chunk,Chunks World. 3.00
11 Return to Earth 3.00
12 Velocity 9 . . . . 3.00
13 Vandal Savage,V:Velocity 9
     Adicts. 3.00
14 V:Vandal Savage 3.00
15 A:Velocity 9 Junkies 3.00
16 C:V.Savage,SpeedMcGeePt.1 . . 3.00
17 GLa,Speed McGee,pt.2 . . . . 3.00
18 GLa,SpeedMcGeePt.3,
     V:V.Savage 3.00
19 JM:+bonus book,R:Rogue
     Gallery,O:Blue/Red Trinity 3.00
20 A:Durlan 3.00
21 A:Manhunter,Invasion x-over . . . 3.00
22 A:Manhunter,Invasion x-over . . . 3.00
23 V:Abrakadabra 3.00
24 GLa,FlashRegainsSpeed,
     A:L.Lane 3.00
25 GLa,Search for Flash 3.00

Flash 2nd Series #21
© DC Comics, Inc.

26 GLa,I:Porcupine Man 3.00
27 GLa,Porcupine Man as Flash . . . 3.00
28 GLa,A:Golden Glider,
     Capt.Cold. 3.00
29 A:New Phantom Lady 3.00
30 GLa,Turtle Saga,pt.1. . . . . 3.00
31 GLa,Turtle Saga,pt.2. . . . . 3.00
32 GLa,Turtle Saga,pt.3,
     R:G.A.Turtle. 3.00
33 GLa,Turtle Saga,pt.4. . . . . 3.00
34 GLa,Turtle Saga,pt.5. . . . . 3.00
35 GLa,Turtle Saga,pt.6,
     D:G.A.Turtle. 3.00
36 GLa,V:Cult 3.00
37 GLa,V:Cult 3.00
38 GLa,V:Cult 3.00
39 GLa,V:Cult 3.00
40 GLa,A:Dr.Alchemy 3.00
41 GLa,A:Dr.Alchemy 3.00
42 GLa,MechanicalTroubles 3.00
43 GLa,V:Kilgore 3.00
44 GLa,V:Velocity 3.00
45 V:Gorilla Grod. 3.00
46 V:Gorilla Grod 3.00
47 V:Gorilla Grod 3.00
48 Persistence of Vision 3.00
49 A:Vandal Savage 3.00
50 N:Flash (double sz)V:Savage . . . 5.00
51 I:Proletariat 3.00
52 I.R.S. Mission 3.00
53 A:Superman,Race to Save
     Jimmy Olsen 3.00
54 Terrorist Airline Attack 3.00
55 War of the Gods x-over 3.00
56 The Way of a Will,pt.1. . . . . 3.00
57 The Way of a Will,pt.2. . . . . 3.00
58 Meta Gene-activated Homeless . 3.00
59 The Last Resort 3.00
60 Love Song of the Chunk. 3.00
61 Wally's Mother's Wedding Day . . 3.00
62 GLa,Year 1,pt.1. . . . . 5.00
63 GLa,Year 1,pt.2. . . . . 4.00
64 GLa,Year 1,pt.3. . . . . 4.00
65 GLa,Year 1,pt.4. . . . . 4.00
66 A:Aq'man,V:Marine Marauder. . . 4.00
67 GLa,V:Abra Kadabra 4.00
68 GLa,V:Abra Kadabra. 4.00
69 GLa,Gorilla Warfare#2 . . . . 4.00
70 Gorilla Warfare#4 . . . . 4.00
71 GLa,V:Dr.Alchemy 4.00
72 GLa,V:Dr.Alchemy,C:Barry
     Allen. 4.00
73 GLa,Xmas Issue,R:Barry Allen . . 6.00
74 GLa,A:Barry Allen? 5.00

75 GLa,A:Reverse Flash,V:Mob
  Violence. 5.00
76 GLa,A:Reverse Flash 5.00
77 GLa,G.A.Flash vs
  Reverse Flash 5.00
78 GLa,V:Reverse Flash 5.00
79 GLa,V:Reverse Flash,48 pgs. . . . 5.00
80 AD(c),V:Frances Kane 5.00
80a Newstand Ed 3.00
81 AD(c). 4.00
82 AD(c),A:Nightwing. 4.00
83 AD(c),A:Nightwing,Starfire 4.00
84 AD(c),I:Razer 4.00
85 AD(c),V:Razer. 4.00
86 AD(c),A:Argus 4.00
86 V:Santa Claus. 4.00
87 Chrismas issue 4.00
88 Mean Streak 4.00
89 On Trial 4.00
90 On Trial#2 . . . . 4.00
91 Out of Time 5.00
92 I:3rd Flash 12.00
93 A:Impulse 6.00
94 Zero Hour 5.00
95 Terminal Velocity,pt.1 . . . . 4.00
96 Terminal Velocity,pt.2 . . . . 5.00
97 Terminal Velocity,pt.3 . . . . 4.00
98 Terminal Velocity,pt.4 . . . . 4.00
99 Terminal Velocity,pt.5 . . . . 4.00
100 I:New Flash. 5.00
100a Collector's Edition 4.00
101 Velocity Aftermath 4.00
102 V:Mongul. 3.00
103 Supernatural threat from
  Linda's Past Secret 3.00
104 Exorcise Demons 3.00
105 Through a Glass Darkly 3.00
106 R:Magenta 3.00
107 MWa,Underworld Unleashed
  tie-in. 3.00
108 MWa,Dead Heat,pt.1 . . . . 3.00
109 MWa,Dead Heat,pt.2 . . . . 3.00
110 MWa,Dead Heat,pt.4. . . . . 3.00
111 MWa,Dead Heat,pt.6. . . . . 3.00
112 MWa,New Flash in town 3.00
113 MWa,F:Linda. 3.00
114 MWa,V:Chillblaine 3.00
115 thru 117 . . . . @3.00
118 MWa&BAu(s),Flash returns
  from the future. 3.00
119 MWa&BAu(s),PR,Final Night
  tie-in. 3.00
120 MWa&BAu(s),PR,Presidential
  Race,pt.1 . . . . 3.00
121 MWa&BAu(s),PR,Presidential
  Race,pt.2 . . . . 3.00
122 MWa&BAu(s),PR, ... 3.00
123 MWa&BAu(s),PR,Flash moves
  to Santa Marta. 3.00
124 MWa&BAu(s),PR,Wally doesn't
  know reality from illusion 3.00
125 MWa&BAu(s),PR,California,
  V:Major Disaster 3.00
126 MWa&BAu(s),PR,V:Major
  Disaster 3.00
127 MWa&Bau(s),PR,Hell to Pay,
  pt.1 . . . . 3.00
128 MWa&BAu(s),PR,Hell to Pay
  pt.2, A:JLA. 3.00
129 MWa&BAu(s),PR,HellPay,pt.3 . 3.00
130 GMo&MMr(s),PR,new menace . 3.00
131 GMo&MMr(s),PR,V:The Suit. . . 3.50
132 GMo&MMr(s),PR,V:The Suit. . . 3.50
133 GMo&MMr(s),PR,V:Mirror
  Master 3.00
134 GMo&MMr(s),PR,V:Weather
  Wizard & Captain Cold 3.00
135 GMo&MMr(s), ... 3.00
136 GMo&MMr(s),PR,Human
  Race,pt.1 . . . . 3.00
137 GMo&MMr(s),PR,Human
  Race,pt.2 . . . . 3.00

Flash 2nd Series #200
© DC Comics, Inc.

138 GMo&MMr(s),PR,Human
  Race,pt.3 . . . . 3.00
139 MMr(s),Clv,Black Flash,pt.1 . . . 3.00
140 MMr(s),Clv,Black Flash,pt.2 . . . 3.00
141 MMr(s),Clv,Black Flash,pt.3 . . . 3.00
142 MWa&BAu(s),Clv,SLi,wedding of
  Wally West & Linda Park 3.00
143 MWa&BAu(s),Clv,V:CobaltBlue 3.00
144 MWa&BAu(s),Clv,O:CobaltBlue 3.00
145 MWa&BAu(s),PaP,VRu,
  Chain Lightning, pt.1 . . . . 3.00
146 MWa&BAu(s),PaP,VRu,
  Chain Lightning, pt.2 . . . . 3.00
147 MWa&BAu(s),PaP,VRu,
  Chain Lightning, pt.3 . . . . 3.00
148 MWa&BAu(s),PaP,VRu,
  Chain Lightning, pt.4 . . . . 3.00
149 MWa&BAu(s),PaP,VRu,
  Chain Lightning, pt.5 . . . . 3.00
150 MWa&BAu(s),PaP,VRu, Chain
  Lightning, pt.6, 48-page. 4.00
151 MWa&BAu(s),PaP,A:Robin
  & Aqualad, flashback issue 2.50
152 MWa&BAu(s),PaP,VRu,
  new costume. 2.50
153 MWa&BAu(s),PaP,JMz,
  V:Folded Man 2.50
154 MWa&BAu(s),PaP,JMz, ... 2.50
155 MWa&BAu(s),PaP,JMz,
  V:Replicant 2.50
156 MWa&BAu(s),PaP,JMz 2.50
157 MWa&BAu(s),PaP,JMz,fate of
  Linda Park. 2.50
158 MWa&BAu(s),PaP,DHz. 2.50
159 MWa&BAu(s),PaP,Dark Flash . 3.00
160 BAu(s),Honeymoon on the Run 2.50
161 PaP,DHz,F:Original JSA 2.50
162 PaP,DHz,R:Felix Faust 2.50
163 RLm,DHz,A:JLA 2.50
164 DHz,BBo(c),Wonderland,pt.1 . . 6.00
165 DHz,Wonderland,pt.2 . . . . 2.50
166 DHz,Wonderland,pt.3 . . . . 2.50
167 DHz,Wonderland,pt.4 . . . . 2.50
168 DHz,Wonderland,pt.5 . . . . 2.50
169 DHz,Wonderland,pt.6 . . . . 2.50
170 DHz,Blood Will Run,pt.1 . . . . . . 2.50
171 DHz,Blood Will Run,pt.2 . . . . . . 2.50
172 DHz,Blood Will Run,pt.3 . . . . . . 2.50
173 DHz,Blood Will Run,pt.4 . . . . . . 2.50
174 DHz,Moving Right Along. 2.50
175 DHz,Deadly storm. 2.50
176 DHz,The Rainmaker 2.50
177 DHz,interdimensional menace . 2.50
178 DHz,Caged,V:Gorilla Grodd . . . 2.50
179 DHz,Joker:Last Laugh 2.50

180 DHz,V:Peekaboo 2.50
181 DHz,BB(c),V:Fallout 2.50
182 DPs,Absolute Zero 2.50
183 DHz,BB(c),new Trickster. 2.50
184 DHz,BB(c),Crossfire,pt.1. . . . . . 2.50
185 DHz,BB(c),Crossfire,pt.2. . . . . . 2.50
186 DHz,BB(c),Crossfire,pt.3. . . . . . 2.50
187 DHz,BB(c),Crossfire,pt.4. . . . . . 2.50
188 DHz,BB(c),Crossfire,pt.5. . . . . . 3.00
189 RBr,DPs,F:Cyborg, ... 2.50
190 Rogues spotlight,Pied Piper . . 2.50
191 ScK,DHz,F:Hawkman 2.50
192 ScK,DHz,Run Riot,pt.1 . . . . 2.50
193 ScK,DHz,Run Riot,pt.2 . . . . 2.50
194 ScK,DHz,Run Riot,pt.3 . . . . 2.50
195 ScK,DHz,The Top 2.50
196 V:Peek-a-Boo 2.50
197 ScK,Blitz,pt.1. . . . . 8.00
198 ScK,Blitz,pt.2. . . . . 5.00
199 ScK,Blitz,pt.3. . . . . 4.00
200 ScK,DHz,Blitz,concl.48-pg. . . . 4.00
201 Ignition,pt.1 . . . . 2.25
202 Ignition,pt.2 . . . . 2.25
203 Ignition,pt.3 . . . . 2.25
204 Ignition,pt.4 . . . . 2.25
205 Ignition,pt.5 . . . . 2.25
206 Ignition,pt.6,concl. 2.25
207 Kid Flash & Jay Garrick 6.00
208 Kid Flash & Jay Garrick 3.50
209 Fastest Hero Alive. 3.00
210 F:New Teen Titans 3.00
211 F:Nightwing 3.00
212 F:Mirror Master 3.00
213 Sins of the Father,pro. 3.00
214 Sins of the Father,pt.1 . . . . 3.00
215 Sins of the Father,pt.2 . . . . 3.00
216 Sins of the Father, pt.3 . . . . . . 3.00
217 Identity Crisis aftermath 3.00
218 F:Heat Wave. 3.00
219 Truth or Dare, x-over, pt.1. . . . . 8.00
220 Rogue War,pt.1 . . . . 4.00
221 Rogue War,pt.2 . . . . 2.50
222 Rogue War,pt.3 . . . . 2.50
223 Rogue War,pt.4 . . . . 2.50
224 Rogue War,pt.5 . . . . 2.50
225 Rogue War,pt.6 . . . . 2.50
226 Wally climbs a mountain 2.50
227 ATi(c),Infinite Crisis approaches 2.50
228 ATi(c),Finish Line 2.50
229 ATi(c),Finish Line, pt.3 . . . . 2.50
230 ATi(c),V:Vandal Savage 2.50
231 . . . . 3.00
232 MWa,Menace beneath home . . 3.00
233 MWa,F:JLA 3.00
234 MWa,The Wild Wests 3.00
235 MWa,The Wild Wests 3.00
236 MWa,The Wild Wests 3.00
237 ATi, West at crossroads 3.00
238 TPe(s),Fast Money, pt.1 . . . . . . 3.00
239 TPe(s),Fast Money, pt.2 . . . . . . 3.00
240 TPe(s),Primate Fear. 3.00
241 TPe(s),Looting the Museum . . . 3.00
242 TPe(s),Gorilla City 3.00
243 TPe(s),Fast Money, concl 3.00
244 This Was Your Life, Wally West 3.00
245 V:Queen Bee,A:Black Lightning 3.00
246 V:Queen Bee 3.00
Ann.#1 JG,The Deathtouch 4.00
Ann.#2 A:Wally's Father. 3.00
Ann.#3 Roots 3.00
Ann.#4 Armageddon,pt7 . . . . 3.00
Ann.#5 TC(1st Full Work),Eclipso,
  V:Rogue's Gallery 8.00
Ann.#6 Bloodlines#4,I:Argus 3.00
Ann.#7 Elseworlds story 3.50
Ann.#8 Year One story. 4.00
Ann.#9 Legends o/t Dead Earth . . . 3.50
Ann.#10 Pulp Heroes (Romance) . . 4.50
Ann.#11 BAu,BWr, Ghosts. 3.50
Ann.#12 DBw,AAd(c),JLApe: Gorilla
  Warfare 3.50
Ann.#13 Planet DC 4.00

Ann.#1 (1963) replica ed.(2001) . . . 7.50
Spec #1,IN,DG,CI,50th Anniv.,
  Three Flash's 5.00
Spec.#1,000,000 MWa(s),JMz,
  A:Capt.Marvel of 853rd-cent. . . 2.50
Spec.#1 Our Worlds at War,48-pg . . 3.50
T.V. Spec.#1,JS,w/episode guide . . 4.25
GN Iron Heights, 48-page 6.00
GN Time Flies, 48-pg. (2002) 6.00
Secret Files #1 MWa,BAu,PRy,
  O:Flash family 6.00
Secret Files #2 (1999) 6.00
Secret Files #3, 48-page (2001) . . . 6.00
Giant #1 MWa,80-page (1998) 5.00
Giant #2 80-page 5.00

FLASH, THE:
FASTEST MAN ALIVE
June, 2006
1 KeL 3.00
1a variant NKu & JKu (c) 3.00
2 Betrayed by his family? 3.00
3 KlK, new hero of Keystone 3.00
4 Secret of the Speed Force 3.00
5 After the Speed Force 3.00
6 Lightning in a Bottle 3.00
7 Speedquest 3.00
8 Smackdown on the Strip 3.00
9 Team player, but which team? . . . 3.00
10 Good cop, bad cop 3.00
11 Full Throttle, V:Rogues 3.00
12 Full Throttle 3.00
13 ATi,Full Throttle 3.00
13a variant (c) 3.00
14 ATi,What happens to the Flash?. 3.00
15 ATi 3.00
15a variant (c) 3.00
Spec. 80-page Giant, Countdown . . 5.00

FLASH & GREEN
LANTERN: THE BRAVE
& THE BOLD
1999
1 (of 6) MWa&TPe(s),BKi 2.50
2 thru 6 MWa&TPe(s),BKi . . . . . @2.50

THE FLASH PLUS
Nov., 1996
1 MWa(s),F:Wally West, Dick
  Grayson 3.50

FLASH GORDON
1988
1 thru 9 DJu,I:New Flash Gordon @3.00

FLASHPOINT
Oct., 1999
1 (of 3) NBy,Elseworlds 3.00
2 NBy,Flash in wheelchair 3.00
3 NBy 3.00

FLINCH
DC/Vertigo, 1999
1 JLe,RCo,horror anthology 2.50
2 thru 16 . . . . @2.50

FLINTSTONES AND
THE JETSONS, THE
Warner Bros./DC, 1997
1 Ancestors & Descendents meet . 3.00
2 thru 21 . . . . @3.00

FLIPPITY & FLOP
1952
1 Funny animal 350.00
2 . . . . 175.00

Flippity & Flop #19
© DC Comics, Inc.

3 thru 5 . . . . @150.00
6 thru 10 . . . . @100.00
11 thru 20 . . . . @125.00
21 thru 47 . . . . @100.00

FLY, THE
Impact, 1991–92
1 I&O:Fly I:Arachnus,Chromium . . . 3.00
2 thru 17 . . . . @2.50
Ann.#1 Earthquest,pt.4,w/card . . . 3.00

FORBIDDEN TALES
OF DARK MANSION
May-June, 1972
5 DH 75.00
6 JK 30.00
7 MK(c&a 25.00
8 MK(c&a) 25.00
9 NA(c),MK,AA 30.00
10 thru 15 Feb.–March, 1974 . . . . 25.00

FOREVER MAELSTROM
Nov., 2002
1 (of 6) HC,EB,time-jumping 3.00
2 HC,EB,time past 3.00
3 HC,EB,V:Praetor 3.00
4 HC,EB,V:Ragnarok 3.00
5 HC,EB,robots 3.00
6 HC,EB,concl. 3.00

FOREVER PEOPLE, THE
1971–72
1 JK,I:Forever People,A:Superman,
  A:Darkseid 125.00
2 JK,A:Darkseid 75.00
3 JK,A:Darkseid 75.00
4 JK,A:Darkseid 75.00
5 JK 50.00
6 thru 11 JK . . . . @45.00

FOREVER PEOPLE
1988
1 Return of Forever People 3.00
2 Return of Earth of Yesterday 3.00
3 A:Mark Moonrider 3.00
4 The Dark controlls M.Moonrider . 3.00
5 R:MotherBox,Infinity Man 3.00
6 Donny's Fate, final issue 3.00

FORGOTTEN REALMS
1989–91
1 A:RealmsMaster, PriamAgrivar . . 4.00
2 Mystic Hand of Vaprak 3.00
3 thru 5 . . . . @2.75
6 thru 13 . . . . @2.50
14 thru 25 . . . . @2.50
Ann.#1 V:Advanced D&D crew 3.50

FORMERLY KNOWN AS
THE JUSTICE LEAGUE
July 2003
1 (of 6) F:Maxwell Lord 2.50
2 JRu,KM 2.50
3 JRu,KM,V:Roulette 2.50
4 JRu,KM,F:Mary Marvel 2.50
5 JRu,R:G'nort 2.50
6 JRu,concl. 2.50

FOUR HORSEMEN
DC/Vertigo, Dec., 1999
1 (of 4) F:Famine 2.50
2 F:War 2.50
3 F:Pestilence 2.50
4 F:Death, concl. 2.50

FOUR STAR
BATTLE TALES
1973
1 MD 40.00
2 RH 25.00
3 MD 25.00
4 MD,JKo 25.00
5 MD,RH,BK 25.00

FOUR STAR
SPECTACULAR
March-April, 1976
1 . . . . 25.00
2 thru 6 . . . . @12.00

FOX AND THE CROW
Dec.–Jan., 1951
1 . . . . 1,750.00
2 . . . . 800.00
3 . . . . 500.00
4 . . . . 500.00
5 . . . . 500.00
6 thru 10 . . . . @350.00
11 thru 20 . . . . @250.00
21 thru 40 . . . . @175.00
41 thru 60 . . . . @150.00
61 thru 80 . . . . @125.00
81 thru 94 . . . . @125.00
95 . . . . 125.00
96 thru 99 . . . . @75.00
100 . . . . 75.00
101 thru 108 . . . . @75.00
Becomes:

STANLEY & HIS
MONSTER
109 thru 112 Oct.Nov.,1968 . . . . @50.00

FREEDOM FIGHTERS
March-April, 1976
1 Freedom Fighters go to Earth-1 50.00
2 . . . . 20.00
3 . . . . 20.00
4 . . . . 20.00
5 A:Wonder Woman 25.00
6 . . . . 20.00
7 . . . . 20.00
8 . . . . 20.00
9 . . . . 20.00
10 O:Doll Man 20.00
11 O:Ray 20.00

12 O:Firebrand. 25.00
13 O:Black Condor 25.00
14 A:Batgirl. 25.00
15 O:Phantom Lady. 25.00

From Beyond the Unknown #19
© DC Comics Inc.

FROM BEYOND THE UNKNOWN
Oct.–Nov., 1969

1 JKu,CI 100.00
2 MA(c),CI,ATh. 60.00
3 NA(c),CI. 50.00
4 MA(c),CI. 50.00
5 MA(c),CI. 50.00
6 NA(c),I:Glen Merrit. 60.00
7 CI,JKu(c) 60.00
8 NA(c),CI. 60.00
9 NA(c),CI. 60.00
10 MA(c),CI 60.00
11 MA(c),CI 60.00
12 JKu(c),CI. 60.00
13 JKu(c),CI,WW 60.00
14 JKu(c),CI. 60.00
15 MA(c),CI 60.00
16 MA(c),CI 60.00
17 MA(c),CI 60.00
18 MK(c),CI,Star Rovers 50.00
19 MK(c),CI,Star Rovers 50.00
20 . . . . 50.00
21 . . . . 50.00
22 MA(c) 55.00
23 CI,Space Museum 50.00
24 CI 50.00

FRONTIER FIGHTERS
1955–56

1 JKu,Davy Crocket, Buffalo Bill. 900.00
2 JKu. 500.00
3 thru 8 JKu. . . . . @475.00

FUNNY FOLKS
1946–1950

1 Nutsy Squirrel 500.00
2 . . . . 250.00
3 . . . . 175.00
4 1st Nutsy Squirrel(c) 175.00
5 HK 175.00
6 . . . . 125.00
7 . . . . 125.00
8 . . . . 125.00
9 . . . . 125.00
10 . . . . 125.00
11 thru 20 . . . . @125.00
21 thru 26 . . . . @125.00

Becomes:

HOLLYWOOD FUNNY FOLKES
1950–54

27 . . . . 150.00
28 thru 40 . . . . @125.00
41 thru 60 . . . . @100.00

FUNNY STOCKING STUFFER
March, 1985

1 . . . . 5.00

FUNNY STUFF
Summer, 1944

1 B:3 Mouseketeers Terrific
　Whatzit 1,500.00
2 . . . . 750.00
3 . . . . 400.00
4 . . . . 400.00
5 . . . . 400.00
6 thru 10 . . . . @300.00
11 thru 20 . . . . @250.00
21 . . . . 175.00
22 C:Superman 600.00
23 thru 30 . . . . @200.00
31 thru 78 . . . . @150.00
79 July-Aug., 1954 . . . . 150.00
Becomes:

DODO AND THE FROG
1954

80 F:Doodles Duck 250.00
81 thru 91 . . . . @150.00
92 scarce 200.00

FURY OF FIRESTORM
June, 1982

1 PB,I:Black Bison 7.00
2 PB,V:Black Bison 3.00
3 PB,V:Pied Piper, Killer Frost . . . 2.50
4 PB,A:JLA,Killer Frost 2.50
5 PB,V:Pied Piper. 2.50
6 V:Pied Piper. 2.50
7 I:Plastique 2.50
8 V:Typhoon 2.50
9 V:Typhoon 2.50
10 V:Hyena 2.50
11 V:Hyena. 2.50
12 PB,V:Hyena 2.50
13 PB,Split 2.50
14 PB,I:Enforcer,A:Multiplex 2.50
15 V:Multiplex 2.50
16 V:Multiplex 2.50
17 I:2000 Committee,Firehawk . . . 2.50
18 I:Tokamak,A:Multiplex 2.50
19 GC,V:Goldenrod 2.50
20 A:Killer Frost 2.50
21 D:Killer Frost 3.00
22 O:Firestorm. 3.00
23 I:Bug & Byte 2.50
24 I:Blue Devil,Bug & Byte 2.75
25 I:Silver Deer 2.50
26 V:Black Bison 2.50
27 V:Black Bison 2.50
28 I:Slipknot 2.50
29 I:2000 C'tee,I:Breathtaker 2.50
30 V:2000 Committee 2.50
31 V:2000 Committee 2.50
32 Phantom Stranger. 2.50
33 A:Plastique 2.50
34 I:Killer Frost 2 . . . . 2.50
35 V:K.Frost/Plastique,I:Weasel . . 2.50
36 V:Killer Frost & Plastique 2.50
37 Not in our Stars but in Ourselves 2.50
38 V:Weasel. 2.50
39 V:Weasel. 2.50
40 Graduation Day. 2.50
41 Crisis 3.00

Fury of Firestorm #22
© DC Comics Inc.

42 Crisis,A:Firehawk 3.00
43 V:Typhoon. 2.50
44 V:Typhoon. 2.50
45 V:Multiplex 2.50
46 A:Blue Devil 2.50
47 A:Blue Devil 2.50
48 I:Moonbow 2.50
49 V:Moonbow 2.50
50 W:Ed Raymond. 2.50
51 A:King Crusher 2.50
52 A:King Crusher 2.50
53 V:Steel Shadow 2.50
54 I:Lava 2.50
55 Legends,V:World's
　Luckiest Man 2.50
56 Legends,A:Hawk. 2.50
57 Due Monday 2.50
58 I:Parasite II 2.50
59 Glasshouse, V:Parasite 2.50
60 Secret behind Hugo's accident. . 2.50
61 V:Typhoon. 2.50
61a Superman Logo 40.00
62 A:Russian Firestorm 2.50
63 A:Capt.Atom 2.50
64 A:Suicide Squad 2.50
Ann.#1 EC,A:Firehawk,
　V:Tokamak. 2.50
Ann.#2 An Illustrated Novella. 2.50
Ann.#3 Spark. 2.50
Ann.#4 KG,CS,GC,DG 2.50
Becomes:

FIRESTORM, THE NUCLEAR MAN
Nov., 1987

65 A:New Firestorm 2.50
66 A:Green Lantern 2.50
67 Millenium, Week 1 . . . . 2.50
68 Millenium. 2.50
69 V:Zuggernaut,Stalnivolk USA . . 2.50
70 V:Flying Dutchman 2.50
71 Trapped in the Timestream. . . . 2.50
72 V:Zuggernaut 2.50
73 V:Stalnivolk & Zuggernaut 2.50
74 Quest for Martin Stein 2.50
75 Return of Martin Stein. 2.50
76 Firestorm & Firehawk
　vs Brimstone 2.50
77 Firestorm & Firehawk in Africa . . 2.50
78 Exile From Eden,pt.1 . . . . 2.50
79 Exile From Eden,pt.2 . . . . 2.50
80 A:Power Girl,Starman,Invasion
　x-over. 2.50
81 A:Soyuz,Invasion aftermath 2.50

82 Invasion Aftermath 2.50
83 V:Svarozhich. 2.50
84 Souls of Fire 2.50
85 Soul of Fire,N:Firestorm 2.50
86 TMd,Janus Directive #7 . . . . 2.50
87 TMd. 2.50
88 TMd,E:Air Wave B:Maser 2.50
89 TMd,V:Firehawk,Vandermeer
    Steel. 2.50
90 TMd,Elemental War #1 . . . . 2.50
91 TMd,Elemental War #2 . . . . 2.50
92 TMd,Elemental War #3 . . . . 2.50
93 TMd,Elemental War concl. 2.50
94 TMd,A:Killer Frost. 2.50
95 TMd,V:Captains of Industry 2.50
96 TMd,A:Shango,African God &
    Obatala,Lord o/t White Cloth. . . 2.50
97 TMd,A:Obatala,V:Shango 2.50
98 TMd,A:Masar 2.50
99 TMd,A:Brimstone,PlasmaGiant. . 2.50
100 TMd,AM,V:Brimstone (Firestorm
    back-up story) final issue 3.00
Ann.#5 JLI,Suicide Squad
    I:New Firestorm 2.50

GAMMARAUDERS
1989
1 I:Animal-Warrior Bioborgs 2.25
2 thru 10 . . . . @2.25

GANG BUSTERS
1947–58
1 DBa,Crime Agency 1,400.00
2 DBa 600.00
3 DBa,Fall Guy 400.00
4 DBa,Jailbreak 400.00
5 DBa 400.00
6 DBa 400.00
7 DBa 400.00
8 DBa 400.00
9 DBa,Ph(c) 300.00
10 DBa,Ph(c) 300.00
11 CS,Ph(c) 250.00
12 DBa,CS,Ph(c) 250.00
13 CS,Ph(c) 250.00
14 FF,Ph(c) 500.00
15 CS 200.00
16 CS, Death on Wheels 200.00
17 Dead Man's Brand 500.00
18 CS, Black Ace Gang 175.00
19 DBa,CS,Broadway Squad . . . 175.00
20 CS 175.00
21 thru 25 . . . . @150.00
26 JK 150.00
27 thru 40 . . . . @150.00
41 thru 44 . . . . @125.00
45 Comics Code 125.00
46 thru 50 . . . . @125.00
51 MD 125.00
52 thru 67 . . . . @125.00

GEMINI BLOOD
DC/Helix, 1996–97
1 Species: Paratwa, pt.1 . . . . 2.50
2 Species: Paratwa, pt.2 . . . . 2.50
3 Species: Paratwa, pt.3 . . . . 2.50
4 Species: Paratwa, pt.4 . . . . 2.50
5 WSi(c),Species: Paratwa,pt.5 . . . 2.50
6 Species: Paratwa, pt.6 . . . . 2.50
7 BSz, Gillian's secret revealed . . . 2.50
8 Loothka Bi-Modal,pt.1 . . . . 2.50
9 Loothka Bi-Modal,pt.2 . . . . 2.50

GENESIS
Aug., 1997
1 (of 4) JBy,RoW,JRu,AD,MFm,
    Marvel x-over 3.00
2 JBy,RoW,JRu,AD,MFm,x-over. . . 3.00
3 JBy,RoW,JRu,AD,MFm,x-over. . . 3.00
4 JBy,RoW,JRu,AD,MFm,concl. . . . 3.00

GHOSTDANCING
DC/Vertigo, 1995
[Mini-Series]
1 I:Snake,Ghost Dancing 2.50
2 Secrets. 2.50
3 I:Father Craft 2.50
4 Coyote prisoner 2.50
5 F:Snot Boy. 2.50

Ghosts #9 © DC Comics, Inc.

GHOSTS
Sept.–Oct., 1971
1 JAp,NC(c),Death's Bride-
    groom! 250.00
2 WW,NC(c),Mission
    Supernatural 125.00
3 TD,NC(c),Death is my Mother . . 90.00
4 GT,NC(c),The Crimson Claw . . . 90.00
5 NC(c),Death, The Pale
    Horseman 90.00
6 NC(c),A Specter Poured
    The Potion 40.00
7 MK(c),Death's Finger Points . . . 40.00
8 NC(c),The Cadaver In
    The Clock 40.00
9 AA,NC(c),The Last Ride
    Of Rosie The Wrecker. 40.00
10 NC(c),A Specter Stalks Saigon. 40.00
11 NC(c),The Devils Lake 25.00
12 NC(c),The Macabre Mummy
    Of Takhem-Ahtem 25.00
13 NC(c),Hell Is One Mile High . . . 25.00
14 NC(c),The Bride Wore
    A Shroud 25.00
15 AA,NC(c),The Ghost That
    Wouldn't Die 25.00
16 NC(c),Death's Grinning Face . . 25.00
17 NC(c),Death Held the
    Lantern High 25.00
18 AA,NC(c),Graveyard of
    Vengeance. 25.00
19 AA,NC(c),The Dead Live On . . 25.00
20 NC(c),The Haunting Hussar
    Of West Point 25.00
21 NC(c),The Ghost In The
    Devil's Chair 15.00
22 NC(c),The Haunted Horns
    Of Death 15.00
23 NC(c),Dead Is My Darling! 15.00
24 AA,NC(c),You Too, Will Die. . . . 15.00
25 AA,NC(c),Three Skulls On
    The Zambezi 15.00
26 DP,NC(c),The Freaky Phantom
    Of Watkins Glen 15.00
27 NC(c),Conversation With
    A Corpse 15.00

28 DP,NC(c),Flight Of The
    Lost Phantom 15.00
29 NC(c),The Haunted Lady
    Of Death 15.00
30 NC(c),The Fangs of
    the Phantom 15.00
31 NC(c),Blood On The Moon 15.00
32 NC(c),Phantom Laughed Last . 15.00
33 NC(c),The Hangman of
    Haunted Island 15.00
34 NC(c),Wrath of the Ghost Apes 15.00
35 NC(c),Feud with a Phantom . . . 15.00
36 NC(c),The Boy Who Returned
    From The Gave 15.00
37 LD(c),Fear On Ice 15.00
38 LD(c),Specter In The Surf. 15.00
39 LD(c),The Haunting Hitchhiker 15.00
40 LD(c),The Nightmare That
    Haunted The World 30.00
41 LD(c),Ship of Specters 20.00
42 LD(c),The Spectral Sentries . . . 20.00
43 LD(c),3 Corpses On A Rope. . . 20.00
44 LD(c),The Case of the
    Murdering Specters 20.00
45 LD(c),Bray of the
    Phantom Beast 20.00
46 LD(c),The World's Most
    Famous Phantom 20.00
47 LD(c),Wrath of the
    Restless Specters 20.00
48 DP,LD(c),The Phantom Head . . 20.00
49 The Ghost in the Cellar. 20.00
50 Home Is Where The Grave Is . . 20.00
51 The Ghost Who Would Not Die 20.00
52 LD(c),Thunderhead Phantom . . 20.00
53 LD(c),Whose Spirit Invades Me 20.00
54 LD(c),The Deadly Dreams
    Of Ernie Caruso. 20.00
55 LD(c),The House That Was
    Built For Haunting 20.00
56 LD(c),The Triumph Of The
    Teen-Age Phantom 20.00
57 LD(c),The Flaming Phantoms
    of Oradour 20.00
58 LD(c),The Corpse in the Closet 20.00
59 LD(c),That Demon Within Me . . 20.00
60 LD(c),The Spectral Smile
    of Death 10.00
61 LD(c),When Will I Die Again . . . 10.00
62 LD(c),The Phantom Hoaxer!. . . 10.00
63 LD(c),The Burning Bride. 10.00
64 LD(c),Dead Men Do Tell Tales . 10.00
65 LD(c),The Imprisoned Phantom 10.00
66 LD(c),Conversation With A
    Corpse. 10.00
67 LD(c),The Spectral Sword 10.00
68 LD(c),The Phantom of the
    Class of '76 . . . . 9.00
69 LD(c),The Haunted Gondola. . . 9.00
70 LD(c),Haunted Honeymoon . . . 9.00
71 LD(c),The Ghost Nobody Knew . 9.00
72 LD(c),The Ghost of
    Washington Monument 9.00
73 LD(c),The Specter Of The
    Haunted Highway 9.00
74 LD(c),The Gem That Haunted
    the World! 9.00
75 LD(c),The Legend Of The
    Lottie Lowry 9.00
76 LD(c),Two Ghosts of
    Death Row. 9.00
77 LD(c),Ghost, Where Do
    You Hide? 9.00
78 LD(c),The World's Most
    Famous Phantom 9.00
79 LD(c),Lure of the Specter 9.00
80 JO(c),The Winged Specter 9.00
81 LD(c),Unburied Phantom 9.00
82 LD(c),The Ghost Who
    Wouldn't Die 9.00
83 LD(c),Escape From the Haunt
    of the Amazon Specter 9.00

84 LD(c),Torment of the
Phantom Face 9.00
85 LD(c),The Fiery Phantom
of Faracutin 9.00
86 LD(c),The Ghostly Garden 9.00
87 LD(c),The Phantom Freak 9.00
88 LD(c),Harem In Hell 9.00
89 JKu(c),Came The Specter
Shrouded In Seaweed 9.00
90 The Ghost Galleon 9.00
91 LD(c),The Haunted Wheelchair . 9.00
92 DH(c),Double Vision 9.00
93 MK(c),The Flaming Phantoms
of Nightmare Alley 9.00
94 LD(c),Great Caesar's Ghost 9.00
95 All The Stage Is A Haunt 9.00
96 DH(c),Dread of the
Deadly Domestic 9.00
97 JAp(c),A Very Special Spirit
A:Spectre 15.00
98 JAp(c),The Death of a Ghost
A:Spectre 15.00
99 EC(c),Till Death Do Us Join
A:Spectre 15.00
100 EC&DG(c),The Phantom's
Final Debt 12.00
101 MK(c),The Haunted Hospital . . 5.00
102 RB&DG(c),The Fine Art
Of Haunting 10.00
103 RB&DG(c),Visions and
Vengeance 10.00
104 LD(c),The First Ghost 10.00
105 JKu(c) 10.00
106 JKu(c) 10.00
107 JKu(c) 10.00
108 JKu(c) 10.00
109 EC(c) 10.00
110 EC&DG(c) 10.00
111 JKu(c) 10.00
112 May, 1982 . . . . 10.00

GIANTKILLER
1999
1 thru 6 . . . . @2.50

G.I. COMBAT
Jan., 1957
Prev: Golden Age
44 RH,JKu,The Eagle and
the Wolves 1,250.00
45 RH,JKu,Fireworks Hill 550.00
46 JKu,The Long Walk
To Wansan 475.00
47 RH, The Walking Weapon . . . 475.00
48 No Fence For A Jet 475.00
49 Frying Pan Seat 475.00
50 Foxhole Pilot 475.00
51 RH,The Walking Grenade 475.00
52 JKu,JKu(c),Call For A Tank . . . 400.00
53 JKu,The Paper Trap 400.00
54 RH,JKu,Sky Tank 400.00
55 Call For A Gunner 400.00
56 JKu,JKu(c),The D.I.-And the
Sand Fleas 450.00
57 RH,Live Wire For Easy 475.00
58 JKu(c),Flying Saddle 475.00
59 JKu,Hot Corner 400.00
60 RH,Bazooka Crossroads 400.00
61 JKu(c),The Big Run 300.00
62 RH,JKu,Drop An Inch 300.00
63 MD,JKu(c),Last Stand 300.00
64 MD,RH,JKu,JKu(c),The
Silent Jet 300.00
65 JKu,Battle Parade 300.00
66 MD,The Eagle of Easy
Company 450.00
67 JKu(c),I:Tank Killer 450.00
68 JKu,RH,The Rock 1,500.00
69 JKu,RH,The Steel Ribbon 350.00
70 JKu,Bull's-Eye Bridge 300.00
71 MD,JKu(c),Last Stand 300.00

G.I. Combat #82
© DC Comics, Inc.

72 MD,JKu(c),Ground Fire 300.00
73 RH,JKu(c),Window War 300.00
74 RH,A Flag For Joey 300.00
75 RH,Dogtag Hill 450.00
76 MD,RH,JKu,Bazooka For
A Mouse 450.00
77 RH,JKu,H-Hour For A Gunner 450.00
78 MD,RH,JKu(c),Who Cares
About The Infantry 450.00
79 JKu,RH,Big Gun-Little Gun . . . 450.00
80 JKu,RH(c),Flying Horsemen . . 450.00
81 Jump For Glory 350.00
82 IN,Get Off My Back 350.00
83 Too Tired To Fight 400.00
84 JKu(c),Dog Company
Is Holding 350.00
85 IN,JKu(c),The T.N.T. Trio 350.00
86 JKu,RH(c),Not Return 350.00
87 RH(c),I:Haunted Tank 1,600.00
88 RH,JKu(c),Haunted Tank Vs.
Ghost Tank 550.00
89 JA,RH,IN,Tank With Wings . . . 350.00
90 JA,IN,RH,Tank Raiders 250.00
91 IN,RH,Tank and the Turtle . . . 250.00
92 JA,IN,The Tank of Doom 250.00
93 RH(c),JA,No-Return Mission . 250.00
94 IN,RH(c),Haunted Tank Vs.
The Killer Tank 250.00
95 JA,RH(c),The Ghost of
the Haunted Tank 250.00
96 JA,RH(c),The Lonesome Tank 250.00
97 IN,RH(c),The Decoy Tank 250.00
98 JA,RH(c),Trap of Dragon's
Teeth 250.00
99 JA,JKu,RH(c),Battle of the
Thirsty Tanks 250.00
100 JA,JKu,Return of the
Ghost Tank 300.00
101 JA,The Haunted Tank Vs.
Attila's Battle Tiger 175.00
102 JKu(c),Haunted Tank
Battle Winton 175.00
103 JKu,JA,RH(c),Rabbit Punch
For A Tiger 175.00
104 JA,JKu,RH(c),Blind
Man's Radar 175.00
105 JA,JKu(c),Time Bomb Tank . 175.00
106 JA,JKu(c),Two-Sided War . . . 175.00
107 JKu(c),The Ghost Pipers . . . 175.00
108 JKu(c),The Wounded
Won't Wait,I:Sgt.Rock 300.00
109 JKu(c),Battle of the Tank
Graveyard 200.00
110 IN,JKu(c),Choose Your War . 200.00
111 JA,JKu(c),Death Trap 200.00

112 JA,JKu(c),Ghost Ace 200.00
113 JKu,RH(c),Tank Fight In
Death Town 250.00
114 JA,RH(c),O:Haunted Tank . . 400.00
115 JA,RH(c),MedalsForMayhem 200.00
116 IN,JA,JKu(c),Battle Cry
For A Dead Man 200.00
117 JA,RH,JKu(c),Tank In
The Ice Box 250.00
118 IN,JA,RH(c),My Buddy-
My Enemy 200.00
119 IN,RH(c),Target For
A Firing Squad 200.00
120 IN,JA,RH(c),Pull a Tiger'sTail 200.00
121 RH(c),Battle of Two Wars . . . 125.00
122 JA,JKu(c),Who Dies Next? . . 125.00
123 IN,RH(c),The Target of Terro 125.00
124 IN,RH(c),Scratch That Tank . 125.00
125 RH(c),Stay Alive-Until Dark . . 125.00
126 JA,RH(c),Tank Umbrella . . . 125.00
127 JA,JKu(c),Mission-Sudden
Death 125.00
128 RH(c),The Ghost of
the Haunted Tank 125.00
129 JA,RH(c),Hold That Town
For A Dead Man 125.00
130 RH(c),Battle of the Generals 125.00
131 JKu&RH(c),Devil For Dinner. 125.00
132 JA,JKu(c),The Executioner . . 125.00
133 JKu(c),Operation:Death Trap 125.00
134 MD,JKu(c),Desert Holocaust 125.00
135 GE,JKu(c),Death is the Joker 125.00
136 JKu(c),Kill Now-Pay Later . . . 125.00
137 JKu(c),We Can't See 125.00
138 JKu(c),I:The Losers 200.00
139 JKu(c),Corner of Hell 100.00
140 RH,MD,JKu(c),The LastTank 100.00
141 MD,JKu(c),Let Me Live..
Let Me Die 50.00
142 RH,JKu(c),Checkpoint-Death . 50.00
143 RH,JKu(c),Iron Horseman . . . 50.00
144 RH,MD,JKu(c),Every
Man A Fort 60.00
145 MD,JKu(c),Sand,Sun
and Death 60.00
146 JKu(c),Move the World 60.00
147 JKu(c),Rebel Tank 60.00
148 IN,JKu(c),The Gold-Plated
General 60.00
149 JKu(c),Leave The
Fighting To Us 50.00
150 JKu(c),The Death of the
Haunted Tank 50.00
151 JKu(c),A Strong Right Arm . . . 50.00
152 JKu(c),Decoy Tank 50.00
153 JKu(c),The Armored Ark 50.00
154 JKu(c),Battle Prize 50.00
155 JKu(c),The Long Journey . . . 25.00
156 JKu(c),Beyond Hell 25.00
157 JKu(c),The Fountain 25.00
158 What Price War. 25.00
159 JKu(c),Mission Dead End . . . 25.00
160 JKu(c),Battle Ghost 25.00
161 JKu(c),The Day of the Goth . 25.00
162 JKu(c),The Final Victor 25.00
163 A Crew Divided 25.00
164 Siren Song 25.00
165 JKu(c),Truce,Pathfinder 25.00
166 Enemy From Yesterday 25.00
167 JKu(c),The Finish Line 25.00
168 NA(c),The Breaking Point . . . 35.00
169 WS(c),The Death of the
Haunted Tank 25.00
170 Chain of Vengeance 25.00
171 JKu(c),The Man Who
Killed Jeb Stuart 25.00
172 RH(c),At The Mercy of
My Foes. 25.00
173 JKu(c),The Final Crash 25.00
174 JKu(c),Vow To A Dead Foe . . 25.00
175 JKu(c),The Captive Tank 25.00
176 JKu(c),A Star Can Cry 25.00

DC COMICS

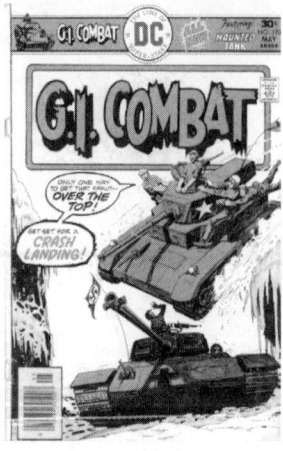

G.I. Combat #190
© DC Comics, Inc.

177 JKu(c),The Tank That
 Missed D-Day 25.00
178 JKu(c),A Tank Is Born 25.00
179 JKu(c),One Last Charge. 25.00
180 JKu(c),The Saints Go
 Riding On 25.00
181 JKu(c),The Kidnapped Tank . . 25.00
182 JKu(c),Combat Clock 25.00
183 JKu(c),6 Stallions To
 Hell- And Back. 25.00
184 JKu(c),Battlefield Bundle 25.00
185 JKu(c),No Taps For A Tank . . . 25.00
186 JKu(c),Souvenir
 From A Headhunter 25.00
187 JKu(c),The General
 Died Twice. 25.00
188 The Devil's Pipers. 25.00
189 The Gunner is a Gorilla 25.00
190 The Tiger and The Terrier 25.00
191 Decoy For Death. 25.00
192 The General Has Two Faces . 25.00
193 JKu(c),The War That
 Had To Wait. 25.00
194 GE(c),Blitzkrieg Brain 25.00
195 JKu(c),The War That
 Time Forgot. 25.00
196 JKu(c),Dead Men Patrol 25.00
197 JKu(c),Battle Ark 25.00
198 JKu(c),The Devil
 Rides A Panzer 25.00
199 JKu(c),A Medal From A Ghost 25.00
200 JKu(c),The Tank That Died . . . 25.00
201 NA&RH(c),The Rocking
 Chair Soldiers 35.00
202 NA&RH(c),Walking Wounded
 Don't Cry 35.00
203 JKu(c),To Trap A Tiger 25.00
204 JKu(c),A Winter In Hell 25.00
205 JKu(c),A Gift From
 The Emperor 25.00
206 JKu(c),A Tomb For A Tank . . . 25.00
207 JKu(c),Foxhole for a Sherman 25.00
208 JKu(c),Sink That Tank. 25.00
209 JKu(c),Ring Of Blood 25.00
210 JKu(c),Tankers Also Bleed . . . 25.00
211 JKu(c),A Nice Day For Killing . 20.00
212 JKu(c),Clay Pigeon Crew 20.00
213 JKu(c),Back Door To War 20.00
214 JKu(c),The Tanker Who
 Couldn't Die. 20.00
215 JKu(c),Last Stand For Losers . 20.00
216 JKu(c),Ghost Squadron 20.00
217 JKu(c), The Pigeon Spies 20.00
218 JKu(c), 48 Hours to Die 20.00

219 thru 230. . . . . @20.00
231 thru 288. . . . . @20.00

GILGAMESH II
1989
1 JSn,O:Gilgamesh. 5.00
2 JSn,V:Nightshadow 4.50
3 JSn,V:Robotic Ninja 4.50
4 JSn,final issue 4.00

Girls Love Stories #17
© DC Comics, Inc.

GIRLS' LOVE STORIES
1949
1 ATh,EK,Romance 800.00
2 EK 400.00
3 thru 10 . . . . @275.00
11 thru 20 . . . . @200.00
21 EK. 150.00
22 thru 83 . . . . @100.00

GIRLS' ROMANCES
1950
1 Ph(c) 800.00
2 ATh,Ph(c). 400.00
3 Ph(c) 300.00
4 thru 6 Ph(c) . . . . @275.00
7 thru 10 . . . . @275.00
11 . . . . 200.00
12 . . . . 200.00
13 ATh(c) 225.00
14 thru 20 . . . . @200.00
21 thru 31 . . . . @150.00
32 thru 50 . . . . @125.00
51 thru 80 . . . . @100.00

GIRL WHO WOULD
BE DEATH, THE
DC/Vertigo, 1998
1 thru 4 F:Plath . . . . @2.50

GODDESS
DC/Vertigo, 1995–96
[Mini-Series]
1 thru 8 . . . . @4.00

GOLDEN AGE
Elseworld 1993–94
1 PS,F:JSA,All-Star Squadron 8.00
2 PS,I:Dynaman 7.00
3 PS,IR:Mr. Terrific is
 Ultra-Humanite. 7.00
4 PS,D:Dynaman,Mr. Terrific 6.00

1 Secret Files,48-page(2000) 5.00

GOTHAM CENTRAL
Dec. 2002
1 MLr,F:Gotham Detectives 3.50
2 MLr,cop murdered 3.00
3 MLr,V:Firebug 3.00
4 MLr,V:Firebug 2.50
5 MLr,two cases 2.50
6 MLr,Half a Life,pt.1 . . . . 2.50
7 MLr,Half a Life,pt.2 . . . . 2.50
8 MLr,Half a Life,pt.3 . . . . 2.50
9 MLr,Half a Life,pt.4 . . . . 2.50
10 MLr,Half a Life,pt.5 . . . . 2.50
11 F:Stacy 2.50
12 A sniper strikes 2.50
13 shadow of the Joker 2.50
14 Joker's reign of terror 2.50
15 Joker sniper spree 2.50
16 Sarge and Crowe 2.50
17 Murder of businesswoman . . . 2.50
18 Hot homicide case 2.50
19 Harvey Bullock 2.50
20 Mad Hatter, Penguin. 2.50
21 Mad Hatter, Penguin, Harvey . . . 2.50
22 High School BB Massacre 2.50
23 War Games tie-in 2.50
24 War Games tie-in 2.50
25 MLr,SGa 2.50
26 MLr(c),F:Catwoman 2.50
27 MLr(c),F:Catwoman 2.50
28 MLr(c) 2.50
29 MLr(c),Keystone Ci ty 2.50
30 MLr(c) 2.50
31 Dr. Alchemy. 2.50
32 Robin's body 2.50
33 Robin's body 2.50
34 F:Teen Titans 2.50
35 Batman's not talking 2.50
36 Dead Robin, concl. 2.50
37 A:Captain Marvel 2.50
38 The Spectre? 2.50
39 A Hero fallen 2.50
40 Another officer gone 2.50

GOTHAM GIRLS
Aug., 2002
1 (of 5) F:Catwoman. 2.50
2 Catwoman,Batgirl,P.Ivy,H.Quinn . 2.50
3 Poison Ivy, Harley Quinn 2.50
4 Batgirl. 2.50
5 Renee Montoya, concl. 2.50

GOTHAM UNDERGROUND
Oct., 2007
1 (of 8) Countdown tie-in 3.00
2 A:Batman, Nightwing. 3.00
3 F:Scarecrow, Penguin 3.00
4 Did Zsasz kill Batman 3.00
5 Flashback, O:Johnny Stitches . . . 3.00
6 F:Vigilante 3.00
7 Penguin's troops 3.00
8 F:Spoiler. 3.00
9 conclusion 3.00

GREATEST HITS
Vertigo, Sept., 2008
1 (of 6) A Day in the Life. 3.00
2 thru 3 A Day in the Life . . . . . . @3.00

GREEN ARROW
[Limited Series], 1983
1 TVE,DG,O:Green Arrow. 5.00
2 TVE,DG,A:Vertigo 4.00
3 TVE,DG,A:Vertigo 4.00
4 TVE,DG,A:Black Canary 4.00
[Regular Series], 1988–97
1 EH,DG,V:Muncie 5.00
2 EH,DG,V:Muncie 4.00

3 EH,DG,FMc,V:Fyres.	4.00
4 EH,DG,FMc,V:Fyres.	4.00
5 EH,DG,FMc,Gauntlet	4.00
6 EH,DG,FMc,Gauntlet	4.00
7 EB,DG,A:Black Canary	4.00
8 DG,Alaska	3.50
9 EH,DG,FMc,R:Shado.	3.50
10 EH,DG,FMc,A:Shado.	3.50
11 EH,DG,FMc,A:Shado	3.50
12 EH,DG,FMc,A:Shado	3.00
13 DJu,DG,FMc,Moving Target	3.00
14 EH,DG,FMc.	3.00
15 EH,DG,FMc,Seattle And Die	3.00
16 EH,DG,FMc,Seattle And Die	3.00
17 DJu,DG,FMc,The Horse Man	3.00
18 DJu,DG,FMc,The Horse Man	3.00
19 EH,DG,FMc,A:Hal Jordan	3.00
20 EH,DG,FMc,A:Hal Jordan	3.00
21 DJu,DG,B:Blood of Dragon,	
A:Shado.	4.00
22 DJu,DG,A:Shado.	3.00
23 DJu,DG,A:Shado.	3.00
24 DJu,DG,E:Blood of Dragon	3.00
25 TVE,Witch Hunt #1	3.00
26 Witch Hunt #2	3.00
27 DJu,DG,FMc,R:Warlord	3.00
28 DJu,DG,FMc,A:Warlord.	3.00
29 DJu,DG,FMc,Coyote Tears	3.00
30 DJu,DG,FMc,Coyote Tears	2.50
31 FMc,V:Drug Dealers	2.50
32 FMc,V:Drug Dealers	2.50
33 DJu,FMc,Psychology Issue	2.50
34 DJu,DG,A:Fryes,Arrested	2.50
35 B:Black Arrow Saga,A:Shade.	2.50
36 Black Arrow Saga,A:Shade.	2.50
37 Black Arrow Saga,A:Shade.	2.50
38 E:Black Arrow Saga,A:Shade	2.50
39 DCw,Leaves Seattle	2.50
40 MGr,Spirit Quest,A:	
Indian Shaman	2.50
41 DCw,I.R.A.	2.50
42 DCw,I.R.A.	2.50
43 DCw,I.R.A.	2.50
44 DCw,Rock'n'Runes,pt.1	2.50
45 Rock'n'Runes,pt.2.	2.50
46 DCw,Africa	2.50
47 DCw,V:Trappers	2.50
48 DCw,V:Trappers	2.50
49 V:Trappers	2.50
50 MGr(c),50th Anniv.,R:Seattle	3.00
51 Tanetti's Murder,pt.1	2.50
52 Tanetti's Murder,pt.2	2.50
53 The List,pt.1,A:Fyres.	2.50
54 The List,pt.2,A:Fyres.	2.50
55 Longbow Hunters tie-in.	2.50
56 A:Lt. Cameron.	2.50
57 And Not A Drop to Drink,pt.1	2.50
58 And Not A Drop to Drink,pt.2	2.50
59 Predator,pt.1	2.50
60 Predator,pt.2	2.50
61 FS,F:Draft Dodgers.	2.50
62 FS	2.50
63 FS,B:Hunt for Red Dragon	2.50
64 FS,Hunt for Red Dragon	2.50
65 MGr(c),Hunt for Red Dragon	2.50
66 MGr(c),E:Hunt for Red Dragon.	2.50
67 MGr(c),FS,V:Rockband Killer	2.50
68 MGr(c),FS,BumRap	2.50
69 MGr(c),Reunion Tour #1	2.50
70 Reunion Tour #2	2.50
71 Wild in the Streets #1	2.50
72 MGr(c),Wild in the Streets#2	2.50
73 MGr(c),F:Vietnam Vet	2.50
74 SAP,MGr(c),V:Sniper	2.50
75 MGr(c),A:Speedy Shado,	
Black Canary	3.00
76 MGr(c),R:Eddie Fyers.	2.50
77 MGr(c),A:Eddie Fyers.	2.50
78 MGr(c),V:CIA	2.50
79 MGr(c),V:CIA	2.50
80 MGr(c),E:MGr(s),V:CIA.	2.50

Green Arrow #81
© DC Comics Inc.

81 B:CDi(s),JAp,V:Shrapnel,	
Nuklon	2.50
82 JAp,I:Rival.	2.50
83 JAp,V:Yakuza	2.50
84 E:CDi(s),JAp,In Las Vegas	2.50
85 AlG(s),JAp,A:Deathstroke.	2.50
86 DgM(s),JAp,A:Catwoman	2.50
87 JAp,V:Factory Owner	2.50
88 JAp,A:M.Manhunter,Bl.Beetle.	2.50
89 JAp,A:Anarky	2.50
90 Zero Hour	2.50
91 Hitman	2.50
92 Partner attacked	2.50
93 Secrets of Red File	2.50
94 I:Camo Rouge.	2.50
95 V:Camo Rouge	2.50
96 I:Slyfox,A:Hal Jordan	3.00
97 Where Angels Fear to Tread.	2.50
98 Where Angels Fear to	
Tread,pt.3, A:Arsenal.	2.50
99 Where Angels Fear to Tread.	2.50
100 JAp,Angels Fear to Tread.	12.00
101 A:Superman,Black Canary	35.00
102 CDi,RbC,Underworld	
Unleashed tie-in	3.00
103 CDi,RbC,Underworld	
Unleashed tie-in	3.00
104 CDi,RbC,A:Green Lantern	3.00
105 CDi,RbC,A:Robin	3.00
106 CDi,RbC	2.50
107 CDi,RbC,protects child-king	2.50
108 CDi,A:Thorn	2.50
109 CDi,JAp,BSz,in Metropolis	2.50
110 CDi(s),RbC,I:Hatchet, Green	
Lantern x-over	3.50
111 CDi(s),RbC,I:Hatchet, Green	
Lantern x-over	3.50
112 CDi(s),RbC,.	2.50
113 CDi(s),RbC,In the Mongolian	
wastes	2.50
114 CDi(s) RbC,airplane downed,	
Final Night tie-in	2.50
115 CDi(s),RbC,IronDeath,pt.1	2.50
116 CDi(s),RbC,IronDeath,pt.2	2.50
117 CDi(s),RbC,IronDeath,pt.3	2.50
118 CDi(s),DBw,RbC,Endangered	
Species,pt.1	2.50
119 CDi(s),DBw,RbC,Endangered	
Species, pt.2	2.50
120 CDi(s),RbC,at grandfather's	
ranch	2.50
121 CDi(s),RbC,V:The Silver	
Monkey	2.50
122 CDi(s),RbC, at Idaho ranch	2.50

123 CDi(s),JAp,KJ,The	
Stormbringers, concl.	2.50
124 CDi(s),RbC,V:Milo Armitage	2.50
125 CDi(s),DBw,Green Lantern	
x-over,pt.1, 48pg	3.50
126 CDi(s),DBw,x-over, pt.3	3.00
127 CDi(s),DBw,to San Francisco.	3.00
128 CDi(s),DWb,Russian Mob.	3.00
129 CDi,DBw,Jansen prisoner,pt.2	3.00
130 CDi,DBw,.	3.00
131 CDi,DBw,F:Crackshot.	3.00
132 CDi,DBw,Eddie Fyers returns.	3.00
133 CDi,DBw,Eddie Fyers pt.2	3.00
134 CDi,DBw,Brotherhood of	
the Fist x-over,pt.1.	3.00
135 CDi,DBw,Brotherhood of the	
Fist x-over, concl.	3.00
136 CDi,DBw,Green Pastures,pt.1	3.00
137 CDi(s),A:Superman.	15.00
Ann.#1 A:Question,FablesII	4.00
Ann.#2 EH,DG,FMc,A:Question.	3.50
Ann.#3 A:Question	3.50
Ann.#4 The Black Alchemist	3.50
Ann.#5 TVE,FS,Eclipso,Batman	3.50
Ann.#6 JBa(c),I:Hook.	3.50
Ann.#7 CDi, Year One	4.25
Spec. #0 Return	2.50
Spec.#1,000,000 CDi(s), A:Superman	
final issue	2.50

Feb., 2001

1 PhH,Quiver,pt.1	15.00
1a 2nd printing	3.00
2 PhH,Quiver,pt.2	8.00
3 PhH,Quiver,pt.3	6.00
4 PhH,Quiver,pt.4,A:JLA	6.00
5 PhH,Quiver,pt.5,A:Batman.	6.00
6 PhH,Quiver,pt.6,F:Arsenal	4.00
7 PhH,Quiver,pt.7	4.00
8 PhH,Quiver,pt.8	4.00
9 PhH,Quiver,pt.9	4.00
10 PhH,Quiver,concl.	4.00
11 KSm(s),PhH,rediscovery.	3.50
12 KSm(s),PhH,Ollie,Connor.	4.00
13 KSm(s),PhH,Oliver & Connor	4.00
14 KSm(s),PhH,Onomatopoeia	4.00
15 KSm(s),PhH,last Smith issue	4.00
16 PhH,Archers Quest,pt.1	5.00
17 PhH,Archers Quest,pt.2	3.50
18 PhH,Archers Quest,pt.3	3.50
19 PhH,Archers Quest,pt.4,F:JLA	3.50
20 PhH,Archers Quest,pt.5	3.50
21 PhH,Archers Quest,pt.6	3.50
22 PhH,V:Count Vertigo.	3.00
23 CAd,Urban Knights,pt.1 x-over.	3.00
24 CAd,Urban Knights,pt.3 x-over.	3.00
25 CAd,Urban Knights,pt.5 x-over.	3.00
26 PhH,Straight Shooter,pt.1	2.50
27 PhH,Straight Shooter,pt.2	2.50
28 PhH,Straight Shooter,pt.3	2.50
29 PhH,Straight Shooter,pt.4	2.50
30 PhH,Straight Shooter,pt.5	2.50
31 PhH,Straight Shooter,pt.6	2.50
32 F:Arsenal,Green Arrow II	2.50
33 SMa,F:Superman,Plastic Man	2.50
34 PhH,City Walls,pt.1	2.50
35 PhH,City Walls,pt.2.	2.50
36 PhH,City Walls,pt.3.	2.50
37 PhH,City Walls,pt.4.	2.50
38 PhH,City Walls,pt.5.	2.50
39 PhH,City Walls,pt.6.	2.50
40 PhH,New Blood,pt.1	2.50
41 PhH,New Blood,pt.2	2.50
42 PhH,New Blood,pt.3	2.50
43 PhH,New Blood,pt.4	5.00
44 PhH,New Blood, pt.5	3.00
45 PhH,New Blood, pt.6	2.50
46 RyR,Team Green road trip	2.50
47 RyR,V:Brick, El Pasan Assassin.	2.50
48 RyR,V:Duke of Oil.	2.50
49 RyR,V:Drakon.	2.50
50 RyR,F:Batman, 40-page.	3.50
51 Anarky returns.	2.50

52 Heading into the Light 2.50
53 Heading into the Light 2.50
54 Heading into the Light 2.50
55 Heading Into the Light 2.50
56 Heading Into the Light, pt.3 . . . . 2.50
57 Heading into the Light, concl . . . 2.50
58 Star City Under Attack 2.50
59 V:Merlyn 2.50
60 SMc,One Year Later 2.50
61 SMc,V:Deathstroke 3.00
62 SMc,V:Deathstroke 3.00
63 SMc,Flesh-eating monsters 3.00
64 SMc,Zombies attack 3.00
65 SMc,Away Game,pt.1 . . . . 3.00
66 SMc,Away Game,pt.2 . . . . 3.00
67 SMc,Deadly mercenaries 3.00
68 SMc,End of Ollie's training 3.00
69 SMc,A:Batman 3.00
70 SMc,A:Batman 3.00
71 SMc,V:Red Hood, A:Batman . . . 3.00
72 SMc,Seeing Red 3.00
73 SMc,Mayor of Star City 3.00
74 SMc,Secrets revealed 3.00
75 SMc,Gr. Arrow proposes, 40-pgs.3.50
Spec. Secret Files #1,64-pg 5.00
GN Green Arrow by Jack Kirby 6.00

GREEN ARROW/
BLACK CANARY
Oct., 2007

1 New team, 40-pgs. 3.50
1a variant (c) (1:10) 3.50
2 Voyage To Amazon Island 3.00
3 Fallout on Paradise Island 3.00
2a thru 5a variant (c)s (1:10) . . @3.00
4 Tragedy for Oliver Queen 3.00
5 Marriage in the light of tragedy . 3.00
6 Rescued from Amazons 3.00
7 To London 3.00
8 V:League of Assassins 3.00
9 F:Ra's Al Ghul 3.00
10 A:Batman 3.00
11 Team Arrow 3.00
12 League of Assassins 3.00
13 Speedy and Dodger 3.00
14 Connor Hawke 3.00
Spec. Wedding Special 4.00

GREEN ARROW
LONGBOW HUNTERS
Aug., 1987

1 MGr,N:GreenArrow,I:Shado 7.00
1a 2nd printing 3.00
2 MGr,Shadow Revealed 5.00
2a 2nd printing 3.00
3 MGr,Tracking Snow 5.00

GREEN ARROW:
THE WONDER YEARS
1993

1 MGr,GM,B:New O:Green Arrow . 2.50
2 MGr,GM,I:Brianna Stone 2.50
3 MGr,GM,A:Brianna Stone 2.50
4 MGr,GM,Conclusion 2.50

GREEN ARROW:
YEAR ONE
July, 2007

1 (of 6) O:Green Arrow 3.00
2 thru 6 . . . . @3.00

GREEN LANTERN
[Original Series], Autumn, 1941

1 O:Green Lantern, V:Master of
   Light, Arson in the Slums . 65,000.00
2 V:Baldy,Tycoon's Legacy . . 12,000.00
3 War cover 10,000.00

Green Lantern, Original Series #6
© DC Comics, Inc.

4 Doiby and Green Lantern
   join the Army 7,000.00
5 V:Nazis and Black
   Prophet,A:General Prophet 5,000.00
6 V:Nordo & Hordes of War Hungry
   Henchmen,Exhile of Exiles,
   A:Shiloh 3,600.00
7 The Wizard of Odds 4,000.00
8 The Lady and Her Jewels,
   A:Hop Harrigan 3,600.00
9 V:The Whistler, The School
   for Vandals 3,500.00
10 V:Vandal Savage,The Man Who
   Wanted the World,O:Vandal
   Savage 3,500.00
11 The Distardly Designs of
   Doiby Dickles' Pals 2,400.00
12 O:The Gambler 2,400.00
13 A:Angela Van Enters 2,400.00
14 Case of the Crooked Cook . 2,400.00
15 V:Albert Zero, One...Two...
   Three...Stop Thinking 2,400.00
16 V:The Lizard 2,400.00
17 V:Kid Triangle, Reward for
   Green Lantern 2,400.00
18 V:The Dandy,The Connoisseur
   of Crime, X-mas(c) 2,700.00
19 V:Harpies, Sing a Song of
   Disaster A:Fate 2,100.00
20 A:Gambler 2,100.00
21 V:The Woodman,The Good
   Humor Man 1,800.00
22 A:Dapper Dan Crocker 1,800.00
23 Doiby Dickles Movie
   Ajax Pictures 1,800.00
24 A:Mike Mattson,OnceA Cop . 1,800.00
25 The Diamond Magnet 1,800.00
26 The Scourge of the Sea 1,800.00
27 V:Sky Pirate 1,900.00
28 The Tricks of the
   Sports Master 1,800.00
29 Meets the Challenge of
   the Harlequin 2,000.00
30 I:Streak the Wonder Dog . . . 3,200.00
31 The Terror of the Talismans . 1,600.00
32 The Case of the
   Astonishing Juggler 1,600.00
33 Crime Goes West 1,600.00
34 Streak meets the Princess . . 1,600.00
35 V:Three-in-One Criminal . . . 1,600.00
36 The Mystery of the
   Missing Messenger 1,900.00
37 A:Sargon 1,900.00
38 DoublePlay,May-June,1949 . 1,900.00

GREEN LANTERN
[1st Regular Series],
1960–72, 1976–86

1 GK,O:Green Lantern 9,000.00
2 GK,I:Qward,Pieface 2,000.00
3 GK,V:Qward 1,000.00
4 GK,Secret of GL Mask 900.00
5 GK,I:Hector Hammond 900.00
6 GK,I:Tomar-Re 900.00
7 GK,I&O:Sinestro 700.00
8 GK,1st Story in 5700 A.D. 600.00
9 GK,A:Sinestro 600.00
10 GK,O:Green Lantern's Oath 2,000.00
11 GK,V:Sinestro 550.00
12 GK,Sinestro,I:Dr.Polaris 550.00
13 GK,A:Flash,Sinestro 750.00
14 GK,I&O:Sonar,1st Jordan
   Brothers story 500.00
15 GK,Zero Hour story 500.00
16 GK,MA,I:Star Saphire,
   O:Abin Sur 500.00
17 GK,V:Sinestro 500.00
18 GK 500.00
19 GK,A:Sonar 500.00
20 GK,A:Flash 500.00
21 GK,O:Dr.Polaris 350.00
22 GK,A:Hector Hammond,Jordan
   Brothers story 350.00
23 GK,I:Tattooed Man 350.00
24 GK,O:Shark 350.00
25 GK,V:Sonar,HectorHammond . 350.00
26 GK,A:Star Sapphire 350.00
27 GK 350.00
28 GK,I:Goldface 350.00
29 GK,I:Black Hand 350.00
30 GK,I:Katma Tui 350.00
31 GK,Jordan brothers story 300.00
32 GK 300.00
33 GK,V:Dr. Light 300.00
34 GK,V:Hector Hammond 300.00
35 GK,I:Aerialist 300.00
36 GK 300.00
37 GK,I:Evil Star 300.00
38 GK,A:Tomar-Re 300.00
39 GK,V:Black Hand 300.00
40 GK,O:Guardians,A:Golden
   Age Green Lantern 1,000.00
41 GK,A:Star Sapphire 200.00
42 GK,A:Zatanna 200.00
43 GK,A:Major Disaster 200.00
44 GK,A:Evil Star 200.00
45 GK,I:Prince Peril,A:Golden
   Age Green Lantern 350.00
46 GK,V:Dr.Polaris 200.00
47 GK,5700 A.D. V:Dr.Polaris . . . 200.00
48 GK,I:Goldface 200.00
49 GK,I:Dazzler 200.00
50 GK,V:Thraxon the Powerful . . 200.00
51 GK,Green Lantern's Evil
   Alter-ego 150.00
52 GK,A:Golden Age Green
   Lantern Sinestro 150.00
53 GK,CI,Jordon brothers story . . 150.00
54 GK,Menace in the Iron Lung . . 150.00
55 GK,Cosmic Enemy #1 . . . . . . 150.00
56 GK 150.00
57 GK,V:Major Disaster 150.00
58 GK,Perils of the Powerless
   Green Lantern 150.00
59 GK,I:Guy Gardner(imaginary
   story) 375.00
60 GK,I:Lamplighter 125.00
61 GK,A:Gold.Age Gr.Lantern . . . 125.00
62 Steel Small,Rob Big 125.00
63 NA(c),This is the Way the
   World Ends 125.00
64 MSy,We Vow Death to Green
   Lantern 125.00
65 MSy,Dry up and Die 125.00
66 MSy,5700 AD story 125.00
67 DD,The First Green Lantern . . 125.00

Green Lantern, 1st Series #76
© DC Comics, Inc.

68 GK,I Wonder Where The
   Yellow Went?. 125.00
69 GK,WW,If Earth Fails the
   Test.. It Means War 125.00
70 GK,A Funny Thing Happened
   on the way to Earth 125.00
71 GK,DD,MA,Jordan brothers . . 100.00
72 GK,Phantom o/t SpaceOpera . 100.00
73 GK,MA,A:Star Sapphire,
   Sinestro 100.00
74 GK,MA,A:Star Sapphire,
   Sinestro 100.00
75 GK,Qward. 100.00
76 NA,Gr.Lantern & Gr.Arrow
   team-up begins 800.00
77 NA,Journey to Desolation. . . . 150.00
78 NA,A:Black Canary,A Kind of
   Loving..A Way to Death. 125.00
79 NA,DA,A:Black Canary,Ulysses
   Star is Still Alive. 125.00
80 NA,DG,Even an Immortal
   can die. 125.00
81 NA,DG,A:Black Canary,Death
   be my Destiny 125.00
82 NA,DG,A:Black Canary,
   V:Sinestro,(BWr 1 page) 125.00
83 NA,DG,A:BlackCanary,Gr.Lantern
   reveals I.D. to Carol Ferris . . 125.00
84 NA,BWr,V:Black Hand 125.00
85 NA,Speedy on Drugs,pt.1,
   rep.Green Lantern #1 . . . . . . 150.00
86 NA,DG,Speedy on Drugs,pt.2,
   ATh(rep)Golden Age G.L. . . . 150.00
87 NA,DG,I:John Stewart,
   2nd Guy Gardner app. 125.00
88 all reprints. 75.00
89 NA,And Through Him Save
   the World. 125.00
90 MGr,New Green Lantern rings 50.00
91 MGr,V:Sinestro 25.00
92 MGr,V:Sinestro 25.00
93 MGr,TA,War Against the
   World Builders. 25.00
94 MGr,TA,DG,Green Arrow
   Assassin,pt.1 . . . . 25.00
95 MGr,Gr.Arrow Assassin,pt.2 . . . 25.00
96 MGr,A:Katma Tui 25.00
97 MGr,V:Mocker. 25.00
98 MGr,V:Mocker. 25.00
99 MGr,V:Mocker. 25.00
100 MGr,AS,I:Air Wave 45.00
101 MGr,A:Green Arrow 30.00
102 AS,A:Green Arrow. 15.00
103 AS,Earth-Asylum for an Alien . 15.00
104 AS,A:Air Wave 15.00

105 AS,Thunder Doom 15.00
106 MGr,Panic..In High Places
   & Low 15.00
107 AS,Green Lantern Corp.story . 15.00
108 MGr,BU:G.A.Green Lantern,
   V:Replikon 20.00
109 MGr,Replicon#2,GA.GL.#2 . . . 15.00
110 MGr,GA.GL.#3 . . . . 15.00
111 AS,O:Green Lantern,
   A:G.A.Green Lantern. 20.00
112 AS,O&A:G.A. Green Lantern. . 30.00
113 AS,Christmas story 15.00
114 AS,I:Crumbler. 15.00
115 AS,V:Crumbler. 15.00
116 Guy Gardner as Gr.Lantern . . 75.00
117 JSon,I:KariLimbo,V:Prof.Ojo . . 15.00
118 AS,V:Prof.Ojo 15.00
119 AS,G.L.& G.A.solo storys. . . . 15.00
120 DH,A:Kari,V:El Espectro 6.00
121 DH,V:El Espectro 6.00
122 DH,A:Guy Gardner,Superman 10.00
123 JSon,DG,E:Green Lantern/Green
   Arrow T.U.,A:G.Gardner,
   V:Sinestro 12.00
124 JSon,V:Sinestro 6.00
125 JSon,FMc,V:Sinestro 6.00
126 JSon,FMc,V:Shark 6.00
127 JSon,FMc,V:Goldface 6.00
128 JSon,V:Goldface 6.00
129 JSon,V:Star Sapphire 6.00
130 JSon,FMc,A:Sonar,B:Tales of the
   Green Lantern Corps. 6.00
131 JSon,AS,V:Evil Star 6.00
132 JSon,AS,E:Tales of GL Corps
   B:B.U.Adam Strange 6.00
133 JSon,V:Dr.Polaris 5.00
134 JSon,V:Dr.Polaris 5.00
135 JSon,V:Dr.Polaris 5.00
136 JSon,A:Space Ranger,
   Adam Strange 5.00
137 JSon,CI,MA,I:Citadel,A:Space
   Ranger,A.Strange 5.00
138 JSon,A&O:Eclipso. 6.00
139 JSon,V:Eclipso 5.00
140 JSon,I:Congressman Block
   Adam Strange 5.00
141 JSon,I:OmegaMen 7.00
142 JSon,A:OmegaMen. 6.00
143 JSon,A:OmegaMen. 6.00
144 JSon,D:Tattooed Man,Adam
   Strange 5.00
145 JSon,V:Goldface 5.00
146 JSon,CI,V:Goldface
   E:B.U.Adam Strange 5.00
147 JSon,CI,V:Goldface 5.00
148 JSon,DN,DA,V:Quardians. . . . 5.00
149 JSon,A:GL.Corps 5.00
150 JSon,anniversary 6.00
151 JSon,GL.Exiled in space. 5.00
152 JSon,CI,GL Exile #2 . . . . 5.00
153 JSon,CI,Gr.Lantern Exile #3 . . . 5.00
154 JSon,Gr.Lantern Exile #4 . . . . 5.00
155 JSon,Gr.Lantern Exile #5 . . . . 5.00
156 GK,Gr.Lantern Exile #6. . . . . . 5.00
157 KP,IN,Gr.Lantern Exile #7 . . . . 5.00
158 KP,IN,Gr.Lantern Exile #8. . . . 5.00
159 KP,Gr.Lantern Exile #9 . . . . . . 5.00
160 KP,Gr.Lantern Exile #10 . . . . . 5.00
161 KP,A:Omega Men,Exile #11 . . . 5.00
162 KP,Gr.Lantern Exile #12 . . . . . 6.00
163 KP,Gr.Lantern Exile #13 . . . . . 6.00
164 KP,A:Myrwhidden,Exile #14 . . 5.00
165 KP,A:John Stewart & Gr.Arrow
   Green Lantern Exile #15 . . . . . 5.00
166 GT,FMc,DGi,Exile #16 . . . . . . 5.00
167 GT,FMc,G.L.Exile #17. . . . . . . 5.00
168 GT,FMc,G.L. Exile #18 . . . . . . 5.00
169 Green Lantern Exile #19. . . . . 5.00
170 GT,MSy,GreenLanternCorps. . . 5.00
171 ATh,TA,DGb,Green Lantern
   Exile #20 . . . . 5.00
172 DGb,E:Gr.Lant.Exile 5.00

173 DGb,I:Javelin,A:Congressman
   Bloch 5.00
174 DGb,V:Javelin. 4.50
175 DGb,A:Flash 4.50
176 DGb,V:The Shark 4.50
177 DGb,rep. Gr.Lant #128 . . . . . . 4.50
178 DGb,A:Monitor,V:Demolition
   Team 4.50
179 DGb,I:Predator 4.50
180 DGb,A:JLA 4.50
181 DGi,Hal Jordan quits as Green
   Lantern 5.00
182 DGi,John Stewart takes over
   V:Major Disaster 10.00
183 DGi,V:Major Disaster 3.50
184 DGi,Rep. Gr.Lant. #59. . . . . . . 4.00
185 DGi,DH,V:Eclipso 5.00
186 DGi,V:Eclipso 4.00
187 BWi,John Stewart meets
   Katma Tui 3.50
188 JSon,C:GrArrow,V:Sonar,John
   Stewart reveals I.D. to world . . . 7.00
189 JSon,V:Sonar 3.50
190 JSon,A:Green Arrow/Black
   Canary,Guy Gardner 3.50
191 JSon,IR:Predator is Star
   Sapphire 3.50
192 JSon,O:Star Sapphire 3.50
193 JSon,V:Replikon,A:G.Gardner . 3.50
194 JSon,Crisis,R:G.Gardner. 6.00
195 JSon,Guy Gardner as Green
   Lantern,develops attitude 12.00
196 JSon,V:Shark,Hal Jordan
   regains ring 4.00
197 JSon,V:Shark,Sonar,
   Goldface 4.00
198 JSon,D:Tomar-Re,Hal returns as
   Green Lantern,(double size) . . . 6.00
199 JSon,V:Star Sapphire 3.50
200 JSon,final Gr.Lantern issue. . . . 5.00
Becomes:

GREEN LANTERN
CORPS
1986–88

201 JSon,I:NewGr.LantCorps,V:Star
   Sapphire, Sonar, Dr.Polaris. . . . 3.50
202 JSon,set up headquarters. 3.50
203 JSon,tribute to Disney. 3.50
204 JSon,Arisia reaches puberty. . . 3.50
205 JSon,V:Black Hand. 3.50
206 JSon,V:Black Hand. 3.00
207 JSon, Legends crossover 3.00

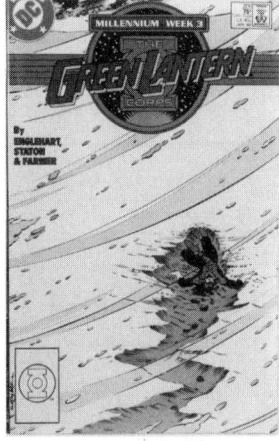

Green Lantern Corps #220
© DC Comics, Inc.

208 JSon,I:Rocket Red Brigade,
   Green Lanterns in Russia#1 . . . 3.00
209 JSon,In Russia #2. . . . . 3.00
210 JSon,In Russia #3. . . . . 3.00
211 JSon,John Stewart proposes
   to Katma Tui 3.00
212 JSon,W:J.Stewart&KatmaTui . . 3.00
213 JSon,For Want of a Male 3.00
214 IG,5700 A.D. Story 3.00
215 IG,Salaak and Chip quit 3.00
216 IG,V:Carl 3.00
217 JSon,V:Sinestro 3.00
218 BWg,V:Sinestro. 3.00
219 BWg,V:Sinestro. 3.00
220 JSon,Millennium,pt.3 . . . . 3.00
221 JSon,Millennium 3.00
222 JSon,V:Sinestro 3.00
223 GK,V:Sinestro 3.00
224 GK,V:Sinestro 3.00
Ann.#1 GK 3.00
Ann.#2 JSa,BWg,S:AnM 3.50
Ann.#3 JBy,JL,JR. 3.00
Spec.#1 A:Superman. 3.00
Spec.#2 MBr,RT,V:Seeker 3.00

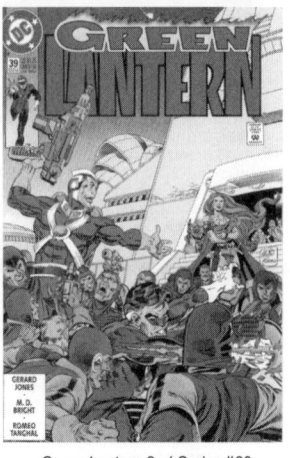

Green Lantern 2nd Series #39
© *DC Comics, Inc.*

GREEN LANTERN
[2nd Regular Series], 1990

1 PB,A:Hal Jordan,John Stuart,
   Guy Gardner 5.00
2 PB,A:Tattooed Man 4.50
3 PB,Jordan vs.Gardner 4.50
4 PB,Vanishing Cities 4.00
5 PB Return to OA 4.00
6 PB 3GL'sCaptive 4.00
7 PB R:Guardians. 4.00
8 PB R:Guardians. 4.00
9 JSon,G.Gardner,pt.1 . . . . 4.00
10 JSon,G.Gardner,pt.2 . . . . 4.00
11 JSon,G.Gardner,pt.3 . . . . 4.00
12 JSon,G.Gardner,pt.4 . . . . 4.00
13 Jordan,Gardner,Stuart(giant) . . . 4.00
14 PB,Mosaic,pt.1 . . . . 4.00
15 RT,Mosaic,pt.2 . . . . 4.00
16 MBr,RT,Mosaic,pt.3. . . . . 4.00
17 MBr,RT,Mosaic,pt.4 . . . . 4.00
18 JSon,JRu,G.Gardner,
   A:Goldface. 4.00
19 MBr,PB,JSon,A:All Four G.L.'s,
   O:Alan Scott,A:Doiby Dickles
   (D.Size-50th Ann.Iss.) 5.00
20 PB,RT,Hal Jordan G.L. Corp
   story begins, A:Flicker 3.00
21 PB,RT,G.L. Corp.,pt.2,
   V:Flicker 3.00
22 PB,RT,G.L. Corp.,pt.3,
   R:Star Sapphire 3.00
23 PB,RT,V:Star Sapphire,
   A:John Stuart. 3.00
24 PB,RT,V:Star Sapphire 3.00
25 MBr,JSon,RT,Hal Vs.Guy,
   A:JLA. 3.00
26 MBr,V:Evil Star,Starlings 3.00
27 MBr,V:Evil Star,Starlings 3.00
28 MBr,V:Evil Star,Starlings 3.00
29 MBr,RT,R:Olivia Reynolds 3.00
30 MBr,RT,Gorilla Warfare#1 . . . . . 3.00
31 MBr,RT,Gorilla Warfare#3 . . . . . . 3.00
32 RT(i),A:Floro,Arisia 3.00
33 MBr,RT,Third Law#1,
   A;New Guardians 3.00
34 MBr,RT,Third Law#2,I:Entropy . . 3.00
35 MBr,RT,Third Law#3,V:Entropy. . 3.00
36 V:Dr.Light 3.00
37 MBg,RT,A:Guy Gardner 3.00
38 MBr,RT,A:Adam Strange 3.00
39 MBr,RT,A:Adam Strange 3.00
40 RT(i),A:Darkstar,
   V:Reverse Flash 3.00
41 MBr,RT,V:Predator,
   C:Deathstroke 3.00
42 MBr,RT,V:Predator,
   Deathstroke 3.00

43 RT(i),A:Itty. 3.00
44 RT(i),Trinity#2,A:L.E.G.I.O.N. . . . 3.00
45 GeH,Trinity#5,A:L.E.G.I.O.N.,
   Darkstars. 3.00
46 MBr,A:All Supermen,
   V:Mongul 8.00
47 A:Green Arrow 6.00
48 KM(c),B:Emerald Twilight,I:Kyle
   Rayner (Last Green Lantern) . 10.00
49 KM(c),GJ(s),A:Sinestro 7.00
50 KM(c),GJ(s),D:Sinestro,Kiliwog,
   Guardians,I:Last Green
   Lantern (in Costume). 8.00
51 V:Ohm,A:Mongul. 6.00
52 V:Mongul. 4.00
53 A:Superman,V:Mongul 4.00
54 D:Alex,V:Major Force 4.00
55 Zero Hour,A:Alan Scott,
   V:Major Force 4.00
56 Green Lantern and ring 3.50
57 Psimon 3.50
58 Donna Troy,Felix Faust. 3.50
59 V:Dr. Polaris 3.50
60 Capital Punishment,pt.3 . . . . 3.50
61 V:Kalibak,A:Darkstar. 3.50
62 V:Duality,R:Ganthet. 3.50
63 Parallax View: The Resurrection
   of Hal Jordan,pt.1 . . . . 3.00
64 Parallax View,pt.2,A:Superman,
   Flash,V:Parallax 3.00
65 Siege of ZiCharan,pt.2 . . . . 3.00
66 V:Sonar. 3.00
67 A:Flash,V:Sonar 3.00
68 RMz,RT,Underworld
   Unleashed tie-in 3.00
69 RMz,RT,Underworld
   Unleashed tie-in 3.00
70 RMz,RT,A:Supergirl 3.00
71 RMz,RT,Hero Quest,pt.1. . . . . . . 3.00
72 RMz,RT,Hero Quest,pt.2. . . . . . . 3.00
73 RMz,RT,Hero Quest,pt.3. . . . . . . 3.00
74 RMz,RT,A:Adam Strange,
   V:Grayven 3.00
75 A:Adam Strange 3.00
76 Green Arrow x-over. 3.00
77 Green Arrow x-over. 3.00
78 RMz(s),A Beginning 3.00
79 V:Sonar. 3.00
80 RMz(s),JWi,MGy,V:Dr. Light,
   Final Night tie-in 3.00
81 RMz(s),DBk,RT,Memorial for
   Hal Jordan 6.00
81a deluxe edition + extra stories,
   foil cover on cardstock 8.00

82 RMz(s),TGb,RT,F:Kyle Rayner,
   Alan Scott, Guy Gardner &
   John Stewart 3.00
83 RMz,Retribution,pt.1 . . . . 3.00
84 Retribution, pt.2 . . . . 3.00
85 Retribution, concl. 3.00
86 RMz,JJ,RT,A:Jade, V:Obsidian. . 3.00
87 RMz,TGb,RT,A:Martian
   Manhunter, vs. Alien Invasion . . 3.00
88 RMz(s),DBk,TA,A:Donna Troy,
   Visit Kyle's Mom 3.00
89 RM(s),TA,V:Machine Messiah . . 3.00
90 RM(s),Why did Kyle Rayner
   become Green Lantern 3.00
91 RMz(s),DBk,TA,V:Desaad. 3.00
92 RMz(s),DBk,TA,A:Green Arrow,
   x-over. 3.00
93 RMz(s),DBk,TA,F:Deadman 3.00
94 RMz(s),PaP,TA,F:Superboy 3.00
95 RMz(s),JSn,TA, deep space. . . . 3.00
96 RMz(s) 3.00
97 RMz(s),MMK,TA,V:Grayven 3.00
98 RMz,DBk,TA,Future Shock,pt.1 . 3.00
99 RMz,DBk,TA,Future Shock,pt.2 . 4.50
100 RMz,DBk,TA,Kyle Rayner and
   Hal Jordan,V:Sinestro, 48pg . . 6.00
100a deluxe edition 4.00
101 RMz(s),JJ,BWi,Emerald
   Knights,pt.1, bi-weekly 4.00
102 RMz(s),PaP,TA,Emerald
   Knights,pt.2, bi-weekly 4.00
103 RMz(s),JJ,BWi,Emerald
   Knights,pt.3, bi-weekly 4.00
104 RMz(s),JJ,BWi,Greener Pastures
   x-over, concl., Emerald
   Knights,pt.4, bi-weekly 4.00
105 RMz(s),JJ,SEa,BWi,Emerald
   Knights,pt.5, bi-weekly 4.00
106 RMz(s),PaP,TA,Emerald
   Knights,concl. 4.00
107 RMz(s),TA,Emerald Knights
   aftermath 2.50
108 DBk,TA,A:Wonder Woman 2.50
109 RMz(s),PaP,TA 2.50
110 RMz(s),TA,A:Green Arrow. 2.50
111 RMz(s),TA,DBk,V:Fatality 2.50
112 RMz(s),TA,DBk,back to Earth . . 2.50
113 RMz(s),TA,DBk,Burning
   in Effigy,pt.1. . . . . 2.50
114 RMz(s),TA,DBk,Burning
   in Effigy,pt.2. . . . . 2.50
115 DJu(s),A:Plastic Man &
   Booster Gold, pt.1 . . . . 2.50
116 DJu(s),A:Plastic Man &
   Booster Gold, pt.1 . . . . 2.50
117 RMz(s),DBk,TA,R:Donna Troy . 2.50
118 RMz(s),DBk,TA,Day of
   Judgment x-over 2.50
119 RMz,DBk,CaS,Day of
   Judgment aftermath 9.00
120 RMz,DBk,CaS. 2.50
121 RMz,DBk,CaS. 2.50
122 RMz,DBk,CaS. 2.50
123 RMz,DBk,V:Controllers. 2.50
124 RMz,DBk,V:Controllers. 2.50
125 RMz,Unmooning secrets 2.50
126 Goes undercover 2.50
127 F:Effigy & Killer Frost 2.50
128 F:Arsenal. 2.50
129 DBk,ASm,V:Manhunters 2.50
130 DBk,ASm,V:Manhunters 2.50
131 DBk,ASm,V:Manhunters 2.50
132 DBk,While Rome Burned,pt.1 . . 2.50
133 DBk,MBr,Rome Burned,pt.2 . . . 2.50
134 DBk,While Rome Burned,pt.3. . 2.50
135 DBk,While Rome Burned,pt.4. . 2.50
136 DBk,While Rome Burned,pt.5. . 2.50
137 DBk,Friends & Lovers. 2.50
138 DBk,Away From Home,pt.1 . . . 2.50
139 DBk,Away From Home,pt.2 . . . 2.50
140 DBk,A:Alan Scott 2.50
141 DBk,A:Jade,V:arsonist 2.50

DC COMICS

142 V:Inferno 2.50
143 JLe,Joker:Last Laugh,tie-in. . . . 2.50
144 Battle to control his powers . . . 2.50
145 V:Nero 7.00
146 incredible metamorphosis. 6.00
147 F:John Stewart 2.50
148 A:Superman,R:Jade 2.50
149 F:JLA. 2.50
150 End of Ion,48-pg. 5.00
151 JLe(c) Hand of God,aftermath . 2.50
152 RbC,uncontrollable madness . . 2.50
153 JLe(c),high school reunion 2.50
154 JLe&SW(c),attacked 2.50
155 JLe&SW(c),A:Flash,JLA 2.50
156 John Stewart back,A:Sentinel . 2.50
157 Girl Talk. 2.50
158 industrialist nomads 2.50
159 Boar Beasts 2.50
160 Child Guardians 2.50
161 V:Amazon 2.50
162 CAd,Urban Knights,pt.2 x-over. 2.50
163 CAd,Urban Knights,pt.4 x-over. 2.50
164 CAd,Urban Knights,pt.6 x-over. 2.50
165 RBr,A Tiny Spark. 2.50
166 RBr,The Blind,pt.1. . . . . 2.50
167 RBr,The Blind,pt.2. . . . . 2.50
168 RBr 2.50
169 RBr,Kilowog's soul 2.50
170 RBr 2.50
171 Wanted, pt.1 . . . . 2.50
172 kidnappers 2.50
173 V:Weaponers of Qward. 2.50
174 V:Black Circle 2.50
175 Qwardians,48-pg. 3.50
176 LRs,RyR,Homecoming,pt.1 . . . 4.00
177 LRs,RyR,Homecoming,pt.2 . . . 4.00
178 LRs,RyR,Homecoming,pt.3 . . . 4.00
179 LRs,RyR,Homecoming,pt.4 . . . 4.00
180 LRs,RyR,Homecoming,pt.5 . . . 4.00
181 LRs,RyR,Homecoming,pt.6 . . . 4.00
Ann.#1 Eclipso,V:Star Sapphire . . 4.00
Ann.#1 80pg, rep. 5.00
Ann.#2 Bloodlines#7,I:Nightblade . . 4.00
Ann.#3 Elseworlds Story 3.50
Ann.#4 Year One story. 4.00
Ann.#5 Legends o/t Dead Earth . . 3.50
Ann.#6 RMz(s),JJ,Low,Pulp
   Heroes, 64pg. 4.50
Ann.#7 SV,RLm,Clv,BWr,Ghosts . . 3.50
Ann.#8 MCa,AAd(c),JLApe:Gorilla
   Warfare 3.50
Ann.#9 Planet DC 4.00
Spec.#1,000,000 RMz(s),BHi,PNe . 2.50
Spec. 3-D #1 V:Dr. Light 4.00
Spec.#1 Our Worlds at War(2001). . 3.00
Secret Files #1. . . . . 5.00
Secret Files Spec.#2 . . . . 5.00
Secret Files #3, 48-pg. 5.00
Green Lantern Plus, 1-shot RMz(s),
   F:The Ray,V:Dr. Polaris 3.00
Green Lantern/Silver Surfer, 1-shot
   DC/Marvel RMz,TA A:Thanos
   vs. Parallax 5.00
Green Lantern Gallery, 1 one-shot . 3.50
Green Lantern: Ganthet's Tale,
   1-shot, JBy,O:Guardians 7.00
Giant #1 80-page 5.50
Giant #2 80-page 5.50
Giant #3 80-page 6.00
GN Ganthet's Tale, JBy 6.00
GN Green Lantern/Superman:
   Legends of the Green Flame . . 6.00
GN 1001 Emerald Nights(2001) . . . 7.00
GN Brightest Day/Blackest Night. . . 6.00

GREEN LANTERN
May, 2005

1 F:Hal Jordan, No Fear,40-page . . 3.50
2 No Fear, pt.2 . . . . 3.00
3 No Fear, pt.3 . . . . 3.00
4 F:Gilowog. 3.00
5 V:Shark 3.00

6 V:Black Hand 3.00
7 A:Green Arrow 3.00
8 A Perfect Life, pt.1 . . . . 3.00
8a Adams (c). 6.00
9 A Perfect Life, pt.2, A:Batman . . 3.00
9a Van Sciver(c). 12.00
10 One Year Later 3.00
11 Revenge of the Green Lanterns . 4.00
12 Revenge of the Green Lanterns . 4.00
13 Wanted: Hal Jordan, pt.1 . . . . . . 3.00
14 Wanted: Hal Jordan, pt.2 . . . . . . 3.00
15 Wanted: Hal Jordan, pt.3 . . . . . . 3.00
16 Wanted: Hal Jordan, pt.4 . . . . . . 3.00
17 Wanted: Hal Jordan, concl. 3.00
18 Mystery of Star Sapphire 5.00
19 Mystery of Star Sapphire 5.00
20 Mystery of Star Sapphire 5.00
21 Sinestro Corps, pt.1 . . . . 5.00
21a variant (c) (1:10) 8.00
22 Sinestro Corps, pt.2 . . . . 4.00
23 Sinestro Corps War. 4.00
24 Sinestro Corps War. 4.00
25 Sinestro Corps War concl.,64-pg.5.00
25a variant GFr(c) (1:10) 12.00
26 The Alpha Lanterns, pt.1 . . . . . . 4.00
27 The Alpha Lanterns, pt.2 . . . . . . 3.00
28 The Alpha Lanterns, concl. 3.00
29 Secret Origin, pt.1 . . . . 3.00
30 Secret Origin, pt.2 . . . . 3.00
31 Secret Origin, pt.3,Sinestro. 3.00
32 Secret Origin, pt.4 . . . . 3.00
33 Secret Origin, pt.5 . . . . 3.00
34 Secret Origin, pt.6 . . . . 3.00
35 Secret Origin, concl. 3.00
36 V:Red Lantern Corps. 3.00
Spec. Sinestro Corps Special #1 . . 5.00
Secret Files 2005, 48-page 5.00
Spec. #1 Green Lantern/Sinestro
   Corp Secret Files, 64-pg.(2007) 5.00

GREEN LANTERN
& SENTINEL:
HEART OF DARKNESS
Feb., 1998

1 (of 3) RMz(s),PaP,DDv 3.00
2 RMz(s),PaP,DDv 3.00
3 RMz(s),PaP,DDv 3.00

GREEN LANTERN:
CIRCLE OF FIRE
Aug., 2000

1 (of 2) NBy,64-pg. x-over 5.00
2 48-pg.x-over concl. 5.00
Spec.Gr.Lant.: Adam Strange #1 . . 2.50
Spec.Gr.Lant.: The Atom #1. . . . . . 2.50
Spec.Gr.Lant.: Firestorm #1. . . . . . 2.50
Spec.Gr.Lant.: Green Lantern #1. . . 2.50
Spec.Gr.Lant.: Power Girl #1 . . . . . 2.50

GREEN LANTERN CORPS
June, 2006

1 DGb 3.00
2 thru 6 DGb . . . . @3.00
7 Dark Side of the Green, pt.1 . . . . 3.00
8 Dark Side of the Green, pt.2 . . . . 3.00
9 Dark Side of the Green, pt.3 . . . . 3.00
10 Lantern vs. Lantern. 3.00
11 Children of the White Lobe 3.00
12 Refuge on Mogo 3.00
13 Mogo's forests. 3.00
14 Mogo under fire. 4.00
15 The Battle of Mogo 4.00
16 Sinestro Corps War. 4.00
17 Sinestro Corps War. 4.00
18 Sinestro Corps War epilogue . . . 4.00
19 F:Guy & Ice. 3.00
20 V:Mongul. 3.00
21 Mongul has a Sinestro ring. 3.00
22 Curse of Lost Lanterns, pt.2 . . . . 3.00

23 Sinestro Corps Rings 3.00
24 Sodam & Arisia captured 3.00
25 F:Black Mercy, Mongul 3.00
26 Ring Quest, concl 3.00
27 Warriors's Bar, Saarek 3.00
28 Scar, Lantern Saarek 3.00
29 Sins of the Star Sapphire,pt.1 . . . 3.00
30 Sins of the Star Sapphire,pt.2 . . . 3.00

GREEN LANTERN
CORPS QUARTERLY
1992–94

1 DAb,JSon,FH,PG,MBr,F:Alan
   Scott G'nort 3.00
2 DAb,JSon,PG,AG,Alan Scott . . . 2.75
3 DAb,RT,F:Alan Scott,G'Nort 2.75
4 TA,AG(i),F:H.Jordan,G'Nort 2.75
5 F:Alan Scott,I:Adam. 2.75
6 JBa,TC,F:Alan Scott 3.25
7 Halloween Issue 3.25
8 GeH,SHa,final issue 3.25

GREEN LANTERN CORPS:
RECHARGE
Sept., 2005

1 (of 5) 40-page 3.50
2 thru 5 . . . . @3.00

GREEN LANTERN:
DRAGON LORD
April, 2001

1 (of 3) PG, 48-page 5.00
2 thru 3 PG, 48-page. . . . . @5.00

GREEN LANTERN:
EMERALD DAWN
[1st Limited Series], 1989–90

1 MBr,RT,I:Mod.Age.Gr.Lantern . . . 5.00
2 MBr,RT,I:Legion (not group) 4.00
3 MBr,RT,V:Legion 3.00
4 MBr,RT,A:Green Lantern Corps. . 3.00
5 MBr,RT,V:Legion 3.00
6 MBr,RT,V:Legion 3.00

[2nd Limited Series], 1991

1 MBr,A:Sinestro,Guy Gardner 2.00
2 MBr,RT,V:Alien Aliance 2.00
3 MBr,RT,Sinestro's Home Planet . 2.00
4 MBr,RT,Korugar Revolt 2.00
5 MBr,RT,A:G.Gardner 2.00
6 MBr,RT,Trial of Sinestro 2.00

Green Lantern Emerald Dawn #6
© DC Comics Inc.

GREEN LANTERN: EVIL'S MIGHT
Aug., 2002
1 (of 3) HC, Elseworlds, 48-pg. 6.00
2 HC,F:Kyle Rayner 6.00
3 HC,concl. 6.00

GREEN LANTERN/ GREEN ARROW
1983–84
1 NA rep. 5.00
2 thru 7 NA,DG rep. . . . . @4.00

GREEN LANTERN: MOSAIC
1992–93
1 F:John Stewart. 2.25
2 thru 18 . . . . @2.25

GREEN LANTERN: THE NEW CORPS
1999
1 (of 2) CDi(s),SEa 5.00
2 CDi(s),SEa, concl. 5.00

GREEN LANTERN: REBIRTH
Oct. 2004
1 (of 6) 40-pg. 3.00
2 F:JLA 3.50
3 V:Spectre 3.50
4 A:JLA,JSA,&Teen Titans 3.00
5 To restore Hal Jordan 3.00
6 Hal Jordan's return 3.00

GREGORY
DC/Piranha
1 MaH, b&w 8.00
2 MaH 5.00
3 MaH Bookshelf Ed. 5.00
3a Platinum Ed. 8.00
4 MaH, b&w 5.00

GRIFFIN
1991–92
1 I:Matt Williams as Griffin 5.50
2 V:Carson 5.25
3 A:Mary Wayne 5.25
4 A:Mary Wayne 5.25
5 Face to Face with Himself 5.25
6 Final Issue 5.25

GRIP: THE STRANGE WORLD OF MEN
DC/Vertigo, Nov., 2001
1 (of 5) GHe 2.50
2 thru 5 GHe . . . . @2.50

GROSS POINT
July, 1997
1 MWa&BAu(s) parody 2.50
2 thru 14 . . . . @2.50

GUARDIAN OF METROPOLIS
Nov., 2008
Spec. #1 New Krypton, pt.3 x-over . 3.00

GUARDIANS OF METROPOLIS
Nov., 1994
1 thru 4 Kirby characters. . . . . . . @2.50

Gunfire #2
© DC Comics, Inc.

GUNFIRE
1994–95
1 B:LWn(s),StE,I:Ricochet 2.50
2 thru 13 . . . . @2.50

GUNS OF THE DRAGON
Aug., 1998
1 (of 4) TT, set in 1920s 2.50
2 TT. 2.50
3 TT. 2.50
4 TT conclusion 2.50

GUY GARDNER
1992–94
1 JSon,A:JLA,JLE 2.50
2 JSon,A:Kilowog 2.50
3 JSon,V:Big,Ugly Alien 2.50
4 JSon,G.Gardner vs Ice 2.50
5 JSon,A:Hal Jordan,V:Goldface . . 2.50
6 JSon,A:Hal Jordan,V:Goldface . . 2.50
7 JSon,V:Goldface 2.50
8 JSon,V:Lobo 2.50
9 JSon,Boodikka 2.50
10 JSon,V:Boodikka. 2.50
11 JSon,B:Year One 2.50
12 JSon,V:Batman,Flash,Green
   Lantern 2.50
13 JSon,Year One#3 . . . . 2.50
14 JSon,E:Year One 2.50
15 V:Bad Guy Gardner 2.50
16 B:CDi(s),MaT,V:Guy's Brother . . 2.50
Becomes:

GUY GARDNER: WARRIOR
1994–96
17 V:Militia 2.50
18 B:Emerald Fallout,N:Guy Gardner,
   V:Militia 4.00
19 A:G.A.Green Lantern,V:Militia . . 4.00
20 A:JLA,Darkstars 2.50
21 E:Emerald Fallout,V:H.Jordan . . 2.50
22 I:Dementor 2.50
23 A:Buck Wargo 2.50
24 Zero Hour 2.50
25 A:Buck Wargo 3.00
26 Zero Hour 2.50
27 Capital Punishment. 2.50
28 Capital Punishment,pt.2 . . . . . . 2.50
29 I:Warriors Bar 2.50
29a Collector's Edition 3.25
30 V:Superman,Supergirl. 2.50

31 A:Sentinel,Supergirl,
   V:Dementor 2.50
32 Way of the Warrior,pt.1,A:JLA . . 2.50
33 Way of the Warrior,pt.4 . . . . 2.50
34 . . . . 2.50
35 Return of an Old Foe 2.50
36 Underworld Unleashed tie-in . . . 2.50
37 Underworld Unleashed tie-in . . . 2.50
38 A new woman 2.50
39 Guest stars galore 2.50
40 . . . . 2.50
41 V:Dungeon 2.50
42 Martika revealed as Seductress . 2.50
43 V:5 Foes 2.50
Ann.#1 Year One Annual, Leechun
   vs. Vuldarians 4.00
Ann.#2 Dead Earth 3.50

GUY GARDNER: COLLATERAL DAMAGE
Nov., 2006
1 (of 2) HC 6.00
2 HC. 6.00

GUY GARDNER: REBORN
1992
1 JSon,JRu,V:Goldface,C:Lobo . . . 6.00
2 JSon,JRu,A:Lobo,V:Weapons
   of Qward 5.50
3 JSon,JRu,A:Lobo,N:G.Gardner
   V:Qwardians 5.50

HACKER FILES
1992–93
1 TS,Soft Wars#1,I:Jack Marshall . 2.50
2 TS,Soft Wars#2 . . . . 2.50
3 TS,Soft Wars#3 . . . . 2.50
4 TS,Soft Wars#4 . . . . 2.50
5 TS,A:Oracle(Batgirl). 2.50
6 TS,A:Oracle,Green Lantern 2.50
7 TS,V:Digitronix 2.50
8 TS,V:Digitronix 2.50
9 TS,V:Digitronix 2.50
10 V:Digitronix 2.50
11 TS,A:JLE 2.50
12 TS,V:Digitronix,final issue 2.50

HAMMER LOCKE
1992–93
1 I:Hammerlocke. 3.00
2 thru 8 . . . . @2.50

HARDCORE STATION
May, 1998
1 (of 6) JSn,JRu,F:Maximillian 3.00
2 JSn,JRu,V:Synnar 3.00
3 JSn,JRu,F:Kyle Rayner 3.00
4 JSn,JRu,V:Synnar 3.00
5 JSn,JRu,F:JLA 3.00
6 JSn,JRu,conclusion 3.00

HARD TIME
DC Focus Feb. 2004
1 F:Ethan Harrow 2.50
2 thru 12 . . . . @2.50

HARD TIME SEASON TWO
Dec., 2005
1 . . . . 2.50
2 . . . . 2.50
3 F:Cutter 2.50
4 F:Cindy 2.50
5 . . . . 2.50
6 . . . . 3.00
7 Finale 3.00

Hardware #41
© DC Comics, Inc.

HARDWARE

DC/Milestone, 1993–96
1 DCw,I:Hardware,Edwin Alva,Reprise,
  Dir.Mark.Ed.,w/A puzzle piece,
  Skybox Card,Poster 4.00
1a NewsstandEd. 2.50
1b Platinum Ed. 6.00
2 thru 15 . . . . @2.50
16 Die-Cut(c),JBy(c),DCw,
  N:Hardware 4.25
16a Newsstand ED. 2.50
17 thru 24 . . . . @2.50
25 V:Death Row, Sanction. 3.00
26 thru 49 . . . . @2.50
50 DGC(s), 48pg. anniversary issue 4.00
51 DMc(s) final issue 2.50

HARLEY QUINN

October, 2000
1 KK,TyD,A:Batman,48 pg. 5.00
2 KK,TyD,A:Two-Face,Poison Ivy. . 2.50
3 KK,TyD,A:Catwoman 2.50
4 KK,TyD,I:Quinntettes 2.50
5 KK,TyD,F:Quinntettes 2.50
6 KK,TyD,A:Oracle 2.50
7 KK,TyD,F:Big Barda. 2.50
8 KK,TyD,Harley's Past 2.50
9 KK,TyD,V:Quinntettes 2.50
10 KK,TyD,F:Barbara Gordon 2.50
11 KK,TyD,F:Nightwing 2.50
12 KK,TyD,40-page 3.50
13 KK,Joker:Last Laugh 2.50
14 KK,TyD,to Metropolis 2.50
15 KK,TyD,Lovers advice 2.50
16 KK,TyD,City of Tomorrow 2.50
17 KK,TyD,F:Bizarro 2.50
18 KK,TyD,F:Bizarro 2.50
19 KK,TyD,A:Superman. 2.50
20 KK,Harley pays price for evil . . . 2.50
21 KK,ultimate prison. 2.50
22 KK,TyD,Highwater. 2.50
23 KK,TyD,World Without Harley. . . 2.50
24 KK,DDv,back from Hell 2.50
25 KK,DDv,F:Batman,A:Joker 2.50
26 wanted for murder. 2.50
27 Harley a psychiatrist 2.50
28 new patient 2.50
29 a stalker 2.50
30 Who framed Harley?. 2.50
31 Harley and Doc. 2.50
32 A:Joker 2.50
33 Behind Blue Eyes,pt.1 . . . . 2.50
34 Behind Blue Eyes,pt.2 . . . . 2.50

35 Behind Blue Eyes,pt.3 . . . . 2.50
36 Behind Blue Eyes,pt.4 . . . . 2.50
37 Behind Blue Eyes,pt.5 . . . . 2.50
38 CAd,final issue 2.50
Spec.#1 Our Worlds at War,48-pg . 3.25
GN Harley & Ivy, Love on the Lam . 6.50

HAVEN:
THE BROKEN CITY
Dec., 2001
1 (of 9) AOI,F:JLA. 2.50
2 AOI,A:JLA 2.50
3 AOI,A:Superman,I:HankVelveeda 2.50
4 AOI,F:Nia 2.50
5 AOI,Eater of Filth 2.50
6 AOI,search for crash survivors. . 2.50
7 AOI,V:Ivas the ultra-powerful . . . 2.50
8 AOI,Anathema 2.50
9 AOI,Valadin 2.50

HAWK & DOVE
[1st Regular Series], 1968–69
1 SD 150.00
2 SD 100.00
3 GK 75.00
4 GK 75.00
5 GK,C:Teen Titans. 75.00
6 GK 75.00

[Limited Series], 1988–89
1 RLd,I:New Dove. 4.00
2 RLd,V:Kestrel. 3.50
3 RLd,V:Kestrel. 3.50
4 RLd,V:Kestrel. 3.50
5 RLd,V:Kestrel,O:New Dove 3.50

[2nd Regular Series], 1989–91
1 A:Superman,Green Lantern
  Hawkman. 2.50
2 V:Aztec Goddess 2.50
3 V:Aztec Goddess 2.50
4 I:The Untouchables 2.50
5 I:Sudden Death, A:1st Dove's
  Ghost. 2.50
6 A:Barter,Secrets o/Hawk&Dove. 2.50
7 A:Barter,V:Count St.Germain. . . 2.50
8 V:Count St.Germain. 2.50
9 A:Copperhead 2.50
10 V:Gauntlet & Andromeda 2.50
11 A:New Titans,V:M.A.C.,
  Andromeda Gauntlet 2.50
12 A:New Titans,V:Scarab 2.50
13 1960's,I:Shellshock. 2.50
14 Prelue to O:Hawk & Dove,
  V:Kestrel 2.50
15 O:Hawk & Dove begins 2.50
16 HawkV:Dove,V:Lord of Chaos . 2.50
17 V:Lords-Order & Chaos 2.50
18 The Creeper #1. . . . . 2.50
19 The Creeper #2. . . . . 2.50
20 KM,DG,Christmas Story 2.50
21 Dove 2.50
22 V:Sudden Death 2.50
23 A:Velv.Tiger,SuddenDeath 2.50
24 A:Velv.Tiger,SuddenDeath 2.50
25 Recap 1st 2 yrs.(48 pg) 2.50
26 Dove's past. 2.50
27 The Hunt for Hawk 2.50
28 War of the Gods,A:Wildebeest
  A:Uncle Sam,final issue,
  double size 3.00
Ann.#1 In Hell 3.00
Ann.#2 CS,KGa,ArmageddonPt.5 . . 3.00

HAWK & DOVE
Sept., 1997
1 (of 5) MBn,DZ,DG,Sasha Martens
  & Wiley Wolverman. 2.50
2 MBn,DZ,DG,Vixen & Vigilante . . 2.50
3 MBn,DZ,DG,grave desecrations . 2.50
4 MBn,DZ,DG,V:Suicide Squad . . 2.50

HAWKMAN
[1st Regular Series], 1964–68
1 MA,V:Chac 1,400.00
2 MA,V:Tralls 500.00
3 MA,V:Sky Raiders 500.00
4 MA,I&O:Zatanna 450.00
5 MA 300.00
6 MA 300.00
7 MA,V:I.Q. 300.00
8 MA 300.00
9 MA,V:Matter Master. 300.00
10 MA,V:Caw 300.00
11 MA. 250.00
12 MA. 200.00
13 MA. 200.00
14 GaF,MA,V:Caw 200.00
15 GaF,MA,V:Makkar. 200.00
16 GaF,MA,V:Ruthvol 200.00
17 GaF,MA,V:Raven 200.00
18 GaF,MA,A:Adam Strange 150.00
19 GaF,MA,A:Adam Strange 150.00
20 GaF,MA,V:Lionmane. 100.00
21 GaF,MA,V:Lionmane. 100.00
22 V:Falcon 100.00
23 V:Dr.Malevolo 100.00
24 Robot Raiders from
  Planet Midnight 100.00
25 DD,V:Medusa,G.A.Hawkman . 100.00
26 RdM,CCu,DD 100.00
27 DD,JKu(c),V:Yeti 100.00

[2nd Regular Series], 1986–87
1 DH,A:Shadow Thief 3.00
2 DH,V:Shadow Thief 2.50
3 DH,V:Shadow Thief 2.50
4 DH A:Zatanna 2.50
5 DH,V:Lionmane. 2.50
6 DH,V:Gentleman Ghost,
  Lionmane. 2.50
7 DH,Honor Wings 2.50
8 DH,Shadow War contd. 2.50
9 DH,Shadow War contd. 2.50
10 JBy(c),D:Hyatis Corp 2.50
11 End of Shadow War 2.50
12 Hawks on Thanagar 2.50
13 DH,Murder Case. 2.50
14 DH,Mystery o/Haunted Masks . 2.50
15 DH,Murderer Revealed. 2.50
16 DH,Hawkwoman lost 2.50
17 EH,DH,final issue 2.50

[3rd Regular Series], 1993–96
1 B:JOs(s),JD,R:Hawkman,
  V:Deadline 5.00
2 JD,A:Gr.Lantern,V:Meta-Tech . . 3.00
3 JD,I:Airstryke 2.75
4 JD,RM 2.50
5 JD(c),V:Count Viper. 2.50
6 JD(c),A:Eradicator 2.50
7 JD(c),PuK(s),LMc,B:King of the
  Netherworld 2.50
8 LMc,E:King of the Netherworld . 2.50
9 BML(s). 2.50
10 I:Badblood. 2.50
11 V:Badblood 2.50
12 V:Hawkgod 2.75
13 V:Hawkgod 2.75
14 New abilities,pt.1. . . . . 2.50
15 New abilities,pt.2. . . . . 2.50
16 Eyes of the Hawk,pt.3. . . . . . . 2.50
17 Eyes of the Hawk,pt.4. . . . . . . 2.50
18 Seagle,Ellis, Pepoy. 2.50
19 F:Hawkman. 2.50
21 RLm,V:Shadow Thief,
  Gentleman Ghost 2.75
22 Way of the Warrior,pt.3
  A:Warrior,JLA 2.75
23 Way of the Warrior,pt.6 . . . . . . 2.75
24 . . . . 2.75
25 V:Lionmane,painted(c) 2.75
26 WML,Underworld
  Unleashed tie-in 2.75

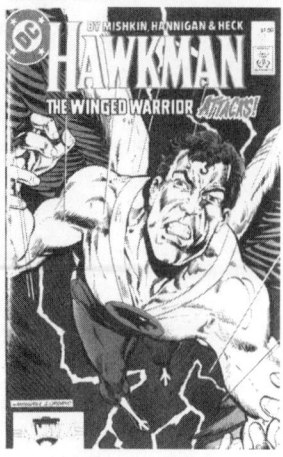

Hawkman 2nd Series #17
© DC Comics, Inc.

27 WML,Underworld
  Unleashed tie-in 2.75
28 WML,V:Doctor Polaris. 2.75
29 HC(c),V:Vandal Savage 2.75
30 . . . . 2.75
31 serial killer has Tangarian
  technology 2.75
32 MC,Search for serial killer 2.75
Ann.#1 JD,I:Mongrel 4.00
Ann.#2 Year One Annual 4.00

[4th Regular Series], 2002
1 RgM,MiB,Hawkman & Hawkgirl. . 5.00
1a 2nd printing 2.50
2 RgM,MiB,F:Hawkgirl 2.50
3 RgM,MiB,inter-dimensional portal 2.50
4 RgM,MiB,trapped in Battlelands . 2.50
5 RgM,MiB,Slings and Arrows,pt.1 . 2.50
6 RgM,MiB,Slings and Arrows,pt.2 . 2.50
7 RgM,TT,Lives past 2.50
8 RgM,MiB,F:Atom 2.50
9 RgM,F:Dr.Fate 2.50
10 RgM,find Speed Saunders 2.50
11 RgM,V:Hath-Set 2.50
12 RgM,V:Darkraven 2.50
13 Hawk vs. Hawk 2.50
14 Hawkgirl's parents' murderer . . . 2.50
15 Shayera Thai 2.50
16 RgM,The Thanagarian,pt.1. . . . . 2.50
17 RgM,The Thanagarian,pt.2. . . . . 2.50
18 RgM,The Thanagarian,pt.3. . . . . 2.50
19 F:Black Adam 2.50
20 RgM,MIB,V:Headhunter,pt.1 . . . . 2.50
21 RgM,MIB,V:Headhunter,pt.2 . . . . 2.50
22 RgM,MIB,V:Headhunter,pt.3 . . . . 2.50
23 Black Reign,pt.2,x-over 2.50
24 Black Reign,pt.4,x-over 2.50
25 Black Reign,pt.6,x-over. 2.50
26 Rabid vampires 2.50
27 SeP,Past Lives 2.50
28 Fate's Warning,pt.1 . . . . 2.50
29 Fate's Warning,pt.2 . . . . 2.50
30 Fate's Warning,pt.3 . . . . 2.50
31 Fate's Warning,pt.4 . . . . 2.50
32 JoB,F:The Atom 2.50
33 ASm,MGy,F:Monolith 2.50
34 V:Manticore 2.50
35 JoB,V:Zombies 2.50
36 JoB,V:Zombies,A:Deadman 2.50
37 JoB,V:Fadeaway Man 2.50
38 previous incarnations visit. 4.00
39 JoB,Hawkman missing 3.00
40 JoB,F:Dr. Fate. 3.00
41 JoB,new Hawkman 5.00
42 JP(s),JoB,V:Pilgrim 2.50

43 JoB,Golden Eagle 2.50
44 JoB,Golden Eagle 2.50
45 JoB,F:JSA 2.50
46 ATi,AKu(c),Rann/Thanagar War . 2.50
47 CsB,CaS,Coalition in Crisis 2.50
48 CsB,CaS,Coalition in Crisis 2.50
49 CsB,CaS,Coalition in Crisis 2.50
Spec. Secret Files #1, 48-pg. 5.00
Becomes:

HAWKGIRL
March, 2006
50 WS,HC, One Year Later 3.00
51 WS,HC,St. Roch Museum 3.00
52 WS,HC,Lizard Kings voodoo . . . 3.00
53 WS,HC,V:Khimaera 3.00
54 WS,HC,Friend from the pst 3.00
55 WS,HC,Hawkman returns. 3.00
56 WS,HC,Truths and Evils 3.00
57 WS,JoB,HC(c). 3.00
58 WS,JoB,HC(c). 3.00
59 WS,JSA Classified x-over, pt.1 . . 3.00
60 WS,JSA Classified x-over, pt.4 . . 3.00
61 WS,HC(c),Search for Hath-Set. . 3.00
62 WS,HC(c),Search for Hath-Set. . 3.00
63 WS,HC(c),Search for Hath-Set. . 3.00
64 WS,HC(c),A:Superman,Oracle . . 3.00
65 WS,HC(c),Fate of the Hawks . . . 3.00
66 WS,V:Hath-Set, final issue 3.00

HAWKMAN
Aug., 2008
Spec. #1 JSn, Holy War tie-in 3.50

HAWKWORLD
1989
1 TT,Hawkman, Origin retold 5.00
2 TT,Katar tried for treason 4.00
3 TT,Hawkgirl's debut 4.00

[1st Regular Series], 1990–93
1 GN,Byth on Earth,R:Kanjar Ro . . 3.00
2 GN,Katar & Shayera in Chicago . 2.50
3 GN,V:Chicago Crime 2.50
4 GN,Byth's Control Tightens 2.50
5 GN,Return of Shadow Thief 2.50
6 GN,Stolen Thanagarian Ship. . . . 2.50
7 GN,V:Byth 2.50
8 GN,Hawkman vs. Hawkwoman . . 2.50
9 GN,Hawkwoman in Prison. 2.50
10 Shayera returns to Thanagar . . . 2.50
11 GN,Blackhawk,Express. 2.50
12 GN,Princess Treska 2.50
13 TMd,A:Firehawk,V:Marauder . . . 2.50
14 GN,Shayera's Father 2.50
15 GN,War of the Gods X-over 2.50
16 GN War of the Gods X-over 2.50
17 GN,Train Terrorists 2.50
18 GN,V:Atilla 2.50
19 GN,V:Atilla 2.50
20 V:Smir'Beau 2.50
21 GN,Thanagar Pt.1,
  A:J.S.A. Hawkman 2.50
22 GN,Thanagar Pt.2. . . . . 2.50
23 GN,Thanagar Pt.3. . . . . 2.50
24 GN,Thanagar Pt.4. . . . . 2.50
25 GN,Thanagar Pt.5. . . . . 2.50
26 GN,V:Attila battle armor 2.50
27 JD,B:Flight's End 2.50
28 JD,Flight's End #2. . . . . 2.50
29 TT(c),JDu,Flight's End #3 . . . . . . 2.50
30 TT,Flight's End #4 . . . . 2.50
31 TT,Flight's End #5 . . . . 2.50
32 TT,V:Count Viper,final issue 3.00
Ann.#1 A:Flash. 4.50
Ann.#2 Armageddon,pt.6 . . . . 4.00
Ann.#2a reprint (Silver) 3.50
Ann.#3 Eclipso tie-in 3.25

HEAVY LIQUID
DC/Vertigo, 1999
1 thru 5 PPo,pt.2 thru pt.5. . . . . . @6.00

HECKLER, THE
1992–93
1 thru 7 KG,MJ,I:The Heckler . . . @2.50

HELLBLAZER
Jan., 1988
1 B:JaD(s),JRy,F:John
  Constantine 15.00
2 JRy,I:Papa Midnight. 9.00
3 JRy,I:Blathoxi 6.00
4 JRy,I:Resurrection Crusade,
  Gemma 6.00
5 JRy,F:Pyramid of Fear. 6.00
6 JRy,V:Resurrection Crusade,
  I:Nergal 5.00
7 JRy,V:Resurrection Crusade,
  I:Richie Simpson 5.00
8 JRy,AA,Constantine receives
  demon blood,V:Nergal. 5.00
9 JRy,A:Swamp Thing 7.00
10 JRy,V:Nergal. 6.00
11 MBu,Newcastle Incident,pt.1 . . . 5.00
12 JRy,D:Nergal. 5.00
13 JRy,John has a Nightmare 5.00
14 JRy,B:The Fear Machine,
  I:Mercury,Marj,Eddie 5.00
15 JRy,Shepard's Warning. 5.00
16 JRy,Rough Justice 5.00
17 MkH,I:Mr. Wester 5.00
18 JRy,R:Zed 5.00
19 JRy,I:Simon Hughes,Sandman. 10.00
20 JRy,F:Mr.Webster 6.00
21 JRy,I:Jallakuntilliokan 6.00
22 JRy,E:The Fear Machine. 6.00
23 I&D:Jerry O'Flynn 5.00
24 E:JaD(s),I:Sammy Morris 5.00
25 GMo(s),DvL,Early Warning. 5.00
26 GMo(s) 5.00
27 NGa(s),DMc,Hold Me 17.00
28 B:JaD(s),RnT,KeW,F:S.Morris . . 5.00
29 RnT,KeW,V:Sammy Morris 5.00
30 RnT,KeW,D:Sammy Morris 5.00
31 E:JaD(s),SeP,Constantine's
  Father's Funeral 5.00
32 DiF(s),StP,I&D:Drummond 4.50
33 B:JaD(s),MPn,I:Pat McDonell . . 4.50
34 SeP,R:Mercury,Marj 4.50
35 SeP,Constantine's Past. 4.50
36 Future Death,(preview of
  World Without End) 4.50
37 Journey to England's Secret
  Mystics. 4.50
38 Constantine's Journey contd. . . . 4.50
39 Journey to Discovery 4.50
40 DMc,I:2nd Kid Eternity 5.00
41 B:GEn(s),WSm,MPn,Dangerous
  Habits 10.00
42 Dangerous Habits. 4.50
43 I:Chantinelle 4.50
44 Dangerous Habits. 4.50
45 Dangerous Habits. 4.50
46 Dangerous Habits epilogue,
  I:Kit(John's girlfriend). 4.50
47 SnW(i),Pub Where I Was Born . . 4.00
48 Love Kills 4.00
49 X-mas issue,Lord o/t Dance 4.00
50 WSm,Remarkable Lives,A:Lord
  of Vampires (48pgs) 6.00
51 JnS,SeP,Laundromat-
  Possession 5.00
52 GF(c),WSm, Royal Blood 5.00
53 GF(c),WSm, Royal Blood 5.00
54 GF(c),WSm, Royal Blood 5.00
55 GF(c),WSm, Royal Blood 5.00
56 GF(c),B:GEn(s),DvL,
  V:Danny Drake 5.00
57 GF(c),SDi,Mortal Clay#1,
  V:Dr. Amis 5.00
58 GF(c),SDi,Mortal Clay#2,
  V:Dr. Amis 5.00

Hellblazer #2
© DC Comics, Inc.

59 GF(c),WSm,MkB(i),KDM,B:Guys
   & Dolls 5.00
60 GF(c),WSm,MkB(i),F:Tali,
   Chantinelle. 5.00
61 GF(c),WSm,MkB(i),E:Guys &
   Dolls, V:First of the Fallen 5.00
62 GF(c),SDi,End of the Line,I:Gemma,
   AIDS storyline insert w/Death . . 6.00

DC/Vertigo, 1993

63 GF(c),SDi,C:Swamp Thing,Zatanna
   Phantom Stranger 5.00
64 GF(c),SDi,B:Fear & Loathing,
   A:Gabriel (Racism) 4.00
65 GF(c),SDi,D:Dez 4.00
66 GF(c),SDi,E:Fear and Loathing . 4.00
67 GF(c),SDi,Kit leaves John 4.00
68 GF(c),SDi,F:Lord of Vampires,
   Darius,Mary 4.00
69 GF(c),SDi,D:Lord of Vampires . . 4.00
70 GF(c),SDi,Kit in Ireland. 4.00
71 GF(c),SDi,A:WWII Fighter Pilot . 4.00
72 GF(c),SDi,B:Damnation's
   Flame,A:Papa Midnight 4.00
73 GF(c),SDi,Nightmare NY,
   A:JFK. 4.00
74 GF(c),SDi,I:Cedella,A:JFK 4.00
75 GF(c),SDi,E:Damnation'sFlame . 4.00
76 GF(c),SDi,R:Brendan 4.00
77 Returns to England. 4.00
78 GF(c),SDi,B:Rake at the
   Gates of Hell 4.00
79 GF(c),SDi,In Hell. 4.00
80 GF(c),SDi,In London. 4.00
81 GF(c),SDi 4.00
82 Kit 4.00
83 Rake,Gates of Hell 4.00
84 John's past 4.00
85 Warped Notions,pt.1 . . . . 4.00
86 Warped Notions,pt.2 . . . . 4.00
87 Warped Notions,pt.3 . . . . 4.00
88 Warped Notions,pt.4 . . . . 4.00
89 Dreamtime 4.00
90 Dreamtime,pt.2 . . . . 4.00
91 Visits Battlefield. 4.00
92 Critical Mass,pt.1 . . . . 4.00
93 Critical Mass,pt.2 . . . . 4.00
94 Critical Mass,pt.3 . . . . 4.00
95 SeP,Critical Mass,pt.4 . . . . 4.00
96 SeP,Critical Mass,pt.5 . . . . 4.00
97 SeP,Critical Mass epilogue 4.00
98 SeP, helps neighbor 4.00
99 SeP 4.00
100 SeP, In a coma 5.00
101 SeP,deal with a demon 3.50

102 SeP,DifficultBeginnings,pt.1 . . . 3.50
103 SeP,DifficultBeginnings,pt.2 . . . 3.50
104 SeP,DifficultBeginnings,pt.3 . . . 3.50
105 . . . . 3.50
106 PJe(s),SEp,In the Line of
   Fire, pt.1 (of 2). 3.50
107 PJe(s),SEp,Line of Fire,pt.2 . . . 3.50
108 PJe(s),SeP,a Bacchic
   celebration. 3.50
109 PJe(s),SeP,cattle mutilations
   in Northern England 3.50
110 PJe(s),SeP,Last Man
   Standing,pt.1 . . . . 3.50
111 PJe(s),SeP,Last Man,pt.2 . . . . . 3.50
112 PJe(s),SeP,Last Man,pt.3 . . . . . 3.50
113 PJe(s),SeP,Last Man,pt.4 . . . . . 3.50
114 PJe(s),SeP,Last Man,pt.5 . . . . . 3.50
115 PJe(s),SeP(s),Dani's ex-
   boyfriend 3.50
116 SeP,Widdershins,pt.1 (of 2) . . . 3.50
117 SeP,Widdershins,pt.2 . . . . 3.50
118 PJe(s),SeP,John's a Godfather . 4.00
119 PJe(s),SeP,disasters 3.50
120 PJe(s),SeP,10th anniv. 48pg . . . 3.00
121 PJe(s),SeP, Up the Down
   Staircase pt.1 . . . . 3.00
122 PJe(s),SeP, Up the Down
   Staircase pt.2 . . . . 3.00
123 PJe(s),SeP, Up the Down
   Staircase pt.3 . . . . 3.00
124 PJe(s),SeP, Up the Down
   Staircase pt.4 . . . . 3.00
125 PJe(s),SeP, How to Play
   with Fire, pt.1 . . . . 3.00
126 PJe(s),SeP,Play/Fire,pt.2 . . . . . 3.00
127 PJe(s),SeP,Play/Fire,pt.3 . . . . . 3.00
128 PJe(s),SeP,Play/Fire,pt.4 . . . . . 3.00
129 . . . . 3.00
130 GEn,JHi,GF,Son of Man,pt.2 . . 3.00
131 GEn,JHi,GF,Son of Man,pt.3 . . 3.00
132 GEn,JHi,GF,Son of Man,pt.4 . . 3.00
133 GEn,JHi,GF,Son of Man,pt.5 . . 3.00
134 WEl(s),JHi,Haunted,pt.1 . . . . . 3.00
135 WEl(s),JHi,Haunted,pt.2 . . . . . 3.00
136 WEl(s),JHi,Haunted,pt.3 . . . . . 3.00
137 WEl(s),JHi,Haunted,pt.4 . . . . . 3.00
138 WEl(s),JHi,Haunted,pt.5 . . . . . 3.00
139 WEl(s),JHi,Haunted,pt.6 . . . . . 3.00
140 WEl(s),Locked. 3.00
141 WEl(s),ALa 3.00
142 WEl,TBd,Setting Sun 3.00
143 WEl,TBd,Telling Tales 3.00
144 GEr,ALa,Ashes & Honey,pt.1 . . 3.00
145 GEr,ALa,Ashes & Honey,pt.2 . . 3.00
146 RC,Hard Time 3.00
147 RC,Hard Time,pt.2 . . . . 3.00
148 RC,Hard Time,pt.3 . . . . 3.00
149 RC,Hard Time,pt.4 . . . . 3.00
150 RC,Hard Time,concl. 3.00
151 Good Intentions,pt.1 . . . . 3.00
152 Good Intentions,pt.2 . . . . 3.00
153 Good Intentions,pt.3 . . . . 3.00
154 Good Intentions,pt.4 . . . . 3.00
155 Good Intentions,pt.5 . . . . 3.00
156 Good Intentions,pt.6 . . . . 3.00
157 SDi,"...and buried?". 3.00
158 Freezes Over,pt.1 . . . . 3.00
159 Freezes Over,pt.2 . . . . 3.00
160 Freezes Over,pt.3 . . . . 3.00
161 Freezes Over,pt.4 . . . . 3.00
162 Lapdogs and Englishmen 3.00
163 Lapdogs and Englishmen 3.00
164 Highwater, pt.1 . . . . 3.00
165 Highwater, pt.2 . . . . 3.00
166 Highwater, pt.3 . . . . 3.00
167 Highwater, pt.4 . . . . 3.00
168 A Fresh Coat of Red Paint 3.00
169 Constantine in LA 3.00
170 Ashes and Dust,pt.1 . . . . 3.00
171 Ashes and Dust,pt.2 . . . . 3.00
172 Ashes and Dust,pt.3 . . . . 3.00
173 Ashes and Dust,pt.4 . . . . 3.00

174 Ashes and Dust,pt.5 . . . . 3.00
175 SDi,JP,High on Life,pt.1 . . . . . . 3.00
176 SDi,JP,High on Life, pt.2 . . . . . 3.00
177 Red Sepulchre,pt.1 . . . . 3.00
178 Red Sepulchre,pt.2 . . . . 3.00
179 Red Sepulchre,pt.3 . . . . 3.00
180 Red Sepulchre,pt.4 . . . . 3.00
181 Red Sepulchre,concl. 3.00
182 MCy(s),Black Flowers,pt.1 . . . . 3.00
183 MCy(s),Black Flowers,pt.2 . . . . 3.00
184 MCy(s),Wild Card 3.00
185 MCy(s),Ordeal. 3.00
186 MCy(s),The Pit 3.00
187 MCy(s),Bred in Bone,pt.1 . . . . . 3.00
188 MCy(s),Bred in Bone,pt.2 . . . . . 3.00
189 MCy(s),Staring at Wall,pt.1 . . . . 3.00
190 MCy(s),Staring at Wall,pt.2 . . . . 3.00
191 MCy(s),Staring at Wall,pt.3 . . . . 3.00
192 MCy(s),Staring at Wall,pt.4 . . . . 3.00
193 MCy(s),Staring at Wall,pt.5 . . . . 3.00
194 MCy(s) 3.00
195 MCy(s),Out of Season,pt.1 . . . . 3.00
196 MCy(s),Out of Season,pt.2 . . . . 3.00
197 Stations of the Cross,pt.1 . . . . . 3.00
198 Stations of the Cross,pt.2 . . . . . 3.00
199 Stations of the Cross,pt.3 . . . . . 3.00
200 Married life 4.50
201 Thieves 3.00
202 Reasons to be Cheerful,pt.1. . . 3.00
203 Reasons to be Cheerful,pt.2. . . 3.00
204 Reasons to be Cheerful,pt.3. . . 3.00
205 Reasons to be Cheerful,pt.4. . . 3.00
206 Chas' rampage 3.00
207 Down in the Ground,pt.1. . . . . . 3.00
208 Down in the Ground,pt.2. . . . . . 3.00
209 Down in the Ground,pt.3. . . . . . 3.00
210 Down in the Ground,pt.4. . . . . . 3.00
211 Down in the Ground,pt.5. . . . . . 3.00
212 Down in the Ground,pt.6. . . . . . 3.00
213 Back from Hell 3.00
214 MCy(s),R.S.V.P., pt.1 . . . . 3.00
215 MCy(s) 3.00
216 Empathy is the Enemy, pt.1 . . . 3.00
217 Empathy is the Enemy, pt.2 . . . 3.00
218 Empathy is the Enemy, pt.3 . . . 3.00
219 Empathy is the Enemy, pt.4 . . . 3.00
220 Empathy is the Enemy, pt.5 . . . 3.00
221 Empathy is the Enemy, pt.6 . . . 3.00
222 Empathy is the Enemy, pt.7 . . . 3.00
223 Empathy is the Enemy, concl . . 3.00
224 The Red Right Hand, pt.1 . . . . 3.00
225 The Red Right Hand, pt.2. . . . . 3.00
226 The Red Right Hand, pt.3 . . . . 3.00
227 The Red Right Hand, pt.4 . . . . 3.00
228 The Red Right Hand, pt.5 . . . . 3.00
229 MCy,JPL 3.00
230 In at the Deep End, pt.1 . . . . . . 3.00
231 In at the Deep End, pt.2 . . . . . . 3.00
232 Wheels of Chance, pt.1 . . . . . . 3.00
233 Wheels of Chance, pt.2 . . . . . . 3.00
234 Joyride, pt. 1 . . . . 3.00
235 Joyride, pt. 2 . . . . 3.00
236 Joyride, pt. 3 . . . . 3.00
237 Joyride, pt. 4 . . . . 3.00
238 Urban Explorers 3.00
239 Sudan to the U.K. 3.00
240 The Laughing Magician, pt.1 . . 3.00
241 The Laughing Magician, pt.2 . . 3.00
242 The Laughing Magician, pt.3 . . 3.00
243 Mortification of the Flesh,pt.1 . . 3.00
244 Mortification of the Flesh,pt.2 . . 3.00
245 Newcastle Calling, pt.1 . . . . . . 3.00
246 Newcastle Calling, pt.2 . . . . . . 3.00
247 Roots of Coincidence, pt.1 . . . . 3.00
248 Roots of Coincidence, pt.2 . . . . 3.00
249 Roots of Coincidence, pt.3 . . . . 3.00
Ann.#1 JaD(s),BT,Raven Scar 7.00
Spec.#1 GF(c),GEn(s),SDi,John
   Constantine's teenage years . . . 4.50
Secret Files #1 . . . . 5.00

All comics prices listed are for *Near Mint* condition.

DC COMICS

HELLBLAZER/
THE BOOKS OF MAGIC
Oct., 1997
1 (of 2) PJe,JNR 2.50
2 PJe,JNR 2.50

HELLBLAZER SPECIAL:

BAD BLOOD
DC/Vertigo, July, 2000
1 (of 4) JaD,PBd 3.50
2 JaD,PBd 3.50
3 JaD,PBd 3.50
4 JaD,PBd,concl. 3.50

...CHAS–THE KNOWLEDGE
Vertigo, July, 2008
1 (of 5) 3.00
2 thru 5 . . . . @3.00

...LADY CONSTANTINE
DC/Vertigo, Dec. 2002
1 (of 4) F:Johanna Constantine . . . 3.00
2 thru 4 . . . . @3.00

HELMET OF FATE, THE
Jan., 2007
Spec. #1 Ibis the Invincible 3.00
Spec. #1 Detective Chimp 3.00
Spec. #1 Sargon the Sorcerer 3.00
Spec. #1 Zauriel 3.00
Spec. #1 Black Alice 3.00

HERCULES UNBOUND
Oct.–Nov., 1975
1 WW 20.00
2 thru 8 . . . . @12.00
9 thru 12 WS,Aug.–Sept.,1977 . . . 10.00

Here's Howie Comics #2
© DC Comics, Inc.

HERE'S HOWIE COMICS
1952–54
1 Teen-age humor 350.00
2 . . . . 200.00
3 & 4 . . . . @150.00
5 Military humor 150.00
6 thru 10 . . . . @125.00
11 thru 18 . . . . @100.00

H-E-R-O
Feb. 2003
1 Jerry Feldon 7.00
2 life-saving mission 4.00

3 F:Molly 4.00
4 Powers and Abilities 4.00
5 F:Matt Allen 3.00
6 F:Andrea Allen 3.00
7 Chaos, Inc. 3.00
8 Chaos, Inc.,pt.2 . . . . 3.00
9 World Made of Glass,pt.1 . . . . . . 3.00
10 World Made of Glass,pt.2 . . . . . 2.50
11 Prehistoric superhero? 2.50
12 Ch-Ch-Ch-Changes,pt.1 . . . . . . 2.50
13 Ch-Ch-Ch-Changes,pt.2 . . . . . . 2.50
14 Ch-Ch-Ch-Changes,pt.3 . . . . . . 2.50
15 Good Guys & Bad Guys,pt.1 . . . 2.50
16 Good Guys & Bad Guys,pt.2 . . . 2.50
17 Good Guys & Bad Guys,pt.3 . . . 2.50
18 Good Guys & Bad Guys,pt.4 . . . 2.50
19 Picking Up the Pieces,pt.1 . . . . 2.50
20 Picking Up the Pieces,pt.2 . . . . 2.50
21 Picking Up the Pieces,pt.3 . . . . 2.50
22 final battle over H-E-R-O device. 2.50
Spec. Double Feature,rep.#1&#2 . . 5.00

HEROES
DC/Milestone, 1996
1 Six heroes join 3.50
2 thru 6 . . . . @2.50

HEROES AGAINST
HUNGER
1986
1 NA,DG,JBy,CS,AA,BWr,BS,
  Superman,Batman 4.00

HERO HOTLINE
1989
1 thru 6, Mini-series . . . . @2.50

HEX
Sept., 1985
1 MT,I:Hex 9.00
2 MT 5.00
3 MT,V:Conglomerate 5.00
4 MT,V:Conglomerate 5.00
5 MT,A:Chainsaw Killer 5.00
6 MT,V:Conglomerate 5.00
7 MT,Tries to Return to own era . . . 5.00
8 MT,The Future 6.00
9 MT,Future Killer Cyborgs 5.00
10 MT,V:Death Cult 5.00
11 MT,V:The Batman 6.00
12 MT,A:Batman,V:Terminators 6.00
13 MT,I:New Supergroup 5.00
14 MT,A:The Dogs of War 5.00
15 KG,V:Chainsaw Killer 5.00
16 KG,V:Dogs of War 5.00
17 KG,Hex/Dogs of War T.U.
  V:XXGG 5.00
18 KGr,Confronting the Past,
  final issue 5.00

HI HI PUFFY AMIYUMI
Jan., 2006
Spec. Photo (c) 2.50
1 thru 3 . . . . @2.50

HISTORY OF
DC UNIVERSE
Sept., 1986
1 GP, From start to WWII 5.00
2 GP, From WWII to present 5.00

HITCHHIKER'S GUIDE TO
THE GALAXY
1993
1 Based on Douglas Adams book . 7.00
2 thru 3 . . . . @6.50

HITMAN
1996–2001
1 GEn, F:Tommy Monaghan 10.00
2 GEn, Attempt to kill Joker 7.00
3 GEn(s),JMC, Mawzin & The
  Arkanonne 5.00
4 GEn(s),JMC, ... 4.00
5 GEn(s),JMC, ... 4.00
6 GEn(s),JMC,A:Johnny Navarone,
  Natt the Hatt 3.00
7 GEn(s),JMC, Pat's dead, Hitman
  wants revenge 3.00
8 GEn(s),JMC,barricaded in
  Noonan's Bar, Final Night tie-in. 3.00
9 GEn(s),JMC,A:Six-Pack 3.00
10 GEn(s),JMC,A:Green Lantern . . . 3.00
11 . . . . 3.00
12 GEn(s),JMC,Local Heroes,
  A:Green Lantern 3.00
13 . . . . 3.00
14 GEn(s),JMC, Zombie Night at
  the Aquarium, concl. 3.00
15 GEn(s),JMC, Ace of
  Killers, pt.1, V:Mawzir 3.00
16 GEn(s),JMC,Ace of Killers,pt.2 . . 3.00
17 GEn(s),JMC,Ace of Killers,pt.3,
  A:Catwoman, Demon Etrigan . . 3.00
18 GEn(s),JMC,Ace of Killers,pt.4,
  A:Demon Etrigan, Baytor 3.00
19 GEn(s),JMC,Ace/Killers,pt.5, . . . 3.00
20 GEn(s),JMC,Ace/Killers,concl. . . 3.00
21 GEn(s),JMC,Romeo & Juliet 2.50
22 GEn(s),JMC,holiday special 2.50
23 GEn(s),JMc,Who Dares
  Wins,pt.1 . . . . 2.50
24 GEn(s),JMc,Dares/Wins,pt.2 . . . 2.50
25 GEn(s),JMc,Dares/Wins,pt.3 . . . 2.50
26 GEn(s),JMc,Dares/Wins,pt.4 . . . 2.50
27 GEn(s),JMc,Dares/Wins,pt.5 . . . 2.50
28 GEn(s),JMC,aftermath 2.50
29 GEn(s),JMC, Tommy's
  Heroes,pt.1 . . . . 2.50
30 GEn(s),JMC,Heroes, pt.2 . . . . . . 2.50
31 GEn(s),JMC,Heroes, pt.3 . . . . . . 2.50
32 GEn(s),JMC,Heroes, pt.4 . . . . . . 2.50
33 GEn(s),JMC,Heroes, pt.5 . . . . . . 2.50
34 GEn(s),A:Superman 2.50
35 GEn(s),Frances Monaghan 2.50
36 GEn(s), ... 2.50
37 GEn(s). 2.50
38 GEn(s),Dead Man's Land, concl. 2.50
39 GEn(s),JMC,A:RingoChen,pt.1 . . 2.50
40 GEn(s),JMC,A:RingoChen,pt.2 . . 2.50
41 GEn(s),JMC,A:RingoChen,pt.3 . . 2.50
42 GEn(s),JMC,A:RingoChen,pt.4 . . 2.50
43 GEn(s),JMC, ... 2.50
44 GEn(s),JMC 2.50
45 GEn(s),JMC 2.50
46 GEn(s),JMC 2.50
47 GEn(s),JMC,Old Dog 2.50
48 GEn(s),JMC,Old Dog,pt.2 . . . . . 2.50
49 GEn(s),JMC,Old Dog,pt.3 . . . . . 2.50
50 GEn(s),JMC,Hitman's future 2.50
51 GEn(s),JMC,Superguy.pt.1 . . . . 2.50
52 GEn(s),JMc,Superguy,pt.2 . . . . 2.50
53 GEn(s),JMc,ClosingTime,pt.1 . . 2.50
54 GEn(s),JMc,ClosingTime,pt.2 . . 2.50
55 GEn(s),JMc,ClosingTime,pt.3 . . 2.50
56 GEn,JMC,GL,O:Tommy
  Monaghan 2.50
57 GEn,JMC,GL,O:Natt 2.50
58 GEn,JMC,GL,Closing time 2.50
59 GEn,JMC,GL,Closing time 2.50
60 GEn,JMC,GL,Closing time,final . 2.50
Ann.#1 Pulp Heroes (Western) 4.00
Spec.#1,000,000 GEn(s),JMC 2.50
Spec. Hitman/Lobo: That
  Stupid Bastich! 4.00

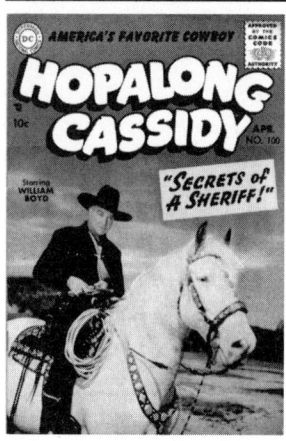

Hopalong Cassidy #100
© DC Comics, Inc.

HOPALONG CASSIDY
Feb., 1954
86 GC,Ph(c):William Boyd & Topper,
Secret o/t Tattooed Burro . . . 500.00
87 GC,Ph(c),Tenderfoot Outlaw. . 300.00
88 Ph(c),GC,15 Robbers of Rimfire
Ridge 175.00
89 GC,Ph(c),One-Day Boom
Town 175.00
90 GC,Ph(c),Cowboy Clown
Robberies 175.00
91 GC,Ph(c),The Riddle of
the Roaring R Ranch. 175.00
92 GC,Ph(c),Sky-RidingOutlaws . 150.00
93 GC,Ph(c),Silver Badge
of Courage. 150.00
94 GC,Ph(c),Mystery of the
Masquerading Lion 150.00
95 GC,Ph(c),Showdown at the
Post-Hole Bank 150.00
96 GC,Ph(c),Knights of
the Range 150.00
97 GC,Ph(c),The Mystery of
the Three-Eyed Cowboy 150.00
98 GC,Ph(c),Hopalong's
Unlucky Day 150.00
99 GC,Ph(c),Partners in Peril . . . 150.00
100 GC,Ph(c),The Secrets
of a Sheriff. 175.00
101 GC,Ph(c),Way Out West
Where The East Begins 125.00
102 GC,Ph(c),Secret of the
Buffalo Hat. 125.00
103 GC,Ph(c),The Train-Rustlers
of Avalance Valley 125.00
104 GC,Ph(c),Secret of the
Surrendering Outlaws 125.00
105 GC,Ph(c),Three Signs
to Danger. 125.00
106 GC,Ph(c),The Secret of
the Stolen Signature 125.00
107 GC,Ph(c),The Mystery Trail
to Stagecoach Town 125.00
108 GC,Ph(c),The Mystery
Stage From Burro Bend 125.00
109 GC,The Big Gun on Saddletop
Mountain 125.00
110 GC,The Dangerous Stunts
of Hopalong Cassidy 100.00
111 GC,Sheriff Cassidy's
Mystery Clue 100.00
112 GC,Treasure Trail to
Thunderbolt Ridge. 100.00

113 GC,The Shadow of the
Toy Soldier. 100.00
114 GC,Ambush at Natural
Bridge 100.00
115 GC,The Empty-Handed
Robberies 100.00
116 GC,Mystery of the
Vanishing Cabin. 100.00
117 GC,School for Sheriffs 100.00
118 GC,The Hero of
Comanche Ridge. 100.00
119 GC,The Dream Sheriff of
Twin Rivers 100.00
120 GC,Salute to a Star-Wearer . 100.00
121 GC,The Secret of the
Golden Caravan 100.00
122 GC,The Rocking
Horse Bandits 100.00
123 GK,Mystery of the
One-Dollar Bank Robbery . . . 100.00
124 GK,Mystery of the
Double-X Brand. 100.00
125 GK,Hopalong Cassidy's
Secret Brother 100.00
126 GK,Trail of the
Telltale Clues. 100.00
127 GK,Hopalong Cassidy's
Golden Riddle 100.00
128 GK,The House That
Hated Outlaws. 100.00
129 GK,Hopalong Cassidy's
Indian Sign 100.00
130 GK,The Return of the
Canine Sheriff 100.00
131 GK&GK(c),The Amazing
Sheriff of Double Creek. 100.00
132 GK,Track of the
Invisible Indians. 100.00
133 GK,Golden Trail to Danger . . 100.00
134 GK,Case of the
Three Crack-Shots 100.00
135 GK,May-June, 1959 . . . . . . 100.00

HORRORIST
DC/Vertigo, 1995
1 I:Horrorist. 6.50
2 conclusion 6.50

HOT WHEELS
March-April, 1970
1 ATh. 200.00
2 ATh. 100.00
3 NA,ATh 125.00
4 ATh. 100.00
5 ATh. 100.00
6 NA(c) 125.00

HOURMAN
1999
1 TPe,RgM,A:JLA 2.50
2 TPe(s),RgM,F:Tomorrow Woman 2.50
3 TPe(s),RgM,Timepoint,pt.1 . . . . 2.50
4 TPe(s),RgM,Timepoint,pt.2 . . . . 2.50
5 TPe(s),RgM,Rex Tyler's life. . . . 2.50
6 TPe,RgM,JLAndroids,pt.1 . . . . . 2.50
7 TPe,RgM,JLAndroids,pt.2 . . . . . 2.50
8 TPe,RgM,Day of Judgment
x-over. 2.50
9 TPe,RgM,F:Rick Tyler 2.50
10 TPe,RgM. 2.50
11 TPe,RgM,One Million,pt.1 . . . . . 2.50
12 TPe,RgM,One Million,pt.2 . . . . . 2.50
13 TPe,RgM,One Million,pt.3 . . . . . 2.50
14 TPe,RgM,V:Undersoul 2.50
15 TPe,RgM,human secrets 2.50
16 TPe,RgM,F:Snapper. 2.50
17 TPe,100 Years of Solitude 2.50
18 TPe,RgM,High Society,pt.1. . . . 2.50
19 TPe,RgM,High Society,pt.2. . . . 2.50
20 TPe,RgM,F:Snapper. 2.50
21 TPe,RgM,reduced to nothing . . . 2.50

22 TPe,TyH 2.50
23 TPe,RgM,Unbelievable
Truth,pt.1 . . . . 2.50
24 TPE,RgM,Unbel.Truth,pt.2 . . . . 2.50
25 TPE,RgM,final issue 2.50

HOUSE OF MYSTERY
Dec.–Jan., 1952
1 I Fell In Love With
a Monster 3,800.00
2 The Mark of X. 1,700.00
3 The Dummy of Death 1,200.00
4 The Man With the Evil Eye . . . 900.00
5 The Man With the Strangler
Hands!. 900.00
6 The Monster in Clay! 750.00
7 Nine Lives of Alger Denham!. . 750.00
8 Tattoos of Doom 750.00
9 Secret of the Little Black Bag . 750.00
10 The Wishes of Doom 750.00
11 Deadly Game of G-H-O-S-T . . 600.00
12 The Devil's Chessboard 600.00
13 The Theater Of A
Thousand Thrills! 600.00
14 The Deadly Dolls 600.00
15 The Man Who Could Change
the World 600.00
16 Dead Men Tell No Tales!. 500.00
17 Man With the X-Ray Eyes 400.00
18 Dance of Doom. 400.00
19 The Strange Faces of Death. . 400.00
20 The Beast Of Bristol 400.00
21 Man Who Could See Death . . 400.00
22 The Phantom's Return 400.00
23 Stamps of Doom. 400.00
24 Kill The Black Cat 400.00
25 The Man With Three Eyes!. . . 400.00
26 The Man with Magic Ears. . . . 350.00
27 Fate Held Four Aces! 350.00
28 The Wings Of Mr. Milo! 350.00
29 CS,Hangman's House 350.00
30 The Demon Gun 350.00
31 The Incredible Illusions! 350.00
32 Pied Piper of the Sea 350.00
33 Mr. Misfortune! 350.00
34 The Hundred Year Duel 350.00
35 The Fatal Superstition. 350.00
36 The Treasure of Montezuma! . 300.00
37 MD,The Statue That
Came to Life 300.00
38 The Voyage Of No Return . . . 300.00
39 Professor Smith's Magic Lamp 300.00
40 The Coins That Came To Life. 300.00
41 The Impossible Tricks! 300.00
42 The Stranger From Out There 300.00

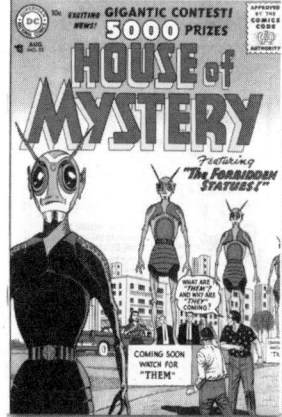

House of Mystery #53
© DC Comics Inc.

House of Mystery #113
© DC Comics, Inc.

43 Imp on the Flying Trapeze . . . 300.00
44 The Secret Of Hill 14 . . . . 300.00
45 The Magic Kite 300.00
46 The Bird of Fate 300.00
47 The Robot Named Think. 300.00
48 The Man Marooned On Earth. 300.00
49 The Mysterious Mr. Omen . . . 300.00
50 The Amazing Swami. 325.00
51 Man Who Stole Teardrops . . . 275.00
52 The Man With The Golden
   Shoes 275.00
53 The Man Who Hated Mirrors . 275.00
54 The Woman Who Lived Twice 275.00
55 I Turned Back Time. 275.00
56 The Thing In The Black Box . . 275.00
57 The Untamed 275.00
58 Haunted Melody 275.00
59 The Tomb Of Ramfis. 275.00
60 The Prisoner On Canvas 275.00
61 JK,Superstition Day 275.00
62 The Haunting Scarecrow 250.00
63 JK,The Lady & The Creature . 275.00
64 The Golden Doom 250.00
65 JK,The Magic Lantern. 350.00
66 JK,Sinister Shadow. 350.00
67 The Wizard of Water. 250.00
68 The Book That Bewitched. . . . 250.00
69 The Miniature Disasters 250.00
70 JK,The Man With Nine Lives . 250.00
71 Menace of the Mole Man 250.00
72 JK,Dark Journey 250.00
73 Museum That Came to Life . . 250.00
74 Museum That Came To Life . . 250.00
75 Assignment Unknown! 250.00
76 JK,Prisoners Of The Tiny
   Universe 250.00
77 The Eyes That Went Berserk . 200.00
78 JK(c),The 13th Hour 250.00
79 JK(c),The Fantastic Sky
   Puzzle 250.00
80 Man With Countless Faces! . . 200.00
81 The Man Who Made Utopia . . 200.00
82 The Riddle of the Earth's
   Second Moon 200.00
83 The Mystery of the
   Martian Eye. 200.00
84 JK,BK,100-Century Doom . . . 275.00
85 JK(c),Earth's Strangest
   Salesman. 265.00
86 The Baffling Bargains 250.00
87 The Human Diamond 250.00
88 Return of the Animal Man. . . . 250.00
89 The Cosmic Plant! 250.00
90 The Invasion Of the Energy
   Creatures! 250.00

91 DD&SMo(c),The Riddle of the
   Alien Satellite. 250.00
92 DD(c),Menace of the
   Golden Globule 250.00
93 NC(c),I Fought The
   Molten Monster 250.00
94 DD&SMo(c),The Creature
   In Echo Lake 250.00
95 The Wizard's Gift 250.00
96 The Amazing 70-Ton Man. . . . 250.00
97 The Alien Who Change
   History 250.00
98 DD&SMo(c),The Midnight
   Creature. 250.00
99 The Secret of the
   Leopard God 250.00
100 The Beast Beneath Earth . . . 275.00
101 The Magnificent Monster . . . 200.00
102 Cellmate to a Monster 200.00
103 Hail the Conquering Aliens . . 200.00
104 I was the Seeing-Eye Man . . 200.00
105 Case of the Creature X-14 . . 200.00
106 Invaders from the Doomed
    Dimension 200.00
107 Captives of the Alien
    Fisherman 200.00
108 RMo,Four Faces of Frank
    Forbes 200.00
109 ATh,JKu,Secret of the Hybrid
    Creatures. 200.00
110 Beast Who Stalked Through
    Time. 200.00
111 Operation Beast Slayer. 200.00
112 Menace of Craven's
    Creatures. 200.00
113 RMo,Prisoners of Beast
    Asteroid 200.00
114 The Movies from Nowhere . . 200.00
115 Prisoner o/t Golden Mask . . . 200.00
116 RMo,Return of the
    Barsfo Beast 200.00
117 Menace of the Fire Furies. . . 150.00
118 RMo,Secret o/SuperGorillas . 150.00
119 Deadly Gift from the Stars. . . 150.00
120 ATh,Catman of KarynPeale . 150.00
121 RMo,Beam that Transformed
    Men 150.00
122 Menace fo the Alien Hero . . . 150.00
123 RMo,Lure o/t Decoy
    Creature. 150.00
124 Secret of Mr. Doom. 150.00
125 Fantastic Camera Creature . 150.00
126 The Human Totem Poles . . . 150.00
127 RMo,Cosmic Game o/Doom. 150.00
128 NC,The Sorcerer's Snares . . 150.00
129 Man in the Nuclear Trap. . . . 150.00
130 The Alien Creature Hunt. . . . 150.00
131 Vengeance o/t GeyserGod . . 125.00
132 MMe,Beware My Invisible
    Master 125.00
133 MMe,Captive Queen of
    Beast Island. 125.00
134 MMe,Secret Prisoner of
    Darkmore Dungeon. 125.00
135 MMe,Alien Body Thief. 125.00
136 MMe,Secret o/t StolenFace . 125.00
137 MMe,Tunnel to Disaster 125.00
138 MMe,Creature Must Die 125.00
139 MMe,Creatures of
    Vengeful Eye 125.00
140 I&Only app.:Astro 125.00
141 MMe,The Alien Gladiator . . . 125.00
142 MMe,The Wax Demons 125.00
143 J'onn J'onzz begins 400.00
144 J'onn J'onzz on Weird
    World of Gilgana 150.00
145 J'onn J'onzz app. 125.00
146 BP,J'onn J'onzz. 125.00
147 J'onn J'onzz 125.00
148 J'onn J'onzz 125.00
149 ATh,J'onn J'onzz. 125.00
150 MMe,J'onn J'onzz. 125.00

151 J'onn J'onzz 125.00
152 MMe,J'onn J'onzz. 125.00
153 J'onn J'onzz 125.00
154 J'onn J'onzz 125.00
155 J'onn J'onzz 125.00
156 JM,I:Dial H for Hero (Giantboy
    Cometeer,Mole)J.J'onzz sty . 125.00
157 JM,Dial H for Hero (Human
    Bullet,Super Charge,Radar
    Sonar Man) J.J'onzz sty 125.00
158 JM,Dial H for Hero (Quake
    MasterSquid)J'onn J'onzz sty 100.00
159 JM,Dial H for Hero (Human
    Starfish,Hypno Man,Mighty
    Moppet) J'onn J'onzz sty. . . . 100.00
160 JM,Dial H for Hero (King Kandy
    A:Plastic Man,I:Marco Xavier (J'onn
    J'onzz new secret I.D.) 125.00
161 JM,Dial H for Hero (Magneto,
    Hornet Man,Shadow Man) . . 75.00
162 JM,Dial H for Hero (Mr.Echo,
    Future Man) J'onnJ'onzz sty . . 75.00
163 JM,Dial H for Hero(Castor&Pollux,
    King Coil) J'onnJ'onzz sty . . . 75.00
164 JM,Dial H for Hero (Super Nova
    Zip Tide) J'onnJ'onzz sty. 75.00
165 JM,Dial H for Hero (Whoozis,
    Whatsis,Howzis) J'onn J'onzz
    story. 75.00
166 JM,Dial H for Hero (Yankee
    Doodle Kid,Chief Mighty Arrow)
    J'onn J'onzz sty. 75.00
167 JM,Dial H for Hero (Balloon Boy,
    Muscle Man,Radar Sonar Man)
    J'onn J'onzz sty. 75.00
168 JM,Dial H for Hero (Thunderbolt,
    Mole,Cometeer,Hoopster)
    J'onn J'onzz sty. 75.00
169 JM,I:Gem Girl in Dial H for
    Hero,J'onn J'onzz sty 75.00
170 JM,Dial H for Hero (Baron
    BuzzSaw,Don Juan,Sphinx
    Man) J'onn J'onzz sty 75.00
171 JM,Dial H for Hero (King Viking
    Whirl-I-Gig)J'onn J'onzz sty. . . 70.00
172 JM,Dial H for Hero 70.00
173 E:Dial H for Hero,F:J'onn
    J'onzz 70.00
174 New direction,SA pg.13 . . . . 300.00
175 I:Cain. 200.00
176 SA,Cain's Game Room. 150.00
177 Curse of the Car. 150.00
178 NA,The Game. 150.00
179 BWr,NA,JO,Widow'sWalk . . . 200.00
180 GK,WW,BWr,SA,Room 13 . . 150.00
181 BWr,The Siren of Satan 150.00
182 ATh,The Devil's Doorway 60.00
183 BWr,WW(i),DeadCanKill . . . 100.00
184 ATh,GK,WW,Eye o/Basilisk . . 60.00
185 AW,The Beautiful Beast 60.00
186 BWr,NA,Nightmare 60.00
187 ATh,Mask of the Red Fox 50.00
188 TD,BWr,NA(c),House of
    Madness 70.00
189 WW(i),NA(c),Eyes of the Cat . 50.00
190 ATh,Fright 50.00
191 BWr,TD,NA(c),Christmas
    Story. 75.00
192 JAp,GM,DH,NA(c),Garnener
    of Eden 50.00
193 BWr(c), Voodoo Vengeance . . 50.00
194 ATh,NR,RH(rep),JK(rep)
    Born Loser. 75.00
195 NR,BWr,ThingsOld..Things
    Forgotten 90.00
196 GM,GK,ATh(rep)A Girl &
    Her Dog. 60.00
197 DD,NR,NA(c),House of
    Horrors. 65.00
198 MSy,NC,Day of the Demon . . 75.00
199 WW,RB,NA(c),Sno'Fun. 85.00
200 MK,TD,The Beast's Revenge . 85.00

DC COMICS

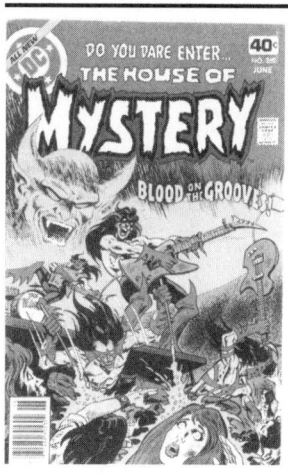

House of Mystery #269
© *DC Comics, Inc.*

201 JAp,The Demon Within 60.00
202 MSy,GC(rep),SA,The Poster
    Plague,John Prentice? 60.00
203 NR,Tower of Prey 60.00
204 BWr,AN,All in the Family 75.00
205 The Coffin Creature 35.00
206 MSy,TP,The Burning 35.00
207 JSn,The Spell 40.00
208 Creator of Evil 35.00
209 AA,JAp,Tomorrow I Hang 40.00
210 The Immortal 35.00
211 NR,Deliver Us From Evil 40.00
212 MA,AN,Ever After 35.00
213 AN,Back from the Realm of
    the Damned 40.00
214 NR,The Shaggy Dog 40.00
215 The Man Who Wanted Power
    over Women 35.00
216 TD,Look into My Eyes & Kill . . 35.00
217 NR,AA,Swamp God 40.00
218 FT,An Ice Place to Visit 35.00
219 AA,NR,BWr(c),Pledge to
    Satan 45.00
220 AA,AN,They Hunt Butterflies
    Don't They? 35.00
221 FT,BWr,MK,He Who Laughs
    Last 45.00
222 AA,Night of the Teddy Bear . . 30.00
223 Demon From the Deep 30.00
224 FR,AA,SheerFear,B:100pg . . . 80.00
225 AA,FT,AN,See No Evil 80.00
226 AA,FR,NR,SA,Monster in House
    Tour of House of Mystery 80.00
227 NR,AA,The Carriage Man 80.00
228 FR,NA(i),The Rebel 80.00
229 NR,Nightmare Castle,
    last 100 page 80.00
230 Experiment In Fear 25.00
231 Cold,Cold Heart 25.00
232 Last Tango in Hell 25.00
233 FR,Cake! 25.00
234 AM,Lafferty's Luck 25.00
235 NR,Wings of Black Death 25.00
236 SD,NA(i),BWr(c),Death
    Played a Sideshow 35.00
237 FT,Night of the Chameleon . . . 25.00
238 A Touch of Death 25.00
239 Day of the Witch 25.00
240 The Murderer 25.00
241 FR,NR,Death Pulls theStrings 25.00
242 FR,The Balloon Vendor 25.00
243 Brother Bear 25.00
244 FT,Kronos..Zagros-Eborak . . . 25.00

245 AN,Check the J.C.Demon
    Catalogue Under...Death 25.00
246 DeathVault of Eskimo Kings . . 25.00
247 SD,Death Rides the Waves . . . 25.00
248 NightJamieGaveUp theGhost . 25.00
249 Hit Parade of Death 25.00
250 AN,Voyage to Hell 25.00
251 WW,AA,NA(c),The Collector,
    68-pages 35.00
252 DP,RT,AA,FR,AN,NA(c),
    ManKillers 35.00
253 TD,AN,GK,KJ,NA(c),Beware
    the Demon Child 35.00
254 SD,AN,MR,NA(c),The
    Devil's Place 35.00
255 RE,GM,BWr(c),Sometimes
    Leopards 35.00
256 DAy,AN,BWr(c),Museum of
    Murders 35.00
257 RE,MGo,TD(i),MBr,Xmas iss. . 35.00
258 SD,RB,BMc,DG(i),The Demon
    and His Boy 35.00
259 RE,RT,MGo,DN,BL,Hair Today,
    Gone Tomorrow, last giant 35.00
260 Go to Hades 15.00
261 The Husker 15.00
262 FreedFrom Infernos of Hell . . . 15.00
263 JCr,Is There Vengeance
    After Death? 15.00
264 Halloween Issue 15.00
265 The Perfect Host 15.00
266 The Demon Blade 15.00
267 A Strange Way to Die 15.00
268 Blood on the Grooves 15.00
269 JSh,JRu,JBi,Black Moss 15.00
270 JSh,JRu,JBi,Black Moss 15.00
271 TS,HellHound of
    Brackenmoor 15.00
272 DN,DA,theSorcerer's Castle . . 15.00
273 The Rites of Inheritance 15.00
274 MR,JBi,Hell Park 15.00
275 JCr,Final Installment 15.00
276 SD,MN,Epode 15.00
277 HC,AMi,Limited Engagement . 15.00
278 TV or Not TV 15.00
279 AS,Trial by Fury 15.00
280 VMK,DAy,Hungry Jaws
    of Death 15.00
281 Now Dying in this Corner 15.00
282 JSw,DG,Superman/Radio
    Shack ins 15.00
283 RT,AN,Kill Me Gently 15.00
284 KG,King and the Dragon 15.00
285 Cold Storage 15.00
286 Long Arm of the Law 15.00
287 NR,AS,BL,Legend o/t Lost . . . 15.00
288 DSp,Piper at Gates of Hell . . . 15.00
289 Brother Bobby's Home for
    Wayward Girls & Boys 15.00
290 TS,I:I..Vampire 27.00
291 TS,DAy,I..Vampire #2 . . . . 15.00
292 TS,MS,TD,RE,DSp,Wendigo . 15.00
293 GT,TS,A:I..Vampire #3 . . . . . . 15.00
294 CI,TY,GT,TD,The Darkness . . 15.00
295 TS,TVE,JCr,I..Vampire #4 . . . . 15.00
296 CI,BH,Night Women 15.00
297 TS,DCw,TD,I..Vampire #5 . . . . 15.00
298 TS,Stalker on a StarlessNight . 15.00
299 TS,DSp,I..Vampire #6 . . . . 15.00
300 GK,DA,JSon,JCr,DSp,Anniv. . 20.00
301 JDu,TVE,KG,TY `...Virginia' . . 17.00
302 TS,NR,DSp,I..Vampire #7 . . . . 17.00
303 TS,DSp,I..Vampire #8 . . . . 17.00
304 EC,RE,I..Vampire #9 . . . . 17.00
305 TVE,EC,I..Vampire #10 . . . . . . 17.00
306 TS,TD,I..Vampire #11,
    A:Jack the Ripper 17.00
307 TS,I..Vampire #12 . . . . 17.00
308 TS,MT,NR,I..Vampire #13 . . . . 17.00
309 TS,I..Vampire #14 . . . . 17.00
310 TS(i),I..Vampire #15 . . . . 17.00
311 I..Vampire #16 . . . . 17.00
312 TS(i),I..Vampire #17 . . . . 17.00

313 TS(i),CI,I..Vampire #18 . . . . . . 17.00
314 TS,I..Vampire #19 . . . . 17.00
315 TS(i),TY,I..Vampire #20 . . . . . . 17.00
316 TS(i),GT,TVE,I..Vampire #21 . 17.00
317 TS(i),I..Vampire #22 . . . . 17.00
318 TS(i),I..Vampire #23 . . . . 17.00
319 TS,JOy,I..Vampire conc. 25.00
320 GM,Project: Inferior 25.00
321 final issue 25.00

Vertigo, May, 2008
1 Room and Boredom 3.00
1a variant (c) (1:10) 3.00
2 thru 5 Room and Boredom . . . @3.00
6 thru 7 . . . . @3.00

HOUSE OF SECRETS
Nov.–Dec., 1956
1 MD,JM,The Hand of Doom . . 2,600.00
2 MMe,RMo,NC,Mask of Fear . . 900.00
3 JM,JK,MMe,The Three
    Prophecies 750.00
4 JM,JK,MMe,Master of
    Unknown 600.00
5 MMe,The Man Who
    Hated Fear 400.00
6 NC,MMe,Experiment 1000 . . . 400.00
7 RMo,Island o/t Enchantress . . 400.00
8 JK,RMo,The Electrified Man . . 450.00
9 JM,JSt,The Jigsaw Creatures . 375.00
10 JSt,NC,I was a Prisoner
    of the Sea 375.00
11 KJ(c),NC,The Man who
    Couldn't Stop Growing 375.00
12 JK,The Hole in the Sky 400.00
13 The Face in the Mist 300.00
14 MMe,The Man who Stole Air . 300.00
15 The Creature in the Camera . . 300.00
16 NC,We Matched Wits with a
    Gorilla Genius 250.00
17 DW,Lady in the Moon 250.00
18 MMe,The Fantastic
    Typewriter 250.00
19 MMe,NC,Lair of the
    Dragonfly 250.00
20 Incredible Fireball Creatures . . 250.00
21 Girl from 50,000 Fathoms 250.00
22 MMe,Thing from Beyond 250.00
23 MMe,I&O:Mark Merlin 275.00
24 NC,Mark Merlin story 250.00
25 MMe,Mark Merlin story 225.00
26 NC,MMe, Mark Merlin story . . 225.00
27 MMe,Mark Merlin 225.00
28 MMe,Mark Merlin 225.00
29 NC,MMe,Mark Merlin 225.00

House of Secrets #17
© *DC Comics Inc.*

30 JKu,MMe,Mark Merlin 225.00
31 DD,MMe,RH,Mark Merlin 200.00
32 MMe,Mark Merlin 200.00
33 MMe,Mark Merlin 200.00
34 MMe,Mark Merlin 200.00
35 MMe,Mark Merlin 200.00
36 MMe,Mark Merlin 200.00
37 MMe,Mark Merlin 200.00
38 MMe,Mark Merlin 200.00
39 JKu,MMe,Mark Merlin 200.00
40 NC,MMe,Mark Merlin 200.00
41 MMe,Mark Merlin 200.00
42 MMe,Mark Merlin 200.00
43 RMo,MMe,CI,Mark Merlin 200.00
44 MMe,Mark Merlin 200.00
45 MMe,Mark Merlin 200.00
46 MMe,Mark Merlin 200.00
47 MMe,Mark Merlin 200.00
48 ATh,MMe,Mark Merlin 200.00
49 MMe,Mark Merlin 200.00
50 MMe,Mark Merlin 200.00
51 MMe,Mark Merlin 200.00
52 MMe,Mark Merlin 200.00
53 CI,Mark Merlin 200.00
54 RMo,MMe,Mark Merlin 200.00
55 MMe,Mark Merlin 200.00
56 MMe,Mark Merlin 200.00
57 MMe,Mark Merlin 200.00
58 MMe,O:Mark Merlin 200.00
59 MMe,Mark Merlin 200.00
60 MMe,Mark Merlin 200.00
61 I:Eclipso,A:Mark Merlin 225.00
62 MMe,Eclipso,Mark Merlin 200.00
63 GC,ATh,Eclipso,Mark Merlin. . 150.00
64 MMe,ATh,M Merlin,Eclipso . . . 150.00
65 MMe,ATh,M Merlin,Eclipso . . . 150.00
66 MMe,ATh,M Merlin,Eclipso . . . 150.00
67 MMe,ATh,M Merlin,Eclipso . . . 150.00
68 MMe,Mark Merlin,Eclipso 150.00
69 MMe,Mark Merlin,Eclipso 150.00
70 MMe,Mark Merlin,Eclipso 150.00
71 MMe,Mark Merlin,Eclipso 150.00
72 MMe,Mark Merlin,Eclipso 150.00
73 MMe,D:Mark Merlin,I:Prince
    Ra-Man; Eclipso 150.00
74 MMe,Prince Ra-Man,Eclipso . 150.00
75 MMe,Prince Ra-Man,Eclipso . 150.00
76 MMe,Prince Ra-Man,Eclipso . 150.00
77 MMe,Prince Ra-Man,Eclipso . 150.00
78 MMe,Prince Ra-Man,Eclipso . 150.00
79 MMe,Prince Ra-Man,Eclipso . 150.00
80 MMe,Prince Ra-Man,Eclipso . 150.00
81 I:Abel, new mystery format
    Don't Move It 300.00
82 DD,NA,One & only, fully guaran–
    teed super-permanent 100%. 100.00
83 ATh,The Stuff that Dreams
    are Made of 100.00
84 DD,If I had but world enough
    and time 100.00
85 DH,GK,NA,Second Chance . . 125.00
86 GT,GM,Strain 125.00
87 DD,DG,RA,MK,BWr,The Coming
    of Ghaglan 135.00
88 DD,The Morning Ghost 125.00
89 GM,DH,Where Dead MenWalk 125.00
90 GT,RB,NA,GM,The Symbionts 135.00
91 WW,MA,The Eagle's Talon . . . 125.00
92 BWr,TD(i),I:Swamp Thing
    (Alex Olson) 1,100.00
93 JAp,TD,ATh(rep.)Lonely in
    Death 100.00
94 TD,ATh(rep.)Hyde.and
    go Seek 100.00
95 DH,NR,The Bride of Death . . . 100.00
96 DD,JAb,WW,BWr,the Monster 100.00
97 JAp,Divide and Murder 100.00
98 MK,ATh(rep),Born Losers 100.00
99 NR,TD(i),BWr,,Beyond His
    Imagination 75.00
100 TP,TD,AA,BWr,Rest in Peace 100.00
101 AN,MK,Small Invasion 40.00

House of Secrets #61
© *DC Comics, Inc.*

102 NR,MK,A Lonely Monstrosity . 40.00
103 AN,BWr,Village on Edge
    of Forever 40.00
104 NR,AA,GT,Ghosts Don't
    Bother Me...But... . . . . 40.00
105 JAp,AA,MK,An Axe to Grind . . 40.00
106 AN,AA,BWr,This Will Kill You . 40.00
107 AA,BWr(c),The Night of
    the Nebbish 40.00
108 A New Kid on the Block 40.00
109 AA,AN...And in Death, there
    is no Escape 40.00
110 Safes Have Secrets, Too 40.00
111 TD,Hair-I-Kari 40.00
112 Case of the Demon Spawn . . . 40.00
113 MSy,NC,NR,Spawns
    of Satan 40.00
114 FBe,Night Game 40.00
115 AA,AN,Nobody Hurts My
    Brother 40.00
116 NR,Like Father,Like Son 40.00
117 AA,AN,Revenge for the Deadly
    Dummy 40.00
118 GE,Very Last Picture Show . . 40.00
119 A Carnival of Dwarves 40.00
120 TD,AA,The Lion's Share 40.00
121 Ms.Vampire Killer 40.00
122 AA,Requiem for Igor 25.00
123 ATh,A Connecticut Ice Cream
    Man in King Arthur's Court . . . 25.00
124 Last of the Frankensteins 25.00
125 AA,FR,Instant Re-Kill 25.00
126 AN,On Borrowed Time 25.00
127 MSy,A Test of Innocence . . . 25.00
128 AN,Freak Out! 25.00
129 Almost Human 25.00
130 All Dolled Up! 25.00
131 AN,Point of No Return 25.00
132 Killer Instinct 25.00
133 Portraits of Death 25.00
134 NR,Inheritance of Blood 25.00
135 BWr,The Vegitable Garden . . . 25.00
136 BWr,NR,Last Voyage of
    Lady Luck 25.00
137 BWr,The Harder They Fall . . 25.00
138 Where Dreams are Born 30.00
139 SD,NR,A Real Crazy Kid 30.00
140 NR,O:Patchwork Man 40.00
141 You Can't Beat the Devil 20.00
142 Playmate 20.00
143 The Evil Side 20.00
144 The Vampire of Broadway . . . 20.00
145 Operation was Successful,But 20.00
146 GM,Snake's Alive 20.00
147 AN,GM,See-Through Thief . . . 20.00

148 GM,SD,Sorcerer's Apprentice. 20.00
149 MK,The Evil One 20.00
150 JSN(c),A:Phantom Stranger
    and Dr.13 . . . . 20.00
151 MGo,MK,Nightmare 20.00
152 Sister Witch 20.00
153 VM,AN,Don't Look Now 20.00
154 TS,MK,JL,Last issue 20.00

DC/Vertigo, Aug., 1996
1 SSe(s),TKr, judgments on your
    darkest secrets 4.00
2 SSe(s),TKr, F:Rain. 3.00
3 SSe(s),TKr,Seattle's citizens
    secrets 3.00
4 SSe(s),TKr,Eric's secrets
    exposed 3.00
5 SSe(s),TKr,Foundation Epilogue. 3.00
6 SSe(s),DFg,Other rooms:
    Meeting 3.00
7 SSe(s),TKr,Blueprint:
    Elevation A 3.00
8 SSe(s),TKr,Road to You,pt.1 . . 3.00
9 SSe(s),TKr,Road to You,pt.2 . . 3.00
10 SSe(s),TKr,Road to You,pt.3 . . . 3.00
11 The Book of Law, pt.1 (of 5) . . 3.00
12 The Book of Law, pt.2 . . . . 3.00
13 SSe,The Book of Law, pt.3 . . . 3.00
14 SSe,The Book of Law, pt.4 . . . 3.00
15 SSe,The Book of Law, pt.5 . . . 3.00
16 SSe,Book of Law, epilogue 3.00
17 SSe,The Road to You, pt.1 . . . 3.00
18 SSe,The Road to You, pt.2 . . . 3.00
19 SSe,The Road to You, pt.3 . . . 3.00
20 SSe,Other Rooms story 3.00
21 SSe,Basement, pt.1 . . . . 3.00
22 SSe,Basement, pt.2 . . . . 3.00
23 SSe,Basement, pt.3 . . . . 3.00
24 SSe,TKr,Attic 3.00
25 SSe,TKr, final issue 3.00

FACADE
DC/Vertigo, March, 2001
1 (of 2) TKr, 48-page 6.00
2 TKr,48-page 6.00

HUMAN DEFENSE CORPS
May 2003
1 (of 6) TTn 2.50
2 TTn,Parasitic aliens 2.50
3 TTn,What dreams may come . . . 2.50
4 TTn,Seance 2.50
5 TTn,War is Hell 2.50
6 TTn,concl. 2.50

HUMAN RACE, THE
March, 2005
1 thru 7 (of 7) . . . . @3.00

HUMAN TARGET
SPECIAL
1991
1 DG(i),Prequel to T.V. Series. . . . 3.00

HUMAN TARGET
DC/Vertigo, 1999
1 (of 4) PrM(s) 3.50
2 PrM(s) 3.00
3 PrM(s) 3.00
4 PrM(s), concl. 3.00

HUMAN TARGET
DC/Vertigo, Aug. 2003
1 PrM(s),40-pg 3.00
2 PrM(s),Unshredded Man,pt.1 . . 3.00
3 PrM(s),Unshredded Man,pt.2 . . 3.00
4 PrM(s),Ball Game, pt.1 . . . . 3.00
5 PrM(s),Ball Game, pt.2 . . . . 3.00
6 PrM(s),For I Have Sinned 3.00
7 PrM(s),Wind Blows,pt.1 . . . . 3.00

8 PrM(s),Wind Blows,pt.2 . . . . 3.00
9 PrM(s),Wind Blows,pt.3 . . . . 3.00
10 PrM(s),Five Days Grace 3.00
11 PrM(s),F:Mary 3.00
12 PrM(s),Crossing the Border 3.00
13 PrM(s),Crossing the Border 3.00
14 PrM(s),Second Coming,pt.1 . . . . 3.00
15 The Second Coming,pt.2 . . . . . . 3.00
16 The Second Coming 3.00
17 You Made Me Love You 3.00
18 Letter From the Front Line 3.00
19 The Stealer, pt.1 . . . . 3.00
20 The Stealer, pt.2 . . . . 3.00
21 The Stealer, pt.3 . . . . 3.00

HUNTER:
THE AGE OF MAGIC
DC/Vertigo, July, 2001
1 R:The Hunter 3.50
10 thru 25 . . . . @3.00

HUNTER'S HEART
1995
1 Cops vs. Serial Killer 5.00
2 thru 3 . . . . @5.00

HUNTRESS, THE
1989–90
1 JSon/DG 2.50
2 JSon,Search for Family's
   Murderer 2.50
3 JSon,A:La Bruja 2.50
4 JSon,Little Italy/Chinatown
   Gangs 2.50
5 JSon,V:Doctor Mandragora 2.50
6 JSon,Huntress'secrets revealed . 2.50
7 JSon,V:Serial Killer 2.50
8 JSon,V:Serial Killer 2.50
9 JSon,V:Serial Killer 2.50
10 JSon,Nuclear Terrorists in NY. . . 2.50
11 JSon,V:Wyvern,Nuclear
   Terrorists contd. 2.50
12 JSon,V:Nuclear Terrorists cont . . 2.50
13 JSon,Violence in NY 2.50
14 JSon,Violence contd.,New
   Mob boss 2.50
15 JSon,I:Waterfront Warrior 2.50
16 JSon,Secret of Waterfront
   Warrior revealed 2.50
17 JSon,Batman+Huntress#1 . . . . . 2.50
18 JSon,Batman+Huntress#2 . . . . . 2.50
19 JSon,Batman+Huntress#3,final
   issue 2.50

[Limited Series], 1994
1 CDi(s),MN,V:Redzone 2.50
2 MN,V:Redzone 2.50
3 MN,V:Redzone 2.50
4 MN,V:Spano,Redzone 2.50

YEAR ONE
May, 2008
1 (of 6) ATi,O:Huntress 3.00
2 thru 6 ATi . . . . @3.00

iCANDY
Sept. 2003
1 DAn&ALa(s) 2.50
2 DAn&ALa(s) thru 6 . . . . @2.50

ICON
DC/Milestone, 1993–96
1 Direct Market Ed.,MBr,MG,I:Icon,
   Rocket,S.H.R.E.D.,w/poster,
   card,C puzzle piece 3.50
1a Newsstand Ed. 2.50
2 thru 24 . . . . @2.50
25 V:Oblivion 3.00
26 thru 45 . . . . @2.50

IDENTITY CRISIS
June 2004
1 (of 7) RgM,MIB,48-pg. 7.50
2 thru 5 RgM,MIB,40-pg. . . . . @6.00
6 RgM,MIB,40-page 4.00
7 RgM,MIB,concl. 4.00
1a thru 7a reps. . . . . @4.00

Impulse #1
© DC Comics, Inc.

IMPULSE
1995–2002
1 Young Flash Adventures 6.00
2 V:Terrorists 3.50
3 thru 12 . . . . @3.00
13 thru 25 . . . . @2.50
26 thru 89 . . . . @2.50
Ann.#2 Pulp Heroes (Western) 4.00
Spec.#1,000,000 BML(s) 2.50
GN Bart Saves the Universe 6.00
Spec. Impulse/Atom Double-Shot
   DJu, x-over concl. (1997) 3.00
Spec. Impulse Plus 48pg.
   with Grossout (1997) 3.00

INDUSTRIAL GOTHIC
DC/Vertigo, 1995
1 Jail Break Plans 2.50
2 thru 5 Jail Break Plans . . . . @2.50

INFERIOR FIVE
March-April, 1967
1 MSy,Super-hero Satire 100.00
2 MSy,A:Plastic Man 45.00
3 MSy,Darwin of the Apes 40.00
4 MSy,Valhallaballoo 40.00
5 MSy,I was a Guillotine-age Hero 40.00
6 MSy,DC Stars and office 25.00
7 WMo,Drainy Day 25.00
8 WMo,V:Dr. Gruesome 25.00
9 WMo,Mummy's the Word 25.00
10 WMo,A:Superman (1968) 35.00
11 JO(c&a) (1972) 25.00
12 JO(c&a) 25.00

INFERNO
Aug., 1997
1 (of 4) SI, from Legion 4.00
2 SI,mall grrls 3.00
3 SI,Legion Month tie-in 3.00
4 SI, concl. 3.00

INFINITE CRISIS
Oct., 2005
1 (of 7) PJ,ALa 5.00
1a variant (c). 6.00
2 (of 7) PJ,ALa 4.00
2a variant (c). 4.00
3 PJ,ALa 4.00
3a variant GP (c) 4.00
4 PJ,ALa, Batman vs. Nightwing . . 4.00
4a variant GP (c) 4.00
5 PJ,ALa,Superman vs. Superman 4.00
5a variant (c). 4.00
6 PJ,ALa,One Year Later 4.00
6a variant (c). 4.00
7 Conclusion 4.00
7a variant (c). 4.00
Spec. Secret Files 64-pg. (2006). . . 6.00
Spec. Villains United 5.00

INFINITY, INC.
March, 1984
1 JOy,O:Infinity Inc. 5.00
2 JOy,End of Origin 4.00
3 JOy,O:Jade 3.00
4 JOy,V:JSA 3.00
5 JOy,V:JSA 3.00
6 JOy,V:JSA 3.00
7 JOy,V:JSA 3.00
8 JOy,V:Ultra Humanite 3.00
9 JOy,V:Ultra Humanite 3.00
10 JOy,V:Ultra Humanite 3.00
11 DN,GT,O:Infinity Inc. 3.00
12 Infinity Unmasks,I:Yolanda
   Montez (New Wildcat) 3.00
13 DN,V:Rose & Thorn 3.00
14 1st TM DC art,V:Chroma 10.00
15 TM,V:Chroma 4.00
16 TM,I:Helix (Mr. Bones) 4.00
17 TM,V:Helix. 4.00
18 TM,Crisis. 4.00
19 TM,JSA,JLA x-over,
   I:Mekanique 4.00
20 TM,Crisis. 4.00
21 TM,Crisis,I:HourmanII,
   Dr.Midnight 4.00
22 TM,Crisis. 4.00
23 TM,Crisis. 4.00
24 TM,Crisis. 4.00
25 TM,Crisis,JSA 4.00
26 TM,V:Carcharo 4.00
27 TM,V:Carcharo 4.00
28 TM,V:Carcharo 4.00
29 TM,V:Helix. 4.00
30 TM,Mourning of JSA 4.00
31 TM,V:Psycho Pirate 4.00
32 TM,V:Psycho Pirate 4.00
33 TM,O:Obsidian 4.00
34 TM,A: Global Guardians 4.00
35 TM,V:Infinitors 4.00
36 TM,V:Injustice Unl. 4.00
37 TM,TD,O:Northwind 4.00
38 Helix on Trial 3.00
39 O:Solomon Grundy 3.00
40 V:Thunderbolt 3.00
41 Jonni Thunder 3.00
42 TD,V:Hastor,L:Fury 3.00
43 TD,V:Hastor,Silver Scarab 3.00
44 TD,D:Silver Scarab 3.00
45 MGu,A:New Teen Titans,
   V:Ultra-Humanite 3.00
46 TD,Millennium,V:Floronic Man . 3.00
47 TD,Millennium,V:Harlequin 3.00
48 TD,O:Nuklon 3.00
49 Silver Scarab becomes
   Sandman 3.00
50 TD,V:The Wizard,O:Sandman . . 3.50
51 W:Fury & Sandman,D:Skyman. . 3.00
52 V:Helix. 3.00
53 V:Justice Unlimited,last issue . . . 3.00
Ann.#1 TM,V:Thorn 4.00

All comics prices listed are for *Near Mint* condition.

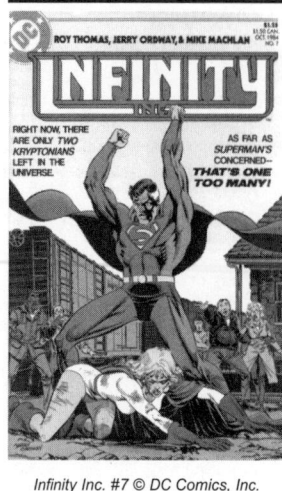

Infinity Inc. #7 © DC Comics, Inc.

Ann.#2 V:Degaton,x-over Young
  All-Stars Annual #1 . . . . 3.00
Spec.#1 TD,A:Outsiders,V:Psycho
  Pirate 3.00

Sept., 2007
1 PrM(s),A:John Henry Irons 3.00
2 PrM(s),A:Superman 3.00
3 PrM(s),V:Kid Empty 3.00
4 PrM(s),V:Kid Empty 3.00
5 PrM(s),Luthor's Monsters 3.00
6 PrM(s),Influencing Machines,pt.1 3.00
7 PrM(s),Influencing Machines,pt.2 3.00
8 PrM(s),The Bogeyman, pt.1 . . . 3.00
9 PrM(s),The Bogeyman, pt.2 . . . 3.00
10 PrM(s),Bogeyman exposed 3.00
11 PrM(s), Dark Side Club 3.00
12 PrM(s), Dark Side Club tie-in . . 3.00

INVASION!
1988–89
1 TM,I:Vril Dox,Dominators
  (20th century) 4.00
2 TM,KG,DG,I:L.E.G.I.O.N. 3.00
3 BS,DG,I:Blasters 3.00
Daily Planet-Invasion! 16p 2.00

INVISIBLES
DC/Vertigo, 1994–96
1 GMo(s). 7.00
2 GMo(s),Down & Out,pt.1 . . . . 4.00
3 GMo(s),Down & Out,pt.2 . . . . 4.00
4 GMo(s),Down & Out,pt.3 . . . . 4.00
5 Arcadia,pt.1 . . . . 4.00
6 Arcadia,pt.2 . . . . 4.00
7 Arcadia,pt.3 . . . . 4.00
8 Arcadia,pt.4 . . . . 4.00
9 SeP(c),L:Dane 3.00
10 SeP(c),CWn,Jim Crow v. 3
  Zombies. 3.00
11 GMo:New Breed of Hunter 3.00
12 GMo,Best Man Fall. 3.00
13 GMo,Sheman,pt.1. . . . . 3.00
14 GMo,SeP,Sheman,pt.2 . . . . 3.00
15 GMo,Sheman,pt.3. . . . . 3.00
16 GMo,An offer from Sir Miles 3.00
17 GMo,Entropy in the U.K.,pt.1 . . . 3.00
18 GMo,Entropy in the U.K.,pt.2 . . . 3.00
19 GMo,Entropy in the U.K.,pt.3 . . . 3.00
20 GMo,F:RaggedRobin,Dane,Boy . 4.00
21 GMo,PuJ,F:Dane 4.00
22 GMo(s),MBu,MPn 4.00
23 GMo(s),MBu,MPn 4.00
24 GMo(s),MBu,MPn 4.00

25 GMo(s),MBu,MPn,final issue
  Aug., 1996 . . . . 5.00
[Volume 2] DC/Vertigo, 1996
1 GMo(s),PJ,Black Science,pt.1 . . . 4.00
2 GMo(s),PJ,Black Science,pt.2 . . . 3.00
3 GMo(s),PJ,Black Science,pt.3 . . . 3.00
4 GMo(s),PJ,Black Science,pt.4 . . . 3.00
5 GMo(s),PJ,In SanFrancisco,pt.1 . 3.00
6 GMo(s),PJ,In SanFrancisco,pt.2 . 3.00
7 GMo(s),PJ,BB(c),Time Machine
  Go, concl. 3.00
8 GMo(s),PJ,BB(c),Sensitive
  Criminals,pt.1. . . . . 3.00
9 GMo(s),PJ,BB(c),Criminals,pt.2 . 3.00
10 GMo(s),PJ,Criminals,pt.3, ... 3.00
11 GMo(s),PJ,BB(c),Hand of Glory
  pt.1 . . . . 3.00
12 GMo(s),PJ,BB(c),Glory,pt.2 . . . 3.00
13 GMo(s),PJ,BB(c),Glory,concl. . . 3.00
14 GMo(s),BB(c),Archons aftermath 3.00
15 GMo(s),BB(c), The Philadelphia
  Experiment, pt.1 . . . . 3.00
16 GMo(s),BB(c),Experiment,pt.2 . . 3.00
17 GMo,CWn,BB,Black Science II
  pt.1. . . . . 3.00
18 GMo,CWn,BB,Science,pt.2. . . . . 3.00
19 GMo,CWn,BB,Science,pt.3. . . . . 3.00
20 GMo,CWn,BB(c),Science,pt.4 . . 2.50
21 GMo,CWn,BB(c),King Mob. 2.50
22 GMo,CWn,BB(c) The Tower 2.50
[Volume 3] DC/Vertigo, 1999
12 GMo,Satanstorm,pt.1 . . . . 3.00
11 GMo,Satanstorm,pt.2 . . . . 3.00
10 GMo,Satanstorm,pt.3 . . . . 3.00
9 GMo,Satanstorm,pt.4. . . . . 3.00
8 GMo,Karmageddon,pt.1 . . . . 3.00
7 GMo,Karmageddon,pt.2 . . . . 3.00
6 GMo,Karmageddon,pt.3 . . . . 3.00
5 GMo 3.00
4 GMo,Invisible Kingdom,pt.1. . . . . 3.00
3 GMo,Invisible Kingdom,pt.2. . . . . 3.00
2 GMo,Invisible Kingdom,pt.3. . . . . 3.00
1 GMo,conclusion 3.00
GN The Mystery Play 10.00

ION
April, 2006
1 RMz, Kyle Rayner returns 3.00
2 RMz, Is Kyle going mad? 3.00
3 RMz, F:Mogo 3.00
4 RMz,F:Green Lantern 3.00
5 RMz,F:Green Lantern 3.00
6 RMz,Guardians of the Universe . 3.00
7 RMz,Return to earth 3.00
8 RMz,A remote world 3.00
9 RMz 3.00
10 RMz,Twilight of Ion 3.00
11 RMz,Kyle Raner & Donna Troy . 3.00
12 RMz,finale 3.00

ISIS
Oct.–Nov., 1976
1 RE/WW 25.00
2 thru 6 . . . . @15.00
7 O:Isis 18.00
8 Dec.–Jan., 1977–78. . . . . 15.00

IT'S GAMETIME
Sept.–Oct., 1955
1 . . . . 1,100.00
2 Dodo and the Frog. 900.00
3 . . . . 900.00
4 March-April, 1956 . . . . 950.00

JACK CROSS
Aug., 2005
1 (of 4) WEI,GEr 2.50
2 WEI,GEr. 2.50
3 WEI,GEr. 2.50

4 WEI,GEr, conclusion 2.50

JACKIE GLEASON AND
THE HONEYMOONERS
June-July, 1956
1 Based on TV show 1,400.00
2 . . . . 800.00
3 thru 11 . . . . @600.00
12 April-May, 1958 . . . . 900.00

JACK KIRBY'S
FOURTH WORLD
Jan., 1997
1 JBy,Worlds of New Genesis &
  Apokolips become one 2.50
2 JBy,F:Big Barda vs. Thor 2.50
3 JBy,at Wall of the Source 2.50
4 JBy,Can Highfather save his son 2.50
5 JBy,conflict between the gods . . . 2.50
6 JBy,Cause of Orion's
  transformation 2.50
7 JBy,Orion taught lesson. 2.50
8 JBy,WS,Genesis aftermath 2.50
9 JBy,WS(c),Genesis aftermath . . . 2.50
10 JBy,WS, ... 2.50
11 JBy,WS,F:Orion. 2.50
12 JBy,WS,F:Mister Miracle. 2.50
13 JBy,WS 2.50
14 JBy,WS,Promethean Giant 2.50
15 JBy,WS,Armaghetto 2.50
16 JBy,WS,Kalibak vs. Darkseid . . . 2.50
17 JBy,WS,Darkseid 2.50
18 JBy,WS,Darkseid freed. 2.50
19 JBy,WS,two stories 2.50
20 JBy,WS,A:Superman,final issue . 2.50

JACK OF FABLES
DC/Vertigo, July, 2006
1 BWg. 3.00
2 BWg,Mr. Revise 3.00
3 BWg,Mr. Revise's prisoner 3.00
4 Great Escape is on 3.00
5 . . . . 3.00
6 Jack Frost, pt.1 . . . . 3.00
7 Jack Frost, pt.2 . . . . 3.00
8 Jack of Hearts, pt.1 . . . . 3.00
9 in Las Vegas 3.00
10 V:Mister Revise. 3.00
11 Jack Frost, pt.2 . . . . 3.00
12 The Bad Prince, pt.1. . . . . 3.00
13 The Bad Prince, pt.2. . . . . 3.00
14 The Bad Prince, pt.3. . . . . 3.00
15 The Bad Prince, pt.4. . . . . 3.00
16 Halloween Issue 3.00
17 Americana, pt.1. . . . . 3.00
18 Americana, pt.2, Bookburner . . . 3.00
19 Americana, pt.3. . . . . 3.00
20 Americana, concl. 3.00
21 Gary, The Pathetic Fallacy 3.00
22 Smiling Jack Candle 3.00
23 Smiling Jack Candle 3.00
24 V:Sheriff without a gun 3.00
25 Turning Pages, pt.1. . . . . 3.00
26 Turning Pages, pt.2. . . . . 3.00
27 Turning Pages, pt.3. . . . . 3.00
28 Jack's Big Book of War, pt.1 . . . . 3.50

JAGUAR
Impact, 1991
1 I&O:Jaguar 2.50
2 thru 14 . . . . @2.50
Ann.#1 Earthquest,w/trading card . . 2.50

JEMM,
SON OF SATURN
Sept., 1984
1 thru 12 GC . . . . @2.50

JIMMY WAKELY
Sept.–Oct., 1949
1 Ph(c),ATh,The Cowboy
  Swordsman. 1,700.00
2 Ph(c),ATh,The Prize Pony. . . . 700.00
3 Ph(c),ATh,The Return of
  Tulsa Tom 650.00
4 Ph(c),ATh,FF,HK,Where There's
  Smoke There's Gunfire 625.00
5 ATh,The Return of the
  Conquistadores 500.00
6 ATh,Two Lives of
  Jimmy Wakely 500.00
7 The Secret of Hairpin Canyon . 500.00
8 ATh,The Lost City of
  Blue Valley 500.00
9 ATh,The Return of the
  Western Firebrands 350.00
10 ATh,Secret of Lantikin'sLight . 350.00
11 ATh,Trail o/a Thousand Hoofs. 350.00
12 ATh,JKU,The King of Sierra
  Valley 350.00
13 ATh,The Raiders of Treasure
  Mountain 350.00
14 ATh(c),JKu,The Badmen
  of Roaring Flame Valley 350.00
15 GK(c),Tommyguns on the
  Range 350.00
16 GK(c),The Bad Luck Boots . . 300.00
17 GK(c),Terror atThunderBasin . 300.00
18 July–Aug., 1952 . . . . 350.00

JLA
Nov., 1996
1 GMo(s),HPo,JhD,V:Hyperclan . . 16.00
2 GMo(s),HPo,JhD,V:Hyperclan . . 12.00
3 GMo(s),HPo,JhD,War of the
  Worlds 10.00
4 GMo(s),HPo,JhD,battle of the
  super-heroes, conc. 10.00
5 GMo(s),HPo,JhD Woman of
  Tomorrow 7.00
6 GMo(s),HPo,JhD,Fire in theSky . 6.00
7 GMo(s),HPo,JhD,Heaven on
  Earth 6.00
8 GMo(s),HPo,JhD,Imaginary
  Stories, F:Green Arrow 6.00
9 GMo(s),V:The Key 6.00
10 GMo(s),HPo,JhD,R:Injustice
  Gang, pt.1 (of 6) 6.00
11 GMo(s),HPo,JhD,Rock of Ages,
  pt.2 . . . . 6.00
12 GMo(s),HPo,JhD,Rock of Ages,
  pt.3, A:Hourman 6.00
13 GMo(s),HPo,JhD,Rock of Ages,
  pt.4 . . . . 6.00
14 GMo(s),HPo,JhD,Rock of Ages,
  pt.5 . . . . 6.00
15 GMo(s),HPo,JhD,Rock of Ages
  pt.6, concl, 48 pg. 6.00
16 GMo(s),HPo,JhD, new member . 6.00
17 GMo(s),HPo,JhD,V:Prometheus . 6.00
18 MWa,Engine of Chance, pt.1 . . . 6.00
19 MWa,Engine of Chance, pt.2 . . . 6.00
20 MWa,F:Adam Strange,pt.1 . . . . 6.00
21 MWa,F:Adam Strange,pt.2 . . . . 6.00
22 GMo(s),The Star Conquerer 2.50
23 GMo,V:Star Conquerer,
  A:Sandman 2.50
24 GMo,HPo,Ultra-Marines,pt.1. . . . 2.50
25 GMo,HPo,Ultra-Marines,pt.2. . . . 2.50
26 GMo,HPo,Ultra-Marines,pt.3. . . . 2.50
27 GMo,HPo,CrisisTimesFive,pt.1. . 2.50
28 GMo,HPo,CrisisTimesFive,pt.2. . 2.50
29 GMo,HPo,CrisisTimesFive,pt.3. . 2.50
30 GMo,HPo,CrisisTimesFive,pt.4. . 2.50
31 GMo,HPo,CrisisTimes
  Five,concl. 2.50
32 MWa(s),No Man's Land 2.50
33 MWa(s),No Man's Land 2.50
34 GMo,Super-villains riot 2.50

JLA A#20 © DC Comics Inc.

35 JMD(s),F:New Spectre 2.50
36 GMo,HPo,World War 3,pt.1 . . . . 2.50
37 GMo,HPo,World War 3,pt.2 . . . . 2.50
38 GMo,HPo,World War 3,pt.3 . . . . 2.50
39 GMo,HPo,World War 3,pt.4 . . . . 2.50
40 GMo,HPo,World War 3,pt.5 . . . . 2.50
41 GMo,HPo,World War 3,
  concl.48-pg. 4.00
42 Miniscule civilization 2.50
43 MWa(s),HPo,V:Ra's al Ghul 2.50
44 HPo,Tower of Babel,pt.2 . . . . . . 2.50
45 HPo,Tower of Babel,pt.3 . . . . . . 2.50
46 HPo,Tower of Babel,concl. 2.50
47 MWa,BHi,PNe,Queen ofFables . 2.50
48 MWa,BHi,PNe,Queen ofFables . 2.50
49 MWa,BHi,PNe,Queen ofFables . 2.50
50 MWa,BHi,PNe,48-page. 5.00
51 MWa,MsM,Man and Superman . 2.50
52 MWa,BHi,PNe. 2.50
53 MWa,BHi,PNe. 2.50
54 MWa,BHi,PNe,Man & Superman 2.50
55 MWa,Terror Incognita,pt.1 . . . . . 2.50
56 MWa,Terror Incognita,pt.2 . . . . . 2.50
57 MWa,Terror Incognita,pt.3 . . . . . 2.50
58 MWa,Terror Incognita,pt.4 . . . . . 2.50
59 CDi,DBk,Joker:Last Laugh 2.50
60 MWa,F:Santa Claus 2.50
61 DoM,TG,+16-pg.PowerCompany 2.50
62 DoM,Golden Perfect,pt.1 . . . . . . 2.50
63 DoM,Golden Perfect,pt.2 . . . . . . 2.50
64 DoM,Golden Perfect,pt.3 . . . . . . 2.50
65 DoM,Batman & Plastic Man 2.50
66 DoM,warrior priests. 2.50
67 DoM,human sacrifice 2.50
68 DoM,Obsidian Age prologue. . . . 2.50
69 Hunt for Aquaman,pt.1 . . . . 2.50
70 DoM,Hunt for Aquaman,pt.2 . . . . 2.50
71 DoM,Hunt for Aquaman,pt.3 . . . . 2.50
72 DoM,Hunt for Aquaman,pt.4 . . . . 2.50
73 DoM,Hunt for Aquaman,pt.5 . . . . 2.50
74 DoM,Hunt for Aquaman,pt.6 . . . . 2.50
75 DoM,Hunt for Aquaman,64-pg. . . 5.00
76 DoM,after Obsidian Age 2.50
77 RV(s),memories stolen 2.50
78 DoM, ... 2.50
79 DoM,F:Faith 2.50
80 White Rage,pt.1 . . . . 2.50
81 White Rage,pt.2 . . . . 2.50
82 White Rage,pt.3 . . . . 2.50
83 Qurac 2.50
84 Trial by Fire,pt.1 . . . . 2.50
85 Trial by Fire,pt.2 . . . . 2.50
86 Trial by Fire,pt.3 . . . . 2.50
87 Trial by Fire,pt.4 . . . . 2.50
88 Trial by Fire,pt.5 . . . . 2.50

89 Trial by Fire,pt.6 . . . . 2.50
90 F:Batman,Wonder Woman 2.50
91 DON(s),Extinction,pt.1 . . . . 2.50
92 DON(s),Extinction,pt.2 . . . . 2.50
93 DON(s),Extinction,pt.3 . . . . 2.50
94 JBy,JOy,10th Circle,pt.1 . . . . 2.50
95 JBy,JOy,10th Circle,pt.2 . . . . 2.50
96 JBy,JOy,10th Circle,pt.3 . . . . 2.50
97 JBy,JOy,10th Circle,pt.4 . . . . 2.50
98 JBy,JOy,10th Circle,pt.5 . . . . 2.50
99 JBy,JOy,10th Circle,pt.6 . . . . 2.50
100 R:The Elite,48-pg. 3.50
101 RG,Pain of the Gods,pt.1 . . . . . 2.50
102 RG,Pain of the Gods,pt.2 . . . . . 2.50
103 RG,Pain of the Gods,pt.3 . . . . . 2.50
104 RG,Pain of the Gods,pt.4 . . . . . 2.50
105 RG,Pain of the Gods,pt.5 . . . . . 2.50
106 RG,Pain of the Gods,pt.6 . . . . . 2.50
107 KBk(s),RG,DGr,space egg 5.00
108 KBk,Syndicate Rules,pt.2 . . . . . 4.00
109 KBk,Syndicate Rules,pt.3 . . . . . 2.50
110 KBk,Syndicate Rules,pt.4 . . . . . 2.50
111 KBk,Syndicate Rules,pt.5 . . . . . 2.50
112 KBk,Syndicate Rules,pt.6 . . . . . 2.50
113 KBk,Syndicate Rules,pt.7 . . . . . 2.50
114 KBk,Syndicate Rules,pt.8 . . . . . 2.50
115 MFm,Crisis of Conscience,pt.1 . 5.00
116 MFm,Crisis of Conscience,pt.2 . 3.00
117 MFm,Crisis of Conscience,pt.3 . 2.50
118 MFm,Crisis of Conscience,pt.4 . 2.50
119 MFm,Crisis of Conscience,pt.5 . 2.50
120 World Without Justice League . 2.50
121 World Without Justice League . 2.50
122 World Without Justice League . 2.50
123 World Without Justice League . 2.50
124 World Without Justice League . 2.50
125 World Without Justice League . 2.50
Ann.#1 Pulp Heroes (Hard Boiled) . 4.50
Ann.#2 TTn,BWr,Ghosts 3.50
Ann.#3 JLApe Gorilla Warfare 3.50
Ann.#4 Planet DC 4.00
Spec.#1,000,000 GMo(s),HPo,
  V:Justice Legion A. 2.50
SuperSpec.#1 Justice League
  of America 6.00
Spec.#1 Our Worlds at War,48-pg. . 3.00
Giant #1, 7 new stories, 80-pg. 5.00
Giant #2, 80-page. 5.00
Giant #3, 80-page oversize. 6.00
SC Secret Origins, oversize. 8.00
JLA: Tomorrow Woman, 1-shot
  TPe,Girlfrenzy (1998) 2.50
GN New World Order GMo(s),HPo,
  JhD, rep. #1–#4. . . . . 6.00
GN American Dreams rep.#5–#9. . . 8.00
GN Secret Files 4.00
GN Secret Files deluxe 5.00
GN Secret Files #2 . . . . 4.00
GN Secret Files #3 How Talia stole
  Batman's Secret Files 5.00
GN Foreign Bodies 6.00
GN JLA/WildC.A.T.S, GMo(s),
  VS,x-over. 6.00
GN JLA/Haven: Arrival (2001) 6.00
GN Gods and Monsters. 7.00
GN Seven Caskets,DIB, 48-page . . 6.00
GN JLA: Superpower. 6.00
GN JLA Primeval 6.00
GN Shogun of Steel,Elseworlds . . . 7.00
GN JLA/Haven:Anathema (2002) . . 6.00
GN The Island of Dr. Moreau,GP
  Elseworlds (2002) 7.00
GN JLA: Liberty and Justice 10.00
JLA/Witchblade, x-over 6.00
JLA Showcase 80-pg Giant #1 . . . . 5.00
Spec. JLA: Workweek 7.00
Spec. Secret Files 2004. . . . . 5.00
Spec. JLA/Cyberforce (2005). 6.00
Spec. Amazing Adventures of JLA. . 4.00

DC COMICS

JLA:

ACT OF GOD
Nov., 2000
1 (of 3) Elseworlds,48-page 5.00
2 powers gone,48-page 5.00
3 concl.,48-page 5.00

...AGE OF WONDER
April 2003
1 (of 2) Elseworlds 6.00
2 concl. 6.00

...BLACK BAPTISM
March, 2001
1 (of 4) F:Faust. 2.50
2 F:Faust. 2.50
3 V:Daiblos 2.50
4 concl. 2.50

JLA Classified #8 © DC Comics, Inc.

...CLASSIFIED
Nov., 2004
1 GMo(s),V:Gorilla Grodd 3.00
2 GMo(s),V:Gorilla Grodd 3.00
3 GMo(s),V:Gorilla Grodd,concl. . . . 3.00
4 KG&JMD(s),KM&JRu, I Can't Believe
  it's Not the Justice League,pt.1 . 3.00
5 KG&JMD(s),KM&JRu, pt.2 . . . . . 3.00
6 KG&JMD(s),KM&JRu, pt.3 . . . . . 3.00
7 KG&JMD(s),KM&JRu, pt.4 . . . . . 3.00
8 KG&JMD(s),KM&JRu, pt.5 . . . . . 3.00
9 KG&JMD(s),KM&JRu, pt.6 . . . . . 3.00
10 WEl(s),New Maps of Hell,pt.1 . . . 3.00
11 WEl(s),New Maps of Hell,pt.2 . . . 3.00
12 WEl(s),New Maps of Hell,pt.3 . . . 3.00
13 WEl(s),New Maps of Hell,pt.4 . . . 3.00
14 WEl(s),New Maps of Hell,pt.5 . . . 3.00
15 WEl(s),New Maps of Hell,concl. . 3.00
16 KJ,Hypothetical Woman,pt.1 . . . 3.00
17 KJ,Hypothetical Woman,pt.2 . . . 3.00
18 KJ,Hypothetical Woman,pt.3 . . . 3.00
19 KJ,Hypothetical Woman,pt.4 . . . 3.00
20 KJ,Hypothetical Woman,pt.5 . . . 3.00
21 KJ,Hypothetical Woman,pt.6 . . . 3.00
22 MFm, A Game of Chance,pt.1 . . . 3.00
23 MFm, A Game of Chance,pt.2 . . . 3.00
24 MFm, A Game of Chance,pt.3 . . . 3.00
25 MFm, A Game of Chance,pt.4 . . . 3.00
26 HC,KPI,Secret Trust, pt.1 . . . . . . 3.00
27 HC,KPI,Secret Trust, pt.2 . . . . . . 3.00
28 HC,KPI,Secret Trust, pt.3 . . . . . . 3.00
29 HC,KPI,Secret Trust, pt.4 . . . . . . 3.00
30 HC,KPI,Sacred Trust, pt.5 . . . . . 3.00
31 HC,KPI,Secret Trust, pt.6 . . . . . . 3.00

32 DJu,4th Parallel, pt.1, 48-pgs. . . 4.00
33 DJu,4th Parallel, pt.2 . . . . 3.00
34 DJu,4th Parallel, pt.3 . . . . 3.00
35 DJu,4th Parallel, pt.4 . . . . 3.00
36 DJu,4th Parallel, pt.5 . . . . 3.00
37 Kid Amazo, pt.1 . . . . 3.00
38 Kid Amazo, pt.2 . . . . 3.00
39 Kid Amazo, pt.3 . . . . 3.00
40 Kid Amazo, pt.4 . . . . 3.00
41 Kid Amazo, pt.5 . . . . 3.00
42 The Ghosts of Mars, pt.1 . . . . . . 3.00
43 The Ghosts of Mars, pt.2 . . . . . . 3.00
44 The Ghosts of Mars, pt.3 . . . . . . 3.00
45 The Ghosts of Mars, pt.4 . . . . . . 3.00
46 The Ghosts of Mars, concl. 3.00
47 JLA bare-handed 3.00
48 V:Weaponers ofQward 3.00
49 Wives and Loved Ones 3.00
50 JBy,MFm,new foe 3.00
51 JBy,MFm,new foe 3.00
52 JBy,MFm, That was Now 3.00
53 JBy,MFm,That was Now 3.00
54 JBy,MFm,That was Now 3.00

...CLASSIFIED: COLD STEEL
Dec., 2005
1 and 2 (0f 2) 48-pg. . . . . @6.00

...CREATED EQUAL
Feb., 2000
1 FaN,KM,JRu,Elseworlds 6.00
2 FaN,KM,JRu 6.00

...DESTINY
June, 2002
1 (of 4) TMd,48-pg 6.00
2 JAr(s),TMd, Elseworlds 6.00
3 JAr(s),TMd,Luthor,Mongul 6.00
4 JAr(s),TMc,concl. 6.00

...GATEKEEPER
Oct., 2001
1 (of 3) TT, 48-page 5.00
2 thru 3 TT, 48-page . . . . @5.00

.../HITMAN
Sept., 2007
1 (of 2) GEn,Hitman is back 4.00
2 finale 4.00

...INCARNATIONS
May, 2001
1 (of 7) JOs,VS,V:Wotan 3.50
2 JOs,VS,Batman joins. 3.50
3 JOs,VS,V:Lex Luthor, Kobra 3.50
4 JOs,VS,F:Aquaman 3.50
5 JOs,VS,F:Aquaman 3.50
6 JOs,VS,two tales 3.50
7 JOs,VS,concl. 3.50

.../JSA
Nov., 2002
1 Secret files, Team-up,
  prelude,64-pg. 5.00

...PARADISE LOST
Nov., 1997
1 (of 3) MMr,AOl,F:Zauriel 2.50
2 MMr,AOl,F:Zauriel,Martian
  Manhunter 2.50

...SCARY MONSTERS
Mar. 2003
1 (of 6) CCl,V:Ancient spirits. 2.50
2 CCl. 2.50
3 CCl,ancient evil 2.50
4 CCl,Kishana secret 2.50
5 CCl,Kishana's origin 2.50
6 CCl,concl. 2.50

.../THE SPECTRE: SOUL WAR
Jan. 2003
1 (of 2) DBk,PNe 6.00
2 DBk,PNe 6.00

.../TITANS
1998
1 (of 3) JLA vs. Teen Titans 3.00
2 . . . . 3.00
3 conclusion, New Titans 3.00

...WEDDING SPECIAL
Sept., 2007
1 ALa,MMK,EBe(c),48-pgs. 4.00

...WORLD WITHOUT GROWN-UPS
June, 1998
1 (of 2) I:Young Justice 48pg 5.00
2 Young Justice, concl. 5.00

...YEAR ONE
Nov., 1997
1 (of 12) MWa,BAu,BKi,48pg. 6.00
1 Platium issue. 9.00
2 MWa,BAu,BKi,V:Vandal Savage . 4.00
3 MWa,BAu,BKi 4.00
4 MWa,BAu,BKi,V:Locus 4.00
5 MWa,BAu,BKi,F:Doom Patrol . . . 4.00
6 MWa,BAu,BKi,V:Doom Patrol . . . 4.00
7 MWa,BAu,BKi,V:Weapon Master 4.00
8 MWa,BAu,BKi,MIB,V:Locus 4.00
9 MWa,BAu,BKi,MIB,V:Locus 3.00
10 MWa,BAu,BKi,MIB,V:Locus 3.00
11 MWa,BAu,BKi,MIB 3.00
12 MWa,BAu,BKi,MIB, concl. 3.50

JLA-Z
Sept. 2003
1 (of 3) handbook 2.50
2 thru 3 . . . . @2.50

JOHN CONSTANTINE—HELLBLAZER SPECIAL: PAPA MIDNITE
DC/Vertigo, Feb., 2005
1 (of 5) 3.00
2 thru 5 . . . . @3.00

JOHNNY THUNDER
Feb.–March, 1973
1 ATh. 30.00
2 GK,MD 15.00
3 ATh,GK,MD,July-Aug., 1973 . . . 15.00

JOKER, THE
1975–76
1 IN,DG,A:TwoFace 90.00
2 IN,JL WillieTheWeeper 40.00
3 JL,A:Creeper 40.00
4 JL,A:GreenArrow 30.00
5 IN,Joker Goes "Wilde" 30.00
6 IN,V:Sherlock Holmes 30.00
7 IN,A:Luthor. 30.00
8 IN,A:Scarecrow 30.00
9 IN,A:Catwoman 40.00

JOKER, THE: LAST LAUGH
Oct., 2001
1 (of 6) CDi,Oracle vs. villains 3.00
2 CDi,Batman,Riot in the Slab 3.00
3 CDi,F:JLA vs. Joker army 3.00
4 CDi,F:Mr. Mind, Lex Luthor 3.00
5 CDi,Harley Quinn is last hope . . . 3.00
6 CDi,Joker's final stand. 3.00
Secret Files #1 64-page. 6.00

JOKER'S ASYLUM, THE
July, 2008
Spec. #1 Joker. 3.00
Spec. #1 Penguin. 3.00

DC COMICS

Spec. #1 Poison Ivy 3.00
Spec. #1: Scarecrow 3.00
Spec. #1 Two-Face 3.00

JONAH HEX
1977–85

1 Vengeance For A Fallen
  Gladiator 200.00
2 The Lair of the Parrot 100.00
3 The Fugitive 75.00
4 The Day of Chameleon 75.00
5 Welcome to Paradise 75.00
6 The Lawman 60.00
7 Son of the Apache 75.00
8 O:Jonah Hex 75.00
9 BWr(c) 50.00
10 GM(c),Violence at Vera Cruz . . 50.00
11 The Holdout 40.00
12 JS(c),Search for 'Gator Hawes . 40.00
13 The Railroad Blaster 40.00
14 The Sin Killer 40.00
15 Saw Dust and Slow Death 40.00
16 The Wyandott Verdict! 35.00
17 Voyage to Oblivion 35.00
18 Amazon Treasure, and Death . . 35.00
19 The Duke of Zarkania! 35.00
20 Phantom Stage to William
  Bend 35.00
21 The Buryin'! 35.00
22 Requiem For A Pack Rat 35.00
23 Massacre of the Celestials 35.00
24 Minister of the Lord 35.00
25 The Widow Maker 35.00
26 Death Race to Cholera Bend! . . 20.00
27 The Wooden Six Gun! 20.00
28 Night of the Savage 20.00
29 The Innocent 20.00
30 O:Jonah Hex 20.00
31 A:Arbee Stoneham 20.00
32 A:Arbee Stoneham 20.00
33 The Crusador 20.00
34 Christmas in an Outlaw Town . . 20.00
35 The Fort Charlotte Brigade 20.00
36 Return to Fort Charlotte 20.00
37 DAy,A:Stonewall Jackson 20.00
38 DSp,Iron Dog's Gold 20.00
39 The Vow of a Samurai! 20.00
40 DAy,The Rainmaker 20.00
41 DAy,Two for the Hangman! 20.00
42 Wanted for Murder 20.00
43 JKu(c),Death by Fire 20.00
44 JKu(c),DAy 20.00
45 DAy,Jonah gets married 20.00
46 JKu(c),DAy,Showdown 20.00
47 DAy,Doom Rides the Sundown
  Town 20.00
48 DAy,A:El Diablo 20.00
49 DAy,Reap the Grim Harvest . . . 20.00
50 DAy,The Hunter 20.00
51 DAy,The Comforter 8.00
52 DAy,Rescue! 8.00
53 DAy,The Haunting 8.00
54 TD,Trapped in the Parrot's Lair . 8.00
55 Trail of Blood 8.00
56 DAy,The Asylum 8.00
57 B:El Diablo backup story 8.00
58 DAy,The Treasure of Catfish
  Pond 8.00
59 DAy,Night of the White Lotus . . . 8.00
60 DAy,Domain of the Warlord 8.00
61 DAy,In the Lair of
  the Manchus 8.00
62 DAy,Belly of the Malay Tiger . . . 8.00
63 DAy,Ship of Doom 8.00
64 DAy,The Pearl! 8.00
65 DAy,The Vendetta! 8.00
66 DAy,Requiem for a Coward 8.00
67 DAy,Deadman's Hand! 8.00
68 DAy,Gunfight at Gravesboro! . . . 8.00
69 DAy,The Gauntlet! 8.00
70 DAy,Mountain of the Manitou . . . 8.00
71 DAy,The Masquerades 8.00

72 DAy,Tarantula 8.00
73 DAy,Jonah in a wheel chair 8.00
74 DAy,A:Railroad Bill 8.00
75 DAy,JAp,A:Railroad Bill 8.00
76 DAy,Jonah goes to Jail 7.00
77 DAy,Over the Wall 7.00
78 DAy,Me Ling returns 7.00
79 DAy,Duel in the Sand 7.00
80 DAy,TD,A:Turnbull 7.00
81 thru 89 DAy . . . . @8.00
90 thru 91 GM . . . . @8.00
92 GM,A Blaze of Glory 25.00

Nov., 2005

1 LRs,Cemetery Without Crosses . 5.00
2 LRs,Cross of solid gold 3.00
3 LRs,F:Bat Lash 3.00
4 LRs,JP 3.00
5 LRs,Nuns with Guns 3.00
6 LRs,V:Nuns with Guns 3.00
7 LRs,Oil Baron 3.00
8 JP,An old acquaintance 3.00
9 JP,TD,Flowers on a grave 3.00
10 JP,Louisiana swamplands 3.00
11 JP,return of El Diablo 3.00
12 JP,Snowstorm 3.00
13 JP,Origin, pt.1 . . . . 3.00
14 JP,Legend of Jonah Hex, pt.2 . . 3.00
15 JP,Legend of Jonah Hex, pt.3 . . 3.00
16 JP,I:Tallulah Black 3.00
17 JP,Tallulah Black's vengeance . 3.00
18 JP,Hex heads to Texas 3.00
19 JP,Friends reunited 3.00
20 JP,Friends reunited 3.00
21 JP,Greatest Inventor 3.00
22 JP,Wizards of Electricity 3.00
23 JP,Two armies out for blood . . . 3.00
24 JP,El Diablo & Bat Lash return . 3.00
25 JP(s),Jonah and Son 3.00
26 JP(s) 3.00
27 JP(s),Star Man 3.00
28 JP(s),Young Man's Revenge . . . 3.00
29 JP(s),Tribe of the Red Scorpion . 3.00
30 JP(s),Desperation 3.00
31 JP(s),RCo(c),Red Mask 3.00
32 JP(s),Dia De los Muertos 3.00
33 JP(s) 3.00
34 JP(s),Peace and Quiet? 3.00
35 JP(s),F:Marshall Roth 3.00
36 JP(s), An old score 3.00
37 JP(s),Trouble Comes in Threes . 3.00

AND OTHER WESTERN TALES
Sept.–Oct., 1979

1 TD,The Hundred Dollar Deal . . . 20.00
2 NA,ATh,SA,GK 25.00
3 Jan.–Feb., 1980 . . . . 20.00

RIDERS OF
THE WORM AND SUCH
[Mini-Series] DC/Vertigo, 1995

1 R:Ronah Hex 4.00
2 At Wildes West Ranch 4.00
3 History Lesson 4.00
4 I:Autumn Brothers 4.00
5 V:Big worm, final issue 4.00

SHADOWS WEST
DC/Vertigo, 1998

1 (of 3) JLd(s),TTn 4.00
2 JLd(s),TTn 4.00
3 JLd(s),TTn concl 4.00

TWO-GUN MOJO
DC/Vertigo, 1993

1 B:JLd(s),TT,SG(i),R:Jonah Hex,
  I:Slow Go Smith 7.00
1a Platinum Ed. 17.00
2 TT,SG(i),D:Slow Go Smith,I:Doc
  Williams,Wild Bill Hickok 4.00
3 TT,SG(i),Jonah captured 4.00
4 TT,SG(i),O:Doc Williams 4.00
5 TT,SG(i),V::Doc Williams 4.00

JONNI THUNDER
Feb., 1985

1 DG,origin issue 2.50
2 DG 2.50
3 DG 2.50

JONNY DOUBLE
DC/Vertigo, July, 1998

1 . . . . 3.00
2 MCo(c) detective 3.00
3 . . . . 3.00
4 . . . . 3.00

JSA
1999

1 JeR,V:Dark Lord 15.00
2 JeR,AD&Mfm(c),A:Hawkgirl 7.00
3 JeR,AD&MFm(c),V:Dark Lord . . 7.00
4 JeR,AD&MFm(c),V:Mordru 7.00
5 JeR,AD&MFm(c), ... 7.00
6 AD&MFm,Justice Like Lightning . 5.00
7 Darkness Falls, pt.1 . . . . 5.00
8 Darkness Falls, pt.2 . . . . 5.00
9 Darkness Falls, pt.3 . . . . 5.00
10 V:Injustice Society 5.00
11 V:Kobra 5.00
12 V:Kobra,Whitehorse project . . . 5.00
13 Hunt for Extant,pt.1 . . . . 5.00
14 Hunt for Extant,pt.2 . . . . 5.00
15 Hunt for Extant,concl 5.00
16 Injustice be Done, pt.1 . . . . 5.00
17 Injustice be Done, pt.2 . . . . 5.00
18 Injustice be Done, pt.3 . . . . 5.00
19 Injustice be Done, pt.4 . . . . 5.00
20 Injustice be Done, pt.5 . . . . 5.00
21 Hawkman prologue 5.00
22 Hawkman prologue 7.00
23 Return of Hawkman,pt.1 . . . . . . 8.00
24 Return of Hawkman,pt.2 . . . . . . 6.00
25 Return of Hawkman,pt.3,48-pg. . 6.50
26 Return of Hawkman,pt.4 . . . . . . 4.00
27 F:Captain Marvel,V:Black Adam . 3.00
28 V:Roulette 3.00
29 PSj,Joker:Last Laugh,tie-in 3.00
30 V:Roulette 3.00
31 RgM(c),MakingWaves,A:Batman 3.00
32 RgM(c),Stealing Thunder,prev. . 3.00
33 RgM(c),Stealing Thunder,pt.1 . . 3.00
34 RgM(c),Stealing Thunder,pt.2 . . 3.00
35 RgM(c),Stealing Thunder,pt.3 . . 3.00
36 RgM(c),Stealing Thunder,pt.4 . . 3.00
37 RgM(c),Thunder,pt.5,40-pg. . . . 4.00

JSA #25
© DC Comics, Inc.

DC

38 RgM(c),F:Rick Tyler 3.00
39 RgM(c),F:Power Girl 3.00
40 RgM(c),Shadower's grandson . . 3.00
41 RgM(c),V:Black Barax. 3.00
42 V:Black Barax 3.00
43 F:JSA B.C. 3.00
44 F:Vandal Savage 3.00
45 F:Doctor Fate 3.00
46 Princes of Darkness,pt.1. . . . . . 3.00
47 Princes of Darkness,pt.2. . . . . . 3.00
48 Princes of Darkness,pt.3. . . . . . 3.00
49 Princes of Darkness,pt.4. . . . . . 3.00
50 Princes of Darkness,concl. 4.50
51 Dr. Fate 3.00
52 F:Black Adam 3.00
53 V:Crimson Avenger 3.00
54 F:Superman,Batman. 3.00
55 F:Original members 3.00
56 Black Reign,pt.1,x-over. 3.00
57 Black Reign,pt.3,x-over. 3.00
58 Black Reign,pt.5,x-over. 3.00
59 SeP,F:Degaton 2.50
60 Redemption Lost,pt.1 . . . . 2.50

JSA #25
© DC Comics, Inc.

61 TMd,Redemption Lost,pt.2 . . . . . 2.50
62 TMc,Redemption Lost,pt.3 . . . . . 2.50
63 JOy,Wake of Sandman,pt.1 . . . . 2.50
64 JOy,Wake of Sandman,pt.2 . . . . 2.50
65 Out of Time,pt.1 . . . . 2.50
66 Out of Time,pt.2 . . . . 2.50
67 DGb,Identity Crisis, tie-in 3.00
68 AxR(c),JSA/JSA 2.50
69 AxR(c),JSA/JSA,pt.2. . . . . 2.50
70 JSA/JSa,pt.3 . . . . 2.50
71 JSA/JSA,pt.4. . . . . 2.50
72 JSA/JSA,pt.5. . . . . 2.50
73 Black Vengeance,pt.1 . . . . 5.00
74 Black Vengeance,pt.2 . . . . 4.00
75 Black Vengeance,pt.3, 40-page . 3.50
76 F:Mr. Terrific, Roulette. 2.50
77 Alan Scott and Hal Jordan 2.50
78 A Day of Vengeance, tie-in 2.50
79 A Day of Vengeance, tie-in 2.50
80 Mordru vs. Dr. Fate. 2.50
81 Stargirl's Past 2.50
82 GP,BWi,Infinite Crisis 2.50
83 RgM,LRs,One Year Later 2.50
84 RGm,LRs. 2.50
85 RGm,LRs,O:Gentleman Ghost. . 3.00
86 RGm,JOy,LRs, A trap 3.00
87 RGm,JOy,LRs,final issue 3.00
Ann.#1 Planet DC 4.00
Spec.#1 Our Worlds at War,48-pg . . 3.50
Secret Files #1 . . . . 7.00
Secret Files #2, 64-page 7.00

JSA: ALL-STARS
May 2003
1 (of 8) SaV,past and present. 2.50
2 JLb,TSe,F:Hawkgirl 2.50
3 Salem Mass. 2.50
4 F:Stargirl 2.50
5 F:Hourman 2.50
6 F:Dr. Mid-Nite. 2.50
7 40 pg.,BU: Mr. Terrific 3.50
8 F:Spectre 2.50

JSA CLASSIFIED
July, 2005
1 JP,ACo,O:Power Girl 5.00
2 JP,ACo,O:Power Girl 3.00
3 JP,ACo,O:Power Girl 3.00
4 JP,ACo,O:Power Girl, concl. 3.00
5 PO,Honor Among Thieves. 2.50
6 PO,Honor Among Thieves,pt.2 . . 2.50
7 PO,Honor Among Thieves,pt.3 . . 2.50
8 F:Wildcat & Flash 2.50
9 F:Wildcat & Flash 2.50
10 PG,JP, One Year Later 2.50
11 Fall & Rise of Vandal Savage . . 2.50
12 Fall & Rise of Vandal Savage . . 3.00
13 Fall & Rise of Vandal Savage . . 3.00
14 Double Trouble,pt.1 . . . . 3.00
15 Double Trouble,pt.2 . . . . 3.00
16 Double Trouble,pt.3 . . . . 3.00
17 SMc,The Venom Connection . . . 3.00
18 SMc,Hourman & Bane 3.00
19 RgM,Skin Game, pt.1 . . . . 3.00
20 RgM,Skin Trade, pt.2 . . . . 3.00
21 WS,Hawkgirl x-over, pt.2 . . . . . 3.00
22 WS,Hawkgirl x-over, pt.3 . . . . . 3.00
23 Unleashed, pt.1. . . . . 3.00
24 Unleashed, pt.2. . . . . 3.00
25 Reformed villain 3.00
26 F:Wildcat, pt.1 . . . . 3.00
27 F:Wildcat, pt.2. . . . . 3.00
28 FaN,F:Jakeem Thunder 3.00
29 Mr. Horrific, pt. 1 . . . . 3.00
30 Mr. Horrific, pt. 2 . . . . 3.00
31 Mr. Horrific, pt. 3 . . . . 3.00
32 Thanksgiving Foregone 3.00
33 Christmas in the DCU. 3.00
34 Hourman, Liberty Belle 3.00
35 Forward Through the Past,pt.1 . . 3.00
36 Forward Through the Past,pt.2 . . 3.00
37 Forward Through the Past,pt.3 . . 3.00
38 Body and Soul, pt.1 . . . . 3.00
39 Body and Soul, pt.2 . . . . 3.00

JSA: THE LIBERTY FILES
Dec., 1999
1 (of 2) Elseworlds 7.00
2 TyH, concl. 7.00

JSA: STRANGE ADVENTURES #3
Aug. 2004
1 (of 6) BKi,GEr,V:Dynamo. 3.50
2 thru 6 BKi,GEr . . . . @3.50

JSA: THE UNHOLY THREE
Feb. 2003
1 (of 2) Elseworlds 7.00
2 concl. 7.00

JUDGE DREDD
1994–96
1 R:Judge Dredd. 3.00
2 Silicon Dreams. 2.50
3 Terrorists 2.75
4 Mega-City One crisis 2.50
5 Solitary Dredd 2.50
6 V:Richard Magg. 2.50
7 48 Hours,Heaven is Hell 2.50

8 V:Ministry of Fear. 2.50
9 V:Mister Synn 2.50
10 D:Judge Dredd 2.50
11 Mega-City One Chaos 2.50
12 V:Wally Squad 2.50
13 Block Wars,pt.1. . . . . 2.50
14 Block Wars,pt.2. . . . . 2.50
15 Block Wars,pt.3. . . . . 2.50
16 R:Judge with a Grudge. 2.50
17 F:Judge Cadet Lewis,
    Nova Scotia 2.50
18 final issue 2.50
Movie Adaptation 6.00

JUDGE DREDD: LEGENDS OF THE LAW
1994–95
1 Organ Donor,pt.1 . . . . 3.00
2 Organ Donor,pt.2 . . . . 2.50
3 Organ Donor,pt.3 . . . . 2.50
4 Organ Donor,pt.4 . . . . 2.50
5 Trial By Gunfire,pt.1 . . . . 2.50
6 Trial By Gunfire,pt.2 . . . . 2.50
7 JHi(c),Trial By Gunfire,pt.3 . . . . . 2.50
8 JBy(s),Fall From Grace,pt.1 . . . . 2.50
9 Fall From Grace,pt.2 . . . . 2.50
10 Fall From Grace,pt.3. . . . . 2.50
11 Dredd of Night,pt.1 . . . . 2.50
12 Dredd of Night,pt.2 . . . . 2.50
13 Dredd of Night,pt.3,final issue . . 2.50

JUSTICE
2005
1 (of 12) DBw,AxR,JLA,40-page . . . 5.00
2 DBw,AxR,Batman, Riddler. 4.00
3 DBw,AxR,Martian Manhunter . . . 4.00
4 DBw,AxR,. 4.00
5 DBw,AxR,Superman 4.00
6 DBw,AxR,. 4.00
7 DBw,AxR,A:Metamorpho 4.00
8 DBw,AxR,. 4.00
9 DBw,AxR,Black Adam 4.00
10 DBw,AxR,F:Green Arrow 4.00
11 DBw,AxR,V:Sinestro 4.00
12 DBw,AxR, finale 4.00

JUSTICE, INC.
May-June, 1975
1 AMc,JKu(c),O:Avenger 25.00
2 JK,The Skywalker 20.00
3 JK,The Monster Bug 20.00
4 JK,JKu(c),Slay Ride in the Sky
    Nov.–Dec., 1975 . . . . 20.00

[Mini-Series], 1989
1 PerfectBound `Trust & Betrayal' . 4.00
2 PerfectBound. 4.00

JUSTICE LEAGUE ADVENTURES
Nov., 2001
1 TTn,based on Cartoon show 3.00
2 . . . . 2.50
3 . . . . 2.50
4 . . . . 2.50
5 . . . . 2.50
6 thru 10 . . . . @2.50
11 thru 34 . . . . @2.50

JUSTICE LEAGUE AMERICA
See: JUSTICE LEAGUE INTERNATIONAL)

JUSTICE LEAGUE ELITE
July 2004
1 (of 12) DoM 2.50
2 thru 4 DoM. . . . . @2.50
5 DoM,I:Aftermath. 2.50

6 DoM,F:JSA 2.50
7 DoM,V:Drug cartel 2.50
8 DoM,V:Drug cartel 2.50
9 DoM,V:Eve. 2.50
10 DoM,V:Aftermath. 2.50
11 DoM,F:Manchester Black 2.50
12 DoM, finale 2.50

JUSTICE LEAGUE
EUROPE
1989–93

1 BS,A:Wonder Woman 4.00
2 BS,Search for Nazi-Killer. 3.00
3 BS,A:Jack O'Lantern,
   Queen Bee 2.50
4 BS,V:Queen Bee 2.50
5 JRu,BS,Metamorpho's Baby,
   A:Sapphire Starr 2.50
6 BS,V:Injustice League 2.50
7 BS,Teasdale Imperative#2,
   A:JLA. 2.50
8 BS,Teasdale Imperative#4,
   A:JLA. 2.50
9 BS,ANi,A:Superman 2.50
10 BS,V:Crimson Fox 2.50
11 BS,C:DocMagnus&Metal Men . . 2.50
12 BS,A:Metal Men 2.50
13 BS,V:One-Eyed Cat, contd
   from JLA #37 . . . . 2.50
14 I:VCR 2.50
15 BS,B:Extremists Vector saga,
   V:One-Eyed Cat,A:BlueJay 2.50
16 BS,A:Rocket Reds, Blue Jay . . . 2.50
17 BS,JLI in Another Dimension . . . 2.50
18 BS,Extremists Homeworld 2.50
19 BS,E:Extremist Vector Saga 2.50
20 MR,I:Beefeater,V:Kilowog 2.50
21 MR,JRu,New JLE embassy in
   London,A:Kilowog 2.50
22 MR,JLE's Cat stolen 2.50
23 BS,O:Crimson Fox 2.50
24 BS,Worms in London 2.50
25 BS,V:Worms 2.50
26 BS,V:Starro 2.50
27 BS,JLE V:JLE,A:JLA,V:Starro . . 2.50
28 BS, JLE V:JLE,A:J'onn J'onzz,
   V:Starro 2.50
29 BS,Breakdowns #2,V:Global
   Guardians 2.50
30 Breakdowns#4,V:J.O'Lantern . . . 2.50
31 Breakdowns #6,War of the
   Gods tie-in 2.50
32 Breakdowns #8,A:Chief(Doom
   Patrol) 2.50

Justice League Europe #44
© DC Comics, Inc.

33 Breakdowns #10,Lobo vs.
   Despero 2.50
34 Breakdowns #12,Lobo
   vs.Despero 2.50
35 Breakdowns #14,V:Extremists,
   D:Silver Sorceress. 2.50
36 Breakdowns #16,All Quit 2.50
37 B:New JLE,I:Deconstructo 2.50
38 V:Deconstructo,A:Batman. 2.50
39 V:Deconstructo,A:Batman. 2.50
40 J:Hal Jordan,A:Metamorpho 2.50
41 A:Metamorpho,Wond.Woman . . . 2.50
42 A:Wonder Woman,V:Echidna . . . 2.50
43 V:Amos Fortune 2.50
44 V:Amos Fortune 2.50
45 Red Winter#1,V:Rocket Reds. . . 2.50
46 Red Winter#2 . . . . 2.50
47 Red Winter#3,V:Sonar 2.50
48 Red Winter#4,V:Sonar 2.50
49 Red Winter #5,V:Sonar 2.50
50 Red Winter#6,Double-sized,
   V:Sonar,J:Metamorpho 3.50
Ann.#1 A:Global Guardians 2.50
Ann.#2 MR,CS,ArmageddonPt.7 . . . 3.00
Ann.#3 RT(i),Eclipso tie-in 2.75
Justice League Spectacular JLE(c)
   New Direction 2.50
Becomes:

JUSTICE LEAGUE
INTERNATIONAL
[2nd Series]

JUSTICE LEAGUE
[INTERNATIONAL]
[1st Series], 1987

1 KM,TA,New Team,I:Max. Lord . . 10.00
2 KM,AG,A:BlueJay & Silver
   Sorceress 6.00
3 KM,AG,J:Booster Gold, V:Rocket
   Lords 5.00
3a Superman Logo 60.00
4 KM,AG,V:Royal Flush 5.00
5 KM,AG,A:The Creeper 5.00
6 KM,AG,A:The Creeper 5.00
Becomes:

JUSTICE LEAGUE
INTERNATIONAL
1988–89

7 KM,AG,L:Dr.Fate,Capt.Marvel,
   J:Rocket Red,Capt.Atom
   (Double size) 4.00
8 KM,AG,KG,Move to Paris Embassy,
   I:C.Cobert,B.U.Glob.Guardians. 3.50
9 KM,AG,KG,Millennium,Rocket
   Red-Traitor 3.50
10 KG,KM,AG,A:G.L.Corps,
   Superman,I:G'Nort. 3.50
11 KM,AG,V:Construct,C:Metron . . . 3.50
12 KG,KM,AG,O:Max Lord. 3.50
13 KG,AG,A:Suicide Squad 3.50
14 SL,AG,J:Fire&Ice,L:Ron,
   I:Manga Kahn 3.50
15 SL,AG,V:Magna Kahn 3.50
16 KM,AG,I:Queen Bee 3.50
17 KM,AG,V:Queen Bee 3.50
18 KM,AG,MPn,A:Lobo,Guy Gardner
   (bonus book) 3.50
19 KM,JRu,A:Lobo vs.Guy Gardner,
   J:Hawkman & Hawkwoman. . . . 3.50
20 KM,JRu(i),A:Lobo,G.Gardner . . . 3.50
21 KM,JRu(i),A:Lobo vs.Guy
   Gardner 3.50
22 KM,JRu,Imskian Soldiers 3.50
23 KM,JRu,I:Injustice League 3.50
24 KM,JRu,DoubleSize + Bonus
   Bk#13,I:JusticeLeagueEurope. . 4.00
25 KM(c),JRu(i),Vampire story. 2.50
Ann.#1 BWg,DG,CR. 2.50
Ann.#2 BWg,JRu,A:Joker 3.00

Justice League International #19
© DC Comics Inc.

Ann.#3 KM(c),JRu,JLI Embassies. . 2.50
Spec.#1 Mr.Miracle 2.00
Spec.#2,The Huntress 3.00
Becomes:

JUSTICE LEAGUE
AMERICA
1989–96

26 KM(c),JRu(i),Possessed Blue
   Beetle 3.00
27 KM(c),JRu,DG(i),'Exorcist',
   (c)tribute 2.50
28 KM(c),JRu(i), A:Black Hand 2.50
29 KM(c),JRu(i),V:Mega-Death 2.50
30 KM(c),BWg,JRu,J:Huntress,
   D:Mega-Death. 2.50
31 ANi,AH,JRu,Teasdale Imperative
   #1,N:Fire,Ice,A:JLE 3.00
32 ANi,AH,Teasdale Imperative
   #3, A:JLE. 3.00
33 ANi,AH,GuyGardner vs.Kilowog . 2.50
34 ANi,AH,`Club JLI,'A:Aquaman . . 2.50
35 ANi,JRu,AH,A:Aquaman 2.50
36 Gnort vs. Scarlet Skier 2.50
37 ANi,AH,L:Booster Gold 2.50
38 JRu,AH,R:Desparo,D:Steel. 2.50
39 JRu,AH,V:Desparo,D:Mr.Miracle,
   Robot. 2.50
40 AH,Mr.Miracle Funeral 2.50
41 MMc,MaxForce 2.50
42 MMc,J:L-Ron. 2.50
43 AH,KG,The Man Who Knew Too
   Much #1. . . . . 2.50
44 AH,Man Knew Too Much #2 . . . . 2.50
45 AH,MJ,JRu,Guy & Ice's 2nd
   date 2.50
46 Glory Bound #1,I:Gen.Glory 2.50
47 Glory Bound #2,J:Gen.Glory. . . . 2.50
48 Glory Bound #3,V:DosUberbot . . 2.50
49 Glory Bound #4. . . . . 2.50
50 Glory Bound #5 (double size). . . 3.00
51 JRu,AH,V:BlackHand,
   R:Booster Gold 2.50
52 TVE,Blue Beetle Vs. Guy Gardner
   A:Batman. 2.50
53 Breakdowns #1, A:JLE 2.50
54 Breakdowns #3, A:JLE 2.50
55 Breakdowns #5,V:Global
   Guardians 2.50
56 Breakdowns #7, U.N. revokes
   JLA charter 2.50
57 Breakdowns #9,A:Lobo,
   V:Despero 2.50

All comics prices listed are for *Near Mint* condition.

58 BS,Breakdowns #11,Lobo
Vs.Despero 2.50
59 BS,Breakdowns #13,
V:Extremists. 2.50
60 KM,TA,Breakdowns #15,
End of J.L.A. 2.50
61 DJu,I:Weapons Master,B:New
JLA Line-up,I:Bloodwynd 3.00
62 DJu,V:Weapons Master 2.50
63 DJu,V:Starbreaker. 2.50
64 DJu,V:Starbreaker. 2.50
65 DJu,V:Starbreaker. 2.50
66 DJu,Superman V:Guy Gardner . . 2.50
67 DJu,Bloodwynd mystery 2.50
68 DJu,V:Alien Land Baron 2.50
69 DJu, Doomsday Pt.1-A 10.00
69a 2nd printing 2.50
70 DJu,Funeral for a Friend#1 . . . . . 6.00
70a 2nd printing 2.50
71 DJu,J:Agent Liberty,Black Condor,
The Ray,Wonder Woman 5.00
71a Newsstand ed. 2.50
71b 2nd Printing. 2.50
72 DJu,A:Green Arrow,Black
Canary,Atom,B:Destiny's Hand . 4.00
73 DJu,Destiny's Hand #2 . . . . 3.00
74 DJu,Destiny's Hand #3 . . . . 2.50
75 DJu,E:Destiny's Hand #4,Martian
Manhunter as Bloodwynd 2.50
76 DJu,Blood Secrets#1,
V:Weaponmaster 2.50
77 DJu,Blood Secrets#2,
V:Weaponmaster. 2.50
78 MC,V:The Extremists 2.50
79 MC,V:The Extremists 2.50
80 KWe,N:Booster Gold 2.50
81 KWe,A:Captain Atom 2.50
82 KWe,A:Captain Atom 2.50
83 KWe,V:Guy Gardner 2.50
84 KWe,A:Ice 2.50
85 KWe,V:Frost Giants 2.50
86 B:Cults of the Machine 2.50
87 N:Booster Gold 2.50
88 E:Cults of the Machine 2.50
89 Judgement Day#1,
V:Overmaster 2.50
90 Judgement Day#4. . . . . 2.50
91 Aftershocks #1 . . . . 2.50
92 Zero Hour,I:Triumph 2.50
93 Power Girl and child 2.50
94 Scarabus 2.50
95 Where the Wild Things Are 2.50
96 Funeral 2.50
97 I:Judgment 2.50
98 J:Blue Devil, Ice Maiden 2.50
99 V:New Metahumes 2.50
100 GJ,Woj,V:Lord Havok,dbl.size . 4.50
100a Collector's Edition. 4.50
101 GJ,Woj,Way of the
Warrior,pt.2 . . . . 2.50
102 Way of the Warrior,pt.5 . . . . 2.50
103 Oh, To Be Nobody 2.50
104 F:Metamorpho. 2.50
105 GJ,Woj,Underworld
Unleashed tie-in 2.50
106 GJ,Woj,Underworld
Unleashed tie-in 2.50
107 GJ,Woj,secret of Power
Girl's son 2.50
108 GJ,Woj,The Arcana revealed . . 2.50
109 GJ,Woj,All That Yazz 2.50
110 GJ,Woj,V:El Diablo 2.50
111 GJ,Woj,The Purge,pt.1 of 3) . . 2.50
112 GJ,Woj,The Purge,pt.2 (of 3) . 2.50
113 GJ,Woj,The Purge,pt.3 (of 3) . 2.50
Ann.#4 KM(c),I:JL Antartica 3.50
Ann.#5 MR,KM,DJu,Armageddon . 3.50
Ann.#5a 2nd Printing,silver 2.50
Ann.#6 DC,Eclipso. 3.00
Ann.#7 I:Terrorsmith. 3.00
Ann.#8 Elseworlds Story 3.50
Ann.#9 Year One Annual 4.00

Ann.#10 CPr(s),SCi,NNa,Legends
of the Dead Earth 3.50
Justice League Spectacular DJu,
JLA(c) New Direction. 2.50
Archives Vol. 4 . . . . 50.00

JUSTICE LEAGUE INTERNATIONAL

[2nd Regular Series], 1993–94
Prev: Justice League Europe

51 Aztec Cult 2.50
52 V:Aztec Cult 2.50
53 R:Fox's Husband 2.50
54 RoR,I:Creator 2.50
55 RoR,A:Creator 2.50
56 RoR,V:Terrorists 2.50
57 RoR,V:Terrorists 2.50
58 RoR,V:Aliens. 2.50
59 RoR,A:Guy Gardner 2.50
60 GJ(s),RoR. 2.50
61 GJ(s),V:Godfrey 2.50
62 GJ(s),N:Metamorpho,V:Godfrey . 2.50
63 GJ(s),In Africa 2.50
64 GJ(s),V:Cadre. 2.50
65 JudgmentDay#3,V:Overmaster. . 2.50
66 JudgmentDay#6,V:Overmaster. . 2.50
67 Aftershock #3 . . . . 2.50
68 Zero Hour, Final Issue 2.50
Ann.#4 Bloodlines#9,I:Lionheart . . . 2.75
Ann.#5 . . . . 3.25
Ann.#6 Elseworlds Story 3.00

JUSTICE LEAGUE [INTERNATIONAL] QUARTERLY

1990–94

1 I:Conglomerate 4.00
2 MJ(i),R:Mr.Nebula 3.50
3 V:Extremists,C:Original JLA. 3.50
4 KM(c),MR,CR,A:Injustice
League. 3.00
5 KM(c),Superhero Attacks. 3.00
6 EB,Elongated Man,B.U.Global
Guardians,Powergirl,B.Beetle . . 3.00
7 EB,DH,MR.Global Guardians . . . 3.00
8 . . . . 3.00
9 DC,F:Power Girl,Booster Gold . . 3.50
10 F:Flash,Fire & Ice 3.50
11 F:JL Women 3.50
12 F:Conglomerate 3.50
13 V:Ultraa 7.00
14 MMi(c),PuK(s),F:Captain Atom,Blue
Beetle,Nightshade,Thunderbolt . 3.75
15 F:Praxis. 3.50
16 F:Gen Glory 3.50
17 Final Issue 3.50

JUSTICE LEAGUE: A MIDSUMMER'S NIGHTMARE

1996

1 (of 3) MWa(s),FaN,JJ,DaR, ... 5.00
2 MWa(s),FaN,JJ,DaR,Batman &
Superman attempt to free
other heroes 4.00
3 MWa&FaN(s), Know-Man's plot
revealed, finale 4.00

JUSTICE LEAGUE OF AMERICA

Oct.–Nov., 1960

1 MSy,I&O:Despero 12,000.00
2 MSy,A:Merlin. 2,500.00
3 MSy,I&O:Kanjar Ro. 2,000.00
4 MSy,J:Green Arrow. 1,400.00
5 MSy,I&O:Dr.Destiny 1,100.00
6 MSy,Prof. Fortune 850.00

Justice League of America #4
© DC Comics, Inc.

7 MSy,Cosmic Fun-House 850.00
8 MSy,For Sale-Justice League . 850.00
9 MSy,O:JLA 1,100.00
10 MSy,I:Felix Faust 850.00
11 MSy,A:Felix Faust 500.00
12 MSy,I&O:Dr Light 500.00
13 MSy,A:Speedy. 500.00
14 MSy,J:Atom. 500.00
15 MSy,V:Untouchable Aliens . . . 500.00
16 MSy,I:Maestro 400.00
17 MSy,A:Tornado Tyrant. 400.00
18 MSy,V:Terrane,Ocana 400.00
19 MSy,A:Dr.Destiny 400.00
20 MSy,V:Metal Being 400.00
21 MSy,R:JSA,1st S.A Hourman,
Dr.Fate 800.00
22 MSy,R:JSA 650.00
23 MSy,I:Queen Bee 350.00
24 MSy,A:Adam Strange 350.00
25 MSy,I:Draad,the Conqueror . . 350.00
26 MSy,A:Despero 350.00
27 MSy,V:I,A:Amazo 350.00
28 MSy,I:Headmaster Mind,
A:Robin 350.00
29 MSy,I:Crime Syndicate,A:JSA,
1st S.A. Starman 400.00
30 MSy,V:Crime Syndicate,
A:JSA. 350.00
31 MSy,J:Hawkman 300.00
32 MSy,I&O:Brain Storm 250.00
33 MSy,I:Endless One 200.00
34 MSy,A:Dr.Destiny,Joker 225.00
35 MSy,A:Three Demons. 200.00
36 MSy,A:Brain Storm,
Handicap story 200.00
37 MSy,A:JSA,x-over,
1st S.A.Mr.Terrific 275.00
38 MSy,A:JSA,Mr. Terrific 275.00
39 Giant 275.00
40 MSy,A:Shark,Penguin. 225.00
41 MSy,I:Key 225.00
42 MSy,A:Metamorpho 150.00
43 MSy,I:Royal Flush Gang 150.00
44 MSy,A:Unimaginable. 150.00
45 MSy,I:Shaggy Man 150.00
46 MSy,A:JSA,Blockbuster,Solomon
Grundy,1st S.A.Sandman . . . 175.00
47 MSy,A:JSA,Blockbuster,
Solomon Grundy 150.00
48 Giant 160.00
49 MSy,A:Felix Faust. 150.00
50 MSy,A:Robin 150.00
51 MSy,A:Zatanna,Elong.Man . . . 150.00
52 MSy,A:Robin,Lord of Time . . . 150.00

53 MSy,A:Hawkgirl 150.00	123 DD,FMc,A:JSA 35.00
54 MSy,A:Royal Flush Gang 150.00	124 DD,FMc,A: JSA 35.00
55 MSy,A:JSA,E-2 Robin 165.00	125 DD,FMc,A:Two-Face 30.00
56 MSy,A:JSA,E-2 Robin 150.00	126 DD,FMc,A:Two-Face 30.00
57 MSy,Brotherhood 150.00	127 DD,FMc,V:Anarchist 30.00
58 Reprint(giant size) 150.00	128 DD,FMc,J:W.Woman 30.00
59 MSy,V:Impossibles 150.00	129 DD,FMC,D:RedTornado 30.00
60 MSy,A:Queen Bee,Batgirl . . . 150.00	130 DD,FMc,O:JLASatellite 30.00
61 MSy,A:Lex Luthor,Penguin . . . 100.00	131 DD,FMc,V:Queen Bee,Sonar . 30.00
62 MSy,V:Bulleters 100.00	132 DD,FMc,A:Supergirl 30.00
63 MSy,A:Key 100.00	133 DD,FMc,A:Supergirl 30.00
64 DD,I:Red Tornado,A:JSA 110.00	134 DD,FMc,A:Supergirl 30.00
65 DD,A:JSA 110.00	135 DD,FMc,A:Squad.of Justice . . 30.00
66 DD,A:Demmy Gog 100.00	136 DD,FMc,A:E-2Joker 35.00
67 MSy,Giant reprints 110.00	137 DD,FMc,Superman vs.
68 DD,V:Choas Maker 100.00	Capt. Marvel 35.00
69 DD,L:Wonder Woman 100.00	138 NA(c),DD,FMc,A:Adam
70 DD,A:Creeper 100.00	Strange 30.00
71 DD,L:J'onn J'onzz 100.00	139 NA(c),DD,FMc,A:AdamStrange,
72 DD,A:Hawkgirl 100.00	Phantom Stranger,doub.size . . 25.00
73 DD,A:JSA 100.00	140 DD,FMc,Manhunters 25.00
74 DD,D:Larry Lance,A:JSA 100.00	141 DD,FMc,Manhunters 25.00
75 DD,J:Black Canary 100.00	142 DD,FMc,F:Aquaman,Atom,
76 Giant,MA,two page pin-up . . . 100.00	Elongated Man 25.00
77 DD,A:Joker,L:Snapper Carr . . . 75.00	143 DD,FMc,V:Injustice Gang 25.00
78 DD,R:Vigilante 75.00	144 DD,FMc,O:JLA 25.00
79 DD,A:Vigilante 75.00	145 DD,FMc,A:Phant.Stranger . . . 25.00
80 DD,A:Tomar-Re,Guardians . . . 75.00	146 J:Red Tornado,Hawkgirl 25.00
81 DD,V:Jest-Master 75.00	147 DD,FMc,A:Legion 25.00
82 DD,A:JSA 70.00	148 DD,FMc,A:Legion 25.00
83 DD,A:JSA,Spectre 90.00	149 DD,FMc,A:Dr.Light 25.00
84 DD,Devil in Paradise 60.00	150 DD,FMc,A:Dr.Light 25.00
85 Giant reprint 90.00	151 DD,FMc,A:Amos Fortune 20.00
86 DD,V:Zapper 60.00	152 DD,FMc 20.00
87 DD,A:Zatanna,I:Silver	153 GT,FMc,I:Ultraa 20.00
Sorceress,Blue Jay 75.00	154 MK(c),DD,FMc 20.00
88 DD,A:Mera 75.00	155 DD,FMc 20.00
89 DD,A:Harlequin Ellis,	156 DD,FMc 20.00
(i.e. Harlan Ellison) 75.00	157 DD,FMc,W:Atom 20.00
90 CI(c),MA(ci),DD,V:Pale People . 75.00	158 DD,FMc,A:Ultraa 20.00
91 DD,A:JSA,V:Solomon Grundy . 75.00	159 DD,FMc,A:JSA,Jonah Hex,
92 DD,A:JSA,V:Solomon Grundy . 75.00	Enemy Ace 18.00
93 DD:A:JSA,(giant size) 75.00	160 DD,FMc,A:JSA,Jonah Hex,
94 DD,NA,O:Sandman,rep.	Enemy Ace 18.00
Adventure #40 . . . . 175.00	161 DD,FMc,J:Zatanna 18.00
95 DD,rep.More Fun Comics #67,	162 DD,FMc 18.00
All American Comics #25 . . . . 90.00	163 DD,FMc,V:Mad Maestro 18.00
96 DD,I:Starbreaker 80.00	164 DD,FMc,V:Mad Maestro 18.00
97 DD,MS,O:JLA 75.00	165 DD,FMc 18.00
98 DD,A:Sargon,Gold.Age reps . . 75.00	166 DD,FMc,V:Secret Society 18.00
99 DD,G.A. reps 75.00	167 DD,FMc,V:Secret Society 18.00
100 DD,A:JSA,Metamorpho,	168 DD,FMc,V:Secret Society 18.00
R:7 Soldiers of Victory 90.00	169 DD,FMc,A:Ultraa 18.00
101 DD,A:JSA,7 Soldiers 50.00	170 DD,FMc,A:Ultraa 18.00
102 DD,DG,A:JSA,7 Soldiers	171 DD,FMc,A:JSA,D:Mr.Terrific . . 18.00
D:Red Tornado 50.00	172 DD,FMc,A:JSA,D:Mr.Terrific . . 18.00
103 DD,DG,Halloween issue,	173 DD,FMc,A:Black Lightning . . . 18.00
A:Phantom Stranger 30.00	174 DD,FMc,A:Black Lightning . . . 18.00
104 DD,DG,A:Shaggy Man,	175 DD,FMc,V:Dr.Destiny 18.00
Hector Hammond 30.00	176 DD,FMc,V:Dr.Destiny 15.00
105 DD,DG,I:ElongatedMan 30.00	177 DD,FMc,V:Desparo 10.00
106 DD,DG,J:RedTornado 30.00	178 JSn(c),DD,FMc,V:Desparo . . . 10.00
107 DD,DG,I:Freedom Fighters,	179 JSn(c),DD,FMc,J:Firestorm . . 10.00
A:JSA 35.00	180 JSn(c),DD,FMc,V:Satin Satan 10.00
108 DD,DG,A:JSA,	181 DD,FMc,L:Gr.Arrow,V:Star . . 11.00
Freedom Fighters 35.00	182 DD,FMc,A:Green Arrow,
109 DD,DG,L:Hawkman 35.00	V:Felix Faust 11.00
110 DD,DG,A:John Stewart,	183 JSn(c),DD,FMc,A:JSA,
Phantom Stranger 75.00	NewGods 11.00
111 DD,DG,I:Injustice Gang 75.00	184 GP,FMc,A:JSA,NewGods 11.00
112 DD,DG,A:Amazo 75.00	185 JSn(c),GP,FMc,A:JSA,
113 DD,DG,A:JSA 75.00	New Gods 10.00
114 DD,DG,A:SnapperCarr 75.00	186 FMc,GP,V:Shaggy Man 7.50
115 DD,FMc,A:J'onn J'onzz 75.00	187 DH,FMc,N:Zatanna 7.50
116 DD,FMc,I:Golden Eagle 75.00	188 DH,FMc,V:Proteus 7.50
117 DD,FMc,R:Hawkman 30.00	189 BB(c),RB,FMc,V:Starro 7.50
118 DD,FMc 30.00	190 BB(c),RB,LMa,V:Starro 7.50
119 DD,FMc,A:Hawkgirl 30.00	191 RB,V:Amazo 7.50
120 DD,FMc,A:Adam Strange . . . 30.00	192 GP,O:Red Tornado 7.50
121 DD,FMc,W:Adam Strange . . . 30.00	193 GP,RB,JOy,I:AllStarSquad . . . 7.50
122 DD,FMc,JLA casebook story	194 GP,V:Amos Fortune 7.50
V:Dr.Light 30.00	195 GP,A:JSA,V:Secret Society . . . 7.50

Justice League of America #164
© DC Comics Inc.

196 GP,RT,A:JSA,V:Secret Soc. . . . 7.50	
197 GP,RT,KP,A:JSA,V:Secret	
Society 7.50	
198 DH,BBr,A:J.Hex,BatLash 7.50	
199 GP(c),DH,BBr,A:Jonah Hex,	
BatLash 7.50	
200 GP,DG,BB (1st Batman),PB,TA,	
BBr,GK,CI,JAp,JKu,Anniv.,A:Adam	
Strange,Phantom Stranger,	
J:Green Arrow 10.00	
201 GP(c),DH,A:Ultraa 5.00	
202 GP(c),DH,BBr,JLA in Space . . 5.00	
203 GP(c),DH,RT,V:Royal	
Flush Gang 5.00	
204 GP(c),DH,RT,V:R.FlushGang . . 5.00	
205 GP(c),DH,RT,V:R.FlushGang . . 5.00	
206 DH,RT,A:Demons 3 . . . . 5.00	
207 GP(c),DH,RT,A:All Star	
Squadron,JSA 6.00	
208 GP(c),DH,RT,A:All Star	
Squadron,JSA 6.00	
209 GP(c),DH,RT,A:All Star	
Squadron,JSA 5.00	
210 RB,RT,JLA casebook #1 . . . . . 5.00	
211 RB,RT,JLA casebook #2 . . . . . 5.00	
212 GP(c),RB,PCu,RT,c.book #3 . . 5.00	
213 GP(c),DH,RT. 5.00	
214 GP(c),DH,RT,I:Siren Sist.h'd . . 5.00	
215 GP(c),DH,RT. 5.00	
216 DH 5.00	
217 GP(c),RT(i) 5.00	
218 RT(i),A:Prof.Ivo 5.00	
219 GP(c),RT(i),A:JSA 5.00	
220 GP(c),RT,O:Bl.Canary,A:JSA . . 4.00	
221 Beasts #1 . . . . 3.00	
222 RT(i),Beasts #2. . . . . 3.00	
223 RT(i),Beasts #3 . . . . 3.00	
224 DG(i),V:Paragon 3.00	
225 V:Hellrazor 3.00	
226 FMc(i),V:Hellrazor 3.00	
227 V:Hellrazor,I:Lord Claw 3.00	
228 GT,AN,R:J'onn J'onzz,War of	
the Worlds,pt.1 . . . . 3.00	
229 War of the Worlds,pt.2 . . . . . . 3.00	
230 War of the Worlds conc. 3.00	
231 RB(i),A:JSA,Supergirl 3.00	
232 A:JSA Supergirl. 3.00	
233 New JLA takes over book,	
B:Rebirth,F:Vibe 3.00	
234 F:Vixen 3.00	
235 F:Steel. 3.00	
236 E:Rebirth,F:Gypsy. 3.00	
237 A:Superman,Flash,WWoman . . 3.00	
238 A:Superman,Flash,WWoman . . 3.00	

239 V:Ox 3.00
240 MSy,TMd. 3.00
241 GT,V:Amazo 3.00
242 GT,V:Amazo,Mask(Toy tie-in)
    insert 3.00
243 GT,L:Aquaman,V:Amazo . . . 3.00
244 JSon,Crisis,A:InfinityInc,JSA . 4.00
245 LMc,Crisis,N:Steel. 4.00
246 LMc,JLA leaves Detroit. 3.00
247 LMc,JLA returns to old HQ . . . 3.00
248 LMc,F:J'onn J'onzz. 3.00
249 LMc,Lead-in to Anniv. 3.00
250 LMc,Anniv.,A:Superman,
    Green Lantern,Green Arrow,
    Black Canary,R:Batman 3.00
251 LMc,V:Despero 3.00
252 LMc,V:Despero,N:Elongated
    Man 3.00
253 LMc,V:Despero 3.00
254 LMc,V:Despero 3.00
255 LMc,O:Gypsy 3.00
256 LMc,Gypsy 3.00
257 LMc,A:Adam,L:Zatanna 3.00
258 LMc,Legends x-over,D:Vibe . . . 3.00
259 LMc,Legends x-over 3.00
260 LMc,Legends x-over,D:Steel. . . 6.00
261 LMc,Legends,final issue 8.00
Ann.#1 DG(i),A:Sandman 3.50
Ann.#2 I:NewJLA 3.00
Ann.#3 MG(i),Crisis 3.00

July, 2006
0 Batman, Superman, W.Woman . . 3.00
0a variant JSC (c). 3.00
1 EBe,The Tornado's Path 3.00
2 EBe, ... 3.00
3 EBe, V:Dr. Impossible 3.00
4 EBe 3.00
5 EBe,The Tornado's Path, pt.5 . . . . 3.00
1a thru 5a variant (c)s . . . . @3.00
6 EBe, 40-pgs. 3.50
7 EBe, New team, new HQ 3.50
8 EBe,Lightning Saga, pt.1 x-over . 3.00
9 EBe,Lightning Saga, pt.3 x-over . 3.00
10 EBe,Lightning Saga,pt.5 x-over . 3.00
11 Two burried alive 3.00
6a thru 11a variant (c)s (1:10). . . @3.00
12 EBe, Monitor Duty. 3.50
12a variant AxR (c) (1:1) 3.50
12b variant (c) (1:10) 3.50
13 JBz,Injustice League Unlimited. . 3.00
13a variant (c) (1:1) 3.00
14 Injustice League 3.00
15 V:Injustice League 3.00
16 A Flash Returns 3.00
17 Double Trouble for the League . . 3.00
18 V:Suicide Squad 3.00
19 Salvation, concl. 3.00
20 V:Queen Bee 3.00
21 Prelude to Final Crisis 3.00
22 Red Tornado's second chance . . 3.00
23 Amazon fury against Amazo. . . . 3.00
24 F:Animal Man 3.00
25 Vixen & Animal Man, 48-pg. 4.00
26 Vixen's Sacrifice 3.00
27 Sightings 3.00
Spec. New Frontier, 48-pg. 5.00
Spec. DC Universe Special rep. . . . 5.00

...ANOTHER NAIL
May 2004
1 AD,MFm,F:Superman 6.00
2 AD,MFm,Darkseid's secrets 6.00
3 AD,MFm,concl. 6.00

...THE NAIL
Elseworlds, June, 1998
1 World without a Superman 5.00
2 AID,MFm,Robin & Batgirl dead . . 5.00
3 AID,MFm,concl. 5.00

JUSTICE LEAGUES
Jan., 2001
Pt.1 Justice Leagues #1,GP(c) 2.50
Pt.2 Just.League of Amazons #1. . . 2.50
Pt.3 Just.League of Atlantis #1 . . . 2.50
Pt.4 Just.League of Arkham #1 . . . . 2.50
Pt.5 Just.League of Aliens #1 . . . . . 2.50

Justice League Task Force #16
© DC Comics, Inc.

Pt.6 Just.League of America #1. . . . 2.50

JUSTICE LEAGUE TASK FORCE
1993–96
1 F:Mart.Manhunter,Nightwing,
    Aquaman,Flash,Gr.Lantern 2.50
2 V:Count Glass,Blitz 2.50
3 V:Blitz,Count Glass 2.50
4 DG,F:Gypsy,A:Lady Shiva 2.50
5 JAl,Knightquest:Crusade,F:Bronze
    Tiger,Green Arrow,Gypsy 2.50
6 JAl,Knightquest:Search,F:Bronze
    Tiger,Green Arrow,Gypsy 2.50
7 PDd(s),F:Maxima,Wonder Woman,
    Dolphin,Gypsy,Vixen,V:Luta . . . 2.50
8 PDd(s),SaV,V:Amazons 2.50
9 GrL,V:Wildman. 2.50
10 Purification Plague #1 . . . . 2.50
11 Purification Plague #2 . . . . 2.50
12 Purification Plague #3 . . . . 2.50
13 Judgement Day #2, ... 2.50
14 Judgement Day#5,
    V:Overmaster 2.50
15 Aftershocks #2 . . . . 2.50
16 Zero Hour,A:Triumph 2.50
17 Savage 2.50
18 Savage 2.50
19 Martian Manhunter 2.50
20 thru 35 . . . . @2.50

JUSTICE LEAGUE UNLIMITED
Sept. 2004
1 From animated series 2.50
2 thru 46 . . . . @2.50

JUSTICE RIDERS
1999
1-shot, Elseworlds 7.00

JUSTICE SOCIETY OF AMERICA
[Limited Series]
April–Nov., 1991
1 B:Veng.From Stars,A:Flash 3.00
2 A:BlackCanary,V:Solomon Grundy,
    C:G.A.Green Lantern. 2.50
3 A:G.A.Green Lantern,Black Canary,
    V:Sol.Grundy 2.50
4 A:G.A.Hawkman,C:G.A.Flash. . . 2.50
5 A:G.A.Hawkman,Flash 2.50
6 FMc(i),A:Bl.Canary,G.A.Gr.Lantern,
    V:Sol.Grundy,V.Savage 2.50
7 JSA united,V:Vandal Savage . . . 2.50
8 E:Veng.FromStar,V:V.Savage,
    Solomon Grundy 2.50
Spec.#1 DR,MG,End of JSA 2.50

[Regular Series], 1992–93
1 V:The New Order. 2.50
2 V:Ultra Gen 2.50
3 R:Ultra-Humanite 2.50
4 V:Ultra-Humanite 2.50
5 V:Ultra-Humanite 2.50
6 F:Johnny Thunderbolt 2.50
7 ..Or give me Liberty 2.50
8 Pyramid Scheme 2.50
9 V:Kulak. 2.50
10 V:Kulak,final issue. 2.50

Dec., 2006
1 ATi,AxR(c),The Next Age, pt.1 . . . 4.00
1a variant (c) (1:10) 4.00
2 ATi,AxR(c),The Next Age, pt.2 . . . 3.00
3 ATi,AxR(c),The Next Age, pt.3 . . . 3.00
4 ATi,AxR(c),The Next Age, pt.4 . . . 3.00
5 ATi,Lightning Saga, pt.2 x-over . . . 3.00
6 Lightning Saga, pt.4 x-over 3.00
7 F:Citizen Steel 3.00
8 F:Liberty Belle 3.00
9 Wildcat vs. Wildcat 3.00
10 AxR(c) Thy Kingdom Come 3.00
2a thru 10a variant (c)s (1:10) . . . @3.00
11 AxR(c),Thy Kingdom Come 3.00
12 Thy Kingdom Come 3.00
13 Thy Kingdom Come 3.00
14 Thy Kingdom Come 3.00
15 Thy Kingdom Come 3.00
16 Gog, pt.1 . . . . 3.00
17 Gog, pt.2 . . . . 3.00
18 Gog, pt.3, F:Magog. 3.00
19 One World, Under Gog 3.00
20 V:Justice Society Infinity 3.00
21 On World, Under Gog 3.00
11a thru 21a variant (c)s (1:10) . . @3.00
Ann. #1 Welcome to Earth-2 . . . . . . 4.00

...KINGDOM COME
Nov., 2008
Spec. 1 Magog 4.00
Spec. 1 The Kingdom 4.00
Spec. 1 Superman 4.00

KAMANDI, THE LAST BOY ON EARTH
Oct.–Nov., 1972
1 JK,O:Kamandi 125.00
2 JK,Year of the Rat 75.00
3 JK,Thing tht Grew on the Moon. 75.00
4 JK,I:Prince Tuftan 60.00
5 JK,The One-Armed Bandit 60.00
6 JK,Flower. 50.00
7 JK,The Monster Fetish 50.00
8 JK,Beyond Reason 50.00
9 JK,Traking Site 50.00
10 JK,Killer Germ. 50.00
11 JK,The Devil 30.00
12 JK,Devil and Mister Sacker . . . 30.00
13 thru 24 JK . . . . @30.00
25 thru 28 JK . . . . @25.00
29 JK,A:Superman. 30.00

Kamandi the Last Boy on Earth #36
© DC Comics, Inc.

30 JK,U.F.O. Wildest Trip Ever ... 25.00
31 JK,The Gulliver Effect........ 25.00
32 JK,Double size 30.00
33 thru 57.................@25.00
58 DAy,A:Karate Kid 30.00
59 JSn,A:Omac, Sept.–Oct,1978. . 30.00

KAMANDI: AT EARTH'S END
[Mini-Series], 1993
1 R:Kamandi................... 2.50
2 V:Kingpin,Big Q 2.50
3 A:Sleeper Zom,Saphira 2.50
4 A:Superman 2.50
5 A:Superman,V:Ben Boxer 2.50
6 final issue................... 2.50

KARATE KID
March-April, 1976
1 I:Iris Jacobs,A:Legion 20.00
2 A:Major Disaster 12.00
3 thru 10 ....@12.00
11 A:Superboy/Legion 12.00
12 A:Superboy/Legion 12.00
13 A:Superboy/Legion 12.00
14 A:Robin 12.00
15 July-Aug., 1978............ 12.00

KENTS, THE
1997
1 (of 12) JOs(s),TT,MiB 3.00
2 JOs(s),TT,MiB, tragedy strikes . . 3.00
3 JOs,TT,MiB,Jed & Nate Kent... 3.00
4 JOs,TT,MiB,Bleeding Kansas,
   concl................... 3.00
5 JOs,TT,Brother vs.Brother pt.1 . 3.00
6 JOs,TT,Brother vs.Brother pt.2 . . 3.00
7 JOs,TT,MiB,Quantrill, Wild
   Bill Hickcock 3.00
8 JOs, ... 3.00
9 JOs,TMd,To the Stars
   by Hard Ways,pt.1.......... 3.00
10 JOs,TMd,To the Stars,pt.2 ..... 3.00
11 JOs,TMd,To the Stars,pt.3 ..... 3.00
12 JOs,TMd,To the Stars,pt.4 ..... 3.00

KID ETERNITY
1991
1 GMo(s),DFg,O:Kid Eternity 5.50
2 GMo(s),DFg,A:Mr.Keeper 5.50
3 GMo(s),DFg, True Origin revealed,
   final issue................. 5.50

KID ETERNITY
DC/Vertigo, 1993–94
1 B:ANo(s),SeP,R:Kid Eternity,
   A:Mdm.Blavatsky,Hemlock 2.75
2 SeP,A:Sigmund Freud,Carl Jung,
   A:Malocchio................ 2.50
3 SeP,A:Malocchio,I:Dr.Pathos.... 2.50
4 SeP,A:Neal Cassady 2.50
5 SeP,In Cyberspace 2.50
6 SeP,A:Dr.Pathos,Marilyn
   Monroe 2.50
7 SeP,I:Infinity................ 2.50
8 SeP,In Insane Asylum 2.50
9 SeP,Asylum,A:Dr.Pathos 2.50
10 SeP,Small Wages 2.50
11 ANi(s),I:Slap 2.50
12 SeP,A:Slap 2.50
13 SeP,Date in Hell,pt.1.......... 2.50
14 SeP,Date in Hell,pt.2.......... 2.50
15 SeP,Date in Hell,pt.3.......... 2.50
16 SeP,The Zone 2.50

KILL YOUR BOYFRIEND
DC/Vertigo, 1995, 1999
GNv PBd(c) (1995) 5.00
1-shot GMo (1999)............. 6.00

KINETIC
DC Focus, March 2004
1 WaP,F:Tom Morell 2.50
2 WaP,newfound super-powers ... 2.50
3 thru 9 WaP................@2.50

KINGDOM, THE
1998
1 (of 2) MWa,AOl 5.00
2 MWa,MZ,JhB,V:Gog 4.00
Spec.#1 Kid Flash 2.50
Spec.#1 Offspring 2.50
Spec.#1 Nightstar............. 2.50
Spec.#1 Planet Krypton 2.50
Spec.#1 Son of the Bat 2.50
DirectCurrents Spec............. free

KINGDOM COME
Elseworlds 1996
1 MWa,AxR.................. 9.00
2 MWa,AxR,R:JLA 9.00
3 MWa,AxR,A:Capt. Marvel 8.00
4 MWa,AxR, final issue.......... 8.00

KOBALT
DC/Milestone, 1994–95
1 JBy(c),I:Kobalt,Richard Page.... 3.00

KoBalt #10 © DC Comics Inc.

2 thru 13 ....@2.50
14 Long Hot Summer, V:Harvester . 3.00
15 Long Hot Summer............ 3.00

KOBRA
1976–77
1 JK,I:Kobra & Jason Burr 15.00
2 I:Solaris 7.50
3 KG/DG,TA,V:Solaris........... 7.50
4 V:Servitor 7.50
5 RB/FMc,A:Jonny Double 7.50
6 MN/JRu,A:Jonny Double 7.50
7 MN/JRu,A:Jonny Double last iss . 7.50

KONG THE UNTAMED
June-July, 1975
1 AA,BWr(c) 20.00
2 AA,BWr(c) 12.00
3 AA 10.00
4 .... 10.00
5 Feb.–March, 1976 .... 10.00

KORAK, SON OF TARZAN
1975
(Prev. published by Gold Key)
46 JKu(c),B:Carson of Venus 25.00
47 JKu(c).................. 12.00
48 JKu(c).................. 12.00
49 JKu(c),Origin of Korak 18.00
50 thru 59 JKu(c),1975 .... 12.00
Becomes:

TARZAN FAMILY

KRYPTON CHRONICLES
1981
1 CS,A:Superman.............. 5.00
2 CS,A:Black Flame 4.00
3 CS,O:Name of Kal-El.......... 4.00

KRYPTO THE SUPERDOG
Aug., 2006
1 thru 6 From TV cartoon ...... @2.50

LAB RATS
April, 2002
1 by the one and only JBy 7.00
1a 2nd printing 4.50
2 JBy, amusement park 6.00
2a 2nd printing 4.50
3 JBy, ... 2.50
4 JBy,time travel,pt.1 .... 2.50
5 JBy,time travel,pt.2 .... 2.50
6 JBy,time travel,pt.3,A:Superman . 2.50
7 JBy,interplanetary adventure 2.50
8 JBy, final issue.............. 2.50

LAST DAYS OF THE JUSTICE SOCIETY
1986
1 .... 5.00

LAST ONE
DC/Vertigo, 1993
1 B:JMD(s),DSw,I:Myrwann,Patrick
   Maguire's Story 3.25
2 DSw,Pat's Addiction to Drugs ... 3.00
3 DSw,Pat goes into Coma....... 3.00
4 DSw,In Victorian age 3.00
5 DSw,Myrwann Memories....... 3.00
6 E:JMD(s),DSw,final Issue 3.00

L.A.W.
1999
1 (of 6) BL,DG,Living Assault
   Weapons 2.50
2 thru 6 BL,DG ....@2.50

LAZARUS FIVE
May, 2000
1 (of 5) THy,F:Inquisitors 2.50
2 thru 5 THy . . . . @2.50

Leading Comics #3
© DC Comics, Inc.

LEADING COMICS
Winter, 1941–42
1 O:Seven Soldiers of Victory,
  B:Crimson Avenger,Green Arrow
  & Speedy,Shining Knight,
  A:The Dummy 8,500.00
2 MMe,V:Black Star 3,500.00
3 V:Dr. Doome 2,500.00
4 Seven Steps to Conquest,
  V:The Sixth Sense 2,000.00
5 The Miracles that Money
  Couldn't Buy. 2,000.00
6 Treasure that Time Forgot . . 1,500.00
7 The Wizard of Wisstark 1,500.00
8 Seven Soldiers Go back
  through the Centuries. 1,500.00
9 V:Mr. X,Chameleon of Crime 1,500.00
10 King of the Hundred Isles . . 1,500.00
11 The Hard Luck Hat! 1,100.00
12 The Million Dollar
  Challenge! 1,100.00
13 The Trophies of Crime 1,100.00
14 Bandits from the Book 1,100.00
15 (fa) King Oscar's Court. 350.00
16 thru 22 (fa) . . . . @150.00
23 (fa),I:Peter Porkchops. 300.00
24 thru 30 (fa) . . . . @125.00
31 (fa). 100.00
32 (fa). 100.00
33 (fa). 100.00
34 thru 40 (fa) . . . . @100.00
41 (fa),Feb.–March, 1950 . . . . . . 100.00
Becomes:

LEADING
SCREEN COMICS
1950
42 thru 50 Funny Animal . . . . . @125.00
51 thru 77 . . . . @100.00

LEAGUE OF JUSTICE
1996
1 (of 2) Elseworlds 6.00
2 (of 2) Elseworlds 6.00

LEAVE IT TO BINKY
1948
1ShM, teen-age 450.00
2 ShM 225.00

---

3 . . . . 135.00
4 . . . . 135.00
5 A:Superman 200.00
6 . . . . 125.00
7 . . . . 125.00
8 . . . . 125.00
9 . . . . 125.00
10 . . . . 125.00
11 thru 13 . . . . @100.00
14 ShM 125.00
15 thru 20 . . . . @90.00
21 thru 27 . . . . @100.00
28 MD 125.00
29 . . . . 100.00
30 thru 60 . . . . @100.00
61 thru 71 . . . . @35.00

LEGEND OF
THE HAWKMAN
July, 2000
1 BRa,Hawkman & Hawkgirl 5.00
2 BRa,V:Thanagarian zealots. 5.00
3 BRa,concl. 5.00

LEGEND OF
THE SHIELD
DC/Impact, 1991–92
1 I:Shield, ... 2.50
2 thru 16 . . . . @2.50
Ann.#1 Earthquest,w/trading card. . 2.50

LEGEND OF
WONDER WOMAN
1986
1 Return of Atomia 4.00
2 A:Queens Solalia & Leila. 3.50
3 Escape from Atomia 3.50
4 conclusion 3.50

LEGENDS
1986–87
1 JBy,V:Darkseid. 5.00
2 JBy,A:Superman 4.00
3 JBy,I:Suicide Squad. 4.00
4 JBy,V:Darkseid. 4.00
5 JBy,A:Dr. Fate 4.00
6 JBy,I:Justice League 5.00

LEGENDS OF
DANIEL BOONE, THE
Oct., 1955–Jan., 1957
1 . . . . 900.00
2 . . . . 600.00
3 thru 8 . . . . 500.00

LEGENDS OF
THE DARK KNIGHT
See: BATMAN

LEGENDS OF
THE DC UNIVERSE
Dec., 1997
1 JeR,VS,PNe,A:Superman, pt.1 . . 3.50
2 JeR,VS,PNe,A:Superman, pt.2 . . 4.00
3 JeR,VS,PNe,A:Superman, pt.3 . . 2.50
4 BML,MD2,VRu,Moments, pt.1 . . 2.50
5 BML,MD2,VRu,Moments, pt.2 . . 2.50
6 DTy,KN,Robin meets Superman . 2.50
7 DON,DG,Peacemakers, pt.1 . . . . 2.50
8 DON,DG,Peacemakers, pt.2 . . . . 2.50
9 DON,DG,Peacemakers, pt.3 . . . . 2.50
10 TyD,KN,F:Batman & Batgirl,pt.1 . 2.50
11 KN,TyD,F:Batman & Batgirl,pt.2 . 2.50
12 CPr(s),Critical Mass,pt.1 . . . . . . 2.50
13 CPr(s),Critical Mass,pt.2 . . . . . . 2.50
14 JK,BR,SR,64-page 5.00

---

15 RCa,Dark Matters, pt.1 . . . . 2.50
16 RCa,Dark Matters, pt.2 . . . . 2.50
17 RCa,Dark Matters, pt.3 . . . . 2.50
18 MWn(s),JG,F:New Teen Titans . . 2.50
19 RT,F:Impulse. 2.50
20 StG(s),MZ,KJ,Trail of the
  Traitor, pt.1 . . . . 2.50
21 StG(s),MZ,KJ,Trail of the
  Traitor, pt.2 . . . . 2.50
22 Transilvane,pt.1. . . . . 2.50
23 Transilvane,pt.2. . . . . 2.50
24 StP,The Jump,pt.1. . . . . 2.50
25 StP,The Jump,pt.2. . . . . 2.50
26 TVE,JRu,Aquaman&Joker,pt.1 . . 2.50
27 TVE,JRu,Aquaman&Joker,pt.2 . . 2.50
28 GK,KJ,pt.1. . . . . 2.50
29 GK,KJ,pt.2,F:Traitor 2.50
30 CPr(s),Wonder Woman,pt.1 . . . . 2.50
31 CPr(s),Wonder Woman,pt.2 . . . . 2.50
32 CPr(s),Wonder Woman,pt.3 . . . . 2.50
33 JMD,MZi,VcL,F:Spectre,pt.1 . . . 2.50
34 JMD,MZi,VcL,F:Spectre,pt.2. . . . 2.50
35 JMD,MZi,VcL,F:Spectre,pt.3 . . . 2.50
36 JMD,MZi,VcL,F:Spectre,pt.4 . . . 2.50
37 ScK,KJ,Traitor Trilogy,pt.1 . . . . . 2.50
38 ScK,KJ,V:Traitor,pt.2. . . . . 2.50
39 RGr,Sole Survivor of Earth 2.50
40 RGr,Lessons in Time,pt.1 . . . . . . 2.50
41 RGr,Lessons in Time,pt.2 . . . . . . 2.50
Giant #1 JKu(c), 80 pg. 5.00
Spec 3-D Gallery #1 . . . . 3.00
GN Crisis on Infinite Earths 5.00

LEGENDS OF
THE LEGION
Dec., 1997
1 (of 4) BKi,TPe,TNu,O:Ultra Boy. . 2.75
2 thru 4 BKi,TPe . . . . @2.50

LEGENDS OF THE
WORLD FINEST
1994
1 WS(s),DIB,V:Silver Banshee,
  Blaze,Tullus,Foil(c) 6.00
2 WS(s),DIB,V:Silver Banshee,
  Blaze,Tullus,Foil(c) 6.00
3 WS(s),DIB,V:Silver Banshee,
  Blaze,Tullus,Foil(c) 6.00

L.E.G.I.O.N. '89-94
1989–94
1 BKi,V:Computer Tyrants 6.00
2 BKi,V:Computer Tyrants 3.50
3 BKi,V:Computer Tyrants,
  A:Lobo. 3.50
4 BKi,V: Lobo 3.50
5 BKi,J:Lobo(in the rest of the
  series),V:Konis-Biz 3.50
6 BKi,V:Konis-Biz 3.50
7 BKi,Stealth vs. Dox 3.50
8 BKi,R:Dox 3.50
9 BKi,J:Phase (Phantom Girl). 3.00
10 BKi,Stealth vs Lobo 3.00
11 BKi,V:Mr.Stoorr 3.00
12 BKi,V:Emerald Eye 3.00
13 BKi,V:Emerald Eye 3.00
14 BKi,V:Pirates. 3.00
15 BKi,V:Emerald Eye 3.00
16 BKi,J:LarGand. 3.00
17 BKi,V:Dragon-Ro 3.00
18 BKi,V:Dragon-Ro 3.00
19 V:Lydea,L:Stealth 3.00
20 Aftermath. 3.00
21 D:Lyrissa Mallor,V:Mr.Starr 3.00
22 V:Mr.Starr 3.00
23 O:R.J.Brande(double sized) 3.50
24 BKi,V:Khunds 3.00
25 BKi,V:Khunds 3.00
26 BKi,V:Khunds 3.00
27 BKi,J:Lydea Mallor 3.00

L.E.G.I.O.N. '89 #6
© *DC Comics Inc.*

28 KG,Birth of Stealth's Babies 3.00
29 BKi,J:Capt.Comet,Marij'n Bek . . 3.00
30 BKi,R:Stealth. 3.00
31 Lobo vs.Capt.Marvel. 4.00
32 V:Space Biker Gang 3.00
33 A:Ice-Man 3.00
34 MPn,V:Ice Man 3.00
35 Legion Disbanded. 3.00
36 Dox proposes to Ignea 3.00
37 V:Intergalactic Ninjas. 3.00
38 BKi,Lobo V:Ice Man 3.00
39 BKi,D:G'odd,V:G'oddSquad 3.00
40 BKi,V:Kyaltic Space Station 3.00
41 BKi,A:Stealth'sBaby 3.00
42 BKi,V:Yeltsin-Beta 3.00
43 BKi,V:Yeltsin-Beta 3.00
44 V:Yeltsin-Beta,C:Gr.Lantern . . . 3.00
45 BKi,New Perspectives 3.00
46 BKi,A:Hal Jordan 3.00
47 BKi,Lobo vs Hal Jordan 3.00
48 BKi,R:Ig'nea 3.00
49 BKi,V:Ig'nea 3.00
50 BKi,V:Ig'nea,A:Legion'67 . . . . . . 4.00
51 F:Lobo,Telepath 3.00
52 BKi,V:Cyborg Skull of Darius . . . 3.00
53 BKi,V:Shadow Creature 3.00
54 BKi,V:Shadow Creature 3.00
55 BKi,V:Shadow Beast 3.00
56 BKi,A:Masked Avenger 3.00
57 BKi,Trinity,V:Green Lantern 3.00
58 BKi,Trinity#6,A:Green Lantern,
    Darkstar. 3.00
59 F:Phase. 3.00
60 V:Phantom Riders. 3.00
61 Little Party. 3.00
62 A:R.E.C.R.U.I.T.S. 3.00
63 A:Superman 3.00
64 BKi(c),V:Mr.B 3.00
65 BKi(c),V:Brain Bandit 3.00
66 Stealth and Dox name child 3.00
67 F:Telepath 3.00
68 Our Porduct is Peace 3.00
69 F:Phase & Jo; Minutes to Go . . . 3.00
70 Zero Hour, last issue. 3.00
Ann.#1 A:Superman,V:Brainiac 5.50
Ann.#2 Armageddon 2001 . . . . 3.50
Ann.#3 Eclipso tie-in 3.25
Ann.#4 SHa(i),I:Pax 3.75
Ann.#5 Elseworlds story 3.50

LEGION, THE
Oct., 2001
1 DAn,ALa, New era dawns 5.00
2 DAn,ALa,F:Oversight Watch 4.00

3 DAn,ALa,new headquarters. 4.00
4 DAn,ALa,Footstep Drive Tech. . . 3.50
5 DAn,ALa,Return to Lost Galaxy . 3.00
6 DAn,ALa,Moon & Inhabitants . . . 3.00
7 DAn,ALa,V:Ra's Al Ghul 3.00
8 DAn,ALa,V:Ra's Al Ghul 3.00
9 DAn,ALa,Apparition,Ultra-Boy . . . 3.00
10 DAn,ALa,Robotica to Earth. 3.00
11 DAn,ALa,F:Robotica 2.75
12 DAn,ALa,F:JLA. 2.75
13 DAn,ALa,V:Robotica 2.75
14 DAn,ALa,V:Robotica 2.75
15 DAn,ALa,F:Timber Wolf 2.75
16 DAn,ALa,F:Lone Wolf 2.75
17 DAn,ALa,The Fittest,pt.1 . . . . . . 2.75
18 DAn,ALa,The Fittest,pt.2 . . . . . . 2.50
19 DAn,MFm,Dream Crime,pt.1 . . . 2.50
20 DAn,MFm,Dream Crime,pt.2 . . . 2.50
21 DAn,MFm,Dream Crime,pt.3 . . . 2.50
22 DAn,MFm,Dream Crime,pt.4 . . . 2.50
23 DAn,MFm,Dream Crime,pt.5 . . . 2.50
24 DAn,ALa,F:Umbra. 2.50
25 Foundations,pt.1,48-pg. 4.00
26 DAn,ALa,Foundations,pt.2 . . . . . 2.50
27 DAn,ALa,Foundations,pt.3 . . . . . 2.50
28 DAn,ALa,Foundations,pt.4 . . . . . 2.50
29 DAn,ALa,Foundations,pt.5 . . . . . 2.50
30 DAn,ALa,Foundations,pt.6 . . . . . 2.50
31 KG,AM,deadly virus 2.50
32 DAn,ALa,V:Credo 2.50
33 DAn,ALa,F:Livewire 2.50
34 SLi,Wildfire,Qward 2.50
35 DJu,ASm,No Better Reason. . . . 2.50
36 DJu,ASm,No Better Reason. . . . 2.50
37 DJu,ASm,No Better Reason. . . . 2.50
38 DJu,ASm,No Better Reason. . . . 2.50
GN Legion Secret Files 3003 . . . . . 5.00

LEGION LOST
March, 2000
1 (of 12) DAn,ALa. 8.00
2 DAn,ALa,V:Progeny. 4.00
3 DAn,ALa,V:Progeny. 4.00
4 DAn,ALa,. 4.00
5 DAn,ALa,Brainiac 5.1 . . . . 4.00
6 DAn,ALa,F:Umbra 3.00
7 DAn,ALa,F:Ultra Boy 3.00
8 DAn,ALa, ... 3.00
9 DAn,ALa 3.00
10 DAn,ALa 3.00
11 DAn,ALa 3.00
12 DAn,ALA conclusion 3.00

LEGIONNAIRES
1992
1 CSp,V:Mano and the Hand,Bagged
    w/SkyBox promo card 4.00
1a w/out card 3.00
2 CSp,V:Mano. 3.00
3 CSp,I:2nd Emerald Empress 3.00
4 CSp,R:Fatal Five 3.00
5 CSp,V:Fatal Five 3.00
6 thru 17 . . . . @2.50
18 Zero Hour, LSH. 3.00
19 thru 49 . . . . @2.50
50 RSt&TMw(s),JMy,The Bride of
    Mordru, 48pg, with poster 5.00
51 thru 81 . . . . @2.50
Ann.#1 Elseworlds Story 3.50
Ann.#2 Year One Story 3.50
Ann.#3 RSt&TMw(s) 4.00
Spec.#1,000,000 TPe(s),SeP, Justice
    Legion L. 2.50

LEGIONNAIRES THREE
1986
1 EC,Saturn Girl,Cosmic Boy 4.00
2 EC,V:Time Trapper,pt.1 . . . . 3.00
3 EC,V:Time Trapper,pt.2 . . . . 3.00
4 EC,V:Time Trapper,pt.3 . . . . 3.00

LEGION OF SUBSTITUTE HEROES
1985
Spec.#1 KG 3.00

LEGION OF SUPER-HEROES
[Reprint Series], 1973
1 rep. Tommy Tomorrow 50.00
2 rep. Tommy Tomorrow 30.00
3 rep. Tommy Tomorrow 30.00
4 rep. Tommy Tomorrow 30.00

[1st Regular Series], 1980–84
Prev: SUPERBOY (& LEGION)
259 JSon,L:Superboy 20.00
260 RE,I:Circus of Death 10.00
261 RE,V:Circus of Death 14.00
262 JSh,V:Engineer. 10.00
263 V:Dagon the Avenger 14.00
264 V:Dagon the Avenger 14.00
265 JSn,DG,Superman/Radio Shack
    insert 10.00
266 R:Bouncing Boy,Duo Damsel . 14.00
267 SD,V:Kantuu 10.00
268 SD,BWi,V:Dr.Mayavale 10.00
269 V:Fatal Five 10.00
270 V:Fatal Five. 10.00
271 V:Tharok (Dark Man) 6.00
272 CI,SD,O:J:Blok, I:New
    Dial `H' for Hero. 6.00
273 V:Stargrave 6.00
274 SD,V:Captain Frake 6.00
275 V:Captain Frake 6.00
276 SD,V:Mordru 6.00
277 A:Reflecto(Superboy) 6.00
278 A:Reflecto(Superboy) 6.00
279 A:Reflecto(Superboy) 6.00
280 R:Superboy 6.00
281 SD,V:Time Trapper 6.00
282 V:Time Trapper 6.00
283 O:Wildfire 6.00
284 PB,V:Organleggor. 6.00
285 PB,KG(1st Legion)V:Khunds . . 8.00
286 PB,KG,V:Khunds. 8.00
287 KG,V:Kharlak. 8.00
288 KG,V:Kharlak. 8.00
289 KG,Stranded 8.00
290 KG,B:Great Darkness Saga,
    J:Invisible Kid II 9.00
291 KG,V:Darkseid's Minions. 9.00
292 KG,V:Darkseid's Minions. 9.00

Legion of Super-Heroes #270
© *DC Comics, Inc.*

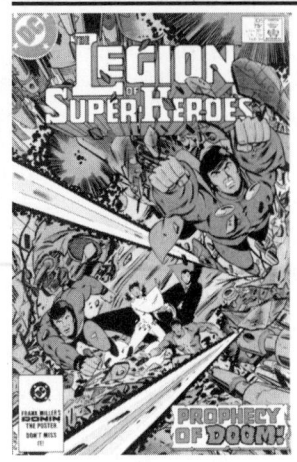

Legion of Super-Heroes #308
© DC Comics, Inc.

293 KG,Daxam destroyed 9.00
294 KG,E:Great Darkness Saga,
V:Darkseid,A:Auron,Superboy. . 9.00
295 KG,A:Green Lantern Corps. . . . 3.50
296 KG,D:Cosmic Boys family 3.50
297 KG,O:Legion,A:Cosmic Boy . . . 3.50
298 KG,EC,I:Amethyst 3.50
299 KG,R:Invisible Kid I 3.50
300 KG,CS,JSon,DC,KS,DG 6.00
301 KG,R:Chameleon Boy 3.50
302 KG,A:Chameleon Boy 3.50
303 KG,V:Fatal Five 3.50
304 KG,V:Fatal Five 3.50
305 KG,V:Micro Lad 3.50
306 KG,CS,RT,O:Star Boy 3.50
307 KG,GT,Omen 3.50
308 KG,V:Omen 3.50
309 KG,V:Omen 3.50
310 KG,V:Omen 3.50
311 KG,GC,New Headquarters 3.50
312 KG,V:Khunds 3.50
313 KG,V:Khunds 3.50
Ann.#1 IT,KG,I:Invisible Kid 4.00
Ann.#2 DGb,W:Karate Kid and
Princess Projectra 3.00
Ann.#3 CS,RT,A:Darkseid 3.00
Ann.#4 thru Ann. #5 reprints . . . . @3.00
Becomes:

TALES OF LEGION OF SUPER HEROES

LEGION OF SUPER-HEROES

[3rd Regular Series], 1984–89
1 KG,V:Legion of Super-Villians . . . 5.00
2 KG,V:Legion of Super-Villians . . . 4.00
3 KG,V:Legion of Super-Villians . . . 4.00
4 KG,D:Karate Kid 4.00
5 KG,D:Nemesis Kid 4.00
6 JO,F:Lightning Lass 3.00
7 SLi,A:Controller 3.00
8 SLi,V:Controller 3.00
9 Sli,V:Sklarians 3.00
10 V:Khunds 3.00
11 EC,KG,L:Orig 3 members 3.00
12 SLi,EC,A:Superboy 3.00
13 SLi,V:Lythyls,F:TimberWolf 3.00
14 SLi,J:Sensor Girl (Princess
Projectra),Quislet,Tellus,Polar
Boy,Magnetic Kid 3.00
15 GLa,V:Dr. Regulus 3.00
16 SLi,Crisis tie-in,F:Braniac5 . . . . 3.00

17 GLa,O:Legion 3.00
18 GLa,Crisis tie-in,V:InfiniteMan . . 3.00
19 GLa,V:Controller 3.00
20 GLa,V:Tyr 3.00
21 GLa,V:Emerald Empress 4.00
22 GLa,V:Restorer,A:Universo 4.00
23 SLi,GLa,A:Superboy,
Jonah Hex 4.00
24 GLa,NBi,A:Fatal Five 4.00
25 GLa,V:FatalFive 4.00
26 GLa,V:FatalFive,O:SensorGirl . . 3.00
27 GLa,GC,A:Mordru 3.00
28 GLa,L:StarBoy 3.00
29 GLa,V:Starfinger 3.00
30 GLa,A:Universo 3.00
31 GLa,A:Ferro Lad,Karate Kid 3.00
32 GLa,V:Universo,I:Atmos 3.00
33 GLa,V:Universo 3.00
34 GLa,V:Universo 3.00
35 GLa,V:Universo,R:Saturn Girl . . . 3.00
36 GLa,R:Cosmic Boy 3.00
37 GLa,V:Universo,I:Superboy
(Earth Prime) 15.00
38 GLa,V:TimeTrapper,
D:Superboy 14.00
39 CS,RT,O:Colossal Boy 3.00
40 GLa,I:New Starfinger 3.00
41 GLa,V:Starfinger 3.00
42 GLa,Millennium,V:Laurel Kent . . 3.00
43 GLa,Millennium,V:Laurel Kent . . 3.00
44 GLa,O:Quislet 3.00
45 GLa,CS,MGr,DC,30th Ann. 4.00
46 GLa,Conspiracy 3.00
47 GLa,PB,V:Starfinger 3.00
48 GLa,Conspiracy,A:Starfinger . . . 3.00
49 PB,Conspiracy,A:Starfinger. . . . 3.00
50 KG,V:Time Trapper,A:Infinite
Man,E:Conspiracy 4.00
51 KG,V:Gorak,L:Brainiac5 . . . . . . 3.00
52 KG,V:Gil'Dishpan 3.00
53 KG,V:Gil'Dishpan 3.00
54 KG,V:Gorak 3.00
55 KG,EC,JL,EL,N:Legion 3.00
56 EB,V:Inquisitor 3.00
57 KG,V:Emerald Empress 3.00
58 KG,V:Emerald Empress 3.00
59 KG,MBr,F:Invisible Kid 3.00
60 KG,B:Magic Wars 3.00
61 KG,Magic Wars 3.00
62 KG,D:Magnetic Lad 3.00
63 KG,E:Magic Wars #4,final iss. . . 4.50
Ann.#1 KG,Murder Mystery 3.00
Ann.#2 KG,CS,O:Validus,
A:Darkseid 3.50
Ann.#3 GLa,I:2nd Karate Kid 3.00
Ann.#4 BKi,V:Starfinger 3.00
Ann #5 I:2nd Legion Sub.Heroes . . 3.00

[4th Regular Series], 1989–97
1 KG,R:Cosmic Boy, Chameleon . . 5.00
2 KG,R:Ultra Boy,I:Kono 4.00
3 KG,D:Block,V:Roxxas 4.00
4 KG,V:Time Trapper 4.00
5 KG,V:Mordru,A:Glorith 4.00
6 KG,I:Laurel Gand 4.00
7 KG,V:Mordru 3.00
8 KG,O:Legion 3.00
9 KG,O:Laurel Gand 3.00
10 KG,V:Roxxas 3.00
11 KG,V:Roxxas 3.00
12 KG,I:Kent Shakespeare 3.00
13 KG,V:Dominators,posters 3.00
14 KG,J:Tenzil Kem 3.00
15 KG,Khund Invasion 3.00
16 KG,V:Khunds 3.00
17 KG,V:Khunds 3.00
18 KG,V:Khunds 3.00
19 KG,cont.from Adv.of Superman
#478,A:Original Dr. Fate 3.00
20 KG,V:Dominators 3.00
21 KG,B:Quiet Darkness,
A:Lobo,Darkseid 3.50
22 KG,A:Lobo,Darkseid 3.00

23 KG,A:Lobo,Darkseid 3.00
24 KG,E:Quiet Darkness,A:Lobo,
Darkseid,C:Legionairres 4.00
25 DAb,I:Legionairres 3.50
26 JPn,B:Terra Mosaic,V:B.I.O.N. . . 2.50
27 JPn,V:B.I.O.N. 2.50
28 JPn,O:Sun Boy 2.50
29 JPn,I:Monica Sade 2.50
30 JPn,V:Dominators 2.50
31 CS,AG,F:Shvaughn as man 2.50
32 JPn,D:Karate Kid,Prin.Projectra,
Chameleon Boy(Legionaires) . . 2.50
33 R:Kid Quantum 2.50
34 R:Sun Boy 2.50
35 JPN,V:Dominators 2.50
36 JPn,E:Terra Mosaic 2.50
37 JBr,R:Star Boy,Dream Girl 2.50
38 JPn,Earth is destroyed 5.00
39 SI,A:Legionnaires 2.50
40 SI,Legion meets Legionnaires . . 2.50
41 SI,F:The Legionnaires 2.50
42 SI,V:Glorith 2.50
43 SI,B:Mordru Arises 2.50
44 SI,R:Karate Kid 2.50
45 SI,R:Roxxas 2.50
46 SI,Battle with the Dead 2.50
47 SI,Last Rites 2.50
48 SI,E:Mordru Arises 2.50
49 F:Matter Eater Lad 2.50
50 W:Tenzil & Saturn Queen,
R:Wildfire,V:B.I.O.N. 4.00
51 R:Kent,Celeste,Ivy,V:Grimbor . . 2.50
52 F:Timber Wolf 2.50
53 SI,V:Glorith 2.50
54 SI,Foil,Die-Cut(c),
N:L.E.G.I.O.N. 5.00
55 SI,On Rimbor 2.50
56 SI,R:Espionage Squad 2.50
57 SI,R:Khund Legionnaires 2.50
58 SI,D:Laurel Gand 2.50
59 SI,R:Valor,Dawnstar 2.50
60 SI,End of an Era#3 . . . . 2.50
61 SI,End of an Era#6 . . . . 2.50
62 I:New Team 2.50
63 Alien Attack 2.50
64 Sibling Rivalry 2.50
65 Breakout 2.50
66 I:New Team Members 2.50
67 F:Leviathan 2.50
68 F:Leviathan 2.50
69 V:Durlan 2.50
70 A:Andromeda, Brainiac 5 . . . . . . 2.50
71 Planet Trom 2.50
72 Absent Friends 2.50

Legion of Super-Heroes 4th Series #65
© DC Comics, Inc.

73 Sibling Rivalry,pt.1 . . . . 2.50
74 Future Tense,pt2. . . . . 2.50
75 Two Timer,pt.1 (of 2). 2.50
76 F:Valor & Triad 2.50
77 F:Brainiac 5. . . . . 2.50
78 The Gathering Doom 2.50
79 Fatal Five attacks 2.50
80 V:Fatal Five. 2.50
81 R:Dirk Morgna. 2.50
82 Lifestyles of the Dead 2.50
83 TPe&TMw(s),Big Tears 2.50
84 TPe&TMw(s),Emerald Legion. . . 2.50
85 TPe&TMw(s),LMd,A:Superman,
   back in 20th century 2.50
86 TPe&TMw(s),LMd,Final Night
   tie-in. 2.50
87 TPe&TMw(s),LMd,F:Deadman . . 2.50
88 TPe&TMw(s),LMd,A:Impulse . . . 2.50
89 TPe&TMw(s),LMd, ... 2.50
90 TPe&TMw(s),LMd,V:Dr. Psycho . 2.50
91 TPe&TMw(s),LMd,Legion back
   together, but trapped in
   timestream. 2.50
92 TPe&TMs(s),LMd,Displaced
   in Time. 2.50
93 TPe&TMw(s),MC, All-tragedy
   issue 2.50
94 TPe&TMw(s),LMd,22 short
   pages about the Legion of
   Super-Heroes 2.50
95 MFm,F:Brainiac 5 . . . . 2.50
96 MFm,wedding 2.50
97 TPe,LMd,Genesis tie-in 2.50
98 TPe&TMC,LMd,C.O.M.P.U.T.O.
   the Conqueror, pt.1 . . . . 2.50
99 TPe&TMw,LMd,Computo, pt.2 . . 2.50
100 TPe&TMw,LMd,Computo, pt.3 . 8.00
101 TPe&TMw(s),AD&MFm(c),
   F:Sparks 2.50
102 TPe&TMw(s), ... 2.50
103 TPe&TMw,AD&MFm(c),Star
   Boy 2.50
104 TPe&TMw,AD&MFm(c),
   changes. 2.50
105 TPe&TMw,AD&MFm(c),
   Adventures in Action x-over . . . 2.50
106 TPe&TMw,AD&MFm(c),Dark
   Circle Rising, x-over pt.2 . . . . . 2.50
107 TPe&TMw,AD&MFm(c),Dark
   Circle Rising, x-over pt.4 . . . . . 2.50
108 TPe&TMw,AD&MFm(c),Dark
   Circle Rising, x-over pt.6 . . . . . 2.50
109 DDv,AD,MFm,F:Violet. 2.50
110 TPe,V:Thunder 2.50
111 TPe&TMw(s),V:Daxamite 2.50
112 TPe&TMw(s),In Space 2.50
113 TPe&TMw(s),Kinetix 2.50
114 TPe&TMw(s),Bizarro
   Legion,pt.1. . . . . 2.50
115 TPe&TMw(s),Bizarro
   Legion, pt.2 . . . . 2.50
116 TPe&TMw(s),V:Pernisius,pt.1 . . 2.50
117 TPe&TMw(s),V:Pernisius,pt.2 . . 2.50
118 TPe&TMw(s),V:Pernisius,pt.3 . . 2.50
119 TPe&TMw(s),A:Valor & Phase . 2.50
120 TPe,TMw,V:Fatal Four,pt.1 . . . . 2.50
121 TPe,TMw,V:Fatal Five,pt.2 . . . . 2.50
122 DAn,ALa,Legion of
   the Damned,pt.1 . . . . 2.50
123 DAn,ALa,Legion of
   the Damned,pt.3 . . . . 2.50
124 DAn,ALa,Legion of the Damned,
   aftermath 10.00
125 DAn,ALa,final issue 6.00
Ann.#1 O:Ultra Boy,V:Glorith 3.50
Ann.#2 O:Valor. 3.50
Ann.#3 N:Timberwolf 4.00
Ann.#4 I:Jamm. 3.50
Ann.#5 SI(c),CDo,MFm,TMC,
   Elseworlds Story 3.75
Ann.#6 Year One Annual + pin-ups . 4.00

Ann.#7 TPe(s),MC,MFm,Legends
   of the Dead Earth 3.50
Spec.#1,000,000 TPe(s),KG,AG . . . 2.50
GN Secret Files, inc.O:Legion 5.00
GN Secret Files #2 . . . . 5.00

Dec., 2004

1 MWa(s),BKi,40-page 3.00
2 MWa(s),BKi,work with the law? . . 3.00
3 MWa(s),BKi,F:Triplicate Girl 3.00
4 MWa(s),DGb,F:Invisible Kid 3.00
5 MWa(s),BKi,ATi,Lightning Lad
   & Saturn Girl 3.00
6 MWa(s),BKi,ATi 3.00
7 MWa(s),BKi,ATi 3.00
8 MWa(s),BKi,ATi, team split 3.00
9 MWa(s),ATi,split widens. 3.00
10 MWa(s),BKi,ATi,V:Terror Firma . 3.00
11 MWa(s),BKi,V:Terror Firma 3.00
12 MWa(s),BKi,Team in shambles. . 3.00
13 MWa(s),BKi,Fifth Dimension. . . . 3.00
14 MWa(s),BKi,I:Atom Girl. 3.00
15 MWa(s),BKi,31st century heroes 3.00
Becomes:

SUPERGIRL
AND THE LEGION
OF SUPERHEROES
March, 2006

16 MWa,BKi 3.00
17 MWa,BKi, newest member 3.00
18 MWa,BKi,Mysteries Unfold 3.00
19 MWa,BKi,F:Chameleon 3.00
20 MWa,BKi,Brainiac & Dream Girl . 3.00
21 MWa,BKi,Colossal Boy's home . 3.00
22 MWa,BKi,Supergirl's Boyfriend . . 3.00
23 MWa,BKi,Supergirl on Krypton . . 3.00
23a variant (c) 3.00
24 MWa,BKi,Super-powered Villains 3.00
25 MWa,BKi 3.00
26 MWa,BKi,V:Dominators 3.00
27 MWa,BKi,F:L.Lad & Mekt Ranzz 3.00
28 MWa,BKi,V:Dominators 3.00
29 MWa,BKi,V:Dominator Empire . . 3.00
30 MWa,BKi,V:Dominators 3.00
31 BKi,Dominators, concl 3.00
32 Quest for Cosmic Boy. 3.00
33 Quest for Cosmic Boy. 3.00
34 Quest for Cosmic Boy. 3.00
35 Quest for Cosmic Boy. 3.00
36 Quest for Cosmic Boy. 3.00
Becomes:

LEGION OF
SUPER-HEROES
Dec., 2007

37 F:Lightning Lad. 3.00
37a variant (c) 3.00
38 Invisible Kid. 3.00
39 F:Princess Projectra 3.00
40 Enemy Rising, pt.1 . . . . 3.00
41 Enemy Rising, pt.2 . . . . 3.00
42 Ultra Boy, on Rimbor 3.00
43 Science Police ransack H.Q. . . . 3.00
44 F:Invisible Kid 3.00
44a variant NA (c) (1:10) 3.00
45 Moving planets 3.00
46 Chameleon's hand amputated . . 3.00
47 F:Meander. 3.00
48 Membership tryouts 3.00

LEGION OF SUPER-
HEROES IN THE 31ST
CENTURY, THE
Apr., 2007

1 . . . . 2.50
2 thru 20 . . . . 2.50

LEGION:
SCIENCE POLICE
June, 1998

1 (of 4) DvM,PR,JRu,set in
   30th century. 2.50
2 DvM,PR,JRu,Jarik Shadder. 2.50
3 DvM,PR,JRu, ... 2.50
4 DvM,PR,JRu 2.50

LEGION WORLDS
April, 2001

1 (of 6) DAn,ALa. 4.00
2 DAn,ALa 4.00
3 DAn,ALa, On Braal 4.00
4 DAn,ALa, heading for Xanthu . . . 4.00
5 DAn,ALa, SDi, on Steele 4.00
6 DAn,ALa, concl 4.00

LEX LUTHOR:
MAN OF STEEL
March, 2005

1 (of 5) Superman, alien villain. . . . 3.00
2 . . . . 3.00
3 F:Batman 3.00
4 and 5 . . . . @3.00

*Life, The Universe and Everything
#1 © DC Comics Inc.*

LIFE, THE UNIVERSE
AND EVERYTHING
1996

1 thru 3 Doug Adams adapt. . . . . @7.00

LIGHT BRIGADE, THE
Feb. 2004

1 thru 4 PSj. . . . . @6.00

LIMITED COLLECTORS
EDITION
Summer, 1973

21 Shazam. 40.00
22 Tarzan. 35.00
23 House of Mystery 45.00
24 Rudolph, the Red-nosed
   Reindeer 125.00
25 NA,NA(c),Batman 60.00
27 Shazam. 35.00
29 Tarzan 35.00
31 NA,O:Superman 35.00
32 Ghosts. 50.00

33 Rudolph. 100.00	
34 X-Mas with Superheroes 35.00	
35 Shazam. 30.00	
36 The Bible 30.00	
37 Batman 40.00	
38 Superman 30.00	
39 Secret Origins 30.00	
40 Dick Tracy 30.00	
41 ATh,Super Friends 30.00	
42 Rudolph 65.00	
43 X-mas with Super-Heroes. 30.00	
44 NA,Batman 30.00	
45 Secret Origins-Super Villians . . 30.00	
46 ATh,JLA 30.00	
47 Superman 30.00	
48 Superman-Flash Race 30.00	
49 Superboy & Legion of	
Super-Heroes 30.00	
50 Rudolph 60.00	
51 NA,NA(c),Batman 35.00	
52 NA,NA(c),The Best of DC 30.00	
57 Welcome Back Kotter 30.00	
59 NA,BWr,Batman,1978 . . . . 35.00	

LOBO
[1st Limited Series], 1990–91
1 SBs,Last Czarnian #1 . . . . 4.00
1a 2nd Printing 2.00
2 SBs,Last Czarnian #2 . . . . 3.00
3 SBs,Last Czarnian #3 . . . . 3.00
4 SBs,Last Czarnian #4 . . . . 3.00
Ann.#1 Bloodlines#1,I:Layla 3.75
Lobo Paramilitary X-Mas SBs 5.50
Lobo:Blazing Chain of Love,DCw . . 2.00

[Regular Series], 1993–97
0 O:Lobo (1994, between #9&#10) 3.00
1 VS,Foil(c),V:Dead Boys 3.25
2 VS,Quigly Affair 3.00
3 VS,Quigly Affair 2.75
4 VS,Quigly Affair 2.75
5 V:Bludhound 2.50
6 I:Bim Simms 2.50
7 A:Losers 2.50
8 A:Losers 2.50
9 V:Lobo 2.50
10 Preacher 2.50
11 Goldstar vs. Rev.Bo 2.50
12 AIG 2.50
13 AIG 2.50
14 Lobo, P.I. 2.50
15 Lobo, P.I.,pt.2 . . . . 2.50
16 Lobo, P.I.,pt.3 . . . . 2.50
17 Lobo, P.I.,pt.4 . . . . 2.50
18 Lobo, P.I.,pt.5 . . . . 2.50
19 AIG 2.50

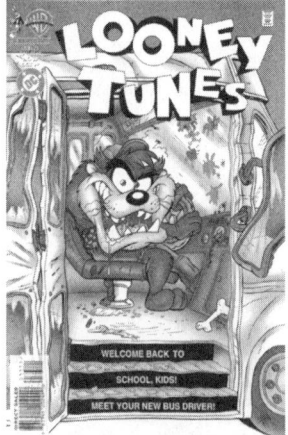

Lobo #0 © DC Comics, Inc.

20 Toilot Fight 2.50	
21 AIG,KON,R:Space Cabby 2.50	
22 AIG,UnderworldUnleashed tie-in . 2.50	
23 AIG,Stargaze Rally,pt.1 . . . . 2.50	
24 AIG,Stargaze Rally,pt.2 . . . . 2.50	
25 AIG 2.50	
26 AIG,V:Erik the Khund 2.50	
27 AIG,V:Billy Krono 2.50	
28 AIG,The Heiress,pt.1 . . . . 2.50	
29 AIG,The Heiress,pt.2 . . . . 2.50	
30 AIG,The Heiress,pt.3 . . . . 2.50	
31 AIG,The Heiress,pt.4 . . . . 2.50	
32 AIG(s),Lobo attends a seance,	
frags himself 2.50	
33 AIG(s),Lobo returns from spirit	
world 2.50	
34 AIG(s),vs. Japan, whaling, ... 2.50	
35 AIG(s), Deathtrek 2.50	
36 AIG(s) 2.50	
37 AIG(s),BKi,Lobo's Guide to Girls 2.50	
38 AIG(s),Bomandi The Last Boy	
on Earth 2.50	
39 AIG(s),In the Belly of the	
Behemoth,pt. 1 . . . . 2.50	
40 AIG(s),Belly of Behemoth,pt.2 . . 2.50	
41 AIG(s),roommates 2.50	
42 AIG(s),A:Perfidia 2.50	
43 AIG(s),A:Jonas 2.50	
44 AIG(s),Genesis tie-in 2.50	
45 AIG(s),battle royale 2.50	
46 AIG(s),Jackie Chin 2.50	
47 AIG(s),V:Kiljoy Riggs. 2.50	
48 AIG(s),F:the penguins 2.50	
49 AIG(s) 2.50	
50 AIG(s),war on DC universe 2.50	
51 AIG(s),Slater and Candy 2.50	
52 AIG(s),Goldstar funeral 2.50	
53 AIG(s),disrupted ceremony 2.50	
54 AIG(s),Good Vibes machine 2.50	
55 AIG(s),Sheepworld 2.50	
56 AIG(s),MPn,GLz,the wedding . . . 2.50	
57 AIG(s),MPn,GLz, Intergalactic	
Police convention 2.50	
58 KG&AIG(s) 2.50	
59 AIG(s),V:Bad Wee Bastards 2.50	
60 AIG(s),All-New, Nonviolent	
Adventures of Superbo, pt.1 . . . 2.50	
61 AIG(s),Superbo, pt.2 . . . . 2.50	
62 AIG(s),Superbo, pt.3 . . . . 2.50	
63 AIG(s),Soul Brothers,pt.1 . . . . . 2.50	
64 AIG(s),Soul Brothers,pt.2 . . . . . 2.50	
Ann.#1 Bloodlines 4.00	
Ann.#2 Elseworlds Story 3.50	
Ann.#3 AIG Year One 5.00	
Spec.#1,000,000 AIG(s),GLz 2.50	
Spec. Lobo's Big Babe Spring Break,	
Miss Voluptuous Contest. 2.50	
Spec. Blazing Chains of Love 2.00	
Spec. Bounty Hunting for Fun	
and Profit, F:Fanboy 5.00	
Spec. Lobo: Chained AIG(s),	
Lobo in prison 2.50	
Spec. Lobo/Demon: Hellowe'en,	
AIG(s),VGi 2.50	
Spec. Lobo In the Chair, AIG(s) . . . 2.50	
Spec. Lobo:I Quit,AIG,	
nicotine withdrawal 2.50	
Spec. Lobo/Judge Dredd: Psycho	
Bikers vs. Mutants From Hell . . 5.00	
Spec. Lobo: Portrait of a Victim	
VS,I:John Doe 2.50	
GN Fragtastic Voyage AGr,	
miniaturized 6.00	
Convention Special, comic con 2.50	

...A CONTRACT ON GAWD
1994
1 AIG(s),KD 2.50
2 AIG(s),KD,A:Dave 2.50
3 AIG(s),KD. 2.50
4 AIG(s),KD,Final Issue 2.50

...'S BACK
1992
1 SBs,w/3(c) inside,V:Loo. 2.50
1a 2nd printing 2.00
2 SBs,Lobo becomes a woman . . . 2.50
3 SBs,V:Heaven 2.50
4 SBs,V:Heaven 2.50

...DEATH & TAXES
[Mini-Series], Aug., 1996
1 (of 4) KG&AIG(s) 2.50
2 KG&AIG(s),Interstellar Revenue
  learns Lobo doesn't pay taxes . 2.50
3 KG&AIG(s),Lobo walks into
  IRS trap 2.50
4 KG&AIG(s),Lobo destroys IRS . . 2.50

...INFANTICIDE
1992–93
1 KG,V:Su,Lobo Bastards 2.50
2 Lobo at Boot Camp 2.50
3 KG,Lobo Vs.his offspring 2.50
4 KG,V:Lobo Bastards 2.50

.../MASK
1 AIG&JAr(s),DoM,Kwi, humorous
  x-over. 6.00
2 AIG&JAr(s),DoM,Kwi, concl. 6.00

...UNAMERICAN GLADIATORS
1993
1 CK,V:Satan's Brothers 2.50
2 CK,V:Jonny Caesar 2.50
3 CK,MMi(c),V:Satan Brothers 2.50
4 CK,MMi(c),V:Jonny Caeser 2.50

...UNBOUND
June 2003
1 (of 6) mass-murder 3.00
2 thru 6 . . . . @3.00

LOBOCOP
1 StG(s). 2.50

LOIS LANE
Aug., 1986
1 and 2 GM . . . . @3.00

LONG HOT SUMMER, THE
Milestone, 1995
1 Blood Syndicate v. G.R.I.N.D. . . . 3.00
2 A:Icon,Xombi,Hardware 2.50

Looney Tunes #33
© DC Comics, Inc.

LOONEY TUNES
1994
1 thru 6 Warner Bros. cartoons. . @3.00
7 thru 11 Warner Bros. . . . . @3.00
12 thru 25. . . . . @2.50
26 thru 168 . . . . @2.25
Spec. Back in Action: Movie 4.00

LOSERS
DC/Vertigo, June 2003
1 crime espionage 4.00
2 thru 6 Goliath,pt.1–pt.5 . . . . . @3.50
7 SMa,Downtime,pt.1 . . . . 3.00
8 SMa,Downtime,pt.2 . . . . 3.00
9 Island Life,pt.1 . . . . 3.00
10 Island Life,pt.2 . . . . 3.00
11 Island Life,pt.3 . . . . 3.00
12 Island Life,pt.4 . . . . 3.00
13 Sheikdown,pt.1 . . . . 3.00
14 Sheikdown,pt.2 . . . . 3.00
15 F:Aisha 3.00
16 The Pass,pt.1 . . . . 3.00
17 The Pass,pt.2 . . . . 3.00
18 The Pass, pt.3 . . . . 3.00
19 The Pass, pt.4 . . . . 3.00
20 London Calling, pt.1 . . . . 3.00
21 London Calling, pt.2 . . . . 3.00
22 London Calling, pt.3 . . . . 3.00
23 Anti-Heist, pt.1 . . . . 3.00
24 Anti-Heist, pt.2 . . . . 3.00
25 Anti-Heist, pt.3 . . . . 3.00
26 CWi,Unamerica,pt.1 . . . . 3.00
27 CWi,Unamerica,pt.2 . . . . 3.00
28 CWi,Unamerica,pt.3 . . . . 3.00
29 Endgame, pt.1 . . . . 3.00
30 Endgame, pt.2 . . . . 3.00
31 Endgame, pt.3 . . . . 3.00
32 final issue 3.00

LOSERS SPECIAL
1985
1 Crisis,D:Losers 4.00

LOVELESS
DC/Vertigo, Oct. 2005
1 Western, A Kin of Homecoming. . 3.00
2 A Kin of Homecoming,pt.2 . . . . . 3.00
3 A Kin of Homecoming,pt.3 . . . . . 3.00
4 A Kin of Homecoming,pt.4 . . . . . 3.00
5 A Kin of Homecoming 3.00
6 A Peace of Iron 3.00
7 F:Ruth Cutter 3.00
8 Born bad? 3.00
9 Thicker Than Blackwater,pt.1 . . . 3.00
10 Thicker Than Blackwater,pt.2 . . . 3.00
11 Thicker Than Blackwater,pt.3 . . . 3.00
12 Thicker Than Blackwater,pt.4 . . . 3.00
13 F:Colonel Silas Redd 3.00
14 . . . . 3.00
15 F:Boyd Johnson 3.00
16 Blackwater Falls, pt.1 . . . . 3.00
17 Blackwater Falls, pt.2 . . . . 3.00
18 Blackwater Falls, pt.3 . . . . 3.00
19 Blackwater Falls, pt.4 . . . . 3.00
20 Blackwater Falls, pt.5 . . . . 3.00
21 Blackwater Falls, concl. 3.00
22 Missouri, 1927 . . . . 3.00
23 F:Jesper 3.00
24 F:Foley 3.00

LUCIFER
DC/Vertigo, Apr., 2000
1 Lucifer strugles to regain power . 7.50
2 Living Tarot Deck 4.50
3 V:Jill Presto 4.50
4 WaP,F:Elaine Belloc 4.00
5 PrG,House of Windowless
   Rooms,pt.1 . . . . 3.50
6 PrG,Windowless Rooms,pt.2 . . . . 3.50
7 PrG,Windowless Rooms,pt.3 . . . . 3.50

8 PrG,Windowless Rooms,pt.4 . . . . 3.50
9 Immortality 3.50
10 Children & Monsters,pt.1 . . . . . 3.50
11 Children & Monsters,pt.2 . . . . . 3.00
12 Children & Monsters,pt.3 . . . . . 3.00
13 Children & Monsters,pt.4 . . . . . 3.00
14 Triptych 3.00
15 Triptych,Two Edge Sword 3.00
16 Triptych,Ancestral Deed 3.00
17 Dalliance with the Dead,pt.1 . . . 3.00
18 Dalliance with the Dead,pt.2 . . . 3.00
19 Dalliance with the Dead,pt.3 . . . 3.00
20 The Thunder Sermon 3.00
21 Paradiso,pt.1 . . . . 3.00
22 Paradiso,pt.2 . . . . 3.00
23 Paradiso,pt.3 . . . . 3.00
24 The Writing on the Wall 3.00
25 Purgatorio,pt.1 . . . . 3.00
26 Purgatorio,pt.2 . . . . 3.00
27 Purgatorio,pt.3 . . . . 3.00
28 F:Gaudium 3.00
29 MCy,Inferno,pt.1 . . . . 3.00
30 MCy,Inferno,pt.2 . . . . 3.00
31 MCy,Inferno,pt.3 . . . . 3.00
32 MCy,Inferno,pt.4 . . . . 3.00
33 MCy,robbery 3.00
34 MCy,Come to Judgment,pt.1 . . . 3.00
35 MCy,Come to Judgment,pt.2 . . . 3.00
36 MCy,Naglfar,pt.1 . . . . 3.00
37 MCy,Naglfar,pt.2 . . . . 3.00
38 MCy,Naglfar,pt.3 . . . . 3.00
39 MCy,Naglfar,pt.4 . . . . 3.00
40 MCy,Naglfar,pt.5 . . . . 3.00
41 MCy,Sisters of Mercy 3.00
42 MCy,Brothers in Arms,pt.1 . . . . . 3.00
43 MCy,Brothers in Arms,pt.2 . . . . . 3.00
44 MCy,Brothers in Arms,pt.3 . . . . . 3.00
45 MCy(s)F:John Sewell 3.00
46 Stitchglass Slide,pt.1 . . . . 3.00
47 Stitchglass Slide,pt.2 . . . . 3.00
48 Stitchglass Slide,pt.3 . . . . 3.00
49 Stitchflass Slide,pt.4 . . . . 3.00
50 CR,48-pg. 4.00
51 Wolf Beneath the Tree,pt.1 . . . . 3.00
52 Wolf Beneath the Tree,pt.2 . . . . 3.00
53 Wolf Beneath the Tree,pt.3 . . . . 3.00
54 Wolf Beneath the Tree,pt.4 . . . . 3.00
55 MCy,MaH,new religion 3.00
56 PrG,Lilith, Elaine,pt.1 . . . . 3.00
57 PrG,Lilith, Elaine,pt.2 . . . . 3.00
58 Escape to new universe 3.00
59 Breach, pt.1 . . . . 3.00
60 Breach, pt.2 . . . . 3.00
61 Breach, pt.3 . . . . 3.00
62 MCy,CDo. 3.00
63 Moringstar,pt.1 . . . . 3.00
64 Moringstar,pt.2 . . . . 3.00
65 Moringstar,pt.3 . . . . 3.00
66 MK,Creation crumbles 3.00
67 Moringstar,pt.4 . . . . 3.00
68 Morningstar,pt.5 . . . . 3.00
69 Morningstar,pt.6 . . . . 3.00
70 MCy. 3.00
71 Evensong, pt.1 . . . . 3.00
72 Evensong, pt.2 . . . . 3.00
73 Someone expendable 3.00
74 Elaine Belloc picks up Godhood. 3.50
75 finale, 48-pg. 4.50
GN Nirvana, 48-pg. 6.00

MADAME XANADU
1981
1 MR/BB 5.00
Vertigo, June, 2008
1 . . . . 3.00
1a variant (c) (1:10) 3.00
2 thru 6 . . . . 3.00

MAJESTIC
Aug. 2004
1 thru 4 (of 4) KIK,F:Mr.Majestic . @3.00

MAJOR BUMMER
June, 1997
1 JAr(s),DoM,I:Major Bummer . . . 2.50
2 thru 15 . . . . @2.50

MAN-BAT
1975–76
1 SD,AM,A:Batman. 40.00
2 V:The Ten-Eyed Man 30.00
Reprint NA(c). 20.00

MAN-BAT
1996
1 CDi,terrorizes city 2.50
2 thru 3 . . . . @2.50

MAN-BAT
April, 2006
1 (of 5) R:Man-Bat 2.50
2 Kirk Langstrom must flee. 3.00
3 Only Man-Bat remains 3.00
4 Batman vs. Man-Bat 3.00
5 finale 3.00

MAN-BAT vs. BATMAN
1 NA,DG,reprint. 4.00

A MAN CALLED AX
Aug., 1997
1 MWn(s),SwM, part rep. 2.50
2 thru 8 MWn(s),SwM, ... @2.50

MANHUNTER
1988–90
1 from Millennium-Suicide Squad. . 2.50
2 in Tokyo,A:Dumas 2.50
3 The Yakuza,V:Dumas 2.50
4 Secrets Revealed-Manhunter,
   Dumas & Olivia 2.50
5 A:Silvia Kandery. 2.50
6 A:Argent,contd.Suicide Squad
   Annual #1 . . . . 2.50
7 Vlatavia, V:Count Vertigo. 2.50
8 FS,A:Flash, Invasion x-over 2.50
9 FS,Invasion Aftermath extra
   (contd from Flash #22) 2.50
10 Finders Keepers 2.50
11 Losers Weepers 2.50
12 Losers Weepers 2.50
13 V:Catman 2.50
14 Janus Directive #5 . . . . 2.50

Manhunter#13
© DC Comics Inc.

15 I:Mirage	2.50
16 V:Outlaw	2.50
17 In Gotham,A:Batman	2.50
18 Saints & Sinners,pt.1,R:Dumas	2.50
19 Saints & Sinners,pt.2,V:Dumas.	2.50
20 Saints & Sinners,pt.3,V:Dumas.	2.50
21 Saints & Sinners,pt.4, A:Manhunter Grandmaster	2.50
22 Saints & Sinners,pt.5, A:Manhunter Grandmaster	2.50
23 Saints & Sinners,pt.6,V:Dumas.	2.50
24 DG,Showdown, final issue	2.50

[2nd Series], 1994–95

0 Here Comes the Night	2.50
1 True Fiction	2.50
2 N:Wild Huntsman	2.50
3 V:Malig	2.50
4 Necrodyne	2.50
5 V:Skin Walker	2.50
6 V:Barbarian,Incarnate	2.50
7 V:Incarnate,A:White Lotus & Capt. Atom	2.50
8 V:Butcher Boys	2.50
9 V:Butcher Boys	2.50
10 V:Necrodyne	2.50
11 Return of Old Enemy	2.50
12 Underworld Unleashed, finale.	2.50

[3rd Series],Aug. 2004

1 JP,JLe(c),Identity Crisis	3.00
2 thru 3 JP,JLe(c)	@4.00
4 JP.	4.00
5 JP,A:JLA	6.00
6 JP,Supervillain Trial	3.00
7 JP,Supervillain Trial	3.00
8 JP,V:Shadow Thief	3.00
9 JP,V:Phobia	3.00
10 Manhunted	3.00
11 JP,Two ex-manhunters	3.00
12 Masks Upon Masks	3.00
13 Kate Spencer & Cameron Chase	3.00
14 Secret of Project Manhunter.	3.00
15 Suit's secret history.	3.00
16 Manhunted aftermath	2.50
17 About to be Unmasked	2.50
18 An Old Foe	2.50
19 V:Her father.	2.50
20 Psychobabble	2.50
21 JSA family connection.	2.50
22 Trial of Dr. Psycho	3.00
23 New villain.	3.00
24 V:Dr. Psycho	3.00
25 F:Kate Spencer, final issue	3.00
26 AAd(c),Unleashed,pt.1.	3.00
26a variant PJ (c).	3.00
27 HC(c), Unleashed, pt.2	3.00
28 KN(c),Unleashed, pt.3	3.00
29 SeP(c),Unleashed, pt.4.	3.00
30 Final issue.	3.00

June, 2008

31 Return of Manhunter.	3.00
32 U.S.-Mexican border	3.00
33 Immigrant workers disappear	3.00
34 V:Suicide Squad	3.00
35 Ciudad Juarez secret	3.00
36 Forgotten.	3.00

MAN OF STEEL
1986

1 JBy,DG,I:Modern Superman	7.00
1a 2nd edition	7.00
2 JBy,DG,R:Lois Lane.	5.00
3 JBy,DG,A:Batman	5.00
4 JBy,DG,V:Lex Luther	5.00
5 JBy,DG,I:Modern Bizarro	5.00
6 JBy,DG,A:Lana Lang	5.00

MANY LOVES OF DOBIE GILLIS
May-June, 1960

1 From TV show	500.00

Man of Steel #1
© DC Comics, Inc.

2	250.00
3	150.00
4	150.00
5 thru 9	@125.00
10 thru 25	@125.00
26 Oct., 1964	125.00

MARTIAN MANHUNTER
1988

1 A:JLI.	3.00
2 A:JLI,V:Death God	2.50
3 V:Death God,A:Dr.Erdel.	2.50
4 A:JLI,final issue	2.50

[Mini-Series]

1 EB,American Secrets #1	5.25
2 EB,American Secrets #2	5.25
3 EB,American Secrets #3	5.25

MARTIAN MANHUNTER
Aug., 1998

0 JOs,TMd,A:Batman,Superman	3.00
1 JOs,TMd,V:Headman	2.50
2 JOs,TMd,V:Antares	2.50
3 JOs,TMd,V:Bette Noir	2.50
4 JOs,TMd,J'emm, Son of Saturn	2.50
5 JAr,JD,A:Chase	2.50
6 JOs,TMd,A:JLA,pt.1.	2.50
7 JOs(s),TMd,A:JLA,pt.2	2.50
8 JOs(s),TMd,A:JLA,pt.3	2.50
9 JOs(s),TMd,A:JLA,pt.4	2.50
10 JOs(s),A:Fire.	2.50
11 JOs,PNe,BHi,	2.50
12 JOs,TMd,Day of Judgment x-over.	2.50
13 JOs,TMd,Rings of Saturn,pt.1	2.50
14 JOs,TMd,Rings of Saturn,pt.2	2.50
15 JOs,TMd,Rings of Saturn,pt.3	2.50
16 JOs,TMd,Rings of Saturn,pt.4	2.50
17 JOs,TMd,Rings of Saturn,pt.5	2.50
18 JOs,TMd,V:Kanto	2.50
19 JOs,TMd,defeated, captured	2.50
20 JOs,TMd,year one on earth	2.50
21 JOs,TT,A:Abin Sur	2.50
22 JOs,TMd,A:Batman.	2.50
23 JOs,TMd,F:Spectre.	2.50
24 JOs,TMd,F:Just.Leag.Int.	2.50
25 JOs,TMd,F:Gypsy.	2.50
26 JOs,TMd,Renegades of Mars.	2.50
27 JOs,TMd,Renegades of Mars..	2.50
28 JOs,TMd,at Stonehenge	2.50
29 JOs,TMd,telepath	2.50
30 JOs,TMd,Altered Egos,pt.1.	2.50
31 JOs,TMd,Altered Egos,pt.2.	2.50

32 TMd,V:Bloodworms of Mars	2.50
33 TMd,J'onn J'onzz hidden life	2.50
34 JOs,V:Darkseid.	2.50
35 JOs,V:Malefic	2.50
36 JOs,final issue	2.50
Ann.#1 TT,AOI,BWr,Ghosts x-over	3.00
Ann.#2 AAd(c),JLApe:Gorilla Warfare	3.00
Spec.#1,000,000 JOs,TMd	2.50

MARTIAN MANHUNTER
Aug., 2006

1 Martian Manhunter's past	3.00
2 Martian artifact.	3.00
3 Truth behind the Lies	3.00
4 Under attack	3.00
5	3.00
6 HC(c),F:Superman, Batman	3.00
7 Betrayal	3.00
8 finale	3.00

MASK
Dec., 1985

1 HC(c),TV tie-in,I:Mask Team	2.50
2 HC(c),In Egypt,V:Venom	2.50
3 HC(c),Anarchy in the U.K.	2.50
4 HC(c),V:Venom, final issue, March, 1986	2.50

[2nd Series], Feb.–Oct., 1987

1 CS/KS,reg.series	2.50
2 CS/KS,V:Venom.	2.50
3 CS/KS,V:Venom.	2.50
4 CS/KS,V:Venom.	2.50
5 CS/KS,Mask operatives hostage.	2.50
6 CS/KS,I:Jacana	2.50
7 CS/KS,Mask gone bad?	2.50
8 CS/KS,Matt Trakker,V:Venom	2.50
9 CS/KS,V:Venom, last issue	2.50

MASTERS OF THE UNIVERSE
May, 1986

1 GT,AA,O:He-Man.	6.00
2 GT,AA,V:Skeletor.	5.00
3 GT,V:Skeletor.	5.00

'MAZING MAN
Jan., 1986

1 I:Maze	3.00
2 Easy Money.	2.50
3 Doing What Married People Do..	2.50
4 The Male Machine	2.50
5 Writer's Block.	2.50
6 Shea Stadium	2.50
7 Shea Stadium	2.50
8 Cat-Sitting	2.50
9 Bank Hold-up.	2.50
10 Big Brother's Watching	2.50
11 Jones Beach	2.50
12 FM(c),last issue, Dec., 1986.	3.00
Spec.#1	2.50
Spec.#2	2.50
Spec.#3 KB/TM	2.50

MEN OF WAR
Aug., 1977

1 I:Gravedigger,Code Name: Gravedigger,I:Enemy Ace	35.00
2 JKu(c),The Five-Walled War	20.00
3 JKu(c),The Suicide Strategem.	20.00
4 JKu(c),Trail by Fire	20.00
5 JKu(c),Valley of the Shadow	20.00
6 JKu(c),A Choice of Deaths	20.00
7 JKu(c),Milkrun	20.00
8 JKu(c),Death-Stroke	20.00
9 JKu(c),Gravedigger-R.I.P.	20.00
10 JKu(c),Crossroads	20.00
11 JKu(c),Berkstaten	15.00
12 JKu(c),Where Is Gravedigger?.	15.00

13 JKu(c),Project Gravedigger -
Plus One 15.00
14 JKu(c),The Swirling
Sands of Death 15.00
15 JKu(c),The Man With the
Opened Eye 15.00
16 JKu(c),Hide and Seek The Spy 15.00
17 JKu(c),The River of Death 15.00
18 JKu(c),The Amiens Assault. . . . 15.00
19 JKu(c),An Angel Named Marie . 15.00
20 JKu(c),Cry:Jerico 15.00
21 JKu(c),Home-Is Where
The Hell Is 15.00
22 JKu(c),Blackout On
The Boardwalk 15.00
23 JKu(c),Mission: Six Feet Under 15.00
24 JKu&DG(c),The Presidential
Peril 15.00
25 GE(c),Save the President. 15.00
26 March, 1980 . . . . 15.00

METAL MEN
1965–78
[1st Regular Series]
1 RA,I:Missile Men. 1,200.00
2 RA,Robot of Terror. 400.00
3 RA,Moon's Invisible Army 275.00
4 RA,Bracelet of Doomed Hero . 275.00
5 RA,Menace of the Mammoth
Robots 275.00
6 RA,I:Gas Gang 175.00
7 RA,V:Solar Brain 150.00
8 RA,Playground of Terror 150.00
9 RA,A:Billy. 150.00
10 RA,A:Gas Gang 150.00
11 RA,The Floating Furies. 150.00
12 RA,A:Missle Men 125.00
13 RA,I:Nameless 125.00
14 RA,A:Chemo 125.00
15 RA,V:B.O.L.T.S. 125.00
16 RA,Robots for Sale 125.00
17 JKu(c),RA,V:Bl.Widow Robot . 125.00
18 JKu(c),RA 125.00
19 RA,V:Man-Horse of Hades . . . 125.00
20 RA,V:Dr.Yes 125.00
21 RA,C:Batman & Robin,Flash
Wonder Woman. 100.00
22 RA,A:Chemo. 100.00
23 RA,A:Sizzler 100.00
24 RA,V:Balloonman 100.00
25 RA,V:Chemo 100.00
26 RA,V:Metal Mods 100.00
27 RA,O:Metal Men,rtd 125.00
28 RA,You Can't Trust a Robot . . 100.00

Metal Men#15
© DC Comics, Inc.

29 RA,V:Robot Eater 100.00
30 RA,GK,in the Forbidden Zone 100.00
31 RA,GK,School for Robots. 75.00
32 RA,Robot Amazon Blues 75.00
33 MS,The Hunted Metal Men. . . . 75.00
34 MS,Death Comes Calling 75.00
35 MS,Danger–Doom Dummies . . 75.00
36 MS,The Cruel Clowns. 75.00
37 MS,To walk among Men 75.00
38 MS,Witch Hunt–1979 . . . . 75.00
39 MS,Beauty of the Beast 75.00
40 MS,Destroy Doc Magnus 75.00
41 MS,Requiem for a Robot(1970) 75.00
1973–78
42 RA,reprint 25.00
43 RA,reprint 25.00
44 RA,reprint,V:Missile Men 25.00
45 WS 25.00
46 WS,V:Chemo 25.00
47 WS,V:Plutonium Man 25.00
48 WS,A:Eclipso 30.00
49 WS,A:Eclipso 30.00
50 WS,JSa 20.00
51 JSn,V:Vox 20.00
52 JSn,V:Brain Children. 20.00
53 JA(c),V:Brain Children 20.00
54 JSn,A:Green Lantern 20.00
55 JSn,A:Green Lantern 20.00
56 JSn,V:Inheritor 20.00
[Limited Series], 1993–94
1 DJu,BBr,Foil(c). 5.00
2 DJu,BBr,O:Metal Men 3.00
3 DJu,BBr,V:Missile Men 3.00
4 DJu,BBr,final issue. 3.00
Aug., 2007
1 (of 8) Le Cabinet Noir 3.00
2 Magnus attemps a rescue 3.00
3 Magnus & Robot Renegades . . 3.00
4 Second Doctor Magnus 3.00
5 . . . . 3.00
6 Terrors of Oolong Island 3.00
7 Robot Renegades return 3.00
8 conclusion 3.00

METAMORPHO
July-Aug., 1965
[Regular Series]
1 A:Kurt Vornok. 300.00
2 Terror from the Telstar 150.00
3 Who stole the USA 150.00
4 V:Cha-Cha Chaves 100.00
5 V:Bulark 100.00
6 JO,SMo 100.00
7 thru 9 . . . . @75.00
10 I:Element Girl 100.00
11 thru 17 March-April, 1968 . . . @75.00
[Mini-Series], 1993
1 GN,V:The Orb of Ra 2.50
2 GN,A:Metamorpho's Son. 2.50
3 GN,V:Elemental Man 2.50
4 GN,final Issue 2.50

METAMORPHO YEAR ONE
Oct., 2007
1 thru 6 DJu, O:Metamorpho . . @3.00

METROPOLIS S.C.U.
Nov., 1994
1 Special Police unit 2.50
2 Eco-terror in Metropolis 2.50
3 Superman 2.50
4 final issue. 2.50

MICHAEL MOORCOCK'S
MULTIVERSE
DC/Helix, Sept., 1997
1 WS. 2.50
2 thru 12 WS. . . . . @2.50

MIDNIGHT, MASS
DC/Vertigo, April, 2002
1 JRz,F:Adam & Julia. 2.50
2 JRz,a lone farmhouse 2.50
3 JRz,JP 2.50
4 JRz,JP,The Four Sisters,pt.1 . . . . 2.50
5 JRz,JP,The Four Sisters,pt.2 . . . . 2.50
6 JRz,JP,The Four Sisters,pt.3 . . . . 2.50
7 JRz,JP,3 uninvited visitors 2.50
8 JRz,Secrets 2.50

MIDNIGHT, MASS:
HERE THERE BE
MONSTERS
DC/Vertigo, Jan. 2004
1 (of 6) 3.00
2 thru 6 . . . . @3.00

Millennium #4
© DC Comics Inc.

MILLENNIUM
Jan., 1988
1 JSa,SEt, The Plan 3.00
2 JSa,SEt, The Chosen 2.50
3 JSa,SEt, Reagen/Manhunters . . 2.50
4 JSa,SEt, Mark Shaw/Batman . . 2.50
5 JSa,SEt, The Chosen 2.50
6 JSa,SEt, Superman 2.50
7 JSa,SEt, Boster Gold. 2.50
8 JSa,SEt,I:New Guardians 2.50

MILLENNIUM FEVER
1995–96
1 Young Love 2.50
2 Nightmares Worsen. 2.50
3 Worst Nightmare 2.50
4 . . . . 2.50

MINX, THE
DC/Vertigo, Aug., 1998
1 PrM,SeP,The Chosen, pt.1 . . . . . 3.00
2 PrM,SeP,The Chosen, pt.2 . . . . . 2.50
3 PrM,SeP,The Chosen, pt.3 . . . . . 2.50
4 PrM,SeP,Monkey Quartet,pt.1 . . 2.50
5 PrM,SeP,Monkey Quartet,pt.2 . . 2.50
6 PrM,SeP,Monkey Quartet,pt.3 . . 2.50
7 PrM,SeP,Monkey Quartet,pt.4 . . 2.50
8 PrM,SeP,final issue 2.50

DC COMICS

MISS BEVERLY HILLS
OF HOLLYWOOD
1949–50

1 Alan Ladd	900.00
2 William Holdun	650.00
3	550.00
4 Betty Hutton	550.00
5 Bob Hope	550.00
6 Lucile Ball	500.00
7	500.00
8 Ronald Reagan	600.00
9 Wendell Corey	500.00

MISS MELODY LANE
OF BROADWAY
1950

1	900.00
2 Sid Caesar	550.00
3 Ed Sullivan	550.00

MISTER E
1991

1 (From Books of Magic)	2.50
2 A:The Shadower	2.50
3 A:The Shadower	2.50
4 A:Tim Hunter, Dr. Fate, Phantom Stranger, final issue	2.50

MISTER MIRACLE
1971–78

1 JK,I:Mr.Miracle	150.00
2 JK,I:Granny Goodness	75.00
3 JK,Paraniod Pill	75.00
4 JK,I:Barda, 52-page	80.00
5 JK,I:Vermin Vundabar, 52-page	80.00
6 JK,I:Female Furies, 52-page	80.00
7 JK,V:Kanto, 52-page	80.00
8 JK,V:Lump, 52-page	80.00
9 JK,O:Mr.Miracle,C:Darkseid	30.00
10 JK,A:Female Furies	30.00
11 JK,V:Doctor Bedlum	30.00
12 JK,Mystivac	30.00
13 JK,The Dictator's Dungeon	30.00
14 JK,I:Madame Evil Eye	30.00
15 JK,O:Shilo Norman	30.00
16 JK,F:Shilo Norman	30.00
17 JK,Murder Lodge	30.00
18 JK,W:Mr.Miracle & Barda	30.00
19 MR,NA,DG,TA,JRu,AM	30.00
20 MR,Eclipse	15.00
21 MR,Command Performance	15.00
22 MR, Midnight of the Gods	15.00
23 MG, As Ethos is my Judge	15.00
24 MG,RH,Double-Bind	15.00
25 MG,RH,Doom Unto Others	15.00
Spec.#1 SR (1987)	3.50

[2nd Series], 1989–91

1 IG,O:Mister Miracle	3.00
2 IG	2.50
3 IG,A:Highfather,Forever People	2.50
4 IG,A:The Dark,Forever People	2.50
5 IG,V:TheDark,A:Forever People	2.50
6 A:G.L. Gnort	2.50
7 A:Blue Beetle,Booster Gold	2.50
8 RM,A:Blue Beetle,Booster Gold	2.50
9 I:Maxi-Man	2.50
10 V:Maxi-Man	2.50
11 What? And Give up Show Biz?	2.50
12 Head of the Clash	2.50
13 Manga Khan Saga begins, A:L-Ron,A:Lobo	3.00
14 A:Lobo	2.50
15 Manga Khan cont	2.50
16 MangaKhan cont.,JLA#39tie-in	2.50
17 On Apokolips,A:Darkseid	2.50
18 On Apokolips	2.50
19 Return to Earth, contd from JLA#42	2.50
20 IG,Oberon	2.50

21 Return of Shilo	2.50
22 New Mr.Miracle revealed	2.50
23 Secrets of the 2 Mr. Miracles revealed, A:Mother Box	2.50
24 Nightmare	2.50
25 Big Barda and Friends	2.50
26 Monster Party,pt.1	2.50
27 Monster Party,pt.2, A:Justice League	2.50
28 final issue	2.50

[3rd Series], 1996

1 JK, new mythology	2.50
2 V:Justice League	2.50
2 How can Scott Free save Big Barda	2.50
3 accepts his powers	2.50
4 corruption throughout the cosmos	2.50
5 SCr	2.50
6 SCr	2.50
7 SCr,final issue	2.50

MR. DISTRICT
ATTORNEY
Jan.–Feb., 1948

1 The Innocent Forger	1,500.00
2 The Richest Man In Prison	700.00
3 The Honest Convicts	500.00
4 The Merchant of Death	500.00
5 The Booby-Trap Killer	500.00
6 The D.A. Meets Scotland Yard	350.00
7 The People vs. Killer Kane	350.00
8 The Rise and Fall of 'Lucky' Lynn	350.00
9 The Case of the Living Counterfeit	350.00
10 The D.A. Takes a Vacation	250.00
11 The Game That Has No Winners	250.00
12 Fake Accident Racket	250.00
13 The Execution of Caesar Larsen	250.00
14 The Innocent Man In Murderers' Row	250.00
15 Prison Train	250.00
16 The Wire Tap Crimes	250.00
17 The Bachelor of Crime	250.00
18 The Case of the Twelve O'Clock Killer	250.00
19 The Four King's Of Crime	250.00
20 You Catch a Killer	250.00
21 I Was A Killer's Bodyguard	175.00
22 The Marksman of Crime	175.00
23 Diary of a Criminal	175.00
24 The Killer In The Iron Mask	175.00

Mr. District Attorney #1
© DC Comics, Inc.

25 I Hired My Killer	175.00
26 The Case of the Wanted Criminals	175.00
27 The Case of the Secret Six	175.00
28 Beware the Bogus Beggars	175.00
29 The Crimes of Mr. Jumbo	175.00
30 Man of a Thousand Faces	175.00
31 The Hot Money Gang	175.00
32 The Case o/t Bad Luck Clues	175.00
33 A Crime Is Born	175.00
34 The Amazing Crimes of Mr. X	175.00
35 This Crime For Hire	175.00
36 The Chameleon of Crime	175.00
37 Miss Miller's Big Case	175.00
38 The Puzzle Shop For Crime	175.00
39 Man Who Killed Daredevils	175.00
40 The Human Vultures	175.00
41 The Great Token Take	175.00
42 Super-Market Sleuth	175.00
43 Hotel Detective	175.00
44 S.S. Justice,B:Comics Code	150.00
45 Miss Miller, Widow	150.00
46 Mr. District Attorney, Public Defender	150.00
47 The Missing Persons Racket	150.00
48 Manhunt With the Mounties	150.00
49 The TV Dragnet	150.00
50 The Case of Frank Bragan, Little Shot	150.00
51 The Big Heist	150.00
52 Crooked Wheels of Fortune	150.00
53 The Courtroom Patrol	150.00
54 The Underworld Spy Squad	150.00
55 The Flying Saucer Mystery	150.00
56 The Underworld Oracle	150.00
57 The Underworld Employment Agency	150.00
58 The Great Bomb Scare	150.00
59 Great Underworld Spy Plot	150.00
60 The D.A.'s TV Rival	150.00
61 SMo(c),Architect of Crime	150.00
62 A-Bombs For Sale	150.00
63 The Flying Prison	150.00
64 SMo(c),The Underworld Treasure Hunt	150.00
65 SMo(c),World Wide Dragnet	150.00
66 SMo(c),The Secret of the D.A.'s Diary	150.00
67 Jan.–Feb., 1959	150.00

MNEMOVORE
DC/Vertigo, Apr., 2005

1 thru 5	@3.00

MOBFIRE
1994–95

1 WaP,Gangsters in London	2.50
2 WaP,	2.50
3 WaP,The Bocor	2.50
4 WaP,V:Bocor	2.50
5 WaP,Voice in My Head	2.50
6 WaP,Genetic Babies, final issue	2.50

MODESTY BLAISE

1 DG,V:Gabriel	5.00
2 DG,V:Gabriel	5.00

MONOLITH, THE
Feb. 2004

1 JP(s),56-pg	3.50
2 JP(s)	3.00
3 JP(s),Heart of Stone	3.00
4 JP(s),Last Rites,pt.1	3.00
5 JP(s),Last Rites,pt.2	3.00
6 JP(s),Friendly Fire,pt.1	3.00
7 JP(s),Friendly Fire,pt.2	3.00
8 JP(s),Friendly Fire,pt.3	3.00
9 JP(s),gangsters retaliate	3.00
10 JP(s)	3.00
11 JP(s),Slavers	3.00
12 JP(s),finale	3.00

All comics prices listed are for *Near Mint* condition.

MOONSHADOW
DC/Vertigo, 1994–95
1 JMD(s),JMu,rep. 2.50
2 thru 4 JMD . . . . @2.50
5 fully painted 2.50
6 . . . . 2.50
7 F:Shady Lady. 2.50
8 Rep. Search for Ira 2.50
9 JMD,JMu,A:Tittletat Twins 2.50
10 JMD,JMu,Interplanetary
   Prostitutes 2.50
11 JMu,Ira's life story. 2.50
12 Rep. w/6pg new material 3.50

MORE FUN COMICS
See: NEW FUN COMICS

MOVIE COMICS
1939
1 Gunga Din. 6,000.00
2 Stagecoach. 4,000.00
3 East Side of Heaven. 3,000.00
4 Captain Fury,B:Oregon Trail . 2,400.00
5 Man in the Iron Mask 2,500.00
6 Phantom Creeps. 3,200.00

Ms. Tree Quarterly #2
© DC Comics, Inc.

MS. TREE QUARTERLY
1990
1 MGr,A:Batman 5.00
2 A:Butcher 4.00
3 A:Butcher 4.00
4 Paper Midnight. 4.50
5 Murder/Rape Investigation. 4.50
6 Gothic House. 4.50
7 The Family Way. 4.50
8 CI,FMc,Ms Tree Pregnant(c),
   B.U. King Faraday. 4.50
9 Child Kidnapped 4.50
10 V:International Mob. 4.00

MUCHA LUCHA
April 2003
1 (of 3) 2.50
2 It's All Buena 2.50
3 Flea loses match 2.50

MUKTUK WOLFSBREATH:
HARD-BOILED SHAMAN
DC/Vertigo, June, 1998
1 (of 3) TLa,SvP,Lady Shaman. . . . 2.50
2 . . . . 2.50
3 TLa, SvP, concl. 2.50

MUTT AND JEFF
1939
1 . . . . 2,200.00
2 . . . . 1,000.00
3 Bucking Broncos 700.00
4 and 5 . . . . @600.00
6 thru 10 . . . . @350.00
11 thru 20 . . . . @250.00
21 thru 30. . . . . @225.00
31 thru 50. . . . . @200.00
51 thru 70. . . . . @150.00
71 thru 80. . . . . @125.00
81 thru 99. . . . . @100.00
100 . . . . 125.00
101 thru 103. . . . . @100.00
104 thru 148. . . . . @100.00

MY GREATEST
ADVENTURE
Jan.–Feb., 1955
1 LSt,I Was King Of
   Danger Island. 3,000.00
2 My Million Dollar Dive. 1,200.00
3 I Found Captain
   Kidd's Treasure 900.00
4 I Had A Date With Doom 900.00
5 I Escaped From Castle Morte . 800.00
6 I Had To Spend A Million 800.00
7 I Was A Prisoner On Island X . 600.00
8 The Day They Stole My Face . 600.00
9 I Walked Through The Doors
   of Destiny 600.00
10 We Found A World Of
   Tiny Cavemen 600.00
11 LSt(c),My Friend, Madcap
   Manning. 500.00
12 MMe(c),I Hunted Big Game
   in Outer Space. 500.00
13 LSt(c),I Hunted Goliath
   The Robot 500.00
14 LSt,I Had the Midas
   Touch of Gold 500.00
15 JK, I Hunted the Worlds
   Wildest Animals. 500.00
16 JK,I Died a Thousand Times . 500.00
17 JK,I Doomed the World 500.00
18 JK(c),We Discovered The
   Edge of the World 700.00
19 I Caught Earth's
   Strangest Criminal. 400.00
20 JK,I Was Big-Game
   on Neptune 400.00
21 JK,We Were Doomed By
   The Metal-Eating Monster. . . 400.00
22 I Was Trapped In The
   Magic Mountains 375.00
23 I Was A Captive In
   Space Prison 375.00
24 NC(c),I Was The Robinson
   Crusoe of Space 375.00
25 I Led Earth's Strangest
   Safari! 375.00
26 NC(c),We Battled The
   Sand Creature 375.00
27 I Was the Earth's First Exile . . 375.00
28 I Stalked the Camouflage
   Creatures. 375.00
29 I Tracked the
   Forbidden Powers 300.00
30 We Cruised Into the
   Supernatural!. 300.00
31 I Was A Modern Hercules. . . . 250.00
32 We Were Trapped In A Freak
   Valley! 250.00
33 I Was Pursued by
   the Elements 250.00
34 DD,We Unleashed The Cloud
   Creatures. 250.00
35 I Solved the Mystery of
   Volcano Valley 250.00

36 I Was Bewitched
   By Lady Doom. 250.00
37 DD&SMo(c),I Hunted the
   Legendary Creatures! 250.00
38 DD&SMo(c),I Was the Slave
   of the Dream-Master 250.00
39 DD&SMo(c),We were Trapped
   in the Valley of no Return . . . 250.00
40 We Battled the StormCreature 250.00
41 DD&SMo(c),I Was Tried
   by a Robot Court. 200.00
42 DD&SMo(c),My Brother
   Was a Robot 200.00
43 DD&SMo(c),I Fought the
   Sonar Creatures 200.00
44 DD&SMo(c),We Fought the
   Beasts of Petrified Island . . . 200.00
45 DD&SMo(c),We Battled the
   Black Narwahl 200.00
46 DD&SMo(c),We Were Prisoners
   of the Sundial of Doom 200.00
47 We Became Partners of the
   Beast Brigade 200.00
48 DD&SMo(c),I Was Marooned
   On Earth 200.00
49 DD&SMo(c),I Was An Ally
   Of A Criminal Creature 200.00
50 DD&SMo(c),I Fought the
   Idol King 200.00
51 DD&SMo(c),We Unleashed
   the Demon of the Dungeon. . 175.00
52 DD&SMo(c),I Was A
   Stand-In For an Alien. 175.00
53 DD&SMo(c),I, Creature Slayer 175.00
54 I Was Cursed With
   an Alien Pal 175.00
55 DD&SMo(c),I Became The
   Wonder-Man of Space. 175.00
56 DD&SMo(c),My Brother-The
   Alien. 175.00
57 DD&SMo(c),Don't Touch Me
   Or You'll Die. 175.00
58 DD&SMo(c),ATh,I was Trapped
   in the Land of L'Oz 200.00
59 DD&SMo(c),Listen Earth-I
   Am Still Alive 200.00
60 DD&SMo(c),ATh,I Lived in
   Two Worlds 200.00
61 DD&SMo(c),ATh,I Battled For
   the Doom-Stone 200.00
62 DD&SMo(c),I Fought For
   An Alien Enemy 150.00
63 DD&SMo(c),We Braved the
   Trail of the Ancient Warrior . . 150.00

My Greatest Adventure #57
© DC Comics Inc.

DC COMICS

64 DD&SMo(c),They Crowned My
   Fiance Their King! 150.00
65 DD&SMo(c),I Lost the Life
   or Death Secret 150.00
66 DD&SMo(c),I Dueled with
   the Super Spirits 150.00
67 I Protected the Idols
   of Idoro! 150.00
68 DD&SMo(c),My Deadly Island
   of Space 150.00
69 DD&SMo(c),I Was A Courier
   From the Past 150.00
70 DD&SMo(c),We Tracked the
   Fabled Fish-Man! 150.00
71 We Dared to open the Door
   of Danger Dungeon 150.00
72 The Haunted Beach 150.00
73 I Defeiller Mountain 150.00
74 GC(c),We Were Challenged
   By The River Spirit 150.00
75 GC(c),Castaway Cave-Men
   of 1950 . . . . 150.00
76 MMe(c),We Battled the
   Micro-Monster 150.00
77 ATh,We Found the Super-
   Tribes of Tomorrow 150.00
78 Destination-'Dead Man's Alley' 150.00
79 Countdown in Dinosaur Valley 125.00
80 BP,I:Doom Patrol 1,000.00
81 BP,ATh,I:Dr. Janus 350.00
82 BP,F:Doom Patrol 300.00
83 BP,F:Doom Patrol 300.00
84 BP,V:General Immortus 300.00
85 BP,ATh,F:Doom Patrol 300.00
Becomes:

DOOM PATROL

March, 1964

86 BP,I:Brogherhood of Evil 200.00
87 BP,O:Negative Man 125.00
88 BP,O:Chief 125.00
89 BP,I:Animal-Veg.-MineralMan . 125.00
90 BP,A:Brotherhood of Evil 125.00
91 BP,I:Manto, Gargvax 125.00
92 BP,I:Dr.Tyme, A:Mento 125.00
93 BP,A:Brotherhood of Evil 125.00
94 BP,I:Dr.Radich, The Claw 125.00
95 BP,A:Animal-Vegetable
   -Mineral Man 125.00
96 MMe(c),A:General Immortus,
   Brotherhood of Evil 125.00
97 BP,A:General Immortus,
   Brotherhood of Evil 125.00
98 BP,I:Mr.103 . . . . 125.00
99 I:Beast Boy 120.00
100 BP,O:Beast Boy,Robotman . . 130.00
101 BP,A:Beast Boy 75.00
102 BP,A:Beast Boy,Challengers
   of the Unknown 70.00
103 BP,A:Beast Boy 70.00
104 BP,W:Elasti-Girl,Mento,
   C:JLA,Teen Titans 70.00
105 BP,A:Beast Boy 70.00
106 BP,O:Negative Man 70.00
107 BP,A:Beast Boy, I:Dr.Death . . . 70.00
108 BP,A:Brotherhood of Evil 70.00
109 BP,I:Mandred 70.00
110 BP,A:Garguax,Mandred,
   Brotherhood of Evil 50.00
111 BP,I:Zarox-13,A:Brotherhood
   of Evil 50.00
112 BP,O:Beast Boy,Madame
   Rouge 50.00
113 BP,A:Beast Boy,Mento 50.00
114 BP,A:Beast Boy 50.00
115 BP,A:Beast Boy 50.00
116 BP,A:Madame Rouge 50.00
117 BP,I:Black Vulture 50.00
118 BP,A:Beast Boy 50.00
119 BP,A:Madam Rouge 50.00
120 I:Wrecker 50.00
121 JO,D:Doom Patrol 150.00
122 rep.Doom Patrol #89 . . . . 15.00

Doom Patrol #92
© *DC Comics, Inc.*

123 rep.Doom Patrol #95 . . . . 15.00
124 rep.Doom Patrol #90 . . . . 15.00

[2nd Series]
See: DOOM PATROL

MY NAME IS CHAOS

1992

1 JRy,Song Laid Waste to Earth . . . 5.00
2 JRy,Colonization of Mars 5.00
3 JRy,Search for Eternal Beings . . . 5.00
4 JRy,final issue 5.00

MY NAME IS HOLOCAUST

DC/Milestone, 1995

[Mini-Series]

1 F:Holocaust (Blood Syndicate) . . 2.50
2 V:Cantano 2.50
3 A:Blood Syndicate 2.50

MYSTERY IN SPACE

April-May, 1951

1 CI&FrG(c),FF,B:Knights of the
   Galaxy,Nine Worlds to
   Conquer 6,000.00
2 CI(c),MA,A:Knights of the
   Galaxy, Jesse James-
   Highwayman of Space 2,500.00
3 CI(c),A:Knights of the
   Galaxy, Duel of the Planets 2,000.00
4 CI(c),S&K,MA,A:Knights of the
   Galaxy, Master of Doom . . . 1,700.00
5 CI(c),A:Knights of the Galaxy,
   Outcast of the Lost World . . 1,700.00
6 CI(c),A:Knights of the Galaxy,
   The Day the World Melted . 1,200.00
7 GK(c),ATh,A:Knights of the Galaxy,
   Challenge o/t Robot Knight 1,200.00
8 MA,It's a Women's World . . . 1,200.00
9 MA(c),The Seven Wonders
   of Space 1,000.00
10 MA(c),The Last Time I
   Saw Earth 1,000.00
11 GK(c),Unknown Spaceman . . . 800.00
12 MA,The Sword in the Sky 800.00
13 MA(c),MD,Signboard
   in Space 800.00
14 MA,GK(c),Hollywood
   in Space 800.00
15 MA(c),Doom from Station X . 800.00
16 MA(c),Honeymoon in Space . . 800.00
17 MA(c),The Last Mile of
   Space 800.00

18 MA(c),GK,Chain Gang
   of Space 800.00
19 MA(c),The Great
   Space-Train Robbery 800.00
20 MA(c),The Man in the
   Martian Mask 750.00
21 MA(c),Interplanetary
   Merry- Go-Round 750.00
22 MA(c),The Square Earth 750.00
23 MA(c),Monkey-Rocket
   to Mars 750.00
24 MA(c),A:Space Cabby,
   Hitchhiker of Space 750.00
25 MA(c),Station Mars on the Air. 700.00
26 GK(c),Earth is the Target 700.00
27 The Human Fishbowl 700.00
28 The Radio Planet 700.00
29 GK(c),Space-Enemy
   Number One 700.00
30 GK(c),The Impossible
   World Named Earth 700.00
31 GK(c),The Day the Earth
   Split in Two 500.00
32 GK(c),Riddle of the
   Vanishing Earthmen 500.00
33 The Wooden World War 500.00
34 GK(c),The Man Who
   Moved the World 500.00
35 The Counterfeit Earth 500.00
36 GK(c),Secret of the
   Moon Sphinx 500.00
37 GK(c),Secret of the
   Masked Martians 500.00
38 GK(c),The Canals of Earth . . . 500.00
39 GK(c),Sorcerers of Space 500.00
40 GK(c),Riddle of the
   Runaway Earth 500.00
41 GK(c),The Miser of Space . . . 450.00
42 GK(c),The Secret of the
   Skyscraper Spaceship 450.00
43 GK(c),Invaders From the
   Space Satellites 450.00
44 GK(c),Amazing Space Flight
   of North America 450.00
45 GK(c),MA,Flying Saucers
   Over Mars 450.00
46 GK(c),MA,Mystery of the
   Moon Sniper 450.00
47 GK(c),MA,Interplanetary Tug
   of War 450.00
48 GK(c),MA,Secret of the
   Scarecrow World 450.00
49 GK(c),The Sky-High Man 450.00
50 GK(c),The Runaway
   Space-Train 450.00
51 GK(c),MA,Battle of the
   Moon Monsters 450.00
52 GK(c),MSy,Mirror Menace
   of Mars 450.00
53 GK(c),B:Adam Strange stories,
   Menace o/t Robot Raiders . 4,000.00
54 GK(c),Invaders of the
   Underground World 1,000.00
55 GK(c),The Beast From
   the Runaway World 900.00
56 GK(c),The Menace of
   the Super-Atom 500.00
57 GK(c),Mystery of the
   Giant Footsteps 500.00
58 GK(c),Chariot in the Sky . . . 500.00
59 GK(c),The Duel of the
   Two Adam Stranges 500.00
60 GK(c),The Attack of the
   Tentacle World 500.00
61 CI&MA(c),Threat of the
   Tornado Tyrant 400.00
62 CI&MA(c),The Beast with
   the Sizzling Blue Eyes 400.00
63 The Weapon that
   Swallowed Men 400.00
64 The Radioactive Menace 400.00

Mystery in Space #55
© DC Comics, Inc.

65 Mechanical Masters of
  Rann 400.00
66 Space-Island of Peril. 400.00
67 Challenge of the
  Giant Fireflies 400.00
68 CI&MA(c),Fadeaway Doom . . 400.00
69 CI&MA(c),Menace of the
  Aqua-Ray Weapon 400.00
70 CI&MA(c),Vengeance of
  the Dust Devil 400.00
71 CI&MA(c),The Challenge of
  the Crystal Conquerors 400.00
72 The Multiple Menace Weapon 300.00
73 CI&MA(c),The Invisible
  Invaders of Rann 300.00
74 CI&MA(c),The Spaceman
  Who Fought Himself 300.00
75 CI&MA(c),The Planet That
  Came to a Standstill 300.00
76 CI&MA(c),Challenge of
  the Rival Starman 300.00
77 CI&MA(c),Ray-Gun in the Sky 300.00
78 CI&MA(c),Shadow People
  of the Eclipse. 300.00
79 CI&MA(c),The Metal
  Conqueror of Rann 300.00
80 CI&MA(c),The Deadly
  Shadows of Adam Strange . . 300.00
81 CI&MA(c),The Cloud-Creature
  That Menaced Two Worlds . . 200.00
82 CI&MA(c),World War on
  Earth and Rann 200.00
83 CI&MA(c),The Emotion-Master
  of Space 200.00
84 CI&MA(c),The Powerless
  Weapons of Adam Strange . . 200.00
85 CI&MA(c),Riddle of the
  Runaway Rockets 200.00
86 CI&MA(c),Attack of the
  Underworld Giants. 200.00
87 MA(c),The Super-Brain of
  Adam Strange,B:Hawkman . . 500.00
88 CI&MA(c),The Robot Wraith
  of Rann 450.00
89 MA(c),Siren o/t Space Ark . . . 400.00
90 CI&MA(c),Planets and
  Peril, E:Hawkman 400.00
91 CI&MA(c),Puzzle of
  the Perilous Prisons 150.00
92 DD&SMo(c),The Alien Invasion
  From Earth,B:Space Ranger . 150.00
93 DD&SMo(c),The Convict
  Twins of Space 150.00
94 DD&SMo(c),The Adam
  Strange Story. 150.00

95 The Hydra-Head From
  Outer Space 150.00
96 The Coins That Doomed
  Two Planets. 150.00
97 The Day Adam Strange
  Vanished 150.00
98 The Wizard of the Cosmos . . . 150.00
99 DD&SMo(c),The World-
  Destroyer From Space 150.00
100 DD&SMo(c),GK,The Death
  of Alanna 150.00
101 GK(c),The Valley of
  1,000 Dooms 150.00
102 GK,The Robot World of Rann 150.00
103 The Billion-Dollar Time-
  Capsule(Space Ranger),I:Ultra
  the Multi-Agent 150.00
104 thru 109. . . . . @100.00
110 Series ends, Sept., 1966 . . . 100.00
[Series Revived], Sept., 1980
111 JAp,SD,MR,DSp. 12.00
112 JAp,TS,JKu(c). 12.00
113 JKu(c),MGo. 12.00
114 JKu(c),JCr,SD,DSp 12.00
115 JKu(c),SD,GT,BB 12.00
116 JSn(c),JCr,SD 12.00
117 DN,GT,March, 1981 . . . . 12.00

MYSTERY IN SPACE
Sept., 2006
1 JSn, 48-pg. 4.00
1a variant NA (c). 4.00
2 JSn, Captain Comet 3.00
3 JSn, Hardcore Station 4.00
4 JSn,V:Lady Styx. 4.00
5 JSn,The Weird. 4.00
6 JSn,League of Insect Assassins . 4.00
7 JSn,Captain Comet must die. . . . 4.00
8 JSn,RLm,finale 4.00

MYTHOS:
THE FINAL TOUR
DC/Vertigo, Oct., 1996
1 JNR(s),GyA,PrG,F:Rock Star
  Adam Case 6.00
2 JNR(s),PSj,F:Rock Star Adam
  Case 6.00
3 JNR(s), finale. 6.00

NAMES OF MAGIC, THE
DC/Vertigo, Dec., 2000
1 (of 5) JBo(c),F:Tim Hunter. 10.00
2 thru 5 JBo(c) . . . . @10.00

NATHANIEL DUSK
Feb., 1984
1 GC(p). 2.50
2 thru 4 GC(p). . . . . @2.50

NATHANIEL DUSK II
Oct., 1985
1 thru 4 GC,Jan., 1986 . . . . @2.50

NATIONAL COMICS
1999
1 MWa(s),AAl,F:Flash &
  Mr. Terrific. 2.50

NAZZ, THE
1990–91
1 Michael's Book. 5.50
2 Johnny's Book 5.00
3 Search for Michael Nazareth. . . . 5.00
4 V:Retaliators,final issue 5.00

NEIL GAIMAN'S
NEVERWHERE
DC/Vertigo, June, 2005
1 (of 9) GF 3.00
2 thru 4 novel adaptation . . . . . . @3.00
5 novel adaptation 3.00
6 thru 9 GF . . . . @3.00

NEVADA
DC/Vertigo, March, 1998
1 thru 6 SvG,SL,show girl . . . . . @2.50

NEW ADVENTURES
OF CHARLIE CHAN
1958
1 GK,SGe,Secret of the Phantom
  Bells 1,100.00
2 SGe,Riddle of the Runaway
  Mummy 700.00
3 SGe,Two Lives of Charlie
  Chan 550.00
4 SGe,Case o/t Vanishing Man . 550.00
5 SGe,Monarch of Monaco. 550.00
6 SGe,Trail Across the Sky. 550.00

NEW ADVENTURES
OF SUPERBOY
See: SUPERBOY

NEW BOOK OF COMICS
1937
1 Dr.Occult. 30,000.00
2 Dr.Occult. 17,000.00

NEW COMICS
1935
1 . . . . 37,000.00
2 . . . . 15,000.00
3 thru 6. . . . . @10,000.00
7 thru 11 . . . . @8,000.00
Becomes:

NEW ADVENTURE
COMICS
Jan., 1937
12 S&S 8,000.00
13 thru 20 . . . . @7,500.00
21 . . . . 6,200.00
22 thru 31 . . . . @4,200.00
Becomes:

ADVENTURE COMICS

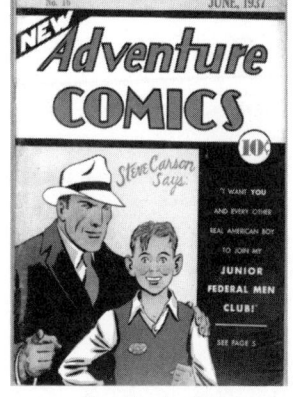

New Adventure #16
© DC Comics Inc.

NEW FUN COMICS
Feb., 1935
1 B:Oswald the Rabbit,
  Jack Woods 75,000.00
2 . . . . 38,000.00
3 . . . . 20,000.00
4 . . . . 20,000.00
5 . . . . 20,000.00
6 S&S,B:Dr.Occult,
  Henri Duval. 40,000.00
Becomes:

MORE FUN COMICS
Jan., 1936
7 S&S,WK 17,000.00
8 S&S,WK 15,000.00
9 S&S,E:Henri Duval 18,000.00
10 S&S 10,000.00
11 S&S,B:Calling all Girls . . . 10,000.00
12 S&S 10,000.00
13 S&S 10,000.00
14 S&S,Color,Dr.Occult. . . . 20,000.00
15 S&S 10,000.00
16 S&S,Christmas(c) 10,000.00
17 S&S,CF 9,000.00
18 S&S,CF 3,500.00
19 S&S,CF 3,500.00
20 HcK,S&S 3,500.00
21 S&S,CF 3,800.00
22 S&S,CF 3,800.00
23 S&S,CF 3,800.00
24 S&S,CF 3,800.00
25 S&S,CF 3,500.00
26 S&S,CF 3,200.00
27 S&S,CF 3,200.00
28 S&S,CF 3,000.00
29 S&S,CF 3,000.00
30 S&S 3,000.00
31 S&S,CF 3,200.00
32 S&S,E:Dr. Occult 3,000.00
33 S&S,BKa 3,000.00
34 S&S,BKa 3,000.00
35 S&S,BKa,CF(c) 3,000.00
36 B:Masked Ranger 3,000.00
37 thru 40 . . . . @3,500.00
41 E:Masked Ranger 4,200.00
42 thru 50 . . . . @3,000.00
51 I:The Spectre 8,000.00
52 O:The Spectre,pt.1,
  E:Wing Brady 120,000.00
53 O:The Spectre,pt.2,
  B:Capt.Desmo 65,000.00
54 E:King Carter,Spectre(c) . . 28,000.00
55 I:Dr.Fate,E:Bulldog Martin,
  Spectre(c). 29,000.00
56 B:Congo Bill,Dr.Fate(c) . . . 13,000.00
57 Spectre(c) 8,000.00
58 Spectre(c) 8,000.00
59 A:Spectre 8,000.00
60 Spectre(c) 8,000.00
61 Spectre(c) 8,000.00
62 Spectre(c) 6,000.00
63 Spectre(c),E:St.Bob Neal. . . 6,000.00
64 Spectre(c),B:Lance Larkin . . 6,000.00
65 Spectre(c) 6,000.00
66 Spectre(c) 6,000.00
67 Spectre(c),O:Dr. Fate,
  E:Congo Bill,Biff Bronson . 14,000.00
68 Dr.Fate(c),B:Clip Carson . . . 5,000.00
69 Dr.Fate(c) 5,000.00
70 Dr.Fate(c),E:Lance Larkin . . 5,000.00
71 Dr.Fate(c),I:Johnny Quick . 10,000.00
72 Dr. Fate has Smaller Helmet,
  E:Sgt. Carey,Sgt.O'Malley . 5,000.00
73 Dr.Fate(c),I:Aquaman,Green
  Arrow,Speedy 27,000.00
74 Dr.Fate(c),A:Aquaman 5,500.00
75 Dr.Fate(c). 5,000.00
76 Dr.Fate(c),MMe,E:Clip Carson,
  B:Johnny Quick 5,000.00
77 MMe,Green Arrow(c) 5,000.00
78 MMe,Green Arrow(c) 5,000.00

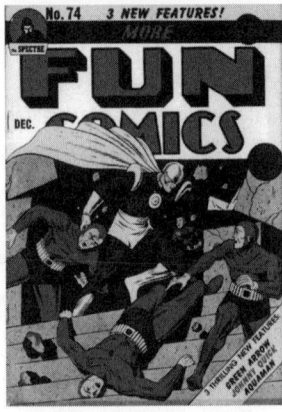

More Fun #74 © DC Comics, Inc.

79 MMe,Green Arrow(c) 5,000.00
80 MMe,Green Arrow(c) 3,500.00
81 MMe,Green Arrow(c) 4,000.00
82 MMe,Green Arrow(c) 4,000.00
83 MMe,Green Arrow(c) 4,000.00
84 MMe,Green Arrow(c) 5,000.00
85 MMe,Green Arrow(c) 2,500.00
86 MMe. 2,500.00
87 MMe,E:Radio Squad 2,500.00
88 MMe,Green Arrow(c) 2,500.00
89 MMe,O:Gr.Arrow&Speedy . . 2,600.00
90 MMe,Green Arrow(c) 3,500.00
91 MMe,Green Arrow(c) 2,000.00
92 MMe,Green Arrow(c) 2,000.00
93 MMe,B:Dover & Clover 3,000.00
94 MMe,Green Arrow(c) 1,500.00
95 MMe,Green Arrow(c) 1,500.00
96 MMe,Green Arrow(c) 1,500.00
97 MMe,JKu,E:Johnny Quick . . 1,700.00
98 E:Dr. Fate 2,000.00
99 Green Arrow(c) 1,800.00
100 Anniversary Issue 1,800.00
101 O&I:Superboy,
  E:The Spectre. 16,000.00
102 A:Superboy 2,500.00
103 A:Superboy 1,800.00
104 Superboy(c) 1,500.00
105 Superboy(c) 1,500.00
106 Superboy(c) 1,500.00
107 E:Superboy 1,500.00
108 A:Genius Jones,Genius
  Meets Genius 500.00
109 A:Genius Jones, The
  Disappearing Deposits 500.00
110 A:Genius Jones, Birds,
  Brains and Burglary. 500.00
111 A:Genius Jones, Jeepers
  Creepers 500.00
112 A:Genius Jones, The
  Tell-Tale Tornado 500.00
113 A:Genius Jones, Clocks
  and Shocks 500.00
114 A:Genius Jones, The
  Milky Way 500.00
115 A:Genius Jones,Foolish
  Questions 500.00
116 A:Genius Jones,Palette
  For Plunder 500.00
117 A:Genius Jones,Battle of
  the Pretzel Benders. 500.00
118 A:Genius Jones,The
  Sinister Siren 500.00
119 A:Genius Jones,A
  Perpetual Jackpot 500.00
120 A:Genius Jones,The Man
  in the Moon 500.00

121 A:Genius Jones,The
  Mayor Goes Haywire. 500.00
122 A:Genius Jones,When Thug-
  Hood Was In Floor 500.00
123 A:Genius Jones,Hi Diddle Diddle,
  the Cat and the Fiddle. 500.00
124 A:Genius Jones,
  The Zany Zoo 500.00
125 Genius Jones,
  Impossible But True 1,500.00
126 A:Genius Jones,The Case
  of the Gravy Spots. 350.00
127 Nov.–Dec., 1947 . . . . 750.00

NEW GODS, THE
Feb.–March, 1971
1 JK,I:Orion. 150.00
2 JK,O'Deadly Darkseid 100.00
3 JK,Death is the Black Racer . . . 50.00
4 JK,O:Manhunter, rep.. . . . . . . 40.00
5 JK,I:Fastbak & Black Racer. . . . 40.00
6 JK,The Glory Boat 40.00
7 JK,O:Orion. 40.00
8 JK,Death Wish of Terrible Turpin 40.00
9 JK,I:Forager. 40.00
10 JK,Earth–The Domed Dominion 40.00
11 JK,Darkseid and Sons (1972) . . 40.00
12 DN,DA,R:New Gods (1977) . . . 10.00
13 DN,DA,AM(c) 10.00
14 DN,DA,RB&AM(c). 10.00
15 RB,BMc,Apocalypse Child . . . 10.00
16 DN,DA,Titan and the Hunter. . . 10.00
17 DN,DA, The Memory Machine . 10.00
18 DN,DA,Song of the Source. . . . 10.00
19 DN,DA,The Secret Within Us . . 10.00

(Reprints) 1984
1 JK reprint 4.00
2 thru 5 JK reprint . . . . @3.50
6 JK rep.+New Material 3.50

[2nd Series], 1989
1 From Cosmic Odyssey 3.00
2 A:Orion of New Genesis 2.50
3 A:Orion. 2.50
4 Renegade Apokolyptian Insect
  Colony 2.50
5 Orion vs. Forager. 2.50
6 A:Eve Donner, Darkseid 2.50
7 Bloodline #1. . . . . 2.50
8 Bloodline #2. . . . . 2.50
9 Bloodline #3. . . . . 2.50
10 Bloodline #4 . . . . 2.50
11 Bloodlines #5 . . . . 2.50
12 Bloodlines #6 . . . . 2.50
13 Back on Earth. 2.50
14 I:Reflektor 2.50
15 V:Serial Killer 2.50
16 A:Fastbak & Metron 2.50
17 A:Darkseid, Metron 2.50
18 A:YugaKhan,Darkseid,
  Moniters. 2.50
19 V:Yuga Khan. 2.50
20 Darkseid Dethroned,
  V:Yuga Khan 2.50
21 A:Orion 2.50
22 A:Metron 2.50
23 A:Forever People 2.50
24 A:Forever People 2.50
25 The Pact #1,R:Infinity Man 2.50
26 The Pact #2 . . . . 2.50
27 Asault on Apokolips,Pact#3 . . . 2.50
28 Pact #4, final issue 2.50

[3rd Series], 1995–97
1 F:Orion vs. Darkseid 2.50
2 RaP,UnderworldUnleashed tie-in. . 2.50
3 RaP,Darkseid destroyed 2.50
4 RaP,F:Lightray. 2.50
5 RaP,F:Orion. 2.50
6 RaP,Destruction of the Beast. . . 2.50
7 RaP,R:Darkseid 2.50
8 RaP,DZ,F:Highfather,Darkseid. . . 2.50
9 thru 11 . . . . @2.50

12 JBy,BWi,F:Metron 2.50
13 JBy,BWi,Orion reappears
   on Earth. 2.50
14 JBy,BWi,A:Forever People,
   Lightray 2.50
Secret Files #1 KK,JBy 5.00

NEW GUARDIANS
1988–89
1 JSon,from Millennium series 3.00
2 JSon,Colombian Drug Cartel. . . . 2.50
3 JSon,in South Africa,
   V:Janwillem's Army 2.50
4 JSon,V:Neo-Nazi Skinheads
   in California 2.50
5 JSon,Tegra Kidnapped 2.50
6 JSon, In China, Invasion x-over . 2.50
7 JSon, Guardians Return Home . . 2.50
8 JSon, V:Janwillem 2.50
9 JSon, A:Tome Kalmaku,
   V:Janwillem 2.50
10 JSon, A:Tome Kalmaku. 2.50
11 PB,Janwillem's secret 2.50
12 PB,New Guardians Future
   revealed, final issue. 2.50

NEW TEEN TITANS
Nov., 1980
1 GP,RT,V:Gordanians (see DC
   Comics Presents #26 . . . . 16.00
2 GP,RT,I:Deathstroke the
   Terminator, I&D:Ravager 36.00
3 GP,I:Fearsome Five 7.00
4 GP,RT,A:JLA,O:Starfire 6.00
5 CS,RT,O:Raven,I:Trigon 6.00
6 GP,V:Trigon,O:Raven. 6.00
7 GP,RT,O:Cyborg 6.00
8 GP,RT,A Day in the Life 6.00
9 GP,RT,A:Terminator,
   V:Puppeteer. 6.00
10 GP,RT,A:Terminator 9.00
11 GP,RT,V:Hyperion 4.00
12 GP,RT,V:Titans of Myth 4.00
13 GP,RT,R:Robotman. 4.00
14 GP,RT,I:New Brotherhood of
   Evil,V:Zahl and Rouge. 4.00
15 GP,RT,D:Madame Rouge 4.00
16 GP,RT,I:Captain Carrot 4.00
17 GP,RT,I:Frances Kane 3.50
18 GP,RT,A:Orig.Starfire 3.50
19 GP,RT,A:Hawkman. 3.50
20 GP,RT,V:Disruptor. 3.50

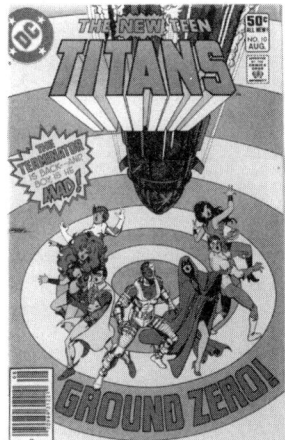

New Teen Titans #10
© DC Comics Inc.

21 GP,RT,GC,I:Brother Blood,
   Night Force 3.50
22 GP,RT,V:Brother Blood 3.50
23 GP,RT,I:Blackfire. 3.50
24 GP,RT,A:Omega Men,I:X-hal . . 3.50
25 GP,RT,A:Omega Men 3.50
26 GP,RT,I:Terra,Runaway #1 . . . . 5.00
27 GP,RT,A:Speedy,Runaway #2. . 3.00
28 GP,RT,V:Terra 4.00
29 GP,RT,V:Broth.of Evil 3.00
30 GP,RT,V:Broth.of Evil,J:Terra . . 3.00
31 GP,RT,V:Broth.of Evil 3.00
32 GP,RT,I:Thunder & Lightning . . 3.00
33 GP,I:Trident 3.00
34 GP,V:The Terminator. 3.00
35 KP,RT,V:Mark Wright. 3.00
36 KP,RT,A:Thunder & Lightning . . 3.00
37 GP,RT,A:Batman/Outsiders(x-over
   BATO#5),V:Fearsome Five 3.00
38 GP,O:Wonder Girl 3.00
39 GP,Grayson quits as Robin. . . . 5.00
40 GP,A:Brother Blood. 3.00
Ann.#1 GP,RT,Blackfire 3.50
Ann.#2 GP,I:Vigilante. 3.00
Ann.#3 GP,DG,D:Terra,A:Deathstroke
   V:The H.I.V.E. 3.50
Ann.#4 rep.Direct Ann.#1. . . . . 2.50

[Special Issues]
Keebler:GP,DG,Drugs 2.50
Beverage:Drugs,RA 2.50
IBM:Drugs 3.00
Becomes:

TALES OF THE
TEEN TITANS
1984–88
41 GP,A:Brother Blood. 3.00
42 GP,DG,V:Deathstroke 5.00
43 GP,DG,V:Deathstroke 5.00
44 GP,DG,I:Nightwing,O:Deathstroke
   Joe Wilson becomes Jericho . . 8.00
45 GP,A:Aqualad,V:The H.I.V.E. . . 3.00
46 GP,A:Aqualad,V:The H.I.V.E. . . 3.00
47 GP,A:Aqualad,V:The H.I.V.E. . . 3.00
48 SR,V:The Recombatants 3.00
49 GP,CI,V:Dr.Light,A:Flash 3.00
50 GP/DG W:Wonder Girl &
   Terry Long,C:Batman,
   Wonder Woman. 4.00
51 RB,A:Cheshire 2.50
52 RB,A:Cheshire 2.50
53 RB,I:Ariel,A:Terminator 2.50
54 RB,A:Terminator 2.50
55 A:Terminator 2.50
56 A:Fearsome Five 2.50
57 A:Fearsome Five 2.50
58 thru 91 rep. . . . . @2.50

NEW TEEN TITANS
[Direct sales series]
Aug., 1984
1 B:MWn(s),GP,L:Raven. 6.00
2 GP,D:Azareth,A:Trigon. 4.00
3 GP,V:Raven 4.00
4 GP,V:Trigon,Raven 4.00
5 GP,D:Trigon,Raven disappears . . 4.00
6 GP,A:Superman,Batman 3.00
7 JL,V:Titans of Myth 3.00
8 JL,V:Titans of Myth 3.00
9 JL,V:Titans of Myth,I:Kole 3.00
10 JL,O:Kole 3.00
11 JL,O:Kole 2.50
12 JL,Ghost story. 2.50
13 EB,Crisis 2.50
14 EB,Crisis 2.50
15 EB,A:Raven 2.50
16 EB,A:OmegaMen 2.50
17 EB,V:Blackfire. 2.50
18 E:MWn(s),EB,V:Blackfire. 2.50
19 EB,V:Mento. 2.50
20 GP(c),EB,V:Cheshire,J.Todd . . 2.50

21 GP(c),EB,V:Cheshire,J.Todd . . 2.50
22 GP(c),EB,V:Blackfire,Mento,
   Brother Blood 2.50
23 GP(c),V:Blackfire 2.50
24 CB,V:Hybrid 2.50
25 EB,RT,V:Hybrid,Mento,A:Flash. . 2.50
26 KGa,V:Mento 2.50
27 KGa,Church of Br.Blood. 2.50
28 EB,RT,V:BrotherBlood,A:Flash . . 2.50
29 EB,RT,V:Brother Blood,
   A:Flash,Robin 2.50
30 EB,Batman,Superman 2.50
31 EB,RT,V:Brother Blood,A:Flash
   Batman,Robin,Gr.Lantern Corps
   Superman 2.50
32 EB,RT,Murder Weekend 2.50
33 EB,V:Terrorists 2.50
34 EB,RT,V:Mento,Hybird 2.50
35 PB,RT,V:Arthur & Eve 2.50
36 EB,RT,I:Wildebeest 2.50
37 EB,RT,V:Wildebeest 2.50
38 EB,RT,A:Infinity. 2.50
39 EB,RT,F:Raven 2.50
40 EB,RT,V:Gentleman Ghost 2.50
41 EB,V:Wildebeest,A:Puppeteer,
   Trident,Wildebeest. 2.50
42 EB,RT,V:Puppeteer,Gizmo,
   Trident,Wildebeest. 2.50
43 CS,RT,V:Phobia 2.50
44 RT,V:Godiva 2.50
45 EB,RT,A:Dial H for Hero 2.50
46 EB,RT,A:Dial H for Hero 2.50
47 O:Titans,C:Wildebeest 2.50
48 EB,RT,A:Red Star 2.50
49 EB,RT,A:Red Star 2.50
Ann.#1 A:Superman,V:Brainiac . . . 2.50
Ann.#2 JBy,JL,O:Brother Blood . . . 3.00
Ann.#3 I:Danny Chase. 2.50
Ann.#4 V:Godiva 2.50
Becomes:

NEW TITANS
1988–96
50 B:MWn(s),GP,BMc,B:Who is
   Wonder Girl?. 7.00
51 GP,BMc. 3.00
52 GP,BMc. 3.00
53 GP,RT 3.00
54 GP,RT,E:Who is Wonder Girl? . 3.00
55 GP,RT,I:Troia. 3.00
56 MBr,RT,Tale of Middle Titans . . 3.00
57 GP,BMc,V:Wildebeast. 3.00
58 GP,TG,BMc,V:Wildebeast 3.00
59 GP,TG,BMc,V:Wildebeast 3.00

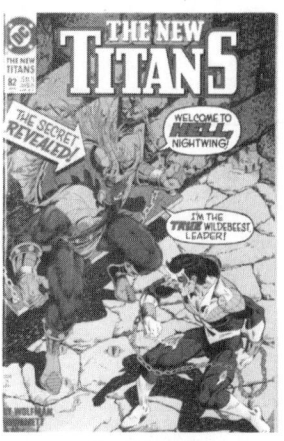

New Titans #82
© DC Comics, Inc.

---

60 GP,TG,BMc,3rd A:Tim Drake
  (Face Revealed),Batman 5.00
61 GP,TG,BMc,A:Tim Drake,
  Batman 5.00
62 TG,AV,A:Deathstroke 3.00
63 TG,AV,A:Deathstroke 3.00
64 TG,AV,A:Deathstroke 3.00
65 TG,AV,A:Deathstroke,Tim Drake,
  Batman 3.00
66 TG,AV,V:Eric Forrester 2.50
67 TG,AV,V:Eric Forrester 2.50
68 SE,V:Royal Flush Gang 2.50
69 SE,V:Royal Flush Gang 2.50
70 SE,A:Deathstroke 3.00
71 TG,AV,B:Deathstroke,
  B:Titans Hunt. 5.00
72 TG,AV,D:Golden Eagle 4.00
73 TG,AV,I:Phantasm. 4.00
74 TG,AV,I:Pantha 3.00
75 TG,AV,IR:Jericho/Wildebeest . . . 3.00
76 TG,AV,V:Wildebeests 2.50
77 TG,AV,A:Red Star,N:Cyborg 2.50
78 TG,AV,V:Cyborg 2.50
79 TG,AV,I:Team Titans 3.00
80 KGa,PC,A:Team Titans. 2.50
81 CS,AV,War of the Gods 2.50
82 TG,AV,V:Wildebeests 2.50
83 TG,AV,D:Jericho 3.00
84 TG,AV,E:Titans Hunt 2.50
85 TG,AV,I:Baby Wildebeest 2.50
86 CS,AV,E:Deathstroke. 2.50
87 TG,AV,A:Team Titans 2.50
88 TG,AV,CS,V:Team Titans 2.50
89 JBr,I:Lord Chaos 2.50
90 TG,AV,Total Chaos#2,A:Team
  Titans,D'stroke,V:Lord Chaos . . 2.50
91 TG,AV,Total Chaos#5,A:Team
  Titans,D'stroke,V:Lord Chaos . . 2.50
92 E:MWn(s),TG,AV,Total Chaos#8,
  A:Team Titans,V:Lord Chaos. . . 2.50
93 TG,AV,Titans Sell-Out#3 . . . . . . 2.50
94 PJ,F:Red Star & Cyborg 2.50
95 PJ,Red Star gains new powers. . 2.50
96 PJ,I:Solar Flare,
  V:Konstantine 2.50
97 TG,AV,B:The Darkening,R:Speedy
  V:Brotherhood of Evil 2.50
98 TG,AV,V:Brotherhood of Evil 2.50
99 TG,AV,I:Arsenal (Speedy) 2.50
100 TG,AV,W:Nightwing&Starfire,
  V:Deathwing,Raven,A:Flash,Team
  Titans,Hologram(c) 4.00
101 AV(i),L:Nightwing. 2.50
102 AV(i),A:Prester John 2.50
103 AV(i),V:Bro. of Evil. 2.50
104 Terminus #1 . . . . 2.50
105 Terminus #2 . . . . 2.50
106 Terminus #3 . . . . 2.50
107 Terminus #4 . . . . 2.50
108 A:Supergirl,Flash. 2.50
109 F:Starfire 2.50
110 A:Flash,Serg.Steele. 2.50
111 A:Checkmate. 2.50
112 A:Checkmate. 2.50
113 F:Nightwing 2.75
114 L:Starfire, Nightwing,Panthra,
  Wildebeest. 2.50
115 A:Trigon 2.50
116 Changling 2.50
117 V:Psimon 2.50
118 V:Raven + Brotherhood 2.50
119 Suffer the Children,pt.1 . . . . . . 2.50
120 Forever Evil,pt.2 . . . . 2.50
121 Forever Evil,pt.3 . . . . 2.50
122 Crimelord/Syndicate War,pt.2
  J:Supergirl 2.50
123 MWn(s),RRa,O:Minion 2.50
124 The Siege of Zi Charan 2.50
125 The Siege of Zi Charan 3.00
126 Meltdown,pt.1 . . . . 2.50
127 MWn,Meltdown, cont. 2.50
128 MWn,Meltdown, cont. 2.50

129 MWn,Meltdown, cont. 2.50
130 MWn,Meltdown,final issue 2.50
Ann.#5 V:Children of the Sun 3.00
Ann.#6 CS,F:Starfire 3.00
Ann.#7 Armageddon 2001,I:Future
  Teen Titans 4.00
Ann.#8 PJ,Eclipso,V:Deathstroke . . 3.75
Ann.#9 Bloodlines#5,I:Anima. 3.75
Ann.#10 Elseworlds story 3.75
Ann.#11 Year One Annual 4.00
#0 Spec. Zero Hour,new team 2.50

NEW T.H.U.N.D.E.R. AGENTS, THE
July, 2003
1 JP 3.00

NEW YEAR'S EVIL:
Dec., 1997
Body Doubles #1 DAn,ALa,JoP,
  JPn(c) 2.50
Dark Nemesis #1 DJu,Ccs,JPn(c). . 2.50
Darkseid #1 JBy,SB,JPn(c) 2.50
Gog #1 MWa,JOy,DJa,JPn(c) 2.50
Mr. Mxyzptlk #1 AIG,TMo,JPn(c) . . . 2.50
Prometheus #1 GMo,JPn(c) 2.50
Scarecrow #1 PrM,DFg,JPn(c) 2.50
The Rogues #1 BAu,RoW,JPn(c) . . 2.50

NEW YORK WORLD'S FAIR
1939–40
1 1939 . . . . 45,000.00
2 1940 . . . . 30,000.00

NEXT, THE
July, 2006
1 Cross-over from other dimension 3.00
2 A:Superman 3.00
3 Trapped in a time anomaly 3.00
4 The Fist of the Iron Ring 3.00
5 Showdown 3.00
6 Finale 3.00

NIGHTFALL: THE BLACK CHRONICLES
Homage/DC, Oct., 1999
1 monsters living among us 3.00
2 . . . . 3.00
3 . . . . 3.00

NIGHT FORCE
Aug., 1982
1 GC,1:Night Force. 5.00
2 thru 13 GC . . . . @3.00
14 GC,Sept.,1983 . . . . 3.00

NIGHT FORCE
Oct., 1996
1 MWn(s),BA,Baron Winters leads . 2.50
2 MWn(s) 2.50
3 MWn(s) 2.50
4 MWn(s),EB,HellSeemsHeaven . . 2.50
5 MWn(s),Low,SMa,Dreamers of
  Dreams,pt.1 . . . . 2.50
6 MWn(s),Low,SMa,Dreamers,pt.2. 2.50
7 MWn(s),Low,SMa,Dreamers,pt.3. 2.50
8 MWn(s),Convergence, x-over . . . 2.50
9 MWn(s),Low,Sma,The Eleventh
  Man pt.1 (of 3). 2.50
10 MWn(s),Eleventh Man, pt.2 . . . . 2.50
11 MWn(s),Eleventh Man, pt.3 . . . . 2.50
12 MWn(s),Lady of the Leopard
  final issue,Sept., 1997 . . . . 2.50

Night Force #1 © DC Comics, Inc.

NIGHTWING
1995
1 R:Nightwing 5.00
2 N:Nightwing 4.00
3 visit to Kravia 4.00
4 conclusion 4.00
1-shot Alfred's Return, DG 5.00

Aug., 1996
1 CDi(s),SMc,KIS,Nightwing goes
  to Bluhaven 15.00
2 CDi(s),SMc,KIS,V:smugglers 8.00
3 CDi(s),SMc,KIS,run-down bank
  iheld up 8.00
4 CDi(s),SMc,KIS,V:Lady Vick 6.00
5 CDi(s),SMc,KIS, ... 6.00
6 CDi(s),SMc,KIS,A:Tim Drake 6.00
7 CDi(s),SMc,KIS,Rough Justice . . 6.00
8 CDi(s),SMc,KIS,V: the kingpin
  of Bluhaven 6.00
9 CDi(s),SMc,KIS,kidnapping, pt.1 . 6.00
10 CDi(s),SMc,KIS,nightmare
  or dream? 6.00
11 CDi(s),SMc,V:Soames,
  Blockbuster 6.00
12 CDi(s),SMc,Mutt 4.00
13 CDi(s),SMc,KIS,A:Batman 4.00
14 CDi(s),SMc,KIS,A:Batman,pt.2 . . 4.00
15 CDi(s),SMc,KIS,A:Batman,pt.3 . . 3.00
16 CDi(s),SMc,KIS,Nightwingmobile 3.00
17 CDi(s),SMc,KIS,V:Man-Bat. 3.00
18 CDi(s),SMc,KIS, ... 3.00
19 CDi(s),SMc,KIS,Cataclysm
  x-over, pt.2. . . . . 4.00
20 CDi(s),SMc,KIS,Cataclysm 4.00
21 CDi(s),SMc,KIS,post Cataclysm 3.00
22 CDi(s),SMc,KIS,V:Lady Vic. 3.00
23 Brotherhood of
  the Fist x-over, pt.4 . . . . 3.00
24 CDi(s),SMc,KIS,cop story 3.00
25 CDi(s),SMc,KIS,A:Robin 3.00
26 CDi(s),SMc,KIS,A:Huntress 3.00
27 CDi(s),SMc,KIS,V:Torque 3.00
28 CDi(s),SMc,KIS,V:Torque 3.00
29 CDi(s),SMc,KIS,A:Huntress 3.00
30 CDi(s),SMc,KIS,A:Superman . . . 3.00
31 CDi(s),SMc,KIS,A:Nite-Wing . . . 3.00
32 CDi(s),SMc,KIS,V:DoubleDare . . 3.00
33 CDi(s),SMc,KIS,
  V:Electrocutioner 3.00
34 CDi(s),SMc,KIS,x-over 3.00
35 CDi(s),SMc,KIS,No
  Man's Land,pt.1. . . . . 3.00
36 CDi(s),SMc,No
  Man's Land,pt.2. . . . . 3.00

37 CDi(s),SMc,KIS,No Man's
   Land, concl. 3.00
38 CDi(s),SMc,KIS,F:Oracle 3.00
39 CDi(s),SMc,KIS 3.00
40 CDi(s),SMc,KIS,R:Tarantula 3.00
41 CDi(s),Police Academy grad. . . . 2.50
42 CDi(s),V:Nite-wing 2.50
43 CDi(s),V:Torque 2.50
44 CDi(s),F:Nite-wing. 2.50
45 CDi(s),Hunt for Oracle,pt.1 . . . . . 2.50
46 CDi(s),Hunt for Oracle,pt.3 . . . . . 2.50
47 CDi(s),showdown 2.50
48 CDi(s),JMz,F:Slyph 2.50
49 CDi(s),JMz,F:Torque. 2.50
50 CDi,JMz,at crossroads,48-pg. . . 4.00
51 CDi,KD,O:Nite-wing 2.50
52 CDi,This issue: Batman dies! . . . 2.50
53 Officer Down x-over,pt.5 . . . . . . 2.50
54 CDi,life-threatening accident. . . . 2.50
55 CDi,A:Blockbuster,Shrike 2.50
56 CDi,V:Blockbuster,Shrike 2.50
57 CDi,RL,MFm,V:Shrike. 2.50
58 CDi,V:Shrike 2.50
59 CDi,RL,Where's Freddy Minh . . . 2.50
60 CDi,Low,V:Transbelvan mob . . . 2.50
61 CDi,V:Bank Robbers. 2.50
62 CDi,Joker:Last Laugh 2.50
63 CDi,Last Laugh, aftermath 2.50
64 CDi,On a Christmas Evening . . . 2.50
65 CDi,BruceWayne:Murderer,pt.3 . 2.50
66 CDi,BruceWayne:Murderer,pt.9 . 2.50
67 CDi,V:Amygdala 2.50
68 CDi,BruceWayne:Fugitive,pt.6 . . 2.50
69 CDi,BruceWayne:Fugitive,pt.9 . . 2.50
70 CDi,in Arizona 2.50
71 RL,Something About Mary,pt.1 . . 2.50
72 RL,Something About Mary,pt.2 . . 2.50
73 RL,Something About Mary,pt.3 . . 2.50
74 RL,Something About Mary,pt.4 . . 2.50
75 RL,MGo,40-pg 3.50
76 MGo(c) 2.50
77 cops go bad 2.50
78 V:new Tarantula 2.50
79 Source of madness. 2.50
80 Venn Diagram,pt.1 . . . . 2.50
81 Venn Diagram,pt.2 . . . . 4.00
82 Venn Diagram,pt.3 . . . . 2.50
83 Murder of Chief Redhorn 2.50
84 RL,Chief Redhorn case 2.50
85 Tarantula or Nite-Wing 2.50
86 Cyber-punks 2.50
87 V:Blockbuster 2.50
88 V:Blockbuster 2.50
89 V:Blockbuster 2.50
90 V:Blockbuster 2.50
91 V:Shrike 2.50
92 V:Blockbuster 2.50
93 V:Blockbuster showdown 2.50
94 F:Tarantula 2.50
95 Tarantula vs. Copperhead. 2.50
96 War Games,Act 1,pt.3 . . . . 2.50
97 War Games,Act 2,pt.3 . . . . 2.50
98 War Games,Act 3,pt.3 . . . . 2.50
99 SMc,Back to the Life. 2.50
100 V:Trantula, 40-page 3.00
101 SMc,Nightwing,Year One,pt.1 . . 8.00
102 SMc,Nightwing,Year One,pt.2 . . 5.00
103 SMc,Nightwing,Year One,pt.3 . . 6.00
104 SMc,Nightwing,Year One,pt.4 . . 5.00
105 SMc,Nightwing,Year One,pt.5 . . 3.00
106 SMc,Nightwing,Year One,pt.6 . . 3.00
107 PhH,Bludhaven left 3.00
108 PhH,in New York. 3.00
109 PhH,V:Black Mask 3.00
110 PhH,F:Robin 3.00
111 Dick Grayson undercover 2.50
112 V:Deathstroke 2.50
113 Villains united 2.50
114 PHe, Nightwing gone 2.50
115 PHe,V:Deathstroke 2.50
116 PHe,V:Deathstroke 2.50
117 PHe,V:Deathstroke 2.50

118 Hiding in New York 2.50
119 Twin Nightwings 2.50
120 V:Pierce Bros. 3.00
121 Dick Grayson to the rescue . . . 3.00
122 Only one Nightwing remaining . 3.00
123 Fire-throwing killer 3.00
124 Heads of the unferworld 3.00
125 MWn,DJu,NRd,V:Raptor. 3.00
126 MWn,DJu,NRd 3.00
127 MWn,DJu,NRd,new villain 3.00
128 MWn,DJu,NRd,Raptor 3.00
129 MWn,Bride and Groom. 3.00
130 MWn,Bride and Groom. 3.00
131 MWn,Bride and Groom. 3.00
132 MWn,Bride and Groom, concl. . 3.00
133 MWn,Grayson's lost year 3.00
134 MWn,The Missing Year. 3.00
135 MWn,O:Vigilante. 3.00
136 MWn,It's a Set-up 3.00
137 MWn,Vigilante, Metal Eddie . . . 3.00
138 Resurrection of Ra's Al Ghul . . 3.00
139 Resurrection of Ra's Al Ghul . . 3.00
140 RgM,A:Batman, Robin 3.00
141 RgM,A:Superman 3.00
142 RgM,Another body stolen 3.00
143 RgM(c),V:League of Assassins . 3.00
144 RgM,Mother of Champions. . . . 3.00
145 RgM,Mother of Champions. . . . 3.00
146 V:Talia nd Dr. Creighton 3.00
147 Batman R.I.P tie-in 3.00
148 Batman R.I.P. tie-in 3.00
149 Batman R.I.P. tie-in 3.00
150 Batman R.I.P. tie-in, 48-pg.. . . . 4.00
Ann.#1 Pulp Heroes (Romance) . . . 4.00
Ann. #2 Nightwing's lost year 4.00
Spec.#1,000,000 CDi(s),SMc,KIS . . 2.50
Secret Files #1 64-page. 5.50
Spec.#1 Our Worlds at War,48-pg . . 3.50
Giant #1 80-pg.CDi,I:Hella. 6.00
GN The Target,CDi,SMc,48-page . . 6.00

NIGHTWING AND HUNTRESS
March, 1998
1 (of 4) BSz,conflict 2.50
2 BSz,good cop, bad cop 2.50
3 BSz,Malfatti 2.50
4 BSz,concl. 2.50

NORTHLANDERS
Vertigo, Dec., 2007
1 Sven the Returned, pt.1. . . . . 3.00
1a variant (c) (1:10) 3.00
2 thru 8 Sven The Returned . . . . @3.00
2a thru 3 variant (c)s (1:10) . . . . @3.00
9 thru 10 Lindisfarne . . . . @3.00
11 thru 12 Cross & the Hammer . @3.00

NUTSY SQUIRREL
Sept.–Oct., 1954
61 SM. 150.00
62 thru 71. . . . . @125.00
72 Nov., 1957. . . . . 125.00

OMAC
Sept.–Oct., 1974
1 JK,I&O:Omac. 75.00
2 JK,I:Mr.Big 30.00
3 JK,100,000 foes. 30.00
4 JK,V:Kafka 30.00
5 JK,New Bodies for Old 30.00
6 JK,The Body Bank. 30.00
7 JK,The Ocean Stealers 30.00
8 JK,Last issue 30.00

[2nd Series], 1991
1 JBy,B&W prestige 5.00
2 JBy,The Great Depression era . . 4.50
3 JBy,To Kill Adolf Hitler 4.50
4 JBy,D:Mr.Big 4.50

OMAC
July, 2006
1 (of 8) Dawn of a new Omac 3.00
2 In Las Vegas 3.00
3 Brother Eye 3.00
4 Mike Costner 3.00
5 Return of Brother Eye 3.00
6 Total Control. 3.00
7 New Omac. 3.00
8 finale 3.00

OMAC PROJECT, THE
Apr., 2005
1 (of 6) Checkmate. 2.50
2 Brother Eye satellite 2.50
3 F:Sasha Bordeaux. 2.50
4 Brother Eye breaks free. 2.50
5 Pawn No More. 2.50
6 concl. 2.50
Spec. Infinite Crisis Special 5.00

OMEGA MEN
Dec., 1982
1 KG,V:Citadol. 3.50
2 KG,O:Broot. 3.00
3 KG,I:Lobo. 9.00
4 KG,D:Demonia,I:Felicity. 3.00
5 KG,V:Lobo 3.00
6 KG,V:Citadel,D:Gepsen. 2.50
7 O:Citadel,L:Auron 2.50
8 R:Nimbus,I:H.Hokum 2.50
9 V:HarryHokum,A:Lobo. 2.50
10 A:Lobo (First Full Story) 6.00
11 V:Blackfire 2.50
12 R:Broots Wife 2.50
13 A:Broots Wife 2.50
14 Karna 2.50
15 Primus Goes Mad. 2.50
16 Spotlight Issue 2.50
17 V:Psions 2.50
18 V:Psions 2.50
19 V:Psions,C:Lobo 2.50
20 V:Psions,A:Lobo 2.50
21 Spotlight Issue 2.50
22 Nimbus 2.50
23 Nimbus 2.50
24 Okaara 2.50
25 Kalista 2.50
26 V:Spiderguild 4.00
27 V:Psions 4.00
28 V:Psions 2.50
29 V:Psions 2.50
30 R:Primus,I:Artin 2.50

Omega Men #13 © DC Comics Inc.

All comics prices listed are for *Near Mint* condition.

31 Crisis tie-in 2.50	60 Staring at the Son,pt.1 . . . . 2.50
32 Felicity. 2.50	61 Staring at the Son,pt.2 . . . . 2.50
33 Regufe World 2.50	62 Staring at the Son,pt.3 . . . . 2.50
34 A:New Teen Titans 2.50	63 The Trust. 2.75
35 A:New Teen Titans 2.50	64 Jack heads to Atlantic City 2.75
36 Last Days of Broot 2.50	65 Loop, Lono & Victor 2.75
37 V:Spiderguild,A:Lobo 5.00	66 Loop, Lono & Victor 2.75
38 A:Tweener Network. 2.50	67 Dizzy & Wylie 2.75
Ann.#1 KG,R:Harpis. 2.50	68 More dead Trust members 2.75
Ann.#2 KG,O:Primus 2.50	69 F:Augustus Medici 2.75
	70 Gambling with their lives. 2.75

OMEGA MEN, THE
Oct., 2006

1 (of 6) Crimes Agains the Galaxy . 3.00	71 A Wake, pt.1 . . . . 2.75
2 . . . . 3.00	72 A Wake, pt.2 . . . . 3.00
3 A:Superman 3.00	73 A Wake, pt.3 . . . . 3.00
4 F:Lady Styx 3.00	74 A Wake, pt.4 . . . . 3.00
5 F:Omega Women 3.00	75 The Briefcase 3.00
6 finale 3.00	76 Secret Armies of the Trust 3.00
	77 On to Mexico. 3.00
	78 In Mexico 3.00
	79 Punch Line, pt.4 . . . . 3.00

100 BULLETS
DC/Vertigo, 1999

1 F:Dizzy Cordova & AgentGraves. 9.00	80 . . . . 3.00
2 Dizzy,pt.2 . . . . 6.00	81 . . . . 3.00
3 F:Mr.Shepard 4.00	82 . . . . 3.00
4 Shot, Water Back,pt.1 . . . . 4.00	83 in Rome 3.00
5 Shot, Water Back,pt.2 . . . . 4.00	84 Lake Tahoe 3.00
6 Short Con, Long Odds,pt.1 . . . . . 3.50	85 The Other woman 3.00
7 Short Con, Long Odds,pt.2 . . . . . 3.50	86 Alone and liking it 3.00
8 F:Agent Graves 3.50	87 A Minuteman to the rescue 3.00
9 Right Ear,Left in the Cold,pt.1 . . . 3.50	88 Mr. Branch and Cole Burns 3.00
10 Right Ear,Left in the Cold,pt.2. . . 3.50	89 South-Side Crime Syndicate. . . . 3.00
11 F:Lilly Roach 3.50	90 F:Pip 3.00
12 Parlez Kung Vous,pt.1 . . . . 3.50	91 F:Pippen 3.00
13 Parlez Kung Vous,pt.2 . . . . 3.50	92 Graves plan? 3.00
14 Parlez Kung Vous,concl. 3.50	93 Graves's war with the Trust 3.00
15 Hang Up on Hang Low,pt.1 . . . . 3.50	94 Old friends meet 3.00
16 Hang Up on Hang Low,pt.2 . . . . 3.50	95 All Hell breaking loose 3.00
17 Hang Up on Hang Low,pt.3 . . . . 3.00	96 . . . . 3.00
18 Hang Up on Hang Low,pt.4 . . . . 3.00	97 . . . . 3.50
19 Hang Up on Hang Low,pt.5 . . . . 3.00	
20 Hot House 3.00	
21 Sell Fish & Out to Sea,pt.1 . . . . 3.00	

100%
DC/Vertigo, June, 2002

22 Sell Fish & Out to Sea,pt.2 . . . . 3.00	1 (of 5) PPo, 48-pg. b&w 6.00
23 Red Prince Blues,pt.1 . . . . 3.00	2 thru 5 PPo, Sci-fi, 48-pg. b&w . @6.00
24 Red Prince Blues,pt.2. . . . . 3.50	

ORION
April, 2000

25 Red Prince Blues,pt.3. . . . . 2.50	1 WS,Darkseid 2.50
26 Mr. Branch & the Family Tree . . . 2.50	2 WS,V:Darkseid. 2.50
27 Idol Chatter 2.50	3 WS,FM,V:Suicide Jockeys. 2.50
28 Contrabandolero,pt.1 . . . . 2.50	4 WS,DGb,V:Darkseid 2.50
29 Contrabandolero,pt.2 . . . . 2.50	5 WS,V:Darkseid. 2.50
30 Contrabandolero,pt.3 . . . . 2.50	6 WS,EL,AG,F:Mortalla. 2.50
31 Counterfeit Detective,pt.1 . . . . . . 2.50	7 WS,HC,V:Kalibak. 2.50
32 Counterfeit Detective,pt.2 . . . . . . 2.50	8 WS,RLe,JLb,V:Kalibak. 2.50
33 Counterfeit Detective,pt.3 . . . . . . 2.50	9 WS,V:Desaad 2.50
34 Counterfeit Detective,pt.4 . . . . . . 2.50	10 WS,AAd,V:Desaad 2.50
35 Counterfeit Detective,pt.5 . . . . . . 2.50	11 WS,New Genesis,Anti-Life 2.50
36 Counterfeit Detective,pt.6 . . . . . . 2.50	12 WS,JLe,return to Apokolips 2.50
37 On Accidental Purpose 2.50	13 WS,TA,JBy,F:Captain Marvel . . . 2.50
38 Cole Burns Slow Hand 2.50	14 WS,TA,JBy,F:Captain Marvel . . . 2.50
39 Ambition's Audition 2.50	15 WS,JPL,48-page. 4.50
40 Night of the Payday 2.50	16 WS,Abysmal Plane,V:Clockwerx 2.50
41 A Crash 2.50	17 WS,Abysmal Plane,V:Clockwerx 2.50
42 V:Wylie Times 2.50	18 WS,AM,F:Rakar 2.50
43 Chill in the Oven,pt.1 . . . . 2.50	19 WS,ECa,Joker-crazed Deep Six. 2.50
44 Chill in the Oven,pt.2 . . . . 2.50	20 WS,fall from Grace 2.50
45 Chill in the Oven,pt.3 . . . . 2.50	21 WS,V:Arnicus Wolfram 2.50
46 Chill in the Oven,pt.4 . . . . 2.50	22 WS,young teen 2.50
47 In Stinked,pt.1 . . . . 2.50	23 WS,BWi,young teen 2.50
48 In Stinked,pt.2 . . . . 2.50	24 WS,BWi,Tactical nuke. 2.50
49 In Stinked,pt.3 . . . . 2.50	25 WS,BWi,48-pg.final issue 4.25
50 Agent Graves,40-pg. 3.50	

OTHER SIDE, THE
DC/Vertigo, Oct., 2006

51 Wylie Runs the Voodoo Down . . 2.50	1 thru 5 (of 5) Vietnam . . . . @3.00
52 Wylie Runs the Voodoo Down . . 2.50	

OTHERWORLD
DC/Vertigo, March, 2005

53 Wylie Runs the Voodoo Down . . 2.50	1 (of 12) PJ,ALa 3.00
54 Wylie Runs the Voodoo Down . . 2.50	2 thru 7 PJ,ALa . . . . @3.00
55 Wylie Runs the Voodoo Down . . 2.50	
56 Wylie Runs the Voodoo Down . . 2.50	
57 Wylie Runs the Voodoo Down . . 2.50	
58 Lono & Loop Hughes 2.50	
59 F:Victor "The Saint". 2.50	

*Our Army at War #7 ©
DC Comics, Inc.*

OUR ARMY AT WAR
Aug., 1952

1 CI(c),Dig Your FoxholeDeep. 3,800.00
2 CI(c),Champ 1,600.00
3 GK(c),No Exit 1,200.00
4 IN(c),Last Man 900.00
5 IN(c),T.N.T. Bouquet 800.00
6 IN(c),Battle Flag. 800.00
7 IN(c),Dive Bomber 800.00
8 IN(c),One Man Army 800.00
9 GC(c),Undersea Raider 800.00
10 IN(c),Soldiers on the
High Wire. 800.00
11 IN(c),Scratch One Meatball. . . 800.00
12 IN(c),The Big Drop 800.00
13 BK(c),Ghost Ace 800.00
14 BK(c),Drummer of Waterloo . 800.00
15 IN(c),Thunder in the Skies . . . 700.00
16 IN(c),A Million To One Shot . . 700.00
17 IN(c),The White Death 700.00
18 IN(c),Frontier Fighter 700.00
19 IN(c),The Big Ditch 700.00
20 IN(c),Abandon Ship 700.00
21 IN(c),Dairy of a Flattop 500.00
22 Jgr(c),Ranger Raid 500.00
23 IN(c),Jungle Navy 500.00
24 IN(c),Suprise Landing 500.00
25 JGr(c),Take 'Er Down 500.00
26 JGr(c),Sky Duel 500.00
27 IN(c),MD,Diary of a Frogman . 500.00
28 JGr(c),Detour-War 500.00
29 IN(c),Grounded Fighter. 500.00
30 JGr(c),Torpedo Raft 500.00
31 IN(c),Howitzer Hill 500.00
32 JGr(c),Battle Mirror 500.00
33 JGr(c),Fighting Gunner 500.00
34 JGr(c),Point-Blank War 500.00
35 JGr(c),Frontline Tackle 500.00
36 JGr(c),Foxhole Mascot 500.00
37 JGr(c),Walking Battle Pin 500.00
38 JGr(c),Floating Pillbox 500.00
39 JGr(c),Trench Trap 500.00
40 RH(c),Tank Hunter 500.00
41 JGr(c),Jungle Target 500.00
42 IN(c),Shadow Targets 400.00
43 JGr(c),A Bridge For Billy 400.00
44 JGr(c),Thunder In The Desert 400.00
45 JGr(c),Diary of a Fighter Pilot. 400.00
46 JGr(c),Prize Package 400.00
47 JGr(c),Flying Jeep 400.00
48 JGr(c),Front Seat 400.00
49 JKu(c),Landing Postponed . . . 400.00
50 JGr(c),RH,Mop-Up Squad . . . 400.00
51 JGr(c),Battle Tag. 400.00
52 JGr(c),Pony Express Pilot. . . . 400.00

Our Army at War #51
© *DC Comics Inc.*

53 JGr(c),One Ringside-For War. 400.00
54 JKu(c),No-Man Secret 400.00
55 JGr(c),No Rest For A Raider. . 400.00
56 JKu(c),You're Next 400.00
57 JGr(c),Ten-Minute Break. 400.00
58 JKu(c),The Fighting SnowBird 400.00
59 JGr(c),The Mustang Had
　My Number 400.00
60 JGr(c),Ranger Raid. 400.00
61 JGr(c),A Pigeon For Easy Co. 300.00
62 JKu(c),Trigger Man 300.00
63 JGr(c),The Big Toss 300.00
64 JKu(c),Tank Rider 300.00
65 JGr(c),Scramble-War Upstairs 300.00
66 RH(c),Gunner Wanted 300.00
67 JGr(c),MD,Boiling Point 300.00
68 JKu(c),MD,End of the Line . . . 300.00
69 JGr(c),Combat Cage. 300.00
70 JKu(c),Torpedo Tank 300.00
71 JGr(c),Flying Mosquitoes 300.00
72 JGr(c),No. 1 Pigeon 300.00
73 JKu(c),Shooting Gallery 300.00
74 JGr(c),Ace Without Guns 300.00
75 JGr(c),Blind Night Fighter . . . 300.00
76 JKu(c),Clipped Hellcat 300.00
77 JGr(c),Jets Don't Dream 300.00
78 IN(c),Battle Nurse 300.00
79 JGr(c),MD,What's the Price
　of a B-17? 300.00
80 JGr(c),The Sparrow And
　The...Hawk 300.00
81 JGr(c),Sgt. Rock in The
　Rock of Easy Co. 5,500.00
82 JGr(c),MD,Gun Jockey 1,500.00
83 JGr(c),MD,B:Sgt.Rock Stories,
　The Rock and the Wall. . . . 4,200.00
84 JKu(c),Laughter On
　Snakehead Hill 650.00
85 JGr(c),Ice Cream Soldier 800.00
86 RH(c),Tank 711. . . . . 600.00
87 RH(c),Calling Easy Co. 600.00
88 JKu(c),The Hard Way 600.00
89 RH(c),No Shoot From Easy . . 600.00
90 RH(c),3 Stripes Hill 600.00
91 JGr(c),No Answer from
　Sarge 1,600.00
92 JGr(c),Luck of Easy 500.00
93 JGr(c),Deliver One Airfield . . . 500.00
94 JKu(c),Target-Easy Company. 500.00
95 JKu(c),Battle of the Stripes . . . 500.00
96 JGr(c),MD,Last Stand
　For Easy 500.00
97 JKu(c),What Makes A
　Sergeant Run? 500.00
98 JKu(c),Soldiers Never Die . . . 500.00

99 JKu(c),Easy's Hardest Battle . 500.00
100 JKu(c),No Exit For Easy 500.00
101 JKu(c),End Of Easy 400.00
102 JKu(c),The Big Star. 400.00
103 RH(c),Easy's Had It 400.00
104 JKu(c),A New Kind Of War . . 400.00
105 JKu(c),T.N.T. Birthday 400.00
106 JKu(c),Meet Lt. Rock 400.00
107 JKu(c),Doom Over Easy. . . . 400.00
108 JGr(c),Unknown Sergeant . . 400.00
109 JKu(c),Roll Call For Heroes . 400.00
110 JKu(c),That's An Order 400.00
111 JKu(c),What's The Price
　Of A Dog Tag. 400.00
112 JKu(c),Battle Shadow 400.00
113 JKu(c),Eyes Of A
　Blind Gunner 400.00
114 JKu(c),Killer Sergeant. 400.00
115 JKu(c),Rock's Battle Family . 400.00
116 JKu(c),S.O.S. Sgt. Rock 400.00
117 JKu(c),Snafu Squad 400.00
118 RH(c),The Tank Vs. The
　Tin Soldier 400.00
119 JKu(c),A Bazooka For
　Babyface 400.00
120 JGr(c),Battle Tags
　For Easy Co. 250.00
121 JKu(c),New Boy In Easy. . . . 200.00
122 JKu(c),Battle of the
　Pajama Commandoes. 200.00
123 JGr(c),Battle Brass Ring 200.00
124 JKu(c),Target-Sgt. Rock 200.00
125 JKu(c),Hold-At All Costs 200.00
126 RH(c),The End Of
　Easy Company 200.00
127 JKu(c),4 Faces of Sgt. Rock. 200.00
128 JKu(c),O:Sgt. Rock. 450.00
129 JKu(c),Heroes Need
　Cowards 200.00
130 JKu(c),No Hill For Easy 200.00
131 JKu(c),One Pair of
　Dogtags For Sale 200.00
132 JKu(c),Young Soldiers
　Never Cry 200.00
133 JKu(c),Yesterday's Hero 200.00
134 JKu(c),The T.N.T. Book. 200.00
135 JKu(c),Battlefield Double . . . 200.00
136 JKu(c),Make Me A Hero 200.00
137 JKu(c),Too Many Sergeants . 200.00
138 JKu(c),Easy's Lost Sparrow . 200.00
139 JKu(c),A Firing Squad
　For Easy 200.00
140 JKu(c),Brass Sergeant 200.00
141 JKu(c),Dead Man's Trigger . . 200.00
142 JKu(c),Easy's New Topkick. . 200.00
143 JKu(c),Easy's T.N.T. Crop . . . 200.00
144 JKu(c),The Sparrow And
　The Tiger 200.00
145 JKu(c),A Feather For
　Little Sure Shot 200.00
146 JKu(c),The Fighting Guns
　For Easy 200.00
147 JKu(c),Book One:Generals
　Don't Die 200.00
148 JKu(c),Book Two:Generals
　Don't Die:Generals Are
　Sergeants With Stars. 200.00
149 JKu(c),Surrender Ticket 200.00
150 JKu(c),Flytrap Hill 200.00
151 JKu(c),War Party,
　I:Enemy Ace 750.00
152 JKu(c),Last Man-Last Shot . . 200.00
153 JKu(c),Easy's Last Stand . . . 400.00
154 JKu(c),Boobytrap Mascot . . . 150.00
155 JKu(c),No Stripes For Me . . . 400.00
156 JKu(c),The Human Tank Trap 150.00
157 JKu(c),Nothin's Ever
　Lost In War 150.00
158 JKu(c),Iron Major-Rock
　Sergeant 150.00
159 JKu(c),The Blind Gun 150.00

160 JKu(c),What's The Color
　Of Your Blood 150.00
161 JKu(c),Dead End
　For A Dogface 150.00
162 JKu(c),The Price and
　The Sergeant. 150.00
163 JKu(c),MD,RE,Kill Me-Kill Me 150.00
164 JKu(c),CE,No Exit For Easy,
　reprint from #100. . . . . 350.00
165 GE,JKu(c),The Return of the
　Iron Major 150.00
166 GE,JKu(c),Half A Sergeant . . 150.00
167 GE,JKu(c),Kill One-
　Save One 150.00
168 GE,JKu(c),I Knew The
　Unknown Soldier. 300.00
169 GE,JKu(c),Nazi On My Back 125.00
170 GE,JKu(c),Buzzard Bait Hill . 125.00
171 GE,JKu(c),The Sergeant
　Must Die 125.00
172 GE,JKu(c),A Slug for a
　Sergeant 125.00
173 GE,JKu(c),Easy's Hardest
　Battle, reprint from #99 . . . . . 125.00
174 GE,JKu(c),One Kill Too
　Many 125.00
175 JKu(c),T.N.T. Letter. 125.00
176 MD,JKu(c),Give Me Your
　Stripes 125.00
177 RH,JKu(c),Target-Easy Company,
　reprint from #94, giant-size . . 200.00
178 RH,JKu(c),Only One Medal
　For Easy 100.00
179 RH,JKu(c),A Penny Jackie
　Johnson. 100.00
180 RH,JKu(c),You Can't
　Kill A General. 100.00
181 RH,Monday's Coward-
　Tuesday's Hero 100.00
182 NA,RH,The Desert Rats
　of Easy 125.00
183 RH,NA,JKu(c),Sergeants
　Don't Stay Dead 150.00
184 RH,JKu(c),Candidate For A
　Firing Squad 100.00
185 RH,JKu(c),Battle Flag For
　A G.I. 100.00
186 RH,NA,JKu(c),3 Stripes Hill
　reprint from #90, Origin 100.00
187 RH,JKu(c),Shadow of a
　Sergeant 90.00
188 RH,JKu(c),Death Comes for
　Easy. 90.00
189 RH,JKu(c),The Mission Was
　Murder. 90.00

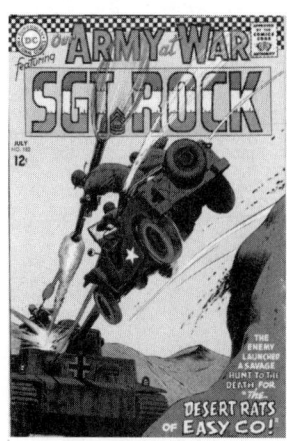

Our Army at War #182
© *DC Comics Inc.*

DC COMICS

190 RH,JKu(c),What Make's A
  Sergeant Run?, reprint
  from #97, giant-size....... 150.00
191 RH,JKu(c),Death Flies High,
  A:Johnny Cloud........... 175.00
192 RH,JKu(c),A Firing Squad
  For A Sergeant 150.00
193 RH,JKu(c),Blood In
  the Desert 150.00
194 RH,JKu(c),Time For
  Vengeance............... 150.00
195 RH,JKu(c),Dead Town 150.00
196 RH,JKu(c),Stop The War-
  I Want To Get Off......... 150.00
197 RH,JKu(c),Last Exit For Easy 150.00
198 RH,JKu(c),Plugged Nickel .. 150.00
199 RH,JKu(c),Nazi Ghost Wolf . 150.00
200 RH,GE,JKu(c),The
  Troubadour 100.00
201 RH,JKu(c),The Graffiti Writer . 75.00
202 RH,JKu(c),Sarge Is Dead.... 75.00
203 RH,MD,JKu(c),Easy's Had It,
  reprint from # 103, giant-size 125.00
204 RH,JKu(c)................. 75.00
205 RH,JKu(c)................. 60.00
206 RH,JKu(c),There's A War On . 60.00
207 RH,JKu(c),A Sparrow's
  Prayer.................. 60.00
208 RH,JKu(c),A Piece of Rag...
  And A Hank of Hair 60.00
209 RH,JKu(c),I'm Still Alive 60.00
210 RH,JKu(c),I'm Kilroy 60.00
211 RH,JKu(c),The Treasure of
  St. Daniel 60.00
212 RH,MD,JKu(c),The Quiet War 60.00
213 RH,JKu(c),A Letter For
  Bulldozer 60.00
214 RH,JKu(c),Where Are You? . 60.00
215 RH,JKu(c),Pied Piper of Peril . 60.00
216 RH,JKu(c),Doom Over Easy,
  reprint from # 107, Giant-size 100.00
217 RH,JKu(c),Surprise Party 50.00
218 RH,JKu(c),Medic! 50.00
219 RH,JKu(c),Yesterday's Hero . 50.00
220 RH,JKu(c),Stone-Age War ... 50.00
221 RH,JKu(c),Hang-Up 50.00
222 RH,JKu(c),Dig In, Easy...... 50.00
223 RH,JKu(c),On Time......... 50.00
224 RH,JKu(c),One For The
  Money 50.00
225 RH,JKu(c),Face Front....... 50.00
226 RH,JKu(c),Death Stop 50.00
227 RH,JKu(c),Traitor's Blood 50.00
228 RH,JKu(c),It's A Dirty War.... 50.00
229 RH,JKu(c),The Battle of the
  Sergeants, reprint #128,
  Giant-size 75.00
230 RH,JKu(c),Home Is The
  Hunter 30.00
231 RH,JKu(c),My Brother's
  Keeper................. 30.00
232 RH,JKu(c),3 Men In A Tub .. 30.00
233 RH,JKu(c),Head Count..... 30.00
234 RH,JKu(c),Summer In Salerno 30.00
235 RH,ATh,JKu(c),Pressure
  Point, giant-size........... 45.00
236 RH,JKu(c),Face The Devil,
  giant-size................ 45.00
237 RH,JKu(c),Nobody Cares,
  giant-size................ 45.00
238 RH,JKu(c),I Kid You Not,
  giant-size................ 45.00
239 RH,JKu(c),The Soldier,
  giant-size................ 45.00
240 RH,JKu(c),NA, giant-size 75.00
241 RH,ATh,JKu(c),War Story,
  giant-size................ 45.00
242 RH,JKu(c),Infantry 45.00
243 RH,MD,JKu(c),24 Hour Pass . 40.00
244 RH,MD,JKu(c),Easy's First
  Tiger 40.00
245 RH,JKu(c),The Prisoner 40.00

246 RH,JKu(c),Naked Combat ... 40.00
247 RH,JKu(c),The Vision 25.00
248 RH,JKu(c),The Firing Squad.. 25.00
249 RH,JKu(c),The Luck of
  Easy,WW................ 30.00
250 RH,JKu(c),90 Day Wonder ... 25.00
251 RH,JKu(c),The Iron Major.... 25.00
252 RH,JKu(c),The Iron Hand 25.00
253 RH,JKu(c),Rock and Iron 25.00
254 RH,ATh,JKu(c),The Town 25.00
255 RH,JKu(c),What's It Like..... 25.00
256 RH,JKu(c),School For
  Sergeants 25.00
257 RH,JKu(c),The Castaway 25.00
258 RH,JKu(c),The Survivors 25.00
259 RH,JKu(c),Lost Paradise 25.00
260 RH,JKu(c),Hell's Island...... 25.00
261 RH,JKu(c),The Medal That
  Nobody Wanted............ 25.00
262 RH,JKu(c),The Return 25.00
263 RH,JKu(c),The Cage 25.00
264 RH,JKu(c),The Hunt 25.00
265 RH,JKu(c),The Brother 25.00
266 RH,GE,JKu(c),The Evacuees . 25.00
267 RH,JKu(c),A Bakers Dozen .. 25.00
268 RH,JKu(c),The Elite 25.00
269 RH,MD,GE,JKu(c), giant-size . 75.00
270 RH,JKu(c),Spawn of the
  Devil................... 25.00
271 RH,JKu(c),Brittle Harvest 20.00
272 RH,JKu(c),The Bloody Flag .. 20.00
273 RH,JKu(c),The Arena 20.00
274 RH,GE,JKu(c),Home Is The
  Hero 20.00
275 RH,MD,JKu(c),Graveyard
  Battlefield, giant-size 75.00
276 RH,GE,JKu(c),A Bullet For
  Rock 22.00
277 RH,JKu(c),Gashouse Gang .. 22.00
278 RH,GE,JKu(c),Rearguard
  Action.................. 22.00
279 JKu(c),Mined City 22.00
280 RH,GE,MD,JKu(c),Mercy
  Mission 40.00
281 RH,JKu(c),Dead Man's Eyes . 20.00
282 JKu(c),Pieces of Time....... 20.00
283 JKu(c),Dropouts 20.00
284 JKu(c),Linkup 20.00
285 JKu(c),Bring Him Back 20.00
286 JKu(c),Firebird 18.00
287 MGr,JKu(c),The Fifth
  Dimension 18.00
288 JKu(c),Defend-Or Destroy .. 18.00
289 JKu(c),The Line 18.00
290 JKu(c),Super-Soldiers....... 18.00
291 JKu(c),Death Squad 18.00
292 JKu(c),A Lesson In Blood.... 18.00
293 JKu(c),It Figures.......... 18.00
294 JKu(c),Coffin For Easy 18.00
295 JKu(c),The Devil in Paradise . 18.00
296 JKu(c),Combat Soldier 18.00
297 JKu(c),Percentages 18.00
298 JKu(c),Return to Chartres.... 18.00
299 JKu(c),Three Soldiers....... 18.00
300 JKu(c),300th Hill 22.00
301 JKu(c),The Farm.......... 18.00
Becomes:

SGT. ROCK
1977–88
302 JKu(c),Anzio-The Bloodbath,
  part I 45.00
303 JKu(c),Anzio, part II 25.00
304 JKu(c),Anzio, part III 20.00
305 JKu(c),Dead Man's Trigger,
  reprint from #141.......... 25.00
306 JKu(c),The Last Soldier 25.00
307 JKu(c),I'm Easy........... 25.00
308 JKu(c),One Short Step 25.00
309 JKu(c),Battle Clowns 25.00
310 JKu(c),Hitler's Wolf Children . 25.00
311 JKu(c),The Sergeant and
  the Lady................. 15.00

Our Army at War #282
© DC Comics, Inc.

312 JKu(c),No Name Hill........ 15.00
313 JKu(c),A Jeep For Joey 15.00
314 JKu(c),Gimme Sky 15.00
315 JKu(c),Combat Antenna 15.00
316 JKu(c),Another Hill.... ..... 15.00
317 JKu(c),Hell's Oven 15.00
318 JKu(c),Stone-Age War 15.00
319 JKu(c),To Kill a Sergeant 15.00
320 JKu(c),Never Salute a
  Sergeant 15.00
321 JKu(c),It's Murder Out Here .. 10.00
322 JKu(c),The Killer........... 10.00
323 JKu(c),Monday's Hero 10.00
324 JKu(c),Ghost of a Tank...... 10.00
325 JKu(c),Future Kill, part I 10.00
326 JKu(c),Future Kill, part II..... 10.00
327 JKu(c),Death Express....... 10.00
328 JKu(c),Waiting For Rock..... 10.00
329 JKu(c),Dead Heat 10.00
330 JKu(c),G.I. Trophy.......... 10.00
331 JKu(c),The Sons of War 10.00
332 JKu(c),Pyramid of Death..... 10.00
333 JKu(c),Ask The Dead 10.00
334 JKu(c),What's Holding Up
  The War................ 10.00
335 JKu(c),Killer Compass 10.00
336 JKu(c),The Red Maple Leaf .. 10.00
337 JKu(c),A Bridge Called Charlie 10.00
338 JKu(c),No Escape From
  the Front 10.00
339 JKu(c),I Was Here Before.... 10.00
340 JKu(c),How To Win A War.... 10.00
341 JKu(c),High-Flyer 10.00
342 JKu(c),The 6 sides of
  Sgt. Rock................ 10.00
343 thru 350................@10.00
351 thru 422................ @7.00

OUR FIGHTING FORCES
Oct.–Nov., 1954
1 IN,JGr(c),Human Booby Trap 2,500.00
2 RH,IN,IN(c),Mile-Long Step ... 900.00
3 RA,JKu(c),Winter Ambush.... 750.00
4 RA,JGr(c),The Hot Seat 600.00
5 IN,RA,JGr(c),The Iron Punch . 600.00
6 IN,RA,JGr(c),The Sitting Tank . 500.00
7 RA,JKu,JGr(c),Battle Fist..... 500.00
8 IN,RA,JGr(c),No War
  For A Gunner.............. 500.00
9 JKu,RH,JGr(c),Crash-
  Landing At Dawn.......... 500.00
10 WW,RA,JGr(c),Grenade
  Pitcher................. 500.00
11 JKu,JGr(c),Diary of a Sub.... 400.00

12 IN,JKu,JGr(c),Jump Seat 400.00
13 RA,JGr(c),Beach Party 400.00
14 JA,RA,IN,JGr(c),Unseen War . 400.00
15 RH,JKu,JGr(c),Target For
    A Lame Duck 400.00
16 RH,JGr(c),Night Fighter 400.00
17 RA,JGr(c),Anchored Frogman 400.00
18 RH,JKu,JGr(c),Cockpit Seat . . 400.00
19 RA,JKu(c),StraightenThatLine 400.00
20 RA,MD,JGr(c),The
    Floating Pilot 500.00
21 RA,JKu(c),The Bouncing
    Baby of Company B 300.00
22 JKu,RA,JGr(c),3 Doorways
    To War 300.00
23 RA,IN,JA,JGr(c),Tin Fish Pilot 300.00
24 RA,RH,JGr(c),Frogman Duel . 300.00
25 RA,JKu(c),Dead End 300.00
26 IN,RH,JKu(c),Tag Day 300.00
27 MD,RA,JKu(c),TNT Escort . . . 300.00
28 RH,MD,JKu(c),AllQuiet atC.P. 300.00
29 JKu,JKu(c),Listen To A Jet . . . 300.00
30 IN,RA,JKu(c),Fort
    For A Gunner 300.00
31 MD,RA,JKu(c),Silent Sub 300.00
32 RH,MD,RH(c),PaperWorkWar 300.00
33 RH,JKu,JKu(c),Frogman
    In A Net 300.00
34 JA,JGr,JKu(c),Calling U-217 . . 300.00
35 JA,JGr,JKu(c),Mask of
    a Frogman 300.00
36 MD,JA,JKu(c),Steel Soldier . . 300.00
37 JA,JGr,JGr(c),Frogman
    In A Bottle 300.00
38 RH,RA,JGr(c),Sub Sinker . 300.00
39 JA,RH,RH(c),Last Torpedo . . . 300.00
40 JGr,JA,JKu,JKu(c),The
    Silent Ones 300.00
41 JGr,RH,JA,JKu(c),Battle
    Mustang 350.00
42 RH,MD,JGr(c),Sorry-
    Wrong Hill 250.00
43 MD,JKu,JGr(c),Inside Battle . . 250.00
44 MD,RH,RA,JGr(c),Big Job
    For Baker 250.00
45 RH,RA,JGr(c),B:Gunner and
    Sarge, Mop-Up Squad 900.00
46 RH,RA,JKu(c),Gunner's
    Squad 350.00
47 RH,JKu(c),TNT Birthday 250.00
48 JA,RH,JGr(c),A Statue
    For Sarge 250.00
49 MD,RH,JGr(c),Blind Gunner . . 300.00
50 JA,RH,JGr(c),I:Pooch,My
    Pal, The Pooch 250.00

51 RA,JA,RH(c),Underwater
    Gunner. 250.00
52 RA,JKu,JKu(c),The Biggest
    Target in the World 200.00
53 MD,JKu,JKu(c),The Gunner
    and the Nurse 200.00
54 JA,RA,An Egg for Sarge 200.00
55 MD,RH,JGr(c),The Last Patrol 200.00
56 RH,RA,JGr(c),Bridge of
    Bullets 200.00
57 JA,IN,JGr(c),A Tank For Sarge 200.00
58 JA,JGr(c),Return of the Pooch 200.00
59 RH,JA,JGr(c),Pooch-Patrol
    Leader 200.00
60 RH,JA,JGr(c),Tank Target 200.00
61 JA,JGr(c),Pass to Peril 200.00
62 JA,JGr(c),The Flying Pooch . . 200.00
63 JA,RH,JGr(c),Pooch-Tank
    Hunter 200.00
64 JK,RH,JGr(c),A Lifeline
    For Sarge 200.00
65 IN,JA,JGr(c),Dogtag Patrol . . . 200.00
66 JKu,JA,JGr(c),Trail of the
    Ghost Bomber 200.00
67 IN,JA,JGr(c),Purple Heart
    For Pooch 200.00
68 JA,JGr(c),Col. Hakawa's
    Birthday Party 200.00
69 JA,JKu,JGr(c),
    Destination Doom 200.00
70 JA,JKu(c),The Last Holdout . . 200.00
71 JA,JGr(c),End of the Marines . 175.00
72 JA,JGr(c),Four-Footed Spy . . . 150.00
73 IN,JGr(c),The Hero Maker . . . 150.00
74 IN,JGr(c),Three On A T.N.T.
    Bull's-Eye. 150.00
75 JKu(c),Purple Heart Patrol . . . 150.00
76 JKu(c),The T.N.T. Seat 150.00
77 JKu(c),No Foxhole-No Home . 150.00
78 JGr(c),The Last Medal 150.00
79 JA,JGr(c),Backs to the Sea . . 150.00
80 JA,JGr(c),Don't Come Back . . 150.00
81 JA,JGr(c),Battle of
    the Mud Marines 150.00
82 JA,JGr(c),Battle of the
    Empty Helmets 150.00
83 RA,JKu(c),Any Marine
    Can Do It 150.00
84 JA,JKu(c),The Gun of Shame. 150.00
85 Ja,JKu(c),The TNT Pin-Points 150.00
86 JKu(c),3 Faces of Combat . . . 150.00
87 JKu(c),Battle of the
    Boobytraps 150.00
88 GC,JKu(c),Devil Dog Patrol . . 150.00
89 JKu(c),TNT Toothache 150.00
90 JKu(c),Stop the War 150.00
91 JKu(c),The Human Shooting
    Gallery 75.00
92 JA,JKu(c),The Bomb That
    Stopped The War. 75.00
93 IN,JKu(c),The Human Sharks. . 75.00
94 RH(c),E:Gunner,Sarge & Pooch,
    The Human Blockbusters 75.00
95 GC,RH(c),B:The Fighting Devil
    Dog, Lt. Rock, The
    Fighting Devil Dog. 75.00
96 JA,RH(c),Battle of Fire 75.00
97 IN(c),Invitation To A
    Firing Squad 75.00
98 IN(c),E:The Fighting Devil
    Dog, Death Wore A Grin 75.00
99 JA,JKu(c),B:Capt. Hunter,
    No Mercy in Vietnam. 75.00
100 GC,IN(c),Death Also
    Stalks the Hunter. 75.00
101 JA,RH(c),Killer of Vietnam . . . 50.00
102 RH,JKu(c),Cold Steel
    For A Hot War 50.00
103 JKu(c),The Tunnels of Death . 50.00
104 JKu(c),Night Raid In Vietnam . 50.00
105 JKu(c),Blood Loyalty 50.00
106 IN(c),Trail By Fury 50.00

107 IN(c),Raid Of The Hellcats . . 50.00
108 IN(c),Kill The Wolf Pack 50.00
109 IN(c),Burn, Raiders, Burn 50.00
110 IN(c),Mountains Full of Death . 50.00
111 IN(c),Train of Terror 50.00
112 IN(c),What's In It For
    The Hellcats? 50.00
113 IN(c),Operation-Survival 50.00
114 IN(c),No Loot For The
    Hellcats 50.00
115 JKu(c),Death In The Desert . . 50.00
116 JKu(c),Peril From the Casbah 50.00
117 JKu(c),Colder Than Death . . . 50.00
118 JKu(c),Hell Underwater. 50.00
119 JKu(c),Bedlam In Berlin 50.00
120 JKu(c),Devil In The Dark 50.00
121 JKu(c),Take My Place. 50.00
122 JKu(c),24 Hours To Die 50.00
123 JKu(c),B:Born Losers,No
    Medals No Graves. 100.00
124 JKu(c),Losers Take All 35.00
125 Daughters of Death. 35.00
126 JKu(c),Lost Town 35.00
127 JKu(c),Angels Over Hell's
    Corner 35.00
128 JKu(c),7 11 War 35.00
129 JKu(c),Ride The Nightmare . . 35.00
130 JKu(c),Nameless Target 35.00
131 JKu(c),Half A Man. 35.00
132 JKu(c),Pooch, The Winner . . . 35.00
133 JKu(c),Heads or Tails,
    giant-size. 50.00
134 JKu(c),The Real Losers,
    giant-size. 50.00
135 JKu(c),Death Picks A Loser,
    giant-size. 50.00
136 JKu(c),Decoy For Death,
    giant-size. 50.00
137 JKu(c),God Of The Losers,
    giant-size. 50.00
138 JKu(c),The Targets 30.00
139 JKu(c),The Pirate 30.00
140 JKu(c),Lost...One Loser 30.00
141 JKu(c),Bad Penny, The. 30.00
142 JKu(c), 1/2 A Man 30.00
143 JKu(c),Diamonds Are
    For Never 30.00
144 JKu(c),The Lost Mission 30.00
145 JKu(c),A Flag For Losers 30.00
146 JKu(c),The Forever Walk 30.00
147 NA(c),The Glory Road 40.00
148 JKu(c),The Last Charge 30.00
149 FT(c),A Bullet For
    A Traitor. 30.00
150 JKu(c),Mark Our Graves. 30.00

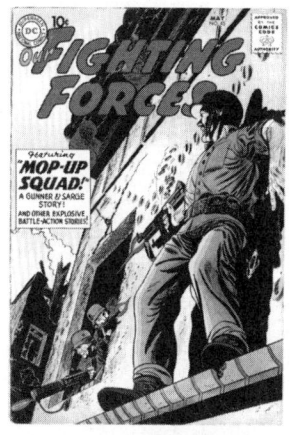

Our Fighting Forces #45
© DC Comics, Inc.

Our Fighting Forces #151
© DC Comics, Inc.

All comics prices listed are for *Near Mint* condition.

151 JKu(c),Kill Me With Wagner . . 32.00
152 JK(c),A Small Place In Hell. . . 32.00
153 JK(c),Big Max 32.00
154 JK(c),Bushido,Live By The
Code, Die By The Code 32.00
155 JK(c),The Partisans 32.00
156 JK(c),Good-Bye Broadway . . . 32.00
157 JK(c),Panama Fattie. 32.00
158 JK(c),Bombing Out On
The Panama Canal 32.00
159 JK(c),Mile-A-Minute Jones . . . 32.00
160 JKu(c),Ivan 32.00
161 JKu(c),The Major's Dream . . . 32.00
162 Gung-Ho 32.00
163 JKu(c),The Unmarked Graves 25.00
164 JKu(c),A Town Full Of Losers . 25.00
165 LD(c),The Rowboat Fleet 25.00
166 LD(c),Sword of Flame. 25.00
167 LD(c),A Front Seat In Hell. . . . 25.00
168 LD(c),A Cold Day To Die. 25.00
169 JKu(c),Welcome Home-And
Die. 25.00
170 JKu(c),A Bullet For
The General 25.00
171 JKu(c),A Long Day...
A Long War 25.00
172 JKu(c),The Two-Headed Spy . 25.00
173 JKu(c),An Appointment
With A Direct Hit 25.00
174 JKu(c),Winner Takes-Death . . 25.00
175 JKu(c),Death Warrant 25.00
176 JKu(c),The Loser Is A
Teen-Ager 25.00
177 JKu(c),This Loser Must Die . . 25.00
178 JKu(c),Last Drop For Losers . 25.00
179 JKu(c),The Last Loser 25.00
180 JKu(c),Hot Seat In A
Cold War 25.00
181 JKu(c),Sept.–Oct., 1978 . . . . . 30.00

OUTCASTS
Oct., 1987
1 thru 11 . . . . @2.50

OUTLAW NATION
DC/Vertigo, Aug., 2000
1 JaD(s),F:pulp-fiction writer. 2.50
2 JaD(s),Southern bayou 2.50
3 JaD,F:Devil Kid 2.50
4 JaD,F:Kid Gloves. 2.50
5 JaD,F:Kid Gloves. 2.50
6 JaD, ... 2.50
7 JaD, ... 2.50
8 JaD,Women,tequila & guns 2.50
9 JaD,Hell Holes. 2.50
10 JaD,V:Gloves 2.50
11 JaD,Hate, Murder and Revenge. 2.50
12 JaD,Temptation. 2.50
13 JaD,Desperado. 2.50
14 JaD,The Devil Kid. 2.50
15 JaD,The Devil Kid. 2.50
16 JaD,Under siege. 2.50
17 JaD,Quicksand 2.50
18 JaD,Old Asa 2.50
19 JaD,final issue 2.50

OUTLAWS
1991
1 LMc,I:Hood 2.50
2 thru 7 LMc . . . . @2.50

OUTSIDERS, THE
Nov., 1985
[1st Regular Series]
1 JAp,I:Looker. 3.00
2 JAp,V:Nuclear Family 2.50
3 JAp,V:Force of July 2.50
4 JAp,V:Force of July 2.50
5 JAp,Christmas Issue 2.50
6 JAp,V:Duke of Oil 2.50

Outsiders #16
© *DC Comics, Inc.*

7 JAp,V:Duke of Oil 2.50
8 JAp,Japan. 2.50
9 JAp/SD/JOp,Bik Lightning 2.50
10 JAp,I:Peoples Heroes 2.50
11 JAp,Imprisoned in death camp . 2.50
12 JAp,Imprisoned in death camp. . 2.50
13 JAp,Desert island 2.50
14 JAp,Looker/murder story 2.50
15 DJu,V:Bio-hazard 2.50
16 Halo vs.Firefly 2.50
17 JAp,J:Batman. 2.50
18 JAp,BB,V:Eclipso 2.50
19 JAp,V:Windfall. 2.50
20 JAp,Masters of Disaster 2.50
21 JAp,V:Kobra,I:Clayface IV 2.50
22 JAp,V:Strike Force Kobra 2.50
23 Return of People's Heroes 2.50
24 TVE,JAp,V:Skull,A:Duke of Oil . . 2.50
25 JAp,V:Skull 2.50
26 JAp,in Markovia 2.50
27 EL,Millennium 2.50
28 EL,Millennium,final issue 2.50
Ann.#1,KN,V:Skull,A:Batman. 2.50
Spec.#1,A:Infinity,Inc. 2.50

[2nd Regular Series], 1993–95
1 Alpha,TC(c),B:MiB(s),PaP,
I:Technocrat,Faust,Wylde 3.00
1a Omega,TC(c),PaP,V:Vampires . 3.00
2 PaP,V:Sanction 2.50
3 PaP,V:Eradicator 2.50
4 PaP,A:Eradicator 2.50
5 PaP,V:Atomic Knight,A:Jihad. . . . 2.50
6 PaP,V:Jihad 2.50
7 PaP,C:Batman 2.50
8 PaP,V:Batman,I:Halo 2.50
9 PaP,V:Batman 2.50
10 PaP,B:Final Blood, R:Looker . . . 2.50
11 PaP,Zero Hour,E:Final Blood . . . 2.50
12 PaP 2.50
13 New base 2.50
14 Martial Arts Spectacular 2.50
15 V:New Year's Evil 2.50
16 R:Windfall 2.50
17 A:Green Lantern 2.50
18 Sins of the Father 2.50
19 Sins of the Father, pt.2 . . . . 2.50
20 DvA,V:Metamorpho. 2.50
21 A:Apokolips. 2.50
22 Alien Assassin. 2.50
23 V:Defilers 2.50
24 finale 2.50

June 2003
1 TR,SHa 10.00
1a 2nd printing 4.00
2 TR,SHa,F:Jade 5.00

3 TR,SHa,Gorilla Grodd 3.00
4 Ccs,V:Brother Blood 3.00
5 CCs,V:Brother Blood 3.00
6 CCs,V:Brother Blood 2.50
7 TR,SHa,two Metamorphos 2.50
8 TR,F:Huntress 2.50
9 TR,F:Black Lightning 2.50
10 TR,F:Captain Marvel Jr. 2.50
11 F:Arsenal. 2.50
12 V:Psimon. 2.50
13 TR,Five by Five,pt.1 . . . . 2.50
14 TR,Five by Five,pt.2 . . . . 2.50
15 TR,Five by Five,pt.3 . . . . 2.50
16 V:Arsenal 2.50
17 TR,Most Wanted 2.50
18 Most Wanted, pt.2. . . . . 2.50
19 Most Wanted, pt.3. . . . . 2.50
20 Shift & Indy on a date 2.50
21 F:Batman 2.50
22 Arsenal vs. Batman. 2.50
23 Lockdown 2.50
24 The Insiders, x-over, pt.2 . . . . . . 2.50
25 The Insdiers, x-over, pt.4 . . . . . . 3.50
26 Tick Tock, pt.1, A:Batman 2.50
27 Tick Tock, pt.2,A:Batman,Katana 2.50
28 ATi,Insider aftermath 2.50
29 ATi,Day of Vengeance tie-in 2.50
30 ATi,Day of Vengeance tie-in 2.50
31 ATi,Infinite Crisis tie-in. 2.50
32 ATi,Infinite Crisis tie-in. 2.50
33 ATi,Infinite Crisis tie-in. 2.50
34 ATi,One Year Later 2.50
35 ATi,Vs brutal regime 3.00
36 ATi,Nightwing's African Mission . 3.00
37 ATi,Monsieur Mallah & Brain. . . . 3.00
38 ATi,Mallah & Brain. 3.00
39 ATi 3.00
40 ATi 3.00
41 ATi, Old foe 3.00
42 ATi. 3.00
43 ATi. 3.00
44 ATi,Pay as You Go, pt.1 . . . . 3.00
45 Pay as you Go, pt.2 . . . . 3.00
46 Pay as you Go, pt.3 . . . . 3.00
47 Checkout,pt.2;Checkmate x-over 3.00
48 Checkout,pt.4;Checkmate x-over 3.00
49 Checkout,finale:x-over 3.00
50 A:Batman, final issue 3.00
Ann. #1 Filling in the Gaps 4.00

OUTSIDERS:
FIVE OF A KIND
Aug., 2007
1 Nightwing/Boomerang 3.00
2 Katana/Shazam 3.00
3 Thunder/Martian Manhunter 3.00
4 Metamorpho/Aquaman 3.00
5 Grace/Wonder Woman 3.00

PARALLAX:
EMERALD NIGHT
Nov., 1996
1 RMz(s),MMK,MkK, pivotal tie-in
to Final Night. 4.50

PAT BOONE
1959
1 Ph(c),Jimmy Rodgers 750.00
2 Edd "Kookie" Byrnes 500.00
3 Fabian, Connie Francis 500.00
4 Bobby Darin, Johnny Mathis . . 500.00
5 Dick Clark, Frankie Avalon . . . 500.00

PEACEMAKER
Jan., 1988
1 A:Dr.Tzin-Tzin. 2.50
2 The Wages of Tzin. 2.50
3 and 4 . . . . @2.50

PENGUIN TRIUMPHANT
1 JSon,A:Batman,Wall Street 6.00

PETER CANNON: THUNDERBOLT
1992–93
1 thru 6 MC . . . . @2.50
7 MC,Battleground 2.50
8 MC,Cairo Kidnapped 2.50
9 MC 2.50
10 MC,A:JLA 2.50
11 MC,V:Havoc,A:Checkmate 2.50
12 MC,final Issue 2.50

PETER PANDA
Aug.–Sept., 1953
1 The Magic Rainbow 600.00
2 The Stolen Wand 300.00
3 thru 30 . . . . @200.00
31 Aug.–Sept., 1958 . . . . 200.00

Peter Porkchops #18
© DC Comics Inc.

PETER PORKCHOPS
Nov.–Dec., 1949
1 . . . . 400.00
2 . . . . 200.00
3 thru 10 . . . . @150.00
11 thru 30 . . . . @100.00
31 thru 61 . . . . @100.00
62 Oct.–Dec., 1960 . . . . 100.00

PHANTOM, THE
Oct., 1987
1 JO,A:Modern Phantom,13th
  Phantom 3.00
2 JO,Murder Trial in Manhattan . . . 3.00
3 JO,A:Chessman 3.00
4 JO,V:Chessman,final issue 3.00

PHANTOM, THE
1989–90
1 LMc,V:Gun Runners 3.00
2 LMc,V:Gun Runners 2.50
3 LMc,V:Drug Smugglers 2.50
4 LMc,In America,A:Diana Palner . . 2.50
5 LMc,Racial Riots 2.50
6 LMc,in Africa,Toxic Waste
  Problem 2.50
7 LMc,Gold Rush 2.50
8 LMc,Train Surfing 2.50
9 LMc,The Slave Trade 2.50

10 LMc,Famine in Khagana 2.50
11 LMc,Phantom/Diana Wedding
  proposal 2.50
12 LMc,Phantom framed for
  murder 2.50
13 W:Phantom & Diana Palner
  C:Mandrake last issue 2.50

PHANTOM STRANGER
Aug.–Sept., 1952
1 . . . . 3,000.00
2 . . . . 1,700.00
3 thru 5 . . . . @1,500.00
6, June-July, 1953 . . . . 1,500.00

PHANTOM STRANGER
May-June, 1969
1 CI rep.&new material 300.00
2 CI rep.&new material 125.00
3 CI rep.&new material 125.00
4 NA,I:Tala,1st All-new issue . . . 150.00
5 MSy,MA,A:Dr.13 . . . . 100.00
6 MSy,A:Dr.13 . . . . 100.00
7 JAp,V:Tala 100.00
8 JAp,A:Dr.13 . . . . 100.00
9 JAp,A:Dr.13 . . . . 100.00
10 JAp,I:Tannarak 100.00
11 JAp,V:Tannarak 50.00
12 JAp,TD,Dr.13 solo story 50.00
13 JAp,TD,Dr.13 solo. 50.00
14 JAp,TD,Dr.13 solo. 50.00
15 JAp,ATh(rep),TD,Iron Messiah,
  giant-size 60.00
16 JAp,TD,MMes(rep)Dr.13 solo
  giant-size 60.00
17 JAp,I:Cassandra Craft,
  giant-size 60.00
18 TD,Dr.13 solo, giant-size 60.00
19 JAp,TD,Dr.13 solo, giant-size . . 60.00
20 JAp,Child Shall Lead Them . . . 50.00
21 JAp,TD,Dr.13 solo. 30.00
22 JAp,TD,I:Dark Circle 30.00
23 JAp,MK,I:Spawn-Frankenstein . 30.00
24 JAp,MA,Spawn Frankenstein . . 50.00
25 JAp,MA,Spawn Frankenstein . . 50.00
26 JAp,A:Frankenstein. 60.00
27 V:Dr. Zorn 50.00
28 BU:Spawn of Frankenstein 50.00
29 V:Dr.Zorn,BU:Frankenstein. . . . 50.00
30 E:Spawn of Frankenstein 50.00
31 B:BU:Black Orchid 55.00
32 NR,BU:Black Orchid 30.00
33 MGr,A:Deadman 40.00
34 BU:Black Orchid 30.00
35 BU:Black Orchid 30.00
36 BU:Black Orchid 30.00
37 Crimson Gold,BU:BlackOrchid . 30.00
38 Images of the Dead 30.00
39 A:Deadman 40.00
40 A:Deadman 40.00
41 A:Deadman 40.00

PHANTOM STRANGER
Oct., 1987–Jan., 1988
1 MMi,CR,V:Eclipso 3.00
2 and 4 MMi,CR,V:Eclipso . . . . . @3.00

PHANTOM ZONE, THE
Jan., 1982
1 GD/TD,A:Jax-Ur. 2.50
2 GC/TD,A:JLA 2.50
3 GC/TD,A:Mon-El 2.50
4 GC/TD 2.50

PICTURE STORIES FROM THE BIBLE
Autumn, 1942–43
1 thru 4 Old Testament . . . . . @300.00
1 thru 3 New Testament . . . . . @400.00

PINKY AND THE BRAIN
Warner Bros./DC, 1996
1 from animated TV series 3.00
2 thru 27 . . . . @3.00

PLASTIC MAN
[1st Series]
Nov.–Dec., 1966
1 GK,I:Dr.Drome (1966 series
  begins). 175.00
2 V:The Spider 75.00
3 V:Whed 75.00
4 V:Dr.Dome 75.00
5 1,001 Plassassins 75.00
6 V:Dr.Dome 60.00
7 O:Plastic Man Jr.,A:Original
  Plastic Man,Woozy Winks 60.00
8 V:The Weasel 60.00
9 V:Joe the Killer Pro 60.00
10 V:Doll Maker(series ends) 60.00
11 (1976 series begins) 15.00
12 I:Carrot-Man 15.00
13 A:Robby Reed. 15.00
14 V:Meat By-Product & Sludge . . 15.00
15 I:Snuffer,V:Carrot-Man 15.00
16 V:Kolonel Kool 15.00
17 O:Plastic Man 15.00
18 V:Professor Klean 15.00
19 I&Only App.Marty Meeker 15.00
20 V:Snooping Sneetches
  Oct.–Nov., 1977. . . . . 15.00

PLASTIC MAN
1988–89
1 Mini-series,Origin retold. 2.50
2 V:The Ooze Brothers 2.50
3 In Los Angeles. 2.50
4 End-series,A:Superman. 2.50

PLASTIC MAN
1999
Spec.#1 TTn(s),ALo,RBr,48-page . . 4.00

PLASTIC MAN
DC Dec. 2003
1 KB,O:Plastic Man. 2.50
2 KB,Eel O'Brien on the Lam 3.00
3 KB,Eel O'Brien on the Lam 3.00
4 KB,Eel O'Brien on the Lam 3.00
5 KB,ghosts of his past. 3.00
6 KB,Eel O'Brien,concl. 3.00
7 Love Makes a Fella Woozy 3.00
8 Continuity Bandit,pt.1. . . . . 3.00
9 Continuity Bandit,pt.2. . . . . 3.00
10 Halloween issue 3.00
11 Homeland Security 3.00
12 KB 3.00
13 KB 3.00
14 KB 3.00
15 thru 18 KB . . . . @3.00
19 Edwina Crisis, pt.2 . . . . 3.00
20 final issue 3.00
GN The Lost Annual, rep. 7.00

PLOP!
Sept.–Oct., 1973
1 SA-AA,GE,ShM 50.00
2 AA,SA 25.00
3 AA,SA 25.00
4 BW,SA 30.00
5 MA,MSy,SA,BWr 22.00
6 MSy,SA 20.00
7 SA 20.00
8 SA 20.00
9 SA 20.00
10 SA 20.00
11 ATh,SA 20.00
12 SA 20.00
13 WW(c),SA. 22.00

DC

14 WW,SA 22.00
15 WW(c),SA 22.00
16 SD,WW,SA 22.00
17 SA 22.00
18 SD,WW,SA 22.00
19 WW,SA 22.00
20 SA,WW 22.00
21 JO,WW 25.00
22 JO,WW,BW 25.00
23 BW,WW. 25.00
24 SA,WW,Nov.–Dec., 1976 . . . . . 25.00

POWER COMPANY, THE
Jan., 2002
1 KBk,TG,V:Doctor Cyber 2.50
2 thru 6 KBk . . . . @2.50
7 thru 18 KBk 2.75

POWER OF SHAZAM!
1995–98
1 R:Captain Marvel 4.00
2 V:Arson Fiend 3.00
3 V:Ibac 3.00
4 JOy,R:Mary Marvel,Tawky,
  Tawny 3.00
5 JOy(c&a),F:Mary Marvel,
  V:Black Adam 3.00
6 R:Captain Marvel 3.00
7 V:Captain Nazi 3.00
8 R:Captain Marvel,Jr. 3.00
9 JOy,MM,V:Black Adam 3.00
10 JOy,MM,V:Seven Deadly
   Enemies of Man 3.00
11 JOy,MM,R:Ibis as Capt.Marvel . . 3.00
12 JOy,MM,How Billy Batson's
   father met Shazam 3.00
13 JOy,MM 3.00
14 JOy,GK,MM,F:CaptainMarvelJr . 3.00
15 JOy,MM,V:Mr.Mind 3.00
16 thru 18 . . . . @3.00
19 JOy(s),GK,MM,Captain Marvel
   Jr. V:Captain Nazi 3.00
20 JOy(s),PKr,MM,A:Superman . . . 3.00
21 JOy(s),PKr,MM,V:Liquidator . . . 3.00
22 JOy(s),PKr,MM,A:Batman 2.50
23 JOy(s),PKr,MM, ... 2.50
24 JOy(s),PKr,MM,V:Baron Blitz-
   krieg, prelude to new family . . . 2.50
25 JOy(s),PKr,MM,The Marvel
   Family '97 . . . . 2.50
26 JOy(s),PKr,MM,new Capt.
   Marvel framed for murder 2.50

Power of Shazam #2
© DC Comics, Inc.

27 JOy(s),PKr,MM,D:Captain
   Marvel 2.50
28 JOy(s),DG, V:Patty Patty
   Bang Bang 2.50
29 JOy(c),DG,F:Hoppy 2.50
30 JOy(c),PKr,DG,V:Mr. Finish 2.50
31 JOy,PKr,DG,Genesis x-over 2.50
32 JOy,PKr,DG,Genesis aftermath . . 2.50
33 JOy,PKr,DG,Madam M, Sin 2.50
34 JOy,PKr,DG,F:Gangbuster 2.50
35 JOy,PKr,DG,Lightning &
   Stars, pt.2 x-over 2.50
36 JOy 2.50
37 JOy,MM,DG,F:Capt.Marvel Jr. . . 2.50
38 JOy,PKr,DG,Monster Society
   of Evil, pt.1 . . . . 2.50
39 JOy,PKr,DG,Monster, pt.2 . . . . . 2.50
40 JOy,PKr,DG,Monster, pt.3 . . . . . 2.50
41 JOy,PKr,DG,Monster, pt.4 . . . . . 2.50
42 JOy,DG,new logo & design 2.50
43 JOy,DG,I:Bulletgirl 2.50
44 JOy,DG,V:Chain Lightning 2.50
45 JOy,DG,A:JLA 2.50
46 JOy,DG,A:Superman 2.50
47 JOy,V:Black Adam, final issue . . . 2.50
Ann.#1 JOy(s),MM,Legends of
   the Dead Earth 3.00
Spec.#1,000,000 JOy,DG 2.50

POWER OF THE ATOM
1988–89
1 1st Issue, Origin retold 2.50
2 Return of Powers 2.50
3 I:Strobe 2.50
4 A:Hawkman+bonus book #8 . . . . 2.50
5 DT,A:Elongated Man 2.50
6 JBy,V:Chronos 2.50
7 GN,Invasion,V:Khunds,Chronos . 2.50
8 GN,Invasion,V:Chronos 2.50
9 GN,A:Justice League 2.50
10 GN,I:Humbug 2.50
11 GN,V:Paul Hoben 2.50
12 GN,V:Edg the Destroyer 2.50
13 GN,Blood Stream Journey 2.50
14 GN,V:Humbug 2.50
15 GN,V:Humbug 2.50
16 GN,V:The CIA 2.50
17 GN,V:The Sting 2.50
18 GN,V:The CIA, last issue 2.50

POWERPUFF GIRLS
Warner Bros./DC March, 2000
1 . . . . 3.50
2 thru 70 . . . . @2.25
Double Whammy, rep. #1 & #2 . . . . 4.00
Spec.Powerpuff Girls movie comic . 3.00

PREACHER
DC/Vertigo, 1995
1 I:Jesse Custer, Genesis 22.00
2 Saint of Killers 18.00
3 GF(c),I:Angels 15.00
4 GF(c),V:Saint of Killers 10.00
5 Naked City,pt.1 . . . . 10.00
6 Naked City,pt.2 . . . . 10.00
7 Naked City,pt.3 . . . . 8.00
8 GEn,SDi,All in the Family,pt.1 . . . 5.00
9 GEn,SDi,All in the Family,pt.2 . . . 5.00
10 GEn,SDi,All in the Family,pt.3 . . 5.00
11 GEn,SDi,All in the Family,pt.4 . . 5.00
12 GEn,SDi,All in the Family,pt.5 . . 6.00
13 GEn,SDi,Hunters,pt.1 . . . . 5.00
14 GEn,SDi,Hunters,pt.2 (of 4) . . . 4.00
15 and 16 . . . . @4.00
17 Star captures Cassidy 3.00
18 GEn(s),SDi,secret of Jesse
   Custer's cigarette lighter 3.00
19 GEn(s),SDi,Crusaders, pt.1 . . . 3.00
20 GEn(s),SDi,Crusaders, pt.2 . . . 3.00
21 GEn(s),SDi,Crusaders, pt.3 . . . 3.00
22 GEn(s),SDi,Crusaders,pt.4 . . . 3.00

23 GEn(s),SDi,Crusaders, pt.5 . . . 3.00
24 GEn(s),SDi,Crusaders, concl . . . 3.00
25 GEn(s),SDi,Cry Blood, Cry
   Erin 3.00
26 GEn(s),SDi,To the Streets of
   Manhattan I Wandered Away . . 2.50
27 GEn(s),SDi, Jessie & Tulip in
   New York, pt.1 . . . . 2.50
28 GEn(s),SDi, Jessie & Tulip in
   New York, pt.2 . . . . 2.50
29 GEn(s),SDi, south to New
   Orleans 2.50
30 GEn,SDi,in New Orleans 2.50
31 GEn,SDi,in New Orleans 2.50
32 GEn,SDi,in New Orleans 2.50
33 GEn,SDi,in New Orleans,concl. . 2.50
34 GEn,SDi,War in the Sun,pt.1 . . . 2.50
35 GEn,SDi,War in the Sun,pt.2 . . . 2.50
36 GEn,SDi,War in the Sun,pt.3 . . . 2.50
37 GEn,SDi,War in the Sun,pt.4 . . . 2.50
38 GEn,SDi,GF,Utah radioactive . . 2.50
39 GEn,SDi,GF,out of the desert . . 2.50
40 GEn,SDi,GF,Arsefaced World . . 2.50
41 . . . . 2.50
42 GEn(s),SDi,GF,V:Meatman 2.50
43 GEn(s),SDi,GF,V:Meat Man . . . 2.50
44 GEn(s),SDi,GF,Gunther Hahn . . 2.50
45 GEn(s),SDi,GF,V:Meat Man . . . 2.50
46 GEn(s),SDi,GF,Miss Oatlash . . 2.50
47 GEn(s),SDi,GF,Salvation 2.50
48 GEn(s),SDi,GF,Salvation 2.50
49 GEn(s),SDi,GF,First Contact . . . 2.50
50 GEn(s),SDi,GF,48-page
   I:100 Bullets 4.00
51 GEn(s),SDi,GF,Tulip's past,pt.1 . 4.00
52 GEn(s),SDi,GF,Tulip's past,pt.2 . 2.50
53 GEn(s),SDi,GF,road trip story . . 2.50
54 GEn(s),SDi,GF,Jesse & Tulip . . . 2.50
55 GEn(s),SKi,GF 2.50
56 GEn(s),GF. 2.50
57 GEn(s), ... 2.50
58 GEn(s),SDi, ... 2.50
59 thru 64 GEn(s),SDi,
   Alamo,pt.1 thru pt.6 . . . . @2.50
65 GEn(s),SDi,Alamo,pt.7 . . . . 5.00
66 GEn(s),SDi,Alamo,pt.8,
   final issue 5.00
GN Preacher Spec. Cassidy: Blood
   and Whisky, GEn(s) (1997) 6.00
GN Tall in the Saddle. 6.00
Spec. The Good Old Boys, parody . 5.50
Spec. The Story of You-Know-Who
   GEn(s),RCa,O:Arseface (1996) 5.00
Spec. One Man's War 5.00

PREACHER SPECIAL: SAINT OF KILLERS
DC/Vertigo, 1996
1 GEn(s),StP 5.00
2 GEn(s),StP 4.50
3 GEn(s),StP 3.50
4 GEn(s),StP 3.00

PREZ
Aug.–Sept., 1973
1 I:Prez (from Sandman #54) 40.00
2 thru 4 F:Prez 20.00

PRIDE & JOY
DC/Vertigo, May, 1997
[Mini-series]
1 (of 4) GEn(s),JHi 2.50
2 thru 4 GEn(s),JHi . . . . @2.50

PRIMAL FORCE
1994–95
O New Team 2.50
1 Claw. 2.50
2 thru 14 . . . . @2.50

All comics prices listed are for *Near Mint* condition.

PRINCE
DC/Piranha Press 1991
1 DCw,KW,based on rock star 7.00
1a Second printing 2.50
1b 3rd printing. 2.00

PRINCESS NATASHA
June, 2006
1 (0f 4) 2.25
2 Undercover cheerleader 2.25
3 Robot Hamsters. 2.25
4 concl. 2.25

PRISONER, THE
1988–89
1 Based on TV series 4.00
2 By Hook or by Crook 4.00
3 Confrontation 4.00
4 Departure, final issue. 4.00

PROPOSITION PLAYER
DC/Vertigo, Oct., 2000
1 (of 6) PGn,BWg, ... 2.50
2 thru 6 PGn,BWg, ... @2.50

PSYBA-RATS, THE
[Mini-Series], 1995
1 CDi,A:Robin 2.50
2 CDi,A:Robin. 2.50
3 CDi,F:Razorsharp,final issue . . . 2.50

PSYCHO, THE
1991
1 I:Psycho 9.00
2 Sonya Rescue 8.00
3 Psycho against the World 7.00

PULP FANTASTIC
DC/Vertigo, Dec., 1999
1 (of 3) HC,RBr,detective 2.50
2 HC,RBr 2.50
3 HC,RBr,conclusion. 2.50

QUESTION, THE
Feb., 1987
1 DCw,R:Question,I:Myra,A:Shiva . 3.00
2 thru 10 . . . . @2.50
11 thru 20 . . . . @2.50
21 thru 36 . . . . @2.50
Ann.#1 DCw,A:Batman,G.A. 3.00
Ann.#2 A:Green Arrow 4.00

QUESTION, THE
Nov., 2004
1 (of 6) F:Vic Sage 3.00
2 in Metropolis 3.00
3 Luthor's Science Spire. 3.00
4 F:Superman 3.00
5 Sceince Spire. 3.00
6 finale 3.00

QUESTION QUARTERLY
1990–92
1 DCw 4.50
2 DCw 4.00
3 DCw(c) Film. 3.00
4 DCw,MM,Waiting for Phil. 3.00
5 DCw,MMi,MM,last issue 3.00

RAGMAN
[1st Limited Series], 1976–77
1 I&O:Ragman 25.00
2 I:Opal 15.00
3 V:Mr. Big 10.00
4 JKu(1st interior on character) . . . 10.00
5 JKu,O:Ragman,final issue 10.00

[2nd Limited Series], 1991–92
1 PB,O:Ragman 3.00
2 PB,O:Ragman Powers. 3.00
3 PB,Original Ragman 3.00
4 PB,Gang War. 3.00
5 PB,V:Golem. 3.00
6 PB,V:Golem,A:Batman 3.00
7 PB,V:Golem,A:Batman 3.00
8 PB,V:Golem,A:Batman 3.00

RAGMAN:
CRY OF THE DEAD
1993–94
1 JKu(c),R:Ragman 3.50
2 JKu(c),A:Marinette 3.00
3 JKu(c),V:Marinette 3.00
4 JKu(c),Exorcism. 3.00
5 JKu(c),V:Marinette 3.00
6 JKu(c),final issue 3.00

RANN/THANAGAR
WAR, THE
May, 2005
1 MCa,F;Adam Strange 6.00
1a 2nd printing 4.00
2 MCa,V:Khund hordes 3.50
3 MCa 3.00
4 MCa 3.00
5 MCa 3.00
6 MCa, Infinite Crisis lead-in. 3.00
Spec. Infinite Crisis 5.00

RANN/THANAGAR:
HOLY WAR
May, 2008
1 (of 8) JSn,RLm, Cosmic Heroes . 3.50
1a variant (c) (1:10) 3.50
2 thru 7 JSn,RLm . . . . @3.50

RAVEN
March, 2008
1 (of 5) MWn(s). 3.00
2 thru 5 . . . . @3.00

THE RAY
[Limited Series], 1992
1 JQ,ANi,I&O:Ray(Ray Torril) 5.00
2 JQ,ANi,I:G.A. Ray 3.00
3 JQ,ANi,A:G.A. Ray. 3.00
4 JQ,ANi,V:Dr.Polaris 4.00
5 JQ,ANi,V:Dr.Polaris 3.00
6 JQ,ANi,C:Lobo,final issue 3.00

[Regular Series], 1994–96
1 JQ(c),RPr,V:Brinestone,
  A:Superboy 3.00
1a Newsstand Ed.. . . . . 2.50
2 RPr,V:Brinestone,A:Superboy . . 2.50
3 RPr,I:Death Masque 2.50
4 JQ(c),RPr,I:Death Masque,
  Dr. Polarus. 2.50
5 JQ(c),RPr,V:G.A.Ray 2.50
6 thru 28 . . . . @2.50
Ann.#1 Year One Annual 4.00

REAL FACT COMICS
March-April, 1946
1 S&K,Harry Houdini story 1,000.00
2 S&K, Rin-Tin-Tin story 650.00
3 H.G. Wells story 500.00
4 Jimmy Stewart story,B:Just
  Imagine 550.00
5 Batman & Robin(c) 3,000.00
6 O:Tommy Tomorrow 2,000.00
7 The Flying White House 300.00
8 VF,A:Tommy Tomorrow. . . . 1,000.00
9 S&K,Glen Miller story 500.00
10 MMe(s),The Vigilante 500.00

Real Fact Comics #11
© DC Comics Inc.

11 EK,How the G-Men Capture
  Public Enemies!. 250.00
12 How G-Men are Trained 250.00
13 Dale Evans story. 700.00
14 Will Rogers Story,Diary of
  Death 300.00
15 A:The Master Magician-
  Thurston,A-Bomb 300.00
16 A:Four Reno Brothers,
  T.Tommorrow. 800.00
17 I Guard an Armored Car 250.00
18 The Mystery Man of
  Tombstone. 250.00
19 Weapon that Won the West . . 250.00
20 JKu,Daniel Boone 275.00
21 JKu,KitCarson,July-Aug.,1949 250.00

REAL SCREEN COMICS
Spring, 1945
1 B:Fox & the Crow,Flippity
  & Flop 1,500.00
2 inc. Tito and His Burrito 700.00
3 (fa) 450.00
4 thru 7 (fa) . . . . @300.00
8 thru 11 (fa) . . . . @300.00
12 thru 20 (fa) . . . . @225.00
21 thru 30 (fa) . . . . @150.00
31 thru 40 (fa) . . . . @125.00
41 thru 128 (fa) . . . . @100.00
Becomes:

TV SCREEN CARTOONS
129 thru 137. . . . . @100.00
138 Jan.–Feb., 1961 . . . . 100.00

REALWORLDS
March, 2000
GN Batman, 48-pg. 6.00
GN Wonder Woman, 48-pg. 6.00
GN JLA, 48-pg. 6.00
GN Superman 6.00

R.E.B.E.L.S. '94–'96
0 New team. 2.50
1 L.E.G.I.O.N.,Green Lantern 2.50
2 Dissent. 2.50
3 Brains. 2.50
4 Ship goes Insane. 2.50
5 F:Dox 2.50
6 Dox Defeated. 2.50
7 John Sin. 2.50
8 V:Galactic Bank 2.50
9 F:Dox,Ignea,Garv,Strata 2.50
10 V:World Bank 2.50
11 Comet's Tail. 2.50

All comics prices listed are for *Near Mint* condition.

12 F:Iceman Assassin 2.50
13 Underworld Unleashed tie-in . . . 2.50
14 F:Lyrl Dox 2.50
15 V:Lyrl Dox 2.50
16 V:Lyrl Dox's satellite 2.50

RED TORNADO
1985
1 thru 4 Cl/FMc . . . . @3.00

REIGN IN HELL
July, 2008
1 (of 8) F:Lord Satanus 3.50
1a variant (c) (1:10) 3.50
2 thru 5 . . . . @3.50
Spec. Reign in Hell 80-pg. giant . . . 5.00

REIGN OF THE ZODIAC
Aug. 2003
1 thru 8 BWi,CDo . . . . @2.75

REMARKABLE WORLDS OF PHINEAS B. FUDDLE
DC/Paradox, 1999
1 (of 4) F:Angus & McKee 6.00
2 . . . . 6.00
3 ancient India 6.00
4 concl. 6.00

RESTAURANT AT THE END OF THE UNIVERSE
1994
1 Adapt. 2nd book in Hitchhikers'
 Guide to the Galaxy,
 I:The Restaurant 7.00
2 V:The Meal 7.00
3 Final issue 7.00

RESURRECTION MAN
March, 1997
1 DAn(s),JG,lenticular death's
 head cover. 6.00
2 DAn(s),JG,V:Amazo 5.00
3 DAn(s),JG,Scorpion Memories
 pt.1 (of 3). 4.00
4 DAn(s),JG,Scorpion,pt.2 . . . . 4.00
5 DAn(s),JG,Scorpion,pt.3, ... 4.00
6 DAn&ALa(s),JoP,Genesis tie-in . . 3.00
7 DAn&ALa(s),TGb,BG,A:Batman . . 3.00
8 DAn&ALa(s),BG,Big Howler. 3.00
9 DAn&ALa(s),F:Hitman, pt.1 . . . . . 3.00

Resurrection Man #8
© DC Comics, Inc.

10 DAn&ALa(s),F:Hitman, pt.2 . . . . 3.00
11 DAn&ALa(s), Origin of the
 Species, pt.1 . . . . 2.50
12 DAn&ALa(s), Origin of the
 Species, pt.2 . . . . 2.50
13 DAn&ALa(s),Candy Man 2.50
14 DAn&ALa(s),really dead? 2.50
15 DAn&ALa(s),JG,V:Rider 2.50
16 DAn&ALa(s),BG,Avenging
 Angels x-over pt.1 . . . . 2.50
17 DAn&ALa(s),BG,Avenging
 Angels x-over pt.3 . . . . 2.50
18 DAn&ALa(s),A:Phantom Stranger,
 Deadman. 2.50
19 DAn&ALa(s),Cape Fear, pt.1 . . . 2.50
20 DAn&ALa(s),Cape Fear, pt.2 . . . 2.50
21 DAn&ALa(s),Cape Fear, pt.3 . . . 2.50
22 DAn&ALa(s) 2.50
23 DAn&ALa(s),Resurrection
 Woman 2.50
24 DAn&ALa(s) 2.50
25 DAn&ALa(s)Millennium
 Meteor,pt.1. . . . . 2.50
26 DAn&ALa(s)Millennium Meteor,
 pt.2,A:Superman, Titans 2.50
27 DAn&ALa(s)Millennium Meteor,
 pt.3,final issue 2.50
Spec.#1,000,000 DAn&ALa(s). 2.50

RICHARD DRAGON, KUNG FU FIGHTER
April-May, 1975
1 O:Richard Dragon 15.00
2 JSn/AM 13.00
3 JK. 11.00
4 thru 8 RE/WW . . . . @10.00
9 thru 17 RE . . . . @8.00
18 Nov.–Dec., 1977 . . . . 8.00

RICHARD DRAGON
May 2004
1 thru 12 CDi(s),SMc . . . . @2.50

RIMA, THE JUNGLE GIRL
April-May, 1974
1 NR,I:Rima,O:Pt. 1 . . . . 25.00
2 NR,O:Pt.2 . . . . 15.00
3 NR,O:Pt.3 . . . . 15.00
4 NR,O:Pt.4 . . . . 15.00
5 NR 15.00
6 NR 15.00
7 April-May, 1975 . . . . 15.00

RING, THE [OF THE NIEBLUNG]
1989
1 GK,Opera Adaption 12.00
2 GK,Sigfried's Father's Sword . . . 7.00
3 GK,to save Brunhilde. 6.00
4 GK, final issue 6.00

RIP HUNTER, TIME MASTER
March-April, 1961
1 . . . . 1,100.00
2 . . . . 500.00
3 thru 5 . . . . @350.00
6 and 7 Ath . . . . @250.00
8 thru 20 . . . . @200.00
21 thru 28. . . . . @150.00
29 Nov.–Dec., 1965 . . . . 150.00

ROBIN
[1st Limited Series], 1991
1 TL,BB(c),Trial,pt.1(&Poster). . . . 5.00
1a 2nd printing 2.50

1b 3rd printing. 2.50
2 TL,BB(c) Trial,pt.2 . . . . 3.00
2a 2nd printing 2.50
3 TL,BB(c) Trial,pt.3 . . . . 3.00
4 TL,Trial,pt.4 . . . . 3.00
5 TL,Final issue,A:Batman 3.00
TPB BB(c),rep. 8.00

[2nd Limited Series], 1991
[ROBIN II: THE JOKER'S WILD]
1 Direct,Hologram(c)Joker face . . . 3.00
1a (c)Joker straightjacket 2.50
1b (c)Joker standing 2.50
1c (c)Batman 2.50
1d Newsstand(no hologram). 2.50
1e collectors set,extra holo. 10.00
2 Direct,Hologram(c) Robin/Joker
 Knife 2.50
2a (c)Joker/Robin-Dartboard 2.50
2b (c)Robin/Joker-Hammer 2.50
2c Newsstand(no hologram). 2.50
2d collectors set,extra holo. 9.00
3 Direct,Holo(c)Robin standing. . . . 2.50
3a (c)Robin swinging 2.50
3b Newsstand(no hologram). 2.50
3c collectors set,extra holo. 7.00
4 Direct,Hologram 2.50
4a Newsstand (no hologram) 2.50
4b collectors set,extra holo. 2.50

[3rd Limited Series], 1992–93
[ROBIN III: CRY OF THE HUNTRESS]
1 TL,A:Huntress,Collector's Ed.
 movable(c),poster 3.00
1a MZ(c),Newsstand Ed. 2.50
2 TL,V:KGBeast,A:Huntress 2.75
2a MZ(c),Newsstand Ed 2.50
3 TL,V:KGBeast,A:Huntress 2.75
3a MZ(c),newsstand Ed. 2.25
4 TL,V:KGBeast,A:Huntress 2.75
4a MZ(c),newsstand Ed. 2.50
5 TL,V:KGBeast,A:Huntress 2.75
5a MZ(c),newsstand Ed. 2.50
6 TL,V:KGBeast,King Snake,
 A:Huntress. 2.75
6a MZ(c),Newsstand Ed 2.50

[Regular Series], 1993–2002
1 B:CDi(s),TG,SHa,V:Speedboyz . . 4.00
1a Newstand Ed. 2.50
2 TG,V:Speedboyz 2.50
3 TG,V:Cluemaster,
 Electrocutioner. 2.50
4 TG,V:Cluemaster,Czonk,
 Electrocutioner. 2.50
5 TG,V:Cluemaster,Czonk,
 Electrocutioner. 2.50
6 TG,A:Huntress 2.50
7 TG,R:Robin's Father 2.50
8 TG,KnightsEnd#5,A:Shiva 3.00
9 TG,Knights End:Aftermath 2.50
10 TG,Zero Hour,V:Weasel 2.50
11 New Batman 2.50
12 Robin vs. thugs. 2.50
13 V:Steeljacket. 2.50
14 CDi(s),TG,Return of Bruce
 Wayne,Troika,pt.4 . . . . 3.00
14a Collector's edition 3.00
15 Cluemaster Mystery 2.50
16 F:Spoiler 2.50
17 I:Silver Monkey,V:King Snake,Lynx
 [New Miraweb format begins] . . 2.50
18 Gotham City sabotaged 2.50
19 V:The General. 2.50
20 F:Robin. 2.50
21 Ninja Camp,pt.1 . . . . 2.50
22 CDi,TG,Ninja Camp,pt.2 . . . . . . 2.50
23 CDi,Underworld Unleashed tie-in 2.50
24 CDi,V:Charaxes 2.50
25 CDi,F:Green Arrow 2.50
26 CDi,The Hard Lessons 2.50
27 CDi,Contagion. 2.50

Robin, Regular Series #15
© DC Comics Inc.

28 CDi,Contagion: conclusion 2.50
29 CDi,FFo,SnW,A:Maxie Zeus. . . . 2.50
30 CDi,FFo,SnW,A:Maxie Zeus . . . 2.50
31 CDi(s),A:Wildcat 2.50
32 CDi(s),Legacy, pt. 3 x-over 2.50
33 CDi(s),Legacy, pt. 7 x-over 2.50
34 CDi(s),JhD,action at a
     Shakespear play 2.50
35 CDi(s),Robin & Spoiler, Final
     Night tie-in 2.50
36 CDi(s),V:Toyman, The General . . 2.50
37 CDi(s),V:The General, Toyman. . 2.50
38 CDi(s),. 2.50
39 CDi(s), pt.2 . . . . 2.50
40 CDi(s),. 2.50
41 CDi(s),F:Tim and Ariana 2.50
42 CDi(s),F:Crocky the Crocodile . . 2.50
43 CDi(s),A:Spoiler 2.50
44 CDi(s) Pt.2 (of 2). 2.50
45 CDi(s) Tim Drake grounded 2.50
46 CDi(s) Genesis tie-in. 2.50
47 CDi,V:General, pt.1 . . . . 2.50
48 CDi,V:General, pt.2. . . . . 2.50
49 CDi,to Paris. 2.50
50 CDi(s),F:Lady Shiva & King
     Snake, 48pg 3.50
51 CDi(s) 2.50
52 CDi(s) Cataclysm x-over,pt.7 . . . 3.00
53 CDi(s),SnW,Cataclysm concl. . . . 3.00
54 CDi(s),SnW,Aftershock 2.50
55 CDi(s),SnW, Brotherhood of
     the Fist x-over, pt.3 . . . . 2.50
56 CDi(s),SnW,tearful turning point . 2.50
57 CDi(s),SnW,A:Spoiler 2.50
58 CDi(s),SnW,A:Spoiler 2.50
59 CDi(s),SnW,V:Steeljacket 2.50
60 CDi(s),SnW,Alvin Draper 2.50
61 CDi(s),SnW,V:Phil Delinger 2.50
62 CDi(s),SnW,A:Flash, pt.1 . . . . . . 2.50
63 CDi(s),SnW,A:Flash, pt.2 . . . . . . 2.50
64 CDi(s),SnW,A:Flash, pt.3 . . . . . . 2.50
65 CDi(s),SnW,A:Spoiler 2.50
66 CDi(s),SnW,V:demons 2.50
67 CDi(s),SnW,No Man's Land 2.50
68 CDi(s),No Man's Land 2.50
69 CDi(s),No Man's Land 2.50
70 CDi(s),No Man's Land 2.50
71 CDi(s),V:Killer Croc. 2.50
72 CDi(s) 2.50
73 CDi(s),F:Batgirl 2.50
74 CDi(s),F:Batman & Nightwing. . . 2.50
75 CDi(s),48-pg. 3.50
76 CDi(s),R:Man-Bat 2.50
77 CDi(s),I:Jaeger 2.50

78 CDi(s),V:Arrakhat 2.50
79 CDi(s),F:Green Arrow 2.50
80 CDi(s),A:Star. 2.50
81 CDi(s),MPn, ... 2.50
82 CDi(s),Spoiler,Star. 2.50
83 CDi,Vacation time 2.50
84 CDi,A:Lagoon Boy 2.50
85 CDi,This issue: Batman dies! . . . 2.50
86 Officer Down x-over,pt.2 . . . . 5.00
87 CDi,A:Spoiler 2.50
88 CDi,Road trip 2.50
89 CDi,to Himalayas 2.50
90 CDi,V:mini-yeti 2.50
91 CDi,F:Danny Temple. 2.50
92 CDi,SBe,A:Batman,Spoiler 2.50
93 CDi,F:Spoiler. 2.50
94 CDi,F:Spoiler,Wesley 2.50
95 CDi,Joker:Last Laugh tie-in 2.50
96 CDi,Last Laugh aftermath. 2.50
97 CDi,F:Normandy 2.50
98 Bruce Wayne:Murderer,pt.8 . . . . 5.00
99 Bruce Wayne:Murderer,pt.11 . . . 5.00
100 CDi,Spoiler,48-pg. 5.00
101 WorldWithoutYoungJustice,pt.3 2.50
102 Spoiler. 2.50
103 Nocturna's secret 2.50
104 Astrology Lady 2.50
105 riddle of Natalia. 2.50
106 A:Batman 2.50
107 F:Charaxis. 2.50
108 F:Charaxis. 2.50
109 V:Charaxis 2.50
110 F:Nightwing. 2.50
111 F:Spoiler 2.50
112 to Pennsylvania. 2.50
113 V:The Riddler 2.50
114 The Wrong Town 2.50
115 The Wrong Town 2.50
116 Identity compromised 2.50
117 Identity compromised 2.50
118 Traitor's identity. 2.50
119 Traitor's identity. 2.50
120 Hell in a handbasket. 2.50
121 BWg(s),Johnny Got His Gun . . 4.00
122 BWg(s),Bad to the Bone. 3.00
123 BWg(s),Nemesis. 3.00
124 F:Spoiler 3.00
125 BWg(s),secret intentity 3.00
126 BWg(s),search for new Robin. . 4.00
127 BWg(s),Girl Wonder,Batman . . 3.00
128 BWg(s),V:Scarab 2.50
129 War Games,Act 1,pt.5 . . . . 2.50
130 War Games,Act 2,pt.5 . . . . 2.50
131 War Games,Act 3,pt.4 . . . . 2.50
132 Fresh Blood, x-over, pt.1 . . . . . 2.50
133 Fresh Blood, x-over, pt.3 . . . . . 2.50
134 Bludhaven. 2.50
135 Rising Sun Archer & Dark Rider 2.50
136 V:Dark Rider 2.50
137 Rising Sun Archer & Dark Rider 2.50
138 V:Penguin 2.50
139 SMc,V:Junkyard Dog 2.50
140 SMc,F:The Veteran. 2.50
141 Black Ops opportunity. 2.50
142 Old Flame 2.50
143 Omac tie-in 2.50
144 Omac tie-in 2.50
145 A:Shadowpact. 2.50
146 F:Teen Titans 2.50
147 F:Teen Titans 2.50
148 Wanted for Murder 2.50
149 Robin: Boy Wanted. 2.50
150 Who Framed Robin?. 3.00
151 League of Assassins job offer. . 3.00
152 V:Captain Boomerang. 3.00
153 V:Captain Boomerang. 3.00
154 Kidnappings 3.00
155 Superhero wannabe 3.00
156 A Life to save 3.00
157 F:Klarion the Witch Boy 3.00
158 F:Klarion the Witch Boy 3.00
159 A first date. 3.00

160 New drug epidemic. 3.00
161 V:Lords of the Avenues. 3.00
162 Save the Lords of the Avenues 3.00
163 V:The Jury. 3.00
164 V:Dodge 3.00
165 Hospital ward hostage 3.00
166 F:Zatara & Ravager 3.00
167 Boy Wonder 3.00
168 Resurrection of Ra's Al Ghul . . 3.00
169 Resurrection of Ra's Al Ghul . . 3.00
170 CDi(s),F:Violet. 3.00
171 CDi(s),F:Girl Trouble. 3.00
172 CDi(s),Casino stakeout. 3.00
173 CDi(s),Violet or Spoiler 3.00
174 V:Sin Fang 3.00
175 Tim Drake turning point, pt.1 . . 3.00
176 Tim Drake now Batman,pt.2 . . . 3.00
177 Spoiler & Cluemaster 3.00
178 Search for a Hero 3.00
179 Search for a Hero 3.00
180 Gotham Youth Gangs 3.00
Ann.#1 TL,Eclipso tie-in,V:Anarky . . 3.00
Ann.#2 KD,JL,Bloodlines#10,
     I:Razorsharp 2.75
Ann.#3 Elsewolds Story 3.25
Ann.#4 Year One Annual 3.00
Ann.#5 CDi,Legends of the Dead
     Earth 3.00
Ann.#5 Legends o/t Dead Earth . . . 3.00
Ann.#6 Pulp Heroes (Western),
     CDi(s) 4.00
Ann. #7 F:Ra's Al Ghul 4.00
Spec.#1,000,000 CDi(s),SnW 2.50
Spec. Robin/Argent Double Shot
     DJu,CDi,V:Spoiler x-over (1997) 2.50
Spec. Robin/Spoiler, CDi (2008) . . . 4.00
80-page Giant #1 CDi 6.00

ROBIN PLUS
1996
1 MWa&BAu(s), F:Bart Allen, skiing
     rips, V:Mystral 3.00
2 LKa,CDi,AWi,ALa,F:Fang 3.00

ROBIN 3000
1992
1 thru 2 CR,Elsewolds,V:Skulpt. @5.25

ROBIN: YEAR ONE
October, 2000
1 CDi,SBe,F:Dick Grayson 5.00
2 CDi,SBe,F:Dick Grayson 5.00
3 CDi,SBe,RbC,F:Dick Grayson . . . 5.00
4 CDi,SBe,concl. 5.00

ROBIN HOOD TALES
1957–58
7 . . . . 500.00
8 thru 14 . . . . @400.00

ROBOTECH
DEFENDERS
1985
1 MA,mini-series 3.50
2 MA 3.00

ROGAN GOSH
DC/Vertigo, 1994
1 PF PrM(s) (From Revolver) 7.25

ROMANCE TRAIL
1949–50
1 EK,ATh. 900.00
2 EK 450.00
3 EK,ATh. 475.00
4 ATh. 350.00
5 . . . . 300.00
6 EK 300.00

RONIN
July, 1983

1 FM,1:Billy 6.00
2 FM,I:Casey 5.00
3 FM,V:Agat 5.00
4 FM,V:Agat 5.00
5 FM,V:Agat 6.00
6 FM,D:Billy 8.00
Paperback, FM inc. Gatefold 12.00

Roots of the Swamp Thing #2
© DC Comics Inc.

ROOTS OF THE SWAMP THING
July, 1986

1 BWr,rep.SwampThing#1&#2 . . . . 3.50
2 BWr,rep.SwampThing#3&#4 . . . . 3.50
3 BWr,rep.SwampThing#5&#6 . . . . 3.50
4 BWr,rep.SwampThing#7&#8 . . . . 3.50
5 BWr,rep.SwampThing#9&#10,
    H.O.S. #92, final issue 3.50

ROSE & THORN
Dec. 2003

1 thru 6 DGr . . . . @3.00

RUDOLPH THE RED–NOSED REINDEER
Dec., 1950

1950 . . . . 275.00
1951 thru 1954 . . . . @150.00
1955 thru 1962 Winter . . . . . . @125.00

RUSH CITY
Nov., 2006

1 CDi, Racing thru New York City . . 3.00
2 CDi, Under the streets 3.00
3 CDi, A:Black Canary 3.00
4 CDi, Missing twin doubles 3.00
5 CDi, Death race with the mob . . . 3.00
6 CDi,finale 3.00

SAGA OF RAS AL GHUL
1988

1 NA,DG,reprints 6.00
2 rep. 5.00
3 rep.Batman #242&#243 . . . . 5.00
4 rep.Batman #244&#245 . . . . 5.00

SAGA OF THE SWAMP THING
1982–85

1 JmP(s),TY,DSp,O:Swamp Thing,
    BU:PhantomStranger 7.00
2 Ph(c),TY,DSp,I:Grasp 4.00
3 TY,DSp,V:Vampires 4.00
4 TY,TD,V:Demon 4.00
5 TY,Scream of Hungry Flesh 4.00
6 TY,I:General Sunderland 4.00
7 TYmHaunting of Amanda Dove . . 4.00
8 TY,Here's Lookin' at You, Kid . . . 4.00
9 TY,Prelude to Holocaust 4.00
10 TY,Number of the Beast 4.00
11 TY,I:Golem 4.00
12 LWn(s),TY 4.00
13 TY,D:Grasp 4.00
14 A:Phantom Stranger 4.00
15 TY,BHa,Empires Made of Sand . 4.00
16 SBi,JTo,TY,Secret Truths 5.00
17 I:Matthew Cable 5.00
18 JmP(s),LWn(s),SBi,JTo,BWr,
    R:Arcane 5.00
19 JmP(s),SBi,JTo,V:Arcane 5.00
20 B:AMo(s),Day,JTo(i),D:Arcane
    (Original incarnation) 24.00
21 SBi,JTo,O:Swamp Thing,I:Floronic
    Man,D:General Sunderland . . . 20.00
22 SBi,JTo,O:Floronic Man 15.00
23 SBi,JTo,V:Floronic Man 15.00
24 SBi,JTo,V:Floronic Man,A:JLA,
    In Arkham 15.00
25 SBi,A:Jason Blood,I:Kamara . . 16.00
26 SBi,A:Demon,
    D:Matthew Cable 10.00
27 SBi,D:Kamara,A:Demon 10.00
28 SwM,Burial of Alec Holland . . . 10.00
29 SBi,JTo,R:Arcane 10.00
30 SBi,AA,D:Abby,C:Joker,V:Arcane 9.00
31 RV,JTo,D:Arcane 9.00
32 SwM,Tribute to WK Pogo strip . . 9.00
33 rep.H.O.S.#92,A:Cain & Abel . . 9.00
34 SBi,JTo,Swamp Thing & Abby
    Fall in Love 9.00
35 SBi,JTo,Nukeface,pt.1 . . . . 9.00
36 SBi,JTo,Nukeface,pt.2 . . . . 9.00
37 RV,JTo,I:John Constantine,
    American Gothic,pt.1 . . . . 35.00
38 SnW,JTo,V:Water-Vampires
    (Pt.1) A:J.Constantine 9.00
39 SBi,JTo,V:Water-Vampires
    (Pt.2) A:J.Constantine 9.00
40 SBi,JTo,C:J.Constantine,
    The Curse 9.00
41 SBi,AA,Voodoo Zombies #1 . . . . 4.00
42 SBi,JTo,RoR,
    Voodoo Zombies #2 . . . . 4.00
43 SnW,RoR,Windfall,
    I:Chester Williams 4.00
44 SBi,JTo,RoR,V:Serial Killer,
    C:Batman,Constantine,Mento . . 5.00
45 SnW,AA,Ghost Dance 4.00
Ann.#1 MT,TD,Movie Adaption 4.00
Ann.#2 AMo(s),E:Arcane,A:Deadman,
    Phantom Stranger,Spectre,
    Demon,Resurrection of Abby . . 8.00
Becomes:

SWAMP THING

SALVATION RUN
Nov. 2007

1 (of 7) DC Universe Villians exiled 3.00
1a variant ScK (c) (1:10) 3.50
2 Villain vs. Villain 3.00
3 Grood & Luthor 3.00
4 Grodd on the rampage 3.00
5 F:Catwoman 3.00
6 Lex Luthor & Joker 3.00
7 conclusion 3.00
7a variant (c) (1:10) 3.00

SAMURAI JACK
Warner Bros./DC July, 2002

Spec. #1 64-pg. 4.00

SANDMAN
[1st Regular Series], 1974–75

1 JK,I&O:Sandman,I:General
    Electric 100.00
2 V:Dr.Spider 50.00
3 Brain that Blanked
    out the Bronx 50.00
4 JK,Panic in the Dream Stream . . 50.00
5 JK,Invasion of the Frog Men 50.00
6 JK,WW,V:Dr.Spider 55.00

[2nd Regular Series], 1989–93

1 B:NGa(s),SK,I:2nd Sandman . . . 45.00
2 SK,A:Cain,Abel 20.00
3 SK,A:John Constantine 15.00
4 SK,A:Demon 15.00
5 SK,A:Mr.Miracle,J'onn J'onzz . . 15.00
6 V:Doctor Destiny 10.00
7 V:Doctor Destiny 10.00
8 Sound of her wings,F:Death 25.00
8a Guest Ed.Pin-Up Cover 50.00
9 Tales in the Sand,Doll's House
    prologue 10.00
10 B:Doll's House,A:Desire
    & Despair,I:Brut & Glob 10.00
11 MovingIn,A:2ndS-man 10.00
12 Play House,D;2ndS'man 10.00
13 Men of Good Fortune,A:Death,
    Lady Constantine 10.00
14 Collectors,D:Corinthian 10.00
15 Into' Night,DreamVortex 10.00
16 E:Doll's House,Lost Hearts 10.00
17 Calliope 10.00
18 Dream of a 1000 Cats 10.00
18a error pg.1 . . . . 25.00
19 Midsummer Nights Dream 6.00
19a error copy 22.00
20 Strange Death Element Girl,
    A:Death 7.00
21 Family Reunion,B:Season
    of Mists 8.00
22 Season of Mists,I:Daniel Hall . . 13.00
23 Season of Mists 7.00
24 Season of Mists 7.00
25 Season of Mists 7.00
26 Season of Mists 6.00
27 E:Season of Mists 6.00
28 Ownership of Hell 6.00
29 A:Lady J.Constantine 5.00
30 Ancient Rome:A:Death,Desire . . 5.00
31 Ancient Rome,pt.2 . . . . 5.00
32 B:The Game of You 5.00
33 The Game of You 5.00
34 The Game of You 4.00
35 The Game of You 4.00
36 The Game of You,48pgs 5.00
37 The Game of You,Epilogue 4.00
38 Convergence 4.00
39 Convergence,A:Marco Polo 4.00
40 Convergence,A:Cain,Abel,Eve,
    Matthew the Raven 4.00
41 JIT,VcL,(i),B:Brief Lives,
    F:Endless 4.00
42 JIT,VcL,(i),F:Delirium,Dream . . . 4.00
43 JIT,VcL,(i),A:Death,Etain 4.00
44 JIT,VcL,(i),R:Corinthian,
    Destruction 4.00
45 JIT,VcL,(i),F:Tiffany,
    Ishtar(Belli) 4.00
46 JIT,VcL,(i),F:Morpheus/Bast,
    A:Aids insert story,F:Death 4.00

DC/Vertigo, 1994–96

47 JIT,VcL,(i),A:Endless 4.00
48 JIT,VcL,(i),L:Destruction 4.00
49 JIT,VcL,(i),E:Brief Lives,
    F:Orpheus 4.00

50 DMc(c),CR,Tales of Baghdad,
pin-upsby TM,DMc,MK 5.00
50a Gold Ed. 22.00
51 BT,MBu(i),B:Inn at the end of
the World,Gaheris' tale 4.00
52 BT,MBu(i),JWk,Cluracan's
Story 4.00
53 BT,DG,MBu(i),MZi,Hob's
Leviathan 4.00
54 BT,MiA,MBu(i),R:Prez. 4.00
55 SAp,VcL,BT,MBu(i),F:Klaproth
Cerements's Story 4.00
56 BT,MBu(i),DG(i),SLi(i),GyA,TyH(i),
E:Inn at the end of the World,
C:Endless 4.00
57 MaH,B:Kindly Ones,Inc.American
Freak Preview 5.00
58 MaH,Kindly Ones,pt.2,
A:Lucifer 5.00
59 MaH,Kindly Ones,pt.3,R:Fury . . . 5.00
60 MaH,Kindly Ones,pt.4 . . . . 5.00
61 MaH,Kindly Ones,pt.5 . . . . 5.00
62 Kindly Ones,pt.6,Murder 5.00
63 MaH,Kindly Ones,pt.7,
A:Rose Walker. 5.00
64 Kindly Ones,pt.8 . . . . 5.00
65 MaH,Kindly Ones,pt.9,Dream
Kingdom 5.00
66 MaH,Kindly Ones,pt.10. . . . . 5.00
67 MaH,Kindly Ones,pt.11 . . . . 5.00
68 MaH,Kindly Ones,pt.12. . . . . 5.00
69 MaH,Kindly Ones finale 6.00
70 The Wake,pt.1. . . . . 4.00
71 The Wake,pt.2. . . . . 4.00
72 NGa,DMc,The Wake,pt.3 . . . . . . 4.00
73 NGa,Sunday Mourning 4.00
74 NGa,V:Lord of Dreams 4.00
75 NGa,last issue 5.00
Sandman Covers, 1989–96 . . . . 40.00
Spec.BT,Glow in the Dark(c),The
Legend of Orpheus,
(inc. Portrait Gallery) 6.00
1 special edition, 48-pg.(2006) 0.50

SANDMAN, THE:
THE DREAM HUNTERS
Vertigo, Nov., 2008
1 NGa . . . . @3.00

SANDMAN MYSTERY
THEATRE
DC/Vertigo, 1993–99
1 B:MWg(s),GyD,R:G.A.Sandman,
B:Tarantula,I:Mr.Belmont,
Dian Belmont. 5.00
2 GyD,V:Tarantula. 3.00
3 GyD,V:Tarantula. 3.00
4 GyD,E:Tarantula 3.00
5 JWk,B:The Face 3.00
6 JWk,The Face #2 . . . . 3.00
7 JWk,The Face #3 . . . . 3.00
8 JWk,E:The Face 3.00
9 RGT,B:The Brute,I:Rocket
Ramsey 3.00
10 RGT,The Brute#2 . . . . 3.00
11 RGT,The Brute#3 . . . . 3.00
12 RGT,E:The Brute 3.00
13 GyD,B:The Vamp 3.00
14 GyD,The Vamp#2 . . . . 3.00
15 GyD,The Vamp#3 . . . . 3.00
16 GyD,E:The Vamp 3.00
17 GyD,B:The Scorpion. 3.00
18 GyD,The Scorpion,pt.2 . . . . 3.00
19 GyD,The Scorpion,pt.3 . . . . 3.00
20 GyD,The Scorpion,pt.4 . . . . 3.00
21 Dr. Death. 3.00
22 Dr. Death,pt.2 . . . . 3.00
23 Dr. Death,pt.3 . . . . 3.00
24 Dr. Death,pt.4 . . . . 3.00
25 The Butcher,pt.1 . . . . 3.00

26 The Butcher,pt.2 . . . . 3.00
27 The Butcher,pt.3 . . . . 3.00
28 The Butcher,pt.4 . . . . 3.00
29 The Hourman,pt.1 . . . . 3.00
30 The Hourman,pt.2 . . . . 3.00
31 The Hourman,pt.3 . . . . 3.00
32 The Hourman,pt.4 . . . . 3.00
33 The Python,pt.1 . . . . 3.00
34 The Python,pt.2 . . . . 3.00
35 The Python,pt.3 . . . . 3.00
36 The Python,pt.4 . . . . 3.00
37 The Mist,pt.1 . . . . 3.00
38 The Mist,pt.2 . . . . 3.00
39 The Mist,pt.3 . . . . 3.00
40 The Mist,pt.4 . . . . 3.00
41 MWg&SSe(s),GyD,Phantom of
the Fair,pt.1 . . . . 2.50
42 MWg&SSe(s),GyD,Phantom of
the Fair,pt.2 . . . . 2.50
43 MWg&SSe(s),GyD,Phantom of
the Fair, pt. 3 . . . . 2.50
44 MWg&SSe(s),GyD,Phantom of
the Fair, pt. 4 . . . . 2.50
45 MWg&SSe(s),Blackhawk,pt.1 . . . 2.50
46 MWg&SSe(s),Blackhawk,pt.2 . . . 2.50
47 MWg&SSe(s),Blackhawk,pt.3 . . . 2.50
48 MWg&SSe(s),RCa,Blackhawk . . 2.50
49 MWg&SSe(s),ScarletGhost,pt.1 . 2.50
50 MWg&SSe(s),The Scarlet
Ghost, pt.2, 48pg. 4.50
51 MWg&SSe(s),ScarletGhost,pt.3 . 2.50
52 MWg&SSe(s),ScarletGhost,pt.4 . 2.50
53 MWg&SSe(s),The Crone,pt.1 . . . 2.50
53 MWg&SSe(s),The Crone,pt.2 . . . 2.50
54 SSe&MWg(s),The Crone,pt.3 . . . 2.50
55 SSe&MWg(s),The Crone,pt.4 . . . 2.50
56 SSe&MWg(s),The Crone, concl.. 2.50
57 SSe&MWg(s),The Cannon,pt.1 . 2.50
58 SSe&MWg(s),The Cannon,pt.2 . 2.50
59 SSe&MWg(s),The Cannon,pt.3 . 2.50
60 SSe&MWg(s),The Cannon,pt.4 . 2.50
61 SSe(s),GyD,The City, pt.1 . . . . . 2.50
62 SSe(s),GyD,The City, pt.2 . . . . . 2.50
63 SSe(s),GyD,The City, pt.3 . . . . . 2.50
64 SSe(s),GyD,The City, pt.4 . . . . . 2.50
65 SSe,GyD,The Goblin, pt.1 . . . . . 2.50
66 SSe,GyD,The Goblin, pt.2 . . . . . 2.50
67 SSe,GyD,The Goblin, pt.3 . . . . . 2.50
68 SSe,GyD,The Goblin, pt.4 . . . . . 2.50
69 SSe,GyD. 2.50
70 SSe,GyD,final issue 2.50
Ann.#1 . . . . 4.00

SANDMAN
MYSTERY THEATRE:
SLEEP OF REASON
Vertigo, Dec., 2006
1 thru 5 . . . . @3.00

SANDMAN PRESENTS:
LOVE STREET
DC/Vertigo, 1999
1 MZi,VcL,F:John Constantine 3.00
2 thru 3 MZi,VcL,Concl. . . . . @3.00

...LUCIFER
DC/Vertigo, 1999
1 (of 3) SHp, Morningstar Option . . 3.00
2 thru 3 SHp . . . . @3.00

...PETREFAX
DC/Vertigo, 2000
1 thru 4 SL . . . . @3.00

...DEAD BOY DETECTIVES
DC/Vertigo, 2001
1 thru 4 SL . . . . @2.50

...CORINTHIAN, THE
DC/Vertigo, 2001
1 thru 3 . . . . @2.50

...THESSALIAD, THE
DC/Vertigo, 2002
1 thru 4 DMc(c) . . . . @2.50

...BAST
DC/Vertigo, 2003
1 thru 3 (of 3) F:Lady Bast . . . . . @3.00
Spec.1-Shot, Merv Pumpkinhead
Agent of Dream,MBu. 6.00
Spec. Everything You've Ever
Wanted to Know About Dreams
But Were Afraid to Ask 4.50

...THESSALY
DC Vertigo, Feb. 2004
1 thru 4 (of 4) Witch for Hire . . . . @3.00

SCALPED
Vertigo, Jan., 2007
1 F:Dashiell Bad Horse. 3.00
2 Life on the Rez 3.00
3 Indian Country 3.00
4 Hoka Hey, pt.1 . . . . 3.00
5 Hoka Hey, pt.2. . . . . 3.00
6 Casino Boogie, pt.1 . . . . 3.00
7 Casino Boogie, pt.2 . . . . 3.00
8 Casino Boogie, pt.3 . . . . 3.00
9 Casino Boogie, pt.4 . . . . 3.00
10 Casino Boogie, pt.5 . . . . 3.00
11 Casino Boogie, concl. 3.00
12 Dash Bad Horse 3.00
13 Dead Mothers, pt.1 . . . . 3.00
14 Dead Mothers, pt.2 . . . . 3.00
15 Dead Mothers, pt.3 . . . . 3.00
16 Dead Mothers, pt.4 . . . . 3.00
17 Dead Mothers, pt.5 . . . . 3.00
18 F:Franklin Falls Down. 3.00
19 F:Dash and Carol 3.00
20 Carol's secret past 3.00
21 Gravel in Your Guts, pt.1 . . . . . . 3.00
22 Gravel in Your Guts, pt.2 . . . . . . 3.00
23 Gravel in Your Guts, pt.3 . . . . . . 3.00

SCARAB
DC/Vertigo, 1993–94
1 GF(c),B:JnS(s),SEa,MkB(i),
R&O:Scarab,V:Halaku-umid . . 2.50
2 thru 8 GF(c),SEa,MkB(i) . . . . . @2.50

SCARE TACTICS
Oct., 1996
1 LKa(s),AWi,ALa, ... 2.50
2 thru 11 . . . . @2.50

Scarlett #3
© DC Comics, Inc.

DC COMICS

SCARLETT
1993–94
1 I:Scarlett,Blood of the Innocent . . 3.50
2 Blood of the Innocent cont. 2.50
3 Blood of the Innocent cont. 2.50
4 thru 14 . . . . @2.50

S.C.I.-SPY
DC/Vertigo, Feb., 2002
1 (of 6) DgM,PG,JP,F:Sebastian
    Starchild secret agent 2.50
2 thru 6 DgM,PG,JP . . . . @2.50

SCOOBY-DOO
Warner Bros./DC June, 1997
1 . . . . 5.00
2 thru 50 . . . . @2.50
51 thru 138 . . . . @2.50
Spooky Spectacular 2000 . . . . 4.00
Spooky Summer Special #1 . . . . 4.00
Spec. Super Scarefest #1 . . . . 4.00
Spec. Dollar Comic, rep.#1 . . . . 2.50

SCRATCH
June 2004
1 thru 5 SK,werewolf v.Batman . . @2.50

Scribbly #4 © DC Comics, Inc.

SCRIBBLY
Aug., 1948–Dec.–Jan., 1951–52
1 SM 1,400.00
2 . . . . 900.00
3 thru 5 . . . . @750.00
6 thru 10 . . . . @500.00
11 thru 15 . . . . @450.00

SEA DEVILS
Sept.–Oct., 1961
1 RH. 1,200.00
2 RH 600.00
3 RH 400.00
4 RH 350.00
5 RH 350.00
6 thru 10 RH . . . . @275.00
11 . . . . 250.00
12 . . . . 250.00
13 JKu,GC,RA 250.00
14 thru 20 . . . . @250.00
21 I:Capt X,Man Fish 150.00
22 thru 35, May-June, 1967 . . . @150.00

SEBASTIAN O
DC/Vertigo, 1993
1 GMo(s),SY,I:Sebastian O,A:Lord
    Lavender,Roaring Boys 2.50

2 GMo(s),SY,V:Roaring Boys,
    Assassins,A:Abbe 2.50
3 GMo(s),SY,D:Lord Lavender 2.50

SECRET FILES & ORIGINS
2000
TPB DAn,ALa,guide to DCU 7.00
GN Secret Files Guide to DCU
    2001-2002 . . . . 5.00

SECRET HEARTS
Sept.–Oct., 1949–July, 1971
1 Make Believe Sweetheart 900.00
2 ATh,Love Is Not A Dream 400.00
3 Sing Me A Love Song 350.00
4 ATh. 350.00
5 ATh. 350.00
6 . . . . 350.00
7 scarce 600.00
8 thru 20 . . . . @250.00
21 thru 26 . . . . @175.00
27 B:Comics Code 150.00
28 thru 30 . . . . @150.00
31 thru 70 . . . . @100.00
71 thru 110 . . . . @50.00
111 thru 120 . . . . @40.00
121 thru 150 . . . . @30.00
151 thru 153 . . . . @25.00

SECRET ORIGINS
Feb., 1973–Oct., 1974
1 O:Superman,Batman,Ghost,
    Flash 65.00
2 O:Green Lantern,Atom,
    Supergirl 35.00
3 O:Wonder Woman,Wildcat 35.00
4 O:Vigilante by MMe 35.00
5 O:The Spectre 35.00
6 O:Blackhawk,Legion of Super
    Heroes 35.00
7 O:Robin, Aquaman 35.00

SECRET ORIGINS
April, 1986
1 JOy,WB,F:Superman 7.00
2 GK,F:Blue Beetle 4.00
3 JBi,F:Captain Marvel 4.00
4 GT,F:Firestorm 4.00
5 GC,F:Crimson Avenger 4.00
6 DG,MR,F:Batman 5.00
7 F:Sandman,Guy Gardner 3.50
8 MA,F:Shadow Lass,Dollman . . . 2.50
9 GT,F:Skyman,Flash 2.50
10 JL,JO,JA,F:Phantom Stranger . . 2.50
11 LMc,TD,F:Hawkman,Powergirl . . 2.50
12 F:Challengers of the Unknown
    I:G.A. Fury 2.50
13 EL,F:Nightwing 3.00
14 F:Suicide Squad 2.50
15 KMo,DG,F:Deadman,Spectre . . 2.50
16 AKu,F:Hourman,Warlord 2.50
17 KGi,F:Green Lantern 2.75
18 KGi,F:Green Lantern, Creeper . . 2.50
19 JM(c),MA,Uncle Sam, Guardian . 2.50
20 RL,DG,F:Batgirl 3.00
21 GM,MA,F:Jonah Hex 2.50
22 F:Manhunter,Millennium tie-in . . 2.50
23 F:Manhunter,Millennium tie-in . . 2.50
24 F:Dr.Fate,Blue Devil 2.50
25 F:The Legion 2.50
26 F:Black Lightning 2.50
27 F:Zatanna,Zatara 2.50
28 RLd,GK,F:Nightshade,Midnight . 2.50
29 F:Atom,Red Tornado 2.50
30 F:Elongated Man 2.50
31 F:Justice Society of America . . . 2.50
32 F:Justice League America 3.00
33 F:Justice League Inter. 2.50
34 F:Justice League Inter. 2.50
35 KSu,F:Justice League Inter. 2.50

36 F:Green Lantern 3.00
37 F:Legion of Subst. Heroes 2.50
38 F:Green Arrow,Speedy 2.50
39 F:Batman,Animal Man 3.50
40 F:Gorilla City 2.50
41 F:Flash Villains 2.75
42 DC,F:Phantom Girl 2.50
43 TVE,TT,F:Hawk & Dove 2.50
44 F:Batman,Clayface tie-in 3.00
45 F:Blackhawk,El Diablo 2.50
46 CS,F:All Headquarters 2.50
47 CS,F:The Legion 2.50
48 KG,F:Ambush Bug 2.50
49 F: The Cadmus Project 2.50
50 GP,CI,DG,F:Batman,Robin,
    Flash,Black Canary 4.00
Ann.#1 JBy,F:Doom Patrol 3.00
Ann.#2 CI,MA,F:Flash 2.50
Ann.#3 F:The Teen Titans 3.00
Spec.#1 SK,PB,DG,F:Batman's worst
    Villians,A:Penguin 4.00
GN DG,New Origin Batman 4.50
GN rep of 1961 Annual 5.00
Replica Edition 80-page 5.00
Vol.3 Even More Secret Origins . . . 7.00

SECRET ORIGINS OF SUPER-VILLAINS
2000
1 80-pg. Giant 5.00

SECRET SIX
May, 2006
1 (of 6) JP 3.00
2 thru 6 JP . . . . @3.00
Sept., 2008
1 DHz 3.00
2 thru 3 DHz . . . . @3.00

SECRET SOCIETY OF SUPER-HEROES
Aug., 2000
1 (of 2) HC,MMK,JP,Elseworlds . . . 6.00
2 HC,MMK,JP,concl. 6.00

SECRET SOCIETY OF SUPER-VILLAINS
May-June, 1976
1 A:Capt.Boomerang, Grodd,
    Sinestro 30.00
2 R:Capt.Comet,A:Green Lantern 15.00
3 A:Mantis, Darkseid 12.00
4 A:Kalibak,Darkseid,Gr.Lantern . . 12.00
5 RB,D:Manhunter,A:JLA 12.00
6 RB/BL,A:Black Canary 12.00
7 RB/BL,A:Hawkgirl,Lex Luthor . . 12.00
8 RB/BL,A:Kid Flash 12.00
9 RB/BMc,A:Kid Flash, Creeper . . 12.00
10 DAy/JAb,A:Creeper 12.00
11 JO,N:Wizard 12.00
12 BMc,A:Blockbuster 12.00
13 A:Crime Syndicate of America . 12.00
14 A:Crime Syndicate of America . 12.00
15 A:G.A.Atom, Dr. Mid Nite 12.00

SECRETS OF HAUNTED HOUSE
April-May, 1975
1 LD(c),Dead Heat 75.00
2 ECh(c),A Dead Man 30.00
3 ECh(c),Pathway To Purgatory . . 30.00
4 LD(c),The Face of Death 30.00
5 BWr(c),Gunslinger! 35.00
6 JAp(c),Deadly Allegiance 25.00
7 JAp(c),It'll Grow On You 25.00
8 MK(c),Raising The Devil 25.00

Secrets of Haunted House #46
© DC Comics Inc.

9 LD(c),The Man Who Didn't
   Believe in Ghosts 25.00
10 MK(c),Ask Me No Questions . . 25.00
11 MK(c),Picasso Fever! 25.00
12 JO&DG(c),Yorick's Skull 25.00
13 JO&DG(c),The Cry of the
   Warewolf 25.00
14 MK(c),Selina 25.00
15 LD(c),Over Your Own Dead
   Body 20.00
16 MK(c),Water, Water Every Fear 20.00
17 LD(c),Papa Don 20.00
18 LD(c),No Sleep For The Dying . 20.00
19 LD(c),The Manner of Execution 20.00
20 JO(c),The Talisman of the
   Serpent 20.00
21 LD(c),The Death's Head
   Scorpion 20.00
22 LD(c),See How They Die 20.00
23 LD(c),The Creeping Red Death 20.00
24 LD(c),Second Chance To Die . . 20.00
25 LD(c),The Man Who Cheated
   Destiny. 20.00
26 MR(c),Elevator to Eternity. 20.00
27 DH(c),Souls For the Master . . . 20.00
28 DH(c),Demon Rum 20.00
29 MK(c),Duel of Darkness 20.00
30 JO(c),For the Love of Arlo 20.00
31 I:Mister E. 25.00
32 The Legend of the Tiger's Paw. 15.00
33 In The Attic Dwells Dark Seth. . 15.00
34 Double Your Pleasure. 15.00
35 Deathwing, Lord of Darkness . . 15.00
36 RB&DG(c),Sister Sinister 15.00
37 RB&DG(c),The Third Wish Is
   Death. 15.00
38 RB&DG(c),Slaves of Satan. . . . 15.00
39 RB&DG(c),The Witch-Hounds
   of Salem 15.00
40 RB&DG(c),The Were-Witch
   of Boston 15.00
41 JKu(c),House at Devil's Tail . . . 15.00
42 JKu(c),Mystic Murder 15.00
43 JO(c),Mother of Invention 15.00
44 BWr(c),Halloween God 15.00
45 EC&JO(c),Star-Trakker. 15.00
46 March, 1982 . . . . 15.00

SINISTER HOUSE OF
SECRET LOVE
Oct.–Nov., 1971–April–May, 1972
1 Curse of the MacIntyres 300.00
2 TD,To Wed the Devil 125.00
3 ATh,Bride of the Falcon 140.00

4 TD,Kiss of the Serpent 125.00
Becomes:

SECRETS OF
SINISTER HOUSE
June-July, 1972
5 NC(c),Death at Castle Dunbar. . 65.00
6 MK,JO,Brief Reunion 40.00
7 NR,MK,Panic 40.00
8 NC,Man Who Cried Werewolf . . 40.00
9 JkS(c),Dance of the Damned . . 40.00
10 JkS(c),Castle Curse 50.00
11 thru 16 . . . . @25.00
17 DBa,NC,HC,WMo 25.00
18 NC,GK,June-July, 1974 . . . . . . 25.00

SECRETS OF THE
LEGION OF
SUPER-HEROES
Jan., 1981
1 O:Legion 3.50
2 O:Brainiac 5. . . . . 3.50
3 March, 1981,O:Karate Kid. 3.50

SEEKERS INTO
THE MYSTERY
1996
1 Pilgrimage of Lucas Hart,pt.1 . . . 2.50
2 Pilgrimage of Lucas Hart,pt.2 . . . 2.50
3 Pilgrimage of Lucas Hart,pt.3 . . . 2.50
4 Pilgrimage of Lucas Hart,pt.4 . . . 2.50
5 Pilgrimage of Lucas Hart,pt.5 . . . 2.50
6 Falling Down to Heaven,pt.1 . . . . 2.50
7 Falling Down to Heaven,pt.2 . . . . 2.50
8 Falling Down to Heaven,pt.3 . . . . 2.50
9 JMD(s),MZi,Falling Down from
   Heaven,pt.4 concl. 2.50
10 JMD(s),JMu,F:Charlie Limbo . . . 2.50
11 JMD(s),JIT,God's Shadow,pt.1 . . 2.50
12 JMD(s),JIT,God's Shadow,pt.2 . . 2.50
13 JMD(s),JIT,God's Shadow,pt.3 . . 2.50
14 JMD(s),JIT,God's Shadow,pt.4 . . 2.50
15 JMD(s),JMu,Hart meets
   Magician, final issue 3.00

SENSATION COMICS
1942–52
1 I:Wonder Woman,Wildcat . . 65,000.00
2 I:Etta Candy & the Holiday
   Girls, Dr. Poison 10,000.00
3 Diana Price joins Military
   Intelligence 5,000.00
4 I:Baroness PaulaVonGunther 4,000.00
5 V:Axis Spies 3,000.00
6 Wonder Woman receives magic
   lasso,V:Baroness Gunther . 3,000.00
7 V:Baroness Gunther 2,200.00
8 Meets Gloria Bullfinch. 2,200.00
9 A:The Real Diana Prince . . . 2,200.00
10 V:Ishti 2,200.00
11 I:Queen Desira 2,200.00
12 V:Baroness Gunther 1,700.00
13 V:Olga,Hitler(c) 2,200.00
14 The Fir Tree's Story 1,700.00
15 V:Simon Slikery 1,700.00
16 V:Karl Schultz 1,700.00
17 V:Princess Yasmini 1,700.00
18 V:Quito 1,700.00
19 Wonder Woman Goes
   Berserk. 1,700.00
20 V:Stoffer 1,700.00
21 V:American Adolf 1,500.00
22 V:Cheetah 1,500.00
23 'War Laugh Mania'. 1,500.00
24 I:Wonder Woman's
   Mental Radio 1,500.00
25 Kidnapper o/t Astral Spirits . 1,500.00
26 A:Queen Hippolyte. 1,500.00

27 V:Ely Close 1,500.00
28 V:Mayor Prude. 1,500.00
29 V:Mimi Mendez 1,500.00
30 V:Anton Unreal. 1,500.00
31 Grow Down Land. 1,100.00
32 V:Crime Chief. 1,100.00
33 Meets Percy Pringle. 1,100.00
34 I:Sargon 1,200.00
35 V:Sontag Henya in Atlantis . 1,000.00
36 V:Bedwin Footh 1,000.00
37 A:Mala((1st app. All-Star #8) 1,000.00
38 V:The Gyp 1,000.00
39 V:Nero 1,000.00
40 I:Countess Draska Nishki . . 1,000.00
41 V:Creeper Jackson 900.00
42 V:Countess Nishki. 900.00
43 Meets Joel Heyday 900.00
44 V:Lt. Sturm 900.00
45 V:Jose Perez. 900.00
46 V:Lawbreakers Protective
   League. 900.00
47 V:Unknown 900.00
48 V:Topso and Teena 900.00
49 V:Zavia 900.00
50 V:'Ears' Fellock 900.00
51 V:Boss Brekel 800.00
52 Meets Prof. Toxino 800.00
53 V:Wanta Wynn 800.00
54 V:Dr. Fiendo 800.00
55 V:Bughumans 800.00
56 V:Dr. Novel 800.00
57 V:Syonide 800.00
58 Meets Olive Norton 800.00
59 V:Snow Man 700.00
60 V:Bifton Jones. 700.00
61 V:Bluff Robust. 700.00
62 V:Black Robert of Dogwood . 700.00
63 V:Prof. Vibrate. 700.00
64 V:Cloudmen 700.00
65 V:Lim Slait. 750.00
66 V:Slick Skeener. 750.00
67 V:Daredevil Dix 750.00
68 Secret of the Menacing
   Octopus 750.00
69 V:Darcy Wells 800.00
70 Unconquerable Woman of
   Cocha Bamba 800.00
71 V:Queen Flaming 800.00
72 V:Blue Seal Gang 800.00
73 Wonder Woman time
   travel story. 800.00
74 V:Spug Spangle 800.00
75 V:Shark 800.00
76 V:King Diamond 800.00
77 V:Boss Brekel 800.00
78 V:Furiosa. 800.00

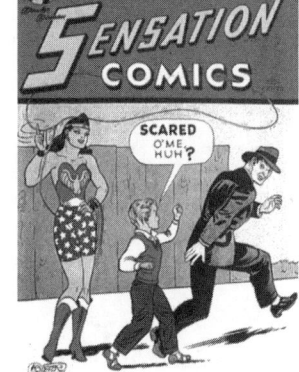

Sensation Comics#66
© DC Comics Inc.

All comics prices listed are for *Near Mint* condition.

DC COMICS

79 Meets Leila and Solala 800.00
80 V:Don Enrago 800.00
81 V:Dr. Frenzi 700.00
82 V:King Lunar 600.00
83 V:Prowd 600.00
84 V:Duke Daxo 600.00
85 Meets Leslie M. Gresham 600.00
86 Secret of the Amazing
    Bracelets 600.00
87 In Twin Peaks(in Old West) . . 600.00
88 Wonder Woman in Holywood . 600.00
89 V:Abacus Rackeett Gang 600.00
90 The Secret of the Modern
    Sphinx 600.00
91 Survivors of the Stone Age . . . 600.00
92 V:Duke of Deceptions 600.00
93 V:Talbot 600.00
94 Girl Issue 750.00
95 CI,Dr. Pat's First Love 750.00
96 CI,W.Woman's RomanticRival 750.00
97 W.Woman Romance Editor . . 750.00
98 Strange Mission 750.00
99 I:Astra 750.00
100 W.Woman Hollywood Star . . 800.00
101 Battle for the Atom World . . . 750.00
102 Queen of the South Seas . . . 750.00
103 V:Robot Archers 750.00
104 The End of Paradise
     Island 750.00
105 Secret of the Giant Forest . . 750.00
106 E:Wonder Woman 750.00
107 ATh,Mystery issue 1,200.00
108 ATh,GK,I:Johnny Peril 1,000.00
109 Ath,GK,A:Johnny Peril 1,500.00
Becomes:

SENSATION MYSTERY
1952–53
110 MA(c),B:Johnny Peril 700.00
111 GK,Spectre in the Flame 650.00
112 GK,Death Has 5 Guesses . . 650.00
113 CI,The End of Death 650.00
114 GK,GC,The Haunted
     Diamond 650.00
115 GK,The Phantom Castle 650.00
116 The Toy Assassins 650.00

SENSATION COMICS
1999
1 JeR(s),ScB, F:Wonder Woman &
    Hawkgirl 2.50

Sensation Comics 1-shot
© DC Comics, Inc.

SERGEANT BILKO
May-June, 1957
1 Based on TV show 1,000.00
2 . . . . 500.00
3 . . . . 400.00
4 . . . . 350.00
5 . . . . 350.00
6 thru 17 . . . . @300.00
18 March-April, 1960 . . . . 300.00

SERGEANT BILKO'S PVT. DOBERMAN
June-July, 1958
1 . . . . 600.00
2 . . . . 300.00
3 and 4 . . . . @225.00
5 photo (c) 225.00
6 thru 10 . . . . @150.00
11 Feb.–March, 1960 . . . . 150.00

SGT. ROCK
See: OUR ARMY AT WAR

SGT. ROCK SPECIAL
Oct., 1988
#1 rep.Our Army at War#162-#63 . 11.00
#2 rep.Brave & Bold #52 . . . . 7.00
#3 rep.Showcase #45 . . . . 7.00
#4 rep.Our Army at War#147-#48 . . 7.00
#5 rep.Our Army at War#81&#103 . 7.00
#6 rep.Our Army at War #160 . . . . 7.00
#7 rep.Our Army at War #85 . . . . . 7.00
#8 thru #20 reprints . . . . @7.00
Spec. #1 TT,MGo,JKu,CR,(new
    stories) 5.00

SGT. ROCK'S PRIZE BATTLE TALES
Winter, 1964
1 . . . . 600.00

SGT. ROCK: THE LOST BATTALION
Nov., 2008
1 (of 6) BTi 3.00

SGT. ROCK: THE PROPHECY
Jan., 2006
1 (of 6) JKu 3.00
1a & b variant (c)s . . . . @3.00
2 JKu 3.00
3 JKu 3.00
4 JKu, Road to Riga 3.00
5 JKu, Farmer's Barn 3.00
6 JKu,concl. 3.00

SEVEN SOLDIERS
Feb., 2005
0 GMo(s),JWi,48-page 3.00
1 48-pg. 4.00
1 GMo(s),JWi,culmination 3.00

SEVEN SOLDIERS: THE BULLETEER
Nov., 2005
1 (of 4) GMo(s) 3.00
2 thru 4 GMo(s) . . . . @3.00

SEVEN SOLDIERS: FRANKENSTEIN
Nov., 2005
1 (of 4) GMo(s),DoM 3.00
2 GMo(s),DoM, on Mars 3.00

3 GMo(s),DoM,A:The Bride 3.00
4 GMo(s),DoM,V:Death Fairies . . . 3.00

SEVEN SOLDIERS: GUARDIAN
March, 2005
1 (of 4) GMo(s),masthead 3.00
2 GMo(s) 3.00
3 GMo(s) 3.00
4 GMo(s) 3.00

SEVEN SOLDIERS: KLARION THE WITCH BOY
Apr., 2005
1 GMo(s),F:Klarion and Teek 3.00
2 GMo(s) 3.00
3 GMo(s) 3.00
4 GMo(s) 3.00

SEVEN SOLDIERS: MISTER MIRACLE
Sept., 2005
1 (of 4) GMo(s),PFe 3.00
2 GMo(s),PFe(c) 3.00
3 GMo(s),I:Baron Bedlam 3.00
4 GMo(s),Forever-Flavored Man . . 3.00

SEVEN SOLDIERS: SHINING KNIGHT
March, 2005
1 (of 4) GMo(s),fantasy epic 3.00
2 GMo(s) 3.00
3 GMo(s) 3.00
4 GMo(s) 3.00

SEVEN SOLDIERS: ZATANNA
Apr., 2005
1 GMo(s),F:Zatanna 3.00
2 thru 4 GMo(s) . . . . @3.00

SHADE
June-July, 1977
[1st Regular Series]
1 SD,I&O: Shade 25.00
2 SD,V:Form 20.00
3 SD,V:The Cloak 15.00
4 SD,Return to Meta-Zone 15.00
5 SD,V:Supreme Decider 15.00
6 SD,V:Khaos 15.00
7 SD,V:Dr.Z.Z. 15.00
8 SD,last issue 15.00

SHADE, THE
Feb., 1997
1 (of 4) JeR(s),GeH,A:Ludlows 3.00
2 JeR(s),JWi,MGy,poisoned by love
    of his life 3.00
3 JeR(s),BBl,Golden Age Flash Jay
    Garrick retiring 3.00
4 JeR(s),MZi,V:last of the Ludlows . 3.00

SHADE, THE CHANGING MAN
July, 1990
1 B:PrM(s),CBa,MPn,I:Kathy George,
    I&D:Troy Grezer 5.00
2 CBa,MPn,Who Shot JFK#1 . . . . . 4.00
3 CBa,MPn,Who Shot JFK#2 . . . . . 3.00
4 CBa,MPn,V:American Scream . . 3.00
5 CBa,MPn,V:Hollywood
    Monsters 3.00
6 CBa,MPn,V:Ed Loot 3.00
7 CBa,MPn,I:Arnold Major 3.00
8 CBa,Mpn,I:Lenny 3.00

9 CBa,MPn,V:Arnold Major 3.00
10 CBa,MPn,Paranioa 2.75
11 CBa,MPn,R:Troy Grezer. 2.50
12 CBa,MPn,V:Troy Grezer. 2.50
13 CBa,MPn,I:Fish Priest 2.50
14 CBa,MPn,V:Godfather of Guilt . . 2.50
15 CBa,MPn,I:Spirit 2.50
16 CBa,MPn,V:American Scream . . 2.50
17 RkB(i),V:Rohug. 2.50
18 MPn,E:American Scream 2.50
19 MPn,V:Dave Messiah Seeker. . . 2.50
20 JD,CBa,MPn,RkB,R:Roger. . . . 2.50
21 MPn,The Road,A:Stringer. 2.50
22 The Road,Childhood. 2.50
23 The Road 2.50
24 The Road 2.50
25 The Road 2.50
26 MPn(i),F:Lenny 2.50
27 MPn(i),Shade becomes female . 2.50
28 MPn(i),Changing Woman #2 . . . 2.50
29 MPn(i),Changing Woman #3 . . . 2.50
30 Another Life. 2.50
31 Ernest & Jim #1 . . . . 2.50
32 Ernest & Jim #2 . . . . 2.50

DC/Vertigo, 1993
33 CBa,B:Birth Pains. 2.50
34 CBa,RkB(i),GID(i),A:Brian Juno,
    Garden of Pain 2.50
35 CBa,RkB(i),E:Birth Pains,
    V:Juno 2.50
36 CBa,PrG(i),RkB(i),B:Passion child,
    I:Miles Laimling 2.50
37 CBa,RkB(i),Shade/Kathy 2.50
38 CBa,RkB(i),Great American
    Novel 2.50
39 CBa,SEa,RkB(i),Pond Life 2.50
40 PBd,at Hotel Shade 2.50
41 GID,Pandora's Story,Kathy is
    pregnant 2.50
42 CBa,RkB(i),SY,B:History Lesson,
    A:John Constantine 3.50
43 CBa,RkB(i),PBd,Trial of William
    Matthieson,A:J.Constantine. . . 3.50
44 CBa,RkB(i),E:History Lesson,
    D:William Matthieson,A:John
    Constantine 3.50
45 CBa,B:A Season in Hell 2.50
46 CBa(c),GID,Season in Hell#2 . . 2.50
47 CBa(c),GID,A:Lenny 2.50
48 CBa(c),GID 2.50
49 CBa(c),GID,Kathy's Past 2.50
50 GID,BBI,MiA,pin-up gallery 3.50
51 GID,BBI,MiA,Masks,pt.1 . . . . . . 2.50

Shade the Changing Man #3
© DC Comics Inc.

52 GID,BBI,MiA,Masks,pt.2 . . . . 2.50
53 GID,BBI,MiA,Masks,pt.3 . . . . 2.50
54 MBu,RkB,Perpetual Motion 2.50
55 MBu,RkB,Life is Short,pt.1 . . . . . 2.50
56 MBu,RkB,Life is Short,pt.2 . . . . . 2.50
57 MBu,PrM,RkB,Life is Short,pt.3 . 2.50
58 PrM,Michael Lark 2.50
59 MBu,PrM,Nasty Infections,pt.1 . . 2.50
60 MBu,PrM,Nasty Infections,pt.2 . . 2.50
61 MBu,PrM,Nasty Infections,pt.3 . . 2.50
62 Nasty Infections,pt.4 . . . . 2.50
63 Nasty Infections,finale. 2.50
64 The Madness 2.50
65 The Roots of Madness,pt.1. . . . . 2.50
66 The Roots of Madness,pt.2. . . . . 2.50
67 The Roots of Madness,pt.3. . . . . 2.50
68 After Kathy,pt.1 . . . . 2.50
69 After Kathy,pt.2 . . . . 2.50
70 After Kathy,pt.3, final issue 2.50

SHADO, SONG OF THE DRAGON
1992
1 GM(i),From G.A. Longbow
    Hunters 5.50
2 GM(i),V:Yakuza 5.00
3 GM(i),V:Yakuza 5.00
4 GM(i),V:Yakuza 5.00

SHADOW, THE
[1st Regular Series], 1973–75
1 MK,The Doom Puzzle 75.00
2 MK,V:Freak Show Killer. 35.00
3 MK,BWr 40.00
4 MK,HC,BWr,Ninja Story. 35.00
5 FR 30.00
6 MK 32.00
7 FR 20.00
8 FR 20.00
9 FR 20.00
10 JCr 22.00
11 A:Avenger 20.00
12 . . . . 20.00

[Limited Series], 1986
1 HC,R:Shadow 5.00
2 HC,O:Shadow 4.00
3 HC,V:Preston Mayrock 4.00
4 HC,V:Preston Mayrock 4.00

[2nd Regular Series], 1987–89
1 BSz,Shadows & Light,pt.1 . . . . . 3.50
2 BSz,Shadows & Light,pt.2 . . . . . 3.50
3 BSz,Shadows & Light,pt.3 . . . . . 3.50
4 BSz,Shadows & Light,pt.4 . . . . . 3.50
5 BSz,Shadows & Light,pt.5 . . . . . 3.50
6 BSz,Shadows & Light,pt.6 . . . . . 3.50
7 MR,KB,Harold Goes to
    Washington 3.00
8 KB,Seven Deadly Finns,pt.1 . . . . 3.00
9 KB,Seven Deadly Finns,pt.2 . . . . 3.00
10 KB,Seven Deadly Finns,pt.3. . . . 3.00
11 KB,Seven Deadly Finns,pt.4. . . . 3.00
12 KB,Seven Deadly Finns,pt.5. . . . 3.00
13 KB,Seven Deadly Finns,pt.6. . . . 3.00
14 KB,Body And Soul,pt.1 . . . . 3.00
15 KB,Body And Soul,pt.2 . . . . 3.00
16 KB,Body And Soul,pt.3 . . . . 3.00
17 KB,Body And Soul,pt.4 . . . . 3.00
18 KB,Body And Soul,pt.5 . . . . 3.00
19 KB,Body And Soul,pt.6 . . . . 3.00
Ann.#1 JO,AA,Shadows & Light
    prologue. 4.00
Ann.#2 KB,Agents 3.50

SHADOW CABINET
Milestone, 1994–95
0 WS(c),3RL,Shadow War,Foil(c),A:All
    Milestone characters 3.00
1 JBy(c),3RW,I&D:Corpsickle 2.50
2 thru 17 . . . . @2.50

Shadow Cabinet #6
© DC Comics Inc.

SHADOWDRAGON
1995
Ann.#1 Year One Annual 3.50

SHADOW OF BATMAN
1 reprints of Detective Comics . . . 10.00
2 thru 4 . . . . @7.50

SHADOW OF THE BATMAN
1985–86
1 WS,AM,MR,rep. 7.00
2 MR,TA,rep.A:Hugo Strange 5.00
3 MR,TA,rep.A:Penguin 5.00
4 MR,TA,rep.A:Joker 6.00
5 MR,DG,rep. 5.00

SHADOWPACT
2006
1 BWg,A:Superman 3.00
2 BWg. 3.00
3 BWg,V:Pentacle. 3.00
4 BWg,F:Blue Devil. 3.00
5 BWg,Killers assemble 3.00
6 Goodbye Ragman & Enchantress 3.00
7 BWg,V:The Congregation 3.00
8 BWg,V:The Congregation 3.00
9 BWg,to Budapest. 3.00
10 BWg,Demon Triptych 3.00
11 BWg,Demon Triptych 3.00
12 BWg, Die by the Sword 3.00
13 BWg,F:Zauriel. 3.00
14 BWg,Blue Devil tries to quit . . . 3.00
15 BWg,Zauriel joins Shadowpact. . 3.00
16 V:Doctor Gotham 3.00
17 DBw,V:Horde of Zombies 3.00
18 Detective Chimp & Enchantress. 3.00
19 Trapped. 3.00
20 Nightshade Dimension 3.00
21 V:Unbound 3.00
22 One less member 3.00
23 Shadowpacts of the past 3.00
24 Three Shadowpacts 3.00
25 Final issue. 3.00

SHADOW'S FALL
1994–95
1 JVF,Voyage of self-discovery. . . . 3.00
2 JVF,More of tale. 3.00
3 JVF,Shen confronts shadow 3.00
4 JVF,Gale wounded. 3.00
5 JVF,Shadow goes Berserk 3.00
6 JVF,F:Warren Gale,final issue . . . 3.00

DC COMICS

SHADOW STRIKES!, THE
1989–92
1 EB,Death's Head 3.00
2 EB,EB,PoliticalKiller,V:Rasputin. . 2.50
3 EB,V:Mad Monk,V:Rasputin 2.50
4 EB,D:Mad Monk,V:Rasputin 4.00
5 EB,Shadow & Doc Savage#1 . . . . 4.00
6 Shadow & Doc Savage #3 . . . . . 2.50
7 RM,A:Wunderkind,O:Shadow's
   Radio Show 2.50
8 EB,A:Shiwan Khan 2.50
9 Fireworks#2 . . . . 2.50
10 EB,Fireworks#3. . . . . 2.50
11 EB,O:Margo Lane 2.50
12 EB,V:Chicago Mob 2.50
13 EB,V:Chicago Mob 2.50
14 EB,V:Chicago Mob 2.50
15 EB,V:Chicago Mob 2.50
16 Assassins,pt.1 . . . . 2.50
17 Assassins,pt.2 . . . . 2.50
18 Shrevvie 2.50
19 NY,NJ Tunnel 2.50
20 Shadow+Margo Vs.Nazis 2.50
21 V:Shiwan Khan 2.50
22 V:Shiwan Khan 2.50
23 V:Shiwan Khan 2.50
24 Search for Margo Lane. 2.50
25 In China 2.50
26 V:Shiwan Khan 2.50
27 V:Shiwan Khan,Margo
   Rescued 2.50
28 SL,In Hawaii 2.50
29 DSp,Valhalla,V:Nazis 2.50
30 The Shadow Year One,pt.1 . . . . 2.50
31 The Shadow Year One,pt.2 . . . . 2.50
Ann.#1 DSp, Crimson Dreams 4.00

SHADOW WAR OF HAWKMAN
May, 1985
1 AA,V:Thangarians 2.50
2 AA,V:Thangarians 2.50
3 AA,V:Thangarians,A:Aquaman,
   Elong.Man 2.50
4 AA,V:Thangarians 2.50
Spec.#1 V:Thangarians 2.50

SHAZAM!
1973–78
[1st Regular Series]
1 B:DON(s),CCB,O:Capt.Marvel . 75.00
2 CCB,A:Mr.Mind. 25.00

Shazam! #1
© DC Comics, Inc.

3 CCB,V:Shagg Naste 25.00
4 E:DON(s),CCB,V:Ibac. 25.00
5 B:ESM(s),CCB,A:Leprechaun . . 25.00
6 B:DON(s),CCB,Dr,Sivana 20.00
7 CCB,A:Capt Marvel Jr. 20.00
8 CCB,O:Marvel Family 90.00
9 E:DON(S)DC,CCB,A:Mr.Mind,
   Captain Marvel Jr. 20.00
10 ESM(s)CCB,BO 20.00
11 ViCKS,BO,rep. 15.00
12 BO,DG 75.00
13 BO,KS,A:Luthor 75.00
14 KS,A:Monster Society 75.00
15 KS,BO,Luther 75.00
16 KS,BO. 75.00
17 KS,BO. 75.00
18 KS,BO. 15.00
19 KS,BO,Mary Marvel 15.00
20 KS,A:Marvel Family 15.00
21 reprint 15.00
22 reprint 15.00
23 reprint 15.00
24 reprint 15.00
25 KS,DG,I&O:Isis 22.00
26 KS 15.00
27 KS,A:Kid Eternity 22.00
28 KS 15.00
29 KS 15.00
30 KS 15.00
31 KS,A:Minute Man 15.00
32 KS 15.00
33 KS 15.00
34 O:Capt.Marvel Jr. 15.00
35 DN,KS,A:Marvel Family 15.00
GN Power of Hope,64-page 15.00

SHAZAM! FAMILY
July, 2002
Annual #1 (1953, rep.) 80-pg. 6.00

SHAZAM: THE MONSTER SOCIETY OF EVIL
Feb., 2007
1 (of 4) JSi,48-pgs. 6.00
2 thru 4 JSi, 48-pgs. . . . . @6.00

SHAZAM, THE NEW BEGINNING
April, 1987
1 O:Shazam & Capt.Marvel 2.50
2 V:Black Adam 2.50
3 V:Black Adam 2.50
4 V:Black Adam 2.50

SHAZAM/SUPERMAN: FIRST THUNDER
Sept., 2005
1 (of 4) V:Cult, Giant Robots 3.50
2 A:Lex Luthor & Dr. Sivana 3.50
3 F:Eclipso 3.50
4 V:Dr. Sivana. 3.50

SHERLOCK HOLMES
Sept.–Oct., 1975
1 ERc,WS 35.00

SHOWCASE
1956–70
1 F:Fire Fighters 7,000.00
2 JKu,F:Kings of Wild 2,000.00
3 F:Frogmen 2,100.00
4 CI,JKu,I&O:S.A. Flash
   (Barry Allen) 50,000.00
5 F:Manhunters 2,000.00
6 JK,I&O:Challengers of the
   Unknown. 7,500.00
7 JK,F:Challengers 4,000.00
8 CI,F:Flash,I:Capt.Cold 20,000.00

9 F:Lois Lane 14,000.00
10 F:Lois Lane 6,000.00
11 JK(c),F:Challengers 3,500.00
12 JK(c),F:Challengers 3,500.00
13 CI,F:Flash,Mr.Element . . . 10,000.00
14 CI,F:Flash,Mr.Element . . . 11,000.00
15 I:Space Ranger 4,000.00
16 F:Space Ranger 2,000.00
17 GK(c),I:Adam Strange 4,500.00
18 GK(c),F:Adam Strange 2,500.00
19 GK(c),F:Adam Strange 2,700.00
20 I:Rip Hunter 2,000.00
21 F:Rip Hunter 1,000.00
22 GK,I&O:S.A. Green Lantern
   (Hal Jordan) 10,000.00
23 GK,F:Green Lantern 3,500.00
24 GK,F:Green Lantern 3,500.00
25 JKu,F:Rip Hunter 750.00
26 JKu,F:Rip Hunter 750.00
27 RH,I:Sea Devils 1,700.00
28 RH,F:Sea Devils 900.00
29 RH,F:Sea Devils 900.00
30 O:Aquaman 2,000.00
31 GK(c),F:Aquaman 1,000.00
32 F:Aquaman 1,000.00
33 F:Aquaman 1,100.00
34 GK,MA,I&O:S.A. Atom 3,000.00
35 GK,MA,F:Atom. 1,500.00
36 GK,MA,F:Atom. 1,000.00
37 RA,I:Metal Man 1,300.00
38 RA,F:Metal Man 800.00
39 RA,F:Metal Man 650.00
40 RA,F:Metal Man 600.00
41 F:Tommy Tomorrow 400.00
42 F:Tommy TOmorrow 400.00
43 F:Dr.No(James Bond 007) . . 1,000.00
44 F:Tommy Tomorrow 300.00
45 JKu,O:Sgt.Rock 300.00
46 F:Tommy Tomorrow 250.00
47 F:Tommy Tomorrow 250.00
48 F:Cave Carson 300.00
49 F:Cave Carson 275.00
50 MA,CI,F:I Spy 225.00
51 MA,CI,F:I Spy 225.00
52 F:Cave Carson 225.00
53 JKu(c),RH,F:G.I.Joe 250.00
54 JKu(c),RH,F:G.I.Joe 250.00
55 MA,F:Dr.Fate,Spectre,1st S.A.
   Gr. Lantern,Solomon Grundy 500.00
56 MA,F:Dr.Fate. 300.00
57 JKu,F:Enemy Ace 700.00
58 JKu,F:Enemy Ace 500.00
59 F:Teen Titans 300.00
60 MA,F:Spectre 600.00
61 MA,F:Spectre 300.00

Showcase #58
© DC Comics Inc.

62 JO,I:Inferior 5 . . . . 200.00
63 JO,F:Inferior 5. . . . . 125.00
64 MA,F:Spectre 300.00
65 F:Inferior 5 . . . . 125.00
66 I:B'wana Beast 100.00
67 F:B'wana Beast. 100.00
68 I:Maniaks. 125.00
69 F:Maniaks 125.00
70 I:Binky 100.00
71 F:Maniaks 90.00
72 JKu,ATh,F:Top Gun 90.00
73 SD,I&O:Creeper 200.00
74 I:Anthro 90.00
75 SD,I:Hawk & Dove 125.00
76 NC,I:Bat Lash 200.00
77 BO,I:Angel & Ape 75.00
78 I:Jonny Double 65.00
79 I:Dolphin 90.00
80 NA(c),F:Phantom Stranger . . . 150.00
81 I:Windy & Willy 75.00
82 I:Nightmaster. 300.00
83 BWr,MK,F:Nightmaster 200.00
84 BWr,MK,F:Nightmaster 200.00
85 JKu,F:Firehair 50.00
86 JKu,F:Firehair 50.00
87 JKu,F:Firehair 50.00
88 F:Jason's Quest 30.00
89 F:Jason's Quest 30.00
90 F:Manhunter 30.00
91 F:Manhunter 30.00
92 F:Manhunter 30.00
93 F:Manhunter (1970) 30.00

[Series Resumes], 1977
94 JA,JSon,I&O:2nd
  Doom Patrol 30.00
95 JA,JSon,F:2nd Doom Patrol . . . 20.00
96 JA,JSon,F:2nd Doom Patrol . . . 20.00
97 JO,JSon,O:Power Girl 12.00
98 JSon,DG,Power Girl 12.00
99 JSon,DG,Power Girl 12.00
100 JSon,all star issue. 20.00
101 JKu(c),AM,MA,Hawkman 12.00
102 JKu(c),AM,MA,Hawkman 12.00
103 JKu(c),AM,MA,Hawkman 12.00
104 RE,OSS Spies 12.00

SHOWCASE '93
1 AAd(c),EH,AV,F:Catwoman,
  Blue Devil,Cyborg 4.00
2 KM(c),EH,AV,F:Catwoman,
  Blue Devil,Cyborg 3.50
3 KM(c),EH,TC,F:Catwoman,
  Blue Devil,Flash 3.00
4 F:Catwoman,Blue Devil,
  Geo-Force 3.00
5 F:KD,DG,BHi,F:Robin,Blue
  Devil,Geo-Force 3.00
6 MZ(c),KD,DG,F:Robin,Blue
  Devil,Deathstroke 3.00
7 BSz(c),KJ,Knightfall#13,F:Two-
  Face,Jade&Obsidian 5.00
8 KJ,Knightfall#14,F:Two-Face,
  Peacemaker,Fire and Ice 4.00
9 F:Huntress,Peacemaker,Shining
  Knight 3.00
10 BWg,SI,F:Huntress,Batman,
  Dr.Light,Peacemaker,Deathstroke,
  Katana,M.Manhunter. 3.00
11 GP(c),F:Robin,Nightwing,
  Peacemaker,Deathstroke,Deadshot,
  Katana,Dr.Light,Won.Woman . . 3.00
12 AD(c),BMc,F:Robin,Nightwing,
  Green Lantern,Creeper 3.00

SHOWCASE '94
1 KN,F:Joker,Gunfire,Orion,Metro . 3.00
2 KON(c),E:Joker,B:Blue Beetle. . . 3.00
3 MMi(c),B:Razorsharpe. 3.00
4 AIG(s),DG,F:Arkham Asylum inmates
  E:Razorsharpe,Blue Bettle 3.00
5 WS(c),CDi(s),PJ,B:Robin&Huntress,
  F:Bloodwynd,Loose Cannon . . . 3.00

Showcase '94 #2
© DC Comics Inc.

6 PJ,KK(s),F:Robin & Huntress . . . 3.00
7 JaL(c),PDd(s),F:Comm. Gordon . 3.00
8 AIG(s),O:Scarface,Ventriloquist,
  F:Monarch,1st Wildcat. 3.25
9 AIG(s),DJ,O:Scarface,Ventriloquist,
  F:Monarch,Waverider 3.00
10 JQ(c),AIG(s),F:Azrael,Zero Hour,
  B:Black Condor 3.25
11 Black Condor, Man-Bat. 3.00
12 Barbara Gordon 3.00

SHOWCASE '95
1 Supergirl 3.00
2 . . . . 3.00
3 F:Eradicator,Claw 3.00
4 A:Catwoman,Hawke 3.00
5 F:Thorne,Firehawk. 3.00
6 thru 12 . . . . @3.00

SHOWCASE '96
1 F:Steel & Warrior 3.00
2 F:Steel and Warrior 3.00
3 thru 7 . . . . @3.00
8 F:Superman, Superboy &
  Supergirl 5.00
9 F:Lady Shiva & Shadowdragon,
  Martian Manhunter 3.00
10 F:Ultra Boy, Captain Comet . . . 3.00
11 Legion of Super-Heroes 3.00
12 10,000 Brainiacs. 3.00

SILVER AGE
DC CLASSICS
Action #252(rep) 3.00
Adventure #247(rep) 3.00
Brave and Bold #28 (rep) 3.00
Detective #225 (rep) 3.00
Detective #327 (rep) 3.00
Green Lantern #76 (rep) 3.00
House of Secrets #92 (rep) 3.00
Showcase #4 (rep). 3.00
Showcase #22 (rep). 3.00
Sugar & Spike #99(1st printing). . . 3.00

SILVER AGE
May, 2000
Secret Files #1. . . . . 5.00
Justice League of America #1 . . . . . 2.50
Challengers of the Unknown #1 . . . 2.50
Teen Titans #1 . . . . 2.50
Doom Patrol #1 . . . . 2.50
Dial "H" For Hero #1 . . . . 2.50

The Flash #1 . . . . 2.50
Green Lantern #1. . . . . 2.50
The Brave and the Bold #1 . . . . . . 2.50
Showcase #1 . . . . 2.50
80-Page Giant #1, 80-pg 6.50
Silver Age #1, 48-pg 4.00

SILVERBLADE
Sept., 1987
1 KJ,GC,maxi-series. 2.50
2 thru 12 GC . . . . @2.50

SIMON DARK
Oct., 2007
1 SHp,Gotham's Newest Defender 3.00
2 thru 14 SHp . . . . @3.00

SINS OF YOUTH
March, 2000
Aquaboy/Lagoon Man #1 x-over . . . 2.50
Batboy & Robin #1 x-over 2.50
JLA/Jr. #1 x-over 2.50
Kid Flash/Impulse #1 x-over 2.50
Secret/Deadboy #1 x-over. 2.50
Starwoman & JSA #1 x-over 2.50
Superman,Jr./Superboy,Sr.#1
  x-over. 2.50
Wonder Girls #1 x-over 2.50

SKIN GRAFT
DC/Vertigo, 1993
1 B:JeP(s),WaP,I:John Oakes,
  A:Tattooed Man(Tarrant) 3.25
2 WaP,V:Assassins 3.00
3 WaP,In Kyoto,I:Mizoguchi Kenji . . 3.00
4 E:JeP(s),WaP,V:Tarrant,Kenji . . . 3.00

SKULL AND BONES
1992
1 EH,I&O:Skull & Bones. 5.00
2 EH,V:KGB 5.00
3 EH,V:KGB 5.00

SLASH MARAUD
Nov., 1987
1 PG. 2.50
2 PG 2.50
3 thru 10 PG . . . . @2.50

SMALLVILLE
Sept., 2002
Spec. TV series 4.00

SMALLVILLE
March 2003
1 Camping trip, from TV show 5.00
2 Miss Smallville Pageant. 4.00
3 F:Lex Luthor. 4.00
4 F:Lex Luthor. 4.00
5 Untold Tales 4.00
6 Lex & Clark,48-pg. 4.00
7 TG,Television x-over,pt.1 . . . . . . 4.00
8 TG,Television x-over,pt.2 . . . . . . 4.00
9 Mysterious men 4.00
10 Who shot Lionel Luthor. 4.00
11 48-page. 4.00

SMASH COMICS
1999
1 TPe(s),F:Doctor Mid-Nite
  & Hourman 2.50

SMAX
DC/Vertigo, 2003
1 (of 5) AMo(s) 3.00
2 thru 4 AMo(s). 3.00

All comics prices listed are for *Near Mint* condition.   **CVA 2009 • Page 147**

SOLO
2004
1 TSe,48-pg.	4.00
2 RCo, 5 stories	5.00
3 PPo	5.00
4 HC	5.00
5 Darwyn Cooke	5.00
6	5.00
7 MiA	5.00
8 NGa(s)	5.00
9 SHp	5.00
10 Five stories	5.00
11 SA	5.00
12 BMc,final issue	5.00

SONIC DISRUPTORS
1987–88
1 thru 10	@3.00

SON OF AMBUSH BUG
July, 1986
1 thru 6 KG	@2.50

SON OF VULCAN
June, 2005
1 (of 6) Mikey Devante	3.00
2	3.00
3 F:Green Lantern & JLA	3.00
4 Vulcan's superpowers	3.00
5 Coalition of Crime	3.00
6 Coalition of Crime, concl.	3.00

Sovereign Seven #19
© DC Comics, Inc.

SOVEREIGN SEVEN
1995–98
1 CCl(s),DT,I:Sovereign Seven, V:Female Furies,A:Darkseid	3.00
2 thru 11 CCl(s)	@2.50
12 thru 36 CCl(s)	@2.50
Ann.#1 CCl, Year One Annual	4.00
Ann.#2 CCl(s),RL,KJ,Legends of the Dead Earth	3.00
1-shot Sovereign Seven Plus (1977)	3.00

SPACE GHOST
Nov., 2004
1 AOl,O:Space Ghost	15.00
2 AOl	6.00
3 thru 6 AOl,V:Zorak	@3.00

SPECIAL EDITION
1944–45
(Reprint giveaways for U.S. Navy)
1 Action Comics #80,WB	750.00
2 Action Comics#81,WB	750.00
3 Superman #33	750.00
4 Detective Comics#97	750.00
5 Superman #34	750.00
6 Action Comics #84,WB	750.00

SPECTRE, THE
1967–69
1 MA,V:Captain Skull	300.00
2 NA,V:Dirk Rawley	175.00
3 NA,A:Wildcat	175.00
4 NA	175.00
5 NA	175.00
6 MA	125.00
7 MA,BU:Hourman	125.00
8 MA,Parchment of Power Perilous	125.00
9 BWr(2nd BWr Art)	200.00
10 MA.	150.00

[2nd Regular Series], 1987–89
1 GC,O:Spectre	5.00
2 GC,Cult of BRM	4.00
3 GC,Fashion Model Murders	3.00
4 GC	3.00
5 GC,Spectre's Murderer	3.00
6 GC,Spectre/Corrigan separated	3.00
7 A:Zatanna,Wotan	3.00
8 A:Zatanna,Wotan	3.00
9 GM,Spectre's Revenge	3.00
10 GM,A:Batman,Millennium	3.00
11 GM,Millennium	3.00
12 GM,The Talisman,pt.1	3.00
13 GM,The Talisman,pt.2	3.00
14 GM,The Talisman,pt.3	3.00
15 GM,The Talisman,pt.4	3.00
16 Jim Corrigan Accused	3.00
17 New Direction,Final Destiny	3.00
18 Search for Host Body	3.00
19 Dead Again	3.00
20 Corrigan Detective Agency	3.00
21 A:Zoran	3.00
22 BS,Sea of Darkness,A:Zoran	3.00
23 A:Lords of Order, Invasion x-over	3.00
24 BWg,Ghosts i/t Machine#1	3.00
25 Ghosts in the Machine #2	3.00
26 Ghosts in the Machine #3	3.00
27 Ghosts in the Machine #4	3.00
28 Ghosts in the Machine #5	3.00
29 Ghosts in the Machine #6	3.00
30 Possession	3.00
31 Spectre possessed, final issue	3.00
Ann.#1, A:Deadman	3.00

[3rd Regular Series], 1992–97
1 B:JOs(s),TMd,R:Spectre, Glow in the dark(c)	7.00
2 TMd,Murder Mystery	6.00
3 TMd,O:Spectre	4.00
4 TMd,O:Spectre	4.00
5 TMd,BB(c),V:Kidnappers	3.50
6 TMd,Spectre prevents evil	3.50
7 TMd	3.50
8 TMd,Glow in the dark(c)	5.00
9 TMd,MWg(c),V:The Reaver	3.00
10 TMd,V:Michael	3.00
11 TMd,V:Azmodeus	3.00
12 V:Reaver	3.00
13 TMd,V:Count Vertigo, Glow in the Dark(c)	4.00
14 JoP,A:Phantom Stranger	2.50
15 TMd,A:Phantom Stranger,Demon, Doctor Fate,John Constantine	2.50
16 JAp,V:I.R.A.	2.50
17 TT(c),TMd,V:Eclipso	2.50
18 TMd,D:Eclipso.	2.50

Spectre 3rd Series #6
© DC Comics, Inc.

19 TMd,V:Hate	2.50
20 A:Lucien	2.50
21 V:Naiad,C:Superman	3.00
22 A:Superman	3.00
23 Book of Judgment, pt.1	2.50
24 Book of Judgment, pt.2	2.50
25 Book of Judgment, pt.3	2.50
26 The Door of the Solstice	2.50
27 R:Azmodus	2.50
28 V:Azmodus	2.50
29 V:Azmodus	2.50
30 V:Azmodus	2.50
31 Descent into Pandemonium	2.50
32 V:Killo	2.50
33 JOs	2.50
34 Power of the Undead	2.50
35 JOs,TMd,Underworld Unleashed tie-in	2.50
36 JOs,TMd,Underworld Unleashed tie-in	2.50
37 JOs,TMd,The Haunting of America,pt.1	2.50
38 JOs,TMd,The Haunting of America,pt.2	2.50
39 JOs,TMd,The Haunting of America,pt.3	2.50
40 JOs,TMd,The Haunting of America,pt.4	2.50
41 JOs,TMd,The Haunting of America,pt.5	2.50
42 JOs,TMd,The Haunting of America,pt.6	2.50
43 Witchcraft	2.50
44 Madame Xanadu	2.50
45 JOs(s),Acts of God	2.50
46 JOs(s),TMd,discovery of the Spear of Destiny	2.50
47 JOs,TMd,The Haunting of America, Final Night tie-in	2.50
48 JOs(s),TMd,The Haunting of America	2.50
49 JOs(s),TMd,The Haunting of America	2.50
50 JOs(s),TMd,	2.50
51 JOs(s),TMd,A:Batman,Joker.	2.50
52 JOs(s),TMd,Nate Kane discovers murder evidence	2.50
53 JOs(s),TMd,Haunting of Jim Corrigan, cont.	2.50
54 JOs(s),TMd,hunt for murderer of Mister Terrific	2.50
55 JOs(s),TMd,Corrigan implicated in murder	2.50

56 JOs(s),TMd,JTo, Haunting of Jim
  Corrigan. 2.50
57 JOs(s),TMd,Spectre & Jim
  Corrigan in Heaven 2.50
58 JOs,TMd,Genesis tie-in 2.50
59 JOs,TMd,BWr(c), alien pod 2.50
60 JOs,TMd,Quest for God, cont. . . 2.50
61 JOs,TMd,Quest for God, concl. . 2.50
62 JOs,TMd,final issue 2.50
Ann.#1 JOs,TMd,Year One 4.00

SPECTRE, THE
Jan., 2001
1 JMD,F:Hal Jordan 3.00
2 JMD,Redeeming the Demon,pt.1 3.00
3 JMD,Redeeming the Demon,pt.2 3.00
4 JMD,Redeeming the Demon,pt.3 3.00
5 JMD,F:Two-Face/Harvey Dent . . 3.00
6 JMD,The Redeemer,pt.1 . . . . 3.00
7 JMD,The Redeemer,pt.2 . . . . 3.00
8 JMD,The Redeemer,pt.3 . . . . 3.00
9 JMD,stolen soul 3.00
10 JMD,Joker:Last Laugh 3.00
11 JMD,F:Phantom Stranger 3.00
12 JMD,Spectre of Christmas 3.00
13 JMD,Eternity in an Hour 3.00
14 JMD,vampire-lord 3.00
15 JMD,NBy,Mystery in Space,pt.1 3.00
16 JMD,NBy,Mystery in Space,pt.2 . 3.00
17 JMD,NBy,Mystery in Space,pt.3 . 3.00
18 JMD,NBy,Abin Sur, Materna 3.00
19 NBy,DJa,V:Darkseid 3.00
20 NBy,DJa,magazine publisher . . . 3.00
21 NBy,DJa,Stigmonus,C.Ferris . . . 3.00
22 NBy,DJa,A:G.Arrow,
  M.Manhunter 3.00
23 JMD,NBy,DJa,Return of
  Sinestro,pt.3 . . . . 3.00
24 JMD,DJa,F:DCU characters . . . 3.00
25 JMD,DJa,F:Rabid 3.00
26 JMD,DJa,terrorist 3.00
27 JMD,DJa,final issue 3.00

SPEED FORCE
Sept., 1997
1 MWa,BAu,JBy,BML,JAp,BSn,
  Flash stories, 64pg. 4.00

SPELLJAMMER
Sept., 1990
1 RogueShip#1 . . . . 3.00
2 RogueShip#2 . . . . 2.50
3 thru 15 . . . . @2.50

SPIRIT, THE
Dec., 2006
1 F:Denny Colt 3.00
2 F:P'Gell 3.00
3 A dead gunman 3.00
4 Mexican bordertown 3.00
5 Spirit Pork & Beans Spread . . . 3.00
6 A fallen meteor. 3.00
7 Three tales. 3.00
8 Time Bomb. 3.00
9 V:El Morte 3.00
10 Murder case 3.00
11 F:El Morte, Central City gangs . . 3.00
12 F:San Sarif 3.00
13 Femmes Fatales. 3.00
14 SA,MP,Murder. 3.00
15 SA,MP,Pageant Diamonds 3.00
16 SA,Murder at the movie studio . . 3.00
17 SA,Impossible mystery 3.00
18 SA,Mummies from Egypt 3.00
19 SA,Cheating death 3.00
20 SA,Swims with dolphins 3.00
21 SA,Dude Ranch 3.00
22 SA,Dude Ranch 3.00
23 SA,Wide open spaces 3.00

STALKER
1975–1976
1 SD,WW,O&I:Stalker 20.00
2 thru 4 SD,WW . . . . @15.00

STANLEY & HIS MONSTER
See: FOX AND THE CROW

STANLEY & HIS MONSTER
1993
1 R:Stanley 2.50
2 I:Demon Hunter 2.50
3 A:Ambrose Bierce 2.50
4 final issue. 2.50

S.T.A.R. CORPS
1993
1 A:Superman 2.50
2 I:Fusion,A:Rampage 2.50
3 thru 6 . . . . @2.50

STAR CROSSED
DC/Helix, April, 1997
1 (of 3) MHo,Dyltah's romance
  with Saa. 2.50
2 MHo,Love During Wartime 2.50
3 concl. 2.50

[NEIL GAIMAN & CHARLES VESS']
STARDUST
DC/Vertigo, Oct., 1997
1 (of 4) NGa(s),CV 6.00
2 NGa(s),CV adult faerie tale 6.00
3 NGa(s),CV 6.00
4 NGa(s),CV. 6.00

STARFIRE
1976–77
1 . . . . 20.00
2 . . . . 12.00
3 thru 8 . . . . @12.00

STAR HUNTERS
Oct.–Nov., 1977
1 DN&BL 15.00
2 LH&BL 12.00
3 MN&BL,D:Donovan Flint 12.00
4 thru 7 . . . . @12.00

STARMAN
1988–92
1 TL,I&O:New Starman. 4.00
2 TL,V:Serial Killer,C:Bolt 3.00
3 TL,V:Bolt 3.00
4 TL,V:Power Elite 2.50
5 TL,Invasion,A:PowerGirl,
  Firestorm 2.50
6 TL,Invasion,A:G.L.,Atom 2.50
7 TL,Soul Searching Issue 2.50
8 TL,V:LadyQuark. 2.50
9 TL,A:Batman,V:Blockbuster. . . . 2.50
10 TL,A:Batman,V:Blockbuster 2.50
11 TL,V:Power Elite 2.50
12 TL,V:Power Elite,A:Superman . . 2.50
13 TL,V:Rampage 2.50
14 TL,A:A:Superman,V:Parasite . . 2.50
15 TL,V:Deadline 2.50
16 TL,O:Starman 2.50
17 TL,V:Dr.Polaris,A:PowerGirl . . . 2.50
18 TL,V:Dr.Polaris,A:PowerGirl . . . 2.50
19 TL,V:Artillery 2.50
20 TL,FireFighting 2.50
21 TL,Starman Quits 2.50
22 TL,V:Khunds 2.50

Starman #25
© DC Comics Inc.

23 TL,A:Deadline 2.50
24 TL,A:Deadline 2.50
25 TL,V:Deadline 2.50
26 V:The Mist. 6.00
27 V:The Mist. 5.00
28 A:Superman 7.00
29 V:Plasmax 2.50
30 Seduction of Starman #1 . . . . . 2.50
31 Seduction of Starman #2 . . . . . 2.50
32 Seduction of Starman #3 . . . . . 2.50
33 Seduction of Starman #4 . . . . . 2.50
34 A:Batman 2.50
35 A:Valor,Mr.Nebula,ScarletSkier . . 2.50
36 A:Les Mille Yeux 2.50
37 A:Les Mille Yeux 2.50
38 War of the Gods X-over 2.50
39 V:Plasmax. 2.50
40 V:Las Vegas 2.50
41 V:Maaldor 2.50
42 Star Shadows,pt.1,A:Eclipso . . . 3.00
43 Star Shadows,pt.2,A:Lobo,
  Eclipso. 2.50
44 Star Shadows,pt.3,A:Eclipso
  V:Lobo. 2.50
45 Star Shadows,pt.4, V:Eclipso . . . 2.50

[2nd Series], 1994
0 New Starman 8.00
1 Sins of the Father,pt.2 . . . . 8.00
2 Sins of the Father,pt.3 . . . . 7.00
3 Sins of the Father,pt.4 . . . . 6.00
4 A Day in the Opal. 6.00
5 V:Starman 6.00
6 Times Past Features 6.00
7 Sinister Circus 6.00
8 TyH(c),Sinister Circus 5.00
9 TyH(c),Mist's daughter breaks
  out of prison. 5.00
10 Sins of the Chile,prelude 5.00
11 JeR,TyH,13 Years Ago:5 Friends 5.00
12 JeR,TyH,Sins of the Child,pt.1 . . 5.00
13 JeR,TyH,Sins of the Child,pt.2 . . 5.00
14 JeR,TyH,Sins of the Child,pt.3 . . 5.00
15 JeR,TyH,Sins of the Child,pt.4 . . 5.00
16 JeR,TyH,Sins of the Child,pt.5 . . 5.00
17 JeR,TyH 5.00
18 JeR,TyH,Orig.Starman
  vs.The Mist 4.00
19 JeR,TyH,Talking with David 2 . . 4.00
20 JeR(s),TyH,GyD,Sand and
  Stars,pt.1 . . . . 4.00
21 JeR,TyH,GyD,Sand/Stars,pt.2 . . 3.00
22 JeR,TyH,GyD,Sand/Stars,pt.3 . . 3.00
23 JeR,TyH,GyD,Sand/Stars,pt.4 . . 3.00
24 JeR(s),TyH,Hell & Back,pt.1 . . . 3.00

25 JeR(s),TyH,Hell & Back,pt.2	3.00
26 JeR(s),TyH,Hell & Back,pt.3	3.00
27 JeR(s),Christmas Knight	3.00
28 JeR(s)Superfreaks and	
Backstabbers	3.00
29 JeR(s),TyH,GyD,V:The Shade,	
Starman history	3.00
30 JeR(s),TyH,Infernal Devices	
pt.1 (of 6).	3.00
31 JeR(s),TyH,Devices,pt.2	3.00
32 JeR(s),TyH,Devices,pt.3	3.00
33 JeR(s),TyH,Infernal Devices	
pt.4,A:Batman, Sentinel.	3.00
34 JeR(s),TyH,A:Batman, Sentinel,	
Floronic Man	3.00
35 JeR(s),TyH,A:Batman, Floronic	
Man, Sentinel	3.00
36 JeR(s),TyH,F:Will Payton	3.00
37 JeR(s),TyH,F:GoldenAgeHeroes	3.00
38 JeR(s),TyH,new JLE	2.50
39 JeR(s),TyH,Lightning &	
Stars, pt.1 x-over	2.50
40 JeR(s),TyH	2.50
41 JeR(s),GEr,TyH	2.50
42 JeR(s),MS,Nazis,Demon	2.50
43 JeR(s),TyH,help from JLA	2.50
44 JeR(s),times past story	2.50
45 JeR(s),search for Will Payton . . .	2.50
46 JeR(s),TyH,Bobo.	2.50
47 JeR,SY,TyH, ...	2.50
48 JeR,SY,A:Swamp Thing	2.50
49 JeR,SY,Talking with David	2.50
50 JeR(s),PSj,48-page.	5.00
51 JeR(s),PSj,to Krypton	2.50
52 JeR(s),PSj,A:Adam Strange	2.50
53 JeR(s),PSj,A:Adam Strange	2.50
54 JeR(s),Times Past tale	2.50
55 JeR(s),PSj,A:Space Cabby.	2.50
56 JeR(s),PSj,A:ElongatedMan	2.50
57 JeR(s),PSj,TyH,AxR,A:Tigorr	
& Fastbak, pt.1	2.50
58 JeR,TyH,AxR, pt.2	2.50
59 JeR,TyH,AxR, pt.3	2.50
60 JeR,TyH,AxR, concl.	2.50
61 JeR,TyH,AxR	2.50
62 JeR,PSj,Grand Guignol,pt.1	2.50
63 JeR,PSj,Grand Guignol,pt.2	2.50
64 JeR,PSj,Grand Guignol,pt.3	2.50
65 JeR,PSj,Grand Guignol,pt.4	2.50
66 JeR,PSj,Grand Guignol,pt.5	2.50
67 JeR,PSj,Grand Guignol,pt.6	2.50
68 JeR,PSj,Grand Guignol,pt.7	2.50
69 JeR,PSj,flashback.	2.50
70 JeR,PSj,Grand Guignol,pt.8	2.50
71 JeR,PSj,Grand Guignol,pt.9	2.50
72 JeR,PSj,Grand Guignol, concl. . . .	2.50
73 JeR,PSj,Grand Guignol,Eulogy .	2.50
74 JeR,RH,Times Past	2.50
75 JeR,A:Superman.	2.50
76 JeR,Talking With David:2001 . .	2.50
77 JeR,1951,pt.1	2.50
78 JeR,1951,pt.2	2.50
79 JeR,1951,pt.3	2.50
80 JeR,48-page final issue	4.50
Ann.#1 Legends o/t Dead Earth . . .	4.00
Ann.#2 Pulp Heroes (Romance) . . .	4.50
Spec.#1,000,000 JeR(s),PSj	2.50
Secret Files #1,O:Starmen.	5.00
Giant #1 80-page.	5.00
Spec. Starman: The Mist, F:Mary	
Marvel, Girlfrenzy (1998).	2.50

STARS AND S.T.R.I.P.E.
1999

0 LMd,DDv,I:Courtney Whitman . . .	3.00
1 LMd, DDv,O:Star-Spangled Kid . .	2.50
2 LMd,DDv,V:Paintball	2.50
3 LMd,DDv,V:Skeeter	2.50
4 LMd,DDv,Day of Judgment	
x-over.	2.50
5 LMd,DDv,F:Young Justice,pt.1 . .	2.50
6	2.50

7 LMd,DDv,F:Mike Dugan.	2.50
8 LMd,DDv	2.50
9 LMd,DDv,R:Nebula Man	2.50
10 LMd,DDv,cheating.	2.50
11 DDv,V:Dr. Graft	2.50
12 DDv,V:Dragon King.	2.50
13 DDv,V:Dragon King.	2.50
14 LMd,DDv,final issue	2.50

STAR SPANGLED
COMICS
Oct., 1941

1 O:Tarantula,B:Captain X of the	
R.A.F.,Star Spangled Kid,	
Armstrong of the Army	9,000.00
2 Star Spang.Kid V:Dr.Weerd .	2,700.00
3 Star Spang.Kid V:Dr.Weerd .	2,000.00
4 V:The Needle	2,000.00
5 V:Dr. Weerd, V:The Needle .	2,000.00
6 E:Armstrong	1,200.00
7 S&K,O&1st app:The Guardian,	
B:Robotman,The Newsboy	
Legion, TNT	12,000.00
8 O:TNT & Dan the Dyna-Mite	3,500.00
9 S&K(c&a),Newsboy Legion .	2,700.00
10 S&K(c&a),Newsboy Legion .	2,700.00
11 S&K(c&a),Newsboy Legion .	2,000.00
12 S&K(c&a),Newsboy Legion,	
Prevue of Peril!	2,000.00
13 S&K(c&a),Suicide Slum . . .	2,000.00
14 S&K,Meanest Man on Earth	2,000.00
15 S&K(c&a),Playmates ofPeril	2,000.00
16 S&K(c&a),Newsboy Legion .	2,000.00
17 S&K(c&a),V:Rafferty Mob .	2,000.00
18 S&K,O:Star Spangled Kid .	2,500.00
19 S&K(c&a),E:Tarantula	2,000.00
20 S&K(c&a),B:Liberty Belle. .	2,000.00
21 S&K,Newsboy Legion	1,800.00
22 S&K,Brains for Sale.	1,800.00
23 S&K,Art for Scrapper'sSake	1,800.00
24 S&K,Death Strikes Bargain .	1,800.00
25 S&K,Victuals for Victory. . .	1,800.00
26 S&K,Newsboy Legion	1,800.00
27 S&K,Turn on the Heat	1,800.00
28 S&K,Poor Man's Rich Man .	1,800.00
29 JK,Cabbages and Comics .	1,800.00
30 JK,Lady of Linden Lake . . .	1,200.00
31 S&K,Questions Please! . . .	1,200.00
32 The Good Samaritan	1,200.00
33 Case of the Baleful Bride. .	1,200.00
34 From Rags to Ruin	1,200.00
35 The Proud Poppa.	1,200.00
36 Cowboy of Suicide Slum . . .	1,200.00
37 Diamonds in the Rough	1,200.00
38 Roll Out the Barrels	1,200.00
39 Two Guardians are a Crowd	1,200.00

Star Spangled Comics #17
© DC Comics, Inc.

40 Farewell to Crime.	1,000.00
41 Time Out for the Guardian . .	900.00
42 JK(c),Power of the Press	900.00
43 CS(c),Trials of a Tenor	900.00
44 Etiquette in Suicide Slum . . .	900.00
45 Crime Gets Clipped	900.00
46 Clothes Make the Criminal . . .	900.00
47 Triumph of Tommy	900.00
48 CS(c),Booty & the Blizzard . . .	900.00
49 CS(c),One Ounce to Victory . .	900.00
50 JKu,Guardian(c)	900.00
51 A:Robot Robber	900.00
52 Rehearsal for Crime	900.00
53 The Poet of Suicide Slum . .	900.00
54 Dead-Shot Dade's Revenge . .	900.00
55 Gabby Strikes a Gusher	900.00
56 The Treasuer of Araby	900.00
57 Recruit for the Legion	900.00
58 Matadors of Suicide Slum. . . .	900.00
59 JK,Answers Inc.	750.00
60 CS(c),Steve Brodie Da 2nd . .	750.00
61 CS,Great Ballroom Race	750.00
62 Prevue of Tomorrow	750.00
63 CS,Code of the Newsstand .	750.00
64 Criminal Cruise	750.00
65 B:Robin,(c) & stories	2,400.00
66 V:No Face	1,300.00
67 The Castle of Doom.	1,100.00
68 WMo(c&a),Octopus (c)	1,100.00
69 The Stolen Atom Bomb . . .	2,000.00
70 V:The Clock	1,100.00
71 Perils of the Stone Age	1,100.00
72 Robin Crusoe.	1,100.00
73 V:The Black Magician	1,100.00
74 V:The Clock	1,100.00
75 The State vs. Robin	1,100.00
76 V:The Fence	1,100.00
77 The Boy who Wanted Robin	
for Christmas	1,100.00
78 Rajah Robin.	1,100.00
79 V:The Clock,The Tick-Tock	
Crimes	1,100.00
80 The Boy Disc Jockey	1,000.00
81 The Seeing-Eye Dog Crimes .	900.00
82 The Boy who Hated Robin . . .	900.00
83 Who is Mr. Mystery,B:Captain	
Compass backup story	900.00
84 How can we Fight Juvenile	
Delinquency?	1,000.00
85 Peril at the Pole	850.00
86 The Barton Brothers	850.00
87 V:Sinister Knight	1,200.00
88 Robin Declares War on	
Batman, B:Batman app. . . .	1,000.00
89 Batman's Utility Belt?	1,000.00
90 Rancho Fear!	1,000.00
91 Cops 'n' Robbers?	1,000.00
92 Movie Hero No. 1?.	1,000.00
93 Riddle of the Sphinx.	1,000.00
94 Underworld Playhouse.	1,100.00
95 The Man with the Midas Touch,	
E:Robin(c),Batman story .	1,100.00
96 B:Tomahawk(c) & stories . . .	750.00
97 The 4 Bold Warriors	600.00
98 Robin's Rival.	600.00
99 The Second Pocahontas . . .	600.00
100 The Frontier Phantom.	750.00
101 Peril on the High Seas	600.00
102 Riddle of Mohawk Valley . .	600.00
103 Tomahawk's Death Duel! . . .	600.00
104 Race with Death!	600.00
105 The Unhappy Hunting	
Grounds.	600.00
106 Traitor in the War Paint. . . .	600.00
107 The Brave who Hunted	
Tomahawk	600.00
108 'The Ghost called Moccasin	
Foot!'	600.00
109 The Land Pirates of	
Jolly Roger Hill!	600.00
110 Sally Raines Frontier Girl . . .	600.00

Star Spangled Comics #120
© DC Comics, Inc.

111 The Death Map of Thunder
    Hill 600.00
112 Coin of Courage 600.00
113 FF,V:The Black Cougar 750.00
114 Return of the Black Cougar . 750.00
115 Journey of a Thousand
    Deaths 600.00
116 The Battle of Junction Fort . 600.00
117 Siege? 600.00
118 V:Outlaw Indians 500.00
119 The Doomed Stockade? 500.00
120 Revenge of Raven Heart! . . . 550.00
121 Adventure in New York! 500.00
122 I:Ghost Breaker,(c)& stories . 700.00
123 The Dolls of Doom 450.00
124 Suicide Tower 450.00
125 The Hermit's Ghost Dog! . . . 450.00
126 The Phantom of Paris! 450.00
127 The Supernatural Alibi! 450.00
128 C:Batman,The Girl who
    lived 5,000 Years! 450.00
129 The Human Orchids 500.00
130 The Haunted Town,
    July, 1952 . . . . 600.00
Becomes:

STAR SPANGLED
WAR STORIES
Aug., 1952

131 CS&StK(c),I Was A Jap
    Prisoner of War 1,600.00
132 CS&StK(c),The G.I. With
    The Million-Dollar Arm . . 1,100.00
133 CS&StK(c),Mission-San
    Marino. 1,000.00
3 CS&StK(c),Hundred-Mission
    Mitchell 750.00
4 CS&StK(c),The Hot Rod Tank . 750.00
5 LSt(c),Jet Pilot 750.00
6 CS(c),Operation Davy Jones . 750.00
7 CS(c),Rookie Ranger,The 700.00
8 CS(c),I Was A
    Hollywood Soldier 700.00
9 CS&StK(c),Sad Sack Squad . . 700.00
10 CS,The G.I. & The Gambler . . 700.00
11 LSt(c),The Lucky Squad 700.00
12 CS(c),The Four Horseman of
    Barricade Hill 700.00
13 No Escape 700.00
14 LSt(c),Pitchfork Army 700.00
15 The Big Fish 700.00
16 The Yellow Ribbon 700.00
17 IN(c),Prize Target 700.00
18 IN(c),The Gladiator 700.00
19 IN(c),The Big Lift 700.00

20 JGr(c),The Battle of
    the Frogmen 700.00
21 JGr(c),Dead Man's Bridge . . . 400.00
22 JGr(c),Death Hurdle 400.00
23 JGr(c),The Silent Frogman . . . 400.00
24 JGr(c),Death Slide 400.00
25 JGr(c),S.S. Liferaft 400.00
26 JGr(c),Bazooka Man 400.00
27 JGr(c),Taps for a Tail Gunner . 400.00
28 JGr(c),Tank Duel. 500.00
29 JGr(c),A Gun Called Slugger . 400.00
30 JGr(c),The Thunderbolt Tank . 400.00
31 IN(c),Tank Block 300.00
32 JGr(c),Bridge to Battle 300.00
33 JGr(c),Pocket War 300.00
34 JGr(c),Fighting...Snowbirds . . 300.00
35 JGr(c),Zero Hour. 300.00
36 JGr(c),A G.I. Passed Here . . . 300.00
37 JGr(c),A Handful of T.N.T. 300.00
38 RH(c),One-Man Army 300.00
39 JGr(c),Flying Cowboy 300.00
40 JGr(c),Desert Duel 300.00
41 IN(c),A Gunner's Hands 250.00
42 JGr(c),Sniper Alley 250.00
43 JGr(c),Top Kick Brother 250.00
44 JGr(c),Tank 711
    Doesn't Answer 250.00
45 JGr(c),Flying Heels 250.00
46 JGr(c),Gunner's Seat 250.00
47 JGr(c),Sidekick 250.00
48 JGr(c),Battle Hills 250.00
49 JGr(c),Payload 250.00
50 JGr(c),Combat Dust 250.00
51 JGr(c),Battle Pigeon 200.00
52 JGr(c),Cannon-Man 200.00
53 JGr(c),Combat Close-Ups . . . 200.00
54 JGr(c),Flying Exit 200.00
55 JKu(c),The Burning Desert . . . 200.00
56 JKu(c),The Walking Sub 200.00
57 JGr(c),Call For a Frogman . . . 200.00
58 JGr(c),MD,Waist Punch 200.00
59 JGr(c),Kick In The Door 200.00
60 JGr(c),Hotbox 200.00
61 JGr(c),MD,Tow Pilot 200.00
62 JGr(c),The Three GIs 200.00
63 JGr(c),Flying Range Rider . . . 200.00
64 JGr(c),MD,Frogman Ambush . 200.00
65 JGr(c),JSe,Frogman Block . . . 200.00
66 JGr(c),Flattop Pigeon 200.00
67 RH(c),MD,Ashcan Alley 200.00
68 JGr(c),The Long Step 200.00
69 JKu(c),Floating Tank, The. . . . 200.00
70 JKu(c),No Medal For
    Frogman 200.00
71 JKu(c),Shooting Star 200.00
72 JGr(c),Silent Fish 200.00
73 JGr(c),MD,The Mouse &
    the Tiger 200.00
74 JGr(c),MD,Frogman Bait. 200.00
75 JGr(c),MD,Paratroop
    Mousketeers 200.00
76 MD,JKu(c),Odd Man 200.00
77 MD,JKu(c),Room to Fight 200.00
78 MD,JGr(c),Fighting Wingman . 200.00
79 MD,JKu(c),Zero Box 200.00
80 MD,JGr(c),Top Gunner 200.00
81 MD,RH(c),Khaki Mosquito . . . 200.00
82 MD,JKu(c),Ground Flier 200.00
83 MD,JGr(c),Jet On
    My Shoulder 200.00
84 MD,IN(c),O:Mademoiselle
    Marie 350.00
85 IN(c),A Medal For Marie 250.00
86 JGr(c),A Medal For Marie 250.00
87 JGr(c),T.N.T. Spotlight 250.00
88 JGr(c),The Steel Trap 250.00
89 IN(c),Trail of the Terror 250.00
90 RA(c),Island of
    Armored Giants 800.00
91 JGr(c),The Train of Terror 200.00
92 Last Battle of the
    Dinosaur Age. 250.00

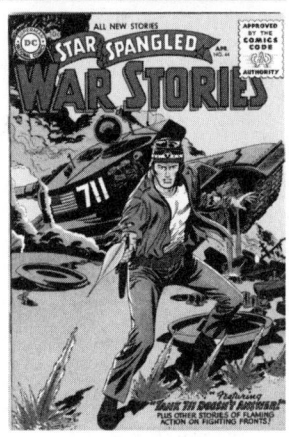

Star Spangled War Stories #44
® DC Comics, Inc.

93 Goliath of the Western Front . 200.00
94 JKu(c),The Frogman and
    the Dinosaur 500.00
95 Guinea Pig Patrol,Dinosaurs . 300.00
96 Mission X,Dinosaur. 300.00
97 The Sub-Crusher, Dinosaur . . 300.00
98 Island of Thunder, Dinosaur . . 300.00
99 The Circus of Monsters,
    Dinosaur 300.00
100 The Volcano of Monsters,
    Dinosaur 350.00
101 The Robot and the Dinosaur 250.00
102 Punchboard War,Dinosaur . . 250.00
103 Doom at Dinosaur Island,
    Dinosaur 250.00
104 The Tree of Terror,
    Dinosaurs 250.00
105 The War of Dinosaur Island . 250.00
106 The Nightmare War,
    Dinosaurs 250.00
107 Battle of the Dinosaur
    Aquarium 250.00
108 Dinosaur D-Day 250.00
109 The Last Soldiers 250.00
110 thru 133 . . . . @250.00
134 NA. 250.00
135 . . . . 250.00
136 . . . . 250.00
137 Dinosaur 250.00
138 Enemy Ace 275.00
139 O:Enemy Ace 200.00
140 . . . . 150.00
141 . . . . 150.00
142 . . . . 150.00
143 . . . . 150.00
144 NA,JKu 200.00
145 . . . . 150.00
146 Enemy Ace(c) 100.00
147 New Enemy Ace 100.00
148 New Enemy Ace 100.00
149 . . . . 100.00
150 JKu,Viking Prince 100.00
151 I:Unknown Soldier. 275.00
152 Rep. New Enemy Ace 100.00
153 . . . . 100.00
154 O:Unknown Soldier. 200.00
155 Rep. New Enemy Ace. 75.00
156 I:Battle Album 75.00
157 thru 160. . . . . 50.00
161 E:Enemy Ace 50.00
162 thru 170 . . . . @40.00
171 thru 200 . . . . @25.00
201 thru 204 . . . . @20.00
Becomes:

UNKNOWN SOLDIER
April-May, 1977
205 thru 247	@17.00
248 and 249 O:Unknown Soldier	@12.00
250	12.00
251 B:Enemy Ace	12.00
252 thru 268	@12.00

STAR SPANGLED COMICS
1999
1 CWn, F:Sandman & Star Spangled Kid	2.50

STAR TREK
1984–88
[1st Regular Series]
1 TS,The Wormhole Connection	15.00
2 TS,The Only Good Klingon	8.00
3 TS,Errand of War	7.00
4 TS,Deadly Allies	7.00
5 TS,Mortal Gods	7.00
6 TS,Who is Enigma?	6.00
7 EB,O:Saavik	6.00
8 TS,Blood Fever	6.00
9 TS,Mirror Universe Saga #1	6.00
10 TS,Mirror Universe Saga #2	6.00
11 TS,Mirror Universe Saga #3	6.00
12 TS,Mirror Universe Saga #4	6.00
13 TS,Mirror Universe Saga #5	5.00
14 TS,Mirror Universe Saga #6	5.00
15 TS,Mirror Universe Saga #7	5.00
16 TS,Mirror Universe Saga end	5.00
17 TS,The D'Artagnan Three	5.00
18 TS,Rest & Recreation	5.00
19 DSp,W.Koenig story	5.00
20 TS,Girl	5.00
21 TS,Dreamworld	5.00
22 TS,The Wolf #1	5.00
23 TS,The Wolf #2	4.00
24 TS,Double Blind #1	4.00
25 TS,Double Blind #2	4.00
26 TSV:Romulans	4.00
27 TS,Day in the Life	4.00
28 GM,The Last Word	4.00
29 Trouble with Bearclaw	4.00
30 CI,F:Uhura	4.00
31 TS,Maggie's World	4.00
32 TS,Judgment Day	4.00
33 TS,20th Anniv.	5.00
34 V:Romulans	3.00
35 GM,Excelsior	3.00
36 GM,StarTrek IV tie-in	3.00
37 StarTrek IV tie-in	3.00
38 AKu,The Argon Affair	3.00
39 TS,A:Harry Mudd	3.00
40 TS,A:Harry Mudd	3.00
41 TS,V:Orions	3.00
42 TS,The Corbomite Effect	3.00
43 TS,Paradise Lost #1	3.00
44 TS,Paradise Lost #2	3.00
45 TS,Paradise Lost #3	3.00
46 TS,Getaway	3.00
47 TS,Idol Threats	3.00
48 TS,The Stars in Secret Influence	3.00
49 TS,Aspiring to be Angels	3.00
50 TS,Anniv.	4.00
51 TS,Haunted Honeymoon	3.00
52 TS,'Hell in a Hand Basket.	3.00
53 You're Dead,Jim	3.00
54 Old Loyalties	3.00
55 TS,Finnegan's Wake	3.00
56 GM,Took place during 5 year Mission	3.00
Ann.#1 All Those Years Ago	4.00
Ann.#2 DJw,The Final Voyage	3.00
Ann.#3 CS,F:Scotty	3.00
Star Trek III Adapt.TS	2.50
Star Trek IV Adapt. TS	2.50
StarTrek V Adapt.	2.50

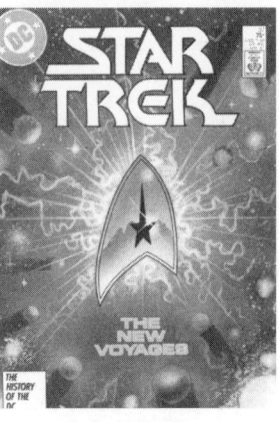

Star Trek #37
© DC Comics, Inc.

[2nd Regular Series], 1989–96
1 The Return	8.00
2 The Sentence	5.00
3 Death Before Dishonor	4.00
4 Reprocussions	4.00
5 Fast Friends	4.00
6 Cure All	4.00
7 Not Sweeney!	4.00
8 Going,Going	3.50
9 ...Gone	3.50
10 Trial of James Kirk #1	3.50
11 Trial of James Kirk #2	3.50
12 Trial of James Kirk #3	3.50
13 Return of Worthy #1	3.50
14 Return of Worthy #2	3.50
15 Return of Worthy #3	3.50
16 Worldsinger	3.00
17 Partners? #1	3.00
18 Partners? #2	3.00
19 Once A Hero	3.00
20	3.00
21 Kirk Trapped	3.00
22 A:Harry Mudd	3.00
23 The Nasgul,A:Harry Mudd	3.00
24 25th Anniv.,A:Harry Mudd	4.00
25 Starfleet Officers Reunion	3.00
26 Pilkor 3	3.00
27 Kirk Betrayed	3.00
28 V:Romulans	3.00
29 Mediators	3.00
30 Veritas #1	3.00
31 Veritas #2	3.00
32 Veritas #3	3.00
33 Veritas #4	3.00
34 JD,F:Kirk,Spock,McCoy	3.00
35 Tabukan Syndrome#1	3.00
36 Tabukan Syndrome#2	3.00
37 Tabukan Syndrome#3	3.00
38 Tabukan Syndrome#4	3.00
39 Tabukan Syndrome#5	3.00
40 Tabukan Syndrome#6	3.00
41 Runaway	3.00
42 Helping Hand	3.00
43 V:Binzalans	3.00
44 Acceptable Risk	3.00
45 V:Trelane	3.00
46 V:Captain Klaa	3.00
47 F:Spock & Saavik	3.00
48 The Neutral Zone	3.00
49 Weapon from Genesis	3.00
50 "The Peacemaker"	4.00
51 "The Price"	3.00
52 V:Klingons	3.00
53 Timecrime #1	3.00
54 Timecrime #2	3.00
55 Timecrime #3	3.00
56 Timecrime #4	3.00
57 Timecrime #5	3.00
58 F:Chekov	3.00
59 Uprising	3.00
60 Hostages	3.00
61 On Talos IV	3.00
62 Alone,pt.1, V:aliens	3.00
63 Alone,pt.2	3.00
64 Kirk	3.00
65 Kirk in Space	3.00
66 Spock	3.00
67 Ambassador Stonn	3.00
68	3.00
69 Wolf in Cheap Clothing,pt.1	3.00
70 Wolf in Cheap Clothing,pt.2	3.00
71 Wolf in Cheap Clothing,pt.3	3.00
72 Wolf in Cheap Clothing,pt.4	3.00
73 Star-crossed,pt.1	3.00
74 Star-crossed,pt.2	2.50
75 Star-crossed,pt.3	4.50
76 Tendar	2.50
77 to the Romulan Neutral Zone	2.50
78 The Chosen,pt.1 (of 3)	2.50
79 The Chosen,pt.2	2.50
80 The Chosen,pt.3	2.50
Ann.#1 GM,sty by G.Takei(Sulu)	4.00
Ann.#2 Kirks 1st Yr At Star Fleet Academy	4.00
Ann #3 KD,F:Ambassador Sarek	4.00
Ann.#4 F:Spock on Pike's ship	4.00
Ann.#6 Convergence,pt.1	4.50
Spec.#1 PDd(s),BSz	4.00
Spec.#2 The Defiant	4.50
Spec.#3 V:Orion pirates	4.50
Spec. 25th Anniv.	7.00
Star Trek VI,movie adapt(direct)	6.00
Star Trek VI,movie(newsstand)	3.00

STAR TREK: THE MODALA IMPERATIVE
1991
1 Planet Modula	6.00
2 Modula's Rebels	4.50
3 Spock/McCoy rescue Attempt	4.00
4 Rebel Victory	4.00

STAR TREK: THE NEXT GENERATION
Feb., 1988
[1st Regular Series]
1 based on TV series,Where No Man Has Gone Before	10.00
2 Spirit in the Sky	8.00
3 Factor Q	5.00
4 Q's Day	5.00
5 Q's Effects	5.00
6 Here Today	5.00

[2nd Regular Series], 1989–95
1 Return to Raimon	15.00
2 Murder Most Foul	9.00
3 Derelict	7.50
4 The Hero Factor	7.50
5 Serafin's Survivors	6.00
6 Shadows in the Garden	6.00
7 The Pilot	5.00
8 The Battle Within	5.00
9 The Pay Off	5.00
10 The Noise of Justice	5.00
11 The Imposter	4.00
12 Whoever Fights Monsters	4.00
13 The Hand of the Assassin	4.00
14 Holiday on Ice	4.00
15 Prisoners of the Ferengi	3.50
16 I Have Heard the Mermaids Singing	3.50
17 The Weapon	3.50
18 MM,Forbidden Fruit	3.50
19 The Lesson	3.50
20 Lost Shuttle	3.50

21 Lost Shuttle cont. 3.50
22 Lost Shuttle cont. 3.50
23 Lost Shuttle cont. 3.50
24 Lost Shuttle conc. 3.50
25 Okona S.O.S. 3.50
26 Search for Okona 3.50
27 Worf,Data,Troi,Okona trapped
   on world. 3.50
28 Worf/K'Ehleyr story 3.50
29 Rift,pt.1 . . . . 3.50
30 Rift,pt.2 . . . . 3.50
31 Rift conclusion 3.50
32 . . . . 3.50
33 R:Mischievous Q. 3.50
34 V:Aliens,F:Mischievous Q 3.50
35 Way of the Warrior 3.50
36 Shore Leave in Shanzibar#1 . . . 3.25
37 Shore Leave in Shanzibar#2 . . . 3.25
38 Shore Leave in Shanzibar#3 . . . 3.25
39 Divergence #1. . . . . 3.25
40 Divergence #2. . . . . 3.25
41 V:Strazzan Warships. 3.25
42 V:Strazzans. 3.25
43 V:Strazzans. 3.25
44 Disrupted Lives 3.25
45 F:Enterprise Surgical Team 3.25
46 Deadly Labyrinth. 3.25
47 Worst of Both World's#1 . . . . . . 3.00
48 Worst of Both World's#2 . . . . . . 3.00
49 Worst of Both World's#3 . . . . . . 3.00
50 Double Sized,V:Borg. 4.00
51 V:Energy Beings 3.00
52 in the 1940's 3.00
53 F:Picard. 3.00
54 F:Picard. 3.00
55 Data on Trial 3.00
56 Abduction 3.00
57 Body Switch 3.00
58 Body Switch 3.00
59 B:Children in Chaos 3.00
60 Children in Chaos#2 . . . . 3.00
61 E:Children in Chaos 3.00
62 V:Stalker 3.00
63 A:Romulans. 3.00
64 Geordie 3.00
65 Geordie. 3.00
66 . . . . 3.00
67 Friends/Strangers 3.00
68 Friends/Strangers,pt.2 . . . . 3.00
69 Friends/Strangers,pt.3 . . . . 3.00
70 Friends/Strangers,pt.4 . . . . 3.00
71 War of Madness,pt.1. . . . . 3.00
72 War of Madness,pt.2. . . . . 3.00
73 War of Madness,pt.3. . . . . 3.00
74 War of Madness,pt.4. . . . . 3.00
75 War of Madness,pt.5. . . . . 4.50
76 F:Geordi 3.00
77 Gateway, pt.1 . . . . 3.00
78 Gateway, pt.2 . . . . 3.00
79 Crew transformed into androids . 3.00
80 Mysterious illness 3.00
Ann.#1 A:Mischievous Q 4.50
Ann.#2 BP,V:Parasitic Creatures . . 4.00
Ann.#3 . . . . 4.00
Ann.#4 MiB(s),F:Dr.Crusher. 4.00
Ann.#6 Convergence,pt.2 . . . . . . 4.50
Series Finale 4.25
Spec.#1 . . . . 3.75
Spec.#2 CCI(s). 4.00
Star Trek N.G.:Sparticus. 5.00

STAR TREK:
THE NEXT GENERATION
DEEP SPACE NINE
1994–95
1 Crossover with Malibu 2.50
2 . . . . 2.50

STAR TREK:
THE NEXT GENERATION
ILL WIND
1995–96
1 Solar-sailing race 2.50
2 Explosion Investigated. 2.50
3 A bomb aboard ship. 2.50
4 finale 2.50

STAR TREK
THE NEXT GENERATION
MODALA IMPERATIVE
1991
1 A:Spock,McCoy 6.00
2 Modula Overrun by Ferengi 5.00
3 Picard,Spock,McCoy & Troi
   trapped 4.00
4 final issue. 4.00

STAR TREK
THE NEXT GENERATION
SHADOWHEART
1994–95
1 thru 3 . . . . @2.50
4 Worf Confront Nikolai 2.50

STATIC
Milestone, 1993–96
1 JPL,I:Static,Hotstreak,Frieda Goren,
   w/poster,card,D puzzle piece . . 4.00
1a Newstand Ed. 2.50
1b Platinum Ed. 8.00
2 thru 13 . . . . @2.50
14 Worlds Collide,V:Rift. 3.00
15 thru 24 . . . . @2.50
25 V:Dusk, 48pgs. 4.00
26 thru 47 . . . . @2.50

STATIC SHOCK!:
REBIRTH OF THE COOL
DC/Milestone, Nov., 2001
1 (of 4) DMD 2.50
2 DMD,F:Hardware. 2.50
3 DMD,A:Hardware,Iron Butterfly . . 2.50
4 DMD,V:Power Junkie. 2.50

STEEL
1994–98
1 JBg(c),B:LSi(s),CsB,N:Steel 3.00
2 JBg(c),CsB,V:Toastmaster. 2.50
3 JBg(c),CsB,V:Amertek 2.50
4 JBg(c),CsB. 2.50
5 JBg(c),CsB,V:Sister's Attacker . . 2.50
6 JBg(c),CsB,Worlds Collide,pt.5 . . 2.50
7 Worlds Collide,pt.6. . . . . 2.50
8 Zero Hour,I:Hazard 2.50
9 F:Steel 2.50
10 F:Steel. 2.50
11 . . . . 2.50
12 . . . . 2.50
13 A:Maxima 2.50
14 A:Superman 2.50
15 R:White Rabbit 2.50
16 V:White Rabbit
   [new Miraweb format begins] . . 2.50
17 Steel controls armor powers . . . 2.50
18 Abduction 2.50
19 . . . . 2.50
20 Body Rejects Armor 2.50
21 LSi,Underworld Unleashed tie-in 2.50
22 Steel separated from Superboy . 2.50
23 Steel attacked 2.50
24 V:Hazard's. 2.50
25 . . . . 2.50
26 Natasha gains superpowers . . . 2.50

Steel #7
© *DC Comics Inc.*

27 LSi,V:Hazard. 2.50
28 . . . . 2.50
29 . . . . 2.50
30 . . . . 2.50
31 LSi(s),V:Armorbeast 2.50
32 V:Blockbuster 2.50
33 JAp,DG,Natasha's drug abuse . . 2.50
34 CPr(s),DCw,TP,A:Natasha, in
   Jersey City. 2.50
35 CPr(s),DCw,TP,. 2.50
36 CPr(s),DCw,TP,Combing the
   sewers of Jersey City 2.50
37 CPr(s),DCw,TP,John Irons,
   Amanda Quick & Skorpio a
   romantic triangle 2.50
38 CPr(s),DCw,TP,A:The Question . 2.50
39 CPr(s),DCw,TP,V:Crash 2.50
40 CPr(s),VGi,Steel tries out
   new hammer 2.50
41 CPr(s),DCw,TMo, John Irons
   guilty of murder? 2.50
42 CPr(s),DCw,TP,Irons and
   Amanda assaulted. 2.50
43 CPr(s),DCw,TP,to Metropolis . . . 2.50
44 CPr(s),DCw,TP,Genesis tie-in . . . 2.50
45 CPr(s),DCw,TP,seek policeman . . 2.50
46 CPr(s),DCw,TP,F:Superboy 2.50
47 CPr(s),DCw,TP,F:Amanda 2.50
48 . . . . 2.50
49 CPr(s),DCw,TP,V:Deadline 2.50
50 CPr(s),DCw,TP,Millennium
   Giants 2.50
51 CPr(s),DCw,TP,bounty hunter. . . 2.50
52 CPr(s),final issue 2.50
1-shot, movie adaptation 5.00
Ann.#1 Elseworlds story 3.00

STEEL, THE
INDESTRUCTIBLE MAN
March, 1978
1 DH,I:Steel. 12.00
2 thru 4 DH . . . . @8.00
5 Oct.–Nov., 1978. . . . . 12.00

STRANGE ADVENTURES
1950–74
1 The Menace of the Green
   Nebula 6,000.00
2 S&K,JM(c),Doom From
   Planet X 2,700.00
3 The Metal World 1,800.00

All comics prices listed are for *Near Mint* condition.   **CVA 2009 • Page 153**

Strange Adventures #12
© DC Comics, Inc.

4 BP,The Invaders From the
   Nth Dimension 1,800.00
5 The World Inside the Atom . . 1,800.00
6 Confessions of a Martian . . . 1,800.00
7 The World of Giant Ants 1,800.00
8 MA,ATh,Evolution Plus 1,800.00
9 MA,B:Captain Comet,The
   Origin of Captain Comet. . . 3,500.00
10 MA,CI,The Air Bandits
   From Space 1,500.00
11 MA,CI,Day the Past
   Came Back. 1,000.00
12 MA,CI,GK(c),The Girl From
   the Diamond Planet 1,000.00
13 MA,CI,GK(c),When the Earth
   was Kidnapped. 1,000.00
14 MA,CI,GK(c),Destination
   Doom 1,000.00
15 MA,CI,GK(c),Captain Comet-
   Enomy of Earth 1,000.00
16 MA,CI,GK(c),The Ghost of
   Captain Comet 1,000.00
17 MA,CI,GK(c),Beware the
   Synthetic Men. 1,000.00
18 CI,MA(c),World of Flying
   Men. 1,000.00
19 CI,MA(c),Secret of the
   Twelve Eternals 1,200.00
20 CI,Slaves of the Sea Master 1,200.00
21 CI,MA(c),Eyes of the
   Other Worlds 800.00
22 CI,The Guardians of the
   Clockwork Universe. 800.00
23 CI,MA(c),The Brain Pirates
   of Planet X. 800.00
24 CI,MA(c),Doomsday on Earth. 800.00
25 CI,GK(c),The Day
   That Vanished 800.00
26 CI,Captain Vs. Miss Universe. 800.00
27 CI,MA(c),The Counterfeit
   Captain Comet 800.00
28 CI,Devil's Island in Space 800.00
29 CI,The Time Capsule From
   1,000,000 B.C. 800.00
30 CI,MA(c),Menace From the
   World of Make-Believe 750.00
31 CI,Lights Camera Action 750.00
32 CI,MA(c),The Challenge of
   Man-Ape the Mighty 750.00
33 CI,MA(c),The Human Beehive 750.00
34 CI,MA(c) 750.00
35 CI,MA(c),Cosmic Chessboard 750.00
36 CI,MA(c),The Grab-Bag
   Planet 750.00

37 CI,MA(c),The Invaders From
   the Golden Atom 750.00
38 CI,MA(c),Seeing-Eye Humans 750.00
39 CI,MA(c),The Guilty Gorilla . . . 750.00
40 CI,MA(c),The Mind Monster . . 750.00
41 CI,MA(c),The Beast From Out
   of Time. 750.00
42 CI,MD,MA(c),The Planet of
   Ancient Children 750.00
43 CI,MD,MA(c),The Phantom
   Prize Fighter 750.00
44 CI,MA(c),The Planet That
   Plotted Murder. 750.00
45 CI,MD,MA(c),Gorilla World . . . 750.00
46 CI,MA(c),E:Captain Comet
   Interplanetary War Base 750.00
47 CI,MA(c),The Man Who Sold
   the Earth 750.00
48 CI,MA(c),Human Phantom . . . 750.00
49 CI,MA(c),The Invasion
   from Indiana 750.00
50 CI,MA(c),The World Wrecker . 600.00
51 CI,MA(c),The Man Who
   Stole Air 600.00
52 CI,MA(c),Prisoner of the
   Parakeets 600.00
53 CI,MA(c),The Human Icicle. . . 600.00
54 CI,MA(c),The Electric Man . . . 400.00
55 CI,MA(c),The Gorilla Who
   Challanged the World,pt.I . . . 400.00
56 CI,The Jungle Emperor,pt.II . . 400.00
57 CI,The Spy from Saturn 400.00
58 CI,I Hunted the Radium Man . 400.00
59 CI,The Ark From Planet X. . . . 400.00
60 CI,Across the Ages 400.00
61 CI,The Mirages From Space. . 400.00
62 CI,The Fireproof Man 400.00
63 CI,I Was the Man in the Moon 400.00
64 CI,GK(c),Gorillas In Space . . . 400.00
65 CI,GK(c),Prisoner From Pluto. 400.00
66 CI,GK(c),The Human Battery . 400.00
67 CI,GK(c),Martian Masquerader 400.00
68 CI,The Man Who Couldn't
   Drown 400.00
69 CI,Gorilla Conquest of Earth. . 400.00
70 CI,Triple Life of Dr. Pluto 400.00
71 CI,MSy,Zero Hour For Earth. . 300.00
72 CI,The Skyscraper That Came
   to Life. 300.00
73 CI,Amazing Rain of Gems . . . 300.00
74 CI,The Invisible Invader
   From Dimension X. 300.00
75 CI,Secret of the Man-Ape. . . . 300.00
76 CI,B:Darwin Jones,The Robot
   From Atlantis 300.00
77 CI,A:Darwin Jones,The World
   That Slipped Out of Space . . 300.00
78 CI,The Secret of the Tom
   Thumb Spaceman 300.00
79 CI,A:Darwin Jones,Invaders
   from the Ice World. 300.00
80 CI,Mind Robbers of Venus . . . 300.00
81 CI,The Secret of the
   Shrinking Twins 300.00
82 CI,Giants of the Cosmic Ray . 250.00
83 CI,Assignment in Eternity 250.00
84 CI,Prisoners of the Atom
   Universe 250.00
85 CI,The Amazing Human Race 250.00
86 CI,The Dog That Saved the
   Earth 250.00
87 CI,New Faces For Old 250.00
88 CI,A:Darwin Jones,The Gorilla
   War Against Earth 250.00
89 CI,Earth For Sale 250.00
90 CI,The Day I Became a
   Martian 250.00
91 CI,Midget Earthmen of Jupiter 250.00
92 CI,GK(c),The Amazing Ray
   of Knowledge. 250.00
93 CI,GK(c),A:Darwin Jones,
   Space-Rescue By Proxy 250.00

94 MA,CI,GK(c),Fisherman of
   Space. 250.00
95 CI,The World at my Doorstep . 250.00
96 CI,MA(c),The Menace of
   Saturn's Rings 250.00
97 CI,MA(c),MSy,Secret of the
   Space-Giant 250.00
98 CI,GK(c),MSy,Attack on Fort
   Satellite 250.00
99 CI,MSy,GK(c),Big Jump Into
   Space. 250.00
100 CI,MSy,The Amazing Trial
   of John (Gorilla) Doe 300.00
101 CI,MSy,GK(c),Giant From
   Beyond 200.00
102 MSy,GK(c),The Three Faces
   of Barry Morrell 200.00
103 GK(c),The Man Who
   Harpooned Worlds. 200.00
104 MSy,GK(c),World of Doomed
   Spacemen 200.00
105 MSy,GK(c),Fisherman From
   the Sea 200.00
106 MSy,CI,GK(c),Genie in the
   Flying Saucer 200.00
107 MSy,CI,GK(c),War of the
   Jovian Bubble-Men 200.00
108 MSy,CI,GK(c),The Human
   Pet of Gorilla Land 200.00
109 MSy,CI,GK(c),The Man Who
   Weighed 100 Tons. 200.00
110 MSy,CI,GK(c),Hand From
   Beyond 200.00
111 MSy,CI,GK(c),Secret of
   the Last Earth-Man 200.00
112 MSy,CI,GK(c),Menace of
   the Size-Changing Spaceman 200.00
113 MSy,CI,GK(c),Deluge From
   Space. 200.00
114 MSy,CI,GK(c),Secret of the
   Flying Buzz Saw 200.00
115 MSy,CI,GK(c),The Great
   Space-Tiger Hunt. 200.00
116 MSy,CI,RH,GK(c),Invasion
   of the Water Warriors 200.00
117 MSy,CI,GK(c),I:Atomic
   Knights 1,000.00
118 MSy,CI,The Turtle-Men of
   Space. . . . . , 225.00
119 MSy,CI,MA(c),Raiders
   From the Giant World 200.00
120 MSy,CI,MA,Attack of the Oil
   Demons 500.00
121 MSy,CI,MA(c),Invasion of the
   Flying Reptiles. 175.00

Strange Adventures #123
© DC Comics Inc.

122 MSy,CI,MA(c),David and the
  Space-Goliath 175.00
123 MSy,CI,MA(c),Secret of the
  Rocket-Destroyer. 300.00
124 MSy,CI,MA(c),The Face-Hunter
  From Saturn 200.00
125 MSy,CI,The Flying Gorilla
  Menace 175.00
126 MSy,CI,MA(c),Return of the
  Neanderthal Man. 300.00
127 MSy,CI,MA(c),Menace
  From the Earth-Globe 175.00
128 MSy,CI,MA(c),The Man
  With the Electronic Brain. . . . 175.00
129 MSy,CI,MA(c),The Giant
  Who Stole Mountains 200.00
130 MSy,CI,MA.War With the
  Giant Frogs 175.00
131 MSy,CI,MA(c),Emperor
  of the Earth 175.00
132 MSy,CI,MA(c),The Dreams
  of Doom. 200.00
133 MSy,CI,MA(c),The Invisible
  Dinosaur 175.00
134 MSy,CI,MA(c), The Aliens
  Who Raided New York 200.00
135 MSy,CI,MA(c) Fishing Hole
  in the Sky. 200.00
136 MSy,CI,MA(c),The Robot
  Who Lost Its Head. 150.00
137 MSy,CI,MA(c),Parade of the
  Space-Toys 150.00
138 MSy,CI,MA(c),Secret of the
  Dinosaur Skeleton. 200.00
139 MSy,CI,MA(c),Space-Roots
  of Evil. 150.00
140 MSy,CI,MA(c),Prisoner of
  the Space-Patch 150.00
141 MSy,CI,MA(c),Battle Between
  the Two Earths 200.00
142 MSy,CI,MA(c),The Return of
  the Faceless Creature 150.00
143 MSy,CI,MA(c),The Face in
  the Atom-Bomb Cloud 150.00
144 MSy,CI,MA(c),A:Atomic
  Knights, When the Earth
  Blacked Out. 200.00
145 MSy,CI,MA,The Man Who
  Lived Forever 150.00
146 MSy,CI,MA(c),Perilous Pet
  of Space 150.00
147 MSy,CI,MA(c),The Dawn-
  World Menace 200.00
148 MSy,CI,MA(c),Earth Hero,
  Number One 150.00
149 MSy,CI,MA(c),Raid of
  the Rogue Star 150.00
150 MSy,CI,MA(c),When Earth
  Turned into a Comet 200.00
151 MSy,CI,MA(c),Invasion Via
  Radio-Telescope 150.00
152 MSy,MA(c),The Martian
  Emperor of Earth. 150.00
153 MSy,MA(c),Threat of the
  Faceless Creature. 150.00
154 CI,MSy,MA,GK(c),Earth's
  Friendly Invaders. 150.00
155 MSy,MA,GK(c),Prisoner
  of the Undersea World 150.00
156 MSy,CI,MA(c),The Man
  With the Head of Saturn 150.00
157 MSy,CI,MA(c),Plight of
  the Human Cocoons 150.00
158 MSy,CI,MA(c),The Mind
  Masters of Space. 150.00
159 MSy,CI,MA(c),The Maze
  of Time. 150.00
160 MSy,CI,MA(c),A:Atomic
  Knights, Here Comes the
  Wild Ones 150.00
161 MSy,CI,MA(c),Earth's Frozen
  Heat Wave,E:Space Museum 100.00

162 CI,MA(c),Mystery of the
  12 O'Clock Man. 100.00
163 MA(c),The Creature in
  the Black Light. 100.00
164 DD&SMo(c),I Became
  a Robot 100.00
165 DD&SMo(c),I Broke the
  Supernatural Barrier 100.00
166 DD&SMo(c),I Lived in
  Two Bodies 100.00
167 JkS(c),The Team That
  Conqured Time 100.00
168 JkS(c),I Hunted Toki
  the Terrible. 100.00
169 DD&SMo(c),The Prisoner
  of the Hour Glass 100.00
170 DD&SMo(c),The Creature
  From Strange Adventures . . . 100.00
171 The Diary of the
  9-Planet Man? 100.00
172 DD&SMo(c),I Became
  the Juggernaut Man 100.00
173 The Secret of the
  Fantasy Films 100.00
174 JkS(c),The Ten Ton Man. . . . 100.00
175 Danger: This Town is
  Shrinking 100.00
176 DD&SMo(c),The Case of
  the Cosmonik Quartet 100.00
177 I Lived a Hundred Lives,
  O:Immortal Man. 100.00
178 JkS(c),The Runaway Comet. 100.00
179 JkS(c),I Buried Myself Alive . 100.00
180 CI,I:Animal Man,I Was the
  Man With Animal Powers . . . 300.00
181 The Man of Two Worlds 100.00
182 JkS(c),The Case of the
  Blonde Bombshell 100.00
183 JM(c),The Plot to Destroy
  the Earth 100.00
184 GK(c),A:Animal Man,The
  Return of the Man With
  Animal Powers 300.00
185 JkS(c),Ilda-Gangsters Inc. . . 100.00
186 Beware the Gorilla Witch . . . 100.00
187 JkS(c),O:The Enchantress . . 120.00
188 SD,JkS(c),I Was the
  Four Seasons 100.00
189 SD,JkS(c),The Way-Out
  Worlds of Bertram Tilley 100.00
190 CI,A:Animal Man,A-Man-the
  Hero with Animal Powers . . . 350.00
191 JkS(c),Beauty vs. the Beast . 100.00
192 Freak Island 100.00
193 The Villian Maker 100.00
194 JkS(c),The Menace of the
  Super- Gloves 100.00
195 JkS(c),Secret of the Three
  Earth Dooms,A:Animal Man . 150.00
196 JkS(c),Mystery of the
  Orbit Creatures 100.00
197 The Hostile Hamlet 75.00
198 JkS(c),Danger! Earth
  is Doomed 75.00
199 Robots of the Round Table . . . 75.00
200 The Guardian Eye. 75.00
201 JkS,Animal Man 100.00
202 Robinson Crusoe of the Sky. . 75.00
203 The Split Man 75.00
204 GK,Crazy Quilt Man 75.00
205 CI,I&O:Deadman. 250.00
206 NA,MSy,F:Deadman 200.00
207 NA,F:Deadman 150.00
208 NA,F:Deadman 150.00
209 NA,F:Deadman 150.00
210 NA,F:Deadman 150.00
211 thru 216 NA,F:Deadman . . @150.00
217 MA,MSy,A:Adam Strange 30.00
218 MA,CI,MSy 50.00
219 CI,JKu 50.00
220 CI,JKu 50.00
221 CI,Two Adam Stranges 50.00

Strange Adventures #213
© *DC Comics, Inc.*

222 MA,New Adam Strange 75.00
223 MA,CI 50.00
224 MA,CI 50.00
225 MA,JKu 50.00
226 MA,JKu,New Adam Strange . . 75.00
227 JKu 50.00
228 NA(c). 70.00
229 MA,The Last Mile of Space. . . 60.00
230 GM(c) 50.00
231 E:Atomic Knights 50.00
232 JKu 50.00
233 JKu 50.00
234 JKu 50.00
235 NA(c). 60.00
236 CI,Human Fishbowl 40.00
237 Ray-Gun in the SKy 25.00
238 MK(c) 25.00
239 Metal Conqueror of Rann 25.00
240 MK(c) 25.00
241 F:Adam Strange 25.00
242 MA. 25.00
243 F:Adam Strange 25.00
244 Oct.–Nov., 1974 . . . . 25.00

STRANGE ADVENTURES
DC/Vertigo, Sept., 1999

1 (of 4) BB,DGb 2.50
2 KJ,Expiration Date. 2.50
3 & 4 . . . . @2.50

STRANGE SPORTS STORIES
Sept.–Oct., 1973

1 CS,DG 40.00
2 thru 6 . . . . @25.00

STREETS
1993

1 Tenderloin 5.00
2 Procurement 5.00
3 . . . . 5.00

SUGAR & SPIKE
April-May, 1956

1 SM 5,000.00
2 SM 1,600.00
3 SM 1,000.00
4 SM 1,000.00
5 SM 1,000.00
6 thru 10 SM . . . . @600.00
11 thru 20 SM. . . . . @500.00
21 thru 29 SM . . . . @350.00
30 SM,A:Scribbly 350.00

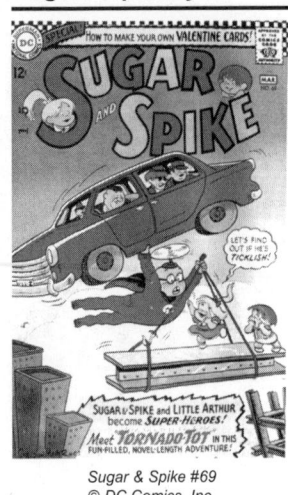

Sugar & Spike #69
© DC Comics, Inc.

31 thru 50 SM	@300.00
51 thru 70 SM	@225.00
71 thru 79 SM	@200.00
80 SM,I:Bernie the Brain	200.00
81 thru 97 SM	@150.00
98 SM,Oct.–Nov., 1971	150.00
1 Facsimile Edition,rep.(2002)	3.00

SUICIDE SQUAD
1987–91

1 LMc,Legends,I:Jihad	4.00
2 LMc,V:The Jihad	2.50
3 LMc,V:Female Furies	2.50
4 LMc,V:William Hell	2.50
5 LM,A:Penguin	3.00
6 LM,A:Penguin	3.00
7 thru 12 LMc	@2.50
13 LMc,X-over,JLI#13	4.00
14 thru 22	@2.50
23 LMc,Invasion	4.00
24 thru 47	@2.50
48 GI,New Thinker	4.00
49 thru 63	@2.50
64 GI,A:Task Force X	4.00
65 GI,Bronze Tiger	2.50
66 GI,Final Iss.E:Suicide Squad	2.50
Ann.#1 GN,V:Argent,A:Manhunter	2.50

[2nd Series] Sept., 2001

1 KG,R:Suicide Squad	2.50
2 thru 12	@2.50

SUICIDE SQUAD: RAISE THE FLAG
Sept., 2007

1 (of 8) F:Rick Flag, Jr.	3.00
2 thru 8	@3.00

SUPERBOY
1949–76

1 WB&StK,Superman(c)	16,000.00
2 The Stunts of Superboy	4,000.00
3 Buperhoy's Hall of Fame	2,900.00
4 The Oracle of Smallville	2,700.00
5 Superboy meets Supergirl, Pre-Adventure #252	2,700.00
6 I:Humpty Dumpty,the Hobby Robber	2,000.00
7 WB,V:Humpty Dumpty	2,000.00
8 CS,I:Superbaby,V:Humpty Dumpty	1,900.00
9 V:Humpty Dumpty	1,900.00
10 CS,I:Lana Lang	1,900.00

11 CS,2nd Lang,V:Humpty Dumpty	1,500.00
12 CS,The Heroes Club	1,400.00
13 CS,Scout of Smallville	1,400.00
14 CS,I:Marsboy	1,400.00
15 CS,A:Superman	1,500.00
16 CS,A:Marsboy	1,300.00
17 CS,Superboy's Double	1,300.00
18 CS,Lana Lang-Hollywood Star	1,300.00
19 CS,The Death of Young Clark Kent	1,300.00
20 CS,The Ghost that Haunted Smallville	1,300.00
21 CS,Lana Lang-Magician	750.00
22 CS,The New Clark Kent	750.00
23 CS,The Super Superboy	750.00
24 CS,The Super Fat Boy of Steel	750.00
25 CS,Cinderella of Smallville	750.00
26 CS,A:Superbaby	750.00
27 CS,Clark Kent-Runaway	750.00
28 CS,The Man Who Defeated Superboy	750.00
29 CS,The Puppet Superboy	750.00
30 CS,I:Tommy Tuttle	600.00
31 CS,The Amazing Elephant Boy From Smallville	600.00
32 CS,His Majesty King Superboy	600.00
33 CS,The Crazy Costumes of the Boy of Steel	600.00
34 CS,Hep Cats o/Smallville	600.00
35 CS,The Five Superboys	600.00
36 CS,The Superboy Souvenirs	600.00
37 CS,I:Thaddeus Lang	600.00
38 CS,Public Chimp #1	600.00
39 CS,Boy w/Superboy Powers	600.00
40 CS,The Magic Necklace	500.00
41 CS,Superboy Meets Superbrave	500.00
42 CS,Gaucho of Smallville	500.00
43 CS,Super-Farmer of Smallville	500.00
44 The Amazing Adventure of Superboy's Costume	500.00
45 A Trap For Superboy	500.00
46 The Battle of Fort Smallville	500.00
47 CS,A:Superman	500.00
48 CS,Boy Without Super-Suit	500.00
49 I:Metallo (Jor-El's Robot)	500.00
50 The Super-Giant of Smallville	500.00
51 I:Krypto	400.00
52 CS,The Powerboy from Earth	400.00
53 CS,A:Superman	400.00
54 CS,The Silent Superboy	400.00
55 CS,A:Jimmy Olson	400.00
56 CS,A:Krypto	400.00
57 CS,One-Man Baseball Team	400.00
58 CS,The Great Kryptonite Mystery	400.00
59 CS,A:Superbaby	400.00
60 The 100,000 Cowboy	400.00
61 The School For Superboys	300.00
62 I:Gloria Kent	300.00
63 CS,The Two Boys of Steel	300.00
64 CS,A:Krypto	300.00
65 Superboy's Moonlight Spell	300.00
66 The Family with X-Ray Eyes	300.00
67 I:Klax-Ar	300.00
68 O&I:Bizarro	1,000.00
69 How Superboy Learned To Fly	250.00
70 O:Superboy's Glasses	250.00
71 A:Superbaby	250.00
72 The Flying Girl of Smallville	250.00
73 CS,A:Superbaby	250.00
74 A:Jor-El & Lara	250.00
75 A:Superbaby	250.00
76 I:Super Monkey	250.00

Superboy #77
© DC Comics, Inc.

77 Superboy's Best Friend	250.00
78 O:Mr.Mzyzptik	350.00
79 A:Jar-El & Lara	250.00
80 Superboy meets Supergirl	300.00
81 The Weakling From Earth	200.00
82 A:Bizarro Krypto	200.00
83 I:Kryptonite Kid	200.00
84 A:William Tell	200.00
85 Secret of Mighty Boy	200.00
86 I:PeteRoss,A:Legion	300.00
87 I:Scarlet Jungle of Krypton	200.00
88 The Invader from Earth	200.00
89 I:Mon-El	200.00
90 A:Pete Ross	200.00
91 CS,Superboy in Civil War	200.00
92 CS,I:Destructo,A:Lex Luthor	200.00
93 A:Legion	225.00
94 I:Superboy Revenge Squad, A:Pete Ross	175.00
95 Imaginary Story,The Super Family From Krypton	175.00
96 A:Pete Ross,Lex Luther	175.00
97 Krypto Story	175.00
98 Legion,I&O:Ultraboy	225.00
99 O: The Kryptonite Kid	150.00
100 I:Phantom Zone	350.00
101 The Handsome Hound of Steel	150.00
102 O:Scarlet Jungle of Krypton	150.00
103 CS,A:King Arthur,Jesse James Red Kryptonite	150.00
104 O:Phantom Zone	150.00
105 CS,The Simpleton of Steel	150.00
106 CS,A:Brainiac	150.00
107 CS,I:Superboy Club of Smallville	175.00
108 The Kent's First Super Son	150.00
109 The Super Youth of Bronze	150.00
110 A:Jor-El	150.00
111 Red Kryptonite Story	125.00
112 CS,A:Superbaby	125.00
113 The Boyhood of Dad Kent	125.00
114 A:Phantom Zone, Mr.Mxyzptlk	125.00
115 A:Phantom Zone,Lex Luthor	125.00
116 The Wolfboy of Smallville	125.00
117 A:Legion	125.00
118 CS,The War Between Superboy and Krypto	125.00
119 V:Android Double	125.00
120 A:Mr.Mxyzptlk	125.00
121 CS,A:Jor-El,Lex Luthor	125.00
122 Red Kryptonite Story	125.00
123 CS,The Curse of the Superboy Mummy	125.00

124 I:Insect Queen 125.00
125 O:Kid Psycho 125.00
126 O:Krypto 125.00
127 A:Insect Queen 100.00
128 A:Phantom Zone,Kryptonite
   Kid,Dev En 100.00
129 rep.A:Mon-El,SuperBaby . . . 150.00
130 CS,Search for a Pet 100.00
131 A;Lex Luthor,Mr.Mxyzptlk,I:
   Space Canine Patrol Agents . 100.00
132, CS,A:Space Canine
   Patrol Agents 100.00
133 A:Robin, repr. 100.00
134 The Scoundrel of Steel 100.00
135 A:Lex Luthor 100.00
136 A:Space Canine Agents 100.00
137 Mysterious Mighty Mites . . . 100.00
138 giant, Superboy's Most
   Terrific Battles 125.00
139 The Samson of Smallville . . . 100.00
140 V:The Gambler 75.00
141 No Mercy for a Hero 75.00
142 A:Super Monkey 75.00
143 NA(c),The Big Fall 75.00
144 Superboy's Stolen Identity . . . 75.00
145 NA(c)Kents become young. . . 75.00
146 NA(c),CS,The Runaway 75.00
147 giant O:Legion 100.00
148 NA(c),CS,C:PolarBoy 75.00
149 NA(c),A:Bonnie & Clyde 75.00
150 JAb,V:Mr.Cipher 75.00
151 NA(c),A:Kryptonite Kid 75.00
152 NA(c),WW 75.00
153 NA(c),WW,A;Prof Mesmer . . . 75.00
154 WW(i),A:Jor-El & Lara
   Blackout For Superboy 75.00
155 NA(c),WW,Revolt of the
   Teenage Robots 75.00
156 Farewell to Smallville,giant . . 75.00
157 WW,NA(c),Get Lost Superboy 75.00
158 WW,A:Jor-El & Lara 50.00
159 WW(i),A:Lex Luthor 50.00
160 WW,I Chose Eternal Exile . . . 50.00
161 WW,The Strange Death of
   Superboy 50.00
162 A:Phantom Zone 50.00
163 NA(c),Reform School Rebel . . 50.00
164 NA(c),Your Death Will
   Destroy Me 50.00
165 CS,Superdog,giant-size 50.00
166 NA(c),A:Lex Luthor 30.00
167 NA(c),MA,A:Superbaby. 30.00
168 NA(c),MA,Hitler. 30.00
169 MA,A:Lex Luthor 30.00
170 MA,A:Genghis Khan 30.00
171 MA,A:Aquaboy 30.00
172 MA(i),GT,A:Legion,
   O:Lightning Lad,Yango 35.00
173 NA(c),GT,DG,O:CosmicBoy . . 30.00
174 CS,Colossal Superdog,giant. . 50.00
175 NA(c),MA,Rejuvenation of
   Ma & Pa Kent 30.00
176 NA(c),MA,GT,WW,A:Legion . 30.00
177 MA,A:Lex Luthor 40.00
178 NA(c),MA,Legion Reprint 40.00
179 MA,A:Lex Luthor 40.00
180 MA,O:Bouncing Boy 40.00
181 MA,CS,Insect Queen 40.00
182 MA,A:Bruce Wayne. 40.00
183 MA,GT,CS(rep),A:Legion 40.00
184 MA,WW,O:Dial H rep. 40.00
185 A:Legion 20.00
186 MA,Mutiny of the Damned . . . 20.00
187 MA,Iron Cage for a Hero 20.00
188 MA,DC,O:Karkan,A:Legn . . . 20.00
189 MA,Runaway Superbaby 20.00
190 MA,WW,Murder the Leader . . 20.00
191 MA,DC,O:SunBoy retold. 20.00
192 MA,The Deadly Dawn. 20.00
193 MA,WW,N:Chameleon Boy,
   Shrinking Violet 20.00
194 MA,Super-Merman of the Sea 20.00

Superboy #206
© DC Comics Inc.

195 MA,WW,I:Wildfire,
   N:Phantom Girl 20.00
196 last Superboy solo 30.00
197 DC,Legion begins, New
   Costumes,I:Tyr 30.00
198 DC,N:Element Lad,
   Princess Projects. 20.00
199 DC,A:Tyr, Otto Orion. 20.00
200 DC,M:Bouncing Boy
   & Duo Damsel. 30.00
201 DC,Wildfire returns 18.00
202 N:Light Lass 75.00
203 MGr,D:Invisible Kid 25.00
204 MGr,A:Supergirl 15.00
205 MGr,CG,100 pages 75.00
206 MGr,A:Ferro Lad 25.00
207 MGr,O:Lightning Lad. 25.00
208 MGr,CS,68pp,Legion of
   Super Villains. 28.00
209 MGr,N:Karate Kid 20.00
210 MGr,O:Karate Kid 25.00
211 MGr,The Ultimate Revenge . . 18.00
212 MGr,L:Matter Eater Lad 18.00
213 MGr,V:Benn Pares 18.00
214 MGr,V:Overseer 18.00
215 MGr,A:Emerald Empress . . . 18.00
216 MGr,I:Tyroc 18.00
217 MGr,I:Laurel Kent 18.00
218 J:Tyroc,A:Fatal Five 18.00
219 MGr,A:Fatal Five. 18.00
220 MGi,BWi 18.00
221 MGr,BWi,I:Grimbor 15.00
222 MGr,BWi,MN,BL,A:Tyroc . . . 15.00
223 MGr,BWi 15.00
224 MGr,BWi,V:Pulsar Stargrave. . 15.00
225 MGr(c),BWi,JSh,MN 15.00
226 MGr(c),MN,JSh,JA,
   I:Dawnstar. 15.00
227 MGr(c),JSon,JA,V:Stargrave. . 15.00
228 MGr(c),JSh,JA,
   D:Chemical King 15.00
229 MGr(c),JSh,JA,V:Deregon . . . 15.00
230 MGr(c),JSh,V:Sden. 15.00
Spec. #147 facsimile (2003) 10.00
Becomes:

SUPERBOY & THE
LEGION OF
SUPER-HEROES
1976–79

231 MGr(c),JSh,MN,JA,doub.size
   begins,V:Fatal Five 18.00
232 MGr(c),JSh,RE,JA,V:
   Dr.Regulus. 18.00

233 MGr(c),JSh,BWi,MN,BL,
   I:Infinite Man 18.00
234 MGr(c),RE,JA,V:Composite
   Creature. 18.00
235 MGr,GT 18.00
236 MGr(c),BMc,JSh,MN,JRu,
   V:Khunds. 18.00
237 MGr(c),WS,JA. 18.00
238 JSn(c),reprint 18.00
239 MGR(c),JSn,JRu,Ultra Boy
   accused 18.00
240 MGr(c),HC,BWi,JSh,BMc,
   O:Dawnstar,V:Grimbor 18.00
241 JSh,BMc,A:Ontir 18.00
242 JSh,BMc,E:Double Size 18.00
243 MGr(c),JA,JSon 18.00
244 JSon,V:Dark Circle 25.00
245 MA,JSon,V:Mordu 25.00
246 MGr(c),JSon,DG,MA,
   V:Fatal Five 15.00
247 JSon,JA,anniv.issue. 15.00
248 JSon 15.00
249 JSon,JA. 15.00
250 JSn,V:Omega 15.00
251 JSn,Brainiac 5 goes insane . . 15.00
252 JSon,V:Starburst bandits 12.00
253 JSon,I:Blok,League of
   Super Assassins 12.00
254 JSon,V:League of Super
   Assassins 12.00
255 JSon,A:Jor-El 12.00
256 JSon 12.00
257 SD,JSon,DA,V:Psycho
   Warrior 12.00
258 JSon,V:Psycho Warrior. 12.00
Becomes:

LEGION OF
SUPER HEROES
[2nd Series]

[NEW ADVENTURES OF]
SUPERBOY
Jan., 1980

1 KS 6.00
2 KS 3.00
3 KS 3.00
4 KS 3.00
5 KS 3.00
6 KS 3.00
7 KS,JSa. 3.00
8 thru 33 KS . . . . @3.00
34 KS,I:Yellow Peri 3.00
35 thru 44 KS . . . . @3.00
45 KS,I:Sunburst 3.00
46 KS,A:Sunburst 3.00
47 KS,A:Sunburst 3.00
48 KS 3.00
49 KS,A:Zatara 3.00
50 KS,KG,A:Legion 3.00
51 KS,FM(c)In Between Years. . . . 3.00
52 KS 3.00
53 KS 3.00
54 KS. 3.00

SUPERBOY
1990–91

1 TV Tie-in,JM,photo(c) 5.00
2 JM,T.J.White Abducted 3.00
3 JM,Fountain of Youth. 3.00
4 JM,Big Man on Campus 3.00
5 JM,Legion Homage 3.00
6 JM,Luthor. 3.00
7 JM,Super Boy Arrested 3.00
8 JM,AAd(i),Bizarro. 3.00
9 JM/CS,PhantomZone#1 . . . . . . 3.00
10 JM/CS,PhantomZone#2 . . . . . . 3.00
11 CS 3.00
12 CS,X-Mas in Smallville 3.00
Becomes:

ADVENTURES OF SUPERBOY
1991
13 A:Mr.Mxyzptlk 3.50
14 CS,A:Brimstone 3.00
15 CS,Legion Homage 3.00
16 CS,Into the Future 3.00
17 CS,A:Luthor 3.00
18 JM,At the Movies 3.00
19 JM,Blood Transfusion 3.00
20 JM,O:Nicknack,(G.Gottfried
    script) 3.00
21 V:Frost Monster 3.00
22 . . . . 3.00
Spec.#1 CS,A:Ma Kent 2.50

SUPERBOY
[2nd Series], 1994
1 B:KK(s),TG,DHz,V:Sidearm 4.00
2 TG,DHz,I:Knockout 2.50
3 TG,DHz,I:Scavenger 2.50
4 TG,DHz,MeP,I:Lock n' Load 2.50
5 TG,DHz,I:Silver Sword 2.50
6 TG,DHz,Worlds Collide,pt.3
    C:Rocket 2.50
7 Worlds Collide, pt.8,V:Rift 2.50
8 Zero Hour,A:Superboy 2.50
9 Silicon Dragon 2.50
10 Monster 2.50
11 Techno 2.50
12 Copperhead 2.50
13 Watery Grave,pt.1 . . . . 2.50
14 Watery Grave,pt.2 . . . . 2.50
15 Watery Grave,pt.3 . . . . 2.50
16 TG,DHz,KK,V:Loose Cannon
    [New Miraweb format begins] . . 2.50
17 TG,DHz,KK Looking for
    Roxy Leech 2.50
18 V:Valor 2.50
19 TG,KK,DHz,T-K-O 2.50
20 R:Scavenger 2.50
21 KK,TG,DHz,Future Tense,Pt.1 . . 2.50
22 KK,TG,DHz,Underworld
    Unleashed x-over 2.50
23 KK,TG,DHz,V:Technician 2.50
24 KK,TG,DHz,V.Silversword 2.50
25 New Gods 4.00
26 KK,DHz,Losin'it,pt.2 . . . . 2.50
27 KK,DHz,Losin'it,pt.3 . . . . 2.50
28 KK,DHz,Losin'it,pt.4 . . . . 2.50
29 KK,DHz,Losin'it,pt.5 . . . . 2.50
30 KK,DHz,Losin'it,pt.6 . . . . 2.50

Superboy 2nd Series #1
© DC Comics Inc.

31 KK,Summer Fun,V:Morpheriste . 2.50
32 RMz(s),RBe,DHz,V:King Shark . 2.50
33 RMz(s),RBe,DHz, survivors flee
    to Hawaii, Final Night tie-in 2.50
34 RMz(s),RBe,DHz, V:Dubbilex . . . 2.50
35 RMz(s),RBe,DHz, Superboy
    abducted 2.50
36 RMz(s),RBe,DHz,V:King SHark . 2.50
37 RMz(s),SB,V:Sledge 2.50
38 RMz,RBe,DHz,Meltdown,pt.1 . . 2.50
39 RMz,RBe,DHz,Meltdown,pt.2 . . 2.50
40 RMz,RBe,DHz,Meltdown,pt.2,
    x-over. 2.50
41 RMz,RBe,DHz,Meltdown,pt.3 . . 2.50
42 SB,Ashes to Ashes 2.50
43 SB,Lanie & Ken 2.50
44 SB,island of teenagers 2.50
45 RMz,DHz,TGu,A:Legion 2.50
46 RMz,DHz,TGu,V:Silver Sword . . 2.50
47 RMz,DHz,TGu,F:Green Lantern . 2.50
48 BKs,DHz,TGu,theme park 2.50
49 DHz,Searching 2.50
50 KK,TGu,Last Boy on Earth pt.1 . 2.50
51 KK,TGu,Last Boy on Earth pt.2 . 2.50
52 KK,TGu,Last Boy on Earth pt.3 . 2.50
53 KK,TGu,Last Boy on Earth pt.4 . 2.50
54 KK,TGu,A:Wild Men 2.50
55 KK,TGu,V:Grokk, Hex. 2.50
56 KK,TGu,Project Cadmus 2.50
57 KK,TGu,Demolition Run,pt.1 . . . 2.50
58 KK,TGu,Demolition Run,pt.2 . . . 2.50
59 KK,DAb,A:Superman 2.50
60 KK,TGu,A:JLA,Hyper-Tension . . 2.50
61 KK,TGu,Hyper-Tension,pt.2 . . . . 2.50
62 KK,TGu,Hyper-Tension,pt.3 . . . . 2.50
63 KK,TGu,Hyper-Tension,pt.4 . . . . 2.50
64 KK,TGu,Hyper-Tension,pt.5 . . . . 2.50
65 KK,TGu,guest-star packed 2.50
66 KK,TGu,Wild Lands 2.50
67 KK,AaL, in Wild Lands 2.50
68 KK,TG,MM,Day of Judgment
    x-over, F:Demon 2.50
69 KK,TG,return to Hawaii 2.50
70 KK,TG,Evil Factory,pt.1 . . . . 2.50
71 KK,TG,Evil Factory,pt.2 . . . . 2.50
72 KK,TG,Evil Factory,pt.3 . . . . 2.50
73 KK,TG,Evil Factory,pt.4 . . . . 2.50
74 KK,TC,Sino of Youth 2.50
75 KK,TG,as normal teenager 2.50
76 KK,TG,still Superboy 2.50
77 KK,TG,MBa,V:Kossak 2.50
78 KK,TG,prisoners 2.50
79 KK,TG,V:Kossak the Slaver 2.50
80 BHr,F:The Titans,pt.1 . . . . 2.50
81 BHr,F:The Titans,pt.2 . . . . 2.50
82 JMz,V:Negative G. 2.50
83 PFe,F:Young Justice 2.50
84 PFe,off to L.A. 2.50
85 PFe,A:Batman,Batgirl 2.50
86 PFe,shotgun wedding 2.50
87 V:Shrapnel,Deadman 2.50
88 PFe,V:DNAngels 2.50
89 PFe,Our Worlds at War, tie-in. . . 2.50
90 PFe,Our Worlds at War, tie-in. . . 2.50
91 PFe,Our Worlds at War, tie-in. . . 2.50
92 PFe,R:Doctor Sin 2.50
93 PFe,Joker:Last Laugh, tie-in. . . . 2.50
94 JMC,finding an apartment. 2.50
95 JP,JMC,Slaughterhouse Six 2.50
96 JP,Trixie & Wipeout. 2.50
97 JP,JMC,F:Wipeout 2.50
98 JP,JMC,F:Jimmy Olsen. 2.50
99 WorldWithoutYoungJustice,pt.4 . 2.50
100 JP,KK,TG,48-pg. 3.50
Ann.#1 Elseworlds Story 3.50
Ann.#2 KK, BKs, Year One 4.50
Ann.#3 Legends o/t Dead Earth . . . 3.50
Ann.#4 Pulp Heroes (High-
    Adventure) 4.50
Spec.#1,000,000 KK,TGu 2.50

SUPERBOY & THE RAVERS
1996–98
1 KK&SMt(s),PaP,DDv, ... 2.50
2 KK&SMt(s),PaP,DDv,InterC.E.P.T.
    pursues Superboy and Kaliber . 2.50
3 KK&SMT(s),PaP,DDv,teleported
    to Rann,V:Half-Life 2.50
4 KK&SMt(s),PaP,DDv,A:Adam
    Strange 2.50
5 KK&SMt(s),PaP,DDv,O:Hero . . . 2.50
6 KK&SMt(s),PaP,DDv, ... 2.50
7 KK&SMt(s),PaP,DDv, Road Trip,
    pt.1,A:Impulse 2.50
8 KK&SMt(s),PaP,DDv, Road Trip,
    pt.2,A:Guy Gardner 2.50
9 KK&SMt(s),PaP,DDv, Road Trip,
    pt.3,A:Aura. 2.50
10 KK&SMt(s),DDv,Meltdown,pt.4 . 2.50
11 KK&SMt(s),PaP,DDv, Superboy
    presumed dead 2.50
12 KK(s),AaL,. 2.50
13 KK(s),SMt,F:Hero,Sparx 2.50
14 KK&SMt(s),Genesis tie-in 2.50
15 KK&SMt(s),new Rave 2.50
16 KK&SMt(s),Half-Life 2.50
17 KK&SMt(s),Kaliber 2.50
18 KK&SMt(s),V:Qward 2.50
19 . . . . 2.50

SUPERBOY PLUS
Nov., 1996
1 RMz(s),ASm,F:Captain
    Marvel Jr.. . . . . 3.50
2 LKa,AWi,ALa,F:Slither. 3.00

SUPERBOY/RISK DOUBLE-SHOT
Dec., 1997
1 DJu,JoP,x-over. 2.50

SUPERBOY'S LEGION
Feb., 2001
1 (of 2) Elseworlds, 48-page. 6.00
2 MFm,AD, concl. 6.00

SUPER DC GIANT
1970–71, 1976
S-13 Binky 200.00
S-14 JKu,GK,Top Guns of
    the West 80.00
S-15 JKu,GK,Western Comics . . . 75.00
S-16 JKu,Best of the Brave
    & the Bold 65.00
S-17 Love 1970 . . . . 500.00
S-18 Three Mouseketeers 150.00
S-19 NA,Jerry Lewis 175.00
S-20 NA,JK,House of Mystery. . . 100.00
S-21 Love 1971 . . . . 600.00
S-22 JKu,Top Guns of the West . . 50.00
S-23 The Unexpected 50.00
S-24 Supergirl 50.00
S-25 Challengers of the Unknown. 50.00
S-26 Aquaman. 45.00
S-27 GK,Strange Flying Saucer
    Adventures (1976). 45.00

SUPER FRIENDS
Nov., 1976
1 ECh(c),JO,RE,Fury of the
    Superfoes,A:Penguin. 60.00
2 RE,A:Penguin 30.00
3 RF(c),RF,A:JLA 25.00
4 RF,V:Riddler,I:Skyrocket 25.00
5 RF(c),RF,V:Greenback. 25.00
6 RF(c),RF,A:Atom 20.00
7 RF(c),RF,I:Zan & Jana,
    A:Seraph 20.00

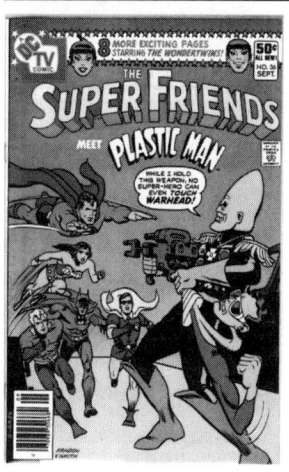

Super Friends #36
© DC Comics, Inc.

8 RF(c),RF,A:JLA 20.00
9 RF(c),RF,A:JLA,I:Iron Maiden . . 20.00
10 RF(c),RFTheMonkeyMenace . . 20.00
11 RF(c),RF 15.00
12 RF(c),RF,A:TNT 15.00
13 RF(c),RF 15.00
14 RF(c),RF 15.00
15 RF(c),RF, A:The Elementals . . . 15.00
16 RF(c),RF,V:The Cvags 15.00
17 RF(c),RF,A:Queen Hippolyte . . 15.00
18 KS(c),V:Tuantra,Time Trapper . 15.00
19 RF(c),RF,V:Menagerie Man . . . 15.00
20 KS(c),KS,V:Frownin' Fritz 15.00
21 RF(c),RF,V:Evil Superfriends
    Doubles 15.00
22 RF(c),RF,V:Matador Mob 15.00
23 FR(c),RF,V:Mirror Master 15.00
24 RF(c),RF,V:Exorians 15.00
25 RF(c),RF,V:Overlord,
    A:Green Lantern, Mera 15.00
26 RF(c),RF,A:Johnny Jones 15.00
27 RF(c),RF,The Spaceman Who
    Stole the Stars 15.00
28 RF(c),RF,A:Felix Faust 15.00
29 RF(c),RF,B.U.KS,Scholar From
    the Stars 15.00
30 RF(c),RF,V:Grodd & Giganta . . 15.00
31 RF(c),RF,A:Black Orchid 18.00
32 KS(c),KS,A:Scarecrow 12.00
33 RF(c),RF,V:Menagerie Man . . . 12.00
34 RF(c)RF,The Creature That
    Slept a Million Years 12.00
35 RT,Circus o/t Super Stars 12.00
36 RF(c),RF,A:Plastic Man
    & Woozy 12.00
37 RF(c),RF,A:Supergirl;
    B.U. A:Jack O'Lantern 12.00
38 RF(c),RF,V:Grax;
    B.U. A:Serpah 12.00
39 RF(c),RF,A:Overlord;
    B.U. A:Wonder Twins 12.00
40 RF(c),RF,V:The Monacle;
    B.U. Jack O'Lantern 12.00
41 RF(c),RF,V:Toyman;
    B.U. A:Seraph 12.00
42 RT,A:Flora,V:Flame; B.U.Wonder
    Twins' Christmas Special 12.00
43 KS(c),RT,V:Futuro; B.U.JSon
    A:Plastic Man 12.00
44 KS(c),RT,Peril o/t Forgotten
    Identities'; B.U.Jack O'Lantern 12.00

45 KS(c),RT,A:Bushmaster,
    Godiva, Rising Sun, Olympian,
    Little Mermaid, Wild Huntsman;
    B.U. Plastic Man,V: Sinestro . . 12.00
46 RT,V:The Conqueror;
    B.U. BO,Seraph 12.00
47 KS(c),RT,A:Green Fury
    Aug., 1981 . . . . 12.00

SUPER FRIENDS
March, 2008
1 From Mattel toy line 2.50
2 thru 9 . . . . @2.50

SUPERGIRL
[1st Regular Series]
Nov., 1972—Sept., 1974
1 Trail of the Madman';
    Superfashions From Fans;
    B.B.U. DG,Zatanna 100.00
2 BO(c)A:Prof.Allan,Bottle
    City of Kandor 50.00
3 BO(c),The Garden of Death . . . 50.00
4 V:Super Scavanger 60.00
5 BO(c),A:Superman,V:Dax; B.U.
    MA:Rep.Hawkman #4 . . . . 65.00
6 BO(c),Love & War 50.00
7 BO(c),A:Zatanna 50.00
8 BO(c),A:Superman,Green
    Lantern, Hawkman 60.00
9 BO(c),V:Sharkman 50.00
10 A:Prey,V:Master Killer 50.00

[DARING NEW ADVENTURES OF] SUPERGIRL
[2nd Regular Series]
Nov., 1982
1 CI,BO,I:Psi; B:B.U.Lois Lane 3.00
2 CI,BO,C:Decay 3.00
3 CI,BO,V:Decay,Decay Day 3.00
4 CI,BO,V:The Gang 3.00
5 CI,BO,V:The Gang 3.00
6 CI,BO,V:The Gang 3.00
7 CI,BO,V:The Gang 3.00
8 CI,BO,A:Doom Patrol 3.00
9 CI,BO,V:Reactron
    A:Doom Patrol 3.00
10 CI,BO,Radiation Fever 3.00
11 CI,BO,V:Chairman 3.00
12 CI,BO,V:Chairman 3.00
13 CI,BO,N:Supergirl,A:Superman
    V:Blackstarr 3.00
Becomes:

SUPERGIRL
Dec., 1983–Sept., 1984
14 GK(c),CI,BO,V:Blackstarr
    A:Rabbi Nathan Zuber 3.00
15 CI,BO,V:Blackstarr,
    A:Blackstarr's Mom 3.00
16 KG/BO(c),CI,BO,
    A:Ambush Bug 3.00
17 CI/DG(c),CI,BO,V:Matrix
    Prime 3.00
18 DG(c),CI,BO, V:Kraken 3.00
19 EB/BO(c),CI,BO,Who Stole
    Supergirl's Life 3.00
20 CI,BO,C:JLA, Teen Titans:
    Teh Parasite 3.00
21 EB/BO(c),EB,Kryptonite Man . . . 3.00
22 EB(c),CI,BO,I Have Seen the
    Future & it is Me 3.00
23 EB(c),CI,BO,The Future
    Begins Today 3.00
Spec.#1 JL/DG(c),GM,MovieAdapt . 3.00
Spec.#1 AT,Honda give-away 3.00

[Limited Series], 1994
1 KGa(c),B:RSt(s),JBr,O:Supergirl . 5.00

2 KGa(c),JBr 4.00
3 KGa(c),JBr,D:Clones 3.00
4 KGa(c),RSt(s),JBr,final Issue 3.00

SUPERGIRL
Sept., 1996
1 PDd(s),GFr,CaS, ... 11.00
1a 2nd printing 3.00
2 PDd(s),GFr,CaS,V:Chakat 5.00
3 PDd(s),GFr,CaS,V:Grodd, Final
    Night tie-in 6.00
4 PDd(s),GFr,CaS,transformed into
    savage 4.00
5 PDd(s),GFr,CaS,Supergirl visits
    the Kents,V:Chemo 4.00
6 PDd(s),GFr,CaS, ... 4.00
7 PDd(s),GFr,CaS,Supergirl learns
    about Linda Danvers 4.00
8 PDd(s),GFr,CaS,Buzz gets date
    with Supergirl. 4.00
9 PDd(s),GFr,CaS,V:Tempus 4.00
10 PDd(s),Linda tries to relax 4.00
11 PDd(s),CaS,V:Silver Banshee . . 4.00
12 PDd(s),Mattie possessed by
    Silver Banshee 4.00
13 CaS, 3 girls dreams invaded by
    incubus 3.00
14 PDa,CaS,Genesis tie-in 3.00
15 PDa,CaS,V:Extremists 3.00
16 PDa,CaS,F:Power Girl 3.00
17 PDa,CaS,L-Ron, Despero 3.00
18 PDa,CaS,V:Despero 3.00
19 . . . . 3.00
20 PDa,CaS,Millennium Giants 3.00
21 PDa,CaS,Comet 3.00
22 PDa, ... 3.00
23 PDa,A:Steel 3.00
24 PDa,Avenging Angels x-over . . . 3.00
25 PDa,truth about Comet. 3.00
26 PDd,truth discovered 3.00
27 PDd(s),V:Female Furies,pt.1 . . . 3.00
28 PDd(s),V:Female Furies,pt.2 . . . 3.00
29 PDd(s),V:Female Furies,pt.3 . . . 3.00
30 PDd(s),V:Matrix. 3.00
31 PDd(s),A:Superman 3.00
32 PDd(s),SeP,V:Mr.Carnivean 3.00
33 PDd(s),V:Mr.Carnivean 3.00
34 PDd(s),V:Parasite 3.00
35 PDd(s),V:Parasite, concl. 3.00
36 PDd(s),Hell's Angel's,pt.2 . . . . . 2.50
37 PDd(s),Hell's Angels,pt.4 . . . . . . 2.50
38 PDd(s),Day of Judgment x-over . 2.50
39 PDd(s),F:Comet 2.50
40 PDd(s). 2.50

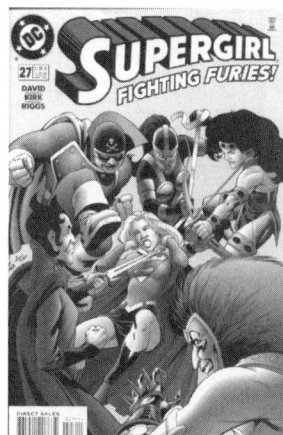

Supergirl #27
© DC Comics, Inc.

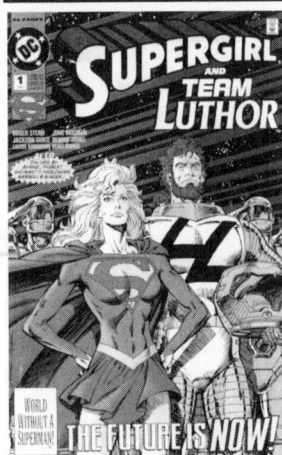

Supergirl Lex Luthor Special
© DC Comics, Inc.

41 PDd(s),F:Ember,V:Satan Girl . . . 2.50
42 PDd(s),dates Dick Malverne. . . . 2.50
43 PDd(s),date become nightmare . 2.50
44 PDd(s),F:Dick Malverne,dying . . 2.50
45 PDd(s),F:Comet,V:Carnivore . . . 2.50
46 PDd(s),V:Comet,Carnivore 2.50
47 PDd(s),V:Carnivore. 2.50
48 PDd(s), ... 2.50
49 PDd(s),V:Carnivore. 2.50
50 PDd(s),48-pg. 4.00
51 PDd(s),to Metropolis, minus
   powers 2.50
52 PDd(s),V:Riot & Prankster 2.50
53 PDd(s),F:Green Lantern 2.50
54 PDd(s),F:Green Lantern 2.50
55 PDd(s),A:Lex Luthor 2.50
56 PDd(s),Buzz's daughter 2.50
57 PDd(s),Daddy's Little Girl 2.50
58 PDd(s),Buzz close to death 2.50
59 PDd(s),Our Worlds at War,tie-in . 2.50
60 PDd(s),Our Worlds at War,tie-in . 2.50
61 PDd(s),Our Worlds at War,tie-in . 2.50
62 PDd(s),A:Two-Face. 2.50
63 PDd(s),Joker:Last Laugh,tie-in . . 5.00
64 PDd(s),A:Lagoon Boy 2.50
65 PDd(s),hearing-impaired kids . . . 2.50
66 PDd(s),F:Demon Etrigan 2.50
67 PDd(s),F:Demon Etrigan 2.50
68 PDd(s),F:Mary Marvel. 4.00
69 PDd(s),F:Capt.Marvel,Jr. 5.00
70 PDd(s),F:Mary Marvel. 2.50
71 PDd(s),V:Tara 2.50
72 PDd(s),V:Quetzlcoatl 2.50
73 PDd(s),Garden of Eden 2.50
74 PDd(s),Linda,Supergirl re-merge 2.50
75 PDd(s),EBe,spacecraft crashes . 8.00
76 PDd(s),F:Superboy,Kara Zor-El 12.00
77 PDd(s),V:Fatalist. 6.00
78 PDd(s),V:Fatalist. 5.00
79 PDd(s),S.A.Supergirl. 5.00
80 PDd(s),V:Kara & Xenon 5.00
Ann.#1 Legends o/t Dead Earth . . . 3.00
Ann.#2 TPe,CDi,ACa, Pulp Heroes . 4.00
Spec.#1,000,000 PDd(s),DAb 2.50
GN Wings, Elseworlds, 48-page . . . 6.00
Spec. Supergirl/Lex Luthor JBr,
   F:Lex Luthor (1993). 4.00
Spec. Supergirl/Prysm Double-Shot
   DJu,TGb,Clv, x-over (1997) . . . 2.50

SUPERGIRL
Aug., 2005
0 JLb(s),IaC,NRd,F:Kara Zor-el . . . 4.00

1 JLb(s),IaC,NRd,V:Power Girl. . . . 5.00
1a variant (c). 5.00
2 JLb(s),IaC,NRd,V:Superboy 4.00
3 JLb(s),IaC,NRd,Spying on Kara . 4.00
4 JLb(s),IaC,NRd,F:JLA 4.00
4a variant (c). 3.00
5 JLb(s),IaC,NRd,Mistress of Might 5.00
5a 2nd printing 3.00
6 JLb(s),IaC,NRd,A:Batman, Wonder
   Woman, F:Superman 5.00
7 IaC,New Flamebird & Nightwing . 3.00
8 EBe,V:Power Girl. 3.00
9 IaC,Supergirl's boyfriend 3.00
10 IaC,New secret identity. 3.00
11 IaC,NRd,A:Outsiders 3.00
12 IaC,NRd,A:Batgirl, League of
   Assassins 3.00
13 IaC,NRd,F:Power Boy 3.00
14 IaC,NRd,V:Batgirl, to the death . 3.00
15 IaC,NRd,F:Powerboy 3.00
16 Sent to kill Superman 3.00
17 F:JLA,Wonder Girl 3.00
18 A:Superman 3.00
19 V:Superman 3.00
20 Amazons Attack tie-in 3.00
21 Countdown tie-in 3.00
22 V:Karate Kid 3.00
23 A:Superman, Batman 3.00
23a variant NKu (c) (1:10) 3.50
24 Ghost of Krypton. 3.00
25 V:Neutron 3.00
26 V:Reactron 3.00
27 V:Reactron 3.00
28 Back from the future 3.00
29 Impossible quest. 3.00
30 Promise to a dying boy 3.00
31 F:Empress. 3.00
32 Promise to a dying boy 3.00
33 At a crossroads 3.00
34 . . . . 3.00
35 New Krypton, pt.5, x-over 3.00
34a thru 35a variant (c) (1:10) . . . @3.00

SUPER HEROES
BATTLE SUPER GORILLA
Winter, 1976
1 Superman Flash rep. 20.00

SUPERMAN
1939–86
1 JoS,O:Superman,reprints Action
   Comics #1–#4 . . . . 425,000.00
2 JoS,I:George Taylor 30,000.00
3 JoS,V:Superintendent
   Lyman 16,000.00
4 JoS,V:Lex Luthor 16,000.00
5 JoS,V:Lex Luthor 12,000.00
6 JoS,V:Brute' Bashby 6,000.00
7 JoS,I:Perry White 6,000.00
8 JoS,V:Jackal 6,000.00
9 JoS,V:Joe Gatson 6,000.00
10 JoS,V:Lex Luthor 5,500.00
11 JoS,V:Rolf Zimba 4,200.00
12 JoS,V:Lex Luthor 4,200.00
13 JoS,I:Jimmy Olsen,V:Lex
   Luthor,The Archer. 4,200.00
14 JoS,I:Lightning Master. 7,000.00
15 JoS,V:The Evolution King . 4,200.00
16 JoS,V:Mr. Sinus 3,500.00
17 JoS,V:Lex Luthor,Lois Lane
   first suspects Clark
   is Superman 3,500.00
18 JoS,V:Lex Luthor 3,500.00
19 JoS,V:Funnyface,
   1st Imaginary story 3,500.00
20 JoS,V:Puzzler,Leopard 3,500.00
21 JoS,V:Sir Gauntlet 2,400.00
22 JoS,V:Prankster 2,400.00
23 JoS,Propaganda story 2,400.00
24 V:Cobra King 4,000.00
25 Propaganda story 4,000.00

26 I:J.Wilbur Wolfingham,
   A:Mercury 4,000.00
27 V:Toyman 4,000.00
28 V:J.Wilbur Wolfingham,
   A:Hercules 4,000.00
29 V:Prankster 4,000.00
30 I&O:Mr. Mxyztplk. 4,200.00
31 V:Lex Luthor. 1,700.00
32 V:Toyman 1,700.00
33 V:Mr. Mxyztplk. 1,700.00
34 V:Lex Luthor. 1,700.00
35 V:J.Wilbur Wolfingham 1,700.00
36 V:Mr. Mxyztplk. 1,700.00
37 V:Prankster,A:Sinbad. 1,700.00
38 V:Lex Luthor. 1,700.00
39 V:J.Wilbur Wolfingham. 1,700.00
40 V:Mr. Mxyzptlk,A:Susie
   Thompkins 1,700.00
41 V:Prankster 1,500.00
42 V:J.Wilbur Wolfingham. 1,500.00
43 V:Lex Luthor. 1,500.00
44 V:Toyman,A:Shakespeare . . 1,500.00
45 A:Hocus & Pocus,Lois Lane
   as Superwoman 1,500.00
46 V:Mr. Mxyzptlk,Lex Luthor,
   Superboy flashback 1,500.00
47 V:Toyman 1,500.00
48 V:Lex Luthor. 1,500.00
49 V:Toyman 1,500.00
50 V:Prankster 1,500.00
51 V:Mr. Mxyztplk 1,200.00
52 V:Prankster 1,200.00
53 WB,O:Superman 5,000.00
54 V:Wrecker 1,200.00
55 V:Prankster 1,200.00
56 V:Prankster 1,200.00
57 V:Lex Luthor. 1,200.00
58 V:Tiny Trix 1,200.00
59 V:Mr.Mxyzptlk. 1,200.00
60 V:Toyman 1,200.00
61 I:Kryptonite,V:Prankster . . . 2,400.00
62 V:Mr.Mxyzptlk,A:Orson
   Welles. 1,200.00
63 V:Toyman 1,200.00
64 V:Prankster 1,200.00
65 V:Mala,Kizo and U-Ban 1,200.00
66 V:Prankster 1,200.00
67 A:Perry Como,I:Brane
   Taylor 1,200.00
68 V:Lex Luthor. 1,200.00
69 V:Prankster,A:Inspector
   Erskine Hawkins. 1,200.00
70 V:Prankster 1,200.00
71 V:Lex Luthor. 1,100.00
72 V:Prankster 1,100.00
72a giveaway 1,200.00
73 Flashback story 1,100.00

Superman #81 © DC Comics, Inc.

74 V:Lex Luthor.	1,100.00
75 V:Prankster	1,100.00
76 A:Batman, Superman & Batman reveal each other's identities	3,500.00
77 A:Pocahontas.	1,100.00
78 V:Kryptonian snagriff, A:Lana Lang	1,100.00
79 V:Lex Luthor,A:Inspector Erskine Hawkins.	1,100.00
80 A:Halk Kar	1,100.00
81 V:Lex Luthor.	1,100.00
82 V:Mr. Mxyzptlk.	900.00
83 V:The Brain.	900.00
84 Time-travel story	900.00
85 V:Lex Luthor	900.00
86 V:Mr.Mxyzptlk	900.00
87 WB,V:The Thing from 40,000 AD	900.00
88 WB,V:Lex Luthor,Toyman, Prankster team	1,000.00
89 V:Lex Luthor	900.00
90 V:Lex Luthor.	1,000.00
91 The Superman Stamp.	900.00
92 Goes back to 12th Century England	900.00
93 V:The Thinker	900.00
94 Clark Kent's Hillbilly Bride.	900.00
95 A:Susie Thompkins.	900.00
96 V:Mr. Mxyzptlk.	700.00
97 Superboy's Last Day In Smallville	700.00
98 Clark Kent, Outlaw!.	700.00
99 V:Midnite gang	700.00
100 F:Superman-Substitute Schoolteacher.	3,500.00
101 A:Lex Luthor	600.00
102 I:Superman Stock Company	600.00
103 A:Mr.Mxyzptlk.	600.00
104 F:Clark Kent,Jailbird	600.00
105 A:Mr.Mxyzptlk	600.00
106 A:Lex Luthor	650.00
107 F:Superman In 30th century (pre-Legion)	600.00
108 I:Perry White Jr.	600.00
109 I:Abner Hokum	600.00
110 A:Lex Luthor	600.00
111 Becomes Mysto the Great.	600.00
112 A:Lex Luthor	600.00
113 A:Jor-El	600.00
114 V:The Great Mento	600.00
115 V:The Organizer	600.00
116 Return to Smallville	600.00
117 A:Lex Luthor	600.00
118 F:Jimmy Olsen	600.00
119 A:Zoll Orr.	600.00
120 V:Gadget Grim	600.00
121 I:XL-49 (Futureman)	450.00
122 In the White House.	450.00
123 CS,pre-Supergirl tryout A:Jor-El & Lara	500.00
124 F:Lois Lane.	450.00
125 F:Superman College Story	450.00
126 F:Lois Lane.	450.00
127 WB,I&O:Titano	500.00
128 V:Vard & Boka.	450.00
129 WB,I&O:Lori Lemaris	500.00
130 A:Krypto,the Superdog	450.00
131 A:Mr. Mxyzptlk.	450.00
132 A:Batman & Robin	450.00
133 F:Superman Joins Army	450.00
134 A:Supergirl & Krypto	450.00
135 A:Lori Lemaris,Mr.Mxyzptlk.	450.00
136 O:Discovery Kryptonite	450.00
137 CS,I:Super-Menace	450.00
138 A:Titano,Lori Lemaris	450.00
139 CS,O:Red Kryptonite	450.00
140 WB,I:Bizarro Jr,Bizarro Supergirl,Blue Kryptonite.	450.00
141 I:Lyla Lerrol,A:Jor-EL & Lara	350.00

142 WB,CS,A:Al Capone	350.00
143 WB,F:Bizarro meets Frankenstein	350.00
144 O:Superboy's 1st Public Appearance	350.00
145 F:April Fool's Issue	350.00
146 F:Superman's life story	400.00
147 CS,I:Adult Legion	350.00
148 CS,V:Mxyzptlk.	300.00
149 CS:A:Luthor,C:JLA	300.00
150 CS,KS,V:Mxyzptlk	250.00
150 CS,KS,V:Mxyzptlk.	250.00
151 CS.	250.00
152 A:Legion	250.00
153 CS.	250.00
154 CS,V:Mzyzptlk.	250.00
155 WB,CS,V:Cosmic Man	250.00
156 CS,A:Legion,Batman	250.00
157 CS,I:Gold kryptonite	250.00
158 CS,I:Nightwing&Flamebird	250.00
159 CS,Imaginary Tale F:Lois Lane	250.00
160 CS,F:Perry White	250.00
161 D:Ma & Pa Kent	250.00
162 A:Legion	250.00
163 CS.	250.00
164 CS,Luthor,I:Lexor	250.00
165 CS,A:Saturn Woman	250.00
166 CS	250.00
167 CS,I:Ardora,Brainiac	275.00
168 CS	200.00
169 Great DC Contest	200.00
170 CS,A:J.F.Kennedy,Luthor	200.00
171 CS,Mxyzptlk	200.00
172 CS,Luthor,Brainiac	200.00
173 CS,A:Batman	200.00
174 Mxyzptlk	200.00
175 CS,Luthor	200.00
176 CS,Green Kryptonite.	200.00
177 Fortress of Solitude.	200.00
178 CS, Red Kryptonite.	200.00
179 CS,Clark Kent in Marines	200.00
180 CS.	200.00
181 Superman 2965	200.00
182 CS,Toyman.	200.00
183 giant	200.00
184 Secrets of the Fortress.	150.00
185 JM,Superman's Achilles Heel.	150.00
186 CS,The Two Ghosts of Superman.	150.00
187 giant	150.00
188 V:Zunial,The Murder Man.	150.00
189 WB,The Mystery of Krypton's Second Doom.	150.00
190 WB,I:Amalak.	150.00
191 The Prisoner of Demon	150.00
192 CS,Imaginary Story, I:Superman Jr.	150.00
193 giant	150.00
194 CS,Imaginary,A:Supes Jr.	150.00
195 CS,V:Amalak.	150.00
196 WB,reprint.	150.00
197 giant	150.00
198 CS,F:The Real Clark Kent	150.00
199 CS,F:Superman/Flash race, A:JLA.	600.00
200 WB,A:Brainiac.	125.00
201 CS,F:Clark Kent Abandons Superman.	100.00
202 A:Bizarro,(giant size).	125.00
203 F:When Superman Killed His Friends.	100.00
204 NA(c),RA,A:Lori Lemaris	100.00
205 NA(c),I:Black Zero	100.00
206 NA(c),F:The Day Superman Became An Assistant	100.00
207 CS,F:The Case Of the Collared Crimefighter	125.00
208 NA(c),CS.	100.00
209 CS,F:The Clark Kent Monster	100.00

210 CS,F:Clark Kent's Last Rites	100.00
211 CS,RA.	100.00
212 giant	150.00
213 CS,JA,V:Luthor,C:Braniac 5.	100.00
214 NA(c),CS,JA,F:The Ghosts That Haunted Superman.	100.00
215 NA(c),CS,JA,V:Luthor, Imaginary Story	100.00
216 JKu(c),RA,Superman in Nam	100.00
217 CS,A:Mr.Mxyzptlk	100.00
218 CS,JA,A:Mr.Mxyzptlk	100.00
219 CS,F:Clark Kent-Hero, Superman Public Enemy.	100.00
220 CS,A:Flash	100.00
221 CS,F:The Two Ton Superman	100.00
222 giant	150.00
223 CS,A:Supergirl	75.00
224 CS,Imaginary Story.	75.00
225 CS,F:The Secret of the Super Imposter	75.00
226 CS,F:When Superman Became King Kong	75.00

Superman #227 © DC Comics Inc.

227 Krypton,(giant)	100.00
228 CS,DA.	75.00
229 WB,CS	75.00
230 CS,DA,Luthor	75.00
231 CS,DA,Luthor	75.00
232 F:Krypton,(giant)	100.00
233 CS,MA,I:Quarrum	75.00
234 NA(c),CS,MA	75.00
235 CS,MA.	75.00
236 CS,MA,DG,A:Green Arrow	75.00
237 NA(c),CS,MA	75.00
238 CS,MA,GM	75.00
239 giant	100.00
240 CS,DG,MK,A:I-Ching.	50.00
241 CS,MA,A:Wonder Woman	50.00
242 CS,MA,A:Wonder Woman	50.00
243 CS,MA.	50.00
244 CS,MA.	50.00
245 100 pg reprints	50.00
246 CS,MA,RB,I.S.T.A.R. Labs	50.00
247 CS,MA,Guardians o/Universe.	50.00
248 CS,MA,A:Luthor,I:Galactic Golem	50.00
249 CS,MA,DD,NA,I:Terra-Man.	75.00
250 CS,MA,Terraman	50.00
251 CS,MA,RB.	50.00
252 NA(c),rep.100pgs	50.00
253 CS,MA.	50.00
254 CS,MA,NA.	75.00
255 CS,MA,DG	30.00
256 CS,MA.	30.00
257 CS,MA,DD,DG,A:Tomar-Re	30.00

All comics prices listed are for *Near Mint* condition.

DC COMICS

258 CS,MA,DC	30.00
259 CS,MA,A:Terra-Man	30.00
260 CS,DC,I:Valdemar	30.00
261 CS,MA,V:Star Sapphire	30.00
262 CS,MA	30.00
263 CS,MA,DD,FMc	30.00
264 DC,CS,I:Steve Lombard	30.00
265 CS,MA	30.00
266 CS,MA,DD,V:Snowman	30.00
267 CS,MA,BO	30.00
268 CS,BO,DD,MA,A:Batgirl	30.00
269 CS,MA	30.00
270 CS,MA,V:Valdemar	30.00
271 CS,BO,DG,V:Brainiac	30.00
272 100pg.reprints	50.00
273 CS,DG	30.00
274 CS	30.00
275 CS,DG,FMc	30.00
276 CS,BO,I&O:Captain Thunder	30.00
277 CS	30.00
278 CS,BO,Terraman,100page	75.00
279 CS,Batgirl,Batman	25.00
280 CS,BO	25.00
281 CS,BO,I:Vartox	25.00
282 CS,KS,N:Luthor	25.00
283 CS,BO,Mxyzptlk	25.00
284 CS,BO,100p reprint	50.00
285 CS,BO	25.00
286 CS,BO	25.00
287 CS,BO,R:Krypto	25.00
288 CS,BO	25.00
289 CS,BO,JL	25.00
290 CS,V:Mxyzptlk	25.00
291 CS,BO	25.00
292 CS,BO,AM,O:Luthor	25.00
293 CS,BO	25.00
294 CS,JL,A:Brain Storm	25.00
295 CS,BO	25.00
296 CS,BO,Identity Crisis #1	25.00
297 CS,BO,Identity Crisis #2	25.00
298 CS,BO,Identity Crisis #3	25.00
299 CS,BO,Identity Crisis #4	
A:Luthor,Brainiac,Bizarro	25.00
300 CS,BO,2001,anniversary	40.00
301 BO,JL,V:Solomon Grundy	15.00
302 JL,BO,V:Luthor,A:Atom	15.00
303 CS,BO,I:Thunder&Lightning	15.00
304 CS,BO,V:Parasite	15.00
305 CS,BO,V:Toyman	15.00
306 CS,BO,V:Bizarro	15.00
307 NA(c),JL,FS,A:Supergirl	15.00
308 NA(c),JL,FS,A:Supergirl	15.00
309 JL,FS,A:Supergirl	15.00
310 CS,V:Metallo	15.00
311 CS,FS,A:Flash	15.00

Superman #299
© *DC Comics, Inc.*

312 CS,FS,A:Supergirl	15.00
313 NA(c),CS,DA,A:Supergirl	15.00
314 NA(c),CS,DA,A:Gr.Lantern	15.00
315 CS,DA,V:Blackrock	12.00
316 CS,DA,V:Metallo	12.00
317 NA(c),CS,DA,V:Metallo	12.00
318 CS	12.00
319 CS,V:Solomon Grundy	12.00
320 CS,V:Solomon Grundy	12.00
321 CS,V:Parasite	20.00
322 CS,V:Solomon Grundy	20.00
323 CS,DA,I:Atomic Skull	15.00
324 CS,A:Atomic Skull	12.00
325 CS	12.00
326 CS,V:Blackrock	12.00
327 CS,KS,V:Kobra,C:JLA	12.00
328 CS,KS,V:Kobra	12.00
329 KS,CS	12.00
330 CS,F:glasses explained	12.00
331 CS,I:Master Jailer	12.00
332 CS,V:Master Jailer	12.00
333 CS,V:Bizarro	12.00
334 CS	7.00
335 CS,W:Mxyzptlk	7.00
336 CS,V:Rose And Thorn	7.00
337 CS,A:Brainiac,Bizarro	7.00
338 CS,F:Kandor enlarged	7.00
339 CS,I:N.R.G.X	7.00
340 CS,V:N.R.G.X	7.00
341 CS,F:Major Disaster	7.00
342 CS,V:Chemo	7.00
343 CS	7.00
344 CS,A:Phantom Stranger	7.00
345 CS,When time ran backward	7.00
346 CS,Streak of Bad Luck	7.00
347 JL	7.00
348 CS	7.00
349 CS,V:Mxyzptlk	7.00
350 CS,Clark Kent's Vanishing	
Classmate	6.00
351 CS,JL,A:Mxyzptlk	6.00
352 CS,RB	6.00
353 CS,origin	6.00
354 CS,JSon,I:Superman 2020	6.00
355 CS,JSon,F:Superman 2020	6.00
356 CS,V:Vartox	6.00
357 CS,DCw,F:Superman 2020	6.00
358 CS,DC,DCw	6.00
359 CS	6.00
360 CS,AS,F:World of Krypton	6.00
361 CS,AS	6.00
362 CS,KS,DA	6.00
363 CS,RB,C:Luthor	6.00
364 GP(c),RB,AS	6.00
365 CS,KS	6.00
366 CS,KS	6.00
367 CS,GK,F:World of Krypton	6.00
368 CS,AS	6.00
369 RB,FMc,V:Parasite	6.00
370 CS,KS,FMc,A:Chemo	6.00
371 CS	6.00
372 CS,GK,F:Superman 2021	6.00
373 CS,V:Vartox	6.00
374 GK(c),CS,DA,KS,V:Vartox	6.00
375 CS,DA,GK,V:Vartox	6.00
376 CS,DA,CI,BO,SupergirlPrev	5.00
377 GK(c),CS,V:Terra-Man	5.00
378 CS	5.00
379 CS,V:Bizarro	5.00
380 CS	5.00
381 GK(c),CS	5.00
382 GK(c),CS	5.00
383 CS	5.00
384 GK(c),CS	5.00
385 GK(c),CS,V:Luthor	5.00
386 GK(c),CS,V:Luthor	5.00
387 GK(c),CS	5.00
388 GK(c),CS	5.00
389 GK(c),CS	5.00
390 GK(c),CS,V:Vartox	5.00
391 GK(c),CS,V:Vartox	5.00
392 GK(c),CS,V:Vartox	5.00

393 IN,DG,V:Master Jailer	5.00
394 CS,V:Valdemar	5.00
395 CS,V:Valdemar	5.00
396 CS	5.00
397 EB,V:Kryptonite Man	5.00
398 CS,AS,DJ	5.00
399 CS,BO,EB	5.00
400 HC(c),FM,AW,JO,JSo,MR,	
TA,WP,MK,KJ,giant	8.00
401 CS,BO,V:Luthor	5.00
402 CS,BO,WB	5.00
403 CS,BO,AS	5.00
404 CI,BO,V:Luthor	5.00
405 KS,KK,AS,F:Super-Batman	5.00
406 IN,AS,KK	5.00
407 IN,V:Mxyzptlk	5.00
408 CS,AW,JRu,F:Nuclear	
Holocaust	5.00
409 CS,AW,KS	5.00
410 CS,AW,V:Luthor	5.00
411 CS,MA,F:End Earth-Prime	5.00
412 CS,AW,V:Luthor	5.00
413 CS,AW,V:Luthor	5.00
414 CS,AW,Crisis tie-in	6.00
415 CS,AW,Crisis,W:Super Girl	6.00
416 CS,AW,Luthor	5.00
417 CS,V:Martians	5.00
418 CS,V:Metallo	5.00
419 CS,V:Iago	5.00
420 CS,F:Nightmares	5.00
421 CS,V:Mxyzptlk	5.00
422 BB(c),CS,TY,LMa,V:Werewolf	5.00
423 AMo(s),CS,GP,F:Last	
Superman	12.00
Ann.#1 I:Supergirl Rep	2,000.00
Ann.#2 I&O:Titano	800.00
Ann.#3 I:Legion	500.00
Ann.#4 O:Legion	450.00
Ann.#5 A:Krypton	350.00
Ann.#6 A:Legion	350.00
Ann.#7 O:Superman,Silver Anniv.	250.00
Ann.#8 F:Secret origins	200.00
Ann.#9 GK(c),ATh,TA,CS,	
A:Batman	7.00
Ann.#10 CS,MA,F:Sword of	
Superman	5.00
Ann.#11 AMo(s),DGb,A:Batman,	
Robin,Wonder Woman	6.00
Ann.#12 BB(c),AS,A:Lex Luthor,	
Last War Suit	4.00
Game Give-away	10.00
Giveaway CS,AT	2.25
Pizza Hut 1977	6.00
Radio Shack 1980 JSw,DG	5.00
Radio Shack 1981 CS	5.00
Radio Shack 1982 CS	5.00
Spec.#1 GK	3.50
Spec.#2 GK,V:Brainiac	3.50
Spec.#3 IN,V:Amazo	3.50
Superman III Movie,CS	2.50
Superman IV Movie,DH,DG,FMc	2.50
Becomes:	

ADVENTURES OF SUPERMAN
1987

424 JOy,I:Man O'War	6.00
425 JOy,Man O'War	3.00
426 JOy,Legends,V:Apokolips	3.00
427 JOy,V:Qurac	3.00
428 JOy,V:Qurac,I:JerryWhite	3.00
429 JOy,V:Concussion	3.00
430 JOy,V:Fearsome Five	3.00
431 JOy,A:Combattor	3.00
432 JOy,I:Jose Delgado	3.00
433 JOy,V:Lex Luthor	3.00
434 JOy,I:Gang Buster	3.00
435 JOy,A:Charger	3.00
436 JOy,Millennium x-over	5.00
437 JOy,Millennium X-over	3.50
438 JOy,N:Brainiac	3.00
439 JOy,R:Superman Robot	3.00

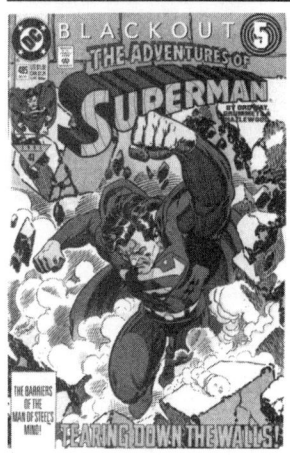

The Adventures of Superman #485
© DC Comics, Inc.

440 JOy,A:Batman,Wond. Woman . . 3.00
441 JOy,V:Mr.Mxyzptlk. 3.00
442 JOy,V:Dreadnaught,A:JLI 3.00
443 JOy,DHz,I:Husque 3.00
444 JOy,Supergirl SagaPt.2 . . . . . . 3.00
445 JOy,V:Brainiac. 3.00
446 JOy,A:Gangbuster,
    A:Luthor's Old Costume 3.00
447 JOy,A:Gangbuster. 3.00
448 JOy,I:Dubbilex,A:Gangbuster . . 3.00
449 JOy,Invasion X-over 3.00
450 JOy,Invasion X-over 3.00
451 JOy,Superman in Space 3.00
452 DJu,V:Wordbringer 3.00
453 JOy,DJu,A:Gangbuster 3.00
454 JOy,DJu,I:New Mongul 4.00
455 DJu,ATb,A:Eradicator 3.50
456 DJu,ATb,V:Turmoil 3.50
457 DJu,V:Intergang 3.50
458 DJu,KJ,R:Elastic Lad
    (Jimmy Olsen) 3.50
459 DJu,V:Eradicator. 3.50
460 DJu,NKu,V:Eradicator. 3.50
461 DJu,GP,V:Eradicator 3.50
462 DJu,ATb,Homeless
    Christmas Story 3.50
463 DJu,ATb,Superman Races
    Flash 3.50
464 DJu,ATb,Day of Krypton
    Man #2,A:Lobo 6.00
465 DJu,ATb,Day of Krypton
    Man #5,V:Draaga 3.00
466 DJu,DG,V:Team Excalibur
    Astronauts,I:Hank Henshaw
    (becomes Cyborg Superman). . 4.50
467 DJu,ATb,A:Batman 3.00
468 DJu,ATb,Man Of Steel's
    Journal,V:Hank Henshaw 3.00
469 DJu,ATb,V:Dreadnaught 3.00
470 DJu,ATb,Soul Search #3,
    D:Jerry White. 3.00
471 CS,Sinbad Contract #2 . . . . . . 3.00
472 DJu,ATb,Krisis of Krimson
    Kryptonite #2 . . . . 3.00
473 DJu,ATb,A:Green Lantern,
    Guy Gardner 3.00
474 DJu,ATb,Drunk Driving issue . . 3.00
475 DJu,ATb,V:Kilgrave,Sleez 3.00
476 DJu,BBr,Time & Time Again,pt.1,
    A:Booster Gold,Legion 3.00
477 DJu,BBr,T & T Again,pt.4,
    A:Legion 3.00
478 DJu,BBr,T & T Again,pt.7,
    A:Legion,Linear Man 3.00

479 EH,Red Glass Trilogy#2 . . . . . . 3.00
480 JOy,DJu,BMc,TG,BBr,CS,
    Revenge of the Krypton
    Man,pt.3. . . . . 3.00
481 1st TG Supes,DHz,V:Parasite . 3.00
482 TG,DHz,V:Parasite 3.00
483 TG,DHz,V:Blindspot 3.00
484 TG,Blackout #1,V:Mr.Z 3.00
485 TG,DHz,Blackout #5,A:Mr.Z . . 3.00
486 TG,V:Purge 3.00
487 TG,DHz,X-mas,A:Agent
    Liberty 3.00
488 TG,Panic in the Sky,pt.3,
    V:Brainiac. 4.00
489 TG,Panic in the Sky,Epiloge . . 4.00
490 TG,A:Agent Liberty,Husque. . . 3.00
491 TG,DHz,V:Cerberus,Metallo . . 3.00
492 WS(c),V:Sons of Liberty,
    A:Agent Liberty 3.00
493 TG,Blaze/Satanus War,pt.1 . . . 3.00
494 TG,DHz,I:Kismet 3.00
495 TG,DHz,A:Forever People,
    Darkseid 3.00
496 V:Mr.Mxyzptlk,C:Doomsday . . . 5.00
496a 2nd printing 2.50
497 TG,Doomsday Pt.3,A:Maxima,
    Bloodwynd. 5.00
497a 2nd printing 2.50
498 TG,Funeral for a Friend#1 . . . . 4.00
498a 2nd Printing. 2.50
499 TG,DHz,Funeral for a
    Friend#5 . . . . 3.50
500 JOy(c),B:KK(s),TG,DJu,JBg,JG,
    BBr,Bagged,Superman in limbo,
    I:Four Supermen,Direct Sales . 3.50
500a Newsstand Ed. 3.00
500b Platinum Ed. 20.00
501 TG,Reign of Supermen#2,Direct
    Sales,Die-Cut(c),Mini-poster
    F:Superboy 3.00
501a Newstand Ed. 2.25
502 TG,A:Supergirl,V:Stinger. 2.25
503 TG,Cyborg Superman Vs.
    Superboy 2.50
504 TG,DHz,A:All Supermen,
    V:Mongul 2.50
505 TG,DHz,Superman returns to
    Metropolis,Holografx(c) 3.00
505a Newstand Ed. 2.25
506 TG,DHz,A:Guardian 2.50
507 Spilled Blood#1,V:Bloodsport . . 2.50
508 BKi,A:Challengers of the
    Unknown 2.50
509 BKi,A:Auron 2.50
510 BKi,Bizarro's World #2,
    V:Bizarro 2.50
511 BKi,A:Guardian 2.50
512 BKi,V:Parasite. 2.50
513 BKi,Battle for Metropolis #4 . . . 2.50
514 BKi,Fall of Metropolis #4. . . . . . 2.50
515 BKi,Massacre in Metropolis . . . 2.50
516 BKi,Zero Hour,I:Alpha
    Centurion. 2.50
517 BKi,deathtrap 2.50
518 BKi 2.50
519 KK,BKi,Secret of Superman's
    Tomb 2.50
520 SI,KK,JMz,100 crimes at
    midnight. 2.50
521 SI,KK,R:Thorn. 2.50
522 SI,KKIdentity known 2.50
523 SI,KK,Death of C.Kent,pt.2 . . . 2.50
524 SI,KK,Death of C.Kent,pt.6
    [New Miraweb format begins] . . 2.50
525 SI,KK. 2.50
526 Bloodsport vs. Bloodsport. 2.50
527 KK,SI,JMz,The Return 2.50
528 Trial of Superman,prelude 2.50
529 Trial of Superman 2.50
530 KK,SI,JMz,Trial of Superman . . 2.50
531 KK,SI,JMz,Trial of Superman,
    concl. 2.50

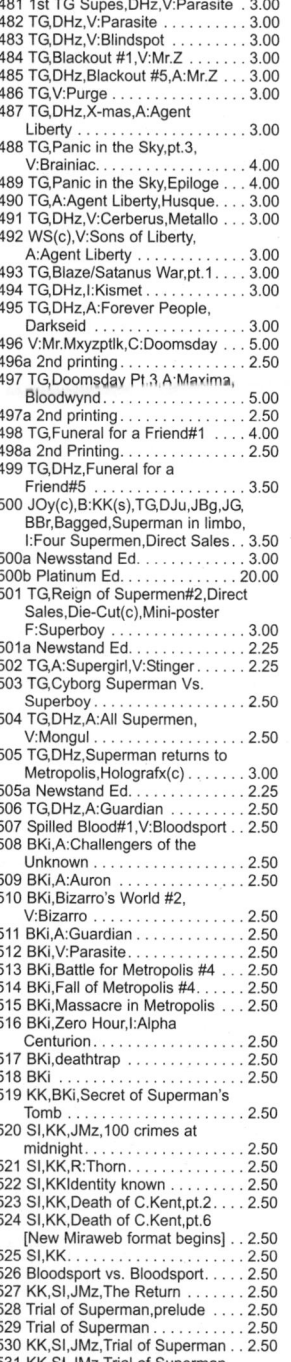

Adventures of Superman #502
© DC Comics Inc.

532 KK,SI,JMz, return of Lori
    Lemaris 2.50
533 KK,SI,JMz. 2.50
534 KK,SI,JMz,V:Lord Satannus . . . 2.50
535 KK,SI,JMz,Lois & LoriLemaris . 2.50
536 Identity Crisis,pt.1:Cages 2.50
537 KK,SI,JMz. 2.50
538 KK,SI,JMz,Fatal Obsession . . . 2.50
539 F:Guardian and the Newsboy
    Legion 2.50
540 KK(s),TyD,KIS,A:Ferro, Final
    Night tie-in 2.50
541 KK(s),SI,JMz,on Honeymoon,
    A:Superboy,Tana Moon,Kekona 2.50
542 KK&JOy(s),PR,JMz,V:Misa. . . . 2.50
543 KK,SI,JMz,Honeymoon's Over . 2.50
544 KK(s),SI,JMz,Who Killed Clark
    Kent in broad daylight? 2.50
545 KK(s),SEa,JMz,Return of the
    Atomic Skull,new blue costume 2.50
546 KK(s),SI,JMz,V:Metallo, uses
    new powers 2.50
547 KK(s),SI,JMz,Superman goes
    to Kandor,A:The Atom 2.50
548 KK(s),SI,JMz,V:Lex Luthor 2.50
549 KK(s),SI,JMz,F:Jimmy Olsen . . 2.50
550 KK(s),SI,TGu,JMz,DRo, 48pg. . 3.50
551 DJu,TGu,DRo,Genesis,
    V:Cyborg 2.50
552 KK,TGu,DRo,V:Parasite 2.50
553 KK,TGu,DRo,disappearances. . 2.50
554 KK,TGu,DRo,disappearances. . 2.50
555 KK,TRu,DRo,Red/Blue x-over . 2.50
556 KK,TRu,DRo,Red & Blue 2.50
557 KK,VS,DRo,Millennium Giants
    x-over. 2.50
558 KK,JOy,DRo,silver age?,pt.1 . . 2.50
559 KK,JOy,DRo,silver age?,pt.2 . . 2.50
560 KK,JOy,DRo,silver age?,pt.3 . . 2.50
561 KK,JOy,TGu,DRo,Waverider. . . 2.50
562 KK(s),JOy,TGu,DRo,Lexcom . . 2.50
563 RMz,TGb,TP,City of the
    Future, pt.4 x-over. 2.50
564 KK&JOy(s),TGu,DRo,
    A:Geo-Force 2.50
565 KK&JOy(s),TGu,DRo,A:JLA . . . 2.50
566 KK&JOy(s),TGu,DRo,V:Lex
    Luthor 2.50
567 KK&JOy(s),DRo,PR,. 2.50
568 LSi(s),TMo,DRo,V:Metallo 2.50
569 LSi(s),TMo,DRo,V:S.C.U. 2.50
570 RMz&TPe(s),TGb,TP,
    A:JLA,pt.2 x-over. 2.50
571 LSi(s),DRo,V:Atomic Skull 2.50

572 RF,SB,Strange Visitor,pt.2	2.50
573 SI,SEp,DRo,flashbacks	2.50
574 SI,F:Obsession	2.50
575 SI,F:Lex Luthor	2.50
576 SI,V:Brainiac 13	2.50
577 SI,JMz,A:Luthor	2.50
578 JMD(s),JMz,alien utopia	2.50
579 JMD(s),Lois has vanished	2.50
580 JMD(s),CriticalCondition,pt.2	2.50
581 JMD(s),V:Adversary,Lex Luthor	2.50
582 JMD(s),Arkham,pt.2	4.00
583 JMD,JMz,Superman:Emperor.	2.50
584 JMD(s),JMz,V:Devouris	2.50
585 JMD,JMz,V:LexLuthor,Satanus	2.50
586 JMD,JMz,V:Satanus	2.50
587 JMD,JMz,V:Satanus	2.50
588 JoC,JMz,V:Satanus	2.50
589 JoC,JMz,Return toKrypton,pt.2	2.50
590 JoC,JMz,Luthor's Lackey?	2.50
591 MWm,Infestation x-over,pt.2	2.50
592 JoC,JMz,F:Jimmy Olson	2.50
593 JoC,JMz,V:Manchester Black	2.50
594 JoC,MeW,All-Out War,x-over	2.50
595 JoC,MeW,Casualties of War	2.50
596 JoC,MeW,No Superman's Job	6.00
597 JoC,Joker:Last Laugh tie-in	2.50
598 JoC,JMz,F:Perry White	2.50
599 JoC,JMz,Russian submarine	2.50
600 JoC,Lex Luthor, 64-pg	5.00
601 JoC,Cult of Persuasion,pt.1	2.50
602 JoC,Cult of Persuasion,pt.2	2.50
603 JoC,F:Superbaby	2.50
604 JoC,V:Ultra-Man	2.50
605 JoC,Superbaby, concl.	2.50
606 JoC,Return to KryptonII,pt.2	2.50
607 F:Argent	2.50
608 JoC,Ending Battle,pt.2	2.50
609 JoC,Ending Battle,pt.6	2.50
610 JoC,in Guatemala	2.50
611 Lost Hearts,pt.2 x-over	2.50
612 JoC,Hollow Man	2.50
613 JoC,Captain Cold	2.50
614 JoC,Hollow Men	2.50
615 JoC,Hollow Men	2.50
616 JoC,Hollow Men	2.50
617 JoC,V:two Mr.Mxyzptlks	2.50
618 JoC,CAd,Mxy Twins	2.50
619 JoC,Lois and Clark	2.50
620 JoC,the Candidate	2.50
621 JoC,Minuteman	2.50
622 prophecy of the Minuteman	2.50
623 Superman & Lois	2.50
624 KIK,Strange New Visitor	2.50
625 Godfall,pt.2	3.00
626 Godfall,pt.5	2.50
627 Special Crimes Unit	2.50
628 F:Wond.Woman & Gr.Lantern	2.50
629 Lois,Replikon	2.50
630 Hostage situation	2.50
631 Lois behind enemy lines	2.50
632 V:Propaganda	2.50
633 ALa, New Parasites	2.50
634 JoC,V:Parasites	2.50
635 ALa,V:Parasites,pt.2	2.50
636 Identity Crisis aftermath	2.50
637 Ruin hunts down Lois	2.50
638 Mr.Mxyzptik returns.	2.50
639 IaC,NRn,Lightning Strikes,pt.2	2.50
640 Unmasking of Ruin	2.50
641 Betrayal	2.50
642 Sacrifice,x-over, pt.3	2.50
643 Where to go from here	2.50
644 V:Zatanna	2.50
645 Omac assault	2.50
646 Myx is back	2.50
647 V:Ruin	2.50
648 KIK,Infinite Crisis tie-in	2.50
649 KIK,This is your life, Superman	3.00

Becomes:

SUPERMAN

650 KBk,Up,Up & Away,pt.1,x-over	2.50
651 KBk,Up,Up & Away,pt.3,x-over	2.50

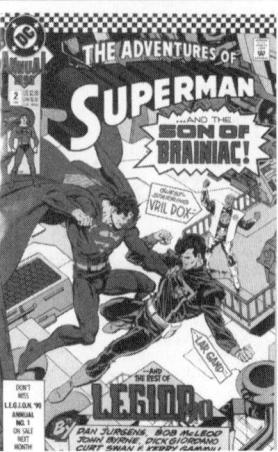

The Adventures of Superman Ann. #2
© DC Comics, Inc.

652 KBk,Up,Up & Away,pt.5,x-over	3.00
653 KBk,Up,Up & Away,pt.7,x-over	3.00
654 KBk,CPa,V:Intergang	3.00
655 KBk,CPa,Time-traveling magic	3.00
656 KBk,CPa,V:Subjekt-17	3.00
657 KBk,CPa, End of Civilization	3.00
658 KBk,CPa, End of Civilization	3.00
659 KBk,RL,CPa,F:Krypto	3.00
660 KBk,CPa,Camelot Falls, pt.1	3.00
661 KBk,CPa,Camelot Falls, pt.2	3.00
662 KBk,CPa,Young Gods.	3.00
663 KBk,CPa,Young Gods.	3.00
664 KBk,CPa,Camelot Falls	3.00
665 KBk,RL,F:Jimmy Olson.	3.00
666 KBk,WS,Goes to Hell, 48-pgs.	4.00
667 KBk,Camelot Falls, pt.1	3.00
668 KBk,Camelot Falls, pt.2	3.00
669 KBk,Third Kryptonian	3.00
670 DGr,RL,Third Kryptonian,pt.2	3.00
671 Insect Queen, pt.1	3.00
672 Insect Queen,pt.2	3.00
673 Final battle on the Moon	3.00
674 V:Paragon	3.00
675 F:Paragon & Daxam,48-pg.	4.00
675a variant (c) (1:10)	4.00
676 Parasite returns	3.00
677 A:Green Lantern	3.00
677a variant (c) (1:10)	3.00
678 V:Atlas, for Metropolis.	3.00
679 Two Supermen	3.00
680 Atlas, pt.4, Krypto to the rescue	3.00
681 New Krypton, pt.2	3.00
682 Humankind vs. Kryptonians	3.00
681a thru 682a variant (c)s (1:10)	3.00
Ann.#1 JSn(c),DJu,I:Word Bringer	3.00
Ann.#2 CS/JBy,KGa/DG,BMc, A:L.E.G.I.O.N.'90 (Lobo)	4.00
Ann.#3 BHi,JRu,DG, Armageddon 2001.	3.00
Ann.#4 BMc,A:Lobo,Guy Gardner, Eclipso tie-in	3.00
Ann.#5 TG,I:Sparx	2.75
Ann.#6 MMi(c),Elseworlds Story	3.00
Ann.#7 Year One Story	4.00
Ann.#8 Legends o/t Dead Earth	3.00
Ann.#9 Pulp Heroes (Western)	4.00
Spec.#1,000,000 ALa&DAn(s)LMa, A:Teen Titans, V:Solaris	3.00
GN Vol. 1 Up, Up and Away	7.00
GN Vol. 2 Never-Ending Battle	7.00
Spec. Superman Through the Ages.	4.00
Spec. Superman: Mongul rep.(2008)	5.00

SUPERMAN'S BUDDY
1954

1 w/costume, giveaway	2,000.00
1 w/out costume, giveaway	1,000.00

SUPERMAN'S CHRISTMAS ADVENTURE

1 (1940) giveaway	6,500.00
2 (1944) giveaway	1,700.00

SUPERMAN AND THE GREAT CLEVELAND FIRE
1948

1 for Hospital Fund, giveaway	900.00

SUPERMAN (miniature)
1942

1 Py-Co-Pay Tooth Powder Give- Away	1,000.00
2 CS,Superman Time Capsule	600.00
3 CS,Duel in Space	500.00
4 CS,Super Show in Metropolis	500.00

SUPERMAN RECORD COMIC
1966

1 w/record	300.00
1 w/out record	150.00

SUPERMAN SPECTACULAR
1982

1 A:Luthor & Terra-Man	2.50

SUPERMAN-TIM STORE PAMPHLETS
1942

Superman-Tim store Monthly Membership Pamphlets, stories, games	
(1942), each	2,000.00
(1943), each	600.00
(1944), each	550.00
(1945), each	450.00
(1946), color(c) each	550.00
(1947), color(c) each	400.00
(1948), color(c) each	350.00
(1949), color(c) each	350.00
(1950), color(c) each	400.00
Superman-Tim stamp albums,	
(1946)	400.00
(1947) Superman story	600.00
(1948)	400.00

SUPERMAN WORKBOOK
1945

1 rep. Superman #14	1,300.00

SUPERMAN
[2nd Regular Series], 1987

1 JBy,TA,I:Metallo	6.00
2 JBy,TA,V:Luthor	3.00
3 JBy,TA,Legends tie-in	3.00
4 JBy,KK,V:Bloodsport	3.00
5 JBy,KK,V:Host	3.00
6 JBy,KK,V:Host	3.00
7 JBy,KK,V:Rampage	3.00
8 JBy,KK,A:Superboy,Legion	3.00
9 JBy,KK,V:Joker	5.00
10 JBy,KK,V:Rampage	3.00
11 JBy,KK,V:Mr.Mxyzptlk	3.00
12 JBy,KK,A:Lori Lemerias	3.00
13 JBy,KK,Millennium	3.00
14 JBy,KK,A:Green Lantern	3.00
15 JBy,KK,I:New Prankster	3.00
16 JBy,KK,A:Prankster.	4.00

Superman, 2nd Series #30
© DC Comics Inc.

17 JBy,KK,O:Silver Banshee 3.00
18 MMi,KK,A:Hawkman 3.00
19 JBy,V:Skyhook 3.00
20 JBy,KK,A:Doom Patrol 3.00
21 JBy,A:Supergirl 4.00
22 JBy,A:Supergirl 4.00
23 MMi,CR,O:Silver Banshee 3.00
24 KGa,V:Rampage 3.00
25 KGa,V:Brainiac 3.00
26 KGa,BBr,V:Baron Sunday 3.00
27 KGa,BBr,V:Guardian 3.00
28 KGa,BBr,Supes Leaves Earth . . 3.00
29 DJu,BBr,V:Word Bringer 3.00
30 KGa,DJu,A:Lex Luthor 3.00
31 DJu,PCu,V:Mxyzptlk 3.00
32 KGa,V:Mongul 3.00
33 KGa,A:Cleric 3.00
34 KGa,V:Skyhook 3.00
35 CS,KGa,A:Brainiac 3.00
36 JOy,V:Prankster 3.00
37 JOy,A:Guardian 3.00
38 JOy,Jimmy Olsen Vanished 3.00
39 JOy,KGa,V:Husque 3.00
40 JOy,V:Four Armed Terror 3.00
41 JOy,Day of Krypton Man #1,
    A:Lobo 3.50
42 JOy,Day of Krypton Man #4,
    V:Draaga 3.50
43 JOy,V:Krypton Man 2.50
44 JOy,A:Batman 2.50
45 JOy,F:Jimmy Olsen's Dairy 2.50
46 DJu,JOy,A:Jade,Obsidian,
    I:New Terra-Man 2.50
47 JOy,Soul Feast #2,V:Blaze 2.50
48 CS,Sinbad Contract #1 . . . . 2.50
49 JOy,Krisis of K.Kryptonite#1 . . . . 3.00
50 JBy,KGa,DJu,JOy,BBr,CS,Krisis
    of Krimson Kryptonite #4,
    Clark Proposes To Lois 6.00
50a 2nd printing 2.50
51 JOy,I:Mr.Z 2.50
52 KGa,V:Terra-Man 2.50
53 JOy,Superman reveals i.d.. . . . . . 3.50
53a 2nd Printing 2.50
54 JOy,KK,Time & Time Again#3. . . 2.50
55 JOy,KK,Time & Time Again#6. . . 2.50
56 EH,KK,Red Glass Trilogy#1 . . . . 2.50
57 JOy,DJu,BBr,ATi,JBg,BMc,TG,
    Revenge o/t Krypton Man #2 . . 3.50
58 DJu,BBr,I:Bloodhounds 2.50
59 DJu,BBr,A:Linear Men 2.50
60 DJu,EB,I:Agent Liberty,
    V:Intergang 2.50

61 DJu,BBr,A:Waverider,
    V:Linear Men 2.50
62 DJu,BBr,Blackout #4,A:Mr.Z 2.50
63 DJu,A:Aquaman 2.50
64 JG,Christmas issue 2.50
65 DJu,Panic in the Sky#2,
    I:New Justice League 3.50
66 DJu,Panic in the Sky#6,
    V:Brainiac 8.00
67 DJu,Aftermath 2.50
68 DJu,V:Deathstroke 2.50
69 WS(c),DJu,A:Agent Liberty 2.50
70 DJu,BBr,A:Robin,V:Vampires 2.50
71 DJu,Blaze/Satanus War 2.50
72 DJu,Crisis at Hand#2 . . . . 2.50
73 DJu,A:Waverider,V:Linear
    Men,C:Doomsday 5.00
73a 2nd printing 2.50
74 DJu,V:Doomsday,A:JLA 8.00
74a 2nd printing 2.00
75 DJu,V:Doomsday,D:Superman,
    Collectors Ed. 20.00
75a newstand Ed. 9.00
75b 2nd printing 4.00
75c 3rd printing 2.50
75d 4th Printing 2.50
75e Platinum Ed. 65.00
76 DJu,BBr,Funeral for Friend#4 . . . 3.00
77 DJu,BBr,Funeral for Friend#8 . . . 3.00
78 DJu,BBr,Reign of Supermen#3,
    Die-Cut(c),Mini poster,F:Cyborg
    Supes,A:Doomsday 3.00
78a Newsstand Ed. 2.50
79 DJu,BBr,Memorial Service for
    Clark 3.00
80 DJu,BBr,Coast City Blows up,
    V:Mongul 4.00
81 DJu,O:Cyborg Superman 3.50
82 DJu,Chromium(c),A:All Supermen,
    V:Cyborg Superman 15.00
82a Newstand Ed. 5.00
83 DJu,A:Batman 3.00
84 DJu,V:Toyman 3.00
85 DJu,V:Toyman 3.00
86 DJu,A:Sun Devils 3.00
87 DJu(c&s),SI,JRu,Bizzaro's
    World#1, R:Bizarro 3.00
88 DJu(c&s),SI,JRu,Bizzaro's
    World#5, D:Bizarro 3.00
89 DJu(c&s),V:Cadmus Project 3.00
90 DJu(c&s),Battle for
    Metropolis#3 . . . . 3.00
91 DJu(c&s),Fall of Metropolis#3. . . 3.00
92 Massacre in Metropolis. 3.00
93 Zero Hour,A:Batman 3.00
94 Conduit 3.00
95 Brainiac 3.00
96 Virtual Reality 3.00
97 Shadow Dragon 3.00
98 R:Shadow Strike 3.00
99 R:Agent Liberty 3.00
100 BBr,DJu,Death of C.Kent,pt.1. . 4.00
100a Collectors Edition 4.00
101 Death of Clark Kent,pt.5
    [New Miraweb format begins] . . 3.00
102 DJu,A:Captain Marvel. 3.00
103 O:Arclight 3.00
104 Revenge of Apokolips. 3.00
105 A:Green Lantern 3.00
106 DJu,RF,The Trial of Superman . 3.00
107 DJu,RF,The Trial of Superman . 3.00
108 DJu,RF,The Trial of Superman . 3.00
109 DJu,RF,V:Kill Fee 3.00
110 F:Plastic Man 3.00
111 DJu,RF,Cat Grant in charge . . . 3.00
112 DJu,RF,Lois & Clark 3.00
113 DJu(s),RF,JRu, ... 3.00
114 DJu(s),RF,JRu,A:Brainiac 3.00
115 DJu(s),RF,JRu,Lois leaves
    Metropolis 3.00

116 DJu(s),RF,JRu,battle city siga
    concl., V:Daxamite,B.U. Teen
    Titans preview 3.00
117 DJu(s),RF,JRu,V: his own
    robots, Final Night tie-in 3.00
118 DJu(s),RF,JRu,F:time-lost
    Legion of Super Heroes 3.00
119 DJu(s),RF,JRu,A:Legion of
    Super Heroes 3.00
120 DJu(s),RF,JRu, ... 3.00
121 DJu(s),RF,JRu,They Call it
    Suicide Slum 3.00
122 DJu(s),RF,JRu,Lois visits
    Fortress of Solitude 3.00
123 DJu(s),RF,Jru,Superman gets
    New Costume 4.00
123a collector's edition, glow-in-
    the-dark cover, ... 6.00
124 DJu(s),RF,JRu,A:Scorn, prince
    of Kandor 2.50
125 DJu(s),RF,JRu,Kandor and
    Metropolis,A:Atom 2.50
126 DJu(s),RF,JRu,A:Batman 2.50
127 DJu(s),RF,JRu,F:Jimmy Olsen . 2.50
128 DJu(s),RF,JRu, Genesis tie-in . 2.50
129 DJu(s),PR,JRu,A:Scorn 2.50
130 DJu(s),RF,JRu,dragon's tooth. . 2.50
131 DJu(s),RF,JRu,Luthor &
    Contessa's kid 2.50
132 DJu,RF,JRu,Red/Blue x-over . . 2.50
133 DJu,RF,JRu,Millennium Guard . 2.50
134 DJu,RF,JRu,Millennium Giants. 2.50
135 DJu,RF,JRu,aftermath. 3.50
136 DJu,PR,JRu,The Superman
    of 2999 A.D., pt.1 . . . . 2.50
137 DJu,PR,JRu,2999 AD,pt.2 . . . . 2.50
138 DJu,PR,JRu,2999 AD,pt.3 . . . . 2.50
139 DJu(s),JSn,JRu,V:Dominus . . . 2.50
140 RMz(s),TGb,TP,City of the
    Future, pt.3 x-over 2.50
141 DJu(s),SEa,JRu,I:Outburst 2.50
142 DJu(s),JRu,F:Outburst 2.50
143 DJu(s),SEp,JRu, ... 2.50
144 DJu(s),SEp,JRu,V:Lex Luthor. . 2.50
145 DJu(s),SEp,JRu,hate mail 2.50
146 DJu(s),SEp,JRu,V:Toyman 2.50
147 RMz(s),TGb,BAn,A:JLA,pt.1 . . 2.50
148 DJu(s),SEp,JRu, ... 2.50
149 RF,SB,Strange Visitor,pt.1 . . . . 2.50
150 DJu(s),SEp,JRu,48-pg. 3.50
150a foil cover 4.50
151 JLb,MMK,Faster than a
    speeding bullet 3.00
152 JLb,MMK. 2.50
153 JLb,MMK,V:Imperiex. 3.00

Superman 2nd Series #137
© DC Comics Inc.

154 JLb,CaS,V:Brainiac 13 . . . . . . 17.00	Ann.#5 Bloodlines#6,DL,I:Myriad. . . 3.00	GN Superman's Metropolis, RLo &
155 JLb,CaS,F:Superboy. 7.00	Ann.#6 Elseworlds Story 3.50	RTs(s),TMK, in Fritz Lang's
156 JLb,CaS,V:Parasite. 5.00	Ann.#7 WS(c),Year One Annual	Metropolis (Elseworlds 1996) . . 6.00
157 JLb,CaS,Lois vs. Superman?. . 5.00	A:Dr. Occult 4.50	GN The Superman Monster. 7.00
158 JLb,CaS,CriticalCondition,pt.1 . 3.00	Ann.#8 Legends o/t Dead Earth . . . 3.00	GN A Nation Divided 5.00
159 JLb,CaS,F:Green Lantern. 3.00	Ann.#9 Pulp Heroes (High-	GN Superman: The Odyssey. 5.00
160 JLb,CaS,Arkham,pt.1 . . . . 10.00	Adventure) DJu 4.50	GN Peace on Earth, oversized . . . 10.00
161 JLb,CaS,Superman:Emperor? . 3.50	Ann.#10 DJu(s),PR,Clv,BWr,	GN Superman Red/Superman Blue,
162 JLb,CaS,A:Aquaman,pt.1 . . . . . 3.00	Ghosts 3.00	V:Toyman, Cyborg, Superman
163 JLb,PaP,CaS,F:Aquaman,pt.2 . 2.50	Ann.#11 JoP,AAd(c),JLApe:Gorilla	split into two entities (1997). . . . 4.00
164 JLb,CaS,V:Bizarro 2.50	Warfare 3.50	Deluxe, 3-D cover 5.00
165 JLb,AAd,A:Linear Man 2.50	Ann.#12 Planet DC 3.50	GN Superman: Silver Banshee, 48pg,
166 JLb,CaS,O:Superman(new) . . 12.00	Ann. #13 DGr,RL,Superman Family 4.00	prestige format (1998). 5.00
166a holofoil(c) 7.00	Spec.#1,000,000 DAn&ALa(s),NBy . 2.50	GN Superman: Speeding Bullets,
167 JLb,CaS,Return toKrypton,pt.1 . 2.50	Giant Ann.#1 Replica edition 5.00	EB (Elseworlds 1993) 6.00
168 JLb,CaS,Lord of the Ring,pt.1 . 6.00	Giant #1 80-page. 5.00	GN Superman, Under a Yellow Sun
169 MWm,Infestation x-over,pt.1 . . 2.50	Giant #2 80-page. 5.00	by Clark Kent,KGa,EB (1994) . . 6.00
170 JLb,CaS,DK,V:Mogul 2.50	Giant #3 80-page. 6.00	GN Superman: The Wedding Album,
171 JLb,OurWorlds atWar,prelude. . 2.50	Spec.#0 PeerPressure,pt.3 (1994) . 2.50	collector's edition, 96 pg.,
172 JLb,All-Out War. 2.50	Spec.King of the World, foil 5.00	cardstock cover 5.00
173 JLb,Casualties of War. 2.50	Spec.King of the World, reg. 4.00	GN War of the Worlds,Elseworlds . . 6.00
174 JLb,CaS,War aftermath 2.50	Spec. Superman: Lois Lane,	GN Superman, Inc. 7.00
175 JLb,CaS,Last Laugh,48-pg . . . 3.50	Girlfrenzy (1998) 2.50	GN Superman: Mann & Superman . 6.00
176 JLb,IaC,NRd,F:Dr. Foster 2.50	Spec.#1 WS,V:L.Luthor,	GN Superman:Where is thy Sting? . 7.00
177 JLb,CaS,F:Toyman,Metallo. . . 2.50	Sandman (1992) 6.00	GN Superman & Savage Dragon:
178 JLb,CaS,F:Uncle Sam 2.50	Spec. Superman Plus One (1997). . 3.00	Chicago, x-over, EL (2002) 6.00
179 JLb,African-American hero 2.50	Spec.#1 Superman: The Earth	Metropolis, x-over,KK,JBg. 5.00
180 JLb,IaC,NRd,V:Dracula. 3.50	Stealers, JBy,CS,JOy (1988). . . 3.50	
181 JLb,CaS,F:Bizarro. 3.50	2nd printing 3.00	**SUPERMAN**
182 JLb,CaS,F:Suicide Squad. . . . 2.50	Spec. Superman:Emperor?(2000). . 3.50	**ADVENTURES**
183 JLb,CaS,Clarke fired from job . 2.50	Spec. Superman Forever,KK,DJu,LSi,	**Sept., 1996**
184 PFe,CaS,Return to Krypton II . . 2.50	JBy,SI,DG, Luthor's kidnapped	1 PDi(s),RBr,TA, from animated
185 BA,PFe(c),baseball game. 2.50	daughter (1998). 5.00	TV show 3.00
186 PFe,CaS,Ending Battle,pt.1 . . . 2.50	Deluxe ed.,AxR(c), lenticular. . . 6.00	2 thru 20 . . . . @2.50
187 PFe,CaS,Ending Battle,pt.5 . . . 2.50	Spec.#1 Superman: The Legacy of	21 Supergirl Adventures, 64pg. . . . 5.50
188 F:Lois Lane. 2.50	Superman,WS,JG,F:Guardian,	22 thru 66 (c) . . . . @2.50
189 PFe,Lost Hearts,pt.1 x-over . . . 2.50	Waverider,Sinbad (1993). 4.00	Ann.#1 JoS,DDv,V:Akamin 4.50
190 SSe(c),SMc,rogue robot 2.50	Spec. Superman & Savage Dragon:	Spec. #1 Superman vs. Lobo –
190a spec.newsstand ed.,56-pg. . . 4.50	Metropolis, KK,JBg,x-over. 5.00	Misery in Space, DvM,MM,
191 F:The Flash. 2.50	Spec. Superman/Toyman (1996). . 2.50	A:Man of Tomorrow 4.00
192 Supergirl vs. Radion 4.00	Spec. Team Superman, MMr(s),	
193 Supergirl vs. Radion 2.50	DHz,48-page,F:Superboy,	**SUPERMAN/BATMAN**
194 SMc,I:Ed 2.50	Supergirl & Steel 3.00	**Aug., 2003**
195 SMc,Futuresmiths. 2.50	Spec. 3-D #1 LSi,V:Mainframe 4.00	1 JLb,V:Metallo 30.00
196 SMc,new adversary 2.50	Spec. Whatever Happened to the	2 JLb,both injured 10.00
197 SMc,deaf Superman,Krypto . . 2.50	Man of Tomorrow. 6.00	3 JLb,V:Gorilla Grodd 10.00
198 SMc,V:Bizarro. 2.50	Spec. Superman Y2K,JBg (1999) . . 5.00	4 F:Captain Atom,Luthor. 6.00
199 SMc,Supergirl origins 2.50	Newstime-The Life and Death of	5 JLb(s),V:Luthor 6.00
200 SMc,Futuresmiths, 48-pg. 5.00	the Man of Steel-Magazine,	6 JLb(s),V:Luthor 13.00
201 KIK,Strange New Visitor 5.00	DJu,BBr,JOy,JG,JBg 3.25	7 JLb(s),F:Robin,Superboy. 8.00
202 Godfall,pt.3 . . . . 5.00	Spec.#1 Superman Gallery (1993) . 3.00	8 Supergirl from Krypton,pt.1 . . . . . 6.00
203 Godfall,pt.6 . . . . 4.00	Superman Secret Files, DJu,JOy,	9 Supergirl from Krypton,pt.2 . . . . . 4.00
204 JLe,SW,I:FatherLeone,40-pg. . 3.00	etc.,inc. O:Superman (1997). . . 10.00	
205 JLe,SW,For Tomorrow,pt.2 . . . 3.50	Secret Files #1 Superman Villains. 10.00	
206 JLe,SW,For Tomorrow,pt.3 . . . 3.00	Secret Files #2. . . . . 10.00	
207 JLe,SW,For Tomorrow,pt.4 . . . 3.00	Secret Files #1 Our Worlds at War 10.00	
208 JLe,SW,For Tomorrow,pt.5 . . . 3.00	Secret Files #1 President Luthor . . 10.00	
209 JLe,SW,For Tomorrow,pt.6 . . . 3.00	Secret Files 2004. . . . . 10.00	
210 JLe,SW,For Tomorrow,pt.7 . . . 2.50	Spec. Secret Files 2005. . . . . 5.00	
211 JLe,SW,For Tomorrow. 2.50	Spec. Metropolis Secret Files #1 . . 5.00	
212 JLe,SW,Superman vanishes. . . 2.50	Spec. Team Superman Secret Files 5.00	
213 JLe,SW,For Tomorrow 2.50	Spec. 1-shot,Superman:Lex 2000,	
214 JLe,SW,For Tomorrow 2.50	JLb,TyH,DoM,Vote for Lex 3.50	
215 JLe,SW,For Tomorrow 3.50	Spec. Superman vs. Darkseid:	
216 IaC,NRd,Lightning Strikes. . . . 3.50	Apokolips Now, MSh(s),48-pg. . 3.00	
217 EBe,new Fortress of Solitude. . 5.00	Spec. Blood of my Ancestors. 7.00	
218 EBe,I:Blackrock. 2.50	GN Death of Superman rep.(1993) . 6.00	
219 EBe,Sacrifice, x-over, pt.1 . . . . 5.00	Later printings 6.00	
220 EBe(c),Return of the Supermen 2.50	Platinum Edition 15.00	
221 EBe,V:Bizarro 2.50	GN Superman At Earth's End	
222 EBe,Crisis Begins. 2.50	(Elseworlds 1995) 5.00	
223 EBe,Infinite Crisis tie-in. 2.50	GN Superman: Distant Fires, HC,GK,	
224 EBe,Infinite Crisis tie-in. 2.50	nuclear winter (1997). 6.00	
225 Infinite Crisis tie-in 2.50	GN Superman: Earth Day 1991, KGa	
226 This is Your Life, Superman . . . 2.50	Metropolis Clean-Up 5.50	
Ann.#1 RF,BBr,A:Titano 4.00	GN Superman For Earth (1991) . . . 5.00	
Ann.#2 RF,BBr,R:Newsboy Legion	GN Superman: Kal, Medieval	
& Guardian 4.00	Superman (Elseworlds 1995) . . 6.00	
Ann.#3 DAb(1st Work),TA,DG,	GN Superman: Last God of Krypton 5.00	
Armageddon 2001. . . . . 9.00	GN Last Stand on Krypton (2003) . . 7.00	
Ann.#3a 2nd printing(silver). 3.00		
Ann.#4 Eclipso 3.00		

Superman/Batman #1
© DC Comics, Inc.

All comics prices listed are for *Near Mint* condition.

10 Supergirl from Krypton,pt.3 . . . . . 4.00
11 Supergirl from Krypton,pt.4 . . . . . 3.50
12 Supergirl from Krypton,pt.5 . . . . . 3.50
13 JLb(s) V:Darkseid 4.00
14 JLb(s),Absolute Power,pt.1 . . . . . 3.50
15 JLb(s),Absolute Power,pt.2 . . . . . 3.25
16 JLb(s),Absolute Power,pt.3 . . . . . 3.25
17 JLb(s),Absolute Power,pt.4 . . . . . 3.25
18 JLb(s),Absolute Power,pt.5 . . . . . 3.25
19 JLb(s),IaC,NRd,F:Supergirl. 3.00
20 JLb(s),With a Vengeance,pt.1 . . . . 6.00
21 JLb(s),With a Vengeance,pt.2. . . 3.00
22 JLb(s),With a Vengeance,pt.3 . . 3.00
23 JLb(s),With a Vengeance,pt.4 . . . 3.00
24 JLb(s),With a Vengeance,pt.5 . . . 3.00
25 JLb(s),With a Vengeance,concl . 3.00
25a variant (c) 3.00
26 40-pg. 4.00
27 F:Power Girl & The Huntress . . . 3.00
28 The Enemies Among Us,pt.1 . . . 3.00
29 The Enemies Among Us,pt.2 . . . 3.00
30 The Enemies Among Us,pt.3 . . . 3.00
31 V:Lex Luthor 3.00
32 ALa,F:Lex Luthor 3.00
33 ALa,V:Aliens 3.00
34 PtL,V:Metal Men 3.00
35 PtL,V:Metal Men 3.00
36 PtL,V:Metal Men, concl. 3.00
37 Torment, pt.1 . . . . 3.00
37a variant (c) (1:10) 3.00
38 Torment, pt.2 . . . . 3.00
39 Torment, pt.3 . . . . 3.00
40 Torment, pt.4 . . . . 3.00
41 Torment, pt.5 . . . . 3.00
42 Torment, concl.,Countdown tie-in 3.00
43 DAn,ALa, MMK,Dr. Light. 3.00
44 Search for (all the) Kryptonite. . . 3.00
45 A:Aquaman 3.00
46 New color Kryptonite. 3.00
47 V:The Last Line. 3.00
48 V:All-American Boy 3.00
49 Search for Kryptonite 3.00
50 Kryptonian artifact, 48-pg.. . . . . . 4.00
50a variant (c) (1:10) 4.50
51 Tiny heroes 3.00
52 Li'l Leaguers, pt.2 . . . . 3.00
53 Super/Bat, pt.1 . . . . 3.00
54 Super/Bat, pt.2 . . . . 3.00
Ann. #1 (2006). 4.00
Ann. #2 V:Nova, 48-pg. 4.00
Spec. Secret Files (2003) 10.00

SUPERMAN & BATMAN: GENERATIONS — AN IMAGINARY TALE
1998
1 (of 4) JBy, Elseworlds 5.00
2 JBy,V:Bat-Mite 5.00
3 JBy. 5.00
4 JBy, conclusion 5.00

SUPERMAN & BATMAN: GENERATIONS II
Aug., 2001
1 (of 4) JBy,Elseworlds,48-page. . . 6.00
2 JBy,48-page. 6.00
3 JBy,48-page. 6.00
4 JBy,48-page, concl. 6.00

SUPERMAN & BATMAN: GENERATIONS III
Jan., 2003
1 (of 12) JBy,Elseworlds 3.00
2 JBy,Super Twins 3.00
3 JBy,22nd Century 3.00
4 JBy,23rd Century 3.00
5 JBy,24th Century 3.00
6 JBy,25th Century 3.00
7 JBy,26th Century 3.00

8 JBy,26th Century 3.00
9 JBy,27th Century 3.00
10 JBy,28th Century 3.00
11 JBy,29th century Superboy 3.00
12 JBy,earth destroyed 3.00

SUPERMAN & BATMAN VS ALIENS & PREDATORS
Jan., 2007
1 MSh(s),AOI 6.00
2 MSh(s),AOI, conclusion 6.00

SUPERMAN & BATMAN VS VAMPIRES AND WEREWOLVES
Oct., 2008
1 thru 4 TMd . . . . @3.00

SUPERMAN & BATMAN: WORLD'S FUNNEST
Nov., 2000
1-shot, Elseworlds,. 7.00

SUPERMAN & BUGS BUNNY
1999
1 thru 4 TP,JSon . . . . @2.50

SUPERMAN: BIRTHRIGHT
July 2003
1 (of 12) F:Jor-El,40-pg. 4.00
2 South Africa,40-pg. 3.50
3 O:retold 3.50
4 Job interview 3.50
5 anti-terrorism weapons 3.50
6 Lex & Clark 3.00
7 Inhuman alien 3.00
8 Lex Luthor 3.00
9 Lex's Plans; Krypton 3.00
10 Threat to Krypton 3.00
11 Krypton Invades Earth 3.00
12 conclusion. 3.00

SUPERMAN CONFIDENTIAL
Nov., 2006
1 TSe,Kryptonite 3.00
2 TSe,Superman vs. a Volcano . . . 3.00
3 TSe,Origin of Kryptonite, pt.1 . . . 3.00
4 TSe,Origin of Kryptonite, pt.2 . . . 3.00
5 TSe,Origin of Kryptonite, pt.3 . . . 3.00
6 TSe,Origin of Kryptonite,concl. . . 3.00
7 JP,F:Lori Lemaris. 3.00
8 JP,F:Lex,Lori, & Lois 3.00
9 F:Emerald Sentinel 3.00
10 F:Darkseid. 3.00
11 PhH,F,Jimmy Olsen, pt.1 . . . . . . 3.00
12 PhH,F:Jimmy Olsen, pt.2 . . . . . . 3.00
13 PhH,Signal to Noise,pt.2. . . . . . . 3.00
14 PhH,Signal to Noise, pt.3 . . . . . . 3.00

SUPERMAN: THE DARK SIDE
Elseworlds, Aug., 1998
1 JFM,KD,First Son of Apokolips . . 5.00
2 . . . . 5.00
3 KD, conclusion. 5.00

SUPERMAN: DAY OF DOOM
Nov., 2002
1 (of 4) DJu,BSz,F:Ty Duffy 3.00

2 DJu,BSz. 3.00
3 DJu,BSz. 3.00
4 DJu,BSz,concl. 3.00

Superman/Doomsday Hunter/Prey #3
© DC Comics, Inc.

SUPERMAN/DOOMSDAY: HUNTER/PREY
1994
1 DJu(a&s),BBr,R:Doomsday,R:Cyborg
    Superman,A:Darkseid 5.50
2 DJu(a&s),BBr,V:Doomsday,Cyborg
    Superman,A:Darkseid 5.25
3 DJu(a&s),BBr,V:Doomsday 5.25

SUPERMAN: THE DOOMSDAY WARS
1998
1 DJu,BBr,R:Doomsday 5.00
2 DJu,BBr,R:Doomsday 5.00
3 DJu,BBr,R:Doomsday 5.00

SUPERMAN FOR ALL SEASONS
June, 1998
1 (of 4) JLb,TSe, from farmboy
    to superhero 7.00
2 JLb,TSe,V:Lex Luthor 5.00
3 JLb,TSe,V:Lex Luthor 5.00
4 JLb,TSe, conclusion 5.00

SUPERMAN/GEN13
DC/Wildstorm April, 2000
1 (of 3) AH, x-over 2.50
1a variant cover (1:4) 2.50
2 AH,x-over. 2.50
2a variant cover (1:4) 2.50
3 AH, 40-pg. 3.50

SUPERMAN: LAST SON OF EARTH
July, 2000
1 (of 2) Elseworlds 6.00
2 Green Lantern's powers 6.00

SUPERMAN: METROPOLIS
Feb. 2003
1 (of 12) F:Jimmy Olsen 3.00
2 Mystery of the Tech 3.00

3 Rebecca	3.00
4 The Tech or the Devil	3.00
5 Jimmy and Lena	3.00
6 Jimmy and Lena	3.00
7 thru 12	@3.00

SUPERMAN:
THE MAN OF STEEL
1991–2003

1 B:LSi(s),DJu,BMc,JOy,BBr,TG, Revenge o/t Krypton Man#1	5.00
2 JBg,V:Cerberus	4.00
3 JBg,War of the Gods X-over	3.00
4 JBg,V:Angstrom	3.00
5 JBg,CS,V:Atomic Skull	3.00
6 JBg,Blackout#3,A:Mr.Z	3.00
7 JBg,V:Cerberus	3.00
8 KD,V:Jolt,Blockhouse	3.00
9 JBg,Panic in the Sky#1, V:Brainiac	3.50
10 JBg,Panic in the Sky#5, D:Draaga	3.00
11 JBg,V:Flashpoint	3.00
12 JBg,V:Warwolves	3.00
13 JBg,V:Cerberus	3.00
14 JBg,A:Robin,V:Vampires	3.00
15 KG,KGa,Blaze/Satanus War	3.00
16 JBg,Crisis at Hand#1	3.00
17 JBg,V:Underworld, C:Doomsday	8.00
17a 2nd printing	2.50
18 JBg,I:Doomsday,V:Underworld	10.00
18a 2nd printing	4.00
18b 3rd printing	2.50
19 JBg,Doomsday,pt.5	7.00
19a 2nd printing	2.50
20 JBg,Funeral for a Friend#3	3.00
21 JBg,Funeral for a Friend#7	3.00
22 JBg,Reign of Supermen#4,Direct Sales,Die-Cut(c),mini-poster, F:Man of Steel	2.50
22a Newsstand Ed.	2.50
23 JBg,V:Superboy	2.50
24 JBg,V:White Rabbit,A:Mongul.	2.50
25 JBg,A:Real Superman	3.00
26 JBg,A:All Supermen,V:Mongul, Cyborg Superman	2.75
27 JBg,A:Superboy,Lex Luthor	2.50
28 JBg(c),A:Steel	2.50
29 LSi(s),JBg,Spilled Blood#3, V:Hi-Tech,Blood Thirst	2.50
30 LSi(s),JBg,V:Lobo,Vinyl(c)	3.50
30a Newstand Ed.	2.50
31 MBr,A:Guardian	2.50
32 MBr,Bizarro's World#4, V:Bizarro	2.50
33 MBr,V:Parasite	2.50
34 JBg,A:Lex Men,Dubbile Men	2.50
35 JBg,Worlds Collide#1, I:Fred Bentson	2.50
36 JBf,Worlds Collide,pt.10,V:Rift A:Icon	2.50
37 JBg,Zero Hour,A:Batman	2.50
38 Mystery	2.50
39 JBg,Luthor	2.50
40 JBg,Mind Games	2.50
41 Locke	2.50
42 F:Locke	2.50
43 V:Deathtrap	2.50
44 Prologue to Death	2.50
45 JGb,DJa,Death of Clark Kent,pt.4 [New Miraweb format begins]	2.50
46 JBg,DJa,A:Shadowdragon	2.50
47 O:Bloodsport	2.50
48 JBg,Here be Monsters	2.50
49 Skyhook	2.50
50 JBg,DJa,The Trial of Superman, 48pg	4.00
51 JBg,DJa,The Trial of Superman	2.50
52 JBg,The Trial of Superman	2.50
53 JBg,DRo,A:Lex Luthor,Contessa	2.50

Superman: The Man of Steel #6
© DC Comics, Inc.

54 JBg	2.50
55 JBg,DJa, Clark dates Lori Lemaris	2.50
56 JBg,DJa, manipulator revealed.	2.50
57 RSt,JBg,DJa, more twisters	2.50
58 LSi(s),JBg,DJa,A:Supergirl	2.50
59 LSi(s),JBg,DJa,Parasite, Steel	2.50
60 LSi(s),JBg,DJa,R:Bottled City of Kandor	2.50
61 LSi(s),JBg,DJa,V:Riot	2.50
62 LSi(s),JBg,DJa, Superman looses powers, Final Night tie-in	2.50
63 LSi(s),JBg,DJa,Clark is kidnapped & revealed identity	2.50
64 LSi(s),JBg,DJa,Superman tries to restore his powers	2.50
65 LSi(s),SB,DJa,V:Superman Revenge Squad	2.50
66 LSi(s),JBg,DJa,V:Rajiv	2.50
67 LSi(s),JBg,DJa,New powers prequel	3.00
68 LSi(s),JBg,DJa,V:Metallo	3.00
69 KK&LSi(s),SEa,DJa,A:Atom, in Kandor	2.50
70 LSi(s),SEa,DJa,V:Saviour	2.50
71 LSi(s),SEa,DJa,V:Mainframe, Superman Revenge Squad	2.50
72 LSi(s),SEa,JP,DJa,JBg,Genesis V:Mainframe	2.50
73 LSi&MWa(s),SEa,DJa,V:Revenge Squad	2.50
74 LSi(s),SEa,DJa,dragon's tooth	2.50
75 LSi(s),DJa,JBg,Mr.Mxyzptlk dies parody of Superman #75	2.50
76 LSi(s),JBb,DJa,V:Mokkari	2.50
77 JBg,Triangles	2.50
78 JBg, Millennium Giants, pt.1 x-over	2.50
79 JBg, Millennium Giants	2.50
80 LSi,JBg,DJa,golden age?,pt.1	2.50
81 LSi,JBg,DJa,golden age?,pt.2	2.50
82 LSi,JBg,DJa,golden age?,pt.3	2.50
83 LSi,SEa,DJa,Dominus	2.50
84 RMz(s),TGb,TP,City of the Future, pt.2 x-over	2.50
85 JBg,DJa,V:Simyan & Mokkari	2.50
86 LSi(s),SEa,DJa,dreams of disasters	2.50
87 MSh,DoM,DJa,A:Steel, Superboy, Supergirl	2.50
88 MSh,DoM,DJa	2.50
89 MSh,DoM,V:Dominus	2.50
90 MSh,V:Superman's Robot	2.50
91 MSh(s),DoM,paranoia	2.50

92 TPe(s),TGb,TP,Secret origins,concl.	2.50
93 MSh,DoM	2.50
94 RF,SB,Strange Visitor,concl.	2.50
95 MSh,DoM,Fortress of Solitude	2.50
96 MSh,DoM,	2.50
97 MSh,DoM,F:Eradicator	2.50
98 MSh,DoM,V:Brainiac 13	2.50
99 MSh,DoM,new armor	2.50
100 MSh,DoM,new Fortress of Solitude, 48-pg.	4.00
100a Collectors edition	4.25
101 MSh,DoM,growing sicker	2.50
102 MSh,DoM,Crit.Condition,pt.3	2.50
103 MSh,DoM,A:Supergirl	2.50
104 MSh,DoM,Arkham,pt.3	2.50
105 MSh,DoM,Superman:Emperor	2.50
106 MSh,HuR,V:Kosnor,Netkon	2.50
107 MSh,DoM, to Phantom Zone	2.50
108 MSh,DoM, from Phantom Zone	2.50
109 MSh,A:Linear Man	2.50
110 MSh,DoM,A:Star-SpangledKid	2.50
111 MSh,DoM,Return-Krypton,pt.3	2.50
112 MSh,A:Superdog	2.50
113 MWm,Infestation x-over,pt.3	2.50
114 MSh,DoM,R:Eradicator	2.50
115 MSh,DoM,Metropolis abducted.	2.50
116 MSh,DoM,JMz,All-out War	2.50
117 MSh,DoM,Casualties of War	2.50
118 MSh,DoM,F:Spectre	2.50
119 MSh,Joker:Last Laugh,tie-in	8.00
120 MSh,V:LexCorp	2.50
121 TNu,Royal Flush Gang	2.50
122 MSh(s),Entropy Aegis Armor	2.50
123 MSh(s),Metropolis Gangs,pt.1	2.50
124 MSh(s),Metropolis Gangs,pt.2	2.50
125 MSh(s),Metropolis Gangs,pt.3	2.50
126 MSh(s),The Pantheon,pt.1	2.50
127 MSh(s),The Pantheon,pt.2	2.50
128 MSh(s),ReturntoKryptonII,pt.3	2.50
129 Bloodsport	2.50
130 MSh(s),Ending Battle,pt.3	2.50
131 MSh(s),Ending Battle,pt.7	2.50
132 MSh,Parade, A:Mr.Mxyzptlk	2.50
133 Lost Hearts,pt.3 x-over	2.50
134 MSh,40-pg.,final issue	3.00
Ann.#1 Eclipso tie-in,A:Starman	3.00
Ann.#2 Bloodlines#2,I:Edge	3.00
Ann.#3 MBr,Elseworlds Story	3.50
Ann.#4 Year One Annual	3.50
Ann.#5 Legends o/t Dead Earth	3.50
Ann.#6 Pulp Heroes (Hard Boiled) LSi(s),DJa	4.50
Spec.#1,000,000 KK&JOy(s), AWi,DJa.	3.00
Gallery 1	3.50

SUPERMAN:
THE MAN OF TOMORROW
1995–96

1 TGu,BBr,RSt(s),V:Lex Luthor	2.50
2 V:Parasite	2.50
3 TG,BBr, The Trial of Superman	2.50
4 RSt(s),PR,BBr,A:Shazam	2.50
5 RSt(s),PR,BBr,Wedding of Lex Luthor	2.50
6 RSt(s),PR,BBr,Superman V: Jackal again	2.50
7 RSt(s),PR,BBr,	2.50
8 RSt(s),PR,BBr,V:Carbide	2.50
9 RSt(s),PR,BBr,Ma and Pa Kent open their album	2.50
10	2.50
11 LSi(s),PR,DJa,BBr	2.50
12 LSi(s),PR,DJa,	2.50
13 LSi(s),PR,DJa,A:JLA	2.50
14 LSi(s),PR,DJa,V:Riot	2.50
15 Day of Judgment x-over,48-pg.	3.00
Spec.#1,000,000 MSh(s),DRo	2.50

SUPERMAN: RED SON
April 2003
1 (of 3) Elseworlds,MMr(s) 6.00
2 MMr(s) 6.00
3 MMr(s),concl 6.00

SUPERMAN:
NEW KRYPTON SPECIAL
Oct., 2008
1 New Krypton, pt.1 x-over 4.00
1a variant (c) (1:10) 4.00

SUPERMAN RETURNS
July, 2006
GN The Movie Adaptation, 72-pg . . . 7.00
Spec: Krypton to Earth, JBy 4.00
Spec: Ma Kent, KIK 4.00
Spec: Lois Lane 4.00
Spec: Lex Luthor, RL 4.00

SUPERMAN:
SECRET IDENTITY
Jan. 2004
1 (of 4) SI 6.00
2 SI Clark Kent gains powers 6.00
3 SI 6.00
4 SI concl 6.00

SUPERMAN'S GIRL
FRIEND, LOIS LANE
1958–74
1 CS,KS,Witch of Metropolis . . 8,500.00
2 CS,KS,Secret Sweetheart . . 2,000.00
3 CS,KS,spanking panel 1,400.00
4 CS,KS,Super-Courtship 1,000.00
5 CS,KS,Greatest Sacrifice . . . 1,000.00
6 CS,KS,Superman Junior 750.00
7 CS,KS,Kiss of Death 750.00
8 CS,KS,Superwoman 650.00
9 CS,KS, A:Pat Boone 650.00
10 CS,KS,Cry-Baby of Metropolis 650.00
11 CS,KS,Leopard Girl of Jungle . 400.00
12 CS,KS,Mermaid of Metropolis . 400.00
13 CS,KS,Lois Lane's Parents . . 400.00
14 KS,Three Nights in the
   Fortress of Solitude 400.00
15 KS,I:Van-Zee 400.00
16 KS, Lois' Signal-Watch 400.00
17 KS,CS,A:Brainiac 400.00
18 KS,A:Astounding Man 400.00
19 KS,Superman of the Past 400.00
20 KS,A:Superman 450.00
21 KS,A:Van-Zee 300.00
22 KS,A:Robin Hood 300.00
23 KS,A:Elastic Lass, Supergirl . 300.00
24 KS,A:Van-Zee, Bizarro 300.00
25 KS,Lois' Darkest Secret 300.00
26 KS,A:Jor-El 300.00
27 KS,CS,A:Bizarro 300.00
28 KS,A:Luthor 300.00
29 CS,A:Aquaman,Batman,Green
   Arrow 300.00
30 KS,A:Krypto,Aquaman 200.00
31 KS,A:Lori Lemaris 200.00
32 KS,CS,A:Bizarro 200.00
33 KS,CS,A:Phantom Zone,Lori
   Lemaris, Mon-El 200.00
34 KS,A:Luthor,Supergirl 200.00
35 KS,CS,A:Supergirl 200.00
36 KS,CS,Red Kryptonite Story . . 200.00
37 KS,CS,The Forbidden Box . . . 200.00
38 KS,CS,A:Prof.Potter,
   Supergirl 200.00
39 KS,CS,A:Supergirl,Jor-El,
   Krypto, Lori Lemaris 200.00
40 KS,Lois Lane, Hag! 200.00
41 KS,CS,The Devil and
   Lois Lane 200.00

Superman's Girl Friend Lois Lane #45
© DC Comics, Inc.

42 KS,A:Lori Lemaris 200.00
43 KS,A:Luthor 200.00
44 KS,A:Lori Lemaris,Braniac,
   Prof. Potter 200.00
45 KS,CS,The Superman-Lois
   Hit Record 200.00
46 KS,A:Luthor 200.00
47 KS,The Incredible Delusion . . 200.00
48 KS,A:Mr. Mxyzptlk 200.00
49 KS,The Unknown Superman . 200.00
50 KS,A:Legion 225.00
51 KS,A:Van-Zee & Lori Lemaris. 150.00
52 KS,Truce Between Lois
   Lane and Lana Lang 150.00
53 KS,A:Lydia Lawrence 150.00
54 KS,CS,The Monster That
   Loved Lois Lane 150.00
55 KS,A:Supergirl 150.00
56 KS,Lois Lane's
   Super-Gamble! 150.00
57 KS,The Camera From
   Outer Space 150.00
58 KS,The Captive Princess 150.00
59 KS,CS,A:Jor-El & Batman 150.00
60 KS,Get Lost,Superman! 150.00
61 KS,A:Mxyzptlk 150.00
62 KS,A:Mxyzptlk 150.00
63 KS,The Satanic Schemes
   of S.K.U.L. 150.00
64 KS,A:Luthor 150.00
65 KS,A:Luthor 150.00
66 KS,They Call Me the Cat! 150.00
67 KS,The Bombshell of
   the Boulevards 150.00
68 giant size 200.00
69 KS,Lois Lane's Last Chance . 150.00
70 KS,I:Silver Age Catwoman,
   A:Batman,Robin,Penguin . . 500.00
71 KS,A:Catwoman,Batman,
   Robin,Penguin 300.00
72 KS,CS,A:Ina Lemaris 100.00
73 KS,The Dummy and
   the Damsel! 100.00
74 KS,A:Justice League & Bizarro
   World,I:Bizarro Flash 125.00
75 KS,The Lady Dictator 100.00
76 KS,A:Hap-El 100.00
77 giant size 150.00
78 KS,Courtship,Kryptonian Style 100.00
79 KS,B:NA(c) 100.00
80 KS,Get Out of My Life,
   Superman 100.00
81 KS,No Witnesses in
   Outerspace 100.00
82 GT,A:Brainiac&Justice League . 60.00

83 GT,Witch on Wheels 60.00
84 GT,KS,Who is Lois Lane? 60.00
85 GT,KS,A:Kandorians 60.00
86 giant size 75.00
87 GT,KS,A:Cor-Lar 60.00
88 GT,KS,Through a Murderer's
   Eyes 60.00
89 CS,A:Batman & Batman Jr. . . . 75.00
90 GT,A:Dahr-nel 60.00
91 GT,A:Superlass 60.00
92 GT,A:Superhorse 60.00
93 GT,A:Wonder Woman 60.00
94 GT,KS,A:Jor 60.00
95 giant size 100.00
96 GT,A:Jor 50.00
97 GT,KS,A:Lori Lemaris,
   Luma Lynai,Lyla Lerrol 50.00
98 GT,A:Phantom Zone 50.00
99 GT,KS,A:Batman 50.00
100 GT,A:Batman 50.00
101 GT,KS,The Super-Reckless
   Lois Lane 50.00
102 GT,KS,When You're Dead,
   You're Dead 50.00
103 GT,KS,A:Supergirl 50.00
104 giant size 75.00
105 RA,I&O:Rose & Thorn 75.00
106 WR,I am Curious Black! 60.00
107 WR,The Snow-Woman Wept . 50.00
108 WR,The Spectre Suitor 50.00
109 WR,I'll Never Fall
   in Love Again 50.00
110 WR,Indian Death Charge! . . . 50.00
111 WR,A:Justice League 50.00
112 WR,KS,A:Lori Lemaris 60.00
113 giant size 75.00
114 WR,KS,A:Rose & Thorn 50.00
115 WR,A:The Black Racer 50.00
116 WR,A:Darkseid & Desaad 50.00
117 WR,S.O.S From Tomorrow! . . 50.00
118 WR,A:Darkseid & Desaad 50.00
119 WR,A:Darkseid & Lucy Lane . 50.00
120 WR,Who Killed Lucy Lane? . . 50.00
121 WR,A:The Thorn 50.00
122 WR,A:The Thorn 50.00
123 JRo,Ten Deadly Division
   of the 100 . . . . 50.00
124 JRo,The Hunters 30.00
125 JRo,Death Rides Wheels! 30.00
126 JRo,The Brain Busters 30.00
127 JRo,Curse of the Flame 30.00
128 JRo,A:Batman & Aquaman . . . 30.00
129 JRo,Serpent in Paradise 30.00
130 JRo,The Mental Murster 30.00
131 JRo,Superman–Marry Me! . . . 30.00
132 JRo,Zatanna B.U. 30.00
133 JRo,The Lady is a Bomb 30.00
134 JRo,A:Kandor 30.00
135 JRo,Amazing After-Life
   of Lois Lane 30.00
136 JRo,A:Wonder Woman 30.00
137 JRo,The Stolen Subway 40.00
Ann.#1 . . . . 500.00
Ann.#2 . . . . 300.00

SUPERMAN:
SILVER BANSHEE
1998
1 (of 2) DIB(s),ALa 2.50
2 DIB(s),ALa, conclusion 2.50

SUPERMAN'S NEMESIS,
LEX LUTHOR
1999
1 (of 4) VS,DJa, ... 2.50
2 VS,DJa. 2.50
3 VS,DJa. 2.50
4 VS,DJa, conclusion 2.50

SUPERMAN'S PAL, JIMMY OLSEN
1954–74

1 CS,The Boy of 100 Faces! . 12,000.00
2 CS,The Flying Jimmy Olsen . 3,500.00
3 CS,The Man Who Collected
   Excitement 2,000.00
4 CS,King For A Day! 1,200.00
5 CS,The Story of Superman's
   Souvenirs 1,200.00
6 CS,Kryptonite story 800.00
7 CS,The King of Marbles 800.00
8 CS,Jimmy Olsen, Crooner. . . . 800.00
9 CS,The Missile of Steel 800.00
10 CS,Jungle Jimmy Olsen 800.00
11 CS,TNT.Olsen,The Champ . . 550.00
12 CS,Invisible Jimmy Olsen. . . . 550.00
13 CS,Jimmy Olsen's
   Super Issue 550.00
14 CS,The Boy Superman. 550.00
15 CS,Jimmy Olsen,Speed
   Demon. 550.00
16 CS,The Boy Superman. 550.00
17 CS,J.Olsen as cartoonist 550.00
18 CS,A:Superboy 550.00
19 CS,Supermam's Kid Brother. . 550.00
20 CS,Merman of Metropolis. . . . 550.00
21 CS,The Wedding of Jimmy
   Olsen 375.00
22 CS,The Super Brain of
   Jimmy Olsen 375.00
23 CS,The Adventure of
   Private Olsen. 375.00
24 CS,The Gorilla Reporter 375.00
25 CS,The Day There Was
   No Jimmy Olsen 375.00
26 CS,Bird Boy of Metropolis . . . 375.00
27 CS,The Outlaw Jimmy Olsen . 375.00
28 CS,The Boy Who Killed
   Superman 375.00
29 CS,A:Krypto 375.00
30 CS,The Son of Superman . . . 375.00
31 CS,I:Elastic Lad 300.00
32 CS,A:Prof.Potter 300.00
33 CS,Human Flame Thrower. . . 300.00
34 CS,Superman's Pal of Steel . . 300.00
35 CS,Superman's Enemy 300.00
36 CS,I:Lois Lane,O:Jimmy Olsen
   as Superman's Pal 300.00
37 CS,O:Jimmy Olsen's SignalWatch,
   A:Elastic Lad(Jimmy Olsen) . 300.00
38 CS,Olsen's Super-Supper . . . 300.00
39 CS,The Super-Lad of Space. . 300.00

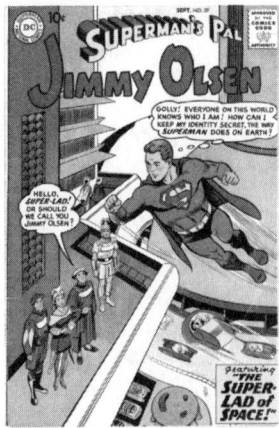

Superman's Pal Jimmy Olsen #39
© DC Comics, Inc.

40 CS,A:Supergirl,Hank White
   (Perry White's son) 300.00
41 CS,The Human Octopus. 200.00
42 CS,Jimmy The Genie 200.00
43 WB,CS,Jimmy Olsen's Private
   Monster 200.00
44 CS,Miss Jimmy Olsen. 200.00
45 CS,A:Kandor. 200.00
46 CS,A:Supergirl,Elastic Lad . . . 200.00
47 CS,Monsters From Earth! 200.00
48 CS,I:Superman Emergency
   Squad 200.00
49 CS,A:Congorilla & Congo Bill . 200.00
50 CS,A:Supergirl,Krypto,Bizarro 200.00
51 CS,A:Supergirl 175.00
52 CS,A:Mr. Mxyzptlk,
   Miss Gzptlsnz 175.00
53 CS,A:Kandor,Lori Lemaris,
   Mr.Mxyztlk. 175.00
54 CS,A:Elastic Lad. 175.00
55 CS,A:Aquaman,Thor. 175.00
56 KS,Imaginary story 175.00
57 KS,A:Supergirl,Imaginary story 125.00
58 CS,C:Batman 125.00
59 CS,A:Titano. 125.00
60 CS,The Fantastic Army of
   General Olsen 125.00
61 CS,Prof. Potter 125.00
62 CS,A:Elastic Lad,Phantom
   Zone 125.00
63 CS,A:Supergirl,Kandor 150.00
64 CS,Jimmy Olsen's
   Super-Romance 125.00
65 CS,A:Miss Gzptlsnz 125.00
66 CS,KS,A:Mr. Mxyzptlk. 125.00
67 CS,The Dummy That Haunted
   Jimmy Olsen 125.00
68 CS,The Helmet of Hate 125.00
69 CS,A:Nightwing,Flamebird . . . 125.00
70 A:Supergirl,Lori Lemaris,
   Element Lad 125.00
71 CS,A:Mr. Mxyzptlk 100.00
72 CS,A:Legion of Super-Heroes,
   Jimmy Olsen becomes honorary
   member 100.00
73 A:Kandor. 100.00
74 CS,A:Mr. Mxyzptlk,Lex Luthor . 75.00
75 CS,A:Supergirl 76.00
76 CS,A:Legion of Super-Heroes . 75.00
77 CS,Jimmy Olsen becomes
   Colossal Boy, A:Titano. 75.00
78 CS,A:Aqualad 75.00
79 CS,The Red-Headed Beetle
   of 1,000 B.C. 75.00
80 CS,A:Bizarro. 75.00
81 CS,KS,A:Lori Lemaris,I&O
   only A:Mighty Eagle. 75.00
82 CS,The Unbeatable Jimmy
   Olsen 75.00
83 CS,A:Kandor. 75.00
84 CS,A:Titano. 75.00
85 CS,C:Legion of Super-Heroes 100.00
86 CS,A:Congorilla,Braniac. 75.00
87 A:Lex Luthor,Brainiac,Legion
   of Super-Villians 100.00
88 C:Legion of Super-Heroes 75.00
89 I:Agent Double-Five,C:John F.
   Kennedy 75.00
90 CS,A:Mr. Mxyzptlk 75.00
91 CS,C:Batman & Robin 75.00
92 JM,A:Batman,Robin,Supergirl. . 75.00
93 The Batman-Superman of
   Earth-X! 75.00
94 O:Insect Queen retold. 75.00
95 Giant 150.00
96 I:Tempus 75.00
97 A:Fortress of Solitude 75.00
98 The Bride of Jungle Jimmy . . . 75.00
99 A:Legion of Super-Heroes 75.00
100 A:Legion of Super-Heroes . . . 100.00
101 A:Jor-El and Lara 75.00

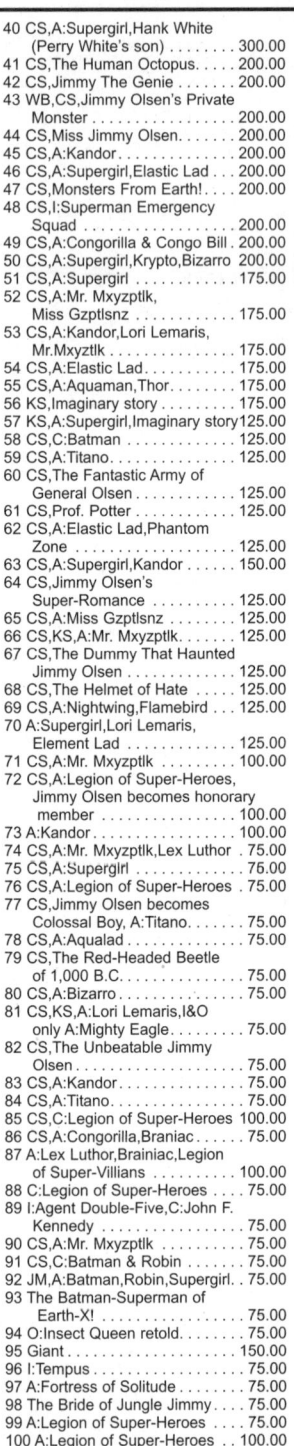

Superman's Pal Jimmy Olsen #141
© DC Comics Inc.

102 Superman's Greatest Double
   Cross! 75.00
103 The Murder of Clark Kent! . . . 75.00
104 Giant 90.00
105 V:Tempus 75.00
106 CS,A:Legion of Super-
   Heroes. 75.00
107 A:Krypto 75.00
108 CS,The Midas of Metropolis . . 75.00
109 A:Lex Luthor 75.00
110 CS,Jimmy Olsen's Blackest
   Deeds! 75.00
111 Jimmy Olsen Boy Wonder. . . . 75.00
112 The Murderous Magnaman. . . 75.00
113 V:Magnaman. 100.00
114 The Wrong Superman! 50.00
115 A:Aquaman 50.00
116 A:Brainiac 50.00
117 Planet of the Capes 50.00
118 A:Lex Luthor 50.00
119 Nine Lives Like a Cat! 50.00
120 V:Climate King 50.00
121 CS&NA(s),Three Lives 50.00
122 CS,Miss Metropolis,giant 50.00
123 CS,Sacrifice of Jimmy Olsen . 50.00
124 CS,Girl Trouble 50.00
125 Superman's Saddest Day 50.00
126 CS,Riddle of Kryptonite Plus . 50.00
127 CS,Jimmy in Revolutionary
   War 50.00
128 I:Mark Olsen(Jimmy'sFather) . 50.00
129 MA,A:Mark Olsen 50.00
130 MA,A:Robin,Brainiac. 50.00
131 CS,Birdboy of Metropolis 75.00
132 MA,When Olsen Sold out
   Superman 50.00
133 JK,B:New Newsboy Legion,
   I:Morgan Edge 100.00
134 JK,I:Darkseid. 125.00
135 JK,I:New Guardian 75.00
136 JK,O:New Guardian,
   I:Dubbilex. 65.00
137 JK,I:Four Armed Terror 50.00
138 JK,V:Four Armed Terror 50.00
139 JK,A:Don Rickles,I:Ugly
   Mannheim 50.00
140 Rep. Jimmy Olsen #69, #72
   and Superman #158 . . . . 50.00
141 JK,A:Don Rickles,Lightray
   B:Newsboy Legion rep 50.00
142 JK,I:Count Dragorian 50.00
143 JK,V:Count Dragorian. 50.00
144 JK,A Big Thing in a Deep
   Scottish Lake. 50.00
145 JK,Brigadoon 50.00

146 JK,Homo Disastrous 50.00
147 JK,Superman on New
   Genesis,A:High Father,
   I:Victor Volcanium 50.00
148 JK,V:Victor Volcanium,
   E:Newsboy Legion rep 50.00
149 BO(i),The Unseen Enemy,
   B:Plastic Man rep 50.00
150 BO(i) A Bad Act to Follow 50.00
151 BO(i),A:Green Lantern 30.00
152 MSy,BO,I:Real Morgan Edge . 30.00
153 MSy,Murder in Metropolis . . . 30.00
154 KS,The Girl Who Was Made
   of Money 30.00
155 KS,Downfall of Judas Olsen . . 30.00
156 KS,Last Jump for
   a Skyjacker 30.00
157 KS,Jimmy as Marco Polo 30.00
158 KS,A:Lena Lawrence
   (Lucy Lane) 30.00
159 KS,Jimmy as Spartacus 30.00
160 KS,A:Lena Lawrence
   (Lucy Lane) 30.00
161 KS,V:Lucy Lane 30.00
162 KS,A:Lex Luthor 30.00
163 KS,Jimmy as Marco Polo 30.00
Becomes:

SUPERMAN FAMILY
1974–82

164 KS,NC(c),Jimmy Olsen:Death
   Bites with Fangs of Stone 75.00
165 KS,NC(c),Supergirl:Princess
   of the Golden Sun 50.00
166 KS,NC(c),Lois Lane:The
   Murdering Arm of Metropolis . . 35.00
167 KS,NC(c),Jimmy Olsen:A
   Deep Death for Mr. Action 35.00
168 NC(c),Supergirl:The Girl
   with the See-Through Mind . . . 35.00
169 NC(c),Lois Lane:Target of
   the Tarantula 35.00
170 KS(c),Jimmy Olsen:The Kid
   Who Adopted Jimmy Olsen . . . 25.00
171 ECh(c),Supergirl:Cleopatra-
   Queen of America 25.00
172 KS(c),Lois Lane:The Cheat
   the Whole World Cheered 25.00
173 KS(c),Jimmy Olsen:Menace
   of the Micro-Monster 25.00
174 KS(c),Supergirl:Eyes of
   the Serpent 25.00
175 KS(c),Lois Lane:Fadeout
   For Lois 25.00
176 KS(c),Jimmy
   Olsen:Nashville, Super-Star . . 25.00
177 KS(c),Supergirl:Bride
   of the Stars 20.00
178 KS(c),Lois Lane:The Girl
   With the Heart of Steel 20.00
179 KS(c),Jimmy Olsen:I Scared
   Superman to Death 20.00
180 KS,Supergirl:The Secret of
   the Spell-Bound Supergirl 20.00
181 ECh(c),Lois Lane:The Secret
   Lois Lane Could Never Tell . . . 20.00
182 CS&NA(c),Jimmy Olsen:
   Death on Ice 20.00
183 NA(c),Supergirl:Shadows
   of Phantoms 20.00
184 NA(c),Supergirl:The
   Visitors From The Void 20.00
185 NA(c),Jimmy Olsen: The
   Fantastic Fists and Fury
   Feet of Jimmy Olsen 20.00
186 JL&DG(c),Jimmy Olsen:
   The Bug Lady 20.00
187 JL(c),Jimmy Olsen:The
   Dealers of Death 20.00
188 JL&DG(c),Jimmy Olsen:
   Crisis in Kandor 20.00
189 JL(c),Jimmy Olsen:The
   Night of the Looter 20.00

190 Jimmy Olsen:Somebody
   Stole My Town 20.00
191 Superboy:The Incredible
   Shrinking Town 20.00
192 RA&DG(c),Superboy:This
   Town For Plunder 20.00
193 RA&DG(c),Superboy:Menace
   of the Mechanical Monster . . . 20.00
194 MR,Superboy:When
   the Sorcerer Strikes 20.00
195 RA&DG(c),Superboy:The Curse
   of the Un-Secret Identity 20.00
196 JL&DG(c),Superboy:The
   Shadow of Jor-El 20.00
197 JL(c),Superboy:Superboy's
   Split Personality 20.00
198 JL(c),Superboy:Challenge
   of the Green K-Tastrophe 20.00
199 RA&DG(c),Supergirl:The
   Case of Cape Caper 20.00
200 RA&DG(c),Lois Lane:
   Unhappy Anniversary 22.00
201 RA&DG(c),Supergirl:The
   Face on Cloud 9 . . . . 8.00
202 RA&DG(c),Supergirl:The
   Dynamic Duel 8.00
203 RA&DG(c),Supergirl:The
   Supergirl From Planet Earth . . . 8.00
204 RA&DG(c),Supergirl:The
   Earth-quake Enchantment 8.00
205 RA&DG(c),Supergirl:Magic
   Over Miami 8.00
206 RA&DG(c),Supergirl:Strangers
   at the Heart's Core 8.00
207 RA&DG(c),Supergirl:Look
   Homeward, Argonian 8.00
208 RA&DG(c),Supergirl:The
   Super-Switch to New York 8.00
209 Supergirl:Strike Three-
   You're Out 8.00
210 Supergirl:The Spoil Sport
   of New York 8.00
211 RA&DG(c):Supergirl:The Man
   With the Explosive Mind 8.00
212 RA&DG(c):Supergirl:Payment
   on Demand 8.00
213 thru 222 . . . . @8.00

SUPERMAN'S PAL, JIMMY OLSEN SPECIAL
Oct., 2008

1 New Krypton, x-over tie-in 4.00
1a variant (c) (1:10) 3.00

SUPERMAN: SAVE THE PLANET
Aug., 1998

1 LSi,SEa,DRo,JP,KN, last
   front page 3.00
1 collector's edition 4.00

SUPERMAN: STRENGTH
Jan., 2005

1 (of 3) TA,48-page 6.00
2 TA 6.00
3 TA,ARo(c) 6.00

SUPERMAN, THE SECRET YEARS
Feb., 1985

1 CS,KS,FM(c) 3.00
2 thru 4 CS,KS,FM(c) . . . . @2.50

SUPERMAN/SUPERGIRL: MAELSTROM
Nov., 2008

1 (of 5) 3.00
2 . . . . 3.00

Superman, The Secret Years #4
© DC Comics Inc.

SUPERMAN VS. AMAZING SPIDER-MAN
DC/Marvel April, 1976

1 RA/DG,oversized 125.00
1a 2nd printing, signed 225.00

SUPERMAN VS. PREDATOR
DC/Dark Horse May, 2000

1 (of 3) weakened by virus 5.00
2 . . . . 5.00
3 conclusion 5.00

SUPERMAN/ WONDER WOMAN: WHOM GODS DESTROY
Elseworlds Oct., 1996

1 CCl(s),DAb, Lois becomes the
   immortal Wonder Woman 5.00
2 CCl(s),DAb, search for Lana
   Lang 5.00
3 . . . . 5.00
4 CCl(s),DAb, romance of the
   century, concl. 5.00

SUPERMEN OF AMERICA
1999

GN with membership kit. 5.00
GN standard edition 4.00
1 (of 6) FaN,DBw, ... 2.50
2 FaN,DBw,V:Lex Luthor 2.50
3 FaN,DBw,F:Brahma 2.50
4 FaN,DBw,F:White Lotus 2.50
5 FaN,F:The Loser 2.50
6 FaN,A:Superman,concl. 2.50

SUPER POWERS
1984

[Kenner Action Figures]
1 A:Batman & Joker 5.50
2 A:Batman & Joker 5.50
3 A:Batman & Joker 5.50
4 A:Batman & Joker 5.50
5 JK(c),JK,A:Batman & Joker 5.50

[2nd Series], 1985–86
1 JK,Seeds of Doom 4.00
2 JK,When Past & Present Meet . . 4.00
3 JK,Time Upon Time 4.00

4 JK,There's No Place Like Rome . 4.00
5 JK,Once Upon a Tomorrow 4.00
6 JK,Darkkseid o/t Moon 4.00

[3rd Series], 1986

1 CI,Threshold 3.50
2 CI,Escape 3.50
3 CI,Machinations 3.50
4 CI,A World Divided 3.50

SUPER-TEAM FAMILY

1975–78

1 Reprints, giant-size 35.00
2 Creeper/Wildcat 18.00
3 RE/WW,Flash & Hawkman 18.00
4 Revenge of Solomon Grundy . . 20.00
5 Batman vs. Eclipso 20.00
6 Return of Composite Superman 20.00
7 To Order is to Destroy 20.00
8 JSh,Challengers 22.00
9 JSh,Challengers 22.00
10 JSh,Challengers 22.00
11 Supergirl,Flash,Atom. 22.00
12 Green Lantern,Hawkman 22.00
13 Aquaman, Capt. Comet 22.00
14 Wonder Woman,Atom. 22.00
15 Flash & New Gods 25.00

SWAMP THING

[1st Regular Series]

Oct.–Nov., 1972

1 B:LWn(s),BWr,O:Swamp Thing 275.00
2 BWr,I:Arcane 125.00
3 BWr,I:Patchwork Man 100.00
4 BWr 75.00
5 BWr 75.00
6 BWr 75.00
7 BWr,A:Batman 80.00
8 BWr,Lurker in Tunnel 13 . . . . . . 60.00
9 BWr 60.00
10 E:BWr,A;Arcane 60.00
11 thru 24 NR . . . . @35.00

SWAMP THING

1986–96

Previously:

SAGA OF THE SWAMP THING

46 B:AMo(s) cont'd,SBi,JTo,Crisis,
    A:John Constantine,Phantom
    Stranger 5.00
47 SBi,Parliment of Trees,Full
    origin,A:Constantine 5.00
48 SBi,JTo,V:Brujeria,
    A:Constantine 4.00
49 SBi,AA,A:Constantine,Demon,Ph.
    Stranger,Spectre,Deadman 4.00
50 SBi,RV,JTo,concl.American
    Gothic,D:Zatara&Sargon,
    Double Size 6.00
51 RV,AA,L:Constantine 4.00
52 RV,AA,Arkham Asylum,A:Flor.
    Man,Lex Luthor,C:Joker,
    2-Face,Darkseid 4.00
53 JTo,V:Batman,Swamp Thing
    Banished to Space 5.00
54 JTo script,RV,AA,C:Batman . . . 4.00
55 RV,AA,JTo,A:Batman,. 4.00
56 RV,AA,My Blue Heaven 4.00
57 RV,AA,A:Adam Strange 4.00
58 RV,AA,A:Adam Strange,GC,
    Spectre preview 4.00
59 JTo,RV,AA,D:Patchwork Man . . . 4.00

Direct Sales Only

60 JTo,Loving the Alien 4.00
61 RV,AA,All Flesh is Grass
    G.L.Corps X-over. 4.00
62 RV(&script),AA,Wavelength,
    A:Metron,Darkseid. 4.00
63 RV,AA,Loose Ends(reprise) 4.00

Swamp Thing #58 © DC Comics, Inc.

64 E:AMo(s),SBi,TY,RV,AA,
    Return of the Good Gumbo. . . . 4.00
65 RV,JTo,A:Constantine 3.50
66 RV,Elemental Energy 3.00
67 RV,V:Solomon Grundy,
    Hellblazer preview. 4.00
68 RV,O:Swamp Thing 3.00
69 RV,O:Swamp Thing 3.00
70 RV,AA,Quest for SwampThing . . 3.00
71 RV,AA,Fear of Flying 3.00
72 RV,AA,Creation. 3.00
73 RV,AA,A:John Constantine 3.50
74 RV,AA,Abbys Secret 3.00
75 RV,AA,Plant Elementals 3.00
76 RV,AA,A:John Constantine 3.50
77 TMd,AA,A:John Constantine. . . . 3.00
78 TMd,AA,Phantom Pregnancy . . . 3.00
79 RV,AA,A:Superman,Luthor 3.00
80 RV,AA,V:Aliends 3.00
81 RV,AA,Invasion x-over 3.00
82 RV,AA,A:Sgt.Rock & Easy Co. . . 3.00
83 RV,AA,A:Enemy Ace 3.00
84 RV,AA,A:Sandman 8.00
85 RV,TY,Time Travel contd. 3.00
86 RV,TY,A:Tomahawk. 3.00
87 RV,TY,Camelot,A:Demon 3.00
88 RV,TY,A:Demon,Golden
    Gladiator 3.00
89 MM,AA,The Dinosaur Age 3.00
90 BP,AA,Birth of Abbys Child
    (Tefe) 3.25
91 PB,AA,Abbys Child (New
    Elemental) 3.00
92 PB,AA,Ghosts of the Bayou 3.00
93 PB,AA,New Power 3.00
94 PB,AA,Ax-Murderer 3.00
95 PB,AA,Toxic Waste Dumpers . . . 3.00
96 PB,AA,Tefes Powers. 3.00
97 PB,AA,Tefe,V:Nergal,
    A:Arcane 3.00
98 PB,AA,Tefe,in Hell 3.00
99 PB,AA,Tefe,A:Mantago,
    John Constantine 3.50
100 PB,AA,V:Angels of Eden,
    (48 pages) 4.00
101 AA,A:Tefe 3.00
102 V:Mantagos Zombies,inc. prev.
    of Worlds Without End. 3.00
103 Green vs. Grey 3.00
104 Quest for Elementals,pt.1 . . . . . 3.00
105 Quest for Elementals,pt.2 . . . . . 3.00
106 Quest for Elementals,pt.3 . . . . . 3.00
107 Quest for Elementals,pt.4 . . . . . 3.00
108 Quest for Elementals,pt.5 . . . . . 3.00
109 Quest for Elementals,pt.6 . . . . . 3.00

110 TMd,A:Father Tocsin 3.00
111 V:Ghostly Zydeco Musician. . . . 3.00
112 TMd,B:Swamp Thing
    for Governor 3.00
113 E:Swamp Thing for Governor . . 3.00
114 TMd,Hellblazer 3.25
115 TMd,A:Hellblazer,V:Dark
    Conrad. 3.25
116 From Body of Swamp Thing . . . 3.00
117 JD,The Lord of Misrule,
    Mardi Gras. 3.00
118 A Childs Garden,A:Matthew
    the Raven 3.00
119 A:Les Perdu 3.00
120 F:Lady Jane 3.00
121 V:Sunderland Corporation 3.00
122 I:The Needleman 3.00
123 V:The Needleman 3.00
124 In Central America 3.00
125 V:Anton Arcane,20th Anniv. . . . 4.00
126 Mescalito. 3.00
127 Project Proteus #1 . . . . 3.00
128 Project proteus #2. . . . . 3.00

DC/Vertigo, 1993

129 CV(c),B:NyC(s),SEa,KDM(i),
    Sw.Thing's Deterioration 3.00
130 CV(c),SEa,KDM(i),A:John
    Constantine,V:Doctor Polygon . 3.00
131 CV(c),SEa,KDM(i),I:Swamp
    Thing's,Doppleganger,
    F:The Folk 3.50
132 CV(c),SEa,KDM(i),
    V:Doppleganger. 3.50
133 CV(c),SEa,KDM(i),R:General
    Sunderland,V:Thunder Petal . . . 3.50
134 CV(c),SEa,KDM(i),Abby Leaves,
    C:John Constantine 3.50
135 CV(c),SEa,KDM(i),A:J.Constantine,
    Swamp Thing Lady Jane meld . 3.50
136 CV(c),RsB,KDM(i),A:Lady Jane,
    Dr.Polygon,John Constantine . . 3.50
137 CV(c),E:NyC(s),RsB,KDM(i),
    IR:Sunderland is Anton Arcane,
    A:J.Constantine 3.50
138 CV(c),DiF(s),RGu,KDM,B:Mind
    Fields. 3.50
139 CV(c),DiF(s),RGu,KDM,A:Black
    Orchid,In Swamp Thing's mind,
    cont'd fr.Black Orchid #5 . . . . . . 3.50
140 B:Bad Gumbo 4.00
140a Platinum Ed. 12.00
141 A:Abigail Arcane 3.00
142 Bad Gumbo#3. . . . . 3.00
143 E:Bad Gumbo 3.00
144 In New York City 3.00
145 In Amsterdam 3.00
146 V:Nelson Strong 3.00
147 Hunter 3.00
148 Sargon 3.00
149 Sargon 3.00
150 V:Sargon 3.50
151 . . . . 3.00
152 River Run,pt.1 . . . . 3.00
153 River Run 3.00
154 River Run 3.00
155 River Run 3.00
156 PJ,River Run. 3.00
157 . . . . 3.00
158 . . . . 3.00
159 Swamp Dog 3.00
160 PhH,KDM,Atmospheres 3.00
161 Atmospheres. 2.50
162 Atmospheres. 2.50
163 Atmospheres. 2.50
164 . . . . 2.50
165 CS,KDM,F:Chester Williams. . . 2.50
166 PhH,KDM,Trial by Fire,pt.1. . . . 2.50
167 PhH,KDM,Trial by Fire,pt.2. . . . 2.50
168 MMr(s),PhH,KDM,Trial,pt.3. . . . 2.50
169 MMr(s),PhH,KDM,Trial,pt.4. . . . 2.50
170 MMr(s),PhH,KDM,Trial,pt.5. . . . 2.50

171 MMr(s),PhH,KDM,Trial by Fire,
  pt.6, last issue 2.50
Ann.#3 AMo(s),Ape issue 4.00
Ann.#4 PB/AA,A:Batman 4.00
Ann.#5 A:BrotherPower Geek 4.00
Ann.#6 Houma 4.00
Ann.#7 CV(c),NyC(s),MBu(i),Childrens
  Crusade,F:Tefe,A:Maxine,BU:
  Beautyand the Beast 7.00

DC/Vertigo, March, 2000
1 JRu,F:Tefe Holland 4.00
2 JRu,new secrets 3.00
3 JRu, ... 3.00
4 Killing Time,pt.1 . . . . 3.00
5 Killing Time,pt.2 . . . . 3.00
6 Killing Time,pt.3 . . . . 3.00
7 RM 3.00
8 RM 3.00
9 RM 3.00
10 RM 3.00
11 RM,Red Harvest, pt.1 . . . . 3.00
12 RM,Red Harvest, pt.2 . . . . 3.00
13 RM,Red Harvest, pt.3 . . . . 3.00
14 RM,Red Harvest, pt.4 . . . . 3.00
15 RM,Red Harvest, pt.5 . . . . 3.00
16 RM,Red Harvest, pt.6 . . . . 3.00
17 Red Harvest, pt.7 . . . . 3.00
18 R:Original Swamp Thing 3.00
19 The Tree of Knowledge 3.00
20 final issue 3.00
Secret Files #1, 64-pg. 5.00

DC/Vertigo, March 2004
1 classic Swamp Thing 3.00
2 Bad Seed,pt.2 . . . . 3.00
3 Bad Seed,pt.3 . . . . 3.00
4 Bad Seed,pt.4 . . . . 3.00
5 Bad Seed,pt.5,40-pg. 3.00
6 Bad Seed,pt.6 . . . . 3.00
7 RCo,Missing Links,pt.1 . . . . 3.00
8 RCo,Missing Links,pt.2 . . . . 3.00
9 Love in Vain, pt.1 . . . . 3.00
10 Love in Vain, pt.2 . . . . 3.00
11 Love in Vain, pt.3 . . . . 3.00
12 Love in Vain, pt.4 . . . . 3.00
13 Measure of Faith, pt.1 . . . . 3.00
14 Measure of Faith, pt.2 . . . . 3.00
15 Healing the Breach,pt.1 . . . . . . 3.00
16 Healing the Breach,pt.2 . . . . . . 3.00
17 Healing the Breach,pt.3 . . . . . . 3.00
18 Healing the Breach,pt.4 . . . . . . 3.00
19 Alec's bizarre mentor 3.00
20 RCo, sub-atomic size 3.00
21 The Bleeding Raconteur 3.00
22 The Bleeding Raconteur 3.00
23 The Bleeding Raconteur 3.00
24 The Bleeding Raconteur 3.00
25 F:Abby. 3.00
26 Unforgivable actions 3.00
27 The Prison Tree, pt.1 . . . . 3.00
28 Floronic Man 3.00
29 final issue 3.00

SWORD OF SORCERY
Feb.–March, 1973
1 MK(c),HC 25.00
2 BWv,NA,Hc 30.00
3 BWv,HC,MK,WS 25.00
4 HC,WS 10.00
5 Nov.–Dec., 1973 . . . . 10.50

SWORD OF THE ATOM
Sept., 1983
1 GK 3.00
2 GK 3.00
3 GK 3.00
4 GK 3.00
Spec.#1 GK 2.50
Spec.#2 GK 2.50
Spec.#3 PB 2.50

TAILGUNNER JO
Sept., 1988
1 . . . . 2.50
2 thru 6 . . . . @2.50

TAKION
1996
1 PuK,AaL,Josh Sanders
  becomes Takion. 2.50
2 thru 4 . . . . @2.50
5 PuK,AaL,Adventures of Source
  Elemental, cont. 2.50
6 PuK,AaL,Final Night tie-in 2.50
7 PuK,AaL,Arzaz trains Takion,
  final issue 2.50

TALES OF THE GREEN LANTERN CORPS
May, 1981
1 JSon,FMc,O:Green Lantern. 2.50
2 JSon,FMc. 2.50
3 JSon,FMc. 2.50

TALES OF THE LEGION OF SUPER HEROES
Aug., 1984
Prev: Legion of Super Heroes)
314 KG,V:Ontiir 2.50
315 KG(i),V:Dark Circle 2.50
316 KG(i),O:White Witch 2.50
317 KG(i),V:Dream Demon 2.50
318 KG(i),V:Persuader. 2.50
319 KG(i),V:Persuader,
  A:Superboy 2.50
320 DJu,V:Magpie 2.50
321 DJu,Exile,V:Kol 2.50
322 DJu,Exile,V:Kol 2.50
323 DJu,Exile,V:Kol 2.50
324 DJu,EC,V:Dev-Em 2.50
325 DJu,V:Dark Circle 2.50
326 thru 354 rep. of Legion of Super
  Heroes, 3rd Series #1–#29 . . . 2.50
Ann.#4 rep. Baxter Ann.#1. . . . . . . 2.50
Ann.#5 rep. Baxter Ann.#2. . . . . . . 2.50

TALES OF THE NEW TEEN TITANS
June, 1982
1 GP, O:Cyborg. 3.50
2 GP, O:Raven 3.50
3 GD, O:Changling 3.50
4 GP/EC,O:Starfire 3.50

TALES OF THE SINESTRO CORPS PRESENTS
Sept., 2007
Spec #1 RMz,Parallax 3.00
Spec #1 The Anti-Monitor 3.00
Spec. #1 Superman 3.00
Spec. #1 RMz(s) Ion 3.00

TALES OF THE TEEN TITANS
See: NEW TEEN TITANS

TALES OF THE UNEXPECTED
1956–68
1 The Out-Of-The-World Club . 2,400.00
2 Gorilla Who Saved the World 1,200.00
3 LSt,Man With 100 Wigs 800.00
4 Seven Steps to the Unknown . 800.00
5 2nd Life of Geoffrey Hawkes . . 800.00
6 The Girl in the Bottle 600.00
7 NC(c),Pen That Never Lied . . . 600.00

Tales of the Unexpected #14
© DC Comics Inc.

8 LSt,Camera that Could Rob . . 600.00
9 LSt(c),The Amazing Cube 600.00
10 MMe(c),The Strangest Show
  On Earth 600.00
11 LSt(c),Who Am I? 400.00
12 JK,Four Threads of Doom . . . 500.00
13 JK(c),Weapons of Destiny . . . 500.00
14 SMo(c),The Forbidden Game . 400.00
15 JK,MMe,Three Wishes
  to Doom. 600.00
16 JK,The Magic Hammer. 600.00
17 JK,Who Is Mr. Ashtar? 600.00
18 JK(c),MMe,A Man Without A
  World 600.00
19 NC,Man From Two Worlds . . . 550.00
20 NC(c),The Earth Gladiator . . . 550.00
21 JK,The Living Phantoms 550.00
22 JK(c),The Man From Robot
  Island 550.00
23 JK,The Invitation From Mars! . 550.00
24 LC,The Secret Of Planetoid
  Zero! 550.00
25 The Sorcerer's Asteroid! 300.00
26 MMe,The Frozem City 300.00
27 MMe,The Prison In Space . . . 300.00
28 The Melting Planet 300.00
29 The Phantom Raider. 300.00
30 The Jinxed Planet. 300.00
31 RH,Keep Off Our Planet 250.00
32 Great Space Cruise Mystery. . 250.00
33 The Man Of 1,000 Planets . . . 250.00
34 Ambush In Outer Space 250.00
35 MMe,I was a Space Refugee . 250.00
36 The Curse Of The
  Galactic Goodess 250.00
37 The Secret Prisoners
  Of Planet 13 . . . . 250.00
38 The Stunt Man Of Space 250.00
39 The Creatures From The
  Space Globe 250.00
40 B:Space Ranger,The Last
  Days Of Planet Mars! 2,400.00
41 SMo(c),The Destroyers From
  The Stars! 800.00
42 The Secret Of The
  Martian Helmet 800.00
43 The Riddle Of The Burning
  Treasures,I:Space Ranger . 1,700.00
44 DD&SMo(c),The Menace Of
  The Indian Aliens. 600.00
45 DD&SMo(c),The Sheriff
  From Jupiter 600.00
46 DD&SMo(c),The
  Duplicate Doom! 600.00

DC COMICS

Tales of the Unexpected #57
© *DC Comics, Inc.*

47 DD(c),The Man Who Stole
    The Solar System 450.00
48 Bring 'Em Back Alive-
    From Space 450.00
49 RH,The Fantastic Lunar-Land 450.00
50 MA,King Barney The Ape 450.00
51 Planet Earth For Sale 450.00
52 Prisoner On Pluto 450.00
53 InterplanetaryTroubleShooter . 450.00
54 The Ugly Sleeper Of Klanth,
    Dinosaur 450.00
55 The Interplanetary
    Creature Trainer 450.00
56 B:Spaceman At Work,Invaders
    From Earth 450.00
57 The Jungle Beasts Of Jupiter . 450.00
58 The Boss Of The
    Saturnian Legion 450.00
59 The Man Who Won A World . . 450.00
60 School For Space Sleuths . . . 450.00
61 The Mystery Of The
    Mythical Monsters 300.00
62 The Menace Of The Red
    Snow Crystals 300.00
63 Death To Planet Earth 300.00
64 Boy Usurper Of Planet Zonn . 300.00
65 The Creature That
    Couldn't Exist 300.00
66 MMe,Trap Of The Space
    Convict. 300.00
67 The Giant That
    Devoured A Village 300.00
68 Braggart From Planet Brax. . . 200.00
69 Doom On Holiday Asteroid . . . 200.00
70 The Hermit Of Planetoid X . . . 200.00
71 Manhunt In Galaxy G-2! 200.00
72 The Creature Of 1,000 Dooms 200.00
73 The Convict Defenders
    Of Space!. 200.00
74 Prison Camp On Asteroid X-3! 200.00
75 The Hobo Jungle Of Space . . 200.00
76 The Warrior Of Two Worlds! . . 200.00
77 Dateline-Outer Space 200.00
78 The Siren Of Space 200.00
79 Big Show On Planet Earth!. . . 200.00
80 The Creature Tamer!. 200.00
81 His Alien Master!. 200.00
82 Give Us Back Our Earth!,
    E:Space Ranger 200.00
83 DD&SMo(c),The Anti-Hex
    Merchant!. 125.00
84 DD&SMo(c),The Menace Of
    The 50-Fathom Men 125.00
85 JkS(c),The Man Who Stole My
    Powers,B:Green Glob 125.00

86 DD&SMo(c),They'll Never
    Take Me Alive! 100.00
87 JkS(c),The Manhunt Through
    Two Worlds 100.00
88 DD&SMo(c),GK,The Fear
    Master 100.00
89 DD,SMo(c),Nightmare on
    Mars. 100.00
90 JkS(c),The Hero Of 5,000 BC. 100.00
91 JkS(c),The Prophetic Mirages,
    I:Automan 125.00
92 The Man Who Dared To Die! . 100.00
93 JkS(c),Prisoners Of Hate
    Island 100.00
94 The Monster Mayor - USA . . . 100.00
95 The Secret Of Chameleo-Man 100.00
96 Wanted For Murder...1966...
    6966. . . . . 100.00
97 One Month To Die. 100.00
98 Half-Man/Half Machine 100.00
99 JkS(c),Nuclear Super-Hero! . . 100.00
100 Judy Blonde, Secret Agent! . 125.00
101 The Man in The Liquid Mask! . 75.00
102 Bang!Bang! You're Dead 75.00
103 JA,ABC To Disaster 75.00
104 NA(c),Master Of The
    Voodoo Machine 75.00

Becomes:

UNEXPECTED, THE

1968–82

105 The Night I Watched
    Myself Die 100.00
106 B:Johnny Peril,The Doorway
    Into Time 75.00
107 MD,JkS(c),The Whip Of
    Fear! 75.00
108 JkS(c),Journey To
    A Nightmare. 75.00
109 JkS(c),Baptism By Starfire!. . . 75.00
110 NA(c),Death Town, U.S.A.! . . . 75.00
111 NC(c),Mission Into Eternity . . 75.00
112 NA(c),The Brain Robbers!. . . . 75.00
113 NA(c),The Shriek Of
    Vengeance. 75.00
114 NA(c),My Self-My Enemy!. . . . 60.00
115 BWr,NA(c),Diary Of
    A Madman 60.00
116 NC(c),Express Train
    To Nowhere! 55.00
117 NC(c),Midnight Summons
    The Executioner! 50.00
118 NA(c),A:Judge Gallows,Play
    A Tune For Treachery 50.00
119 BWr,NC(c),Mirror,Mirror
    On The Wall. 75.00
120 NC(c),Rambeau's Revenge . . 50.00
121 BWr,NA(c),Daddy's
    Gone-A-Hunting. 50.00
122 WW,DG(c),The Phantom
    Of The Woodstock Festival . . . 50.00
123 NC(c),Death Watch! 40.00
124 NA(c),These Walls Shall
    Be Your Grave. 40.00
125 NC(c),Screech Of Guilt! 40.00
126 ATh,NC(c),You Are Cordially
    Invited To Die! 40.00
127 GT,JK,ATh,NC(c),Follow The
    Piper To Your Grave 40.00
128 DW,BWr,NC(c),Where Only
    The Dead Are Free!. 40.00
129 NC(c),Farewell To A
    Fading Star 40.00
130 NC(c),One False Step 40.00
131 NC(c),Run For Your Death! . . . 40.00
132 MD,GT,NC(c),The Edge Of
    Madness 40.00
133 WW,JkS(c),A:Judge Gallows,
    Agnes Doesn't Haunt Here
    Anymore! 40.00
134 GT,NC(c),The Restless Dead . 40.00
135 NC(c),Death, Come
    Walk With Me! 40.00

136 SMo,GT,NC(c),An Incident
    of Violence. 40.00
137 WW,NC(c),Dark Vengeance! . 25.00
138 WW,NC(c),Strange Secret of
    the Huan Shan Idol 30.00
139 GT,NC(c),The 2 Brains of
    Beast Bracken! 25.00
140 JkS(c),The Anatomy of Hate. . 25.00
141 NC(c),Just What Did Eric
    See? 25.00
142 NC(c),Let The Dead Sleep! . . 25.00
143 NC(c),Fear is a Nameless
    Voice 25.00
144 NC(c),The Dark Pit of
    Dr. Hanley 25.00
145 NC(c),Grave of Glass 25.00
146 NC(c),The Monstrosity!. 25.00
147 NC(c),The Daughter of
    Dr. Jekyll 25.00
148 NC(c),Baby Wants Me Dead! . 25.00
149 NC(c),To Wake the Dead 25.00
150 NC(c),No One Escapes From
    Gallows Island 25.00
151 NC(c),Sorry, I'm Not Ready
    To Die! 25.00
152 GT,NC(c),Death Wears Many
    Faces. 25.00
153 NC(c),Who's That Sleeping
    In My Grave?. 25.00
154 NC(c),Murder By Madness . . . 25.00
155 NC(c),Non-Stop Journey
    Into Fear 25.00
156 NC(c),A Lunatic Is Loose
    Among Us!. 25.00
157 NC(c),The House of
    the Executioner 60.00
158 NC(c),Reserved for Madmen
    Only. 60.00
159 NC(c),A Cry in the Night 60.00
160 NC(c),Death of an Exorcist . . . 60.00
161 BWr,NC(c),Has Anyone
    Seen My Killer 60.00
162 JK,NC(c),I'll Bug You
    To Your Grave 60.00
163 DD,LD(c),Room For Dying . . . 20.00
164 House of the Sinister Sands . . 20.00
165 LD(c),Slayride in July 20.00
166 LD(c),The Evil Eyes of Night . 20.00
167 LD(c),Scared Stiff 20.00
168 LD(c),Freak Accident 20.00
169 LD(c),What Can Be Worse
    Than Dying? 20.00
170 LD(c),Flee To Your Grave . . . 20.00
171 LD(c),I.O.U. One Corpse 20.00
172 LD(c),Strangler in Paradise . . 20.00
173 LD(c),What Scared Sally? . . . 20.00
174 LD(c),Gauntlet of Fear 20.00
175 LD(c),The Haunted Mountain . 20.00
176 JkS(c),Having A
    Wonderful Crime 20.00
177 ECh(c),Reward for the Wicked 20.00
178 LD(c),Fit To Kill! 20.00
179 LD(c),My Son, The Mortician . 20.00
180 GT,LD(c),The Loathsome
    Lodger of Nightmare Inn 22.00
181 LD(c),Hum of the Haunted . . . 20.00
182 LD(c),Sorry, This Coffin
    is Occupied 20.00
183 LD(c),The Dead Don't
    Always Die. 20.00
184 LD(c),Wheel of Misfortune!. . . 20.00
185 LD(c),Monsters from a
    Thousand Fathoms 20.00
186 LD(c),To Catch a Corpse 20.00
187 LD(c),Mangled in Madness. . . 20.00
188 LD(c),Verdict From The Grave 20.00
189 SD,LD(c),Escape From The
    Grave. 20.00
190 LD(c),The Jigsaw Corpse 20.00
191 MR,JO(c),Night of the Voodoo
    Curse. 22.00
192 LD(c),A Killer Cold & Clammy. 18.00

193 DW,LD(c),Don't Monkey the
　　Murder 18.00
194 LD(c),Have I Got a Ghoul
　　For You 18.00
195 JCr,LD(c),Whose Face is at
　　My Window 18.00
196 LD(c),The Fear of Number 13　15.00
197 LD(c),Last Laugh of a Corpse　15.00
198 JSn(c),Rage of the
　　Phantom Brain. 15.00
199 LD(c),Dracula's Daughter . . . 15.00
200 GT,RA&DG(c),A:Johnny Peril,
　　House on the Edge of Eternity　15.00
201 Do Unto Others. 15.00
202 JO,LD(c),Death Trap. 15.00
203 MK(c),Hang Down Your
　　Head, Joe Mundy 15.00
204 DN,JKu(c),Twinkle, Twinkle
　　Little Star 15.00
205 JkS,A:Johnny Peril,The Second
　　Possession of Angela Lake . . . 15.00
206 JkS,A:Johnny Peril,The
　　Ultimate Assassin 15.00
207 JkS,A:Johnny Peril,Secret of
　　the Second Star. 15.00
208 JkS,A:Johnny Peril,Factory
　　of Fear 15.00
209 JkS,Game for the Ghastly . . . 15.00
210 Vampire of the Apes,Time
　　Warp 15.00
211 A:Johnny Peril,The Temple
　　of the 7 Stars 15.00
212 JkS,MK(c),A:Johnny Peril,The
　　Adventure of the Angel's Smile　15.00
213 A:Johnny Peril,The Woman
　　Who Died Forever 15.00
214 JKu(c),Slaughterhouse Arena.　15.00
215 JKu(c),Is Someone
　　Stalking Sandra 15.00
216 GP,JKu(c),Samurai Nightmare　15.00
217 ShM,DSp,EC(c),Dear Senator　15.00
218 KG,ECh&DG(c),I'll Remember
　　You Yesterday 15.00
219 JKu(c),A Wild Tale. 15.00
220 ShM,JKu(c),The Strange
　　Guide 15.00
221 SD,ShM,JKu(c),Em the
　　Energy Monster. 15.00
222 KG,SD(c). 15.00

TALES OF THE UNEXPECTED
Oct., 2006
1 F:Spectre 4.00
2 thru 8 . . . . @4.00

TANGENT COMICS
(All Oct., 1997)
The Atom #1 DJu,PR,V:Fatal Five. . 3.00
The Flash #1, TDz,GFr,CaS 3.00
Doom Patrol #1 DJu,SCh. 3.00
Green Lantern #1 JeR,JWi,MGy . . . 3.00
The Joker #1 KK,MHy, ... 3.00
Metal Men #1 MRz,MkK 3.00
Nightwing #1 JOs,JD 3.00
Sea Devils #1 KBk,VGi,TP 3.00
The Secret Six #1 CDi,TG, ... 3.00

TANGENT COMICS: SUPERMAN'S REIGN
Mar., 2008
1 (of 12) Tangent Joker. 3.00
2 thru 9 . . . . @3.00

TANGENT '98
(All June, 1998)
The Batman #1 DJu,KJ 2.50
JLA #1 DJu,DBk,V:UltraHumanites . 2.50
Joker's Wild #1 KK 2.50

Tangent The Joker #1
© *DC Comics, Inc.*

Nightwing: Night Force #1 JOs . . 2.50
Powergirl #1 RMz 2.50
The Superman #1 Harvey Dent. . . 2.50
Tales of the Green Lantern #1 . . . . 2.50
The Trials of the Flash #1,
　V:Plastic Man. 2.50
Wonder Woman #1 PDa, ... 2.50

TANK GIRL
1995
1 Movie Adaptation 6.00

TANK GIRL: APOCALYPSE
1995–96
1 AIG,BBo(c) 3.00
2 AIG,BBo(c)Tank Girl Pregnant . . . 3.00
3 AIG,BBo(c) 3.00
4 AIG, finale. 3.00

TANK GIRL: THE ODYSSEY
DC/Vertigo, 1995
1 New Limited Series 3.00
2 BBo(c),Land of Milk & Honey . . . 3.00
3 I:The Sirens 3.00

TARZAN
April, 1972
(Prev. published by Gold Key)
207 JKu,O:Tarzan,pt.1 . . . . 100.00
208 thru 210 JKu,O:Tarzan,pt.2–4.　40.00
211 thru 229 . . . . @30.00
230 RH. 50.00
231 thru 235 . . . . @45.00
236 and 237 . . . . @20.00
238 giant-size. 30.00
239 thru 258 Feb., 1977. . . . . . . @20.00

TARZAN FAMILY
Nov.–Dec., 1975
(Prev.: Korak, Son of Tarzan)
60 B:Korak 20.00
61 thru 66 Nov.–Dec.,1976 . . . . @15.00

TATTERED BANNERS
1998
1 (of 4) AIG(s),MMc 3.00
2 AIG&KG(s),MMc 3.00
3 AIG(s),MMc 3.00
4 AIG(s),MMc, conclusion 3.00

TEAM TITANS
1992–94
1 KM,Total Chaos#3,A:New Titans,
　Deathstroke,V:Lord Chaos,
　BU:KGa,Killowat 4.00
1a thru 1d variant (c)s. . . . . @2.50
2 thru 24 . . . . @2.50
Ann.#1 I:Chimera. 3.50
Ann.#2 PJ,Elseworlds Story. 3.75

TEEN BEAT
Nov.–Dec., 1967
1 Monkees photo 250.00
Becomes:

TEEN BEAM
2 Monkees 250.00

TEEN TITANS
[1st Series]
Jan., 1966
1 NC,Titans join Peace Corps . . 600.00
2 NC,I:Garn Akaru 250.00
3 NC,I:Ding Dong Daddy 150.00
4 NC,A:Speedy 150.00
5 NC,I:Ant 150.00
6 NC,A:Beast Boy. 125.00
7 NC,I:Mad Mod 125.00
8 IN/JAb,I:Titans Copter 125.00
9 NC,A:Teen Titan Sweatshirts. . 125.00
10 NC,I:Bat-Bike 125.00
11 IN/NC A:Speedy 100.00
12 NC,in Spaceville 125.00
13 NC,Christmas story. 100.00
14 NC,I:Gargoyle 100.00
15 NC,I:Capt. Rumble 100.00
16 NC,I:Dimension X 100.00
17 NC,A:Mad Mod 100.00
18 NC,1:Starfire (Russian). 100.00
19 GK,WW,J:Speedy 100.00
20 NA,NC J:Joshua. 125.00
21 NA,NC,A:Hawk,Dove 125.00
22 NA,NC,O:Wondergirl. 125.00
23 GK,NC,N:Wondergirl. 75.00
24 GK,NC. 75.00
25 NC,I:Lilith,A:J.L.A 75.00
26 NC,I:Mal 75.00
27 NC,Nightmare in Space 75.00
28 NC,A:Ocean Master 75.00
29 NC,A:Ocean Master 75.00
30 NC,A:Aquagirl 75.00
31 NC,GT,A:Hawk,Dove 75.00
32 NC,I:Gnarrk. 40.00
33 GT,NS,A:Gnarrk 40.00
34 GT,NC 40.00

Teen Titans #9© DC Comics, Inc.

35 GT,NC,O:Mal 40.00
36 GT,NC,JAp,V:Hunchback 40.00
37 GT,NC 40.00
38 GT,NC 40.00
39 GT,NC,Rep.Hawk & Dove 40.00
40 NC,A:Aqualad 40.00
41 NC,DC,Lilith Mystery 40.00
42 NC,Slaves o/t Emperor Bug . . . 40.00
43 NC,Inherit the Howling Night . . 40.00
44 C:Flash (1976) 40.00
45 IN,V:Fiddler 40.00
46 IN,A:Fiddler 40.00
47 C:Two-Face 20.00
48 I:Bumblebee,Harlequin,
    A:Two-Face 40.00
49 R:Mal As Guardian 20.00
50 DH,I:Teen Titans West 35.00
51 DH,A:Teen Titans West 20.00
52 DH,A:Teen Titans West 20.00
53 O:Teen Titans, A:JLA 20.00

Aug., 1996

1 DJu(s),GP,Titan's Children,
    pt.1 (of 3) 5.00
2 DJu(s),GP,Titan's Children,
    pt.2,V:Prysm 4.00
3 DJu(s),GP,Titan's Children,
    pt.3 . . . . 4.00
4 DJu(s),GP,Coming Out,pt.1,
    A:Robin 3.00
5 DJu(s),GP,Coming Out,pt.2 . . . . 3.00
6 DJu(s),DJu,GP,F:Risk 3.00
7 DJu(s),DJu,GP,The Atom quits
    team. 3.00
8 DJu(s),DJu,GP,J:Atom,V:Dark
    Nemesis. 3.00
9 DJu(s),DJu,GP,Lost World of
    Skartaris, pt.1 . . . . 3.00
10 DJu(s),DJu,GP,Lost World of
    Skartaris, pt.2 . . . . 3.00
11 DJu(s),DJu,GP,Lost World of
    Skartaris, concl.,A:Warlord, . . . 3.00
12 DJu(s),DJu,GP,Original Titans,
    pt.1 (of 4) 48pg 4.00
13 DJu,GP,Original Titans, pt.2
    Genesis tie-in 3.00
14 DJu,GP,Original Titans, pt.3 . . . 3.00
15 DJu,GP,Original Titans, pt.4 . . . 3.00
16 DJu,GP,aftermath 3.00
17 DJu,PJ,team reunites 3.00
18 DJu,PR 3.00
19 DJu,PJ,Millennium Giants,
    A:Superman Red 3.00
20 DJu, night with the Titans 3.00
21 DJu,Titans Hunt,pt.1 . . . . 3.00
22 DJu,Titans Hunt,pt.2 . . . . 3.00
23 DJu,Titans Hunt,pt.3 . . . . 3.00
24 DJu,Titans Hunt,pt.4 . . . . 3.00
Ann.#1 Pulp Heroes (High-
    Adventure) 4.50
Ann.#1 (1967) 80-page, rep. 5.00

July 2003

1 MMK 8.00
1a 2nd printing 3.50
2 MMK,Cyborg 4.00
3 MMK, ... 7.00
4 MMK,disobey order 4.00
5 MMk,Infighting 4.00
6 MMk, ... 2.50
7 MMk,F:Superman 2.50
8 TG,F:Raven 2.50
9 Raven Rising,pt.1 . . . . 2.50
10 Raven Rising,pt.2 . . . . 2.50
11 Raven Rising,pt.3 . . . . 2.50
12 Raven Rising,pt.4 . . . . 2.50
13 Raven Rising,pt.5 . . . . 2.50
14 Beast Boys and Girls,pt.1 . . . . 2.50
15 Beast Boys and Girls,pt.2 . . . . 2.50
16 MMk,Lost to the Legion,pt.1 . . . 5.00
17 MMk,Titans Tomorrow,pt.1 . . . . 5.00
18 MMK,Titans Tomorrow, pt.2 . . 10.00
19 MMk,Titans Tomorrow, pt.3 . . . 5.00
20 TG,Nel,V:Warp,Electrocutioner . . 4.00

21 MMK,Lights Out,pt.1 . . . . 8.00
22 MMK,Lights Out,pt. 2 . . . . 5.00
23 MMK,Lights Out,pt. 3 . . . . 5.00
24 MFm,The Insiders,x-over,pt.1 . . 4.00
25 MFm,The Insiders,x-over,pt.3 . . 3.50
26 TnD,F:Superboy,Raven 2.50
27 RLd,Cosmic chaos 2.50
28 RLd,Cosmic chaos, pt.2 . . . . . . 2.50
29 V:Red Hood 2.50
30 Brother Blood Returns, pt.1 . . . 2.50
31 V:Brother Blood. 2.50
32 Infinite Crisis tie-in 2.50
33 MWm(s),Infinite Crisis tie-in . . . 2.50
34 One Year Later, New Teen
    Titans, pt.1 . . . . 2.50
34a variant (c) 2.50
35 New Teen Titans, pt.2 . . . . 2.50
36 New Teen Titans, pt.3 . . . . 3.00
37 New Teen Titans, pt.4 . . . . 3.00
38 Titans Around the World,pt.1 . . 3.00
39 Titans Around the World,pt.2 . . 3.00
40 Titans Around the World,pt.3 . . 3.00
41 Titans Around the World, concl. . 3.00
42 F:Kid Devil V:BLue Devil. 3.00
43 Titans East, pt.1 . . . . 3.00
44 Titans East, pt.2 . . . . 3.00
45 Titans East, pt.3 . . . . 3.00
46 Titans East, pt.4 . . . . 3.00
47 Countdown begins 3.00
48 Amazon's Attack tie-in. 3.00
49 Amazon's Attack x-over 3.00
50 48-pgs. 4.00
50a variant (c) (1:10) 4.00
51 Titans of Tomorrow 3.00
52 V:Starro 3.00
53 Titans of Tomorrow, Today 3.00
54 Titans of Tomorrow 3.00
55 New Clock King 3.00
56 New Bolt 3.00
57 Attack on Titans Tower 3.00
58 Miss Martian, M'gann M'orzz . . . 3.00
59 V:Clock King Terror Titans 3.00
60 V:Terror Titans. 3.00
61 The Red and the Blue. 3.00
62 F:Cyborg, Wonderdog 3.00
63 F:Bombshell 3.00
64 F:Bombshell 3.00
65 F:Wonder Girl 3.00
Ann. #1 MWm(s), 48-pg.(2006) . . . 5.00
Ann. The Lost Annual (2008). 5.00
Spec. Swingin' Elseworlds Spec. . . 6.00
Spec. Teen Titans/Legion 4.00
Spec. Teen Titans Outsiders,
    Secret Files 6.00
Spec. Teen Titans/Secret
    Files 2005 . . . . 5.00

TEEN TITANS EAST

Nov., 2008

Spec. #1 Cyborg and New Team . . . 4.00

TEEN TITANS GO!

Nov. 2003

1 F:Robin,Cyborg,Beast Boy 2.50
2 thru 55 . . . . @2.50

TEEN TITANS SPOTLIGHT

Aug., 1986

1 DCw,DG,Starfire Apartheid 4.00
2 DCw,DG,Starfire Apartheid#2. . . 3.00
3 RA,Jericho 3.00
4 RA,Jericho 3.00
5 RA,Jericho 3.00
6 RA,Jericho 3.00
7 JG,Hawk. 4.00
8 JG,Hawk 3.00
9 Changeling. 3.00
10 EL,Aqualad And Mento 3.00
11 JO,Brotherhood of Evil 3.00

*Teen Titans Spotlight #10 ©
DC Comics, Inc.*

12 EC,Wondergirl. 3.00
13 Cyborg 3.00
14 1st Nightwing/BatmanTeam-up. . 4.00
15 EL,Omega Men. 3.00
16 Thunder And Lightning 3.00
17 DH,Magennta 3.00
18 ATi,Aqualad,A:Aquaman 3.00
19 Starfire,A:Harbinger,Millennium
    X-over 3.00
20 RT(i),Cyborg 3.00
21 DSp,Flashback sty w/orig.Teen
    Titans 3.00

TEEN TITANS: YEAR ONE

Jan., 2008

1 (of 6) KK 3.00
2 A:Flash, Aquaman, Green Arrow . . 3.00
3 V:Possessed Justice League. . . . 3.00
4 F:Wally West 3.00
5 Wonder Girl, Speedy 3.00
6 conclusion 3.00

TEMPEST

Mini-series Sept., 1996

1 thru 4 (of 4) from Aquaman . . . @2.50

TEMPUS FUGITIVE

1990

1 KSy,Time Travel,I:Ray 27 . . . . . . 6.00
2 KSy,Viet Nam. 6.00
3 KSy,World War I. 6.00
4 KSy,final issue 6.00

TERMINAL CITY

DC/Vertigo, 1996–97

1 thru 3 DMt(s),MLr, ... @2.50
4 DMt(s),MLr,I:Kid Gloves. 2.50
5 DMt(s),MLr,Missing link is loose . 2.50
6 DMt(s),MLr, ... 2.50
7 DMt(s),MLr,A:Lady in Red 2.50
8 DMt(s),MLr, ... 2.50
9 (of 9) DMt(s),MLr,finale 2.50

TERMINAL CITY: AERIAL GRAFFITI

DC/Vertigo, Sept., 1997

1 (of 5) DMt,MLr,MCo(c). 2.50
2 DMt,MLr,MCo(c),F:Cosmo Quinn 2.50
3 DMt,MLr,MCo(c), ... 2.50
4 DMt,MLr,MCo(c) 2.50

TERRA
Nov., 2008
1 JP,Power Girl, Doctor Mid-Nite . . 3.00
2 . . . . 3.00

TERROR TITANS
Oct., 2008
1 (of 6) V:Ravager 3.00
2 F:Ravager 3.00

TESTAMENT
DC/Vertigo, Dec., 2005
1 thru 5 LSh . . . . @3.00
6 thru 22 . . . . @3.00

3-D Adventures of Superman
© DC Comics Inc.

3-D ADVENTURES OF SUPERMAN
1953
N# O:Superman 1,600.00

3-D BATMAN ADVENTURES
1953, 1966
1 with Bat-glasses 1,600.00
1a A:Tommy Tomorrow (1966) . . 500.00

THE THREE MOUSEKETEERS
1956–60
1 . . . . 300.00
2 . . . . 150.00
3 thru 10 . . . . @125.00
11 thru 20 . . . . @100.00
21 thru 26 . . . . @100.00

THRILLER
Nov., 1983
1 TVE 2.50
2 TVE,O:Thriller 2.50
3 TVE 2.50
4 TVE 2.50
5 TVE,DG,Elvis satire 2.50
6 TVE,Elvis satire 2.50
7 thru 10 TVE . . . . @2.50
11 & 12 AN . . . . @2.50

THRILLING COMICS
1999
1 CDi(s),RH,F:Hawkman & Wildcat. 2.50

THRILLKILLER
Elseworlds 1997
1 HC(s),DIB,F:Robin and Batgirl. . . 3.50
2 HC(s),DIB, ... 3.00
3 HC(s),DIB,conl. 3.00

THRILLKILLERS '62
Feb., 1998
GN HC,DIB. 5.00

TIMBER WOLF
1992–93
1 AG(i),V:Thrust 2.50
2 V:Captain Flag 2.50
3 AG(i),V:Creeper 2.50
4 AG(i),V:Captain Flag 2.50
5 AG(i),V:Dominators,Capt.Flag . . . 2.50

TIME BREAKERS
DC/Helix, 1997
1 (of 5) RaP(s),CWn,time paradoxes created. 2.50
2 RaP(s),CWn, ... 2.50
3 RaP(s),CWn,expedition to 20th century England 2.50
4 RaP(s),CWn,Angela travels back in time 2.50
5 RaP(s),CWn,final issue 2.50

TIME MASTERS
Feb., 1990
1 ATi,O:Rip Hunter,A:JLA 2.50
2 ATi,A:Superman 2.50
3 ATi,A:Jonah Hex, Cave Carson . . 2.50
4 thru 8 ATi, ... @2.50

TIME WARP
Oct.–Nov., 1979
1 JAp,RB,SD,MK(c),DN,TS 20.00
2 DN,JO,TS,HC,SD,MK(c),GK . . . 15.00
3 DN,SD,MK(c),TS 15.00
4 MN,SD,MK(c),DN 15.00
5 DN,MK(c),July, 1980 . . . . 12.00

TINY TITANS
Feb., 2008
1 . . . . 2.50
2 thru 10 . . . . @2.50

TITANS
1999
1 MBu, new team, two covers 3.50
2 MBu,A:Superman 3.00
3 MBu 3.00
4 MBu,V:Goth 3.00
5 MBu,A:Siren. 3.00
6 MBu,A:Green Lantern 3.00
7 MBu,Velocity 10, pt.1 . . . . 3.00
8 MBu,Velocity 10, pt.2. . . . . 3.00
9 Day of Judgment x-over 3.00
10 MBu,F:Changeling & Deathstroke 3.00
11 MBu. 3.00
12 MBu,This Immortal Coil,pt.3 . . . 3.50
13 internal fight 3.00
14 to Scotland 3.00
15 MBu,pt.1 . . . . 3.00
16 MBu,V:Gargoyle 3.00
17 ALa,into space 3.00
18 ALa,into space,pt.2 . . . . 3.00
19 ALa,into space,pt.3 . . . . 3.00
20 ALa,end of Cyborg 3.00
21 PaP,Hangmen. 3.00
22 PaP,Arsenal vs. Deathstroke . . 3.00
23 PaP,Who's Troia?,pt.1. . . . . 3.00
24 PaP,Who's Troia?,pt.2. . . . . 3.00
25 MWn,GP,48-page 4.00
26 PaP,V:Shockwave 3.00

27 PaP,F:Cheshire,Epsilon 3.00
28 PaP,The All-Nighter. 3.00
29 PaP,tower of troublemakers 3.00
30 JP,Sins of the Past 3.00
31 JP,V:Theta. 3.00
32 V:Dakota Jameson 3.00
33 V:Theta 3.00
34 Cheshire Smile,Last Laugh. 3.00
35 F:Beast Boy & Flamebird 3.00
36 V:Wildebeests. 3.00
37 BKi,in the Orphanage 3.00
38 BKi,V:Epsilon,final stand. 3.00
39 BKi,V:Dark Nemesis 3.00
40 BKi,F:The Favored 3.00
41 PGr,F:Nikki 3.00
42 BKi,Chemical World,pt.1 . . . . 3.00
43 BKi,Chemical World,pt.2 . . . . 3.00
44 BKi,JmP,Chemical World,pt.3 . . . 3.00
45 BKi,JmP,F:Damage. 3.00
46 BKi,JmP,F:Damag,Jesse 3.00
47 TPe,BKi,PGr,JmP 3.00
48 TPe,BKi,JmP,Murder,pt.1 . . . . . . 3.00
49 TPe,BKi,JmP,Murder,pt.2 . . . . . . 3.00
50 TPe,BKi,JmP,final issue 3.00
Ann.#1 Planet DC 4.00
Spec. Secret Files #1. . . . . 5.50
Spec. Secret Files #2. . . . . 5.50
GN Scissors, Paper, Stone, manga style (1997) 5.50

TITANS SELL-OUT SPECIAL
1 SE,AV,I:Teeny Titans, w/Nightwing poster 3.75

TITANS
April, 2008
1 New team of Titans, 40-pg. 3.50
1a variant (c) (1:10) 3.50
2 Titans under fire. 3.00
3 Internal fighting 3.00
4 Sons of Trigon 3.00
5 Raven's half-brothers. 3.00
6 Raven missing 3.00
7 F:Match 3.00

TITANS, THE/LEGION OF SUPER-HEROES: UNIVERSE ABLAZE
Jan., 2000
1 (of 4) DJu,PJ 5.00
2 thru 4 DJu,PJ . . . . @5.00

TITANS, THE/ YOUNG JUSTICE: GRADUATION DAY
May 2003
1 (of 3) 20.00
2 Indigo 11.00
3 Concl.. 13.00

TOE TAGS FEATURING GEORGE ROMERO
2004
1 . . . . 3.00
2 thru 6 . . . . @3.00

TOMAHAWK
1950
1 Prisoner Called Tomahawk. . 2,700.00
2 FF(4pgs),Four Boys Against the Frontier 1,000.00
3 Warpath 750.00
4 Tomahawk Wanted: Dead or Alive. 750.00
5 The Girl Who Was Chief 750.00
6 Tomahawk-King of the Aztecs . 600.00
7 Punishment of Tomahawk 600.00
8 The King's Messenger 600.00

9 The Five Doomed Men 600.00
10 Frontied Sabotage 600.00
11 Girl Who Hated Tomahawk . . . 400.00
12 Man From Magic Mountain . . . 400.00
13 Dan Hunter's Rival 400.00
14 The Frontier Tinker 400.00
15 The Wild Men of
  Wigwam Mountain 400.00
16 Treasure of the Angelique 400.00
17 Short-Cut to Danger 400.00
18 Bring In M'Sieur Pierre 400.00
19 The Lafayette Volunteers 400.00
20 NC(c),The Retreat of
  Tomahawk 400.00
21 NC(c),The Terror of the
  Wrathful Spirit 300.00
22 CS(c),Admiral Tomahawk . . . 300.00
23 CS(c),The Indian Chief
  from Oxford 300.00
24 NC(c),Adventure In the
  Everglades. 300.00
25 NC(c),The Star-Gazer of
  Freemont 300.00
26 NC(c),Ten Wagons For
  Tomahawk 300.00
27 NC(c),Frontier Outcast 300.00
28 I:Lord Shilling 325.00
29 Conspiracy of Wounded Bear. 350.00
30 The King of the Thieves 300.00
31 NC(c),The Buffalo Brave
  From Misty Mountain. 300.00
32 NC(c),The Clocks That
  Went to War. 300.00
33 The Paleface Tribe 300.00
34 The Capture of General
  Washington 300.00
35 Frontier Feud 300.00
36 NC(c),A Cannon for Fort
  Reckless 300.00
37 NC(c),Feathered Warriors. . . . 300.00
38 The Frontier Zoo. 300.00
39 The Redcoat Trickster. 300.00
40 Fearless Fettle-Daredevil 300.00
41 The Captured Chieftain. 300.00
42 The Prisoner Tribe 300.00
43 Tomahawk's Little Brother. . . . 300.00
44 Tho Brave Named Tomahawk 300.00
45 The Last Days of Chief Tory . . 300.00
46 The Chief With 1,000 Faces . . 200.00
47 The Frontier Rain-Maker. 200.00
48 Indian Twin Trouble. 200.00
49 The Unknown Warrior. 200.00
50 The Brave Who Was Jinxed . . 200.00
51 General Tomahawk. 200.00
52 Tom Thumb of the Frontier . . . 200.00
53 The Four-Footed Renegade . . 200.00
54 Mystery of the 13th Arrows . . . 200.00
55 Prisoners of the Choctaw 200.00
56 The Riddle of the
  Five Little Indians 200.00
57 The Strange Fight
  at Fort Bravo 250.00
58 Track of the Mask 150.00
59 The Mystery Prisoner of
  Lost Island. 150.00
60 The Amazing Walking Fort . . . 150.00
61 Tomahawk's Secret Weapons. 135.00
62 Strongest Man in the World . . 135.00
63 The Frontier Super Men 135.00
64 The Outcast Brave 135.00
65 Boy Who Wouldn't Be Chief . . 135.00
66 DD&SMo(c),A Trap For
  Tomahawk 135.00
67 DD&SMo(c),Frontier Sorcerer 135.00
68 DD&SMo(c),Tomahawk's
  Strange Ally 135.00
69 DD&SMo(c),Tracker-King
  of the Wolves. 135.00
70 DD&SMo(c),Three Tasks
  for Tomahawk 135.00
71 DD&SMo(c),The Boy Who
  Betrayed His Country 135.00

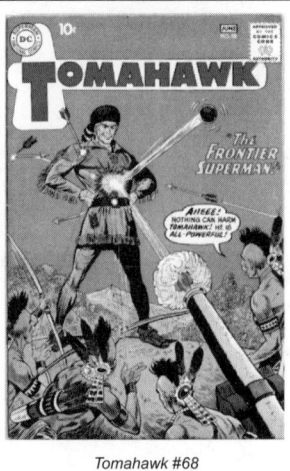

Tomahawk #68
© DC Comics, Inc.

72 DD&SMo(c),The Frontier Pupil 135.00
73 DD&SMo(c),The Secret of
  the Indian Sorceress 135.00
74 DD&SMo(c),The Great
  Paleface Masquerade 135.00
75 DD&SMo(c),The Ghost of
  Lord Shilling. 135.00
76 DD&SMo(c),The Totem-Pole
  Trail 135.00
77 DD&SMo(c),The Raids of
  the One-Man Tribe 135.00
78 DD&SMo(c),The Menace
  of the Mask 125.00
79 DD&SMo(c),Eagle Eye's
  Debt of Honor 125.00
80 DD&SMo(c),The Adventures
  of Tracker 85.00
81 The Strange Omens of
  the Indian Seer 85.00
82 The Son of the Tracker. 85.00
83 B:Tomahawk Rangers,
  Against the Tribe 85.00
84 There's a Coward Among
  the Rangers. 85.00
85 The Wispering War 85.00
86 Rangers vs. King Colossus . . . 75.00
87 The Secrets of Sgt.
  Witch Doctor 75.00
88 The Rangers Who Held
  Back the Earth. 75.00
89 The Terrible Tree-Man 75.00
90 The Prisoner In The Pit. 75.00
91 The Tribe Below the Earth 75.00
92 The Petrified Sentry of
  Peaceful Valley 75.00
93 The Return of King Colosso . . . 75.00
94 Rip Van Ranger 75.00
95 The Tribe Beneath the Sea. . . . 75.00
96 The Ranger Killers 75.00
97 The Prisoner Behind the
  Bull's-Eye. 75.00
98 The Pied Piper Rangers 75.00
99 The Rangers vs.ChiefCobweb . 75.00
100 The Weird Water-Tomahawk . 85.00
101 Tomahawk, Enemy Spy 60.00
102 The Dragon Killers 60.00
103 The Frontier Frankenstein . . . 60.00
104 The Fearful Freak of
  Dunham's Dungeon. 60.00
105 The Attack of the Gator God . . 60.00
106 The Ghost of Tomahawk. 60.00
107 Double-Cross of the
  Gorilla Ranger. 60.00
108 New Boss For the Rangers . . 60.00
109 The Caveman Ranger 60.00

110 Tomahawk Must Die 60.00
111 Vengeance of the Devil-Dogs . 60.00
112 The Rangers vs. Tomahawk . . 60.00
113 The Mad Miser of
  Carlisle Castle 60.00
114 The Terrible Power of
  Chief Iron Hands 60.00
115 The Deadly Flaming Ranger . . 60.00
116 NA(c),The Last Mile of
  Massacre Trail. 90.00
117 NA(c),Rangers'Last Stand. . . . 60.00
118 NA(c),Tomahawk, Guilty
  of Murder. 60.00
119 NA(c),Bait For a Buzzard 60.00
120 NC(c),The Coward Who
  Lived Forever 60.00
121 NA(c),To Kill a Ranger 60.00
122 IN(c),Must the Brave Die 60.00
123 NA(c),The Stallions of Death . 60.00
124 NA(c),The Valley of
  No Return 60.00
125 NA(c),A Chief's Feather
  For Little Bear 60.00
126 NA(c),The Baron of
  Gallows Hill 60.00
127 NA(c),The Devil is Waiting . . . 60.00
128 NA(c),Rangers-Your 9
  Lives For Mine. 60.00
129 NA(c),Treachery at
  Thunder Ridge. 60.00
130 NA(c),Deathwatch at
  Desolation Valley. 60.00
131 JKu(c),B:Son of Tomahawk,
  Hang Him High 60.00
132 JKu(c),Small Eagle...Brother
  Hawk 30.00
133 JKu(c),Scalp Hunter 30.00
134 JKu(c),The Rusty Ranger 30.00
135 JKu(c),Death on Ghost
  Mountain 30.00
136 JKu(c),A Piece of Sky 40.00
137 JKu(c),Night of the Knife. 40.00
138 JKu(c),A Different Kind
  of Christmas 40.00
139 JKu(c),Death Council 50.00
140 Jku(c),The Rescue 40.00

TOR
May-June, 1975
1 JKu,O:Tor. 20.00
2 thru 6, Tor reprints . . . . @12.00
May, 2008
1 (of 6) JKu,Prehistoric adventure . 3.00
2 thru 6 JKu . . . . @3.00

TOTAL JUSTICE
Sept., 1996
1 thru 6 CPr(s),RBe,DG, toy
  line tie-in . . . . @2.50

TOTAL RECALL
1990
1 Movie Adaption 3.00

TOUCH
DC Focus Apr. 2004
1 Rory Goodman, Las Vegas 2.50
2 thru 6 . . . . @2.50

TRANSMETROPOLITAN
DC/Helix, July, 1997
1 WEI,DaR,JeM, gonzo journalism
  in 21st century. 15.00
2 WEI,DaR,Angels 8 district 8.00
3 WEI,DaR, riot in Angels 8 . . . . . 7.00
4 WEI,DaR, Vs President of US . . . 4.00
5 WEI,DaR, Watches TV 4.00
6 WEI,DaR,evangelicals 4.00
7 WEI,DaR 4.00

Transmetropolitan #8
© DC Comics Inc.

8 WEI,DaR,AnotherColdMorning . . 4.00
9 WEI,DaR,Wild in the Country . . . 3.00
10 WEI,DaR,Freeze Me with
   Your Kiss, pt.1 . . . . 3.00
11 WEI,DaR,Freeze Me, pt.2 . . . . . . 3.00
12 WEI,DaR,Freeze Me, pt.3 . . . . . . 3.00
13 WEI,DaR,JaL(c),Year of the
   Bastard, pt.1 . . . . 3.00
14 WEI,DaR,JaL(c),Bastard,pt.2 . . . 3.00
15 WEI,DaR,JaL(c),Bastard,pt.3 . . . 3.00
16 WEI,DaR,Bastard,pt.4 . . . . 3.00
17 WEI,DaR,Bastard,pt.5 . . . . 3.00
18 WEI,DaR,Bastard, concl. 3.00
19 WEI,DaR,New Scum,pt.1 . . . . . . 3.00
20 WEI,DaR,New Scum,pt.2 . . . . . . 3.00
21 WEI,DaR,New Scum,pt.3 . . . . . 2.50
22 WEI,DaR,New Scum,pt.4 . . . . . 2.50
23 WEI,DaR,New Scum,pt.5 . . . . . 2.50
24 WEI,DaR,New Scum,pt.6 . . . . . 2.50
25 WEI,DaR,JLe(c),Days in
   the City #1 . . . . 2.50
26 WEI,DaR,RyR,JLe(c),Days in
   the City #2 . . . . 2.50
27 WEI,DaR,RyR,JLe(c) 2.50
28 WEI,DaR,RyR,LonelyCity,pt.1. . . 2.50
29 WEI,DaR,RyR,LonelyCity,pt.2. . . 2.50
30 WEI,DaR,RyR,LonelyCity,pt.3. . . 2.50
31 WEI,DaR,RyR,F:Spider. 2.50
32 WEI,DaR,RyR, ... 2.50
33 WEI,DaR,RyR 2.50
34 WEI,DaR,RyR,Gouge Away,pt.1 . 2.50
35 WEI,DaR,RyR,Gouge Away,pt.2 . 2.50
36 WEI,DaR,RyR,Gouge Away,pt.3 . 2.50
37 WEI,DaR,Back to Basics,pt.1 . . . 2.50
38 WEI,DaR,Back to Basics,pt.2 . . . 2.50
39 WEI,DaR,Back to Basics,pt.3 . . . 2.50
40 WEI,DaR,Streets atNight,pt.1 . . . 2.50
41 WEI,DaR,Streets atNight,pt.2 . . . 2.50
42 WEI,DaR,Streets atNight,pt.3 . . . 2.50
43 WEI,DaR,Dirge,pt.1. . . . . 2.50
44 WEI,DaR,Dirge,pt.2. . . . . 2.50
45 WEI,DaR,Dirge,pt.3. . . . . 2.50
46 WEI,DaR,Dirge aftermath 2.50
47 WEI,DaR,A Disaster Zone 2.50
48 WEI,DaR,Year Four begins 2.50
49 WEI,DaR,rebuild Spider's case. . 2.50
50 WEI,DaR,Filthy Assistants 2.50
51 WEI,DaR,F:Mitchell Royce 2.50
52 WEI,DaR,The Cure,pt.1 . . . . 2.50
53 WEI,DaR,The Cure,pt.2 . . . . 2.50
54 WEI,DaR,The Cure,pt.3 . . . . 2.50
55 WEI,DaR,Vita Severn Zone 2.50
56 WEI,DaR,Martial law. 2.50
57 WEI,DaR,White House siege . . . 2.50

58 WEI,DaR,martial law. 2.50
59 WEI,DaR,final meeting 2.50
60 WEI,DaR,final issue 2.50
GN I Hate it Here. 6.00
GN Filth of the City 6.00

TRENCHCOAT BRIGADE
DC/Vertigo, 1999
1 (of 4) JNR(s),F:John Constantine,
   Mister E, Dr.Occult, Phantom
   Stranger 2.50
2 JNR 2.50
3 JNR 2.50
4 JNR, conclusion. 2.50

TRIALS OF SHAZAM
Aug., 2006
1 (of 12) HPo, The Boy & The Man 3.00
2 thru 9 HPo . . . . @3.00
10 thru 12. . . . . @3.00

TRIGGER
DC/Vertigo, Dec., 2004
1 JWk,F:Deirdre Myers. 3.00
2 JWk 3.00
3 JWk 3.00
4 JWk 3.00
5 JWk 3.00
6 JWk, concl. 3.00
7 JWk, I:Leonard. 3.00
8 JWk 3.00

TRINITY
June, 2008
1 KBk&FaN(s),weekly, 40-pg.. . . . 3.00
2 MBa,ATi,V:Konvikt 3.00
3 MBa,ATi,V:Konvikt 3.00
4 MBa,ATi,JOy,V:Konvikt 3.00
5 MBa,ATi,V:Konvikt 3.00
6 MBa,ATi 3.00
7 MBa,ATi 3.00
8 MBa,ATi,Cosmic Egg. 3.00
9 MBa,ATi,Batman vs. Howlers . . 3.00
10 MBa,ATi,Antimatter Earth 3.00
11 MBa,ATi,The Crime Syndicate . . 3.00
12 MBa,ATi,V:The Crime Syndicate 3.00
13 MBa,ATi,JLe&SW(c),Ultraman . . 3.00
14 MBa,ATi,JLe&SW(c),Superman . 3.00
15 MBa,ATi,JLe&SW(c),Batman . . . 3.00
16 MBa,ATi,JLe&SW(c),W.Woman . 3.00
17 MBa,ATi,JLe&SW(c),Superman . 3.00
18 MBa,ATi,JLe&SW(c) 3.00
19 MBa,ATi. 3.00
20 MBa,ATi. 3.00
21 MBa,ATi. 3.00
22 MBa,ATi,NKu(c) 3.00
23 MBa,ATi. 3.00
24 MBa,ATi. 3.00
25MBa,ATi 3.00
26 MBa,ATi. 3.00

TRIUMPH
[Mini-Series], 1995
1 From Zero Hour. 2.50
2 Teamates Peril. 2.50
3 V:Mind Readers. 2.50

TROUBLE MAGNET
Dec., 1999
1 (of 4) KPI, F:robot whose mind
   has been stolen. 2.50
2 KPI 2.50
3 KPI 2.50
4 KPI,concl. 2.50

TV SCREEN CARTOONS
See: REAL SCREEN COMICS

2020 VISIONS
DC/Vertigo, April, 1997
1 (of 12) the Disunited States
   of America 2.50
2 JaD(s), ... 2.50
3 JaD(s), ... 2.50
4 JaD(s),WaP,La Tormenta,pt.1 . . . 2.50
5 JaD(s),WaP,La Tormenta,pt.2 . . . 2.50
6 JaD(s),WaP,La Tormenta,pt.3 . . . 2.50
7 JaD(s),Renegade,pt.1 . . . . 2.50
8 JaD(s),Renegade,pt.2 . . . . 2.50
9 JaD(s),Renegade,pt.3 . . . . 2.50
10 JaD(s),Repro-Man,pt.1 . . . . 2.50
11 JaD(s),Repro-Man,pt.2 . . . . 2.50
12 JaD(s),Repro-Man,pt.3 . . . . 2.50

TWILIGHT
1990–91
1 JL,Last Frontier 5.50
2 JL,K.SorensenVs.T.Tomorrow . . . 5.00
3 JL,K.SorensenVs.T.Tomorrow . . . 5.00

TWO-FACE YEAR ONE
July, 2000
1 (of 2) 48-pg. 6.00
2 . . . . 6.00

UNAUTHORIZED BIO
OF LEX LUTHOR
1989
1 EB 4.00

UNCLE SAM
DC/Vertigo, Nov, 1997
GN 1 (of 2) AxR. 5.00
GN 2 AxR. 5.00

UNCLE SAM AND
THE FREEDOM FIGHTERS
July, 2006
1 (of 8) JP, Shade task force 3.00
2 JP, Wanted: Uncle Sam. 3.00
3 JP, Arizona Desert. 3.00
4 JP. 3.00
5 JP. 3.00
6 thru 8JP . . . . @3.00
Vol. 2, 2007
1 (of 8) JP 3.00
2 JP. 3.00
3 JP,O:Doll Man 3.00
4 JP,V:Doll Man. 3.00
5 JP,Human Bomb 3.00
6 JP,Red Bee's powers. 3.00
7 JP,V:Red Bee. 3.00
8 JP,conclusion. 3.00

UNDERWORLD
Dec., 1987
1 EC,New Yorks Finest. 2.50
2 EC,A:Black Racer 2.50
3 EC,V:Black Racer 2.50
4 EC,final issue. 2.50

UNDERWORLD
UNLEASHED
1995–96
1 PWa,F:Neron 5.00
2 PWa,Neron Vs.Green Lantern. . . 4.00
3 PWa,conclusion 4.00
Abyss—Hell's Sentinel 1-shot . . . 3.00
Apokolips-Dark Uprising 1-shot . . . 3.00
Batman—Devil's Asylum 1-shot
   AIG,BSz 3.00
Patterns of Fear 1-shot 3.00

All comics prices listed are for *Near Mint* condition.

Untold Legend of Batman #1
© DC Comics, Inc.

UNEXPECTED, THE
See: TALES OF
THE UNEXPECTED

UNKNOWN SOLDIER
See: STAR SPANGLED

UNKNOWN SOLDIER

April, 1988
1 True Origin revealed,Viet
  Nam 1970 . . . . 4.00
2 Origin contd.,Iran 1977 . . . 3.00
3 Origin contd.Afghanistan1982 . . . 3.00
4 Nicaragua 3.00
5 Nicaragua contd. 3.00
6 . . . . 3.00
7 Libia 3.00
8 Siberia, U.S.S.R. 3.00
9 North Korea 1952 . . . . 3.00
10 C.I.A. 3.00
11 C.I.A., Army Intelligence 3.00
12 final issue,1989. . . . . 3.00

DC/Vertigo, Feb., 1997
1 (of 4) GEn(s),KPI,F:maverick
  CIA agent. 7.00
2 GEn(s),KPI,search for Unknown
  Soldier continues. 5.00
3 GEn(s),KPI,search for Unknown
  Soldier continues. 5.00
4 GEn(s),KPI,intrigue, finale 5.00

DC/Vertigo, Oct., 2008
1 . . . . 3.00
1a variant RCo(c) (1:10). 3.50
2 . . . . 3.00

UN-MEN, THE

DC/Vertigo, Aug., 2007
1 Get Your Freak On, pt.1 . . . . . . 3.00
2 Get Your Freak On, pt.2 . . . . . . 3.00
3 Get Your Freak On, pt.3 . . . . . . 3.00
4 Get Your Freak On, pt.4 . . . . . . 3.00
5 Get Your Freak On, concl. 3.00
6 Domestic Disturbances 3.00
7 Children of Paradox, pt.1. . . . . . 3.00
8 Children of Paradox, pt.2. . . . . . 3.00
9 A shocking secret. 3.00
10 Sickening secret 3.00
11 Kilcrop's secret past 3.00
12 Uncorp Asunder, pt.1 . . . . 3.00
13 Uncorp Asunder, pt.2 . . . . 3.00

UNTOLD LEGEND
OF BATMAN

July, 1980
1 JA,JBy,(1st DC work)O:Batman . 6.00
2 JA,O:Joker&Robin 4.50
3 JA,O:Batgirl 4.50

USER

DC/Vertigo, Jan., 2001
1 (of 3) 48-page 6.00
2 JBo,SeP,48-page 6.00
3 JBo,SeP,48-page 6.00

V

(TV Adaptation)
Feb., 1985
1 Cl/TD 3.00
2 thru 5 Cl/TD . . . . @2.50
6 thru 16 Cl/TD . . . . @2.50
17 & 18 DG . . . . @2.50

VALOR

1992–94
1 N:Valor,A:Lex Luthor Jr 3.00
2 thru4 MBr,AGI . . . . @2.50
5 thru 23 . . . . @2.50

VERMILLION

DC/Helix, Aug., 1996
1 ADv,MKu(c) Lucius Shepard
  story. 2.50
2 ADv,MKu(c) Jonathan Cave's
  cover blown 2.50
3 ADv,riot aboard space ship,
  Ildiko's tale. 2.50
4 ADv,Starship's engines run wild. . 2.50
5 ADv 2.50
6 ADv,Creation of Vermillion 2.50
7 ADv,Jonathan Cave discovers
  hiding place of enemy 2.50
8 ADv,Joyland 2.50
9 GEr, the library in Kaia Mortai . . . 2.50
10 GEr, Lord Iron and Lady
  Manganese, pt.2 . . . . 2.50
11 GEr,Lord Iron and Lady
  Manganese, concl. 2.50
12 final issue 2.50

VERTICAL

DC/Vertigo, Dec. 2003
Spec. MiA,64-pg. 5.00

VERTIGO JAM

1993
1 GF(c),NGa(s),ANo(s),PrM(s),GEn(s),
  JaD(s),KN,SDi,SEa,NyC(s),EiS,PhH,
  KDM(i),SeP,MiA,RaP(s),MPn(i),
  Vertigo Short Stories 4.50

VERTIGO POP!

TOKYO
DC/Vertigo, July, 2002
1 (of 4) by Seth Fisher 3.00
2 thru 4 . . . . @3.00

LONDON
DC/Vertigo, Nov., 2002
1 (of 4) PrM,PBd. 3.00
2 thru 4 PrM,PBd . . . . @3.00

BANGKOK
DC/Vertigo, May 2003
1 (of 4) 3.00
2 thru 4 . . . . @3.00

VERTIGO PREVIEW

1992
Preview of new Vertigo titles,
  new Sandman story. 2.50

VERTIGO SECRET FILES:
HELLBLAZER

Jan., 2005
1 rep. 5.00

VERTIGO VERITE:

HELL ETERNAL
Feb., 1998
1-shot JaD,SeP 7.00

...THE SYSTEM
1 thru 3 . . . . @3.00
GN Seven Miles a Second 8.00

...THE UNSEEN HAND
DC/Vertigo, 1996
1 thru 3 TLa. . . . . @2.50
4 TLa, final issue 2.50

...DR. OCCULT
1 F:Dr. Occult 4.00

...DR. THIRTEEN
DC/Vertigo, July, 1998
GN evil artificial intelligence. 6.00

VERTIGO VISIONS:

THE GEEK
1993
1 RaP(s),MiA,V:Dr.Abuse 4.00

...PHANTOM STRANGER
1993
1 AaK(s),GyD,The Infernal House . 4.00

...THE EATERS
1995
1 I:The Quills. 5.00

...TOMAHAWK
DC/Vertigo, May, 1998
GN RaP,TY 5.00

VEXT

1999
1 KG,MMK,MkM 2.50
2 th`ru 6 KG,MMK,MkM. . . . . . . @2.50

V FOR VENDETTA

Sept., 1988
1 Reps.Warrior Mag(U.K.),I:V,
  A:M.Storm (Moore scripts). 6.00
2 Murder Spree. 5.00
3 Govt. Investigators close in 4.00
4 T.V. Broadcast take-over 4.00
5 Govt.Corruption Expose 4.00
6 Evey in Prison 4.00
7 Evey released 4.00
8 Search for V,A:Finch 4.00
9 V:Finch. 4.00
10 D:V 4.00

VIGILANTE

Oct., 1983
1 KP,DG,F:Adrian Chase 3.50
2 KP 3.00
3 KP,Cyborg 2.50
4 DN,V:Exterminator. 2.50
5 KP 2.50
6 O:Vigilante 3.00
7 O:Vigilante 3.00
8 thru 16 . . . . @2.50
17 Moore 4.00
18 Moore 4.00
19 thru 49. . . . . @2.50

Vigilante #47 © DC Comics, Inc.

50 KSy(c)D:Vigilante 3.00
Ann.#1 . . . . 3.00
Ann.#2 V:Cannon 2.50

Sept., 2005

1 (of 6) 3.00
2 thru 6 . . . . @3.00

VIGILANTE: CITY LIGHTS, PRAIRIE JUSTICE

1995–96

1 JeR,MCo,(of 4) 2.50
2 JeR,V:Bugsy Siegel 2.50
3 JeR 2.50
4 finale 2.50

VILLAINS UNITED

May, 2005

1 (of 6) F:Mockingbird 10.00
1a 2nd printing 4.00
2 . . . . 3.50
2a 2nd printing 3.00
3 The Six 3.00
4 . . . . 3.00
5 Catman vs. Deadshot 3.00
6 F:Mockingbird, concl. 3.00

VIMANARAMA!

DC/Vertigo, Feb., 2005

1 (of 3) GMo(s),PBd 3.00
2 thru 3 GMo(s),PBd . . . . @3.00

VINYL UNDERGROUND, THE

Vertigo, Oct., 2007

1 Snogging for England 3.00
2 Watching the Detectives 3.00
3 Another Occult case 3.00
4 Trail of Joshua's killers 3.00
5 Morrison and hsi mother 3.00
6 Pretty young dead things 3.00
7 Vengeance 3.00
8 Separate theories 3.00
9 Ritual Killings 3.00
10 Morrison's checkered past 3.00
11 Detective Caulfield 3.00
12 London's Burning 3.00

VIPER

1994

1 thru 4 Based on the TV Show . @2.50

VIXEN: RETURN OF THE LION

Oct., 2008

1 (of 5) Murderer from the past . . . 3.00
2 Wounded and alone 3.00

WANDERERS

June, 1988

1 I:New Team 3.00
2 thru 13 . . . . @3.00

WANTED: THE WORLD'S MOST DANGEROUS VILLIANS

July-Aug., 1972

1 GK,rep. Batman,Green Lantern. 50.00
2 CI,Batman/Joker/Penguin 40.00
3 JK,MMe,Dr. Fate 30.00
4 Green Lantern 30.00
5 GK,Dollman/Green Lantern 30.00
6 JK,Starman 30.00
7 JK,MMe,Hawkman/Flash 30.00
8 Dr. Fate/Flash 30.00
9 Sandman/Superman 30.00

WARLORD

Jan., 1976

1 MGr,O:Warlord 40.00
2 MGr,I:Machiste 20.00
3 MGr,War Gods of Skartaris 15.00
4 MGr,Duel of the Titans 15.00
5 MGr,The Secret of Skartaris . . . 15.00
6 MGr,I:Mariah,Stryker 9.00
7 MGr,O:Machiste 9.00
8 MGr,A:Skyra 9.00
9 MGr,N:Warlord 9.00
10 MGr,I:Ashiya 9.00
11 MGr,rep.1st Issue special #8 . . 6.00
12 MGr,I:Aton 6.00
13 MGr,D:Stryker 6.00
14 MGr,V:Death 6.00
15 MGr,I:Joshua 6.00
16 MGr,I:Saaba 6.00
17 MGr,Citadel of Death 6.00
18 MGr,I:Shadow 6.00
19 MGr,Wolves of the Steppes 6.00
20 MGr,I:Joshua clone 7.00
21 MGr,D:Joshua clone,Shadow . . 5.00
22 MGr,Beast in the Tower 10.00
23 MGr,Children of Ba'al 5.00
24 MGr,I:ligia 5.00
25 MGr,I:Ahir 5.00
26 MGr,The Challenge 5.00
27 MGr,Atlantis Dying 5.00
28 MGr,I:Wizard World 5.00
29 MGr,I:Mongo Ironhand 5.00
30 MGr,C:Joshua 5.00
31 MGr,Wing over Shamballah 5.00
32 MGr,I:Shakira 5.00
33 MGr,Birds of Prey,A:Shakira . . . 5.00
34 MGr,Sword of the Sorceror,
    I:Hellfire 5.00
35 MGr,C:Mike Grell 5.00
36 MGr,Interlude 5.00
37 MGr,JSn,I:Firewing,B:Omac . . . 6.00
38 MGr,I:Jennifer,A:Omac 5.00
39 MGr,JSn,Feast of Agravar 5.00
40 MGr,N:Warlord 5.00
41 MGr,A:Askir 5.00
42 MGr,JSn,A:Tara,Omac 5.00
43 MGr,JSn,Berserk'A:Omac 5.00
44 MGr,The Gamble 5.00
45 MGr,Nightmare in Vista
    Vision,A:Omac 5.00
46 MGr,D:Shakira 5.00
47 MGr,I:Mikola,E:Omac 5.00
48 MGr,EC,TY,I:Arak,Claw(B) 5.00
49 MGr,TY,A:Shakira,E:Claw 3.00
50 MGr,By Fire and Ice 3.00

51 MGr,TY,rep.#1,
    I(B):Dragonsword 3.00
52 MGr,TY,Back in the U.S.S.R. . . . 3.00
53 MT,TY,Sorcerer's Apprentice . . . 3.00
54 MT,Sorceress Supreme,
    E:Dragonsword 3.00
55 MT,Have a Nice Day 3.00
56 MT,JD,I:Gregmore,(B:)Arion . . . 3.00
57 MT,The Two Faces of
    Travis Morgan 3.00
58 MT,O:Greamore 3.00
59 MGr,A:Joshua 3.00
60 JD,Death Dual 3.00
61 JD,A:Greamore 3.00
62 JD,TMd,A:Mikola,E:Arion 3.00
63 JD,RR,I(B):Barren Earth 4.00
64 DJu,RRElsewhere 3.00
65 DJu,RR,A:Wizard World,
    No Barren Earth 3.00
66 DJuWizard World,
    No Barren Earth 3.00
67 DJu,RR,The Mark 3.00
68 DJu,RR 3.00
69 DJu,RR 3.00
70 DJu,Outback 3.00
71 DJu/DA,The Journey Back
    No Barren Earth 3.00
72 DJu,DA,I:Scarhart,No Barren
    Earth 3.00
73 DJ,DA,Cry Plague 3.00
74 DJu,No Barren Earth 3.00
75 DJu,All Dreams Must Pass
    No Barren Earth 3.00
76 DJu,DA,RR,A:Sarga 3.00
77 DJu,DA,RR,Let My People Go . . 3.00
78 DJu,RR,Doom's Mouth 3.00
79 PB,RM,Paradox,No Barren
    Earth 3.00
80 DJu,DA,RR,Future Trek 3.00
81 DJu,DA,RR,Thief's Magic 3.00
82 DJu,DA,RR,Revolution 3.00
83 DJu,RR,All the President's
    Men 3.00
84 DJu,DA,RR,Hail to the Chief . . . 3.00
85 DJu,RR,The Price of Change . . . 3.00
86 DJ,DA,No Barren Earth 3.00
87 DJu,RB,RR,I:Hawk 3.00
88 DJu,RB,RR,I:Patch,E:Barren
    Earth 3.00
89 RB,I:Sabertooth 3.00
90 RB,Demon's of the Past 3.00
91 DJu,DA,I:Maddox,O:Warlord
    O:Jennifer 3.00
92 NKu,Evil in Ebony 3.00
93 RR,A:Sabertooth 3.00

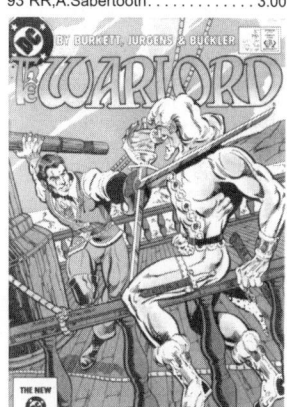

Warlord #87 © DC Comics Inc.

94 Assassin's Prey. 3.00
95 AKu,Dragon's Doom 3.00
96 Nightmare Prelude 3.00
97 RB,A:Saaba,D:Scarhart 3.00
98 NKu,Crisis tie-in 3.00
99 NKuFire and Sword 3.00
100 AKu,D:Greamore,Sabertooth . . 4.00
101 MGr,Temple of Demi-god 3.00
102 I:Zuppara,Error-Machiste
    with two hands. 3.00
103 JBi,Moon Beast. 3.00
104 RR,Dragon Skinner. 3.00
105 RR,Stalilers of Skinner 3.00
106 RR,I:Daimon 3.00
107 RR,Bride of Yano 3.00
108 RR,I:Mortella. 3.00
109 RR,A:Mortella 3.00
110 RR,A:Skyra III 3.00
111 RR,Tearing o/t Island Sea 3.00
112 RR,Obsession 3.00
113 RR,Through Fiends
    Destroy Me 3.00
114 RR,Phenalegeno Dies 3.00
115 RR,Citadel of Fear 3.00
116 RR,Revenge of the Warlord . . . 3.00
117 RR,A:Power Girl 3.00
118 RR,A:Power Girl 3.00
119 RR,A:Power Girl 3.00
120 ATb,A:Power Girl 3.00
121 ATb,A:Power Girl 3.00
122 ATb,A:Power Girl 3.00
123 JD,TMd,N:Warlord 3.00
124 JD,TMd,I:Scavenger 3.00
125 JD,TMd,D:Tara 3.00
126 JD,TMd,A:Machiste. 3.00
127 JD,The Last Dragon 3.00
128 JD,I:Agife 3.00
129 JD,Vision of Quest 3.00
130 JD,A:Maddox 3.00
131 JD,RLd,Vengeful Legacies 5.00
132 A New Beginning. 3.00
133 JD,final issue (44pg) 4.00
Ann.#1 MGr,A:Shakira 4.00
Ann.#2 I:Krystovar 3.00
Ann.#3 DJu,Full Circle 3.00
Ann.#4 A:New Gods,
    Legends tie-in 3.00
Ann.#5 AKu,Hellfire 3.00
Ann.#6 F:New Gods 3.00

[Limited Series], 1992
1 Travis Morgan retrospective 2.50
2 Fate of T. Morgan revealed 2.50
3 Return of Deimos. 2.50
4 V:Deimos 2.50
5 MGr(c),Skartaros at War 2.50
6 finale 2.50

WARLORD, THE
Feb., 2006
1 BS, F:Travis Morgan 3.00
2 BS, Return of the Warlord 3.00
3 BS, Travis Morgan 3.00
4 BS, In Skartaris 3.00
5 BS, Sword of Truth 3.00
6 BS,Somewhere in Skartaris. 3.00
7 BS,F:Brovis 3.00
8 BS, Someone dies. 3.00
9 BS, Revenge 3.00
10 Final Issue 3.00

WAR OF THE GODS
1991
1 GP,A:Lobo,Misc.Heroes,Circe . . . 2.50
2 GP,A:Misc.Heroes,V:Circe,
    w/poster. 2.50
3 GP,A:Misc.Heroes,V:Circe,
    w/poster. 2.50
4 GP,A:Misc.Heroes,V:Circe,
    w/poster. 2.50
2a thru 4a Newsstand . . . . @2.50

WAR STORY
DC/Vertigo, Sept., 2001
Spec. Johann's Tiger,GEn 5.00
Spec. D-Day Dodgers,GEn 5.00
Spec. Screaming Eagles,GEn 5.00
Spec. The Reivers 5.00
Spec. Nightingale,GEn. 5.00
Spec. J for Jenny 5.00
Spec. Condors 5.00
Spec. Archangel. 5.00
Spec. Johann's Tiger 5.00

WAR THAT TIME FORGOT, THE
May, 2008
1 (of 8) JP,NA(c),Enemy Ace,Dinos 3.00
2 thru 7 JP. . . . . @3.00

WASTELAND
Dec., 1987
1 Selection of Horror stories 2.50
2 thru 10 . . . . @2.50
11 thru 18 . . . . @2.50

WATCHMEN
Sept., 1986
1 B:AMo,DGb,D:Comedian 11.00
2 DGb,Funeral for Comedian 9.00
3 DGb,F:Dr.Manhattan 8.00
4 DGb,O:Dr.Manhattan 8.00
5 DGb,F:Rorschach 8.00
6 DGb,O:Rorschach 8.00
7 DGb,F:Nite Owl 8.00
8 DGb,F:Silk Spectre 8.00
9 DGb,O:Silk Spectre 8.00
10 DGb,A:Rorschach 8.00
11 DGb,O:Ozymandius 8.00
12 DGb,D:Rorsharch 8.00

WEB, THE
DC/Impact, 1991–92
1 I:Gunny, Bill Grady, Templar . . . 2.50
2 thru 14 . . . . @2.50
Ann.#1 Earthquest,w/trading card . . 2.50

WEIRD, THE
April, 1988
1 BWr,A:JLI. 4.00
2 BWr,A:JLI 3.00
3 BWr,V:Jason 3.00
4 final issue. 3.00

WEIRD
DC/Paradox Press, 1997
1 B&W magazine 3.00
2 . . . . 3.00
3 . . . . 3.00

WEIRD SECRET ORIGINS
Aug. 2004
Spec. 80-page giant. 6.00

WEIRD WAR TALES
Sept.–Oct., 1971
1 JKu(c),JKu,RH,Fort which
    Did Not Return. 475.00
2 JKu,MD,Military Madness 200.00
3 JKu(c),RA,The Pool 200.00
4 JKu(c),Ghost of Two Wars. . . . 150.00
5 JKu(c),RH,Slave 150.00
6 JKu(c),Pawns, The Sounds
    of War 100.00
7 JKu(c),JKu,RH,Flying Blind . . . 100.00
8 NA(c),The Avenging Grave 125.00
9 NC(c),The Promise 100.00
10 NC(c),Who is Haunting
    the Haunted Chateau 100.00

Weird War Tales#42
© *DC Comics, Inc.*

11 NC(c),ShM,Oct. 30, 1918:
    The German Trenches, WWI . 50.00
12 MK(c),God of Vengeance 50.00
13 LD(c),The Die-Hards. 50.00
14 LD(c),ShM,The Ghost of
    McBride's Woman 50.00
15 LD(c),Ace King Just Flew
    In From Hell. 50.00
16 LD(c),More Dead Than Alive . . 50.00
17 GE(c),Dead Man's Hands. 50.00
18 GE(c),Captain Dracula 50.00
19 LD(c),The Platoon That
    Wouldn't Die 50.00
20 LD(c),Operation Voodoo 50.00
21 LD(c),One Hour To Kill 30.00
22 LD(c),Wings of Death 30.00
23 LD(c),The Bird of Death 30.00
24 LD(c),The Invisible Enemy 30.00
25 LD(c),Black Magic...White
    Death. 30.00
26 LD(c),Jump Into Hell 30.00
27 LD(c),Survival of the
    Fittest. 30.00
28 LD(c),Isle of Forgotten
    Warriors 30.00
29 LD(c),Breaking Point. 30.00
30 LD(c),The Elements of Death . . 30.00
31 LD(c),Death Waits Twice 30.00
32 LD(c),The Enemy, The Stars . . 30.00
33 LD(c),Pride of the Master
    Race 30.00
34 LD(c),The Common Enemy . . . 30.00
35 LD(c),The Invaders 30.00
36 JKu(c),Escape. 35.00
37 LD(c),The Three Wars of
    Don Q 20.00
38 JKu(c),Born To Die 20.00
39 JKu(c),The Spoils of War 20.00
40 ECh(c),Back From The Dead . . 20.00
41 JL(c), The Dead Draftees of
    Regiment Six 20.00
42 JKu(c),Old Soldiers Never
    Die 20.00
43 ECh(c),Bulletproof. 20.00
44 JKu(c),ShM,The Emperor
    Weehawken. 20.00
45 JKu(c),The Battle of Bloody
    Valley 20.00
46 Kill Or Be Killed. 20.00
47 JKu(c),Bloodbath of the Toy
    Soldiers 20.00
48 JL(c),Ultimate Destiny 20.00
49 The Face Of The Enemy 20.00

50 ECh(c),-An Appointment With
  Destiny. 20.00
51 JKu(c),Secret Weapon 20.00
52 JKu(c),The Devil Is A
  Souvenir Hunter 20.00
53 JAp(c), Deadly Dominoes. 20.00
54 GM(c),Soldier of Satan 20.00
55 JKu(c),A Rebel Shall Rise
  From The Grave 20.00
56 AM(c),The Headless Courier . . 20.00
57 RT(c),Trial By Combat 20.00
58 JKu(c),Death Has A Hundred
  Eyes. 20.00
59 The Old One 20.00
60 JKu(c),Night Flight 20.00
61 HC(c),Mind War 15.00
62 JKu(c),The Grubbers 15.00
63 JKu(c),Battleground 15.00
64 JKu(c),FM(1st DC),D-Day. 50.00
65 JKu(c),The Last Cavalry
  Charge 15.00
66 JKu(c),The Iron Star 15.00
67 JKu(c),The Attack of the
  Undead 15.00
68 FM,JKu(c),The Life and Death of
  Charlie Golem 35.00
69 JKu(c),Day After Doomsday . . . 10.00
70 LU(c),The Blood Boat. 10.00
71 LD(c),False Prophet 10.00
72 JKu(c),Death Camp 10.00
73 GE(c),The Curse of Zopyrus . . 10.00
74 GE(c),March of the Mammoth . 10.00
75 JKu(c),The Forgery. 10.00
76 JKu(c),The Fire Bug 10.00
77 JKu(c),Triad 10.00
78 JKu(c),Indian War In Space . . . 10.00
79 JKu(c),The Gods Themselves . 10.00
80 JKu(c),An Old Man's Profession 10.00
81 JKu(c),It Takes Brains To
  Be A Killer 10.00
82 GE(c),Funeral Fire 10.00
83 GE(c),Prison of the Mind 10.00
84 JKu(c),Devil's Due 10.00
85 thru 124 June, 1983 . . . . @10.00

WEIRD WAR TALES
DC/Vertigo, April, 1997
1 (of 4) anthology 3.00
2 MK(c) 3.00
3 . . . . 3.00
4 final issue. 3.00
Spec.#1 GEn (2000) 5.00

Weird Western Tales #28
© DC Comics, Inc.

ALL-STAR WESTERN
Aug.–Sept., 1970
1 NA(c),CI 75.00
2 NA(c),GM,B:Outlaw 60.00
3 NA(c),GK,O:El Diablo 60.00
4 NA(c),GK,JKu,GM 60.00
5 NA(c),JAp,E:Outlaw. 60.00
6 GK,B:Billy the Kid 60.00
7 JKu. 50.00
8 E:Billy the Kid 50.00
9 FF 50.00
10 GM,I:Jonah Hex 750.00
11 GM,A:Jonah Hex. 350.00
Becomes:

WEIRD WESTERN TALES
June-July, 1972
12 NA,BWr,JKu 250.00
13 . . . . 150.00
14 ATh 100.00
15 NA(c),GK. 75.00
16 thru 17. . . . . @60.00
18 Jonah Hex 100.00
19 thru 28. . . . . @60.00
29 O:Jonah Hex. 100.00
30 thru 38. . . . . @05.00
39 I&O:Scalphunter 35.00
40 thru 70. . . . . @20.00

WEIRD WESTERN TALES
DC/Vertigo, Feb., 2001
1 (of 4) 2.50
2 thru 4 . . . . @2.50

WEIRD WORLDS
Aug.–Sept., 1971
1 JO,MA,John Carter 50.00
2 NA,JO(c),MA,BWr 40.00
3 MA,NA 25.00
4 MK(c),MK. 20.00
5 MK(c),MK. 20.00
6 MK(c),MK. 20.00
7 John Carter ends. 20.00
8 HC,I:Iron Wolf 20.00
9 and 10 HC . . . . @20.00

WESTERN COMICS
Jan.–Feb., 1948
1 MMe,B:Vigilante,Rodeo Rick,
  Wyoming Kid, Cowboy
  Marshal. 1,500.00
2 MMe,Vigilante vs. Dirk Bigger . 600.00
3 MMe,Vigilante vs. Pecos Kid . . 650.00
4 MMe,Vigilante as Pecos Kid . . 650.00
5 I:Nighthawk 500.00
6 Wyoming Kid vs. The
  Murder Mustang 300.00
7 Wyoming Kid in The Town
  That Was Never Robbed. . . . 300.00
8 O:Wyoming Kid 500.00
9 Wyoming Kid vs. Jack
  Slaughter 300.00
10 Nighthawk in Tunnel ofTerror . 300.00
11 Wyoming Kid vs. Mayor Brock 275.00
12 Wyoming Kid vs. Baldy Ryan . 275.00
13 I:Running Eagle 275.00
14 Wyoming Kid in The Siege
  of Prairie City. 275.00
15 Nighthawk in Silver, Salt
  and Pepper 275.00
16 Wyoming Kid vs. Smilin' Jim. . 275.00
17 BP,Wyoming Kid vs. Prof.
  Penny 275.00
18 LSt on Nighthawk,Wyoming Kid
  in Challenge of the Chiefs. . . 275.00
19 LSt,Nighthawk in The
  Invisible Rustlers 275.00
20 LSt,Nighthawk in The Mystery
  Mail From Defender Dip 225.00

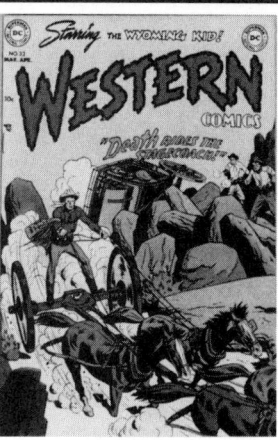
Western Comics #33
© DC Comics Inc.

21 LSt,Nighthawk in Rattlesnake
  Hollow 225.00
22 LSt,I:Jim Pegton 225.00
23 LSt,Nighthawk reveals
  ID to Jim 225.00
24 The $100,000 Impersonation . 225.00
25 V:Souix Invaders. 225.00
26 The Storming of the Sante
  Fe Trail 225.00
27 The Looters of Lost Valley . . . 225.00
28 The Thunder Creek Rebellion. 225.00
29 Six Guns of the Wyoming Kid. 225.00
30 V:Green Haired Killer 225.00
31 The Sky Riding Lawman. 225.00
32 Death Rides the Stage Coach 225.00
33 Wyoming Kid's Magic Finger . 225.00
34 Prescription For Killers 225.00
35 The River of Rogues. 225.00
36 Nighthawk(c),Duel in the Dark 200.00
37 The Death Dancer 200.00
38 Warpath in the Sky 200.00
39 Death to Fort Danger 200.00
40 Blind Man's Bluff. 200.00
41 thru 60. . . . . @175.00
61 thru 85. . . . . @150.00

WHO'S WHO
1985–87
1 . . . . 5.00
2 thru 26 . . . . @4.00

WHO'S WHO IN
THE DC UNIVERSE
1990–92
1 inc. Superman 6.00
1a 2nd printing 5.50
2 inc. Flash 5.50
2a 2nd printing 5.00
3 inc. Green Lantern. 5.50
4 inc. Wonder Woman 5.50
5 inc. Batman. 5.50
6 inc. Hawkman 5.50
7 inc. Shade 5.50
8 inc. Lobo 6.00
9 inc. Legion of Super-Heroes . . . 5.50
10 inc. Robin 5.50
11 inc. L.E.G.I.O.N. '91 . . . . 5.50
12 inc. Aquaman 5.50
13 Villains issue, inc. Joker 6.00
14 inc. New Titans 5.50
15 inc. Doom Patrol 5.50
16 inc. Catwoman,final issue. 5.00

WHO'S WHO IN IMPACT
1991
1 Shield 5.00
2 Black Hood 5.00

WHO'S WHO IN THE LEGION
1987–88
1 History/Bio of Legionnaires 3.50
2 inc. Dream Girl. 3.50
3 inc. Karate Kid 3.50
4 inc. Lightning Lad 3.50
5 inc. Phantom Girl 3.50
6 inc. Timber Wolf. 3.50
7 wraparound(c) 3.50

WHO'S WHO IN STAR TREK
1987
1 HC(c) 6.00
2 HC(c) 6.00

WHO'S WHO UPDATE '87
1 inc. Blue Beetle 3.00
2 inc. Catwoman 3.00
3 inc. Justice League 3.00
4 . . . . 3.00
5 inc. Superboy. 3.00

WHO'S WHO UPDATE '88
1 inc. Brainiac. 3.00
2 inc. JusticeLeagueInternational . . 3.00
3 inc. Shado 3.00
4 inc. Zatanna 3.00

WHO'S WHO UPDATE '93
1 F:Eclipso,Azrael. 5.25

WILD DOG
Sept., 1987
1 mini series DG(i),I:Wild Dog 3.00
2 DG(i),V:Terrorists 2.50
3 DG(i) 2.50
4 DG(i),O:Wild Dog, final issue. . . . 2.50
Spec.#1 . . . . 2.50

WILD WILD WEST
1999
1-shot movie adaptation 5.00

WINDY & WILLY
May-June, 1969
1 . . . . 65.00
2 thru 4 . . . . @40.00

WISE SON: THE WHITE WOLF
DC/Milestone, Sept., 1996
1 thru 4 by Ho Che Anderson . . . @2.50

WITCHCRAFT
DC/Vertigo, 1994
1 CV(c),Three Witches from
    Sandman 4.00
2 F:Mildred 3.50
3 Final issue 3.25

WITCHCRAFT: LA TERREUR
Feb., 1998
1 thru 3 JeR, sequel . . . . @2.50

WITCHING, THE
DC/Vertigo, June 2004
1 Triple Goddess. 3.00
2 thru 4 . . . . @3.00
5 MBu 3.00
6 thru 10 . . . . @3.00

Witching Hour #47
© *DC Comics, Inc.*

WITCHING HOUR
1969–78
1 NA,ATh,Let the Judge Be You . 250.00
2 ATh, The Trip of Fools 100.00
3 ATh,BWr. 100.00
4 ATh,A Matter of Conscience . . . 65.00
5 ATh,BWr. 100.00
6 ATh,A Face in the Crowd 100.00
7 ATh. 75.00
8 NA,ATh,3 Day Free Home Trial . 75.00
9 ATh,The Lonely Road Home . . . 75.00
10 ATh,Hold Softly, Hand of Death 75.00
11 ATh,The Mark of the Witch . . . 75.00
12 ATh,Double Edge 75.00
13 NA. 100.00
14 AW,CG,NA(c) 90.00
15 thru 20 . . . . @40.00
21 thru 30 . . . . @25.00
31 thru 37 . . . . @25.00
38 100-pg. 90.00
39 thru 60 . . . . @20.00
61 thru 85 . . . . @15.00

THE WITCHING HOUR
DC/Vertigo, Dec., 1999
1 (of 3) JLb,CBa,ATi 6.00
2 JLb,CBa,ATi 6.00
3 JLb,CBa,ATi, concl. 6.00

WONDER GIRL
Sept., 2007
1 (of 6) 3.00
2 F:Hercules 3.00
3 F:Warriors of the Fourth World . . 3.00
4 thru 6 . . . . @3.00

WONDER WOMAN
1942–86
1 O:Wonder Woman,A:Paula
    Von Gunther 50,000.00
2 I:Earl of Greed,Duke of Deception
    and Lord Conquest. 7,700.00
3 Paula Von Gunther reforms . 4,000.00
4 A:Paula Von Gunther 3,000.00
5 I:Dr. Psycho,A:Mars 3,000.00

6 I:Cheetah 2,400.00
7 Adventure of the Life Vitamin 2,400.00
8 I:Queen Clea. 2,400.00
9 I:Giganto 2,400.00
10 I:Duke Mephisto Saturno . . . 2,500.00
11 I:Hypnota 1,700.00
12 I:Queen Desira. 1,700.00
13 V:King Rigor & the Seal Men 1,700.00
14 I:Gentleman Killer 1,700.00
15 I:Solo 1,700.00
16 I:King Pluto 1,700.00
17 Wonder Woman goes to
    Ancient Rome. 1,700.00
18 V:Dr. Psycho 1,700.00
19 V:Blitz. 1,700.00
20 V:Nifty and the Air Pirates . . 1,700.00
21 I:Queen Atomia 1,500.00
22 V:Saturno. 1,500.00
23 V:Odin and the Valkyries . . . 1,500.00
24 I:Mask 1,500.00
25 V:Purple Priestess 1,500.00
26 I:Queen Celerita. 1,500.00
27 V:Pik Socket. 1,500.00
28 V:Cheetah,Clea,Dr. Poison,
    Giganta,Hypnata,Snowman,
    Zara (Villainy,Inc.). 2,000.00
29 V:Paddy Gypso 2,000.00
30 The Secret of the
    Limestone Caves 2,000.00
31 V:Solo 1,000.00
32 V:Uvo 1,000.00
33 V:Inventa 1,000.00
34 V:Duke of Deception 1,000.00
35 Jaxo,Master of Thoughts . . . 1,000.00
36 V:Lord Cruello 1,000.00
37 A:Circe 1,000.00
38 V:Brutex 1,000.00
39 The Unmasking of Wonder
    Woman 1,000.00
40 Hollywood Goes To Paradise
    Island 1,000.00
41 Wonder Woman,Romance
    Editor. 900.00
42 V:General Vertigo 900.00
43 The Amazing Spy Ring
    Mystery 900.00
44 V:Master Destroyer. 900.00
45 The Amazon and the
    Leprechaun. 1,800.00
46 V:Prof. Turgo. 900.00
47 V:Duke of Deception 900.00
48 V:Robot Woman 900.00
49 V:Boss. 900.00
50 V:Gen. Voro 900.00
51 V:Garo. 650.00
52 V:Stroggo 650.00
53 V:Crime Master of Time 650.00
54 A:Merlin. 650.00
55 The Chessmen of Doom. 650.00
56 V:Plotter Gang 650.00
57 V:Mole Men. 650.00
58 V:Brain 650.00
59 V:Duke Dozan. 650.00
60 A:Paula Von Gunther 650.00
61 Earth's Last Hour 600.00
62 V:Angles Andrews. 600.00
63 V:Duke of Deception 600.00
64 V:Thought Master 600.00
65 V:Duke of Deception 600.00
66 V:Duke of Deception 600.00
67 Confessions of a Spy 600.00
68 Landing of the Flying
    Saucers 600.00
69 A:Johann Gutenberg,Chris.
    Columbus, Paul Revere
    and the Wright Brothers 600.00
70 I:Angle Man. 600.00
71 One-Woman Circus 600.00
72 V:Mole Goldings 600.00
73 V:Prairie Pirates 600.00
74 The Carnival of Peril. 500.00
75 V:Angler 500.00

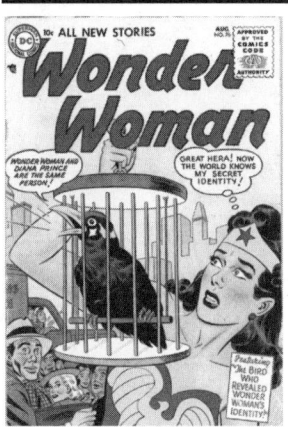

Wonder Woman #76
© DC Comics, Inc.

Wonder Woman #236
© DC Comics Inc.

76 Bird Reveals Secret Identity	500.00
77 V:Smokescreen gang	500.00
78 V:Angle Man	500.00
79 V:Spider	500.00
80 V:Machino	500.00
81 V:Duke of Deception, Angle Man	500.00
82 A:Robin Hood	500.00
83 The Boy From Nowhere	500.00
84 V:Duke of Deception, Angle Man	500.00
85 V:Capt. Virago	500.00
86 V:Snatcher	500.00
87 The Day the Clocks Stopped	500.00
88 V:Duke of Deception	500.00
89 The Triple Heroine	500.00
90 Wonder Woman on Jupiter	500.00
91 The Interplanetary Olympics	400.00
92 V:Angle Man	400.00
93 V:Duke of Deception	400.00
94 V:Duke of Deception, A:Robin Hood	400.00
95 O:Wonder Woman's Tiara	400.00
96 V:Angle Man	400.00
97 The Runaway Time Express	400.00
98 The Million Dollar Penny	400.00
99 V:Silicons	400.00
100 Anniversary Issue	450.00
101 V:Time Master	400.00
102 F:Steve Trevor	400.00
103 V:Gadget-Maker	400.00
104 A:Duke of Deception	400.00
105 O,I:Wonder Woman	2,000.00
106 W.Woman space adventure	400.00
107 Battles space cowboys	550.00
108 Honored by U.S. Post Off.	400.00
109 V:Slicker	400.00
110 I:Princess 1003	400.00
111 I:Prof. Menace	400.00
112 V:Chest of Monsters	300.00
113 A:Queen Mikra	300.00
114 V:Flying Saucers	300.00
115 A:Angle Man	300.00
116 A:Professor Andro	300.00
117 A:Etta Candy	300.00
118 A:Merman	300.00
119 A:Mer Boy	300.00
120 A:Hot & Cold Alien	300.00
121 A:Wonder Woman Family	250.00
122 I:Wonder Tot	250.00
123 A:Wonder Girl,Wonder Tot	250.00
124 A:Wonder Girl,Wonder Tot	250.00
125 WW-Battle Prize	250.00
126 I:Mr.Genie	250.00
127 Suprise Honeymoon	200.00
128 O:InvisiblePlane	200.00

129 A:WonderGirl,WonderTot	200.00
130 A:Angle Man	200.00
131 Proving of Wonder Woman	250.00
132 V:Flying Saucer	250.00
133 A:Miss X	275.00
134 V:Image-Maker	250.00
135 V:Multiple Man	250.00
136 V:Machine Men	300.00
137 V:Robot Wonder Woman	275.00
138 V:Multiple Man	275.00
139 Amnesia revels Identity	275.00
140 A:Morpheus,Mr.Genie	300.00
141 A:Angle Man	250.00
142 A:Mirage Giants	275.00
143 A:Queen Hippolyte	250.00
144 I:Bird Boy	250.00
145 V:Phantom Sea Beast	250.00
146 $1,000 Dollar Stories	250.00
147 Wonder Girl becomes Bird Girl and Fish Girl	225.00
148 A:Duke of Deception	250.00
149 Last Day of the Amazons	275.00
150 V:Phantome Fish Bird	250.00
151 F:1st Full Wonder Girl story	200.00
152 F:Wonder Girl	200.00
153 V:Duke of Deception	200.00
154 V:Doiling Man	200.00
155 I married a monster	200.00
156 V:Brain Pirate	225.00
157 A:Egg Fu,the First	225.00
158 A:Egg Fu,the First	225.00
159 Origin	250.00
160 A:Cheetah,Dr. Psycho	150.00
161 A:Angle Man	150.00
162 O:Diana Prince	150.00
163 A:Giganta	150.00
164 A:Angle Man	150.00
165 A:Paper Man,Dr.Psycho	125.00
166 A:Egg Fu,The Fifth	125.00
167 A:Crimson Centipede	125.00
168 RA,ME,V:Giganta	125.00
169 RA,ME,Crimson Centipede	125.00
170 RA,ME,V:Dr.Pyscho	125.00
171 A:Mouse Man	125.00
172 IN,A:Android Wonder Woman	125.00
173 A:Tonia	125.00
174 A:Angle Man	125.00
175 V:Evil Twin	125.00
176 A:Star Brothers	125.00
177 A:Super Girl	150.00
178 MSy,DG,I:New Wonder Woman	150.00
179 D:Steve Trevor,I:Ching	100.00
180 MSy,DG,wears no costume I:Tim Trench	100.00
181 MSy,DG,A:Dr.Cyber	100.00
182 MSy,DG	100.00
183 MSy,DG,V:War	100.00
184 MSy,DG,A:Queen Hippolyte	75.00
185 MSy,DG,V:Them	75.00
186 MSy,DG,I:Morgana	75.00
187 MSy,DG,A:Dr.Cyber	75.00
188 MSy,DG,A:Dr.Cyber	75.00
189 MSy,DG	75.00
190 MSy,DG	75.00
191 MSy,DG	75.00
192 MSy,DG	75.00
193 MSy,DG	75.00
194 MSy,DG	75.00
195 MSy,WW	75.00
196 MSy,DG,giant,Origin rep.	80.00
197 MSy,DG	80.00
198 MSy,DG	80.00
199 JJ(c),DG	125.00
200 JJ(c),DG	150.00
201 DG,A:Catwoman	50.00
202 DG,A:Catwoman,I:Fafhrd & the Gray Mouser	50.00
203 DG,Womens lib	35.00
204 DH,BO,rewears costume	60.00
205 DH,BO,Target WonderWoman	35.00

206 DH,O:Wonder Woman	35.00
207 RE,The Four Dooms	35.00
208 RE,The Titanic Trials	35.00
209 RE,Planet of Plunder	35.00
210 RE,The Shrinking Formula	35.00
211 RE,giant	100.00
212 CS,A:Superman,tries to rejoin JLA	30.00
213 IN,A:Flash	30.00
214 CS,giant,A:Green Lantern	100.00
215 A:Aquaman	25.00
216 A:Black Canary	25.00
217 DD,A:Green Arrow,giant	40.00
218 KS,Red Tornado	25.00
219 CS,A:Elongated Man	25.00
220 DG,NA,A:Atom	25.00
221 CS,A:Hawkman	25.00
222 A:Batman	25.00
223 R:Steve Trevor	25.00
224 Wonder Woman vs. USA	25.00
225 Maximus, Emperor	25.00
226 A Life in Flames	25.00
227 My World in Ashes	25.00
228 B:War stories	25.00
229 Tomorrow Belongs to Me	25.00
230 V:Cheetah	25.00
231 This War has Been Cancelled	25.00
232 MN,A:JSA	25.00
233 GM,Seadeath	25.00
234 And Death my Destiny	25.00
235 The Biology Bomb	25.00
236 Armageddon Day	25.00
237 RB(c),O:Wonder Woman	30.00
238 RB(c),Assassin	20.00
239 RB(c),Duke named Deception	20.00
240 Wanted Dead or Alive	20.00
241 JSon,DG,A:Spectre	22.00
242 Tomorrow's Gods & Demons	15.00
243 The Five-Sided Square	15.00
244 The Terrorist Dooms	15.00
245 Vengeance From Ice to Fire	15.00
246 Darkness Everywhere	15.00
247 The Inside-Out Man	15.00
248 D:Steve Trevor	20.00
249 A:Hawkgirl	15.00
250 I:Orana	15.00
251 O:Orana	15.00
252 Empress of the Silver Snake	20.00
253 Spirit of Silver Spirit of Gold	15.00
254 The Angle in the Stars	15.00
255 V:Bushmaster	15.00
256 V:Royal Flush Gang	15.00
257 Case o/t Impossible Crimes	15.00

DC COMICS

DC COMICS

311 DH,Huntress 7.00
312 DH,DSp,A:Gremlins 7.00
313 DH,V:Circe 7.00
314 DH,Huntress 7.00
315 DH,Huntress 7.00
316 DH,Huntress 7.00
317 DH,V:Cereberus 7.00
318 DH,V:Space Aliens 7.00
319 DH,V:Dr.Cyber 7.00
320 DH,Launch on Warning 7.00
321 DH,Huntress 7.00
322 IN,Bid Time Return 7.00
323 DH,A:Cheetah, Angle Man . . 7.00
324 DH,The Cassandra Complex . 7.00
325 DH,Gremlin from the Kremlin . . 7.00
326 DH,Tropidor Heat 7.00
327 DH,Crisis. 7.00
328 DH,Crisis. 7.00
329 DH,Crisis, giant. 15.00

[2nd Regular Series], 1987

1 GP,O:Amazons,Wonder Woman . 8.00
2 GP,I:Steve Trevor. 6.00
3 GP,I:Julia Vanessa. 6.00
4 GP,V:Decay 6.00
5 GP,V:Deimos,Phobos 6.00
6 GP,V:Ares 5.00
7 GP,I:Myndi Mayer 5.00
8 GP,O:Legends,A:JLA,Flash 5.00
9 GP,I:New Cheetah 5.00
10 GP,V:Seven Headed Hydra,
    Challenge of the Gods,pt.1,
    gatefold(c) 4.00
10a regular(c). 3.00
11 GP,V:Echidna,Challenge
    of the Gods,pt.3. . . . . 4.00
12 GP,Millennium,V:Pan, Challenge
    of the Gods,pt.3,
    Millennium x-over 4.00
13 GP,Millennium,A:Ares,Challenge
    of the Gods,pt.4. . . . . 4.00
14 GP,A:Hercules. 4.00
15 GP,I:New Silver Swan. 4.00
16 GP,V:Silver Swan 4.00
17 GP,DG,V:Circe. 4.00
18 GP,DG,V:Circe,+Bonus bk#4 . . 4.00
19 GP,FMc,V:Circe. 4.00
20 GP,BMc,D:Myndi Mayer 4.00
21 CP,BMc,L:Greek Gods,
    Destruction of Olympus. 3.00
22 GP,BMc,F:Julia, Vanessa 3.00
23 GP,R:Hermes,V:Phobos,
    Prelude to New Titans #50 . . . . 3.00
24 GP,V:Ixion, Phobos 3.00
25 CMa,Invasion,A:JLA 3.00
26 CMa,Invasion,V:Capt.Atom. . . . 3.00
27 CMa,V:Khunds,A:Cheetah 3.00
28 CMa,V:Cheetah. 3.00
29 CMa,V:Cheetah. 3.00
30 CMa,V:Cheetah. 3.00
31 CMa,V:Cheetah. 3.00
32 TG,V:Amazons,A:Hermes 3.00
33 CMa,V:Amazons,Cheetah. 3.00
34 CMa,I:Shim'Tar 3.00
35 CMa,V:Shim'Tar 3.00
36 CMa,A:Hermes 3.00
37 CMa,V:Discord,A:Superman. . . 3.00
38 CMa,V:Eris 3.00
39 CMa,V:Eris,A:Lois Lane 3.00
40 CMa,V:Eris,A:Lois Lane 3.00
41 CMa,RT,F:Julia,Ties that Bind . . 3.00
42 CMa,RT,V:Silver Swan 3.00
43 CMA,RT,V:Silver Swan 3.00
44 CMa,RT,V:SilverSwan. 3.00
45 CM,RT,Pandora's Box. 3.00
46 RT,Suicide Issue,D:Lucy. 3.00
47 RT,A:Troia 3.00
48 RTP,A:Troia. 3.00
49 recap of 1st four years 3.00
50 RT,SA,BB,AH,CM,KN,PCR,MW
    A:JLA,Superman 4.00
51 RT,V:Mercury 3.00
52 CM,KN,Shards,V:Dr.Psycho . . . 3.00

Wonder Woman #248
© *DC Comics, Inc.*

258 Long Grey Line of Death 15.00
259 A Power Gone Mad. 15.00
260 A Warrior in Chains. 15.00
261 Palace at the Edge of Time . . 15.00
262 RE,A:Bushmaster 15.00
263 Power and the Pampas 15.00
264 A Bomb in the Bird 15.00
265 Land of the Scaled Gods 15.00
266 The Uninvited 15.00
267 R:Animal Man 20.00
268 A:Animal Man 20.00
269 WW(i),Rebirth of Wonder
    Woman,pt.1 . . . . 12.00
270 Rebirth,pt.2 . . . . 12.00
271 JSon,B:Huntress,Rebirth,pt.3 . 12.00
272 JSon 12.00
273 JSon,A:Angle Man 12.00
274 JSon,I:Cheetah II 12.00
275 JSon,V:Cheetah II. 12.00
276 JSon,V:Kobra 12.00
277 JSon,V:Kobra 12.00
278 JSon,V:Kobra 12.00
279 JSon,A:Demon,Catwoman . . 12.00
280 JSon,A:Demon,Catwoman . . 12.00
281 JSon,Earth 2 Joker 10.00
282 JSon,Earth 2 Joker 10.00
283 Earth 2 Joker 10.00
284 Shadow of the Dragon 7.00
285 JSon,V:Red Dragon 7.00
286 Be Wonder Woman and Die. . . 7.00
287 DH,RT,JSon,Teen Titans. 8.00
288 GC,RT,New Wonder Woman . . 8.00
289 GC,RT,JSon,New W.Woman . . 7.00
290 GC,RT,JSon,New W.Woman . . 7.00
291 GC,FMc,A:Zatanna. 8.00
292 GC,FMc,RT,Supergirl 8.00
293 GC,FMc,Starfire,Raven. 8.00
294 GC,FMc,JSon,V:Blockbuster . . 7.00
295 GC,FMc,JSon,Huntress 7.00
296 GC,Fmc,JSon 7.00
297 MK(c),GC,FMc,JSon. 7.00
298 GC,FMc,JSon 7.00
299 GC,FMc,JSon 7.00
300 GC,FMc,RA,DG,KP,RB,KG
    C:New Teen Titans 9.00
301 GC,FMc. 7.00
302 GC,FMc,V:Artemis 7.00
303 GC,FMc,Huntress. 7.00
304 GC,FMc,Huntress. 7.00
305 GC,Huntress,I:Circe 8.00
306 DH,Huntress. 7.00
307 DH,Huntress,Black Canary. . . . 7.00
308 DH,Huntress,Black Canary. . . . 7.00
309 DH,Huntress. 7.00
310 DH,Huntress. 7.00

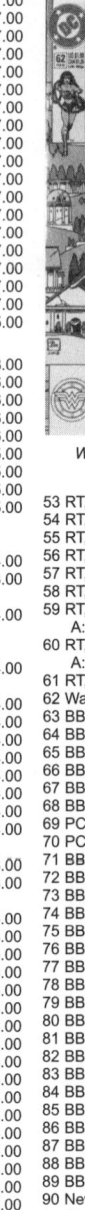

Wonder Woman 2nd Series #62
© *DC Comics, Inc.*

53 RT,A:Pariah. 3.00
54 RT,V:Dr.Psycho. 3.00
55 RT,V:Dr.Psycho. 3.00
56 RT,A:Comm.Gordon 3.00
57 RT,A:Clark Kent,Bruce Wayne . 3.00
58 RT,War of the Gods,V:Atlas . . . 3.50
59 RT,War of the Gods,
    A:Batman Robin 3.50
60 RT,War of the Gods,
    A:Batman, Lobo. 3.50
61 RT,War of the Gods,V:Circe . . . 3.50
62 War o/t Gods,Epilogue. 3.00
63 BB(c)A:Deathstroke,Cheetah . . 5.00
64 BB(c),Kidnapped Child 2.50
65 BB(c),PCu,V:Dr.Psycho 2.50
66 BB(c),PCu,Exodus In Space#1 . 2.50
67 BB(c),PCu,Exodus In Space#2. . 2.50
68 BB(c),PCu,Exodus In Space#3. . 2.50
69 PCu, Exodus In Space#4 . . . . . 2.50
70 PCu,Exodus In Space#5. . . . . . 2.50
71 BB(c),DC,RT,Return fr.space . . . 2.50
72 BB(c),O:retold 16.00
73 BB(c),Diana gets a job 3.00
74 BB(c),V:White Magician 2.50
75 BB(c),A:The White Magician. . . 2.50
76 BB(c),A:Doctor Fate 2.50
77 BB(c). 2.50
78 BB(c),A:Flash 2.50
79 BB(c),V:Mayfly,A:Flash 2.50
80 BB(c),V:Ares Buchanan 2.50
81 BB(c),V:Ares Buchanan 2.50
82 BB(c),V:Ares Buchanan 2.50
83 BB(c),V:Ares Buchanan 2.50
84 BB(c),V:Ares Buchanan 2.50
85 BB(c). 13.00
86 BB(c),Turning Point. 6.00
87 BB(c),No Quarter,NoSanctuary . 6.00
88 BB(c),A:Superman 10.00
89 BB(c),A:Circle 10.00
90 New Direction 7.00
91 Choosing Wonder Woman 4.00
92 New Wonder Woman 4.00
93 New Wonder Woman 4.00
94 . . . . 5.00
95 V:Cheetah 5.00
96 V:The Joker. 5.00
97 V:The Joker. 5.00
98 BB(c),F:Artemis. 3.00
99 BB(c),A:White Magician 3.00
100 BB(c) White Magician defeats
    Artemis 6.00
100a Collector's ed., holo(c) 6.00
101 V:White Magician 3.00
102 V:Metron,Darkseid 2.50

---

103 JBy,A:Darkseid 2.50
104 JBy,Diana takes crown? 2.50
105 JBy,Grecian artifact comes
    to life 2.50
106 JBy,A:The Demon,Phantom
    Stranger. 2.50
107 . . . . 2.50
108 JBy,F:The Demon,Arion,The
    Phantom Stranger 2.50
109 JBy,V:The Flash,I:Champion . . 2.50
110 JBy,V:Sinestro. 2.50
111 JBy,I:New Wonder Girl,
    V:Doomsday 2.50
112 JBy,V:Doomsday,A:Superman . 3.00
113 JBy,Wonder Girl vs. Decay . . . 2.50
114 JBy,V:Doctor Psycho. 2.50
115 JBy,beneath the Arctic ice. . . . 2.50
116 JBy,beneath the Arctic ice. . . . 2.50
117 JBy,V:Earth Moovers. 2.50
118 JBy 2.50
119 JBy,fight to regain Cheetah's
    humanity, cont. 2.50
120 JBy,48pg., pin-ups 4.00
121 JBy,Wonder Woman reverting
    to clay 2.50
122 JBy,Gods of Olympus are back 2.50
123 JBy,R:Artemis 2.50
124 JBy,A:Demon 2.50
125 JBy,A:Donna Troy & JLA 2.50
126 JBy,JL,Genesis tie-in 2.50
127 JBy,JL(c),new era 2.50
128 JBy,JL,V:Egg Fu 2.50
129 JBy,JL,Hippolyta debuts as
    replacement Wonder Woman . . 2.50
130 JBy,JL,pt.1,A:Golden-age
    Flash 2.50
131 JBy,pt.2 . . . . 2.50
132 JBy,pt.3,A:Justice Society. . . . 2.50
133 . . . . 2.50
134 JBy,Who is Donna Troy? 2.50
135 JBy,secret revealed 2.50
136 JBy,back to Earth 2.50
137 CPr,V:Circe, pt.1 . . . . 2.50
138 MBr,F:Hippolyta,V:Circe,pt.2. . 2.50
139 MBr, ... 2.50
140 BMc,A:Superman & Batman. . . 2.50
141 BMc,A:Superman & Batman. . . 2.50
142 BMc,The Wonder Dome 2.50
143 BMc,Devastation,pt.1 . . . . 2.50
144 BMc,Devastation,pt.2 . . . . 2.50
145 BMc,Devastation,pt.3 . . . . 2.50
146 BMc,Devastation,pt.4 . . . . 2.50
147 BMc,GodWar begins. 2.50
148 BMc,GodWar, pt.2. . . . . 2.50
149 RBr,BMc,GodWar,pt.3. . . . . . . 2.50
150 GodWar, 48-pg 4.00
151 AH(c),V:Dr. Poison 2.50
152 . . . . 2.50
153 MMr,F:Wonder Girl 2.50
154 Three Hearts,pt.1 . . . . 2.50
155 Three Hearts,pt.2 . . . . 2.50
156 Devastation Returns,pt.1 . . . . 2.50
157 Devastation Returns,pt.2 . . . . 2.50
158 Devastation Returns,concl. . . . 2.50
159 WonderDome comes to Earth . 2.50
160 A Piece of You,pt.1 . . . . 3.00
161 A Piece of You,pt.2 . . . . 3.00
162 GodComplex,pt.1,A:Aquaman . 2.50
163 GodComplex,pt.2,A:Aquaman . 2.50
164 Gods of Gotham,pt.1 . . . . 6.00
165 Gods of Gotham,pt.2 . . . . 3.00
166 Gods of Gotham,pt.3 . . . . 3.00
167 Gods of Gotham,pt.4 . . . . 3.00
168 GP,Paradise Island Lost,pt.1 . . 2.50
169 GP,Paradise Island Lost,pt.2 . . 2.50
170 PJ,ALa,Lois & Diana. 2.50
171 Our Worlds at War, tie-in 2.50
172 Our Worlds at War, tie-in 3.00
173 Our Worlds at War, tie-in 2.50
174 PJ,ALa,Witch & Warrior,pt.1 . . 2.50
175 PJ,ALa,Witch & Warrior,pt.2 . . 8.00
176 PJ,ALa,Witch & Warrior,pt.3 . . 2.50

Wonder Woman 2nd Series #99
© DC Comics Inc.

177 PJ,ALa,Our Worlds at War 2.50
178 PJ,ALa,date with Trevor 2.50
179 PJ,ALa,V:Villainy,Inc. 2.50
180 PJ,ALa,O:new Villainy, Inc.. . . . 2.50
181 PJ,ALa,prisoners of Skartaris . . 2.50
182 PJ,ALa,Shamballa 2.50
183 PJ,ALa,Skartaris mastermind . . 2.50
184 PJ,ALa,Diana,pt.1 . . . . 2.50
185 PJ,ALa,Diana in '40s,pt.2 . . . . 2.50
186 PJ,ALa,V:Barbara Minerva 2.50
187 PJ,ALa,Cat fight 2.50
188 PJ,ALa,Day in the Life 2.50
189 WS,JOy,CR,Game Gods,pt.1 . . 2.50
190 WS,JOy,CR,Game Gods,pt.2 . . 4.00
191 WS,JOy,CR,Game Gods,pt.3 . . 2.50
192 WS,JOy,CR,Game Gods,pt.4 . . 2.50
193 WS,JOy,CR,Game Gods,pt.5 . . 2.50
194 WS,JOy,CR,Game Gods,pt.6 . . 2.50
195 AH 3.00
196 Down to Earth,pt.1 . . . . 2.50
197 Down to Earth,pt.2 . . . . 2.50
198 Down to Earth,pt.3 . . . . 2.50
199 Down to Earth,pt.4 . . . . 2.50
200 Down to Earth, 64-pg. 4.00
201 Themyscira 2.50
202 V:Veronica Cale 2.50
203 Bitter Pills,pt.1 . . . . 2.50
204 Bitter Pills,pt.2. . . . . 2.50
205 Bitter Pills,pt.3 . . . . 2.50
206 Stoned,pt.1 . . . . 2.50
207 Stoned,pt.2 . . . . 2.50
208 Stoned,pt.3 . . . . 2.50
209 Stoned,pt.4 . . . . 2.50
210 Stoned, concl. 2.50
211 SeP 2.50
212 F:JLA 2.50
213 War on Olympus 2.50
214 Truth or Dare, F:Flash, x-over 15.00
215 RgM,MIB,Tartarus, pt.1 . . . . . . 2.50
216 RgM,MIB,The Bronze Doors. . . 2.50
217 RgM,MIB,The Bronze Doors. . . 2.50
218 RgM,MIB, ... 2.50
219 Sacrifice,Superman,x-over,pt.4 10.00
220 A:Checkmate. 2.50
221 RgM,Power of Omac 2.50
222 RgM,F:Donna Troy, Cheetah . . 2.50
223 RgM,V:Omacs. 2.50
224 RgM,Omacs attack 2.50
225 Uncertain Future. 2.50
226 Final issue. 2.50
Ann.#1,GP,AAd,RA,BB,JBo,JL,CS
    Tales of Paradise Island 4.00
Ann.#2 CM,F:Mayer Agency 4.00
Ann.#3 Eclipso tie-in 3.00
Ann.#4 Year One Annual 4.00

Ann.#5 JBy,DC,NBy,Legends of the
    Dead Earth 3.50
Ann.#6 Pulp Heroes (Macabre). . . . 4.50
Ann.#7 Ghosts 3.50
Ann.#8 JLApe Gorilla Warfare. 3.50
Annual #1 (1967) (rep.2003) 5.00
Spec.#1,000,000 CPr(s),MC,BMc . . 3.00
Spec #1 A:Deathstroke,Cheetah . . 2.50
Spec.#0 History of Amazons 7.00
Spec.#1 Our Worlds at War,48-pg . . 3.00
GN Amazonia, BML 8.00
GN Amazonia, Elseworlds 8.00
GN The Once and Future Story. . . . 5.00
GN The Gods of Gotham, rep. 6.00
Secret Files #2. . . . . 5.00
Secret Files #3, 48-pg 5.00
Spec. Wonder Woman: Donna Troy
    Girlfrenzy (1998) 2.50
Spec. Wonder Woman Plus CPr(s),
    MC, TP,Jesse Quick & Wonder
    Woman (1996). 3.00
Spec. The Blue Amazon (2003). . . . 7.00

WONDER WOMAN
June, 2006
1 TyD, Who is Wonder Woman . . . 3.00
1a variant (c). 3.00
2 TyD,F:Wonder Girl. 3.00
3 TyD,Who is Wonder Woman . . . 3.00
4 TyD,Cheetah, Giganta 3.00
5 TyD,Who is Wonder Woman,pt.5 3.00
6 TyD(c),F:The Amazons 3.00
7 TyD(c),F:The Amazons 3.00
8 TyD,Amazon's Attack prequel . . 3.00
9 TyD,Amazon's Attack tie-in 3.00
10 TyD,Crossing the line 3.00
11 TyD,Sarge Steel missing. 3.00
12 TyD,Amazons Attack tie-in 3.00
13 TyD,The Circle 3.00
14 TyD, The Circle, pt.1 . . . . 3.00
14a variant (c) (1:10) 3.00
15 TyD,The Circle, pt. 2 . . . . 3.00
16 TyD,The Circle, pt.3 . . . . 3.00
17 TyD,The Circle, concl. 3.00
18 TyD,V:Khund, pt.1 . . . . 3.00
19 TyD,V:Khund, pt.2. . . . . 3.00
20 AaL,Ends of the Earth, pt.1. . . . 3.00
21 AaL,Ends of the Earth, pt.2. . . . 3.00
22 AaL,Ends of the Earth, pt.3. . . . 3.00
23 AaL,Ends of the Earth, pt.4. . . . 3.00
24 Hollywood comes calling 3.00
25 Her name in lights. 3.00
26 Rise of the Olympian 3.00
Ann. #1 Who is W.Woman,48-pgs. . 4.00

WORLD OF KRYPTON
July, 1979
1 HC/MA.O:Jor-El. 10.00
2 HC/MA,A:Superman 6.00
3 HC 6.00
[2nd Series], 1987–88
1 MMi,John Byrne script. 3.00
2 MMi,John Byrne script. 3.00
3 MMi,John Byrne script. 3.00
4 MMi,A:Superman 3.00

WORLD OF METROPOLIS
1988
1 DG(i),O:Perry White. 2.50
2 DG(i),O:Lois Lane 2.50
3 DG(i),Clark Kent 2.50
4 DG(i),O:Jimmy Olsen. 2.50

WORLD OF SMALLVILLE
1988
1 KS/AA,Secrets of Ma&Pa Kent . . 3.00
2 KS/AA,Stolen Moments 3.00
3 KS/AA,Lana Lang/Manhunter . . . 3.00
4 KS/AA,final issue 3.00

All comics prices listed are for *Near Mint* condition.

WORLDS COLLIDE
1994
1 MBr(c),3RW,CsB,Ccs,DCw,
  TG,A:Blood Syndicate,Icon,
  Hardware,Static,Superboy,
  Superman,Steel,Vinyl Cling(c). . 4.25
1a Newsstand Ed.. . . . . 2.75

WORLD'S BEST COMICS
Oct. 2003
Spec. G.A. DC Archives Sampler. . . 1.00
Spec. S.A. DC Archives Sampler. . . 1.00

WORLD'S BEST COMICS
Spring, 1941
1 Superman vs. the Rainmaker,
  Batman vs. Wright 27,000.00
Becomes:

WORLD'S FINEST
COMICS
1941–86
2 Superman V:The Unknown X,
  Batman V:Ambrose Taylor 12,000.00
3 I&O:Scarecrow 7,000.00
4 Superman V:Dan Brandon,
  Batman V:Ghost Gang 5,000.00
5 Superman V:Lemuel P.Potts,
  Batman V:Brains Kelly 4,500.00
6 Superman V:Metalo,Batman
  meets Scoop Scanlon 3,500.00
7 Superman V:Jenkins,Batman
  V:Snow Man Bandits 3,500.00
8 Superman:Talent Unlimited
  Batman V:Little Nap Boyd,
  B:Boy Commandos 3,000.00
9 Superman:One Second to
  Live,Batman V:Bramwell B.
  Bramwell. 3,500.00
10 Superman V:The Insect Master,
  Batman reforms OliverHunt 3,000.00
11 Superman V:Charlie Frost,
  Batman V:Rob Calendar . . 2,500.00
12 Superman V:Lynx,Batman:
  Alfred Gets His Man 2,500.00
13 Superman V:Dice Dimant,
  Batman,V:Swami Pravhoz . 2,500.00
14 Superman V:Al Bandar,Batman
  V:Jib Buckler. 2,500.00
15 Superman V:Derby Bowser,
  Batman V:Mennekin 2,500.00
16 Superman:Music for the Masses,
  Batman V:Nocky Johnson . 2,500.00

World's Finest #7
© *DC Comics, Inc.*

17 Superman:The Great Godini,
  Batman V:Dr.Dreemo 2,500.00
18 Superman:The Junior Reporters,
  Batman V:Prof.Brane 2,200.00
19 A:The Joker 2,200.00
20 A:Toyman 2,200.00
21 Superman:Swindle in
  Sweethearts!. 1,800.00
22 Batman V:Nails Finney 1,800.00
23 Superman:The Colossus
  of Metropolis. 1,800.00
24 . . . . 1,800.00
25 Superman V:Ed Rook,Batman:
  The Famous First Crimes. . 1,800.00
26 Confessions of Superman . . 1,800.00
27 The Man Who Out-Supered
  Superman. 1,800.00
28 A:Lex Luther,Batman V:Glass
  Man. 1,800.00
29 Superman:The Books that
  Couldn't Be Bound 1,800.00
30 Superman:Sheriff Clark Kent,
  Batman V:Joe Coyne 1,800.00
31 Superman's Super-Rival,Batman:
  Man with the X-Ray Eyes. . 1,500.00
32 Superman Visits
  Ancient Egypt. 1,500.00
33 Superman Press, Inc.,
  Batman V:James Harmon . 1,500.00
34 The Un-Super Superman. . . 1,500.00
35 Daddy Superman,A:Penguin 1,500.00
36 Lois Lane,Sleeping Beauty . 1,500.00
37 The Superman Story,Batman
  V:T-Gun Jones 1,500.00
38 If There were No Superman 1,500.00
39 Superman V:Big Jim Martin,
  Batman V:J.J.Jason 1,500.00
40 Superman V:Check,Batman:
  Four Killers Against Fate! . . 1,100.00
41 I:Supermanium,
  E:Boy Commandos 1,100.00
42 Superman goes to Uranus,
  A:Marco Polo & Kubla Khan1,100.00
43 A:J.Wilbur Wolfingham. . . . 1,100.00
44 Superman:The Revolt of the
  Thought Machine 1,100.00
45 Superman:Lois Lane and Clark
  Kent,Private Detectives . . . 1,100.00
46 Superman V:Mr. 7 . . . . 1,100.00
47 Superman:The Girl Who
  Hated Reporters. 1,100.00
48 A:Joker. 1,100.00
49 Superman Meets the
  Metropolis Shutterbug
  Society, A:Penguin 1,100.00
50 Superman Super Wrecker . . 1,100.00
51 Superman:The Amazing
  Talents of Lois Lane 1,100.00
52 A:J.Wilbur Wolfingham. 1,100.00
53 Superman V:Elias Toomey. . 1,100.00
54 The Superman Who Avoided
  Danger!. 1,100.00
55 A:Penguin. 1,100.00
56 Superman V:Dr.Vallin,Batman
  V:Big Dan Hooker. 1,100.00
57 The Artificial Superman 1,100.00
58 Superman V:Mr.Fenton. . . . 1,100.00
59 A:Lex Luthor,Joker. 1,100.00
60 A:J.Wilbur Wolfingham. 1,100.00
61 A:Joker,Superman's
  Blackout. 900.00
62 A:Lex Luthor 900.00
63 Superman:Clark Kent,
  Gangster 900.00
64 Superman:The Death of Lois
  Lane,Batman:Bruce Wayne...
  Amateur Detective. 900.00
65 The Confessions of Superman,
  Batman V:The Blaster 1,300.00
66 Superman,Ex-Crimebuster;
  Batman V:Brass Haley 900.00

World's Finest Comics #91
© *DC Comics, Inc.*

67 Superman:Metropolis-Crime
  Center!. 900.00
68 Batman V:The Crimesmith . . . 900.00
69 A:Jor-El,Batman
  V:Tom Becket 900.00
70 The Two Faces of Superman,
  Batman:Crime Consultant . . . 900.00
71 B:Superman/Batman
  team-ups. 2,200.00
72 V:Heavy Weapon gang 1,400.00
73 V:Fang 1,400.00
74 The Contest of Heroes 1,100.00
75 V:The Purple Mask Mob . . . 1,000.00
76 When Gotham City
  Challenged Metropolis. 800.00
77 V:Prof.Pender 800.00
78 V:Varrel mob 800.00
79 A:Aladdin. 800.00
80 V:Mole. 800.00
81 Meet Ka Thar from future . . . 600.00
82 A:Three Musketeers 600.00
83 The Case of the Mother
  Goose Mystery 600.00
84 V:Thad Linnis Gang 600.00
85 Meet Princess Varina 600.00
86 V:Henry Bartle. 600.00
87 V:Elton Craig. 600.00
88 1st team-up Luthor & Joker . 650.00
89 I:Club of Heroes 600.00
90 A:Batwoman 600.00
91 V:Rohtul,Descendent of Lex
  Luthor 400.00
92 1st & only A:Skyboy. 400.00
93 V:Victor Danning. 400.00
94 O:Superman/Batman team,
  A:Lex Luthor. 1,200.00
95 Battle o/t Super Heroes 400.00
96 Super-Foes from Planet X . . 400.00
97 V:Condor Gang. 400.00
98 I:Moonman 400.00
99 JK,V:Carl Verril 400.00
100 A:Kandor, Lex Luthor. 1,000.00
101 A:Atom Master 300.00
102 V:Jo-Jo Groff gang,
  B:Tommy Tomorrow. 300.00
103 The Secrets of the
  Sorcerer's Treasure. 300.00
104 A:Lex Luthor 300.00
105 V:Khalex 300.00
106 V:Duplicate Man 300.00
107 The Secret of the Time
  Creature. 300.00
108 The Star Creatures 300.00
109 V:Fangan 300.00

110 The Alien Who Doomed
  Robin! 300.00
111 V:Floyd Frisby 300.00
112 Menace of Superman's Pet. . 300.00
113 1st Bat-Mite/Mr.Mxyzptlk
  team-up 300.00
114 Captives o/t Space Globes . . 300.00
115 The Curse That Doomed
  Superman 250.00
116 V:Vance Collins 250.00
117 A:Batwoman,Lex Luthor . . . 250.00
118 V:Vath-Gar. 250.00
119 V:General Grambly 250.00
120 V:Faceless Creature 250.00
121 I:Miss Arrowette 250.00
122 V:Klor 175.00
123 A:Bat-Mite & Mr. Mxyzptlk. . . 175.00
124 V:Hroguth,E:Tommy
  Tomorrow. 175.00
125 V:Jundy,B:Aquaman 175.00
126 A:Lex Luthor 175.00
127 V:Zerno 175.00
128 V:Moose Morans. 175.00
129 Joker/Luthor T.U. 175.00
130 Riddle of the Four Planets . . 175.00
131 V:Octopus 175.00
132 V:Denny Kale,Shorty Biggs . 175.00
133 Deasls of the Supernatural . . 175.00
134 V:Band of Super-Villians. . . . 175.00
135 V:The Future Man. 175.00
136 The Batman Nobody
  Remembered. 175.00
137 A:Lex Luthor 175.00
138 V:General Grote 175.00
139 V:Sphinx Gang,E:Aquaman . 175.00
140 CS,V:Clayface. 175.00
141 CS,A:Jimmy Olsen 175.00
142 CS,O:Composite Man. 175.00
143 CS,A:Kandor,I:Mailbag 125.00
144 CS,A:Clayface,Brainiac. 125.00
145 CS,Prison for Heroes 125.00
146 CS,Batman,Son of Krypton. . 125.00
147 CS,A:Jimmy Olsen 125.00
148 CS,A:Lex Luthor,Clayface. . . 125.00
149 CS,The Game of the
  Secret Identities. 125.00
150 CS,V:Rokk and Sorban. 125.00
151 CS,A:Krypto,BU:Congorilla . . 125.00
152 CS,A:The Colossal Kids,Bat-
  mite,V:Mr.Mxyzptlk 125.00
153 CS,V:Lex Luthor 125.00
154 CS,The Sons of Batman &
  Superman(Imaginary) 125.00
155 CS,The 1000th Exploit of
  Batman & Superman. 125.00
156 CS,I:BizarroBatman,V:Joker . 125.00
157 CS,The Abominable Brats
  (Imaginary story) 110.00
158 CS,V:Brainiac 110.00
159 CS,A:Many Major villians,I:Jim
  Gordon as Anti-Batman & Perry
  White as Anti-Superman 110.00
160 V:Dr Zodiac. 110.00
161 CS,80 page giant 125.00
162 V:The Jousting Master 75.00
163 CS,The Court of No Hope . . . 75.00
164 CS,I:Genia,V:Brainiac. 75.00
165 CS,The Crown of Crime 75.00
166 CS,V:Muto & Joker 100.00
167 CS,The New Superman &
  Batman(Imaginary) V:Luthor . 75.00
168 CS,R:Composite Superman . . 75.00
169 The Supergirl/Batgirl Plot;
  V:Batmite,Mr.Mxyzptlk. 75.00
170 80 page giant,reprint. 125.00
171 CS,V:The Executioners. 75.00
172 CS,Superman & Batman
  Brothers (Imaginary) 75.00
173 CS,The Jekyll-Hyde
  Heroes. 150.00
174 CS,Secrets of the Double
  Death Wish 100.00

World's Finest Comics #210
© DC Comics Inc.

175 NA(1st Batman),C:Flash. . . . 100.00
176 NA,A:Supergirl & Batgirl 100.00
177 V:Joker & Luthor 100.00
178 CS,The Has-Been Superman . 75.00
179 CS,giant 125.00
180 RA,ME,Supermans Perfect
  Crime. 75.00
181 RA,ME. 75.00
182 RA,ME,The Mad Manhunter. . 75.00
183 RA,ME,Superman's Crimes
  of the Ages 75.00
184 RA,ME,A:JLA,Robin 75.00
185 CS,The Galactic Gamblers. . . 75.00
186 RA,ME,The Bat Witch. 75.00
187 RA,ME,Demon Superman . . . 75.00
188 giant,reprint. 100.00
189 RA,ME,V:Lex Luthor 50.00
190 RA,V:Lex Luthor 40.00
191 RA,A:Jor-El,Lara. 40.00
192 RA,The Prison of No Escape . 40.00
193 The Breaking of Batman
  and Superman. 40.00
194 RA,ME,Inside the Mafia 40.00
195 RA,ME,Dig Now-Die Later . . . 40.00
196 CS,The Kryptonite Express,
  E:Batman. 40.00
197 giant 100.00
198 DD,B:Superman T.U.,
  A:Flash 125.00
199 DD,Superman & Flash race . 125.00
200 NA(c),DD,Prisoners of the
  Immortal World; A:Robin 50.00
201 NA(c),DD,A Prize of Peril,
  A:Green Lantern,Dr. Fate. . . . 35.00
202 NA(c),DD,Vengeance of the
  Tomb Thing,A:Batman. 35.00
203 NA(c),DD,Who's Minding the
  Earth,A:Quamar. 35.00
204 NA(c),DD,Journey to the End
  of Hope,A:Wonder Woman . . 35.00
205 NA(c),DD,The Computer that
  Captured a Town,Frazetta Ad,
  A:Teen Titans. 40.00
206 DD,giant reprint. 75.00
207 DD,Superman,A:Batman,
  V:Dr.Light. 40.00
208 NA(c),DD,A:Dr Fate 40.00
209 NA(c),DD,A:Green Arrow,
  Hawkman,I&V:The Temper. . . 40.00
210 NA(c),DD,A:Batman 40.00
211 NA(c),DD,A:Batman 40.00
212 CS(c),And So My World
  Begins,A:Martian Manhunter. . 40.00
213 DD,Peril in a Very Small
  Place,A:The Atom 40.00

214 DD,A:Vigilante. 40.00
215 DD,Saga of the Super Sons
  (Imaginary story) 60.00
216 DD,R:Super Sons,Little Town
  with a Big Secret 20.00
217 DD,MA,Heroes with
  Dirty Hands 20.00
218 DD,DC,A:Batman,
  BU:Metamorpho 20.00
219 DD,Prisoner of Rogues Rock;
  A:Batman. 20.00
220 DD,MA,Let No Man Write My
  Epitaph,BU:Metamorpho 20.00
221 DD,Cry Not For My Forsaken
  Son; R:Super Sons 20.00
222 DD,Evil In Paradise. 20.00
223 DD,giant,A:Deadman,Aquaman
  Robotman 60.00
224 DD,giant,A:Super Sons,
  Metamorpho,Johnny Quick . . 60.00
225 giant,A:Rip Hunter,Vigilante,
  Black Canary,Robin 60.00
226 A:Sandman,Metamorpho,
  Deadman,Martian Manhunter . 60.00
227 MGr,BWi,A:The Demonic Duo,
  Vigilante,Rip Hunter,Deadman,
  I:Stargrave 60.00
228 ATh,A:Super Sons,Aquaman,
  Robin,Vigilante 60.00
229 I:Powerman,A:Metamorpho . . 30.00
230 A:Super-Sons,Deadman,
  Aquaman, giant-size 50.00
231 A:Green Arrow,Flash. 18.00
232 DD,The Dream Bomb. 18.00
233 A:Super-Sons 18.00
234 CS,Family That Fled Earth . . . 18.00
235 DD,V:Sagitaurus. 18.00
236 DD,A:The Atom. 18.00
237 Intruder from a Dead World . . 18.00
238 DD,V:Luthor,A:Super-Sons. . . 18.00
239 CS,A:Gold(from Metal Men) . . 18.00
240 DD,A:Kandor. 18.00
241 Make Way For a New World. . 15.00
242 EC,A:Super-Sons 15.00
243 CS,AM,A:Robin. 15.00
244 NA(c),JL,MA,MN,TA,giant
  B:Green Arrow. 25.00
245 NA(C),CS,MA,MN,TA,
  GM,JSh,BWi,giant 25.00
246 NA(c),KS,MA,MN,TA,GM,
  DH,A:JLA. 25.00
247 KS,GM,giant 25.00
248 KS,GM,DG,TVE,A:Sgt.Rock . . 20.00
249 KS,SD,TVE,A:Phantom
  Stranger,B:Creeper 20.00
250 GT,SD,Superman,Batman,
  Wonder Woman,Green Arrow,
  Black Canary,team-up 22.00
251 GT,SD,JBi,BL,TVE,RE,
  JA,A:Poison Ivy,Speedy,
  I:CountVertigo 22.00
252 GT,TVE,SD,JA,giant 22.00
253 KS,DN,TVE,SD,B:Shazam . . . 15.00
254 GT,DN,TVE,SD,giant 15.00
255 JL,DA,TVE,SD,DN,KS,
  E:Creeper 15.00
256 MA,DN,KS,DD,Hawkman,Black
  Lightning,giant 15.00
257 DD,FMc,DN,KS,GT,RB,
  RT,giant 15.00
258 NA(c),RB,JL,DG,DN,KS,RT,
  giant. 17.00
259 RB,DG,MR,MN,DN,KS 15.00
260 RB,DG,MN,DN 15.00
261 RB,DG,AS,RT,EB,DN,
  A:Penguin, Terra Man 15.00
262 DG,DN,DA,JSon,RT,
  Aquaman 15.00
263 RB,DG,DN,TVE,JSh,Aquaman,
  Adam Strange 15.00
264 RB,DG,TVE,DN,Aquaman . . . 15.00
265 RB,DN,RE,TVE. 15.00

World's Finest Comics #303
© DC Comics, Inc.

266 RB,TVE,DN 15.00
267 RB,DG,TVE,AS,DN,
    A:Challengers of the Unknown 15.00
268 DN,TVE,BBr,RT,AS 15.00
269 RB,FMc,TVE,BBr,AS,DN,DA . 15.00
270 NA(c),RB,RT,TVE,AS,
    DN,LMa 15.00
271 GP(c),RB,FMc,O:Superman/
    Batman T.U. 15.00
272 RB,DN,TVE,BBr,AS 14.00
273 TVE,LMa,JSon,AS,DN,DA,
    A:Plastic Man 14.00
274 TVE,LMa,BBr,GC,AS,DN,
    Green Arrow 14.00
275 RB,FMc,TVE,LMa,DSp,AS,
    DN,DA,A:Mr.Freeze. 14.00
276 GP(c),RB,TVE,LMa,DSp,CI,
    DN,DA 14.00
277 GP(c),RT,TVE,DSp,AS,DN,
    DH,V:Dr.Double X 14.00
278 GP(c),RB,TVE,LMa,DSp,DN . 14.00
279 KP,TVE,LMa,AS,DN,
    B:Kid Eternity. 14.00
280 RB,TVE,LMa,AS,DN 14.00
281 GK(c),IN,TVE,LMa,AS,DN . . . 14.00
282 IN,FMc,GK,CI,last giant
    E:Kid Eternity. 14.00
283 GT,FMc,GK 14.00
284 GT,DSp,A:Legion,E:G.Arrow . 14.00
285 FM(c),RB,A:Zatanna 14.00
286 RB,A:Flash 14.00
287 TVE,A:Flash 14.00
288 A:JLA. 14.00
289 GK(c),Kryll way of Dying. . . . 14.00
290 TD(i),I:Stalagron 14.00
291 WS(c),TD(i),V:Stalagron 14.00
292 . . . . 14.00
293 . . . . 14.00
294 . . . . 14.00
295 FMc(i) 14.00
296 RA 14.00
297 GC,V:Pantheon 14.00
298 V:Pantheon 14.00
299 GC,V:Pantheon 14.00
300 RA,GP,KJ,MT,FMc,A:JLA . . . 14.00
301 Rampage 7.00
302 DM,NA(rep). 7.00
303 Plague. 7.00
304 SLi,O:Null&Void 7.00
305 TVE,V:Null&Void 7.00
306 SLi,I:Swordfish & Barracuda . . 7.00
307 TVE,V:Null&Void 7.00
308 GT,Night and Day 7.00
309 MT,AA,V:Quantum 7.00

310 I:Sonik. 7.00
311 A:Monitor 7.00
312 AA,I:Network 7.00
313 AA(i),V:Network. 7.00
314 AA(i),V:Executrix 7.00
315 V:Cathode 7.00
316 LSn,I:Cheapjack 7.00
317 LSn,V:Cheapjack 7.00
318 AA(i),A:Sonik. 7.00
319 AA(i),I:REM 7.00
320 AA(i),V:REM 7.00
321 AA,V:Chronos 7.00
322 KG,The Search 7.00
323 AA(i),final issue 7.00
Spec.#1 Our Worlds at War,48-pg . . 6.00

WORLD'S FINEST
[Limited Series], 1990
1 SR,KK,Worlds Apart 8.00
2 SR,KK,Worlds Collide 6.00
3 SR,KK,Worlds At War 6.00

WORLD'S FINEST:
SUPERBOY/ROBIN
Oct., 1996
1 (of 2) CDi&KK(s),TG,SHa,
    V:Poison Ivy, Metallo. 5.00
2 CDi&KK(s),TG,SHa, V:Poison
    Ivy, Metallo. 5.00

WORLD'S GREATEST
SUPER-HEROES
1977
1 A:Batman,Robin. 35.00

WORLD WAR III
Apr., 2007
Pt. 1 A Call to Arms 2.50
Pt. 2 The Valiant 2.50
Pt. 3 Hell is For Heroes 2.50
Pt. 4 United We Stand 2.50

WORLD WITHOUT END
1990
1 The Host, I:Brother Bones. . . . 5.00
2 A:Brother Bones. 3.50
3 . . . . 3.50
4 House of Fams 2.50
5 Female Fury 2.50
6 conclusion 2.50

WRATH OF THE
SPECTRE
May, 1988
1 JAp,rep.Adventure #431-#433 . . . 4.00
2 JAp,rep.Adventure #434-#436 . . . 4.00
3 JAp,rep.Adventure #437-#440 . . . 4.00
4 JAp,reps.,final issue. 5.00

XENOBROOD
1994–95
0 New team. 2.50
1 Battles 2.50
2 Bestiary 2.50
3 A:Superman 2.50
4 V:Bestiary. 2.50
5 V:Vimian. 2.50
6 final issue. 2.50

XERO
March, 1997
1 Cpr(s),Ccs,Trane Walker/Xero . . 3.00
2 CPr(s),Ccs,The Rookie 2.50
3 Cpr(s),Ccs,The Beast 2.50
4 CPr(s) 2.50
6 CPr, Genesis tie-in 2.50

7 CPr(s),O:Zero, pt.1 . . . . 2.50
8 CPr,O:Zero. 2.50
9 CPr(s), ... 2.50
10 CPr,a matter of ethics 2.50
11 . . . . 2.50
12 CPr, final issue, Xero dead 2.50

XOMBI
Milestone, 1994–96
0 WS(c),DCw,Shadow War,Foil(c),
    I:Xombi,Twilight 2.50
1 JBy(c),B:Silent Cathedrals 2.50
1a Platinum ed. 7.00
2 I:Rabbi Simmowitz,Golms,Liam
    Knight of the Spoken Fire 2.50
3 A:Liam 2.50
4 Silent Cathedrals 2.50
5 thru 20 . . . . @2.50
21 final issue 3.50

Y: THE LAST MAN
DC/Vertigo, July, 2002
1 JMz,UnManned,pt.1,40-pg 30.00
2 JMz,UnManned,pt.2. . . . . 25.00
3 JMz,UnManned,pt.3. . . . . 20.00
4 JMz,UnManned,pt.4. . . . . 12.00
5 JMz,UnManned,pt.5. . . . . 10.00
6 JMz,Cycles,pt.1 . . . . 7.00
7 JMz,Cycles,pt.2 . . . . 6.00
8 JMz,Cycles,pt.3 . . . . 6.00
9 JMz,Cycles,pt.4 . . . . 6.00
10 JMz,Cycles,pt.5. . . . . 4.00
11 JMz,One Small Step,pt.1 . . . . . 4.00
12 JMz,One Small Step,pt.2 . . . . . 4.00
13 JMz,One Small Step,pt.3 . . . . . 4.00
14 JMz,One Small Step,pt.4 . . . . . 3.50
15 JMz,One Small Step,pt.5 . . . . . 3.50
16 JMz,Comedy&Tragedy,pt.1. . . . 3.50
17 JMz,Comedy&Tragedy,pt.2. . . . 3.00
18 JMz,Safeword,pt.1 . . . . 3.00
19 JMz,Safeword,pt.2 . . . . 3.00
20 JMz,Safeword,pt.3 . . . . 3.00
21 JMz,Widow's Pass,pt.1 . . . . 3.00
22 JMz,Widow's Pass,pt.2 . . . . 3.00
23 JMz,Widow's Pass,pt.3 . . . . 3.00
24 JMz,Tongues of Flame,pt.1 . . . . 3.00
25 JMz,Tongues of Flame,pt.2 . . . . 3.00
26 JMz,Hero's Journey 3.00
27 JMz,Ring of Truth,pt.1 . . . . 3.00
28 Ring of Truth, pt.2 . . . . 3.00
29 Ring of Truth, pt.3 . . . . 3.00
30 Ring of Truth, pt.4 . . . . 3.00
31 Ring of Truth, pt.5 . . . . 3.00
32 thru 35 Girl on Girl, pt.1–pt.4 . @3.00
36 F:Beth Deville 3.00
37 Paper Dolls, pt.1 . . . . 3.00
38 Paper Dolls, pt.2 . . . . 3.00
39 Paper Dolls, pt.3 . . . . 3.00
40 The Women Left Behind 3.00
41 O:Agent 355 . . . . 3.00
42 F:Ampersand 3.00
43 A trip to Japan. 3.00
44 Kimono Dragons 3.00
45 Kimono Dragons 3.00
46 Kimono Dragons, concl. 3.00
47 Secret origin of Dr. Allison Mann 3.00
48 O:Alter Tse'elon 3.00
49 Motherland, pt.1 . . . . 3.00
50 Motherland, pt.2 . . . . 3.00
51 Motherland, pt.3 . . . . 3.00
52 Motherland, pt.4 . . . . 3.00
53 . . . . 3.00
54 Fish & Bicycle Theatre Troupe . . 3.00
55 Whys and Wherefores, pt.1 . . . . 3.00
56 Whys and Wherefores, pt.2 . . . . 3.00
57 Whys and Wherefores, pt.3 . . . . 3.00
58 Whys and Wherefores, pt.4 . . . . 3.00
59 Whys and Wherefores, pt.5 . . . . 3.00

YEAR ONE: BATMAN/RA'S AL GHUL
June, 2005
1 (of 2) PG,JP48-page 6.00
2 PG,JP. 6.00

YEAR ONE: BATMAN/SCARECROW
May, 2005
1 (of 2) 48-page 6.00
2 . . . . 6.00

YEAH!
Homage/DC, 1999
1 GHe 3.00
2 GHe 3.00
3 GHe 3.00
4 GHe,Origins of Yeah,pt.1. . . . . . . 3.00
5 GHe,Origins of Yeah,pt.2. . . . . . . 3.00
6 thru 9 GHe, ... @3.00

YOUNG ALL STARS
June, 1987
1 I:IronMunro&FlyingFox,D:TNT. . . 1.60
2 V:Axis Amerika. 2.50
3 V:Axis Amerika. 2.50
4 I:The Tigress 2.50
5 I:Dyna-mite,O:Iron Munro 2.50
6 . . . . 2.50
7 Baseball Game,A:Tigress 2.50
8 Millennium 2.50
9 Millennium 2.50
10 Hugo Danner 2.50
11 Birth of Iron Munro 2.50
12 Secret of Hugo Danner 2.50
13 V:Deathbolt,Ultra-Humanite 2.50
14 Fury+Ultra Humanite. 2.50
15 IronMunro At high school 2.50
16 Ozyan Inheritance. 2.50
17 Ozyan Inheritance. 2.50
18 Ozyan Inheritance. 2.50
19 Ozyan 2.50
20 O:Flying Fox 2.50
21 Atom & Evil#1 . . . . 2.50
22 Atom & Evil#2 . . . . 2.50
23 Atom & Evil#3 . . . . 2.50
24 Atom & Evil#4 . . . . 2.50
25 . . . . 2.50
26 End of the All Stars? 2.50
27 Sons of Dawn' begins 2.50
28 Search for Hugo Danner. 2.50
29 A:Hugo Danner 2.50
30 V:Sons of Dawn 2.50
31 V:Sons of Dawn,last issue 2.50
Ann.#1 MG,V:Mekanique 2.50

YOUNG HEROES IN LOVE
April, 1997
1 DeM,F:Hard Drive 3.00
2 DeM,sex, lies and superheroics . 2.50
3 A:Superman. 2.50
4 F:Hard Drive. 2.50
5 Genesis tie-in. 2.50
6 The Rat Pack. 2.50
7 Secret Identity Issue 2.50
8 V:Scarecrow. 2.50
9 F:Frostbite & Bonfire 2.50
10 V:Grundo'mu. 2.50
11 V:Grundo'mu 2.50
12 Hard Drive dead? 2.50
13 New leader picked 2.50
14 Man of Inches vs. Man
    of Candles. 2.50
15 Junior vs. Birthday Boy. 2.50
16 DeM,Zip-Kid. 2.50
17 DeM,Monstergirl's Uncle. 2.50
Spec.#1,000,000 DeM final issue . . 3.00

YOUNG JUSTICE
July, 1998
1 PDd,TNu,Robin,Superboy,
    Impulse 5.00
2 PDd,TNu,V:Super-Cycle 3.00
3 PDd(s),TNu,V:Mr.Mxyzptlk. 3.00
4 PDd(s),TNu,Girls join team 3.00
5 PDd(s),TNu,V:Harm. 3.00
6 PDd(s),TNu,F:JLA. 3.00
7 PDd(s),TNu,A:Nightwing 3.00
8 CDi(s),TNu,A:Razorsharp 3.00
9 PDd(s),V:Huggathugees 3.00
10 PDd(s),V:The Acolyte 3.00
11 PDd(s),Rescue Red Tornado . . . 3.00
12 PDd(s),TNu,Supergirl x-over
    Hell's Angels,pt.1 . . . . 3.00
13 PDd(s), Hell's Angels,pt.3. . . . . . 3.00
14 PDd(s),Day of Judgment x-over . 3.00
15 PDd(s),F:Arrowette 3.00
16 PDd(s). 3.00
17 PDd(s),A:A.P.E.S. 3.00
18 PDd(s),Young Injustice 3.00
19 PDd(s),I:Empress 3.00
20 PDd(s),new team 3.00
21 PDd(s),all new? 2.75
22 Day in the life 2.75
23 PDd,TNu,AustraliaGames,pt.1 . . 2.75
24 PDd,TNu,AustraliaGames,pt.2 . . 2.75
25 PDd,TNu,Into space,pt.1 . . . . . . 2.75
26 PDd,TNu,Into space,pt.2 . . . . . . 2.75
27 PDd,TNu,Into space,pt.3 . . . . . . 2.75
28 PDd,TNu,New Genesis. 2.75
29 PDd,TNu,F:Forever People 2.75
30 PDd,TNu,Secret vs. Spoiler 2.75
31 PDd,TNu,F:Empress. 2.75
32 PDd,TNu,F:Empress. 2.75
33 PDd,TNu,WendyWerewolfHunter 2.75
34 PDd,TNu,wolf bites. 2.75
35 PDd,TNu,Worlds at War,tie-in. . . 2.75
36 PDd,TNu,Worlds at War,tie-in. . . 2.75
37 PDd,TNu,stuck in Hell 2.75
38 PDd,TNu,jokerized Match 2.75
39 PDd,TNu,V:New Genesis 2.75
40 PDd(s),TNu,Christmas Past 2.75
41 PDd(s),TNu,F:Ray 2.75
42 PDd(s),TNu,F:Hal Jordan 2.75
43 PDd(s),TNu,F:Traya 2.75
44 PDd(s),TNu,WorldWithoutYJ,pt.1 2.75
45 PDd(s),TNu,WorldWithoutYJ,pt.5 2.75
46 PDd(s),TNu,election day at HQ . 2.75
47 PDd(s),TNu,Fighting MAAD,pt.1. 2.75
48 PDd(s),TNu,Fighting MAAD,pt.2. 2.75
49 PDd(s),TNu,Fighting MAAD,pt.3. 2.75
50 PDd(s),TNu,F.MAAD,pg.4,48-pg. 4.00
51 PDd(s),TNu, on Zandia. 2.75
52 PDd(s),TNu,Real World 2.75
53 PDd(s),TNu,V:Secret 2.75
54 PDd(s),TNu,V:Secret 2.75
55 PDd(s),TNu,final issue 2.75
Spec.#1,000,000 PDd(s),TNu 3.00
Giant#1 Secret Origins, 80-page . . . 5.00
Giant#1 80-page 5.00
Secret Files #1. . . . . 5.00
Spec.#1 Young Justice in
    No Man's Land, CDi(s) 4.00
Spec.#1 Young Justice: The Secret
    Impulse,Superboy,Robin (1998) 2.50
Spec.#1 Our Worlds at War 3.00

YOUNG JUSTICE: SINS OF YOUTH
March, 2000
1 (of 2) PDd,x-over. 4.00
2 PDd,x-over. 4.00
Secret Files #1. . . . . 5.00
TPB Sins of Youth 20.00

YOUNG LIARS
Vertigo, March 2008
1 thru 9 by David Lapham. . . . . . @3.00

Young Love #125
© DC Comics Inc.

YOUNG LOVE
Sept.–Oct., 1963
39 . . . . 75.00
40 thru 50. . . . . @50.00
51 thru 60 . . . . @40.00
61 thru 68 . . . . @40.00
69 giant size. 90.00
70 thru 80 . . . . @40.00
81 thru 99 giants, 52-page. . . . . @35.00
100 . . . . 45.00
101 thru 106 . . . . @30.00
107 GC, Giant, 100-page. 125.00
108 thru 114 Giant, 100-page . @100.00
115 thru 126 52-page. . . . . @50.00

Y: THE LAST MAN
60 56-pg. final issue. 5.00

ZATANNA
1987
1 R:Zatanna 2.50
2 N:Zatanna 2.50
3 Come Together 2.50
4 V:Xaos 2.50

ZERO GIRL
DC/Homage Dec., 2000
1 (of 5) SK,F:Amy Snooster 3.00
2 SK. 3.00
3 SK,Vice Principal Hooly 3.00
4 SK,Mr. Foster. 3.00
5 SK, concl. 3.00

...FULL CIRCLE
DC/Vertigo, Nov., 2002
1 (of 5) SK 3.00

ZERO HOUR: CRISIS IN TIME
1994
4 DJu(a&s),JOy,A:All DC Heroes,
    D;2nd Flash 4.50
3 DJu(a&s),JOy,D:G.A.Sandman,
    G:A.Atom,Dr.Fate,1st Wildcat
    IR:Time Trapper is Rokk Krinn,
    Hawkmen merged 2.50
2 DJu(a&s),JOy 2.50
1 DJu(a&s),JOy,b:Power Gir's
    Child 2.50
0 DJu(A&s),JOy,Gatefold(c),Extant
    vs. Spectre. 2.50

Dark Claw Adventures #1
© DC/Marvel

Magneto & The Magnetic Men #1
© DC/Marvel

X-Patrol #1
© DC/Marvel

AMAZON
DC, 1996–97
1 JBy,TA 3.00
1 one-shot JBy,Princess Ororo
   is Wonder Woman 2.50

ASSASSINS
DC, 1996–97
1 DGC,SMc. 3.00
1 one-shot DGC(s),SMc,F:Dare
   and Catsai 2.50

BAT-THING
DC, 1997
1 one-shot LHa(s),RDm,BSz,
   V:motorcycle gang 2.50

BRUCE WAYNE:
AGENT OF S.H.I.E.L.D.
Marvel, 1996
1 CDi, ... 3.00

BULLETS & BRACELETS
Marvel, 1996
1 JOs,GFr,CaS 3.00

CHALLENGERS OF
THE FANTASTIC
Marvel, 1997
1 KK,TGu,AV 2.50

DARK CLAW
ADVENTURES, THE
DC, 1997
1 one-shot TTy,RBr,V:Ladia Talia . . 2.50

DC VERSUS MARVEL
MARVEL VERSUS DC
1 (DC)DJu 6.00
1a 2nd printing 4.00
2 (Marvel)PDd,DJu 5.00
2a 2nd printing 4.00
3 (Marvel)DJu 4.00
4 (DC)PDd,DJu 4.00
TPB rep. mini series #1–#4 . . . . . . 13.00

DOCTOR STRANGEFATE
DC, 1996–97
1 RMz,KN 3.00
1 one-shot RMz(s),JL,KN,Supreme
   Lord of Order 2.50

EXCITING X-PATROL
Marvel, 1997
1 BKs,BHi 2.50

GENERATION HEX
DC, 1997
1 one-shot,PrM(s),AdP,F:Jono Hex,
   Madam Banshee 2.50

IRON LANTERN
Marvel, 1997
1 KB,PSm,AW. 2.50

JLX
DC 1996–97
1 MWa,GJ, ... 3.00
1 one-shot,MWa(s),GJ,HPo,JhD . . 2.50

JLX UNLEASHED
DC, 1997
1 one-shot, CPr,The Inextinguish-
   able Flame. 2.50

LEGENDS OF
THE DARK CLAW
DC, 1996–97
1 LHa,JBa, ... 3.00
1 one-shot LHa(s),JBa, ... 2.50
1 2nd printing 2.50

LOBO THE DUCK
DC, 1997
1 one-shot, AlG,VS, ... 2.50

MAGNETO &
THE MAGNETIC MEN
Marvel, 1996
1 MWa,GJ,JMs,ATi 3.00

MAGNETIC MEN
FEATURING MAGNETO
Marvel, 1997
1 TPe,BKi,DPs 2.50

SPEED DEMON
Marvel, 1996
1 HMe,SvL,AM 3.00

SPIDER-BOY
Marvel, 1996
1 KK,MeW. 3.00

SPIDER-BOY TEAM-UP
Marvel, 1997
1 KK,RSt 2.50

SUPER-SOLDIER
DC, 1996–97
1 MWa,DGb 3.00
1-shot MWa(s),DGb,V:Ultra-
   Metallo, Green Skull, Hydra . . . 2.50

SUPER SOLDIER:
MAN OF WAR
DC, 1997
1 one-shot MWa(s),DGb,JP,
   V:Nazis 2.50

THORION OF
THE NEW ASGODS
Marvel, 1997
1 KG,JR2. 2.50

X-PATROL
Marvel, 1996
1 KK,BKs, ... 3.00
The Amalgam Age of Comics: The DC
   Comics Collection TPBs 13.00
The Amalgam Age of Comics: The
   Marvel Comics Collection TPBs . . 13.00
Return to the Amalgam Age of Comics:
   The DC Comics Collection TPB . . 13.00

MARVEL

ABRAHAM STONE
1995
1 JKu, Early 20th century 7.00
2 Wandering Man in the 20s. 7.00

ACTUAL CONFESSIONS
See: LOVE ADVENTURES

ACTUAL ROMANCES
Oct., 1949
1 . . . . 150.00
2 Photo Cover. 100.00

ADAM: LEGEND OF THE BLUE MARVEL
Nov., 2008
1 (of 4) 3.00

ADVENTURE INTO FEAR
See: FEAR

Adventure Into Mystery #1
© Marvel Entertainment Group

ADVENTURE INTO MYSTERY
Marvel Atlas, 1956–57
1 BP,BEv(c),Future Tense 600.00
2 Man on the 13th Floor 300.00
3 Next Stop Eternity 300.00
4 BP,AW, The Hex 300.00
5 JO,BEv,The People Who
  Weren't 300.00
6 The Wax Man 300.00
7 AT,BEv(c) 300.00
8 AT,JWo,TSe 300.00

ADVENTURES INTO TERROR
See: JOKER COMICS

ADVENTURES INTO WEIRD WORLDS
Jan., 1952–June, 1954
1 RH,GT,The Walking Death . . 1,200.00
2 GT,JMn,Thing in the Bottle . . . 600.00
3 JMn,The Thing That Waited . . 450.00
4 BEv,RH,TheVillageGraveyard . 450.00
5 BEv,I Crawl Thru Graves 450.00

6 The Ghost Still Walks 450.00
7 OW,Monsters In Disguise 450.00
8 DAy,Nightmares 450.00
9 Do Not Feed 450.00
10 BEv,Down In The Cellar 450.00
11 JMn,Phantom 400.00
12 GT,Lost In the Graveyard 400.00
13 JeR,DRi,Where Dead Men
  Walk 400.00
14 A Shriek In the Night 400.00
15 GT,Terror In Our Town 400.00
16 The Kiss of Death 400.00
17 RH,He Walks With A Ghost . . 400.00
18 Ivan & Petroff 400.00
19 It Happened One Night. 400.00
20 JMn,The Doubting Thomas . . 400.00
21 JF,What Happened In
  the Cave,Hitler. 450.00
22 JMn,RH,Vampire's Partner . . . 400.00
23 JMn,The Kiss of Death 300.00
24 JF,Halfway Home 300.00
25 BEv,JSt,The Mad Mamba 300.00
26 DAy,Good-Bye Earth. 300.00
27 The Dwarf of Horror Moor. . . . 600.00
28 DW,Monsters From the Grave 400.00
29 Bone Dry. 250.00
30 JSt,The Impatient Ghost 250.00

ADVENTURES OF CAPTAIN AMERICA
Sept., 1991
1 KM,JRu,O:Capt. America. 6.00
2 KM,KWe,TA,O:Capt.America. . . 5.50
3 KM,KWe,JRu,D:Lt.Col.Fletcher . 5.50
4 KWe,JRu,V:Red Skull 5.50

ADVENTURES OF CYCLOPS & PHOENIX
1994
1 SLo(s),GeH,AV,O:Cable 5.00
2 thru 4 SLo(s),GeH,AV,O:Cable @4.00

ADVENTURES OF HOMER GHOST
Atlas, June–Aug., 1957
1 and 2 . . . . @150.00

ADVENTURES OF PINKY LEE
Marvel Atlas, July, 1955
1 . . . . 400.00
2 . . . . 300.00
3 thru 5 . . . . @250.00

ADVENTURES OF SPIDER-MAN
1996
1 from animated TV show. 3.00
2 V:Hammerhead 3.00
3 thru 8 . . . . 3.00
8 AS,V:Kingpin 3.00
9 MHi,A:Dr. Strange, ... 3.00
10 AS,V:The Beetle 3.00
11 AS,V:Doctor Octopus, Venom. . 3.00
12 AS,V:Doctor Octopus, Venom. . 3.00

THE ADVENTURES OF BIG BOY
Marvel Timely Comics, 1956
1 . . . . 1,500.00

2 . . . . 750.00
3 . . . . 300.00
Becomes:

ADVENTURES OF THE BIG BOY
Marvel Timely Comics, 1956
4 . . . . 250.00
5 . . . . 250.00
6 . . . . 200.00
7 . . . . 200.00
8 thru 10 . . . . @200.00
11 thru 20 . . . . @150.00
21 thru 30 . . . . @100.00
31 thru 40 . . . . @50.00
41 thru 50 . . . . @35.00
51 thru 60 . . . . @25.00
61 thru 70 . . . . @25.00

ADVENTURES OF THE X-MEN
1996–97
1 from animated TV show. 3.00
2 X-Factor vs. X-Men 3.00
3 thru 12 . . . . @3.00

ADVENTURES ON THE PLANET OF THE APES
Oct., 1975
1 GT,Planet of the Apes Movie
  Adaptation 50.00
2 GT,Humans Captured 20.00
3 GT,Man Hunt 20.00
4 GT,Trial By Fear. 20.00
5 GT, Fury in the Forbidden Zone 20.00
6 GT,The Forbidden Zone,Cont'd. 35.00
7 AA,Man Hunt Cont'd 35.00
8 AA,Brent & Nova Enslaved 20.00
9 AA,Mankind's Demise 15.00
10 AA,When Falls the Lawgiver. . . 20.00
11 AA,Final Chapter,Dec.,1976 . . 25.00

AGENT X
July, 2002–Oct., 2003
1 Taskmaster trainee,40-pg. 3.50
2 thru 4 . . . . @3.00
5 thru 15 . . . . @2.50

AGENTS OF ATLAS
Aug., 2006
1 F:The Spaceman, The Goddess,
  The Robot, The Gorilla, The Spy3.00
2 A:Venus 3.00
3 A:Marvel Boy 3.00
4 A:Namora 3.00
5 The Temple of Atlas 3.00
6 finale, The Temple of Atlas 3.00

AGE OF THE SENTRY, THE
Sept., 2008
1 (of 6) 3.00
2 Man vs. Nature 3.00
3 . . . . 3.00
3a variant SB(c) 3.00

AKIRA
Epic, Sept., 1988
1 The Highway,I:Kaneda,Tetsuo,
  Koy,Ryu,Colonel,Takaski 35.00
1a 2nd printing 5.00
2 Pursuit,I:Number27,(Masaru) . . 17.00
2a 2nd printing 5.00

MARVEL

3 Number 41,V:Clown Gang 12.00
4 King of Clowns,V:Colonel 12.00
5 Cycle Wars,V:Clown Gang 12.00
6 D:Yamagota 10.00
7 Prisoners and Players,I:Miyo . . . 10.00
8 Weapon of Vengeance 10.00
9 Stalkers 10.00
10 The Awakening 10.00
11 Akira Rising 7.00
12 Enter Sakaki 7.00
13 Desperation 7.00
14 Caught in the Middle 7.00
15 Psychic Duel 7.00
16 Akira Unleashed 7.00
17 Emperor of Chaos 7.00
18 Amid the Ruins 6.00
19 To Save the Children 6.00
20 Revelations 6.00
21 . . . . 6.00
22 . . . . 6.00
23 . . . . 6.00
24 Clown Gang 6.00
25 Search For Kay 6.00
26 Juvenile A Project 6.00
27 Kay and Kaneda 6.00
28 Tetsuo 6.00
29 Tetsuo 6.00
30 Tetsuo,Kay,Kaneda 6.00
31 D:Kaori,Kaneda,Vs.Tetsuo 6.00
32 Tetsuo'sForces vs.U.S.Forces . . 6.00
33 Tetsuo V:Kaneda 6.00
34 64pt. R:Otomo 14.00
35 Leads toward final battle 14.00
36 Lady Miyako 14.00
37 ghost of Tetsuo 14.00
38 conclusion 14.00

ALF
Star, March, 1988
1 Photo Cover 4.00
1a 2nd printing 2.50
2 thru 19 . . . . @2.50
20 thru 22 . . . . @3.00
23 thru 30 . . . . @2.50
31 thru 43 . . . . @3.00
44 thru 45 . . . . @4.00
46 thru 49 . . . . @3.00
50 giant size 4.00
Ann.#1 Evol.War 3.00
Ann.#2 . . . . 3.00
Spring Spec.#1 . . . . 3.00
Holiday Spec.#2 . . . . 3.00

ALIAS
Marvel Max, Sept., 2001
1 BMB(s) 10.00
2 BMB(s), F:Jessica Jones 6.00
3 BMB(s) 6.00
4 BMB(s),DMk(c) 6.00
5 BMB(s),DMk(c) 4.00
6 BMB(s),DMk(c), ... 4.00
7 BMB(s),BSz 4.00
8 BMB(s),BSz 4.00
9 BMB(s),2nd story, concl. 4.00
10 BMB(s),J.J.Jameson,Jessica . . 3.50
11 BMB(s),to small town 3.50
12 BMB(s),in small town 3.50
13 BMB(s) 3.50
14 BMB(s),DMk(c),case concludes . 3.50
15 BMB(s),DMk(c),Cage again 3.50
16 BMB(s),DMk(c),Underneath 3.50
17 BMB(s),DMk(c),Underneath 3.50
18 BMB(s),DMk(c),Underneath 3.50
19 BMB(s),DMk(c),Underneath 3.50
20 BMB(s),DMk(c),Underneath 3.50
21 BMB(s),DMk(c),Underneath 3.50
22 BMB(s),DMk(c),Jessica Jones . . 3.25
23 BMB(s),DMk(c),Jessica Jones . . 3.25
24 BMB(s),DMk(c),Purple,pt.1 . . . . 3.25
25 BMB(s),DMk(c),Purple,pt.2 . . . . 3.25
26 BMB(s),DMk(c),Purple,pt.3 . . . . 3.25
27 BMB(s),DMk(c),Purple,pt.4 . . . . . 3.25
28 BMB(s),DMk(c),Purple,pt.5 . . . . . 4.00

ALIEN LEGION
Epic, April, 1984
1 FC,TA,I:Sarigar,Montroc 4.00
2 FC,TA,CP,V:Harkilons 3.50
3 thru 20 . . . . @3.00

[2nd Series], Aug., 1987
1 LSn,I:Guy Montroc 3.00
2 thru 18 . . . . @2.50
GN Grimrod 6.00
1-shot Alien Legion: Binary Deep
  with trading card (1993) 3.50
Spec. Alien Legion: Jugger Grimron
  Book One, (8-1992) 6.00

ALIEN LEGION: ONE PLANET AT A TIME
Epic, Heavy Hitters May, 1993
1 HNg,CDi,One Planet at a Time . . 5.00
2 HNg,CDi 5.00
3 HNg,CDi 5.00

ALIEN LEGION: ON THE EDGE
Epic, Nov., 1990
1 LSn,V:B'Be No N'ngth 5.00
2 LSn,V:B'Be No N'ngth 5.00
3 LSn,V:B'Be No N'ngth 5.00
4 LSn,V:B'Be No N'ngth 5.00

ALIEN LEGION: TENANTS OF HELL
Epic, 1991
1 LSn,Nomad Squad On
  Combine IV 5.00
2 LSn,L:Torie Montroc,I:Stagg . . . 5.00

ALL-NEW OFFICIAL HANDBOOK OF THE MARVEL UNIVERSE A to Z
Jan., 2006
1 . . . . 4.00
2 thru 12 . . . . @4.00
Update #1 thru #4 . . . . @4.00

ALL SELECT COMICS
Marvel Timely, (Daring Comics) Fall, 1943
1 ASh(c),B:Capt.America,Sub-Mariner,
  Human Torch;WWII 25,000.00
2 ASh(c),A:Red Skull,V:Axis
  Powers 8,000.00
3 ASh(c),B:Whizzer,V:Axis 5,000.00
4 ASh(c),V: Axis 3,500.00
5 ASh(c),E:Sub-Mariner,V:Axis 3,500.00
6 ASh,A:The Destroyer,V:Axis . 2,500.00
7 ASh,MSu,E:Whizzer,V:Axis. . 2,500.00
8 ASh(c),MSu,V:Axis Powers . 2,500.00
9 ASh(c),V:Axis Powers 2,500.00
10 ASh(c),E:Capt.America,Human
  Torch;A:The Destroyer 2,500.00
11 SSh, I:Blonde Phantom,
  A:Miss America 4,200.00
Becomes:

BLONDE PHANTOM
1946
12 SSh, B:Miss America;
  The Devil's Playground . . . 2,500.00
13 SSh,B:Sub-Mariner;Horror
  In Hollywood 1,600.00
14 SSh,E:Miss America;Horror
  At Haunted Castle 1,500.00
15 SSh,The Man Who Deserved
  To Die 1,500.00
16 SSh,A:Capt.America,Bucky;
  Modeled For Murder 2,000.00
17 Torture & Rescue 1,400.00
18 SSh,Jealously,Hate&Cruelty . 1,400.00
19 SSh(c),Killer In the Hospital. 1,400.00
20 Blonde Phantom's Big Fall . 1,400.00
21 SSh,Murder At the Carnival . 1,400.00
22 V: Crime Bosses 1,400.00
Becomes:

LOVERS
1949
23 Love Stories 275.00
24 My Dearly Beloved 150.00
25 The Man I Love 150.00
26 thru 29 . . . . @125.00
30 MK 150.00
31 thru 36 . . . . @125.00
37 . . . . 175.00
38 BK 175.00
39 . . . . 125.00
40 . . . . 125.00
41 BEv 150.00
42 thru 65 . . . . @125.00
66 . . . . 100.00
67 ATh 125.00
68 thru 86 Aug., 1957 . . . . @100.00

All Surprise #2
© Marvel Entertainment Group

ALL SURPRISE
Marvel Timely, Fall, 1943
1 (fa),F:Super Rabbit,Gandy,
  Sourpuss 450.00
2 . . . . 200.00
3 . . . . 150.00
4 thru 10 . . . . @150.00
11 HK 165.00
12 Winter, 1946 . . . . 150.00

ALL-TRUE CRIME
See: OFFICIAL TRUE CRIME CASES

ALL WINNERS COMICS
Marvel Timely, Summer, 1941
1 S&K,BEv,B:Capt.America & Bucky,
  Human Torch & Toro,Sub-Mariner
  A:The Angel,Black Marvel 42,000.00
2 S&K,SSh, B:Destroyer,
  Whizzer 10,000.00
3 BEv,Bucky & Toro Captured . 6,000.00

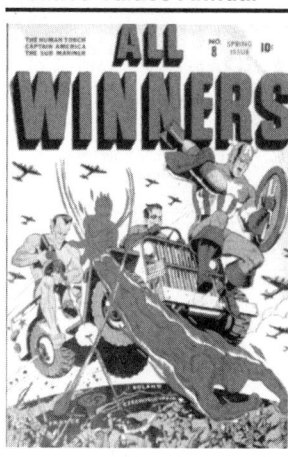

All Winners #8
© Marvel Entertainment Group

4 BEv,AAv,Battle For Victory
  For America 6,500.00
5 AAv,V:Nazi Invasion Fleet. . . 4,500.00
6 SSh,AAv,V:Axis Powers,
  A:Black Avenger. 5,000.00
7 V:Axis Powers. 3,600.00
8 V:Axis Powers. 3,500.00
9 V:Nazi Submarine Fleet 3,500.00
10 V:Nazi Submarine Fleet. . . . 3,600.00
11 V: Nazis 2,500.00
12 ASh(c),A:Red Skull,E:Destroyer;
   Jap P.O.W. Camp. 3,500.00
13 ASh(c),V:Japanese Fleet . . . 2,500.00
14 ASh(c),V:Japanese Fleet . . . 2,500.00
15 ASh(c),Jap Supply Train . . . 2,500.00
16 ASh(c),In Alaska
   V:Gangsters 2,500.00
17 V:Gansters;Atomic
   Research Department 2,500.00
18 ASh(c),V:Robbers;Internal
   Revenue Department. 2,600.00
19 ASh(c),SSh,I:All Winners Squad,
   Fall, 1946 . . . . 10,000.00
21 SSh,AAv,A:All-Winners Squad;
   Riddle of Demented Dwarf. 8,000.00
Becomes:

ALL TEEN COMICS
1947
20 F:Georgie,Willie,
   Mitzi,Patsy Walker. 200.00
Becomes:

TEEN COMICS
1947
21 HK,A:George,Willie,Mitzi,
   Patsy Walker, Hey Look 200.00
22 A:George,Willie,Margie,
   Patsy Walker 125.00
23 SSh,A:P.Walker,Cindy,George 125.00
24 . . . . 150.00
25 thru 27. . . . . @150.00
28 . . . . 150.00
29 . . . . 125.00
30 HK,Hey Look. 150.00
31 thru 34. . . . . @125.00
35 May, 1950 . . . . 125.00
Becomes:

JOURNEY INTO
UNKNOWN WORLDS
Marvel Atlas, Sept., 1950
36(1) RH,End of the Earth. . . . 4,000.00
37(2) BEv,GC,When Worlds
   Collide. 1,700.00

38(3) GT,Land of Missing Men 1,500.00
4 MSy,RH,Train to Nowhere. . . . 900.00
5 MSy,Trapped in Space. 900.00
6 GC,RH,World Below
  the Atlantic. 900.00
7 BW,RH,JMn,House That
  Wasn't. 1,500.00
8 RH,JMn,The Stone Thing . . 1,000.00
9 MSy,JSt,The People Who
  Couldn't Exist 1,000.00
10 The Undertaker 1,000.00
11 BEv,Frankie Was Afraid 700.00
12 BK,Last Voice You Hear 700.00
13 The Witch Woman 600.00
14 BW,BEv,CondemnedBuilding 1,200.00
15 JMn,They Crawl By Night . . 1,200.00
16 JMn,Scared to Death 600.00
17 BEv,GC,RH,The Ice
   Monster Cometh 700.00
18 The Broth Needs Somebody . 700.00
19 MF,GC,The Long Wait 700.00
20 GC,RH,The Race That
   Vanished 600.00
21 MF,JMn,JSt,Decapitation 400.00
22 thru 32. . . . . @400.00
33 SD,The Man in the Box 400.00
34 MK,AT,DAy 350.00
35 AT,MD 350.00
36 thru 44 . . . . @300.00
45 AW,SD. 300.00
46 & 47. . . . . @300.00
48 GW,GM. 300.00
49 JF,JMn. 300.00
50 JDa,RC 300.00
51 WW,SD,JSe 300.00
52 . . . . 300.00
53 RC,BP. 300.00
54 AT,BP 300.00
55 AW,RC,BEv. 300.00
56 BEv. 300.00
57 JO 250.00
58 MD,JMn. 250.00
59 AW,Aug., 1957 . . . . 350.00

ALL WINNERS COMICS
[2nd Series], Aug., 1948
1 SSh,F:Blonde Phantom,A:Capt.Am.
  Sub-Mariner,Human Torch 5,000.00
Becomes:

ALL WESTERN
WINNERS
1948–49
2 SSh,B,I&O:Black Rider,
  B:Two-Gun Kid, Kid-Colt . . 1,200.00

All Western Winners #2
© Marvel Entertainment Group

3 Black Rider V: Satan 600.00
4 Black Rider Unmasked 600.00
Becomes:

WESTERN WINNERS
1949
5 I Challenge the Army 500.00
6 The Mountain Mystery 450.00
7 Ph(c) Randolph Scott 450.00
Becomes:

BLACK RIDER
1950–55
8 Ph(c) of Stan Lee,B:Black Rider;
  Valley of Giants 750.00
9 SSh,JMn,Wrath of the Redskin 400.00
10 O:Black Rider 425.00
11 Redmen on the Warpath. 300.00
12 GT,The Town That Vanished. . 300.00
13 SSh,The Terrified Tribe 300.00
14 The Tyrant of Texas 300.00
15 Revolt of the Redskins 250.00
16 . . . . 250.00
17 . . . . 250.00
18. . . . . 250.00
19 SSh,GT,A:Two-Gun Kid 250.00
20 GT. 300.00
21 SSh,GT,A:Two-Gun Kid 250.00
22 SSh,DAy(c),A:Two-Gun Kid . . 250.00
23 SSh,A:Two-Gun Kid 250.00
24 SSh,JSt. 250.00
25 SSh,JSt,A:Arrowhead 250.00
26 SSh,A:Kid-Colt 250.00
27 SSh,JMn(c),A:Kid-Colt 300.00
Becomes:

WESTERN TALES OF
BLACK RIDER
1955
28 JSe,D:Spider. 300.00
29 . . . . 200.00
30 . . . . 200.00
31 . . . . 200.00
Becomes:

GUNSMOKE WESTERN
1955–63
32 MD,MB,F:Kid Colt,Billy
   Buckskin 300.00
33 MD 200.00
34 MB. 175.00
35 GC. 200.00
36 AW,GC 200.00
37 JDa 175.00
38 . . . . 150.00
39 GC. 150.00
40 AW 175.00
41 thru 43. . . . . @125.00
44 AT 125.00
45 & 46. . . . . @125.00
47 JK 150.00
48 & 49. . . . . @125.00
50 JK,RC 200.00
51 JK 150.00
52 thru 54. . . . . @125.00
55 & 56 MB . . . . @125.00
57 Two Gun Kid 100.00
58 & 59. . . . . @100.00
60 Sam Hawk (Kid Colt) 125.00
61 RC. 150.00
62 thru 67 JK . . . . @100.00
68 . . . . 100.00
69 JK 100.00
70 . . . . 100.00
71 JK 125.00
72 O:Kid Colt 125.00
73 JK 135.00
74 thru 76. . . . . @100.00
77 JK,July, 1963 . . . . 150.00

All comics prices listed are for *Near Mint* condition.

ALPHA FLIGHT
Aug., 1983

1 JBy,I:Puck,Marrina,Tundra 5.00
2 JBy,I:Master,Vindicator Becomes
    Guardian,B:O:Marrina 3.00
3 JBy,O:Master,A:Namor,Invisible
    Girl, ... 3.00
4 JBy,A:Namor,Invisible Girl,
    E:O:Marrina,A:Master 3.00
5 JBy,B:O:Shaman,F:Puck 3.00
6 JBy,E:O:Shaman,I:Kolomag 3.00
7 JBy,B:O:Snowbird,I:Delphine
    Courtney & Deadly Ernest 3.00
8 JBy,E:O:Snowbird,O:Deadly
    Ernest,I:Nemesis 3.00
9 JBy,O:Aurora,A:Wolverine,
    Super Skrull 3.00
10 JBy,O:Northstar,A:LokI,SuperSkrull . . 3.00
11 JBy,I:Omega Flight,Wild Child
    O:Sasquatch 3.00
12 JBy,D:Guardian,V:Omega
    Flight 3.00
13 JBy,C:Wolverine,Nightmare 3.50
14 JBy,V:Genocide. 3.00
15 JBy,R:Master. 3.00
16 JBy,BWi,V:Master,C:Wolverine
    I:Madison Jeffries 3.00
17 JBy,BWi,A:Wolverine,X-Men. . . . 3.50
18 JBy,BWi,J:Heather,I:Ranaq. 3.00
19 JBy,I:Talisman,V:Ranaq 3.00
20 JBy,I:Gilded Lily,N:Aurora 3.00
21 JBy,BWi,O:Gilded Lily,Diablo . . . 3.00
22 JBy,BWi,I:Pink Pearl 3.00
23 JBy,BWi,D:Sasquatch,
    I:Tanaraq 3.00
24 JBy,BWi,V:Great Beasts,J:Box . . 3.00
25 JBy,BWi,V:Omega Flight
    I:Dark Guardian 3.00
26 JBy,BWi,A:Omega Flight,Dark
    Guardian 3.00
27 JBy,V:Omega Flight 3.00
28 JBy,Secret Wars II,V:Omega
    Flight,D:Dark Guardian 3.00
29 MMi,V:Hulk,A:Box 2.50
30 MMi,I&O:Scramble,R:Deadly
    Ernest 2.50
31 MMi,D:Deadly Ernest,
    O:Nemesis 2.50
32 MMi(c),JBg,O:Puck,I:2nd
    Vindicator 2.50
33 MMi(c),SB,X-Men,I:Deathstrike . 4.00
34 MMi(c),SB,Wolverine,V:
    Deathstrike 4.00
35 DR,R:Shaman. 2.50
36 MMi(c),DR,A:Dr.Strange 2.50

Alpha Flight #15
© Marvel Entertainment Group

37 DR,O:Pestilence,N:Aurora 2.50
38 DR,A:Namor,V:Pestilence. 2.50
39 MMi(c),DR,WPo,A:Avengers 2.75
40 DR,WPo,W:Namor & Marrina . . . 2.75
41 DR,WPo,I:Purple Girl,
    J:Madison Jeffries 2.75
42 DR,WPo,I:Auctioneer,J:Purple
    Girl,A: Beta Flight 2.75
43 DR,WPo,V:Mesmero,Sentinels. . . 2.75
44 DR,WPo,D:Snowbird,
    A:Pestilence. 2.75
45 JBr,WPo,R:Sasquatch,
    L:Shaman 2.75
46 JBr,WPo,I:2nd Box 2.75
47 MMi,WPo,TA,Vindicator solo . . . 2.75
48 SL(i),I:Omega 2.75
49 JBr,WPo,I:Manikin,D:Omega . . . 2.75
50 WS(c),JBr,WPo,L:Northstar,Puck,
    Aurora,A:Loki,Double size 3.00
51 JLe(1st Marv),WPo(i),V:Cody . . . 7.00
52 JBr,WPo(i),I:Bedlam,
    A:Wolverine 3.00
53 JLe,WPo(i),I:Derangers,Goblyn
    D&V:Bedlam,A:Wolverine 4.00
54 WPo(i),O&J:Goblyn. 2.50
55 JLe,TD,V:Tundra. 2.50
56 JLe,TD,V:Bedlamites 3.50
57 JLe,TD,V:Crystals,
    C:Dreamqueen 3.50
58 JLe,AM,V:Dreamqueen. 3.50
59 JLe,AM,I:Jade Dragon,R:Puck . . 3.50
60 JLe,AM,V:J.Dragon,D.Queen . . . 3.50
61 JLe,AM,on Trial
    (1st JLe X-Men). 3.50
62 JLe,AM,V:Purple Man 3.50
63 MG,V:U.S.Air Force. 2.50
64 JLe,AM,V:Great Beasts 3.00
65 JLe(c),AM(i),Dream Issue 3.00
66 JLe(c),I:China Force 3.00
67 JLe(c),O:Dream Queen 3.00
68 JLe(c),V:Dream Queen 3.00
69 JLe(c),V:Dream Queen 3.00
70 MM(i),V:Dream Queen 2.50
71 MM(i),I:Sorcerer 2.50
72 V:Sorcerer. 2.50
73 MM(i),V:Sorcerer. 2.50
74 MM(i),Alternate Earth 3.00
75 JLe(c),MMi(i),Double Size 3.00
76 MM(i),V:Sorcerer. 2.50
77 MM(i),V:Kingpin 2.50
78 MM(i),A:Dr.Strange,Master 2.50
79 MM(i),AofV,V:Scorpion,Nekra . . 2.50
80 MM(i),AofV,V:Scorpion,Nekra . . 2.50
81 JBy(c),MM(i),B:R:Northstar. 2.50
82 JBy(c),MM(i),E:R:Northstar. 2.50
83 JSh 2.50
84 MM(i),Northstar. 2.50
85 MM(i). 2.50
86 MBa,MM,V:Sorcerer 2.50
87 JLe(c),MM(i),A:Wolverine 3.00
88 JLe(c),MM(i),A:Wolverine 3.00
89 JLe(c),MM(i),R:Guardian,A:
    Wolverine. 3.00
90 JLe(c),MM(i),A:Wolverine 3.00
91 MM(i),A:Dr.Doom 2.50
92 Guardian vs.Vindicator 2.50
93 MM(i),A:Fant.Four,I:Headlok . . . 2.50
94 MM(i),V:Fant.Four,Headlok. 2.50
95 MM(i),Lifelines. 2.50
96 MM(i),A:Master 2.50
97 B:Final Option,A:Her. 2.50
98 A:Avengers 2.50
99 A:Avengers 2.50
100 JBr,TMo,DR,LMa,E:Final Option
    A:Galactus,Avengers,D:
    Guardian,G-Size 3.00
101 TMo,Final Option Epilogue,
    A:Dr.Strange,Avengers 2.50
102 TMo,I:Weapon Omega,. 2.50
103 TMo,V:Diablo,U.S.Agent. 2.50
104 TMo,N:Alpha Flight,Weapon
    Omega is Wild Child 2.50

105 TMo,V:Pink Pearl 2.50
106 MPa,Aids issue,Northstar
    acknowledges homosexuality . . 3.00
106a 2nd printing 2.50
107 A:X-Factor,V:Autopsy 2.50
108 A:Soviet Super Soldiers 2.50
109 V:Peoples Protectorate 2.50
110 PB,Infinity War,I:2nd Omega
    Flight,A:Wolverine 2.50
111 PB,Infinity War,V:Omega
    Flight,A:Wolverine 2.50
112 PB,Infinity War,V:Master 2.50
113 V:Mauler 2.50
114 A:Weapon X 2.50
115 PB,I:Wyre,A:Weapon X. 2.50
116 PB,I:Rok,V:Wyre 2.50
117 PB,V:Wyre 2.50
118 PB,V:Thunderball 2.50
119 PB,V:Wrecking Crew. 2.50
120 PB,10th Anniv.,V:Hardliners,
    w/poster. 3.00
121 PCu,V:Brass Bishop,A:Spider-
    Man,Wolverine,C:X-Men 2.50
122 PB,BKi,Inf.Crusade. 2.50
123 PB,BKi,Infinity Crusade 2.50
124 PB,BKi,Infinity Crusade 2.50
125 PB,V:Carcass 2.50
126 V:Carcass 2.50
127 SFu(s),Infinity Crusade. 2.50
128 B:No Future 2.50
129 C:Omega Flight. 2.50
130 E:No Future,last issue,
    Double Sized 3.00
Ann.#1 LSn,V:Diablo,Gilded Lily . . . 3.00
Ann.#2 JBr,BMc 2.50
Spec.#1 PB,A:Wolverine,
    O:First Team,V:Egghead 3.75
Spec.#1–#3 Newsstand versions
    of #97–#99. . . . . @2.50
Spec.#4 Newsstand ver.of #100 . . 2.50

[2nd Series] 1997

1 SSe,ScC, former team kidnapped,
    I:Murmur, Radius,Flex,Guardian 5.00
2 SSe,ScC 4.00
2 variant cover 3.50
3 SSe,ScC, ... 3.50
4 SSe,ScC,V:Mesmero. 3.00
5 SSe,ScC,A:Mesmero. 3.00
6 SSe,What's up with Sasquatch? . 3.00
7 SSe,Evils explode 3.00
8 SSe,ScC,North & South prelude . 3.00
9 SSe,ScC,North & South pt.1,
    X-Men x-over. 3.00
10 SSe,Flung into Prometheus Pit . 3.00
11 SSe,race to save 2 worlds 3.00
12 SSe,Alphan dies,48pg. 3.50
13 SSe,F:Basil Killbrew. 2.50
14 SSe,I:Brass Bishop 2.50
15 SSe 2.50
16 SSe,V:Brass Bishop 2.50
17 SSe,V:X the Unknown 2.50
18 SSe,Alpha:Omega,pt.1 . . . . 2.50
19 SSe,Alpha:Omega,pt.2 . . . . 2.50
20 SSe,Alpha:Omega,pt.3 . . . . 2.50
Spec. #1 SSe,In the Beginning,
    Flashback, A:Wolverine 2.50
Ann.1998 Alpha Flight/Inhumans. . 3.50

[3rd Series] March, 2004

1 SLo,You Gotta Be Kiddin,pt.1 . . 3.00
2 SLo,You Gotta Be Kiddin,pt.2 . . 3.00
3 SLo,You Gotta Be Kiddin,pt.3 . . 3.00
4 SLo,You Gotta Be Kiddin,pt.4 . . 3.00
5 SLo,You Gotta Be Kiddin,pt.5 . . 3.00
6 SLo,You Gotta Be Kiddin,pt.6 . . 3.00
7 Waxing Poetic,pt.1 . . . . 3.00
8 Waxing Poetic,pt.2. . . . . 3.00
9 Days of Future Present,pt.1 . . . . 3.00
10 Days of Future Present,pt.2 . . . 3.00
11 Days of Future Present,pt.3 . . . 3.00
12 Days of Future Present,pt.4 . . . 3.00

AMAZING ADVENTURES
June, 1961
1 JK,SD,O&B:Dr.Droom;Torr . 2,700.00
2 JK,SD,This is Manoo 1,000.00
3 JK,SD,Trapped in the
   Twilight World 850.00
4 JK,SD, I Am X 800.00
5 JK,SD, Monsteroso 800.00
6 JK,SD,E:Dr.Droom; Sserpo . . . 800.00
Becomes:

AMAZING ADULT FANTASY
Dec., 1961
7 SD,Last Man on Earth 1,000.00
8 SD,The Coming of the Krills . . 900.00
9 SD,The Terror of Tim Boo Ba . 700.00
10 SD,Those Who Change 700.00
11 SD,In Human Form 700.00
12 SD,Living Statues 700.00
13 SD,At the Stroke of Midnight . 700.00
14 SD,Beware of the Giants 750.00
Becomes:

AMAZING FANTASY
Aug., 1962
15 JK(c),SD,I&O:Spider-Man,I:Aunt
   May, Flash Thompson, Burglar,
   I&D:Uncle Ben 55,000.00
Marvel Milestone rep.#15 (1992). . . 4.00

[Second Series], 1995
15a gold Rep. (1995). 25.00
16 KBk, O:Spider-Man,painted . . . 4.00
17 KBk, More early adventures 4.00
18 KBk,conclusion 4.00

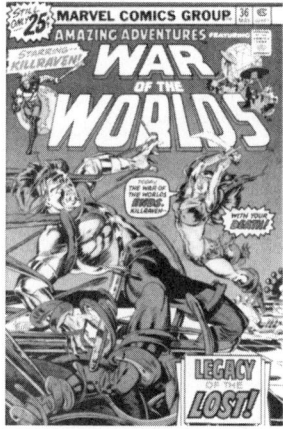

Amazing Adventures #36
© Marvel Ent. Group (Killraven)

AMAZING ADVENTURES
Aug., 1970
[1st Regular Series]
1 JK,JB,B:Inhumans,Bl.Widow . . . 90.00
2 JK,JB,A:Fantastic Four 45.00
3 JK,GC,BEv,V:Mandarin 45.00
4 JK,GC,BEv,V:Mandarin 45.00
5 NA,TP,DH,BEv,V:Astrologer . . . 75.00
6 NA,DH,SB,V:Maximus 75.00
7 NA,DH,BEv 75.00
8 NA,DH,BEv,E:Black Widow,
   A:Thor,(see Avengers #95) . . . 75.00
9 MSy,BEv,V:Magneto 40.00
10 GK(c),MSy,V:Magneto,
   E:Inhumans 40.00
11 GK(c),TS,B:O:New Beast,
   A:X-Men. 275.00

12 GK(c),TS,MP,A:Iron Man 100.00
13 JR(c),TS,V:New Br'hood
   Evil Mutants,I:Buzz Baxter
   (Mad Dog) 100.00
14 GK(c),TS,JM,V:Quasimodo . . 100.00
15 JSn(c),TS,A:X-Men,V:Griffin . . 100.00
16 JSn(c),FMc(i),V:Juggernaut . . 100.00
17 JSn,A:X-Men,E:Beast 100.00
18 HC,NA,B:Killraven. 100.00
19 HC,Sirens on 7th Avenues 12.00
20 Coming of the Warlords 12.00
21 Cry Killraven 12.00
22 Killraven 12.00
23 Killraven 12.00
24 New Year Nightmare-2019AD. . 12.00
25 RB,V:Skar 12.00
26 GC,V:Ptson-Rage Vigilante . . 12.00
27 CR,JSn,V:Death Breeders 12.00
28 JSn,CR,V:Death Breeders 12.00
29 CR,Killraven 12.00
30 CR,Killraven 12.00
31 CR,Killraven 12.00
32 CR,Killraven 12.00
33 CR,Killraven 12.00
34 CR,D:Hawk 12.00
35 KG,Killraven Continued. 12.00
00 CR,Killraven Continued 12.00
37 CR,O:Old Skull 12.00
38 CR,Killraven Continued. 12.00
39 CR,E:Killraven. 12.00

[2nd Regular Series], 1979
1 rep.X-Men#1,38,Professor X . . 10.00
2 thru 14 reps. . . . . @8.00

AMAZING COMICS
Marvel Timely, 1944
1 ASh(c),F:Young Allies,Destroyer,
   Whizzer, Sergeant Dix 4,000.00
Becomes:

COMPLETE COMICS
2 ASh(c),F:Young Allies,Destroyer,
   Whizzer Sergeant Dix; 3,000.00

AMAZING DETECTIVE CASES
Marvel Atlas, Nov., 1950
3 Detective/Horror Stories 400.00
4 Death of a Big Shot 250.00
5 . . . . 250.00
6 Danger in the City 250.00
7 . . . . 200.00
8 . . . . 200.00
9 GC, The Man Who Wasn't . . . 200.00
10 GT. 200.00
11 The Black Shadow 500.00
12 MSy,BK, Harrigan's Wake. . . . 500.00
13 BEv,JSt,. 500.00
14 Hands Off; Sept., 1952 . . . . . 400.00

AMAZING FANTASY
June, 2004
1 (of 6) 4.00
2 thru 5 . . . . @4.00
6 . . . . 3.00
7 F:Scorpion,pt.1 . . . . 3.00
8 Motherless Country 3.00
9 Identity Politics. 3.00
10 F:all-new Scorpion 3.00
11 The New Pollution 3.00
12 Poison Tomorrow 3.00
13 KK,I:Vegas 3.00
14 KK,F:Vegas 3.00
15 48-pg. 4.00
16 Unnatural Selection,pt.1 . . . . . . 3.00
17 Unnatural Selection,pt.2 . . . . . . 3.00
18 Unnatural Selection,pt.3 . . . . . . 3.00
19 Unnatural Selection,pt.4 . . . . . . 3.00
20 Unnatural Selection,pt.5 . . . . . . 3.00
Digest Scorpion: Poison Tomorrow . 8.00

AMAZING MYSTERIES
Marvel-Comics, 1949–50
32 The Isle of No Return 1,400.00
33 The Thing in the Vault. 700.00
34 Photo(c) 300.00
35 Photo(c) 300.00

AMAZING SPIDER-GIRL
Oct., 2006
0 RF,TDF,Spec., F:Mayday Parker . 2.00
1 RF,TDF, V:Black Tarantula. 3.00
2 RF,TDF, V:Hobgoblin 3.00
3 RF,TDF,V:Hobgoblin 3.00
4 RF,TDF,V:Mad Dog 3.00
5 RF,TDF,V:Black Tarantula 3.00
6 RF,TDF,V:Mad Dog, Hobgoblin . . 3.00
7 RF,TDF,Obsession. 3.00
8 RF,TDF,Midtown High 3.00
9 RF,TDF,V:Carnage, pt.1. . . . . 3.00
10 RF,TDF,V:Carnage, pt.2 . . . . . . 3.00
11 RF,TDF,V:Carnage, pt.3 . . . . . . 3.00
12 RF,TDF,V:Carnage, pt.4 . . . . . . 3.00
13 RF,TDF,I, Hobgoblin 3.00
14 RF,TDF,Know Thy Enemy. 3.00
15 RF,TDF,48-pg, Happy Birthday. . 4.00
16 RF,TDF 3.00
17 RF,TDF,Betrayed, pt.1 . . . . 3.00
18 RF,TDF,Betrayed, pt.2 . . . . 3.00
19 RF,TDF,There Can Be Only One 3.00
20 RF,TDF,V:Moose. 3.00
21 RF,TDF,A Brand New May,pt.1 . . 3.00
22 RF,TDF,A Brand New May,pt.2 . . 3.00
23 RF,TDF,A Brand New May,pt.3 . . 3.00
24 RF,TDF,The End of May 3.00
25 RF,TDF, 48-pg. 4.00
25a Zombie Variant (c) 4.00
26 RF,TDF, The Replacement 3.00

AMAZING SPIDER-MAN
March, 1963
1 JK(c),SED,I:Chameleon,J.Jonah &
   John Jameson,A:F.Four . . 45,000.00
2 SD,I:Vulture,Tinkerer
   C:Mysterio(disguised). . . . 10,000.00
3 SD,I&O:Dr.Octopus. 7,500.00
4 SD,I&O:Sandman,I:Betty
   Brant,Liz Allen 7,000.00
5 SD,V:Dr.Doom,C:Fant.Four . 7,000.00
6 SD,I&O:Lizard,The Connors. 4,000.00
7 SD,V:Vulture 3,000.00
8 SD,JK,I:Big Brain,V:Human
   Torch,A:Fantastic Four 2,500.00
9 SD,I&O:Electro 3,000.00

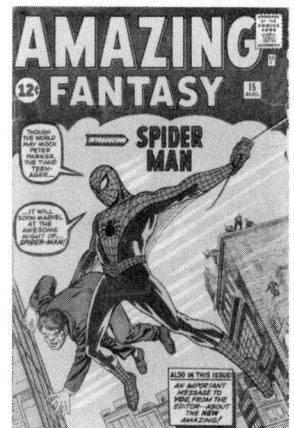

Amazing Fantasy #15
© Marvel Entertainment Group

10 SD,I:Enforcers,Big Man 2,600.00	
11 SD,V:Dr.Octopus,	
D:Bennett Brant 2,000.00	
12 SD,V:Dr.Octopus 2,000.00	
13 SD,I:Mysterio 2,500.00	
14 SD,I:Green Goblin,	
V:Enforcers, Hulk 4,700.00	
15 SD,I:Kraven,A:Chameleon . . 2,400.00	
16 SD,A:Daredevil,	
V:Ringmaster 1,700.00	
17 SD,2nd A:Green Goblin,	
A:Human Torch. 2,200.00	
18 SD,V:Sandman,Enforcers,	
C:Avengers,F.F.,Daredevil . 1,200.00	
19 SD,V:Sandman,I:Ned Leeds	
A:Human Torch. 1,000.00	
20 SD,I&O:Scorpion 1,800.00	
21 SD,A:Beetle,Human Torch. . 1,100.00	
22 SD,V:The Clown,Masters of	
Menace 900.00	
23 SD,V:GreenGoblin(3rd App.) 1,200.00	
24 SD,V:Mysterio 800.00	
25 SD,I:Spider Slayer,Spencer	
Smythe,C:Mary Jane 850.00	
26 SD,I:CrimeMaster,V:Green	
Goblin 1,000.00	
27 SD,V:CrimeMaster,	
Green Goblin 1,000.00	
28 SD,I:Molten Man,Peter Parker	
Graduates High School . . . 2,000.00	
29 SD,V:Scorpion 750.00	
30 SD,I:Cat Burglar 750.00	
31 SD,I:Gwen Stacy,Harry Osborn	
Prof.Warren,V:Dr.Octopus . . . 750.00	
32 SD,V:Dr.Octopus 450.00	
33 SD,V:Dr.Octopus. 450.00	
34 SD,V:Kraven 450.00	
35 SD,V:Molten Man 450.00	
36 SD,I:The Looter 450.00	
37 SD,V:Professor Stromm,	
I:Norman Osborn. 450.00	
38 SD,V:Joe Smith(Boxer). 450.00	
39 JR,IR:Green Goblin is Norman	
Osborn 1,100.00	
40 JR,O:Green Goblin 1,200.00	
41 JR,I:Rhino,C:Mary Jane 750.00	
42 JR,V:John Jameson,I:Mary	
Jane (Face Revealed). 450.00	
43 JR,O:Rhino 400.00	
44 JR,V:Lizard(2nd App.). 400.00	
45 JR,V:Lizard 400.00	
46 JR,I&O:Shocker 425.00	
47 JR,V:Kraven 400.00	
48 JR,I:Fake Vulture,A:Vulture . . 400.00	
49 JR,V:Fake Vulture,Kraven . . . 400.00	
50 JR,I:Kingpin,Spidey Quits,	
C:Johnny Carson 1,500.00	
51 JR,V:Kingpin 750.00	
52 JR,V:Kingpin,I:Robbie	
Robertson,D:Fred Foswell. . . 300.00	
53 JR,V:Dr.Octopus 350.00	
54 JR,V:Dr.Octopus 350.00	
55 JR,V:Dr.Octopus 350.00	
56 JR,V:Dr.Octopus,I:Capt.Stacy. 350.00	
57 JR,DH,A:Ka-Zar 350.00	
58 JR,DH,V:Spencer Smythe,	
Spider Slayer. 350.00	
59 JR,DH,V:Kingpin 350.00	
60 JR,DH,V:Kingpin 350.00	
61 JR,DH,V:Kingpin 350.00	
62 JR,DH,V:Medusa 200.00	
63 JR,DH,V:1st & 2nd	
Vulture 200.00	
64 JR,DH,V:Vulture 200.00	
65 JR,JM,V:Prisoners 200.00	
66 JR,DH,V:Mysterio 200.00	
67 JR,JM,V:Mysterio,I:Randy	
Robertson 200.00	
68 JR,JM,V:Kingpin 225.00	
69 JR,JM,V:Kingpin 225.00	
70 JR,JM,V:Kingpin 225.00	

Amazing Spider-Man #20
© *Marvel Ent. Group (Scorpion)*

71 JR,JM,V:Scarlet Witch,C:Scarlet	
Witch,Toad,A:Kingpin 200.00	
72 JR,JB,JM,V:Shocker 200.00	
73 JR,JB,JM,I:Man Mountain Marko,	
Silvermane. 200.00	
74 JR,JM,V:Silvermane 160.00	
75 JR,JM,V:Silvermane,A:Lizard . 150.00	
76 JR,JM,V:Lizard,A:H.Torch. . . . 150.00	
77 JR,JM,V:Lizard,A:H.Torch. . . . 150.00	
78 JR,JM,I&O:Prowler. 135.00	
79 JR,JM,V:Prowler 135.00	
80 JR,JB,JM,V:Chameleon 135.00	
81 JR,JB,JM,I:Kangaroo 135.00	
82 JR,JM,V:Electro 135.00	
83 JR,I:Richard Fisk(as Schemer),	
Vanessa(Kingpin's wife) 135.00	
84 JR,JB,JM,V:Schemer,Kingpin . 135.00	
85 JR,JB,JM,V:Schemer,Kingpin . 135.00	
86 JR,JM,V:Black Widow, C:Iron	
Man, Hawkeye. 135.00	
87 JR,JM,Reveals ID to his	
friends,changes mind 135.00	
88 JR,JM,V:Dr.Octopus 135.00	
89 GK,JR,V:Dr.Octopus 135.00	
90 GK,JR,V:Dr.Octopus	
D:Capt.Stacy 150.00	
91 GK,JR,I:Bullit. 135.00	
92 GK,JR,V:Bullit,A:Iceman 135.00	
93 JR,V:Prowler 135.00	
94 JR,SB,V:Beetle,O:Spider-Man 150.00	
95 JR,SB,London,V:Terrorists . . . 135.00	
96 GK,JR,A:Green Goblin,Drug	
Mention,No Comic Code 150.00	
97 GK,V:Green Goblin,Drugs . . . 150.00	
98 GK,V:Green Goblin,Drugs . . . 150.00	
99 GK,Prison Riot,A:Carson 135.00	
100 JR(c),GK,Spidey gets four	
arms from serum 350.00	
101 JR(c),GK,I:Morbius,the	
Living Vampire,A:Lizard. . . . 325.00	
101a Reprint,Metallic ink 5.00	
102 JR(c),GK,O:Morbius,	
V:Lizard 135.00	
103 GK,V:Kraven,A:Ka-Zar 100.00	
104 GK,V:Kraven,A:Ka-Zar 100.00	
105 GK,V:Spenser Smythe,	
Spider Slayer. 100.00	
106 JR,V:Spenser Smythe,	
Spider Slayer. 100.00	
107 JR,V:Spenser Smythe,	
Spider Slayer 100.00	
108 JR,R:Flash Thompson,	
I:Sha-Shan,V:Vietnamese . . . 100.00	
109 JR,A:Dr.Strange,	
V:Vietnamese 100.00	

110 JR,I:The Gibbon 100.00	
111 JR,V:The Gibbon,Kraven . . . 100.00	
112 JR,Spidey gets an Ulcer . . . 100.00	
113 JSn,JR,I:Hammerhead	
V:Dr.Octopus 100.00	
114 JSn,JR,V:Hammerhead,Dr.	
Octopus,I:Jonas Harrow 100.00	
115 JR,V:Hammerhead,	
Dr.Octopus. 100.00	
116 JR,JM,V:The Smasher 100.00	
117 JR,JM,V:Smasher,Disruptor . 100.00	
118 JR,JM,V:Smasher,Disruptor . 100.00	
119 JR,A:Hulk 125.00	
120 GK,JR,V:Hulk 125.00	
121 GK,JR,V:Green Goblin	
D:Gwen Stacy,Drugs 375.00	
122 GK,JR,D:Green Goblin 400.00	
123 GK,JR,A:Powerman 100.00	
124 GK,JR,I:Man-Wolf 110.00	
125 RA,JR,O:Man-Wolf 100.00	
126 JM(c),RA,JM,V:Kangaroo,	
A: Human Torch. 100.00	
127 JR(c),RA,V:3rd Vulture,	
A:Human Torch 100.00	
128 JR(c),RA,V:3rd Vulture 100.00	
129 K&R(c),RA,I:Punisher,Jackal 750.00	
130 JR(c),RA,V:Hammerhead,	
Dr.Octopus,I:Spider-Mobile . . . 75.00	
131 GK(c),RA,V:Hammerhead,	
Dr.Octopus. 75.00	
132 GK(c),JR,V:Molten Man 75.00	
133 JR(c),RA,V:Molten Man 75.00	
134 JR(c),RA,I:Tarantula,C:	
Punisher(2nd App.) 80.00	
135 JR(c),RA,V:Tarantula,	
A:Punisher. 150.00	
136 JR(c),RA,I:2nd GreenGoblin . 150.00	
137 GK(c),RA,V:Green Goblin . . . 110.00	
138 K&R(c),RA,I:Mindworm. 50.00	
139 K&R(c),RA,I:Grizzly,V:Jackal . 50.00	
140 GK(c),RA,I:Gloria Grant,	
V:Grizzly,Jackal. 50.00	
141 JR(c),RA,V:Mysterio 50.00	
142 JR(c),RA,V:Mysterio 50.00	
143 K&R(c),RA,I:Cyclone 50.00	
144 K&R(c),RA,V:Cyclone. 50.00	
145 K&R(c),RA,V:Scorpion 50.00	
146 RA,JR,V:Scorpion 50.00	
147 JR(c),RA,V:Tarantula 50.00	
148 GK(c),RA,V:Tarantula,IR:Jackal	
is Prof.Warren 60.00	
149 K&R(c),RA,D:Jackal 100.00	
150 GK(c),RA,V:Spenser Smythe . 70.00	
151 RA,JR,V:Shocker 60.00	
152 K&R(c),RA,V:Shocker. 40.00	
153 K&R(c),RA,V:Paine. 40.00	
154 JR(c),SB,V:Sandman 40.00	
155 JR(c),SB,V:Computer 40.00	
156 JR(c),RA,I:Mirage,W:Ned	
Leeds & Betty Brant 40.00	
157 JR(c),RA,V:Dr.Octopus 40.00	
158 JR(c),RA,V:Dr.Octopus 40.00	
159 JR(c),RA,V:Dr.Octopus 40.00	
160 K&R(c),RA,V:Tinkerer. 40.00	
161 K&R(c),RA,A:Nightcrawler,	
C:Punisher 50.00	
162 JR(c),RA,Nightcrawler,	
Punisher,I:Jigsaw. 50.00	
163 JR(c),RA,V:Kingpin 35.00	
164 JR(c),RA,V:Kingpin 35.00	
165 JR(c),RA,Lizard. 35.00	
166 JR(c),RA,Lizard. 35.00	
167 JR(c),RA,V:Spiderslayer,	
I:Will-o-the Wisp 35.00	
168 JR(c),KP,V:Will-o-the Wisp . . . 40.00	
169 RA,V:Dr.Faustas 35.00	
170 RA,V:Dr.Faustas. 35.00	
171 RA,A:Nova 40.00	
172 RA,V:Molten Man 35.00	
173 JR(c),RA,JM,V:Molten Man . 35.00	
174 RA,TD,JM,A:Punisher. 40.00	
175 RA,JM,A:Punisher,D:Hitman. . 40.00	

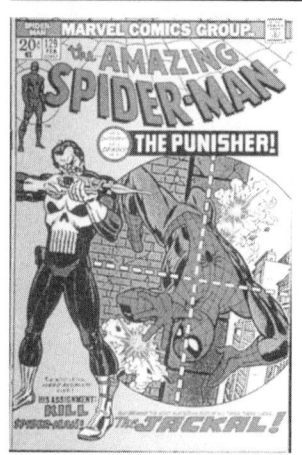

Amazing Spider-Man #129
® Marvel Ent. Group (1ˢᵗ Punisher)

176 RA,TD,V:Green Goblin 40.00
177 RA,V:Green Goblin 40.00
178 RA,JM,V:Green Goblin 40.00
179 RA,V:Green Goblin 40.00
180 RA,IR&V:Green Goblin is Bart
  Hamilton) 40.00
181 GK(c),SB,O:Spider-Man 35.00
182 RA,A:Rocket Racer. 35.00
183 RA,BMc,V:Rocket Racer. 35.00
184 RA,V:White Tiger 35.00
185 RA,V:White Tiger 35.00
186 KP,A:Chameleon,Spidey
  cleared by police of charges . . 35.00
187 JSn,BMc,A:Captain
  America,V:Electro 35.00
188 KP,A:Jigsaw 35.00
189 JBy,JM,A:Man-Wolf. 35.00
190 JBy,JM,A:Man-Wolf. 35.00
191 KP,V:Spiderslayer 35.00
192 KP,JM,V:The Fly 35.00
193 KP,JM,V:The Fly 35.00
194 KP,I:Black Cat 65.00
195 KP,AM,JM,O:Black Cat 35.00
196 AM,JM,D:Aunt May,A:Kingpin . 25.00
197 KP,JM,V:Kingpin 25.00
198 SB,JM,V:Mysterio 25.00
199 SB,JM,V:Mysterio 25.00
200 JR(c),KP,JM,D:Burglar,Aunt May
  alive,O:Spider-Man 55.00
201 KP,JM,A:Punisher 25.00
202 KP,JM,A:Punisher 25.00
203 FM(c),KP,A:Dazzler. 15.00
204 JR2(c),KP,V:Black Cat 15.00
205 KP,JM,V:Black Cat 15.00
206 JBy,GD,V:Jonas Harrow 15.00
207 JM,V:Mesmero 15.00
208 JR2,AM,BBr,V:Fusion(1stJR2
  SpM art),I:Lance Bannon. 15.00
209 KJ,BMc,JRu,BWi,AM,
  I:Calypso, V:Kraven. 25.00
210 JR2,JSt,I:Madame Web 15.00
211 JR2,JM,A:Sub-mariner 15.00
212 JR2,JM,I:Hydro-Man 15.00
213 JR2,JM,V:Wizard 15.00
214 JR2,JM,V:Frightful Four,
  A: Namor,Llyra. 15.00
215 JR2,JM,V:Frightful Four,
  A: Namor,Llyra. 15.00
216 JR2,JM,A:Madame Web 15.00
217 JR2,JM,V:Sandman,
  Hydro-Man. 15.00
218 FM(c),JR2,JM,AM,V:Sandman
  Hydro-Man. 15.00

219 FM(c),LMc,JM,V:Grey
  Gargoyle,A:Matt Murdock 15.00
220 BMc,A:Moon Knight 12.00
221 JM(i),A:Ramrod. 12.00
222 WS(c),BH,JM,I:SpeedDemon . 12.00
223 JR2,AM,A:Red Ghost 12.00
224 JR2,V:Vulture 12.00
225 JR2,BWi,V:Foolkiller 12.00
226 JR2,JM,A:Black Cat 12.00
227 JR2,JM,A:Black Cat 12.00
228 RL,Murder Mystery 12.00
229 JR2,JM,V:Juggernaut 12.00
230 JR2,JM,V:Juggernaut 12.00
231 JR2,AM,V:Cobra 12.00
232 JR2,JM,V:Mr.Hyde 12.00
233 JR2,JM,V:Tarantula 12.00
234 JR2,DGr,V:Tarantula 12.00
235 JR2,V:Tarantula,C:Deathlok
  O:Will-o-the Wisp 12.00
236 JR2,D:Tarantula 12.00
237 BH,A:Stilt Man. 12.00
238 JR2,JR,I:Hobgoblin (inc.
  Tattoo transfer) 120.00
238a w/out Tattoo 12.00
239 JR2,V:Hobgoblin 60.00
240 JR2,BL,Vulture 12.00
241 JR2,O:Vulture 12.00
242 JR2,Mad Thinker 12.00
243 JR2,Peter Quits School 12.00
244 JR2,KJ,V:Hobgoblin 18.00
245 JR2,V:Hobgoblin 20.00
246 JR2,DGr,Daydreams issue . . . 12.00
247 JR2,JR,V:Thunderball 12.00
248 JR2,BBr,RF,TA,V:Thunderball,
  Kid who Collects Spider-Man . 12.00
249 JR2,DGr,V:Hobgoblin,
  A:Kingpin 20.00
250 JR2,KJ,V:Hobgoblin 20.00
251 RF,KJ,V:Hobgoblin,Spidey
  Leaves for Secret Wars. 20.00
252 RF,BBr,returns from Secret
  Wars,N:Spider-Man 50.00
253 RL,I:Rose 12.00
254 RL,JRu,V:Jack O'Lantern 10.00
255 RF,JRu,Red Ghost 10.00
256 RF,JRu,I:Puma,A:Black Cat . . 10.00
257 RF,JRu,V:Puma,
  A:Hobgoblin 10.00
258 RF,JRu,A:Black Cat,Fant.Four,
  Hobgoblin,V:Black Costume . . 15.00
259 RF,JRu,A:Hobgoblin,O:
  Mary Jane 15.00
260 RF,JRu,BBr,V:Hobgoblin 12.00
261 CV(c),RF,JRu,V:Hobgoblin . . . 12.00
262 Ph(c),BL,Spidey Unmasked . . 13.00
263 RF,BBr,I:Spider-Kid 10.00
264 Paty,V:Red Nine 10.00
265 RF,JRu,V:Black Fox,
  I:Silver Sable 18.00
265a 2nd printing 3.00
266 RF,JRu,I:Misfits,Toad 10.00
267 BMc,PDd(s),A:Human Torch. . 10.00
268 JBy(c),RF,JRu,Secret WarsII . 10.00
269 RF,JRu,V:Firelord 10.00
270 RF,BMc,V:Firelord,
  A:Avengers,I:Kate Cushing . . . 10.00
271 RF,JRu,A:Crusher Hogan,
  V:Manslaughter 10.00
272 SB,KB,I&O:Slyde 10.00
273 RF,JRu,Secret Wars II,
  A:Puma 10.00
274 TMo,JR,Secret Wars II,
  Beyonder V:Mephisto,A:1st
  Ghost Rider 10.00
275 RF,JRu,V:Hobgoblin,O:Spidey
  (From Amaz.Fantasy#15) 25.00
276 RF,BBr,V:Hobgoblin 15.00
277 RF,BL,CV,A:Daredevil,Kingpin 10.00
278 A:Hobgoblin,V:Scourge,
  D:Wraith. 10.00
279 RL,A:Jack O'Lantern,
  2nd A:Silver Sable 10.00

Amazing Spider-Man #252
© Marvel Ent. Group (Black Csotume)

280 RF,BBr,V:Sinister Syndicate,
  A:Silver Sable,Hobgoblin,
  Jack O'Lantern 10.00
281 RF,BBr,V:Sinister Syndicate,
  A:Silver Sable,Hobgoblin,
  Jack O'Lantern 15.00
282 RL,BL,A:X-Factor 10.00
283 RF,BL,V:Titania,Absorbing
  Man,C:Mongoose 10.00
284 RF,BBr,JRu,B:Gang War,
  A: Punisher,Hobgoblin. 15.00
285 MZ(c),A:Punisher,Hobgoblin . . 15.00
286 ANi(i),V:Hobgoblin,A:Rose . . . 15.00
287 EL,ANi,A:Daredevil,Hobgoblin. 15.00
288 E:Gang War,A:Punisher,
  Falcon,Hobgoblin,Daredevil,
  Black Cat, Kingpin. 15.00
289 TMo,IR:Hobgoblin is Ned Leeds,
  I:2nd Hobgoblin (Jack O'
  Lantern) 30.00
290 JR2,Peter Proposes 10.00
291 JR2,V:Hobgoblin 10.00
292 AS,V:Spiderslayer,Mary
  Jane Accepts proposal 10.00
293 MZ,BMc,V:Kraven. 12.00
294 MZ,BMc,D:Kraven. 12.00
295 BSz(c),KB(i),Mad Dog,pt.#2 . . 10.00
296 JBy(c),AS,V:Dr.Octopus 10.00
297 AS,V:Dr.Octopus 10.00
298 TM,BMc,V:Chance,C:Venom
  (not in costume). 75.00
299 TM,BMc,V:Chance,I:Venom . . 40.00
300 TM,O:Venom. 150.00
301 TM,A:Silver Sable 20.00
302 TM,V:Nero,A:Silver Sable 20.00
303 TM,A:Silver Sable,Sandman. . 20.00
304 TM,JRu,V:Black Fox,Prowler
  I:Jonathan Caesar. 18.00
305 TM,JRu,V:BlackFox,Prowler. . 18.00
306 TM,V:Humbug,Chameleon. . . 15.00
307 TM,O:Chameleon 15.00
308 TM,V:Taskmaster,J.Caesar . . . 15.00
309 TM,I:Styx & Stone 15.00
310 TM,V:Killershrike 15.00
311 TM,Inferno,V:Mysterio 15.00
312 TM,Inferno,Hobgoblin V:
  Green Goblin 22.00
313 TM,Inferno,V:Lizard. 15.00
314 TM,X-mas issue,V:J.Caesar . . 15.00
315 TM,V:Venom,Hydro-Man. 22.00
316 TM,V:Venom 22.00
317 TM,V:Venom,A:Thing 22.00
318 TM,V:Scorpion 22.00
319 TM,V:Scorpion,Rhino 15.00

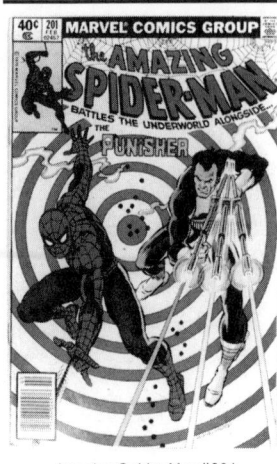

Amazing Spider-Man #201
© Marvel Entertainment Group

320 TM,B:Assassin Nation Plot
A:Paladin,Silver Sable. 15.00
321 TM,A:Paladin,Silver Sable . . . 12.00
322 TM,A:Silver Sable,Paladin . . . 12.00
323 TM,A:Silver Sable,Paladin,
Captain America 12.00
324 TM(c),EL,AG,V:Sabretooth,A:
Capt.America,Silver Sable . . . 12.00
325 TM,E:Assassin Nation Plot,
V:Red Skull,Captain America,
Silver Sable 12.00
326 V:Graviton,A of V. 7.00
327 EL,AG,V:Magneto,A of V. 7.00
328 TM,V:Hulk,A of V. 12.00
329 EL,V:Tri-Sentinel. 7.00
330 EL,A:Punisher,Black Cat. 7.00
331 EL,A:Punisher,C:Venom 6.00
332 EL,V:Venom,Styx & Stone 7.00
333 EL,V:Venom,Styx & Stone 7.00
334 EL,B:Sinister Six,A:Iron Man . . . 5.00
335 EL,TA,A:Captain America 5.00
336 EL,D:Nathan Lubensky,
A:Dr.Strange,Chance. 5.00
337 WS(c),EL,TA,A:Nova 5.00
338 EL,A:Jonathan Caesar 5.00
339 EL,JR,E:Sinister Six,A:Thor
D:Jonathan Caesar 5.00
340 EL,V:Femme Fatales 5.00
341 EL,V:Tarantula,Powers Lost . . . 5.00
342 EL,A:Blackcat,V:Scorpion 5.00
343 EL,Powers Restored,
C:Cardiac,V:Chameleon 5.00
344 EL,V:Rhino,I:Cardiac,Cletus
Kassady(Carnage),A:Venom . . 15.00
345 MBa,V:Boomerang,C:Venom,
A:Cletus Kassady(infected
with Venom-Spawn). 15.00
346 EL,V:Venom 12.00
347 EL,V:Venom 10.00
348 EL,A:Avengers 4.00
349 EL,A:Black Fox 4.00
350 EL,V:Doctor Doom,Black Fox . . 6.00
351 MBa,A:Nova,V:Tri-Sentinal 6.00
352 MBa,A:Nova,V:Tri-Sentinal 4.00
353 MBa,B:Round Robin:The Side
Kick's Revenge,A:Punisher,
Nova,Moon Knight,Darkhawk . . 4.00
354 MBa,A:Nova,Punisher,
Darkhawk,Moon Knight 4.00
355 MBa,A:Nova,Punisher,
Darkhawk,Moon Knight 4.00
356 MBa,A:Moon Knight,
Punisher,Nova. 4.00

357 MBa,A:Moon Knight,
Punisher,Darkhawk,Nova 4.00
358 MBa,E:Round Robin:The Side
Kick's Revenge,A:Darkhawk,
Moon Knight,Punisher,Nova,
Gatefold(c). 4.00
359 CMa,A:Cardiac,C:Cletus
Kasady (Carnage) 5.00
360 CMa,V:Cardiac,C:Carnage 6.00
361 MBa,I:Carnage 16.00
361a 2nd printing. 3.00
362 MBa,V:Carnage,Venom 10.00
362a 2nd printing. 3.00
363 MBa,V:Carnage,Venom. 10.00
364 MBa,V:Shocker. 6.00
365 MBa,JR,V:Lizard,30th Anniv.,
Hologram(c),w/poster,Prev.of
Spider-Man 2099 by RL 6.00
366 JBi,A:Red Skull,Taskmaster . . . 3.00
367 JBi,A:Red Skull,Taskmaster . . . 3.00
368 MBa,B:Invasion of the Spider
Slayers #1,BU:Jonah Jameson . 3.00
369 MBa,V:Electro,BU:Green
Goblin 3.00
370 MBa,V:Scorpion,BU:A.May 3.00
371 MBa,V:Spider-Slayer,
BU:Black Cat. 3.00
372 MBa,V:Spider-Slayer. 3.00
373 MBa,V:Sp.-Slayer,BU:Venom . . 4.00
374 MBa,V:Venom 5.00
375 MBa,V:Venom,30th Anniv.,Holo
graphx(c). 6.00
376 V:Styx&Stone,A:Cardiac 3.00
377 V:Cardiac,O:Styx&Stone 3.00
378 MBa,Total Carnage#3,V:Shriek,
Carnage,A:Venom,Cloak. 3.00
379 MBa,Total Carnage#7,
V:Carnage,A:Venom 3.00
380 MBa,Maximum Carnage#11 . . . 3.00
381 MBa,V:Dr.Samson,A:Hulk. 3.00
382 MBa,V:Hulk,A:Dr.Samson. 3.00
383 MBa,V:Jury 3.00
384 MBa,AM,V:Jury. 3.00
385 B:DvM(s),MBa,RyE,V:Jury 3.00
386 MBa,RyE,B:Lifetheft,V:Vulture . 3.00
387 MBa,RyE,V:Vulture 3.00
388 Blue Foil(c),MBa,RyE,RLm,TP,
E:Lifetheft,D:Peter's Synthetic
Parents,BU:Venom,Cardiac,
Chance,. 5.00
388a Newsstand Ed. 3.00
389 MBa,RyE,E:Pursuit,
V:Chameleon. 3.00
390 MBa,RyE,B:Shrieking,
A:Shriek,w/cel 4.00
390a Newsstand Ed. 3.00
391 MBa,RyE,V:Shriek,Carrion 3.00
392 MBa,RyE,V:Shriek,Carrion 3.00
393 MBa,RyE,E:Shrieking,
V:Shriek,Carrion 3.00
394 MBa,RyE,Power & Responsibility,
pt.2,V:Judas Traveller, ... 4.00
394a w/flip book,2 covers 3.00
395 MBa,RyE,R:Puma. 3.00
396 MBa,RyE,V:Daredevil,
V:Vulture, Owl 3.00
397 MBa,Web of Death,pt.1,
V:Stunner,Doc Ock 3.50
398 MBa,Web of Death,pt.3 . . . . . . 3.00
399 MBa,Smoke and Mirrors,pt.2 . . 2.50
400 MBa,Death of a Parker. 6.00
400a die-cut cover. 10.00
401 MBa,The Mark of Kaine,pt.2. . . 3.00
402 MBa,R:Judas Travellor 3.00
403 MBa,JMD,LMa The Trial of
Peter Parker, pt.2 . . . . 3.00
404 Maximum Clonage 3.00
405 JMD,DaR,LMa,Exiled,pt.2, ... 3.00
406 I:New Doc Ock 3.00
407 TDF,MBa,LMa,Return of
Spider-Man,pt.2 . . . . 3.00

408 TDF,MBa,LMa,Media
Blizzard,pt.2. . . . . 3.00
409 . . . . 3.00
410 . . . . 3.00
411 TDF,MBa,LMa,Blood
Brothers,pt.2 . . . . 3.00
412 . . . . 3.00
413 . . . . 3.00
414 A:The Rose 3.00
415 Onslaught saga,V:Sentinels . . . 3.00
416 Onslaught epilogue. 3.00
417 TDF,RG,secrets of Scrier &
Judas Traveler. 3.00
418 Revelations,pt.3, R:Norman
Osborn. 3.00
419 TDF,SSr,V:Black Tarantula 3.00
420 TDF,SSr,X-Man x-over,pt.1 . . . . 3.00
421 TDF,SSr,I:Dragonfly; Electro
Kidnapped 3.00
422 TDF,SSr,V:Electro,Tarantula . . . 3.00
423 TDF,V:Electro 3.00
424 TDF,JoB,V:Black Tarantula, The
Hand, Dragonfly, Delilah,
The Rose, Elektra 3.00
425 TDF,SSr, V:Electro,double size. 4.00
426 TDF,SSr,V:Doctor Octopus 3.00
427 TDF,SSr,JR gatefold cover,
V:Doctor Octopus 4.00
428 TDF,SSr,V:Doctor Octopus 3.00
429 TDF,A:Daredevil, X-Man,
Absorbing Man, Titania 3.00
430 TDF,SSr,V:Carnage,A:Silver
Surfer. 3.00
431 TDF,SSr,V:Carnage (with Silver
Surfer's powers) 3.00
432 SSr,JR2,Spider-Hunt,pt.2
x-over. 4.00
432a variant cover. 4.00
433 TDF,TL,Identity Crisis prelude,
good-bye to Joe Robertson. . . . 3.00
434 TDF,JoB,Identity Crisis, as
Ricochet vs. Black Tarantula . . . 3.00
435 TDF,MD2,Ricochet,A:Delilah . . . 3.00
436 TDF,JoB,V:Black Tarantula 3.00
437 TDF,JoB,V:Plant Man 3.00
Bi-weekly
438 TDF,V:Daredevil 3.00
439 TDF,future history chronicle . . . 3.00
440 JBy,The Gathering of the Five,
Pt.2 (of 5) x-over 3.00
441 JBy,V:Green Goblin, The
Final Chapter, pt.1. . . . . 5.00
Minus 1 Spec., TDF,JBe, flashback,
early Kingpin 2.50

Amazing Spider-Man #266
© Marvel Entertainment Group

Amazing Spider-Man #406
© *Marvel Entertainment Group*

Ann.#1 SD,I:Sinister Six 2,000.00
Ann.#2 SD,A:Dr.Strange 700.00
Ann.#3 JR,DH,A:Avengers 300.00
Ann.#4 A:H.Torch,V:Mysterio,
    Wizard 250.00
Ann.#5 JR(c),A:Red Skull,I:Peter
    Parker's Parents 250.00
Ann.#6 JR(c),Rep.Ann.#1,Fant.
    Four Ann.#1,SpM #8 . . . . 75.00
Ann.#7 JR(c),Rep.#1,#2,#38 . . . . 75.00
Ann.#8 Rep.#46,#50 . . . . 75.00
Ann.#9 JR(c),Rep.Spec.SpM #2 . . 75.00
Ann.#10 JR(c),GK,V:Human Fly . . 30.00
Ann.#11 GK(c),DP,JM,JR2,AM, . . 20.00
Ann.#12 JBy(c),KP,Rep.#119,
    #120. . . . . 25.00
Ann.#13 JBy,TA,V:Dr.Octopus . . . 25.00
Ann.#14 FM,TP,A:Dr.Strange,
    V:Dr.Doom,Dormammu 25.00
Ann.#15 FM,KJ,BL,Punisher 25.00
Ann.#16 JR2,JR,I:New Captain
    Marvel,A:Thing 10.00
Ann.#17 EH,JM,V:Kingpin 10.00
Ann.#18 RF,BL,JG,V:Scorpion 10.00
Ann.#19 JR(c),MW,V:Spiderslayer . 10.00
Ann.#20 BWi(i),V:Iron Man 2020 . . 10.00
Ann.#21 JR(c),PR,W:SpM,direct . . 20.00
Ann.#21a W:SpM,news stand 15.00
Ann.#22 JR(c),MBa(1stSpM),SD,
    JG,RLm,TD,Evolutionary War,
    I:Speedball,New Men 8.00
Ann.#23 JBy(c),RLd,MBa,RF,
    AtlantisAttacks#4,A:She-Hulk . . 7.00
Ann.#24 GK,SD,MZ,DGr,
    A:Ant Man 4.00
Ann.#25 EL(c),SB,PCu,SD,
    Vibranium Vendetta#1,Venom . . 6.00
Ann.#26 Hero Killers#1,A:New
    Warriors,BU:Venom,Solo. 6.00
Ann.#27 TL,I:Annex,w/card 4.00
Ann.#28 SBt(s),V:Carnage,BU:Cloak
    & Dagger,Rhino 4.00
Ann. '96 two new stories, 48pg,. . . 3.50
Ann. '97 RSt,TL,RJn, 48pg,. 3.50
Ann. '98 TL,TDF,F:Spider-Man &
    Devil Dinosaur, 48pg. 3.00
G-Size Superheroes #1 GK,
    A:Morbius,Man-Wolf 75.00
G-Size #1 JR(c),RA,DH,
    A:Dracula. 40.00
G-Size #2 K&R(c),RA,AM,
    A:Master of Kung Fu 40.00
G-Size #3 GK(c),RA,DocSavage. . 40.00
G-Size #4 GK(c),RA,Punisher 75.00
G-Size #5 GK(c),RA,V:Magnum . . 30.00

G-Size #6 Rep.Ann.#4. . . . . 30.00
G-Size Spec.#1 O:Symbiotes 5.00
Marvel Milestone rep. #1 (1993) . . . 3.00
Marvel Milestone rep. #3 (1995) . . . 3.00
Marvel Milestone rep. #129 (1992) . 3.00
Marvel Milestone rep. #149 (1994) . 3.00
Nothing Can Stop the Juggernaut . . 4.00
Sensational Spider-Man,reps. 5.00
Skating on Thin Ice(Canadian) . . . 15.00
Skating on Thin Ice(US). 2.00
Soul of the Hunter MZ,BMc,
    R:Kraven 7.00
Unicef:Trial of Venom,
    A:Daredevil,V:Venom 50.00
See Also:
PETER PARKER;
SPECTACULAR SPIDER-MAN;
WEB OF SPIDER-MAN

AMAZING SPIDER-MAN
Jan., 1999
1 HMe,JBy,DHz,V:Scorpion,48-page
    prismatic etched (c). 7.00
1a Dynamic Forces JR2 . . . . 12.00
2 HMe,JBy,DHz,I:Shadrac 5.00
2a variant BiT cover 6.00
3 HMe,JBy,DHz,V:Shadrac,
    A:Iceman 3.00
4 HMe,JBy,SHa,A:Fantastic Four . . 3.00
5 HMe,JBy,SHa,I:new
    Spider-Woman. 3.00
6 JBy,HMe,SHa,F:Spider-Woman. . 3.00
7 JBy,HMe,SHa,Reality Bent 3.00
8 JMy,HMe,SHa,JR2(c),
    Reality Bent x-over 3.00
9 JMy,HMe,SHa,JR2(c),V:Scorpion 3.00
10 JMy,HMe,SHa,JR2(c),MaryJane. 3.00
11 HMe,SHa,JBy,marital problems . 3.00
12 HMe,SHa,JBy,48-pg. 4.00
13 HMe,JBy 3.00
14 HMe,JBy,A:Sp.-Woman,x-over . . 3.00
15 HMe,JBy,DGr,x-over 3.00
16 HMe,JBy,DGr,Mary Jane gone . . 3.00
17 HMe,JBy,DGr,A:Sandman 3.00
18 HMe,JBy,JR,V:Green Goblin . . . 3.00
19 HMe,EL,DGr,Eddie Brock,
    Venom 5.00
20 HMe,EL,JBy,100-pg 3.50
21 HMe,EL,JhB,AlistairSmythe 3.00
22 HMe,JR2,SHa,Senator Ward . . . 3.00
23 HMe,JR2,SHa,Ranger 3.00
24 HMe,JR2,SHa,Max.Security 3.00
25 HMe,JR2,SHa,A:Green Goblin . . 3.00
25a holographic foil(c) 15.00
26 HMe,JR2,SHa,F:Spidey's dad . . 3.00
27 HMe,JR2,SHa,V:A.I.M. 3.00
28 HMe,JR2,SHa,Enforcers. 10.00
29 HMe,JR2,SHa,x-over 15.00
30 B:MSz(s),JR2,JSC(c) 10.00
31 MSz(s),JR2,JSC(c). 8.00
32 MSz(s),JR2,SHa,Ezekiel. 8.00
33 MSz(s),JR2,SHa,Morlun 8.00
34 MSz(s),JR2,SHa,V:Morlun 8.00
35 MSz(s),JR2,SHa,pt.1 . . . . 8.00
36 MSz(s),JR2,SHa 25.00
37 MSz(s),JR2,SHa 5.00
38 MSz(s),JR2,SHa,'Nuff Said 3.00
39 MSz(s),JR2,SHa,Aunt May. 3.00
40 MSz(s),JR2,SHa,Aunt May. 3.00
41 MSz(s),JR2,SHa 3.00
42 MSz(s),JR2,SHa 3.00
43 MSz(s),JR2,SHa 3.00
44 MSz(s),JR2,SHa 3.00
45 MSz(s),JR2,SHa 3.00
46 MSz(s),JR2,SHa 3.00
47 MSz(s),JR2,SHa 3.00
48 MSz(s),JR2,SHa 3.00
49 MSz(s),JR2,SHa 3.00
50 MSz(s),JR2,SHa,F:Mary Jane . . 4.50
51 MSz(s),JR2,SHa,F:Mary Jane . . 2.50
52 MSz(s),JR2,SHa,F:Mary Jane . . 2.50
53 MSz(s),JR2,SHa,F:Mary Jane . . 2.50

54 MSz(s),JR2,Digger 2.50
55 MSz(s),JR2,Consequences,pt.1 . 2.50
56 MSz(s),JR2,Consequences,pt.2 . 2.50
57 MSz(s),JR2,pt.1 . . . . 2.50
58 MSz(s),JR2,pt.2 . . . . 2.50
Resumes original numbering
500 MSz(s),JR2,48-pg. 5.00
501 MSz(s),JR2 . . . . 2.50
502 MSz(s),JR2. . . . . 2.50
503 JR2,A Dark Shadow,pt.1. . . . . 2.50
504 JR2,A Dark Shadow,pt.2. . . . . 2.50
505 MSz(s),JR2,Ezekiel,pt.1 . . . . . 2.50
506 MSz(s),JR2,Ezekiel,pt.2 . . . . . 2.50
507 MSz(s),JR2,Ezekiel,pt.3 . . . . . 2.50
508 MSz(s),JR2,Ezekiel,pt.4 . . . . . 2.50
509 MSz(s),MD2,Sins Past,pt.1. . . . 2.50
510 MSz(s),MD2,Sins Past,pt.2. . . . 2.50
511 MSz(s),MD2,Sins Past,pt.3. . . . 2.50
512 MSz(s),MD2,Sins Past,pt.4. . . . 2.50
513 MSz(s),MD2,Sins Past,pt.5. . . . 2.50
514 MSz(s),MD2. . . . . 2.50
515 MSz(s),MD2,Skin Deep 2.50
516 MSz(s),MD2,Skin Deep 2.50
517 MSz(s),MD2,Skin Deep 2.50
518 MSz(s),MD2,JJu(c),Skin Deep . 2.50
519 MSz(s),MD2,NewAvengers,pt.1 2.50
520 MSz(s),MD2,NewAvengers,pt.2 2.50
521 MSz(s),MD2,Moving Up 2.50
522 MSz(s),MD2,V:Hydra 2.50
523 MSz(s),MD2,Moving Up 2.50
524 MSz(s),MD2,Acts of Aggression 2.50
525 PDd(s),The Other,x-over,pt. 3. . 4.00
525a second printing (var). 4.50
526 MD2,The Other,x-over,pt.6 . . . . 4.00
526a 2nd printing. 7.00
527 MSz(s),The Other,x-over,pt.9 . . 2.50
527a 2nd printing. 7.00
528 MSz(s),The Other,x-over,pt.12 . 2.50
528a 2nd printing. 5.00
529 MSz,RG, new outfit. 12.00
529a 2nd printing 8.00
530 MSz(s),RG 6.00
531 Mr. Parker Goes to Washington 8.00
532 MSz(s),RG,War at Home,pt.1 . 12.00
533 MSz(s),RG,War at Home,pt.2 . . 5.00
534 MSz(s),RG,War at Home,pt.3 . . 5.00
535 MSz(s),RG,War at Home,pt.4 . . 5.00
536 MSz(s),RG,War at Home,pt.5 . . 5.00
537 MSz(s),RG,War at Home,pt.6 . . 5.00
538 MSz,RG,The War at Home 5.00
539 MSz,RG,Back in Black, pt.1 . . . 3.00
540 MSz,RG,Back in Black, pt.2 . . . 3.00
541 MSz,RG,Back in Black, pt.3 . . . 3.00
542 MSz,RG,Back in Black, pt.4 . . . 3.00
543 MSz,RG,V:Kingpin 3.00
544 MSz,JQ,One More Day, pt.1. . . 4.50
544a variant (c) 4.00
545 MSz,JQ,One More Day,pt.4. . . . 4.00
545a variant (c) 4.00
546 48-pg. thrice monthly launch . . 4.00
547 Brand new day 3.00
548 Brand new day 3.00
549 SvL,Brand New Day 3.00
549a variant (c) 15.00
550 SvL, Brand New Day 3.00
551 SvL, Brand New Day 3.00
552 PJ, Brand New Day 3.00
552a variant (c) 15.00
553 PJ, Brand New Day 3.00
554 PJ, Brand New Day 3.00
555 CBa, Brand New Day 3.00
555a variant (c) 3.00
556 Sometimes It Snows in April. . . 3.00
557 Sometimes It Snows in April. . . 3.00
558 BKi 3.00
558a variant (c) 15.00
559 BKi,Peter Parker: Paparazzi . . 3.00
560 BKi,Peter Parker: Paparazzi . . . 3.00
561 Peter Parker: Paparazzi,pt.3. . . 3.00
562 The Other Spider-Man 3.00
563 Bar Room Brawl 3.00
564 Traffic Jam 3.00

MARVEL

MARVEL

565 . . . . 3.00
566 . . . . 3.00
567 PJ 3.00
568 JR2,New Ways to Die. 3.00
568a variant (c) 3.00
568b variant JR (c) 3.00
569 JR2,New Ways to Die. 3.00
570 JR2,New Ways to Die. 3.00
571 JR2,New Ways to Die. 3.00
572 JR2,New Ways to Die. 3.00
573 JR2,New Wayst to Die,48-pg. . 4.00
574 BKi,Flash Thompson. 3.00
575 CBa,Hammerhead 3.00
576 CBa,Hammerhead 3.00
577 F:Punisher. 3.00
577a variant SB (c) 3.00
578 MWa(s),Earthquake 3.00
Ann.1999 JB,HMe, 48-page 4.00
Ann.2000 HMe,48-pg. 4.00
Ann.2001 48-page 4.00
Ann. #1 Brand New Day (2008). . . 4.00
Giant Sized 80-pg. 4.50
King-Size Summer Special (2008). . 5.00
Spec. Must Have,Rep. #30–#32 . . . 4.00
Spec.Spider-Man/Sentry,PJe,RL,TA 3.00
Spec.Spider-Man/Marrow,SLo 3.00
Spec.Coll. ed.,rep #30–#32 . . . . . . 4.00
Spec. Brand New Day extra 4.00
Coll.Classics rep. #300 . . . . 2.50
Coll.Classics rep. Sp-M #1. . . . . . . 2.50

AMAZING SPIDER-MAN FAMILY
Aug., 2008
1 thru 2 RFz . . . . @5.00

AMAZING X-MEN, THE
March–June, 1995
1 X-Men after Xavier. 4.00
2 Exodus,Dazzler,V:Abyss 3.00
3 F:Bishop. 3.00
4 V:Apocalypse. 2.50

AMERICAN DREAM
May, 2008
1 thru 5 (of 5) TNu,RF(c) . . . . . . @3.00

A-NEXT
Aug., 1998
1 TDF,RF,BBr,Next Generation of
   Avengers 3.00
2 thru 12 . . . . @2.50

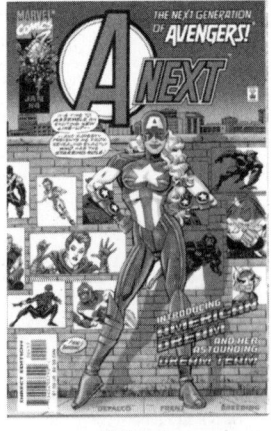

A-Next 4
© *Marvel Entertainment Group*

ANGEL: REVELATIONS
May, 2008
1 (of 5) AdP,The Annunciation 3.00
2 thru 5 AdP . . . . @4.00

ANIMATED MOVIE-TUNES
Marvel-Margood Publ., 1945
1 Super Rabbit 350.00
2 Super Rabbit 350.00
Becomes:

MOVIE TUNES
Marvel-Margood Publ., 1946
3 . . . . 150.00
Becomes:

FRANKIE
Marvel-Margood, 1946–48
4 . . . . 200.00
5 thru 9 . . . . @125.00
10 . . . . 100.00
11 . . . . 100.00
Becomes:

FRANKIE & LANA
Marvel-Margood, 1949
12 . . . . 100.00
13 . . . . 100.00
14 . . . . 100.00
15 . . . . 100.00
Becomes:

FRANKIE FUDDLE
Marvel-Margood, 1949
16 . . . . 100.00
17 . . . . 100.00

ANITA BLAKE, VAMPIRE HUNTER: GUILTY PLEASURES
Prev. See Color section
9a variant (c) 3.00
10 thru 12 RLm . . . . @3.00
Spec. Handbook 4.00

ANITA BLAKE, VAMPIRE HUNTER: FIRST DEATH
July, 2007
1 of 2 (of 2) . . . . @4.00

ANITA BLAKE, VAMPIRE HUNTER: THE LAUGHING CORPSE
Book One, Oct., 2008
1 (of 5) RLm 4.00
1a monkey variant (c) 4.00
2 RLm. 4.00

ANNIE OAKLEY
Marvel Timely, Spring, 1948
1 A:Hedy Devine 700.00
2 CCB,I:Lana,A:Hedy Devine . . 450.00
3 . . . . 300.00
4 . . . . 300.00
5 JMn(c) 250.00
6 . . . . 250.00
7 . . . . 250.00
8 GWb 250.00
9 AW, ... 250.00
10 GWb 200.00
11 JSe(c), June, 1956 . . . . 200.00

ANNIHILATION
Sept., 2006
1 Silver Surfer, Super-Skrull, Ronan
   & Nova, V:Annihilus. 3.00

2 F:Nova Ronan & Drax 3.00
3 F:Nova, Ronan. 3.00
4 F:Drax, Thanos, Nova 3.50
5 . . . . 3.00
6 finale 3.00
Spec. Annihilation Saga 2.50
Spec. Conquest Prologue 4.00

...CONQUEST
Nov., 2007
1 (of 6) Phalanx vs. Kree Empire . . 3.00
2 thru 5 TR . . . . @3.00
6 TR, 48-pg. 4.00

...CONQUEST – QUASAR
July, 2007
1 (of 4) F:Phyla-Vell 3.00
2 thru 4 . . . . @3.00

...CONQUEST – STAR-LORD
July, 2007
1 (of 4) F:Peter Quill. 3.00
2 thru 4 KG(s) . . . . @3.00

...CONQUEST – WRAITH
July, 2007
1 (of 4) 3.00
2 thru 4 . . . . @3.00

...HERALDS OF GALACTUS
Feb., 2007
1 Terrax & Stardust 4.00
2 Tenebrous & Aegis. 4.00
(3) Silver Surfer/Firelord 4.00

...NOVA
April, 2006
1 V:Annihilation Wave. 3.00
2 thru 4 . . . . @3.00

...THE NOVA CORPS
Aug., 2006
1 Nova Corps files 4.00

...PROLOGUE
March, 2006
1 KG,V:Annihilation Wave 4.00

...RONAN
April, 2006
1 V:Annihilation Wave. 3.00
2 thru 4 . . . . @3.00

...SILVER SURFER
April, 2006
1 V:Annihilation Wave. 7.00
2 thru 3 . . . . @5.00
4 . . . . @7.00

...SUPER-SKRULL
April, 2006
1 thru 4 V:Annihilation Wave. . . . @3.00

ANT-MAN
Dec., 2003
1 thru 5 (of 5) Size does matter . @3.00
Oct., 2006
1 & 2 PhH . . . . @3.00
3 thru 12 PhH . . . . @3.00

ANT-MAN'S BIG CHRISTMAS
Dec., 1999
GN 48-pg. 6.00

A-1
1993
1 The Edge 8.00
2 Cheeky,Wee Budgie Boy 8.00
3 King Leon. 8.00
4 King Leon. 8.00

Western Gunfighters #23
© Marvel Entertainment Group

APACHE KID
Marvel-Comics, 1950–52
1 (53)	500.00
2	275.00
3	200.00
4	200.00
5	200.00
6	150.00
7 RH	200.00
8 thru 10	@150.00
11 RH	100.00
12 JMn	100.00
13 RH	100.00
14 thru 19	@100.00

Becomes:

WESTERN GUNFIGHTERS
Marvel Atlas, 1956–57
20 GC,JSe	150.00
21 RC	150.00
22 WW,BP	250.00
23 AW	200.00
24 ATh	200.00
25 GM	100.00
26 GC	100.00
27 GC,JSe	100.00

APACHE SKIES
July, 2002
1 (of 4) JOs,Apache Kid,wild west	3.00
2 thru 4 JOs	@3.00

ARANA: THE HEART OF THE SPIDER
Jan., 2005
1 Freshman Flu.	3.00
1a variant JQ(c)	3.00
2 A Tangled Web.	3.00
3 Ultimatum.	3.00
4 Between Life and Death, A:Spider-Man.	3.00
5 Heart of the Spider	3.00
6 Heart of the Spider,concl.	3.00
7 thru 10 Unexpected Pasts	@3.00
11 V:Jade	3.00
12 V:Wasps	3.00

ARIZONA KID
Atlas, March, 1951
1 RH,Coming of the Arizons Kid.	300.00
2 RH,Code of the Gunman	150.00
3 RH(c)	125.00
4 PMo	125.00
5 PMo	125.00

6 PMo,JSt,Jan., 1952	125.00

ARRGH!
Dec., 1974
Satire
1 MSy,TS,Vampire Rats	35.00
2 AA,TS.	25.00
3 TS,AA(c),Beauty and the Big Foot	25.00
4 The Night Gawker	25.00
5 Sept., 1975	25.00

ARROWHEAD
April, 1954
1 JSt,Indian Warrior Stories	200.00
2 JSt, JMn(c).	125.00
3 JSt, RH(c).	125.00
4 JSt, Nov., 1954	125.00

MARVEL BOY
Dec., 1950
1 RH,O:Marvel Boy,Lost World	1,700.00
2 BEv,The Zero Hour	1,200.00

Becomes:

ASTONISHING
1951
3 BEv,Marvel Boy,V:Mr Death	1,500.00
4 BEv,Stan Lee,The Screaming Tomb	1,100.00
5 BEv,Horror in the Caves of Doom	1,100.00
6 BEv,My Coffin is Waiting E:Marvel Boy	1,100.00
7 JR,JMn,Nightmare	500.00
8 RH,Behind the Wall	500.00
9 RH(c),The Little Black Box	500.00
10 BEv,Walking Dead	500.00
11 BF,JSt.Mr Mordeau	350.00
12 GC,BEv,Horror Show	350.00
13 BK,MSy,Ghouls Gold	500.00
14 BK,The Long Jump Down.	500.00
15 BEv(c),Grounds for Death	375.00
16 BEv(c),DAy,SSh,Don't Make a Ghoul of Yourself	375.00
17 Who Was the Wilmach Werewolf?	375.00
18 BEv(c),JR,Vampire at My Window	375.00
19 BK,Back From the Grave	375.00
20 GC,Mystery at Midnight	375.00
21 Manhunter.	325.00
22 RH(c),Man Against Werewolf	325.00
23 The Woman in Black.	350.00
24 JR,The Stone Face.	350.00
25 RC,I Married a Zombie	350.00
26 RH(c),I Died Too Often	300.00
27	300.00
28 TLw,No Evidence	300.00
29 BEv(c),GC,Decapitation(c)	325.00
30 Tentacled eyeball story	650.00
31 JMn	250.00
32 A Vampire Takes a Wife	250.00
33 SMo,JMn.	250.00
34 JMn,Transformation	250.00
35	250.00
36 Pithecanthrope Giant	250.00
37 BEv,TLw,Poor Pierre.	250.00
38 The Man Who Didn't Belong.	200.00
39	200.00
40	200.00
41 MD	200.00
42 TLw	200.00
43 BP,JR	200.00
44 RC,BP	225.00
45 BK	225.00
46	225.00
47 BK,JO,BEv	225.00
48 BP	200.00
49 BEv	200.00
50 DCn	200.00

51	200.00
52 GM	200.00
53 SD,JF,BEv.	225.00
54 BEv	225.00
55 BEv	250.00
56 JMn,JK	200.00
57 JR	225.00
58 JF,JO.	200.00
59 TSe,BEv	225.00
60 JF,BEv.	200.00
61 GM,JO,JR,BEv	200.00
62 MD,BEv.	225.00
63 BEv,August, 1957	225.00

ASTONISHING TALES
Aug., 1970
1 BEv(c),JK,WW,Ka-Zar,Dr.Doom	90.00
2 JK,WW,Ka-Zar,Dr.Doom	50.00
3 BWS,WW,Ka-Zar,Dr.Doom	60.00
4 BWS,WW,Ka-Zar,Dr.Doom	60.00
5 BWS,GT,Ka-Zar,Dr.Doom	60.00
6 BWS,BEv,GT,I:Bobbi Morse	60.00
7 HT,GC,Ka-Zar,Dr.Doom	30.00
8 HT,TS,GT,GC,Ka-Zar,Dr.Doom	30.00
9 GK(c),JR Ka-Zar,Dr.Doom	20.00
10 GK(c),BWS,SB,Ka-Zar	25.00
11 GK,O:Ka-Zar.	25.00
12 JB,DA,NA,V:Man Thing	50.00
13 JB,RB,DA,V:Man Thing	40.00
14 GK(c),rep. Ka-Zar.	15.00
15 GK,TS,Ka-Zar.	15.00
16 RB,AM,A:Ka-Zar.	15.00
17 DA,V:Gemini.	15.00
18 JR(c),DA,A:Ka-Zar	15.00
19 JR(c),DA,JSn,JA,I:Victorious	15.00
20 JR(c),A:Ka-Zar	15.00
21 RTs(s),DAy,B:It	45.00
22 RTs(s),DAy,V:Granitor.	30.00
23 RTs(s),DAy,A:Fin Fang Foom	30.00
24 RTs(s),DAy,E:It	30.00
25 RB(a&s),B:I&O:Deathlok, GP(1st art).	75.00
26 RB(a&s),I:Warwolf	20.00
27 RB(a&s),V:Warwolf	20.00
28 RB(a&s),V:Warwolf	20.00
29 rep.Marv.Super Heroes #18	15.00
30 RB(a&s),KP,	15.00
31 RB(a&s),BW,KP,V:Ryker.	18.00
32 RB(a&s),KP,V:Ryker	18.00
33 RB(a&s),KJ,I:Hellinger	18.00
34 RB(a&s),KJ,V:Ryker	18.00
35 RB(a&s),KJ,I:Doomsday-Mech.	75.00
36 RB(a&s),KP,E:Deathlok, I:Godwulf	75.00

ASTONISHING X-MEN
March–June, 1995
1 Uncanny X-Men.	5.00
2 V:Holocaust	3.50
3 V:Abyss	3.00
4 V:Beast,Infinities	3.00

July, 1999
1 (of 3) BPe,HMe,new X-Men team	2.50
2 BPe,HMe,The Shattering x-over	2.50
3 BPe,HMe,Shattering,concl.	2.50

May, 2004
1 Gifted,pt.1	6.00
1a variant (c).	6.00
1b Director's Cut.	10.00
2 thru 6 Gifted,pt.2 thru pt.6	@6.00
7 thru 12 JoW(s),Dangerous,pt.1 thru pt. 6	@4.00
13 thru 18 JoW(s), Torn, pt.1 thru pt. 6	@4.00
19 JoW(s) Unstoppable, pt.1	3.00
19a variant (c)	3.00
20 JoW(s),Unstoppable, pt.2	3.00
21 JoW(s),Unstoppable, pt.3	3.00
22 JoW(s),Unstoppable, pt.4	3.00
23 JoW(s),Unstoppable, pt.5	3.00
24 JoW(s),Unstoppable	3.00

MARVEL

Astonishing Tales #1
© Marvel Entertainment Group

20a thru 24a variant (c)s . . . . @3.00
25 WEI(s),Ghost Box, pt.1 . . . . 3.00
26 WEI(s),Ghost Box, pt.2 . . . . 3.00
27 WEI(s),Ghost Box, pt.3 . . . . 3.00
Giant-Size #1 JoW(s). 5.00
1-shot Astonishing X-Men Saga
  48-pg. 4.00

ASTONISHING X-MEN: GHOST BOXES
Oct., 2008
1 thru 2 (of 2) WEI(s) . . . . @4.00

A-TEAM
March, 1984
1 thru 3 . . . . @5.00

AVENGERS
Sept., 1963
1 JK,O:Avengers,V:Loki. 8,500.00
2 JK,V:Space Phantom 2,000.00
3 JK,V:Hulk,Sub-Mariner 1,100.00
4 JK,R&J:Captain America 3,500.00
5 JK,L:Hulk,V:Lava Men 850.00
6 JK,I:Masters of Evil 850.00
7 JK,V:BaronZemo,Enchantress. 850.00
8 JK,I:Kang 750.00
9 JK(c),DH,I&D:Wonder Man . . . 750.00
10 JK(c),DH,I:Immortus 450.00
11 JK(c),DH,A:Spider-Man,
  V:Kang. 750.00
12 JK(c),DH,V:Moleman,
  Red Ghost 350.00
13 JK(c),DH,I:Count Nefaria 350.00
14 JK,DH,V:Count Nefaria 350.00
15 JK,DH,D:Baron Zemo. 300.00
16 JK,J:Hawkeye,Scarlet Witch,
  Quicksilver. 400.00
17 JK(c),DH,V:Mole Man,A:Hulk . 250.00
18 JK(c),DH,V:The Commisar . . . 250.00
19 JK(c),DH,I&O:Swordsman,
  O:Hawkeye 250.00
20 JK(c),DH,WW,V:Swordsman,
  Mandarin 200.00
21 JK(c),DH,WW,V:Power Man
  (not L.Cage),Enchantress . . . 200.00
22 JK(c),DH,WW,V:Power Man . . 200.00
23 JK(c),DH,JR,V:Kang 150.00
24 JK(c),DH,JR,V:Kang 150.00
25 JK(c),DH,V:Dr.Doom. 150.00
26 DH,V:Attuma. 150.00
27 DH,V:Attuma,Beetle 150.00

28 JK(c),DH,I:1st Goliath,
  I:Collector 150.00
29 DH,V:Power Man,Swordsman 150.00
30 JK(c),DH,V:Swordsman 150.00
31 DH,V:Keeper of the Flame . . . 125.00
32 DH,I:Bill Foster 100.00
33 DH,V:Sons of the Serpent
  A:Bill Foster 100.00
34 DH,V:Living Laser 100.00
35 DH,V:Mandarin 100.00
36 DH,V:The Ultroids 100.00
37 GK(c),DH,V:Ultroids 150.00
38 GK(c),DH,V:Enchantress,
  Ares,J:Hercules 100.00
39 DH,V:Mad Thinker 100.00
40 DH,V:Sub-Mariner. 100.00
41 JB,V:Dragon Man,Diablo 80.00
42 JB,V:Dragon Man,Diablo 80.00
43 JB,V:Red Guardian. 80.00
44 JB,V:Red Guardian,
  O:Black.Widow 80.00
45 JB,V:Super Adoptoid. 80.00
46 JB,V:Whirlwind 80.00
47 JB,GT,V:Magneto 150.00
48 GT,I&O:New Black Knight. . . . 150.00
49 JB,V:Magneto 125.00
50 JB,V:Typhon 125.00
51 JB,GT,R:Iron Man,Thor,
  V:Collector 125.00
52 JB,J:Black Panther,
  I:Grim Reaper 125.00
53 JB,GT,A:X-Men; x-over
  X-Men #45. . . . . 180.00
54 JB,GT,V:Masters of Evil
  I:Crimson Cowl(Ultron) 150.00
55 JB,I:Ultron,V:Masters of Evil . . 150.00
56 JB,D:Bucky retold,
  V:Baron Zemo 150.00
57 JB,I:Vision,V:Ultron 300.00
58 JB,O&J:Vision. 125.00
59 JB,I:Yellowjacket 125.00
60 JB,W:Yellowjacket & Wasp. . . 125.00
61 JB,A:Dr.Strange,x-over
  Dr. Strange #178 . . . . 125.00
62 JB,I:Man-Ape,A:Dr.Strange. . 125.00
63 GC,I&O:2nd Goliath(Hawkeye)
  V:Egghead. 125.00
64 GC,V:Egghead,O:Hawkeye . . 125.00
65 GC,V:Swordsman,Egghead . . 125.00
66 BWS,I:Ultron 6,Adamantium . 135.00
67 BWS,V:Ultron 6. . . . . 135.00
68 SB,V:Ultron 120.00
69 SB,I:Nighthawk,Grandmaster,
  Squadron Supreme, V:Kang . 120.00
70 SB,O:Squadron Supreme
  V:Kang. 120.00
71 SB,I:Invaders,V:Kang 150.00
72 SB,A:Captain Marvel,
  I:Zodiac 75.00
73 HT(i),V:Sons of Serpent 75.00
74 JB,TP,V:Sons of Serpent,
  IR:Black Panther on TV. 75.00
75 JB,TP,I:Arkon 75.00
76 JB,TP,V:Arkon 75.00
77 JB,TP,V:Split-Second Squad.. . 75.00
78 SB,TP,V:Lethal Legion 75.00
79 JB,TP,V:Lethal Legion 75.00
80 JB,TP,I&O:Red Wolf 75.00
81 JB,TP,A:Red Wolf 75.00
82 JB,TP,V:Ares,A:Daredevil . . . 75.00
83 JB,TP,I:Valkyrie,
  V:Masters of Evil 75.00
84 JB,TP,V:Enchantress,Arkon . . 75.00
85 JB,V:Squadron Supreme 75.00
86 JB,JM,A:Squad Supreme 75.00
87 SB(i),O:Black Panther,
  V: A.I.M. 100.00
88 SB,JM,V:Psyklop,A:Hulk,
  Professor.X 95.00
88a 2nd Printing. 12.00
89 SB,B:Kree/Skrull War 65.00

Avengers #10
© Marvel Entertainment Group

90 SB,V:Sentry #459,Ronan,
  Skrulls 65.00
91 SB,V:Sentry #459,Ronan,
  Skrulls 65.00
92 SB,V:Super Skrull,Ronan,. . . . 80.00
93 NA,TP,V:Super-Skrull,G-Size . 225.00
94 NA,JB,TP,V:Super-Skrull,
  I:Mandroids 125.00
95 NA,TP,V:Maximus,Skrulls,
  A:Inhumans,O:Black Bolt . . . 100.00
96 NA,TP,V:Skrulls,Ronan 100.00
97 GK&BEv(c),JB,TP,E:Kree-Skrull
  War,V:Annihilus,Ronan,Skrulls,
  A:Golden Age Heroes 75.00
98 BWS,SB,V:Ares,R:Hercules,
  R&N:Hawkeye 75.00
99 BWS,TS,V:Ares 75.00
100 BWS,JSr,V:Ares & Kratos. . . 150.00
101 RB,DA,A:Watcher 50.00
102 RB,JSt,V:Grim Reaper,
  Sentinels 45.00
103 RB,JSt,V:Sentinels 45.00
104 RB,JSt,V:Sentinels 45.00
105 JB,JM,V:Savage Land
  Mutates; A:Black Panther . . . 45.00
106 GT,DC,RB,V:Space Phantom . 45.00
107 GT,DC,JSn,V:Space
  Phantom, Grim Reaper 45.00
108 DH,DC,JSt,V:Space
  Phantom,Grim Reaper 45.00
109 DH,FMc,V:Champion,
  L:Hawkeye 45.00
110 DH,V:Magneto,A:X-Men 65.00
111 DH,J:Bl.Widow,A:Daredevil,
  X-Men,V:Magneto 65.00
112 DH,I:Mantis,V:Lion-God,
  L:Black Widow 60.00
113 FBe(i),V:The Living Bombs . . . 30.00
114 JR(c),V:Lion-God,J:Mantis,
  Swordsman 30.00
115 JR(c),A:Defenders,V:Loki,
  Dormammu 30.00
116 JR(c),A:Defenders,S.Surfer
  V:Loki,Dormammu. 30.00
117 JR(c),FMc(i),A:Defenders,Silv.
  Surfer,V:Loki,Dormammu 30.00
118 JR(c),A:Defenders,S.Surfer
  V:Loki,Dormammu. 30.00
119 JR(c),DH(i),V:Collector 30.00
120 JSn(c),DH(i),V:Zodiac. 30.00
121 JR&JSn(c),JB,DH,V:Zodiac . . 30.00
122 K&R(c),V:Zodiac. 30.00
123 JR(c),DH(i),O:Mantis. 30.00
124 JR(c),JB,DC,V:Kree,O:Mantis. 30.00

All comics prices listed are for *Near Mint* condition.

125 JR(c),JB,DC,V:Thanos 40.00
126 DC(i),V:Klaw,Solarr 30.00
127 GK(c),SB,JSon,A:Inhumans,
    V:Ultron,Maximus 30.00
128 K&R(c),SB,JSon,V:Kang 30.00
129 SB,JSon,V:Kang 30.00
130 GK(c),SB,JSon,V:Slasher,
    Titanic Three 30.00
131 GK(c),SB,JSon,V:Kang,
    Legion of the Unliving 30.00
132 SB,JSon,Kang,Legion
    of the Unliving 30.00
133 GK(c),SB,JSon,O:Vision 30.00
134 K&R(c),SB,JSon,O:Vision . . . 30.00
135 JSn&JR(c),GT,O:Mantis,
    Vision,C:Thanos 40.00
136 K&R(c),rep Amazing Adv#12 . 20.00
137 JR(c),GT,J:Beast,
    Moondragon 20.00
138 GK(c),GT,V:Toad 20.00
139 K&R(c),GT,V:Whirlwind 18.00
140 K&R(c),GT,V:Whirlwind 18.00
141 GK(c),GP,V:Squad.Sinister . . . 12.00
142 K&R(c),GP,V:Squadron
    Sinister,Kang 12.00
143 GK(c),GP,V:Squadron
    Sinister,Kang 12.00
144 GK,GK(c),V:Squad.Sinister,
    O&J:Hellcat,O:Buzz Baxter . . 30.00
145 GK(c),DH,V:Assassin 12.00
146 GK(c),DH,KP,V:Assassin 12.00
147 GP,V:Squadron Supreme 12.00
148 JK(c),GP,V:Squad.Supreme . . 12.00
149 GP,V:Orka 15.00
150 GP,JK,rep.Avengers #16 . . . . . 15.00
151 GP,new line-up,
    R:Wonder Man 15.00
152 JB,JSt,I:New Black Talon 15.00
153 JB,JSt,V:L.Laser,Whizzer 12.00
154 GP,V:Attuma 12.00
155 SB,V:Dr.Doom,Attuma 12.00
156 SB,I:Tyrak,V:Attuma 12.00
157 DH,V:Stone Black Knight 12.00
158 JK(c),SB,I&O:Graviton, ... 12.00
159 JK(c),SB,V:Graviton, ... 12.00
160 GP,V:Grim Reaper 100.00
161 GP,V:Ultron,A:Ant-Man 100.00
162 GP,V:Ultron,I:Jocasta 100.00
163 GT,A:Champions,V:Typhon . . 100.00
164 JBy,V:Lethal Legion 15.00
165 JBy,V:Count Nefario 14.00
166 JBy,V:Count Nefario 14.00
167 GP,A:Guardians,A:Nighthawk,
    Korvac,V:Porcupine 8.00
168 GP,A:Guardians,V:Korvac,
    I:Gyrich 8.00
169 SB,I:Eternity Man 8.00
170 GP,R:Jocasta,C:Ultron,
    A:Guardians. 8.00
171 GP,V:Ultron,A:Guardians,
    Ms Marvel 8.00
172 SB,KJ,V:Tyrak 8.00
173 SB,V:Collector. 8.00
174 GP(c),V:Collector. 8.00
175 V&O:Korvac,A:Guardians 8.00
176 V:Korvac,A:Guardians 8.00
177 DC(c),D:Korvac,A:Guardians . . 8.00
178 CI,V:Manipulator 8.00
179 JM,AG,V:Stinger,Bloodhawk . . 8.00
180 JM,V:Monolith,Stinger,
    D:Bloodhawk 8.00
181 JBy,GD,I:Scott Lang 10.00
182 JBy,KJ,V:Maximoff 10.00
183 JBy,KJ,J:Ms.Marvel. 10.00
184 JBy,KJ,J:Falcon,
    V:Absorbing Man 10.00
185 JBy,DGr,O:Quicksilver & Scarlet
    Witch,I:Bova,V:Modred 10.00
186 JBy,DGr,V:Modred,Chthon . . 10.00
187 JBy,DGr,V:Chthon,Modred . . 10.00
188 JBy,DGr,V:The Elements 10.00
189 JBy,DGr,V:Deathbird 10.00

190 JBy,DGr,V:Grey Gargoyle,
    A:Daredevil 10.00
191 JBy,DGr,V:Grey Gargoyle,
    A:Daredevil 10.00
192 I:Inferno. 8.00
193 FM(c),SB,DGr,O:Inferno 10.00
194 GP,JRu,J:Wonder Man 10.00
195 GP,JRu,A:Antman,
    I&C:Taskmaster 12.00
196 GP,JA,A:Antman,
    V:Taskmaster. 12.00
197 CI,JAb,V:Red Ronin 10.00
198 GP,DGr,V:Red Ronan 10.00
199 GP,DGr,V:Red Ronan 10.00
200 GP,DGr,V:Marcus,
    L:Ms.Marvel. 12.00
201 GP,DGr,F:Jarvis 5.00
202 GP,V:Ultron 5.00
203 CI,V:Crawlers,F:Wonderman . . 5.00
204 DN,DGr,V:Yellow Claw 5.00
205 DGr,V:Yellow Claw 5.00
206 GC,DGr,V:Pyron 5.00
207 GC,DGr,V:Shadowlord 5.00
208 GC,DGr,V:Berserker 5.00
209 DGr,A:Mr.Fantastic,V:Skrull . . 5.00
210 GC,DGr,V:Weathermen 5.00
211 GC,DGr,Moon Knight,J:Tigra . . 5.00
212 DGr,V:Elfqueen 5.00
213 BH,DGr,L:Yellowjacket 5.00
214 BH,DGr,V:Gh.Rider,A:Angel . . 7.00
215 DGr,A:Silver Surfer,
    V:Molecule Man. 5.00
216 DGr,A:Silver Surfer,
    V:Molecule Man 5.00
217 BH,DGr,V:Egghead,
    R:Yellowjacket,Wasp3 . . . . 5.00
218 DP,V:M.Hardy 5.00
219 BH,A:Moondragon,Drax 5.00
220 BH,DGr,D:Drax,V:MnDragon . . 5.00
221 J:She Hulk 5.00
222 V:Masters of Evil. 5.00
223 A:Antman 5.00
224 AM,A:Antman 5.00
225 A:Black Knight. 5.00
226 A:Black Knight. 5.00
227 J:2nd Captain Marvel,
    O:Avengers 5.00
228 V:Masters of Evil. 5.00
229 JSt,V:Masters of Evil. 5.00
230 A:Cap.Marvel,L:Yellowjacke . . 5.00
231 AM,JSi,J:2nd Captain Marvel,
    Starfox 5.00
232 AM,JSi. 5.00
233 JBy,V:Annihilus 5.00
234 AM,JSi,O:ScarletWitch 5.00
235 AM,JSi,V:Wizard 5.00
236 AM,JSi,A:SpM,V:Lava Men . . . 4.50
237 AM,JSi,A:SpM,V:Lava Men . . . 4.50
238 AM,JSi,V:Moonstone,
    O:Blackout. 4.00
239 AM,JSi,A:David Letterman . . . 4.00
240 AM,JSi,A:Dr.Strange 4.00
241 AM,JSi,V:Morgan LeFey 4.00
242 AM,JSi,Secret Wars 4.00
243 AM,JSi,Secret Wars 4.00
244 AM,JSi,V:Dire Wraiths. 4.00
245 AM,JSi,V:Dire Wraiths. 4.00
246 AM,JSi,V:Eternals 4.00
247 AM,JSi,A:Eternals,V:Deviants . . 4.00
248 AM,JSi,A:Eternals,V:Deviants. . 4.00
249 AM,JSi,A:Maelstrom 4.00
250 AM,JSi,A:W.C.A.
    V:Maelstrom 5.00
251 BH,JSi,A:Paladin. 4.00
252 BH,JSi,J:Hercules
    V:Blood Brothers 4.00
253 BH,JSi,J:Black Knight 4.00
254 BH,JSi,A:W.C.A. 4.00
255 TP,p(c),JB,Legacy of
    Thanos/Sanctuary II 4.00
256 JB,TP,A:Ka-Zar 4.00

Avengers #28
© *Marvel Entertainment Group*

257 JB,TP,D:Savage Land,
    I:Nebula 4.00
258 JB,TP,A:SpM,Firelord,Nebula . . 4.00
259 JB,TP,V:Nebula. 4.00
260 JB,TP,SecretWarsII, IR:Nebula
    is Thanos' Granddaughter. 4.00
261 JB,TP,Secret Wars II. 4.00
262 JB,TP,J:Submariner 4.00
263 JB,TP,X-Factor tie-in,
    Rebirth,Marvel Girl,pt.1 . . . . . . 7.00
264 JB,TP,I:2nd Yellow Jacket. . . . 4.00
265 JB,TP,Secret Wars II 3.50
266 JB,TP,Secret Wars II,A:
    Silver Surfer. 3.50
267 JB,TP,V:Kang 3.50
268 JB,TP,V:Kang 3.50
269 JB,TP,V:Kang,A:Immortus. . . . 3.50
270 JB,TP,V:Moonstone. 3.50
271 JB,TP,V:Masters of Evil. 3.50
272 JB,TP,A:Alpha Flight 3.50
273 JB,TP,V:Masters of Evil. 3.50
274 JB,TP,V:Masters of Evil. 3.50
275 JB,TP,V:Masters of Evil. 3.50
276 JB,TP,V:Masters of Evil. 3.50
277 JB,TP,V:Masters of Evil. 3.50
278 JB,TP,V:Tyrok,J:Dr.Druid. 3.50
279 JB,TP,new leader 3.50
280 BH,KB,O:Jarvis. 3.50
281 JB,TP,V:Olympian Gods 3.50
282 JB,TP,V:Cerberus 3.50
283 JB,TP,V:Olympian Gods 3.50
284 JB,TP,V:Olympian Gods 3.50
285 JB,TP,V:Zeus 3.50
286 JB,TP,V:Fixer 3.50
287 JB,TP,V:Fixer 3.50
288 JB,TP,V:Sentry 459. . . . . 3.50
289 JB,TP,J:Marrina. 3.50
290 JB,TP,V:Adaptoid 3.50
291 JB,TP,V:Marrina 3.50
292 JB,TP,V:Leviathon. 3.50
293 JB,TP,V:Leviathon. 3.50
294 JB,TP,V:Nebula. 3.50
295 JB,TP,V:Nebula. 3.50
296 JB,TP,V:Nebula. 3.50
297 JB,TP,V:Nebula. 3.50
298 JB,TP,Inferno,Edwin Jarvis . . . 3.50
299 JB,TP,Inferno,V:Orphan
    Maker,R:Gilgemesh 3.50
300 JB,TP,WS,Inferno,V:Kang,
    O:Avengers,J:Gilgemesh,
    Mr.Fantastic,Invis.Woman 5.00
301 BH,DH,A:SuperNova 3.50
302 RB,TP,V:SuperNova,
    A:Quasar 3.50

303 RB,TP,V:SuperNova,A:FF.....3.50
304 RB,TP,V:U-Foes,Puma.......3.50
305 PR,TP,V:Lava Men..........5.00
306 PR,TP,O:Lava Men..........3.50
307 PR,TP,V:Lava Men..........3.50
308 PR,TP,A:Eternals,J:Sersi.....3.50
309 PR,TP,V:Blastaar...........3.50
310 PR,TP,V:Blastaar...........3.50
311 PR,TP,Acts of Veng.,V:Loki....3.50
312 PR,TP,Acts of Vengeance,
    V:Freedom Force............3.50
313 PR,TP,Acts of Vengeance,
    V:Mandarin,Wizard..........3.50
314 PR,TP,J:Sersi,A:Spider-Man,
    V:Nebula.................4.00
315 PR,TP,A:SpM,V:Nebula......4.00
316 PR,TP,J:Spider-Man........4.00
317 PR,TP,A:SpM,V:Nebula......4.00
318 PR,TP,A:SpM,V:Nebula......4.00
319 PR,B:Crossing Line.........3.00
320 PR,TP,A:Alpha Flight.......3.00
321 PR,Crossing Line#3.........3.00
322 PR,TP,Crossing Line#4.......3.00
323 PR,TP,Crossing Line#5.......3.00
324 PR,TP,E:Crossing Line.......3.00
325 V:MotherSuperior,3
    Machinesmith..............3.00
326 TP,I:Rage.................5.00
327 TP,V:Monsters.............3.00
328 TP,O:Rage................4.00
329 TP,J:Sandman,Rage.........3.00
330 TP,V:Tetrarch of Entropy......3.00
331 TP,J:Rage,Sandman.........3.00
332 TP,V:Dr.Doom.............3.00
333 HT,V:Dr.Doom.............3.00
334 NKu,TP,B:Collector,
    A:Inhumans...............3.00
335 RLm(c),SEp,TP,V:Thane
    Ector,A:Collector,...........3.00
336 RLm(c),SEp,TP...........3.00
337 RLm(c),SEp,TP,V:ThaneEctor.3.00
338 RLm(c),SEp,TP,A:Beast,......3.00
339 RLm(c),SEp,TP,E:Collector...3.00
340 RLm(c),F:Capt.Amer.,Wasp...3.00
341 SEp,TP,A:New Warriors,V:Sons
    of Serpents...............3.00
342 SEp,TP,A:New Warriors,
    V:Hatemonger............3.00
343 SEp,TP,J:Crystal,C&I:2nd
    Swordsman,Magdalene.......3.00
344 SEp,TP,I:Proctor...........3.00
345 SEp,TP,Oper. Galactic Storm
    Pt.5,V:Kree................3.00
346 SEp,TP,Oper. Galactic Storm
    Pt.12,I:Star Force...........3.00
347 SEp,TP,Oper. Galactic Storm
    Pt.19,D:Kree Race,Conclusion.3.00
348 SEp,TP,F:Vision............3.00
349 SEp,TP,V:Ares............3.00
350 SEp,TP,rep.Avengers#53,A:Prof.
    X,Cyclops,V:StarJammers.....4.00
351 KWe,V:Star Jammers........3.00
352 V:Grim Reaper............3.00
353 V:Grim Reaper............3.00
354 V:Grim Reaper............3.00
355 BHs(s),SEp,I:Gatherers,
    Coal Tiger................3.00
356 B:BHs(s),SEp,TP,A:Bl.Panther
    D:Coal Tiger..............3.00
357 SEp,TP,A:Watcher.........3.00
358 SEp,TP,V:Arkon...........3.00
359 SEp,TP,A:Arkon...........3.00
360 SEp,TP,V:Proctor,double-size,
    bronze foil(c).............4.50
361 SEp,I:Alternate Vision.......2.50
362 SEp,TP,V:Proctor..........3.00
363 SEp,TP,V:Proctor,D:Alternate
    Vision,C:Deathcry,Silver Foil(c),
    30th Anniv.,..............4.00
364 SEp,TP,I:Deathcry,V:Kree.....3.00
365 SEp,TP,V:Kree............3.00
366 SEp,TP,V:Kree,N:Dr.Pym,Foil(c)5.00

367 F:Vision.................3.00
368 SEp,TP,Bloodties#1,
    A:X-Men.................4.00
369 SEp,TP,E:BHs(s),Bloodties#5,
    D:Cortez,V:Exodus,Platinum
    Foil(c)..................4.00
370 SEp(c),TP(c),GI,V:Deviants,
    A:Kro,I:Delta Force.........3.00
371 GM,TP,V:Deviants,A:Kro......3.00
372 B:BHs(s),SEp,TP,I:2nd
    Gatherers,A:Proctor.........3.00
373 SEp,TP,I:Alternate Jocasta,
    V:Sersi.................3.00
374 SEp,TP,O&IR:Proctor is Alternate
    Black Knight..............3.00
375 SEp,TP,Double Sized,D:Proctor,
    L:Sersi,Black Knight.........3.50
376 F:Crystal,I:Terrigen.........3.00
377 F:Quicksilver.............3.00
378 TP,I:Butcher.............3.00
379 TP,Hercules,V:Hera.........3.00
379a Avengers Double Feature #1
    flip-book with Giant-Man #1...3.50
380 Hera...................6.00
380a Avengers Double Feature #2
    flip-book with Giant Man #2...5.00
381 Quicksilvr, Scarlet Witch......4.00
381a Avengers Double Feature #3
    flip-book with Giant Man #3...3.00
382 Wundagore...............2.50
382a Avengers Double Feature #4
    flip-book with Giant Man #4...3.00
383 A:Fantastic Force,V:Arides....3.00
384 Hercules Vs. Stepmom.......4.00
385 V:Red Skull..............3.00
386 F:Black Widow............3.00
387 Taking A.I.M.,pt.2..........3.00
388 Taking A.I.M.,pt.4..........3.00
389 B:Mike Deodato...........3.00
390 BHs,TP,The Crossing, prelude.3.00
391 BHs,Cont. From Avg. Crossing.3.00
392 BHs,TP,The Crossing........3.00
393 BHs,TP,The Crossing........3.00
394 BHs,TP,The Crossing........3.00
395 BHs,TP,Timeslide concludes..3.00
396 ....3.00
397 TP,Incred.Hulk #440 x-over...3.00
390 TP,V:Unknown foe.........3.00
399 ....3.00
400 MeW,MWa,double size.......4.50
401 MeW,MWa,Onslaught saga.....4.00
402 MWa,MD2,Onslaught, finale...4.00
Ann.#1 DH,V:Mandarin,
    Masters of Evil...........250.00

Avengers #133
© Marvel Entertainment Group

Ann.#2 DH,JB,V:Scar.Centurion.150.00
Ann.#3 rep.#4,T.ofSusp.#66-68..100.00
Ann.#4 rep.#5,#6............50.00
Ann.#5 JK(c),rep.#8,#11.......25.00
Ann.#6 GP,HT,V:Laser,Nuklo,
    Whirlwind................20.00
Ann.#7 JSn,JRu,V:Thanos,A:Captain
    Marvel,D:Warlock(2nd)......65.00
Ann.#8 GP,V:Dr.Spectrum.......15.00
Ann.#9 DN,V:Arsenal..........10.00
Ann.#10 MGo,A:X-Men,Spid.Woman,
    I:Rogue,V:Br.o/Evil Mutants...40.00
Ann.#11 DP,V:Defenders........6.00
Ann.#12 JG,V:Inhumans,Maximus..5.00
Ann.#13 JBy,V:Armin Zola.......5.00
Ann.#14 JBy,KB,V:Skrulls.......5.00
Ann.#15 SD,KJ,V:Freedom Force..5.00
Ann.#16 RF,BH,TP,JR2,BSz,KP,AW,
    MR,BL,BWi,JG,KN,A:Silver
    Surfer,Rebirth Grandmaster...5.00
Ann.#17 MBr,MG,Evol.Wars,J:2nd
    Yellow Jacket.............5.00
Ann.#18 MBa,MG,Atlan.Attack#8,
    J:Quasar................4.00
Ann.#19 HT,Terminus Factor.....4.00
Ann.#20 Subterran.Odyssey#1...4.00
Ann.#21 Citizen Kang#4........4.00
Ann.#22 I:Bloodwraith,w/card....4.00
Ann.#23 JB.................4.00
G-Size#1 JR(c),RB,DA,I:Nuklo...35.00
G-Size#2 JR(c),DC,O:Kang,
    D:Swordsman,O:Rama-Tut...20.00
G-Size#3 GK(c),DC,V:Kang,Legion
    of the Unliving............20.00
G-Size#4 K&R(c),DH,W:Scarlet Witch
    &Vision,O:Mantis,Moondragon 25.00
G-Size#5 rep,Annual #1........15.00
GNv Death Trap:The Vault RLm,
    A:Venom................20.00
Marvel Milestone rep. #1 (1993)...3.00
Marvel Milestone rep. #4 (1995)...3.00
Marvel Milestone rep. #16 (1993)..3.00
Spec. Avengers Log,GP(c), History
    of the Avengers (1994).......2.50
Spec. Avengers Strikefile, BHa(s),
    Avengers pin-ups (1994)......2.50
Spec. Avengers: The Crossing,BHs,
    Death of an Avenger (1995)...6.00
Spec. Avengers/Ultraforce x-over
    V:Malibu's Ultraforce (1995)...4.00

[2nd Series] Nov., 1996
1 RLd,JV,CYp,JSb,Heroes Reborn,
    F:Thor, Captain America,
    V:Loki...................6.00
1A Variant cover..............8.00
1 gold signature edition, bagged.20.00
2 RLd,JV,CYp,JSb,V:Kang......4.00
3 RLd,JV,CYp,JSb,V:Kang,A:Nick
    Fury...................4.00
4 RLd,JLb,CYp,JSb...........4.00
4A variant cover..............4.00
5 RLd,CYp,JSb,V:Hulk,concl.....5.00
6 RLd,JLb,CYp,JSb,Industrial
    Revolution, pt.1 x-over.......5.00
7 RLd,JLb,IaC,JSb,...........4.00
8 RLd,JLb,IaC,JSb,F:Simon
    Williams (Wonder Man),V:Ultron,
    Lethal Legion.............4.00
9 JLb,RLd,IaC,F:Vision, Wonder
    Man...................5.00
10 WS...................4.00
11 ....4.00
12 WS,Galactus Saga, x-over....4.00
13 JeR, Wildstorm x-over........4.00
Minus 1 Spec., JLb,RLd,IaC,JSb,
    flashback................2.50

[3rd Series] Dec., 1997
1 GP,KBk,AV,F:Everyone,48 pg....5.00
1a Variant (c)...............10.00
2 KBk,GP,AV,A:Scarlet Witch.....5.00
3 KBk,GP,AV,trapped in midieval
    present.................4.00

Avengers Vol 3 #12
© Marvel Entertainment Group

4 KBk,GP,AV,who makes the
team?.................... 5.00
5 KBk,GP,AV,Squadron Supreme .. 5.00
6 KBk,GP,AV,V:SquadronSupreme. 5.00
7 KBk,GP,AV,Live Kree or Die,pt.4 . 2.50
8 KBk,GP,AV,I:Triathlon 2.50
9 KBk,GP,AV,V:Moses Magnum ... 2.50
10 KBk,GP,AV,V:Grim Reaper 2.50
11 KBk,GP,AV,V:Grim Reaper 2.50
12 KBk,GP,AV,V:Thunderbolts,
48-page 40.00
12a Variant, white background 3.00
13 KBk,GP,AV,R:New Warriors 2.50
14 KBk,GP,AV,R:Beast.......... 2.50
15 KBk,GP,AV,A:Iron Man 2.50
16 JOy,AG,R:Photon 5.00
16a variant JOy,GP cover 2.50
17 JOy,AG,A:Warbird &
Black Knight 2.50
18 JOy,AG,V:Wrecking Crew 2.50
19 KBk,GP,AV,Ultron,pt.1 .... 2.50
19a signed 30.00
20 KBk,GP,AV,Ultron,pt.2........ 2.50
21 KBk,GP,AV,Ultron,pt.3........ 2.50
22 KBk,GP,AV,Ultron,pt.4........ 2.50
23 KBk,GP,AV,V:Wonder Man 2.50
24 KBk,GP,AV 2.50
25 KBk,GP,AV, 48-pg. 3.50
26 KBk,GP,AV,SI,V:Triune 2.50
27 KBk,GP,AV,100-pg........... 3.50
28 KBk,GP,AV,Kulan Gath,pt.1 .... 2.50
29 KBk,GP,AV,Kulan Gath,pt.2 .... 2.50
30 KBk,GP,AV,Kulan Gath,pt.3 .... 2.50
31 KBk,GP,AV,F:Vision 2.50
32 KBk,GP,AV,F:Black Widow 2.50
33 KBk,GP,AV,Thunderbolts 2.50
34 KBk,GP,AV,Thunderbolts 3.50
35 KBk,JR2,AV,MaximumSecurity .. 2.50
36 KBk,SEp,AV,A:Capt.Am.+poster. 2.50
37 KBk,SEp,AV,F:Capt.Am........ 2.50
38 KBk,AD,MFm 2.50
39 KBk,AD,MFm,F:Silverclaw 2.50
40 KBk,AD,MFm,F:Hulk,Silverclaw . 2.50
41 KBk,AD,MFm,A:Kang 2.50
42 KBk,AD,MFm,A:Kang 2.50
43 KBk,AD,MFm,V:Kang 2.50
44 KBk,KK,V:Kang,Thor berserk ... 2.50
45 KBk,KK,V:Conqueror 2.50
46 KBk,Kang Dynasty 2.50
47 KBk,Kang Dynasty 2.50
48 KBk,KD,100-page........... 4.00
49 KBk,KD,F:Kang,'Nuff Said 2.50
50 KBk,KD,V:Kang, 48-pg. 4.00
51 KBk,KD,F:Wonder Man,
Scarlet Witch 2.50

52 KBk,KD,Kang War 2.50
53 KBk,KD,Avengers Avenge 2.50
54 KBk,KD,Kang War,concl. 2.50
55 KBk,KD,Kang War,aftermath 2.50
56 KBk,F:Beast,She-Hulk,USAgent. 2.50
57 KD,World Trust, pt.1 .... 3.00
58 KD,World Trust, pt.2 .... 2.50
59 KD,World Trust, pt.3 .... 2.50
60 KD,World Trust, concl.,40-pg ... 4.00
61 GFr,.................... 2.50
62 GFr 2.50
63 AD,MFm,Standoff,pt.3,x-over ... 3.00
64 F:Falcon 2.50
65 ALa,Red Zone,pt.1 .... 2.50
66 ALa,Red Zone,pt.2 .... 2.50
67 ALa,Red Zone,pt.3 .... 2.50
68 ALa,Red Zone,pt.4 .... 2.50
69 ALa,Red Zone,pt.5 .... 2.50
70 ALa,Red Zone,pt.6 .... 2.50
71 V:Wasp, Yellowjacket 2.50
72 ScK,Search for She-Hulk,pt.1 .. 2.50
73 ScK,Search for She-Hulk,pt.2 .. 2.50
74 ScK,Search for She-Hulk,pt.3 .. 2.50
75 ScK,Search for She-Hulk,pt.4 .. 2.50
76 JaL(c),an Avenger falls 2.50
77 Lionheart of Avalon,pt 1 ......2.50
78 Lionheart of Avalon,pt.2 ...... 2.50
79 Lionheart of Avalon,pt.3 ...... 2.50
80 Lionheart of Avalon,pt.4 ...... 2.50
81 Lionheart of Avalon, concl. 2.50
82 Once an Invader,pt.1 .... 2.50
83 Once an Invader,pt.2 .... 2.50
84 Once an Invader,pt.3 .... 2.50
500 BMB,Disassembled,pt.1,48-pg. 5.00
500a Director's Cut,64-pg....... 8.00
501 BMB,Disassembled,pt.2,48-pg. 5.00
502 BMB,Disassembled,pt.3,48-pg. 5.00
503 BMB,Disassembled,pt.4,48-pg. 4.00
Ann. '98 Avengers/Squadron Supreme
KBk,CPa,GP, 48pg 2.50
Ann.1999 KBk,JFM, Why Avengers
disbanded, 48-page......... 3.50
Ann.2000 KBk,NBy,48-pg 3.50
Ann.2001 KBk,IaC,NRd........ 3.00
Rough Cut Edition KBk,GP, 48pg,
original pencils of #1, b&w 3.00
Spec. 1-1/2, 32-pg.RSt.......... 2.50
Spec. Avengers: Year in Review ... 3.00
Spec. Avengers Finale (2004) 3.00

AVENGERS AND POWER PACK ASSEMBLE
Apr., 2006
1 thru 4 .... @3.00

AVENGERS: CELESTIAL QUEST
Sept., 2001
1 (of 8) SEt,SHa.............. 2.50
2 SEt,SHa,F:Mantis 3.00
3 SEt,SHa,F:Quoi,Mantis 3.00
4 SEt,SHa,F:Quoi,Thanos 2.50
5 SEt,SHa,F:Thanos 2.50
6 SEt,SHa,F:Mantis & Vision 2.50
7 SEt,SHa,F:Mantis,Quoi,Vision .. 2.50
8 SEt,SHa,finale,48-pg. 3.50

AVENGERS CLASSIC
June, 2007
1 reps 4.00
2 thru 12 .... @3.00
Spec. #1 Giant-Size, 96-pg........ 5.00

AVENGERS: EARTH'S MIGHTIEST HEROES
Nov., 2004
1 JoC,ScK, Avengers early days .. 3.50
2 thru 8 JoC,ScK............. @3.50

AVENGERS: EARTH'S MIGHTIEST HEROES II
Nov., 2006
1 JoC, Avengers early days 4.00
2 JoC 4.00
3 thru 8 JoC .... @4.00

AVENGERS FAIRY TALES
Mar., 2008
1 (of 4) 3.00
2 thru 4 .... @3.00

AVENGERS FOREVER
Oct., 1998
1 (of 12) GP,KBk,CPa,Rick Jones
radiation poisoning 4.00
2 GP,KBk,CPa,new Avengers..... 3.00
3 GP,KBk,CPa,Kang/Immortus.... 3.00
4 KBk,different eras 3.00
4a, b & c variant covers .... @3.00
5 KBk,RSt,A:1950s Avengers 3.00
6 KBk,RSt,V:Immortus 3.00
7 KBk,RSt,reunited 3.00
8 KBk,Immortus' plan 3.00
9 KBk,RSt,Kang the Conqueror ... 3.00
10 KBk,RSt,V:Immortus.......... 3.00
11 KBk,RSt,V:Avengers Battalion .. 3.00
12 KBk,RSt,concl.............. 3.00

AVENGERS HANDBOOK
June, 2007
Spec. F:Mighty Avengers 4.00

AVENGERS ICONS: TIGRA
March, 2002
1 (of 4) MD2,................ 3.00
2 MD2,Brethren of the Blue Fist... 3.00
3 MD2,Brethren of the Blue Fist... 3.00
4 MD2,concl................. 3.00

AVENGERS ICONS: THE VISION
Aug., 2002
1 (of 4) 3.00
2 thru 4 .... @3.00

AVENGERS INDEX
See: OFFICIAL MARVEL INDEX TO THE AVENGERS

AVENGERS INFINITY
July, 2000
1 (of 4) RSt,SCh,SHa 3.00
2 RSt,SCh,SHa,Servitors 3.00
3 RSt,SCh,SHa,Infinites 3.00
4 RSt,SCh,SHa,concl 3.00

AVENGERS/INVADERS
May, 2008
1 (of 12) Legends Live Again 3.00
1a variant (c)................ 3.00
2 thru 6 .... @3.00
2a thru 6a variant (c)........... @3.00
5a variant sketch (c) 3.00
Giant-Size #1 (2008) 4.00

AVENGERS NEXT
Nov. 2006
1 RLm,V:Zombie Avengers,A:Nova 3.00
2 RLm..................... 3.00
3 RLm..................... 3.00
4 RLm..................... 3.00
5 RLm, finale................. 3.00

AVENGERS SPOTLIGHT
Aug., 1989
Formerly: Solo Avengers

21 AM,DH,TMo,JRu,Hawkeye, Starfox	3.00
22 AM,DH,Hawkeye,O:Swordsman	2.50
23 AM,DH,KD,Hawkeye,Vision	2.50
24 AM,DH,Hawkeye,O:Espirita	2.50
25 AM,TMo,Hawkeye,Rick Jones	2.50
26 A of V,Hawkeye,Iron Man	2.50
27 A of V,AM,DH,DT,Hawkeye Avengers	2.50
28 A of V,AM,DH,Hawkeye, Wonder Man,Wasp	2.50
29 A of V,DT,Hawkeye,Iron Man	2.50
30 AM,DH,Hawkeye,New Costume	2.50
31 AM,DH,KW,Hawkeye,US.Agent	2.50
32 AM,KW,Hawkeye,U.S.Agent	2.50
33 AM,DH,KW,Hawkeye,US.Agent	2.50
34 AM,DH,KW,SLi(c),Hawkeye U.S.Agent	2.50
35 JV,Gilgamesh	2.50
36 AM,DH,Hawkeye	2.50
37 BH,Dr.Druid	2.50
38 JBr,Tigra	2.50
39 GCo,Black Knight	2.50
40 Vision,Last Issue	2.50

AVENGERS: THE INITIATIVE
April, 2007

1 Classified	3.00
1a variant (c)	3.00
2 Hero Moment	3.00
3 Bug Hunt	3.00
4 Green Zone	3.00
5 Green Zone	3.00
6 The Gauntlet	3.00
7 Triple Threat	3.00
8 Killed in Action, pt.1	3.00
9 Killed in Action, pt.2	3.00
10 Killed in Action, pt.3	3.00
11 Killed in Action, pt.4	3.00
12 Changing of the Guard	3.00
13 Dutterball	3.00
14 Secret Invasion tie-in	3.00
15 Secret Invasion tie-in	3.00
16 Secret Invasion tie-in	3.00
17 Secret Invasion tie-in	3.00
18 Secret Invasion tie-in	3.00
19 V-S Day, Secret Invasion tie-in	3.00
Ann. #1	4.00
Spec. 48-pg. (2008)	4.00

AVENGERS: THE TERMINATRIX OBJECTIVE
1993

1 B:MGu(s),MG,Holografx(c), V:Terminatrix	3.00
2 MG,V:Terminatrix,A:Kangs	2.50
3 MG,V:Terminatrix,A:Kangs	2.50
4 MG,Last issue	2.50

AVENGERS/ THUNDERBOLTS
March, 2004

1 (of 6) FaN&KBk(s),BKi	3.00
2 FaN&KBk(s),BKi	3.00
3 thru 6 FaN&KBk(s),TG	@3.00

AVENGERS: TIMESLIDE
1996

1 BHs,TKa,End of the Crossing Megallic chrome cover	5.00

AVENGERS TWO: WONDER MAN & THE BEAST
Mar., 2000

1 (of 3) RSt,MBa,	3.00
2 RSt,MBa,	3.00
3 RSt,MBa,concl.	3.00

AVENGERS: UNITED THEY STAND
Sept., 1999

1 TTn,RCa, Cartoon tie-in	3.00
2 TTn,	2.50
3 TTn,	2.50
4 TTn,	2.50
5 TTn,Hawkeye&Black Widow	2.50
6 TTn,A:Capt.America	2.50
7 TTn,F:Devil Dinosaur,Moonboy	3.50

AVENGERS UNLEASHED
1995

1 V:Count Nefarious	2.50

Becomes:

AVENGERS UNPLUGGED
1996

2 Crushed by Graviton	2.50
3 x-over with FF Unplugged	2.50
4 The Old Ball and Chain	2.50
5 A:Captain Marvel	2.50
6 final issue	2.50

Avengers West Coast-96
© Marvel Entertainment Group

AVENGERS WEST COAST
Sept., 1989
Prev: West Coast Avengers

47 JBy,V:J.Random	3.00
48 JBy,V:J.Random	3.00
49 JBy,V:J.Random,W.Man	3.00
50 JBy,R:G.A.Human Torch	4.00
51 JBy,R:Iron Man	2.50
52 JBy,V:MasterPandmonum.	2.50
53 JBy,Acts ofVeng.,V:U-Foes	2.50
54 JBy,Acts ofVeng.,V:MoleMan	2.50
55 JBy,Acts ofVeng.finale,V:Loki Magneto kidnaps Sc.Witch	4.00
56 JBy,V:Magneto	11.00
57 JBy,V:Magneto	5.00
58 V:Vibro,	2.50
59 TMo,V:Hydro-Man,A:Immortus	2.50
60 PR,V:Immortus,	2.50
61 PR,V:Immortus	2.50

62 V:Immortus	2.50
63 PR,I:Living Lightning	2.50
64 F:G.A.Human Torch	2.50
65 PR,V:Ultron,Grim Reaper	2.50
66 PR,V:Ultron,Grim Reaper	2.50
67 PR,V:Ultron,Grim Reaper	2.50
68 PR,V:Ultron	2.50
69 PR,USAgent vs Hawkeye, I:Pacific Overlords	2.50
70 DR,V:Pacific Overlords	3.00
71 DR,V:Pacific Overlords	3.00
72 DR,V:Pacific Overlords	3.00
73 DR,V:Pacific Overlords	3.00
74 DR,J:Living Lightning,Spider Woman,V:Pacific Overlords	3.00
75 HT,A:F.F,V:Arkon,double	3.00
76 DR,Night Shift,I:Man-Demon	2.50
77 DR,A:Satannish & Nightshift	2.50
78 DR,V:Satannish & Nightshift	2.50
79 DR,A:Dr.Strange,V:Satannish	2.50
80 DR,Galactic Storm,pt.2	2.50
81 DR,Galactic Storm,pt.9	2.50
82 DR,Galactic Storm,pt.16 A:Lilandra	2.50
83 V:Hyena	2.50
84 DR,I:Deathweb,A:SpM, O:Spider-Woman	3.00
85 DR,A:SpM,V:Death Web	2.50
86 DR,A:SpM,V:Death Web.	2.50
87 DR,A:Wolverine,V:Bogatyri	3.00
88 DR,A:Wolverine,V:Bogatyri	2.50
89 DR,V:Ultron	2.50
90 DR,A:Vision,V:Ultron	2.50
91 DR,V:Ultron,I:War Toy	2.50
92 DR,V:Goliath(Power Man)	2.50
93 DR,V:Doctor Demonicus	2.50
94 DR,J:War Machine	2.50
95 DR,A:Darkhawk,V:Doctor Demonicus	2.50
96 DR,Inf.Crusade x-over	2.50
97 ACe,Inf.Crusade,V:Power Platoon	2.50
98 DR,I:4th Lethal Legion	2.50
99 DR,V:4th Lethal Legion	2.50
100 DR,D:Mockingbird,V:4th Lethal Legion,Red Foil(c)	4.50
101 DR,Bloodties#3,V:Exodus	4.00
102 DR,L:Iron Man,Spider-Woman, US Agent,Scarlet Witch,War Machine,last issue	4.00
Ann.#4 JBy,TA,MBa,Atlan.Attacks #12,V:Seven Brides of Set	4.00
Ann.#5 Terminus Factor	3.50
Ann.#6 Subterranean Odyssey#5	2.50
Ann.#7 Assault on Armor City#4	2.50
Ann.#8 DR,I:Raptor w/card	3.25

BALDER THE BRAVE
Nov., 1985

1 WS,SB,V:Frost Giants	3.00
2 WS,SB,V:Frost Giants	3.00
3 WS,SB,V:Frost Giants	3.00
4 WS,SB,V:Frost Giants;Feb,1986	3.00

BANNER
Startling Stories, July, 2001

1 (of 4) RCo, F:Hulk	3.00
2 RCo,	3.00
3 RCo,	3.00
4 RCo, concl.	3.00

BARBIE
Jan., 1991

1 polybagged with Credit Card	16.00
2	10.00
3 thru 49	@9.00
50 Anniv. issue, Disney World(c)	12.00
51 thru 66	@7.00

Barbie #52
© Marvel Entertainment Group

BARBIE FASHION
Jan., 1991
1 bagged with doorknob hanger . . 15.00
2 thru 63 . . . . @10.00

BATTLE
Marvel Atlas, March, 1951
1 They called Him a Coward . . . 450.00
2 The War Department Secrets . 250.00
3 The Beast of the Bataan 150.00
4 JMn,I:Buck Private O'Toole . . 150.00
5 Death Trap Of Gen. Wu. 150.00
6 RH, JMn. 150.00
7 Enemy Sniper 150.00
8 A Time to Die 150.00
9 RH 100.00
10 . . . . 100.00
11 SC 100.00
12 thru 21 . . . . @110.00
22 . . . . 100.00
23 BK 100.00
24 . . . . 100.00
25 . . . . 100.00
26 JR 100.00
27 . . . . 100.00
28 JSe 100.00
29 . . . . 100.00
30 . . . . 100.00
31 RH,JMn 100.00
32 JSe,GT 100.00
33 GC,JSe,JSt 100.00
34 JSe 100.00
35 . . . . 100.00
36 BEv 100.00
37 RA,JSt. 125.00
38 thru 46 . . . . @100.00
47 JO 100.00
48 . . . . 100.00
49 JDa 100.00
50 BEv 100.00
51 . . . . 100.00
52 GWb 100.00
53 BP 100.00
54 . . . . 100.00
55 GC,AS,BP,AW,GWb 125.00
56 . . . . 100.00
57 . . . . 100.00
58 . . . . 100.00
59 AT 100.00
60 A:Combat Kelly 100.00
61 JMn,A:Combat Kelly 100.00
62 A:Combat Kelly 100.00
63 SD 150.00
64 JK 150.00
65 JK 150.00

66 JSe,JK,JDa 150.00
67 JSe,JK,AS,JDa 150.00
68 JSe,JK,AW,SD 150.00
69 RH,JSe,JK,SW 175.00
70 BEv,SD; June, 1960 . . . . 175.00

BATTLE ACTION
Marvel Atlas, Feb., 1952
1 . . . . 350.00
2 . . . . 200.00
3 JSt,RH 100.00
4 . . . . 100.00
5 . . . . 100.00
6 JeR 100.00
7 JeR 100.00
8 RH 125.00
9 thru 15 . . . . @100.00
16 thru 27 . . . . @100.00
28 GWb 100.00
29 . . . . 100.00
30 GWb,Aug., 1957 . . . . 100.00

BATTLEBOOKS
Nov., 1998
Captain America, BiT(c) 4.00
Citizen V, BiT(c) 4.00
Colossus, BiT(c). 4.00
Elektra, BiT(c) 4.00
Gambit, BiT(c) 4.00
Iron Man, BiT(c) 4.00
Rogue, BiT(c). 4.00
Spider-Girl, BiT(c) 4.00
Spider-Man, BiT(c). 4.00
Storm, BiT(c) 4.00
Thor, BiT(c) 4.00
Wolverine, BiT(c) 4.00

BATTLE BRADY
See: MEN IN ACTION

BATTLEFIELD
Marvel Atlas, April, 1952
1 RH, Slaughter on Suicide
   Ridge 275.00
2 RH 150.00
3 Ambush Patrol 150.00
4 . . . . 150.00
5 Into the Jaws of Death 150.00
6 thru 10 . . . . @100.00
11 GC,May, 1953 . . . . 100.00

BATTLEFRONT
Marvel Atlas, June, 1952
1 JeR,RH(c),Operation Killer . . . 400.00
2 JeR 200.00
3 JeR,Spearhead 150.00
4 JeR,Death Trap of General
   Chun 150.00
5 JeR,Terror of the Tank Men . . . 150.00
6 A:Combat Kelly 150.00
7 A:Combat Kelly 150.00
8 A:Combat Kelly 150.00
9 A:Combat Kelly 150.00
10 A:Combat Kelly 150.00
11 thru 20 . . . . @125.00
21 thru 39 . . . . @125.00
40 AW 125.00
41 . . . . 125.00
42 AW 125.00
43 thru 48 Aug.,1957 . . . . @135.00

BATTLEGROUND
Marvel Atlas, Sept., 1954
1 . . . . 300.00
2 JKz 150.00
3 thru 8 . . . . @125.00
9 BK 125.00
10 . . . . 125.00
11 AW,GC,GT. 135.00

12 MD,JSe. 125.00
13 AW 125.00
14 JD 135.00
15 thru 17 . . . . @125.00
18 AS 135.00
19 JMn,JSe 125.00
20 Aug., 1957 . . . . 125.00

Battlestar Galactica-1
© Marvel Entertainment Group

BATTLESTAR GALACTICA
March, 1979
1 EC,B:TV Adaptation;
   Annihalation 12.00
2 EC,Exodus 9.00
3 EC,Deathtrap 9.00
4 WS,Dogfight 9.00
5 WS,E:TV Adaptation;Ambush . . . 9.00
6 Nightmare 8.00
7 Commander Adama Trapped . . . 8.00
8 Last Stand 8.00
9 Space Mimic 8.00
10 This Planet Hungers 8.00
11 WS,Starbuck's Dilemma 8.00
12 WS,Memory Ends. 8.00
13 WS,All Out Attack 8.00
14 Radiation Threat 8.00
15 Ship of Crawling Death. 8.00
16 . . . . 8.00
17 Animal on the Loose 8.00
18 Battle For the Forbidden Fruit. . . 8.00
19 Starbuck's Back 8.00
20 Duel to the Death 8.00
21 To Slay a Monster..To Deatroy
   a World 8.00
22 WS,A Love Story?. 8.00
23 Dec., 1981 . . . . 8.00

BEAST
March, 1997
1 (of 3) KG,CNn,F:Karma, Cannonball, V:Viper & Spiral 3.00
2 KG,CNn,V:Spiral. 3.00
3 KG,CNn, concl. 3.00

BEAUTY AND THE BEAST
Jan., 1985
1 DP,Beast & Dazzler,direct 3.00
1a DP,Beast & Dazzler,UPC 3.00
2 thru 4 DP,Beast & Dazzler . . . . @3.00

BEAVIS & BUTT-HEAD
March, 1994
1 Based on the MTV Show	5.00
1a 2nd Printing	2.50
2 Dead from the Neck up	3.50
3 Break out at Burger World	3.00
4 thru 28	@2.50

BEFORE THE FANTASTIC 4:
GRIMM AND LOGAN
May, 2000
1 (of 3) LHa,Wolverine&Thing	3.25
2 LHa,A:Carol Danvers	3.25
3 LHa,concl.	3.25

...REED RICHARDS
July, 2000
1 (of 3) PDa,DFg,V:Dr.Doom	3.25
2 PDa,DFg	3.25
3 PDa,DFg,concl.	3.25

...THE STORMS
Oct., 2000
1 (of 3) TKa,CAd,F:Sue & J. Storm	3.25
2 V:St. Germaine	3.25
3 TKa,CaD,concl.	3.25

BEST LOVE
Marvel-Manvis Publ., 1949
(Formerly: Sub-Mariner #32)
33 JKu	150.00
34	100.00
35 BEv	125.00
36 BEv	125.00

BEST WESTERN
June, 1949
58 A:KidColt,BlackRider,Two-Gun Kid; Million Dollar Train Robbery	325.00
59 A:BlackRider,KidColt,Two-Gun Kid;The Black Rider Strikes.	300.00
Becomes:

WESTERN OUTLAWS & SHERIFFS
1949
60 PH(c),Hawk Gaither	300.00
61 Ph(c),Pepper Lawson	250.00
62 Murder at Roaring House Bridge.	250.00
63 thru 65	@250.00
66 Hanging.	250.00
67 Cannibalism	250.00
68 thru 72	@225.00
73 June, 1952	225.00

BEWARE
March, 1973
1 Reprints	35.00
2 thru 8	@20.00
Becomes:

TOMB OF DARKNESS
1974
9 Reprints	35.00
10 thru 22	@20.00
23 November, 1976	25.00

BEYOND!
July, 2006
1 DMD,ScK, Nine heroes vs. Space Phantom	3.00
2 thru 6	@3.00

BIBLE TALES FOR YOUNG FOLK
Marvel/Atlas, 1953
1	350.00
2 BEv,BK.	250.00
3	200.00
4 JeR	225.00
5	200.00

BIG HERO SIX
Sept., 2008
1 CCl(s).	4.00
1a variant (c)	4.00
2 CCl(s).	4.00
3 CCl(s).	4.00

BILLY BUCKSKIN WESTERN
Marvel Atlas, Nov., 1955
1 MD,Tales of the Wild Frontier	250.00
2 MD,Ambush	150.00
3 MD,AW, Thieves in the Night	200.00
Becomes:

2-GUN KID
1956
4 SD,A: Apache Kid	200.00
Becomes:

TWO-GUN WESTERN
1956
5 B:Apache Kid,Doc Holiday, Kid Colt Outlaw	250.00
6	225.00
7	225.00
8 RC	200.00
9 AW	200.00
10	200.00
11 AW	225.00
12 Sept., 1957,RC	200.00

BISHOP
1994
1 Mountjoy, foil cover	4.00
2 foil stamped cover	4.00
3 JOs	3.50
4 V:Mountjoy	3.50

BISHOP: THE LAST X-MAN
Aug., 1999
1 R:Bishop, 48-page debut	6.00
2A I:Nom,Link,Jinx & Scorch	2.50
2B variant (c)	2.50
3 thru 15	@2.50
16 NMa,Dream'sEnd,pt.3,x-over	8.00

BISHOP: XAVIER'S SECURITY ENFORCER
Nov., 1997
1 (of 3) JOs,SEp	3.00
2 JOs,SEp,hunted by X.S.E.	3.00
3 JOs,SEp,Bishop v. Rook, concl.	3.00

BIZARRE ADVENTURES
See: MARVEL PREVIEW

BLACK AXE
1993
1 JR2(c),A:Death's Head II	3.00
2 JR2(2),A:Sunfire,V:The Hand	3.00
3 A:Death's Head II,V:Mesphisto	3.00
4 in ancient Egypt	3.00
5 KJ(c),In Wakanda	3.00
6 KJ(c),A:Black Panther	3.00
7 KJ(c),A:Black Panther	3.00
8 thru 13	@3.00

BLACK GOLIATH
Feb., 1976—Nov., 1976
1 GT,O:Black Goliath,Cont's From Powerman #24	30.00
2 GT,V:Warhawk	15.00
3 GT,D:Atom-Smasher	15.00
4 KP,V:Stilt-Man	15.00
5 D:Mortag	15.00

BLACK KNIGHT, THE
Marvel Atlas, 1955–56
1 JMn,O: Crusader;The Black Knight Rides	1,500.00
2 JMn,Siege on Camelot	900.00
3 JMn,Black Knight Unmasked	750.00
4 JMn,Betrayed	750.00
5 JMn,SSh,The Invincible Tartar.	750.00

Black Panther #15
© Marvel Entertainment Group

BLACK PANTHER
[1st Series]
Jan., 1977—May, 1979
1 JK,V:Collectors	40.00
2 JK,V:Six Million Year Man	20.00
3 JK,V:Ogar	20.00
4 JK,V:Collectors	20.00
5 JK,V:Yeti	20.00
6 JK,V:Ronin	20.00
7 JK,V:Mister Little	20.00
8 JK,D:Black Panther	20.00
9 JK,V:Jakarra	20.00
10 JK,V:Jakarra	20.00
11 JK,V:Kilber the Cruel.	20.00
12 JK,V:Kilber the Cruel	20.00
13 JK,V:Kilber the Cruel	20.00
14 JK,A:Avengers,V:Klaw	25.00
15 JK,A:Avengers,V:Klaw	25.00

BLACK PANTHER
July, 1988—Oct., 1988
[1st Mini-Series]
1 I:Panther Spirit	4.00
2 V:Supremacists	4.00
3 A:Malaika	4.00
4 V:Panther Spirit	4.00

[2nd Mini-Series]
PANTHER'S PREY
May, 1991
1 thru 4 DT,V:Solomon Prey	@5.00

BLACK PANTHER
[2nd Series] Sept., 1998
1 CPr,MT,A:T'Challa 7.00
2 CPr,MT,A:Mephisto 3.00
2a variant cover 3.00
3 CPr,MT,JQ,I:Achebe 3.00
4 CPr,MT,JQ,V:Mephisto. 3.00
5 CPr,V:Mephisto 3.00
6 thru 35 CPr. . . . . @2.50
36 CPr,SaV,100-page 4.00
37 thru 56 . . . . @2.50
57 thru 63 . . . . @3.00
[3rd Series] Feb., 2005
1 JR2 . . . . 5.00
2 thru 6 JR2 . . . . @3.00
7 thru 17 . . . . @3.00
18 SEa,Bride of the Panther, 48-pg. 6.00
18a variant (c) 8.00
19 thru 20 . . . . @3.00
21 Civil War 10.00
22 Civil War 4.50
23 Foreign Affairs, pt.1, Civil War . 4.00
24 Foreign Affairs, pt.2, Civil War . 4.00
25 Foreign Affairs, pt.3, Civil War . 9.00
26 Two Plus Two 3.00
27 Classified 3.00
28 Good Eatin', pt. 1 . . . . 3.00
29 Good Eatin', pt. 2 . . . . 3.00
30 Good Eatin', pt. 3 . . . . 3.00
31 Size Matters 3.00
32 Little Green Men 3.00
33 Little Green Men, pt.2 . . . . 3.00
34 . . . . 3.00
35 Back to Africa 3.00
36 Back to Africa, pt.2 . . . . 3.00
37 R:Killmonger 3.00
38 Back to Africa, concl. 3.00
39 Secret Invasion tie-in 3.00
40 Secret Invasion tie-in 3.00
41 Secret Invasion tie-in 3.00
Ann. #1 Black to the Future. 4.00

BLACK RIDER
See: ALL WINNERS COMICS

BLACK RIDER RIDES AGAIN
Marvel Atlas, Sept., 1957
1 JK,Treachery at Hangman's
Ridge 350.00

BLACKSTONE, THE MAGICIAN
May, 1948—Sept., 1948
2 B:Blonde Phantom 1,000.00
3 BO(c),bondage (c) 650.00
4 Bondage(c) 650.00

BLACK WIDOW
Apr. 1999
1 (of 3) Black Widow replaced? . . . 6.00
1a variant cover (1:4) 7.00
2 A:Daredevil 4.00
3 conclusion 4.00
Nov., 2000
1 thru 3 SHp,Natasha vs.Yelena. @3.00
Sept., 2004
1 (of 6) BSz,F:Natasha Romanova. 3.00
2 thru 6 BSz . . . . @3.00

BLACK WIDOW: PALE LITTLE SPIDER
Marvel Max, April, 2002
1 (of 3) F:Belova 3.25
2 thru 3 . . . . @3.25

BLACK WIDOW 2
Sept., 2005
1 (of 6) BSz,Things They Say 3.00
2 thru 6 BSz,Things They Say
About Her. . . . . @3.00

BLACKWULF
1994–95
1 AMe,Embossied(c),I:Mammoth,
Touchstone,Toxin,D:Pelops,
V:Tantalus, ... 3.00
2 AMe,I:Sparrow,Wildwind 2.50
3 AMe,I:Scratch 2.50
4 AMe,I:Giant-man 2.50
5 AMe 2.50
6 AMe,Tantalus 2.50
7 AMe,V:Tantalus 2.50
8 AMe 2.50
9 Seven Worlds of Tantalus,pt.1
A:Daredevil 2.50
10 Seven Worlds of Tantalus,pt.2,
last issue 2.50

BLADE, THE VAMPIRE HUNTER
1994–95
1 Foil(c),Clv(i),R:Dracula 3.50
2 Clv(i),V:Dracula 2.50
3 Clv(i) 2.50
4 Clv(i) 2.50
5 Clv(i) 2.50
6 Clv(i) 2.50
7 Clv(i) 2.50
8 Bible John, Morbius 2.50
9 . . . . 2.50
10 R:Dracula 2.50
11 Dracula Untombed,pt.2 . . . . 2.50

BLADE
Sept., 1998
1 (of 6) DMG,40-page, photo(c) . . . 3.50
1a variant cover (1:4) 3.50
2 DMG,A:Morbius,Dominique 3.00
2a variant cover 3.00
3 DMG, ... 3.00
4 DMG,F:Morbius 3.00
1-shot Blade: Crescent City Blues,
MPe,V:Deacon Frost (1998) . . . 3.50
1-shot DMG, movie tie-in (1998) . . . 3.00
1-shot movie adaptation,48 pg 6.00

BLADE: VAMPIRE HUNTER
Oct., 1999
1 (of 6) BS, 48-pg. 4.00
2 BS 3.00
3 BS,V:Reaper 3.00
4 BS,V:Hrolf 3.00
5 BS,V:Reaper 3.00
6 BS,V:Reaper, concl. 3.00

BLADE
Marvel Max, March, 2002
1 StP,V:Tryks. 3.25
2 StP,F:Tryks,Seven 3.25
3 StP,date with Susan 3.25
4 StP,Fofo's missing fingers 3.25
5 StP,V:Rowks. 3.25
6 horror hits home 3.25
GN Bloodhunt, movie adapt. 6.00

BLADE
Sept., 2006
1 HC, A:Spider-Man 3.00
2 HC, V:Dr. Doom 3.00
3 HC 3.00
4 HC,Night before X-mas 3.00

Blade The Vampire Hunter #6
© Marvel Entertainment Group

5 HC,Casualties of War, Civil War . 3.00
6 HC,Blade's Father 3.00
7 HC,Blade dies 3.00
8 HC,F:Hannibal King 3.00
9 HC,F:Union Jack 3.00
10 HC,V:Spider-Man 3.00
11 HC,V:father 3.00
12 HC finale issue 3.00

BLADE RUNNER
Oct., 1982
1 AW, Movie Adaption 4.00
2 AW, ... 4.00

BLAZE
[Limited Series], 1993–94
1 HMe(s),RoW,A:Clara Menninger . 2.50
2 HMe(s),RoW,I:Initiate. 2.50
3 HMe(s),RoW, ... 2.50
4 HMe(s),RoW,D:Initiate 2.50
[Regular Series], Aug., 1994
1 HMz,LHa,foil (c) 3.50
2 thru 5 HMz,LHa . . . . @2.50
6 thru 12 . . . . @2.50

BLAZE CARSON
Sept., 1948
1 SSh(c),Fight,Lawman
or Crawl 350.00
2 Guns Roar on Boot Hill 250.00
3 A:Tex Morgan 250.00
4 SSh,A:Two-Gun Kid 250.00
5 A:Tex Taylor 275.00
Becomes:

REX HART
1949
6 CCB,Ph(c),B:Rex Hart,
A:Black Rider 350.00
7 Ph(c),Mystery at Bar-2 Ranch 250.00
8 Ph(c),The Hombre Who
Killed His Friends 250.00
Becomes:

WHIP WILSON
1950
9 Ph(c),B:Whip Wilson,O:Bullet;
Duel to the Death 800.00
10 Ph(c),Wanted for Murder 400.00
11 Ph(c) 400.00
Becomes:

Blaze (Rex Hart) #6
© *Marvel Entertainment Group*

GUNHAWK, THE
1950
12 The Redskin's Revenge 350.00
13 GT,The Man Who Murdered
Gunhawk 300.00
14 . . . . 250.00
15 . . . . 250.00
16 EC 250.00
17 . . . . 250.00
18 JMn,Dec., 1951. . . . . 250.00

BLAZE OF GLORY
Dec., 1999
1 (of 4) JOs,F:John Woo 3.00
2 JOs, ... 3.00
3 JOs, ... 3.00
4 JOs,concl. 3.00

BLAZE,
THE WONDER COLLIE
Oct., 1949
2 Ph(c),Blaze-Son of Fury 300.00
3 Ph(c), Lonely Boy;Feb.,1950 . . 300.00

BLINK
Dec., 2000
1 (of 4) SLo,AKu(c). 3.25
2 SLo,Age of Apocalypse story. . . . 3.25
3 SLo,AKu(c),in love. 3.25
4 SLo,AKu(c),V:Blastaar. 3.25

BLONDE PHANTOM
See: ALL-SELECT
COMICS

BLOOD
Feb., 1988—April, 1988
1 . . . . 6.00
2 thru 4 . . . . @5.00

BLOOD & GLORY
1993
1 KJ Cap & the Punisher 6.00
2 KJ Cap & the Punisher 6.00
3 KJ Cap & the Punisher 6.00

BLOODLINES
Epic, 1992
1 F:Kathy Grant-Peace Corps 6.00

BLOODSEED
1993
1 LSh,I:Bloodseed 2.50
2 LSh,V:Female Bloodseed 2.50

BLOODSTONE
Oct., 2001
1 DAn,ALa,SHa,F:Elsa Bloodstone 3.25
2 DAn,ALa,SHa,F:Dracula 3.25
3 DAn,ALa,SHa,Living Mummy . . . 3.25
4 DAn,ALa,SHa, concl. 3.25

BOOK OF LOST SOULS
Icon, Oct., 2005
1 thru 6 MSz,CDo,Dragons in the
Dishwater. . . . . @3.00

BOOK OF THE DEAD
1993–94
1 thru 5 Horror rep . . . . @4.00

BOOKS OF DOOM
Nov., 2005
1 F:Victor von Doom, early years . . 3.00
2 thru 6 . . . . @3.00

BORN
June, 2003
1 (of 4) GEn(s),O:Punisher. 6.00
2 GEn(s),Capt. Frank Castle 4.00
3 GEn(s),attacked. 4.00
4 GEn(s),concl. 4.00

BREAK THE CHAIN
1 KB,KRS-One,w/audio tape 7.00

BROTHERHOOD, THE
May, 2001
1 BSz(c),F:Magneto 2.75
2A BSz(c), ... 2.50
2B variant cover 2.50
3 BSz(c) 2.50
4 JP,BWS(c) 2.50
5 JP,GF(c). 2.50
6 JP,GF(c) message to daddy 2.50
7 SeP,KW, X speaks out. 2.50
8 SeP,KW, ... 2.50
9 SeP,KW, final issue 2.50

BRUTE FORCE
Aug., 1990
1 JD/JSt 2.50
2 thru 3 . . . . @2.50
4 November, 1990 . . . . 2.50

B-SIDES
Sept., 2002
1 SK, super-team from New Jersey 3.00
2 SK, F:Fantastic Four 3.00
3 SK, F:Fantastic Four 3.00

BUCK DUCK
Marvel Atlas, June, 1953
1 (fa) stories 200.00
2 thru 4 Dec., 1953 . . . . @100.00

BUCKAROO BANZAI
Dec., 1984
1 Movie Adaption 3.00
2 Conclusion, Feb., 1985 . . . . 2.50

BUG
1997
1-shot 48pg. 3.25

BULLET POINTS
Nov., 2006
1 thru 5 MSz(s) . . . . @3.00

BULLSEYE:
GREATEST HITS
Sept., 2004
1 thru 5 SDi,O:Bullseye. . . . . @3.00

BULLWINKLE & ROCKY
Star, Nov., 1987
1 EC&AM,Based on 1960's TV . . . 4.00
2 thru 9 EC&AM . . . . @3.00

CABLE
[Limited Series], 1992
1 JR2,DGr,V:Mutant Liberation
Front,A:Weapon X 4.00
2 JR2,DGr,V:Stryfe,O:Weapon X . . 3.00
[Regular Series], 1993
1 B:FaN(s),ATi,O:Cable,V:New
Canaanites,A:Stryfe,foil(c) 5.00
2 ATi,V:Stryfe. 4.00
3 ATi,A:Six Pack 4.00
4 ATi,A:Six Pack 4.00
5 DaR,V:Sinsear. 4.00
6 DT,A:Tyler,Zero,Askani,
Mr.Sinister,C:X-Men. 4.00
7 V:Tyler,A:Askani,X-Men,Domino . 4.00
8 O:Cable,V:Tyler,A:X-Men,Cable is
Nathan Summers 4.00
9 MCW,B:Killing Field,A:Excalibur,
V:Omega Red 4.00
10 MCW,A:Acolytes,Omega Red. . . 4.00
11 MCW,E:Killing Field,D:Katu 4.00
12 SLo(s),B:Fear & Loathing,
V:Senyaka 4.00
13 V:D'Spayre 4.00
14 V:S'yM. 4.00
15 A:Thorn 4.00
16 Foil(c),Dbl-size,A:Jean,Scott
Logan,V:Phalanx 9.00
16a Newsstand ed. 3.00
17 Deluxe ed. 3.00
17a Newsstand ed. 2.50
18 Deluxe ed. 3.00
18a Newsstand ed. 2.50
19 Deluxe ed. 3.00
19a Newsstand ed. 2.50
20 V:Legion, Deluxe ed. w/card . . . 5.00
20a Newsstand ed. 2.50
21 Cable makes tough decisions,
A:Domino 3.00
22 V:Fortress 3.00
23 IaC,A:Domino 3.00
24 F:Blaquesmith 3.00
25 IaC,SHa,F:Cable's Wife,foil(c) . . 5.00
26 Tries to return to X-Mansion 3.00
27 IaC, A:Domino. 3.00
28 IaC,SHa,concl. war in Genosha . 3.00
29 . . . . 3.00
30 . . . . 3.00
31 IaC, cont.X-Men/Cable war. 3.00
32 Onslaught saga. 3.50
33 Onslaught saga. 3.00
34 Onslaught saga. 3.00
35 Onslaught saga. 3.00
36 . . . . 3.00
37 JLb,IaC,SHa,V:Askani'son,Kane. 3.00
38 JLb,IaC,SHa,V:PSycho-Man,
A:Kane. 3.00
39 JLb,IaC,SHa,V:Psycho-Man 3.00
40 TDz,IaC,SHa,A:Renee Majcomb 3.00
41 TDz,SHa,F:Bishop 3.00
42 TDz,RGr,SHa,The Prophecy
of the Twelve 3.00
43 TDz,RGr,Images of Nathan's
past 3.00

44 TDz,RGr,SHa,A:Madelyne Pryor
(Cable's mom) 3.00
45 JeR,RGr,Zero Tolerance,
No Escape,pt.2 . . . . 3.00
46 JeR,RGr,SHa,Zero Tolerance,
No Escape, pt.2 (of 3) 3.00
47 JeR,RGr,SHa, Operation Zero
Tolerance, V:Batsion 3.00
48 JeR,SHa,V:Hellfire Club 3.00
49 JeR,SHa,V:Hellfire Club 3.00
50 JeR,SHa,A:Cyclops, Phoenix,
Union Jack, 48pg. 4.00
51 JeR,Hellfire Hunt. 2.50
52 JeR,Hellfire Hunt, pt.5. . . . . 2.50
53 JoC,Hellfire Hunt, concl. 2.50
54 JoC,A:Black Panther,V:Klaw. . . . 2.50
55 JoC,A:Irene Merryweather,
Domino 2.50
56 JoC,V:Stilt-Man & Hydro-Man. . . 2.50
57 JoC,Cable powers altered by
EMP wave 2.50
58 JoC,Persecution, pt.1 . . . . 2.50
59 JoC,I:Agent 18,V:Zzaxx 2.50
60 JoC,Nemesis Contract,pt.2. . . . . 2.50
61 JoC,Nemesis Contract,pt.3. . . . . 2.50
62 JoC,Nemesis Contract,pt.4. . . . . 2.50
63 JoC,Blood Brothers,pt.2,x over. . 2.50
64 JoC,O:Cable. 2.50
65 JoC,Millennium countdown 2.50
66 JoC,Sign of the End Times,pt.1 . 2.50
67 JoC,Sign of the End Times,pt.2 . 2.50
68 JoC,Sign of the End Times,pt.3 . 2.50
69 JoC,A:Blaquesmith,Archangel . . 2.50
70 JoC,A:Archangel. 2.50
71 RLd,abandons his destiny,
with RLd poster 2.50
72 RLd,reunited with X-force 2.50
73 RLd,reunited 2.50
74 V:Caliban 2.50
75 RLd,Apocalypse 11.00
76 Apocalypse The 12:pt.6 . . . . . . 8.00
77 Ages of Apocalypse,pt.2 . . . . . 15.00
78 mutant no more. 3.00
79 X-Men: Revolution 3.00
79a variant (c) 3.50
80 Apocalypse gone 2.50
81 The Undying 2.50
82 Nathan Summers, murderer?. . . 2.50
83 R:Domino 2.50
84 Phoenix & Beast. 2.50
85 Mother Askani, Gaunt. 2.50
86 Gaunt 2.50
87 Dream'sEnd,pt.2,x-over 8.00
88 F:Nightcrawler. 2.50
89 in Washington DC. 2.50
90 Dark Sisterhood 2.50
91 Dark Sisterhood 2.50
92 Cable quits X-Men? 2.50
93 V:Dark Sisterhood. 2.50
94 V:Dark Sisterhood. 2.50
95 V:Dark Sisterhood,concl. 2.50
96 Old Man Coll. 2.50
97 Path of Most Resistance. 2.50
98 Shining Path 2.50
99 V:Shining Path 2.50
100 V:Techno-OrganicVirus,64-pg. . 4.50
101 Macedonian Plot. 2.50
102 Albanians' deadly plan 2.50
103 shot in the head 2.50
104 on the wrong side? 2.50
105 in Rio. 2.50
106 In Kazakhstan 2.50
107 final issue 2.50
Ann. '98 AOl(c) F:Cable vs. Machine
Man, O:Bastion 3.00
Ann.1999 48-page 3.50
Minus 1 Spec., TDz,JeR, flashback. 2.50
GN Cable/Wolverine Guts 'N' Glory. 6.00
Cable: Second Genesis. 4.00

CABLE
Mar., 2008
1 Arms, pt.1. . . . . 3.00
1a variant RLd (c). 3.00
2 Divided We Stand, tie-in 3.00
3 Divided We Stand, tie-in 3.00
4 Divided We Stand, tie-in 3.00
5 Messiah CompleX tie-in. 3.00
5a variant MS(c) 3.00
6 Manifest Destiny 3.00
7 F:X-Force. 3.00
8 Waiting for the end of the world. . 3.00
King-Size #1 Cable Spectacular . . . 5.00

CABLE & DEADPOOL
Nov., 2003
1 RLd(c),Looks Could Kill,pt.1 . . . 3.50
2 RLd(c),Looks Could Kill,pt.2 . . . 3.50
3 RLd(c),Looks Could Kill,pt.3 . . . 3.00
4 RLd(c),Looks Could Kill,pt.4 . . . 3.00
5 RLd(c),Looks Could Kill,pt.5 . . . 3.00
6 Looks Could Kill,pt.6 . . . . 3.00
7 Passion of the Cable,pt.1 . . . . . 3.00
8 Passion of the Cable,pt.2 . . . . . 3.00
9 Passion of the Cable,pt.3 . . . . . 3.00
10 Passion of the Cable,pt.4 . . . . . 3.00
11 FaN,Thirty Pieces,pt.1 . . . . 3.00
12 FaN,Thirty Pieces,pt.2 . . . . 3.00
13 A Murder in Paradise,pt.1 . . . . . 3.00
14 A Murder in Paradise,pt.2 . . . . . 3.00
15 Enema of the State,pt.1 . . . . . . 3.00
16 Enema of the State,pt.2 . . . . . . 3.00
17 Enema of the State,pt.3 . . . . . . 3.00
18 Enema of the State,pt.4 . . . . . . 3.00
19 FaN,Why, When I Was Your Age 3.00
20 FaN, Bosom Buddies 3.00
21 FaN, Bosom Buddies 3.00
22 FaN,Bosom Buddier 3.00
23 FaN,Bosom Buddies. 3.00
24 FaN,V:Spider-Man 3.00
25 FaN,Living Legends 3.00
26 FaN,Born Again, pt.1 . . . . 3.00
27 FaN,Born Again, pt.2 . . . . 3.00
28 FaN, ... 3.00
29 FaN, ... 3.00
30 FaN,The Hero Hunter 3.00
31 FaN,For King and Country 3.00
32 FaN, ... 3.00
33 FaN,RLd(c) Domino Principle. . . 3.00
34 FaN,RLd(c). 3.00
35 FaN 3.00
36 FaN,Unfinished Business,pt.1 . . 3.00
37 FaN,Unfinished Business,pt.2 . . 3.00
38 FaN,Unfinished Business,pt.3 . . 3.00
39 FaN,Unifinished Business,pt.4 . . 3.00
40 FaN,Unifinished Business,pt.5 . . 3.00
41 FaN,Fractured, pt.1. . . . . 3.00
42 FaN,Fractured, pt.2. . . . . 3.00
43 FaN,Deadpool & Wolverine 3.00
44 FaN,Deadpool & Wolverine 3.00
45 FaN,F:Capt. America 3.00
46 . . . . 3.00
47 FaN 3.00
48 FaN 3.00
49 . . . . 3.00
50 48-pgs.,series finale 4.00

CABLE & X-FORCE
1995–97
Cable & X-Force '95 Spec. 4.00
Cable & X-Force '96 Spec.48pg. . . 3.50
Cable & X-Force '97 Spec.#1
JFM,CJ,V:Malekith,48pg. 3.50

CADILLACS & DINOSAURS
Epic, Nov., 1990
1 Rep.Xenozoic Tales. 5.00
2 thru 6 Rep.Xenozoic Tales. . . . @3.00

Cage #5
© Marvel Entertainment Group

CAGE
1992–93
1 DT,R:Luke Cage,I:Hardcore, ... 3.00
2 thru 20 . . . . @2.50

CAGE
Marvel Max, Feb., 2002
1 (of 5) RCo,Justice isn't cheap . . . 5.00
2 RCo,teen-age girl murdered 4.00
3 RCo, ... 4.00
4 RCo,secret shame. 4.00
5 RCo,Hammerhead. 4.00

CALL, THE
April, 2003
1 PO, everyday heroes. 2.50
2 thru 4 PO . . . . @2.50

CALL OF DUTY, THE: THE BROTHER HOOD
June, 2002
1 (of 6) ATi,F:FDNY,48-pg. 4.00
2 thru 6 ATi,F:FDNY . . . . @2.50
The Call of Duty, Must Have ed. . . . 3.00

THE CALL OF DUTY: THE PRECINCT
July, 2002
1 (of 5) TMd,F:NYPD 3.00
2 thru 5 TMd . . . . @2.50

THE CALL OF DUTY: THE WAGON
Marvel Aug., 2002
1 (of 4) F:NYC EMS 2.50
2 thru 4 . . . . @2.50

CAMP CANDY
May, 1990
1 thru 6, Oct., 1990 . . . . @4.00

CAPTAIN AMERICA COMICS
Timely/Atlas, 1941–54
1 S&K,SSh,JK(c),Hitler(c),I&O:Capt.
America & Bucky,A:Red Skull,
B:Hurricane, Tuk 190,000.00

Captain America #1
© *Marvel Entertainment Group*

2 S&K,RC,AAv,Hitler(c),
  I:Circular Shield;Trapped
  in the Nazi Stronghold . . . 30,000.00
3 ASh(c),S&K,RC,AAv,Stan Lee's
  1st Text,A:Red Skull,
  Bondage(c) 25,000.00
4 ASh(c),S&K,AAv,Horror
  Hospital 14,000.00
5 S&K,AAv,SSh,Ringmaster's
  Wheel of Death 13,000.00
6 S&K,AAv,SSh,O:Father Time,
  E:Tuk 13,000.00
7 S&K,SSh,A: Red Skull . . . 14,000.00
8 S&K, The Tomb 9,500.00
9 S&K,RC,V:Black Talon 9,500.00
10 S&K,RC,Chamber
  of Horrors 9,500.00
11 AAv,SSh,E:Hurricane;Feuding
  Mountaneers. 9,000.00
12 AAv,SSh,B:Imp,E:Father Time;
  Pygmie's Terror. 7,000.00
13 AAv,O:Secret Stamp,All Out
  For America 8,000.00
14 AAv,V:Japs;Pearl Harbor
  Symbol cover 8,000.00
15 AAv,Den of Doom 8,000.00
16 AAv,A:R.Skull;Captain America
  Unmasked 9,000.00
17 AAv,I:Fighting Fool;
  Graveyard. 6,000.00
18 AAv,SSh,V:Japanese 6,000.00
19 AAv,V:Ghouls,
  B:Human Torch. 5,000.00
20 AAv,A:Sub-Mariner,V:Nazis . 5,000.00
21 SSh(c),Bucky Captured 4,500.00
22 SSh(c),V:Japanese 4,500.00
23 SSh(c),V:Nazis. 4,500.00
24 SSh(c),V:Black
  Dragon Society. 4,500.00
25 SSh(c),V:Japs;Drug Story . . 4,500.00
26 ASh(c),SSh,V:Nazi Fleet . . 4,500.00
27 ASh(c),SSh,AAv,CapAm&Russians
  V:Nazis, E:Secret Stamp . . 4,300.00
28 ASh(c),SSh,Nazi Torture
  Chamber. 4,300.00
29 ASh(c),SSh,V:Nazis;French
  Underground. 4,300.00
30 SSh(c),Bucky Captured 4,300.00
31 ASh(c),Bondage(c). 4,000.00
32 SSh(c),V: Japanese Airforce 4,000.00
33 ASh(c),V:Nazis;BrennerPass 4,000.00
34 SSh(c),Bondage(c) 4,000.00
35 SSh(c),CapA in Japan 4,000.00
36 SSh(c),V:Nazis;Hitler(c). . . . 5,500.00
37 ASh(c),SSh,Captain America
  in Berlin, A:Red Skull 5,000.00
38 ASh(c),V:Japs;Bondage(c). . 4,200.00

39 ASh(c),SSh,V:Japs;Boulder
  Dam 4,200.00
40 ASh(c),V:Japs;Ammo Depot 4,200.00
41 ASh(c),FinalJapaneseWar(c) 4,000.00
42 ASh(c),SSh,V:BankRobbers 4,000.00
43 ASh(c),V:Gangsters 4,000.00
44 ASh(c),V:Gangsters 4,000.00
45 ASh(c),V:Bank Robbers . . . 4,000.00
46 ASh(c),Holocaust(c). 4,500.00
47 ASh(c),Final Nazi War(c) . . . 4,500.00
48 ASh(c),V:Robbers 3,500.00
49 ASh(c),V:Saboteurs 3,500.00
50 ASh(c),V:Gorilla Gang 3,600.00
51 ASh(c),V:Gangsters 3,500.00
52 ASh(c),V:AtomBombThieves 3,500.00
53 ASh(c),V:Burglars 3,500.00
54 ASh(c),TV Studio,
  V:Gangsters 3,500.00
55 SSh,V:Counterfeiters 3,500.00
56 SSh(c),V:Art Theives 3,500.00
57 SSh,AAv,Symbolic CapA(c). 3,500.00
58 ASh(c),V:Bank Robbers 2,600.00
59 SSh(c)O:CapA Retold;Private
  Life of Captain America . . . 5,500.00
60 SSh,V:The Human Fly 2,600.00
61 SSh(c),V:Red Skull;
  Bondage(c). 5,000.00
62 SSh(c),Kingdom of Terror . . 2,600.00
63 SSh(c),AAv,I&O:Asbestos Lady;
  The Parrot Strikes. 3,100.00
64 SSh,Diamonds Spell Doom . 3,200.00
65 SSh,AAv,Friends Turn Foes 3,200.00
66 SSh,O:Golden Girl;Bucky
  Shot 3,800.00
67 SSh,E:Toro(in Human Torch);
  Golden Girl Team-Up 3,500.00
68 A:Golden Girl;Riddle of
  the Living Dolls. 3,500.00
69 Weird Tales of the Wee
  Males, A:Sun Girl 3,500.00
70 A:Golden Girl,Sub-Mariner,
  Namora;Worlds at War. . . . 3,500.00
71 A:Golden Girl; Trapped 3,500.00
72 AAv,Murder in the Mind 3,500.00
73 The Outcast of Time 3,500.00
74 A:Red Skull;Capt.America's
  Weird Tales. 12,000.00
75 Thing in the Chest 3,700.00
76 JR(c),Capt.America,Commie
  Smasher 3,700.00
77 Capt.A,Commie Smasher . . 2,000.00
78 JR(c),V:Communists 2,000.00

CAPTAIN AMERICA
Prev: Tales of Suspense
April, 1968

100 JK,A:Avengers 500.00
101 JK,I:4th Sleeper 150.00
102 JK,V:Red Skull,4th Sleeper . 150.00
103 JK,V:Red Skull 150.00
104 JK,DA,JSo,V:Red Skull. . . . 150.00
105 JK,DA,A:Batroc. 150.00
106 JK,Cap.Goes Wild 150.00
107 JK,Red Skull 150.00
108 JK,Trapster 150.00
109 JK,O:Captain America 200.00
110 JSo,JSt,A:Hulk,Rick Jones
  in Bucky Costume 175.00
111 JSo,JSt,I:Man Killer 175.00
112 JK,GT,Album. 125.00
113 JSo,TP,Avengers,
  D:Madame Hydra 150.00
114 JR,SB,C:Avengers 75.00
115 JB,SB,A:Red Skull 75.00
116 GC,JSt,A:Avengers 75.00
117 JR(c),GC,JSt,I:Falcon 150.00
118 JR(c),GC,JSt,A:Falcon 50.00
119 GC,JSt,O:Falcon 50.00
120 GC,JSt,A:Falcon 50.00
121 GC,JSt,V:Man Brute 35.00
122 GC,JSt,Scorpion 35.00

123 GC,JSt,A:NickFury,
  V:Suprema. 35.00
124 GC,JSt,I:Cyborg 35.00
125 GC,Mandarin. 35.00
126 JK&BEv(c),GC,A:Falcon 35.00
127 GC,WW,A:Nick Fury 35.00
128 GC,V:Satan's Angels 35.00
129 GC,Red Skull 35.00
130 GC,I:Batroc. 35.00
131 GC,V:Hood 35.00
132 GC,A:Bucky Barnes 35.00
133 GC,O:Modok,B:Capt.America/
  Falcon Partnership 35.00
134 GC,V:Stone Face 35.00
135 JR(c),GC,TP,A:Nick Fury 35.00
136 GC,BEv,V:Tyrannus 35.00
137 GC,BEv,A:Spider-Man 40.00
138 JR,A:Spider-Man. 40.00
139 JR,Falcon solo 35.00
140 JR,O:Grey Gargoyle 35.00
141 JR,JSt,V:Grey Gargoyle 25.00
142 JR,JSt,Nick Fury 25.00
143 JR,Red Skull 25.00
144 GM,JR,N:Falcon,V:Hydra 25.00
145 GK,JR,V:Hydra 25.00

Captain America #100
© *Marvel Entertainment Group*

146 JR(c),SB,V:Hydra 22.00
147 GK(c),SB,V:Hydra 22.00
148 SB,JR,Red Skull 22.00
149 GK(c),SB,JM,V:Batroc 22.00
150 K&R(c),SB,V:The Stranger . . . 22.00
151 SB,V:Mr.Hyde 22.00
152 SB,V:Scorpion,Mr.Hyde 22.00
153 SB,JM,V:50's Cap. 22.00
154 SB,V:50's Cap. 22.00
155 SB,FMc,O:50's Cap 22.00
156 SB,FMc,V:50's Cap. 22.00
157 SB,I:The Viper 22.00
158 SB,V:The Viper 22.00
159 SB,V:PlantMan,Porcupine 22.00
160 SB,FMc,V:Solarr 22.00
161 SB,V:Dr.Faustus 22.00
162 JSn(c),SB,V:Dr.Faustus 22.00
163 SB,I:Serpent Squad 22.00
164 JR(c),I:Nightshade 22.00
165 SB,FMc,V:Yellow Claw 22.00
166 SB,FMc,V:Yellow Claw 22.00
167 SB,V:Yellow Claw 22.00
168 SB,I&O:Phoenix
  (2nd Baron Zemo). 22.00
169 SB,FMc,C:Black Panther 22.00
170 K&R(c),SB,C:Black Panther . . 22.00
171 JR(c),SB,A:Black Panther. . . . 22.00
172 GK(c),SB,C:X-Men 25.00
173 GK(c),SB,A:X-Men 28.00
174 GK(c),SB,A:X-Men 28.00

MARVEL

175 SB,A:X-Men	28.00
176 JR(c),SB,O:Capt.America	18.00
177 JR(c),SB,A:Lucifer,Beast	15.00
178 SB,A:Lucifer	15.00
179 SB,A:Hawkeye	15.00
180 GK(c),SB,I:1st Nomad(Cap)	25.00
181 GK(c),SB,I&O:New Cap	20.00
182 FR,Madam Hydra	10.00
183 GK(c),FR,R:Cap,D:New Cap	10.00
184 K&R(c),HT,A:Red Skull	10.00
185 GK(c),SB,FR,V:Red Skull	10.00
186 GK(c),FR,O:Falcon	15.00
187 K&R(c),FR,V:Druid	10.00
188 GK(c),SB,V:Druid	10.00
189 GK(c),FR,V:Nightshade	10.00
190 GK(c),FR,A:Nightshade	10.00
191 FR,A:Stilt Man,N.Fury	10.00
192 JR(c),FR,A:Dr.Faustus	10.00
193 JR(c),JK,`Mad Bomb'	20.00
194 JK,I:Gen.Heshin	22.00
195 JK,1984	22.00
196 JK,Madbomb	22.00
197 JK,Madbomb	22.00
198 JK,Madbomb	22.00
199 JK,Madbomb	22.00
200 JK,Madbomb	20.00
201 JK,Epilogue	13.00
202 JK,Night People	15.00
203 JK,Night People	15.00
204 JK,I:Argon	15.00
205 JK,V:Argon	15.00
206 JK,I:Swine	15.00
207 JK,V:Swine	15.00
208 JK,I:Arnim Zola,D:Swine	15.00
209 JK,O:Arnim Zola,I:Primus	15.00
210 JK,A:Red Skull	15.00
211 JK,A:Red Skull	15.00
212 JK,A:Red Skull	15.00
213 JK,I:Night Flyer	15.00
214 JK,D:Night Flyer	15.00
215 GT,Redwing	10.00
216 Reprint,JK	10.00
217 JB, I:Quasar(Marvel Boy) I:Vamp	10.00
218 SB,A:Iron Man	6.00
219 SB,JSt,V:TheCorporation	6.00
220 SB,D:L.Dekker	6.00
221 SB,Ameridroid	6.00
222 SB,I:Animus(Vamp)	6.00
223 SB,Animus	6.00
224 MZ,V:Animus	6.00
225 SB,A:Nick Fury	6.00
226 SB,A:Nick Fury	6.00
227 SB,A:Nick Fury	6.00
228 SB,Constrictor	6.00
229 SB,R:SuperAgents of Shield	6.00
230 SB,A:Hulk	8.00
231 SB,DP,A:Grand Director	6.00
232 SB,DP,V:Grand Director	6.00
233 SB,DP,D:Sharon Carter	6.00
234 SB,DP,A:Daredevil	6.00
235 SB,FM,A:Daredevil	8.00
236 SB,V:Dr.Faustus	6.00
237 SB,`From the Ashes'	6.00
238 SB,V:Hawk Riders	6.00
239 JBy(c),SB,V:Hawk Riders	6.00
240 SB,V:A Guy Named Joe	6.00
241 A:Punisher	30.00
241a 2nd printing	4.00
242 JSt,A:Avengers	6.00
243 GP(c),RB,V:Adonis	6.00
244 TS,`A Monster Berserk',RRegan	7.00
245 CI,JRn,Nazi Hunter	6.00
246 GP(c),JBi,V:Joe	6.00
247 JBy,V:BaronStrucker	10.00
248 JBy,JRu,Dragon Man	10.00
249 JBy,O:Machinesmith, A:Air-Walker	10.00
250 JBy,Cap for Pres	10.00
251 JBy,V:Mr.Hyde	10.00
252 JBy,V:Batrok	10.00
253 JBy,V:Baron Blood	10.00

254 JBy,D:B.Blood,UnionJack,I:3rd Union Jack	10.00
255 JBy,40th Anniv.,O:Cap	10.00
256 GC,V:Demon Druid	3.50
257 A:Hulk	3.50
258 MZ,V:Blockbuster	3.50
259 MZ,V:Dr. Octopus	3.50
260 AM,In Jail	3.50
261 MZ,A:Nomad	4.00
262 MZ,V:Ameridroid	3.50
263 MZ,V:Red Skull	3.50
264 MZ,X-Men	4.00
265 MZ,A:Spider-Man,N.Fury	3.50
266 MZ,A:Spider-Man	3.50
267 MZ,V:Everyman	3.00
268 MZ,A:Defenders(x-over from Def.#106)	3.00
269 MZ,A:Team America	3.00
270 MZ,V:Tess-One	3.00
271 MZ,V:Mr.X	3.00
272 MZ,I:Vermin	3.50
273 MZ,A:Nick Fury	3.00
274 MZ,D:SamSawyer	3.00
275 MZ,V:Neo-Nazis	3.00
276 MZ,V:Baron Zemo	3.00
277 MZ,V:Baron Zemo	3.00
278 MZ,V:Baron Zemo	3.00
279 MZ,V:Primus	3.00
280 MZ,V:Scarecrow	3.00
281 MZ,A:Spider Woman, R:`50's Bucky	3.00
282 MZ,I:2nd Nomad	6.00
282a (second primting)	2.50
283 MZ,A:Viper	4.00
284 SB,Nomad	3.00
285 MZ,V:Porcupine	3.00
286 MZ,V:Deathlok	5.00
287 MZ,V:Deathlok	5.00
288 MZ,V:Deathlok,D:Hellinger	5.00
289 MZ,A:Red Skull	3.00
290 JBy(c),RF,A:Falcon	3.00
291 JBy(c),HT,V:Tumbler	3.00
292 I&O:Black Crow	3.00
293 V:Mother Superior	3.00
294 R:Nomad	3.00
295 V:Sisters of Sin	3.00
296 V:Baron Zemo	4.00
297 O:Red Skull	4.00
298 V:Red Skull	4.00
299 V:Red Skull	3.00
300 D:Red Skull	4.00
301 PNe,A:Avengers	3.00
302 PNe,I:Machete,V:Batroc	3.00
303 PNe,V:Batroc	3.00
304 PNe,V:Stane Armor	3.00
305 PNe,A:Capt.Britain,V:Modred	3.00
306 PNe,A:Capt.Britain,V:Modred	3.00
307 PNe,I:Madcap	3.00
308 PNe,V:Armadillo, Secret Warsll	3.00
309 PNe,V:Madcap	3.00
310 PNe,V:Serpent Society,I:Cotton Mouth,Diamondback	3.00
311 PNe,V:Awesome Android	3.00
312 PNe,I:Flag Smasher	3.00
313 PNe,D:Modok	3.00
314 PNe,A:Nighthawk	3.00
315 PNe,V:Serpent Society	3.00
316 PNe,A:Hawkeye	3.00
317 PNe,I:Death-Throws	3.00
318 PNe,V&D:Blue Streak	3.00
319 PNe,V:Scourge,D:Vamp	3.00
320 PNe,V:Scourge	3.00
321 PNe,V:Flagsmasher, I:Ultimatum	3.00
322 PNe,V:Flagsmasher	3.00
323 PNe,I:Super Patriot (US Agent)	5.00
324 PNe,V:Whirlwind,Trapster	3.00
325 I:Slug,A:Nomad	3.00
326 V:Dr.Faustus	3.00
327 MZ(c)V:SuperPatriot	4.00

328 MZ(c),I:Demolition Man	3.00
329 MZ(c),A:Demolition Man	3.00
330 A:Night Shift,Shroud	3.00
331 A:Night Shift,Shroud	3.00
332 BMc,Rogers resigns	8.00
333 B:John Walker Becomes 6th Captain America	5.00
334 I:4th Bucky	5.00
335 V:Watchdogs	4.00
336 A:Falcon	3.00
337 TMo,I:The Captain	3.00
338 KD,AM,V:Professor Power	3.00
339 KD,TD,Fall of Mutants, V:Famine	3.00
340 KD,AM,A:Iron Man,	3.00
341 KD,AM,I:Battlestar,A:Viper	3.00
342 KD,AM,A:D-Man,Falcon,	3.00
343 KD,AM,A:D-Man,Falcon, Nomad,Viper	3.00
343 KD,AM,A:D-Man,Falcon, Nomad	3.00
344 KD,AM,A:D-Man,Nomad	4.00
345 KD,AM,V:Watchdogs	4.00
346 KD,AM,V:Resistants	4.00
347 KD,AM,V:RWinger&LWinger	4.00
348 KD,AM,V:Flag Smasher	4.00
349 KD,AM,V:Flag Smasher	4.00
350 KD,AM,doub-size,Rogers Ret. as Captain Am,V:Red Skull, E:6th Cap	5.00
351 KD,AM,A:Nick Fury	3.00
352 KD,AM,I:Supreme Soviets	3.00
353 KD,AM,V:Supreme Soviets	3.00
354 KD,AM,I:USAgent, V:Machinesmith	3.50
355 RB,AM,A:Falcon,Battlestar	3.00
356 AM,V:Sisters of Sin	3.00
357 KD,AM,V:Sisters of Sin Baron Zemo,Batroc	3.00
358 KD,B:Blood Stone Hunt	3.00
359 KD,V:Zemo,C:Crossbones	3.00
360 KD,I:Crossbones	3.00
361 KD,V:Zemo,Batroc	3.00
362 KD,V:Zemo,Crossbones	3.00
363 KD,E:Blood Stone Hunt, V:Crossbones,C:Wolverine	3.00
364 KD,V:Crossbones	3.00
365 KD,Acts of Vengeance, V:SubMariner,Red Skull	3.00
366 1st RLm Capt.Amer.,Acts of Vengeance,V:Controller	3.00
367 KD,Acts of Vengeance, Magneto Vs. Red Skull	3.00
368 RLm,V:Machinesmith	3.00
369 RLm,I:Skeleton Crew	3.00

Captain America #366 ©
© Marvel Entertainment Group

370 RLm,V:Skeleton Crew....... 3.00
371 RLm,V:Trump,Poundcakes.... 3.00
372 RLm,B:Streets of Poison,
　Cap on Drugs,C:Bullseye 3.00
373 RLm,V:Bullseye,A:Bl.Widow ... 3.00
374 RLm,V:Bullseye,A:Daredevil... 3.00
375 RLm,V:Daredevil............ 3.00
376 RLm,A:Daredevil............ 3.00
377 RLm,V:Crossbones,Bullseye .. 3.00
378 RLm,E:Streets of Poison,Red
　Skull vs Kingpin,V:Crossbones . 3.00
379 RLm(c),V:Serpent Society 3.00
380 RLm,V:Serpent Society...... 3.00
381 RLm,V:Serpent Society...... 3.00
382 RLm,V:Serpent Society...... 3.00
383 RLm(c),RLm,50th Anniv.
　64Pages 5.00
384 RLm,A:Jack Frost........... 2.50
385 RLm,A:USAgent 2.50
386 RLm,Cap./USAgent T.U...... 2.50
387 B:Superia Strategem 2.50
388 A:Paladin................. 2.50
389 Superia Strategem #3....... 2.50
390 Superia Strategem #4....... 2.50
391 Superia Strategem #5....... 2.50
392 E:Superia Strategem........ 2.50
393 V:Captain Germany 2.50
394 A:Red Skull,Diamondback ... 2.50
395 A:Red Skull,Crossbones 2.50
396 I:2nd Jack O'Lantern........ 2.50
397 V:Red Skull,X-Bones,Viper.... 2.50
398 Operation:Galactic Storm
　Pt.1,V:Warstar 2.50
399 Operation Galactic Storm
　Pt.8,V:Kree Empire 2.50
400 Operation Galactic Storm
　Pt.15,BU:rep.Avengers #4..... 4.00
401 R:D-Man,A:Avengers 2.50
402 RLe,B:Man & Wolf,
　A:Wolverine............... 2.50
403 RLe,A:Wolverine........... 2.50
404 RLe,A:Wolverine........... 2.50
405 RLe,A:Wolverine........... 2.50
406 RLe,A:Wolverine........... 2.50
407 RLe,A:Wolverine,Cable....... 2.50
408 RLe,E:Man & Wolf........... 2.50
409 RLe,V:Skeleton Crew 2.50
410 RLe,V:Crossbones,Skel.Crew . 2.50
411 RLe,V:Snapdragon.......... 2.50
412 RLe,V:Batroc,A:Shang-Chi.... 2.50
413 A:Shang-Chi,V:Superia...... 2.50
414 RLe,A:Ka-Zar,Black Panther... 2.50
415 Rle,A:Black Panther,Ka-Zar ... 2.50

416 RLe,Savage Land Mutates,
　A:Black.Panther,Ka-Zar....... 2.50
417 RLe,A:Black Panther,Ka-Zar,
　V:AIM................... 2.50
418 RLe,V:Night People 2.50
419 RLe,V:Viper................ 2.50
420 RLe,I:2nd Blazing Skull,
　A:Nightshift 3.00
421 RLe,V:Nomad............. 2.50
422 RLe,I:Blistik.............. 2.50
423 RTs(s),MCW,V:Namor........ 2.50
424 MGv(s),A:Sidewinder 2.50
425 B:MGu(s),DHv,Embossed(c),
　I:2nd SuperPatriot,DeadRinger . 4.00
426 DHv,A:Super Patriot,Dead
　Ringer,V:Resistants 2.50
427 DHv,V:Super Patriot,Dead
　Ringer 2.50
428 DHv,I:Americop............ 2.50
429 DHv,V:Kono.............. 2.50
430 Daemon Dran, Americop 2.50
431 DHv,I:Free Spirit 2.50
432 DHv,Fighting Chance 2.50
433 DHv,Baron Zemo 2.50
434 DHv,A:Fighting Spirit,
　V:King Cobra 2.50
435 DHv,Fighting Chance 2.50
436 V:King Cobra, Mister Hyde,
　Fighting Chance conclusion .. 2.50
437 Cap in a Coma 2.50
438 I:New Body Armor.......... 2.50
439 Dawn's Early Light,pt.2 ...... 2.50
440 Taking A.I.M.,pt.1 .... 2.50
441 Taking A.I.M.,pt.3 .... 2.50
442 Batroc, Cap,V:Zeitgeist...... 2.50
443 MGu,24 hours to live 2.50
444 MWa,RG,President Kidnapped . 6.00
445 MWa,RG,R:Captain America... 4.00
446 MWa,RG,Operation
　Rebirth,pt.2 .... 4.00
447 MWa,RG,Op.Rebirth,pt.3 ..... 4.00
448 MWa,RG,Operation
　Rebirth,pt.4,double size..... 6.00
449 MWa,RG,A:Thor 4.00
450 MWa,RG,Man Without a
　Country, pt,1 .... 4.00
450a alternate cover 4.00
451 MWa,RG,DRo,Man Without
　A Country,pt.2,new costume .. 3.50
452 MWa,RG,Man Without a
　Country, pt.3 A. B Clinton 4.00
453 MWa,RG Man Without a
　Country, concl.,old costume .. 3.50
454 MWa,RG,A:Avengers 3.50
Ann.#1 rep. 75.00
Ann.#2 rep. 40.00
Ann.#3 JK,.................. 30.00
Ann.#4 JK,V:Magneto,I:Mutant
　Force 30.00
Ann.#5 `Deathwatcher' 6.00
Ann.#6 A:Contemplator 6.00
Ann.#7 O:Shaper of Worlds...... 6.00
Ann.#8 MZ,A:Wolverine 45.00
Ann.#9 MBa,SD,Terminus Factor
　#1,N:Nomad 4.50
Ann.#10 MM,Baron Strucker,pt.3
　(see Punisher Ann.#4)........ 4.00
Ann.#11 Citizen Kang#1 .... 4.00
Ann.#12 I:Bantam,w/card......... 4.00
Ann.#13 RTs(s),MCW,......... 4.00
Drug Wars PDd(s),SaV,A:New
　Warriors.................. 3.00
G-Size#1 GK(c),rep.O:Cap Amer.. 7.00
Medusa Effect RTs(s),MCW,RB,
　V:Master Man 3.50
Movie Adapt 3.00
Spec.#1 Rep.Cap.A #110,#111 .... 2.50
Spec.#2 Rep.Cap.A.#113
　& Strange Tales #169 .... 2.50
Collector's Preview 2.50
Ashcan 2.50

Captain America Vol 2 #7
© *Marvel Entertainment Group*

[2nd Series], Nov., 1996

1 RLd,CDi,JSb, Heroes Reborn,
　I:Nick Fury,48pg.............. 7.00
1A Stars and stripes background
　variant cover 7.50
1b gold signature edition,
　cardstock cover............ 15.00
1c San Diego Con edition....... 25.00
2 RLd,JLb,JSb,Falcon & Red Skull 3.00
3 RLd,JLb,JSb,A:Hulk,V:Red Skull
　& Master Man 3.00
4 RLd,JLb,JSb,F:Prince Namor,... 3.00
5 RLd,JLb,JSb,V:Crossbones..... 3.00
6 RLd,JLb,JSb,Industrial
　Revolution, epilogue,A:Cable .. 3.00
7 RLd,JLb,DaF,................ 3.00
8 RLd,JLb,SPa,A:Nick Fury,
　WWII story................ 3.00
9 JLb,RLd,SPa,WWII story....... 3.00
10 JLb,RLd,SPa,WWII story, concl.. 3.00
11 JeR,JoB,Odyssey acrose
　America, pt.4, concl. 3.00
12 JeR,JoB,Heroes Reborn, Galactus
　concl..................... 4.00
13 JeR,RLm,Wildstorm x-over..... 3.00
Ashcan, ComicCon 5.00

[3rd Series], Nov., 1997

1 MWa,RG,BWi,A:Lady Deathstrike,
　Red Skull, Sharon Carter, 48pg 4.00
1a variant cover 8.00
2 MWa,RG,BWi,A devastating loss. 5.00
2a variant cover 4.00
3 MWa,RG,BWi,V:Hydra......... 4.00
4 MWa,RG,BWi,F:Batroc......... 3.00
5 MWa,RG,BWi,V:Hordes of Hydra 3.00
6 MWa,RG,V:Skrulls 3.00
7 MWa,NKu,Power & Glory concl. . 3.00
8 MWa,Nku,Live Kree or Die, pt.2
　x-over.................... 3.50
9 MWa,NKu,American Nightmare,
　pt.1..................... 3.00
10 MWa,NKu,American Nightmare,
　pt.2..................... 3.00
11 MWa,NKu,American
　Nightmare, pt.3 .... 3.00
12 MWa,NKu,American Night-
　mare, pt.4, 48-page.......... 4.00
13 MWa,MFm,R:Red Skull 2.50
14 MWa,MFm,R:Red Skull 2.50
15 MWa,NKu,V:Red Skull 2.50
16 MWa,NKu,V:Red Skull 2.50
17 MWa,NKu,V:Red Skull 2.50
18 MWa,LW,RbC,V:Cosmic Cube
　double-size 3.50

Captain America #436
© *Marvel Entertainment Group*

19 MWa,NKu,V:2 foes	2.50
20 MWa,NKu,Shield secrets	2.50
21 MWa,NKu,A:Black Panther	2.50
22 MWa,NKu,A:Black Panther	2.50
23 MWa,Capt.America convict?.	2.50
24 TDF,RF,V:Hydra	2.50
25 DJu,NKu,DGr,Twisted Tomorrows,pt.1	4.00
26 DJu,NKu,DGr,Twisted,pt.2	2.50
27 DJu,NKu,DGr,Twisted,pt.3	2.50
28 DJu,NKu,DGr,V:CountNefaria	2.50
29 DJu,DGr,A:Ka-Zar	2.50
30 DJu,DGr,NKu,Savage Land	2.50
31 DJu,NKu,DGr,F:Sharon Carter	2.50
32 DJu,JO,kidnapped	2.50
33 DJu,ATi,Protocide	2.50
34 DJu,ATi,Cache	2.50
35 DJu,ATi,Protocide	2.50
36 DJu,ATi,Maximum Security	2.50
37 DJu,ATi,V:Protocide	2.50
38 DJu,ATi,Capt.Am. unleashed	2.50
39 DJu,V:A.I.M.	2.50
40 DJu,V:A.I.M.	2.50
41 DJu,Batroc the Leaper	2.50
42 DJu,BL,V:Crimson Dynamo	2.50
43 DJu,DR,BL,A:David Ferrari.	2.50
44 DJu,BL,A:Taskmaster	2.50
45 DJu,BL,America Lost,pt.1	2.50
46 DJu,BL,America Lost,pt.2	2.50
47 DJu,BL,America Lost,pt.3	2.50
48 DJu,BL,America Lost,pt.4	2.50
49 DJu,BL,F:Sam Wilson.	2.50
50 96-page, last issue	6.50
Ann.1998 Captain America/ Citizen V,KBk,KK, 48-page	4.00
Ann. 1999 JoC,V:Flag Smasher	4.00
Ann.2000 DJu,DGr,48-pg.	4.00
Ann.2001 DJu,48-page	3.50
Spec.#1 Captain America (2000).	2.50
Spec.Cap: A Universe X Special	4.00
GN Captain America/Nick Fury: The Otherworld War (2001).	7.00

CAPTAIN AMERICA
April, 2002

1 JNR(s), terrorism, 48-pg.	4.00
2 JNR(s), terrorism,pt.2	3.50
3 JNR(s), terrorism,pt.3	3.50
4 JNR(s), terrorism,pt.4	3.50
5 JNR(s), terrorism,pt.5	3.50
6 JNR(s), terrorism,concl.	3.50
7 JNR(s)	3.50
8 JNR(s),Extremists,pt.2	3.50
9 JNR(s),Extremists,pt.3	3.50
10 JNR(s),Extremists,pt.4	3.50
11 JNR(s),Extremists,pt.5	3.50
12 JNR(s),JaL,Ice,pt.1	3.50
13 JNR(s),JaL,Ice,pt.2	3.50
14 JNR(s),JaL,Ice,pt.3	3.50
15 JNR(s),JaL,Ice,pt.4	3.50
16 JNR(s),JaL,Ice,pt.5	3.50
17 LW,Cap.Am Lives Again,pt.1	3.50
18 LW,Cap.Am Lives Again,pt.2	3.50
19 LW,Cap.Am Lives Again,pt.3	3.50
20 LW,Cap.Am Lives Again,pt.4	3.50
21 CBa,Homeland,pt.1.	3.00
22 CBa,Homeland,pt.2.	3.00
23 CBa,Homeland,pt.3.	3.00
24 CBa,Homeland,pt.4.	3.00
25 CBa,Homeland,pt.5.	3.00
26 CBa,F:Bucky Barnes	3.00
27 ECa.	3.00
28 ECa.	3.00
29 Avengers Disassembled tie-in	3.00
30 Avengers Disassembled,pt.2	3.00
31 Avengers Disassembled,pt.3	3.00
32 SEa,Disassembled,tie-in,pt.4	3.00

CAPTAIN AMERICA
Nov., 2004

1 SEp,V:Red Skull	6.00

Captain America #00
© Marvel Entertainment Group

2 SEp,	5.00
3 SEp,F:Sharon Carter	4.00
4 SEp,home from Europe	4.00
5 SEp,flash-backs	4.00
6 SEp,Out of Time, finale	4.00
7 SEp,Winter Soldier,pt.1	4.00
7a variant (c).	3.00
8 SEp,Winter Soldier,pt.1	4.00
8a variant (c).	3.00
9 SEp,Winter Soldier,pt.2	3.00
10 SEp,Winter Soldier,pt.3.	3.00
11 SEp,Winter Soldier,pt.4	3.00
12 SEp,Winter Soldier,pt.5.	3.00
13 SEp,Winter Soldier,pt.	3.00
14 SEp,Winter Soldier,pt.	3.00
15 A:Crossbones, Sin	3.00
16 F:Crossbones, Sin	3.00
17 F:Corssbones, Sin	3.00
18 SEp,Twenty-First Century Blitz	3.00
19 SEp,Twenty-First Century Blitz	3.00
20 SEp,Twenty-First Century Blitz	3.00
21 SEp,Twenty-First Century Blitz	3.00
22 Civil War tie-in.	3.00
23 Civil War tie-in.	3.00
24 Civil War tie-in.	3.00
25 SEp, Death of a Dream, pt.1	4.00
25a variant (c)	4.00
25b director's cut	4.00
26 SEp, Death of a Dream, pt.2	3.00
27 SEp, Death of a Dream, pt.3	3.00
28 SEp, New Serpent Squad.	3.00
29 SEp, Winter Soldier	3.00
30 SEp, Winter Soldier	3.00
31 SEp,Prisoner of Red Skull	3.00
32 SEp,Death of Capt. America.	3.00
33 SEp,V:Iron Man.	3.00
34 SEp,Death of Capt.America	3.00
35 SEp,A city gone insane.	3.00
36 SEp,Second act concl.	3.00
37 SEp,Act three	3.00
38 SEp,New Captain America	3.00
39 SEp,Two Captain Americas?	3.00
40 SEp,Two Captain Americas	3.00
41 SEp,Death of Captain America	3.00
42 SEp,Death of Captain America	3.00
43 LRs,New Captain America	3.00
44 LRs,New Captain America,pt 2.	3.00
44a variant SB (c)	3.00
Spec. 65th Anniversary #1, 48-pg.	5.00
Spec. Captain America White #0.	4.00
Ann. #1 Ultimate Captain America.	4.00
Spec. Theater of War, Operation Zero Point	4.00

CAPTAIN AMERICA & THE FALCON
March, 2004

1 BS,Two Americas,pt.1	3.00
2 BS,Two Americas,pt.2	3.00
3 BS,Two Americas,pt.3	3.00
4 BS,Two Americas,pt.4	3.00
5 Avengers Disassembled tie-in	3.00
6 Avengers Disassembled,pt.2	3.00
7 Avengers Disassembled,pt.3	3.00
8 JoB,Brothers & Keepers,pt.1	3.00
9	3.00
10	3.00
11 CPr(s),JoB,Brothers & Keepers	3.00
12 CPr(s),JoB,Brothers & Keepers	3.00
13 CPr(s),DJu,American Psycho	3.00
14 CPr(s),DJu,finale.	3.00

CAPTAIN AMERICA: DEAD MAN RUNNING
Jan., 2002

1 (of 3) distress call	3.25
2	3.25
3 concl.	3.25

CAPTAIN AMERICA: SENTINEL OF LIBERTY
July, 1998

1 MWa,RG,new foe, in future	2.50
1 signed by MWa & RG	5.00
2A MWa,RG(c&a) F:Invaders, V:Nazis	2.50
2B variant JSm(c).	2.50
3 MWa,RG,DGr,A:Sub-Mariner.	2.50
4 MWa,RG,DGr,A:Human Torch	2.50
5 MWa,RG,MFm,Tales of Suspense,pt.1	2.50
6 MWa,RG,MFm,Tales of Suspense pt.2	3.50
7 RSt,RF,civil war tale concl.	2.50
8 MWa,R:Falcon	2.50
9 MWa,A:Falcon	2.50
10 psychedelic look back.	2.50
11 MWa,A:Human Torch	2.50
12 MWa,DGr,F:Bucky,48-page	3.50
Spec.RoughCut #1,MWa,RG,48-pg	3.00

CAPTAIN AMERICA: THE CHOSEN
Sept., 2007

1 thru 6 (of 6)	@4.00
1a thru 5a variant (c)	@4.00

CAPTAIN AMERICA: WHAT PRICE GLORY
March, 2003

1 thru 4 SR	@3.25

CAPTAIN AMERICA: WHITE
Oct., 2008

1 (of 6) JLb(s).	4.00
0 Director's Cut.	4.00

CAPTAIN BRITAIN AND MI13
May, 2008

1 Secret Invasion tie-in.	3.00
2 Secret Invasion tie-in.	3.00
3 Secret Invasion tie-in.	3.00
4 Secret Invasion tie-in.	3.00
5 Blade is Back.	3.00
5a Monkey variant	3.00
6 Hell Comes to Birmingham,pt.1.	3.00
7 Hell Comes to Birmingham,pt.2.	3.00

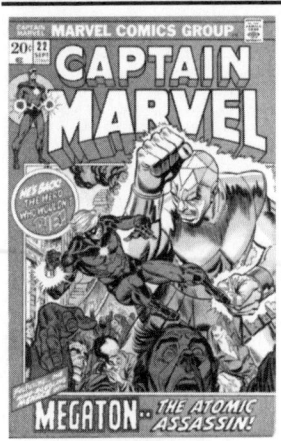

Captain Marvel-#22
© *Marvel Entertainment Group*

CAPTAIN MARVEL
May, 1968
1 GC,O:retold,V:Sentry#459 .... 225.00
2 GC,V:Super Skrull 100.00
3 GC,V:Super Skrull 60.00
4 GC,Sub-Mariner............. 60.00
5 DH,I:Metazoid 60.00
6 DH,I:Solam 40.00
7 JR(c),DH,V:Quasimodo 40.00
8 DH,I:Cuberex 40.00
9 DH,D:Cuberex 40.00
10 DH,V:Number 1............. 40.00
11 BWS(c),I:Z0................ 40.00
12 K&R(c),I:Man-Slayer......... 25.00
13 FS,V:Man-Slayer 25.00
14 FS,Iron Man 25.00
15 TS,DA,Z0 .... 22.00
16 DH,Ronan 22.00
17 GK,DA,O;R.Jones ret,N:Capt.
    Marvel 25.00
18 GK,JB,DA,I:Mandroid 22.00
19 GK,DA,Master.of.MM 22.00
20 GK,DA,I:Rat Pack........... 22.00
21 GK,DA,Hulk................ 22.00
22 GK(c),WB,V:Megaton 22.00
23 GK(c),WB,FMc,V:Megaton 22.00
24 GK(c),WB,ECh,I:L.Mynde..... 22.00
25 1st JSn,Cap.Marvel,Cosmic
    Cube Saga Begins 50.00
26 JSn,DC,Thanos(2ndApp.)
    A:Thing 50.00
27 JSn,V:Thanos,A:Mentor,
    Starfox, I:Death 45.00
28 JSn,DGr,Thanos Vs.Drax,
    A:Avengers 45.00
29 JSn,AM,O:Zeus,C:Thanos
    I:Eon,O:Mentor 30.00
30 JSn,AM,Controller,C:Thanos .. 30.00
31 JSn,AM,Avengers,
    Thanos,Drax,Mentor 35.00
32 JSn,AM,DGr,O:Drax,
    Moondragon,A:Thanos 35.00
33 JSn,KJ,E:Cosmic Cube Saga
    1st D:Thanos 45.00
34 JSn,JA,V:Nitro(leads to
    his Death) 30.00
35 GK(c),AA,Ant Man 10.00
36 AM,Watcher,Rep.CM#1 ...... 10.00
37 AM,KJ,Nimrod.............. 10.00
38 AM,KJ,Watcher 10.00
39 AM,KJ,Watcher 10.00
40 AM,AMc,Watcher 10.00
41 AM,BWr,CR,BMc,TA,Kree..... 12.00
42 AM,V:Stranger,C:Drax....... 10.00
43 AM,V:Drax................. 10.00

44 GK(c),AM,V:Drax 12.00
45 AM,I:Rambu 12.00
46 AM,TA,D:Fawn 10.00
47 AM,TA,A:Human Torch 10.00
48 AM,TA,I:Chetah............. 10.00
49 AM,V:Ronan,A:Cheetah 10.00
50 AM,TA,Avengers,
    V:Super Adaptiod........... 11.00
51 AM,TA,V:Mercurio,4-D Man ... 12.00
52 AM,TA,V:Phae-dor 10.00
53 AM,TA,A:Inhumans.......... 10.00
54 PB,V:Nitro 10.00
55 PB,V:Death-grip 10.00
56 PB,V:Death-grip 10.00
57 PB,V:Thor,A;Thanos 15.00
58 PB,Drax/Titan 10.00
59 PB,Drax/Titan,I:Stellarax..... 10.00
60 PB,Drax/Titan 10.00
61 PB,V:Chaos 10.00
62 PB,V:Stellarax............. 10.00
G-Size #1 reprints 10.00

CAPTAIN MARVEL
1989
1 MBr,I:Powerkeg,V:Moonstone ... 3.00
1 DyM(s),MBr,V:Skinhead(1993) .. 2.50
PF Death of Captain Marvel 8.00
1995
1 FaN,R:Captain Marvel(son of)... 4.00
2 FaN,V:X-Treme,Erik the Red.... 3.00
3 FaN,V:X-treme............... 3.00
4 thru 6 FaN .... @3.00
Jan., 2000
1A PDd,Ccs,A:Rick Jones 5.00
1B variant JOy (c).............. 5.50
2 PDd,Ccs.................. 7.00
3 PDd,Ccs,V:Wendigo 3.00
4 PDd,Ccs,A:Moondragon 3.00
5 PDd,Ccs,V:Drax............. 3.00
6 PDd,Ccs,V:Marlo 3.00
7 PDd,Ccs,A:Comet Man 3.00
8 PDd,Ccs,V:Super-Skrull....... 3.00
9 PDd,Ccs,V:Hyssta 3.00
10 PDd,Ccs,V:Genis 3.00
11 PDd,JSn 3.00
12 PDd,Ccs,Maximum Security.... 3.00
13 PDd,Ccs,V:klds of Yon-Rogg ... 3.00
14 PDd,Ccs,F:Psycho-Man 3.00
15 PDd,Ccs,F:Psycho-Man 3.00
16 PDd,Ccs,V:Psycho-Man 3.00
17 PDd,JSn,AM,V:Thanos........ 3.00
18 PDd,JSn,AM,A:Thor,Thanos.... 3.00
19 PDd,Ccs,A:Thor,Thanos 3.00
20 PDd,Ccs,.................. 3.00
21 PDd,Ccs,.................. 3.00
22 PDd,Ccs,Supreme Intelligence.. 3.00
23 PDd,Ccs,.................. 3.00
24 PDd,Ccs,Negative Zone 3.00
25 PDd,Ccs,V:Quasar,.......... 3.00
26 PDd,F:Rick Jones,'Nuff Said ... 3.00
27 PDd,CCs,Time Flies,pt.1 ...... 3.00
28 PDd,Time Flies, pt.2 .... 3.00
29 PDd,Time Flies, pt.3 .... 3.00
30 PDd,Time Flies, pt.4 .... 3.00
31 PDd,Ccs,F:Marlo,V:Mephisto... 3.00
32 PDd,Ccs,F:Moondragon 3.00
33 PDd,Ccs,V:Magus........... 3.50
34 PDd,Ccs,V:Magus,Rick Jones .. 3.00
35 PDd, last issue 3.00
Sept., 2002
1 PDd,Ccs, U-Decide.......... 3.00
1b Variant JJu(c)............... 2.50
1c Variant AxR(c) 2.50
2 PDd,Ccs,F:Punisher 2.50
3 PDd,Ccs,AxR............... 2.50
3a Director's Cut, AxR, 40-pg. 3.50
4 PDd,CCs 2.50
5 PDd,CCs 2.50
6 PDd,CCs 2.50
7 PDd,A:Thor,pt.1 .... 2.50
8 PDd,A:Thor,pt.2 .... 3.00

9 PDd,Coven,pt.1 .... 3.00
10 PDd,Coven,pt.2............. 3.00
11 PDd,Coven,pt.3............. 3.00
12 PDd,Coven,pt.4............. 3.00
13 PDd,Pop,V:Badoon........... 3.00
14 PDd,accidents do happen. 3.00
15 PDd,NA(c),V:Kree........... 3.00
16 PDd,Crazy Like a Fox,pt.2 ..... 3.00
17 PDd,Crazy Like a Fox,pt.3 ..... 3.00
18 PDd,Crazy Like a Fox,pt.4 ..... 3.00
19 PDd,Odyssey,pt.1 .... 3.00
20 PDd,Odyssey,pt.2 .... 3.00
21 PDd,Odyssey,pt.3 .... 3.00
22 PDd,AsL,Odyssey,pt.4 .... 3.00
23 PDd,AsL,Odyssey,pt.5 .... 3.00
24 PDd,Odyssey,pt.6 .... 3.00
25 PDd,Exit Strategy 3.00
Nov., 2007
1 (of 5) 3.00
2 thru 5 Secrt Infiltration .... @3.00

CAPTAIN PLANET
Oct., 1991
1 I&O:Captain Planet 5.00
2 thru 12 .... @3.00

Capt Savage #1
© *Marvel Entertainment Group*

CAPT. SAVAGE & HIS LEATHERNECK RAIDERS
Jan., 1968
1 SSh(c),C:Sgt Fury;The Last
    Bansai 75.00
2 SSh(c),O:Hydra;Return of Baron
    Strucker 35.00
3 SSh,Two Against Hydra....... 35.00
4 SSh,V:Hydra;The Fateful Finale 35.00
5 SSh,The Invincible Enemy 35.00
6 Mission;Save a Howler 35.00
7 SSh,Objective:Ben Grimm 35.00
8 Mission:Foul Ball 35.00
Becomes:

CAPT. SAVAGE & HIS BATTLEFIELD RAIDERS
1968
9 .... 35.00
10 To the Last Man 35.00
11 A:Sergeant Fury 35.00
12 V:The Japanese 35.00
13 The Junk Heap Juggernauts... 35.00
14 Savage's First Mission 35.00
15 Within the Temple Waits Death. 30.00
16 V:The Axis Powers 30.00
17 V:The Axis Powers 30.00

18 V:The Axis Powers 30.00
19 March, 1970 . . . . 30.00

CAPTAIN UNIVERSE
Nov., 2005
1 F:Hulk 3.00
2 F:Daredevil 3.00
3 F:X-23 . . . . 3.00
4 F:Invisible Woman 3.00
5 F:Silver Surfer 3.00

CARE BEARS
Star, Nov., 1985
1 . . . . 4.00
2 thru 14 . . . . @4.00
Marvel 1988
15 thru 20 . . . . @4.00

CARNAGE
1-shot Carnage: Its a Wonderful
　Life (1996). 3.00
1-shot Carnage: Mindbomb
　foil cover (1996). 3.50

CARTOON KIDS
Marvel Atlas, 1957
1 JMn,A:Dexter the Demon, Little
　Zelda,Willie,Wise Guy 150.00

CAR WARRIORS
Epic, 1990
1 Based on Roll Playing Game . . . 2.50
2 Big Race Preparations. 2.50
3 Ft.Deloranian-Lansing Race begin. 2.50
4 Race End, Final issue 2.50

CASEY–CRIME
PHOTOGRAPHER
Aug., 1949
1 Ph(c),Girl on the Docks 325.00
2 Ph(c),Staats Cotsworth 250.00
3 Ph(c),He Walked With Danger 250.00
4 Ph(c),Lend Me Your Life 250.00
Becomes:
TWO GUN WESTERN
[1st Series], 1950
5 JB,B,I&O:Apache Kid 300.00
6 JMn,The Outcast 225.00
7 Human Sacrifice 225.00
8 JR,DW,A:Kid Colt,Texas Kid,
　Doc Holiday 225.00
9 JMn,GM,A:Kid Colt,Marshall
　'Frosty' Bennet Texas Kid . . . 225.00
10 . . . . 225.00
11 thru 14 JMn,June, 1952 . . . @150.00

CAT, THE
Nov., 1972—June, 1973
1 JM,I&O:The Cat 50.00
2 JM,V:The Owl 25.00
3 BEv,V:Kraken 25.00
4 JSn,V:Man-Bull 30.00

CAUGHT
Marvel-Vista Publications, 1956
1 JSe,Crime 350.00
2 MD,JSe 200.00
3 MMe,Al,JSe 200.00
4 MMe,JSe 200.00
5 RC,JSe,BK. 200.00

CENTURY:
DISTANT SONS
1996
1-shot DAn,48pg. 3.25

Cat #1
© Marvel Entertainment Group

CHAMBER OF CHILLS
Nov., 1972
1 SSh,A Dragon Stalks By
　Night,(H.Ellison Adapt.) 40.00
2 FB,BEv,SD,Monster From the
　Mound,(RE Howard Adapt.) . . 20.00
3 FB,BEv,SD, Thing on the Roof . 20.00
4 FB,BEv,SD, Opener of the
　Crypt,(J.Jakes,E.A.Poe Adapt) 20.00
5 FB,BEv,SD, Devils Dowry 20.00
6 FB,BEv,SD, Mud Monster 20.00
7 thru 24 FB,BEv,SD . . . . @20.00
25 FB,BEv,SD Nov., 1976 . . . . . . 20.00

CHAMBER OF DARKNESS
Oct., 1969
1 JB, Tales of Maddening Magic 125.00
2 NA(script),Enter the Red Death. 75.00
3 JK, BWS,JB, Something Lurks
　on Shadow Mountain. 60.00
4 JK Monster Man Came Walking,
　BU:BWS 125.00
5 JCr,JK,SD, And Fear Shall
　Follow, plus Lovecraft adapt. . . 50.00
6 SD 50.00
7 SD,JK,BWr, Night of the
　Gargoyle 75.00
8 BWr(c),DA,BEv, Beast that Walks
　Like a Man Special, 5 Tales of
　Maddening Magic, Jan.,1972 125.00
Becomes:
MONSTERS ON
THE PROWL
1971
9 SAD,BWS,Monster Stories
　Inc,Gorgilla 45.00
10 JK,Roc 25.00
11 JK,A Titan Walks the Land 25.00
12 HT,JK,Gomdulla The Living
　Pharoah 25.00
13 HT,JK,Tragg 30.00
14 JK,SD,Return of the Titan. 30.00
15 FrG,JK,The Thing Called It 25.00
16 JSe,SD,JK, Serpent God of
　Lost Swamp,A:King Kull 25.00
17 JK,SD,Coming of Colossus . . . 25.00
18 JK,SD,Bruttu 25.00
19 JK,SD,Creature From the
　Black Bog 25.00
20 JK,SD,Oog Lives Again 25.00
21 JK,SD,A Martian Stalks
　the City 25.00
22 JK,SD,Monster Runs Amok . . 18.00

23 JK,The Return of Grogg 18.00
24 JK,SD, Magnetor 18.00
25 JK,Colossus Lives Again 18.00
26 JK,SD,The Two Headed Thing . 18.00
27 JK,Sserpo 18.00
28 JK,The Coming of Monsteroso. 18.00
29 JK,SD Monster at my Window . 18.00
30 JK,Diablo Demon from the 5th
　Dimension, Oct., 1974. . . . . . . 18.00

CHAMPIONS
Oct., 1975
1 GK(c),DH,I&O:Champions. 50.00
2 DH,O:Champions. 20.00
3 GT,Assault on Olympus 20.00
4 GT,'Murder at Malibu' 20.00
5 DH,I:Rampage 20.00
6 JK(c),GT,V:Rampage 20.00
7 GT,O:Black Widow,I:Darkstar . 20.00
8 BH,O:Black Widow 20.00
9 BH,BL,V:Crimson Dynamo 20.00
10 BH,BL,V:Crimson Dynamo 20.00
11 JBy,A:Black Goliath,Hawkeye . 25.00
12 JBy,BL,V:Stranger. 25.00
13 JBy,BL V:Kamo Tharn. 25.00
14 JBy,I:Swarm 25.00
15 JBy,V:Swarm. 25.00
16 BH,A:Magneto,Dr.Doom,
　Beast 20.00
17 GT,JBy,V:Sentinels,last issue . . 20.00

CHAMPIONS, THE
Sept., 2007
1 . . . . 3.00

CHILI
May, 1969
1 Millie's Rival. 125.00
2 . . . . 75.00
3 Millie and Chilli. 80.00
4 . . . . 75.00
5 . . . . 75.00
6 thru 15 . . . . @50.00
16 thru 20 . . . . @40.00
21 thru 25 . . . . @35.00
26 Dec., 1973. . . . . 35.00
Spec.#1, 1971. . . . . 45.00

CHUCK NORRIS
Star, Jan.–Sept., 1987
1 SD 4.00
2 thru 5 . . . . @5.00

CINDY COMICS
See: KRAZY COMICS

CITIZEN V
April, 2001
1 (of 3) FaN,F:V-Battalion. 3.25
2 FaN,. 3.25
3 FaN,F:Iron Cross 3.25

CITIZEN V
& THE V BATTALION:
THE EVERLASTING
Feb., 2002
1 (of 4) FaN, ... 3.25
2 FaN,Marduk 3.25
3 FaN,. 3.25
4 FaN, concl. 3.25

CIVIL WAR
May, 2006
1 F: everybody, x-over-48-pg 8.00
1a Turner variant (c) 32.00
1b director's cut, 64-pg. 6.00
1c Turner sketch (c) 50.00

All comics prices listed are for *Near Mint* condition.

2 Spider-Man 7.00
2a Turner variant (c) 6.00
2b 2nd printing 6.00
3 Thor 5.00
3a Turner variant (c) 15.00
4 Goliath 3.50
4a Turner variant (c) 7.00
5 . . . . 4.00
5a Turner variant (c) 7.00
6 . . . . 4.00
6a Turner variant (c) 7.00
7 . . . . 3.00
7a Turner variant (c) 3.00
Spec. Civil War Files #1 . . . . 4.00
Spec. Daily Bugle Civil War issue 0.50
Spec. Battle Damage Report 4.00
Spec. The Initiative, BMB,WEI,MS .5.00
Spec. The Return, PJe (2007) 3.00
Spec. War Crimes (2006) 4.00

CIVIL WAR CHRONICLES
July, 2007
1 PJe 5.00
2 MSz(s),RG 5.00
3 MSz(s),RG 5.00
4 PJe 5.00
5 MSz(s),RG 5.00
6 thru 12 MSz(s) . . . . @5.00

CIVIL WAR: FRONT LINE
June, 2006
1 Embeded 5.00
2 thru 10 . . . . @4.00
11 PJe 4.00

CIVIL WAR: HOUSE OF M
Sept., 2008
1 thru 3 (of 5) . . . . @3.00

CIVIL WAR: X-MEN
July, 2006
1 . . . . 4.00
1a variant (c) 10.00
2 thru 4 . . . . @3.50

CIVIL WAR: YOUNG
AVENGERS & RUNAWAYS
July, 2006
1 . . . . 4.00
2 thru 4 . . . . @3.50

CLANDESTINE
Oct., 1994–Sept., 1995
Preview issue, Intro (1994) 2.50
1 MFm,AD,foil(c). 3.25
2 Wraparound (c),A:Silver Surfer . . 2.75
3 I:Argent,Kimera,A:SilverSurfer . . . 2.75
4 R:Adam 2.75
5 MFm,AD,O:Adam Destine 2.75
6 A:Spider-Man 2.75
7 A:Spider-Man 2.75
8 A:Dr.Strange. 2.75
9 thru 14 . . . . @2.75

Feb., 2008
1 thru 5 AD . . . . @3.00

CLASSIC CONAN
See: CONAN SAGA

CLASSIC X-MEN
See: X-MEN

CLAWS
Aug., 2006
1 JP,F:Wolverine & Black Cat 4.00
2 JP 4.00
3 JP 4.00

CLIVE BARKER'S
BOOK OF THE DAMNED
Epic, Nov., 1991
1 JBo,Hellraiser companion 5.00
2 MPa,Hellraiser Companion 5.00

CLIVE BARKER'S
HELLRAISER
Epic, 1989–93
1 BWr,DSp 7.00
2 . . . . 6.00
3 . . . . 6.50
4 . . . . 6.00
5 . . . . 6.00
6 . . . . 7.00
7 The Devil's Brigade #1 . . . . 7.00
8 The Devil's Brigade #2&3 . . . . . 7.00
9 The Devil's Brigade #4&5 . . . . . 7.00
10 The Devil's Brigade #6&7
   foil Cover 7.00
11 The Devil's Brigade #8&9 . . . . . 6.00
12 The Devil's Brigade #10-12 . . . . 6.00
13 MMi,RH,Devil's Brigade #13 . . . . 6.00
14 The Devil's Brigade #14 . . . . . . 6.00
15 The Devil's Brigade #15 . . . . . . 6.00
16 E:Devil's Brigade 6.00
17 BHa,DR,The Harrowing 10.00
18 O:Harrowers 6.00
19 A:Harrowers 6.00
20 NGa(s),DMc,Last Laugh 9.00
Dark Holiday Spec.#1 (1992) 6.00
Spring Slaughter Spec.#1 (1994). . . 7.00
Summer Spec.#1 (1992 . . . . 6.00

CLOAK & DAGGER
(Limited Series) Oct., 1983
1 RL,TA,I:Det.O'Reilly,
   Father Delgado 3.00
2 RL,TA,V:Duane Hellman 3.00
3 RL,TA,V:Street Gang 3.00
4 RL,TA,O:Cloak & Dagger, ... 3.00

CLOAK & DAGGER
[1st Regular Series], July, 1985
1 RL,Pornography. 3.00
2 RL,Dagger's mother 2.50
3 RL,A:Spider-Man 2.50
4 RL,Secret Wars II 2.50
5 RL,I:Mayhem 2.50
6 RL,A:Mayhem 2.50
7 RL,A:Mayhem 2.50
8 TA, Drugs. 2.50
9 AAd,TA,A:Mayhem. 2.75
10 BBI,TA,V:Dr. Doom 2.50
11 BBI,TA,Last Issue 2.50

[Mutant Misadventures of]
CLOAK & DAGGER
[2nd Regular Series]
Oct., 1988
1 CR(i),A:X-Factor 3.00
2 CR(i),C:X-Factor,V:Gromitz 2.50
3 SW(i),JLe(c),A:Gromitz 2.50
4 TA(i),Inferno,R:Mayhem 2.50
5 TA(i),R:Mayhem 2.50
6 TA(i),A:Mayhem 2.50
7 A:Crimson Daffodil,V:Ecstacy . . . 2.50
8 Acts of Vengeance prelude 2.50
9 Acts of Vengeance. 2.50
10 Acts of Vengeance,X-Force
   name used,Dr.Doom 2.50
11 . . . . 2.50
12 A:Dr.Doom. 2.50
13 A:Dr.Doom. 2.50
14 & 15 RL . . . . @2.50
16 RL,A:Spider-Man 2.50
17 A:Spider-Man, ... 2.50

18 Inf.Gauntlet X-over,
   A:Spider-Man, Ghost Rider 2.50
19 O:Cloak & Dagger,final issue . . . 2.50

Codename Genetix #1
© Marvel Entertainment Group

CODENAME: GENETIX
1993
1 PGa,A:Wolverine 3.00
2 PGa,V:Prime EvilA:Wolverine . . . 3.00
3 . . . . 3.00
4 A:Wolverine,Ka-Zar 3.00

CODE OF HONOR
1996
1 thru 4 (of 4) CDi,TnS,I:Jeff Piper,
   fully painted . . . . @6.00

CODE NAME: SPITFIRE
See: SPITFIRE AND
THE TROUBLESHOOTERS

COLOSSUS
Aug., 1997
1-shot BRa,Colossus & Meggan
   V:Arcade, 48pg 3.50

COLOSSUS:
GOD'S COUNTRY
PF V:Cold Warriors 7.00

COMBAT
Marvel Atlas, June, 1952
1 JMn,War Stories, Bare
   Bayonets 350.00
2 RH, Break Thru,(Dedicated to
   US Infantry) 200.00
3 JMn(c) 150.00
4 BK 160.00
5 thru 10 . . . . @150.00
11 April, 1953 . . . . 200.00

COMBAT CASEY
See: WAR COMBAT

COMBAT KELLY AND
THE DEADLY DOZEN
Marvel Atlas, Nov., 1951
1 RH,Korean War Stories 400.00
2 Big Push 200.00
3 The Volunteer 175.00
4 JMn,V:Communists 175.00
5 JMn,OW,V:Communists 175.00

MARVEL

MARVEL

6 V:Communists 175.00	
7 JMn,V:Communists 175.00	
8 JMn,Death to the Reds 175.00	
9 . . . . 175.00	
10 JMn(c). 175.00	
11 . . . . 150.00	
12 thru 16. . . . . @150.00	
17 A:Combat Casey. 175.00	
18 A:Battle Brady. 125.00	
19 V:Communists. 125.00	
20 V:Communists 125.00	
21 Transvestite Cover 75.00	
22 thru 40 . . . . @100.00	
41 thru 44 Aug., 1957 . . . . @100.00	

COMBAT KELLY
June, 1972
1 JM, Stop the Luftwaffe. 40.00
2 The Big Breakout. 20.00
3 O:Combat Kelly 25.00
4 Mutiny,A:Sgt.Fury and the
   Howling Commandoes 25.00
5 Escape or Die 20.00
6 The Fortress of Doom 20.00
7 Nun Hostage,V:Nazis 20.00
8 V:Nazis. 20.00
0 Oct., 1973 . . . . 20.00

COMBAT ZONE
Jan., 2005
1 (of 5) DJu,G.I.s in Iraq 3.00
2 DJu 3.00
3 DJu,Hellfires to Avoid Damnation 3.00
4 and 5 . . . . @3.00

COMEDY COMICS
Marvel Timely, 1942
9 BEv,BW,The Fin,Capt Dash. 5,000.00
10 Fourth Musketeer. 3,500.00
11 Vagabonds 750.00
12 . . . . 250.00
13 Funny animal 250.00
14 Super Rabbit 750.00
15 . . . . 200.00
16 . . . . 200.00
17 . . . . 200.00
18 . . . . 200.00
19 . . . . 200.00
20 . . . . 200.00
21 thru 32 . . . . @150.00
33 HK 200.00
34 BW 300.00
Becomes:

MARGIE COMICS
Marvel Comics, 1946
35 thru 39 Glamour Girl . . . . . @250.00
40 . . . . 200.00
41 thru 49 . . . . @225.00
Becomes:

RENO BROWNE
Marvel Comics, 1950
50 Photo(c); Western babe 400.00
51 Photo(c); 350.00
52 Photo(c); 350.00

COMEDY COMICS
Marvel Animirth 1948–49
1 HK, Romance,F:Hedy, Millie,
   Tessie 500.00
2 . . . . 200.00
3 . . . . 200.00
4 HK, 'Hey Look'. 225.00
5 . . . . 125.00
6 . . . . 125.00
7 . . . . 125.00
8 . . . . 125.00
9 . . . . 125.00
10 . . . . 125.00

COMET MAN
Feb., 1987
1 BSz(c),I:Comet Man 2.50
2 BSz(c),A:Mr.Fantastic 2.50
3 BSz(c),A:Hulk 2.50
4 BSz(c),A:Fantistic Four 2.50
5 BSz(c),A:Fantastic Four. 2.50
6 BSz(c),Last issue, July,1987 . . . 2.50

COMIC CAPERS
Marvel Comics, 1944
1 Funny animal, Super Rabbit . . 350.00
2 . . . . 200.00
3 . . . . 150.00
4 . . . . 150.00
5 . . . . 150.00
6 . . . . 150.00

COMICS FOR KIDS
Marvel Timely, 1945
1 Funny animal 300.00
2 . . . . 300.00

COMIX BOOK
(black & white magazine) 1974
1 BW. 40.00
2 BW. 30.00
3 . . . . 25.00
4 & 5 . . . . @30.00

COMIX ZONE
1 thru 2 video game tie-in . . . . . @2.50

COMMANDO ADVENTURES
Marvel Atlas, June, 1957
1 Seek, Find and Destroy. 200.00
2 MD, Hit 'em and Hit 'em
   Hard, Aug.,1957 . . . . 125.00

COMPLETE COMICS
See: AMAZING COMICS

COMPLETE MYSTERY
Aug., 1948
1 Seven Dead Men 650.00
2 Jigsaw of Doom 500.00
3 Fear in the Night 500.00
4 A Squealer Dies Fast. 500.00
Becomes:

TRUE COMPLETE MYSTERY
1949
5 Rice Mancini,
   The Deadly Dude 325.00
6 Ph(c),Frame-up that Failed . . . 250.00
7 Ph(c),Caught 250.00
8 Ph(c),The Downfall of Mr.
   Anderson, Oct., 1949 . . . . . . 250.00

CONAN
1995–96
1 Pit Fighter 3.00
2 LHa,Hyborean tortue factory 3.00
3 V:Cannibals 3.00
4 LHa,JP,Rune Conan Prelude. . . . 3.00
5 LHa,V:yeti 3.00
6 LHa, the plague 3.00
7 LHa,BBI,V:The Iron Man 3.00
8 thru 11 . . . . @3.00

...DEATH COVERED IN GOLD
July, 1999
1 (of 3) RTs. 3.00
2 RTs. 3.00
3 RTs,JB,concl. 3.00

CONAN THE ADVENTURER
1994–95
1 RT(s),RK,Red Foil(c). 3.00
2 RT(s),RK 2.50
3 RT(s),RK 2.50
4 thru 14 . . . . @2.50

CONAN THE BARBARIAN
Oct., 1970
1 BWS/DA,O:Conan,A:Kull. 400.00
2 BWS/SB,Lair o/t Beast-Men . . 150.00
3 BWS,SB,Grey God Passes . . . 250.00
4 BWS,SB,Tower o/t Elephant . . 125.00
5 BWS,Zukala's Daughter 125.00
6 BWS,SB,Devil Wings Over
   Shadizar 100.00
7 BWS,SB,DA,C:Thoth-Amon,
   I:Set. 100.00
8 BWS,TS,TP,Keepers o/t Crypt. 100.00
9 BWS,SB,Garden of Fear 100.00
10 BWS,SB,JSe,Beware Wrath of
   Anu;BU:Kull 125.00
11 BWS,SB,Talons of Thak 125.00
12 BWS,GK,Dweller in the Dark,
   Blood of the Dragon B.U. 75.00
13 BWS,SB,Web o/t Spider-God . 75.00
14 BWS,SB,Green Empress of
   Melnibone 75.00
15 BWS,SB 75.00
16 BWS,Frost Giant's Daughter . . 70.00
17 GK,Gods of Bal-Sagoth,
   A:Fafnir 50.00
18 GK,DA,Thing in the Temple,
   A:Fafnir 50.00
19 BWS,DA,Hawks from
   the Sea 70.00
20 BWS,DA,Black Hound of
   Vengeance,A:Fafnir. 70.00
21 BWS,CR,VM,DA,SB, Monster
   of the Monoliths. 60.00
22 BWS,DA,rep.Conan #1. . . . . . 60.00
23 BWS,DA,Shadow of the
   Vulture,I:Red Sonja 85.00
24 BWS,Song of Red Sonja 85.00
25 JB,SB,JSe,Mirrors of Kharam
   Akkad,A:Kull 30.00
26 JB,Hour of the Griffin 20.00
27 JB,Blood of Bel-Hissar 20.00
28 JB,Moon of Zembabwei 20.00
29 JB,Two Against Turan. 20.00
30 JB,The Hand of Nergal 20.00
31 JB,Shadow in the Tomb 15.00

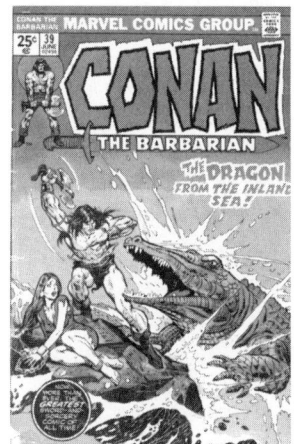

Conan the Barbarian #39
© Marvel Entertainment Group

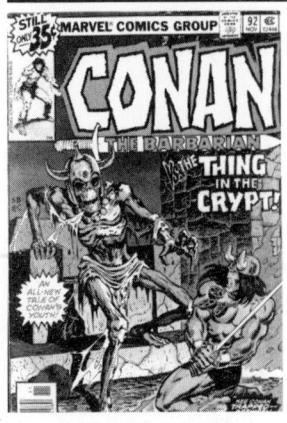

Conan the Barbarian #92
© Marvel Entertainment Group

32 JB,Flame Winds of Lost Khitai . 15.00
33 JB,Death & 7 Wizards 15.00
34 JB,Temptress in the Tower
   of Flame 15.00
35 JB,Hell-Spawn of Kara-Shehr . . 15.00
36 JB,Beware of Hyrkanians
   bearing Gifts 15.00
37 NA,Curse of the Golden Skull . . 30.00
38 JB,Warrior & Were-Woman . . . 12.00
39 JB,Dragon from the
   Inland Sea 12.00
40 RB,Fiend from Forgotten City . . 12.00
41 JB,Garden of Death & Life 15.00
42 JB,Night of the Gargoyle 15.00
43 JB,Tower o/Blood,A:RedSonja . 15.00
44 JB,Flame&Fiend,A:RedSonja . . 15.00
45 JB,NA,Last Ballad of
   Laza-Lanti 12.00
46 JB,NA,JSt,Curse of the
   Conjurer. 12.00
47 JB,DA,Goblins in the
   Moonlight 12.00
48 JB,DG,DA,Rats Dance at Raven
   gard,BU:Red Sonja 12.00
49 JB,DG,Wolf-Woman 12.00
50 JB,DG,Dweller in the Pool 12.00
51 JB,DG,Man Born of Demon 8.00
52 JB,TP,Altar and the Scorpion . . . 8.00
53 JB,FS,Brothers of the Blade 8.00
54 JB,TP,Oracle of Ophir 8.00
55 JB,TP,Shadow on the Land 8.00
56 JB,High Tower in the Mist 8.00
57 MP,Incident in Argos 8.00
58 JB,Queen o/tBlackCoast,
   2nd A:Belit 10.00
59 JB,Ballad of Belit,O:Belit. 7.00
60 JB,Riders o/t River Dragons 7.00
61 JB,She-Pirate,I:Amra 7.00
62 JB,Lord of the Lions,O:Amra . . . 7.00
63 JB,Death Among Ruins,
   V&D:Amra 7.00
64 JSon,AM,rep.Savage Tales#5 . . 7.00
65 JB,Fiend o/tFeatheredSerpent . . 7.00
66 JB,Daggers & Death Gods,
   C:Red Sonja 6.00
67 JB,Talons of the Man-Tiger,
   A:Red Sonja 6.00
68 JB,Of Once & Future Kings,
   V:KingKull,A:Belit,Red Sonja . . 6.00
69 VM,Demon Out of the Deep 6.00
70 JB,City in the Storm 6.00
71 JB,Secret of Ashtoreth 6.00
72 JB,Vengeance in Asgalun 6.00
73 JB,..In the Well of Skelos 6.00
74 JB,Battle at the Black Walls
   C:Thoth-Amon 6.00

75 JB,Hawk-Riders of Harakht 7.00
76 JB,Swordless in Stygia 7.00
77 JB,When Giants Walk
   the Earth 7.00
78 JB,rep.Savage Sword #1,
   A:Red Sonja 7.00
79 HC,Lost Valley of Iskander 7.00
80 HC,Trial By Combat 6.00
81 HC,The Eye of the Serpent 5.00
82 HC,The Sorceress o/t Swamp . . 5.00
83 HC,The Dance of the Skull 5.00
84 JB,Two Against the Hawk-City,
   I:Zula 5.00
85 JB,Of Swordsmen & Sorcerers,
   O:Zulu 5.00
86 JB,Devourer of the Dead 5.00
87 TD, rep. Savage Sword #3. . . . . 5.00
88 JB,Queen and the Corsairs 5.00
89 JB,Sword & the Serpent,
   A:Thoth-Amon 5.00
90 JB,Diadem of the Giant-Kings . . 5.00
91 JB,Savage Doings in Shem 5.00
92 JB,The Thing in the Crypt. 5.00
93 JB,Of Rage & Revenge 5.00
94 JB,BeastKing ofAbombi,L:Zulu . . 5.00
95 JB,The Return of Amra 5.00
96 JB,Long Night of Fang
   & Talon,pt.1 . . . . 5.00
97 JB,Long Night of Fang
   & Talon,pt.2 . . . . 5.00
98 JB,Sea-Woman 5.00
99 JB,Devil Crabs o/t Dark Cliffs . . . 5.00
100 JB,Death on the Black Coast,
   D:Belit (double size) 7.00
101 JB,The Devil has many Legs . . 3.00
102 JB,The Men Who
   Drink Blood. 3.00
103 JB,Bride of the Vampire 3.00
104 JB,The Vale of Lost Women . . . 3.00
105 JB,Whispering Shadows. 3.00
106 JB,Chaos in Kush 3.00
107 JB,Demon of the Night 3.00
108 JB,Moon-Eaters of Darfar. 3.00
109 JB,Sons of the Bear God 3.00
110 JB,Beward the Bear of Heaven 3.00
111 JB,Cimmerian Against a City. . . 3.00
112 JB,Buryat Besieged 3.00
113 JB,A Devil in the Family 3.00
114 JB,The Shadow of the Beast . . 3.00
115 JB,A War of Wizards, A:Red
   Sonja Double size 10th Anniv.
   (L:Roy Thomas script). 4.00
116 JB,NA,Crawler in the Mist. 5.00
117 JB,Corridor of Mullah-Kajar. . . . 3.00
118 JB,Valley of Forever Night 3.00
119 JB,Voice of One Long Gone . . . 3.00
120 JB,The Hand of Erlik. 3.00
121 JB,BMc,Price of Perfection 3.00
122 JB,BMc,The City Where Time
   Stood Still. 3.00
123 JB,BMc,Horror Beneath the
   Hills 3.00
124 JB,BMc,the Eternity War. 3.00
125 JB,BMc,the Witches ofNexxx . . 3.00
126 JB,BMc,Blood Red Eye
   of Truth 3.00
127 GK,Snow Haired Woman
   of the Wastes 3.00
128 GK,And Life Sprang Forth
   From These 3.00
129 GK,The Creation Quest 3.00
130 GK,The Quest Ends 3.00
131 GK,The Ring of Rhax 3.00
132 GK,Games of Gharn 3.00
133 GK,The Witch of Windsor 3.00
134 GK,A Hitch in Time 3.00
135 MS,JRu,Forest of the Night . . . 3.00
136 JB,The River of Death 3.00
137 AA,Titans Gambit 3.00
138 VM,Isle of the Dead 3.00
139 VM,In the Lair of
   the Damned 3.00

140 JB,Spider Isle 3.00
141 JB,The Web Tightens 3.00
142 JB,The Maze,the Man,
   the Monster 3.00
143 JB,Life Among the Dead 3.00
144 JB,The Blade & the Beast 3.00
145 Son of Cimmeria 3.00
146 JB,Night o/t Three Sisters 3.00
147 JB,Tower of Mitra 3.00
148 JB,The Plague of Forlek 3.00
149 JB,Deathmark 3.00
150 JB,Tower of Flame 3.00
151 JB,Vale of Death 3.00
152 JB,Dark Blade of
   Jergal Zadh 3.00
153 JB,Bird Men of Akah Ma'at 3.00
154 JB,the Man-Bats of
   Ur-Xanarrh. 3.00
155 JB,SL,The Anger of Conan 3.00
156 JB,The Curse 3.00
157 JB,The Wizard 3.00
158 JB,Night of the Wolf 3.00
159 JB,Cauldron of the Doomed . . . 3.00
160 Veil of Darkness 3.00
161 JB,House of Skulls,A:Fafnir . . . 3.00
162 JB,Destroyer in the Flame,
   A:Fafnir 3.00
163 JB,Cavern of the Vines of
   Doom,A:Fafnir 3.00
164 The Jeweled Sword of Tem . . . 3.00
165 JB,V:Nadine 3.00
166 JB,GI,Blood o/t Titan,A:Fafnir . . 3.00
167 JB,Creature From Time's
   Dawn,A:Fafnir 3.00
168 JB,Bird Woman & the Beast . . . 3.00
169 JB,Tomb of the Scarlet Mage . . 3.00
170 JB,Dominion of the Dead,
   A&D:Fafnir 3.00
171 JB,Barbarian Death Song 3.00
172 JB,Reavers in Borderland 3.00
173 JB,Honor Among Thieves 3.00
174 JB,V:Tetra 3.00
175 JB,V:Spectre ofDeath 3.00
176 JB,Argos Rain 2.50
177 JB,V:Nostume 2.50
178 JB,A:Tetra,Well of Souls 2.50
179 JB,End of all there is,A:Kiev . . . 2.50
180 JBV:AnitRenrut 2.50
181 JB,V:KingMaddoc II 2.50
182 JB,V:King of Shem 2.50
183 JB,V:Imhotep 2.50
184 JB,V:Madoc. 2.50
185 JB,R:Tetra 2.50
186 JB,The Crimson Brotherhood . . 2.50

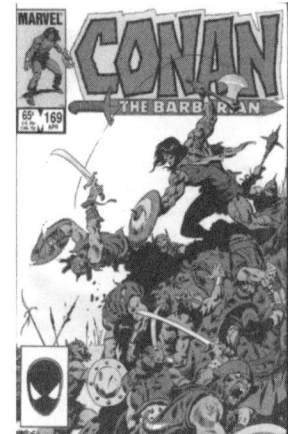

Conan The Barbarian #169
© Marvel Entertainment Group

MARVEL

187 JB,V:Council of Seven	2.50
188 JB,V:Devourer-Souls	2.50
189 JB,V:Devourer-Souls	2.50
190 JB,Devourer-Souls	2.50
191 Deliverance	2.50
192 JB,V:TheKeeper	2.50
193 Devourer-Souls	2.50
194 V:Devourer-Souls	2.50
195 Blood of Ages	2.50
196 V:Beast	2.50
197 A:Red Sonja	2.50
198 A:Red Sonja	2.50
199 O:Kaleb	2.50
200 JB,D.sizeV:Dev-Souls	5.00
201 NKu,GI,Thulsa Doom	2.50
202	2.50
203 V:Thulsa Doom	2.50
204 VS,GI,A:Red Sonja,I:Strakkus	2.50
205 A:Red Sonja	2.50
206 VS,GI,Heku trilogy,pt.1	2.50
207 VS,GI,Heku,pt.2,O:Kote	2.50
208 VS,GI,Heku,pt.3	2.50
209 VS,GI,Heku epilogue	2.50
210 VS,GI,V:Sevante	2.50
211 VS,GI,V:Sevante	2.50
212 EC,GI	2.50
213 V:Ghamud Assassins	2.50
214 AA	2.50
215 VS,AA,Conan Enslaved	2.50
216 V:Blade of Zed	2.50
217 JLe(c),V:Blade of Zed	2.50
218 JLe(c),V:Picts	2.50
219 JLe(c),V:Forgotten Beasts	2.50
220 Conan the Pirate	2.50
221 Conan the Pirate	2.50
222 AA,DP,Revenge	2.50
223 AA,Religious Cult	2.50
224 AA,Cannibalism	2.50
225 AA,Conan Blinded	2.50
226 AA,Quest for Mystic Jewel	2.50
227 AA,Mystic Jewel,pt.2	2.50
228 AA,Cannibalism,pt.1	2.50
229 AA,Cannibalism,pt.2	2.50
230 FS,SDr,Citadel,pt.1	2.50
231 FS,DP,Citadel,pt.2	2.50
232 RLm,Birth of Conan	3.00
233 RLm,DA,B:Conan as youth	2.50
234 RLm,DA	2.50
235 RLm,DA	2.50
236 RLm,DA	2.50
237 DA,V:Jormma	2.50
238 DA,D:Conan	2.50
239 Conan Possessed	2.50
240 Conan Possessed	2.50
241 TM(c),R:RoyThomasScript	3.50
242 JLe(c),A:Red Sonja	2.50
243 WPo(c),V:Zukala	2.50
244 A:Red Sonja,Zula	2.50
245 A:Red Sonja,V:King of Vampires	2.50
246 A:Red Sonja,V:MistMonster	2.50
247 A:Red Sonja,Zula	2.50
248 V:Zulu	2.50
249 A:Red Sonja,Zula	2.50
250 A:RedSonja,Zula,V:Zug double size	5.00
251 Cimmeria,V:Shumu Gorath	3.00
252 ECh	3.00
253 ECh,V:Kulan-Goth(X-Men Villain)	3.00
254 ECh,V:Shuma-Gorath (Dr. Strange Villain)	3.00
255 ECh,V:Shuma-Gorath	3.00
256 ECh,D:Nemedia's King	3.00
257 ECh,V:Queen Vammator	3.00
258 AA(i),A:Kulan Gath	3.00
259 V:Shuma-Gorath	3.00
260 AA(i),V:Queen Vammatar	3.00
261 V:Cult of the Death Goddess	3.00
262 V:The Panther	3.00
263 V:Malaq	3.00
264 V:Kralic	3.00

Conan The Barbarian Movie Special #2 © Marvel Entertainment Group

265 V:Karlik	3.00
266 Conan the Renegade (adapt.)	3.00
267 adapt.,pt.2	3.00
268 adapt.,pt.3	3.00
269 V:Agohoth,Prince Borin	3.00
270 Devourer of the Dead	3.00
271 V:Devourer of Souls	3.00
272 V:Devourer	3.00
273 V:Purple Lotus	3.00
274 V:She-Bat	3.00
275 RTs(s),Last Issue cont. in Savage Sword of Conan	25.00
G-Size#1 GK,TS,Hour of the Dragon, inc.rep.Conan#3, I:Belit	35.00
G-Size#2 GK,TS,Conan Bound, inc. rep Conan #5	15.00
G-Size#3 GK,TS,To Tarantia & the Tower,inc.rep.Conan#6	10.00
G-Size#4,GK,FS,Swords of the South,inc.rep.Conan #7	10.00
G-Size#5 rep.Conan #14,#15 & Back-up story #12	10.00
KingSz.#1 rep.Conan #2,#4	13.00
Ann.#2 BWS,Phoenix on the Sword A:Thoth-Amon	10.00
Ann.#3 JB,HC,Mountain of the Moon God, B.U.Kull story	8.00
Ann.#4 JB,Return of the Conqueror,A:Zenobia	8.00
Ann.#5 JB,W:Conan/Zenobia	5.00
Ann.#6 GK,King of the Forgotten People	5.00
Ann.#7 JB,Red Shadows & Black Kraken	4.00
Ann.#8 VM,Dark Night of the White Queen	4.00
Ann.#9	4.00
Ann.#10 Scorched Earth (Conan #176 x-over)	4.00
Ann.#11	4.00
Conan-Barbarian Movie Spec.#1	3.00
Conan-Barbarian Movie Spec.#2	3.00
Conan-Destroyer Movie Spec.#1	3.00
Conan-Destroyer Movie Spec.#2	3.00
Red Nails Special Ed.BWS	4.00

CONAN: THE FLAME AND THE FIEND
June, 2000

1 (of 3) RTs,GI,V:Kulan Gath	3.00
2 RTs,GI,Bone Dragon	3.00
3 RTs,GI,concl	3.00

CLASSIC CONAN
June, 1987

1 BWS,rep	7.00
2 BWS,rep	5.00
3 BWS,rep	5.00

Becomes:

CONAN SAGA
1987

4 thru 10 rep	@3.50
11 thru 98 rep	@3.00

CONAN CLASSICS
1994–95

1 rep. Conan #1	2.50
2 rep. Conan #2	2.50
3 rep. Conan #3	2.50
2 thru 11 rep	@2.50

CONAN/RUNE
1995

1 BWS,Conan Vs. Rune	3.50

CONAN
1997

1 CCt,	2.50
2 CCt,V:Sorcerer	2.50
3 (of 3) CCt,	2.50

CONAN: RIVER OF BLOOD
April, 1998

1 (of 3) Valeria, vs. giant crocs	2.50
2 Caught in the middle of a war	2.50
3 Lord of the Crocodiles, concl	2.50

CONAN THE BARBARIAN VS. THE LORD OF THE SPIDERS
Jan., 1998

1 (of 3) RTs,V:Harpagus	2.50
2 RTs,	2.50
3 RTs,V:Harpagus	2.50

CONAN: THE RETURN OF STYRM
July, 1998

1 (of 3) V:Mecora	2.50
2 (of 3) V:Mecora	3.00
3 conclusion	3.00

CONAN: THE SCARLET SWORD
Oct., 1998

1 (of 3) RTs,V:Thun'da	3.00
2 RTs,A:Helliana	3.00
3 RTs,conclusion	3.00

CONAN: THE USURPER
Oct., 1997

1 (of 3) CDi,KJ,Conan attacks Cimmeria?	2.50
2 CDi,KJ,	2.50
3 CDi,KJ, concl	2.50

KING CONAN
March, 1980

1 JB/ECh,I:Conn,V:Thoth-Amon	7.00
2 thru 19	@4.00

Becomes:

CONAN THE KING
1984

20 MS,The Prince is Dead	4.00
21 thru 55	@3.00

MARVEL

CONAN THE SAVAGE
(B&W Magazine), 1995–96
1 New Series 3.00
2 thru 10 . . . . @3.00

Coneheads #2
© Marvel Entertainment Group

CONEHEADS
1994
1 Based Saturday Night Live 2.50
2 There Goes the Neighborhood . . 2.50
3 In Paris. 2.50

CONSPIRACY
Dec., 1997
1 (of 2) DAn,Were the origins of
Marvel's superheroes really a
conspiracy, not an accident?. . . 3.00
2 DAn,concl. 3.00

CONTEST OF CHAMPIONS
June, 1982
1 JR2,Grandmaster vs. Mistress
Death, A:Alpha Flight. 8.00
2 JR2,Grandmaster vs. Mistress
Death, A:X-Men. 7.00
3 JR2,D:Grandmaster, Rebirth
Collector, A:X-Men. 7.00

CONTEST OF CHAMPIONS II
July, 1999
1 (of 5) CCI,Marvel vs. Marvel 3.00
2 CCI,Atlas vs. Storm 3.00
3 CCI,super hero slugfest. 3.00
4 CCI. 3.00
5 CCI, conclusion 3.00

COPS: THE JOB
1992
1 MGo(c),V:Serial killer. 2.50
2 MGo(c). 2.50
3 MGo(c),V:Eviscerator. 2.50
4 MGo(c),D:Eviscerator,Nick 2.50

COSMIC POWERS
1994
1 RMz(s),RLm,JP,F:Thanos 2.75
2 RMz(s),JMr,F:Terrax 2.75
3 RMz(s),F:Jack of Hearts 2.75
4 RMz(s),RLm,F:Legacy. 2.75
5 RMz(s),F&O:Morg 2.75
6 RMz(s),F&O:Tyrant 2.75

COSMIC POWERS UNLIMITED
1995–96
1 Surfer vs. Thanos 4.25
2 Jack of Hearts vs. Jakar 4.25
3 GWt,JB,F:Lunatik,64pg. 4.25
4 GWt,SEa,cont.StarMasters#3 . . 4.25
5 GWt,SEa,R:Captain Universe . . . 4.25

COUNT DUCKULA
Star, Nov., 1988
1 O:CountDuckula,B:DangerMouse 4.00
2 A:Danger Mouse 3.00
3 thru 15 . . . . @3.00

COWBOY ACTION
See: WESTERN THRILLERS

COWBOY ROMANCES
Oct., 1949
1 Ph(c),Outlaw and the Lady . . . 300.00
2 Ph(c),William Holden/Mona
Freeman,Streets of Laredo . . 250.00
3 Phc,Romance in
Roaring Valley 175.00
Becomes:

YOUNG MEN
1950
4 A Kid Names Shorty. 250.00
5 Jaws of Death 200.00
6 Man-Size 200.00
7 The Last Laugh 200.00
8 Adventure stories continued . . 200.00
9 Draft Dodging story 200.00
10 JMn,US Draft Story. 200.00
11 Adventure stories continued . . 200.00
12 JMn,B:On the Battlefield,
inc.Spearhead 200.00
13 RH,Break-through. 200.00
14 GC,RH,Fox Hole. 200.00
15 GC,JMn,Battlefield stories
cont. 200.00
16 Sniper Patrol. 200.00
17 Battlefield stories cont, ... 200.00
18 BEv,Warlord 200.00
19 BEv 200.00
20 BEv,E:On the Battlefield 200.00
21 B:Flash Foster and his High
Gear Hot Shots 200.00
22 Screaming Tires 200.00
23 E:Flash Foster and his High
Gear Hot Shots 200.00
24 BEv,B:Capt. America,Human
Torch,Sub-Mariner,O:Capt.
America,Red Skull 4,500.00
25 BEv,JR, Human Torch,Capt.
America,Sub-Mariner 1,800.00
26 BEv,Human Torch, Capt.
America,Sub Mariner 1,800.00
27 Bev, Human Torch/Toro
V:Hypnotist 1,600.00
28 E:Human Torch, Capt.America,
Sub Mariner,June, 1954 . . . 1,800.00

COWGIRL ROMANCES
See: DARING MYSTERY

COYOTE
Epic, June, 1983
1 SL, ... 3.00
2 SL 2.50
3 BG 2.50
4 thru 6 SL . . . . @2.50
7 SL,SD 2.50
8 SL 2.50
9 SL,SD 2.50
10 SL 2.50

11 FS,1st TM art,O:Slash 7.00
12 TM. 4.00
13 TM. 4.00
14 FS,TM,A:Badger. 4.00
15 SL 3.00
16 SL,A:Reagan,Gorbachev 3.00

CRAZY
Marvel Atlas, Dec., 1953
1 JMn,BEv,satire, Frank N.
Steins Castle 450.00
2 JMn,BEv,Beast from 1000
Fathoms. 300.00
3 JMn,BEv,RH,Madame Knock-
wurst's Whacks Museum. . . . 250.00
4 JMn,BEv,DAv,I Love Lucy
satire 250.00
5 JMn,BEv,Censorship satire . . . 250.00
6 JMn,BEv,MD,satire 300.00
7 JMn,BEv,RH,satire,July, 1954 250.00

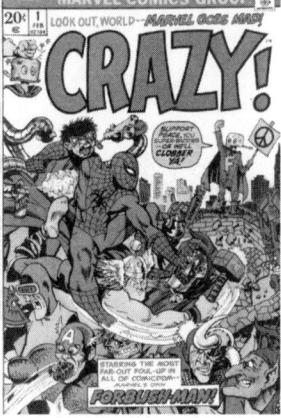

Crazy #1
© Marvel Entertainment Group

CRAZY
Feb., 1973–June, 1973
1 Not Brand Echh reps,
Forbushman 35.00
2 Big,Batty Love & Hisses issue . 25.00
3 Stupor-Man,A:FantasticalFour. . 25.00

CREATURES ON THE LOOSE
See: TOWER OF SHADOWS

CREW
May, 2003
1 JoB,DaM,Big Trouble,pt.1 . . . . . . 2.50
2 thru 7 JoB,Big Trouble,pt.2–7 . @2.50

CRIME CAN'T WIN
See: KRAZY COMICS

CRIME CASES COMICS
Marvel Atlas, 1950–52
(Formerly: WILLIE COMICS)
(See: IDEAL)
1 (24) Police 250.00
2 (25) 200.00
3 (26) 150.00
4 (27) 150.00
5 . . . . 150.00
6 . . . . 150.00
7 . . . . 150.00

8	150.00
9	150.00
10	150.00
11	150.00
12	150.00

CRIME EXPOSED
Marvel Atlas Comics, 1948–52
1	450.00
2	250.00
3 GT	150.00
4 GT	150.00
5 thru 7	@150.00
8 MMe(c)	175.00
9	150.00
10	150.00
11 JeR	175.00
12 BK,JeR	200.00
13 BK	200.00
14	125.00

CRIMEFIGHTERS
April, 1948–Nov., 1949
1 Police Stories	350.00
2 Jewelry Robbery	200.00
3 The Nine Who Were Doomed, addiction	225.00
4 Human Beast at Bay	150.00
5 V:Gangsters	150.00
6 Pickpockets	150.00
7 True Cases, Crime Can't Win	150.00
8 True Cases, Crime Can't Win	150.00
9 Ph(c),It Happened at Night	150.00
10 Ph(c),Killer at Large	150.00
Becomes:

CRIME FIGHTERS ALWAYS WIN
Marvel Atlas, 1954–1955
11 JMn,V:Gangsters	175.00
12 V:Gangsters	150.00
13 Clay Pidgeon	150.00

CRIME MUST LOSE!
Marvel Atlas, 1950
4	250.00
5	175.00
6	175.00
7	175.00
8	175.00
9 JeR	200.00
10	175.00
11	175.00
12	175.00

CRIMINAL
Icon, Oct., 2006
1 SeP	3.00
2 SeP	3.00
3 thru 10	@3.00
Vol. 2
2 40-pg.	3.50
3 thru 7 40-pg.	@3.50

CRITICAL MASS
Epic, Jan.–July, 1990
1 KS,GM,BSzF:ShadowlineSaga	5.00
2 thru 7	@5.00

CRYPT OF SHADOWS
Jan., 1973
1 BW,RH,GK,Midnight on Black Mountain	40.00
2 GT,BEv,JMn,Monster at the Door.	30.00
3 Dead Man's Hand	25.00
4 CI,Secret in the Vault.	25.00
5 JM,The Graveyard Ghoul	25.00

6 BEv,GK,Don't Bury Me Deep.	30.00
7 JSt,The Haunting of Bluebeard	30.00
8 How Deep my Grave	25.00
9 Beyond Death	25.00
10 A Scream in the Dark	25.00
11 The Ghouls in my Grave	20.00
12 BP,Behind the Locked Door	25.00
13 BEv,SD,Back From the Dead	25.00
14 The Thing that Creeps	20.00
15 My Coffin is Crowded	20.00
16	20.00
17 In the Hands of Shandu	20.00
18 SD,Face of Fear	25.00
19 SD,Colossus that Challenged the World	25.00
20 A Monster walks Among Us	20.00
21 SD,Death Will Be Mine, Nov., 1975	25.00

CUPID
Dec., 1949–March, 1950
1 Ph(c),Cora Dod's Amazing Decision	250.00
2 Ph(c),BP,Bettie Page	550.00

CYBERSPACE 3000
1993
1 A:Dark Angel,Galactus,V:Badoon, Glow in the dark(c)	3.25
2 thru 11	@2.50

CYCLOPS
Aug., 2001
1 (of 4) MT,JP	2.75
2 MT,JP,I:Ulysses	2.75
3 MT,JP,in a savage land	2.75
4 MT,JP,V:Ulysses	2.75

DAILY BUGLE
B&W 1996
1 (of 3) KIK,GA	2.75
2 thru 3 KIK,GA	@2.75

DAKOTA NORTH
1986–87
1 (Now in Cage)	2.50
2 thru 5	@2.50

DAMAGE CONTROL
May, 1989
1 EC/BWi;A:Spider-Man	3.00
2 EC/BWi;A:Fant.Four	2.50
3 EC/BWi;A:Iron Man	2.50

Damage Control Vol. 2 #1
© Marvel Entertainment Group

4 EC/BWi;A:X-Men	2.50

[2nd Series], 1989–90
1 EC,A:Capt.America&Thor	3.00
2 EC,A:Punisher	2.50
3 EC	2.50
4 EC,Punisher	2.50

[3rd Series], 1991
1 Clean-up Crew Returns	2.50
2 A:Hulk,New Warriors	2.50
3 A:Avengers W.C.,Wonder Man, Silver Surfer.	2.50
4 A:SilverSurfer & others	2.50

DANCES WITH DEMONS
Frontier 1993
1 CAd	3.50
2 CAd,V:Manitou	2.50
3 CAd,V:Manitou	2.50
4 CAd,last issue	2.50
5 Okay, there's more!	2.50
6	2.50

DAREDEVIL
April, 1904
1 B:StL(s),JK(c),BEv,I&O:Daredevil, I:Karen Page,Foggy Nelson	6,500.00
2 JK(c),JO,V:Electro	1,500.00
3 JK(c),JO,I&O:The Owl	1,200.00
4 JK(c),JO,I&O:Killgrave	1,000.00
5 JK(c),WW,V:Masked Matador	800.00
6 WW,I&O Original Mr. Fear.	500.00
7 WW,I:Red Costume,V:Namor	1,500.00
8 WW,I&O:Stiltman	350.00
9 WW(i),Killers Castle.	350.00
10 WW(i),V:Catman	350.00
11 WW(i),R:Cat	250.00
12 JK,JR,2nd A:Ka-Zar	250.00
13 JK,JR,O:Ka-Zar.	250.00
14 JR,If This Be Justice.	250.00
15 JR,A:Ox.	250.00
16 JR,A:Spider-Man, I:Masked Marauder	300.00
17 JR,A:Spider-Man.	300.00
18 DON(s),JR,I:Gladiator.	225.00
19 JR,V:Gladiator.	150.00
20 JR(c),GC,V:Owl	150.00
21 GC,BEv,V:Owl.	150.00
22 GC,V:Tri-man	150.00
23 GC,V:Tri-man	125.00
24 GC,A:Ka-Zar	160.00
25 GC,V:Leapfrog	150.00
26 GC,V:Stiltman	150.00
27 GC,Spider-Man	150.00
28 GC,V:Aliens	150.00
29 GC,V:The Boss.	150.00
30 BEv(c),GC,A:Thor.	150.00
31 GC,V:Cobra	100.00
32 GC,V:Cobra	100.00
33 GC,V:Beetle	100.00
34 BEv(c),GC,O:Beetle	100.00
35 BEv(c),GC,A:Susan Richards.	100.00
36 GC,A:FF	100.00
37 GC,V:Dr.Doom	100.00
38 GC,A:FF	100.00
39 GC,GT,V:Unholy Three.	100.00
40 GC,V:Unholy Three.	100.00
41 GC,D:Mike Murdock.	85.00
42 GC,DA,I:Jester	85.00
43 JK(c),GC,A:Capt.America.	85.00
44 JSo(c),GC,V:Jester.	75.00
45 GC,V:Jester	75.00
46 GC,V:Jester	75.00
47 GC,`Brother Take My Hand'	75.00
48 GC,V:Stiltman	75.00
49 GC,V:Robot,I:Starr Saxon.	75.00
50 JR(c),BWS,JCr,V:Robot	85.00
51 B:RTs(s),BWS,V:Robot	85.00
52 BWS,JCr,A:Black Panther	85.00
53 GC,O:Daredevil.	75.00
54 GC,V:Mr.Fear,A:Spidey.	75.00
55 GC,V:Mr.Fear	50.00

56 GC,V:Death Head	50.00
57 GC,V:Death Head	50.00
58 GC,V:Stunt Master	50.00
59 GC,V:Torpedo	50.00
60 GC,V:Crime Wave	50.00
61 GC,V:Cobra	50.00
62 GC,O:Night Hawk	40.00
63 GC,V:Gladiator	40.00
64 GC,A:Stuntmaster	40.00
65 GC,V:BrotherBrimstone	40.00
66 GC,V:BrotherBrimstone	40.00
67 BEv(c),GC,Stiltman	40.00
68 AC,V:Kragg Blackmailer, a:Bl.Panther,DD'sID Rev.	40.00
69 E:RTs(s),GC,V:Thunderbolts, A:Bl.Panther(DD's ID Rev)	40.00
70 GC,V:Terrorists	40.00
71 RTs(s),GC,V:Terrorists	40.00
72 GyC(s),GC,Tagak,V:Quother	40.00
73 GC,V:Zodiac	40.00
74 B:GyC(s),GC,I:Smasher	40.00
75 GC,V:El Condor	40.00
76 GC,TP,V:El Condor	40.00
77 GC,TP,V:Manbull	40.00
78 GC,TP,V:Manbull	40.00
79 GC,TP,V:Manbull	40.00
80 GK(c),GC,TP,V:Owl	40.00
81 GK(c),GC,JA,A:Black Widow	60.00

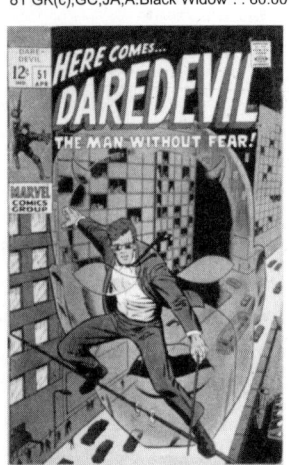

Daredevil #51
© Marvel Entertainment Group

82 GK(c),GC,JA,V:Scorpion	30.00
83 JR(c),BWS,BEv,V:Mr.Hyde	35.00
84 GK(c),GC,Assassin	30.00
85 GK(c),GC,A:Black Widow	30.00
86 GC,TP,V:Ox	30.00
87 GC,TP,V:Electro	30.00
88 GK(c),GC,TP,O:Black Widow	30.00
89 GC,TP,A:Black Widow	30.00
90 E:StL(s),GK(c),GC,TP,V:Ox	30.00
91 GK(c),GC,TP,I:Mr. Fear III	30.00
92 GK(c),GC,TP,A:BlackPanther	30.00
93 GK(c),GC,TP,A:Black Widow	30.00
94 GK(c),GC,TP,V:Damon Dran	30.00
95 GK(c),GC,TP,V:Manbull	30.00
96 GK(c),GC,ECh,V:Manbull	30.00
97 GK(c),V:Dark Messiah	30.00
98 E:GyC(s),GC,ECh,V:Dark Messiah	30.00
99 B:SvG(s),JR(c),V:Hawkeye	30.00
100 GC,V:Angar the Screamer	45.00
101 RB,A:Angar the Screamer	22.00
102 A:Black Widow	22.00
103 JR(c),DH,A:Spider-Man	22.00
104 GK(c),DH,V:Kraven	22.00

105 DH,JSn,DP,C:Thanos	25.00
106 JR(c),DH,A:Black Widow	22.00
107 JSn(c),JB(i),A:Capt.Marvel	22.00
108 K&R(c),PG(i),V:Beetle	22.00
109 GK(c),DH(i),V:Beetle	22.00
110 JR(c),GC,A:Thing,O:Nekra	22.00
111 JM(i),I:Silver Samurai	25.00
112 GK(c),GC,V:Mandrill	22.00
113 JR(c),V:Gladiator	22.00
114 GK(c),I:Death Stalker	22.00
115 V:Death Stalker	22.00
116 GK(c),GC,V:Owl	22.00
117 E:SvG(s),K&R(c),V:Owl	22.00
118 JR(c),DH,I:Blackwing	22.00
119 GK(c),DH(i),V:Crusher	22.00
120 GK(c),V:Hydra,I:El Jaguar	22.00
121 GK(c),A:Shield	20.00
122 GK(c),V:Blackwing	20.00
123 V:Silvermane,I:Jackhammer	20.00
124 B:MWn(s),GK(c),GC,KJ, I:Copperhead	20.00
125 GK(c),KJ(i),V:Copperhead	20.00
126 GK(c),KJ(i),D: 2nd Torpedo	20.00
127 GK(c),KJ(i),V:3rd Torpedo	20.00
128 GK(c),KJ(i),V:Death Stalker	20.00
129 KJ(i),V:Man Bull	20.00
130 KJ(i),V:Brother Zed	20.00
131 KJ(i),I&O:2nd Bullseye	125.00
132 KJ(i),V:Bullseye	75.00
133 JM(i),GK(c),V:Jester	20.00
134 JM(i),V:Chamelon	20.00
135 JM(i),V:Jester	20.00
136 JB,JM,V:Jester	20.00
137 JB,V:Jester	20.00
138 JBy,A:Ghost Rider	25.00
139 SB,V:A Bomber	20.00
140 SB,V:Gladiator	20.00
141 GC,Bullseye	35.00
142 GC,V:Cobra	20.00
143 E:MWn(s),GC,V:Cobra	20.00
144 GT,V:Manbull	20.00
145 GT,V:Owl	20.00
146 GC,V:Bullseye	40.00
147 GC,V:Killgrave	20.00
148 GC,V:Deathstalker	20.00
149 KI,V:Smasher	20.00
150 GC,KJ,I:Paladin	20.00
151 CC,Daredevil I Inmasked	20.00
152 KJ,V:Paladin	20.00
153 GC,V:Cobra	20.00
154 GC,V:Mr. Hyde	20.00
155 V:Avengers	20.00
156 GC,V:Death Stalker	20.00
157 GC,V:Death Stalker	20.00
158 FM,V:Death Stalker	125.00
159 FM,V:Bullseye	60.00
160 FM,Bullseye	50.00
161 FM,V:Bullseye	50.00
162 SD,JRu,`Requiem'	15.00
163 FM,V:Hulk,I:Ben Urich	30.00
164 FM,KJ,A:Avengers	30.00
165 FM,KJ,V:Dr.Octopus	25.00
166 FM,KJ,V:Gladiator	25.00
167 FM,KJ,V:Mauler	25.00
168 FM,KJ,I&O:Elektra	165.00
169 FM,KJ,V:Bullseye	60.00
170 FM,KJ,V:Bullseye	25.00
171 FM,KJ,V:Kingpin	22.00
172 FM,KJ,V:Kingpin	22.00
173 FM,KJ,V:Gliadator	22.00
174 FM,KJ,A:Gladiator	26.00
175 FM,KJ,A:Elektra,V:Hand	30.00
176 FM,KJ,A:Elektra	25.00
177 FM,KJ,A:Stick	30.00
178 FM,KJ,A:PowerMan&I.Fist	25.00
179 FM,KJ,V:Elektra	25.00
180 FM,KJ,V:Kingpin	25.00
181 FM,KJ,V:Bullseye,D:Elektra, A:Punisher	45.00
182 FM,KJ,A:Punisher	20.00
183 FM,KJ,V:PunisherDrug	20.00
184 FM,KJ,V:PunisherDrug	20.00

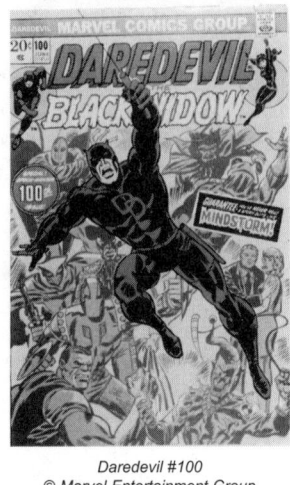

Daredevil #100
© Marvel Entertainment Group

185 FM,KJ,V:King Pin	12.00
186 FM,KJ,V:Stiltman	12.00
187 FM,KJ,A:Stick	12.00
188 FM,KJ,A:Black Widow	12.00
189 FM,KJ,A:Stick,A:BlackWidow	12.00
190 FM,KJ,R:Elektra	12.00
191 FM,TA,A:Bullseye	12.00
192 KJ,V:Kingpin	6.00
193 KJ,Betsy	6.00
194 KJ,V:Kingpin	6.00
195 KJ,Tarkington Brown	6.00
196 KJ,A:Wolverine	16.00
197 V:Bullseye	6.00
198 V:Dark Wind	6.00
199 V:Dark Wind	6.00
200 JBy(c),V:Bullseye	7.00
201 JBy(c),A:Black Widow	6.00
202 I:Micah Synn	6.00
203 JBy(c),I:Trump	6.00
204 BSz(c),V:Micah Synn	6.00
205 I:Gael	6.00
206 V:Micah Synn	6.00
207 BSz(c),A:Black Widow	6.00
208 Harlan Ellison	7.00
209 Harlan Ellison	7.00
210 DM,V:Micah Synn	6.00
211 DM,V:Micah Synn	6.00
212 DM,V:Micah Synn	6.00
213 DM,V:Micah Synn	6.00
214 DM,V:Micah Synn	6.00
215 DM,A:Two-Gun Kid	6.00
216 DM,V:Gael	6.00
217 BS(c),V:Gael	6.00
218 KP,V:Jester	6.00
219 FM,JB	7.00
220 DM,D:Heather Glenn	6.00
221 DM,Venice	6.00
222 DM,A:Black Widow	6.00
223 DM,Secret Wars II	6.00
224 DM,V:Sunturion	6.00
225 DM,V:Vulture	6.00
226 FM(plot),V:Gladiator	6.00
227 FM,Kingpin,Kar.Page	10.00
228 FM,DM,V:Kingpin	8.00
229 FM,Kingpin,Turk	8.00
230 R:Matt's Mother	8.00
231 FM,DM,V:Kingpin	8.00
232 FM,V:Kingpin,Nuke	8.00
233 FM,Kingpin,Nuke,Capt.Am.	8.00
234 SD,KJ,V:Madcap	5.00
235 SD,KJ,V:Mr. Hyde	5.00
236 BWS,A:Black Widow	6.00
237 AW(i),V:Klaw	5.00
238 SB,SL,AAd(c)V:Sabretooth	7.00

239 AAd(c),AW,GI(i),V:Rotgut 5.00
240 AW,V:Rotgut 5.00
241 MZ(c),TM,V:Trixter 6.00
242 KP,V:Caviar Killer 5.00
243 AW,V:Nameless One 5.00
244 TD(i),V:Nameless One 5.00
245 TD(i),A:Black Panther 5.00
246 TD(i),V:Chance 5.00
247 KG,A:Black Widow 5.00
248 RL,AW,A:Wolverine,
    V:Bushwhacker 7.00
249 RL,AW,V:Wolverine,
    Bushwhacker 7.00
250 JR2,AW,I:Bullet 5.00
251 JR2,AW,V:Bullet 5.00
252 JR2,AW,Fall o/Mutants 6.00
253 JR2,AW,V:Kingpin 5.00
254 JR2,AW,I:Typhoid Mary 13.00
255 JR2,AW,A:Kingpin,TMary 6.00
256 JR2,AW,A:Kingpin,TMary 6.00
257 JR2,AW,A:Punisher 10.00
258 RLm,V:Bengal 6.00
259 JR2,AW,V:TyphoidMary 5.00
260 JR2,AW,V:T.Mary,K.pin 5.00
261 JR2,AW,HumanTorch 5.00
262 JR2,AW,Inferno 5.00
263 JR2,AW,Inferno 6.00
264 SD,AW,MM,V:The Owl 5.00
265 JR2,AW,Inferno 5.00
266 JR2,AW,V:Mephisto 5.00
267 JR2,AW,V:Bullet 5.00
268 JR2,AW,V:TheMob 5.00
269 JR2,AW,V:Pyro&Blob 5.00
270 JR2,AW,A:Spider-Man,
    I:Blackheart 5.00
271 JR2,AW,I:Number9 . . . . 5.00
272 JR2,AW,I:Shotgun 5.50
273 JR2,AW,V:Shotgun 5.00
274 JR2,AW,V:Inhumans 5.00
275 JR2,AW,ActsOfVen.,V:Ultron . 5.00
276 JR2,AW,ActsOfVen.,V:Ultorn . 5.00
277 RL,AW,Vivian's Story 5.00
278 JR2,AW,V:Blackheart,
    A:Inhumans 5.00
279 JR2,AW,V:Mephisto,
    A:Inhumans 5.00
280 JR2,AW,V:Mephisto,
    A:Inhumans 5.00
281 JR2,AW,V:Mephisto,
    A:Inhumans 5.00
282 JR2,AW,V:Mephisto,
    A:Silver Surfer, Inhumans 5.00
283 MBa,AW,A:Captain America . . 5.00
284 LW,AW,R:Bullseye 5.00
285 LW,AW,B:Bullseye
    become DD#1 . . . . 5.00
286 LW,AW,GCa,Fake
    Daredevil #2 . . . . 5.00
287 LW,AW,Fake Daredevil #3 . . . . 5.00
288 LW,AW,A:Kingpin 5.00
289 LW,AW,A:Kingpin 5.00
290 LW,AW,E:Fake Daredevil 5.00
291 LW,AW,V:Bullet 5.00
292 LW,A:Punisher,V:Tombstone . . 5.00
293 LW,A:Punisher,V:Tombstone . . 5.00
294 LW,V:The Hand 5.00
295 LW,V:The Hand,A:GhostRider . 5.00
296 LW,AW,V:The Hand 5.00
297 B:DGC(s),LW,AW,B:Last Rites,
    V:Typhoid Mary,A:Kingpin 5.00
298 LW,AW,A:Nick Fury,Kingpin . . . 5.00
299 LW,AW,A:Nick Fury,Kingpin . . . 5.00
300 LW,AW,E:Last Rites, ... 8.00
301 V:The Owl 5.00
302 V:The Owl 5.00
303 V:The Owl. 5.00
304 AW,Non-action issue 5.00
305 AW,A:Spider-Man 5.00
306 AW,A:Spider-Man 5.00
307 1st SMc DD,Dead Man's
    Hand #1,A:Nomad 6.00

308 SMc,Dead Man's Hand #5,
    A:Punisher,V:Silvermane 5.00
309 SMc,Dead Man's Hand#7,
    A:Nomad,Punisher 5.00
310 SMc,Inf.War,V:Calipso 5.00
311 SMc,V:Calypso 5.00
312 Firefighting issue 5.00
313 SMc,V:Pyromaniac 5.00
314 SMc,V:Mr.Fear,I:Shock 5.00
315 SMc,V:Mr.Fear 5.00
316 Goes Underground 5.00
317 SMc,Comedy Issue. 5.00
318 SMc,V:Taskmaster 5.00
319 SMc,Fall from Grace Prologue,
    A:Silver Sable,Garrett,Hand . . . 7.00
319a 2nd Printing. 3.00
320 SMc,B:Fall from Grace,
    V:Crippler,S.Sable,A:Stone . . . 7.00
321 SMc,N:Daredevil,A:Venom,
    Garret, V:Hellspawn,Glow
    in the Dark(c). 6.00
321a Newsstand Ed. 5.00
322 SMc,A:Venom,Garret,Siege . . 4.00
323 SMc,V:Venom,A:Siege,Garret,
    I:Erynys 4.00
324 SMc,A:Garret,R:Elektra,
    A:Stone, Morbius 4.00
325 SMc,E:Fall from Grace,A:Garret,
    Siege,Elektra,Morbius,V:Hand,
    D:Hellspawn,Double size 4.00
326 SMc,B:Tree of Knowledge,
    I:Killobyte,A:Capt.America. 3.00
327 E:DGC(s),SMc,A:Capt.Amer. . . 3.00
328 GtW(s),V:Wirehead,A:Captain
    America,S.Sable,Wild Pack. . . . 3.00
329 B:DGC(s),SMc,A:Captain
    America, S.Sable,Iron Fist. 3.00
330 SMc,A:Gambit. 3.00
331 SMc,A:Captain America,
    VLHydra. 3.00
332 A:Captain America,Gambit 3.00
333 TGb,GWt. 3.00
334 TGb,GWt. 3.00
335 . . . . 3.00
336 . . . . 3.00
337 V:Kingpin,A:Blackwulf 3.00
338 Wages of Sin,pt.1 . . . . 3.00
339 Wages of Sin,pt.2 . . . . 3.00
340 R:Kingpin 3.00
341 Kingpin 3.00
342 DGc,KP,V:Kingpin 3.00
343 Without Costume 3.00
344 Identity Crisis,pt.1 . . . . 3.00
345 Identity Crisis,pt.2 . . . . 3.00

Daredevil #225
© Marvel Entertainment Group

346 V:Sir 3.00
347 V:mystery man 3.00
348 In NY City 3.50
349 Retreats to the Chaste 3.50
350 Double size. 4.00
351 . . . . 3.00
352 Return of Matt Murdock 3.00
353 KK,CNr,A:Mr. Hyde. 3.00
354 KK,CNr,A:Spider-Man 3.00
355 KK,CNr,A:Pyro 3.00
356 KK,CNr, ... 3.00
357 KK,CNr, ... 3.00
358 KK,CNr,MRy,A:Mysterio 3.00
359 KK,CNr,A:Absorbing Man 3.00
360 KK,CNr,MRy,V:Onslaught 3.00
361 KK,CNr,MRy,A:Black Widow. . . 3.00
362 KK,CNr,Romance 3.00
363 KK,GC,CaS,V:Insomnia 3.00
364 KK,CNr,MRy,V:Insomnia 3.00
365 CNr,MRy,V:Mr. Fear,
    A:Molten Man 3.00
366 GC,V:Gladiator 3.00
367 GC,V:Gladiator, concl. 3.00
368 GC,A:Black Widow and Omega
    Red 3.00
369 AOI,V:Soviet Super Soldiers . . 3.00
370 GC,Black Widow, concl. 3.00
371 AOI,Matt Murdock & Karen
    Page's relationship 3.00
372 AOI,Killers after Karen Page. . . 3.00
373 AOI,V:The 3. . . . . 3.00
374 AOI,V:Mr. Fear 3.00
375 AOI,RL,V:Mr. Fear,double size . 4.00
376 SLo,CHm,Daredevil deep
    undercover. 3.00
377 SLo,TMo,SHa,Flying Blind,pt.2 3.00
378 SLo,TMo,SHa,Flying Blind,pt.3. 3.00
379 SLo,CHm,Flying Blind,concl. . . 3.00
380 DGC,LW,RbC, V:Bullseye,Bush-
    wacker,Kingpin, double size . . . 5.00
Minus 1 Spec., GC, flashback 3.00
Ann.#1 GC 275.00
Ann.#2 reprints. 200.00
Ann.#3 reprints. 150.00
Ann.#4 (1976)GT,A:Black
    Panther,Namor 7.00
Ann.#5 (1989)MBa,JLe,JR2,KJ,
    WPo,AM,Atlantis Attacks,
    A:Spider-Man. 5.00
Ann.#6 TS,Lifeform#2,A:Typhoid
    Mary. 5.00
Ann.#7 JG,JBr,Von Strucker
    Gambit,pt.1,A:Nick Fury 5.00
Ann.#8 Sys.Bytes#2,A:Deathlok . . . 5.00
Ann.#9 MPa,I:Devourer,w/card,tie-in
    to Fall From Grace 5.00
Ann.#10 I:Ghostmaker,A:Shang
    Chi, Elektra 4.00
G-Size #1 GK(c),reprints 12.00

DAREDEVIL
Sept., 1998

1 JP,JQ,F:Matt Murdock 14.00
1a Deluxe edition 10.00
2 JP,JQ,blind faith dilemma 10.00
2a variant JSC cover 10.00
3 JP,JQ,Guardian Devil,pt.3 . . . . . . 6.00
4 JP,JQ,Guardian Devil,pt.4 . . . . . . 6.00
5 JP,JQ,Guardian Devil,pt.5 . . . . . . 6.00
5a Variant (c) 7.00
6 JP,JQ,Guardian Devil,pt.6 . . . . . . 4.00
7 JP,JQ,Guardian Devil,pt.7 . . . . . . 5.00
8 JP,JQ,Guardian Devil,concl. 5.00
8a signed 20.00
9 JP,JQ,DmK,V:Kingpin. 5.00
9a signed 15.00
10 JP,JQ,DmK,I:Echo. 4.00
11 JP,JQ,DmK,A:Kingpin 4.00
12 JP,JQ,DmK,V:Kingpin 4.00
13 JP,JQ,DmK,V:Kingpin 4.00
14 JQ,DmK,V:Kingpin 5.00
15 JQ,DmK,V:Echo 4.00

MARVEL

MARVEL

16 BMB,DMk,. 5.00
17 BMB,DMk,F:Ben Urich 5.00
18 BMB,DMk,F:Ben, Timmy 4.00
19 BMB,DMk,F:Ben, Timmy 5.00
20 40-page,BU:F:Spider-Man 5.00
21 A:Jester. 4.00
22 Matt Murdock vs. Daredevil 4.00
23 Matt Murdock vs. Daredevil 4.00
24 MPn,the trial begins 4.00
25 Playing to the Camera 4.00
26 BMB,V:Nitro 10.00
27 BMB,V:Silke,Kingpin 5.00
28 BMB,Elektra x-over,'Nuff Said . . 5.00
29 BMB,Kingpin's Empire 5.00
30 BMB,Kingpin's Secrets 5.00
31 BMB,plot twist. 5.00
32 BMB,Kingpin's Empire 7.00
33 BMB,F:Matt Murdock 4.00
34 BMB, anger's terms 4.00
35 BMB,V:Mr. Hyde 4.00
36 BMB,F:Luke Cage 4.00
37 BMB,F:Elektra. 4.00
38 BMB,Trial of White Tiger,pt.1 . . 4.00
39 BMB,Trial of White Tiger,pt.2 . . 4.00
40 BMB,Trial of the Century 4.00
41 BMB,Lowlife,pt.1 . . . . 3.00
42 BMB,Lowlife,pt.2. . . . . 3.00
43 BMB,Lowlife,pt.3. . . . . 3.00
44 BMB,Lowlife,pt.4. . . . . 3.00
45 BMB,Lowlife,concl. 3.00
46 BMB,Hardcore,pt.1 . . . . 3.00
47 BMB,Hardcore,pt.2 . . . . 3.00
48 BMB,Hardcore,pt.3 . . . . 3.00
49 BMB,Hardcore,pt.4 . . . . 3.00
50 BMB,Hardcore,pt.5 . . . . 5.00
51 DMk,R:Echo,pt.1. . . . . 3.00
52 DMk,V:Echo,pt.2. . . . . 3.00
53 DMk,V:Echo,pt.3. . . . . 3.00
54 DMk,V:Echo,pt.4,F:Wolverine . . 3.00
55 DMk,Echo's vision quest. 3.00
56 BMB,New Kingpin. 3.00
57 BMB,A:Spider-Man 3.00
58 BMB,King of Hell's Kitchen,pt.3 . 3.00
59 BMB,King of Hell's Kitchen,pt.4 . 3.00
60 BMB,King of Hell's Kitchen,pt.5 . 3.00
61 BMB,The Widow,pt.1 . . . . 3.00
62 BMB,The Widow,pt.2 . . . . 3.00
63 BMB,The Widow,pt.3 . . . . 3.00
64 BMB,The Widow,pt.4 . . . . 3.00
65 BMB,Anniversary Spec.,48-pg. . . 4.50
66 BMB,Golden Age,pt.1 . . . . 3.00
67 BMB,Golden Age,pt.2 . . . . 3.00
68 BMB,Golden Age,pt.3 . . . . 3.00
69 BMB,Golden Age,pt.4 . . . . 3.00
70 BMB,Golden Age,pt.5 . . . . 3.00

71 BMB,Decalogue,pt.1 . . . . 3.00
72 BMB,Decalogue,pt.2 . . . . 3.00
73 BMB,Decalogue,pt.3 . . . . 3.00
74 BMB,Decalogue,pt.4 . . . . 3.00
75 BMB,Decalogue,pt.5, 48-pg. . . . 4.50
76 BMB,The Murdock Papers,pt.1 . . 3.00
77 BMB,The Murdock Papers,pt.2 . . 3.00
78 BMB,The Murdock Papers,pt.3 . . 3.00
79 BMB,The Murdock Papers,pt.4 . . 3.00
80 BMB, The Murdock Papers,pt.5 . 3.00
81 BMB Murdock in prison 4.00
82 MLr,Devil in Cell Block D,36-pg . 5.00
82a Variant. 10.00
83 MLr,Devil in Cell Block D 4.00
84 MLr,Devil in Cell Block D 4.00
85 MLr,Devil in Cell Block D 4.00
86 MLr,Devil in Cell Block D 3.00
87 MLr,Devil in Cell Block D 3.00
88 MLr,Secret Life of Foggy Nelson 3.00
89 MLr,Devil Takes A Ride, pt.1. . . 3.00
90 MLr,Devil Takes A Ride, pt.2. . . 3.00
91 MLr,Devil Takes A Ride, pt.3. . . 3.00
92 MLr 3.00
93 MLr,Devil Takes a Ride. 3.00
94 JR(c), Blind Love 3.00
95 MLr,To the Devil, His Due 3.00
96 MLr,To the Devil, His Due 3.00
97 MLr,To the Devil, His Due 3.00
98 MLr,To the Devil, His Due 3.00
99 MLr,To the Devil, His Due 3.00
100 MLr,Without Fear, 104-pgs. . . . 4.50
100a variant (c) 5.00
100b variant wraparound (c) 5.00
101 MLr,Without Fear, pt.2 . . . . 3.00
102 MLr,V:Mr. Fear 3.00
103 MLr,V:Mr. Fear 3.00
104 MLr,V:Mr. Fear 3.00
105 MLr,V:Mr. Fear 3.00
106 Long Night of the Soul 3.00
107 Other People's Problems, pt.1 . 3.00
108 Cruel and Unusual, pt.2 . . . . . 3.00
109 Cruel and Unusual, pt.3 . . . . . 3.00
110 Cruel and Unusual, pt.4 . . . . . 3.00
111 V:Lady Bullseye,pt.1 . . . . 3.00
111a variant (c) 3.00
112 MLr,Lady Bullseye,pt.2 . . . . . . 3.00
112a Zombie variant (c) 3.00
113 V:Lady Bullseye,pt.3 . . . . 3.00
Ann. #1 . . . . 4.00
Spec.Daredevil vs. Punisher 3.50
Spec. Daredevil/Deadpool, BCh, JHo,
Two annuals in one,48pg.(1997)5.00
Spec. Daredevil/Batman, DGC,
SMc, 48pg. (1997). 6.00
Spec.#1 Daredevil (2000) 2.50
Spec. Daredevil Movie adapt. 3.50
Spec. Blood of the Tarantula 4.00
Spec. Daredevil & Captain America
Dead on Arrival, 48-pg. (2008) . 5.00

DAREDEVIL: BATTLIN' JACK MURDOCK
June, 2007
1 thru 4 . . . . @4.00

DAREDEVIL: FATHER
April, 2004
1 (of 5) JQ,DaM 3.50
#1 Director's Cut. 3.00
2 thru 6 JQ . . . . @3.00

DAREDEVIL: THE MAN WITHOUT FEAR
1993–94
1 B:FM(s),JR2,AW,O:Daredevil,
  A:Stick,D:Daredevil's Father . . . 7.00
2 JR2,AW,A:Stick,Stone,Elektra . . . 6.00
3 JR2,AW,A:Elektra,Kingpin 6.00
4 JR2,AW,A:Kingpin,I:Mickey 6.00
5 JR2,AW,A:Mickey,Last Issue 6.00

Daredevil -Vol 2 #6
© Marvel Entertainment Group

DAREDEVIL: NINJA
Oct., 2000
1 (of 3) BMB,Stick. 5.00
2 BMB,V:Hand 5.00
3 BMB,concl.. . . . . 5.00

DAREDEVIL: REDEMPTION
Feb., 2005
1 (of 6) Redemption Valley murder. 3.00
2 thru 6 BSz(c) . . . . @3.00

DAREDEVIL/SHI SHI/DAREDEVIL
Marvel/Crusade 1996
1 (Daredevil/Shi) TSg,AW,
  x-over,pt.1 . . . . 5.00
1 (Shi/Daredevil) x-over, pt.2 . . . . . 5.00

DAREDEVIL/SPIDER-MAN
Nov., 2000
1 (of 4) AxR,PJe, ... 4.00
2 AxR,PJe,Gladiator,Stilt-Man. 4.00
3 AxR,PJe,Owl,Copperhead. 4.00
4 AxR,PJe,TP,concl. 4.00

DAREDEVIL: THE TARGET
Nov., 2002
1 (of 4) KSm,GF,V:Bullseye 3.50

DAREDEVIL VS. PUNISHER
July, 2005
1(of 6) DL,Means and Ends 3.00
2 DL,Means and End 3.00
3 DL 3.00
4 DL 3.00
5 DL 3.00
6 DL 3.00

DAREDEVIL: YELLOW
March, 2001
1 (of 6) JLb,TSe,O:Daredevil 10.00
2 JLb,TSe,Vengeance 7.00
3 JLb,TSe,F:Fantastic Four 7.00
4 JLb,TSe,V:Electro 7.00
5 JLb,TSe,V:Owl. 7.00
6 JLb,TSe,last yellow costume. . . . 7.00

DARING MYSTERY COMICS
Marvel Timely, Jan., 1940
1 ASh(c),JSm,O:Fiery Mask,
  A:Monako John Steele,Doc Doyle,
  Flash FosterBarney Mullen,
  Sea Rover, Bondage (c). . 40,000.00
2 ASh(c),JSm,O:Phantom Bullet
  A:Zephyr Jones & K4,Laughing
  Mask Mr.E,B:Trojak 25,000.00
3 ASh(c),JSm,A:Phantom
  Reporter,Marvex,Breeze
  Barton, B:Purple Mask . . 10,000.00
4 ASh(c),A:G-Man Ace,K4,
  Monako,Marvex,E:Purple
  Mask,B:Whirlwind Carter . . 6,000.00
5 ASh(c),JSm,B:Falcon,A:Fiery
  Mask,K4, Little Hercules,
  Bondage(c) 6,000.00
6 S&K,O:Marvel Boy,A:Fiery
  Mask, Flying Fame,Dynaman,
  Stuporman,E:Trojak 9,000.00
7 ASh(c),S&K,O:Blue Diamond,
  A:The Fin, Challenger,Captain
  Daring, Silver Scorpion,
  Thunderer. 6,000.00

Daring #10
© *Marvel Entertainment Group*

8 S&K,O:Citizen V,A:Thunderer,
    Fin Silver Ocorplon,Captain
    Daring Blue Diamond 5,000.00
Becomes:

DARING COMICS
1944
9 ASh(c),B:Human Torch,Toro,
    Sub Mariner 2,500.00
10 ASh(c),A;The Angel 2,000.00
11 ASh(c),A:The Destroyer 2,000.00
12 E:Human Torch,Toro,Sub-
    Mariner, Fall, 1945 . . . . 2,000.00
Becomes:

JEANIE COMICS
1947
13 B:Jeanie,Queen of the
    Teens Mitzi,Willie 300.00
14 Baseball(c) 200.00
15 Schoolbus(c) 200.00
16 Swimsuit(c) 225.00
17 HK,Fancy Dress Party(c),
    Hey Look 175.00
18 HK,Jeanie's Date(c), Hey
    Look 150.00
19 Ice-Boat(c),Hey Look 175.00
20 Jukebox(c) 150.00
21 . . . . 150.00
22 HK,Hey Look 175.00
23 thru 25 . . . . @150.00
26 . . . . 150.00
27 E:Jeanie,Queen of Teens 150.00
Becomes:

COWGIRL ROMANCES
1950
28 Ph(c),Mona Freeman/MacDonald
    Carey,Copper Canyon 300.00

DARK ANGEL
See: HELL'S ANGEL

DARK CRYSTAL
April, 1983
1 movie adaption 3.00
2 movie adaption,May, 1983 . . . . . 3.00

DARK GUARD
1993–94
1 A:All UK Heroes 3.00
2 A:All UK Heroes 2.50
3 V:Leader,MyS-Tech 2.50
4 V:MyS-Tech 2.50
5 . . . . 2.50
6 and 7 . . . . @2.50

DARKHAWK
March, 1991
1 MM,I&O:Darkhawk,
    A:Hobgoblin 5.00
2 MM,A:Spider-Man,V:Hobgoblin . . 3.00
3 MM,A:Spider-Man,V:Hobgoblin . . 3.00
4 MM,I:Savage Steel 3.00
5 MM,I:Portal 3.00
6 MM,A:Cap.Am,D.D.,Portal,
    V:U-Foes 3.00
7 MM,I:Lodestone 2.50
8 MM,V:Lodestone 2.50
9 MM,A:Punisher,V:Savage Steel . . 2.50
10 MM,A&N:Tombstone 2.50
11 MM,V:Tombstone 2.50
12 MM,V:Tombstone,R:Dark
    Hawks'Father 2.50
13 MM,V:Venom 3.00
14 MM,V:Venom,D:Dark
    Hawks Father 3.00
15 thru 24 . . . . @2.50
25 MM,O:Darkhawk,V:Evilhawk,
    Holo-graphx(c) 3.50
26 thru 49 . . . . @2.50
50 V:Overhawk 3.00
Ann.#1 MM Assault on ArmorCity . . 3.00
Ann.#2 GC,AW,I:Dreamkiller,
    w/Trading card 3.00
Ann.#3 I:Damek 3.00

Darkhold #7
© *Marvel Entertainment Group*

DARKHOLD
1992–94
1 RCa,I:Redeemers,Polybagged
    w/poster,A:Gh.Rider,Blaze 3.00
2 RCa,R:Modred 2.50
3 thru 16 . . . . @2.50

DARK MAN
MOVIE ADAPTION
Sept., 1990
1 BH/MT/TD 3.00
2 thru 3 BH/TD . . . . @2.50

DARKMAN
Sept., 1990
1 JS,R:Darkman 4.50
2 JS,V:Witchfinder 3.00
3 JS,Witchfinder 3.00
4 JS,V:Dr.West 3.00
5 JS,Durant 3.00
6 JS,V:Durant 3.00

DARK TOWER:
THE GUNSLINGER BORN
Feb., 2007
1 (of 7) PDd(s),JaL 5.00
1a JaL variant sketch (c) 75.00
1b JQ variant (c) 15.00
1c 2nd printing 4.00
2 PDd(s),JaL 8.00
2a variant (c) 15.00
3 PDd(s),JaL 4.00
3a variant (c) 10.00
4 PDd(s),JaL 4.00
4a variant JaL sketch (c) 35.00
4b variant (c) 15.00
5 PDd(s),JaL 4.00
5a variant JaL sketch (c) 30.00
5b variant (c) 15.00
6 . . . . 5.00
6a variant (c) 15.00
7 PDd(s),JaL 4.00
7a variant JaL sketch (c) 20.00
7b variant (c) 10.00
Spec. Gunslinger's Guidebook 4.00
Spec. Sketchbook (2006) freebee . 1.00

DARK TOWER:
THE LONG ROAD HOME
Mar., 2008
1 (of 5) PDd(s),JaL, S.King adapt. . 4.00
1a variant JQ(c) 15.00
1b variant JaL sketch (c) 25.00
2 thru 5 Stephen King adapt. . . . @4.00
2a thru 5a variant(c)s . . . . @15.00
2b thru 5b variant JaL sketch(c) @25.00

DARK TOWER:
TREACHERY
Sept., 2008
1 (of 5) 4.00
1a variant (c) 5.00
1b variant JaL sketch (c) 8.00
2 thru 3 JaL . . . . @4.00
3a variant (c) 5.00
3b variant JaL sketch (c)s 8.00

A DATE WITH MILLIE
Marvel Atlas, Oct., 1956
[1st Series]
1 . . . . 350.00
2 . . . . 200.00
3 thru 7 . . . . @150.00

[2nd Series], Oct., 1959
1 . . . . 200.00
2 thru 7 . . . . @150.00
Becomes:

LIFE WITH MILLIE
1960
8 . . . . 100.00
9 & 10 . . . . @60.00
11 thru 20 . . . . @50.00
Becomes:

MODELING WITH MILLIE
1963
21 . . . . 100.00
22 thru 54 June, 1967 . . . . @50.00

A DATE WITH PATSY
Sept., 1957
1 A:Patsy Walker 150.00

DAUGHTERS
OF THE DRAGON
Jan., 2006
1 thru 6 JP . . . . @3.00
Spec. #1 Deadly Hands, 80-pg. . . . 4.00

MARVEL

DAYDREAMERS
Aug., 1997
1 (of 3) JMD,MEg,HSm 2.75
2 JMD,MEg,HSm, ... 2.75
3 JMD,TDz,MEg,HSm,concl. 2.75

DAZZLER
March, 1981
1 AA,JR2,A:X-Men,Spm,
O:Dazzler. 5.00
2 WS,JR2,AA,X-Men,A:SpM. 3.00
3 JR2,Dr.Doom 3.00
4 FS,Dr.Doom 3.00
5 FS,I:Blue Shield 3.00
6 FS,Hulk 3.00
7 FS,Hulk 3.00
8 FS,Quasar 3.00
9 FS,D:Klaw 3.00
10 FS,Galactus 3.00
11 FS,Galactus 3.00
12 FS,The Light That Failed 3.00
13 FS,V:Grapplers 3.00
14 FS,She Hulk 3.00
15 FS,BSz,Spider Women 3.00
16 FS,BSz,Enchantress 3.00
17 FS,Angel,V:Doc Octopus 3.00
18 FS,BSz,A:Fantastic Four,Angel,
V:Absorbing Man 3.00
19 FS,Blue Bolt,V:Absorbing Man . 3.00
20 FS,V:Jazz and Horn 3.00
21 FS,A:Avengers,F.F.,C:X-Men,
(double size) 3.00
22 FS,V:Rogue,Mystique 4.00
23 FS,V:Rogue,A:Powerman,
Iron Fist 3.00
24 FS,V:Rogue,A:Powerman,
Iron Fist 4.00
25 FS,'The Jagged Edge' 3.00
26 FS,Lois London. 3.50
27 FS,Fugitive 3.50
28 FS,V:Rogue 4.00
29 FS,Roman Nekoboh 3.00
30 FS,Moves to California 3.00
31 FS,The Last Wave 3.00
32 FS,A:Inhumans 3.00
33 Chiller 3.50
34 FS,Disappearance 3.00
35 FS,V:Racine Ramjets 3.00
36 JBy(c),FS,V:Tatterdemalion . . . 3.00
37 JBy(c),FS 3.00
38 PC,JG,X-Men 5.00
39 PC,JG,Caught in the grip of
death 3.00
40 PC,JG,Secret Wars II 3.50
41 PC,JG,A:Beast 3.50
42 PC,JG,A:Beast,last issue 3.50

Dazzler #3
© Marvel Entertainment Group

DEADLIEST HEROES OF KUNG FU
Summer, 1975
1 Magazine size 30.00

DEADLINE
April, 2002
1 (of 4) GyD, F:Katherine Farrell
Daily Bugle reporter. 3.25
2 thru 3 GyD,The Judge . . . . . . @3.25
4 GyD,finale 3.25

DEADLY FOES OF SPIDER-MAN
May, 1991
1 AM,KGa,V:Sinister Syndicate . . . 4.00
2 AM,Boomerang on Trial 3.00
3 AM,Deadly Foes Split 3.00
4 AM,Conclusion. 3.00

DEADLY HANDS OF KUNG FU
April, 1974
1 NA(c),JSa,JSon,O:Sons of
the Tiger, B:Shang-Chi,
Bruce Lee Pin-up 75.00
2 NA(c),JSa 50.00
3 NA(c),JSon,A:Sons of the Tiger. 40.00
4 NA(Bruce Lee)(c),JSon,Bruce
Lee biography 40.00
5 BWS,PG 35.00
6 GP,JSon,A:Sons of the Tiger . 35.00
7 GP,JSon,A:Sons of the Tiger . 40.00
8 GP,JSon,A:Sons of the Tiger . . 30.00
9 GP,JSon,A:Sons of the Tiger . . 30.00
10 GP,JSon,A:Sons of the Tiger . . 35.00
11 NA(c),GP,JSon,A:Sons
of the Tiger 30.00
12 NA(c),GP,JSon,A:Sons
of the Tiger 30.00
13 GP,JSon,A:Sons of the Tiger . . 30.00
14 NA(c),GP,HC,JSon,A:Sons
of the Tiger 90.00
15 JS,PG,JSn,,Annual #1 . . . . 30.00
16 JSn,A:Sons of the Tiger 30.00
17 NA(c),JSn,KG,A:Sons
of the Tiger 60.00
18 JSn,A:Sons of the Tiger 30.00
19 JSn,I:White Tiger 35.00
20 GP,O:White Tiger 30.00
21 . . . . 30.00
22 KG,C:Jack of Hearts 30.00
23 GK,Jack of Hearts. 35.00
24 KG,Ironfist 35.00
25 I:Shimaru 35.00
26 . . . . 35.00
27 . . . . 30.00
28 Bruce Lee Special. 125.00
29 Ironfist vs. Shang Chi 40.00
30 Swordquest. 35.00
31 JSon, Jack of Hearts 35.00
32 MR,JSon,Daughters of the
Dragon. 35.00
33 MR,Feb., 1977 . . . . 32.00
Spec. Album Ed.,NA, Sum.,1974. . 35.00

DEAD OF NIGHT
Dec., 1973–Aug., 1975
1 JSt,Horror reprints,A Haunted
House is not a Home. 35.00
2 BEv(c),House that Fear Built . . 20.00
3 They Lurk Below 20.00
4 Warewolf Beware. 20.00
5 Deep Down 20.00
6 Jack the Ripper 20.00
7 SD,The Thirteenth Floor 20.00
8 Midnight Brings Dark Madness 20.00
9 Deathride 20.00

10 SD,I Dream of Doom 20.00
11 GK/BWr(c),I:Scarecrow, Fires
of Rebirth,Fires of Death. 45.00

DEAD OF NIGHT FEATURING DEVIL-SLAYER
Marvel Max, Sept., 2008
1 thru 3 (of 4) . . . . @4.00

DEAD OF NIGHT FEATURING MAN-THING
Marvel Max, Feb., 2008
1 (of 4) 4.00
2 thru 4 . . . . @4.00

DEADPOOL
1993
1 B:FaN(s),JMd,MFm(i),
V:Slayback,Nyko 7.00
2 JMd,MFm(i),V:Black Tom
Cassidy,Juggernaut. 5.00
3 JMd,MFm(i),I:Comcast,
Makeshift,Rive,A:Slayback 5.00
4 E:FaN(s),JMd,MFm(i),
A:Slayback,Kane 5.00

[2nd Limited Series], 1994
1 A:Banshee,Syrin,Juggernaut
Black Tom 4.00
2 A:Banshee,Syrin,V:Juggernaut . . 4.00
3 A:Syrin,Juggernaut 4.00
4 Final issue 4.00

DEADPOOL
1996
1 NMa,V:Sasquatch,48pg, ... 12.00
2 NMa,A:Copycat 7.00
3 NMa,A:Siryn. 6.00
4 NMa,Will Hulk cure him? 6.00
5 NMa,A:Siryn,T-Ray 6.00
6 NMa,I: 6.00
7 AaL,A:Typhoid Mary. 7.00
8 NMa, cont. from Daredevil/
Deadpool '97,A:Gerry 9.00
9 NMa, new villain 9.00
10 NMa,A:Great Lake Avengers . . . 8.00
11 NMa,Fall through time, A:Alfred 18.00
12 NMa,Typhoid Mary, Zoe
Cullodon & Siryn return 6.00
13 NMa,V:T-Ray 5.00
14 WMc,Deal of a Lifetime 5.00
15 WMc,A:Landau, Luckman
& Lake 5.00
16 WMc, in middle east 5.00
17 WMc, Landau, Luckman
& Lake's plan. 5.00
18 WMc,V:Ajax 5.00
19 WMc,more secrets of blind Al . . . 5.00
20 Cosmic Messiah 5.00
21 . . . . 6.00
22 WMc,A:Cable 6.00
23 WMc,Dead Reckoning,pt.1
48-page 6.00
24 WMc,Dead Reckoning,pt.2 . . . . . 6.00
25 WMc,Dead Reckoning,pt.3 . . . . . 6.00
26 Dead Reckoning,aftermath 6.00
27 V:A.I.M. concl. 6.00
28 R:Weasel 4.00
29 V:Bullseye 4.00
30 A:Mercedes,T Ray 4.00
31 V:T-Ray 5.00
32 V:T-Ray,A:Mercedes 5.00
33 V:T-Ray 7.00
34 CPr,Chapter Pt.1 . . . . 4.00
35 CPr 4.00
36 CPr 4.00
37 CPr,Chapter X,Addendum 4.00
38 CPr,F:Taskmaster 4.00

Deadpool #1
© *Marvel Entertainment Group*

39 CPr,F:Taskmaster 4.00
40 CPr,space station 4.00
41 CPr,V:Dirty Wolf 4.00
42 V:Humbug 18.00
43 CPr,JCf,V:Rasputin 4.00
44 CPr,JCf,CatTrap,pt.1,x-over . . . 25.00
45 CPr,JCf,Constrictor 4.00
46 JJu,JP,PC,CruelSummer,pt.1 . . . 7.00
47 JP,PC,CruelSummer,pt.2 . . . . . . 7.00
48 JP,PC,CruelSummer,pt.3 . . . . . . 7.00
49 JP,dating? 4.00
50 AAd,JP,DaR,I:Kid Deadpool 4.00
51 JP,DaR,F:Kid Deadpool 4.00
52 JP,AWi,ALa,V:Mercy Sisters 4.00
53 JP,AWi,ALa,V:Mercy Sisters 4.00
54 JP,V:Punisher 40.00
55 JP,V:Punisher, round two 30.00
56 F:Siryn 4.00
57 JHo,BWS(c),Agent of Weapon X 10.00
58 JHo,BWS(c),Agent of Weapon X 10.00
59 JHo,BWS(c),Agent of Weapon X 10.00
60 JHo,BWS(s),Agent of Weapon X 10.00
61 Funeral For a Freak 1. . . . . 10.00
62 Funeral For a Freak 2. . . . . 8.00
63 Funeral For a Freak 3. . . . . 8.00
64 Funeral For a Freak 4. . . . . 8.00
65 Did Deadpool survive 7.00
66 steal from Rhino? 7.00
67 R:Dazzler 10.00
68 V:Black Swan, insanity 10.00
69 V:Black Swan 10.00
Ann. '98 BCh(c) F:Deadpool & Death,
   48pg. 14.00
Minus 1 Spec., ALo, flashback,
   O:Deadpool 7.00
Spec. Deadpool Team-Up,2
   Deadpools,F:Widdle Wade . . . 10.00
Spec. Baby's First Deadpool Book . 7.00
Spec. Encyclopedia Deadpoolica . 25.00

DEADPOOL
Sept., 2008
1 Secret Invasion tie-in 4.00
1a variant RLd(c) 4.00
2 Secret Invasion tie-in 3.00
2a variant (c)s . . . . @3.00
3 Secret Invasion tie-in 3.00
4 Say Hi to the Bad Guy, pt.1 . . . . . 3.00

DEADPOOL/GLI
July, 2007
Summer Fun Spectacular 4.00

DEATH3
1993
1 I:Death Metal,Death Wreck 3.00
2 V:Ghost Rider 2.50
3 A:Hulk,Cable,Storm,Thing 2.50
4 Last issue. 2.50

DEATHLOK
[Limited Series], July, 1990
1 JC,SW,I:Michael Colins
   (2nd Deathlok) 5.00
2 JC,SW,V:Wajler 4.00
3 DCw,SW,V:Cyberants 4.00
4 DCw,SW,V:Sunfire,final issue . . . 4.00

[Regular Series], 1991–94
1 DCw,MM,V:Warwolf 3.00
2 DCw,MM,A:Dr.Doom,Machine
   Man,Forge 2.50
3 DCw,MM,V:Dr.Doom,
   A:Mr.Fantastic 2.50
4 DCw,MM,A:X-Men,F.F.,Vision,
   O:Mechadoom 2.50
5 DCw,MM,V:Mechadoom,
   A:X-Men,Fantastic Four. 2.50
6 DCw,MM,A:Punisher,
   V:Silvermane 2.50
7 DCw,MM,A:Punisher,
   V:Silvermane 2.50
8 A:Main Frame,Ben Jacobs 2.00
9 DCw,MM,A:Ghost Rider,
   V:Nightmare. 2.50
10 DCw,MM,A:GhR,V:Nightmare. . . 2.50
11 DCw,MM,V:Moses Magnum 2.50
12 DCw,MM,Biohazard Agenda. . . . 2.50
13 DCw,MM,Biohazard Agenda. . . . 2.50
14 DCw,MM,Biohazard Agenda. . . . 2.50
15 DCw,MM,Biohazard Agenda. . . . 2.50
16 DCw,MM,Inf.War,V:Evilok 2.50
17 WMc,MM,B:Cyberwar. 2.50
18 WMc,A:Silver Sable 2.50
18a Newstand Ed. 2.50
19 SMc,Cyberwar#3 . . . . 3.50
20 SMc,Cyberwar#4 . . . . 2.50
21 E:Cyberwar,A:Cold Blood
   Nick Fury 2.50
22 V:MosesMagnum,A:Bl.Panther. . 2.50
23 A:Bl.Panther,V:Phreak,Stroke . . 2.50
24 V:MosesMagnum,A:Bl.Panther. . 2.50
25 WMc,V:MosesMagnum,A:Black
   Panther,holo-grafx(c) 3.50
26 V:Hobogoblin 2.50
27 R:Siege 2.50
28 Infinty Crusade 2.50

Deathlok #10
© *Marvel Entertainment Group*

29 Inner Fears 2.50
30 KHd,V:Hydra 2.50
31 GWt(s),KoK,B:Cyberstrike,
   R:1st Deathlok. 2.50
32 GWt(s),KoK,A:Siege 2.50
33 GWt(s),KoK,V:Justice Peace . . . 2.50
34 GWt(s),KoK,E:Cyberstrike,V:Justice
   Peace,final issue 2.50
Ann.#1 JG,I:Timestream 3.00
Ann.#2 I:Tracer,w/card. 3.25

DEATHLOK
July, 1999
1 JoC,JQ&JaL(c),Marvel Tech 2.50
2 JoC,A:Nick Fury. 2.50
2a variant cover 2.50
3 JoC,I:Billy Bailey 2.50
4 JoC,R:Clown 2.50
5 JoC,I:Jack Truman. 2.50
6 JoC,. 2.50
7 JoC,V:Serpent Society. 2.50
8 JoC,Nick Fury 2.50
9 JoC,V:Ringmaster 2.50
10 JoC,V:Clown 2.50
11 JoC,V:Clown 2.50

DEATHLOK: DETOUR
Jan., 2004
1 (of 4) DaR 3.00
2 thru 4 DaR . . . . @3.00

DEATHLOK SPECIAL
1991
1 Rep.Mini Series 2.50
2 Rep.Mini Series 2.50
3 Rep.Mini Series 2.50
4 Rep.Mini Series, final issue 2.50

DEATH METAL
Marvel UK, 1994
1 JRe,I:Argon,C:Alpha Flight 2.50
2 JRe,V:Alpha Flight. 2.50
3 JRe,I:Soulslug 2.50
4 Re,Last Issue. 2.50

DEATH METAL
VS. GENETIX
Marvel UK, 1993–94
1 and 2 PaD,w/card . . . . @3.00

DEATH'S HEAD
Marvel UK, Dec., 1988
1 V:Backbreaker 5.00
2 A:Dragons Claws. 4.00
3 . . . . 4.00
4 V:Plague Dog. 3.00
5 V:Big Shot 3.00
6 V:Big Shot 3.00
7 & 8 . . . . @3.00
9 A:Fantastic Four. 3.50
10 A:Iron Man 3.50

DEATH'S HEAD
[Limited Series]
1 A:`Old' Death's Head 2.50

DEATH'S HEAD II
Marvel UK, March, 1992
[Limited Series]
1 LSh,I:2nd Death's Head,
   D:1st Death's Head. 4.00
1a 2nd printing,Silver 2.50
2 LSh,A:Fantastic Four. 3.00
2a 2nd printing,Silver 3.00
3 LSh,I:Tuck 3.50
4 LSh,A:Wolverine,Spider-Man,
   Punisher 3.50

Deaths Head II- 9
© *Marvel Entertainment Group*

[Regular Series], 1992
1 LSh,A:X-Men,I:Wraithchilde	3.00
2 LSh,A:X-Men	2.50
3 LSh,A:X-Men,V:Raptors	2.50
4 LSh,A:X-Men,V:Wraithchilde	2.50
5 V:UnDeath's Head II, A:Warheads	2.50
6 R:Tuck,V:Major Oak	2.50
7 V:Major Oak	2.50
8 V:Wizard Methinx	2.50
9 BHi,V:Cybernetic Centaurs	2.50
10 DBw,A:Necker	2.50
11 SCy,R:Charnel	2.50
12 DAn(s),SvL,V:Charnel	2.50
13 SvL,A:Liger	2.50
14 SvL,Brain Dead Cold,Blue Foil(c)	3.25
15 SvL,V:Duplicates	2.50
16 SvL,DAn	2.50
17 SvL,DAn	2.50
18 SvL,DAn	2.50
Spec. Gold Ed. LSh(a&s)	4.00

DEATH'S HEAD II/DIE CUT
Marvel UK, 1993
1 I:Die Cut	3.25
2 O:Die Cut	2.50

DEATH'S HEAD II/ KILLPOWER: BATTLETIDE
[1st Limited Series]
1 GSr,A:Wolverine	2.50
2 thru 4 GSr,A:Wolverine	@2.50

[2nd Limited Series]
1 A:Hulk	3.25
2 V:Hulk	2.50
3 A:Hulk	2.50
4 last issue	2.50

DEATH-WRECK
Marvel UK, 1994
1 A:Death's Head II	2.50
2 V:Gangsters	2.50
3 A:Dr.Necker	2.50
4 last issue	2.50

DECIMATION: HOUSE OF M
Nov., 2005
Spec. The Day After	4.00

DEEP, THE
Nov., 1977
1 CI,Movie Adaption	15.00

DEFENDERS
Aug., 1972
1 SB,I&D:Necrodames	200.00
2 SB,V:Calizuma	100.00
3 GK(c),SB,JM,V:UndyingOne	65.00
4 SB,FMc,Bl.Knight,V:Valkyrie	65.00
5 SB,FMc,D:Omegatron	65.00
6 SB,FMc,V:Cyrus Black	40.00
7 SB,FBe,A:Hawkeye	35.00
8 SB,FBe,Avengers,SilverSurfer	45.00
9 SB,FMc,Avengers	45.00
10 SB,FBe,Thor vs. Hulk	125.00
11 SB,FBe,A:Avengers	45.00
12 SB,JA,Xemnu	20.00
13 GK(c),SB,KJ,J:Night Hawk	20.00
14 SB,DGr,O:Hyperion	20.00
15 SB,KJ,A:Professor X,V:Magneto, Savage Land Mutates	25.00
16 GK(c),SB,Professor X,V:Magneto, Savage Land Mutates	25.00
17 SB,DGr,Power Man	12.00
18 GK(c),SB,DGr,A:Power Man	12.00
19 GK(c),SB,KJ,A:Power Man	12.00
20 K&R(c),SB,A:Thing	12.00
21 GK(c),SB,O:Valkyrie	8.00
22 GK(c),SB,V:Sons o/t Serpent	8.00
23 GK(c),SB,A:Yellow Jacket	8.00
24 GK(c),SB,BMc,A:Daredevil	8.00
25 GK(c),SB,JA,A:Daredevil	8.00
26 K&R(c),SB,A:Guardians	10.00
27 K&R(c),SB,A:Guardians C:Starhawk	10.00
28 K&R(c),SB,A:Guardians I:Starhawk	10.00
29 K&R(c),SB,A:Guardians	10.00
30 JA(i),A:Wong	6.00
31 GK(c),SB,JM,Nighthawk	6.00
32 GK(c),SB,JM,O:Nighthawk	6.00
33 GK(c),SB,JM,V:Headmen	6.00
34 SB,JM,V:Nebulon	6.00
35 GK(c),SB,KJ,I:Red Guardian	6.00
36 GK(c),SB,KJ,A:Red Guardian	12.00
37 CK(o),SB,KJ,J:Luke Cage	7.00
38 SB,KJ,V:Nebulon	12.00
39 SB,KJ,V:Felicia	5.00
40 SB,KJ,V:Assassin	5.00
41 KG,KJ,Nighthawk	5.00
42 KG,KJ,V:Rhino	5.00
43 KG,KJ,Cobalt Man,Egghead	5.00
44 KG,KJ,J:Hellcat,V:Red Rajah	5.00
45 KG,KJ,Valkyrie V:Hulk	5.00
46 KG,KJ,L:DrStrange,LukeCage	5.00
47 KG,KJ,Moon Knight	5.00
48 KG,A:Wonder Man	5.00
49 KG,O:Scorpio	5.00
50 KG,Zodiac,D:Scorpio	5.00
51 KG,Moon Knight	5.00
52 KG,Hulk,V:Sub Mariner	5.00
53 KG,DC,MG,TA,C&I:Lunatik	4.00
54 MG,Nigh Fury	4.00
55 CI,O:Red Guardian	4.00
56 CI,KJ,Hellcat,V:Lunatik	4.00
57 DC,Ms.Marvel	4.00
58 Return of Dr.Strange	4.00
59 I:Belathauzer	4.00
60 V:Vera Gemini	4.00
61 Spider-Man,A:Lunatik	5.00
62 Hercules,C:Polaris	3.00
63 Mutli Heroes	3.00
64 Mutli Heroes	3.00
65 Red Guardian	3.00
66 JB,Valkyrie I	3.00
67 Valkryie II	3.00
68 HT,When Falls the Mountain	3.00
69 HT,A:The Anything Man	3.00
70 HT,A:Lunatik	3.00
71 HT,O:Lunatik	3.00

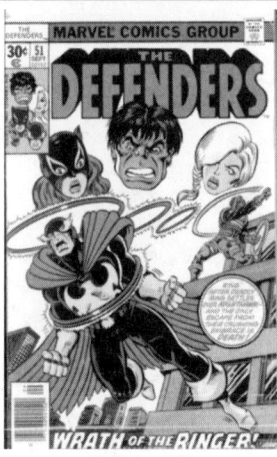

Defenders #51
© *Marvel Entertainment Group*

72 HT,V:Lunatik	3.00
73 HT,Foolkiller,V:WizardKing	5.00
74 HT,Foolkiller,L:Nighthawk	5.00
75 HT,Foolkiller	4.00
76 HT,O:Omega	3.00
77 HT,Moon Dragon	3.00
78 HT,Yellow Jacket	3.00
79 HT,Tunnel World	3.00
80 HT,DGr,Nighthawk	3.00
81 HT,Tunnel World	3.00
82 DP,JSt,Tunnel World	3.00
83 DP,JSt,Tunnel World	3.00
84 DP,JSt,Black Panther	3.00
85 DP,JSt,Black Panther	3.00
86 DP,JSt,Black Panther	3.00
87 DP,JSt,V:Mutant Force	3.00
88 DP,JSt,Matt Mardock	3.00
89 DP,JSt,D:Hellcat's Mother, O:Mad-Dog	3.00
90 DP,JSt,Daredevil	3.00
91 DP,JSt,Daredevil	3.00
92 DP,JSt,A:Eternity, Son of Satan	3.00
93 DP,JSt,Son of Satan	3.00
94 DP,JSt,I:Gargoyle	4.00
95 DP,JSt,V:Dracula,O:Gargoyle	2.50
96 DP,JSt,Ghost Rider	4.00
97 DP,JSt,False Messiah	2.50
98 DP,JSt,A:Man Thing	2.50
99 DP,JSt,Conflict	2.50
100 DP,JSt,DoubleSize,V:Satan	6.00
101 DP,JSt,Silver Surfer	4.00
102 DP,JSt,Nighthawk	2.50
103 DP,JSt,I:Null	2.50
104 DP,JSt,Devilslayer,J:Beast	2.50
105 DP,JSt,V:Satan	2.50
106 DP,Daredevil,D:Nighthawk	2.50
107 DP,JSt,Enchantress,A:D.D.	2.50
108 DP,A:Enchantress	2.50
109 DP,A:Spider-Man	3.00
110 DP,A:Devilslayer	2.50
111 DP,A:Hellcat	2.50
112 DP,A:SquadronSupreme	2.50
113 DP,A:SquadronSupreme	2.50
114 DP,A:SquadronSupreme	2.50
115 DP,A:Submariner	2.50
116 DP,Gargoyle	2.50
117 DP,Valkyrie	2.50
118 DP,V:Miracleman	2.50
119 DP,V:Miracleman	2.50
120 DP,V:Miracleman	4.00
121 DP,V:Miracleman	4.00
122 DP,A:Iceman	4.00
123 DP,I:Cloud,V:Secret Empire	2.50
124 DP,V:Elf	2.50

125 DP,New Line-up:Gargoyle,Moon
   dragon,Valkyrie,Iceman,Beast,
   Angel,W:Son of Satan & Hellcat
   I:Mad Dog 5.00
126 DP,A:Nick Fury 2.50
127 DP,V:Professor Power 2.50
128 DP,V:Professor Power 2.50
129 DP,V:Professor Power,New
   Mutants X-over 2.50
130 DP,V:Professor Power 2.50
131 DP,V:Walrus,A:Frogman 2.50
132 DP,V:Spore Monster 2.50
133 DP,V:Spore Monster 2.50
134 DP,I:Manslaughter. 2.50
135 DP,V:Blowtorch Brand. 2.50
136 DP,V:Gargoyle. 2.50
137 DP,V:Gargoyle. 2.50
138 DP,O:Moondragon 2.50
139 DP,A:Red Wolf,V:Trolls 2.50
140 DP,V:Asgardian Trolls 2.50
141 DP,All Flesh is Grass 2.50
142 DP,V:M.O.N.S.T.E.R. 2.50
143 DP,I:Andromeda,Runner. 2.50
144 DP,V:Moondragon. 2.50
145 DP,V:Moondragon 2.50
146 DP,Cloud. 2.50
147 DP,A:Andromeda,I:Interloper . . 2.50
148 DP,A:Nick Fury 2.50
149 DP,V:Manslaughter,O:Cloud . . . 2.50
150 DP,O:Cloud,double-size 5.00
151 DP,A:Interloper 2.50
152 DP,Secret Wars II,D:Moon-
   dragon,Valkyrie,Gargoyle 5.00
G-Size#1 GK(c),JSn,AM,O:Hulk . . 22.00
G-Size#2 GK,KJ,Son of Satan. . . . 15.00
G-Size#3 JSn,DA,JM,DN,A:D.D.. . 10.00
G-Size#4 GK(c),DH,A:YellowJack . 20.00
G-Size#5 K&R(c),DH,A:Guardians 25.00
Ann.#1 SB,KJ. 30.00

DEFENDERS
Jan., 2001
1 EL,KBk,KJ,48-page 6.00
2A EL,KBk,KJ, ... 3.00
2B variant AAd(c) 3.50
3 EL,KBk,KJ,V:Pluto 2.50
4 EL,KBk,KJ,V:Pluto 2.50
5 EL,KBk,KJ,A:Dr.Strange 2.50
6 EL,KBk,KJ,A:Red Raven 2.50
7 EL,KBk,KJ,A:Red Raven 2.50
8 EL,KBk,AG,V:Headmen 2.50
9 EL,KBk,RF,V:Headmen 2.50
10 EL,KBk,SB,V:Headmen 2.50
11 EL,KBk,SB,V:Attuma,DeepSix . . 2.50
12 EL,KBk,'Nuff Said,48-pg. 3.50
Spec.Day of the Defenders, mag. . . 3.50
July, 2005
1(of 5) KG,JMD 3.00
2 KG,Hulk vs. Mindless Ones 3.00
3 thru 5 KG,JMD . . . . @3.00

DEFENDERS OF DYNATRON CITY
1992
1 FC,I:Defenders of Dynatron City
   (from video game & TV ser.) . . . 3.00
2 FC,O:Defender of D.City 3.00
3 FC,A:Dr Mayhem 3.00
4 FC 3.00
5 FC,V:Intelligent Fleas 3.00
6 FC,V:Dr.Mayhem. 3.00

DEFENDERS OF THE EARTH
Jan., 1987—Sept., 1984
1 AS,Flash Gordon & Mandrake. . . 5.00
2 AS,Flash Gordon & Mandrake. . . 4.00
3 AS,O:Phantom. 4.00
4 AS,O:Mandrake 4.00

DELLA VISION
Marvel Atlas, April, 1955
1 The Television Queen 250.00
2 . . . . 200.00
3 . . . . 200.00
Becomes:

PATTY POWERS
1955
4 . . . . 200.00
5 & 6 . . . . @125.00
7 Oct., 1956 . . . . 100.00

Dennis the Menace #1
© Marvel Entertainment Group

DENNIS THE MENACE
Nov., 1981–Nov., 1982
1 . . . . 12.00
2 thru 13 . . . . @7.00

DESTROYER, THE
1989–90
1 Black & White Mag. 3.50
2 thru 10 . . . . @2.50

THE DESTROYER: TERROR
Dec., 1991
1 V:Nuihc 2.50
2 V:Nuihc 2.50
3 GM,V:Nuihc 2.50
4 DC,'The Last Dinosaur'. 2.50

DEVIL DINOSAUR
April, 1978—Dec., 1978
1 JK,I:Devil Dinosaur,Moon Boy . 25.00
2 JK,War With the Spider God . . . 15.00
3 JK,Giant 15.00
4 JK,Objects From the Sky 15.00
5 JK,The Kingdom of the Ants . . . 15.00
6 JK,The Fall 15.00
7 JK,Prisoner of the Demon Tree 15.00
8 JK,V:Dino Riders 15.00
9 JK,Lizards That Stand 15.00

DEVIL DINOSAUR SPRING FLING
1997
Spec. F:Devil Dinosaur,Moon-Boy . . 3.00

DEVIL-DOG DUGAN
Marvel Atlas, July, 1956
1 War Stories 200.00
2 JSe(c) 150.00
3 . . . . 100.00
Becomes:

TALES OF THE MARINES
4 BP,War Stories 100.00
Becomes:

MARINES AT WAR
5 War Stories 125.00
6 . . . . 125.00
7 The Big Push, Aug., 1957 . . . . 125.00

DEXTER THE DEMON
See: MELVIN THE MONSTER

DIE-CUT
Marvel UK, 1993–94
1 A:Beast. 2.50
2 V:X-Beast. 2.50
3 A:Beast,Prof.X 2.50
4 V:Red Skull 2.50

DIE-CUT VS. G-FORCE
Marvel UK, 1993
1 SFr(s),LSh(c),I:G-Force 3.00
2 SFr(s),LSh(c),Last issue 3.00

DIGITEK
Marvel UK, 1992–93
1 DPw,I:Digitek,C:Deathlok. 2.50
2 DPw,A:Deathlok,V:Bacillicons . . . 2.50
3 DPw,A:Deathlok,V:Bacillicons . . . 2.50
4 DPw,V:Bacillicons 2.50

DINOSAURS: A CELEBRATION
Epic, 1992
Horns and Heavy Armor 5.00
Bone-Heads and Duck-Bills. 5.00
Terrible Claws and Tyrants 5.00
Egg Stealers and Earth Shakers . . . 5.00

DIPPY DUCK
Marvel Atlas, 1957
1 Funny animal 100.00

DISNEY AFTERNOON
1994–95
1 DarkwingDuck vs.FearsomeFive. 3.50
2 thru 10 . . . . @3.00

DISNEY COMIC HITS
1995
1 . . . . 5.00
2 thru 9 . . . . 4.00
10 Hunchback of Notre Dame 5.00
11 thru 17 . . . . @4.00

DISNEY PRESENTS
1 F:Aladdin 2.50
2 F:Timon & Pummba. 2.50
3 . . . . 2.50

DISTRICT X
May, 2004
1 Mr.M,pt.1,F:Bishop,Ismael 3.00
2 thru 6 Mr.M,pt.2 thru pt.6 . . . . . @3.00
7 Underground,pt.1. . . . . 3.00
8 Underground,pt.2. . . . . 3.00
9 Underground,pt.3. . . . . 3.00
10 Underground,pt.4 . . . . 3.00
11 Underground,pt.5 . . . . 3.00

MARVEL

12 Underground, concl. 3.00
13 One of Us,pt.1. . . . . 3.00
14 One of Us,pt.2. . . . . 3.00

DOC SAMSON
1996
1 From The Incredible Hulk 2.50
2 A:She-Hulk. 2.50
3 . . . . 2.50
4 . . . . 2.50

DOC SAMSON
Jan., 2006
1 thru 5 . . . . @3.00

Doc Savage #7
© Marvel Entertainment Group

DOC SAVAGE
Oct., 1972
1 JM,Pulp Adapts,Death Eighty
   Stories High. 35.00
2 JSo(c),The Feathered Serpent
   Strikes 20.00
3 JSo(c),Silver Death's Head 20.00
4 JSo(c),The Hell Diver 15.00
5 GK(c),Night of the Monsters . . . 15.00
6 JSo(c),Where Giants Walk 15.00
7 JSo(c),Brand of the Werewolfs . 15.00
8 In the Lair of the Werewolf
   Jan., 1974 . . . . 15.00
G-Size#1 thru #2 Reprints 12.00

DOC SAVAGE
Aug., 1975
(black & white magazine)
1 JB,Ph(c),Ron Ely 25.00
2 JB 15.00
3 JB 15.00
4 thru 7 . . . . @15.00
8 Spring 1977 . . . . 15.00

DOCTOR OCTOPUS: NEGATIVE EXPOSURE
Oct., 2003
1 (of 5) 2.50
2 V:Vulture 2.50
3 thru 5 . . . . @3.00

DOCTOR SPECTRUM
Aug., 2004
1 (of 6) F:Corporal Joe Ledger 3.00
2 thru 6 . . . . @3.00

DR. STRANGE
[1st Series], June, 1968
Prev: Strange Tales
169 DA,O:Dr.Strange 225.00
170 DA,A:Ancient One. 75.00
171 TP,DA,V:Dormammu. 65.00
172 GC,TP,V:Dormammu 65.00
173 GC,TP,V:Dormammu 65.00
174 GC,TP,I:Satannish 65.00
175 GC,TP,I:Asmodeus 65.00
176 GC,TP,V:Asmodeus 65.00
177 GC,TP,D:Asmodeus,
   N:Dr.Strange. 65.00
178 GC,TP,A:Black Knight 65.00
179 BWS(c),rep.Amazing Spider-
   Man Ann.#2 . . . . 65.00
180 GC,TP,V:Nightmare. 65.00
181 FB(c),GC,TP,I:Demons of
   Despair 65.00
182 GC,TP,V:Juggernaut 60.00
183 BEv(c),GC,TP,
   I:Undying Ones 60.00

[2nd Regular Series], 1974–87
1 FB,DG,I:Silver Dagger 100.00
2 FB,DG,I:Soul Eater . . . . ,. . 50.00
3 FB,A:Dormammu 30.00
4 FB,DG,V:Death 30.00
5 FB,DG,A:Silver Dagger 30.00
6 FB(c),GC,KJ,A:Umar,I:Gaea . . . 15.00
7 GC,JR,A:Dormammu 15.00
8 GK(c),GC,TP,O:Clea 15.00
9 GK(c),GC,A:Dormammu,O:Clea 15.00
10 B:MWn(s),GK(c),GC,A:Eternity. 15.00
11 JR(c),GC,TP,A:Eternity 9.00
12 GC,TP,A:Eternity. 9.00
13 GC,TP,A:Eternity. 9.00
14 GC,TP,A:Dracula. 9.00
15 GC,TP,A:Devil. 9.00
16 GC,TP,A:Devil. 9.00
17 GC,TP,A:Styggro. 9.00
18 GC,A:Styggro 9.00
19 GC,AA,I:Xander 9.00
20 A:Xander. 9.00
21 DA,O:Dr.Strange 8.00
22 I:Apalla 8.00
23 E:MWn(s),JSn,A:Wormworld . . 8.00
24 JSn,A·Apalla,I;Visamajoris 8.00
25 AM,V:Dr.Strange Yet 8.00
26 JSn,A:The Ancient One 8.00
27 TS,A:Stygyro,Sphinx 8.00
28 TS,A:Ghost Rider,
   V:In-Betweener 6.00
29 TS,A:Nighthawk 5.00
30 I:Dweller 5.00
31 TS,A:Sub Mariner 5.00
32 A:Sub Mariner. 5.00
33 TS,A:The Dreamweaver 5.00
34 TS,A:Nightmare,D:CyrusBlack . . 5.00
35 TS,V:Dweller,I:Ludi 5.00
36 Thunder of the Soul 5.00
37 Fear,the Final Victor 5.00
38 GC,DG,A:Baron Mordo 5.00
39 GC,DG,A:Baron Mordo 5.00
40 GC,A:Asrael 5.00
41 GC,A:Man Thing 4.00
42 GC,A:Black Mirror. 4.00
43 V:Shadow Queen 4.00
44 GC,A:Princess Shialmar. 4.00
45 GC,A:Demon in the Dark 4.00
46 FM,A:Sibylis 4.00
47 MR,TA,I:Ikonn 4.00
48 MR,TA,Brother Voodoo 4.00
49 MR,TA,A:Baron Mordo 4.00
50 MR,TA,A:Baron Mordo 4.00
51 MR,TA,A:Sgt. Fury,
   V:Baron Mordo 4.00
52 MR,TA,A:Nightmare 5.00
53 MR,TA,A:Nightmare,Fantastic
   Four,V:Rama-Tut 5.00
54 PS,V:Tiboro. 5.00
55 MGo,TA,V:Madness 5.00

56 PS,TA,O:Dr.Strange 6.00
57 KN,TA,A:Dr.Doom. 5.00
58 DGr,TA,V:Dracula. 5.00
59 DGr,TA,V:Dracula 6.00
60 DGr,TA,Scarlet Witch 6.00
61 DGr,TA,V:Dracula 6.00
62 SL,V:Dracula. 6.00
63 CP,V:Topaz 5.00
64 TSa,`Art Rage' 5.00
65 PS,Charlatan. 5.00
66 PS,`The Cosen One'. 5.00
67 SL,A:Jessica Drew,Shroud 5.00
68 PS,A:Black Knight. 5.00
69 PS,A:Black Knight. 5.00
70 BBI,V:Umar. 5.00
71 DGr,O:Dormammu 4.00
72 PS,V:Umar 4.00
73 PS,V:Umar 4.00
74 MBg,Secret Wars II. 4.00
75 A:Fantastic Four 4.00
76 A:Fantastic Four 4.00
77 A:Topaz 4.00
78 A:Cloak,I:Ecstacy 3.50
79 A:Morganna. 3.00
80 A:Morganna,C:Rintah 3.00
81 V:Urthona,I:Rintah. 3.00
Ann.#1 CR,`Doomworld' 20.00
GN Dr.Strange: What is it that
   Distrubs you, Stephen?, CR,
   revised from Dr.Strange Ann.#1,
   48pg bookshelf (Aug., 1997). . 10.00
G-Size#1 K&R(c),reps Strange
   Tales#164–#168 . . . . 10.00

[3rd Regular Series], 1988–96
1 V:Dorammu 4.00
2 V:Dorammu 3.00
3 I:Dragon Force. 3.00
4 EL(c),A:Dragon Force 3.00
5 JG,V:Baron Mordo 3.50
6 JG,I:Mephista 3.00
7 JG,V:Agamotto,Mephisto 3.00
8 JG,V:Mephisto & Satanish 3.00
9 JG,O:Dr.Strange. 3.00
10 JG,V:Morbius. 3.50
11 JG,A of V,V:Hobgoblin,
   C:Morbius 4.00
12 JG,A of V,V:Enchantress. 2.75
13 JG,A of V,V:Arkon 2.75
14 JG,B:Vampiric Verses,
   A:Morbius 3.50
15 JG,A:Morbius,Amy Grant(C) 5.00
16 JG,A:Morbius,Brother Voodoo . . 3.50
17 JV,TD,A:Morbius,Br.Voodoo . . . 3.50
18 JG,E:Vampiric Verses,A:Morbius,
   Brother Voodoo,R:Varnae 3.50
19 GC,A:Azrael 2.50
20 JG,TD,A:Morbius,V:Zom 3.50
21 JG,TD,B:Dark Wars,
   R:Dormammu 2.50
22 JG,TD,LW,V:Dormammu. 2.50
23 JG,LW,V:Dormammu. 2.50
24 JG,E:Dark Wars,V:Dormammu . . 2.50
25 RLm,A:Red Wolf, Black Crow. . . 2.50
26 GI,V:Werewolf By Night 2.50
27 GI,V:Werewolf By Night 2.50
28 X-over Ghost Rider #12,
   V:Zodiac 3.00
29 A:Baron Blood. 2.50
30 Topaz' Fate 2.50
31 TD,Inf.Gauntlet,A:Silver Surfer . . 3.00
32 Inf.Gauntlet,A:Warlock,Silver
   Surfer,V:Silver Dagger. 2.50
33 Inf.Gauntlet,V:Thanos,
   Zota,A:Pip 2.50
34 Inf.Gauntlet,V:Dr.Doom,
   A:Pip,Scarlet Witch. 2.50
35 Inf.Gauntlet,A:Thor,Pip,
   Scarlet Witch 2.50
36 Inf.Gauntlet,A:Warlock(leads
   into Warlock&Inf.Watch#1) 3.00
37 GI,V:Frankensurfer 2.50
38 GI,Great Fear #1. . . . . 2.50

Doctor Strange #29
© *Marvel Entertainment Group*

39 GI,Great Fear #2.	2.50
40 GI,Great Fear #3,A:Daredevil	2.50
41 GI,A:Wolverine	3.00
42 GI,Infinity War,V:Galactus,A:	
Silver Surfer.	2.50
43 GI,Infinity War,Galactus Vs.	
Agamotto,A:Silver Surfer.	2.50
44 GI,Infinity War,V:Juggernaut	2.50
45 GI,Inf.War,O:Doctor Strange	2.50
46 GI,Inf.War,R:old costume	2.50
47 GI,Inf.War,V:doppleganger	2.50
48 GI,V:The Vishanti	2.50
49 GI,R:Dormammu.	2.50
50 GI,A:Hulk,Ghost Rider,Silver	
Surfer,V:Dormammu(leads into	
Secret Defenders)holo-grafx(c).	3.50
51 GI,V:Religious Cult	2.50
52 GI,A:Morbius.	2.50
53 GI,Closes Mansion,L:Wong	2.50
54 GI,Infinity Crusade	2.50
55 GI,Inf.Crusade.	2.50
56 GI,Inf.Crusade.	2.50
57 A:Kyllian,Urthona	2.50
58 V:Urthona	2.50
59 GI,V:Iskelior	2.50
60 B:DQ(s),Siege of	
Darkness,pt.#7	4.00
61 Siege of Darkness,pt.#15	3.25
62 V:Dr.Doom	2.50
63 JJ(c),V:Morbius.	2.50
64 MvR,V:Namor	2.50
65 MvR,V:Namor,Vengeance.	2.75
66 A:Wong	2.75
67 R:Clea.	2.75
68 MvR.	2.50
69 MvR.	2.50
70 A:Hulk	2.50
71 V:Hulk	2.50
72 Metallic(c),Last Rites,pt.1	2.50
73 Last Rites,pt.2.	2.50
74 SY,DQ,Last Rites,pt.3	2.50
75 Prismatic cover	4.00
76 I:New Costume.	2.50
77 Mob Clean-up	2.50
78 R:Chton.	2.50
79 Doc's new Asylum.	2.50
80 Missing for four months?	2.50
81 A:Nick Fury	2.50
82 A:Hellstorm	2.50
83 V:Tempo Mob,Dormammu	2.50
84 The Homecoming,pt.1	2.50
85 The Homecoming,pt.2	2.50
86 The Homecoming,pt.3	2.50
87 The Homecoming,pt.4	2.50
88 The Fall of the Tempo,pt.1	2.50

89 The Fall of the Tempo,pt.2	2.50
90 final issue	2.50
Ann #2 Return of Defenders,Pt4	5.00
Ann #3 GI,I:Killiam,w/card	3.50
Ann.#4 V:Salome	3.50
Spec. Dr. Strange/Ghost Rider#1	
Newsstand vers. of Dr.	
Strange #28 (1991)	6.00
Spec.#1 Dr. Strange vs. Dracula	
rep. MWn(s),GC (1994).	2.50

DOCTOR STRANGE
Dec., 1998

1 (of 4) TyH,killer pursued	3.00
2 TyH,secrets in Topaz	3.00
3 TyH,magic in Manhattan	3.00
4 TyH,PC,conclusion	3.00

DR. STRANGE CLASSICS
March, 1984

1 thru 4 SD,Reprints	@3.50

DOCTOR STRANGE: THE OATH
Oct., 2006

1 thru 5	@3.00

DOCTOR WHO
1984–86

1 BBC TV Series,UK reprints,	
Return of the Daleks	7.00
2 Star Beast	6.00
3 Transformation	5.00
4 A:K-9,Daleks	5.00
5 V:Time Witch,Colin Baker	
interview	5.00
6 B:Ancient Claw saga	5.00
7	5.00
8 The Collector	5.00
9 The Life Bringer	5.00
10 This is your Life	5.00
11 The Deal	5.00
12 End of the Line	5.00
13 V:The Cybermen.	5.00
14 Clash of the Neutron Knight	5.00
15 B:Peter Davison-Dr. Who	5.00
16 Into the Realm of Satan,	5.00
17 Peter Davison Interview	5.00
18 A:Four Dr.Who's	5.00
19 A:The Sontarans	5.00
20–22 The Stockbridge Horror.	@5.00
23 The Unearthly Child	5.00

DR. ZERO
Epic, April, 1988

1 BSz,DCw,I:Dr.Zero.	2.50
2 thru 8	@2.50

DOLLY DILL
1945

1 Newsstand	250.00

DOMINATION FACTOR
Sept., 1999

1.1 Fantastic Four (of 4) DJu,	
JOy,BMc,x-over	2.50
1.2 Avengers, DJu,JO,DJa, x-over	2.50
2.3 Fantastic Four, DJu,BMc	2.50
2.4 Avengers, DJu,JOy,DJa	2.50
3.5 Fantastic Four, DJu,BMc	2.50
3.6 Avengers, JOy,DJa	2.50
4.7 Fantastic Four, DJu,BMc	2.50
4.8 Avengers, DJa,JOy,concl	2.50

DOMINO
1996

1 thru 3	@2.50

DOMINO
May, 2003

1 (of 4) BSf	2.50
2 thru 4 BSf.	@2.50

DOOM 2099
1993–96

1 PB,I:Doom 2099,V:Tiger Wylde,	
foil(c)	3.00
2 I:Rook Seven	2.50
3 PB,V:Tiger Wylde.	2.50
4 PB,V:Tiger Wylde.	2.50
5 PB,I:Fever	2.50
6 I:Duke Stratosphear.	2.50
7 PB,I:Paloma,V:Duke,Fever Haze	2.50
8 PB,C:Ravage.	2.50
9 EC,V:Jack the Ripper	2.50
10 PB,w/Poster	2.50
11 PB,I:Thandaza	2.50
12 PB,V:Thandaza.	2.50
13 PB(c),JFm(s),V:Necrotek	2.50
14 RLm(c),PB,Fall o/t Hammer#4	2.50
15 PB,I:Radian.	2.50
16 EC(a&s),	2.50
17 PR,V:Radian,w/card	2.50
18 PB,	2.50
19 PB,C:Bloodhawk.	2.50
20 PB,A:Bloodhawk.	2.50
21 PB,Shadow King.	2.50
22 PB,R:Duke Stratosphere.	2.50
23 PB,R:Tyger Wylde	2.50
24 PB	2.50
25 PB	3.50
25a foil cover	4.00
26	2.50
27 Revolution.	2.50
28 Prologue to D-Day	2.50

Becomes:

DOOM 2099 A.D.
1995

29 Doom Invades America.	4.00
29a Chromium Cover.	4.00
30 D:Corporate Head.	2.50
31 PB,One Nation Under Doom	2.50
32 Ravage Aftermath.	2.50
33	2.50
34 I:Anthony Herod	2.50
35 E:One Nation Under Doom.	2.50
36 thru 39.	@2.50
40 Rage Against Time,pt.1.	2.50
41 Rage Against Time,pt.2.	2.50

Doom 2099 #5
© *Marvel Entertainment Group*

DOOM
Aug., 2000
1 (of 3) CDi,F:Dr.Doom 3.00
2 CDi,Al Khalad 3.00
3 CDi,concl. 3.00

DOOM:
THE EMPEROR RETURNS
Nov., 2001
1 CDi,F:Dr. Doom 2.50
2 CDi,center of Counter-Earth 2.50
3 CDi, ... 2.50

DOPEY DUCK COMICS
Marvel Timely, Fall, 1945
1 A:Casper Cat,Krazy Krow 250.00
2 A:Casper Cat,Krazy Krow 225.00
Becomes:
WACKY DUCK
1946
3 Paperchase(c) 225.00
4 Wacky Duck(c) 200.00
5 Duck & Devil(c) 175.00
6 Cliffhanger(c) 175.00
1 Baketball(c) 125.00
2 Traffic Light(c) 125.00
Becomes:
JUSTICE COMICS

DOUBLE DRAGON
July, 1991
1 I:Billy&Jimmy Lee 2.50
2 Dragon Statue Stolen,V:Stelth . . . 2.50
3 Billy Vs. Jimmy 2.50
4 Dragon Force out of control. 2.50
5 V:Stealth. 2.50
6 V:Nightfall, final issue 2.50

DOUBLE EDGE
1995
Alpha Punisher vs. Nick Fury 5.00
Omega D:Major Character. 5.00

D.P. 7
Nov., 1986
1 O:DP7 . . . . 2.50
2 thru 20 V:Headhunter. . . . . @2.50
21 thru 32. . . . . @3.00
Ann.#1,I:Witness 3.00

DRACULA LIVES
B&W Magazine, 1973—75
1 GC 100.00
2 NA,GC,JSn,O:Dracula. 65.00
3 NA,JB, ... 60.00
4 MP 50.00
5 GC 50.00
6 JB,GC 50.00
7 GE 50.00
8 GC 50.00
9 AA,RG 50.00
10 . . . . 60.00
11 thru 13 . . . . @50.00

DRACULA:
LORD OF THE UNDEAD
Oct., 1998
1 (of 3) PO,TP,R:Dracula 3.00
2 PO,TP,V:Seward 3.00
3 PO,TP,conclusion 3.00

DRAFT, THE
1988
1 Sequel to The Pit. 3.75

DRAGON LINES
Epic, *Heavy Hitters* 1993
[1st Limited Series]
1 RLm,V:Terrorist on Moon,
 Embossed(c) 3.00
2 RLm,V:Kuei Emperor. 2.50
3 RLm,V:Spirit Boxer 2.50
4 RLm,K:Kuei Emperor. 2.50
[Regular Series]
1 B:PQ(s),RLm,I:Tao. 2.50
2 RLm, ... 2.50

DRAGONSLAYER
Oct.–Nov., 1981
1 and 2 Movie adapt. . . . . @3.00

DRAGON STRIKE
1994
1 Based on TSR Game 2.50

DRAGON'S TEETH/
DRAGON'S CLAWS
July, 1988
1 GSr,I:Mercy Dragon,
 Scavenger,Digit Steel 2.50
2 GSr,V:Evil Dead. 2.50
3 GSr,Go Home 2.50
4 GSr 2.50
5 GSr,I:Death's Head 18.00
6 thru 10 GSr . . . . @2.00

DRAX THE DESTROYER
Sept., 2005
1 (of 4) KG(s) 4.00
2 thru 4 KG(s) . . . . @3.00

DREADLANDS
Epic, 1992
1 Post-Apocalyptic Mini-series 4.00
2 Trapped in Prehistoric Past 4.00
3 V:Alien Time Travelers. 4.00
4 Final Issue 4.00

DREADSTAR
Epic, Nov., 1982
1 JSn,I:Lord Papal 5.00
2 thru 5 . . . . @3.50
6 thru 7 . . . . @4.00
8 thru 26 . . . . @3.00
Ann.#1 JSn,The Price 3.00
See COLOR COMICS section

Dreadstar and Company #1
© Marvel Entertainment Group

DREADSTAR & COMPANY
July, 1985
1 JSo,reprint 2.50
2 thru 5 JSo,rep. . . . . @2.50

DREAM POLICE
June, 2005
1 MD2, 48-pg. 4.00

DROIDS
Star, April, 1986
1 JR 25.00
2 AW 15.00
3 JR/AW 15.00
4–5 AW 15.00
5 AW 15.00
6 EC/AW,A:Luke Skywalker 15.00
7 EC/AW,A:Luke Skywalker 15.00
8 EC/AW,A:Luke Skywalker 15.00

DRUID
1995
1 R:Dr. Druid Surprise!!! 3.50
2 F:Nekra 3.00
3 deranged canibal wisemen 3.00
4 Why Must He Die?. 3.00

DUNE
April–June, 1985
1 Movie Adapt,Rep. Marvel
 Super Spec,BSz 3.50
2 Movie Adapt,BSz 3.50
3 Movie Adapt,BSz 3.50

DYNOMUTT
Nov., 1977
1 Based on TV series 50.00
2 thru 5 . . . . @30.00
6 Sept., 1978 . . . . 30.00

EARTHWORM JIM
1995–96
1 I:Earthworm Jim. 3.00
2 Cow tipping 3.00
3 V:Lawyers,conclusion 3.00

EARTH X
Jan., 1999
0 (of 14) AxR,JPL,Machine Man
 & Watcher 6.00
0a signed 25.00
1 AxR,JPL,V:Inhumans,32-page. . . 8.00
1a signed 30.00
2 AxR,JPL,fate of Fant.Four. 4.00
3 AxR,JPL,World Super Powers . . . 4.00
4 JPL,AxR(c),A:new Hulk 4.00
5 JPL,AxR(c),V:Doombots 4.00
6 JPL,AxR(c),different X-Men 4.00
7 JPL,AxR(c),A:Hulk 4.00
8 JPL,AxR(c),A:Venom 4.00
9 JPL,AxR(c),Revelations 4.00
10 JPL,AxR(c) 4.00
11 JPL,AxR(c),V:Skull 4.00
12 JPL,AxR(c),concl 4.00
Spec.X AxR(c) concl.,48-pg 6.00
Sketchbook 6.00

ECTOKID
Razorline 1993–94
1 I:Dex Mungo,BU:Hokum & Hex. . 3.50
2 O:Dex. 2.50
3 I:Ectosphere. 2.50
4 I:Brothers Augustine 2.50
5 A:Saint Sinner 2.50
6 Highway 61 Revisited 2.50
7 . . . . 2.50
8 V:Ice Augustine 2.50

MARVEL

9 Love is like a Bullet 2.50
10 . . . . 2.50
Ectokid Unleashed 3.25

EDEN'S TRAIL
Nov., 2002
1 (of 6) western 3.00
2 thru 5 . . . . @3.00

ELECTRIC UNDERTOW
Dec., 1989
1 MBa,Strike Force 4.00
2 thru 5 MBa . . . . @4.00

ELEKTRA
Nov., 1996
1 PrM,MD2, ... 3.50
1A variant (c). 5.00
2 PrM,MD2,V:Bullseye, round two . 3.00
3 PrM,MD2, ... 3.00
4 PrM,MD2 . . . . 3.00
5 PrM,MD2, ... 3.00
6 PrM,MD2 . . . . 3.00
7 PrM,MD2,A:Konrad,The Architect 3.00
8 PrM,MD2,V:The Architect 3.00
9 PrM,MD2,V:The Four Winds 3.00
10 PrM,MD2,V:Daredevil,American
   Samurai, pt.1 . . . . 3.00
11 PrM,MD2,F:Daredevil 3.00
12 PrM,MD2,F:Daredevil,V:American
   Samuri 3.00
13 PrM,MD2,F:Daredevil, concl. . . . 3.00
14 LHa,MD2,A:Wolverine 3.00
15 LHa,MD2,A:Silver Samurai. . . . 3.00
16 LHa,MD2,A Hole in the Soul. . . 3.00
17 LHa,MD2,V:The Hand. 3.00
18 LHa,MD2,A:Shang-Chi&Kingpin. 3.00
19 LHa,MD2,last issue. 3.00
Minus 1 Spec.,PMg,MD2,flashback. 3.00

ELEKTRA
July, 2001
1 BMB,non-comics code series . . 5.00
2A BMB,A:S.H.I.E.L.D. 3.00
2B variant BSz(c) 3.00
3 BMB,A:Hydra 3.50
3a nude 20.00
4 BMB,A:Nick Fury 3.50
5 BMB,concl 3.50
6 BMB,F:Daredevil,'Nuff Said 3.50
7 Hubris, pt.1 . . . . 3.50
8 Hubris, pt.2 . . . . 3.50

Elektra #1
© *Marvel Entertainment Group*

9 Hubris, pt.3 . . . . 3.00
10 Hubris, concl. 3.00
11 Elektra between jobs. 3.00
12 F:Mr. Locke. 3.00
13 DaM 3.00
14 DaM,Elektra fights back 3.00
15 DaM 3.00
16 DaM 3.00
17 DaM 3.00
18 DaM 3.00
19 DaM 3.00
20 DaM,V:The Hand 3.00
21 V:The Hand 3.00
22 V:The Hand, concl. 3.00
23 BSz(c),pt.1 . . . . 3.00
24 BSz(c),pt.2 . . . . 3.00
25 BSz(c),How to,pt.1 . . . . 3.00
26 How to,pt.2 . . . . 3.00
27 How to,pt.3,concl. 3.00
28 Tables turned 3.00
29 Assassination 3.00
30 Prophet & Loss,pt.2 . . . . 3.00
31 Prophet & Loss,pt.3 . . . . 3.00
32 Fever,pt.1 . . . . 3.00
33 Fever,pt.2 . . . . 3.00
34 Fever,pt.3 . . . . 3.00
35 Visits grave 3.00
36 JoB,pt.1. . . . . 3.00
Spec., Elektra: The Movie 3.00

ELEKTRA: ASSASSIN
Aug., 1986
1 FM,BSz,V:Shield 8.00
2 FM,BSz,I:Garrett 5.00
3 FM,BSz,V:Shield,A:Garrett 5.00
4 FM,BSz,V:Shield,A:Garrett 5.00
5 FM,BSz,I:Chastity,A:Garrett. . . . 5.00
6 FM,BSz,A:Nick Fury,Garrett . . . 5.00
7 FM,BSz,V:Ken Wind,A:Garrett . . 5.00
8 FM,BSz,V:Ken Wind,A:Garrett . . 6.00

ELEKTRA: GLIMPSE & ECHO
July, 2002
1 (of 4) F:The Hand 3.50
2 thru 4 . . . . @3.50

ELEKTRA: THE HAND
Sept., 2004
1 (of 5) The First Impression 3.00
2 thru 5 . . . . @3.00

ELEKTRA: ROOT OF EVIL
1 V:Snakeroot 3.00
2 V:Snakeroot 3.00
3 Elektra's Brother 3.00
4 V:The Hand 3.00

ELEKTRA: SAGA
Feb., 1984
1 FM,rep.Daredevil 7.00
2 FM,rep.Daredevil 7.00
3 FM,rep.Daredevil 7.00
4 FM,rep.Daredevil 7.00
GN Book One FM,KJ, rep. from
   Daredevil, 96pg 4.00
GN Book Two FM,KJ, rep. from
   Daredevil, 96pg 4.00

ELEKTRA & WOLVERINE: THE REDEEMER
Nov., 2001
GN#1 painted, 48-page 6.50
GN#2 48-page 6.50
GN#3 concl., 48-page 6.50

ELEKTRA/WITCHBLADE
1-shot Devil's Reign,
   pt.6, x-over 3.00

ELFQUEST
Star, Aug., 1985
1 WP,reprints. 4.00
2 thru 31 WP. . . . . @2.50
32 WP,Conclusion, March, 1988 . . . 2.50

Elsewhere Prince #1
© *Marvel Entertainment Group*

ELSEWHERE PRINCE
Epic, May–Oct., 1990
1 thru 6 . . . . @3.00

ELVIRA
Oct., 1988
Spec.B&W, Movie Adapt. 3.00

EMMA FROST
July, 2003
1 RGr,Higher Learning,pt.1. . . . . . . 7.00
2 RGr,Higher Learning,pt.2. . . . . . . 4.00
3 RGr,Higher Learning,pt.3. . . . . . . 4.00
4 RGr,Higher Learning,pt.4. . . . . . . 4.00
5 RGr,Higher Learning,pt.5. . . . . . . 4.00
6 RGr,White Queen 4.00
7 Mind Games,pt.1 . . . . 3.50
8 Mind Games,pt.2 . . . . 3.50
9 Mind Games,pt.3 . . . . 3.50
10 Mind Games,pt.4 . . . . 3.50
11 Mind Games,pt.5. . . . . 3.50
12 Mind Games,pt.6 . . . . 3.50
13 Bloom,pt.1. . . . . 3.50
14 Bloom,pt.2. . . . . 3.50
15 Bloom,pt.3. . . . . 3.50
16 Bloom,pt.4. . . . . 3.50
17 Bloom,pt.5. . . . . 3.50
18 Bloom,pt.6. . . . . 3.50
Digest Vol. 1: Higher Learning. 8.00
Digest Vol. 2: Mind Games 8.00
Digest Vol. 3: Bloom 8.00

ENDER'S GAME
Oct., 2008
1 PFe,Orson Scott Card adapt. . . . 4.00
1a variant (c) 4.00
1b variant sketch (c) 4.00
2 PFe 4.00
2a variant (c) 4.00
2b variant PFe sketch (c) 4.00

All comics prices listed are for *Near Mint* condition.

EPIC
1992
1 Wildcards,Hellraiser 6.00
2 Nightbreed,Wildcards 6.00
3 DBw,MFm,Alien Legion, ... 6.00
4 Stalkers,Metropol,Wildcards 6.00

EPIC ANTHOLOGY
April, 2004
1 . . . . 6.00

Epic Illustrated #28
© *Marvel Entertainment Group*

EPIC, ILLUSTRATED
Spring, 1980
1 Black and White/Color Mag. . . . 14.00
2 thru 10 . . . . @8.00
11 thru 20 . . . . @10.00
21 thru 25 . . . . @12.00
26 thru 34, March, 1986. . . . . . @14.00

EPIC, LITE
Epic, Nov., 1991
One-shot short stories 4.00

ETERNAL
Marvel Max, June, 2003
1 thru 6 Gift of the Gods,pt.2–6 . @3.00

ETERNALS
[1st Series], July, 1976
1 JK,I:Ikaris,25 cent edition 30.00
2 JK,I:Ajak,25 cent edition 15.00
3 JK,I:Sersi 10.00
4 JK,Night of the Demons. 10.00
5 JK,I:Makarri,Zuras Thena,Domo 10.00
6 JK,Gods & Men at City College. 10.00
7 JK,V:Celestials. 10.00
8 JK,I:Karkas, Reject 10.00
9 JK,I:Sprite,Reject vs. Karkas . . . 10.00
10 JK,V:Celestials 10.00
11 JK,I:Kingo Sunen 10.00
12 JK,I:Uni-Mind 15.00
13 JK,I:ForgottenOne(Gilgamesh). 15.00
14 JK,V:Hulk 15.00
15 JK,V:Hulk 15.00
16 JK,I:Dromedan 15.00
17 JK,I:Sigmar. 10.00
18 JK,I:Nerve Beast. 10.00
19 JK,Secret o/t Pyramid 10.00
Ann.#1 JK,V:Timekillers 12.00

[2nd Series], Oct., 1985
1 SB,I:Cybele 3.00
2 thru 10 SB,V:Deviants. . . . . . @2.50
11 &12 WSKP,V:Deviants. . . . . . @2.50

ETERNALS
June, 2006
1 NGa,JR2 . . . . 4.00
2 thru 7 NGa,JR2 . . . . @4.00
2a variant (c) 8.00
7a variant JR2(c) 4.00

ETERNALS
June, 2008
1 . . . . 4.00
1a variant (c) 4.00
2 . . . . 4.00
3 Dreaming Celestial 4.00
4 Tremble, Mortals 4.00
5 A Spy Revealed 4.00
5a Zombie variant (c) 4.00
6 . . . . 4.00
7 NGa(s),JR2, finale 4.00
7a variant JR2(c) 4.00
Ann #1 . . . . 4.00

ETERNALS:
HEROD FACTOR
Nov., 1991
1 MT/BMc,A:Sersi (giant size) 2.50

EVERYMAN
Epic, 1991
1-shot Supernatural Story 8.00

EWOKS
Star, June, 1985—Sept., 1987
1 Based on TV Series. 18.00
2 . . . . 15.00
3 . . . . 15.00
4 A:Foonars 15.00
5 Wicket vs. Ice Demon. 15.00
6 Mount Sorrow, A:Teebo 15.00
7 A:Logray,V:Morag 15.00
8 . . . . 15.00
9 Lost in Time 15.00
10 AW,Lost in Time 18.00
11 thru 15 . . . . @15.00

EXCALIBUR
April, 1988
1 AD,Special,O:Excalibur,
  V:Technet. 5.00
1a 2nd Printing 2.50
1b 3rd Printing 2.00
2 AAd,Mojo Mayhem,A:X-Babies . . 4.00
3 Air Apparent Spec.RLm,KJ,JG,TP,
  RL,EL,JRu,A:Coldblood. 4.00

[Regular Series]
1 B:CCl(s),AD,V:Warwolves,
  I:Widget. 6.00
2 AD,V:Warwolves,I:Kylun 5.00
3 AD,V:Juggernaut 4.00
4 AD,V:Arcade,Crazy Gang 4.00
5 AD,V:Arcade 3.00
6 AD,Inferno,I:Alistaire Stuart 3.00
7 AD,Inferno 3.00
8 RLm,JRu,A:New Mutants 3.00
9 AD,I:Nazi-Excalibur 3.00
10 MR,V:Nazi-Excalibur. 3.00
11 MR,V:Nazi-Excalibur 3.00
12 AD,Fairy Tale Dimension 3.00
13 AD,The Prince,N:Capt.Britian . . 3.00
14 AD,Too Many Heroes 2.50
15 AD,I:US James Braddock 2.50
16 AD,V:Anjulie 2.50
17 AD,C:Prof.X,Starjammers 2.50
18 DJ,DA,V:Jamie Braddock 2.50
19 RL,TA,AM,V:Jamie Braddock . . 2.50
20 RLm,JRu,V:Demon Druid 2.50
21 I:Crusader X 2.50
22 V:Crusader X 2.50
23 AD,V:Magik 2.50

24 AD,Return Home,C:Galactus . . . 2.50
25 E:CCl(s),AM,A:Galactus,Death,
  Watcher 2.50
26 RLm,JRu,V:Mastermind 2.50
27 BWS,BSz,A:Nth Man 3.00
28 BBl,Night at Bar 2.50
29 JRu,V:Nightmare,A:PowerPack . 2.50
30 DR,AM,A:Doctor Strange 2.50
31 DR,AM,V:Son of Krakoa 2.50
32 V:Mesmero 2.50
33 V:Mesmero 2.50
34 V:Mesmero 2.50
35 AM,Missing Child 2.50
36 AM,V:Silv.Sable,Sandman 2.50
37 A:Avengers W.C.,Dr.Doom 2.50
38 A:Avengers W.C.,Dr.Doom 2.50
39 A:Avengers W.C.,Dr.Doom 2.50
40 O:Excalibur,Trial-Lockheed. 2.50
41 V:Warwolves,C:Cable 3.00
42 AD,Team Broken Up 3.50
43 AD,Nightcrawler,V:Capt.Brit 3.00
44 AD,Capt.Britain On Trial 3.00
45 AD,I:N-Men. 3.00
46 AD,Return of Kylun,C:Cerise . . . 3.00
47 AD,I:Cerise 3.00
48 AD,A:Anti-Phoenix 3.00
49 AD,MFm,V:Necrom,R:Merlyn . . . 3.00
50 AD,Phoenix,V:Necrom,Merlyn . . 5.00
51 V:Giant Dinosaurs. 2.50
52 O:Phoenix,A:Prof X,MarvGirl . . . 2.50
53 A:Spider-Man,V:The Litter. 2.50
54 AD,MFm,V:Crazy Gang 2.50
55 AD,MFm,A:Psylocke 2.50
56 AD,MFm,A:Psylocke,
  V:Saturyne,Jamie Braddock . . . 2.50
57 A:X-Men,Alchemy,V:Trolls. 2.75
58 A:X-Men,Alchemy,V:Trolls. 2.75
59 A:Avengers 2.50
60 A:Avengers 2.50
61 AD,MFm,Phoenix Vs.Galactus . 2.50
62 AD,MFm,A:Galactus 2.50
63 AD,MFm,V:Warpies. 2.50
64 AD,MFm,V:RCX,R:Rachel 2.50
65 AD,MFm,V:Dark Phoenix 2.50
66 AD,MFm,V:Ahab,Sentinels,
  O:Widget 2.50
67 AD,MFm,V:Ahab,Sentinels 2.50
68 V:Starjammers 2.50
69 A:Starjammers. 2.50
70 A:Starjammers. 2.50
71 DaR,Hologram(c),N:Excalibur. . . 5.00
72 KeL,V:Siena Blaze 2.50
73 TSr,V:Siena Blaze. 2.50
74 InC,A:Mr.Sinster,Siena Blaze . . . 2.50

Excalibur #1
© *Marvel Entertainment Group*

75 SLo(s),KeL,I:Daytripper(Amanda
  Sefton),Britannic(Capt.Britain),
  BU:Nightcrawler............ 4.00
75a Newstand Ed............... 2.50
76 KeL,V:D'spayre 2.50
77 KeL,R:Doug Ramsey 2.50
78 A:Zero,Doug Ramsey 2.50
79 A:Zero,Doug Ramsey 2.50
80 A:Zero,Doug Ramsey 2.50
81 Doug Ramsey............... 2.50
82 .... 3.00
82a foil(c).................. 4.00
83 regular ed................. 2.25
83a Deluxe ed. Kitty,Nightcrawler .. 2.50
84 regular ed................. 2.25
84a Deluxe ed................. 2.50
85 regular ed................. 2.25
85a Deluxe ed................. 2.50
86 regular ed................. 2.25
86a Deluxe ed................. 2.50
87 KeL,Secrets of the Genoshan
  Mutate Technology 2.50
88 Dream Nails,pt.1 .... 2.50
89 Dream Nails,pt.2 .... 2.50
90 Between Uncreated,Phalanx .. 4.00
91 F:Colossus 2.50
92 F:Colossus 2.50
93 F:Wolfsbane 2.50
94 A:Karma & Psylocke......... 2.50
95 .... 2.50
96 .... 2.50
97 BWi,B.Braddock's secrets told .. 2.50
98 .... 2.50
99 European Hellfire Club,
  Onslaught 2.50
100 Onslaught saga, double size .. 4.00
101 .... 2.50
102 .... 2.50
103 WEI,F:Colossus,Kitty &
  Nichtcrawler............... 2.50
104 JAr,BHi,PNe,Douglock's
  dark side 2.50
105 JAr,BHi,PNe,V:Moonstar, ... 2.50
106 .... 2.50
107 SvL,New direction.......... 2.50
108 Dragons of the Crimson Dawn . 2.50
109 V:Spiral,A:Captain Britain 2.50
110 V:The Dragons of the
  Crimson Dawn.............. 2.50
111 F:Shadowcat,R:Rory Cambell
  (Ahab?) 2.50
112 Quicksilver tie-in 2.50
113 BRa,Colossus & Meggan 2.50
114 BRa,Vanisher 2.50
115 BRa,Quarantine,F:GenerationX . 2.50
116 BRa,Legacy Virus, cont. 2.50
117 BRa,F:Kitty Pryde, Colossus &
  Nightcrawler............... 2.50
118 BRa,V:Creatures from the
  Shadows 2.50
119 BRa,V:Nightmare 2.50
120 BRa,F:Kitty Pryde & Pete
  Wisdom 2.50
121 BRa,to Egypt.............. 2.50
122 BRa,V:Original X-Men?...... 2.50
123 BRa,V:Mimic 2.50
124 BBr,Captain Britain's bachelor
  party..................... 2.50
125 TvS,SHa, W:Captain Britain &
  Meggan, final issue 4.00
Minus 1 Spec., flashback,
  F:Nightcrawler.............. 2.50
Ann.#1 I:Khaos,w/card......... 3.25
Spec #1 The Possession 4.00
Spec #2 RLm,DT,JG,RL,
  A:Original X-Men............ 3.00
PF Cold Blood 5.00

EXCALIBUR
May, 2004
1 CCI,Forging the Sword,pt.1 .... 3.00
2 CCI,Forging the Sword,pt.2 ..... 3.00

Excalibur #99
© Marvel Entertainment Group

3 CCI,Forging the Sword,pt.3 ..... 3.00
4 CCI,Forging the Sword,pt.4 ..... 3.00
5 CCI,Food Fight,pt.1 .... 3.00
6 CCI,Food Fight,pt.2 .... 3.00
7 CCI,Food Fight,pt.3 .... 3.00
8 ALo,Saturday Night Fever,pt.1. . 3.00
9 ALo,Saturday Night Fever,pt.2.. . 7.00
10 CCI,ALo,Saturday Night Fever .. 3.00
11 CCI,ALo,Save My Child,pt.1 ... 3.00
12 CCI,ALo,Save My Child,pt.2 ... 3.00
13 CCI,ALo,House of M, prelude .. 5.00
14 CCI,ALo,A:Dr. Strange 4.00

EXCALIBUR:
SWORD OF POWER
Dec., 2000
1 (of 4) IaC,BRa,F:Capt.Britain... 3.00
2 thru 4 BRa,................. @3.00

EXILES
June, 2001
1 MkK,F:Blink, 48-page 10.00
2A MkK, ... 7.00
2B variant JWi(c) 6.00
3 MkK,trial of Phoenix........... 4.00
4 MkK,trial of Phoenix........... 4.00
5 MkK,JCf,F:Hulk 4.00
6 MkK,JCf,F:Alpha Flight 4.00
7 MkK,'Nuff Said (no words)...... 4.00
8 MkK,A World Apart,pt.1 .... 4.00
9 MkK,A World Apart,pt.2 .... 4.00
10 MkK,A World Apart,pt.3....... 4.00
11 MkK,F:Morph............... 3.50
12 MkK,New team 3.50
13 MkK,team must kill 3.50
14 MkK,V:Dr. Doom 3.50
15 MkK,Mimic vs. Namor........ 3.50
16 MkK, ... 3.50
17 world gone reptile 3.50
18 MkK,F:Morph 3.50
19 MkK,JHo 3.50
20 JCf,V:Legacy Virus,pt.1 ...... 3.00
21 JCf,V:Legacy Virus,pt.2 ...... 3.00
22 JCf,One goew down 3.00
23 With an Iron Fist,pt.1 .... 3.00
24 With an Iron Fist,pt.2 .... 3.00
25 With an Iron Fist,pt.3 .... 3.50
26 Hard Choices,pt.1 .... 3.00
27 Hard Choices,pt.2 .... 3.00
28 Unnatural Selection,pt.1 ...... 3.00
29 Unnatural Selection,pt.2 ...... 3.00
30 Unnatural Selection,pt.3 ...... 3.00

31 Avengers Forever,pt.1........ 3.00
32 Avengers Forever,pt.2........ 3.00
33 A Second Farewell,pt.1 ...... 3.00
34 A Second Farewell,pt.2 ...... 3.00
35 Fantastic Voyage,pt.1 .... 3.00
36 Fantastic Voyage,pt.2 .... 3.00
37 Fantastic Voyage,pt.3 .... 4.00
38 King Hyperion,pt.1 .... 4.00
39 King Hyperion,pt.2 .... 4.00
40 King Hyperion,pt.3 .... 4.00
41 A Nocturne's Tale,pt.1 .... 3.00
42 A Nocturne's Tale,pt.2 .... 3.00
43 Blink in Time,pt.1 .... 3.00
44 Blink in Time,pt.2 .... 3.00
45 Blink in Time,pt.3 .... 3.00
46 Earn Your Wings,pt.1 .... 3.00
47 Earn Your Wings,pt.2 .... 3.00
48 Earn Your Wings,pt.3 .... 3.00
49 Capitol dome dump........... 3.00
50 The Big M,pt.1 .... 3.00
51 The Big M,pt.2 .... 3.00
52 Living Planet,pt.1 .... 3.00
53 Living Planet,pt.2 .... 3.00
54 Chain Lightning............. 3.00
55 Bump in the Night, pt.1....... 3.00
56 Bump in the Night, pt.2 ...... 3.00
57 Bump in the Night, pt.3....... 3.00
58 F:Sasquatch, Tanaraq........ 3.00
59 F:Blink..................... 3.00
60 Son of Apocalypse,pt.1 ...... 4.00
61 Son of Apocalypse,pt.2 ...... 4.00
62 Timebreakers,pt.1 .... 4.00
63 Timebreakers,pt.2 .... 4.00
64 Timebreakers,pt.3 .... 3.00
65 Timebreakers,pt.4 .... 3.00
66 Destroy All Monsters,pt.1 .... 3.00
67 Destroy All Monsters,pt.2 .... 3.00
68 Destroy All Monsters,pt.3 .... 3.00
69 PaP,World Tour: Earth 616 ... 3.00
70 PaP,World Tour: Earth 616 .... 3.00
71 World Tour: House of M 3.00
72 World Tour: New Universe, pt. 1. 3.00
73 World Tour: New Universe, pt. 2. 3.00
74 World Tour: New Universe, pt. 3. 3.00
75 World Tour: 2099, pt. 1 ...... 3.00
76 World Tour: 2099, pt. 2 ...... 3.00
77 World Tour: Squadron Supreme . 3.00
78 World Tour: Squadron Supreme . 3.00
79 World Tour: Future Imperfect ... 3.00
80 World Tour: Future Imperfect .. 3.00
81 World Tour: Heroes Reborn 3.00
82 World Tour: Heroes Reborn ... 3.00
83 It's Your Funeral 3.00
84 Back in the Saddle 3.00
85 The New Exiles.............. 3.00
86 Countdown to Infinite Wolverines 3.00
87 Superguardians, pt.1 .... 3.00
88 Superguardians, pt.2 .... 3.00
89 JCf, Wallflower 3.00
90 CCI,PaP,J:Psylocke 3.00
91 CCI,PaP,F:Blink............. 3.00
92 CCI,PaP,V:Hand 3.00
93 .... 3.00
94 CCI,PaP,Enemy of the Stars.... 3.00
95 CCI 3.00
96 CCI, Dream of Two Good Men .. 3.00
97 CCI 3.00
98 CCI 3.00
99 Dream of Two Good Men 3.00
100 CCI(s), TG, 64-pg. 4.00
Ann. #1 JCf 4.00
Spec. Days of Then and Now 3.00

FACTOR X
1995
1 After Xavier................. 4.00
2 Scott vs. Alex Summers........ 3.00
3 Cyclops vs. Havok............ 3.00
4 Jean & Scott 3.00

FAFHRD AND THE GRAY MOUSER
Epic, Oct., 1990
1 MMi,Fritz Leiber adapt. 5.00
2 thru 4 MMi, Feb., 1991. . . . . . @5.00

FAITHFUL
Nov., 1949
1 Ph(c),I Take This Man 150.00
2 Ph(c),Love Thief,Feb.,1950 . . . 150.00

FALCON
Nov., 1983
1 PS,V:Nemesis 3.00
2 V:Sentinels. 3.00
3 V:Electro 3.00
4 A:Capt.America, Feb., 1984 . . 3.00

FALLEN ANGELS
April, 1987
1 KGa,TP,A:Sunspot,Warlock 3.00
2 KGa,TP,I:Gomi,Fallen Angels . . . 2.50
3 KGa,TP,A:X-Factor 2.50
4 KGa,TP,A:Moon Boy, Devil
  Dinosaur 2.50
5 JSon,D:Angel,Don 2.50
6 JSon,Coconut Grove 2.50
7 KGa,Captured in CoconutGrove . 2.50
8 KGa,L:Sunspot,Warlock. 2.50

FALLEN SON: THE DEATH OF CAPTAIN AMERICA
May, 2007
1-shot Capt. America, JLb,JR2 . . . . 3.00
1-shot-a variant (c). 3.00
1-shot JLb, Spider-Man 3.00
1-shot-a variant (c) 3.00
1-shot JLb, Iron Man 3.00
1-shot-a variant (c) 3.00

FANTASTIC FIVE
Aug., 1999
1 TDF,PR,AM,New Team:Human Torch
  Thing,Ms.Fantastic,Psilord
  & Big Brain 2.50
2A TDF,PR,AM,Bloody
  Reunions x-over 2.50
2B variant MSh(c). 2.50
3 TDF,PR,AM,A:Spider-Girl 2.50
4 TDF,PR,AM 2.50
5 TDF,PR,AM,A:Kristoff 2.50
Digest In Search of Doom 8.00

July, 2007
1 RLm, The Final Doom 3.00
2 RLm, The Final Doom 3.00
3 RLm, The Final Doom 3.00
4 RLm, The Final Doom 3.00
5 RLm, The Final Doom 3.00

FANTASTIC FORCE
1994–96
1 Foil stamped cover 3.00
2 thru 18 . . . . @2.50

FANTASTIC FOUR
Nov., 1961
1 JK,I&O:Mr.Fantastic,Thing
  Invisible Girl,Human Torch
  Mole Man 46,000.00
2 JK,I:Skrulls 10,000.00
3 JK,I:Miracleman 6,500.00
4 JK,R:Submariner 7,500.00
5 JK,JSt,I&O:Doctor Doom . 10,000.00
6 JK,V:Doctor Doom 5,000.00
7 JK,I:Kurrgo 3,000.00
8 JK,I:Alicia Masters,I&O:
  Puppet Master 3,000.00

Fantastic Four #4
© *Marvel Entertainment Group*

9 JK,V:Submariner. 3,000.00
10 JK,V:Doctor Doom,I:Ovoids . 3,000.00
11 JK,I:Impossible Man. 2,500.00
12 JK,V:Hulk 5,000.00
13 JK,SD,I&O:Red Ghost,
  I:Watcher 1,500.00
14 JK,SD,V:Submariner 1,200.00
15 JK,I:Mad Thinker 1,200.00
16 JK,V:Doctor Doom 1,200.00
17 JK,V:Doctor Doom 1,200.00
18 JK,I:Super Skrull 1,200.00
19 JK,I&O:Rama Tut. 1,200.00
20 JK,I:Molecule Man 1,000.00
21 JK,I:Hate Monger 900.00
22 JK,V:Mole Man 600.00
23 JK,V:Doctor Doom 600.00
24 JK,I:Infant Terrible 600.00
25 JK,Thing vs.Hulk 1,200.00
26 JK,V:Hulk,A:Avengers 1,200.00
27 JK,A:Doctor Strange 750.00
28 JK,1st X-Men x-over 1,000.00
29 JK,V:Red Ghost 500.00
30 JK,I&O:Diablo 500.00
31 JK,V:Mole Man 400.00
32 JK,V:Superskrull 400.00
33 JK,I:Attuma 400.00
34 JK,I:Gideon 400.00
35 JK,I:Dragon Man,A:Diablo . . 400.00
36 JK,I:Medusa,Frightful Four . . 400.00
37 JK,V:Skrulls. 375.00
38 JK,V:Frightful Four,I:Trapster . 375.00
39 JK,WW,A:Daredevil. 375.00
40 JK,A:Daredevil,Dr.Doom. . . . 375.00
41 JK,V:Fright.Four,A:Medusa. . . 250.00
42 JK,V:Frightful Four 250.00
43 JK,V:Frightful Four 250.00
44 JK,JSt,I:Gorgon,
  V:Dragon Man 250.00
45 JK,JSt,I:Inhumans(Black Bolt,
  Triton,Lockjaw,Crystal,
  Karnak) 500.00
46 JK,JSt,V:Seeker 275.00
47 JK,JSt,I:Maximus,Attilan,
  Alpha Primitives. 275.00
48 JK,JSt,I:Silver Surfer,
  C:Galactus 1,500.00
49 JK,JSt,A:Silver Surfer,
  V:Galactus 750.00
50 JK,JSt,V:Galactus,Silver
  Surfer,I:Wyatt Wingfoot 900.00
51 JK,JSt,I:Negative Zone 500.00
52 JK,JSt,I:Black Panther 750.00
53 JK,JSt,I:Klaw,Vibranium 325.00
54 JK,JSt,I:Prester John 200.00

55 JK,JSt,A:Silver Surfer 400.00
56 JK,JSt,O:Klaw,A:Inhumans,
  C:Silver Surfer. 200.00
57 JK,JSt,V:DocDoom,A:S.Surfer. 200.00
58 JK,JSt,V:DocDoom,A:S.Surfer. 200.00
59 JK,JSt,V:DocDoom,A:S.Surfer. 200.00
60 JK,JSt,V:DocDoom,A:S.Surfer. 200.00
61 JK,JSt,V:Sandman,A:S.Surfer 200.00
62 JK,JSt,I:Blastaar 150.00
63 JK,JSt,V:Blastaar 150.00
64 JK,JSt,I:The Kree,Sentry . . . 150.00
65 JK,JSt,I:Ronan,Supreme
  Intelligence 150.00
66 JK,JSt,O:Him,A:Crystal 225.00
67 JK,JSt,I:Him 225.00
68 JK,JSt,V:Mad Thinker 150.00
69 JK,JSt,V:Mad Thinker 150.00
70 JK,JSt,V:Mad Thinker 150.00
71 JK,JSt,V:Mad Thinker 150.00
72 JK,JSt,A:Watcher,S.Surfer . . . 200.00
73 JK,JSt,A:SpM,DD,Thor 200.00
74 JK,JSt,A:Silver Surfer 150.00
75 JK,JSt,A:Silver Surfer 150.00
76 JK,JSt,V:Psycho Man,S.Surf. . 150.00
77 JK,JSt,V:Galactus,S.Surfer. . . 100.00
78 JK,JSt,V:Wizard 100.00
79 JK,JSt,A:Crystall,V:Mad
  Thinker. 100.00
80 JK,JSt,A:Crystal 100.00
81 JK,JSt,J:Crystal,V:Wizard . . . 100.00
82 JK,JSt,V:Maximus 100.00
83 JK,JSt,V:Maximus 100.00
84 JK,JSt,V:Doctor Doom 100.00
85 JK,JSt,V:Doctor Doom 75.00
86 JK,JSt,V:Doctor Doom 75.00
87 JK,JSt,V:Doctor Doom 75.00
88 JK,JSt,V:Mole Man 75.00
89 JK,JSt,V:Mole Man 75.00
90 JK,JSt,V:Skrulls. 75.00
91 JK,JSt,V:Skrulls,I:Torgo. 75.00
92 JK,JSt,V:Torgo,Skrulls. 75.00
93 JK,V:Torgo,Skrulls. 75.00
94 JK,JSt,I:Agatha Harkness 75.00
95 JK,JSt,I:Monocle 75.00
96 JK,JSt,V:Mad Thinker 75.00
97 JK,JSt,V:Monster from
  Lost Lagoon. 75.00
98 JK,JSt,V:Kree Sentry 75.00
99 JK,JSt,A:Inhumans 75.00
100 JK,JSt,V:Puppetmaster 200.00
101 JK,JSt,V:Maggia 75.00
102 JK,JSt,V:Magneto 75.00
103 JR,V:Magneto 75.00
104 JR,V:Magneto 75.00
105 JR,L:Crystal 75.00
106 JR,JSt,'Monster's Secret' . . . 75.00
107 JB,JSt,V:Annihilus. 75.00
108 JK,JB,JR,JSt, V:Annihilus . . . 75.00
109 JB,JSt,V:Annihilus. 75.00
110 JB,JSt,V:Annihilus 75.00
111 JB,JSt,A:Hulk. 75.00
112 JB,JSt,Thing vs. Hulk 250.00
113 JB,JSt,I:Overmind 60.00
114 JR(c),JB,V:Overmind. 60.00
115 JR(c),JB,JSt,I:Eternals 60.00
116 JB,JSt,O:Stranger 75.00
117 JB,JSt,V:Diablo 50.00
118 JR(c),JB,JM,V:Diablo 50.00
119 JB,JSt,V:Klaw 50.00
120 JB,JSt,I:Gabriel(Airwalker)
  (Robot). 50.00
121 JB,JSt,V:Silver Surfer,D:
  Gabriel Destroyer 75.00
122 JR(c),JB,JSt,V:Galactus,
  A:Silver Surfer 75.00
123 JB,JSt,V:Galactus,
  A:Silver Surfer 75.00
124 JB,JSt,V:Monster 50.00
125 E:StL(s),JB,JSt,V:Monster. . . 50.00
126 B:RTs(s),JB,JSt,
  O:FF,MoleMan. 50.00
127 JB,JSt,V:Mole Man 50.00

128 JB,JSt,V:Mole Man 50.00	177 JP,JS,A:Frightful Four
129 JB,JSt,I:Thundra,	I:Texas Twister,Capt.Ultra 15.00
V:Frightful Four 50.00	178 GP,V:Frightful Four,Brute 15.00
130 JSo(c),JB,JSt,V:Frightful Four. 50.00	179 JSt,V:Annihilus 15.00
131 JSo(c),JB,JSt,V:QuickSilver . . 50.00	180 reprint #101. . . . . 15.00
132 JB,JSt,J:Medusa 50.00	181 E:RTs(s),JSt,V:Brute,
133 JSt(i),V:Thundra 50.00	Annihilus 15.00
134 JB,JSt,V:Dragon Man 50.00	182 SB,JSt,V:Brute,Annihilus. 15.00
135 JB,JSt,V:Gideon 50.00	183 SB,JSt,V:Brute,Annihilus. 15.00
136 JB,JSt,A:Shaper 50.00	184 GP,JSt,V:Eliminator. 15.00
137 JB,JSt,A:Shaper 50.00	185 GP,JSt,V:Nich.Scratch 15.00
138 JB,JSt,O:Miracle Man 50.00	186 GP,JSi,I:Salem's Seven 15.00
139 JB,V:Miracle Man 50.00	187 GP,JSt,V:Klaw,Molecule Man . 15.00
140 JB,JSt,O:Annihilus 50.00	188 GP,JSt,V:Molecule Man 15.00
141 JR(c),JB,JSt,V:Annihilus 50.00	189 reprint FF Annual #4 . . . . 15.00
142 RB,JSt,A:Doc Doom 50.00	190 SB,O:Fantastic Four 15.00
143 GK(c),RB,V:Doc Doom 50.00	191 GP,JSt,V:Plunderer,
144 RB,JSt,V:Doc Doom 50.00	Team Breaks Up 15.00
145 JSt&GK(c),RA,I:Ternak 50.00	192 GP,JSt,V:Texas Twister 15.00
146 RA,JSt,V:Ternak 50.00	193 KP,V:Darkoth,Diablo 15.00
147 RB,JSt,V:Subby 50.00	194 KP,V:Darkoth,Diablo 15.00
148 RB,JSt,V:Frightful Four 50.00	195 KP,A:Sub-Mariner 15.00
149 RB,JSt,V:Sub-Mariner. 50.00	196 KP,V:Invincible Man (Reed),
150 GK(c),RB,JSt,W:Crystal &	A:Dr.Doom,Team Reunited . . . 15.00
Quicksilver,V:Ultron 60.00	197 KP,JSt,Red Ghost 15.00
151 RB,JSt,O:Thundra. 25.00	198 KP,JSt,V:Doc Doom 15.00
152 JR(c),RB,JM,A:Thundra 25.00	199 KP,JSt,V:Doc Doom 15.00
153 GK(c),RB,JSt,A: I hundra. . . . 25.00	200 KP,JSt,V:Doc Doom 25.00
154 GK(c),rep.Str.Tales #127. . . . 25.00	201 KP,JSt,FF's Machinery 8.00
155 RB,JSt,A:Surfer. 30.00	202 KP,JSt,V:Quasimodo. 8.00
156 RB,JSt,A:Surfer,V:Doom 30.00	203 KP,JSt,V:Mutant 8.00
157 RB,JSt,A:Surfer. 30.00	204 KP,JSt,V:Skrulls 8.00
158 RB,JSt,V:Xemu 25.00	205 KP,JSt,V:Skrulls 8.00
159 RB,JSt,V:Xemu 25.00	206 KP,JSt,V:Skrulls,A:Nova 8.00
160 K&R(c),JB,V:Arkon 25.00	207 SB,JSt,V:Monocle,A:SpM 8.00
161 RB,JSt,V:Arkon 15.00	208 SB,V:Sphinx,A:Nova 8.00
162 RB,DA,JSt,V:Arkon 15.00	209 JBy,JSt,I:Herbie,A:Nova 10.00
163 RB,JSt,V:Arkon 15.00	210 JBy,JS,A:Galactus 8.00
164 JK(c),GP,JSt,V:Crusader,R:	211 JBy,JS,I:Terrax,A:Galactus . . . 10.00
Marvel Boy,I:Frankie Raye . . . 15.00	212 JBy,JSt,V:Galactus,Sphinx . . . 8.00
165 GP,JSt,O:Crusader,	213 JBy,JSt,V:Terrax,Galactus
O&D:Marvel Boy 15.00	Sphinx 8.00
166 GP,V:Hulk 30.00	214 JBy,JSt,V:Skrull. 8.00
167 JK(c),GP,JSt,V:Hulk 30.00	215 JBy,JSt,V:Blastaar. 8.00
168 RB,JSt,J:Luke Cage 15.00	216 JBy,V:Blastaar. 8.00
169 RB,JSt,V:Puppetmaster 15.00	217 JBy,JSt,A:Dazzler 8.00
170 GP,JSt,L:Luke Cage 15.00	218 JBy,JSt,V:FrightfulFour,
171 JK(c),RB,GP,JSt,I:Gor. 15.00	A:Spider-Man. 8.00
172 JK(c),GP,JSt,V:Destroyer 15.00	219 BSz,JSt,A:Sub-Mariner 7.00
173 JB,V:Galactus,O:Heralds 15.00	220 JBy,JSt,A:Vindicator 7.00
174 JB,V:Galactus 15.00	221 JBy,JSt,V:Vindicator 7.00
175 JB,A:High Evolutionary 15.00	222 BSz,JSt,V:Nicholas Scratch . . . 7.00
176 GP,JSt,V:Impossible Man 15.00	223 BSz,JSt,V:Salem's Seven 7.00
	224 BSz,A:Thor 7.00
	225 BSz,A:Thor 7.00
	226 BSz,A:Shogun. 7.00
	227 BSz,JSt,V:Ego-Spawn. 7.00
	228 BSz,JSt,V:Ego-Spawn. 7.00
	229 BSz,JSt,I:Firefrost,Ebon
	Seeker 7.00
	230 BSz,JSt,A:Avengers,
	O:Firefrost & Ebon Seeker 7.00
	231 BSz,JSt,V:Stygorr 7.00
	232 JBy,New Direction,V:Diablo . . . 8.00
	233 JBy,V:Hammerhead 7.00
	234 JBy,V:Ego 7.00
	235 JBy,O:Ego. 7.00
	236 JBy,V:Dr.Doom,A:Puppet
	Master, 20th Anniv. 7.00
	237 JBy,V:Solons. 6.00
	238 JBy,O:Frankie Raye,
	new Torch. 6.00
	239 JBy,I:Aunt Petunia,
	Uncle Jake. 6.00
	240 JBy,A:Inhumans,b:Luna 6.00
	241 JBy,A:Black Panther 6.00
	242 JBy,A:Daredevil,Thor,Iron Man
	Spider-Man,V:Terrax 6.00
	243 JBy,A:Daredevil,Dr.Strange,
	Spider-Man,Avengers,V:Galactus,
	Terrax. 6.00

Fantastic Four #219
© *Marvel Entertainment Group*

244 JBy,A:Avengers,Dr.Strange,
Galactus, Becomes Nova 6.00
245 JBy,V:Franklin Richards 6.00
246 JBy,V:Dr.Doom,
A:Puppet Master 6.00
247 JBy,A:Dr.Doom,I:Kristoff,
D:Zorba 6.00
248 JBy,A:Inhumans 6.00
249 JBy,V:Gladiator 6.00
250 JBy,A:Capt.Am.,SpM,
V:Gladiator. 6.00
251 JBy,A:Annihilus 6.00
252 JBy,1st sideways issue,V:
Ootah,A:Annihilus,w/tattoo 6.00
252a w/o tattoo 6.00
253 JBy,V:Kestorans,A:Annihilus. . . 6.00
254 JBy,V:Mantracora,
A:She-Hulk,Wasp 6.00
255 JBy,A:Daredevil,Annihilus,
V:Mantracora. 6.00
256 JBy,A:Avengers,Galactus,
V:Annihilus,New Costumes 6.00
257 JBy,A:Galactus,Death,Nova,
Scarlet Witch 5.00
258 JBy,A:Dr.Doom,D:Hauptmann . 5.00
259 JBy,V:Terrax,Dr.Doom,
C:Silver Silver 5.00
260 JBy,V:Terrax, Dr.Doom,
A:Silver Surfer,Sub-Mariner. . . . 6.00
261 JBy,A:Sub-Mariner,Marrina,
Silver Surfer,Sc.Witch,Lilandra . 6.00
262 JBy,O:Galactus,A:Odin,
(J.Byrne in story) 5.00
263 JBy,V:Messiah,A:Mole Man . . . 5.00
264 JBy,V:Messiah,A:Mole Man . . . 5.00
265 JBy,A:Trapster,Avengers,
J:She-Hulk,Secret Wars 5.00
266 KGa,JBy,A:Hulk,Sasquatch,
V:Karisma 5.00
267 JBy,A:Hulk,Sasquatch,Morbius,
V:Dr.Octopus,Sue miscarries . . 5.00
268 JBy,V:Doom's Mask 5.00
269 JBy,R:Wyatt Wingfoot,
I:Terminus 5.00
270 JBy,V:Terminus 5.00
271 JBy,V:Gormuu 5.00
272 JBy,I:Warlord (Nathaniel
Richards) 5.00
273 JBy,V:Warlord 5.00
274 JBy,AG,cont.from Thing#19,
A:Spider-Man's Black Costume. 5.00
275 JBy,AG,V:T.J.Vance. 5.00
276 JBy,JOy,V:Mephisto,
A:Dr.Strange 5.00

Fantastic Four #158
© *Marvel Entertainment Group*

All comics prices listed are for *Near Mint* condition.

MARVEL

Fantastic Four #285
© *Marvel Entertainment Group*

277 JBy,JOy,V:Mephisto,
    A:Dr.Strange,R:Thing 5.00
278 JBy,JOy,O:Dr.Doom,A:Kristoff
    (as Doom) 5.00
279 JBy,JOy,V:Dr.Doom(Kristoff),
    I:New Hate-Monger 5.00
280 JBy,JOy,I:Malice,
    V:Hate-Monger 5.00
281 JBy,JOy,A:Daredevil,V:Hate
    Monger,Malice 5.00
282 JBy,JOy,A:Power Pack,Psycho
    Man,Secret Wars II 5.00
283 JBy,JOy,V:Psycho-Man 5.00
284 JBy,JOy,V:Psycho-Man 5.00
285 JBy,JOy,Secret Wars II
    A:Beyonder 5.00
286 JBy,TA,R:Jean Grey,
    A:Hercules Capt.America 6.00
287 JBy,JSt,A:Wasp,V:Dr.Doom . . . 5.00
288 JBy,JSt,V:Dr.Doom,Secret
    Wars II 6.00
289 JBy,AG,D:Basilisk,V:Blastaar,
    R:Annihilus 5.00
290 JBy,AG,V:Annihilus 5.00
291 JBy,CR,A:Nick Fury 5.00
292 JBy,AG,A:Nick Fury,V:Hitler . . . 5.00
293 JBy,AG,A:Avengers.W.C. 5.00
294 JOy,AG,V:FutureCentralCity . . . 3.00
295 JOy,AG,V:Fut.Central City 3.00
296 BWS,KGa,RF,BWi,AM,KJ,JB,
    SL,MS,JRu,JOy,JSt,25th
    Anniv.,V:MoleMan 5.00
297 JB,SB,V:Umbra-Sprite 3.00
298 JB,SB,V:Umbra-Sprite 3.00
299 JB,SB,She-Hulk,V:Thing,
    A:Spider-Man,L:She-Hulk 3.00
300 JB,SB,W:Torch & Fake Alicia
    (Lyja),A:Puppet-Master,Wizard,
    Mad Thinker,Dr.Doom 4.00
301 JB,SB,V:Wizard,MadThinker . . 3.00
302 JB,SB,V:Project Survival. 3.00
303 JB,RT,A:Thundra,V:Machus . . . 3.00
304 JB,JSt,V:Quicksilver,
    A:Kristoff 3.00
305 JB,JSt,V:Quicksilver,
    J:Crystal,A:Dr.Doom 3.00
306 JB,JSt,A:Capt.America,
    J:Ms.Marvel,V:Diablo. 3.00
307 JB,JSt,L:Reed&Sue,V:Diablo . . 3.00
308 JB,JSt,I:Fasaud. 3.00
309 JB,JSt,V:Fasaud 3.00
310 KP,JSt,V:Fasaud,N:Thing
    & Ms.Marvel 3.00

311 KP,JSt,A:Black Panther,
    Dr.Doom,V:THRob. 3.00
312 KP,JSt,A:Black Panther,
    Dr.Doom,X-Factor 3.00
313 SB,JSt,V:Lava Men,
    A:Moleman 3.00
314 KP,JSt,V:Belasco 3.00
315 KP,JSt,V:Mast.Pandem. 3.00
316 KP,JSt,A:CometMan 3.00
317 KP,JSt,L:Crystal 3.00
318 KP,JSt,V:Dr.Doom. 3.00
319 KP,JSt,G-Size,O:Beyonder 3.00
320 KP,JSt,Hulk vs Thing. 3.00
321 RLm,RT,A:She-Hulk 3.00
322 KP,JSt,Inferno,V:Graviton 3.00
323 KP,JSt,RT,Inferno A:Mantis 3.00
324 KP,JSt,RT,A:Mantis 3.00
325 RB,RT,A:Silver Surfer,
    D:Mantis 3.00
326 KP,RT,I:New Frightful Four 3.00
327 KP,RT,V:Frightful Four. 3.00
328 KP,RT,V:Frightful Four. 3.00
329 RB,RT,V:Mole Man 3.00
330 RB,RT,V:Dr.Doom. 3.00
331 RB,RT,V:Ultron 3.00
332 RB,RT,V:Aron 3.00
333 RB,RT,V:Aron,Frightful Four . . . 3.00
334 RB,Acts of Vengeance 3.00
335 RB,RT,Acts of Vengeance 3.00
336 RLm,Acts of Vengeance, ... 3.00
337 WS,A:Thor,Iron Man,
    B:Timestream saga 4.00
338 WS,V:Deathshead,A:Thor,
    Iron Man 3.00
339 WS,V:Gladiator 3.00
340 WS,V:Black Celestial 3.00
341 WS,A:Thor,Iron Man 3.00
342 A:Rusty,C:Spider-Man 3.00
343 WS,V:Stalin 3.00
344 WS,V:Stalin 3.00
345 WS,V:Dinosaurs 3.00
346 WS,V:Dinosaurs 3.00
347 AAd,ATi(i)A:Spider-Man,
    GhostRider,Wolverine,Hulk 4.00
347a 2nd printing 3.00
348 AAd,ATi(i)A:Spider-Man,
    GhostRider,Wolverine,Hulk 4.00
348a 2nd printing. 3.00
349 AAd,ATi(i),AM(i)A:Spider-Man,
    Wolverine,GhostRider,Hulk,
    C:Punisher. 3.50
350 WS,Am(i),R:Ben Grimm as
    Thing,(48p) 3.50
351 MBa,Kubic. 3.00
352 WS,Reed Vs.Dr.Doom 3.00
353 WS,E:Timestream Saga,
    A:Avengers, ... 3.00
354 WS,Secrets of the Time
    Variance Authority 3.00
355 AM,V:Wrecking Crew 3.00
356 B:TDF(s),PR,A:New Warriors,
    V:Puppet Master 3.00
357 PR,V:Mad Thinker,
    Puppetmaster, ... 3.00
358 PR,AAd,30th Anniv.,1st Marv.
    Die Cut(c),D:Lyja,V:Paibok,
    BU:Dr.Doom 3.50
359 PR,I:Devos the Devastator 3.00
360 PR,V:Dreadface 3.00
361 PR,V:Dr.Doom,X-masIssue . . . 3.00
362 PR,A:Spider-Man,
    I:WildBlood 3.00
363 PR,I:Occulus,A:Devos 3.00
364 PR,V:Occulus 3.00
365 PR,V:Occulus 3.00
366 PR,Infinity War,R:Lyja 3.00
367 PR,Inf.War,A:Wolverine 3.00
368 PR,V:Infinity War X-Men 3.00
369 PR,Inf.War,R:Malice,
    A:Thanos 3.00
370 PR,Inf.War,V:Mr.Fantastic
    Doppleganger 3.00

371 PR,V:Lyja,foil(c) 4.00
371a 2nd Printing. 3.00
372 PR,A:Spider-Man,Silver
    Sable 3.00
373 PR,V:Aron,Silver sable 3.00
374 PR,V:Secret Defenders 3.00
375 V:Dr.Doom,A:Inhumans,Lyja,
    Holo-Grafix(c) 3.50
376 PR,A:Nathan Richards,V:Paibok,
    Devos,w/Dirt Magazine 3.50
376a w/out Dirt Magazine 2.50
377 PR,V:Paibok,Devos,Klaw,
    I:Huntara 2.50
378 PR,A:Sandman,SpM,DD. 2.50
379 PR,V:Ms.Marvel 2.50
380 PR,A:Dr.Doom,V:Hunger 2.50
381 PR,D:Dr.Doom,Mr.Fantastic,
    V:Hunger 5.00
382 PR,V:Paibok,Devos,Huntara . . 3.00
383 PR,V:Paibok,Devos,Huntara . . 2.50
384 PR,A:Ant-Man,V:Franklin
    Richards 2.50
385 PR,A:Triton,Tiger Shark,
    Starblast#7. . . . . 2.50
386 PR,Starblast#11,A:Namor,Triton,
    b:Johnny & Lyja child 2.50
387 Die-Cut & Foil (c),PR,N:Invisible
    Woman,J:Ant-Man,A:Namor . . . 4.00
387a Newsstand Ed. 2.50
388 PR,I:Dark Raider,V:FF,
    Avengers,w/cards 2.50
389 PR,I:Raphael Suarez,A:Watcher,
    V:Collector 2.50
390 PR,A:Galactus 2.50
391 PR,I:Vibraxas 2.50
392 Dark Raider. 2.50
393 . . . . 2.50
394 Neon(c) w/insert print 3.00
394a Newsstand ed.,no bag/inserts 2.50
395 Thing V:Wolverine. 2.50
396 . . . . 2.50
397 Resurrection,pt.1. . . . . 2.50
398 regular edition 2.50
398a Enhanced cover 3.00
399 Watcher's Lie 3.00
399a Foil stamped cover 3.00
400 Watcher's Lie,pt.3 . . . . 5.00
401 V:Tantalus 2.50
402 Atlantis Rising,Namor
    vs. Black Bolt. 2.50
403 TDF,PR,DBi,F:Thing,Medusa . . 2.50
404 R:Namor,I:New Villian 2.50
405 J:Namor 2.50

Fantastic Four #414
© *Marvel Entertainment Group*

406 TDF,PR,DBI,R:Dr. Doom,
    I:Hyperstorm 2.50
407 TDF,PR,DBi,Return of
    Reed Richards. 2.50
408 TDF,PR,DBi,Original FF unite. . 2.50
409 TDF,PR,DBi,All new line-up . . . 2.50
410 . . . . 2.50
411 . . . . 2.50
412 TDF,PR,DBi,Mr.Fantastic
    vs. Sub-Mariner. 2.50
413 . . . . 2.50
414 Galactus vs. Hyperstorm 2.50
415 Onslaught saga, A:X-Men. 4.00
416 Onslaught saga, A:Dr. Doom,
    double size, finale 5.00
Ann.#1 JK,SD,I:Atlantis,Dorma,
    Krang,V:Namor,O:FF 1,700.00
Ann.#2 JK,JSt,O:Dr.Doom 1,000.00
Ann.#3 JK,W:Reed and Sue 400.00
Ann.#4 JK,JSt,I:Quasimodo. 250.00
Ann.#5 JK,JSt,A:Inhumans,Silver
    Surfer,Black Panther,
    I:Psycho Man. 250.00
Ann.#6 JK,JSt,I:Annihilus,
    Franklin Richards 250.00
Ann.#7 JK(c),reprints 100.00
Ann.#8 JR(c),reprints 50.00
Ann.#9 JK(c),reprints. 50.00
Ann.#10 reprints Ann.#3 . . . . 50.00
Ann.#11 JK(c),JB,A:The Invaders . . 12.00
Ann.#12 A:The Invaders 12.00
Ann.#13 V:The Mole Man 12.00
Ann.#14 GP,V:Salem's Seven 12.00
Ann.#15 GP,V:Dr.Doom,Skrulls . . . 10.00
Ann.#16 V:Dragonlord 10.00
Ann.#17 JBy,V:Skrulls 10.00
Ann.#18 KGa,V:Skrulls,W:Black
    Bolt and Medusa,A:Inhumans . 10.00
Ann.#19 JBy,V:Skrulls 10.00
Ann.#20 TD(i),V:Dr.Doom 4.00
Ann.#21 JG,JSt,Evol.Wars 4.00
Ann.#22 RB,Atlantis Attacks,
    A:Avengers 4.00
Ann.#23 JG,GCa,Days of Future
    Present #1. . . . . 5.00
Ann.#24 JG,AM,Korvac Quest #1,
    A:Guardians of the Galaxy 3.00
Ann.#25 Citizen Kang #3 . . . . 3.00
Ann.#26 HT,I:Wildstreak,
    V:Dreadface,w/card 3.50
Ann.#27 MGu,V:Justice Peace 3.50
G-Size#1 RB,Thing/Hulk 17.00
G-Size#2 K&R(c),JB,Time to Kill . . 15.00
G-Size#3 RB,JSt,Four Horseman . 15.00
G-Size#4 JB,JSt,I:Madrox 15.00
G-Size#5 JK(c),V:Psycho Man,
    Molecule Man 12.00
G-Size#6 V:Annihilus 12.00
Spec.#1 Rep.Ann.#1 JBy(c). 2.50
Marvel Milestone rep. #1 (1991) . . 3.00
Marvel Milestone rep. #5 (1992) . . 3.00
Ashcan. 75
Spec. The Origin of Galactus. . . . 2.50
Spec. Marvel's Greatest Comic:
    rep. #52: I:Black Panther (2006) 3.00

[2nd Series], Nov., 1996
1 JLe,BCi,SW, 48pg 5.00
1A Mole Man cover. 12.00
1B Gold signature, bagged,
    limited 25.00
2 JLe,BCi,V:Namor 5.00
3 JLe,BCi,SW,A:Avengers 4.00
4 JLe,BCi,SW,I:Black Panther . . . 4.00
4A x-mas cover. 5.00
5 JLe,BCi,SW,V:Dr. Doom 4.00
6 JLe,BCi,SW,Industrial Revolution
    prologue. 3.00
7 JLe,BCi,BBh,V:Blastaar 3.00
8 JLe,BCi,BBh,V:Inhumans 3.00
9 JLe,BCi,BBh,V:Inhumans 3.00
10 JLe,BCi,BBh,A:Silver Surfer,
    Tyrax 3.00

Fantastic Four 2nd Series #5
© Marvel Entertainment Group

11 JLe,BCi,BBh,A:Silver Surfer,
    Firelord, Terrax 3.00
12 JLe,BCi,BBh,GalactusSaga,pt.1,
    reunited 5.00
13 JeR,Wildstorm x-over 3.00
Ashcan, signed, numbered 10.00

[3rd Series], Nov., 1997
1 SLo,AD,MFm, The Ruined, 48pg
    debut 5.00
2 SLo,AD,MFm,A:Iconoclast. 4.00
3 SLo,AD,MFm,V:Red Ghost 4.00
4 SLo,SvL,ATi,A:Silver Surfer,
    double size 4.00
4 signed by SLo, (500 copies) . . . 20.00
5 SLo,SvL,ATi,V:The Crucible . . . 3.00
6 CCI,SvL, new villains 3.00
7 CCI,SvL,ATi,V:Technet. 3.00
8 CCI,SvL,V:Captain Britain corp. . 3.00
9 CCI,SvL,A:Spider-Man. 3.00
10 CCI,SvL,ATi. 3.00
11 CCI,SvL,ATi,Crucible—unleashed
    in Genosha 3.00
12 CCI,SvL,ATi,V:Fantastic Four
    double-size 4.50
13 CCI,SvL,A:Ronan the Accuser . . 2.50
14 CCI,SvL,V:Ronan 2.50
15 CCI,SvL,ATi,Iron Man x-over . . . 2.50
16 CCI,SvL,ATi,V:Kree Avengers. . 2.50
17 CCI,SvL,ATi,I:Lockdown 2.50
18 CCI,SvL,ATi,Jail Break 2.50
19 CCI,SvL,ATi,V:Annihilus 2.50
20 CCI,SvL,ATi,V:Ruined 2.50
21 CCI,SvL,ATi,V:Hades 2.50
22 CCI,SvL,ATi,V:Valeria
    Von Doom 2.50
23 CCI,SvL,ATi,A:She-Hulk 2.50
24 CCI,SvL,ATi,F:FranklinRichards . 2.50
25 CCI,SvL,ATi,V:Dr.Doom 3.50
26 CCI,SvL,ATi,F:ValeriaVonDoom . 3.00
27 CCI,SvL,F:Invisible Woman . . . 3.00
28 CCI,SvL,ATi,Planet Doom. 3.00
29 CCI,SvL,ATi,Frightful Four 2.50
30 CCI,SvL,ATi,Castle Doom. 2.50
31 CCI,SvL,ATi,InvisibleWoman . . . 2.50
32 CCI,SvL,ATi,InvisibleWoman . . . 2.50
33 JFM,SvL,ATi,Kid Colt 2.50
34 JFM,SvL,ATi,aliens. 2.50
35A CPa,Diablo,foil (c). 5.00
35B painted (c) 2.50
36 CPa,Diablo triumphant 2.50
37 CPa,F:Johnny Storm. 2.50
38 CPa,JLb,V:Grey Gargoyle 2.50
39 CPa,JLb,V:Grey Gargoyle 2.50
40 CPa,JLb,Negative Zone 2.50

41 CPa,JLb,Hellscout 2.50
42 CPa,JLb,SI,V:Namor. 2.50
43 CPa,JLb,JoB,new Fant.Four. . . 2.50
44 CPa,JLb,Negative Zone,concl. . 2.50
45 CPa,JLb,one new costume. . . . 2.50
46 CPa,JLb,Abraxas Saga 2.50
47 CPa,JLb,Abraxas,pt.3 . . . . 2.50
48 CPa,JLb,Abraxas,pt.4 . . . . 2.50
49 CPa,JLb,Abraxas,pt.5 . . . . 2.50
50 Four new stories,BWS(c),64-pg. . 5.00
51 MBa,KK,F:Inhumans. 3.50
52 MBa,KK,F:Dr. Doom 2.50
53 MBa,KK,Inhumans 2.50
54 MBa,KK,Inhumans, 100-pg. 4.00
55 KK,SI,Thing,Human Torch 2.50
56 F:Thing 2.50
57 AWa,F:Thing,pt.1 . . . . 2.50
58 AWa,F:Thing,pt.2 . . . . 2.50
59 AWa,F:Thing,pt.3 . . . . 2.50
60 MWa,KK 2.50
61 MWa,KK 3.00
62 MWa,KK,Sentient,pt.1, 48-pg . . 3.00
63 MWa,KK,Sentient,pt.2. . . . . 3.00
64 MWa,KK,Sentient,pt.3. . . . . 3.00
65 MWa,MBu,Small Stuff/Big Stuff. . 3.00
66 MWa,MBu,Small Stuff/Big Stuff. . 3.00
67 MWa,KK,Unthinkable 5.00
68 MWa,KK,Unthinkable 3.50
69 MWa,KK,Unthinkable 3.50
70 MWa,Unthinkable 3.50
Resumes original numbering
500 MWa,Unthinkable,48-pg. 5.00
500a Director's Cut, foil 6.00
501 MWa,CJ,Fifth Wheel,pt.1 . . . . 2.50
502 MWa,CJ,Fifth Wheel,pt.2 . . . . 2.50
503 MWa,Authoritative Action,pt.1 . 2.50
504 MWa,Authoritative Action,pt.2. . 2.50
505 MWa,Authoritative Action,pt.3 . 2.50
506 MWa,Authoritative Action,pt.4 . 2.50
507 MWa,Authoritative Action,pt.5. . 2.50
508 MWa,Authoritative Action,pt.6. . 2.50
509 MWa,Hereafter,pt.1 . . . . 2.50
510 MWa,Hereafter,pt.2. . . . . 2.50
511 MWa,Hereafter,pt.3 . . . . 2.50
512 MWa,Spider Sense,pt.1 . . . . . 2.50
513 MWa,Spider Sense,pt.2 . . . . . 2.50
514 MWa&KK(s),Dysfunctional,pt.1. 2.50
515 MWa&KK(s),Dysfunctional,pt.2. 2.50
516 MWa,KK(s),Dysfunctional,pt.3 . 2.50
517 MWa(s),Fourtitude,pt.1 . . . . . . 3.00
518 Fourtitude,pt.2. . . . . 3.00
519 Fourtitude,pt.3. . . . . 3.00
520 . . . . 3.00
521 . . . . 3.00
522 MWa,MeW,Galactus 3.00
523 MWa,MeW,Rising Storm, concl. 3.00
524 MWa,MeW, ... 3.00
525 KK,TGu,Dream Fever,pt.1 . . . 3.00
526 KK,TGu,Dream Fever,pt.2 . . . 3.00
527 MMK,Distant Music, Entity . . . 5.00
528 MMK,Random Factors, Entity. . 3.00
529 MMK,Appointment Overdue . . . 3.00
530 MMK,Reunion with destiny . . . 3.00
531 MSz(s),MMK,V:The Entity,pt.5 . 3.00
532 MSz(s),MMK,V:The Entity,pt.6 . 3.00
533 MSz(s),MMK,A:Hulk 3.00
534 MSz(s),MMK,A:Hulk 3.00
535 MSz(s),MMK,A:Hulk 3.00
536 MSz(s),MMK,Road to Civil War 7.00
537 MSz(s),MMK,Road to Civil War 7.00
538 MSz(s),MMK,Civil War tie-in. . 3.50
539 MSz(s),MMK,Civil War tie-in. . 3.50
540 MSz(s),MMK,Civil War tie-in. . 3.50
541 MSz(s),MMK,Civil War tie-in. . 3.50
542 MSz(s),MMK,Civil War tie-in. . 3.50
543 MSz(s),MMK,Civil War tie-in. . 3.50
544 DMD(s),PaP 3.00
545 DMD(s),PaP 3.00
546 DMD(s),PaP,V:Epoch 3.00
547 DMD(s),PaP,V:The Wizard . . . 3.00
548 . . . . 3.00
549 DMD(s),PaP 3.00

550 DMD(s),PaP 3.00
551 . . . . 3.00
552 DMD(s),PaP,V:Dr. Doom. 3.00
553 . . . . 3.00
554 MMr(s),BHi,F:Mrs. Fantastic . . 3.00
555 MMr(s),BHi,World's Greatest . . 3.00
556 MMr(s),BHi,World's Greatest . . 3.00
557 MMr(s),BHi,World's Greatest . . 3.00
558 MMr(s),BHi,Doctor Doom 3.00
559 MMr(s),BHi,Psionics 3.00
560 MMr(s),BHi,Exodus. 3.00
561 MMr(s),BHi,Death of Invisible
   Woman 3.00
561a monkey variant (c) 3.00
562 BHi,Wedding & Funeral 3.00
563 Mister & Mrs. Thing 3.00
Ann.1998 Fant.Four & Fant.Four. . 4.00
Ann.1999 CCI,I:Mechamage 4.00
Ann.2000 LSi,SvL,48-pg. 4.00
Ann.2001 Galactus,48-page 3.50
Spec.#1 KIK FantasticFour (2000). . 2.50
Spec. Fantastic Four/Sentry 3.00
Spec. Fantastic Fourth Voyage
  of Sinbad, 48-page (2001) . . 6.00
Spec. The Movie,DJu (2005). 5.00
Spec. Franklin Richards, Son
  Of a Genius, Rep. Power Pack . 3.00
Spec. The Wedding (2006) 5.00
Spec. Isla de la Muerte (2008) . . . 4.00

FANTASTIC FOUR: ATLANTIS RISING
1995
1 B:Atlantis Rising. 5.00
2 TDF,MCW,finale, acetate(c). 5.00

FANTASTIC FOUR: A DEATH IN THE
May, 2006
1 64-pg. 4.00

FANTASTIC FOUR INDEX
See: OFFICIAL MARVEL INDEX TO THE FANTASTIC FOUR

FANTASTIC FOUR: FIRST FAMILY
Mar., 2006
1 CWn. 3.00
2 thru 6 CWn . . . . @3.00

FANTASTIC FOUR: FOES
Jan., 2005
1 (of 6) Puppet Master & Mad
  Thinker. 3.00
2 Annihilus 3.00
3 Green Goblin 3.00
4 Mole Man. 3.00
5 Red Ghost 3.00
6 conclusion 3.00

FANTASTIC FOUR: HOUSE OF M
July, 2005
1 (of 3) SEa, A:Magneto, Doom . . . 3.00
2 Sea 3.00
3 SEa, concl.. . . . . 3.00

FANTASTIC FOUR/ IRON MAN: BIG IN JAPAN
Oct., 2005
1 . . . . 3.50
2 All-out Monster Riot 3.50
3 Do you know kung fu. 3.50
4 Chock Full'O Monsters 3.50

FANTASTIC FOUR: 1 2 3 4
June, 2001
1 (of 4) GMo,JaL,F:Thing 3.00
2 GMo,JaL,F:Invisible Woman 3.00
3 GMo,JaL,F:Human Torch. 3.00
4 GMo,JaL,F:Mr. Fantastic 3.00

FANTASTIC FOUR AND POWER PACK
July, 2007
1 Attack of the Super-Bullies 3.00
2 thru 4 . . . . @3.00

FANTASTIC FOUR ROAST
May, 1982
1 FH/MG/FM/JB/MA/TA 5.00

FANTASTIC FOUR'S BIG TOWN
Nov., 2000
1 (of 4) SEt,MMK,MkK,48-page . . . 3.50
2 SEt,MMK,MkK 3.00
3 SEt,MMK,MkK 3.00
4 SEt,MMK,MkK,48-page 3.50

FANTASTIC FOUR: THE END
Nov., 2006
1 AD 4.00
1a 3.00
2 thru 6 AD . . . . @3.00

FANTASTIC FOUR: TRUE STORY
July, 2008
1 thru 4. . . . . @3.00

FANTASTIC FOUR 2099
1996
1 Cont. from 2099 Genesis. 4.00
2 thru 5 . . . . @2.50

FANTASTIC FOUR UNLIMITED
1993–96
1 HT,A:Bl.Panther,V:Klaw 4.50
2 HT,JQ(c),A:Inhumans 4.25
3 HT,V:Blastaar,Annihilus 4.25
4 RTs(s),HT,V:Mole Man,A:Hulk . . . 4.25
5 RTs(s),HT,V:Frightful Four 4.25
6 RTs(s),HT,V:Namor 4.00
7 HT,V:Monsters 4.00
8 . . . . 4.00
9 A:Antman 4.00
10 RTs,HT,V:Maelstrom,A:Eternals . 4.00
11 RTs,HT,Atlantis Rising fallout . . . 4.00
12 RTs,TDF,V:Hyperstorm 4.00
13 . . . . 4.00

FANTASTIC FOUR UNPLUGGED
1995–96
1 comic for a buck 2.50
2 Reed Richard's Will 2.50
3 F:Mr. Fantastic. 2.50
4 . . . . 2.50
5 Back in NY,V:Blastaar 2.50

FANTASTIC FOUR: UNSTABLE MOLECULES
Jan., 2003
1 (of 4) GyD 3.00
2 thru 3 GyD . . . . @3.00

FANTASTIC FOUR VS. X-MEN
Feb., 1987
1 JBg,TA,V:Dr.Doom. 5.00
2 JBg,TA,V:Dr.Doom. 4.00
3 JBg,TA,V:Dr.Doom. 4.00
4 JBg,TA,V:Dr.Doom, June, 1987. . 4.00

FANTASTIC FOUR THE WORLD'S GREATEST COMIC MAGAZINE
Dec., 2000
1 (of 12) EL,ErS,V:Dr.Doom 3.00
2 F:Dr.Doom,Crystal 3.00
3 A:X-Men,Spider-Man 3.00
4 A:X-Men,Capt.America 3.00
5 EL(c),Hulk vs. Thing 3.00
6 MGo(c),A:Silver Surfer. 3.00
7 KG(c),A:Dr.Doom,Inhumans 3.00
8 KG(c),F:Avengers 3.00
9 EL,KG,A:Dr.Doom 3.00
10 EL,KG,Cosmic Cube 3.00
11 RF,Planet Doom 3.00
12 StL,EL,JSt, concl. 3.00

FANTASTIC WORLD OF HANNA-BARBERA
Dec., 1977
1 . . . . 30.00
2 . . . . 20.00
3 June, 1978 . . . . 20.00

Fantasy Masterpieces #12
© Marvel Entertainment Group

FANTASY MASTERPIECES
Feb., 1966
1 JK/DH/SD,reprints 200.00
2 JK,SD,DH,Fin Fang Foom. . . . 100.00
3 GC,DH,JK,SD,Capt.A rep. 100.00
4 JK,Capt.America rep. 100.00
5 JK,Capt.America rep. 100.00
6 JK,Capt.America rep. 100.00
7 SD,Sub Mariner rep. 100.00
8 H.Torch & Sub M.rep. 100.00
9 SD,MF,O:Human Torch Rep . . 125.00
10 rep.All Winners #19 . . . . 100.00
11 JK,(rep),O:Toro 100.00
Becomes:

MARVEL SUPER-HEROES

FANTASY MASTERPIECES
[Volume 2], Dec., 1979
1 JB,JSt,Silver Surfer rep. 5.00
2 thru 7 JB,JSt,Silver Surfer rep. @5.00
8 thru 11 JB/JSn,.Strange Tales . @4.00
12 thru 14 JB,JSn,rep.Warlock . . @4.00

FAREWELL TO WEAPONS
1 DirtBag,W/Nirvana Tape 3.50

FEAR
Nov., 1970
1 JK,1950's Monster rep.B:I
 Found Monstrum,The Dweller
 in the Black Swamp. 75.00
2 JK,X The Thing That Lived . . 40.00
3 JK,Zzutak, The Thing That
 Shouldn't Exist. 40.00
4 JK,I Turned Into a Martian 40.00
5 JK,I Am the Gorilla Man. 40.00
6 JK,SD,The Midnight Monster. . . 40.00
7 JK,SD,I Dream of Doom 25.00
8 JK,SD,It Crawls By Night! 25.00
9 JK,Dead Man's Escape 25.00
Becomes:

ADVENTURE INTO FEAR
1972
10 HC,GM,B:Man-Thing 60.00
11 RB,I:Jennifer Kale,Thog 25.00
12 JSn,RB 25.00
13 VM,Where World's Collide 18.00
14 VM,Plague o/t Demon Cult. . . . 18.00
15 VM,Lord o/t Dark Domain. 18.00
16 VM,ManThing in Everglades. . . 18.00
17 VM,I:Wundarr(Aquarian). 18.00
18 VM. 18.00
19 VM,FMc,I:Howard the Duck,
 E:Man-Thing 55.00
20 PG,GK,B:Morbius 55.00
21 GK,V:Uncanny Caretaker 20.00
22 RB,V:Cat-Demond 20.00
23 GC,GK,1st CR art,A World He
 Never Made. 20.00
24 CR,SMn,V:Blade, The Vampire
 Slayer 35.00
25 FR,GK,You Always Kill the
 One You Love 15.00
26 FR,GK,V:Uncanny Caretaker . . 15.00
27 FR,GK,V:Simon Stroud. 15.00
28 GK,Doorway Down into Hell. . . 15.00
29 Death has a Thousand Eyes . . 15.00
30 Bloody Sacrifice 15.00
31 FR,GK,last issue,Dec., 1975 . . 15.00

Adventure Into Fear # 24
© *Marvel Entertainment Group*

FEUD
Epic, 1993
1 I:Skids,Stokes,Kite 3.00
2 thru 4 . . . . @2.50

FIGHT MAN
1993
1 I:Fight Man. 2.50

FILM FUNNIES
Marvel Chipiden Publ., 1949–50
1 Funny animal. 250.00
2 . . . . 175.00

FIRESTAR
March, 1986
1 MW,SL,O:Firestar,A:X-Men,
 New Mutants 5.00
2 MW,BWI,A:New Mutants 4.00
3 AAd&BSz(c),MW,SL,
 A:White Queen 4.00
4 MW,SL,V:White Queen 4.00
Digest X-Men: Firestar (2006) 8.00

FISH POLICE
1992–93
1 V:S.Q.U.I.D,Hook. 2.50
2 thru 6 . . . . @2.50

FLASH GORDON
1995
1 R:Flash Gordon 3.00
2 AW,V:Ming, final issue 3.00

FLINTSTONE KIDS
Star, Aug., 1987
1 thru 10 . . . . @5.00
11 April, 1989. . . . . 5.00

FLINTSTONES
Oct., 1977–Feb., 1979
1 From TV Series 75.00
2 . . . . 50.00
3 . . . . 30.00
4 A:Jetsons 30.00
5 thru 7 . . . . @35.00

FLYING HERO BARBIE
1 Super Hero Barbie. 2.50

FOOFUR
Star, Aug., 1987
1 thru 6 . . . . @3.00

FOOLKILLER
Oct., 1990
1 I:Kurt Gerhardt (Foolkiller III). . . . 3.50
2 O:Foolkiller I & II 3.00
3 Old Costume 3.00
4 N:Foolkiller. 2.50
5 Body Count 2.50
6 thru 10 . . . . @2.50
Marvel Max, Oct., 2007
1 (of 5) Fool's Paradise 4.00
2 Fool's Paradise, pt.2 . . . . 4.00
3 Fool's Paradise, pt.3 . . . . 4.00
4 . . . . 4.00
5 . . . . 4.00

FOOLKILLER: SHORT TIME
Marvel Max, July, 2008
1 (of 5) 4.00

FOOLKILLER: WHITE ANGELS
Marvel Max
1 (of 5) Short Time, pt.1 . . . . 4.00
2 Punishment Fits the Crime 4.00
3 Fool's Gold. 4.00
4 Good Night, Moon 4.00
5 Play the Fool 4.00

FORCE WORKS
1994–96
1 TmT,Pop-up(c),I:Century,V:Kree,
 N:US Agent 4.00
2 thru 11 . . . . @2.50
12 V:Recorder 3.00
13 thru 20. . . . . @2.50

411
April, 2003
1 thru 3 . . . . @3.50

FOR YOUR EYES ONLY
1 HC,James Bond rep. 3.00
2 HC,James Bond rep. 3.00

Fraggle Rock #4
© *Marvel Entertainment Group*

FRAGGLE ROCK
1985
1 thru 8 . . . . @5.00
[Volume 2], April, 1988
1 thru 5 rep. . . . . @2.50
6 Sept., 1988 . . . . 2.50

FRANCIS, BROTHER OF THE UNIVERSE
1980
1-shot SB 5.00

FRANKLIN RICHARDS
Mar, 2007
Spec. March Madness! 3.00
Spec. World Be Warned 3.00
Spec. Monster Mash 3.00
Spec. Fall Football Fiasco! 3.00
Spec. Spring Break (3-2008) 3.00
Spec. Not So Secret Invasion
 (5-2008). 3.00
Spec. Summer Smackdown (8-08) . 4.00
Spec. Sons of Geniuses (11-2008) . 4.00

All comics prices listed are for *Near Mint* condition.

Fred Hembeck Destroys the Marvel Universe #1 © Marvel Ent. Group

FRANKENSTEIN
See: MONSTER OF
FRANKENSTEIN

FRED HEMBECK
1-shot Destroys the Marvel
  Universe, parody (1989) 2.50
1-shot Sells the Marvel Universe
  parody (1990) 2.50

FRIENDLY NEIGHBOR-
HOOD SPIDER-MAN
Oct., 2005
1 PDd(s),The Other, x-over,pt.1 . . . 6.00
1a 2nd printing 7.00
2 PDd(s),The Other, x-over,pt.4 . . . 6.00
2a 2nd printing 6.00
3 PDd(s),The Other, x-over,pt.7 . . . 3.00
3a 2nd printing 6.00
4 PDd(s),The Other, x-over,pt.10 . . 3.00
5 PDd(s),Weblog 3.00
6 PDd(s),Wrestling 3.00
7 PDd(s),Wrestling 3.00
8 PDd(s),MeW 3.00
9 PDd(s),Jumping the Tracks 3.00
10 PDd(s),Jumping the Tracks 3.00
11 PDd(s),I Hate a Mystery,pt.1 . . . 3.00
12 PDd(s),I Hate a Mystery,pt.2 . . . 3.00
13 PDd(s),I Hate a Mystery,pt.3 . . . 3.00
14 PDd(s),A:Deb Whitman,V:Vulture 3.00
15 PDd(s),SEa,V:Vulture 3.00
16 PDd(s),SEa,V:Vulture 3.00
17 PDd(s),TNu,Back in Black 3.00
17a variant (c) 5.00
18 PDd(s),TNu,Back in Black 3.00
19 PDd(s),TNu,Back in Black 3.00
20 PDd(s),TNu,Back in Black 3.00
21 PDd(s),TNu,Back in Black 3.00
22 PDd(s),TNu,Back in Black 3.00
23 PDd(s),TNu,Back in Black 3.00
24 MSz,JQ,One More Day, pt.2 . . . . 4.00
24a variant (c) 4.00
Ann. #1 PDd(s) 4.00

FRIGHT
June, 1975
1 Son of Dracula 15.00

FRONTIER WESTERN
Feb., 1956
1 RH, ... 275.00

2 AW,GT,GC,JMn 200.00
3 MD 200.00
4 MD,Ringo Kid 150.00
5 RC,DW,JDa 200.00
6 AW,GC 175.00
7 JR,JMn 150.00
8 RC,DW. 150.00
9 JMn 150.00
10 SC,Aug., 1957 . . . . 150.00

FUNNY FROLICS
Summer, 1945
1 Shardy Fox,KrazyKroid,(fa) . . . 300.00
2 . . . . 150.00
3 . . . . 100.00
4 . . . . 100.00
5 HK 125.00

FUNNY TUNES
Marvel Timely, 1944–46
(KRAZY KOMICS spinoff)
16 Animated Funny
  Comic-Tunes 250.00
17 . . . . 200.00
18 . . . . 200.00
19 . . . . 200.00
20 . . . . 200.00
21 . . . . 200.00
22 . . . . 200.00
23 HK 200.00
Becomes:

OSCAR

FURTHER ADVENTURES
OF CYCLOPS
AND PHOENIX
1996
1 thru 4 . . . . @3.00

FURY
1994
1 MCW,O:Fury,A:S.A. Heroes 3.25

FURY
Marvel Max, Sept., 2001
1 (of 6) GEn,DaR,JP,F:Nick Fury . . 6.00
2 GEn,DaR,JP,F:Rudi Gagarin 4.00
3 GEn,DaR,JP, ... 4.00
4 thru 6 GEn,DaR,JP . . . . @4.00

FURY/AGENT 13
March, 1998
1 (of 2) TKa,is Nick Fury alive? . . . 3.00
2 TKa,MZ(c),Sharon Carter's searches
  for Nick 3.00

FURY OF S.H.I.E.L.D.
1995
1 Foil etched cover 3.00
2 A:Iron Man 2.50
3 J:Hydra 2.50
4 w/decoder card 3.00

FURY: PEACEMAKER
Feb., 2006
1 GEn,DaR,JP, Kasserine Pass . . . 3.50
2 GEn,DaR,JP, War Without Army . 3.50
3 thru 6 GEn,DaR,JP . . . . @3.50

GALACTIC GUARDIANS
1994
1 KWe,C:Woden 2.50
2 KWe,I:Hazmat,Savant,Ganglia . . 2.50
3 KWe 2.50
4 KWe,final issue 2.50

GALACTUS
THE DEVOURER
April, 1999
1 (of 6) JMu,LSi,A:Silver Surfer,
  Fant.Four & Avengers,48-page . 4.00
2 LSi,JB,BSz 3.00
3 LSi,JB,BSz 3.00
4 LSi,JB,BSz,A:Silver Surfer 3.00
5 LSi,JB,BSz 3.00
6 LSi,JB,BSz,concl 3.50

GAMBIT
1997
1 HMe(c),LW,KJ,V:Assassin'sGuild,
  D:Henri LeBeau,Embossed(c). . 5.00
1a Gold Ed. 15.00
2 LW,KJ,C:Gideon,A:Rogue 3.00
3 LW,KJ,A:Candra,Rogue,
  D:Gambit's Father 3.00
4 LW,KJ,A:Candra,Rogue,D:Tithe
  Collector 3.00

GAMBIT
1997
1 (of 4) HMe,KJ,In Miami 3.50
2 HMe,KJ, ... 3.00
3 HMe,KJ,in the Vatican 3.00
4 HMe V:Stoker, concl. 3.00

GAMBIT
Dec., 1998
1 FaN,SSr,O:Gambit,48-page. 4.00
1a signed 25.00
2 FaN,SSr,V:Storm 3.00
2a variant cover 3.00
3 FaN,SSr,V:Mengo Brothers 2.50
4 FaN,SSr,A:Blade 2.50
5 FaN,SSr,R:Rogue 2.50
6 FaN,SSr,I:The Pig 2.50
7 FaN,SSr, ... 2.50
8 FaN,A:Sinister,Sabretooth 2.50
9 FaN,The Shattering,x-over 2.50
10 FaN,V:Candra & Fenris 2.50
11 FaN,A:Daredevil 2.50
12 FaN 2.50
13 FaN,Black Womb 2.50
14 FaN,ALa,A:Mr. Sinister 2.50
15 FaN,F:Rogue 2.50
16 FaN,X-Men: Revolution 2.50
16a variant (c) 2.50
17 FaN,AssassinationGame,pt.1 . . 2.50
18 FaN,AssassinationGame,pt.2 . . 2.50
19 FaN,AssassinationGame,pt.3 . . 2.50
20 FaN,Fontanelle 2.50
21 FaN,Remy LeBeau 2.50
22 FaN,Neo,Remy LeBeau,Rax . . . 2.50
23 FaN,X-Cutioner 2.50
24 FaN,V:New Son 2.50
25 SLo, 48-page 3.50
Ann.1999 48-page 3.50
Ann.2000 FaN,F:X-Men 3.50
Giant Sized Gambit, 96-page, rep. . 4.00

GAMBIT
Sept., 2004
1 House of Cards,pt.1 . . . . 3.00
2 House of Cards,pt.2 . . . . 3.00
3 House of Cards,pt.3 . . . . 3.00
4 House of Cards,pt.4 . . . . 3.00
5 House of Cards,pt.5 . . . . 3.00
6 House of Cards, Concl. 3.00
7 Voodoo Economics,pt.1 . . . . 3.00
8 Voodoo Economics,pt.2 . . . . 3.00
9 Voodoo Economics,pt.3 . . . . 3.00
10 Hath No Fury,pt.1 . . . . 3.00
11 Hath No Fury,pt.2 . . . . 3.00
12 Hath No Fury,pt.3 . . . . 3.00

MARVEL

GAMBIT & BISHOP: SONS OF THE ATOM
Jan., 2001
1 SLo,Bishop captured 2.50
2 SLo,on the run 2.50
3 SLo,common enemy 2.50
4 SLo, ... 2.50
5 SLo,Ultimate sacrifice 2.50
6 SLo,finale 2.50
Spec. Alpha, SLo,CNr 2.50
Spec. Genesis,CCl 3.50

GAMBIT AND THE X-TERNALS
1995
1 X-Force after Xavier 3.50
2 V:Deathbird,Starjammers 2.50
3 V:Imperial Guard 2.50
4 Charles Kidnapped 2.50

Gargoyle #4
© Marvel Entertainment Group

GARGOYLE
June, 1985
1 BWr(c),from `Defenders' 4.00
2 thru 4 . . . . @3.00

GARGOYLES
1995–96
1 TV Series 4.00
2 TV Series 3.00
3 F:Broadway 3.00
4 V:Statues 3.00
5 Humanoid Gargoyles 3.00
6 Medusa Project concl 3.00
7 Demona & Triad 3.00
8 I:The Pack 3.00
9 V:Demonia,Triad 3.00
10 Demonia gains magical powers . 3.00
11 Elisa turns to Xanatos 3.00
12 Sorceress traps Gargoyles 3.00
13 Behind Enemy Lines 3.00
14 thru 16 . . . . @3.00

GAY COMICS
Marvel Timely, 1944
1 BW,Guys and gals humor 800.00
18 BW 450.00
19 BW 400.00
20 BW 400.00
21 BW 400.00
22 BW 400.00

23 BW 400.00
24 BW,HK,Hey Look 400.00
25 BW 400.00
26 BW 400.00
27 BW 400.00
28 BW 400.00
29 BW,HK,Hey Look 400.00
30 HK,Hey Look 200.00
31 HK,Hey Look 200.00
32 . . . . 125.00
33 HK,Hey Look 200.00
34 HK,Hey Look 200.00
35 thru 40 . . . . @125.00
Becomes:

HONEYMOON
Marvel Comics, 1950
41 Photo(c) 125.00

GENE DOGS
Marvel UK, 1993–94
1 I:Gene DOGS,w/cards 3.00
2 V:Genetix 2.50
3 V:Hurricane 2.50
4 last issue 2.50

GENERATION M
Nov., 2005
1 Decimation 3.00
2 thru 5 . . . . @3.00

GENERATION NEXT
1995
1 Generation X AX 3.50
2 Genetic Slave Pens 2.50
3 V:Sugar Man 2.50
4 V:Sugar Man 2.50

GENERATION X
Oct., 1994
1 CBa,Banshee & White Queen . . . 7.00
2 CBa,SLo 4.00
2a Deluxe edition 4.00
3 CBa 3.00
3a Deluxe edition 4.00
4 CBa,V:Nanny,Orphanmaker 3.00
4a Deluxe edition 4.00
5 SLo,CBa,MBu,two new young
   mutants at the Academy 3.50
6 A:Wolverine 3.50
7 SLo,F:Banshee,A:White Queen . 3.50
8 F:Banshee 3.50
9 SLo,TG,Chamber in a kilt 3.50
10 SLo,TG,MBu,Banshee vs.
   OmegaRed 3.50
11 SLo,TG,V:Omega Red 3.00
12 SLo,TG,V:Emplate 3.00
13 . . . . 3.00
14 . . . . 3.00
15 SLo,MBu,Synch goes psycho . . 3.00
16 . . . . 3.00
17 SLo,CBa,Onslaught saga,
   X-Cutioner vs. Skin 3.00
18 SLo,CBa,Onslaught saga 3.00
19 SLo,CBa, ... 3.00
20 SLo,CBa, ... 3.00
21 SLo,CBa,MBu,F:Skin & Chamber,
   A:Beverly Switzer, Howard
   the Duck 3.00
22 SLo,CBa, ... 3.00
23 SLo,CBa,V:Black Tom Cassidy . . 3.00
24 SLo,MBy,F:Monet,Emplate 3.00
25 SLo,CBa,double size 4.00
26 SLo,CBa,Shot down over the
   Atlantic 3.00
27 SLo,CBa,on nuclear sub. 3.00
28 SLo,CBa,No Exit prelude 3.00
29 JeR,CBa, V:Sentinels 3.00
30 JeR, CBa, V:Zero Tolerance 3.00
31 JeR,CBa, ... 3.00

32 TDF,MBu,F:Banshee, Moira
   McTaggert 3.00
33 LHa,MBu,new direction 3.00
34 LHa,Truth behind M 3.00
35 LHa,Jubilee,V:Emplate 3.00
36 LHa,Final Fate of M 3.00
37 LHa,Final Fate of M 3.00
38 LHa,TyD,kids save universe 2.50
39 LHa,TyD, multi-dimensional trip . 2.50
40 LHa,TyD,Penance mystery
   revealed 2.50
41 LHa,TyD,Jubilee,V:Bastion,
   Omega Red, Sabretooth 2.50
42 LHa,TyD,results of EMP wave . . 2.50
43 LHa,TyD,V:Bianca LaNiege 2.50
44 LHa,TyD,V:White Queen 2.50
45 LHa,TyD,F:Banshee 2.50
46 LHa,TyD,F:Forge 2.50
47 LHa,TyD,Danger Room 2.50
48 TyD,Jubilee vs. M 2.50
49 TyD,V:Maggott 2.50
50 TyD,War of the Mutants,pt.1 . . . 3.50
50a signed 20.00
51 V:Hunter Brawn 2.50
52 TyD,blackmail 2.50
53 TyD V:Rising Sons,A:Paladin . . . 2.50
54 TyD,A:Paladin 2.50
55 TyD,in bodies of Hellions 2.50
56 TyD,A:X-Men of past. 2.50
57 TyD, double sized 3.50
58 TyD, new Penance 2.50
59 TyD, ... 2.50
60 TyD,F:Siryn 2.50
61 TyD,ATi,R:Mondo 2.50
62 TyD,F:Monet St. Croix. 2.50
63 WEI,X-Men Revolution 2.50
63a variant (c) 2.50
64 WEI,Correction,pt.2 . . . . 2.50
65 WEI,Correction,pt.3 . . . . 2.50
66 WEI,Correction,pt.4 . . . . 2.50
67 WEI,Come On Die Young,pt.1 . . 2.50
68 WEI,Come On Die Young,pt.2 . . 2.50
69 WEI,Come On Die Young,pt.3 . . 2.50
70 WEI,Come On Die Young,pt.4 . . 2.50
71 WEI,Four Days,pt.1 . . . . 2.50
72 AAd(c),StP,Four Days,pt.2 . . . . 2.50
73 AAd(c),StP,Four Days,pt.3 . . . . 2.50
74 AAd(c),StP,Four Days,pt.4 . . . . 2.50
75 AAd(c),StP,final issue 3.50
Minus 1 Spec., JeR,CBa, flashback,
   F:Banshee 2.50
Ann. '95 SLo,J:Mondo,
   V:Hellfire Club 4.50
Ann. '96 GN MGo,JJ,DPs,V:Fenris . 3.50

Generation X/Gen 13
© Marvel Entertainment Group

All comics prices listed are for *Near Mint* condition.

Ann. '97, Haunted by Ghosts
of Hellions 3.50
Ann.1998 Generation X/Dracula . . . 4.00
Ann.1999 48-pg. 4.00
Holliday Spec. 48-page 1-shot 4.00

GENERATION X/GEN 13
Dec., 1997
1-shot JeR,SvL,V:Mr. Pretorious . . . 4.00
1a variant cover CBa (1:4). 4.00

GENERATION X:
UNDERGROUND
March, 1998
1-shot by Jim Mahfood, b&w 2.50

GENETIX
Marvel UK, 1993–94
1 B:ALa(s),w/cards 3.00
2 I:Tektos 2.50
3 V:Tektos 2.50
4 PGa,V:MyS-Tech 2.50
5 PGa,V:MyS-Tech 2.50
6 V:Tektos 2.50

GENEXT
May, 2008
1 thru 5 CCl . . . . @4.00

GEORGIE COMICS
Spring, 1945
1 Georgie stories begin 350.00
2 Pet Shop (c) 175.00
3 Georgie/Judy(c) 135.00
4 Wedding Dress(c) 135.00
5 Monty/Policeman(c) 135.00
6 Classroom(c) 150.00
7 Fishing(c) 135.00
8 Soda Jerk(c) 135.00
9 Georgie/Judy(c),HK,Hey Look 135.00
10 Georgie/Girls(c),HK,Hey Look 135.00
11 Table Tennis(c),A:Margie,Millie 100.00
12 Camping(c) 100.00
13 Life Guard(c),HK,Hey Look. . . 150.00
14 Classroom(c),HK,Hey Look . . 150.00
15 Winter Sports(c) 100.00
16 . . . . 100.00
17 HK,Hey Look. 150.00
18 . . . . 100.00
19 Baseball(c) 100.00
Becomes:

Georgie #11
© *Marvel Entertainment Group*

GEORGIE & JUDY COMICS
20 . . . . 125.00
21 . . . . 100.00
Becomes:
GEORGIE COMICS
22 Georgie comics 100.00
23 & 24. . . . . @100.00
25 Driben painted (c). 125.00
26 thru 28. . . . . @100.00
29 . . . . 125.00
30 thru 38. . . . . @100.00
39 Oct., 1952 . . . . 100.00

GETALONG GANG
May, 1985—March, 1986
1 thru 6 . . . . @3.50

GHOST RIDER
1967
1 O&I:Ghost Rider (western) . . . 150.00
2 V:Tarantula. 75.00
3 Cougar's Circus of Fear 50.00
4 Sting Ray 50.00
5 Tarantula Strikes Back 50.00
6 Behold a Falling Star 50.00
7 Mystery of Massacre Mountain . 50.00

GHOST RIDER
[1st Regular Series], Sept., 1973
1 GK,JSt,C:Son of Satan 250.00
2 GK,I:Son of Satan,A:Witch
Woman 100.00
3 JR,D:Big Daddy Dawson,
new Cycle 75.00
4 GK,A:Dude Jensen 75.00
5 GK,JR,I:Roulette 75.00
6 JR,O:Ghost Rider 50.00
7 JR,A:Stunt Master 50.00
8 GK,A:Satan,I:Inferno 50.00
9 GK,TP,O:Johnny Blaze 50.00
10 JSt,A:Hulk 50.00
11 GK,KJ,SB,A:Hulk 50.00
12 GK,KJ,FR,A:Phantom Eagle. . . 20.00
13 GK,JS,GT,A:Trapster 20.00
14 GT,A:The Orb 20.00
15 SB,O:The Orb 20.00
16 DC,GT,Blood in the Water 20.00
17 RB,FR,I:Challenger. 20.00
18 RB,FR,A:Challenger,
Spider-Man 20.00
19 GK,FR,A:Challenger 20.00
20 GK,KJ,JBy,A:Daredevil 22.00
21 A:Gladiator,D:Eel. 12.00
22 AM,DH,KP,JR,A:Enforcer 12.00
23 JK,DH,DN,I:Water Wiz.. . . . . . 12.00
24 GK,DC,DH,A:Enforcer 12.00
25 GK,DH,A:Stunt Master 12.00
26 GK,DP,A:Dr. Druid 12.00
27 SB,DP,A:Hawkeye 12.00
28 DP,A:The Orb 12.00
29 RB,DP,A:Dormammu 12.00
30 DP,A:Dr.Strange 12.00
31 FR,DP,BL,A:Bounty Hunt.. . . . . 12.00
32 KP,BL,DP,A:Bounty Hunt. 12.00
33 DP,I:Dark Riders 12.00
34 DP,C:Cyclops 12.00
35 JSn,AM,A:Death 16.00
36 DP,Drug Mention. 12.00
37 DP,I:Dick Varden 12.00
38 DP,A:Death Cult 12.00
39 DP,A:Death Cult 12.00
40 DP,I:Nuclear Man 12.00
41 DP,A:Jackal Gang. 12.00
42 DP,A:Jackal Gang. 12.00
43 CI:Crimson Mage 12.00
44 JAb,CI,A:Crimson Mage 12.00
45 DP,I:Flagg Fargo 12.00
46 DP,A:Flagg Fargo 12.00
47 AM,DP. 12.00
48 BMc,DP. 12.00

49 DP,I:The Manitou 12.00
50 DP,A:Night Rider. 15.00
51 AM,PD,A:Cycle Gang 7.00
52 AM,DP. 7.00
53 DP,I:Lord Asmodeus 7.00
54 DP,A:The Orb 7.00
55 DP,A:Werewolf By Night 7.00
56 DP,A:Moondark,I:Night Rider . . . 7.00
57 AM,DP,I:The Apparition. 7.00
58 DP,FM,A:Water Wizard 7.00
59 V:Water Wizard,Moon Dark 7.00
60 DP,HT,A:Black Juju 7.00
61 A:Arabian Knight. 7.00
62 KJ,A:Arabian Knight 7.00
63 LMc,A:The Orb 7.00
64 BA,V:Azmodeus 7.00
65 A:Fowler 7.00
66 BL,A:Clothilde 7.00
67 DP,A:Sally Stantop 7.00
68 O:Ghost Rider. 7.00
69 . . . . 7.00
70 I:Jeremy 7.00
71 DP,I:Adam Henderson 7.00
72 A:Circus of Crime 7.00
73 A:Circus of Crime 7.00
74 A:Centurions 7.00
75 I:Steel Wind. 7.00
76 DP,A:Mephisto,I:Saturnine 7.00
77 O:Ghost Rider's Dream 7.00
78 A:Nightmare 7.00
79 A:Man Cycles 7.00
80 A:Centurions 7.00
81 D:Ghost Rider. 15.00

[2nd Regular Series], 1990–98
1 JS,MT,I:2nd Ghost Rider,
Deathwatch 7.00
1a 2nd printing 3.00
2 JS,MT,I:Blackout 3.00
3 JS,MT,A:Kingpin,V:Blackout,
Deathwatch 3.00
4 JS,MT,V:Mr.Hyde 3.00
5 JLe(c),JS,MT,A:Punisher 3.00
5a rep.Gold. 2.50
6 JS,MT,A:Punisher 3.00
7 MT,V:Scarecrow. 3.00
8 JS,MT,V:H.E.A.R.T 3.00
9 JS,MT,A:Morlocks,X-Factor 2.50
10 JS,MT,V:Zodiac. 2.50
11 LSn,MI,V:Nightmare,
A:Dr.Strange 2.50
12 JS,MT,A:Dr.Strange 2.50
13 MT,V:Snow Blind,R:J.Blaze . . . 2.50
14 MT,Blaze Vs.Ghost Rider.. . . . . 2.50
15 MT,A:Blaze,V:Blackout
Glow in Dark(c) 3.00
15a 2nd printing (gold). 2.50
16 MT,A:Blaze,Spider-Man,
V:Hobgoblin 2.50
17 MT,A:Spider-Man,Blaze,
V:Hobgoblin 2.50
18 MT,V:Reverend Styge 2.50
19 MT,A:Mephisto 2.50
20 MT(i),O:Zodiac 2.50
21 MT(i),V:Snowblind,
A:Deathwatch 2.50
22 MT,A:Deathwatch,Ninjas. 2.50
23 MT,I:Hag & Troll,A:Deathwatch. . 2.50
24 MT,V:Deathwatch,D:Snowblind,
C:Johnny Blaze 2.50
25 V:Blackout (w/Center spread
pop-up) 3.00
26 A:X-Men,V:The Brood 3.00
27 A:X-Men,V:The Brood 3.00
28 NKu,JKu,Rise of the Midnight
Sons#1,V:Lilith,w/poster 3.00
29 NKu,JKu,A:Wolverine,Beast . . . 2.50
30 NKu,JKu,V:Nightmare. 2.50
31 NKu,JKu,Rise o/t Midnight Sons#6,
A:Dr.Strange,Morbius,Nightstalkers,
Redeemers, V:Lilith,w/poster. . . 3.00
32 BBi,A:Dr.Strange 2.50

Ghost Rider 2nd Series Ann. #1
© *Marvel Entertainment Group*

33 BBI,AW,V:Madcap (inc.Superman
    tribute on letters page) 2.50
34 BBI,V:Deathwatchs' ninja 2.50
35 BBI,AW,A:Heart Attack 2.50
36 BBI,V:Mr.Hyde,A:Daredevil 2.50
37 BBI,A:Archangel,V:HeartAttack . . . 2.50
38 MM,V:Scarecrow 2.50
39 V:Vengeance 2.50
40 Midnight Massacre#2,
    D:Demoglbin 3.00
41 Road to Vengeance#1 . . . . 2.50
42 Road to Vengeance#2 . . . . 2.50
43 Road to Vengeance#3 . . . . 2.50
44 Siege of Darkness,pt.#2 . . . . 2.50
45 Siege of Darkness,pt.#10 . . . . . . 2.50
46 HMe(s),New Beginning 2.50
47 HMe(s),RG, ... 2.50
48 HMe(s),RG,A:Spider-Man 2.50
49 HMe(s),RG,A:Hulk,w/card 2.50
50 Red Foil(c),AKu,SMc,A:Blaze,
    R:2nd Ghost Rider 3.25
50a Newsstand Ed. 2.75
51 SvL 2.50
52 SvL 2.50
53 SvL,V:Blackout 2.50
54 SvL,V:Blackout 2.50
55 V:Mr. Hyde 2.50
56 The Next Wave 2.50
57 A:Wolverine 2.50
58 HMe,SvL,Betrayal,pt.1 . . . . 2.50
59 Betrayal,pt.2 . . . . 2.50
60 Betrayal,pt.3 . . . . 2.50
61 Betrayal,pt.4 . . . . 3.00
62 EventInChains,pt.1,A:Fury 2.50
63 EventInChains,pt.2 . . . . 2.50
64 EventInChains,pt.3 . . . . 2.50
65 EventInChains,pt.4,R:Blackout . . 2.50
66 V:Blackout 2.50
67 A:Gambit,V:Brood 2.50
68 A:Gambit,Wolverine,V:Brood . . . 2.50
69 Domestic Violence 2.50
70 New Home in Bronx 2.50
71 . . . . 2.50
72 . . . . 2.50
73 John Blaze is back 2.50
74 A:Blaze, Vengeance 2.50
75 . . . . 2.50
76 V:Vengeance 2.50
77 A:Dr. Strange 2.50
78 new costume, A:Dr. Strange 2.50
79 IV,New costume, A:Valkyrie, . . . 2.50
80 IV,V:Furies,Valkyrie
    A:Black Rose 2.50

81 IV,A:Howard the Duck,
    Devil Dinosaur 2.50
82 IV,A:Devil Dinosaur, ... 2.50
83 IV,A:Scarecrow,Lilith 2.50
84 IV,A:Scarecrow, Lilith 2.50
85 IV,V:Lilith, Scarecrow 2.50
86 IV,rampage through the Bronx . . 2.50
87 IV,KIK,AM, ... 2.50
88 IV, V:Pao Fu,Blackheart 2.50
89 IV,JS, ... 2.50
90 IV,JS,Last Temptation, pt.1 . . . . . 5.00
91 IV,JS,A:Blackheart 5.00
92 IV,JS,Journey into the past 5.00
93 IV,JS,MT,Last Temptation concl.,
    double sized 10.00
94 IV,JS,MT,Becomes Lord of the
    Underworld, last issue 2.00
Ann.#1 I:Night Terror,w/card 3.25
Ann.#2 F:Scarecrow 3.00
GN Ghost Rider/Captain America:
    Fear, AW, V:Scarecrow (1992) . 6.25
GN Ghost Rider/Wolverine/Punisher:
    Dark Design (1994) 6.00
GN Ghost Rider/Wolverine/Punisher:
    Hearts of Darkness, JR2/KJ,V:
    Blackheart, gatefold(c) (1991) . . 5.50
Poster Book 5.00
Spec. Crossroads 4.00
Minus 1 Spec., IV,JS, flashback 2.00

GHOST RIDER

1 Director's Cut, GEn(s),48-pg. . . . 4.00

GHOST RIDER
Sept., 2005

1 (of 6) GEn(s),Road to Damnation 3.00
2 thru 6 Gen(s),Road to
    Damnation . . . . @3.00

GHOST RIDER
July., 2006

1 (of 6) MT,JS,Vicious Cycle 3.00
1a variant (c) 3.00
2 thru 5 MT, JS,Vicious Cycle . . . @3.00
6 RCo,Hell to Pay, pt.1 . . . . 3.00
7 RCo,Hell to Pay, pt.2 . . . . 3.00
8 MT,JS,Sleepy Hollow Illinois . . . 3.00
9 MT,JS,Sleepy Hollow Illinois 3.00
10 MT,JS,Sleepy Hollow Illinois . . . 3.00
11 MT,JS,Sleepy Hollow Illinois . . . 3.00
12 JS,Apocalypse Soon, pt.1 . . . . . 3.00
12a 2nd printing 3.00
13 JS,Apocalypse Soon, pt.2 . . . . . 3.00
14 JS,MT,Revelations, pt.1 . . . . 3.00
15 JS,MT,Revelations, pt.2 . . . . 3.00
16 JS,MT,Revelations, pt.3 . . . . 3.00
17 JS,MT,Revelations, pt.4 . . . . 3.00
18 JS,MT,Revelations, pt.5 . . . . 3.00
19 . . . . 3.00
20 Hell-to Pay, pt.1 . . . . 3.00
21 Hell-to Pay, pt.2 . . . . 3.00
22 Hell to Pay, pt.3 . . . . 3.00
23 Hell to Pay, pt.4 . . . . 3.00
24 Maximum security prison 3.00
25 Caged Heat 3.00
26 Danny Ketch is back 3.00
27 I:Caretaker 3.00
28 Last Stand of Spirits of Veng. . . 3.00
29 Johnny Blaze vs. Danny Ketch . . 3.00
Ann. #1 I:Mr. Eleven 4.00
Ann. #2 Mercy 4.00

GHOST RIDER/
BALLISTIC/CYBLADE
Marvel/Top Cow 1996

1-shot IV,ACh,Devil's Reign,
    pt.2, x-over 3.25
1-shot WEI,BTn,Devil's
    Reign, pt.3, x-over 3.00

Ghost Rider Spirits of Vengeance #2
© *Marvel Entertainment Group*

GHOST RIDER/BLAZE
SPIRITS OF VENGEANCE
1992–94

1 AKu,polybagged w/poster,V:Lilith,
    Rise of the Midnight Sons#2 . . . 3.50
2 AKu,V:Steel Wind 3.00
3 AKu,CW,V:The Lilin 3.00
4 AKu,V:Hag & Troll,C:Venom 3.00
5 AKu,BR,Spirits of Venom#2,
    A:Venom,Spidey,Hobgoblin 5.00
6 AKu,Spirits of Venom#4,A:Venom,
    Spider-Man,Hobgoblin 3.50
7 AKu,V:Steel Vengeance 2.50
8 V:Mephisto 2.50
9 I:Brimstone 2.50
10 AKu,V:Vengeance 2.50
11 V:Human Spider Creature 2.50
12 AKu,BR,Vengeance,glow in the
    dark(c) 3.25
13 AKu,Midnight Massacre#5 . . . . . 2.50
14 Missing Link#2 . . . . 2.50
15 Missing Link#3 . . . . 2.50
16 V:Zarathos,Lilith 2.50
17 HMe(s),Siege/Darkness,pt.8 . . . 2.50
18 HMe(s),Siege/Darkness,pt.13 . . 2.50
19 HMe(s),HMz,V:Vampire 2.50
20 HMe(s),A:Steel Wind 2.50
21 HMe(s),HMz,V:Werewolves 2.50
22 HMe(s),HMz,V:Cardiac 2.50
23 HMe(s),HMz,A:Steel Wind 2.50

GHOST RIDER:
DANNY KETCH
Oct., 2008

1 (of 5) 4.00
2 . . . . 3.00

GHOST RIDER FINALE
Jan., 2007

Inc. Ghost Rider #93 reprint 4.00

GHOST RIDER:
THE HAMMER LANE
June, 2001

1 (of 6) TKn 3.00
2 TKn,DaM 3.00
3 TKn,DaM,Gunmetal Gray 3.00
4 TKn,DaM,Gunmetal Gray 3.00
5 TKn,DaM,Gunmetal Gray 3.00
6 TKn,DaM,Gunmetal Gray 3.00

MARVEL

GHOST RIDER:
HIGHWAY TO HELL
June, 2001
Spec. 64-pages 3.50

GHOST RIDER:
TRAIL OF TEARS
Feb., 2007
1 (of 6) GEn, Trail of Tears, pt.1 . . 3.00
2 thru 5 GEn . . . . @3.00

GHOST RIDER 2099
1994–96
1 Holografx(c),LKa,CBa,MBu,I:Ghost
Rider 2099,w/card 3.00
1a Newsstand Ed. 2.50
2 LKa,CBa,MBu 2.50
3 LKa,CBa,MBu,I:Warewolf 2.50
4 LKa,CBa,MBu,V:Warewolf. 2.50
5 LKa,CBa,MBu 2.50
6 LKa,CBa,MBu 2.50
7 LKa,CBa,MBu 2.50
8 LKa,CBa,MBu 2.50
9 . . . . 2.50
10 . . . . 2.50
11 V:Bloodsport Society. 2.50
12 I:Coda 2.50
Becomes:

GHOST RIDER 2099 A.D.
1995
13 F:Doom 2.50
14 Deputized by Doom 2.50
15 One Nation Under Doom 2.50
16 V:Max Synergy 2.50
17 . . . . 2.50
18 V:L-Cipher. 2.50
19 V:L-Cipher. 2.50
20 . . . . 2.50
21 V:Vengeance 2099 . . . . 2.50
22 V:Vengeance 2099 . . . . 2.50
23 . . . . 2.50
24 . . . . 2.50
25 Double size final issue 3.50

GIANT-SIZE CHILLERS
1975
1 AA, ... 75.00
2 . . . . 40.00
3 BWr,Night of the Gargoyle. 50.00

GIANT-SIZE CHILLERS
1974
1 I&O:Lilith,F:Curse of Dracula. . . 75.00
Becomes:

GIANT-SIZE DRACULA
2 Vengeance of the Elder Gods . . 40.00
3 rep. Uncanny Tales #6. . . . . . . 40.00
4 SD,Demon of Devil's Lake. 40.00
5 JBy, 1st Marvel art. 60.00

GIANT-SIZE
MINI-MARVELS:
STARRING SPIDEY
Dec., 2001
1 F:Hawkeye, 48-pg.. . . . . 3.50

G.I. JOE:
A REAL AMERICAN HERO
June, 1982
1 HT,BMc,Baxter paper. 35.00
2 DP,JAb,North Pole 30.00
3 HT,JAb,Trojan Robot 22.00
4 HT,JAb,Wingfield 22.00
5 DP,Central Park 22.00
6 HT,V:Cobra 22.00

7 HT,Walls of Death 22.00
8 HT,Sea Strike. 22.00
9 The Diplomat 22.00
10 Springfield. 22.00
11 thru 20 . . . . @20.00
21 SL(i),Silent Interlude 35.00
22 V:Destro 15.00
23 I:Duke 10.00
24 RH,I:Storm Shadow 10.00
25 FS,I:Zartan 10.00
26 SL(i),O:Snake Eyes 20.00
27 FS,O:Snake Eyes 20.00
28 Swampfire 10.00
29 FS,V:Destro 10.00
30 JBy(c),FS,V:Dreddnoks 10.00
31 thru 60 . . . . @6.00
2a to 36a 2nd printings . . . . @3.00
60 TM,I:Zanzibar 6.00
61 thru 90 . . . . @5.00
91 TSa,V:Red Ninjas,D:Blind
Masters 6.00
92 MBr,V:Cobra Condor. 6.00
93 MBr,V:Baroness 20.00
94 MBr,A:Snake Eyes 6.00
95 MBr,A:Snake Eyes 6.00
96 MBr,A:Snake Eyes 6.00
97 thru 109 . . . . @6.00
110 Mid-East Crisis 6.00
111 thru 119 . . . . @10.00
120 V:Red Ninjas,Slice & Dice. . . . 11.00
121 thru 134 . . . . @10.00
135 thru 143 . . . . @11.00
144 O: Snake Eyes 15.00
145 thru 147 . . . . @12.00
148 F:Star Brigade. 15.00
149 . . . . 15.00
150 Cobra Commander vs.
Snake Eyes 32.00
151 V:Cobra. 30.00
152 First G.I. Joe 30.00
153 V:Cobra. 30.00
154 . . . . 38.00
155 final issue 60.00
SC GI Joe and the Transformers. . . 5.00
Spec. TM rep.#61 . . . . 40.00
Ann.#1 . . . . 40.00
Ann.#2 . . . . 10.00
Ann.#3 . . . . 10.00
Ann.#4 . . . . 10.00
Ann.#5 . . . . 10.00
Yearbook #1 (1985) 10.00
Yearbook #2 (1986) 10.00
Yearbook #3 (1987) 10.00
Yearbook #4 (1988) 10.00

G. I. Joe #52
© Marvel Entertainment Group

G.I. JOE
EUROPEAN MISSIONS
June, 1988
1 British rep. 12.00
2 . . . . 7.00
3 . . . . 12.00
4 thru 15 . . . . @6.00

G.I. JOE
SPECIAL MISSIONS
Oct., 1986
1 HT,New G.I. Joe. 4.00
2 thru 20 HT . . . . @4.00
21 thru 28. . . . . @5.00

G.I. JOE AND
THE TRANSFORMERS
1987
1 thru 4 HT,mini-series . . . . @3.00

G.I. JOE UNIVERSE
1 Biographies rep.#1. . . . . 3.50
2 thru 4 . . . . @2.50

G.I. TALES
See: SERGEANT BARNEY
BARKER

GIRL COMICS
Marvel Atlas, Nov., 1949
1 Ph(c),True love stories,I Could
Escape From Love 300.00
2 Ph(c),JKu,Blind Date 150.00
3 BEv,Ph(c),Liz Taylor 350.00
4 PH(c),Borrowed Love 125.00
5 Love stories 125.00
6 same 125.00
7 same 125.00
8 same 125.00
9 same 125.00
10 The Deadly Double-Cross 125.00
11 Love stories. 125.00
12 BK,The Dark Hallway 150.00
Becomes:

GIRL CONFESSIONS
1952
13 . . . . 150.00
14 . . . . 125.00
15 . . . . 125.00
16 BEv 150.00
17 BEv 150.00
18 BEv 150.00
19 . . . . 110.00
20 . . . . 110.00
21 thru 34 . . . . @100.00
35 Aug., 1954. . . . . 100.00

GIRLS' LIFE
Marvel Atlas, Jan., 1954
1 . . . . 150.00
2 . . . . 125.00
3 . . . . 100.00
4 . . . . 100.00
5 . . . . 100.00
6 November, 1954 . . . . 100.00

G.L.A.
April, 2005
1 (of 4) F:Great Lakes Avengers . . 3.00
2 Dis-membership Drive 3.00
3 . . . . 3.00
4 Countdown to a Miscount 3.00

GLADIATOR/SUPREME
1997
1 KG,ASm,x-over 5.00

X — Men
Supergirl
Super Klutz
Soldier of Freedom
1 + 2

GLX-MAS
Dec., 2005
1-shot X-mas special 4.00

GODZILLA
Aug., 1977
1 HT,JM,Based on Movie Series . 30.00
2 HT,FrG,GT,Seattle Under Seige   12.00
3 HT,TD,A;Champions 20.00
4 TS,TD,V;Batragon 12.00
5 TS,KJ,Isle of the Living
    Demons 12.00
6 HT,A Monster Enslaved 12.00
7 V:Red Ronin 12.00
8 V:Red Ronin 12.00
9 Las Gamble in Las Vegas 12.00
10 V:Yetrigar 12.00
11 V;Red Ronin,Yetrigar. 10.00
12 Star Sinister 10.00
13 V:Mega-Monster 10.00
14 V:Super-Beasts. 10.00
15 Stampede 10.00
16 Jaws of Fear 10.00
17 Godzilla Shrunk 10.00
18 Battle Beneath Eighth Avenue . 10.00
19 Panic on the Pier 10.00
20 A;Fantastic Four 12.00
21 V;Devil Dinosaur. 10.00
22 V:Devil Dinosaur 10.00
23 A;Avengers 12.00
24 July, 1979 . . . . 15.00

GRAVITY
June, 2005
1(of 5) F:Greg Willis 3.00
2 . . . . 3.00
3 V:Black Death 3.00
4 . . . . 3.00
5 Finale. 3.00

GREEN GOBLIN
1995–96
1 I:New Green Goblin 4.00
2 thru 13 . . . . @2.50

GROO CHRONICLES
Epic, 1989
1 SA 5.00
2 thru 6 SA . . . . @4.00

Groo, The Wanderer #18
© Marvel Entertainment Group

[SERGIO ARAGONE'S] GROO, THE WANDERER
(see Pacific, Eclipse)
Epic, 1985–95
1 SA,I:Minstrel 15.00
2 SA,A:Minstrel 8.00
3 SA,Medallions 8.00
4 SA,Airship 8.00
5 SA,Slavers 8.00
6 SA,The Eye of the Kabala 8.00
7 SA,A:Sage 8.00
8 SA,A:Taranto 8.00
9 SA,A:Sage 8.00
10 SA,I:Arcadio 8.00
11 thru 18 SA . . . . @6.00
19 thru 29 SA . . . . @4.00
30 thru 49. . . . . @4.00
50 SA,double size 4.00
51 thru 87 SA . . . . @3.00
88 SA,V:Cattlemen,B.U. Sage 4.00
89 thru 99 SA . . . . @3.00
100 SA,Groo gets extra IQ points . . 8.00
101 thru 120 SA . . . . @4.00

GROOVY
March, 1968—July, 1968
1 Monkeys,Ringo Starr,Photos . . 140.00
2 Cartoons,Gags,Jokes 100.00
3 . . . . 100.00

GUARDIANS
2004
1 (of 5) Reach for the Stars 3.00
2 thru 5 Reach for the Stars . . . . @3.00

GUARDIANS OF THE GALAXY
June, 1990
1 B:JV(a&s),I:Taserface,R:Aleta . . . 4.00
2 MZ(c),JV,V:Stark,C:Firelord 3.00
3 JV,V:Stark,I:Force,C:Firelord 3.00
4 JV,V:Stark,A:Force,Firelord 3.00
5 JV,TM(c),V:Force,I:Mainframe
    (Vision) 3.00
6 JV,V:Force,Vance Possesses
    Capt.America Shield 3.00
7 GP(c),JV,I:Malevolence,
    O:Starhawk 3.00
8 SLi(c),JV,V:Yondu,C:Rancor 3.00
9 RLd(c),JV,I:Replica,Rancor 3.00
10 JLe(c),JV,V:Rancor,The Nine
    I&C:Overkill(Taserface) 3.00
11 BWi(c),JV,V:Rancor,I:Phoenix . . . 3.00
12 ATb(c),JV,V:Overkill
    A:Firelord 3.00
13 JV,A:Ghost Rider,Force,
    Malevolence 3.00
14 JS(c),JV,A:Ghost Rider,Force,
    Malevolence 3.00
15 JSn(c),JV,I:Protege,V:Force 3.00
16 JV,V:Force,A:Protege,
    Malevolence,L:Vance Astro 3.00
17 JV,V:Punishers(Street Army),
    L:Martinex,N:Charlie-27, ... 2.50
18 JV,V:Punishers,I&C:Talon,A:
    Crazy Nate 3.00
19 JV,V:Punishers,A:Talon. 2.50
20 JV,I:Major Victory (Vance Astro)
    J:Talon & Krugarr. 2.50
21 JV,V:Rancor 2.50
22 JV,V:Rancor 2.50
23 MT,V:Rancor,C:Silver Surfer. . . . 2.50
24 JV,A:Silver Surfer 3.00
25 JV, Prismatic Foil(c)
    V:Galactus,A:SilverSurfer 3.50
25a 2nd printing,Silver. 2.50
26 JV,O:Guardians(retold) 2.50
27 JV,Infinity War,O:Talon,
    A:Inhumans 2.50

Guardians of the Galaxy #8
© Marvel Entertainment Group

28 JV,Inf.War,V:Various Villians 2.50
29 HT,Inf.War,V:Various Villians. . . . 2.50
30 KWe,A:Captain America 2.50
31 KWe,V:Badoon,A:Capt.A. 2.50
32 KWe,V:Badoon Gladiator 2.50
33 KWe,A:Dr.Strange,R:Aleta 2.50
34 KWe,J:Yellowjacket II 2.50
35 KWe,A:Galatic Guardians,
    V:Bubonicus 2.50
36 KWe,A:Galatic Guardians,
    V:Dormammu 2.50
37 KWe,V:Dormammu,A:Galatic
    Guardians 2.50
38 KWe,N:jacket,A:Beyonder 2.50
39 KWe,Rancor Vs. Dr.Doom,Holo-
    grafx(c) 3.25
40 KWe,V:Loki,Composite 2.50
41 KWe,V:Loki,A:Thor 2.50
42 KWe,I:Woden 2.50
43 KWe,A:Woden,V:Loki 2.50
44 KWe,R:Yondu 2.50
45 KWe,O:Starhawk. 2.50
46 KWe,N:Major Victory. 2.50
47 KWe,A:Beyonder,Protoge,
    Overkill. 2.50
48 KWe,V:Overkill 2.50
49 KWe,A:Celestial 2.50
50 Foil(c),R:Yondu,Starhawk sep-
    arated,BU:O:Guardians. 3.25
51 KWe,A:Irish Wolfhound. 2.50
52 KWe,A:Drax 2.50
53 KWe,V:Drax 2.50
54 KWe,V:Sentinels 2.50
55 KWe,Ripjack 2.50
56 Ripjack 2.50
57 R:Keeper 2.50
58 . . . . 2.50
59 A:Keeper 2.50
60 F:Starhawk 2.50
61 F:Starhawk 2.50
62 Guardians Stop War of the Worlds
    last issue 2.50
Ann.#1 Korvac Quest #4,I:Krugarr. . 3.25
Ann.#2 HT,I:Galactic Guardians,
    System Bytes #4 . . . . 3.25
Ann.#3 CDo,I:Irish Wolfhound,
    w/Trading card. 3.25
Ann.#4 V:Nine 3.25

GUARDIANS OF THE GALAXY
May., 2008
1 DAn&ALa(s), PaP 3.00
2 DAn&ALa(s),PaP 3.00

MARVEL

3 DAn&ALa(s),PaP,Starhawk 3.00
4 DAn&ALA(s),PaP,Secret Invasion 3.00
5 DAn&ALA(s),PaP,Secret Invasion 3.00
5a Monkey variant 3.00
6 DAn&ALA(s),PaP,Secret Invasion 3.00
7 DAn&ALa(s), Star-Lord Missing. . 3.00

GUNHAWK, THE
See: BLAZE CARSON

GUNHAWKS
Oct., 1972
1 SSh,B:Reno Jones & Kid
　Cassidy Two Rode Together . . 35.00
2 Ride out for Revenge. 30.00
3 Indian Massacre 30.00
4 Trial by Ordeal 30.00
5 The Reverend Mr. Graves 30.00
6 E:Reno Jones & Kid Cassidy
　D:Kid Cassidy 30.00
7 A Gunhawks Last Stand
　A;Reno Jones, Oct., 1973 . . . 30.00

GUNRUNNER
Marvel UK, 1993–94
1 I:Gunrunner,w/trading cards 3.00
2 A:Ghost Rider 2.50
3 V:Cynodd 2.50
4 . . . . 2.50
5 A:Enhanced 2.50
6 final issue. 2.50

GUNSLINGERS
Dec., 1999
1-shot 64-pg. 3.00

GUNSLINGER
See: TEX DAWSON,
GUNSLINGER

GUNSMOKE WESTERN
See: ALL WINNERS
COMICS

GUN THEORY
Marvel Epic, Aug., 2003
1 thru 4 . . . . @2.50

HALO: UPRISING
July, 2007
1 BMB(s). 8.00
1a Second printing 5.00
2 . . . . 5.00
3 thru 4 BMB(s), finale . . . . @4.00

HARROWERS
1993–94
1 MSt(s),GC,F:Pinhead. 3.50
2 thru 4 GC,AW(i),. . . . . @3.00
5 GC,AW(i),Devil's Pawn#1 . . . . . 3.00
6 GC,AW(i),Devil's Pawn#2 . . . . . 3.00

HARVEY
Oct., 1970–Dec., 1972
1 . . . . 150.00
2 thru 6 . . . . @100.00

HARVEY PRESENTS:
CASPER
1 . . . . 2.50

HAUNT OF HORROR:
LOVECRAFT
June, 2008
1 (of 3) RCo 4.00
2 thru 3 RCo . . . . @4.00

Harvey #1
© *Marvel Entertainment Group*

HAUNT OF HORRORS:
EDGAR ALLAN POE
May, 2006
1 RCo, b&w, inc. The Raven 4.00
2 RCo, b&w, inc. Tell-Tale Heart. . . 4.00
3 RCo, b&w, three stories. 4.00

HAVOK & WOLVERINE
Epic, March, 1988
1 JMu,KW,V:KGB,Dr.Neutron. 5.00
2 JMu,KW,V:KGB,Dr.Neutron 4.00
3 JMu,KW,V:Meltdown 4.00
4 JMu,KW,V:Meltdown,Oct.1989 . . 4.00

HAWKEYE
[1st Limited Series], Sept., 1983
1 A:Mockingbird 3.00
2 I:Silencer 3.00
3 I:Bombshell,Oddball. 3.00
4 V:Crossfire,W:Hawkeye &
　Mockingbird, Dec., 1983 . . . . . . 3.00
[2nd Limited Series], 1994
1 B:CDi(s),ScK,V:Trickshot,
　I:Javelynn,Rover 2.50
2 ScK,V:Viper 2.50
3 ScK,A:War Machine,N:Hawkeye,
　V:Secret Empire 2.50
4 E:CDi(s),ScK,V:Trickshot,Viper,
　Javelynn 2.50

HAWKEYE
Oct., 2003
1 FaN(s),High,Hard Shaft,pt.1 . . . . 3.00
2 FaN(s),High,Hard Shaft,pt.2 . . . . 3.00
3 FaN(s),High,Hard Shaft,pt.3 . . . . 3.00
4 FaN(s),High,Hard Shaft,pt.4 . . . . 3.00
5 FaN(s),High,Hard Shaft,pt.5 . . . . 3.00
6 FaN(s),High,Hard Shaft,pt.6 . . . . 3.00
7 FaN(s),A Little Murder,pt.1. . . . . 3.00
8 FaN(s),A Little Murder,pt.2. . . . . 3.00

HAWKEYE: EARTH'S
MIGHTIEST MARKSMAN
Aug., 1998
1-shot TDF,MBa,JJ,DR,AM 48pg. . . 3.00

HEADMASTERS
Star, July, 1987
1 FS,Transformers 2.50
2 and 4 . . . . @2.50

HEATHCLIFF
Star, April, 1985
1 . . . . 7.00
2 thru 10 . . . . @4.00
11 thru 16 . . . . @3.00
17 Masked Moocher 5.00
18 thru 49 . . . . @3.00
50 Double-size. 3.00
51 thru 55 . . . . @3.00

HEATHCLIFF'S
FUNHOUSE
Star, May, 1987
1 thru 9 . . . . @3.00
10 1988 . . . . 3.00

HEAVY HITTERS
Ann.#1 (1993) 4.00

HEDGE KNIGHT II:
SWORN SWORD
Apr., 2007
1 thru 6 . . . . @3.00

HEDY DEVINE COMICS
Aug., 1947—Sept., 1952
22 I:Hedy Devine 350.00
23 BW,Beauty and the Beach,
　HK,Hey Look 225.00
24 High Jinx in Hollywood,
　HK, Hey Look 225.00
25 Hedy/Bull(c),HK,Hey Look . . . 225.00
26 Skating(c),HK,Giggles&Grins . 250.00
27 Hedy at Show(c),HK,HeyLook 225.00
28 Hedy/Charlie(c),HK,HeyLook . 225.00
29 Tennis(c),HK,Hey Look 225.00
30 . . . . 175.00
31 thru 35. . . . . @175.00
Becomes:

Hedy of Hollywood #40
© *Marvel Entertainment Group*

HEDY HOLLYWOOD
36 thru 50 . . . . @175.00

HEDY WOLFE
Marvel Atlas, Aug., 1957
1 Patsy Walker's Rival 125.00

HELLCAT
July, 2000
1 (of 3) SEt,NBy,F:PatsyWalker . . . 3.00
2 thru 3 SEt,NBy, ... @3.00

HELLHOUND
1993–94
1 Hellhound on my Trial 3.00
2 Love in Vain 3.00
3 Last Fair Deal Gone Down 3.00

HELLRAISER
See: CLIVE BARKER'S HELLRAISER

HELLRAISER III HELL ON EARTH
1 Movie Adaptation,(prestige) 5.00
1a Movie Adapt.(magazine) 3.00

HELLSTORM, PRINCE OF LIES
1993
1 R:Daimon Hellstrom,
    Parchment(c) 3.50
2 A:Dr.Strange,Gargoyle 3.00
3 O:Hellstorm 2.75
4 V:Ghost Rider 2.75
5 MB, ... 2.50
6 MB,V:Dead Daughter 2.50
7 A:Armaziel 2.50
8 Hell is where the heart is 2.50
9 LKa(s),Highway to Heaven 2.50
10 LKa(s),Heaven's Gate 2.50
11 LKa(s),PrG,Life in Hell 2.50
12 Red Miracles 2.50
13 Red Miracles Sidewalking 2.50
14 Red Miracles Murder is Easy . . . 2.50
15 Cigarette Dawn 3.00
16 Down Here 2.50
17 The Saint of the Pit 2.50
18 thru 21 . . . . @2.50

HELLSTORM: SON OF SATAN
Oct., 2006
1 Equinox, pt.1 . . . . 4.00
2 thru 5 Equinox, pt.2 thru pt.5 . . @4.00

HELL'S ANGEL
1992
1 GSr,A:X-Men,O:Hell's Angel 3.00
2 GSr,A:X-Men,V:Psycho Warriors . 2.50
3 GSr,A:X-Men,V:MyS-Tech 2.50
4 GSr,A:X-Men,V:MyS-Tech 2.50
5 GSr,A:X-Men,V:MyS-Tech 2.50
6 Gfr,A:X-Men,V:MyS-Tech 2.50
Becomes:

DARK ANGEL
1992
7 DMn,A:Psylocke,V:MyS-Tech . . . 2.50
8 DMn,A:Psylocke 2.50
9 A:Punisher 2.50
10 MyS-Tech Wars tie-in 2.50
11 A:X-Men,MyS-Tech wars tie-in . 2.50
12 A:X-Men 2.50
13 A:X-Men,Death's Head II 2.50
14 Aftermath#2 . . . . 2.50
15 Aftermath#3 . . . . 2.50
16 SvL,E:Aftermath,last issue 2.50

HERCULES
April, 2005
1 (of 5) MT 3.00
2 MT,v:king Eurytheses 3.00
3 MT,12 Labors for Reality TV 3.00
4 MT,Final four labors 3.00
5 MT,final Four Labors 3.00

HERCULES AND THE HEART OF CHAOS
Limited Series Aug., 1997
1 (of 3) TDF,RF,PO, ... 2.50
2 TDF,RF,PO, ... 2.50
3 TDF,RF,PO,V:Ares, concl. 2.50

HERCULES PRINCE OF POWER
Sept., 1982
1 BL,I:Recorder 5.00
2 BL,I:Layana Sweetwater 3.00
3 BL,V:The Brothers,C:Galactus . . 3.00
4 BL,A:Galactus 3.00

[2nd Series], March, 1984
1 BL,I:Skyypi 3.00
2 BL,A:Red Wolf 2.50
3 BL,A:Starfox 2.50
4 BL,D:Zeus, June, 1984 . . . . 2.50

HERO
May, 1990
1 . . . . 2.50
2 thru 6 . . . . @2.50

HERO FOR HIRE
June, 1972
1 GT,JR,I&O:Power Man 135.00
2 GT,A:Diamond Back 60.00
3 GT,I:Mace 40.00
4 V:Phantom of 42nd St. 40.00
5 GT,A:Black Mariah 40.00
6 V:Assassin 35.00
7 GT,Nuclear Bomb issue 35.00
8 GT,A:Dr.Doom 35.00
9 GT,A:Dr.Doom,Fant.Four 35.00
10 GT,A:Dr.Death,Fant.Four 35.00
11 GT,A:Dr.Death 25.00
12 GT,C:Spider-Man 25.00
13 A:Lion Fang 25.00
14 V:Big Ben 25.00
15 Cage Goes Wild 25.00
16 O:Stilletto,D:Rackham 25.00
Becomes:

POWER MAN

HEROES FOR HIRE
July, 1997
1 JOs,PFe,F:Iron Fist 5.00

Hero For Hire #15
© Marvel Entertainment Group

2 JOs,PFe,V:Nitro 3.00
2A Variant PFe cover 3.00
3 JOs,PFe,V:Nitro 3.00
4 JOs,Power Man vs. Iron Fist 3.00
5 JOs,V:Sersi, Diabolical Deviants . 3.00
6 JOs,PFe, Deviants 3.00
7 JOs V:Thunderbolts 3.00
8 JOs,Iron Fist's agenda revealed . 3.00
9 JOs,Search for Punisher 3.00
10 JOs,Deadpool hired 3.00
11 JOs,PFe,A:Deadpool, V:Silver
    Sable and Wild Pack 3.00
12 JOs,PFe,Traitor revealed, 48pg . 3.50
13 JOs,PFe,V:Master 3.00
14 JOs,F:Black Knight 3.00
15 JOs,PFe,Siege of Wundagore,
    pt.1 (of 5) 3.00
16 JOs,PFe,Siege of Wundagore,
    pt.3 . . . . 3.00
17 JOs,DBw,F:Luke Cage
    & She-Hulk 3.00
18 JOs,PFe,A:Wolverine 3.00
19 JOs,PFe,F:Wolverine 3.00
Ann.'98 JOs,BWi,PFe,Heroes For
    Hire/Quicksilver, Siege of
    Wundagore, pt.5 (of 5) 48pg . . . 3.00

HEROES FOR HIRE
Aug., 2006
1 JP,BiT,Civil War tie-in 3.00
2 thru 4 JP,BiT . . . . @3.00
5 JP,BiT 3.00
6 JP,BiT(c) 3.00
7 JP,BiT(s) 3.00
8 TP 3.00
9 . . . . 3.00
10 . . . . 3.00
11 World War Hulk 3.00
11a 2nd printing 3.00
12 World War Hulk 3.00
13 World War Hulk 3.00
14 World War Hulk 3.00
15 World War Hulk 3.00

HEROES FOR HOPE
1985
1 TA/JBy/HC/RCo/BWr,A:XMen . . . 7.00

HEROES REBORN: THE RETURN
Oct., 1997
? Heroes Reborn prequel, (Marvel/
    Wizard 1996) 7.50
1 (of 4) PDd,ATi,SvL,F:Franklin
    Richards 4.00
2 PDd,ATi,SvL, F:Spider-Man,
    Thunderbolts & Doctor Strange . 4.00
3 PDd,SvL,ATi,A UniverseMayDie . 4.00
4 PDd,SvL,ATi, crossover to Marvel
    Universe? 4.00

HOKUM & HEX
Razorline 1993–94
1 BU:Saint Sinner 3.00
2 thru 9 . . . . @2.50

HOLIDAY COMICS
Marvel Star, Jan., 1951
1 LbC(c),Christmas(c) 500.00
2 LbC(c),Easter Parade(c) 525.00
3 LbC(c),4th of July(c) 325.00
4 LbC(c),Summer Vacation 300.00
5 LbC(c),Christmas(c) 300.00
6 LbC(c),Birthday(c) 300.00
7 LbC(c),Rodeo (c) 300.00
8 LbC(c),Xmas(c) Oct., 1952 . . . 300.00
Becomes:

FUN COMICS
Marvel Star, 1953
9 LbC	300.00
10 LbC	250.00
11 LbC	250.00
12 LbC	250.00

Becomes:

MIGHTY BEAR
Marvel Star, 1954
13 LbC	100.00
14 LbC	100.00

Becomes:

UNSANE
Marvel Star, 1954
15	475.00

HOLLYWOOD SUPERSTARS
Epic, Nov., 1990
1 DSp	3.00
2 thru 5 DSp, March, 1991	@2.50

Homer the Happy Ghost #1
© Marvel Entertainment Group

HOMER, THE HAPPY GHOST
March, 1955
1	300.00
2	200.00
3	175.00
4 thru 15	@175.00
16 thru 22	@150.00

[2nd Series], Nov., 1969
1	200.00
2 thru 5	@125.00

HOMER HOOPER
Marvel Atlas, 1953
1 Teen-age romance humor	125.00
2	100.00
3	100.00
4	100.00

HONEYMOON
See: GAY COMICS

HOOD, THE
Marvel Max, May, 2002
1 (of 6) F:Parker Robbins,40-pg.	6.00
2 FBI attention	6.00
3 diamond heist	5.00

---

4 thru 5	@5.00
6 concl.	6.00

HOOK
1992
1 JRy,GM,movie adaption.	2.50
2 JRy,Return to Never Land	2.50
3 Peter Pans Magic	2.50
4 conclusion	2.50
Hook Super Spec.#1	3.00

HORRORS, THE
Marvel Star Publications, Jan., 1953–April, 1954
11 LbC(c),JyD,Horrors of War	400.00
12 LbC(c),Horrors of War	375.00
13 LbC(c),Horrors of Mystery	350.00
14 LbC(c),Horrors of the Underworld	375.00
15 LbC(c),Horrors of the Underworld	375.00

HOUSE II
1 1987, Movie Adapt. 2.50

HOUSE OF M
June, 2005
1 (of 8) F:X-Men, New Avengers	3.00
2 BMB,V:the Scarlet Witch	3.00
3 BMB,F:Wolverine	3.00
4 BMB,F:Layla Miller.	3.00
5 BMB,F:Spider-man	3.00
6 BMB	3.00
7 BMB	3.00
8 BMB	3.00
1a thru 8a variant (c).	@3.00
Spec. Secrets of the House of M.	4.00

HOUSE OF M: AVENGERS
Nov., 2007
1 (of 5)	3.00
2 V:Shang-Chi's Dragons	3.00
3 thru 5	@3.00

HOWARD THE DUCK
Jan., 1976
1 FB,SL,A:Spider-Man,I:Beverly	45.00
2 FB,V:TurnipMan&Kidney Lady.	20.00
3 JB,Learns Quack Fu	15.00
4 GC,V:Winky Man	15.00
5 GC,Becomes Wrestler.	15.00
6 GC,V:Gingerbread Man	10.00
7 GC,V:Gingerbread Man.	10.00
8 GC,A:Dr.Strange,ran for Pres.	10.00
9 GC,V:Le Beaver.	10.00
10 GC,A:Spider-Man	10.00
11 GC,V:Kidney Lady.	10.00
12 GC,I:Kiss.	45.00
13 GC,A:Kiss	50.00
14 thru 32 GC	@5.00
33 BB(c),The Material Duck.	8.00
Ann.#1, V:Caliph of Bagmom	10.00
Holiday Spec. LHa,ATi,PFe (1996)	3.50

HOWARD THE DUCK
Marvel Max, Jan., 2002
1 (of 6) SvG,Making the Band	4.00
2 SvG,Beverly's ex	3.00
3 SvG,GF,The former Duck.	3.00
4 SvG,GF,House of Mystery	3.00
5 SvG,GF,House of Mystery,pt.2.	3.00
6 SvG,GF,Duck or Mouse	3.00

HOWARD THE DUCK
Oct., 2006
1 (of 4) TTn.	3.00
2	3.00

Howard the Duck #10
© Marvel Entertainment Group

3 TTn, Howard in prison	3.00
4	3.00

[NICK FURY'S] HOWLING COMMANDOS
Oct., 2005
1 KG,F:horror characters	3.00

HULK, THE
Feb., 1999
1 JBy,RG,DGr,48-page	4.00
1a signed	20.00
1b gold foil cover	10.00
2 JBy,RG,DGr,Hulk unleashed	4.00
2a variant AdP cover	4.00
3 JBy,RG,DGr,Hulk berserk	4.00
4 JBy,RG,DGr,old foe	4.00
5 JBy,RG,DGr,V:Man-Thing	4.00
6 JBy,RG,DGr,V:Man-Thing	4.00
7 JBy,RG,DGr,A:Avengers	4.00
8 JBy,RG,DGr,V:Wolverine	20.00
9 RG,V:Thing.	3.00
10 RG.	3.00
11 PJe,RG,SB,A:DocSamson	3.00

Becomes:

INCREDIBLE HULK
2000
12 PJe,RG,SB,48-pg	3.00
13 PJe,RG,SB,new Hulk	2.50
14 PJe,RG,SB,V:Ryker	2.50
15 PJe,RG,SB,Dogs of War,pt.2	2.50
16 PJe,RG,SB,Dogs of War,pt.3	2.50
17 PJe,RG,SB,Dogs of War,pt.4	2.50
18 PJe,RG,SB,Dogs of War,pt.5	2.50
19 PJe,RG,SB,Dogs of War,pt.6	2.50
20 PJe,RG,SB,Dogs of War,pt.7	2.50
21 PJe,Maximum Security	2.50
22 PJe,Joe Fixit's Money.	2.50
23 PJe,Nobby Stiles.	2.50
24 PJe,JR2,V:Abomination	2.50
25 PJe,JR2,V:Abomination	3.50
26 Psyche of child-like Hulk.	2.50
27 PJe,JR2,TP.	2.50
28 PJe,JR2,TP,V:Devil Hulk.	2.50
29 FaN,A:Angela,Doc Samson	2.50
30 PJe,JoB,TP,	2.50
31 PJe,JoB,TP,Banner gone	2.50
32 PJe,JoB,TP,Ant-Man inside	2.50
33 CPr,JBg,100-page.	4.00
34 JR2,TP,The beast within	5.00
35 JR2,TP,crosses the line?	3.00
36 JR2,TP,Gangs All Here,pt.1	3.00

MARVEL

37 JR2,TP,Remember This,pt.2 . . . . 3.00	
38 JR2,TP, ... 3.00	
39 JR2,TP,Tag-You're Dead. 3.00	
40 LW,TP,madman with gun 3.00	
41 JR2,TP,madman with gun. 3.00	
42 LW,TP,hostage crisis. 3.00	
43 JR2,TP,hostage crisis,concl. 3.00	
44 SI. 3.00	
45 SI,dream lover 3.00	
46 SI. 3.00	
47 SI. 3.00	
48 SI. 3.00	
49 SI. 3.00	
50 MD2,R:Abomination,pt.1 . . . . . . 4.00	
51 MD2,R:Abomination,pt.2 . . . . . . 3.00	
52 MD2,R:Abomination,pt.3. . . . . . 3.00	
53 MD2,R:Abomination,pt.4. . . . . . 3.00	
54 MD2,R:Abomination,pt.5. . . . . . 3.00	
55 Hide in Plain Sight,pt.1 . . . . 3.00	
56 Hide in Plain Sight,pt.2 . . . . 3.00	
57 Hide in Plain Sight,pt.3 . . . . 3.00	
58 Hide in Plain Sight,pt.4 . . . . 3.00	
59 Hide in Plain Sight,pt.5 . . . . 3.00	
60 MD2,Split Decisions,pt.1. . . . . . 3.00	
61 MD2,Split Decisions,pt.2. . . . . . 3.00	
62 MD2,Split Decisions,pt.3 . . . . . . 3.00	
63 MD2,Split Decisions,pt.4. . . . . . 3.00	
64 MD2,Split Decisions,pt.5. . . . . . 3.00	
65 MD2,Split Decisions,concl. 3.00	
66 MD2,Bury Me Not,pt.1 . . . . 3.00	
67 DBw,MD2(c),Bury Me Not,pt.2 . . 3.00	
68 DBw,MD2(c),Bury Me Not,pt.3 . . 3.00	
69 DBw,MD2(c),Bury Me Not,pt.4 . . 3.00	
70 MD2, Marvel Knights Hulk 3.00	
71 MD2,Big Things,pt.1 . . . . 3.00	
72 MD2,Big Things,pt.2 . . . . 3.00	
73 MD2,Big Things,pt.3 . . . . 3.00	
74 DBw,Big Things,pt.4 . . . . 3.00	
75 DaR,Wake to Nightmare,48-pg. . 3.50	
76 DBw,Shattered,48-pg. 3.50	
77 PDd(s),LW,Tempest Fugit,pt.1 . . 4.00	
78 PDd(s),LW,Tempest Fugit,pt.2 . . 3.00	
79 PDd(s),LW,Tempest Fugit,pt.3 . . 3.00	
80 PDd(s),LW,Tempest Fugit,pt.4 . . 3.00	
81 PDd(s),LW,Tempest Fugit,pt.5 . . 3.00	
82 PDd(s),JaL,vengeance 3.00	
83 PDd(s),The Last Refuge,pt.1 . . . 3.00	
84 PDd(s),The Last Refuge,pt.2 . . . 3.00	
85 PDd(s),The Last Refuge,pt.3 . . . 3.00	
86 PDd(s),The Last Refuge,pt.4 . . . 3.00	
87 PDd(s),AKu,F:New Scorpion . . . 3.00	
88 Peace in Our Time, pt.1 . . . . 3.50	
89 Peace in Our Time, pt.2 . . . . 3.50	
90 Peace in Our Time, pt.3 . . . . 3.50	
91 Peace in Our Time, pt.4 . . . . 3.50	
92 Planet Hulk: Exile, pt.1 . . . . 6.00	
93 Planet Hulk: Exile, pt.2 . . . . 3.00	
94 Planet Hulk: Exile, pt.3 . . . . 3.00	
95 Planet Hulk: Exile, pt.4 . . . . 3.00	
96 AaL,Planet Hulk: Anarchy, pt.1 . . 3.00	
97 AaL,Planet Hulk: Anarchy, pt.2 . . 3.00	
98 AaL,Planet Hulk: Anarchy, pt.3. . 3.00	
99 AaL,Planet Hulk: Anarchy, pt.4 . . 3.00	
100 Hulk sized 104-pg. 4.00	
100a variant (c) 4.00	
101 AaL,Allegiance,pt.2 . . . . 3.00	
102 AaL,Allegiance,pt.3 . . . . 3.00	
103 AaL,Allegiance,pt.4 . . . . 3.00	
104 Planet Hulk 3.00	
105 . . . . 3.00	
106 Warbound, pt.1 . . . . 3.00	
106a later printing 3.00	
107 GFr,F:Amadeus Cho. 3.00	
107a 2nd printing 3.00	
108 F:Amadeus Cho 3.00	
109 F:Amadeus Cho 3.00	
110 F:Amadeus Cho 3.00	
111 . . . . 3.00	
112 AAd(c) 3.00	
Giant-Size #1 48-pg. 4.00	
Ann. 1999 JBy,DGr,48-page 4.00	
Ann. 2001 EL,V:Thor 3.50	

Spec. Hulk/Sentry 3.50
GN The End, DK, ... 6.00
Spec. Must Have, rep. #34–#36 . . . 4.00
Spec. Planet Hulk: Gladiator
   Guidebook (2006) 4.00
Becomes:

INCREDIBLE HERCULES
Jan., 2008
113 AAd(c) 3.00
114 AAd(c) 3.00
115 AAd(c), V: Ares 3.00
116 . . . . 3.00
117 Secret Invasion tie-in 3.00
118 Secret Invasion tie-in 3.00
119 Secret Invasion tie-in 3.00
120 Secret Invasion tie-in 3.00
121 Love and War, pt.1 . . . . 3.00
122 Love and War, pt.2 . . . . 3.00
123 Love and War, pt.3 . . . . 3.00

HULK
Jan., 2008
1 JLb(s),Who is The Red Hulk? . . . 3.00
2 JLb(s),Who is The Red Hulk? . . . 3.00
3 JLb(s),V:Abomination. 3.00
4 JLb(s). 3.00
5 JLb(s),Two Hulks 3.00
6 JLb(s),Hulk vs. Hulk. 3.00
7 AAd,What Happens in Vegas . . . 3.00
8 AAd,V:Wendigo, Lady Liberators . 3.00
2a thru 8a variant (c)s . . . . @3.00
1-shot Hulk vs. Fin Fang Foom 4.00
Spec. Hulk vs. Hercules, When
   Titans Clash, 64-pgs. 4.00
King Size #1 96-pgs. 5.00
Spec. Raging Thunder (2008) 4.00
Ann. #1 Ultimate Hulk Annual 4.00
Monster Size #1 Hulk (2008). 4.00

HULK AND POWER PACK
Mar., 2007
1 (of 4) 3.00
2 thru 4 . . . . 3.00

HULK CHRONICLES: WWH
July, 2008
1 JR2(c) 5.00
2 thru 5 . . . . @5.00

HULK: DESTRUCTION
July, 2005
1 (of 4) PDd 3.00
2 PDd,v:Abomination 3.00
3 PDd 3.00
4 PDd 3.00

HULK: GRAY
Oct., 2003
1 thru 6 JLb,TSe . . . . @3.50

HULK: THE MOVIE
June, 2003
Spec. Movie adaptation, 48-pg. . . . 3.50

HULK: NIGHTMERICA
June, 2003
1 thru 6 . . . . @3.00

HULK SMASH
Jan., 2001
1 thru 2 GEn,JMC . . . . @3.00

HULK & THING: HARD KNOCKS
Sept., 2004
1 (of 4) JaL 3.50

2 JaL 3.50
3 . . . . 3.00
4 . . . . 3.00

HULK 2099
1994–95
1 GJ,Foil(c),V:Draco 3.00
2 GJ,V:Draco 2.50
3 I:Golden Boy 2.50
4 . . . . 2.50
5 Ultra Hulk. 2.50
Becomes:

HULK 2099 A.D.
1995
6 Gamma Ray Scientist 2.50
7 A:Doom,Dr.Apollo 2.50
8 One Nation Under Doom. 2.50
9 California Quake 2.50

HULK/WOLVERINE: 6 HOURS
Jan., 2003
1 (of 4) ScK,SBs(c),rescue. 3.00
2 ScK,SBs(c) 3.00
3 ScK,SBs(c) 3.00
4 ScK,SBs(c),concl. 3.00

HUMAN FLY
July, 1987
1 I&O:Human Fly,A:Spider-Man . 10.00
2 A:Ghost Rider 12.00
3 DC,JSt(c),DP,Fortress of Fear . . . 5.00
4 JB/TA(c),David Drier 5.00
5 V:Makik 5.00
6 Fear in Funland 5.00
7 ME,Fury in the Wind 5.00
8 V:White Tiger 5.00
9 JB/TA(c),ME,V:Copperhead,A:
   White Tiger,Daredevil 7.00
10 ME,Dark as a Dungeon 5.00
11 ME,A:Daredevil 5.00
12 ME,Suicide Sky-Dive 5.00
13 BLb/BMc(c),FS,V:Carl Braden . . 5.00
14 BLb/BMc(c),SL,Fear Over
   Fifth Avenue. 5.00
15 BLb/BMc(c),War in the
   Washington Monument 5.00
16 BLb/BMc(c),V:Blaze Kendall. . . . 5.00
17 BLb,DP,Murder on the Midway . . 5.00
18 V:Harmony Whyte. 5.00
19 BL(c),V:Jacopo Belbo
   March, 1979 . . . . 10.00

Human Fly #2
© Marvel Entertainment Group

RED RAVEN COMICS

Marvel Timely Comics Aug., 1940

1 JK,O:Red Raven,I:Magar,A:Comet Pierce & Mercury,Human Top, Eternal Brain 25,000.00

Becomes:

HUMAN TORCH

Marvel Comics, 1940–49

2 (#1)ASh(c),BEv,B:Sub-Mariner A:Fiery Mask,Falcon,Mantor, Microman 65,000.00
3 (#2)Ash(c),BEv,V:Sub-Mariner,Bondage(c) 10,000.00
4 (#3)ASh(c),BEv,O:Patriot . . . 8,000.00
5 (#4)V:Nazis,A:Patriot,Angel crossover 6,500.00
5a(#5)ASh(c),V:Sub-Mariner . 10,000.00
6 ASh(c),Doom Dungeon 4,500.00
7 ASh(c),V:Japanese 4,700.00
8 ASh(c),BW,V:Sub-Mariner . . 6,500.00
9 ASh(c),V:General Rommel . . 5,000.00
10 ASh(c),BW,V:Sub-Mariner . . 5,000.00
11 ASh(c),Nazi Oil Refinery . . . 3,500.00
12 ASh(c),V:Japanese, Bondage(c) 5,500.00
13 ASh(c),V:Japanese, Bondage(c) 3,500.00
14 ASh(c),V:Nazis 3,500.00

Human Torch #12
© *Marvel Entertainment Group*

15 ASh(c),Toro Trapped 3,500.00
16 ASh(c),V:Japanese 2,500.00
17 ASh(c),V:Japanese 2,500.00
18 ASh(c),V:Japanese, MacArthurs HQ. 2,500.00
19 ASh(c),Bondage(c). 2,700.00
20 ASh(c),Last War Issue 2,500.00
21 ASh(c),V:Organized Crime. . 2,200.00
22 ASh(c),V:Smugglers. 2,200.00
23 ASh(c),V:Giant Robot. 2,800.00
24 SSh(c),V:Mobsters. 2,700.00
25 The Masked Monster 2,500.00
26 SSh(c),Her Diary of Terror . . 2,500.00
27 SSh(c),BEv,V:The Asbestos Lady. 2,500.00
28 BEv,The Twins Who Weren't 2,500.00
29 SSh(c),You'll Die Laughing . 2,500.00
30 SSh(c),BEv,The Stranger, A:Namora 2,500.00
31 A:Namora 2,000.00
32 SSh(c),A:Sungirl,Namora. . . 2,000.00
33 Capt.America crossover . . . 2,000.00
34 The Flat of the Land 2,000.00
35 A;Captain America,Sungirl . 2,200.00

Becomes:

LOVE TALES

Revived As:

HUMAN TORCH

Marvel Comics, 1954

36 A:Submariner. 2,000.00
37 BEv,A:Submariner 1,800.00
38 BEv,A:Submariner 1,800.00

HUMAN TORCH

Sept., 1974

1 JK,rep.StrangeTales #101 . . . . . 30.00
2 rep.Strange Tales #102 . . . . . . 25.00
3 rep.Strange Tales #103 . . . . . . 25.00
4 rep.Strange Tales #104 . . . . . . 25.00
5 rep.Strange Tales #105 . . . . . . 25.00
6 rep.Strange Tales #106 . . . . . . 25.00
7 rep.Strange Tales #107 . . . . . . 25.00
8 rep.Strange Tales #108 . . . . . . 25.00

HUMAN TORCH

April, 2003

1 KK(s),Burn,pt.1 . . . . 2.50
2 KK(s),Burn,pt.2 . . . . 2.50
3 KK(s),Burn,pt.3 . . . . 2.50
4 KK(s),Burn,pt.4 . . . . 2.50
5 KK(s),Burn,pt.5 . . . . 2.50
6 KK(s),Burn,concl. 2.50
7 KK(s),Plague of Locusts,pt.1 . . . 2.50
8 KK(s),Plague of Locusts,pt.2 . . . 3.00
9 KK(s),Plague of Locusts,pt.3 . . . 3.00
10 KK(s),Plague of Locusts,pt.4 . . . 3.00
11 KK(s),F:Namorita 3.00
12 KK(s),series finale. 3.00

HUMAN TORCH COMICS

Feb., 1999

1-shot V:Sub-Mariner, 48-page 4.00

HYPERKIND

Marvel/Razorline 1993

1 I:Hyperkind,BU:EctoKid 3.00
2 thru 9 . . . . @2.50

HYPERKIND UNLEASHED

1994

1 BU,V:Thermakk 3.25

ICEMAN

Dec., 1984

1 DP,mini-series 3.00
2 DP,V:Kali 3.00
3 DP,A:Original X-Men,Defenders Champions 3.00
4 DP,Oblivion,June, 1985 . . . . 4.00

ICEMAN

Oct., 2001

1 (of 4) DAn,ALa,KIK 3.00
2 DAn,ALa,KIK,A:Augmen 3.00
3 DAn,ALa,KIK,F:Foe-Dog,Augmen 3.00
4 DAn,ALa, concl. 3.00

IDEAL

Marvel Timely, July, 1948

1 Antony and Cleopatra 500.00
2 The Corpses of Dr.Sacotti . . . 375.00
3 Joan of Arc 350.00
4 Richard the Lionhearted A:The Witness 550.00
5 Phc,Love and Romance 250.00

Becomes:

LOVE ROMANCES

6 Ph(c),I Loved a Scoundrel . . . 250.00
7 Ph(c) 175.00
8 Ph(c) 200.00

Love Romances #87
© *Marvel Entertainment Group*

9 thru 12 Ph(c) . . . . @150.00
13 thru 20 . . . . @150.00
21 BK 125.00
22 . . . . 125.00
23 . . . . 125.00
24 BK 125.00
25 . . . . 125.00
26 thru 35 . . . . @125.00
36 BK 125.00
37 . . . . 150.00
38 BK 150.00
39 thru 44 . . . . @125.00
45 MB. 150.00
46 . . . . 150.00
47 . . . . 150.00
48 . . . . 125.00
49 ATh 150.00
50 . . . . 125.00
51 . . . . 125.00
52 . . . . 125.00
53 ATh 14U.UU
54 . . . . 125.00
55 . . . . 125.00
56 . . . . 125.00
57 MB. 135.00
58 thru 74 . . . . @135.00
75 MB. 135.00
76 . . . . 125.00
77 MB. 135.00
78 . . . . 125.00
79 . . . . 125.00
80 RH(c). 125.00
81 . . . . 125.00
82 MB,JK(c). 150.00
83 JSe,JK(c) 150.00
84 JK 150.00
85 JK 150.00
86 thru 95 . . . . @100.00
96 JK 150.00
97 . . . . 150.00
98 JK 160.00
99 JK 160.00
100 thru 104 . . . . @160.00
105 JK 160.00
106 JK,July, 1963 . . . . 160.00

IDEAL COMICS

Marvel Timely, Fall, 1944

1 B:Super Rabbit,Giant Super Rabbit V:Axis(c) 300.00
2 Super Rabbit at Fair(c) 200.00
3 Super Rabbit(c). 200.00
4 How to Catch Robbers 200.00

Becomes:

WILLIE COMICS
1946
5 B:Willie,George,Margie,Nellie
  Football(c) 250.00
6 Record Player(c) 175.00
7 Soda Fountain(c),HK 175.00
8 Fancy Dress(c) 150.00
9 . . . . 150.00
10 HK,Hey Look. 175.00
11 HK,Hey Look. 175.00
12 . . . . 150.00
13 . . . . 150.00
14 . . . . 150.00
15 . . . . 150.00
16 thru 18. . . . . @150.00
19 . . . . 175.00
20 Li'L Willie Comics 150.00
21 Li'L Willie Comics 150.00
22 . . . . 150.00
23 May, 1950 . . . . 150.00
Becomes:

CRIME CASES

I ♥ MARVEL
Feb., 2006
Marvel AI 3.00
Masked Intentions #1 . . . . 3.00
My Mutant Heart 3.00
Outlaw Love #1 . . . . 3.00
Web of Romance #1 . . . . 3.00

ILLUMINATOR
1993
1 . . . . 5.50
2 . . . . 5.50
3 thru 4 . . . . @3.25

IMMORTAL IRON FIST
Nov., 2006
1 . . . . 3.00
1a Director's Cut. 4.00
2 . . . . 3.00
3 . . . . 3.00
4 . . . . 3.00
5 . . . . 3.00
6 . . . . 3.00
7 F:Wu Ao-Shi. 3.00
8 Seven Capital Cities of Heaven. . 3.00
9 Seven Capital Cities of Heaven. . 3.00
10 . . . . 3.00
11 Seven Capital Cities of Heaven . 3.00
12 Seven Capital Cities of Heaven . 3.00
13 Seven Capital Cities of Heaven . 3.00
14 Seven Capital Cities of Heaven . 3.00
15 Tales of the Iron Fist. 3.00
16 Happy Birthday Danny 3.00
17 Mortal Iron Fist, pt.1 . . . . 3.00
18 Mortal Iron Fist, pt.2 . . . . 3.00
19 Mortal Iron Fist, pt.3 . . . . 3.00
20 Mortal Iron Fist, pt.4 . . . . 3.00
Ann. #1 . . . . 4.00
Spec. Orson Randall and the Green
  Mist of Death 4.00
Spec. The Origin of Danny Rand. . . 4.00
Spec. Orson Randall and the Death
  Queen of California 4.00

IMPOSSIBLE MAN
SUMMER VACATION
1990–91
1 GCa,DP 2.50
2 . . . . 2.50
Summer Fun Spec. TPe, Vacation
  on Earth. 2.50

INCAL, THE
Epic, Nov., 1988
1 Moebius,Adult 12.00

---

2 Moebius,Adult 12.00
3 Moebius,Adult, Jan., 1989 . . . 12.00

INCOMPLETE
DEATH'S HEAD
1993
1 . . . . 3.50
2 thru 11 rep.Death's Head #1
  thru #11 . . . . @2.50

INCREDIBLE HULK
May, 1962
1 JK,I:Hulk(Grey Skin),Rick Jones,
  Thunderbolt Ross,Betty Ross,
  Gremlin,Gamma Base . . . 35,000.00
2 JK,SD,O:Hulk,(Green skin). . 6,500.00
3 JK,O:rtd.,I:Ring Master,
  Circus of Crime. 4,000.00
4 JK,V:Mongu 3,500.00
5 JK,I:General Fang. 3,500.00
6 SD,I:Metal Master. 4,000.00
See: Tales to Astonish #59-#101

April, 1968
102 MSe,GT,O:Retold 700.00
103 MSe,I:Space Parasite 250.00
104 MSe,O&N:Rhino 200.00
105 MSe,GT,I:Missing Link 150.00
106 MSe,HT,GT 150.00
107 HT,V:Mandarin 150.00
108 HT,JMe,A:Nick Fury 150.00
109 HT,JMe,A:Ka-Zar 125.00
110 HT,JMe,A:Ka-Zar. 125.00
111 HT,DA,I:Galaxy Master 100.00
112 HT,DA,O:Galaxy Master 80.00
113 HT,DA,V:Sandman 80.00
114 HT,DA 80.00
115 HT,DA,A:Leader 80.00
116 HT,DA,V:Super Humanoid . . . 80.00
117 HT,DA,A:Leader 80.00
118 HT,V:Sub-Mariner 80.00
119 HT,V:Maximus 75.00
120 HT,V:Maximus 75.00
121 HT,I:The Glob 75.00
122 HT,V:Thing 125.00
123 HT,V:Leader 75.00
124 HT,SB,V:Rhino,Leader 75.00
125 HT,V:Absorbing Man 75.00
126 HT,A:Dr.Strange 75.00
127 HT,Moleman vs.Tyrannus
  I:Mogol. 50.00
128 HT,A:Avengers 50.00
129 HT,V:Glob 50.00
130 HT,Banner vs. Hulk. 50.00
131 HT,A:Iron Man. 50.00
132 HT,JSe,V:Hydra 50.00
133 HT,JSe,I:Draxon 50.00
134 HT,SB,I:Golem 50.00
135 HT,SB,V:Kang 50.00
136 HT,SB,I:Xeron 50.00
137 HT,V:Abomination 50.00
138 HT,V:Sandman 50.00
139 HT,V:Leader 50.00
140 HT,V:Psyklop. 50.00
141 HT,JSe,I&O:Doc.Samson . . . 150.00
142 HT,JSe,V:Valkyrie,A:Doc
  Samson 60.00
143 DA,JSe,V:Dr.Doom 60.00
144 DA,JSe,V:Dr.Doom 60.00
145 HT,JSe,O:Retold 65.00
146 HT,JSe,Leader 30.00
147 HT,JSe,Doc.Samson loses
  Powers. 30.00
148 HT,JSe,I:Fialan 30.00
149 HT,JSe,I:Inheritor 30.00
150 HT,JSe,I:Viking,A:Havoc. . . . 30.00
151 HT,JSe,C:Ant Man 30.00
152 HT,DA,Many Cameos 30.00
153 HT,JSe,C:Capt.America 30.00
154 HT,JSe,A:Ant Man,
  V:Chameleon. 30.00

Incredible Hulk #116
© Marvel Entertainment Group

155 HT,JSe,I:Shaper of Worlds . . . 30.00
156 HT,V:Hulk 30.00
157 HT,I:Omnivac,Rhino 30.00
158 HT,C:Warlock,V:Rhino 30.00
159 HT,V:Abomination,Rhino. 30.00
160 HT,V:Tiger Shark. 30.00
161 HT,V:Beast. 40.00
162 HT,I:Wendigo I 100.00
163 HT,I:Gremlin 25.00
164 HT,I:Capt.Omen 25.00
165 HT,I:Aquon 25.00
166 HT,I:Zzzax 25.00
167 HT,JAb,V:Modok 25.00
168 HT,JAb,I:Harpy 25.00
169 HT,JAb,I:Bi-Beast 25.00
170 HT,JAb,V:Volcano 25.00
171 HT,JAb,A:Abomination,Rhino . 25.00
172 HT,JAb,X:X-Men 50.00
173 HT,V:Cobolt Man. 22.00
174 HT,V:Cobolt Man. 22.00
175 JAb,V:Inhumans 22.00
176 HT,JAb,A:Man-Beast,C:Warlock
  Crisis on Counter-Earth. 25.00
177 HT,JAb,D:Warlock. 25.00
178 HT,JAb,Warlock Lives. 25.00
179 HT,JAb 22.00
180 HT,JAb,I:Wolverine
  V:Wendigo I 400.00
181 HT,JAb,A:Wolverine (1st
  Full Story),V:Wendigo II . . 1,500.00
182 HT,JAb,I&D:Crackajack
  Jackson,C:Wolverine. 200.00
183 HT,V:Zzzax 18.00
184 HT,V:Living Shadow 18.00
185 HT,V:General Ross 18.00
186 HT,I:Devastator 18.00
187 HT,JSt,V:Gremlin. 18.00
188 HT,JSt,I:Droog. 18.00
189 HT,JSt,I:Datrine. 18.00
190 HT,MSe,Toadman 18.00
191 HT,JSt,Toadman,I:Glorian. . . . 18.00
192 HT,V:The Lurker 18.00
193 HT,JSt,Doc.Samson regains
  Powers. 18.00
194 SB,JSt,V:Locust 18.00
195 SB,JSt,V:Abomination. 18.00
196 SB,JSt,V:Army 18.00
197 BWr(c),SB,JSt,A:Man-Thing . . 18.00
198 SB,JSt,A:Man-Thing 18.00
199 SB,JSt,V:Shield,Doc.Samson . 18.00
200 SB,JSt,Multi,Hulk in Glenn
  Talbots Brain 40.00
201 SB,JSt,V:Fake Conan 7.00
202 SB,JSt,A:Jarella 7.00
203 SB,JSt,A:Jarella 7.00
204 SB,JStI:Kronus 7.00

All comics prices listed are for *Near Mint* condition.

205 SB,JSt,D:Jarella 7.00	279 SB,JSt,C:X-Men,	328 AM,1st PDd(s),Outcasts 8.00
206 SB,JSt,C:Dr.Strange 7.00	Avengers,Fantastic Four 6.00	329 AM,V:Enigma 5.00
207 SB,JSt,A:Dr.Strange 7.00	280 SB,JSt,Jack Daw 5.00	330 1st TM Hulk,D:T-bolt Ross . . . 27.00
208 SB,JSt,V:Absorbing Man. 7.00	281 SB,JSt,Trapped in Space 5.00	331 TM,V:Leader. 27.00
209 SB,JSt,V:Absorbing Man. 7.00	282 SB,JSt,A:She Hulk 5.00	332 TM,V:Leader. 15.00
210 SB,A:Dr.Druid,O:Merlin II 7.00	283 SB,JSt,A:Avengers 5.00	333 TM,V:Leader. 15.00
211 SB,A:Dr.Druid 7.00	284 SB,JSt,A:Avengers 5.00	334 TM,I:Half-life 15.00
212 SB,I:Constrictor. 8.00	285 SB,JSt,Northwind,V:Zzzax 5.00	335 Horror Issue 6.00
213 SB,TP,I:Quintronic Man 7.00	286 SB,JSt,V:Soldier 5.00	336 TM,A:X-Factor. 15.00
214 SB,Jack of Hearts. 7.00	287 SB,JSt,V:Soldier 5.00	337 TM,A:X-Factor, A:DocSamson 15.00
215 SB,V:Bi-Beast 6.00	288 SB,JSt,V:Abomination. 5.00	338 TM,I:Mercy,V:Shield 15.00
216 SB,Gen.Ross 6.00	289 SB,JSt,V:Modok 5.00	339 TM,A:RickJones 15.00
217 SB,I:Stilts,A:Ringmaster 6.00	290 SB,JSt,V:Modok 5.00	340 TM,Hulk vs Wolverine 50.00
218 SB,KP,Doc.Samson versus	291 SB,JSt,V:Thunderbolt Ross . . . 5.00	341 TM,V:Man Bull 9.00
Rhino. 6.00	292 SB,JSt,V:Dragon Man 5.00	342 TM,V:Leader. 9.00
219 SB,V:Capt.Barravuda 6.00	293 SB,V:Nightmare 5.00	343 TM,V:Leader. 9.00
220 SB,Robinson Crusoe 6.00	294 SB,V:Boomerang 5.00	344 TM,V:Leader. 9.00
221 SB,AA,A:Sting Ray 6.00	295 SB,V:Boomerang 5.00	345 TM,V:Leader,Double-Size. . . . 10.00
222 JSn,AA,Cavern of Bones 6.00	296 SB,A:Rom 5.00	346 TM,EL,L:Rick Jones 9.00
223 SB,V:Leader 6.00	297 SB,V:Nightmare 5.00	347 In Las Vegas,I:Marlo Chandler,
224 SB,V:The Leader 6.00	298 KN(c),SB,V:Nightmare 5.00	V:Absorbing Man. 5.00
225 SB,V:Leader,A:Doc.Samson. . . 6.00	299 SB,A:Shield. 5.00	348 V:Absorbing Man 4.00
226 SB,JSt,A:Doc.Samson 6.00	300 SB,A:Spider-Man,Avengers	349 A:Spider-Man 4.00
227 SB,JK,A:Doc.Samson. 6.00	Doctor Strange 8.00	350 Hulk vs Thing,A:Beast
228 SB,BMc,I:Moonstone,V:Doc	301 SB,Crossroads 4.00	V:Dr.Doom 5.00
Samson 8.00	302 SB,Crossroads 4.00	351 R:Jarella's World. 3.00
229 SB,O:Moonstone,V:Doc	303 SB,V:The Knights 4.00	352 V:Inquisitor 3.00
Samson 6.00	304 SB,V:U-Foes. 4.00	353 R:Bruce Banner 3.00
230 JM,BL,A:Bug Thing. 6.00	305 SB,V:U-Foes. 4.00	354 V:Maggia. 3.00
231 SB,I:Fred Sloan 6.00	306 SB,V:Klaatu. 4.00	355 V:Glorian. 3.00
232 SB,A:Capt.America 6.00	307 SB,V:Klaatu. 4.00	356 V:Glorian,Cloot 3.00
233 SB,A:Marvel Man 6.00	308 SB,V:Puffball Collective 4.00	357 V:Glorian,Cloot 3.00
234 SB,Marvel Man Changes name	309 SB,V:Goblin & Glow 4.00	358 V:Glorian,Cloot 3.00
to Quasar. 6.00	310 Crossroads 4.00	359 JBy(c),C:Wolverine(illusion) . . . 4.00
235 SB,A:Machine Man 6.00	311 Crossroads 4.00	360 V:Nightmare & Dyspare 3.00
236 SB,A:Machine Man 6.00	312 Secret Wars II,O:Bruce. 4.50	361 A:Iron Man,V:Maggia 3.00
237 SB,A:Machine Man 6.00	313 A:Alpha Flight 4.00	362 V:Werewolf By Night. 3.00
238 SB,JAb,Jimmy Carter 6.00	314 JBy,V:Doc.Samson 6.00	363 Acts of Vengeance 3.00
239 SB,I:Gold Bug 6.00	315 JBy,A:Doc.Samson,Banner	364 A:Abomination,B:Countdown . . 3.00
240 SB,Eldorado 6.00	& Hulk Separated 4.00	365 A:Fantastic Four 3.00
241 SB,A:Tyrannus 6.00	316 JBy,A:Avengers,N:Doc	366 A:Leader,I:Riot Squad. 3.00
242 SB,Eldorado 6.00	Samson 4.00	367 1st DK Hulk,I:Madman(Leader's
243 SB,A:Gammernon. 6.00	317 JBy,I:Hulkbusters,A:Doc	brother),E:Countdown 10.00
244 SB,A:It. 6.00	Samson 4.00	368 SK,V:Mr.Hyde. 5.00
245 SB,A:Super Mandroid 6.00	318 JBy,A:Doc.Samson 5.00	369 DK,V:Freedom Force 3.00
246 SB,V:Capt.Marvel 6.00	319 JBy,W:Bruce & Betty. 6.00	370 DK,R:Original Defenders 3.00
247 SB,A:Bat Dragon 6.00	320 AM,A:Doc.Samson 3.00	371 DK,BMc,A:Orig.Defenders 3.00
248 SB,V:Gardener 6.00	321 AM,A:Avengers. 3.00	372 DK,R:Green Hulk 10.00
249 SD,R:Jack Frost 6.00	322 AM,A:Avengers. 3.00	373 DK,Green Hulk & Grey Hulk. . . 4.00
250 SB,A:Silver Surfer. 15.00	323 AM,A:Avengers. 3.00	374 DK,BMc,Skrulls,
251 MG,A:3-D Man 5.00	324 AM,R:Grey Hulk(1st since #1),	R:Rick Jones 4.00
252 SB,A:Woodgod 5.00	A:Doc.Samson. 15.00	375 DK,BMc,V:Super Skrull. 4.00
253 SB,A:Woodgod 5.00	325 AM,Rick Jones as Hulk. 6.00	376 DK,BMc,Green Hulk,Grey
254 SB,I:U-Foes 5.00	326 A:Rick Jones,New Hulk. 7.00	Hulk & Banner fight 5.00
255 SB,V:Thor 5.00	327 AM,F:General Ross 3.00	377 DK,BMc,New Green Hulk,
256 SB,I&O:Sabra 5.00		combination of green, grey, and
257 SB,I&O:Arabian Knight 5.00		Bruce Banner,A:Ringmaster . 11.00
258 I:Soviet Super Soldiers 5.00		377a 2nd printing (gold). 5.00
259 SB,A:Soviet Super-Soldiers,		378 V:Rhino,Christmas Issue 3.00
O:Darkstar 5.00		379 DK,MFm,I:Pantheon 4.00
260 SB,Sugata. 5.00		380 A:Nick Fury,D:Crazy-8 . . . . . . 3.00
261 SB,V:Absorbing Man. 5.00		381 DK,MFm,Hulk,J:Pantheon 4.00
262 SB,I:Glazer 5.00		382 DK,MFm,A:Pantheon 4.00
263 SB,Avalanche 5.00		383 DK,MFm,Infinity Gauntlet 4.00
264 SB,A:Corruptor 5.00		384 DK,MFm,Infinity Gauntlet 4.00
265 SB,I:Rangers. 5.00		385 DK,MFm,Infinity Gauntlet 4.00
266 SB,V:High Evolutionary. 5.00		386 DK,MFm,V:Sabra,A:Achilles . . . 4.00
267 SB,V:Rainbow,O:Glorian. 5.00		387 DK,MFm,V:Sabra,A:Achilles . . . 4.00
268 SB,I:Pariah 5.00		388 DK,MFm,I:Speed Freak,Jim
269 SB,I:Bereet 5.00		Wilson,revealed to have AIDS. . 5.00
270 SB,A:Abomination. 5.00		389 1st Comic art By Gary Barker
271 SB,I:Rocket Raccoon,		(Garfield),A:Man-Thing,Glob . . . 4.00
20th Anniv.. . . . . 5.00		390 DK,MFm,B:War & Pieces,
272 SB,C:X-Men,I:Wendigo III. 6.00		C:X-Factor 4.00
273 SB,A:Alpha Flight 5.00		391 DK,MFm,V:X-Factor 4.00
274 SB,Beroct 5.00		392 DK,MFm,E:War & Pieces,
275 SB,JSt,I:Megalith 5.00		A:X-Factor 4.00
276 SB,JSt,V:U-Foes. 5.00		393 DK,MFm,R:Igor,A:Soviet Super
277 SB,JSt,U-Foes 5.00		Soldiers,30th Ann.,Green foil(c) 6.00
278 SB,JSt,C:X-Men,		393a 2nd printing,Silver. 2.50
Avengers,Fantastic Four 6.00		394 MFm(i),F:Atalanta,I:Trauma . . . 3.00

Incredible Hulk #313
© Marvel Entertainment Group

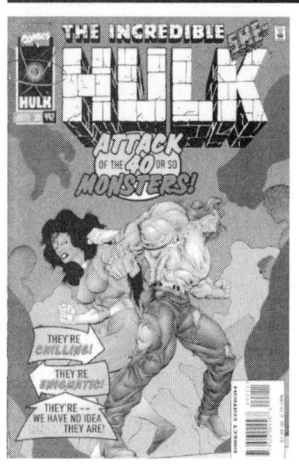

Incredible Hulk #442
© *Marvel Entertainment Group*

395 DK,MFm,A:Punisher,
I:Mr.Frost 3.00
396 DK,MFm,A:Punisher,
V:Mr.Frost 3.00
397 DK,MFm,B:Ghost of the
Past,V:U-Foes,A:Leader 3.00
398 DK,MFm,D:Marlo,V:Leader. . . . 3.00
399 JD,A:FF,Dr.Strange 3.00
400 JD,MFm,E:Ghost of the Past,
V:Leader,1st Holo-grafx(c),1st
GFr Hulk(pin-up) 3.50
400a 2nd Printing. 4.00
401 JDu,O:Agememnon 3.00
402 JDu,V:Juggernaut 3.00
403 GFr,V:Red Skull,A:Avengers. . . 3.00
404 GFr,V:Red Skull,Juggernaut,
A:Avengers 3.50
405 GFr,Ajax vs. Achilles. 3.00
406 GFr,V:Captain America 3.00
407 GFr,I:Piecemeal,A:Madman,
B:O:Ulysses. 3.00
408 GFr,V:Madman,Piecemeal,
D:Perseus,A:Motormouth,
Killpower. 3.00
409 GFr,A:Motormouth,Killpower,
V:Madman 3.00
410 GFr,A:Nick Fury,S.H.I.E.L.D.,
Margo agrees to marry Rick . . . 3.00
411 GFr,V:Nick Fury,S.H.I.E.L.D. . . 3.00
412 PaP,V:Bi-Beast,A:She-Hulk. . . . 3.00
413 GFr,CaS,B:Troyjan War,
I:Cassiopea,Armageddon,
V:Trauma. 3.00
414 GFr,CaS,V:Trauma,C:S.Surfer . 3.00
415 GFr,CaS,V:Trauma,A:Silver
Surfer,Starjammers 3.00
416 GFr,CaS,E:Troyjan War,D:Trauma,
A:S.Surfer,Starjammers 3.00
417 GFr,CaS,Rick's/Marlo's Bachelor/
Bachelorette Party. 5.00
418 GFr,CaS,W:Rick & Marlo,
A:Various Marvel persons,
Die Cut(c) 5.00
418a Newsstand ed. 4.00
419 CaS,V:Talos 3.00
420 GFr,CaS,AIDS Story,
D:Jim Wilson 3.50
421 CaS,B:Myth Conceptions 3.00
422 GFr,Myth Conceptions,pt.2 . . . . 3.00
423 GFr,CaS,Myth Concept.,pt.3 . . . 3.00
424 B:Fall of the Hammer 3.00
425 Regular edition 3.00
425a Enhanced cover 4.00
426 PDa,LSh,R:Mercy 3.00

426a Deluxe edition 3.00
427 A:Man-Thing 4.00
427a Deluxe edition 8.00
428 Suffer The Children. 3.00
429 Abortion Issue 3.00
430 A:Speed Freak 3.00
431 PDd,LSh R:Abomination 3.00
432 V:Abomination. 3.00
433 PDd,V:Abomination. 3.00
434 Funeral of the Year 3.00
435 Hulk vs. Rhino baseball 4.00
436 PDd,AMe,Ghosts of the
Future,pt.1 . . . . 3.00
437 PDd,AMe,Ghosts of the
Future,pt.2 . . . . 3.00
438 PDd,AMe,Ghosts of the
Future,pt.3 . . . . 3.00
439 PDd,AMe,Ghosts of the
Future,pt.4 . . . . 3.00
440 PDd,AMe. 3.00
441 PDd,AMe,A:She-Hulk 3.00
442 A:Molecule Man, She-Hulk 3.00
443 Janis 3.00
444 Onslaught saga, V:Cable 4.50
445 Onslaught saga 4.00
446 Blamed for loss of Fantastic
Four and Avengers 3.50
447 PDd,MD2,F:Unleashed Hulk. . . 4.00
447a Variant Tank Smashing cover . 7.50
448 PDd,MD2,V:The Pantheon . . . 3.00
449 PDd,MD2,I:Thunderbolts 9.00
450 PDd,MD2,F:Doctor Strange,
56pg. 6.00
451 PDd,MD2, ... 3.00
452 PDd,MD2, ... 3.00
453 PDd,MD2,V:Future Hulk 3.00
454 PDd,AKu,MFm,A God,
In Savage Land 3.00
455 PDd,AKu,MFm,in X-Mansion . . 3.00
456 PDd,AKu,MFm,A:Apocalypse. . 3.00
457 PDd,Hulk vs. Juggernaut 3.00
458 PDd,AKu,MFm,V:Mercy 3.00
459 PDd,AKu,MFm,V:Abomination . 3.00
460 PDa,AKu,MFm, Return of Bruce
Banner 4.00
461 PDa,V:Thunderbolt Ross 3.00
462 PDa,AKu,MFm,V:Thunderbolt
Ross 3.00
463 PDa,AKu,MFm,V:Thunderbolt
Ross 3.00
464 PDa,AKu,MFm,V:Troygens &
Silver Surfer. 3.00
465 PDa,MFm,Poker game 3.00
466 PDa,AKu,MFm,tragic loss. 5.00
467 PDa,AKu,MFm,Hulk attempts
suicide 5.00
468 JoC,new direction 2.50
469 JoC,LMa,F:Super-Adaptoid . . . 3.00
470 JoC,NMa,V:Ringmaster
& Circus of Crime 2.50
471 JoC,NMa,Circus of
Crime,concl. 2.50
472 JoC,Great Astonishment,pt.1 . . 2.50
473 JoC,Great Astonishment,pt.2 . . 2.50
474 JoC,Great Astonishment,pt.3 . . 6.00
Spec.#1 A:Inhumans (1968) 175.00
Spec.#2 rep.O:Hulk,A:Leader
(1969) 90.00
Spec.#3 rep.A:Leader (1971). 40.00
Spec.#4 IR:Hulk/Banner (1972). . . 40.00
Ann.#5 V:Xemnu,Diablo (1976) . . . 18.00
Ann.#6 HT,A:Dr.Strange,I:Paragon
(Her) (1977). 15.00
Ann.#7 JBy,BL,A:Angel,Iceman
A:Doc.Samson (1978) 15.00
Ann.#8 Alpha Flight (1979) 15.00
Ann.#9 Checkmate (1980). 6.00
Ann.#10 A:Captain Universe (1981) 6.00
Ann.#11 RB,JSt,A:Spider-Man,
Avengers,V:Unis (1982) 5.00
Ann.#12 (1983) 4.00
Ann.#13 (1984) 4.00

Ann.#14 JBy,SB (1985) 4.00
Ann.#15 V:Abomitation (1986). 4.00
Ann.#16 HT,Life Form #3,
A:Mercy (1990) 4.00
Ann.#17 Subterran.Odyssey #2
(1991) 4.00
Ann #18 KM,TA,TC(1st Work),Return
of the Defenders,Pt.1 (1992). . . 7.00
Ann.#19 I:Lazarus,w/card (1993). . . 4.00
Ann.#20 SvL,SI (1994) 4.00
Ann.'98 F:Hulk&Sub-Mariner, 48pg . 3.00
Ann. Hulk 1999 . . . . 3.50
Marvel Milestone rep. #1 (1991) . . . 3.00
G-Size#1 rep. Greatest Foes. 10.00
Minus 1 Spec., PDd,AKu,MFm,
flashback. 3.00
Spec. '97 Onslaught aftermath 3.00
Spec. Incredible Hulk
vs. Superman, 48-pg. 6.00
Spec. Hulk vs. Superman, signed . 20.00
Milestone #181, F:Wolverine 3.00
Hulk vs. Thing, rep. 4.00

INCREDIBLE HULK:
FUTURE IMPERFECT
1993
1 GP,V:Maestro 10.00
2 GP,V:Maestro 8.00

INCREDIBLE HULK/PITT
1997
Spec. PDd,DK,x-over. 6.00

INCREDIBLE HULK
VS. WOLVERINE
Oct., 1986
1 HT,rep. #181 B:,V:Wolverine. . . 12.00
1a 2nd printing 4.00

INDEPENDENCE DAY
1996
0 . . . . 5.00
1 and 2 . . . . @2.50

[Further Adventures of]
INDIANA JONES
Jan., 1983–Mar., 1986
1 JBy/TA 3.00
2 JBy/TA 2.50
3 . . . . 2.50

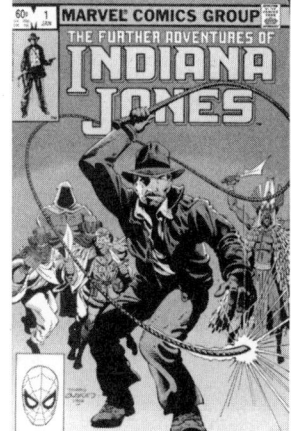

Indiana Jones #1
© *Marvel Entertainment Group*

4 KGa	2.50
5 KGa	2.50
6 HC/TA	2.50
7 thru 24 KGa	@2.50
25 thru 34 SD	@2.50

INDIANA JONES AND THE LAST CRUSADE
1 B&W,Mag.,movie adapt, 1989. . . 3.00

[Mini-Series], 1989
1 Rep., Movie adapt., 1989.	3.50
2 Rep., Movie adapt.	3.50
3 Rep., Movie adapt.	3.50
4 Rep., Movie adapt.	3.50

INDIANA JONES AND THE TEMPLE OF DOOM
1984
1 Movie adapt.	3.00
2 Movie adapt.	3.00
3 Movie adapt.	3.00

INFINITY ABYSS
June, 2002
1 (of 6) JSn,AM,V:Thanos	3.00
2 JSn,AM,F:Adam Warlock	3.00
3 JSn,AM,Spider-Man,Capt.Marvel	3.00
4 JSn,AM,Eternity & Infinity	3.00
5 JSn,AM	3.00
6 48-pg.	3.50

INFINITY CRUSADE
1993
1 RLm,AM,I:Goddess,A:Marvel Heroes,foil(c).	4.00
2 RLm,AM,V:Goddess	3.00
3 RLm,AM,V:Goddess,Mephisto.	3.00
4 RLm,AM,V:Goddess,A:Magnus.	3.00
5 RLm,AM,V:Goddess	3.00
6 RLm,AM,V:Goddess	3.00

INFINITY GAUNTLET
July, 1991
1 GP,O:Infinity Gauntlet	5.00
2 GP,JRu,2nd Rebirth:Warlock	4.00
3 GP,JRu,I:Terraxia	4.00
4 GP,JRu,RLm,V:Thanos	4.00
5 JRu,RLm,V:Thanos,D:Terraxia	4.00
6 RLm,JRu,V:Nebula	4.00

INFINITY WAR
1992
1 RLm,AM,R:Magus,Thanos	5.00
2 RLm,AM,V:Magus,A:Everyone	3.00
3 RLm,AM,V:Magus,A:Everyone	2.50
4 RLm,AM,Magus gets Gauntlet	2.50
5 RLm,AM,V:Magus	2.50
6 RLm,AM,V:Magus	2.50

INHUMANOIDS
Star, Jan.–July, 1987
1 Hasbro Toy.	3.00
2 O:Inhumanoids	3.00
3 V:D'Compose.	3.00
4 A:Sandra Shore	3.00

INHUMANS
Oct., 1975
1 GP,V:Blastaar.	28.00
2 GP,V:Blastaar.	15.00
3 GP,I:Kree S	20.00
4 GK,Maximus	20.00
5 GK,V:Maximus	20.00
6 GK,Maximus	20.00
7 GK,DP,I:Skornn	20.00
8 GP,DP,Skornn	20.00
9 rep., V:Mor-Tog	20.00

10 KP,D:Warkon.	20.00
11 KP,JM,I:Pursuer	20.00
12 KP,Hulk	20.00
Spec.#1(The Untold Saga), O:Inhumans.	4.00
Spec. Atlantis Rising story	3.00

INHUMANS
Sept., 1998
1 (of 12) PJe,JaL,F:Black Bolt, Medusa, Karnak, Triton, Gorgon, Crystal, Lockjaw	9.00
2 PJe,JaL,F:Tonaje	4.00
2a Variant cover	3.00
3 PJe,JaL,Attilan's dark side	3.00
4 PJe,JaL,War against Attilan	3.00
5 PJe,JaL,Earth vs. Attilan	3.00
6 PJe,JaL,V:Maximus	3.00
7 PJe,JaL,F:Black Bolt	3.00
8 PJe,JaL,F:Lockjaw	3.00
9 PJe,JaL,F:Triton.	3.00
10 PJe,JaL,F:Woz & Medusa	3.00
11 PJe,JaL,F:Black Bolt.	3.00
12 PJe,JaL,concl.	3.00

INHUMANS
Apr. 2000
1 (of 4) V:Ronan the Accuser	3.00
2 A:Kree	3.00
3 Maximus the Mad	3.00
4 concl.	3.00

INHUMANS
May, 2003
1 Lunar,pt.1	2.50
2 Lunar,pt.2.	2.50
3 Lunar,pt.3	2.50
4 Culture Shock,pt.1	2.50
5 Culture Shock,pt.2	2.50
6 Culture Shock,pt.3	2.50
7 San finds love	3.00
8 Alaris	3.00
9 No Matter the Cost,pt.1	3.00
10 No Matter the Cost,pt.2	3.00
11 No Matter the Cost,pt.3.	3.00
12 No Matter the Cost,pt.4	3.00

INTERFACE
Epic, Dec., 1989
1 ESP	2.50
2 thru 8	@2.25

INVADERS
Aug., 1975
1 FR,JR(c),A:Invaders, A:Mastermind	75.00
2 FR,JR(c),I:Brain Drain	30.00
3 FR,JR(c),I:U-Man.	30.00
4 FR,O&V:U-Man	30.00
5 RB,JM,V:Red Skull	30.00
6 FR,V:Liberty Legion	30.00
7 FR,I:Baron Blood, 1st Union Jack.	30.00
8 FR,FS,J:Union Jack.	18.00
9 FR,FS,O:Baron Blood	18.00
10 FR,FS,rep.Captain America Comics #22	18.00
11 FR,FS,I:Blue Bullet	12.00
12 FR,FS,I:Spitfire	12.00
13 FR,FS,GK(c),I:Golem, Half Face	12.00
14 FR,FS,JK(c),I:Crusaders.	12.00
15 FR,FS,JK(c),V:Crusaders	12.00
16 FR,JK(c),V:Master Man	12.00
17 FR,FS,GK(c),I:Warrior Woman.	12.00
18 FR,FS,GK(c),R:1st Destroyer	12.00
19 FR,FS,V:Adolph Hitler.	12.00
20 FR,FS,GK(c),I&J:2nd Union Jack, BU:rep.Marvel Comics #1	18.00

Invaders #6
© Marvel Entertainment Group

21 FR,FS,GK(c),BU:rep.Marvel Mystery #10.	15.00
22 FR,FS,GK(c),O:Toro	8.00
23 FR,FS,GK(c),I:Scarlet Scarab	8.00
24 FR,FS,GK(c),rep.Marvel Mystery #17.	10.00
25 FR,FS,GK(c),V:Scarlet Scarab	8.00
26 FR,FS,GK(c),V:Axis Agent	8.00
27 FR,FS,GK(c),V:Axis Agent	8.00
28 FR,FS,I:2nd Human Top, Golden Girl,Kid Commandos.	8.00
29 FR,FS,I:Teutonic Knight	8.00
30 FR,FS,V:Teutonic Knight.	8.00
31 FR,FS,V:Frankenstein	8.00
32 FR,FS,JK(c),A:Thor	10.00
33 FR,FS,JK(c),A:Thor	10.00
34 FR,FS,V:Master Man	8.00
35 FR,FS,I:Iron Cross	8.00
36 FR,FS,O:Iron Cross	8.00
37 FR,FS,V:Iron Cross.	8.00
38 FR,FS,V:Lady Lotus	8.00
39 FR,FS,O:Lady Lotus.	8.00
40 FR,FS,V:Baron Blood	8.00
41 E:RTs(s)FR,FS,V:Super Axis, double-size	18.00
Ann.#1 A:Avengers,R:Shark	65.00
G-Size#1 FR,rep.Submariner #1	25.00

[Limited Series], 1993
1 R:Invaders	2.50
2 V:Battle Axis.	2.50
3 R:Original Vison (1950's).	2.50
4 V:The Axis	2.50

INVADERS
June, 2004
0 Once an Invader,pt.4	3.00
1 To End All Wars,pt.1	3.00
2 To End All Wars,pt.2	3.00
3 To End All Wars,pt.3	3.00
4 To End All Wars,pt.4	3.00
5 To End All Wars,pt.5	3.00

Becomes:
NEW INVADERS
6 Oil & Water,pt.1,A:Wolverine	3.00
7 Cruel and Unusual,pt.1	3.00
8 Cruel and Unusual,pt.2	3.00
9 Cruel and unusual, concl.	3.00

INVINCIBLE IRON MAN
May, 2008
1 SvL.	3.00
1a variant (c)s	@3.00

MARVEL

2 thru 7 SvL................ @3.00	
2a thru 6a variant (c) .... @3.00	
7 SvL,F:Spider-Man 3.00	

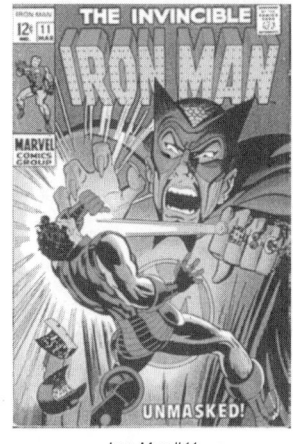

Iron Fist #3
© *Marvel Entertainment Group*

IRON FIST
Nov., 1975

1 JBy,A:Iron Man 90.00	
2 JBy,V:H'rythl................. 50.00	
3 JBy,KP,KJ,V:Ravager........ 30.00	
4 JBy,V:Radion 30.00	
5 JBy,V:Scimitar 30.00	
6 JBy,O:Misty Knight.......... 30.00	
7 JBy,V:Khimbala Bey......... 30.00	
8 JBy,V:Chaka 30.00	
9 JBy,V:Chaka 30.00	
10 JBy,DGr,A:Chaka 30.00	
11 JBy,V:Wrecking Crew 30.00	
12 JBy,DGr,V:Captain America .. 30.00	
13 JBy,A:Boomerang 25.00	
14 JBy,I:Sabretooth 250.00	
15 JBy,A&N:Wolverine,A:X-Men	
Sept., 1977 .... 100.00	
Marvel Milestone rep. #14 (1992) .. 4.00	

IRON FIST
May, 1998

1 (of 3) DJu,JG, from Heroes For	
Hire 3.00	
2 DJu,JG,search for Scorpio Key,	
V:S.H.I.E.L.D. 3.00	
3 DJu,JG,concl. 3.00	

IRON FIST
March, 2004

1 Breathless,pt.1.............. 3.00	
2 thru 6 Breathless,pt.2–pt.6.. @3.00	

IRON FIST/WOLVERINE
Sept., 2000

1 (of 4) F:DannyRand,Junzo Moto . 3.00	
2 K'un L'un 3.00	
3 A:Capt.America,Dragon Kings... 3.00	
4 concl..................... 3.00	

IRON MAN
May, 1968

1 B:StL,AGw(s),JCr,GC,	
I:Mordius 750.00	
2 JCr,I:Demolisher 250.00	
3 JCr,V:The Freak............ 200.00	
4 JCr,A:Unicorn.............. 150.00	

5 JCr,GT,I:Cerebos 150.00	
6 JCr,GT,V:Crusher........... 125.00	
7 JCr,GT,V:Gladiator 125.00	
8 JCr,GT,O:Whitney Frost...... 125.00	
9 JCr,GT,A:Mandarin 125.00	
10 JCr,GT,V:Mandarin 125.00	
11 JCr,GT,V:Mandarin 100.00	
12 JCr,GT,I:Controller 100.00	
13 JCr,GT,A:Nick Fury 100.00	
14 JCr,V:Night Phantom 100.00	
15 JCr,GT,A:Red Ghost 100.00	
16 JCr,GT,V:Unicorn 75.00	
17 JCr,GT,I:Madam Masque,	
Midas.................. 75.00	
18 JCr,GT,V:Madame Masque.... 75.00	
19 JCr,GT,V:Madame Masque.. 75.00	
20 JCr,I:Charlie Gray 75.00	
21 JCr,I:Eddie 40.00	
22 JCr,D:Janice Cord.......... 40.00	
23 JCr,I:Mercenary........... 40.00	
24 JCr,GT,V:Madame Masque... 40.00	
25 JCr,A:Sub-Mariner 50.00	
26 JCr,DH,J:Val-Larr.......... 40.00	
27 JCr,DH,I:Firebrand 40.00	
28 E:AGw(s),JCr,DH,	
V:Controller 40.00	
29 B:StL,AyB(s),DH,V:Myrmidon .. 40.00	
30 DH,I:Monster Master........ 40.00	
31 DH,I:Mastermind........... 40.00	
32 GT,I:Mechanoid............ 40.00	
33 DH,I:Spy Master 40.00	
34 DH,A:Spy Master 40.00	
35 DH,A:Daredevil,Spy Master .. 40.00	
36 E:AyB(s),DH,I:Ramrod 40.00	
37 DH,A:Ramrod 40.00	
38 GT,Jonah................. 40.00	
39 HT,I:White Dragon 30.00	
40 GT,A:White Dragon......... 30.00	
41 GT,JM,I:Slasher 30.00	
42 GT,I:Mikas................ 30.00	
43 GT,JM,A:Mikas,I:Guardsmen . 50.00	
44 GT,A:Capt.America......... 30.00	
45 GT,A:Guardsman 30.00	
46 GT,D:Guardsman 30.00	
47 BS,JM,O:Iron Man 35.00	
48 GT,V:Firebrand 22.00	
49 GT,V:Adaptoid............. 22.00	
50 B:RTs(s),GT,V:Prin.Python ... 22.00	
51 GT,C:Capt.America......... 22.00	
52 GT,I:Raga 22.00	
53 GT,JSn,I:Black Lama 22.00	
54 GT,BEv,Sub-Mariner,I:Madame	
MacEvil (Moondragon) 60.00	
55 JSn,I:Destroyer,Thanos,Mentor	
Starfox(Eros),Blood Bros. ... 250.00	
56 JSn,I:Fangor 60.00	
57 GT,R:Mandarin 20.00	
58 GT,V:Mandarin 20.00	
59 GT,A:Firebrand 20.00	
60 GT,C:Daredevil 20.00	
61 GT,Marauder.............. 20.00	
62 whiplash 20.00	
63 GT,A:Dr.Spectrum 20.00	
64 GT,I:Rokk 20.00	
65 GT,O:Dr.Spectrum 20.00	
66 GT,V:Thor 30.00	
67 GT,V:Freak 20.00	
68 GT,O:Iron Man 18.00	
69 GT,V:Mandarin 16.00	
70 GT,A:Sunfire 16.00	
71 GT,V:Yellow Claw 16.00	
72 E:RTs(s),GT,V:Black Lama ... 16.00	
73 B:LWn(s),KP,JM,V:Titanic	
Three.................. 16.00	
74 KP,V:Modok............... 16.00	
75 V:Black Lama 16.00	
76 Rep., A:Hulk.............. 16.00	
77 V:Thinker................. 16.00	
78 GT,V:Viet Cong 16.00	
79 GT,I:Quasar(not Current one).. 16.00	
80 JK(c),O:Black Lama 16.00	
81 A:Black Lama 16.00	

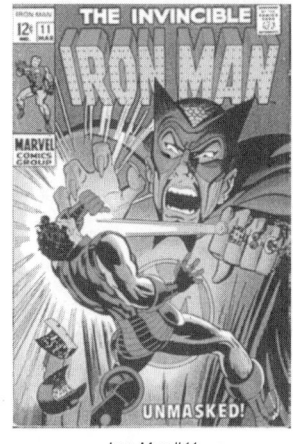

Iron Man #11
© *Marvel Entertainment Group*

82 MSe,A:Red Ghost........... 16.00	
83 E:LWn(s),HT,MSe,Red Ghost.. 16.00	
84 HT,A:Dr.Ritter 16.00	
85 HT,MSe,A:Freak 16.00	
86 B:MWn(s),GT,I:Blizzard....... 16.00	
87 GT,V:Blizzard 16.00	
88 E:MWn(s),GT,	
V:Blood Brothers 16.00	
89 GT,A:D.D.,Blood Bros. 16.00	
90 JK(c),GT,Controller,A:Thanos . 14.00	
91 GT,BL,A:Controller 12.00	
92 JK(c),GT,V:Melter 12.00	
93 JK(c),HT,V:Kraken 12.00	
94 JK(c),HT,V:Kraken 12.00	
95 JK(c),GT,PP,V:Ultimo 12.00	
96 GT,DP,V:Ultimo 12.00	
97 GT,DP,I:Guardsman II....... 12.00	
98 GT,DP,A:Sunfire 12.00	
99 GT,V:Mandarin 12.00	
100 JSn(c),GT,V:Mandarin....... 35.00	
101 GT,I:Dread Knight 14.00	
102 GT,O:Dread Knight......... 14.00	
103 GT,V:Jack of Hearts 14.00	
104 GT,V:Midas............... 9.00	
105 GT,V:Midas............... 9.00	
106 GT,V:Midas............... 9.00	
107 KP,V:Midas............... 9.00	
108 CI,A:Growing Man 9.00	
109 JBy(c),CI,V:Van Guard 9.00	
110 KP,I:C.Arcturus 9.00	
111 KP,O:Rigellians 9.00	
112 AA,KP,V:Punisher from	
Beyond 9.00	
113 KP,HT,V:Unicorn,Spy Master.. 10.00	
114 KG,I:Arsenal 9.00	
115 JR2,O:Unicorn,V:Ani-men..... 9.00	
116 JR2,BL,V:Madame Masque ... 9.00	
117 BL,JR2,1st Romita Jr 11.00	
118 JBy,BL,A:Nick Fury 14.00	
119 BL,JR2,Alcoholic Plot 11.00	
120 JR2,BL,A:Sub-Mariner,I:Rhodey	
(becomes War Machine),	
Justin Hammer........... 11.00	
121 BL,JR2,A:Submariner....... 10.00	
122 DC,CI,BL,O:Iron Man 10.00	
123 BL,JR2,V:Blizzard 10.00	
124 BL,JR2,A:Capt.America 10.00	
125 BL,JR2,A:Ant-Man 10.00	
126 JR2,V:Hammer 10.00	
127 BL,JR2,Battlefield 10.00	
128 BL,JR2,Alcohol 20.00	
129 SB,A:Dread Night 7.00	
130 BL,V:Digital Devil 7.00	
131 BL,V:Hulk 10.00	
132 BL,V:Hulk 10.00	

133 BL,A:Hulk,Ant-Man 7.00	212 DT,V:Iron Monger 3.00	262 JR2,BWi,A:Mandarin. 2.50
134 BL,V:Titanium Man 7.00	213 A:Dominic Fortune 3.00	263 JR2,BWi,A:Wonderman,
135 BL,V:Titanium Man 7.00	214 A:Spider-Woman. 4.00	V:Living Laser 2.50
136 V:Endotherm. 7.00	215 BL,A.I.M. 4.00	264 JR2,BWi,A:Mandarin. 2.50
137 BL,Fights oil rig fire. 7.00	216 BL,MBr,D:Clymenstra 3.00	265 JR2,BWi,V:Dewitt 2.50
138 BL,Dreadnought,Spymaster . . 7.00	217 BL,MRr,V:Hammer 3.00	266 JR2,BWi,E:Armor Wars II 2.50
139 BL,Dreadnought,Spymaster . . 7.00	218 BL,MBr,Titanic. 3.00	267 PR,BWi,B:New O:Iron Man,
140 BL,V:Force 7.00	219 BL,V:The Ghost 3.00	Mandarin,V:Vibro. 2.50
141 BL,JR2,V:Force. 7.00	220 BL,MBr,V:The Ghost,	268 PR,BWi,E:New O:Iron Man. . . . 2.50
142 BL,JR2,Space Armor 7.00	D:Spymaster 3.00	269 PR,BWi,A:Black Widow 2.50
143 BL,JR2,V:Sunturion 7.00	221 BL,MBr,V:The Ghost. 3.00	270 PR,BWi,V:Fin Fang Foom 2.50
144 BL,JR2,Sunturion,O:Rhodey . . 7.00	222 BL,MBr,R:Abrogast 3.00	271 PR,BWi,V:Fin Fang Foom 2.50
145 BL,JR2,A:Raiders 7.00	223 BL,MBr,V:Blizzard,Beetle 3.00	272 PR,BWi,O:Mandarin 2.50
146 BL,JR2,I:Black Lash 7.00	224 BL,V:Justin Hammer,Force 3.00	273 PR,BWi,V:Mandarin 2.50
147 BL,JR2,V:Black Lash 7.00	225 BL,MBr,B:Armor Wars. 5.00	274 MBr,BWi,V:Mandarin. 2.50
148 BL,JR2,V:Terrorists 7.00	226 BL,MBr,V:Stingray. 4.50	275 PR,BWi,A:Mandarin,Fin Fang
149 BL,JR2,V:Dr.Doom 7.00	227 BL,MBr,V:Mandroids, ... 4.00	Foom, double-size. 4.00
150 BL,JR2,V:Dr.Doom,Dble 10.00	228 BL,MBr,V:Guardsmen. 4.00	276 PR,BWi,A:Black Widow 2.50
151 TA,BL,A:Ant-Man 5.00	229 BL,D:Titanium Man 4.00	277 PR,BWi,A:Black Widow 2.50
152 BL,JR2,New Armor 5.00	230 V:Firepower, ... 4.00	278 BWi,Galactic Storm,pt.6
153 BL,JR2,V:Living Laser 5.00	231 V:Firepower,N:Iron Man 4.00	A:Capt.America,V:Shatterax . . . 2.50
154 BL,JR2,V:Unicorn 5.00	232 BWS,Nightmares,E:Armor	279 BWi,Galactic Storm,pt.13,
155 JR2,V:Back-Getters 5.00	Wars 4.50	V:Ronan,A:Avengers 2.50
156 JR2,I:Mauler 5.00	233 JG,BL,A:Ant-Man 2.50	280 KHd,V:The Stark 2.50
157 V:Spores 5.00	234 JG,BL,A:Spider-Man 4.00	281 KHd,I&V:Masters of Silence,
158 CI,AM,Iron Man Drowning 5.00	235 JG,BL,V:Grey Gargoyle. 3.00	C:War Machine Armor. 5.00
159 PS,V:Diablo. 5.00	236 JG,BL,V:Grey Gargoyle. 3.00	282 KHd,I:War Machine Armor,
160 SD,V:Serpent'sSquad 5.00	237 JG,BL,V:SDI Monster 3.00	V:Masters of Silence 4.00
161 A:Moon Knight 5.00	238 JG,BL,V:Rhino,D:M.Masque . . . 2.50	283 KHd,V:Masters of Silence. 2.50
162 V:Space Ships. 5.00	239 JG,BL,R:Ghost 2.50	284 KHd,Stark put under Cryogenic
163 V:Chessmen 5.00	240 JG,BL,V:Ghost 2.50	Freeze,B:Rhodey as Iron Man . 3.50
164 LMc,A:Bishop 5.00	241 BL,V:Mandarin 2.50	285 KHd,BWi(i),Tony's Funeral 2.50
165 LMc,Meltdown 5.00	242 BL,BWS,V:Mandarin 3.00	286 KHd,V:Avengers West Coast . . 2.50
166 LMc,V:Melter. 5.00	243 BL,BWS,Stark Paralyzed 3.00	287 KHd,I:New Atom Smasher 2.50
167 LMc,Alcoholic Issue 5.00	244 BL,V:Fixer,A:Force,double-size 5.00	288 KHd,30th Anniv.,V:Atom
168 LMc,A:Machine Man 5.00	245 BL(c),V:Dreadnaughts. 2.50	Smasher,foil(c). 4.50
169 LMc,B:Rhodey as 2nd	246 BL,HT,V:A.I.M.,Maggia 2.50	289 KHd,V:Living Laser,
Iron Man 10.00	247 BL,A:Hulk 4.00	R:Tony Stark 2.50
170 LMc,2nd Iron Man. 8.00	248 BL,Tony Stark Cured. 2.50	290 KHd,30th Anniv.,N:Iron Man,
171 LMc,2nd Iron Man. 5.00	249 BL,V:Dr.Doom 2.50	Gold foil(c). 5.00
172 LMc,V:Firebrand 3.00	250 BL,V:Dr.Doom,A of V 3.00	291 KHd,E:Rhodey as Iron Man,
173 LMc,Stane International 3.00	251 HT,AM,V:Wrecker,A of V 2.50	Becomes War Machine 2.50
174 LMc,Alcoholism. 3.50	252 HT,AM,V:Chemistro,A of V 2.50	292 KHd,Tony reveals he is alive . . 2.50
175 LMc,Alcoholism. 3.50	253 BL,V:Slagmire. 2.50	293 KHd,V:Controller. 2.50
176 LMc,Alcoholism. 3.50	254 BL,V:Spymaster 2.50	294 KHd,Infinity Crusade. 2.50
177 LMc,Alcoholism. 3.00	255 HT,V:Devestator	295 KHd,Infinity Crusade. 2.50
178 LMc,V:Wizard 3.00	I:2nd Spymaster 2.50	296 KHd,V:Modam,A:Omega Red. . 2.50
179 LMc,V:Mandarln 3.00	266 JR2,V:Space Station 2.50	297 KHd,V:Modam,Omega Red . . . 2.50
180 LMc,V:Mandarin 3.00	257 V:Samurai Steel 2.50	298 KHd(c),I:Earth Mover 2.50
181 LMc,V:Mandarin 3.00	258 JR2,BWi,B:Armor Wars II,V:	299 KHd(c),R:Ultimo 2.50
182 LMc,Secret Wars 3.00	Titanium Man 2.50	300 KHd,TMo,N:Iron Man,I:Iron
183 LMc,Turning Point. 3.00	259 JR2,BWi,V:Titanium Man 2.50	Legion,A:War Machine,V:Ultimo
184 LMc,Moves to California 3.00	260 JR2,BWi,V:Living Laser 2.50	Foil(c). 5.00
185 LMc,V:Zodiac Field 3.00	261 JR2,BWi,A:Mandarin. 2.50	300a Newsstand ed. 2.75
186 LMc,I:Vibro 3.00		301 KHd,B:Crash and Burn,
187 LMc,V:Vibro. 3.00		A:Deathlok,C:Venom 2.50
188 LMc,I:New Brother's Grimm . . . 3.00		302 KHd,V:Venom 2.50
189 LMc,I:Termite 3.00		303 KHd,V:New Warriors,
190 LMc,O:Termite,A:Scar.Witch . . 3.00		C:Thundrstrike. 2.50
191 LMc,New Grey Armor 5.00		304 KHd,C:Hulk,V:New Warriors,
192 LMc,V:Iron Man(Tony Stark) . . . 5.00		Thundrstrike,N:Iron Man 2.50
193 LMc,V:Dr.Demonicus 3.00		305 KHd,V:Hulk. 2.50
194 LMc,I:Scourge,A:West Coast		306 KHd,E:Stark Enterprise. 2.50
Avengers 3.00		307 TMo,I:Vor/Tex,R:Mandarin . . . 2.50
195 LMc,A:Shaman 3.00		308 TMo,Vor/Tex 2.50
196 LMc,V:Dr.Demonicus 3.00		309 TMo,Vor/Tex 2.50
197 LMc,Secret Wars II 3.00		310 regular. 3.00
198 SB,V:Circuit Breaker. 3.00		310a Neon(c),with insert print 3.50
199 LMc,E:Rhodey as 2nd Iron Man,		311 V:Mandarin 2.50
V:Obadiah Stone. 3.00		312 double-size 3.00
200 LMc,D:Obadiah Stone. 6.00		313 LKa,TMo,AA Meeting 2.50
201 MBr,V:Madam Masque 3.00		314 LKa,TMo,new villain 2.50
202 A:Ka-Zar 3.00		315 A:Black Widow 2.50
203 MBr,A:Hank Pym 3.00		316 I:Slag,A:Crimson Dynamo 2.50
204 MBr,V:Madame Masque 3.00		317 In Dynamos Armor 3.00
205 MBr,V:A.I.M. 3.00		318 LKa,TMo,V:Slag 2.50
206 MBr,V:Goliath 3.00		319 LKa,TMo,New Space Armor . . . 2.50
207 MBr,When the Sky Rains Fire . 3.00		320 F:Hawkeye 2.50
208 MBr,V:A.I.M. 3.00		321 Cont. From Avg. Crossing 2.50
209 V:Living Laser 3.00		322 TKa,TheCrossing,V:JackFrost . 2.50
210 MBr,V:Morgan LeFey 3.00		323 TKa,V:Avengers 2.50
211 AS,V:Living Laser 3.00		324 TKa,The Crossing. 2.50

Iron Man #212
© *Marvel Entertainment Group*

325 TKa,Avengers:Timeslide after. . 3.50
326 First Sign,pt.3 . . . . 2.50
327 Frostbite 2.50
328 TKa,Tony Stark at ColumbiaU. . 2.50
329 Stark Enterprises taken over . . 2.50
330 & 331. . . . . @2.50
332 final issue 4.00
Ann.#1 rep.Iron Man #25. . . . . . . 60.00
Ann.#2 rep.Iron Man #6. . . . . 35.00
Ann.#3 SB,Manthing 20.00
Ann.#4 DP,GT,V:Modok,
   A:Champions. 20.00
Ann.#5 JBr,A:Black Panther 7.00
Ann.#6 A:Eternals,V:Brother
   Tode. 7.00
Ann.#7 LMc,A:West Coast
   Avengers, I:New Goliath 7.00
Ann.#8 A:X-Factor 7.00
Ann.#9 V:Stratosfire,A:Sunturion . . 5.00
Ann.#10 PS,BL,Atlantis Attacks #2
   A:Sub-Mariner. 4.00
Ann.#11 SD,Terminus Factor #2 . . 4.00
Ann.#12 Subterran.Odyssey #4. . . 4.00
Ann.#13 GC,AW,Assault on Armor
   City,A:Darkhawk 4.00
Ann.#14 TMo,I:Face Theif,w/card,
   BU:War Machine. 4.00
Ann.#15 GC,V:Controller. 4.00
Spec.#1 rep.Sub-Mariner x-over . . 40.00
Spec.#2 rep.(1971) 20.00
Marvel Milestone rep. #55 (1992) . . 3.00
G-Size#1 Reprints 15.00
1-shot Iron Manual,Guide
   to Iron Man's technology 2.50
1-shot Iron Man/Force Works Collec-
   tors' Preview, Neon wrap-around
   cover, double size, X-over. 2.50
GN Iron Man 2020 . . . . 6.00

[2nd Series], Nov., 1996
1 JLe,SLo,WPo,SW,A:Bruce
   Banner, New O:Hulk,48pg. 4.00
1A variant Hulk showing cover 5.00
1 gold signature ed., bagged 18.00
2 JLe,SLo,WPo,SW 4.00
3 JLe,SLo,WPo,SW,Heroes brawl . . 3.00
4 JLe,SLo,WPo,SW,V:Laser. 3.00
4A X-mas cover 5.00
5 JLe,SLo,WPo,SW, Whirlwind. . . . 3.00
6 JLe,SLo,WPo,SW,Industrial
   Revolution, pt.2 x-over 3.00
7 JLe,SLo,WPo,SW,A:Pepper
   Potts,Villain revealed. 3.00
8 JLe,SLo,RBn,fate of Rebel 3.00
9 JLe,SLo,RBn,V:Mandarin 3.00

Iron Man Vol. 2 #7
© Marvel Entertainment Group

10 JLe,SLo,RBn,F:The Hulk 3.00
11 JLb,RBn,V:Dr. Doom,A:Hydra. . . 3.00
12 WPo,JLe,JLb,F:Dr. Doom,
   Galactus 3.00
13 JeR,LSn,Wildstorm x-over 3.00

[3rd Series], 1997
1 SCh,KBk,V:Mastermind,48-pg. . . 5.00
2 KBk,SCh,in Switzerland. 3.50
3 KBk,SCh,V:Hydra Dreadnought
   Robot. 3.00
4 KBk,SCh,R:Firebrand 3.00
5 KBk,SCh,V:Firebrand. 3.00
6 KBk,F:Black Widow 3.00
7 KBk,SCh,Live Kree or Die,pt.1
   x-over. 3.00
8 KBk,SCh,secret identity out. 3.00
9 KBk,SCh,A:Black Widow 3.00
10 KBk,SCh,A:Avengers 3.00
11 KBk,SCh,A:Warbird &
   War Machine. 3.00
12 KBk,V:War Machine 3.00
13 KBk,SCh,V:Controller,48-pg. . . . 4.00
13a signed 20.00
14 KBk,SCh,Fant.Four x-over 3.00
15 KBk,SCh,V:Nitro 3.00
16 KBk,RSt,V:Dragon Lord 3.00
17 KBk,RSt,SCh,V:Fin Fang Foom . 3.00
18 KBk,RSt,SCh,V:War Machine. . . 3.00
19 KBk,RSt,SCh,V:War Machine. . . 3.00
20 KBk,RSt,SCh,V:War Machine. . . 3.00
21 KBk,RSt,TGu,MBa,
   Eighth Day prologue 3.00
22 KBk,RSt,Eighth Day,pt.2,
   I:Carnivore 3.00
23 KBk,RSt,UltimateDanger,pt.1 . . 3.00
24 KBk,RSt,UltimateDanger,pt.2 . . 3.25
25 KBk,RSt,Ultimate
   Danger,pt.3, 48-pg. 3.50
26 JQ,Mask of Iron Man,pt.1 . . . . . 2.50
27 JQ,Mask of Iron Man,pt.2 . . . . . 2.50
28 JQ,Mask of Iron Man,pt.3 . . . . . 2.50
29 JQ,Mask of Iron Man,pt.4 . . . . . 2.50
30 JQ,Mask of Iron Man,pt.5 . . . . . 2.50
31 JQ,Sons of Yinsen,pt.1 . . . . 2.50
32 JQ,Sons of Yinsen,pt.2 . . . . 2.50
33 JQ,Sons of Yinsen,pt.3 . . . . 2.50
34 JQ,Dr. Power 2.50
35 JQ,Maximum Security. 2.50
36 CDi,PR 2.50
37 JQ,F:Tyberius Stone 2.50
38 R:classic foe 2.50
39 MPn,Remote Control 2.50
40 MPn,Remote Control 2.50
41 new art team. 2.50
42 Big Bang Theory,pt.1 . . . . 2.50
43 Big Bang Theory,pt.2 . . . . 2.50
44 Big Bang,pt.3,new armor 2.50
45 Big Bang Theory,pt.4 . . . . 2.50
46 Frankenstein Syndrome,pt.1
   100-pages 4.00
47 IaC,Frankenstein Syndrome . . . 2.50
48 IaC,Frankenstein Syndrome . . . 2.50
49 CsB,V:Titanium Man 2.50
50 MGr,48-pg. 4.00
51 MGr,Jane Doe,pt.1 . . . . 2.50
52 MGr,Jane Doe,pt.2 . . . . 2.50
53 MGr,Book of Ten Rings. 2.50
54 MGr,Temugin. 2.50
55 MGr,would be #400 issue,54-pg. 4.00
56 MGr,fall-out begins 2.50
57 MGr,fight on, fight on 2.50
58 MGr. 2.50
59 MGr,In Shining Armor. 2.50
60 MGr,In Shining Armor,pt.2. . . . . 2.50
61 MGr,In Shining Armor,pt.3. . . . . 2.50
62 MGr,You Can't Always Get,pt.1 . 2.50
63 MGr,You Can't Always Get,pt.2 . 2.50
64 AD,MFm,MGr,Standoff,pt.1 . . . . 2.50
65 MGr,Manhunt,pt.1 . . . . 2.50
66 MGr,Manhunt,pt.2. . . . . 2.50
67 MGr,Manhunt,pt.3. . . . . 3.00
68 MGr,Manhunt,pt.4 . . . . 3.00

69 MGr,Manhunt,pt.5 . . . . 3.00
70 Vegal Bleeds Neon,pt.1. . . . . . . 3.00
71 Vegas Bleeds Neon,pt.2 . . . . . . 3.00
72 Vegas Bleeds Neon,pt.3 . . . . . . 3.00
73 The Best Defense,pt.1 . . . . 3.00
74 The Best Defense,pt.2 . . . . 3.00
75 Secretary of Defense? 3.00
76 The Best Defense,pt.4 . . . . 3.00
77 The Best Defense,pt.5 . . . . 3.00
78 The Best Defense,pt.6 . . . . 3.00
79 The Deep End,pt.1 . . . . 3.00
80 The Deep End,pt.2 . . . . 3.00
81 The Deep End,pt.3 . . . . 3.00
82 The Deep End,pt.4 . . . . 3.00
83 F:Titanium Man 3.00
84 Top-secret materials 5.00
85 Top-secret materials 5.00
86 Singularity,pt.1 . . . . 3.00
87 Singularity,pt.2 . . . . 3.00
88 Singularity,pt.3 . . . . 3.00
89 Singularity,pt.4 . . . . 3.00
Ann.1998 Iron Man/Captain
   America, KBk,MWa, 48-pg. 3.50
Ann.1999 KBk,JoC,48-pg. 3.50
Ann.2000 Sons of Yin-Sen,pt.3 . . . 3.50
Ann.2001 CCl,48 pg. 0.00
Spec.#1 Age of Innocence, Avengers:
   Timeslide. 2.50

IRON MAN
Nov., 2004
1 WEl,Extremis 4.00
2 WEl,Extremis 3.00
3 WEl,Extremis 3.00
4 WEl,Extremis 3.00
5 WEl,Extremis 3.00
6 WEl,Extremis 3.00
7 The List 3.00
7a variant (c) 7.00
8 The List 3.00
9 SHa,Execute Program 3.00
10 SHa,Execute Program 3.00
11 SHa,Execute Program 3.00
12 SHa,Execute Program 3.00
13 SHa,Civil War tie-in. 3.00
14 SHa,Civil War tie-in. 3.00
15 Civil War The Initiative 3.00
15 variant (c) 3.00
16 Civil War: The Initiative 3.00
17 Civil War: The Initiative 3.00
18 Civil War: The Initiative 3.00
19 World War Hulk tie-in 3.00
19a 2nd printing 3.00
20 World War Hulk tie-in 3.00
21 thru 23. . . . . @3.00
24 Haunted 3.00
25 . . . . 3.00
26 V:Mandarin 3.00
27 Red Rain, pt.1 . . . . 3.00
28 V:Mandarin, 48-pgs. 4.00
Spec. Iron Manual (5-2008). 5.00
Becomes:

IRON MAN:
DIRECTOR OF S.H.I.E.L.D.
May, 2008
29 Damasqus, pt.1. . . . . 3.00
30 Damasqus, pt.2,With Iron Hands 3.00
31 Damasqus, pt.3,With Iron Hands 3.00
32 Damasqus, pt.4,With Iron Hands 3.00
33 Secret Invasion tie-in 3.00
Spec. Golden Avenger. 3.00
Spec. BL,The End, 48-pg. 5.00
becomes:

WAR MACHINE:
WEAPON OF SHIELD
Oct., 2008
34 Secret Invasion tie-in 3.00
35 Secret Invasion tie-in 3.00

All comics prices listed are for *Near Mint* condition.

MARVEL

IRON MAN

AND POWER PACK
Nov., 2007
1 (of 4) 3.00
2 thru 4 . . . . @3.00

...AND SUBMARINER
April, 1968
1 GC, 2 stories 300.00

...BAD BLOOD
July, 2000
1 (of 4) BL,DvM,V:JustinHammer . . 3.00
2 BL,DvM,Spymaster 3.00
3 BL,DvM,James Rhodes 3.00
4 BL,DvM,Justin Hammer 3.00

...CAPTAIN AMERICA:
CASUALTIES OF WAR
Dec., 2006
1-shot Civil War 4.00
1-shot-a variant (c) 4.00

...DIRECTOR OF S.H.I.E.L.D.
Nov., 2007
Ann. #1 V: Madame Hydra 4.00

...ENTER THE MANDARIN
Aug., 2007
1 JoC 3.00
2 thru 6 JoC . . . . @3.00

...HOUSE OF M
July, 2005
1 (of 3) 3.00
2 . . . . 3.00
3 finale 3.00

...HYPERVELOCITY
Jan., 2007
1 (of 6) AWa(s&c) 3.00
2 thru 6 AWa(s) . . . . @3.00

...INEVITABLE
Dec., 2005
1 JoC 3.00
2 thru 6 . . . . @3.00

...LEGACY OF DOOM
Apr., 2008
1 (of 4) RLm,BL 3.00
2 thru 4 RLm,BL . . . . @3.00

...THE IRON AGE
June, 1998
1 (of 2) KBk,48pg bookshelf 6.50
2 KBk,48pg bookshelf, concl. 6.50

...VIVA LAS VEGAS
May, 2008
1 (of 4) 3.00
2 thru 3 . . . . @4.00

ISLAND OF DR. MOREAU
Oct., 1977
1 GK(c),movie adapt. 8.00

IT'S A DUCK'S LIFE
Feb., 1950
1 F;Buck Duck,Super Rabbit . . . 150.00
2 . . . . 100.00
3 thru 11 . . . . @100.00

JACK KIRBY'S GALACTIC
BOUNTY HUNTERS
Icon, July, 2006
1 JK, 56-pg. 4.00
2 thru 6 JK. . . . . @3.00

JACK OF HEARTS
Jan., 1984
1 thru 4 . . . . @2.50

JAMES BOND JR.
1992
1 I&O:JamesBondJr.(TVseries) . . . 3.00
2 thru 12 . . . . @2.50

JANN OF THE JUNGLE
See: JUNGLE TALES

JEANIE COMICS
See: DARING MYSTERY

JIHAD
Epic
1 Cenobites vs. Nightbreed 4.50
2 E:Cenobites vs. Nightbreed. 4.50

JLA/AVENGERS
Marvel/DC, Sept., 2003
1 KBk,GP(c),x-over,48-pg. 6.00
3 KBk,GP,x-over,48-pg. 6.00

JOHN CARTER,
WARLORD OF MARS
June, 1977
1 GK,DC,O:John Carter,Created
  by Edgar Rice Burroughs 15.00
2 GK/DC(c),GK,RN, White Apes
  of Mars 7.00
3 GK,RN,Requiem for a Warlord . . 7.00
4 GK,RN, Raiding Party 7.00
5 GK,RN,Giant Battle Issue 7.00
6 GK/DC(c),GK,Alone Against a
  World 7.00
7 GK,TS,Showdown 7.00
8 GK,RN,Beast With Touch of
  Stone 7.00
9 GK,RN,Giant Battle Issue 7.00
10 GK,The Death of Barsoom? . . 7.00
11 RN,O:Dejah Thoris 7.00
12 RN,City of the Dead 7.00
13 RN,March of the Dead 7.00
14 RN,The Day Helium Died 7.00
15 RN,GK,Prince of Helium
  Returns 7.00
16 RN,John Carters Dilemna 7.00
17 BL,What Price Victory 10.00
18 FM,Tars Tarkas Battles Alone . . 7.00
19 RN(c),War With the Wing Men . . 7.00

John Carter Warlord of Mars #2
© Marvel Entertainment Group

20 RN(c),Battle at the Bottom
  of the World 7.00
21 RN(c),The Claws of the Banth . . 7.00
22 RN(c),The Canyon of Death 7.00
23 Murder on Mars 7.00
24 GP/TA(c),Betrayal 7.00
25 Inferno. 7.00
26 Death Cries the Guild of
  Assassins 7.00
27 Death Marathon 7.00
28 Guardians of the Lost
  City Oct., 1979 . . . . 7.00
Ann.#1 RN(c),GK,Battle story 7.00
Ann.#2 RN(c),GK,Outnumbered . . . 7.00
Ann.#3 RN(c),GK,Battle story 7.00

JOHN ROMITA JR 30TH
ANNIVERSARY SPECIAL
Dec., 2006
Spec. 4.00

JOKER COMICS
Marvel Timely, April, 1942
1 BW,I&B:Powerhouse Pepper,
  A:Stuporman 4,700.00
2 BW,I:Tessie the Typist 1,600.00
3 BW,A:Tessie the Typist,
  Squat Car Squad 1,000.00
4 BW,Squat Car (c) 900.00
5 BW,same 900.00
6 BW, ... 750.00
7 BW 750.00
8 BW 750.00
9 BW 750.00
10 BW,Shooting Gallery (c) 750.00
11 BW 750.00
12 BW 750.00
13 BW 750.00
14 BW 750.00
15 BW 750.00
16 BW 750.00
17 BW 750.00
18 BW 750.00
19 BW 750.00
20 BW 750.00
21 BW 750.00
22 DW 750.00
23 BW,HK,Hey Look 750.00
24 BW,HK,Laff Favorites 800.00
25 BW,HK,same. 800.00
26 BW,HK,same. 800.00
27 BW 800.00
28 . . . . 250.00
29 BW 500.00
30 BW 500.00
31 BW 500.00
32 B:Millie,Hedy. 200.00
33 HK 225.00
34 . . . . 200.00
35 HK 225.00
36 HK 200.00
37 . . . . 200.00
38 . . . . 200.00
39 . . . . 200.00
40 . . . . 200.00
41 A:Nellie the Nurse 200.00
42 I:Patty Pin-up 225.00
Becomes:

ADVENTURES INTO
TERROR
1950
43(1)AH,B:Horror Stories 1,000.00
44(2)AH,Won't You Step Into
  My Palor 600.00
3 GC,I Stalk By Night 400.00
4 DR,The Torture Room 400.00
5 GC,DR,The Hitchhiker 450.00
6 RH,The Dark Room 350.00

7 GT(c),BW,JMn,Where Monsters Dwell	900.00
8 JSt,Enter... the Lizard	400.00
9 RH(c),JSt,The Dark Dungeon	375.00
10 JMn,When the Vampire Calls	375.00
11 JMn,JSt,Dead Man's Escape	325.00
12 BK,Man Who Cried Ghost	350.00
13 BEv(c),The Hands of Death	350.00
14 GC,GT,The Hands	300.00
15 Trapped by the Tarantula	300.00
16 RH(c),Her Name Is Death	300.00
17 I Die Too Often,Bondage(c)	350.00
18 He's Trying To Kill Me	300.00
19 The Girl Who Couldn't Die	275.00
20	275.00
21 GC,JMn	250.00
22 JMn	250.00
23	250.00
24 MF,GC	250.00
25 MF	300.00
26 GC	250.00
27	250.00
28 GC	250.00
29 GC,JMn	250.00
30	250.00
31 May, 1954	250.00

JOURNEY INTO MYSTERY
June, 1952

1 RH(c),B:Mystery/Horror stories	5,500.00
2 Don't Look	2,000.00
3 I Didn't See Anything	1,500.00
4 RH,BEv(c),I'm Drowning, Severed Hand (c)	1,500.00
5 RH,BEv(c),Fright	1,000.00
6 BEv(c),Till Death Do Us Part	1,000.00
7 BEv(c),Ghost Guard	1,000.00
8 He Who Hesitates	1,000.00
9 BEv(c),I Made A Monster	1,000.00
10 The Assassin of Paris	1,000.00
11 RH,GT,Meet the Dead	900.00
12 A Night At Dragmoor Castle	750.00
13 The Living and the Dead	750.00
14 DAy,RH,The Man Who Owned A World	750.00
15 RH(c),Till Death Do Us Part	750.00
16 DW,Vampire Tale	750.00
17 SC,Midnight On Black Mountain	750.00
18 He Wouldn't Stay Dead	750.00
19 JF,The Little Things	750.00
20 BEv,BP,After Man, What	750.00
21 JKu,The Man With No Past	750.00
22 Haunted House	750.00
23 GC,Gone, But Not Forgotten	500.00
24 The Locked Drawer	500.00
25 The Man Who Lost Himself	500.00
26 The Man From Out There	500.00
27 BP,JSe,Masterpiece	500.00
28 The Survivor	500.00
29 Three Frightened People	500.00
30 JO,The Lady Who Vanished	500.00
31 The Man Who Had No Fear	500.00
32 Elevator In The Sky	500.00
33 SD,AW,There'll Be Some Changes Made	600.00
34 BP,BK,The Of The Mystic Ring	500.00
35 LC,JF,Turn Back The Clock	500.00
36 I, The Pharaoh	500.00
37 BEv(c),The Volcano	500.00
38 SD,Those Who Vanish	500.00
39 BEv(c),DAy,WW,The Forbidden Room	500.00
40 BEv(c),JF,The Strange Secret Of Henry Hill	500.00
41 BEv(c),GM,RC,I Switched Bodies	450.00

42 BEv(c),GM,What Was Farley's Other Face	450.00
43 AW,Ghost Ship	450.00
44 SD,JK,BEv	450.00
45 BEv,JO	400.00
46	400.00
47 BEv	400.00
48	400.00
49	400.00
50 SD	400.00
51 SD,JK	450.00
52 JK	400.00
53 DH	400.00
54 AW	450.00
55	450.00
56 thru 61 SD,JK	@400.00
62 SD,JK,I:Xemnu	450.00
63 SD,JK	450.00
64 SD,JK	450.00
65 SD,JK	450.00
66 Hulk Type	500.00
67 SD,JK	350.00
68 SD,JK	350.00
69 SD,JK	350.00
70 Sandman Type	450.00
71 JK,SD	350.00
72 JK,SD	350.00
73 JK,DH,Spider-Man type	700.00
74	350.00
75 JK,DH	350.00
76 JK,DH	300.00
77 DH,SD,JK	300.00
78 DH,Dr.Strange Type	450.00
79 JK,DH,SD	400.00
80 JK,DH,SD	300.00
81 JK,DH,SD	300.00
82 JK,DH,SD	300.00
83 JK,SD,I&O:Thor	16,000.00
84 JK,SD,DH,I:Executioner	4,000.00
85 JK,SD,I:Loki,Heimdall,Balder, Tyr,Odin,Asgard	2,500.00
86 JK,SD,DH,V:Tomorrow Man	1,500.00
87 JK,SD,V:Communists	1,200.00
88 JK,SD,V:Loki	1,200.00
89 JK,SD,O:Thor(rep)	1,200.00
90 SD,I:Carbon Copy	900.00
91 JSt,SD,I:Sandu	900.00
92 JSt,SD,V:Loki,I:Frigga	900.00
93 DAy,JK,SD,I:Radioactive Man	850.00
94 JSt,SD,V:Loki	700.00
95 JSt,SD,I:Duplicator	700.00
96 JSt,SD,I:Merlin II	700.00
97 JK,I:Lava Man,O:Odin	900.00
98 DH,JK,I&O:Cobra	600.00

Journey Into Mystery #96
© Marvel Entertainment Group

99 DH,JK,I:Mr.Hyde,Surtur	600.00
100 DH,JK,V:Mr.Hyde	600.00
101 JK,V:Tomorrow Man	400.00
102 JK,I:Sif,Hela	400.00
103 JK,I:Enchantress, Executioner	400.00
104 JK,Giants	400.00
105 JK,V:Hyde,Cobra	400.00
106 JK,O:Balder	400.00
107 JK,I:Grey Gargoyle,Karnilla	400.00
108 JK,A:Dr.Strange	400.00
109 JK,V:Magneto	800.00
110 JK,V:Hyde,Cobra,Loki	400.00
111 JK,V:Hyde,Cobra,Loki	400.00
112 JK,V:Hulk,O:Loki	850.00
113 JK,V:Grey Gargoyle	350.00
114 JK,I&O:Absorbing Man	350.00
115 JK,O:Loki,V:Absorbing Man	400.00
116 JK,V:Loki,C:Daredevil	350.00
117 JK,V:Loki	350.00
118 JK,I:Destroyer	350.00
119 JK,V:Destroyer,I:Hogun, Fandrall,Volstagg	350.00
120 JK,A:Avengers,Absorbing Man	350.00
121 JK,V:Absorbing Man	350.00
122 JK,V:Absorbing Man	350.00
123 JK,V:Absorbing Man	350.00
124 JK,A:Hercules	375.00
125 JK,A:Hercules	375.00
Annual #1, JK,I:Hercules	450.00

Becomes:

THOR

JOURNEY INTO MYSTERY
[2nd series], Oct., 1972

1 GK,TP,MP,Dig Me No Grave	45.00
2 GK,Jack the Ripper	30.00
3 JSn,TP,Shambler From the Stars	30.00
4 GC,DA,Haunter of the Dark, H.P. Lovecraft adaptation	30.00
5 RB,FrG,Shadow From the Steeple,R. Bloch adaptation	30.00
6 thru 19 Mystery Stories	@25.00

JOURNEY INTO UNKNOWN WORLDS
See: ALL WINNERS COMICS

JUBILEE
Sept., 2004

1 In Los Angeles	3.00
2 F:Meg Devereaux	3.00
3 thru 6	@3.00

J-2
Aug., 1998

1 TDF,RLm,AM,F:J2 with the powers of Juggernaut	2.50
2 thru 12 TDF,RLm,AM	@2.50

JUGGERNAUT
1997
1-shot 48pg. ... 3.00

JUGGERNAUT: THE EIGHTH DAY
Sept., 1999
1-shot JoC,TSr,AKu(c),x-over,pt.4 ... 3.00

JUNGLE ACTION
Marvel Atlas, Oct., 1954

1 JMn,JMn(c),B:Leopard Girl	450.00
2 JMn,JMn(c)	475.00
3 thru 6 JMn,JMn(c)	@300.00

JUNGLE ACTION
Oct., 1972—Nov., 1976
1 JB(c),Lorna,Tharn,Jann
   reprints 25.00
2 GK(c),same 15.00
3 JSn(c),same 15.00
4 GK(c),same 15.00
5 JR(c),JB,B:Black Panther,
   V:Man-Ape 30.00
6 RB/FrG(c),RB,V:Kill-Monger . . . 25.00
7 RB/KJ(c),RB,V:Venomn 15.00
8 RB/KJ(c),RB,GK,
   O:Black Panther 20.00
9 GK/KJ(c),RB,V:Baron Macabre 15.00
10 GK/FrG(c),RB,V:King Cadaver . . 15.00
11 GK(c),V:Baron Macabre,Lord
   Karnaj 15.00
12 RB/KJ(c),V:Kill Monger 10.00
13 GK/JK(c),V:White Gorilla,
   Sombre 10.00
14 GK(c),V:Prehistoric Monsters . 10.00
15 GK(c),V:Prehistoric Monsters . 10.00
16 GK(c),V:Venomn 10.00
17 GK(c),V:Kill Monger 10.00
18 JKu(c),V:Madame Slay 10.00
19 GK(c),V:KKK,Sacrifice of Blood 10.00
20 V:KKK,Slaughter In The
   Streets 10.00
21 V:KKK,Cross Of Fire, Cross
   Of Death 9.00
22 JB(c),V:KKK,Soul Stranger 9.00
23 JBy(c),V:KKK 9.00
24 GK(c),I:Wind Eagle 9.00

JUNGLE TALES
Marvel Atlas, Sept., 1954
1 B:Jann of the Jungle,Cliff
   Mason,Waku 500.00
2 GT,Jann Stories cont. 350.00
3 Cliff Mason,White Hunter,
   Waku Unknown Jungle 350.00
4 Cliff Mason,Waku,Unknown
   Jungle 350.00
5 RH(c),SSh,Cliff Mason,Waku,
   Unknown Jungle 350.00
6 DH,SSh,Cliff Mason,Waku,
   Unknown Jungle 350.00
7 DH,SSh,Cliff Mason,Waku,
   Unknown Jungle 350.00
Becomes:

JANN OF THE JUNGLE
1955
8 SH,SSh,The Jungle Outlaw . . . 450.00
9 With Fang and Talons 250.00
10 AW,The Jackal's Lair. 250.00
11 Bottomless Pit 250.00
12 The Lost Safari 250.00
13 When the Trap Closed 250.00
14 V:Hunters 250.00
15 BEv(c),DH,V:Hunters 250.00
16 BEv(c),AW,JungleVengeance. 275.00
17 BEv(c),DH,AW,June, 1957 . . . 275.00

JUSTICE
Nov., 1986
1 I:Justice 2.50
2 thru 31. . . . . @2.50
32 Last issue,A:Joker 2.50

JUSTICE COMICS
Marvel Atlas, Fall, 1947
7(1) B:FBI in Action,Mystery of
   White Death. 400.00
8(2),HK,Crime is For Suckers . . 250.00
9(3),FBI Raid 225.00
4 Bank Robbery 225.00
5 Subway(c) 200.00
6 E:FBI In Action 200.00

Justice #8
© Marvel Entertainment Group

7 Symbolic(c) 200.00
8 Funeral(c) 200.00
9 B:True Cases Proving Crime
   Can't Win. 200.00
10 Ph(c),Bank Hold Up 200.00
11 Ph(c),Behind Bars. 200.00
12 Ph(c),The Crime of
   Martin Blaine 135.00
13 Ph(c),The Cautious Crook . . . 135.00
14 Ph(c). 135.00
15 Ph(c) 135.00
16 F:"Ears"Karpik-Mobster. 125.00
17 The Ragged Stranger 125.00
18 Criss-Cross 125.00
19 Death Of A Spy 125.00
20 Miami Mob 125.00
21 Trap. 125.00
22 The Big Break. 125.00
23 thru 40 . . . . @100.00
41 Electrocution cover 225.00
42 thru 51 . . . . @100.00
52 Flare Up 100.00
Becomes:

TALES OF JUSTICE
May, 1955—Aug., 1957
53 BEv,Keeper Of The Keys 200.00
54 thru 57. . . . . @175.00
58 BK 150.00
59 BK. 150.00
60 thru 63. . . . . @100.00
64 RC,DW,JSe. 125.00
65 RC. 125.00
66 JO,AT 125.00
67 DW 125.00

JUSTICE: FOUR BALANCE
1994
1 A:Thing, Yancy Street Gang . . . 2.50
2 V:Hate Monger 2.50
3 the story continues. 2.50
4 ...to its conclusion 2.50

KATHY
Marvel Atlas, Oct., 1959—Feb., 1964
1 Teenage Tornado. 160.00
2 . . . . 125.00
3 thru 15 . . . . @75.00
16 thru 27 . . . . @60.00

KA-ZAR
[Reprint Series], Aug., 1970
1 X-Men ID 50.00
2 Daredevil 12, 13 . . . . 35.00
3 DDH,Spider-Man,March, 1971 . 35.00

[1st Series], Jan., 1974
1 O:Savage Land 20.00
2 DH,JA,A:Shanna The She-Devil 10.00
3 DH,V:Man-God,A:El Tigre 10.00
4 DH,V:Man-God 10.00
5 DH,D:El-Tigre. 8.00
6 JB/AA,V:Bahemoth 8.00
7 JB/BMcRevenge of the
   River-Gods 8.00
8 JB/AA,Volcano of
   Molten Death. 8.00
9 JB,Man Who Hunted Dinosaur . . 8.00
10 JB,Dark City of Death. 8.00
11 DH/FS,Devil-God of Sylitha 7.00
12 RH,Wizard of Forgotten
   Death. 7.00
13 V:Lizard Men. 7.00
14 JAb,V:Klaw 7.00
15 VM,V:Klaw,Hellbird 7.00
16 VM,V:Klaw 7.00
17 VM,V:Klaw 7.00
18 VM,V:Klaw,Makrum. 7.00
19 VM,V:Klaw,Raknor the Slayer. . . 7.00
20 VM,V:Klaw,Fortress of Fear 7.00

[2nd Series], Apr. 1981
1 BA,O:Ka-Zar 4.00
2 thru 7 BA . . . . @3.00
8 BA,Ka-Zar Father. 2.50
9 BA 2.50
10 BA,Direct D. 2.50
11 BA/GK,Zabu 2.50
12 BA,Panel Missing 2.50
12a Scarce Reprint 2.50
13 BA 2.50
14 BA/GK,Zabu 2.50
15 BA 2.50
16 . . . . 2.50
17 Detective 2.50
18 & 19. . . . . @2.50
20 A:Spider-Man 3.00
21 . . . . 3.00
22 A:Spider-Man 3.00
23 A:Spider-Man 3.00
24 A:Spider-Man 3.00
25 A:Spider-Man 3.00
26 A:Spider-Man 3.00
27 A:Buth 3.00
28 Pangea 3.00
29 W:Ka-Zar & Shanna, Doub.Size. 3.00
30 V:Pterons 3.00
31 PangeaWarII 3.00
32 V:Plunderer 3.00
33 V:Plunderer. 3.00
34 Last Issue Doub.Size 3.00

[3rd Series], 1997
1 MWa,NKu,Ka-Zar, Shanna, Zabu,
   V:Gregor, 40pg 5.00
1a 2nd printing 2.50
2 MWa,NKu,V:Gregor. 4.00
2A NKu variant cover 3.00
3 MWa,NKu,Ka-Zar's son dead? . . 3.00
4 MWa,NKu,in New York City 3.00
5 MWa,NKu,. 2.50
6 MWa,V:Rampaging Rhino 2.50
7 MWa,NKu,F:Shanna the
   She-Devil. 2.50
8 MWa,NKu, Urban Jungle, pt.1 . . . 2.50

KABUKI
Icon, July, 2004
1 DMk,The Alchemy,pt.1 . . . . 3.00
2 thru 6 DMk,The Alchemy,pt.2–6 @3.00
7 DMk 3.00
8 DMk 3.00
9 Kabuki Reflections. 5.00
10 DMk. 6.00
11 DMk 6.00

Ka-Zar 3rd Series #2
© Marvel Entertainment Group

9 MWa,NKu, Urban Jungle, pt.2 . . 2.50
10 MWa,NKu, Urban Jungle, pt.3 . . 2.50
11 MWa,NKu, Urban Jungle, pt.4,
   concl 2.50
12 MWa,A:High Evolutionary 2.50
13 MWa,A:High Evolutionary 2.50
14 MWa,NKu,end old & begin new
   storyline, double size 3.50
15 A:Punisher 3.00
16 A:Punisher 2.50
17 Ka-Zar clears his name,
   A:Jameka 2.50
18 People of the Savage Land
   revolt 2.50
19 V:Gregor 2.50
20 A:Gregor,Zira, final issue 2.50
Ann. '97 V:Garrok, Petrified Man . . . 2.50
Ann. '98 Ka-Zar/Daredevil heroes
   unite 3.00
1-shot Ka-Zar of the Savage Land,
   CDi,V:Sauron, 48-pg., prelude to
   3rd series (1996) 3.00
1-shot Ka-Zar: Sibling Rivalry,
   MWa,TDz,Flashback (1997) . . . 2.50

KELLYS, THE
See: KID KOMICS

KENT BLAKE OF THE
SECRET SERVICE
May, 1951—July, 1953
1 U.S. Govt. Secret Agent
   stories,Bondage cover 300.00
2 JSt,Drug issue,Man with
   out A Face 200.00
3 JMn,Trapped By The Chinese
   Reds 125.00
4 Secret Service Stories 125.00
5 RH(c),Condemned To Death . . 125.00
6 Cases from Kent Blake files . . . 125.00
7 RH(c),Behind Enemy Lines . . 125.00
8 GT,V:Communists 125.00
9 thru 14 . . . . @125.00

KICK-ASS
Marvel Icon, Feb., 2008
1 MMr,JR2 . . . . 3.00
1a variant (c) 3.00
1b variant JR2 sketch (c) 3.00
1c director's cut 4.00
2 thru 6 MMr,JR2 . . . . @3.00

KICKERS INC.
Nov., 1986
1 SB,O:Kickers 2.50
2 SB 2.50
3 RF,Witches 2.50
4 RF,FIST 2.50
5 RF,A:D.P.7 . . . . 2.50
6 thru 12 . . . . @2.50

KID & PLAY
1 Based on Rap Group 2.50
2 thru 9 . . . . @2.50

KID COLT OUTLAW
Marvel Atlas, Aug., 1948
1 B:Kid Colt,A:Two-Gun Kid . . 1,700.00
2 Gun-Fighter and the Girl 800.00
3 SSh,Colt-Quick Killers
   For Hire 600.00
4 Wanted,A:Tex Taylor 600.00
5 Mystery of the Misssing
   Mine,A:Blaze Carson 600.00
6 A:Tex Taylor,Valley of
   the Werewolf 400.00
7 B:Nimo the Lion 400.00
8 . . . . 400.00
9 . . . . 400.00
10 The Whip Strikes,E:Nimo
   the Lion 400.00
11 O:Kid Colt 500.00
12 . . . . 250.00
13 DRi 250.00
14 . . . . 250.00
15 Gun Whipped in ShotgunCity . 250.00
16 . . . . 250.00
17 . . . . 250.00
18 DRi 250.00
19 . . . . 225.00
20 The Outlaw 225.00
21 thru 30 . . . . @225.00
31 . . . . 225.00
32 . . . . 225.00
33 thru 45 A:Black Rider . . . . . @200.00
46 RH(c) 200.00
47 DW 200.00
48 RH(c),JKu 200.00
49 . . . . 200.00
50 . . . . 200.00
51 thru 56 . . . . @125.00
57 AW 125.00
58 AW 125.00
59 AW 125.00
60 AW 125.00
61 . . . . 100.00
62 . . . . 100.00
63 . . . . 100.00
64 RC 110.00
65 RC 110.00
66 AW 150.00
67 thru 78 . . . . @100.00
79 Origin Retold 110.00
80 thru 86 . . . . @100.00
87 JDa(reprint) 110.00
88 AW 120.00
89 AW,Matt Slade 120.00
90 thru 99 . . . . @100.00
100 JK 120.00
101 JK 75.00
102 JK 75.00
103 JK,The Great Train Robbery . . 75.00
104 JKu(c),DH,Trail of
   Kid Colt 75.00
105 DH,V:Dakota Dixon 75.00
106 JKu(c),The Circus
   of Crime 75.00
107 JK,SciFi(c) 100.00
108 BEv 75.00
109 DAy,V:The Barracuda 75.00
110 GC,V:Iron Mask 100.00
111 JKu(c),V:Sam Hawk, The
   Man Hunter 65.00

Kid Colt #103 (Marvel 1970s)
© Marvel Entertainment Group

112 JKu(c),V:Mr. Brown 65.00
113 JKu(c),GC,V:Bull Barton 65.00
114 JKu(c),Return of Iron Mask . . . 65.00
115 JKu(c),V:The Scorpion 65.00
116 JKu(c),GC,V:Dr. Danger &
   Invisible Gunman 65.00
117 JKu(c),GC,V:The Fatman &
   His Boomerang 65.00
118 V:Scorpion,Bull Barton,
   Dr. Danger 65.00
119 DAy(c),JK,V:Bassett The
   Badman 65.00
120 Cragsons Ride Again 65.00
121 A:Rawhide Kid,Iron Mask 50.00
122 V:Rattler Ruxton 50.00
123 V:Ringo Barker 50.00
124 A:Phantom Raider 50.00
125 A:Two-Gun Kid 50.00
126 V:Wes Hardin 50.00
127 thru 129 . . . . @50.00
130 O:Kid Colt 65.00
131 thru 150 . . . . @30.00
151 thru 200 reprints . . . . @25.00
201 thru 228 reprints . . . . @20.00
229 April, 1979 . . . . 20.00

KID FROM DODGE CITY
Marvel Atlas, July, 1957—Sept.,
1957
1 . . . . 150.00
2 . . . . 100.00

KID FROM TEXAS
Marvel Atlas, June, 1957—Aug.,
1957
1 . . . . 125.00
2 . . . . 100.00

KID KOMICS
Marvel Timely, Feb., 1943
1 SSh(c),BW,O:Captain Wonder
   & Tim Mulrooney I:Whitewash,
   Knuckles,Trixie Trouble,
   Pinto Pete Subbie 7,500.00
2 AsH(c),F:Captain Wonder
   Subbie, B:Young Allies,
   B:Red Hawk,Tommy Tyme 3,500.00
3 ASh(c),AAv,SSh,A:The Vision
   & Daredevils 3,000.00
4 ASh(c),B:Destroyer,A:Sub-Mariner,
   E:Red Hawk,Tommy Tyme 2,200.00
5 ASh(c),V:Nazis 1,800.00
6 ASh(c),V:Japanese 1,800.00

7 ASh(c),B;Whizzer 1,600.00
8 ASh(c),V:Train Robbers 1,600.00
9 ASh(c),V:Elves 1,600.00
10 ASh(c),E:Young Allies,
   The Destoyer,The Whizzer 1,600.00
Becomes:

Kid Movie Comics #11
© Marvel Entertainment Group

KID MOVIE KOMICS
1946
11 F:Silly Seal,Ziggy Pig
   HK,Hey Look 300.00
Becomes:

RUSTY COMICS
1947
12 F:Rusty,A:Mitzi 225.00
13 Do not Disturb(c). 125.00
14 Beach(c),BW,HK,Hey Look. . . 250.00
15 Picnic(c),HK,Hey Look 175.00
16 Juniors Grades,HK,HeyLook . 175.00
17 John in Trouble,HK,HeyLook . 175.00
18 John Fired. 125.00
19 Fridge raid(c),HK 125.00
20 And Her Family,HK 200.00
21 And Her Family,HK 250.00
22 HK. 250.00
Becomes:

KELLYS, THE
1950
23 F:The Kelly Family(Pop,
   Mom,Mike,Pat & Goliath) . . 125.00
24 Mike's Date,A;Margie 75.00
25 Wrestling(c). 75.00
Becomes:

SPY CASES
1950
26(#1) Spy stories 350.00
27(#2) BEv,Bondage(c) 300.00
28(#3) Sabotage,A:Douglas
   Grant Secret Agent. 175.00
4 The Secret Invasion 150.00
5 The Vengeance of Comrade
   de Casto 150.00
6 A:Secret Agent Doug Grant . . 150.00
7 GT,A:Doug Grant 150.00
8 Atom Bomb(c),Frozen
   Horror 250.00
9 Undeclared War 125.00
10 Battlefield Adventures 125.00
11 Battlefield Adventures 125.00
12 Battlefield Adventures 125.00
13 Battlefield Adventures 125.00
14 Battlefield Adventures 125.00

15 Doug Grant 125.00
16 Doug Grant 125.00
17 Doug Grant 125.00
18 Contact in Ankara 125.00
19 Final Issue,Oct., 1953. . . . . . . 125.00

KID SLADE GUNFIGHTER
See: MATT SLADE

KILLFRENZY
1 . . . . 2.50
2 Castle Madspike 2.50

KILLPOWER:
THE EARLY YEARS
1993
1 B:MiB,Goes on Rampage 3.25
2 thru 3 O:Killpower . . . . @2.50
4 E:MiB,last issue 2.50

KILLRAVEN
Dec., 2000
Spec. JLi,R:Killraven 3.00

KILLRAVEN
Oct., 2002
1 (of 6) AD,MFm,V:Martians 3.00
2 thru 6 AD,MFm. . . . . @3.00

KING ARTHUR & THE
KNIGHTS OF JUSTICE
1993–94
1 thru 3 Based on Cartoon . . . . . @2.50

KING CONAN:
See: CONAN THE KING

KINGPIN
Nov., 1997
1-shot StL,JR, bookshelf 48pg. 6.00

KINGPIN
June, 2003
1 SeP,KJ,Wilson Fixk 2.50
2 thru 7 SeP,KJ. . . . . @2.50

KISSNATION
1997
1 Rock & Roll, A:X-Men 10.00

KITTY PRYDE:
AGENT OF S.H.I.E.L.D.
Oct., 1997
1 (of 3) LHa,V:Ogun 2.50
2 LHa,V:Ogun 2.50
3 LHa,Ogun's Slave? 2.50

KITTY PRYDE
& WOLVERINE
Nov., 1984
1 AM,V:Ogun. 6.00
2 AM,V:Ogun. 5.00
3 thru 5 AM,V:Ogun. . . . . @5.00
6 AM,D:Ogun, April, 1985. . . . . . . 5.00

KNIGHTS OF
PENDRAGON
[1st Regular Series], July, 1990
1 GEr 2.75
2 thru 18 . . . . @2.50
[2nd Regular Series], 1992
1 GEr,A:Iron Man,R:Knights of
   Pendragon. 2.50
2 thru 15 . . . . @2.50

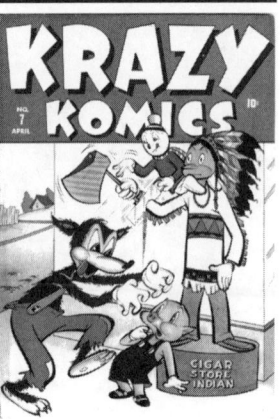

Krazy Komics #7
© Marvel Entertainment Group

KOMIC KARTOONS
Marvel Timely, 1945
1 Funny Animal. 225.00
2 . . . . 225.00

KRAZY KOMICS
Marvel Timely, July, 1942
1 B:Ziggy Pig,Silly Seal 800.00
2 Toughy Tomcat(c) 325.00
3 Toughy Tomcat/Bunny(c) 250.00
4 Toughy Tomcat/Ziggy(c) 250.00
5 Ziggy/Buzz Saw(c) 250.00
6 Toughy/Cannon(c) 250.00
7 Cigar Store Indian(c) 250.00
8 Toughy/Hammock(c) 250.00
9 Hitler(c) 275.00
10 Newspaper(c). 225.00
11 Canoe(c). 225.00
12 Circus(c) 300.00
13 Pirate Treasure(c). 200.00
14 Fishing(c) 200.00
15 Ski-Jump(c) 175.00
16 Airplane(c). 125.00
17 Street corner(c). 125.00
18 Mallet/Bell(c) 125.00
19 Bicycle(c) 125.00
20 Ziggy(c) 125.00
21 Toughy's date(c) 125.00
22 Crystal Ball(c) 125.00
23 Sharks in bathtub(c) 150.00
24 Baseball(c) 125.00
25 HK,Krazy Krow(c) 150.00
26 Super Rabbit(c). 125.00
Becomes:

CINDY COMICS
1947
27 HK,B:Margie,Oscar. 250.00
28 HK,Snow sled(c). 150.00
29 . . . . 150.00
30 . . . . 150.00
31 HK. 150.00
32 . . . . 100.00
33 A;Georgie 100.00
34 thru 40. . . . . @100.00
Becomes:

CRIME CAN'T WIN
1950
41 Crime stories. 350.00
42 . . . . 200.00
43 GT,Horror story 250.00
4 thru 11 . . . . @150.00
12 Sept., 1953 . . . . 125.00

MARVEL

KRAZY KOMICS
Marvel Timely
[2nd Series], 1948
1 BW,HK,B:Eustice Hayseed . . . 650.00
2 BW,O:Powerhouse Pepper . . . 450.00

KRAZY KROW
Summer, 1945
1 B:Krazy Krow 250.00
2 . . . . 150.00
3 Winter, 1945-46 . . . . 150.00

KREE-SKRULL WAR
Sept.–Oct., 1983
1 & 2 JB,NA,reprints . . . . @5.00

KRULL
Nov.–Dec., 1983
1 Ph(c),BBI,movie adapt. 2.50
2 BBI,rep.,Marvel Super Spec. 2.50

KULL THE CONQUEROR
[1st Series], June, 1971
1 MSe,RA,WW,A King Comes
Riding,O:Kull 75.00
2 MSe,JSe,Shadow Kingdom 30.00
3 MSe,JSe,Death Dance of
Thulsa Doom 30.00
4 MSe,JSe,Night o/t Red Slayers . 30.00
5 MSe,JSe,Kingdom By the Sea . 30.00
6 MSe,JSe,Lurker Beneath
the Sea 15.00
7 MSe,JSe,Delcardes'Cat,
A:Thulsa Doom 15.00
8 MSe,JSe,Wolfshead 15.00
9 MSe,JSe,The Scorpion God . . . 15.00
10 MSe,Swords o/t White Queen . 15.00
11 MP,King Kull Must Die, O:Kull
cont.,A:Thulsa Doom 12.00
12 MP,SB,Moon of Blood,V:Thulsa
Doom,B:SD,B.U.stories 12.00
13 MP,AM,Torches From Hell,
V:Thulsa Doom 12.00
14 MP,JA,The Black Belfry,
A:Thulsa Doom 12.00
15 MP,Wings o/t Night-Beast,
E:SD,B.U.stories 12.00
16 EH,Tiger in the Moon,
A:Thulsa Doom 15.00
17 AA,EH,Thing from Emerald
Darkness 10.00
18 EH,AA,Keeper of Flame
& Frost. 10.00
19 EH,AA,The Crystal Menace . . . 10.00
20 EH,AA,Hell Beneath Atlantis. . . 10.00
21 City of the Crawling Dead. 10.00
22 Talons of the Devil-Birds. 10.00
23 Demon Shade. 10.00
24 Screams in the Dark. 9.00
25 A Lizard's Throne 9.00
26 Into Death's Dimension. 9.00
27 The World Within 9.00
28 Creature and the Crown,
A:Thulsa Doom 9.00
29 To Sit the Topaz Throne,
V:Thulsa Doom, final issue 9.00
[2nd Series], 1982
1 JB,Brule 4.00
2 Misareenia 3.00
[3rd Series], 1983–85
1 JB,BWi,DG,Iraina 3.50
2 JB,Battle to the Death 3.00
3 JB. 3.00
4 JB. 3.00
5 JB 3.00
6 JB 3.00
7 JB,Masquerade Death 3.00
8 thru 10 JB . . . . @3.00

KULL AND THE BARBARIANS
May, 1975
1 NA,GK,reprint Kull #1 . . . . 30.00
2 BBI,reprint,Dec., 1983 . . . . 25.00
3 NA,HC,O:Red Sonja 25.00

LABRYNTH
1986–87
1 Movie adapt. 3.00
2 and 3 . . . . @3.00

LAFF-A-LYMPICS
1978–79
1 F;Hanna Barbera 45.00
2 thru 5 . . . . @30.00
6 thru 13 . . . . @35.00

LANA
Aug., 1948
1 F:Lana Lane The Show Girl,
A:Rusty,B:Millie 275.00
2 HK,Hey Look,A:Rusty . . . . . , , , 200.00
3 Ohow(c),B:Nellie 100.00
4 Ship(c) 100.00
5 Audition(c) 100.00
6 Stop sign(c) 100.00
7 Beach(c) 100.00
Becomes:

LITTLE LANA
1949
8 Little Lana(c) 100.00
9 Final Issue,March, 1950 . . . . 100.00

LANCE BARNES: POST NUKE DICK
Epic, 1993
1 I:Lance Barnes. 2.50
2 Cigarettes 2.50
3 Warring Mall Tribe 2.50
4 V:Ex-bankers,last issue 2.50

LAST AMERICAN
Epic, 1990–91
1 . . . . 3.50
2 . . . . 3.00
3 . . . . 2.50
4 Final issue.. . . . . 2.50

THE LAST AVENGERS STORY
1995
1 PDd, Alterverse,Future world. . . . 6.00
2 PDd, Final fate,fully painted. 6.00

LAST DEFENDERS, THE
Mar., 2008
1 (of 6) JoC(s). 3.00
2 JoC(s),MD2(c) 3.00
3 thru 6 JoC(s) . . . . @3.00

LAST FANTASTIC FOUR STORY, THE
Aug., 2007
Spec. StL(s),JR2 . . . . 5.00

LAST HERO STANDING
June, 2005
1 thru 5 Po . . . . @3.00

LAST PLANET STANDING
May, 2006
1 thru 5 (of 5) PO . . . . @3.00

Last Starfighter-3 (Marvel 1984)
© Marvel Entertainment Group

LAST STARFIGHTER, THE
Oct.–Dec., 1984
1 thru 3 JG(c),BBI,Movie adapt. . @2.50

LAWBREAKERS ALWAYS LOSE
Marvel Crime Bureau Stories, 1948–49
1 HK; FBI Reward Poster Photo
Adam and Eve, HK,Giggles
and Grins. 500.00
2 FBI V:Fur Theives 250.00
3 . . . . 200.00
4 AyB(c),Vampire 200.00
5 AyB(c) 200.00
6 Anti Wertham Edition 225.00
7 Crime at Midnight 350.00
8 Prison Break 150.00
9 Ph(c),He Prowled at Night . . . 150.00
10 Phc(c),I Met My Murderer. . . . 150.00

LAWDOG
1993
1 B:CDi(s),FH,I:Lawdog 2.50
2 thru 10 FH . . . . @2.50
1-shot Lawdog & Grimrod: Terror
at the Crossroads 3.50

LEGION OF MONSTERS
Sept., 1975
(black & white magazine)
1 NA(c),GM,I&O:Legion of
Monsters,O:Manphibian 40.00

LEGION OF MONSTERS
2007
Spec.#1 Werewolf by Night (2-2007) 3.00
Spec.#1 Man-Thing (3-2007). 3.00
Spec.#1 Morbius (5-2007) 3.00
Spec.#1 Satana (6-2007). 3.00

LEGION OF NIGHT
Oct., 1991
1 WPo/SW,A:Fin Fang Foom 5.50
2 WPo,V:Fin Fang Foom 5.50

LETHAL FOES OF SPIDER-MAN
1993
1 B:DFr(s),SMc,R:Stegron 3.00
2 SMc,A:Stegron. 3.00

MARVEL

3 SMc,V:Spider-Man 3.00
4 E:DFr(s),SMc,Last Issue 3.00

LIFE OF CAPTAIN MARVEL
Aug., 1985
1 rep.Iron Man #55,
   Capt.Marvel #25,26 . . . . 7.00
2 rep.Capt.Marvel#26-28 . . . . 5.00
3 rep.Capt.Marvel#28-30
   Marvel Feature #12 . . . . 5.00
4 rep.Marvel Feature #12,Capt.
   Marvel #31,32,Daredevil#105 . . 5.00
5 rep.Capt.Marvel #32-#34 . . . . . . 5.00

LIFE OF CHRIST
1993
1 Birth of Christ 5.00
2 MW,The Easter Story 5.00

LIFE OF POPE JOHN-PAUL II
1983
1 JSt, Jan., 1983 . . . . 6.00
1a Special reprint 4.00

LIFE WITH MILLIE
See: DATE WITH MILLIE

LIGHT AND DARKNESS WAR
Epic, Oct., 1988
1 . . . . 4.00
2 . . . . 3.00
3 thru 6 Dec., 1989 . . . . @2.50

LINDA CARTER, STUDENT NURSE
Atlas, Sept., 1961
1 . . . . 100.00
2 thru 9, Jan., 1963 . . . . @60.00

LION KING
1 based on Movie 2.75

LI'L KIDS
Aug., 1970–June, 1973
1 . . . . 125.00
2 thru 12 . . . . @60.00

Li'l Kids #1)
© *Marvel Entertainment Group*

LI'L PALS
Sept., 1972
1 . . . . 90.00
2 thru 5, May, 1973 . . . . @50.00

LITTLE ASPIRIN
Marvel Comics, 1949
1 HK 200.00
2 HK 125.00
3 . . . . 100.00

LITTLE LANA
See: LANA

LITTLE LENNY
Marvel Classic Detective, 1949
1 . . . . 135.00
2 . . . . 100.00
3 . . . . 100.00

LITTLE LIZZIE
June, 1949
1 Roller Skating(c) 150.00
2 Soda(c) 100.00
3 Movies(c) 100.00
4 Lizzie(c) 100.00
5 Lizzie/Swing(c) April,1950 . . . 100.00

[2nd Series] Sept., 1953
1 . . . . 100.00
2 . . . . 75.00
3 Jan., 1954 . . . . 75.00

LITTLE MERMAID, THE
1993
1 . . . . 3.50
2 thru 13 . . . . @2.50

LIVEWIRES
Feb., 2005
1 (of 6) AWa(s), ... 3.00
2 Awa(s&c) 3.00
3 AWa(s&c) 3.00
4 AWa(s&c) 3.00
5 Awa(c&c) 3.00
6 AWa(s&c), finale 3.00
Digest Vol. 1: Clockwork Thugs, Yo. 8.00

LOGAN
1-shot HMe,48pg 6.00
1-shot Logan: Path of the
   Warrior (1996) 5.00
1-shot Logan: Shadow Society,
   HMe,TCk Early life of
   Wolverine (1996) 5.00

LOGAN
Mar., 2008
1 (of 3) 3.00
2 and 3 . . . . @4.00
3a black and white variant (c) 4.00

LOGAN'S RUN
Jan., 1977
1 GP,From Movie 16.00
2 GP,Cathedral Kill 10.00
3 GP,Lair of Laser Death 10.00
4 GP,Dread Sanctuary 10.00
5 GP,End Run 10.00
6 MZ,B.U.Thanos/Drax 25.00
7 TS,Cathedral Prime 10.00

LOKI
July, 2004
1 (of 4) 7.50
2 thru 4 . . . . @7.50

LONERS, THE
Apr., 2007
1 . . . . 3.00
2 thru 6 . . . . @3.00

LONGSHOT
Sept., 1985
1 AAd,WPo(i),BA,I:Longshot 8.00
2 AAd,WPo(i),I:RicoshetRita 6.00
3 AAd,WPo(i),I:Mojo,Spiral 6.00
4 AAd,WPo(i),A:Spider-Man 6.00
5 AAd,WPo(i),A:Dr. Strange 6.00
6 AAd,WPo(i),A:Dr. Strange 6.00
1-shot, JMD,MZi,AW (1997) 4.00

LOOSE CANNONS
1 and 2 DAn . . . . @2.50
3 DAn 2.75

LORDS OF AVALON: KNIGHT OF DARKNESS
Nov., 2008
1 (of 5) 4.00

LORDS OF AVALON: SWORD OF DARKNESS
Feb., 2008
1 (of 6) 3.00
1a variant TG (c) 3.00
1b variant TG sketch (c) 3.00
2 thru 6 . . . . @3.00

Lorna, The Jungle Girl #6
© *Marvel Entertainment Group*

LORNA, THE JUNGLE GIRL
Marvel Atlas, 1953–57
1 Terrors of the Jungle,O:Lorna . 600.00
2 Headhunter's Strike
   I:Greg Knight 300.00
3 . . . . 225.00
4 . . . . 225.00
5 . . . . 225.00
6 RH(c),GT 200.00
7 RH(c) 200.00
8 Jungle Queen Strikes Again . . 200.00
9 . . . . 200.00
10 White Fang 200.00
11 Death From the Skies 200.00
12 Day of Doom 150.00
13 thru 17 . . . . @150.00
18 AW(c) 165.00
19 thru 26 . . . . @150.00

LOVE ADVENTURES
Marvel Atlas, Oct., 1949
1 Ph(c) 250.00
2 BP,Ph(c),Tyrone Power/
   Gene Tierney 225.00
3 thru 12 . . . . @150.00
Becomes:

ACTUAL CONFESSIONS
1952
13 . . . . 100.00
14 Dec., 1952 . . . . 100.00

LOVE CLASSICS
Marvel Classic Detective, 1949
1 . . . . 200.00
2 . . . . 200.00

LOVE DRAMAS
Oct., 1949
1 Ph(c),JKa 250.00
2 Jan., 1950 . . . . 150.00

LOVELAND
1949
1 Ph(c) 150.00
2 Ph(c) 150.00

LOVE ROMANCES See: IDEAL

LOVERS
See: ALL-SELECT COMICS

LOVE SECRETS
Oct., 1949
1 . . . . 200.00
2 Jan., 1950 . . . . 150.00

LOVE TALES
Marvel Atlas, 1949–56
(Formerly: The Human Torch)
36 Ph(c) 250.00
37 . . . . 175.00
38 . . . . 150.00
39 thru 41 . . . . @150.00
42 thru 44 . . . . @125.00
45 BP 150.00
46 thru 51 . . . . @125.00
52 BK 150.00
53 thru 68 . . . . @125.00
69 BEv 150.00
70 thru 75 . . . . @100.00

LOVE TRAILS
Marvel Current Detective, 1949
1 western romance 200.00
2 . . . . 200.00

LUNATIK
1995
1 KG 2.50
2 V:The Avengers 2.50
3 conclusion 2.50

MACHINE MAN
April, 1978
1 JK,From 2001 . . . . 20.00
2 JK 12.00
3 JK,V:Ten-For,The Mean
   Machine 12.00
4 JK,V:Ten-For,Battle on A
   Busy Street 12.00
5 JK,V:Ten-For,Day of the
   Non-Hero 12.00
6 JK,V:Ten-For 12.00
7 JK,With A Nation Against Him . . 12.00
8 JK,Escape:Impossible 12.00

9 JK,In Final Battle 12.00
10 SD,Birth of A Super-Hero 7.00
11 SD,V:Binary Bug 7.00
12 SD,Where walk the Gods 7.00
13 SD,Xanadu 7.00
14 SD,V:Machine Man 7.00
15 SD,A:Thing,Human Torch 7.00
16 SD,I:Baron Brimstone And the
   Satan Squad 7.00
17 SD,Madam Menace 7.00
18 A:Alpha Flight 25.00
19 I:Jack o'Lantern 25.00

MACHINE MAN
[Limited-Series]
Oct., 1984
1 HT,BWS,V:Baintronics 4.00
2 HT,BWS,C:Iron Man of 2020 . . . . 4.00
3 HT,BWS,I:Iron Man of 2020 . . . . 4.00
4 HT,BWS,V:Iron Man of 2020 . . . . 4.00

MACHINE MAN 2020
1994
1 rep. limited series #1–#2 . . . . . . 2.50
2 rep. limited series #3–#4 . . . . . . 2.50

MACHINE TEEN
May, 2005
1 (of 5) F:Adam Aaronson 3.00
2 History 101001 . . . . 3.00
3 History 101001 . . . . 3.00
4 Trust no one 3.00
5 Finale 3.00

MAD ABOUT MILLIE
April, 1969
1 . . . . 125.00
2 thru 3 . . . . @100.00
4 thru 10 . . . . @50.00
11 thru 16 . . . . @45.00
17 Dec., 1970 . . . . 45.00
Ann.#1 . . . . 50.00

MADBALLS
Star, Sept., 1986
1 Based on Toys 4.00
2 thru 9 . . . . @4.00
10 June, 1988 . . . . 4.00

MAD DOG
1 from Bob TV Show 2.50
2 V:Trans World Trust Corp 2.50
3 V:Cigarette Criminals 2.50
4 V:Dogs of War 2.50
5 thru 6 . . . . @2.50

MADE MEN
May, 1998
1-shot HMe gangster epic 6.00

MADROX
Sept., 2004
1 (of 5) PDd(s),F:Jamie Madrox . . 3.00
2 PDd(s) 3.00
3 . . . . 3.00
4 . . . . 3.00
5 PDd(c),V:Clay,concl. 3.00

MAGIK
Dec., 1983
1 JB,TP,F:Storm and Illyana 4.00
2 JB,TP,A:Belasco,Sym 3.00
3 TP,A:New Mutants,Belasco 3.00
4 TP,V:Belasco,A:Sym 3.00

MAGNETO
1993
0 JD,JBo,rep. origin stories 6.00
0a Gold ed 8.00
0b Platinum ed 10.00

MAGNETO
1996
1 (of 4) PrM,KJo,JhB, Joseph 2.50
2 PrM,KJo,JhB, Joseph's search
   for his past life 2.50
3 PrM,KJo,JhB 2.50
4 PrM,KJo,JhB, concl. 2.50

MAGNETO: DARK SEDUCTION
April, 2000
1 (of 4) FaN,X-Men: Revolution . . . 3.00
2 FaN,Scarlet Witch 3.00
3 FaN,RCz,V:Scarlet Witch 3.00
4 FaN,RCz,concl. 3.00

MAGNETO REX
March, 1999
1 (of 3) BPe,takes over Genosha . . 2.50
1a signed 20.00
2 BPe,V:Rogue 2.50
3 BPe,A:Rogue,Quicksilver 2.50
GN Magneto Ascendant,
   96-page rep. 4.00

Man Comics #9
© Marvel Entertainment Group

MAN COMICS
Marvel Atlas, 1949–53
1 GT 350.00
2 GT 250.00
3 . . . . 200.00
4 . . . . 200.00
5 . . . . 200.00
6 . . . . 200.00
7 JeR 200.00
8 BEv 200.00
9 EC,TSe,War format begins 150.00
10 JeR,MMe(c) 150.00
11 RH,TSe,MMe 150.00
12 . . . . 150.00
13 . . . . 150.00
14 GT,JeR 175.00
15 . . . . 150.00
16 . . . . 150.00
17 RH 175.00
18 . . . . 150.00
19 . . . . 150.00

All comics prices listed are for *Near Mint* condition.

20	150.00
21 EC-RH	175.00
22 BEv(c),BK	175.00
23 GT,JSt	175.00
24	150.00
25 BEv(c)	175.00
26	150.00
27	150.00
28 Where Mummies Prowl	150.00

MANDRAKE
1995
1 fully painted series	3.25
2 V:Octon	3.25
3 final issue	3.25

MAN FROM ATLANTIS
Feb., 1978–Aug., 1978
1 TS,From TV Series,O:Mark Harris	20.00
2 FR,FS,The Bermuda Triangle Trap	12.00
3 FR,FS,Undersea Shadow	12.00
4 FR,FS,Beware the Killer Spores	12.00
5 FR,FS,The Ray of the Red Death	12.00
6 FR,FS,Bait for the Behemoth	12.00
7 FR,FS,Behold the Land Forgotten	12.00

MAN-THING
[1st Series] Jan., 1974
1 FB,JM,A:Howard the Duck	75.00
2 VM,ST,Hell Hath No Fury	30.00
3 VM,JA,I:Original Foolkiller	25.00
4 VM,JA,O&D:Foolkiller	20.00
5 MP,Night o/t Laughing Dead	20.00
6 MP,V:Soul-Slayers,Drug Issue	20.00
7 MP,A Monster Stalks Swamp	20.00
8 MP,Man Into Monster	20.00
9 MP,Deathwatch	20.00
10 MP,Nobody Dies Forever	20.00
11 MP,Dance to the Murder	20.00
12 KJ,Death-Cry of a Dead Man	12.00
13 TS,V:Captain Fate	12.00
14 AA,V:Captain Fate	12.00
15 A Candle for Saint Cloud	12.00
16 JB,TP,Death of a Legend	12.00
17 JM,Book Burns in Citrusville	12.00
18 JM,Chaos on the Campus	12.00
19 JM,FS,I:Scavenger	12.00
20 JM,A:Spider-Man,Daredevil, Shang-Chi,Thing	14.00

Man-Thing-2nd Series-1 (Marvel 1979)
© Marvel Entertainment Group

21 JM,O:Scavenger,Man Thing	12.00
22 JM,C:Howard the Duck	12.00
G-Size #1 MP,SD,JK,rep.TheGlob.	10.00
G-Size #2 JB,KJ,The Monster Runs Wild	10.00
G-Size #3 AA,A World He Never Made	10.00
G-Size #4 FS,EH,inc.Howard the Duck vs.Gorko	10.00
G-Size #5 DA,EH,inc.Howard the Duck vs.Vampire	12.00

[2nd Series] 1979–1981
1 JM,BWi	11.00
2 BWi,JM,Himalayan Nightmare	10.00
3 BWi.JM,V:Snowman	10.00
4 BWi,DP,V:Mordo,A:Dr Strange	10.00
5 DP,BWi,This Girl is Terrified	10.00
6 DP,BWi,Fraternity Rites	10.00
7 BWi,DP Return of Captain Fate	10.00
8 BWi,DP,V:Captain Fate	10.00
9 BWi(c),Save the Life of My Own Child	10.00
10 BWi,DP,Swampfire	10.00
11 Final issue	10.00

[3rd Series] Oct., 1997
1 JMD,LSh, non-code	3.00
2 JMD,LSh, reunion with ex-wife, A:Dr. Strange	3.00
3 JMD,LSh, visit to Devil Slayer	3.00
4 JMD,LSh, V:Devil-Slayer	3.00
5 JMD,LSh, new abilities revealed	3.00
6 JMD,LSh, V:Cult of Entropy	3.00
7 JMD,LSh, Muck Monster, Namor.	3.00
8 JMD,LSh, Muck Monster turned back into Ted Sallis	3.00

Storyline continues in Strange Tales

MAN-THING
July, 2004
1 (of 3) movie prequel	3.00
2 movie prequel,pt.2	3.00
3 movie prequel,pt.3	3.00

MARINES AT WAR
See: DEVIL-DOG DUGAN

MARINES IN ACTION
Marvel Atlas, June, 1955
1 B:Rock Murdock,Boot Camp Brady	150.00
2 thru 13	@100.00
14 Sept., 1957	100.00

MARINES IN BATTLE
Marvel Atlas, Aug., 1954
1 RH,B:Iron Mike McGraw	275.00
2	150.00
3 thru 6	@125.00
7 thru 17	@125.00
18 thru 22	@100.00
23	125.00
24	100.00
25 Sept., 1958	125.00

MARK HAZZARD: MERC
Nov., 1986–Oct., 1987
1 GM,O:Mark Hazard	2.50
2 GM	2.50
3 M,Arab Terrorists	2.50
4 thru 8 GM	@2.50
9 NKu/AKu	2.50
10 thru 12	@2.50
Ann.#1 D:Merc	2.50

MARSHALL LAW
Epic, 1987–89
1	4.50
2	3.00
3 thru 6	@2.50

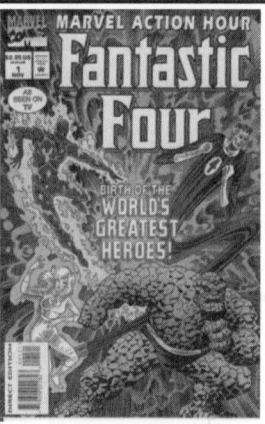

Marvel Action Hour-Fantastic Four #1
© Marvel Entertainment Group

MARVEL ACTION HOUR: FANTASTIC FOUR
1994–95
1 regular	2.50
1a bagged with insert print from animated series	3.00
2 thru 8	@2.50

MARVEL ACTION HOUR: IRON MAN
1994–95
1 regular	2.50
1a bagged with insert print from animated series	3.25
2 thru 8	@2.50

MARVEL ACTION UNIVERSE
TV Tie-in, Jan., 1989
1 Rep.Spider-Man & Friends	4.00

MARVEL ADVENTURES
Feb., 1997
1 RMc,F:The Hulk	2.50
2 thru 20 RMc	@2.50

MARVEL ADVENTURES
Flipbook, June, 2005
1 Marvel Adventures Spider-Man #1 & Fantastic Four #1	4.00
2 thru 13	@4.00
14 thru 17	@5.00

...FANTASTIC FOUR
May, 2005
0 SEa,Dr. Doom	2.50
1	2.50
2 thru 10	@2.50
11 thru 18	@3.00
19 thru 30	@3.00
31 thru 42	@3.00

...HULK
July, 2007
1	3.00
2 thru 16	@3.00

...IRON MAN
May, 2007
1	3.00
2 thru 7	@3.00
8 thru 13	@3.00

All comics prices listed are for *Near Mint* condition.

...SPIDER-MAN

March, 2005

1 Birth of Spider-Man	2.50
2 thru 13	@2.50
14 thru 21	@3.00
22 thru 33	@3.00
34 thru 45	@3.00

...STARRING DAREDEVIL

Dec., 1975–Oct., 1976

1 Rep,Daredevil #22	15.00
2 thru 6, Rep.,Daredevil	@10.00

...SUPER HEROES

July, 2008

1 F:Orthus & Cerberus	3.00
2 V:Meteor Men	3.00
3 V:Kang the Conqueror	3.00
4 F:Klaw	3.00
5 F:Doctor Strange	3.00

...THE AVENGERS

May, 2006

1	3.00
2 thru 7	@3.00
8 thru 18	@3.00
19 thru 30	@3.00
Giant Sz #1	5.00
Digest Vol. 1 Heroes Assembled	7.00

...THE THING

March, 2005

1 (of 4) Destiny's Song	2.50
2 Thing Vs. Hulk	2.50
3 Invisible Things	2.50

...TWO-IN-ONE

July, 2007

1	5.00
2 thru 5	@5.00
6 thru 17	@5.00

MARVEL AGE:

FANTASTIC FOUR

April, 2004

1 V:Mole Man	2.50
2 thru 12	@2.50
Digest #1 All for One	6.00
Digest #2 Doom	6.00
Digest #3 Return of Doctor Doom	6.00

...FANTASTIC FOUR TALES

Feb., 2005

1 V:Black Panther	2.50
Digest Vol. 1: Fantastic Four Tales	8.00

...HULK

Sept., 2004

1	2.50
2	2.50
3 thru 4	@3.00
Digest, rep. #1–#4	6.00

...RUNAWAYS

Digest #3 The Good Die Young	8.00

...SENTINEL

2004

1 Salvage, digest	8.00
2 No Hero, digest	8.00

...SPIDER-MAN

March, 2004

1 V:Vulture	2.50
2 thru 20	@2.50
Digest #1 thru #4	@6.00
Digest, rep. #17–#20	6.00

...SPIDER-MAN TALES

Feb., 2005

1 O:Spider-Man	2.50

...SPIDER-MAN TEAM-UP

Sept., 2004

1 F:Fantastic Four	2.50
2 F:Captain America	2.50
3	2.50
4	2.50
5 F:storm	2.50
Digest, rep. #1–4	6.00
Digest Vol. 1: A Little Helf From My Friends	8.00

MARVEL & DC PRESENTS

Nov., 1982

1 WS,TA,X-Men & Titans,A:Darkseid, Deathstroke(3rd App.),	25.00

MARVEL BOY

See: ASTONISHING

MARVEL APES

Sept., 2008

1 (of 4) KK(s)	4.00
2 thru 4 KK(s)	@4,00
1a thru 4a variant (c)s	@4.00

MARVEL ATLAS

Nov., 2007

1 thru 2 (of 2)	@4.00

MARVEL BOY

June, 2000

1 (of 6) GMo,F:Noh-Varr	5.00
2 GMo,V:Human Race	3.50
3 GMo,Hexus	3.50
4 GMo,Exterminatrix	3.50
5 GMo,Oubliette	3.50
6 GMo,V:Dr. Midas,concl.	3.50

MARVEL CHILLERS

Oct., 1975

1 GK(c),I:Mordred the Mystic	20.00
2 E:Mordred	12.00
3 HC/BWr(c),B:Tigra,The Were Woman	22.00
4 V:Kraven The Hunter	12.00
5 V:Rat Pack,A:Red Wolf	12.00
6 RB(c),JBy,V:Red Wolf	12.00
7 JK(c),GT,V:Super Skrull E:Tigra,Oct., 1976	12.00
GN MGu(s),LSh,F:The Hulk	10.00
GN LHa(s) F:Wolverine	10.00

MARVEL CHRISTMAS SPECIAL

1 DC/AAd/KJ/SB/RLm,A:Ghost Rider X-Men,Spider-Man.	2.50

MARVEL CLASSICS COMICS

1976–78

1 GK/DA(c),B:Reprints from Pendulum Illustrated Comics Dr.Jekyll & Mr. Hyde	30.00
2 GK(c),AN,Time Machine	20.00
3 GK/KJ(c) The Hunchback of Notre Dame	20.00
4 GK/DA(c),20,000 Leagues– Beneath the Sea by Verne	20.00
5 GK(c),RN,Black Beauty	20.00
6 GK(c),Gullivers Travels	20.00
7 GK(c),Tom Sawyer	20.00
8 GK(c),AN,Moby Dick	20.00
9 GK(c),NR,Dracula	20.00
10 GK(c),Red Badge of Courage	20.00
11 GK(c),Mysterious Island	15.00
12 GK/DA(c),AN,3 Musketeers	15.00

Marvel Classic Comics 14
© Marvel Entertainment Group

13 GK(c),Last of the Mohicans	15.00
14 GK(c),War of the Worlds	15.00
15 GK(c),Treasure Island	15.00
16 GK(c),Ivanhoe	12.00
17 JB/ECh(c),The Count of Monte Cristo	12.00
18 ECh(c),The Odsyssey	12.00
19 JB(c),Robinson Crusoe	12.00
20 Frankenstein	12.00
21 GK(c),Master of the World	12.00
22 GK(c),Food of the Gods	12.00
23 Moonstone by Wilkie Collins	12.00
24 GK/RN(c),She	12.00
25 The Invisible Man by H.G.Wells	12.00
26 JB(c),The Illiad by Homer	12.00
27 Kidnapped	12.00
28 MGo(1st art) The Pit and the Pendulum	15.00
29 The Prisoner of Zenda	12.00
30 The Arabian Nights	12.00
31 The First Men in the Moon	12.00
32 GK(c),White Fang	12.00
33 The Prince and the Pauper	12.00
34 AA,Robin Hood	12.00
35 FBe,Alice in Wonderland	12.00
36 A Christmas Carol	12.00

MARVEL COLLECTORS ITEM CLASSICS

Feb., 1965

1 SD,JK,reprint FF #2	200.00
2 SD,JK,reprint FF #3	100.00
3 SD,JK,reprint FF #4	135.00
4 SD,JK,reprint FF #7	135.00
5 thru 10 SD,JK,rep.F.Four	@100.00
11 thru 22 SD,JK,rep.F.Four	@75.00

Becomes:

MARVEL'S GREATEST COMICS

1969–81

23 thru 34 SD,JK,rep.F.Four	@30.00
35 thru 37 JK,rep.F.Four	@20.00
38 thru 50 JK,rep.F.Four	@15.00
51 thru 75 JK,rep.F.Four	@10.00
76 thru 96 rep.F.Four	@9.00

MARVEL COMICS

Oct.-Nov., 1939

1 FP(c),BEv,CBu,O:Sub-Mariner I&B:The Angel,A:Human Torch, Ka-Zar,Jungle Terror, B:The Masked Raider	450,000.00

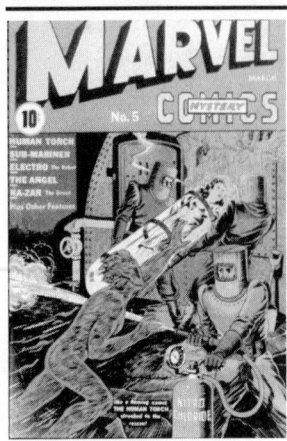

Marvel Mystery Comics #5
© Marvel Entertainment Group

Becomes:

MARVEL MYSTERY COMICS

2 CSM(c),BEv,CBu,PGv,
  B:American, Ace,Human
  Torch,Sub-Mariner,Ka-Zar 60,000.00
3 ASh(c),BEv,CBu,PGv,
  E:American Ace 33,000.00
4 ASh(c),BEv,CBu,PGv,
  I&B:Electro,The Ferret,
  Mystery Detective. 25,000.00
5 ASh(c),BEv,CBu,PGv,
  Human Torch(c) 48,000.00
6 ASh(c),BEv,CBu,PGv,
  Angle!(c) 15,000.00
7 ASh(c),BEv,CBu,PGv,
  Bondage(c) 15,000.00
8 ASh(c),BEv,CBu,PGv,Human
  TorchV:Sub-Mariner 22,000.00
9 ASh(c),BEv,CBu,PGv,Human
  Torch V:Sub-Mariner(c) . . 55,000.00
10 ASh(c),BEv,CBu,PGv,B:Terry
  Vance Boy Detective 18,000.00
11 ASh(c),BEv,CBu,PGv,
  Human Torch V:Nazis(c). . . 6,500.00
12 ASh(c),BEv,CBu,
  PGv,Angel(c) 7,500.00
13 ASh(c),BEv,CBu,PGv,S&K,
  I&B:The Vision 10,000.00
14 ASh(c),BEv,CBu,PGv,S&K,
  Sub-Mariner V:Nazis 4,800.00
15 ASh(c),BEv,CBu,PGv,S&K,
  Sub-Mariner(c) 5,000.00
16 ASh(c),BEv,CBu,PGv,S&K,
  HumanTorch/NaziAirbase. . 5,000.00
17 ASh(c),BEv,CBu,PGv,S&K,
  Human Torch/Sub-Mariner 5,000.00
18 ASh(c),BEv,CBu,PGv,S&K,
  Human Torch & Toro(c) . . . 4,500.00
19 ASh(c),BEv,CBu,PGv,S&K,
  O:Toro,E:Electro 4,500.00
20 ASh(c),BEv,CBu,PGv,S&K,
  O:The Angel 4,500.00
21 ASh(c),BEv,CBu,PGv,S&K,
  I&B:The Patriot. 4,500.00
22 ASh(c),BEv,CBu,PGv,S&K,
  AAv,Toro/Bomb(c). 4,000.00
23 ASh(c),BEv,CBu,PGv,S&K,
  O:Vision,E:The Angel 4,000.00
24 ASh(c),BEv,CBu,S&K,
  AAv,Human Torch(c). 4,000.00
25 BEv,CBu,S&K,ASh Nazi(c) . 4,000.00
26 ASh(c),BEv,CBu,S&K,
  Sub-Mariner(c) 3,800.00

27 ASh(c),BEv,CBu,
  S&K,E:Ka-Zar 3,800.00
28 ASh(c),BEv,CBu,S&K,Bondage
  (c),B:Jimmy Jupiter 3,800.00
29 ASh(c),BEv,CBu,SSh,
  Bondage(c) 3,800.00
30 BEv,CBu,SSh,Pearl
  Harbor(c) 3,800.00
31 BEv,CBu,Human Torch(c) . . 4,200.00
32 CBu,I:The Boboes 3,500.00
33 ASh(c),CBu,SSh,Jap(c) 3,200.00
34 ASh(c),CBu,SSh,V:Hitler . . . 4,000.00
35 ASh(c),SSh,BeachAssault(c) 3,300.00
36 ASh(c),Nazi Invasion of NY . 3,300.00
37 SSh(c),Nazi(c) 3,300.00
38 SSh(c),Battlefield(c). 3,300.00
39 ASh(c),Nazis/U.S(c) 3,300.00
40 ASh(c),SSh,Zeppelin(c) . . . 3,300.00
41 ASh(c),Jap. Command(c) . . 2,800.00
42 ASh(c),Japanese Sub(c) . . . 2,800.00
43 ASh(c),SSh,Destroyed
  Bridge(c). 2,800.00
44 ASh(c),Nazi Super Plane(c). 2,800.00
45 ASh(c),SSh,Nazi(c) 2,800.00
46 ASh(c),Hitler Bondage(c). . . 2,800.00
47 ASh(c),Ruhr Valley Dam(c) . 2,800.00
48 ASh(c),E:Jimmy Jupiter,
  Vision,Allied Invasion(c) . . . 2,800.00
49 SSh(c),O:Miss America,
  Bondage(c) 3,500.00
50 ASh(c),Bondage(c),Miss
  Patriot 2,800.00
51 ASh(c),Nazi Torture(c) 2,400.00
52 ASh(c),Bondage(c). 2,400.00
53 ASh(c),Bondage(c). 2,400.00
54 ASh(c),Bondage(c). 2,400.00
55 ASh(c),Bondage(c). 2,400.00
56 ASh(c),Bondage(c). 2,400.00
57 ASh(c),Torture/Bondage(c) . 2,400.00
58 ASh(c),Torture(c) 2,400.00
59 ASh(c),Testing Room(c). . . . 2,400.00
60 ASh(c),Japanese Gun(c) . . 2,400.00
61 ASh(c),Torturer Chamber(c). 2,400.00
62 ASh(c),Violent(c) 2,400.00
63 ASh(c),Nazi High
  Command(c). 2,400.00
64 ASh(c),Last Nazi(c) 2,400.00
65 ASh(c),Bondage(c). 2,400.00
66 ASh(c),Last Japanese(c) . . . 2,400.00
67 ASh(c),Treasury raid(c) 2,400.00
68 ASh(c),Torture Chamber(c) . 3,000.00
69 ASh(c),Torture Chamber(c) . 2,200.00
70 Cops & Robbers(c) 2,200.00
71 ASh(c),Egyptian(c). 2,200.00
72 Police(c) 2,200.00
73 Werewolf Headlines(c). 2,200.00
74 ASh(c),Robbery(c),E:The
  Patriot 2,200.00
75 SSh,Tavern(c),B:YoungAllies 2,200.00
76 ASh(c),Shoot-out(c),B:Miss
  America 2,200.00
77 SSh,Human Torch/Sub-
  Mariner(c). 2,200.00
78 SSh,Safe Robbery(c). 2,200.00
79 SSh,Super Villians(c),E:The
  Angel 2,200.00
80 SSh,I:Capt.America
  (in Marvel) 2,500.00
81 SSh,Mystery o/t Crimson
  Terror 2,000.00
82 SSh,I:Sub-Mariner/Namora
  Team-up, O:Namora,A:Capt.
  America 4,500.00
83 SSh,The Photo Phantom,
  E;Young Allies. 1,700.00
84 SSh,BEv,B:Blonde Phantom 2,500.00
85 SSh,BEv,A:Blonde Phantom,
  E;Miss America. 1,800.00
86 BEv,Blonde Phantom ID
  Revealed,E:Bucky 1,700.00
87 SSh,BEv,I:Capt.America/Golden
  Girl Team-up. 2,500.00

88 SSh,BEv,E:Toro 1,700.00
89 SSh,BEv,AAv,I:Human Torch/
  Sun Girl Team-up 1,700.00
90 BEv,Giant of the Mountains 1,700.00
91 BEv,I:Venus,E:Blonde
  Phantom,Sub-Mariner 1,700.00
92 BEv,How the Human Torch was
  Born,D:Professor Horton,I:The
  Witness,A:Capt.America. . . 5,500.00
92a Marvel #33(c)rare,reps. . . 40,000.00
Becomes:

MARVEL TALES
Aug., 1949

93 The Ghoul Strikes 2,200.00
94 BEv,The Haunted Love 1,400.00
95 The Living Death 1,100.00
96 MSy,SSh(c),Monster Returns 1,100.00
97 DRi,MSy,The Wooden
  Horror 1,200.00
98 BEv,BK,MSy,The Curse of
  the Black Cat 1,000.00
99 DRi,The Secret of the Wax
  Museum. 900.00
100 The Eyes of Doom. 1,000.00
101 The Man Who Died Twice . . 900.00
102 BW,A Witch Among Us . . . 1,300.00
103 RA,A Touch of Death 1,000.00
104 RH(c),BW,BEv,The Thing
  in the Mirror 1,300.00
105 RH(c),GC,JSt,The Spider. . 1,000.00
106 RH(c),BK,BEv,In The Dead of
  the Night 750.00
107 GC,OW,BK,The Thing in the
  Sewer 750.00
108 RH(c),BEv,JR,Horror in the
  Moonlight. 500.00
109 BEv(c),Sight for Sore Eyes. . 500.00
110 RH,SSh,A Coffin for Carlos . 500.00
111 BEv,Horror Under the Earth . 500.00
112 The House That Death Built . 500.00
113 RH,Terror Tale. 500.00
114 BEv(c),GT,JM,2 for Zombie. . 500.00
115 The Man With No Face. 500.00
116 JSt 500.00
117 BEv(c),GK,Terror in the
  North. 500.00
118 RH,DBr,GC,A World
  Goes Mad 500.00
119 RH,They Gave Him A Grave. 500.00
120 GC,Graveyard(c) 500.00
121 GC,Graveyard(c). 400.00
122 JKu,Missing One Body 400.00
123 No Way Out 400.00
124 He Waits at the Tombstone. . 400.00
125 JF,Horror House 400.00
126 DW,It Came From Nowhere . 375.00

Marvel Comics Presents #127
© Marvel Entertainment Group

127 BEv(c),GC,MD,Gone is the
   Gargoyle 375.00
128 Emily,Flying Saucer(c) 375.00
129 You Can't Touch Bottom . . 375.00
130 RH(c),JF,The Giant Killer . . . 375.00
131 GC,BEv,Five Fingers 375.00
132 . . . . 250.00
133 . . . . 250.00
134 BK,JKu,Flying Saucer(c) . . . 250.00
135 thru 143 . . . . @250.00
144 AW 265.00
145 . . . . 250.00
146 MD 200.00
147 BEv 250.00
148 thru 151 BEv . . . . @225.00
152 JMn 225.00
153 BEv 250.00
154 thru 158 . . . . @200.00
159 Aug., 1957 . . . . 225.00

MARVEL COMICS PRESENTS
Sept., 1988

1 WS(c),B:Wolverine(JB,KJ),Master
   of Kung Fu(TS),Man-Thing(TGr,DC)
   F:Silver Surfer(AM) 10.00
2 F:The Captain(AM) 5.00
3 JR2(c),F:The Thing(AM) 5.00
4 F:Thor(AM) 5.00
5 F:Daredevil(DT,MG) 5.00
6 F:Hulk 4.00
7 F:Submariner(SD) 4.00
8 CV(c),E:Master of Kung Fu,F:
   Iron Man(JS) 4.00
9 F:Cloak,El Aquila 4.00
10 E:Wolverine,B:Colossus(RL,CR),
   F:Machine Man(SD,DC) 4.00
11 F:Ant-Man(BL),Slag(RWi) 3.00
12 E:Man-Thing,F:Hercules(DH),
   Namorita(FS) 3.00
13 B:Black Panther(GC,TP),F:
   Shanna,Mr.Fantastic &
   Invisible Woman 3.00
14 F:Nomad(CP),Speedball(SD) . . . 3.00
15 F:Marvel Girl(DT,MG),Red
   Wolf(JS) 3.00
16 F:Ka-Zar(JM),Longshot(AA) 3.00
17 E:Colossus,B:Cyclops(RLm),
   F:Watcher(TS) 4.00
18 F:She-Hulk(JBy,BWi),Willie
   Lumpkin(JSt) 3.00
19 RLd(c)B:Dr.Strange(MBg),
   I:Damage Control(EC,AW) 3.00
20 E:Dr.Strange,F:Clea(RLm) 3.00
21 F:Thing,Paladin(RWi,DA) 3.00
22 F:Starfox(DC),Wolfsbane &
   Mirage 3.00
23 F:Falcon(DC),Wheels(RWi) 3.00
24 E:Cyclops,B:Havok(RB,JRu),
   F:Shamrock(DJ,DA) 3.00
25 F:Ursa Major,I:Nth Man 4.00
26 B&I:Coldblood(PG),F:Hulk 2.50
27 F:American Eagle(RWi) 2.50
28 F:Triton(JS) 2.50
29 F:Quasar(PR) 2.50
30 F:Leir(TMo) 2.50
31 EL,E:Havok,B:Excalibur
   (EL,TA) 4.00
32 TM(c),F:Sunfire(DH,DC) 3.00
33 F:Namor(JLe 4.00
34 F:Captain America(JsP) 3.00
35 E:Coldblood,F:Her(EL,AG) 4.00
36 BSz(c),F:Hellcat(JBr) 4.00
37 E:Bl.Panther,F:Devil-Slayer . . . 3.00
38 E:Excalibur,B:Wonderman(JS),
   Wolverine(JB),F:Hulk(MR,DA) . . 4.00
39 F:Hercules(BL),Spider-Man 3.50
40 F:Hercules(BL),Overmind(DH) . . 3.50
41 F:Daughters of the Dragon(DA),
   Union Jack(KD) 3.50
42 F:Iron Man(MBa),Siryn(LSn) 3.50

43 F:Iron Man(MBa),Siryn(LSn) 3.50
44 F:Puma(BWi),Dr.Strange 3.50
45 E:Wonderman,F:Hulk(HT),
   Shooting Star 3.50
46 RLd(c),B:Devil-Slayer,F:Namor,
   Aquarian 3.50
47 JBy(c),E:Wolverine,F:Captain
   America,Arabian Knight(DP) . . . 3.50
48 B:Wolverine&Spider-Man(EL),
   F:Wasp,Storm&Dr.Doom 5.00
49 E:Devil-Slayer,F:Daredevil(RWi),
   Gladiator(DH) 4.50
50 E:Wolverine&Spider-Man,B:Comet
   Man(KJo),F:Captain Ultra(DJ),
   Silver Surfer(JkS) 4.50
51 B:Wolverine(RLd),F:Iron Man
   (MBr,DH),Le Peregrine 4.00
52 F:Rick Jones,Hulk(RWi,TMo) . . . 4.00
53 E:Wolverine,Comet Man,F:
   Silver Sable&Black Widow
   (RLd,BWi),B:Stingray 4.00
54 B:Wolverine&Hulk(DR),
   Werewolf,F:Shroud(SD,BWi) . . 6.00
55 F:Collective Man(GLa) 6.00
56 E:Stingray,F:Speedball(SD) 6.00
57 DK(c),B:Submariner(MC,MFm),
   Black Cat(JRu) 6.00
58 F:Iron Man(SD) 6.00
59 E:Submariner,Werewolf,
   F:Punisher 6.00
60 B:Poison,Scarlet Witch,
   F:Captain America(TL) 6.00
61 E:Wolverine&Hulk,
   F:Dr.Strange 6.00
62 F:Wolverine(PR),Deathlok(JG) . . 6.00
63 F:Wolverine(PR),E:Scarlet
   Witch,Thor(DH) 4.00
64 B:Wolverine&Ghost Rider(MT),
   Fantastic Four(TMo),F:Blade . . 4.00
65 F:Starfox(ECh) 3.50
66 F:Volstagg 3.50
67 E:Poison,F:Spider-Man(MG) 3.50
68 B:Shanna(PG),E:Fantastic Four
   F:Lockjaw(JA,AM) 3.50
69 B:Daredevil(DT),F:Silver Surfer . 3.50
70 F:BlackWidow&Darkstar(AM) . . . 3.50
71 E:Wolverine&Ghost Rider,F:
   Warlock(New Mutants),SMc . . . 3.50
72 B:Weapon X(BWS),E:Daredevil,
   F:Red Wolf(JS) 7.00
73 F:Black Knight(DC),
   Namor(JM) 5.00
74 F:Constrictor(SMc),Iceman &
   Human Torch(JSon,DA) 5.00

Marvel Comics Presents #149
© Marvel Entertainment Group

75 F:Meggan & Shadowcat,
   Dr.Doom(DC) 5.00
76 F:Death's Head(BHi,MFm),
   A:Woodgod(DC) 5.00
77 E:Shanna,B:Sgt.Fury&Dracula
   (TL,JRu),F:Namor 4.50
78 F:Iron Man(KSy),Hulk&Selene . . 4.50
79 E:Sgt.Fury&Dracula,F:Dr.Strange,
   Sunspot(JBy) 4.50
80 F:Daughters of the Dragon,Mister
   Fantastic(DJ),Captain America
   (SD,TA) 4.50
81 F:Captain America(SD,TA),
   Daredevil(MR,AW),Ant-Man . . . 4.00
82 B:Firestar(DT),F:Iron Man(SL),
   Power Man 4.00
83 F:Hawkeye,Hum.Torch(SD,EL) . 4.00
84 E:Weapon X 4.00
85 B:Wolverine(SK),Beast(RLd,JaL-
   1st Work),F:Speedball(RWi),
   I:Cyber 7.00
86 F:PaladinE:RLd on Beast 5.00
87 E:Firestar,F:Shroud(RWi) 5.00
88 F:Solo,Volcana(BWi) 5.00
89 F:Spitfire(JSn),Mojo(JMa) 5.00
90 D:Ghost Rider & Cable,F:
   Nightmare 4.50
91 F:Impossible Man 3.50
92 E:Wolverine,Beast,
   F:Northstar(JMa) 3.50
93 SK(c),B:Wolverine,Nova,
   F:Daredevil 3.00
94 F:Gabriel 3.00
95 SK(c),E:Wolverine,F:Hulk 3.00
96 B:Wolverine(TT),E:Nova,
   F:Speedball 3.00
97 F:Chameleon,Two-Gun Kid,
   E:Ghost Rider/Cable 3.00
98 E:Wolverine,F:Ghost Rider,
   Werewolf by Night 2.50
99 F:Wolverine,Ghost Rider,
   Mary Jane,Captain America 2.50
100 SK,F:Ghost Rider,Wolverine,
   Dr.Doom,Nightmare 3.00
101 SK(c),B:Ghost Rider&Doctor
   Strange,Young Gods,Wolverine
   &Nightcrawler,F:Bar With
   No Name 2.50
102 RL,GC,AW,F:Speedball 2.50
103 RL,GC,AW,F:Puck 2.50
104 RL,GC,AW,F:Lockheed 2.50
105 RL,GC,AW,F:Nightmare 2.50
106 RL,GC,AW,F:Gabriel,E:Ghost
   Rider&Dr.Strange 2.50
107 GC,AW,TS,B:Ghost Rider&
   Werewolf 2.50
108 GC,AW,TS,SMc,E:Wolverine&
   Nightcrawler,B:Thanos 2.50
109 SLi,TS,SMc,B:Wolverine&
   Typhoid Mary,E:Young Gods . . . 2.50
110 SLi,SMc,F:Nightcrawler 2.50
111 SK(c),SLi,RWi,F:Dr.Strange,
   E:Thanos 2.50
112 SK(c),SLi,F:Pip,Wonder Man,
   E:Ghost Rider&Werewolf 2.50
113 SK(c),SLi,B:Giant Man,
   Ghost Rider&Iron Fist 2.50
114 SK(c),SLi,F:Arabian Knight 2.50
115 SK(c),SLi,F:Cloak&Dagger 2.50
116 SK(c),SLi,E:Wolverine &
   Typhoid Mary 2.50
117 SK,PR,B:Wolverine&Venom,
   I:Ravage 2099 . . . . 4.00
118 SK,PB,RWi,E:Giant Man,
   I:Doom 2099 . . . . 3.00
119 SK,GC,B:Constrictor,E:Ghost
   Rider&Iron Fist,F:Wonder Man . 3.00
120 SK,GC,E:Constrictor,B:Ghost
   Rider/Cloak & Dagger,
   F:Spider-Man 2.50
121 SK,GC,F:Mirage,Andromeda . . 2.50

122 SK(c),GK,E:Wolverine&Venom,
    Ghost Rider&Cloak&Dagger,F:
    Speedball&Rage,Two-Gun Kid . 2.50
123 SK(c),DJ,SLi,B:Wolverine&Lynx,
    Ghost Rider&Typhoid Mary,
    She-Hulk,F:Master Man 2.50
124 SK(c),DJ,MBa,SLi,F:Solo 2.50
125 SLi,SMc,DJ,B:Iron Fist 2.50
126 SLi,DJ,E:She-Hulk 2.50
127 SLi,DJ,DP,F:Speedball 2.50
128 SLi,DJ,RWi,F:American Eagle . 2.50
129 SLi,DJ,F:Ant Man 2.50
130 DJ,SLi,RWi,E:Wolverine&Lynx,
    Ghost Rider&Typhoid Mary,Iron
    Fist,F:American Eagle 2.50
131 MFm,B:Wolverine,Ghost Rider&
    Cage,Iron Fist&Sabretooth,
    F:Shadowcat 2.50
132 KM(c),F:Iron Man 2.50
133 F:Cloak & Dagger 2.50
134 SLi,F:Vance Astro 2.50
135 SLi,F:Daredevil 2.50
136 B:Gh.Rider&Masters of Silence,
    F:Iron Fist,Daredevil 2.50
137 F:Ant Man 2.50
138 B:Wolverine,Spellbound 2.50
139 F:Foreigner 2.50
140 F:Captain Universe 2.50
141 BCe(s),F:Iron Fist 2.50
142 E:Gh.Rider&Masters of Silence,
    F:Mr.Fantastic 2.50
143 Siege of Darkness,pt.#3,
    B:Werewolf,Scarlet Witch,
    E:Spellbound 2.50
144 Siege of Darkness,pt.#6,
    B:Morbius 2.50
145 Siege of Darkness,pt.#11 . . . . 2.50
146 Siege of Darkness,pt.#14 . . . . 2.50
147 B:Vengeance,F:Falcon,Masters of
    Silence,American Eagle 2.50
148 E:Vengeance,F:Capt.Universe,
    Black Panther 2.50
149 F:Daughter o/t Dragon,Namor,
    Vengeance,Starjammers 2.50
150 ANo(s),SLi,F:Typhoid Mary,DD,
    Vengeance,Wolverine 2.50
151 ANo(s),F:Typhoid Mary,DD,
    Vengeance. 2.50
152 CDi(s),PR,B:Vengeance,Wolverine,
    War Machine,Moon Knight . . 2.50
153 CDi(s),A:Vengeance,Wolverine,
    War Machine,Moon Knight 2.50
154 CDi(s),E:Vengeance,Wolverine,
    War Machine,Moon Knight 2.50
155 CDi(s),B:Vengeance,Wolverine,
    War Machine,Kymaera 2.50
156 B:Shang Chi,F:Destroyer 2.50
157 F:Nick Fury 2.50
158 AD,I:Clan Destine,E:Kymaera,
    Shang Chi,Vengeance. 2.50
159 B:Hawkeye, New Warriors,
    F:Fun,E:Vengeance. 2.50
160 B:Vengeance,Mace. 2.50
161 E:Hawkeye 2.50
162 B:Tigra,E:Mace 2.50
163 E:New Warriors 2.50
164 Tigra, Vengeance 2.50
165 Tigra, Vengeance 2.50
166 Turbo, Vengeance. 2.50
167 Turbo, Vengeance. 2.50
168 Thing, Vengeance. 2.50
169 Mandarin, Vengeance. 2.50
170 Force, Vengeance. 2.50
171 Nick Fury. 2.50
172 Lunatik 2.50
173 thru 175. . . . . @2.50

MARVEL COMICS
PRESENTS
Sept., 2007
1 F:Hellcat. 4.00

---

2 F:Hellcat. 4.00
3 F:Magneto 4.00
4 F:Weapon Omega 4.00
5 . . . . 4.00
6 F:Captain America 4.00
7 F:Vanguard 4.00
8 F:Machine Man 4.00
9 F:The Hulk 4.00
10 F:Deadpool 4.00
11 Vanguard. 4.00
12 Vanguard and Weapon Omega . 4.00

MARVEL COMICS
SUPER SPECIAL
[Magazine, 1977]
1 JB,WS,Kiss,Features &Photos 200.00
2 JB,Conan(1978) 25.00
3 WS,Close Encounters 15.00
4 GP,KJ,Beatles story 65.00
Becomes:
MARVEL SUPER SPECIAL
5 Kiss 1978 . . . . 200.00
6 GC,Jaws II 25.00
7 Does Not Exist in US
8 Battlestar Galactica(Tabloid) . . . 22.00
9 Conan 20.00
10 GC,Starlord 15.00
11 JB,RN,Weirdworld, ... 15.00
12 JB,Weirdworld, ... 15.00
13 JB,Weirdworld. 15.00
14 GC,Meteor,adapt. 15.00
15 Star Trek 15.00
15a Star Trek 17.00
16 AW,B:Movie Adapts,Empire
    Strikes Back. 17.00
17 Xanadu 7.00
18 HC(c),JB,Raiders of the Lost
    Ark 7.00
19 HC,For Your Eyes Only 9.00
20 Dragonslayer 7.00
21 JB,Conan 7.00
22 JSo(c),AW,Bladerunner 9.00
23 Annie 9.00
24 Dark Crystal 9.00
25 Rock and Rule 9.00
26 Octopussy. 8.00
27 AW,Return of the Jedi. 9.00
28 PH(c),Krull. 8.00
29 DSp,Tarzan of the Apes 8.00
30 Indiana Jones and the Temple
    of Doom 9.00
31 The Last Star Fighter 9.00
32 Muppets Take Manhattan 9.00
33 Buckaroo Banzai. 11.00
34 GM,Sheena. 9.00

Marvel Comics Super Special #3
© *Marvel Entertainment Group*

---

35 JB,Conan The Destroyer 9.00
36 Dune 9.00
37 2010 . . . . 9.00
38 Red Sonja. 9.00
39 Santa Claus 9.00
40 JB,Labrynth 9.00
41 Howard the Duck,Nov.,1986. . . . 9.00

MARVEL DOUBLE
FEATURE
Dec., 1973
1 JK,GC,B:Tales of Suspense
    Reprints,Capt.America,
    Iron-Man 20.00
2 JK,GC ,A:Nick Fury 15.00
3 JK,GC 15.00
4 JK,GC,Cosmic Cube 15.00
5 JK,GC,V:Red Skull 15.00
6 JK,GC,V:Adaptoid 15.00
7 JK,GC,V:Tumbler. 15.00
8 JK,GC,V:Super Adaptoid 15.00
9 GC,V:Batroc 15.00
10 GC. 15.00
11 GC,Capt.America Wanted. 10.00
12 GC,V:Powerman,Swordsman . . 10.00
13 GC,A:Bucky 10.00
14 GC,V:Red Skull. 10.00
15 GK,GC,V:Red Skull. 10.00
16 GC,V;Assassin 10.00
17 JK,GC,V:Aim,Iron Man &
    Sub-Mariner #1 . . . . 10.00
18 JK,GC,V:Modok,Iron Man #1 . . 10.00
19 JK,GC,E:Capt.America. 10.00
20 JK(c) 9.00
21 Capt.America,Black Panther
    March, 1977 . . . . 9.00

MARVEL DOUBLE-SHOT
Nov., 2002
1 JJu(c),Hulk, Thor. 3.00
2 JJu(c),Doom & Avengers. 3.00
3 JJu(c),F:Mr. Fantastic 3.00
4 JJu(c),F:Iron Man. 3.00

MARVEL FANFARE
March, 1972
1 MG,TA,PS,F:Spider-Man,
    Daredevil,Angel. 15.00
2 MG,SM,FF,TVe,F:SpM,Ka-Zar . . 10.00
3 DC,F:X-Men. 10.00
4 PS,TA,MG,F:X-Men,Deathlok . . 10.00
5 MR,F:Dr.Strange 8.00
6 F:Spider-Man,Scarlet Witch. . . . 9.00
7 F:Hulk/Daredevil 6.00
8 CI,TA,GK,F:Dr.Strange 6.00
9 GM,F:Man Thing 6.00
10 GP,B:Black Widow 7.00
11 GP,D:M.Corcoran . . . . `.` 7.00
12 GP,V:Snapdragon 7.00
13 GP,E:B.Widow,V:Snapdragon . 7.00
14 F:Fantastic Four,Vision 3.00
15 BWS,F:Thing,Human Torch 3.00
16 DC,JSt,F:Skywolf 2.50
17 DC,JSt,F:Skywolf 2.50
18 FM,JRu,F:Captain America. . . . 3.00
19 RL,F:Cloak and Dagger 2.50
20 JSn,F:Thing&Dr.Strange 3.00
21 JSn,F:Thing And Hulk. 3.00
22 KSy,F:Iron Man 2.50
23 KSy,F:Iron Man 2.50
24 F:Weird World 3.00
25 F:Weird World 2.50
26 F:Weird World 2.50
27 F:Daredevil 2.50
28 KSy,F:Alpha Flight 3.00
29 JBy,F:Hulk. 3.00
30 BA,AW,F:Moon Knight 2.50
31 KGa,F:Capt.America,
    Yellow Claw. 2.50

Marvel Fanfare #1 (Marvel 1982)
© *Marvel Entertainment Group*

32 KGa,PS,F:Capt.America,
   Yellow Claw 2.50
33 JBr,F:X-Men 5.00
34 CV,F:Warriors Three 2.50
35 CV,F:Warriors Three 2.50
36 CV,F:Warriors Three 2.50
37 CV,F:Warriors Three 2.50
38 F:Captain America 2.50
39 JSon,F:Hawkeye,Moon Knight . 2.50
40 DM,F:Angel,Storm,Mystique . . . 3.00
41 DGb,F:Dr.Strange 2.50
42 F:Spider-Man 3.00
43 F:Sub-Mariner,Human Torch. . . 2.50
44 KSy,F:Iron Man vs.Dr.Doom . . . 2.50
45 All Pin-up Issue,WS,AAd,MZ,
   JOy,BSz,KJ,HC,PS,JBy. 3.00
46 F:Fantastic Four 2.50
47 MG,F:Spider-Man,Hulk 3.00
48 KGa,F:She-Hulk 2.50
49 F:Dr.Strange 2.50
50 JSon,JRu,F:Angel. 3.00
51 JB,JA,GC,AW,F:Silver Surfer . . . 4.00
52 F:Fantastic Four 2.50
53 GC,AW,F:Bl.Knight,Dr.Strange . 2.50
54 F:Black Knight,Wolverine 3.50
55 F:Powerpack,Wolverine 3.50
56 CI,DH,F:Shanna t/She-Devil. . . 2.50
57 BBl,AM,F:Shanna,Cap.Marvel . 2.50
58 BBl,F:Shanna,Vision/Sc.Witch . 2.50
59 BBl,F:Shanna,Hellcat 2.50
60 PS,F:Daredevil,Capt.Marvel . . . 2.50

Second Series 1996
1 Captain America, Falcon 2.50
2 New Fantastic Four 2.50
3 BbB,F:Spider-Man, Ghost Rider,. 2.50
4 F:Longshot. 2.50
5 F:Longshot. 2.50
6 F:Power Man & Iron Fist V:
   Sabretooth. 2.50

MARVEL FEATURE
[1st Regular Series]
Dec., 1971
1 RA,BE,NA,I&O:Defenders &
   Omegatron. 300.00
2 BEv,F:The Defenders 150.00
3 BEv,F:The Defenders 100.00
4 F:Ant-Man 45.00
5 F:Ant-Man 25.00
6 F:Ant-Man 20.00
7 CR,F:Ant-Man 20.00
8 JSc,CR,F:Ant-Man,O:Wasp. . . . 20.00
9 CR,F:Ant-Man 20.00

10 CR,F:Ant-Man. 20.00
11 JSn,JSt,F:Thing & Hulk. 90.00
12 JSn,JSt,F:Thing,Iron Man,
   Thanos,Blood Brothers 60.00

[2nd Regular Series]
(All issues feature Red Sonja)
1 DG,The Temple of Abomination. 12.00
2 FT,Blood of the Hunter. 7.00
3 FT,Balek Lives 7.00
4 FT,Eyes of the Gorgon. 8.00
5 FT,The Bear God Walks 8.00
6 FT,C:Conan,Belit 8.00
7 FT,V:Conan,A:Belit,Conan#68 . . 12.00

MARVEL FRONTIER
COMICS SPECIAL
1 All Frontier Characters. 3.25
1994 . . . . 3.00

MARVEL GRAPHIC NOVEL
1982
1 JSn,D:Captain Marvel,A:Most
   Marvel Characters. 30.00
1a 2nd printing 12.00
1b 3rd-5th printing. 8.00
2 F:Elric,Dreaming City. 12.00
2a 2nd printing 7.00
3 JSn,F:Dreadstar. 15.00
3a 2nd-3rd printing 7.00
4 BMc,I:New Mutants,Cannonball
   Sunspot,Psyche,Wolfsbane. . . 22.00
4a 2nd printing 10.00
4b 3rd-4th printing. 8.00
5 BA,F:X-Men 27.00
5a 2nd printing 9.00
5b 3rd-5th printing. 7.00
6 WS,F:Starslammers 10.00
6a 2nd printing 7.00
7 CR,F:Killraven 10.00
8 RWi,AG,F:Super Boxers 10.00
8a 2nd printing 7.00
9 DC,F:Futurians 12.00
9a 2nd printing 7.00
10 RV,F:Heartburst 10.00
10a 2nd printing 6.00
11 VM,F:Void Indigo. 12.00
12 F:Dazzler the Movie 10.00
12a 2nd printing 6.00
13 MK,F:Starstruck 10.00
14 JG,F:SwordsofSwashbucklers . 10.00
15 CV,F:Raven Banner 10.00
16 GLa,F:Alladin Effect 10.00
17 MS,F:Living Monolith 10.00
18 JBy,F:She-Hulk 15.00
18 later printings 14.00
19 F:Conan 15.00
20 F:Greenberg the Vampire 10.00
21 JBo,F:Marada the She-wolf . . . 10.00
22 BWr,Hooky,F:Spider-Man 16.00
23 DGr,F:Dr.Strange 10.00
24 FM,BSz,F:Daredevil 15.00
25 F:Dracula 10.00
26 FC,TA,F:Alien Legion 15.00
27 BH,F:Avengers 15.00
28 JSe,F:Conan the Reaver 16.00
29 BWr,F:Thing & Hulk 10.00
30 F:A Sailor's Story 10.00
31 F:Wolf Pack 10.00
32 SA,F:Death of Groo 17.00
33 F:Thor. 10.00
34 AW,F:Cloak & Dagger. 10.00
35 MK/RH,F:The Shadow 18.00
36 F:Willow movie adaption. 10.00
37 BL,F:Hercules 15.00
38 JB,F:Silver Surfer 20.00
39 F:Iron Man,Crash 14.50
40 JZ,F:The Punisher 12.00
41 F:Roger Rabbit 10.00
42 F:Conan of the Isles 15.00
43 EC,F:Ax. 12.00

44 BJ,F:Arena 10.00
45 JRy,F:Dr.Who 12.00
46 TD,F:Kull 10.00
47 GM,F:Dreamwalker. 10.00
48 F:Sailor's Storm II 10.00
49 MBd,F:Dr.Strange&Dr.Doom. . 25.00
50 F:Spider-Man,Parallel Lives . . . 12.00
51 F:Punisher,Intruder 14.00
52 DSp,F:Roger Rabbit 12.00
53 PG,F:Conan 12.00
54 HC,F:Wolverine & Nick Fury. . . 20.00

MARVEL HALLOWEEN:
THE SUPERNATURALS
TOUR BOOK
Sept., 1999
1-shot, 16-page, cardstock cov 3.00

MARVEL HEROES
1 StL,FaN,Mega-Jam,48-pg.. . . . . 3.00

MARVEL HEROES
Flipbook, June, 2005
1 New Avengers #1
   & Captain America #1 . . . . 4.00
2 thru 13 . . . . @4.00
14 thru 17 . . . . @5.00

MARVEL: HEROES
AND LEGENDS 1997
Aug., 1997
1-shot, Stan Lee, JR(c) 6.00

MARVEL HOLIDAY
SPECIAL
1991–2007
1 AAd (1991). 4.00
n/n RLm,JSn,TA (1993) 3.50
n/n StG(s),PDd(s),RLm,PB (1994). . 3.25
1-shot MWa,KK (1996) 3.00
1-shot Marvel Holiday Special 2004 3.00
1-shot Marvel Holiday (2006). 8.00
1-shot Marvel Holiday (2007). 4.00

MARVEL ILLUSTRATED
May, 2007
LAST OF THE MOHICANS
1 thru 6 Last of the Mohicans . . . @3.00
TREASURE ISLAND
1 thru 6 Treasure Island . . . . @3.00
MAN IN THE IRON MASK
1 thru 6 Man in the Iron Mask. . . @3.00
PICTURE OF DORIAN GRAY
1 thru 6 Picture of Dorian Gray. . @3.00
ILIAD, THE
1 thru 8 The Iliad. . . . . @3.00
MOBY DICK
1 thru 6 Moby Dick . . . . @3.00
THREE MUSKETEERS, THE
1 thru 6 The Three Musketeers . @3.00
ODYSSEY, THE
1 thru 3 The Odyssey . . . . @3.00
KIDNAPPED
1 (of 5) 3.00

MARVEL KIDS
1999
Fantastic Four: Franklin's
   Adventures 3.50
Incredible Hulk: Project Hide 3.50
Spider-Man Mysteries. 3.50
X-Men: Mutant Search R.U.1. . . . . 3.50

MARVEL KNIGHTS
May, 2000
1 JQ,JP,KJ 3.50
2A JQ,KJ,CDi,EB,V:Ulik 3.00
2B variant EB(c) 3.00
3 JQ,KJ,CDi,EB,V:Ulik 3.00
4 JQ,KJ,CDi,EB,Zaran 3.00
5 JQ,KJ,CDi,EB,DaddyWronglegs . 3.00
6 JQ,KJ,CDi,EB,MaximumSecurity. 3.00
7 JQ,KJ,CDi,EB,F:Dr.Strange 3.00
8 JQ,CDi,EB,V:Cloak 3.00
9 JQ,CDi,EB,Dagger vs. Cloak. . . . 3.00
10 JQ,CDi,EB,Punisher 3.00
11 CDi,EB,Luke Cage,Power Man. . 3.00
12 CDi,EB,A:Cloak. 3.00
13 CDi,EB,A:Black Widow,Dagger . 3.00
14 CDi,EB,one quits 3.00
15 CDi,EB,V:S.H.I.E.L.D.. . . . . 3.00
GN Millennial Visions,TyH,48-pg. . . 4.00

March, 2002
1 Punisher,Daredevil,Black Widow. 3.00
2 thru 6 . . . . @3.00

MARVEL KNIGHTS:
DOUBLE-SHOT
Oct., 2001
1 GEn,JQ,Daredevil & Punisher. . . 3.00
2 GEn,Nick Fury & Man-Thing 3.00
3 GF(c),Elektra & Cloak&Daggar . . 3.00
4 GeH,GF(c),Iron Fist 3.00
5 GeH,GF(c),Daredevil 3.00

MARVEL KNIGHTS 4
Feb., 2004
1 Wolf at the Door,pt.1 . . . . 3.00
2 thru 4 Wolf at the Door. . . . . . . @3.00
5 thru 7 The Pine Barrens. . . . . . @3.00
8 Frozen,pt.1. . . . . 3.00
9 Frozen,pt.2. . . . . 3.00
10 Stuff of Dreams,pt.1 . . . . 3.00
11 Stuff of Dreams,pt.2 . . . . 3.00
12 Stuff of Dreams,pt.3 . . . . 3.00
13 Eyes Without a Face 3.00
14 Eyes Without a Face 3.00
15 Divine Time, prologue 3.00
16 Divine Time. 3.00
17 Divine Time. 3.00
18 Divine Time. 3.00
19 Inhumane,pt.1 . . . . 3.00
20 Inhumane,pt.2. . . . . 3.00
21 Desperate Housewife 3.00
22 The Yancy Street Golem. 3.00
23 F:Impossible Man 3.00
24 F:Impossible Man 3.00
25 Resurrection of Nicholas Scratch 3.00
26 Resurrection of Nicholas Scratch 3.00
27 Resurrection of Nicholas Scratch 3.00
28 Private Lives/Public Faces 3.00
29 Super Hero's Apprentice, pt.1. . . 3.00
30 Super Hero's Apprentice, pt.2. . . 3.00

MARVEL KNIGHTS
SPIDER-MAN
April, 2004
1 TyD,Down Among the Dead,pt.1 . 3.00
2 TyD,Down Among the Dead,pt.2 . 3.00
3 TyD,Down Among the Dead,pt.3 . 3.00
4 TyD,Down Among the Dead,pt.4 . 3.00
5 Venomous,pt.1. . . . . 3.00
6 TyD,Venomous,pt.2 . . . . 3.00
7 TyD,Venomous,pt.3 . . . . 3.00
8 TyD,Venomous,pt.4 . . . . 3.00
9 TyD,The Last Stand,pt.1 . . . . 3.00
10 MMr,TyD,The Last Stand 4.00
11 MMr,TyD,V:Sinister Twelve 3.00
12 MMr,TyD,The Last Stand 3.00
13 BTn,Wild Blue Yonder. 3.00
14 BTn,Wild Blue Yonder. 3.00
15 BTn,Wild Blue Yonder. 3.00

16 BTn,Wild Blue Yonder. 3.00
17 BTn,Wild Blue Yonder. 3.00
18 BTn,Wild Blue Yonder. 3.00
19 PDd(s), The Other,x-over,pt.2 . . 5.00
19a 2nd printing 7.00
20 PDd(s), The Other,x-over,pt.5. . . 5.00
21 PDd(s), The Other,x-over,pt.8. . . 5.00
22 PDd(s), The Other,x-over,pt.11 . . 6.00
Digest Marvel Age, Vol. 1 . . . . 8.00
Becomes:

Sensational Spider-Man 33
© Marvel Entertainment Group

SENSATIONAL
SPIDER-MAN
Feb., 2006
23 AMe, Feral, pt.1 . . . . 3.00
24 AMe, Feral, pt.2 . . . . 3.00
25 AMe, Feral, pt.3 . . . . 3.00
26 AMe, Feral, pt.4 . . . . 3.00
27 AMe, Feral, pt.5 . . . . 3.00
28 AMe,War at Home tie-in 3.00
29 AMe,Deadly Foes of Spider-Man 3.00
30 AMe,Deadly Foes of Spider-Man 3.00
31 AMe,Deadly Foes of Spider-Man 3.00
32 The Husband or the Spider?. . . . 3.00
33 Wounds. 3.00
34 V:Black Cat. 3.00
35 Strange Case of, pt.1 . . . . 4.00
36 Strange Case of, pt.2 . . . . 4.00
37 . . . . 4.00
38 Last Temptation, pt.1 . . . . 4.00
39 Last Temptation, pt.2 . . . . 4.00
40 The Book of Peter. 4.00
41 One More Day, pt.3 . . . . 4.00
Ann. #1 SvL, Till Death Do Us Part . 4.00

MARVEL KNIGHTS
TOUR BOOK
Aug., 1998
1-shot, cardstock cover 3.00

MARVEL KNIGHTS 2009
Sept., 2004
Spec. Daredevil #1 . . . . 3.00
Spec. Black Panther #1 . . . . 3.00
Spec. Inhumans #1 . . . . 3.00
Spec. Punisher #1 . . . . 3.00
Spec. Mutant #1. . . . . 3.00

MARVEL LEGACY
Feb., 2006
1 The 1960s Handbook 5.00

2 The 1970s Handbook 5.00
3 The 1980s Handbook 5.00
4 The 1990s Handbook 5.00

MARVEL:
THE LOST GENERATION
Jan., 2000
12 (of 12) JBy,AM,Fireball, Flatiron,
   Cassandra, Oxbow, etx. 3.00
11 JBy,AM,F:Justice. 3.00
10 JBy,AM,O:Walkabout 3.00
9 JBy,AM,Effigy,Black Fox 3.00
8 JBy,AM,Nocturne. 3.00
7 JBy,AM,Knight Templar 3.00
6 JBy,AM,First Line. 3.00
5 JBy,AM,F:Thor. 3.00
4 JBy,AM,Yankee Clipper 3.00
3 JBy,AM,Liberty Girl 3.00
2 JBy,AM,V:Yankee Clipper 3.00
1 JBy,AM,concl. 3.00

MARVEL MANGAVERSE
Jan., 2002
New Dawn #1 BDn 3.00
Avengers #1 . . . . 2.50
Fantastic Four #1 AWa 2.50
Ghost Rider #1 . . . . 2.50
Punisher #1 PDd(s) 2.50
Spider-Man #1 . . . . 2.50
X-Men #1 JMs 2.50
Eternal Twilight #1 BDn 3.00

MARVEL MANGAVERSE
April, 2002
1 BDn, F:Marvin Elwood. 3.00
2 BDn, Inhumans 2.50
3 BDn, V:Galactus 2.50
4 BDn, UN held hostage. 2.50
5 BDn 2.50
6 BDd, only Doom knows 2.50

MARVEL MASTERPIECES
COLLECTION
1993
1 Joe Jusko Masterpiece Cards . . . 3.25
2 F:Wolverine,Thanos,Apocalypse . 3.00
3 F:Gambit,Venom,Hulk 3.00
4 F:Wolverine Vs. Sabretooth. 3.00

MARVEL MASTERPIECES
II COLLECTION
1994
1 thru 3 w/cards . . . . @3.00

MARVEL MILESTONES
March, 2005
1 Iron Man, silver-age reps. 4.00
2 Venom & Hercules, reps. 4.00
3 Wolverine, X-Men, Tuk
   The Cave Boy, Silver Age Reps. 4.00
4 Dr. Doom, Sub-Mariner
   & Red Skull, silver-age reps. . . . 4.00
5 Dr. Strange, Silver Surfer
   Sub-mariner & Hulk, Reps. 4.00
6 Captain Britain, Psylocke
   Golden Age Sub-Mariner, reps. . 4.00
7 Ghost Rider, Black Widow
   Iceman, Silver-age Reps. 4.00
8 Blade, Man-Thing, and
   Satanna, silver-age reps. 4.00
9 Ultimate Spider-Man, Ultimate
   X-Men, Microman 4.00
10 Bloodstone, X-51 & Captain
   Marvel II. 4.00
11 Dragon Lord, Speedball
   and The Man in the Sky 4.00
12 Star Brand & Quasar 4.00
13 Beast & Kitty 4.00

14 Black Panther & Storm 4.00
15 Rawhid Kid & Two-Gun 4.00
16 Millie the Model & Patsy
  Walker 4.00
17 X-Men & The Starjammers 4.00
18 X-Men & The Starjammers 4.00
19 Legion of Monsters, Spider-
  Man and Brother Voodoo 4.00
20 Onslaught 4.00

MARVEL MINI-BOOKS
1966
(black & white)
1 F:Capt.America,Spider-Man,Hulk
  Thor,Sgt.Fury 75.00
2 F:Capt.America,Spider-Man,Hulk
  Thor,Sgt.Fury 75.00
3 F:Capt.America,Spider-Man,Hulk
  Thor,Sgt.Fury 75.00
4 thru 6 F:Capt.America,Spider-Man,
  Hulk,Thor,Sgt.Fury . . . . @75.00

MARVEL MONSTERS
Oct., 2005
1-shot Devil Dinosaur,rep. 4.00
1-shot Where Monsters Dwell, rep . . 4.00
1-shot Fin Fang Four, rep. 4.00
1-shot Monsters on the Prowl, rep. . . 4.00
1-shot Marvel Monsters 4.00

MARVEL MOVIE
PREMIERE
B&W Magazine, 1975
1 Land That Time Forgot 20.00

MARVEL MOVIE
SHOWCASE FEATURING
STAR WARS
Nov., 1982
1 Rep,Stars Wars #1-6 . . . . 5.00
2 Dec., 1982 . . . . 5.00

MARVEL MOVIE
SPOTLIGHT FEATURING
RAIDERS OF
THE LOST ARK
Nov., 1982
1 Rep,Raiders of Lost Ark#1-3 . . . 3.00

MARVEL
MYSTERY COMICS
See: MARVEL COMICS

MARVEL NEMESIS:
THE IMPERFECTS
May, 2005
1 (of 6) Rise of the Imperfects 3.00
2 Rise of the Imperfects 3.00
3 Birth of the Imperfects 3.00
4 JaL(c). 3.00
5 Jal(c) 3.00
6 Rise of the Imperfects, finale. . . . 3.00

MARVEL 1985
May, 2008
1 (of 6) MMr(s) 4.00
1a variant (c) 4.00
2 MMr(s),Clyde Wyncham 4.00
3 MMr(s),The Visitors 4.00
4 MMr(s),Small-Town Mutie 4.00
5 MMr(s),The Odyssey 4.00
6 MMr(s),concl 4.00

MARVEL NO-PRIZE BOOK
Jan., 1983
1 MGo(c),Stan Lee as
  Dr.Doom(c) 7.00

MARVEL: PORTRAITS
OF A UNIVERSE
1 Fully painted moments 3.00
2 Fully painted moments. 3.00
3 F:Death of Elektra 3.00
4 final issue. 3.00

MARVEL POSTER BOOK
June, 2001
Summer 2001, 64-page 3.50
Winter 2001, 64-page 3.50

MARVEL PREMIERE
April, 1972
1 GK,O:Warlock,Receives Soul Gem,
  Creation of Counter Earth . . . 100.00
2 GK,JK,F:Warlock 50.00
3 BWS,F:Dr.Strange 90.00
4 FB,BWS,F:Dr.Strange 35.00
5 MP,CR,F:Dr.Strange,I:Silgguth . 30.00
6 MP,FB,F:Dr.Strange 25.00
7 MP,CR,F:Dr.Strange,I:Dagoth . . 25.00
8 JSn,F:Dr.Strange 25.00
9 NA,FB,F:Dr.Strange 25.00
10 FB,F:Dr.Strange,
  D:Ancient One. 30.00
11 NA,FB,F:Dr.Strange,I:Shuma . . 15.00
12 NA,FB,F:Dr.Strange 15.00
13 NA,FB,F:Dr.Strange 15.00
14 NA,FB,F:Dr.Strange 15.00
15 GK,DG,I&O:Iron Fist,pt.1 . . . . 140.00
16 DG,O:Iron Fist,pt.2,V:Scythe. . 50.00
17 DG,Citadel on the
  Edge of Vengeance 30.00
18 DG,V:Triple Irons. 30.00
19 DG,A:Ninja 30.00
20 I:Misty Knight 30.00
21 V:Living Goddess 30.00
22 V:Ninja 30.00
23 PB,V:Warhawk 30.00
24 PB,V:Monstroid 30.00
25 1st JBy,AMc,E:Iron Fist. 35.00
26 JK,GT,F:Hercules 10.00
27 F:Satana 15.00
28 F:Legion Of Monsters,A:Ghost
  Rider,Morbius,Werewolf. 25.00
29 JK,I:Liberty Legion,
  O:Red Raven. 6.00
30 JK,F:Liberty Legion. 6.00
31 JK,I:Woodgod 6.00
32 HC,F:Monark. 5.00
33 HC,F:Solomon Kane. 5.00
34 HC,F:Solomon Kane. 5.00
35 I&O:Silver Age 3-D Man 5.00
36 F:3-D Man. 5.00
37 F:3-D Man. 5.00
38 AN,MP,I:Weird World 5.00
39 AM,I:Torpedo(1st solo) 5.00
40 AM,F:Torpedo. 5.00
41 TS,F:Seeker 3000. . . . . 5.00
42 F:Tigra. 5.00
43 F:Paladin. 5.00
44 KG,F:Jack of Hearts(1stSolo) . . 5.00
45 GP,F:Manwolf 5.00
46 GP,F:Manwolf 5.00
47 JBy,I:2nd Antman(Scott Lang) . 10.00
48 JBy,F:2nd Antman. 10.00
49 F:The Falcon. 5.00
50 TS,TA,F:Alice Cooper 20.00
51 JBi,F:Black Panther,V:Klan 5.00
52 JBi,F:B.Panther,V:Klan 5.00
53 JBi,F:B.Panther,V:Klan 5.00
54 GD,TD,I:Hammer 5.00
55 JSt,F:Wonderman(1st solo) 6.00
56 HC,TA,F:Dominic Fortune. 5.00

Marvel Premiere #35
© *Marvel Entertainment Group*

57 WS(c),I:Dr.Who. 7.00
58 TA(c),FM,F:Dr.Who. 5.00
59 F:Dr.Who. 5.00
60 WS(c),DGb,F:Dr.Who 5.00
61 TS,F:Starlord. 5.00

MARVEL PRESENTS
Oct., 1975
1 BMc,F:Bloodstone 15.00
2 BMc,O:Bloodstone. 9.00
3 AM,B:Guardians/Galaxy 20.00
4 AM,I:Nikki 12.00
5 AM,Planet o/t Absurd 12.00
6 AM,V:Karanada 12.00
7 AM,Embrace the Void 12.00
8 AM,JB,JSt,reprint.S.Surfer#2 . . 15.00
9 AM,O:Starhawk 12.00
10 AM,O:Starhawk 12.00
11 AM,D:Starhawk's Children . . . 12.00
12 AM,E:Guardians o/t Galaxy . . 12.00

MARVEL PREVIEW
Feb., 1975
(black & white magazine)
1 NA,AN,Man Gods From
  Beyond the Stars 25.00
2 GM(c),O:Punisher 150.00
3 GM(c),Blade the VampireSlayer 30.00
4 GM(c),I&O:Starlord 20.00
5 Sherlock Holmes 20.00
6 Sherlock Holmes 20.00
7 KG,Satana,A:Sword in the Star . 20.00
8 GM,MP,Legion of Monsters 30.00
9 Man-God,O:Starhawk 15.00
10 JSn,Thor the Mighty 30.00
11 JBy,I:Starlord 15.00
12 MK,Haunt of Horror. 10.00
13 JSn(c),Starhawk 10.00
14 JSn(c),Starhawk 10.00
15 MK(c),Starhawk. 10.00
16 GC,Detectives. 10.00
17 GK,Black Mask 6.00
18 GC,Starlord 6.00
19 Kull 6.00
20 HC,NA,GP,Bizarre Adventures . . 7.00
21 SD,Moonlight 10.00
22 JB,King Arthur. 6.00
23 JB,GC,FM,Bizarre Adventures . . 7.00
24 Debut Paradox 6.00
Becomes:

BIZARRE ADVENTURES
1981
25 MG,TA,MR,Lethal Ladies 12.00
26 JB(c),King Kull 12.00

27 JB,AA,GP,Phoenix,A:Ice-Man . . 15.00
28 MG,TA,FM,NA,The Unlikely
    Heroes,Elektra 15.00
29 JB,WS,Horror 10.00
30 JB,Tomorrow 10.00
31 JBy,After the Violence Stops . . . 12.00
32 Gods 12.00
33 Ph(c),Horror 12.00
34 PS,Christmas Spec,Son of Santa
    Howard the Duck,Feb.,1983 . . 10.00

MARVEL PREVIEW
1993
Preview of 1993 . . . . 4.00

MARVEL REMIX
Nov., 1998
1 (of 3) Fantastic Four 3.00
1a signed 20.00
2 Fantastic Four:Fireworks 3.00
3 Fantastic Four:Fireworks 3.00

MARVEL ROMANCE REDUX
March., 2006
1 . . . . 3.00
2 Guys & Dolls 3.00
3 Restraining Orders for Other Girls 3.00
4 I Should Have Been A 3.00
5 Love is a Four Letter Word 3.00

MARVELS
1994
1 B:KBk(s),AxR,I:Phil Sheldon,
    A:G.A.Heroes,Human Torch Vs
    Namor 10.00
2 AxR,A:S.A.Avengers,FF,X-Men . . 8.00
3 AxR,FF vs Galactus 8.00
4 AxR,Final issue 8.00

Marvel Saga #1
© Marvel Entertainment Group

MARVEL SAGA
Dec., 1985
1 JBy,Fantastic Four,Wolv. 3.00
2 Hulk 2.50
3 Spider-Man 3.00
4 X-Men 3.00
5 thru 24 . . . . @2.50
25 O:Silver Surfer,Dec.,1987 . . . . . 2.75

MARVEL SELECT
Flipbook, June, 2005
1 Astonishing X-Men #1
    & New X-men: Academy X #1 . . 4.00
2 Aston.X-Men#2 & Acad.X#2 . . . . 4.00
3 Aston.X-Men#3 & Acad.X#3 . . . . 4.00
4 Aston.x-men#4 & Acad.x#4 . . . . . 4.00
5 Aston.X-Men#5 & Acad.X#5 . . . . 4.00
6 thru 18 . . . . @4.00

MARVEL SELECTS: FANTASTIC FOUR
Nov., 1999
1 (of 12) 2.75
2 rep. Vol. 1, #108, AD(c) 2.75
3 rep. Vol. 1, #109, AD(c) 2.75
4 rep. Vol. 1, #110, AD(c) 2.75
5 rep. Vol. 1, #111, AD(c) 2.75
6 rep. Vol. 1, #112, AD(c) 2.75

MARVEL SELECTS: SPIDER-MAN
Nov., 1999
1 (of 12) 2.75
2 rep. Amaz.Sp-M #101 . . . . 2.75
3 rep. Amaz.Sp-M #102 . . . . 2.75
4 rep. Amaz.Sp-M #103 . . . . 2.75
5 rep. Amaz.Sp-M #104 . . . . 2.75
6 rep. Amaz.Sp-M #105 . . . . 2.75

MARVEL: SHADOWS & LIGHT
B&W 1996
1-shot MGo,JPL,KJ,48-pg. 3.00

MARVEL 1602
Aug., 2003–March, 2004
1 thru 7 NGa(s),NKu . . . . @3.50
8 NGa(s),NKu,48-pg. 4.00

MARVEL 1602: FANTASTICK FOUR
Sept., 2006
1 V:Count Otto von Doom 3.50
2 thru 3 . . . . @3.50
4 PDd(s) 3.50
5 PDd(s) 3.50

MARVEL 1602: NEW WORLD
Aug., 2005
1 (of 5) Bruce David Banner 3.50
2 Peter Parquagh 3.50
3 Superpowers outlawed 3.50
4 Lord Iron vs. Hulk 3.50
5 War in Roanoke 3.50

MARVEL 65th ANNIVERSARY
Sept., 2004
Spec. F:Sub-Mariner,Human
    Torch,48-pg. 5.00

MARVEL SPECTACULAR
Aug., 1973–Nov., 1975
1 JK,rep Thor #128 . . . . 15.00
2 thru 10 rep.Thor#129–#139 . . . @7.00
11 thru 19 rep Thor #140–#148 . . @6.00

MARVEL SPOTLIGHT
[1st Regular Series] Nov., 1971
1 NA(c)WW,F:Red Wolf 75.00
2 MP,BEv,NA,I&O:Werewolf 375.00
3 MP,F:Werewolf 100.00

4 SD,MP,F:Werewolf 100.00
5 SD,MP,I&O:Ghost Rider 450.00
6 MP,TS,F:Ghost Rider 75.00
7 MP,TS,F:Ghost Rider 75.00
8 JM,MB,F:Ghost Rider 75.00
9 TA,F:Ghost Rider 50.00
10 SD,JM,F:Ghost Rider 50.00
11 SD,F:Ghost Rider 50.00
12 SD,2nd A:Son of Satan 50.00
13 F:Son of Satan 18.00
14 JM,F:Son of Satan,I:Ikthalon . . 18.00
15 JM, F:Son of Satan,
    I:Baphomet 15.00
16 JM,F:Son of Satan 15.00
17 JM,F:Son of Satan 15.00
18 F:Son of Satan, I:Allatou 15.00
19 F:Son of Satan 15.00
20 F:Son of Satan 15.00
21 F:Son of Satan 15.00
22 F:Son of Satan, Ghost Rider . . 18.00
23 F:Son of Satan 15.00
24 JM,F:Son of Satan 15.00
25 GT,F:Sinbad 15.00
26 F:The Scarecrow 12.00
27 F:The Sub-Mariner 22.00
28 F:Moon Knight (1st full solo) . . 50.00
29 F:Moon Knight 40.00
30 JSt,JB,F:Warriors Three 22.00
31 HC,JSn,F:Nick Fury 22.00
32 I:Spiderwoman, Jessica Drew . 22.00
33 F:Deathlok, I:Devilslayer 10.00

[2nd Regular Series] 1979
1 PB,F:Captain Marvel 4.00
1a No`1' on Cover 12.00
2 FM(c),F:Captain Marvel,A:Eon . . 3.00
3 PB,F:Captain Marvel 3.00
4 PB,F:Captain Marvel 3.00
5 FM(c),SD,F:Dragon Lord 3.00
6 F:Star Lord 3.00
7 FM(c),F:StarLord 3.00
8 FM,F:Captain Marvel 7.00
9 FM(c),SD,F:Captain Universe . . . 3.00
10 SD,F:Captain Universe 3.00
11 SD,F:Captain Universe 3.00

Dec., 2005
1 John Cassady & Saen McKeever 3.00
2 Warren Ellis, Jim Cheung 3.00
3 Joss Whedon & Michael Lark . . . 3.00
4 David Finch & Roberto
    Aquirre-Sacasa 3.00
5 Daniel Way & Olivier Coipel 3.00
6 Mark Millar & Steve McNiven . . . 3.00
7 Neil Gaiman & Salvador Laroca . 3.00

Marvel Spotlight-2nd Series #3
© Marvel Entertainment Group

---

8 Robert Kirkman & Greg Land . . . 3.00	
9 Ed Brubaker & Billy Tan. 3.00	
10 Stan Lee & Jack Kirby 3.00	
11 Brian Michael Bendis &	
Mark Bagley 3.00	

Dec., 2006

Spec. Ghost Rider (2006) 3.00
Spec. Dark Tower (2007) 3.00
Spec. Spider-Man, Back in Black. . . 3.00
Spec. Fantastic Four (2007) 3.00
Spec. Halo (2007) 3.00
Spec. World War Hulk (2007) 3.00
Spec. Thor (2007) JR2. . . . . 3.00
Spec. Marvel Zombies (2007) 3.00
Spec. Spider-Man One More Day/
    Brand New Day 3.00
Spec. Messiah Complex (2008). . . . 3.00
Spec. Ultimates 3 (2008) 3.00
Spec. Laurell K. Hamilton/ George
    R.R. Martin 3.00
Spec. Iron Man Movie (2008) 3.00
Spec. Hulk Movie (5-2008) 3.00
Spec. Secret Invasion (6-2008) . . . 3.00
Spec. Uncanny X-Men 500 issues
    Celebration (7-2008) 3.00
Spec. Spider-Man Brand New Day . 3.00
Spec. Marvel Knights 10th Anniv. . . 3.00
Spec. Ultimatum (10-2008) 3.00
Spec. Punisher Movie (11-2008) . . . 3.00

MARVEL SPOTLIGHT:
CIVIL WAR
May, 2007

1-shot Civil War Remembered. . . . 12.00
1-shot, Aftermath, 48-pgs. 12.00

MARVEL SPOTLIGHT ON

CAPTAIN AMERICA
1 thru 4, Captain America rep. . . @3.00

...DR. STRANGE
1 thru 4, Dr. Strange, rep. . . . . . . @3.00

...SILVER SURFER
1 thru 4, Silver Surfer, rep. . . . . . @3.00

MARVEL SUPER ACTION
Jan., 1976

1-shot TD,GE,FS,MP,HC,F:Punisher,
    Weirdworld,Dominic Fortune,
    I:Huntress(Mockingbird) 100.00

May, 1977–Nov., 1981

1 JK,reprint,Capt.America #100 . . 15.00
2 JK,reprint,Capt.America #101 . . 10.00
3 JK,reprint,Capt.America #102 . . 10.00
4 BEv,RH,reprint,Marvel Boy #1. . 10.00
5 JK,reprint,Capt.America #103 . . 10.00
6 JK,reprint,Capt.America #104 . . . 8.00
7 JK,reprint,Capt.America #105 . . . 8.00
8 JK,reprint,Capt.America #106 . . . 8.00
9 JK,reprint,Capt.America #107 . . . 8.00
10 JK,reprint,Capt.America #108. . . 8.00
11 JK,reprint,Capt.America #109 . . . 8.00
12 JSo,reprint,Capt.America #110. . 8.00
13 JSo,reprint,Capt.America #111 . . 8.00
14 JB,reprint,Avengers #55 . . . . . . 8.00
15 JB,reprint,Avengers #56 . . . . . . 8.00
16 Reprint,Avengers,annual #2 . . . 5.00
17 Reprint,Avengers # 5.00
18 JB(c),reprint,Avengers #57 . . . . 5.00
19 JB(c),reprint,Avengers #58 . . . . 5.00
20 JB(c),reprint,Avengers #59 . . . . 5.00
21 Reprint,Avengers #60 . . . . 4.00
22 JB(c),reprint,Avengers #61 . . . . 4.00
23 Reprint,Avengers #63 . . . . 4.00
24 Reprint,Avengers #64 . . . . 4.00
25 Reprint,Avengers #65 . . . . 4.00
26 Reprint,Avengers #66 . . . . 4.00
27 BWS,Reprint,Avengers #67 . . . . 4.00
28 BWS,Reprint,Avengers #68 . . . . 4.00

29 Reprint,Avengers #69 . . . . 4.00
30 Reprint,Avengers #70 . . . . 4.00
31 Reprint,Avengers #71 . . . . 4.00
32 Reprint,Avengers #72 . . . . 4.00
33 Reprint,Avengers #73 . . . . 4.00
34 Reprint,Avengers #74 . . . . 4.00
35 JB(c),Reprint,Avengers #75 . . . . 4.00
36 JB(c),Reprint,Avengers #75 . . . . 4.00
37 JB(c),Reprint,Avengers #76 . . . . 4.00

MARVEL SUPERHEROES
Oct., 1966

1-shot Rep. D.D. #1, Avengers #2,
    Marvel Mystery #8 . . . . 200.00

MARVEL SUPER-HEROES
[1st Regular Series] 1967–71
(Prev.: Fantasy Masterpieces)

12 GC,I&O:Captain Marvel 225.00
13 GC,2nd A:Captain Marvel. . . . 125.00
14 F:Spider-Man 175.00
15 GC,F:Medusa 75.00
16 I:Phantom Eagle 75.00
17 O:Black Knight 75.00
18 GC,I:Guardians o/t Galaxy . . . 100.00
19 F:Ka-Zar 45.00
20 F:Dr.Doom,Diablo 65.00
21 thru 31 reprints . . . . @25.00
32 thru 55 rep. Hulk/Submariner
    from Tales to Astonish . . . . . @10.00
56 reprints Hulk #102. . . . . 7.00
57 thru 105 reps.Hulk issues . . . . @7.00

MARVEL SUPERHEROES
[2nd Regular Series] May, 1990

1 RLm,F:Hercules,Moon Knight,
    Magik,Bl.Panther,Speedball. . . . 7.00
2 . . . . 3.50
3 F:Captain America,Hulk,Wasp. . . 4.00
4 AD,F:SpM,N.Fury,D.D.,Speedball
    Wond.Man,Spitfire,Bl.Knight . . . 3.50
5 F:Thor,Thing,Speedball,
    Dr.Strange 3.50
6 RB,SD,F:X-Men,Power Pack,
    Speedball,Sabra 3.00
7 RB,F:X-Men,Cloak & Dagger . . . 2.75
8 F:X-Men,Iron Man,Namor 2.75
9 F:Avengers W.C,Thor,Iron Man . . 3.00
10 DH,F:Namor,Fantastic Four,
    Ms.Marvel#24 . . . . 3.50
11 F:Namor,Ms.Marvel#25 . . . . . . 3.00
12 F:Dr.Strange,Falcon,Iron Man. . . 3.00
13 F:Iron Man 3.00
14 BMc,RWi,F:Iron Man,
    Speedball, Dr.Strange 3.00
15 KP,DH,F:Thor,Iron Man,Hulk . . . 3.00
Holiday Spec.#1 AAd,DC,JRu,F:FF,
    X-Men,Spider-Man,Punisher . . . 3.25
Holiday Spec.#2 AAd(c),SK,MGo,
    RLm,SLi,F:Hulk,Wolverine,
    Thanos,Spider-Man 3.25
Fall Spec.RB,A:X-Men,Shroud,
    Marvel Boy,Cloak & Dagger . . . 3.00

MARVEL SUPERHEROES
MEGAZINE

1 thru 6 rep.. . . . . @3.00

MARVEL SUPER SPECIAL
See: MARVEL COMICS

MARVEL SWIMSUIT
1992

1 Schwing Break. 10.00

MARVEL TAILS
Nov., 1983

1 ST,Peter Porker 5.00

Marvel Tales #40
© *Marvel Entertainment Group*

MARVEL TALES
1964

1 All reprints,O:Spider-Man. 600.00
2 rep.Avengers #1,X-Men #1,
    Hulk #3 . . . . 300.00
3 rep.Amaz.SpM.#6 . . . . 150.00
4 rep.Amaz.SpM.#7 . . . . 100.00
5 rep.Amaz.SpM.#8 . . . . 100.00
6 rep.Amaz.SpM.#9 . . . . 100.00
7 rep.Amaz.SpM.#10 . . . . 100.00
8 rep.Amaz.SpM.#13 . . . . 75.00
9 rep.Amaz.SpM.#14 . . . . 75.00
10 rep.Amaz.SpM.#15 . . . . 75.00
11 rep.Amaz.SpM.#16 . . . . 75.00
12 rep.Amaz.SpM.#17 . . . . 75.00
13 rep.Amaz.SpM.#18
    rep.1950's Marvel Boy 75.00
14 rep.Amaz.SpM.#19,
    reps.Marvel Boy 50.00
15 rep.Amaz.SpM.#20,
    reps.Marvel Boy 50.00
16 rep.Amaz.SpM.#21,
    reps.Marvel Boy. 50.00
17 thru 22 rep.Amaz.SpM.
    #22-#27 . . . . @50.00
23 thru 27 rep.Amaz.SpM.
    #30-#34 . . . . @50.00
28 rep.Amaz.SpM.#35&36 . . . . . . 50.00
29 rep.Amaz.SpM.#39&40 . . . . . . 50.00
30 rep.Amaz.SpM.#58&41 . . . . . . 50.00
31 rep.Amaz.SpM.#42 . . . . 50.00
32 rep.Amaz.SpM.#43&44 . . . . . . 50.00
33 rep.Amaz.SpM.#45&47 . . . . . . 50.00
34 rep.Amaz.SpM.#48 . . . . 15.00
35 rep.Amaz.SpM.#49 . . . . 15.00
36 thru 41 rep.
    Amaz.SpM#51-#56 . . . . @15.00
42 thru 53 rep.
    Amaz.SpM#59-#70 . . . . @15.00
54 thru 80 rep.
    Amaz.SpM#73-#99 . . . . @15.00
81 rep.Amaz.SpM.#103 . . . . 15.00
82 rep.Amaz.SpM.#103-4 . . . . . . 15.00
83 thru 97 rep.
    Amaz.SpM.#104-#118. . . . . . @15.00
98 rep.Amaz.SpM.#121 . . . . 15.00
99 rep.Amaz.SpM.#122 . . . . 15.00
100 rep.Amaz.SpM.#123,BU:Two
    Gun Kid,Giant-Size 4.00
101 thru 105 rep.Amaz.
    SpM.#124-#128 . . . . @4.00
106 rep.Amaz.SpM.#129,
    (I:Punisher) 4.00

Marvel Tales #188
© Marvel Entertainment Group

107 thur 110 rep.Amaz.
  SpM.#130-133 . . . . @4.00
111 Amaz.SpM#134,A:Punisher. . . 4.00
112 Amaz.SpM#135,A:Punisher . . . 4.00
113 thru 125 rep.Amaz.Spider
  Man #136-#148 . . . . @4.00
126 rep.Amaz.Spider-Man#149 . . . . 4.00
127 rep.Amaz.Spider-Man#150 . . . . 4.00
128 rep.Amaz.Spider-Man#151 . . . . 4.00
129 thru 136 rep.Amaz.Spider
  Man #152-#159 . . . . @4.00
137 rep.Amaz.Fantasy#15 . . . . 7.00
138 rep.Amaz.SpM.#1 . . . . 7.00
139 thru 149 rep.
  AmazSpM#2-#12 . . . . @4.00
150 rep.AmazSpM Ann#1 . . . . 4.00
151 rep.AmazSpM#13 . . . . 4.00
152 rep.AmazSpM#14 . . . . 4.00
153 thru 190
  rep.AmazSpM#15 52 . . . . @2.50
191 rep. #96-98 . . . . 2.50
192 rep. #121-122 . . . . 2.50
193 thru 198 rep.Marv.Team
  Up#59-64 . . . . @2.50
199 . . . . 2.50
200 rep. SpM Annual 14 . . . . 2.50
201 thru 206 rep.Marv.
  Team Up#65-70 . . . . @2.50
207 thru 208 . . . . @2.50
209 MZ(c),rep.SpM#129,Punisher. . 3.00
210 MZ(c),rep.SpM#134 . . . . 4.00
211 MZ(c),rep.SpM#135 . . . . 4.00
212 MZ(c),rep.Giant-Size#4. . . . . . 4.00
213 MZ(c),rep.Giant-Size#4 . . . . . . 4.00
214 MZ(c),rep.SpM#161 . . . . 4.00
215 MZ(c),rep.SpM#162 . . . . 3.00
216 MZ(c),rep.SpM#174 . . . . 3.00
217 MZ(c),rep.SpM#175 . . . . 3.00
218 MZ(c),rep.SpM#201 . . . . 3.00
219 MZ(c),rep.SpM#202 . . . . 3.00
220 MZ(c),rep.Spec.SpM #81 . . . . . 3.00
221 MZ(c),rep.Spec.SpM #82 . . . . . 3.00
222 MZ(c),rep.Spec.SpM #83 . . . . . 2.50
223 thru 227 TM(c),rep.
  SpM #88-92 . . . . @2.50
228 TM(c),rep.Spec.SpM.#17 . . . . . 2.50
229 TM(c),rep.Spec.SpM.#18 . . . . . 2.50
230 TM(c),rep.SpM #203 . . . . 2.50
231 TM(c),rep.Team-Up#108 . . . . . 2.50
232 TM(c),rep. 2.50
233 thru 236 TM(c),rep. X-Men . . @2.50
237 TM(c),rep. 2.50
238 TM(c),rep. 2.50
239 TM(c),rep.SpM,Beast 2.50
240 rep.SpM,Beast,MTU#90 . . . . . 2.50

241 rep.MTU#124 . . . . 2.50
242 rep.MTU#89,Nightcrawler 2.50
243 rep.MTU#117,SpM,Wolverine . . 2.50
244 MR(c),rep. 2.50
245 MR(c),rep. 2.50
246 MR(c),rep. 2.50
247 MR(c),rep.MTU Annual #6 . . . . 2.50
248 MR(c),rep. 2.50
249 MR(c),rep.MTU #14 . . . . 2.50
250 MR(c),rep.MTU #100 . . . . 2.50
251 rep.Amaz.SpM.#100 . . . . 2.50
252 rep.Amaz.SpM.#101 . . . . 3.50
253 rep.Amaz.SpM.#102 . . . . 3.00
254 rep.MTU #15,inc.2 Ghost
  Rider pin-ups by JaL 3.00
255 SK(c),rep.MTU #58,
  BU:Ghost Rider 2.25
256 rep. MTU 2.25
257 rep.Amaz.SpM.#238 . . . . 2.25
258 rep.Amaz.SpM.#239 . . . . 2.25
259 thru 261 rep.Amaz.SpM.#249
  thru #251 . . . . @2.25
262 rep Marvel Team-Up #53 . . . . . 2.25
263 rep Marvel Team-Up #54 . . . . . 2.25
264 rep.B:Amaz.SpM.Ann.#5 . . . . . 2.25
265 rep.E:Amaz.SpM.Ann.#5 . . . . . 2.25
266 thru 275 rep.Amaz.SpM#252
  thru #261 . . . . @2.25
276 rep.Amaz.SpM#263 . . . . 2.25
277 rep.Amaz.SpM#265 . . . . 2.25
278 thru 282 rep.Amaz.SpM #268
  thru #272 . . . . @2.25
283 rep.Amaz.SpM#273 . . . . 2.25
284 thru 287 rep.Amaz.SpM#275
  thru #278 . . . . @2.25
288 rep.Amaz.SpM#280 . . . . 2.25
289 rep.Amaz.SpM#281 . . . . 2.25
290 & 291 rep.Amaz.SpM 2.25

MARVEL TALES
Flipbook, June, 2005

1 Amazing Spider-Man #34
  & Amazing Fantasy #1 . . . . 4.00
2 Amaz.Sp-M#35 & Amaz.Fant.#2 . 4.00
3 Amaz.Sp-M#33 & Amaz.Fant.#3 . 4.00
4 Amaz.sp-m#33 & Amaz.fant.#4 . . 4.00
5 thru 16 . . . . @4.00

MARVEL TALES
See: MARVEL COMICS

MARVEL TEAM-UP
March, 1972
(Spider-Man in all,unless *)

1 RA,F:Hum.Torch,V:Sandman. . 250.00
2 RA,F:Hum.Torch,V:Sandman. . 90.00
3 F:Human Torch,V:Morbius 100.00
4 GK,F:X-Men,A:Morbius 100.00
5 GK,F:Vision 40.00
6 GK,F:Thing,O:Puppet Master,
  V:Mad Thinker 40.00
7 RA,F:Thor 40.00
8 JM,F:The Cat 40.00
9 RA,F:Iron Man 40.00
10 JM,F:Human Torch 40.00
11 JM,F:The Inhumans 20.00
12 RA,F:Werewolf 40.00
13 GK,F:Captain America 30.00
14 GK,F:Sub-Mariner 20.00
15 RA,F:Ghostrider 40.00
16 GK,JM,F:Captain Marvel 20.00
17 GK,F:Mr.Fantastic,
  A:Capt.Marvel 20.00
18 *F:Hulk,Human Torch 20.00
19 SB,F:Ka-Zar 20.00
20 SB,F:Black Panther 17.00
21 SB,F:Dr.Strange 12.00
22 SB,F:Hawkeye 12.00
23 *F:Human Torch,Iceman,
  C:Spider-Man,X-Men 12.00
24 JM,F:Brother Voodoo 12.00

25 JM,F:Daredevil 12.00
26 *F:H.Torch,Thor,V:Lavamen . . . 12.00
27 JM,F:The Hulk 12.00
28 JM,F:Hercules 12.00
29 *F:Human Torch,Iron Man. 12.00
30 JM,F:The Falcon. 12.00
31 JM,F:Iron Fist 12.00
32 *F:Hum.Torch,Son of Satan . . . 12.00
33 SB,F:Nighthawk 12.00
34 SB,F:Valkyrie 12.00
35 SB,*F:H.Torch,Dr.Strange 12.00
36 SB,F:Frankenstein 10.00
37 SB,F:Man-Wolf 10.00
38 SB,F:Beast 10.00
39 SB,F:H.Torch,I:Jean Dewolff. . . 10.00
40 SB,F:Sons of the Tiger 10.00
41 SB,F:Scarlet Witch 10.00
42 SB,F:Scarlet Witch,Vision 10.00
43 SB,F:Dr.Doom. 10.00
44 SB,F:Moon Dragon 10.00
45 SB,F:Killraven 10.00
46 SB,F:Deathlok. 8.00
47 F:The Thing 7.00
48 SB,F:Iron Man,I:Wraith 7.00
49 SB,F:Iron Man 7.00
50 SB,F:Dr.Strange 7.00
51 SB,F:Iron Man. 7.00
52 SB,F:Captain America 7.00
53 1st JBy New X-Men,F:Hulk. . . . 35.00
54 JBy,F:Hulk,V:Woodgod 10.00
55 JBy,F:Warlock,I:Gardener 10.00
56 SB,F:Daredevil 10.00
57 SB,F:Black Widow 10.00
58 SB,F:Ghost Rider,V:Trapster . . 10.00
59 JBy,F:Yellowjacket,V:Equinox . 10.00
60 JBy,F:Wasp,V:Equinox 10.00
61 JBy,F:Human Torch. 10.00
62 JBy,F:Ms.Marvel 10.00
63 JBy,F:Iron Fist. 10.00
64 JBy,F:Daughters o/t Dragon . . 10.00
65 JBy,I:Captain Britain(U.S.)
  I:Arcade 9.00
66 JBy,F:Captain Britain 8.00
67 JBy,F:Tigra,V:Kraven 8.00
68 JBy,F:Man-Thing,I:D'Spayre . . 8.00
69 JBy,F:Havok 8.00
70 JBy,F:Thor. 8.00
71 F:The Falcon,V:Plantman 6.00
72 F:Iron Man 6.00
73 F:Daredevil 6.00
74 BH,F:Not ready for prime time
  players(Saturday Night Live). . . 6.00
75 JBy,F:Power Man 7.00
76 HC,F:Dr.Strange 6.00
77 HC,F:Ms.Marvel 6.00
78 DP,F:Wonderman 6.00
79 JBy,TA,F:Red Sonja 6.00
80 SpM,F:Dr.Strange,Clea 5.00
81 F:Satana 5.00
82 SB,F:Black Widow 6.00
83 SB,F:Nick Fury 5.00
84 SB,F:Master of Kung Fu 5.00
85 SB,F:Bl.Widow,Nick Fury 5.00
86 BMc,F:Guardians o/t Galaxy. . . 4.00
87 GC,F:Black Panther 4.00
88 SB,F:Invisible Girl 4.00
89 RB,F:Nightcrawler 4.50
90 BMc,F:The Beast 4.00
91 F:Ghost Rider 4.00
92 CI,F:Hawkeye,I:Mr.Fear IV . . . 3.50
93 CI,F:Werewolf
  I:Tatterdemalion (named) 4.00
94 MZ,F:Shroud. 3.50
95 I:Mockingbird(Huntress) 4.00
96 F:Howard the Duck 3.50
97 *F:Hulk,Spider-Woman 3.50
98 F:Black Widow 3.50
99 F:Machine Man 3.50
100 FM,JBy,F:F.F.,I:Karma,
  BU:Storm & Bl.Panther 8.00
101 F:Nighthawk 3.00
102 F:Doc Samson,Rhino 3.00

103 F:Antman	3.00
104 *F:Hulk,Ka-zar.	3.00
105 *F:Powerman,Iron Fist,Hulk	3.00
106 HT,F:Captain America	3.00
107 HT,F:She-Hulk.	3.00
108 HT,F:Paladin	3.00
109 HT,F:Dazzler	3.00
110 HT,F:Iron Man	3.00
111 HT,F:Devil Slayer.	3.00
112 HT,F:King Kull	3.00
113 HT,F:Quasar,V:Lightmaster.	3.00
114 KGa,F:Falcon.	3.00
115 HT,F:Thor	3.00
116 HT,F:Valkyrie.	3.00
117 HT:Wolv,V:Prof Power	12.00
118 HT,F:Professor X.	4.00
119 KGa,F:Gargoyle	3.00
120 KGa,F:Dominic Fortune	3.00
121 KGa,F:Human Torch,I:Leap Frog(Frog Man)	3.00
122 KGa,F:Man-Thing.	3.00
123 KGa,F:Daredevil	3.00
124 KGa,F:Beast	3.50
125 KGa,F:Tigra	3.00
126 BH,F:Hulk	3.00
127 KGa,F:Watcher,X-mass issue.	3.00
128 Ph(c)KGa,F:Capt.America.	3.00
129 KGa,F:The Vision	3.00
130 KGa,F:The Scarlet Witch	3.00
131 KGa,F:Leap Frog	3.00
132 KGa,F:Mr.Fantastic.	3.00
133 KGa,F:Fantastic Four	3.00
134 F:Jack of Hearts	3.00
135 F:Kitty Pryde	3.00
136 F:Wonder Man	3.00
137 *F:Aunt May & F.Richards	3.00
138 F:Sandman,I:New Enforcers.	3.00
139 F:Sandman,Nick Fury	3.00
140 F:Black Widow	3.00
141 SpM(2nd App Black Costume) F:Daredevil	12.00
142 F:Captain Marvel(2nd one).	3.00
143 F:Starfox	3.00
144 F:M.Knight,V:WhiteDragon	3.00
145 F:Iron Man	3.00
146 F:Nomad	3.50
147 F:Human Torch	3.00
148 F:Thor	3.00
149 F:Cannonball.	3.00
150 F:X-Men,V:Juggernaut	5.50
Ann.#1 SB,F:New X-Men.	40.00
Ann.#2 F:The Hulk.	10.00
Ann.#3 F:Hulk,PowerMan	7.00
Ann.#4 F:Daredevil,Moon Knight.	5.00
Ann.#5 F:Thing,Scarlet Witch, Quasar,Dr.Strange	5.00
Ann.#6 F:New Mutants,Cloak & Dagger(cont.New Mutants#22)	5.00
Ann.#7 F:Alpha Flight	5.00

MARVEL TEAM-UP
1997

1 TPe,PO,AW, F:Spider-Man, Generation X	2.50
2 TPe,PO,AW, F:Spider-Man & Hercules	2.50
3 TPe,DaR,AW, F:Spider-Man & Sandman	2.50
4 TPe,DaR,F:Spider-Man & Man-Thing	2.50
5 TPe,DaR,F:Spider-Man & Mystery guest	2.50
6 TPe,F:Spider-Man & Sub-Mariner	2.50
7 MWn,TPe,F:Spider-Man & Blade	2.50
8 TPe,F:Sub-Mariner & Doctor Strange	2.50
9 TPe,F:Sub-Mariner & Captain America	2.50
10 TPe,AW,F:Sub Mariner & Thing	2.50
11 TPe,AW,PO,F:Sub-Mariner & Iron Man, final issue	2.50

MARVEL TEAM-UP
Nov., 2004

1 ScK, Golden Child, pt.1	2.50
2 ScK, Golden Child, pt.2	2.50
3 ScK, Fant. Four & Dr. Strange	2.50
4 ScK, Iron Man, Hulk.	2.50
5 Sck, Spider-man, X-23.	2.50
6 ScK,The Golden Child	2.50
7 ScK,Ring of the Master	2.50
8 Sck,Master of the Ring,pt.2	3.00
9 ScK,Master of the Ring,pt.3.	3.00
10 ScK,Master of the Ring,pt.4	3.00
11 Titannus War,pt.1	3.00
12 Titannus War,pt.2	3.00
13 Titannus War,pt.3	3.00
14 F:Spider-Man	3.00
15 League of Losers, pt.1	3.00
16 League of Losers, pt.2	3.00
17 League of Losers, pt.3	3.00
18 League of Losers, pt.4	3.00
19 Wolv. & Cable vs. Ringmaster	3.00
20 Freedom Ring	3.00
21 Freedom Ring	3.00
22 Freedom Ring	3.00
23 Freedom Ring	3.00
24 Freedom Ring	3.00
25 Final Issue	3.00

MARVEL TEAM-UP INDEX
See: OFFICIAL MARVEL
INDEX TO
MARVEL TEAM-UP

MARVEL
Treasury Edition
Sept., 1974

1 SD,Spider-Man,I:Contemplator	75.00
2 JK,F:Fant.Four,Silver Surfer	35.00
3 F:Thor	30.00
4 BWS,F:Conan	30.00
5 O:Hulk	30.00
6 GC,FB,SD,F:Dr.Strange.	30.00
7 JB,JK,F:The Avengers	30.00
8 F:X-Mass stories	30.00
9 F:Super-Hero Team-Up	30.00
10 F:Thor	30.00
11 F:Fantastic Four	20.00
12 F:Howard the Duck	20.00
13 F:X-Mas stories.	20.00
14 F:Spider-Man	22.00
15 BWS,F:Conan,Red Sonja	22.00
16 F:Defenders	20.00
17 F:The Hulk	20.00
18 F:Spider Man,X-Men.	25.00
19 F:Conan	22.00
20 F:Hulk	22.00
21 F:Fantastic Four	22.00
22 F:Spider-Man	25.00
23 F:Conan	22.00
24 F:The Hulk	22.00
25 F:Spider-Man,Hulk	22.00
26 GP,F:Hulk,Wolverine,Hercules	25.00
27 HT,F:Hulk,Spider-Man.	22.00
28 JB,JSt,F:SpM/Superman.	50.00

MARVEL TREASURY
OF OZ
(oversized) 1975

1 JB,movie adapt.	30.00

MARVEL TREASURY
SPECIAL

Vol. I Spider-Man, 1974	30.00
Vol. II Capt. America, 1976	35.00

MARVEL TRIPLE ACTION
Feb., 1972

1 Rep.	40.00

2 thru 5 rep.	@20.00
6 thru 10 rep.	@15.00
11 thru 47 rep.	@9.00
G-Size#1 F:Avengers	10.00
G-Size#2 F:Avengers.	10.00

MARVEL TWO-IN-ONE
Jan., 1974
(Thing in all, unless *)

1 GK,F:Man-Thing	100.00
2 GK,JSt,F:Namor,Namorita	35.00
3 F:Daredevil	35.00
4 F:Capt.America,Namorita	25.00
5 F:Guardians of the Galaxy.	25.00
6 F:Dr.Strange.	25.00
7 F:Valkyrie.	15.00
8 F:Ghost Rider	25.00
9 F:Thor	15.00
10 KJ,F:Black Widow	15.00
11 F:Golem	10.00
12 F:Iron Man	10.00
13 F:Power Man	10.00
14 F:Son of Satan	11.00
15 F:Morbius	11.00
16 F:Ka-Zar	10.00
17 F:Spider-Man	10.00
18 F:Spider-Man	10.00
19 F:Tigra	10.00
20 F:The Liberty Legion.	10.00
21 F:Doc Savage	7.00
22 F:Thor,Human Torch	7.00
23 F:Thor,Human Torch	7.00
24 SB,F:Black Goliath	7.00
25 F:Iron Fist	7.00
26 F:Nick Fury	7.00
27 F:Deathlok.	7.00
28 F:Sub-Mariner.	8.00
29 F:Master of Kung Fu	7.00
30 JB,F:Spiderwoman	15.00
31 F:Spiderwoman.	7.00
32 F:Invisible girl	7.00
33 F:Modred the Mystic.	7.00
34 F:Nighthawk,C:Deathlok.	7.00
35 F:Skull the Slayer	7.00
36 F:Mr.Fantastic.	7.00
37 F:Matt Murdock.	7.00
38 F:Daredevil.	7.00
39 F:The Vision	7.00
40 F:Black Panther	7.00
41 F:Brother Voodoo	5.00
42 F:Captain America	5.00
43 JBy,F:Man-Thing.	6.00
44 GD,F:Hercules	4.00

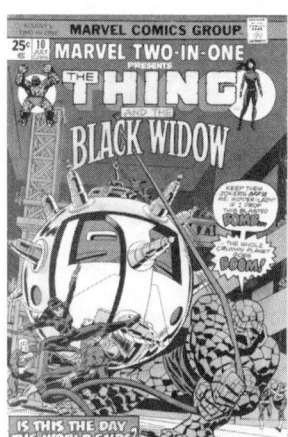

Marvel Two-In-One #10
© Marvel Entertainment Group

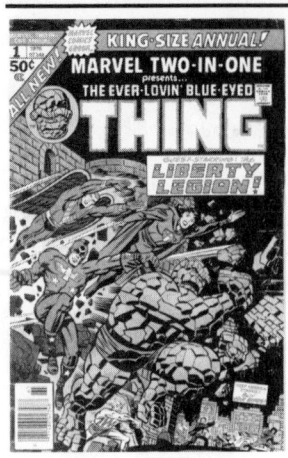

Marvel Two-In-One-Ann. #1
© Marvel Entertainment Group

45 GD,F:Captain Marvel 5.00
46 F:The Hulk 12.00
47 GD,F:Yancy Street Gang,
   I:Machinesmith 4.00
48 F:Jack of Hearts 4.00
49 GD,F:Dr.Strange 4.00
50 JBy,JS,F:Thing & Thing 4.00
51 FM,BMc,F:Wonderman,Nick
   Fury, Ms.Marvel 8.00
52 F:Moon Knight,I:Crossfire 4.00
53 JBy,JS,F:Quasar,C:Deathlok . . . 4.00
54 JBy,JS,D:Deathlok,
   I:Grapplers 11.00
55 JBy,JS,I:New Giant Man 4.00
56 GP,GD,F:Thundra 3.00
57 GP,GD,F:Wundarr 3.00
58 GP,GD,I:Aquarian,A:Quasar . . . 3.00
59 F:Human Torch 3.00
60 GP,GD,F:Impossible Man,
   I:Impossible Woman 3.00
61 GD,F:Starhawk,I&O:Her 4.00
62 GD,F:Moondragon 4.00
63 GD,F:Warlock 4.00
64 DP,GD,F:Stingray,
   I:Serpent Squad 3.00
65 GP,GD,F:Triton 3.00
66 GD,F:Scarlet Witch,
   V:Arcade 3.00
67 F:Hyperion,Thundra 3.00
68 F:Angel,V:Arcade 3.00
69 GD,F:Guardians o/t Galaxy . . . 3.00
70 F:The Inhumans 3.00
71 F:Mr.Fantastic,I:Deathurge,
   Maelstrom 3.00
72 F:Stingray 3.00
73 F:Quasar 3.00
74 F:Puppet Master,Modred 3.00
75 F:The Avengers,O:Blastaar 4.00
76 F:Iceman,O:Ringmaster 3.00
77 F:Man-Thing 3.00
78 F:Wonder Man 3.00
79 F:Blue Diamond,I:Star Dancer . . 3.00
80 F:Ghost Rider 3.50
81 F:Sub-Mariner 2.50
82 F:Captain America 2.50
83 F:Sasquatch 3.50
84 F:Alpha Flight 3.50
85 F:Giant-Man 3.00
86 O:Sandman 3.00
87 F:Ant-Man 3.00
88 F:She-Hulk 3.00
89 F:Human Torch 3.00
90 F:Spider-Man 4.00
91 V:Sphinx 3.00

92 F:Jocasta,V:Ultron 3.00
93 F:Machine Man,D:Jocasta 3.00
94 F:Power Man,Iron Fist 3.00
95 F:Living Mummy 3.00
96 F:Sandman,C:Marvel Heroes . . 3.00
97 F:Iron Man 3.00
98 F:Franklin Richards 3.00
99 JBy(c),F:Rom 3.00
100 F:Ben Grimm 4.00
Ann.#1 SB,F:Liberty Legion 15.00
Ann.#2 JSn,2nd D:Thanos,A:Spider
   Man,Avengers,Capt.Marvel,
   I:Lord Chaos,Master Order . . . 60.00
Ann.#3 F:Nova 7.00
Ann.#4 F:Black Bolt 7.00
Ann.#5 F:Hulk,V:Pluto 5.00
Ann.#6 I:American Eagle 4.00
Ann.#7 I:Champion,A:Hulk,Thor,
   DocSamson,Colossus,Sasquatch,
   Wonder Man 4.00

MARVEL TWO-IN-ONE
July, 2007
1 . . . . 5.00
2 thru 5 64-pg . . . . @5.00
6 thru 17 . . . . @5.00

MARVEL UNIVERSE:
OFFICIAL HANDBOOK TO
Jan., 1983
1 Abomination-Avengers'
   Quintet 7.50
2 BaronMordo-Collect.Man 6.00
3 Collector-Dracula 5.00
4 Dragon Man-Gypsy Moth 5.00
5 Hangman-Juggernaut 5.00
6 K-L 4.00
7 Mandarin-Mystique 4.00
8 Na,oria-Pyro 4.00
9 Quasar to She-Hulk 4.00
10 Shiar-Sub-Mariner 4.00
11 Subteraneans-Ursa Major 4.00
12 Valkyrie-Zzzax 4.00
13 Book of the Dead 4.00
14 Book of the Dead 4.00
15 Weaponry 4.00

[2nd Series] 1985
1 Abomination-Batroc 5.00
2 Beast-Clea 4.00
3 Cloak & D.-Dr.Strange 4.00
4 Dr.Strange-Galactus 4.00
5 Gardener-Hulk 4.00
6 Human Torch-Ka-Zar 3.25
7 Kraven-Magneto 3.25
8 Magneto-Moleman 3.25
9 Moleman-Owl 3.25
10 . . . . 3.25
11 . . . . 3.00
12 S-T 3.00
13 . . . . 3.00
14 V-Z 3.00
15 . . . . 3.00
16 Book of the Dead 3.00
17 Handbook of the Dead,inc.
   JLe illus. 3.00
18 . . . . 3.00
19 . . . . 3.00
20 Inc.RLd illus. 3.00

Marvel Universe Update
1 thru 8 . . . . @3.00

Marvel Universe Packet
1 inc. Spider-Man 5.50
2 inc. Captain America 4.50
3 inc. Ghost Rider 5.00
4 inc. Wolverine 4.50
5 inc. Punisher 4.25
6 inc. She-Hulk 4.00
7 inc. Daredevil 4.00
8 inc. Hulk 4.00
9 inc. Moon Knight 4.00

10 inc. Captain Britain 4.00
11 inc. Storm 4.00
12 inc. Silver Surfer 4.00
13 inc. Ice Man 4.50
14 inc. Thor 4.00
15 thru 22 . . . . @4.50
23 inc. Cage 4.50
24 inc. Iron Fist 4.50
25 inc.Deadpool,Night Thrasher . . . 4.50
26 inc. Wonder Man 5.00
27 inc.Beta Ray Bill,Pip 5.00
28 inc.X-Men 5.00
29 inc.Carnage 5.00
30 thru 36 . . . . @5.00

MARVEL UNIVERSE
1996
1 Post Onslaught 3.25
April, 1998
1 CPa(c),RSt,SEp,AW,F:Human
   Torch,Capt.Am.,Namor,48-pg . . . 3.00
2A JBy(c),RSt,SEp,AW,V:Hydra,
   Baron Strucker 2.50
2B DGb(c) 2.50
3 RSt,SEp,AW,V:Hydra 2.50
4 RSt,MM, all-star jam cover,
   F:Monster Hunters 2.50
5 MM,RSt,F:The Monster Hunters . 2.50
6 MM,RSt,F:Monster Hunters,pt.3 . 2.50
7 MM,RSt,F:Monster Hunters,pt.4 . 2.50

MARVEL UNIVERSE:
MILLENNIAL VISIONS
Dec., 2001
Spec.2001 48-page 4.00

MARVEL UNIVERSE:
THE END
March, 2003
1 (of 6) JSn,AM 2.50
2 JSn,AM 2.50
3 thru 6 JSn,AM . . . . @3.00

MARVEL
VALENTINE'S SPECIAL
1997
1-shot MWa,TDF, 48-pg 3.00

MARVEL WESTERNS
July., 2006
1 Three new tales 4.00
2 Kid Colt & Arizona Annie 4.00
3 Two-Gun Kid 4.00
4 The Black 4.00
Spec. Outlaw Files #1 . . . . 4.00

MARVEL X-MEN
COLLECTION
1994
1 thru 3 JL from the 1st series
   X-Men Cards . . . . @3.25

MARVEL YOUNG GUNS
SKETCH BOOK
Dec., 2004
2004 . . . . 3.00

MARVEL ZOMBIES
Dec., 2005
1 . . . . 3.50
1a 2nd printing 10.00
1b 3rd & 4th printing . . . . @5.00
2 Avengers 5.00
3 Hulk 10.00
4 X-Men 7.00

5 Spider-Man 9.00
2 thru 5 2nd printings . . . . @3.00

MARVEL ZOMBIES
Mar., 2007
1 Army of Darkness x-over 10.00
1a 2nd printing 4.00
2 Army of Darkness x-over 4.00
3 Army of Darkness x-over 4.00
4 Army of Darkness x-over 4.00
5 Army of Darkness x-over 4.00
Spec. Dead Days 4.00
Spec. Book of Angels, Demons 4.00

MARVEL ZOMBIES 2
Oct., 2007
1 (of 5) Marvel Zombies Civil War . 4.00
2 thru 5 . . . . @4.00

MARVEL ZOMBIES 3
Oct., 2008
1 (of 4) 4.00
2 . . . . 4.00

MARVELOUS ADVENTURES OF GUS BEEZER
April, 2003
Spec. F:Spider-Man 3.00
Spec. F:X-Men 3.00
Spec. F:The Hulk 3.00

MARVILLE
Sept., 2002
1 U-Decide 3.00
1b foil (c) 40-pg. 4.00
1c variant foil (c) 4.00
2 thru 6 . . . . @2.50
5a thru 6a MBr,variant (c) . . . . . . @2.50
7 . . . . 3.00

MARVIN MOUSE
Marvel Atlas, Sept., 1957
1 BEv,F:Marvin Mouse 150.00

MARY JANE
June, 2004
1 thru 4 . . . . 2.50
Digest Vol. 1 Circle of Friends 6.00

Mary Jane #2
© Marvel Entertainment Group

MARY JANE: HOMECOMING
March, 2005
1 (of 4) The Cheating Thing 3.00
2 the Friendship Thing 3.00
3 The Regret Thing 3.00
4 The Homecoming Thing 3.00
Digest Vol. 2 Homecoming 7.00

MASTER OF KUNG FU, SPECIAL MARVEL ED.
April, 1974
Prev: Special Marvel Edition
17 JSn,I:Black Jack Tarr 40.00
18 PG,1st Gulacy Art 20.00
19 PG,A:Man-Thing 22.00
20 GK(c),PG,AM,V:Samurai 15.00
21 AM,Season of Vengeance..
　Moment of Death 12.00
22 PG,DA,Death 12.00
23 AM,KJ,River of Death 12.00
24 JSn,WS,AM,ST,Night of the
　Assassin 15.00
25 JSt(c),PG,ST,Fists Fury...
　Rites of Death 12.00
26 KP,ST,A:Daughter of
　Fu Manchu 12.00
27 SB,FS,A:Fu Manchu 12.00
28 EH,ST,Death of a Spirit 12.00
29 PG,V:Razor-Fist 12.00
30 PG,DA,Pit of Lions 12.00
31 GK&DA(c),PG,DA,Snowbuster . 12.00
32 GK&ME(c),SB,ME,Assault on an
　Angry Sea 12.00
33 PG,Messenger of Madness,
　I:Leiko Wu 12.00
34 PG,Captive in A Madman's
　Crown 12.00
35 PG,V:Death Hand 12.00
36 The Night of the Ninja's 12.00
37 V:Darkstrider & Warlords of
　the Web 5.00
38 GK(c),PG,A:The Cat 5.00
39 GK(c),PG,A:The Cat 5.00
40 PG,The Murder Agency 5.00
41 . . . . 5.00
42 GK(c),PG,TS,V:Shockwave 5.00
43 PG,V:Shockwave 5.00
44 SB(c),PG,V:Fu Manchu 5.00
45 GK(c),PG,Death Seed 5.00
46 PG,V:Sumo 5.00
47 PG,The Cold White
　Mantle of Death 5.00
48 PG,Bridge of a 1,000 Dooms . . 5.00
49 PG,V:Shaka Kharn,The
　Demon Warrior 5.00
50 PG,V:Fu Manchu 5.00
51 PG(c),To End...To Begin 5.00
52 Mayhem in Morocco 5.00
53 . . . . 5.00
54 JSn(c),Death Wears Three
　Faces 5.00
55 PG(c),The Ages of Death 5.00
56 V:The Black Ninja 5.00
57 V:Red Baron 5.00
58 Behold the Final Mask 5.00
59 GK(c),B:Phoenix Gambit,
　Behold the Angel of Doom 5.00
60 A:Dr.Doom,Doom Came 5.00
61 V:Skull Crusher 4.50
62 Coast of Death 4.50
63 GK&TA(c),Doom Wears
　Three Faces 4.50
64 PG(c),To Challenge a Dragon . . 4.50
65 V:Pavane 4.50
66 V:Kogar 4.50
67 PG(c),Dark Encounters 4.50
68 Final Combats,V:The Cat 4.50
69 . . . . 4.50

Master of Kung Fu #26
© Marvel Entertainment Group

70 A:Black Jack Tarr,Murder
　Mansion 4.50
71 PG(c),Ying & Yang (c) 4.50
72 V:Shockwave 4.50
73 RN(c),V:Behemoths 4.50
74 TA(c),A:Shockwave 4.50
75 Where Monsters Dwell 4.50
76 GD,Battle on the Waterfront 4.00
77 GD,I:Zaran 4.00
78 GD,Moving Targets 4.00
79 GD,This Side of Death 4.00
80 GD,V:Leopard Men 4.00
81 GD,V:Leopard Men 4.00
82 GD,Flight into Fear 4.00
83 GD, ... 4.00
84 GD,V:Fu Manchu 4.00
85 GD,V:Fu Manchu 4.00
86 GD,V:Fu Manchu 4.00
87 GD,V:Zaran, ... 4.00
88 GD,V:Fu Manchu 4.00
89 GD,D:Fu Manchu 4.00
90 MZ,Death in Chinatown 4.00
91 GD,Gang War,drugs 5.00
92 GD,Shadows of the Past 4.00
93 GD,Cult of Death 4.00
94 GD,V:Agent Synergon 4.00
95 GD,Raid 4.00
96 GD,I:Rufus Carter 4.00
97 GD,V:Kung Fu's Dark Side 4.00
98 GD,Fight to the Finish 4.00
99 GD,Death Boat 4.00
100 GD,Doublesize 6.00
101 GD,Not Smoke,Nor Beads,
　Nor Blood 3.75
102 GD,Assassins,1st GD(p) 4.00
103 GD,V:Assassins 3.75
104 GD,Fight without Reason,
　C:Cerberus 3.75
105 GD,I:Razor Fist 3.75
106 GD,C:Velcro 3.75
107 GD,A:Sata 3.75
108 GD 3.75
109 GD,Death is a Dark Agent 3.75
110 GD,Perilous Reign 3.75
111 GD 3.75
112 GD(c),Commit and Destroy 3.75
113 GD(c),V:Panthers 3.75
114 Fantasy o/t Autumn Moon 3.75
115 GD 3.75
116 GD 3.75
117 GD,Devil Deeds Done
　in Darkness 3.75
118 GD,D:Fu Manchu,double 4.50
119 GD 3.75
120 GD,Dweller o/t Dark Stream . . . 3.75

MARVEL

121 Death in the City of Lights	3.00
122	3.00
123 V:Ninjas.....................	3.00
124	3.00
125 double-size	6.00
G-Size#1,CR,PG	20.00
G-Size#2 PG,V:Yellow Claw	3.00
G-Size#3	3.00
G-Size#4 JK,V:Yellow Claw	3.00
Spec.#1 Bleeding Black..........	3.00

MASTER OF KUNG FU:
BLEEDING BLACK
1 V:ShadowHand, 1991 .... 3.00

MASTERS OF TERROR
July–Sept., 1975
1 GM(c),FB,BWS,JSn,NA	30.00
2 JSn(c),GK,VM, ...	25.00

MASTERS OF
THE UNIVERSE
Star, May, 1986—March, 1988
1 I:Hordak....................	7.00
2 thru 11	@4.00
12 D:Skeletor	8.00
Movie #1 GT	2.00

MATT SLADE,
GUNFIGHTER
Atlas, May, 1956
1 AW,AT,F:Matt Slade,Crimson Avenger	250.00
2 AW,A:Crimson Avenger	175.00
3 A:Crimson Avenger	150.00
4 A:Crimson Avenger	125.00
Becomes:	

KID SLADE GUNFIGHTER
5 F:Kid Slade	125.00
6	100.00
7 AW,Duel in the Night	110.00
8 July, 1957	100.00

MAVERICK
1997
1 JGz,F:Christopher Nord/David North/Maverick, 48-pg.	3.50
2 JGz,A:Victor Creed and Logan ..	3.00
2a variant cover	3.00
3 JGz,V:Puck & Vindicator	3.00
4 JGz,A:Wolverine	3.00

Maverick #3
© Marvel Entertainment Group

5 JGz,A:The Blob	3.00
6 JGz,V:Sabretooth...........	3.00
7 JGz,V:Sabretooth...........	3.00
8 JGz,V:The Confessor	3.00
9 JGz,Maverick's secrets	3.00
10 JGz,V:Ivan the Terrible, Chris Bradley becomes Bolt	3.00
11 JGz,A:Darkstar,Vanguard, Ursa Major..................	3.00
12 JGz, double sized last issue ...	3.50
1-shot LHa, V:Sabretooth,48-pg....	3.00

MAXIMUM SECURITY
Oct., 2000
1 (of 3) KBk,JOy,x-over	3.00
2 KBk,JOy,x-over	3.00
3 KBk,JOy,x-over,concl.	3.00
Spec. Thor vs. Ego, 64-pg.,SL,JK ..	3.00
Spec. Dangerous Planet	3.00

MEET MISS BLISS
Marvel Atlas, 1955
1	150.00
2 thru 4	@100.00

MEGA MORPHS
Aug., 2005
1 (of 4) Toy tie-in.............	3.00
2	3.00
3 Red Rampage	3.00
4 The Pawns and the Power	3.00

MEKANIX
Oct., 2002
1 (of 6) CCI,F:Kitty Pryde	3.00
2 CCI,back in school...........	3.00
3 thru 6 CCI.	@3.00

MELVIN THE MONSTER
Marvel Atlas, July, 1956
1 JMn	175.00
2 thru 6	@125.00
Becomes:	

DEXTER THE DEMON
Sept., 1957
7 .... 100.00

MEMORIES
Epic
1 Space Adventures 2.50

MENACE
Marvel Atlas, May, 1953
1 RH,BEv,GT,One Head Too Many	1,200.00
2 RH,BEv,GT,JSt,Burton'sBlood .	750.00
3 BEv,RH,JR,The Werewolf	550.00
4 BEv,RH,The Four Armed Man.	550.00
5 BEv,RH,GC,GT,I&O:Zombie ..	800.00
6 BEv,RH,JR,The Graymoor Ghost	500.00
7 JSt,RH,Fresh out of Flesh	450.00
8 RH,The Lizard Man	450.00
9 BEv,The Walking Dead	500.00
10 RH(c),Half Man,Half....	450.00
11 JKz,JR,Locked In,May, 1954 .	450.00

MEN IN ACTION
Marvel Atlas, April, 1952
1 Sweating it Out	250.00
2 US Infantry stories	150.00
3 RH	125.00
4 War stories	100.00
5 JMn,Squad Charge	100.00
6 War stories	100.00
7 RH(c),BK,No Risk Too Great .	150.00
8 JRo(c),They Strike By Night ..	100.00

9 SSh(c),Rangers Strike Back ..	100.00
Becomes:	

BATTLE BRADY
10 SSh(c),F:Battle Brady.......	150.00
11 SSh(c)...................	100.00
12 SSh(c),Death to the Reds....	100.00
13	100.00
14 Final Issue,June, 1953	100.00

MEN IN BLACK
1 ANi, prequel to movie (1997)....	4.00
Spec. Movie Adaptation (1997)	4.00

MEN IN BLACK:
RETRIBUTION
Aug., 1997
1 continuation from movie 4.00

MEN'S ADVENTURES
See: TRUE WESTERN

MEPHISTO vs.
FOUR HEROES
April–July, 1987
1 JB,BWi,A:Fantastic Four	3.50
2 JB,BWi,A:X-Factor...........	3.00
3 JB,AM,A:X-Men.............	3.00
4 JB,BWi,A:Avengers	3.00

METEOR MAN
1993–94
1 R:Meteor Man	2.50
2 V:GhostStrike,Malefactor,Simon .	2.50
3 A:Spider-Man	2.50
4 A:Night Thrasher	2.50
5 Exocet	2.50
6 final issue.................	2.50

[TED McKEEVER'S}
METROPOL
Epic, 1991–92
1 Ted McKeever	3.00
2 thru 12	@3.00

METROPOL A.D.
Epic, 1992
1 R:The Angels...............	3.50
2 V:Demons	3.50
3 V:Nuclear Arsenal	3.50

MICRONAUTS
[1st Series] Jan., 1979
1 MGo,JRu,O:Micronauts........	5.00
2 thru 36 MGo,JRu,Earth	@3.00
37 KG,Nightcrawler	4.00
38 thru 59 GK,1st direct........	@2.50
Ann.#1,SD	2.50
#2 SD......................	2.50

[2nd Series] 1984
1 V:The Makers	2.50
2 thru 20	@2.50

MICRONAUTS
(Special Edition) Dec., 1983
1 MGo/JRu,rep.	3.00
2 MGo/JRu,rep.	3.00
3 & 4 Rep.MG/JRu	@3.00
5 Rep.MG/JRu,April, 1984	3.00

MIDNIGHT MEN
Epic *Heavy Hitters*, 1993
1 HC,I:Midnight Men............	3.00
2 HC,J:Barnett	2.50
3 HC,Pasternak is Midnight Man ..	2.50
4 HC,Last issue	2.50

MIDNIGHT SONS UNLIMITED
1993–95
1 JQ,JBi,MT(c),A:Midnight Sons. . . 4.25
2 BSz(c),F:Midnight Sons. 4.25
3 JR2(c),JS,A:Spider-Man 4.25
4 Siege of Darkness #17,
   D:2nd Ghost Rider. 4.25
5 DQ(s),F:Mordred,Vengeance,
   Morbius,Werewolf,Blaze,
   I:Wildpride 4.25
6 DQ(s),F:Dr.Strange 4.00
7 DQ(s),F:Man-Thing 4.00
8 . . . . 4.00
9 J:Mighty Destroyer. 4.00

MIGHTY AVENGERS
Mar., 2007
1 BMB(s). 5.00
1a 2nd printing 4.00
2 thru 8 BMB(s). . . . . @4.00
9 BMB(s),MBa,A:Doctor Doom. . . 3.00
10 BMB(s),MBa,A:Doctor Doom . . 3.00
11 BMB(s),MBa,V:Doctor Doom . . 3.00
12 BMB(s),Secret Invasion tie-in . . 4.00
13 BMB(s),Secret Invasion tie-in . . 3.00
14 BMB(s),Secret Invasion tie-in . . 3.00
15 BMB(s),Secret Invasion tie-in . . 3.00
16 BMB(s),Secret Invasion tie-in . . 3.00
17 BMB(s),Secret Invasion tie-in . . 3.00
18 BMB(s),Secret Invasion tie-in . . 3.00
19 BMB(s),Secret Invasion tie-in . . 3.00
20 BMB(s),Secret Invasion after . . 3.00

MIGHTY HEROES
Nov., 1997
1-shot SLo, Diaper Man, Rope Man,
   Cuckoo Man, Tornado Man, Strong
   Man, etc. 3.00

MIGHTY MARVEL WESTERN
Oct., 1968
1 JK,All reprints,B:Rawhide Kid
   Kid Colt,Two-Gun Kids 100.00
2 JK,DAy,Beware of the Barker
   Brothers 75.00
3 HT(c),JK,DAy,Walking Death. . . 75.00
4 HT(c),DAy 75.00
5 HT(c),DAy,Ambush 75.00
6 HT(c),DAy Doom in the Desert . 75.00

Mighty Marvel Western #2
© Marvel Entertainment Group

7 DAy,V:MurderousMasquerader . 75.00
8 HT(c),DAy,Rustler's on the
   Range 75.00
9 JSe(c),JK,DAy,V:Dr Danger . . . 75.00
10 OW,DH,Cougar. 75.00
11 V:The Enforcers 50.00
12 JK,V:Blackjack Bordon 55.00
13 V:Grizzly 55.00
14 JK.V:The Enforcers. 55.00
15 Massacre at Medicine Bend . . . 55.00
16 JK,Mine of Death 55.00
17 Ambush at Blacksnake Mesa . . 35.00
18 Six-Gun Thunderer 35.00
19 Reprints cont. 35.00
20 same 35.00
21 same 25.00
22 . . . . 25.00
23 same 25.00
24 JDa,E:Kid Colt 25.00
25 B:Matt Slade 25.00
26 thru 31 Reprints . . . . @25.00
32 JK,AW,Ringo Kid #23 . . . . 20.00
33 thru 36 Reprints . . . . @20.00
37 JK, AW Two-Gun #51 . . . . 20.00
38 thru 45 Reprints . . . . @20.00
46 same,Sept., 1976 . . . . 20.00

[SABAN'S] MIGHTY MORPHIN POWER RANGERS
1 SLo,FaN,New ongoing series . . . 2.50
2 thru 7 . . . . @2.50
Photo Adaptation 3.00

[SABAN'S] MIGHTY MORPHIN POWER RANGERS: NINJA RANGERS/ VR TROOPERS
1 FaN,RLm,JP,flip book 2.50
2 JP,flip book. 2.50
3 thru 6 . . . . @2.50

MIGHTY MOUSE
[1st Series] Fall, 1946
1 Terrytoons Presents 2,400.00
2 . . . . 1,000.00
3 . . . . 600.00
4 Summer, 1947 . . . . 600.00

MIGHTY MOUSE
Oct., 1990
1 EC,Dark Mite Returns 3.00
2 EC,V:The Glove. 2.50
3 EC/JBr(c)Prince Say More 2.50
4 EC/GP(c)Alt.Universe #1. . . . . . 2.50
5 EC,Alt.Universe #2 . . . . 2.50
6 Ferment',A:MacFurline 2.50
7 EC,V:Viral Worm 2.50
8 EC,BAT-BAT:Year One,
   O:Bug Wonder. 2.50
9 EC,BAT-BAT:Year One,
   V:Smoker. 2.50
10 Night o/t Rating Lunatics 2.50

MILLIE THE MODEL
Winter, 1945
1 O:Millie the Model,
   Bowling(c) 1,500.00
2 Totem Pole(c) 750.00
3 Anti-Noise(c) 500.00
4 Bathing Suit(c) 500.00
5 Blame it on Fame 500.00
6 Beauty and the Beast 500.00
7 Bathing Suit(c) 500.00
8 Fancy Dress(c),HK,Hey Look . 500.00
9 Paris(c),BW 600.00

10 Jewelry(c),HK,Hey Look 500.00
11 HK,Giggles and Grins 350.00
12 A;Rusty,Hedy Devine 250.00
13 A;Hedy Devine,HK,Hey Look . 275.00
14 HK,Hey Look. 275.00
15 HK,Hey Look. 250.00
16 HK,Hey Look. 250.00
17 thru 20 . . . . @275.00
21 thru 75. . . . . @225.00
76 thru 99. . . . . @150.00
100 . . . . 200.00
101 thru 126. . . . . @150.00
127 Millie/Clicker. 165.00
128 A:Scarlet Mayfair. 125.00
129 The Truth about Agnes 125.00
130 thru 153. . . . . @125.00
154 B:New Millie 125.00
155 thru 206. . . . . @125.00
207 Dec., 1973 . . . . 125.00
Ann.#1 How Millie Became
   a Model 450.00
Ann.#2 Millies Guide to
   the World of Modeling 300.00
Ann.#3 Many Lives of Millie. . . . 200.00
Ann.#4 Many Lives of Millie. . . . 175.00

MISS AMERICA COMICS
1944
1 Miss America(c),pin-ups . . . 2,700.00

MISS AMERICA MAGAZINE
Nov., 1944—Nov., 1958
2 Ph(c),Miss America costume
   I;Patsy Walker,Buzz Baxter,
   Hedy Wolfe 2,000.00
3 Ph(c),A:Patsy Walker,Miss
   America 800.00
4 Ph(c),Betty Page,A:Patsy
   Walker,Miss America 800.00
5 Ph(c),A:Patsy Walker,Miss
   America 800.00
6 Ph(c),A:Patsy Walker. 350.00
7 Patsy Walker stories 175.00
8 same 175.00
9 same 175.00
10 same 175.00
11 same 175.00
12 same 175.00
13 thru 18 . . . . @175.00
21 . . . . 200.00
22 thru 93 . . . . @125.00

MISS FURY COMICS
Marvel Timely, Winter, 1942-43
1 Newspaper strip reprints,
   ASh(c) O:Miss Fury 6,500.00
2 V:Nazis(c) 3,000.00
3 Hitler/Nazi Flag(c) 2,500.00
4 ASh(c),Japanese(c) 2,000.00
5 ASh(c),Gangster(c) 1,600.00
6 ASh(c),Gangster(c). 1,600.00
7 Gangster(c) 1,200.00
8 Atom-Bomb Secrets(c)
   Winter, 1946 . . . . 1,200.00

MISSION: IMPOSSIBLE
May, 1996
1 RLd,MWn(s),Movie adapt. 3.00

MISTY
Star, Dec., 1985
1 F:Millie the Models Niece 3.50
2 thru 5 . . . . @3.50
6 May, 1986 . . . . 3.50

MITZI COMICS
Marvel Timely, Spring, 1948
1 HK:Hey Look,Giggles
　and Grins 350.00
Becomes:

MITZI'S BOYFRIEND
2 F:Chip,Mitzi/Chip(c) 200.00
3 Chips adventures 125.00
4 thru 7 same . . . . @125.00
Becomes:

MITZI'S ROMANCES
8 Mitzi/Chip(c) 125.00
9 . . . . 100.00
10 Dec., 1949 . . . . 100.00

MODELING WITH MILLIE
See: DATE WITH MILLIE

MOEBIUS
Epic, Oct., 1987
1 . . . . 12.00
2 . . . . 12.00
3 . . . . 15.00
4 . . . . 12.00
5 . . . . 12.00
6 1988 . . . . 12.00

MOEBIUS: FUSION
1 128-pg. Sketchbook 20.00

Molly Manton's Romances #1
© Marvel Entertainment Group

MOLLY MANTON'S ROMANCES
Sept., 1949
1 Ph(c),Dare Not Marry 225.00
2 Ph(c),Romances of 150.00
Becomes:

ROMANTIC AFFAIRS
3 Ph(c) 125.00

MOMENT OF SILENCE
Dec., 2001
Spec. 9-11-01 tribute issue 3.50

THE MONKEY AND THE BEAR
Marvel Atlas, 1953
1 . . . . 100.00
2 . . . . 65.00

MONSTER MENACE
1 thru 4 SD,rep . . . . @3.00

MONSTER OF FRANKENSTEIN
Jan., 1973
1 MP,Frankenstein's Monster 75.00
2 MP,Bride of the Monster 50.00
3 MP,Revenge 50.00
4 MP,Monster's Death 50.00
5 MP,The Monster Walks
　Among Us 50.00
Becomes:

FRANKENSTEIN
1973–75
6 MP,Last of the Frankensteins . . 30.00
7 JB,The Fiend and the Fury 30.00
8 JB,A:Dracula 45.00
9 JB,A:Dracula 45.00
10 JB,Death Strikes Frankenstein . 25.00
11 Carnage at CastleFrankenstein 20.00
12 Frankenstein's Monster today . . 20.00
13 Undying Fiend 20.00
14 Fury of the Night Creature 20.00
15 Trapped in a Nightmare 20.00
16 The Brute and the Berserker . . 20.00
17 Phoenix Aflame 20.00
18 Children of the Damned 20.00

MONSTERS ON THE PROWL
See: CHAMBER OF DARKNESS

MONSTERS UNLEASHED
July, 1973
1 GM(c),GC,DW,B&W Mag 65.00
2 JB,FB,BEv,B:Frankenstein 50.00
3 NA(c),GK,GM,GT,B:Man-Thing 50.00
4 JB,GC,BK,I:Satana 50.00
5 JB 35.00
6 MP 25.00
7 AW 35.00
8 GP,NA 40.00
9 A:Wendigo 40.00
10 O:Tigra 40.00
11 FB(C),April, 1975 . . . . 40.00
Ann.#1 CK 40.00

MOON KNIGHT
[1st Regular Series] Nov., 1980
1 BSz,O:Moon Knight 7.00
2 BSz,V:Slasher 3.50
3 BSz,V:Midnight Man 3.50
4 BSz,V:Committee of 5 . . . . 3.50
5 BSz,V:Red Hunter 3.50
6 BSz,V:White Angels 3.50
7 BSz,V:Moon Kings 3.50
8 BSz,V:Moon Kings, Drug 3.00
9 BSz,V:Midnight Man 3.00
10 BSz,V:Midnight Man 3.00
11 BSz,V:Creed (Angel Dust) 3.00
12 BSz,V:Morpheus 3.00
13 BSz,A:Daredevil & Jester 3.00
14 BSz,V:Stained Glass Scarlet . . 3.00
15 FM(c),BSz,1st Direct 4.00
16 V:Blacksmith 3.00
17 BSz,V:Master Sniper 3.00
18 BSz,V:Slayers Elite 3.00
19 BSz,V:Arsenal 3.00
20 BSz,V:Arsenal 3.00
21 A:Bother Voodoo 2.50
22 BSz,V:Morpheus 2.50
23 BSz,V:Morpheus 2.50
24 BSz,V:Stained Glass Scarlet . . 2.50
25 BSz,Black Specter 2.50
26 KP,V:Cabbie Killer 2.50
27 A:Kingpin 2.50
28 BSz,Spirits in the Sands 2.50
29 BSz,V:Werewolf 2.50
30 BSz,V:Werewolf 2.50
31 TA,V:Savage Studs 2.50

32 KN,Druid Walsh 2.50
33 KN,V:Druid Walsh 2.50
34 KN,Marc Spector 2.50
35 KN,X-Men,FF,V:The Fly
　DoubleSized 3.00
36 A:Dr.Strange 2.50
37 V:Zohar 2.50
38 V:Zohar 2.50

[2nd Regular Series] 1985
1 O:Moon Knight,DoubleSize 2.50
2 Yucatan 2.50
3 V:Morpheus 2.50
4 A:Countess 2.50
5 V:Lt.Flint 2.50
6 GI,LastIssue 2.50

[3rd Regular Series] 1989–94
1 V:Bushmaster 4.00
2 A:Spider-Man 3.00
3 V:Bushmaster 2.50
4 RH,A:Midnight,Black Cat 2.50
5 V:Midnight,BlackCat 2.50
6 A:BrotherVoodoo 2.50
7 A:BrotherVoodoo 2.50
8 TP,A:Punisher,A of V 3.00
9 TP,A:Punisher,A of V 3.00
10 V:Killer Shrike,A of V 2.50
11 TP,V:Arsenal 2.50
12 TP,V:Bushman,A:Arsenal 2.50
13 TP,V:Bushman 2.50
14 TP,V:Bushman 2.50
15 TP,Trial o/Marc Spector #1,A:
　Silv.Sable,Sandman,Paladin . . . 3.00
16 TP,Trial o/Marc Spector #2,A:
　Silv.Sable,Sandman,Paladin . . . 3.00
17 TP,Trial o/Marc Spector #3 . . . . 3.00
18 TP,Trial o/Marc Spector #4 . . . . 3.00
19 RLd(c),TP,SpM,Punisher 3.00
20 TP,A:Spider-Man,Punisher 3.00
21 TP,Spider-Man,Punisher 3.00
22 I:Harbinger 2.50
23 Confrontation 2.50
24 A:Midnight 2.50
25 MBa,TP,A:Ghost Rider 3.00
26 BSz(c),TP,B:Scarlet Redemption
　V:Stained Glass Scarlet 2.50
27 TP,V:Stained Glass Scarlet 2.50
28 TP,V:Stained Glass Scarlet 2.50
29 TP,V:Stained Glass Scarlet 2.50
30 TP,V:Stained Glass Scarlet 2.50
31 TP,E:Scarlet Redemption,
　A:Hobgoblin 2.75
32 TP,V:Hobgoblin,SpM(in Black) . . 3.00
33 TP,V:Hobgoblin,A:Spider-Man . . 3.00
34 V:Killer Shrike 2.50
35 TP,Return of Randall Spector
　Pt.1,A:Punisher 2.50
36 TP,A:Punisher,Randall 2.50
37 TP,A:Punisher,Randall 2.50
38 TP,A:Punisher,Randall 2.50
39 TP,N:Moon Knight,A:Dr.Doom . . 2.50
40 TP,V:Dr.Doom 2.50
41 TP,Infinity War,I:Moonshade . . . 2.50
42 TP,Infinity War,V:Moonshade . . 2.50
43 TP(i),Infinity War 2.50
44 Inf.War,A:Dr.Strange.FF 2.50
45 V:Demogoblin 2.50
46 V:Demogoblin 2.50
47 Legacy Quest Scenario 2.50
48 I:Deadzone 2.50
49 V:Deadzone 2.50
50 A:Avengers,I:Hellbent,
　Die-cut(c) 3.50
51 A:Gambit,V:Hellbent 2.50
52 A:Gambit,Werewolf 2.50
53 Pang 2.50
54 . . . . 2.50
55 SPa,V:Sunstreak 15.00
56 SPa,V:Seth 8.00
57 SPa,Inf.Crusade 12.00
58 SPa(c),A:Hellbent 10.00
59 SPa(c) 8.00
60 E:TKa(s),SPa,D:Moonknight . . . 10.00

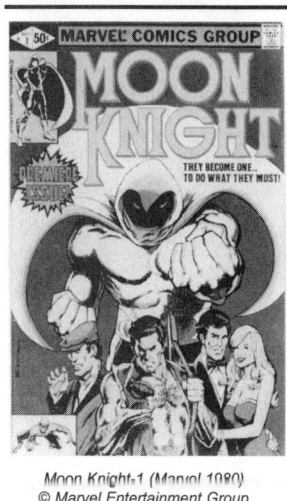

Moon Knight-1 (Marvel 1980)
© Marvel Entertainment Group

Spec.#1 ANi,A:Shang-Chi 2.50
1-shot Moon Knight: Divided We Fall
   DCw,V:Bushman (1992) 5.00

MOON KNIGHT
(Special Edition) Nov., 1983
1 BSz,reprints 2.50
2 BSz,reprints 2.50
3 BSz,reprints,Jan., 1984 . . . . 2.50

MOON KNIGHT
Nov., 1997–Feb., 1998
1 (of 4) DgM, Moon Knight returns . 2.50
1A signed by Tommy Lee Edwards
   (250 copies). 20.00
2 DgM,A:Scarlet 2.50
3 DgM,Resurrection War,V:Black
   Spectre 2.50
4 DgM,Resurrecton War, concl. . . . 2.50

MOON KNIGHT
Dec., 1998
1 (of 4) DgM,MT,A:Marlene 3.00
2 DgM,MT 3.00
3 DgM,MT 3.00
4 DgM,MT,concl. 3.00

MOON KNIGHT
April, 2006
1 The Bottom, pt.1 . . . . 3.00
2 thru 6 The Bottom, pt.2 – pt.6 . @3.00
7 Midnight Sun, pt.1 . . . . 3.00
8 Mignight Sun, pt.2, Civil War . . . 3.00
9 Midnight Sun, pt.3, Civil War . . . 3.00
10 Midnight Sun, pt.4, Civil War . . . 3.00
11 Midnight Sun, pt.5, Civil War. . . 3.00
12 Midnight Sun, concl. 3.00
13 48-pgs. 4.00
14 MT,God and Country, pt.1. . . . . 3.00
15 MT,God and Country, pt.2. . . . . 3.00
16 MT,God and Country, pt.3. . . . . 3.00
17 MT,God and Country, pt.4. . . . . 3.00
18 MT V:Black Spectre 3.00
19 God and Country, concl. 3.00
20 In the Company of Wolves 4.00
21 Death of Marc Spector,pt.1 . . . . 3.00
22 Death of Marc Spector,pt.2 . . . . 3.00
23 Death of Marc Spector,pt.3 . . . . 3.00
24 Death of Marc Spector,pt.4 . . . . 3.00
Ann. #1 . . . . 4.00

MOONSHADOW
Epic, May, 1985
1 JMu,O:Moonshadow 6.00
2 thru 12 . . . . @4.00

MORBIUS
1992–95
1 V:Lilith,Lilin,A:Blaze,Gh.Rider,
   Rise o/t Midnight Sons #3,
   polybagged w/poster 3.00
2 V:Simon Stroud 2.50
3 A:Spider-Man 2.50
4 I:Dr.Paine,C:Spider-Man 2.50
5 V:Basilisk,(inc Superman tribute
   on letters page) 2.50
6 V:Basilisk 2.50
7 V:Vic Slaughter 2.50
8 V:Nightmare 2.50
9 V:Nightmare 2.50
10 Two Tales 2.50
11 A:Nightstalkers 2.50
12 Midnight Massacre#4 . . . . 2.50
13 R:Martine,A:Lilith. 2.50
14 RoW,V:Nightmare,A:Werewolf . . 2.50
15 A:Ghost Rider,Werewolf 2.50
16 GWt(s),Siege of Darkness#5 . . . 2.50
17 GWt(s),Siege of Darkness#17 . . 2.50
18 GWt(s),A:Deathlok 2.50
19 GWt(s),A:Deathlok 2.50
20 GWt(s),I:Bloodthirst. 2.50
21 B:Dance of the Hunter,A:SpM. . 2.50
22 A:Spider-Man 2.50
23 E:Dance of the Hunter,A:SpM. . 2.50
24 Return of the Dragon 2.50
25 RoW 2.50
26 . . . . 2.50
27 . . . . 2.50
28 A:Werewolf 2.50
29 . . . . 2.50
30 New Morbius 2.50
31 A:Mortine. 2.50
32 Another Kill 2.50

MORBIUS REVISITED
1993
1 WMc,rep.Fear #20 . . . . 2.50
2 WMc,rep.Fear #28 . . . . 2.50
3 WMc,rep.Fear #29 . . . . 2.50
4 WMc,rep.Fear #30 . . . . 2.50
5 WMc,rep.Fear #31 . . . . 2.50

MORLOCKS
April, 2002
1 (of 4) SMa, outsiders 2.50
2 SMa,mutants stay hidden 2.50
3 SMa,where lurk the Morlocks . . . 2.50
4 SMa,concl 2.50

MORT THE DEAD TEENAGER
1993–94
1 LHa(s),I:Mort 2.50
2 thru 4 LHa(s), ... @2.50

MOTHER TERESA
1984
1 Mother Teresa Story 5.00

MOTOR MOUTH & KILLPOWER
Marvel UK, 1992–93
1 GFr,A:Nick Fury,I:Motor
   Mouth,Killpower . . . . : 2.50
2 GFr,A:Nick Fury, ... 2.50
3 GFr,V:Killpower,A:Punisher 2.50
4 GFr,A:Nick Fury,Warheads,
   Hell's Angel,O:Killpower 2.50

5 GFr,A:Excalibur,Archangel. 2.50
6 GFr,A:Cable,Punisher 2.50
7 EP,A:Cable,Nick Fury 2.50
8 JFr,A:Cable,Nick Fury 2.50
9 JFr,A:Cable,N.Fury,V:Harpies . . . 2.50
10 V:Red Sonja 2.50
11 V:Zachary Sorrow 2.50
12 A:Death's Head II 2.50
13 A:Death's Head II 2.50

MS. MARVEL
Jan., 1977
1 JB,O:Ms Marvel 15.00
2 JB,JSt,V:Scorpion 8.00
3 JB,JSt,V:Doomsday Man 8.00
4 JM,JSt,V:Destructor 8.00
5 JM,JSt,A:V:Vision 8.00
6 JM,JSt,V:Grotesk 8.00
7 JM,JSt,V:Modok 8.00
8 JM,JSt,GF(c),V:Grotesk. 8.00
9 KP,JSt,I:Deathbird 9.00
10 JB,TP,V:Deathbird,Modok. 7.00
11 V:Elementals 6.00
12 JSn(c),V:Hecate 6.00
13 Bedlam in Boston 6.00
14 CI,TA(c),V:Steeplejack 6.00
15 V:Tigershark 6.00
16 TA,V:Tigershark,A:Beast. 15.00
17 TA,C:Mystique. 12.00
18 I:Mystique,A,:Avengers 22.00
19 A:Captain Marvel 6.00
20 V:Lethal Lizards,N:Ms.Marvel . . 6.00
21 V:Lethal Lizards 6.00
22 TA,V:Deathbirds 6.00
23 The Woman who Fell to Earth
   April, 1979 . . . . 6.00

MS. MARVEL
Mar., 2006
1 . . . . 10.00
2 thru 9 . . . . @3.00
10 A:Rogue, Beast. 3.00
11 V:Doomsday Man 3.00
12 V:Doomsday Man 3.00
13 AaL,The Deal,pt.1 . . . . 3.00
14 AaL,The Deal,pt.1 . . . . 3.00
15 AaL,Ready, A.I.M., Fire, pt.1 . . . 3.00
16 AaL,Ready, A.I.M., Fire, pt.2 . . . 12.00
17 AaL,Ready, A.I.M., Fire, pt.3 . . . 3.00
18 Puppets,pt.1 . . . . 18.00
19 AaL,Puppets,pt.2. . . . . 3.00
20 Puppets,pt.3 . . . . 3.00
21 Monster Island 3.00
22 AaL,The Brood Return 3.00
23 AaL,V:The Brood. 3.00
24 AaL,V:The Brood. 3.00
25 Secret Invasion, 48-pg. 4.00
26 Secret Invasion tie-in 3.00
27 V:Skrull 3.00
28 Secret Invasion tie-in 3.00
29 Secret Invasion tie-in 3.00
30 Secret Invasion tie-in 3.00
31 Ms.Marvel's New Life 3.00
31a monkey variant (c) 3.00
32 Air Force Secret Agent 3.00
33 Secret Agent tales. 3.00
Spec.F:Wonder Man 3.00
Ann. #1 . . . . 4.00
Spec.F:Wonder Man 3.00
Spec. Storyteller, Pirate 3.00

MUPPET BABIES
Star, Aug., 1984
1 thru 10 . . . . @2.50
11 thru 25 July, 1989 . . . . @2.50

MUPPETS TAKE MANHATTAN
1 movie adapt,November, 1984 . . . 3.00
2 thru 3 movie adapt. . . . . @3.00

MARVEL

MUTANTS: THE AMAZING X-MEN

1 X-Men After Xavier	3.50
2 Exodus, Dazzler,V:Abyss	2.50
3 F:Bishop	2.50
4 V:Apocalypse	2.50

MUTANTS: THE ASTONISHING X-MEN

1 Uncanny X-Men	3.50
2 V:Holocaust	2.50
3 V:Abyss	2.50
4 V:Beast,Infinitio	2.50

MUTANTS: GENERATION NEXT

1 Generation X Ax	3.50
2 Genetic Slave Pens	2.50
3 V:Sugar Man	2.50
4 V:Sugar Man	2.50

MUTANT 2099
Sept., 2004

1	3.00

MUTANT X
Aug., 1998

1 HMe,TR,F:Havok, 48-pg	3.00
2 HMe,TR,F:Havok	2.50
2a variant cover	2.50
3 HMe,TR,V:Pack	2.50
4 HMe,TR,V:Goblin Queen	2.50
5 HMe,F:Brute, Fallen	2.50
6 HMe,A:Mutant-X Spider-Man	2.50
7 HMe,Trial of the Brute	2.50
8 HMe,V:Goblin Queen	2.50
9 HMe,V:Sentinels	2.50
10 HMe,V:The Six	2.50
11 HMe,Bloodstorm vs. Havok	2.50
12 HMe,O:Goblin Queen,Havok, 48-page	3.50
13 O:Bloodstorm	2.50
14 HMe,CNr,I:Cyclops	2.50
15 HMe,F:Havok	2.50
16 HMe	2.50
17 HMe,CNr,V:Cyclops	2.50
18 HMe,CNr,A:Punisher	2.50
19 HMe,A:Professor X	2.50
20 HMe,A:Havok	2.50
21 HMe,BS,Prof.X & Apocalypse	2.50
22 HMe,BS,Galactus	2.50

Mutant X #4
© *Marvel Entertainment Group*

23 HMe,TL,Apocalypse	2.50
24 HMe,TL,Master Planner	2.50
25 HMe,TL,The Six,48-pg	3.50
26 HMe,TL,The Six,Bloodstorm	2.50
27 HMe,TL,Dagger,Outcasts	2.50
28 HMe,TL,F:Wolverine	2.50
29 HMe,TL,F:Wolverine	2.50
30 HMe,RLm,F:Capt.America	2.50
31 HMe,RLm,F:Capt.America	2.50
32 HMe,RLm,48-page, final	3.00
GN Mutant X, rep.#1 & #2	6.00
Ann.1999, 48-page	3.50
Ann.2000 HMe,secrets	3.50
Ann.2001 HMe,48-page	3.00

Oct., 2001

1 HC,JHo, TV show tie-in	3.00
2 HC,JHo	2.50
Spec.#1 48-pg.,photo(c) (2002)	3.50
Spec.Dangerous Discoveries (2002)	3.50

MUTANT X: FUTURE SHOCK
May, 2002

1 CCI,F:Shalimar,54-pg	3.50

MUTATIS
Epic

1 I:Mutatis	2.50
2 O:Mutatis	2.50
3 A:Mutatis	2.50

MUTIES
Feb., 2002

1 (of 6) F:Jared	2.50
2 in Japan, I:Seiji	2.50
3 F:Riek Bukenya	2.50
4	2.50
5	2.50
6 concl	2.50

MUTOPIA X
July, 2005

1 (of 5) House of M tie-in	3.00
2 House of M Tie-in	3.00
3 thru 5	@3.00

MY DIARY
Dec., 1949–March, 1950

1 Ph(c),The Man I Love	200.00
2 Ph(c),I Was Anybody's Girl	175.00

WESTERN LIFE ROMANCES
Marvel Comics, 1949

1	300.00
2	250.00

Becomes:

MY FRIEND IRMA
Marvel Atlas, 1950

3	250.00
4 HK	265.00
5 HK	200.00
6	150.00
7 HK	150.00
8	150.00
9 Paper dolls	175.00
10	150.00
11	100.00
12 thru 22	@100.00
23 FF(one page)	125.00
24 thru 48	@100.00

MY GIRL PEARL
Marvel Atlas, 1955–61

1	200.00
2	150.00

3	125.00
4	125.00
5	125.00
6	125.00
7	100.00
8	100.00
9	100.00
10	100.00
11	100.00

MY LOVE
July, 1949

1 Ph(c),One Heart to Give	200.00
2 Ph(c),Hate in My Heart	125.00
3 Ph(c),	125.00
4 Ph(c),Betty Page, April,1950	500.00

MY LOVE
Sept., 1969

1 Love story reprints	100.00
2 thru 9	@50.00
10	65.00
11 thru 38	@45.00
39 March, 1976	45.00

MY ROMANCE
Sept., 1948

1 Romance Stories	250.00
2	150.00
3	150.00

Becomes:

MY OWN ROMANCE

4 Romance Stories Continue	250.00
5 thru 10	@150.00
11 thru 20	@150.00
21 thru 50	@125.00
51 thru 54	@100.00
55 ATh	125.00
56 thru 60	@100.00
61 thru 70	@100.00
71 AW	125.00
72 thru 76	@100.00

Becomes:

TEENAGE ROMANCE

77 Romance Stories Continue	100.00
78 thru 85	@100.00
86 March, 1962	100.00

MYS-TECH WARS
Marvel UK, 1993

1 BHi,A:FF,X-Men,Avengers	2.50
2 A:FF,X-Men,X-Force	2.50
3 BHi,A:X-Men,X-Force	2.50
4 A:Death's Head II	2.50

MYSTERY TALES
Marvel Atlas, March, 1952

1 GC,Horror Strikes at Midnight	1,400.00
2 BK,BEv,OW,The Corpse is Mine	700.00
3 RH,GC,JM, Vampire Strikes	600.00
4 Funeral of Horror	600.00
5 Blackout at Midnight	600.00
6 A-Bomb Picture	600.00
7 JRo,The Ghost Hunter	600.00
8 BEv	600.00
9 BEv(c),the Man in the Morgue	600.00
10 BEV(c),GT,What Happened to Harry	600.00
11 BEv(c)	450.00
12 GT,MF	475.00
13	400.00
14 BEv(c),GT	400.00
15 RH(c),EK	400.00
16	400.00
17 RH(c)	400.00
18 AW,DAy,GC	475.00
19	400.00

All comics prices listed are for *Near Mint* condition.

20 Electric Chair	400.00
21 JF,MF,BP,Decapitation	400.00
22 JF,MF	400.00
23 thru 27	@350.00
28	300.00
29 thru 32	@325.00
33 BEv	300.00
34	300.00
35 BEv,GC	300.00
36	325.00
37 DW,BP,JR	300.00
38 BP,BEv	300.00
39 BK,BEv	325.00
40 JM	325.00
41 MD,BEv	300.00
42 JeR	300.00
41 GC	300.00
44 AW	300.00
45 SD	275.00
46 RC,SD,JP	275.00
47 DAy,BP	275.00
48 BEv	300.00
49 GM,AT,DAy	300.00
50 JO,AW,GM	275.00
51 DAy,JO	275.00
52 DAy	275.00
53 BEv	275.00
54 RC,Aug., 1957	300.00

MYSTICAL TALES
Marvel Atlas, June, 1956

1 BEv,BP,JO,Say the Magical Words	750.00
2 BEv(c),JO,Black Blob	500.00
3 BEv(c),RC,Four Doors To	550.00
4 BEv(c).The Condemned	550.00
5 AW,Meeting at Midnight	550.00
6 BK,AT,He Hides in the Tower	400.00
7 BEv,JF,JO,AT,FBe,The Haunted Tower	400.00
8 BK,SC, Stone Walls Can't Stop Him,Aug., 1957	400.00

MYSTIC ARCANA
June 2007

Spec. Magik	3.00
Spec. Black Knight	3.00
Spec. Scarlet Witch	3.00
Spec. Sister Grimm	3.00

MYSTIC COMICS
Marvel Timely, March, 1940
[1st Series]

1 ASh(c),SSh,O;Blue Blaze,Dynamic, Man,Flexo,B:Dakor the Magician, A:Zephyr Jones,3X's, Deep Sea, Demon,bondage(c)	27,000.00
2 ASh(c),B:The Invisible Man Mastermind,Blue Blaze	9,000.00
3 ASh(c),O:Hercules	6,000.00
4 ASh(c),O:Thin Man,Black Widow E:Hercules,Blue Blazes,Dynamic Man,Flexo,Invisible Man	6,500.00
5 ASh(c)O:The Black Marvel, Blazing Skull,Super Slave Terror,Sub-Earth Man	6,000.00
6 ASh(c),O:The Challenger, B:The Destroyer	7,000.00
7 S&K(c),B:The Witness,O:Davey and the Demon,E;The Black Widow,Hitler(c)	7,500.00
8 Bondage(c)	4,000.00
9 MSy,DRi,Hitler/Bondage(c)	4,500.00
10 E:Challenger,Terror	4,000.00

[2nd Series] Oct., 1944

1 SSh,B:The Angel,Human Torch, Destroyer,Terry Vance, Tommy Tyme,Bondage(c)	4,000.00
2 E:Human Torch,Terry Vance,Bondage(c)	2,000.00

3 E:The Angel,Tommy Tyme Bondage(c)	2,000.00
4 ASh(c),A:Young Allies Winter, 1944-45	1,800.00

MYSTIC
[3rd Series] March, 1951

1 MSy,Strange Tree	1,700.00
2 MSy,Dark Dungeon	800.00
3 GC,Jaws of Creeping Death	700.00
4 BW,MSy,The Den of the Devil Bird	1,500.00
5 MSy,Face	600.00
6 BW,She Wouldn't Stay Dead	1,600.00
7 GC,Untold Horror waits in the Tomb	500.00
8 DAy(c),BEv,GK,A Monster Among Us	500.00
9 BEv	500.00
10 GC	500.00
11 JR,The Black Gloves	400.00
12 GC	400.00
13 In the Dark	400.00
14 The Corpse and I	400.00
15 GT,JR,House of Horror	350.00
16 A Scream in the Dark	350.00
17 BEv,Behold the Vampire	350.00
18 BEv(c),The Russian Devil	350.00
19 Swamp Girl	350.00
20 RH(c)	350.00
21 BEv(c),GC	325.00
22 RH(c)	325.00
23 RH(c),RA,RMn,Chilling Tales	325.00
24 GK,RMn,How Many Times Can You Die	325.00
25 RH(c),RA,E.C.Swipe	325.00
26 Severed Head(c)	325.00
27 Who Walks with a Zombie	300.00
28 DW,RMn(c),Not Enough Dead	300.00
29 SMo,RMn(c),The Unseen	300.00
30 RH(c),DW	300.00
31 SC,JKz,RMn(c)	300.00
32 The Survivor	300.00
33 thru 36	@300.00
37 thru 51	@275.00
52 WW,RC	300.00
53 thru 57	@275.00
58 thru 60	@300.00
61	250.00

MYTHOS
2007

Spec. Ghost Rider, PJe (1-2007)	4.00
Spec. Spider-Man, PJe (6-2007)	4.00
Spec. Hulk, PJe (8-2007)	4.00
Spec. Fantastic Four,PJe (10-2007)	4.00
Spec. Captain America (3-2008)	4.00
Spec. Captain America (6-2008)	4.00

MYSTIQUE
April, 2003

1 JLi(c),Drop Dead Gorgeous,pt.1	3.00
2 JLi(c),Drop Dead Gorgeous,pt.2	3.00
3 JLi(c),Drop Dead Gorgeous,pt.3	3.00
4 JLi(c),Drop Dead Gorgeous,pt.4	3.00
5 JLi(c),Drop Dead Gorgeous,pt.5	3.00
6 JLi(c),Drop Dead Gorgeous,pt.6	3.00
7 Tinker,Tailor,Mutant,Spy,pt.1	3.00
8 Tinker,Tailor,Mutant,Spy,pt.2	3.00
9 Tinker,Tailor,Mutant,Spy,pt.3	3.00
10 Tinker,Tailor,Mutant,Spy,pt.4	3.00
11 Maker's Mark,pt.1	3.00
12 Maker's Mark,pt.2	3.00
13 F:Shortpack	3.00
14 Unnatural,pt.1	3.00
15 Unnatural,pt.2	3.00
16 Unnatural,pt.3	3.00
17 Unnatural,pt.4	3.00
18 Unnatural,pt.5	3.00
19 Assassin's bullet	3.00
20 Quiet,pt.1	3.00

21 Quiet,pt.2	3.00
22 Quiet,pt.3	3.00
23 Quiet,pt.4	3.00
24 Quiet, concl.	3.00

MYTHOS
Jan., 2006

1 PJe,X-Men	4.00
2 PJe,Hulk	4.00

The Nam #15
© Marvel Entertainment Group

'NAM, THE
Dec., 1986

1 MGo,Vietnam War	3.00
1a 2nd printing	2.50
2 MGo,Dust Off	2.50
3 thru 8 MGo	@2.50
9 MGo,Action Issue,Tunnel Rat	3.50
10 thru 49 MGo	@2.50
52 Frank Castle(Punisher)#1	3.00
52a 2nd printing	2.50
53 Punisher #2	2.50
54 thru 84	@2.50

'NAM MAGAZINE, THE
(B&W) Aug., 1988–May, 1989

1 Reprints	3.00
2 thru 10	@2.50

NAMOR
April, 2003

1 MiS,manga	2.50
2 MiS	2.50
3 SvL	2.50
4 SvL,F:Sandy	2.50
5 SvL,F:Sandy	2.50
6 SvL,Namor's choice	2.50
7 PO, In Deep, pt.1	2.50
8 PO, In Deep, pt.2	2.50
9 PO, In Deep, pt.3	3.00
10 PO,In Deep, pt.4	3.00
11 JoB,In Deep,pt.5	3.00
12 JoB,finale	3.00

NAMORA
Fall, 1948–Dec., 1948

1 BEv,DR	4,000.00
2 BEv,A:Sub-Mariner,Blonde Phantom	2,200.00
3 BEv,A:Sub-Mariner	2,400.00

All comics prices listed are for *Near Mint* condition.

Namor the Sub-Mariner #22
© Marvel Entertainment Group

NAMOR THE SUB-MARINER
April, 1990

1 JBy,BWi,I:Desmond
  & Phoebe Marrs 5.00
2 JBy,BWi,V:Griffin 3.00
3 JBy,BWi,V:Griffin 3.00
4 JBy,A:Reed & Sue Richards,
  Tony Stark 3.00
5 JBy,A:FF,IronMan,C:Speedball . . 3.00
6 JBy,V:Sluj 3.00
7 JBy,V:Sluj 3.00
8 JBy,V:Headhunter,R:D.Rand 3.00
9 JBy,V:Headhunter 3.00
10 JBy,V:Master Man,Warrior
  Woman 2.50
11 JBy,V:Mast.Man,War.Woman . . . 2.50
12 JBy,R:Invaders,Spitfire 2.50
13 JBy,Namor on Trial,A:Fantastic
  Four,Captain America,Thor . . . 2.50
14 JBy,R:Lady Dorma,A:Ka-Zar
  Griffin 2.50
15 JBy,A:Iron Fist 2.50
16 JBy,A:Punisher,V:Iron Fist 2.50
17 JBy,V:Super Skrull(Iron Fist) . . . 2.50
18 JBy,V:SuperSkrull,A:Punisher . . 2.50
19 JBy,V:Super Skrull,D:D.Marrs . . 2.50
20 JBy,Search for Iron Fist,
  O:Namorita 2.50
21 JBy,Visit to K'un Lun 2.50
22 JBy,Fate of Iron Fist,
  C:Wolverine 2.50
23 JBy,BWi,Iron Fist Contd.,
  C:Wolverine 2.50
24 JBy,BWi,V:Wolverine 3.00
25 JBy,BWi,V:Master Khan 2.50
26 JaL,BWi,Search For Namor 5.00
27 JaL,BWi,V:Namorita 4.00
28 JaL,BWi,A:Iron Fist 3.00
29 JaL,BWi,After explosion 3.00
30 JaL,A:Doctor Doom 3.00
31 JaL,V:Doctor Doom 3.00
32 JaL,V:Doctor Doom,
  Namor regains memory 3.00
33 JaL,V:Master Khan 2.50
34 JaL,R:Atlantis 2.50
35 JaL,V:Tiger Shark 2.50
36 JaL,I:Suma-Ket,A:Tiger Shark . . 2.50
37 JaL,Blue Holo-Grafix,Altantean
  Civil War,N:Namor 2.75
38 JaL,O:Suma-Ket 2.50
39 A:Tigershark,V:Suma-Ket 2.50
40 V:Suma-Ket 2.50
41 V:War Machine 2.50

42 MCW,A:Stingray,V:Dorcas 2.50
43 MCW,V:Orka,Dorcas 2.50
44 I:Albatross 2.50
45 GI,A:Sunfire,V:Attuma 2.50
46 GI, ... 2.50
47 GI,Starblast #2 . . . . 2.50
48 GI,Starblast #9,A:FF 2.50
49 GI,A:Ms. Marrs 2.50
50 GI,Holo-grafx(c),A:FF 4.00
50a Newsstand Ed. 2.50
51 AaL, ... 2.50
52 GI,I:Sea Leopard 2.50
53 GI,V:Sea Leopard 2.50
54 GI,I:Llyron 2.50
55 GI,V:Llyron 2.50
56 GI,V:Llyron 2.50
57 A:Capt. America, V:Llyron 2.50
58 . . . . 2.50
59 GI,V:Abomination 2.50
60 A:Morgan Le Fay 2.50
61 Atlantis Rising 2.50
62 V:Triton 2.50
Ann.#1 Subterran.Odyssey #3. . . . 3.00
Ann.#2 Return o/Defenders,pt.3 . . 4.00
Ann.#3 I:Assassin,A:Iron Fist,
  w/Trading card 3.25
Ann.#4 V:Hydra 3.25

NAVY ACTION
Aug., 1954

1 BP,US Navy War Stories 250.00
2 TLn,Navy(c) 125.00
3 BEv 100.00
4 and 5 . . . . @100.00
6 JH(c) 100.00
7 MD,JMn 100.00
8 JMn,GC. 100.00
9 thru 15 . . . . @100.00
16 BEv(c) 100.00
17 MD,BEv(c). 100.00
18 Aug., 1957. . . . . 100.00

NAVY COMBAT
Marvel Atlas, June, 1955

1 DH,JMn(c),B:Torpedo Taylor . . 250.00
2 DH 125.00
3 DH,BEv 100.00
4 DH 100.00
5 DH 100.00
6 JMn,A:Battleship Burke 100.00
7 thru 10 . . . . @100.00
11 MD,GC,JMn 100.00
12 RC. 125.00
13 GT 100.00
14 AT,GT 100.00
15 GT 100.00
16 . . . . 100.00
17 AW,AT,JMn 110.00
18 . . . . 100.00
19 . . . . 100.00
20 BEv,BP,AW,Oct., 1958 . . . . . . 110.00

NAVY TALES
Marvel Atlas, Jan., 1957

1 BEv(c),BP,Torpedoes 200.00
2 AW,RC,JMn(c),One Hour
  to Live 175.00
3 JSe(c) 150.00
4 JSe(c),GC,JSt,RC,July, 1957 . 150.00

NELLIE THE NURSE
Marvel Atlas, 1945

1 Beach(c) 600.00
2 Nellie's Date(c) 300.00
3 Swimming Pool(c) 225.00
4 Roller Coaster(c) 225.00
5 Hospital(c),HK,Hey Look 225.00
6 Bedside Manner(c) 225.00
7 Comic book(c)A:Georgie 225.00
8 Hospital(c),A:Georgie 225.00

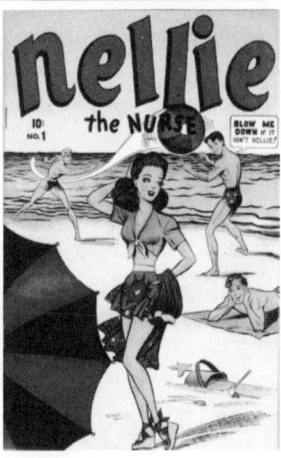

Nellie the Nurse #1 (Marvel Timely
1945) © Marvel Entertainment Group

9 BW,Nellie/Swing(c)A:Millie . . . 225.00
10 Bathing Suit(c),A:Millie 225.00
11 HK,Hey Look 250.00
12 HK,Giggles 'n' Grins 225.00
13 HK. 150.00
14 HK. 165.00
15 HK. 165.00
16 HK. 165.00
17 HK.A:Annie Oakley 165.00
18 HK. 165.00
19 . . . . 150.00
20 . . . . 150.00
21 . . . . 125.00
22 . . . . 125.00
23 . . . . 125.00
24 . . . . 125.00
25 . . . . 125.00
26 . . . . 125.00
27 . . . . 125.00
28 HK,Rusty Reprint 125.00
29 thru 35. . . . . @125.00
36 Oct., 1952. . . . . 125.00

NEW ADVENTURES OF CHOLLY & FLYTRAP
Epic

1 . . . . 5.00
2 . . . . 4.00
3 . . . . 4.00

NEW AVENGERS
Nov., 2004

1 BMB, The Breakout 5.00
1a variant (c). 6.00
2 BMB, The Breakout 3.00
2a variant (c). 4.00
3 BMB,The Breakout,pt.3 . . . . 3.00
3a variant (c). 15.00
4 BMB, The Breakout,pt.4 . . . . 3.00
5 BMB,The Breakout,pt.5 . . . . 2.50
6 BMB,F:Captain America 2.50
7 BMB,the Sentry,pt.1. . . . . 2.50
8 BMB,SB, The Sentry,pt.2. . . . . . 2.50
9 BMB,The Sentry,pt.3 . . . . 2.50
5a thru 9a Variant(c) . . . . @2.50
10 BMB,The Sentry,pt.4. . . . . 2.50
11 BMB,Ronin,pt.1 . . . . 2.50
12 BMB,Ronin,pt.2. . . . . 2.50
13 BMB,Ronin,pt.3. . . . . 2.50
14 BMB,F:Spider-Woman 2.50
15 BMB,V:J. Jonah Jameson 2.50
16 BMB,The Collective, prologue . . 2.50
17 BMB,The Collective 3.50

18 BMB,The Collective 3.00	
19 BMB,The Collective 3.00	
20 BMB,The Collective 3.00	
21 BMB,Civil War tie-in 4.00	
22 BMB,Civil War tie-in 4.00	
23 BMB,Civil War tie-in 4.00	
24 BMB,Civil War tie-in 4.00	
25 BMB,Civil War tie-in 4.00	
26 BMB,A:Dr. Strange 3.00	
27 BMB(s) 3.00	
28 BMB(s),Team is formed 5.00	
29 BMB(s) 3.00	
30 BMB(s),V:The Hand 3.00	
31 BMB(s) 3.00	
32 BMB(s) 3.00	
33 BMB(s) 3.00	
34 BMB(s),Wolverine vs. The Hood 3.00	
35 BMB(s) The Hood 3.00	
36 BMB(s), Symbiote 3.00	
37 BMB(s),V:Hood's gang 3.00	
38 BMB(s),Secret Invasion 3.00	
39 BMB(s),DMk,Secret Invasion . . . 3.00	
40 BMB(s),Secret Invasion tie-in . . . 3.00	
41 BMB(s),Secret Invasion tie-in . . . 3.00	
42 BMB(s),Secret Invasion tie-in . . . 3.00	
43 BMB(s),Secret Invasion tie-in . . . 3.00	
44 BMB(s),Secret Invasion tie-in . . . 3.00	
45 BMB(s),Secret Invasion tie-in . . . 3.00	
46 BMB(s),Secret Invasion tie-in . . . 3.00	
47 BMB(s),Secret Invasion tie-in . . . 3.00	
Ann. #1 BMB 4.00	
Spec.#1 Director's Cut (2004) 3.00	
Spec. Handbook bios. 4.00	
Spec. Illuminati. 7.00	
New Avengers: Must-Haves 4.00	
Ann. #2 (2008) 4.00	

NEW AVENGERS: ILLUMINATI
Dec., 2006

1 (of 5) BMB(s) 7.00	
2 thru 5 BMB(s) . . . . @4.00	

NEW AVENGERS/ TRANSFORMERS
July, 2007

1 . . . . 3.00	
2 thru 4 . . . . @3.00	

NEW ETERNALS: APOCALYPSE NOW
Dec., 1999

1-shot JoB,SHa,64-pg. 4.00	

NEW EXCALIBUR
Nov., 2005

1 CCI. 3.00	
2 CCI,Defenders of the Realm 3.00	
3 CCI,V: Original X-Men 3.00	
4 CCI,Choose Your Destiny 3.00	
5 CCI,Choose Your Destiny 3.00	
6 CCI,Black Monday 3.00	
7 CCI,Black Monday. 3.00	
8 CCI,So Why is it I'm Not Dead . . 3.00	
9 Chest Pains 3.00	
10 The Last Days of Camelot 3.00	
11 The Last Days of Camelot 3.00	
12 The Last Days of Camelot 3.00	
13 Unredeemed,pt.1. . . . . 3.00	
14 JCf,Unredeemable 3.00	
15 JCf,Unredeemable 3.00	
16 CCI,SEa,Fallen Friend, pt.1 . . . 3.00	
17 CCI,SEa,Fallen Friend, pt.2 . . . 3.00	
18 CCI,SEa,Battle for Eternity,pt.1. . 3.00	
19 CCI,SEa,Battle for Eternity,pt.2. . 3.00	
20 CCI,SEa,Battle for Eternity,pt.3. . 3.00	
21 CCI,Battle for Eternity,pt.4 . . . . 3.00	
22 CCI,Battle for Eternity,pt.5 . . . . 3.00	
23 CCI,Battle for Eternity,pt.6 . . . . 3.00	

24 CCI,Battle for Eternity,pt.7 . . . . 3.00	

NEW EXILES
Jan., 2008

1 CCI,TG 3.00	
2 CCI,TG 3.00	
3 CCI,TG,Panther's Vengeance . . . 3.00	
4 CCI,TG,War between Atlanteens . 3.00	
5 CCI,TG,Royalty and Dragons . . . 3.00	
6 CCI,AD(c),F:Morph, Cat, Sage . . 3.00	
7 CCI,TG 3.00	
8 CCI,TG 3.00	
9 CCI,TG. 3.00	
10 CCI,TG 3.00	
11 CCI,F:Sabretooth 3.00	
12 CCI(s),V:Madam Hydra. 3.00	
13 CCI(s),End of All 3.00	
14 CCI(s),TG 3.00	

NEW MANGAVERSE
Jan., 2006

1 Rings of Fate 3.00	
2 thru 5 . . . . @5.00	

NEW MUTANTS, THE
March, 1983

1 BMc,MG,O:New Mutants 5.00	
2 BMc,MG,V:Sentinels 4.00	
3 BMc,MG,V:Brood Alien 3.50	
4 SB,BMc,A:Peter Bristow 3.50	
5 SB,BMc,A:Dark Rider 3.50	
6 SB,AG,V:Viper 3.50	
7 SB,BMc,V:Axe 3.50	
8 SB,BMc,I:Amara Aquilla. 3.50	
9 SB,TMd,I:Selene 3.50	
10 SB,BMc,C:Magma 3.50	
11 SB,TMd,I:Magma 3.50	
12 SB,TMd,J:Magma 3.50	
13 SB,TMd,I:Cypher(Doug Ramsey)	
A:Kitty Pryde,Lilandra 4.00	
14 SB,TMd,J:Magik,A:X-Men. 3.00	
15 SB,TMd,Mass.Academy 3.00	
16 SB,TMd,V:Hellions,I:Warpath	
I:Jetstream 18.00	
17 SB,TMd,V:Hellions,A:Warpath . . 4.00	
18 BSz,V:Demon Bear,I:New	
Warlock,Magus 5.00	
19 BSz,V:Demon Bear. 3.00	
20 BSz,V:Demon Bear. 3.00	
21 BSz,O&J:Warlock,doub.sz 5.00	
22 BSz,A:X-Men 3.50	
23 BSz,Sunspot,Cloak & Dagger. . 3.00	
24 BSz,A:Cloak & Dagger 3.00	
25 BSz,A:Cloak & Dagger 6.00	
26 BSz,I:Legion(Prof.X's son) 7.00	
27 BSz,V:Legion 4.00	
28 BSz,O:Legion 4.00	
29 BSz,V:Gladiators,I:Guido	
(Strong Guy) 3.00	
30 BSz,A:Dazzler. 3.00	
31 BSz,A:Shadowcat 3.00	
32 SL,V:Karma. 3.00	
33 SL,V:Karma. 3.00	
34 SL,V:Amahl Farouk. 3.00	
35 BSz,J:Magneto 3.00	
36 BSz,A:Beyonder 3.00	
37 BSz,D:New Mutants 3.00	
38 BSz,A:Hellions 3.00	
39 BSz,A:White Queen 3.00	
40 JG,KB,V:Avengers. 3.00	
41 JG,TA,Mirage 3.00	
42 JG,KB,A:Dazzler 3.00	
43 SP,V:Empath,A:Warpath 3.00	
44 JG,V:Legion. 5.00	
45 JG,A:Larry Bodine. 3.00	
46 JG,KB,Mutant Massacre 3.50	
47 JG,KB,V:Magnus 3.00	
48 JG,CR,Future 3.00	
49 VM,Future 3.00	
50 JG,V:Magus,R:Prof.X 4.00	
51 KN,A:Star Jammers 3.00	

52 RL,DGr,Limbo. 3.00	
53 RL,TA,V:Hellions. 3.00	
54 SB,TA,N:New Mutants 3.00	
55 BBI,TA,V:Aliens. 3.00	
56 JBr,TA,V:Hellions,A:Warpath. . . 3.00	
57 BBI,TA,I&J:Bird-Boy. 3.00	
58 BBI,TA,Bird-Boy 3.00	
59 BBI,TA,Fall of Mutants,	
V:Dr.Animus. 3.00	
60 BBI,TA,F.of M.,D:Cypher. 2.50	
61 BBI,TA,Fall of Mutants 2.50	
62 JMu,A:Magma,Hellions. 2.50	
63 BHa,JRu,Magik. 2.50	
64 BBI,TA,R:Cypher. 2.50	
65 BBI,TA,V:FreedomForce 2.50	
66 BBI,TA,V:Forge 2.50	
67 BBI,I:Gosamyr. 2.50	
68 BBI,V:Gosamyr 2.50	
69 BBI,AW,I:Spyder 2.50	
70 TSh,AM,V:Spyder 2.50	
71 BBI,AW,V:N'Astirh 2.50	
72 BBI,A,Inferno. 2.50	
73 BBI,W,A:Colossus. 3.00	
74 BBI,W,A:X-Terminators 2.50	
75 JBy,Mc,Black King,V:Magneto . 3.50	
76 RB,TP,J:X-Terminators 2.50	
77 RB,V:Mirage 2.50	
78 RL,AW,V:FreedomForce 2.50	
79 BBI,AW,V:Hela 2.50	
80 BBI,AW,Asgard. 2.50	
81 LW,TSh,JRu,A:Hercules 2.50	
82 BBI,AW,Asgard 2.50	
83 BBI,Asgard 2.50	
84 TSh,AM,A:QueenUla 2.50	
85 RLd&TMc(c),BBI,V:Mirage 5.00	
86 RLd,BWi,V:Vulture,C:Cable . . . 6.00	
87 RLd,BWi,I:Mutant Liberation	
Front,Cable 25.00	
87a 2nd Printing. 3.00	
88 RLd,2nd Cable,V:Freedom	
Force 7.50	
89 RLd,V:Freedom Force 6.00	
90 RLd,A:Caliban,V:Sabretooth. . . . 6.00	
91 RLd,A:Caliban,Masque,	
V:Sabretooth. 6.00	
92 RLd(c),BH,V:Skrulls 4.00	
93 RLd,A:Wolverine,Sunfire,	
V:Mutant Liberation Front 6.00	
94 RLd,A:Wolverine,Sunfire,	
V:Mutant Liberation Front 5.00	
95 RLd,Extinction Agenda,V:Hodge	
A:X-Men,X-Factor,D:Warlock . . 5.00	
95a 2nd printing(gold) 5.00	

New Mutants #32
© Marvel Entertainment Group

96 RLd,ATb,JRu,Extinction Agenda
   V:Hodge,A:X-Men,X-Factor . . 5.00
97 E:LSi(s),RLd(c),JRu,Extinction
   Agenda,V:Hodge 5.00
98 FaN(s),RLd,I:Deadpool,Domino,
   Gideon,L:Rictor 40.00
99 FaN(s),RLd,I:Feral,Shatterstar,
   L:Sunspot,J:Warpath 5.00
100 FaN(s),RLd,J:Feral,Shatterstar,
   I:X-Force,V:Masque,Imperial
   Protectorate,A:MLF 6.00
100a 2nd Printing(Gold). 4.00
100b 3rd Printing(Silver) 3.50
Ann.#1 BMc,TP,L.Cheney 7.00
Ann.#2 AD,V:Mojo,I:Psylocke,Meggan
   (American App.). 10.00
Ann.#3 AD,PN,V:Impossible Man . . 4.00
Ann.#4 JBr,BMc,Evol.Wars 6.00
Ann.#5 RLd,JBg,MBa,KWi,Atlantis
   Attacks,A:Namorita,I:Surf 8.00
Ann.#6 RLd(c),Days o/Future Present
   V:FranklinRichards,(Pin-ups) . . 6.00
Ann.#7 JRu,RLd,Kings of Pain,
   I:Piecemeal & Harness,
   Pin-ups X-Force. 5.00
Spec #1,AAd,TA,Asgard War. 6.00
Summer Spec.#1 BBl,Megapolis . . . 3.50

Sept., 1997
1 (of 3) BRa,BCh,F:Cannonball,
   Moonstar, Wolfsbane,Karma &
   Sunspot 2.50
2 BRa,BCh,meeting with mutants
   of the past 2.50
3 BRa,BCh, will Magik return
   for good? 2.50

May, 2003
1 R:Original New Mutants. 2.50
2 F:Dani Moonstar 2.50
3 new student 2.50
4 F:Karma 2.50
5 mutant teens 2.50
6 V:Reavers 2.50
7 CBa(c),Ties That Bind,pt.1 . . . . . 2.50
8 CBa(c),Ties That Bind,pt.2 . . . . . 2.50
9 CBa(c),Ties That Bind,pt.3 . . . . . 2.50
10 CBa(c),Ties That Bind,pt.4 . . . . 3.00
11 CBa(c),Ties That Bind,pt.5 . . . . 3.00
12 CBa(c),Ties That Bind,pt.6 . . . . 3.00
13 The More Things Change. 3.00

NEW THUNDERBOLTS
See: THUNDERBOLTS

NEW UNIVERSAL
Dec., 2006
1 WEI,SvL. 3.00
2 WEI,SvL,Trauma 3.00
3 WEI,SvL,Mathematics 3.00
4 WEI,SvL,The White Event 3.00
5 WEI,SvL 3.00
6 WEI,SvL 3.00

NEWUNIVERSAL:
SHOCKFRONT
May, 2008
1 (of 6) WEI. 3.00
2 thru 4 WEI . . . . @3.00
Spec. Newuniversal: 1959 . . . . 4.00
Spec. Newuniversal Conqueror 4.00

NEW WARRIORS
July, 1990
1 B:FaN(s),MBa,AW,V:Terrax,
   O:New Warriors 5.00
1a Gold rep. 2.50
2 thru 10 . . . . @3.50
11 thru 49 . . . . @2.50
50 reg. (c) 2.50
50a Glow-in-the-dark(c),V:Sphinx . . 3.25

New Warriors #11
© *Marvel Entertainment Group*

51 thru 59 . . . . @2.50
60 Nova Omega,pt.2 . . . . 2.50
61 thru 71 . . . . @2.50
Ann.#1 MBa,A:X-Force,V:Harness,
   Piecemeal,Kings of Pain #2 . . . 4.00
Ann.#2 Hero Killers #4,V:Sphinx . . . 2.75
Ann.#3 LMa(i),E:Forces of Light,
   Forces of Darkness,I:Darkling
   w/card 3.25
Ann.#4 DaR(s),V:Psionex 3.25

Aug., 1999
1 F:Speedball,48-page 3.00
2 thru 10 . . . . @2.50

June, 2005
1 (of 6) 3.00
2 thru 6 . . . . @3.00

June, 2007
1 . . . . 3.00
2 thru 6 . . . . @3.00
7 F:Sofia Mantega 3.00
8 J:Sofia Mantega. 3.00
9 Thrashed, pt.1 . . . . 3.00
10 Thrashed, pt.2. . . . . 3.00
11 Thrashed, pt.3. . . . . 3.00
12 Thrashed, pt.4. . . . . 3.00
13 Thrashed, concl. 3.00
14 Secret Invasion tie-in 3.00
15 Secret Invasion tie-in 3.00
16 Beginning of the End 3.00
17 F:Night Thrasher. 3.00
18 F:Night Thrasher. 3.00

NEW X-MEN
See: X-MEN

NEW X-MEN
May, 2004
1 Choosing Sides,pt.1. . . . . 3.00
2 Choosing Sides,pt.2. . . . . 3.00
3 Choosing Sides,pt.3. . . . . 3.00
4 Choosing Sides,pt.4. . . . . 3.00
5 Choosing Sides,pt.5. . . . . 3.00
6 Choosing Sides,pt.6. . . . . 3.00
7 Haunted 3.00
8 Haunted 3.00
9 Haunted, Concl. 3.00
10 Too Much Information,pt.1 . . . . . 3.00
11 Too Much Information 3.00
12 X-Posed 3.00
13 Campfire 3.00
14 Year's End,pt.1 . . . . 3.00
15 Year's End,pt.2 . . . . 3.00

16 AaL,House Divided,pt.1 . . . . 3.00
17 AaL,House Divided,pt.2 . . . . 3.00
18 AaL,House Divided,pt.3 . . . . 3.00
19 AaL,House Divided,pt.4 . . . . 3.00
20 Childhood's End,pt.1. . . . . 5.00
21 Childhood's End,pt.2. . . . . 3.00
22 Childhood's End,pt.3. . . . . 3.00
23 Childhood's End,pt.4. . . . . 3.00
24 Crusade,pt.1 . . . . 3.00
25 Crusade,pt.2 . . . . 3.00
26 Crusade,pt.3 . . . . 3.00
27 Crusade,pt.4 . . . . 3.00
28 Nimrod,pt.1 . . . . 3.00
29 Nimrod,pt.2 . . . . 3.00
30 Nimrod,pt.3 . . . . 3.00
31 Nimrod,pt.4 . . . . 3.00
32 Whatever Happened to Wither . . 3.00
33 Mercury Falling, pt.1 . . . . 3.00
34 Mercury Rising 3.00
35 Mercury Falling 3.00
36 Mercury Rising, concl. 3.00
37 Quest For Magik, prelude 3.00
38 Quest For Magik, pt.1 . . . . 3.00
39 Quest For Magik, pt.2 . . . . 3.00
40 Quest For Magik, pt.3 . . . . 3.00
41 Quest For Magik, pt.4 . . . . 3.00
42 Children of X-Men. 3.00
43 Children of X-Men. 3.00
44 Messiah Complex, pt.4 x-over . . 5.00
45 Messiah Complex, pt.8 x-over . . 3.00
45a var 12.00
46 . . . . 12.00
Spec. Academy X Yearbook,AaL . . . 4.00

NEW X-MEN: HELLIONS
May, 2005
1 (of 4) 3.00
2 . . . . 3.00
3 Fortune and Glory 3.00
4 Fortune and Glory 3.00

NEXTWAVE
Jan., 2006
1 WEI,SI 3.00
2 thru 5 WEI,SI . . . . @3.00
Becomes:

NEXTWAVE:
AGENTS OF H.A.T.E.
6 thru 10 Agents of H.A.T.E. . . . . @3.00
11 WEI,SI,Not a Civil War tie-in 3.00
12 WEI,SI 3.00

NFL SUPERPRO
1 . . . . 7.00
Spec.#1 reprints 2.50
[Regular Series] Oct., 1991
1 A:Spider-Man,I:Sanzionaire 2.50
2 V:Quickkick 2.50
3 I:Instant Replay 2.50
4 V:Sanction 2.50
5 A:Real NFL Player 2.50
6 Racism Iss.,recalled by Marvel . . 6.00
7 thru 11 . . . . @2.50
12 V:Nefarious forces of evil 2.50

NICK FURY, AGENT
OF S.H.I.E.L.D.
[1st Regular Series] June, 1968
1 JSo/JSt,I:Scorpio 200.00
2 JSo,A:Centaurius 125.00
3 JSo,DA,V:Hell Hounds. 125.00
4 FS,O:Nick Fury 125.00
5 JSo,V:Scorpio 150.00
6 FS,Doom must Fall 100.00
7 FS,V:S.H.I.E.L.D. 100.00
8 FS,Hate Monger 60.00
9 FS,Hate Monger 60.00
10 FS,JCr,Hate Monger 60.00
11 BS(c),FS,Hate Monger 60.00

12 BS	65.00
13	65.00
14	65.00
15 I:Bullseye	125.00
16 JK,rep	40.00
17 JK,rep	40.00
18 JK,rep	40.00

[Limited Series] 1983–94

1 JSo,rep	4.00
2 JSo,rep	3.50

[2nd Regular Series] 1989–93

1 BH,I:New Shield,V:Death's Head(not British hero)	3.00
2 KP,V:Death's Head	2.50
3 KP,V:Death's Head	2.50
4 KP,V:Death's Head	2.50
5 KP,V:Death's Head	2.50
6 KP,V:Death's Head	2.50
7 KP,Chaos Serpent #1	2.50
8 KP,Chaos Serpent #2	2.50
9 KP,Chaos Serpent #3	2.50
10 KP,Chaos Serpent ends, A:Capt.America	2.50
11 D:Murdo MacKay	2.50
12 Hydra Affair #1	2.50
13 Hydra Affair #2	2.50
14 Hydra Affair #3	2.50
15 Apogee of Disaster #1	2.50
16 Apogee of Disaster #2	2.50
17 Apogee of Disaster #3	2.50
18 Apogee of Disaster #4	2.50
19 Apogee of Disaster #5	2.50
20 JG,A:Red Skull	2.50
21 JG,R:Baron Strucker	2.50
22 JG,A:Baron Strucker,R:Hydra	2.50
23 JG,V:Hydra	2.50
24 A:Capt.Am,Thing,V:Mandarin	2.50
25 JG,Shield Vs. Hydra	2.50
26 JG,A:Baron Strucker, C:Wolverine	2.50
27 JG,V:Hydra,A:Wolverine	2.50
28 V:Hydra,A:Wolverine	2.50
29 V:Hydra,A:Wolverine	2.50
30 R:Leviathan,A:Deathlok	2.50
31 A:Deathlok,V:Leviathan	2.50
32 V:Leviathan	2.50
33 Super-Powered Agents	2.50
34 A:Bridge(X-Force),V:Balance of Terror	2.50
35 A:Cage,V:Constrictor	2.50
36	2.50
37	2.50
38 Cold War of Nick Fury #1	2.50
39 Cold War of Nick Fury #2	2.50
40 Cold War of Nick Fury #3	2.50
41 Cold War of Nick Fury #4	2.50
42 I:Strike Force Shield	2.50
43 R:Clay Quatermain	2.50
44 A:Captain America	2.50
45 A:Bridge	2.50
46 V:Gideon,Hydra	2.50
47 V:Baron Strucker,last issue	2.50

NICK FURY, VERSUS S.H.I.E.L.D.

June, 1988

1 JSo(c),D:Quartermail	6.00
2 BSz(c),Into The Depths	5.00
3 Uneasy Allies	4.00
4 V:Hydra	4.00
5 V:Hydra	4.00
6 V:Hydra, Dec., 1988	4.00

NICK FURY'S HOWLING COMMANDOS

Oct., 2005

1 KG	3.00
1a expanded edition	4.00
2 thru 6 KG	@3.00

Nick Fury vs SHIELD #1
© Marvel Entertainment Group

NIGHTBREED

Epic, April, 1990

1	4.00
2	3.00
3 thru 10	@2.50
11 thru 20	@2.50
21 thru 25	@2.50
Nightbreed:Genesis, Rep.#1-#4	10.00

NIGHTCAT

1 DCw,I&O:Night Cat	4.50

NIGHTCRAWLER

Nov., 1985

1 DC,A;Bamfs	4.00
2 DC	3.50
3 DC,A:Other Dimensional X-Men	3.50
4 DC,A:Lockheed,V:Dark Bamf	3.50

NIGHTCRAWLER

Nov., 2001

1 (of 4) Passion Play	2.50
2 thru 4	@2.50

NIGHTCRAWLER

Sept., 2004

1 DaR,Diabolique,pt.1	3.00
2 DaR,Diabolique,pt.2	3.00
3 DaR,The Devil Inside	3.00
4 DaR,The Devil Inside	3.00
5 DaR,Ghosts on the Rails,pt.1	3.00
6 DaR,Ghosts on the Rails	3.00
7 DaR,The Winding Way, Pt.1	3.00
8 DaR,The Winding Way, Pt.2	3.00
9 DaR,The Winding Way, pt.3	3.00
10 DaR,The Winding Way, pt.4	3.00
11 DaR,The Winding Way, pt.5	3.00
12 DaR,Loose Ends	3.00

NIGHTHAWK

July, 1998

1 (of 3) RCa,BWi,Nighthawk shake off coma	3.00
2 (of 3) RCa,BWi,V:Mephisto	3.00
3 RCa,BWi,conclusion	3.00

NIGHTMARE ON ELM STREET

Oct., 1989

1 RB/TD/AA.,Movie adapt	3.00
2 AA,Movie adapt,Dec., 1989	2.50

NIGHT NURSE

Nov., 1972

1 The Making of a Nurse	200.00
2 Moment of Truth	150.00
3	150.00
4 Final Issue,May, 1973	150.00

NIGHT RIDER

Oct., 1974–Aug., 1975

1 Reprint Ghost Rider #1	20.00
2 Reprint Ghost Rider #2	15.00
3 Reprint Ghost Rider #3	15.00
4 Reprint Ghost Rider #4	15.00
5 Reprint Ghost Rider #5	15.00
6 Reprint Ghost Rider #6	15.00

NIGHT THRASHER

[Limited Series] 1992–93

1 B:FaN(s),DHv,N:Night Thrasher, V:Bengal	2.50
2 thru 4	@2.50

[Regular Series] 1993–95

1 B:FaN(s),MBa,JS,V:Poison Memories	3.50
2 thru 21	@2.50

NIGHTWATCH

1994–95

1 RLm,I:Salvo,Warforce Holo(c)	3.00
1a Newsstand ed	2.50
2 thru 12	@2.50

NO ESCAPE

1994

1 & 2 Movie adaptation	@2.50

NOMAD

[Limited Series] Nov., 1990

1 B:FaN(s),A:Capt.America	3.00
2 thru 4	@2.50

[Regular Series] 1992–94

1 B:FaN(s),R:Nomad,[Gatetfold(c), map]	3.00
2 V:Road Kill Club	2.50
3 thru 25	@2.50

NORTHSTAR

1994

1 SFr,DoC,V:Weapon:P.R.I.M.E.	2.50
2 SFr,DoC,V:Arcade	2.50
3 SFr,DoC,V:Arcade	2.50
4 SFr,DoC,final issue	2.50
N Presents James O'Barr	2.50

NOT BRAND ECHH

Aug., 1967

1 JK(c),BEv,Forbush Man(c)	150.00
2 MSe,FrG,Spidey-Man,Gnat-Man & Rotten	75.00
3 MSe(C),TS,JK,FrG,O:Charlie America	75.00
4 GC,JTg,TS,Scaredevil, ECHHs-Men	75.00
5 JK,TS,GC,I&O:Forbush Man	75.00
6 MSe(c),GC,TS,W:Human Torch	75.00
7 MSe(c),JK,GC,TS,O:Fantastical Four,Stupor Man	75.00
8 MSe(c),GC,TS,C:Beatles	75.00
9 MSe,GC,TS,Bulk V:Sunk-Mariner	75.00
10 JK,TS,MSe,The Worst of	100.00
11 King Konk	100.00
12 MSe,Frankenstein, A:Revengers	100.00
13 GC,MSe,Stamp Out Trading Cards(c)	100.00

NOVA

[1st Regular Series] Sept., 1976

1 B:MWn(s),JB,JSt,I&O:Nova	20.00
2 JB,JSt,I:Condor,Powerhouse	12.00
3 JB,JSt,I:Diamondhead	12.00
4 SB,TP,A:Thor,I:Corruptor	12.00
5 SB,V:Earthshaker	10.00
6 SB,V:Condor,Powerhouse,	
Diamondhead,I:Sphinx	10.00
7 SB,War in Space,O:Sphinx	10.00
8 V:Megaman	10.00
9 V:Megaman	10.00
10 V:Condor,Powerhouse,	
Diamond-head Sphinx	10.00
11 V:Sphinx	11.00
12 A:Spider-Man	12.00
13 I:Crimebuster,A:Sandman	7.00
14 A:Sandman	7.00
15 CI,C:Spider-Man, Hulk	7.00
16 CI,A:Yellow Claw	7.00
17 A:Yellow Claw	7.00
18 A:Yellow Claw, Nick Fury	7.00
19 CI,TP,I:Blackout	7.00
20 What is Project X?	7.00
21 JB,BMc,JRu	7.00
22 CI,I:Comet	7.00
23 CI,V:Dr.Sun	7.00
24 CI,I:New Champions,V:Sphinx	7.00
25 E:MWn(s),CI,A:Champions,	
V:Sphinx	7.00

[2nd Regular Series] 1994–95

1 B:FaN(s),ChM,V:Gladiator,Foil	
Embossed(c)	3.50
2 ChM,V:Tail Hook Rape	2.50
3 ChM,A:Spider-Man,Corruptor	2.50
4 ChM,I:NovaO:O	2.50
5 ChM,R:Condor,w/card	2.50
6 ChM,Time & Time Again,pt.3	2.50
7 ChM,Time & Time Again,pt.6	2.50
8 ChM,I:Shatterforce	2.50
9 ChM,V:Shatterforce	2.50
10 ChM,V:Diamondhead	2.50
11 ChM,V:Diamondhead	2.50
12 ChM,A:Inhumans	2.50
13 ChM,A:Inhumans	2.50
14 A:Condor	2.50
15 V:Brethern of Zorr	2.50
16 Countdown Conclusion	2.50
17 Nova Loses Powers	2.50
18 Nova Omega,pt.1	2.50

NOVA

March, 1999

1 EL,JoB,F:Rich Rider,48-page	3.00
2 EL,JoB,A:Capt.America	2.50
2a variant JoB cover	2.50
3 EL,JoB,A:Capt.America & Hulk	2.50
4 EL,JoB,A:Mr.Fantastic	2.50
5 EL,JoB,A:Spider-Man	2.50
6 EL,JoB,V:Sphinx	2.50
7 EL,JoB, final issue	2.50

NOVA

Apr., 2007

1 DAn	5.00
2 DAn,ALa,A:Iron Man	4.00
3 DAn,ALa,A:Thunderbolts	4.00
4 DAn,ALa,Annihilation: Conquest	4.00
5 DAn,ALa,Annihilation: Conquest	4.00
6 DAn,ALa,Annihilation: Conquest	4.00
7 DAn,ALa	3.00
8 DAn,ALa	3.00
9 DAn,ALa	3.00
10 DAn,ALa,PaP	3.00
11	3.00
12 DAn,ALa,PaP	3.00
13 DAn,ALa,F:Galactus,pt.1	3.00
14 DAn,ALa,F:Galactus,pt.2	3.00
15 DAn,ALa,F:Galactus,pt.3	3.00
16 DAn,ALa,Secret Invasion tie-in	3.00

Nova #9
© Marvel Entertainment Group

17 DAn,ALa,Secret Invasion tie-in	3.00
18 DAn,ALa,Secret Invasion tie-in	3.00
19 DAn,ALa(s),Nova Corps?	3.00
Ann. #1 DAn,ALa(s)	4.00

Nth MAN

Aug., 1989

1	2.50
2 thru 7	@2.50
8 DK	2.50
9 thru 16, finale, Sept., 1990	@2.50

NYX

Oct., 2003

1 JQ,gutterpunks	7.00
2 JQ,self-preservation's price	6.00
3 JQ,Y-23	40.00
4 JQ,F:Tatiana	6.00
5 JQ	4.00
6 JQ	3.00
7 JQ,finale	3.00
NYX Must Have, rep.#1–#3	5.00
NYX Must Have, rep.#4 & #5	4.00

NYX: NO WAY HOME

Aug., 20087

1 (of 6)	3.00
2 thru 3	@3.00

OBNOXIO THE CLOWN

April, 1983

1 X-Men	3.50

OFFCASTES

Epic *Heavy Hitters,* 1993

1 MV,I:Offcastes	2.50
2 MV,V:Kaoro	2.50
3 MV,Last Issue	2.50

OFFICIAL HANDBOOK OF THE MARVEL UNIVERSE

Avengers 2004	4.00
Daredevil 2004	4.00
Hulk 2004	4.00
Spider-Man 2004	4.00
Wolverine 2004	4.00
X-Men 2004	4.00
Book of the Dear 2004	4.00
Golden Age Marvel 2004	4.00
Horror 2005	4.00
Women of Marvel 2005	4.00

Marvel Knights 2005	4.00
Age of Apocalypse 2005	4.00
Spider-Man 2005	4.00
Teams 2005	4.00
Fantastic Four 2005	4.00
Avengers 2005	4.00
Spider-Man & Fantastic Four (2005)	4.00
Alternate Universes (2005)	4.00
X-Men (2005)	4.00
Squadron Supreme (2005)	4.00
Ultimate Marvel Universe #2	4.00

OFFICIAL MARVEL INDEX:

1985–88

TO THE AMAZING SPIDER-MAN

Index 1	3.00
Index 2 thru 9	@2.50

TO THE AVENGERS

Index 1 thru 7	@2.50

TO THE FANTASTIC FOUR

Index 1 thru 12	@2.50

TO MARVEL TEAM-UP

Index 1 thru 6	@2.50

TO THE X-MEN

Index 1 thru 7	@3.00

[Vol. 2] 1994

Index 1 thru 5	@2.50

OFFICIAL MARVEL TIMELINE

1-shot, 48-pg.	6.00

OFFICIAL TRUE CRIME CASES

Fall, 1947

24 (1)SSh(c),The Grinning Killer	300.00
25 (2)She Made Me a Killer,HK	250.00
Becomes:	

ALL-TRUE CRIME

1948

26 SSh(c),The True Story of Wilbur	
Underhill	450.00
27 Electric Chair(c),Robert Mais	350.00
28 Cops V:Gangsters(c)	150.00
29 Cops V:Gangsters(c)	150.00
30 He Picked a Murderous Mind	150.00
31 Hitchiking Thugs(c)	150.00
32 Jewel Thieves(c)	150.00
33 The True Story of Dinton	
Phillips	150.00
34 Case of the Killers Revenge	150.00
35 Ph(c),Date with Danger	150.00
36 Ph(c)	150.00
37 Ph(c),Story of Robert Marone	150.00
38 Murder Weapon,Nick Maxim	150.00
39 Story of Vince Vanderee	150.00
40	150.00
41 Lou 'Lucky' Raven	150.00
42 BK,Baby Face Nelson	175.00
43 Doc Channing Paulson	140.00
44 Murder in the Big House	140.00
45 While the City Sleeps	140.00
46	140.00
47 Gangster Terry Craig	140.00
48 GT,They Vanish By Night	140.00
49 BK,Squeeze Play	175.00
50 Shoot to Kill	140.00
51 Panic in the Big House	140.00
52 Prison Break, Sept., 1952	140.00

OMEGA FLIGHT

April, 2007

1 ScK	3.00
2 thru 5 ScK	@3.00

OMEGA THE UNKNOWN
March, 1976
1 JM,I:Omega	15.00
2 JM,A:Hulk	10.00
3 JM,A:Electro	10.00
4 JM,V:Yellow Claw	9.00
5 JM,V:The Wrench	9.00
6 JM,V:Blockbuster	9.00
7 JM,V:Blockbuster	9.00
8 JM,C:New Foolkiller,V:Nitro	10.00
9 JM,A:New Foolkiller,	
D:Blockbuster	14.00
10 JM,D:Omega the Unknown	8.00

OMEGA: THE UNKNOWN
Oct., 2007
1 (of 10)	3.00
2	3.00
3 thru 10	@3.00

ONE, THE
Epic, July, 1985
1 thru 5	@2.50
6 Feb., 1986	2.50

100 GREATEST MARVELS
Sept., 2001
1 (of 5) weekly, 112-pages	8.00
2 thru 5 112-pages	@8.00
5 Top 5 #5, 32-pages	4.00
4 Top 5 #4, 32-pages	4.00
3 Top 5 #3, 48-pages	4.00
2 Top 5 #2, 48-pages	4.00
1 Top 5 #1, 48-pages	4.00

101 WAYS TO END THE CLONE SAGA
1-shot (1997)	2.50

ONSLAUGHT
1996–97
Marvel Universe: AKu,SLo,MWd,	
Marvel Heroes vs. Onslaught	8.00
Marvel Universe: Gold edition	100.00
X-Men: AKu,SLo,MWd (1996)	7.00
X-Men: Gold editon	75.00
Onslaught: Epilogue (1997)	9.00

ONSLAUGHT REBORN
Nov., 2006
1 RLd	3.00
1a variant (c)	3.00
2 thru 5 JLb,RLd	@3.00
2a thru 5a variant (c)	@3.00

ONYX OVERLORD
Epic, 1992–93
1 JBi,Sequel to Airtight Garage	3.00
2 JBi,The Joule	3.00
3 JBi,V:Overlord	3.00
4 V:Starbilliard	3.00

OPEN SPACE
Dec., 1989–Aug., 1990
1	6.00
2 thru 4	@5.25

ORDER, THE
Feb., 2002
1 (of 6) KBk,JDy,MHy,F:Hulk, Namor,	
Dr. Strange, & Silver Surfer	2.50
2 KBk,JDy,MHy,A:Avengers	2.50
3 KBk,JDy,MHy,DPs,V:Avengers	2.50
4 KBk,JDy,DPs,Hulk,Nighthawk	2.50
5 KBk,JDy,DPs,F:Nighthawk	2.50
6 KBk,JDy,DPs,V:everybody	2.50

ORDER, THE
July, 2007
1 BKi	3.00
2 thru 5 BKi	@3.00
6 thru 10 BKi	@3.00

ORIGIN
Aug., 2001
1 (of 6) PJe,NKu,F:Wolverine	3.50
2 thru 6 PJe,NKu,JQ(c)	@3.50

ORIGINAL GHOST RIDER
1992–94
1 MT(c),rep.	2.50
2 thru 23 rep.	@2.50

ORIGINAL GHOST RIDER RIDES AGAIN
July, 1991
1 rep.GR#68+#69(O:JohnnyBlaze)	3.00
2 thru 7 rep.Ghost Rider.	@2.50

ORORO: BEFORE THE STORM
June, 2005
1 (of 4) Ororo Monroe in Cairo	3.00
2 thru 4	@3.00

OSBORN JOURNALS, THE
1997
1-shot KHt,F:Norman Osborn	3.00

OSCAR COMICS
Marvel USA Comics, 1947–49
(FUNNY TUNES spin-off)
1 (24)	250.00
2 (25) BW,HK,Hey Look	275.00
3	150.00
4 thru 9	@150.00
10 HK	175.00

Becomes:

AWFUL OSCAR
Marvel USA Comics, 1949
11	125.00
12	125.00

Becomes:

OSCAR
13	135.00

Oscar #5
© Marvel Entertainment Group

OUR LOVE
Sept., 1949
1 Ph(c),Guilt of Nancy Crane	200.00
2 Ph(c),My Kisses Were Cheap	150.00

OUR LOVE STORY
Oct., 1969
1 JB	100.00
2 JB	50.00
3 JB	50.00
4	50.00
5 JSo,JB	150.00
6 thru 13	@50.00
14 Gary Friedrich &Tarpe Mills	55.00
15 thru 37	@30.00
38 Feb., 1976.	30.00

OUTLAW FIGHTERS
Marvel Atlas, Aug., 1954
1 GT,Western Tales	150.00
2 GT ,JMn(c)	100.00
3	100.00
4 A;Patch Hawk	100.00
5 RH, Final Issue,April, 1955	100.00

OUTLAW KID
Atlas, Sept., 1954
1 SSh,DW,JMn(c),B&O:Outlaw Kid,	
A;Black Rider	350.00
2 DW,JMn(c),A:Black Rider	175.00
3 DW,AW,GWb,JMN(c)	175.00
4 DW(c),Death Rattle	150.00
5 JMn	150.00
6 JMn	150.00
7 JMn	150.00
8 AW,DW,JMn	150.00
9	125.00
10 JSe	125.00
11 thru 17	@100.00
18 AW,JMn	100.00
19 JSe,Sept., 1957	100.00

[2nd series] Aug., 1970
1 JSe(c),DW,Jo,Showdown,rep	40.00
2 DW,One Kid Too Many	25.00
3 HT(c),DW,Six Gun Double	
Cross	25.00
4 DW	20.00
5 DW	20.00
6 DW	20.00
7 HT(c),DW,Treachery on	
the Trail	20.00
8 HT(c),DW,RC,Six Gun Pay Off	30.00
9 JSe(c),DW,GWb,The Kids	
Last Stand	20.00
10 GK(c),DAy,NewO:Outlaw Kid	40.00
11 GK(c),Thunder Along the	
Big Iron	20.00
12 The Man Called Bounty Hawk	20.00
13 The Last Rebel	20.00
14 The Kid Gunslingers of	
Calibre City	20.00
15 GK(c),V:Madman of Monster	
Mountain	20.00
16 The End of the Trail	20.00
17 thru 29	@20.00
30 Oct., 1975	20.00

OVER THE EDGE AND UNDER A BUCK
1995–96
1 F:Daredevil vs. Mr. Fear	2.50
2 F:Doctor Strange	2.50
3 F:Hulk	2.50
4 in Cypress Hills	2.50
5	2.50
6 F:Daredevil	2.50
7 Doc & Nightmare	2.50

PARADISE X: THE HERALDS

Oct., 2001

1 (of 3) AxR, Earth X trilogy	3.50
2 AxR,	3.50
3 AxR,StP,concl.	3.50

PARADISE X

Feb., 2002

1 (of 13) AxR,Earth X trilogy	3.50
2 AxR,DBw,F:Captain Mar-Vell	3.50
3 AxR,DBw,King Britain,Medusa	3.00
4 AxR,DBw,nature of new Paradise	3.00
5 AxR,DBw	3.00
6 AxR,DBw,the new Death	3.00
7 AxR,DBw	3.00
8 AxR,DBw	3.00
9 AxR,DBw,O:Ghost Rider	3.00
10 AxR,DBw,F:Matt Murcock	3.00
11 AxR,DBw,F:Harry Pym	3.00
12 AxR,DBw,concl.	3.00
Spec.#0, AxR, prologue to series	3.50
Special A DBw	3.00
Special 1-shot, AxR	3.00
GN Paradise X:Xen, 56-pg.	4.50
GN Devils AxR, 48-pg.	4.50

PARADISE X/RAGNAROK

Jan., 2003

1 (of 2) AxR.	3.00
2 AxR	3.00

PARAGON

1 I:Paragon,Nightfire.	5.00

PATSY & HEDY

Marvel Atlas, Feb., 1952

1 AJ(c),B:Patsy Walker & Hedy Wolfe	300.00
2 Skating(c)	175.00
3 Boyfriend Trouble	150.00
4 Swimsuit(c)	150.00
5 Patsy's Date(c)	150.00
6 Swimsuit/Picnic(c)	150.00
7 Double-Date(c)	150.00
8 AJ(c),The Dance	150.00
9	150.00
10	150.00
11 thru 25	@125.00
26 thru 50	@100.00
51 thru 60	@100.00
61 thru 109	@100.00
110 Feb., 1967	100.00

PATSY & HER PALS

May, 1953

1 MWs(c),F:Patsy Walker	250.00
2 MWs(c),Swimsuit(c)	125.00
3 MWs(c),Classroom(c)	100.00
4 MWs(c),Golfcourse(c)	100.00
5 MWs(c).Patsy/Buzz(c)	100.00
6 thru 28	@100.00
29 Aug., 1957.	100.00

PATSY WALKER

1945

1 F:Patsy Walker Adventures	800.00
2 Patsy/Car(c)	400.00
3 Skating(c)	300.00
4 Perfume(c)	300.00
5 Archery Lesson, Eye Injury(c)	325.00
6 Bus(c)	300.00
7 Charity Drive(c)	300.00
8 Organ Driver Monkey(c)	300.00
9 Date(c)	300.00
10 Skating(c),Wedding Bells, A:Millie	300.00
11 Date with a Dream,A:Mitzi	175.00

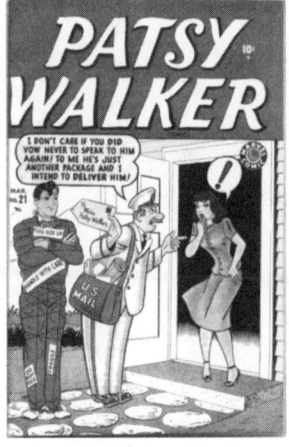

Patsy Walker #21
© Marvel Entertainment Group

12 Love in Bloom,Artist(c), A:Rusty	175.00
13 Swimsuit(c),There Goes My Heart;HK,Hey Look	175.00
14 An Affair of the Heart, HK,Hey Look	175.00
15 Dance(c)	175.00
16 Skating(c)	175.00
17 Patsy's Diary(c),HK,Hey Look	225.00
18 Autograph(c)	200.00
19 HK,Hey Look	200.00
20 HK,Hey Look	200.00
21 HK,Hey Look	200.00
22 HK,Hey Look	200.00
23	150.00
24	150.00
25 HK,Rusty	200.00
26 thru 29	@125.00
30 HK,Egghead Double	125.00
31	125.00
32 thru 56	@100.00
57 thru 58 AJ(c)	@125.00
59 thru 99	@100.00
100	100.00
Fashion Parade #1	150.00

PATSY WALKER: HELLCAT

July, 2008

1 (of 5) SI(s),Agent of the Initiative.	3.00
2 SI(c)	3.00
3 SI(c)	3.00
3a monkey variant SI (c).	3.00
4 SI(c)	3.00

PENANCE: RELENTLESS

Sept., 2007

1 (of 5)PJe,PG	3.00
2 thru 3	@3.00
4 PJe,PG	3.00
5	3.00

PETER PARKER, THE SPECTACULAR SPIDER-MAN

Dec., 1976

1 SB,V:Tarantula	90.00
2 SB,V:Kraven,Tarantula	30.00
3 SB,I:Lightmaster	25.00

4 SB,V:Vulture,Hitman	25.00
5 SB,V:Hitman,Vulture	25.00
6 SB,V:Morbius,rep.M.T.U.#3	27.00
7 SB,V:Morbius,A:Human Torch	28.00
8 SB,V:Morbius.	28.00
9 SB,I:White Tiger.	20.00
10 SB,A:White Tiger	15.00
11 JM,V:Medusa	15.00
12 SB,V:Brother Power	15.00
13 SB,V:Brother Power	15.00
14 SB,V:Brother Power	15.00
15 SB,V:Brother Power	15.00
16 SB,V:The Beetle	15.00
17 SB,A:Angel & Iceman Champions disbanded.	15.00
18 SB,A:Angel & Iceman	15.00
19 SB,V:The Enforcers	12.00
20 SB,V:Lightmaster	12.00
21 JM,V:Scorpion	10.00
22 MZ,A:Moon Knight,V:Cyclone	12.00
23 A:Moon Knight,V:Cyclone	12.00
24 FS,A:Hypno-Hustler	10.00
25 JM,FS,I:Carrion	11.00
26 JM,A:Daredevil,V:Carrion	10.00
27 DC,FM,I:Miller Daredevil, V:Carrion	60.00
28 FM,A:Daredevil,V:Carrion	50.00
29 JM,FS,V:Carrion	7.00
30 JM,FS,V:Carrion	7.00
31 JM,FS,D:Carrion	7.00
32 BL,JM,FS,V:Iguana	7.00
33 JM,FS,O:Iguana	7.00
34 JM,FS,V:Iguana,Lizard	7.00
35 V:Mutant Mindworm	7.00
36 JM,V:Swarm	7.00
37 DC,MN,V:Swarm	7.00
38 SB,V:Morbius	7.00
39 JM,JR2,V:Schizoid Man	8.00
40 FS,V:Schizoid Man	8.00
41 JM,V:Meteor Man,A:GiantMan	7.00
42 JM,A:Fant.Four,V:Frightful 4	7.00
43 JBy(c),MZ,V:The Ringer, V:Belladonna	7.00
44 JM,V:The Vulture	7.00
45 MSe,V:The Vulture	7.00
46 FM(c),MZ,V:Cobra	7.00
47 MSe,A:Prowler II.	7.00
48 MSe,A:Prowler II.	7.00
49 MSe,I:Smuggler	7.00
50 JR2,JM,V:Mysterio	7.00
51 MSe&FM(c),V:Mysterio	7.00
52 FM(c),D:White Tiger	7.00
53 JM,FS,V:Terrible Tinkerer	7.00
54 FM,WS,MSe,V:Silver Samurai	7.00
55 LMc,JM,V:Nitro	7.00
56 FM,JM,V:Jack-o-lantern	12.00

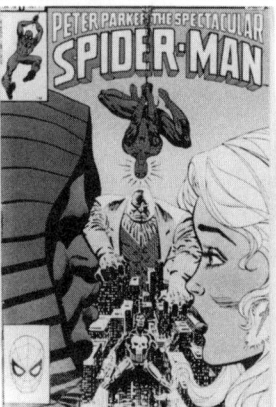

Peter Parker, The Spectacular Spider-Man #82 © Marvel Entertainment Group

57 JM,V:Will-o-the Wisp. 6.00
58 JBy,V:Ringer,A:Beetle. 7.00
59 JM,V:Beetle. 6.00
60 JM&FM(c),O:Spider-Man,
   V:Beetle. 7.00
61 JM,V:Moonstone 5.00
62 JM,V:Goldbug 5.00
63 JM,V:Molten Man 5.00
64 JM,I:Cloak & Dagger. 15.00
65 BH,JM,V:Kraven,Calypso 5.00
66 JM,V:Electro 5.00
67 AMb,V:Boomerang 5.00
68 LMc,JM,V:Robot of Mendell
   Stromm 5.00
69 AM,A:Cloak & Dagger. 10.00
70 A:Cloak & Dagger 10.00
71 JM,Gun Control issue 5.00
72 AM,V:Dr.Octopus 5.00
73 AM,JM,V:Dr.Octopus,A:Owl 5.00
74 AM,JM,V:Dr.Octopus,R:Bl.Cat . . 5.00
75 AM,JM,V:Owl,Dr.Octopus 6.00
76 AM,Black Cat on deathbed 5.00
77 AM,V:Gladiator,Dr.Octopus 5.00
78 AM,V:Dr.Octopus,C:Punisher . . . 5.00
79 AM,V:Dr.Octopus,A:Punisher . . . 5.00
80 AM,F:J.Jonah Jameson 5.00
81 A:Punisher 6.00
82 A:Punisher. 8.00
83 A:Punisher. 8.00
84 AM,F:Black Cat 4.00
85 AM,O:Hobgoblin powers
   (Ned Leeds) 11.00
86 FH,V:Fly 4.00
87 AM,Reveals I.D.to Black Cat . . . 4.00
88 AM,V:Cobra,Mr.Hyde 4.00
89 AM,Secret Wars,A:Kingpin 5.00
90 AM,Secret Wars 6.00
91 AM,V:Blob 4.00
92 AM,I:Answer 4.00
93 AM,V:Answer 4.00
94 AM,A:Cloak & Dagger,V:
   Silver Mane. 4.00
95 AM,A:Cloak & Dagger,V:
   Silvermane. 4.00
96 AM,A:Cloak & Dagger,V:
   Silvermane. 4.00
97 HT,JM,A:Black Cat 4.00
98 HT,JM,I:Spot 4.00
99 HT,JM,V:Spot 4.00
100 AM,V:Kingpin,C:Bl.Costume . . . 6.00
101 JBy(c),AM,V:Killer Shrike 3.00
102 JBy(c),AM,V:Backlash 3.00
103 AM,V:Blaze;Not John Blaze . . . 3.00
104 JBy(c),AM,V:Rocket Racer 3.00
105 AM,A:Wasp 3.00
106 AM,A:Wasp 3.00
107 RB,D:Jean DeWolf,I:SinEater . . 4.00
108 RB,A:Daredevil,V:Sin-Eater . . . 3.00
109 RB,A:Daredevil,V:Sin-Eater . . . 3.00
110 RB,A:Daredevil,V:Sin-Eater . . . 3.00
111 RB,Secret Wars II 3.00
112 RB,A:Santa Claus,Black Cat. . . 3.00
113 RB,Burglars,A:Black Cat. 3.00
114 BMc,V:Lock Picker 3.00
115 BMc,A:Black Cat,Dr.Strange,
   I:Foreigner 4.00
116 A:Dr.Strange, Foreigner,
   Black Cat, Sabretooth 10.00
117 DT,C:Sabretooth,A:Foreigner,
   Black Cat,Dr.Strange 4.00
118 MZ,D:Alexander,V:SHIELD 3.00
119 RB,BMc,V:Sabretooth,
   A:Foreigner,Black Cat 10.00
120 KG 3.00
121 RB,BMc,V:Mauler 3.00
122 V:Mauler 3.00
123 V:Foreigner,Black Cat 3.00
124 V:Dr.Octopus. 3.00
125 V:Wr.Crew,A:Spiderwoman 3.00
126 JM,A:Sp.woman,V:Wrecker . . . 3.00
127 AM,V:Lizard. 3.00
128 C:DDevil,A:Bl.Cat,Foreigner . . . 3.50

129 A:Black Cat,V:Foreigner 3.00
130 A:Hobgoblin. 6.00
131 MZ,BMc,V:Kraven 7.00
132 MZ,BMc,V:Kraven. 7.00
133 BSz(c),Mad Dog,pt.3 . . . . 5.00
Ann.#1 RB,JM,V:Dr.Octopus 15.00
Ann.#2 JM,I&O:Rapier 7.00
Ann.#3 JM,V:Manwolf 5.00
Ann.#4 AM,O:Aunt May,A:Bl.Cat . . . 5.00
Ann.#5 I:Ace,Joy Mercado. 5.00
Ann.#6 V:Ace 4.50
Ann.#7 Honeymoon iss,A:Puma . . . 4.50
Becomes:

SPECTACULAR
SPIDER-MAN

PETER PARKER:
SPIDER-MAN
Nov., 1998

1 JR2,HMe,SHa,A:new Spider-Man,
   V:Ranger,48-page 3.00
1a signed 15.00
2 JR2,HMe,SHa,A:Thor 4.00
2a variant cover 4.00
3 HMe,JR2,SHa,A:Iceman
   V:Shadrac 3.00
4 HMe,JR2,SHa,V:Marrow 3.00
5 HMe,SHa,BS,JBy(c),F:Spider-
   Woman,Aunt May, Black Cat. . . 3.00
6 HMe,SHa,RJ2,JBy(c),V:Kingpin . 3.00
7 JR2,HMe,SHa,Reality Bent 3.00
8 JR2,HMe,SHa,V:Bullseye 3.00
9 JR2,HMe,SHa,R:Venom 3.00
10 JR2,HMe,SHa,R:Carnage. 3.00
11 JR2,HMe,SHa,Eighth Day,pt.3
   x-over. 3.00
12 JR2,HMe,SHa, 48-pg. 3.50
13 JR2,HMe 3.00
14 JR2,HMe,A:Hulk 3.50
15 JR2,HMe,x-over 3.50
16 JR2,HMe,V:Sinister Six. 3.00
17 JR2,HMe,SHa,V:Kraven. 2.50
18 HMe,JR2,SHa,V:Green Goblin . . 2.50
19 HMe,JR2,SHa,Mary Jane dies . . 2.50
20 PJe,MBu,Mary Jane dead. . . 3.00
21 PJe,MBu,DGr,HumanTorch. 2.50
22 PJe,MBu,DGr,FlintMarko 2.50
23 PJe,MBu,DGr,Type Face 2.50
24 PJe,MBu,DGr,Max.Security 2.50
25 PJe,MBu,DGr,V:Green Goblin . . 3.50
26 PJe,JoB,DGr,F:NYPD 2.50
27 PJe,MBu,DGr,F:NYPD 2.50
28 PJe,MBu,DGr,. 2.50
29 PJe,CAd,DGr,x-over 7.00
30 PJe,MBu,HuR(c),I:Terminal 7.00
31 PJe,MBu,HuR(c),I:Fusion 3.50
32 PJe,MBu,HuR(c),V:Fusion 2.50
33 PJe,MBu,HuR(c),ballpark 2.50
34 PJe,MBu,cleanse the city 2.50
35 PJe,MBu,Jamal. 2.50
36 PJe,MBu,private-eye. 2.50
37 PJe,slice-of-life 2.50
38 PJe,MBu,V:Mimes,'Nuff Said . . . 2.50
39 PJe,MBu,return of Dr. Octopus . . 2.50
40 PJe,MBu,Doc Octopus,pt.2 . . . . 2.50
41 PJe,MBu,Doc Octopus,pt.3 . . . . 2.50
42 Spring Break,pt.1 . . . . 2.50
43 Spring Break,pt.2 . . . . 2.50
44 PJe,HuR,R:Green Goblin 6.00
45 PJe,HuR,R:Green Goblin,pt.2 . . 4.00
46 PJe,HuR,R:Green Goblin,pt.3 . . 2.50
47 PJe,HuR,R:Green Goblin,pt.4 . . 2.50
48 PJe,MBu 2.50
49 PJe,MBu 2.50
50 PJe,MBu 4.00
51 pt.1 . . . . 2.50
52 pt.2 . . . . 2.50
53 pt.1 . . . . 2.50
54 pt.2 . . . . 2.50
55 pt.3 . . . . 2.50

56 SK,Reborn,pt.1,F:Sandman 2.50
57 SK,Reborn,pt.2,F:Sandman 2.50
Ann.1999,CCs, 48-pg. 4.00
Ann.2000 CCl,JoB,80-pg. 4.00
Ann.2001 South America, 28-pg. . . . 3.50
Spec. Peter Parker, Spider-
   Man 2000 . . . . 4.00

PETER PORKER
Star, May, 1985

1 Parody 4.50
2 thru 17 . . . . @3.00

PETER, THE LITTLE PEST
Nov., 1969–May, 1970

1 F:Peter 100.00
2 Rep,Dexter & Melvin 60.00
3 Rep,Dexter & Melvin 60.00
4 Rep,Dexter & Melvin 60.00

PHANTOM
1995

1 Lee Falk's Phantom. 4.00
2 V:General Babalar 4.00
3 final issue. 4.00

The Phantom 2040 #3
© *Marvel Entertainment Group*

PHANTOM 2040
1995

1 Based on cartoon 2.50
2 V:Alloy 2.50
3 MPa,V:Crime Syndicate. 2.50
4 Vision Quest 2.50

PHOENIX
(UNTOLD STORY)
April, 1984

1 JBy,O:Phoenix (R.Summers). . . 15.00

PILGRIM'S PROGRESS
1 adapts John Bunyans novel . . . 10.00

PINHEAD
1993–94

1 Red Foil(c),from Hellraiser. 3.00
2 DGC(s),V:Cenobites 2.50
3 DGC(s),V:Cenobites 2.50
4 DGC(s),V:Cenobites 2.50
5 DGC(s),Devil in Disguise 2.50
6 DGC(s), ... 2.50

PINHEAD VS. MARSHALL LAW
1993
1 and 2 KON,In Hell . . . . @3.00

PINOCCHIO & THE EMPEROR OF THE NIGHT
March, 1988
1 Movie adapt. 3.00

PINT-SIZED X-BABIES: MURDERAMA
June, 1998
1-shot, Mojo, Arcade, 48-pg. 3.00

PIRATES OF DARK WATERS
Nov., 1991
1 based on T.V. series 3.00
2 Search for 13 Treasures 3.00
3 V:Albino Warriors,Konk 3.00
4 A:Monkey Birds 3.00
5 Tula Steals 1st Treasuer 3.00
6 thru 9 . . . . @3.00

PITT, THE
March, 1988
1 SB,SDr,A:Spitfire 4.00

PLANET OF THE APES
Aug., 1974–Feb., 1977
(black & white magazine)
1 MP 45.00
2 MP 30.00
3 thru 10 . . . . @25.00
11 thru 20 . . . . @30.00
21 thru 29 . . . . @65.00

PLANET TERRY
Star, April, 1985
1 thru 12 . . . . @3.00

PLASMER
Marvel UK, 1993–94
1 A:Captain America 3.50
2 A:Captain Britain,Black Knight. . . 2.50
3 A:Captain Britain 2.50
4 A:Captain Britain 2.50
5 thru 7 . . . . @2.50

PLASTIC FORKS
Epic, 1990
1 . . . . 6.00
2 thru 5 . . . . @5.50

POLICE ACADEMY
Nov., 1989
1 Based on TV Cartoon 2.50
2 thru 6 . . . . @2.50

POLICE ACTION
Jan., 1954
1 JF,GC,JMn(c),Riot Squad 275.00
2 JF,Over the Wall 150.00
3 JMn 125.00
4 DAy 125.00
5 DAy,JMn 125.00
6 . . . . 125.00
7 BPNov., 1954 . . . . 125.00

POLICE BADGE #479
Marvel Atlas, 1955
5 . . . . 125.00

POLICE STRIKE BACK AT GANGLAND!

Police Action #1
© *Marvel Entertainment Group*

POLICE BADGE
See: SPY THRILLERS

POPPLES
Star, Dec., 1986
1 Based on Toys 3.00
2 thru 5 . . . . @3.00

POWDERED TOAST-MAN
Spec. F:Powder Toast-Man. 3.25

POWERHOUSE PEPPER COMICS
1943—Nov., 1948
1 BW,Movie Auditions(c) 3,000.00
2 BW,Dinner(c) 1,300.00
3 BW,Boxing Ring(c) 1,200.00
4 BW,Subway(c) 1,200.00
5 BW,Bankrobbers(c) 1,400.00

POWERLESS
June, 2004
1 thru 6 . . . . @3.00

POWER LINE
Epic, May, 1988
1 BMc(i) 2.50
2 Aw(i) 2.50
3 A:Dr Zero 2.50
4 . . . . 2.50
5 thru 8 GM. . . . . @2.50

POWER MAN
Prev: Hero for Hire
Feb., 1974
17 GT,A:Iron Man. 25.00
18 GT,V:Steeplejack. 15.00
19 GT,V:Cottonmouth 15.00
20 GT,Heroin Story 15.00
21 V:Original Power Man. 10.00
22 V:Stiletto & Discus 10.00
23 V:Security City 10.00
24 GT,I:BlackGoliath(BillFoster). . . 10.00
25 A:Circus of Crime 10.00
26 GT,V:Night Shocker 10.00
27 GP,AMc,V:Man Called X 10.00
28 V:Cockroach 10.00
29 V:Mr.Fish. 10.00
30 RB,KJ,KP,I:Piranha 10.00
31 SB,NA(i),V:Piranha 10.00
32 JSt,FR,A:Wildfire. 8.00

33 FR,A:Spear 8.00
34 FR,A:Spear,Mangler 8.00
35 DA,A:Spear,Mangler 8.00
36 V:Chemistro 8.00
37 V:Chemistro 8.00
38 V:Chemistro 8.00
39 KJ,V:Chemistro,Baron 8.00
40 V:Baron 8.00
41 TP,V:Thunderbolt,Goldbug 8.00
42 V:Thunderbolt,Goldbug. 8.00
43 AN,V:Mace 8.00
44 TP,A:Mace. 8.00
45 JSn,A:Mace. 8.00
46 GT,I:Zzzax(recreated) 8.00
47 BS,A:Zzzax 10.00
48 JBy,A:Iron Fist. 15.00
49 JBy,A:Iron Fist. 15.00
Becomes:

POWER MAN & IRON FIST
1978
50 JBy,I:Team-up with Iron Fist . . . 15.00
51 MZ,Night on the Town. 4.00
52 MZ,V:Death Machines 4.00
53 SB,O:Nightshade 4.00
54 TR,O:Iron Fist 4.00
55 Chaos at the Coliseum 4.00
56 Mayhem in the Museum 4.00
57 X-Men,V:Living Monolith. 40.00
58 1st El Aguila(Drug) 4.00
59 BL(c),TVE,V:Big Apple
    Bomber. 4.00
60 BL(c),V:Terrorists 4.00
61 BL(c),V:The Maggia 4.00
62 BL(c),KGa,V:Man Mountain
    D:Thunerbolt 4.00
63 BL(c),Cage Fights Fire 4.00
64 DGr&BL(c),V:Suetre,Muertre . . . 4.00
65 BL(c),A:El Aquila. 4.00
66 FM(c),Sabretooth(2nd App.) . . . 60.00
67 V:Bushmaster 4.00
68 FM(c),V:Athur Nagan 4.00
69 V:Soldier 4.00
70 FM(c)V:El Supremo 4.00
71 FM(c),I:Montenegro 4.00
72 FM(c),V:Chako 4.00
73 FM(c),V:Rom. 4.00
74 FM(c),V:Ninja 4.00
75 KGa,O:IronFist 4.00
76 KGa,V:Warhawk 4.00
77 KGa,A:Daredevil 4.00
78 KGa,A:El Aguila,Sabretooth
    (Slasher)(3rd App.) 35.00
79 V:Dredlox 3.00
80 KJ(c),V:Montenegro 3.00
81 V:Black Tiger. 3.00
82 V:Black Tiger. 3.00
83 V:Warhawk 3.00
84 V:Constrictor,A:Sabertooth
    (4th App.). 35.00
85 KP,V:Mole Man 3.00
86 A:Moon Knight 3.00
87 A:Moon Knight 3.00
88 V:Scimtar. 3.00
89 V:Terrorists 3.00
90 V:Unus BS(c) 3.00
91 Paths and Angles 3.00
92 V:Hammeread,I:New Eel 3.00
93 A:Chemistro 3.00
94 V:Chemistro 3.00
95 Danny Rand 3.00
96 V,Chemistro 3.00
97 K'unlun,A:Fera 3.00
98 V:Shades & Commanche 3.00
99 R:Daught.of Dragon 3.00
100 O:K'unlun,DoubleSize. 5.00
101 A:Karnak 3.00
102 V:Doombringer 3.00
103 O:Doombringer 3.00
104 V:Dr.Octopus,Lizard 3.00
105 F:Crime Buster 3.00
106 Luke Gets Shot. 3.00
107 JBy(c),Terror issue 3.00

MARVEL

Power Man & Iron Fist #125
© Marvel Entertainment Group

108 V:Inhuman Monster. 3.00
109 V:The Reaper 3.00
110 V:Nightshade,Eel. 3.00
111 I:Captain Hero 3.00
112 JBy(c),V:Control7 . . . . 3.00
113 JBy(c),A:Capt.Hero 3.00
114 JBy(c),V:Control7 . . . . 3.00
115 JBy(c),V:Stanley 3.00
116 JBy(c),V:Stanley 3.00
117 R:K'unlun. 3.00
118 A:Colleen Wing 3.00
119 A:Daught.of Dragon 3.00
120 V:Chiantang 3.00
121 Secret Wars II. 3.00
122 V:Dragonkin 3.00
123 V:Race Killer. 3.00
124 V:Yellowclaw 3.00
125 MBr,LastIssue;D:Iron Fist 5.00
G-Size#1 reprints. 4.00
Ann.#1 Earth Shock. 20.00

POWER PACHYDERMS
Sept., 1989
1 Elephant Superheroes 2.50

POWER PACK
Aug., 1984
1 JBr,BWi,I&O:Power Pack,
  I:Snarks 2.50
2 JBr,BWi,V:Snarks. 2.50
3 JBr,BWi,V:Snarks. 2.50
4 JBr,BWi,V:Snarks. 2.50
5 JBr,BWi,V:Bogeyman. 2.50
6 JBr,BWi,A:Spider-Man 2.50
7 JBr,BWi,A:Cloak & Dagger 2.50
8 JBr,BWi,A:Cloak & Dagger 2.50
9 BA,BWi,A:Marrina 2.50
10 BA,BWi,A:Marrina. 2.50
11 JBr,BWi,V:Morlocks 2.50
12 JBr,BWi,A:X-Men,V:Morlocks . . . 3.00
13 BA,BWi,Baseball issue 2.50
14 JBr,BWi,V:Bogeyman 2.50
15 JBr,BWi,A:Beta Ray Bill 2.50
16 JBr,BWi,I&O:Kofi,J:Tattletale
  (Franklin Richards) 2.50
17 JBr,BWi,V:Snarks 2.50
18 BA,SW,Secret Wars II,V:Kurse. . 2.50
19 BA,SW,Doub.size,Wolverine. . . . 4.00
20 BMc,A:NewMutants 2.50
21 BA,TA,C:Spider-Man 2.50
22 JBg,BWi,V:Snarks. 2.50
23 JBg,BWi,V:Snarks,C:FF 2.50
24 JBg,BWi,V:Snarks,C:Cloak. 2.50

25 JBg,BWi,A:FF,V:Snarks 2.50
26 JBg,BWi,A:Cloak & Dagger 2.50
27 JBg,AG,A:Wolverine,X-Factor,
  V:Sabretooth 5.00
28 A:Fantastic Four,Hercules. 2.50
29 JBg,DGr,A:SpM,V:Hobgoblin . . . 2.50
30 VM,Crack 2.50
31 JBg,I:Trash 2.50
32 JBg,V:Trash 2.50
33 JBg,A:Sunspot,Warlock,
  C:Spider-Man. 2.50
34 TD,V:Madcap 2.50
35 JBg,A:X-Factor,D:Plague 2.50
36 JBg,V:Master Mold 2.50
37 SDr(i),I:Light-Tracker 2.50
38 SDr(i),V:Molecula 2.50
39 V:Bogeyman 2.50
40 A:New Mutants,V:Bogeyman . . . 2.50
41 SDr(i),V:The Gunrunners 2.50
42 JBg,SDr,Inferno,V:Bogeyman . . . 2.50
43 JBg,SDr,AW,Inferno,
  V:Bogeyman 2.50
44 JBr,Inferno,A:New Mutants 2.50
45 JBr,End battle w/Bogeyman 2.50
46 WPo,A:Punisher,Dakota North . . 2.50
47 JBg,I:Bossko. 2.50
48 JBg,Toxic Waste #1 . . . . 2.50
49 JBg,JSh,Toxic Waste #2 . . . . . . 2.50
50 AW(i),V:Snarks 2.50
51 GM,I:Numinus 2.50
52 AW(i),V:Snarks,A:Numinus 2.50
53 EC,A of V,A:Typhoid Mary 2.50
54 JBg,V:Mad Thinker 2.50
55 DSp,V:Mysterio 2.50
56 TMo,A:Fant.Four,Nova 2.50
57 TMo,A:Nova,V:Star Stalker 2.50
58 TMo,A:Galactus,Mr.Fantastic . . . 2.50
59 TMo,V:Ringmaster 2.50
60 TMo,V:Puppetmaster 2.50
61 TMo,V:Red Ghost & Apes. 2.50
62 V:Red Ghost & Apes
  (last issue). 2.50
Holiday Spec.JBr,Small Changes . . 2.50

April, 2005
1 (of 4) I know what we did
  That Summer. 3.00
2 Misadventures in Babysitting. . . . 3.00
3 F:Fantastic Four. 3.00
4 End of the Rainbow 3.00
Digest Vol. 1. . . . . 7.00

...DAY ONE
Mar., 2008
1 (of 4) O:Power Pack 3.00
2 thru 4 . . . . @3.00

...PEER PRESSURE
June, 2000
1 (of 4) TA,CDo. 3.00
2 TA,CDo,V:Snarks. 3.00
3 TA,CDo, ... 3.00
4 Ta,CDo,concl 3.00

POWERS
Marvel Icon, July, 2004
1 BMB,F:Deena Pilgrim 3.00
2 thru 5 BMB . . . . @3.00
6 thru 12 . . . . @3.00
13 thru 18 Cosmic . . . . @3.00
19 thru 24 Secret Identity. . . . . . . @3.00
25 25 Coolest Dead Super Heroes . 3.00
25a variant (c) 3.00
26 25 Coolest Dead Superheroes. . 3.00
27 25 Coolest Dead Superheroes . . 4.00
28 25 Coolest Dead Superheroes. . 4.00
28 25 Coolest Dead Superheroes. . 4.00
29 25 Coolest Dead Superheroes. . 4.00
30 Redemption of Deena Pilgrim. . . 4.00
31 Z 4.00
32 Z, pt.2 . . . . 4.00
Spec. Encyclopedia, Vol. 1 . . . . . . 4.00
Ann. 2008. . . . . 5.00

PRINCE NAMOR,
THE SUB-MARINER
Sept., 1984
1 I:Dragonrider, Dara 3.00
2 I:Proteus 2.50
3 . . . . 2.50
4 Dec., 1984 . . . . 2.50

PRINCE VALIANT
1994–95
1 JRy,CV,Thule, Camelot
  and the Misty Isles 4.00
2 JRy,CV. 4.00
3 JRy,CV. 4.00

Prince Valiant #4
© Marvel Entertainment Group

4 JRy,CV, final issue. 4.00

PRIVATE EYE
Marvel Atlas, Jan., 1951
1 . . . . 275.00
2 . . . . 175.00
3 GT 175.00
4 . . . . 125.00
5 . . . . 125.00
6 JSt 125.00
7 . . . . 125.00
8 March, 1952. . . . . 125.00

PROFESSOR XAVIER
AND THE X-MEN
1995
1 1st Year Together. 3.00
2 V:The Vanisher 2.50
3 FaN,F:The Blob 2.50
4 V:Magneto & Brotherhood 2.50
5 & 6 . . . . @2.50
7 FdS,Sub-Mariner 2.50
8 thru 12 . . . . @2.50
13 AHo,F:Juggernaut. 2.50
14 JGz,V:Juggernaut. 2.50
15 JGz,F:Quicksilver & Scarlet
  Witch 2.50
16 . . . . 2.50
17 JGz,V:Sentinels,F:Beast 2.50
18 JGz,X-Men vs. Sentinels,
  final issue 2.50

PROWLER, THE
1994
1 Creatures of the Night, pt.1 . . . . 2.50
2 V:Nightcreeper, Creatures, pt.2 . . 2.50

3 Creatures of the Night, pt.3 . . . . . 2.50	
4 V:Vulture, Creatures, pt.4 . . . . . . 2.50	

PSI FORCE
Nov., 1986
1 MT,O:PSI Force 2.50
2 thru 9 MT . . . . @2.50
10 thru 32 . . . . @2.50
Ann.#1 . . . . 3.00

PSYCHONAUTS
Epic, 1993–94
1 thru 4 War in the Future . . . . . . @5.50

PSYLOCKE & ANGEL:
CRIMSON DAWN
1997
1 SvL,ATi,V:Obsideon 3.00
2 SvL,ATi, ... 3.00
3 BRa,SvL,ATi 3.00
4 (of 4) BRa,SvL,ATi 3.00

PULSE, THE
Feb., 2004
1 BMB,MBa,Thin Air,pt.1 . . . . 5.00
2 BMB,MBa,Thin Air,pt.2,F:Vulture . 3.50
3 BMB,MBa,Thin Air,pt.3 . . . . 3.00
4 BMB,MBa,Thin Air,pt.4 . . . . 3.00
5 BMB,MBa,Thin Air,pt.5 . . . . 3.00
6 BMB,BA,Secret War,pt.1 . . . . . . 3.00
7 BMB,BA,Secret War,pt.2 . . . . . . 3.00
8 BMB,Secret War,pt.3 . . . . 3.00
9 BMB,Secret War,pt.4, concl. 3.00
10 BMB,House of M tie-in 4.00
11 BMB,Birth of Jessica Jones &
    Luke Cage's Baby 3.00
12 BMB, A:D-Man 3.00
13 BMB,F:Jessica Jones, baby 3.00
14 BMB,F:Luke Cage 3.00
Spec. BMB,House of M 2.50

PUNISHER
[Limited Series] Jan., 1986
1 MZ,Circle of Blood,double size . 25.00
2 MZ,Back to the War. 15.00
3 MZ,V:The Right 12.00
4 MZ,V:The Right 12.00
5 V:Jigsaw,end Mini-Series. 12.00
[Regular Series] 1987–95
1 KJ,V:Wilfred Sobel,Drugs 15.00

Punisher #25
© Marvel Entertainment Group

2 KJ,V:General Trahn,Bolivia 6.00	
3 KJ,V:Colonel Fryer. 6.00	
4 KJ,I:The Rev,Microchip Jr. 6.00	
5 KJ,V:The Rev. 6.00	
6 DR,KN,V:The Rosettis 5.00	
7 DR,V:Ahmad,D:Rose. 5.00	

8 WPo,SW(1st Punisher),
    V:Sigo & Roky 4.00
9 WPo,SW,D:MicrochipJr,V:Sigo . . 4.00
10 WPo,SW,A:Daredevil (x-over
    w/Daredevil #257) 7.00
11 WPo,SW,O:Punisher. 3.00
12 WPo,SW,V:Gary Saunders. 3.00
13 WPo,SW,V:Lydia Spoto 3.00
14 WPo,SW,I:McDowell,Brooks. . . . 3.00
15 WPo,SW,V:Kingpin 3.00
16 WPo,SW,V:Kingpin. 3.00
17 WPo,SW,V:Kingpin 3.00
18 WPo,SW,V:Kingpin,C:X-Men . . . 3.00
19 LSn,In Australia. 3.00
20 WPo(c),In Las Vegas 3.00
21 EL,SW,Boxing Issue 3.00
22 EL,SW,I:Saracen. 3.00
23 EL,SW,V:Scully 3.00
24 EL,SW,A:Shadowmasters. 3.00
25 EL,AW,A:Shadowmasters. 3.00
26 RH,Oper.Whistle Blower#1 . . . . 3.00
27 RH,Oper.Whistle Blower#2 . . . . 3.00
28 BR,A:Dr.Doom,A of Veng 3.00
29 BR,A:Dr.Doom,A of Veng. 3.00
30 BR,V:Geltrate 3.00
31 BR,V:Bikers #1 . . . . 2.50
32 BR,V:Bikers #2 . . . . 2.50
33 BR,V:The Reavers 2.50
34 BR,V:The Reavers 2.50
35 BR,MF,Jigsaw Puzzle #1 . . . . . 2.50
36 MT,MF,Jigsaw Puzzle #2 . . . . . 2.50
37 MT,Jigsaw Puzzle #3 . . . . 2.50
38 BR,MF,Jigsaw Puzzle #4 . . . . . 2.50
39 JSh,Jigsaw Puzzle #5. . . . . 2.50
40 BR,JSh,Jigsaw Puzzle #6. . . . . 2.50
41 BR,TD,V:Terrorists 2.50
42 MT,V:Corrupt Mili. School 2.50
43 BR,Border Run 2.50
44 Flag Burner. 2.50
45 One Way Fare 2.50
46 HH,Cold Cache 2.50
47 HH,Middle East #1 . . . . 2.50
48 HH,Mid.East #2,V:Saracen 2.50
49 HH,Punisher Hunted 2.50
50 HH,MGo(c),I:Yo Yo Ng 2.50
51 Chinese Mafia. 2.50
52 Baby Snatchers 2.50
53 HH,in Prison 2.50
54 HH,in Prison 2.50
55 HH,in Prison 2.50
56 HH,in Prison 2.50
57 HH,in Prison 2.50
58 V:Kingpin's Gang,A:Micro 2.50
59 MT(c),V:Kingpin 2.50
60 VM,AW,Black Punisher,
    A:Luke Cage 2.50
61 VM,A:Luke Cage. 2.50
62 VM,AW,A:Luke Cage 2.50
63 MT(c),VM,V:Thieves 2.50
64 Eurohit #1 . . . . 2.50
65 thru 70 Eurohit . . . . @2.50
71 AW(i) 2.50
72 AW(i) 2.50
73 AW(i),Police Action #1 . . . . 2.50
74 AW(i),Police Action #2 . . . . 2.50
75 AW(i),Police Action #3,foil(c),
    double size 3.00
76 LSn,in Hawaii 2.50
77 VM,Survive#1 . . . . 2.50
78 VM,Survive#2 . . . . 2.50
79 VM,Survive#3 . . . . 2.50
80 Goes to Church. 2.50
81 V:Crooked Cops 2.50
82 B:Firefight 2.50
83 Firefight#2 . . . . 2.50
84 E:Firefight 2.50

85 Suicide Run 2.50
86 Suicide Run#3,Foil(c), ... 3.00
87 Suicide Run#6 . . . . 2.50
88 LSh(c),Suicide Run#9. . . . . 2.50
89 . . . . 2.50
90 Hammered 2.50
91 Silk Noose. 2.50
92 Razor's Edge 2.50
93 Killing Streets 2.50
94 B:No Rules 2.50
95 No Rules 2.50
96 . . . . 2.50
97 CDi 2.50
98 . . . . 2.50
99 . . . . 2.50
100 New Punisher 4.00
100a Enhanced ed. 5.00
101 CC,Raid's Franks Tomb 3.00
102 A:Bullseye 3.00
103 Countdown 4. . . . . 3.00
104 CDi,Countdown 1, V:Kingpin,
    final issue 4.00
Ann.#1 MT,A:Eliminators,
    Evolutionary War. 4.00
Ann.#2 JLe,Atlantis Attacks #5,
    A:Moon Knight 3.50
Ann.#3 LS,MT,Lifeform #1 . . . . . . 3.50
Ann.#4 Baron Strucker,pt.2
    (see D.D.Annual #7) 3.50
Ann.#5 System Bytes #1 . . . . 3.50
Ann.#6 I:Eradikator,w/card. 3.50
GNv 5.00
Summer Spec.#1 VM,MT. 3.50
Summer Spec.#2 SBs(c) 2.50
Summer Spec.#3 V:Carjackers . . . 2.50
Summer Spec.#4 . . . . 3.25
Spec. Punisher/Batman,CDi,JR2,
    48-pg. (1994) 5.00
Spec.#1 Punisher/Daredevil, rep.
    Daredevil 6.00
Punisher:No Escape A:USAgent,
    Paladin (1990) 5.50
Punisher Movie Spec.BA (1989) . . 6.00
GNv Punisher: The Prize (1990) . . 5.50
Punisher:Bloodlines DC 6.25
Punisher:Blood on the Moors . . . 17.00
Punisher:G-Force. 5.25
Punisher:Origin of Mirco Chip #1,
    O:Mirco Chip 2.50
Punisher:Origin of Mirco Chip #2
    V:The Professor. 2.50
Punisher:Back To School Spec.
    #1 JRy,short stories. 3.25
    #2 BSz. 3.00

Punisher Ann. #6
© Marvel Entertainment Group

MARVEL

Classic Punisher rep early
  B&W magazines 7.00
Punisher:Die Hard in the Big
  Easy Mardi Gras 5.25
Holiday Spec.#1 V:Young
  Mob Capo 3.25
Holiday Spec #2. . . . . 3.00
Punisher:Ghosts of the Innocent#1
  TGr, V:Kingpin's Dead Men. . . . 6.00
Punisher:Ghosts of the Innocent#2
  TGr, V:Kingpin,Snake 6.00

[2nd Regular Series] 1995
1 JOs,TL,Clv,Punisher sent to
  the Electric Chair, foil(c) 3.00
2 JOs,TL,Clv,Crime family boss . . . 2.50
3 JOs,TL,Clv,V:Hatchetman 2.50
4 JOs,TL,Clv,A:Daredevil,Jigsaw . . 2.50
5 . . . . 2.50
6 . . . . 2.50
7 JOs,TL,Clv,V:Son of Nick Fury . . 2.50
8 . . . . 2.50
9 . . . . 2.50
10 . . . . 2.50
11 Onslaught saga. 2.50
12 A:X-Cutioner 3.00
13 JOs,TL, Working for S.H.I.E.L.D.?,
  A:X-Cutioner 2.50
14 . . . . 2.50
15 JOs,TL, X-Cutioner. 2.50
16 JOS,TL, concl.? 2.50
17 JOS,TL,A:Daredevil,Doc Samson,
  Spider-Man 2.50
18 JOS, TL,Frank Castle amnesia? . 2.50
19 JOS,TL,V:Taskmaster. 2.50
20 JOS,TL, fugitive Punisher. 2.50

Sept., 1998
1 (of 4) BWr,JP,TSg,F:Frank
  Castle 3.00
2 BWr,JJu,JP,A:Hellstrom 3.00
3 BWr,JJu,TSg,JP,A:Gadriel 7.00
4 BWr,JJu,TSg,JP,Hell on Earth . . 3.00

Jan., 2000
1 (of 12) JP,GEn,SDi,R:Punisher . . 3.00
2A JP,GEn,SDi,V:Ma Gnucci 3.00
2B variant SDi(c). 3.00
3 GEn,JP,SDi,polybaged 8.00
4 GEn,JP,SDi,Gnuccis 3.00
5 GEn,JP,SDi,Mr.Payback 3.00
6 GEn,JP,SDi,Elite 3.00
7 GEn,JP,SDi,Mr.Payback 3.00
8 GEn,JP,SDi,Gnuccis 3.00
9 GEn,JP,SDi,Russian 3.00
10 GEn,JP,SDi,Russian 3.00
11 GEn,JP,SDi,Russian. 3.00
12 GEn,JP,SDi,concl. 3.00
Spec. Punisher/Painkiller Jane 3.50
GN Punisher Kills the Marvel
  Universe, 48-pg. GEn,DBw 6.00

June, 2001
1 GEn,JP,SDi,pt.1 . . . . 5.00
2A GEn,JP,SDi,pt.2. . . . . 3.00
2B variant SDi(c). 3.00
3 GEn,JP,SDi,Grand Nixon Island . 3.00
4 GEn,JP,SDi,Survivor 3.00
5 GEn,JP,SDi,V:Kriegkopf. 3.00
6 GEn,JP,Viet Nam 3.00
7 SDi,JP,'Nuff Said 3.00
8 TPe,Taxi Wars 3.00
9 TPe,Taxi Wars 3.00
10 TPe,Taxi Wars. 3.00
11 TPe,Taxi Wars, Medallion 3.00
12 TPE,Taxi Wars, concl. 3.00
13 GeN,SDi, to South America 3.00
14 GeN,SDi, in Columbia. 3.00
15 GeN,SDi,F:Wolverine 3.00
16 GeN,SDi,F:Wolverine 3.00
17 GeN,DaR,F:Wolverine 3.00
18 GeN,SDi,Northern Ireland. 3.00
19 GeN,SDi,. 3.00
20 GEn,SDi,Brotherhood,pt.1 . . . . 3.00
21 GEn,SDi,Brotherhood,pt.2 . . . . 3.00

Punisher Vol. 2, #4
© Marvel Entertainment Group

22 GEn,SDi 3.00
23 GEn,SDi,Giant Squid 3.00
24 GEn,TMd,Hidden,pt.1 . . . . 3.00
25 GEn,TMd,Hidden,pt.2 . . . . 3.00
26 GEn,TMd,Hidden,pt.3 . . . . 3.00
27 GEn,SDi,F:Elektra. 3.00
28 GEn,CK,Streets of Loredo,pt.1 . 3.00
29 GEn,CK,Streets of Loredo,pt.2 . 3.00
30 GEn,CK,Streets of Loredo,pt.3 . 3.00
31 GEn,CK,Streets of Loredo,pt.4 . 3.00
32 GEn,CK,Streets of Loredo,pt.5 . 3.00
33 GEn,JMC,Dunces,pt.1 . . . . 3.00
34 GEn,JMC,Dunces,pt.2 . . . . 3.00
35 GEn,JMC,Dunces,pt.3 . . . . 3.00
36 GEn,JMC,Dunces,pt.4 . . . . 3.00
37 GEn,JMC,Dunces,pt.5 . . . . 4.00

Max, 2004
1 GEn,In the Beginning,pt.1 . . . . . 9.00
2 GEn,In the Beginning,pt.2 . . . . . 5.00
3 GEn,In the Beginning,pt.3 . . . . . 5.00
4 GEn,In the Beginning,pt.4 . . . . . 5.00
5 GEn,In the Beginning,pt.5 . . . . . 3.00
6 GEn,In the Beginning,pt.6 . . . . . 3.00
7 GEn,Kitchen Irish,pt.1 . . . . 3.00
8 GEn,Kitchen Irish,pt.2 . . . . 3.00
9 GEn,Kitchen Irish,pt.3 . . . . 3.00
10 GEn,Kitchen Irish,pt.4. . . . . 3.00
11 GEn,Kitchen Irish,pt.5. . . . . 3.00
12 GEn,Kitchen Irish,pt.6. . . . . 3.00
13 GEn,DBw,Mother Russia, pt.1 . . 3.00
14 GEn,DBw,Mother Russia, pt.2 . . 3.00
15 GEn,DBw,Mother Russia, pt. 3. . 3.00
16 GEn,DBw,Mother Russia, pt.4 . . 3.00
17 GEn,DBw,Mother Russia 3.00
18 GEn,DBw,Mother Russia 3.00
19 GEn,DBw,Up is Down and
  Black Is White,pt.1. . . . . 3.00
20 GEn,Up is Down, Black is White 3.00
21 GEn,Up is Down, Black is White 3.00
22 GEn,Up is Down, Black is White 3.00
23 GEn,Up is Down, Black is White 3.00
24 GEn,Up is Down, Black is White 3.00
25 GEn,The Slavers,pt.1 . . . . 3.00
26 GEn,The Slavers,pt.2 . . . . 3.00
27 GEn,The Slavers,pt.3 . . . . 3.00
28 GEn,The Slavers,pt.4 . . . . 3.00
29 GEn,The Slavers,pt.5 . . . . 3.00
30 GEn,The Slavers,pt.6 . . . . 3.00
31 GEn,Barracuda,pt.1 . . . . 3.00
32 GEn,Barracuda,pt.2 . . . . 3.00
33 GEn,Barracuda,pt.3 . . . . 3.00
34 GEn,Barracuda,pt.4 . . . . 3.00
35 GEn,Barracuda,pt.5 . . . . 3.00
36 GEn,Barracuda,pt.6 . . . . 3.00

37 GEn,Man of Stone, pt.1 . . . . . . 3.00
38 GEn,Man of Stone, pt.2 . . . . . . 3.00
39 GEn,Man of Stone, pt.3 . . . . . . 3.00
40 GEn,Man of Stone, pt.4 . . . . . . 3.00
41 GEn. 3.00
42 GEn,Man of Stone 3.00
43 GEn,Widowmaker, pt.1 . . . . . . 3.00
44 GEn,Widowmaker, pt.2 . . . . . . 3.00
45 GEn,Widowmaker, pt.3 . . . . . . 3.00
46 GEn,Widowmaker, pt.4 . . . . . . 3.00
47 GEn,Widowmaker, pt.5 . . . . . . 3.00
48 GEn,Widowmaker, pt 6 . . . . . . 3.00
49 GEn,Widowmaker, pt.7 . . . . . . 3.00
50 GEn,Long Cold Dark, pt.1 . . . . 4.00
51 GEn,Long Cold Dark, pt.2 . . . . 3.00
52 GEn,Long Cold Dark, pt.3 . . . . 3.00
53 GEn,Long Cold Dark, pt.4 . . . . 3.00
54 GEn. 3.00
55 GEn,Valley Forge, pt.1 . . . . 3.00
56 GEn,Valley Forge, pt.2 . . . . 3.00
57 GEn,Valley Forge, pt.3 . . . . 3.00
58 GEn,Valley Forge, pt.4 . . . . 3.00
59 GEn,Valley Forge, pt.5 . . . . 3.00
60 GEn,Valley Forge, concl. 3.00
61 Girls in White Dresses, pt.1 . . . 3.00
62 Girls in White Dresses, pt.2 . . . 3.00
63 Girls in White Dresses, pt.3 . . . 3.00
64 Girls in White Dresses, pt.4 . . . 3.00
Ann. #1 The Hunted. 4.00
Spec. Punisher: Red X-Mas (2004). 3.00
Spec. Punisher: The End,RCo. 5.00
Spec. X-Mas Special, The List. . . . 4.00
Spec. Little Black Book 4.00
Spec. Punisher Kills the Marvel
  Universe, DBw. 5.00
1-shot The Cell, GEn,56-pg. 5.00
1-shot Punisher Valentine's One . . . 4.00
1-shot Punisher Silent Night (2005). 4.00
1-shot Punisher: The Tyger (2006) . 5.00
1-shot Punisher: Force of Nature . . 5.00

PUNISHER ARMORY
July, 1990
1 JLe(c). 3.00
2 JLe(c). 2.50
3 . . . . 2.50
4 thru 6 . . . . @2.50
7 thru 10 . . . . @2.50

PUNISHER/
CAPTAIN AMERICA:
BLOOD AND GLORY
1 thru 3 KJ,V:Drug Dealers. . . . . @6.25

CLASSIC PUNISHER
1 TDz 5.00

PUNISHER KILLS
THE MARVEL UNIVERSE
1995
1-shot Alterniverse 20.00

PUNISHER
MEETS ARCHIE
1994
1 JB. 4.25
1a newsstand ed. 3.25

PUNISHER MOVIE COMIC
Nov., 1989
1 Movie adapt. 2.50
2 thru 3 Movie adapt. . . . . @2.50

PUNISHER: THE MOVIE
March, 2004
1 (of 3) PO 3.00
2 and 3 PO . . . . @3.00

PUNISHER PRESENTS: BARRACUDA MAX
Feb., 2007
1 (of 5) GEn(s) 4.00
2 thru 5 GEn(s) . . . . @4.00

PUNISHER P.O.V.
July, 1991
1 BWr,Punisher/Nick Fury 5.50
2 BWr,A:Nick Fury,Kingpin 5.50
3 BWr,V:Mutant Monster,
  A:Vampire Slayer 5.50
4 BWr,A:Nick Fury 5.25

PUNISHER 2099
1993–95
1 TMo,Jake Gallows family
  Killed, foil(c) 2.50
2 TMo,I:Fearmaster,Kron,Multi
  Factor 2.50
3 TMo,V:Frightening Cult 2.50
4 TMo,V:Cyber Nostra 2.50
5 TMo,V:Cyber Nostra,Fearmaster. 2.50
6 TMo,V:Multi-Factor 2.50
7 TMo,Love and Bullets#1 . . . . . 2.50
8 TMo,Love and Bullets#2 . . . . . 2.50
9 TMo,Love and Bullets#3 . . . . . 2.50
10 TMo,I:Jigsaw 2.50
11 TMo,V:Jigsaw 2.50
12 TMo,A:Spider-Man 2099 . . . . . 2.50
13 TMo,Fall of the Hammer#5 . . . . 2.50
14 WSm, ... 2.50
15 TMo,V:Fearmaster,
  I:Public Enemy 2.50
16 TMo,V:Fearmaster,
  Public Enemy 2.50
17 TMo,V:Public Enemy 2.50
18 TMo,I:Goldheart 2.50
19 TMo,I:Vendetta 2.50
20 . . . . 2.50
21 . . . . 2.50
22 V:Hotwire 2.50
23 I:Synchron,V:Hotwire 2.50
24 V:Synchron 2.50
25 Enhanced cover 3.50
25a newsstand ed. 2.50
26 V:Techno-Shaman 2.50
27 R:Blue Max 2.50
Becomes:

PUNISHER 2099 A.D.
28 Minister of Punishment 2.50

Punisher 2099 #25
© Marvel Entertainment Group

29 Minister of Punishment 2.50
30 One Nation Under Doom 2.50
31 . . . . 2.50
32 Out of Ammo. 2.50
33 Counddown to final issue 2.50
34 final issue 2.50

PUNISHER VS. BULLSEYE
Nov., 2005
1 The Man's Got Style 3.00
2 The Drop 3.00
3 Massacre on 34th Street 3.00
4 Two of a Kind. 3.00
5 Profit and Loss. 3.00

PUNISHER WAR JOURNAL
Nov., 1988
1 CP,JLe,O:Punisher 5.00
2 CP,JLe,A:Daredevil 4.00
3 CP,JLe,A:Daredevil 4.00
4 CP,JLeV:The Sniper. 4.00
5 CP,JLe,V:The Sniper 4.00
6 CP,JLe,A:Wolverine 4.00
7 CP,JLe,A:Wolverine 4.00
8 JLe,I:Shadowmasters 4.00
9 JLe,A:Black Widow 4.00
10 JLe,V:Sniper 4.00
11 JLe,Shock Treatment 3.50
12 JLe,AM,V:Bushwacker 3.50
13 JLe(c),V:Bushwacker 3.50
14 JLe(c),DR,RH,A:Spider-Man. . . 3.50
15 JLe(c),DR,RH,A:Spider-Man. . . 3.50
16 MT(i),Texas Massacre 3.50
17 JLe,AM,Hawaii 3.00
18 JLe,AM,Kahuna,Hawaii. 3.00
19 JLe,AM,Traume in Paradise . . . 3.00
20 AM. 3.00
21 TSm,AM 3.00
22 TSm,AM,Ruins #1. . . . . 3.00
23 TSm,AM,Ruins #2. . . . . 3.00
24 . . . . 3.00
25 MT. 3.00
26 MT,A:Saracen 3.00
27 MT,A:Saracen 3.00
28 MT. 3.00
29 MT,A:Ghostrider 3.00
30 MT,A:Ghostrider 3.00
31 NKu,Kamchatkan
  Konspiracy#1. . . . . 3.00
32 Kamchatkan Konspiracy #2 . . . 3.00
33 Kamchatkan Konspiracy #3 . . . 3.00
34 V:Psycho. 3.00
35 Movie Stuntman 3.00
36 Radio Talk Show #1 . . . . 3.00
37 Radio Talk Show #2 . . . . 3.00
38 . . . . 3.00
39 DGr,V:Serial Killer. 3.00
40 MWg 3.00
41 Armageddon Express 3.00
42 Mob run-out 3.00
43 JR2(c) 3.00
44 Organ Donor Crimes. 3.00
45 Dead Man's Hand #3,V:Viper . . 3.00
46 Dead Man's Hand #6,V:Chainsaw
  and the Praetorians. 3.00
47 Dead Man's Hand #7,A:Nomad,
  D.D,V:Hydra,Secret Empire. . . . 3.00
48 B:Payback. 3.00
49 JR2(c),V:Corrupt Cop 3.00
50 MT,V:Highjackers,I:Punisher
  2099. . . . . 3.00
51 E:Payback. 3.00
52 A:Ice(from The'Nam). 3.00
53 A:Ice(from the Nam) 3.00
54 Hyper#1 . . . . 3.00
55 Hyper#2 . . . . 3.00
56 Hyper#3 . . . . 3.00
57 A:Ghost Rider,Daredevil 3.00
58 A:Ghost Rider,Daredevil 3.00
59 F:Max the Dog 3.00

60 CDi(s),F:Max the Dog 3.00
61 CDi(s),Suicide Run#1,Foil(c) . . 3.00
62 CDi(s),Suicide Run#4 . . . . 2.50
63 CDi(s),Suicide Run#7 . . . . 2.50
64 CDi(s),Suicide Run#10 . . . . . . 3.00
64a Newsstand Ed. 2.50
65 B:Pariah 2.50
66 A:Captain America 2.50
67 Pariah#3 . . . . 2.50
68 A:Spider-Man 2.50
69 E:Pariah 2.50
70 . . . . 2.50
71 . . . . 2.50
72 V:Fake Punisher 2.50
73 E:Frank Castle 2.50
74 . . . . 2.50
75 MT(c). 3.00
76 First Entry 2.50
77 R:Stone COld 2.50
78 V:Payback,Heathen 2.50
79 Countdown 3. . . . . 6.00
80 Countdown 0, A:Nick Fury,
  V:Bullseye, final issue 10.00

PUNISHER WAR JOURNAL
Nov., 2006
1 . . . . 5.00
2 Civil War 5.00
3 Civil War tie-in 7.00
4 MD2,Small Wake for a Tall Man . 4.00
5 AOI, ... 4.00
6 AOI, Blood and Sand, pt.1 . . . . 4.00
7 AOI, Blood and Sand, pt.2 . . . . 3.00
7a variant AOI (c) 3.00
8 AOI, Blood and Sand, pt.3 . . . . 3.00
9 AOI, Blood and Sand, pt.4 . . . . 3.00
10 AOI 3.00
11 . . . . 3.00
12 World War Hulk. 4.00
13 Hunter/Hunted, pt.1 . . . . 4.00
14 Hunter/Hunted, pt.2 . . . . 3.00
15 . . . . 3.00
16 HC,F:The Gibbon 3.00
17 HC,Misfits, pt.2 . . . . 3.00
18 HC,Jigsaw, pt.1. . . . . 3.00
19 HC,Jigsaw, pt.2. . . . . 3.00
20 HC,Jigsaw, pt.3. . . . . 3.00
21 HC,Jigsaw, pt.4. . . . . 3.00
22 HC,Jigsaw, pt.5. . . . . 3.00
23 HC,Jigsaw, concl. 3.00
23 monkey variant (c) 3.00
24 HC, Secret Invasion tie-in. 3.00
25 HC, Secret Invasion tie-in. 3.00
Ann. #1 If I Die Before I Wake. . . . 4.00

PUNISHER WAR ZONE
1992
1 JR2,KJ,Punisher As Johnny Tower
  Die-Cut Bullet Hole(c) 3.00
2 JR2,KJ,Mafia Career 2.50
3 JR2,KJ,Punisher/Mafia,contd . . 2.50
4 JR2,KJ,Cover gets Blown 2.50
5 JR2,KJ,A:Shotgun 2.50
6 JR2,KJ,A:Shotgun 2.50
7 JR2,V:Rapist in Central Park. . . 2.50
8 JR2,V:Rapist in Central Park. . . 2.50
9 JR2,V:Magnificent Seven 2.50
10 JR2,V:Magnificent Seven 2.50
11 JR2,MM,V:Magnificent Seven. . 2.50
12 Punisher Married 2.50
13 Self-Realization. 2.50
14 Psychoville#3 . . . . 2.50
15 Psychoville#4 . . . . 2.50
16 Psychoville#5 . . . . 2.50
17 Industrial Esponiage 2.50
18 Jerico Syndrome#2. . . . . 2.50
19 Jerico Syndrome#3. . . . . 2.50
20 B:2 Mean 2 Die. 2.50
21 2 Mean 2 Die#2 . . . . 2.50
22 A:Tyger Tyger 2.50
23 Suicide Run#2,Foil(c) 3.25

24 Suicide Run#5,	2.50
25 Suicide Run#8,	3.00
26 CDi(s),JB,Pirates	2.50
27 CDi(s),JB,	2.50
28 CDi(s),JB,Sweet Revenge	2.50
29 CDi(s),JB,The Swine	2.50
30 CDi(s),JB,	2.50
31 CDi(s),JB,River of Blood,pt.1	2.50
32 CDi(s),JB,River of Blood,pt.2	2.50
33 CDi(s),JB,River of Blood,pt.3	2.50
34 CDi(s),JB,River of Blood,pt.4	2.50
35 River of Blood,pt.5	2.50
36 River of Blood,pt.6	2.50
37 O:Max	2.50
38 Dark Judgment,pt.1	2.50
39 Dark Judgment,pt.2	2.50
40 In Court	2.50
41 CDi,Countdown 2, final issue	2.50
Ann.#1 Jb,MGo,(c),I:Phalanx, w/Trading card	3.25
Ann.#2 CDi(s),DR	3.00

PUNISHER: YEAR ONE
1994

1 O:Punisher	2.50
2 thru 4	@2.50

PUSSYCAT
(B&W Magazine) Oct., 1968

1 BEv,BWa,WW	300.00

QUASAR
Oct., 1989

1 O:Quasar	3.00
2 V:Deathurge,A:Eon	2.50
3 A:Human Torch,V:The Angler	2.50
4 Acts of Vengeance,A:Aquarian	2.50
5 A of Veng,V:Absorbing Man	2.50
6 V:Klaw,Living Laser,Venom, Red Ghost	3.00
7 MM,A:Cosmic SpM,V:Terminus	2.50
8 MM,A:New Mutants,BlueShield	2.50
9 MM,A:Modam	2.50
10 MM,A:Dr.Minerva	2.50
11 MM,A:Excalibur,A:Modred	2.50
12 MM,A:Makhari,Blood Bros	2.50
13 JLe(c)MM,J.into Mystery #1	2.50
14 TM(c)MM,J.into Mystery #2	2.50
15 MM,Journey into Mystery #3	2.50
16 MM,Double sized	2.50
17 MM,Race,A:Makkari,Whizzer, Quicksilver,Capt.Marv,Super Sabre,Barry Allen Spoof	2.50

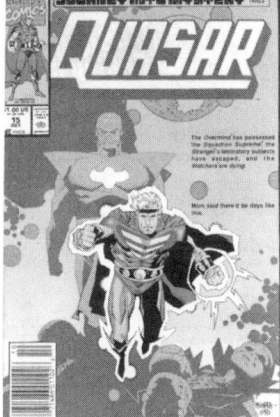

Quasar #15
© Marvel Entertainment Group

18 GCa,N:Quasar	2.50
19 GCa,B:Cosmos in Collision, C:Thanos	2.50
20 GCa,A:Fantastic Four	2.50
21 GCa,V:Jack of Hearts	2.50
22 GCa,D:Quasar,A:Ghost Rider	2.50
23 GCa,A:Ghost Rider	2.50
24 GCa,A:Thanos,Galactus, D:Maelstrom	2.50
25 GCa,A:Eternity & Infinity,N:Quasar, E:Cosmos Collision	2.50
26 GCa,Inf.Gauntlet,A:Thanos	2.50
27 GCa,Infinity Gauntlet,I:Epoch	2.50
28 GCa,A:Moondragon,Her, X-Men	2.50
29 GCa,A:Moondragon,Her	2.50
30 GCa,What If? tie-in	2.50
31 GCa,R:New Universe	2.50
32 GCa,Op.GalacticStorm,pt.3	2.50
33 GCa,Op.GalacticStorm,pt.10	2.50
34 GCa,Op.GalacticStorm,pt.17	2.50
35 GCa,Binary V:Her	2.50
36 GCa,V:Soul Eater	2.50
37 GCa,V:Soul Eater	2.50
38 GCa,Inf.War,V:Warlock	2.50
39 SLi,Inf.War,V:Deathurge	2.50
40 SLi,Inf.War V:Deathurge	2.50
41 R:Marvel Boy	2.50
42 V:Blue Marvel	2.50
43 V:Blue Marvel	2.50
44 V:Quagmire	2.50
45 V:Quagmire,Antibody	2.50
46 Neutron,Presence	2.50
47 1st Full Thunderstrike Story	2.50
48 A:Thunderstrike	2.50
49 Kalya Vs. Kismet	2.50
50 A:Man-Thing,Prism(c)	3.50
51 V:Angler,A:S.Supreme	2.50
52 V:Geometer	2.50
53	2.50
54 MGu(s),Starblast #2	2.50
55 MGu(s),A:Stranger	2.50
56 MGu(s),Starblast #10	2.50
57 MGu(s),A:Kismet	2.50
58	2.50
59 A:Thanos,Starfox	2.50
60 final issue	2.50

QUEST
June, 2003

1 (of 6) Manga,F:Katherine West	2.50
2 Quest & Kaori	2.50

QUESTPROBE
Aug., 1984

1 JR,A:Hulk,I:Chief Examiner	3.00
2 AM,JM,A:Spider-Man	3.00
3 JSt,A:Thing & Torch	3.00

QUICKSILVER
Sept., 1997

1 CJ,TPe, V:Exodus, cont. from Excalibur #113	3.00
2 TPe,CJ,A:Knights of Wundagore	2.50
3 TPe,CJ,V:Arkon	2.50
4 TPe, Crystal returns	2.50
5 TPe,V:Inhumans	2.50
6 TPe,Inhumands trilogy concl.	2.50
7 JOs,F:The Black Knight	2.50
8 JOs,F:Pietro,V:Pyro	2.50
9 JOs,Savage Land concl.,A:High Evolutionary	2.50
10 JOS,Live Kree or Die, pt.3, x-over	2.50
11 JOs,The Seige of Wundagore, pt.2 (of 5)	2.50
12 JOs,The Seige of Wundagore, pt.4 (of 5) 48-pg.	3.00
13 JOs,Seige of Wundagore,pt.5, final issue	2.50

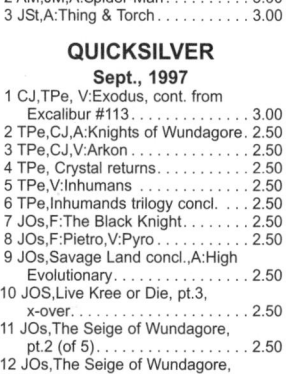

QUICK-TRIGGER WESTERN
See: WESTERN THRILLERS

RAIDERS OF THE LOST ARK
Sept., 1981

1 JB/KJ,movie adaption	3.00
2 JB/KJ,	3.00
3 JB/KJ,Nov.,1981	3.00

RAMPAGING HULK, THE
May, 1998

1 RL,double size, savage Hulk era.	3.00
2A RL,DGr,I:Ravage	2.50
2B JQ,JP,variant cover	2.50
3 RL,DGr,V:Ravage, concl.	2.50
4 DR,Trapped by an Avalanche	2.50
5 RL,F:Fantastic Four	2.50
6 RL,DGr,V:Puma	2.50

RANGELAND LOVE
Marvel Comics, 1949

1 Robert Taylor	250.00
2	200.00

RAVAGE 2099
1992–95

1 PR,I:Ravage	3.00
2 PR,V:Deathstryk	2.50
3 PR,V:Mutroids	2.50
4 PR,V:Mutroids	2.50
5 PR,Hellrock	2.50
6 PR,N:Ravage	2.50
7 PR,New powers	2.50
8 V:Deathstryke	2.50
9 PR,N:Ravage	2.50
10 V:Alchemax	2.50
11 A:Avatarr	2.50
12 Ravage Transforms	2.50
13 V:Fearmaster	2.50
14 V:Punisher 2099	2.50
15 Fall of the Hammer #2	2.50
16 I:Throwback	2.50
17 GtM,V:Throwback,O:X-11	2.50
18 GtM,w/card	2.50
19 GtM,	2.50
20 GtM,V:Hunter	2.50
21 Savage on the Loose	2.50

Ravage 2099 #1
© Marvel Entertainment Group

---

22 Exodus 2.50
23 Blind Justice 2.50
24 Unleashed 2.50
25 Flame Bearer 2.50
25a Deluxe ed. 3.00
26 V:Megastruck 2.50
27 V:Deathstryke 2.50
28 R:Hela 2.50
29 V:Deathstryke 2.50
30 King Ravage 2.50
Becomes:

RAVAGE 2099 A.D.
31 V:Doom 2.50
32 One Nation Under Doom 2.50
33 Final issue. 2.50

RAWHIDE KID
Atlas, March, 1955—May, 1979
1 JMn,B:Rawhide Kid & Randy,
  A:Wyatt Earp 1,400.00
2 JMn,Shoot-out(c) 600.00
3 V:Hustler 400.00
4 Rh(c) 400.00
5 GC,JMn 400.00
6 JMn,Six-Gun Lesson 350.00
7 AW 350.00
8 . . . . 350.00
9 . . . . 350.00
10 thru 16 Sept. 1957 . . . . . @300.00
17 JK,O:Rawhide Kid; Aug. 1960 300.00
18 thru 20 . . . . @300.00
21 . . . . 300.00
22 . . . . 300.00
23 JK,O:Rawhide Kid Retold 350.00
24 thru 30 . . . . @250.00
31 JK,DAy,No Law in Mesa 250.00
32 JK,DAy,Beware of the
  Parker Brothers 250.00
33 JK(c),JDa,V:Jesse James. . . . 250.00
34 JDa,JK,V:Mister Lightning. . . . 250.00
35 JK(c),GC,JDa,
  I&D:The Raven 250.00
36 DAy,A Prisoner in
  Outlaw Town 150.00
37 JK(c),DAy,GC,V:The Rattler . . 150.00
38 DAy,V:The Red Raven 200.00
39 DAy 150.00
40 JK(c),DAy,A:Two Gun Kid . . . 150.00
41 JK(c),The Tyrant of
  Tombstone Valley 150.00
42 JK 150.00
43 JK 200.00
44 JK(c),V:The Masked Maverick 150.00
45 JK(c),O:Rawhide Kid Retold . . 175.00

Rawhide Kid #1
© Marvel Entertainment Group

46 JK(c),ATh 150.00
47 JK(c),The Riverboat Raiders. . 110.00
48 GC,V:Marko the Manhunter . . 100.00
49 The Masquerader 100.00
50 A;Kid Colt,V:Masquerader . . . 100.00
51 DAy,Trapped in the
  Valley of Doom 100.00
52 DAy,Revenge at
  Rustler's Roost 100.00
53 Guns of the Wild North 100.00
54 DH,BEv,The Last Showdown . 100.00
55 . . . . 100.00
56 DH,JTgV:The Peacemaker. . . 100.00
57 V:The Scorpion 100.00
58 DAy 100.00
59 V:Drako 100.00
60 DAy,HT,Massacre at Medicine
  Bend 100.00
61 DAy,TS,A:Wild Bill Hickok. . . . 75.00
62 Gun Town,V:Drako 75.00
63 Shootout at Mesa City 75.00
64 HT,Duel of the Desparadoes . . 75.00
65 JTg,HT,BE. 75.00
66 JTg,BEv,Death of a Gunfighter. 75.00
67 Hostage of Hungry Hills 75.00
68 JB,V:The Cougar 75.00
69 JTg,The Executioner. 75.00
70 JTg,The Night of the Betrayers. 50.00
71 JTg,The Last Warrior 50.00
72 JTg,The Menace of Mystery
  Valley 50.00
73 JTg,The Manhunt 50.00
74 JTg,The Apaches Attack 50.00
75 JTg,The Man Who Killed
  The Kid 50.00
76 JTg,V:The Lynx 50.00
77 JTg,The Reckoning. 50.00
78 JTg 50.00
79 JTg,AW,The Legion of the Lost 50.00
80 Fall of a Hero 50.00
81 thru 85. . . . . @50.00
86 JK,O:Rawhide Kid retold. 55.00
87 thru 89 . . . . @75.00
90 Kid Colt 80.00
91 . . . . 30.00
92 & 93 giants . . . . @35.00
94 thru 99 . . . . @40.00
100 O:Rawhide Kid retold 30.00
101 thru 124. . . . . @25.00
125 JDa 28.00
126 thru 151 . . . . @25.00

RAWHIDE KID
Aug., 1985
1 JSe,mini-series 6.00
2 thru 4 . . . . @5.00

RAWHIDE KID
Marvel Max, Feb., 2003
1 (of 5) JSe. 3.00
2 thru 5 JSe. . . . . @3.00
3 JSe. 3.00
4 JSe. 3.00
5 JSe,concl. 3.00

RAZORLINE FIRST CUT
1993
1 Intro Razorline 2.50

REAL EXPERIENCES
See: TESSIE THE TYPIST

RED RAVEN
See: HUMAN TORCH

RED SONJA
[1st Series] Jan., 1977
1 FT,O:Red Sonja,Blood of the
  Unicorn 20.00
2 FT,Demon of the Maze 10.00

3 FT,The Games of Gita 10.00
4 FT,The Lake of the Unknown . . 10.00
5 FT,Master of the Bells 10.00
6 FT,The Singing Tower 10.00
7 FT,Throne of Blood 10.00
8 FT,Vengeance o/t Golden Circle 10.00
9 FT,Chariot o/t Fire-Stallions 10.00
10 FT,Red Lace,pt.1 . . . . 10.00
11 FT,Red Lace,pt.2. . . . . 9.00
12 JB/JRu,Ashes & Emblems 9.00
13 JB/AM,Shall Skranos Fall 9.00
14 SB/AM,Evening on the Border . . 9.00
15 JB/TD,Tomb of 3 Dead Kings
  May, 1979 . . . . 9.00

[2nd Series] Feb., 1983
1 TD,GC, The Blood That Binds . . 4.00
2 GC, March,1983 . . . . 4.00

[3rd Series] Aug., 1983
1 . . . . 3.00
2 thru 13 . . . . @3.00
1 movie adaption, 1985 . . . . 2.50
2 movie adaption, 1985 . . . . 2.50

RED SONJA
1-shot Bros.Hildebrandt(c),48-pg. . . 3.00

RED WARRIOR
Atlas, Jan.–Dec., 1951
1 GT,Indian Tales 200.00
2 GT(c),The Trail of the Outcast 125.00
3 The Great Spirit Speaks 100.00
4 O:White Wing 100.00
5 . . . . 100.00
6 JMn(c) final issue. 100.00

RED WOLF
May, 1972–Sept., 1973
1 SSh(c),GK,JSe,F:Red Wolf
  & Lobo 35.00
2 GK(c),SSh,Day of the Dynamite
  Doom 20.00
3 SSh,War of the Wolf Brothers . 20.00
4 SSh,V:Man-Bear 20.00
5 GK(c),SSh 20.00
6 SSh,JA,V;Devil Rider 20.00
7 SSh,JA,Echoes from a Golden
  Grave 20.00
8 SSh,Hell on Wheels 20.00
9 DAy,To Die Again,O:Lobo 20.00

REN AND STIMPY SHOW
1992–96
1 Polybagged w/Air Fowlers,
  Ren(c) 5.00
1a Stimpy(c) 4.00
1b 2nd Printing 3.00
1c 3rd Printing. 2.50
2 Frankenstimpy 3.00
2a 2nd Printing 2.50
3 Christmas issue 3.00
3a 2nd Printing 2.50
4 thru 12 . . . . @3.00
13 Halloween issue 2.50
14 Mars needs Vecro. 2.50
15 thru 24 . . . . @2.50
25 regular (c) 2.50
25a die-cut(c),A new addition . . . 3.00
26 thru 42 . . . . @2.50
Spec.#1 . . . . 3.25
Spec.#2 . . . . 3.25
Spec.#3 Powder Toast Man 3.25
Spec.#4 . . . . 3.25
Spec.#5 Virtual Stupidity 3.25
Spec.#6 History of Music 3.25
Holiday Special 3.00
Spec. Radio Dazed & Confused . . . 2.50
Spec. Around the World in a Daze . 3.00

RETURN OF THE JEDI
1 thru 4 AW,movie adapt. . . . . . @3.00

MARVEL

REX HART
See: BLAZE CARSON

RICHIE RICH
1 Movie Adaptation 3.00

RINGO KID
[2nd Series] Jan., 1970
1 AW,Reprints 35.00
2 JSe,Man Trap 20.00
3 JR,Man from the Panhandle . . . 20.00
4 HT(c),The Golden Spur 20.00
5 JMn,Ambush 20.00
6 Capture or Death 20.00
7 HT(c),JSe,JA,Terrible Treasure
   of Vista Del Oro 20.00
8 The End of the Trail 20.00
9 JSe,Mystery of the Black
   Sunset 20.00
10 Bad day at Black Creek 20.00
11 Bullet for a Bandit 20.00
12 A Badge to Die For 30.00
13 DW,Hostage at Fort Cheyenne. 15.00
14 Showdown in the Silver
   Cartwheel 15.00
15 Fang,Claw, and Six-Gun. 15.00
16 Battle of Cattleman's Bank 15.00
17 Gundown at the Hacienda . . . 15.00
18 . . . . 15.00
19 Thunder From the West 15.00
20 AW 15.00
21 thru 29. . . . . @15.00
30 Nov., 1973. . . . . 15.00

RINGO KID WESTERN
Atlas, Aug., 1954
1 JMn,JSt,O:Ringo Kid,
   B:Ringo Kid 400.00
2 JMn,I&O:Arab,A:Black Rider . 200.00
3 JMn 125.00
4 JMn 125.00
5 JMn 125.00
6 & 7 . . . . @125.00
8 JSe. 125.00
9 . . . . 100.00
10 JSe(c),AW. 125.00
11 JSe(c) 100.00
12 JO 100.00
13 AW 125.00
14 thru 20. . . . . @100.00
21 Sept., 1957 . . . . 100.00

RIOT
Marvel Atlas, 1954–56
1 RH,MMe,GC,BEv. 450.00
2 MMe,Li'l Abner. 300.00
3 MMe(c). 350.00
4 JSe,MMe,BEv,Marilyn Monroe 350.00
5 JSe,MMe,BEv,Marilyn Monroe 350.00
6 MMe,JSe 250.00

ROBOCOP
March, 1990
1 LS,I:Nixcops. 6.00
2 LS,V:Nixcops. 4.00
3 LS 3.00
4 LS 3.00
5 LS,WarzonePt1 . . . . 3.00
6 LS,WarzonePt2 . . . . 3.00
7 thru 10 LS . . . . @2.50
11 HT 2.50
12 thru 23. . . . . @2.50
Robocop Movie Adapt 5.00
Robocop II Movie Adapt. 5.00

ROBOCOP II
Aug., 1990
1 MBa,rep.Movie Adapt 2.50
2 and 3 MBa,rep.Movie adapt. . . @2.50

ROBOTIX
Feb., 1986
1 Based on toys 3.00

ROCKET RACCOON
May, 1985—Aug., 1985
1 thru 4 MM. . . . . @3.00

ROCKO'S MODERN LIFE
1994
1 and 2 . . . . @2.50
3 and 4 . . . . @2.50

ROGUE
1995
1 Enhanced cover. 4.50
2 A:Gambit 4.00
3 Gamtit or Rogue? 3.00
4 final issue. 3.00

ROGUE
Aug., 2001
1 (of 4) AaL,RyE, ... 2.50
2 AaL,RyE 2.50
3 AaL,RyE, leaves school. 2.50
4 AaL,RyE,JuB(c) 2.50

ROGUE
July, 2004
1 Going Rogue,pt.1 . . . . 3.00
2 Going Rogue,pt.2. . . . . 3.00
3 Going Rogue,pt.3. . . . . 3.00
4 Going Rogue,pt.4. . . . . 3.00
5 Going Rogue,pt.5. . . . . 3.00
6 Going Rogue,pt.6. . . . . 3.00
7 Forget-Me-Not 3.00
8 Forget-Me-Not,A:Sunfire 3.00
9 Forget-Me-Not 3.00
10 Forget-Me-Not,V:Lady
   Deathstrike 3.00
11 Forget-Me-Not. 3.00
12 Forget-Me-Not, concl. 3.00

ROM
Dec., 1979
1 SB,I&O:Rom 17.00
2 thru 16 . . . . @6.00
17 SB,A:X-Men 10.00
18 SB,A:X-Men 10.00
19 thru 23 . . . . @5.00
24 thru 27 . . . . @7.00
28 thru 30 . . . . @4.00
31 thru 49. . . . . @3.00
50 SB,D:Torpedo,V:Skrulls 4.00
51 thru 55 . . . . @3.00
56 A:Alpha Flight 3.00
57 A:Alpha Flight 3.00
58 JG(c),A:Antman 3.00
59 SD,BL,V:Microbe Menace. . . . 3.00
60 SD,TP,V:Dire Wraiths 3.00
61thru 74 . . . . @2.50
75 SD,CR,Doublesize,last issue . . 7.00
Ann.#1 PB,A:Stardust 3.00
Ann.#2 I:Knights of Galador. 3.00
Ann.#3 A:New Mutants 3.00
Ann.#4 V:Gladiator. 3.00

ROMANCE DIARY
Dec., 1949
1 . . . . 175.00
2 March, 1950 . . . . 150.00

THE ROMANCES OF
NURSE HELEN GRANT
Marvel Atlas, 1957
1 . . . . 100.00

ROMANCES OF
THE WEST
Nov., 1949
1 Ph(c),Calamity Jane,
   Sam Bass 300.00
2 March, 1950 . . . . 175.00

ROMANCE TALES
Oct., 1949
(no #1 thru 6)
7 . . . . 175.00
8 . . . . 100.00
9 March, 1950 . . . . 100.00

ROMANTIC AFFAIRS
See: MOLLY MANTON'S
ROMANCES

ROYAL ROY
Star, May, 1985
1 thru 5 . . . . @3.00
6 March, 1986 . . . . 3.00

Rugged Action #1
© *Marvel Entertainment Group*

RUGGED ACTION
Atlas, Dec., 1954
1 AyB,Man-Eater 150.00
2 JSe,DAy,JMn(c),Manta-Ray . . 100.00
3 DAy,JMn(c) 100.00
4 . . . . 100.00
Becomes:

STRANGE STORIES
OF SUSPENSE
5 RH,JMn(c),Little Black Box . . . 550.00
6 BEv,The Illusion 350.00
7 JSe(c),BEv,Old John's House . 375.00
8 AW,BP,TYhumbs Down 375.00
9 BEv(c),Nightmare 400.00
10 RC,MME,AT 400.00
11 BEv(c) 275.00
12 AT 275.00
13 BEv,GM. 275.00
14 AW 300.00
15 BK 300.00
16 MF,BP, Aug., 1957 . . . . 300.00

RUINS
1995
1 Marvel's Alterverse 5.00
2 Fully painted, 32-pg. 5.00

MARVEL

RUNAWAYS
April, 2003

1 Pride & Joy, pt.1	10.00
2 Pride & Joy, pt.2	7.00
3 Pride & Joy, pt.3	7.00
4 Pride & Joy, pt.4	7.00
5 Pride & Joy, pt.5	4.00
6 Pride & Joy, pt.6	4.00
7 Teenage Wasteland,pt.1	4.00
8 Teenage Wasteland,pt.2	4.00
9 Teenage Wasteland,pt.3	4.00
10 Teenage Wasteland,pt.4	4.00
11 Lost & Found,pt.1	4.00
12 Lost & Found,pt.2	4.00
13 thru 17 The Good Die Young	@4.00
18 Season Finale	4.00
Spec Runaways/Sentinel flip book	4.00

RUNAWAYS
Feb., 2005

1 True Believers, pt.1	6.00
2 True Believers, Pt.2	5.00
3 True Believers, pt.3	4.00
4 True Believers, pt.4	4.00
5 True Believers, Pt.5	4.00
6 True Believers, pt.6	4.00
7 Sinister plan, Part 1	4.00
8 Sinister Plan, Part 2	4.00
9 East Coast/West Coast	3.00
10 East Coast/West Coast	3.00
11 East Coast/West Coast	3.00
12 East Coast/West Coast	3.00
13 Molly Hayes alone	3.00
14 Parental Guidance,pt.1	3.00
15 Parental Guidance,pt.2	3.00
16 Parental Guidance,pt.3	3.00
17 Parental Guidance,pt.4	3.00
18 Parental Guidance,pt.5	3.00
19 Dead Means Dead,pt.1	3.00
20 Dead Means Dead,pt.2	3.00
21 Dead Means Dead,pt.3	3.00
22 Live Fast, pt.1	3.00
23 Live Fast, pt.2	3.00
24 Live Fast, pt.3	3.00
25	3.00
26 JoW,Dead End Kids	3.00
27 JoW,Dead End Kids	3.00
28 JoW,Dead End Kids	3.00
29 JoW,Dead End Kids, pt.5	3.00
30 JoW,Dead End Kids, concl.	3.00
Spec. Runaways Saga	@4.00

RUNAWAYS
Aug., 2008

1 thru 4 TMo,HuR	@3.00

RUSTY COMICS
See: KID KOMICS

SABLE & FORTUNE
Jan., 2006

1 F:Silver Sable & Dominic Fortune	3.00
2 thru 4	@3.00

SABRETOOTH
[Limited Series] 1993

1 B:LHa(s),MT,A:Wolverine	5.00
2 MT,A:Mystique,C:Wolverine	4.00
3 MT,A:Mystique,Wolverine	4.00
4 E:LHa(s),MT,D:Birdy	4.00

Oct., 2004

1 (of 5) BS,F:Sasquatch	3.00
2 thru 4 BS,F:Sasquatch	@3.00

SABRETOOTH CLASSICS
1994–95

1 rep. Power Man/Iron Fist #66	4.00
2 rep. Power Man/Iron Fist #78	3.00

Sabretooth Classics #1
© Marvel Entertainment Group

3 rep. Power Man/Iron Fist #84	3.00
4 rep. Spider-Man #116	3.00
5 rep. Spider-Man #119	3.00
6 reprints	3.00
7 reprints	3.00
8 reprints	3.00
9 reprints	3.00
10 Morlock Massacre	3.00
11 rep. Daredevil #238	3.00
12 rep. V:Wolverine	3.00
13 rep.	3.00
14 A:Mauraders	3.00
15 Mutant Massacre, rep. Uncanny X-Men #221	3.00

SABRETOOTH
Spec.#1 FaN, cont.from X-Men#48 . 5.00

SABRETOOTH
Oct., 1997

1-shot,F:Wildchild 2.50

SABRETOOTH & MYSTIQUE

1 JGz,AOI,	2.50
2 thru 4 JGz,AOI	@2.50

SABRETOOTH: MARY SHELLEY OVERDRIVE
June, 2002

1 (of 4) F:Creed	3.00
2 TyH	3.00
3	3.00
4 TyH	3.00

SACHS & VIOLENS
Epic, 1993–94

1 GP,PDd(s)	3.00
2 GP,PDd(s),V:Killer	2.50
3 GP,PDd(s),V:White Slavers	2.50
4 GP,PDd(s),D:Moloch	2.50

SAGA OF CRYSTAR
May, 1983

1 O:Crystar	5.00
2 A:Ika	4.00
3 A:Dr.Strange	4.00
4 thru 10	@4.00
11 Alpha Flight,Feb., 1985	4.00

SAGA OF ORIGINAL HUMAN TORCH

1 RB,O:Original Human Torch	3.00
2 RB,A:Toro	2.50
3 RB,V:Adolph Hitler	2.50
4 RB,Torch vs. Toro	2.50

ST. GEORGE
Epic, June, 1988

1 KJ,Shadow Line	2.50
2 thru 8	@2.50

SAINT SINNER
Razorline 1993–94

1 I:Phillip Fetter	2.75
2 thru 8	@2.50

SAM & MAX GO TO THE MOON
1 Dirtbag Special,w/Nirvana Tape. . 4.00

[Regular Series]

1 MMi,AAd,F:Skull Boy	3.25
2 thru 3 AAd,MMi	@3.25

SAMURAI CAT
Epic, 1991

1 I:MiaowaraTomokato	2.50
2 I:Con-Ed,V:Thpaghetti-Thoth	2.50
3 EmpireStateStrikesBack	2.50

SAMURAI: LEGEND
Sept., 2008

1 thru 3 . . . . @6.00

SATANA
Nov., 1997

1 JaL,WEI,AOI,V:Doctor Strange, non-code series	3.00
2 WEI,AOI,to the gates of Hell	3.00

SAVAGE SWORD OF CONAN
Aug., 1974
(black & white magazine)

1 BWS,JB,NA,GK,O:Blackmark, 3rdA:Red Sonja,Boris(c)	175.00
2 NA(c),HC,GK,Black Colossus, B.U.King Kull;B.U.Blackmark	90.00
3 JB,BWS,GK,At The Mountain of the Moon God;B.U.s: Kull;Blackmark	75.00
4 JB,RCo,GK,Iron Shadows in the Moon B.U.Blackmark,Boris(c)	50.00
5 JB,Witch Shall be born,Boris(c)	35.00
6 AN,Sleeper`Neath the Sands	35.00
7 JB,Citadel at the Center of Time Boris(c)	35.00
8 inc.GK,Corsairs against Stygia	35.00
9 Curse of the Cat-Goddess, Boris(c),B.U.King Kull	35.00
10 JB,Sacred Serpent of Set Boris(c)	35.00
11 JB,The Abode of the Damned	25.00
12 JB,Haunters of Castle Crimson Boris(c)	25.00
13 GK,The Thing in the Temple, B.U. Solomon Kane	25.00
14 NA,Shadow of Zamboula, B.U.Solomon Kane	25.00
15 JB,Boris(c),Devil in Iron	25.00
16 JB,BWS,People of the Black Circle,B.U.Bran Mak Morn	25.00
17 JB,On to Yimsha!, B.U.Bran Mak Morn	25.00
18 JB,The Battle of the Towers B.U. Solomon Kane	25.00

19 JB,Vengeance in Vendhya
  B.U. Solomon Kane. 25.00
20 JB,The Slithering Shadow
  B.U. Solomon Kane. 20.00
21 JB,Horror in the Red Tower . . . 20.00
22 JB,Pool o/t Black One
  B.U. Solomon Kane. 20.00
23 JB,FT,Torrent of Doom
  B.U. Solomon Kane. 20.00
24 JB,BWS,Tower of the
  Elephant,B.U.Cimmeria. 20.00
25 DG,SG,Jewels of Gwahlur,
  B.U.Solomon Kane. 20.00
26 JB/TD,Beyond the Black River,
  B.U.Solomon Kane 20.00
27 JB/TD,Children of Jhebbal Sag 20.00
28 JB/AA,Blood of the Gods 20.00
29 ECh,FT,Child of Sorcery,
  B.U. Red Sonja 20.00
30 FB,The Scarlet Citadel 20.00
31 JB/TD,The Flaming Knife,pt.1 . . 15.00
32 JB/TD,Ghouls of Yanaldar,pt.2 . 15.00
33 GC,Curse of the Monolith,
  B.U.Solomon Kane 15.00
34 GI/AA,MP,Lair o/t Ice Worm,B.U.
  Solomon Kane,B.U.King Kull. . 15.00
35 ECh,Black Tears 15.00
36 JB,AA,Hawks over Shem 15.00
37 SB,Sons of the White Wolf
  B.U. Solomon Kane. 15.00
38 JB/TD,The Road of the Eagles. 15.00
39 SB/TD,The Legions of the Dead,
  B.U.Solomon Kane concl. 15.00
40 JB/TD,A Dream of Blood 15.00
41 JB/TD,Quest for the Cobra Crown
  A:Thoth-Amon,B.U.Sol.Kane. . 15.00
42 JB/TD,Devil-Tree of Gamburu,
  A:Thoth-Amon,B.U.Sol.Kane. . 15.00
43 JB/TD,King Thoth-Amon,
  B.U.King Kull 15.00
44 SB/TD,The Star of Khorala 15.00
45 JB/TD,The Gem in the Tower,
  B.U. Red Sonja 15.00
46 EC/TD,Moon of Blood,
  B.U. Hyborian Tale 15.00
47 GK/JB/JRu,Treasure of Tranicos
  C:Thoth-Amon 15.00
48 JB/KJ,A Wind Blows from Stygia
  C:Thoth-Amon 15.00
49 JB/TD,When Madness Wears the
  Crown, B.U.Hyborian Tale 15.00
50 JB/TD,Swords Across the
  Alimane 18.00
51 JB/TD,Satyrs' Blood 10.00
52 JB/TD,Conan the Liberator. . . . 10.00

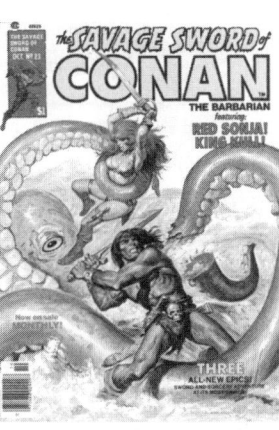

Savage Sword of Conan #23
© Marvel Entertainment Group

53 JB,The Sorcerer and the Soul,
  B.U. Solomon Kane. 10.00
54 JB,The Stalker Amid the Sands,
  B.U. Solomon Kane. 10.00
55 JB,Black Lotus & Yellow Death
  B.U. King Kull 10.00
56 JB/TD,The Sword of Skelos . . . 10.00
57 JB/TD,Zamboula. 10.00
58 JB/TD,KGa,For the Throne of
  Zamboula,B.U.OlgerdVladislav 10.00
59 AA,ECh,City ofSkulls,B.U.Gault 10.00
60 JB,The Ivory Goddess 10.00
61 JB,Wizard Fiend of Zingara . . . 10.00
62 JB/ECh,Temple of the Tiger,
  B.U. Solomon Kane. 10.00
63 JB/ECh,TP/BMc,GK,Moat of Blood
  I:Chane of the Elder Earth. . . . 10.00
64 JB/ECh,GK,Children of Rhan,
  B.U. Chane 10.00
65 GK,JB,Fangs of the Serpent,
  B.U. Bront 10.00
66 thru 80 . . . . @10.00
81 JB/ECh,Palace of Pleasure,
  B.U. Bront 10.00
82 AA,BWS,Devil in the Dark,Pt.1
  B.U.repConan#24,Swamp Gas 10.00
83 AA,MW,NA,ECh,Devil in the Dark
  Pt.2,B.U. Red Sonja,Sol.Kane. 10.00
84 VM,Darksome Demon of
  Rabba Than. 10.00
85 GK,Daughter of the God King. . 10.00
86 GK,Revenge of the Sorcerer . . 10.00
87 . . . . 10.00
88 JB,Isle of the Hunter 10.00
89 AA,MW,Gamesman of Asgalun,
  B.U. Rite of Blood 10.00
90 JB,Devourer of Souls 10.00
91 JB,VM,Forest of Friends,
  B.U. The Beast,The Chain . . . 10.00
92 JB,The Jeweled Bird. 10.00
93 JB/ECh,WorldBeyond the Mists 10.00
94 thru 101. . . . . @10.00
102 thru 161. . . . . @8.00
162 thru 175. . . . . @7.00
176 thru 235. . . . . @5.00
Ann.#1 SB,BWS,inc.Beware the
  Wrath of Anu,B.U. King
  Kull Vs.Thulsa Doom. 5.00

SAVAGE TALES
May, 1971
(black & white magazine)
1 GM,BWS,JR,I&O:Man-Thing,
  B:Conan,Femizons,A:Ka-Zar 350.00
2 GM,FB,BWS,AW,BWr,A:King
  Kull rep,Creatures on
  the Loose #10 . . . . 90.00
3 FB,BWS,AW,JSo 60.00
4 NA(c),E:Conan 50.00
5 JSn,JB,B:Brak the Barbarian . . 50.00
6 NA(c),JB,AW,B:Ka-Zar 35.00
7 GM,NA 30.00
8 JB,A:Shanna,E:Brak 30.00
9 MK,A:Shanna 30.00
10 RH,NA,AW,A:Shanna 30.00
11 RH. 30.00
12 Summer, 1975 . . . . 30.00
Ann.#1 GM,GK,BWS,O:Ka-Zar . . . 30.00

SAVAGE TALES
Nov., 1985–March, 1987
(black & white magazine)
1 MGo,I:The `Nam 6.00
2 thru 9 MGo . . . . @4.00

SCARLET SPIDER
1995–96
1 HMe,GK,TP,VirtualMortality,pt.3 . 2.50
2 HMe,JR2,AW,CyberWar,pt.3 . . . . 2.50
3 and 4 HMe . . . . @2.50

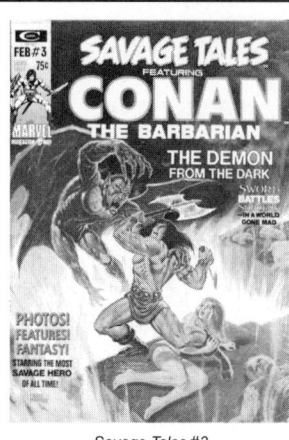

Savage Tales #3
© Marvel Entertainment Group

SCARLET SPIDER
UNLIMITED
1995
1 True Origin,64-pg. 4.50

SCARLET WITCH
1994
1 ALa(s),DAn(s),JH,I:Gargan,
  C:Master Pandemonium 2.50
2 C:Avengers West Coast 2.50
3 A:Avengers West Coast. 2.50
4 V:Lore,last issue 2.50

SCOOBY-DOO
Oct., 1977
1 B:DynoMutt 40.00
2 thru 9 Feb., 1979 . . . . @30.00

SECRET DEFENDERS
1993–95
1 F:Dr.Strange(in all),Spider
  Woman,Nomad,Darkhawk,
  Wolverine,V:Macabre 3.25
2 F:Spider Woman,Nomad,Darkhawk,
  Wolverine,V:Macabre 2.50
3 F:Spider Woman,Nomad,Darkhawk,
  Wolverine,V:Macabre 2.50
4 F:Namorita,Punisher,
  Sleepwalker,V:Roadkill 2.50
5 F:Naromita,Punisher,
  Sleepwalker, V:Roadkill. 2.50
6 F:Spider-Man,Scarlet Witch,Captain
  America,V:Suicide Pack 2.50
7 F:Captain America,Scarlet Witch,
  Spider-Man 2.50
8 F:Captain America,Scarlet Witch,
  Spider-Man 2.50
9 F:War Machine,Thunderstrike,
  Silver Surfer. 2.50
10 F:War Machine,Thunderstrike,
  Silver Surfer. 2.50
11 TGb,F:Hulk,Nova,Northstar. . . . 2.50
12 RMz(s),TGb,F:Thanos 2.75
13 RMz(s),TGb,F:Thanos,Super Skrull,
  Rhino,Nitro,Titanium Man 2.50
14 RMz(s),TGb,F:Thanos,Super Skrull,
  Rhino,Nitro,Titanium Man,
  A:Silver Surfer. 2.50
15 thru 17 F:Dr.Druid,Cage,
  Deadpool 2.50
18 F:Iron Fist,Giant Man 2.50
19 F:Dr.Druid,Cadaver,
  Shadowoman. 2.50

20 V:Venom 2.50
21 V:Slaymaker 2.50
22 thru 24 Final Defense,pt.1–pt.2@2.50
25 V:Dr.Druid 2.50

SECRET INVASION
Apr., 2008
1 (of 8) BMB(s),48-pg. 4.00
1a director's cut 64-pgs. (7-2008) . 5.00
2 thru 8 BMB(s). . . . . @4.00
2a thru 8a variant (c)s . . . . @4.00
2b thru 8b variant sketch (c)s . . @4.00
Spec. Secret Invasion Saga . . . . . . free
Spec. Who Do You Trust? 4.00

...FANTASTIC FOUR
May, 2008
1 (of 3) No One Gets Back Alive . . 3.00
2 He's Just Not That Into You 3.00
3 Operation Break-in. 3.00

...FRONT LINE
July, 2008
1 (of 5) 3.00
2 thru 5 . . . . @3.00

...INHUMANS
Aug., 2008
1 (of 4) TR 3.00
2 thru 4 TR, Hunt for Black Bolt . @3.00

...RUNAWAYS/
YOUNG AVENGERS
June, 2008
1 (of 3) 3.00
2 thru 3 . . . . @3.00

...SPIDER-MAN:
BRAND NEW DAY
Aug., 2008
1 (of 3) 3.00
2 . . . . 3.00
3 Amazing Spider-Man 3.00

...THOR
Aug., 2008
1 (of 3) DBw 3.00
2 thru 3 DBw . . . . @3.00

...X-MEN
Aug., 2008
1 (of 4) CNr, Manifest Destiny 3.00
2 thru 4 CNr, Manifest Destiny . . @3.00

SECRET STORY
ROMANCES
Marvel Atlas, 1953
1 BEv 200.00
2 . . . . 125.00
3 thru 9 . . . . @100.00
10 thru 21 ViC (in many) . . . . . @100.00

SECRET WAR
Feb., 2004
Book One BMB 8.00
Book One, Commemorative ed. . . . 6.00
Book Two BMB 5.00
Book Three BMB 4.00

SECRET WAR
2005
1 (of 5) BMB, 48-pg. 4.00
2 thru 5 BMB, 48-pg. 4.00
Spec. From the Files of Nick Fury . 4.00

SECRET WARS
May, 1984
1 MZ,A:X-Men,Fant.Four,Avengers,
Hulk,SpM in All,I:Beyonder 7.00

Secret Wars II #1
© Marvel Entertainment Group

2 MZ,V:Magneto 6.00
3 MZ,I:Titania & Volcana. 6.00
4 BL,V:Molecule Man 6.00
5 BL,F:X-Men 6.00
6 MZ,V:Doctor Doom 6.00
7 MZ,I:New Spiderwoman. 7.00
8 MZ,I:Alien Black Costume
(for Spider-Man) 25.00
9 MZ,V:Galactus 5.00
10 MZ,V:Dr.Doom 5.00
11 MZ,V:Dr.Doom. 5.00
12 MZ,Beyonder Vs. Dr.Doom. . . . 7.00

SECRET WARS II
July, 1985
1 AM,SL,A:X-Men,New Mutants . . . 5.00
2 AM,SL,A:Fantastic Four. 3.00
3 AM,SL,A:Daredevil. 3.00
4 AM,I:Kurse 3.00
5 AM,SL,I:Boom Boom 3.50
6 AM,SL,A:Mephisto 3.00
7 AM,SL,A:Thing. 3.00
8 AM,SL,A:Hulk. 3.00
9 AM,SL,A:Everyone,double-size . . 5.00

SECTAURS
June, 1985
1 Based on toys 3.00
2 . . . . 3.00
3 . . . . 3.00
4 . . . . 3.00
5 thru 10 1986. . . . . @3.00

SEEKER 3000
April, 1998
1 (of 4) DAn,IEd,sci-fi adventure,
48-pg. 3.00
2 DAn,IEd,encounter with aliens . . 3.00
3 DAn,IEd,V:Hkkkt,. 3.00
4 DAn,IEd,V:Hkkkt, concl. 3.00

SEMPER FI
Dec., 1988
1 JSe. 2.50
2 JSe. 2.50
3 JSe. 2.50
4 JSe. 2.50
5 JSe. 2.50
6 and 9 . . . . @2.50

SENSATIONAL
SPIDER-MAN
May, 1984
1 KM/TP/KJ,rep. (1989) 6.00

SENSATIONAL
SPIDER-MAN
Jan., 1996
0 DJu,KJ,Return of Spider-Man,pt.1
Lenticular cover 6.00
1 DJu,KJ,Media Blizzard,pt.1,
V:New Mysterio 5.00
2 DJu,KJ,Return of Kaine,pt.2 . . . . 4.00
3 DJu,KJ,Web of Carnage,pt.1 . . . 4.00
4 DJu,KJ,Blood Brothers,pt.1 . . . . 4.00
5 DJu 4.00
6 DJu 3.00
7 TDz,A:Onslaught 3.00
8 TDz,The Looter 3.00
9 TDz,Onslaught tie-in 3.00
10 TDz,RCa,V:Swarm 3.00
11 TDz,Revelations, pt.2 . . . . 3.00
11A bagged with card, etc. 5.00
12 TDz,SwM, V:Trapster 3.00
13 TDz,RCa,A:Ka-Zar, Shanna . . . 3.00
14 TDz,RCa,Savage Land saga . . . 3.00
15 TDz,RCa,Savage Land saga . . . 3.00
16 TDz,RCa,R:Black Cat,
V:Prowler,Vulture. 3.00
17 TDz,RCa,V:Black Cat,
Prowler,Vulture 3.00
18 TDz,RCa,V:Vulture 3.00
19 TDz,RCa,R:Living Monolith . . . 2.50
20 TDz,RCa,Living Pharoah, concl.. 2.50
21 TDz,RCa,Techomancers. 2.50
22 TDz,RCa,A:Doctor Strange. . . . 2.50
23 TDz,RCa,A:Doctor Strange. . . . 2.50
24 TDz,RCa,A:S.H.I.E.L.D., Looter . 3.00
25 TDz,RCa,Spider-Hunt,pt1 x-over 4.00
26 TDz,RCa,JoB,Identity Crisis
prelude. 2.50
27 TDz,RCa,MeW,Identity Crisis,
as Hornet V:Phaeton 2.50
28 TDz,RCa,as Hornet, V:Vulture . . 2.50
29 TDz,RCa,V:Arcade, Black Cat . . 2.50
30 TDz,A:Black Cat,V:Arcade 2.50
31 TDz,MeW,RCa,V:Rhino 2.50
32 TDz,JoB,The Gathering of the
Five, pt.1 (of 5) 2.50
33 TDz,JoB,Gathering of
the Five,pt.5. . . . . 2.50
Minus 1 Spec.,TDz,RCa, flashback . 3.00

SENSATIONAL SPIDER-MAN
See: MARVEL KNIGHTS
SPIDER-MAN

SENTINEL
April, 2003
1 thru 6 Salvage,pt.1–6 . . . . @3.00
7thru 9 No Hero,pt.1–3 . . . . @2.50
10 thru 12 Awakening,pt.1–3 . . . . @3.00

SENTINEL
Nov., 2005
1 V:Stealth Sentinel 3.00
2 thru 5 . . . . @3.00
Digest Past Imperfect 8.00

SENTINEL SQUAD O*N*E
Jan., 2006
1 Decimation tie-in 3.00
2 thru 5 . . . . @3.00

SENTRY
July, 2000
1 (of 5) PJe,JaL 15.00
2 PJe,JaL,Unicorn 10.00
3 PJe,JaL,Hulk,Spider-Man 10.00
4 PJe,JaL,Prof.X. 10.00
5 PJe,JaL, ... 10.00
Spec.#1 Sentry vs. The Void,
JaL,PJe (2001) 20.00

MARVEL

SENTRY, THE
Sept., 2005
1 JR2,V:Hords of Attuma 3.00
1a Rough Cut, Jr2 . . . . 4.00
2 thru 8 JR2 . . . . @3.00

SERGEANT BARNEY BARKER
Aug., 1956
1 JSe,Comedy 250.00
2 JSe,Army Inspection(c) 150.00
3 JSe,Tank(c) 150.00
Becomes:

G.I. TALES
4 JSe,At Grips with the Enemy . 125.00
5 . . . . 100.00
6 JO,BP,GWb, July, 1957 . . . . . 100.00

SGT. FURY & HIS HOWLING COMMANDOS
May, 1963–Dec., 1981
1 Seven Against the Nazis . . . 4,000.00
2 JK,Seven Doomed Men 000.00
3 JK,Midnight on Massacre
 Mountain 500.00
4 JK,V:Lord Ha-Ha,D:Junior
 Juniper 500.00
5 JK,V:Baron Strucker 500.00
6 JK,The Fangs of the Fox . . . 300.00
7 JK,Fury Court Martial 300.00
8 JK,V:Dr Zemo,I:Percival
 Pinkerton 300.00
9 DAy,V:Hitler 300.00
10 DAy,On to Okinwawa,I:Capt.
 Savage 300.00
11 DAy,V:Capt.Flint 150.00
12 DAy,Howler deserts 150.00
13 DAy,JK,A;Capt.America 700.00
14 DAy,V:Baron Strucker 150.00
15 DAy,SD,Too Small to Fight
 Too Young to Die 150.00
16 DAy,In The Desert a Fortress
 Stands 150.00
17 DAy,While the Jungle Sleeps . 150.00
18 DAy,Killed in Action 150.00
19 DAy,An Eye for an Eye 150.00
20 DAy,V:the Blitz Squad 150.00
21 DAy,To Free a Hostage. 100.00
22 DAy,V:Bull McGiveney 100.00
23 DAy,The Man who Failed 100.00
24 DAy,When the Howlers Hit
 the Home Front 100.00
25 DAy,Every Man my Enemy . . . 110.00
26 DAy,Dum Dum Does it the
 Hard Way. 100.00
27 DAy,O:Fury's Eyepatch. 100.00
28 DAy,Not a Man Shall Remain
 Alive. 100.00
29 DAy,V:Baron Strucker 100.00
30 DAy,Incident in Italy 100.00
31 DAy,Into the Jaws of Death . . . 75.00
32 DAy,A Traitor in Our Midst 75.00
33 DAy,The Grandeur That was
 Greece. 75.00
34 DAy,O:Howling Commandoes . 60.00
35 DAy,Berlin Breakout,J:Eric
 Koenig 60.00
36 DAy,My Brother My Enemy. . . 60.00
37 DAy,In the Desert to Die 60.00
38 This Ones For Dino 60.00
39 Into the Fortress of Fear. 60.00
40 That France Might be Free . . . 60.00
41 V:The Blitzers 60.00
42 Three Were AWOL 60.00
43 Scourge of the Sahara,A:Bob
 Hope,Glen Miller 60.00
44 DAy,The Howlers First Mission . 60.00
45 JSe,I:The War Lover. 60.00
46 JSe,They Also Serve 60.00

47 Tea and Sabotage. 60.00
48 A:Blitz Squad 60.00
49 On to Tarawa 60.00
50 The Invasion Begins 60.00
51 The Assassin 60.00
52 Triumph at Treblinka 60.00
53 To the Bastions of Bavaria . . . 60.00
54 Izzy Shoots the Works 60.00
55 Cry of Battle, Kiss of Death . . 50.00
56 Gabriel Blow Your Horn 50.00
57 TS,The Informer 50.00
58 Second Front 50.00
59 D-Day for Dum Dum 50.00
60 Authorised Personnel Only . . . 50.00
61 The Big Breakout 50.00
62 The Basic Training of Fury . . . 50.00
63 V:Nazi Tanks. 50.00
64 The Peacemonger,A:Capt
 Savage 50.00
65 Eric Koenig,Traitor 50.00
66 Liberty Rides the Underground. 50.00
67 With a Little Help From My
 Friends. 75.00
68 Welcome Home Soldier 50.00
69 While the City Sleeps 50.00
70 The Missouri Marauders 50.00
71 Burn,Bridge,Burn 50.00
72 Battle in the Sahara 50.00
73 Rampage on the
 Russian Front 50.00
74 Each Man Alone 50.00
75 The Deserter. 30.00
76 He Fought the Red Baron. 30.00
77 A Traitor's Trap,A:Eric Koenig. . 30.00
78 Escape or Die. 30.00
79 Death in the High Castle. 30.00
80 To Free a Hostage 30.00
81 The All American. 30.00
82 Howlers Hit The
 Home Front,rep. 25.00
83 Dum DumV:Man-Mountain
 McCoy 25.00
84 The Devil's Disciple 25.00
85 Fury V:The Howlers 25.00
86 Germ Warfare 25.00
87 Dum Dum does it...rep 25.00
88 Save General Patton 25.00
89 O:Fury's eyepatch,rep. 25.00
90 The Chain That Binds 25.00
91 Not A Man...rep. 25.00
92 Some Die Slowly, giant-sz. . . . 28.00
93 A Traitor... . . . . 20.00
94 GK(c),Who'll Stop the Bombs. . 20.00
95 7 Doomed Men, rep 20.00

Sgt. Fury & His Howling Commandos
#126 © Marvel Entertainment Group

96 GK(c),Dum-Dum Sees it
 Through. 20.00
97 Till the Last Man Shall Fail . . . 20.00
98 A:Deadly Dozen 20.00
99 Guerillas in Greece. 20.00
100 When a Howler Falls 30.00
101 Pearl Harbor 18.00
102 Death For A Dollar 18.00
103 Berlin Breakout. 18.00
104 The Tanks Are Coming 18.00
105 My Brother,My Enemy 18.00
106 Death on the Rhine. 18.00
107 Death-Duel in the Desert 18.00
108 Slaughter From the Skies 18.00
109 This Ones For Dino,rep 18.00
110 JSe(c),The Reserve 18.00
111 V:Colonel Klaw 18.00
112 V:Baron Strucker. 18.00
113 That France Might
 Be Free,rep 18.00
114 Jungle Bust Out 18.00
115 V:Baron Strucker. 18.00
116 End of the Road 18.00
117 Blitz Over Britain 18.00
118 War Machine 18.00
118 War Machine 18.00
119 They Strike by Machine. 18.00
120 Trapped in the Compound of
 Death 18.00
121 An Eye for an Eye. 12.00
122 A;The Blitz Squad 12.00
123 To Free a Hostage 12.00
124 A:Bull McGiveney 12.00
125 The Man Who Failed 12.00
126 When the Howlers Hit Home.. 12.00
127 Everyman My Enemy,rep 12.00
128 Dum Dum does it...rep 12.00
129 O:Fury's Eyepatch 12.00
130 A:Baron Strucker 12.00
131 Armageddon 12.00
132 Incident in Italy 12.00
133 thru 140 . . . . @12.00
141 thru 150. . . . . @12.00
151 thru 167 . . . . @12.00
Ann.#1 Korea #4,#5. . . . . 300.00
Ann.#2 This was D-Day 100.00
Ann.#3 Vietnam 60.00
Ann.#4 Battle of the Bulge. 40.00
Ann.#5 Desert Fox. 30.00
Ann.#6 Blaze of Battle 30.00
Ann.#7 Armageddon 30.00

SERGIO ARAGONES MASSACRES MARVEL
1996
1-shot Parody. 5.00

SHADOWMASTERS
Oct., 1989–Jan., 1990
1 RH 7.00
2 . . . . 5.00
3 . . . . 4.00
4 . . . . 4.00

SHADOWRIDERS
1993
1 I:Shadowriders,A:Cable,
 Ghost Rider 3.00
2 A:Ghost Rider 2.50
3 A:Cable 2.50
4 A:Cable 2.50

SHADOWS & LIGHT
Dec., 1997
1 BSf,RMz,LWn,BWr,GeH,SD,B&W
 anthology series 3.00
2 JSn,LW,LSh,GK 3.00
3 BL,JSn 3.00
4 three new tales 3.00

SHANNA, THE SHE-DEVIL
Dec., 1972–Aug., 1973
1 GT,F:Shanna	40.00
2 RA,The Dungeon of Doom	30.00
3 RA,The Hour of the Bull	20.00
4 RA,Mandrill	20.00
5 JR(c),RA,V:Nekra	20.00

SHANNA, THE SHE-DEVIL
Feb., 2005
1 (of 7) by Frank Cho	3.50
2 thru 7	@3.50

SHANNA THE SHE DEVIL: SURVIVAL OF THE FITTEST
Aug., 2007
1 thru 4 JP	@3.00

SHEENA
Dec., 1984–Feb., 1985
1 and 2 Movie adapt	@3.00

SHE-HULK
[1st Regular Series] Feb., 1980
1 JB,BWi,I&O:She-Hulk	10.00
2 BWi,D:She-Hulk's best friend	7.00
3 BWi,Wanted for Murder	7.00
4 BWi,V:Her Father	7.00
5 BWi,V:Silver Serpent	7.00
6 A:Iron Man	5.00
7 BWi,A:Manthing	5.00
8 BWi,A:Manthing	5.00
9 BWi,Identity Crisis	5.00
10 V:The Word	5.00
11 BWi,V:Dr.Morbius	5.00
12 V:Gemini	5.00
13 V:Man-Wolf	5.00
14 V:Hellcat	5.00
15 V:Lady Kills	5.00
16 She Hulk Goes Berserk	5.00
17 V:Man-Elephant	5.00
18 V:Grappler	5.00
19 V:Her Father	5.00
20 A:Zapper	5.00
21 V:Seeker	5.00
22 V:Radius	5.00
23 V:Radius	5.00
24 V:Zapper	5.00
25 Double-sized,last issue	5.00

[2nd Regular Series] 1989–94
1 JBy,V:Ringmaster	4.00
2 JBy	2.50
3 JBy,A:Spider-Man	2.50
4 JBy,I:Blond Phantom	3.00
5 JBy	2.50
6 JBy,A:U.S.1,Razorback	2.50
7 JBy,A:U.S.1,Razorback	2.50
8 JBy,A:Saint Nicholas	2.50
9 AM(i)	2.50
10 AM(i)	2.50
11	2.50
12	2.50
13 SK(c)	2.50
14 MT(c),A:Howard the Duck	3.00
15 SK(c)	3.00
16 SK(c)	3.00
17 SK(c),V:Dr.Angst	3.00
18 SK(c)	2.50
19 SK(c),V:Nosferata	2.50
20 SK(c),Darkham Asylum	2.50
21 SK(c),V:Blonde Phantom	3.00
22 SK(c),V:Blonde Phantom,A:All Winners Squad	3.00
23 V:Blonde Phantom	3.00
24 V:Deaths'Head	4.00
25 A:Hercules,Thor	2.50
26 A:Excalibur	2.50

She-Hulk #49
© Marvel Entertainment Group

27 Cartoons in N.Y.	2.50
28 Game Hunter Stalks She-Hulk	2.50
29 A:Wolv.,Hulk,SpM,Venom	2.50
30 MZ(c),A:Silver Surfer,Thor Human Torch	2.50
31 JBy,V:Spragg the Living Hill	2.50
32 JBy,A:Moleman,V:Spragg	2.50
33 JBy,A:Moleman,V:Spragg	2.50
34 JBy,Returns to New York	2.50
35 JBy,V:X-Humed Men	2.50
36 JBy,X-mas issue (#8 tie-in)	2.50
37 JBy,V:Living Eraser	2.50
38 JBy,V:Mahkizmo	2.50
39 JBy,V:Mahkizmo	2.50
40 JBy,V:Spraggs,Xemnu	2.50
41 JBy,V:Xemnu	2.50
42 JBy,V:USArcher	2.50
43 JBy,V:Xemnu	2.50
44 JBy,R:Rocket Raccoon	2.50
45 JBy,A:Razorback	2.50
46 JBy,A:Rocket Raccoon	2.50
47 V:D'Bari	2.50
48 JBy,A:Rocket Raccoon	2.50
49 V:Skrulls,D'Bari	2.50
50 JBy,WS,TA,DGb,AH,HC, D:She-Hulk	4.00
51 TMo,V:Savage She-Hulk	2.50
52 D:She-Hulk,A:Thing,Mr.Fantastic, I:Rumbler,V:Titania	2.50
53 AH(c),A:Zapper	2.50
54 MGo(c),A:Wonder Man	2.50
55 V:Rumbler	2.50
56 A:War Zone	2.50
57 A:Hulk	2.50
58 V:Electro	2.50
59 V:Various Villains	2.50
60 last issue	2.50

March, 2004
1 F:Avengers	8.00
2 Class Action Comics	5.00
3 Dead Certain,F:The Thing	4.00
4 Web of Lies	3.00
5 The Big Picture,pt.1	3.00
6 The Big Picture,pt.2	3.00
7 Space Cases,pt.1	3.00
8 Engagement Ring,pt.2	3.00
9 A:Hercules	3.00
10 Titania	3.00
11 Balance of Power	3.00
12 Acceptable Losses	3.00

SHE-HULK 2
Nov., 2005
1 A:New Avengers,Titan	6.00

2 Cause & Effect	3.00
3 104-pg. special	4.00
Becomes:	

SHE-HULK
4 Return to Bone	3.00
5 New Kid in Town	3.00
6 I'm With Cupid	3.00
7 Beaus & Eros	3.00
8 Civil War tie-in	12.00
8a 2nd printing	6.00
9 My Spoiler with Spoiler	3.00
10 V:Man-Wolf	3.00
11 Creature Comforts	3.00
12 F:Starfox, A:Thanos	3.00
13 Remember the Titans	3.00
14 RBr,Awesome Andy	3.00
15 RBr,Planet Without a Hulk,pt.1	3.00
16 RBr,Planet Without a Hulk,pt.2	3.00
17 RBr,Planet Without a Hulk,pt.3	3.00
18 RBr,Planet Without a Hulk,pt.4	3.00
19 RBr,The Gamma Defense	3.00
20 RBr,What the @#*%?!!	3.00
21	3.00
22 PDd(s), Jaded, pt.1	8.00
23 PDd(s), Jaded, pt.2	3.00
24 PDd(s)	3.00
25 PDd(s),Whole Hero Thing	3.00
26 PDd(s),Whole Hero Thing, concl	3.00
27 PDd(s),MD2(c)	3.00
28 PDd(s),MD2(c),Here Today	3.00
29 PDd(s),Savage She-Hulk	3.00
30 PDd(s),A:Hercules	3.00
31 PDd(s),Secret Invasion tie-in	3.00
32 PDd(s),Secret Invasion tie-in	3.00
33 PDd(s),Secret Invasion tie-in	3.00
34 PDd(s),Lady Liberators	3.00
35 PDd(s),I:Valkayrie,Thundra	3.00

SHE HULK: CEREMONY
1989
1 JBr/SDr	4.00
2 JBr/FS	4.00

SHERRY THE SHOWGIRL
Marvel Atlas, 1956
1	225.00
2	135.00
3	125.00
4	125.00
5 thru 7	@125.00

SHIELD
Feb., 1973
1 JSo	25.00
2 JSo	20.00
3 JB,JSo,JK	20.00
4 JSo	20.00
5 JSo,Oct., 1973	20.00

SHOGUN WARRIORS
Feb., 1979
1 HT,DGr,F:Raydeen, Combatra, Dangard Ace	15.00
2 HT,DGr,V:Elementals of Evil	10.00
3 AM(c),HT,DGr,V:Elementals of Evil	10.00
4 HT,DGr,Menace of the Mech Monsters	10.00
5 HT,DGr,Into The Lair of Demons	10.00
6 HT,ME	10.00
7 HT,ME	10.00
8 HT,ME	10.00
9 War Beneath The Waves	10.00
10 Five Heads of Doom	10.00
11 TA(c)	8.00
12 WS(c)	8.00
13 Demons on the Moon	8.00
14 V:Dr. Demonicus	8.00
15	8.00

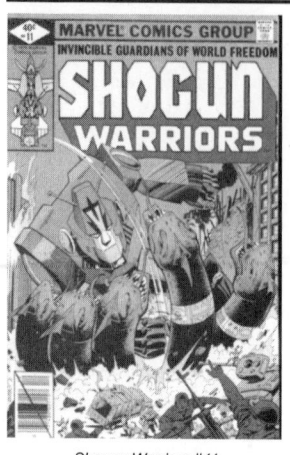

Shogun Warriors #11
© *Marvel Entertainment Group*

16	8.00
17	8.00
18	8.00
19 A:Fantastic Four	8.00
20 Sept., 1980	8.00

SHOWGIRLS
Marvel Atlas, 1957

1	150.00
2	125.00

SHROUD
Limited Series 1994

1 B:MiB(s),MCW,A:Spider-Man, V:Scorpion	2.50
2 MCW	@2.50

SILENT WAR
Jan., 2007

1 (of 6) Fant.Four V:Gorgon	3.00
2 thru 4	3.00
5 Sentry vs. Black Bolt	@3.00
6 F:Black Bolt	3.00

SILLY TUNES
Marvel Timely, 1945–47

1 Ziggy Pig	300.00
2	150.00
3 thru 7	@125.00

SILVERHAWKS
Aug., 1987

1 thru 5	@3.00
6 June, 1988	3.00

SILVER SABLE
1992–95

1 Foil stamped(c),A:Sandman, Spider-Man	3.00
2 I:Gattling	2.50
3 V:Gattling,Foreigner	2.50
4 Infinity War,V:Doctor Doom	2.50
5 Infinity War,V:Doctor Doom	2.50
6 A:Deathlok	2.50
7 A:Deathlok	2.50
8 V:Hydra	2.50
9 O:Silver Sable	2.50
10 A:Punisher,Leviathan	2.50
11 Cyber Warriors,Hydra	2.50
12 V:Cyberwarriorss,R:Sandman	2.50
13 For Love Nor Money#3, A:Cage,Terror	2.50

14 For Love Nor Money#6, A:Cage,Terror	2.50
15 V:Viper,A:Captain America	2.50
16 SBt,Infinty Crusade	2.50
17 Infinity Crusade	2.50
18 A:Venom	2.50
19 Siege of Darkness x-over	2.50
20 GWt(s),StB,BU:Sandman,Fin	2.50
21 Gang War	2.50
22	2.50
23 GWt(s),A:Deadpool,Daredevil, BU:Sandman	2.50
24 GWt(s),BU:Crippler,w/card	2.50
25 V:Hydra	3.00
26 F:Sandman	2.50
27 A:Code Blue	2.50
28 F:Chen	2.50
29 A:Wild Pack	2.50
30 problems with law	2.50
31 V:terrorists	2.50
32 A:The Foreigner	2.50
33 V:Hammerhead	2.50
34	2.50
35 Li'l Silvie Tale	2.50

SILVER SURFER
[1st Series] Aug., 1968

1 B:StL(s),JB,JSr,GC,O:Silver Surfer, O:Watcher,I:Shala Bal	850.00
2 JB,JSr,GC,A:Watcher	500.00
3 JB,JSr,GC,I:Mephisto	400.00
4 JB,A:Thor,low distribution scarce	800.00
5 JB,A:Fant.Four,V:Stranger	250.00
6 JB,FB,A:Watcher	300.00
7 JB,A:Watcher,I:Frankenstein's Monster	275.00
8 JB,DA,A:Mephisto,I:Ghost	250.00
9 JB,DA,A:Mephisto,A:Ghost	250.00
10 JB,DA,South America	300.00
11 JB,DA	300.00
12 JB,DA,V:The Abomination	250.00
13 JB,DA,V:Doomsday Man	250.00
14 JB,DA,A:Spider-Man	275.00
15 JB,DA,A:Human Torch	150.00
16 JB,V:Mephisto	150.00
17 JB,V:Mephisto	150.00
18 E:StL(s),JK,V:Inhumans	150.00

[2nd Regular Series] 1982

1 JBy,TP,Direct Only,V:Mephisto	12.00

[3rd Regular Series] July, 1987

1 MR,JRu,A:Fantastic Four, Galactus,V:Champion	12.00
2 MR,A:Shalla Bal,V:Skrulls	6.00
3 MR,V:Collector & Runner	5.00
4 MR,JRu,A:Elders,I:Obliterator	5.00
5 MR,JRu,V:Obliterator	5.00
6 MR,JRu,O:Obliterator,A:Kree, Skrulls	5.00
7 MR,JRu,V:Supremor,Elders/ Soul Gems	5.00
8 MR,JRu,V:Supremor	5.00
9 MR,Elders Vs.Galactus	5.00
10 MR,A:Galactus,Eternity	5.00
11 JSon,JRu,V:Reptyl	4.50
12 MR,JRu,V:Reptyl,A:Nova	4.50
13 JSon,DC,V:Ronan	4.50
14 JSon,JRu,V:Skrull Surfer	4.50
15 RLm,JRu,A:Fantastic Four	6.00
16 RLm,Inbetweener possesses Soul Gem,A:Fantastic Four	4.00
17 RLm,A:Inbetweener,Galactus, Fantastic Four,D:Trader, Possessor,Astronomer	4.00
18 RLm,Galactus V:Inbetweener	4.00
19 RLm,MR,V:Firelord	4.00
20 RLm,A:Superskrull,Galactus	4.00
21 MR,DC,V:Obliterator	4.00
22 RLm,V:Ego	4.00
23 RLm,V:Dragon	4.00
24 RLm,V:G.I.G.O.	4.00

25 RLm,V:Ronan,Kree Skrull War	4.00
26 RLm,V:Nenora	4.00
27 RLm,V:Stranger	4.00
28 RLm,D:Super Skrull,V:Reptyl	4.00
29 RLm,V:Midnight Sun	4.00
30 RLm,V:Midnight Sun	4.00
31 RLm,O:Living Tribunal & Stranger (double size)	4.50
32 RF,JSt,A:Mephisto	4.00
33 Rlm,V:Impossible Man	4.00
34 RLm,(1stJSn),2nd R:Thanos	5.00
35 RLm,A:Thanos,R:Drax	4.00
36 RLm,V:Impossible Man,A:Warlock Capt.Marvel,C:Thanos	4.00
37 RLm,V:Drax,A:Mentor	4.00
38 RLm,V:Thanos(continued in Thanos Quest)	4.00
39 JSh,V:Algol	3.00
40 RLm,V:Dynamo City	3.00
41 RLm,V:Dynamo City,A:Thanos	4.00
42 RLm,V:Dynamo City,A:Drax	3.00
43 RLm,V:DynamoCity	3.00
44 RLm,R:Thanos,Drax, O:Inf.Gems	4.00
45 RLm,Thanos vs. Mephisto	4.00
46 RLm,R:Warlock,A:Thanos	4.00
47 RLm,Warlock V:Drax, A:Thanos	4.00
48 RLm,A:Galactus,Thanos	4.00
49 RLm,V:Thanos Monster	4.00
50 RLm,Silver Stamp(D.size), V:Thanos Monster	8.00
50a 2nd printing	3.00
50b 3rd printing	3.00
51 RLm,Infinity Gauntlet x-over	3.00
52 RLm,Infinity Gauntlet x-over	3.00
53 RLm,Infinity Gauntlet x-over	3.00
54 RLm,I.Gauntlet x-over,V:Rhino	3.00
55 RLm,I.Gauntlet x-over,Universe According to Thanos,pt.1	3.00
56 RLm,I.Gauntlet x-over,Universe According to Thanos,pt.2	3.00
57 RLm,Infinity Gauntlet x-over	3.00
58 RLm(c),Infinity Gauntlet x-over, A:Hulk,Namor,Dr.Strange	3.00
59 RLm(c),TR,Infinity Gauntlet, Thanos V:Silver Surfer	3.00
60 RLm,V:Midnight Sun, A:Inhumans	2.50
61 RLm,I:Collection.Agency	2.50
62 RLm,O:Collection Agency	2.50
63 RLm,A:Captain Marvel	2.50
64 RLm,V:Dark Silver Surfer	2.50

Silver Surfer, 3rd Series, #34
© *Marvel Entertainment Group*

65 RLm,R:Reptyl,I:Princess
  Alaisa. 2.50
66 RLm,I:Avatar,Love & Hate 2.50
67 RLm(c),KWe,Inf.War,V:Galactus
  A:DrStrange. 2.50
68 RLm(c),KWe,Inf.War,O:Nova . . . 2.50
69 RLm(c),KWe,Infinity War,
  A:Galactus. 2.50
70 RLm(c),Herald War#1,I:Morg . . . 2.50
71 RLm(c),Herald War#2,V:Morg . . 2.50
72 RLm(c),Herald War#3,R:Nova . . 2.50
73 RLm,R:Airwalker. 2.50
74 RLm,V:Terrax 2.50
75 RLm,E:Herald Ordeal,V:Morg,
  D:Nova. 3.00
76 RLm,A:Jack of Hearts. 2.50
77 RLm,A:Jack of Hearts. 2.50
78 RLm,R:Morg,V:Nebula 2.50
79 RLm,V:Captain Atlas. 2.50
80 RLm,I:Ganymede,Terrax
  Vs.Morg. 2.50
81 RLm,O:Ganymedel:Tyrant 2.50
82 RLm,V:Tyrant,double sized. 2.50
83 Infinity Crusade. 2.50
84 RLm(c),Infinity Crusade 2.50
85 RLm(c),Infinity Crusade 2.50
86 RLm(c), Blood & Thunder,pt.2
  V:Thor,A:Beta Ray Bill. 2.50
87 RLm(c),Blood & Thunder,pt.7 . . . 2.50
88 RLm(c),Blood & Thunder,pt.10 . . 2.50
89 RLm(c),CDo,C:Legacy 2.50
90 RLm(c),A:Legacy,C:Avatar 2.50
91 RLm 2.50
92 RLm,V:Avatar 2.50
93 V:Human Torch 2.50
94 A:Fantastic Four, Warlock. 2.50
95 SEa,A:Fantastic Four 2.50
96 A:Fantastic Four,Hulk 2.50
97 A:Fantastic Four,R:Nova. 2.50
98 R:Champion 2.50
99 A:Nova 2.50
100 V:Mephisto 2.50
100a enhanced ed. 5.00
101 RMz,JoP,A:Shalla Bal. 2.50
102 V:Galactus 2.50
103 I:Death quad 2.50
104 Surfer Rampage 2.50
105 V:Super Skrull. 2.50
106 A:Legacy,Morg 2.50
107 TGb,BAn,A:Galactus,Morg,
  Tyrant. 2.50
108 Galactus Vs. Tyrant 2.50
109 Morg has Ultimate Nulifier 2.50
110 JB,F:Nebula 2.50
111 GP,TGb,BAn,to Other Side
  of Galaxy. 2.50
112 GP,TGb,BAn,. 2.50
113 GP,TGb,BAn,V:Blackbody. 2.50
114 . . . . 2.50
115 GP,TGb,BAn,Surfer in pieces . . 2.50
116 GP,TGb,BAn,Pieces cause
  trouble 2.50
117 thru 119 . . . . @2.50
120 . . . . 2.50
121 A:Quasar, Beta Ray Bill 2.50
122 GP,SEa, returns to Marvel
  Universe 2.50
123 GP,RG. 2.50
124 GP,RG. 2.50
125 RG,V:Hulk, double size 3.50
126 JMD,RG,BWi,A:Dr. Strange . . . 2.50
127 JMD,RG,BWi,A:Alicia Masters . . 2.50
128 JMD,RG,BWi,V:Puppet Master . 2.50
129 JMD,RG,BWi,back in time,
  late 1940s 2.50
130 JMD,CNr,BWi, trapped in past . 2.50
131 JMD,RG,BWi, ... 2.50
132 JMD,PaP,Puppet Master
  missing 2.50
133 JMD,MRy,PaP,V:PuppetMaster 2.50
134 JMD,TGm,MRy,Regains his
  memories,pt.1 (of 4). 2.50

Silver Surfer #101
© Marvel Entertainment Group

135 JMD,TGm,MRy,Alicia summons
  Scrier. 2.50
136 JMD,TGm,MRy, ... 2.50
137 JMD,TGm,MRy,Mephisto v.
  Scrier. 2.50
138 JMD,RCz,MRy,A:The Thing,
  tie-in. 2.50
139 JMD,RCz,MRy,V:Gargoyle 2.50
140 JMD,JMu,on Zenn-La untouched
  by Galactus 2.50
141 JMD,JMu,A:Sama-D,Alicia
  Masters 2.50
142 JMD,JMu,Tenebrae,The Union,
  Cipher 2.50
143 JMD,DCw,Tenebrae,V:Psycho
  Man 2.50
Bi-Weekly Issues
144 JMD,JMu,V:Psycho-Man,
  A:Tenebrae 2.50
145 JMD,JMu,A:Psycho-Man,
  Tenebrae,Cypphyrr 2.50
146 TDF,DCw,V:Firelord 2.50
Minus 1 Spec., JMD,RG,BWi,
  flashback, first human contact. . 2.50
Spec. Silver Surfer: Dangerous Arti-
  facts,RMz, Galactus,Thanos
  (1996) 4.00
Spec. Silver Surfer: Inner Demons,
  rep. JMD,RGa,BWi (1998) 3.00
Ann.#1 RLm,JSon,Evolution War . . 7.00
Ann.#2 RLm,Atlantis Attacks 5.00
Ann.#3 RLm,Lifeform #4 . . . . 4.00
Ann.#4 RLm,Korvac Quest #3,A:
  Guardians of Galaxy 3.00
Ann.#5 RLm,Ret.o/Defenders #3. . . 3.00
Ann.#6 RLm(c),I:Legacy,w/card. . . . 3.75
Ann.'97 1 JMD,VS,KJ,V:Scrier,
  48-pg. 3.00
Ann.'98 MPe,RBe,TDF,F:Thor 3.00
Epic, Dec., 1988
1 Moebius,V:Galactus. 5.00
2 Moebius,V:Galactus. 5.00
Graphic Novel 15.00

July, 2003
1 JJu(c),children disappear. 2.50
2 JaL(c),Denise Waters 2.50
3 Denise Waters 2.50
4 thru 6 Communion,pt.4–6 . . . . @2.50
7 thru 14 Revelation,pt.1–8. . . . . @3.00

...IN THY NAME
Nov., 2007
1 thru 4 . . . . @3.00

...LOFTIER THAN MORTALS
Aug., 1999
1 MFr,V:Dr. Doom. 2.50
2 MFr,V:Dr. Doom, concl. 2.50

...REQUIEM
May, 2007
1 (of 4) MSz(s) 4.00
2 MSz(s), Kyrie 4.00
3 MSz(s),Sanctus 4.00
4 MSz(s),Agnus Dei 4.00

...SUPERMAN
Marvel/DC 1996
Spec. GP,RLm,TA, x-over 6.00

...DRACULA
1994
1 rep,MWn(s),GC,TP 2.50

...WARLOCK: RESURRECTION
1993
1 JSn,V:Mephisto,Death 3.50
2 JSn,TA,V:Death 3.00
3 & 4 JSn,TA,V:Mephisto . . . . . . @3.00

...WEAPON ZERO
Marvel/Top Cow 1997
1-shot Devil's Reign, pt.8 . . . . 4.00

SISTERHOOD OF STEEL
Epic, Dec., 1984
1 I:Sisterhood 4.00
2 thru 8 . . . . @3.00

SIX FROM SIRIUS
Epic, July, 1984
1 PG,limited series 3.00
2 thru 4 PG . . . . @2.50

SIX FROM SIRIUS II
Epic, Feb., 1986
1 PG 2.50

SIX-GUN WESTERN
Marvel Atlas, Jan., 1957
1 JSe(c),RC,JR,Kid Yukon
  Gunslinger 250.00
2 SSh,AW,DAy,JO,His Guns
  Hang Low 175.00
3 AW,BP,DAy 175.00
4 JSe(c),JR,GWb 125.00

SKAAR: SON OF HULK
June, 2008
1 RG,Destined to smash. 3.00
1a variant BV&JuB(c) 3.00
2 RG, ... 3.00
3 RG,Princess Omaka 3.00
4 RG,The Prophet. 3.00
4a Zombie variant (c) 3.00
5 RG,Battle for Prophet Rock 3.00
Spec. Savage World of Skaar 4.00

SKELETON WARRIORS
1995
1 based on cartoon. 2.50
2 Legion of Light. 2.50
3 V:Grimstar 2.50
4 Grimskull abandons Legion
  of Light. 2.50

SKRULL KILL CREW
1995
1 I:Kill Crew. 3.00
2 V:Hydra 3.00
3 V:Captain America 3.00
4 V:Fantastic Four. 3.00
5 Conclusion. 3.00

SKRULLS
July, 2008
One-shot 5.00

SKRULLS VS. POWER PACK
July, 2008
1 thru 4 . . . . @3.00

SKULL, THE SLAYER
Aug., 1975
1 GK(c),O:Skull the Slayer 15.00
2 GK(c),Man Against Gods 10.00
3 Trapped in the Tower
   of Time 10.00
4 Peril of the Pyramids,
   A:Black Knight 10.00
5 A:Black Knight 10.00
6 The Savage Sea 10.00
7 Dungeon of Blood 10.00
8 JK(c),Nov., 1976 . . . . 10.00

SKY DOLL
May, 2008
1 (of 3) 64-pgs. 6.00
1a variant (c) 6.00
2 thru 3 . . . . @6.00

SLAPSTICK
1992–93
1 TA(i),I:Slapstick 2.50
2 TA(i),A:Spider-Man,V:Overkill . . . 2.50
3 V:Dr.Denton 2.50
4 A:GR,DD,FF,Cap.America 2.50

SLEDGE HAMMER
Feb., 1988
1 . . . . 5.00
2 March, 1988. . . . . 3.00

SLEEPWALKER
June, 1991
1 BBl,I:Rick Sheridan,C:8-Ball 3.00
2 BBl,V:8-Ball 2.50
3 BBl,A:Avengers,X-Men,X-Factor,
   FF,I:Cobweb,O:Sleepwalker . . . 2.50
4 RL,I:Bookworm 2.50
5 BBl,A:SpM,K.Pin,V:Ringleader . . 2.50
6 BBl,A:SpM,Inf.Gauntlet x-over . . . 2.50
7 BBl,Infinity Gauntlet x-over,
   V:Chain Gang 2.50
8 BBl,A:Deathlok. 2.50
9 BBl,I:Lullabye. 2.50
10 BBl,MM,I:Dream-Team 2.50
11 BBl,V:Ghost Rider 2.50
12 JQ,A:Nightmare 3.00
13 BBl,MM,I:Spectra 2.50
14 BBl,MM,V:Spectra 2.50
15 BBl,MM,I:Thought Police 2.50
16 BBl,MM,A:Mr.Fantastic,Thing . . . 2.50
17 BBl,A:Spider-Man,Darkhawk,
   V:Brotherhood o/Evil Mutants . . 2.50
18 JQ(c),Inf.War,A:Prof.X 2.50
19 V:Cobweb,w/pop out Halloween
   Mask 2.50
20 V:Chain Gang,Cobweb 2.50
21 V:Hobgoblin 2.50
22 V:Hobgoblin,8-Ball 2.50
23 V:Cobweb,Chain Gang 2.50
24 Mindfield#6 . . . . 2.50
25 O:Sleepwalker,Holo-grafx(c). . . . 3.50
26 V:Mindspawn. 2.50
27 A:Avengers 2.50
28 I:Psyko 2.50
29 DG,V:Psyko. 2.50
30 V:Psyko. 2.50
31 DG(ci),A:Spectra 2.50
32 V:Psyko. 2.50

Sleepwalker #31
© Marvel Entertainment Group

33 V:Mindspawn,Last issue 2.50
Holiday Spec.#1 JQ(c). 2.50

SLEEZE BROTHERS
Aug., 1989
1 Private Eyes 2.50
2 thru 6 . . . . @2.50

SLINGERS
Oct., 1998
1 Ccs,F:Ricochet, Hornet,
   Prodigy & Dusk, 48-page:
1a Ricochet edition 3.00
1b Hornet edition 3.00
1c Prodigy edition 3.00
1d Dusk edition. 3.00
2 CCs,V:Maggia 2.50
2a variant cover 2.50
3 CCs,F:Prodigy 2.50
4 CCs,F:Prodigy 2.50
5 CCs,F:Black Marvel 2.50
6 CCs,Truth or Dare 2.50
7 CCs,V:The Griz 2.50
8 CCs,V:The Griz 2.50
9 CCs,A:Ricochet 2.50
10 CCs,Raising Hell'sChildren,pt.1 . 2.50
11 CCs,Raising Hell'sChildren,pt.2 . 2.50
12 CCs,Hell's Children,pt.3 final . . . 2.50

SMURFS
Dec., 1982
1 . . . . 9.00
2 . . . . 6.00
3 . . . . 6.00
Treasury Edition 30.00

SOLARMAN
Jan., 1989
1 JM 3.00
2 MZ/NR,A:Dr.Doom, May, 1990 . . 3.00

SOLDIER X
July, 2002
1 Cable's future, 40-pg. 3.00
2 . . . . 2.50
3 to Russia without love 2.50
4 Geo debuts 2.50
5 . . . . 2.50
6 . . . . 2.50
7 . . . . 2.50
8 Askani religion 2.50
9 V:Racist militia group 2.50

10 V:Racism. 3.00
11 SEa,Dead Ends,pt.1 . . . . 3.00
12 SEa,Dead Ends,pt.2 . . . . 3.00

SOLO
[Limited Series] 1994
1 RoR,I:Cygnus 2.50
2 RoR,V:A.R.E.S. 2.50
3 RoR,V:Spidey. 2.50
4 final issue. 2.50

SOLO AVENGERS
Dec., 1987
1 MBr,JRu,JLe,AW,Hawkeye;
   Mockingbird 4.00
2 MBr,JRu,KD,BMc,Hawkeye;
   Capt.Marvel. 2.50
3 MBr,JRu,BH,SDr,Hawkeye;
   Moon Knight 2.50
4 RLm,JRu,PR,BL,Hawkeye;
   Black Knight 2.50
5 MBr,JRu,JRy,Hawkeye;
   Scarlet Witch 2.50
6 MBi,JRu,TGr,Hawkeye;Falcon . . 2.50
7 MBr,JG,BL,Hawkeye;Bl.Widow . . 2.50
8 MBr,Hawkeye;Dr.Pym 2.50
9 MBr,JBr,SDr,Hawkeye;Hellcat . . 2.50
10 MBr,LW,Hawkeye;Dr.Druid 2.50
11 MBr,JG,BL,Hawkeye;Hercules . . 2.50
12 RLm,SDr,Hawkeye; New
   Yellow Jacket. 2.50
13 RLm,JG,Hawkeye;WonderMan. . 2.50
14 AM,AD,JRu,Hawkeye;She-Hulk . 2.50
15 AM,Hawkeye;Wasp. 2.50
16 AM,DP,JA,Hawkeye;
   Moondragon 2.50
17 AM,DH,DC,Hawkeye;
   Sub-Mariner. 2.50
18 RW,DH,Hawkeye;Moondragon . . 2.50
19 RW,DH,Hawkeye,BlackPanther . 2.50
20 RW,DH,Hawkeye;Moondragon . . 2.50
Becomes:

AVENGERS SPOTLIGHT

SOLOMON KANE
Sept., 1985
1 F:Solomon Kane 3.00
2 . . . . 3.00
3 BBl,Blades of the Brotherhood . . 3.00
4 MMi 3.00
5 Hills of the Dead 3.00
6 . . . . 3.00

Solomon Kane #1
© Marvel Entertainment Group

SON OF M
Dec., 2005
1 F:Quicksilver 3.00
2 thru 5 . . . . @3.00

SON OF SATAN
Dec., 1975–Feb., 1977
1 GK(c),JM,F:Daimon Hellstrom. . 32.00
2 Demon War,O:Possessor 20.00
3 . . . . 20.00
4 The Faces of Fear 15.00
5 V:Mind Star 15.00
6 A World Gone Mad 15.00
7 Mirror of Judgement 15.00
8 RH,To End in Nightmare 15.00

SOVIET SUPER SOLDIERS
1 AMe,JS,I:Redmont 4 . . . . 2.50

SPACEKNIGHTS
Aug., 2000
1 (of 5) JSn,R:Spaceknights 3.00
2 JSn,Terminator. 3.00
3 JSn,Deathwings. 3.00
4 JSn,Wraith Knights 3.00
5 JSn,concl. 3.00

SPACEMAN
Marvel Atlas, Sept., 1953
1 BEv(c),F:Speed Carter and
    the Space Sentinals 1,000.00
2 JMn,Trapped in Space. 650.00
3 BEv(c),JMn,V:Ice Monster. . . . 550.00
4 JMn, A-Bomb. 600.00
5 GT 550.00
6 JMn,Thing From Outer Space 550.00

SPACE SQUADRON
Atlas, June, 1951
1 AyB,F:Capt. Jet Dixon,Blast,
    Dawn,Revere,Rusty Blake 1,000.00
2 GT(c),. 800.00
3 Planet of Madness,GT. 700.00
4 . . . . 700.00
5 AyB 700.00
Becomes:

SPACE WORLDS
April, 1952
6 Midnight Horror 650.00

Space Squadron #5
© Marvel Entertainment Group

SPECIAL COLLECTOR'S EDITION
Dec., 1975
1 Kung-Fu,Iron Fist 10.00

SPECIAL MARVEL EDITION
Jan., 1971
1 JK,B:Thor,B:Reprints 40.00
2 JK,V:Absorbing Man 25.00
3 JK,While a Universe
    Trembles 25.00
4 JK,Hammer and the Holocaust,
    E:Thor 25.00
5 JSe(c),JK,DAy,B:Sgt. Fury 25.00
6 HT(c),DAy,Death Ray of
    Dr. Zemo 12.00
7 DAy,V:Baron Strucker 12.00
8 JSe(c),DAy,On To Okinawa 12.00
9 DAy,Crackdown-CaptainFlint . . 12.00
10 DAy 12.00
11 JK,DAy,A:Captain
    America & Bucky. 12.00
12 DAy,V:Baron Strucker 12.00
13 JK/DAy(c),DAy,SD,Too Small
    to Fight, Too Young To Die . . . 12.00
14 DAy,E:Reprints,Sgt. Fury 12.00
15 JSn,AM,I:Shang-Chi & Master of
    Kung Fu,I&O:Nayland Smith,
    Dr. Petrie 200.00
16 JSn,AM,I&O:Midnight 75.00
KingSz.Ann.#1 A:Iron Fist 18.00
Becomes:

MASTER OF KUNG FU

SPECTACULAR SCARLET SPIDER
1995
1 SB,BSz,Virtual Morality,pt.4 . . . . 2.50
2 SB,BSz,CyberWar,pt.4. . . . . 2.50

SPECTACULAR SPIDER-MAN
(Magazine) July, 1968
1 JR,JM. 200.00
2 JR,JM,V:Green Goblin. 175.00

SPECTACULAR SPIDER-MAN
Dec., 1976
Prev: Peter Parker
134 SB,A:Sin-Eater,V:Electro 4.00
135 SB,A:Sin-Eater,V:Electro 3.00
136 SB,D:Sin-Eater,V:Electro 3.00
137 SB,I:Tarantula II 3.00
138 SB,A:Capt.A.,V:TarantulaII 3.00
139 SB,O:Tombstone. 4.00
140 SB,A:Punisher,V:Tombstone. . . 3.50
141 SB,A:Punisher,V:Tombstone. . . 5.00
142 SB,A:Punisher,V:Tombstone. . . 5.00
143 SB,A:Punisher,D:Persuader,
    I:Lobo Brothers. 5.00
144 SB,V:Boomerang 3.00
145 SB,A:Boomerang 3.00
146 SB,R:Green Goblin 5.00
147 SB,V:Hobgoblin (Demonic
    Power) 14.00
148 SB,Inferno. 3.00
149 SB,V:Carrion II 5.00
150 SB,A:Tombstone,Trial
    J.Robertson 3.00
151 SB,V:Tombstone 3.00
152 SB,O:Lobo Bros.,A:Punisher,
    Tombstone. 4.00
153 SB,V:Hammerhead,A:
    Tombstone. 3.00

154 SB,V:Lobo Bros.,Puma. 3.00
155 SB,V,Tombstone 3.00
156 SB,V:Banjo,A:Tombstone 3.00
157 SB,V:Shocker,Electro,
    A:Tombstone 3.00
158 SB,Super Spider Spec.,
    I:Cosmic Spider-Man 9.00
159 Cosmic Powers,V:Brothers
    Grimm 5.00
160 SB,A:Hydro Man,Shocker,
    Rhino,Dr.Doom 4.00
161 SB,V:Hobgoblin,Hammerhead,
    Tombstone. 3.00
162 SB,V:Hobgoblin,Carrion II. 3.00
163 SB,V:Hobgoblin,D:Carrion II . . . 3.00
164 SB,V:Beetle. 3.00
165 SB,SDr,D:Arranger,I:Knight
    & Fogg. 3.00
166 SB,O:Knight & Fogg 3.00
167 SB,D:Knight & Fogg 3.00
168 SB,A:Kingpin,Puma,
    Avengers 3.00
169 SB,I:Outlaws,A:R.Racer,
    Prowler,Puma,Sandman 3.00
170 SB,A:Avengers,Outlaws 3.00
171 SB,V:Puma 2.50
172 SB,V:Puma 2.50
173 SB,V:Puma 2.50
174 SB,A:Dr.Octopus. 2.50
175 SB,A:Dr.Octopus. 2.50
176 SB,I:Karona. 2.50
177 SB,V:Karona,A:Mr.Fantastic. . . 2.50
178 SB,B:Child Within,V:Green
    Goblin, A:Vermin 2.50
179 SB,V:Green Goblin,Vermin 2.50
180 SB,V:Green Goblin,Vermin 2.50
181 SB,V:Green Goblin 2.50
182 SB,V:Green Goblin 2.50
183 SB,V:Green Goblin 2.50
184 SB,E:Child Within,V:Green
    Goblin 2.50
185 SB,A:Frogman,White Rabbit. . . 2.50
186 SB,B:FuneralArrangements
    V:Vulture 2.50
187 SB,V:Vulture 2.50
188 SB,E:Funeral Arrangements
    V:Vulture 2.50
189 SB,30th Ann.,Hologram(c),
    V:Green Goblin 6.00
189a Gold 2nd printing 3.00
190 SB,V:Rhino,Harry Osborn. 2.50
191 SB,Eye of the Puma 2.50
192 SB,Eye of the Puma 2.50
193 SB,Eye of the Puma 2.50
194 SB,Death of Vermin#1 . . . . 2.50
195 SB,Death of Vermin#2 . . . . 4.00
195a Dirtbag Spec,w/Dirt#2 tape. . 2.50
196 SB,Death of Vermin#3 . . . . 2.50
197 SB,A:X-Men,V:Prof.Power 2.50
198 SB,A:X-Men,V:Prof.Power 2.50
199 SB,A:X-Men,Green Goblin 2.50
200 SB,V:Green Goblin,D:Harry
    Osborn,Holografx(c) 5.00
201 SB,Total Carnage,V:Carnage,
    Shriek,A:Black Cat,Venom 4.00
202 SB,Total Carnage#9,A:Venom,
    V:Carnage 4.00
203 SB,Maximum Carnage#13 . . . . 4.00
204 SB,A:Tombstone 2.50
205 StG(s),SB,V:Tombstone,
    A:Black Cat 2.50
206 SB,V:Tombstone 2.50
207 SB,A:The Shroud 2.50
208 SB,A:The Shroud 2.50
209 StB,SB,I:Dead Aim,
    BU:Black Cat 2.50
210 StB,SB,V:Dead Aim,
    BU:Black Cat. 2.50
211 Pursuit#2,V:Tracer 2.50
212 . . . . 2.50
213 ANo(s),V:Typhiod Mary,w/cel . . 3.50
213a Newsstand Ed. 2.50

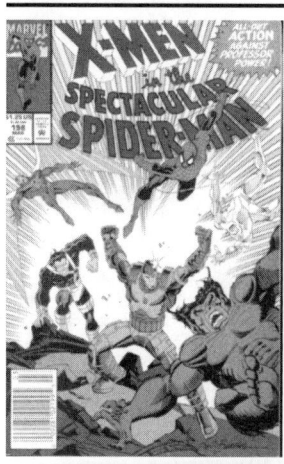

Spectacular Spider-Man #198
© Marvel Entertainment Group

214 V:Bloody Mary. 2.50
215 V:Scorpion 2.50
216 V:Scorpion 2.50
217 V:Judas Traveller,clone. 3.00
217a Foil(c),bonus stuff 5.00
218 V:Puma 3.00
219 Back from the Edge,pt.2 . . . . . . 3.00
220 Web of Death,pt.3. . . . . 3.00
221 Web of Death,finale 3.00
222 The Price of Truth 2.50
223 Aftershocks,pt.4 . . . . 3.00
223a enhanced cover 3.00
224 The Mark of Kaine,pt.4 . . . . 2.50
225 SB,TDF,BSz,I:New Green
    Goblin, 48-pg. 3.00
225a 3-D HoloDisk Cover 5.00
226 SB,BSz,The Trial of Peter
    Parker,pt.4, identity revealed. . . 3.00
227 TDF,SB,BSz,Maximum
    Clonage,pt.5 . . . . 2.50
228 Timebomb,pt.1 . . . . 2.50
229 Greatest Responsibility,pt.3 . . . 3.00
229a Special cover 5.00
230 SB,Return of Spider-Man,pt.4. . 2.50
231 SB,Return of Kaine,pt.1 . . . . . . 2.50
232 . . . . 2.50
233 SB,JP,Web of Carnage,pt.4 . . . 2.50
234 SB,Blood Brothers,pt.4 . . . . 2.50
235 . . . . 2.50
236 . . . . 2.50
237 V:Lizard. 2.50
238 V:Lizard. 2.50
239 V:Lizard. 2.50
240 TDz,LRs,Book of Revelations,
    pt.1 (of 4). 3.00
241 Revelations epilogue 2.50
242 JMD,LRs,R:Chameleon,
    A:Kangaroo 2.50
243 JMD,LRs,R:Chameleon 2.50
244 JMD,LRs,V:Chameleon 2.50
245 JMD,LRs,V:Chameleon,
    A:Kangaroo 2.50
246 JMD,LRs,V:Kangaroo,Grizzly . . 2.50
247 JMD,LRs,F:JackO'Lantern,pt.1. 2.50
248 JMD,LRs,DGr,F:Jack O'
    Lantern, pt.2 . . . . 2.50
249 JMD,LRs,DGr, Last Temptation
    of Flash Thompson 2.50
250 JR, V:Original Green Goblin,
    double gatefold cover 3.50
251 JMD,LRs,DGr,V:Kraven the
    Hunter 2.50
252 JMD,LRs,DGr,V:Norman
    Osborn. 2.50

253 JMD,LRs,DGr,V:Norman Osborn,
    Gibbon, Grizzly 2.50
254 JMD,LRs,DGr,V:Prof.Angst. . . . 2.50
255 JMD,LRs,DGr,Spider-Hunt,pt.4
    x-over, double size 3.00
256 JMD,LRs,DGr,Identity Crisis
    prelude, A:Prodigy. 2.50
257 JMD,LRs,DGr,Identity Crisis,
    as Prodigy, V:Conundrum 2.50
258 JMD,LRs,DGa,as Prodigy. 2.50
259 RSt,LRs,DGa,V:Hobgoblin 2.50
260 JR,RSt,LRs,DGa,Green Goblin
    vs. Hobgoblin. 2.50
261 RSt,LRs,AM,Goblins at the
    Gate,pt.3 . . . . 2.50
262 JBy, AM, LRs, The Gathering of
    the Five, pt.4 (of 5) x-over. 2.50
263 JBy,AM,LRs,The Final
    Chapter,pt.3 x-over 4.00
Ann.#8 MBa,RLm,TD,Evolutionary
    Wars,O:Gwen Stacy Clone 7.00
Ann.#9 DR,MG,DJu,MBa,Atlantis
    Attacks. 4.00
Ann.#10 SLi(c),RB,MM,TM,RA 6.00
Ann #11 EL(c),RWi,Vib.Vendella . . . 3.00
Ann.#12 Hero Killers#2,A:New
    Warriors,BU:Venom. 4.50
Ann.#13 I:Noctune,w/Card. 3.25
Ann.#14 V:Green Goblin 3.00
Super-Size Spec.#1 Planet of the
    Symbiotes,pt.4,64-pg.flip-book . 4.00
Minus 1 Spec., JMD,LRs,DGr,
    flashback, F:Flash Thompson . . 2.00

SPECTACULAR
SPIDER-MAN
June, 2003

1 HuR,V:Venom,pt.1 . . . . 3.00
2 HuR,V:Venom,pt.2 . . . . 2.50
3 HuR,V:Venom,pt.3 . . . . 2.50
4 HuR,V:Venom,pt.4 . . . . 2.50
5 HuR,V:Venom,pt.5 . . . . 2.50
6 HuR,Countdown,pt.1,V:Doc Ock . 2.50
7 HuR,Countdown,pt.2 . . . . 2.50
8 HuR,Countdown,pt.3 . . . . 2.50
9 HuR,Countdown,pt.4 . . . . 2.50
10 HuR,Countdown,concl. 2.50
11 The Lizard's Tale,pt.1 . . . . 2.50
12 The Lizard's Tale,pt.2 . . . . 2.50
13 The Lizard's Tale,pt.3 . . . . 2.50
14 F:Morbius 2.50
15 F:Captain America 2.50
16 F:Captain America 2.50
17 Changes,pt.1. . . . . 2.50
18 Changes,pt.2. . . . . 2.50
19 Changes,pt.3. . . . . 2.50
20 Disassembled, tie-in,pt.4 . . . . . . 2.50
21 . . . . 2.50
22 . . . . 2.50
23 SEa,Sins Remembered,pt.1 . . . . 2.50
24 SEa,Sins Remembered,pt.2 . . . . 2.50
25 SEa,Sins Remembered,pt.3 . . . . 2.50
26 SEa,Sins Remembered,pt.4 . . . . 2.50
27 PJe,MBu,finale 3.00

SPEEDBALL
Sept., 1988

1 SD,JG,O:Speedball 2.50
2 thru 10 . . . . @2.50

SPELLBINDERS
March, 2005

1 (of 6) F:Witches of Salem 3.00
2 Salem Ghosts 3.00
3 Pillar of Smoke 3.00
4 Pillar of Smoke 3.00
5 The Halls of the Dead 3.00
6 World of the Dead, finale. 3.00
Digest Vol. 1: Signs and Wonders. . 8.00

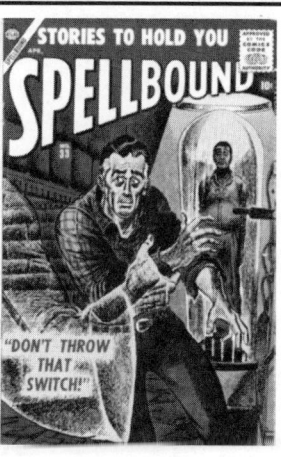

Spellbound #33
© Marvel Entertainment Group

SPELLBOUND
Marvel Atlas, March, 1952

1 AyB(c),Step into my Coffin . . 1,200.00
2 BEv,RH,Horror Story,
    A:Edgar A. Poe 600.00
3 RH(c),OW 500.00
4 RH,Decapitation story 500.00
5 AyB,BEv,JM,Its in the Bag. . . . 500.00
6 AyB,BK,The Man Who Couldn't
    be Killed. 500.00
7 AyB,BEv,JMn,Don't Close
    the Door. 400.00
8 BEv(c),RH,JSt,DAy,
    The Operation 400.00
9 BEv(c),RH,The Death of
    Agatha Slurl. 400.00
10 AyB,BEv,RH,JMn(c),The Living
    Mummy 400.00
11 The Empty Coffin 350.00
12 RH,My Friend the Ghost. 350.00
13 JM,AyB,The Dead Men. 350.00
14 BEv(c),RH,JMn,Close Shave . 350.00
15 AyB,CI,Get Out of my
    Graveyard 350.00
16 RH,BEv,JF,JSt,Behind
    the Door. 350.00
17 BEv(c),GC,BK,Goodbye
    Forever 350.00
18 BEv(c),JM 325.00
19 BEv(c),BP,Witch Doctor 325.00
20 RH(c),BP 325.00
21 RH(c). 400.00
22 . . . . 400.00
23 . . . . 400.00
24 JMn(c),JR 375.00
25 JO,AyB,Look Into My Eyes. . . 375.00
26 JR,AyB,Things in the Box. . . . 375.00
27 JMn,JR,AyB,Trap in the
    Mirage 375.00
28 BEv 375.00
29 JSe(c),SD 400.00
30 BEv(c) 375.00
31 JMn 375.00
32 BP,AyB,Almost Human 375.00
33 AT 375.00
34 June, 1957 . . . . 375.00

SPELLBOUND
Jan., 1988

1 thru 5 . . . . 2.50
6 double-size 3.00

SPIDER-GIRL
Aug., 1998
0 TDF,RF,BSz, cont. from What-If?
  #105, Peter & Mary Jane's
  daughter 7.00
1 TDF,PO,AW, F:Mayday Parker,
  V:Mr. Nobody 7.00
2 TDF,PO,AW,V:Crazy Eight
  & Darkdevil 4.00
2a variant cover 4.00
3 TDF,PO,AW,A:Fantastic Five 2.50
4 TDF,PO,AW,turning points 2.50
5 TDF,PO,AW,Ghosts of the Past . . 2.50
6 TDF,PO,AW,Majority Rules 2.50
7 TDF,PO,AW,Last Days of
  Spider-Man 2.50
8 TDF,PO,AW,A:Spider-Man,
  Uneasy Allies 2.50
8a autographed 20.00
9 TDF,PO,AW,Critical Choices 2.50
10 TDF,PO,AW,Incredible Journeys 2.50
11 TDF,PO,AW,V:Spider-Man 2.50
12 TDF,PO,AW,A:Darkdevil 2.50
13 TDF,Po,AW,Joins A-Next 2.50
14 TDF,PO,AW,Bloody Reunions
  x-over. 2.50
15 TDF,PO,AW,A:Speedball 2.50
16 TDF,PO,AW. 2.50
17 TDF,PO,AW,48-pg. 3.00
18 TDF,SB,RF,A:Buzz 2.50
19 TDF,AW,PO,V:A-Next foes 2.50
20 TDF,AW,PO,R:Green Goblin. . . . 2.50
21 TDF,AW,PO,V:Earthshaker. 2.50
22 TDF,AW,PO,Darkdevil. 2.50
23 TDF,AW,PO,Basketball 2.50
24 TDF,AW,PO,Dragonfist 2.50
25 TDF,AW,PO,Savage Six 3.50
26 TDF,AW,PO,Phil Urich 2.50
27 TDF,AW,PO,Parker/Osborn War. 2.50
28 TDF,AW,PO,V:Raptor 2.50
29 TDF,AW,PO,A:Nova 2.50
30 TDF,AW,PO,V:Avengers 2.50
31 TDF,AW,PO,V:Avengers 2.50
32 TDF,PO,Steel Spider. 2.50
33 TDF,PO,AW,A:Spider-Man 2.50
34 TDF,AW,PO,A:Fant.Five 2.50
35 TDF,AW,PO,V:Canis 2.50
36 TDF,AW,PO,V:Canis 2.50
37 TDF,AW,PO,V:Green Goblin. . . . 2.50
38 TDF,AW,PO,V:Green Goblin 2.50
39 TDF,AW,PO,Green Goblin 2.50
40 TDF,AW,PO,Death in the family . 2.50
41 TDF,AW,PO,V:Canis,'Nuff Said. . 2.50

Spider-Girl #38
© *Marvel Entertainment Group*

42 TDF,RF,mothers 2.50
43 TDF,AW,PO,original Spider-Man. 2.50
44 TDF,AW,PO,F:Ben Reilly 2.50
45 TDF,AW,PO,A:Big Brain,H.Torch 2.50
46 TDF,AW,PO,F:Fantastic Five . . . 2.50
47 TDF,RF,V:Apox,+ Chapter 1 . . . 2.50
48 TDF,AW,PO,Spider-Man,Kaine . . 2.50
49 TDF,AW,PO,V:Green Goblin. . . . 2.50
50 TDF,AW,PO,48-pg. 4.00
51 CJ,. 2.50
52 TDF,AW,RF 2.50
53 TDF,AW,PO. 2.50
54 TDF,AW,PO,Serpent,pt.1 . . . . . . 2.50
55 TDF,AW,PO,Serpent,pt.2 . . . . . . 2.50
56 TDF,AW,PO,Serpent,pt.3 . . . . . . 2.50
57 TDF,AW,PO,Serpent,pt.4 . . . . . . 2.50
58 TDF,AW,PO,Serpent,pt.5 . . . . . . 2.50
59 TDF,RF,Serpent,pt.6 . . . . 3.00
60 TDF,RF,finale 3.00
61 TDF,RF,Marked for Death,pt.1 . . 3.00
62 TDF,RF,Marked for Death,pt.2 . . 3.00
63 TDF,RF,Marked for Death,pt.3 . . 3.00
64 TDF,RF,Marked for Death,pt.4 . . 3.00
65 TDF,RF,Marked for Death,pt.5 . . 3.00
66 TDF,RF,Marked for Death,pt.6 . . 3.00
67 TDF,RF,Monsters 3.00
68 TDF,RF,The Rules 3.00
69 TDF,RF,Truth,pt.1 . . . . 3.00
70 TDF,RF,Truth,pt.2 . . . . 3.00
71 TDF,RF,F:Doc Magus 3.00
72 TDF,RF,Whispers in the Night . . 3.00
73 TDF,RF,PO,F:Claw,the Cat 3.00
74 TDF,RF,PO,F:Claw,the Cat 3.00
75 TDF,RF,Team Spider. 3.00
76 TDF,RF,Spider-Girl Must Die. . . . 3.00
77 TDF,RF,Betrayed. 3.00
78 TDF,RF,People Played
  by Games 3.00
79 RF,If this be my destiny 3.00
80 TDF(s),PO,V:Dragon King 3.00
81 TDF(s),PO F:Electro 3.00
82 TDF(s),RF,V:Venom 3.00
83 TDF(s),RF,Back in Black. 3.00
84 TDF(s),RF,V:New Venom 3.00
85 TDF(s),RF,V:Funny Face 3.00
86 TDF(s),RF,Family Business,pt.1 . 3.00
87 TDF(s),RF,Family Business,pt.2 . 3.00
88 TDF(s),RF,Family Business,pt.3 . 3.00
89 TDF(s),RF,. 3.00
90 TDF(s),RF, spider-creature 3.00
91 TDF(s),RF,The Sinister Secret
  Of the Spider Shoppe 3.00
92 TDF(s),RF,In the Shadow of Evil 3.00
93 TDF(s),RF,Something Osborn This
  Way Comes. 3.00
94 TDF(s),RF,V:Avengers 3.00
95 TDF(s),RF,A:Green Goblin 3.00
96 TDF(s),RF,A:Kaine 3.00
97 TDF(s),RF,Here Comes
  Hobgoblin 3.00
98 TDF(s),RF,In black costume 3.00
99 TDF(s),RF,A:Tarantula 3.00
100 TDF(s),RF,A:Spider-man,
  104-pg. 4.00
Ann.#1 TDF,PO,AW,A:Green Goblin 6.00
Digest Marvel Age, Vol. 1 . . . . 8.00
Digest Vol. 1: Legacy 8.00
Digest Vol. 2: Like Father, Like
  Daughter 8.00
Digest Vol. 3: Avenging Allies 8.00
Digest Vol. 4: Turning Point 8.00
Digest Vol. 5: Endgame. 8.00
Digest Vol. 6: Too Many Spiders . . 8.00
Digest Vol. 7: Betrayed 8.00

SPIDER-GIRL PRESENTS:
THE BUZZ
May, 2000
1 (of 3) TDF,RF,SB 3.00
2 TDF,RF,SB,A:Spider-Girl 3.00
3 TDF,RF,SB,Dr.Jade 3.00

SPIDER-GIRL PRESENTS:
DARKDEVIL
Sept., 2000
1 (of 3) TDF,RF,AM,Kingpin 3.00
2 TDF,RF,AM,O:Darkdevil. 3.00
3 TDF,RF,AM, concl 3.00

SPIDER-MAN
Aug., 1990
1 TM Purple Web(c),V:Lizard,
  A:Calypso,B:Torment. 5.00
1a Silver Web(c). 6.00
1b Bag,Purple Web. 12.00
1c Bag,Silver Web 15.00
1d 2nd print,Gold(c) 5.00
1e 2nd print Gold UPC(rare). . . . 150.00
1f Platinum Ed. 125.00
2 TM,V:Lizard,A:Calypso 6.00
3 TM,V:Lizard,A:Calypso 6.00
4 TM,V:Lizard,A:Calypso 6.00
5 TM,V:Lizard,A:Calypso,
  E:Torment 6.00
6 TM,A:Ghost Rider,V:Hobgoblin . . 6.00
7 TM,A:Ghost Rider,V:Hobgoblin . . 6.00
8 TM,B:Perceptions,A:Wolverine
  I:Wendigo IV 8.00
9 TM,A:Wolverine,Wendigo 8.00
10 TM,RLd,SW,JLe(i),A:Wolv. 8.00
11 TM,A:Wolverine,Wendigo. 8.00
12 TM,E:Perceptions,A:Wolv. 8.00
13 TM,V:Morbius,R:Black Cost. . . . 6.00
14 TM,V:Morbius,A:Black Cost. . . . 6.00
15 EL,A:Beast 6.00
16 TM,RLd,A:X-Force,V:Juggernaut,
  Black Tom,cont.in X-Force#4 . . 6.00
17 RL,AW,A:Thanos,Death 4.00
18 EL,B:Return of the Sinister Six,
  A:Hulk 4.00
19 EL,A:Hulk,Deathlok. 4.00
20 EL,A:Nova. 4.00
21 EL,A:Hulk,Deathlok,Solo. 4.00
22 EL,A:Ghost Rider,Hulk 4.00
23 EL,E:Return of the Sinister Six,
  A:Hulk,G.Rider,Deathlok,FF. . . . 4.00
24 Infinity War,V:Hobgoblin,
  Demogoblin. 4.00
25 CMa,A:Excalibur,V:Arcade 4.00
26 RF,MBa,Hologram(c),30th Anniv.
  I:New Burglar. 5.00
26a 2nd print 4.00
27 MR,Handgun issue 3.00
28 MR,Handgun issue 3.00
29 CMa,Ret.to Mad Dog Ward#1 . . 3.00
30 CMa,Ret.to Mad Dog Ward#2 . . 3.00
31 CMa,Ret.to Mad Dog Ward#3 . . 3.00
32 BMc,A:Punisher,V:Master of
  Vengeance. 3.00
33 BMc,A:Punisher,V:Master of
  Vengeance. 3.00
34 BMc,A:Punisher,V:Master of
  Vengeance. 3.00
35 TL,Total Carnage#4,V:Carnage,
  Shriek,A:Venom,Black Cat 4.00
36 TL,Total Carnage#8,V:Carnage,
  A:Venom,Morbius 4.00
37 TL,Total Carnage#12,
  V:Carnage 4.00
38 thru 40 KJ,V:Electro 3.00
41 TKa(s),JaL,I:Platoon,
  A:Iron Fist 3.00
42 TKa(s),JaL,V:Platoon,
  A:Iron Fist 3.00
43 TKa(s),JaL,V:Platoon,
  A:Iron Fist 3.00
44 HMe(s),TL,V:Hobgoblin 3.00
45 HMe(s),TL,SHa,Pursuit#1,
  V:Chameleon. 2.50
46 HMe(s),TL,V:Hobgoblin,w/cel . . 3.25
46a Newsstand Ed. 2.50
47 TL,SHa,V:Demogoblin 2.50

48 TL,SHa,V:Hobgoblin,
  D:Demogoblin 2.50
49 TL,SHa,I:Coldheart 2.50
50 TL,SHa,I:Grim Hunter,foil(c) 5.00
50a newsstand ed. 2.50
51 TL,SHa,Power,pt.3,foil(c) 4.00
51a newsstand ed. 2.50
52 TL,SHa,Spide-clone,V:Venom . . 2.50
53 TL,SHa,Clone,V:Venom 2.50
54 Web of Life,pt.3 . . . . 3.00
55 Web of Life,finale 2.50
56 Smoke and Mirrors 2.50
57 Aftershocks,pt.1 . . . . 2.50
57a enhanced cover 3.00
58 The Mark of Kaine,pt.3 . . . . 2.50
59 F:Travellor,Host. 2.50
60 TL,SHa,HMa,The Trial of
  Peter Parker,pt.3 . . . . 2.50
61 TL,Maximum Clonage,pt.4 . . . . . 2.50
62 HMe,TL,Exiled,pt.3 . . . . 2.50
63 HMe,TL,Greatest
  Responsibility,pt.2 . . . . 2.50
64 HMe,JR2,Return of
  Spider-Man,pt.3 . . . . 2.50
65 HMe,JR2,AW,Media
  Blizzard,pt.3 . . . . 2.50
66 HMe,JR2,Return of Kaine,pt.4 . . 2.50
67 HMe,JR2,Web of Carnage,pt.3. . 2.50
68 HMe,JR2,AW,Blood
  Brothers,pt.3 . . . . 2.50
69 HMe,JR2,Blood Brothers
  aftermath 2.50
70 HMe,JR2,A:Onslaught 3.00
71 HMe,JR2, ... 3.00
72 HMe,JR2,Onslaught saga. 3.00
73 HMe,JR2, ... 3.00
74 HMe,JR2,AW,A:Daredevil,
  V:Fortunato 3.00
75 HMe,JR2,Revelations, #4 . . . . . . 3.50
76 HMe,JR2,SHa,Post-Onslaught
  world,I:Shoc. 2.50
77 HMe,JR2,SHa,V:Morbius 2.50
Becomes:

PETER PARKER,
SPIDER-MAN
78 HMe,JR2,SHa,F:Mary Jane
  Parker 2.50
79 HMe,JR2,SHa,V:Hydra,A:Captain
  Arthur Stacy 2.50
80 HMe,JR2,SHa,V:S.H.O.C. 2.50
81 HMe,JR2,SHa,V:Shang-Chi,pt.1. 2.50
82 HMe,JR2,SHa,Anti-Mutant
  Movement 2.50

Peter Parker Spider-Man #96
© Marvel Entertainment Group

83 HMe,JR2,SHa,V:Morbius 2.50
85 HMe,JR2,SHa,V:Friends of
  Humanity 2.50
86 HMe,JR2,SHa,F:Jimmy Six,
  Hammerhead. 2.50
87 HMe,JR2,SHa,A:Trapster &
  Shocker 2.50
88 HMe,JR2,SHa,Spider-Man is
  Public Enemy #1 . . . . 2.50
89 HMe,JR2,SHa,Spider-Hunt,pt.3
  x-over. 3.00
90 HMe,JR2,SHa,Identity Crisis
  prelude. 2.50
91 HMe,JR2,SHa,Identity Crisis,
  as Dusk 2.50
92 HMe,JR2,as Dusk, V:Trapster . . 2.50
93 HMe,JS,R:Ghost Rider 2.50
94 HMe,JR2,SHa,Who wasJoeyZ? . 2.50
95 HMe,JR2,SHa,Trapped in
  elevator shaft. 2.50
96 HMe,JR2,SHa,The Gathering of
  the Five (pt. 3 (of 5)x-over. 2.50
97 HMe,JR2,SHa,JBy(c),The Final
  Chapter,pt.2 x-over 2.50
98 HMe,JR2,SHa,JBy(c),The Final
  Chapter,pt.4 x-over 2.50
98a alternate JBy(c) (1:2) 2.50
Minus 1 Spec., HMe,JR2,SHa,
  flashback, A:Stacys 2.50
Ann.'97 Simon Garth—Zombie 3.50
Ann.'98 HMe, Spider-Man/Elektra,
  V:The Silencer, 48-pg. 3.00
Spec. Chaos in Calgary 2.50
Spec. Double Trouble 2.50
Spec. Hit and Run, Canadian 2.50
Spec. Skating on Thin Ice 2.50
Spec. Trial of Venom,UNICEF 15.00
Spec.#1 Spider-Man (2000). 2.50
Spec. Spider-Man vs. Punisher 3.00
Spec. Year in Review(1999)48-pg. . 3.00
Holiday Spec.'95 . . . . 3.00
Sup.Sz.Spec#1 Planet of the
  Symbiotes, pt.2;
  flipbook F:Scarlet Spider 4.00
Giant-Sized CCI,JBy 4.00
1-shot Spider-Man Startling Stories:
  Megalomaniacal Spider-Man. . . 3.00
Spec.#1 Spider-Man/Daredevil . . . 3.00
GN Fear Itself 13.00
GN Nothing Stops Juggernaut. 4.00
GN Parallel Lives. 9.00
GN JMD,MZ,Soul of the Hunter. . . . 6.00
GN Spider-Man: Made Men
  HMe,gangster epic (1998). 6.00
GN Spider-Man ParallelLives(2002) 6.00
GN Sweet Charity,Scorpion,64-pg. . 5.00

SPIDER-MAN
ADVENTURES
1994–96
1 From animated series 2.50
1a foil (c). 3.00
2 thru 15 . . . . @2.50

SPIDER-MAN AND
AMAZING FRIENDS
Dec., 1981
1 DSp,A:Iceman,I:Firestar. 10.00

...POWER PACK
Nov., 2006
1 V: Sandman & Vulture 3.00
2 thru 4 . . . . @3.00

...WOLVERINE
June, 2003
1 (of 4) Stuff of Legends 3.00
2 . . . . 3.00
3 . . . . 3.00
4 concl. 3.00

Spider-Man Adventures #1
© Marvel Entertainment Group

SPIDER-MAN: BACK IN
BLACK HANDBOOK
Mar., 2007
Spec. 4.00

SPIDER-MAN/BADROCK
Marvel/Maximum Press 1997
1 x-over, pt.1. . . . . 3.00
2 x-over, pt. 2 . . . . 3.00

SPIDER-MAN/BATMAN
1995
1 JMD,MBa,MFm,V:Carnage,Joker 6.00

SPIDER-MAN/BLACK CAT:
THE EVIL THAT MEN DO
June, 2002
1 (of 5) KSm,TyD 3.00
2 KSm,TyD 3.00
3 KSm,TyD 3.00
4 KSm,TyD,concl.(2005 . . . . 3.00
5 KSm,TyD,concl.,pt.2 (2005). 3.00
6 KSm,TyD,concl., pt.3 (2006) 3.00

SPIDER-MAN: BLUE
May, 2002
1 (of 6) JLb,TSe,Green Goblin 5.00
2 JLb,TSe,Gwen Stacy,Rhino. 4.00
3 JLb,TSe,Gwen & Mary Jane 4.00
4 JLb,TSe,college years 4.00
5 thru 6 JLb,TSe, ... @4.00

SPIDER-MAN:
BRAND NEW DAY
Oct., 2008
1 56-pg. 5.00
2 . . . . 4.00

SPIDER-MAN: BREAKOUT
April, 2005
1 (of 5) MD2(c) 3.00
2 MD2(c) 3.00
3 MD2(c) 3.00
4 . . . . 3.00
5 Finale 3.00

All comics prices listed are for *Near Mint* condition.

SPIDER-MAN, CHAPTER 1
Oct., 1998
1 (of 13) JBy,formative years 2.50
1a signed 20.00
2 JBy,A:Fantastic Four 2.50
2a variant JBy cover 5.00
2b signed, both covers 30.00
3 JBy,V:J.Jonah Jameson. 2.50
4 JBy,V:Dr.Octopus & Dr.Doom . . . 2.50
5 JBy,V:Lizard 2.50
6 JBy,V:Electro 2.50
7 JBy,V:Mysterio 2.50
8 JBy,V:Green Goblin 2.50
9 JBy,V:Circus of Crime 2.50
10 JBy,V:Green Goblin 2.50
11 JBy,V:Giant-Man 2.50
12 JBy,V:Sandman, double size
  final issue 4.00
Spec.#0 JBy,O:Sandman,Vulture
  & Lizard 2.50

SPIDER-MAN CLASSICS
1993–94
1 rep.Amazing Fantasy#15. . . . . . 2.50
2 thru 14 rep.Amaz.SpM . . . . . . @2.50
15 rep.Amaz.SpM#14,w/cel 3.25
15a Newsstand Ed. 2.50

SPIDER-MAN COMICS MAGAZINE
Jan., 1987
1 . . . . 7.00
2 thru 13 . . . . @6.00

SPIDER-MAN: DEAD MAN'S HAND
1997
1-shot, RSt,DaR,JeM,V:Carrion . . . 3.00

SPIDER-MAN: DEATH & DESTINY
June, 2000
1 (of 3) LW,RCa,F:Gwen Stacy 3.00
2 LW,RCa,Doctor Octopus 3.00
3 LW,RCa,concl. 3.00
Spec.Death of Gwen Stacy,64-pg.
  rep. of Amaz.Sp-M #88–#90 . . . 3.50

SPIDER-MAN/ DOCTOR OCTOPUS: OUT OF REACH
2004
1 (of 5) 3.00
2 thru 5 concl. . . . . @3.00
Digest. 8.00

SPIDER-MAN/DOCTOR OCTOPUS: YEAR ONE
June, 2004
1 (of 5) First battle 3.00
2 thru 5 concl. . . . . @3.00

SPIDER-MAN FAIRY TALES
May, 2007
1 (of 4) 3.00
2 thru 4 . . . . @3.00

SPIDER-MAN FAMILY
Oct., 2005
1-shot,TDF(s),RLm, Spider-Man
  Family 5.00
1-shot Featuring Spider-Clan 5.00
1-shot Featuring Amazing Friends. . 5.00

Feb., 2007
1 104-pgs. 5.00
2 thru 5 F:Dr. Strange, 104 pgs. . @5.00
6 A:Frog Thor, 104-pgs. 5.00
7 F:The Looter 104-pgs. 5.00
8 F:Invincible Iron Man 5.00
9 F:Mr. & Mrs. Spider-Man 5.00

SPIDER-MAN/ FANTASTIC FOUR
April, 2007
1 (of 4) 3.00
2 thru 3 . . . . 3.00

SPIDER-MAN: THE FINAL ADVENTURE
1995–96
1 FaN,DaR,Clv,I:Tendril 3.00
2 FaN,DaR,JAl,V:Tendril 3.00
3 FaN,DaR,JAl,V:Tendril 3.00
4 FaN,DaR,JAl,V:Tendril,concl. 3.00

SPIDER-MAN: FRIENDS AND ENEMIES
1995
1 V:Metahumes 2.50
2 A:Nova,Darkhawk,Speedball 2.50
3 V:Metahumes 2.50
4 F:Metahumes 2.50

SPIDER-MEN: FUNERAL FOR AN OCTOPUS
1995
1 Doc Oc Dead 2.50
2 A:Sinister Six 2.50
3 Final Issue 2.50

SPIDER-MAN/GEN13
Marvel/Wildstorm 1996
1-shot PDd,SI,CaS x-over 5.00

SPIDER-MAN: GET KRAVEN
June, 2002
1 (of 7) F:Alyosha Kravinoff 3.00
2 wants to make a movie 2.50
3 thru 6 JQ(c) . . . . @2.50

SPIDER-MAN: HOBGOBLIN LIVES
1997
1 (of 3) RSt,RF,GP 2.50
2 RSt,RF,GP,Who was the original
  Hobgoblin? 2.50
3 RSt,RF,GP,Original identity
  revealed. 2.50

SPIDER-MAN: HOUSE OF M
June, 2005
1 (of 5) MWa&TPe(s),SvL 3.00
2 MWa&tpe(s),Svl 3.00
3 MWa&TPe(s),SvL 3.00
4 MWa&TPe(s),SvL 3.00
5 MWa&TPe(s),Svl 3.00

SPIDER-MAN/ HUMAN TORCH
Jan., 2005
1 (of 5) TTn. 3.00
2 TTn,catch You on the Flip-side . . 3.00
3 TTn 3.00
4 TTn,A:Black Cat. 3.00

Spider-Man Hobgoblin Lives #1
© Marvel Entertainment Group

5 TTn,together Again 3.00
Digest I'm With Stupid 8.00

SPIDER-MAN & THE INCREDIBLE HULK
A.C.T.O.R./Marvel Epic, 2003
1-shot benefit issue 2.50

SPIDER-MAN: INDIA
Nov., 2004
1 (of 5) F:Pavitr Prabhakar 3.00
2 . . . . 3.00
3 V:Doc Ock 3.00
4 V:Green Goblin 3.00
5 . . . . 3.00

SPIDER-MAN: LEGEND OF THE SPIDER-CLAN
Marvel Mangaverse Oct., 2002
1 (of 3) 2.50
2 F:Manga Daredevil 2.50
3 F:Manga Green Govlin 2.50
4 . . . . 2.50
5 concl. 2.50

SPIDER-MAN: LIFELINE
Feb., 2001
1 (of 3) FaN,SR,BWi, ... 3.00
2 FaN,SR,BWi,V:Hammerhead . . . 3.00
3 FaN,SR,BWi,concl. 3.00

SPIDER-MAN LOVES MARY JANE
Dec., 2005
1 The Boyfriend Thing 3.00
2 thru 19 . . . . @3.00
Digest Vol. 1: Super Crush 8.00

SPIDER-MAN LOVES MARY JANE
Aug., 2008
1 thru 4 TMr . . . . @3.00

SPIDER-MAN: THE MANGA
B&W, Oct., 1997
1 imported, translated 4.00
2 thru 14 . . . . @3.00

All comics prices listed are for *Near Mint* condition.

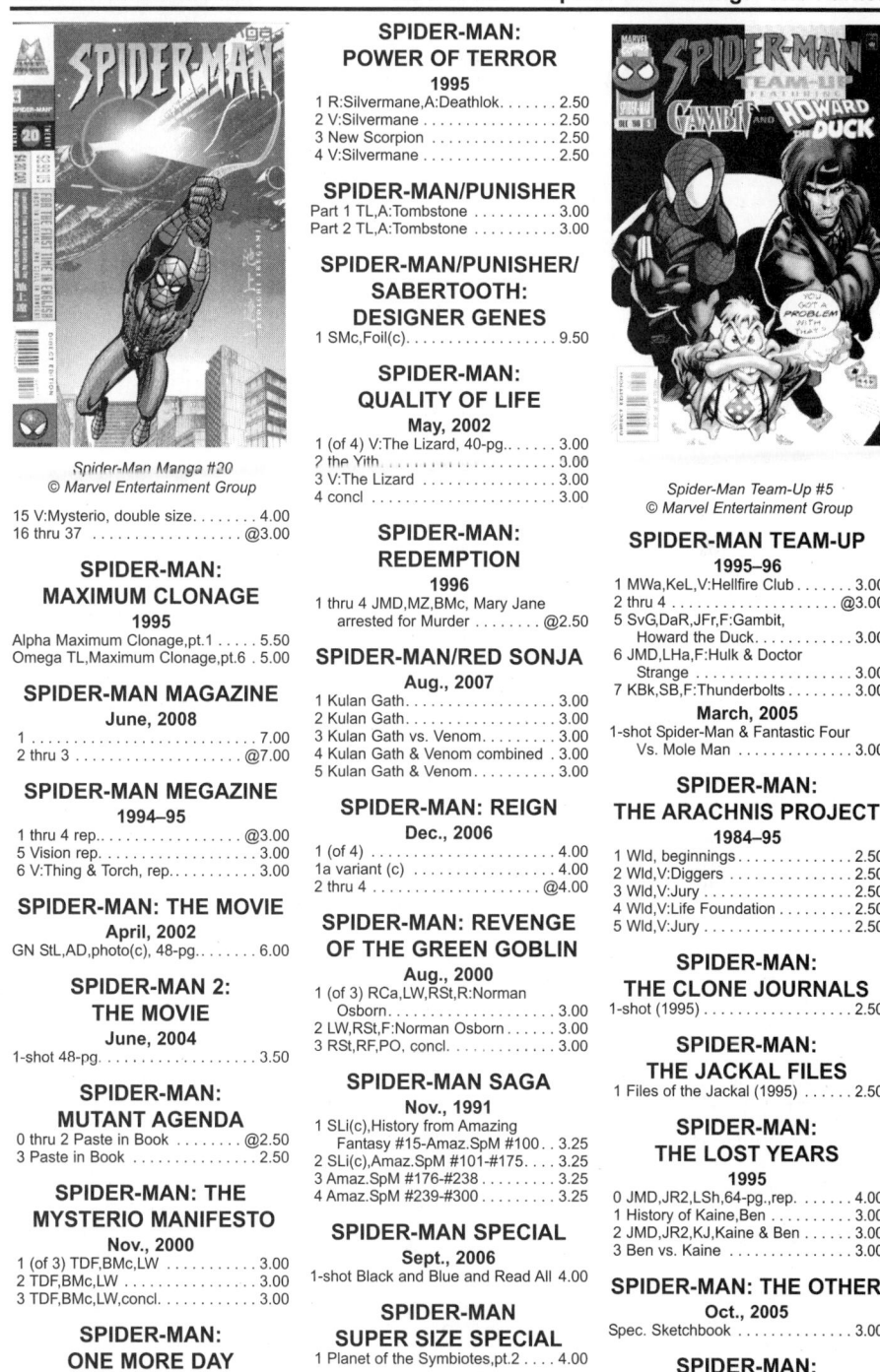

Spider-Man Manga #20
© *Marvel Entertainment Group*

15 V:Mysterio, double size........ 4.00
16 thru 37 .... @3.00

SPIDER-MAN: MAXIMUM CLONAGE
1995
Alpha Maximum Clonage,pt.1 ..... 5.50
Omega TL,Maximum Clonage,pt.6 . 5.00

SPIDER-MAN MAGAZINE
June, 2008
1 .... 7.00
2 thru 3 .... @7.00

SPIDER-MAN MEGAZINE
1994–95
1 thru 4 rep................. @3.00
5 Vision rep.................. 3.00
6 V:Thing & Torch, rep.......... 3.00

SPIDER-MAN: THE MOVIE
April, 2002
GN StL,AD,photo(c), 48-pg........ 6.00

SPIDER-MAN 2: THE MOVIE
June, 2004
1-shot 48-pg. 3.50

SPIDER-MAN: MUTANT AGENDA
0 thru 2 Paste in Book .... @2.50
3 Paste in Book 2.50

SPIDER-MAN: THE MYSTERIO MANIFESTO
Nov., 2000
1 (of 3) TDF,BMc,LW 3.00
2 TDF,BMc,LW 3.00
3 TDF,BMc,LW,concl............ 3.00

SPIDER-MAN: ONE MORE DAY
Aug., 2007
Sketchbook JQ................ 3.00

SPIDER-MAN: POWER OF TERROR
1995
1 R:Silvermane,A:Deathlok....... 2.50
2 V:Silvermane 2.50
3 New Scorpion 2.50
4 V:Silvermane 2.50

SPIDER-MAN/PUNISHER
Part 1 TL,A:Tombstone 3.00
Part 2 TL,A:Tombstone 3.00

SPIDER-MAN/PUNISHER/ SABERTOOTH: DESIGNER GENES
1 SMc,Foil(c)................. 9.50

SPIDER-MAN: QUALITY OF LIFE
May, 2002
1 (of 4) V:The Lizard, 40-pg...... 3.00
2 the Yith................... 3.00
3 V:The Lizard 3.00
4 concl 3.00

SPIDER-MAN: REDEMPTION
1996
1 thru 4 JMD,MZ,BMc, Mary Jane
 arrested for Murder .... @2.50

SPIDER-MAN/RED SONJA
Aug., 2007
1 Kulan Gath................. 3.00
2 Kulan Gath................. 3.00
3 Kulan Gath vs. Venom........ 3.00
4 Kulan Gath & Venom combined . 3.00
5 Kulan Gath & Venom......... 3.00

SPIDER-MAN: REIGN
Dec., 2006
1 (of 4) 4.00
1a variant (c) 4.00
2 thru 4 .... @4.00

SPIDER-MAN: REVENGE OF THE GREEN GOBLIN
Aug., 2000
1 (of 3) RCa,LW,RSt,R:Norman
 Osborn................... 3.00
2 LW,RSt,F:Norman Osborn...... 3.00
3 RSt,RF,PO, concl............ 3.00

SPIDER-MAN SAGA
Nov., 1991
1 SLi(c),History from Amazing
 Fantasy #15-Amaz.SpM #100.. 3.25
2 SLi(c),Amaz.SpM #101-#175.... 3.25
3 Amaz.SpM #176-#238 .... 3.25
4 Amaz.SpM #239-#300 .... 3.25

SPIDER-MAN SPECIAL
Sept., 2006
1-shot Black and Blue and Read All 4.00

SPIDER-MAN SUPER SIZE SPECIAL
1 Planet of the Symbiotes,pt.2 .... 4.00

SPIDER-MAN: SWING SHIFT
Dec., 2007
1-shot Director's Cut, 48-pg. 4.00

Spider-Man Team-Up #5
© *Marvel Entertainment Group*

SPIDER-MAN TEAM-UP
1995–96
1 MWa,KeL,V:Hellfire Club....... 3.00
2 thru 4 .... @3.00
5 SvG,DaR,JFr,F:Gambit,
 Howard the Duck............ 3.00
6 JMD,LHa,F:Hulk & Doctor
 Strange 3.00
7 KBk,SB,F:Thunderbolts 3.00
March, 2005
1-shot Spider-Man & Fantastic Four
 Vs. Mole Man 3.00

SPIDER-MAN: THE ARACHNIS PROJECT
1984–95
1 Wld, beginnings............. 2.50
2 Wld,V:Diggers 2.50
3 Wld,V:Jury 2.50
4 Wld,V:Life Foundation 2.50
5 Wld,V:Jury 2.50

SPIDER-MAN: THE CLONE JOURNALS
1-shot (1995) 2.50

SPIDER-MAN: THE JACKAL FILES
1 Files of the Jackal (1995) 2.50

SPIDER-MAN: THE LOST YEARS
1995
0 JMD,JR2,LSh,64-pg.,rep. 4.00
1 History of Kaine,Ben 3.00
2 JMD,JR2,KJ,Kaine & Ben 3.00
3 Ben vs. Kaine 3.00

SPIDER-MAN: THE OTHER
Oct., 2005
Spec. Sketchbook 3.00

SPIDER-MAN: THE PARKER YEARS
1995
1 JR2,JPi,F:The Real Clone...... 2.50

MARVEL

SPIDER-MAN 2099
1992–96

1 RL,AW,I:Spider-Man 2099	4.00
2 RL,AW,O:Spider-Man 2099	3.00
3 RL,AW,V:Venture	2.50
4 RL,AW,I:Specialist,	
A:Doom 2099	2.50
5 RL,AW,V:Specialist	2.50
6 RL,AW,I:New Vulture	2.50
7 RL,AW,Vulture of 2099	2.50
8 RL,AW,V:New Vulture	2.50
9 KJo,V:Alchemax	2.50
10 RL,AW,O:Wellvale Home	2.50
11 RL,AW,V:S.I.E.G.E.	2.50
12 RL,AW,w/poster	2.50
13 RL,AW,V:Thanatos	2.50
14 PDd(s),RL(c),TGb,Downtown	2.50
15 PDd(s),RL,I:Thor 2099,	
Heimdall 2099	2.50
16 PDd(s),RL,Fall of the	
Hammer #1	2.50
17 PDd(s),RL,V:Bloodsword	2.50
18 PDd(s),RLm,V:Lyla	2.50
19 PDd(s),RL,w/card	2.50
20 PDd(s),RL,Crash & Burn	2.50
21 V:Gangs	2.50
22 V:Gangs	2.50
23 RL,I:Risque	3.00
24 Kasey	2.50
25 A:Hulk 2099, dbl-size,foil(c)	4.00
25a Newsstand ed.	2.50
26 V:Headhunter, Travesty	2.50
27 V:Travesty	2.50
28 V:Travesty	2.50
29 V:Foragers	2.50
30 V:Flipside	2.50
31 I:Dash	2.50

Becomes:

SPIDER-MAN 2099 A.D.

32 I:Morgue	2.50
33 One Nation Under Doom	2.50
34 V:Alchemex	2.50
35	2.50
36a Spider-Man 2099(c)	2.50
36b Venom 2099(c)	2.50
37a Venom 2099	2.50
37b variant cover	2.50
38	2.50
39 A:Venom 2099	2.50
40 V:Goblin 2099	2.50
41 and 42	@2.50
43 V:Sub-Mariner 2099	2.50
Ann.#1 PDd(s),RL	3.00
Spec.#1 I:3 new villains	4.00

SPIDER-MAN UNLIMITED
1993

1 RLm,Maximun Carnage #1,	
I:Shriek,R:Carnage	6.00
2 RLm,Maximum Carnage #14.	4.50
3 RLm,O:Doctor Octopus	4.50
4 RLm,V:Mystrerio,Rhino	4.25
5 RLm,A:Human Torch,	
I:Steel Spider	4.25
6 RLm,A:Thunderstrike	4.25
7 RLm,A:Clone	4.25
8 Tom Lyle	4.25
9 The Mark of Kaine,pt.5	4.25
10 SwM,Exiled,pt.4	4.25
11 FaN,V:Black Cat	4.25
12 Blood Brother,tie-in	4.25
13	3.25
14 JoB, an ally dies	3.25
15 TDF,JoB,F:Puma	3.25
16 cont. from X-Force #64	3.25
17 JoB, Revelations, sequel	3.25
18 TDF,JoB,F:Doctor Octopus	3.25
19 JoB,F:Lizard	3.25
20 JoB,A:Hannibal King, V:Lilith	3.25
21 MD2,Frankenstein Monster Lives	3.25
22 MD2,V:The Scorpion	3.25

SPIDER-MAN UNLIMITED
Nov., 1999

1 cartoon, tie-in	3.50
2 thru 4	@2.50

Jan., 2004

1 V:Slyde	3.00
2 F:Mary Jane	3.00
3 thru 10	@3.00
11 thru 15	@3.00

SPIDER-MAN UNIVERSE
Jan., 2000

1 rep. 3 stories, 80-pg.	5.00
2 thru 6 rep. 3 stories, 80-pg.	@5.00
7 thru 9 rep. 3 stories, 80-pg	@4.00

SPIDER-MAN UNMASKED
1996

1-shot 64-pg. information source	6.00

SPIDER-MAN VS. DRACULA
1994

1 rep.	2.50

SPIDER-MAN VS. VENOM
1990

1 TM(c)	9.00

SPIDER-MAN: THE VENOM AGENDA
Nov., 1997

1-shot LHa,TL, J. Jonah Jameson,	
V:Venom	3.00

SPIDER-MAN VS. WOLVERINE
1990

1 MBr,AW,D:Ned Leeds(the original	
Hobgoblin),V:Charlie	25.00
1a reprint.	5.00

SPIDER-MAN: WEB OF DOOM
1994

1 3-part series	2.50
2 Spidey falsely accused	2.50
3 conclusion	2.50

SPIDER-MAN: WITH GREAT POWER
Jan., 2008

1 (of 5) TyH	4.00
2 thru 5 TyH	@4.00

SPIDER-MAN & X-FACTOR: SHADOW GAMES

1 PB,I:Shadowforce	2.50
2 PB,V:Shadowforce	2.50
3 PB,V:Shadowforce, final issue	2.50

SPIDER-WOMAN
April, 1978

1 CI,TD,O:Spider-Woman	22.00
2 CI,TD,I:Morgan LeFey	6.00
3 CI,TD,I:Brothers Grimm	6.00
4 CI,TD,V:Hangman	6.00
5 CI,TD,Nightmares	6.00
6 CI,A:Werewolf By Night	7.00
7 CI,SL,AG,V:Magnus	6.00
8 CI,AG,Man Who Would Not Die	6.00
9 CI,AG,A:Needle,Magnus	6.00

Spider-Woman #7
© *Marvel Entertainment Group*

10 CI,AG,I:Gypsy Moth	6.00
11 CI,AG,V:Brothers Grimm	6.00
12 CI,AG,V:Brothers Grimm	6.00
13 CI,AG,A:Shroud	6.00
14 BSz(c),CI,AG,A:Shroud	6.00
15 BSz(c),CI,AG,A:Shroud	6.00
16 BSz(c),CI,AG,V:Nekra	6.00
17 CI,Death Plunge	6.00
18 CI,A:Flesh	6.00
19 CI,A:Werewolf By Night,	
V:Enforcer	7.00
20 FS,A:Spider-Man	7.00
21 FS,A:Bounty Hunter	6.00
22 FS,A:Killer Clown	6.00
23 TVE,V:The Gamesmen	6.00
24 TVE,V:The Gamesmen	6.00
25 SL,Two Spider-Women	6.00
26 JBy(c),SL,V:White Gardenia	6.00
27 BSz(c),JBi,A:Enforcer	6.00
28 BSz(c),SL,A:Enforcer,Spidey	7.00
29 JR2(c),ECh,FS,A:Enforcer,	
Spider-Man	7.00
30 FM(c),SL,JM,I:Dr.Karl Malus	6.00
31 FM(c),SL,JM,A:Hornet	6.00
32 FM(c),SL,JM,A:Werewolf	6.00
33 SL,V:Yesterday's Villain	6.00
34 SL,AM,V:Hammer and Anvil	6.00
35 SL,AG,V:Angar the Screamer	6.00
36 SL,Spider-Woman Shot	6.00
37 SL,TA,BWi,AM,FS,A:X-Men,I:	
Siryn,V:Black Tom	10.00
38 SL,BWi,A:X-Men,Siryn	10.00
39 SL,BWi,Shadows	5.00
40 SL,BWi,V:The Flying Tiger	5.00
41 SL,BWi,V:Morgan LeFay	5.00
42 SL,BWi,V:Silver Samurai	5.00
43 SL,V:Silver Samurai	5.00
44 SL,V:Morgan LeFay	5.00
45 SL,Spider-Man Thief cover	5.00
46 SL,V:Mandroids,A:Kingpin	5.00
47 V:Daddy Longlegs	5.00
48 O:Gypsy Moth	5.00
49 A:Tigra	5.00
50 PH(c),D:Spider-Woman	15.00

[Limited Series] 1993–94

1 V:Therak	2.50
2 O:Spider-Woman	2.50
3 V:Deathweb	2.50
4 V:Deathweb, last issue	2.50

May, 1999

1 JBy,BS,48-pg.	3.00
1a signed	20.00
2 BS,JBy,A:Dr. Octopus	2.50
2a variant JR2 cover	2.50

3 BS,JBy,V:Flesh & Bones 2.50
4 BS,JBy,V:Flesh & Bones 2.50
5 BS,JBy,I:Shadowcaster 2.50
6 BS,JBy,V:Shadowcaster 2.50
7 BS,JBy 2.50
8 BS,JBy,A:Cluster,x-over. 2.50
9 BS,JBy,A:Mattie 2.50
10 BS,JBy,A:Rhino. 2.50
11 BS,JBy,V:Exomorph 2.50
12 BS,JBy,F:J.Jonah Jameson 2.50
13 BS,JBy,V:Werewolf 2.50
14 JBy,GN,BS(c),V:Nighteyes 2.50
15 JBy,BS,Itch & Scratch. 2.50
16 JBy,BS,Flesh. 2.50
17 JBy,BS,Flesh & Bones 2.50
18 JBy,BS,final issue 2.50

July, 2005
Giant Size #1 classic reprints 5.00

SPIDER-WOMAN: ORIGIN
Dec., 2005
1 BMB(s). 3.00
2 thru 5 BMB(s) 3.00

SPIDEY AND THE MINI MARVELS
April, 2003
Spec. Bullpen bits, 40-pg. 3.50

SPIDEY SUPER STORIES
Oct., 1974
1 Younger reader's series in
association with the Electric
Company,O:Spider-Man . . . 65.00
2 A:Kraven 35.00
3 A:Ringleader 25.00
4 A:Medusa 25.00
5 A:Shocker 25.00
6 A:Iceman 25.00
7 A:Lizard, Vanisher 25.00
8 A:Dr. Octopus 25.00
9 A:Dr. Doom 25.00
10 A:Green Goblin 25.00
11 A:Dr. Octopus 22.00
12 A:The Cat,V:The Owl 22.00
13 A:Falcon 22.00
14 A:Shanna 22.00
15 A:Storm 25.00
16 . . . . 22.00
17 A:Captain America 22.00
18 A:Kingpin. 22.00
19 A:Silver Surfer,Dr. Doom. 22.00
20 A:Human Torch,Invisible Girl . . 22.00
21 A:Dr. Octopus 22.00
22 A:Ms. Marvel,The Beetle. 22.00
23 A:Green Goblin 22.00
24 A:Thundra 22.00
25 A:Dr. Doom 22.00
26 A:Sandman 22.00
27 A:Thor,Loki 22.00
28 A:Medusa 22.00
29 A:Kingpin. 22.00
30 A:Kang 22.00
31 A:Moondragon,Dr. Doom 18.00
32 A:Spider-Woman,Dr. Octopus . . 18.00
33 . . . . 18.00
34 A:Sub-Mariner 18.00
35 . . . . 18.00
36 A:Lizard 18.00
37 A:White Tiger 18.00
38 A:Fantastic Four 18.00
39 A:Hellcat,Thanos. 20.00
40 A:Hawkeye 18.00
41 A:Nova,Dr. Octopus 18.00
42 A:Kingpin. 18.00
43 A:Daredevil,Ringmaster 18.00
44 A:Vision 18.00
45 A:Silver Surfer,Dr. Doom. 18.00

46 A:Mysterio. 18.00
47 A:Spider-Woman,Stilt-Man 18.00
48 A:Green Goblin 18.00
49 Spidey for President 18.00
50 A:She-Hulk 18.00
51 and 52. . . . . @18.00
53 A:Dr. Doom 18.00
54 Attack of the Bird-Man 18.00
55 A:Kingpin. 18.00
56 A:Captain Britain,
Jack O'Lantern 18.00
57 March, 1982 . . . . 18.00

SPITFIRE AND THE TROUBLESHOOTERS
Oct., 1986
1 HT/JSt 2.50
2 HT 2.50
3 HT,Macs Armor 2.50
4 TM/BMc(Early TM work) 3.50
5 HT/TD,A:Star Brand. 2.50
6 HT,Trial. 2.50
7 HT 2.50
8 HT,New Armor 2.50
9 . . . . 2.50
Becomes:

CODE NAME: SPITFIRE
10 MR/TD. 2.50
11 thru 13 . . . . @2.50

SPOOF
Oct., 1970
1 MSe 25.00
2 MSe,Brawl in the Family 15.00
3 MSe,Richard Nixon cover 15.00
4 MSe,Blechhula. 15.00
5 MSe,May, 1973 . . . . 20.00

SPORT STARS
Nov., 1949
1 The Life of Knute Rockne 650.00
Becomes:

SPORTS ACTION
2 BP(c),Life of George Gipp. . . . 650.00
3 BEv,Hack Wilson 350.00
4 Art Houtteman 300.00
5 Nile Kinnick 300.00
6 Warren Gun 300.00
7 Jim Konstanty 300.00
8 Ralph Kiner 325.00
9 Ed 'Strangler' Lewis 300.00
10 JMn,The Yella-Belly 300.00
11 The Killers 300.00
12 BEv,Man Behind the Mask . . . 300.00
13 BEv,Lew Andrews. 310.00
14 MWs,Ken Roper,Sept.,1952 . . 310.00

SPOTLIGHT
Sept., 1978
1 F:Huckleberry Hound,Yogi Bear 50.00
2 Quick Draw McGraw 35.00
3 The Jetsons 35.00
4 Magilla Gorilla, March, 1979 . . 30.00

SPUMCO COMIC BOOK
1 I:Jimmy the Hapless Boy 7.00
2 . . . . 7.00
3 64-pgs. of sick humor 7.00
4 More sick humor 7.00

SPY CASES
See: KID KOMICS

SPY FIGHTERS
March, 1951
1 GT 350.00
2 GT 200.00
3 . . . . 150.00

4 thru 13 . . . . @150.00
14 thru 15 July, 1953 . . . . @165.00

SPYKE
Epic Heavy Hitters, 1993
1 MBn,BR,I:Spyke. 2.75
2 MBn,BR,V:Conita. 2.75
3 thru 4 MBn,BR . . . . @2.50

Spy Thrillers #2
© Marvel Entertainment Group

SPY THRILLERS
Atlas, Nov., 1954
1 AyB(c),The Tickling Death 300.00
2 V:Communists 150.00
3 thru 4 . . . . @125.00
Becomes:

POLICE BADGE
5 Sept., 1955 . . . . 125.00

SQUADRON SUPREME
Sept., 1985
1 BH,L:Nighthawk. 5.00
2 BH,F:Nuke,A:Scarlet Centurion . . 4.00
3 BH,D:Nuke. 4.00
4 BH,L:Archer. 4.00
5 BH,L:Amphibian. 4.00
6 PR,J:Institute of Evil 4.00
7 JB,JG,V:Hyperion. 4.00
8 BH,V:Hyperion. 4.00
9 BSz(c),PR,D:Tom Thumb 4.00
10 PR,V:Quagmire. 4.00
11 PR,V:Redeemers 4.00
12 PR,D:Nighthawk,Foxfire,
Black Archer 4.00
GN Death of a Universe 12.00

March, 2006
1 MSz(s) 3.00
2 thru 7 MSz(s) . . . . @3.00
8 MSz(s),MD2. . . . . 3.00
9 MSz(s),MD2. . . . . 3.00
Spec.#1 Saga of the Squadron
Supreme (Feb., 2006). 4.00

July, 2008
1 HC(s),Power to the People, pt.1 . 3.00
2 thru 5 HC(s),Power to the
People, pt.2 thru pt.5 . . . . . . @3.00

SQUADRON SUPREME: HYPERION VS. NIGHTHAWK
1 (of 4) PG 3.00
2 thru 4 PG . . . . @3.00

Stalkers #11
© *Marvel Entertainment Group*

STALKERS
Epic, 1990–91
1 MT 2.50
2 thru 12 MT . . . . @2.50

STAND, THE:
CAPTAIN TRIPS
Sept., 2008
1 . . . . 4.00
1a variant (c) 4.00
1b variant sketch (c) 4.00
2 thru 3 . . . . @4.00
2a thru 3a variant (c)s . . . . @4.00
3a thru 3b variant sketch (c)s . . @4.00

STAN LEE MEETS...
Sept., 2006
Spider-Man #1 . . . . 4.00
Dr. Strange #1 . . . . 4.00
The Thing #1 . . . . 4.00
Silver Surfer #1 . . . . 4.00
Dr. Doom #1 . . . . 4.00

STARBLAST
1994
1 MGu(s),HT,After the Starbrand . . 2.50
2 MGu(s),HT,After the Starbrand . . 2.50
3 MGu(s),HT,After the Starbrand . . 2.50
4 MGu(s),HT,final issue 2.50

STARBRAND
Oct., 1986
1 JR2,O:Starbrand 2.50
2 thru 8 JR2/AW . . . . @2.50
9 thru 15 . . . . @2.50
16 thru 19 . . . . @3.00
Ann.#1 . . . . 3.00

STAR COMICS
MAGAZINE
Dec., 1986 (digest size)
1 F:Heathcliff,Muppet Babies,
Ewoks 2.50
2 thru 13 1988 . . . . @2.50

STARJAMMERS
1995–96
1 I:The Uncreated 3.00
2 thru 4 . . . . @3.00

STARJAMMERS
July, 2004
1 (of 6) Cadet & Corsairs,pt.1 . . . . 3.00
2 thru 6 Cadet and the Corsairs,
pt.2 thru pt.6 . . . . @3.00

STAR-LORD,
SPECIAL EDITION
Feb., 1982
1 JBy reprints 6.00

STARLORD
Mini-Series 1996
1 (of 3) DLw 2.50
2 DLw 2.50
3 DLw,V:Damyish 2.50

STAR MASTER
1 MGu,Cosmic Avengers assemble 2.50
2 MGu,World Engine saga 2.50
3 MGu,Cauldron of Conversion . . . 2.50

STARSTRUCK
March, 1985
1 MK 3.00
2 thru 8 MK, Feb., 1986 . . . . @3.00

STARTLING STORIES:
THE THING–NIGHT FALLS
ON YANCY ST.
May, 2003
1 (of 4) EDo(s),40-pg 3.50
2 EDo(s),40-pg. 3.50
3 EDo(s),40-pg. 3.50
4 EDo(s),concl. 3.50
Spec. Last Line of Defense 3.50

STARTLING STORIES:
THE INCORRIGIBLE HULK
Jan., 2004
1-shot 3.00

STAR TREK
April, 1980
1 DC,KJ,rep.1st movie adapt 17.00
2 DC,KJ,rep.1st movie adapt 9.00
3 DC,KJ,rep.1st movie adapt 9.00
4 thru 16 . . . . @9.00
17 EH,TP,The Long Nights Dawn . 15.00
18 A Thousand Deaths,last issue . 20.00

STAR TREK:
DEEP SPACE NINE
1996
1 HWe(s),TGb,AM,DS9 in the
Gamma Quadrant,pt.1 (of 2) . . 3.00
2 thru 15 . . . . @2.50

STAR TREK:
EARLY VOYAGES
Dec., 1996
1 DAn,IEd,Captain Pike's crew,
double size premier 4.00
2 thru 17 . . . . @2.50

STAR TREK
GN Star Trek, First Contact
Movie adapt. 6.00
1-shot Mirror, Mirror (1996) 4.00
1-shot Operation Assimilation 3.00
1-shot Telepathy War, pt.4
x-over, 48-pg.(1997) 3.00

STAR TREK: THE NEXT
GENERATION
RIKER SPECIAL
May, 1998
1-shot, DAn,IEd,Riker photo cover . 3.50

STAR TREK: THE NEXT
GENERATION/X-MEN:
SECOND CONTACT
March, 1998
1-shot, DAn,IEd,64-pg. 5.00
1-shot, variant CNr cover (1:5) 5.00

STAR TREK:
STARFLEET ACADEMY
1996
1 Cadets vs. Gorns 2.50
2 thru 19 . . . . @2.50

STAR TREK: UNLIMITED
1996
1 DAn,IEd,MBu,JeM,AW, Classic
series & TNG 5.00
2 thru 10 . . . . @4.00

STAR TREK:
THE UNTOLD VOYAGES
Jan., 1998
1 . . . . 3.00
2 . . . . 3.00
3 . . . . 3.00
4 . . . . 3.00
5 48-pg. finale 3.50

STAR TREK: VOYAGER
1996
1 . . . . 3.00
2 thru 15 . . . . @3.00

STAR TREK: VOYAGER:
SPLASHDOWN
Jan., 1998
1 thru 4 AM . . . . @3.00

STAR TREK/X-MEN
1-shot SLo,MS, 64-pg. 5.00
1a rep. of STAR TREK/X-MEN 5.00

STAR WARS
July, 1977
1 HC,30 Cent,movie adaption. . . . 90.00
1a HC,35 Cent(square Box). . . . 725.00
1b "Reprint" 7.50
2 HC,movie adaptation 40.00
2b "Reprint" 4.00
3 HC,movie adaptation 35.00
3b "Reprint" 4.00
4 HC,SL,movie adapt.(low dist.) . . 35.00
4b "Reprint" 4.00
5 HC,SL,movie adaptation 25.00
5b "Reprint" 3.00
6 HC,DSt,E:movie adaption 25.00
6b "Reprint" 3.00
7 HC,FS,F:Luke & Chewbacca. . . 20.00
8 HC,TD,Eight against a World . . 20.00
9 HC,TP,V:Cloud Riders 20.00
7b thru 9b "Reprint" . . . . @2.50
10 HC,TP,Dehemoth From Below . 22.00
11 CI,TP,Fate of Luke Skywalker . . 20.00
12 TA,CI,Doomworld 20.00
13 TA,JBy,CI,Deadly Reunion 20.00
14 TA,CI 20.00
15 CI,V:Crimson Jack 20.00
16 WS,V:The Hunter 20.00

17 Crucible, low dist. 20.00
18 CI,Empire Strikes,low dist. 20.00
19 CI,Ultimate Gamble,low dist . . . 20.00
20 CI,Death Game, scarce 20.00
21 TA,CI,Shadow of a Dark
 Lord(Scarce) 20.00
22 CI,Han Solo vs.Chewbacca . . . 15.00
23 CI,Flight Into Fury 15.00
24 CI,Ben Kenobi Story 15.00
25 CI,Siege at Yavin 15.00
26 CI,Doom Mission 15.00
27 CI,V:The Hunter 15.00
28 CI,Cavern o/t Crawling Death. . 15.00
29 CI,Dark Encounter 15.00
30 CI,A Princess Alone 15.00
31 CI,Return to Tatooine 15.00
32 CI,The Jawa Express 15.00
33 CI,GD,V:Baron Tagge 15.00
34 CI,Thunder in the Stars. 15.00
35 CI,V:Darth Vader. 15.00
36 CI,V:Darth Vader. 15.00
37 CI,V:Darth Vader. 15.00
38 TA,MG,Riders in the Void 15.00
39 AW,B:Empire Strikes Back . . . 25.00
40 AW,Battleground Hoth. 25.00
41 AW,Imperial Pursuit. 25.00
42 AW,Bounty Hunters. 25.00
43 AW,Betrayal at Bespin 25.00
44 AW,E:Empire Strikes Back . . . 25.00
45 CI,GD,Death Probe. 15.00
46 DI,TP,V:Dreamnaut Devourer . 15.00
47 CI,GD,Droid World 15.00
48 CI,Leia vs.Darth Vader 15.00
49 SW,TP,The Last Jedi 15.00
50 WS,AW,TP,G-Size issue 15.00
51 WS,TP,Resurrection of Evil. . . . 12.00
52 WS,TP,D:Death Star II 12.00
53 CI,WS,Gift of Alderaan 12.00
54 CI,WS,Starfire Rising 12.00
55 thru 66 WS,TP . . . . @12.00
67 TP, The Darker 12.00
68 GD,TP,O:Boba Fett. 20.00
69 GD,TP,Death in City of Bone . . 20.00
70 A:Han Solo 20.00
71 A:Han Solo 20.00
72 Fool's Boontu 20.00
73 Secret of Planet Lansbane . . . 20.00
74 thru 91 . . . . @20.00
92 BSz(c),The Dream 22.00
93 thru 97 . . . . @20.00
98 AW,Supply & Demand 20.00
99 Touch of Goddess 20.00
100 Painted(c),double-size 22.00
101 BSz, Far,Far Away 22.00
102 KRo's Back 15.00

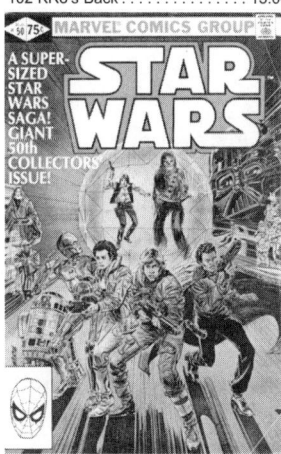

Star Wars #50
© *Marvel Entertainment Group*

103 thru 106 . . . . @15.00
107 WPo(i),last issue 90.00
Ann.#1 WS(c),V:Winged Warlords100.00
Ann.#2 RN 15.00
Ann.#3 RN,Darth Vader(c) 15.00

STEELGRIP STARKEY
Epic, July, 1986
1 . . . . 2.50
2 thru 5 . . . . @2.50
6 June, 1987 . . . . 2.50

STEELTOWN ROCKERS
April, 1990—Sept., 1990
1 SL 2.50
2 thru 6 SL . . . . @2.50

STOKER'S DRACULA
Oct., 2004
1 (of 4) RTs,DG. 4.00
2 . . . . 4.00
3 RTs(s),DG 4.00
4 Rts(s),Dg 4.00

STORIES OF ROMANCE
Marvel Atlas, 1956
5 MB,ViC(c) 150.00
6 . . . . 100.00
7 . . . . 100.00
8 . . . . 100.00
9 ViC 125.00
10 . . . . 100.00
11 MB,ViC,JR. 150.00
12 . . . . 120.00
13 ABr 150.00

STORM
1 TyD,KIS,V:Candra 4.00
2 . . . . 4.00
3 . . . . 4.00
4 TyD,KIS, conclusion,foil cover . . . 4.00

STORM
Feb., 2006
1 Storm & Black Panther 3.00
2 thru 6 . . . . @3.00

STORMBREAKER: THE SAGA OF BETA RAY BILL
Jan., 2005
1 (of 6) 3.00
2 I:stardust 3.00
3 V:Stardust 3.00
4 . . . . 3.00
5 Return to Asgard 3.00
6 Vs. Spider-Man 3.00

STRANGE
Sept., 2004
1 MSz,BPe,O:Dr.Strange 3.50
2 MSz,BPe, ... 3.50
3 . . . . 3.50
4 MSz(s),BPe 3.50
5 MSz(s),Bpe,new Costume 3.50
6 MSz(s),BPe, finale 3.50

STRANGE COMBAT TALES
1 and 2 . . . . @2.75
3 Tiger by the Tail 2.50
4 Midnight Crusade. 2.50

STRANGE STORIES OF SUSPENSE
See: RUGGED ACTION

Strange Tales #3
© *Marvel Entertainment Group*

STRANGE TALES
[1st Regular Series] June, 1951
1 The Room. 5,000.00
2 Trapped In A Tomb 1,700.00
3 JMn,Man Who Never Was . . 1,300.00
4 BEv,Terror in the Morgue . . 1,400.00
5 A Room Without A Door 1,300.00
6 RH(c),The Ugly Man 900.00
7 Who Stands Alone 900.00
8 BEv(c),Something in the Fog. . 900.00
9 Drink Deep Vampire 900.00
10 BK,Hidden Head. 1000.00
11 BEv(c),GC,'O'Malley's Friend . 600.00
12 Graveyard At Midnight 600.00
13 BEv(c),Death Makes A Deal . . 600.00
14 GT,Horrible Herman 600.00
15 BK,Don't Look Down. 600.00
16 Decapitation cover 600.00
17 DBr,JRo,Death Feud. 600.00
18 Witch Hunt 600.00
19 RH(c),The Rag Doll 600.00
20 RH(c),GC,SMo,Lost World . . . 600.00
21 BEv 500.00
22 BK,JF 500.00
23 Strangest Tale in the World. . . 500.00
24 The Thing in the Coffin 500.00
25 . . . . 500.00
26 . . . . 500.00
27 JF,The Garden of Death 500.00
28 Come into my Coffin 500.00
29 Witch-Craft 500.00
30 The Thing in the Box 500.00
31 Man Who Played with Blocks . 500.00
32 . . . . 500.00
33 JMn(c),Step Lively Please . . . 500.00
34 Flesh and Blood 475.00
35 The Man in the Bottle 400.00
36 . . . . 400.00
37 Out of the Storm 400.00
38 . . . . 400.00
39 Karnoff's Plan 400.00
40 BEv,Man Who Caught
 a Mermaid 400.00
41 BEv,Riddle of the Skull 425.00
42 DW,BEv,JMn,Faceless One . . 425.00
43 JF,The Mysterious Machine . . 400.00
44 . . . . 400.00
45 JKa,Land of Vanishing Men . . 425.00
46 thru 57 . . . . @400.00
58 AW 400.00
59 BK 400.00
60 . . . . 375.00
61 BK 400.00
62 . . . . 375.00

63	400.00
64 AW	400.00
65	375.00
66	375.00
67 thru 78	@450.00
79 SD,JK,Dr.Strange Prototype	450.00
80 thru 83 SD,JK	@350.00
84 SD,JK,Magneto Prototype	350.00
85 SD,JK	350.00
86 SD,JK,I Created Mechano	350.00
87 SD,JK,Return of Grogg	350.00
88 SD,JK,Zzutak	350.00
89 SD,JK,Fin Fang Foom	900.00
90 SD,JK,Orrgo Unconquerable	350.00
91 SD,JK,The Sacrifice	350.00
92 SD,JK,Thing That Waits	350.00
93 SD,JK,The Wax People	350.00
94 SD,JK,Pildorr the Plunderer	350.00
95 SD,JK,Two-Headed Thing	350.00
96 SD,JK,I Dream of Doom	350.00
97 SD,JK,When A Planet Dies	700.00
98 SD,JK,No Human Can Beat Me	350.00
99 SD,JK,Mister Morgan's Monster	350.00
100 SD,JK,I Was Trapped in the Crazy Maze	350.00
101 B:StL(s),SD,JK, B:Human Torch	2,500.00
102 SD,JK,I:Wizard	900.00
103 SD,JK,I:Zemu	700.00
104 SD,JK,I:The Trapster	700.00
105 SD,JK,V:Wizard	700.00
106 SD,A:Fantastic Four	600.00
107 SD,V:Sub-Mariner	750.00
108 SD,JK,A:FF,I:The Painter	600.00
109 SD,JK,I:Sorcerer	600.00
110 SD,I&B:Dr.Strange, Nightmare	3,000.00
111 SD,I:Asbestos,BaronMordo	900.00
112 SD,I:The Eel	325.00
113 SD,I:Plant Man	325.00
114 SD,JK,A:Captain America	1,000.00
115 SD,O:Dr.Strange	1,000.00
116 SD,V:Thing	400.00
117 SD,V:The Eel	300.00
118 SD,V:The Wizard	400.00
119 SD,C:Spider-Man	400.00
120 SD,1st Iceman/Torch T.U.	450.00
121 SD,V:Plant Man	200.00
122 SD,V:Dr.Doom	175.00
123 SD,A:Thor,I:Beetle	200.00
124 SD,I:Zota	175.00
125 SD,V:Sub-Mariner	200.00
126 SD,I:Dormammu,Clea	175.00
127 SD,V:Dormammu	175.00
128 SD,I:Demon	175.00
129 SD,I:Tiboro	175.00
130 SD,C:Beatles	175.00
131 SD,I:Dr.Vega	175.00
132 SD,I:Orini	175.00
133 SD,I:Shazana	175.00
134 SD,E:Torch,I:Merlin	175.00
135 SD,JK:I:Shield & Hydra B:Nick Fury	300.00
136 SD,JK,V:Dormammu	135.00
137 SD,JK,A:Ancient One	150.00
138 SD,JK,I:Eternity	150.00
139 SD,JK,V:Dormammu	150.00
140 SD,JK,V:Dormammu	150.00
141 SD,JK,I:Fixer,Mentallo	100.00
142 SD,JK,I:THEM,V:Hydra	100.00
143 SD,JK,V:Hydra	100.00
144 SD,JK,V:Druid,I:Jasper Sitwell	100.00
145 SD,JK,I:Mr.Rasputin	100.00
146 SD,JK,V:Dormammu,I:A.I.M.	100.00
147 BEv,JK,F:Wong	100.00
148 BEv,JK,O:Ancient One	90.00
149 BEv,JK,V:Kaluu	100.00
150 BEv,JK,JB(1st Marvel Art) I:Baron Strucker,Umar	100.00

Strange Tales #170
© Marvel Entertainment Group

151 JK,JSo(1st Marvel Art), I:Umar	150.00
152 BEv,JK,JSo,V:Umar	100.00
153 JK,JSo,MSe,V:Hydra	100.00
154 JSo,MSe,I:Dreadnought	100.00
155 JSo,MSe,A:L.B.Johnson	100.00
156 JSo,MSe,I:Zom	100.00
157 JSo,MSe,A:Zom,C:Living Tribunal	100.00
158 JSo,MSe,A:Zom,I:Living Tribunal(full story)	100.00
159 JSo,MSe,O:Nick Fury,A:Capt. America,I:Val Fontaine	125.00
160 JSo,MSe,A:Captain America, I:Jimmy Woo	100.00
161 JSo,I:Yellow Claw	100.00
162 JSo,DA,A:Captain America	100.00
163 JSo,DA,V:Yellow Claw	90.00
164 JSo,DA,V:Yellow Claw	90.00
165 JSo,DA,V:Yellow Claw	90.00
166 DA,GT,JSo,A:AncientOne	90.00
167 JSo,DA,V:Doctor Doom	125.00
168 JSo,DA,E:Doctor Strange,Nick Fury,V:Yandroth	100.00
169 JSo,I&O:Brother Voodoo	30.00
170 JSo,O:Brother Voodoo	25.00
171 GC,V:Baron Samed	25.00
172 GC,DG,V:Dark Lord	25.00
173 GC,DG,I:Black Talon	25.00
174 JB,JM,O:Golem	20.00
175 SD,R:Torr	20.00
176 F:Golem	20.00
177 FB,F:Golem	20.00
178 JSn,B&O:Warlock,I:Magus	60.00
179 JSn,I:Pip,I&D:Capt.Autolycus	55.00
180 JSn,I:Gamora,Kray-tor	55.00
181 JSn,E:Warlock	55.00
182 SD,GK,rep. Str.Tales #123,124	20.00
183 SD,rep.Str.Tales #130,131	20.00
184 SD,rep.Str.Tales #132,133	20.00
185 SD,rep.Str.Tales #134,135	20.00
186 SD,rep.Str.Tales #136,137	20.00
187 SD,rep.Str.Tales #138,139	20.00
188 SD,rep.Str.Tales #140,141	20.00
Ann.#1 V:Grottu,Diablo	1,100.00
Ann.#2 A:Spider-Man	1,800.00
Marvel Milestone rep. stories from #110–#111, #114–#115 (1995)	3.00

[2nd Regular Series] 1987–88

1 BBl,CW,B:Cloak&Dagger,Dr. Strange,V:Lord of Light	3.00
2 BBl,CW,V:Lord of Light,Demon	2.50
3 BBl,AW,CW,A:Nightmare,Khat	2.50
4 BBl,CW,V:Nightmare	2.50
5 BBl,V:Rodent,A:Defenders	2.50
6 BBl,BWi,V:Erlik Khan, A:Defenders	2.50
7 V:Nightmare,A:Defenders	2.50
8 BBl,BWi,V:Kaluu	2.50
9 BBl,BWi,A:Dazzler,I:Mr.Jip, V:Kaluu	2.50
10 BBl,BWi,RCa,A:Black Cat, V:Mr.Jip,Kaluu	2.50
11 RCa,BWi,V:Mr.Jip,Kaluu	2.50
12 WPo,BWi,A:Punisher,V:Mr.Jip	2.50
13 JBr,BWi,RCa,Punisher, Power Pack	2.50
14 JBr,BWi,RCa,Punisher,P.Pack	2.50
15 RCa,BMc,A:Mayhem	2.50
16 RCa,BWi,V:Mr.Jip	2.50
17 RCa,BWi,V:Night	2.50
18 RCa,KN,A:X-Factor,V:Night	2.50
19 MMi(c),EL,TA,RCa,A:Thing	2.50

STRANGE TALES
June, 1998

1 JMD,PJe,LSh,Man-Thing, 64-pg.	5.00
2A JMD,PJe,LSh,Man-Thing, Werewolf, 64-pg.	5.00
2B variant cover	5.00
3 JMD,PJe,NA(c),Man-Thing, Werewolf, 64-pg.	5.00
4 JMD,PJe,LSh,F:Man-Thing final issue	5.00

STRANGE TALES: DARK CORNERS
March, 1998

1-shot JEs, three stories, 48-pg.	4.00

STRANGE TALES OF THE UNUSUAL
Dec., 1955—Aug., 1957

1 JMn(c),BP,DH,JR,Man Lost	650.00
2 BEv,Man Afraid	400.00
3 AW,The Invaders	400.00
4 The Long Wait	275.00
5 RC,SD,The Threat	300.00
6 BEv	275.00
7 JK,JO	275.00
8	275.00
9 BEv(c),BK	300.00
10 GM,AT	275.00
11 BEv(c),Aug., 1957	275.00

STRANGE WORLDS
Dec., 1958

1 JK,SD,Flying Saucer	1,300.00
2 SD	750.00
3 JK	600.00
4 AW	550.00
5 SD	450.00

STRAWBERRY SHORTCAKE
Star, June, 1985—April, 1986

1	3.00
2 thru 7	@3.00

STRAY TOASTERS
Epic, Jan., 1988

1 BSz	5.00
2 BSz	4.50
3 and 4 BSz	@4.00

STRIKEFORCE MORITURI
Dec., 1986

1 BA,SW,WPo(1st pencils-3 pages),I:Blackwatch	3.00
2 BA,SW,V:The Horde	2.50
3 BA,SW,V:The Horde	2.50

4 BA,SW,WPo,V:The Horde 2.50
5 BA,SW,V:The Horde 2.50
6 BA,SW,V:The Horde 2.50
7 BA,SW,V:The Horde 2.50
8 BA,SW,V:The Horde 2.50
9 BA,SW,V:THe Horde 2.50
10 WPo(1st pencils-full story),
    SW,R:Black Watch,O:Horde . . . 3.00
11 BA,SW,V:The Horde 2.50
12 BA,SW,D:Jelene 2.50
13 BA,SW,Old vs. NewTeam 2.50
14 BA,AW,V:The Horde 2.50
15 BA,AW,V:The Horde 2.50
16 WPo,SW,V:The Horde 2.50
17 WPo(c),SW,V:The Horde 2.50
18 BA,SW,V:Hammersmith 2.50
19 BA,SW,V:THe Horde,D:Pilar. . . . 2.50
20 BA,SW,V:The Horde 2.50
21 MMi(c),TD(i),V:The Horde. 2.50
22 TD(i),V:The Horde. 2.50
23 MBa,VM,V:The Horde 2.50
24 VM(i),I:Vax,V:The Horde 2.50
25 TD(i),V:The Horde. 3.00
26 MBa,VM,V:The Horde 3.00
27 MBa,VM,O:Morituri Master 3.00
28 MBa,V:The Tiger. 3.00
29 MBa,V:Zakir Shastri 3.00
30 MBa,V:Andre Lamont,The Wind . 3.00
31 MBa(c),V:The Wind,last issue . . 3.00

STRONG GUY REBORN
Spec. TDz,ASm,ATi (1997) 3.00

STRYFE'S STRIKE FILE
1 LSn,NKu,GCa,BP,C:Siena
    Blaze,Holocaust (1993). 4.00
1a 2nd printing 2.50

SUB-MARINER
May, 1968
1 JB,O:Sub-Mariner 400.00
2 JB,A:Triton 150.00
3 JB,A:Triton 100.00
4 JB,V:Attuma. 100.00
5 JB,I&O:Tiger Shark 100.00
6 JB,DA,V:Tiger Shark 125.00
7 JB,I:Ikthon 100.00
8 JB,V:Thing 135.00
9 MSe,DA,A:Lady Dorma 100.00
10 GC,DA,O:Lemuria. 100.00
11 GC,V:Capt.Barracuda 60.00
12 MSe,I:Lyna 60.00
13 MSe,JS,A:Lady Dorma 60.00

Sub-Mariner #40
© Marvel Entertainment Group

14 MSe,V:Fake Human Torch 75.00
15 MSe,V:Dragon Man 60.00
16 MSe,I:Nekaret,Thakos 65.00
17 MSe,I:Stalker,Kormok 60.00
18 MSe,A:Triton 35.00
19 MSe,I:Stingray 35.00
20 JB,V:Dr.Doom 35.00
21 MSe,D:Lord Seth 35.00
22 MSe,A:Dr.Strange 35.00
23 MSe,I:Orka 35.00
24 JB,JM,V:Tiger Shark 35.00
25 SB,JM,O:Atlantis. 30.00
26 SB,A:Red Raven. 30.00
27 SB,I:Commander Kraken 30.00
28 SB,V:Brutivae 30.00
29 SB,V:Hercules. 25.00
30 SB,A:Captain Marvel 28.00
31 SB,A:Triton 25.00
32 SB,JM,I&O:Llyra 28.00
33 SB,JM,I:Namora 30.00
34 SB,JM,AK,1st Defenders 125.00
35 SB,JM,A:Silver Surfer. 100.00
36 BWr,SB,W:Lady Dorma 35.00
37 RA,D:Lady Dorma. 35.00
38 RA,JSe,O:Rec,I:Thakorr,Fen . . 35.00
39 RA,JM,V:Llyra 35.00
40 GC,I:Turalla,A:Spidey 25.00
41 GT,V:Rock 22.00
42 GT,JM,V:House Named Death . 22.00
43 GC,V:Tunal,king-sz. 30.00
44 MSe,JM,V:Human Torch 25.00
45 MSe,JM,V:Tiger Shark 25.00
46 GC,D:Namor's Father. 20.00
47 GC,A:Stingray,V:Dr.Doom 20.00
48 GC,V:Dr.Doom 20.00
49 GC,V:Dr.Doom 20.00
50 BEv,I:Namorita 22.00
51 BEv,O:Namorita,C:Namora. . . . 20.00
52 GK,V:Sunfire 20.00
53 BEv,V:Sunfire 18.00
54 BEv,AW,V:Sunfire,I:Lorvex 18.00
55 BEv,V:Torg 18.00
56 DA,I:Coral 18.00
57 BEv,I:Venus. 18.00
58 BEv,I:Tamara 18.00
59 BEv,V:Tamara,A:Thor 25.00
60 BEv,V:Tamara 15.00
61 BEv,JM,V:Dr.Hydro 15.00
62 HC,JSt,I:Tales of Atlantis. 15.00
63 HC,JSt,V:Dr.Hydro,I:Arkus 15.00
64 HC,JSe,I:Maddox 15.00
65 DH,DP,V:She-Devil,inc.BEv
    Eulogy pin-up 15.00
66 DH,V:Orka,I:Raman 15.00
67 DH,A:FF,V:Triton,N:Namor
    I&O:Force 15.00
68 DH,O:Force. 15.00
69 GT,V:Spider-Man. 18.00
70 GT,I:Piranha 15.00
71 GT,V:Piranha. 15.00
72 DA,V:Slime/Thing 15.00
Spec.#1 rep. Tales to Astonish
    #70-#73 . . . . 30.00
Spec.#2 rep. Tales to Astonish
    #74-#76 . . . . 25.00

[Limited Series]
1 RB,BMc,Namor's Birth. 2.50
2 RB,BMc,Namor Kills Humans . . 2.50
3 RB,BMc,V:Surface Dwellers . . . 2.50
4 RB,BMc,V:Human Torch 2.50
5 RB,BMc,A:Invaders 2.50
6 RB,BMc,V:Destiny 2.50
7 RB,BMc,A:Fantastic Four 2.50
8 RB,BMc,A:Hulk,Avengers 2.50
9 RB,BMc,A:X-Men,Magneto 2.50
10 RB,BMc,V:Thing 2.50
11 RB,BMc,A:Namorita,Defenders . 2.50
12 RB,BMc,A:Dr.Doom,
    Alpha Flight 2.50

Saga of the Sub-Mariner #7
© Marvel Entertainment Group

(SAGA OF THE) SUB-MARINER
[Mini-Series] Nov., 1988
1 RB,BMc,Namor's Birth. 3.00
2 RB,BMc,Namor Kills Humans . . 3.00
3 RB,BMc,V:Surface Dwellers . . . 3.00
4 RB,BMc,V:Human Torch 3.00
5 RB,BMc,A:Invaders 3.00
6 RB,BMc,V:Destiny 3.00
7 RB,BMc,A:Fantastic Four 3.00
8 RB,BMc,A:Hulk,Avengers 3.00
9 RB,BMc,A:X-Men,Magneto 3.50
10 RB,BMc,V:Thing 3.00
11 RB,BMc,A:Namorita,Defenders . 3.00
12 RB,BMc,A:Dr.Doom,Alp.Flight . . 3.00

SUB-MARINER COMICS
Marvel Timely, Spring, 1941
1 ASh(c),BEv,PGv,B:Sub-
    Mariner, The Angel 65,000.00
2 ASh(c),BEv,Nazi
    Submarine (c) 10,000.00
3 ASh(c),BEv,Churchill. 9,500.00
4 ASh(c),BEv,BW 6,500.00
5 V:Axis Powers. 5,000.00
6 ASh(c),Panama Canal 4,500.00
7 ASm&FrG(c). 4,500.00
8 ASh(c),PGv 4,500.00
9 ASh(c),BW,Flag(c) 4,500.00
10 ASh(c),GS 4,500.00
11 ASh(c),Dragon(c) 4,500.00
12 ASh(c) 3,500.00
13 ASh(c),Bondage(c). 3,500.00
14 ASh(c) 3,500.00
15 ASh(c),V:Japs 3,500.00
16 ASh(c),CI,ASm,GS. 2,500.00
17 ASh(c),V:Japs 2,500.00
18 ASh(c),ASm 2,500.00
19 . . . . 2,500.00
20 ASh(c),V:Crooks 2,500.00
21 SSh(c),BEv,Last Angel. . . . 2,200.00
22 SSh(c),BEv,A:Young Allies. . 2,200.00
23 SSh(c),BEv,Human Torch . . 2,200.00
24 MSy(c),BEv,A:Namora,
    bondage cover 2,200.00
25 MSy(c),HK,B:The Blonde
    Phantom, A:Namora,
    bondage(c). 2,400.00
26 BEv,SSh,A:Namora 2,000.00
27 DRi(c),BEv,A:Namora 2,000.00
28 DRi(c),BEv,A:Namora 2,000.00
29 BEv,SSh,A:Namora,Human
    Torch. 2,000.00

MARVEL

30 DRi(c),BEv,Slaves Under
  the Sea 2,000.00
31 BEv,The Man Who Grew,
  A:Capt. America,E:Blonde
  Phantom 2,000.00
32 BEv,O:Sub-Mariner 2,700.00
33 BEv,O:Sub-Mariner,A:Human
  Torch,B:Namora 2,200.00
34 BEv,A:Human Torch,bondage
  cover 2,000.00
35 BEv,A:Human Torch 2,000.00
36 BEv,Hidden World 2,000.00
37 JMn(c),BEv 2,000.00
38 SSh(c),BEv,JMn,
  O:Sub-Mariner 2,300.00
39 JMn(c),BEv,Commie
  Frogman 2,000.00
40 JMn(c),BEv,Secret Tunnel . . 2,000.00
41 JMn(c),BEv,A:Namora 2,000.00
42 BEv,Oct., 1955 . . . . 2,400.00

SUB-MARINER
June, 2007
1 (of 6) Revolution 3.00
2 thru 6 . . . . @3.00

SUB-MARINER:
THE DEPTHS
Sept., 2008
1 (of 4) PrM(s) 4.00
2 thru 3 . . . . @4.00

SUBURBAN JERSEY
NINJA SHE-DEVILS
1 I:Ninja She-Devils 2.50

SUNFIRE & BIG HERO 6
July, 1998
1 (of 3) SLo,from Alpha Flight 2.50
2 SLo,V:Everwraith 2.50
3 SLO,conclusion 2.50

SUN GIRL
Marvel Comics, 1948
1 Miss America 2,500.00
2 Blonde Phantom 1,700.00
3 . . . . 1,700.00

SUPERNATURALS
Oct., 1998
1 (of 4) BnP,JBa(c),F:Brother Voodoo,
  V:Jack O'Lantern, with mask . . . 4.00
1a signed 30.00
2 BnP,JBa(c), with mask 4.00
3 BnP,JBa(c), with mask 4.00
4 BnP,JBa(c), with mask, concl. . . . 4.00

SUPERNATURAL
THRILLERS
Dec., 1972
1 JSo(c),JSe,FrG,IT! 50.00
2 VM,DA,The Invisible Man 30.00
3 GK,The Valley of the Worm . . . 30.00
4 Dr. Jekyll and Mr. Hyde 30.00
5 RB,The Living Mummy 75.00
6 GT,JA,The Headless Ho.seman 40.00
7 VM,B:The Living Mummy,
  Back From The Tomb 40.00
8 VM,He Stalks Two Worlds 40.00
9 GK/AM(c),VM,DA,Pyramid of
  the Watery Doom 40.00
10 VM,A Choice of Dooms 40.00
11 VM,When Strikes the ASP 40.00
12 VM,KJ,The War That Shook
  the World 40.00
13 VM,DGr,The Tomb of the
  Stalking Dead 40.00

Supernatural Thrillers #8
© *Marvel Entertainment Group*

14 VM,AMc,All These Deadly
  Pawns 40.00
15 TS, E:The Living Mummy,Night
  of Armageddon, Oct.,1975 . . . 40.00

SUPER RABBIT
Marvel Timely, 1943
1 Hitler 1,200.00
2 . . . . 500.00
3 . . . . 350.00
4 . . . . 350.00
5 . . . . 350.00
6 Origin of Super Rabbit 325.00
7 . . . . 225.00
8 . . . . 225.00
9 . . . . 225.00
10 . . . . 225.00
11 HK,Hey Look 250.00
12 . . . . 250.00
13 . . . . 250.00
14 . . . . 250.00

SUPER SOLDIERS
Marvel UK, 1993
1 I:Super Soldier,A:USAgent 2.75
2 A:USAgent 2.50
3 A:USAgent 2.50
4 A:USAgent,Avengers 2.50
5 A:Captain America,AWC 2.50
6 O:Super Soldiers 2.50
7 in Savage Land 2.50

SUPER-VILLAIN
CLASSICS
May, 1983
1 O:Galactus 6.00

SUPER-VILLAIN
TEAM-UP
Aug., 1975
1 GT/BEv(c),B:Dr.Doom/Sub-
  Mariner,A:Attuma,Tiger Shark 50.00
2 SB,A:Tiger Shark, Attuma 20.00
3 EH(c),JA,V:Attuma 20.00
4 HT,JM,Dr.Doom vs. Namor . . . 20.00
5 RB/JSt(c),HT,DP,A:Fantastic
  Four,I:Shroud 20.00
6 HT,JA,A:Shroud,Fantastic Four . 18.00
7 RB/KJ(c),HT,O:Shroud 18.00
8 KG,V:Ringmaster 18.00
9 ST,A:Avengers,Iron Man 18.00

10 BH,DP,A:Capt.America,
  V:Attuma,Red Skull 18.00
11 DC/JSt(c),BH,DP,B:Dr. Doom,
  Red Skull,A:Capt. America . . . 18.00
12 DC/AM(c),BH,DP,Dr.Doom vs.
  Red Skull 18.00
13 KG,DP,Namor vs. Krang 18.00
14 JBy/TA(c),BH,DP,V:Magneto,
  x-over with Champions #15 . . . 18.00
15 GT,ME,A:Red Skull 18.00
16 CI,A:Dr. Doom 18.00
17 KP(c),Red Skull Vs.Hatemonger
  June, 1976 . . . . 18.00
G-Size#1 F:Namor, Dr.Doom 18.00
G-Size#2 F:Namor, Dr.Doom 18.00

SUPER-VILLAIN TEAM-
UP/M.O.D.O.K.'S 11
July, 2007
1 (of 5) 3.00
2 thru 5 . . . . @3.00

SUPREME POWER
Marvel Max, July, 2003
1 MSz(s),GFr 7.00
1a special edition, JQ(c) 10.00
2 MSz(s),GFr 4.00
3 MSz(s),GFr 4.00
4 thru 10 MSz(s),GFr . . . . @3.00
11 thru 18 MSz(s),GFr . . . . @3.00

SUPREME POWER:
HYPERION
Sept., 2005
1 (of 5) MSz(s),DJu 3.00
2 DJu,MD2,Hunting the Alien 3.00
3 thru 5 . . . . @3.00

SUPREME POWER:
NIGHTHAWK
Sept., 2005
1 SDi,F:Kyle Richmond 3.00
2 SDi,put on a Happy Face 3.00
3 thru 6 . . . . @3.00

SUSPENSE
Marvel Atlas, Dec., 1949
1 BP,Ph(c),Sidney Greenstreet/
  Peter Lorne (Maltese Falcon) 900.00
2 Ph(c),Dennis O'Keefe/Gale
  Storm (Abandoned) 450.00
3 B:Horror stories,The Black
  Pit 550.00
4 Thing In Black 350.00
5 BEv,GT,RH,BK,DBr,
  Hangman's House 400.00
6 BEv,GT,PMo,RH,Madness
  of Scott Mannion 400.00
7 DBr,GT,DR,Murder 350.00
8 GC,DRi,RH,Don't Open
  the Door 350.00
9 GC,DRi,Back From The Dead . 350.00
10 JMn(c),WIP,RH,Trapped
  In Time 350.00
11 MSy,The Suitcase 325.00
12 GT,Dark Road 325.00
13 JMn(c),Strange Man,
  bondage cover 325.00
14 RH,Death And Doctor Parker . 450.00
15 JMn(c),OW,The Machine 325.00
16 OW,Horror Backstage 325.00
17 Night Of Terror 325.00
18 BK,The Cozy Coffin 350.00
19 BEv,RH 325.00
20 . . . . 300.00
21 BEv(c) 300.00
22 BEv(c),BK, OW 300.00
23 BEv 300.00

24 RH,GT. 350.00
25 I Died At Midnight 400.00
26 BEv(c). 275.00
27 DBr 300.00
28 BEv 300.00
29 JMn,BF,JRo,April, 1953 . . . . . 300.00

SWORDS OF THE SWASHBUCKLERS
Epic, 1985–87
1 JG,Adult theme 3.00
2 thru 7 JG . . . . @2.50
8 thru 12, June, 1987 . . . . @2.50

TALE OF THE MARINES
See: DEVIL-DOG DUGAN

TALES OF ASGARD
Oct., 1968
1 . . . . 75.00
Vol.2 #1 Feb,1984. . . . . 6.00

TALES OF G.I. JOE
Jan., 1988
1 reprints,#1 . . . . 3.00
2 thru 7 reprints . . . . @2.50

TALES OF JUSTICE
See: JUSTICE COMICS

TALES OF THE AGE OF APOCALYPSE
1996
1-shot SLo,JoB,Age of Apocalypse
stories 5.00
GN, rep. 6.00

TALES OF THE AGE OF APOCALYPSE: SINISTER BLOODLINE
Dec., 1997
GN JFM,SEp, 48-pg. bookshelf. . . . 6.00

TALES OF THE MARVELS: BLOCKBUSTER
Fully painted (1995). 6.00

TALES OF THE MARVELS: INNER DEMONS
Fully painted, 48-pg. (1996). 6.00

TALES OF THE MARVELS: WONDER YEARS
1 & 2 DAb (1995) . . . . @5.00

TALES OF SUSPENSE
Jan., 1959
1 AW,DH,JB,SD,JK 3,300.00
2 SD,JK,RH,Robot. 1,200.00
3 SD,JK,JB(c),Flying Saucer . . 1,200.00
4 AW,JK,BEv,SD 1,000.00
5 JK,SD,JF 700.00
6 SD,JK. 700.00
7 SD,JK, ... 750.00
8 SD,BEv,JK,Lava Man 700.00
9 SD,JK,TF,Iron man type 750.00
10 SD,RH,JK 700.00
11 SD,JK 600.00
12 RC,SD,JK 600.00
13 SK,JK,Elektro 600.00
14 SD,JK,Colossus (1) 700.00
15 SD,JK 600.00
16 JK,Metallo (1) 650.00
17 JK 550.00
18 JK 550.00

Tales of Suspense #1
© Marvel Entertainment Group

19 JK 550.00
20 JK,Colossus (2) 550.00
21 JK/DAy(c),SD,This Is Klagg . . 400.00
22 JK/DAy(c),SD,Beware
Of Bruttu 400.00
23 JK,DAy,SD,The Creature
in the Black Bog 400.00
24 JK,DAy,SD,Insect Man 400.00
25 JK,DAy,SD,The Death of
Monstrollo 400.00
26 JK,DAy,SD,The Thing That
Crawled By Night. 350.00
27 JK,DAy,SD,When Oog Lives
Again 350.00
28 JK,DAy,SD,Back From
the Dead 350.00
29 JK,DAy,SD,DH,The Martian
Who Stole A City 350.00
30 JK,DAy,SD,DH,The Haunted
Roller Coaster 350.00
31 JK,DAy,SD,DH,The Monster
in the Iron Mask. 375.00
32 JK,DAy,SD,DH,The Man in
the Bee-Hive 600.00
33 JK,DAy,SD,DH,Chamber of
Fear. 350.00
34 JK,DAy,SD,DH,Inside The
Blue Glass Bottle. 350.00
35 JK,DAy,SD,DH,The Challenge
of Zarkorr. 400.00
36 SD,Meet Mr. Meek 350.00
37 DH,SD,Hagg 350.00
38 JDa,The Teenager Who Ruled
the World 350.00
39 JK,O&I:Iron Man 14,000.00
40 JK,C:Iron Man 3,500.00
41 JK,A:Iron Man,V:Dr.Strange. 2,200.00
42 DH,SD,I:Red Pharoah 1,200.00
43 JK,DH,I:Kala,A:Iron Man . . . 1,200.00
44 DH,SD,V:Mad Pharoah 1,200.00
45 DH,V:Jack Frost. 1,200.00
46 DH,CR,I:Crimson Dynamo . . 700.00
47 SD,V:Melter. 700.00
48 SD,N:Iron Man 800.00
49 SD,A:Angel 1,400.00
50 DH,I:Mandarin. 550.00
51 DH,I:Scarecrow. 450.00
52 DH,I:Black Widow. 650.00
53 DH,O:Watcher. 450.00
54 DH,V:Mandarin 300.00
55 DH,V:Mandarin 300.00
56 DH,I:Unicorn 300.00
57 DH,I&O:Hawkeye 650.00
58 DH,GT,B:Captain America . . . 700.00

59 DH,1st S.A. Solo Captain
America,I:Jarvis. 700.00
60 DH,JK,V:Assassins 400.00
61 DH,JK,V:Mandarin 250.00
62 DH,JK,O:Mandarin 250.00
63 JK,O:Captain America 500.00
64 DH,JK,A:Black Widow,
Hawkeye 225.00
65 DH,JK,I:Red Skull. 400.00
66 DH,JK,O:Red Skull 400.00
67 DH,JK,V:Adolph Hitler. 150.00
68 DH,JK,V:Red Skull 150.00
69 DH,JK,I:Titanium Man. 150.00
70 DH,JK,GT,V:Titanium Man . . 150.00
71 DH,JK,WW,GT,V:TitaniumMan 125.00
72 DH,JK,GT,V:The Sleeper 125.00
73 JA,JK,GT,A:Black Knight 125.00
74 JA,JK,GT,V:The Sleeper. 125.00
75 JA,JK,I:Batroc,Sharon Carter . 125.00
76 JA,JR,V:Mandarin 125.00
77 JA,JK,JR,V:Ultimo,I:Peggy
Carter. 125.00
78 JA,GC,JK,V:Ultimo 125.00
79 JA,GC,JK,V:Red Skull,
I:Cosmic Cube. 150.00
80 JA,GC,JK,V:Red Skull 160.00
81 JA,GC,JK,V:Red Skull 125.00
82 GC,JK,V:The Adaptoid 125.00
83 GC,JK,V:The Adaptoid 125.00
84 GC,JK,V:Mandarin 125.00
85 GC,JK,V:Batroc. 125.00
86 GC,JK,V:Mandarin 125.00
87 GC,V:Mole Man 125.00
88 GK,JK,GC,V:Power Man. 125.00
89 GK,JK,GC,V:Red Skull 125.00
90 GK,JK,GC,V:Red Skull 125.00
91 GK,GC,JK,V:Crusher 125.00
92 GC,JK,A:Nick Fury 125.00
93 GC,JK,V:Titanium Man 125.00
94 GC,JK,I:Modok 125.00
95 GC,JK,V:Grey Gargoyle,
IR:Captain America 125.00
96 GC,JK,V:Grey Gargoyle 125.00
97 GC,JK,I:Whiplash,
A:Black Panther. 125.00
98 GC,JK,I:Whitney Frost
A:Black Panther. 175.00
99 GC,JK,A:Black Panther 200.00
Marvel Milestone rep. #39 (1993) . . 3.00
Becomes:

CAPTAIN AMERICA

TALES OF SUSPENSE: CAPTAIN AMERICA/ IRON MAN
Dec., 2004
1 Commemorative Edition 3.00

TALES OF THE ZOMBIE
Aug., 1973
(Black & White Magazine)
1 Reprint Menace #5,O:Zombie . 60.00
2 GC,GT 50.00
3 . . . . 50.00
4 Live and Let Die. 50.00
5 BH 50.00
6 . . . . 50.00
7 thru 9 AA . . . . @50.00
10 March, 1975 . . . . 50.00

TALES TO ASTONISH
Marvel Atlas, Jan., 1959
1 JDa,Ninth Wonder of the
World 3,500.00
2 SD,Capture A Martian. 1,400.00
3 SD,JK,The Giant From
Outer Space 1,000.00

MARVEL

4 SD,JK,The Day The
  Martians Struck. 1,000.00
5 SD,AW,The Things on
  Easter Island 1,000.00
6 SD,JK,Invasion of the
  Stone Men 750.00
7 SD,JK,The Thing on Bald
  Mountain 750.00
8 DAy,SD,JK,Mmmex, King of
  the Mummies. 750.00
9 DAy,JK(c),SD,Droom, the
  Living Lizard 750.00
10 DAy,JK,SD,Titano 750.00
11 DAy,JK,SD,Monstrom, the Dweller
  in the Black Swamp. 600.00
12 JK/DAy(c),SD,Gorgilla 600.00
13 JK,SD,Groot, the Monster
  From Planet X 600.00
14 JK,SD,Krang 600.00
15 JK/DAy,The Blip 650.00
16 DAy,JK,SD,Thorr. 600.00
17 JK,SD,Vandoom 600.00
18 DAy,JK,SD,Gorgilla Strikes
  Again 600.00
19 DAy,JK,SD,Rommbu. 600.00
20 JK,SD,X, The Thing
  That Lived 600.00
21 JK,SD,Trull the Inhuman. 600.00
22 JK,SD,The Crawling
  Creature. 450.00
23 JK,SD,Moomba is Here!. 450.00
24 JK,SD,The Abominable
  Snowman. 450.00
25 JK,SD,The Creature From
  Krogarr. 450.00
26 JK,SD,Four-Armed Things . . . 450.00
27 StL(s),SD,JK,I:Ant-Man . . 9,500.00
28 JK,SD,I am the Gorilla Man . . 400.00
29 JK,SD,When the Space
  Beasts Attack. 400.00
30 JK,SD,Thing From the
  Hidden Swamp 400.00
31 JK,SD,The Mummy's Secret. . 400.00
32 JK,SD,Quicksand 400.00
33 JK,SD,Dead Storage. 400.00
34 JK,SD,Monster at Window . . . 400.00
35 StL(s),JK,SD, B:Ant-Man
  (2nd App.). 4,000.00
36 JK,SD,V:Comrade X 1,800.00
37 JK,SD,V:The Protector 900.00
38 JK,SD,Betrayed By the Ants. . 900.00
39 JK,DH,V:Scarlet Beetle. 900.00
40 JK,SD,DH,The Day Ant-Man
  Failed. 900.00
41 DH,St,SD,V:Kulla 700.00
42 DH,JSe,SD,Voice of Doom. . . 700.00
43 DH,SD,Master of Time 700.00
44 JK,SD,I&O:Wasp 1,000.00
45 DH,SD,V:Egghead 400.00
46 DH,SD,I:Cyclops(robot) 400.00
47 DH,SD,V:Trago 400.00
48 DH,SD,I:Porcupine 400.00
49 JK,DH,AM,Ant-Man Becomes
  Giant-Man 500.00
50 JK,SD,I&O:Human Top 300.00
51 JK,V:Human Top 300.00
52 I&O:Black Knight. 300.00
53 DH,V:Porcupine 300.00
54 DH,I:El Toro 250.00
55 V:Human Top 250.00
56 V:The Magician. 250.00
57 A:Spider-Man 600.00
58 V:Colossus(not X-Men one) . . 250.00
59 V:Hulk,Black Knight 600.00
60 SD,B:Hulk,Giant Man 600.00
61 SD,I:Glenn Talbot,
  V:Egghead 250.00
62 I:Leader,N:Wasp 250.00
63 SD,O:Leader(1st full story) . . 250.00
64 SD,V:Leader 300.00
65 BP,DH,SD,N:Giant-Man,. . . . 250.00

66 BP,JK,SD,V:Leader,
  Chameleon 250.00
67 BP,JK,SD,I:Kanga Khan 250.00
68 BP,JK,N:Human Top,V:Leader 250.00
69 BP,JK,V:Human Top,Leader,
  E:Giant-Man 250.00
70 GC,JK,B:Sub-Mariner/Hulk,I:
  Neptune. 275.00
71 GC,JK,V:Leader,I:Vashti 100.00
72 GC,JK,V:Leader 100.00
73 GC,JK,V:Leader,A:Watcher . . 100.00
74 GC,JK,V:Leader,A:Watcher . . 100.00
75 GC,JK,A:Watcher 100.00
76 GC,GK,JK,Atlantis 100.00
77 JK,V:Executioner 100.00
78 BEv,GC,JK,Prince and
  the Puppet. 100.00
79 BEv,GC,JK,Hulk vs.Hercules . 100.00
80 BEv,GC,JK,Moleman vs.
  Tyrannus 100.00
81 BEv,GC,JK,I:Boomerang,Secret
  Empire,Moleman vs.Tyrannus 100.00
82 BEv,GC,JK,V:Iron Man 110.00
83 BEv,JK,V:Boomerang 100.00
84 BEv,GC,JK,Like a Beast
  at Bay 100.00
85 BEv,GC,JB,Missile &
  the Monster 100.00
86 BEv,JB,V:Warlord Krang 100.00
87 BEv,JB,IR:Hulk 100.00
88 BEv,GK,V:Boomerang. 100.00
89 BEv,GK,V:Stranger 100.00
90 JK,GK,BEv,I:Abomination 100.00
91 GK,BEv,DA,V:Abomination . . . 100.00
92 MSe,C:Silver Surfer x-over . . 110.00
93 MSe,Silver Surfer x-over. 150.00
94 BEv,MSe,V:Dragorr,High
  Evolutionary. 100.00
95 BEv,MSe,V:High Evolutionary. 100.00
96 MSe,Skull Island,High Evol. . . 100.00
97 MSe,C:Ka-Zar,X-Men 110.00
98 DA,MSe,I:Legion of the Living
  Lightning,I:Seth 100.00
99 DA,MSe,V:Legion of the Living
  Lighting 100.00
100 MSe,DA,Hulk vs.Sub-Mariner 250.00
101 MSe,GC,V:Loki 125.00
Becomes:

INCREDIBLE HULK

TALES TO ASTONISH
[2nd Series] Dec., 1979
1 JB,rep.Sub-Mariner#1 . . . . 5.00
2 thru 14 JB,rep.Sub-Mariner . . . @3.00

TANGLED WEB
April, 2001
1 GEn,JMC,The Thousand 3.00
2 GEn,JMC,The Thousand 3.00
3 GEn,JMC,V:The Thousand 3.00
4 Severance Package. 3.00
5 PrM,DFg,Flowers for Rhino 3.00
6 PrM,DFg,Flowers/Rhino,pt.2 . . . 3.00
7 Gentlemen's Agreement 3.00
8 Gentlemen's Agreement 3.00
9 LW,Gentlemen's Agreement,pt.3 . 3.00
10 Impact on Kids 3.00
11 Open All Night, 48-pg. 3.50
12 I Was A Teenaged Frog-Man . . . 3.00
13 SeP,Double Shots 3.00
14 The Last Shoot 3.00
15 The Collaborator 3.00
16 F:Tombstone, Kangaroo 3.00
17 Tombstone in jail. 3.00
18 TMK 3.00
19 F:Grizzly & Rhino 3.00
20 J.Jonah Jameson 3.00
21 . . . . 3.00
22 The System. 3.00

Tarzan #2
© Marvel Entertainment Group

TARZAN
June, 1977
1 JB,Edgar Rice Burroughs Adapt. 20.00
2 JB,O:Tarzan 15.00
3 JB,The Alter of the Flaming
  God,I:LA 15.00
4 JB,TD,V:Leopards 15.00
5 JB,TD,Vengeance,A:LA 10.00
6 JB,TD,Rage of Tantor,A:LA . . . 10.00
7 JB,TD,Tarzan Rescues The
  Moon 10.00
8 JB,Battle For The Jewel Of
  Opar. 10.00
9 JB,Histah, the Serpent. 10.00
10 JB,The Deadly Peril of
  Jane Clayton 10.00
11 JB 10.00
12 JB,Fangs of Death 10.00
13 JB,Lion-God 10.00
14 JB,The Fury of Fang and Claw. 10.00
15 JB,Sword of the Slaver. 10.00
16 JB,Death Rides the Jungle
  Winds. 10.00
17 JB,The Entrance to the
  Earths Core 10.00
18 JB,Corsairs of the Earth's Core 10.00
19 Pursuit. 10.00
20 Blood Bond 10.00
21 Dark and Bloody Sky 8.00
22 JM,RN,War In Pellucidar 8.00
23 To the Death 8.00
24 The Jungle Lord Returns 8.00
25 RB(c),V:Poachers 8.00
26 RB(c),Caged. 8.00
27 RB(c),Chaos in the Caberet . . . 8.00
28 A Savage Against A City 8.00
29 Oct., 1979 . . . . 8.00
Ann.#1 JB 7.00
Ann.#2 Drums of the
  Death-Dancers 7.00
Ann.#3 Ant-Men and the
  She-Devils. 7.00

TARZAN OF THE APES
July, 1984
1 and 2 (movie adapt.) . . . . . . @4.00

TASKMASTER
Feb., 2002
1 (of 4) F:Iron Man 3.00
2 crime syndicates 3.00
3 syndicates catch on 3.00
4 concl. 3.00

All comics prices listed are for *Near Mint* condition.

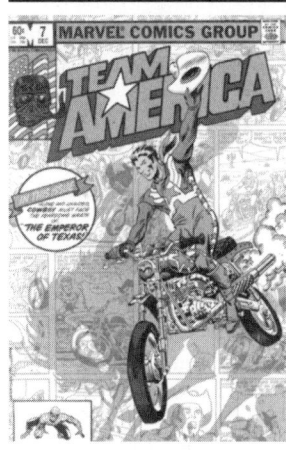

Team America #7
© Marvel Entertainment Group

TEAM AMERICA
June, 1982
1 O:Team America 2.50
2 V:Marauder 2.50
3 LMc,V:Mr.Mayhem. 2.50
4 LMc,V:Arcade Assassins 2.50
5 A:Marauder 2.50
6 A:R.U. Ready 2.50
7 LMc,V:Emperor of Texas 2.50
8 DP,V:Hydra 2.50
9 A:Iron Man 2.50
10 V:Minister Ashe. 2.50
11 A:Marauder,V:Ghost Rider 3.00
12 DP,Marauder unmasked,
    May, 1983 . . . . 2.50

TEAM HELIX
1993
1 A:Wolverine 2.50
2 A:Wolverine 2.50

TEAM X/TEAM 7
1996
1-shot LHa,SEp,MRy 5.00

TEAM X 2000
Dec., 1998
1-shot, 48-page. 3.50

TEEN COMICS
See: ALL WINNERS COMICS

TEENAGE ROMANCE
See: MY ROMANCE

TEK WORLD
See: WILLIAM SHATNER'S TEK WORLD

TERMINATOR 2
Sept., 1991
1 KJ,movie adaption 3.00
2 KJ,movie adaption 3.00
3 KJ,movie adaption 3.00
Terminator II (bookshelf format). . . . 5.00
Terminator II (B&W mag. size). 2.50

TERRARISTS
Epic, 1993–94
1 thru 4 w/card . . . . @2.50
5 thru 7 . . . . @2.50

TERROR INC.
1992–93
1 JZ,I:Hellfire. 3.00
2 JZ,I:Bezeel,Hellfire. 2.50
3 JZ,A:Hellfire 2.50
4 JZ,A:Hellfire,V:Barbados 2.50
5 JZ,V:Hellfire,A:Dr. Strange. 2.50
6 JZ,MT,A:Punisher 2.50
7 JZ,V:Punisher 2.50
8 Christmas issue 2.50
9 JZ,V:Wolverine. 2.50
10 V:Wolverine. 2.50
11 A:Silver Sable,Cage 2.50
12 For Love Nor Money#4,A:Cage,
    Silver Sable 2.50
13 Inf.Crusade,A:Gh.Rider. 2.50

TERROR, INC.
Aug., 2007
1 . . . . 4.00
2 thru 5 Mr. Terror . . . . @4.00

TESSIE THE TYPIST
Marvel Timely, Summer, 1944
1 BW,Doc Rockblock 1,000.00
2 BW,Powerhouse Pepper 500.00
3 Football cover 200.00
4 BW 350.00
5 BW 350.00
6 BW,HK,Hey Look. 350.00
7 BW 350.00
8 BW 350.00
9 BW,HK,Powerhouse Pepper . . 375.00
10 BW,A:Rusty. 375.00
11 BW,A:Rusty. 375.00
12 BW,HK 375.00
13 BW,A:Millie The Model,Rusty . 375.00
14 BW 375.00
15 HK,A:Millie,Rusty 375.00
16 HK. 225.00
17 HK,A:Millie, Rusty. 225.00
18 HK. 225.00
19 Annie Oakley story 150.00
20 . . . . 150.00
21 A:Lana, Millie 150.00
22 . . . . 150.00
23 . . . . 150.00
Becomes:

TINY TESSIE
24 . . . . 100.00
Becomes:

REAL EXPERIENCES
25 Ph(c),Jan., 1950 . . . . 100.00

TEXAS KID
Marvel Atlas, Jan., 1951
1 GT,JMn,O:Texas Kid 300.00
2 JMn 200.00
3 JMn,Man Who Didn't Exist . . . 150.00
4 thru 9 JMn . . . . @150.00
10 JMn,July, 1952 . . . . 150.00

TEX DAWSON, GUN-SLINGER
Jan., 1973
1 JSo(c) 35.00
Becomes:

GUNSLINGER
2 . . . . 25.00
3 June, 1973 . . . . 25.00

TEX MORGAN
Aug., 1948
1 Tex Morgan & Lobo 400.00
2 Boot Hill Welcome For A
    Bad Man 225.00
3 A:Arizona Annie 175.00

---

4 SSh,Trapped in the Outlaw's
    Den, A:Arizona Annie 150.00
5 Valley of Missing Cowboys . . . 150.00
6 Never Say Murder,
    A:Tex Taylor 175.00
7 CCB,Ph(c),Captain Tootsie,
    A:Tex Taylor 225.00
8 Ph(c),Terror Of Rimrock
    Valley, A:Diablo 225.00
9 Ph(c),Death to Tex Taylor,
    Feb., 1950 . . . . 225.00

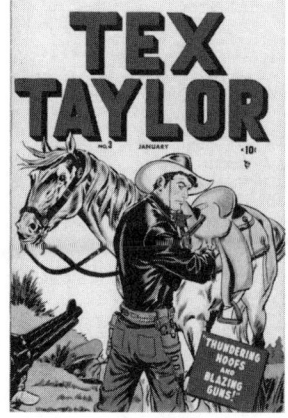

Tex Taylor #3
© Marvel Entertainment Group

TEX TAYLOR
Sept., 1948
1 SSh,Boot Hill Showdown 400.00
2 When Two-Gun Terror Rides
    the Range 200.00
3 SSh,Thundering Hooves and
    Blazing Guns. 150.00
4 Ph(c),Draw or Die Cowpoke . . 200.00
5 Ph(c),The Juggler of Yellow
    Valley,A:Blaze Carson 200.00
6 Ph(c),Mystery of Howling Gap. 200.00
7 Ph(c),Trapped in Time's Lost
    Land,A:Diablo 225.00
8 Ph(c),The Mystery of Devil-
    Tree Plateau,A:Diablo 225.00
9 Ph(c),Guns Along the Border,
    A:Nimo,March, 1950 . . . . . . 225.00

THANOS
Oct., 2003
1 JSn. 3.00
2 JSn,Galactus,Adam Warlock. . . . 3.00
3 JSn,F:Moondragon 3.00
4 JSn,Epiphany,pt.4 . . . . 3.00
5 JSn,Epiphany,pt.5 . . . . 3.00
6 JSn,concl. 3.00
7 KG,RLm 3.00
8 KG,RLm 3.00
9 KG,RLm 3.00
10 KG,RLm,V:The Maker. 3.00
11 KG,RLm. 3.00
12 KG,RLm. 3.00

THANOS QUEST
1990
1 JSn,RLm,V:Elders,
    for Soul Gems 8.00
2 JSn,RLm,O:SoulGems,I: Infinity
    Gauntlet (story cont.in Silver
    Surfer #44) 8.00
1a & 2a 2nd printings . . . . @4.00

MARVEL

THANOS QUEST
Jan., 2000
GN JSn,RLm,96-pg.. . . . . .4.00

THING, THE
July, 1983
1 JBy,O:Thing 3.50
2 JBy,Woman from past 2.50
3 JBy,A:Inhumans. 2.50
4 JBy,A:Lockjaw. 2.50
5 JBy,A:Spider-Man,She-Hulk 2.50
6 JBy,V:Puppet Master 2.50
7 JBy,V:Goody Two Shoes 2.50
8 JBy,V:Egyptian Curse 2.50
9 JBy,F:Alicia Masters 2.50
10 JBy,Secret Wars 2.50
11 JBy,B:Rocky Grimm 2.50
12 JBy,F:Rocky Grimm 2.50
13 JBy,F:Rocky Grimm 2.50
14 F:Rocky Grimm. 2.50
15 F:Rocky Grimm. 2.50
16 F:Rocky Grimm. 2.50
17 F:Rocky Grimm. 2.50
18 F:Rocky Grimm. 2.50
19 F:Rocky Grimm. 2.50
20 F:Rocky Grimm. 2.50
21 V:Ultron. 2.50
22 V:Ultron. 2.50
23 R:Thing to Earth,A:Fant. Four . . 2.50
24 V:Rhino,A:Miracle Man. 2.50
25 V:Shamrock 2.50
26 A:Vance Astro. 2.50
27 I:Sharon Ventura 2.50
28 A:Vance Astro 2.50
29 A:Vance Astro 2.50
30 Secret Wars II,A:Vance Astro . . . 2.50
31 A:Vance Astro 2.50
32 A:Vance Astro 2.50
33 A:Vance Astro,I:New Grapplers . 2.50
34 V:Titania,Sphinx 2.50
35 I:New Ms.Marvel,Power Broker . 2.50
36 Last Issue,A:She-Hulk 2.50

[Mini-Series]
1 rep.Marvel Two-in-One #50. . . . . 2.50
2 rep Marvel Two-in-One,V:GR . . . 2.50
3 rep Marvel Two-in-One #51. . . . . 2.00
4 rep Marvel Two-in-One #43. . . . . 2.00

Nov., 2005
1 Money Changes Every Thing . . . 3.00
2 Fun 'N Games 3.00
3 Fun 'N Games 3.00
4 Paws ...and Fast Forward. 3.00
5 Give Till It Hurts 3.00
6 Friendly Neighborhood Brouhaha 3.00
7 On the Way to the Forum 3.00
8 Poker game 3.00

THING/SHE-HULK
March, 1998
1-shot TDz,V:Dragon Man, 48-pg . . 3.00
1-shot The Long Night, 48-pg. 3.00

THING, THE: FREAKSHOW
June, 2002
1 (of 4) ALa,grumpiest super-hero . 3.00
2 ALa,people are enthralled 3.00
3 ALa,ScK 3.00
4 ALa,ScK,concl. 3.00

THOR, THE MIGHTY
Prev: Journey Into Mystery
March, 1966
126 JK,V:Hercules 400.00
127 JK,I:Pluto,Volla 200.00
128 JK,V:Pluto,A:Hercules. 200.00
129 JK,V:Pluto,I:Ares. 200.00
130 JK,V:Pluto,A:Hercules. 200.00
131 JK,I:Colonizers 200.00

Thor #233
© Marvel Entertainment Group

132 JK,A:Colonizers,I:Ego. 200.00
133 JK,A:Colonizers,A:Ego 200.00
134 JK,I:High Evolutionary,
    Man-Beast. 225.00
135 JK,O:High Evolutionary. 150.00
136 JK,F:Odin 150.00
137 JK,I:Ulik. 150.00
138 JK,V:Ulik,A:Sif. 150.00
139 JK,V:Ulik 150.00
140 JK,V:Growing Man 150.00
141 JK,V:Replicus 100.00
142 JK,V:Super Skrull 100.00
143 JK,BEv,V:Talisman 100.00
144 JK,V:Talisman. 100.00
145 JK,V:Ringmaster. 100.00
146 JK,O:Inhumans Part 1 . . . . . 150.00
147 JK,O:Inhumans Part 2 . . . . . 150.00
148 JK,I:Wrecker,O:Black Bolt. . . 150.00
149 JK,O:Black Bolt,Medusa. . . . 150.00
150 JK,A:Triton 150.00
151 JK,V:Destroyer 125.00
152 JK,V:Destroyer 125.00
153 JK,F:Dr.Blake 125.00
154 JK,I:Mangog 125.00
155 JK,V:Mangog 125.00
156 JK,V:Mangog 125.00
157 JK,D:Mangog 125.00
158 JK,O:Don Blake Part 1 . . . . . 160.00
159 JK,O:Don Blake Part 2 . . . . . 125.00
160 JK,I:Travrians 100.00
161 JK,Shall a God Prevail 100.00
162 JK,O:Galactus. 110.00
163 JK,I:Mutates,A:Pluto 75.00
164 JK,A:Pluto,V:Greek Gods 75.00
165 JK,V:Him/Warlock 150.00
166 JK,V:Him/Warlock 125.00
167 JK,F:Sif 70.00
168 JK,O:Galactus. 100.00
169 JK,O:Galactus. 100.00
170 JK,BEv,V:Thermal Man. 75.00
171 JK,BEv,V:Wrecker. 75.00
172 JK,BEv,V:Ulik 75.00
173 JK,BEv,V:Ulik,Ringmaster. . . . 75.00
174 JK,BEv,V:Crypto-Man 75.00
175 JK,Fall of Asgard,V:Surtur . . . 75.00
176 JK,V:Surtur 75.00
177 JK,I:Igon,V:Surtur 75.00
178 JK,C:Silver Surfer. 90.00
179 JK,MSe,C:Galactus. 75.00
180 NA,JSi,V:Loki 90.00
181 NA,JSi,V:Loki 90.00
182 JB,V:Dr.Doom 50.00
183 JB,V:Dr.Doom 50.00
184 JB,I:The Guardian. 50.00
185 JB,JSt,V:Silent One. 50.00

186 JB,JSt,V:Hela 50.00
187 JB,JSt,V:Odin 50.00
188 JB,JM,F:Odin 50.00
189 JB,JSt,V:Hela 50.00
190 JB,I:Durok. 50.00
191 JB,JSt,V:Loki. 50.00
192 JB 50.00
193 JB,SB,V:Silver Surfer 100.00
194 JB,SB,V:Loki. 50.00
195 JB,JR,V:Mangog 50.00
196 JB,NR,V:Kartag. 50.00
197 JB,V:Mangog 50.00
198 JB,V:Pluto 50.00
199 JB,V:Pluto,Hela. 50.00
200 JB,Ragnarok. 75.00
201 JB,JM,Odin resurrected. 40.00
202 JB,V:Ego-Prime 40.00
203 JB,V:Ego-Prime 40.00
204 JB,JM,Demon from t/Depths. . 40.00
205 JB,V:Mephisto. 40.00
206 JB,V:Absorbing Man 30.00
207 JB,V:Absorbing Man 30.00
208 JB,V:Mercurio 30.00
209 JB,I:Druid 30.00
210 JB,DP,I:Ulla,V:Ulik. 30.00
211 JB,DP,V:Ulik 30.00
212 JB,JSt,V:Sssthgar 30.00
213 JB,DP,I:Gregor 30.00
214 SB,JM,V:Dark Nebula 30.00
215 JB,JM,J:Xorr 30.00
216 JB,JM,V:4D-Man 30.00
217 JB,SB,I:Krista,V:Odin 30.00
218 JB,JM,A:Colonizers. 30.00
219 JB,I:Protector 30.00
220 JB,V:Avalon. 30.00
221 JB,V:Olympus 30.00
222 JB,JSe,A:Hercules,V:Pluto . . . 30.00
223 JB,A:Hercules,V:Pluto. 30.00
224 JB,V:Destroyer 30.00
225 JB,JSi,I:Fire Lord 35.00
226 JB,A:Watcher,Galactus 25.00
227 JB,JSi,V:Ego. 25.00
228 JB,JSi,A:Galactus,D:Ego 25.00
229 JB,JSi,A:Hercules,I:Dweller . . 25.00
230 JB,A:Hercules 25.00
231 JB,DG,V:Armak 25.00
232 JB,JSi,A:Firelord 25.00
233 JB,Asgard Invades Earth 25.00
234 JB,V:Loki. 25.00
235 JB,JSi,I:Possessor
    (Kamo Tharnn) 25.00
236 JB,JSi,V:Absorbing Man 25.00
237 JB,JSi,V:Ulik 25.00
238 JB,JSi,V:Ulik 25.00
239 JB,JSi,V:Ulik 25.00
240 SB,KJ,V:Seth 25.00
241 JB,JGi,I:Geb 25.00
242 JB,JSi,V:Servitor. 25.00
243 JB,JSt,V:Servitor. 25.00
244 JB,JSt,V:Servitor. 25.00
245 JB,JSt,V:Servitor. 25.00
246 JB,JSt,A:Firelord 25.00
247 JB,JSt,A:Firelord 25.00
248 JB,V:Storm Giant 25.00
249 JB,V:Odin 25.00
250 JB,D:Igron,V:Mangog 25.00
251 JB,A:Sif 15.00
252 JB,V:Ulik 15.00
253 JB,I:Trogg 15.00
254 JK,O:Dr.Blake rep. 15.00
255 Stone Men of Saturn rep. 15.00
256 JB,I:Sporr 15.00
257 JK,JB,I:Fee-Lon 15.00
258 JK,JB,V:Grey Gargoyle 15.00
259 JB,A:Spider-Man. 15.00
260 WS,I:Doomsday Star 15.00
261 WS,I:Soul Survivors 15.00
262 WS,Odin Found,I:Odin Force . 15.00
263 WS,V:Loki. 15.00
264 WS,V:Loki 15.00
265 WS,V:Destroyer 15.00
266 WS,Odin Quest. 15.00

267 WS,F:Odin 15.00	
268 WS,V:Damocles 15.00	
269 WS,V:Stilt-Man 15.00	
270 WS,V:Blastaar. 15.00	
271 Avengers,Iron Man x-over. . . . 15.00	
272 JB,Day the Thunder Failed. . . 15.00	
273 JB,V:Midgard Serpent. 15.00	
274 JB,D:Balder,I:Hermod,Hoder . 15.00	
275 JB,V:Loki,I:Sigyn. 15.00	
276 JB,Trial of Loki 15.00	
277 JB,V:Fake Thor. 15.00	
278 JB,V:Fake Thor. 15.00	
279 A:Pluto,V:Ulik 15.00	
280 V:Hyperion 15.00	
281 O:Space Phantom. 10.00	
282 V:Immortus,I:Tempus 10.00	
283 JB,V:Celestials 10.00	
284 JB,V:Gammenon. 10.00	
285 JB,R:Karkas 10.00	
286 KP,KRo,D:Kro,I:Dragona. . . . 10.00	
287 KP,2nd App. & O:Forgotten	
One(Hero) 10.00	
288 KP,V:Forgotten One 10.00	
289 KP,V:Destroyer 10.00	
290 I:Red Bull(Toro Rojo) 10.00	
291 KP,A:Eternals,Zeus. 10.00	
292 KP,V:Odin 10.00	
293 KP,Door to Mind's Eye 10.00	
294 KP,O:Odin & Asgard,I:Frey . . 10.00	
295 KP,I:Fafnir,V:Storm Giants . . . 10.00	
296 KP,D:Siegmund. 10.00	
297 KP,V:Sword of Siegfried 10.00	
298 KP,V:Dragon(Fafnir) 10.00	
299 KP,A:Valkyrie,I:Hagen 10.00	
300 KP,giant,O:Odin & Destroyer,	
Rindgold Ring Quest ends,D:	
Uni-Mind,I:Mother Earth 20.00	
301 KP,O:Mother Earth,V:Apollo . . 10.00	
302 KP,V:Locus 10.00	
303 Whatever Gods There Be. . . . 10.00	
304 KP,V:Wrecker 10.00	
305 KP,R:Gabriel(Air Walker) 10.00	
306 KP,O&V:Firelord,O:Air Walker. 10.00	
307 KP,I:Dream Demon 10.00	
308 KP,V:Snow Giants. 10.00	
309 V:Bomnardiers 10.00	
310 KP,V:Mephisto. 10.00	
311 KP,GD,A:Valkyrie. 10.00	
312 KP,V:Tyr 10.00	
313 KP,Thor Trial 7.00	
314 KP,A:Drax,Moondragon 7.00	
315 KP,O:Bi-Beast 7.00	
316 KP,A:Iron Man,Man Thing,	
V:Man-Beast 7.00	

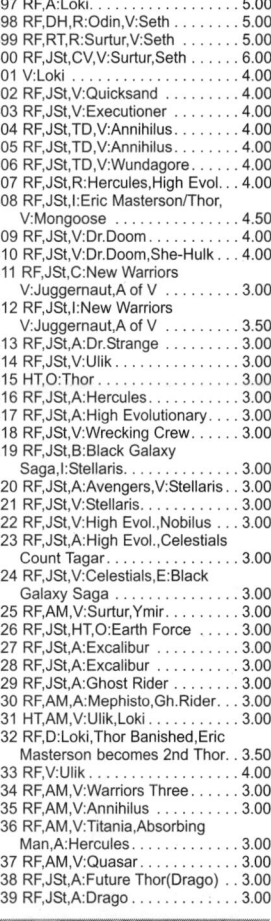

Thor #338
© Marvel Entertainment Group

317 KP,V:Man-Beast 7.00	
318 GK,V:Fafnir 7.00	
319 KP,I&D:Zaniac. 7.00	
320 KP,V:Rimthursar 7.00	
321 I:Menagerie. 7.00	
322 V:Heimdall. 7.00	
323 V:Death 7.00	
324 V:Graviton. 7.00	
325 JM,O:Darkoth,V:Mephisto. . . . 7.00	
326 I:New Scarlet Scarab 7.00	
327 V:Loki & Tyr. 7.00	
328 I:Megatak 7.00	
329 HT,V:Hrungnir 7.00	
330 BH,I:Crusader. 7.00	
331 Threshold of Death 7.00	
332 V:Dracula 7.00	
333 BH,V:Dracula 7.00	
334 Quest For Rune Staff 7.00	
335 V:Possessor 7.00	
336 A:Captain Ultra 7.00	
337 WS,I:Beta Ray Bill,A:Surtur . . 10.00	
338 WS,O:Beta Ray Bill,I:Lorelei. . 9.00	
339 WS,V:Beta Ray Bill 6.00	
340 WS,A:Beta Ray Bill 6.00	
341 WS,V:Fafnir. 6.00	
342 WS,V:Fafnir,I:Eilif 6.00	
343 WS,V:Fafnir. 6.00	
344 WS,Balder vs. Loki,I:Malekith. . 6.00	
345 WS,V:Malekith 6.00	
346 WS,V:Malekith 6.00	
347 WS,V:Malekith,I:Algrim	
(Kurse). 6.00	
348 WS,V:Malekith 6.00	
349 WS,R:Beta Ray Bill,O:Odin,	
I&O:Vili & Ve(Odin's brothers). . 6.00	
350 WS,V:Surtur 6.00	
351 WS,V:Surtur 6.00	
352 WS,V:Surtur 6.00	
353 WS,V:Surtur,D:Odin 6.00	
354 WS,V:Hela 5.00	
355 WS,SB,A:Thor's Great	
Grandfather 5.00	
356 BL,BG,V:Hercules. 5.00	
357 WS,A:Beta Ray Bill 5.00	
358 WS,A:Beta Ray Bill 5.00	
359 WS,V:Loki 5.00	
360 WS,V:Hela 5.00	
361 WS,V:Hela 5.00	
362 WS,V:Hela 5.00	
363 WS,Secret Wars II,V:Kurse. . . 5.00	
364 WS,I:Thunder Frog 5.00	
365 WS,A:Thunder Frog 5.00	
366 WS,A:Thunder Frog 5.00	
367 WS,D:Malekith,A:Kurse 5.00	
368 WS,F:Balder t/Brave,Kurse. . . 5.00	
369 WS,F:Balder the Brave. 5.00	
370 JB,V:Loki. 5.00	
371 SB,I:Justice Peace,V:Zaniac. . . 5.00	
372 SB,V:Justice Peace 5.00	
373 SB,A:X-Factor,(Mut.Mass) . . . 5.00	
374 WS,SB,A:X-Factor,(Mut.Mass)	
A:Sabretooth 6.00	
375 WS,SB,N:Thor(Exoskeleton) . . 4.00	
376 WS,SB,V:Absorbing Man 4.00	
377 WS,SB,N:Thor,A:Ice Man 4.00	
378 WS,SB,V:Frost Giants 4.00	
379 WS,V:Midgard Serpent 4.00	
380 WS,V:Midgard Serpent 4.00	
381 WE,SB,A:Avengers. 4.00	
382 WS,SB,V:Frost Giants,Loki. . . 5.00	
383 BBr,Secret Wars story 4.00	
384 RF,BBr,I:Future Thor(Dargo). . 6.00	
385 EL,V:Hulk 4.00	
386 RF,BBr,I:Leir 4.00	
387 RF,BBr,V:Celestials. 4.00	
388 RF,BBr,V:Celestials. 4.00	
389 RF,BBr,V:Celestials. 4.00	
390 RF,BBr,A:Avengers,V:Seth . . . 4.00	
391 RF,BBr,I:Mongoose,Eric	
Masterson,A:Spider-Man. 6.00	
392 RF,I:Quicksand 5.00	
393 RF,BBr,V:Quicksand,A:DD . . . 5.00	

394 RF,BBr,V:Earth Force 5.00	
395 RF,V:Earth Force 5.00	
396 RF,A:Black Knight. 5.00	
397 RF,A:Loki. 5.00	
398 RF,DH,R:Odin,V:Seth 5.00	
399 RF,RT,R:Surtur,V:Seth 5.00	
400 RF,JSt,CV,V:Surtur,Seth 6.00	
401 V:Loki 4.00	
402 RF,JSt,V:Quicksand 4.00	
403 RF,JSt,V:Executioner 4.00	
404 RF,JSt,TD,V:Annihilus. 4.00	
405 RF,JSt,TD,V:Annihilus. 4.00	
406 RF,JSt,TD,V:Wundagore 4.00	
407 RF,JSt,R:Hercules,High Evol. . . 4.00	
408 RF,JSt,I:Eric Masterson/Thor,	
V:Mongoose 4.50	
409 RF,JSt,V:Dr.Doom 4.00	
410 RF,JSt,V:Dr.Doom,She-Hulk . . 4.00	
411 RF,JSt,C:New Warriors	
V:Juggernaut,A of V 3.00	
412 RF,JSt,I:New Warriors	
V:Juggernaut,A of V 3.50	
413 RF,JSt,A:Dr.Strange 3.00	
414 RF,JSt,V:Ulik 3.00	
415 HT,O:Thor 3.00	
416 RF,JSt,A:Hercules. 3.00	
417 RF,JSt,A:High Evolutionary. . . 3.00	
418 RF,JSt,V:Wrecking Crew. 3.00	
419 RF,JSt,B:Black Galaxy	
Saga,I:Stellaris. 3.00	
420 RF,JSt,A:Avengers,V:Stellaris . . 3.00	
421 RF,JSt,V:Stellaris. 3.00	
422 RF,JSt,V:High Evol.,Nobilus . . 3.00	
423 RF,JSt,A:High Evol.,Celestials	
Count Tagar. 3.00	
424 RF,JSt,V:Celestials,E:Black	
Galaxy Saga 3.00	
425 RF,AM,V:Surtur,Ymir. 3.00	
426 RF,JSt,HT,O:Earth Force 3.00	
427 RF,JSt,A:Excalibur 3.00	
428 RF,JSt,A:Excalibur 3.00	
429 RF,JSt,A:Ghost Rider 3.00	
430 RF,AM,A:Mephisto,Gh.Rider. . . 3.00	
431 HT,AM,V:Ulik,Loki 3.00	
432 RF,D:Loki,Thor Banished,Eric	
Masterson becomes 2nd Thor. . 3.50	
433 RF,V:Ulik 4.00	
434 RF,AM,V:Warriors Three 3.00	
435 RF,AM,V:Annihilus 3.00	
436 RF,AM,V:Titania,Absorbing	
Man,A:Hercules. 3.00	
437 RF,AM,V:Quasar. 3.00	
438 RF,JSt,A:Future Thor(Drago) . . 3.00	
439 RF,JSt,A:Drago 3.00	

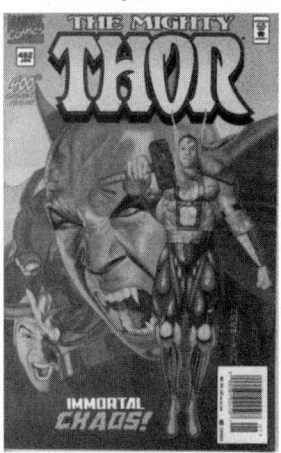

Thor #482
© Marvel Entertainment Group

MARVEL

440 RF,AM,I:Thor Corps 4.00
441 RF,AM,Celestials vs.Ego 4.00
442 RF,AM,Don Blake,Beta Ray
    Bill,Mephisto 3.00
443 RF,AM,A:Dr.Strange,Silver
    Surfer,V:Mephisto 3.00
444 RF,AM,Special X-mas tale 3.00
445 AM,Galactic Storm,pt.7,
    V:Gladiator 3.00
446 AM,Galactic Storm,pt.14,
    A:Avengers 3.00
447 RF,AM,V:Absorbing Man,
    A:Spider-Man. 3.00
448 RF,AM,V:Titania,A:SpM. 3.00
449 RF,AM,V:Ulik. 3.00
450 RF,AM,V:Heimdall,A:Code Blue
    Double-Sized,Gatefold(c),rep.
    Journey Into Mystery#87. . . . . . 3.00
451 RF,AM,I:Bloodaxe 3.00
452 RF,AM,V:Bloodaxe 3.00
453 RF,AM,V:Mephisto 3.00
454 RF,AM,V:Mephisto,Loki,
    Karnilla. 3.00
455 AM(i),V:Loki,Karnilla,R:Odin,
    A:Dr.Strange 3.00
456 RF,AM,V:Bloodaxe 3.00
457 RF,AM,R:1st Thor 3.00
458 RF,AM,Thor vs. Eric 3.00
459 RF,AM,C&I:Thunderstrike(Eric
    Masterson). 3.00
460 I:New Valkyrie 3.00
461 V:Beta Ray Bill 3.00
462 A:New Valkyrie 3.00
463 Infinity Crusade. 3.00
464 Infinity Crusade,V:Loki 3.00
465 Infinity Crusade. 3.00
466 Infinity Crusade. 3.00
467 Infinity Crusade. 3.00
468 RMz(s),Blood & Thunder#1 . . . 3.00
469 RMz(s),Blood & Thunder#5 . . . 3.00
470 MCW,Blood & Thunder#9 . . . . 3.00
471 MCW,E:Blood & Thunder 3.00
472 B:RTs(s),MCW,I:Godling,C:High
    Evolutionary 3.00
473 MCW,V:Godling,High Evolutionary,
    I&C:Karnivore(Man-Beast) 3.00
474 MCW,C:High Evolutionary 3.00
475 MCW,Foil(c),A:Donald Blake,
    N:Thor 3.50
475a Newsstand ed. 3.00
476 V:Destroyer 3.00
477 V:Destroyer,A:Thunderstrike. . . 3.00
478 V:Norvell Thor 3.00
479 V:Norvell Thor 3.00
480 V:High Evolutionary 3.00
481 V:Grotesk 3.00
482 Don Blake construct 3.00
483 RTs,MCW,V:Loki 3.00
484 Badoy and Soul 3.00
485 V:The Thing 3.00
486 High Evolutionary,Godpack. . . . 3.00
487 V:Kurse 3.00
488 RTs,MCW,Kurse Saga concl. . . 3.00
489 RTs,V:Kurse,A:Hulk. 3.00
490 TDF,after Thunderstrike 3.00
491 N:Thor. 7.50
492 Worldengine's Secrets 5.00
493 Worldengine trigers Ragnarok . 3.00
494 Worldengine saga conclusion. . 3.00
495 BML,Avengers:Timeslide 3.00
496 MD2,BML,A:Capt.America 3.00
497 MD2,BML,Thor Must Die 3.00
498 BML,V:Absorbing Man 3.00
499 MD2,BML 3.00
500 MD2,BML,double size,A:Dr.
    Strange 3.50
501 MD2,BML,I:Red Norvell 3.00
502 MD2,BML,Onslaught tie-in, A:Red
    Norvell, Jane Foster, Hela. 3.00
Becomes:

JOURNEY INTO MYSTERY
[Third Series] Nov., 1996

503 TDF,MD2, The Lost Gods, New
    Norse gods? 2.50
504 TDF,Golden Realm in ruins,
    V:Ulik the Troll 2.50
505 TDF,MD2, V:Wrecker,
    A:Spider-Man. 2.50
506 TDF,MD2, R:Heimdall 2.50
507 TDF,Odin kidnapped 2.50
508 TDF 2.50
509 TDF,Battle for the Future
    of Asgard 2.50
510 TDF,Return of Loki,A:Seth 2.50
511 TDF,EBe,Lost Gods reunited
    with Odin 2.50
512 EBe, Odin vs. Seth 2.50
513 TDF,SB,AM, Odin vs.
    Seth, concl. 2.50
514 BRa,VRu,F:Shang Chi, Master
    of Kung Fu. 2.50
515 BRa,VRu,F:Shang Chi, Master
    of Kung Fu, pt.2. . . . . 2.50
516 BRa,VRu,F:Shang Chi, Master
    of Kung Fu, pt.3. . . . . 2.50
517 SLo,RGr,F:Black Widow 2.50
518 SLo,RGr,F:Black Widow 2.50
519 SLo,RGr,F:Black Widow, concl. 2.50
520 MWn,F:Hannibal King, pt.1. . . . 2.50
521 MWn,F:Hannibal King, pt.2. . . . 2.50
Ann.#2 JK,V:Destroyer 125.00
Ann.#3 JK,rep,Grey Gargoyle. . . . 50.00
Ann.#4 JK,rep,TheLivingPlanet. . . 30.00
Ann.#5 JK,JB,Hercules,O:Odin . . . 30.00
Ann.#6 JK,JB,A:Guardians of the
    Galaxy,V:Korvac 30.00
Ann.#7 WS,Eternals. 25.00
Ann.#8 JB,V:Zeus 25.00
Ann.#9 LMc,Dormammu 25.00
Ann.#10 O:Chthon,Gaea,A:Pluto. . 15.00
Ann.#11 O:Odin 15.00
Ann.#12 BH,I:Vidar(Odin's son). . . 15.00
Ann.#13 JB,V:Mephisto 15.00
Ann.#14 AM,DH,Atlantis Attacks . . . 7.00
Ann.#15 HT,Terminus Factor #3 . . . 5.00
Ann.#16 Korvac Quest,pt.2,
    Guardians of Galaxy 3.00
Ann.#17 Citizen Kang#2 . . . . 3.00
Ann.#18 TGr,I:The Flame,w/card. . . 3.50
Ann.#19 V:Flame 3.00
G-Size.#1 Battles,A:Hercules 14.00
Minus 1 Spec., TDF,EBe,flashback . 2.00
1-shot, Rough Cut, DJu,JR,original
    pencils, b&w 48-pg. 3.00

Journey Into Mystery #510
© *Marvel Entertainment Group*

THOR
May, 1998

1 JR2,KJ,DJu,The hero returns,
    48-pg. 6.00
2A JR2,KJ,DJu,V:Destroyer,A:Hela,
    Marnot 3.50
2B JR2,KJ variant cover. 3.50
3 DJu,JR2,KJ,A:Marnot,V:Sedna . 3.00
4 DJu,JR2,KJ,A:Namor,Sedna . . . 3.00
5 DJu,JR2,KJ,V:Charles Diamond . 3.00
6 DJu,JR2,KJ,V:Hercules 3.00
7 DJu,JR2,KJ,V:Zeus 4.00
8 DJu,JR2,KJ,PeterParker x-over. . 4.00
9 DJu,JB,JOy,War on
    Asgard,prelude 4.00
10 DJu,JR2,KJ,War on Asgard,pt.1 . 4.00
11 DJu,JR2,KJ,War on Asgard,pt.2 . 4.00
12 DJu,JR2,KJ,War on
    Asgard,concl. 48-page 4.00
12a signed 20.00
13 DJu,JR2,KJ,A:Marnot 4.00
14 DJu,Hammer secret 4.00
15 DJu,KJ,JR2(c),A:Warriors 3 . . . . 4.00
16 DJu,KJ,JR2,A:Warriors 3 . . . . . . 3.00
17 DJu,KJ,JR2,Eighth
    Day,pt.1, x-over 5.00
18 DJu,KJ,JR2,V:Enrakt 3.00
19 DJu 3.00
20 DJu,V:Loki. 3.00
21 DJu,JR2,KJ,R:Thanos 5.00
22 DJu,JR2,KJ,V:Thanos. 5.00
23 DJu,JR2,DG,V:Thanos 5.00
24 DJu,JR2,DG,V:Thanos 5.00
25A DJu,JR2,DG,48-pg.,foil(c). 6.00
25B variant (c) 3.00
26 DJu,EL,KJ,V:AbsorbingMan 3.00
27 DJu,EL,KJ,Dr.Jane Foster 5.00
28 DJu,EL,KJ,WarriorsThree 3.00
29 DJu,NKu,SHa,Jagrfelm. 3.00
30 DJu,NKu,SHa,MaxSecurity. 3.00
31 DJu,NKu,SHa,V:Malekith 3.00
32 DJu,NKu,SHa,100-page 4.00
33 DJu,SI,I:new 3.00
34 DJu,NKu,SHa 5.00
35 DJu,NKu,SHa,V:Gladiator,
    48-page 5.00
36 DJu,R:Loki,A:Destroyer 5.00
37 DJu,JSn,AM,A:Watcher 5.00
38 DJu,SI,BWS(c),V:Destroyer 3.00
39 DJu,SI,BWS(c),V:Surtur 3.00
40 DJu,SI,V:Surtur. 4.00
41 DJu,SI,V:Surtur,concl. 3.00
42 DJu,SI,Asgard,Midgard. 3.00
43 DJu,JoB,Thor:King of Asgard . . . 3.00
44 DJu,SI,Odin funeral,'Nuff Said . . 3.00
45 TR,new King in Asgard 3.00
46 DJu,SHa,TR,F:Thor-Girl 3.00
47 DJu,SHa,TR,Enchantress. 3.00
48 DJu,JoB,TP,V:Desak. 3.00
49 DJu,TR,SHa,V:Desak 3.00
50 DJu,TR,SHa,64-pg. 6.00
51 DJu,TR,SHa,F:Spider-Man 3.00
52 DJu,TP 3.00
53 DJu 3.00
54 DJu,TR,SHa 3.00
55 DJu,TR,SHa 3.00
56 DJu,TR, ... 3.00
57 DJu,JoB 3.00
58 DJu,AD,Standoff,pt.1,x-over 3.00
59 CPr(s) 3.00
60 DJu,JoB,Spiral,pt.1 . . . . 3.00
61 DJu,Spiral,pt.2 . . . . 3.00
62 DJu,Spiral,pt.3 . . . . 3.00
63 DJu,Spiral,pt.4 . . . . 3.00
64 DJu,Spiral,pt.5 . . . . 3.00
65 DJu,Spiral,pt.6 . . . . 3.00
66 DJu,Spiral,pt.7 . . . . 3.00
67 DJu,Spiral,concl. 3.00
68 DJu,SEa,The Reigning,prologue 3.00
69 DJu,SEa,The Reigning,pt.1 . . . . 3.00
70 DJu,SEa,The Reigning,pt.2 . . . . 3.00
71 DKi,SEa,The Reigning,pt.3. . . . . 3.00

72 DJu,SEa,The Reigning,pt.4 . . . . 3.00	2 GEn(s),GF,F:Doctor Strange 4.00
73 DJu,SEa,The Reigning,pt.5 . . . . 3.00	3 GEn(s),GF 4.00
74 DJu,SEa,The Reigning,concl. . . . 3.00	4 GEn(s),GF,back in time 4.00
75 DJu,SEa,Gods & Men,pt.1 . . . . 3.00	5 GEn(s),GF,Zombie Vikings 4.00
76 DJu,SEa,Gods & Men,pt.2 . . . . 3.00	
77 DJu,SEa,Gods & Men,pt.3 . . . . 3.00	

3-D ACTION
Marvel Atlas 1954
1 Battle Brady 500.00

78 DJu,SEa,Gods & Men,pt.4 . . . . 3.00	
79 DJu,SEa,Gods & Men,pt.5 . . . . 3.00	
80 F:The Avengers 15.00	

3-D TALES OF THE WEST
Marvel Atlas, 1954
1 . . . . 500.00

81 F:The Avengers 10.00	
82 Avengers Disassembled tie-in . . 7.00	
83 Ragnarok,pt.3 . . . . 7.00	

THREE MUSKETEERS
1 thru 2 movie adapt. 2.50

84 Ragnarok,pt.4 . . . . 6.00	
85 Ragnarok,pt.5 . . . . 9.00	
Ann.1999 DJu,KJ, 48-page 3.50	
Ann.1999 signed 20.00	
Ann.2000, 48-pg. 3.50	
Ann.2001 TG,DJu,48-page 3.50	
Spec.#1 Thor (2000) 3.00	
Spec. rep.#1 & #2 . . . . 6.00	

THUNDERBOLTS
Feb., 1997
1 KBk,MBa,VRu,Post-onslaught new
  team:Citizen V, Meteroite, Techno,
  Songbird, Atlas & Mach-1 . . . . 10.00
1 rep. 3.00
2 KBk,MBa,VRu,V;Mad Thinker . . . 6.00
2a variant cover by MBa&VRu 6.00
2 rep. 4.50
3 KBk,MBa,VRu,Freedom's Plaza . 4.50
4 KBk,MBa,VRu,I:Jolt 4.50
5 KBk,MBa,VRu,V:Elements-Doom 4.50
6 KBk,MBa,VRu,V:Elements-Doom 4.50
7 KBk,MBa,VRu,F:Citizen V 4.00
8 KBk,MBa,VRu,Songbird alone. . . 4.00
9 KBk,MBa,VRu,Black Widow 4.00
10 KBk,MBa,VRu,Identy discovered 4.00
11 KBk,MBa,VRu,V:Citizen V 4.00

THOR
July, 2007
1 MSz(s) 8.00
2 thru 5 MSz(s) . . . . @5.00
2a thru 5a variant (c) . . . . @5.00
6 MSz(s),AAd(c) 5.00
6a variant (c) 4.00
7 MSz(s),pt.1 (of 2). 5.00
7a variant (c) 4.00
8 MSz(s),pt.2 . . . . 5.00
8a variant (c) 4.00
9 thru 12 MSz(s) . . . . @3.00
1-Shot Thor: Ages of Thunder 4.00
Spec. Ages of Thunder-Reign
  of Blood 4.00
1-Shot Thor: The Truth of History . . 4.00
1-Shot Thor: Man of War (2008) . . . 4.00

THOR: BLOOD OATH
Sept., 2005
1 (of 6) Classic Thor 3.00
2 Thor & Warriors 3.00
3 V:Hercules 3.00
4 thru 6 . . . . @3.00

THOR CORPS
[Limited Series]
1 TDF(s),PO,V:Demonstaff. 2.50
2 TDF(s),PO,A:Invaders 2.50
3 TDF(s),PO,A:Spider-Man 2099 . . 2.50
4 TDF(s),PO,last issue 2.50

THOR: GODSTORM
Sept., 2001
1 (of 3) KBk,SR. 3.50
2 KBk,SR,V:Loki. 3.50
3 KBk,SR,V:Loki,concl. 3.50

THOR: SON OF ASGARD
March, 2004
1 (of 6) The Warriors Teen,pt.1 . . . . 3.00
2 The Warriors Teen,pt.2 . . . . 3.00
3 The Warriors Teen,pt.3 . . . . 3.00
4 The Warriors Teen,pt.4 . . . . 3.00
5 The Warriors Teen,pt.5 . . . . 3.00
6 The Warriors Teen,pt.6 . . . . 3.00
7 Enchanted,pt.1. . . . . 3.00
8 Enchanted,pt.2 . . . . 3.00
9 Enchanted,pt.3 . . . . 3.00
10 . . . . 3.00
11 . . . . 3.00
12 Worthy, finale 3.00
Digest,Vol. 1 Warriors Teen 8.00
Digest,Vol. 2 Worthy 8.00

THOR: VIKINGS
Marvel Max, July, 2003
1 GEn(s),GF,Zombie Vikings 5.00

12 KBk,MBa,VRu,A:FF,Avengers . 10.00
13 KBk,MBa,SHa,on trial 3.00
14 KBk,MBa,VRu,V:Citizen V 3.00
15 KBk,MBa,VRu,V:S.H.I.E.L.D. . . 3.00
16 KBk,MBa,SHa,V:Lightningrods . . 3.00
17 KBk,MBa,SHa,V:Graviton 3.00
18 KBk,MBa,SHa,villains again? . . . 3.00
19 KBk,MBa,SHa 3.00
20 KBk,MBa,SHa,V:Masters-Evil . . 3.00
21 KBk,MBa,SHa,F:Songbird 3.00
22 KBk,MBa,SHa,A:Hercules 3.00
23 KBk,MBa,SHa,V:U.S.Agent 3.00
24 KBk,MBa,SHa,R:Citizen V 3.00
25 KBk,MBa,SHa,48-page. 3.50
25a signed 20.00
26 KBk,MBa,SHa,JoC,A:Mach-1 . . 2.50
27 KBk,MBa,SHa,A:Archangel 2.50
28 KBk,MBa,SHa,V:Graviton 2.50
29 KBk,MBa,SHa,V:Graviton 2.50
30 KBk,MBa,SHa,V:Graviton 2.50
31 KBk,MBa,SHa,R:Citizen V 2.50
32 KBk,MBa,SHa,V:Citizen V 2.50
33 KBk,MBa,SHa,F:Jolt 2.50
34 MBa,SHa. 2.50
35 FaN,MBa,SHa. 2.50
36 FaN,MBa,SHa,V:Beetle 2.50
37 FaN,MBa,SHa,A:Hawkeye 2.50
38 FaN,MBa,SHa,V:Citizen V 2.50
39 FaN,MBa,SHa,100-pg. 3.00
40 FaN,MBa,SHa,V:Citizen V 2.50
41 FaN,MBa,Sandman 2.50
42 FaN,MBa,Avengers x-over 2.50
43 FaN,MBa,Avengers x-over 2.50
44 FaN,MBa,Avengers x-over 2.50
45 FaN,MBa,Maximum Security . . . 2.50
46 FaN,MBa,V:Scourge 2.50
47 FaN,MBa,A:Songbird 2.50
48 FaN,MBa,V:Scourge,pt.1 . . . . . 2.50
49 FaN,V:Scourge,face shown 2.50
50 FaN,MBa,48-page. 4.00
51 FaN,AV,rescue mission 2.50
52 FaN,AV,V:Dr.Doom 2.50
53 FaN,AV,F:Charcoal 2.50
54 FaN,AV,F:Fixer 2.50
55 FaN,AV,V:Redeemers 2.50
56 FaN,AV,V:Graviton 2.50
57 FaN,AV,V:Graviton 2.50

Thunderbolts #28
© Marvel Entertainment Group

58 FaN,AV,V:Graviton 2.50
59 FaN,MBa,AV,Songbird,'NuffSaid. 2.50
60 FaN,MBa,AV,Chain Gang 2.50
61 FaN,Heroes Return,pt.2 . . . . 2.50
62 FaN,Heroes Return,pt.3 . . . . 2.50
63 FaN,Hawkeye,Screaming Mimi . . 2.50
64 FaN,F:Zemo 2.50
65 FaN,V:Masters of Evil 2.50
66 FaN,F:Baron Zemo,Jolt 2.50
67 FaN,F:Harrier, Hawkeye 2.50
68 FaN,F:Moonstone,PhantomEagle2.50
69 FaN,AV 2.50
70 FaN, ... 2.50
71 FaN 2.50
72 FaN 2.50
73 Fan,AV 2.50
74 FaN 2.50
75 FaN,48-pg. 3.50
76 Fight club 2.50
77 JAr(s) 2.50
78 JAr(s) 3.00
79 JAr(s) 3.00
80 JAr(s),F:Spider-Man,pt.1. . . . . . 2.50
81 JAr(s),F:Spider-Man,pt.2. . . . . . 2.50
Continued As:

NEW THUNDERBOLTS
Nov., 2004
1 FaN,TG,Zeroes to Heroes,pt.1 . . 3.00
2 FaN,TG,Zeroes to Heroes,pt.2 . . 3.00
3 FaN,TG,Zeroes to Heroes,pt.3 . . 3.00
4 FaN,TG,Enemy of the State,
  Wolverine X-over. 3.00
5 FaN,TG,V:Fathom 5. . . . . 3.00
6 FaN,TG,V:Hydra. 3.00
7 FaN,TG,modern Marvels 3.00
8 FaN,TG,F:Speed Demon,Blizzard 3.00
9 FaN,TG,F:Photon. 3.00
10 FaN,TG,Purple Reign,pt.1. . . . . 3.00
11 FaN,TG,Purple Reign,pt.2. . . . . 3.00
12 FaN,TG,Purple Reign,pt.3. . . . . 3.00
13 FaN,TG,A:New Avengers 3.00
14 FaN,TG,A:New Avengers 3.00
15 FaN,TG,F:Songbird. 3.00
16 FaN,TG,New Squadron Sinister . 3.00
17 FaN,TG,V:Baron Zemo 3.00
18 FaN,TG,R:Moonstone 3.00
Becomes:

THUNDERBOLTS
March, 2006
100 FaN,TG, V:Photon, 104-pg. . . . 4.00
101 FaN,TG, Zemo & Songbird 3.00
102 FaN,TG, V:Speed Demon 3.00
103 FaN,TG, Civil War tie-in 6.00

103a 2nd printing 3.50
104 FaN,TG, Civil War tie-in 4.00
105 FaN,TG, Civil War tie-in 3.00
106 FaN,TG, Supervillain Army 3.00
107 FaN,TG, Supervillain Army 3.00
108 FaN,TG, V:Grandmaster 3.00
109 FaN,TG, Weight of the World . . 3.00
110 MD2,Faith in Monsters, pt.1 . . . 3.00
111 MD2,Faith in Monsters, pt.2 . . . 3.00
112 MD2,Faith in Monsters, pt.3 . . . 3.00
112a variant PFe (c) 3.00
113 MD2,Faith in Monsters, pt.4 . . . 3.00
114 MD2,Faith in Monsters, pt.5 . . . 3.00
115 MD2,Faith in Monsters, pt.6 . . . 3.00
115a variant (c) 3.00
116 WEI,MD2,Caged Angels 3.00
117 WEI,MD2,Caged Angels 3.00
118 . . . . 3.00
119 . . . . 3.00
120 WEI,MD2, ... 3.00
121 WEI,MD2,Green Goblin 3.00
122 Secret Invasion tie-in 3.00
123 Secret Invasion tie-in 3.00
124 Secret Invasion tie-in 3.00
125 Secret Invasion tie-in 3.00
126 Bullseye & Songbird 3.00
Ann. '97 KBk,MBa,TGu,GP,
   O:Thunderbolts, 48-pg. . . . 3.00
Ann.2000 FaN,NBy, 48-pg. 3.50
Spec.#0 Wizard Nov., 1998 . . . . . . 5.00
Spec.First Strikes, rep.#1 & #2 . . . 5.00
Spec #1 Distant Rumblings KBk,
   SEp,Flashback,F:Citizen V . . . 2.50
Spec.Life Sentences (2001). 3.50
Spec. Desperate Measures 3.00
Spec. Breaking Point (2007) 3.00
Spec. International Incident 3.00
Spec. Reason in Madness 3.00

THUNDERBOLTS PRESENTS: ZEMO – BORN BETTER
1 (of 4) FaN,TG 3.00
2 thru 4 FaN,TG . . . . @3.00

THUNDERCATS
Star, Dec., 1985
1 JM,TV tie-in 10.00
1a 2nd printing 7.00
2 thru 10 . . . . @7.00
11 thru 24 . . . . @7.00

THUNDERSTRIKE
1993–95
1 B:TDF(s),RF,Holografx(c),
   V:Bloodaxe,I:Car Jack 3.25
2 RF,V:Juggernaut 2.50
3 RF,I:Sangre 2.50
4 RF,A:Spider-Man,I:Pandora 2.50
5 RF,A:Spider-Man,V:Pandora 2.50
6 RF,I:Blackwulf,Bristle,Schizo,Lord
   Lucian,A:SpM,Code:Blue,Stellaris,
   V:SHIELD,Pandora,C:Tantalus . 2.50
7 KP,V:Tantalus,D:Jackson 2.50
8 RF,I&V:Officer ZERO 2.50
9 RF,V:Bloodaxe 2.50
10 RF,A:Thor 2.50
11 RF,A:Wildstreak. 2.50
12 RF,A:Whyte Out 2.50
13 RF,Inferno 42 . . . . 2.50
13a Double Feature flip book
   with Code Blue #1 . . . . 2.50
14 RF, Inferno 42 . . . . 2.50
14a Double Feature flip book 2.50
15 RF,V:Methisto 2.50
15a Double Feature flip book
   with Code Blue #3 . . . . 2.50
16 . . . . 2.50
17 V:Bloodaxe 2.50
18 V:New Villain 2.50

Thunderstrike #1
© *Marvel Entertainment Group*

19 Shopping Network 2.50
20 A:Black Panther 2.50
21 A:War Machine,V:Loki. 2.50
22 TDF,AM,RF,Mystery of Bloodaxe
   blows open 2.50
23 TDF,A:Avengers 2.50
24 TDF,V:Bloodaxe, final issue 2.50

TIMELY PRESENTS: HUMAN TORCH COMICS
Aug., 1998
1-shot GN. 6.00

TIMESLIP COLLECTION
Sept., 1998
1-shot, 48-page 3.00

TIMESLIP: THE COMING OF THE AVENGERS
Aug., 1998
1-shot GN. 6.00

TIMESPIRITS
Epic, Jan., 1985
1 TY 3.00
2 thru 8 . . . . @2.50

TIMESTRYKE
1 . . . . 2.50
2 . . . . 2.50

TINY TESSIE
See: TESSIE THE TYPIST

TOMB OF DARKNESS
See: BEWARE

TOMB OF DRACULA
April, 1972
1 GC,Night of the Vampire 300.00
2 GC,Who Stole My Coffin? 125.00
3 GC,TP,I:Rachel Van Helsing . . 100.00
4 GC,TP,Bride of Dracula! 100.00
5 GC,TP,To Slay A Vampire 100.00
6 GC,TP,Monster of the Moors . . . 75.00
7 GC,TP,Child is Slayer of
   the Man 75.00
8 GC(p),The Hell-Crawlers 75.00
9 The Fire Cross. 75.00
10 GC,I:Blade Vampire Slayer. . . 350.00

11 GC,TP,Master of the Undead
   Strikes Again! 50.00
12 GC,TP,House that Screams . . . 75.00
13 GC,TP,O:Blade 100.00
14 GC,TP,Vampire has Risen
   from the Grave 50.00
15 GC,TP,Stay Dead 50.00
16 GC,TP,Back from the Grave . . . 50.00
17 GC,TP,A Vampire Rides This
   Train! 50.00
18 GC,TP,A:Werewolf By Night . . . 60.00
19 GC,TP,Snowbound in Hell 50.00
20 GC,TP,Manhunt For A Vampire. . 50.00
21 GC,TP,A:Blade 50.00
22 GC,TP,V:Gorna 30.00
23 GC,TP,Shadow over Haunted
   Castle 30.00
24 GC,TP,I am your Death 35.00
25 GC,TP,Blood Stalkers of Count
   Dracula. 35.00
26 GC,TP,A Vampire Stalks the
   Night 30.00
27 GC,TP,...And the Moon Spews
   Death!. 30.00
28 GC,TP,Five came to Kill a
   Vampire 35.00
29 GC,TP,Vampire goes Mad? . . . 30.00
30 GC,TP,A:Blade 30.00
31 GC,TP,Child of Blood 30.00
32 GC,TP,The Vampire Walks
   Among Us. 30.00
33 GC,TP,Blood on My Hands. . . . 30.00
34 GC,TP,Bloody Showdown. 30.00
35 GC,TP,A:Brother Voodoo 30.00
36 GC,TP,Dracula in America 30.00
37 GC,TP,The Vampire Walks
   Among Us. 30.00
38 GC,TP,Bloodlust for a Dying
   Vampire 30.00
39 GC,TP,Final Death of Dracula . 30.00
40 GC,TP,Triumph of Dr.Sun 30.00
41 GC,TP,A:Blade 30.00
42 GC,TP,V:Dr.Sun 30.00
43 GC,TP,A:NewYear'sNightmare . 75.00
44 GC,TP,A:Dr.Strange 75.00
45 GC,TP,A:Hannibal King 75.00
46 GC,TP,W:Dracula & Domini . . . 20.00
47 GC,TP,Death-Bites 20.00
48 GC,TP,A:Hannibal King 20.00
49 GC,TP,A:Robin Hood,
   Frankenstein's Monster. 20.00
50 GC,TP,A:Silver Surfer. 35.00
51 GC,TP,A:Blade 15.00
52 GC,TP,V:Demon 15.00
53 GC,TP,A:Hannibal King,Blade . 15.00
54 GC,TP,Twas the Night Before
   Christmas 15.00
55 GC,TP,Requiem for a Vampire . 15.00
56 GC,TP,Harold H. Harold 15.00
57 GC,TP,The Forever Man. 15.00
58 GC,TP,A:Blade 35.00
59 GC,TP,The Last Traitor. 15.00
60 GC,TP,The Wrath of Dracula . 15.00
61 GC,TP,Resurrection 20.00
62 GC,TP,What Lurks Beneath . . . 20.00
63 GC,TP,A:Janus 20.00
64 GC,TP,A:Satan 20.00
65 GC,TP,Where No Vampire
   Has Gone Before. 20.00
66 GC,TP,Marked for Death 20.00
67 GC,TP,A:Lilith 20.00
68 GC,TP,Dracula Turns Human . . 20.00
69 GC,TP,Cross of Fire 20.00
70 GC,TP,double size,last issue . . 40.00
Savage Return of Dracula. rep.
   Tomb of Dracula #1,#2 . . . . . . 2.50
Wedding of Dracula. rep.Tomb
   of Dracula #30,#45,#46. . . . . . 2.50
Requiem for Dracula. rep.Tomb
   of Dracula #69,#70 . . . . 2.50

TOMB OF DRACULA
(B&W Mag.) Nov., 1979
1 . . . . 25.00
2 SD 18.00
3 FM 18.00
4 . . . . 15.00
5 . . . . 15.00
6 Sept., 1980 . . . . 15.00

TOMB OF DRACULA
[Mini-Series] Nov., 1991
1 GC,AW,Day of Blood 6.00
2 GC,AW,Dracula in D.C. 5.50
3 GC,AW,A:Blade 5.50
4 GC,AW,D:Dracula 5.50

TOMB OF DRACULA
2004
1 BSz(c) F:Blade. 3.00
2 . . . . 3.00
3 . . . . 3.00
4 Bsz(c). 3.00

TOMORROW KNIGHTS
Epic, June, 1990
1 . . . . 2.50
2 thru 6 . . . . @2.50

TOP DOG
Star, April, 1985
1 . . . . 3.00
2 thru 14, June, 1987 . . . . @3.00

TOR
Epic *Heavy Hitters,* 1993
1 JKu,R:Tor,magazine format 6.25
2 JKu. 6.25
3 JKu,V:The Iduard Ring 6.25

TOUGH KID SQUAD COMICS
Marvel Timely, March, 1942
1 AAv,SSh,O:The Human Top,
Tough Kid Squad,A:The Flying
Flame, V:Doctor Klutch . . 18,000.00

TOWER OF SHADOWS
Sept., 1969
1 JR(c),JSo,JCr,At The Stroke
of Midnight. 150.00

Tough Kid Squad Comics #1
© Marvel Entertainment Group

2 JR(c),DH,DA,NA,The Hungry
One 100.00
3 GC,BWs,GT,Midnight in the
Wax Museum. 100.00
4 DH,Within The Witching Circle . 75.00
5 DA,BWS,WW,Demon That
Stalks Hollywood 75.00
6 WW,SD,Pray For the Man in
the Rat-Hole 75.00
7 BWS,WW,Titano 75.00
8 WW,SD,Demons of
Dragon-Henge 75.00
9 BWr(c),TP,Lovecraft story 75.00
Becomes:

CREATURES ON THE LOOSE
March, 1971
10 BWr,A:King Kull 100.00
11 DAy,rep. Moomba is Here 30.00
12 JK,I Was Captured By Korilla . . 30.00
13 RC,The Creature
From Krogarr 30.00
14 MSe,Dead Storage 30.00
15 SD,Spragg the Living Mountain 30.00
16 GK,BEv,GK,B&O:Gullivar Jones,
Warrior of Mars. 25.00
17 GK,Slaves o/t Spider Swarm . . 25.00
18 RA,The Fury of Phra 25.00
19 WB,JM,GK,Red Barbarian
of Mars 25.00
20 GK(c),GM,SD,The Monster...
And the Maiden 25.00
21 JSo(c),GM,Two Worlds To
Win,E:Gulliver. 25.00
22 JSo(c),SD,VM,B:Thongor,
Warrior of Lost Lemuria 28.00
23 VM,The Man-Monster Strikes . . 12.00
24 VM,Attack of the Lizard-Hawks 12.00
25 VM,GK(c),Wizard of Lemuria . . 12.00
26 VM,Doom of the Serpent Gods 12.00
27 VM,SD,Demons Dwell in the
Crypts of Yamath 12.00
28 SD,The Hordes of Hell 12.00
29 GK(c),Day of the Dragon Wings,
E:Thongor,Warrior of Lemuria . 12.00
30 B:Man-Wolf,Full Moon, Dark
Fear. 30.00
31 GT,The Beast Within. 15.00
32 GT,V:Kraven the Hunter 15.00
33 GK(c),GP,The Name of the
Game is Death 15.00
34 GP,Nightflight to Fear 12.00
35 GK(c),GP 12.00
36 GK(c),GP,Murder by Moonlight. 12.00
37 GP,Sept., 1975 . . . . 12.00

TOXIC AVENGER
March, 1991
1 VM(i),I&O:Toxic Avenger 2.50
2 VM(i) 2.50
3 VM(i),Night of Living H.bodies . . 2.50
4 Legend of Sludgeface 2.50
5 I:Biohazard. 2.50
6 V:Biohazard. 2.50
7 Sewer of Souviaki 2.50
8 Sewer of Souviaki' conc. 2.50
9 Abducted by Aliens 2.50
10 Die,Yuppie Scum,pt.1 . . . . 2.50

TOXIC CRUSADERS
1992
1 F:Toxic Avengers & Crusaders . . 2.50
2 SK(c),V:Custard-Thing. 2.50
3 SK(c),V:Custard-Thing. 2.50
4 V:Giant Mutant Rats 2.50
5 V:Dr.Killemoff. 2.50
6 V:Dr.Killemoff. 2.50
7 F:Yvonne 2.50
8 V:Psycho 2.50

[2nd Series]
1 . . . . 2.50
2 . . . . 2.50

TOXIN
April, 2005
1 (of 6) DaR 3.00
2 Dar,cut to the Chase 3.00
3 The Answer, My Friend 3.00
4 Zero Hour. 3.00
5 Razor Fist 3.00
6 DaR,V:Razor-Fist,concl. 3.00

TRANSFORMERS
[1st Regular Series] Sept., 1984
1 FS,Toy Comic 22.00
2 FS,OptimusPrime V:Megatron . . 13.00
3 FS.A:Spider-Man 11.00
4 MT(c),FS 10.00
5 Transformers Dead? 10.00
6 Autobots vs Decepticons 10.00
7 KB,V:Megatron. 10.00
8 KB,A:Dinobots 10.00
9 MM,A:Circuit Breaker. 10.00
10 Dawn of the Devastator 10.00
11 HT 9.00
12 HT,V:Shockwave. 9.00
13 DP,Return of Megatron 9.00
14 DP,V:Decepticons 9.00
15 DP 9.00
16 KN,A:Bumblebee 9.00
17 DP,I:New Transformers,pt.1 . . . . 9.00
18 DP,I:New Transformers,pt.2 . . . . 9.00
19 DP,I:Omega Supreme 9.00
20 HT,Skid vs.Ravage 9.00
21 DP,I:Aerialbots 9.00
22 DP,I:Stuntacons(Menasor) 9.00
23 DP,Return of Circuit Breaker . . . 9.00
24 DP,D:Optimus Prime. 9.00
25 DP,Decpticons (full story) 9.00
26 DP 9.00
27 DP,V:Head Hunter. 9.00
28 DP 9.00
29 DP,I:Scraplets, Triplechangers . . 9.00
30 DP,V:Scraplets 9.00
31 DP,Humans vs. Decepticons . . . 9.00
32 DP,Autobots for Sale. 9.00
33 DP,Autobots vs.Decepticons. . . . 9.00
34 V:Sky Lynx 9.00
35 JRy,I:U.K.version Transformers . 9.00
36 . . . . 9.00
37 . . . . 9.00
38 . . . . 9.00

Transformers #9
© Marvel Entertainment Group

39	9.00
40 Autobots' New Leader	9.00
41	9.00
42 Return of Optimus Prime	9.00
43 Optimus Prime,Goldbug	9.00
44 FF,Return of Circuit Breaker	9.00
45 V:The Jammers	9.00
46 I:New Transformers	9.00
47 B:Underbase saga,I:Seacons	9.00
48 Optimus Prime/Megatron (past story)	9.00
49 Underbase saga cont.	9.00
50 E:Underbase saga,I:new characters	10.00
51 I:Pretender Decepticon Beasts	10.00
52 I:Mecannibles,pt.1	10.00
53 Mecannibles,pt.2	10.00
54 I:Micromasters	10.00
55 MG	10.00
56 Return of Megatron	10.00
57 Optimus Prime vs.Scraponok	10.00
58 V:Megatron	10.00
59 A:Megatron,D:Ratchet	10.00
60 Battle on Cybertron	11.00
61 O:Transformers	11.00
62 B:Matrix Quest,pt.1	11.00
63	11.00
64 I:The Klud	11.00
65 GSr	15.00
66 E:Matrix Quest,pt.5	15.00
67 V:Unicorn,also Alternative World	15.00
68 I:Neoknights	15.00
69 Fate of Ratchet & Megatron revealed	15.00
70 Megatron/Ratchet fused together	15.00
71 Autobots Surrender to Decepticons	17.00
72 Decepticon Civil War, I:Gravitron	17.00
73 I:Unicron,A:Neoknights	17.00
74 A:Unicron & Brothers of Chaos	17.00
75 V:Thunderwing & Dark Matrix	17.00
76 Aftermath of War	17.00
77 Unholy Alliance	17.00
78 Galvatron vs.Megatron	22.00
79 Decepticons Invade Earth	22.00
80 Return of Optimus Prime,final	35.00

[2nd Regular Series]

1 Split Foil(c),A:Dinobots	3.00
2 A:G.I.Joe,Cobra	2.50
3	2.50

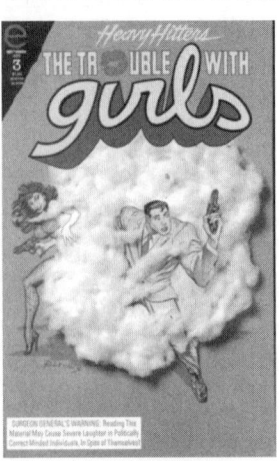

Trouble With Girls #3
© Marvel Entertainment Group

4 MaG,V:Jhiaxus	2.50
5	2.50
6 V:Megatron	2.50
7 V:Darkwing	2.50
8 V:Darkwing	2.50
9	2.50
10 Total War	2.50
11	2.50

TRANSFORMERS COMICS MAGAZINE
1986–88

1 thru 11 Digest-size	@2.50

TRANSFORMERS, THE MOVIE
Dec., 1986–Feb., 1987

1 thru 3 Animated movie adapt.	@2.50

TRANSFORMERS UNIVERSE
Dec., 1986

1 thru 4	@3.00

TRANSMUTATION OF IKE GARUDA
Epic, 1991

1 JSh,I:Ike Garuda	4.00
2 JSh,conclusion	4.00

TROUBLE
Marvel Epic, June, 2003

1 MMr(s),Tyd,Teenage Romance	3.50
2 MMr(s),Tyd,photo (c)	3.00
3 MMr(s),Tyd,consequences	3.00
4 MMr(s),TyD,consequences	3.00
5 MMr(s),TyD,concl.	3.00

TROUBLE WITH GIRLS: NIGHT OF THE LIZARD
Epic *Heavy Hitters,* 1993

1 BBl,AW,R:Lester Girls	2.75
2 BBl,AW,V:Lizard Lady	2.50
3 BBl,AW,V:Lizard Lady	2.50
4 BBl,AW,last issue	2.50

TRUE BELIEVERS
July, 2008

1 (of 5) Payback is a Bitch	3.00
2 PG, Daddy Issues	3.00
3 PG, F:Luke Cage	3.00
4 PG,F:Armadillo & Madam Hydra	3.00
5 PG,F:Iron Man	3.00

TRUE COMPLETE MYSTERY
See: COMPLETE MYSTERY

TRUE LIFE TALES
Marvel Comics, 1949

1 (8) Ph(c)	125.00
2 Ph(c)	125.00

TRUE SECRETS
Marvel Atlas, 1950–56
Previously LOVE DIARY or OUR LOVE, depending on who you believe.

3	175.00
4	100.00
5	100.00
6 BEv	125.00
7	100.00
8 thru 10	@100.00
11 thru 21	@90.00
22 BEv	100.00

23	90.00
24 ViC	100.00
25 thru 28	@90.00
29 thru 39	@75.00
40 Sept., 1956	75.00

TRUE WESTERN
Dec., 1949

1 Ph(c),Billy the Kid	225.00
2 Ph(c),Alan Ladd,Badmen vs. Lawmen	250.00

Becomes:

TRUE ADVENTURES

3 BP,MSy,Boss of Black Devil	200.00

Becomes:

MEN'S ADVENTURES

4 AvB,He Called me a Coward	400.00
5 AvB,Brother Act	250.00
6 AvB,Heat of Battle	225.00
7 AvB,The Walking Death	225.00
8 AvB,RH,Journey Into Death	225.00
9 AvB,Bullets,Blades and Death	150.00
10 BEv,The Education of Thomas Dillon	150.00
11 Death of A Soldier	150.00
12 Firing Squad	150.00
13 RH(c),The Three Stripes	150.00
14 GC,BEv,Steel Coffin	150.00
15 JMn(c)	150.00
16 AyB	150.00
17 AyB	150.00
18 AyB	150.00
19 JRo	125.00
20 GC,RH(c)	125.00
21 BEv(c),JSt,The Eye of Man	250.00
22 BEv,JR,Mark of the Witch	250.00
23 BEv(c),RC,The Wrong Body	275.00
24 RH,JMn,GT,Torture Master	250.00
25 SSh(c),Who Shrinks My Head	450.00
26 Midnight in the Morgue	250.00
27 BP,CBu(c),A:Capt.America, Human Torch,Sub-Mariner	1,500.00
28 BEv,A:Capt.America,Human Torch, Sub-Mariner,July, 1954	1,400.00

TRUTH: RED WHITE BLACK
Nov., 2002

1 (of 7) untold Capt. America	3.50
2 thru 7 KB	@3.50
GN Truth, Red White & Black	4.00

TRY-OUT WINNER BOOK
March, 1988

1 Spider-Man vs. Doc Octopus	15.00

TV STARS
Aug., 1978

1 A:Great Grape Ape	40.00
2	35.00
3 ATh,DSt	35.00
4 A:Top Cat,Feb., 1979	30.00

TWELVE, THE
Jan., 2008

1 (of 12) MSz(s)	3.00
2 thru 9 MSz(s)	@3.00
Spec. 0 preview (2007)	3.00
Spec. 1/2 48-pg.	4.00

2-GUN KID
See: BILLY BUCKSKIN

TWO-GUN KID
Atlas, March, 1948—April, 1977

1 SSh,B:Two-Gun Kid,The Sheriff	1,800.00

2 Killers of Outlaw City 750.00
3 RH,SSh,A:Annie Oakley 600.00
4 RH,A:Black Rider 600.00
5 RH 700.00
6 . . . . 600.00
7 RH,Brand of a Killer 600.00
8 Secret of the Castle of Slaves 600.00
9 JSe,SSh,Trapped in Hidden
   Valley, A:Black Rider 600.00
10 JK(c),The Horrible Hermit
   of Hidden Mesa 600.00
11 JMn(c),GT,A:Black Rider. . . . 350.00
12 JMn(c),GT,A:Black Rider 350.00
13 . . . . 300.00
14 . . . . 300.00
15 thru 24 . . . . @300.00
25 AW,JMn 300.00
26 DAy,JMn 200.00
27 DAy,JMn 200.00
28 JMn 200.00
29 . . . . 200.00
30 AW 200.00
31 thru 44 . . . . @150.00
45 JDa 125.00
46 JDa 125.00
47 JDa 125.00
48 . . . . 125.00
49 JMn 125.00
50 . . . . 125.00
51 AW 125.00
52 thru 59 . . . . @125.00
60 DAy,New O:Two-Gun Kid . . . 150.00
61 JK,DAy,The Killer and The Kid 100.00
62 JK,DAy,At the Mercy of Moose
   Morgan 100.00
63 DAy,The Guns of Wild Bill
   Taggert. 75.00
64 DAy,Trapped by Grizzly
   Gordon. 75.00
65 DAy,Nothing Can Save Fort
   Henry 75.00
66 DAy,Ringo's Raiders 75.00
67 DAy,The Fangs of the Fox 75.00
68 DAy,The Purple Phantom 75.00
69 DAy,Badman Called Goliath . . . 75.00
70 DAy,Hurricane 75.00
71 DAy,V:Jesse James 75.00
72 DAy,V:Geronimo 75.00
73 Guns of the Galloway Gang . . . 75.00
74 Dakota Thompson. 75.00
75 JK,Remember the Alamo 100.00
76 JK,Trapped on the Doom 100.00
77 JK,V:The Panther 100.00
78 V:Jesse James 60.00
79 The River Rats 60.00
80 V:The Billy Kid 60.00

Two-Gun Kid #52
© Marvel Entertainment Group

81 The Hidden Gun 60.00
82 BEv,Here Comes the Conchos . 60.00
83 Durango,Two-Gun
   Kid Unmasked 60.00
84 Gunslammer 60.00
85 Fury at Falcon Flats,
   A:Rawhide Kids 60.00
86 V:Cole Younger 60.00
87 OW,The Sidewinder and the
   Stallion 60.00
88 thru 101 . . . . @50.00
102 thru 136 . . . . @40.00

TWO-GUN KID: SUNSET RIDERS
1995
1 FaN,R:Two-Gun Kid,64-pg. 7.00
2 FaN,concl. 64-pg. 7.00

TWO GUN WESTERN
See: CASEY–CRIME PHOTOGRAPHER

2001: A SPACE ODYSSEY
Oct., 1976
1 JK,FRg,Based on Movie 10.00

2001: A SPACE ODYSSEY
Dec., 1976—Sept., 1977
1 JK,Based on Movie 25.00
2 JK,Vira the She-Demon 15.00
3 JK,Marak the Merciless 15.00
4 JK,Wheels of Death 15.00
5 JK,Norton of New York 15.00
6 JK,Immortality ...Death 15.00
7 JK,The New Seed 15.00
8 JK,Capture of X-51,I&O:Mr.
   Machine(Machine-Man) 20.00
9 JK,A:Mr Machine 15.00
10 Hotline to Hades,A:Mr Machine 15.00

2010
April, 1985
1 TP,movie adapt 2.50
2 TP,movie adapt,May, 1985 . . . . . 2.50

2099 A.D.
1995
1 Chromium cover 4.00

2099 APOCALYPSE
1995
1 . . . . 5.00

2099 GENESIS
1996
1 Chromium Cover 4.00

2099: MANIFEST DESTINY
March, 1998
GN LKa,MMK,F:Miguel
   O'Hara, 48-pg. 6.00

2099 SPECIAL: THE WORLD OF DOOM
1995
1 The World of Doom 2.50

2099 UNLIMITED
1993–96
1 DT,I:Hulk 2099,A:Spider-Man 2099,
   I:Mutagen. 4.50
2 DT,F:Hulk 2099,Spider-Man 2099,
   I:R-Gang 4.25
3 GJ(s),JJB,F:Hulk & SpM 2099. . . 4.25

4 PR(c),GJ(s),JJB,I:Metalscream
   2099,Lachryma 2099 . . . . 4.25
5 GJ(s),I:Vulx,F:Hazarrd 2099 . . . . 4.25
6 . . . . 4.25
Becomes:

2099 A.D. UNLIMITED
7 . . . . 4.25
8 F:Public Enemy 4.25
9 One Nation Under Doom 4.25
10 V:Chameleon 2099 . . . . 4.25
Spec. #1 The World of Doom 2.50

2099: WORLD OF TOMORROW
1996–97
1 . . . . 2.50
2 . . . . 2.50
3 MMk,MsM,ATi,F:Spider-Man,
   X-Men 2.50
4 ATi,X-Men 2099 discover secret . 2.50
5 ATi 2.50
6 PFe&ATi(c),Phalanx's final
   assault 2.50
7 Spider-Man 2099 searches for his
   brother: Green Goblin 2.50
8 Phalanx invasion aftermath 2.50
9 Humanity vs. Lunatika 2.50

TYPHOID
1995–96
1 ANo,JVF,Painted series 4.00
2 ANo,JVF,Hunt for serial killer. . . . 4.00
3 ANo,JVF,sex,blood & videotapes. 4.00
4 ANo,JVF,conclusion 4.00

ULTIMATE ADVENTURES (OF HAWK-OWL & ZIPPY)
Sept., 2002
1 JQ designs,U-Decide. 2.50
2 DFg 2.50
3 DFg 2.50
4 DFg,Hawk-Owl & Zippy 2.50
5 & 6 DFg . . . . @3.00

ULTIMATE CIVIL WAR SPIDER-HAM CRISIS
Jan., 2007
Spec. F:Wolver-Ham 3.00

ULTIMATE DAREDEVIL & ELEKTRA
Nov., 2002
1 (of 4) DaM, at Columbia U. 5.00
2 SvL,DaM 3.50
3 SvL,DaM 3.50
4 SvL,concl. 3.50

ULTIMATE ELEKTRA
Aug., 2004
1 (of 5) SvL,Devil's Due,pt.1 . . . . . . 2.50
2 SvL,Devil's Due,pt.2 . . . . 2.50
3 SvL,Devil's Due,pt.3 . . . . 2.50
4 SvL,Devil's Due,pt.4 . . . . 3.00
5 SvL,Devil's Due,pt.5 . . . . 3.00

ULTIMATE EXTINCTION
Jan., 2006
1 WEI,BPe 3.00
2 thru 5 . . . . @3.00

ULTIMATE FANTASTIC FOUR
Dec., 2003
1 BMB,AKu,The Fantastic,pt.1 . . . . 5.00
2 BMB,AKu,The Fantastic,pt.2 . . . . 5.00

---

3 BMB,AKu,The Fantastic,pt.3 . . . . 4.00
4 BMB,AKu,The Fantastic,pt.4 . . . . 4.00
5 BMB,AKu,The Fantastic,pt.5 . . . . 4.00
6 BMB,AKu,The Fantastic,pt.6 . . . . 4.00
7 WEl(s),SI,Doom,pt.1 . . . . 4.00
8 WEl(s),SI,Doom,pt.2 . . . . 2.50
9 WEl(s),SI,Doom,pt.3 . . . . 2.50
10 WEl(s),SI,Doom,pt.4 . . . . 2.50
11 WEl(s),SI,Doom,pt.5 . . . . 2.50
12 WEl(s),SI,Doom,pt.6 . . . . 2.50
13 WEl,AKu,N-Zone,pt.1 . . . . 2.50
14 WEl,AKu,N-Zone,pt.2 . . . . 2.50
15 WEl,AKu,N-Zone,pt.3 . . . . 2.50
16 WEl,AKu,N-Zone,pt.4 . . . . 2.50
17 WEl,AKu,N-Zone,pt.5 . . . . 2.50
18 WEl,AKu,N-Zone,pt.6 . . . . 2.50
19 JaL,Think Tank,pt.1 . . . . 2.50
20 JaL,Think Tank,pt.2 . . . . 2.50
21 MMr(s),Crossover,pt.1 . . . . 6.00
22 MMr(s),Crossover,pt.2 . . . . 8.00
23 MMr(s),Crossover,pt.3 . . . . 7.00
24 MMr(s),,Tomb of Namor,pt.1 . . 2.50
25 MMr(s),Tomb of Namor. 2.50
26 MMr(s),Tomb of Namor. 2.50
27 MMr(s),President Thor, pt.1 . . . 2.50
28 MMr(s),President Thor, pt.2 . . . 2.50
29 MMr(s),President Thor, pt.3 . . . 3.00
30 MMr(s),Frightful, pt.1 . . . . 7.00
31 MMr(s),Frightful, pt.2 . . . . 7.00
32 MMr(s),Frightful, pt.3 . . . . 3.00
33 PFe,God War, pt.1 . . . . 3.00
34 PFe,God War, pt.2 . . . . 3.00
35 PFe,God War, pt.3 . . . . 3.00
36 PFe,God War, pt.4 . . . . 3.00
37 PFe, God War, pt.5 . . . . 3.00
38 PFe, God War, pt.6 . . . . 3.00
39 MCy(s),Diablo, pt.1 . . . . 3.00
40 MCy(s),Devils, pt.2 . . . . 3.00
41 MCy(s),Diablo, pt.3 . . . . 3.00
42 MCy(s),PFe,Silver Surfer,pt.1 . . 3.00
43 MCy(s),PFe,Silver Surfer,pt.2 . . 3.00
44 MCy(s),PFe,Silver Surfer,pt.3 . . 3.00
45 MCy(s),PFe,Silver Surfer,pt.4 . . 3.00
46 MCy(s),PFe,Silver Surfer,pt.5 . . 3.00
47 Ghosts, pt.1 (of 3). 3.00
48 MCy(s),Ghosts, pt. 2. . . . . 3.00
49 MCy(s),V:Red Ghost. 3.00
50 . . . . 4.00
51 MCy(s),Mr. Fantastic V:Thanos . 3.00
52 MCy(s),Thanos saga 3.00
53 MCy(s),Cosmic Cube Thanos. . . 3.00
54 MCy(s),Mole Man 3.00
55 MCy(s),Ultimate Salem Seven . 3.00
56 MCy(s),Ultimate Salem Seven . 3.00
57 MCy(s),Ultimate Salem Seven . 3.00
58 PFe(c) Ultimatum x-over. 3.00
Ann. #1 Enter the Inhumans 4.00
Ann. #2 Nursery Two 4.00
Ann. #1 Ultimate Fantastic Four/
    Ultimate X-Men x-over. 4.00

ULTIMATE HUMAN
Jan., 2008
1 (of 4) WEl(s),CNr 3.00
2 thru 4 WEl(s),CNr. . . . . @3.00

ULTIMATE IRON MAN
March, 2005
1 (of 5) AKu, Orson Scott Card(s) . 6.00
1a Variant Foil (C). 6.00
2 AKu,O:Ultimate Iron Man. 3.00
3 AKu,F:Rhodey Rhodes 3.00
4 AKu 3.00
5 AKu 3.00

ULTIMATE
IRON MAN II
1 (of 4) PFe, O:Iron Man 3.00
1 variant (c) 3.00
2 thru 5 PFe . . . . @3.00

ULTIMATE MARVEL
Flipbook, June, 2005
1 Ultimate X-Men #1
    & Ultimate Fantastic Four #1. . . 4.00
2 Ult.X-Men#2 & Ult. F.Four#2 . . . 4.00
3 Ult.X-Men#3 & Ult. F.Four#3 . . . 4.00
4 Ult.x-men#4 & Ult. F.four#4 . . . . 4.00
5 Ult.X-Men#5 & Ult. F.Four#5 . . . 4.00
6 thru 11 . . . . @4.00
12 thru 20 . . . . 5.00

Ultimate Marvel Team-Up #11
© Marvel Entertainment Group

ULTIMATE
MARVEL TEAM-UP
Feb., 2001
1 Spider-Man & Wolverine 5.00
2 Spider-Man & The Hulk 4.00
3 Spider-Man & The Hulk 4.00
4 Spider-Man & Iron Man 4.00
5 Spider-Man & Iron Man,MiA 4.00
6 Spider-Man & Punisher,BSz . . . 3.50
7 Spider-Man & Daredevil,BSz. . . . 3.50
8 Spider-Man,Daredevil,Punisher. . 3.50
9 Spider-Man & Fantastic Four. . . . 3.50
10 Spider-Man & Man-Thing 3.50
11 BMB(s),Spider-Man & X-Men . . 3.50
12 Spider-Man & Dr. Strange. 3.50
13 Spider-Man & Dr. Strange. 3.50
14 Spider-Man & Black Widow . . . 3.50
15 Spider-Man & Shang-Chi 3.50
16 Spider-Man & Shang-Chi 3.50

ULTIMATE NIGHTMARE
Aug., 2004
1 (of 5) Tunguska 2.50
2 WEl(s) 2.50
3 WEl(s) 2.50
4 WEl(s) 3.00
5 WEl(s) 3.00

ULTIMATE ORIGINS
Nov., 2007
1 (of 6) BMB 3.00
1a variant (c) 3.00
2 thru 5 BMB(s) . . . . @3.00
2a thru 5a variant (c)s. . . . . @3.00

ULTIMATE POWER
Oct., 2006
1 BMB(s),V:Squadron Supreme . . . 3.00
1a Director's Cut. 4.00

2 BMB(s),V:Squadron Supreme . . . 3.00
3 BMB(s). 3.00
4 MSz(s) 3.00
5 MSz(s) 3.00
6 MSz(s) 3.00
7 JLb(s), ... 3.00
8 JLb(s). 3.00
9 finale 3.00

ULTIMATES, THE
Jan., 2002
1 MMr,BHi,Nick Fury, heroes 6.00
2 MMr,BHi,Search for Cap.Am. . . 10.00
3 MMr,BHi,Cap.America lives. 8.00
4 MMr,BHi,no one to fight. 8.00
5 MMr,BHi 10.00
6 MMr,BHi,celebrities 5.00
7 MMr,BHi,new additions 5.00
8 MMr,Quicksilver&ScarletWitch. . 3.00
9 MMr,BHi 3.00
10 MMr,BHi,F:Hawkeye 3.00
11 BHi,PNe 4.00
12 BHi,PNe 3.00
13 BHi,Chitauri,concl.48-pg. 3.50
Spec. Must Have rep. #1–#3 . . . . . 4.00
Vol. 2
1 BHi. 3.00

ULTIMATES SAGA
Nov., 2007
Spec. 4.00

ULTIMATE SECRET
Dec., 2004
1 (of 4) WEl(s) 3.00
2 Wel(s), Mahr Vehl 3.00
3 WEl(s),V:Kree 3.00
4 WEl(s), conc. 3.00

ULTIMATES SECRETS
Jan., 2008
Spec. 4.00

ULTIMATE SIX
Sept., 2003
1 BMB,JQ,F:Villains 3.00
2 BMB,Sinister Six 3.00
3 BMB,Ultimate Spidey. 3.00
4 BMB,F:The Ultimates. 3.00
5 BMB,Spidey kidnapped 3.00
6 BMB,V:Sinister Six. 3.00
7 BMB,Green Goblin. 3.00

ULTIMATE SPIDER-MAN
Sept., 2000
1 BMB,JQ,MBa,ATi,A:Mary Jane
    48-pg.red card(c) 110.00
1A variant white (c) 175.00
1B Dynamic Forces (c) 65.00
2A BMB,MBa,ATi,Dr.Otto Octopus,
    car 50.00
2B Dynamic Forces JaL(c),
    Spider-Man swinging. 40.00
3 BMB,ATi,MBa,A:Mary Jane 40.00
4 BMB,ATi,MBa,D:Uncle Ben 40.00
5 BMB,ATi,MBa,hand of fate,
    scarce 75.00
6 BMB,ATi,MBa,V:Green Goblin . 40.00
7 BMB,ATi,MBa,V:Green Goblin . 25.00
8 BMB,ATi,MBa,V:Shocker 20.00
9 BMB,ATi,MBa,V:Kingpin 12.00
10 BMB,ATi,MBa,V:Kingpin 12.00
11 BMB,ATi,MBa,V:Kingpin 12.00
12 BMB,ATi,MBa,V:Kingpin 12.00
13 BMB,ATi,MBa,Mary Jane 11.00
14 BMB,MBa,ATi,Doctor Octopus . . 9.00
15 BMB,MBa,ATi,Doctor Octopus . . 8.00
16 BMB,MBa,ATi,F:Ock,Kraven.. . . 8.00
17 BMB,MBa,ATi,F:Justin Hammer . 7.00

Ultimate Spider-Man 318
© Marvel Entertainment Group

18 BMB,MBa,ATi,Doc Oc kicks butt 7.00
19 BMB,MBa,ATi,Justin Hammer . . 7.00
20 BMB,MBa,ATi,Doc Oc,Kraven . . 7.00
21 BMB,MBa,ATi,vs. the press . . . 7.00
22 BMB,MBa,ATi,R:Green Goblin
 + Chapter 1, 54-pg. 7.00
23 BMB,MBa,ATi,G.Goblin,G.Stacy . 7.00
24 BMB,MBa,ATi,Green Goblin deal 4.00
25 BMB,MBa,ATi 4.00
26 BMB,MBa,ATi,S.H.I.E.L.D. 3.00
27 BMB,MBa,ATi 3.00
28 BMB,MBa,ATi 3.00
29 BMB,MBa,ATi 3.00
30 BMB,MBa,ATi 3.00
31 BMB,MBa,ATi 3.00
32 BMB,MBa,ATi 3.00
33 BMB,MBa,ATi,V:Venom 10.00
34 BMB,MBa,ATi,V:Venom 8.00
35 BMB,MBa,ATi,V:Venom 8.00
36 BMB,MBa,ATi,V:Venom 5.00
37 BMB,MBa,ATi,V:Venom 5.00
38 BMB,MBa,ATi,V:Venom,concl. . . 5.00
39 BMB,MBa,ATi,F:Nick Fury 3.00
40 BMB,MBa,Irresponsible,pt.1 . . . . 3.00
41 BMB,MBa,Irresponsible,pt.2 . . . . 3.00
42 BMB,MBa,Irresponsible,pt.3 . . . . 3.00
43 BMB,MBa,Irresponsible,pt.4 . . . . 3.00
44 BMB,MBa,Irresponsible,pt.5 . . . . 3.00
45 BMB,MBa,Irresponsible,pt.6 . . . . 3.00
46 BMB,MBa,F:S.H.I.E.L.D.,40-pg . 3.00
47 BMB,MBa,Unfair,pt.1 . . . . 3.00
48 BMB,MBa,Unfair,pt.2 . . . . 3.00
49 BMB,MBa,Unfair,pt.3 . . . . 3.00
50 BMB,MBa,Claws,pt.1 . . . . 3.00
51 BMB,MBa,Claws,pt.2 . . . . 3.00
52 BMB,MBa,Claws,pt.3 . . . . 3.00
53 BMB,MBa,Claws,concl. 3.00
54 BMB,MBa,Goes Hollywood,pt.1 . 3.00
54a Arachnoman variant 12.00
55 BMB,MBa,Goes Hollywood,pt.2 . 2.50
56 BMB,MBa,Goes Hollywood,pt.3 . 2.50
57 BMB,MBa,Goes Hollywood,pt.4 . 2.50
58 BMB,MBa,Goes Hollywood,pt.5 . 2.50
59 BMB,MBa,Goes Hollywood,pt.6 . 2.50
60 BMB,MBa,Carnage,pt.1 . . . . 6.00
61 BMB,MBa,Carnage,pt.2 . . . . 3.50
62 BMB,MBa,Carnage,pt.3 . . . . 5.00
63 BMB,MBa,Carnage,pt.4 . . . . 2.50
64 BMB,MBa,Carnage,pt.5 . . . . 2.50
65 BMB,MBa,Carnage,pt.6 . . . . 2.50
66 BMB,MBa,Switcheroo,pt.1 . . . . . 2.50
67 BMB,MBa,Switcheroo,pt.2 . . . . . 2.50
68 BMB,MBa,F:Johnny Storm 2.50
69 BMB,MBa,F:Johnny Storm 2.50
70 BMB,MBa,Sorcerer Supreme . . . 2.50

71 BMB,MBa,Sorcerer Supreme . . . 2.50
72 BMB,MBa,Hobgoblin,pt.1 . . . . . . 2.50
73 BMB,MBa,Hobgoblin,pt.2 . . . . . . 2.50
74 BMB,MBa,Hobgoblin,pt.3 . . . . . . 2.50
75 BMB,MBa,Hobgoblin,pt.4 . . . . . . 2.50
76 BMB,MBa,Hobgoblin,pt.5 . . . . . . 2.50
77 BMB,MBa,Hobgoblin,pt.6 . . . . . . 2.50
78 BMB,MBa,I:Mark Raxton 2.50
79 BMB,MBa,Warriors,pt.1 . . . . 3.00
80 BMB,MBa,Warriors,pt.2 . . . . 2.50
81 BMB,MBa,Warriors,pt.3 . . . . 2.50
82 MBa,Warriors,pt.4, Gang War. . . 2.50
83 MBa,Warriors,pt.5, Gang War. . . 2.50
84 BMB,MBa,Warriors,pt.6 . . . . 2.50
85 BMB,MBa,Warriors,pt.7 . . . . 2.50
86 BMB,MBa,Silver Sable,pt.1 . . . . 2.50
87 BMB,MBa,Silver Sable,pt.2 . . . . 2.50
88 BMB,MBa,Silver Sable,pt.3 . . . . 2.50
89 BMB,MBa,Silver Sable,pt.4 . . . . 2.50
90 BMB,MBa,Silver Sable,pt.5 . . . . 2.50
91 BMB,MBa,Deadpool,pt.1 . . . . . . 2.50
92 BMB,MBa,Deadpool,pt.2 . . . . . . 2.50
93 BMB,MBa,Deadpool,pt.3 . . . . . . 3.00
94 BMB,MBa,Deadpool,pt.4 . . . . . . 3.00
95 BMB,MBa,Morbius 3.00
96 BMB,MBa,Morbius V:Blade 3.00
97 BMB,MBa,Clone Saga,pt.1 . . . . . 3.00
98 BMB,MBa,Clone Saga,pt.2 . . . . . 3.00
99 BMB,MBa,Clone Saga,pt.3 . . . . . 4.00
100 MBa,Clone Saga,pt.4, 64-pg. . . 4.00
100a variant (c) 10.00
101 BMB,MBa,Clone Saga,pt.5 . . . . 3.00
102 BMB,MBa,Clone Saga,pt.6 . . . . 3.00
103 BMB(s),MBa,Clone Saga,pt.7. . 3.00
104 BMB(s),MBa,Clone Saga,pt.8. . 4.00
105 BMB(s),MBa,Clone Saga 4.00
106 BMB(s),MBa,Ultimate Knights . 4.00
107 BMB(s),MBa,Ultimate Knights . 3.00
108 BMB(s),MBa,Ultimate Knights . 3.00
109 BMB(s),MBa,Ultimate Knights . 3.00
110 BMB(s),MBa,Ultimate Knights. . 3.00
110a variant (c) 3.00
111 BMB(s),SI 3.00
111a variant (c) 3.00
112 BMB(s),SI,Death of a Goblin . . 3.00
113 BMB(s),SI,Death of a Goblin . . 3.00
114 BMB(s),SI,Death of a Goblin . . 3.00
115 BMB(s),SI,Death of a Goblin . . 3.00
116 BMB(s),SI,Death of a Goblin . . 3.00
117 BMB(s),SI,Death of a Goblin . . 3.00
118 BMB(s),SI 3.00
119 BMB(s),SI,V:Magneto 3.00
120 BMB(s),SI,I:X-Men 3.00
121 BMB(s),SI,F:Omega Red 4.00
122 BMB(s),SI 3.00
123 BMB(s),SI,War of Symbiotes . . 3.00
124 BMB(s),SI,War of Symbiotes . . 3.00
125 BMB(s),SI,War of Symbiotes . . 3.00
126 Ultimatum x-over. 3.00
127 Ultimatum x-over. 3.00
128 BMB(s),SI,Ultimatum x-over . . . 3.00
Ann.#1 More than you
 Bargained for (2005) 6.00
Ann.#2 (2006) 4.00
Ann.#3 BMB(s). 4.00
Spec.1 Collected, rep.#1–#3 . . . . . 4.00
Spec.#1-#2-#3, 96-pg. 4.00
Spec.#1 all-star artists, 54-pg. 3.50
Spec. Must Have, rep. 4.00

ULTIMATES SAGA
Nov., 2007
Spec. 4.00

ULTIMATE TALES
Flipbook, June, 2005
1 Ultimate Spider-Man #0
 & Ultimate Spider-Man #1 . . . . 4.00
2 Ultimate Spider-Man #2 & #3 . . . 4.00
3 Ultimate Spider-Man #4 & #5 . . . 4.00
4 Ultimate Spider-Man #6 & #7 . . . 4.00

5 Ultimate Spider-Man #7 & #8 . . . 4.00
6 thru 13 . . . . @4.00
14 thru 18. . . . . @5.00

ULTIMATES 2
Dec., 2004
1 MMr,BHi. 3.00
2 MMr,BHi,Gods & Monsters 3.00
3 MMr,BHi,Trial of Incredible Hulk . 3.00
4 MMr,BHi,Nick Fury vs. Thor. 3.00
5 MMr,BHi,v:Thor 3.00
6 MMr,BHi,F:Hank Pym 3.00
7 MMr,BHi,Wolf in the Fold. 3.00
8 MMr,BHi,Grand Theft America . . . 4.00
9 MMr,BHi,Grand Theft America . . . 3.00
10 MMr,BHi,Grand Theft America . . 3.00
11 MMr,BHi,Grand Theft America . . 3.00
12 MMr,BHi,Grand Theft America . . 4.00
13 BHi,Grand Theft America 4.00
Ann.#1 The Reserves (2005). 5.00
Ann.#2 F:Arnim Zola (2006) 4.00
Spec. Must Have, rep. #1–#3 . . . . 5.00

ULTIMATES 3
Dec., 2007
1 (of 5) JLb(s). 3.00
2 thru 5 JLb(s). . . . . @3.00
5a variant (c). 3.00

ULTIMATE VISION
Nov., 2006
1-shot Visions 3.00
1 (of 5) BPe 3.00
2 BPe 3.00
3 BPe 3.00
4 BPe 3.00
5 . . . . 3.00

ULTIMATE WAR
Marvel Dec. 2002
1 (of 4) CBa,X-Men vs. Ultimates. . 5.00
2 CBa 4.00
3 CBa 4.00
4 CBa,concl. 4.00

ULTIMATE
WOLVERINE VS. HULK
Dec., 2005
1 . . . . 3.00
2 . . . . 3.00
3 . . . . 3.00

ULTIMATE X-MEN
Dec., 2000
1 AKu,ATi,MMr,48-page, card (c) . 25.00
1A Dynamic Forces (c) 30.00
1B Preview 30.00
2 AKu,ATi,MMr,F:Wolverine 22.00
3 AKu,ATi,MMr,V:Magneto 7.00
4 AKu,ATi,MMr,V:Magneto 7.00
5 AKu,ATi,MMr,One traitor? 7.00
6 AKu,ATi,MMr,V:Magneto 7.00
7 AKu,ATi,MMr,Weapon X,pt.1 . . . 10.00
8 AKu,ATi,MMr,Weapon X,pt.2 . . . . 7.00
9 MMr,TR,SHa,Weapon X,pt.3 . . . . 7.00
10 MMr,TR,SHa,Weapon X,pt.4 . . . 7.00
11 MMr,AKu,ATi,Weapon X,pt.5. . . 5.00
12 MMr,AKu,Weapon X,pt.6 . . . . . 5.00
13 AKu(c),F:Gambit 5.00
14 AKu(c),F:Gambit,pt.2 . . . . 4.00
15 AKu,MMr,Xavier's teachings. . . . 4.00
16 AKu,MMr,to Scotland 4.00
17 AKu,MMr,Proteus Saga,pt.2 . . . . 4.00
18 AKu,MMr,World Tour. 4.00
19 AKu,MMr,World Tour,concl. 4.00
20 AKu,MMr,World Tour,epilogue. . 3.75
21 MMr,DaM,Hellfire & Brimstone . . 3.75
22 MMr,DaM,Hellfire & Brimstone . . 3.75
23 MMr,DaM,Hellfire & Brimstone . . 3.75

Ultimate X-Men #3
© Marvel Entertainment Group

24 MMr,DaM,Hellfire&Brimstone . . .	3.75
25 MMr,DaM,AKu(c), Hellfire &	
Brimstone, 48-pg.	5.00
26 MMr,AKu,Professor-X	5.00
27 MMr,AKu,V:Brotherhood	5.00
28 MMr,AKu,V:Brotherhood	5.00
29 MMr,AKu,Missing X-Man	5.00
30 MMr,AKu,Storm's gang	5.00
31 MMr,AKu,V:Magneto	5.00
32 MMr,AKu,Ultimate fate	4.50
33 MMr,AKu,Return of the King	3.50
34 BMB,Blockbuster,pt.1	6.00
35 BMB,Blockbuster,pt.2	3.25
36 BMB,Blockbuster,pt.3	3.25
37 BMB,Blockbuster,pt.4	3.25
38 BMB,Blockbuster,pt.5	3.25
39 BMB,Blockbuster,pt.6	2.75
40 BMB,New Mutants,pt.1	3.00
41 BMB,New Mutants,pt.2	2.75
42 BMB,New Mutants,pt.3	3.50
43 BMB,New Mutants,pt.4	2.50
44 BMB,New Mutants,pt.5	4.00
45 BMB,New Mutants,pt.6	2.50
46 BPe,The Tempest,pt.1	2.50
47 BPe,The Tempest,pt.2	2.50
48 BPe,The Tempest,pt.3	2.50
49 BPe,The Tempest,pt.4	2.50
50 NKu,Cry Wolf,pt.1	4.00
51 NKu,Cry Wolf,pt.2	2.50
52 NKu,Cry Wolf,pt.3	2.50
53 NKu,Cry Wolf,pt.4	2.50
54 Sl,Longshot, pt.1	2.50
55 Sl,Longshot, pt.2	2.50
56 Sl,Longshot, pt.3	2.50
57 Sl,The Most Dangerous Game . .	2.50
58 Sl, A Hard Lesson	2.50
59 Sl,F:Wolverine,pt.1	2.50
60 Sl,F:Wolverine & Storm,pt.2 . . .	2.50
61 Sl,Magnetic North,pt.1	15.00
62 Sl,Magnetic North,pt.2	2.50
63 Sl,Magnetic North,pt.3	2.50
64 Sl,Magnetic North,pt.4	2.50
65 Sl,Magnetic North,pt.5	2.50
66 TR,Date Night,pt.1	2.50
67 TR,Date Night,pt.2	2.50
68 TR,Date Night,pt.3	2.50
69 Phoenix, pt.1	3.00
70 Phoenix, pt.2	3.00
71 Phoenix, pt.3	3.00
72 TR,Magical,pt.1	3.00
73 TR,Magical,pt.2	3.00
74 TR,Magical,pt.3	3.00
75 TR,Ultimate Cable,pt.1	4.00
76 TR,Ultimate Cable,pt.2	4.00

77 F:Ultimate Cable,pt.3	4.00
78 F:Ultimate Cable,pt.4	4.00
79 Aftermath, pt.1	3.00
80 Aftermath.	3.00
81	3.00
82 The Underneath, pt.1	3.00
83 The Underneath, pt.2	3.00
84 Sentinels, pt.1	3.00
85 Sentinels, pt.2	3.00
86 Sentinels, pt.3	3.00
87 Sentinels, pt.4	3.00
88 Sentinels, pt. 5	3.00
89 F:Storm	3.00
90 F:Sinister.	3.00
91 F:Apocalypse	3.00
92 F:Stryfe & Onslaught	3.00
93 F:Apocalypse	3.00
94	3.00
95 I:Ultimate Alpha Flight.	3.00
96 X-Men vs. X-Men	3.00
97 Ultimatum x-over.	3.00
98 Ultimatum x-over.	3.00
Ann.#1 Ultimate Sacrifice (2005) . . .	5.00
Ann.#2 F:Dazzler (2006)	4.00
Spec. #1-#2-#3, 96-pg.	4.00
Spec. rep. Must Have #1-#3	4.00

ULTIMATE X-MEN/
FANTASTIC FOUR
Dec., 2005

1 x-over.	3.00
1 Ultimate F.Four/X-Men x-over	3.00
Ann. #1 Ultimate X-Men/Ultimate	
Fantastic Four x-over	4.00

ULTRAFORCE/AVENGERS

1 V:Loki,A:Malibu's Ultraforce.	4.00

ULTIMATUM
Nov., 2008

1 (of 5) x-over	4.00
2	4.00
1a thru 2a variant (c)s. . . . . @4.00

ULTRAGIRL
[Mini-series] 1996

1 thru 3 BKs,I&O:Ultra Girl . . . . . @2.50

UNCANNY ORIGINS
Sept., 1996

1 F:Cyclops.	2.50
2 F:Quicksilver	2.50
3 DHv,BAn,F:Archangel	2.50
4 F:Firelord	2.50
5 MHi,F:Hulk	2.50
6 F:Beast	2.50
7 F:Venom	2.50
8 F:Nightcrawler	2.50
9 F:Storm	2.50
10 F:Black Cat	2.50
11 F:Luke Cage	2.50
12 F:Black Knight.	2.50
13 LWn,MCa,F:Doctor Strange	2.50
14 LWn,MCW,F:Iron Fist	2.50

UNCANNY TALES
Marvel Atlas, June, 1952

1 RH,While the City Sleeps . .	1,400.00
2 JMn,BEv	750.00
3 Escape to What	600.00
4 JMn,Nobody's Fool	600.00
5 Fear	600.00
6 He Lurks in the Shadows	600.00
7 BEv,Kill,Clown,Kill	600.00
8 JMn,Bring Back My Face.	500.00
9 BEv,RC,The Executioner.	500.00
10 JMn,RH(c),JR,The Man Who	
Came Back To Life	500.00
11 GC,The Man Who Changed . .	400.00

Uncanny Tales #35
© Marvel Entertainment Group

12 BP,BEv,Bertha Gets Buried . .	400.00
13 RH,Scared Out of His Skin . .	400.00
14 RH,TLw,Victims of Vonntor . . .	400.00
15 RA,JSt,The Man Who	
Saw Death.	400.00
16 JMn,GC,Zombie at Large	400.00
17 GC,TLw,I Live With Corpses .	400.00
18 JF,BP,Clock Face(c)	400.00
19 DBr,RKr,TLw,The Man Who	
Died Again	400.00
20 DBr,Ted's Head	400.00
21	350.00
22 DAy	350.00
23 TLw	350.00
24	350.00
25 MSy.	350.00
26 Spider-Man prototype story . .	450.00
27 RA,TLw	300.00
28 TLw	325.00
29 JMn	300.00
30	300.00
31	300.00
32 BEv	300.00
33	300.00
34 BP	300.00
35 TLw,JMn	300.00
36 BP,BEv	300.00
37 MD	300.00
38 BP	300.00
39 BEv	300.00
40	300.00
41	300.00
42 MD	300.00
43	250.00
44	250.00
45 MD	250.00
46 GM	250.00
47 TSe	250.00
48 BEv	250.00
49 JO	250.00
50 JO	250.00
51 GM	275.00
52 GC.	250.00
53 JO,AT	250.00
54	250.00
55	250.00
56 Sept., 1957	275.00

UNCANNY TALES
FROM THE GRAVE
Dec., 1973—Oct., 1975

1 RC,Room of no Return	35.00
2 DAy,Out of the Swamp	25.00
3 No Way Out	25.00

4 JR,SD,Vampire 25.00
5 GK,GT,Don't Go in the Cellar . . 25.00
6 JR,SD,The Last Kkrul 25.00
7 RH,SD,Never Dance With a
     Vampire 25.00
8 SD,Escape Into Hell 25.00
9 JA,The Nightmare Men 25.00
10 SD,DH,Beware the Power of
     Khan 25.00
11 SD,JF,RH,Dead Don't Sleep . . 25.00
12 SD,Final Issue 25.00

UNCANNY X-MEN
See: X-MEN

UNDERWORLD
Feb., 2006
1 F:Jackie Dio 3.00
2 thru 5 . . . . @3.00

UNION JACK
Oct., 1998
1 (of 3) BRa,F:Joey Chapman 3.00
2 BRa,V:Baroness 3.00
3 BRa,conclusion 3.00
Sept., 2006
1 thru 4 . . . . @3.00

UNIVERSAL WAR ONE
July, 2008
1 thru 3 (of 6) 56-pgs. . . . . @6.00

UNIVERSE X
July, 2000
0 AxR,DBw,48-pg. 4.00
1 (of 12) AxR,DBw,Capt.MarVell . . 3.50
2 AxR,DBw, ... 3.50
3 AxR,DBw, ... 3.50
4 AxR,DBw,Cap.Am vs. Hydra 3.50
5 AxR,DBw,Mar-Vell vs.Death 3.50
6 AxR,DBw,Moonknight 3.50
7 AxR,DBw,Supreme Intelligence . . 3.50
8 AxR,DBw,Monster Generation . . . 3.50
9 AxR,DBw,Supreme Intelligence . . 3.50
10 AxR,DBw,V:Mephisto 3.50
11 AxR,DBw,A:Belasco 3.50
12 AxR,DBw,V:Absorbing Man . . . 3.50
Spec."4",F:Fantastic Four 4.00
Spec. Spidey,AxR,JG,JR,48-page . . 4.00
Spec. Beasts,AxR,48-page 4.00
Spec. Omnibus,AxR. 4.00
Spec. Iron Men, 48-page 4.00
Spec. Universe X:X 48-page 4.00

USA #11
© *Marvel Entertainment Group*

UNKNOWN WORLDS OF SCIENCE FICTION
Jan., 1975
(Black & White Magazine)
1 AW,RKr,AT,FF,GC 30.00
2 FB,GP 25.00
3 GM,AN,GP,GC 25.00
4 . . . . 25.00
5 GM,NC,GC 25.00
6 FB,AN,GC,Nov., 1975 . . . . 25.00
Spec.#1 AN,NR,JB. 30.00

UNTAMED
Epic *Heavy Hitters*, 1993
1 I:Griffen Palmer 2.75
2 V:Kosansui 2.50
3 V:Kosansui 2.50

UNTOLD LEGEND OF CAPTAIN MARVEL, THE
1997
1 (of 3) Early days of Captain
     Marvel 2.50
2 Early days of Captain Marvel . . . 2.50
3 V:Kree 2.50

UNTOLD TALES OF SPIDER-MAN
Sept., 1995 – Sept., 1997
1 F:Young Spider-Man 3.00
2 V:Batwing 2.50
3 V:Sandman 2.50
4 V:J.Jonah Jameson 2.50
5 V:Vulture 2.50
6 A:Human Torch 2.50
7 . . . . 2.50
8 . . . . 2.50
9 A:Batwing,Lizard 2.50
10 KBk,PO,I:Commanda 2.50
11 thru 14 KBk,PO, ... @2.50
15 KBk,PO,AV,Gordon's plan to
     control the Bugle 2.50
16 Re-I:Mary Jane Watson 2.50
17 KBk,PO,AV,V:Hawkeye 2.50
18 KBk,PO,AV,A:Green Goblin,
     Headsman 2.50
19 KBk,PO,AW,F:Doctor Octopus . . 2.50
20 KBk,PO,AW,V:Vulture 2.50
21 KBk,PO,AW,V:Menace,A:Original
     X-Men 2.50
22 KBk,PO,AW,V:Scarecrow, ... 2.50
23 KBk,PO,AW,V:Crime Master,
     A:Green Goblin 2.50
24 KBk,PO,BMc, Fate of Batwing . . 2.50
25 LBI,PO,BMc, V:Green Goblin,
     final issue 2.50
Minus 1 Spec., RSt,JR, flashback,
     Peter's parents 2.50
Ann.'96 1 KBk,MiA,JSt,A date with
     Invisible Girl? 2.50
Ann.'97 KBk,TL,A:everyone, 48-pg. 3.00
one-shot GN KBk,SL,Encounter,
     A:Dr. Strange 48-pg. 6.00

UNTOLD TALES OF THE NEW UNIVERSE
March, 2006
D.P. 7 #1 . . . . 3.00
Justice #1 . . . . 3.00
Nightmask #1 . . . . 3.00
Starbrand #1 . . . . 3.00
PSI-Force #1 . . . . 3.00

U.S.A. COMICS
Marvel Timely, Aug., 1941
1 S&K(c),BW,AAv,SSh,Bondage(c),
     The Defender(c) 24,000.00

2 S&K(c),BW,SSh, Capt.
     Terror(c) 7,000.00
3 S&K(c),SSh,Capt.Terror(c) . . 5,000.00
4 SSh,Major Liberty 4,500.00
5 Hitler(c),O:AmericanAvenger 4,200.00
6 ASh(c),Capt.America(c) 6,000.00
7 BW,O:Marvel Boy 6,000.00
8 ASh(c),Capt.America (c). . . . 4,000.00
9 ASh(c),Bondage(c), Captain
     America 4,000.00
10 ASh(c),Bondage(c), Captain
     America 4,000.00
11 SSh(c),Bondage(c), Captain
     America 3,000.00
12 ASh(c),Capt.America 3,000.00
13 ASh(c),Capt.America 3,000.00
14 AyB(c),Capt.America 2,000.00
15 Capt.America 2,000.00
16 ASh(c),Bondage(c),
     Capt.America 2,000.00
17 Bondage(c),Capt.America . . 2,000.00

U.S. 1
May, 1983–Oct., 1984
1 AM(c),HT,Trucking Down the
     Highway 3.00
2 HT,Midnight 3.00
3 FS,ME,Rhyme of the Ancient
     Highwayman 3.00
4 FS,ME 3.00
5 FS,ME,Facing The Maze 3.00
6 FS,ME 3.00
7 FS,ME 3.00
8 FS,ME 3.00
9 FS,ME,Iron Mike-King of
     the Bike 3.00
10 thru 12 FS,ME. . . . . @3.00

U.S. AGENT
June–Dec., 1993
1 V:Scourge,O:U.S.Agent 2.50
2 V:Scourge 2.50
3 V:Scourge 2.50
4 last issue 2.50

U.S. AGENT
May, 2001
1 (of 3) JOy,KK,Maximum Security. 3.00
2 JOy,KK, ... 3.00
3 JOy,KK,A:Capt.America 3.00

U.S. WAR MACHINE
Marvel Max, Sept., 2001
1 (of 12) Weekly series,24-page. . . 2.50
2 thru 12 . . . . @2.50

U.S. WAR MACHINE 2.0
June, 2003
1 (of 3) V:Iron Man 3.00
2 thru 3 concl. . . . . @3.00

VAMPIRE TALES
Aug., 1973
(black & white magazine)
1 BEv,B:Morbius the Living
     Vampire 125.00
2 JSo,I:Satana 75.00
3 A:Satana 65.00
4 GK 65.00
5 GK,O:Morbius The Living
     Vampire 65.00
6 AA,I:Lilith 50.00
7 HC,PG 50.00
8 AA,A:Blade The Vampire
     Slayer 75.00
9 RH,AA 50.00
10 . . . . 50.00
11 June, 1975 . . . . 50.00
Ann.#1 . . . . 50.00

MARVEL

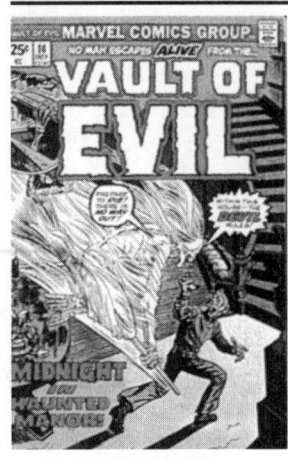

Vault of Evil #14
© *Marvel Entertainment Group*

VAULT OF EVIL
Feb., 1973—Nov., 1975
1 GK,B:1950's reps,Come
　Midnight,Come Monster 35.00
2 The Hour of the Witch 25.00
3 The Woman Who Wasn't 25.00
4 Face that Follows 25.00
5 Ghost 25.00
6 GT,The Thing at the Window . . 25.00
7 Monsters 25.00
8 The Vampire is my Brother 25.00
9 Giant Killer 25.00
10 MD,The Lurkers in the Caves. . 25.00
11 JK,BEv,Two Feasts For
　a Vampire 25.00
12 Midnight in the
　Haunted Mansion 25.00
13 Hot as the Devil 25.00
14 SD,Midnight in the Haunted
　Manor 25.00
15 SD,Don't Shake Hands with
　the Devil 25.00
16 A Grave Honeymoon. 25.00
17 Grave Undertaking 25.00
18 The Deadly Edge 25.00
19 Vengeance of Ahman Ra 25.00
20 SD. 25.00
21 Victim of Valotorr. 25.00
22 SD. 25.00
23 Black Magician Lives Again . . . 25.00

VENOM
April, 2003
1 SK(c),Shiver,pt.1 . . . . 3.00
2 Shiver,pt.2 . . . . 2.50
3 SK(c),Shiver,pt.3 . . . . 2.50
4 SK(c),Shiver,pt.4 . . . . 2.50
5 SK(c),Shiver,pt.5 . . . . 2.50
6 . . . . 2.50
7 SK(c) 2.50
8 SK(c) Run,pt.3,F:Wolverine 3.00
9 SK(c) Run,pt.4 . . . . 3.00
10 Run,pt.5 . . . . 3.00
11 Patterns,pt.1 . . . . 3.00
12 Patterns,pt.2 . . . . 3.00
13 Patterns,pt.3 . . . . 3.00
14 thru 18 Twist,pt.1–5. . . . . @3.00

VENOM: ALONG
CAME A SPIDER
1996
1 LHA,GLz,V:New Spider-Man 8.00

2 LHa,JPi,V:New Spider-Man 8.00
3 . . . . 5.00
4 conclusion, 48-pg. 5.00

VENOM: CARNAGE
UNLEASHED
1995
1 Venom vs. Carnage 3.00
2 Venom vs. Carnage 3.00
3 No Spider-Help 3.00
4 JRu,Wld,LHa,cardstock(c) 3.00

VENOM: DARK ORIGIN
Aug., 2008
1 (of 5) AMe 3.00
2 thru 4 AMe . . . . @3.00

VENOM:
THE ENEMY WITHIN
1994
1 BMc,Glow-in-the-dark(C),
　A:Demogoblin,Morbius 3.25
2 BMc,A:Demogoblin,Morbius 3.25
3 BMc,V:Demogoblin,A:Morbius . . . 3.25

VENOM: FINALE
1997–98
1 (of 3) LHa, ... 6.00
2 LJa, ... 5.00
3 LJa 5.00

VENOM: FUNERAL PYRE
1993
1 TL,JRu,A:Punisher. 3.50
2 TL,JRu,AM,V:Gangs 3.50
3 TL,JRu,Last issue 3.50

VENOM: THE HUNGER
1996
1 thru 4 LKa,TeH,V:Dr. Paine . . . @2.50

VENOM: THE HUNTED
1996
1 LHa,3 part mini-series 3.00

VENOM:
LETHAL PROTECTOR
1993
1 MBa,A:Spider-Man.holo-grafx(c) . 7.00
1a Gold Ed. 30.00
2 MBa,A:Spider-Man. 3.50
3 MBa,Families of Venom's
　victims 3.50
4 RLm,A:Spider-Man,V:Life
　Foundation. 3.50
5 RLm,V:Five Symbiotes,A:SpM. . . 3.50
6 RLm,V:Spider-Man. 3.50
Super Size Spec.#1 Planet of
　the Symbiotes,pt.3. . . . . 4.00
Venom:Deathtrap:The Vault,RLm,
　A:Avengers,Freedom Force . . . 7.00

VENOM: LICENSE TO KILL
1997
1 (of 3) LHa,KHt, sequel to Venom
　on trial 2.50
2 LHa,V:Dr. Yes 2.50
3 LHa,V:Dr. Yes 2.50

VENOM: THE MACE
1994
1 Embossed(c),CP(s),LSh,I:Mace . 3.25
2 CP(s),LSh,V:Mace 3.25
3 CP(s),LSh,V:Mace,final issue . . . 3.25

VENOM: THE MADNESS
1993–94
1 B:ANi(s),KJo,V:Juggernaut 3.50
2 KJo,V:Juggernaut 3.25
3 E:ANi(s),KJo,V:Juggernaut 3.25

VENOM: NIGHTS
OF VENGEANCE
1994
1 RLm,I:Stalkers,A:Vengeance 3.25
2 RLm,A:Vengeance,V:Stalkers . . . 3.25
3 RLm,V:Stalkers 3.25
4 RLm,final issue 3.25

VENOM: ON TRIAL
Jan.–May, 1997
1 LHa,Tries to break out 5.00
2 LHa,Defended by Matt Murdock
　(Daredevil),A:Spider-Man 4.00
3 LHa,A:Spider-Man, Carnage,
　Daredevil 4.00

VENOM:
SEED OF DARKNESS
1997
1 LKa,JFy,Flashback, early Eddie
　Brock 2.50

VENOM:
SEPARATION ANXIETY
1994–95
1 Embossed(c) 5.00
2 V:Symbiotes. 5.00
3 . . . . 5.00
4 . . . . 5.00

VENOM: SIGN
OF THE BOSS
1997
1 (of 2) IV,TDr,V:Ghost Rider 5.00
2 (of 2) IV,TDr,conclusion 4.00

VENOM: SINNER
TAKES ALL
1995
1 LHa,GLz,I:New Sin-Eater 3.00
2 V:Sineater 3.00
3 Wrong Man 3.00
4 LHa,GLz,V:Sin-Eater 3.00
5 LHa, finale 3.00

VENOM: TOOTH
AND CLAW
1996–97
1 (of 3) LHa,JPi,AM, Dirtnap usurps
　Venom's body 5.00
2 LHa,JPi,AM,V:Wolverine 4.00
3 LHa,JPi,AM,V:Wolverine,
　Chimera. 4.00

VENOM VS. CARNAGE
June, 2004
1 (of 4) 3.00
2 F:Black Cat 3.00
3 . . . . 3.00
4 F:Toxin 3.00

VENUS
Marvel Atlas, Aug., 1948
1 B:Venus,Hedy Devine,HK,Hey
　Look 2,200.00
2 Venus(c) 1,300.00
3 Carnival(c) 1,100.00
4 Cupid(c).HK,Hey Look 1,100.00

Venus #10
© Marvel Entertainment Group

5 Serenade(c) 1,100.00
6 SSh(c),Wrath of a Goddess,
   A:Loki. 900.00
7 Romance that Could Not Be . . 900.00
8 The Love Trap 900.00
9 Whom the Gods Destroy 900.00
10 JMn,B:Science Fiction/Horror,
   Trapped On the Moon 1,200.00
11 RH,The End of the World. . . 1,300.00
12 GC,The Lost World 1,200.00
13 BEv,King o/t Living Dead . . . 1,200.00
14 BEv,The Fountain of Death . 1,200.00
15 BEv,The Empty Grave 1,200.00
16 BEv,Where Gargoyles Dwell 1,300.00
17 BEv,Tower of Death,
   Bondage(c). 1,200.00
18 BEv,Terror in the Tunnel . . . 1,200.00
19 BEv,PMo, Kiss Of Death . . . 1,200.00

VERY BEST OF
MARVEL COMICS
1-shot reps Marvel Artists
   Favorite Stories 13.00

VIDEO JACK
Nov., 1987
1 KGi,O:Video Jack 3.00
2 KGi. 2.50
3 KGi. 2.50
4 KGi. 2.50
5 KGi. 2.50
6 KGi,NA,BWr,AW 2.50

VISION, THE
1994–95
1 BHs,mini-series 2.50
2 BHs 2.50
3 BHs 2.50
4 BHs 2.50

VISION &
SCARLET WITCH
[1st Series] Nov., 1982
1 RL,V:Halloween 3.00
2 RL,V:Isbisa,D:Whizzer. 3.00
3 RL,A:Wonderman,V:GrimReaper 3.00
4 RL,A:Magneto,Inhumans. 3.00
[2nd Series] 1985–86
1 V:Grim Reaper. 2.50
2 V:Lethal Legion,D:Grim Reaper. . 2.50
3 V:Salem's Seven 2.50
4 I:Glamor & Illusion 2.50
5 A:Glamor & Illusion 2.50

6 A:Magneto 2.50
7 V:Toad 2.50
8 A:Powerman 2.50
9 V:Enchantress 2.50
10 A:Inhumans. 2.50
11 A:Spider-Man. 2.50
12 Birth of V&S's Child 8.00

VISIONARIES
Star, Nov., 1987
1 thru 5 . . . . @2.50
6 Sept., 1988 . . . . 2.50

VOID INDIGO
Epic, Nov., 1984
1 VM,Epic Comics 2.50
2 VM,Epic Comics,March, 1985 . . . 2.50

WACKY DUCK
See: DOPEY DUCK

WALLY THE WIZARD
Star, April, 1985
1 . . . . 4.00
2 thru 12 . . . . @4.00

WAR, THE
1989
1 Sequel to The Draft & The Pit . . 4.00
2 thru 4 . . . . @4.00

WAR ACTION
Marvel Atlas, April, 1952
1 JMn,RH,War Stories, Six Dead
   Men 300.00
2 GT 150.00
3 Invasion in Korea 100.00
4 thru 10 . . . . @100.00
11 and 12 . . . . @125.00
13 BK 125.00
14 Rangers Strike,June, 1953 . . . 100.00

WAR ADVENTURES
Marvel Atlas, Jan., 1952
1 GT,Battle Fatigue 250.00
2 The Story of a Slaughter 125.00
3 JRo 100.00
4 RH(c) 100.00
5 RH,Violent(c) 100.00
6 Stand or Die 100.00
7 JMn(c) 100.00
8 BK 125.00
9 RH(c) 100.00
10 JRo(c),Attack at Dawn 100.00
11 Red Trap 200.00
12 . . . . 100.00
13 RH(c),The Commies Strike
   Feb., 1953 . . . . 100.00

WAR COMBAT
Marvel Atlas, March, 1952
1 JMn,Death of Platoon Leader . 200.00
2 . . . . 125.00
3 JMn(c) 100.00
4 JMn(c) 100.00
5 The Red Hordes 100.00
Becomes:

COMBAT CASEY
6 BEv,Combat Casey cont 175.00
7 . . . . 125.00
8 JMn(c) 100.00
9 . . . . 100.00
10 RH(c). 125.00
11 . . . . 100.00
12 . . . . 100.00
13 thru 19. . . . . @125.00
20 thru 33. . . . . @100.00
34 July, 1957 . . . . 100.00

War Comics #4
© Marvel Entertainment Group

WAR COMICS
Marvel Atlas, Dec., 1950
1 You Only Die Twice 350.00
2 Infantry's War 200.00
3 . . . . 125.00
4 GC,The General Said Nuts . . 125.00
5 . . . . 125.00
6 The Deadly Decision of
   General Kwang 125.00
7 RH,JMn 125.00
8 RH,No Survivors 125.00
9 RH,JMn 125.00
10 . . . . 125.00
11 Flame thrower 150.00
12 thru 21 . . . . @100.00
22 . . . . 125.00
23 thru 37 . . . . @100.00
38 JKu 125.00
39 . . . . 100.00
40 . . . . 100.00
41 . . . . 100.00
42 JO 100.00
43 AT,MD 125.00
44 . . . . 100.00
45 . . . . 125.00
46 RC 125.00
47 . . . . 100.00
48 MD,JO 100.00
49 Sept., 1957 . . . . 125.00

WARHEADS
Marvel UK, 1992–93
1 GEr,I:Warheads,A:Wolverine, . . . 2.50
2 GEr,V:Nick Fury 2.50
3 DTy,A:Iron Man 2.50
4 SCy,A:X-Force 2.50
5 A:X-Force,C:Deaths'Head II 2.50
6 SCy,A:Death's Head II. 2.50
7 SCy,A:Death's Head II,S.Surfer. . 2.50
8 SCy,V:Mephisto 2.50
9 SCy,V:Mephisto 2.50
10 JCz,V:Mephisto 2.50
11 A:Death's Head II 2.50
12 V:Mechanix 2.50
13 Xenophiles Reptiles 2.50
14 last issue. 2.50

WARHEADS: BLACK
DAWN
1 A:Gh.Rider,Morbius 3.25
2 V:Dracula. 2.50

WAR IS HELL
Jan., 1973—Oct., 1975
1 BP,B:reps.,Decision at Dawn . . 35.00
2 Anytime,Anyplace,War is Hell . . 20.00
3 Retreat or Die 20.00
4 Live Grenade 20.00
5 Trapped Platoon 20.00
6 We Die at Dawn 20.00
7 While the Jungle Sleeps,A:Sgt
   Fury 20.00
8 Killed in Action,A;Sgt Fury 20.00
9 B:Supernatural,War Stories . . . 75.00
10 Death is a 30 Ton Tank. 20.00
11 thru 15 . . . . @20.00

WAR IS HELL:
THE FIRST FLIGHT OF
THE PHANTOM EAGLE
Mar., 2008
1 (of 5) GEn,HC 4.00
2 thru 5 GEn,HC . . . . @4.00

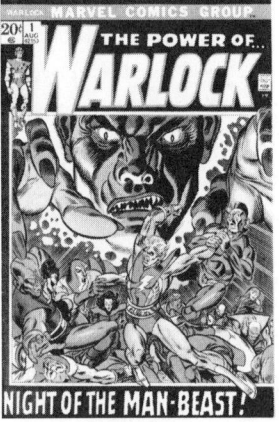

Warlock #1
© Marvel Entertainment Group

WARLOCK
[1st Regular Series] Aug., 1972
1 MGr,GK,I:Counter Earth,
   A:High Evolutionary. 100.00
2 MGr,JB,TS,V:Man Beast 50.00
3 MGr,GK,TS,V:Apollo 50.00
4 MGr,JK,TS,V:Triax 25.00
5 MGr,GK,TS,V:Dr.Doom 25.00
6 MGr,TS(i),O:Brute 25.00
7 MGr,TS(i),V:Brute,D:Dr.Doom . . 25.00
8 MGr,TS(i),R:Man-Beast(cont.
   in Hulk #176). 25.00
9 MGr,JSn,1st`Rebirth`Thanos,
   O:Magnus,N:Warlock,
   I:In-Betweener. 40.00
10 MGr,JSn,SL,O:Thanos,V:Magus,
   A:In-Betweener 50.00
11 MGr,JSn,SL,D:Magus,A:Thanos,
   In-Betweener 40.00
12 MGr,JSn,SL,O:Pip,V:Pro-Boscis
   A:Starfox 25.00
13 MGr,JSn,SL,I&O:Star-Thief. . . . 25.00
14 MGr,JSn,SL,V:Star-Thief. 25.00
15 MGr,JSn,A:Thanos,V:Soul-Gem 40.00

[2nd Regular Series] 1992
1 JSn,rep.Strange Tales #178-180
   Baxter Paper 5.00
2 JSn,rep.Strange Tales #180
   & Warlock #9. . . . . 4.00
3 JSn,rep.Warlock #10-#12 . . . . . 4.00

4 JSn,rep.Warlock #13-#15 . . . . . . 4.00
5 JSn,rep.Warlock #15 . . . . 4.00
6 JSn,rep. 4.00

WARLOCK
[Limited Series]
1 Rep.Warlock Series 3.50
2 thru 6 Rep.Warlock Series . . . @3.00

WARLOCK
Sept., 1998
1 (of 4) TL,RJn,R:Adam Warlock . . 3.00
2 TL,murderer revealed 3.00
3 TL,V:Drax. 3.00
4 TL,Concl. 3.00

Aug., 1999
1 LSi,PFe,Marvel Tech 3.00
2 LSi,PFe,A:Iron Man 2.50
2a variant PFe cover 2.50
3 LSi,PFe,MMo,F:Psiren. 2.50
4 LSi,PFe,MMo,V:Mole Man 2.50
5 LSi,PFe,MMo. 2.50
6 LSi,PFe,MMo,A:Kitty Pryde 2.50
7 LSi,PFe,MMo,R:Wolfsbane,
   Magus 2.50
8 LSi,PFe,MMo,V:Bastion. 2.50
9 LSi,PFe,MMo,F:Bastion. 2.50

Sept., 2004
1 CAd,F:Adam Warlock 3.00
2 CAd 3.00
3 CAd 3.00
4 CAd 3.00

WARLOCK AND THE
INFINITY WATCH
1992–95
1 AMe,Trial of the Gods(from
   Infinity Gauntlet) 3.00
2 AMe,I:Infinity Watch(Gamora,Pip,
   Moondragon,Drax & 1 other). . . 2.75
3 RL,TA,A:High Evolutionary,
   Nobilus,I:Omega 2.75
4 RL,TA,V:Omega. 2.50
5 AMe,TA,V:Omega 2.50
6 AMe,V:Omega(Man-Beast) 2.50
7 TR,TA,V:Mole Man,A:Thanos . . . 2.50
8 TR,TA,Infinity War,A:Thanos 2.50
9 AMe,TA,Inf.War,O:Gamora 2.50
10 AMe,Inf.War,Thanos vs
   Doppleganger 2.50
11 O:Pip,Gamora,Drax,M'dragon. . 2.50
12 TR,Drax Vs.Hulk 2.50
13 TR,Drax vs Hulk 2.50
14 AMe,V:United Nations. 2.50
15 AMe,Magnus,Him 2.50
16 TGr,I:Count Abyss 2.50
17 TGr,I:Maxam 2.50
18 AMe,Inf.Crusade,N:Pip 2.50
19 TGr,A:Hulk,Wolverine,Infinity
   Crusade. 2.50
20 AMe,Inf.Crusade 2.50
21 V:Thor 2.50
22 AMe,Infinity Crusade. 2.50
23 JSn(s),TGb,Blood &
   Thunder#4 . . . . 2.50
24 JSn(s),TGb,V:Geirrodur 2.50
25 JSn(s),AMe,Die-Cut(c),Blood &
   Thunder #12 . . . . 3.50
26 A:Avengers 2.50
27 TGb,V:Avengers 2.50
28 TGb,V:Man-Beast 2.50
29 A:Maya 2.50
30 PO. 2.50
31 . . . . 2.50
32 Heart & Soul 2.50
33 V:Count Abyss 2.50
34 V:Count Abyss 2.50
35 V:Tyrannus 2.50
36 . . . . 2.50

Warlock and the Infinity Watch #3
© Marvel Entertainment Group

37 A:Zaharius. 2.50
38 . . . . 2.50
39 V:Domitron 2.50
40 A:Thanos. 2.50
41 Monster Island 2.50
42 Warlock vs. Maxam, Atlantis
   Rising, final issue 2.50

WARLOCK CHRONICLES
1993–94
1 TR,F:Adam Warlock,holo-grafx(c),
   I:Darklore,Meer'lyn 3.25
2 TR,Infinity Crusade,Thanos revealed
   to have the Reality Gem 2.50
3 TR,A:Mephisto 2.50
4 TR,A:Magnus 2.50
5 TR(c),Inf.Crusade 2.50
6 TR,Blood & Thunder,pt.#3 . . . . . 2.50
7 TR,Blood & Thunder,pt.#7 . . . . . 2.50
8 TR,Blood & Thunder,pt.#11 . . . . 2.50
9 TR 2.50
10 TR. 2.50
11 TR 2.50

WAR MACHINE
1994–96
1 GG,Foil Embossed(c),B:LKa&StB,
   O:War Machine,V:Cable,
   C:Deathlok. 3.25
1a Newstand Ed. 2.50
2 GG,V:Cable,Deathlok,w/card . . . 3.25
3 GG,V:Cable,Deathlok. 3.25
4 GG,C:Force Works. 3.25
5 GG,I:Deachtoll 3.25
6 GG,V:Deathtoll 3.25
7 GG,A:Hawkeye 3.25
8 reg ed. 3.25
8a neon(c),w/insert print 3.00
9 Hands of Mandarin,pt.2 . . . . 2.50
10 Hands of Mandarin,pt.5 . . . . . . 2.50
11 X-Mas Party 2.50
12 V:Terror Device 2.50
13 V:The Rush Team 2.50
14 A:Force Works 2.50
15 In The Past of WWII 2.50
16 DAn,A:Rick Fury,Cap.America . . 2.50
17 The Man Who Won WWII 2.50
18 DAn,N:War Machine 2.50
19 DAn,A:Hawkeye 2.50
20 DAn,The Crossing 2.50
21 DAn,The Crossing 2.50
22 DAn,V:Iron Man 2.50
23 DAn,Avengers:Timeslide. 2.50

MARVEL

WAR MAN
Epic, 1993
1 thru 2 CDi(s) 2.50

WEAPON X
1995
1 Wolverine After Xavier 4.00
2 Full Scale War 2.50
3 Jean Leaves 2.50
4 F:Gateway 2.50

WEAPON X
Aug., 2002
1-shot Wild Child #1, JWi 3.00
1-shot Sauron #1, JWi,KIK 3.00
1-shot Kane #1, JWi 3.00
1-shot Marrow #1, JWi 3.00
1-shot Agent Zero #1, JWi 3.00
1 . . . . 3.00
2 F:Marrow 3.00
3 . . . . 3.00
4 Hunt for Sabretooth 3.00
5 Evil plans,D.Maggot 3.00
6 NRd,special mission 3.00
7 The Underground,pt.1 . . . . 3.00
8 The Underground,pt.2 . . . . 3.00
9 The Underground,pt.3 . . . . 3.00
10 The Underground,pt.4 . . . . 3.00
11 The Underground,pt.5 . . . . 3.00
12 The Underground,pt.6 . . . . 3.00
13 The Underground,concl. 3.00
14 R:Mr. Sinister 3.00
15 Defection,pt.1,F:X-Man 3.00
16 Defection,pt.2 . . . . 3.00
17 Defection,pt.3 . . . . 3.00
18 Defection,pt.4 . . . . 3.00
19 Countdown to Zero,pt.1 . . . . . . 3.00
20 Countdown to Zero,pt.2 . . . . . . 3.00
21 Countdown to Zero,pt.3 . . . . . . 3.00
22 Mutant feared 3.00
23 TMd,War of the Programs,pt.1 . . 3.00
24 TMd,War of the Programs,pt.2 . . 3.00
25 TMd,War of the Programs,pt.3 . . 3.00
26 TMd,Man and Superman,pt.1 . . 3.00
27 TMd,Man and Superman,pt.2 . . 3.00
28 TMd,Man and Superman,pt.3 . . 3.00

WEAPON X: DAYS OF FUTURE NOW
July, 2005
1 (of 5) BS 3.00
2 Bs. 3.00
3 BS(c), ... 3.00
4 BS,Lord Magnus 3.00
5 BS 3.00

WEAPON X: FIRST CLASS
Nov., 2008
1 (of 3) 4.00
1a variant (c) 4.00

WEAVEWORLD
Epic, 1991–92
1 MM, Clive Barker adaptation 5.00
2 MM,Into the Weave 5.00
3 MM. 5.00

WEB OF SCARLET SPIDER
1995–96
1 TDF,Virtual Mortality,pt.1 . . . . . . 2.50
2 TDF,CyberWar,pt.2 . . . . 2.50
3 Nightmare in Scarlet,pt.1 . . . . . . 2.50
4 Nightmare in Scarlet,pt.3 . . . . . . 2.50

WEB OF SPIDER-MAN
April, 1985
1 JM,V:New Costume 20.00
2 JM,V:Vulture 15.00
3 JM,V:Vulture 15.00
4 JM,JBy,V:Dr.Octopus 7.00
5 JM,JBy,V:Dr.Octopus 7.00
6 MZ,BL,JM,Secret Wars II 7.00
7 SB,A:Hulk,V:Nightmare,
     C:Wolverine 7.00
8 V:Smithville Thunder 7.00
9 V:Smithville Thunder 7.00
10 JM,A:Dominic Fortune,
     V:Shocker 7.00
11 BMc,V:Thugs 7.00
12 BMc,SB,V:Thugs 7.00
13 BMc,V:J.JonahJameson 7.00
14 KB,V:Black Fox 7.00
15 V:Black Fox,I:Chance 6.00
16 MS,KB,V:Magma 6.00
17 MS,V:Magma 7.00
18 MS,KB,Where is Spider-Man? . 10.00
19 MS,BMc,I:Solo,Humbug 7.00
20 MS,V:Terrorists 7.00
21 V:Fake Spider-Man 7.00
22 MS,V:Terrorists 7.00
23 V:Slyde 7.00
24 SB,V:Vulture,Hobgoblin 7.00
25 V:Aliens 7.00
26 V:Thugs. 7.00
27 V:Headhunter 7.00
28 BL,V:Thugs 7.00
29 A:Wolverine,2nd App:New
     Hobgoblin 9.00
30 KB,O:Rose,C:Daredevil,Capt.
     America,Wolverine,Punisher . . 9.00
31 MZ,BMc,V:Kraven 8.00
32 MZ,BMc,V:Kraven 8.00
33 BSz(c),SL,V:Kingpin,Mad
     Dog Ward,pt.#1 . . . . 6.00
34 SB,A:Watcher 6.00
35 AS,V:Living Brain 6.00
36 AS,V:Phreak Out,I:Tombstone . . 7.00
37 V:Slasher 7.00
38 AS,A:Tombstone,V:Hobgoblin . . 7.00
39 AS,V:Looter(Meteor Man) 6.00
40 AS,V:Cult of Love 6.00
41 AS,V:Cult of Love 6.00
42 AS,V:Cult of Love 6.00
43 AS,V:Cult of Love 6.00
44 AS,V:Warzone,A:Hulk 5.00
45 AS,V:Vulture 5.00
46 A:Dr.Pym,V:Nekra 5.00
47 AS,V:Hobgoblin 6.00

Web of Spider-Man #24
© *Marvel Entertainment Group*

48 AS,O:New Hobgoblin's Demonic
     Power 10.00
49 VM,V:Drugs 5.00
50 AS,V:Chameleon(double size) . . 7.00
51 MBa,V:Chameleon,Lobo Bros. . . 5.00
52 FS,JR,O:J.Jonah Jameson
     V:Chameleon 5.00
53 MBa,V:Lobo Bros.,C:Punisher
     A:Chameleon 5.00
54 AS,V:Chameleon,V:Lobo Bros. . . 5.00
55 AS,V:Chameleon,Hammerhead,
     V:Lobo Bros. 5.00
56 AS,I&O:Skin Head,
     A:Rocket Racer 5.00
57 AS,D:SkinHead,
     A:Rocket Racer 5.00
58 AS,V:Grizzly 5.00
59 AS,Acts of Vengeance,V:Titania
     A:Puma,Cosmic Spider-Man . . . 7.00
60 AS,A of V,V:Goliath 5.00
61 AS,A of V,V:Dragon Man. 5.00
62 AS,V:Molten Man 3.00
63 AS,V:Mister Fear. 3.00
64 AS,V:Graviton,Titania,Trapster . . 3.00
65 AS,V:Goliath,Trapster,Graviton . . 3.00
66 AS,V:Tombstone,A:G.Goblin 3.00
67 AS,A:GreenGoblin,
     V:Tombstone 3.00
68 AS,A:GreenGoblin,
     V:Tombstone 3.00
69 AS,V:Hulk 4.00
70 AS,I:The Spider/Hulk. 4.00
71 A:Silver Sable 3.00
72 AM,A:Silver Sable 3.00
73 AS,A:Human Torch,
     Colossus,Namor 3.00
74 AS,I:Spark,V:Bora 3.00
75 AS,C:New Warriors 3.00
76 AS,Spidey in Ice 3.00
77 AS,V:Firebrand,Inheritor 3.00
78 AS,A:Firebrand,Cloak&Dagger . . 3.00
79 AS,V:Silvermane 3.00
80 AS,V:Silvermane 3.00
81 I:Bloodshed 3.00
82 V:Man Mountain Marko. 3.00
83 V:A.I.M. Supersuit. 3.00
84 AS,B:Name of the Rose 3.00
85 AS,Name of the Rose 3.00
86 AS,I:Demogoblin 3.00
87 AS,I:Praetorian Guard. 3.00
88 AS,Name of the Rose 3.00
89 AS,E:Name of the Rose,
     I:Bloodrose 3.00
90 AS,30th Ann.,w/hologram,
     polybagged,V:Mysterio 3.50
90a Gold 2nd printing 3.00
91 AS,V:Whisper And Pulse 3.00
92 AS,V:Foreigner 3.00
93 AS,BMc,V:Hobgoblin,A:Moon
     Knight,Foreigner 3.00
94 AS,V:Hobgoblin,A:MoonKnight . . 3.00
95 AS,Spirits of Venom#1,A:Venom,
     J.Blaze,GR,V:Hag & Troll 3.00
96 AS,Spirits of Venom#3, A:G.R,
     J.Blaze,Venom,Hobgoblin 3.00
97 AS,I:Dr.Trench,V:Bloodrose . . . 3.00
98 AS,V:Bloodrose,Foreigner 3.00
99 I:Night Watch,V:New Enforcer . . 3.00
100 AS,JRu,V:Enforcers,Bloodrose,
     Kingpin(Alfredo),I:Spider Armor,
     O:Night Watch,Holografx(c). . . 4.00
101 AS,Total Carnage,V:Carnage,
     Shriek,A:Cloak and Dagger,
     Venom 3.00
102 Total Carnage#6,V:Carnage,
     A:Venom,Morbius 3.00
103 AS,Maximum Carnage#10,
     V:Carnage 3.00
104 AS,Infinity Crusade 2.50
105 AS,Infinity Crusade 2.50
106 AS,Infinity Crusade 2.75
107 AS,A:Sandman,Quicksand 2.50

108 B:TKa(s),AS,I:Sandstorm,
    BU:Cardiac 2.50
109 AS,V:Shocker,A:Night Thrasher,
    BU:D:Calypso 2.50
110 AS,I:Warrant,A:Lizard 2.50
111 AS,V:Warrant,Lizard 2.50
112 AS,Pursuit#3,V:Chameleon,
    w/card 2.50
113 AS,A:Gambit,Black Cat,w/cel . . 3.50
113a Newsstand Ed. 2.50
114 AS 2.50
115 AS,V:Facade 2.50
116 AS,V:Facade 2.50
117 Foil(c), flip book with
    Power & Responsibility #1 . . . . 5.00
117a Newsstand ed. 2.50
118 Spider-clone, V:Venom 3.00
119 Clone,V:Venom 3.00
119a bagged with Milestone rep.
    Amazing Sp-Man #150,checklist 8.00
120 Web of Life,pt.1 . . . . 2.50
121 Web of Life,pt.3 . . . . 2.50
122 Smoke and Mirrors,pt.1 . . . . . . 2.50
123 The Price of Truth,pt.2 . . . . 2.50
124 The Mark of Kaine,pt.1 . . . . 2.50
125 R:Gwen Stacy 3.00
125a 3-D Holodisk cover 4.25
126 The Trial of Peter Parker,pt.1 . . 2.50
127 Maximum Clonage,pt.2 . . . . 2.50
128 TDF,Exiled,pt.1 . . . . 2.50
129 Timebomb,pt.2 . . . . 3.00
Ann.#1 V:Future Max 7.00
Ann.#2 AAd,MMi,A:Warlock 10.00
Ann.#3 AS,DP,JRu,JM,BL 4.50
Ann.#4 AS,TM,RLm,Evolutionary
    Wars,A:Man Thing,V:Slug 5.00
Ann.#5 AS,SD,JS,Atlantis
    Attacks,A:Fantastic Four 4.00
Ann.#6 SD,JBr,SB,A:Punisher 4.50
Ann.#7 Vibranium Vendetta #3 . . . . 3.50
Ann.#8 Hero Killers#3,A:New
    Warriors,BU:Venom,Black Cat . 3.50
Ann.#9 CMa,I:Cadre,w/card. 3.50
Ann.#10 V:Shriek 4.00
Super Size Spec.#1 Planet of
    the Symbiotes,pt.5 . . . . 4.00

WEBSPINNERS: TALES
OF SPIDER-MAN
Nov., 1998

1 JMD,JR,MZi,A:Mysterio,seq.to
    Amaz.Sp-M#38, 48-page 3.00
1a signed 7.00
2 JMD,JR,V:J.Jonah Jameson 2.50
2a variant SR cover 2.50
3 JMD,V:Mysterio, concl. 2.50
4 KG,ErS,seq.to Silver Surfer#18 . . 2.50
5 KG,ErS,A:Silver Surfer 2.50
6 KG,ErS,F:Silver Surfer,
    Psycho-Man & Annihilus 2.50
7 BS,MPn,V:Sandman 2.50
8 BS,MPn,V:Sandman 2.50
9 V:Sandman 2.50
10 V:Chameleon, pt.1 . . . . 2.50
11 V:Chameleon, pt.2 . . . . 2.50
12 conclusion, 48-pg.. . . . . 3.50
13 . . . . 2.50
14 HMe,BS,A:Carnage 2.50
15 V:Vulture 2.50
16 V:Vulture 2.50
17 TDF, black costume 2.50
18 TDF, Silversable 2.50

WEIRD WONDERTALES
Dec., 1973

1 B:Reprints 45.00
2 I Was Kidnapped by a Flying
    Saucer 25.00
3 BP,The Thing in the Bog 25.00
4 SD,SK,It Lurks Behind
    the Wall 25.00

5 SD 25.00
6 The Man Who Owned a Ghost . 25.00
7 BP,The Apes That Walked
    like Men 25.00
8 JMn,Reap A Deadly Harvest . 25.00
9 The Murder Mirror 25.00
10 SD,SK,Mister Morgan's
    Monster 25.00
11 SD,SK,Slaughter in
    Shrangri-La 20.00
12 SD,MD,The Stars Scream
    Murder 20.00
13 SD,The Totem Strikes 20.00
14 Witching Circle 20.00
15 . . . . 20.00
16 GC,The Shark 20.00
17 Creature From Krogarr 20.00
18 Krang 20.00
19 SD,A:Dr Druid 20.00
20 SD,MD,The Madness 20.00
21 SD,A:Dr Druid 20.00
22 The World Below,May, 1975 . . . 20.00

WENDY PARKER COMICS
Marvel Atlas, 1953

1 . . . . 150.00
2 . . . . 100.00
3 . . . . 125.00
4 . . . . 125.00
5 . . . . 125.00
6 . . . . 125.00
7 . . . . 125.00
8 . . . . 125.00

WEREWOLF BY NIGHT
Sept., 1972

1 MP(cont from Marvel Spotlight)
    FullMoonRise..WerewolfKill . . 200.00
2 MP,Like a Wild Beast at Bay . . . 90.00
3 MP,Mystery of the Mad Monk . . 60.00
4 MP,The Danger Game 60.00
5 MP,A Life for a Death 60.00
6 MP,Carnival of Fear 50.00
7 MP,JM,Ritual of Blood 50.00
8 MP,Krogg,Lurker from Beyond . 50.00
9 TS,V:Tatterdemalion 50.00
10 TS,bondage cover 50.00
11 GK,TS,Full Moon..Fear Moon . 35.00
12 GK,Cry Monster 35.00
13 MP,ManMonsterCalledTaboo . . 30.00
14 MP,Lo,the Monster Strikes 30.00
15 MP,(new)O:Werewolf,
    V:Dracula 50.00
16 MP,TS,A:Hunchback of Notre
    Dame 35.00
17 Behold the Behemoth 35.00
18 War of the Werewolves 35.00
19 V:Dracula 32.00
20 The Monster Breaks Free 30.00
21 GK(c),To Cure a Werewolf 20.00
22 GK(c),Face of a Friend 20.00
23 Silver Bullet for a Werewolf . . . 20.00
24 GK(c),V:The Brute 20.00
25 GK(c),Eclipse of Evil 20.00
26 GK(c),A Crusade of Murder . . . 20.00
27 GK(c),Scourge o/t Soul-Beast . 20.00
28 GK(c),V:Dr.Glitternight 20.00
29 GK(c),V:Dr.Glitternight 20.00
30 GK(c),Red Slash across
    Midnight 20.00
31 Death in White 20.00
32 I&O:Moon Knight 175.00
33 Were-Beast..Moon Knight
    A:Moon Knight(2nd App) 175.00
34 GK(c),TS,House of Evil..House
    of Death 20.00
35 TS,JS,BWi,Jack Russell vs.
    Werewolf 20.00
36 Images of Death 20.00
37 BWr(c),BW,A:Moon Knight,
    Hangman,Dr.Glitternight 35.00

38 . . . . 50.00
39 V:Brother Voodoo 50.00
40 A:Brother Voodoo,V:Dr.
    Glitternight 20.00
41 V:Fire Eyes 20.00
42 A:IronMan,Birth of a Monster . . 20.00
43 Tri-Animal Lives,A:Iron Man . . . 20.00
G-Size#2,SD,A:Frankenstein
    Monster (reprint) 20.00
G-Size#3 GK(c),Transylvania 20.00
G-Size#4 GK(c),A:Morbius 20.00
G-Size#5 GK(c),Peril of
    Paingloss 15.00

WEREWOLF BY NIGHT
Dec., 1997

1 PJe,F:Jack Russell returns 3.00
2 PJe,Search for wolf Amulet 3.00
3 PJe,Stuck between man & wolf . . 3.00
4 PJe,to the depths of hell 3.00
5 PJe, confronts demon 3.00
6 PJe, visit Underworld nightclub . . 3.00
Storyline continues in Strange Tales

WEST COAST AVENGERS
[Limited Series] Sept., 1984

1 BH,A:Shroud,J:Hawkeye,IronMan,
    WonderMan,Mockingbird,Tigra . 4.00
2 BH,V:Blank 3.00
3 BH,V:Graviton 3.00
4 BH,V:Graviton 3.00

[Regular Series] 1985–89

1 AM,JSt,V:Lethal Legion 4.00
2 AM,JSt,V:Lethal Legion 3.00
3 AM,JSt,V:Kraven 3.00
4 AM,JSt,A:Firebird,Thing,I:Master
    Pandemonium 3.00
5 AM,JSt,A:Werewolf,Thing 3.00
6 AM,KB,A:Thing 3.00
7 AM,JSt,V:Ultron 3.00
8 AM,JSt,V:Rangers,A:Thing 3.00
9 AM,JSt,V:Master Pandemonium . 3.00
10 AM,JSt,V:Headlok,Griffen 3.00
11 AM,JSt,A:Nick Fury 3.00
12 AM,JSt,V:Graviton 3.00
13 AM,JSt,V:Graviton 3.00
14 AM,JSt,V:Pandemonium 3.00
15 AM,JSt,A:Hellcat 3.00
16 AM,JSt,V:Tiger Shark,
    Whirlwind 3.00
17 AM,JSt,V:Dominus' Minions 3.00
18 AM,JSt,V:The Wild West 3.00
19 AM,JSt,A:Two Gun Kid 3.00

20 AM,JSt,A:Rawhide Kid 3.00
21 AM,JSt,A:Dr.Pym,Moon Knight . . 3.00
22 AM,JSt,A:Fant.Four,Dr.Strange,
   Night Rider 3.00
23 AM,RT,A:Phantom Rider 3.00
24 AM,V:Dominus 3.00
25 AM,V:Abomination 3.00
26 AM,V:Zodiac 3.00
27 AM,V:Zodiac 3.00
28 AM,V:Zodiac 3.00
29 AM,V:Taurus,A:Shroud 3.00
30 AM,C:Composite Avenger 3.00
31 AM,V:Arkon 3.00
32 AM,TD,V:Yetrigar,J:Wasp 3.00
33 AM,O:Ant-Man,Wasp;
   V:Madam X,El Toro 3.00
34 AM,V:Quicksilver,J:Vision &
   Scarlet Witch 3.00
35 AM,V:Dr.Doom,Quicksilver 3.00
36 AM,V:The Voice 3.00
37 V:The Voice,A:Mantis 3.00
38 AM,TMo,V:Defiler 3.00
39 AM,V:Swordsman 3.00
40 AM,MGu,V:NightShift,
   A:Shroud 3.00
41 TMo,I:New Phantom Rider,
   L:Moon Knight 3.00
42 JBy,Visionquest#1,V:Ultron 3.50
43 JBy,Visionquest#2, ... 3.00
44 JBy,Visionquest#3,J:USAgent . . 3.00
45 JBy,Visionquest#4,
   I:New Vision. 3.50
46 JBy,I:Great Lakes Avengers 3.00
Ann. #1 MBr,GI,V:Zodiak 3.25
Ann. #2 AM,A:SilverSurfer,V:Death,
   Collector,R:Grandmaster 3.00
Ann. #3 AM,RLm,TD,Evolutionary
   Wars,R:Giant Man 3.50
Becomes:

AVENGERS WEST COAST

WESTERN GUNFIGHTERS
[2nd series] Aug., 1970
1 JK,JB,DAy,B:Ghost Rider
   A:Fort Rango,The Renegades
   Gunhawk 75.00
2 HT(c),DAy,JMn,O:Nightwind,
   V:Tarantula 35.00
3 DAy,MD,V:Hurricane, rep. 35.00
4 HT(c),DAy,TS,B:Gunhawk,
   Apache Kid,A:Renegades . . . 45.00
5 DAy,FrG,A:Renegades 35.00

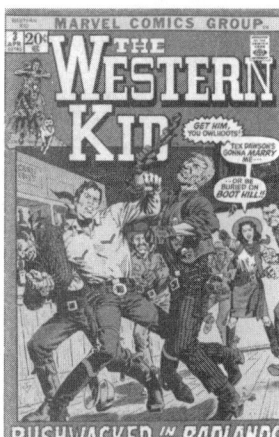
Western Kid #3
© *Marvel Entertainment Group*

6 HT(c),DAy,SSh,Death of
   Ghost Rider 30.00
7 HT(c),DAy,SSh,O:Ghost Rider
   retold,E:Ghost Rider,Gunhawk 30.00
8 DAy,SSh,B:Black Rider,Outlaw
   Kid(rep) 25.00
9 DW,Revenge rides the Range. . 25.00
10 JK,JMn,O:Black Rider,B:Matt
   Slade,E:Outlaw Kid 25.00
11 JK,Duel at Dawn 25.00
12 JMn,O:Matt Slade 30.00
13 Save the Gold Coast Expires . . 25.00
14 JSo(c),Outlaw Town 25.00
15 E:Matt Slade,Showdown in
   Outlaw Canyon 25.00
16 B:Kid Colt,Shoot-out in Silver
   City 25.00
17 thru 20 . . . . @25.00
21 thru 24 . . . . @15.00
25 . . . . 15.00
26 F:Kid Colt,Gun-Slinger,
   Apache Kid 15.00
27 thru 32 . . . . @15.00
33 Nov., 1975 . . . . 15.00

WESTERN KID
[1st Series] Dec., 1954
1 JR,B:Western Kid,O:Western Kid
   (Tex Dawson) 250.00
2 JMn,JR,Western Adventure . . . 125.00
3 JMn(c),JR,Gunfight(c) 100.00
4 JMn(c),JR,The Badlands 100.00
5 JR 100.00
6 JR 100.00
7 JR 100.00
8 JR 100.00
9 JR,AW 125.00
10 JR,AW,Man in the Middle 125.00
11 thru 16 . . . . @100.00
17 Aug., 1957 . . . . 100.00

[2nd Series]
Dec., 1971–Aug., 1972
1 Reprints 35.00
2 . . . . 20.00
3 AW 25.00
4 . . . . 20.00
5 . . . . 20.00

WESTERN OUTLAWS
Marvel Atlas,
Feb., 1954—Aug., 1957
1 JMn(c),RH,BP,The Greenville
   Gallows,Hanging(c) 300.00
2 . . . . 150.00
3 thru 10 . . . . @125.00
11 AW,MD 150.00
12 JMn 100.00
13 MB,JMn 125.00
14 AW 125.00
15 AT,GT 100.00
16 BP,JMn,JSe,AW 100.00
17 JMn,AW 100.00
18 JSe 100.00
19 JMn,JSe,RC 100.00
20 and 21 JSe . . . . @100.00

WESTERN OUTLAWS
& SHERIFFS
See: BEST WESTERN

WESTERN TALES
OF BLACK RIDER
See: ALL WINNERS COMICS

WESTERN TEAM-UP
Nov., 1973
1 Rawhide Kid/Dakota Kid 50.00

WESTERN THRILLERS
Nov., 1954
1 JMn,Western tales 200.00
2 . . . . 100.00
3 . . . . 100.00
4 . . . . 100.00
Becomes:

COWBOY ACTION
March, 1955–March, 1956
5 JMn(c),The Prairie Kid 150.00
6 thru 10 . . . . @100.00
11 MN,AW,The Manhunter 125.00
Becomes:

QUICK-TRIGGER
WESTERN
May, 1956–Sept., 1957
12 Bill Larson Strikes 200.00
13 AW,The Man From Cheyenne 200.00
14 BEv,RH(c) 200.00
15 AT,RC 175.00
16 JK,JD 150.00
17 GT 150.00
18 GM 150.00
19 JSe 100.00

WESTERN TRAILS
Marvel Atlas, 1957
1 MMe,FBe,JSe(c),Ringo Kid . . . 165.00
2 MMe,FBe,JSe(c) 100.00

WESTERN WINNERS
See: ALL WINNERS COMICS

WHAT IF?
[1st Regular Series] Feb., 1977
1 Spider-Man joined Fant.Four . . . 30.00
2 GK(c),Hulk had Banner brain . . 15.00
3 GK,KJ,F:Avengers 12.00
4 GK(c),F:Invaders 12.00
5 F:Captain America 12.00
6 F:Fantastic Four 12.00
7 GK(c),F:Spider-Man 10.00
8 GK(c),F:Daredevil 10.00
9 JK(c),F:Avengers of the '50s . . 10.00
10 JB,F:Thor 10.00
11 JK,F:FantasticFour 8.00
12 F:Hulk 8.00
13 JB,Conan Alive Today 10.00
14 F:Sgt. Fury 6.00
15 CI,F:Nova 6.00

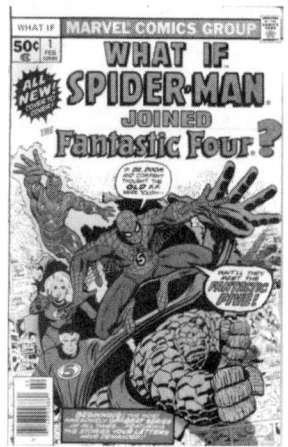
What If #1
© *Marvel Entertainment Group*

MARVEL

16 F:Master of Kung Fu......... 6.00
17 CI,F:Ghost Rider............. 6.00
18 TS,F:Dr.Strange 5.00
19 PB,F:Spider-Man 6.00
20 F:Avengers 6.00
21 GC,F:Sub-Mariner............. 6.00
22 F:Dr.Doom................... 5.00
23 JB,F:Hulk 6.00
24 GK,RB,Gwen Stacy had lived... 10.00
25 F:Thor,Avengers,O:Mentor 5.00
26 JBy(c),F:Captain America 8.00
27 FM(c),Phoenix hadn't died ... 22.00
28 FM,F:Daredevil,Ghost Rider. .. 10.00
29 MG(c),F:Avengers............. 6.00
30 RB,F:Spider-Man 10.00
31 Wolverine killed the Hulk 25.00
32 Avengers lost to Korvac 5.00
33 BL,Dazzler herald of Galactus .. 5.00
34 FH,FM,JBy,BSz:Humor issue ... 5.00
35 FM,Elektra had lived.......... 10.00
36 JBy,Fant.Four had no powers... 5.00
37 F:Thing,Beast,Silver Surfer..... 5.00
38 F:Daredevil,Captain America ... 5.00
39 Thor had fought Conan....... 5.00
40 F:Dr.Strange 5.00
41 F:Sub-Mariner................ 5.00
42 F:Fantastic Four 5.00
43 F:Conan 6.00
44 F:Captain America 5.00
45 F:Hulk,Berserk 5.00
46 Uncle Ben had lived 7.00
47 F:Thor,Loki 5.00
Spec.#1 F:Iron Man,Avengers..... 6.00
Best of What If? rep.#1,#24,
    #27,#28 .... 13.00

[2nd Regular Series]
1 RWi,MG,The Avengers had lost
    the Evolutionary War........ 5.00
2 GCa,Daredevil Killed Kingpin,
    A:Hobgoblin, The Rose 4.00
3 Capt.America Hadn't Given Up
    Costume,A:Avengers......... 3.50
4 MBa,Spider-Man kept Black
    Costume,A:Avengers,Hulk 9.00
5 Vision Destroyed Avengers,
    A:Wonder Man.............. 3.50
6 RLm,X-Men Lost Inferno,
    A:Dr.Strange 6.00
7 RLd,Wolverine Joined Shield,
    A:Nick Fury,Black Widow 7.00
8 Iron Man Lost The Armor Wars,
    A:Ant Man 3.50
9 RB,New X-Men Died 6.00
10 MZ(c),BMc,Punisher's Family
    Didn't Die,A:Kingpin 3.00
11 TM(c),JV,SM,Fant.Four had the
    Same Powers,A:Nick Fury ... 3.50
12 JV,X-Men Stayed in Asgard,
    A:Thor,Hela 5.00
13 JLe(c),Prof.X Became
    Juggernaut,A:X-Men 3.50
14 RLm(c),Capt.Marvel didn't die
    A:Silver Surfer............. 3.50
15 GCa,Fant.Four Lost Trial of
    Galactus,A:Gladiator 3.00
16 Wolverine Battled Conan,
    A:X-Men,Red Sonja.......... 5.00
17 Kraven Killed Spider-Man,
    A:Daredevil,Captain America .. 3.00
18 LMc,Fant.Four fought Dr.Doom
    before they gained powers ... 3.00
19 RW,Vision took over Earth,
    A:Avengers,Dr.Doom........ 3.00
20 Spider-Man didn't marry Mary
    Jane,A:Venom,Kraven........ 5.00
21 Spider-Man married Black Cat,
    A:Vulture,Silver Sable 5.00
22 RLm,Silver Surfer didn't escape
    Earth,A:F.F,Mephisto,Thanos . 4.00
23 New X-Men never existed,
    A:Eric the Red,Lilandra 3.00

24 Wolverine Became Lord of
    Vampires,A:Punisher......... 3.00
25 Marvel Heroes lost Atlantis
    Attacks,double size 3.50
26 LMc,Punisher Killed Daredevil,
    A:Spider-Man.............. 3.00
27 Submariner Joined Fantastic
    Four,A:Dr. Doom 3.00
28 RW,Capt.America led Army of
    Super-Soldiers,A:Submariner .. 3.00
29 RW,Capt.America formed the
    Avengers 3.00
30 Inv.Woman's 2nd Child had
    lived,A:Fantastic Four 3.00
31 Spider-Man/Captain Universe
    Powers................... 3.00
32 Phoenix Rose Again,pt.1 ..... 4.00
33 Phoenix Rose Again,pt.2 ..... 4.00
34 Humor Issue 3.00
35 B:Time Quake,F.F. vs.Dr. Doom
    & Annihilus............... 3.00
36 Cosmic Avengers,V:Guardians
    of the Galaxy.............. 3.00
37 X-Vampires,V:Dormammu 4.00
38 Thor was prisoner of Set 3.00
39 E:Time Quake,Watcher saved the
    Universe 3.00
40 Storm remained A thief?...... 3.00
41 JV,Avengers fought Galactus ... 3.00
42 KWe,Spidey kept extra arms ... 3.00
43 Wolverine married Mariko...... 3.50
44 Punisher possessed by Venom . 5.00
45 Barbara Ketch became G.R..... 3.00
46 Cable Killed Prof.X,Cyclops &
    Jean Grey 4.00
47 Magneto took over USA 3.00
48 Daredevil Saved Nuke 3.00
49 Silver Surfer had Inf.Gauntlet?.. 3.50
50 Hulk killed Wolverine 10.00
51 PCu,Punisher is Capt.America . 15.00
52 BHi,Wolverine led Alpha Flight.. 3.50
53 F:Iron Man,Hulk 3.00
54 F:Death's Head.............. 3.00
55 LKa(s),Avengers lose G.Storm .. 3.00
56 Avengers lose G.Storm#2 ..... 3.00
57 Punisher a member of SHIELD . 3.00
58 Punisher kills SpM 5.00
59 Wolverine lead Alpha Flight 5.00
60 RoR,Scott & Jean's Wedding ... 5.00
61 Spider-Man's Parents 3.00
62 Woverine vs Weapon X 3.50
63 F:War Machine,Iron Man 3.00
64 Iron Man sold out 3.00
65 Archangel fell from Grace...... 3.00
66 Rogue and Thor 3.00
67 Cap.America returns.......... 3.00
68 Captain America story......... 3.00
69 Stryfe Killed X-Men 3.00
70 Silver Surfer 3.50
71 The Hulk 3.00
72 Parker Killed Burglar.......... 3.00
73 Daredevil,Kingpin 3.00
74 Sinister Formed X-Men........ 7.00
75 Gen-X's Blink had lived 3.00
76 Flash Thompson Spider-Man ... 3.00
77 Legion had killed Magneto 10.00
78 FF had stayed together 7.00
79 Storm had Phoenix's Power 3.00
80 KGa,Hulk was Cured 4.00
81 Age of Apocalypse didn't end .. 11.00
82 WML,J.JonahJameson
    adopted Spider-Man 3.00
83 Daredevil.................. 3.00
84 Shard 3.00
85 Magneto Ruled all mutants..... 3.00
86 Scarlet Spider vs. Spider-Man .. 3.00
87 Sabretooth 3.00
88 Spider-Man 3.00
89 Fantastic Four.............. 4.00
90 Cyclops & Havok 3.00
91 F:Hulk, nice guy, Banner violent. 3.00
92 F:Cannonball,Husk 3.00

What If, 2nd Series, Minus 1 Special
© Marvel Entertainment Group

93 F:Wolverine................. 3.50
94 JGz,F:Juggernaut............ 3.00
95 IV,F:Ghost Rider 3.00
96 CWo,F:Quicksilver........... 3.00
97 F:Black Knight.............. 3.00
98 F:Nightcrawler & Rogue 3.00
99 F:Black Cat................ 3.00
100 IV,KJ,F:Gambit &
    Rogue, 48-pg............. 7.00
101 ATi,F:Archangel............. 3.00
102 F:Daredevil's Dad........... 3.00
103 DaF,F:Captain America....... 3.00
104 F:Silver Surver,ImpossibleMan. 3.00
105 TDF,RF,F:Spider-Man and
    Mary Jane's Daughter....... 25.00
106 TDF,F:X-Men,Gambit
    sentenced to death 3.00
107 TDF,RF,BSz,F:Thor......... 3.00
108 TDF,F:The Avengers........ 3.00
109 TA,F:Fantastic Four 3.00
110 TDF,F:Wolverine........... 3.00
111 TDF,F:Wolverine........... 3.00
112 F:Ka-Zar 3.00
113 F:Iron Man, Dr. Strange, ... 3.00
114 F:Secret Wars, 32-page,
    final issue 12.00
Minus 1 Spec., AOI, flashback,
    F:Bishop 3.00

WHAT IF
Dec., 2004
1-shot Aunt May Had Died Instead
    Of Uncle Ben.............. 3.00
1-shot Karen Page Had Lived 3.00
1-shot Jessica Jones Had Joined
    The Avengers 3.00
1-shot Magneto Had Formed the
    X-Men with Professor X 3.00
1-shot Dr. Doom Had Become
    The Thing 3.00
1-shot General Ross Had Become
    The Hulk 3.00
1-shot Wha...Huh? (2005) 4.00

WHAT IF?
Dec., 2005
1 Fantastic Four were cosmonauts 3.00
2 Stephen Rogers/Captain America 3.00
3 Thor transformed into Herald
    of Galactus 3.00
4 Public Enemy Number One..... 3.00
5 Namor grew up on land........ 3.00
6 Samurai Devil Who Dares...... 3.00

WHAT IF?
Nov., 2006
Avengers Disassembled #1 . . . . . . 4.00
Spider-Man #1 . . . . 5.00
Wolverine Enemy of the State #1 . . 3.00
X-Men Age of Apocalypse 5.00
X-Men Deadly Genesis 3.00
Planet Hulk. 4.00
Annihilation (2007). 3.00
X-Men Age of Apocalypse 4.00
X-Men Deadly Genesis 4.00
Civil War. 4.00
X-Men Rise & Fall of Shi'ar Empire. 3.00
Spider-Man vs. Wolverine 3.00

WHAT THE -?!
[Parodies]
Aug., 1988
1 . . . . 5.00
2 JBy,JOy,AW,. 4.00
3 TM,. 5.00
4 . . . . 3.00
5 EL,JLe,WPo,Wolverine 5.00
6 Wolverine,Punisher 3.00
7 . . . . 2.50
8 DK 2.50
9 . . . . 2.50
10 JBy,X-Men,Dr.Doom, Cap.
   America 2.50
11 DK,RLd(part). 2.50
12 Conan, F.F.,Wolverine. 2.50
13 Silver Burper,F.F.,Wolverine. . . . 2.50
14 Spittle-Man 2.50
15 Capt.Ultra,Wolverina 2.50
16 Ant Man,Watcher 2.50
17 Wulverean/Pulverizer,Hoagg/
   Spider-Ham,Sleep Gawker,F.F. . 2.50
18. . . . . 2.50
19. . . . . 2.50
20 Infinity Wart Crossover 2.50
21 Weapon XX,Toast Rider 2.50
22 F:Echs Farce 2.50
23. . . . . 2.50
24 Halloween issue 2.50
25 . . . . 2.50
26 Spider-Ham 2099 . . . . 2.50
Summer Spec. 2.50
Fall Spec. 2.50

WHERE CREATURES ROAM
July, 1970—Sept., 1971
1 JK,SD,DAy,B:Reprints
   The Brute That Walks 40.00
2 JK,SD,Midnight/Monster 25.00
3 JK,SD,DAy,Thorg 25.00
4 JK,SD,Vandoom 25.00
5 JK,SD,Gorgilla 25.00
6 JK,SD,Zog 25.00
7 SD 25.00
8 The Mummy's Secret,E:Reprints 25.00

WHERE MONSTERS DWELL
Jan., 1970
1 JK,SD,B:Reprints,Cyclops 50.00
2 JK,Sporr 35.00
3 JK,Grottu 35.00
4 . . . . 35.00
5 JK,Taboo 35.00
6 JK,Groot 35.00
7 JK,Rommbu 35.00
8 JK,SD,The Four-Armed Men . . 35.00
9 JK,Bumbu 35.00
10 JK,SD,Monster That Walks
   Like A Man. 35.00
11 JK,Gruto 25.00
12 JK,GC,SD,Orogo,giant-size . . 40.00
13 JK,The Thing That Crawl 25.00

14 JK,The Green Thing 25.00
15 JK,JSe,Kraa- The Inhuman . . . 25.00
16 JK,Beware the Son Of Goom . . 25.00
17 SD,The Hidden Vampires 25.00
18 SD,The Mask of Morghum 25.00
19 SD,The Insect Man. 25.00
20 Klagg 25.00
21 Fin Fang Foom 25.00
22 Elektro. 25.00
23 SD,The Monster Waits For Me . 25.00
24 SD,The Things on
   Easter Island 25.00
25 SD,The Ruler of the Earth 25.00
26 . . . . 25.00
27 . . . . 25.00
28 Droom,The Living Lizard. 25.00
29 thru 37 Reprints . . . . @25.00
38 AW,reprints, Oct., 1975. . . . . . 25.00

WHIP WILSON
See: BLAZE CARSON

WHITE TIGER
Nov., 2006
1 A Hero's compulsion 3.00
2 thru 6 . . . . @3.00

WILD
Marvel Atlas, Feb., 1954
1 BEv,JMn,Charlie Chan
   Parody 350.00
2 BEv,RH,JMn,Witches(c). 200.00
3 CBu(c),BEv,RH,JMn, ... 175.00
4 GC,Didja Ever See a Cannon
   Brawl 175.00
5 RH,JMn,Aug., 1954 . . . . 175.00

WILD CARDS
Epic, Sept., 1990
1 JG 5.50
2 JG,V:Jokers 4.50
3 A:Turtle. 4.50

WILDC.A.T.S/X-MEN: THE DARK AGE
Dec., 1997
1-shot MtB,WEl,V:Daemonites
   & Sentinels, 48-pg. 4.50
1a variant cover MGo 4.50

WILD THING
Marvel UK, 1993
1 A:Virtual Reality Venom and
   Carnage. 3.00
2 A:VR Venom and Carnage 2.50
3 A:Shield 2.50
4 . . . . 2.50
5 Virtual Reality Gangs. 2.50
6 Virtual Reality Villians 2.50
7 V:Trask. 2.50
8 thru 13 . . . . @2.50

WILD THING
Aug., 1999
1 RLm,AM,LHa,F:Wolverine's
   daughter Rina 2.50
2A RLm,AM,LHa,Bloody
   Reunions 2.50
2B variant AW (c) 2.50
3 RLm,AM,LHa,A:Rina 2.50
4 RLm,AM,LHa 2.50
5 RLm,AM,LHa,V:Robot monster . 2.50

WILD WEST
Spring, 1948
1 SSh(c),B:Two Gun Kids,Tex
   Taylor,Arizona Annie. 450.00
2 SSh(c),CCb, Captain Tootsie. . 300.00

Wild Western #3
© *Marvel Entertainment Group*

Becomes:

WILD WESTERN
1948
3 SSh(c),B:Tex Morgan,Two Gun
   Kid,Tex Taylor,Arizona Annie 350.00
4 Rh,SSh,CCB,Capt. Tootsie.
   A:Kid Colt,E:Arizona Annie . . 250.00
5 RH,CCB,SSh,Captain Tootsie
   A;Black Rider,Blaze Carson . 300.00
6 A:Blaze Carson,Kid Colt 200.00
7 Two-Gun Kid 200.00
   Kid,Tex Taylor,Arizona Annie 350.00
8 RH 200.00
9 Ph(c),B:Black Rider,
   Tex Morgan 225.00
10 Ph(c), Black Rider. 250.00
11 Black Rider 200.00
12 Black Rider 200.00
13 Black Rider 200.00
14 Prairie Kid,Black Rider 175.00
15 Black Rider 175.00
16 thru 18 Black Rider . . . . . . @175.00
19 Black Rider 185.00
20 thru 29 Kid Colt . . . . @150.00
30 JKa, Kid Colt. 150.00
31 thru 40. . . . . @100.00
41 thru 47. . . . . @100.00
48 AW 125.00
49 thru 53. . . . . @100.00
54 AW 125.00
55 AW 125.00
56 and 57 Sept., 1957 . . . . . . @100.00

WILLIAM SHATNER'S TEK WORLD
1992–94
1 LS,Novel adapt. 2.50
2 LS,Novel adapt.cont. 2.50
3 LS,Novel adapt.cont. 2.50
4 LS,Novel adapt.cont. 2.50
5 LS,Novel adapt.concludes. 2.50
6 LS,V:TekLords 2.50
7 E:The Angel 2.50
8 . . . . 2.50
9 . . . . 2.50
10 thru 17. . . . . @2.50
18 . . . . 2.50
19 Sims of the Father#1 . . . . 2.50
20 Sims of the Father#2 . . . . 2.50
21 Who aren't in Heaven. 2.50
22 Father and Guns. 2.50
23 We'll be Right Back 2.50
24 . . . . 2.50

WILLIE COMICS
See: IDEAL COMICS

WILLIE THE WISE-GUY
Marvel Atlas, 1957
1 MMe 100.00

WILLOW
Aug., 1988
1 thru 3 Movie adapt. . . . . @3.00

WINTER SOLDIER: WINTER KILLS
Dec., 2006
Civil War 3.00

WISDOM
Nov., 2006
1 F:Pete Wisdom 4.00
2 thru 6 . . . . 4.00

WITCHES
June, 2004
1 MD2,F:Kale,Topaz,Satana 3.00
2 MD2,F:Kale,Topaz,Satana 3.00
3 MD2 . . . . 3.00
4 MD2 . . . . 3.00

Witness #1
© *Marvel Entertainment Group*

WITNESS, THE
Sept., 1948
1 . . . . 3,500.00

WOLFPACK
Aug., 1988
1 I:Wolfpack 8.00
2 thru 11 . . . . @2.50
12 July, 1988 . . . . 2.50

WOLVERINE
[Limited Series] Sept., 1982
1 B:CCl(s),FM,JRu,A:Mariko,
   I:Shingen 75.00
2 FM,JRu,A:Mariko,I:Yukio 50.00
3 FM,JRu,A:Mariko,Yukio 50.00
4 B:CCl(s),FM,JRu,A:Mariko,
   D:Shingen 55.00

[Regular Series] 1988
1 JB,AW,V:Banipur 50.00
2 JB,KJ,V:Silver Samurai 25.00

3 JB,AW,V:Silver Samurai 10.00
4 JB,AW,I:Roughouse,
   Bloodsport 10.00
5 JB,AW,V:Roughouse,
   Bloodsport 10.00
6 JB,AW,V:Roughouse,
   Bloodsport 10.00
7 JB,A:Hulk 10.00
8 JB,A:Hulk 10.00
9 GC,Old Wolverine Story 10.00
10 JB,BSz,V:Sabretooth
   (1st battle) 32.00
11 JB,BSz,B:Gehenna Stone 10.00
12 JB,BSz,Gehenna Stone 10.00
13 JB,BSz,Gehenna Stone 10.00
14 JB,BSz,Gehenna Stone 10.00
15 JB,BSz,Gehenna Stone 10.00
16 JB,BSz,E:Gehenna Stone 10.00
17 JBy,KJ,V:Roughouse 10.00
18 JBy,KJ,V:Roughouse 10.00
19 JBy,KJ,A of V,I:La Bandera 10.00
20 JBy,KJ,A of V,V:Tigershark 7.00
21 JBy,KJ,V:Geist 7.00
22 JBy,KJ,V:Geist,Spore 7.00
23 JBy,KJ,V:Geist,Spore 7.00
24 GC,Snow Blind 6.00
25 JB,O:Wolverine(part) 6.00
26 KJ,Return to Japan 6.00
27 thru 30 Lazarus Project 6.00
31 MS,DGr,A:Prince o'Mandripoor . 6.00
32 MS,DGr,V:Ninjas 6.00
33 MS,Wolverine in Japan 6.00
34 MS,DGr,Wolverine in Canada. . . 6.00
35 MS,DGr,A:Puck 6.00
36 MS,DGr,A:Puck,Lady D'strike . . 6.00
37 MS,DGr,V:Lady Deathstrike 6.00
38 MS,DGr,A:Storm,I:Elsie Dee . . . 6.00
39 MS,DGr,Wolverine Vs. Clone . . . 6.00
40 MS,DGr,Wolverine Vs. Clone . . . 6.00
41 MS,DGr,R:Sabretooth,
   A:Cable 8.00
41a 2nd printing 2.50
42 MS,DGr,A:Sabretooth,Cable . . . 9.00
42a 2nd printing 2.50
43 MS,DGr,A:Sabretooth,C:Cable . . 7.00
44 LSn,DGr 6.00
45 MS,DGr,A:Sabretooth 7.00
46 MS,DGr,A:Sabretooth 7.00
47 V:Tracy 6.00
48 LHa(s),MS,DGr,B:Shiva
   Scenario 6.00
49 LHa(s),MS,DGr, ... 6.00
50 LHa(s),MS,DGr,A:X-Men,Nick Fury,
   I:Shiva,Slash-Die Cut(c) 7.00
51 MS,DGr,A:Mystique,X-Men 5.00
52 MS,DGr,A:Mystique,V:Spiral . . . 5.00
53 MS,A:Mystique,V:Spiral,Mojo . . 5.00
54 A:Shatterstar 5.00
55 MS,V:Cylla,A:Gambit,Sunfire . . . 5.00
56 MS,A:Gambit,Sunfire,V:Hand,
   Hydra 5.00
57 MS,D:Lady Mariko,A:Gambit . . . 5.50
58 A:Terror 5.00
59 A:Terror 5.00
60 Sabretooth vs.Shiva,
   I:John Wraith 5.00
61 MT,History of Wolverine and
   Sabretooth,A:John Wraith 5.00
62 MT,A:Sabretooth,Silver Fox . . . 5.00
63 MT,V:Ferro,D:Silver Fox 5.00
64 MPa,V:Ferro,Sabretooth 5.00
65 MT,A:Professor X 5.00
66 MT,A:X-Men 5.00
67 MT,A:X-Men 5.00
68 MT,V:Epsilon Red 5.00
69 DT,A:Rogue,V:Sauron,tie-in to
   X-Men#300 . . . . 5.00
70 DT,Sauron,A:Rogue,Jubilee . . . 5.00
71 DT,V:Sauron,Brain Child,
   A:Rogue, Jubilee 5.00
72 DT,Sentinels 5.00
73 DT,V:Sentinels 5.00

Wolverine #71
© *Marvel Entertainment Group*

74 ANi,V:Sentinels 5.00
75 AKu,Hologram(c),Wolv.has
   Bone Claws,leaves X-Men . . . 10.00
76 DT(c),B:LHa(s),A:Deathstrike,
   Vindicator,C:Puck 5.00
77 AKu,A:Vindicator,Puck,V:Lady
   Deathstrike 5.00
78 AKu,V:Cylla,Bloodscream 5.00
79 AKu,V:Cyber,I:Zoe Culloden . . . 5.00
80 IaC,V:Cyber, ... 5.00
81 IaC,V:Cyber,A:Excalibur 5.00
82 AKu,BMc,A:Yukio,Silver
   Samurai 5.00
83 AKu,A:Alpha Flight 5.00
84 A:Alpha Flight 5.00
85 Phalanx Covenant, Final Sanction,
   V:Phalanx,holografx(c) 5.50
85a newsstand ed 5.00
86 AKu,V:Bloodscream 3.00
87 AKu,deluxe,V:Juggernaut 3.00
87a newsstand ed 3.00
88 AKu,deluxe ed 3.00
88a newsstand ed 3.00
89 deluxe ed 3.00
89a newsstand ed 2.00
90 V:Sabretooth, deluxe ed. 4.00
90a newsstand ed 2.00
91 LHa,Logan's future unravels . . . 3.00
92 LHa,AKu,DGr,A:Sabretooth . . . 3.00
93 R:Cyber 3.00
94 Feral Wolverine 3.00
95 LHa,AKu,DGr,V:Dark Riders . . . 3.00
96 LHa,Aku,DGr,Death of Cyber . . 3.00
97 LHa,AKu,DGr,A:Genesis 3.00
98 LHa,AKu,F:Genesis 3.00
99 . . . . 3.00
100 LHa,AKu,DGA,Elektra;double-
   size, Foil Hologram cover 12.00
100a regular edition 4.00
101 LHa,AKu,A:Elektra 3.00
102 LHa 3.00
103 LHa,Elektra,A:Onslaught 3.00
104 LHa,Gateway, Onslaught 3.00
105 LHa,Gateway, Elektra 3.00
106 LHa 3.00
107 LHa,VS,prologue to Elektra#1 . 3.00
108 LHa,back to Tokyo,A:Yukio . . . 3.00
109 LHa,DG, ... 3.00
110 LHa,DG,Who's spying on
   Logan 3.00
111 LHa,DG,Logan moves to NYC . 3.00
112 LHa,DG,Logan in NYC 3.00
113 LHa,R:Ogun,A:Lady Deathstrike
   & Spiral 3.00

114 LHa,back in costume,V:Cyborg	187 JMC 2.50	53 B&W 3.00
Donald Pierce 4.00	188 pt.1 . . . . 2.50	54 JLb 3.00
115 LHa,Zero Tolerance,V:Bastion . 4.00	189 pt.2 . . . . 2.50	54a in B&W 3.00
116 LHa,Zero Tolerance, ... 4.00	Ann. '97 JOs,V:Volk 4.00	55 JLb,V:Sabretooth 3.00
117 LHa,Zero Tolerance, V:Prime	Ann.1999 F:Deadpool, 48-pg. 4.00	55a in B&W 3.00
Sentinels 4.00	Ann.2000 48-page 4.00	56 HC,Man in the Pit, 48-pgs. 4.00
118 LHa,Zero Tolerance aftermath . 4.00	Ann.2001 48-page 3.50	57 ScK 3.00
119 WEI,Pt.1 (of 4). 4.00	Spec. '95 LHa,F:Nightcrawler 4.00	58 Logan Dies, pt.2 . . . . 3.00
120 WEI,The White Ghost 4.00	Spec.Minus 1, LHa,CNn, flashback,	59 Logan Dies, pt.3 . . . . 3.00
121 WEI,Not Yet Dead,pt.3 . . . . . . 4.00	F:Weapon X. 2.50	60 Logan Dies, pt. 3.00
122 WEI,Not Yet Dead, pt.4 . . . . . . 4.00	Spec.Global Jeapordy,PDd(s) 3.00	61 . . . . 3.00
123 TDF,DCw,R:Roughouse,	Spec.Save the Tiger,rep. 3.00	62 Get Mystique, pt.1. . . . . 3.00
Bloodscream 4.00	Spec.Winter Spec. MWa B&W 3.00	63 Get Mystique, pt.2. . . . . 3.00
124 TDF,DCw,A:Captain America,	Spec.JungleAdventure,MMi,deluxe . 5.50	64 Get Mystique, pt.3. . . . . 3.00
V:Rascal 3.00	1-shot Bloodlust,AD,V:Siberian	65 Get Mystique, pt.4. . . . . 3.00
125 CCI,V:Viper,48-pg. 7.50	Were-Creatures. 6.00	66 Old Man Logan, pt.1 . . . . 3.00
125a Dynamic Forces (c). 6.50	GN Acts of Vengeance, rep. 7.00	66a variant (c) 3.00
126 CCI,V:Sabretooth 5.00	GN Black Rio, 48-page 6.00	67 Old Man Logan, pt.2 . . . . 3.00
127 CCI,Sabretooth takes over 5.00	GN Bloody ChoicesJB,A:N.Fury . . 13.00	68 Old Man Logan, pt.3 . . . . 3.00
128 CCI,V:Hydra, The Hand 3.00	GN Inner Fury,BSz,V:Nanotech	69 Old Man Logan, pt.4 . . . . 3.00
129 TDz,A:Wendigo. 3.00	Machines 6.25	Ann. Deathsong 4.00
130 TDz,V:Viper. 3.00	GN Killing, KSW,JNR. 6.00	Spec. Marvel Must Have, rep.
131 TDz,V:Viper. 3.00	GN Rahne of Terror, C:Cable 8.00	#20–#22 Enemy of the State. . . 4.00
131a Uncensored. 12.00	GN Scorpio Rising, T.U.Fury 6.00	One-shot Wolverine: Chop Shop. . . 3.00
132 TDz,Halloween in SalemCenter 3.00	GN Typhoid's Kiss,rep. 7.00	One-shot Fire Break 4.00
133 EL,JMs,F:Warbird 3.00	GN Bloodhungry SK 7.00	One-shot Amazing Immortal Man . . 4.00
133a variant EL cover (1:4) 6.00		Spec. Wolverine Dangerous Game . 4.00
134 EL,JMs,V:Big Apple heroes . . . 3.00	**May, 2003**	Spec. Killing Made Simple 4.00
135 EL,JMs,Joins Starjammers 3.00	1 DaR,Brothers,pt.1, relaunch 5.00	Spec. Wolverine: Saudade 5.00
136 EL,JMs,on prison planet 3.00	2 DaR,Brothers,pt.2 . . . . 3.00	Spec. Wolverine: Roar. 4.00
137 EL,JMs,V:The Collector 3.00	3 DaR,Brothers,pt.3 . . . . 3.00	
138 EL,JMs,Great Escape concl. . . 3.00	4 DaR,Brothers,pt.4 . . . . 3.00	**WOLVERINE**
139 EL,A:Cable 3.00	5 DaR,Brothers,pt.5 . . . . 3.00	**AND POWER PACK**
140 EL,Xavier paranoid 3.00	6 DaR,F:Nightcrawler 3.00	**Nov., 2008**
141 EL,Wolverine paranoid 3.00	7 Coyote Crossing,pt.1 . . . . 3.00	1 (of 4) 3.00
142 EL,R:Alpha Flight 3.00	8 Coyote Crossing,pt.2 . . . . 3.00	
143 EL,A:Alpha Flight 3.00	9 Coyote Crossing,pt.3 . . . . 3.00	
144 EL,A:Hercules,V:Leader 3.00	10 Coyote Crossing,pt.4 . . . . 3.00	
145 EL,25th Anniv. 48-pg. 8.00	11 Coyote Crossing,concl. 3.00	
145A Foil Stamped (c) 20.00	12 Dreams 3.00	
146 EL,Ages of Apocalypse,pt.1 . . 20.00	13 DaR,Feral,pt.1. . . . . 3.00	
147 FaN,Ages of Apocalypse,pt.2 . 10.00	14 DaR,Feral,pt.2. . . . . 3.00	
148 EL,Ages of Apocalypse,pt.3 . . . 7.00	15 DaR,Return of the Native,pt.3 . . 3.00	
149 EL,mutant no more? 3.00	16 DaR,Return of the Native,pt.4 . . 3.00	
150 X-Men: Revolution 5.00	17 DaR,Return of the Native,pt.5 . . 3.00	
150a variant (c) 8.00	18 DaR,Return of the Native,pt.6 . . 3.00	
151 SSr,V:Lord Haan 3.00	19 DaR,Return of the Native,pt.7 . . 3.00	
152 SSr,Lord Haan, Gom 3.00	20 JR2,Enemy of the State,pt.1. . . 5.00	
153 SSr,Kia 3.00	21 JR2,Enemy of the State,pt.2. . . 3.00	
154 RLd,ErS,Deadpool 3.00	22 MMr,JR2,Enemy of the State . . 3.00	
155 RLd,Watchtower,Siryn 3.00	23 MMr,JR2,Enemy of the State . . 3.00	
156 RLd,IaC,F:Spider-Man 3.00	24 MMr,JR2,Enemy of the State . . 3.00	
157 RLd,IaC,F:Spider-Man 3.00	25 MMr,JR2,Enemy of the State . . 3.00	
158 RLd,IaC,V:Administrator 3.00	26 MMr,JR2,Agent of S.H.I.E.L.D. . 3.00	
159 SCh,V:Mr.X 3.00	26a variant MS(c) 10.00	
160 SCh,V:Lady Killers,Mr.X 3.00	27 MMr,JR2,Agent of S.H.I.E.L.D.. 3.00	
161 SCh,V:Mr.X 3.00	28 MMr,JR2,Agent of S.H.I.E.L.D.. 3.00	
162 SCh,A:Sabretooth. 3.00	29 MMr,JR2,Agent of S.H.I.E.L.D.. 3.00	
163 SCh,F:Beast 3.00	30 MMr,JR2,Agent of S.H.I.E.L.D.. 3.00	
164 SCh,F:Beast 3.00	31 MMr,JR2,Agent of S.H.I.E.L.D.. 3.00	
165 SCh,NRd,trapped 3.50	32 MMr,Prisoner Number Zero 3.00	
166 SCh,NRd,BWS,48-page 10.00	33 Chasing Ghosts,pt.1 . . . . 3.00	
167 DaF,NRd,BWS(c),V:Viper 2.50	34 Chasing Ghosts,pt.2 . . . . 3.00	
168 DaF,NRd,F:Patch 2.50	35 Chasing Ghosts,pt.3 . . . . 3.00	
169 DaF,NRd,Bloodsport,concl.. . . . 2.50	36 Origins and Endings,pt.1 . . . . . 3.00	
170 SCh,NRd,Stay Alive,pt.1 . . . . . 2.50	37 Origins and Endings,pt.2 . . . . . 3.00	
171 SCh,NRd,V:Wendigo,'Nuff Said 2.50	38 Origins and Endings,pt.3 . . . . . 4.00	**WOLVERINE & PUNISHER:**
172 SCh,NRd,Stay Alive,pt.3 . . . . . 2.50	39 Origins and Endings,pt.4 . . . . . 4.00	**DAMAGING EVIDENCE**
173 SCh,NRd,in Las Vegas. 2.50	40 Origins and Endings,pt.5 . . . . . 4.00	**1993**
174 SCh,NRd,Amiko & Yukio 2.50	41 The Package, 48-pg. 4.00	1 B:CP(s),GEr,A:Kingpin. 3.00
175 SCh,NRd,Omega Red,48-pg. . . 4.00	42 Vendetta,pt.1, Civil War tie-in . 10.00	2 GEr,A:Kingpin,Sniper. 3.00
176 SCh,NRd, ... 2.50	43 Vendetta,pt.2, Civil War tie-in . . 6.00	3 GEr,Last issue 3.00
177 SCh,DaF,Shadow Pulpit,pt.1 . . 2.50	44 Vendetta,pt.3, Civil War tie-in . . 4.00	
178 SCh,DaF,Shadow Pulpit,pt.2 . . 2.50	45 Vendetta,pt.4, Civil War tie-in . . 4.00	**WOLVERINE/ CAPTAIN**
179 SCh&MRd(c),R:Alpha Flight . . . 2.50	46 Vendetta,pt.5, Civil War tie-in . . 4.00	**AMERICA**
180 AKu(c). 2.50	47 Vendetta,pt.6, Civil War tie-in . . 3.50	**March, 2004**
181 SCh, new direction 2.50	48 Vendetta epilogue 3.00	1 Alien technology stolen 3.00
182 SCh,TP 2.50	49 Better to Give, 48-pgs. 4.00	2 thru 4 . . . . 3.00
183 SCh,, 48-pg. 3.50	50 JLb,Evolution, pt.1 . . . . 4.00	
184 SCh,When Animals Attack 2.50	50a in B&W 4.00	
185 SCh,When Animals Attack 2.50	51 JLb,Evolution, pt.2 . . . . 3.00	
186 SCh,V:Punisher, Round 2. . . . . 3.00	52 JLb,Evolution, pt.3 . . . . 3.00	
	53 . . . . 3.00	

Wolverine & Punisher: Damaging Evidence #2 © Marvel Ent. Group

WOLVERINE: DAYS OF FUTURE PAST
Oct., 1997
1 (of 3) JFM,JoB,JHo, Logan &
  Magneto in far future 2.50
2 JFM,JoB,JHo,with Jubilee 2.50
3 JFM,JoB,JHo,V:Council of the
  Chosen, concl. 2.50

WOLVERINE: DOOMBRINGER
Nov., 1997
1-shot DgM,JP,F:Silver Samurai . . . 3.00

WOLVERINE/DOOP
May, 2003
1 thru 2 (of 2) . . . . @3.00

WOLVERINE ENCYCLOPEDIA
Vol. 1 AKu(c) 48-pg. 8.50
Vol. 2 thru Vol. 3 48-pg. . . . . @6.50

WOLVERINE: THE END
Nov., 2003
1 (of 6) CCt. 10.00
2 thru 3 CCt. . . . . @5.00
4 thru 6 CCt. . . . . @3.50

WOLVERINE: FIRST CLASS
Mar., 2008
1 F:Kitty Pryde 3.00
2 F:Sabretooth 3.00
3 Last Knights of Wundagore, pt.1 3.00
4 Last Knights of Wundagore, pt.2 . 3.00
5 To Me, My X-Men 3.00
6 Tonight 3.00
7 Soviet Super Soldiers 3.00
8 Kitty Pryde is Dead 3.00
9 . . . . 3.00

WOLVERINE/GAMBIT: VICTIMS
1995
1 Takes Place in London 3.00
2 Is Wolverine the Killer? 3.00
3 V:Mastermind. 3.00
4 conclusion 3.00

WOLVERINE/HULK
Feb., 2002
1 (of 4) SK, and a girl named Po . . 3.50
2 SK,snowy wasteland 3.50
3 SK,ghostly little girl 3.50
4 SK,concl. 3.50

WOLVERINE: MANIFEST DESTINY
Oct., 2008
1 (of 4) 3.00
2 Back in Chinatown. 3.00

WOLVERINE/NETSUKE
Sept., 2002
1 (of 4) GgP, Wolverine Samurai . . 3.00
2 thru 4 GgP . . . . @4.00

WOLVERINE ORIGINS
Apr., 2006
1 SDi. 45.00
2 SDi. 20.00
3 SDi,Born in Blood 10.00
4 SDi,Born in Blood 6.00

---

5 SDi,Born in Blood 6.00
6 SDi,Savior, pt.1 . . . . 6.00
7 SDi,Savior, pt.2 . . . . 4.00
8 SDi,Savior, pt.3 . . . . 4.00
9 SDi,Savior, pt.4 . . . . 3.00
10 SDi,Wolverine's son 3.00
10a variant (c) 3.00
11 SDi,Swift and Terrible, pt.1 . . . . 3.00
12 SDi,Swift and Terrible, pt.2 . . . . 3.00
13 SDi,Swift and Terrible, pt.3 . . . . 3.00
14 SDi,Swift and Terrible, pt.4 . . . . 3.00
15 SDi,Swift and Terrible, pt.5 . . . . 3.00
16 SDi,Our War, pt.1 . . . . 3.00
16a variant (c) 3.00
17 SDi,Our War, pt.2 . . . . 3.00
18 SDi,Our War, pt.3 . . . . 3.00
19 SDi,Our War, pt.4 . . . . 3.00
20 SDi,Our War, pt.5 . . . . 3.00
21 SDi,The Deep End, pt.1 . . . . . . 3.00
22 SDi,The Deep End, pt.2 . . . . . . 3.00
23 SDi,The Deep End, pt.3 . . . . . . 3.00
24 SDi,The Deep End, pt.4 . . . . . . 3.00
25 SDi,The Deep End, pt.5 . . . . . . 3.00
26 Son of X, pt.1 . . . . 3.00
27 Son of X, pt.2 . . . . 3.00
28 MD2,Dark Deception: Prologue . 3.00
29 MD2,Original Sin x-over, pt.3 . . . 3.00
30 MD2,Original Sin. 3.00
Ann. #1 Return to Madripoor 4.00

WOLVERINE/PUNISHER
March 2004
1 (of 5) LW 3.00
2 thru 5 LW . . . . @3.00

WOLVERINE/PUNISHER: REVELATION
Apr. 1999
1 (of 4) TSg,PtL,Revelation 3.00
1a signed 30.00
2 TSg,PtL,V:Revelation. 3.00
3 TSg,PtL,V:Revelation. 3.00
4 TsG,PtL,V:Revelation,concl. 3.00

WOLVERINE SAGA
Sept., 1989
1 RLd(c), ... 6.50
2 . . . . 5.50
3 . . . . 5.50
4 Dec., 1989 . . . . 5.50

WOLVERINE: SNIKT!
May, 2003
1 (of 5) 3.00
2 alien landscape 3.00
3 . . . . 3.00
4 V:Mandate aliens 3.00
5 Concl. 3.00

WOLVERINE: SOULTAKER
March, 2005
1 (of 5) Mark of Mana 3.00
2 Mark of Mana. 3.00
3 V:demon-lord Ryuki 3.00
4 V:Hana,Ryuki 3.00
5 Finale 3.00

WOLVERINE: X-ISLE
April, 2003
1 (of 5) A:Amiko 2.50
2 thru 5 . . . . @2.50

WONDER DUCK
Sept., 1949
1 Whale(c) 200.00
2 . . . . 125.00
3 March, 1950 . . . . 125.00

WONDERMAN
March, 1986
1 KGa,one-shot special 3.00

WONDER MAN
Sept., 1991
1 B:GJ(s),JJ,V:Goliath 2.50
2 JJ,A:West Coast Avengers 2.50
3 JJ,V:Abominatrix,I:Spider. 2.50
4 JJ,I:Splice,A:Spider 2.50
5 JJ,A:Beast,V:Rampage 2.50
6 JJ,A:Beast,V:Rampage 2.50
7 JJ,Galactic Storm,pt.4,
  A:Hulk & Rich Jones 2.50
8 JJ,GalacticStorm,pt.11,A:Vision. . 2.50
9 JJ,GalacticStorm,pt.18,A:Vision. . 2.50
10 JJ,V:Khmer Rouge 2.50
11 V:Angkor 2.50
12 V:Angkor 2.50
13 Infinity War 2.50
14 Infinity War,V:Warlock 2.50
15 Inf.War,V:Doppleganger 2.50
16 JJ,I:Armed Response,
  A:Avengers West Coast 2.50
17 JJ,A:Avengers West Coast 2.50
18 V:Avengers West Coast 2.50
19 . . . . 2.50
20 V:Splice,Rampage 2.50
21 V:Splice,Rampage 2.50
22 JJ,V:Realm of Death 2.50
23 JJ,A:Grim Reaper,Mephisto 2.50
24 JJ,V:Grim Reaper,Goliath 2.50
25 JJ,N:Wonder Man,D:Grim Reaper,
  V:Mephisto. 3.25
26 A:Hulk,C:Furor,Plan Master 2.50
27 A:Hulk 2.50
28 RoR,A:Spider-Man 2.50
29 RoR,A:Spider-Man 2.50
30 V:Hate Monger 2.50
31 . . . . 2.50
32 . . . . 2.50
33 . . . . 2.50
Spec.#1 (1985),KGa 3.00
Ann.#1 System Bytes #3 . . . . 2.50
Ann.#2 I:Hit-Maker,w/card 3.00

WONDER MAN
Dec., 2006
1 PDd,My Fair Super Hero 3.00
2 PDd,My Fair Super Hero 3.00
3 PDd,My Fair Super Hero 3.00
4 PDd, ... 3.00
5 . . . . 3.00

Wonder Man #29
© Marvel Ent. Group

WORLD CHAMPIONSHIP WRESTLING
1 F:Lex Luger,Sting. 2.50
2 . . . . 2.50
3 . . . . 2.50
4 Luger Vs El Gigante 2.50
5 Rick Rude Vs. Sting. 2.50
6 F:Dangerous Alliance,R.Rude . . . 2.50
7 F:Steiner Brothers 2.50
8 F:Sting,Dangerous Alliance 2.50
9 Bunkhouse Brawl. 2.50
10 Halloween Havoc 2.50
11 Sting vs Grapplers. 2.50
12 F:Ron Simmons 2.50

WORLD OF FANTASY
Marvel Atlas, May, 1956
1 The Secret of the Mountain . . . 750.00
2 JMn,AW,Inside the Tunnel. . . . 400.00
3 DAy,SC, The Man in the Cave. 350.00
4 BEv(c),BP,JF,Back to the
   Lost City 275.00
5 BEv(c),BP,In the Swamp 275.00
6 BEv(c),BP,The Strange Wife
   of Henry Johnson 275.00
7 BEv(c),GM,Man in Grey 275.00
8 GM,JO,MF,The Secret of the
   Black Cloud 300.00
9 BEv,BK. 275.00
10 . . . . 275.00
11 AT 200.00
12 BEv(c). 200.00
13 BEv,JO 200.00
14 JMn(c),GM,JO,CI,JM 200.00
15 JK(c) 200.00
16 AW,SD,JK 275.00
17 JK(c),SD 275.00
18 JK(c) 275.00
19 JK(c),SD,Aug., 1959. . . . . 275.00

WORLD OF MYSTERY
Marvel Atlas, 1956–57
1 BEv(c),AT,JO,The Long Wait . 700.00
2 BEv(c),The Man From
   Nowhere 300.00
3 SD,AT,JDa, The Bugs 325.00
4 SD(c),BP,What Happened in
   the Basement 325.00
5 JO,She Stands in Shadows . . 250.00
6 AW,SD,GC,Sinking Man 325.00
7 GC,JSe,Pick A Door 250.00

WORLD OF SUSPENSE
Marvel Atlas, April, 1956
1 JO,BEv,JMn,A Stranger
   Among Us 550.00
2 SD,LC,JMN(c),When Walks
   the Scarecrow 350.00
3 AW,JMN(c),The Man Who
   Couldn't Be Touched 350.00
4 Something is in This House . . 250.00
5 BEv,DH,JO. 250.00
6 BEv(c),BP 250.00
7 AW,The Face 300.00
8 Prisoner of the Ghost Ship . . . 250.00

WORLD'S GREATEST SONGS
Marvel Atlas, 1954
1 Eddie Fisher, Frank Sinatra. . . 550.00

WORLDS UNKNOWN
May, 1973
1 GK,AT,The Coming of the
   Martians,Reprints 25.00
2 GK,TS,A Gun For A Dinosaur . . 20.00
3 The Day the Earth Stood
   Still. 20.00

---

4 JB,Arena 20.00
5 DA,JM,Black Destroyer 20.00
6 GK(c),The Thing Called It 20.00
7 GT,The Golden Voyage of
   Sinbad,Part 1 . . . . 20.00
8 The Golden Voyage of
   Sinbad,Part 2, Aug., 1974 . . . 20.00

WORLD WAR HULK
May, 2007
1 JR2 . . . . 4.00
2 thru 5 JR2,finale. . . . . @4.00
1a thru 4a variant JR2 (c) . . . . . . @4.00
Spec. Prologue: World Breaker 4.00
Spec. Aftersmash. 4.00

...AFTERSMASH: DAMAGE CONTROL
Jan., 2008
1 thru 3 JR(c) . . . . @3.00

...FRONT LINE
June, 2007
1 PJe. 3.00
2 thru 6 PJe 3.00

...GAMMA CORPS
July, 2007
1 . . . . 3.00
2 thru 4 finale 3.00
Spec. Gamma Files 4.00

...WARBOUND
Dec., 2007
1 thru 5 . . . . @3.00

...X-MEN
June, 2007
1 thru 3 . . . . @3.00

WYATT EARP
Marvel Atlas, Nov., 1955
1 JMn,F:Wyatt Earp 300.00
2 AW,Saloon(c). 150.00
3 JMn(c),The Showdown,
   A:Black Bart 125.00
4 Ph(c),Hugh O'Brian,JSe,
   India Sundown 125.00
5 Ph(c),Hugh O'Brian,DW,
   Gun Wild Fever 125.00
6 BEv(c) 125.00
7 AW 125.00
8 JMn,Wild Bill Hickok 125.00
9 and 10 . . . . @125.00
11 . . . . 125.00
12 AW,JMn. 125.00
13 . . . . 100.00
14 . . . . 100.00
15 thru 20. . . . . @100.00
21 JDa(c). 100.00
22 thru 29. . . . . @100.00
30 AW,Reprints 35.00
31 thru 33 Reprints . . . . @30.00
34 June, 1973 . . . . 30.00

WYRMS
Feb., 2007
1 (of 6) Orson Scott Card adapt. . . 3.00
2 thru 6 . . . . @3.00

XAVIER INSTITUTE ALUMNI YEARBOOK
GN 48-pg. (1996). 6.00

X-CALIBRE
1995
1 Excaliber After Xavier 4.00
2 V:Callisto & Morlock Crew 3.00
3 D:Juggernaut 3.00
4 Secret Weapon 3.00

X-FACTOR
Feb., 1986
1 WS(c),JG,BL,JRu,I:X-Factor,
   Rusty 8.00
2 JG,BL,I:Tower. 5.00
3 JG,BL,V:Tower 5.00
4 KP,JRu,V:Frenzy 5.00
5 JG,JRu,I:Alliance of Evil,
   C:Apocalypse 7.00
6 JG,BMc,I:Apocalypse. 10.00
7 JG,JRu,V:Morlocks,I:Skids. 5.00
8 MS,JRu,V:Freedom Force 5.00
9 JRu(i),V:Freedom Force
   (Mutant Massacre). 5.00
10 WS,BWi,V:Marauders(Mut.Mass),
   A:Sabretooth 6.00
11 WS,BWi,A:Thor(Mutant Mass) . . 5.00
12 MS,BWi,V:Vanisher. 4.00
13 WS,DGr,V:Mastermold 4.00
14 WS,BWi,V:Mastermold 4.00
15 WS,BWi,D:Angel. 5.00
16 DM,JRu,V:Masque 4.00
17 WS,BWi,I:Rictor 5.00
18 WS,BWi,V:Apocalypse 4.00
19 WS,BWi,V:Horsemen of
   Apocalypse 3.50
20 JBr,A:X-Terminators 3.50
21 WS,BWi,V:The Right. 3.50
22 SB,BWi,V:The Right 3.50
23 WS,BWi,C:Archangel 7.00
24 WS,BWi,Fall of Mutants,
   I:Archangel 12.00
25 WS,BWi,Fall of Mutants 3.50
26 WS,BWi,Fall of Mutants,
   N:X-Factor 3.50
27 WS,BWi,Christmas Issue 3.50
28 WS,BWi,V:Ship. 3.50
29 WS,BWi,V:Infectia. 3.50
30 WS,BWi,V:Infectia,Free.Force . . 3.50
31 WS,BWi,V:Infectia,Free.Force . . 3.50
32 SLi,A:Avengers 3.50
33 WS,BWi,V:Tower & Frenzy,
   R:Furry Beast 3.50
34 WS,BWi,I:Nanny,
   Orphan Maker 3.50
35 JRu(i),WS(c),V:Nanny,
   Orphan Maker 3.50
36 WS,BWi,Inferno,V:Nastirh. 3.50
37 WS,BWi,Inferno,V:Gob.Queen . 3.50
38 WS,AM,Inferno,A:X-Men,D:
   MadelynePryor(GoblinQueen). . 3.50
39 WS,AM,Inferno,A:X-Men,
   V:Mr.Sinister 3.50
40 RLd,AM,O:Nanny,Orphan Maker
   1st Liefeld Marvel work 6.00

X-Factor #9
© Marvel Entertainment Group

---

41 AAd,AM,I:Alchemy 3.50
42 AAd,AM,A:Alchemy. 3.50
43 PS,AM,V:Celestials. 3.50
44 PS,AM,V:Rejects. 3.50
45 PS,AM,V:Rask 3.50
46 PS,AM,V:Rejects. 3.50
47 KD,AM,V:Father 3.50
48 thru 49 PS,AM,V:Rejects 3.50
50 RLd&TM(c),RB,AM,A:Prof.X
   (double sized),BU:Apocalypse . 5.00
51 AM,V:Sabretooth,Caliban 4.00
52 RLd(c),AM,V:Sabretooth,
   Caliban 3.00
53 AM,V:Sabretooth,Caliban 3.00
54 MS,AM,A:Colossus,I:Crimson. . . 3.00
55 MMi(c),CDo,AM,V:Mesmero. . . . 3.00
56 AM,V:Crimson 3.00
57 NKu,V:Crimson 3.00
58 JBg,AM,V:Crimson 3.00
59 AM,V:Press Gang 3.00
60 JBg,AM,X-Tinction Agenda#3. . . 4.00
60a 2nd printing(gold) 2.50
61 JBg,AM,X-Tinction Agenda#6. . . 3.50
62 JBg,AM,JLe(c),E:X-Agenda 3.50
63 WPo,I:Cyberpunks 3.50
64 WPo,ATb,V:Cyberpunks 3.00
65 WPo,ATb,V:Apocalypse 3.00
66 WPo,ATb,I:Askani,
   V:Apocalypse. 3.00
67 WPo,ATb,V:Apocalypse,I:Shinobi
   Shaw,D:Sebastian Shaw. 3.00
68 WPo,ATb,JLe(c),V:Apocalypse,
   L:Nathan,(taken into future). . . . 3.00
69 WPo,V:Shadow King. 3.00
70 MMi(c),JRu,Last old team. 3.00
71 LSn,AM,New Team 4.00
71a 2nd printing 2.50
72 LSn,AM,Who shot Madrox
   revealed. 3.00
73 LSn,AM,Mob Chaos in D.C.. . . . 3.00
74 LSn,AM,I:Slab. 3.00
75 LSn,AM,I:Nasty Boys(doub.sz). . 3.50
76 LSn,AM,A:Hulk,Pantheon. 3.25
77 LSn,AM,V:Mutant Lib. Front. . . . 3.25
78 LSn,AM,V:Mutant Lib. Front 3.25
79 LSn,AM,V:Helle's Belles 3.25
80 LSn,AM,V:Helle's Belles,
   C:Cyber 3.25
81 LSn,AM,V:Helle's Belles,Cyber. . 3.25
82 JQ(c),LSn,V:Brotherhood of Evil
   Mutants,I:X-iles 3.25
83 MPa,A:X-Force,X-iles 3.25
84 JaL,X-Cutioners Song #2,
   V:X-Force,A:X-Men 3.25

X-Factor #109
© *Marvel Entertainment Group*

85 JaL,X-Cutioners Song #6,
   Wolv.& Bishop,V:Cable 3.25
86 JaL,AM,X-Cutioner's Song#10,
   A:X-Men,X-Force,V:Stryfe 3.25
87 JQ,X-Cutioners Song
   Aftermath 3.00
88 JQ,AM,V:2nd Genegineer,
   I:Random. 4.00
89 JQ,V:Mutates,Genosha. 3.00
90 JQ,AM,Genosha vs. Aznia 3.00
91 AM,V:Armageddon 3.00
92 JQ,AM,V:Fabian Cortez,
   Acolytes,hologram(c). 6.00
93 Magneto Protocols 3.00
94 PR,J:Forge 3.00
95 B:JMD(s),AM,Polaris
   Vs. Random. 3.00
96 A:Random. 3.00
97 JD,I:Haven,A:Random 3.00
98 GLz,A:Haven,A:Random. 3.00
99 JD,A:Haven,Wolfsbane returns
   to human 3.00
100 JD,Red Foil(c),V:Haven,
   D:Madrox. 6.00
100a Newstand Ed. 3.00
101 JD,AM,Aftermath. 2.50
102 JD,AM,V:Crimson Commando,
   Avalanche 2.50
103 JD,AM,A:Malice 2.50
104 JD,AM,V:Malice,
   C:Mr. Sinister. 2.50
105 JD,AM,V:Malice 2.50
106 Phalanx Covenant,Life Signs
   Holografx(c). 3.50
106a newsstand ed 2.50
107 A:Strong Guy. 2.50
108 A:Mystique, deluxe ed. 2.50
108a newsstand ed. 2.00
109 A:Mystique,V:Legion, deluxe. . . 3.00
109a newsstand ed. 2.50
110 Invasion. 2.50
110a deluxe ed. 2.50
111 Invasion. 3.00
111a deluxe ed. 2.50
112 AM,JFM,SEp,F:Guido,Havok . . 2.50
113 A:Mystique. 2.50
114 AM,Wild Child & Mystique. 2.50
115 F:Wild Child,Havok 2.50
116 F:Wild Child. 2.50
117 HMe,AM,F:Cyclops 2.50
118 HMe,AM,A:Random,Shard 2.50
119 HMe,AM,F:Sabretooth 2.50
120 A:Sabretooth 2.50
121 A:Sabretooth 2.50
122 HMe,SEp,AM,J:Sabretooth. . . . 2.50
123 A:Hound 2.50
124 A:Onslaught 3.50
125 Onslaught saga, double size . . 4.00
126 Beast vs. Dark Beast 2.50
127 Mystique 2.50
128 HMe,JMs,AM,Hound Program . 2.50
129 HMe,JMs,AM,Graydon Creed's
   campaign. 2.50
130 HMe,JMs,AM,Assassination of
   Graydon Creed 2.50
131 HMe,JMs,ATi,Havok strikes
   back. 2.50
132 HMe,JMs,ATi,Break away from
   government 2.50
133 HMe,JMs,ATi,A:Multiple Man &
   Strong Guy 2.50
134 HMe,JMs,Ati,Operation X-Factor
   Underground, cont. 2.50
135 HMe,JMs,Strong Guy awakes . 2.50
136 HMe,JMs,ATi, A:Sabretooth . . . 2.50
137 HMe,JMs,ATi, Final fate of
   Shard and Polaris 2.50
138 HMe,JMs,ATi,Sabertooth,
   V:Maberick. 2.50
139 HMe,ATi,Who killed Graydon
   Creed. 2.50

140 HMe,ATi,Who killed Graydon
   Creed, A:Mystique. 2.50
141 HMe,ATi,Shard's Plan. 2.50
142 ATi,F:Wild Child. 2.50
143 HMe,ATi,Havok vs.DarkBeast. . 2.50
144 HMe,ATi,V:Brotherhood,
   Dark Beast. 2.50
145 HMe,ATi,Havok vs. X.U.E. 2.50
146 HMe,ATi,Havok, Multiple
   Man,V:Polaris 2.50
147 HMe,Havok v. Mandroids 2.50
148 F:Shard 2.50
149 HMe,Polaris & Madrox rejoin . . 3.50
Spec #1 JG,Prisoner of Love 5.00
Ann.#1 BL,BBr,V:CrimsonDynamo . 5.00
Ann.#2 TGr,JRu,A:Inhumans. 4.00
Ann.#3 WS(c),AM,JRu,PC,TD,
   Evolutionary War. 3.50
Ann.#4 JBy,WS,JRu,MBa,Atlantis
   Attacks,BU:Doom & Magneto . 3.50
Ann.#5 JBg,AM,DR,GI,Days of Future
   Present,A:Fant.Four,V:Ahab. . . 4.00
Ann.#6 Flesh Tears Saga,pt.4,
   A:X-Force, New Warriors 4.00
Ann #7 JQ,JRu,Shattershot,pt.3 . . 4.00
Ann.#8 I:Charon,w/card 3.25
Ann.#9 JMD(s),MtB,V:Prof.Power,
   A:Prof.X,O:Haven 3.25
Minus 1 Spec., HMe,JMs,ATi,
   flashback,F:Havok. 2.50
GN X-Men: Wrath of Apocalypse,
   rep.X-Factor#65-#68 . . . . 5.00

April, 2002

1 (of 4) When will it stop 2.50
2 FBI agents 2.50
3 in San Francisco 2.50
4 Concl. 2.50

Dec., 2005

1 PDd(s) 4.50
2 PDd(s), Decimation tie-in. 3.00
3 PDd(s), Decimation tie-in. 3.00
4 PDd(s), Strong Guy & Wolfsbane 3.00
5 PDd(s) 3.00
6 PDd(s), The Butterfly Defect 3.00
7 PDd(s), Two Meetings 3.00
8 PDd(s), Civil War tie-in 5.00
9 PDd(s), Civil War tie-in 4.00
10 PDd(s). 3.00
11 PDd(s) 3.00
12 PDd(s), V:Mr. Tryp & Singularity 3.00
13 PDd(s), Re-X-Aminations 3.00
14 PDd(s),F:Jamie Madrox 3.00
15 PDd(s),Agent of Hydra 3.00
16 PDd(s),The Multiple Man 3.00
17 PDd(s),I:X-MAD 3.00
18 . . . . 3.00
19 PDd(s). 3.00
20 PDd(s). 3.00
21 PDd(s), The Isolationist, pt.1 . . . 3.00
22 PDd(s), The Isolationist, pt.2 . . . 3.00
23 PDd(s), The Isolationist, pt.3 . . . 3.00
24 PDd(s), The Isolationist, pt.4 . . . 3.00
25 Messiah Complex, pt.3 x-over . . 3.00
26 Messiah Complex, pt.7 x-over . . 3.00
27 . . . . 3.00
28 PDd(s),Only Game in Town, pt.1 3.00
29 PDd(s),Only Game in Town, pt.2 3.00
30 PDd(s),Only Game in Town, pt.3 3.00
31 PDd(s),Only Game in Town, pt.4 3.00
32 PDd(s),Only Game in Town, pt.5 3.00
33 PDd(s),Secret Invasion tie-in . . 3.00
34 PDd(s),Secret Invasion tie-in . . 3.00
35 PDd(s),Karma Project. 3.00
35a Monkey variant (c) 3.00
36 PDd(s),Darwin. 3.00
37 PDd(s),V:Karma 3.00
Spec. The Quick and the Dead 3.00
Spec. Layla Miller PDd(s) 4.00

X-51

July, 1999

1 JQ&JP(c) Marvel Tech	2.50
2 JoB,V:Brotherhood of Mutants	2.50
2a variant cover	2.50
3 JoB,A:X.E.R.O.	2.50
4 JoB,A:Avengers	2.50
5 JoB,V:Vision	2.50
6 JoB	2.50
7 JoB,A:Sebastian Shaw	2.50
8 JoB,F:X-Men	2.50
9 JoB	2.50
10 JoB,F:Machine Man	2.50
11 JoB,F:Celestial	2.50
12 JoB,final issue	2.50

X-FORCE

Aug., 1991

1 RLd,V:Stryfe,Mutant Liberation Front,bagged, white on black graphics with X-Force Card	4.00
1a with Shatterstar Card	4.00
1b with Deadpool Card	4.00
1c with Sunspot & Gideon Card	4.00
1d with Cable Card	5.00
1e Unbagged Copy	2.75
1f 2nd Printing	2.50
2 RLd,I:New Weapon X,V:Deadpool	3.50
3 RLd,C:Spider-Man, V:Juggernaut,Black Tom	3.00
4 RLd,SpM/X-Force team-up, V:Juggernaut(cont.from SpM#16) Sideways format	3.00
5 RLd,A:Brotherhood Evil Mutants	3.00
6 RLd,V:Bro'hood Evil Mutants	3.00
7 RLd,V:Bro'hood Evil Mutants	3.00
8 MMi,O:Cable(Part)	3.50
9 RLd,D:Sauron,Masque	3.00
10 MPa,V:Mutant Liberation Front	3.00
11 MPa,Deadpool Vs Domino	3.00
12 MPa,A:Weapon Prime,Gideon	2.50
13 MPa,V:Weapon Prime	2.50
14 TSr,V:Weapon Prime,Krule	2.50
15 GCa,V:Krule,Deadpool	2.50
16 GCa,X-Cutioners Song #4, X-Factor V:X-Force	3.00
17 GCa,X-Cutioners Song#8, Apocalypse V:Stryfe	3.00
18 GCa,X-Cutioners Song#12, Cable vs Stryfe	3.00
19 GCa,X-Cutioners Song Aftermath,N:X-Force	2.50

X-Force #1
© Marvel Entertainment Group

20 GCa,O:Graymalkin	2.50
21 GCa,V:War Machine,SHIELD	2.50
22 GCa,V:Externals	2.50
23 GCa,V:Saul,Gigeon,A:Six Pack	2.50
24 GCa,A:Six Pack,A:Deadpool	2.50
25 GCa,A:Mageneto,Exodus, R:Cable	5.00
26 GCa(c),MtB,I:Reignfire	2.50
27 GCa(c),MtB,V:Reignfire,MLF, I:Moonstar,Locus	2.50
28 MtB,V:Reignfire,MLF	2.50
29 MtB,V:Arcade,C:X-Treme	2.50
30 TnD,V:Arcade,A:X-Treme	2.50
31 F:Siryn	2.50
32 Child's Play#1,A:New Warriors	2.50
33 Child's Play#3,A:New Warriors, V:Upstarts	2.50
34 F:Rictor,Domino,Cable	3.00
35 TnD,R:Nimrod	2.50
36 TnD,V:Nimrod	2.50
37 PaP,I&D:Absalom	2.50
38 TaD,Life Signs,pt.2, I:Generation X, foil(c)	5.00
38a newsstand ed.	2.50
39 TaD	2.50
40 TaD, deluxe	2.50
40a newsstand ed.	2.50
41 TaD,O:feral,deluxe	2.50
41a newsstand ed.	2.50
42 Emma Frost, deluxe	3.00
42a newsstand ed.	2.50
43 Home is Where Heart	2.50
43a deluxe ed.	2.50
44 AdP,Prof.X,X-Mansion	2.50
45 AdP,Caliban vs. Sabretooth	2.50
46 R:The Mimic	2.50
47 A:Deadpool	2.50
48 AdP,Siryn Takes Charge	2.50
49 ADp,MBu,Holocaust is here	2.50
50 AdP,MPn,F:Sebastian Shaw	3.00
50a prismatic foil cover	4.50
50b variant RLd(c)	6.00
51 AdP,MPn,V:Risque	2.50
52 A:Onslaught	3.50
53	2.50
54 AdP, Can X-Force protect X-Ternals?	2.50
55 V:S.H.I.E.L.D.	2.50
56 Deadpool, A:Onslaught	4.00
57 Onslaught saga.	2.50
58 Onslaught saga.	2.50
59 Longshot, with card.	2.50
60 JLb,,F:Shatterstar,A:Long Shot.	2.50
61 JLb,R:Longshot,O:Shatterstar	2.50
62 JLb,F:Sunspot.	2.50
63 JFM,AdP,F:Risque,Cannonball	2.50
64 JFM,AdP,In Latveria, searching for Doctor Doom's weapons	2.50
65 JFM,AdP,Warpath follows Risque to Florida	2.50
66 JFM,AdP,A:Risque,James Proudstar	2.50
67 JFM,AdP,F:Warpath, Risque	2.50
68 JFM,AdP,Zero Tolerance	2.50
69 JFM,AdP,Zero Tolerance aftermath	2.50
70 JFM,AdP,new direction starts	2.50
71 JFM,AdP,new direction	2.50
72 JFM,AdP,on the road	2.50
73 JFM,AdP,in New Orleans	2.50
74 JFM,ASm,Skids is back	2.50
75 JFM,AdP,A:Reignfire, double size	3.00
76 JFM,AdP,F:Shatterstar	2.50
77 JFM,AdP,F:Sunfire & Meltdown	2.50
78 JFM,AdP,Reignfire makes his move	2.50
79 JFM,AdP,O:Reignfire	2.50
80 JFM,AdP,V:Reignfire	2.50
81 JFM,AdP,trip to Hawaii, V:Lava Men, AdP Poster	2.50

82 JFM,V:Griffin, Damocles Foundation	2.50
83 JFM,F:Cannonball	2.50
84 JFM,V:Deviants	2.50
85 JFM,Return of Skids	2.50
86 JFM,A:Hulk	2.50
87 JFM,V:new Hellions	2.50
88 JFM,V:new Hellions	2.50
89 JFM,prisoners of the Hellions	2.50
90 JFM,Hellion War,concl.	2.50
91 JFM,home to San Francisco.	2.50
92 JFM,F:Domino	2.50
93 JFM,Domino returns	2.50
94 JFM,destination Genosha.	2.50
95 JFM,F:Magneto.	2.50
96 JFM,A:Selene	2.50
97 JFM,V:Reignfire	2.50
98	2.50
99 JFM,F:Dani Moonstar	2.50
100 JFM,Four Personas,48-pg.	3.00
101 new members,some gone	2.50
102 WPo,X-Men: Revolution	2.50
102a variant (c)	5.00
103 WPo,WEI,Games Without Frontiers,pt.2	2.50
104 WPo,WEI,Games,pt.3	2.50
105 WPo,WEI,Games,pt.4	2.50
106 WEI,IEd,WPo,Murder Ballads,pt.1	2.50
107 WEI,IEd,MurderBallads,pt.2	2.50
108 WEI,IEd,Ballads,pt.3	2.50
109 WEI,IEd,Ballads,pt.4	2.50
110 WEI,IEd,Rage War,pt.1	2.50
111 WEI,IEd,Rage War,pt.2	2.50
112 WEI,IEd,Rage War,pt.3	2.50
113 WEI,IEd,Rage War,pt.4	2.50
114	2.50
115 IEd,final issue?	2.50
116 PrM,MiA,new team	5.00
117 PrM,MiA,new members.	5.00
118 PrM,MiA,F:U-Go Girl.	2.50
119 PrM,MiA,F:U-Go Girl.	2.50
120 PrM,MiA,A:Wolverine	2.50
121 PrM,MiA,I:Lacuna	2.50
122 PrM,MiA,F:Lacuna	2.50
123 PrM,MiA,'Nuff Said	2.50
124 PrM,Orphan & U-Go Girl	2.50
125 PrM,Anarchist, Doop.	2.50
126 PrM,MiA,one won't come home	2.50
127 PrM,MiA,who won't come home	2.50
128 PrM,MiA,body bag time	2.50
129 PrM,DFg,something even worse	2.50
Ann.#1 Shattershot,pt1	3.00
Ann.#2 JaL,LSn,I:X-Treme,w/card.	3.25
Ann.#3	3.50
Ann.1998 X-Force/Champions.	6.00
Ann.1999 R:Shatterstar & Rictor	3.50
Spec.#102 Rough cut edition.	3.00
Minus 1 Spec., JFM,AdP, flashback, F:John Proudstar	2.50

X-FORCE

Aug., 2004

1 RLd,X-Men: Reload Wave	3.00
2 RLd,Cable completes team	3.00
3 RLd,Cable vs. Cannonball	3.00
4 RLd,F:Wolverine & Deadpool	3.00
5 RLd,F:Fantastic Four	3.00
6 Fan,rld, V:skornn,concl.	3.00

X-FORCE

Feb., 2008

1 Angels and Demons, pt.1	3.00
1a variant (c)	3.00
2 Angels and Demons, pt.2	3.00
3 Angels and Demons, pt.3	3.00
4 Angels and Demons, pt.4	3.00
4a variant bloody(c)	3.00
5 Angels and Demons, pt.5	3.00
6 Angels and Demons, pt.6	3.00

MARVEL

7 Old Ghosts, pt.1	3.00
8 Old Ghosts, pt.2	3.00
9 Old Ghosts, pt.3	3.00
Spec. Ain't No Dog	4.00

X-FORCE: SHATTERSTAR
Feb., 2005

1 (of 4) RLd(c),MMy	3.00
2 Rld(c),Mmy	3.00
3 RLd(c),MMy	3.00
4 RLd(c),MMy,finale	3.00

X-MAN
March, 1995

1 Cable after Xavier	5.00
2 Sinister's Plan	4.00
3 V:Domino	3.00
4 V:Sinister	3.00
5 Into this World	3.00
6 V:X-Men	2.50
7 Evil from Age of Apocalypse	2.50
8 Crossover Adventure	2.50
9 F:Nate's Past	2.50
10 Nate's Past	2.50
11 Young Nate seeks out X-Men	2.50
12 F:Excalibur	2.50
13	2.50
14	2.50
15 JOs,X-Men/Cable war aftermath	3.00
16 Holocaust,A:Onslaught	2.50
17 Holocaust,Quicksilver,Scarlet Witch, A:Onslaught	2.50
18 Onslaught saga	2.50
19 Onslaught saga	2.50
20	2.50
21 TKa,RCz,F:Nate	2.50
22 TKa,RCz,F:Threnody,A:Madelyne Pryor	2.50
23 TKa,RCz,F:Bishop	2.50
24 TKa,RCz,Spider-Man vs. Nate	2.50
25 TKa,RCz,Madelyne Pryor, double size	4.00
26 TKa,RCz,Nate limps to Muir Isle,A:Moira Mactaggert	2.50
27 TKa,RCz,Hellfire Club, concl.	2.50
28 TKa,RCz,Dark Beast's offer	2.50
29 TKa,RCz,Back in New York,	2.50
30 TKa,RCz,F:Nate Grey	2.50
31 RL,DGr,F:Nate Grey	2.50
32 TKa,V:Jacknife	2.50
33 TKa,V:Jacknife	2.50
34 TKa,Secret of Nate's popularity	2.50
35 TKa,Terrorists Strike	2.50

36 TKa,V:Purple Man	2.50
37 TKa,Nate leaves N.Y., A:Spider-Man	2.50
38 TKa,A:Spider-Man, Gwen Stacy	2.50
39 TKa,AOl,Nate & Madeline Pryor	2.50
40 TKa,RPc,V:Great Beasts	2.50
41 TKa,RCz,Madelyne Pryor	2.50
42 TKa,RCz,hunted by leprechauns	2.50
43 TKa,RCz,Nate Grey–murderer?!	2.50
44 TKa,RCz,F:Nate Grey,Gauntlet	2.50
45 TKa,prelude to X-Man/Cable x-over	2.50
46 TKa,Cable x-over	2.50
47 TKa,Blood Brothers,pt.3	2.50
48 LRs,V:Crusader	2.50
49 LRs,TKa,F:Nate	2.50
50 TKa,LRs,War of the Mutants,pt.2, 48-page	3.50
51 TKa,LRs,V:Psi-Ops	2.50
52 TKa,LRs,V:Psi-Ops	2.50
53 TKa,Strange Relations,pt.1	2.50
54 TKa,Strange Relations,pt.2	2.50
55 TKa,M'Kraan Crystal	2.50
56 TKa,Nate in Greyville	2.50
57 TKa,V:Mysterio	2.50
58 TKa,V:Threnody	2.50
59 TKa	2.50
60 TKa	2.50
61 TKa,	2.50
62 TKa,trapped	2.50
63 WEI,X-Men: Revolution	3.00
63a variant(c)	2.50
64 WEI,No Direction Home,pt.2	2.50
65 WEI,No Direction Home,pt.3	2.50
66 WEI,No Direction Home,pt.4	2.50
67 WEI,Down the Spiral,pt.1	2.50
68 WEI,Down the Spiral,pt.2	2.50
69 WEI,Down the Spiral,pt.3	2.50
70 WEI,Down the Spiral,pt.4	2.50
71 AOl,StG,Fearful Symmetries,pt.1	2.50
72 AOl,StG,Symmetries,pt.2	2.50
73 AOl,StG,Symmetries,pt.3	2.50
74 AOl,StG,Symmetries,pt.4	2.50
75 Anti-Man, final issue	3.00
Minus 1 Spec., TKa,RCz, flashback,O:Nate Grey	2.00
Spec.#1 X-Man '96	3.50
Ann. '97 RBe, Nate, Sugar Man, Dark Beast, Holocaust.	3.00
Ann. '98 X-Man, The Hulk, Thanos, 48-pg.	3.00
GNv X-Man,BRa,TyD, 48-pg.	6.00

X-MEN
Sept., 1963

1 JK,O:X-Men,I:Professor X,Beast Cyclops,Marvel Girl,Iceman Angel,Magneto	20,000.00
2 JK,I:Vanisher	5,000.00
3 JK,I:Blob	2,000.00
4 JK,I:Quicksilver,Scarlet Witch Mastermind,Toad	2,500.00
5 JK,V:Broth. of Evil Mutants	1,500.00
6 JK,V:Sub-Mariner	1,100.00
7 JK,V:Broth. of Evil Mutants, Blob	1,100.00
8 JK,I:Unus,1st Ice covered Iceman	1,100.00
9 JK,A:Avengers,I:Lucifer	1,200.00
10 JK,I:Modern Ka-Zar	1,200.00
11 JK,I:Stranger	900.00
12 JK,O:Prof.X,I:Juggernaut	1,200.00
13 JK,JSt,V:Juggernaut	650.00
14 JK,I:Sentinels	650.00
15 JK,O:Beast,V:Sentinels	650.00
16 JK,V:Mastermold,Sentinels	650.00
17 JK,V:Magneto	400.00
18 V:Magneto	400.00
19 I:Mimic	400.00
20 V:Lucifer	400.00
21 V:Lucifer,Dominus	250.00

22 V:Maggia	250.00
23 V:Maggia	250.00
24 I:Locust(Prof.Hopper)	250.00
25 JK,I:El Tigre	250.00
26 V:El Tigre	240.00
27 C:Fant.Four,V:Puppet Master	240.00
28 I:Banshee	400.00
29 V:Super-Apaptoid	240.00
30 JK,I:The Warlock	240.00
31 JK,I:Cobalt Man	225.00
32 V:Juggernaut	225.00
33 GK,A:Dr.Strange,Juggernaut	225.00
34 V:Tyrannus,Mole Man	225.00
35 JK,A:Spider-Man,Banshee	225.00
36 V:Mekano	225.00
37 DH,V:Blob,Unus	225.00
38 DH,A:Banshee,O:Cyclops	250.00
39 DH,GT,A:Banshee,V:Mutant Master,O:Cyclops	300.00
40 DH,GT,V:Frankenstein, O:Cyclops	250.00
41 DH,GT,I:Grotesk,O:Cyclops	250.00
42 DH,GT,JB,V:Grotesk, O:Cyclops,D:Prof.X	165.00
43 GT,JB,V:Magneto,Quicksilver, Scarlet Witch,C:Avengers	200.00
44 V:Magneto,Quicksilver,Sc.Witch, R:Red Raven,O:Iceman	200.00
45 PH,JB,V:Magneto,Quicksilver, Scarlet Witch,O:Iceman	200.00
46 DH,V:Juggernaut,O:Iceman	225.00
47 DH,I:Maha Yogi	210.00
48 DH,JR,V:Quasimodo	210.00
49 JSo,DH,C:Magneto,I:Polaris, Mesmero,O:Beast	210.00
50 JSo,V:Magneto,O:Beast	200.00
51 JSo,V:Magneto,Polaris, Erik the Red,O:Beast	200.00
52 DH,MSe,JSt,O:Lorna Dane V:Magneto,O:Beast	175.00
53 1st BWS,O:Beast	175.00
54 BWS,DH,I:Havok,O:Angel	175.00
55 BWS,DH,O:Havok,Angel	175.00
56 NA,V:LivingMonolith,O:Angel	175.00
57 NA,V:Sentinels,A:Havok	175.00
58 NA,A:Havoc,V:Sentinels	250.00
59 NA,V:Sentinels,A:Havoc	225.00
60 NA,I:Sauron	200.00
61 NA,V:Sauron	200.00
62 NA,A:Ka-Zar,Sauron,Magneto	200.00
63 A:Ka-Zar,V:Magneto	200.00
64 DH,A:Havok,I:Sunfire	200.00
65 NA,MSe,A:Havok,Shield, Return of Prof.X	200.00
66 SB,MSe,V:Hulk,A:Havok	200.00

X-Man #53
© *Marvel Entertainment Group*

X-Men #93
© *Marvel Entertainment Group*

67 rep.X-Men #12,#13 . . . . 150.00
68 rep.X-Men #14,#15 . . . . 150.00
69 rep.X-Men #16,#19 . . . . 150.00
70 rep.X-Men #17,#18 . . . . 150.00
71 rep.X-Men #20 . . . . 150.00
72 rep.X-Men #21,#24 . . . . 150.00
73 thru 93 rep.X-Men #25-45. . @125.00
94 GK(c),B:CCl(s),DC,BMc,B:2nd
  X-Men,V:Count Nefaria . . . 1,400.00
95 GK(c),DC,V:Count Nefaria,
  Ani-Men,D:Thunderbird 300.00
96 DC,I:Moira McTaggert,
  Kierrok. 150.00
97 DC,V:Havok,Polaris,Eric
  the Red,I:Lilandra 150.00
98 DC,V:Sentinels,Stephen Lang 140.00
99 DC,V:Sentinels,S.Lang 140.00
100 DC,V:Stephen Lang 200.00
101 DC,I:Phoenix,Black Tom,
  A:Juggernaut. 225.00
102 DC,O:Storm,V:Juggernaut,
  Black Tom 125.00
103 DC,V:Juggernaut,Bl.Tom . . . 125.00
104 DC,V:Magneto,I:Star
  Jammers,A:Lilandra. 125.00
105 DC,BL,V:Firelord 110.00
106 DC,TS,V:Firelord 110.00
107 DC,DGr,I:Imperial Guard,Star
  Jammers,Gladiator,Corsair . . 125.00
108 JBy,TA,A:Star Jammers,
  C:Fantastic Four,Avengers. . . 125.00
109 JBy,TA,I:Vindicator 110.00
110 TD,DC,V:Warhawk 100.00
111 JBy,TA,V:Mesmero,A:Beast,
  Magneto. 100.00
112 GP(c),JBy,TA,V:Magneto,
  A:Beast 100.00
113 JBy,TA,V:Magneto,A:Beast . . 100.00
114 JBy,TA,A:Beast,R:Sauron 90.00
115 JBy,TA,V:Sauron,Garokk,
  A:Ka-Zar,I:Zaladane 75.00
116 JBy,TA,V:Sauron,Garokk,
  A:Ka-Zar 75.00
117 JBy,TA,O:Prof.X,I:Amahl
  Farouk (Shadow King). 65.00
118 JBy,I:Moses Magnum,A:Sunfire
  C:Iron Fist,I:Mariko 65.00
119 JBy,TA,V:Moses Magnum,
  A:Sunfire 65.00
120 JBy,TA,I:AlphaFlight (Shaman,
  Sasquatch,Northstar,Snowbird,
  Aurora). 125.00
121 JBy,TA,V:Alpha Flight 100.00
122 JBy,TA,A:Juggernaut,Black
  Tom,Arcade,Power Man 65.00
123 JBy,TA,V:Arcade,A:SpM 60.00
124 JBy,TA,V:Arcade 60.00
125 JBy,TA,A:Beast,Madrox the
  Multiple Man,Havok,Polaris. . . 65.00
126 JBy,TA,I:Proteus,
  A:Havok,Madrox 65.00
127 JBy,TA,V:Proteus,A:Havok,
  Madrox. 65.00
128 GP(c),JBy,TA,V:Proteus,
  A:Havok,Madrox 65.00
129 JBy,TA,I:Shadow Cat,White
  Queen,C:Hellfire Club 90.00
130 JR2(c),JBy,TA,I:Dazzler
  V:White Queen. 65.00
131 JBy,TA,V:White Queen,
  A:Dazzler. 65.00
132 JBy,TA,I:Hellfire Club,
  V:Mastermind 65.00
133 JBy,TA,V:Hellfire Club,
  Mastermind,F:Wolverine 65.00
134 JBy,TA,V:Hellfire Club,Master
  mind,I:Dark Phoenix,A:Beast . 75.00
135 JBy,TA,V:Dark Phoenix,C:SpM,
  Fant.Four,Silver Surfer 65.00
136 JBy,TA,V:Dark Phoenix,
  A:Beast 65.00

137 JBy,TA,D:Phoenix,V:Imperial
  Guard,A:Beast. 70.00
138 JBy,TA,History of X-Men,
  L:Cyclops,C:Shadow Cat 55.00
139 JBy,TA,A:Alpha Flight,R:Wendigo,
  N:Wolverine,J:Shadowcat 60.00
140 JBy,TA,V:Wendigo,A:Alpha
  Flight 55.00
141 JBy,TA,I:2nd Brotherhood of Evil
  Mutants,I:Rachel (Phoenix II) . 70.00
Becomes:

UNCANNY X-MEN

142 JBy,TA,V:Evil Mutants,
  A:Rachel (Phoenix II) 80.00
143 JBy,TA,V:N'Garai,I:Lee
  Forrester 60.00
144 BA,JRu,A:Man-Thing,
  O:Havok, V:D'Spayre. 20.00
145 DC,JRu,V:Arcade,A:DrDoom . 20.00
146 DC,JRu,V:Dr.Doom,Arcade . . 20.00
147 DC,JRu,V:Dr.Doom,Arcade . . 20.00
148 DC,JRu,I:Caliban,A:Dazzler
  Spiderwoman. 20.00
149 DC,JRu,A:Magneto. 20.00
150 DC,JRu,BWi,V:Magneto 22.00
151 JSh,BMc,JRu,V:Sentinels 20.00
152 BMc,JRu,V:White Queen 20.00
153 DC,JRu,I:Bamf 20.00
154 DC,JRu,BWi,I:Sidrian Hunters
  A:Corsair,O:Cyclops(part) . . . 20.00
155 DC,BWi,V:Deathbird,I:Brood. . 20.00
156 DC,BWi,V:Death Bird,
  A:Tigra, Star Jammers. 20.00
157 DC,BWi,V:Deathbird 20.00
158 DC,BWi,2nd A:Rogue,
  Mystique 30.00
159 BSz,BWi,V:Dracula 20.00
160 BA,BWi,V:Belasco,I:Magik . . . 20.00
161 DC,BWi,I:Gabrielle Haller,
  O:Magneto,Professor X. 20.00
162 DC,BWi,V:Brood 25.00
163 DC,BWi,V:Brood 20.00
164 DC,BWi,V:Brood,I:Binary 18.00
165 PS,BWi,V:Brood 20.00
166 PS,BWi,V:Brood,A:Binary,
  I:Lockheed. 18.00
167 PS,BWi,V:Brood,A:N.Mutants . 22.00
168 PS,BWi,I:Madelyne Pryor 20.00
169 PS,BWi,I:Morlocks 18.00
170 PS,BWi,A:Angel,V:Morlocks . . 18.00
171 WS,BWi,J:Rogue,V:Binary . . . 28.00
172 PS,BWi,V:Viper,Silver
  Samurai, ... 20.00
173 PS,BWi,V:Viper,Silver
  Samurai, ... 18.00
174 PS,BWi,A:Mastermind 18.00
175 PS,JR2,BWi,W:Cyclops and
  Madelyne,V:Mastermind 20.00
176 JR2,BWi,I:Val Cooper. 12.00
177 JR2,JR,V:Brotherhood of
  Evil Mutants. 12.00
178 JR2,BWi,BBr,V:Brotherhood
  of Evil Mutants. 12.00
179 JR2,DGr,V:Morlocks 12.00
180 JR2,DGr,BWi,Secret Wars . . . 15.00
181 JR2,DGr,A:Sunfire 12.00
182 JR2,DGr,V:S.H.I.E.L.D. 12.00
183 JR2,DGr,V:Juggernaut 12.00
184 JR2,DGr,V:Selene,I:Forge . . . 16.00
185 JR2,DGr,V:Shield,U.S.
  Govt.,Storm loses powers 12.00
186 BWS,TA,Lifedeath,
  V:Dire Wraiths 14.00
187 JR2,DGr,V:Dire Wraiths 12.00
188 JR2,DGr,V:Dire Wraiths 12.00
189 JR2,SL,V:Selene,A:Magma . . 12.00
190 JR2,DGr,V:Kulan Gath,A:SpM,
  Avengers,New Mutants 12.00
191 JR2,DGr,A:Avengers,Spider-Man,
  New Mutants,I:Nimrod. 12.00
192 JR2,DGr,V:Magus 12.00

Uncanny X-Men #195
© Marvel Entertainment Group

193 JR2,DGr,V:Hellions,I:Firestar
  Warpath,20th Anniv. 20.00
194 JR2,DGr,SL,V:Nimrod. 12.00
195 BSz(c),JR2,DGr,A:Power
  Pack,V:Morlocks 12.00
196 JR2,DGr,J:Magneto 15.00
197 JR2,DGr,V:Arcade 12.00
198 BWS,F:Storm,Lifedeath II 12.00
199 JR2,DGr,I:Freedom Force,
  Rachel becomes 2nd Phoenix 12.00
200 JR2,DGr,A:Magneto,I:Fenris. . 20.00
201 RL,WPo(i),I:Nathan
  Christopher (Cyclops son). . . . 22.00
202 JR2,AW,Secret Wars II 12.00
203 JR2,AW,Secret Wars II 12.00
204 JBr,WPo,V:Arcade 12.00
205 BWS,A:Lady Deathstrike 22.00
206 JR2,DGr,V:Freedom Force. . . 12.00
207 JR2,DGr,V:Selene. 12.00
208 JR2,DGr,V:Nimrod,
  A:Hellfire Club 12.00
209 JR2,CR,V:Nimrod,A:Spiral . . . 12.00
210 JR2,DGr,I:Marauders,
  (Mutant Massacre). 25.00
211 JR2,BBI,AW,V:Marauders,
  (Mutant Massacre). 25.00
212 RL,DGr,V:Sabretooth,
  (Mutant Massacre). 35.00
213 AD,V:Sabretooth (Mut.Mass) . 35.00
214 BWS,BWi,V:Malice,A:Dazzler. 12.00
215 AD,DGr,I:Stonewall,Super
  Sabre,Crimson Commando. . . 12.00
216 BWS(c),JG,DGr,V:Stonewall . . 12.00
217 WS(c),JG,SL,V:Juggernaut . . . 12.00
218 AAD(c),MS,DGr,V:Juggernaut 12.00
219 BBI,DGr,V:Marauders,Polaris
  becomes Malice,A:Sabertooth 12.00
220 MS,DGr,A:Naze 12.00
221 MS,DGr,I:Mr.Sinister,
  V:Maruaders 24.00
222 MS,DGr,V:Marauders,Eye
  Killers,A:Sabertooth. 28.00
223 KGa,DGr,A:Freedom Force . . 12.00
224 MS,DGr,V:Adversary. 15.00
225 MS,DGr,Fall of Mutants
  I:1st US App Roma 16.00
226 MS,DGr,Fall of Mutants 16.00
227 MS,DGr,Fall of Mutants 16.00
228 RL,TA,A:OZ Chase. 14.00
229 MS,DGr,I:Reavers,Gateway . . 14.00
230 RL,DGr,Xmas Issue 14.00
231 RL,DGr,V:Limbo 12.00
232 MS,DGr,V:Brood 12.00
233 MS,DGr,V:Brood 12.00

234 MS,JRu,V:Brood 15.00	273 JLe,WPo,JBy,KJ,RL,MS,MGo,	320 deluxe ed. 5.00
235 RL,CR,V:Magistrates 12.00	LSn,SW,A:Cable,N.Mutants . . 10.00	320 newsstand ed. 3.00
236 MS,DGr,V:Magistrates 12.00	274 JLe,SW,V:Zaladane,A:Magneto,	321 R:Lilandra, deluxe ed. 5.00
237 RL,TA,V:Magistrates 12.00	Nick Fury,Ka-Zar 10.00	321 newsstand ed. 3.00
238 MS,DGr,V:Magistrates 12.00	275 JLe,SW,R:Professor X,A:Star	322 SLo,TGu,Rogue,Iceman run from
239 MS,DGr,Inferno,A:Mr.Sinister . 12.00	Jammers,Imperial Guard. . . . 12.00	Gambit's Secret. 8.00
240 MS,DGr,Inferno,V:Marauders . 15.00	275a 2nd Printing (Gold) 3.00	323 I:Onslaught 5.00
241 MS,DGr,Inferno,O:Madeline	276 JLe,SW,V:Skrulls,Shi'ar 10.00	324 SLo,F:Cannonball 5.00
Pryor,V:Marauders. 12.00	277 JLe,SW,V:Skrulls,Shi'ar 10.00	325 R:Colossus 7.00
242 MS,DGr,Inferno,D:N'Astirh,	278 PS,Professor X Returns to	326 SLo,JMd,F:Gambit,Sabretooth . 4.00
A:X-Factor,Double-sized 12.00	Earth,V:Shadowking 8.00	327 SLo,JMd,Magneto's Fate 4.00
243 MS,Inferno,A:X-Factor. 12.00	279 NKu,SW,V:Shadowking 7.00	328 SLo,JMd,Sabretooth freed . . . 4.00
244 MS,DGr,I:Jubilee. 30.00	280 E:CCl(s),NKu,A:X-Factor,	329 SLo,JMd,A:Doctor Strange . . . 4.00
245 RLd,DGr,Invasion Parody . . . 12.00	D:Shadowking,Prof.X Crippled . 7.00	330 Dr.Strange. 4.00
246 MS,DGr,V:Mastermold,	281 WPo,ATi,new team (From X-Men	331 White Queen. 4.00
A:Nimrod 12.00	#1),D:Pierce,Hellions,V:Sentinels,	332 SLo,JMd, cont from
247 MS,DGr,V:Mastermold 12.00	I:Trevor Fitzroy,Upstarts 10.00	Wolverine #100 . . . . 4.00
248 JLe(1st X-Men Art),DGr,	281a 2nd printing,red(c). 3.00	333 SLo,JMd, Operation: Zero
V:Nanny & Orphan Maker 30.00	282 WPo,ATi,V:Fitzroy,C:Bishop . . 15.00	Tolerance, Onslaught saga 4.00
248a 2nd printing 3.00	282a 2nd printing,gold(c) of #281	334 SLo,JMd, Onslaught saga 4.00
249 MS,DGr,C:Zaladane,	inside 3.00	335 SLo,JMd, Onslaught saga 4.00
V:Savage Land Mutates. 10.00	283 WPo,ATi,I:Bishop,Malcolm,	336 Apocalypse vs. Onslaught . . . 4.00
250 MS,SL,I:Zaladane. 10.00	Randall 15.00	337 Operation: Zero Tolerance . . . 4.00
251 MS,DGr,V:Reavers 14.00	284 WPo,ATi,SOS from USSR. . . . 5.00	338 SLo,JMd,R:Angel 4.00
252 JLe,BSz(c),RL,SW,V:Reavers 10.00	285 WPo,I:Mikhail(Colossus'	339 SLo,JMd,F:Cyclops, J.J.
253 MS,SL,V:Amahl Farouk 10.00	brother from Russia) 5.00	Jameson, Havok 4.00
254 JLe(c),MS,DGr,V:Reavers . . . 10.00	286 JLe,WPo,ATi,A:Mikhail 5.00	340 SLo,JMd,F:Iceman 4.00
255 MS,DGr,V:Reavers,D:Destiny. 10.00	287 JR2,O:Bishop,	341 SLo,JMd,Rogue gets gift 4.00
256 JLe,SW,Acts of Vengeance,	D:Malcolm,Randall 6.00	342 SLo,JMd, Shi'ar Empire, pt.1 . . 5.00
V:Manderin,A:Psylocke 15.00	288 NKu,BSz,A:Bishop 5.00	342a Rogue cover 12.00
257 JLe,JRu,AofV,V:Manderin . . . 12.00	289 WPo,ATi,Forge proposes	343 SLo,JMd, Shi'ar Empire, pt.2 . . 4.00
258 JLe,SW,AofV,V:Manderin . . . 12.00	to Storm 5.00	344 SLo,JMd, Shi'ar Empire, pt.3 . . 4.00
259 MS,DGr,V:Magistrates 8.00	290 WPo,SW,V:Cyberpunks,	345 SLo,JMd, trip home, A:Akron . . 5.00
260 JLe(c),MS,DGr,A:Dazzler 8.00	L:Forge 5.00	346 SLo,JMd,Zero Tolerance,
261 JLe(c),MS,DGr,V:Hardcase &	291 TR,V:Morlocks. 5.00	A:Spider-Man. 4.00
Harriers 8.00	292 TR,V:Morlocks. 5.00	347 SLo,JMd,Zero Tolerance 4.00
262 KD,JRu,V:Masque,Morlocks . . 8.00	293 TR,D:Morlocks,Mikhail 5.00	348 SLo,JMd,at Magneto's base . . . 4.00
263 JRu(i),O:Forge,V:Morlocks . . . 8.00	294 BP,TA,X-Cutioner's Song#1,	349 SLo,JMd,Maggot vs. Psylocke
264 JLe(c),MC,JRu,V:Magistrate. . 8.00	Stryfe shoots Prof X,A:X-Force,	& Archangel 4.00
265 JRu(i),SW,V:Shadowking 8.00	X-Factor,polybag.w/ProfX card . 5.00	350 SSe,JMd,Trial of Gambit,
266 NKu(c),MC,JRu,I:Gambit 50.00	295 BP,TA,X-Cutioners Song #5,	double-sized 5.00
267 JLe,WPo,SW,V:Shadowking . . 20.00	V:Apocalypse. 5.00	350a Gambit (c) 12.00
268 JLe,SW,A:Captain America,	296 BP,TA,X-Cutioners Song #9,	351 SSe,JMd,Dr. Cecilia Reyes. . . 3.00
Black Widow,V:The Hand,	A:X-Force,X-Factor,V:Stryfe . . . 5.00	352 SSe,EBe,Cyclops & Phoenix
Baron Strucker. 20.00	297 BP,X-Cutioners Song	leave, Facade arrives 3.00
269 JLe,ATi,Rogue V:Ms.Marvel . . 10.00	Aftermath. 5.00	353 SSe,CBa,Rogues Anguish . . . 3.00
270 JLe,ATi,SW,X-Tinction Agenda	298 BP,TA,V:Acolytes 5.00	354 SSe,CBa,F:Rogue 10.00
#1, A:Cable,New Mutants 12.00	299 BP,A:Forge,Acolytes,I:Graydon	354a Jean Gray (c) 12.00
270a 2nd printing(Gold) 4.00	Creed (Sabretooth's son) 5.00	355 SSe,CBa, North & South
271 JLe,SW,X-Tinction Agenda	300 JR2,DGr,BP,V:Acolytes,A:Forge,	pt.2 x-over 5.00
#4,A:Cable,New Mutants. 10.00	Nightcrawler,Holografx(c) 10.00	356 SSe,CBa, originals V:Phoenix . 3.00
272 JLe,SW,X-Tinction Agenda	301 JR2,DGr,I:Sienna Blaze,	357 SSe,Cyclops & Phoenix 3.00
#7,A:Cable,New Mutants. 10.00	V:Fitzroy 5.00	358 SSe,CBa,Phoenix collapses . . 3.00
	302 JR2,V:Fitzroy 5.00	359 SSe,CBa,Rogue 3.00
	303 JR2,V:Upstarts,D:Illyana 6.00	360A SSe,CBa, I:New X-Men, foil
	304 JR2,JaL,PS,L:Colossus,	etched cover 5.00
	V:Magneto,Holo-grafx(c) 8.00	360B regular cover 4.00
	305 JD,F:Rogue,Bishop. 5.00	361 SSe,SSr,R:Gambit 3.50
	306 JR2,V:Hodge. 5.00	362 SSe,CBa,Hunt for Xavier,pt.1 . 3.50
	307 JR2,Bloodties#4,A:Avengers,	363 SSe,CBa,Hunt for Xavier,pt.3 . . 3.50
	V:Exodus,Cortez 6.00	364 SSe,Hunt for Xavier,pt.5 . . . . . 5.00
	308 JR2,Scott & Jean announce	365 SSe,CBa,A:Professor X 3.00
	impending marriage. 5.00	366 AD,BPe,Magneto War,pt.1 . . . . 3.00
	309 JR2,O:Professor X & Amelia . . 5.00	367 AD,Magneto War,pt.3 . . . . 3.00
	310 JR2,DG,A:Cable,V:X-Cutioner,	368 AD,AKu,Requiem for an X-Man 3.00
	w/card 5.00	368a signed 20.00
	311 JR2,DG,AV,V:Sabretooth,	369 AD,AKu,V:Juggernaut. 3.00
	C:Phalanx 5.00	370 AD,AKu,in the past 3.00
	312 JMd,DG,A:Yukio,I:Phalanx,	371 AD,AKu(c),Rage Against
	w/card 5.00	the Machine, pt.1 x-over 3.00
	313 JMd,DG,V:Phalanx 5.00	371a signed 20.00
	314 LW,BSz,R:White Quen 5.00	372 AKu,AD,The Shattering,pt.1 . . . 3.00
	315 F:Acolytes 5.00	373 AKu,AD,The Shattering,pt.2 . . . 3.00
	316 V:Phalanx,I:M,Phalanx Covenant	374 AKu,AD,The Shattering. 3.00
	Generation Next,pt.1, holo(c) . 5.00	375 AKu,AD,48-pg. 5.00
	316a newsstand ed. 3.00	376 AKu,AD 7.00
	317 JMd,V:Phalanx,prism(c) 5.00	377 AKu,AD,Apocalypse12,pt.5. . . 7.00
	317a newsstand ed. 3.00	378 AKu,AD,TTn,Ages of
	318 JMd,L:Jubilee, deluxe 5.00	Apocalypse,pt.1,x-over 3.00
	318a newsstand ed. 3.00	379 AKu,AD,TTn,mutants no more . 3.00
	319 R:Legion, deluxe 5.00	380 AD,TR,poly-bagged w/Genesis. 4.00
	319a newsstand ed. 3.00	

Uncanny X-Men #296
© *Marvel Entertainment Group*

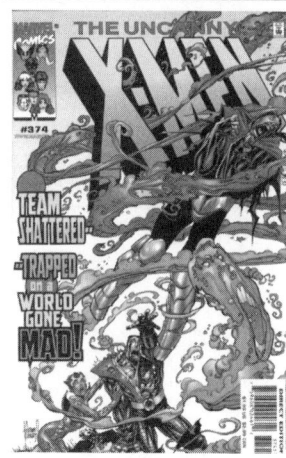

Uncanny X-Men #374
© Marvel Entertainment Group

381 CCl,AKu,TTn,X-Men:
  Revolution 7.00
381a foil (c) 12.00
382 CCl,TTn,Shockwave Riders . . . 3.00
383 CCl,AKu,TTn,48-pg. 3.50
384 CCl,AKu,TTn,I:Killion 3.00
385 CCl,TR,Red Pirates 3.00
386 CCl,TR,Phoenix 3.00
387 CCl,TTn,Maximum Security . . . 3.00
388 CCl,SvL,Dream's End,pt.1 . . . . 5.00
389 CCl,SvL,F:Cecilia Reyes 3.00
390 CCl,SvL,Legacy Virus,
  D:Colossus 10.00
391 SLo,SvL,return 3.00
392 SLo,SvL,Eve of Destruction . . 3.00
393 SLo,SvL,Eve of Destruction . . 5.00
394 JoC,IaC,F:Warp Savant 5.00
395A JoC,IaC,Poptopia,pt.1 . . . . . . 3.00
395B variant BWS(c) 3.00
396 JoC,IaC,Poptopia,pt.2 . . . . 3.00
397 JoC,IaC,Poptopia,pt.3 . . . . 3.00
398 JoC,IaC,Poptopia,pt.4 . . . . 3.00
399 JoC,SHa,X-Ranch 3.00
400 F:XStacy,48-page 5.00
401 JoC,RG,F:Banshee,'Nuff Said . 3.50
402 JoC,RG,vs.X-Corp. 3.00
403 JoC,AaL,DaM,X-Corp's secret . 3.00
404 JoC,RG,V:Multiple Men. 3.00
405 JoC,SeP,V:Banshee 3.00
406 JoC,AaL,X-Corps,concl. 3.00
407 JoC,SeP,Nightcrawler 3.00
408 JoC,SeP,V:Vanisher 3.00
409 JoC,SeP,V:Vanisher 3.00
410 RG,Hope 3.00
411 RG,Hope,pt.2 . . . . 3.00
412 RG,Hope,pt.3 . . . . 3.00
413 RG,Annie's Moving 3.00
414 Northstar Joins team. 3.00
415 SeP,F:Nightcrawler 3.00
416 KiA,F:Juggernaut 4.00
417 KiA,Dominant Species 3.00
418 KiA,Dominant Species 3.00
419 KiA,Archangel and Husk. 3.00
420 KiA,Dominant Species,concl. . . 3.00
421 RG,V:Alpha Flight,pt.1 . . . . 3.00
422 RG,V:Alpha Flight,pt.2,48-pg. . . 3.50
423 RG,Holy War,pt.1 . . . . 3.00
424 RG,Holy War,pt.2 . . . . 3.00
425 Sacred Vows,pt.1 . . . . 3.00
426 Sacred Vows,pt.2 . . . . 3.00
427 F:Jubilee, Angel, Husk 3.00
428 O:Nightcrawler,F:Mystique 3.00
429 Draco,pt.1 . . . . 3.00
430 Draco,pt.2 . . . . 3.00

431 Draco,pt.3 . . . . 3.00
432 Draco,pt.4 . . . . 3.00
433 Draco,pt.5 . . . . 3.00
434 Draco,pt.6 . . . . 3.00
435 Trial of the Juggernaut,pt.1 . . . 3.00
436 Trial of the Juggernaut,pt.2 . . . 3.00
437 She Lies With Angels,pt.1 . . . . 3.00
438 She Lies With Angels,pt.2 . . . . 3.00
439 She Lies With Angels,pt.3 . . . . 3.00
440 She Lies With Angels,pt.4 . . . . 3.00
441 She Lies With Angels,pt.5 . . . . 3.00
442 Of Darkest Nights,pt.1 . . . . . . 3.00
443 Of Darkest Nights,pt.2 . . . . . . 3.00
444 The End of History,pt.1 . . . . . . 3.00
445 The End of History,pt.2 . . . . . . 3.00
446 The End of History,pt.3 . . . . . . 3.00
447 The End of History,pt.4 . . . . . . 3.00
448 CCl,Guess Who's Back,pt.1 . . 3.00
449 CCl,Guess Who's Back,pt.2 . . 3.00
450 CCl,AD,Cruelest Cut,pt.1 . . . . 3.00
451 CCl,AD,Cruelest Cut,pt.2 . . . . 3.00
452 CCl(s),Chasing Hellfire 3.00
453 CCl(s),Chasing Hellfire 3.00
454 CCl(s),Chasing Hellfire, concl. . 3.00
455 CCl(s),On Ice,pt.1 . . . . 3.00
456 CCl(s),On Ice,pt.2 . . . . 3.00
457 CCl(s),AD,On Ice 3.00
458 CCl(s),AD,On Ice,A:Ka-Zar. . . . 3.00
459 CCl(s),AD,On Ice 3.00
460 CCl(s),TR,Mojo Rising,pt.1 . . . . 3.00
461 CCl(s),TR,Mojo Rising,pt.2 . . . . 5.00
462 CCl(s),AD,Season of the Witch . 3.00
463 CCl(s),AD,Season of the Witch 3.00
464 CCl,CBa,Season of the Witch . 3.00
465 CCl,CBa,Season of the Witch . 3.00
466 Grey's End, Decimation tie-in . . 3.00
467 Grey's End, Decimation tie-in . . 3.00
468 Grey's End, Decimation tie-in . . 3.00
469 CCl,Wand'ring Star,pt.1 . . . . . . 3.00
470 CCl,Wand'ring Star,pt.2 . . . . . . 3.00
471 CCl,Wand'ring Star,pt.3 . . . . . . 3.00
472 CCl,CBa,First Foursaken, pt.1 . 3.00
473 CCl,CBa,First Foursaken, pt.2 . 3.00
474 CCl,CBa,First Foursaken, pt.3 . 3.00
475 Rise and Fall of Shi'ar Empire . 3.00
476 Rise and Fall of Shi'ar Empire . 3.00
477 Rise and Fall of Shi'ar Empire . 3.00
478 Rise and Fall of Shi'ar Empire . 3.00
479 Rise and Fall of Shi'ar Empire . 3.00
480 Rise and Fall of Shi'ar Empire . 3.00
481 BTn,Rise & Fall Shi'ar Empire . 3.00
482 BTn,Rise & Fall Shi'ar Empire . 3.00
483 BTn,Rise & Fall Shi'ar Empire . 3.00
484 BTn,Rise & Fall Shi'ar Empire . 3.00
485 BTn,Rise & Fall Shi'ar Empire . 3.00
486 BTn,Rise & Fall Shi'ar Empire . 3.00
487 SvL,The Extremists,pt.1 . . . . . . 3.00
488 SvL,The Extremists,pt.2 . . . . . . 3.00
489 SvL,The Extremists,pt.3 . . . . . . 3.00
490 SvL,The Extremists,pt.4 . . . . . . 3.00
491 SvL,The Extremists,pt.5 . . . . . . 3.00
492 Messiah Complex, pt.2 x-over . 3.00
493 Messiah Complex, pt.6 x-over . 3.00
494 . . . . 3.00
495 Divided We Stand, pt.1 . . . . . . 3.00
496 Divided We Stand, pt.2 . . . . . . 3.00
497 Divided We Stand, pt.3 . . . . . . 3.00
498 Divided We Stand, pt.4 . . . . . . 3.00
499 Divided We Stand, pt.5 . . . . . . 3.00
500 TDo,Manifest Destiny,48-pg. . . 4.00
500a variant (c)s . . . . @4.00
500b variant wraparound (c)s . . . @4.00
501 Manifest Destiny 3.00
502 Manifest Destiny 3.00
503 Manifest Destiny 3.00
504 TDo,Lovelorn, pt.1 . . . . 3.00
Ann.#1 rep.#9,#11 . . . . 200.00
Ann.#2 rep.#22,#23 . . . . 125.00
Ann.#3 GK(c),GP,TA,A:Arkon . . . 65.00
Ann.#4 JR2,BMc,A:Dr.Strange . . . 25.00
Ann.#5 BA,BMc,A:F.F. 20.00
Ann.#6 BSz,BWi,Dracula. 20.00

Ann.#7 MGo,TMd,BWi,TA,BBr,
  BA,JRu,BBI,SL,AM,
  V:Impossible Man 15.00
Ann.#8 SL,Kitty's story. 15.00
Ann.#9 AAd,AG,MMi,Asgard,V:Loki,
  Enchantress,A:New Mutants . . 20.00
Ann.#10 AAd,TA,V:Mojo,
  J:Longshot,A:New Mutants . . . 18.00
Ann.#11 AD,V:Horde,A:CaptBrit. . . 7.00
Ann.#12 AAd,BWi,RLm,TD,Evol.
  War,V:Terminus,Savage Land . . 7.00
Ann.#13 MBa,JRu,Atlantis Attacks . 6.00
Ann.#14 AAd,DGr,BWi,AM,ATi,
  V:Ahab,A:X-Factor. 25.00
Ann.#15,TR,JRu,MMi(c),Flesh Tears,
  Pt.3,A:X-Force,New Warriors . . 6.00
Ann.#16 JaL,JRu,Shattershot
  Part.2. . . . . 5.00
Ann.#17 JPe,MFm,I:X-Cutioner,
  D:Mastermind,w/card. 5.00
Ann.#18 JR2,V:Caliban,
  BU:Bishop 4.00
Ann.1999 AD 3.50
Ann.2000 SLo,F:Professor X 3.50
Ann.2001 JoC,48-pg. 3.50
Ann. #1 (2006) 4.00
Marvel Milestone rep. #1 (1991) . . . 3.00
Marvel Milestone rep. #9 (1993) . . . 3.00
Marvel Milestone rep. #28 (1994) . . 3.00
G-Size #1,GK,DC,I:New X-Men
  (Colossus,Storm,Nightcrawler,
  Thunderbird,3rd A:Wolv.) . . 1,500.00
G-Size #2,rep.#57-59. . . . . 150.00
Marvel Milestone rep. Giant
  Size #1 (1991). 4.00
Spec.#1 X-Men: Earth Fall,
  rep.#232–#234 (1996) 3.00
Spec.#1 X-Men vs. Dracula, rep.
  X-Men Ann.#6 (1993) 2.00
GN X-Men: Days of Future Past
  rep. X-Men #141-142 . . . . 5.00
GN Pryde of the X-Men 11.00
GN God Loves,Man Kills,
  (1994) prestige 7.00
GN X-Men Firsts, I:Wolverine,Rogue,
  Gambit & Mr. Sinister, rep.
  Avengers Ann.#10, Uncanny
  X-Men 221,#266 & Incredible
  Hulk #181 (1996). 5.00
GN X-Men Rarities,F:Classic
  Stories (1995) 6.00

X-MEN

[2nd Regular Series] Oct., 1991
1A(c);Storm,Beast,B:CCl(s),JLe,SW
  I:Fabian Cortez,Acolytes,
  V:Magneto 5.00
1B(c);Colossus,Psylocke 8.00
1C(c);Cyclops,Wolverine 8.00
1D(c);Magneto 8.00
1E(c);Gatefold w/pin-ups 9.00
2 JLe,SW,V:Magneto Contd. 5.00
3 E:CCl(s),JLe,SW,V:Magneto . . . 5.00
4 JBy(s),JLe,SW,I:Omega Red,
  V:Hand. 6.00
5 B:SLo(s),JLe,SW,V:Hand,
  Omega Red,I:Maverick 5.00
6 JLe,SW,V:Omega Red, Hand,
  Sabretooth. 7.00
7 JLe,SW,V:Omega Red,Hand,
  Sabretooth 5.00
8 JLe,SW,Bishop vs. Gambit 5.00
9 JLe,SW,A:Ghost Rider,V:Brood. . 4.50
10 JLe,SW,MT,Longshot Vs. Mojo,
  BU:Maverick 4.50
11 E:SLo(s)JLe,MT,V:Mojo,
  BU:Maverick 4.50
12 B:FaN(s),ATb,BWi,I:Hazard 4.00
13 ATb,BWi,V:Hazard 4.00
14 NKu,X-Cutioners Song#3,A:X-Fact.
  X-Force,V:Four Horsemen 4.00

X-Men 2nd Series #24
© Marvel Entertainment Group

15 NKu,X-Cutioners Song #7,
   V:Mutant Liberation Front 4.00
16 NKu,MPn,X-Cutioners Song #11,
   A:X-Force,X-Factor,V:Dark Riders,
   Apocalypse Vs.Archangel,IR:Stryfe
   is Nathan Summers. 4.00
17 NKu,MPn,R:Illyana,A:Darkstar . . 4.00
18 NKu,MPn,R:Omega Red,V:Soul
   Skinner 4.00
19 NKu,MPn,V:Soul Skinner,
   Omega Red 4.00
20 NKu,MPn,J.Grey vs Psylocke . . 4.00
21 NKu,V:Silver Samurai,Shinobi . . 4.00
22 BPe,V:Silver Samurai,Shinobi . . 4.00
23 NKu,MPn,V:Dark Riders,
   Mr.Sinister 4.00
24 NKu,BSz,A Day in the Life 4.00
25 NKu,Hologram(c),V:Magneto,
   Wolverine's Adamantium skeleton
   pulled out. 15.00
25a Gold Edition 25.00
25b B&W version 35.00
26 NKu,Bloodties#2,A:Avengers,
   I:Unforgiven 4.00
27 RiB,I:Threnody 4.00
28 NKu,MRy,F:Sabretooth 4.00
29 NKu,MRy,V:Shinobi. 4.00
30 NKu,MRy,W:Cyclops&Jean Grey,
   w/card 6.00
31 NKu,MRy,A:Spiral,Matsuo,
   D:Kwannon 4.00
32 NKu,MRy,A:Spiral,Matsuo. 3.50
33 NKu,MRy,F:Gambit &
   Sabretooth 3.50
34 NKu,MRy,A:Riptide 3.50
35 LSh,A:Nick Fury 3.50
36 NKu,MRy,I:Synch,PhalanxCovenant
   Generation Next,pt.2, deluxe. . . 5.00
36a Newsstand ed. 2.50
37 NKu,MRy,Generation Next,pt.3
   foil(c) 5.00
37a newsstand ed. 2.50
38 NKu,MRy,F:Psylocke 3.50
38a newsstand ed. 3.00
39 X-Treme, deluxe 3.50
39a newsstand ed. 3.00
40 deluxe 3.50
40a newsstand ed. 3.00
41 V:Legion, deluxe 3.50
41a newsstand ed. 3.00
42 PS,PaN,Mysterious Visitor 3.00
43 Rogue and Iceman 3.00
44 FaN,Mystery of Magneto 3.00
45 20th Anniv.pt.2 . . . . 5.00

46 FaN,Aku,V:Comcast 3.00
47 SLo,AKu,CaS,F:Dazzler 3.00
48 SLo,AKu,CaS,F:Sabretooth 3.00
49 SLo,AKu,Bishop wanted 3.00
50 Onslaught(c) 7.00
50a regular edition 8.00
51 MWa,Onslaught 6.00
52 MWa,AKu,CaS,V:Sinister 6.00
53 Onslaught saga. 7.00
54 Onslaught saga. 5.00
54a Foil cover 25.00
55 Onslaught saga. 3.50
56 Onslaught saga. 3.50
57 Operation: Zero Tolerence 3.50
58 SLo,NKu 3.50
59 . . . . 3.50
60 SLo,NKu,F:Ororo, V:Candra 3.50
61 SLo,CNn,F:Storm, V:Candra. . . . 3.50
62 SLo,CPa,F:Sebastian Shaw,
   Shang Chi 3.50
62A variant Storm/Wolverine(c) . . . 15.00
63 SLo,CPa,ATi,A:Sebastian Shaw,
   Inner Circle 3.00
64 SLo,CPa,ATi,V:Hellfire Club 3.00
65 SLo,CPa,ATi, No Exit prelude. . . 3.00
66 SLo,CPa,ATi, Zero Tolerance,
   A:Bastion 3.00
67 SLo,CPa,ATi, Zero Tolerance,
   F:Iceman, Cecilia Reyes 3.00
68 SLo,CPa,ATi, Operation: Zero
   Tolerance 3.00
69 SLo,CPa, Operation: Zero
   Tolerance, concl. 3.50
70 ATi,Who will join X-Men?,
   double-sized 5.00
71 ATi,Cyclops banished 4.00
72 ATi,Professor Logan's School of
   Hard Knocks 3.00
73 ATi,Marrow visits Callisto 3.00
74 ATi,Terror in Morlock Tunnels . . . 3.00
75 ATi,V:N'Garai, double size 4.00
76 CCl,V:Sabretooth, 35th anniv
   kickoff 3.00
77 ATi,A:Black Panther,Maggott . . . 3.00
78 Return of Professor X. 3.00
79 ATi,Cannonball must leave team 3.00
80A BPe, ATi, cont. from Uncanny
   X-Men #360, etched foil (c). . . . 7.50
80B regular cover 6.00
81 AKu,MFm,Search for Prof.X . . . 3.00
82 AKu,MFm, Hunt for Xavier. 3.00
83 AKu,MFm,Hunt for Xavier,pt.4 . . 3.00
84 AJu,Hunt for Xavier,concl. 3.50
85 AD,MFm,R:Magneto 3.00
85a signed 30.00
86 AD,MFm,Magneto War,pt.2,
   O:Joseph 3.50
87 AD,MFm,Magneto War,pt.4. . . . 3.50
88 AD,MFm,R:Juggernaut 3.00
89 AD,MFm,In the past 3.00
90 AD,MFm,In the past,concl. 3.00
91 AD,AKu,Rage Against
   the Machine, pt.2 x-over 3.00
91a signed 30.00
92 AD,MFm,The Shattering x-over . 3.00
93 AD,MFm,The Shattering x-over . 3.00
94 AD,MFm,Shattering,x-over 4.00
95 AD,TR,A:Death, ... 3.00
96 AD 9.00
97 AD,MFm,Apocalypse12,pt.7 . . . 8.00
97a variant (c) 20.00
98 AD,MFm,Ages of Apocalypse . . 9.00
99 AD,BBh,mutants no more? 3.00
100 CCl,X-Men:Revolution,48-pg. . 6.00
100a variant covers 7.00
101 CCl,X-Men:Revolution 3.00
102 CCl,R:Wolverine 3.00
103 CCl,Wolverine v. Rogue 3.00
104 CCl,V:Killion 3.00
105 CCl,Archangel,Psylocke 3.00
106 CCl,Neo,Cecelia Reyes 3.50
107 CCl,Cadre K 4.00

108 CCl,Dream'sEnd,pt.4,x-over . . . 5.00
109 CCl,at X-Mansion, 100-page . . 4.00
110 SLo,F:Kitty Pryde 8.00
111 SLo,F:Trish Tilby 5.00
112 SLo,Eve of Destruction,pt.2 . . . 5.00
113 SLo,Eve of Destruction,pt.4 . . . 8.00
Becomes:

NEW X-MEN

114 GMo,E is for Extinction,pt.1 . . . 8.00
115A GMo,E for Extinction,pt.2 . . . . 6.00
115B variant BWS(c) 4.00
116 GMo,E for Extinction,pt.3 . . . . 3.50
117 GMo,F:Beast. 3.50
118 GMo,GermFreeGeneration,pt.1 3.50
119 GMo,Germ Free Gen.,pt.2 . . . 3.50
120 GMo,Germ Free Gen.,concl. . . 3.00
121 GMo,Xavier's mind,'Nuff Said. . 3.00
122 GMo,Imperial,pt.1 . . . . 3.00
123 GMo,Imperial,pt.2 . . . . 3.00
124 GMo,Imperial,pt.3 . . . . 3.00
125 GMo,Imperial,pt.4 . . . . 3.00
126 GMo,Imperial,pt.5 . . . . 3.50
127 GMo,F:Xorn 3.00
128 GMo,Jean Grey, Emma Frost . . 3.00
129 GMo,Weapon XII 3.00
130 GMo 3.00
131 GMo,JPL,BSz 3.00
132 GMo,PJ,F:Storm 3.00
133 . . . . 3.00
134 GMo,NRd,no Magneto 3.00
135 GMo,Riot At Xavier's 3.00
136 GMo,Riot At Xavier's 3.00
137 GMo,Riot At Xavier's 3.00
138 GMo,Riot At Xavier's,concl. . . . 3.00
139 GMo,PJ,Murder at Mansion . . . 3.00
140 GMo,PJ,Murder at Mansion . . . 3.00
141 GMo,PJ,Murder at Mansion . . . 3.00
142 GMo,CBa,Weapon Plus,pt.1. . . 3.00
143 GMo,CBa,Weapon Plus,pt.2. . . 3.00
144 GMo,CBa,Weapon Plus,pt.3. . . 3.00
145 GMo,CBa,Weapon Plus,pt.4. . . 3.00
146 PJ,Planet X,pt.1 . . . . 3.00
147 PJ,Planet X,pt.2 . . . . 3.00
148 PJ,Planet X,pt.3 . . . . 3.00
149 PJ,Planet X,pt.4 . . . . 3.00
150 PJ,Planet X,finale,48-pg. 3.50
151 MS,Here Comes Tomorrow . . . 3.00
152 MS,Here Comes Tomorrow . . . 3.00
153 MS,Here Comes Tomorrow . . . 3.00
154 MS,Here Comes Tomorrow . . . 3.00
155 SvL,Bright New Mourning,pt.1 . 3.00
156 SvL,Bright New Mourning,pt.2 . 3.00
becomes:

X-MEN

157 SvL,Day of the Atom,pt.1 . . . . . 3.00
158 SvL,Day of the Atom,pt.2 . . . . . 3.00
159 SvL,Day of the Atom,pt.3 . . . . . 3.00
160 SvL,Day of the Atom,pt.4 . . . . . 3.00
161 SvL,Heroes & Villains,pt.1 . . . . 3.00
162 SvL,Heroes & Villains,pt.2 . . . . 3.00
163 SvL,Heroes & Villains,pt.3 . . . . 3.00
164 SvL,Heroes & Villains,pt.4 . . . . 3.00
165 . . . . 3.00
166 SvL,Golgotha,pt.1 . . . . 3.00
167 SvL,Golgotha,pt.2 . . . . 3.00
168 SvL,Golgotha,pt.3 . . . . 3.00
169 SvL,Golgotha,pt.4 . . . . 3.00
170 SvL,Golgotha,pt.5, concl. 3.00
171 SvL,Bizarre Love Triangle,pt.1 . 3.00
172 SvL,Bizarre Love Triangle,pt.2 . 3.00
173 SvL,Bizarre Love Triangle,pt.3 . 3.00
174 SvL,Bizarre Love Triangle,pt.4 . 3.00
175 SvL,Wild Kingdom,x-over,pt.1 . . 3.00
176 SvL,Wild Kingdom,x-over,pt.3 . . 3.00
177 SvL,House Arrest, pt.1 . . . . 4.00
178 SvL,House Arrest, pt.2 . . . . 4.00
179 SvL,House Arrest, pt.3 . . . . 4.00
180 SvL,What Lorna Saw,pt.1 . . . . . 3.00
181 SvL,What Lorna Saw,pt.2 . . . . . 3.00
182 SvL,Blood of Apocalypse, pt.1 . 3.00
183 SvL,Blood of Apocalypse, pt.2 . 3.00

MARVEL

184 SvL,Blood of Apocalypse, pt.3 . 3.00
185 SvL,Blood of Apocalypse, pt.4 . 3.00
186 SvL,Blood of Apocalypse, pt.5 . 3.00
187 SvL,Blood of Apocalypse, after. 3.00
188 CBo,Supernovas,pt.1 . . . . 4.00
189 CBo,Supernovas,pt.2 . . . . 3.00
190 CBo,Supernovas,pt.3 . . . . 3.00
191 CBo,Supernovas,pt.4 . . . . 3.00
192 CBo,Supernovas,pt.5 . . . . 3.00
193 CBo,Supernovas,pt.6 . . . . 3.00
194 CBo,Primary Infection. 3.00
195 HuR,Primary Infection. 3.00
196 HuR,Primary Infection. 3.00
197 MCy,CBa,Condition Critical,pt.1 3.00
198 MCy,CBa,Condition Critical,pt.2 3.00
199 MCy,CBa,Condition Critical,pt.3 3.00
200 CBa,Blinded by the Light,pt.1 . 4.00
200a variant (c) 4.00
200b variant gatefold (c) 4.00
201 MCy,HuR. 4.00
202 MCy,HuR. 3.00
203 MCy,HuR. 3.00
204 Blinded by the Light 3.00
205 Messiah Complex, pt.5 x-over . 3.00
205a, 206a, 207a Variant. . . . . . @15.00
206 Messiah Complex,pt.9 x-over . . 3.00
207 . . . . 3.00
1-shot Endangered Species. 4.00
Ann.#1 JLe,Shattershot,pt.1,
    I:Mojo II 4.00
Ann.#2 I:Empyrean,w/card. 4.00
Ann.#3 F:Storm 4.00
Ann. Uncanny X-Men '97, V:Brother-
    hood, 48-pg. 3.50
Ann. '98 RMz, F:X-Men & Doctor
    Doom. 3.50
Ann. '98 X-Men/Fantastic Four, JoC,
    PaP, 48-pg. 3.50
Ann.1999 Rage Against the
    Machine, pt.3 x-over, 48-pg. . . . 3.50
Ann.2000 CCl,SHa,SEa,48-pg. 4.00
Ann. 2001 GMo,Marvelscope 7.50
Ann. 1 F:Northstar & Aurora (2007). 4.00
Uncanny X-Men'95 Spec. F:Husk . . 4.00
Giant Size X-Men #3 (2005) 5.00
Giant Size X-Men #4 (2005) 5.00
Spec.X-Men'95, F:Mr.Sinister 5.00
Spec.X-Men'96 LHa, 64-pg., F:Gambit,
    Rogue, Magneto, Jubilee
    & Wolverine 4.00
Spec. X-Men'97,JFM,SEp,F:Gambit,
    Joesph & Phoenix 4.00
Minus 1 Spec., SLo,JMd,, flashback,
    discovery of mutants 2.00
Spec.#1 X-Men: Road to Onslaught
    (1996) 2.50
Spec. X-Men Universe: Past,
    Present and Future 3.00
Spec. X-Men:Year in Review 3.00
Spec.#1 X-Men (2000). 3.50
Spec. Millennial Visions 4.00
Spec.2001, Millennial Vision
    48-page 3.50
Spec. X-Men:Declassified,48-pg . . 3.50
Spec. Unearthed Archives
    Sketchbook 3.00
Spec. X-Men/Sentry, PJe,MT. 3.00
Spec. God Loves, Man Kills. 5.00
Spec. rep. Must Have #114–#116 . 4.00
Chrom.Classics GN,TKa,AD,MFm,
    Age of Apocalypse. 3.00
Becomes

X-MEN: LEGACY

208 MCy(s),SEa, Legacy. 3.00
209 Divided We Stand, tie-in 3.00
210 Divided We Stand, tie-in 3.00
211 Divided We Stand, tie-in 3.00
212 Divided We Stand, tie-in 3.00
213 Divided We Stand, tie-in 3.00
214 MCy(s),SEa,A:Gambit. 3.00
215 MCy(s),SEa,Manifest Destiny. . 3.00
216 MCy(s),SEa. 3.00

X-Men Adventures Vol. 2, #2
© *Marvel Entertainment Group*

217 MCy(s),SEa,Original Sin x-over 3.00
218 F:Wolverine & Professor X 3.00
219 MCy(s) 3.00
Ann. 1 F:Northstar & Aurora 4.00
One-shot Endangered Species 4.00
One-shot Odd Men Out 4.00
Spec. X-Men: Return of Magik. 4.00

X-MEN ADVENTURES
[1st Season] 1992–94

1 V:Sentinals, Based on TV
    Cartoon 6.00
2 V:Sentinals,D:Morph 5.00
3 V:Magneto,A:Sabretooth 4.00
4 V:Magneto 4.00
5 V:Morlocks 4.00
6 V:Sabretooth 3.50
7 V:Cable,Genosha,Sentinels. 3.00
8 A:Colossus,A:Juggernaut 3.00
9 I:Colossus(on cartoon),
    V:Juggernaut 3.00
10 A:Angel,V:Mystique. 3.00
11 I:Archangel(on cartoon) 3.00
12 V:Horsemen of Apocalypse. 3.00
13 RMc(s),I:Bishop(on cartoon). . . . 3.00
14 V:Brotherhood of Evil Mutants . . 3.00
15 . . . . 3.00

[2nd Season] 1994–95

1 R:Morph,I:Mr. Sinister
    (on cartoon). 3.00
2 I:Nasty Boys (on cartoon) 3.00
3 I:Shadow King (on cartoon). 3.00
4 I:Omega Red (on cartoon). 3.00
5 I:Alpha Flight (on cartoon). 3.00
6 F:Gambit 3.00
7 A:Cable,Bishop,Apocalypse. 3.00
8 A:Cable,Biship,Apocalypse 3.00
9 O:Rogue 3.00
10 . . . . 3.00
11 F:Mojo,Longshot 3.00
12 Reunions,pt.1 . . . . 3.00
13 Reunions,pt.1 . . . . 3.00

[3rd Season] 1995–96

1 Out of the Past,pt.1 . . . . 3.00
2 V:Spirit Drinker. 3.00
3 Phoenix Saga,pt.1 . . . . 3.00
4 Phoenix Saga,pt.2 . . . . 3.00
5 Phoenix Saga,pt.3 . . . . 3.00
6 Phoenix Saga,pt.4 . . . . 3.00
7 Phoenix Saga,pt.5 . . . . 3.00
8 War in The Savage Land. 3.00
9 F:Ka-Zar. 3.00

10 thru 13 Dark Phoenix,Saga. . . @3.00

X-MEN: AGE OF APOCALYPSE
March, 2005

1-shot Age of Apocalypse, 48-pg. . . 4.00
1 thru 6 CBa . . . . @3.00

X-MEN: ALPHA
1994

1 Age of Apocalypse, double size. . 9.00
1a gold edition, 48pp 50.00

X-MEN/ALPHA FLIGHT
Jan., 1986

1 PS,BWi,V:Loki 5.00
2 PS,BWi,V:Loki 5.00

X-MEN/ALPHA FLIGHT: THE GIFT
Jan., 1998

1-shot CCl,PS, rep. of limited series 6.00

X-MEN AND POWER PACK
Oct., 2005

1 thru 4 . . . . @3.00
Digest The Power of X. 8.00

X-MEN/ ANIMATION SPECIAL

TV Screenplay Adapt 11.00

X-MEN: APOCALYPSE/ DRACULA
Feb., 2006

1 thru 4 . . . . @3.00

X-MEN ARCHIVES: CAPTAIN BRITAIN
1995

1 AMo,AD,Secret History 3.00
2 AMo,AD,F:Captain Britain 3.00
3 AMo,AD,Trial of Captain Britain. . 3.00
4 AMo,AD,Trial cont. 3.00
5 AD,AMo,F:Captain Britain 3.00
6 AMo,AD,Final Apocalypse? 3.00
7 AMo,AD,conclusion 3.00

X-Men Archives #5
© *Marvel Entertainment Group*

X-MEN: ASKANI'SON
1 SLo,GeH,sequel to Adventures of
  Cyclops & Phoenix 3.00
2 SLo,GeH,A:Stryfe 3.00
3 SLo,GeH 3.00
4 SLo,GeH,conclusion 3.00
Books of Askani, portraits (1995). . . 3.00

X-MEN AT STATE FAIR
1 KGa,Dallas Times Herald 65.00

X-MEN: BLACK SUN
Sept., 2000
1 (of 5) CCI,New X-Men 3.00
2 CCI,Storm 3.00
3 CCI,RT,Banshee & Sunfire 3.00
4 CCI,LSi,Colossus&Nightcrawler . 3.00
5 CCI,Wolverine & Thunderbird . . . 3.00

X-MEN: CHILDREN
OF THE ATOM
Jan., 2000
1 (of 6) JoC,SR,O:X-Men 5.00
2 JoC,SR,F:Professor X 3.00
3 thru 6 JoC,SR . . . . @3.00

X-MEN CHRONICLES
1995
1 X-Men Unlimited AX 5.00
2 V:Abbatoir 5.00

X-MEN/CLANDESTINE
1996
1 & 2 AD,MFm,48-pg. . . . . @3.00

X-MEN CLASSICS
Dec., 1983
1 NA,rep. 7.00
2 NA,rep. 7.00
3 NA,rep. 7.00

CLASSIC X-MEN
Sept., 1986
1 AAd(c),JBo,New stories, rep.
  giant size X-Men 1 . . . . 9.00
2 rep.#94,JBo/AAd(c) 6.00
3 thru 9 rep#95-101,JBo/AAd(c) . @4.00
10 rep.#102,JBo/AAd(c),BU:Wolv.. 8.00
11 rep.#103,JBo/BL(c), ... 3.00
12 rep.#104,JBo/AAd(c),BU:
  O:Magneto. 7.00
13 thru 16 rep.,JBo/AAd(c) . . . . . @3.00
17 rep.#111,JBo/TA(c). 5.00
18 rep.#112,JBo/AAd(c). 4.00
19 rep.#113,JBo/AAd(c). 4.00
20 thru 22 rep.,JBo/AAd(c) . . . . . @3.00
23 thru 25 rep.,JBo/KGa(c) . . . . . @3.00
26 rep.#120,JBo/KGa(c). 4.00
27 thru 29 rep.,JBo/KD(c) . . . . . . @3.00
30 thru 35 rep.,JBo/SLi(c) . . . . . . @3.00
36 rep.#130,MBr/SLi(c) 3.00
37 rep.#131,RL/SLi(c) 3.00
38 rep.#132,KB/SLi(c) 3.00
39 rep.#133,2nd JLe X-Men/SLi(c) 11.00
40 thru 42 rep.,SLi(c) . . . . @3.00
43 rep.#137,JBy(c). 3.00
Becomes:

X-MEN CLASSICS
1990
44 rep.#138,KD/SLi(c) 3.00
45 thru 49 rep.#139-#145,SLi(c) . @3.00
50 thru 69 rep.#146-#165 . . . . . . @3.00
70 thru 105 rep.#166-#201 . . . . . @3.00
106 Phoenix vs. Beyonder. 3.00
107 F:Rogue 3.00
108 F:Nightcrawler. 3.00
109 Rep. Uncanny X-Men #205 . . . 3.00

X-Men Classics #93
© Marvel Entertainment Group

110 Rep. Uncanny X-Men #206 . . . 3.00

X-MEN:
COLOSSUS–BLOODLINE
Sept., 2005
1 (of 5) Colossus 3.00
2 Russia 3.00
3 thru 5 . . . . @3.00

X-MEN: DEADLY GENESIS
Nov., 2005
1 . . . . 4.00
2 Decimation tie-in 3.50
3 thru 5 . . . . @3.50

X-MEN:
DIE BY THE SWORD
Oct., 2007
1 (of 5) 3.00
2 thru 3 . . . . @3.00
4 thru 5 CCI(s) . . . . @3.00

X-MEN:
DIVIDED WE STAND
Apr., 2008
1 and 2 (of 2) . . . . @4.00

X-MEN:
EMPEROR VULCAN
Sept., 2007
1 thru 5 . . . . @3.00

X-MEN: THE END
Aug., 2004
1 Dreamers and Demons,pt.1 . . . . 3.00
2 thru 6 Dreamers and Demons . @3.00

X-MEN: THE END–
HEROES AND MARTYRS
March, 2005
1 (of 6) CCI(s) 3.00
2 thru 6 CCI(s) . . . . @3.00

X-MEN: THE END–
MEN AND X-MEN
Jan., 2006
1 CCI. 3.00

2 thru 6 CCI. . . . . @3.00

X-MEN EVOLUTION
Nov., 2001
1 cartoon series tie-in 3.00
2 F:Cyclops. 3.00
3 F:Jean Grey. 3.00
4 F:Nigntcrawler, Shadowcat,
  Spyke, Rogue 3.00
5 F:Mystique, Rogue. 3.00
6 I:Mimic 3.00
7 new recruits, Beast 3.00
8 F:Angel, Storm. 3.00
9 F:Professor X, Brotherhood. 3.00
10 . . . . 3.00
Digest. 6.00

X-MEN FAIRY TALES
May, 2006
1 Kitty's Fairy Tale. 3.00
2 Professor X and Magneto 3.00
3 Rogue and Gambit 3.00
4 Logan. 3.00

X-MEN/FANTASTIC FOUR
Dec., 2004
1 (of 5) PtL 3.50
2 PtL 3.50
3 PtL 3.50
4 PtL,Brood attack 3.50
5 PtL,Finale. 3.50

X-MEN FIRST CLASS
Sept., 2006
1 . . . . 3.00
2 V:The Lizard 3.00
3 . . . . 3.00
June, 2007
1 RCz 3.00
4 thru 6 RCz . . . . @3.00
7 RCz 3.00
8 RCz 3.00
9 RCz 3.00
10 JR2(c),F:Cyclops 3.00
11 V:Mysterio 3.00
12 F:Angel 3.00
13 F:Machine Man 3.00
14 F:Aaron 3.00
15 KK,F:Medusa 3.00
16 Iceman & Human Torch 3.00
Spec. 4.00
Giant-Size #1 (2008) 4.00

X-MEN FOREVER
Nov., 2000
1 (of 6) FaN,KM. 5.00
2 FaN,KM,displaced in time 4.00
3 FaN,KM, crucial points 4.00
4 FaN,KM,Toad. 3.50
5 FaN,KM,Prosh. 3.50
6 FaN,KM, concl. 3.50

X-MEN: HELLFIRE CLUB
Nov., 1999
1 (of 4) AKu,BRa,CAd. 3.00
2 AKu,BRa,CAd,O:Inner Circle. . . . 3.00
3 AKu,BRa,CAd,O:cont. 3.00
4 AKu,BRa,O:Concl. 3.00

X-MEN:
THE HIDDEN YEARS
Oct., 1999
1 JBy,TP,Original team,48-pg. 4.00
2 thru 11 JBy,TP . . . . @3.00
12 JBy,TP,48-pg. 4.00
13 thru 22 . . . . @3.00

MARVEL

X-MEN ICONS: CHAMBER
Aug., 2002
1 (of 4) NRd 3.50
2 thru 4 NRd . . . . @3.00

X-MEN INDEX
See: OFFICIAL MARVEL INDEX TO THE X-MEN

X-MEN: KITTY PRYDE– SHADOW & FLAME
June, 2005
1 (of 5),Kitty Pryde & Lockhead . . . 3.00
2 thru 5 Finale . . . . @3.00

X-MEN: LIBERATORS
Sept., 1999
1 (of 4) PJ,F:Wolverine,Nightcrawler
  & Colossus 3.00
2 PJ,V:Russian army 3.00
3 PJ,V:Nikolas 3.00
4 PJ,V:Omega Red 3.00

X-MEN: LOST TALES
1997
1 CCl,JBo,rep. from Classic X-Men 3.00
2 CCl,JBo,rep. from Classic X-Men 3.00

X-MEN: MAGIK
Oct., 2000
1 (of 4) DAn,ALa,LSh 3.00
2 DAn,ALa,LSh,V:Mephisto 3.00
3 DAn,ALa,LSh,F:Limbo 3.00
4 DAn,ALa,LSh,concl. 3.00

X-MEN: MAGNETO – TESTAMENT
Sept., 2008
1 thru 3 (of 5) . . . . @4.00

X-MEN: MANIFEST DESTINY
Sept., 2008
1 (of 4) MCy(s),HuR(c) 4.00
2 thru 3 F:Iceman . . . . @4.00

X-MEN: MESSIAH COMPLEX
Oct., 2007
One-shot x-over, pt.1 . . . . 4.00
One-shot Mutant Files 4.00

X-MEN/MICRONAUTS
Jan., 1984
1 JG,BWi,Limited Series 4.00
2 JG,BWi,KJo,V:Baron Karza 3.00
3 JG,BWi,V:Baron Karza 3.00
4 JG,BWi,V:Baron Karza,Apr.1984 . 3.00

X-MEN: THE MAGNETO WAR
Jan., 1999
1-shot AD, Joseph vs. Magneto 3.00
1a signed 20.00

X-MEN: THE MANGA
Jan., 1998
1 b&w,translated,F:Jubilee 4.00
2 Jubilee joins, V:Sentinels 3.00
3 Agent Gyrich strikes 3.00
4 Beast captured, morph dead 3.00
5 Magneto attempts to rescue
  Beast 3.00

X-Men Manga #15
© Marvel Entertainment Group

6 Beast on trial, A:Sabretooth 3.00
7 V:Magneto 3.00
8 V:Magneto 3.00
9 V:Morlocks 3.00
10 V:Morlocks, 40-pg. finale 3.00
11 Wolverine vs. Sabretooth 3.00
12 Wolverine vs. Sabretooth 3.00
13 F:Storm, Jubilee & Gambit 3.00
14 &15 . . . . @3.00
16 A:Colossus,V:Juggernaut,
  double-size 4.00
17 F:Cable & Angel 3.00
18 Angel becomes Archangel 3.00
19 Angel becomes Death 3.00
20 Rogue vs. Apocalypse 3.00
21 V:Four Horsemen 3.00
22 V:Sentinels 3.00
23 RGr(c),F:Bishop 3.00
24 RGr(c),V:Nimrod 3.00
25 Bishop vs. Gambit 3.00
26 V:Brotherhood of Evil Mutants . . 3.00
27 Magneto Returns 3.00
28 V:Master Mold,A:Magneto 3.00
29 thru 32 . . . . @3.00

X-MEN: THE MOVIE
June, 2000
Magneto, photo(c) 6.00
Rogue, photo(c) 6.00
Wolverine, photo(c) 6.00
X-Men The Movie, photo(c) 6.00

X-MEN OMEGA
1995
1 FaN,Slo,After Xavier, concl 10.00
1a Gold ed. Chromium(c) 48-pg. . . 50.00

X-MEN ORIGIN
May, 2008
Spec. Colossus (4-2008) 4.00
Spec. Jean Grey (8-2008) 4.00
Spec. Beast (9-2008) 4.00

X-MEN: ORIGINAL SIN
Oct., 2008
1 Original Sin x-over pt.1 . . . . 4.00

X-MEN: PHOENIX
Oct., 1999
1 (of 3) JFM,F:Rachel Summers . . 3.00
2 thru 3 JFM . . . . @3.00

May, 2003
1 (of 3) Legacy of Fire 3.00
2 Sword of Limbo 3.00
3 Concl 3.00

...ENDSONG
Jan., 2005
1 thru 5 (of 5) Phoenix Force . . . @5.00

..WARSONG
Sept., 2006
1 thru 3 . . . . @5.00
4 thru 5 . . . . @3.00

X-MEN: PIXIES AND DEMONS
2008
1 Director's Cut 4.00

X-MEN PRIME
1995
1 SLo,FaN,BHi,major plotlines for
  all X books begin, chromium(c)10.00

X-MEN: PRYDE & WISDOM
1996
1 WEI,TyD,KIS 3.00
2 & 3 Wel,TyD,KIS 3.00

X-MEN: RONIN
March, 2003
1 (of 5) manga mania 3.00
2 thru 5 . . . . @3.00

X-MEN/SPIDER-MAN
Nov., 2008
1 (of 4) 4.00

X-MEN: THE 198
Jan., 2006
1 thru 5 Decimation tie-in . . . . . . @3.00

X-MEN: THE EARLY YEARS
1 rep. X-Men (first series) #1 . . . . . 3.00
2 rep. X-Men (first series) #2 . . . . . 3.00
3 rep. X-Men (first series) #3 . . . . . 3.00
4 thru 16 rep. X-Men (first series)
  #4 to #16 . . . . @3.00
17 Rep. X-Men #17 & #18 . . . . 3.00

X-Men The Early Years #7
© Marvel Entertainment Group

X-MEN: THE RISE OF APOCALYPSE

1 TKa,AdP, ancient history of
  X-Men 5.00
2 thru 4 TKa,AdP, ... @5.00

X-MEN: THE SEARCH FOR CYCLOPS

Oct., 2000

1A (of 4) TR,SHa, ... 5.00
1B variant AdP (c). 5.00
2A TR,SHa,Scott alive? 3.00
2B variant AdP(c) 3.00
3A TR,SHa, ... 3.00
3B variant AdP(c) 3.00
4A TR,SHa, concl. 5.00

X-MEN SPOTLIGHT ON STARJAMMERS

1990

1 DC,F:Starjammers,A:Prof.X. 5.00
2 DC,F:Starjammers,A:Prof.X. 5.00

X-MEN: TRUE FRIENDS

July, 1999

1 (of 3) CCI,RL,JP,F:Shadowcat . . 3.00
2 CCI,RL,JP,A:Kitty Pryde. 3.00
3 CCI,RL,JP,A:Wolverine,concl. . . 3.00

X-MEN 2099

1993–96

1 B:JFM(s),RLm,JP,I:X-Men 2099 . 4.00
1a Gold Ed. 5.00
2 RLm,JP,V:Rat Pack 3.00
3 RLm,JP,D:Serpentina 3.00
4 RLm,JP,I:Theatre of Pain. 3.00
5 RLm,JP,Fall of the Hammer#3. . 3.00
6 RLm,JP,I:Freakshow 3.00
7 RLm,JP,V:Freakshow. 3.00
8 RLm(c),JS3,JP,N;Metalhead,
  I:2nd X-Men 2099 . . . . 3.00
9 RLm,JP,V:2nd X-Men 2099 . . . . 3.00
10 RLm,JP,A:La Lunatica 3.00
11 RLm,JP,V:2nd X-Men 2099. . . . 3.00
12 RLm,JP,A:Junkpile 3.00
13 RLm,JP 3.00
14 RLm,JP,R:Loki 3.00
15 RLm,JP,F:Loki,I:Haloween Jack . 3.00
16 . . . . 3.00
17 X'ian 3.00
18 Haloween Jack 3.00
19 Conclusion Halloween Jack 3.00
Becomes:

X-MEN 2099 A.D.

20 F:Bloodhawk 3.00
21 Doom Factor 3.00
22 One Nation Under Doom 3.00
23 V:Junkpile 3.00
24 . . . . 3.00
25 X-Men Reunited 3.00
25a variant cover 4.25
26 V:Graverobber 3.00
27 . . . . 3.00
28 X-Nation x-over. 3.00
29 X-Nation x-over. 3.00
30 & 31. . . . . @3.00
32 V:Foolkiller 3.00
Spec.#1 Bros.Hildebrandt(c) 4.50
GN X-Men 2099: Oasis, rep., Greg
  Hildebrandt(c) 64-pg., (1998) . . 6.00

X-MEN 2: THE MOVIE

March, 2003

Prequel Wolverine, TMd 3.50
Prequel Nightcrawler 3.50
Spec. Movie Adapt., 48-pg. 3.50

X-Men Unlimited #5
© Marvel Entertainment Group

X-MEN UNIVERSE

Oct., 1999

1 rep. July 99 stories, 80-pg. 5.00
2 thru 11 rep., 80-pg. . . . . @5.00
12 thru 17,rep., 80-pg. . . . . @4.00

X-MEN UNLIMITED

1993

1 CBa,BP,O:Siena Blaze 7.00
2 JD,O:Magneto 6.00
3 FaN(s),BSz(c),MMK,Sabretooth
  joins X-Men,A:Maverick. 7.00
4 SLo(s),RiB,O:Nightcrawler,Rogue,
  Mystique,IR:Mystique is
  Nightcrawler's mother 5.00
5 JFM(s),LSh,After Shi'ar/
  Kree War 4.50
6 JFM(s),PS,Sauron 4.50
7 JR2,HMe,O:Storm 4.50
8 Legacy Virus Victim 4.50
9 LHa,Wolverine & Psylocke 4.50
10 MWa,Dark Beast,Beast,
  double-size 8.00
11 Rogue & Magneto, double-size . 8.00
12 Onslaught x-over,A:Juggernaut . 3.00
13 GP,Binary gone berserk 3.00
14 TKa, Onslaught fallout 3.00
15 HMe,F:Wolverine, Iceman &
  Maverick 3.00
16 MvR,F:Banshee, White Queen,
  I:Primal 3.00
17 TKa,Wolverine vs. Sabretooth,
  minds are switched 4.00
18 TDF,V:Hydro Man 3.00
19 BRa,Nightcrawler v. Belasco . . . 3.00
20 F:Generation X 3.00
21 TDz,Strong Guy returns 3.00
22 into Marrow's World 4.00
23 F:Professor X 3.00
24 F:Wolverine & Cecilia Reyes . . . 3.00
25 BBh,48-pg. 3.00
26 BBh,Ages of Apocalypse,pt.4 . . 7.00
27 BBh,X-Men: Revolution 3.00
28 BBh,Russia 3.00
29 BBh,Maximum Security 3.00
30 BBh, ... 3.00
31 MGo(c) three stories 3.00
32 JIT(c). 3.00
33 MK(c),Sabretooth,Blob 3.00
34 Marvel Girl vs. Sabretooth 3.50
35 F:Emma Frost, Jubilee 3.50
36 three stories 3.50
37 multiple dimensions, 48-pg. 3.50

---

38 DaR,F:Colossus 2.50
39 KIS,48-pg. 3.50
40 All evil issue, 48-pg. 3.50
41 I:MC Mystik,48-pg. 3.50
42 F:Prof. X, Jean Grey,48-pg. . . . 3.50
43 CCI,BSz 3.00
44 animal cruelty 3.00
45 V:Alpha Flight 3.00
46 SB,F:Wolverine. 3.00
47 Return of Psylocke 3.00
48 Mystique returns 3.00
49 F:Nightcrawler. 3.00
50 PS,Japan connections 3.00

X-MEN UNLIMITED

March, 2004

1 TMd 3.00
2 F:Bishop. 3.00
3 F:Gambit 3.00
4 F:Juggernaut 3.00
5 F:Wolverine 3.00
6 Ladies of X. 3.00
7 F:nightcrawler, Kitty Pryde. 3.00
8 F:Angel, Beast. 3.00
9 F:Wolverine, Iceman 3.00
10 F:The Beast 3.00
11 MD2(c),Rachel & Havok 3.00
12 F:Wolverine. 3.00
13 Decimation tie-in 3.00
14 F:Colossus. 3.00

X-MEN VS. AVENGERS

April, 1987

1 MS,JRu,V:Soviet SuperSoldiers . 5.00
2 MS,JRu,V:Sov.Super Soldiers . . 3.50
3 MS,JRu,V:Sov.Super Soldiers . . 3.50
4 KP,JRu,BMc,AW,AM,V:Magneto
  July, 1987 . . . . 3.50

X-MEN VS. THE BROOD

1996

1 and 2 Day of Wrath . . . . @3.00

X-MEN WORLD'S APART

Oct., 2008

1 and 2 (of 4) F:Storm . . . . @4.00

X-MEN: YOUNG AVENGERS PRESENTS

Jan., 2008

1 (of 6) 3.00
2 . . . . 3.00
3 The Lost Boys 3.00
4 F:The Vision 3.00
5 F:Stature 3.00
6 F:Kate Bishop 3.00

X-NATION 2099

1996

1 . . . . 4.00
2 thru 3 . . . . @3.00

X-STATIX

July, 2002

1 PrM,MiA,super-team, 40-pg. 3.00
2 PrM,MiA, ... 2.50
3 PrM,MiA. 2.50
4 PrM,MiA, sex = death? 2.50
5 PrM,PPo 2.50
6 PrM,MiA,pt.1 . . . . 2.50
7 PrM,MiA 2.50
8 PrM,MiA,Orphan's New Love . . . 2.50
9 PrM,MiA, ... 2.50
10 PrM,Diaries of Edie Sawyer . . . 3.00
11 PrM,F:Latino 3.00
12 PrM,If You Think I'm Sexy 3.00
13 PrM,MiA,Di Another Day,pt.1 . . . 3.00

---

14 PrM,MiA,Di Another Day,pt.2 . . . 3.00
15 PrM,MiA,Di Another Day,pt.3 . . . 3.00
16 PrM,MiA,Di Another Day,pt.4 . . . 3.00
16 PrM,MiA,Back from Dead,pt.4 . . 3.00
17 PrM,MiA,Back from Dead,pt.5 . . 3.00
18 PrM,MiA,Back from Dead,pt.6 . . 3.00
19 PrM,MiA,The Cure,pt.1 . . . . 3.00
20 PrM,MiA,The Cure,pt.2 . . . . 3.00
21 PrM,MiA,V:Avengers,pt.1 . . . . . 3.00
22 PrM,MiA,V:Avengers,pt.2 . . . . . 3.00
23 PrM,MiA,V:Avengers,pt.3 . . . . . 3.00
24 PrM,MiA,V:Avengers,pt.4 . . . . . 3.00
25 PrM,MiA,V:Avengers,pt.5 . . . . . 3.00
26 PrM,MiA,finale. 3.00

X-TERMINATORS
Oct., 1988—Jan., 1989
1 JBg,AW,AM,I:N'astirh. 4.00
2 JBg,AM,V:N'astirh 3.50
3 JBg,AM,V:N'astirh 3.00
4 JBg,AM,A:New Mutants. 3.00

X-TREME X-MEN
June, 2001
1 CCI,SvL,Destiny,48-page. 4.50
2A CCI,SvL,Guardia,Vargas 3.50
2B variant CPa(c) 3.50
3 CCI,SvL,V:Vargas 3.00
4 CCI,SvL,V:Vargas 3.00
5 CCI,SvL,F:Gambit 3.00
6 CCI,SvL,F:Gambit,Rogue 3.00
7 CCI,SvL 3.00
8 CCI,SvL,concl.'Nuff Said 3.00
9 CCI,SvL,V:Lady Mastermind 3.00
10 CCI,SvL,Dimension X,pt.1 . . . . . 3.00
11 CCI,SvL,Dimension X,pt.2 . . . . . 3.00
12 CCI,SvL,V:Shaitan,Khan. 3.00
13 CCI,SvL,F:Gambit,Lifeguard. . . . 3.00
14 CCI,SvL,F:Storm, Sage. 3.00
15 CCI,SvL,F:Storm,Rogue 3.00
16 CCI,SvL,F:Rogue, Gambit 3.00
17 CCI,SvL. 3.00
18 CCI,SvL,F:Jean Grey,Beast,
   Nightcrawler. 3.00
19 CCI,F:Jean Grey 3.00
20 CCI,SvL,Scism,pt.1 . . . . 3.00
21 CCI,SvL,Scism,pt.2 . . . . 3.00
22 CCI,SvL,Scism,pt.3 . . . . 3.00
23 CCI,SvL,Scism,pt.4 . . . . 3.00
24 CCI,SvL,R:Cannonball 3.00
25 CCI,SvL,God Loves,Man Kills2. . 3.00
26 CCI,SvL,God Loves,Man Kills2. . 3.00
27 CCI,SvL,God Loves,Man Kills2. . 3.00
28 CCI,SvL,God Loves,Man Kills2. . 3.00
29 CCI,SvL,God Loves,Man Kills2. . 3.00
30 CCI,SvL,God Loves,Man Kills2. . 3.00
31 CCI,SHa,Intifada,pt.1 . . . . 3.00
32 CCI,SHa,Intifada,pt.2 . . . . 3.00
33 CCI,SHa,Intifada,pt.3 . . . . 3.00
34 CCI,SHa,Intifada,pt.4 . . . . 3.00
35 CCI,SHa,Intifada,pt.5 . . . . 3.00
36 Storm: The Arena,pt.1. . . . . 3.00
37 Storm: The Arena,pt.2. . . . . 3.00
38 Storm: The Arena,pt.3. . . . . 3.00
39 Storm: The Arena,pt.4. . . . . 3.00
40 CCI,Bogan,pt.1,Prisoner of Fire . 3.00
41 CCI,Bogan,pt.2,Prisoner of Fire . 3.00
42 CCI,Bogan,pt.3,Prisoner of Fire . 3.00
43 CCI,Bogan,pt.4,Prisoner of Fire . 3.00
44 CCI,Prisoner of Fire,pt.5 . . . . 3.00
45 CCI,Prisoner of Fire,pt.6 . . . . 3.00
46 CCI,finale 3.50
Ann.2001 CCI,SvL,64-pg. 5.00

X-TREME X-MEN:
SAVAGE LAND
July, 2001
1 (of 4) CCI,F:Rogue 3.50
2 CCI,Velociraptors & T-Rexes. . . . 3.00
3 CCI. 3.00

4 CCI,concl. 3.00

X-TREME X-MEN:
X-POSE
Nov., 2002
1 (of 2) Ccl, two reporters. 3.00
2 CCI,Forbidden Mutant Love. 3.00

X-23
Jan., 2005
1 (of 6) BTn,Innocence Lost,pt.1 . . 6.00
2 Btn,o:x-23 . . . . 4.00
3 BTn,Innocence Lost. 3.00
4 BTn,Innocence Lost. 3.00
5 BTn,Innocence Lost. 3.00
6 BTn,Innocence Lost,concl. 3.00

X-23: TARGET X
Dec., 2006
1 (of 6) 3.00
2 thru 6 . . . . @3.00

X-UNIVERSE
1995
1 The Other Heroes 5.00
2 F:Ben Grimm,Tony Stark 5.00

YELLOW CLAW
Marvel Atlas, 1956
1 MMe 1,500.00
2 JK,JSe 1,200.00
3 BEv 1,200.00
4 JK,JSe 1,200.00

YOGI BEAR
Nov., 1977
1 A:Flintstones 40.00
2 thru 9 March, 1979 . . . . @25.00

YOUNG ALLIES COMICS
Timely,
Summer, 1941—Oct., 1946
1 S&K,SSh,Hitler(c),I&O:Young Allies
   1st meeting Capt. America &
   Human Torch,A:Red Skull 30,000.00
2 S&K,A;Capt.America,Human
   Torch. 7,500.00
3 Remember Pearl Harbor(c) . 5,500.00
4 A;Capt. America,Torch,Red Skull
   ASh(c),Horror In Hollywood
   A:Capt.America,Torch. 8,000.00
5 ASh(c),AAv,Capt.America . . 3,500.00
6 ASh(c) 2,500.00
7 ASh(c),SSh 2,500.00
8 ASh(c),WW2,Bondage 2,500.00
9 ASh(c),Axis leaders(c),
   B:Tommy Type,Hitler 2,800.00
10 ASh(c),O:Tommy Type. 2,500.00
11 ASh(c) 1,600.00
12 ASh(c),Decapitation 1,600.00
13 ASh(c) 1,600.00
14 ASh(c) 1,600.00
15 ASh(c),AAv. 1,600.00
16 ASh(c) 1,600.00
17 ASh(c),SSh 1,600.00
18 ASh(c) 1,500.00
19 ASh(c),E:Tommy Type 1,500.00
20 SSh 1,500.00

YOUNG AVENGERS
Feb., 2005
1 Sidekicks 5.00
2 Sidekicks 3.00
3 Sidekicks 3.00
4 Sidekicks 3.00
5 Sidekicks 3.00
6 Sidekicks,concl. 3.00

7 Secret Identities,pt.1 . . . . 3.00
8 Secret Identities,pt.2 . . . . 3.00
9 New team member 3.00
10 Family Matters 3.00
11 Kree-Skrull War II 3.00
12 Family Matters 3.00
Spec. #1 Secret History (2005) 3.00

YOUNG HEARTS
Nov., 1949—Feb., 1950
1 . . . . 150.00
2 Feb., 1950 . . . . 100.00

YOUNG MEN
See: COWBOY ROMANCES

YOUNG X-MEN
Apr., 2008
1 Divided We Stand, tie-in 3.00
1a variant MS (c) 5.00
2 Divided We Stand, tie-in 3.00
3 V:Brotherhood of Evil Mutants. . . 3.00
4 New Genesis, pt.4 . . . . 3.00
5 New Genesis, pt.5 . . . . 3.00
6 Manifest Destiny 3.00
6a Monkey variant (c) 3.00
7 Manifest Destiny 3.00
8 Manifest Destiny 3.00

ZIGGY PIG,
SILLY SEAL
Marvel Timely, 1944
1 Funny Animals vs. Japs. 350.00
2 . . . . 175.00
3 thru 5 . . . . @125.00
6 . . . . 175.00

ZOMBIE
Sept., 2006
1 thru 4 . . . . @4.00

ZOMBIE, THE:
SIMON GARTH
Marvel Max, Nov., 2007
2 thru 4 . . . . @4.00

ZORRO
Marvel UK, 1990
1 Don Diego 3.00
2 thru 12 . . . . @3.00

Ziggy Pig Silly Seal #5
© Marvel Entertainment Group

GOLDEN AGE

A-1 COMICS
Magazine Enterprises, 1944
N# F:Kerry Drake,BU:Johnny
  Devildog & Streamer Kelly . . 300.00
1 A:Dotty Driple,Mr. EX,Bush
  Berry and Lew Loyal 165.00
2 A:Texas Slim & Dirty Dalton,
  The Corsair,Teddy Rich, Dotty
  Dripple,Inca Dinca,Tommy Tinker
  Little Mexico and Tugboat . . . 100.00
3 same 100.00
4 same 100.00
5 same 100.00
6 same 100.00
7 same 100.00
8 same 100.00
9 Texas Slim Issue 125.00
10 Same characters as
  issues #2–#8 . . . . 100.00
11 Teena 150.00
12 Teena 100.00
13 JCr,Guns of Fact and Fiction,
  narcotics & junkies featured . 400.00
14 Tim Holt #1 . . . . 1,100.00
15 Teena 100.00
16 Vacation Comics 75.00
17 Tim Holt #2, E:"A-1" on cover . 600.00
18 Jimmy Durante, Ph(c) 700.00
19 Tim Holt #3 . . . . 400.00
20 Jimmy Durante Ph(c) 600.00
21 OW,Joan of Arc movie adapt. . 400.00
22 Dick Powell (1949) 350.00
23 Cowboys N' Indians #6 . . . . . . 175.00
24 FF(c),LbC,Trail Colt #1 . . . . . . 600.00
25 Fibber McGee & Molly (1949). 125.00
26 LbC, Trail Colt #2 . . . . 500.00
27 GhostRider#1,O:GhostRider 1,700.00
28 Christmas (Koko & Kola #6) . . . 75.00
29 FF(c), Ghost Rider #2 . . . . . 1,200.00
30 BP, Jet Powers #1 . . . . 500.00
31 FF,Ghost Rider #3,O:Ghost
  Rider 1, 200.00
32 AW,GE,Jet Powers #2 . . . . . . 500.00
33 Muggsy Mouse #1 . . . . 100.00
34 FF(c),Ghost Rider #4 . . . . . . 1,100.00
35 AW,Jet Powers#3 . . . . 550.00
36 Muggsy Mouse #2 . . . . 150.00
37 FF(c),Ghost Rider #5 . . . . . . 1,100.00
38 AW,WW,Jet Powers#4, Drugs 700.00
39 Muggsy Mouse #3 . . . . 75.00
40 Dogface Dooley #1 . . . . 100.00
41 Cowboys 'N' Indians #7 . . . . . 100.00
42 BP,Best of the West #1 . . . . . 650.00
43 Dogface Dooley#2 . . . . 75.00
44 Ghost Rider #6 . . . . 450.00
45 American Air Forces #5 . . . . . 150.00
46 Best of the West #2 . . . . 400.00
47 FF,Thunda #1 . . . . 2,200.00
48 Cowboys N' Indians #8 . . . . . 100.00
49 Dogface Dooley #3 . . . . 75.00
50 BP,Danger is Their
  Business #11 . . . . 200.00
51 Ghost Rider #7 . . . . 450.00
52 Best of the West #3 . . . . 300.00
53 Dogface Dooley #4 . . . . 75.00
54 BP,American Air Forces #6 . . . 100.00
55 BP,U.S. Marines #5 . . . . 100.00
56 BP,Thunda #2 . . . . 350.00
57 Ghost Rider #8, Drugs 500.00
58 American Air Forces #7 . . . . . 100.00
59 Best of the West #4 . . . . 250.00
60 The U.S. Marines #6 . . . . 100.00
61 Space Ace #5 . . . . 900.00
62 Starr Flagg, Undercover
  Girl #5 . . . . 600.00

A-1 Comics #31
© *Magazine Enterprises*

63 FF,Manhunt #13 . . . . 550.00
64 Dogface Dooley #5 . . . . 75.00
65 BP,American Air Forces #8 . . . 100.00
66 Best of the West #5 . . . . 250.00
67 American Air Forces #9 . . . . . 100.00
68 U.S. Marines #7 . . . . 100.00
69 Ghost Rider #9, Drugs 500.00
70 Best of the West #6 . . . . 200.00
71 Ghost Rider #10 . . . . 400.00
72 U.S. Marines #8 . . . . 100.00
73 BP,Thunda #3 . . . . 250.00
74 BP,American Air Forces #10 . . 100.00
75 Ghost Rider #11 . . . . 350.00
76 Best of the West #7 . . . . 200.00
77 LbC,Grl,Manhunt #14 . . . . 450.00
78 BP,Thunda #4 . . . . 250.00
79 American Air Forces #11 . . . . . 100.00
80 Ghost Rider #12, Bondage(c). 500.00
81 Best of the West #8 . . . . 200.00
82 BP,Cave Girl #11 . . . . 700.00
83 BP,Thunda #5 . . . . 225.00
84 Ghost Rider #13 . . . . 400.00
85 Best of the West #9 . . . . 200.00
86 BP,Thunda #6 . . . . 250.00
87 Best of the West #10 . . . . 200.00
88 Bobby Benson's B-Bar-B #29. 150.00
89 BP,Home Run #3,Stan Musial. 275.00
90 Red Hawk #11 . . . . 200.00
91 BP,American Air Forces #12 . . 100.00
92 Dream Book of Romance #5 . 175.00
93 BP,Great Western #8 . . . . 300.00
94 FF,White Indian #11 . . . . 350.00
95 BP,Muggsy Mouse #4 . . . . 75.00
96 BP,Cave Girl #12 . . . . 500.00
97 Best of the West #11 . . . . 200.00
98 Starr Flagg Undercover
  Girl #6 . . . . 550.00
99 Muggsy Mouse #5 . . . . 75.00
100 Badmen of the West #1 . . . . . 325.00
101 FF,White Indian #12 . . . . 325.00
101(a) BP(c),FGu, Dream Book of
  Romance #6, Marlon Brando 300.00
103 BP,Best of the West #12 . . . 200.00
104 FF,White Indian #13 . . . . 325.00
105 Great Western #9 . . . . 200.00
106 BP,Dream Book of Love #1 . 200.00
107 Hot Dog #1 . . . . 125.00
108 BP,LbC,Red Fox #15 . . . . . . 350.00
109 BP,Dream Book of Romance 150.00
110 Dream Book of Romance #8 150.00

111 BP,I'm a Cop #1 . . . . 200.00
112 Ghost Rider #14 . . . . 350.00
113 BP,Great Western #11 . . . . . 175.00
114 Dream Book of Love #2 . . . . 150.00
115 Hot Dog #2 . . . . 100.00
116 BP,Cave Girl #13 . . . . 500.00
117 White Indian #14 . . . . 175.00
118 BP(c),Starr Flagg–
  Undercover Girl #7 . . . . 550.00
119 Straight Arrow's Fury #1 . . . 225.00
120 Badmen of the West #2 . . . . 250.00
121 Mysteries of the
  Scotland Yard #1 . . . . 250.00
122 Black Phantom #1 . . . . 550.00
123 Dream Book of Love #3 . . . . 125.00
124 Hot Dog #3 . . . . 100.00
125 BP,Cave Girl #14 . . . . 500.00
126 BP,I'm a Cop #2 . . . . 150.00
127 BP,Great Western 200.00
128 BP,I'm a Cop #3 . . . . 150.00
129 The Avenger #1 . . . . 600.00
130 BP,Strongman #1 . . . . 325.00
131 BP,The Avenger #2 . . . . 400.00
132 Strongman #2 . . . . 300.00
133 BP,The Avenger #3 . . . . 400.00
134 Strongman #3 . . . . 300.00
135 White Indian #15 . . . . 175.00
136 Hot Dog #4 . . . . 100.00
137 BP,Africa #1 . . . . 350.00
138 BP,Avenger #4 . . . . 400.00
139 BP,Strongman #4, 1955 . . . . 300.00

ABBIE AN' SLATS
United Features Syndicate, March–Aug., 1948
1 RvB(c) 250.00
2 RvB(c) 175.00
3 RvB(c) 150.00
4 Aug., 1948 . . . . 150.00
N# 1940,Earlier Issue 600.00
N# 500.00

ABBOTT AND COSTELLO
St. John Publishing Co., Feb., 1948
1 PP(c), Waltz Time 900.00
2 Jungle Girl and Snake(c) 450.00
3 Outer Space (c) 300.00
4 MD, Circus (c) 250.00
5 MD,Bull Fighting (c) 250.00
6 MD,Harem (c) 250.00
7 MD,Opera (c) 250.00
8 MD,Pirates (c) 250.00
9 MD,Polar Bear (c) 250.00
10 MD,PP(c),Son of Sinbad tale . 325.00
11 MD 200.00
12 PP(c), Movie issue 250.00
13 Fire fighters (c) 200.00
14 Bomb (c) 200.00
15 Bubble Bath (c) 200.00
16 thru 29 MD . . . . @175.00
30 thru 39 MD . . . . @150.00
40 MD,Sept., 1956 . . . . 150.00
3-D #1, Nov., 1953 . . . . 500.00

ACE COMICS
David McKay Publications, April, 1937
1 JM, F:Katzenjammer Kids . . 5,500.00
2 JM, A:Blondie 1,500.00
3 JM, A:Believe It Or Not 1,000.00
4 JM, F:Katzenjammer Kids . . 1,000.00
5 JM, A:Believe It Or Not 1,000.00
6 JM, A:Blondie 750.00

7 JM, A:Believe It Or Not 750.00
8 JM, A:Jungle Jim 750.00
9 JM, A:Blondie. 750.00
10 JM, F:Katzenjammer Kids. . . . 700.00
11 I:The Phantom series. 1,200.00
12 A:Blondie, Jungle Jim 600.00
13 A:Ripley's Believe It Or Not . . 500.00
14 A:Blondie, Jungle Jim 500.00
15 A:Blondie. 500.00
16 F:Katzenjammer Kids 500.00
17 A:Blondie. 500.00
18 A:Ripley's Believe It Or Not . . 500.00
19 F:Katzenjammer Kids 500.00
20 A:Jungle Jim 500.00
21 A:Blondie. 450.00
22 A:Jungle Jim 450.00
23 F:Katzenjammer Kids 450.00
24 A:Blondie. 450.00
25 . . . . 450.00
26 O:Prince Valiant. 1,500.00
27 thru 36. . . . . @450.00
37 Krazy Kat Ends. 350.00
38 thru 40 . . . . @350.00
41 thru 59. . . . . @300.00
60 thru 69. . . . . @250.00
70 thru 89. . . . . @150.00
90 thru 99 . . . . @125.00
100 F:The Phantom. 165.00
101 thru 109. . . . . @125.00
110 thru 127 . . . . @100.00
128 Brick Bradford begins 100.00
129 thru 143. . . . . @100.00
144 Phantom covers begin 125.00
145 thru 150 . . . . @100.00
151 Oct.–Nov., 1949 . . . . 125.00

ACES HIGH
E.C. Comics, March–April, 1955
1 GE(a&c),JDa,WW,BK 500.00
2 GE(a&c),JDa,WW,BK 300.00
3 GE(a&c),JDa,WW,BK 250.00
4 GE(a&c),JDa,WW,BK 250.00
5 GE(c),JDa,WW,BK. 250.00

ADVENTURE IS MY CAREER
Street & Smith Publ., 1944
n# U.S.Coast Guard Academy. . . 300.00

ADVENTURES
**St. John Publishing Co.,
Nov. 1949–Feb. 1950**
1 Adventures in Romance 350.00
2 Spectacular Adventures 500.00

ADVENTURES IN 3-D
**Harvey Publications,
Nov. 1953–Jan 1954**
1 with glasses 350.00
1a rep. O'Dells Adventures
in 3-D 300.00
2 with glasses 300.00

ADVENTURES INTO DARKNESS
Standard Pub., Aug., 1952
5 JK(c), ATh 650.00
6 GT, JK 450.00
7 JK(c) 450.00
8 ATh. 450.00
9 JK,ATh 450.00
10 JK,ATh,MSy 400.00
11 JK,ATh,MSy 400.00
12 JK,ATh,MSy 400.00
13 Cannibalism feature 550.00
14 Frozen Death 300.00

ADVENTURES INTO THE UNKNOWN!
**American Comics Group,
Fall 1948**
1 FGu, Haunted House (c) . . . 4,000.00
2 Haunted Island (c) 1,500.00
3 AF, Sarcophagus (c) 1,500.00
4 Monsters (c). 750.00
5 Monsters (c). 750.00
6 Giant Hands (c) 600.00
7 Skeleton Pirate (c). 600.00
8 Horror. 600.00
9 Snow Monster 600.00
10 Red Bats 600.00
11 Death Shadow 600.00
12 OW(c) 600.00
13 OW(c),Dinosaur 400.00
14 OW(c),Cave 400.00
15 Red Demons. 400.00
16 OW(c) 300.00
17 OW(c),The Thing Type 500.00
18 OW(c),Wolves. 400.00
19 OW(c),Graveyard 400.00
20 OW(c),Graveyard 400.00
21 OW(c),Bats and Dracula. . . . 350.00
22 Witches' Wrath 350.00
23 OW(c),Bats 350.00
24 Swamp Monster 350.00
25 The Were-Tiger of Assam. . . . 350.00
26 DW(s) 350.00
27 AW,RKu,OW(c) 400.00
28 thru 37. . . . . @350.00
38 A-Bomb. 500.00
39 thru 49. . . . . @400.00
50 Giant fly (c) 400.00
51 H. Lazarus 500.00
52 H. Lazarus, 3-D-ish. 500.00
53 thru 55 . . . . @500.00
56 H. Lazarus 500.00
57 SMo,OW(c). 500.00
58 H. Lazarus 500.00
59 3-D-ish 400.00
60 Hospitality; Tomb for Titus. . . . 200.00
61 OW,Rocket ship (c). 200.00
62 thru 69. . . . . @150.00
70 thru 79. . . . . @150.00
80 thru 90. . . . . @125.00
91 AW 150.00
92 thru 95. . . . . @100.00
96 AW 150.00
97 thru 99 . . . . @100.00
100 JB 125.00
101 thru 106. . . . . @100.00
107 AW 150.00
108 thru 115 . . . . @125.00
116 AW,AT 150.00
117 thru 127 . . . . @125.00
128 AW,Forbidden Worlds 125.00
129 thru 151. . . . . @125.00
152 JCr 125.00
153 A:Magic Agent. 125.00
154 O:Nemesis 150.00
155 Nemesis 125.00
156 A:Magic Agent. 125.00
157 thru 167. . . . . @125.00
168 JB,SD, Nemesis 125.00
169 Nemesis vs. Hitler. 150.00
170 thru 174, Aug., 1967 . . . . . @125.00

ADVENTURES IN WONDERLAND
**Lev Gleason Publications,
April, 1955**
1 . . . . 150.00
2 . . . . 100.00
3 and 4 . . . . @75.00
5 Christmas. 125.00

ADVENTURES OF ALICE
Civil Service Publ., 1945–46
1 In Wonderland 200.00
2 Through the Looking Glass . . . 125.00
3 Monkey Island 125.00

THE ADVENTURES OF HOMER COBB
Say/Bart Prod., Sept. 1947
1 . . . . 500.00

ADVENTURES OF LITTLE ORPHAN ANNIE COMICS
Giveaway 1940–42
N#(1) 600.00
N#(2) 500.00
N#(3) 500.00

MIGHTY MOUSE ADVENTURES
**St. John Publishing Co.,
Nov., 1951**
1 Mighty Mouse Adventures 400.00
Becomes:

ADVENTURES OF MIGHTY MOUSE
**St. John Publishing Co.,
Nov., 1951**
2 Menace of the Deep 400.00
3 Storm Clouds of Mystery 300.00
4 Thought Control Machine 300.00
5 Jungle Peril 300.00
6 'The Vine of Destruction' 250.00
7 Space Ship(c) 250.00
8 Charging Alien(c). 250.00
9 Meteor(c) 150.00
10 'Revolt at the Zoo'. 150.00
11 Jungle(c) 150.00
12 A:Freezing Terror 150.00
13 A:Visitor from Outer Space . . . 150.00
14 V:Cat 150.00
15 . . . . 150.00
16 . . . . 150.00
17 . . . . 150.00
18 May, 1955 . . . . 150.00

ADVENTURES OF MIGHTY MOUSE
See: TERRY-TUNES COMICS

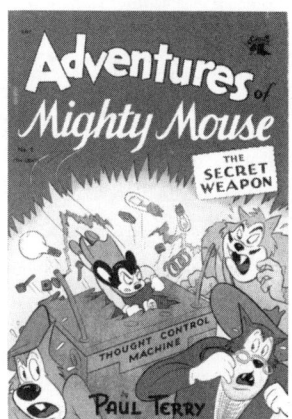

*Adventures of Mighty Mouse #4
© St John Publishing*

Air Fighters-10
© Hillman Periodicals

AGGIE MACK
Four Star Comics/
Superior Comics, Jan., 1948
1 AF,HR(c),Johnny Prep 600.00
2 JK(c) 300.00
3 AF,JK(c) 300.00
4 AF, Johnny Prep 400.00
5 AF,JK(c) 300.00
6 AF,JK(c) 275.00
7 AF,Burt Lancaster on cover . . . 325.00
8 AF,JK(c), Aug., 1949 . . . . 275.00

BILL BARNES
Street & Smith Publ.,July, 1940
1 (Bill Barnes Comics) 1,500.00
Becomes:

BILL BARNES,
AMERICA'S AIR ACE
Street & Smith Publ., 1940
2 Second Battle Valley Forge . . . 650.00
3 A:Aviation Cadets 500.00
4 Shotdown(c) 500.00
5 A:Air Warden, Danny Hawk . . . 500.00
6 A:Danny Hawk,RocketRodney . 400.00
7 How to defeat the Japanese . . 400.00
8 Ghost Ship 400.00
9 Flying Tigers, John Wayne . . . 425.00
10 I:Roane Waring 400.00
11 Flying Tigers 400.00
12 War Workers 400.00
Becomes:

AIR ACE
Street & Smith Publ., Jan., 1944
2-1 Invades Germany 600.00
2-2 Jungle Warfare 650.00
2-3 A:The Four Musketeers 250.00
2-4 A:Russell Swann 250.00
2-5 A:The Four Musketeers 250.00
2-6 Raft(c) 250.00
2-7 BP, What's New In Science . 250.00
2-8 XP-59 . . . . 250.00
2-9 The Northrop P-61 . . . . 250.00
2-10 NCG-14 . . . . 250.00
2-11 Whip Launch 250.00
2-12 PP(c) 250.00
3-1 . . . . 175.00
3-2 Atom and Its Future 175.00
3-3 Flying in the Future 175.00
3-4 How Fast Can We Fly 175.00
3-5 REv(c) 175.00
3-6 V:Wolves 175.00
3-7 BP(c), Vortex of Atom Bomb 350.00
3-8 BP,Feb.–March, 1947 . . . . . 200.00

AIR FIGHTERS COMICS
Hillman Periodicals, Nov., 1941
1 I:Black Commander
(only App) 4,500.00
2 O:Airboy A:Sky Wolf 7,000.00
3 O:Sky Wolf and Heap 3,500.00
4 A:Black Angel, Iron Ace 3,000.00
5 A:Sky Wolf and Iron Ace 2,200.00
6 Airboy's Bird Plane 2,700.00
7 Airboy Battles Kultur 2,500.00
8 A:Skinny McGinty 2,200.00
9 A:Black Prince, Hatchet Man 2,200.00
10 I:The Stinger 2,200.00
11 Kida(c) 2,200.00
12 A:Misery 2,200.00
2-1 A:Flying Dutchman 2,400.00
2-2 I:Valkyrie 2,700.00
2-3 Story Panels (c) 1,000.00
2-4 V:Japanese 1,000.00
2-5 Air Boy in Tokyo 1,000.00
2-6 'Dance of Death' 1,000.00
2-7 A:Valkyrie 1,000.00
2-8 Airboy Battles Japanese . . . 1,000.00
2-9 Airboy Battles Japanese . . . 1,000.00
2-10 O:Skywolf 1,200.00
Becomes:

AIRBOY COMICS
Hillman Periodicals, Dec., 1945
2-11 . . . . 1,200.00
2-12 A:Valkyrie 800.00
3-1 . . . . 600.00
3-2 . . . . 600.00
3-3 Never published
3-4 I:The Heap 500.00
3-5 Airboy 500.00
3-6 A:Valkyrie 500.00
3-7 AMc,Witch Hunt 500.00
3-8 A:Condor 550.00
3-9 O:The Heap 550.00
3-10 . . . . 500.00
3-11 . . . . 500.00
3-12 Airboy missing 650.00
4-1 Elephant in chains (c) 600.00
4-2 I:Rackman 400.00
4-3 Airboy profits on name 400.00
4-4 S&K 500.00
4-5 S&K,The American Miracle . 400.00
4-6 S&K,A:Heap and
Flying Fool 400.00
4-7 S&K 400.00
4-8 S&K,Girlfriend captured 400.00
4-9 S&K,Airboy in Quick Sand . . 400.00
4-10 S&K,A:Valkyrie 400.00
4-11 S&K,A:Frenchy 400.00
4-12 FBe 500.00
5-1 LSt 350.00
5-2 I:Wild Horse of Calabra 350.00
5-3 . . . . 350.00
5-4 CI 350.00
5-5 Skull on cover 350.00
5-6 . . . . 350.00
5-7 . . . . 350.00
5-8 Bondage (c) 350.00
5-9 Zoi,Row 350.00
5-10 A:Valkyrie,O:The Heap 450.00
5-11 Airboy vs. The Rats 350.00
5-12 BK,Rat Army captures
Airboy 350.00
6-1 . . . . 350.00
6-2 . . . . 350.00
6-3 . . . . 350.00
6-4 Airboy boxes 500.00
6-5 A:The Ice People 350.00
6-6 . . . . 350.00
6-7 Airboy vs. Chemical Giant . . 350.00
6-8 O:The Heap 350.00
6-9 . . . . 350.00
6-10 . . . . 350.00
6-11 . . . . 350.00
6-12 . . . . 350.00
7-1 . . . . 300.00

7-2 BP 300.00
7-3 BP 300.00
7-4 I:Monsters of the Ice 300.00
7-5 V:Monsters of the Ice 300.00
7-6 . . . . 300.00
7-7 Mystery of the Sargasso
Sea 300.00
7-8 A:Centaur 300.00
7-9 I:Men of the StarlightRobot . . 300.00
7-10 O:The Heap 300.00
7-11 . . . . 300.00
7-12 Airboy visits India 300.00
8-1 BP,A:Outcast and Polo
Bandits 250.00
8-2 BP,Suicide Dive (c) 250.00
8-3 BK, I:The Living Fuse 250.00
8-4 A:Death Merchants of
the Air 250.00
8-5 A:Great Plane from Nowhere 250.00
8-6 . . . . 250.00
8-7 . . . . 250.00
8-8 . . . . 250.00
8-9 . . . . 250.00
8-10 A:Mystery Walkers 250.00
8-11 . . . . 250.00
8-12 . . . . 250.00
9-1 . . . . 250.00
9-2 A:Valkyrie 200.00
9-3 A:Heap (c) 200.00
9-4 A:Water Beast, Frog Headed
Riders 250.00
9-5 A:Heap vs.Man of Moonlight 200.00
9-6 Heap (c) 200.00
9-7 Heap (c) 200.00
9-8 Heap (c) 250.00
9-9 . . . . 250.00
9-10 Space (c) 250.00
9-11 . . . . 250.00
9-12 Heap (c) 250.00
10-1 Heap (c) 250.00
10-2 Ships on Space 200.00
10-3 . . . . 250.00
10-4 May, 1953 . . . . 250.00

AL CAPP'S
DOGPATCH COMICS
Toby Press, June, 1949
1 . . . . 300.00
2 A:Daisy 250.00
3 . . . . 225.00
4 Dec., 1949 . . . . 225.00

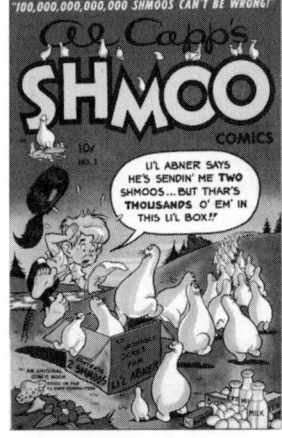

Al Capps Shmoo #1
© Toby Perss

AL CAPP'S SHMOO
Toby Press, July, 1949
1 100 Trillion Schmoos	500.00
2 Super Shmoo(c).	400.00
3	400.00
4	400.00
5 April, 1950	400.00

AL CAPP'S WOLF GAL
Toby Press, 1951
1 Pin-Up	450.00
2 1952.	400.00

ALICE
Ziff-Davis Publ. Co., 1952
10 New Adventures in Wonderland	400.00
11 (#2)	350.00

ALLEY OOP
Standard Comics, Sept. 1947–Oct. 1949
10	350.00
11 thru 18	@300.00

(The Adventures of) ALLEY OOP
Argo Publications, 1955–56
1	225.00
2	150.00
3	150.00

ALL-FAMOUS CRIME
Star Publications, May, 1951
1 LbC(c) (8).	350.00
2 LbC(c) (9).	500.00
3 LbC(c) (10).	325.00
4 LbC(c) (4) Law Crime	300.00
5 LbC(c) (5).	300.00

Becomes:

ALL-FAMOUS POLICE CASES
Feb., 1952
6 LbC(c)	300.00
7 LbC(c)	275.00
8 LbC(c) Marijuana	275.00
9 LbC(c)	250.00
10 thru 15 LbC(c).	@250.00
16 Sept., 1954	250.00

All-Famous Police Cases #15, Star Publications © Fox Features

ALL GOOD COMICS
Fox Publications, 1946
1	400.00

ALL GOOD
R. W. Voight/ St. John Publishing, 1949
N# Giant.	1,000.00

ALL GREAT
Fox Features, 1946
1 Crazy Horse, etc.	600.00

ALL GREAT COMICS
See: DAGAR, DESERT HAWK

ALL HERO COMICS
Fawcett Publications, March, 1943
1 A:Capt. Marvel Jr.,Capt. Midnight,Ibis, Golden Arrow and Spy Smasher.	3,000.00

ALL HUMOR COMICS
Comic Favorites, Inc. (Quality Comics) Spring 1946
1	350.00
2 PG Atomic Tot	200.00
3 I:Kelly Poole.	125.00
4 thru 7	@ 125.00
8 PG	125.00
9	125.00
10	125.00
11 thru 17	@100.00

ALL-NEGRO COMICS
June,1947
1	10,000.00

ALL-NEW COMICS
Family Comics (Harvey Publ.) Jan., 1943
1 A:Steve Case, Johnny Rebel I:Detective Shane.	5,000.00
2 JKu,O:Scarlet Phantom	2,000.00
3 Nazi War.	1,800.00
4 AdH	1,500.00
5 Flash Gordon	1,700.00
6 ASh(c),I:Boy Heroes and Red Blazer	1,700.00
7 JKu,ASh(c),A:Black Cat & Zebra	1,700.00
8 JKu,A:Shock Gibson.	1,700.00
9 JKu,A:Black Cat	1,700.00
10 ASh(c),JKu,A:Zebra	1,700.00
11 BP,A:Man in Black, Girl Commandos.	1,700.00
12 JKu.	1,200.00
13 Stuntman by S&K, A:Green Hornet&(c)	1,300.00
14 BP,A:Green Hornet	1,000.00
15 Smaller size, Distributed by Mail, March–April, 1947.	2,000.00

ALL PICTURE ALL TRUE LOVE STORY
St. John Publ. Co. 1952
1 MB,Romance on Route 202	800.00
2 MB	500.00

REAL SPORTS COMICS
Hillman Periodicals, 1948
1 BP,Boxing (c)	600.00

Becomes:

ALL SPORTS COMICS
Hillman Periodicals, 1949
2 BP,BK,Football (c)	550.00
3 Basketball (c).	450.00

Becomes:

ALL-TIME SPORTS COMICS
Hillman Periodicals, 1949
4 Auto Racing (c)	350.00
5 BP,Baseball (c), Ty Cobb.	325.00
6 Horse Racing (c)	300.00
7 BK, Baseball (c), W. Johnson	300.00

ALL TOP
William H. Wise Co., 1944
N# 132pgs.,A:Capt. V,Red Robbins	450.00

ALL TOP COMICS
Fox Features Syndicate, Spring 1946
1 A:Cosmo Cat, Flash Rabbit.	350.00
2	150.00
3 thru 6	@125.00
7	125.00
7a	125.00
8 JKa(c),I:Blue Beetle	4,500.00
9 JKa(c),A:Rulah	2,200.00
10 JKa(c),A:Rulah.	2,200.00
11 A:Rulah,Blue Beetle	1,800.00
12 A:Rulah,Jo Jo,Blue Beetle	1,800.00
13 A:Rulah	1,800.00
14 A:Rulah,Blue Beetle	2,500.00
15 A:Rulah	2,100.00
16 A:Rulah,Blue Beetle.	1,800.00
17 A:Rulah,Blue Beetle.	1,800.00
18 A:Dagar,Jo Jo	1,300.00

Becomes:

MY EXPERIENCE
Fox Features Syndicate 1949–50
19 WW.	450.00
20	125.00
21 WW	450.00
22 WW.	400.00

Becomes:

JUDY CANOVA
Fox Features Syndicate, May, 1950–Sept., 1950
23 (1)WW(a&c)	400.00
24 (2)WW(a&c)	400.00
3 JO,WW(a&c)	400.00

ALL TOP COMICS
Green Publ., 1957–59
6 1957 Patoruzu the Indian	75.00
6 1958 Cosmo Cat.	75.00
6 1959 Atomic Mouse	75.00
6 1959 Little Eva	75.00
6 Supermouse (c)	75.00

ALL-TRUE DETECTIVE CASES
Avon Periodicals, 1954
1 WW	350.00
2 EK(c),JKa.	250.00
3 JKa.	250.00
4 JKa.	300.00
N# (5) JK,JKu	700.00

ALL YOUR COMICS
R.W. Voight, 1944
1 Red Robbins	350.00

All comics prices listed are for *Near Mint* condition.

ALL YOUR COMICS
Fox Features, 1946
1 . . . . 300.00

AMAZING ADVENTURE FUNNIES
Centaur Publ,. 1940
1 BEv,The Fantom of the Fair . 3,500.00
2 rep.After Fantoman 2,000.00
Becomes:

FANTOMAN
Aug., 1940
2 The Fantom of the Fair 3,000.00
3 . . . . 2,500.00
4 Red Blaze 2,500.00

AMAZING ADVENTURES
Ziff-Davis Publ., Co., 1950
1 MA,WW, Asteroid Witch 1,400.00
2 MA,ASh(c),Masters of Living
  Flame 650.00
3 MA,The Evil Men Do 650.00
4 Invasion of the Love Robots . . 650.00
5 MA,Secret of the Crater-Men . . 650.00
6 BK,Man Who Killed a World . . 700.00

AMAZING GHOST STORIES
See: WEIRD HORRORS

AMAZING-MAN COMICS
**Centaur Publications,
Sept., 1939–Feb., 1942**
5 BEv,O:Amazing Man 35,000.00
6 BEv,FT,B:The Shark 6,500.00
7 BEv,I:Magician From Mars . . 5,000.00
8 BEv, Cat-Man as Woman . . . 4,000.00
9 BEv,FT,A:Eternal Monster . . . 4,000.00
10 BEv,FT 2,800.00
11 BEv,I:Zardi 2,800.00
12 SG(c) 2,500.00
13 SG(c) 2,500.00
14 FT,B:Reef Kinkaid, Dr. Hypo 2,000.00
15 FT,A:Zardi 2,000.00
16 AAv,Mighty Man's Powers
  Revealed 2,000.00
17 FT,A:Dr. Hypo 2,000.00
18 FT,BLb(a),SG(c) 2,000.00
19 FT,BLb(a),SG(c) 2,000.00
20 FT,BLb(a),SG(c) 2,000.00
21 FT,O:Dash Dartwell 2,000.00
22 A:Silver Streak, The Voice . . 2,500.00
23 I&O:Tommy the AmazingKid 1,600.00
24 B:King of Darkness,
  Blue Lady 1,600.00
25 A:Meteor Marvin 2,500.00
26 A:Meteor Marvin,ElectricRay 2,500.00

AMAZING MYSTERY FUNNIES
Centaur Publications, 1938
1 Skyrocket Steele in Year X . . 7.000.00
2 WE,Skyrocket Steele 4,000.00
3 . . . . 2,000.00
(#4) WE,bondage (c) 1,900.00
2-1(#5) 1,800.00
2-2(#6) Drug use 1,500.00
2-3(#7) Air Sub DX 1,500.00
2-4(#8) Sand Hog 1,500.00
2-5(#9) 2,500.00
2-6(#10) 1,500.00
2-7(#11) Fantom of Fair, scarce 7,000.00
2-8(#12) Speed Centaur 3,000.00
2-9(#13) 1,800.00
2-10(#14) 1,800.00
2-11(#15)Robot(c) 1,800.00
2-12(#16) BW,I:Space Patrol . 3,800.00

3-1(#17) I:Bullet 1,800.00
18 Fantom of Fair 1,800.00
19 BW,Space Patrol 2,000.00
20 . . . . 1,500.00
21 thru 24 BW,Space Patrol . @2,000.00

AMAZING WILLIE MAYS
Famous Funnies, 1954
1 Willie Mays(c) 1,500.00

AMERICA IN ACTION
Dell Publishing Co., 1942
1 . . . . 300.00

THE AMERICAN AIR FORCES
Flying Cadet Publ., 1944–45
1 War (c) 300.00
2 War (c) 400.00
3 War (c) 400.00
4 War (c) 250.00
Continues in *A-1 Comics*. See #45,
#54, #58, #65, #67, #74, #79, #91

AMERICAN GRAPHICS
Henry Stewart, 1954
1 Indian Legends 175.00
2 . . . . 125.00

AMERICAN LIBRARY
David McKay Publ., 1943
(#1) Thirty Seconds Over
  Tokyo, movie adapt. 550.00
(#2) Guadalcanal Diary 400.00
3 Look to the Mountain 250.00
4 The Case of the Crooked
  Candle (Perry Mason) 250.00
5 Duel in the Sun 250.00
6 Wingate's Raiders 250.00

AMERICA'S BEST COMICS
**Nedor/Better/Standard
Publications, Feb., 1942**
1 ASh(c),B:Black Terror, Captain Future,
  The Liberator,Doc Strange . 4,500.00
2 O:American Eagle 2,000.00
3 B:Pyroman 1,500.00
4 A:Doc Strange, Jimmy Cole . 1,100.00
5 ASh(c),A:LoneEagle,
  Cap.Future 1,100.00

Americas Best Comics #1
© *Nedor/Better/Standard*

6 A:American Crusader 1,100.00
7 ASh(c),A:Hitler,Hirohito 2,000.00
8 The Liberator ends 1,100.00
9 ASh(c),Fighting Yank 1,500.00
10 ASh(c),American Eagle 1,100.00
11 ASh(c) Hirihito & Tojo(c) . . . 1,500.00
12 Red Cross (c) 1,100.00
13 Fighting Yank 1,100.00
14 Last American Eagle app. . . . 1,100.00
15 ASh(c),Fighting Yank 1,100.00
16 ASh(c),Fighting Yank 1,100.00
17 ASh(c),Doc Strange
  carries football 1,100.00
18 Fighting Yank,Bondage(c) . . 1,100.00
19 ASh(c),Fighting Yank 1,100.00
20 ASh(c),vs. the Black Market 1,100.00
21 ASh(c),Infinity (c) 1,100.00
22 A:Captain Future 1,000.00
23 B:Miss Masque 1,150.00
24 Miss Masque,Bondage (c) . . 1,150.00
25 A:Sea Eagle 750.00
26 A:The Phantom Detective 750.00
27 Pyroman,ASh(c) 750.00
28 A:Commando Cubs,
  Black Terror 750.00
29 ASh(c),A:Doc Strange 750.00
30 ASh(c).Xela 750.00
31 ASh(c),Xela,July, 1949 . . . . . 750.00

AMERICA'S BIGGEST COMICS BOOK
William H. Wise, 1944
1 196 pgs. A:Grim Reaper, Zudo,
  Silver Knight, Thunderhoof,
  Jocko and Socko,Barnaby
  Beep,Commando Cubs 700.00
Becomes:

AMERICA'S FUNNIEST COMICS
William H. Wise, 1944
2 Funny Animal 500.00
N# (3) 500.00

AMERICA'S GREATEST COMICS
Fawcett Publications, Fall 1941
1 MRa(c),A:Capt. Marvel,
  Bulletman,Spy Smasher and
  Minute Man 6,500.00
2 F:Capt. Marvel 3,000.00
3 F:Capt. Marvel 2,500.00
4 B:Commando Yank 2,000.00
5 Capt.Marvel in 'Lost Lighting' 2,000.00
6 Capt.Marvel fires
  Machine Gun 2,000.00
7 A:Balbo the Boy Magician . . . 1,800.00
8 A:Capt.Marvel Jr.,Golden
  Arrow, Summer 1943 . . . . . 1,800.00

ANCHORS ANDREWS
St. John Publ. Co. 1953
1 MB,Navy Humor 275.00
2 thru 4 . . . . @100.00

ANDY COMICS
See: SCREAM COMICS

ANDY DEVINE WESTERN
Fawcett Publ. 1950
1 Photo (c) 900.00
2 . . . . 700.00

ANGEL
Dell Publishing Co., Aug., 1954
(1) see Dell Four Color #576
2 . . . . 90.00
3 thru 16 . . . . @75.00

ANIMAL ADVENTURES
Timor Publ./Accepted Publ.
1953–54
1 Funny Animal 90.00
1a rep. 75.00
2 . . . . 75.00

ANIMAL ANTICS
Dell Publishing Co., 1946
1 B: Racoon Kids 650.00
2 . . . . 300.00
3 thru 10 . . . . @175.00
11 thru 23 . . . . @125.00

ANIMAL COMICS
Dell Publishing Co., 1942
1 WK,Pogo. 1,700.00
2 Uncle Wiggily(c),A:Pogo. . . . 1,000.00
3 Muggin's Mouse(c),A:Pogo . . . 750.00
4 Uncle Wiggily(c). 500.00
5 WK,Pogo(c). 750.00
6 Uncle Wiggily 500.00
7 Uncle Wiggily 500.00
8 WK,Pogo 600.00
9 WK,War Bonds(c),A:Pogo 600.00
10 WK,Pogo. 600.00
11 WK,Pogo. 400.00
12 WK,Pogo. 400.00
13 WK,Pogo. 400.00
14 WK,Pogo. 400.00
15 WK,Pogo. 400.00
16 Uncle Wiggily 250.00
17 WK,Pogo(c). 300.00
18 WK,Pogo(c). 300.00
19 WK,Pogo(c). 300.00
20 WK,Pogo. 250.00
21 WK,Pogo(c). 300.00
22 WK,Pogo. 200.00
23 WK,Pogo. 200.00
24 WK,Pogo(c). 200.00
25 WK,Pogo(c). 200.00
26 WK,Pogo(c). 200.00
27 thru 30 WK,Pogo(c) . . . . . . @200.00

ANIMAL FABLES
E.C. Comics, July–Aug., 1946
1 B:Korky Kangaroo,Freddy Firefly
  Petey Pig & Danny Demon . 750.00
2 B:Aesop Fables 450.00
3 . . . . 350.00
4 . . . . 350.00
5 Firefly vs. Red Ants 350.00
6 . . . . 350.00
7 O:Moon Girls,Nov.–Dec.1947 1,100.00

ANIMAL FAIR
Fawcett Publications,
March, 1946
1 B:Captain Marvel Bunny,
  Sir Spot 500.00
2 A:Droopy, Colonel Walrus 350.00
3 . . . . 250.00
4 A:Kid Gloves, Cub Reporter . 250.00
5 thru 7 . . . . @250.00
8 thru 10 . . . . @150.00
11 Feb., 1947 . . . . 200.00

ANIMATED COMICS
E.C. Comics, 1948
1 Funny Animal 1,250.00

ANNIE OAKLEY & TAGG
Dell Publishing Co., 1953
(1) see Dell Four Color #438
(2) see Dell Four Color #481
(3) see Dell Four Color #575
4 . . . . 250.00
5 . . . . 200.00

---

6 thru 10 . . . . @175.00
11 thru 18 . . . . @135.00

APACHE
Fiction House Magazines, 1951
1 . . . . 300.00

APACHE TRAIL
America's Best, 1957
1 . . . . 125.00
2 GT 85.00
3 . . . . 75.00
4 . . . . 75.00

APPROVED COMICS
St. John Publishing Co., 1954
1 The Hawk. 125.00
2 Invisible Boy. 225.00
3 Wild Boy of the Congo. 100.00
4 Kid Cowboy 100.00
5 Flyboy 100.00
6 MB,BK,Daring Adventures. . . . 150.00
7 The Hawk. 100.00
8 BP,Crime on the Run 125.00
9 MB,Western Bandit Trails 150.00
10 Dinky Duck 100.00
11 MB,Fighting Marines 175.00
12 Northwest Mounties 175.00

Archie #4 © Archie Publishing

ARCHIE COMICS
MLJ Magazines,
Winter, 1942-43
1 I:Jughead & Veronica 35,000.00
2 rare 7,500.00
3 scarce 5,000.00
4 . . . . 2,800.00
5 . . . . 2,800.00
6 Christmas issue 2,000.00
7 thru 10 . . . . @2,200.00
11 thru 15 . . . . @1,500.00
16 thru 19 . . . . @1,300.00
Archie Publications, 1946
20 . . . . 1,300.00
21 . . . . 800.00
22 thru 31 . . . . @750.00
32 thru 42 . . . . @500.00
43 thru 50 . . . . @400.00
51 A:Katy Keene 250.00
52 thru 64 . . . . @225.00
65 thru 70 A:Katy Keene . . . . @225.00
71 . . . . 150.00
72 thru 74 A:Katy Keene . . . . @175.00
75 thru 99 . . . . @150.00
100 . . . . 150.00

---

101 thru 122 . . . . @150.00
123 UFO,Vampire 100.00
124 thru 130 . . . . @100.00
131 thru 145 . . . . @60.00
146 thru 182 . . . . @60.00
183 Caveman Archie 60.00
184 . . . . 60.00
185 I:The Archies Band 75.00
186 thru 195 . . . . @50.00
196 I:Cricket O'Dell 75.00
197 thru 200 . . . . @50.00
201 thru 228 . . . . @50.00
229 Lost Child 50.00
230 thru 260 . . . . @30.00
261 thru 300 . . . . @30.00

ARCHIE'S GIANT
SERIES MAGAZINE
Archie Publications, 1954
1 . . . . 2,400.00
2 . . . . 1,400.00
3 . . . . 900.00
4 . . . . 850.00
5 . . . . 850.00
6 thru 10 . . . . @850.00
11 thru 20 . . . . @400.00
21 thru 29 . . . . @200.00
30 thru 35 . . . . @150.00

ARCHIE'S GIRLS
BETTY AND VERONICA
Archie Publications, 1950
1 . . . . 3,600.00
2 . . . . 1,500.00
3 . . . . 900.00
4 . . . . 850.00
5 . . . . 850.00
6 thru 10 . . . . @750.00
11 thru 15 . . . . @550.00
16 thru 20 . . . . @400.00
21 . . . . 350.00
22 thru 29 . . . . @325.00
30 thru 40 . . . . @250.00
41 thru 50 . . . . @200.00
51 thru 60 . . . . @150.00
61 thru 70 . . . . @135.00
71 thru 74 . . . . @125.00
75 Devil 300.00
76 thru 90 . . . . @125.00
91 thru 99 . . . . @125.00
100 . . . . 125.00

ARCHIE'S JOKE
BOOK MAGAZINE
Archie Publications, 1953
1 . . . . 1,700.00
2 . . . . 750.00
3 . . . . 600.00
15 thru 19 . . . . @350.00
20 thru 25 . . . . @250.00
26 thru 35 . . . . @200.00
36 thru 40 . . . . @175.00
41 1st NA art 400.00
42 & 43 TV Personalities . . . . . @125.00
44 thru 48 NA . . . . @150.00
49 thru 60 . . . . @75.00

ARCHIE'S MECHANICS
Archie Publications, 1954
1 . . . . 1,300.00
2 . . . . 750.00
3 . . . . 600.00

ARCHIE'S PAL,
JUGHEAD
Archie Publications, 1949
1 . . . . 3,000.00
2 . . . . 1,500.00

All comics prices listed are for *Near Mint* condition.

3	700.00
4	650.00
5	650.00
6	500.00
7 thru 10	@450.00
11 thru 15	@300.00
16 thru 20	@300.00
21 thru 30	@250.00
31 thru 39	@150.00
40 thru 50	@150.00
51 thru 70	@100.00
71 thru 80	@45.00
81 thru 100	@40.00

ARCHIE'S PALS 'N' GALS
Archie Publications, 1952–53

1	1,400.00
2	750.00
3	500.00
4	450.00
5	450.00
6	275.00
7	275.00
8 thru 10	@275.00
11 thru 15	@150.00
16 thru 18	@125.00
19 Marilyn Monroe	275.00
20 thru 30	@100.00

ARCHIE'S RIVAL REGGIE
Archie Publications, 1950

1	1,350.00
2	700.00
3	500.00
4	450.00
5	450.00
6	350.00
7 thru 9	@250.00
10 thru 14 A: Katy Keen	@225.00
15	200.00
16 Aug., 1954	200.00

ARMY & NAVY COMICS
See: SUPERSNIPE COMICS

ARROW, THE
Centaur Publications, Oct., 1940–Oct., 1941
1 B:Arrow, BLb(c)	5,700.00

Atom-Age Combat #1
© St John Publications

2 BLb(c)	2,500.00
3 O:Dash Dartwell,Human Meteor, Rainbow, Bondage(c)	2,500.00

ATOM-AGE COMBAT
St. John Publ. Co., 1952–53
1 Buck Vinson	900.00
1a rep. (1958)	500.00
2 Flying Saucer	500.00
3	450.00
4	500.00
5 Flying Saucer	350.00

ATOMAN
Spark Publications, Feb., 1946
1 JRo,MMe,O:Atoman,A:Kid Crusaders	1,200.00
2 JRo,MMe	700.00

ATOMIC BOMB
Jay Burtis Publ., 1945
1	1,300.00

ATOMIC COMICS
Green Publishing Co., Jan., 1946
1 S&S,A:Radio Squad, Barry O'Neal	2,200.00
2 MB,A:Inspector Dayton, Kid Kane	1,100.00
3 MB,A:Zero Ghost Detective	800.00
4 JKa(c), July–Aug., 1946	800.00

ATOMIC COMICS
Daniels Publications, 1946 (Reprints)
1 A:Rocketman,Yankee Boy, Bondage (c),rep.	700.00

ATOMIC MOUSE
Capital Stories/ Charlton Comics, March, 1953
1 AFa,O:Atomic Mouse	500.00
2 AFa,Ice Cream (c)	150.00
3 AFa,Genie and Magic Carpet (c)	125.00
4 AFa	125.00
5 AFa,A:Timmy the Timid Ghost	125.00
6 thru 10 Funny Animal	@100.00
11 thru 14 Funny Animal	@100.00
15 A:Happy the Marvel Bunny	100.00
16 Funny Animal,Giant	75.00
17 thru 30 Funny Animal	@75.00
31 thru 36 Funny Animal	@75.00
37 A:Atom the Cat	75.00
38 thru 40 Funny Animal	@50.00
41 thru 53 Funny Animal	@30.00
54 June, 1963	30.00

ATOMIC THUNDERBOLT, THE
Regor Company, Feb., 1946
1 I:Atomic Thunderbolt, Mr. Murdo	1,200.00

ATOMIC WAR!
Ace-Junior Books, 1952–53
1 Atomic explosion (c)	1,700.00
2	1,200.00
3 A-Bomb	1,200.00
4	1,200.00

ATOM THE CAT
See: BO

ATTACK
Youthful Mag./Trojan, 1952
1 Violence	500.00
2	250.00
3 Bondage	300.00
4 RKu	250.00
Becomes:

ATOMIC ATTACK
Youthful Magazines, 1953
5	250.00
6 thru 8	@ 200.00

AUTHENTIC POLICE CASES
St. John Publ. Co., 1948
1 Hale the Magician	700.00
2 Lady Satan, Johnny Rebel	400.00
3 A:Avenger	700.00
4 Masked Black Jack	400.00
5 JCo	400.00
6 JCo,MB(c)	750.00
7 thru 10	@350.00
11 thru 15	@350.00
16 thru 23	@250.00
24 thru 28 Giants	@500.00
29 thru 38	@175.00

AVIATION CADETS
Street & Smith Publ., 1943
1	200.00

AVON ONE-SHOTS
Avon Periodicals, 1949-1953
{Listed in Alphabetical Order}
1 Atomic Spy Cases	500.00
N# WW,Attack on Planet Mars	1,400.00
1 Bachelor's Diary	750.00
1 Badmen of the West	600.00
N# Badmen of Tombstone	225.00
1 EK,Behind Prison Bars	500.00
2 Betty and Her Steady	125.00
N# EK,Blackhawk Indian Tomahawk War	250.00
1 EK,Blazing Sixguns	250.00
1 EK,Butch Cassidy	250.00
N# Chief Crazy Horse	300.00
N# FF,AW,EK,Chief Victorio's Apache Massacre	700.00
N# City of the Living Dead	750.00
1 Complete Romance	600.00
N# Custer's Last Fight	225.00
1 EK(c),Dalton Boys	225.00
N# GT(c),Davy Crockett	250.00
N# The Dead Who Walk	800.00
1 Diary of Horror,Bondage(c)	700.00
N# WW,Earth Man on Venus	2,000.00
1 Eerie, bondage (c)	1,400.00
1 EK,Escape from Devil's Island	550.00
N# EK,Fighting Daniel Boone	250.00
N# EK(c),For a Night of Love	400.00
1 WW,Flying Saucers	1,400.00
N# Flying Saucers	700.00
1 Going Steady with Betty	200.00
N# Hooded Menace	800.00
N# EK,King of the Badmen of Deadwood	200.00
1 King Solomon's Mines	600.00
N# EK(c),Kit Carson & the Blackfeet Warriors	150.00
N# EK,Last of the Comanches	200.00
N# EK,Masked Bandit	250.00
1 WW,Mask of Dr. Fu Manchu	1,500.00
N# EK,Night of Mystery	700.00
1 WW,JKu,Outlaws of the Wild West	500.00
1 JKu,Out of this World	1,100.00
N# EK,Pancho Villa	300.00
1 EK,Phantom Witch Doctor	700.00

1 Pixie Puzzle Rocket
  to Adventureland 175.00
1 EK,Prison Riot,drugs 500.00
N# EK,Red Mountain Featuring
  Quantrell's Raiders 350.00
N# Reform School Girl 5,000.00
1 Robotmen of the Lost Planet 1,700.00
N# JO,WW(c),Rocket to
  the Moon 1,700.00
N# JKu,Secret Diary of
  Eerie Adventures 3,200.00
1 EK,Sheriff Bob Dixon's
  Chuck Wagon 175.00
1 Sideshow 500.00
1 JKu,Sparkling Love 300.00
N# Speedy Rabbit 100.00
1 EK(c)Teddy Roosevelt &
  His Rough Riders 250.00
N# The Underworld Story 400.00
N# EK(c),The Unknown Man. . . . 400.00
1 EK,War Dogs of the U.S. Army 175.00
N# EK(c),White Chief of the
  Pawnee Indians. 250.00
N# Women to Love 700.00

BABE
Prize/Headline Feature,
June–July, 1948
1 BRo 350.00
2 BRo 200.00
3 BRo 175.00
4 thru 9 BRo . . . . @165.00

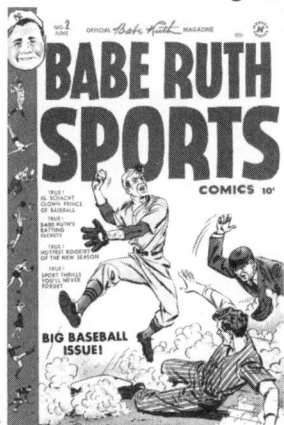

Babe Ruth Sports Comics #2
© Harvey Publications

BABE RUTH
SPORTS COMICS
Harvey Publications,
April, 1949
1 BP 600.00
2 BP,Baseball 400.00
3 BP,Joe DiMaggio(c) 400.00
4 BP,Bob Feller(c). 325.00
5 BP,Football(c) 325.00
6 BP,Basketball(c). 325.00
7 BP 275.00
8 BP,Yogi Berra. 325.00
9 BP,Stan Musial(c). 300.00
10 . . . . 300.00
11 Feb., 1951. . . . . 275.00

BADGE OF JUSTICE
See: CRIME AND JUSTICE

INDIAN BRAVES
Ace Periodicals, 1951
1 Green Arrow. 150.00
2 . . . . 75.00
3 . . . . 65.00
4 . . . . 65.00
Becomes:

BAFFLING MYSTERIES
Periodical House/
Ace Mag., 1951–55
5 GC,MSy 550.00
6 MSy 400.00
7 . . . . 325.00
8 LC 325.00
9 . . . . 325.00
10 . . . . 325.00
11 GC. 325.00
12 thru 15. . . . . @300.00
16 LC 300.00
17 LC 300.00
18 LC 300.00
19 . . . . 300.00
20 LC,Bondage 450.00
21 LC 300.00
22 LC,MSy 325.00
23 Bondage 325.00
24 reprint 200.00
25 reprint 200.00
Becomes:

HEROES OF
THE WILD FRONTIER
Ace Periodicals, 1956
27 (1) 100.00
2 . . . . 100.00

BANG-UP COMICS
Progressive Publ., 1941
1 CosmoMan, Lady Fairplay,
  O:Buzz Balmer 1,700.00
2 Buzz Balmer 1,000.00
3 Buzz Balmer 1,000.00

BANNER COMICS
Ace Magazines, Sept., 1941
3 B:Captain Courageous,
  Lone Warrior 1,700.00
4 JM(c),Flag(c) 1,200.00
5 . . . . 1,200.00
Becomes:

CAPTAIN COURAGEOUS
COMICS
March, 1942
6 I:The Sword 1,500.00

THE BARKER
Quality Comics Group, 1946–49
1 Circus. 250.00
2 thru 14 . . . . @150.00
15 JCo 110.00

BARNEY BAXTER
Argo Publ., 1956
1 . . . . 125.00
2 . . . . 125.00

BARNEY GOOGLE &
SNUFFY SMITH
Toby Press, 1951–52
1 . . . . 150.00
2 thru 3 . . . . @100.00
4 HK 100.00

BARNYARD COMICS
Animated Cartoons, June, 1944
1 (fa) 300.00

2 (fa) 250.00
3 (fa) 150.00
4 (fa) 150.00
5 (fa) 150.00
6 thru 12 (fa) . . . . @125.00
13 FF(ti) 150.00
14 FF(ti) 150.00
15 FF(ti) 150.00
16 . . . . 125.00
17 FF(ti) 125.00
18 FF,FF(ti) 150.00
19 FF,FF(ti) 150.00
20 FF(ti) 125.00
21 FF(ti) 125.00
22 FF,FF(ti) 150.00
23 FF(ti) 125.00
24 FF,FF(ti) 150.00
25 FF,FF(ti) 150.00
26 FF(ti) 125.00
27 FF(ti) 125.00
28 . . . . 100.00
29 FF(ti) 125.00
30 and 31 . . . . @100.00
Becomes:

DIZZY DUCK
32 Funny Animal 125.00
33 thru 39. . . . . @100.00

BASEBALL COMICS
Will Eisner Productions,
Spring, 1949
1 WE,A:Rube Rocky 1,100.00

BASEBALL HEROS
Fawcett Publications, 1952
N# Babe Ruth (c) 1,500.00

BASEBALL THRILLS
Ziff-Davis Publ. Co., 1951
10 Bob Feller Predicts Pennant
  Winners 700.00
2 BP, Yogi Berra story 500.00
3 EK, Joe DiMaggio story,
  Summer 1952 . . . . 600.00

BASIL
St. John Publishing, 1953
1 F:Basil, The Royal Cat. 65.00
2 . . . . 40.00
3 . . . . 20.00
4 . . . . 20.00

BATTLE ATTACK
Stanmor Publications, 1952–55
1 War Combat. 150.00
2 thru 8 . . . . @100.00

BATTLE CRY
Stanmor Publications, 1952–55
1 Flame-thrower (c) 200.00
2 . . . . 125.00
3 . . . . 125.00
4 EC Copy 125.00
5 . . . . 125.00
6 thru 20 . . . . @100.00

BATTLEFIELD ACTION
See: DYNAMITE

BATTLE FIRE
Stamfor Publications, 1955
1 War 150.00
2 thru 7 . . . . @100.00

BATTLEFRONT
Standard Comics, 1952
5 ATh. 175.00

GOLDEN AGE

BATTLE REPORT

**Excellent Publ./
Ajax-Farrell, 1952--53**
1 . . . . 150.00
2 thru 6 . . . . @100.00

BATTLE SQUADRON

Stanmor Publications, 1955
1 . . . . 125.00
2 . . . . 100.00
3 Iwo Jima flag 100.00
4 . . . . 100.00
5 . . . . 100.00

BATTLE STORIES

Fawcett Publications 1952–53
1 GE 200.00
2 . . . . 100.00
3 . . . . 100.00
4 . . . . 100.00
5 . . . . 100.00
6 thru 11 . . . . @100.00

BEANY & CECIL

Dell Publishing Co., Jan., 1952
1 . . . . 250.00
2 thru 5 . . . . @150.00

BEE 29,
THE BOMBARDIER

Neal Publications, 1945
1 Funny Animal 400.00

BEN BOWIE & HIS
MOUNTAIN MEN

Dell Publishing Co., 1952
(1) see Dell Four Color #443
(2 thru 6) see Dell Four Color
7 . . . . 100.00
8 thru 10 . . . . @75.00
11 I:Yellow Hair 60.00
12 thru 17 . . . . @60.00

BEST COMICS

Better Publications, Nov., 1939
1 B:Red Mask 1,800.00
2 A:Red Mask, Silly Willie 1,200.00
3 A:Red Mask 1,200.00
4 Cannibalism story,
Feb., 1940 . . . . 1,500.00

BEWARE

See: CAPTAIN SCIENCE

BEWARE TERROR TALES

Fawcett Publications, 1952–53
1 BP 800.00
2 RA,BP,MSy 500.00
3 . . . . 400.00
4 . . . . 600.00
5 . . . . 600.00
6 . . . . 480.00
7 . . . . 350.00
8 BP 600.00

THE BEYOND

Ace Magazines, 1950–55
1 Werewolf 650.00
2 . . . . 500.00
3 thru 10 . . . . @350.00
11 thru 20 . . . . @300.00
21 thru 30 . . . . @300.00

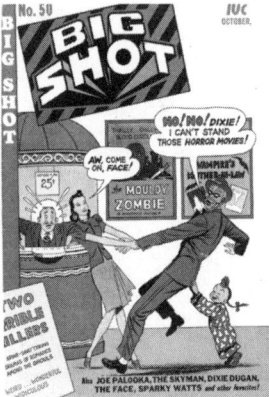

Best Comics #4 © Better Publications

BIG CHIEF WAHOO

**Eastern Color Printing,
1942–43**
1 . . . . 600.00
2 BWa(c),Three Ring Circus . . . 300.00
3 BWa(c) 225.00
4 BWa(c) 225.00
5 BWa(c),Wild West Rodeo 225.00
6 A:Minnie-Ha-Cha 175.00
7 . . . . 150.00
8 . . . . 100.00
9 . . . . 100.00
10 . . . . 125.00
11 thru 23 . . . . @100.00

BIG SHOT COMICS

**Columbia Comics Group,
May, 1940**
1 MBI,OW,Skyman,B:The Face,
Joe Palooka, Rocky Ryan . 4,000.00
2 MBi,OW,Marvelo (c) 1,500.00
3 MBi,Skyman (c) 1,400.00
4 MBi,OW,Joe Palooka (c) . . . 1,000.00
5 MBi,Joe Palooka (c) 800.00
6 MBi,Joe Palooka (c) 750.00
7 MBi,Elect Joe Palooka
and Skyman 700.00
8 MBi,Joe Palooka and Skyman
dress as Santa 700.00
9 MBi,Skyman 700.00
10 MBi,Skyman 700.00
11 MBi 600.00
12 MBi,OW 600.00
13 MBi,OW 600.00
14 MBi,OW,O:Sparky Watts 600.00
15 MBi,OW,O:The Cloak 800.00
16 MBi,OW 500.00
17 MBi(c),OW 500.00
18 MBi,OW 500.00
19 MBi,OW,The Face (c) 475.00
20 MBi,OW,OW(c),Skyman cov. . 475.00
21 MBi,OW,A:Raja the Arabian
Knight 475.00
22 MBi,OW,Joe Palooka (c) 475.00
23 MBi,OW,Sparky Watts (c) 400.00
24 MBi,OW,Uncle Sam (c) 700.00
25 MBi,OW,Hitler,Sparky Watts(c) 600.00
26 MBi,OW,Hitler,Devildog (c) . . . 450.00
27 MBi,OW,Skyman (c) 450.00
28 MBi,OW,Hitler (c) 800.00
29 MBi,OW,I:Captain Yank 450.00
30 MBi,OW,Santa (c) 450.00
31 MBi,OW,Sparky Watts (c) 400.00
32 MBi,OW,B:Vic Jordan
newspaper reps 450.00

33 MBi,OW,Sparky Watts (c) 400.00
34 MBi,OW 400.00
35 MBi,OW 400.00
36 MBi,OW,Sparky Watts (c) 350.00
37 MBi,OW 350.00
38 MBi,Uncle Slap Happy (c) . . . 350.00
39 MBi,Uncle Slap Happy (c) . . . 350.00
40 MBi,Joe Palooka Happy (c) . . 350.00
41 MBi,Joe Palooka 300.00
42 MBi,Joe Palooka parachutes . 300.00
43 MBi,V:Hitler 500.00
44 MBi,Slap Happy (c) 300.00
45 MBi,Slap Happy (c) 300.00
46 MBi,Uncle Sam (c),V:Hitler . . 500.00
47 MBi,Uncle Slap Happy (c) . . . 300.00
48 MBi 300.00
49 MBi 250.00
50 MBi,O:The Face 250.00
51 MBi 250.00
52 MBi,E:Vic Jordan (Hitler cov)
newspaper reps 450.00
53 MBi,Uncle Slap Happy (c) . . . 225.00
54 MBi,Uncle Slap Happy (c) . . . 225.00
55 MBi,Happy Easter (c) 225.00
56 MBi 225.00
57 MBi 225.00
58 MBi 225.00
59 MBi,Slap Happy 225.00
60 MBi,Joe Palooka 225.00
61 MBi 200.00

*Big Shot #50
© Columbia Comics Group*

62 MBi 200.00
63 MBi 200.00
64 MBi,Slap Happy 200.00
65 MBi,Slap Happy 200.00
66 MBi,Slap Happy 200.00
67 MBi 200.00
68 MBi,Joe Palooka 200.00
69 MBi 200.00
70 MBi,OW,Joe Palooka (c) 200.00
71 MBi,OW 200.00
72 MBi,OW 200.00
73 MBi,OW,The Face (c) 200.00
74 MBi,OW 200.00
75 MBi,OW,Polar Bear Swim
    Club (c) 200.00
76 thru 80 MBi,OW . . . . @175.00
81 thru 84 MBi,OW . . . . @175.00
85 MBi,OW,Dixie Dugan (c) 175.00
86 thru 95 MBi,OW . . . . @150.00
96 MBi,OW,X-Mas (c) 150.00
97 thru 99 MBi,OW . . . . @150.00
100 MBi,OW,Special issue 175.00
101 thru 103 MBi,OW . . . . . . @150.00
104 MBi, Aug., 1949 . . . . 175.00

BIG-3
**Fox Features Syndicate,
Fall 1940**
1 B:BlueBeetle,Flame,Samson 4,000.00
2 A:BlueBeetle,Flame,Samson 1,600.00
3 same 1,500.00
4 same 1,400.00
5 same 1,400.00
6 E:Samson, bondage (c) . . . 1,300.00
7 A:V-Man, Jan., 1942 . . . . . 1,300.00

THE BIG TOP COMICS
Toby Press, 1951
1 . . . . 135.00
2 . . . . 100.00

BILL BARNES,
AMERICA'S AIR ACE
See: AIR ACE

BILL BATTLE,
THE ONE-MAN ARMY
Fawcett Publications 1952–53
1 . . . . 200.00
2 . . . . 150.00
3 . . . . 150.00
4 . . . . 150.00

BILL BOYD WESTERN
Fawcett Publications, 1950
1 B:Bill Boyd, Midnite,Ph(c) 700.00
2 P(c) 500.00
3 B:Ph(c) 350.00
4 . . . . 300.00
5 . . . . 300.00
6 . . . . 300.00
7 thru 11 . . . . @250.00
12 thru 21 . . . . @235.00
22 E:Ph(c) 235.00
23 June, 1952 . . . . 250.00

BILL STERN'S
SPORTS BOOK
**Approved Comics,
Spring-Summer, 1951**
1 Ewell Blackwell 300.00
2 . . . . 250.00
2-2 EK Giant 300.00

BILLY AND BUGGY BEAR
I.W. Enterprises, 1958
1 Funny animal 50.00

BILLY BUNNY
Excellent Publications, 1954
1 . . . . 100.00
2 . . . . 75.00
3 . . . . 75.00
4 . . . . 75.00
Ann. #1 Christmas Frolics 150.00

*Billy the Kid Adventure Magazine #3
© Toby Press*

BILLY THE KID
ADVENTURE MAGAZINE
Toby Press, Oct., 1950
1 AW(a&c),FF(a&c) 500.00
2 Photo (c) 200.00
3 AW,FF 500.00
4 . . . . 125.00
5 . . . . 125.00
6 FF,Photo (c) 250.00
7 Photo (c) 125.00
8 . . . . 125.00
9 HK Pot-Shot Pete 150.00
10 . . . . 125.00
11 . . . . 100.00
12 . . . . 100.00
13 HK 100.00
14 AW,FF 150.00
15 thru 21 . . . . @100.00
22 AW,FF 125.00
23 thru 29 . . . . @100.00
30 1955 . . . . 100.00

BILLY THE KID
AND OSCAR
Fawcett Publications, 1945–46
1 Funny animal 250.00
2 . . . . 200.00
3 . . . . 200.00

BILLY WEST
**Visual Editions (Standard
Comics), 1949–51**
1 . . . . 200.00
2 . . . . 150.00
3 thru 8 . . . . @100.00
9 . . . . 125.00

BINGO COMICS
Howard Publications, 1945
1 LbC,Drug 600.00

BLACK CAT COMICS
**Harvey Publications
(Home Comics),June–July, 1946**
1 JKu 1,300.00
2 JKu,JSm(c) 700.00
3 JSm(c) 550.00
4 B:Red Demon 550.00
5 S&K 600.00
6 S&K,A:Scarlet Arrow,
    O:Red Demon 600.00
7 S&K 600.00
8 S&K,B:Kerry Drake 600.00
9 S&K,O:Stuntman 650.00
10 JK,JSm 550.00
11 . . . . 550.00
12 'Ghost Town Terror' 550.00
13 LEI 500.00
14 LEI 500.00
15 LEI 500.00
16 LEI 500.00
17 A:Mary Worth, Invisible
    Scarlet 500.00
18 LEI 500.00
19 LEI 500.00
20 A:Invisible Scarlet 500.00
21 LEI 500.00
22 LEI thru 26 . . . . @500.00
27 X-Mas issue 450.00
28 I:Kit,A:Crimson Raider 450.00
29 Black Cat bondage (c) 450.00
Becomes:

BLACK CAT MYSTERY
Aug., 1951
30 RP,Black Cat(c) 600.00
31 RP 500.00
32 BP,RP,Bondage (c) 550.00
33 BP,RP,Electrocution (c) 550.00
34 BP,RP,Bondage 400.00
35 BP,RP,OK, Atomic Storm 500.00
36 RP 500.00
37 RP 400.00
38 RP 400.00
39 RP 450.00
40 RP 400.00
41 . . . . 400.00
42 . . . . 400.00
43 BP,Bondage 400.00
44 BP,HN,JkS,Oil Burning (c) . . . 500.00
45 BP,HN,Classic (c) 600.00
46 BP,HN 500.00
47 BP,HN 500.00
48 BP,HN 500.00
49 BP,HN 500.00
50 BP,Rotting Face 1,500.00
51 BP,HN,MMe 400.00
52 BP 350.00
53 BP 350.00
Becomes:

BLACK CAT WESTERN
Feb., 1955
54 A:Black Cat & Story 600.00
55 A:Black Cat 400.00
56 same 400.00
Becomes:

BLACK CAT MYSTIC
Sept., 1956
58 JK,Starts Comic Code 500.00
59 KB 400.00
60 JK 450.00
61 Colorama, HN 400.00
62 . . . . 300.00
63 JK 350.00
64 JK 350.00
65 April, 1963 . . . . 350.00

BLACK COBRA
**Farrell Publications (Ajax),
1954–55**
1 . . . . 500.00

All comics prices listed are for *Near Mint* condition.

2 (6) 350.00
3 . . . . 300.00
Becomes:

BRIDES DIARY
Farrell Publications, 1955
4 . . . . 150.00
5 thru 8 . . . . @100.00
9 . . . . 125.00
10 . . . . 125.00

BLACK DIAMOND
WESTERN
See: DESPERADO

UNCLE SAM QUARTERLY
Quality Comics Group,
Fall, 1941
1 BE,LF(c),JCo,O:Uncle Sam . 7,000.00
2 LF&WE(c),DBe, Ray,
  Black Condor 2,500.00
3 GT(a&c) 2,000.00
4 GT,GF(c) 1,900.00
5 RC,GT. 2,000.00
6 GT. 1,900.00
7 Hitler, Tojo, Mussolini 2,000.00
8 GT 1,900.00
Becomes:

BLACKHAWK
Comic Magazines, Winter, 1944
9 Bait for a Death Trap 6,500.00
10 RC 1,850.00
11 RC 1,300.00
12 Flies to thrilling adventure . . 1,200.00
13 Blackhawk Stalks Danger . . 1,200.00
14 BWa 1,300.00
15 Patrols the Universe 1,200.00
16 RC,BWa,Huddles for
  Action 1,200.00
17 BWa,Prepares for Action . . 1,500.00
18 RC(a&c),BWa,One for All
  and All for One 1,800.00
19 RC(a&c),BWa,Calls
  for Action 2,000.00
20 RC(a&c),BWa,Smashes
  Rugoth the Ruthless God . . 1,700.00
21 BWa,Battles Destiny
  Written in Blood 1,000.00
22 RC(a&c),BWa,Fear battles
  Death and Destruction 1,000.00
23 RC(a&c),BWa,Batters
  Down Oppression. 1,000.00
24 RC(a&c),BWa 1,000.00
25 RC(a&c),BWa,V:The Evil
  of Mung 1,000.00
26 RC(a&c),V:Menace of a
  Sunken World 900.00
27 BWa,Destroys a War-Mad
  Munitions Magnate 900.00
28 BWa,Defies Destruction in the
  Battle of the Test Tube 900.00
29 BWa,Tale of the Basilisk
  Supreme Chief 900.00
30 BWa,RC(a&c),The Menace
  of the Meteors 900.00
31 BWa,RC(a&c),JCo,Treachery
  among the Blackhawks 800.00
32 BWa,RC(a&c),A:Delya,
  Flying Fish. 800.00
33 RC,BWa,A:The Mockers. . . . 800.00
34 BWa,A:Tana,Mavis 800.00
35 BWa,I:Atlo,Strongest Man
  on Earth. 800.00
36 RC(a&c),BWa,V:Tarya 650.00
37 RC(a&c),BWa,V:Sari,The
  Rajah of Ramastan 650.00
38 BWa 650.00
39 RC(a&c),BWa,V:Lilith 650.00
40 RC(a&c),BWa,Valley of
  Yesterday. 650.00
41 RC(a&c),BWa 550.00

42 RC(a&c),BWa,V:Iron Emperor 550.00
43 RC(a&c),BWa,Terror
  from the Catacombs 550.00
44 RC(a&c),BWa, King of Winds . 550.00
45 BWa,The Island of Death 550.00
46 RC(a&c),BWa,V:DeathPatrol . 550.00
47 RC(a&c),BWa,War! 550.00
48 RC(a&c),BWa,A:Hawks of
  Horror,Port of Missing Ships . 550.00
49 RC(a&c),BWa,A:Valkyrie,
  Waters of Terrible Peace. . . 550.00
50 RC(a&c),BWa,I:Killer Shark,
  Flying Octopus 650.00
51 BWa,V:The Whip, Whip of
  Nontelon 550.00
52 RC(a&c),BWa,Traitor in
  the Ranks 550.00
53 RC(a&c),BWa,V:Golden
  Mummy 550.00
54 RC(a&c),BWa,V:Dr. Deroski,
  Circles of Suicide. 550.00
55 RC(a&c),BWa,V:Rocketmen . 550.00
56 RC(a&c),BWa,V:The Instructor,
  School for Sabotage 550.00
57 RC(a&c),BWa,Paralyzed City
  of Armored Men. 550.00
58 RC(a&c),BWa,V:King Cobra,
  The Spider of Delanza. 550.00
59 BWa,V:Sea Devil 550.00
60 RC(a&c),BWa,V:Dr. Mole and
  His Devils Squadron 550.00
61 V:John Smith, Stalin's
  Ambassador of Murder 500.00
62 V:General X, Return of
  Genghis Kahn 500.00
63 RC(a&c),The Flying
  Buzz-Saws. 500.00
64 RC(a&c),V:Zoltan Korvas,
  Legion of the Damned. 500.00
65 Olaf as a Prisoner in Dungeon
  of Fear. 500.00
66 RC(a&c),V:The Red
  Executioner, Crawler. 500.00
67 RC(a&c),V:Future Fuehrer . . . 500.00
68 V:Killers of the Kremlin 400.00
69 V:King of the Iron Men,
  Conference of the Dictators . 400.00
70 V:Killer Shark 400.00
71 V:Von Tepp, The Man Who
  could Defeat Blackhawk
  O:Blackhawk 500.00
72 V:Death Legion 400.00
73 V:Hangman,The Tyrannical
  Freaks 300.00
74 Plan of Death 300.00

Blackhawk #80
© Comic Magazines

75 V:The Mad Doctor Baroc,
  The Z Bomb Menace. 300.00
76 The King of Blackhawk Island 300.00
77 V:The Fiendish
  Electronic Brain 300.00
78 V:The Killer Vulture,
  Phantom Raider 300.00
79 V:Herman Goering, The
  Human Bomb 300.00
80 V:Fang, the Merciless,
  Dr. Death 300.00
81 A:Killer Shark, The Sea
  Monsters of Killer Shark 300.00
82 V:Sabo Teur, the Ruthless
  Commie Agent. 300.00
83 I:Hammmer & Sickle, V:Madam
  Double Cross. 300.00
84 V:Death Eye,Dr. Genius,
  The Dreaded Brain Beam . . . 300.00
85 V:The Fiendish Impersonator . 300.00
86 V:The Human Torpedoes 300.00
87 A:Red Agent Sovietta,V:Sea
  Wolf, Le Sabre,Comics Code 300.00
88 V:Thunder the Indestructible,
  The Phantom Sniper 300.00
89 V:The Super Communists. . . . 400.00
90 V:The Storm King, Villainess
  Who Smashed the Blackhawk
  Team 400.00
91 Treason in the Underground . . 400.00
92 V:The World Traitor. 400.00
93 V:Garg the Destroyer,
  O:Blackhawk 350.00
94 V:Black Widow, Darkk the
  Destroyer. 350.00
95 V:Madam Fury, Queen of the
  Pirates 350.00
96 Doom in the Deep. 350.00
97 Revolt of the Slave Workers. . 300.00
98 Temple of Doom 300.00
99 The War That Never Ended . . 300.00
100 The Delphian Machine 325.00
101 Satan's Paymaster 275.00
102 The Doom Cloud 275.00
103 The Super Race 275.00
104 The Jet Menace 275.00
105 The Red Kamikaze Terror . . 275.00
106 The Flying Tank Platoon 275.00
107 The Winged Menace 275.00
Continued by: DC Comics

BLACK HOOD
See: LAUGH COMICS

BLACK KNIGHT, THE
Toby Press, 1953
1 Bondage 400.00

BLACK MAGIC
Crestwood Publ., 1950–51
1 S&K,MMe. 2,400.00
2 S&K,MMe 1,200.00
3 S&K,MMe 1,100.00
4 S&K,MMe 1,100.00
5 S&K,MMe 1,100.00
6 S&K,MMe 1,100.00
Volume 2, 1951
1 S&K,MMe. 600.00
2 MMe. 500.00
3 . . . . 500.00
4 S&K,MMe. 600.00
5 S&K,MMe. 600.00
6 . . . . 500.00
7 S&K,MMe. 600.00
8 MMe 500.00
9 S&K,MMe 600.00
10 . . . . 500.00
11 MMe 500.00
12 S&K,MMe. 500.00
Volume 3, 1953
1 S&K,MMe. 500.00

2 S&K,MMe,AMc	500.00
3 S&K	500.00
4 S&K	500.00
5 S&K,MMe	500.00
6 S&K,MMe	500.00

Volume 4, 1954

1 S&K	500.00
2 S&K	500.00
3 S&K,SD(2nd work)	800.00
4 S&K,SD,eye damage	650.00
5 S&K,SD	500.00
6 S&K,BP	400.00

Volume 5, 1956

1 S&K,MMe	350.00
2 S&K,MMe	350.00
3 S&K	350.00
4 S&K	350.00
5 S&K	350.00
6 S&K	350.00

Volume 6, 1957

1 JO	300.00
2 JO(c)	300.00
3 JO(c),GT	300.00
4 JO	300.00
5 JO(c)	300.00
6 JO(c)	300.00

Volume 7, 1958

1 LSt	300.00
2 JO	300.00
3 & 4	@300.00
5 AT,Hitler(c)	350.00
6 BP	250.00

Volume 8, 1961

1 BP	250.00
2 BP,SD	250.00
3 thru 5 BP	@250.00

BLACKSTONE, MASTER MAGICIAN COMICS
Vital/Street & Smith Publ. 1946

1	900.00
2	700.00
3	700.00

BLACKSTONE, THE MAGICIAN DETECTIVE
EC Comics, 1947

1 Happy Houlihans	750.00

See: Marvel Listings

BLACK TERROR
Better Publications/ Standard, Winter, 1942-43

1 Bombing (c)	5,000.00

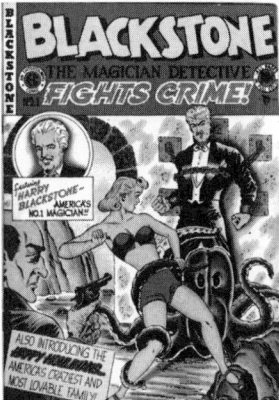

Blackstone The Magician Detective #1
© EC Comics

2 V:Arabs,Bondage(c)	2,000.00
3 V:Nazis,Bondage(c)	1,200.00
4 ASh(c),V:Sub Nazis	1,000.00
5 V:Japanese	1,000.00
6 Air Battle	900.00
7 Air Battle,V:Japanese, A:Ghost	900.00
8 V:Nazis	900.00
9 V:Japanese,Bondage(c)	1,000.00
10 ASh(c),V:Nazis	900.00
11 & 12	@800.00
13 ASh(c)	725.00
14 ASh(c)	800.00
15 ASh(c)	725.00
16 ASh(c)	725.00
17 ASh(c),Bondage(c)	800.00
18 ASh(c)	700.00
19 & 20 ASh	@700.00
21 ASh(c)	800.00
22 FF,ASh	700.00
23 ASh	700.00
24 Bondgae(c)	800.00
25 ASh	700.00
26 GT,ASh(c)	700.00
27 MME,GT,ASh	700.00

BLAZING COMICS
Enwil Associates/Rural Home, June, 1944

1 B:Green Turtle, Red Hawk, Black Buccaneer	1,000.00
2 Green Turtle (c)	700.00
3 Green Turtle (c)	650.00
4 Green Turtle (c)	650.00
5 March, 1945	650.00
5a Black Buccaneer(c),1955.	400.00
6 Indian-Japanese(c), 1955	400.00

BLAZING WEST
B & I Publ./American Comics 1948

1	300.00
2	150.00
3	150.00
4 O&I: Little Lobo	125.00
5 thru 13	@100.00
14 O&I: The Hooded Horseman	150.00
15 thru 20	@125.00

Becomes:

HOODED HORSEMAN
American Comics, 1952–54

21	250.00
22	200.00
23	150.00
24	150.00
25	125.00
26	150.00
27	135.00

BLAZING WESTERN
Timor Publications, 1954

1	200.00
2 thru 5	@100.00

BLONDIE COMICS
David McKay, Spring, 1947

1	400.00
2	200.00
3	150.00
4	150.00
5	150.00
6 thru 10	@100.00
11 thru 15	@100.00

Harvey Publications, 1950

16	150.00
17 thru 20	@125.00
21 thru 30	@100.00
31 thru 50	@100.00
51 thru 80	@100.00

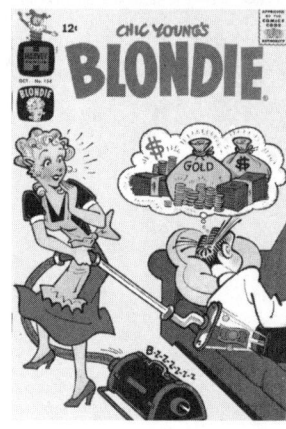

Blondie #154 (Harvey
© Harvey Publications

81 thru 99	@100.00
100	110.00
101 thru 124	@100.00
125 Giant, 80-pg.	125.00
126 thru 136	@100.00
137 Giant, 80-pg.	125.00
138 thru 139	@100.00
140 Giant, 80-pg.	125.00
141 thru 147	@100.00
148 Giant, 68-pg.	125.00
149 thru 154	@100.00
155 Giant, 68-pg.	125.00
156	100.00
157 thru 159 Giant, 68-pg.	@125.00
160	100.00
161 thru 163 Giant, 68-pg.	@125.00

See also: DAISY AND HER PUPS

BLOOD IS THE HARVEST
Catechetical Guild 1950

N# Comunist menace	1,800.00

BLUE BEETLE, THE
Fox Features Syndicate/ Holyoke Publ., Winter 1939

1 O:Blue Beetle,A:Master Magician	8,500.00
2 BP,Wonder World	2,500.00
3 JSm(c)	1,600.00
4 Mentions marijuana	1,500.00
5 GT,A:Zanzibar the Magician	1,300.00
6 B:Dynamite Thor, O:Blue Beetle	1,300.00
7 A:Dynamo	1,200.00
8 E:Thor,A:Dynamo	1,200.00
9 BP(c),A:Black Bird,Gorilla	1,200.00
10 BP(c),A:Black Bird, bondage(c)	1,200.00
11 BP(c),A:Gladiator, Bondage	900.00
12 A:Black Fury, Bondage	900.00
13 B:V-Man	900.00
14 JKu,I:Sparky	900.00
15 JKu	900.00
16	900.00
17 AyB,A:Mimic	900.00
18 JKu,E:V-Man,A:Red Knight	900.00
19 JKu,A:Dascomb Dinsmore	900.00
20 I&O:Flying Tiger Squadron	900.00
21	700.00
22 A:Ali-Baba	700.00
23 A:Jimmy DooLittle	700.00
24 I:The Halo	700.00
25	700.00
26 General Patton story	800.00
27 A:Tamoa	700.00

GOLDEN AGE

28	700.00
29	700.00
30 L:Holyoke	700.00
31 F:Fox.	775.00
32 Hitler (c)	800.00
33 Fight for Freedom	600.00
34 A:Black Terror,Menace of K-4	600.00
35 Threat From Saturn	600.00
36 The Runaway House	600.00
37 Inside the House.	600.00
38 Revolt of the Zombies.	600.00
39	600.00
40	600.00
41 A:O'Brine Twins	550.00
42	550.00
43	550.00
44	550.00
45	550.00
46 BP,A:Puppeteer, Bondage	550.00
47 JKa,V:Junior Crime Club	2,000.00
48 JKa,A:Black Lace.	1,500.00
49 JKa.	1,500.00
50 JKa,The Ambitious Bride	1,500.00
51 JKa, Shady Lady	1,500.00
52 BP,JKa(c),Bondage (c)	1,900.00
53 JKa,A:Jack "Legs" Diamond,Bondage(c)	1,300.00
54 JKa,The Vanishing Nude	2,200.00
55 JKa.	1,250.00
56 JKa,Tri-State Terror	1,250.00
57 JKa,The Feagle Bros.	1,250.00
58	250.00
59	250.00
60 Aug., 1960	275.00

BLUE BEETLE
See: THING!, THE

BLUE BOLT
Funnies, Inc./Novelty Press/ Premium Service Co, 1940

1 JSm,PGv,O:Blue Bolt	6,000.00
2 JSm,S&K	3,000.00
3 S&K,A:Space Hawk	2,500.00
4 S&K,BEv(c).	2,000.00
5 BEv,S&K,B:Sub Zero	2,000.00
6 JK,JSm	1,900.00
7 S&K,BEv	1,900.00
8 PGv,S&K(c)	1,900.00
9	1,700.00
10 PGv,S&K(c)	1,700.00
11 BEv(c)	1,700.00
12 PGv	1,700.00
2-1 BEv(c),PG,O:Dick Cole & V:Simba.	700.00
2-2 BEv(c),FGu,C:Twister	550.00
2-3 PGv,Cole vs Simba	400.00
2-4 BD	400.00
2-5 I:Freezum.	400.00
2-6 PGv,O:Sgt.Spook, Dick Cole	350.00
2-7 BD,Lois Blake	350.00
2-8 BD	350.00
2-9 JW	350.00
2-10 JW	350.00
2-11 JW	350.00
2-12 E:Twister	350.00
3-1 A:115th Infantry	350.00
3-2 A:Phantom Sub	350.00
3-3	350.00
3-4 JW(c)	250.00
3-5 Jor	250.00
3-6 Jor	250.00
3-7 X-Mas (c)	250.00
3-8	250.00
3-9 A:Phantom Sub	250.00
3-10 DBa	250.00
3-11 April Fools (c).	250.00
3-12	250.00
4-1 Hitler,Tojo,Mussolini (c)	600.00
4-2 Liberty Bell (c)	200.00

4-3 What are You Doing for Your Country	200.00
4-4 I Fly for Vengence	200.00
4-5 TFH(c)	200.00
4-6 HcK	200.00
4-7 JWi(c).	200.00
4-8 E:Sub Zero	200.00
4-9	200.00
4-10	200.00
4-11	200.00
4-12	200.00
5-1 thru 5-12.	@175.00
6-1	175.00
6-2 War Bonds (c)	175.00
6-3	175.00
6-4 Racist(c).	300.00
6-5 Soccer (c)	175.00
6-6 thru 6-12.	@175.00
7-1 thru 7-12.	@175.00
8-1 Baseball (c)	175.00
8-2 JHa	175.00
8-3 JH	175.00
8-4 JHa	175.00
8-5 JH	175.00
8-6 JDo	175.00
8-7 LbC(c).	350.00
8-8	175.00
8-9 AMc(c)	175.00
8-10	175.00
8-11 Basketball (c)	200.00
8-12	175.00
9-1 AMc,Baseball (c)	175.00
9-2 AMc	175.00
9-3	175.00
9-4 JH	175.00
9-5 JH	175.00
9-6 LbC(c),Football (c)	300.00
9-7 JH	175.00
9-8 Hockey (c)	185.00
9-9 LbC(c),3-D effect	275.00
9-10	175.00
9-11	175.00
9-12	175.00
10-1 Baseball (c),3-D effect	200.00
10-2 3-D effect	200.00

Star Publications, 1949

102 LbC(c),Chameleon	550.00
103 LbC(c),same	500.00
104 LbC(c),same	500.00
105 LbC(c),O:Blue Bolt Space, Drug Story	900.00
106 S&K,LbC(c),A:Space Hawk	800.00
107 S&K,LbC(c),A:Space Hawk	800.00
108 S&K,LbC(c),A:Blue Bolt	800.00
109 BW,LbC(c).	800.00
110 B:Horror (c)s,A:Target	800.00
111 Weird Tales of Terror, A:Red Rocket	800.00
112 JyD	700.00
113 BW,JyD,A:Space Hawk	700.00
114 LbC(c),JyD	700.00
115 LbC(c),JyD,A:Sgt.Spook	700.00
116 LbC(c),JyD,A:Jungle Joe	700.00
117 LbC(c),A:Blue Bolt,Jo-Jo.	700.00
118 WW,LbC(c),A:White Spirit.	700.00
119 LbC(c)	700.00

Becomes:

GHOSTLY WEIRD STORIES
Star Publications, Sept., 1953

120 LbC,A:Jo-Jo.	750.00
121 LbC,A:Jo-Jo	700.00
122 LbC,A:The Mask,Sci-Fi.	750.00
123 LbC,A:Jo-Jo	600.00
124 LbC, Sept., 1954.	600.00

BLUE CIRCLE COMICS
Enwil Associates/ Rural Home, June, 1944

1 B:Blue Circle,O:Steel Fist	500.00

2	350.00
3 Hitler parody (c)	400.00
4	300.00
5 E:Steel Fist,A:DriftwoodDavey.	300.00
6	300.00

Blue Ribbon Comics #1
© MLJ Magazines

BLUE RIBBON COMICS
MLJ Magazines, Nov., 1939

1 JCo,B:Dan Hastings, Richy-Amazing Boy	6,000.00
2 JCo,B:Bob Phantom, Silver Fox	2,500.00
3 JCo,A:Phantom,Silver Fox	1,500.00
4 O:Fox,Ty Gor,B:Doc Strong, Hercules	1,700.00
5 Gattling Gun (c)	1,500.00
6 Amazing Boy Richy (c)	1,400.00
7 A:Fox (c),Corporal Collins V:Nazis	1,400.00
8 E:Hercules	1,400.00
9 SCp,O&I:Mr. Justice	5,200.00
10 SCp,Mr. Justice (c)	2,200.00
11 CBi,MMe,SCp(c)	2,200.00
12 SCp,MMe,CBi,E:Doc Strong	2,200.00
13 CBi,IN,MMe,B:Inferno	2,200.00
14 MMe,CBi,SCp(c),A:Inferno	2,000.00
15 A:Inferno,E:Green Falcon	2,000.00
16 SCp(c),O:Captain Flag	2,500.00
17 Captain Flag, V:Black Hand.	2,000.00
18 SCp(c),Captain Flag	1,600.00
19 Captain Flag (c)	1,600.00
20 Captain Flag V:Nazis (c)	2,000.00
21 Captain Flag V:Death	1,600.00
22 Circus (c), March, 1942.	1,600.00

BLUE RIBBON COMICS
St. John Publications, Feb., 1949

1 Heckle & Jeckle	150.00
2 MB(c),Diary Secrets	300.00
3 MB,MB(c),Heckle & Jeckle	150.00
4 Teen-age Diary Secrets	275.00
5 MB,Teen-age Diary Secrets.	350.00
6 Dinky Duck	100.00

BO
Charlton Comics, June, 1955

1	100.00
2	100.00
3 Oct., 1955	100.00

Becomes:

TOM CAT
Charlton Comics, 1956
4 Funny animal-cat 100.00
5 thru 8 . . . . @75.00
Becomes:

ATOM THE CAT
Charlton Comics, 1957–58
9 . . . . 100.00
10 . . . . 75.00
11 Atomic Mouse 125.00
12 Atomic Mouse 125.00
13 thru 17 . . . . @75.00

BOB & BETTY & SANTA'S WISHING WELL
Sears-Roebuck Co., 1941
N# Giveaway 300.00

BOBBY BENSON'S B-BAR-B RIDERS
Parkway Publ. Co. (M.E. Entertainment), 1950
1 BP, Teen-age cowboy 700.00
2 BP 300.00
3 BP 250.00
4 BP, Lemonade Kid (c) 250.00
5 BP 250.00
6 BP 250.00
7 BP 250.00
8 BP 250.00
9 BP, FF(c) 500.00
10 BP 200.00
11 BP, FF(c) 500.00
12 BP 150.00
13 DAy, FF(c), A: Ghost Rider 500.00
14 DAy, A: Ghost Rider, bondage . . 400.00
15 DAy, A: Ghost Rider 350.00
16 photo(c) 200.00
17 . . . . 150.00
18 . . . . 150.00
19 . . . . 150.00

BOBBY COMICS
Universal Phoenix Features, 1946
1 . . . . 150.00

BOB COLT
Fawcett Publications, Nov., 1950
1 B: Bob Colt, Buck Skin 600.00

Bob Colt #1
© Fawcett Publications

2 Death Round Train 400.00
3 Mysterious Black Knight of the Prairie 300.00
4 Death Goes Downstream 300.00
5 The Mesa of Mystery 300.00
6 The Mysterious Visitors 300.00
7 Dragon of Disaster 250.00
8 Redman's Revenge 250.00
9 Hidden Hacienda 250.00
10 Fiend from Vulture Mountain 250.00

BOB STEELE WESTERN
Fawcett Publications, 1950–52
1 Photo(c) 750.00
2 Ph(c); Dynamite Death 400.00
3 Ph(c); The Perilous Deadline . . 300.00
4 Ph(c); Six-Gun Menace 300.00
5 Ph(c); Murder on the Hoof 300.00
6 Ph(c); Range War 250.00
7 Ph(c); Tall Timber Terror 250.00
8 Ph(c); The Race of Death 250.00
9 Ph(c); Death Rides the Storm . 250.00
10 Ph(c); Draw...Or Die 250.00

BOB SWIFT
Fawcett Publications 1951–52
1 Boy sportsman 150.00
2 thru 5 . . . . @100.00

BOLD STORIES
Kirby Publishing Co., 1950
1 WW, Near nudity (c) 2,200.00
2 GI, Cobra's Kiss 1,800.00
3 WW, Orge of Paris 1,500.00
4 Case of the Winking Buddha . . 800.00
5 It Rhymes with Lust 800.00
6 Candid Tales, April, 1950 . . . . 800.00

BOMBER COMICS
Elliot Publishing Co., 1944
1 B: Wonder Boy, Kismet, Eagle Evans 1,400.00
2 Wonder Boy(c) Hitler 1,100.00
3 Wonder Boy-Kismet (c) 650.00
4 Hitler, Tojo, Mussolini (c) . . . 1,200.00

BOOK OF ALL COMICS
William H. Wise, 1945
1 A: Green Mask, Puppeteer 650.00

BOOK OF COMICS, THE
William H. Wise, 1945
N# A: Captain V 600.00

BOOTS AND HER BUDDIES
Visual Editions (Standard Comics), 1948–49
5 Cowgirl 250.00
6 . . . . 200.00
7 . . . . 225.00
8 . . . . 200.00
9 FF 450.00

BORDER PATROL
P.L. Publishing Co., 1951
1 Wild West 200.00
2 . . . . 150.00
3 . . . . 150.00

THE BOUNCER
Fox Features Syndicate, 1944
N# (10) 500.00
11 O: The Bouncer 400.00

12 . . . . 300.00
13 . . . . 300.00
14 rep. #(10) 300.00

BOY COMICS
Comic House, Inc. (Lev Gleason Publ.) April, 1942
3 O: Crimebuster, Bombshell, Young Robin, B: Yankee Longago, Swoop Storm 5,700.00
4 Hitler, Tojo, Mussolini (c) 2,200.00
5 Crimebuster saves day (c) . . 1,600.00
6 O: Iron Jaw & Death of Son, B: Little Dynamite 5,000.00
7 Hitler, Tojo, Mussolini (c) 1,600.00
8 D: Iron Jaw 1,700.00
9 I: He-She 1,600.00
10 Iron Jaw returns 2,300.00
11 Iron Jaw falls in love 1,700.00
12 Crimebuster V: Japanese . . . 1,000.00
13 V: New, more terrible Iron Jaw 1,000.00
14 V: Iron Jaw 1,000.00
15 I: Rodent, D: Iron Jaw 1,200.00
16 Crimebuster V: Knight 600.00
17 Flag (c), Crimebuster V: Moth 600.00
18 Smashed car (c) 550.00
19 Express train (c) 550.00
20 Coffin (c) 550.00
21 Boxing (c) 400.00
22 Under Sea (c) 400.00
23 Golf (c) 400.00
24 County insane asylum (c) . . . 400.00
25 52 pgs 400.00
26 68 pgs 400.00
27 Express train (c) 450.00
28 E: Yankee Longago 450.00
29 Prison break (c) 450.00
30 O: Crimebuster, Murder (c) . . . 600.00
31 68 pgs 400.00
32 E: Young Robin Hood 400.00
33 . . . . 400.00
34 Suicide (c) & story 350.00
35 . . . . 300.00
36 . . . . 300.00
37 . . . . 300.00
38 . . . . 300.00
39 E: Little Dynamite 300.00
40 . . . . 300.00
41 thru 50 . . . . @275.00
51 thru 56 . . . . @250.00
57 B: Dilly Duncan 275.00
58 . . . . 250.00
59 . . . . 250.00
60 Iron Jaw returns 275.00
61 O: Iron Jaw, Crimebuster 300.00
62 A: Iron Jaw 275.00
63 thru 70 . . . . @200.00
71 E: Dilly Duncan 200.00
72 . . . . 200.00
73 . . . . 200.00
74 thru 79 . . . . @200.00
80 I: Rocky X 150.00
81 thru 88 . . . . @150.00
89 A: The Claw 175.00
90 same 175.00
91 same 175.00
92 same 175.00
93 The Claw(c), A: Rocky X 175.00
94 . . . . 125.00
95 . . . . 125.00
96 . . . . 125.00
97 . . . . 125.00
98 A: Rocky X 125.00
99 . . . . 125.00
100 . . . . 150.00
101 thru 118 . . . . @150.00
119 March, 1956 . . . . 150.00

BOY DETECTIVE
Avon Periodicals, 1951–52
1 F:Dan Tayler 300.00
2 Vice Lords of Crime 200.00
3 Spy Menace 200.00
4 The Death Trap 200.00

BOY EXPLORERS
See: TERRY AND THE PIRATES

BOYS' RANCH
Harvey Publications, 1950–51
1 S&K,F:Clay Duncan 1,000.00
2 S&K 750.00
3 S&K,MMe. 700.00
4 S&K 600.00
5 S&K,MMe. 400.00
6 S&K,MMe. 400.00

THE BRAIN
Sussex Publ. Co./Magazine
Enterprises, 1956–58
1 . . . . 150.00
2 thru 7 . . . . @100.00

BRENDA STARR
Four Star Comics Corp., 1947
13(1) 1,600.00
14(2) JKa,Bondage (c) 3,000.00
Superior Comics Ltd., 1948
2-3 . . . . 1,800.00
2-4 JKa,Operating table (c). . . . 1,800.00
2-5 Swimsuit (c) 1,500.00
2-6 . . . . 1,500.00
2-7 . . . . 1,500.00
2-8 Cosmetic (c) 1,500.00
2-9 Giant Starr (c) 1,500.00
2-10 Wedding (c) 1,500.00
2-11 . . . . 1,500.00
2-12 . . . . 1,500.00
Becomes:

BRENDA STARR
REPORTER
Charlton Comics, 1955
13 . . . . 700.00
14 & 15. . . . . @600.00

BRICK BRADFORD
Best Books
(Standard Comics) July, 1949
5 . . . . 300.00

Bruce Gentry #2
© *Superior Comics*

6 Robot (c) 400.00
7 ASh(c) 150.00
8 . . . . 150.00

BRIDES DIARY
See: BLACK COBRA

BROADWAY ROMANCES
Quality Comics Group, 1950
1 PG,BWa(a&c). 600.00
2 BWa,Glittering Desire 400.00
3 Bl.,Stole My Love. 200.00
4 Enslaved by My Past. 200.00
5 Flame of Passion,Sept.,1950 . 200.00

BRONCHO BILL
Visual Editions
(Standard Comics) Jan., 1948
5 . . . . 250.00
6 ASh(c) 125.00
7 ASh(c) 100.00
8 . . . . 75.00
9 thru 13 ASh(c) . . . . @100.00
14 and 15. . . . . @75.00
16 ASh(c). 100.00

BRUCE GENTRY
Four Star Publ./
Visual Editions/
Superior, Jan., 1948
1 B:Ray Bailey reprints 900.00
2 Plane crash (c) 500.00
3 E:Ray Bailey reprints 500.00
4 Tiger attack (c) 400.00
5 . . . . 400.00
6 Help message (c) 400.00
7 . . . . 400.00
8 End of Marriage (c),July, 1949 400.00

BUCCANEERS
See: KID ETERNITY

BUCK JONES
Dell Publishing Co., 1950
1 Buck Jones & Horse Silver . . . 250.00
2 . . . . 150.00
3 thru 8 . . . . @100.00

BUCK ROGERS
Eastern Color Printing,
Winter 1940
1 Partial Painted(c) 6,000.00
2 . . . . 2,300.00
3 Living Corpse from Crimson
  Coffin 2,000.00
4 One man army of greased
  lightning 1,900.00
5 Sky Roads 1,700.00
6 Sept., 1943 . . . . 1,700.00
Toby Press
100 Flying Saucers. 700.00
101 . . . . 600.00
9 MA 600.00

BUDDIES IN
THE U.S. ARMY
Avon Periodicals, 1952–53
1 Fightin' Guys & Fabulous Gals 200.00
2 . . . . 125.00

BUFFALO BILL
Youthful Magazines, 1950–51
2 Annie Oakley 200.00
3 thru 9 . . . . @150.00

BUFFALO BILL
PICTURE STORIES
Street & Smith Publ. 1949
1 . . . . 250.00
2 . . . . 250.00

BUFFALO BILL JR.
Dell Publishing Co., 1956
1 . . . . 200.00
2 thru 6 . . . . @150.00
7 thru 13 . . . . @125.00

BUGHOUSE
Ajax/Farrell, 1954
1 . . . . 250.00
2 . . . . 150.00
3 . . . . 150.00
4 . . . . 150.00

BUG MOVIES
Dell Publishing Co., 1931
1 . . . . 600.00

BUGS BUNNY
DELL GIANT EDITIONS
Dell Publishing Co.
Christmas
1 Christmas Funnies (1950). . . . 350.00
2 Christmas Funnies (1951). . . . 300.00
3 Christmas Funnies (1952). . . . 250.00
4 Christmas Funnies (1953). . . . 200.00
5 Christmas Funnies (1954). . . . 200.00
6 Christmas Party (1955) 175.00
7 Christmas Party (1956) 185.00
8 Christmas Funnies (1957). . . . 185.00
9 Christmas Funnies (1958). . . . 185.00
1 County Fair (1957). 200.00
Halloween
1 Halloween Parade (1953) 200.00
2 Halloween Parade (1954) 175.00
3 Trick 'N' Treat
  Halloween Fun (1955). 185.00
4 Trick 'N' Treat
  Halloween Fun (1956). 185.00
Vacation
1 Vacation Funnies (1951) 325.00
2 Vacation Funnies (1952) 275.00
3 Vacation Funnies (1953) 250.00
4 Vacation Funnies (1954) 200.00
5 Vacation Funnies (1955) 200.00
6 Vacation Funnies (1956) 175.00
7 Vacation Funnies (1957) 175.00
8 Vacation Funnies (1958) 175.00
9 Vacation Funnies (1959) 175.00

BUGS BUNNY
Dell Publishing Co., 1942
see Four Color for early years
28 thru 30. . . . . @130.00
31 thru 50 . . . . @120.00
51 thru 70. . . . . @100.00
71 thru 85. . . . . @100.00
86 Giant-Show Time 125.00
87 thru 100. . . . . @100.00
101 thru 120. . . . . @75.00
121 thru 140. . . . . @50.00
141 thru 190. . . . . @50.00
191 thru 245. . . . . @50.00

BULLETMAN
Fawcett Publications,
Summer, 1941
1 I:Bulletman & Bulletgirl 7,000.00
2 MRa(c) 2,800.00
3 MRa(c) 2,300.00
4 V:Headless Horror,
  Guillotine (c). 1,800.00

5 Riddle of Dr. Riddle. 2,300.00	21 thru 24 . . . . @100.00	23 V:Billy the Kid 100.00
6 V:Japanese 1,500.00	25 RC 150.00	24 A:Hector, Sept., 1949 . . . . . . 100.00
7 V:Revenge Syndicate 1,500.00	26 thru 36. . . . . @100.00	
8 V:Mr. Ego 1,500.00	37 RC 150.00	

CALLING ALL GIRLS
Parent Magazine Press, Inc.,
Sept., 1941

9 V:Canine Criminals 1,500.00	38 . . . . 100.00	1 . . . . 300.00
10 I:Bullet Dog 1,700.00	39 . . . . 100.00	2 Virginia Weidler (c) 250.00
11 V:Fiendish Fiddler 1,100.00	40 RC 150.00	3 Shirley Temple (c) 300.00
12 . . . . 1,000.00	41 RC 150.00	4 Darla Hood (c) 150.00
13 . . . . 1,000.00	42 . . . . 100.00	5 Gloria Hood (c) 150.00
14 V:Death the Comedian 1,000.00	43 . . . . 100.00	6 . . . . 150.00
15 V:Professor D. 1,000.00		7 . . . . 150.00
16 VanishingElephant,Fall 1946 1,000.00		8 . . . . 150.00

BULLS-EYE
Charlton Comics, 1954

BUSTER BUNNY
Animated Cartoons
(Standard)/Pines, 1949

1 S&K,Western Scout. 850.00	1 FF,Funny animal 150.00	9 Flag (c) 150.00
2 S&K 700.00	2 thru 5 . . . . @100.00	10 . . . . 150.00
3 thru 5 S&K . . . . @550.00	6 thru 10 . . . . @100.00	11 Gary Cooper as Lou Gerrig . 200.00
6 S&K 500.00	11 thru 14 . . . . @100.00	12 thru 20. . . . . @125.00
7 S&K 600.00	15 racist(c). 125.00	21 thru 39. . . . . @125.00
Becomes:	16 . . . . 100.00	40 Liz Taylor. 250.00

CODY OF THE
PONY EXPRESS
Charlton Comics, 1955

BUSTER CRABBE
Famous Funnies, Nov., 1951

	1 The Arrow of Death 650.00	41 . . . . 100.00
8 F:Buffalo Bill Cody 125.00	2 AW&GE(c) 700.00	42. . . . . 100.00
9 . . . . 100.00	3 AW&GE(c) 750.00	43 Oct., 1945 . . . . 100.00
10 . . . . 100.00	4 FF(c) 900.00	
Becomes:	5 AW,FF(a&c) 1,800.00	

OUTLAWS OF THE WEST

BULLS-EYE
See: SCOOP COMICS

CALLING ALL KIDS
Quality Comics, Inc.,
Dec./Jan., 1946

	6 Sharks (c) 300.00	1 Funny Animal stories 150.00
	7 FF 350.00	2 . . . . 125.00
	8 Gorilla (c) 300.00	3 thru 5 . . . . @100.00
	9 FF 350.00	6 thru 10 . . . . @100.00
	10 . . . . 250.00	11 thru 25. . . . . @100.00
	11 Snakes (c) 200.00	26 Aug., 1949. . . . . 100.00
	12 Sept., 1953 . . . . 200.00	

BUSTER BEAR
Arnold Publications/
Quality Comics Group, 1953

BUSTER CRABBE
Lev Gleason Pub., 1953

CAMERA COMICS
U.S. Camera Publishing Corp.,
July–Sept., 1944

1 Funny animal 150.00	1 Ph(c) 300.00	1 Airfighter,Grey Comet 300.00
2 . . . . 125.00	2 ATh 275.00	2 How to Set Up a Darkroom . . 275.00
3 thru 10 . . . . @100.00	3 ATh 275.00	3 Linda Lens V:Nazi (c) 275.00
	4 F. Gordon(c) 275.00	4 Linda Lens (c) 250.00

BUSTER BROWN COMICS
Brown Shoe Co., 1945–59

BUZ SAWYER
Standard Comics, June, 1948

1 . . . . 1,000.00		5 Diving (c) 250.00
2 . . . . 350.00	1 . . . . 350.00	6 Jim Lane (c) 250.00
3 . . . . 250.00	2 I:Sweeney 250.00	7 Linda Lens (c) 250.00
4 scarce 400.00	3 . . . . 250.00	8 Linda Lens (c) 250.00
5 . . . . 250.00	4 . . . . 250.00	9 Summer, 1946 . . . . 250.00
6 . . . . 250.00	5 June, 1949 . . . . 250.00	
7 . . . . 250.00		

CALLING ALL BOYS
Parents Magazine Institute
Jan., 1946

CAMP COMICS
Dell Publishing Co., 1942

8 . . . . 250.00		1 Ph(c),WK,A:Bugs Bunny. . . . 1,500.00
9 . . . . 250.00	1 Skiing 200.00	2 Ph(c),WK,A:Bugs Bunny. . . . 1,200.00
10 . . . . 250.00	2 Roy Rogers Story 150.00	3 Ph(c),WK 1,000.00
11 thru 20. . . . . @100.00	3 Peril Out Post 150.00	
	4 Model Airplane 150.00	
	5 Fishing 150.00	
	6 Swimming 150.00	
	7 Baseball 175.00	
	8 School 150.00	
	9 The Miracle Quarterback . . . 150.00	
	10 Gary Cooper (c) 200.00	
	11 Rin-Tin-Tin (c) 150.00	
	12 Bob Hope (c). 250.00	
	13 Bing Cosby (c) 225.00	
	14 J. Edgar Hoover (c) 150.00	
	15 Tex Granger (c). 125.00	
	16 . . . . 125.00	
	17 Tex Granger (c), May, 1948 . . 125.00	
	Becomes:	

Buz Sawyer #3
© Standard Comics

TEX GRANGER
June, 1948

18 Bandits of the Badlands 125.00
19 The Seven Secret Cities. 100.00
20 Davey Crockett's Last Fight . . 100.00
21 Canyon Ambush 100.00
22 V:Hooded Terror 100.00

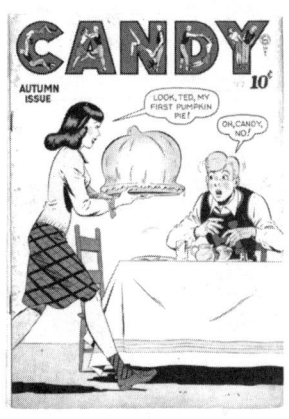

Candy #1
© Quality Comics

GOLDEN AGE

CAMPUS LOVES
**Comic Magazines
(Quality Comics Group), 1949**
1 BWa,PGv 500.00
2 BWa,PGv 400.00
3 PGv,Photo(c) 250.00
4 PGv,Photo(c) 250.00
5 PGv,Photo(c) 250.00

CAMPUS ROMANCES
**Avon Periodicals/
Realistic Publ., 1949**
1 Walter Johnson 350.00
2 . . . . 300.00
3 . . . . 300.00

CANDY
William H. Wise, 1944–45
1 BW,Two-Scoop 600.00
1a rep.BW 100.00
2 BW 500.00
3 BW 500.00

CANDY
Quality Comics Group, 1947–56
1 JCo,PGv,Teen-age 350.00
2 JCo,PGv 300.00
3 JCo 150.00
4 JCo 150.00
5 JCo 150.00
6 thru 10 JCo . . . . @150.00
11 thru 20 JCo . . . . @125.00
21 thru 40 . . . . @100.00
41 thru 64 . . . . @100.00

CANNONBALL COMICS
Rural Home Publ. Co., 1945
1 Superhero, Crash Kid 1,400.00
2 Captive Prince 1,200.00

CANTEEN KATE
St. John Publishing Co., 1952
1 MB,Sexy babe 1,000.00
2 MB 650.00
3 MB 750.00

CAPTAIN AERO COMICS
Holyoke Publishing Co., 1941
1 B:Flag-Man&Solar,Master
 of Magic Captain Aero,
 Captain Stone 4,000.00
2 A:Pals of Freedom 1,600.00
3 JKu,B:Alias X,A:Pals of
 Freedom 1,600.00
4 JKu,O:Gargoyle,
 Parachute jump 1,600.00
5 JKu 1,500.00
6 JKu,Flagman,A:Miss Victory . 1,400.00
7 Alias X 900.00
8 O:Red Cross,A:Miss Victory . . 900.00
9 A:Miss Victory,Alias X 800.00
10 A:Miss Victory,Red Cross . . . 750.00
11 A:Miss Victory 750.00
12 A:Miss Victory 750.00
13 A:Miss Victory 750.00
14 A:Miss Victory 750.00
15 AS(c),A:Miss Liberty 750.00
16 AS(c),Leather Face 500.00
17 LbC(c) 900.00
21 LbC(c) 900.00
22 LbC(c),I:Mighty Mite 900.00
23 LbC(c) 900.00
24 LbC(c) American Planes Dive
 Bomb Japan 1,200.00
25 LbC(c),Science Fiction(c) 700.00
26 LbC(c) 1,600.00

Captain Easy #13
© *Standard Comics*

CAPTAIN ATOM
**Nationwide Publishers, 1951
Mini-size**
1 Scientific adventure 600.00
2 thru 7 . . . . @300.00

CAPTAIN BATTLE
**New Friday Publ./
Magazine Press, Summer, 1941**
1 B:Captain Battle,O:Blackout 2,700.00
2 Pirate Ship (c) 1,700.00
3 Dungeon (c) 1,500.00
4 *may not exist*
5 V:Japanese, Summer, 1943 . . 900.00

CAPTAIN BATTLE, Jr.
Comic House, Fall, 1943
1 Claw V:Ghost, A:Sniffer 2,200.00
2 Man who didn't believe
 in Ghosts 2,000.00

CAPTAIN COURAGEOUS
See: BANNER COMICS

CAPTAIN EASY
Standard Comics, 1939
N# Swash Buckler 1,400.00
10 . . . . 300.00
11 . . . . 150.00
12 . . . . 150.00
13 ASh(c) 150.00
14 . . . . 150.00
15 . . . . 150.00
16 ASh(c) 150.00
17 Sept., 1949 . . . . 150.00

CAPTAIN FEARLESS COMICS
Helnit Publishing Co., 1941
1 O:Mr. Miracle,Alias X,Captain
 Fearless Citizen Smith,
 A:Miss Victory 1,500.00
2 A:Border Patrol, Sept.,1941 . . 800.00

CAPTAIN FLASH
Sterling Comics, Nov., 1954
1 O:Captain Flash 600.00
2 V:Black Knight 300.00
3 Beasts from 1,000,000 BC . . . 300.00
4 Flying Saucer Invasion 300.00

CAPTAIN FLEET
Approved Comics, Fall, 1952
1 Storm and Mutiny ...Typhoon . 250.00

CAPTAIN FLIGHT COMICS
**Four Star Publications,
March, 1944–Feb.-March, 1947**
N# B:Captain Flight,Ace
 Reynolds, Dash the Avenger,
 ProfessorX 800.00
2 . . . . 450.00
3 . . . . 450.00
4 B:Rock Raymond Salutes
 America's Wartime Heroines . 450.00
5 Bondage (c),B:Red Rocket
 A:The Grenade 2,000.00
6 Girl tied at the stake 500.00
7 LbC(c),Dog Fight (c) 900.00
8 LbC(c),B:Yankee Girl,
 A:Torpedoman 900.00
9 LbC(c),Dog Fight (c) 900.00
10 LbC(c),Bondage (c) 900.00
11 LbC(c),Future(c) 2,000.00

CAPTAIN GALLANT
Charlton Comics, 1955
1 Ph(c),Buster Crabbe 150.00
2 . . . . 125.00
3 . . . . 125.00
4 Sept., 1956 . . . . 125.00

CAPTAIN JET
Four Star Publ., May, 1952
1 Factory bombing (c) 300.00
2 Parachute jump (c) 200.00
3 Tank bombing (c) 175.00
4 Parachute (c) 175.00
5 . . . . 175.00

CAPTAIN KIDD
**See: DAGAR,
DESERT HAWK**

CAPTAIN MARVEL ADVENTURES
Fawcett Publications, 1941
N# JK, B:Captain Marvel &
 Sivana 55,000.00
2 GT,JK(c),Billy Batson (c) 7,500.00
3 JK(c),Thunderbolt (c) 4,500.00
4 Shazam(c) 3,500.00
5 V:Nazis 2,500.00
6 Solomon, Hercules, Atlas, Zeus,
 Achilles & Mercury (c) 2,000.00
7 Ghost of the White Room . . . 2,000.00
8 Forward America 2,000.00
9 A:Ibac the Monster, Nippo
 the Nipponese, Relm of
 the Subconscious 2,000.00
10 V:Japanese 2,000.00
11 V:Japanese and Nazis 1,500.00
12 Joins the Army 1,400.00
13 V:Diamond-Eyed Idol of
 Doom 1,400.00
14 Nippo meets his Nemesis . . 1,400.00
15 Big "Paste the Axis" contest. 1,400.00
16 Uncle Sam (c), Paste
 the Axis 1,400.00
17 P(c), Paste the Axis 1,200.00
18 P(c), O:Mary Marvel 3,600.00
19 Mary Marvel & Santa (c) . . . 1,500.00
20 Mark of the Black
 Swastika 6,000.00
21 Hitler (c) 1,700.00
22 B:Mr. Mind serial,
 Shipyard Sabotage 1,500.00
23 A:Steamboat 1,100.00

24 Minneapolis Mystery 1,100.00
25 Sinister Faces (c). 1,100.00
26 Flag (c). 1,100.00
27 Joins Navy 800.00
28 Uncle Sam (c). 800.00
29 Battle at the China Wall 800.00
30 Modern Robinson Crusoe . . . 800.00
31 Fights his own Conscience. . . 800.00
32 V:Mole Men, Dallas. 800.00
33 Mt. Rushmore parody
　　(c), Omaha 800.00
34 Oklahoma City 800.00
35 O:Radar the International
　　Policeman, Indianapolis 700.00
36 Missing face contest,
　　St. Louis. 700.00
37 V:Block Busting Bubbles,
　　Cincinnati. 700.00
38 V:Chattanooga Ghost,
　　Rock Garden City 700.00
39 V:Mr. Mind's Death Ray,
　　Pittsburgh 700.00
40 V:Ghost of the Tower,Boston . 700.00
41 Runs for President, Dayton . . 600.00
42 Christmas special, St. Paul. . . 600.00
43 V:Mr. Mind,I:Uncle Marvel,
　　Chicago 600.00
44 OtherWorlds,Washington,D.C. 600.00
45 V:Blood Bank Robbers 600.00
46 E: Mr. Mind Serial, Tall
　　Stories of Jonah Joggins. . . . 600.00
47 CCB,Shazam(c) 550.00
48 Signs Autographs (c) 550.00
49 V: An Unknown Killer 550.00
50 Twisted Powers 550.00
51 Last of the Batsons. 450.00
52 O&I:Sivana Jr.,V:Giant
　　Earth Dreamer. 450.00
53 Gets promoted 450.00
54 Marooned in the Future,
　　Kansas City 450.00
55 Endless String, Columbus . . . 450.00
56 Goes Crazy, Mobile 450.00
57 A:Haunted Girl, Rochester . . . 450.00
58 V:Sivana 450.00
59 CCB(c),PrC 450.00
60 Man who made Earthquakes . 450.00
61 I&V: Oggar, the Worlds
　　Mightiest Immortal 450.00
62 The Great Harness Race 450.00
63 Stuntman. 450.00
64 CCB(c&a),I:Lester the Imp . . . 450.00
65 V:Invaders from Outer Space . 450.00
66 Atomic War (c) 450.00
67 Hartford 350.00

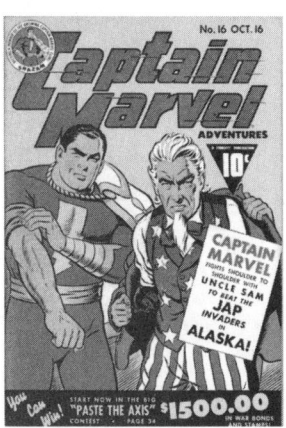

Captain Marvel Adventures #16
© *Fawcett Publications*

68 Scenes from the Past,
　　Baltimore 400.00
69 Gets Knighted 350.00
70 Horror in the Box 350.00
71 Wheel of Death 350.00
72 CCB,Empire State Bldg.Ph(c). 350.00
73 Becomes a Petrophile. 350.00
74 Who is the 13th Guest 350.00
75 V:Astonishing Yeast Menace . 350.00
76 A:Atom Ambassador 350.00
77 The Secret Life 350.00
78 O:Mr. Tawny 450.00
79 O:Atom,A:World's Worst
　　Actor 400.00
80 Twice told story 900.00
81 A:Mr. Atom 800.00
82 A:Mr. Tawny 400.00
83 Indian Chief. 400.00
84 V:Surrealist Imp 400.00
85 Freedom Train 400.00
86 A:Mr. Tawny 400.00
87 V:Electron Thief 400.00
88 Billy Batson's Boyhood 400.00
89 V:Sivana 400.00
90 A:Mr. Tawny 400.00
91 A:Chameleon Stone 400.00
92 The Land of Limbo 400.00
93 Book of all Knowledge 400.00
94 Battle of Electricity 400.00
95 The Great Ice Cap 400.00
96 V:Automatic Weapon 400.00
97 Wiped Out. 400.00
98 United Worlds 400.00
99 Rain of Terror 400.00
100 V:Sivana,Plot against
　　the Universe 750.00
101 Invisibility Trap 350.00
102 Magic Mix-up 350.00
103 Ice Covered World of
　　1,000,000 AD. 350.00
104 Mr. Tawny's Masquerade . . 350.00
105 The Dog Catcher 350.00
106 V:Menace of the Moon 350.00
107 V:Space Hunter. 350.00
108 V:Terrible Termites 350.00
109 The Invention Inventor 350.00
110 CCB(c),V:Sivana 350.00
111 The Eighth Sea,V:Vikings . . . 350.00
112 Worrybird. 350.00
113 Feud with Mr. Tawny 350.00
114 V:The Ogre 350.00
115 Mr. Tawny 350.00
116 Flying Saucer 450.00
117 Mr. Tawny bondage (c) 350.00
118 V:Weird Water Man 350.00
119 Invisibility. 350.00
120 Voice heard round the world. 350.00
121 Origin retold 350.00
122 Atomic Fire 350.00
123 Dinosaur Dilemma 350.00
124 V:Discarded Instincts 350.00
125 V:Ancient Villain 350.00
126 The Creeping Horror. 350.00
127 Sivana's Voodoo Spell 350.00
128 . . . . 350.00
129 Robot Hunt 350.00
130 Double Doom 350.00
131 Station Whiz gets Atomic
　　Powers. 350.00
132 V:Flood 350.00
133 The Pressure Peril 350.00
134 Sivana's Capsule Kingdom. . 350.00
135 Perplexing Past Puzzle. 325.00
136 Witch of Haven Street. 325.00
137 Seven Deadly Sins 325.00
138 V:Haunted Horror 400.00
139 V:Red Crusher 325.00
140 Hand of Horror 325.00
141 Man Without a World 325.00
142 The Beauty in Black 325.00
143 Great Stone Face on Moon . 325.00
144 Stolen Shazam Powers 325.00

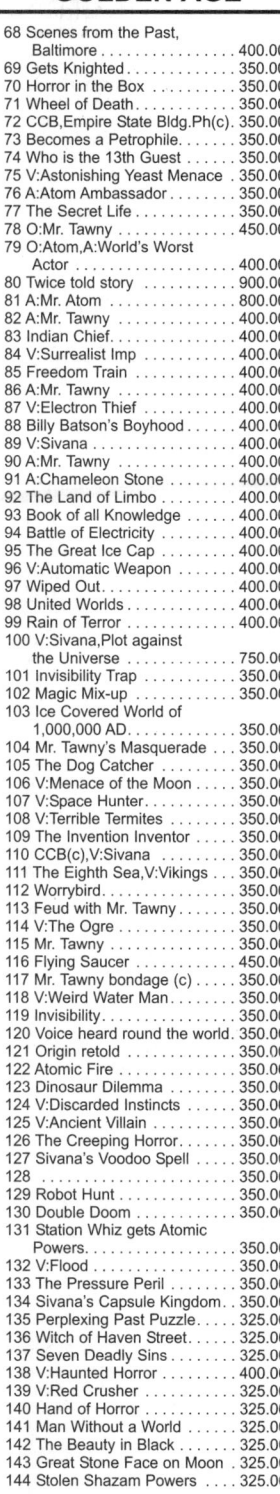

Captain Marvel Jr. #107
© *Fawcett Publications*

145 The Machines of Murder. . . . 325.00
146 The Unholy Spider 325.00
147 Thief From the Past 325.00
148 V:The World 325.00
149 Mr. Tawny Hermit 325.00
150 Captain Marvel's Wedding,
　　Nov., 1953 . . . . 650.00

CAPTAIN MARVEL JR.
Fawcett Publications, 1942

1 MRa(c),O:Captain Marvel, Jr.,
　　A:Capt. Nazi 9,700.00
2 MRa(c),O:Capt.Nippon,
　　V:Capt. Nazi 3,500.00
3 MRa(c),Parade to
　　Excitement 2,000.00
4 MRa(c),V:Invisible Nazi 1,800.00
5 MRa(c),V:Capt. Nazi 1,500.00
6 MRa(c),Adventure of Sabbac 1,300.00
7 MRa(c),City under the Sea . 1,300.00
8 MRa(c),Dangerous Double . 1,300.00
9 MRa(c),Independence (c) . . 1,400.00
10 Hitler (c). 1,600.00
11 MRa(c) 1,100.00
12 MRa(c),Scuttles the Axis
　　Isle in the Sky. 1,200.00
13 MRa(c),V:The Axis,Hitler,(c) 1,600.00
14 MRa(c),X-Mas (c), Santa wears
　　Capt. Marvel uniform 1,000.00
15 MRa(c),V:Capt. Nazi 1,100.00
16 MRa(c),A:Capt. Marvel,
　　Sivana, Pogo 1,000.00
17 MRa(c),Meets his future self 1,000.00
18 MRa(c),V:Birds of Doom . . . 1,000.00
19 MRa(c),A:Capt. Nazi &
　　Capt. Nippon 1,000.00
20 MRa(c),Goes on the Warpath 900.00
21 MRa(c),Buy War Stamps . . . 700.00
22 MRa(c),Rides World's oldest
　　steamboat 700.00
23 MRa(c) 700.00
24 MRa(c),V:Weather Man 700.00
25 MRa(c),Flag (c). 700.00
26 MRa(c),Happy New Year . . . 700.00
27 MRa(c),Jungle Thrills 700.00
28 MRa(c),V:Sivana's Crumbling
　　Crimes 700.00
29 MRa(c),Blazes a Wilderness
　　Trail 700.00
30 MRa(c) 700.00
31 MRa(c) 500.00
32 Keeper of the Lonely Rock . . 500.00
33 . . . . 500.00
34/35 I&O:Sivana Jr. 500.00
36 Underworld Tournament 500.00

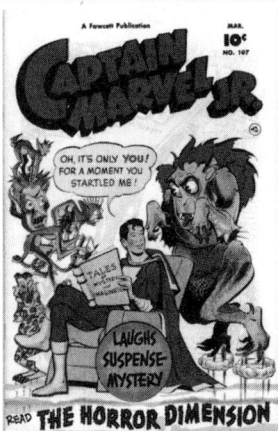

GOLDEN AGE

37 FreddyFreeman'sNews-stand . 500.00
38 A:Arabian Knight 500.00
39 V:Sivana Jr., Headline Stealer 500.00
40 Faces Grave Situation 500.00
41 I:The Acrobat 400.00
42 V:Sivana Jr. 400.00
43 BTh(c),V:Beasts on Broadway 400.00
44 Key to the Mystery 400.00
45 A:Icy Fingers 400.00
46 BTh(c&a) 400.00
47 BTh(c),V:Giant o/t Beanstalk . 400.00
48 Whale of a Fish Story 400.00
49 BTh(c),V:Dream Recorder . . . 400.00
50 Wanted: Freddy Freeman . . . 400.00
51 The Island Riddle 350.00
52 A:Flying Postman 350.00
53 Atomic Bomb on the Loose. . . 400.00
54 V:Man with 100 Heads 350.00
55 Pyramid of Eternity 350.00
56 Blue Boy's Black Eye 350.00
57 MRa(c),Magic Ladder 350.00
58 BTh(c),Amazing Mirror Maze . 350.00
59 MRa(c) 350.00
60 V:Space Menace 350.00
61 V:Himself. 300.00
62 V:Mr. Hydro 300.00
63 V:Witch of Winter . . . . @300.00
64 thru 74 . . . . @300.00
75 V:Outlaw of Crooked Creek . . 300.00
76 thru 85 . . . . @300.00
86 Defenders of time 300.00
87 thru 89 . . . . @300.00
90 The Magic Trunk 300.00
91 thru 99 . . . . @300.00
100 V:Sivana Jr 300.00
101 thru 106 . . . . @300.00
107 The Horror Dimension 400.00
108 thru 118 . . . . @250.00
119 Condemned to Die, Electric
     Chair, June, 1953 . . . . 250.00

CAPTAIN MIDNIGHT
Fawcett Publications, 1942
1 O:Captain Midnight,
     Capt. Marvel (c) 6,000.00
2 Smashes Jap Juggernaut. . . 2,500.00
3 Battles Phantom Bomber . . . 2,400.00
4 Grapples the Gremlins 2,000.00
5 Double Trouble in Tokyo . . . 2,000.00
6 Blasts the Black Mikado . . . 1,400.00
7 Newspaper headline (c) 1,400.00
8 Flying Torpedoes
     Berlin-Bound 1,400.00
9 MRa(c), Subs in Mississippi 1,400.00
10 MRa(c), Flag (c). 1,500.00
11 MRa(c), Murder in Mexico . . 1,200.00
12 V:Sinister Angels 1,200.00
13 Non-stop around the World . 1,200.00
14 V:King of the Villains 1,200.00
15 V:Kimberley Killer. 1,200.00
16 Hitler's Fortress Breached . . 1,200.00
17 MRa(c), Hello Adolf 1,200.00
18 Death from the Skies 1,200.00
19 Hour of Doom for the Axis . . 1,200.00
20 Brain & Brawn against Axis 1,200.00
21 Trades with Japanese. 800.00
22 Plea for War Stamps. 800.00
23 Japanese Prison (c) 800.00
24 Rising Sun Flag (c). 800.00
25 Amusement Park Murder 800.00
26 Hotel of Horror 800.00
27 Death Knell for Tyranny 800.00
28 Gliderchuting to Glory. 800.00
29 Bomb over Nippon 800.00
30 . . . . 800.00
31 and 32 . . . . @500.00
33 V:Shark 500.00
34 thru 40 . . . . @500.00
41 thru 63 . . . . @400.00
64 V:XOG, Ruler of Saturn. 400.00
65 . . . . 400.00
66 V:XOG. 400.00

67 Fall, 1948 . . . . 400.00
Becomes:

SWEETHEARTS
Oct., 1948
68 Robert Mitchum 250.00
69 thru 110 . . . . @125.00
111 Ronald Reagan story 175.00
112 thru 118 . . . . @125.00
119 WW,Marilyn Monroe 600.00
120 Atomic Bomb story . . . . . . @150.00
121 Liz Taylor. 200.00
122 Marjuana,1954 . . . . 150.00

CAPTAIN ROCKET
P.L. Publications, 1951
1 Sci-Fi 650.00

CAPTAIN SCIENCE
Youthful Magazines, 1950
1 WW,O:Captain Science,
     V:Monster God of Rogor . . 1,400.00
2 V:Cat Men of Phoebus,
     Space Pirates 650.00
3 Ghosts from the Underworld . 650.00
4 WW,Vampires 1,200.00
5 WW,V:Shark Pirates of
     Pisces. 1,200.00
6 V:Invisible Tyrants,
     bondage (c) 700.00
7 Bondage(c) Dec., 1951 . . . . . 700.00
Becomes:

FANTASTIC
Feb., 1952
8 Isle of Madness 500.00
9 Octopus (c) 400.00
Becomes:

BEWARE
June, 1952
10 SHn,Doll of Death. 900.00
11 SHn,Horror Head 500.00
12 SHn,Body Snatchers 500.00
Becomes:

CHILLING TALES
Dec., 1952
13 MF,Screaming Skull 1,000.00
14 SHn,Smell of Death 700.00
15 SHn,Curse of the Tomb 750.00
16 HcK,Mark of the Beast
     Bondage(c) 600.00
17 MFc(c),Wandering Willie,
     Oct.,1953 . . . . 700.00

CAPTAIN STEVE SAVAGE
Avon Periodicals
[1st Series] 1950
N# WW 550.00
2 EK(c),The Death Gamble 300.00
3 EK(c),Crash Landing in
     Manchuria 250.00
4 EK(c),V:Red Raiders from
     Siang-Po 150.00
5 EK(c),Rockets of Death 150.00
6 Operation Destruction 150.00
7 EK(c),Flight to Kill 150.00
8 EK(c),V:Red Mystery Jet 150.00
9 EK(c) 150.00
10 . . . . 150.00
11 EK(c) 150.00
12 WW 225.00
13 . . . . 150.00

[2nd Series] Sept./Oct., 1954
5 . . . . 150.00
6 WW 200.00
7 thru 13 . . . . @150.00

CAPTAIN TOOTSIE
& THE SECRET LEGION
Toby Press, 1950
1 Sci-Fi 450.00
2 . . . . 250.00

CAPTAIN VIDEO
Fawcett Publications, 1951
1 GE,Ph(c) From TV series . . . 1,800.00
2 Time When Men Could Not
     Walk 1,200.00
3 GE,Indestructible Antagonist 1,000.00
4 GE,School of Spies 1,000.00
5 GE,Missiles of Doom,
     photo (c) 1,000.00
6 GE,Island of Conquerors,
     Photo (c); Dec., 1951 . . . . . 1,000.00

CAPTAIN WIZARD
Rural Home, 1946
1 Impossible Man 500.00

CARNIVAL
See: SCOOP COMICS

CASPER, THE
FRIENDLY GHOST
St. John Publishing, 1949
1 O:Baby Huey 3,700.00
2 . . . . 1,500.00
3 . . . . 1,400.00
4 . . . . 1,000.00
5 . . . . 1,000.00

Harvey Publications, 1952
7 Baby Huey 800.00
8 thru 9 Baby Huey . . . . @500.00
10 I:Spooky 550.00
11 A:Spooky 300.00
12 thru 18 . . . . @300.00
19 I:Nightmare 400.00
20 I:Wendy the Witch 2,000.00
21 thru 30 . . . . @250.00
31 thru 40 . . . . @200.00
41 thru 50 . . . . @150.00
51 thru 60 . . . . @150.00
61 thru 69 . . . . @150.00
70 July, 1958 . . . . 150.00

CATHOLIC COMICS
Catholic Publications, 1946–49
1 Sports. 500.00
2 Sports. 350.00

Captain Video #2)
© *Fawcett Publications*

3 Sports 300.00
4 thru 10 . . . . @300.00
11 thru 20 . . . . @250.00
21 thru 34 . . . . @275.00

CATMAN COMICS
Helnit Publ. Co./
Holyoke Publ. Co./
Continental Magazine, 1941
1 O:Deacon&Sidekick Mickey,
  Dr. Diamond & Ragman,A:Black
  Widow, B:Blaze Baylor 7,500.00
2 Ragman 2,800.00
3 B:Pied Piper 2,500.00
4 CQ 2,000.00
5 I&O: The Kitten 1,500.00
6 CQ 1,500.00
7 CQ 1,500.00
8 JKa, I:Volton 1,800.00
9 JKa 1,200.00
10 JKa,O:Blackout,
  B:Phantom Falcon 1,200.00
11 JKa,DRi,BF,PzF 1,200.00
12 Volton 1,000.00
13 rare 1,500.00
14 CQ 1,000.00
15 Rajah of Destruction 1,000.00
16 Bye-Bye Axis, Hitler 1,500.00
17 Buy Bonds and Stamps 1,000.00
18 Buy Bonds and Stamps 1,000.00
19 CQ,Hitler,Tojo &Mussolini(c) 1,500.00
20 CQ,Hitler,Tojo &Mussolini(c) 1,500.00
21 CQ 1,000.00
22 CQ 1,000.00
23 CQ 1,000.00
N# DRiV:Japanese,Bondage(c) 1,200.00
N# V:Demon 1,000.00
N# LbC(c),A:Leather Face 1,400.00
27 LbC(c),Flag (c),O:Kitten 1,500.00
28 LbC(c),Horror (c) 1,500.00
29 LbC(c),BF,RP 1,500.00
30 LbC(c),BF,Bondage(c) 1,600.00
31 LbC(c) 1,500.00
32 LbC(c),RP,Aug., 1946 . . . . . 1,500.00

CAVALIER COMICS
Sture Ashberg Publ. 1945
1 Historic adventure 250.00

CENTURY OF COMICS
Eastern Color Printing Co., 1933
N# Giveaway, very early 60,000.00

CHALLENGER, THE
Interfaith Publications, 1945
N# O:The Challenger Club 750.00
2 and 3 JKa . . . . @600.00
4 JKa,BF 600.00

CHAMBER OF CHILLS
Harvey Publications/
Witches Tales, June, 1951
21 (1) AAv 900.00
22 (2) AAv 600.00
23 (3) Eyes Ripped Out 600.00
24 (4) LEI,Bondage (c) 700.00
5 LEI,Shrunken Skull,
  Operation Monster 700.00
6 LEI,Seven Skulls of Magondi . 600.00
7 LEI,Pit of the Damned 600.00
8 LEI,Formula for Death 600.00
9 LEI,Bondage (c) 500.00
10 LEI,AAv,Cave of Death 500.00
11 AAv,Curse of Morgan Kilgane . 400.00
12 AAv,Swamp Monster 400.00
13 AAv,The Lost Race 550.00
14 LEI,Down to Death 500.00
15 LEI,AAv,Nightmare of Doom . . 550.00
16 LEI,Cycle of Horror 550.00

17 LEI,Amnesia 550.00
18 LEI,Hair Cut-Atom Bomb 600.00
19 LEI,Happy Anniversary 500.00
20 Shock is Struck 500.00
21 LEI,BP,RP,Decapitation 600.00
22 LEI,Is Death the End? 550.00
23 LEI,BP,RP,Heartline 550.00
24 LEI,BP,Bondage(c) 600.00
25 LEI, ... 400.00
26 LEI,HN,AAv,Captains Return . 400.00
Becomes:

CHAMBER OF CLUES
Feb., 1955
27 BP,A:Kerry Drake 250.00
28 A:Kerry Drake 150.00

CHAMPION COMICS
Worth Publishing Co., 1939
2 B:Champ, Blazing Scarab, Neptina,
  Liberty Lads, Jingleman . . . 3,200.00
3 . . . . 1,500.00
4 Bailout(c) 1,500.00
5 Jungleman(c) 1,500.00
6 MNe 1,500.00
7 MNe,Human Meteor 1,500.00
8 JK 3,000.00
9 JK,S&K 3,000.00
10 JK,Bondage (c) 3,000.00
Becomes:

CHAMP COMICS
Oct. 1940
11 Human Meteor 2,000.00
12 Human Heteor 1,800.00
13 Dragon's Teeth 1,700.00
14 Liberty Lads 1,700.00
15 RC,Liberty Lads 1,700.00
16 Liberty Lads 1,700.00
17 Liberty Lads 1,700.00
18 Liberty Lads 2,000.00
19 JSm,A:The Wasp 2,100.00
20 S&K,A:The Green Ghost . . . 1,700.00
21 S&K 1,200.00
22 A:White Mask 1,500.00
23 Flag (c) 1,400.00
24 Hitler,Tojo & Mussolini 1,200.00
25 thru 29 . . . . @1,200.00

CHARLIE CHAN
Crestwood, 1948–55
1 S&K(c),CI,Detective 1,500.00
2 S&K 1,000.00
3 S&K 1,000.00
4 S&K 1,000.00
5 S&K 1,000.00
Charlton Comics, 1955
6 S&K 750.00
7 . . . . 500.00
8 . . . . 500.00
9 . . . . 500.00
Becomes:

ZAZA THE MYSTIC
Charlton Comics, 1956
10 Psychic revelations 300.00
11 . . . . 300.00
Becomes:

THIS MAGAZINE IS HAUNTED
Charlton Comics, 1957
12 . . . . 450.00
13 . . . . 650.00
14 The Green Man 400.00
15 . . . . 350.00
16 . . . . 700.00
Becomes:

OUTER SPACE
Charlton Comics, 1958
17 AS,WW,Sci-Fi 300.00
18 SD 450.00
19 SD 450.00
20 SD 450.00
21 SD 450.00
22 . . . . 300.00
23 . . . . 300.00
24 SD Machine Men of Mars 300.00
25 . . . . 300.00

CHARLIE McCARTHY
Dell Publishing Co., 1947
1 Ph(c) 300.00
2 . . . . 200.00
3 thru 9 . . . . @200.00

CHEYENNE
Dell Publishing Co., 1956
1 Ph(c) all 350.00
2 . . . . 200.00
3 . . . . 150.00
4 thru 12 . . . . @135.00
13 thru 25 . . . . @125.00

CHIEF, THE
Dell Publishing Co., 1950
(1) see Dell Four Color #290
2 . . . . 125.00

CHILLING TALES
See: CAPTAIN SCIENCE

CHOICE COMICS
Great Comics, 1941
1 O:Secret Circle 2,500.00
2 . . . . 1,500.00
3 The Lost City 2,100.00

CHRISTMAS CARNIVAL
Approved Comics (Ziff-Davis)/
St. John Publ., 1955
N# Santa 500.00
2 . . . . 300.00

CHUCKLE THE GIGGLY BOOK OF COMIC ANIMALS
R. B. Leffing Well Co., 1944
1 . . . . 300.00

Charlie Chan #1
© Crestwood

Clue #10
© Hillman Periodicals.

CINEMA COMICS HERALD
Paramount/Universal/RKO/
20th Century Fox
Giveaways, 1941-43
N# Mr. Bug Goes to Town 200.00
N# Bedtime Story 150.00
N# Lady for a Night,J.Wayne ... 325.00
N# Reap the Wild Wind 150.00
N# Thunderbirds 150.00
N# They All Kissed Me 150.00
N# Bombardier 175.00
N# Crash Dive 135.00
N# Arabian Nights............ 150.00

CIRCUS COMICS
Farm Women's Publ., 1945
1 Clown, Funny Animal....... 200.00
2 .... 150.00

CIRCUS COMICS
D.S. Publications, 1948
1 FF 400.00

CIRCUS OF FUN COMICS
A.W. Nugent Publ. Co., 1946
1 Funny animal............. 250.00
2 .... 150.00
3 .... 150.00

CIRCUS THE COMIC RIOT
Globe Syndicate, June, 1938
1 BKa,WE,BW 10,000.00
2 BKa,WE,BW 6,000.00
3 BKa,WE,BW, Aug., 1938 ... 5,000.00

CISCO KID COMICS
Bernard Bailey/
Swappers Quarterly, 1944
1 .... 700.00

CISCO KID, THE
Dell Publishing Co., 1951
(1) *See Dell Four Color #292*
2 Jan., 1951 .... 500.00
3 thru 5 .... @300.00
6 thru 10 .... @250.00
11 thru 20 .... @225.00
21 thru 36 .... @175.00
37 thru 41 Ph(c)'s.......... @350.00

CLAIRE VOYANT
Leader Publ./Visual Ed./
Pentagon Publ., 1946-47
N# 1,100.00
2 JKa(c) 800.00
3 Case of the Kidnapped
    Bride 1,000.00
4 Bondage (c) 800.00

CLAY CODY, GUNSLINGER
Better Publications, 1957
1 Western hero............. 100.00

CLEAN FUN, STARRING 'SHOOGAFOOTS JONES'
Specialty Book Co., 1945
N# 200.00

CLIMAX!
Gilmor Magazines, 1955
1 Mystery 250.00
2 .... 200.00

CLOAK AND DAGGER
Approved Comics
(Ziff-Davis), Fall, 1952
1 NS(c),Al Kennedy of the Secret
    Service 400.00

CLOWN COMICS
Harvey Publications, 1945
N# 225.00
2 .... 150.00
3 .... 150.00

CLUE COMICS
Hillman Periodicals, 1943
1 O:Boy King,Nightmare,Micro-Face,
    Twilight,Zippo........... 2,700.00
2 rare 1,600.00
3 Boy King V:The Crane 1,100.00
4 V:The Crane 900.00
5 V:The Crane 900.00
6 Hells Kitchen 600.00
7 V:Dr. Plasma,Torture(c) 600.00
8 RP,A:The Gold Mummy King . 550.00
9 I:Paris 550.00
10 O:Gun Master 550.00
11 A:Gun Master 550.00
12 O:Rackman............. 550.00
2-1 S&K,O:Nightro,A:Iron Lady. 1,100.00
2-2 S&K,Bondage(c)........ 1,600.00
2-3 S&K................. 1,100.00
Becomes:

REAL CLUE CRIME STORIES
June, 1947
2-4 DBw,S&K,True Story of
    Ma Barker............. 1,100.00
2-5 S&K, Newface surgery(c) ... 800.00
2-6 S&K, Breakout (c) 800.00
2-7 S&K, Stick up (c) 800.00
2-8 Kidnapping (c) 200.00
2-9 DBa,Boxing fix (c) 200.00
2-10 DBa,Murder (c) 200.00
2-11 Attempted bankrobbery (c) . 200.00
2-12 Murder (c) 200.00
3-1 thru 3-12............... @200.00
4-1 thru 4-12............... @200.00
5-1 thru 5-12............... @150.00
6-1 thru 6-12............... @150.00
6-10 Bondage(c) 200.00
7-1 thru 7-12............... @135.00
8-1 thru 8-5, May, 1953 ...... @135.00

THE CLUTCHING HAND
American Comics, 1954
1 Horror.................. 600.00

CLYDE BEATTY
Commodore Productions, 1953
1 Photo(c)................. 400.00

C-M-O COMICS
Comic Corp. of America
(Centaur), May, 1942
1 Invisible Terror 2,000.00
2 Super Ann.............. 1,200.00

COCOMALT BIG BOOK OF COMICS
Harry A. Chesler, 1938
1 BoW,PGv,FGu,JCo,(Give away)
    Little Nemo 4,000.00

CODY OF THE PONY EXPRESS
See: BULLS-EYE

CODY OF THE PONY EXPRESS
Fox Features Syndicate, 1950
1 Western................ 200.00

COLOSSAL FEATURES MAGAZINE
Fox Features Syndicate, 1950
1 (33) Cody of the Pony Express 200.00
2 (34) Cody of the Pony Express 200.00
3 Crime.................. 200.00

COLOSSUS COMICS
Sun Publications
March, 1940
1 A:Colossus 12,000.00

COLUMBIA COMICS
William H. Wise Co., 1944
1 Joe Palooka,Charlie Chan ... 400.00

COMIC BOOKS
Metropolitan Printing Co. 1950
1 Boots & Saddles 125.00
1 Green Lama-The Green Jet .. 500.00

Clown Comics #3
© Harvey Periodicals

1 My Pal Dizzy 60.00
1 Talullah. 150.00
1 New World 60.00

COMIC COMICS
Fawcett Publications, 1946
1 Captain Kidd 250.00
2 . . . . 275.00
3 thru 10 BW . . . . @275.00

COMIC LAND
Fact and Fiction, 1946
1 Sandusky and the Senator . . . 250.00

COMICS, THE
Dell Publishing Co., March, 1937
1 I:Tom Mix & Arizona Kid 3,200.00
2 A:Tom Mix & Tom Beaty 2,500.00
3 A:Alley Oop 1,500.00
4 thru 11 same . . . . @1,500.00

THE COMICS CALENDAR
True Comics Press, 1946
1 . . . . 650.00

COMICS NOVEL
Fawcett Publications, 1947
1 Anarcho Dictator of Death 500.00

COMICS ON PARADE
United Features Syndicate, April, 1938–Feb., 1955
1 B:Tarzan,Captain and the Kids,
  Little Mary, Mixup,Abbie & Slats,
  Broncho Bill,Li'l Abner 6,500.00
2 Circus Parade of all 2,500.00
3 . . . . 1,900.00
4 On Rocket 1,200.00
5 All at the Store 1,200.00
6 All at Picnic 900.00
7 Li'l Abner(c) 900.00
8 same 900.00
9 same 900.00
10 same 900.00
11 same 800.00
12 same 800.00
13 same 800.00
14 Abbie n' Slats (c). 800.00
15 Li'l Abner(c). 800.00
16 Abbie n' Slats(c) 800.00
17 Tarzan,Abbie n' Slats(c). . . . 1,000.00
18 Li'l Abner(c). 800.00
19 same 800.00
20 same 800.00
21 Li'l Abner(c). 700.00
22 Tail Spin Tommy(c) 700.00
23 Abbie n' Slats(c) 700.00
24 Tail Spin Tommy(c) 700.00
25 Li'l Abner(c). 700.00
26 Abbie n' Slats(c) 700.00
27 Li'l Abner(c). 700.00
28 Tail Spin Tommy(c) 700.00
29 Abbie n' Slats(c) 700.00
30 Li'l Abner(c). 400.00
31 The Captain & the Kids(c) . . . 300.00
32 Nancy and Fritzi Ritz(c) 250.00
33 Li'l Abner(c). 300.00
34 The Captain & the Kids(c) . . . 300.00
35 Nancy and Fritzi Ritz(c) 300.00
36 Li'l Abner(c). 300.00
37 The Captain & the Kids(c) . . . 250.00
38 Nancy and Fritzi Ritz(c) 250.00
39 Li'l Abner(c). 300.00
40 The Captain & the Kids(c) . . . 250.00
41 Nancy and Fritzi Ritz(c) 200.00
42 Li'l Abner(c). 300.00
43 The Captain & the Kids(c) . . . 250.00
44 Nancy and Fritzi Ritz(c) 200.00

45 Li'l Abner(c). 250.00
46 The Captain & the Kids(c) . . . 200.00
47 Nancy and Fritzi Ritz(c) 200.00
48 Li'l Abner(c). 250.00
49 The Captain & the Kids(c) . . . 200.00
50 Nancy and Fritzi Ritz(c) 200.00
51 Li'l Abner(c). 250.00
52 The Captain & the Kids(c) . . . 200.00
53 Nancy and Fritzi Ritz(c) 200.00
54 Li'l Abner(c). 250.00
55 Nancy and Fritzi Ritz(c) 200.00
56 The Captain & the Kids(c) . . . 200.00
57 Nancy and Fritzi Ritz(c) 200.00
58 Li'l Abner(c). 250.00
59 The Captain & the Kids(c) . . . 200.00
60 thru 76 Nancy &
  Fritzi Ritz(c) . . . . @150.00
77 Nancy & Sluggo(c) 125.00
78 thru 104 Nancy & Sluggo(c) @125.00

COMICS REVUE
St. John Publ. Co., 1947
1 Ella Cinders and Blackie 200.00
2 Hap Hopper 125.00
3 Iron Vic. 125.00
4 Eva Cinders 125.00
5 Gordo. 125.00

COMMANDER BATTLE AND THE ATOMIC SUBMARINE
American Comics Group, 1954
1 3-D(c) 1,000.00
2 . . . . 700.00
3 H-Bomb-3-D type. 800.00
4 . . . . 700.00
5 . . . . 700.00
6 . . . . 700.00
7 . . . . 700.00

COMPLETE BOOK OF COMICS AND FUNNIES
William H. Wise & Co., 1945
1 Wonderman-Magnet 700.00

COMPLETE BOOK OF TRUE CRIME COMICS
William H. Wise & Co., 1945
1 rep. Crime Does Not Pay . . . 2,000.00

CONFESSIONS ILLUSTRATED
E.C. Comics, 1956
1WW,JO,JCr,JKa,Adult romance 400.00
2 JCr,RC,JKa,JO 300.00

CONQUEROR COMICS
Albrecht Publications, Winter, 1945
1 . . . . 300.00

CONQUEST
Famous Funnies, 1955
1 Historical adventure 90.00

CONTACT COMICS
Aviation Press, July, 1944
N# LbC(c),B:Black Venus,
  Golden Eagle. 900.00
2 LbC(c),Peace Jet. 700.00
3 LbC(c),LbC,E:Flamingo 650.00
4 LbC(c),LbC 600.00
5 LbC(c),A:Phantom Flyer 650.00
6 LbC(c),HK 750.00
7 LbC(c),Flying Tigers. 600.00

Complete Book of True Crime Comics
N# © Wm Wise

8 LbC(c),Peace Jet 600.00
9 LbC(c),LbC,A:Marine Flyers . . 600.00
10 LbC(c),A:Bombers of the AAF 600.00
11 LbC(c),HK,AF,Salutes Naval
  Aviation 700.00
12 LbC(c),A:Sky Rangers, Air Kids,
  May, 1946. . . . . 1,600.00

COO COO COMICS
Nedor/Animated Cartoons (Standard), Oct., 1942
1 O&I:Super Mouse 500.00
2 . . . . 250.00
3 . . . . 200.00
4 . . . . 225.00
5 . . . . 225.00
6 thru 10 . . . . @150.00
11 thru 33 . . . . @150.00
34 thru 40 FF illustration . . . . . @250.00
41 FF 400.00
42 FF 350.00
43 FF illustration 250.00
44 FF illustration 250.00
45 FF illustration 250.00
46 FF illustration 250.00
47 FF 350.00
48 FF illustration 250.00
49 FF illustration 250.00
50 FF illustration 250.00
51 thru 61 . . . . @125.00
62 April, 1952. . . . . 100.00

"COOKIE"
Michel Publ./Regis Publ. (American Comics Group) April, 1946
1 . . . . 350.00
2 . . . . 250.00
3 thru 5 . . . . @200.00
6 thru 20 . . . . @150.00
21 thru 30 . . . . @100.00
31 thru 54 . . . . @100.00
55 Aug., 1955. . . . . 100.00

COSMO CAT
Fox Features Syndicate, 1946
1 . . . . 325.00
2 . . . . 200.00
3 O:Cosmo Cat 225.00
4 thru 10 . . . . @150.00

COSMO
THE MERRY MARTIAN
Radio Comics/Archie Publ., 1958
1 Funny alien 250.00
2 thru 6 . . . . @200.00

COURAGE COMICS
J. Edward Slavin, 1945
1 . . . . 250.00
2 Boxing (c). 250.00
77 Naval rescue, PT99 (c) 250.00

COWBOY COMICS
See: STAR RANGER

COWBOYS 'N' INJUNS
Compix (M.E. Enterprises), 1946-47
1 Funny Animal Western 300.00
2 thru 5 . . . . @250.00
6 thru 8 See: *A-1 Comics*, #23,#41,#48

COWBOY WESTERN/ COMICS/HEROES
See: YELLOWJACKET

COW PUNCHER
Avon Periodicals/ Realistic Publ., Jan., 1947
1 JKu 650.00
2 JKu,JKa(c),Bondage (c) 550.00
3 AU(c) 350.00
4 . . . . 350.00
5 . . . . 350.00
6 WJo(c),Drug story 500.00
7 . . . . 350.00
1 JKu 350.00

CRACK COMICS
Comic Magazines (Quality Comics Group) 1940
1 LF,O:Black Condor,Madame Fatal, Red Torpedo, Rock Bradden, Space Legion, B:The Clock,Wizard Wells . 9,000.00
2 Black Condor (c) 3,800.00
3 The Clock (c) 2,800.00
4 Black Condor (c) 2,500.00
5 LF,The Clock (c) 1,700.00
6 PG,Black Condor (c) 1,600.00
7 Clock (c) 1,600.00
8 Black Condor (c) 1,600.00
9 Clock (c) 1,600.00
10 Black Condor (c) 1,600.00
11 LF,PG,Clock (c) 1,400.00
12 LF,PG,Black Condor (c) 1,400.00
13 LF,PG,Clock (c) 1,400.00
14 AMc,LF,PG,Clack Condor(c) 1,400.00
15 AMc,LF,PG,Clock (c) 1,400.00
16 AMc,LF,PG,Black Condor(c) 1,400.00
17 FGu,AMc,LF,PG,Clock (c) . . 1,400.00
18 AMc,LF,PG,Black Condor(c) 1,400.00
19 AMc,LF,PG,Clock (c) 1,400.00
20 AMc,LF,PG,BlackCondor(c) 1,400.00
21 AMc,LF,PG,same 1,200.00
22 LF,PG,same 1,200.00
23 AMc,LF,PG,same 1,200.00
24 AMc,LF,PG,same 1,200.00
25 AMc,same 900.00
26 AMc,same 900.00
27 AMc,I&O:Captain Triumph . . 1,800.00
28 Captain Triumph (c) 1,000.00
29 A:Spade the Ruthless 1,000.00
30 I:Biff 800.00
31 Helps Spade Dig His Own Grave. 500.00
32 Newspaper (c) 500.00

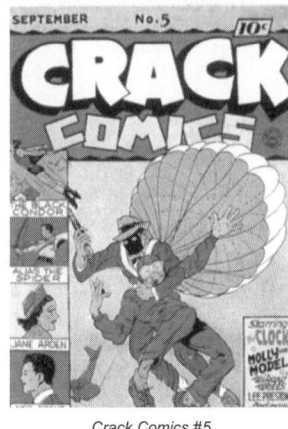
Crack Comics #5
© *Comic Magazines*

33 V:Men of Darkness 500.00
34 . . . . 500.00
35 V:The Man Who Conquered Flame. 500.00
36 Good Neighbor Tour 500.00
37 V:The Tyrant of Toar Valley. . . 500.00
38 Castle of Shadows 500.00
39 V:Crime over the City 500.00
40 Thrilling Murder Mystery 350.00
41 . . . . 350.00
42 All that Glitters is Not Gold . . . 350.00
43 Smashes the Evil Spell of Silent 350.00
44 V:Silver Tip 350.00
45 V:King-The Jack of all Trades. 350.00
46 V:Mr. Weary 350.00
47 V:Hypnotic Eyes Khor. 400.00
48 Murder in the Sky 400.00
49 . . . . 400.00
50 A Key to Trouble 400.00
51 V:Werewolf 400.00
52 V:Porcupine 400.00
53 V:Man Who Robbed the Dead 400.00
54 Shoulders the Troubles of the World. 400.00
55 Brain against Brawn 400.00
56 Gossip leads to Murder 400.00
57 V:Sitok–Green God of Evil . . . 400.00
58 V:Targets 300.00
59 A Cargo of Mystery 300.00
60 Trouble is no Picnic 300.00
61 V:Mr. Pointer-Finger of Fear . . 300.00
62 V:The Vanishing Vandals 300.00
Becomes:

CRACK WESTERN
Nov., 1949–May, 1951
63 PG, I&O:Two-Gun Lil, B:Frontier Marshal,Arizona Ames, ... 350.00
64 RC,Arizona AmesV:Two-Legged Coyote 225.00
65 RC,Ames Tramples on Trouble 225.00
66 Arizona Ames Arizona Raines, Tim Holt,Ph(c) 150.00
67 RC, Ph(c),Randolph Scott . . . 225.00
68 Ph(c) 150.00
69 RC. 150.00
70 O&I:Whip and Diablo 175.00
71 Bob Allen, Marshall,RC(c). . . . 200.00
72 RC,Tim Holt,Ph(c). 150.00
73 Tim Holt,Ph(c). 100.00
74 RC(c). 150.00
75 RC(c). 150.00
76 RC(c),Stage Coach to Oblivion 150.00
77 RC(c),Comanche Terror 150.00

78 RC(c),Killers of Laurel Ridge . 150.00
79 RC(c),Fires of Revenge 150.00
80 RC(c),Mexican Massacre . . . 150.00
81 RC(c),Secrets of Terror Canyon 150.00
82 The Killer with a Thousand Faces. 125.00
83 Rattlesnake Pete's Revenge . 125.00
84 PG(c),Revolt at Broke Creek . 125.00

CRACKAJACK FUNNIES
Dell Publishing Co., 1938
1 AMc,A:Dan Dunn,The Nebbs, Don Winslow 4,000.00
2 AMc,same. 2,000.00
3 AMc,same. 1,500.00
4 AMc,same. 1,200.00
5 AMc,Naked Women(c) 1,400.00
6 AMc,same. 1,100.00
7 AMc,same. 1,100.00
8 AMc,same. 1,100.00
9 AMc,A:Red Ryder 3,000.00
10 AMc,A:Red Ryder 850.00
11 AMc,A:Red Ryder 750.00
12 AMc,A:Red Ryder 750.00
13 AMc,A:Red Ryder 750.00
14 AMc,A:Red Ryder 750.00
15 AMc,A:Tarzan 850.00
16 AMc. 700.00
17 AMc. 700.00
18 AMc,A:Stratosphere Jim 700.00
19 AMc. 700.00
20 AMc. 700.00
21 AMc. 700.00
22 AMc. 700.00
23 AMc,A:Ellery Queen 700.00
24 AMc. 700.00
25 AMc,I:The Owl 1,500.00
26 AMc 1,000.00
27 AMc 1,000.00
28 AMc,A:The Owl 1,000.00
29 AMc,A:Ellery Queen. 1,000.00
30 AMc,A:Tarzan. 1,000.00
31 AMc,A:Tarzan. 1,000.00
32 AMc,O:Owl Girl 1,100.00
33 AMc,A:Tarzan 900.00
34 AMc,same 900.00
35 AMc,same 900.00
36 AMc,same 900.00
37 AMc. 900.00
38 AMc. 900.00
39 AMc,I:Andy Panada 1,100.00
40 AMc,A:Owl(c) 750.00
41 AMc. 750.00
42 AMc. 750.00
43 AMc,Terry & The Pirates, A:Owl(c). 700.00

CRASH COMICS
Tem Publishing Co., May, 1940
1 S&K,O:Strongman, B:Blue Streak, Perfect Human, Shangra . . 6,000.00
2 S&K 3,000.00
3 S&K 2,400.00
4 S&K,O&I:Catman 6,000.00
5 S&K, Nov., 1940 . . . . 2,300.00

CRIME AND JUSTICE
Capitol Stories/ Charlton Comics 1951–55
1 . . . . 450.00
2 . . . . 250.00
3 . . . . 200.00
4 . . . . 200.00
5 . . . . 200.00
6 Negligee. 250.00
7 . . . . 200.00
8 . . . . 200.00
9 Comics vs. Crime story 350.00
10 . . . . 175.00

11 thru 13 Bondage . . . . @250.00
14 Woman Beheaded 300.00
15 Negligee 250.00
16 . . . . 200.00
17 . . . . 200.00
18 SD 350.00
19 thru 21 . . . . @200.00
Becomes:

BADGE OF JUSTICE
Charlton Comics, 1955
22 (1) 200.00
23 (2) 150.00
24 (3) 150.00
25 (4) 150.00
Revived as:

CRIME AND JUSTICE
Charlton Comics, 1955
23 thru 26 . . . . @150.00

CRIME AND PUNISHMENT
Lev Gleason Publications, April, 1948
1 CBi(c),Mr.Crime(c) 500.00
2 CBi(c) 250.00
3 CBi(c),BF 275.00
4 CBi(c),BF 200.00
5 CBi(c) 200.00
6 thru 10 CBi(c) . . . . @125.00
11 thru 15 CBi(c) . . . . @100.00
16 thru 27 CBi(c) . . . . @100.00
28 thru 38 . . . . @100.00
39 Drug issue 150.00
40 thru 44 . . . . @100.00
45 Drug issue 150.00
46 thru 58 . . . . @100.00
59 . . . . 350.00
60 thru 65 . . . . @100.00
66 ATh 550.00
67 Drug Storm 600.00
68 ATh(c) 400.00
69 Drug issue 150.00
74 Aug., 1955 . . . . 100.00

CRIME CLINIC
Approved Publ. (Ziff-Davis), 1951
1 (10) F:Dr. Tom Rogers 375.00
2 (11) 250.00
3 . . . . 250.00
4 . . . . 250.00
5 . . . . 250.00

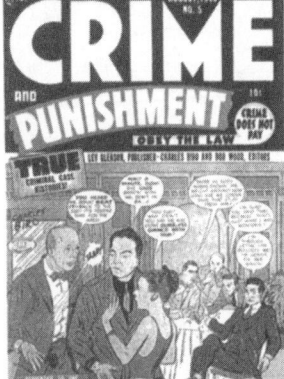

Crime & Punishment #5
© Lev Gleason

CRIME DETECTOR
Timor Publications, 1954
1 . . . . 300.00
2 . . . . 250.00
3 . . . . 200.00
4 . . . . 200.00
5 . . . . 250.00

CRIME DETECTIVE COMICS
Hillman Publications, March–April, 1948
1 BF(c),A:Invisible 6 . . . . 400.00
2 Jewel Robbery (c) 200.00
3 Stolen Cash (c) 175.00
4 Crime Boss Murder (c) 175.00
5 BK,Maestro (c) 175.00
6 AMc,Gorilla (c) 150.00
7 GMc,Wedding (c) 150.00
8 . . . . 150.00
9 Safe Robbery (c) (a classic) . . 500.00
10 BP 150.00
11 BP 150.00
12 BK 150.00
2-1 GT,Bluebird Captured 200.00
2-2 . . . . 150.00
2-3 . . . . 150.00
2-4 BK 175.00
2-5 . . . . 150.00
2-6 . . . . 150.00
2-7 BK,GMc 175.00
2-8 . . . . 150.00
2-9 . . . . 150.00
2-10 . . . . 150.00
2-11 . . . . 150.00
2-12 . . . . 150.00
3-1 Drug Story 150.00
3-2 thru 3-7 . . . . @150.00
3-8 May/June, 1953 . . . . 100.00

CRIME DOES NOT PAY
See: SILVER STREAK COMICS

CRIME-FIGHTING DETECTIVE
See: CRIMINALS ON THE RUN

CRIME FILES
Standard Comics, 1952
5 ATh 300.00
6 . . . . 200.00

CRIME ILLUSTRATED
E.C. Comics, Nov.–Dec., 1955
1 Grl,RC,GE,JO 350.00
2 Grl,RC,JCr,JDa,JO 250.00

CRIME INCORPORATED
Fox Features Syndicate, 1950
(Formerly: WESTERN THRILLERS; MY PAST CONFESSIONS)
1 (12) Crimes Incorporated 300.00
2 . . . . 225.00
3 . . . . 225.00

CRIME MUST PAY THE PENALTY
Ace Magazines, 1948–56
1 "True cases of actual crimes" . 550.00
2 Violent 350.00
3 . . . . 300.00
4 . . . . 300.00
5 . . . . 200.00
6 . . . . 200.00
7 . . . . 200.00
8 Transvestite 300.00

9 . . . . 150.00
10 . . . . 150.00
11 . . . . 150.00
12 . . . . 150.00
13 thru 19 . . . . @150.00
20 GC,Drugs 250.00
21 thru 32 . . . . @150.00
33 Drug story 225.00
34 thru 48 . . . . @150.00

CRIME MUST STOP
Hillman Periodicals, Oct., 1952
1 BK 1,100.00

CRIME MYSTERIES
Ribage Publishing Corp., May, 1952
1 Transvestism,Bondage(c) . . . 1,000.00
2 A:Manhunter, Lance Storm, Drug 750.00
3 FF-one page, A:Dr. Foo 500.00
4 HcK,A:Queenie Star, BondageStar 850.00
5 Claws of the Green Girl 450.00
6 . . . . 450.00

Crime Incorporated #12
© Fox Features

7 Sons of Satan 450.00
8 Death Stalks the Crown, Bondage(c) 450.00
9 You are the Murderer 375.00
10 The Hoax of the Death 375.00
11 The Strangler 375.00
12 Bondage(c) 450.00
13 AT,6 lives for one 500.00
14 Painted in Blood 375.00
15 Feast of the Dead,Acid Face . 650.00
Becomes:

SECRET MYSTERIES
Nov., 1954
16 Hiding Place,Horror 400.00
17 The Deadly Diamond,Horror . . 300.00
18 Horror 350.00
19 Horror,July, 1955 . . . . 350.00

INTERNATIONAL COMICS
E.C. Publ. Co., Spring, 1947
1 KS,I:Manhattan's Files 1,000.00
2 KS,A: Van Manhattan & Madelon 750.00
3 KS,same 600.00
4 KS,same 600.00
5 I:International Crime-Busting Patrol 600.00

GOLDEN AGE

Becomes:

INTERNATIONAL CRIME PATROL
Spring, 1948
6 A:Moon Girl & The Prince . . 1,000.00
Becomes:

CRIME PATROL
Summer, 1948
7 SMo,A:Capt. Crime Jr.,Field
  Marshall of Murder 1,200.00
8 JCr,State Prison (c) 1,000.00
9 AF,JCr,Bank Robbery 1,000.00
10 AF,JCr,Wanted:James Dore. 1,000.00
11 AF,JCr. 1,000.00
12 AF,Grl,JCr,Interrogation(c) . . 1,000.00
13 AF,JCr 1,000.00
14 AF,JCr,Smugglers (c) 1,000.00
15 AF,JCr,Crypt of Terror . . . 5,200.00
16 AF,JCr,Crypt of Terror 3,200.00
Becomes:

CRYPT OF TERROR
E.C. Comics, April, 1950
17 JCr(a&c),AF,'Werewolf
  Strikes Again' 4,800.00
18 JCr(a&c),AF,WW,HK
  'The Living Corpse' 3,000.00
19 JCr(a&c),AF,Grl,
  'Voodoo Drums' 2,900.00
Becomes:

TALES FROM THE CRYPT
Oct., 1950
20 JCr(a&c),AF,Gl,JKa
  'Day of Death'. 2,500.00
21 JCr(a&c),WW,HK,Gl,'Cooper
  Dies in the Electric Chair . . 2,000.00
22 AF, JCr(c). 1,700.00
23 AF(a&c),JCr,JDa,Grl
  'Locked in a Mausoleum' . . 1,200.00
24 AF(c),WW,JDa,JCr,Grl
  'Danger...Quicksand' 1,200.00
25 AF(c),WW,JDa,JKa,Grl
  'Mataud Waxworks' 1,200.00
26 WW(c),JDa,Grl,
  'Scared Graveyard'. 1,100.00
27 JKa, WW(c), Guillotine (c) . . 1,100.00
28 AF(c),JDa,JKa,Grl,JO
  'Buried Alive' 1,100.00
29 JDa(a&c),JKa,Grl,JO
  'Coffin Burier' 1,100.00
30 JDa(a&c),JO,JKa,Grl
  'Underwater Death' 1,100.00
31 JDa(a&c),JKa,Grl,AW
  'Hand Chopper' 1,200.00
32 JDa(a&c),GE,Grl,'Woman
  Crushed by Elephant' 1,200.00
33 JDa(a&c),GE,JKa,Grl,'Lower
  Berth',O:Crypt Keeper 1,200.00
34 JDa(a&c),JKa,GE,Grl,'Jack the
  Ripper,'RayBradbury adapt. 1,200.00
35 JDa(a&c),JKa,JO,Grl,
  'Werewolf'. 1,100.00
36 JDa(a&c),JKa,GE,Grl, Ray
  Bradbury adaptation 800.00
37 JDa(c),JO,BE 800.00
38 JDa(c),BE,RC,Grl,'Axe Man' . 800.00
39 JDa(c),JKa,JO,Grl,'Children
  in the Graveyard'. 800.00
40 JDa(a&c),GE,BK,Grl,
  'Underwater Monster' 1,200.00
41 JDa(a&c),JKa,GE,Grl,
  'Knife Thrower' 1,200.00
42 JDa(c),JO,Vampire (c) 1,200.00
43 JDa(c),JO,GE. 1,100.00
44 JO,RC,Guillotine (c). 1,100.00
45 JDa(a&c),JKa,BK,Gl,'Rat
  Takes Over His Life' 1,100.00
46 JDa(a&c),GE,JO,Gl,Werewolf
  man being hunted,Feb.'55 . 1,100.00

CRIME REPORTER
**St. John Publishing Co.,
Aug., 1948**
1 Death Makes a Deadline . . . 1,000.00
2 GT,MB(c),Matinee Murders . 1,100.00
3 GT,MB(c),Dec., 1948 . . . . . . 900.00

CRIMES BY WOMEN
**Fox Features Syndicate,
June, 1948**
1 Bonnie Parker 2,000.00
2 Vicious Female 1,300.00
3 Prison Break (c) 1,200.00
4 Murder (c) 1,200.00
5 . . . . 1,200.00
6 Girl Fight (c) 1,200.00
7 . . . . 900.00
8 . . . . 900.00
9 . . . . 900.00
10 Girl Fight (c) 800.00
11 . . . . 800.00
12 . . . . 800.00
13 ACME Jewelry Robbery (c) . . 800.00
14 Prison break (c) 800.00
15 Aug., 1951. . . . . 800.00

CRIME SMASHER
**Fawcett Publications,
Summer, 1948**
1 The Unlucky Rabbit's Foot . . . 700.00

CRIME SMASHERS
**Ribage Publishing Corp.,
Oct., 1950**
1 Girl Rape. 1,400.00
2 JKu,A:Sally the Sleuth, Dan
  Turner, Girl Friday, Rat Hale . 750.00
3 MFa 550.00
4 Zak(c) 550.00
5 WW 900.00
6 . . . . 450.00
7 Bondage (c),Drugs. 550.00
8 . . . . 450.00
9 Bondage (c). 550.00
10 . . . . 450.00
11 . . . . 450.00
12 FF, Eye Injury 550.00
13 . . . . 550.00
14 & 15. . . . . @450.00

CRIME ON THE WATERFRONT
See: FAMOUS GANGSTERS

CRIME SUSPENSTORIES
**L.L. Publishing Co.
(E.C. Comics), Oct.–Nov., 1950**
1a JCr,Grl 2,700.00
1 JCr,WW,Grl 2,000.00
2 JCr,JKa,Grl 1,400.00
3 JCr,WW,Grl,Poe Story 800.00
4 JCr,Gln,Grl,JDa 800.00
5 JCr,JKa,Grl,JDa. 800.00
6 JCr,JDa,Grl 700.00
7 JCr,Grl. 700.00
8 JCr,Grl 700.00
9 JCr,Grl 700.00
10 JCr,Grl. 700.00
11 JCr,Grl. 500.00
12 JCr,Grl. 500.00
13 JCr,AW 600.00
14 JCr 500.00
15 JCr,Old Witch 500.00
16 JCr,AW 600.00
17 JCr,FF,AW, Ray Bradbury. . . 800.00
18 JCr,RC,BE. 550.00
19 JCr,RC,GE,AF(c) 550.00
20 RC,JCr, Hanging (c) 600.00
21 JCr 500.00

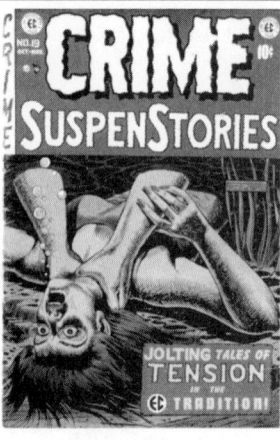

Crime SuspenseStories #19
© EC Comics

22 RC,JO,JCr(c),
  Severed head (c). 600.00
23 JKa,RC,GE 550.00
24 BK,RC,JO 500.00
25 JKa,(c),RC 600.00
26 JKa,(c),RC,JO. 700.00
27 JKa,(c),GE,Grl,March, 1955 . . 500.00

CRIMINALS ON THE RUN
**Premium Group of Comics,
Aug., 1948**
4-1 LbC(c) 500.00
4-2 LbC(c), A:Young King Cole . 400.00
4-3 LbC(c), Rip Roaring Action
  in Alps 400.00
4-4 LbC(c), Shark (c) 400.00
4-5 AMc 400.00
4-6 LbC,Dr. Doom 400.00
4-7 LbC 900.00
5-1 LbC 350.00
5-2 LbC 350.00
10 LbC 350.00
Becomes:

CRIME-FIGHTING DETECTIVE
April–May, 1950
11 LbC, Brodie Gang Captured . . 350.00
12 LbC(c), Jail Break Genius . . . 300.00
13 . . . . 250.00
14 LbC(c), A Night of Horror 300.00
15 LbC(c). 300.00
16 LbC(c), Wanton Murder 300.00
17 LbC(c), The Framer
  was Framed. 300.00
18 LbC(c), A Web of Evil 300.00
19 LbC(c), Lesson of the Law . . . 300.00
Becomes:

SHOCK DETECTIVE CASES
**Star Publications,
Sept., 1952**
20 LbC(c), The Strangler 400.00
21 LbC(c), Death Ride. 400.00
Becomes:

SPOOK DETECTIVE CASES
Star Publications, Jan., 1953
22 Headless Horror 500.00
Becomes:

SPOOK SUSPENSE AND MYSTERY

23 LbC,Weird Picture of Murder	350.00
24 LbC(c),Mummy's Case	400.00
25 LbC(c),Horror Beyond Door	350.00
26 LbC(c),JyD,Face of Death	350.00
27 LbC(c),JyD,Ship of the Dead	350.00
28 LbC(c),JyD,Creeping Death	350.00
29 LbC(c),JyD,Solo for Death	350.00
30 LbC(c),JyD,Nightmare, Oct.,1954	350.00

CROWN COMICS

Golfing/McCombs Publ., Winter 1944

1 Edgar Allen Poe adapt.	700.00
2 MB,I:Mickey Magic	500.00
3 MB,Jungle adventure (c)	500.00
4 MB(c),A:Voodah.	550.00
5 MB(c),Jungle Adventure (c)	550.00
6 MB(c),Jungle Adventure (c)	550.00
7 JKa,AF,MB(c),Race Car (c)	550.00
8 MB	500.00
9	300.00
10 Plane crash (c),A:Voodah	300.00
11 LSt,A:Voodah	250.00
12 LSt,AF,Master Marvin	250.00
13 LSt,AF,A:Voodah	250.00
14 A:Voodah	275.00
15 FBe,A:Voodah	250.00
16 FBe,A:Voodah,Jungle Adventure(c)	250.00
17 FBe,A:Voodah	250.00
18 FBe,A:Voodah	250.00
19 BP,A:Voodah,July, 1949	250.00

CRUSADER FROM MARS

Approved Publ. (Ziff-Davis), Jan.–March, 1952

1 Mission Thru Space, Death in the Sai	1,300.00
2 Beachhead on Saturn's Ring, Bondage(c),Fall, 1952	1,000.00

CRYIN' LION, THE

William H. Wise Co., Fall, 1944

1 Funny Animal	300.00
2 A. Hitler	200.00
3 Spring, 1945	150.00

CRYPT OF TERROR

See: CRIME PATROL

CURLY KAYOE COMICS

United Features Syndicate, 1946–50

1 Boxing	300.00
2	250.00
3 thru 8	@200.00
1a United Presents ..... (1948)	200.00

CYCLONE COMICS

Bibara Publ. Co., June, 1940

1 O:Tornado Tom	2,500.00
2	1,800.00
3	2,000.00
4 Voltron.	1,200.00
5 A:Mr. Q,Oct., 1940	1,600.00

DAFFY

Dell Publishing Co., March, 1953

(1) see Dell Four Color #457	
(2) see Dell Four Color #536	
(3) see Dell Four Color #615	
4 thru 7	@100.00
8 thru 11	@75.00

Cyclone Comics #4
© Bilbara Publ. Co.

12 thru 17	@60.00

Becomes:

DAFFY DUCK

July, 1959

18	60.00
19	60.00
20	60.00
21 thru 30	@60.00

DAFFY TUNES COMICS

Four Star Publications, 1947

12 Funny Animal	125.00

ALL GREAT COMICS

Fox Features Syndicate, Oct., 1947

12 A:Brenda Starr	1,200.00
13 JKa,O:Dagar, Desert Hawk	1,300.00

Becomes:

DAGAR, DESERT HAWK

Feb., 1948

14 JKa,Monster of Mura	1,400.00
15 JKa,Curse of the Lost Pharaoh,Bondage	900.00
16 JKa,Wretched Antmen	800.00
19 Pyramid of Doom	700.00
20	700.00
21 JKa(c),The Ghost of Fate, Bondage (c)	750.00
22	700.00
23 Bondage (c)	750.00

Becomes:

CAPTAIN KIDD

June, 1949

24 Blackbeard the Pirate	250.00
25 Sorceress of the Deep	250.00

Becomes:

MY SECRET STORY

Oct., 1949

26 He Wanted More Than Love.	250.00
27 My Husband Hated Me	200.00
28 I Become a Marked Women	200.00
29 My Forbidden Rapture, April, 1950	200.00

DAGWOOD

Harvey Publications, 1950

1	300.00
2	200.00
3	175.00
4	175.00

5	175.00
6 thru 10	@175.00
11 thru 20	@150.00
21 thru 30	@125.00
31 thru 50	@100.00
51 thru 70	@100.00
71 thru 109	@75.00
110 thru 140	@75.00

DAISY AND HER PUPS

Harvey Publications, 1951–1954

1 (21) F:Blondie & Dagwood's dog.	100.00
2 (22)	60.00
3 (23)	60.00
4 (24)	60.00
5 (25)	60.00
6 (26)	60.00
7 (27)	60.00
8 thru 18	@50.00

DAISY COMICS

Eastern Color Printing Co., 1936

N#	750.00

DAISY HANDBOOK

Daisy Manufacturing Co., 1946

1 Buck Rogers, Red Ryder.	475.00
2 Capt. Marvel	475.00
N# (1955)	400.00

DANDY COMICS

E.C. Comics 1947–48

1 Funny Animal.	475.00
2	325.00
3 thru 7	@250.00

DANGER

Comic Media, 1953–54

1 DH(c&a)	350.00
2 PMo	200.00
3 PMo	200.00
4 Marijuana (c) & story	250.00
5 PMo	200.00
6 Drug	250.00
7	200.00
8 Torture (c)	250.00
9 thru 11	200.00

Charlton Comics, 1955

12	150.00
13	125.00
14	125.00

Becomes:

JIM BOWIE

15	100.00
16	100.00
17	100.00
18	100.00
19 April, 1957.	100.00

DANGER AND ADVENTURE

See: THIS MAGAZINE IS HAUNTED

DANGER IS OUR BUSINESS

Toby Press/ I.W. Enterprises, 1953

1 AW,FF,Men Who Defy Death for a Living.	750.00
2 Death Crowds the Cockpit	300.00
3 Killer Mountain	250.00
4	250.00
5 thru 9	@200.00
10 June, 1955	250.00

DAN'L BOONE
Sussex Publ. Co. 1955–57
1 F:Dan'l Boone Greatest
  Frontiersman 200.00
2 . . . . 150.00
3 . . . . 100.00
4 thru 8 . . . . @100.00

DANNY BLAZE
Charlton Comics, 1955
1 . . . . 150.00
2 . . . . 125.00
Becomes:

NATURE BOY
3 JB,O:Blue Beetle 300.00
4 . . . . 125.00
5 Feb., 1957 . . . . 100.00

DAREDEVIL COMICS
**Lev Gleason Publications,
July, 1941**
1 Daredevil Battles Hitler, A:Silver
  Streak, Lance Hale, Dickey Dean,
  Cloud Curtis,V:The Claw,
  O:Hitler 25,000.00
2 I:The Pioneer, Champion of
  American,B:London,Pat
  Patriot,Pirate Prince 5,500.00
3 CBi(c),O:Thirteen 3,500.00
4 CBi(c),Death is the Referee . 3,000.00
5 CBi(c),I:Sniffer&Jinx, Claw
  V:Ghost,Lottery of Doom . . 2,700.00
6 CBi(c) 1,800.00
7 CBi(c), What Ghastly Sight Lies
  within the Mysterious Trunk 1,600.00
8 V:Nazis (c), E:Nightro 1,500.00
9 V:Double 1,500.00
10 America will Remember
  Pearl Harbor 1,500.00
11 Bondage (c), E:Pat
  Patriot, London 1,800.00
12 BW,CBi(c), O:The Law. 2,200.00
13 BW,I:Little Wise Guys 1,700.00
14 BW,CBi(c) 1,200.00
15 BW,CBi(c), D:Meatball 1,400.00
16 BW,CBi(c) 1,100.00
17 BW,CBi(c), Into the Valley
  of Death 1,100.00
18 BW,CBi(c), O:Daredevil,
  double length story 2,000.00
19 BW,CBi(c), Buried Alive 900.00
20 BW,CBi(c), Boxing (c) 900.00
21 CBi(c), Can Little Wise Guys
  Survive Blast of Dynamite? 1,500.00

Daredevil #37
© Lev Gleason Publications

22 CBi(c) 750.00
23 CBi(c), I:Pshyco 750.00
24 CBi(c), Punch and Judy
  Murders 750.00
25 CBi(c), Baseball (c) 750.00
26 CBi(c) 700.00
27 CBi(c), Bondage (c) 750.00
28 CBi(c) 700.00
29 CBi(c) 700.00
30 CBi(c), Ann Hubbard White
  1922-1943 . . . . 700.00
31 CBi(c), D:The Claw 1,400.00
32 V:Blackmarketeers 500.00
33 CBi(c) 500.00
34 CBi(c) 500.00
35 B:Two Daredevil stories
  every issue 550.00
36 CBi(c) 550.00
37 CBi(c) 550.00
38 CBi(c), O:Daredevil. 800.00
39 CBi(c) 500.00
40 CBi(c) 500.00
41 . . . . 500.00
42 thru 50 CBi(c) . . . . @500.00
51 CBi(c) 350.00
52 CBi(c),Football (c). 400.00
53 thru 57 . . . . @350.00
58 Football (c) 400.00
59 . . . . 350.00
60 . . . . 350.00
61 thru 68 . . . . @350.00
69 E:Daredevil 350.00
70 . . . . 250.00
71 thru 78 . . . . @150.00
79 B:Daredevil 250.00
80 . . . . 275.00
81 . . . . 150.00
82 . . . . 150.00
83 thru 99 . . . . @150.00
100 . . . . 175.00
101 thru 133 . . . . @150.00
134 Sept., 1956 . . . . 150.00

DARING LOVE
Gilmore Magazines, 1953
1 SD,1st work 1,200.00

DARK MYSTERIES
**Merit Publications,
June–July, 1951**
1 WW(a&c), Curse of the
  Sea Witch 1,800.00
2 WW(a&c), Vampire Fangs
  of Doom 1,200.00
3 Terror of the Unwilling
  Witch 800.00
4 Corpse that Came Alive 800.00
5 Horror of the Ghostly Crew . . . 650.00
6 If the Noose Fits Wear It! 650.00
7 Terror of the Cards of Death . . 650.00
8 Terror of the Ghostly Trail 650.00
9 Witch's Feast at Dawn 650.00
10 Terror of the Burning Witch. . 650.00
11 The River of Blood 600.00
12 Horror of the Talking Dead . . 600.00
13 Terror of the Hungry Cats . . . 600.00
14 Horror of the Fingers of Doom 650.00
15 Terror of the Vampires Teeth. . 550.00
16 Horror of the Walking Dead . . 550.00
17 Terror of the Mask of Death . . 550.00
18 Terror of the Burning Corpse . 550.00
19 The Rack of Terror 750.00
20 Burning Executioner 650.00
21 The Sinister Secret 500.00
22 The Hand of Destiny. 500.00
23 The Mardenburg Curse. 350.00
24 Give A Man Enough Rope,
  July, 1955 . . . . 350.00

DARK SHADOWS
**Steinway Publications/Ajax
1957–58**
1 . . . . 350.00
2 and 3 . . . . @300.00

DATE WITH DANGER
**Visual Editions
(Standard Comics), 1952**
5 Secret Agent 150.00
6 Atom Bomb 175.00

DAVY CROCKETT
Avon Periodicals, 1951
1 . . . . 250.00

FRONTIER FIGHTER
Charlton Comics, 1955
1 JK,Davy Crocket-Buffalo Bill . . 150.00
2 JK. 100.00
Becomes:

DAVY CROCKETT
Charlton Comics, 1956
3 thru 7 JK. . . . . @100.00
8 Jan., 1957 JK. 90.00
Becomes:

KID MONTANA

DEAD END
CRIME STORIES
**Kirby Publishing Co.,
April, 1949**
N# BP 750.00

DEAD-EYE
WESTERN COMICS
**Hillman Periodicals
Nov.–Dec., 1948**
1 BK 300.00
2 . . . . 250.00
3 . . . . 200.00
4 thru 12 . . . . @150.00
2-1 . . . . 125.00
2-2 . . . . 125.00
2-3 . . . . 150.00
2-4 . . . . 150.00
2-5 thru 2-12 . . . . @125.00
3-1 . . . . 125.00

DEADWOOD GULCH
Dell Publishing Co., 1931
1 . . . . 750.00

DEAR BEATRICE
FAIRFAX
**Best Books
(Standard Comics), Nov., 1950**
5 AsH(c) 200.00
6 thru 9 AsH(c) . . . . @125.00

DEATH VALLEY
**Comic Media/
Charlton Comics, 1953**
1 Cowboys & Indians 200.00
2 DH(c) 150.00
3 PMo 125.00
4 . . . . 125.00
5 PMo 125.00
6 . . . . 125.00
7 . . . . 125.00
8 BW 125.00
9 . . . . 125.00
Becomes:

GOLDEN AGE

Desperado #1 (1948)
© Lev Gleason

FRONTIER SCOUT
DANIEL BOONE
Charlton Comics
10 . . . . 150.00
11 thru 13 . . . . @100.00

DEBBIE DEAN,
CAREER GIRL
Civil Service Publishing,
April, 1945
1 . . . . 250.00
2 . . . . 200.00

DELL GIANT EDITIONS
Dell Publishing Co.,
1952-58
Abe Lincoln Life Story 175.00
Cadet Gray of West Point 175.00
Golden West Rodeo Treasury . . . 200.00
Life Stories of
   American Presidents 175.00
Lone Ranger Golden West 400.00
Lone Ranger Movie Story 850.00
Lone Ranger Western
   Treasury('53) 400.00
Lone Ranger Western
   Treasury('54) 500.00
Moses & Ten Commandments. . . 150.00
Nancy & Sluggo Travel Time 200.00
Pogo Parade 700.00
Raggedy Ann & Andy 350.00
Santa Claus Funnies 200.00
Tarzan's Jungle Annual #1 . . . . . . 350.00
Tarzan's Jungle Annual #2 . . . . . . 225.00
Tarzan's Jungle Annual #3 . . . . . . 200.00
Tarzan's Jungle Annual #4 . . . . . . 200.00
Tarzan's Jungle Annual #5 . . . . . . 200.00
Tarzan's Jungle Annual #6 . . . . . . 200.00
Tarzan's Jungle Annual #7 . . . . . . 200.00
Treasury of Dogs 160.00
Treasury of Horses 160.00
Universal Presents-Dracula-
   The Mummy & Other Stories. 500.00
Western Roundup #1 . . . . 600.00
Western Roundup #2 . . . . 350.00
Western Roundup #3 . . . . 275.00
Western Roundup #4 thru #5. . @250.00
Western Roundup #6 thru #10. @250.00
Western Roundup #11 thru #17 @225.00
Western Roundup #18 . . . . 225.00
Western Roundup #19 thru #25 @180.00
Woody Woodpecker Back
   to School #1 (1952). 250.00

Woody Woodpecker Back
   to School #2 (1953). 225.00
Woody Woodpecker Back
   to School #3 (1954). 225.00
Woody Woodpecker Back
   to School #4 (1955). 225.00
Woody Woodpecker County
   Fair #5 (1956) 225.00
Woody Woodpecker Back
   to School #6 (1957). 200.00
Woody Woodpecker County
   Fair #2 (1958) 200.00
Also See: Bugs Bunny; Marge's Little
Lulu; Tom and Jerry, and Walt Disney
Dell Giant Editions

DELL GIANT COMICS
Dell Publishing Co.,
Sept., 1959
21 M.G.M. Tom & Jerry
   Picnic Time 250.00
22 W.Disney's Huey, Dewey & Louie
   Back to School (Oct 1959) . . 400.00
23 Marge's Little Lulu &
   Tubby Halloween Fun 350.00
24 Woody Woodpeckers
   Family Fun. 250.00
25 Tarzan's Jungle World. 250.00
26 W.Disney's Christmas
   Parade,CB 550.00
27 W.Disney's Man in
   Space (1960). 250.00
28 Bugs Bunny's Winter Fun . . . 250.00
29 Marge's Little Lulu &
   Tubby in Hawaii. 325.00
30 W.Disney's DisneylandU.S.A.. 300.00
31 Huckleberry Hound
   Summer Fun 300.00
32 Bugs Bunny Beach Party 250.00
33 W.Disney's Daisy Duck &
   Uncle Scrooge Picnic Time. . 300.00
34 Nancy&SluggoSummerCamp. 200.00
35 W.Disney's Huey, Dewey &
   Louie Back to School 350.00
36 Marge's Little Lulu & Witch
   Hazel Halloween Fun 300.00
37 Tarzan, King of the Jungle . . . 250.00
38 W.Disney's Uncle Donald and
   his Nephews Family Fun . . . 350.00
39 W.Disney's Merry Christmas. . 350.00
40 Woody Woodpecker
   Christmas Parade 200.00
41 Yogi Bear's Winter Sports. . . . 300.00
42 Marge's Little Lulu &
   Tubby in Australia 375.00
43 Mighty Mouse in OuterSpace . 500.00
44 Around the World with
   Huckleberry & His Friends . . 350.00
45 Nancy&SluggoSummerCamp. 150.00
46 Bugs Bunny Beach Party 175.00
47 W.Disney's Mickey and
   Donald in Vacationland 250.00
48 The Flintstones #1
   (Bedrock Bedlam) 500.00
49 W.Disney's Huey, Dewey &
   Louie Back to School 325.00
50 Marge's Little Lulu &
   Witch Hazel Trick 'N' Treat . . 325.00
51 Tarzan, King of the Jungle . . . 200.00
52 W.Disney's Uncle Donald &
   his Nephews Dude Ranch . . 350.00
53 W.Disney's Donald Duck
   Merry Christmas 300.00
54 Woody Woodpecker
   Christmas Party. 225.00
55 W.Disney's Daisy Duck & Uncle
   Scrooge Show Boat (1961). . 250.00

DELL JUNIOR TREASURY
Dell Publishing Co.,
June, 1955
1 Alice in Wonderland 175.00
2 Aladdin 125.00
3 Gulliver's Travels 100.00
4 Adventures of Mr. Frog 125.00
5 Wizard of Oz 125.00
6 Heidi 135.00
7 Santa & the Angel 135.00
8 Raggedy Ann 135.00
9 Clementina the Flying Pig . . . 125.00
10 Adventures of Tom Sawyer. . . 125.00

DENNIS THE MENACE
Visual Editions/Literary Ent.
(Standard, Pines), Aug., 1953
1 . . . . 1,200.00
2 . . . . 500.00
3 . . . . 300.00
4 . . . . 300.00
5 thru 10 . . . . @200.00
11 thru 20 . . . . @175.00
21 thru 31 . . . . @150.00
Hallden (Fawcett Publications)
32 thru 40 . . . . @100.00
41 thru 50 . . . . @100.00
51 thru 60 . . . . @75.00
61 thru 70 . . . . @75.00
71 thru 90 . . . . @75.00
91 thru 140 . . . . @40.00
141 thru 166 . . . . @25.00

DESPERADO
Lev Gleason Publications,
June, 1948
1 CBi(c) 250.00
2 CBi(c) 150.00
3 CBi(c) 200.00
4 CBi(c) 100.00
5 CBi(c) 100.00
6 CBi(c) 100.00
7 CBi(c) 100.00
8 CBi(c) 100.00
Becomes:

BLACK DIAMOND
WESTERN
March, 1949
9 CBi(c) 300.00
10 CBi(c) 200.00
11 CBi(c) 150.00
12 CBi(c) 150.00

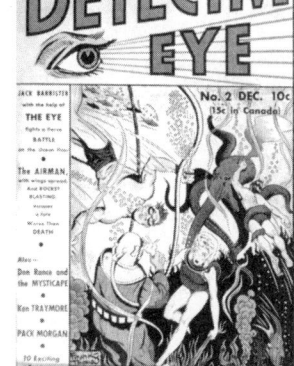

Detective Eye #2
© Centaur Publications

GOLDEN AGE

GOLDEN AGE

13 CBi(c) 150.00
14 CBi(c) 150.00
15 CBi(c) 150.00
16 thru 28 BW,Big Bang Buster @150.00
29 thru 40. . . . . @175.00
41 thru 50. . . . . @125.00
51 thru 52 3-D Luse . . . . @250.00
53 thru 60 . . . . @100.00

DETECTIVE DAN, SECRET OP, 48
Humor Publ. Co., 1933
N# 10"x13", 36 pg. b&w 25,000.00

DETECTIVE EYE
Centaur Publications, Nov., 1940
1 B:Air Man, The Eye Sees,
  A:Masked Marvel 3,500.00
2 O:Don Rance, Mysticape,
  Dec., 1940 . . . . 2,500.00

DETECTIVE PICTURE STORIES
Comics Magazine Co., Dec., 1936
1 The Phantom Killer 6,500.00
2 The Clock 3,000.00
3 . . . . 2,000.00
4 WE, Muss Em Up 2,000.00
5 Trouble, April, 1937. . . . . 2,200.00

DEVIL DOGS
Street & Smith Publ., 1942
1 U.S. Marines 500.00

DEXTER COMICS
Dearfield Publications, Summer, 1948–July, 1949
1 Teen Age 150.00
2 Sunie Prom 125.00
3 thru 5 . . . . @100.00

DICK COLE
Curtis Publ./ Star Publications, Dec.–Jan., 1949
1 LbC(a&c),CS,All sports(c) 500.00
2 LbC 250.00
3 LbC(a&c) 275.00
4 LbC(a&c),Rowing (c) 275.00
5 LbC(a&c) 275.00
6 LbC(a&c), Rodeo (c) 275.00
7 LbC(a&c) 250.00
8 LbC(a&c), Football (c) 250.00
9 LbC(a&c), Basketball (c) 250.00
10 Joe Louis 300.00
Becomes:

SPORTS THRILLS
Nov., 1950–Nov., 1951
11 Ted Williams & Ty Cobb 500.00
12 LbC, Joe DiMaggio & Phil
  Rizzuto, Boxing (c) 450.00
13 LbC(c),Basketball (c) 350.00
14 LbC(c),Baseball (c). 375.00
15 LbC(c),Baseball (c). 375.00

DICKIE DARE
Eastern Color Printing Co., 1941–42
1 BEv(c),M.Caniff 1,000.00
2 . . . . 500.00
3 . . . . 500.00
4 H. Scorcery Smith 550.00

Dick Tracy Comics Monthly #38
© Harvey Publ. Co.

DICK TRACY MONTHLY
Dell Publishing Co., Jan., 1948
1 ChG,AAv,Dick Tracy & the Mad
  Doctor'. 800.00
2 ChG,A:MarySteele,BorisArson 450.00
3 ChG,A:Spaldoni,Big Boy 450.00
4 ChG,A:Alderman Zeld 450.00
5 ChG,A:Spaldoni,Mrs.Spaldoni . 375.00
6 ChG,A:Steve the Tramp 375.00
7 ChG,A:Boris Arson,Mary
  Steele 375.00
8 ChG,A:Boris & Zora Arson . . . 375.00
9 ChG,A:Chief Yellowpony 375.00
10 ChG,A:Cutie Diamond. 375.00
11 ChG,A:Toby Townly,
  Bookie Joe. 325.00
12 ChG,A:Toby Townly,
  Bookie Joe. 325.00
13 ChG,A:Toby Townly, Blake . . . 350.00
14 ChG,A:Mayor Waite Wright. . . 300.00
15 ChG,A:Bowman Basil 300.00
16 ChG,A:Maw,'Muscle'
  & 'Cut' Famon 300.00
17 ChG,A:Jim Trailer,
  Mary Steele 300.00
18 ChG,A:Lips Manlis,
  Anthel Jones 300.00
19 I:Sparkle Plenty. 350.00
20 'Black Cat Mystery' 300.00
21 'Tracy Meets Number One'. . . 300.00
22 'Tracy and the Alibi Maker' . . . 275.00
23 'Dick Tracy Meets Jukebox' . . 275.00
24 'Dick Tracy and Bubbles' 275.00
Becomes:

DICK TRACY COMICS MONTHLY
Harvey, May, 1950
25 ChG,A:Flattop 300.00
26 ChG,A:Vitamin Flintheart. 200.00
27 ChG,'Flattop Escapes Prision' 200.00
28 ChG,'Case of the Torture
  Chamber'. 200.00
29 ChG,A:Brow,Gravel Gertie . . . 250.00
30 ChG,'Blackmail Racket'. 200.00
31 ChG,A:Snowflake Falls 175.00
32 ChG,A:Shaky,Snowflake Falls 175.00
33 ChG,'Strange Case
  of Measles' 225.00
34 ChG,A:Measles,Paprika 200.00
35 ChG,'Case of Stolen $50,000'. 200.00
36 ChG,'Case of the
  Runaway Blonde' 225.00

37 ChG,'Case of Stolen Money'. . 200.00
38 ChG,A:Breathless Mahoney . . 200.00
39 ChG,A:Itchy,B.O.Plenty 200.00
40 ChG,'Case of Atomic Killer'. . . 200.00
41 ChG,Pt.1'Murder by Mail' 175.00
42 ChG,Pt.2'Murder by Mail' 175.00
43 ChG,'Case of the
  Underworld Brat' 175.00
44 ChG,'Case of the Mouthwash
  Murder' 175.00
45 ChG,'Case of the Evil Eyes' . . 175.00
46 ChG,'Case of the
  Camera Killers' 175.00
47 ChG,'Case of the
  Bloodthirsty Blonde'. 175.00
48 ChG,'Case of the
  Murderous Minstrol'. 175.00
49 ChG,Pt.1 'Killer Who Returned
  From the Dead 175.00
50 ChG,Pt.2 'Killer Who
  Returned From the Dead' . . . 175.00
51 ChG, 'Case of the
  High Tension Hijackers'. 150.00
52 ChG, 'Case of the
  Pipe-Stem Killer. 150.00
53 ChG,Pt.1 'Dick Tracy Meets
  the Murderous Midget'. 150.00
54 ChG,Pt.2 'Dick Tracy Meets
  the Murderous Midget'. 150.00
55 ChG,Pt.3 'Dick Tracy Meets
  the Murderous Midget' 150.00
56 ChG,'Case of the
  Teleguard Terror'. 150.00
57 ChG,Pt.1 'Case of the
  Ice Cold Killer'. 175.00
58 ChG,Pt.2 'Case of the
  Ice Cold Killer' 150.00
59 ChG,Pt.1 'Case of the
  Million Dollar Murder' 150.00
60 ChG,Pt.2 'Case of the
  Million Dollar Murder' 150.00
61 ChG,'Case of the
  Murderers Mask' 150.00
62 ChG,Pt.1 'Case of the
  White Rat Robbers'. 150.00
63 ChG,Pt.2 'Case of the
  White Rat Robbers'. 150.00
64 ChG,Pt.1 'Case of the
  Interrupted Honeymoon' 150.00
65 ChG,Pt.2 'Case of the
  Interrupted Honeymoon' 150.00
66 ChG,Pt.1 'Case of the
  Killer's Revenge' 150.00
67 ChG,Pt.2 'Case of the
  Killer's Revenge' 150.00
68 ChG,Pt.1'Case o/t TV Terror' . 150.00
69 ChG,Pt.2'Case o/t TV Terror' . 150.00
70 ChG,Pt.3'Case o/t TV Terror' . 135.00
71 ChG,A:Mrs. Forchune,Opal. . . 135.00
72 ChG,A:Empty Wiliams,Bonny . 135.00
73 ChG,A:Bonny Braids. 135.00
74 ChG,A:Mr. & Mrs.
  Fortson Knox. 135.00
75 ChG,A:Crewy Lou, Sphinx . . . 135.00
76 ChG,A:Diet Smith,Brainerd . . . 135.00
77 ChG,A:Crewy Lou,
  Bonny Braids. 135.00
78 ChG,A:Spinner Records 135.00
79 ChG,A:Model Jones,
  Larry Jones 135.00
80 ChG,A:Tonsils,Dot View 135.00
81 ChG,A:Edward Moppet,Tonsils 135.00
82 ChG,A:Dot View,Mr. Crime . . . 135.00
83 ChG,A:RifleRuby,NewsuitNan. 135.00
84 ChG,A:Mr.Crime,NewsuitNan . 135.00
85 ChG,A:NewsuitNan, Mrs.Lava 135.00
86 ChG,A:Mr. Crime,Odds Zonn . 135.00
87 ChG,A:Odds Zonn,Wingy . . . 135.00
88 ChG,A:Odds Zonn,Wingy 135.00
89 ChG,Pt.1'Canhead' 135.00
90 ChG,Pt.2'Canhead' 135.00
91 ChG,Pt.3'Canhead' 135.00

92 ChG,Pt.4'Canhead' 135.00
93 ChG,Pt.5'Canhead' 135.00
94 ChG,Pt.6'Canhead' 135.00
95 ChG,A:Mrs. Green,Dewdrop . . 135.00
96 ChG,A:Dewdrop,Sticks 135.00
97 ChG,A:Dewdrop,Sticks 135.00
98 ChG,A:Open-Mind Monty,
Sticks 135.00
99 ChG,A:Open-Mind Monty,
Sticks 150.00
100 ChG,A:Half-Pint,Dewdrop . . . 175.00
101 ChG,A:Open-Mind Monty . . . 150.00
102 ChG,A:Rainbow Reiley,
Wingy. 150.00
103 ChG,A:Happy,Rughead. 150.00
104 ChG,A:Rainbow Reiley,
Happy 150.00
105 ChG,A:Happy,Rughead. 150.00
106 ChG,A:Fence,Corny,Happy . . 150.00
107 ChG,A:Rainbow Reiley 150.00
108 ChG,A:Rughead,Corny,
Fence. 150.00
109 ChG,A:Rughead,Mimi,Herky. 150.00
110 ChG,A:Vitamin Flintheart. . . . 150.00
111 ChG,A:Shoulders,Roach . . . 150.00
112 ChG,A:Brilliant,Diet Smith . . . 150.00
113 ChG,A:Snowflake Falls 150.00
114 ChG,A:'Sketch'Paree, ... 150.00
115 ChG,A:Rod & Nylon Hoze . . . 150.00
116 ChG,A:Empty Williams 150.00
117 ChG,A:Spinner Records 150.00
118 ChG,A:Sleet. 150.00
119 ChG,A:Coffyhead 150.00
120 ChG,'Case Against
Mumbles Quartet' 150.00
121 ChG,'Case of the Wild Boys'. 150.00
122 ChG,'Case of the
Poisoned Pellet'. 150.00
123 ChG,'Case of the Deadly
Treasure Hunt'. 150.00
124 ChG,'Case of Oodles
Hears Only Evil'. 150.00
125 ChG,'Case of the Desparate
Widow' 150.00
126 ChG,'Case of Oodles'
Hideout'. 150.00
127 ChG,'Case Against
Joe Period' 150.00
128 ChG,'Case Against Juvenile
Delinquent'. 150.00
129 ChG,'Case of Son of Flattop' 150.00
130 ChG,'Case of Great
Gang Roundup' 150.00
131 ChG,'Strange Case of
Flattop's Conscience' 150.00

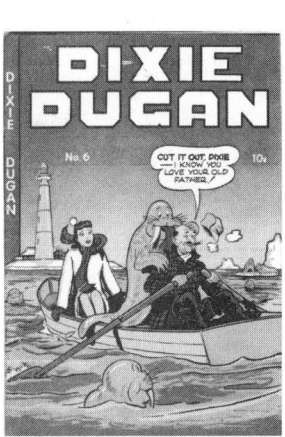

Dixie Dugan #6
© Columbia Publ./Publication

132 ChG,'Case of Flattop's
Big Show' 150.00
133 ChG,'Dick Tracy Follows Trail
of Jewel Thief Gang' 150.00
134 ChG,'Last Stand of
Jewel Thieves'. 150.00
135 ChG,'Case of the
Rooftop Sniper' 150.00
136 ChG,'Mystery of the
Iron Room'. 150.00
137 ChG,'Law Versus Dick Tracy' 150.00
138 ChG,'Mystery of Mary X' . . . 150.00
139 ChG,'Yogee the Merciless' . . 150.00
140 ChG,'The Tunnel Trap' 150.00
141 ChG,'Case of Wormy &
His Deadly Wagon' 150.00
142 ChG,'Case of the
Killer's Revenge' 150.00
143 ChG,'Strange Case of
Measles' 150.00
144 ChG,'Strange Case of
Shoulders' 150.00
145 ChG,'Case of the Fiendish
Photographers'; April, 1961. . 150.00

DICK WINGATE
OF THE U.S. NAVY
Superior Publ./
Toby Press, 1951
N# 200.00
N# reprint. 150.00

DIME COMICS
Newsbook Publ. Corp., 1945
1 LbC,A:Silver Streak 1,300.00

DING DONG
Compix
(Magazine Enterprises), 1947
1 (fa). 300.00
2 (fa). 150.00
3 thru 5 (fa) . . . . @100.00

DINKY DUCK
St. John Publ. Co./Pines,
Nov., 1951
1 . . . . 150.00
2 . . . . 125.00
3 thru 10 . . . . @100.00
11 thru 15 . . . . @100.00
16 thru 18. . . . . @75.00
19 Summer, 1958 . . . . 75.00

DIXIE DUGAN
Publication Enterprises,
July, 1942
1 Boxing (c),Joe Palooka 500.00
2 . . . . 250.00
3 . . . . 175.00
4 . . . . 150.00
5 . . . . @150.00
6 thru 12 . . . . @100.00
13 1949 . . . . 100.00

DIZZY DON COMICS
Howard Publications/
Dizzy Dean Ent., 1943
1 B&W interior. 300.00
2 B&W Interior 150.00
3 B&W Interior 125.00
4 B&W Interior 125.00
5 thru 21 . . . . @125.00
22 Oct., 1946. . . . . 275.00
1a thru 3a. . . . . @300.00

DOC CARTER
V.D. COMICS
Health Publ. Inst., 1949
N# 350.00
N# 250.00

Doc Savage Vol. #5
© Street & Smith Publications

DOC SAVAGE COMICS
Street & Smith Publ., May, 1940
1 B:Doc Savage, Capt. Fury, Danny
Garrett, Mark Mallory, Whisperer,
Capt. Death, Treasure
Island, A: The Magician . . . 9,000.00
2 O:Ajax,The Sun Man,E:The
Whisperer. 3,200.00
3 Artic Ice Wastes 2,000.00
4 E:Treasure Island, Saves
U.S. Navy 1,600.00
5 O:Astron, the Crocodile
Queen, Sacred Ruby 1,500.00
6 E: Capt. Fury, O:Red Falcon,
Murderous Peace Clan . . 1,000.00
7 V:Zoombas 1,000.00
8 Finds the Long Lost Treasure1,000.00
9 Smashes Japan's Secret Oil
Supply. 1,000.00
10 O:Thunder Bolt, The Living
Dead A:Lord Manhattan . . . 1,000.00
11 V:Giants of Destruction 800.00
12 Saves Merchant Fleet from
Complete Destruction 800.00
2-1 The Living Evil 800.00
2-2 V:Beggar King 800.00
2-3 . . . . 800.00
2-4 Fight to Death 800.00
2-5 Saves Panama Canal from
Blood Raider 800.00
2-6 . . . . 800.00
2-7 V:Black Knight 800.00
2-8 Oct., 1943 . . . . 800.00

DR. ANTHONY KING
HOLLYWOOD LOVE
DOCTOR
Harvey, Publ., 1952
1 . . . . 250.00
2 . . . . 200.00
3 . . . . 200.00
4 BP,May, 1954. . . . . 200.00

DO-DO
Nationwide Publishers, 1950
1 Funny Animal Circus Humor	300.00
2	150.00
3	150.00
4	150.00
5 thru 7	@150.00

DOLL MAN
**Comic Favorites
(Quality Comics Group),
Fall, 1941–Oct., 1953**
1 RC,B:Doll Man & Justine Wright	6,000.00
2 B:Dragon	2,200.00
3 Five stories	1,400.00
4 Dolls of Death, Wanted: The Doll Man	1,300.00
5 RC,Four stories	1,200.00
6 Buy War Stamps (c)	900.00
7 Four stories	900.00
8 BWa,Three stories,A:Torchy	2,500.00
9 Torchy	900.00
10 RC,V:Murder Marionettes, Grim, The Good Sport	750.00
11 Shocks Crime Square in the Eye	750.00
12 Torchy	750.00
13 RC,Blows Crime Sky High	750.00
14 Spotlight on Comics	750.00
15 Faces Danger	750.00
16 Torchy	600.00
17 Deals Out Punishment for Crime	600.00
18 Redskins Scalp Crime	600.00
19 Fitted for a Cement Coffin	600.00
20 Destroys the Black Heart of Nemo Black	600.00
21 Problem of a Poison Pistol	500.00
22 V:Tom Thumb	500.00
23 V:Minstrel, Musician of Menace	500.00
24 V:Elixir of Youth	500.00
25 V:Thrawn, Lord of Lightning	500.00
26 V:Sultan of Satarr & Wonderous Runt	500.00
27 Space Conquest	500.00
28 V:The Flame	500.00
29 V:Queen MAB	500.00
30 V:Lord Damion	500.00
31 I:Elmo, the Wonder Dog	450.00
32 A:Jeb Rivers	450.00
33 & 34	@450.00
35 Prophet of Doom	450.00
36 Death Trap in the Deep	450.00
37 V:The Skull,B:Doll Girl, Bondage(c)	700.00
38 The Cult of Death	400.00
39 V:The Death Drug, Narcotics	400.00
40 Giants of Crime	400.00
41 The Headless Horseman	300.00
42 Tale of the Mind Monster	300.00
43 The Thing that Kills	300.00
44 V:Radioactive Man	300.00
45 What was in the Doom Box?	300.00
46 Monster from Tomorrow	300.00
47 V:Mad Hypnotist	300.00

FAMOUS GANG, BOOK OF COMICS
Firestone Tire & Rubber Co., 1942
N# Porky Pig,Bugs Bunny	1,200.00

Becomes:

DONALD AND MICKEY MERRY CHRISTMAS
N# (2),CB, 1943	1,200.00
N# (3),CB, 1944	1,100.00
N# (4),CB, 1945	1,700.00

N# (5),CB, 1946	1,200.00
N# (6),CB, 1947	1,200.00
N# (7),CB, 1948	1,200.00
N# (8),CB, 1949	1,100.00

DONALD DUCK
Whitman
W.Disney's Donald Duck ('35)	6,000.00
W.Disney's Donald Duck ('36)	5,000.00
W.Disney's Donald Duck ('38)	5,000.00

DONALD DUCK GIVEAWAYS
Donald Duck Surprise Party (Icy Frost Ice Cream 1948)WK	4,000.00
Donald Duck (Xmas Giveaway 1944)	1,500.00
Donald Duck Tells About Kites (P.G.&E., Florida 1954)	4,000.00
Donald Duck Tells About Kites (S.C.Edison 1954)	3,500.00
Donald Duck and the Boys (Whitman 1948)	1,200.00
Donald Ducks Atom Bomb (Cherrios 1947)	1,200.00

(WALT DISNEY'S) DONALD DUCK
Dell Publishing Co., Nov., 1952
(#1-#25) See *Dell Four Color*	
26 CB;"Trick or Treat" (1952)	800.00
27 CB(c);"Flying Horse"('53)	300.00
28 CB(c); Robert the Robot	250.00
29 CB(c)	250.00
30 CB(c)	250.00
31 thru 39	@200.00
40	150.00
41	150.00
42	150.00
43	150.00
44	150.00
45 CB	400.00
46 CB; "Secret of Hondorica"	500.00
47 thru 51	@200.00
52 CB; "Lost Peg-Leg Mine"	400.00
53	200.00
54 CB; "Forbidden Valley"	500.00
55 thru 59	@150.00
60 CB; "Donald Duck & the Titanic Ants"	400.00
61 thru 67	@150.00
68 CB	225.00

*Donald and Mickey Merry Christmas
N# (#6) © Firestone*

69 thru 78	@150.00
79 CB (1 page)	200.00
80	125.00
81 CB (1 page)	150.00
82	125.00
83	125.00
84	125.00

DON FORTUNE MAGAZINE
Don Fortune Publ. Co., Aug., 1946
1 CCB	400.00
2 CCB	225.00
3 CCB,Bondage(c)	200.00
4 CCB	150.00
5 CCB	150.00
6 CCB, Jan., 1947	150.00

DON NEWCOMBE
Fawcett Publications, 1950
1 Baseball Star	650.00

DON WINSLOW OF THE NAVY
Fawcett Publ./ Charlton Comics, Feb., 1943
1 Captain Marvel (c)	2,000.00
2 Nips the Nipponese in the Solomons	850.00
3 Single-Handed invasion of the Philippines	600.00
4 Undermines the Nazis!	500.00
5 Stolen Battleship Mystery	500.00
6 War Stamps for Victory,Flag(c)	500.00
7 Coast Guard	400.00
8 U.S. Marines	400.00
9 Fighting Marines	400.00
10 Fighting Seabees	400.00
11	350.00
12 Tuned for Death	350.00
13 Hirohito's Hospitality	350.00
14 Catapults against the Axis	350.00
15 Fighting Merchant Marine	300.00
16 V:The Most Diabolical Villain of all Time	300.00
17 Buy War Stamps (c)	300.00
18 The First Underwater Convoy	300.00
19 Bonape Excersion	300.00
20 The Nazi Prison Ship	300.00
21 Prisoner of the Nazis	225.00
22 Suicide Football	225.00
23 Peril on the High Seas	225.00
24 Adventures on the High Seas	225.00
25 Shanghaied Red Cross Ship	225.00
26 V:The Scorpion	225.00
27 Buy War Stamps	225.00
28	225.00
29 Invitation to Trouble	225.00
30	225.00
31 Man or Myth?	175.00
32 Return of the Renegade	175.00
33 Service Ribbons	175.00
34 Log Book	175.00
35	175.00
36 V:Octopus	175.00
37 V: Sea Serpent	175.00
38 Climbs Mt. Everest	175.00
39 Scorpion's Death Ledger	175.00
40 Kick Off!	175.00
41 Rides the Skis!	150.00
42 Amazon Island	150.00
43 Ghastly Doll Murder Case	150.00
44 The Scorpions Web	150.00
45 V:Highwaymen of the Seas	150.00
46 Renegades Jailbreak	150.00
47 The Artic Expedition	150.00
48 Maelstrom of the Deep	150.00
49 The Vanishing Ship!	150.00
50 V:The Snake	150.00

51 A:Singapore Sal 150.00
52 Ghost of the Fishing Ships . . . 150.00
53 . . . . 150.00
54 . . . . 150.00
55 . . . . 150.00
56 Far East 150.00
57 A:Singapore Sal 150.00
58 thru 63 . . . . @150.00
64 MB 150.00
65 Ph(c),Flying Saucer 250.00
66 Ph(c) 225.00
67 Ph(c) 225.00
68 Ph(c) 225.00
69 Ph(c), Jaws of Destruction . . . 225.00
70 . . . . 125.00
71 . . . . 125.00
72 . . . . 125.00
73 Sept., 1955 . . . . 125.00

DOROTHY LAMOUR
See: JUNGLE LIL

DOUBLE COMICS
Elliot Publications
1 ('40),Masked Marvel 4,000.00
2 ('41),Tornado Tim 3,000.00
3 ('42) 2,500.00
4 ('43) 2,000.00
5 ('44) 2,000.00

DOUBLE TALK
Feature Publications
1 Anti-communist 150.00

DOUBLE TROUBLE
St. John Publishing Co., 1957
1 Funny kids 100.00

DOUBLE UP
Elliot Publications, 1941
1 . . . . 1,500.00

DOWN WITH CRIME
Fawcett Publications, Nov., 1951
1 A:Desarro 600.00
2 BP, A:Scanlon Gang 300.00
3 H-is for Heroin 300.00
4 BP, A:Desarro 275.00
5 No Jail Can Hold Me 275.00
6 The Puncture-Proof Assassin . 275.00
7 The Payoff, Nov., 1952 . . . . . . 275.00

DO YOU BELIEVE IN NIGHTMARES
St. John Publ. Co., 1957
1 SD 800.00
2 DAy 500.00

DUDLEY
Prize Publications, Nov.–Dec., 1952
1 . . . . 175.00
2 . . . . 125.00
3 March–April, 1950 . . . . 100.00

DUMBO WEEKLY
The Walt Disney Co., 1942
1 Gas giveaways 1,500.00
2 thru 16 . . . . @600.00

DURANGO KID
Magazine Enterprises, Oct.–Nov., 1949
1 FF, Charles Starrett photo (c)
    B:Durango Kid & Raider . . 1,200.00
2 FF, Charles Starrett Ph(c) 600.00

Dynamic #13
© *Harry A Chesler*

3 FF, Charles Starrett Ph(c) 500.00
4 FF, Charles Starrett Ph(c),
    Two-Timing Guns 450.00
5 FF, Charles Starrett Ph(c),
    Tracks Across the Trail 450.00
6 FF 300.00
7 FF,Atomic(c) 350.00
8 FF 300.00
9 FF 300.00
10 FF 300.00
11 FF 250.00
12 FF 250.00
13 FF 250.00
14 thru 16 FF . . . . @250.00
17 O:Durango Kid 300.00
18 FMe,DAy(c) 200.00
19 FMe,FGu 175.00
20 FMe,FGu 175.00
21 FMe,FGu 175.00
22 FMe,FGu 200.00
23 FMe,FGu,I:Red Scorpion 200.00
24 thru 30 FMe,FGu . . . . @200.00
31 FMe,FGu 200.00
32 thru 40 FGu . . . . @150.00
41 FGu,Oct., 1941 . . . . 150.00

DYNAMIC COMICS
Dynamic Publications (Harry 'A' Chesler), Oct., 1941
1 EK,O:Major Victory, Dynamic Man,
    Hale the Magician, A:Black
    Cobra 3,500.00
2 O:Dynamic Boy & Lady
    Satan,I:Green Knight,
    Lance Cooper 1,800.00
3 GT 1,600.00
8 Horror (c) 2,000.00
9 MRa,GT,B:Mr.E 2,000.00
10 . . . . 1,000.00
11 GT 900.00
12 GT 800.00
13 GT 900.00
14 . . . . 800.00
15 Sky Chief 800.00
16 GT,Bondage(c),Marijuana 900.00
17 . . . . 1,000.00
18 Ric 700.00
19 A:Dynamic Man 700.00
20 same,Nude Woman 1,500.00
21 same,Dinosaur(c) 700.00
22 same 700.00
23 A:Yankee Girl,1.0948 . . . . . . 700.00

DYNAMITE
Comic Media/Allen Hardy Publ., May, 1953
1 DH(c),A:Danger#6 . . . . 450.00
2 . . . . 250.00
3 PMo(a&c),B:Johnny
    Dynamite,Drug 300.00
4 PMo(a&c),Prostitution 350.00
5 PMo(a&c) 200.00
6 PMo(a&c) 200.00
7 PMo(a&c),Prostitution 250.00
8 PMo(a&c) 200.00
9 PMo(a&c) 200.00
Becomes:

JOHNNY DYNAMITE
Charlton Comics, June, 1955
10 PMo(c) 150.00
11 . . . . 125.00
12 . . . . 125.00
Becomes:

FOREIGN INTRIGUES
1956
13 A:Johnny Dynamite 150.00
14 same 125.00
15 same 125.00
Becomes:

BATTLEFIELD ACTION
Nov., 1957
16 . . . . 150.00
17 . . . . 100.00
18 . . . . 100.00
19 . . . . 100.00
20 . . . . 100.00
21 thru 30 . . . . @100.00

EAGLE, THE
Fox Features Syndicate, July, 1941
1 B:The Eagle,A:Rex Dexter
    of Mars 3,500.00
2 B:Spider Queen 1,500.00
3 B:Joe Spook 1,200.00
4 Jan., 1942 . . . . 1,200.00

EAGLE
Rural Home Publ., Feb.–March, 1945
1 LbC 800.00
2 LbC,April–May, 1945 . . . . 500.00

EAT RIGHT TO WORK AND WIN
Swift Co., 1942
N# Flash Gordon,Popeye 750.00

EDDIE STANKY
Fawcett Publications, 1951
N# New York Giants 500.00

EERIE
Avon Periodicals, May–June, 1951– Aug.–Sept., 1954
1 JKa,Horror from the Pit,
    Bondage(c), 1947 . . . . 7,500.00
1a reprint, 1951 . . . . 1,200.00
2,WW(a&c), Chamber of Death 1,200.00
3 WW(a&c),JKa,JO
    Monster of the Storm 1,300.00
4 WW(c),Phantom of Reality . 1,200.00
5 WW(c), Operation Horror . . . 1,000.00
6 Devil Keeps a Date 450.00
7 WW(c),JKa,JO,Blood for
    the Vampire 700.00
8 EK, Song of the Undead 500.00
9 JKa, Hands of Death 500.00

10 EK,Castle of Terror 450.00
11 Anatomical Monster 450.00
12 Dracula 600.00
13 . . . . 500.00
14 Master of the Dead 500.00
15 Reprint #1 . . . . 350.00
16 WW, Chamber of Death 350.00
17 WW(c),JO,JKa, ... 450.00

EERIE ADVENTURES
**Approved Comics
(Ziff-Davis), Winter, 1951**
1 BP,JKa,Bondage 700.00

EGBERT
**Arnold Publications/
Comic Magazine, Spring, 1946**
1 I:Egbert & The Count 350.00
2 . . . . 250.00
3 . . . . 200.00
4 . . . . 200.00
5 . . . . 200.00
6 . . . . 250.00
7 thru 10 . . . . @200.00
11 thru 17 . . . . @150.00
18 1950 . . . . 150.00

EH!
**Charlton Comics,
Dec., 1953–Nov., 1954**
1 DAy(c),DG,Atomic Mouse 500.00
2 DAy(c) 300.00
3 DAy(c) 275.00
4 DAy(c),Sexual 300.00
5 DAy(c) 275.00
6 DAy(c),Sexual 300.00
7 DAy(c) 275.00

EL BOMBO COMICS
Frances M. McQueeny, 1945
1 . . . . 175.00

ELLA CINDERS
St. John Publishing Co. 1948
1 . . . . 200.00
2 . . . . 150.00
3 . . . . 100.00
4 . . . . 100.00
5 . . . . 100.00

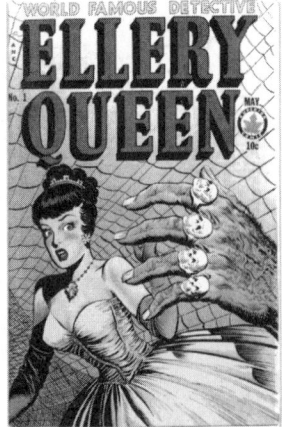

*Ellery Queen #1
© Superior Comics*

ELLERY QUEEN
**Superior Comics,
May–Nov., 1949**
1 LbC(c),JKa,Horror 800.00
2 . . . . 550.00
3 Drug issue 650.00
4 The Crooked Mile 550.00

ELLERY QUEEN
**Approved Comics
(Ziff-Davis),
Jan.–March, 1952**
1 NS(c),The Corpse the Killed . . 700.00
2 NS,Killer's Revenge,
   Summer, 1952 . . . . 550.00

ELSIE THE COW
**D.S. Publishing Co.,
Oct.–Nov., 1949**
1 P(c) 450.00
2 Bondage(c) 300.00
3 July–Aug., 1950 . . . . 200.00

ENCHANTING LOVE
**Kirby Publishing Co.
Oct., 1949**
1 Branded Guilty, Ph(c) 250.00
2 Ph(c),BP 125.00
3 Ph(c),Utter Defeat was Our
   Victory; Jimmy Stewart 150.00
4 . . . . 125.00
5 Ph(c) GRi 200.00
6 . . . . 125.00

ERNIE COMICS
See: SCREAM COMICS

ESCAPE FROM FEAR
**Planned Parenthood
of America, 1956**
1 . . . . 150.00
2 (1962) 100.00

ETTA KETT
**Best Books, Inc.
(Standard Comics),
Dec., 1948**
11 . . . . 150.00
12 . . . . 100.00
13 . . . . 100.00
14 Sept., 1949 . . . . 100.00

EXCITING COMICS
**Better Publ./Visual Editions
(Standard Comics),
April, 1940**
1 O:Mask, Jim Hatfield,
   Dan Williams 7,000.00
2 B:Sphinx 3,500.00
3 V:Robot 2,500.00
4 V:Sea Monster 2,000.00
5 V:Gargoyle 2,000.00
6 . . . . 2,000.00
7 AS(c) 1,500.00
8 . . . . 1,500.00
9 O:Black Terror & Tim,
   Bondage(c) 17,000.00
10 A:Black Terror 5,000.00
11 same 2,800.00
12 Bondage(c) 2,200.00
13 Bondage(c) 2,200.00
14 O:Sphinx 1,700.00
15 O:Liberator 1,800.00
16 Black Terror 1,600.00
17 same 1,600.00
18 same 1,600.00
19 same 1,600.00
20 E:Mask,Bondage(c) 1,200.00

21 A:Liberator 1,200.00
22 O:The Eaglet,B:American
   Eagle 1,200.00
23 Black Terror 900.00
24 Black Terror 900.00
25 Bondage(c) 900.00
26 ASh(c) 900.00
27 ASh(c) 900.00
28 ASh(c),B:Crime Crusader . . 1,100.00
29 ASh(c) 1,000.00
30 ASh(c),Bondage(c) 1,100.00
31 ASh(c) 1,200.00
32 ASh(c) 1,200.00
33 ASh(c) 1,200.00
34 ASh(c) 1,200.00
35 ASh(c),E:Liberator 1,200.00
36 ASh(c) 1,200.00
37 ASh(c) 1,200.00
38 ASh(c) 1,200.00
39 ASh(c)O:Kara, Jungle
   Princess 1,700.00
40 ASh(c) 1,200.00
41 ASh(c) 1,200.00
42 ASh(c),B:Scarab 1,200.00
43 ASh(c) 1,000.00
44 ASh(c) 1,000.00
45 ASh(c),V:Robot 1,000.00
46 ASh(c) 1,000.00
47 ASh(c) 1,000.00
48 ASh(c) 1,000.00
49 ASh(c),E:Kara &
   American Eagle 1,000.00
50 ASh(c),E:American Eagle . . 1,000.00
51 ASh(c),B:Miss Masque . . . 1,200.00
52 ASh(c),Miss Masque 900.00
53 ASh(c),Miss Masque 900.00
54 ASh(c),E:Miss Masque 900.00
55 ASh(c),O&B:Judy o/t Jungle . . 900.00
56 ASh(c) 900.00
57 ASh(c) 900.00
58 ASh(c) 900.00
59 ASh(c),FF,Bondage(c) 1,000.00
60 ASh(c),The Mystery Rider . . . 800.00
61 ASh(c) 800.00
62 ASh(c),CQ 800.00
63 ASh(c) 800.00
64 ASh(c) 800.00
65 ASh(c),CQ 800.00
66 . . . . 800.00
67 GT 800.00
68 . . . . 800.00
69 Sept., 1949 . . . . 800.00

*Exciting #62
© Standard Comics*

EXCITING ROMANCES
Fawcett Publications, 1949
1 Ph(c) 200.00
2 Ph(c) 150.00
3 WW,Ph(c). 150.00
4 Ph(c) 150.00
5 thru 7 .... @100.00
8 thru 10 BP .... @120.00
11 thru 12 .... @100.00

EXCITING WAR
**Visual Editions
(Standard Comics), 1952**
5 Korean war 150.00
6 .... 100.00
7 .... 100.00
8 ATh..................... 125.00

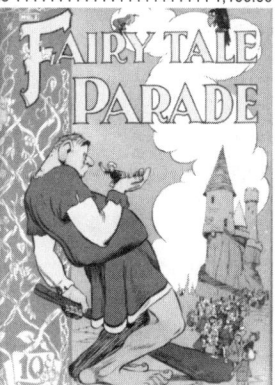

Exploits of Daniel Boone #1
© Quality Comics

EXPLOITS OF DANIEL BOONE
**Comic Magazines
(Quality Comics Group), 1955**
1 Frontier hero 350.00
2 .... 225.00
3 thru 6 .... @175.00

EXPLORER JOE
**Approved Comics
(Ziff-Davis), Winter, 1951**
1 NS,The Fire Opal
 of Madagscar 150.00
2 BK, Oct.–Nov., 1952 .... 165.00

EXPOSED
**D.S. Publishing Co.,
March–April, 1948**
1 Corpses Cash and Carry 400.00
2 Giggling Killer 500.00
3 One Bloody Night 200.00
4 JO,Deadly Dummy 200.00
5 Body on the Beach 200.00
6 Fatal Masquerade 500.00
7 The Midnight Guest........ 500.00
8 Grl,The Secret in the Snow .. 500.00
9 The Gypsy Baron,
 July–Aug., 1949 .... 500.00

EXTRA COMICS
Magazine Enterprises, 1947
1 .... 900.00

EXTRA!
**E.C. Comics,
March–April, 1955**
1 JCr,RC,JSe 400.00
2 JCr,RC,JSe 300.00
3 JCr,RC,JSe 300.00
4 JCr,RC,JSe 300.00
5 Nov.–Dec., 1955 .... 300.00

FACE, THE
**Publication Enterprises
(Columbia Comics), 1942**
1 MBi(c),The Face.......... 1,600.00
2 MBi(c) 1,200.00
Becomes:

TONY TRENT
1948
3 MBi,A:The Face........... 350.00
4 1949 .... 300.00

FAIRY TALE PARADE
Dell Publishing Co., 1942
1 WK,Giant 2,500.00
2 WK,Flying Horse.......... 1,500.00
3 WK 1,000.00
4 WK................... 800.00
5 WK................... 800.00
6 WK................... 500.00
7 WK................... 500.00
8 WK................... 500.00
9 WK,Reluctant Dragon 500.00

FAIRY TALES
**Approved Comics
(Ziff-Davis), 1951**
10 .... 300.00
11 .... 250.00

FAMILY FUNNIES
Harvey Publications, 1950
1 Mandrake................ 200.00
2 Flash Gordon............ 150.00
3 .... 125.00
4 Flash Gordon............ 125.00
5 Flash Gordon............ 125.00
6 .... 125.00
7 Flash Gordon............ 125.00
8 .... 125.00
Becomes:

TINY TOT FUNNIES
Harvey Publications, 1951
9 Dagwood (c),Flash Gordon ... 150.00
Becomes:

JUNIOR FUNNIES
Harvey Publications, 1951–52
10 Blondie, Popeye 100.00
11 .... 100.00
12 .... 100.00
13 .... 100.00

FAMOUS COMICS
Whitman Publ. Co., 1934
1 3"x8", three per box 1,200.00
2 .... 1,000.00
3 .... 1,000.00

FAMOUS COMICS
Zain-Eppy Publ.
N# Joe Palooka 600.00

FAMOUS CRIMES
**Fox Features Syndicate,
June, 1948**
1 Cold Blooded Killer 800.00
2 Near Nudity (c) 550.00

3 Crime Never Pays 700.00
4 .... 350.00
5 .... 350.00
6 .... 350.00
7 Drug issue 550.00
8 thru 19 .... @300.00
20 Aug., 1951 .... 250.00
51 1952 .... 180.00

FAMOUS FAIRY TALES
K.K. Publication Co., 1942
N# WK, Giveaway........... 600.00
N# WK, Giveaway 400.00
N# WK, Giveaway 400.00

FAMOUS FEATURE STORIES
Dell Publishing Co., 1938
1A:Tarzan, Terry and the Pirates
 Dick Tracy,Smilin' Jack.... 2,500.00

FAMOUS FUNNIES
**Eastern Color Printing Co.,
1933**
N# A Carnival of Comics 60,000.00
N# Feb., 1934,
 1st 10-cent comic....... 50,000.00
1 July, 1934 .... 35,000.00
2 .... 15,000.00
3 B:Buck Rogers 12,000.00
4 Football (c) 5,000.00
5 Christmas 4,500.00
6 .... 3,000.00
7 .... 3,000.00
8 .... 3,000.00
9 .... 3,000.00
10 .... 3,000.00
11 Four pages of Buck Rogers . 1,500.00
12 Four pages of Buck Rogers. 1,500.00
13 .... 1,200.00
14 .... 1,200.00
15 Football (c). 1,200.00
16 .... 1,200.00
17 Christmas (c) 1,200.00
18 Four pages of Buck Rogers. 1,500.00
19 .... 1,200.00
20 .... 1,200.00
21 Baseball 1,000.00
22 Buck Rogers 1,100.00
23 .... 1,100.00
24 B: War on Crime 1,100.00
25 .... 1,100.00
26 .... 1,100.00
27 G-Men (c). 1,100.00
28 .... 1,100.00

Fairy Tale Parade #1
© Dell Publishing

GOLDEN AGE

29 Christmas. 1,100.00
30 . . . . 1,100.00
31 . . . . 700.00
32 Phantom Magician. 1,000.00
33 A:Baby Face Nelson &
   John Dillinger. 700.00
34 . . . . 700.00
35 Buck Rogers 800.00
36 . . . . 700.00
37 . . . . 700.00
38 Portrait,Buck Rogers. 800.00
39 . . . . 700.00
40 . . . . 700.00
41 thru 50. . . . . @600.00
51 thru 57. . . . . @500.00
58 Baseball (c). 500.00
59 . . . . 500.00
60 . . . . 500.00
61 . . . . 400.00
62 . . . . 400.00
63 . . . . 400.00
64 . . . . 400.00
65 JK 400.00
66 . . . . 400.00
67 . . . . 400.00
68 JK 400.00
69 . . . . 400.00
70 . . . . 400.00
71 BEv 300.00
72 BEv,B:Speed Spaulding 300.00
73 BEv 300.00
74 BEv 300.00
75 BEv 300.00
76 BEv 300.00
77 BEv,Merry Christmas (c). . . . 300.00
78 BEv 300.00
79 BEv 300.00
80 BEv,Buck Rogers 300.00
81 O:Invisible Scarlet O'Neil . . . 325.00
82 Buck Rogers (c) 300.00
83 Dickie Dare 250.00
84 Scotty Smith 250.00
85 Eagle Scout,Roy Rogers . . . 250.00
86 Moon Monsters 250.00
87 Scarlet O'Neil 250.00
88 Dickie Dare 250.00
89 O:Fearless Flint 250.00
90 Bondage (c) 350.00
91 . . . . 250.00
92 . . . . 250.00
93 . . . . 250.00
94 War Bonds 275.00
95 Invisible Scarlet O'Neil 200.00
96 . . . . 200.00
97 War Bonds Promo 200.00
98 . . . . 200.00
99 . . . . 200.00
100 Anniversary issue 200.00
101 thru 110 . . . . @200.00
111 thru 130 . . . . @150.00
131 thru 150 . . . . @125.00
151 thru 162. . . . . @125.00
163 Valentine's Day (c) 100.00
164 . . . . 100.00
165 . . . . 100.00
166 . . . . 100.00
167 . . . . 100.00
168 . . . . 100.00
169 AW 135.00
170 AW 135.00
171 thru 190. . . . . @150.00
191 thru 203. . . . . @135.00
204 War (c) 100.00
205 . . . . 100.00
206 . . . . 100.00
207 . . . . 100.00
208 . . . . 100.00
209 FF(c),Buck Rogers. 2,500.00
210 FF(c),Buck Rogers. 2,500.00
211 FF(c),Buck Rogers. 2,500.00
212 FF(c),Buck Rogers. 2,500.00
213 FF(c),Buck Rogers. 2,500.00

214 FF(c),Buck Rogers. 2,500.00
215 FF(c),Buck Rogers. 2,500.00
216 FF(c),Buck Rogers. 2,500.00
217 . . . . 100.00
218 July, 1955 . . . . 100.00

Famous Gangsters #1
© Avon Periodicals

FAMOUS GANGSTERS
Avon Periodicals, 1951
1 Al Capone, Dillinger,
  Luciano & Shultz 550.00
2 WW(c),Dillinger Machine-
  Gun Killer 500.00
3 Lucky Luciano & Murder Inc. . 500.00
Becomes:

CRIME ON
THE WATERFRONT
May, 1952
4 Underworld Gangsters who
  Control the Shipment of
  Drugs! 450.00

FAMOUS STARS
Ziff-Davis Publ. Co., 1950
1 OW,Shelley Winter,Susan
  Peters & Shirley Temple . . . 700.00
2 BEv,Betty Hutton, Bing Crosby 600.00
3 OW,Judy Garland, Alan Ladd . 700.00
4 RC,Jolson, Bob Mitchum . . . 600.00
5 BK,Elizabeth Taylor,
  Esther Williams 800.00
6 Gene Kelly, Spring, 1952 . . . 500.00

FAMOUS STORIES
Dell Publishing Co., 1942
1 Treasure Island 450.00
2 Tom Sawyer 400.00

FAMOUS WESTERN
BADMEN
See: REDSKIN

FANTASTIC
See: CAPTAIN SCIENCE

FANTASTIC COMICS
Fox Features Syndicate, 1939
1 LF(c),I&O:Samson,B:Star
  Dust, Super Wizard, Space
  Smith & Capt. Kid. 9,000.00
2 BP,LF(c),Samson Destroyed the
  Battery & Routed the Foe. . 4,500.00

3 BP,LF(c),Slays the Iron
  Monster. 14,000.00
4 GT,LF(c),Demolishes the
  Closing Torture Walls 3,000.00
5 GT,LF(c),Crumbles the
  Mighty War Machine. 2,700.00
6 JSm(c),Bondage(c) 2,500.00
7 JSm(c) 2,500.00
8 GT,Destroys the Mask of
  Fire,Bondage(c) 1,600.00
9 Mighty Muscles saved the
  Drowning Girl 1,600.00
10 I&O:David. 1,600.00
11 Wrecks the Torture Machine
  to save his fellow American 1,500.00
12 Heaved the Huge Ship high
  into the Air 1,500.00
13 Samson(c) 1,500.00
14 Samson(c) 1,500.00
15 Samson(c) 1,500.00
16 E:Stardust 1,500.00
17 Samson(c) 1,500.00
18 I:Black Fury & Chuck 1,500.00
19 Samson(c) 1,300.00
20 Samson(c) 1,300.00
21 B&I: The Banshee,Hitler(c) . 1,600.00
22 Hittler & Samson(c) 1,500.00
23 O:The Gladiator, Hitler (c)
  Nov., 1941 . . . . 1,800.00

FANTASTIC FEARS
**Farrell Publications
(Ajax), 1953
(Formerly: CAPTAIN JET)**
1 (7) Tales of Stalking Terror. . . . 750.00
2 (8) 500.00
3 . . . . 400.00
4 . . . . 400.00
5 SD,1st art 1,400.00
6 Decapitation. 850.00
7 . . . . 400.00
8 Decapitation. 500.00
9 . . . . 325.00
Becomes:

FANTASTIC COMICS
Ajax, 1954
10 Tales of Enchantment 300.00
11 Amazing Adventures 400.00

FANTASTIC WORLDS
**Visual Editions
(Standard Comics), 1952–53**
5 ATh,Triumph Over Terror, Sci-fi 500.00
6 ATh,The Cosmic Terror 450.00
7 The Asteroid God. 300.00

FANTOMAN
See: AMAZING
ADVENTURE FUNNIES

FARGO KID
See: JUSTICE TRAPS
THE GUILTY

FAST FICTION
**Seaboard Publ.,
Oct., 1949**
1 Scarlet Pimpernel 500.00
2 HcK,Captain Blood 400.00
3 She 500.00
4 The 39 Steps 350.00
5 HcK,Beau Geste 350.00
Becomes:

GOLDEN AGE

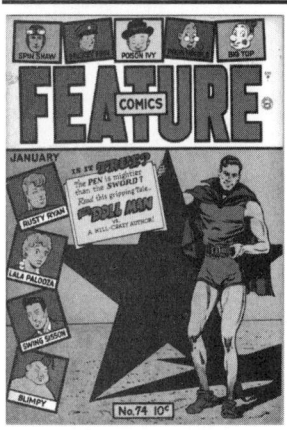

Feature Comics #74
© *Quality Publications*

STORIES BY FAMOUS AUTHORS ILLUSTRATED

Famous Author Illustrated, Aug., 1950

1a Scarlet Pimpernel	400.00
2a Captain Blood	400.00
3a She	500.00
4a The 39 Steps	325.00
5a Beau Geste	300.00
6 HcK,MacBeth.	325.00
7 HcK,Window	275.00
8 HcK,Hamlet	300.00
9 Nicholas Nickleby	275.00
10 HcK,Romeo & Juliet	275.00
11 GS,Ben Hur.	290.00
12 GS,La Svengali.	275.00
13 HcK,Scaramouche	275.00

FAT AND SLAT JOKE BOOK

William H. Wise, 1944

N#	500.00

FAT AND SLAT

Fables Publ., Inc. (E.C. Comics), 1947

1 I&O:Voltage, Man of Lightning.	500.00
2	350.00
3	350.00
4	350.00

Becomes:

GUNFIGHTER

Fables Publ., Inc. (E.C. Comics), 1948–50

5 JCr(c),Wild West	800.00
6 Grl,JCr(c),Moon Girl	700.00
7 AF,Grl.	600.00
0 AF,Gıl.	600.00
9 AF,Grl.	600.00
10 JCr,AF,Grl	600.00
11 AF,Grl	600.00
12 Grl.	600.00
13 JCr,WW,Grl.	625.00
14 JCr,WW,Grl,Bondage	700.00

Becomes:

HAUNT OF FEAR

FAVORITE COMICS

1934

1 Giveaways,Nebbs,Joe Palooka.	1,500.00

---

2 same.	1,000.00
3 same.	1,000.00

FAWCETT FUNNY ANIMALS

Fawcett Publications, Dec., 1942

1 I:Hoppy the Marvel Bunny, Captain Marvel (c)	1,000.00
2 X-Mas Issue	500.00
3 Spirit of '43	400.00
4 and 5 . . . . @400.00
6 Buy War Bonds and Stamps . .	300.00
7	300.00
8 Flag (c).	300.00
9 and 10 . . . . @300.00
11 thru 20 . . . . @200.00
21 thru 30 . . . . @150.00
31 thru 40 . . . . @150.00
41 thru 83 . . . . @125.00

Charlton Comics

84	125.00
85 thru 91 Feb., 1956. . . . . . . @100.00

FAWCETT MINIATURES

Fawcett Publ. (Wheaties Giveaways), 1946

1 Capt. Marvel	250.00
2 Capt. Marvel	250.00
3 Capt. Marvel Jr.	250.00
4 Delecta of the Planets	400.00

FAWCETT MOVIE COMICS

Fawcett Publications, 1949

N# Dakota Lil	400.00
N#a Copper Canyon	300.00
N# Destination the Moon	1,200.00
N# Montana	300.00
N# Pioneer Marshal	300.00
N# Powder River Rustlers	450.00
N# Singing Guns	275.00
7 Gunmen of Abilene	325.00
8 King of the Bull Whip	450.00
9 BP,The Old Frontier	300.00
10 The Missourians	300.00
11 The Thundering Trail.	400.00
12 Rustlers on Horseback	325.00
13 Warpath.	250.00
14 Last Outpost,RonaldReagan .	550.00
15 The Man from Planet-X . . .	4,000.00
16 10 Tall Men	200.00
17 Rose Cimarron	150.00
18 The Brigand	175.00
19 Carbine Williams.	175.00
20 Ivanhoe, Dec., 1952	300.00

FEATURE BOOKS

David McKay Publications, May, 1937

N# Dick Tracy	17,000.00
N# Popeye	11,000.00
1 Zane Grey's King of the Royal Mounted	1,500.00
2 Popeye	1,500.00
3 Popeye and the "Jeep" . . .	1,400.00
4 Dick Tracy	2,500.00
5 Popeye and his Poppa . . .	1,200.00
6 Dick Tracy	1,500.00
7 Little Orphan Annie	1,600.00
8 Secret Agent X-9	750.00
9 Tracy & the Famon Boys . .	1,500.00
10 Popeye & Susan	1,200.00
11 Annie Rooney	400.00
12 Blondie.	1,300.00
13 Inspector Wade.	400.00
14 Popeye in Wild Oats	1,400.00
15 Barney Baxter in the Air . . .	600.00
16 Red Eagle	400.00

---

17 Gang Busters.	1,100.00
18 Mandrake the Magician . . .	1,100.00
19 Mandrake.	1,100.00
20 The Phantom	1,500.00
21 Lone Ranger	1,400.00
22 The Phantom	1,000.00
23 Mandrake in Teibe Castle .	1,100.00
24 Lone Ranger	1,400.00
25 Flash Gordon on the Planet Mongo	1,900.00
26 Prince Valiant.	1,500.00
27 Blondie	300.00
28 Blondie and Dagwood.	300.00
29 Blondie at the Home Sweet Home	300.00
30 Katzenjammer Kids	275.00
31 Blondie Keeps the Home Fires Burning.	300.00
32 Katzenjammer Kids.	250.00
33 Romance of Flying	200.00
34 Blondie Home is Our Castle .	300.00
35 Katzenjammer Kids.	250.00
36 Blondie on the Home Front. .	275.00
37 Katzenjammer Kids.	275.00
38 Blondie the ModelHomemaker	275.00
39 The Phantom	800.00
40 Blondie	275.00
41 Katzenjammer Kids.	275.00
42 Blondie in Home-Spun Yarns .	275.00
43 Blondie Home-Cooked Scraps	275.00
44 Katzenjammer Kids in Monkey Business	275.00
45 Blondie in Home of the Free and the Brave	275.00
46 Mandrake in Fire World	800.00
47 Blondie in Eaten Out of House and Home	275.00
48 The Maltese Falcon	1,300.00
49 Perry Mason - The Case of the Lucky Legs	350.00
50 The Shoplifters Shoe, P. Mason	350.00
51 Rip Kirby - Mystery of the Mangler	350.00
52 Mandrake in the Land of X . .	600.00
53 Phantom in Safari Suspense .	600.00
54 Rip Kirby - Case of the Master Menace	425.00
55 Mandrake in 5-Numbers Treasue Hunt.	600.00
56 Phantom Destroys the Sky Band	600.00
57 Phantom in the Blue Gang, 1948.	600.00

FEATURE FUNNIES

Harry A. Chesler Publ./ Comic Favorites, Oct., 1937

1 RuG(a&c),A:Joe Palooka, Mickey Finn, Bungles, Dixie Dugan, Big Top, Strange as It Seems, Off the Record . .	3,600.00
2 A: The Hawk	1,700.00
3 WE,Joe Palooka,The Clock .	1,400.00
4 RuG,WE,RuG(c),JoePalooka	1,200.00
5 WE, Joe Palooka drawing . .	1,200.00
6 WE,Joe Palooka (c)	1,200.00
7 WE,LLe, Gallant Knight story by Vernon Henkel	900.00
8 WE	900.00
9 WE, Joe Palooka story & (c)	1,200.00
10 WE,Micky Finn(c).	1,000.00
11 WE,LLe,The Bungles(c). . . .	1,000.00
12 WE, Joe Palooka(c).	1,000.00
13 WE,LLe, World Series(c) . . .	1,100.00
14 WE,Ned Brant(c).	700.00
15 WE,Joe Palooka(c).	800.00
16 Mickey Finn(c)	700.00
17 WE	700.00
18 Joe Palooka (c).	800.00
19 WE,LLe,Mickey Finn(c).	700.00
20 WE,LLe	700.00

GOLDEN AGE

All comics prices listed are for *Near Mint* condition.

GOLDEN AGE

Becomes:

FEATURE COMICS
Quality Comics Group,
June. 1939–May, 1950

21 Joe Palooka(c). 1,000.00
22 LLe(c),Mickey Finn(c) 650.00
23 B:Charlie Chan 650.00
24 AIA,Joe Palooka(c) 650.00
25 AIA,The Clock(c). 650.00
26 AIA, The Bundles(c). 650.00
27 WE,AIA,I:Doll Man 9,000.00
28 LF,AIA,The Clock(c). 3,000.00
29 LF,AIA,The Clock(c). 1,800.00
30 LF,AIA,Doll Man(c) 2,500.00
31 LF,AIA,Mickey Finn(c) 1,200.00
32 PGv,LF,GFx,Doll Man(c) . . . 1,000.00
33 PGv,LF,GFx,Bundles(c) 850.00
34 PGv,LF,GFx,Doll Man(c) . . . 1,000.00
35 PGv,LF,GFx,Bundles(c) 850.00
36 PGv,LF,GFx,Doll Man(c) . . . 1,000.00
37 PGv,LF,GFx,Bundles(c) 850.00
38 PGv,GFx,Doll Man(c) 800.00
39 PGv,GFx,Bundles(c). 800.00
40 PGv,GFx,WE(c),Doll Man(c) . 800.00
41 PGv,GFx,WE(c),Bundles(c) . . 600.00
42 GFx,Doll Man(c) 600.00
43 RC,GFx,Bundles(c). 425.00
44 RC,GFx,Doll Man(c) 800.00
45 RC,GFx,Bundles(c). 400.00
46 RC,PGv,GFx,Doll Man(c) 600.00
47 RC,GFx,Bundles(c). 400.00
48 RC,GFx,Doll Man(c) 600.00
49 RC,GFx,Bundles(c). 400.00
50 RC,GFx,Doll Man(c) 600.00
51 RC,GFx,Bundles(c). 400.00
52 RC,GFx,Doll Man(c) 500.00
53 RC,GFx,Bundles(c). 325.00
54 RC,GFx,Doll Man(c) 500.00
55 RC,GFx,Bundles(c). 325.00
56 RC,GFx,Doll Man(c) 500.00
57 RC,GFx,Bundles(c). 325.00
58 RC,GFx,Doll Man (c) 500.00
59 RC,GFx,Mickey Finn(c) 325.00
60 RC,GFx,Doll Man(c) 500.00
61 RC,GFx,Bundles(c). 300.00
62 RC,GFx,Doll Man(c) 400.00
63 RC,GFx,Bundles(c). 300.00
64 BP,GFx,Doll Man(c) 400.00
65 BP,GFx(c),Bundles(c) 300.00
66 BP,GFx,Doll Man(c) 400.00
67 BP. 300.00
68 BP,Doll Man vs.Bearded
    Lady. 400.00
69 BP,GFx(c),Devil (c). 350.00
70 BP,Doll Man(c) 500.00
71 BP,GFx(c) 350.00
72 BP,Doll Man(c) 400.00
73 BP,GFx(c),Bundles(c) 250.00
74 Doll Man(c) 400.00
75 GFx(c). 300.00
76 GFx(c). 300.00
77 Doll Man (c) until #140 . . . . . 400.00
78 Knows no Fear but the
    Knife Does. 300.00
79 Little Luck God 300.00
80 . . . . 300.00
81 Wanted for Murder 250.00
82 V:Shawunkas the Shaman . . . 250.00
83 V:Mechanical Man 250.00
84 V:Masked Rider, Death
    Goes to the Rodeo 250.00
85 V:King of Beasts. 250.00
86 Is He A Killer?. 250.00
87 The Maze of Murder 250.00
88 V:The Phantom Killer 250.00
89 Crook's Goose 250.00
90 V:Whispering Corpse 250.00
91 V:The Undertaker 250.00
92 V:The Image 250.00
93 . . . . 250.00
94 V:The Undertaker 250.00

95 Flatten's the Peacock's Pride . 250.00
96 Doll Man Proves
    Justice is Blind. 250.00
97 V:Peacock. 250.00
98 V:Master Diablo 250.00
99 On the Warpath Again! 250.00
100 Crushes the City of Crime . . 300.00
101 Land of the Midget Men!. . . . 200.00
102 The Angle 200.00
103 V:The Queen of Ants 200.00
104 V:The Botanist 200.00
105 Dream of Death 200.00
106 V:The Sword Fish 200.00
107 Hand of Horror!. 200.00
108 V:Cateye 200.00
109 V:The Brain. 200.00
110 V:Fat Cat 200.00
111 V:The Undertaker 200.00
112 I:Mr. Curio & His Miniatures . 200.00
113 V:Highwayman 200.00
114 V:Tom Thumb 200.00
115 V:The Sphinx. 200.00
116 V:Elbows 200.00
117 Polka Dot on the Spot. 200.00
118 thru 144 . . . . @ 200.00

A FEATURE PRESENTATION
Fox Features Syndicate, 1950

1 (5) The Black Tarantula 700.00
2 (6) WW,Moby Dick. 600.00
3 Jungle Thrills, bondage 500.00

FEDERAL MEN COMICS
Gerard Publ. Co., 1942

2 S&S,Spanking 800.00

Felix the Cat #11
© *Toby Press*

FELIX THE CAT
Dell Publishing Co.,
Feb.–March, 1948

1 . . . . 550.00
2 . . . . 300.00
3 . . . . 200.00
4 . . . . 200.00
5 . . . . 200.00
6 thru 10 . . . . @150.00
11 thru 19 . . . . @150.00

Toby Press

20 thru 30 . . . . @350.00
31 . . . . 150.00
32 . . . . 350.00
33 . . . . 350.00
34 . . . . 150.00

35 . . . . 150.00
36 . . . . 350.00
37 Giant, Christmas(c). 750.00
38 . . . . 350.00
39 . . . . 350.00
40 thru 60 . . . . @350.00
61 . . . . 350.00

Harvey, 1955

62 thru 80. . . . . @125.00
81 thru 99. . . . . @100.00
100 . . . . 125.00
101 thru 118. . . . . @100.00
Spec., 100 pgs, 1952. . . . . 350.00
Summer Ann., 100 pgs. 1953 . . 650.00
Winter Ann.,#2 100 pgs, 1954. . 600.00

FELIX AND HIS FRIENDS
Toby, 1953

1 F:Felix the Cat 350.00
2 . . . . 400.00
3 . . . . 400.00

FERDINAND THE BULL
Dell Publishing Co., 1938

1 . . . . 400.00

FIGHT AGAINST CRIME
Story Comics, May, 1951

1 Scorpion of Crime Inspector
    "Brains" Carroway 600.00
2 Ganglands Double Cross 350.00
3 Killer Dolan's Double Cross . . 300.00
4 Hopped Up Killers - The
    Con's Slaughter,Drug issue . 350.00
5 FF,Horror o/t Avenging Corpse 350.00
6 Terror of the Crazy Killer 250.00
7 . . . . 250.00
8 Killer with the Two-Bladed
    Knife 250.00
9 Rats Die by Gas,Horror 600.00
10 Horror of the Con's Revenge . 600.00
11 Case of the Crazy Killer 600.00
12 Horror,Drug issue 700.00
13 The Bloodless Killer 600.00
14 Electric Chair (c). 700.00
15 Violence 600.00
16 RA,Bondage(c) 700.00
17 Knife in Neck(c) 700.00
18 Attempted Hanging (c) 700.00
19 Bondage(c) 700.00
20 Severed Head (c) 1,200.00
21 Violence 500.00
Becomes:

FIGHT AGAINST THE GUILTY
Dec., 1954

22 RA,Electric Chair 500.00
23 March, 1955 . . . . 350.00

FIGHT COMICS
Fiction House Magazines,
Jan., 1940

1 LF,GT,WE(c),O:Spy Fighter . 6,500.00
2 GT,WE(c),Joe Lewis 2,500.00
3 WE(c),GT,B:Rip Regan,
    The Powerman 2,000.00
4 GT,LF(c). 1,500.00
5 WE(c) 1,500.00
6 GT,BP(c) 900.00
7 GT,BP(c),Powerman-Blood
    Money 900.00
8 GT,Chip Collins-Lair of
    the Vulture 900.00
9 GT,Chip Collins-Prey of the
    War Eagle 900.00
10 GT,Wolves of the Yukon 900.00
11 . . . . 800.00

Fight Comics-12
© *Fiction House*

12 RA,Powerman-Monster of
 Madness................1,000.00
13 Shark Broodie-Legion
 of Satan.................900.00
14 Shark Broodie-Lagoon
 of Death.................900.00
15 Super-American-Hordes of
 the Secret Dicator........1,200.00
16 B:Capt. Fight, Swastika
 Plague 1,200.00
17 Super-American-Blaster of
 the Pig-Boat Pirates......1,200.00
18 Shark Broodie-Plague of
 the Yellow Devils 1,200.00
19 E:Capt. Fight 1,200.00
20 ....800.00
21 Rip Carson-Hell's Sky-Riders . 600.00
22 Rip Carson-Sky Devil's
 Mission 600.00
23 Rip Carson-Angels of
 Vengeance..............600.00
24 Baynonets the Banzai
 Breed! Bondage(c) 800.00
25 Rip Carson-Samurai
 Showdown..............600.00
26 Rip Carson-Fury of
 the Sky-Brigade..........600.00
27 War-Loot for the Mikado
 Bondage(c) 800.00
28 Rip Carson 600.00
29 Rip Carson-Charge of the
 Lost Region.............600.00
30 Rip Carson-Jeep-Raiders of
 the Torture Jungle 600.00
31 Gangway for the Gyrenes,
 Decapitation (c).........800.00
32 Vengeance of the Hun-
 Hunters, Bondage(c).......800.00
33 B:Tiger Girl.............400.00
34 Bondage(c)..............500.00
35 MB.....................400.00
36 MB.....................400.00
37 MB.....................400.00
38 MB,Bondage(c)...........500.00
39 MB,Senorita Rio-Slave Brand
 of the Spider Cult..........400.00
40 MB,Bondage (c) 500.00
41 MB,Bondage (c) 500.00
42 MB.....................350.00
43 MB,Senorita Rio-The Fire-Brides of
 the Lost Atlantis, Bondage(c) 400.00
44 MB,R:Capt. Fight 500.00
45 MB,Tonight Don Diablo Rides. 500.00
46 MB.....................500.00
47 MB,SenoritaRio-Horror's
 Hacienda...............500.00

48 MB......................500.00
49 MB,JKa,B:Tiger Girl(c) 500.00
50 MB......................500.00
51 JKa,MB,O:Tiger Girl 700.00
52 JKa,MB,Winged Demons
 of Doom................375.00
53 JKa,MB,Shadowland Shrine.. 375.00
54 JKa,MB,Flee the Cobra Fury . 375.00
55 JKa,MB,Jungle Juggernaut... 375.00
56 JKa,MB,Bondage 375.00
57 JKa,MB,Jewels of Jeopardy .. 375.00
58 JKa,MB,Bondage 375.00
59 JKa,MB,Vampires of Crystal
 Cavern................375.00
60 JKa,MB,Kraal of Deadly
 Diamonds 375.00
61 JKa,MB,Seekers of the Sphinx,
 O:Tiger Girl 500.00
62 JKa,MB,Graveyard of the
 Tree Tribe 400.00
63 JKa,MB,Bondage 400.00
64 JKa,MB,DawnBeast from
 Karama-Zan!............400.00
65 JKa,Beware the Congo Girl . 300.00
66 JKa,Man or Ape!..........300.00
67 Head-Hunters of Taboo Trek . 300.00
68 Fangs of Dr. Voodoo.......300.00
69 Cage of the Congo Fury.....300.00
70 Kraal of Traitor Tusks 300.00
71 Captives for the Golden
 Crocodile..............300.00
72 Land of the Lost Safaris 300.00
73 War-Gods of the Jungle 300.00
74 Advengers of the Jungle.....300.00
75 Perils of Momba-Kzar......300.00
76 Kraal of Zombi-Zaro 300.00
77 Slave-Queen of the Ape Man . 300.00
78 Great Congo Diamond
 Robbery...............400.00
79 A:Space Rangers 500.00
80 ....225.00
81 E:Tiger Girl(c) 225.00
82 RipCarson-CommandoStrike . 225.00
83 NobodyLoves a Minesweeper 225.00
84 Rip Carson-Suicide Patrol ... 225.00
85 ....225.00
86 GE,Tigerman,Summer,1954 .. 250.00

FIGHTIN' AIR FORCE
Charlton Comics, 1956–60
3 ....125.00
4 thru 10 ....@75.00
11 giant 100.00
12 US,Russia Nuclear attack.... 150.00
13 thru 20 ....@75.00
21 thru 30 ....@75.00

FIGHTING AMERICAN
**Headline Publications
(Prize), April–May, 1954**
1 S&K,O:Fighting American &
 Speedboy 2,700.00
2 S&K(a&c) 1,200.00
3 S&K(a&c) 1,000.00
4 S&K(a&c) 900.00
5 S&K(a&c) 900.00
6 S&K(a&c),O:Fighting
 American 900.00
7 S&K(a&c), April–May, 1955 .. 800.00

FIGHTING FRONTS!
Harvey Publications, 1952–53
1 War 150.00
2 BP,violence 200.00
3 BP 125.00
4 ....100.00
5 ....100.00

FIGHTING DAVY
CROCKETT
See: KIT CARSON

FIGHTING INDIANS OF
THE WILD WEST
**Avon Periodicals,
March, 1952**
1 EK,EL,Geronimo, Crazy Horse,
 Chief Victorio 250.00
2 EK,Same, Nov., 1952 ....150.00

FIGHTING
LEATHERNECKS
Toby Press, Feb., 1952
1 JkS,Duke's Diary 175.00
2 ....150.00
3 ....125.00
4 ....125.00
5 ....125.00
6 Dec., 1952 ....125.00

THE FIGHTING MAN
**Excellent Publications
(Ajax/Farrell), 1952–53**
1 War 175.00
2 ....125.00
3 thru 8 ....@100.00
Ann.#1 (1952) 325.00

FIGHTIN' TEXAN
See: TEXAN, THE

FIGHTING UNDERSEA
COMMANDOS
Avon Periodicals, 1952–53
1 Navy Frogmen............200.00
2 ....125.00
3 ....100.00
4 BK 110.00
5 ....100.00

FIGHTING WAR STORIES
Men's Publications, 1952
1 ....150.00
2 thru 5 ....@100.00

FIGHTING YANK
**Nedor Publ./Better Publ.
(Standard Comics) Sept., 1942**
1 JaB,B:Fighting Yank, A:Wonder
 Man, Mystico, bondage (c). 6,000.00
2 JaB...................2,200.00
3 Shark, bondage (c).......2,000.00
4 ASh(c), bondage (c) 2,000.00

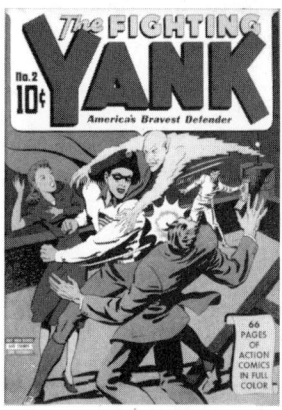

Fighting Yank #2
© *Nedor Publications*

GOLDEN AGE

5 ASh(c) 1,200.00
6 ASh(c) 1,200.00
7 ASh(c),Bomb(c) 1,100.00
8 ASh(c), bondage(c) 1,200.00
9 ASh(c) 1,100.00
10 ASh(c),bondage-torture(c) . . 1,200.00
11 ASh(c), A:Grim Reaper,
  bondage (c) 1,100.00
12 ASh(c), Hirohito bondage (c) 1,100.00
13 ASh(c),kid bondage,snake(c)1,100.00
14 ASh(c) 900.00
15 ASh(c),bondage-torture(c) . . 1,100.00
16 ASh(c), ... 900.00
17 ASh(c),bondage(c) 1,100.00
18 ASh(c), A:American Eagle . . 1,000.00
19 ASh(c) 900.00
20 ASh(c) Shark 900.00
21 ASh(c) A:Kara,Jungle
  Princess 900.00
22 ASh(c) A:Miss Masque-
  (c) story 1,000.00
23 ASh(c) Klu Klux Klan
  parody (c) 1,500.00
24 ASh(c),A:Miss Masque 800.00
25 ASh(c),JRo,MMe,A:Cavalier 1,100.00
26 ASh(c),JRo,MMe,A:Cavalier . . 800.00
27 ASh(c),JRo,MMe,A:Cavalier . . 800.00
28 ASh(c),JRo,MMe,AW
  A:Cavalier 900.00
29 ASh(c),JRo,MMe,Aug., 1949 . 900.00

FILM STAR ROMANCES
Star Publications, 1950
1 LbC(c), Rudy Valentino story . 650.00
2 Liz Taylor & Robert Taylor,
  photo (c) 850.00
3 May–June, 1950, photo(c) . . . 375.00

FIREHAIR COMICS
**Flying Stories, Inc.
(Fiction House Magazine),
Winter, 1948–Spring, 1952**
1 I:Firehair, Riders on the
  Pony Express 750.00
2 Bride of the Outlaw Guns 400.00
3 Kiss of the Six-Gun Siren! . . . 350.00
4 . . . . 350.00
5 . . . . 350.00
6 . . . . 325.00
7 War Drums at Buffalo Bend . . 250.00
8 Raid on the Red Arrows 250.00
9 French Flags and Tomahawks . 250.00
10 Slave Maiden of the Crees . . . 250.00
11 Wolves of the Overland Trail . . 250.00

5 CENT COMICS
Fawcett Publications, 1940
1 B&W, I:Dan Dare, very rare 15,000.00

FLAME, THE
**Fox Feature Syndicate,
Summer, 1940**
1 LF,O:The Flame 6,000.00
2 GT,LF,Wing Turner 2,500.00
3 BP,Wonderworld 1,600.00
4 . . . . 1,600.00
5 GT 1,600.00
6 GT 1,600.00
7 A:The Yank 1,600.00
8 The Finger of the Frozen
  Death!, Jan., 1942 . . . . 1,600.00

FLAME, THE
Ajax/Farrell, 1954–55
1 (#5) superhero,O:Flame 700.00
2 . . . . 450.00
3 . . . . 400.00

Flame #1
© Fox Features

FLAMING LOVE
**Comic Magazines
(Quality Comics Group),
Dec., 1949**
1 BWa,BWa(c),The Temptress
  I Feared in His Arms 600.00
2 Torrid Tales of Turbulent
  Passion 250.00
3 BWa,RC,My Heart's at Sea . . 350.00
4 One Women Who Made a
  Mockery of Love, Ph(c) 250.00
5 Bridge of Longing, Ph(c) 250.00
6 Men Both Loved & Feared Me,
  Oct., 1950 . . . . 250.00

FLAMING WESTERN
ROMANCES
Star Publ., 1950
3 LbC,Robert Taylor Photo(c) . . . 550.00

FLASH GORDON
Harvey Publications, Oct., 1950
1 AR,Bondage(c) 600.00
2 AR 350.00
3 AR Bondage(c) 400.00
4 AR, April, 1951 . . . . 300.00

FLASH GORDON
Dell Publishing Co., 1953
2 . . . . 200.00
See also FOUR COLOR

FLIP
Harvey Publications, April, 1954
1 HN 300.00
2 HN,BP,June, 1954 . . . . 300.00

FLY BOY
**Approved Comics
(Ziff-Davis) Spring, 1952**
1 NS(c),Angels without Wings . . 300.00
2 NS(c),Flyboy's Flame-Out,
  Oct.–Nov., 1952 . . . . 200.00

FLYING ACES
Key Publications, 1955–56
1 War 125.00
2 . . . . 100.00
3 . . . . 100.00
4 . . . . 100.00
5 . . . . 100.00

FLYING A'S
RANGE RIDER, THE
**Dell Publishing Co.,
June–Aug., 1953**
(1) = *Dell Four Color #404*
2 Ph(c) all 200.00
3 . . . . 150.00
4 thru 10 . . . . @125.00
11 thru 16 . . . . @100.00
17 ATh 150.00
19 thru 24 . . . . @100.00

FLYING CADET
Flying Cadet Publ. Co., 1943
1 Aviation for student Airmen . . . 200.00
2 . . . . 150.00
3 Photo(c) 125.00
4 Photo(c) 125.00
5 Photo(c) 125.00
6a Photo(c) 125.00
6b Photo(c) 125.00
7 Photo(c) 125.00
8 Photo(c) 125.00
9 Photo(c) 125.00
10 thru 16 . . . . @100.00
17 nudity-woman 300.00

FLYIN' JENNY
Pentagon Publ. Co, 1946
N# 300.00
2 . . . . 350.00

FLYING MODELS
**Health-Knowledge
Publications, 1954**
1 . . . . 150.00

FOODINI
**Continental Publications,
March, 1950**
1 TV Puppet 300.00
2 Jingle Dingle 150.00
3 . . . . 125.00
4 Aug., 1950 . . . . 125.00

FOOTBALL THRILLS
**Approved Comics
(Ziff-Davis),
Fall-Winter, 1952**
1 BP,NS(c),Red Grange story . . 375.00
2 NS(c),Bronko Nagurski,
  Spring,1952 . . . . 250.00

FORBIDDEN LOVE
**Comic Magazine
(Quality Comics Group),
March, 1950**
1 RC,Ph(c),Heartbreak Road . 1,300.00
2 Ph(c),I Loved a Gigolo 1,000.00
3 Kissless Bride 650.00
4 BWa,Brimstone Kisses,
  Sept., 1950 . . . . 700.00

FORBIDDEN WORLDS
**American Comics Group,
July–Aug., 1951**
1 AW,FF 2,500.00
2 . . . . 1,200.00
3 AW,WW,JD 1,400.00
4 Werewolf (c) 800.00
5 AW 850.00
6 AW,King Kong (c) 800.00
7 . . . . 500.00
8 . . . . 500.00
9 Atomic Bomb 600.00
10 JyD 450.00
11 The Mummy's Treasure 300.00

12 Chest of Death	300.00
13 Invasion from Hades	300.00
14 Million-Year Monster	300.00
15 The Vampire Cat	300.00
16 The Doll	300.00
17	300.00
18 The Mummy	300.00
19 Pirate and the Voodoo Queen	300.00
20 Terror Island	300.00
21 The Ant Master	250.00
22 The Cursed Casket	250.00
23 Nightmare for Two	250.00
24	250.00
25 Hallahan's Head	250.00
26 The Champ	250.00
27 SMo,The Thing with the Golden Hair	250.00
28 Portrait of Carlotta	250.00
29 The Frogman	250.00
30 The Things on the Beach	250.00
31 SMo,The Circle of the Doomed	225.00
32 The Invasion of the Dead Things	225.00
33	225.00
34 Atomic Bomb	300.00
35 Comics Code	275.00
36 thru 62	@175.00
63 AW	175.00
64	125.00
65	125.00
66	125.00
67	125.00
68 OW(c)	125.00
69 AW	175.00
70	125.00
71	125.00
72	125.00
73 OW,I:Herbie	600.00
74	125.00
75 JB	125.00
76 AW	175.00
77	125.00
78 AW,OW(c)	150.00
79 thru 85 JB	@125.00
86 Flying Saucer	160.00
87	125.00
88	125.00
89	125.00
90	125.00
91	125.00
92	125.00
93	125.00
94 OW(c),A:Herbie	175.00
95	125.00
96 AW	175.00

Forbidden Worlds #102
© American Comics Group

97 thru 115	@150.00
116 OW(c)A:Herbie	175.00
117	125.00
118	125.00
119	125.00
120 thru 124	@125.00
125 I:O:Magic Man	125.00
126 A:Magic Man	125.00
127 same	125.00
128 same	125.00
129 same	125.00
130 same	125.00
131 same	125.00
132 same	125.00
133 I:O:Dragona	125.00
134 A:Magic Man	125.00
135 A:Magic Man	125.00
136 A:Nemesis	125.00
137 SD,A:Magic Man	150.00
138 SD,A:Magic Man	150.00
139 A:Magic Man	125.00
140 SD,A:Mark Midnight	150.00
141 thru 145	@125.00

FOREIGN INTRIGUES
See: DYNAMITE

Four Color #23 — Gang Busters
© Dell Publishing

FOUR COLOR
Dell Publishing Co., 1939

N# Dick Tracy	17,000.00
N# Don Winslow of the Navy	3,000.00
N# Myra North	1,500.00
4 Disney's Donald Duck (1940)	25,000.00
5 Smilin' Jack	1,100.00
6 Dick Tracy	3,200.00
7 Gang Busters	700.00
8 Dick Tracy	1,700.00
9 Terry and the Pirates	1,000.00
10 Smilin' Jack	950.00
11 Smitty	700.00
12 Little Orphan Annie	1,000.00
13 Walt Disney's Reluctant Dragon (1941)	3,300.00
14 Moon Mullins	700.00
15 Tillie the Toiler	750.00
16 W.Disney's Mickey Mouse Outwits the Phantom Blob (1941)	25,000.00
17 W.Disney's Dumbo the Flying Elephant (1941)	4,000.00
18 Jiggs and Maggie	700.00
19 Barney Google and Snuffy Smith	700.00
20 Tiny Tim	500.00
21 Dick Tracy	1,200.00
22 Don Winslow	700.00
23 Gang Busters	550.00
24 Captain Easy	750.00

25 Popeye	1,400.00

[Second Series, 1942]

1 Little Joe	1,200.00
2 Harold Teen	600.00
3 Alley Oop	1,000.00
4 Smilin' Jack	800.00
5 Raggedy Ann and Andy	1,000.00
6 Smitty	500.00
7 Smokey Stover	600.00
8 Tillie the Toiler	500.00
9 Donald Duck finds Pirate Gold!	20,000.00
10 Flash Gordon	2,000.00
11 Wash Tubs	600.00
12 Bambi	1,200.00
13 Mr. District Attorney	600.00
14 Smilin' Jack	700.00
15 Felix the Cat	1,800.00
16 Porky Pig	2,000.00
17 Popeye	900.00
18 Little Orphan Annie's Junior Commandos	700.00
19 W.Disney's Thumper meets the Seven Dwarfs	1,200.00
20 Barney Baxter	500.00
21 Oswald the Rabbit	1,000.00
22 Tillie the Toiler	400.00
23 Raggedy Ann and Andy	700.00
24 Gang Busters	500.00
25 Andy Panda	1,200.00
26 Popeye	850.00
27 Mickey Mouse and the Seven Colored Terror	2,200.00
28 Wash Tubbs	400.00
29 CB,Donald Duck and the Mummy's Ring	14,000.00
30 Bambi's Children	1,000.00
31 Moon Mullins	350.00
32 Smitty	300.00
33 Bugs Bunny	2,500.00
34 Dick Tracy	1,000.00
35 Smokey Stover	350.00
36 Smilin' Jack	450.00
37 Bringing Up Father	400.00
38 Roy Rogers	4,200.00
39 Oswald the Rabbit	650.00
40 Barney Google and Snuffy Smith	450.00
41 WK,Mother Goose	475.00
42 Tiny Tim	350.00
43 Popeye	650.00
44 Terry and the Pirates	750.00
45 Raggedy Ann	650.00
46 Felix the Cat and the Haunted House	900.00
47 Gene Autry	850.00
48 CB,Porky Pig of the Mounties	2,200.00
49 W.Disney's Snow White and the Seven Dwarfs	1,400.00
50 WK,Fairy Tale Parade	500.00
51 Bugs Bunny Finds the Lost Treasure	700.00
52 Little Orphan Annie	550.00
53 Wash Tubbs	275.00
54 Andy Panda	600.00
55 Tillie the Toiler	275.00
56 Dick Tracy	800.00
57 Gene Autry	800.00
58 Smilin' Jack	450.00
59 WK,Mother Goose	400.00
60 Tiny Folks Funnies	300.00
61 Santa Claus Funnies	500.00
62 CB,Donald Duck in Frozen Gold	5,000.00
63 Roy Rogers-photo (c)	1,000.00
64 Smokey Stover	250.00
65 Smitty	250.00
66 Gene Autry	800.00
67 Oswald the Rabbit	400.00
68 WK,Mother Goose	400.00
69 WK,Fairy Tale Parade	500.00

70 Popeye and Wimpy 500.00
71 WK,Walt Disney's
 Three Caballeros 1,500.00
72 Raggedy Ann 500.00
73 The Grumps 250.00
74 Marge's Little Lulu 3,000.00
75 Gene Autry and the Wildcat . . 600.00
76 Little Orphan Annie 450.00
77 Felix the Cat 800.00
78 Porky Pig & the Bandit Twins . 700.00
79 Mickey Mouse in the Riddle
 of the Red Hat 2,400.00
80 Smilin' Jack 300.00
81 Moon Mullins 200.00
82 Lone Ranger 800.00
83 Gene Autry in Outlaw Trail . . 600.00
84 Flash Gordon 900.00
85 Andy Panda and the
 Mad Dog Mystery 350.00
86 Roy Rogers-photo (c) 700.00
87 WK,DNo(c),Fairy Tale Parade 500.00
88 Bugs Bunny 450.00
89 Tillie the Toiler 275.00
90 WK,Christmas with
 Mother Goose 375.00
91 WK,Santa Claus Funnies 375.00
92 WK,W.Disney's Pinocchio . . 1,200.00
93 Gene Autry 600.00
94 Winnie Winkle 250.00
95 Roy Rogers,Ph(c) 700.00
96 Dick Tracy 500.00
97 Marge's Little Lulu 1,200.00
98 Lone Ranger 600.00
99 Smitty 200.00
100 Gene Autry Comics-photo(c) 600.00
101 Terry and the Pirates 500.00
102 WK,Oswald the Rabbit 275.00
103 WK,Easter with
 Mother Goose 350.00
104 WK,Fairy Tale Parade 375.00
105 WK,Albert the Alligator 1,300.00
106 Tillie the Toiler 200.00
107 Little Orphan Annie 375.00
108 Donald Duck in the
 Terror of the River 3,500.00
109 Roy Rogers Comics 500.00
110 Marge's Little Lulu 800.00
111 Captain Easy 300.00
112 Porky Pig's Adventure in
 Gopher Gulch 500.00
113 Popeye 300.00
114 WK,Fairy Tale Parade 400.00
115 Marge's Little Lulu 800.00
116 Mickey Mouse and the
 House of Many Mysteries . . 600.00
117 Roy Rogers Comics, Ph(c) . . 400.00
118 Lone Ranger 600.00
119 Felix the Cat 700.00
120 Marge's Little Lulu 700.00
121 Fairy Tale Parade 225.00
122 Henry 275.00
123 Bugs Bunny's Dangerous
 Venture 300.00
124 Roy Rogers Comics,Ph(c) . . 400.00
125 Lone Ranger 450.00
126 WK,Christmas with
 Mother Goose 250.00
127 Popeye 275.00
128 WK,Santa Claus Funnies . . . 300.00
129 W.Disney's Uncle Remus
 & His Tales of Brer Rabbit . . 600.00
130 Andy Panda 250.00
131 Marge's Little Lulu 700.00
132 Tillie the Toiler 200.00
133 Dick Tracy 400.00
134 Tarzan and the Devil Ogre . 1,400.00
135 Felix the Cat 500.00
136 Lone Ranger 400.00
137 Roy Rogers Comics 400.00
138 Smitty 175.00
139 Marge's Little Lulu 600.00

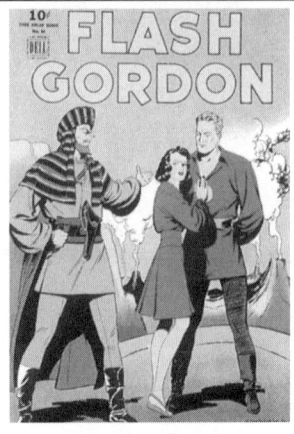

Four Color #84 — Flash Gordon
© Dell Publishing Co.

140 WK,Easter with
 Mother Goose 300.00
141 Mickey Mouse and the
 Submarine Pirates 500.00
142 Bugs Bunny and the
 Haunted Mountain 300.00
143 Oswald the Rabbit & the
 Prehistoric Egg 175.00
144 Poy Rogers Comics,Ph(c) . . 400.00
145 Popeye 275.00
146 Marge's Little Lulu 650.00
147 W.Disney's Donald Duck
 in Volcano Valley 2,400.00
148 WK,Albert the Alligator
 and Pogo Possum 1,000.00
149 Smilin' Jack 200.00
150 Tillie the Toiler 175.00
151 Lone Ranger 350.00
152 Little Orphan Annie 300.00
153 Roy Rogers Comics 350.00
154 Andy Panda 250.00
155 Henry 200.00
156 Porky Pig and the Phantom . 600.00
157 W.Disney's Mickey Mouse
 and the Beanstalk 500.00
158 Marge's Little Lulu 650.00
159 CB,W.Disney's Donald Duck
 in the Ghost of the Grotto . 3,000.00
160 Roy Rogers Comics,Ph(c) . . 400.00
161 Tarzan & the Fires of Tohr . 1,100.00
162 Felix the Cat 350.00
163 Dick Tracy 350.00
164 Bugs Bunny Finds the
 Frozen Kingdom 300.00
165 Marge's Little Lulu 650.00
166 Roy Rogers Comics,Ph(c) . . 350.00
167 Lone Ranger 350.00
168 Popeye 300.00
169 Woody Woodpecker,Drug . . . 400.00
170 W.Disney's Mickey Mouse
 on Spook's Island 400.00
171 Charlie McCarthy 500.00
172 WK,Christmas with
 Mother Goose 250.00
173 Flash Gordon 400.00
174 Winnie Winkle 150.00
175 WK,Santa Claus Funnies . . . 275.00
176 Tillie the Toiler 200.00
177 Roy Rogers Comics,Ph(c) . . 350.00
178 CB,W.Disney's Donald
 Duck Christmas on Bear
 Mountain 2,800.00
179 WK,Uncle Wiggily 300.00
180 Ozark the Ike 200.00
181 W.Disney's Mickey Mouse
 in Jungle Magic 500.00

182 Porky Pig in Never-
 Never Land 600.00
183 Oswald the Rabbit 225.00
184 Tillie the Toiler 175.00
185 WK,Easter with
 Mother Goose 250.00
186 W.Disney's Bambi 300.00
187 Bugs Bunny and the
 Dreadful Bunny 250.00
188 Woody Woodpecker 250.00
189 W.Disney's Donald Duck in
 The Old Castle's Secret . . . 1,800.00
190 Flash Gordon 400.00
191 Porky Pig to the Rescue 500.00
192 WK,The Brownies 275.00
193 Tom and Jerry 400.00
194 W.Disney's Mickey Mouse
 in the World Under the Sea . . 500.00
195 Tillie the Toiler 125.00
196 Charlie McCarthy in The
 Haunted Hide-Out 350.00
197 Spirit of the Border 250.00
198 Andy Panda 225.00
199 W.Disney's Donald Duck in
 Sheriff of Bullet Valley 2,000.00
200 Bugs Bunny, Super Sleuth . . 250.00
201 WK,Christmas with
 Mother Goose 225.00
202 Woody Woodpecker 150.00
203 CB,W.Disney's Donald Duck in
 The Golden Christmas Tree 1,400.00
204 Flash Gordon 300.00
205 WK,Santa Claus Funnies . . . 275.00
206 Little Orphan Funnies 200.00
207 King of the Royal Mounted . . 275.00
208 W.Disney's Brer Rabbit
 Does It Again 225.00
209 Harold Teen 100.00
210 Tippe and Cap Stubbs 100.00
211 Little Beaver 150.00
212 Dr. Bobbs 90.00
213 Tillie the Toiler 125.00
214 W.Disney's Mickey Mouse
 and his Sky Adventure 400.00
215 Sparkle Plenty 250.00
216 Andy Panda and the
 Police Pup 150.00
217 Bugs Bunny in Court Jester . 250.00
218 W.Disney's 3 Little Pigs 225.00
219 Swee'pea 150.00
220 WK,Easter with
 Mother Goose 275.00
221 WK,Uncle Wiggly 175.00
222 West of the Pecos 125.00
223 CB,W.Disney's Donald Duck in
 Lost in the Andes 1,800.00
224 Little Iodine 250.00
225 Oswald the Rabbit 125.00
226 Porky Pig and Spoofy 400.00
227 W.Disney's Seven Dwarfs . . . 225.00
228 The Mark of Zorro 400.00
229 Smokey Stover 125.00
230 Sunset Press 125.00
231 W.Disney's Mickey Mouse
 and the Rajah's Treasure . . . 400.00
232 Woody Woodpecker 150.00
233 Bugs Bunny 200.00
234 W.Disney's Dumbo in Sky
 Voyage 250.00
235 Tiny Tim 90.00
236 Heritage of the Desert 125.00
237 Tillie the Toiler 125.00
238 CB,W.Disney's Donald Duck
 in Voodoo Hoodoo 1,300.00
239 Adventure Bound 100.00
240 Andy Panda 150.00
241 Porky Pig 300.00
242 Tippie and Cap Stubbs 90.00
243 W.Disney's Thumper
 Follows His Nose 250.00
244 WK,The Brownies 200.00

GOLDEN AGE

245 Dick's Adventures in
    Dreamland 100.00
246 Thunder Mountain 90.00
247 Flash Gordon 500.00
248 W.Disney's Mickey Mouse
    and the Black Sorcerer 300.00
249 Woody Woodpecker 150.00
250 Bugs Bunny in
    Diamond Daze 225.00
251 Hubert at Camp Moonbeam . 100.00
252 W.Disney's Pinocchio 225.00
253 WK,Christmas with
    Mother Goose 225.00
254 W,Santa Claus Funnies,
    A:Pogo. 250.00
255 The Ranger. 100.00
256 CB,W.Disney's Donald Duck in
    Luck of the North 1,100.00
257 Little Iodine 150.00
258 Andy Panda and the
    Ballon Race 150.00
259 Santa and the Angel 100.00
260 Porky Pig, Hero of the
    Wild West 250.00
261 W.Disney's Mickey Mouse
    and the Missing Key 300.00
262 Raggedy Ann and Andy 175.00
263 CB,W.Disney's Donald Duck in
    Land of the Totem Poles . . 1,000.00
264 Woody Woodpecker in
    the Magic Lantern 150.00
265 King of the Royal Mountain . 150.00
266 Bugs Bunny on the Isle of
    Hercules 175.00
267 Little Beaver 150.00
268 W.Disney's Mickey Mouse's
    Surprise Visitor 300.00
269 Johnny Mack Brown,Ph(c) . . 450.00
270 Drift Fence 100.00
271 Porky Pig 250.00
272 W.Disney's Cinderella 225.00
273 Oswald the Rabbit 100.00
274 Bugs Bunny 175.00
275 CB,W.Disney's Donald Duck
    in Ancient Persia. 1,000.00
276 Uncle Wiggly. 175.00
277 PorkyPig in DesertAdventure 250.00
278 Bill Elliot Comics,Ph(c) 250.00
279 W.Disney's Mickey Mouse &
    Pluto Battle the Giant Ants . . 300.00
280 Andy Panda in the Isle
    of the Mechanical Men 150.00
281 Bugs Bunny in The Great
    Circus Mystery. 175.00
282 CB,W.Disney's Donald Duck in
    The Pixilated Parrot 1,000.00
283 King of the Royal Mounted . . 150.00
284 Porky Pig in the Kingdom
    of Nowhere 250.00
285 Bozo the Clown. 350.00
286 W.Disney's Mickey Mouse
    and the Uninvited Guest 300.00
287 Gene Autry's Champion in the
    Ghost of BlackMountain,Ph(c)250.00
288 Woody Woodpecker 150.00
289 BugsBunny in IndianTrouble. 175.00
290 The Chief 125.00
291 CB,W.Disney's Donald Duck In
    The Magic Hourglass 1,000.00
292 The Cisco Kid Comics 450.00
293 WK,The Brownies 200.00
294 Little Beaver 100.00
295 Porky Pig in President Pig . . 250.00
296 W.Disney's Mickey Mouse
    Private Eye for Hire 200.00
297 Andy Panda in The
    Haunted Inn. 150.00
298 Bugs Bunny in Sheik
    for a Day 175.00
299 Buck Jones & the Iron Trail . 250.00
300 CB,W.Disney's Donald Duck in
    Big-Top Bedlam 1,000.00

301 The Mysterious Rider 100.00
302 Santa Claus Funnies 125.00
303 Porky Pig in The Land of
    the Monstrous Flies. 200.00
304 W.Disney's Mickey Mouse
    in Tom-Tom Island 250.00
305 Woody Woodpecker 125.00
306 Raggedy Ann 125.00
307 Bugs Bunny in Lumber
    Jack Rabbit 150.00
308 CB,W.Disney's Donald Duck in
    Dangerous Disguise 900.00
309 Dollface and Her Gang 100.00
310 King of the Royal Mounted . 125.00
311 Porky Pig in Midget Horses
    of Hidden Valley 200.00
312 Tonto 225.00
313 W.Disney's Mickey Mouse in
    the Mystery of the Double-
    Cross Ranch 250.00
314 Ambush. 90.00
315 Oswald Rabbit 100.00
316 Rex Allen,Ph(c). 275.00
317 Bugs Bunny in Hare Today
    Gone Tomorrow 150.00
318 CB,W.Disney's Donald Duck in
    No Such Varmint 900.00
319 Gene Autry's Champion 125.00
320 Uncle Wiggly 150.00
321 Little Scouts 75.00
322 Porky Pig in Roaring Rockies 150.00
323 Susie Q. Smith 75.00
324 I Met a Handsome Cowboy . 150.00
325 W.Disney's Mickey Mouse
    in the Haunted Castle 250.00
326 Andy Panda 100.00
327 Bugs Bunny and the
    Rajah's Treasure 150.00
328 CB,W.Disney's Donald Duck
    in Old California 1,000.00
329 Roy Roger's Trigger,Ph(c) . . 300.00
330 Porky Pig meets the
    Bristled Bruiser 150.00
331 Disney's Alice in
    Wonderland 300.00
332 Little Beaver 100.00
333 Wilderness Trek 100.00
334 W.Disney's Mickey Mouse
    and Yukon Gold. 250.00
335 Francis the Famous
    Talking Mule 200.00
336 Woody Woodpecker 125.00
337 The Brownies 100.00
338 Bugs Bunny and the
    Rocking Horse Thieves 200.00
339 W.Disney's Donald Duck
    and the Magic Fountain. 400.00

Four Color # 411 — Mickey Mouse
© Dell Publishing Co.

340 King of the Royal Mountain . 150.00
341 W.Disney's Unbirthday Party
    with Alice in Wonderland 300.00
342 Porky Pig the Lucky
    Peppermint Mine 150.00
343 W.Disney's Mickey Mouse in
    Ruby Eye of Homar-Guy-Am 150.00
344 Sergeant Preston from
    Challenge of the Yukon. 250.00
345 Andy Panda in Scotland Yard 100.00
346 Hideout 200.00
347 Bugs Bunny the Frigid Hare . 150.00
348 CB,W.Disney's Donald Duck
    The Crocodile Collector. 600.00
349 Uncle Wiggly. 125.00
350 Woody Woodpecker 100.00
351 Porky Pig and the Grand
    Canyon Giant 150.00
352 W.Disney's Mickey Mouse
    Mystery of Painted Valley . . . 200.00
353 CB(c),W.Disney'sDuckAlbum 300.00
354 Raggedy Ann & Andy 125.00
355 Bugs Bunny Hot-Rod Hair . . 150.00
356 CB(c),W.Disney's Donald
    Duck in Rags to Riches. 500.00
357 Comeback. 75.00
358 Andy Panada 100.00
359 Frosty the Snowman. 175.00
360 Porky Pig in Tree Fortune . . 100.00
361 Santa Claus Funnies 100.00
362 W.Disney's Mickey Mouse &
    the Smuggled Diamonds. . . . 250.00
363 King of the Royal Mounted. . 125.00
364 Woody Woodpecker 90.00
365 The Brownies 90.00
366 Bugs Bunny Uncle
    Buckskin Comes to Town . . . 150.00
367 CB,W.Disney's Donald Duck in
    A Christmas for Shacktown. . 800.00
368 Bob Clampett's
    Beany and Cecil 750.00
369 Lone Ranger's Famous
    Horse Hi-Yo Silver. 500.00
370 Porky Pig in Trouble
    in the Big Trees. 200.00
371 W.Disney's Mickey Mouse
    the Inca Idol Case 200.00
372 Riders of the Purple Sage . . . 75.00
373 Sergeant Preston 150.00
374 Woody Woodpecker 75.00
375 John Carter of Mars 600.00
376 Bugs Bunny 200.00
377 Susie Q. Smith 75.00
378 Tom Corbett, Space Cadet . . 350.00
379 W.Disney's Donald Duck in
    Southern Hospitality 300.00
380 Raggedy Ann & Andy 125.00
381 Marge's Tubby 375.00
382 W.Disney's Show White and
    the Seven Dwarfs 200.00
383 Andy Panda 75.00
384 King of the Royal Mounted . . 100.00
385 Porky Pig 100.00
386 CB,W.Disney's Uncle Scrooge
    in Only A Poor Old Man . . . 3,800.00
387 W.Disney's Mickey Mouse
    in High Tibet 200.00
388 Oswald the Rabbit 100.00
389 Andy Hardy Comics 75.00
390 Woody Woodpecker 75.00
391 Uncle Wiggly. 125.00
392 Hi-Yo Silver. 100.00
393 Bugs Bunny 150.00
394 CB(c),W.Disney's Donald Duck
    in Malayalaya 500.00
395 Forlorn River. 75.00
396 Tales of the Texas Rangers,
    Ph(c) 200.00
397 Sergeant Preston o/t Yukon . 150.00
398 The Brownies 75.00
399 Porky Pig in the Lost
    Gold Mine 100.00

GOLDEN AGE

GOLDEN AGE

400 AMc,Tom Corbett 200.00	
401 W.Disney's Mickey Mouse &	
Goofy's Mechanical Wizard . . 150.00	
402 Mary Jane and Sniffles 100.00	
403 W.Disney's Li'l Bad Wolf 150.00	
404 The Ranger Rider,Ph(c) 200.00	
405 Woody Woodpecker 75.00	
406 Tweety and Sylvester 125.00	
407 Bugs Bunny, Foreign-	
Legion Hare 125.00	
408 CB,W.Disney's Donald Duck	
and the Golden Helmet 750.00	
409 Andy Panda 75.00	
410 Porky Pig in the	
Water Wizard 100.00	
411 W.Disney's Mickey Mouse	
and the Old Sea Dog 150.00	
412 Nevada 75.00	
413 Disney's Robin Hood(movie),	
Ph(c) 200.00	
414 Bob Clampett's Beany	
and Cecil 300.00	
415 Rootie Kazootie 200.00	
416 Woody Woodpecker 90.00	
417 Double Trouble with Goober . . 75.00	
418 Rusty Riley 75.00	
419 Sergeant Preston 150.00	
420 Bugs Bunny 125.00	
421 AMc,Tom Corbett 200.00	
422 CB,W.Disney's Donald Duck	
and the Gilded Man 750.00	
423 Rhubarb 100.00	
424 Flash Gordon 225.00	
425 Zorro 250.00	
426 Porky Pig 100.00	
427 W.Disney's Mickey Mouse &	
the Wonderful Whizzix 150.00	
428 Uncle Wiggily 100.00	
429 W.Disney's Pluto in	
Why Dogs Leave Home 200.00	
430 Marge's Tubby 225.00	
431 Woody Woodpecker 100.00	
432 Bugs Bunny and the	
Rabbit Olympics 125.00	
433 Wildfire 75.00	
434 Rin Tin Tin,Ph(c) 300.00	
435 Frosty the Snowman 100.00	
436 The Brownies 75.00	
437 John Carter of Mars 400.00	
438 W.Disney's Annie	
Oakley (TV) 275.00	
439 Little Hiawatha 100.00	
440 Black Beauty 75.00	
441 Fearless Fagan 75.00	
442 W.Disney's Peter Pan 200.00	
443 Ben Bowie and His	
Mountain Men 150.00	
444 Marge's Tubby 225.00	
445 Charlie McCarthy 100.00	
446 Captain Hook and Peter Pan 175.00	
447 Andy Hardy Comics 75.00	
448 Beany and Cecil 300.00	
449 Tappan's Burro 75.00	
450 CB(c),W.Disney's Duck	
Album 200.00	
451 Rusty Riley 65.00	
452 Raggedy Ann and Andy 125.00	
453 Susie Q. Smith 65.00	
454 Krazy Kat Comics 65.00	
455 Johnny Mack Brown Comics,	
Ph(c) 125.00	
456 W.Disney's Uncle Scrooge	
Back to the Klondike 2,000.00	
457 Daffy 200.00	
458 Oswald the Rabbit 75.00	
459 Rootie Kazootie 150.00	
460 Buck Jones 175.00	
461 Marge's Tubby 200.00	
462 Little Scouts 50.00	
463 Petunia 75.00	
464 Bozo 175.00	
465 Francis the Talking Mule 100.00	

466 Rhubarb, the Millionaire Cat . . 75.00	
467 Desert Gold 75.00	
468 W.Disney's Goofy 300.00	
469 Beetle Bailey 200.00	
470 Elmer Fudd 100.00	
471 Double Trouble with Goober . . 40.00	
472 Wild Bill Elliot,Ph(c) 150.00	
473 W.Disney's Li'l Bad Wolf 75.00	
474 Mary Jane and Sniffles 125.00	
475 M.G.M.'s the Two	
Mouseketeers 125.00	
476 Rin Tin Tin,Ph(c) 150.00	
477 Bob Clampett's Beany and	
Cecil 300.00	
478 Charlie McCarthy 100.00	
479 Queen o/t West Dale Evans . 400.00	
480 Andy Hardy Comics 65.00	
481 Annie Oakley and Tagg 200.00	
482 Brownies 90.00	
483 Little Beaver 75.00	
484 River Feud 75.00	
485 The Little People 150.00	
486 Rusty Riley 75.00	
487 Mowgli, the Jungle Book 100.00	
488 John Carter of Mars 350.00	
489 Tweety and Sylvester 100.00	
490 Jungle Jim 125.00	
491 EK,Silvertip 150.00	
492 W.Disney's Duck Album 150.00	
493 Johnny Mack Brown,Ph(c) . . 125.00	
494 The Little King 175.00	
495 CB, W.Disney's Uncle	
Scrooge 1,400.00	
496 The Green Hornet 750.00	
497 Zorro, (Sword of) 250.00	
498 Bugs Bunny's Album 100.00	
499 M.G.M.'s Spike and Tyke . . . 100.00	
500 Buck Jones 100.00	
501 Francis the Famous	
Talking Mule 90.00	
502 Rootie Kazootie 135.00	
503 Uncle Wiggily 90.00	
504 Krazy Kat 75.00	
505 W.Disney's the Sword and	
the Rose (TV),Ph(c) 150.00	
506 The Little Scouts 50.00	
507 Oswald the Rabbit 100.00	
508 Bozo 175.00	
509 W.Disney's Pluto 100.00	
510 Son of Black Beauty 60.00	
511 EK,Outlaw Trail 75.00	
512 Flash Gordon 150.00	
513 Ben Bowie and His	
Mountain Men 60.00	
514 Frosty the Snowman 100.00	
515 Andy Hardy 50.00	
516 Double Trouble With Goober . 40.00	
517 Walt Disney's Chip 'N' Dale . 200.00	
518 Rivets 50.00	
519 Steve Canyon 150.00	
520 Wild Bill Elliot,Ph(c) 125.00	
521 Beetle Bailey 100.00	
522 The Brownies 75.00	
523 Rin Tin Tin,Ph(c) 150.00	
524 Tweety and Sylvester 100.00	
525 Santa Claus Funnies 100.00	
526 Napoleon 50.00	
527 Charlie McCarthy 100.00	
528 Queen o/t West Dale Evans,	
Ph(c) 200.00	
529 Little Beaver 75.00	
530 Bob Clampett's Beany	
and Cecil 300.00	
531 W.Disney's Duck Album 150.00	
532 The Rustlers 60.00	
533 Raggedy Ann and Andy 125.00	
534 EK,Western Marshal 125.00	
535 I Love Lucy,Ph(c) 1,100.00	
536 Daffy 100.00	
537 Stormy, the Thoroughbred . . . 75.00	
538 EK,The Mask of Zorro 250.00	
539 Ben and Me 75.00	

Four Color #447 — Andy Hardy
© Dell Publishing Co.

540 Knights of the Round Table,	
Ph(c) 150.00	
541 Johnny Mack Brown,Ph(c) . . 125.00	
542 Super Circus Featuring	
Mary Hartline 125.00	
543 Uncle Wiggly 100.00	
544 W.Disney's Rob Roy(Movie),	
Ph(c) 150.00	
545 The Wonderful Adventures	
of Pinocchio 150.00	
546 Buck Jones 100.00	
547 Francis the Famous	
Talking Mule 90.00	
548 Krazy Kat 75.00	
549 Oswald the Rabbit 75.00	
550 The Little Scouts 50.00	
551 Bozo 175.00	
552 Beetle Bailey 100.00	
553 Susie Q. Smith 60.00	
554 Rusty Riley 70.00	
555 Range War 70.00	
556 Double Trouble with Goober . . 40.00	
557 Ben Bowie and His	
Mountain Men 75.00	
558 Elmer Fudd 75.00	
559 I Love Lucy,Ph(c) 600.00	
560 W.Disney's Duck Album 150.00	
561 Mr. Magoo 200.00	
562 W.Disney's Goofy 150.00	
563 Rhubarb, the Millionaire Cat . 100.00	
564 W.Disney's Li'l Bad Wolf 100.00	
565 Jungle Jim 75.00	
566 Son of Black Beauty 60.00	
567 BF,Prince Valiant,Ph(c) 250.00	
568 Gypsy Cat 90.00	
569 Priscilla's Pop 75.00	
570 Bob Clampett's Beany	
and Cecil 300.00	
571 Charlie McCarthy 100.00	
572 EK,Silvertip 90.00	
573 The Little People 100.00	
574 The Hand of Zorro 250.00	
575 Annie and Oakley and Tagg,	
Ph(c) 175.00	
576 Angel 60.00	
577 M.G.M.'s Spike and Tyke 60.00	
578 Steve Canyon 90.00	
579 Francis the Talking Mule 75.00	
580 Six Gun Ranch 75.00	
581 Chip 'N' Dale 100.00	
582 Mowgli, the Jungle Book 100.00	
583 The Lost Wagon Train 75.00	
584 Johnny Mack Brown,Ph(c) . . 125.00	
585 Bugs Bunny's Album 100.00	
586 W.Disney's Duck Album 160.00	
587 The Little Scouts 50.00	

GOLDEN AGE

588 MB,King Richard and the
  Crusaders,Ph(c) 175.00
589 Buck Jones. 100.00
590 Hansel and Gretel. 125.00
591 EK,Western Marshal. 100.00
592 Super Circus. 125.00
593 Oswald the Rabbit 60.00
594 Bozo 175.00
595 Pluto 75.00
596 Turok, Son of Stone. 1,200.00
597 The Little King. 100.00
598 Captain Davy Jones 90.00
599 Ben Bowie and His
  Mountain Men 75.00
600 Daisy Duck's Diary 150.00
601 Frosty the Snowman. 100.00
602 Mr. Magoo and the Gerald
  McBoing-Boing 225.00
603 M.G.M.'s The Two
  Mouseketeers 90.00
604 Shadow on the Trail 75.00
605 The Brownies 75.00
606 Sir Lancelot. 150.00
607 Santa Claus Funnies 125.00
608 EK,Silver Tip 75.00
609 The Littlest Outlaw,Ph(c). . . . 125.00
610 Drum Beat,Ph(c) 175.00
611 W.Disney's Duck Album 150.00
612 Little Beaver 65.00
613 EK,Western Marshal. 100.00
614 W.Disney's 20,000 Leagues
  Under the Sea (Movie) 200.00
615 Daffy 100.00
616 To The Last Man. 75.00
617 The Quest of Zorro 225.00
618 Johnny Mack Brown,Ph(c) . . 125.00
619 Krazy Kat 65.00
620 Mowgli, Jungle Book 90.00
621 Francis the Famous
  Talking Mule 65.00
622 Beetle Bailey. 100.00
623 Oswald the Rabbit 65.00
624 Treasure Island,Ph(c) 150.00
625 Beaver Valley 125.00
626 Ben Bowie and His
  Mountain Men 75.00
627 Goofy 150.00
628 Elmer Fudd 65.00
629 Lady & The Tramp with Jock 150.00
630 Priscilla's Pop 65.00
631 W.Disney's Davy Crockett
  Indian Fighter (TV),Ph(c). . . . 375.00
632 Fighting Caravans. 75.00
633 The Little People. 75.00
634 Lady and the Tramp Album. . 100.00
635 Bob Clampett's Beany
  and Cecil 300.00
636 Chip 'N' Dale. 100.00
637 EK,Silvertip 75.00
638 M.G.M.'s Spike and Tyke 60.00
639 W.Disney's Davy Crockett
  at the Alamo (TV),Ph(c). . . . 300.00
640 EK,Western Marshal 100.00
641 Steve Canyon 110.00
642 M.G.M.'s The Two
  Mouseketeers 80.00
643 Wild Bill Elliott,Ph(c). 75.00
644 Sir Walter Raleigh,Ph(c) 125.00
645 Johnny Mack Brown,Ph(c) . . 125.00
646 Dotty Dripple and Taffy 75.00
647 Bugs Bunny's Album. 100.00
648 Jace Pearson of the
  Texas Rangers,Ph(c). 100.00
649 Duck Album. 100.00
650 BF,Prince Valiant 125.00
651 EK,King Colt 75.00
652 Buck Jones 75.00
653 Smokey the Bear 200.00
654 Pluto 75.00
655 Francis the Famous
  Talking Mule 75.00
656 Turok, Son of Stone 650.00

657 Ben Bowie and His
  Mountain Men 75.00
658 Goofy 150.00
659 Daisy Duck's Diary 125.00
660 Little Beaver 75.00
661 Frosty the Snowman. 100.00
662 Zoo Parade. 100.00
663 Winky Dink 150.00
664 W.Disney's Davy Crockett in
  the Great Keelboat
  Race (TV),Ph(c) 300.00
665 The African Lion 100.00
666 Santa Claus Funnies 100.00
667 EK,Silvertip and the Stolen
  Stallion. 100.00
668 W.Disney's Dumbo 325.00
668a W.Disney's Dumbo 2nd print 300.00
669 W.Disney's Robin Hood
  (Movie),Ph(c). 125.00
670 M.G.M.'s Mouse Musketeers . 75.00
671 W.Disney's Davey Crockett &
  the River Pirates(TV),Ph(c). . 275.00
672 Quentin Durward,Ph(c) 125.00
673 Buffalo Bill Jr.,Ph(c) 150.00
674 The Little Rascals 150.00
675 EK,Steve Donovan,Ph(c) . . . 150.00
676 Will-Yum!. 60.00
677 Little King 100.00
678 The Last Hunt,Ph(c) 150.00
679 Gunsmoke. 350.00
680 Out Our Way with the
  Worry Wart 60.00
681 Forever, Darling,Lucile
  Ball Ph(c). 225.00
682 When Knighthood Was
  in Flower,Ph(c) 150.00
683 Hi and Lois 60.00
684 SB,Helen of Troy,Ph(c) 200.00
685 Johnny Mack Brown,Ph(c) . . 150.00
686 Duck Album. 150.00
687 The Indian Fighter,Ph(c). . . . 150.00
688 SB,Alexander the Great,
  Ph(c) 150.00
689 Elmer Fudd 75.00
690 The Conqueror,
  John Wayne Ph(c). 350.00
691 Dotty Dripple and Taffy 50.00
692 The Little People. 75.00
693 W.Disney's Brer Rabbit
  Song of the South 175.00
694 Super Circus,Ph(c) 125.00
695 Little Beaver 75.00
696 Krazy Kat 75.00
697 Oswald the Rabbit 60.00
698 Francis the Famous
  Talking Mule 75.00
699 BA,Prince Valiant 150.00
700 Water Birds and the
  Olympic Elk 100.00
701 Jimmy Cricket 175.00
702 The Goofy Success Story . . . 135.00
703 Scamp. 175.00
704 Priscilla's Pop 60.00
705 Brave Eagle,Ph(c). 150.00
706 Bongo and Lumpjaw. 100.00
707 Corky and White Shadow,
  Ph(c) 135.00
708 Smokey the Bear 100.00
709 The Searchers,John
  Wayne Ph(c) 600.00
710 Francis the Famous
  Talking Mule 75.00
711 M.G.M.'s Mouse Musketeers. . 60.00
712 The Great Locomotive
  Chase, Ph(c) 135.00
713 The Animal World 60.00
714 W.Disney's Spin
  & Marty (TV) 250.00
715 Timmy 75.00
716 Man in Space 150.00
717 Moby Dick,Ph(c) 150.00
718 Dotty Dripple and Taffy 50.00

Four Color #671 — Davy Crockett
© Dell Publishing Co.

719 BF,Prince Valiant. 125.00
720 Gunsmoke,Ph(c). 175.00
721 Captain Kangaroo,Ph(c) . . . 325.00
722 Johnny Mack Brown,Ph(c) . . 125.00
723 EK,Santiago 175.00
724 Bugs Bunny's Album. 75.00
725 Elmer Fudd. 60.00
726 Duck Album. 100.00
727 The Nature of Things 110.00
728 M.G.M.'s Mouse Musketeers . 60.00
729 Bob Son of Battle 75.00
730 Smokey Stover 100.00
731 EK,Silvertip and The
  Fighting Four 80.00
732 Zorro, (the Challenge of) . . . 250.00
733 Buck Rogers 100.00
734 Cheyenne,C.Walker Ph(c) . . 300.00
735 Crusader Rabbit 575.00
736 Pluto 75.00
737 Steve Canyon 100.00
738 Westward Ho, the Wagons,
  Ph(c) 200.00
739 MD,Bounty Guns 75.00
740 Chilly Willy 125.00
741 The Fastest Gun Alive,Ph(c). 150.00
742 Buffalo Bill Jr.,Ph(c) 100.00
743 Daisy Duck's Diary 110.00
744 Little Beaver 65.00
745 Francis the Famous
  Talking Mule 65.00
746 Dotty Dripple and Taffy 50.00
747 Goofy 135.00
748 Frosty the Snowman. 100.00
749 Secrets of Life,Ph(c). 100.00
750 The Great Cat 125.00
751 Our Miss Brooks,Ph(c) 150.00
752 Mandrake, the Magician 200.00
753 Walt Scott's Little People 75.00
754 Smokey the Bear 125.00
755 The Littlest Snowman 100.00
756 Santa Claus Funnies 100.00
757 The True Story of
  Jesse James,Ph(c) 175.00
758 Bear Country. 100.00
759 Circus Boy,Ph(c). 250.00
760 W.Disney's Hardy Boys(TV) . 250.00
761 Howdy Doody 250.00
762 SB,The Sharkfighters,Ph(c) . 150.00
763 GrandmaDuck'sFarmFriends 150.00
764 M.G.M.'s Mouse Musketeers . 60.00
765 Will-Yum!. 60.00
766 Buffalo Bill,Ph(c) 100.00
767 Spin and Marty 175.00
768 EK,Steve Donovan, Western
  Marshal,Ph(c) 125.00
769 Gunsmoke. 200.00

GOLDEN AGE

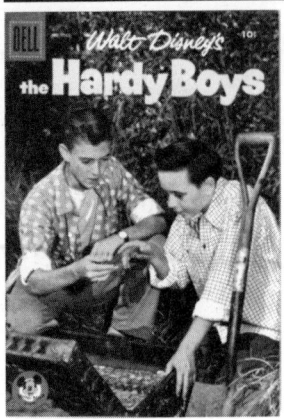

Four Color #760 — Hardy Boys
© *Dell Publishing Co.*

770 Brave Eagle,Ph(c) 65.00
771 MD,Brand of Empire 65.00
772 Cheyenne,C.Walker Ph(c) . . 150.00
773 The Brave One,Ph(c) 100.00
774 Hi and Lois 50.00
775 SB,Sir Lancelot and
    Brian,Ph(c). 200.00
776 Johnny Mack Brown,Ph(c) . . 125.00
777 Scamp. 135.00
778 The Little Rascals 100.00
779 Lee Hunter, Indian Fighter . . 100.00
780 Captain Kangaroo,Ph(c) 275.00
781 Fury,Ph(c) 150.00
782 Duck Album. 100.00
783 Elmer Fudd 60.00
784 Around the World in 80
    Days,Ph(c). 125.00
785 Circus Boys,Ph(c) 250.00
786 Cinderella 125.00
787 Little Hiawatha 100.00
788 BF,Prince Valiant. 125.00
789 EK,Silvertip-Valley Thieves . . 100.00
790 ATh,The Wings of Eagles,
    J.Wayne Ph(c) 300.00
791 The 77th Bengal Lancers,
    Ph(c) 150.00
792 Oswald the Rabbit 65.00
793 Morty Meekle 50.00
794 SB,The Count of Monte
    Cristo 150.00
795 Jiminy Cricket 125.00
796 Ludwig Bemelman's
    Madeleine and Genevieve. . . . 60.00
797 Gunsmoke,Ph(c). 175.00
798 Buffalo Bill,Ph(c) 100.00
799 Priscilla's Pop 60.00
800 The Buccaneers,Ph(c) 150.00
801 Dotty Dripple and Taffy 50.00
802 Goofy 150.00
803 Cheyenne,C.Walker Ph(c) . . 150.00
804 Steve Canyon 100.00
805 Crusader Rabbit 450.00
806 Scamp. 125.00
807 MB,Savage Range 65.00
808 Spin and Marty,Ph(c) 175.00
809 The Little People. 75.00
810 Francis the Famous
    Talking Mule 65.00
811 Howdy Doody 225.00
812 The Big Land,A.Ladd Ph(c) . 225.00
813 Circus Boy,Ph(c) 225.00
814 Covered Wagon,A:Mickey
    Mouse 125.00
815 Dragoon Wells Massacre . . 150.00
816 Brave Eagle,Ph(c) 65.00
817 Little Beaver 65.00

818 Smokey the Bear 125.00
819 Mickey Mouse in Magicland . 100.00
820 The Oklahoman,Ph(c) 175.00
821 Wringle Wrangle,Ph(c) 150.00
822 ATh,W.Disney's Paul Revere's
    Ride (TV). 175.00
823 Timmy 50.00
824 The Pride and the Passion,
    Ph(c) 175.00
825 The Little Rascals 100.00
826 Spin and Marty and Annette,
    Ph(c) 450.00
827 Smokey Stover 90.00
828 Buffalo Bill, Jr,Ph(c) 90.00
829 Tales of the Pony Express,
    Ph(c) 90.00
830 The Hardy Boys,Ph(c) 175.00
831 No Sleep 'Til Dawn,Ph(c) . . . 125.00
832 Lolly and Pepper. 65.00
833 Scamp. 125.00
834 Johnny Mack Brown,Ph(c) . . 125.00
835 Silvertip- The Fake Rider 90.00
836 Man in Fight 135.00
837 All-American Athlete
    Cotton Woods 65.00
838 Bugs Bunny's Life
    Story Album 75.00
839 The Vigilantes 125.00
840 Duck Album 100.00
841 Elmer Fudd 60.00
842 The Nature of Things 100.00
843 The First Americans 150.00
844 Gunsmoke,Ph(c). 175.00
845 ATh,The Land Unknown 250.00
846 ATh,Gun Glory 175.00
847 Perri 90.00
848 Marauder's Moon 65.00
849 BF,Prince Valiant. 125.00
850 Buck Jones 75.00
851 The Story of Mankind,
    V.Price Ph(c) 135.00
852 Chilly Willy 100.00
853 Pluto 75.00
854 Hunchback of Notre Dame,
    Ph(c) 275.00
855 Broken Arrow,Ph(c). 100.00
856 Buffalo Bill, Jr.,Ph(c) 100.00
857 The Goofy Adventure Story . 150.00
858 Daisy Duck's Diary 90.00
859 Topper and Neil. 80.00
860 Wyatt Earp,Ph(c) 200.00
861 Frosty the Snowman. 75.00
862 Truth About Mother Goose . . 135.00
863 Francis the Famous
    Talking Mule 60.00
864 The Littlest Snowman 90.00
865 Andy Burnett,Ph(c) 175.00
866 Mars and Beyond 150.00
867 Santa Claus Funnies 125.00
868 The Little People. 90.00
869 Old Yeller,Ph(c) 110.00
870 Little Beaver 75.00
871 Curly Kayoe 60.00
872 Captain Kangaroo,Ph(c) 250.00
873 Grandma Duck's
    Farm Friends. 90.00
874 Old Ironsides. 125.00
875 Trumpets West 60.00
876 Tales of Wells Fargo,Ph(c) . . 175.00
877 ATh,Frontier Doctor,Ph(c). . . 175.00
878 Peanuts. 400.00
879 Brave Eagle,Ph(c). 60.00
880 MD,Steve Donovan,Ph(c) . . . 75.00
881 The Captain and the Kids. . . . 60.00
882 ATh,W.DisneyPresentsZorro. 300.00
883 The Little Rascals 100.00
884 Hawkeye and the Last
    of the Mohicans,Ph(c) 135.00
885 Fury,Ph(c). 125.00
886 Bongo and Lumpjaw. 90.00
887 The Hardy Boys,Ph(c) 175.00
888 Elmer Fudd 60.00

889 ATh,W.Disney's Clint
    & Mac(TV),Ph(c) 250.00
890 Wyatt Earp,Ph(c) 135.00
891 Light in the Forest,
    C.Parker Ph(c). 135.00
892 Maverick,J.Garner Ph(c). . . . 500.00
893 Jim Bowie,Ph(c) 100.00
894 Oswald the Rabbit 60.00
895 Wagon Train,Ph(c) 225.00
896 Adventures of Tinker Bell . . . 150.00
897 Jiminy Cricket 125.00
898 EK,Silvertip 90.00
899 Goofy 100.00
900 BF,Prince Valiant 125.00
901 Little Hiawatha 90.00
902 Will-Yum!. 60.00
903 Dotty Dripple and Taffy 50.00
904 Lee Hunter, Indian Fighter . . . 60.00
905 W.Disney's Annette (TV),
    Ph(c) 575.00
906 Francis the Famous
    Talking Mule 60.00
907 Ath,Sugarfoot,Ph(c). 250.00
908 The Little People
    and the Giant. 75.00
909 Smitty 60.00
910 ATh,The Vikings,
    K.Douglas Ph(c) 150.00
911 The Gray Ghost,Ph(c). 150.00
912 Leave it to Beaver,Ph(c). . . . 325.00
913 The Left-Handed Gun,
    Paul Newman Ph(c) 175.00
914 ATh,No Time for Sergeants,
    Ph(c) 200.00
915 Casey Jones,Ph(c) 100.00
916 Red Ryder Ranch Comics . . 150.00
917 The Life of Riley,Ph(c) 225.00
918 Beep Beep, the Roadrunner. 200.00
919 Boots and Saddles,Ph(c) . . . 135.00
920 Ath,Zorro,Ph(c) 225.00
921 Wyatt Earp.Ph(c) 135.00
922 Johnny Mack Brown,Ph(c) . . 135.00
923 Timmy 50.00
924 Colt .45,Ph(c) 200.00
925 Last of the Fast Guns,Ph(c) . 135.00
926 Peter Pan 75.00
927 SB,Top Gun 60.00
928 Sea Hunt,L.Bridges Ph(c) . . . 250.00
929 Brave Eagle,Ph(c). 60.00
930 Maverick,J. Garner Ph(c) . . . 250.00
931 Have Gun, Will Travel,Ph(c). 300.00
932 Smokey the Bear 100.00
933 ATh,W.Disney's Zorro 225.00
934 Restless Gun 225.00
935 King of the Royal Mounted . . . 65.00
936 The Little Rascals 100.00
937 Ruff and Ready. 250.00
938 Elmer Fudd 60.00
939 Steve Canyon 90.00
940 Lolly and Pepper 50.00
941 Pluto 75.00
942 Pony Express 90.00
943 White Wilderness 125.00
944 SB,7th Voyage of Sinbad . . . 250.00
945 Maverick,J.Garner Ph(c) . . . 250.00
946 The Big Country,Ph(c) 150.00
947 Broken Arrow,Ph(c). 90.00
948 Daisy Duck's Diary 90.00
949 High Adventure,Ph(c) 100.00
950 Frosty the Snowman 75.00
951 ATh,Lennon Sisters
    Life Story,Ph(c) 275.00
952 Goofy 90.00
953 Francis the Famous
    Talking Mule 60.00
954 Man in Space 150.00
955 Hi and Lois 50.00
956 Ricky Nelson,Ph(c) 375.00
957 Buffalo Bee 175.00
958 Santa Claus Funnies 90.00
959 Christmas Stories 75.00
960 ATh,W.Disney's Zorro 225.00

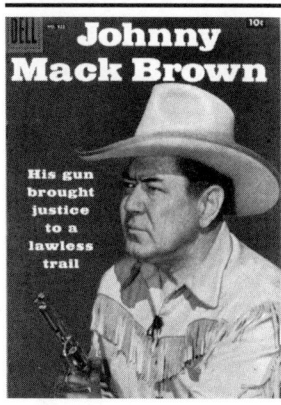

Four Color #922 — Johnny Mack Brown © Dell Publishing Co.

961 Jace Pearson's Tales of
  Texas Rangers,Ph(c)........ 90.00
962 Maverick,J.Garner Ph(c)... 250.00
963 Johnny Mack Brown,Ph(c).. 125.00
964 The Hardy Boys,Ph(c) 175.00
965 GrandmaDuck'sFarmFriends . 90.00
966 Tonka,Ph(c)............... 150.00
967 Chilly Willy 90.00
968 Tales of Wells Fargo,Ph(c) . 150.00
969 Peanuts.................. 225.00
970 Lawman,Ph(c)............. 250.00
971 Wagon Train,Ph(c) 125.00
972 Tom Thumb............... 175.00
973 SleepingBeauty & the Prince 250.00
974 The Little Rascals......... 125.00
975 Fury,Ph(c)............... 125.00
976 ATh,W.Disney's Zorro,Ph(c) . 225.00
977 Elmer Fudd 60.00
978 Lolly and Pepper.......... 50.00
979 Oswald the Rabbit 60.00
980 Maverick,J.Garner Ph(c).... 250.00
981 Ruff and Ready 150.00
982 The New Adventures of
  Tinker Bell 150.00
983 Have Gun, Will Travel,Ph(c) . 175.00
984 Sleeping Beauty's Fairy
  Godmothers.............. 165.00
985 Shaggy Dog,Ph(c) 150.00
986 Restless Gun,Ph(c)........ 150.00
987 Goofy 90.00
988 Little Hiawatha 90.00
989 Jimmy Cricket............ 125.00
990 Huckleberry Hound 250.00
991 Francis the Famous
  Talking Mule 60.00
992 ATh,Sugarfoot,Ph(c) 250.00
993 Jim Bowie,Ph(c).......... 90.00
994 Sea HuntL.Bridges Ph(c) ... 150.00
995 Donald Duck Album 125.00
996 Nevada 75.00
997 Walt Disney Presents,Ph(c) . 150.00
998 Ricky Nelson,Ph(c)........ 375.00
999 Leave It To Beaver,Ph(c) ... 300.00
1000 The Gray Ghost,Ph(c)..... 150.00
1001 Lowell Thomas' High
  Adventure,Ph(c)........... 90.00
1002 Buffalo Bee 125.00
1003 ATh,W.Disney's Zorro,Ph(c) 225.00
1004 Colt .45,Ph(c) 150.00
1005 Maverick,J.Garner Ph(c)... 225.00
1006 SB,Hercules 175.00
1007 John Paul Jones,Ph(c) 90.00
1008 Beep, Beep, the
  Road Runner............. 125.00
1009 CB,The Rifleman,Ph(c) ... 475.00
1010 Grandma Duck's Farm
  Friends................. 250.00
1011 Buckskin,Ph(c) 150.00

1012 Last Train from Gun
  Hill,Ph(c) 155.00
1013 Bat Masterson,Ph(c)...... 225.00
1014 ATh,The Lennon Sisters,
  Ph(c) 250.00
1015 Peanuts................. 225.00
1016 Smokey the Bear 75.00
1017 Chilly Willy 90.00
1018 Rio Bravo,J.Wayne Ph(c) . 450.00
1019 Wagoon Train,Ph(c) 125.00
1020 Jungle 60.00
1021 Jace Pearson's Tales of
  the Texas Rangers,Ph(c).... 90.00
1022 Timmy 55.00
1023 Tales of Wells Fargo,Ph(c) . 150.00
1024 ATh,Darby O'Gill and
  the Little People,Ph(c)...... 175.00
1025 CB,W.Disney's Vacation in
  Disneyland............... 350.00
1026 Spin and Marty,Ph(c) 135.00
1027 The Texan,Ph(c) 150.00
1028 Rawhide,
  Clint Eastwood Ph(c)...... 450.00
1029 Boots and Saddles,Ph(c) .. 100.00
1030 Spanky and Alfalfa, the
  Little Rascals 100.00
1031 Fury,Ph(c)............... 125.00
1032 Elmer Fudd 55.00
1033 Steve Canyon,Ph(c) 90.00
1034 Nancy and Sluggo
  Summer Camp 75.00
1035 Lawman,Ph(c)........... 150.00
1036 The Big Circus,Ph(c)...... 125.00
1037 Zorro,Ph(c) 275.00
1038 Ruff and Ready........... 150.00
1039 Pluto 75.00
1040 Quick Draw McGraw 275.00
1041 ATh,Sea Hunt,
  L.Bridges Ph(c) 150.00
1042 The Three Chipmunks 125.00
1043 The Three Stooges,Ph(c) .. 550.00
1044 Have Gun,Will Travel,Ph(c) 175.00
1045 Restless Gun,Ph(c)....... 150.00
1046 Beep Beep, the
  Road Runner............. 100.00
1047 CB,W.Disney's
  GyroGearloose 350.00
1048 The Horse Soldiers
  J.Wayne Ph(c)........... 275.00
1049 Don't Give Up the Ship
  J.Lewis Ph(c)............ 150.00
1050 Huckleberry Hound 150.00
1051 Donald in Mathmagic Land. 150.00
1052 RsM,Ben-Hur 200.00
1053 Goofy 90.00
1054 Huckleberry Hound
  Winter Fun.............. 150.00
1055 CB,Daisy Duck's Diary 175.00
1056 Yellowstone Kelly,
  C.Walker Ph(c) 120.00
1057 Mickey Mouse Album 100.00
1058 Colt .45,Ph(c) 175.00
1059 Sugarfoot 175.00
1060 Journey to the Center of the
  Earth, P.Boone Ph(c) 225.00
1061 Buffalo Bill.............. 125.00
1062 Christmas Stories 75.00
1063 Santa Claus Funnies 90.00
1064 Bugs Bunny's Merry
  Christmas 90.00
1065 Frosty the Snowman....... 75.00
1066 ATh,77 Sunset Strip,Ph(c). 235.00
1067 Yogi Bear 220.00
1068 Francis the Famous
  Talking Mule 60.00
1069 ATh,The FBI Story,Ph(c)... 175.00
1070 Soloman and Sheba,Ph(c) . 160.00
1071 ATh,TheRealMcCoys,Ph(c). 175.00
1072 Blythe 90.00
1073 CB,Grandma Duck's Farm
  Friends................. 250.00
1074 Chilly Willy 90.00

1075 Tales of Wells Fargo,Ph(c) . 150.00
1076 MSy,The Rebel,Ph(c) 250.00
1077 SB,The Deputy,
  H.Fonda Ph(c)........... 350.00
1078 The Three Stooges,Ph(c) .. 275.00
1079 The Little Rascals........ 100.00
1080 Fury,Ph(c).............. 125.00
1081 Elmer Fudd............. 55.00
1082 Spin and Marty 150.00
1083 Men into Space,Ph(c)..... 150.00
1084 Speedy Gonzales 125.00
1085 ATh,The Time Machine.... 300.00
1086 Lolly and Pepper......... 50.00
1087 Peter Gunn,Ph(c) 175.00
1088 A Dog of Flanders,Ph(c) ... 90.00
1089 Restless Gun,Ph(c)....... 150.00
1090 Francis the Famous
  Talking Mule 60.00
1091 Jacky's Diary............ 90.00
1092 Toby Tyler,Ph(c)......... 125.00
1093 MacKenzie's Raiders,Ph(c) 125.00
1094 Goofy 150.00
1095 CB,W.Disney's
  GyroGearloose 170.00
1096 The Texan,Ph(c) 150.00
1097 Rawhide,C.Eastwood Ph(c) 375.00
1098 Sugarfoot,Ph(c)......... 150.00
1099 CB(c),Donald Duck Album . 150.00
1100 W.Disney's Annette's
  Life Story (TV),Ph(c) 450.00
1101 Robert Louis Stevenson's
  Kidnapped,Ph(c) 125.00
1102 Wanted: Dead or Alive,
  Ph(c) 250.00
1103 Leave It To Beaver,Ph(c). . 300.00
1104 Yogi Bear Goes to College . 150.00
1105 ATh,Gale Storm,Ph(c)..... 225.00
1106 ATh,77 Sunset Strip,Ph(c). . 175.00
1107 Buckskin,Ph(c) 125.00
1108 The Troubleshooters,Ph(c) . 90.00
1109 This Is Your Life, Donald
  Duck,O:Donald Duck....... 300.00
1110 Bonanza,Ph(c) 700.00
1111 Shotgun Slade........... 125.00
1112 Pixie and Dixie
  and Mr. Jinks............ 150.00
1113 Tales of Wells Fargo,Ph(c) . 165.00
1114 Huckleberry Finn,Ph(c) 90.00
1115 Ricky Nelson,Ph(c) 300.00
1116 Boots and Saddles,Ph(c) ... 90.00
1117 Boy and the Pirate,Ph(c).. . 125.00
1118 Sword and the Dragon, Ph(c)135.00
1119 Smokey and the Bear
  Nature Stories 65.00
1120 Dinosaurus,Ph(c) 150.00
1121 RC,GE,HerculesUnchained 175.00
1122 Chilly Willy............. 80.00
1123 Tombstone Territory,Ph(c) . 175.00
1124 Whirlybirds,Ph(c)........ 165.00
1125 GK,RH,Laramie,Ph(c)..... 175.00
1126 Sundance,Ph(c) 125.00
1127 The Three Stooges,Ph(c) . 350.00
1128 Rocky and His Friends ... 650.00
1129 Pollyanna,H.Mills Ph(c).... 150.00
1130 SB,The Deputy,
  H.Fonda Ph(c) 175.00
1131 Elmer Fudd 55.00
1132 Space Mouse 100.00
1133 Fury,Ph(c) 125.00
1134 ATh,Real McCoys,Ph(c) ... 175.00
1135 M.G.M.'s Mouse Musketeers100.00
1136 Jungle Cat,Ph(c) 120.00
1137 The Little Rascals 100.00
1138 The Rebel,Ph(c) 165.00
1139 SB,Spartacus,Ph(c)....... 250.00
1140 Donald Duck Album 200.00
1141 Huckleberry Hound for
  President............... 150.00
1142 Johnny Ringo,Ph(c) 135.00
1143 Pluto 100.00
1144 The Story of Ruth,Ph(c) ... 150.00
1145 GK,The Lost World,Ph(c) .. 175.00

GOLDEN AGE

1146 Restless Gun,Ph(c). 150.00
1147 Sugarfoot,Ph(c). 175.00
1148 I aim at the Stars,Ph(c). . . . 135.00
1149 Goofy. 125.00
1150 CB,Daisy Duck's Diary 200.00
1151 Mickey Mouse Album 100.00
1152 Rocky and His Friends 400.00
1153 Frosty the Snowman. 90.00
1154 Santa Claus Funnies. 175.00
1155 North to Alaska 325.00
1156 Walt Disney Swiss
    Family Robinson 135.00
1157 Master of the World. 125.00
1158 Three Worlds of Gulliver . . . 125.00
1159 ATh,77 Sunset Strip 170.00
1160 Rawhide 300.00
1161 CB,Grandma Duck's
    Farm Friends. 300.00
1162 Yogi Bera joins the Marines 135.00
1163 Daniel Boone 90.00
1164 Wanted: Dead or Alive 175.00
1165 Ellery Queen 200.00
1166 Rocky and His Friends 475.00
1167 Tales of Wells Fargo,Ph(c) . 150.00
1168 The Detectives,
    R.Taylor Ph(c) 200.00
1169 New Adventures of
    Sherlock Holmes 300.00
1170 The Three Stooges,Ph(c) . . 300.00
1171 Elmer Fudd 60.00
1172 Fury,Ph(c) 125.00
1173 The Twilight Zone 450.00
1174 The Little Rascals 75.00
1175 M.G.M.'s Mouse Musketeers. 50.00
1176 Dondi,Ph(c). 75.00
1177 Chilly Willy. 80.00
1178 Ten Who Dared 135.00
1179 The Swamp Fox,
    L.Nielson Ph(c) 150.00
1180 The Danny Thomas Show . 300.00
1181 Texas John Slaughter,Ph(c) 135.00
1182 Donald Duck Album 100.00
1183 101 Dalmatians 225.00
1184 CB,W.Disney's
    Gyro Gearloose 175.00
1185 Sweetie Pie 75.00
1186 JDa,Yak Yak 145.00
1187 The Three Stooges,Ph(c) . . 300.00
1188 Atlantis the Lost
    Continent,Ph(c) 200.00
1189 Greyfriars Bobby,Ph(c) 135.00
1190 CB(c),Donald and
    the Wheel 135.00
1191 Leave It to Beaver,Ph(c) . . . 400.00
1192 Rocky Nelson,Ph(c) 300.00
1193 The Real McCoys,Ph(c) . . . 150.00
1194 Pepe,Ph(c) 50.00
1195 National Velvet,Ph(c) 125.00
1196 Pixie and Dixie
    and Mr. Jinks 100.00
1197 The Aquanauts,Ph(c) 135.00
1198 Donald in Mathmagic Land . 125.00
1199 Absent-Minded Professor,
    Ph(c) 150.00
1200 Hennessey,Ph(c) 125.00
1201 Goofy 90.00
1202 Rawhide,C.Eastwood Ph(c) 325.00
1203 Pinocchio 100.00
1204 Scamp. 75.00
1205 David & Goliath,Ph(c) 125.00
1206 Lolly and Pepper. 40.00
1207 MSy,The Rebel,Ph(c) 175.00
1208 Rocky and His Friends 400.00
1209 Sugarfoot,Ph(c). 150.00
1210 The Parent Trap,
    H.Mills Ph(c) 175.00
1211 RsM,77 Sunset Strip,Ph(c) . 150.00
1212 Chilly Willy 80.00
1213 Mysterious Island,Ph(c) . . . 150.00
1214 Smokey the Bear 65.00
1215 Tales of Wells Fargo,Ph(c) . 135.00
1216 Whirlybirds,Ph(c). 135.00

1218 Fury,Ph(c) 125.00
1219 The Detectives,
    Robert Taylor Ph(c) 150.00
1220 Gunslinger,Ph(c) 150.00
1221 Bonanza,Ph(c) 350.00
1222 Elmer Fudd 60.00
1223 GK,Laramie,Ph(c) 125.00
1224 The Little Rascals 75.00
1225 The Deputy,H.Fonda Ph(c) . 175.00
1226 Nikki, Wild Dog of the North . 90.00
1227 Morgan the Pirate,Ph(c) . . . 135.00
1229 Thief of Bagdad,Ph(c). 125.00
1230 Voyage to the Bottom
    of the Sea,Ph(c) 225.00
1231 Danger Man,Ph(c) 200.00
1232 On the Double. 75.00
1233 Tammy Tell Me True 125.00
1234 The Phantom Planet. 135.00
1235 Mister Magoo 175.00
1235a Mister Magoo 2nd print. . . 100.00
1236 King of Kings,Ph(c). 135.00
1237 ATh,The Untouchables,
    Ph(c) 400.00
1238 Deputy Dawg 200.00
1239 CB(c),Donald Duck Album . 150.00
1240 The Detectives,
    R.Taylor Ph(c) 150.00
1241 Sweetie Pies 50.00
1242 King Leonardo and
    His Short Subjects. 250.00
1243 Ellery Queen 150.00
1244 Space Mouse 200.00
1245 New Adventures of
    Sherlock Holmes 275.00
1246 Mickey Mouse Album 100.00
1247 Daisy Duck's Diary 150.00
1248 Pluto 125.00
1249 The Danny Thomas Show,
    Ph(c) 300.00
1250 Four Horseman of the
    Apocalypse,Ph(c) 125.00
1251 Everything's Ducky 85.00
1252 The Andy Griffith Show,
    Ph(c) 750.00
1253 Spaceman. 135.00
1254 'Diver Dan' 90.00
1255 The Wonders of Aladdin . . . 125.00
1256 Kona, Monarch of
    Monster Isle. 135.00
1257 Car 54, Where Are You?,
    Ph(c) 175.00
1258 GE,The Frogmen 135.00
1259 El Cid,Ph(c). 135.00
1260 The Horsemasters,Ph(c) . . 250.00
1261 Rawhide,C.Eastwood Ph(c) 325.00
1262 The Rebel,Ph(c) 175.00
1263 RsM,77 Sunset Strip,Ph(c) . 150.00
1264 Pixie & Dixie & Mr.Jinks . . . 175.00
1265 The Real McCoys,Ph(c) . . . 150.00
1266 M.G.M.'s Spike and Tyke . . . 50.00
1267 CB,GyroGearloose 125.00
1268 Oswald the Rabbit 60.00
1269 Rawhide,C.Eastwood Ph(c) 325.00
1270 Bullwinkle and Rocky 375.00
1271 Yogi Bear Birthday Party. . . . 90.00
1272 Frosty the Snowman. 90.00
1273 Hans Brinker,Ph(c) 125.00
1274 Santa Claus Funnies 100.00
1275 Rocky and His Friends 400.00
1276 Dondi. 50.00
1278 King Leonardo and
    His Short Subjects. 225.00
1279 Grandma Duck's Farm
    Friends. 75.00
1280 Hennessey,Ph(c) 110.00
1281 Chilly Willy 80.00
1282 Babes in Toyland,Ph(c). . . . 250.00
1283 Bonanza,Ph(c) 375.00
1284 RH,Laramie,Ph(c) 125.00
1285 Leave It to Beaver,Ph(c). . . 375.00
1286 The Untouchables,Ph(c). . . 300.00
1287 Man from Wells Fargo,Ph(c)100.00

Four Color #1313 — Moon Pilot
© Dell Publishing Co.

1288 RC,GE,The Twilight Zone . . 250.00
1289 Ellery Queen 150.00
1290 M.G.M.'s Mouse
    Musketeers 50.00
1291 RsM,77 Sunset Strip,Ph(c) . 150.00
1293 Elmer Fudd 55.00
1294 Ripcord 125.00
1295 Mr. Ed, the Talking Horse,
    Ph(c) 250.00
1296 Fury,Ph(c) 125.00
1297 Spanky, Alfalfa and the
    Little Rascals. 75.00
1298 The Hathaways,Ph(c) 75.00
1299 Deputy Dawg 200.00
1300 The Comanchero 275.00
1301 Adventures in Paradise 100.00
1302 JohnnyJason,TeenReporter . 50.00
1303 Lad: A Dog,Ph(c). 75.00
1304 Nellie the Nurse 125.00
1305 Mister Magoo 150.00
1306 Target: The Corruptors,
    Ph(c) 100.00
1307 Margie. 90.00
1308 Tales of the Wizard of Oz . . 225.00
1309 BK,87th Precinct,Ph(c) 175.00
1310 Huck and Yogi Winter
    Sports 150.00
1311 Rocky and His Friends 375.00
1312 National Velvet,Ph(c) 75.00
1313 Moon Pilot.Ph(c). 135.00
1328 GE,The Underwater
    City,Ph(c). 125.00
1330 GK,Brain Boy 225.00
1332 Bachelor Father 135.00
1333 Short Ribs. 90.00
1335 Aggie Mack. 60.00
1336 On Stage. 75.00
1337 Dr. Kildare,Ph(c) 150.00
1341 The Andy Griffith Show,
    Ph(c) 700.00
1348 JDa,Yak Yak 150.00
1349 Yogi Berra Visits the U.N. . . 175.00
1350 Commanche,Ph(c) 90.00
1354 Calvin and the Colonel 150.00

FOUR FAVORITES
Ace Magazines, Sept., 1941
1 B:Vulcan, Lash Lighting, Magno
    the Magnetic Man, Raven,
    Flag (c),Hitler 2,700.00
2 A: Black Ace 1,300.00
3 E:Vulcan 1,000.00
4 E:Raven,B:Unknown
    Soldiers 900.00
5 B:Captain Courageous 900.00
6 A: The Flag, B: Mr. Risk 800.00

All comics prices listed are for *Near Mint* condition.

GOLDEN AGE

7 JM	800.00
8	800.00
9 RP,HK	900.00
10 HK	1,000.00
11 HK,LbC,UnKnown Soldier	1,200.00
12 LbC	600.00
13 LbC	500.00
14 Fer	500.00
15 Fer	500.00
16 Bondage(c)	600.00
17 Magno Lighting	500.00
18 Magno Lighting	500.00
19 RP(a&c)	400.00
20 RP(a&c)	400.00
21 RP(a&c)	400.00
22 RP(c)	350.00
23 RP(c)	350.00
24 RP(c)	350.00
25 RP(c)	350.00
26 RP(c)	350.00
27 RP(c)	300.00
28	300.00
29	300.00
30 thru 32	@250.00

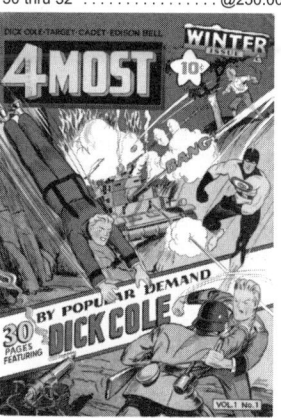

4 Most #1
© *Novelty Press*

4MOST
Novelty Publ./Star Publ.,
Winter 1941

1 The Target, The Cadet	2,500.00
2 The Target	1,200.00
3 Dan'l Flannel, Flag(c)	700.00
4 Dr. Seuss (1pg.)	700.00
2-1	400.00
2-2	400.00
2-3	400.00
2-4 Hitler,Tojo,Mussolini (c)	600.00
3-1	300.00
3-2	300.00
3-3	300.00
3-4	300.00
4-1	250.00
4-2 Walter Johnson(c)	250.00
4-3	250.00
4-4	250.00
5-1 The Target, Football(c)	200.00
5-2	200.00
5-3	200.00
5-4 Football(c)	200.00
6-1 Skiing(c)	200.00
6-2 LbC(c)	500.00
6-3 Tennis(c)	200.00
6-4 Football(c)	200.00
6-5	300.00
7-1 Basketball(c)	200.00
7-2 LbC(c)	500.00
7-3	250.00

7-4 LbC(c)	500.00
7-5	250.00
7-6 LbC(c)	500.00
Becomes:	

FOREMOST BOYS
Jan., 1949

8-1	250.00
8-2 LbC(c),Surfing(c)	500.00
8-3 LbC(c)	500.00
8-4 LbC	500.00
8-5 LbC(c)	500.00
8-6 LbC	500.00
38 LbC(c), Johnny Weissmuller	500.00
39 LbC(c), Johnny Weissmuller	500.00
40 LbC(c), White Rider	500.00
Becomes:	

THRILLING CRIME CASES

FOXHOLE
Mainline Publ., 1954

1 JK	700.00
2 JK	500.00
3 JK(c)	400.00
4 JK(c)	400.00

Charlton Comics, 1955–56

5 JK(c)	400.00
6 JK	400.00
7	150.00

FOXY FAGAN
Dearfield Publ. Co., 1946–48

1	175.00
2	125.00
3	100.00
4	100.00
5	100.00
6 Rocket	100.00
7	100.00

FRANK BUCK
Fox Features Syndicate, 1950

1 (70) WW	450.00
2 (71) WW	250.00
3	175.00

FRANKENSTEIN COMICS
Crestwood Publications
(Prize Publ.), Summer, 1945

1 B:Frankenstein,DBr(a&c)	2,000.00
2 DBr(a&c)	1,000.00
3 DBr(a&c)	750.00
4 DBr(a&c)	750.00
5 DBr(a&c)	750.00
6 DBr(a&c),S&K	600.00
7 DBr(a&c),S&K	600.00
8 DBr(a&c),S&K	600.00
9 DBr(a&c),S&K	600.00
10 DBr(a&c),S&K	600.00
11 DBr(a&c)A:Boris Karloff	500.00
12 DBr(a&c)	500.00
13 DBr(a&c)	500.00
14 DBr(a&c)	500.00
15 DBr(a&c)	500.00
16 DBr(a&c)	600.00
17 DBr(a&c)	500.00
18 DBr,B:Horror	750.00
19 DBr	400.00
3-4 DBr	350.00
3-5 DBr	350.00
3-6 DBr	350.00
4-1 thru 4-6 DBr	@350.00
5-1 thru 5-4 DBr	@350.00
5-5 DBr, Oct.–Nov., 1954	350.00

FRANK MERRIWELL
AT YALE
Charlton Comics, 1955–56

1	100.00
2 thru 4	@75.00

FREEDOM TRAIN
Street & Smith Publications

1 BP	250.00

FRISKY ANIMALS
ON PARADE
Ajax-Farrell Publ., 1957

1 LbC(c)	250.00
2	125.00
3 LbC(c)	250.00

FRISKY FABLES
Novelty Press/Premium Group/
Star Publ., Spring, 1945

1 AFa	250.00
2 AFa	150.00
3 AFa	150.00
4 AFa	125.00
5 AFa	125.00
6 AFa	125.00
7 AFa,Flag (c)	150.00
2-1 AFa,Rainbow(c)	150.00
2-2 AFa	135.00
2-3 AFa	135.00
2-4 AFa	135.00
2-5 AFa	135.00
2-6 AFa	135.00
2-7 AFa	135.00
2-8 AFa,Halloween (c)	135.00
2-9 AFa,Thanksgiving(c)	125.00
2-10 AFa,Christmas (c)	135.00
2-11 AFa	135.00
2-12 AFa,Valentine's Day (c)	125.00
3-1 AFa	125.00
3-2 AFa	125.00
3-3 AFa	135.00
3-4 AFa	125.00
3-5 AFa	125.00
3-6 AFa	125.00
3-7 AFa	125.00
3-8 AFa,Turkey (c)	125.00
3-9 AFa	125.00
3-10 AFa	125.00
3-11 AFa,1948(c)	125.00
3-12 AFa	125.00
4-1 thru 4-7 AFa	@125.00
5-1 AFa	125.00

Frisky Animals #52
© *Star Publishing*

All comics prices listed are for *Near Mint* condition.

5-2 AFa 125.00
5-3 . . . . 125.00
5-4 Star Publications 125.00
39 LbC(c) 300.00
40 LbC(c), Christmas 300.00
41 LbC(c) 300.00
42 LbC(c) 300.00
43 LbC(c) 300.00
Becomes:

FRISKY ANIMALS
Star Publications Jan., 1951
44 LbC, Super Cat 300.00
45 LbC 375.00
46 LbC,Baseball 275.00
47 LbC 275.00
48 LbC 275.00
49 LbC 275.00
50 LbC 275.00
51 LbC(c) 275.00
52 LbC(c), Christmas 300.00
53 LbC(c) 275.00
54 LbC(c),Supercat(c) 275.00
55 LbC(c),same 275.00
56 LbC(c),same 275.00
57 LbC(c),same 275.00
58 LbC(c),same,July, 1954 . . . . . 275.00

FRITZI RITZ
United Features Syndicate/
St. John Publications,
Fall, 1948
N# Special issue 250.00
2 . . . . 150.00
3 . . . . 125.00
4 and 5 . . . . @125.00
6 A:Abbie & Slats 150.00
7 . . . . 125.00
Becomes:

UNITED COMICS
United Features, 1950
8 thru 26 Bushmiller(c) . . . . . . @125.00
Becomes:

FRITZI RITZ
United Features, 1953
27 thru 59 . . . . @100.00

FROGMAN COMICS
Hillman Periodicals,
Jan.–Feb., 1952–May, 1953
1 . . . . 200.00
2 . . . . 150.00
3 . . . . 150.00
4 MMe 150.00
5 BK,AT 150.00
6 thru 11 . . . . @100.00

FROM HERE TO INSANITY
Charlton Comics, 1955
8 . . . . 300.00
9 . . . . 250.00
10 SD(c) 350.00
11 JK 350.00
12 JK 350.00
3-1 . . . . 600.00

FRONTIER FIGHTER
See: DAVY CROCKETT

FRONTIER ROMANCES
Avon Periodicals,
Nov.–Dec., 1949
1 She Learned to Ride and Shoot,
　and Kissing Came Natural . . 700.00
2 Bronc-Busters Sweetheart,
　Jan.–Feb., 1950 . . . . 500.00

FRONTIER SCOUT
DANIEL BOONE
See: DEATH VALLEY

FRONTIER TRAIL
See: RIDER, THE

Frontline Combat #10
© EC Comics

FRONTLINE COMBAT
Tiny Tot Publications
(E.C. Comics),
July–Aug., 1951
1 HK(c),WW, JSe,JDa,Hanhung
　Changjn (c) 1,400.00
2 HK(c),WW,Tank Battle (c) 650.00
3 HK(c),WW,Naval Battleship
　fire (c) 700.00
4 HK(c),WW, Bazooka (c) 600.00
5 HK(c),JSe 700.00
6 HK(c),WW,JSe 450.00
7 HK(c),WW,JSe,Document of the
　Action at Iwo Jima 450.00
8 HK(c),WW,ATh 450.00
9 HK(c),WW,JSe,Civil War iss. . . 450.00
10 GE,HK(c),WW,
　Crying Child (c) 400.00
11 GE 300.00
12 GE,Air Force issue 300.00
13 JSe,GE,WW(c), Bi-Planes (c). 300.00
14 JKu,GE,WW(c) 300.00
15 JSe,GE,WW(c), Jan., 1954 . . 300.00

FRONT PAGE
COMIC BOOK
Front Page Comics, 1945
1 JKu,BP,BF(c),I:Man in Black . . 600.00

FUGITIVES FROM
JUSTICE
St. John Publishing Co.,
Feb., 1952
1 . . . . 300.00
2 MB, Killer Boomerang 300.00
3 GT 275.00
4 . . . . 175.00
5 Bondage (c), Oct., 1952 . . . . . 250.00

FUNLAND
Approved Comics
(Ziff-Davis), 1949
N# 225.00

FUNLAND COMICS
Croyden Publ., 1945
1 Funny Animal 250.00

FUNNIES, THE
(1ST SERIES)
Dell Publishing Co., 1929-30
1 B:Foxy Grandpa, Sniffy 2,500.00
2 thru 21 . . . . @700.00
N#(22) thru (36) . . . . @800.00

FUNNIES, THE
(2ND SERIES)
Dell Publishing Co., Oct., 1936
1 Tailspin Tommy,Mutt & Jeff,
　Capt. Easy,D.Dixon 5,500.00
2 Scribbly 2,700.00
3 . . . . 2,000.00
4 Christmas issue 1,500.00
5 . . . . 1,500.00
6 thru 10 . . . . @1,200.00
11 thru 22 . . . . 1,000.00
23 thru 29 . . . . @800.00
30 B:John Carter of Mars 2,500.00
31 inc. Dick Tracy 1,400.00
32 . . . . 1,400.00
33 . . . . 1,400.00
34 . . . . 1,400.00
35 AMc,John Carter (c) 1,500.00
36 AMc,John Carter (c) 1,400.00
37 AMc,John Carter (c) 1,400.00
38 Rex King of the Deep (c) . . . 1,400.00
39 Rex King (c) 1,400.00
40 AMc,John Carter (c) 1,400.00
41 Sky Ranger (c) 1,400.00
42 Rex King (c) 1,400.00
43 Rex King (c) 1,400.00
44 Rex King (c) 1,400.00
45 AMc,I&O:Phantasmo:Master
　of the World 1,600.00
46 AMc,Phantasmo (c) 900.00
47 AMc,Phantasmo (c) 800.00
48 AMc,ShM,Phantasmo (c) 800.00
49 AMc,Phantasmo (c) 800.00
50 AMc,Phantasmo (c) 800.00
51 AMc,Phantasmo (c) 800.00
52 AMc,Phantasmo (c) 750.00
53 AMc,Phantasmo (c) 750.00
54 AMc,Phantasmo (c) 750.00
55 AMc,Phantasmo (c) 750.00
56 AMc,Phantasmo (c)
　E:John Carter 750.00
57 AMc,I&O:Captain Midnight . . 6,000.00
58 AMc,Captain Midnight (c) . . . 1,800.00
59 AMc,Captain Midnight (c) . . . 1,800.00
60 AMc,Captain Midnight (c) . . . 1,800.00
61 AMc,Captain Midnight (c) . . . 1,500.00
62 AMc,Captain Midnight (c) . . . 1,200.00
63 AMc,Captain Midnight (c) . . . 1,200.00
64 B: Woody Woodpecker 1,650.00
Becomes:

NEW FUNNIES
Dell Publishing Co. July, 1942
65 Andy Panda, Raggedy Ann &
　Andy, Peter Rabbit 1,600.00
66 same 750.00
67 Felix the Cat 750.00
68 . . . . 750.00
69 WK, The Brownies 750.00
70 . . . . 750.00
71 . . . . 500.00
72 WK 500.00
73 . . . . 500.00
74 . . . . 500.00
75 WK,Brownies 500.00
76 CB,Andy Panda, Woody
　Woodpecker 2,000.00
77 same 500.00
78 Andy Panda 500.00

79 .... 350.00	7 WE 1,500.00
80 .... 350.00	8 WE 1,500.00
81 .... 350.00	9 .... 1,500.00
82 WK,Brownies 400.00	10 WE 1,500.00
83 WK,Brownies 400.00	11 .... 1,500.00
84 WK,Brownies 400.00	12 .... 1,000.00
85 WK,Brownies 400.00	13 FGu,BoW 1,000.00
86 .... 300.00	14 JCo,FGu,BoW 1,000.00
87 Woody Woodpecker 250.00	15 JCo. 1,000.00
88 same................... 250.00	16 JCo,FGu. 1,000.00
89 same................... 250.00	17 Centaur 1,500.00
90 same................... 250.00	18 .... 1,000.00
91 thru 99................. @200.00	19 .... 1,000.00
100 .... 175.00	20 .... 1,000.00
101 thru 110............. @150.00	21 B:The Arrow 6,000.00
111 thru 118............. @150.00	22 BEv,GFx. 2,000.00
119 Christmas 150.00	23 .... 2,000.00
120 thru 142............. @150.00	24 BKa,B.Wayne prototype. 2,600.00
143 Christmas (c) 150.00	25 JCo. 1,800.00
144 thru 149............. @150.00	26 .... 1,800.00
150 thru 154............. @100.00	27 .... 1,800.00
155 Christmas (c) 150.00	28 .... 1,800.00
156 thru 167............. @100.00	29 JCo,BoW 1,800.00
168 Christmas (c) 150.00	30 BoW,The Arrow(c) 4,400.00
169 thru 181............. @100.00	31 .... 4,000.00
182 I&O:Knothead & Splinter.... 100.00	32 JCo,BoW 2,000.00
183 thru 200............. @100.00	33 JCo,BoW,The Arrow(c) 3,500.00
201 thru 240............. @100.00	34 JCo,The Arrow(c)........ 4,400.00
241 thru 288............. @75.00	35 BoW,The Arrow(c) 4,400.00
	36 Mad Ming (c) 2,000.00

THE FUNNIES ANNUAL
Avon Periodicals, 1959
1 Best newspaper strips 700.00

FUNNIES ON PARADE
Eastern Color Printing Co., 1933
N# Mutt & Jeff, Joe Palooka.. 18,000.00

FUNNY BOOK
**Funny Book Publ. Corp.,
(Parents Magazine) Dec., 1952**
1 Alec, the Funny Bunny,
  Alice in Wonderland 200.00
2 Gulliver in Giant-Land 150.00
3 .... 125.00
4 Adventures of Robin Hood ... 100.00
5 thru 9 .... @100.00

FUNNY FILMS
**Best Syndicated Features
(American Comics Group),
Sept.–Oct., 1949**
1 B:Puss An' Boots,
  Blunderbunny 250.00
2 .... 125.00
3 Christmas(c) 125.00
4 thru 10 .... @100.00
11 thru 20................. @100.00
21 thru 28................. @75.00
29 May–June, 1954........... 100.00

FUNNY FUNNIES
**Nedor Publ. Co.,
April, 1943**
1 Funny Animals............. 250.00

COMICS MAGAZINE
**Comics Magazine/Centaur,
May, 1936**
1 S&S, Dr. Mystic........... 25,000.00
2 S&S, Federal Agent 4,000.00
3 .... 3,000.00
4 .... 3,000.00
5 .... 3,000.00
Becomes:

FUNNY PAGES
Centaur, Nov., 1936
6 I:The Clock,1st masked hero 3,900.00

37 JCo,Mad Ming (c) 2,000.00
38 Mad Ming(c)............ 2,000.00
39 The Arrow(c) 3,500.00
40 BoW,The Arrow(c) 3,500.00
41 BoW,The Arrow(c) 3,500.00
42 BoW,The Arrow(c) 3,500.00

FUNNY PICTURE STORIES
**Comics Magazine/Centaur
Publ., Nov., 1936**
1 B:The Clock 6,000.00
2 The Spinner Talks........ 2,000.00
3 Tyrant Gold 1,300.00
4 WE,The Brothers Three 1,300.00
5 Timber Terror 1,300.00
6 War in Asia (c) 1,300.00
7 Racist Humor (c)......... 1,300.00
Vol 2
#1(10) 900.00
#2 (11) BoW................ 900.00
#3 (12)BoW 800.00
#4 (13) Christmas (c)...... 900.00
#5 (14) BoW................ 800.00
#6 (15) Centaur........... 1,200.00
#7 (16)................... 700.00
#8 (17)................... 700.00
#9 (18)................... 700.00
#10 (19).................. 700.00
#11 (20).................. 700.00
Vol 3
#1 .... 700.00
#2 .... 700.00
#3 .... 700.00
Becomes:

COMIC PAGES
July, 1939
4 BoW..................... 850.00
5 .... 650.00
6 .... 650.00

FUNNYMAN
**Magazine Enterprises
of Canada, Dec., 1947**
1 S&K(a&c)................. 700.00
2 S&K(a&c) 400.00
3 S&K(a&c) 300.00
4 S&K(a&c) 300.00
5 S&K(a&c) 300.00
6 S&K(a&c), Aug., 1948 ..... 300.00

Funny Tunes #2
© Star Publications

FUNNY TUNES
**Avon Periodicals,
July, 1953**
1 (fa),Space Mouse, Peter Rabbit
  Merry Mouse,Cicero the Cat. 150.00
2 same 100.00
3 same 100.00
Becomes:

SPACE COMICS
**Avon Periodicals,
March–April, 1954**
4 (fa),F:Space Mouse 125.00
5 (fa),F:Space Mouse 100.00

FUTURE COMICS
**David McKay Publications,
June, 1940**
1 Lone Ranger,Phantom 4,500.00
2 Lone Ranger............. 2,000.00
3 Lone Ranger............. 1,600.00
4 Lone Ranger,Sept., 1940 ... 1,500.00

FUTURE WORLD COMICS
**George W. Dougherty,
Summer, 1946**
1 .... 600.00
2 Fall, 1946 .... 500.00

GABBY HAYES WESTERN
Fawcett Publ., Nov., 1948
1 Ph(c) 700.00
2 Ph(c) 350.00
3 The Rage of the Purple Sage,
  Ph(c) 225.00
4 Ph(c) 225.00
5 Ph(c) 175.00
6 Ph(c) 175.00
7 Ph(c) 150.00
8 Ph(c) 150.00
9 Ph(c),V:The Kangaroo Crook . 150.00
10 Ph(c) 150.00
11 Ph(c), Chariot Race 150.00
12 V:Beaver Ben, The Biting
  Bandit,Ph(c). 125.00
13 thru 50................. @125.00

Charlton Comics
51 .... 125.00
52 thru 59 Dec., 1954 ...... @100.00

GOLDEN AGE

GANGSTERS AND GUN MOLLS

Realistic Comics (Avon), Sept., 1951
1 WW,A:Big Jim Colosimo,
  Evelyn Ellis 700.00
2 JKa, A:Bonnie Parker, The
  Kissing Bandit 550.00
3 EK, A:Juanita Perez, Crimes
  Homicide Squad 500.00
4 A:Mara Hite, Elkins Boys,
  June, 1952 .... 400.00

GANGSTERS CAN'T WIN

D.S. Publishing Co., Feb.–March, 1948
1 Shot Cop (c) 500.00
2 A:Eddie Bentz 275.00
3 Twin Trouble Trigger Man 250.00
4 Suicide on SoundStageSeven 275.00
5 Trail of Terror 250.00
6 Mystery at the Circus 250.00
7 Talisman Trail 200.00
8 .... 200.00
9 Suprise at Buoy 13,
  June–July, 1949 .... 200.00

GANG WORLD

Literary Enterprises (Standard Comics), Oct., 1952
5 Bondage (c) 300.00
6 Mob Payoff, Jan., 1953 ..... 150.00

GASOLINE ALLEY

Star Publications, Oct., 1950
1 .... 275.00
2 LBc 325.00
3 LBc(c), April, 1950 .... 250.00

GEM COMICS

Spotlight Publ. April, 1945
1 A:Steve Strong,Bondage(c) .. 700.00

GENE AUTRY COMICS

Fawcett Publications, Jan., 1942
1 The Mark of Cloven Hoof . 15,000.00
2 .... 2,500.00
3 Secret o/t Aztec Treasure .. 1,700.00
4 .... 1,600.00
5 Mystery of Paint Rock
  Canyon 1,600.00
6 Outlaw Round-up 1,300.00
7 Border Bullets 1,300.00
8 Blazing Guns 1,300.00
9 Range Robbers 1,300.00
10 Fightin' Buckaroo, Danger's
  Trail, Sept., 1943 .... 1,300.00
11 .... 1,200.00
12 .... 1,200.00

GENE AUTRY COMICS

Dell Publishing Co., May/June, 1946
1 .... 1,000.00
2 Ph(c) 600.00
3 Ph(c) 400.00
4 Ph(c),I:Flap Jack 400.00
5 Ph(c), all................. 400.00
6 thru 10 .... @300.00
11 thru 19................. @300.00
20 .... 275.00
21 thru 29................. @200.00
30 thru 40, B:Giants........ @175.00
41 thru 56 E:Giants .... @150.00
57 .... 150.00

Gene Autry Comics #6
© Dell Publishing Co.

58 Christmas (c) 125.00
59 thru 66................. @125.00
67 thru 80, B:Giant......... @125.00
81 thru 90, E:Giant......... @100.00
91 thru 93................. @100.00
94 Christmas (c) 100.00
95 thru 99................. @100.00
100 .... 150.00
101 thru 111............... @125.00
112 thru 121............... @125.00

GENE AUTRY'S CHAMPION

Dell Publishing Co., Aug., 1950
(1) *see Dell Four Color #287*
(2) *see Dell Four Color #319*
3 .... 150.00
4 thru 19 .... @125.00

GENERAL DOUGLAS MACARTHUR

Fox Features Syndicate, 1950
N# True life story 275.00

GEORGE PAL'S PUPPETOON'S

Fawcett Publications, Dec., 1945
1 Captain Marvel (c) 700.00
2 .... 400.00
3 .... 300.00
4 thru 17 .... @250.00
18 Dec., 1947 .... 200.00

GERALD McBOING-BOING AND THE NEARSIGHTED MR. MAGOO

Dell Publishing Co., Aug.–Oct., 1952
1 .... 225.00
2 thru 5 .... @175.00

GERONIMO

Avon Periodicals, 1950
1 Massacre at San Pedro Pass . 250.00
2 EK(c), Murderous Battle
  at Kiskayah 150.00
3 EK(c) 150.00
4 EK(c),Apache Death Trap,
  Feb., 1952 .... 125.00

GET LOST

Mikeross Publications, Feb.–March, 1954
1 .... 400.00
2 .... 300.00
3 June–July, 1954 .... 225.00

GHOST

Fiction House Magazine, Winter, 1951–Summer, 1954
1 The Banshee Bells 1,400.00
2 I Woke In Terror 800.00
3 The Haunted Hand of X 700.00
4 Flee the Mad Furies 350.00
5 The Hex of Ruby Eye 600.00
6 The Sleepers in the Crypt 600.00
7 When Dead Rogues Ride ... 600.00
8 Curse of the Mist-Thing 600.00
9 It Crawls by Night,
  Bondage(c) 700.00
10 Halfway to Hades 600.00
11 GE, The Witch's Doll....... 600.00

GHOST BREAKERS

Street & Smith Publ., 1948
1 BP(a&c), A:Dr. Neff 800.00
2 BP(a&c), Breaks the Voodoo
  Hoodoo,Dec., 1948 .... 600.00

GHOSTLY WEIRD STORIES

See: BLUE BOLT

GIANT BOY BOOK OF COMICS

Newsbook Publ. (Lev Gleason), 1945
1 A:Crime Buster & Young
  Robin Hood 1,500.00

GIANT COMICS EDITION

St. John Publ., 1948
1 Mighty Mouse 750.00
2 Abbie and Slats 400.00
3 Terry Toons 600.00
4 Crime Comics 850.00
5 MB, Police Case Book 850.00
6 MB(a&c), Western
  Picture Story 700.00
7 Mopsy 450.00
8 Adventures of Mighty Mouse .. 450.00
9 JKu,MB,Romance & Confession
  Stories,Ph(c) 750.00
10 Terry Toons 500.00
11 MB(a&c),JKu,Western
  Picture Stories 700.00
12 MB(a&c),Diary Secrets,
  Prostitute 2,700.00
13 MB,JKu, Romances 750.00
14 Mighty Mouse Album 500.00
15 MB(c),Romance 900.00
16 Little Audrey 550.00
N#, Mighty Mouse Album 500.00

GIANT COMICS EDITION

United Features Syndicate, 1945
1 A:Abbie & Slats, Jim Hardy,
  Ella Cinders,Iron Vic 600.00
2 Elmo, Jim Hardy, Abbie &
  Slats, 1945 .... 400.00

G.I. COMBAT

Quality Comics Group, 1952
1 RC(c), Beyond the Call
  of Duty 1,100.00
2 RC(c), Operation Massacre .. 500.00

3 An Indestructible Marine 400.00
4 Bridge to Blood Hill 400.00
5 Hell Breaks loose on
  Suicide Hill. 400.00
6 Beachhead Inferno 375.00
7 Fire Power Assault 300.00
8 RC(c),Death-trap Hill 300.00
9 Devil Riders 300.00
10 RC(c), Two-Ton Booby Trap . . 400.00
11 Hell's Heroes 250.00
12 Hand Grenade Hero 250.00
13 Commando Assault. 250.00
14 Spear Head Assault 250.00
15 Vengeance Assault 250.00
16 Trapped Under Fire. 225.00
17 Attack on Death Mountain. . . . 225.00
18 Red Battle Ground 225.00
19 Death on Helicopter Hill 225.00
20 Doomed Legion-Death Trap . 225.00
21 Red Sneak Attack 200.00
22 Vengeance Raid 200.00
23 No Grandstand in Hell 200.00
24 Operation Steel
  Trap,Comics Code. 200.00
25 Charge of the Commie
  Brigade 200.00
26 Red Guerrilla Trap 200.00
27 Trapped Behind Commie
  Lines 200.00
28 Atomic Battleground 200.00
29 Patrol Ambush 200.00
30 Operation Booby Trap 200.00
31 Human Fly on Heartbreak
  Hill 200.00
32 Atomic Rocket Assault 225.00
33 Bridge to Oblivion 200.00
34 RC,Desperate Mission 225.00
35 Doom Patrol 200.00
36 Fire Power Assault 200.00
37 Attack at Dawn 200.00
38 Get That Tank 200.00
39 Mystery of No Man's Land . . 200.00
40 Maneuver Battleground 200.00
41 Trumpet of Doom 200.00
42 March of Doom 200.00
43 Operation Showdown 200.00
See: DC Comics

GIFT COMICS
**Fawcett Publications,
March, 1942**
1 A:Captain Marvel, Bulletman,
  Golden Arrow,Ibis, the
  Invincible, Spy Smasher. . . 4,500.00
2 . . . . 2,700.00
3 . . . . 1,800.00
4 A:Marvel Family, 1949 . . . . . 1,400.00

GIGGLE COMICS
**Creston Publ./
American Comics Group,
Oct., 1943**
1 (fa)same. 500.00
2 KHu 250.00
3 KHu 225.00
4 KHu 200.00
5 KHu 200.00
6 KHu 150.00
7 KHu 150.00
8 KHu 150.00
9 I:Super Katt 175.00
10 KHu 125.00
11 thru 20 KHu . . . . @125.00
21 thru 30 KHu . . . . @125.00
31 thru 40 KHu . . . . @100.00
41 thru 94 KHu . . . . @100.00
95 A:Spencer Spook 100.00
96 KHu 100.00
97 KHu 100.00
98 KHu 100.00
99 KHu 100.00

100 and 101 March–April,1955 @100.00

G.I. IN BATTLE
Ajax/Farrell, 1952
1 War stories. 150.00
2 thru 9 . . . . @100.00
Ann #1 100 pgs. (1952) 350.00

Ajax, 1957
1 . . . . 125.00
2 . . . . 100.00
3 thru 6 . . . . @100.00

G.I. JANE
**Stanhall Publ.,
May, 1953**
1 . . . . 150.00
2 thru 6 . . . . @125.00
7 thru 9 . . . . @100.00
10 Dec., 1954 . . . . 100.00

G.I. JOE
**Ziff-Davis Publication Co.,
1950**
10 NS(c),Red Devils of Korea,
  V:Seoul City Lou 250.00
11 NS(c),The Guerrilla's Lair 125.00
12 NS(c). 125.00
13 NS(c),Attack at Dawn 125.00
14 NS(c),Temple of Terror,
  A:Peanuts the Great 135.00
2-6 It's a Foot Soldiers Job,
  I:Frankie of the Pump 125.00
2-7 BP,NS(c),The Rout at
  Sugar Creek 125.00
8 BP,NS(c),Waldo'sSqueezeBox 125.00
9 NS(c),Dear John 125.00
10 NS(c),Joe Flies the Payroll . 125.00
11 NS(c),For the Love of Benny . 125.00
12 NS(c),Patch work Quilt 125.00
13 NS(c). 125.00
14 NS(c),The Wedding Ring 125.00
15 The Lacrosse Whoopee 125.00
16 Mamie's Mortar 125.00
17 A Time for Waiting. 125.00
18 Giant 300.00
19 Old Army Game..Buck Passer 125.00
20 General Confusion 125.00
21 Save 'Im for Brooklyn 125.00
22 Portrait of a Lady 125.00
23 Take Care of My Little Wagon 125.00
24 Operation 'Operation' 125.00
25 The Two-Leaf Clover 125.00
26 NS(c),Nobody Flies Alone
  Mud & Wings. 125.00

GI Joe #24
© Ziff-Davis

27 'Dear Son...Come Home' 125.00
28 They Alway's Come Back
  Bondage (c). 135.00
29 What a Picnic 100.00
30 NS(c),The One-Sleeved
  Kimono 125.00
31 NS(c),Get a Horse 100.00
32 thru 47. . . . . @100.00
48 Atom Bomb 125.00
49 thru 51 June, 1957 . . . . . . @100.00

GINGER
**Close-Up Publ.
(Archie Publications),
Jan., 1951**
1 GFs,Teen-age 200.00
2 . . . . 150.00
3 . . . . 125.00
4 . . . . 125.00
5 . . . . 100.00
6 . . . . 100.00
7 thru 9 . . . . @125.00
10 A:Katy Keene,Summer,1954. . 150.00

GIRLS IN LOVE
**Fawcett Publications,
May, 1950**
1 Ph(c) 150.00
2 Ph(c),July, 1950 . . . . 100.00

GOLDEN ARROW
**Fawcett Publications,
Spring, 1942**
1 B:Golden Arrow 1,250.00
2 . . . . 600.00
3 . . . . 425.00
4 . . . . 400.00
5 Spring, 1947 . . . . 400.00
6 BK 425.00
6a 1944 Well Known Comics
  (Giveaway) 450.00

GOLDEN LAD
**Spark Publications,
July, 1945–June, 1946**
1 MMe(a&c),A:Kid Wizards,
  Swift Arrow,B:Golden Ladd. 1,200.00
2 MMe(a&c) 600.00
3 MMe(a&c) 600.00
4 MMe(a&c), The Menace of
  the Minstrel 600.00
5 MMe(a&c),O:Golden Girl 600.00

GOLDEN WEST LOVE
**Kirby Publishing Co.,
Sept.–Oct., 1949**
1 BP,I Rode Heartbreak Hill,
  Ph(c) 300.00
2 BP 200.00
3 BP,Ph(c) 200.00
4 BP,April, 1950 . . . . 200.00

GOLD MEDAL COMICS
Cambridge House, 1945
N# Captain Truth, Lucky Man. . . 500.00

GOOFY COMICS
**Nedor Publ. Co./
Animated Cartoons
(Standard Comics),
June, 1943**
1 (fa) 400.00
2 . . . . 250.00
3 VP 250.00
4 VP 225.00
5 VP 225.00
6 thru 10 VP . . . . @225.00
11 thru 15 . . . . @200.00

15 thru 19 . . . . @200.00
20 thru 35 FF . . . . @150.00
36 thru 48 . . . . @100.00

GREAT AMERICAN COMICS PRESENTS– THE SECRET VOICE
4 Star Publ., 1944
1 Hitler,Secret Weapon 600.00

GREAT COMICS
Novak Publ. Co., 1945
1 LbC(c) 650.00

GREAT COMICS
Great Comics Publications, Nov., 1941
1 I:The Great Zarro,Madame
    Strange 2,400.00
2 Buck Johnson 1,100.00
3 The Lost City, Hitler,
    Jan., 1942 . . . . 5,000.00

GREEN GIANT COMICS
Pelican Publications, 1941
1 Black Arrow, Dr. Nerod
    O:Colossus, Green Giant . 19,000.00

GREEN HORNET COMICS
Helnit Publ. Co./ Family Comics (Harvey Publ.), Dec., 1940
1 B:Green Hornet,P(c) 10,000.00
2 Radio Stories 3,500.00
3 BWh(c) 2,500.00
4 BWh(c) 2,000.00
5 BWh(c) 2,000.00
6 . . . . 2,000.00
7 BP, O:Zebra, B:Robin
    Hood & Spirit of 76 . . . . . . 1,700.00
8 BP,Bondage (c). 1,800.00
9 BP,JK(c),Behind the (c) 2,000.00
10 BP 1,800.00
11 Who is Mr. Q? 1,500.00
12 BP,A:Mr.Q 1,500.00
13 Hitler (c) 1,800.00
14 BP,Spirit of 76-Twinkle
    Twins, Bondage(c) 1,200.00
15 ASh(c),Nazi Ghost Ship . . . 1,200.00
16 BP,Prisoner of War 1,200.00
17 BP,ASh(c),Nazis' Last Stand 1,200.00
18 BP,ASh(c),Jap's Treacherous
    Plot,Bondage (c). 1,200.00
19 BP,ASh(c),Clash with the
    Rampaging Japs. 1,200.00
20 BP,ASh(c),Tojo's
    Propaganda Hoax 1,400.00
21 BP,ASh(c),Unwelcome
    Cargo 1,000.00
22 ASh(c),Rendezvous with
    Jap Saboteurs 800.00
23 BF,ASh(c),Jap's Diabolical
    Plot #B2978 . . . . 800.00
24 BF,Science Fiction (c) 1,000.00
25 thru 29 . . . . @750.00
30 BP,JKu,AAv 750.00
31 BP,JKu 750.00
32 BP,JKu 600.00
33 BP,JKu,AAv 600.00
34 BP,JKu 600.00
35 BP,JKu 600.00
36 BP,JKu,Bondage (c) 800.00
37 BP,JKu,AAv,S&K 500.00
38 BP,JKu 500.00
39 S&K,AAv 800.00
40 thru 45 . . . . @500.00
46 Drug 600.00

Green Hornet Comics #33
© Harvey Publications

47 AAv,Sept., 1949 . . . . 500.00

GREEN LAMA
Spark Publications/Prize Publ., Dec., 1944
1 I:Green Lama, Lt. Hercules
    & Boy Champions 2,200.00
2 MRa,Forward to Victory
    in 1945 . . . . 1,500.00
3 MRa,The Riddles of Toys . . 1,200.00
4 MRa,Dive Bombs Japan . . . 1,100.00
5 MRa(a&c),Fights for
    the Four Freedoms 1,100.00
6 MRa,Smashes a Plot
    against America 1,100.00
7 MRa,Merry X-Mas 600.00
8 MRa,Smashes Toy Master
    of Crime, March, 1946 . . . . . 600.00

GREEN MASK, THE
Fox Features Syndicate, Summer, 1940
1 LF(c),O:Green Mask &
    Domino 6,500.00
2 A:Zanzibar 2,200.00
3 BP 1,500.00
4 B:Navy Jones 1,200.00
5 . . . . 1,000.00
6 B:Nightbird,E:Navy Jones,
    Bondage (c) 800.00
7 B:Timothy Smith &
    The Tumbler 800.00
8 JSs 600.00
9 E:Nightbird, Death Wields
    a Scalpel! 600.00
10 . . . . 500.00
11 The Banshee of Dead
    Man's Hill 500.00
2-1 Election of Skulls 400.00
2-2 Pigeons of Death 400.00
2-3 Wandering Gold Brick 350.00
2-4 Time on His Hands 350.00
2-5 JFe,SFd 450.00
2-6 Adventure of the Disappearing
    Trains, Oct.–Nov., 1946 . . . . 450.00

GUMPS, THE
Dell Publishing Co., 1945
1 . . . . 250.00
2 . . . . 200.00
3 thru 5 . . . . @150.00

GUNFIGHTER
See: FAT AND SLAT

GUNS AGAINST GANGSTERS
Curtis Publ./Novelty Press, Sept.–Oct., 1948
1 LbC(a&c),B:Toni Gayle 600.00
2 LbC(a&c) 400.00
3 LbC(a&c) 350.00
4 LbC(a&c) 350.00
5 LbC(a&c) 350.00
6 LbC(a&c),Shark 350.00
2-1 LbC(a&c),Sept.–Oct., 1949 . 350.00

GUNSMOKE
Western Comics, Inc., April–May, 1949
1 Grl(a&c),Gunsmoke & Masked
    Marvel,Bondage (c) 700.00
2 Grl(a&c) 400.00
3 Grl(a&c),Bondage(c) 350.00
4 Grl(c) 250.00
5 Grl(c) 250.00
6 . . . . 225.00
7 . . . . 150.00
8 . . . . 150.00
9 . . . . 150.00
10 . . . . 150.00
11 thru 15 . . . . @135.00
16 Horror, Jan., 1952 . . . . 150.00

GUNSMOKE
Dell Publishing Co., 1957
6 J.Arness Ph(c) all 200.00
7 . . . . 200.00
8 . . . . 200.00
9 . . . . 200.00
10 AW,RC 225.00
11 . . . . 200.00
12 AW 225.00
13 thru 27 . . . . @175.00

GUNSMOKE TRAIL
Four Star Comic. Corp (Ajax/Farrell), 1957
1 Western action 125.00
2 . . . . 100.00
3 . . . . 100.00
4 . . . . 100.00

HA HA COMICS
Creston Publ. (American Comics Group), Oct., 1943
1 Funny Animal, all 450.00
2 . . . . 200.00
3 . . . . 150.00
4 . . . . 150.00
5 . . . . 150.00
6 thru 10 . . . . @125.00
11 . . . . 100.00
12 KHu 100.00
13 KHu 100.00
14 KHu 100.00
15 KHu 100.00
16 thru 20 KHu . . . . @100.00
21 thru 30 KHu . . . . @100.00
31 thru 101 . . . . @100.00
102 Feb.–March, 1955 . . . . 100.00

MISTER RISK
Humor Publ., Oct., 1950
1 (7) B:Mr. Risk 150.00
2 . . . . 150.00
Becomes:

MEN AGAINST CRIME
Ace Magazines, Feb., 1951
3 A:Mr. Risk, Case of the Carnival
  Killer 150.00
4 Murder-And the Crowd Roars 125.00
5 . . . . 125.00
6 . . . . 125.00
7 Get Them! 125.00
Becomes:

HAND OF FATE
Ace Magazines, Dec., 1951
8 MSy 600.00
9 LC 400.00
10 LC 400.00
11 Genie(c) 300.00
12 . . . . 275.00
13 MSy,Hanging(c) 400.00
14 MSy, ... 275.00
15 . . . . 275.00
16 . . . . 275.00
17 . . . . 275.00
18 . . . . 275.00
19 LC,Drug issue,Quicksand(c). . 400.00
20 LC 300.00
21 LC,Drug issue 400.00
22 LC 300.00
23 LC,Graveyard(c) 400.00
24 LC,Electric Chair. 500.00
25 Nov., 1954. . . . . 250.00
25a Dec., 1954 . . . . 275.00

HANGMAN COMICS
See: LAUGH COMICS

HAP HAZARD COMICS
**A.A. Wyn/Red Seal Publ./
Readers Research,
Summer, 1944**
1 Funny Teen 250.00
2 Dog Show 200.00
3 Sgr, ... 150.00
4 Sgr, ... 150.00
5 thru 10 Sgr, ... @150.00
11 thru 13 Sgr, ... @75.00
14 AF(c) 100.00
15 . . . . 75.00
16 thru 24 . . . . @75.00
Becomes:

REAL LOVE
April, 1949
25 Dangerous Dates 200.00
26 . . . . 150.00
27 LbC(c), Revenge Conquest . . 175.00
28 thru 40 . . . . @125.00
41 thru 66 . . . . @100.00
67 Comics code 75.00
68 thru 76, Nov., 1956 . . . . @75.00

HAPPY COMICS
**Nedor Publications/
Animated Cartoons,
Aug., 1943**
1 Funny Animal in all 400.00
2 . . . . 250.00
3 . . . . 150.00
4 . . . . 150.00
5 thru 10 . . . . @150.00
11 thru 20 . . . . @125.00
21 thru 31 . . . . @125.00
32 FF 300.00
33 FF 500.00
34 thru 37 FF . . . . @150.00
38 thru 40 . . . . @100.00
Becomes:

HAPPY RABBIT
Standard Comics, Feb., 1951
41 Funny Animal in all 100.00
42 thru 50 . . . . @75.00

HARVEY COMIC HITS
**Harvey Publications, Oct., 1951
(Formerly: JOE PALOOKA)**
51 Phantom 400.00
52 Steve Canyon's Air Power . . . 200.00
53 Mandrake 300.00
54 Tim Tyler's Tales of Jungle
  Terror. 175.00
55 Love Stories of Mary Worth . . 125.00
56 Phantom, Bondage (c) 400.00
57 AR,Kidnap Racket 250.00
58 Girls in White 150.00
59 Tales of the Invisible 200.00
60 Paramount Animated Comics 600.00
61 Casper the Friendly Ghost . . . 750.00
62 Paramount Animated Comics,
  April, 1953 . . . . 225.00

HARVEY COMICS LIBRARY
Harvey Publications, 1952
1 Teen-age dope slaves 2,200.00
2 Sparkle Plenty 350.00

HAUNTED THRILLS
**Four Star Publ.
(Ajax/Farrell), June, 1952**
1 Ellery Queen 900.00
2 LbC,Ellery Queen 550.00
3 Drug Story 500.00
4 Ghouls Castle 450.00
5 Fatal Scapel 450.00
6 Pit of Horror 450.00
7 Trail to a Tomb, Hitler 425.00
8 Vanishing Skull 400.00
9 Madness of Terror 400.00
10 . . . . 400.00
11 Nazi Concentration Camp. . . . 450.00
12 RWb 400.00
13 . . . . 300.00
14 RWb, Jesus Christ 325.00
15 The Devil Collects 300.00
16 . . . . 300.00
17 Mirror of Madness. 300.00
18 No Place to Go, Lingerie
  Nov.–Dec., 1954 . . . . 325.00

HAUNT OF FEAR
**Fables Publ. (E.C. Comics) ,
May–June, 1950**
15 JCr(a&c),AF,WW 5,000.00

*Haunted Thrills #1
© Farrell*

16 JCr(a&c),AF,WW 2,500.00
17 JCr(a&c),AF,WW,O:Crypt
  of Terror,Vault of Horror
  & Haunt of Fear 2,400.00
4 AF(c),WW,JDa 1,500.00
5 JCr(a&c),WW,JDa,Eye Injury 1,200.00
6 JCr(a&c),WW,JDa. 1,000.00
7 JCr(a&c),WW,JDa. 1,000.00
8 AF(c),JKa,JDa,
  Shrunken Head 1,000.00
9 AF(c),JCr,JDa 1,000.00
10 AF(c),Grl,JDa 900.00
11 JKa,Grl,JDa 1,000.00
12 JCr,Grl,JDa 800.00
13 Grl,JDa 800.00
14 Grl(a&c),JDa,O:Old Witch . . . 900.00
15 JDa 700.00
16 Grl(c),JDa,Ray Bradbury
  adaptation 700.00
17 JDa,Grl(c),Classic
  Ghastly (c) 700.00
18 JDa,Grl(c),JKa,Ray Bradbury
  adaptation 700.00
19 JDa,Guillotine (c),
  Bondage (c). 900.00
20 RC,JDa,Grl(a&c) 900.00
21 JDa,Grl(a&c) 800.00
22 JDa,Grl(a&c) 700.00
23 JDa,Grl(a&c) 700.00
22 JDa,Grl(a&c) 700.00
23 JDa,Grl(a&c) 700.00
24 JDa,Grl(a&c) 700.00
25 JDa,Grl(a&c) 700.00
26 RC,JDa,Grl(a&c) 800.00
27 JDa,Grl(a&c), Cannibalism. . . 800.00
28 Dec., 1954 . . . . 750.00

HAWK, THE
**Approved Comics
(Ziff-Davis), Winter, 1951**
1 MA,The Law of the Colt,P(c) . 275.00
2 JKu,Iron Caravan of the
  Mojave, P(c) 150.00
3 Leverett's Last Stand,P(c) . . . 135.00
4 Killer's Town,P(c) 125.00
5 . . . . 125.00
6 . . . . 125.00
7 . . . . 125.00
8 MB(c),Dry River Rampage . . . 175.00
9 MB(a&c),JKu 175.00
10 MB(c) 175.00
11 MB(c). 175.00
12 MB(a&c), May, 1955 . . . . 175.00

HEADLINE COMICS
**American Boys Comics/
Headline Publ. (Prize Publ.),
Feb., 1943**
1 B:Jr. Rangers 1,000.00
2 JaB(a&c) 500.00
3 JaB(a&c) 450.00
4 . . . . 350.00
5 HcK 350.00
6 HcK 350.00
7 HcK,Jr. Rangers 350.00
8 HcK,Hitler (c) 1,200.00
9 HcK 350.00
10 HcK,Hitler story,Wizard(c). . . 400.00
11 . . . . 275.00
12 HcK,Heroes of Yesterday . . . 275.00
13 HcK,A:Blue Streak 275.00
14 HcK,A:Blue Streak 275.00
15 HcK,A:Blue Streak 275.00
16 HcK,O:Atomic Man 450.00
17 Atomic Man(c) 250.00
18 Atomic Man(c) 250.00
19 S&K,Atomic Man(c) 500.00
20 Atomic Man(c) 250.00
21 E:Atomic Man 250.00
22 HcK 200.00

23 S&K(a&c),Valentines Day
    Massacre 400.00
24 S&K(a&c),You Can't Forget
    a Killer 400.00
25 S&K(a&c),Crime Never Pays . 400.00
26 S&K(a&c),Crime Never Pays . 400.00
27 S&K(a&c),Crime Never Pays . 400.00
28 S&K(a&c),Crime Never Pays . 400.00
29 S&K(a&c),Crime Never Pays . 400.00
30 S&K(a&c),Crime Never Pays . 400.00
31 S&K(a&c),Crime Never Pays . 400.00
32 S&K(a&c),Crime Never Pays . 400.00
33 S&K(a&c),Police and FBI
    Heroes 400.00
34 S&K(a&c),same 400.00
35 S&K(a&c),same 400.00
36 S&K,same,Ph(c) 350.00
37 S&K,MvS,same,Ph(c) 400.00
38 S&K,same,Ph(c) 150.00
39 S&K,same,Ph(c) 150.00
40 S&K,Ph(c)Violent Crime 150.00
41 Ph(c),J.Edgar Hoover(c) 150.00
42 Ph(c) 125.00
43 Ph(c) 125.00
44 MMe,MvS,WE,S&K 250.00
45 JK 200.00
46 . . . . 150.00
47 . . . . 150.00
48 . . . . 150.00
49 MMe 150.00
50 . . . . 150.00
51 JK 150.00
52 . . . . 150.00
53 . . . . 150.00
54 . . . . 150.00
55 . . . . 150.00
56 S&K 250.00
57 . . . . 100.00
58 . . . . 100.00
59 . . . . 100.00
60 MvS(c). 100.00
61 MMe,MvS(c) 100.00
62 MMe(a&c) 100.00
63 MMe(a&c) 100.00
64 MMe(a&c) 100.00
65 MMe(a&c) 100.00
66 MMe(a&c) 100.00
67 MMe(a&c) 100.00
68 MMe(a&c) 100.00
69 MMe(a&c) 100.00
70 MMe(a&c) 100.00
71 MMe(a&c) 100.00
72 MMe(a&c) 100.00
73 MMe(a&c) 100.00
74 MMe(a&c) 100.00

Heckle and Jeckle #14
© *St John Publishing*

75 MMe(a&c) 100.00
76 MMe(a&c) 100.00
77 MMe(a&c),Oct., 1956 . . . . . . 100.00

HECKLE AND JECKLE
St. John Publ./Pines,
Nov., 1951
1 Blue Ribbon Comics 350.00
2 Blue Ribbon Comics 150.00
3 . . . . 125.00
4 . . . . 125.00
5 . . . . 125.00
6 . . . . 125.00
7 . . . . 125.00
8 thru 14 . . . . @100.00
15 . . . . 125.00
16 thru 20 . . . . @100.00
21 thru 33 . . . . @100.00
34 June, 1959 . . . . 100.00

HELLO PAL COMICS
Harvey Publications,
Jan., 1943
1 B:Rocketman & Rocket Girl,
    Mickey Rooney, Ph(c) 1,400.00
2 Charlie McCarthy, Ph(c) 1,000.00
3 Bob Hope, Ph(c), May, 1943 1,400.00

HE-MAN
Approved Comics
(Ziff-Davis)/Toby Press, 1952
1 "Real-Life Adventure". 200.00
1a 175.00
2a 175.00

HENRY
Dell Publishing Co.,
Oct., 1946
2 . . . . 150.00
3 thru 10 . . . . @150.00
11 thru 20 . . . . @125.00
21 thru 30 . . . . @125.00
31 thru 40 . . . . @100.00
41 thru 50 . . . . @75.00
51 thru 65 . . . . @50.00

HENRY ALDRICH COMICS
Dell Publishing Co.,
Aug.–Sept., 1950
1 . . . . 200.00
2 . . . . 150.00
3 thru 5 . . . . @125.00
6 thru 10 . . . . @100.00
11 thru 22 . . . . @75.00

HEROES OF
THE WILD FRONTIER
See: BAFFLING MYSTERIES

HEROIC COMICS
Eastern Color Printing Co./
Famous Funnies Aug., 1940
1 BEv(a&c),O:Hydroman,Purple
    Zombie, B:Man of India . . . 3,000.00
2 BEv(a&c),B:Hydroman (c)s. . 1,500.00
3 BEv(a&c) 750.00
4 BEv(a&c) 750.00
5 BEv(a&c) 650.00
6 BEv(a&c) 650.00
7 BEv(a&c),O:Man O'Metal . . . 750.00
8 BEv(a&c) 500.00
9 BEv 500.00
10 BEv 500.00
11 BEv,E:Hydroman (c)s 500.00
12 BEv,B&0:Music Master 550.00
13 BEv,RC,LF 500.00
14 BEv 550.00
15 BEv,I:Downbeat 550.00

16 BEv,BTh,CCB(c),A:Lieut
    Nininger, Major Heidger,
    Lieut Welch,B:P(c) 350.00
17 BEv,A:JohnJames Powers,Hewitt
    T.Wheless, Irving Strobing. . . 350.00
18 HcK,BEv,Pass the Ammunition 350.00
19 HcK,BEv,A:Barney Ross 350.00
20 HcK,BEv 350.00
21 HcK,BEv 250.00
22 HcK,BEv,Howard Gilmore 250.00
23 HcK,BEv 250.00
24 HcK,BEv 250.00
25 HcK,BEv, Rainbow Boy 250.00
26 HcK,BEv 250.00
27 HcK,BEv 250.00
28 HcK,BEv,E:Man O'Metal 250.00
29 HcK,BEv,E:Hydroman 250.00
30 BEv 250.00
31 BEv,CCB,Capt. Tootsie 125.00
32 ATh,CCB,WWII(c),
    Capt. Tootsie 150.00
33 ATh, ... 175.00
34 WWII(c) 125.00
35 Ath,B:Rescue(c) 175.00
36 HcK,ATh 150.00
37 same 75.00
38 ATh 150.00
39 HcK,ATh 125.00
40 ATh,Boxing 125.00
41 Grl(c),ATh 125.00
42 ATh 125.00
43 ATh 100.00
44 HcK,ATh 100.00
45 HcK 100.00
46 HcK 100.00
47 HcK 125.00
48 HcK 125.00
49 HcK 100.00
50 HcK 100.00
51 HcK,ATh,AW 150.00
52 HcK,AW 125.00
53 HcK 125.00
54 . . . . 125.00
55 ATh 125.00
56 ATh(c) 100.00
57 ATh(c) 100.00
58 ATh(c) 100.00
59 ATh(c) 100.00
60 ATh(c) 100.00
61 BEv(c) 100.00
62 BEv(c) 100.00
63 BEv(c) 100.00
64 GE,BEv(c) 100.00
65 HcK(c),FF,ATh,AW,GE 150.00
66 HcK(c),FF 125.00
67 HcK(c),FF,Korean War(c) 125.00
68 HcK(c),Korean War(c). 100.00
69 HcK(c),FF 150.00
70 HcK(c),FF,B:Korean War(c) . . 100.00
71 HcK(c),FF 100.00
72 HcK(c),FF 150.00
73 HcK(c),FF 100.00
74 HcK(c). 100.00
75 HcK(c),FF 100.00
76 thru 80 HcK,HcK(c) . . . . . . @100.00
81 FF,HcK(c) 100.00
82 FF,HcK(c) 100.00
83 FF,HcK(c) 100.00
84 HcK(c). 100.00
85 HcK(c). 100.00
86 FF,HcK(c) 120.00
87 FF,HcK(c) 120.00
88 HcK(c),E:Korean War (c)s . . . 100.00
89 HcK(c). 100.00
90 HcK(c). 100.00
91 HcK(c). 100.00
92 HcK(c). 100.00
93 HcK(c). 100.00
94 HcK(c). 120.00
95 HcK(c). 100.00
96 HcK(c). 100.00
97 HcK(c),E:P(c),June, 1955. . . . 100.00

HICKORY
**Comic Magazine
(Quality Comics Group),
Oct., 1949**
1 HSa, ... 250.00
2 HSa, ... 125.00
3 HSa, ... 100.00
4 HSa, ... 100.00
5 HSa, ... 100.00
6 HSa,Aug., 1950 . . . . 100.00

HI-HO COMICS
Four Star Publications, 1946
1 LbC(c) 600.00
2 LbC(c) 300.00
3 1946 . . . . 250.00

HI-JINX
**B & I Publ. Co. (American
Comics Group),
July–Aug., 1947**
1 (fa) all. 325.00
2 . . . . 200.00
3 . . . . 125.00
4 thru 7 . . . . @100.00
N# 150.00

HI-LITE COMICS
E.R. Ross Publ. Fall, 1945
1 . . . . 300.00

HILLBILLY COMICS
Charlton Comics, 1955
1 . . . . 125.00
2 thru 4 July 1956 . . . . @100.00

HI-SCHOOL ROMANCE
Harvey Publications, 1949–58
1 BP,Ph(c). 200.00
2 BP,Ph(c). 150.00
3 BP,Ph(c). 125.00
4 Ph(c) 125.00
5 BPPh(c). 125.00
6 and 7 . . . . @125.00
8 BP 125.00
9 . . . . 125.00
10 Rare 150.00
11 thru 20 BP(in many) . . . . . . @100.00
21 thru 50 . . . . @100.00
51 thru 75 . . . . @75.00

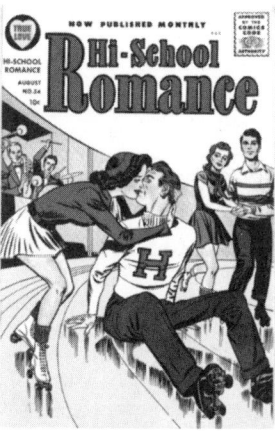

*Hi-School Romance #54
© Harvey Publications*

HI-SPOT COMICS
See: RED RYDER COMICS

HIT COMICS
**Comics Magazine
(Quality Comics Group),
July, 1940**
1 LF(c),O:Neon,Hercules,I:The
    Red Bee, B:Bob & Swab,
    Blaze Barton Strange
    Twins,X-5 Super Agent
    Casey Jones,Jack & Jill . . 12,000.00
2 GT,LF(c),B:Old Witch 4,000.00
3 GT,LF(c),E:Casey Jones. . . . 3,800.00
4 GT,LF(c),B:Super Agent &
    Betty Bates,E:X-5 . . . . 3,500.00
5 GT,LF(c),B:Red Bee (c) . . . 11,000.00
6 GT,LF(c) 3,000.00
7 GT,LF(c),E:Red Bee (c) 2,800.00
8 GT,LF(c),B:Neon (c) 2,800.00
9 JCo,LF(c),E:Neon (c) 2,800.00
10 JCo,RC,LF(c),B:Hercules(c) 2,800.00
11 JCo,RC,LF(c),A:Hercules. . 2,700.00
12 JCo,RC,LF(c),A:Hercules . . 2,200.00
13 JCo,RC,LF(c),A:Hercules . . 2,200.00
14 JCo,RC,LF(c),A:Hercules . . 2,200.00
15 JCo,RC,A:Hercules 1,800.00
16 JCo,RC,LF(c),A:Hercules . . 1,800.00
17 JCo,RC,LF(c),E:Hercules(c) 1,800.00
18 JCo,RC(a&c),O:Stormy
    Foster,B:Ghost of Flanders 1,900.00
19 JCo,RC(c),B:Stormy
    Foster(c) 1,500.00
20 JCo,RC(c),A:Stormy Foster . 1,600.00
21 JCo,RC(c) 1,500.00
22 JCo. 1,500.00
23 JCo,RC(a&c) 1,400.00
24 JCo,E:Stormy Foster (c) . . . 1,400.00
25 JCo,RP,O:Kid Eternity 2,700.00
26 JCo,RP,A:Black Hawk 1,500.00
27 JCo,RP,B:Kid Eternity (c)s . . . 700.00
28 JCo,RP,A:Her Highness 700.00
29 JCo,RP 700.00
30 JCo,RP,HK,V:Julius Caesar
    and his Legion of Warriors . . 650.00
31 JCo,RP 650.00
32 JCo,RP,V:Merlin the Wizard . . 450.00
33 JCo,RP 400.00
34 JCo,RP,E:Stormy Foster 400.00
35 JCo,Kid Eternity Accused
    of Murder 400.00
36 JCo,The Witch's Curse 400.00
37 JCo,V:Mr. Silence 400.00
38 JCo 400.00
39 JCo,Runaway River Boat 400.00
40 PG,V:Monster from the Past . 400.00
41 PG,Did Kid Eternity Lose
    His Power? 300.00
42 PG,Kid Eternity Loses Killer
    Cronson 300.00
43 JCo,PG,V:Modern
    Bluebeard 300.00
44 JCo,PG,Trips up the Shoe . . . 300.00
45 JCo,PG,Pancho Villa against
    Don Pablo 300.00
46 JCo,V:Mr. Hardeel. 300.00
47 A Polished Diamond Can Be
    Rough on Rats 300.00
48 EhH,A Treasure Chest
    of Trouble 300.00
49 EhH,V:Monsters from
    the Mirror 300.00
50 EhH,Heads for Trouble 300.00
51 EhH,Enters the Forgotten
    World 250.00
52 EhH,Heroes out of the Past . . 250.00
53 EhH,V:Mr. Puny 250.00
54 V:Ghost Town Killer. 250.00
55 V:The Brute. 250.00
56 V:Big Odds 250.00

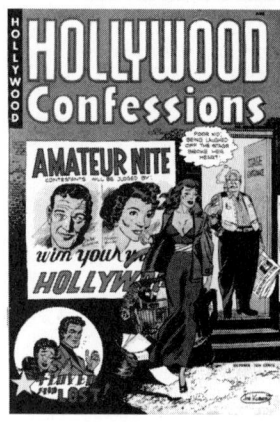

*Hollywood Confessions #1
© St John Publishing*

57 Solves the Picture in
    a Frame 250.00
58 Destroys Oppression! 250.00
59 Battles Tomorrow's Crimes
    Today! 250.00
60 E:Kid Eternity (c)s,
    V:The Mummy 250.00
61 RC(a&c),I:Jeb Rivers 300.00
62 RC(c). 250.00
63 RC(c),A:Jeb Rivers 300.00
64 RC,A:Jeb Rivers 300.00
65 Bondage (c),RC,July, 1950. . . 350.00

HOLIDAY COMICS
Fawcett Publ., Nov., 1942
1 Captain Marvel (c) 2,900.00

HOLLYWOOD COMICS
**New Age Publishers,
Winter, 1944**
1 (fa) 225.00

HOLLYWOOD
CONFESSIONS
**St. John Publ. Co.,
Oct., 1949**
1 JKu(a&c) 450.00
2 JKu(a&c), Dec., 1949 . . . . . . 475.00

HOLLYWOOD DIARY
**Comics Magazine
(Quality Comics), Dec., 1949**
1 . . . . 275.00
2 Photo (c) 200.00
3 Photo (c) 150.00
4 . . . . 150.00
5 Photo (c), Aug., 1950 . . . . . . 150.00

HOLLYWOOD FILM
STORIES
**Feature Publications,
(Prize) April, 1950**
1 June Allison,Ph(c) 300.00
2 Lizabeth Scott,Ph(c) 175.00
3 Barbara Stanwick,Ph(c) 175.00
4 Beth Hutton, Aug., 1950 . . . . . 175.00

HOLLYWOOD SECRETS
**Comics Magazine
(Quality Comics Group),
Nov., 1949**
1 BWa,BWa(c) 450.00

GOLDEN AGE *(side tab)*

2 BWa,BWa(c),RC 300.00
3 Ph(c) 200.00
4 Ph(c),May, 1950 . . . . 200.00
5 Ph(c) 200.00
6 Ph(c) 200.00

HOLYOKE ONE-SHOT
Tem Publ.
(Holyoke Publ. Co.), 1944
1 Grit Grady 300.00
2 Rusty Dugan 300.00
3 JK,Miss Victory,O:Cat Woman. 400.00
4 Mr. Miracle 250.00
5 U.S. Border Patrol 250.00
6 Capt. Fearless 250.00
7 Strong Man 300.00
8 Blue Streak 200.00
9 S&K, Citizen Smith 300.00
10 S&K, Capt. Stone 300.00

THE HOODED HORSEMAN
See: OUT OF THE NIGHT

HOORAY COMICS
Tendon Publishing Co., 1946
1 Funny animal 250.00

HOOT GIBSON WESTERN
Fox Features Syndicate, 1950
(Formerly: MY LOVE STORY)
1 (5) Ph(c). 350.00
2 (6) 325.00
3 WW 350.00

HOPALONG CASSIDY
Fawcett Publications,
Feb., 1943
1 B:Hopalong Cassidy & Topper,
  Captain Marvel (c) 9,000.00
2 . . . . 1,200.00
3 Blazing Trails 600.00
4 5-full length story 500.00
5 Death in the Saddle, Ph(c) . . . 450.00
6 . . . . 450.00
7 . . . . 450.00
8 Phantom Stage Coach,Ph(c) . 450.00
9 The Last Stockade 450.00
10 4-spine tingling adventures. . . 450.00
11 Desperate Jetters! Ph(c). 300.00
12 The Mysterious Message 300.00
13 The Human Target, Ph(c). . . . 300.00
14 Land of the Lawless, Ph(c). . . 300.00
15 Death holds the Reins, Ph(c) . 300.00
16 Webfoot's Revenge, Ph(c) . . . 300.00
17 The Hangman's Noose, Ph(c) 300.00
18 The Ghost of Dude Ranch,
  Ph(c) 300.00
19 A:William Boyd,Ph(c) 300.00
20 The Notorious Nellie Blaine!,
  B:P(c). 225.00
21 V:Arizona Kid 225.00
22 V:Arizona Kid 225.00
23 Hayride Horror 225.00
24 Twin River Giant 225.00
25 On the Trails of the Wild
  and Wooly West 225.00
26 thru 30. . . . . @200.00
31 52 pages 150.00
32 36 pages 150.00
33 52 pages 150.00
34 52 pages 150.00
35 52 pages 150.00
36 36 pages 125.00
37 thru 40, 52 pages . . . . @150.00
40 36 pages 150.00
41 E:P(c) 150.00
42 B:Ph(c) 150.00
43 . . . . 150.00
44 . . . . 125.00
45 . . . . 135.00

---

46 thru 51. . . . . @125.00
52 . . . . 100.00
53 . . . . 125.00
54 . . . . 125.00
55 . . . . 100.00
56 . . . . 125.00
57 thru 70. . . . . @125.00
71 thru 84, Ph(c)s . . . . @100.00
85 E:Ph(c),Jan., 1954 . . . . 125.00

HOPPY THE MARVEL BUNNY
Fawcett Publications,
Dec., 1945
1 A:Marvel Bunny 500.00
2 . . . . 250.00
3 . . . . 225.00
4 . . . . 225.00
5 . . . . 225.00
6 thru 14 . . . . @200.00
15 Sept., 1947 . . . . 200.00

HORRIFIC
Artful/Comic Media/
Harwell Publ./Mystery,
Sept., 1952
1 Conductor in Flames(c) 900.00
2 Human Puppets(c). 500.00
3 DH(c),Bullet hole in
  head(c) 1,000.00
4 DH(c),head on a stick (c) 400.00
5 DH(c) 400.00
6 DH(c),Jack the Ripper 500.00
7 DH(c),Shrunken Skulls 400.00
8 DH(c),I:The Teller 500.00
9 DH(c),Claws of Horror, Wolves
  of Midnight 400.00
10 DH(c),The Teller-Four
  Eerie Tales of Horror 400.00
11 DH(c),A:Gary Ghoul,Freddie,
  Demon,Victor Vampire
  Walter Werewolf 350.00
12 DH(c),A:Gary Ghoul,Freddie
  Demon,Victor Vampire,
  Walter Werewolf 350.00
13 DH(c),A:Gary Ghoul,Freddie
  Demom,Victor Vampire,
  Walter Werewolf 350.00
Becomes:

TERRIFIC COMICS
Dec., 1954
14 Eye Injury 900.00
15 . . . . 400.00
16 B:Wonderboy 400.00
Becomes:

WONDERBOY
Ajax/Farrell Publ., May, 1955
17 The Enemy's Enemy. 700.00
18 Success is No Accident,
  July, 1955 . . . . 550.00

HORROR FROM THE TOMB
See: MYSTERIOUS STORIES

HORSE FEATHER COMICS
Lev Gleason Publications,
Nov., 1947
1 BW 300.00
2 . . . . 200.00
3 . . . . 150.00
4 Summer, 1948 . . . . 150.00

Hot Rod and Speedway Comics #2
© Hillman Publications

HOT ROD AND SPEEDWAY COMICS
Hillman Periodicals
Feb.–March, 1952
1 . . . . 400.00
2 BK 250.00
3 . . . . 200.00
4 . . . . 200.00
5 April–May, 1953 . . . . 200.00

HOT ROD COMICS
Fawcett Publications,
Feb., 1952–53
N# BP,BP(c),F:Clint Curtis 500.00
2 BP,BP(c),Safety comes First . . 275.00
3 BP,BP(c),The Racing Game . . 200.00
4 BP,BP(c),Bonneville National
  Championships 200.00
5 BP,BP(c), ... 200.00
6 BP,BP(c),Race to Death 200.00

HOT ROD KING
Approved Comics
(Ziff-Davis), Fall, 1952
1 P(c) 350.00

HOT RODS AND RACING CARS
Motor Mag./
Charlton Comics, 1951
1 Speedy Davis. 400.00
2 . . . . 200.00
3 thru 10 . . . . @150.00
11 thru 20 . . . . @125.00
21 thru 70 . . . . @100.00

HOWDY DOODY
Dell Publishing Co.,
Jan., 1950
1 Ph(c). 1,900.00
2 Ph(c) 800.00
3 Ph(c) 450.00
4 Ph(c) 450.00
5 Ph(c) 450.00
6 P(c) 450.00
7 thru 10 . . . . @300.00
11 . . . . 250.00
12. 250.00
13 Christmas (c) 250.00
14 thru 20. . . . . @250.00
21 thru 38. . . . . @200.00

HOW STALIN HOPES WE WILL DESTROY AMERICA
Pictorial News, 1951
N# (Giveaway) 750.00

HOW TO SHOOT
Remington, 1952
N# (promotional) 100.00

HUMBUG
Harvey Kurtzman, 1957
1 JDa,WW,WE,End of the World 400.00
2 JDa,WE,Radiator. 200.00
3 JDa,WE 150.00
4 JDa,WE,Queen Victoria(c). . . . 150.00
5 JDa,WE 150.00
6 JDa,WE 150.00
7 JDa,WE,Sputnik(c). 175.00
8 JDa,WE,Elvis/George
  Washington(c) 150.00
9 JDa,WE 150.00
10 JDa,Magazine. 250.00
11 JDa,WE,HK,Magazine 200.00

HUMDINGER
Novelty Press/Premium
Service, May–June, 1946
1 B:Jerkwater Line,Dink,
  Mickey Starlight 500.00
2 . . . . 250.00
3 . . . . 200.00
4 . . . . 200.00
5 . . . . 200.00
6 . . . . 200.00
2-1 . . . . 175.00
2-2 July–Aug., 1947 . . . . 175.00

HUMPHREY COMICS
Harvey Publications,
Oct., 1948
1 BP,Joe Palooka 200.00
2 BP 125.00
3 BP 110.00
4 BP,A:Boy Heroes 125.00
5 BP 100.00
6 BP 100.00
7 BP,A:Little Dot 100.00
8 BP,O:Humphrey 100.00
9 BP 100.00
10 BP 100.00
11 thru 21 . . . . @100.00
22 April, 1952. . . . . 100.00

HUNTED
Fox Features Syndicate, 1950
(Formerly: MY LOVE MEMOIRS)
1 (13) Famous Crime Cases . . . 500.00
2 . . . . 250.00

HURRICANE COMICS
Cambridge House, 1945
1 F:Hurry Kane 350.00

HYPER MYSTERY COMICS
Hyper Publications, May, 1940
1 B:Hyper 3,200.00
2 June, 1940 . . . . 2,000.00

IBIS, THE INVINCIBLE
Fawcett Publications,
Jan., 1942–Spring, 1948
1 MRa(c),O:Ibis 3,500.00

---

2 Bondage (c) 1,800.00
3 BW 1,500.00
4 BW,A:Mystic Snake People . . 900.00
5 BW,Bondage (c),The
  Devil's Ibistick 1,000.00
6 BW, The Book of Evil 1,000.00

IF THE DEVIL WOULD TALK
Catechetical Guild, 1950
N# Rare 1,200.00
N#, 1958 Very Rare 850.00

ILLUSTRATED STORIES OF THE OPERAS
B. Bailey Publ. Co., 1943
N# Faust 900.00
N# Aida 850.00
N# Carman 850.00
N# Rigoletto 850.00

I LOVED
See: ZOOT COMICS

I Love Lucy #4
© *Dell Publishing Co.*

I LOVE LUCY COMICS
Dell Publishing Co., 1954
(1) *see Dell Four Color #535*
(2) *see Dell Four Color #559*
3 Lucile Ball Ph(c) all 400.00
4 . . . . 350.00
5 . . . . 350.00
6 thru 10 . . . . @300.00
11 thru 20 . . . . @200.00
21 thru 35 . . . . @175.00

IMPACT
E.C. Comics,
March–April, 1955
1 RC,GE,BK,Grl 400.00
2 RC,JDu,Grl,BK,JO. 275.00
3 JO,RC,JDU,Grl,JKa,BK. 250.00
4 RC,JO,JDa,GE,Grl,BK. 250.00
5 Nov.–Dec., 1955 . . . . 250.00

INCREDIBLE SCIENCE FANTASY
See: WEIRD SCIENCE

INCREDIBLE SCIENCE FICTION
E.C. Comics, July–Aug., 1955
30 JDa,BK,JO,WW 800.00
31 AW,WW,BK 750.00
32 AW,JDa,BK,JO 750.00
33 JDa,BK,JO,WW 750.00

INDIAN BRAVES
See: BAFFLING MYSTERIES

INDIAN CHIEF
Dell Publishing Co.,
July–Sept., 1951
3 P(c) all 125.00
4 . . . . 100.00
5 . . . . 100.00
6 A:White Eagle 100.00
7 . . . . 100.00
8 . . . . 100.00
9 . . . . 100.00
10 . . . . 100.00
11 . . . . 100.00
12 I:White Eagle 125.00
13 thru 29 . . . . @75.00
30 SB 75.00
31 thru 33 SB . . . . @75.00

INDIAN FIGHTER
Youthful Magazines,
May, 1950
1 Revenge of Chief Crazy
  Horse 200.00
2 Bondage (c) 200.00
3 . . . . 100.00
4 Cheyenne Warpath 100.00
5 . . . . 100.00
6 Davy Crockett in Death Stalks
  the Alamo 100.00
7 Tom Horn-Bloodshed at
  Massacre Valley 100.00
8 Tales of Wild Bill Hickory,
  Jan., 1952 . . . . 100.00

INDIANS
Wings Publ. Co.
(Fiction House), Spring, 1950
1 B:Long Bow, Manzar, White
  Indian & Orphan 400.00
2 B:Starlight 200.00
3 Longbow(c) 175.00
4 Longbow(c) 150.00
5 Manzar(c). 175.00
6 Captive of the Semecas 150.00
7 Longbow(c) 150.00
8 A:Long Bow 150.00
9 A:Long Bow 150.00
10 Manzar(c) 150.00
11 thru 16 . . . . @125.00
17 Spring, 1953,Longbow(c) 125.00

INDIANS ON THE WARPATH
St. John Publ. Co., 1950
N# MB(c). 500.00

INDIAN WARRIORS
See: OUTLAWS, THE

INFORMER, THE
Feature Television
Productions, April, 1954
1 MSy,The Greatest Social
  Menace of our Time! 200.00
2 MSy 150.00
3 MSy 100.00
4 MSy 100.00
5 Dec., 1954 . . . . 100.00

GOLDEN AGE

All comics prices listed are for *Near Mint* condition.

INSIDE CRIME
Hero Books/
Fox Feature Syndicate, 1950
1	400.00
2	300.00
N#	150.00

INTERNATIONAL COMICS
See: CRIME PATROL

INTERNATIONAL CRIME PATROL
See: CRIME PATROL

INTIMATE CONFESSIONS
Fawcett Publ./
Realistic Comics, 1951
1a P(c) all, Unmarried Bride	1,400.00
1 EK,EK(c),Days of Temptation... Nights of Desire	300.00
2 Doomed to Silence	300.00
3 EK(c), The Only Man For Me	200.00
3a Robert Briffault	400.00
4 EK(c),Tormented Love	300.00
5 Her Secret Sin	300.00
6 Reckless Pick-up	300.00
7 A Love Like Ours,Spanking	300.00
8 Fatal Woman, March, 1953	250.00

INTRIGUE
Comics Magazine (Quality Comics Group), 1955
1 LbC,Ghost Ship	450.00

INVISIBLE SCARLET O'NEIL
Harvey Publications, Dec., 1950
1	200.00
2	150.00
3 April, 1951	150.00

IRON VIC
United Features Syndicate/
St. John Publ. Co., 1940
1-shot	500.00

IS THIS TOMORROW?
Catechetical Guild, 1950
1 Communist threat	250.00
2 (1) Canada	150.00
3 (1) America	200.00
4 (1) Turkey	100.00
5 (1) Australia	150.00

IT REALLY HAPPENED
William H. Wise/
Visual Editions, 1945
1 Benjamin Franklin, Kit Carson	300.00
2 The Terrible Tiddlers	200.00
3 Maid of the Margiris	150.00
4 Chaplain Albert J. Hoffman	150.00
5 AS(c),Monarchs of the Sea,Lou Gehrig, Amelia Earhart	275.00
6 AS(c),Ernie Pyle	150.00
7 FGu,Teddy Roosevelt,Jefferson Davis,Story of the Helicopter.	150.00
8 FGu,Man O' War,Roy Rogers	250.00
9 AS(c),The Story of Old Ironsides	150.00
10 AS(c),Honus Wagner, The Story of Mark Twain	200.00
11 AS(c),MB,Queen of the Spanish Main, Oct., 1947	175.00

IT'S FUN TO STAY ALIVE
Nat.'l Auto Dealers Assoc., 1947
1 Bugs Bunny	250.00

JACE PEARSON OF THE TEXAS RANGERS
Dell Publishing Co., May, 1952
(1) *see Dell Four Color #396*
2 Ph(c),Joel McRae	150.00
3 Ph(c),Joel McRae	150.00
4 Ph(c),Joel McRae	150.00
5 Ph(c),Joel McRae	150.00
6 Ph(c),Joel McRae	150.00
7 Ph(c),Joel McRae	150.00
8 Ph(c),Joel McRae	150.00
9 Ph(c),Joel McRae	150.00
(10) *see Dell Four Color #648*
Becomes:

TALES OF JACE PEARSON OF THE TEXAS RANGERS
Feb., 1955
11	125.00
12	125.00
13	125.00
14	125.00
15 ATh	150.00
16 ATh	150.00
17 thru 20	@100.00

Jack Armstrong #2
© Parents Magazine

JACK ARMSTRONG
Parents' Institute, Nov., 1947
1 Artic Mystery	700.00
2 Den of the Golden Dragon	275.00
3 Lost Valley of Ice	200.00
4 Land of the Leopard Men	200.00
5 Fight against Racketeers of the Ring	200.00
6	175.00
7 Baffling Mystery on the Diamond	175.00
8	175.00
9 Mystery of the Midgets	175.00
10 Secret Cargo	175.00
11	175.00
12 Madman's Island, rare	200.00
13 Sept., 1949	175.00

JACKIE GLEASON
St. John Publishing Co., Sept., 1955
1 Ph(c)	1,000.00
2	650.00
3	600.00
4 Dec., 1955	600.00

JACKIE ROBINSON
Fawcett Publications, May, 1950
N# Ph(c) all issues	1,800.00
2	1,000.00
3	900.00
4	900.00
5	900.00
6 May, 1952	900.00

JACK IN THE BOX
See: YELLOW JACKET COMICS

JACKPOT COMICS
MLJ Magazines, Spring, 1941
1 CBi(c),B:Black Hood,Mr.Justice, Steel Sterling,Sgt.Boyle	5,500.00
2 SCp(c),	2,400.00
3 Bondage (c)	1,800.00
4 First Archie	8,000.00
5 Hitler(c)	3,000.00
6 Son of the Skull v:Black Hood, Bondage(c)	1,800.00
7 Bondage (c)	1,800.00
8 Sal(c),	1,600.00
9 Sal(c),	1,600.00
Becomes:

JOLLY JINGLES
Summer, 1943
10 Super Duck,(fa)	500.00
11 Super Duck	250.00
12 Hitler parody (c),A:Woody Woodpecker	350.00
13 thru 15 Super Duck	@150.00
16 Dec., 1944	150.00

JACK THE GIANT KILLER
Bimfort & Co., Aug.–Sept., 1953
1 HcK,HcK(c)	350.00

JAMBOREE
Round Publishing Co., Feb., 1946
1	350.00
2 March, 1946	200.00

JANE ARDEN
St. John Publ. Co., March, 1948
1	200.00
2 June, 1948	150.00

JEEP COMICS
R.B. Leffingwell & Co., Winter, 1944
1 B;Captain Power	900.00
2	600.00
3 LbC(c),March–April, 1948	700.00

JEFF JORDAN, U.S. AGENT
D.S. Publ. Co., Dec., 1947
1	250.00

GOLDEN AGE

JERRY DRUMMER
Charlton Comics, 1957
1 Revolutionary War 100.00
2 . . . . 100.00

JESSE JAMES
Avon Periodicals/
Realistic Publ., Aug., 1950
1 JKu,The San Antonio Stage
  Robbery 250.00
2 JKu,The Daring Liberty Bank
  Robbery 175.00
3 JKu,The California Stagecoach
  Robberies 175.00
4 EK(c),Deadliest Deed! 100.00
5 JKu,WW,Great Prison Break . 175.00
6 JKu,Wanted Dead or Alive . . . 175.00
7 JKu,Six-Gun Slaughter at
  San Romano! 150.00
8 EK,Daring Train Robbery! 125.00
9 EK 100.00
10 thru 14 {Do not exist}
15 EK 125.00
16 EK, Butch Cassidy 100.00
17 EK, Jessie James 100.00
18 JKu 100.00
19 JKu 100.00
20 AW,FF,A:Chief Vic,Kit West . . 200.00
21 EK, Two Jessie James 100.00
22 EK,Chuck Wagon 100.00
23 EK 100.00
24 EK,B:New McCarty 100.00
25 EK 100.00
26 EK 100.00
27 EK,E:New McCarty 100.00
28 Quantrells Raiders 100.00
29 Aug., 1956 . . . . 100.00

JEST
Harry 'A' Chesler, 1944
10 J. Rebel,Yankee Boy 300.00
11 1944,Little Nemo 350.00

JET ACES
Real Adventure Publ. Co.
(Fiction House), 1952
1 Set 'em up in MIG Alley 250.00
2 Kiss-Off for Moscow Molly . . . 125.00
3 Red Task Force Sighted 125.00
4 Death-Date at 40,000, 1953 . . 125.00

JET FIGHTERS
Standard Magazines,
Nov., 1953
5 ATh,Korean War Stories 150.00
6 Circus Pilot 125.00
7 ATh, Iron Curtains for Ivan,
  March, 1953 . . . . 150.00

JETTA OF THE 21st CENTURY
Standard Comics, Dec., 1952
5 Teen Stories 300.00
6 Robot (c) 250.00
7 April, 1953 . . . . 150.00

JIGGS AND MAGGIE
Best Books (Standard)/
Harvey Publ., June, 1949
11 . . . . 150.00
12 thru 21 . . . . @100.00
22 thru 25 . . . . @100.00
26 Part 3-D 200.00
27 Feb.–March, 1954 . . . . 100.00

JIM BOWIE
See: DANGER

JIM DANDY
Dandy Magazine
(Lev Gleason), 1956
1 Teen-age humor 125.00
2 . . . . 100.00
3 . . . . 100.00

JIM HARDY
Spotlight Publ., 1944
N# Dynamite Jim,Mirror Man . . . 600.00

JIM RAY'S AVIATION SKETCH BOOK
Vital Publishers, Feb., 1946
1 Radar, the Invisible eye 550.00
2 Gen.Hap Arnold, May, 1946 . . 350.00

JINGLE JANGLE COMICS
Eastern Color Printing Co.,
Feb., 1942
1 B:Benny Bear,Pie Face Prince,
  Jingle Jangle Tales,Hortense 700.00
2 GCn 350.00
3 GCn 300.00
4 GCn,Pie Face (c) 300.00
5 GCn,B:Pie Face 300.00
6 GCn, ... 250.00
7 . . . . 250.00
8 . . . . 250.00
9 . . . . 250.00
10 . . . . 250.00
11 . . . . 200.00
12 . . . . 200.00
13 . . . . 200.00
14 . . . . 200.00
15 E:Pie Face . . . . @200.00
16 thru 20 . . . . @175.00
21 thru 25 . . . . @150.00
26 thru 30 . . . . @150.00
31 thru 41 . . . . @100.00
42 Dec., 1949 . . . . 100.00

JING PALS
Victory Publ. Corp.,
Feb., 1946
1 Johnny Rabbit 250.00
2 . . . . 200.00
3 . . . . 200.00
4 Aug., 1948 . . . . 200.00

Joe Louis #2
© Fawcett Publishing

JOE COLLEGE
Hillman Periodicals,
Fall, 1949
1 BP,DPr 150.00
2 BP, Winter, 1949 . . . . 125.00

JOE LOUIS
Fawcett Periodicals,
Sept., 1950
1 Ph(c),Life Story 850.00
2 Ph(c),Nov., 1950 . . . . 550.00

JOE PALOOKA
Publication Enterprises
(Columbia Comics Group) 1943
1 Lost in the Desert 1,500.00
2 Hitler (c) 850.00
3 KO's the Nazis! 600.00
4 Eiffel tower (c), 1944 . . . . 450.00

JOE PALOOKA
Harvey Publications,
Nov., 1945–March, 1961
1 Joe Tells How He Became
  World Champ 700.00
2 Skiing (c) 350.00
3 . . . . 200.00
4 Welcome Home Pals! 200.00
5 S&K,The Great Carnival
  Murder Mystery 275.00
6 Classic Joe Palooka (c) 200.00
7 BP,V:Grumpopski 200.00
8 BP,Mystery of the Ghost Ship . 150.00
9 Drooten Island Mystery 150.00
10 BP 150.00
11 . . . . 125.00
12 BP,Boxing Course 125.00
13 . . . . 110.00
14 BP,Palooka's Toughest Fight . . 110.00
15 BP,O:Humphrey 200.00
16 BP,A:Humphrey 110.00
17 BP,I:Little Max,A:Humphrey . . 200.00
18 A:Little Max 110.00
19 BP,Freedom Train(c) 125.00
20 Punch Out(c) 110.00
21 . . . . 100.00
22 V:Assassin 100.00
23 Big Bathing Beauty Issue . . . 100.00
24 . . . . 100.00
25 . . . . 100.00
26 BP,Big Prize Fight Robberies . 100.00
27 BP,Mystery of Bal
  Eagle Cabin,A:Little Max 110.00
28 BP,Fights Out West, Babe
  Ruth 100.00
29 BP,Joe Busts Crime
  Wide Open 100.00
30 BP,V:Hoodlums, Nude
  Painting 125.00
31 BP, Dizzy Dean 125.00
32 BP,Fight Palooka Was Sure
  to Lose 100.00
33 BP,Joe finds Ann 100.00
34 BP,How to Box like a Champ . 100.00
35 BP,More Adventures of Little
  Max, Joe Louis 125.00
36 BP 100.00
37 BP,Joe as a Boy 100.00
38 BP 100.00
39 BP,Original Hillbillies with
  Big Leviticus 100.00
40 BP,Joe's Toughest Fight 100.00
41 BP,Humphrey's Grudge Fight . 100.00
42 BP 100.00
43 BP 100.00
44 BP,M:Ann Howe, Markies . . . 125.00
45 BP 90.00
46 Champ of Champs 90.00
47 BreathtakingUnderwaterBattle . 90.00
48 BP,Exciting Indian Adventure . . 90.00

Joe Palooka–Judo

49 BP 90.00
50 BP,Bondage(c) 90.00
51 BP, Babe Ruth 90.00
52 BP,V:Balonki 90.00
53 BP 90.00
54 V:Bad Man Trigger McGehee . . 90.00
55 . . . . 90.00
56 Foul Play on the High Seas . . . 90.00
57 Curtains for the Champ 90.00
58 V:The Man-Eating Swamp
    Terror 90.00
59 The Enemy Attacks 90.00
60 Joe Fights Escaped Convict . . 90.00
61 . . . . 90.00
62 S&K, Boy Explorers 125.00
63 . . . . 90.00
64 . . . . 90.00
65 . . . . 90.00
66 Drug 125.00
67 Drug 150.00
68 . . . . 90.00
69 Torture 150.00
70 BP, Vs. "Gooks" 90.00
71 Bloody Bayonets 90.00
72 Tank 90.00
73 BP 90.00
74 thru 115 . . . . @90.00
116 thru 117 giants . . . . @150.00
118 Giant, Jack Dempsey . . . . @150.00
Giant 1 Body Building 150.00
Giant 2 Fights His Way Back 200.00
Giant 3 Visits Lost City 125.00
Giant 4 All in Family 150.00

JOE YANK
**Visual Editions
(Standard Comics),
March, 1952**

5 ATh,WE,Korean Jackpot! 150.00
6 Bacon and Bullets,
    G.I.Renegade 150.00
7 Two-Man War,A:Sgt. Glamour . 150.00
8 ATh(c),Miss Foxhole of 1952, . 125.00
9 G.I.'s and Dolls,Colonel Blood . 75.00
10 A Good Way to Die,
    A:General Joe 75.00
11 . . . . 75.00
12 RA 75.00
13 . . . . 75.00
14 . . . . 75.00
15 . . . . 75.00
16 July, 1954 . . . . 75.00

JOHN HIX SCRAPBOOK
**Eastern Color Printing Co.,
1937**

1 Strange as It Seems 600.00
2 Strange as It Seems 400.00

JOHNNY DANGER
Toby Press, Aug., 1954
1 Ph(c),Private Detective 225.00

JOHNNY DYNAMITE
See: DYNAMITE

JOHNNY HAZARD
**Best Books
(Standard Comics),
Aug., 1948**

5 FR 250.00
6 FR,FR(c) 225.00
7 FR(c) 200.00
8 FR,FR(c), May, 1949 . . . . 225.00

JOHNNY LAW, SKY RANGER
**Good Comics (Lev Gleason),
April, 1955**

1 . . . . 125.00
2 . . . . 75.00
3 . . . . 75.00
4 Nov., 1955 . . . . 75.00

JOHNNY MACK BROWN
Dell Publishing Co., 1950–52
1 See: FOUR COLOR
2 Western hero 225.00
3 . . . . 175.00
4 thru 10 . . . . @125.00

JOHN WAYNE ADVENTURE COMICS
Toby Press, Winter, 1949
1 Ph(c),The Mysterious Valley
    of Violence 2,500.00
2 AW,FF,Ph(c) 1,200.00
3 AW,FF,Flying Sheriff 1,200.00
4 AW,FF,Double-Danger,Ph(c) 1,200.00
5 Volcano of Death,Ph(c) 750.00
6 AW,FF,Caravan of Doom,
    Ph(c) 900.00
7 AW,FF,Ph(c) 800.00
8 AW,FF,Duel of Death,Ph(c) . 1,100.00
9 Ghost Guns,Ph(c) 525.00
10 Dangerous Journey,Ph(c) . . . 500.00
11 Manhunt!,Ph(c) 500.00
12 HK,Joins the Marines,Ph(c) . . 500.00
13 V:Frank Stacy 450.00
14 Operation Peeping John 450.00
15 Bridge Head 450.00
16 AW,FF,Golden Double-Cross . 450.00
17 Murderer's Music 450.00
18 AW,FF,Larson's Folly 550.00
19 . . . . 400.00
20 Whale (c) 400.00
21 . . . . 400.00
22 Flash Flood! 400.00
23 Death on Two Wheels 400.00
24 Desert 400.00
25 AW,FF,Hondo!,Ph(c) 550.00
26 Ph(c) 450.00
27 Ph(c) 450.00
28 Dead Man's Boots! 450.00
29 AW,FF,Ph(c),Crash in
    California Desert 500.00
30 The Wild One, Ph(c) 450.00
31 AW,FF,May, 1955 . . . . 500.00

*John Wayne Adventure Comics
© Toby Press*

JO-JO COMICS
**Fox Features Syndicate,
Spring, 1946**

N# (fa) JoJo 250.00
2 (fa) Electro 150.00
3 (fa) 150.00
4 (fa) 150.00
5 (fa) 150.00
6 (fa) 150.00
7 B:Jo-Jo Congo King 1,400.00
8 (7)B:Tanee,V:The
    Giant Queen 900.00
9 (8)The Mountain of Skulls 750.00
10 (9)Death of the Fanged Lady . 750.00
11 (10) 750.00
12 (11)Bondage(c),
    Water Warriors 650.00
13 (12) Jade Juggernaut 625.00
14 The Leopards of Learda 625.00
15 The Flaming Fiend 700.00
16 Golden Gorilla,bondage(c) . . . 625.00
17 Stark-Mad Thespian,
    bondage(c) 700.00
18 The Death Traveler 625.00
19 Gladiator of Gore 625.00
20 . . . . 625.00
21 . . . . 625.00
22 . . . . 625.00
23 . . . . 625.00
24 . . . . 625.00
25 Bondage(c) 700.00
26 . . . . 625.00
27 . . . . 625.00
28 . . . . 625.00
29 July, 1949 . . . . 650.00

JOLLY JINGLES
See: JACKPOT

JON JUAN
Toby Press, 1950
1 ASh(c),Superlover 1,000.00

JOURNEY INTO FEAR
**Superior Publications,
May, 1951–Sept., 1954**

1 MB,Preview of Chaos 1,000.00
2 Debt to the Devil 650.00
3 Midnight Prowler 550.00
4 Invisible Terror 550.00
5 Devil Cat 375.00
6 Partners in Blood 375.00
7 The Werewolf Lurks 375.00
8 Bells of the Damned 375.00
9 Masked Death 375.00
10 Gallery of the Dead 375.00
11 Beast of Bedlam 350.00
12 No Rest for the Dead 350.00
13 Cult of the Dead 350.00
14 Jury of the Undead 350.00
15 Corpse in Make-up 375.00
16 Death by Invitation 325.00
17 Deadline for Death 325.00
18 Here's to Horror 325.00
19 This Body is Mine! 325.00
20 Masters of the Dead 325.00
21 Horror in the Clock 325.00

JUDGE PARKER
Argo, Feb., 1956

1 . . . . 100.00
2 . . . . 75.00

JUDO JOE
**Jay-Jay Corp.,
Aug., 1952**

1 Drug 150.00
2 . . . . 100.00
3 Drug, Dec., 1953 . . . . 125.00

GOLDEN AGE

JUDY CANOVA
See: ALL TOP COMICS

JUKE BOX
Famous Funnies,
March, 1948
1 ATh(c),Spike Jones 600.00
2 Dinah Shore,Transvestitism. . . 400.00
3 Vic Damone, Peggie Lee. 300.00
4 Jimmy Durante. 300.00
5 . . . . 300.00
6 Jan., 1949,Desi Arnaz 325.00

JUMBO COMICS
Real Adventure Publ. Co.
(Fiction House),
Sept., 1938
1 LF,BKa,JK,WE(a&c),B:Sheena
 Queen of the Jungle,The Hawk
 The Hunchback 40,000.00
2 LF,JK,WE,BKa,BP,
 O:Sheena 18,000.00
3 JK,WE(a&c),BP,LF,BKa . . . 10,000.00
4 WE(a&c),MMe,LF,BKa,
 O:The Hawk 9,000.00
5 WE(a&c),BP,BKa 8,000.00
6 WE(a&c),BP,BKa 7,000.00
7 WE,BKa,BP 7,000.00
8 LF(c),BP,BKa,World of
 Tommorow 7,000.00
9 LF(c),BP 6,000.00
10 WE,LF(c),BKa,Regular size
 issues begin 3,000.00
11 LF(c),WE&BP,War of the
 Emerald Gas 2,000.00
12 WE(c),WE&BP,Hawk in Buccaneer
 Vengeance,Bondage(c) . . . 2,500.00
13 WE(c),BP,Sheena in The
 Thundering Herds. 2,000.00
14 WE(c),LF,BP,Hawk in Siege
 of Thunder Isle,B:Lightning 2,100.00
15 BP(a&c),Sheena(c) 1,200.00
16 BP(a&c),The Lightning
 Strikes Twice 1,500.00
17 BP(c), B:Sheena covers
 and lead stories 1,200.00
18 BP 1,200.00
19 BP(c),BKa,Warriors of
 the Bush. 1,200.00
20 BP,BKa,Spoilers of the
 Wild. 1,200.00
21 BP,BKa,Prey of the
 Giant Killers. 900.00
22 BP,BKa,Victims of the
 Super-Ape,O:Hawk. 1,000.00
23 BP,BKa,Swamp of the
 Green Terror. 1,000.00
24 BP,BKa,Curse of the Black
 Venom 1,000.00
25 BP,BKa,Bait for the Beast. . . . 900.00
26 BP,BKa,Tiger-Man Terror 900.00
27 BP,BKa,Sabre-Tooth Terror. . . 900.00
28 BKa,RWd,The Devil of
 the Congo 900.00
29 BKa,RWd,Elephant-Scourge . 900.00
30 BKa,RWd,Slashing Fangs . . . 900.00
31 BKa,RWd,Voodoo Treasure
 of Black Slave Lake. 800.00
32 BKa,RWd,AB,Captives of
 the Gorilla-Men 800.00
33 BKa,RWd,AB,Stampede
 Tusks. 800.00
34 BKa,RWd,AB,Claws of the
 Devil-Cat 800.00
35 BKa,RWd,AB,Hostage of the
 Devil Apes 800.00
36 BKa,RWd,AB,Voodoo Flames 800.00
37 BKa,RWd,AB,Congo Terror . . 800.00
38 BKa,RWd,AB,Death-Trap of
 the River Demons 800.00

39 BKa,RWd,AB,Cannibal Bait . . 800.00
40 BKa,RWd,AB,
 Assagai Poison 800.00
41 BKa,RWd,AB,Killer's Kraal,
 Bondage(c) 700.00
42 BKa,RWd,AB,Plague of
 Spotted Killers 700.00
43 BKa,RWd,AB,Beasts of the
 Devil Queen. 700.00
44 BKa,RWd,AB,Blood-Cult of
 K'Douma 700.00
45 BKa,RWd,AB,Fanged
 Keeper of the Fire-Gem 700.00
46 BKa,RWd,AB,Lair of the
 Armored Monsters. 700.00
47 BKa,RWd,AB,The Bantu
 Blood-Monster 700.00
48 BKa,RWd,AB,Red Meat for
 the Cat-Pack 700.00
49 BKa,RWd,AB,Empire of the
 Hairy Ones 700.00
50 BKa,RWd,AB,Eyrie of the
 Leopard Birds 700.00
51 BKa,RWd.AB,Monsters with
 Wings. 500.00
52 BKa,RWd,AB,Man-Eaters
 Paradise 500.00
53 RWd,AB,Slaves of the
 Blood Moon 500.00
54 RWd,AB,Congo Kill. 500.00
55 RWd,AB,Bait for the Silver
 King Cat. 500.00
56 RWd,AB,Sabre Monsters of
 the Aba-Zanzi,Bondage(c). . . 700.00
57 RWd,AB,Arena of Beasts 500.00
58 RWd,AB,Sky-Atlas of the
 Thunder-Birds 500.00
59 RWd,AB,Kraal of Shrunken
 Heads 500.00
60 RWd,AB,Land of the
 Stalking Death 400.00
61 RWd,AB,King-Beast of
 the Masai. 400.00
62 RWd,AB,Valley of Golden
 Death. 400.00
63 RWd,AB,The Dwarf Makers . . 400.00
64 RWd,The Slave-Brand of Ibn
 Ben Satan,Male Bondage . . . 600.00
65 RWd,The Man-Eaters of
 Linpopo 400.00
66 RWd,Valley of Monsters 400.00
67 RWd,Land of Feathered Evil . 400.00
68 RWd,Spear of Blood Ju-Ju . . . 400.00
69 RWd,AB,MB,Slaves for the
 White Sheik 400.00

Jumbo Comics #10
© Fiction House

70 RWd,AB,MB,The Rogue
 Beast's Prey 400.00
71 RWd,AB,MB,The Serpent-
 God Speaks. 350.00
72 RWd,AB,MB,Curse of the
 Half-Dead 350.00
73 RWd,AB,MB,War Apes of
 the T'Kanis. 350.00
74 RWd,AB,MB,Drums of the
 Voodoo God 350.00
75 RWd,AB,MB,Terror Trail of
 the Devil's Horn 350.00
76 RWd,AB,MB,Fire Gems of
 Skull Valley 350.00
77 RWd,AB,MB,Blood Dragons
 from Fire Valley 350.00
78 RWd,AB,MB,Veldt of the
 Vampire Apes 350.00
79 RWd,AB,MB,Dancing
 Skeletons. 350.00
80 RWd,AB,MB,Banshee
 Cats 350.00
81 RWd,MB,AB,JKa,Heads for
 King' Hondo's Harem. 300.00
82 RWd,MB,AB,JKa,Ghost Riders
 of the Golden Tuskers 300.00
83 RWd,MB,AB,JKa,Charge of
 the Condo Juggernauts. 300.00
84 RWd,MB,AB,JKa,Valley of
 the Whispering Fangs 300.00
85 RWd,MB,AB,JKa,Red Tusks
 of Zulu-Za'an 300.00
86 RWd,MB,AB,JKa,Witch-Maiden
 of the Burning Blade 300.00
87 RWd,AB,MB,JKa,Sargasso of
 Lost Safaris 300.00
88 RWd,AB,MB,JKa,Kill-Quest
 of the Ju-Ju Tusks. 300.00
89 RWd,AB,MB,JKa,Ghost Slaves
 of Bwana Rojo. 300.00
90 RWd,AB,MB,JKa,Death Kraal
 of the Mastadons 300.00
91 RWd,AB,MB,JKa,Spoor of
 the Sabre-Horn Tiger. 300.00
92 RWd,MB,JKa,Pied Piper
 of the Congo 300.00
93 RWd,MB,JKa,The Beasts
 that Dawn Begot 300.00
94 RWd,MB,JKa,Wheel of a
 Thousand Deaths 350.00
95 RWd,MB,JKa,Flame Dance
 of the Ju-Ju Witch 275.00
96 RWd,MB,JKa,Ghost
 Safari. 275.00
97 RWd,MB,JKa,Banshee Wail
 of the Undead,Bondage(c) . . 400.00
98 RWd,MB,JKa,Seekers of
 the Terror Fangs 300.00
99 RWd,MB,JKa,Shrine of
 the Seven Souls 300.00
100 RWd,MB,Slave Brand
 of Hassan Bey. 350.00
101 RWd,MB,Quest of the
 Two-Face Ju Ju 300.00
102 RWd,MB,Viper Gods of
 Vengeance Veldt 300.00
103 RWd,MB,Blood for the
 Idol of Blades. 300.00
104 RWd,MB,Valley of Eternal
 Sleep 300.00
105 RWd,MB,Man Cubs from
 Momba-Zu. 350.00
106 RWd,MB,The River of
 No-Return. 350.00
107 RWd,MB,Vandals of
 the Veldt 300.00
108 RWd,MB,The Orphan of
 Vengeance Vale. 300.00
109 RWd,MB,The Pygmy's Hiss
 is Poison 300.00
110 RWd,MB,Death Guards the
 Congo Keep 300.00

111 RWd,MB,Beware of the
Witch-Man's Brew 300.00
112 RWd,MB,The Blood-Mask
from G'Shinis Grave 275.00
113 RWd,MB,The Mask's of
Zombi-Zan 275.00
114 RWd,MB 275.00
115 RWd,MB,Svengali of
the Apes 275.00
116 RWd,MB,The Vessel of
Marbel Monsters 275.00
117 RWd,MB,Lair of the Half-
Man King 275.00
118 RWd,MB,Quest of the
Congo Dwarflings 275.00
119 RWd,MB,King Crocodile's
Domain 275.00
120 RWd,MB,The Beast-Pack
Howls the Moon 275.00
121 RWd,MB,The Kraal of
Evil Ivory 275.00
122 RWd,MB,Castaways of
the Congo 250.00
123 RWd,MB, ... 250.00
124 RWd,MB,The Voodoo Beasts
of Changra-Lo 250.00
125 RWd,MB,JKa(c),The Beast-
Pack Strikes at Dawn 250.00
126 RWd,MB,JKa(c),Lair of the
Swamp Beast 250.00
127 RWd,MB,JKa(c),The Phantom
of Lost Lagoon 250.00
128 RWd,MB,JKa(c),Mad Mistress
of the Congo-Tuskers 250.00
129 RWd,MB,JKa(c),Slaves of
King Simbas Kraal. 250.00
130 RWd,MB,JKa(c),Quest of
the Pharaoh's Idol 250.00
131 RWd,JKa(c),Congo Giants
at Bay 250.00
132 RWd,JKa(c),The Doom of
the Devil's Gorge. 250.00
133 RWd,JKa(c),Blaze the
Pitfall Trail 250.00
134 RWd,JKa(c),Catacombs of
the Jackal-Men 250.00
135 RWd,JKa(c),The 40 Thieves
of Ankar-Lo 250.00
136 RWd,JKa(c),The Perils of
Paradise Lost 250.00
137 RWd,JKa(c),The Kraal of
Missing Men 250.00
138 RWd,JKa(c),The Panthers
of Kajo-Kazar. 250.00
139 RWd,JKa(c),Stampede of
the Congo Lancers 250.00
140 RWd,JKa(c),The Moon
Beasts from Vulture Valley . . 250.00
141 RWd,JKa(c),B:Long
Bow 275.00
142 RWd,JKa(c),Man-Eaters
of N'Gamba 250.00
143 RWd,JKa(c),The Curse of
the Cannibal Drum 250.00
144 RWd,JKa(c),The Secrets of
Killers Cave 250.00
145 RWd,JKa(c),Killers of
the Crypt 250.00
146 RWd,JKa(c),Sinbad of the
Lost Lagoon. 250.00
147 RWd,JKa(c),The Wizard of
Gorilla Glade 250.00
148 RWd,JKa(c),Derelict of
the Slave King 250.00
149 RWd,JKa(c),Lash Lord of
the Elephants 250.00
150 RWd,JKa(c),Queen of
the Pharaoh's Idol 250.00
151 RWd,The Voodoo Claws
of Doomsday Trek. 250.00
152 RWd,Red Blades of Africa . . 250.00

153 RWd,Lost Legions of the
Nile 250.00
154 RWd,The Track of the
Black Devil. 250.00
155 RWd,The Ghosts of
Blow- Gun Trail 250.00
156 RWd,The Slave-Runners
of Bambaru 250.00
157 RWd,Cave of the
Golden Skull 250.00
158 RWd,Gun Trek to
Panther Valley 250.00
159 RWd,A:Space Scout 225.00
160 RWd,Savage Cargo,
E:Sheena covers 225.00
161 RWd,Dawns of the Pit 225.00
162 RWd,Hangman's Haunt 225.00
163 RWd,Cagliostro Cursed
Thee 225.00
164 RWd,Death Bars the Door . . 225.00
165 RWd,Day off from a Corpse . 225.00
166 RWd,The Gallows Bird 225.00
167 RWd,Cult of the Clawmen,
March, 1953 . . . . 225.00

JUNGLE COMICS
Glen Kel Publ./Fiction House,
Jan., 1940

1 HcK,DBr,LF(c),O:The White
Panther,Kaanga,Tabu, B:The
Jungle Boy,Camilla, all
Kaanga covers & stories . . 9,000.00
2 HcK,DBr,WE(c),B:Fantomah 2,500.00
3 HcK,DBr,GT,The Crocodiles
of Death River 2,200.00
4 HcK,DBr,Wambi in
Thundering Herds. 2,000.00
5 WE(c),GT,HcK,DBr,Empire
of the Ape Men 2,400.00
6 WE(c),GT,DBr,HcK,Tigress
of the Deep Jungle Swamp 1,400.00
7 BP(c),DBr,GT,HcK,Live
Sacrifice,Bondage(c) 1,200.00
8 BP(c),GT,HcK,Safari into
Shadowland 1,200.00
9 GT,HcK,Captive of the
Voodoo Master 1,200.00
10 GT,HcK,BP,Lair of the
Renegade Killer 1,200.00
11 GT,HcK,V:Beasts of Africa's Ancient
Primieval Swamp Land 900.00
12 GT,HcK,The Devil's
Death-Trap 900.00
13 GT(c),GT,HcK,Stalker of
the Beasts 950.00

Jungle Comics #15
© Fiction House

14 HcK,Vengeance of the
Gorilla Hordes 900.00
15 HcK,Terror of the Voodoo
Cauldron 900.00
16 HcK,Caveman Killers 900.00
17 HcK,Valley of the Killer-Birds . 900.00
18 HcK,Trap of the Tawny
Killer, Bondage(c). 1,000.00
19 HcK,Revolt of the Man-Apes . 900.00
20 HcK,One-offering to
Ju-Ju Demon 900.00
21 HcK,Monster of the Dismal
Swamp, Bondage(c) 750.00
22 HcK,Lair o/t Winged Fiend . . . 700.00
23 HcK,Man-Eater Jaws 700.00
24 HcK,Battle of the Beasts. . . . 700.00
25 HcK,Kaghis the Blood God,
Bondage(c) 750.00
26 HcK,Gorillas of the
Witch-Queen 700.00
27 HcK,Spore o/t Gold-Raiders . . 700.00
28 HcK,Vengeance of the Flame
God, Bondage(c). 750.00
29 HcK,Juggernaut of Doom . . . 625.00
30 HcK,Claws o/t Black Terror . . 625.00
31 HcK,Land of Shrunken
Skulls. 500.00
32 HcK,Curse of the King-Beast . 500.00
33 HcK,Scaly Guardians of
Massacre Pool,Bondage(c). . 600.00
34 HcK,Bait of the Spotted
Fury,Bondage(c) 600.00
35 HcK,Stampede of the
Slave-Masters 500.00
36 HcK,GT,The Flame-Death of
Ju Ju Mountain 500.00
37 HcK,GT,Scaly Sentinel of
Taboo Swamp 500.00
38 HcK,GT,Duel of the Congo
Destroyers. 500.00
39 HcK,Land of Laughing Bones. 500.00
40 HcK,Killer Plague 500.00
41 Hck,The King Ape
Feeds at Dawn 450.00
42 Hck,RC,Master of the
Moon-Beasts 475.00
43 HcK,The White Shiek 450.00
44 HcK,Monster of the
Boiling Pool 450.00
45 HcK,The Bone-Grinders of
B'Zambi, Bondage(c). 500.00
46 HcK,Blood Raiders of
Tree Trail 450.00
47 HcK,GT,Monsters of the Man
Pool, Bondage(c). 500.00
48 HcK,GT,Strangest Congo
Adventure 400.00
49 HcK,GT,Lair of the King
-Serpent. 400.00
50 HcK,GT,Juggernaut of
the Bush 400.00
51 HcK,GT,The Golden Lion of
Genghis Kahn 400.00
52 HcK,Feast for the River
Devils, Bondage(c) 500.00
53 HcK,GT,Slaves for Horrors
Harem 375.00
54 HcK,GT,Blood Bride of
the Crocodile 350.00
55 HcK,GT,The Tree Devil. 350.00
56 HcK,Bride for the
Rainmaker Raj. 350.00
57 HcK,Fire Gems of T'ulaki 350.00
58 HcK,Land of the
Cannibal God 350.00
59 HcK,Dwellers of the Mist
Bondage(c) 450.00
60 HcK,Bush Devil's Spoor 400.00
61 HcK,Curse of the Blood
Madness 400.00
62 Bondage(c) 450.00

63 HcK,Fire-Birds for the
Cliff Dwellers 350.00
64 Valley of the Ju-Ju Idols 350.00
65 Shrine of the Seven Ju Jus,
Bondage(c) 400.00
66 Spoor of the Purple Skulls . . . 350.00
67 Devil Beasts of the Golden
Temple 350.00
68 Satan's Safari 350.00
69 Brides for the Serpent King . . 350.00
70 Brides for the King Beast,
Bondage(c) 400.00
71 Congo Prey,Bondage(c) 400.00
72 Blood-Brand o/t Veldt Cats . . . 350.00
73 The Killer of M'omba Raj,
Bondage(c) 400.00
74 AgF,GoldenJaws,
Bondage(c) 400.00
75 AgF,Congo Kill 350.00
76 AgF,Blood Thirst of the
Golden Tusk 350.00
77 AgF,The Golden Gourds
Shriek Blood,Bondage(c) . . . 400.00
78 AgF,Bondage(c) 400.00
79 AgF,Death has a
Thousand Fangs 375.00
80 AgF,Salome of the
Devil-Cats Bondage(c) 400.00
81 AgF,Colossus of the Congo . . 375.00
82 AgF,Blood Jewels of the
Fire-Bird 375.00
83 AgF,Vampire Veldt,
Bondage(c) 400.00
84 AgF,Blood Spoor of the
Faceless Monster 375.00
85 AgF,Brides for the Man-Apes
Bondage(c) 400.00
86 AgF,Firegems of L'hama
Lost, Bondage(c). 400.00
87 AgF,Horror Kraal of the
Legless One,Bondage(c). . . . 400.00
88 AgF,Beyond the Ju-Ju Mists . . 375.00
89 AgF,Blood-Moon over the
Whispering Veldt 350.00
90 AgF,The Skulls for the
Altar of Doom,Bondage(c) . . 425.00
91 AgF,Monsters from the Mist
Lands, Bondage(c) 425.00
92 AgF,Vendetta of the
Tree Tribes 400.00
93 AgF,Witch Queen of the
Hairy Ones 400.00
94 AgF,Terror Raid of
the Congo Caesar 400.00
95 Agf,Flame-Tongues of the
Sky Gods 400.00
96 Agf,Phantom Guardians of the
Enchanted Lake,Bondage(c). 400.00
97 AgF,Wizard of the Whirling
Doom,Bondage(c) 375.00
98 AgF,Ten Tusks of Zulu Ivory . . 450.00
99 AgF,Cannibal Caravan,
Bondage(c) 375.00
100 AgF,Hate has a
Thousand Claws 375.00
101 AgF,The Blade of
Buddha, Bondage(c) 375.00
102 AgF,Queen of the
Amazon Lancers 350.00
103 AgF,The Phantoms of
Lost Lagoon. 350.00
104 AgF 350.00
105 AgF,The Red Witch
of Ubangi-Shan 350.00
106 AgF,Bondage(c) 375.00
107 Banshee Valley 375.00
108 HcK,Merchants of Murder. . . 375.00
109 HcK,Caravan of the
Golden Bones 350.00
110 HcK,Raid of the Fire-Fangs . 350.00
111 HcK,The Trek of the
Terror-Paws 350.00

112 HcK,Morass of the
Mammoths. 350.00
113 HcK,Two-Tusked Terror 350.00
114 HcK,Mad Jackals Hunt
by Night 350.00
115 HcK,Treasure Trove in
Vulture Sky 350.00
116 HcK,The Banshees of
Voodoo Veldt 350.00
117 HcK,The Fangs of the
Hooded Scorpion. 350.00
118 HcK,The Muffled Drums
of Doom. 350.00
119 HcK,Fury of the Golden
Doom. 350.00
120 HcK,Killer King Domain 350.00
121 HcK,Wolves of the
Desert Night 350.00
122 HcK,The Veldt of
Phantom Fangs. 350.00
123 HcK,The Ark of the
Mist-Maids 350.00
124 HcK,The Trail of the
Pharaoh's Eye 350.00
125 HcK,Skulls for Sale on
Dismal River 350.00
126 HcK,Safari Sinister 300.00
127 HcK,Bondage(c) 300.00
128 HcK,Dawn-Men of the
Congo 300.00
129 HcK,The Captives of
Crocodile Swamp 300.00
130 HcK,Phantoms of the Congo 300.00
131 HcK,Treasure-Tomb of the
Ape-King 300.00
132 HcK,Bondage(c) 350.00
133 HcK,Scourge of the Sudan
Bondage(c) 350.00
134 HcK,The Black Avengers of
Kaffir Pass. 300.00
135 HcK 300.00
136 HcK,The Death Kraals
of Kongola 300.00
137 BWg(c),HcK,The Safari of
Golden Ghosts 300.00
138 BWg(c),HcK,Track of the
Black Terror Bondage(c) 350.00
139 BWg(c),HcK,Captain Kidd
of the Congo 300.00
140 BWg(c),HcK,The Monsters
of Kilimanjaro 300.00
141 BWg(c)HcK,The Death Hunt
of the Man Cubs 300.00
142 BWg(c),Hck,Sheba of the
Terror Claws,Bondage(c). . . . 350.00
143 BWg(c)Hck,The Moon of
Devil Drums. 300.00

144 BWg(c)Hck,Quest of the
Dragon's Claw 300.00
145 BWg(c)Hck,Spawn of the
Devil's Moon 300.00
146 BWg(c),HcK,Orphans of
the Congo 300.00
147 BWG(c),HcK,The Treasure
of Tembo Wanculu. 300.00
148 BWg(c),HcK,Caged Beasts
of Plunder-Men,Bondage(c) . 350.00
149 BWg(c),HcK 275.00
150 BWg(c),HcK,Rhino Rampage,
Bondage(c) 350.00
151 BWg(c),HcK 275.00
152 BWg(c),HcK,The Rogue of
Kopje Kull 275.00
153 BWg(c),HcK,The Wild Men
of N'Gara 275.00
154 BWg(c),HcK,The Fire Wizard 275.00
155 BWg(c),HcK,Swamp of
the Shrieking Dead 275.00
156 BWg(c),HcK 275.00
157 BWg(c),HcK 275.00
158 BWg(c),HcK,A:Sheena 275.00
159 BWg(c),HcK,The Blow-Gun
Kill 275.00
160 BWg,HcK,King Fang. 275.00
161 BWg(c),HcK,The Barbarizi
Man-Eaters 275.00
162 BWg(c) 275.00
163 BWg(c),Jackals at the
Kill, Summer,1954 . . . . 275.00

JUNGLE JIM
Best Books
(Standard Comics), Jan., 1949
11 . . . . 125.00
12 Mystery Island. 100.00
13 Flowers of Peril. 100.00
14 thru 19. . . . . @100.00
20 1951 . . . . 100.00

JUNGLE JIM
Dell Publishing Co., Aug., 1953
(1) *see Dell Four Color #490*
(1) *see Dell Four Color #565*
3 P(c) all 125.00
4 . . . . 125.00
5 . . . . 125.00
6 . . . . 100.00
7 . . . . 100.00
8 thru 12 . . . . @100.00
13 'Mystery Island' 100.00
14 'Flowers of Peril' 100.00
15 thru 20. . . . . @100.00

JUNGLE JO
Hero Books
(Fox Features Syndicate),
March, 1950
N# Congo King 700.00
1 WW,Mystery of Doc Jungle . . 750.00
2 Tangl 600.00
3 The Secret of Youth,
Sept., 1950 . . . . 600.00

JUNGLE LIL
Hero Books, April, 1950
1 Betrayer of the Kombe Dead. . 550.00
Becomes:

DOROTHY LAMOUR
Fox Features Syndicate,
June 1950
2 WW,Ph(c)The Lost Safari 500.00
3 WW,Ph(c), Aug., 1950 . . . . . . 350.00

JUNGLE THRILLS
See: TERRORS OF
THE JUNGLE

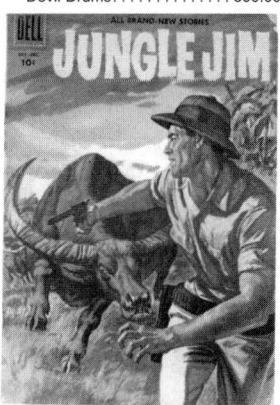

Jungle Jim #10
© Dell Publishing

All comics prices listed are for *Near Mint* condition.

JUNIE PROM
Dearfield Publishing Co.
Winter, 1947
1 Teenage Stories	150.00
2	125.00
3	100.00
4	100.00
5	100.00
6 June, 1949	100.00

JUNIOR COMICS
Fox Features Syndicate,
Sept., 1947
9 AF(a&c),Teenage Stories	1,700.00
10 AF(a&c)	1,500.00
11 AF(a&c)	1,500.00
12 AF(a&c)	1,500.00
13 AF(a&c)	1,500.00
14 AF(a&c)	1,500.00
15 AF(a&c)	1,500.00
16 AF(a&c),July,1948	1,500.00

JUNIOR FUNNIES
See: FAMILY FUNNIES

JUNIOR HOPP COMICS
Stanmor Publications,
Jan., 1952
1 Teen-age	125.00
2	100.00
3 July, 1952	100.00

JUNIOR MISS
Marvel Timely, 1944, 1947–50
1 F:Frank Sinatra &June Allyson	400.00
24	200.00
25 thru 38 Cindy	@125.00
39 HK	150.00

JUSTICE TRAPS THE GUILTY
Headline Publications,
(Prize) Oct.–Nov., 1947
2-1 S&K(a&c),Electric chair (c)	900.00
2 S&K(a&c)	500.00
3 S&K(a&c)	450.00
4 S&K(a&c),True Confession of a Girl Gangleader	450.00
5 S&K(a&c)	450.00
6 S&K(a&c),JSe,AF	475.00
7 S&K(a&c)	400.00
8 S&K(a&c),WE,BK	400.00
9 S&K(a&c)	400.00
10 S&K(a&c),BK	400.00
11 S&K(a&c),JSe	200.00
12	125.00
13	150.00
14 JSe,WE	125.00
15	125.00
16	125.00
17	125.00
18 S&K(a&c)	200.00
19 S&K(a&c)	200.00
20	200.00
21 S&K.	200.00
22 S&K(c),MMe	200.00
23 S&K(c).	200.00
24	100.00
25	100.00
26	100.00
27 S&K(c),MMe	175.00
28	100.00
29	100.00
30 S&K.	150.00
31 thru 49	@100.00
50	100.00
51 thru 54	@100.00
55	100.00
56	100.00

57	100.00
58 Drug	300.00
59 thru 92	@100.00

Becomes:

FARGO KID
Headline Publications
(Prize), June–July. 1958
93 AW,JSe,O:Kid Fargo	175.00
94 JSe	125.00
95 June–July, 1958,JSe	125.00

KA'A'NGA COMICS
Glen-Kel Publ.
(Fiction House),
Spring, 1949–Summer, 1954
1 Phantoms of the Congo	800.00
2 V:The Jungle Octopus	400.00
3	300.00
4 The Wizard Apes of Inkosi-Khan	350.00
5 A:Camilla	225.00
6 Captive of the Devil Apes	200.00
7 GT,Beast-Men of Mombassa	200.00
8 The Congo Kill-Cry	200.00
9 Tabu-Wizard.	200.00
10 Stampede for Congo Gold	200.00
11 Claws of the Roaring Congo.	150.00
12 Bondage(c)	250.00
13 Death Web of the Amazons	150.00
14 Slave Galley of the Lost Nile Bondage(c).	250.00
15 Crocodile Moon,Bondage(c).	250.00
16 Valley of Devil-Dwarfs,Sheena	150.00
17 Tembu of the Elephants	125.00
18 The Red Claw of Vengeance	125.00
19 The Devil-Devil Trail	125.00
20 The Cult of the Killer Claws	125.00

KASCO COMICS
Kasco Grainfeed
(Giveaway), 1945
1 BWo	250.00
2 1949,BWo	200.00

KATY KEENE
Archie Publications/Close-Up
Radio Comics, 1949
1 BWo	2,200.00
2 BWo	1,000.00
3 BWo	900.00
4 BWo	900.00
5 BWo	800.00
6 BWo	700.00
7 BWo	500.00
8 thru 12 BWo	@500.00
13 thru 20 BWo	@400.00
21 thru 29 BWo	@300.00
30 thru 38 BWo	@300.00
39 thru 62 BWo	@300.00
Ann.#1	900.00
Ann.#2 thru #6	@500.00

KATZENJAMMER KIDS
David McKay Publ., 1947–50
1	275.00
2	125.00
3	100.00
4	100.00
5 thru 11	@100.00

Standard Comics, 1950–53
12 thru 22	@100.00

Harvey Publ., 1953–54
22 thru 25	@100.00

KAYO
See: SCOOP COMICS

Keen Detective Funnies #13
© Centaur Publications

KEEN DETECTIVE FUNNIES
Centaur Publications,
July, 1938
1-8 B:The Clock,	3,700.00
1-9 WE	1,300.00
1-10	1,200.00
1-11 Dean Denton	1,200.00
2-1 The Eye Sees	1,100.00
2-2 JCo	1,100.00
2-3 TNT	1,100.00
2-4 MGv,Gabby Flynn	1,100.00
5 MGv	1,100.00
6 MGv,BEv.	1,000.00
7 BEv,Masked Marvel	3,800.00
8 PGv,Gabby Flynn,Nudity Expanded 16 pages	1,400.00
9 BEv,Dean Denton	1,200.00
10 BEv	1,200.00
11 BEv,Sidekick	1,200.00
12 BEv,Masked Marvel(c).	1,400.00
3-1 Masked Marvel(c).	1,100.00
3-2 Masked Marvel(c).	1,100.00
3-3 BEv	1,100.00
16 BEv	1,100.00
17 JSm	1,100.00
18 The Eye Sees,Bondage(c).	1,200.00
19 LFe	950.00
20 BEv,The Eye Sees.	1,400.00
21 Masked Marvel(c)	1,000.00
22 Masked Marvel(c)	1,000.00
23 B:Airman	1,500.00
24 Airman	1,600.00

KEEN KOMICS
Centaur Publications,
May, 1939
1 Teenage Stories	1,500.00
2 PGv,JaB,CBu,Cut Carson.	1,000.00
3 JCo,Saddle Sniffl	1,000.00

KEEN TEENS
Life's Romances Publ./Leader/
Magazine Enterprises, 1945
N# P(c),Claire Voyant	600.00
N# Ph(c),Van Johnson	400.00
3 Ph(c),	200.00
4 Ph(c),Glenn Ford	200.00
5 Ph(c),Perry Como	200.00
6	200.00

KEN MAYNARD WESTERN
Fawcett Publications, Sept., 1950–Feb., 1952
1 B:Ken Maynard & Tarzan (horse)
   The Outlaw Treasure Trail . . 800.00
2 Invasion of the Badmen 500.00
3 Pied Piper of the West 350.00
4 Outlaw Hoax 350.00
5 Mystery of Badman City 350.00
6 Redwood Robbery 350.00
7 Seven Wonders of the West . . 350.00
8 Mighty Mountain Menace 350.00

KEN SHANNON
Quality Comics Group, Oct., 1951–April, 1953
1 RC, Evil Eye of Count Ducrie . 550.00
2 RC, Cut Rate Corpses 400.00
3 RC, Corpse that Wouldn't
   Sleep 350.00
4 RC, Stone Hatchet Murder . . . 300.00
5 RC, Case of the Carney Killer 300.00
6 Weird Vampire Mob 300.00
7 RC,Ugliest Man in the World . 250.00
8 Chinatown Murders,Drug. 350.00
9 RC, Necklace of Blood 250.00
10 RC, Shadow of the Chair 250.00

KEN STUART
Publication Enterprises, 1949
1 . . . . 150.00

KERRY DRAKE DETECTIVE CASES
Life's Romances/M.E., 1944
(1) see N# A-1 Comics
2 A:The Faceless Horror 250.00
3 . . . . 200.00
4 A:Squirrel, Dr. Zero, Caresse . 200.00
5 Bondage (c) 400.00

Harvey Publ., Jan., 1952
6 A:Stitches 250.00
7 A:Shuteye 275.00
8 Bondage (c) 350.00
9 Drug 350.00
10 BP,A:Meatball,Drug. 350.00
11 BP,I:Kid Gloves 150.00
12 BP 150.00
13 BP,A:Torso 125.00
14 BP,Bullseye Murder Syndicate 125.00
15 BP,Fake Mystic Racket. 125.00
16 BP,A:Vixen 100.00
17 BP,Case of the $50,000
   Robbery. 100.00
18 BP,A:Vixen 100.00
19 BP,Case of the Dope
   Smugglers 250.00
20 BP,Secret Treasury Agent. . . . 100.00
21 BP,Murder on Record 100.00
22 BP,Death Rides the Air Waves 100.00
23 BP,Blackmailer's Secret
   Weapon. 100.00
24 Blackmailer's Trap 100.00
25 Pretty Boy Killer 100.00
26 . . . . 100.00
27 . . . . 100.00
28 BP 100.00
29 BP 100.00
30 Mystery Mine,Bondage(c) . . . 250.00
31 . . . . 100.00
32 . . . . 100.00
33 Aug., 1952. . . . . 100.00

KEWPIES
Will Eisner Publications, Spring, 1949
1 . . . . 700.00

KEY COMICS
Consolidated Magazines Jan., 1944
1 B:The Key, Will-O-The-Wisp . . 600.00
2 . . . . 325.00
3 . . . . 275.00
4 WJo(c) O:John Quincy,
   B:The Atom 275.00
5 HoK,Aug., 1946 . . . . 350.00

KEY RING COMICS
Dell Publishing Co., 1941
1 Sky Hawk,Viking Carter. 250.00
(1) Radior. 300.00

KID COWBOY
Approved Comics/ St. John Publ. Co., 1950
1 B:Lucy Belle & Red Feather . . 250.00
2 JMr,Six-Gun Justice 150.00
3 Shadow on Hangman's Bridge 125.00
4 Red Feather V:Eagle of Doom 100.00
5 Killers on the Rampage 100.00
6 The Stovepipe Hat 100.00
7 Ghost Town of Twin Buttes . . 100.00
8 Thundering Hoofs 100.00
9 Terror on the Salt Flats 100.00
10 Valley of Death 100.00
11 Vanished Herds,Bondage(c). . 200.00
12 . . . . 100.00
13 . . . . 100.00
14 1954 . . . . 100.00

KIDDIE KARNIVAL
Approved Comics, 1952
N# Little Bit 500.00

KID ETERNITY
Comics Magazine, Spring, 1946
1 . . . . 1,600.00
2 . . . . 550.00
3 Follow Him Out of This World . 575.00
4 Great Heroes of the Past 350.00
5 Don't Kid with Crime 325.00
6 Busy Battling Crime 325.00
7 Protects the World 325.00
8 Fly to the Rescue 325.00
9 Swoop Down on Crime 325.00
10 Golden Touch from Mr. Midas. 325.00
11 Aid the Living by Calling
   the Dead 250.00
12 Finds Death 250.00

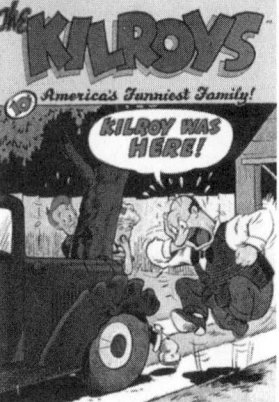

Kilroys #2
© American Comics

KILLERS, THE
Magazine Enterprises, 1947
1 LbC(c),Thou Shall Not Kill . . 1,700.00
2 Grl,OW,Assassins Mad Slayers
   of the East,Hanging(c),Drug 1,400.00

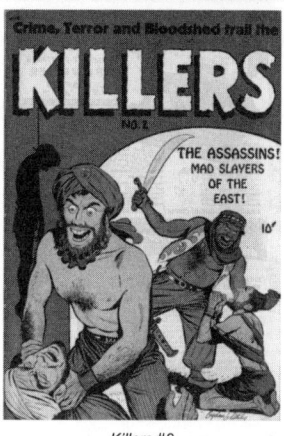

Killers #2
© Magazine Enterprises

13 Invades General Poschka. . . . 250.00
14 Battles Double 250.00
15 A: Master Man. 250.00
16 Balance Scales of Justice. . . . 225.00
17 A:Baron Roxx 225.00
18 A:Man with Two Faces 225.00
Becomes:

BUCCANEERS
Quality Comics Group, Jan., 1950
19 RC,Sword Fight(c) 750.00
20 RC,Treasure Chest 500.00
21 RC,Death Trap 550.00
22 A:Lady Dolores,Snuff,
   Bondage(c) 400.00
23 RC,V:Treasure Hungry
   Plunderers of the Sea 500.00
24 A:Adam Peril,Black Roger,
   Eric Falcon 350.00
25 V:Clews 350.00
26 V:Admiral Blood 350.00
27 RC(a&c)May, 1951 . . . . 500.00

KID ZOO COMICS
Street & Smith Publ., 1948
1 (fa) 350.00

KILLERS, THE
Magazine Enterprises, 1947
1 LbC(c),Thou Shall Not Kill . . 1,700.00
2 Grl,OW,Assassins Mad Slayers
   of the East,Hanging(c),Drug 1,400.00

KILROYS, THE
B&L Publishing Co./ American Comics, June–July, 1947
1 Three Girls in Love(c) 300.00
2 Flat Tire(c) 150.00
3 Right to Swear(c) 125.00
4 Kissing Booth(c) 125.00
5 Skiing(c),Moronica 125.00
6 Prom(c) 100.00
7 To School 100.00
8 . . . . 100.00
9 . . . . 100.00
10 B:Solid Jackson solo. 100.00
11 . . . . 100.00
12 Life Guard(c). 100.00
13 thru 21. . . . . @100.00
22 thru 30. . . . . @100.00
31 thru 40. . . . . @100.00
41 thru 47. . . . . @100.00

All comics prices listed are for *Near Mint* condition.

GOLDEN AGE

48 3-D effect 200.00
49 3-D effect 200.00
50 thru 54, July, 1954. . . . . . . @100.00

KING COMICS
**David McKay Publications,
April, 1936
(all have Popeye covers)**
1 AR,EC,B:Popeye,Flash Gordon,B:
   Henry,Mandrake 20,000.00
2 AR,EC,Flash Gordon 4,000.00
3 AR,EC,Flash Gordon 2,500.00
4 AR,EC,Flash Gordon 2,000.00
5 AR,EC,Flash Gordon 1,500.00
6 AR,EC,Flash Gordon 1,100.00
7 AR,EC,King Royal Mounties 1,050.00
8 AR,EC,Thanksgiving(c) 1,000.00
9 AR,EC,Christmas(c) 1,000.00
10 AR,EC,Flash Gordon 1,000.00
11 AR,EC,Flash Gordon 800.00
12 AR,EC,Flash Gordon 800.00
13 AR,EC,Flash Gordon 800.00
14 AR,EC,Flash Gordon 800.00
15 AR,EC,Flash Gordon 800.00
16 AR,EC,Flash Gordon 800.00
17 AR,EC,Flash Gordon 750.00
18 AR,EC,Flash Gordon 750.00
Covers say: "Starring Popeye"
19 AR,EC,Flash Gordon 750.00
20 AR,EC,Football(c). 750.00
21 AR,EC,Flash Gordon 600.00
22 AR,EC,Flash Gordon 600.00
23 AR,EC,Flash Gordon 600.00
24 AR,EC,Flash Gordon 600.00
25 AR,EC,Flash Gordon 600.00
26 AR,EC,Flash Gordon 550.00
27 AR,EC,Flash Gordon 550.00
28 AR,EC,Flash Gordon 550.00
29 AR,EC,Flash Gordon 550.00
30 AR,EC,Flash Gordon 550.00
31 AR,EC,Flash Gordon 550.00
32 AR,EC,Flash Gordon 550.00
33 AR,EC,Skiing(c) 550.00
34 AR,Ping Pong(c) 500.00
35 AR,Flash Gordon 500.00
36 AR,Flash Gordon 500.00
37 AR,Flash Gordon 500.00
38 AR,Flash Gordon 500.00
39 AR,Baseball(c) 500.00
40 AR,Flash Gordon 500.00
41 AR,Flash Gordon 450.00
42 AR,Flash Gordon 450.00
43 AR,Flash Gordon 450.00
44 AR,Popeye golf(c). 450.00
45 AR,Flash Gordon 450.00
46 AR,B:Little Lulu 450.00
47 AR,Flash Gordon 450.00
48 AR,Flash Gordon 450.00
49 AR,Weather Vane 450.00
50 AR,B:Love Ranger 450.00
51 AR,Flash Gordon 300.00
52 AR,Flash Gordon 300.00
53 AR,Flash Gordon 300.00
54 AR,Flash Gordon 300.00
55 AR,Magic Carpet. 300.00
56 AR,Flash Gordon 300.00
57 AR,Cows Over Moon(c) 300.00
58 AR,Flash Gordon 300.00
59 AR,Flash Gordon 300.00
60 AR,Flash Gordon 300.00
61 AR,B:Phantom,Baseball(c) . . . 300.00
62 AR,Flash Gordon 300.00
63 AR,Flash Gordon 250.00
64 AR,Flash Gordon 250.00
65 AR,Flash Gordon 250.00
66 AR,Flash Gordon 250.00
67 AR,Sweet Pea. 250.00
68 AR,Flash Gordon 250.00
69 AR,Flash Gordon 250.00
70 AR,Flash Gordon 250.00
71 AR,Flash Gordon 250.00
72 AR,Flash Gordon 250.00

73 AR,Flash Gordon 250.00
74 AR,Flash Gordon 250.00
75 AR,Flash Godron 250.00
76 AR,Flag(c). 250.00
77 AR,Flash Gordon 250.00
78 AR,Popeye,Olive Oil(c). 250.00
79 AR,Sweet Pea. 250.00
80 AR,Wimpy(c). 250.00
81 AR,B:Blondie(c). 250.00
82 thru 91 AR. . . . . @200.00
92 thru 98 AR . . . . @200.00
99 AR,Olive Oil(c) 200.00
100 . . . . 200.00
101 thru 116 AR . . . . @175.00
117 O:Phantom 200.00
118 Flash Gordon 175.00
119 Flash Gordon 150.00
120 Wimpy(c). 125.00
121 thru 140 . . . . @125.00
141 Flash Gordon 125.00
142 Flash Gordon 125.00
143 Flash Gordon 125.00
144 Flash Gordon 125.00
145 Prince Valiant 100.00
146 Prince Valiant 100.00
147 Prince Valiant 100.00
148 thru 154 . . . . @100.00
155 E:Flash Gordon. 100.00
156 Baseball(c) 100.00
157 thru 159 . . . . @100.00

KING OF THE ROYAL MOUNTED
**Dell Publishing Co.,
Dec., 1948–1958**
(1) *see Dell Four Color #207*
(2) *see Dell Four Color #265*
(3) *see Dell Four Color #283*
(4) *see Dell Four Color #310*
(5) *see Dell Four Color #340*
(6) *see Dell Four Color #363*
(7) *see Dell Four Color #384*
8 Zane Grey adapt. 150.00
9 . . . . 125.00
10 . . . . 125.00
11 thru 28 . . . . @100.00

KIT CARSON
Avon Periodicals, 1950
N# EK(c) Indian Scout 200.00
2 EK(c),Kit Carson's Revenge,
   Doom Trail. 150.00
3 EK(c),V:Comanche Raiders . . 100.00
4 . . . . 100.00
5 EK(c),Trail of Doom 100.00

AMERICA'S GREATEST INDIAN FIGHTER!

KIT CARSON

AND THE TRAIL OF DOOM

Kit Carson #5
© Avon Periodicals

6 EK(c) 100.00
7 EK(c) 100.00
8 EK(c) 100.00
Becomes:

FIGHTING DAVY CROCKETT
Oct.–Nov, 1955
9 EK(c) 100.00

KO KOMICS
**Gerona Publications,
Oct., 1945**
1 . . . . 1,100.00

KOMIK PAGES
See: SCOOP COMICS

KRAZY KAT COMICS
**Dell Publishing Co.,
May–June, 1951**
1 . . . . 150.00
2 . . . . 100.00
3 . . . . 100.00
4 . . . . 100.00
5 . . . . 100.00

KRAZY LIFE
See: PHANTOM LADY

LABOR IS A PARTNER
**Catechetical Guild
Educational Society, 1949**
1 Anti-Communism 250.00

LADY LUCK
See: SMASH

LAFFY-DAFFY COMICS
**Rural Home Publ. Co.,
Feb., 1945**
1 (fa) 150.00
2 . . . . 150.00

LANCE O'CASEY
Fawcett, 1946–47
1 High Seas Adventure
   from Whiz comics 450.00
2 thru 4 . . . . @300.00

LAND OF THE LOST
**E.C. Comics,
July–Aug., 1946–Spring 1948**
1 Radio show adapt. 500.00
2 . . . . 300.00
3 thru 9 . . . . @250.00

LARGE FEATURE COMICS
Dell Publishing Co., 1939
1 Dick Tracy vs. the Blank. . . . 2,700.00
2 Terry and the Pirates 1,400.00
3 Heigh-Yo Silver!
   the Lone Ranger. 2,400.00
4 Dick Tracy gets his man 1,500.00
5 Tarzan of the Apes 2,700.00
6 Terry and the Pirates 1,200.00
7 Lone Ranger to the rescue. . . 2,200.00
8 Dick Tracy, Racket Buster . . 1,500.00
9 King of the Royal Mounted . . . 800.00
10 Gang Busters 1,000.00
11 Dick Tracy, Mad Doc Hump . 1,400.00
12 Smilin' Jack. 950.00
13 Dick Tracy and Scottie
   of Scotland Yard 1,300.00
14 Smilin' Jack helps G-Men 950.00

15 Dick Tracy and	
the Kidnapped Princes	1,300.00
16 Donald Duck, 1st Daisy.	10,000.00
17 Gang Busters	700.00
18 Phantasmo The Master	
of the World	500.00
19 Walt Disney's Dumbo	4,500.00
20 Donald Duck	11,000.00
21 Private Buck	225.00
22 Nuts and Jolts	225.00
23 The Nebbs	300.00
24 Popeye in 'Thimble Theatre'	1,100.00
25 Smilin'Jack	900.00
26 Smitty	450.00
27 Terry and the Pirates	900.00
28 Grin and Bear It	250.00
29 Moon Mullins	500.00
30 Tillie the Toiler	450.00

[Series 2]

1 Peter Rabbit	900.00
2 Winnie Winkle	350.00
3 Dick Tracy	1,200.00
4 Tiny Tim	550.00
5 Toots and Casper	300.00
6 Terry and the Pirates	850.00
7 Pluto saves the Ship	2,500.00
8 Bugs Bunny	2,700.00
9 Bringing Up Father	425.00
10 Popeye	850.00
11 Barney Google&SnuffySmith	500.00
12 Private Buck	250.00
13 1001 Hours of Fun	400.00

LARRY DOBY, BASEBALL HERO
Fawcett Publications, 1950

1 Ph(c),BW	1,200.00

LARS OF MARS
Ziff-Davis Publishing Co., April–May, 1951

10 MA,'Terror from the Sky'	1,500.00
11 GC, The Terror Weapon	1,000.00

LASH LARUE WESTERN
Fawcett Publications, Summer, 1949

1 Ph(c),The Fatal Roundups	1,600.00
2 Ph(c),Perfect Hide Out	750.00
3 Ph(c),The Suspect	600.00
4 Ph(c),Death on Stage	600.00
5 Ph(c),Rustler's Haven	600.00
6 Ph(c)	500.00
7 Ph(c),Shadow of the Noose	425.00
8 Ph(c),Double Deadline	425.00
9 Ph(c),Generals Last Stand	425.00
10 Ph(c)	425.00
11 Ph(c)	350.00
12 thru 20 Ph(c)	@300.00
21 thru 29 Ph(c)	@250.00
30 thru 46 Ph(c)	@225.00
46 Ph(c),Lost Chance	225.00

LASSIE
Dell Publishing Co., Oct.–Dec., 1950

1 Ph(c) all	300.00
2	150.00
3 thru 10	@125.00
11	100.00
12 Rocky Langford	100.00
13	100.00
14	100.00
15 I:Timbu	100.00
16	100.00
17	100.00
18	100.00
19	100.00
20 MB	125.00

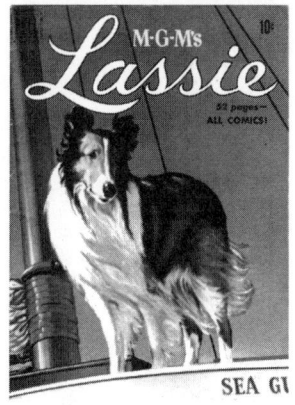

Lassie #2
© Dell Publishing Co.

21 MB	125.00
22 MB	125.00
23 thru 38	@100.00
39 I:Timmy	100.00
40 thru 62	@100.00
63 E:Timmy	100.00
64 thru 70	@100.00

LATEST COMICS
Spotlight Publ./ Palace Promotions, March, 1945

1 Funny Animal-Super Duper	250.00
2	200.00

SPECIAL COMICS
MLJ Magazines, Winter, 1941

1 O:Boy Buddies & Hangman,	
D:The Comet	5,000.00

Becomes:

HANGMAN COMICS
Spring, 1942

2 B:Hangman & Boy Buddies	3,000.00
3 V:Nazis (c),Bondage(c)	2,000.00
4 V:Nazis (c)	1,800.00
5 Bondage (c)	1,800.00
6 HSa	1,800.00
7 BF,Graveyard (c)	1,800.00
8 BF	1,800.00

Becomes:

BLACK HOOD
Winter, 1943–44

9 BF, Hang Man	1,600.00
10 BF,A:Dusty, Boy Detective	1,000.00
11 Here lies the Black Hood	800.00
12	700.00
13 EK(c)	700.00
14 EK(c)	600.00
15 EK	600.00
16 EK(c)	600.00
17 Bondage (c)	650.00
18	650.00
19 I.D. Revealed	800.00

Becomes:

LAUGH COMICS
Archie Comics, Fall, 1946

20 BWo,B:Archie,Katy Keene	1,000.00
21 BWo	500.00
22 BWo	500.00
23 Bwo	500.00
24 BWo,JK,Pipsy	500.00
25 BWo	500.00

26 BWo	275.00
27 BWo	275.00
28 BWo	275.00
29 BWo	275.00
30 BWo	275.00
31 thru 40 BWo	@200.00
41 thru 50 BWo	@175.00
51 thru 60 BWo	@150.00
61 thru 80 BWo	@150.00
81 thru 99 BWo	@150.00
100 BWo	150.00
101 thru 126 BWo	@125.00
127 A:Jaguar	150.00
128 A:The Fly	150.00
129 A:The Fly	150.00
130 A:Jaguar	150.00
131 A:Jaguar	150.00
132 A:The Fly	150.00
133 A:Jaguar	150.00
134 A:The Fly	150.00
135 A:Jaguar	150.00
136 A:Fly Girl	150.00
137 A:Fly Girl	150.00
138 A:The Fly	150.00
139 A:The Fly	150.00
140 A:Jaguar	150.00
141 A:Jaguar	150.00
142 thru 144	@150.00

LAUGH COMIX
See: TOP-NOTCH COMICS

LAUREL AND HARDY
St. John Publishing Co., March, 1949

1	1,100.00
2	600.00
3	400.00
26 Rep #1	225.00
27 Rep #2	225.00
28 Rep #3	225.00

LAWBREAKERS
Law & Order Magazines (Charlton), March, 1951

1	600.00
2	300.00
3	250.00
4 Drug, White Death	350.00
5	225.00
6 LM(c)	250.00
7 Drug, Deadly Dopester	350.00
8	225.00
9 StC(c)	225.00

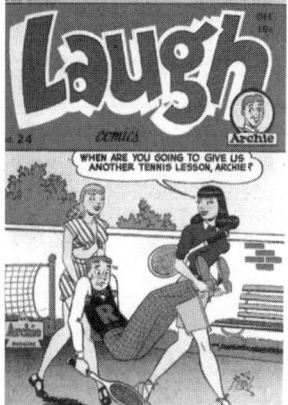

Laugh Comis #24
© Archie Comics

Becomes:

LAWBREAKERS SUSPENSE STORIES
Jan., 1953

10 StC(c)	600.00
11 LM(c),Negligee(c)	1,800.00
12 LM(c)	350.00
13 DG(c)	350.00
14 DG(c),Sharks	350.00
15 DG(c),Acid in Face(c)	800.00

Becomes:

STRANGE SUSPENSE STORIES
Jan., 1954

16 DG(c)	400.00
17 DG(c)	300.00
18 SD,SD(c)	600.00
19 SD,SD(c),Electric Chair	800.00
20 SD,SD(c)	600.00
21 SD,SD(c)	300.00
22 SD,SD(c)	450.00

Becomes:

THIS IS SUSPENSE
Feb., 1955

23 WW; Comics Code	350.00
24 GE,DG(c)	175.00
25 DG(c)	150.00
26 DG(c)	150.00

Becomes:

STRANGE SUSPENSE STORIES
Oct., 1955

27	200.00
28	150.00
29	150.00
30	150.00
31 SD	300.00
32 SD	300.00
33 SD	300.00
34 SD	800.00
35 SD	350.00
36 SD	350.00
37 SD	350.00
38	150.00
39 SD	250.00
40 SD	300.00
41 SD	250.00
42	100.00
43	100.00
44	100.00
45	100.00
46	100.00
47 SD	250.00
48 SD	250.00
49	100.00
50 SD	250.00
51 SD	250.00
52 SD	250.00
53 SD	250.00
54 thru 60	@100.00
61 thru 74	@100.00
75 SD,SD(c), Captain Atom	250.00
77 Oct 1965	125.00

LAW-CRIME
Essenkay Publications, April, 1948

1 LbC,LbC-(c);Raymond Hamilton Dies In The Chair	1,100.00
2 LbC,LbC-(c);Strangled Beauty Puzzles Police	900.00
3 LbC,LbC-(c);Lipstick Slayer Sought; Aug., 1943	1,100.00

MISS LIBERTY
Burten Publishing, circa 1944

1 Reprints-Shield,Wizard	450.00

Becomes:

LIBERTY COMICS
Green Publishing, May, 1946

10 Reprints,Hangman	300.00
11 Wilbur in women's clothes	225.00
12 Black Hood, Skull(c)	900.00
14 Patty of Airliner	200.00
15 Patty of Airliner	200.00

LIBERTY GUARDS
Chicago Mail Order (Comic Corp of America), Circa 1942

1 PG(c),Liberty Scouts	500.00

Becomes:

Liberty Scouts #3
© Centaur

LIBERTY SCOUTS
June, 1941–Aug., 1941

PG(a&c)O:Fireman,Liberty Scouts	2,000.00
3 PG,PG(c),O:Sentinel	1,500.00

LIFE STORY
Fawcett Publications, April, 1949

1 Ph(c)	200.00
2 Ph(c)	150.00
3 Ph(c)	125.00
4 Ph(c)	125.00
5 Ph(c)	125.00
6 Ph(c)	125.00
7 Ph(c)	100.00
8 Ph(c)	100.00
9 Ph(c)	100.00
10 Ph(c)	100.00
11	100.00
12	100.00
13 WW, BP,Drug	250.00
14	100.00
15	100.00
16 thru 21	@100.00
22 Drug	200.00
23 BP	100.00
24 BP	100.00
25 thru 35	@100.00
36 Drug	200.00
37	100.00
38	100.00
39 BP,Drug	125.00
40	100.00
41	100.00
42	100.00
43 GE	125.00

44	100.00
45 1952	100.00

LIFE WITH SNARKY PARKER
Fox Feature Syndicate, Aug., 1950

1	350.00

SURE-FIRE
Ace Magazines, 1940

1 O:Flash Lightning	2,700.00
2 Whiz Wilson	1,250.00
3 The Raven,Sept., 1940	900.00
3a Ace McCoy,Oct., 1940	900.00

Becomes:

LIGHTNING COMICS
Dec., 1940

4 Sure-Fire Stories	1,600.00
5 JM	1,000.00
6 JM,Dr. Nemesis	1,000.00

Vol. 2

1 JM	800.00
2 JM,Flash Lightning	800.00
3 JM	800.00
4 JM	800.00
5 JM	800.00
6 JM, bondage(c)	900.00

Vol. 3

1 I:Lightning Girl	800.00

LINDA
Ajax/Farrell Publications, 1954

1	200.00
2 Lingerie	150.00
3	125.00
4	125.00

LINDA
See: PHANTOM LADY

LI'L ABNER
Harvey Publications, Dec., 1947

61 BP,BW,Sadie Hawkins Day	500.00
62	300.00
63	300.00
64	300.00
65 BP	300.00
66	250.00
67	250.00
68 FearlessFosdick V:Any Face	300.00
69	300.00
70	250.00

Toby Press

71	200.00
72	200.00
73	200.00
74	200.00
75 HK	250.00
76	200.00
77 HK	250.00
78 HK	250.00
79 HK	250.00
80	225.00
81	200.00
82	200.00
83 Baseball	225.00
84	200.00
85	200.00
86 HK	250.00
87	200.00
88	200.00
89	200.00
90	200.00
91 Rep. #77	225.00
92	200.00
93 Rep. #71	225.00

GOLDEN AGE

94 . . . . 200.00
95 Fearless Fosdick 225.00
96 . . . . 200.00
97 Jan., 1955 . . . . 200.00

LITTLE AL OF THE F.B.I.
**Approved Comics
(Ziff Davis), 1950**

10 . . . . 225.00
11 . . . . 150.00

LITTLE AL OF THE SECRET SERVICE
**Approved Comics
(Ziff Davis), 1951**

1 . . . . 225.00
2 . . . . 150.00
3 . . . . 150.00

LITTLE ANGEL
Standard Comics, 1954–59

5 . . . . 125.00
6 thru 16 . . . . @100.00

LITTLE ANNIE ROONEY
**St. John Publishing
Co./Standard, 1948**

1 . . . . 225.00
2 . . . . 125.00
3 . . . . 125.00

LITTLE AUDREY
**St. John Publ. Co./
Harvey Comics, April, 1948**

1 . . . . 700.00
2 . . . . 350.00
3 thru 6 . . . . @250.00
7 thru 10 . . . . @175.00
11 thru 20 . . . . @150.00
21 thru 24 . . . . @125.00
25 B:Harvey Comics 250.00
26 A: Casper 150.00
27 A: Casper 150.00
28 A: Casper 150.00
29 thru 31 . . . . @125.00
32 A: Casper 125.00
33 A: Casper 125.00
34 A: Casper 125.00
35 A: Casper 125.00
36 thru 53 . . . . @100.00

LITTLE BEAVER
Dell Publishing Co., 1951

3 . . . . 100.00
4 thru 8 . . . . @100.00

LITTLE BIT
**Jubilee Publishing Company,
March, 1949**

1 . . . . 125.00
2 June, 1949 . . . . 100.00

LITTLE DOT
**Harvey Publications,
Sept., 1953**

1 I; Richie Rich & Little Lotta . . 3,600.00
2 . . . . 1,400.00
3 . . . . 800.00
4 . . . . 750.00
5 O:Dots on Little Dot's Dress . . 750.00
6 1st Richie Rich(c) 750.00
7 . . . . 550.00
8 . . . . 500.00
9 . . . . 500.00
10 . . . . 500.00
11 thru 20 . . . . @350.00
21 thru 30 . . . . @250.00

31 thru 39 . . . . @200.00
40 thru 50 . . . . @150.00
51 thru 60 . . . . @150.00
61 thru 70 . . . . @150.00
71 thru 80 . . . . @150.00
81 thru 100 . . . . @150.00
101 thru 130 . . . . @100.00
131 thru 140 . . . . @100.00
141 thru 145, 52 pages . . . . @100.00
146 thru 163 . . . . @75.00

LITTLE EVA
**St. John Publishing Co.,
May, 1952**

1 . . . . 200.00
2 . . . . 150.00
3 . . . . 125.00
4 . . . . 125.00
5 thru 10 . . . . @100.00
11 thru 30 . . . . @100.00
31 Nov., 1956 . . . . 100.00

LI'L GENIUS
Charlton Comics, 1955

1 . . . . 125.00
2 . . . . 80.00
3 . . . . 80.00
4 . . . . 80.00
5 . . . . 80.00
6 thru 15 . . . . @80.00
16 Giants 125.00
17 Giants 125.00
18 Giants,100 pages 150.00
19 thru 40 . . . . @75.00
41 thru 54 . . . . @60.00
55 1965 . . . . 50.00

LI'L GHOST
**St. John Publishing/
Fago Magazine Co.**

1 . . . . 125.00
2a 75.00
3 . . . . 75.00

LITTLE GIANT COMICS
**Centaur Publications,
July, 1938**

1 PG, B&W with Color(c) 1,500.00
2 B&W with Color(c) 1,000.00
3 B&W with Color(c) 1,000.00
4 B&W with Color(c) 1,000.00

LITTLE GIANT DETECTIVE FUNNIES
**Centaur Publications,
Oct., 1938–Jan., 1939**

1 B&W 1,500.00
2 B&W 1,000.00
3 B&W 1,000.00
4 WE 1,000.00

LITTLE GIANT MOVIE FUNNIES
**Centaur Publications,
Aug., 1938**

1 Ed Wheelan-a 1,500.00
2 Ed Wheelan-a, Oct., 1938 . . 1,000.00

LITTLE GROUCHO
Reston Publ., Co. 1955

1 . . . . 100.00
2 . . . . 75.00

LITTLE IKE
**St. John Publishing Co.,
April, 1953**

1 . . . . 100.00

2 . . . . 75.00
3 . . . . 75.00
4 Oct., 1953 . . . . 75.00

LITTLE IODINE
**Dell Publishing Co.,
April, 1949**

1 . . . . 250.00
2 . . . . 150.00
3 . . . . 150.00
4 . . . . 150.00
5 . . . . 150.00
6 thru 10 . . . . @100.00
11 thru 30 . . . . @100.00
31 thru 50 . . . . @100.00
51 thru 56 . . . . @100.00

LITTLE JACK FROST
Avon Periodicals, 1951

1 . . . . 125.00

LI'L JINX
Archie Publications, 1956

11 . . . . 150.00
12 thru 16 . . . . @125.00

LITTLE JOE
St. John Publishing Co., 1953

1 . . . . 75.00

LITTLE LULU
See: MARGE'S LITTLE LULU

LI'L MENACE
Fago Magazine Co., 1958

1 Peter Rabbit 100.00
2 . . . . 75.00
3 . . . . 75.00

LITTLE MAX COMICS
**Harvey Publications,
Oct., 1949**

1 I: Little Dot,Joe Palooka(c) . . . 300.00
2 A: Little Dot,Joe Palooka(c) . . . 250.00
3 A: Little Dot,Joe Palooka(c) . . 150.00
4 . . . . 100.00
5 C: Little Dot 100.00
6 thru 10 . . . . @100.00
11 thru 22 . . . . @75.00
23 A: Little Dot 75.00

Little Lotta #1
© Harvey Publications

GOLDEN AGE

24 thru 37 .... @60.00
38 Rep. #20 .... 60.00
39 thru 72 .... @50.00
73 A: Richie Rich; Nov.'61 ...... 50.00

LITTLE MISS MUFFET
**Best Books
(Standard Comics),
Dec., 1948**
11 Strip Reprints 250.00
12 Strip Reprints 75.00
13 Strip Reprints; Mar.'49 .... 75.00

LITTLE MISS SUNBEAM
COMICS
**Magazine Enterprises,
June–July, 1950**
1 .... 250.00
2 .... 100.00
3 .... 100.00
4 Dec.–Jan., 1951 .... 100.00

LITTLE ORPHAN ANNIE
Dell Publishing Co., 1948
1 .... 250.00
2 Orphan Annie and the Rescue 150.00
3 .... 150.00
See also: *Four Color*

LI'L PAN
**Fox Features Syndicate,
Dec.–Jan., 1946-47**
6 .... 125.00
7 .... 100.00
8 April–May, 1947 .... 100.00

LITTLE ROQUEFORT
**St. John Publishing Co.,
June,1952**
1 .... 125.00
2 .... 100.00
3 thru 9 .... @100.00
Pines
10 Summer 1958 .... 100.00

LITTLE SCOUTS
**Dell Publishing Co.,
March, 1951**
(1) see Dell Four Color #321
2 .... 100.00
3 thru 6 .... @75.00

LITTLEST SNOWMAN
**Dell Publishing Co.,
Dec., 1956**
1 .... 100.00

LIVING BIBLE, THE
**Living Bible Corp.
Autumn, 1945**
1 LbC-(c) Life of Paul 525.00
2 LbC-(c) Joseph &His Brethern. 400.00
3 LbC-(c) Chaplains At War 575.00

LONE EAGLE
**Ajax/Farrell,
April–May, 1954**
1 .... 200.00
2 .... 150.00
3 Bondage(c) 200.00
4 Oct.–Nov., 1954 .... 150.00

LONELY HEART
**Excellent Publications
(Ajax/Farrell), 1955**
9 .... 150.00

---

10 thru 14 .... @100.00
Becomes:

DEAR HEART
Ajax/Farrell Publ., 1956
15 .... 100.00
16 .... 100.00

LONE RANGER
**Dell Publishing Co.,
Jan.–Feb., 1948**
1 B:Lone Ranger & Tonto
   B:Strip Reprint 1,400.00
2 .... 600.00
3 .... 400.00
4 .... 400.00
5 .... 400.00
6 .... 350.00
7 .... 350.00
8 O:Retold 400.00
9 .... 350.00
10 .... 350.00
11 B:Young Hawk 250.00
12 thru 20 .... @250.00
21 .... 200.00
22 .... 200.00
23 O:Retold 275.00
24 thru 30 .... @200.00
31 (1st Mask Logo) 250.00
32 thru 36 .... @175.00
37 (E:Strip reprints) 150.00
38 thru 50 .... @150.00
51 thru 75 .... @150.00
76 thru 99 .... @125.00
100 .... 150.00
101 thru 111 .... @150.00
112 B:Clayton Moore Ph(c) 350.00
113 thru 117 .... @200.00
118 O:Lone Ranger & Tonto
   retold, Anniv. issue 450.00
119 thru 144 .... @200.00
145 final issue,May/July, 1962 ... 200.00

THE LONE RANGER'S
COMPANION TONTO
Dell Publishing Co., Jan., 1951
(1) see Dell Four Color #312
2 P(c) all 225.00
3 .... 150.00
4 .... 125.00
5 .... 125.00
6 thru 10 .... @125.00
11 thru 20 .... @100.00
21 thru 25 .... @100.00
26 thru 33 .... @100.00

THE LONE RANGER'S
FAMOUS HORSE
HI-YO SILVER
Dell Publishing Co., Jan., 1952
(1) see Dell Four Color #369
(1) see Dell Four Color #392
3 P(c) all 200.00
4 .... 125.00
5 .... 125.00
6 thru 10 .... @125.00
11 thru 36 .... @100.00

LONE RIDER
**Farrell (Superior
Comics), April, 1951**
1 .... 400.00
2 I&O: Golden Arrow; 52 pgs. .. 225.00
3 .... 200.00
4 .... 200.00
5 .... 200.00
6 E: Golden Arrow 200.00
7 G.Arrow Becomes Swift Arrow 200.00
8 O: Swift Arrow 225.00

Lone Ranger #72
© *Dell Publishing*

9 thru 14 .... @125.00
15 O: Golden Arrow Rep. #2 .... 135.00
16 thru 19 .... @100.00
20 .... 100.00
21 3-D (c) 250.00
22 .... 100.00
23 A: Apache Kid 100.00
24 .... 100.00
25 .... 100.00
26 July, 1955 .... 100.00

LONG BOW
**Real Adventures Publ.
(Fiction House), Winter, 1950**
1 .... 250.00
2 .... 125.00
3 'Red Arrows Means War' 125.00
4 'Trial of Tomahawk' 125.00
5 .... 125.00
6 'Rattlesnake Raiders' 100.00
7 .... 100.00
8 .... 100.00
9 Spring, 1953 .... 100.00

LONG JOHN SILVER
AND THE PIRATES
**See: TERRY
AND THE PIRATES**

LOONEY TUNES AND
MERRIE MELODIES
Dell Publishing Co., 1941
1 B:&1st Comic App. Bugs Bunny
   Daffy Duck,Elmer Fudd .. 21,000.00
2 Bugs/Porky(c) 4,000.00
3 Bugs/Porky(c) B:WK,
   Kandi the Cave 3,000.00
4 Bugs/Porky(c),WK 3,000.00
5 Bugs/Porky(c),WK,
   A:Super Rabbit 2,400.00
6 Bugs/Porky/Elmer(c),E:WK,
   Kandi the Cave 1,800.00
7 Bugs/Porky(c) 1,500.00
8 Bugs/Porky swimming(c),F:WK,
   Kandi the Cave 1,800.00
9 Porky/Elmer car painted(c) .. 1,300.00
10 Porky/Bugs/Elmer Parade(c) 1,300.00
11 Bugs/Porky(c),F:WK,
   Kandi the Cave 1,300.00
12 Bugs/Porky rollerskating(c) .. 900.00
13 Bugs/Porky(c) 900.00
14 Bugs/Porky(c) 900.00
15 Bugs/Porky X-Mas(c),F:WK
   Kandi the Cave 1,000.00
16 Bugs/Porky ice-skating(c) .. 1,000.00

17 Bugs/Petunia Valentines(c) . 1,000.00	
18 Sgt.Bugs Marine(c) 1,000.00	
19 Bugs/Painting(c). 1,000.00	
20 Bugs/Porky/ElmerWarBonds(c),	
B:WK,Pat,Patsy&Pete 1,000.00	
21 Bugs/Porky 4th July(c). 1,000.00	
22 Porky(c). 1,000.00	
23 Bugs/Porky Fishing(c) 1,000.00	
24 Bugs/Porky Football(c) 1,000.00	
25 Bugs/Porky/Petunia Halloween	
(c),E:WK,Pat, Patsy & Pete 1,000.00	
26 Bugs Thanksgiving(c) 750.00	
27 Bugs/Porky New Years(c). . . . 750.00	
28 Bugs/Porky Ice-Skating(c) . . 750.00	
29 Bugs Valentine(c) 750.00	
30 Bugs(c) 750.00	
31 Bugs(c) 600.00	
32 Bugs/Porky Hot Dogs(c). 600.00	
33 Bugs/Porky War Bonds(c) . . 750.00	
34 Bugs/Porky Fishing(c). 500.00	
35 Bugs/Porky Swimming(c) 500.00	
36 Bugs/Porky(c) 500.00	
37 Bugs Halloween(c) 500.00	
38 Bugs Thanksgiving(c) 500.00	
39 Bugs X-Mas(c) 500.00	
40 Bugs(c) 500.00	
41 Bugs Washington's	
Birthday(c) 400.00	
42 Bugs Magician(c) 400.00	
43 Bugs Dream(c) 400.00	
44 Bugs/Porky(c) 400.00	
45 Bugs War Bonds(c). 400.00	
46 Bugs/Porky(c) 400.00	
47 Bugs Beach(c) 350.00	
48 Bugs/Porky Picnic(c). 350.00	
49 Bugs(c) 350.00	
50 Bugs(c) 350.00	
51 thru 60 . . . . @300.00	
61 thru 80 . . . . @250.00	
81 thru 86 . . . . @150.00	
87 Bugs X-Mas(c) 175.00	
88 thru 99 . . . . @150.00	
100 . . . . 150.00	
101 thru 110 . . . . @150.00	
111 thru 125 . . . . @150.00	
126 thru 150 . . . . @150.00	
151 thru 165 . . . . @100.00	

Becomes:

LOONEY TUNES
Aug., 1955

166 thru 200 . . . . @100.00
201 thru 245 . . . . @100.00
246 final issue,Sept.1962 . . . . . . 100.00

LOST WORLDS
Literary Enterprises
(Standard Comics),
Oct., 1952

5 ATh, Alice in Terrorland 700.00
6 ATh 500.00

LUCKY COMICS
Consolidated Magazines,
Jan., 1944–Summer 1946

1 Lucky Star 300.00
2 HcK(c) 200.00
3 . . . . 200.00
4 . . . . 200.00
5 Devil(c) 200.00

LUCKY DUCK
Standard Comics
(Literary Enterprises),
Jan.–Sept., 1953

5 IS(a&c) 125.00
6 IS(a&c) 100.00
7 IS(a&c) 100.00
8 IS(a&c) 100.00

LUCKY FIGHTS IT THROUGH
Educational Comics, 1949

N# HK-a, V.D. Prevention 1,800.00

LUCKY "7" COMICS
Howard Publications, 1944

1 Bondage(c) Pioneer 600.00

LUCKY STAR
Nationwide Publications, 1950

1 JDa,B:52 pages western 225.00
2 JDa 150.00
3 JDa 150.00
4 JDa 125.00
5 JDa 125.00
6 JDa 125.00
7 JDa 125.00
8 thru 13 . . . . @100.00
14 1955,E:52 pages western 100.00

LUCY, THE REAL GONE GAL
St. John Publishing Co., June, 1953

1 Negligee Panels,Teenage 250.00
2 . . . . 125.00
3 MD-a 100.00
4 Feb., 1954 . . . . 75.00

Becomes:

MEET MISS PEPPER
April, 1954

5 JKu-a 250.00
6 JKu (a&c), June,1954 . . . . 200.00

MAD
E.C. Comics, Oct.–Nov., 1952

1 JSe,HK(c),JDa,WW 12,000.00
2 JSe,JDa(c),JDa,WW 3,500.00
3 JSe,HK(c),JDa,WW 2,200.00
4 JSe,HK(c),JDa-Flob Was
    A Slob,JDa,WW 2,100.00
5 JSe,BE(c).JDa,WW 3,000.00
6 JSe,HK(c),Jda,WW 1,200.00
7 HK(c),JDa,WW 1,200.00
8 HK(c),JDa,WW 1,200.00
9 JSe,HK(c),JDa,WW 1,200.00
10 JSe,HK(c),JDa,WW 1,300.00
11 BW,BW(c),JDa,WW,Life(c). . 1,200.00
12 BK,JDa,WW. 1,000.00
13 HK(c),JDa,WW,Red(c). 1,000.00
14 RH,HK(c),JDa,WW,
    Mona Lisa(c). 1,000.00

Mad Magazine #57
© E.C. Comics

15 JDa,WW,Alice in	
Wonderland(c) 1,000.00	
16 HK(c),JDa,WW,	
Newspaper(c). 1,000.00	
17 BK,BW,JDa,WW 1,000.00	
18 HK(c),JDa,WW. 1,000.00	
19 JDa,WW,Racing Form(c) 800.00	
20 JDa,WW,Composition(c). 900.00	
21 JDa,WW,1st A.E.Neuman(c) 1,000.00	
22 BE,JDa,WW,Picasso(c) 1,000.00	
23 Last Comic Format Edition,	
JDa,WW Think(c) 800.00	
24 BK,WW, HK Logo & Border;	
1st Magazine Format 1,800.00	
25 WW,AlJaffee Becomes Reg. 1,000.00	
26 BK,WW,WW(c) 750.00	
27 WWa,RH,JDa(c) 700.00	
28 WW,BE(c),RH Back(c) 550.00	
29 JKa,BW,WW,WW(c);	
1st Don Martin Artwork 550.00	
30 BE,WW,RC; 1st A.E.	
Neuman(c) By Mingo 750.00	
31 JDa,WW,BW,Mingo(c) 500.00	
32 MD,JO 1st as reg.;Mingo(c);	
WW-Back(c) 400.00	
33 WWa,Mingo(c);JO Back(c) . . 500.00	
34 WWa,Mingo(c);1st Berg	
as Reg. 400.00	
35 WW,RC,Mingo	
Wraparound(c). 400.00	
36 WW,BW,Mingo(c),JO,MD . . . 400.00	
37 WW,Mingo(c)JO,MD 400.00	
38 WW,JO,MD 400.00	
39 WW,JO,MD 400.00	
40 WW,BW,JO,MD 400.00	
41 WW,JO,MD 250.00	
42 WW,JO,MD 250.00	
43 WW,JO,MD 250.00	
44 WW,JO,MD 250.00	
45 WW,JO,MD 250.00	
46 JO,MD 250.00	
47 JO,MD 250.00	
48 JO,MD 250.00	
49 JO,MD 250.00	
50 JO,MD 250.00	
51 JO,MD 200.00	
52 JO,MD 200.00	
53 JO,MD 200.00	
54 JO,MD 200.00	
55 JO,MD 200.00	
56 JO,MD 200.00	
57 JO,MD 200.00	
58 JO,MD 200.00	
59 WW,JO,MD 250.00	
60 JO,MD 250.00	

MAD HATTER, THE
O.W. Comics, 1946

1 Freddy the Firefly 1,300.00
2 V:Humpty Dumpty 600.00

MADHOUSE
Ajax/Farrell Publ., 1954

1 . . . . 400.00
2 . . . . 200.00
3 . . . . 200.00
4 . . . . 300.00

Second Series, 1957

1 . . . . 150.00
2 . . . . 125.00
3 . . . . 125.00

MAGIC COMICS
David McKay Publications,
Aug.,1939–Nov.-Dec., 1949

1 Mandrake the Magician, Henry,
    Popeye,Blondie, Barney Baxter,
    Secret Agent X-9, Bunky,
    Henry on(c) 4,200.00
2 Henry on(c). 1,500.00

3 Henry on(c) 1,100.00
4 Henry on(c),Mandrake-Logo . . 850.00
5 Henry on(c),Mandrake-Logo . . 750.00
6 Henry on(c),Mandrake-Logo . . 600.00
7 Henry on(c),Mandrake-Logo . . 600.00
8 B:Inspector Wade,Tippie 550.00
9 Henry-Mandrake Interact(c) . . 525.00
10 Henry-Mandrake Interact(c) . . 550.00
11 Henry-Mandrake Interact(c) . . 500.00
12 Mandrake on(c). 500.00
13 Mandrake on(c). 500.00
14 Mandrake on(c). 500.00
15 Mandrake on(c). 500.00
16 Mandrake on(c). 500.00
17 B:Lone Ranger 550.00
18 Mandrake on(c) 450.00
19 Mandrake/Robot on(c) 750.00
20 Mandrake on(c). 500.00
21 Mandrake on(c). 400.00
22 Mandrake on(c). 400.00
23 Mandrake on(c). 400.00
24 Mandrake on(c). 400.00
25 B:Blondie; Mandrake in
    Logo for Duration. 400.00
26 Blondie (c). 350.00
27 Blondie(c); HighSchoolHeroes 350.00
28 Blondie(c); HighSchoolHeroes 350.00
29 Blondie(c); HighSchoolHeroes 350.00
30 Blondie (c) 350.00
31 Blondie(c);High School
    Sports Page. 250.00
32 Blondie (c);Secret Agent X-9 . 250.00
33 C.Knight's-Romance of Flying 250.00
34 ClaytonKnight's-War in the Air 250.00
35 Blondie (c). 250.00
36 July'42; Patriotic-(c) 250.00
37 Blondie (c). 250.00
38 ClaytonKnight's-Flying Tigers . 250.00
39 Blondie (c). 250.00
40 Jimmie Doolittle bombs Tokyo 250.00
41 How German Became
    British Censor 200.00
42 Joe Musial's-Dollar-a-Dither . . 200.00
43 Clay Knight's-War in the Air . . 200.00
44 Flying Fortress in Action 200.00
45 Clayton Knight's-Gremlins . . . 200.00
46 Adventures of Aladdin Jr. 200.00
47 Secret Agent X-9. . . . . 200.00
48 General Arnold U.S.A.F. 200.00
49 Joe Musial's-Dollar-a-Dither . . 200.00
50 The Lone Ranger 200.00
51 Joe Musial's-Dollar-a-Dither . 150.00
52 C. Knights-Heroes on Wings . 150.00
53 C. Knights-Heroes on Wings . 150.00
54 High School Heroes 150.00
55 Blondie (c). 175.00
56 High School Heroes 150.00
57 Joe Musial's-Dollar-a-Dither . . 150.00
58 Private Breger Abroad 150.00
59 . . . . 150.00
60 . . . . 150.00
61 Joe Musial's-Dollar-a-Dither . . 125.00
62 . . . . 125.00
63 B:Buz Sawyer, Naval Pilot . . . 125.00
64 thru 70. . . . . @125.00
71 thru 80 . . . . @125.00
81 thru 90 . . . . @125.00
91 thru 99 . . . . @100.00
100 . . . . 125.00
101 thru 108. . . . . @100.00
108 Flash Gordon 125.00
109 Flash Gordon 125.00
110 thru 113 . . . . @125.00
114 The Lone Ranger 125.00
115 thru 119 . . . . @125.00
120 Secret Agent X-9 . . . . 150.00
121 Secret Agent X-9. . . . . 150.00
122 Secret Agent X-9. . . . . 150.00
123 Sec. Agent X-9 . . . . 150.00

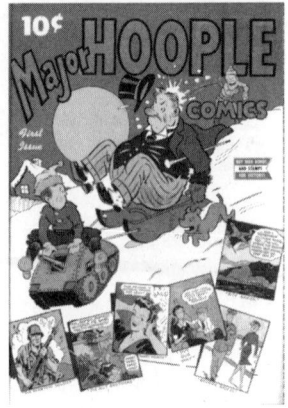

Major Hoople Comics #1
© Nedor Publications

MAJOR HOOPLE COMICS
Nedor Publications, 1942
1 Mary Worth,Phantom Soldier;
    Buy War Bonds On(c) 500.00

MAJOR INAPAK THE SPACE ACE
Magazine Enterprises, 1951
1 BP,Sci-Fi 200.00

MAJOR VICTORY COMICS
**H. Clay Glover Svcs./
Harry A. Chestler, 1944**
1 O:Major Victory,I:Spider
    Woman 1,000.00
2 A: Dynamic Boy 600.00
3 A: Rocket Boy 500.00

MAMMOTH COMICS
K.K. Publications, 1938
1 Alley Oop, Dick Tracy, etc. . . 3,000.00

MANHUNT!
Magazine Enterprises, 1953
1 LbC,FGu,OW(c);B:Red Fox,
    Undercover Girl, Space Ace . 750.00
2 LbC,FGu,OW(c);
    Electrocution(c) 550.00
3 LbC,FGu,OW,OW(c) 450.00
4 LbC,FGu,OW,OW(c) 450.00
5 LbC,FGu,OW,OW(c) 450.00
6 LbC,OW,OW(c) 400.00
7 LbC,OW; E:Space Ace 375.00
8 LbC,OW,FGu(c);B:Trail Colt . . 375.00
9 LbC,OW 375.00
10 LbC,OW,OW(c),Gwl 375.00
11 LbC,FF,OW;B:The Duke,
    Scotland Yard 600.00
12 LbC,OW 300.00
13 See: *A-1 Comics* #63
14 See: *A-1 Comics* #77

MAN OF WAR
**Comic Corp. of America
(Centaur Publ.), Nov., 1941**
1 PG,PG(c);Flag(c);B:The Fire-
    Man,Man of War,The Sentinel,
    Liberty Guards,Vapoman . . 2,700.00
2 PG,PG(c);I: The Ferret 2,100.00

MAN O'MARS
**Fiction House/
I.W. Enterprises, 1953**
1 MA, Space Rangers 700.00
1 MA, Rep. Space Rangers 100.00

MARCH OF COMICS
**K.K. Publications/
Western Publ., 1946
(All were Giveaways)**
N# WK back(c),Goldilocks 700.00
N# WK,How Santa got His
    Red Suit 400.00
N# WK,Our Gang 600.00
N# CB,Donald Duck;
    'Maharajah Donald' 14,000.00
5 Andy Panda 250.00
6 WK,Fairy Tales 300.00
7 Oswald the Lucky Rabbit 250.00
8 Mickey Mouse 700.00
9 Gloomey Bunny 150.00
10 Santa Claus 150.00
11 Santa Claus. 125.00
12 Santa's Toys 125.00
13 Santa's Suprise. 125.00
14 Santa's Kitchen. 125.00
15 Hip-It-Ty Hop. 125.00
16 Woody Woodpecker 175.00
17 Roy Rogers. 350.00
18 Fairy Tales 125.00
19 Uncle Wiggily 125.00
20 CB,Donald Duck 5,700.00
21 Tom and Jerry. 150.00
22 Andy Panda 125.00
23 Raggedy Ann and Andy 175.00
24 Felix the Cat; By
    Otto Messmer 300.00
25 Gene Autrey 300.00
26 Our Gang 275.00
27 Mickey Mouse. 500.00
28 Gene Autry 300.00
29 Easter 75.00
30 Santa 75.00
31 Santa. 75.00
32 Does Not Exist
33 A Christmas Carol. 75.00
34 Woody Woodpecker 150.00
35 Roy Rogers. 325.00
36 Felix the Cat 250.00
37 Popeye 175.00
38 Oswald the Lucky Rabbit 100.00
39 Gene Autry 275.00
40 Andy and Woody 100.00
41 CB,DonaldDuck,SouthSeas. 5,500.00

March of Comics #41
© Walt Disney

42 Porky Pig	125.00
43 Henry	100.00
44 Bugs Bunny	125.00
45 Mickey Mouse	400.00
46 Tom and Jerry	125.00
47 Roy Rogers	300.00
48 Santa	100.00
49 Santa	100.00
50 Santa	100.00
51 Felix the Cat	225.00
52 Popeye	150.00
53 Oswald the Lucky Rabbit	100.00
54 Gene Autrey	250.00
55 Andy and Woody	100.00
56 CB back(c),Donald Duck	450.00
57 Porky Pig	100.00
58 Henry	100.00
59 Bugs Bunny	125.00
60 Mickey Mouse	400.00
61 Tom and Jerry	100.00
62 Roy Rogers	250.00
63 Santa	75.00
64 Santa	75.00
65 Jingle Bells	75.00
66 Popeye	125.00
67 Oswald the Lucky Rabbit	100.00
68 Roy Rogers	250.00
69 Donald Duck	400.00
70 Tom and Jerry	100.00
71 Porky Pig	100.00
72 Krazy Kat	125.00
73 Roy Rogers	250.00
74 Mickey Mouse	300.00
75 Bugs Bunny	100.00
76 Andy and Woody	100.00
77 Roy Rogers	250.00
78 Gene Autrey; last regular sized issue	250.00
79 Andy Panda,5"x7" format	100.00
80 Popeye	150.00
81 Oswald the Lucky Rabbit	75.00
82 Tarzan	250.00
83 Bugs Bunny	75.00
84 Henry	75.00
85 Woody Woodpecker	75.00
86 Roy Rogers	175.00
87 Krazy Kat	100.00
88 Tom and Jerry	75.00
89 Porky Pig	75.00
90 Gene Autrey	150.00
91 Roy Rogers and Santa	175.00
92 Christmas w/Santa	50.00
93 Woody Woodpecker	50.00
94 Indian Chief	125.00
95 Oswald the Lucky Rabbit	50.00
96 Popeye	125.00
97 Bugs Bunny	75.00
98 Tarzan,Lex Barker Ph(c)	200.00
99 Porky Pig	50.00
100 Roy Rogers	125.00
101 Henry	50.00
102 Tom Corbet,P(c)	175.00
103 Tom and Jerry	50.00
104 Gene Autrey	125.00
105 Roy Rogers	125.00
106 Santa's Helpers	50.00
107 Not Published	
108 Fun with Santa	50.00
109 Woody Woodpecker	50.00
110 Indian Chief	50.00
111 Oswald the Lucky Rabbit	50.00
112 Henry	50.00
113 Porky Pig	50.00
114 Tarzan,RsM	225.00
115 Bugs Bunny	50.00
116 Roy Rogers	125.00
117 Popeye	125.00
118 Flash Gordon, P(c)	150.00
119 Tom and Jerry	50.00
120 Gene Autrey	125.00
121 Roy Rogers	125.00
122 Santa's Suprise	50.00

March of Comics #205
© Western Publications

123 Santa's Christmas Book	50.00
124 Woody Woodpecker	50.00
125 Tarzan, Lex Barker Ph(c)	200.00
126 Oswald the Lucky Rabbit	50.00
127 Indian Chief	75.00
128 Tom and Jerry	50.00
129 Henry	50.00
130 Porky Pig	50.00
131 Roy Rogers	125.00
132 Bugs Bunny	50.00
133 Flash Gordon,Ph(c)	125.00
134 Popeye	75.00
135 Gene Autrey	125.00
136 Roy Rogers	125.00
137 Gifts from Santa	40.00
138 Fun at Christmas	40.00
139 Woody Woodpecker	40.00
140 Indian Chief	75.00
141 Oswald the Lucky Rabbit	40.00
142 Flash Gordon	125.00
143 Porky Pig	40.00
144 RsM,Ph(c),Tarzan	175.00
145 Tom and Jerry	40.00
146 Roy Rogers,Ph(c)	125.00
147 Henry	40.00
148 Popeye	75.00
149 Bugs Bunny	40.00
150 Gene Autrey	125.00
151 Roy Rogers	125.00
152 The Night Before Christmas	40.00
153 Merry Christmas	40.00
154 Tom and Jerry	40.00
155 Tarzan,Ph(c)	175.00
156 Oswald the Lucky Rabbit	40.00
157 Popeye	75.00
158 Woody Woodpecker	40.00
159 Indian Chief	75.00
160 Bugs Bunny	40.00
161 Roy Rogers	100.00
162 Henry	40.00
163 Rin Tin Tin	125.00
164 Porky Pig	40.00
165 The Lone Ranger	125.00
166 Santa & His Reindeer	40.00
167 Roy Rogers and Santa	100.00
168 Santa Claus' Workshop	40.00
169 Popeye	75.00
170 Indian Chief	75.00
171 Oswald the Lucky Rabbit	40.00
172 Tarzan	175.00
173 Tom and Jerry	40.00
174 The Lone Ranger	125.00
175 Porky Pig	40.00
176 Roy Rogers	100.00
177 Woody Woodpecker	40.00
178 Henry	40.00

179 Bugs Bunny	40.00
180 Rin Tin Tin	75.00
181 Happy Holiday	30.00
182 Happi Tim	40.00
183 Welcome Santa	30.00
184 Woody Woodpecker	40.00
185 Tarzan, Ph(c)	150.00
186 Oswald the Lucky Rabbit	30.00
187 Indian Chief	75.00
188 Bugs Bunny	30.00
189 Henry	30.00
190 Tom and Jerry	30.00
191 Roy Rogers	100.00
192 Porky Pig	30.00
193 The Lone Ranger	125.00
194 Popeye	75.00
195 Rin Tin Tin	100.00
196 Not Published	
197 Santa is Coming	30.00
198 Santa's Helper	30.00
199 Huckleberry Hound	100.00
200 Fury	75.00
201 Bugs Bunny	50.00
202 Space Explorer	100.00
203 Woody Woodpecker	30.00
204 Tarzan	125.00
205 Mighty Mouse	75.00
206 Roy Rogers,Ph(c)	100.00
207 Tom and Jerry	30.00
208 The Lone Ranger,Ph(c)	150.00
209 Porky Pig	30.00
210 Lassie	75.00
211 Not Published	
212 Christmas Eve	30.00
213 Here Comes Santa	30.00
214 Huckleberry Hound	125.00
215 Hi Yo Silver	100.00
216 Rocky & His Friends	125.00
217 Lassie	75.00
218 Porky Pig	30.00
219 Journey to the Sun	100.00
220 Bugs Bunny	30.00
221 Roy and Dale,Ph(c)	125.00
222 Woody Woodpecker	30.00
223 Tarzan	125.00
224 Tom and Jerry	30.00
225 The Lone Ranger	100.00
226 Christmas Treasury	30.00
227 Not Published	
228 Letters to Santa	30.00
229 The Flintstones	150.00
230 Lassie	75.00
231 Bugs Bunny	30.00
232 The Three Stooges	250.00
233 Bullwinkle	150.00
234 Smokey the Bear	40.00
235 Huckleberry Hound	100.00
236 Roy and Dale	100.00
237 Mighty Mouse	50.00
238 The Lone Ranger	100.00
239 Woody Woodpecker	30.00
240 Tarzan	125.00
241 Santa Around the World	30.00
242 Santa Toyland	30.00
243 The Flintstones	150.00
244 Mr.Ed,Ph(c)	75.00
245 Bugs Bunny	30.00
246 Popeye	50.00
247 Mighty Mouse	50.00
248 The Three Stooges	200.00
249 Woody Woodpecker	30.00
250 Roy and Dale	100.00

MARGE'S LITTLE LULU
Dell Publishing Co., 1948

1 B:Lulu's Diary	1,500.00
2 I:Gloria,Miss Feeny	600.00
3	600.00
4	550.00
5	550.00
6	450.00
7 I:Annie,X-Mas (c)	450.00

All comics prices listed are for *Near Mint* condition.

GOLDEN AGE

8	450.00
9	450.00
10	450.00
11 thru 18	@350.00
19 I:Wilbur	350.00
20 I:Mr.McNabbem	350.00
21	300.00
22	300.00
23	300.00
24	300.00
25	300.00
26 rep.Four Color #110	300.00
27 thru 29	@300.00
30 Christmas (c)	300.00
31 thru 34	@250.00
35 B:Mumday Story	250.00
36	250.00
37	250.00
38	250.00
39 I:Witch Hazel	275.00
40 Halloween (c)	250.00
41	225.00
42 Christmas (c)	225.00
43 Skiing (c)	225.00
44 Valentines Day (c)	225.00
45 2nd A:Witch Hazel	225.00
46 thru 60	@200.00
61	200.00
62	200.00
63 I:Chubby	200.00
64 thru 67	@200.00
68 I:Professor Cleff	200.00
69 thru 77	@200.00
78 Christmas (c)	200.00
79	200.00
80	200.00
81 thru 89	@150.00
90 Christmas (c)	150.00
91 thru 99	@150.00
100	175.00
101 thru 122	@100.00
123 I:Fifi	110.00
124 thru 164	@100.00
165 giant sized	200.00
166 giant sized	200.00

MARGE'S TUBBY
Dell Publishing Co., 1953

1	400.00
2	250.00
3 & 4	@200.00
5 thru 10	@150.00
11 thru 20	@125.00
21 thru 49	@100.00

MARK TRAIL
Standard Magazines/
Fawcett/Pines, 1955

1	125.00
5	75.00
A1	150.00

MARMADUKE MOUSE
Quality Comics Group
(Arnold Publications), 1946

1 Funny Animal	250.00
2 Funny Animal	200.00
3 thru 8 Funny Animal	@125.00
9 Funny Animal	100.00
10 Funny Animal	100.00
11 thru 20 Funny Animal	@75.00
21 thru 50 Funny Animal	@60.00
51 thru 65 Funny Animal	@50.00

MARTIN KANE
Hero Books (Fox Features
Syndicate), June, 1950

1 WW,WW-(c)	400.00
2 WW,JO, Auguat, 1950	300.00

MARVEL FAMILY, THE
Fawcett Publications,
Dec., 1945–Jan., 1954

1 O:Captain Marvel,Captain Marvel Jr., Mary Marvel,Uncle Marvel; V:Black Adam	2,700.00
2 Uncle Marvel	1,300.00
3	900.00
4 The Witch's Tale	700.00
5 Civilization of a Prehistoric Race	600.00
6	550.00
7 The Rock of Eternity,Shazam	550.00
8 The Marvel Family Round Table	500.00
9 V: The Last Vikings	500.00
10 CCB(c),JaB,BTh,V:Sivana Family	500.00
11 V: The Well of Evil	400.00
12 V: The Iron Horseman	400.00
13 BTh,CCB,PrC(c)	400.00
14 Captain Marvel Invalid	400.00
15 V: Mr. Triangle	425.00
16 World's Mightiest Quarrell	425.00
17	425.00
18	425.00
19 V: The Monster Menace	425.00
20 The Marvel Family Feud	425.00
21 V: The Trio of Terror	400.00
22 V: The Triple Threat	400.00
23 March of Independence (c)	425.00
24 V: The Fighting Xergos	400.00
25 Trial of the Marvel Family	400.00
26 V: Mr. Power	400.00
27 V: The Amoeba Men	400.00
28	400.00
29 V: The Monarch of Money	400.00
30 A:World's Greatest Magician	400.00
31 V:Sivana & The Great Hunger	300.00
32 The Marvel Family Goes Into Buisness	300.00
33 I: The Hermit Family	300.00
34 V: Sivana's Miniature Menace	300.00
35 V: The Berzerk Machines	300.00
36 V: The Invaders From Infinity	300.00
37 V: The Earth Changer	300.00
38 V: Sivana's Instinct Exterminator Gun	300.00
39 The Legend of Atlantis	300.00
40 Seven Wonders of the Modern World	300.00
41 The Great Oxygen Theft	300.00
42 V: The Endless Menace	250.00
43	250.00

The Marvel Family #17
© Fawcett Publications

44 V: The Rust That Menaced the World	250.00
45 The Hoax City	250.00
46 The Day Civilization Vanished	250.00
47 V: The Interplanetary Thieves	300.00
48 V: The Four Horsemen	250.00
49 ...Proves Human Hardness	250.00
50 The Speech Scrambler Machine	250.00
51 The Living Statues	275.00
52 The School of Witches	250.00
53 V:Man Who Changed World	250.00
54	250.00
55	250.00
56 The World's Mightiest Project	250.00
57	250.00
58 The Triple Time Plot	250.00
59	250.00
60	250.00
61	250.00
62	250.00
63 V: The Pirate Planet	250.00
64	250.00
65	250.00
66 The Miracle Stone	250.00
67	250.00
68	250.00
69 V: The Menace of Old Age	250.00
70 V: The Crusade of Evil	250.00
71	250.00
72	250.00
73	250.00
74	250.00
75 The Great Space Struggle	250.00
76	225.00
77 Anti-Communist	400.00
78 V: The Red Vulture	300.00
79 Horror	250.00
80	250.00
81	250.00
82	250.00
83 V: The Flying Skull	250.00
84 thru 87	@250.00
88 Jokes of Jeopardy	250.00
89 And Then There Were None	250.00

MARVELS OF SCIENCE
Charlton Comics, 1946

1 1st Charlton Book; Atomic Bomb Story	350.00
2	250.00
3	250.00
4 President Truman(c); Jun.'6	250.00

MARY MARVEL COMICS
Fawcett Publications,
Dec., 1945

1 Intro: Mary Marvel	3,500.00
2	1,300.00
3	900.00
4 On a Leave of Absence	800.00
5 Butterfly (c) Bullet Girl	600.00
6 A:Freckles,Teenager of Mischief	600.00
7 The Kingdom Undersea	600.00
8 Holiday Special Issue	600.00
9 Air Race (c)	500.00
10 A: Freckles	500.00
11 A: The Sad Dryads	350.00
12 Red Cross Appeal on(c)	350.00
13 Keep the Homefires Burning	350.00
14 Meets Ghosts (c)	350.00
15 A: Freckles	350.00
16 The Jukebox Menace	325.00
17 Aunt Agatha's Adventures	325.00
18	325.00
19 Witch (c)	325.00
20	325.00
21 V: Dice Head	300.00
22 The Silver Slippers	300.00
23 The Pendulum Strikes	300.00

24 V: The Nightowl. 300.00
25 A: Freckles 300.00
26 A:Freckles dressed as Clown . 300.00
27 The Floating Oceanliner 300.00
28 Western, Sept., 1948 . . . . 300.00
Becomes:

MONTE HALE WESTERN
**Fawcett Publications,
Oct., 1948**
29 Ph(c),B:Monte Hale & His
　　Horse Pardner. 700.00
30 Ph(c),B:Big Bow-Little
　　Arrow; CCB,Captain Tootsie . 300.00
31 Ph(c),Giant 250.00
32 Ph(c),Giant 250.00
33 Ph(c),Giant 250.00
34 Ph(c),E:Big Bow-Little
　　Arrow;B:Gabby Hayes,Giant . 250.00
35 Ph(c),Gabby Hayes, Giant . . . 250.00
36 Ph(c),Gabby Hayes, Giant . . . 250.00
37 Ph(c),Gabby Hayes 200.00
38 Ph(c),Gabby Hayes, Giant . . . 200.00
39 Ph(c);CCB, Captain Tootsie;
　　Gabby Hayes, Giant 200.00
40 Ph(c),Gabby Hayes, Giant . . . 200.00
41 Ph(c),Gabby Hayes 200.00
42 Ph(c),Gabby Hayes, Giant . . . 175.00
43 Ph(c),Gabby Hayes, Giant . . . 175.00
44 Ph(c),Gabby Hayes, Giant . . . 175.00
45 Ph(c),Gabby Hayes 175.00
46 Ph(c),Gabby Hayes, Giant . . . 200.00
47 Ph(c),A:Big Bow-Little Arrow;
　　Gabby Hayes, Giant 200.00
48 Ph(c),Gabby Hayes, Giant . . . 200.00
49 Ph(c),Gabby Hayes 175.00
50 Ph(c),Gabby Hayes, Giant . . . 175.00
51 Ph(c),Gabby Hayes, Giant . . . 135.00
52 Ph(c),Gabby Hayes, Giant . . . 135.00
53 Ph(c),A:Slim Pickens;
　　Gabby Hayes. 125.00
54 Ph(c),Gabby Hayes, Giant . . . 135.00
55 Ph(c),Gabby Hayes, Giant . . . 135.00
56 Ph(c),Gabby Hayes, Giant . . . 125.00
57 Ph(c),Gabby Hayes 125.00
58 Ph(c),Gabby Hayes, Giant . . . 125.00
59 Ph(c),Gabby Hayes, Giant . . . 125.00
60 thru 79 Ph(c),Gabby Hayes @100.00
80 Ph(c),E: Gabby Hayes 100.00
81 Ph(c). 100.00
82 Final Ph(c) 125.00

Charlton Comics, Feb., 1955
83 R:G. Hayes Back B&W Ph(c) . 150.00
84 . . . . 100.00
85 . . . . 100.00
86 E: Gabby Hayes 100.00
87 . . . . 100.00
88 Jan., 1956. . . . . 100.00

MASK COMICS
**Rural Home Publications,
Feb.–March, 1945**
1 LbC,LbC-(c), Evil (c). 4,500.00
2 LbC-(c),A:Black Rider,The
　Collector The Boy Magician;
　Apr-May'45, Devil (c) 2,500.00

MASKED MARVEL
**Centaur Publications,
Sept., 1940**
1 I: The Masked Marvel 2,500.00
2 PG, ... 1,800.00
3 Dec., 1940 . . . . 1,700.00

THE MASKED RAIDER
Charlton Comics, 1955
1 . . . . 150.00
2 . . . . 125.00
3 . . . . 100.00
4 thru 7 . . . . @100.00

8 Billy the Kid 100.00
*Continued as Billy the Kid,
see Color Pub. section*

MASKED RANGER
**Premier Magazines,
April, 1954**
1 FF,O&B:The Masked Ranger,
　Streak the Horse,The
　Crimson Avenger. 600.00
2 . . . . 200.00
3 . . . . 200.00
4 B: Jessie James,Billy the Kid,
　Wild Bill Hickok,
　Jim Bowie's Life Story 200.00
5 . . . . 200.00
6 . . . . 200.00
7 . . . . 200.00
8 . . . . 200.00
9 AT,E:All Features; A:Wyatt
　Earp Aug., 1955. . . . . 250.00

MASTER COMICS
**Fawcett Publications,
March, 1940**
1-6 Oversized,7-Normal Format
1 O:Master Man; B:The Devil's
　Dagger, El Carin-Master of
　Magic, Rick O'Say, Morton
　Murch, White Rajah, Shipwreck
　Roberts, Frontier Marshall,
　Mr. Clue, Streak Sloan . . . 16,000.00
2 Master Man (c) 4,500.00
3 Master Man (c) Bondage . . . 3,600.00
4 Master Man (c) 3,500.00
5 Master Man (c) 3,500.00
6 E: All Above Features 3,600.00
7 B:Bulletman,Zorro,The Mystery
　Man, Lee Granger, Jungle
　King,Buck Jones 5,000.00
8 B:The Red Gaucho,Captain
　Venture, Planet Princess . . 3,000.00
9 Bulletman & Steam Roller . . 2,800.00
10 E: Lee Granger 4,000.00
11 O: Minute Man 5,500.00
12 Minute Man (c). 3,000.00
13 O:Bulletgirl; E:Red Gaucho . 3,500.00
14 B: The Companions Three. . 2,500.00
15 MRa, Bulletman & Girl (c) . 2,500.00
16 MRa, Minute Man (c). 2,500.00
17 B:MRa on Bulletman 2,200.00
18 MRa, ... 2,200.00
19 MRa, Bulletman & Girl (c) . 2,200.00
20 MRa,C:Cap.Marvel-
　Bulletman 2,200.00

*Master Comics #46
© Fawcett Publications*

21 MRa-(c),Capt. Marvel in
　Bulletman,I&O:Captain
　Nazi 9,000.00
22 MRa-(c),E:Mystery Man,Captain
　Venture; Bondage(c);Capt.
　Marvel Jr. X-Over In
　Bulletman; A:Capt. Nazi . . 8,200.00
23 MRa(a&c),B:Capt. Marvel Jr.
　V:Capt. Nazi 4,800.00
24 MRa(a&c),Death By Radio . 2,200.00
25 MRa(a&c),The Jap Invasion 2,200.00
26 MRa(a&c),Capt. Marvel Jr.
　Avenges Pearl Harbor 2,200.00
27 MRa(a&c),V For Victory(c). . 2,200.00
28 MRa(a&c)Liberty Bell(c). . . . 2,200.00
29 MRa(a&c),Hitler &
　Hirohito(c). 2,900.00
30 MRa(a&c),Flag (c);Capt.
　Marvel Jr, V: Capt. Nazi . . 2,000.00
31 MRa(a&c),E:Companions
　Three,Capt.Marvel Jr,
　V:Mad Dr. Macabre 1,500.00
32 MRa(a&c),E: Buck Jones;
　CMJr Strikes Terror Castle . 1,500.00
33 MRa(a&c),B:Balbo the Boy
　Magician,Hopalong Cassidy 1,500.00
34 MRa(a&c),Capt.Marvel Jr
　V: Capt.Nazi 2,000.00
35 MRa(a&c),CMJr Defies
　the Flame 1,500.00
36 MRa(a&c),Statue Of
　Liberty(c). 1,500.00
37 MRa(a&c),CMJr Blasts
　the Nazi Raiders 1,500.00
38 MRa(a&c),CMJr V:the Japs . 1,500.00
39 MRa(a&c),CMJr Blasts
　Nazi Slave Ship 1,500.00
40 MRa(a&c),Flag (c) 1,500.00
41 MRa(a&c),Bulletman,Bulletgirl,
　CMJr X-over In Minuteman 1,500.00
42 MRa(a&c),CMJr V: Hitler's
　Dream Soldier 700.00
43 MRa(c),CMJr Battles For
　Stalingrad. 700.00
44 MRa(c),CMJr In Crystal City
　of the Peculiar Penguins 700.00
45 MRa(c), ... 700.00
46 MRa(c), ... 700.00
47 MRa(c),A:Hitler; E: Balbo 750.00
48 MRa(c),I:Bulletboy;Capt.
　Marvel A: in Minuteman. 800.00
49 MRa(c),E: Hopalong Cassidy,
　Minuteman. 700.00
50 I&O: Radar,A:Capt. Marvel,
　B:Nyoka the Jungle Girl 700.00
51 MRa(c),CMJr V: Japanese . . . 500.00
52 MRa(c),CMJr & Radar Pitch
　War Stamps on (c). 500.00
53 CMJR V: Dr. Sivana 500.00
54 MRa(c),Capt.Marvel Jr
　Your Pin-Up Buddy 500.00
55 . . . . 500.00
56 MRa(c) 400.00
57 CMJr V: Dr. Sivana 400.00
58 MRa(a&c), ... 400.00
59 MRa(c),A:The Upside
　Downies. 500.00
60 MRa(c) 500.00
61 CMJr Meets Uncle Marvel . . . 500.00
62 Uncle Sam on (c) 500.00
63 W/ Radar (c) 400.00
64 W/ Radar (c) 400.00
65 BTh(c),JkS 400.00
66 CMJr & Secret Of the Sphinx . 400.00
67 Knight (c) 400.00
68 CMJr in the Range of
　the Beasts 400.00
69 . . . . 400.00
70 . . . . 400.00
71 CMJr,V:Man in Metal Mask. . . 350.00
72 CMJr V: Sivana & The Whistle
　That Wouldn't Stop 350.00

73 CMJr V: The Ghost of Evil . . . 350.00
74 CMJr & The Fountain of Age . 350.00
75 CMJr V: The Zombie Master. . 350.00
76 . . . . 350.00
77 BTh(c),BK,Pirate Treasure . . . 350.00
78 CMJr in Death on the Scenic
  Railway 350.00
79 CMJr V: The Black Shroud . . . 350.00
80 CMJr-The Land of Backwards 350.00
81 CMJr & The Voyage 'Round
  the Horn. 300.00
82 CMJr,IN,Death at the
  Launching 300.00
83 . . . . 300.00
84 BTh(c&a) CMJr V: The Human
  Magnet. 300.00
85 CMJr-Crime on the Campus . 250.00
86 CMJr & The City of Machines. 250.00
87 CMJr & The Root of Evil. 250.00
88 CMJr V: The Wreckers;
  B: Hopalong Cassidy. 250.00
89 . . . . 250.00
90 CMJr V: The Caveman 250.00
91 CMJr V: The Blockmen. 250.00
92 CMJr V: The Space Slavers . 250.00
93 BK,CMJr,V:TheGrowingGiant. 250.00
94 E: Hopalong Cassidy 250.00
95 B: Tom Mix; CMJr Meets
  the Skyhawk 250.00
96 CMJr Meets the World's
  Mightiest Horse 250.00
97 CMJr Faces the Doubting
  Thomas 250.00
98 KKK Type 250.00
99 Witch (c) 250.00
100 CMJr V: The Ghost Ship. . . . 275.00
101 thru 105 . . . . @225.00
106 E: Bulletman 225.00
107 CMJr Faces the Disappearance
  of the Statue of Liberty 250.00
108 . . . . 250.00
109 . . . . 250.00
110 CMJr & The Hidden Death . . 250.00
111 thru 122 . . . . @250.00
123 CMJr V: The Flying
  Desperado. 250.00
124 . . . . 250.00
125 CMJr & The Bed of Mystery . 250.00
126 thru 131. . . . . @250.00
132 V: Migs 250.00
133 E: Tom Mix; April, 1953. . . . . 300.00

MAZIE
Nationwide Publ./
Magazine Publ./
Harvey Publ., 1951–58
1 . . . . 150.00
2 . . . . 75.00
3 . . . . 75.00
4 . . . . 75.00
5 . . . . 75.00
6 thru 10 . . . . @75.00
11 thru 20. . . . . @50.00
21 thru 28 . . . . @50.00

MD
E.C. Comics,
April, 1955–Jan., 1956
1 RC,GE,Grl,JO,JCr(c). 500.00
2 thru 5 RC,GE,Grl,JO,JCr(c). @350.00

MEDAL OF
HONOR COMICS
Stafford Publication,
Spring, 1947
1 True Stories of Medal of Honor
  Recipients 200.00

MEET CORLISS
ARCHER
Fox Features Syndicate,
March, 1948
1 AF,AF(c), Teenage 1,600.00
2 AF(c) 750.00
3 . . . . 700.00
Becomes:

MY LIFE
Sept., 1948
4 JKa,AF, ... 550.00
5 JKa, ... 300.00
6 JKa,AF, ... 275.00
7 WW,Watercolor & Ink Drawing
  on(c) 325.00
8 . . . . 150.00
9 . . . . 150.00
10 WW, July, 1950. . . . . 300.00

MEET MERTON
Toby Press, Dec., 1953
1 DBe,Teen Stories. 125.00
2 DBe 75.00
3 DBe 75.00
4 DBe; June, 1954 . . . . 75.00

MEET THE NEW
POST GAZETTE
SUNDAY FUNNIES
Pittsburg Post Gazette, 1949
N# One Shot Insert F: Several
  Syndicated Characters in Stories
  Exclusive to This Edition . . 9,000.00

MEL ALLEN
SPORTS COMICS
Visual Editions, 1949
1 GT 300.00
2 Lou Gehrig. 200.00

MEN AGAINST CRIME
See: HAND OF FATE

MEN IN ACTION
Ajax/Farrell Publ., 1957
1 AyB 250.00
2 . . . . 150.00
3 RH 150.00
4 AyB 150.00
5 AyB,JMn. 150.00
6 AyB 150.00
7 RH 125.00
8 SSh 125.00
9 . . . . 125.00

MEN OF COURAGE
Catechetical Guild
N# 100.00

MERRY COMICS
Carlton Comics, 1945
N# A:Boogeyman. 300.00

MERRY-GO-ROUND
COMICS
LaSalle/Croyden/
Rotary Litho., 1944
1 LaSalle Publications Edition . . 250.00
1a 1946, Croyden Edition 100.00
1b Sept-Oct.'47,Rotary Litho Ed. 125.00
2 . . . . 125.00

Mickey Mouse Magazine V1 #1
© Fox Features Syndicate

MERRY MOUSE
Avon Periodicals,
June, 1953
1 (fa),F. Carin (a&c) 150.00
2 (fa),F. Carin (a&c) 75.00
3 (fa),F. Carin (a&c) 75.00
4 (fa),F. Carin (a&c);Jan.'54 . . . . . 75.00

METEOR COMICS
Croyden Publications,
Nov., 1945
1 Captain Wizard & Baldy Bean . 550.00

MICKEY FINN
Eastern Color/
Columbia Comics Group, 1942
1 . . . . 400.00
2 . . . . 250.00
3 A: Charlie Chan 200.00
4 . . . . 150.00
5 thru 9 . . . . @100.00
10 thru 15. . . . . @80.00

(WALT DISNEY'S)
MICKEY MOUSE
Dell Publishing Co., Dec., 1952
#1-#27 Dell Four Color
28 . . . . 125.00
29 . . . . 100.00
30 . . . . 100.00
31 . . . . 100.00
32 thru 34 . . . . @100.00
35 thru 50 . . . . @100.00
51 thru 73 . . . . @100.00
74 . . . . 125.00
75 thru 99 . . . . @100.00
100 thru 105 rep. . . . . @125.00
106 thru 120. . . . . @150.00
121 thru 130. . . . . @100.00
131 thru 146. . . . . @30.00
147 rep,Phantom Fires 30.00
148 rep. 100.00
149 thru 158. . . . . @60.00
159 rep. 60.00
160 thru 170. . . . . @60.00
171 thru 199. . . . . @25.00
200 rep. 25.00
201 thru 218. . . . . @25.00

MICKEY MOUSE
MAGAZINE
Kay Kamen, 1933
1 scarce 25,000.00
2 . . . . 6,000.00

3 thru 8 . . . . @5,000.00
9 . . . . 4,500.00

MICKEY MOUSE MAGAZINE
Kay Kamen, 1933–34
1 digest size (1933) 4,000.00
2 dairy give-away promo 2,000.00
3 dairy give-away promo 1,500.00
4 dairy give-away promo 1,500.00
5 dairy give-away promo 1,500.00
6 dairy give-away promo 1,500.00
7 dairy give-away promo 1,500.00
8 dairy give-away promo 1,500.00
9 dairy give-away promo 1,500.00
10 dairy give-away promo. . . . 1,500.00
11 dairy give-away promo. . . . 1,500.00
12 dairy give-away promo. . . . 1,500.00

Volume II, 1934–35
1 dairy give-away promo 1,500.00
2 Christmas issue 1,500.00
3 dairy give-away promo 1,500.00
4 dairy give-away promo 1,500.00
5 1st Donald Duck as Sailor . . 5,000.00
6 dairy give-away promo 1,500.00
7 dairy give-away promo 1,500.00
8 dairy give-away promo 1,500.00
9 dairy give-away promo 1,500.00
10 dairy give-awaypromo 1,500.00
11 dairy give-awaypromo 1,500.00
12 dairy give-awaypromo 1,500.00

MICKEY MOUSE MAGAZINE
K.K. Pub./Westen Pub., 1935
1 (1935) 13¼"x10¼" 35,000.00
2 OM, new size 11½"x8½". . . . 6,000.00
3 OM 3,000.00
4 OM 3,000.00
5 (1936) Donald Duck solo . . . 5,000.00
6 Donald Duck editor 4,500.00
7 . . . . 3,000.00
8 Donald Duck solo 4,500.00
9 1st Minnie & Minnie 4,500.00
10 . . . . 3,000.00
11 Mickey & Pluto 3,500.00
12 . . . . 3,000.00

Volume II
1 OM 2,500.00
2 OM 2,500.00
3 OM,Christmas issue, 100pg . 7,500.00
4 OM (1937) Roy Ranger
   adv.strip 2,000.00
5 Ted True strip 1,200.00
6 Mickey Mouse cut-outs. . . . 1,200.00
7 Mickey Mouse cut-outs. . . . 1,200.00
8 Mickey Mouse cut-outs. . . . 1,200.00
9 Mickey Mouse cut-outs. . . . 1,200.00
10 Full color 2,200.00
11 . . . . 1,200.00
12 Hiawatha 1,500.00
13 . . . . 1,200.00

Volume III
2 Big Bad Wolf (c) 1,700.00
3 CB,First Snow White 4,000.00
4 CB,(1938) Snow White. . . . 2,500.00
5 Snow White (c) 2,500.00
6 Snow White ends 1,600.00
7 CB,7 Dwarfs Easter (c). . . . 1,400.00
8 . . . . 1,200.00
9 CB,Dopey(c) 1,100.00
10 Goofy(c) 1,100.00
11 Mickey Mouse Sheriff. . . . 1,100.00
12 CB,A:Snow White 1,100.00

Volume IV
1 OM,Practile Pig & Brave
   Little Tailor 1,200.00
2 I:Huey,Louis & Dewey(c) . . . 1,500.00
3 Ferdinand the Bull 1,200.00

4 (1939),B:Spotty 1,100.00
5 Pluto solo 1,200.00
7 Ugly Duckling 1,200.00
7a Goofy & Wilber 1,200.00
8 Big Bad Wolf(c). 1,200.00
9 CB,The Pointer 1,200.00
10 CB,July 4th 1,400.00
11 Slick, oversize 1,200.00
12 CB,Donald's Penguin. 1,300.00

Volume V
1 Black Pete. 1,300.00
2 Goofy(c),I:Pinocchio 1,500.00
3 Pinocchio 1,500.00
4 (1940) 1,200.00
5 Jiminy Cricket(c) 1,200.00
6 Tugboat Mickey 1,200.00
7 Huey, Louis & Dewey(c) 1,200.00
8 Figaro & Cleo 1,200.00
9 Donald(c),J.Cricket 1,300.00
10 July 4th 1,300.00
11 Mickey's Tailor 1,300.00
12 Change of comic format . . . 8,000.00
becomes:
WALT DISNEY COMICS & STORIES

MICKEY MOUSE
Whitman
904 W.Disney's Mickey Mouse
   and His Friends (1934). . . . 3,000.00
948 Disney'sMickeyMouse('34) 3,000.00

MIDGET COMICS
St. John Publishing Co., Feb., 1950
1 MB(c),Fighting Indian Stories . 250.00
2 April, 1950;Tex West-Cowboy
   Marshall 150.00

MIDNIGHT
Ajax/Farrell, 1957
1 Voodoo & Strange Fantasy . . . 175.00
2 . . . . 125.00

MIGHTY ATOM, THE
See: PIXIES

MIGHTY MIDGET COMICS
4"x5" Format
Samuel E. Lowe & Co./ Fawcett, 1942-43
1 Bulletman. 500.00
2 Captain Marvel 500.00
3 Captain Marvel Jr. 500.00
4 Golden Arrow 400.00
5 Ibis the Invincible 500.00
6 Spy Smasher 450.00
7 Balbo, The Boy Magician 250.00
8 Bulletman 300.00
9 Commando Yank 200.00
10 Dr. Voltz, The Human
   Generator 250.00
11 Lance O'Casey 250.00
12 Leatherneck the Marine 250.00
13 Minute Man 250.00
14 Mister Q 275.00
15 Mr. Scarlet & Pinky 250.00
16 Pat Wilson & His
   Flying Fortress. 225.00
17 Phantom Eagle 250.00
18 State Trooper Stops Crime . . 250.00
19 Tornado Tom 250.00

MIGHTY MOUSE
St. John Publishing, Aug., 1947
5 . . . . 600.00
6 thru 10 . . . . @300.00
11 thru 20 . . . . @200.00

Mighty Mouse #37
© St. John Publishing

21 thru 25 . . . . @150.00
26 thru 30 . . . . @125.00
31 thru 34 . . . . @100.00
35 Flying Saucer 150.00
36 . . . . 100.00
37 . . . . 100.00
38 thru 45 Giant 100 pgs . . . . @250.00
46 thru 66 . . . . @100.00
67 P(c), ... 100.00

Pines
68 thru 81 Funny Animal . . . . @100.00
82 Infinity (c) 100.00
83 June, 1959 . . . . 100.00

MIGHTY MOUSE ADVENTURES
See: ADVENTURES OF MIGHTY MOUSE

MIGHTY MOUSE ADVENTURE STORIES
St. John Publishing Co., 1953
N# 384 Pages,Rebound 700.00

MIKE BARNETT, MAN AGAINST CRIME
Fawcett Publications, Dec., 1951
1 The Mint of Dionysosi 250.00
2 Mystery of the Blue Madonna . 150.00
3 Revenge Holds the Torch 125.00
4 Special Delivery 125.00
5 Market For Morphine Drug . . . 175.00
6 Oct., 1952 . . . . 125.00

MILITARY COMICS
Comics Magazines (Quality Comics Group), Aug., 1941
1 JCo,CCu,FGu,BP,WE(c),O:Black-
   hawk, Miss America, Death Patrol,
   Blue Tracer; B:X of the Underground, Yankee Eagle,Q-Boat,
   Shot & Shell, Archie Atkins,
   Loops & Banks 20,000.00
2 JCo,FGu,BP,CCu,CCu(c),B:
   Secret War News 5,000.00
3 JCo,FGu,BP,AMc,CCu,CCu(c),
   I&O:Chop Chop 4,000.00
4 FGu,BP,AMc,CCu,CCu(c) . . 3,500.00
5 FGu,BP,AMc,CCu,CCu(c)
   B: The Sniper 3,000.00
6 FGu,BP,AMc,CCu,CCu(c) . . 2,500.00

7 FGu,BP,AMc,CCu,CCu(c)
E:Death Patrol 2,500.00
8 FGu,BP,AMc,CCu,CCu(c) . . 2,500.00
9 FGu,BP,AMc,CCu,CCu(c),
B: The Phantom Clipper . . 2,500.00
10 FGu,BP,CCu,AMc,WE(c) . . 2,700.00
11 FGu,BP,CCu,AMc,
WE(c),Flag(c) 2,200.00
12 FGu,BP,AMc,RC(a&c) 2,300.00
13 FGu,BP,AMc,RC(a&c),E:X of
the Underground 2,000.00
14 FGu,AMc,RC(a&c),B:Private
Dogtag 2,000.00
15 FGu,AMc,RC(a&c), ... 2,000.00
16 FGu,AMc,RC(a&c),E:The Phantom
Clipper,Blue Tracer. 1,500.00
17 FGu,AMc,RC(a&c),
B:P.T. Boat 1,500.00
18 FGu,AMc,RC(a&c), V:
The Thunderer 1,500.00
19 FGu,RC(a&c), V:King Cobra 1,500.00
20 GFx,RC(a&c), Death Patrol 1,500.00
21 FGu,GFx 1,200.00
22 FGu,GFx 1,200.00
23 FGu,GFx 1,200.00
24 FGu,GFx,V: Man-Heavy
Glasses. 1,200.00
25 FGu,GFx,V: Wang The Tiger 1,200.00
26 FGu,GFx,V: Skull 1,000.00
27 FGu,JCo,R:The Death Patrol1,000.00
28 FGu,JCo, Dungeon of Doom 1,000.00
29 FGu,JCo,V: Xanukhara . . . 1,000.00
30 FGu, JCo,BWa(a&c),Blackhawk
V: Dr. Koro 1,000.00
31 FGu,JCo,BWa,E:Death
Patrol; I: Captain Hitsu 1,000.00
32 JCo,A: Captain Hitsu 900.00
33 W/ Civil War Veteran. 900.00
34 A: Eve Rice 900.00
35 Shipwreck Island. 900.00
36 Cult of the Wailing Tiger 900.00
37 Pass of Bloody Peace 900.00
38 B.Hawk Faces Bloody Death . 900.00
39 A: Kwan Yin. 900.00
40 V: Ratru 800.00
41 W/ Chop Chop (c). 800.00
42 V: Jap Mata Hari. 800.00
43 . . . . 800.00

Becomes:

MODERN COMICS
Nov., 1945

44 Duel of Honor. 1,000.00
45 V: Sakyo the Madman 750.00
46 RC, Soldiers of Fortune 750.00
47 RC,PG,V:Count Hokoy 750.00
48 RC,PG,V:Pirates of Perool . . . 750.00
49 RC,PG,I:Fear,Lady
Adventuress. 750.00
50 RC,PG 750.00
51 RC,PG, Ancient City of Evil. . . 550.00
52 PG,BWa,V: The Vulture. 550.00
53 PG,BWa,B: Torchy 850.00
54 PG,RC,RC/CCu,BWa 500.00
55 PG,RC,RC/CCu,BWa 500.00
56 PG,RC/CCu,BWa 500.00
57 PG,RC,RC/CCu,BWa 500.00
58 PG,RC,RC/CCu,BWa,
V:The Grabber. 500.00
59 PG,RC,RC/CCu,BWa 500.00
60 PG,RC/CCu,BWa,RC(c),
V:Green Plague. 500.00
61 PG,RC/CCu,BWa,RC(c) 475.00
62 PG,RC/CCu,BWa,RC(c) 475.00
63 PG,RC/CCu,BWa,RC(c) 450.00
64 PG,RC/CCu,BWa,RC(c) 450.00
65 PG,RC/CCu,BWa,RC(c) 450.00
66 PG,RC/CCu,BWa 450.00
67 PG,RC/CCu,BWa,RC(c) 450.00
68 PG,RC/CCu,BWa,RC(c);
I:Madame Butterfly 450.00
69 PG,RC/CCu,BWa,RC(c) 450.00
70 PG,RC/CCu,BWa,RC(c) 450.00

Milt Gross Funnies 32
© *Milt Gross*

71 PG,RC/CCu,BWa,RC(c) 450.00
72 PG,RC/CCu,BWa,RC(c) 450.00
73 PG,RC/CCu,BWa,RC(c) 450.00
74 PG,RC/CCu,BWa,RC(c) 450.00
75 PG,RC/CCu,BWa,RC(c) 450.00
76 PG,RC/CCu,BWa,RC(c) 450.00
77 PG,RC/CCu,BWa,RC(c) 450.00
78 PG,RC/CCu,BWa,JCo,RC(c) . 500.00
79 PG,RC/CCu,BWa,JCo,RC(c) . 450.00
80 PG,RC/CCu,BWa,JCo,RC(c) . 475.00
81 PG,RC/CCu,BWa,JCo,RC(c) . 475.00
82 PG,RC/CCu,BWa,JCo,RC(c) . 450.00
83 PG,RC/CCu,BWa,JCo,RC(c);
E: Private Dogtag 450.00
84 PG,RC/CCu,BWa,RC(c) 450.00
85 PG,RC/CCu,BWa,RC(c) 450.00
86 PG,RC/CCu,BWa,RC(c) 450.00
87 PG,RC/CCu,BWa,RC(c) 450.00
88 PG,RC/CCu,BWa,RC(c) 450.00
89 PG,RC/CCu,BWa,RC(c) 450.00
90 PG,RC/CCu,GFx,RC(c) 450.00
91 RC/CCu,GFx,RC(c) 450.00
92 RC/CCu,GFx,RC(c) 450.00
93 RC/CCu,GFx,RC(c) 450.00
94 RC/CCu,GFx,RC(c) 450.00
95 RC/CCu,GFx,RC(c) 450.00
96 RC/CCu,GFx,RC/CCu(c) 450.00
97 RC/CCu,GFx,RC/CCu(c) 450.00
98 RC/CCu,GFx,RC/CCu(c) 450.00
99 RC/CCu,GFx,JCo,RC/CCu(c). 450.00
100 GFx,JCo,RC/CCu(c) 475.00
101 GFx,JCo,RC/CCu(c) 450.00
102 GFx,JCo,WE,BWa,
RC/CCu(c). 600.00

MILT GROSS FUNNIES
Milt Gross, Inc., Aug., 1947

1 Gag Oriented Caricature 250.00
2 Gag Oriented Caricature 175.00

MINUTE MAN
Fawcett Publications,
Summer, 1941

1 V: The Nazis 3,000.00
2 V: The Mongol Horde 2,000.00
3 V: The Black Poet;Spr'42 . . 2,000.00

MIRACLE COMICS
E.C. Comics, Feb.,1940

1 B:Sky Wizard,Master of Space,
Dash Dixon,Man of Might,Dusty
Doyle,Pinkie Parker, The Kid
Cop,K-7 Secret Agent,Scorpion
& Blandu,Jungle Queen . . 3,000.00
2 . . . . 1,500.00

3 B:Bill Colt,The Ghost Rider . 1,400.00
4 A:The Veiled Prophet,
Bullet Bob; Mar'41 . . . . 1,200.00

MISS CAIRO JONES
Croyden Publishers, 1944

1 BO,Rep. Newspaper Strip . . . 250.00

MISS LIBERTY
See: LIBERTY COMICS

MR. ANTHONY'S
LOVE CLINIC
Hillman Periodicals, 1945

1 Ph(c) 250.00
2 . . . . 150.00
3 . . . . 100.00
4 . . . . 100.00
5 Ph(c),Apr/May'50 . . . . 100.00

MR. MUSCLES
See: THING, THE

MISTER MYSTERY
Media Publ./SPM Publ./
Aragon Publ., Sept., 1951

1 HK,RA,Horror 1,500.00
2 RA,RA(c) 950.00
3 RA(c) 950.00
4 Bondage(c) 1,000.00
5 Lingerie(c) 900.00
6 Bondage(c) 900.00
7 BW,Bondage(c);The Brain
Bats of Venus 1,900.00
8 Lingerie(c) 800.00
9 HN 800.00
10 . . . . 800.00
11 BW,Robot Woman 2,000.00
12 Flaming Object to Eye 800.00
13 . . . . 600.00
14 . . . . 600.00
15 The Coffin & Medusa's Head . 600.00
16 Bondage(c) 600.00
17 Severed Heads. 600.00
18 BW,Bondage(c). 900.00
19 Reprints. 600.00

MISTER RISK
See: HAND OF FATE

MISTER UNIVERSE
Mr. Publ./Media Publ./
Stanmore, July, 1951

1 . . . . 300.00
2 RA(c);Jungle That time Forgot 200.00
3 Marijuana Story 200.00
4 Mr. Universe Goes to War . . . 150.00
5 Mr. Universe Goes to War;
April, 1952 . . . . 150.00

MODERN COMICS
See: MILITARY COMICS

MODERN LOVE
Tiny Tot Comics
(E.C. Comics), June–July, 1949

1 Grl,AF,Stolen Romance 1,200.00
2 Grl,JcR,AF(c),I Craved
Excitement 750.00
3 AF(c);Our Families Clashed . . 650.00
4 AF(c);I Was a B Girl, panties . 800.00
5 RP,AF(c);Saved From Shame 800.00
6 AF(c);The Love That
Might Have Been 800.00
7 Grl,WW,AF(c);They Won't Let
Me Love Him 600.00
8 Grl,AF(c);Aug-Sept'50 . . . . . . 600.00

MOLLY O'DAY
Avon Periodicals,
Feb., 1945
1 GT;The Enchanted Dagger . . . 850.00

MONSTER
Fiction House Magazines, 1953
1 Dr. Drew 800.00
2 . . . . 600.00

MONSTER CRIME COMICS
Hillman Periodicals,
Oct., 1952
1 52 Pgs,15 Cent (c) Price . . . 2,000.00

MONTE HALL WESTERN
See: MARY MARVEL COMICS

MONTY HALL OF THE U.S. MARINES
Toby Press, Aug., 1951
1 JkS,:Monty Hall,Pin-Up Pete;
  (All Issues) 150.00
2 JkS 125.00
3 thru 5 JkS . . . . @100.00
6 JkS 100.00
7 JkS,The Fireball Express 100.00
8 JkS 100.00
9 JkS 100.00
10 The Vial of Death 100.00
11 Monju Island Prison Break . . . 100.00

MOON GIRL AND THE PRINCE
E.C. Comics, Autumn, 1947
1 JCr(c),O:Moon Girl 1,500.00
Becomes:

MOON GIRL
E.C. Comics, 1947
2 JCr(c),Battle of the Congo . . 1,000.00
3 . . . . 750.00
4 V: A Vampire 750.00
5 1st E.C. Horror-Zombie
  Terror 1,700.00
6 . . . . 900.00
Becomes:

MOON GIRL FIGHTS CRIME
E.C. Comics, 1949
7 O:Star;The Fiend Who
  Fights With Fire 900.00
8 True Crime Feature 900.00
Becomes:

A MOON, A GIRL ...ROMANCE
Sept.–Oct., 1949
9 AF,Grl,AF(c),C:Moon Girl;
  Spanking Panels 1,200.00
10 AF,Grl,WW,AF(c),Suspicious
  of His Intentions 900.00
11 AF,Grl,WW,AF(c),Hearts
  Along the Ski Trail 900.00
12 AF,Grl,AF(c),
  March–April, 1950 . . . . 1,100.00
Becomes:

WEIRD FANTASY

MOON MULLINS
Michael Publ. (American Comics Group), 1948
1 . . . . 300.00
2 thru 8 . . . . @150.00

Moon Mullins #1
© ACG

MOPSY
St. John Publishing Co.,
Feb., 1948
1 Paper Dolls Enclosed 800.00
2 . . . . 550.00
3 . . . . 550.00
4 Paper Dolls Enclosed 550.00
5 Paper Dolls Enclosed 550.00
6 Paper Dolls Enclosed 550.00
7 . . . . 525.00
8 Paper Dolls Enclosed;
  Lingerie Panels 550.00
9 . . . . 500.00
10 . . . . 500.00
11 . . . . 500.00
12 . . . . 500.00
13 Paper Dolls Enclosed 500.00
14 thru 18 . . . . @500.00
19 Lingerie(c);Paper
  Dolls Enclosed 500.00

MOTION PICTURE COMICS
Fawcett Publications,
Nov., 1950
101 Ph(c),Monte Hale's-
  Vanishing Westerner 450.00
102 Ph(c),Rocky Lane's-Code
  of the Silver Sage 400.00
103 Ph(c),Rocky Lane's-Covered
  Wagon Raid 400.00
104 BP,Ph(c),Rocky Lane's-
  Vigilante Hideout 400.00
105 BP,Ph(c),Audie Murphy's-
  Red Badge of Courage 500.00
106 Ph(c),George Montgomery's-
  The Texas Rangers 450.00
107 Ph(c),Rocky Lane's-Frisco
  Tornado 400.00
108 Ph(c),John Derek's-Mask
  of the Avenger 350.00
109 Ph(c),Rocky Lane's-Rough
  Rider of Durango 375.00
110 GE,Ph(c), When Worlds
  Collide 1,700.00
111 Ph(c),Lash LaRue's-The
  Vanishing Outpost 500.00
112 Ph(c),Jay Silverheels'-
  Brave Warrior 300.00
113 KS,Ph(c),George Murphy's-
  Walk East on Beacon 250.00
114 Ph(c),George Montgomery's-
  Cripple Creek;Jan, 1953 . . . . 250.00

MOTION PICTURES FUNNIES WEEKLY
1st Funnies Incorporated, 1939
1 BEv,1st Sub-Mariner 35,000.00
2 Cover Only 1,500.00
3 Cover Only 1,500.00
4 Cover Only 1,500.00

MOVIE COMICS
Fiction House Magazines,
Dec., 1946
1 Big Town on(c) 800.00
2 MB,White Tie & Tails 550.00
3 MB,Andy Hardy Laugh Hit . . . 550.00
4 MB,Slave Girl 650.00

MOVIE LOVE
Famous Funnies Publ.,
Feb., 1950
1 Ph(c),Dick Powell(c) 250.00
2 Ph(c),Myrna Loy(c) 150.00
3 Ph(c),Cornell Wilde(c) 125.00
4 Ph(c),Paulette Goddard(c) . . . 125.00
5 Ph(e),Joan Fontaine(c) 125.00
6 Ph(c),Ricardo Montalban(c) . . 125.00
7 Ph(c),Fred Astaire(c) 150.00
8 AW,FF,Ph(c),Corinne
  Calvert(c) 700.00
9 Ph(c),John Lund(c) 125.00
10 FF,Ph(c),Mona Freeman(c) . . 700.00
11 Ph(c),James Mason(c) 150.00
12 Ph(c),Jerry Lewis &
  Dean Martin(c) 200.00
13 Ph(c),Ronald Reagan(c) 300.00
14 Ph(c),Janet Leigh,Gene Kelly. 125.00
15 Ph(c),John Payne 125.00
16 Ph(c),Angela Lansbury 150.00
17 Ph(c),Leslie Caron 150.00
18 Ph(c),Cornel Wilde 125.00
19 Ph(c),John Derek 125.00
20 Ph(c),Debbie Reynolds 150.00
21 Ph(c),Patricia Medina 125.00
22 Ph(c),John Payne 125.00

MOVIE THRILLERS
Magazine Enterprises 1949
1 Ph(c),Burt Lancaster's-
  Rope of Sand 375.00

MURDER, INCORPORATED
Fox Features Incorporated,
Jan., 1948–Aug., 1951
1 For Adults Only-on(c) 800.00
2 For Adults Only-on(c);Male
  Bondage(c),Electrocution sty 600.00
3 Dutch Schultz-Beast of Evil . . 350.00
4 The Ray Hamilton Case,
  Lingerie(c) 350.00
5 . . . . 350.00
6 . . . . 350.00
7 . . . . 350.00
8 . . . . 375.00
9 Bathrobe (c) 350.00
9a Lingerie (c) 350.00
10 . . . . 250.00
11 . . . . 250.00
12 . . . . 250.00
13 . . . . 275.00
14 Bill Hale-King of the
  Murderers 250.00
15 . . . . 250.00
16(5),Second Series 200.00
17(2) 200.00
18(3), Bondage(c) with Lingerie. . 300.00

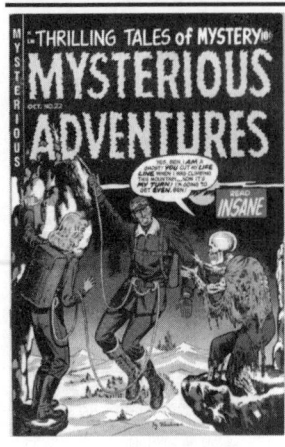

Mysterious Adventures #22
© Story Comics

MURDEROUS GANGSTERS

Avon Periodicals/Realistic, July, 1951
1 WW,Pretty Boy Floyd,
Leggs Diamond 700.00
2 WW,Baby Face Nelson,Mad
Dog Esposito 400.00
3 P(c),Tony & Bud Fenner,
Jed Hawkins 350.00
4 EK(c),Murder By Needle-
Drug Story, June, 1952 . . . . . 400.00

MUTINY

Aragon Magazines, Oct., 1954
1 AH(c),Stormy Tales of the
Seven Seas 200.00
2 AH(c) 150.00
3 Bondage(c),Feb., '55 . . . . 300.00

MY CONFESSION
See: WESTERN TRUE CRIME

MY PAST CONFESSIONS
See: WESTERN THRILLERS

MY SECRET LIFE

Fox Features Syndicate, July, 1949
22 I Loved More Than Once 150.00
23 WW 250.00
24 Love Was a Habit 100.00
25 . . . . 100.00
Becomes:

ROMEO TUBBS
Dec., 1952
26 WW,That Lovable Teen-ager . 250.00

MY SECRET STORY
See: DAGAR, DESERT HAWK

MYSTERIES WEIRD AND STRANGE

Superior Comics/ Dynamic Publ., May, 1953
1 The Stolen Brain 600.00
2 The Screaming Room,
Atomic Bomb 350.00
3 SD,The Avenging Corpse 300.00

---

4 SD,Ghost on the Gallows 300.00
5 SD,Horror a la Mode 300.00
6 SD,Howling Horror 300.00
7 SD,Demon in Disguise 275.00
8 SD,The Devil's Birthmark 275.00
9 SD 275.00
10 SD 300.00
11 SD 300.00

MYSTERIOUS ADVENTURES

Story Comics, March, 1951
1 WJo(c),Wild Terror of the
Vampire Flag 1,100.00
2 Terror of the Ghoul's Corpse . 600.00
3 Terror of the Witche's Curse . . 500.00
4 The Little Coffin That Grew . . . 500.00
5 LC,Curse of the Jungle,
Bondage(c) 600.00
6 LC,Ghostly Terror in the
Cave 500.00
7 LC,Terror of the Ghostly
Castle 700.00
8 Terror of the Flowers of Death . 800.00
9 The Ghostly Ghouls-
Extreme Violence 600.00
10 Extreme Violence 550.00
11 The Trap of Terror 600.00
12 SHn,Vultures of Death-
Extreme Violence 600.00
13 Extreme Violence 600.00
14 Horror of the Flame Thrower
Extreme Violence 600.00
15 DW,Ghoul Crazy 650.00
16 Chilling Tales of Horror 650.00
17 DW,Bride of the Dead 650.00
18 Extreme Violence 650.00
19 The Coffin 650.00
20 Horror o/t Avenging Corpse . 650.00
21 Mother Ghoul's Nursery
Tales, Bondage (c) 650.00
22 RA,Insane 500.00
23 RA,Extreme Violence 500.00
24 KS 400.00
25 KS,Aug., 1955 . . . . 400.00

HORROR FROM THE TOMB

Premier Magazines, Sept., 1954
1 AT,GWb,The Corpse Returns . 600.00
Becomes:

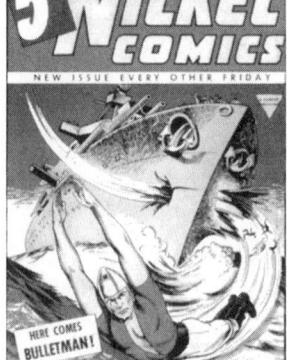

Nickel Comics #1
© Fox Features Syndicate

MYSTERIOUS STORIES

Dec., 1954–Jan., 1955
2 GWb(c),Eternal Life 700.00
3 GWb,The Witch Doctor 450.00
4 That's the Spirit 400.00
5 King Barbarossa 400.00
6 GWb,Strangers in the Night . . 450.00
7 KS,The Pipes of Pan;Dec'55 . . 400.00

MYSTERIOUS TRAVELER COMICS

Trans-World Publications, Nov., 1948
1 BP,BP(c),Five Miles Down 900.00

MYSTERY COMICS

William H. Wise & Co., 1944
1 ASh(c),B:Brad Spencer-Wonderman,
King of Futeria,The Magnet, Zudo-
Jungle Boy,Silver Knight . . . 1,900.00
2 ASh(c),Bondage (c) 1,100.00
3 ASh(c),Robot(c),Lance Lewis,
Brad Spencer, Wonderman 1,000.00
4 ASh(c),E:All Features,
KKK Type(c) 1,000.00

MYSTERY MEN COMICS

Fox Features Syndicate, Aug., 1939
1 GT,DBr,LF(c),I:Blue
Beetle,Green Mask,Rex Dexter
of Mars,Zanzibar,Lt.Drake,D-13
Secret Agent,Chen Chang,
Wing Turner,Capt. Denny 18,000.00
2 GT,BP,DBr,LF(c),
Rex Dexter (c) 6,000.00
3 LF(c) 7,500.00
4 LF(c),B:Captain Savage 4,000.00
5 GT,BP,LF(c),Green Mask . 4,000.00
6 GT,BP 3,500.00
7 GT,BP,Bondage(c),
Blue Beetle(c) 4,500.00
8 GT,BP,LF(c),Bondage(c),
Blue Beetle 3,800.00
9 GT,BP,DBr,B:The Moth . . . 2,000.00
10 GT,BP,JSm(c),A:Wing
Turner; Bondage(c) 1,500.00
11 GT,BP,JSm(c),I:The Domino 1,500.00
12 GT,BP,JSm(c),BlueBeetle(c) 1,500.00
13 GT,I:The Lynx & Blackie . . 1,000.00
14 GT,Male Bondage (c) 950.00
15 GT,Blue Beetle (c) 900.00
16 GT,Hypo(c),MaleBondage(c) . 950.00
17 GT,BP,Blue Beetle (c) 900.00
18 GT,Blue Beetle (c) 900.00
19 GT,I&B:Miss X 1,000.00
20 GT,DBr,Blue Beetle (c) 900.00
21 GT,E:Miss X 900.00
22 GT,CCu(c),Blue Beetle (c) . . . 900.00
23 GT,Blue Beetle (c) 900.00
24 GT,BP,DBr, Blue Beetle (c) . . . 900.00
25 GT,Bondage(c);
A:Private O'Hara 950.00
26 GT,Bondage(c);B:The Wraith . 950.00
27 GT,Bondage(c),BlueBeetle(c). 950.00
28 GT,Bondage(c);Satan's
Private Needlewoman 950.00
29 GT,Bondage(c),Blue
Beetle (c) 950.00
30 Holiday of Death 900.00
31 Bondage(c);Feb'42 . . . . 950.00

MY STORY
See: ZAGO, JUNGLE PRINCE

NANCY AND SLUGGO
See: SPARKLER COMICS

Negro Romance #1
© *Fawcett Publications`*

NAPOLEON AND UNCLE ELBY
Eastern Color Printing, 1942
1 . . . . 650.00

NATIONAL COMICS
**Comics Magazines
(Quality Comics Group),
July, 1940**
1 GT,HcK,LF(c),B:Uncle Sam,
 Wonder Boy,Merlin the Magician,
 Cyclone, Kid Patrol,Sally O'Neil-
 Police-woman, Pen Miller,
 Prop Powers,PaulBunyan 10,000.00
2 WE,GT,HcK,LF&RC(c) 4,200.00
3 GT,HcK,LF,WE&RC(c) 3,000.00
4 GT,HcK,LF&RC(c),E:Cyclone;
 Torpedo Islands of Death . . 3,100.00
5 GT,LF&RC(c),B:Quicksilver;
 O:Uncle Sam 2,800.00
6 GT,LF&RC(c) 2,100.00
7 GT,LF&RC(c) 3,800.00
8 GT,LF&RC(c) 2,100.00
9 JCo,LF&RC(c) 2,100.00
10 RC,JCo,LF&RC(c) 2,100.00
11 RC,JCo,LF&RC(c) 2,100.00
12 RC,JCo,LF&RC(c) 1,600.00
13 RC,JCo,LF,LF&RC(c). 1,500.00
14 RC,JCo,LF,PG,LF&RC(c). . . 1,600.00
15 RC,JCo,LF,PG,LF&RC(c). . . 1,600.00
16 RC,JCo,LF,PG,LF&RC(c). . . 1,600.00
17 RC,JCo,LF,PG,LF&RC(c). . . 1,700.00
18 JCo,LF,PG,LF&RC(c),
 Pearl Harbor. 2,200.00
19 JCo,LF,PG,RC(c),The Black
 Fog Mystery 1,700.00
20 JCo,LF,PG,LF&RC(c) 1,700.00
21 LF,JCo,PG,LF(c). 1,700.00
22 JCo,LF,PG,FGu,GFx,LF(c),
 E:Jack & Jill,Pen Miller,
 Paul Bunyan 1,700.00
23 JCo,PG,FGu,GFx,AMc,LF
 & GFx(c),B:The Unknown,
 Destroyer 171. . . . . 1,800.00
24 JCo,PG,RC,AMc,FGu,
 GFx,RC(c) 1,800.00
25 AMc,RC,JCo,PG,FGu,
 GFx,RC(c) 1,300.00
26 AMc,Jco,RC,PG,RC(c),
 E:Prop Powers,WonderBoy 1,300.00
27 JCo,AMc 1,300.00
28 JCo,AMc 1,300.00
29 JCo,O:The Unknown;U.Sam
 V:Dr. Dirge 1,400.00

30 JCo,RC(c) 900.00
31 JCo,RC(c) 1,000.00
32 JCo,RC(c) 1,000.00
33 JCo,GFx,RC(c),B:Chic Carter;
 U.Sam V:Boss Spring. 1,000.00
34 JCo,GFx,U.Sam V:Big John
 Fales. 1,000.00
35 JCo,GFx,E:Kid Patrol 900.00
36 JCo 900.00
37 JCo,FGu,A:The Vagabond . . . 900.00
38 JCo,FGu,Boat of the Dead . . . 900.00
39 JCo,FGu,Hitler(c);U.Sam
 V:The Black Market 1,300.00
40 JCo,FGu,U.Sam V:The
 Syndicate of Crime 750.00
41 JCo,FGu 750.00
42 JCo,FGu,JCo(c),B:The Barker 600.00
43 JCo,FGu,JCo(c) 600.00
44 JCo,FGu 600.00
45 JCo,FGu,E:Merlin Magician . . 600.00
46 JCo,JCo(c),Murder is no Joke 600.00
47 JCo,JCo(c),E:Chic Carter 600.00
48 JCo,O:The Whistler 600.00
49 JCo,JCo(c),A Corpse
 for a Cannonball 600.00
50 JCo,JCo(c),V:Rocks Myzer . . 600.00
51 JCo,BWa,JCo(c),
 A:Sally O'Neil 700.00
52 JCo,A Carnival of Laughs. . . . 500.00
53 PG,V:Scramolo 500.00
54 PG,V:Raz-Ma-Taz 500.00
55 JCo,AMc,V:The Hawk. 500.00
56 GFx,JCo,AMc,V:The Grifter . . 500.00
57 GFx,JCo,AMc,V:Witch Doctor. 500.00
58 GFz,JCo,AMc,Talking Animals 500.00
59 GFx,JCo,AMc,V:The Birdman. 500.00
60 GFx,JCo,AMc,V:Big Ed Grew 500.00
61 GFx,AMc,Trouble Comes in
 Small Packages. 300.00
62 GFx,AMc,V:Crocodile Man . . . 300.00
63 GFx,AMc,V:Bearded Lady . . . 300.00
64 GFx,V:The Human Fly 300.00
65 GFx,GFx(c)V:The King 300.00
66 GFx,GFx(c)V:The Man Who
 Hates the Circus 300.00
67 GFx,Gfx(c),A:Quicksilver;
 V:Ali Ben Riff Raff 300.00
68 GFx,GFx(c),V:Leo theLionMan 300.00
69 GFx,Gfx(c),A:Percy the
 Powerful. 300.00
70 GFx,GFx(c),Barker Tires
 of the Big Top 300.00
71 PG,GFx(c),V:SpellbinderSmith 300.00
72 PG,GFx(c),The Oldest Man
 in the World 300.00
73 PG,GFx(c),V:A CountrySlicker 300.00
74 PG,GFx(c),V:Snake Oil Sam. . 300.00
75 PG,GFx(c),Barker Breakes the
 Bank at Monte Marlo;Nov'49. 300.00

NAVY HEROES
Almanac Publ. Co., 1945
1 Propaganda 150.00

NAVY PATROL
Key Publications, 1955
1 . . . . 125.00
2 thru 4 . . . . @100.00

NAVY TASK FORCE
**Stanmor Publ./
Aragon Publ., 1953**
1 . . . . 125.00
2 thru 8 . . . . @75.00

NEGRO HEROES
National Urban League, 1947
1 . . . . 1,900.00
2 Jackie Robinson 2,000.00

NEGRO ROMANCE
**Fawcett Publications,
June, 1950**
1 GE,Ph(c), Love's Decoy 1,900.00
2 GE,Ph(c), A Tragic Vow 1,500.00
3 GE,Ph(c), My Love
 Betrayed Me 1,500.00
Charlton Comics
4 Rep.FawcettEd.#2;May,1955 1,200.00

NEW ROMANCES
**Standard Comics,
May, 1951**
5 Ph(c), The Blame I Bore 200.00
6 Ph(c), No Wife Was I 150.00
7 Ph(c), My Runaway Heart,
 Ray Miland 125.00
8 Ph(c) 125.00
9 Ph(c) 125.00
10 ATh,Ph(c) 150.00
11 ATh,Ph(c) of Elizabeth Taylor . 350.00
12 Ph(c) 125.00
13 Ph(c) 125.00
14 ATh,Ph(c) 150.00
15 Ph(c) 125.00
16 ATh,Ph(c) 150.00
17 Ath, ... 150.00
18 and 19. . . . . @125.00
20 GT, ... 125.00
21 April, 1954. . . . . 125.00

NICKEL COMICS
Dell Publishing Co., 1938
1 Bobby & Chip 1,200.00

NICKEL COMICS
**Fawcett Publications,
May, 1940**
1 JaB(c),O&I: Bulletman 7,000.00
2 JaB(c), ... 2,000.00
3 JaB(c), ... 1,500.00
4 JaB(c), B: Red Gaucho 1,300.00
5 CCB(c),Bondage(c) 1,300.00
6 and 7 CCB(c) . . . . @1,200.00
8 CCB(c),Aug. 23, 1940,
 World's Fair 1,400.00

NIGHTMARE
See: WEIRD HORRORS

NIGHTMARE
Ziff-Davis Publishing Co., 1952
1 EK,GT,P(c),The Corpse That
 Wouldn't Stay Dead 900.00
2 EK,P(c),Vampire Mermaid . . . 550.00
St. John Publishing Co.
3 EK,P(c),The Quivering Brain . 450.00
4 P(c),1953 . . . . 350.00

NORTHWEST MOUNTIES
**Jubilee Publications/
St. John Publ. Co.,
Oct., 1948**
1 MB,DLb(c),Rose of the Yukon 700.00
2 MB,BLb(c),A:Ventrilo 550.00
3 MB, Bondage(c) 600.00
4 MB(c),A:Blue Monk,July'49 . . 550.00

NUTS!
**Premere Comics Group,
March, 1954**
1 . . . . 400.00
2 . . . . 300.00
3 Mention of "Reefers" 325.00
4 . . . . 250.00
5 Captain Marvel Spoof;Nov.'54 250.00

GOLDEN AGE

NUTTY COMICS
Harvey Publications, 1945
1 BW,Funny animal 125.00
2 . . . . 125.00
3 . . . . 110.00
4 thru 8 . . . . @75.00

NUTTY LIFE
See: PHANTOM LADY

NYOKA THE JUNGLE GIRL
Fawcett Publications, Winter, 1945
2 Bondage(c);Partial Ph(c) of
   Kay Aldridge as Nyoka 800.00
3 . . . . 450.00
4 Bondage(c) 500.00
5 Barbacosi Madness;
   Bondage(c) 500.00
6 . . . . 275.00
7 North Pole Jungle;
   Bondage(c) 400.00
8 Bondage(c) 400.00
9 . . . . 250.00
10 . . . . 250.00
11 Danger! Death! in an
   Unexplored Jungle 250.00
12 . . . . 225.00
13 The Human Leopards 250.00
14 The Mad Witch Doctor;
   Bondage(c) 400.00
15 Sacred Goat of Kristan 225.00
16 BK,The Vultures of Kalahari . . 250.00
17 BK 250.00
18 BK,The Art of Murder 250.00
19 The Elephant Battle 250.00
20 Explosive Volcano Action . . . 250.00
21 . . . . 175.00
22 The Weird Monsters 175.00
23 Danger in Duplicate 175.00
24 The Human Jaguar;
   Bondage(c) 400.00
25 Hand Colored Ph(c) 150.00
26 A Jungle Stampede 150.00
27 Adventure Laden 150.00
28 The Human Statues of
   the Jungle 150.00
29 Ph(c) 150.00
30 Ph(c) 150.00
31 thru 40 Ph(c) . . . . @125.00
41 thru 50 Ph(c) . . . . @135.00
51 thru 59 Ph(c) . . . . @100.00
60 Ph(c) 100.00
61 Ph(c),The Sacred Sword of
   the Jungle 100.00
62 & 63 Ph(c) . . . . @100.00
64 Ph(c), The Jungle Idol 100.00
65 Ph(c) 100.00
66 Ph(c) 100.00
67 Ph(c), The Sky Man 100.00
68 thru 74 Ph(c) . . . . @100.00
75 Ph(c), The Jungle Myth
   of Terror 100.00
76 Ph(c) 100.00
77 Ph(c),The Phantoms of the
   Elephant Graveyard;Jun'53 . . 100.00

OAKY DOAKS
Eastern Color Printing Co., July, 1942
1 Humor Oriented 450.00

OKAY COMICS
United Features Syndicate, 1940
1 . . . . 650.00

OK COMICS
United Features Syndicate, July, 1940
1 B:Pal Peyton,Little Giant, Phantom
   Knight,Sunset Smith,Teller Twins,
   Don Ramon, Jerrry Sly,Kip Jaxon,
   Leatherneck,Ulysses 1,200.00
2 O:Master Mist,Oct., 1940 . . . 1,300.00

OKLAHOMA KID
Ajax/Farrell Publ., 1957
1 . . . . 150.00
2 . . . . 125.00
3 . . . . 125.00
4 . . . . 125.00

100 PAGES OF COMICS
Dell Publishing Co., 1937
101 Alley Oop,OG,Wash Tubbs,
   Tom Mix,Dan Dunn 2,500.00

ON THE AIR
NBC Network Comics, 1947
1 Giveaway, no cover 300.00

ON THE SPOT
Fawcett Publications, Autumn, 1948
N# Bondage(c),PrettyBoyFloyd . . 450.00

OPERATION PERIL
American Comics Group (Michel Publ.), Oct.–Nov., 1950
1 LSt,OW,OW(c),B:TyphoonTyler,
   DannyDanger,TimeTravellers 600.00
2 OW,OW(c),War (c) 350.00
3 OW,OW(c),Horror 300.00
4 OW,OW(c), Flying Saucers . . . 350.00
5 OW,OW(c), Science Fiction . . . 350.00
6 OW, Tyr. Rex 275.00
7 OW,OW(c),Sabretooth 275.00
8 OW,OW(c) 250.00
9 OW,OW(c) 250.00
10 OW,OW(c),science fiction 275.00
11 OW,OW(c), War 250.00
12 OW,OW(c),E:Time Travellers . 250.00
13 OW,OW(c),War Stories 150.00
14 OW,OW(c),War Stories 150.00
15 OW,OW(c),War Stories 150.00
16 OW,OW(c),April–May,1953,
   War Stories 150.00

OUR FIGHTING MEN IN ACTION
Ajax/Farrell, 1957
1 . . . . 125.00
2 thru 6 . . . . @100.00

OUR FLAG COMICS
Ace Magazines, Aug., 1941–April, 1942
1 MA,JM,B:Capt.Victory,Unknown
   Soldier,The Three Cheers . 3,900.00
2 JM,JM(c),O:The Flag 1,700.00
3 Tank Battle (c) 1,300.00
4 MA 1,300.00
5 I:Mr. Risk, Male Bondage . . . 1,400.00

OUR GANG COMICS
Dell Publishing Co., Sept.–Oct., 1942
1 WK,Barney Bear, Tom &
   Jerry 1,700.00
2 WK 750.00
3 WK,Benny Burro 500.00
4 WK 500.00

5 WK 550.00
6 WK 750.00
7 WK 400.00
8 WK,CB,Benny Burro 1,000.00
9 WK,CB,Benny Burro 900.00
10 WK,CB,Benny Burro 650.00
11 WK,I:Benny Bear 900.00
12 thru 20 WK . . . . @400.00
21 thru 29 WK . . . . @300.00
30 WK,Christmas(c) 250.00
31 thru 34 WK . . . . @250.00
35 WK,CB 200.00
36 WK,CB 200.00
37 thru 40 WK . . . . @125.00
41 thru 50 WK . . . . @100.00
51 thru 56 WK . . . . @100.00
57 . . . . 100.00
58 Our Gang 100.00
59 Our Gang 100.00

Tom & Jerry #83
© Dell Publishing Co.

Becomes:

TOM AND JERRY
July, 1949
60 . . . . 200.00
61 . . . . 150.00
62 . . . . 100.00
63 . . . . 100.00
64 . . . . 100.00
65 . . . . 100.00
66 Christmas (c) 120.00
67 thru 70 . . . . @125.00
71 thru 76 . . . . @125.00
77 Christmas (c) 125.00
78 thru 80 . . . . @125.00
81 thru 89 . . . . @100.00
90 Christmas (c) 125.00
91 thru 99 . . . . @100.00
100 . . . . 125.00
101 thru 120 . . . . @100.00
121 thru 150 . . . . @100.00
151 thru 212 . . . . @100.00

OUTER SPACE
See: CHARLIE CHAN

OUTLAWS
D.S. Publishing Co., Feb.–March, 1948
1 HcK,Western Crime Stories . . 500.00
2 Grl,Doc Dawson's Dilema . . . 500.00
3 Cougar City Cleanup 200.00
4 JO,Death Stakes A Claim 250.00
5 RJ,RJ(c),Man Who Wanted
   Mexico 200.00

6 AMc,RJ,RJ(c),The Ghosts of
Crackerbox Hill 200.00
7 Grl,Dynamite For Boss Cavitt . 350.00
8 Grl,The Gun & the Pen 350.00
9 FF,Shoot to Kill;June–
July, 1949 . . . . 700.00

WHITE RIDER AND SUPER HORSE
**Star Publications,
Sept., 1950**
1 LbC(c) 250.00
2 LbC(c) 200.00
3 LbC(c) 200.00
4 LbC(c) 200.00
5 LbC(c),Stampede of Hard
Riding Thrills 225.00
6 LbC(c),Drums of the Sioux . . . 225.00
Becomes:

INDIAN WARRIORS
June, 1951
7 LbC(c),Winter on the Great
Plains 250.00
8 LbC(c) 225.00
Becomes:

Outlaws #3
© DS Publishing

WESTERN CRIME CASES
Dec., 1951
9 LbC(c),The Card Sharp Killer . 275.00
Becomes:

OUTLAWS, THE
May, 1952
10 LbC(c),Federated Express . . . 275.00
11 LbC(c),Frontier Terror!!! 225.00
12 LbC(c),Ruthless Killer!!! 225.00
13 LbC(c),The Grim Avengers. . . 225.00
14 AF,JKa,LbC(c),Trouble in
Dark Canyon,April, 1954. . . . 225.00

OUT OF THE NIGHT
**American Comics Group/
Best Synd. Feature,
Feb.–March, 1952**
1 AW 1,000.00
2 AW 700.00
3 . . . . 400.00
4 AW 550.00
5 . . . . 400.00
6 The Ghoul's Revenge 400.00

7 . . . . 400.00
8 The Frozen Ghost 400.00
9 Death Has Wings,
Science Fiction 400.00
10 Ship of Death 400.00
11 . . . . 275.00
12 Music for the Dead 275.00
13 HN,From the Bottom of
the Well 275.00
14 Out of the Screen 275.00
15 The Little Furry Thing 250.00
16 Nightmare From the Past 250.00
17 The Terror of the Labyrinth . . . 250.00
Becomes:

HOODED HORSEMAN
Dec., 1954–Jan., 1955
18 B: The Hooded Horseman . . . 125.00
19 The Horseman's Strangest
Adventure 175.00
20 OW,O:Johnny Injun. 125.00
21 OW,OW(c). 175.00
22 OW 125.00
23 . . . . 125.00
24 . . . . 125.00
25 . . . . 100.00
26 O&I:Cowboy Sahib 125.00
27 Jan.–Feb., 1953 . . . . 110.00

OUT OF THE SHADOWS
**Visual Editions
(Standard Comics),
July, 1952–Aug., 1954**
5 ATh,GT,The Shoremouth
Horror 900.00
6 ATh,JKz,Salesman of Death . . 600.00
7 JK,Plant of Death 400.00
8 Mask of Death 800.00
9 RC,Till Death Do Us Part 400.00
10 MSy,We Vowed,Till Death
Do Us Part. 400.00
11 ATh,Fountain of Fear. 400.00
12 ATh,Hand of Death 600.00
13 MSy,The Cannibal 400.00
14 ATh,The Werewolf. 400.00

OXYDOL-DREFT
**Giveaways, 1950
The Set is More Valuable if the
Original Envelope is Present**
1 L'il Abner 150.00
2 Daisy Mae 150.00
3 Shmoo 200.00
4 AW&FF(c),John Wayne 200.00
5 Archie 200.00
6 Terry Toons Comics 150.00

OZARK IKE
**Visual Editions
(Standard Comics), 1948**
11 . . . . 175.00
12 thru 20 . . . . @100.00
21 thru 25 . . . . @100.00

OZZIE AND BABS
**Fawcett Publications,
Winter, 1946**
1 Humor Oriented, Teenage 150.00
2 Humor Oriented 100.00
3 thru 12 Humor Oriented . . . @100.00
13 Humor Oriented;1949 . . . . . . 100.00

PAGEANT OF COMICS
**St. John Publishing Co.,
Sept., 1947**
1 Rep. Mopsy 150.00
2 Rep. Jane Arden,Crime
Reporter. 150.00

Out of the Night #12
© American Comics

PANHANDLE PETE AND JENNIFER
**J. Charles Lave
Publishing Co., July, 1951**
1 (fa) 125.00
2 (fa) 100.00
3 (fa),Nov.'51 . . . . 100.00

PANIC
**Tiny Tot Publications
(E.C. Comics), March, 1954
"Humor in a Jugular Vein"**
1 BE,JKa,JO,JDa,AF(c) 750.00
2 BE,JO,WW,JDa,A:Bomb 400.00
3 BE,JO,BW,WW,JDa,AF(c) . . . 300.00
4 BE,JO,WW,JDa,BW(c),
Infinity(c) 300.00
5 BE,JO,WW,JDa,AF(c) 250.00
6 BE,JO,WW,JDa,Blank (c) 250.00
7 BE,JO,WW,JDa 250.00
8 BE,JO,WW,JDa,Eye Chart (c). 200.00
9 BE,JO,WW,JDa,Ph(c),
Confidential(c) 500.00
10 BE,JDa, Postal Package(c) . . 350.00
11 BE,WW,JDa,Wheaties parody
as Weedies (c) 300.00
12 BE,WW,JDa,JDa(c);
Dec.–Jan., 1955–56 . . . . 300.00

PARAMOUNT ANIMATED COMICS
**Family Publications
(Harvey Publ.), June, 1953**
1 (fa),B:Baby Herman & Katnip,
Baby Huey,Buzzy the Crow . 300.00
2 (fa) 150.00
3 (fa) 100.00
4 thru 6 (fa) . . . . @100.00
7 (fa), Baby Huey (c) 300.00
8 (fa), Baby Huey (c) 100.00
9 (fa), Infinity(c),Baby Huey (c) . . 100.00
10 thru 21 (fa),Baby Huey(c) . . @100.00
22 (fa), July, 1956, Baby Huey (c) 100.00

PAROLE BREAKERS
**Avon Periodicals/Realistic,
Dec., 1951–July, 1952**
1 P(c),Hellen Willis,Gun
Crazed Gun Moll 650.00
2 JKu,P(c),Vinnie Sherwood,
The Racket King 400.00
3 EK(c),John "Slicer" Berry,
Hatchetman of Crime 350.00

GOLDEN AGE

PATCHES

**Rural Home Publ./
Patches Publ.,
March–April, 1945**

1 LbC(c),Imagination In Bed(c). . 600.00
2 Dance (c). 225.00
3 Rocking Horse (c) 200.00
4 Music Band (c). 200.00
5 LbC(c),A:Danny Kaye,Football 275.00
6 A: Jackie Kelk 200.00
7 A: Hopalong Cassidy 225.00
8 A: Smiley Burnettte 175.00
9 BK,A: Senator Claghorn 175.00
10 A: Jack Carson 175.00
11 A: Red Skeleton; Dec'47. . . . . 200.00

PAT THE BRAT

**Radio Comics (Archie
Publications), 1955–59**

1 . . . . 175.00
2 . . . . 150.00
3 . . . . 125.00
4 . . . . 125.00
15 thru 20. . . . . @75.00
21 thru 33 . . . . @75.00

PAUL TERRY'S COMICS

**See: TERRY-TOONS
COMICS**

PAWNEE BILL

**Story Comics,
Feb.–July, 1951**

1 A:Bat Masterson,Wyatt Earp,
Indian Massacre
at Devil's Gulch 150.00
2 Blood in Coffin Canyon 100.00
3 LC,O:Golden Warrior,Fiery
Arrows at Apache Pass. . . . 100.00

PAY-OFF

**D.S. Publishing Co.,
July–Aug., 1948–
March–April, 1949**

1 True Crime 1 & 2 . . . . 350.00
2 The Pennsylvania Blue-Beard 250.00
3 The Forgetful Forger 200.00
4 RJ(c),Lady and the Jewels . . 200.00
5 The Beautiful Embezzeler 200.00

PEDRO

**Fox Features Syndicate,
Jan., 1950**

1 WW,WW(c),Humor Oriented . 300.00
2 Aug., 1950 . . . . 200.00

PENNY

Avon Publications, 1947

1 The Slickest Chick of 'em All . 200.00
2 . . . . 100.00
3 America's Teen-age
Sweetheart 100.00
4 . . . . 100.00
5 . . . . 100.00
6 Perry Como Ph(c),Sept.–
Oct., 1949 . . . . 125.00

PEP COMICS

**MJL Magazines/
Archie Publications,
Jan., 1940**

1 IN,JCo,MMe,IN(c),I:Shield,
O:Comet,Queen of Diamonds,
B:The Rocket,Press Guardian,
Sergeant Boyle Chang,Bently
of Scotland Yard. . 19,000.00
2 CBi,JCo,IN,IN(c),O:Rocket . . 4,500.00
3 JCo,IN,IN(c),Shield (c) 3,000.00

4 Cbi,JCo,MMe,IN,IN(c),
C:Wizard(not Gareb) 2,400.00
5 Cbi,JCo,MMe,IN,IN(c),
C:Wizard. 2,400.00
6 IN,IN(c), Shield (c) 1,800.00
7 IN,IN(c),Bondage(c),Shield(c)1,800.00
8 JCo,IN, Shield (c) 1,800.00
9 IN, Shield (c). 1,800.00
10 IN,IN(c), Shield (c) 1,800.00
11 MMe,IN,IN(c),I:Dusty,
Boy Detective 2,000.00
12 IN,IN(c),O:Fireball
Bondage(c), E:Rocket,
Queen of Diamonds 2,200.00
13 IN,IN(c),Bondage(c). 1,500.00
14 IN,IN(c). 1,500.00
15 IN,Bondage(c) 1,500.00
16 IN,O:Madam Satan 2,400.00
17 IN,IN(c),O:Hangman,
D:Comet. 6,500.00
18 IN,IN(c),Bondage(c) 1,500.00
19 IN 1,500.00
20 IN,IN(c),Fireball 1,500.00
21 IN,IN(c),Bondage(c),
E: Madam Satan. 1,500.00
22 IN,IN(c)I:Archie,
Jughead, Betty 35,000.00
23 IN,IN(c). 3,500.00
24 IN,IN(c). 2,300.00
25 IN,IN(c). 2,300.00
26 IN,IN(c),I:Veronica. 3,500.00
27 IN,IN(c),Bill of Rights (c) . . . 1,800.00
28 IN,IN(c), V:Capt. Swastika . . 1,900.00
29 ASh (c). 1,800.00
30 B:Capt.Commando 1,800.00
31 Bondage(c) 1,800.00
32 Bondage(c) 1,500.00
33 . . . . 1,500.00
34 Bondage(c) 1,500.00
35 . . . . 1,500.00
36 1st Archie(c). 4,000.00
37 Bondage(c) 1,000.00
38 ASh(c) 1,000.00
39 ASh(c), Human Shield 1,000.00
40 . . . . 1,000.00
41 2nd Archie; I:Jughead. 750.00
42 F:Archie & Jughead 750.00
43 F:Archie & Jughead 750.00
44 . . . . 750.00
45 . . . . 750.00
46 . . . . 750.00
47 E:Hangman,Infinity(c) 750.00
48 B:Black Hood 750.00
49 . . . . 750.00
50 . . . . 750.00

Peter Rabbit Comics #1
© Avon Periodicals

51 . . . . 450.00
52 B:Suzie 450.00
53 . . . . 450.00
54 E:Captain Commando 450.00
55 . . . . 450.00
56 thru 58 . . . . @400.00
59 E:Suzie 400.00
60 B:Katy Keene 400.00
61 . . . . 350.00
62 I L'il Jinx 350.00
63 . . . . 350.00
64 . . . . 350.00
65 E:Shield. 350.00
66 thru 71 . . . . @250.00
72 thru 80. . . . . @200.00
81 thru 90 . . . . @150.00
91 thru 99 . . . . @125.00
100 . . . . 200.00
101 thru 110 . . . . @125.00
111 thru 120 . . . . @100.00
121 thru 130 . . . . @125.00
131 thru 140 . . . . @100.00
141 thru 150 . . . . @100.00
151 thru 160,A:Super Heroes . @100.00

PERFECT CRIME, THE

**Cross Publications,
Oct., 1949**

1 BP,DW 450.00
2 BP 250.00
3 . . . . 225.00
4 BP 225.00
5 DW 225.00
6 . . . . 225.00
7 B:Steve Duncan 225.00
8 Drug Story 300.00
9 . . . . 200.00
10 . . . . 200.00
11 Bondage (c) 300.00
12 . . . . 200.00
13 . . . . 200.00
14 Poisoning (c). 350.00
15 'The Most Terrible Menace,'
Drug. 300.00
16 . . . . 150.00
17 . . . . 150.00
18 Drug (c). 400.00
19 . . . . 150.00
20 thru 25 . . . . @125.00
26 Drug w/ Hypodermic (c) 400.00
27 . . . . 150.00
28 . . . . 150.00
29 . . . . 150.00
30 E:Steve Duncan, Rope
Strangulation (c) 400.00
31 . . . . 125.00
32 . . . . 125.00
33 . . . . 125.00

PETER PAUL'S 4 IN 1 JUMBO COMIC BOOK

Capitol Stories, 1953

1 F: Racket Squad in Action,
Space Adventures,Crime &
Justice,Space Western 500.00

PETER PENNY AND HIS MAGIC DOLLAR

American Bakers Assn., 1947

1 History from Colonial
America to the 1950's 200.00
2 . . . . 125.00

PETER RABBIT

Avon Periodicals, 1947

1 HCa 450.00
2 HCa 325.00
3 HCa 275.00
4 HCa 275.00

5 HC 275.00
6 HCa 275.00
7 thru 10 . . . . @100.00
11 . . . . 100.00

KRAZY LIFE
Fox Features Syndicate, 1945
1 (fa) 100.00
Becomes:

NUTTY LIFE
Summer, 1946
2 (fa) 100.00
Becomes:

WOTALIFE
**Fox Features Synd./
Green Publ., Aug.–Sept., 1946**
3 (fa)B:L'il Pan,Cosmo Cat 150.00
4 . . . . 100.00
5 thru 11 . . . . @100.00
12 July, 1947 . . . . 100.00
9a rep (1959) 100.00
Becomes:

PHANTOM LADY
**Fox Features Syndicate,
Aug., 1947**
13(#1) MB,MB(c) Knights of
    the Crooked Cross 7,500.00
14(#2) MB,MB(c) Scoundrels
    and Scandals 3,900.00
15 MB,MB(c) The Meanest
    Crook In the World 3,900.00
16 MB,MB(c) Claa Peete The
    Beautiful Beast, Negligee . . 3,900.00
17 MB.MB(c) The Soda Mint
    Killer, Bondage (c) 12,000.00
18 MB,MB(c) The Case of
    Irene Shroeder 2,500.00
19 MB,MB(c) The Case of
    the Murderous Model 2,500.00
20 MB,MB(c) Ace of Spades. . . 2,200.00
21 MB,MB(c). 2,200.00
22 MB,JKa 2,200.00
23 MB,JKa Bondage (c) 2,400.00
Becomes:

MY LOVE SECRET
June, 1949
24 JKa, My Love Was For Sale. . 250.00
25 Second Hand Love 150.00
26 WW I Wanted Both Men 250.00
27 I Was a Love Cheat 125.00
28 WW, I Gave Him Love 250.00
29 . . . . 125.00
30 Ph(c) 125.00

LINDA
Ajax/Farrell, April–May, 1954
1 . . . . 200.00
2 Lingerie section 150.00
3 . . . . 100.00
4 Oct.–Nov.,1954 . . . . 100.00
Becomes:

PHANTOM LADY
Dec., 1954–Jan., 1955
5(1) MB 1,700.00
2 Last Pre-Code Edition 1,300.00
3 Comics Code 1,000.00
4 Red Rocket,June, 1955 . . . . 1,000.00

PHIL RIZZUTO
Fawcett Publications, 1951
Ph(c) The Sensational Story of
    The American League MVP 1,150.00

PICTURE CRIMES
1937
1 . . . . 1,500.00

PICTURE NEWS
**299 Lafayette Street Corp.,
Jan., 1946–Jan.-Feb., 1947**
1 Will The Atom Blow The
    World Apart 750.00
2 Meet America's 1st Girl Boxing
    Expert,Atomic Bomb 500.00
3 Hollywood's June Allison Shows
    You How to be Beautiful,
    Atomic Bomb 400.00
4 Amazing Marine Who Became
    King of 10,000 Voodoos,
    Atomic Bomb 450.00
5 G.I.Babies,Hank Greenberg. . 400.00
6 Joe Louis(c) 450.00
7 Lovely Lady, Englands
    Future Queen 350.00
8 Champion of them All 350.00
9 Bikini Atom Bomb,
    Joe DiMaggio 400.00
10 Dick Quick, Ace Reporter,
    Atomic Bomb 400.00

PICTURE PARADE
Gilberton Co., 1953
1 A-Bomb 300.00
2 United Nations 150.00
3 American Indians 150.00
4 Christmas issue 150.00
Becomes:

PICTURE PROGRESS
Gilberton Co., 1954
5 1953 News 100.00
6 Birth of America 100.00
7 Four Seasons 100.00
8 Paul Revere 100.00
9 Hawaian Islands 100.00
10 Flight 100.00
11 thru 20 . . . . @100.00

PICTURE SCOPE
JUNGLE ADVENTURES
Star Publications, 1954
7 LbC(c) 700.00

PICTURE STORIES FROM
AMERICAN HISTORY
E.C. Comics, 1946–47
1 . . . . 600.00
2 thru 4 . . . . @450.00

PICTURE STORIES
FROM SCIENCE
**Educational Comics,
Spring, 1947**
1 Understanding Air and Water . 500.00
2 Fall '47 Amazing Discoveries
    About Food & Health 400.00

PICTURE STORIES
FROM WORLD HISTORY
E.C. Comics, Spring, 1947
1 Ancient World to the
    Fall of Rome 400.00
2 Europes Struggle for
    Civilization 375.00

PINHEAD AND
FOODINI
**Fawcett Publications,
July, 1951–Jan., 1952**
1 Ph(c) 400.00
2 Ph(c) 250.00
3 Ph(c) Too Many Pinheads 150.00
4 Foodini's Talking Camel 150.00

PIN-UP PETE
Toby Publishers, 1952
1 Loves of a GI Casanova 250.00

PIONEER PICTURE
STORIES
**Street & Smith Publ.,
Dec., 1941**
1 Red Warriors in Blackface 400.00
2 Life Story Of Errol Flynn 350.00
3 Success Stories of Brain
    Muscle in Action 250.00
4 Legless Ace & Boy Commando
    Raid Occupied France 250.00
5 How to Tell Uniform and
    Rank of Any Navy Man 250.00
6 General Jimmy Doolittle 300.00
7 Life Story of Admiral Halsey . . 300.00
8 Life Story of Timoshenko 250.00
9 Dec., '43,Man Who Conquered
    The Wild Frozen North 250.00

Piracy #2
© EC Comics

PIRACY
E.C. Comics, Oct.–Nov., 1954
1 WW,JDa,AW,WW(c),RC,AT . . 650.00
2 RC,JDa(c),WW,AW,AT. 500.00
3 RC,GE, RC(c),Grl 400.00
4 RC,GE,RC(c),Grl 350.00
5 RC,GE,BK(c),Grl 350.00
6 JDa,RC,GE,BK(c),Grl 350.00
7 Oct Nov GE(c),RC,GE,Grl . . . 350.00

PIRATES COMICS
Hillman Periodicals, Feb., 1950
1 . . . . 350.00
2 . . . . 250.00
3 . . . . 200.00
4 Aug–Sept., 1950 . . . . 200.00

PIXIES, THE
**Magazine Enterprises,
Winter, 1946**
1 Mighty Atom 150.00
2 thru 5 . . . . @100.00
Becomes:

MIGHTY ATOM, THE
1949
6 . . . . 125.00

PLANET COMICS
Love Romance Publ.
(Fiction House Magazines),
Jan., 1940–Winter, 1953

1 AB,DBr,HcK, Planet Comics,
  WE&LF,O:Aura,B:Flint Baker,
  Red Comet,Spurt Hammond,
  Capt. Nelson Cole 24,000.00
2 HcK,LF(c) 8,000.00
3 WE(c),HcK 5,000.00
4 HcK,B:Gale Allan and
  the Girl Squad 4,500.00
5 BP,HcK 4,000.00
6 BP,HcK,BP(c),The Ray
  Pirates of Venus 4,000.00
7 BP,AB,HcK,BP(c) B:Buzz
  Crandall Planet Payson ... 3,200.00
8 BP,AB HcK 3,200.00
9 BP,AB,GT,HcK,B:Don
  Granville Cosmo Corrigan . 3,200.00
10 BP,AB,GT HcK 3,200.00
11 HcK, B:Crash Parker 3,200.00
12 Dri,B:Star Fighter 3,200.00
13 Dri,B:Reef Ryan 2,300.00
14 Dri B:Norge Benson 2,300.00
15 B: Mars,God of War 5,000.00
16 Invasion From The Void ... 2,200.00
17 Warrior Maid of Mercury ... 2,200.00
18 Bondage(c) 2,300.00
19 Monsters of the Inner
  World 2,200.00
20 RP, Winged Man Eaters
  of the Exile Star 2,200.00
21 RP,B:Lost World
  Hunt Bowman 2,300.00
22 Inferno on the Fifth Moon .. 2,200.00
23 GT,Lizard Tyrant of
  the Twilight World 2,000.00
24 GT,Grl Raiders From
  The Red Moon 2,000.00
25 Grl,B:Norge Benson 2,000.00
26 Grl,B:The Space Rangers
  Bondage(c) 2,100.00
27 Grl, The Fire Eaters of
  Asteroid Z 1,600.00
28 Grl, Bondage (c) 2,200.00
29 Grl,Dragon Raiders of Aztla. 2,600.00
30 GT,Grl City of Lost Souls ... 2,000.00
31 Grl,Fire Priests of Orbit6X . 1,600.00
32 Slaver's Planetoid 1,700.00
33 MA 1,600.00
34 MA,Bondage 1,700.00
35 MA B:Mysta of The Moon .. 1,600.00
36 MA Collosus of the
  Blood Moon 1,600.00
37 MA, Behemoths of the
  Purple Void 1,600.00
38 MA 1,400.00
39 MA.Death Webs Of Zenith 3 1,400.00
40 Chameleon Men from
  Galaxy 9 .... 1,400.00
41 MA,AgF,New O: Auro
  Bondage (c) 1,400.00
42 MA,AgF,E:Gale Allan 1,400.00
43 MA,AgF Death Rays
  From the Sun.. .... 1,400.00
44 MA,Bbl,B:Futura 1,400.00
45 Ma,Bbl,Her Evilness
  from Xanado 1,400.00
46 MA,Bbl,GE The Mecho-Men
  From Mars 1,400.00
47 MA,Bbl,GE,The Great
  Green Spawn 1,100.00
48 MA,GE 1,100.00
49 MA,GE, Werewolves From
  Hydra Hell. 1,100.00
50 MA,GE,The Things of Xeves 1,100.00
51 MA,GE, Mad Mute X-Adapts 1,000.00
52 GE,Mystery of the Time
  Chamber. 1,000.00
53 MB,GE,Bondage(c)
  Dwarflings From Oceania .. 1,000.00

54 MB,GE,Robots From Inferno 1,000.00
55 MB,GE,Giants of the
  Golden Atom. 1,000.00
56 MB,GE,Grl 900.00
57 MB,GE,Grl 900.00
58 MB,GE,Grl 900.00
59 MB,GE,Grl,LSe. 900.00
60 GE,Grl,Vassals of Volta ... 900.00
61 GE,Grl, The Brute in the
  Bubble 800.00
62 GE,Musta,Moon Goddess ... 800.00
63 GE,Paradise or Inferno 800.00
64 GE,Monkeys From the Blue . 800.00
65 The Lost World 800.00
66 The Plague of the
  Locust Men 800.00
67 The Nymphs of Neptune 800.00
68 Synthoids of the 9th Moon ... 800.00
69 The Mentalists of Mars 800.00
70 Cargo For Amazonia 800.00
71 Sandhogs of Mars. 700.00
72 Last Ship to Paradise 700.00
73 The Martian Plague 700.00

PLASTIC MAN
Comics Magazines
(Quality Comics Group),
Summer, 1943–Nov., 1956

1 JCo(a&c)Game of Death ... 7,500.00
2 JCo(a&c)The Gay Nineties
  Nightmare 2,700.00
3 JCo(a&c). 1,800.00
4 JCo(a&c). 1,500.00
5 JCo(a&c). 1,400.00
6 JCo(a&c). 1,500.00
7 JCo(a&c). 1,500.00
8 JCo(a&c). 1,500.00
9 JCo(a&c). 1,500.00
10 JCo(a&c) 1,500.00
11 JCo(a&c) 1,500.00
12 JCo(a&c),V:Spadehead 1,500.00
13 JCo(a&c),V:Mr.Hazard 1,500.00
14 JCo(a&c),Words,Symbol
  of Crime 1,500.00
15 JCo(a&c),V:BeauBrummel.. 1,500.00
16 JCo(a&c),Money
  Means Trouble 1,500.00
17 JCo(a&c),A:The Last
  Man on Earth 1,200.00
18 JCo(a&c),Goes Back
  to the Farm 1,200.00
19 JCo(a&c),V:Prehistoric
  Plunder 1,200.00
20 JCo(a&c),A:Sadly,Sadly.... 1,200.00

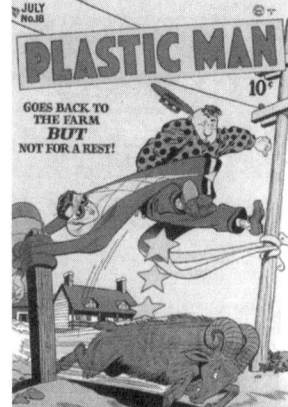

Plastic Man-18
© Quality Comics

21 JCo(a&c),V:Crime Minded
  Mind Reader 800.00
22 JCo(a&c), Which Twin
  is the Phony. 800.00
23 JCo(a&c),The Fountain
  of Age 800.00
24 JCo(a&c),The Black Box
  of Terror 800.00
25 JCo(a&c),A:Angus
  MacWhangus 800.00
26 JCo(a&c),On the Wrong
  Side of the Law? 800.00
27 JCo(a&c),V:The Leader 800.00
28 JCo(a&c),V:Shasta 800.00
29 JCo(a&c),V:Tricky Toledo 800.00
30 JCo(a&c),V:Weightless
  Wiggins 800.00
31 JCo(a&c),V:Raka the
  Witch Doctor 600.00
32 JCo(a&c),V:Mr.Fission 600.00
33 JCo(a&c),V:The Mad
  Professor 600.00
34 JCo(a&c),Smuggler'sHaven . 600.00
35 JCo(a&c),V:The Hypnotist ... 600.00
36 JCo(a&c),The Uranium
  Underground 600.00
37 JCo(a&c),V:Gigantic Ants 600.00
38 JCo(a&c),The Curse of
  Monk Mauley 600.00
39 JCo(a&c),The Stairway
  to Madness 600.00
40 JCo(a&c),The Ghoul of
  Ghost Swamp 600.00
41 JCo(a&c),The Beast with
  the Bloody Claws. 500.00
42 JCo(a&c),The King of
  Thunderbolts 500.00
43 JCo(a&c),The Evil Terror 500.00
44 JCo(a&c),The Magic Cup 500.00
45 The Invisible Raiders 500.00
46 V:The Spider. 500.00
47 The Fiend of a
  Thousand Faces 500.00
48 Killer Crossbones 500.00
49 JCo,The Weapon for Evil 500.00
50 V:Iron Fist 500.00
51 Incredible Sleep Weapon 500.00
52 V:Indestructible Wizard 500.00
53 V:Dazzia,Daughter of
  Darkness 500.00
54 V:Dr.Quomquat 500.00
55 The Man Below Zero 500.00
56 JCo, The Man Who Broke
  the Law of Gravity 500.00
57 The Chemist's Cauldron 500.00
58 JCo,The Amazing
  Duplicating Machine 500.00
59 JCo,V:The Super Spy 500.00
60 The Man in the Fiery
  Disguise. 450.00
61 V:King of the Thunderbolts ... 450.00
62 V:The Smokeweapon 450.00
63 V:Reflecto 450.00
64 The Invisible Raiders 450.00

PLAYFUL LITTLE AUDREY
Harvey Publications, 1957

1 .... 450.00
2 .... 250.00
3 .... 135.00
4 .... 135.00
5 .... 135.00
6 thru 9 .... @100.00
10 thru 30 .... @100.00

POCAHONTAS
Pocahontas Fuel Co.,
Oct., 1941

N# 300.00
2 .... 275.00

POCKET COMICS
Harvey Publications, Aug., 1941

1 100 pages,O:Black Cat,Spirit of '76,Red Blazer Phantom Sphinx & Zebra,B:Phantom Ranger,British Agent #99, Spin Hawkins,Satan 1,500.00
2 . . . . 1,000.00
3 . . . . 750.00
4 Jan.'42,All Features End 750.00

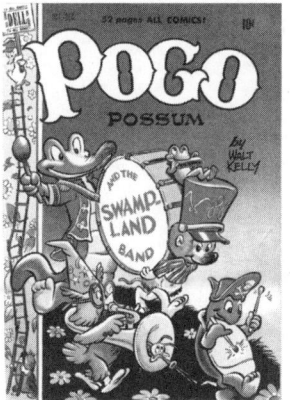

Pogo Possum #1
© Dell Publishing

POGO POSSUM
Dell Publishing Co., 1949

1 WK,A:Swamp Land Band . . . 1,500.00
2 WK 1,000.00
3 WK 600.00
4 WK 600.00
5 WK 600.00
6 thru 10 WK . . . . @450.00
11 WK, Christmas (c) . . . . @400.00
12 thru 16 WK . . . . @500.00

POLICE AGAINST CRIME
Premier Magazines, 1954

1 JyD,Knife in Face 400.00
2 . . . . 200.00
3 . . . . 150.00
4 thru 9 . . . . @150.00

POLICE COMICS
Comic Magazines (Quality Comics Group), Aug., 1941

1 JCo,WE.PGv,RC,FGu,AB, GFx(a&c),B&O:Plastic Man The Human Bomb,#711,I&B, Chic Canter,The Firebrand Mouthpiece,Phantom Lady The Sword 15,000.00
2 JCo,PGv,WE,RC,FGu, GFx(a&c) 5,500.00
3 JCo,PGv,WE,RC,FGu, GFx(a&c) 3,500.00
4 JCo,GFx,PGv,WE,RC,FGu, GFx&WEC(c) 3,000.00
5 JCo,PGv,WE,RC,FGu, GFx(a&c) 3,000.00
6 JCo,PGv,WE,RC,FGu, GFx(a&c) 2,500.00
7 JCo,PGv,WE,RC,FGu, GFx(a&c) 2,500.00
8 JCo,PGv,WE,RC,FGu, GFx(a&c),B&O:Manhunter 3,000.00

9 JCo,PGv,WE,RC,FGu, GFx(a&c) 2,000.00
10 JCo,PGv,WE,RC,FGu, GFx(a&c) 2,000.00
11 JCo,PGv,WE,RC,FGu,GFx(a&c), B:Rep:Rep.Spirit Strips 4,000.00
12 JCo,GFx,PGv,WE,FGu,AB, RC(c) I:Ebony 2,000.00
13 JCo,GFx,PGv,WE,FGu,AB,RC(c) E:Firebrand,I:Woozy Winks 2,000.00
14 JCo,PGv,WE,Jku,GFx(a&c) . 1,500.00
15 JCo,PGv,WE,Jku,GFx(a&c) E#711,B:Destiny 1,500.00
16 JCo,PGv,WE,JKu 1,500.00
17 PGv,WE,JKu,JCo(a&c) 1,500.00
18 PGv,WE,JCo(a&c) 1,500.00
19 PGv,WE,JCo(a&c) 1,500.00
20 PGv,WE,JCo(a&c),A:Jack Cole in Phantom Lady 1,500.00
21 PGv,WE,JCo(a&c) 1,400.00
22 PGv,WE,RP,JCo(a&c) The Eyes Have it 1,400.00
23 WE,RP,JCo(a&c),E:Phantom Lady 1,200.00
24 WE,HK,JCo(a&c),B:Flatfoot Burns 1,200.00
25 WE,HK,RP,JCo(a&c),The Bookstore Mysrery 1,200.00
26 WE,Hk,JCo(a&c)E:Flatfoot Burns 1,200.00
27 WE,JCo(a&c) 1,200.00
28 WE,JCo(a&c) 1,200.00
29 WE,JCo(a&c) 1,200.00
30 WE,JCo(a&c),A Slippery Racket 1,200.00
31 WE,JCo(a&c),Is Plastic Man Washed Up? 1,000.00
32 WE,JCo(a&c),Fiesta Turns Into a Fracas 1,000.00
33 JCo,WE 1,000.00
34 WE,JCo(a&c) 1,000.00
35 WE,JCo(a&c) 1,000.00
36 WE,JCo(a&c),Rest In Peace 1,000.00
37 WE,PGv,JCo(a&c),Love Comes to Woozy 1,000.00
38 WE,PGv,JCo(a&c) 1,000.00
39 WE,PGv,JCo(a&c) 1,000.00
40 WE,PGv,JCo(a&c) 1,000.00
41 WE,PGv,JCo(a&c),E:Reps. of Spirit Strip 900.00
42 LF&WE,PGv,JCo(a&c), Woozy Cooks with Gas 900.00
43 LF&WE,PGv,JCo(a&c) 900.00
44 PGv,LF,JCo(a&c) 900.00
45 PGv,LF,JCo(a&c) 900.00
46 PGv,LF,JCo(a&c) 900.00
47 PGv,LF,JCo(a&c),V:Dr.Slicer . 900.00
48 PGv,LF,JCo(a&c),V:Big Beaver 900.00
49 PGv,LF,JCo(a&c),V:Thelma Twittle 900.00
50 PGv,LF,JCo(a&c) 900.00
51 PGv,LF,JCo(a&c),V:The Granite Lady 700.00
52 PGv,LF,JCo(a&c) 700.00
53 PGv,LF,JCo(a&c),V:Dr. Erudite 700.00
54 PGv,LF,JCo(a&c) 700.00
55 PGv,LF,JCo(a&c),V:The Sleepy Eyes 700.00
56 PGv,LF,JCo(a&c),V:The Yes Man 700.00
57 PGv,LF,JCo(a&c),V:Mr.Misfit . . 700.00
58 PGv,LF,JCo(a&c),E:The Human Bomb 700.00
59 PGv,LF,JCo(a&c),A:Mr. Happiness 700.00
60 PGv,LF,JCo(a&c) 500.00
61 PGv,LF,JCo(a&c) 500.00
62 PGv,LF,JCo(a&c) 500.00
63 PGv,LF,JCo(a&c),V:The Crab 500.00

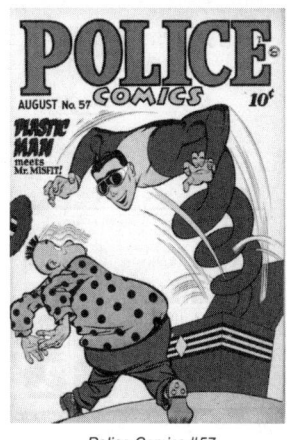

Police Comics #57
© Quality Comics Group

64 PGv,LF,HK,JCo(a&c) 500.00
65 PGv,LF,JCo(a&c) 500.00
66 PGv,LF,JCo(a&c) Love Can Mean Trouble 500.00
67 LF,JCo(a&c), V:The Gag Man 500.00
68 LF,JCo(a&c) 500.00
69 LF,JCo(a&c),V:Strecho 500.00
70 LF,JCo(a&c) 500.00
71 LF,JCo(a&c) 400.00
72 LF,JCo(a&c),V:Mr.Cat 400.00
73 LF,JCo(a&c) 400.00
74 LF,JCo(a&c),V:Prof.Dimwit . . . 400.00
75 LF,JCo(a&c) 400.00
76 LF,JCo(a&c),V:Mr.Morbid . . . 400.00
77 LF,JCo(a&c),V:Skull Face & Eloc 400.00
78 LF,JCo(a&c),A Hot Time In Dreamland 400.00
79 LF,JCo(a&c),V:Eaglebeak . . . 400.00
80 LF,JCo(a&c),V:Penetro 400.00
81 LF,JCo(a&c),V:A Gorilla 400.00
82 LF,JCo(a&c) 400.00
83 LF,JCo(a&c) 400.00
84 LF,JCo(a&c) 400.00
85 LF,JCo(a&c),V:Lucky 7 . . . . . . 400.00
86 LF,JCo(a&c),V:The Baker 400.00
87 LF,JCo(a&c) 400.00
88 LF,JCo(a&c),V:The Seen 400.00
89 JCo(a&c),V:The Vanishers . . . 350.00
90 LF,JCo(a&c),V:Capt.Rivers . . . 350.00
91 JCo(a&c),The Forest Primeval 400.00
92 LF,JCo(a&c),V:Closets Kennedy 400.00
93 JCo(a&c),V:The Twinning Terror 350.00
94 JCo(a&c),WE 600.00
95 JCo(a&c),WE,V:Scowls 600.00
96 JCo(a&c),WE,V:Black Widow . 600.00
97 JCo(a&c),WE,V:The Mime . . . 600.00
98 JCo(a&c),WE 600.00
99 JCo(a&c),WE 600.00
100 JCo(a&c) 700.00
101 JCo(a&c) 700.00
102 JCo(a&c),E:Plastic Man 700.00
103 JCo,LF,B&I:Ken Shannon; Bondage(c) 550.00
104 The Handsome of Homocide 350.00
105 Invisible Hands of Murder . . . 350.00
106 Museum of Murder 350.00
107 Man with the Shrunken Head 350.00
108 The Headless Horse Player . 350.00
109 LF,Bondage(c),Blood on the Chinese Fan 350.00
110 Murder with a Bang 350.00

111 Diana, Homocidal Huntress . 350.00
112 RC,The Corpse on the
      Sidewalk 400.00
113 RC(a&c), The Dead Man
      with the Size 13 Shoe 400.00
114 The Terrifying Secret of
      the Black Bear. 350.00
115 Don't Let Them Kill Me 350.00
116 Stage Was Set For Murder . . 350.00
117 Bullet Riddled Bookkeeper . . 350.00
118 Case of the Absent Corpse. . 350.00
119 A Fast & Bloody Buck 350.00
120 Death & The Derelict 350.00
121 Curse of the Clawed Killer . . 350.00
122 The Lonely Hearts Killer . . . 350.00
123 Death Came Screaming 350.00
124 Masin Murder 350.00
125 Bondage(c),The Killer of
      King Arthur's Court 400.00
126 Hit & Run Murders 350.00
127 Oct'53,Death Drivers 350.00

POLICE LINE-UP
Avon Periodicals/
Realistic Comics, Aug., 1951
1 WW,P(c). 550.00
2 P(c),Drugs 400.00
3 JKu,EK,P(c) 300.00
4 July, '52;EK 300.00

POLICE TRAP
Mainline, Sept., 1954
1 S&K(c). 400.00
2 S&K(c) 250.00
3 S&K(c) 250.00
4 S&K(c) 250.00

Charlton Comics, July, 1955
5 S&K,S&K(c) 350.00
6 S&K,S&K(c) 350.00
Becomes:

PUBLIC DEFENDER
IN ACTION
Charlton Comics, March, 1956
7 . . . . 150.00
8 and 9 . . . . @100.00
10 thru 12, ... @100.00

POPEYE
Dell Publishing Co., 1948
1 . . . . 600.00
2 . . . . 300.00
3 'Welcome to Ghost Island'. . . . 225.00
4 thru 10 . . . . @225.00
11 . . . . 200.00
12 . . . . 200.00
13 . . . . 200.00
14 thru 20 . . . . @200.00
21 thru 30 . . . . @150.00
31 thru 40 . . . . @135.00
41 thru 45 . . . . @125.00
46 O:Swee' Pea 150.00
47 thru 50 . . . . @125.00
51 thru 65 . . . . @100.00

POPULAR COMICS
Dell Publishing Co.,
Feb., 1936
1 Dick Tracy, Little Orphan
   Annie 9,000.00
2 Terry Pirates 4,000.00
3 Terry,Annie,Dick Tracy 3,000.00
4 . . . . 2,000.00
5 B:Tom Mix 2,000.00
6 I:Scribbu 1,800.00
7 . . . . 1,500.00
8 Scribbu & Reg Fellers 1,500.00
9 . . . . 1,500.00
10 Terry,Annie,Tracy 1,500.00

Popeye #1
© Dell Publishing Co.

11 Terry,Annie,Tracy 1,200.00
12 Christmas(c). 1,200.00
13 Terry,Annie,Tracy 1,200.00
14 Terry,Annie,Tracy 1,200.00
15 Terry,Annie,Tracy 1,200.00
16 Terry,Annie,Tracy 1,200.00
17 Terry,Annie,Tracy 1,200.00
18 Terry,Annie,Tracy 1,200.00
19 Terry,Annie,Tracy 1,200.00
20 Terry,Annie,Tracy 1,200.00
21 Terry,Annie,Tracy 900.00
22 Terry,Annie,Tracy 900.00
23 Terry,Annie,Tracy 900.00
24 Terry,Annie,Tracy 900.00
25 Terry,Annie,Tracy 900.00
26 Terry,Annie,Tracy 900.00
27 E:Terry,Annie,Tracy. 900.00
28 A:Gene Autry. 700.00
29 . . . . 700.00
30 . . . . 700.00
31 A:Jim McCoy 750.00
32 A:Jim McCoy 750.00
33 . . . . 750.00
34 . . . . 750.00
35 Christmas(c),Tex Ritter 750.00
36 . . . . 750.00
37 . . . . 750.00
38 B:Gang Busters 750.00
39 . . . . 600.00
40 . . . . 600.00
41 . . . . 600.00
42 . . . . 600.00
43 F:Gang Busters. 600.00
44 . . . . 500.00
45 Tarzan(c). 500.00
46 O:Martan the Marvel Man . . . 600.00
47 F:Martan the Marvel Man . . . 500.00
48 F:Martan the Marvel Man . . . 500.00
49 F:Martan the Marvel Man . . . 500.00
50 . . . . 500.00
51 B&O:Voice. 500.00
52 A:Voice 550.00
53 F:The Voice. 450.00
54 F:Gang Busters,A:Voice 450.00
55 F:Gang Busters. 450.00
56 F:Gang Busters. 450.00
57 F:The Marvel Man. 450.00
58 F:The Marvel Man. 450.00
59 F:The Marvel Man. 450.00
60 O:Prof. Supermind 450.00
61 Prof. Supermind & Son. 350.00
62 Supermind & Son 350.00
63 B:Smilin' Jack 350.00
64 Smilin'Jack,Supermind 350.00
65 Professor Supermind 350.00
66 . . . . 350.00
67 Gasoline Alley 350.00

68 F:Smilin' Jack 350.00
69 F:Smilin' Jack 350.00
70 F:Smilin' Jack 350.00
71 F:Smilin' Jack 350.00
72 B:Owl,Terry & the Pirates 550.00
73 F:Terry and the Pirates 400.00
74 F:Smilin' Jack 400.00
75 F:Smilin'Jack,A:Owl 400.00
76 Captain Midnight. 500.00
77 Captain Midnight. 500.00
78 Captain Midnight. 500.00
79 A:Owl 350.00
80 F:Smilin' Jack,A:Owl 350.00
81 F: Terry&thePirates,A:Owl . . . 350.00
82 F:Smilin' Jack,A:Owl 350.00
83 F:Smilin' Jack,A:Owl 350.00
84 F:Smilin' Jack,A:Owl 350.00
85 F:ThreeLittleGremlins,A:Owl . . 350.00
86 F:Three Little Gremlins 250.00
87 F:Smilin' Jack 250.00
88 F:Smilin' Jack 250.00
89 F:Smokey Stover 250.00
90 F:Terry and the Pirates 250.00
91 F:Smokey Stover 250.00
92 F:Terry and the Pirates 250.00
93 F:Smilin' Jack 250.00
94 F:Terry and the Pirates 250.00
95 F:Smilin' Jack 250.00
96 F:Gang Busters. 250.00
97 F:Smilin' Jack 250.00
98 B:Felix Cat 250.00
99 F:Bang Busters 250.00
100 . . . . 275.00
101 thru 141 . . . . @175.00
142 E:Terry & the Pirates. 125.00
143 . . . . 125.00
144 . . . . 125.00
145 F:Harold Teen 125.00

POWER COMICS
Holyoke/Narrative Publ., 1944
1 LbC(c). 2,200.00
2 B:Dr.Mephisto,Hitler(c) 2,300.00
3 LbC(c) 2,500.00
4 LbC(c) 2,200.00

PRIDE OF THE
YANKEES
Magazine Enterprises, 1949
1 N#,OW,Ph(c),The Life
   of Lou Gehrig 1,400.00

PRISON BREAK
Avon Periodicals/Realistic,
Sept., 1951
1 WW(c),WW 600.00
2 WW(c),WW,JKu 400.00
3 JD,JO. 350.00
4 EK 275.00
5 EK,CI 275.00

PRIZE COMICS
Feature Publications
(Prize Publ.), March, 1940
1 O&B:Power Nelson,Jupiter.
   B:Ted O'Neil,Jaxon of
   the Jungle,Bucky Brady,
   Storm Curtis, Rocket(c) . . . 5,000.00
2 B:The Owl 2,500.00
3 Power Nelson(c). 2,100.00
4 Power Nelson(c) 2,100.00
5 A:Dr.Dekkar. 1,500.00
6 A:Dr.Dekkar. 1,500.00
7 S&K,DBr,JK(c),O&B DR Frost,
   Frankenstein,B:GreenLama,
   Capt Gallant,Voodini
   Twist Turner 3,500.00
8 S&K,DBr 1,800.00
9 S&K,DBr,Black Owl(c) 1,700.00
10 DBr,Black Owl(c) 1,500.00

GOLDEN AGE

11 DBr,O:Bulldog Denny 1,200.00	
12 DBr. 1,200.00	
13 DBr,O&B:Yank and	
Doodle,Bondage(c). 1,400.00	
14 DBr,Black Owl(c) 1,200.00	
15 DBr,Black Owl(c) 1,200.00	
16 DBr,JaB,B:Spike Mason. . . . 1,200.00	
17 DBr,Black Owl(c) 1,200.00	
18 DBr,Black Owl(c) 1,200.00	
19 DBr,Yank&Doodle(c) 1,200.00	
20 DBr,Yank&Doodle(c) 1,200.00	
21 DBr,JaB(c),Yank&Doodle(c) . . 900.00	
22 DBr,Yank&Doodle(c). 900.00	
23 DBr,Uncle Sam(c). 900.00	
24 DBr,Abe Lincoln(c) 900.00	
25 DBr,JaB,Yank&Doodle(c) 900.00	
26 DBr,JaB,JaB(c),Liberty	
Bell(c) 900.00	
27 DBr,Yank&Doodle(c). 700.00	
28 DBr,Yank&Doodle(c). 600.00	
29 DBr,JaB(c)Yank&Doodle(c). . . 600.00	
30 DBr,Yank&Doodle(c). 700.00	
31 DBr,Yank&Doodle(c). 600.00	
32 DBr,Yank&Doodle(c). 600.00	
33 DBr,Bondage(c),Yank	
& Doodle 700.00	
34 DBr,O:Airmale;New	
Black Owl 700.00	
35 DBr,B:Flying Fist & Bingo 500.00	
36 DBr,Yank&Doodle(c). 500.00	
37 DBr,I:Stampy,Hitler(c) 550.00	
38 DBr,B.Owl,Yank&Doodle(c) . . 500.00	
39 DBr,B.Owl,Yank&Doodle(c) . . 500.00	
40 DBr,B.Owl,Yank&Doodle(c) . . 500.00	
41 DBr,B.Owl,Yank&Doodle(c) . . 500.00	
42 DBr,B.Owl,Yank&Doodle(c) . . 300.00	
43 DBr,B.Owl,Yank&Doodle(c) . . 300.00	
44 DBr, B&I:Boom Boom	
Brannigan 300.00	
45 DBr 300.00	
46 DBr 300.00	
47 DBr 300.00	
48 DBr,B:Prince Ra;Bondage(c) . 400.00	
49 DBr,Boom Boom(c). 300.00	
50 DBr,Frankenstein(c) 300.00	
51 DBr 300.00	
52 DBr, B:Sir Prize. 300.00	
53 DBr, The Man Who Could	
Read Features. 300.00	
54 DBr 300.00	
55 DBr,Yank&Doodle(c). 300.00	
56 DBr,Boom Boom (c) 300.00	
57 DBr,Santa Claus(c). 300.00	
58 DBr,The Poisoned Punch 300.00	
59 DBr,Boom Boom(c). 300.00	
60 DBr,Sir Prise(c). 300.00	
61 DBr,The Man wih the	
Fighting Feet 300.00	
62 DBr,Hck(c),Yank&Doodle(c) . . 300.00	
63 DBr,S&K(c),S&K(c),Boom	
Boom(c). 350.00	
64 DBr,Blackowl Retires 250.00	
65 DBr,DBr(c),Frankenstein. 250.00	
66 DBr,DBr(c),Frankenstein. 250.00	
67 DBr,B:Brothers in Crime 250.00	
68 DBr,RP(c) 250.00	
Becomes:	

PRIZE COMICS
WESTERN
Feature Publ., April–May, 1948

69 ACa(c),B:Dusty Ballew 175.00	
70 ACa(c). 150.00	
71 ACa(c). 150.00	
72 ACa(c),JSe 150.00	
73 ACa(c). 150.00	
74 ACa(c). 150.00	
75 JSe,S&K(c),6-Gun Showdown	
at Rattlesnake Gulch 160.00	
76 Ph(c),Randolph Scott 175.00	
77 Ph(c),JSe,Streets of	
Laredo,movie. 160.00	

78 Ph(c),JSe,HK,Bullet	
Code, movie 250.00	
79 Ph(c),JSe,Stage to	
China, movie 250.00	
80 Ph(c),Gunsmoke Justice. 175.00	
81 Ph(c),The Man Who Shot	
Billy The Kid 175.00	
82 Ph(c),MBi,JSe&BE,Death	
Draws a Circle. 175.00	
83 JSe,S&K(c) 150.00	
84 JSe 125.00	
85 JSe,B:American Eagle 325.00	
86 JSe 150.00	
87 JSe&BE 150.00	
88 JSe&BE. 150.00	
89 JSe&BE. 150.00	
90 JSe&Be 150.00	
91 JSe&BE,JSe&BE(c) 150.00	
92 JSe,JSe&BE(c) 150.00	
93 JSe,JSe&BE(c), ... 150.00	
94 JSe&BE,JSe&BE(c) 150.00	
95 JSe,JSe&BE(c) 150.00	
96 JSe,JSe&BE,JSe&BE(c). 150.00	
97 JSe,JSe&BE,JSeBE(c). 150.00	
98 JSe&BE,JSe&BE(c) 150.00	
99 JSe&BE,JSe&BE(c) 150.00	
100 JSe,JSe(c) 175.00	
101 JSe 150.00	
102 JSe 150.00	
103 JSe 150.00	
104 JSe 150.00	
105 JSe 150.00	
106 JSe 100.00	
107 JSe 100.00	
108 JSe 110.00	
109 JSe&AW 125.00	
110 JSe&BE. 125.00	
111 JSe&BE 125.00	
112 . . . . 100.00	
113 AW&JSe 125.00	
114 MMe,B:The Drifter. 100.00	
115 MMe 100.00	
116 MMe 100.00	
117 MMe 100.00	
118 MMe,E:The Drifter. 100.00	
119 Nov/Dec'56 . . . . 100.00	

PRIZE MYSTERY
Key Publications, 1955

1 . . . . 125.00	
2 . . . . 100.00	
3 . . . . 100.00	

PSYCHOANALYSIS
E.C. Comics,
March–April, 1955

1 JKa,JKa(c). 350.00	
2 JKa,JKa(c). 275.00	
3 JKa,JKa(c). 250.00	
4 JKa,JKa(c) Sept.–Oct., 1955. . 250.00	

PUBLIC DEFENDER
IN ACTION
See: POLICE TRAP

PUBLIC ENEMIES
D.S. Publishing Co., 1948

1 AMc 350.00	
2 AMc 300.00	
3 AMc 200.00	
4 AMc 200.00	
5 AMc 200.00	
6 AMc 175.00	
7 AMc,Eye Injury. 200.00	
8 . . . . 175.00	
9 . . . . 175.00	

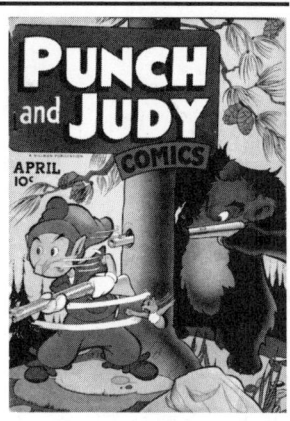

Punch and Judy 4
© Hillman Periodicals

PUNCH AND JUDY
COMICS
Hillman Periodicals, 1944

1 (fa) 300.00	
2 . . . . 250.00	
3 . . . . 200.00	
4 thru 12 . . . . @175.00	
2-1 . . . . 150.00	
2-2 JK. 300.00	
2-3 . . . . 150.00	
2-4 . . . . 150.00	
2-5 . . . . 150.00	
2-6 . . . . 150.00	
2-7 . . . . 150.00	
2-8 . . . . 150.00	
2-9 . . . . 150.00	
2-10 JK. 300.00	
2-11 JK. 300.00	
2-12 JK. 300.00	
3-1 JK. 300.00	
3-2 . . . . 275.00	
3-3 . . . . 100.00	
3-4 . . . . 100.00	
3-5 . . . . 100.00	
3-6 . . . . 100.00	
3-7 . . . . 100.00	
3-8 . . . . 100.00	
3-9 . . . . 100.00	

PUNCH COMICS
Harry 'A' Chesler, Dec., 1941

1 B:Mr.E,The Sky Chief,Hale	
the Magician,Kitty Kelly . . . 2,500.00	
2 A:Capt.Glory 2,000.00	
3-8 Do Not Exist	
9 B:Rocket Man & Rocket	
girl,Master Ken 2,000.00	
10 JCo,A:Sky Chief 1,200.00	
11 JCo,O:Master Key,A:Little	
Nemo 1,200.00	
12 A:Rocket Boy,Capt.Glory . . . 4,000.00	
13 Ric(c) 1,200.00	
14 GT. 900.00	
15 FSm(c) 900.00	
16 . . . . 900.00	
17 . . . . 900.00	
18 FSm(c),Bondage(c),Drug. . . 1,200.00	
19 FSm(c) 900.00	
20 Women semi-nude(c) 1,600.00	
21 Drug 1,200.00	
22 I:Baxter,Little Nemo 500.00	
23 A:Little Nemo 500.00	

GOLDEN AGE

PUPPET COMICS
Dougherty, Co., Spring, 1946
1 Funny Animal 150.00
2 . . . . 125.00

PURPLE CLAW, THE
Minoan Publishing Co./
Toby Press, Jan., 1953
1 O:Purple Claw 450.00
2 and 3 . . . . @300.00

Queen of the West Dale Evans #20
© Dell Publishing Co.

QUEEN OF THE WEST, DALE EVANS
Dell Publishing Co.,
July, 1953
(1) *see Dell Four Color #479*
(1) *see Dell Four Color #528*
3 ATh, Ph(c) all 150.00
4 ATh,RsM 135.00
5 RsM 125.00
6 RsM 125.00
7 RsM 125.00
8 RsM 125.00
9 RsM 125.00
10 RsM. 125.00
11 . . . . 90.00
12 RsM. 100.00
13 RsM. 100.00
14 RsM. 100.00
15 RsM. 100.00
16 RsM. 100.00
17 RsM. 100.00
18 RsM. 100.00
19 . . . . 90.00
20 RsM. 100.00
21 . . . . 90.00
22 RsM. 100.00

RACKET SQUAD IN ACTION
Capitol Stories/
Charlton Comics,
May–June, 1952
1 Carnival(c) 400.00
2 . . . . 200.00
3 Roulette 200.00
4 FFr(c) 350.00
5 Just off the Boat 300.00
6 The Kidnap Racket 200.00
7 . . . . 150.00
8 . . . . 150.00
9 2 Fisted fix 150.00
10 Explosion Blast (c) 250.00

---

11 SD(a&c),Racing(c) 425.00
12 JoS,SD(c),Explosion(c). 900.00
13 JoS(c),The Notorious Modelling
    Agency Racket,Acid 150.00
14 DG(c),Drug 200.00
15 Photo Extortion Racket. 150.00
16 thru 28 . . . . @150.00
29 March, 1958 . . . . 150.00

RAGGEDY ANN AND ANDY
Dell Publishing Co., 1946
1 Billy & Bonnie Bee 650.00
2 . . . . 350.00
3 DNo,B:Egbert Elephant 350.00
4 DNo,WK 400.00
5 DNo 300.00
6 DNo 300.00
7 Little Black Sambo 300.00
8 . . . . 300.00
9 . . . . 300.00
10 . . . . 300.00
11 thru 20 . . . . @250.00
21 Alice in Wonderland 300.00
22 thru 27 . . . . @200.00
28 WK 225.00
29 thru 39. . . . . @200.00

RAGS RABBIT
Harvey Publications, 1957
11 . . . . 75.00
12 thru 18. . . . . @60.00

RALPH KINER HOME RUN KING
Fawcett Publications, 1950
1 N#, Life Story of the
    Famous Pittsburgh Slugger 1,000.00

RAMAR OF THE JUNGLE
Toby Press/
Charlton Comics, 1954
1 Ph(c),TV Show. 300.00
2 Ph(c) 200.00
3 . . . . 200.00
4 . . . . 200.00
5 Sept '56 . . . . 200.00

RANGE BUSTERS
Charlton Comics, 1955
8 . . . . 100.00
9 & 10 . . . . @75.00

RANGE ROMANCES
Comics Magazines
(Quality Comics), Dec., 1949
1 PGv(a&c) 350.00
2 RC(a&c) 350.00
3 RC,Ph(c) 300.00
4 RC,Ph(c) 250.00
5 RC,PGv,Ph(c) 250.00

RANGERS OF FREEDOM
Flying Stories, Inc.
(Fiction House), Oct., 1941
1 I:Ranger Girl & Rangers
    of Freedom;V:Super-Brain . 5,500.00
2 V:Super -Brain 1,700.00
3 Bondage(c) The Headsman
    of Hate 1,300.00
4 Hawaiian Inferno 1,000.00
5 RP,V:Super-Brain 1,000.00
6 RP,Bondage(c);Bugles
    of the Damned 1,000.00
7 RP,Death to Tojo's Butchers . . 750.00
Becomes:

RANGERS COMICS
Dec., 1942
8 RP,B:US Rangers 750.00
9 GT,BLb,Commando Steel
    for Slant Eyes 750.00
10 BLb,Bondage (c). 750.00
11 Raiders of the
    Purple Death 700.00
12 A:Commando Rangers 700.00
13 Grl,B:Commando Ranger. . . . 800.00
14 Grl,Bondage(c) 850.00
15 GT,Grl,Bondage(c) 850.00
16 Grl,GT;Burma Raid 600.00
17 GT,GT,Bondage(c),Raiders
    of the Red Dawn 750.00
18 GT. 600.00
19 GE,BLb,GT,Bondage(c) 750.00
20 GT. 600.00
21 GT,Bondage(c) 650.00
22 GT,B&O:Firehair 500.00
23 GT,BLb,B:Kazanda 450.00
24 Bondage(c) 450.00
25 Bondage(c) 450.00
26 Angels From Hell 400.00
27 Bondage(c) 500.00
28 BLb,E:Kazanda;B&O Tiger
    Man 450.00
29 Bondage(c) 500.00
30 BLb,B:Crusoe Island. 450.00
31 BLb,Bondage(c) 400.00
32 BLb 400.00
33 BLb,Drug. 550.00
34 BLb 300.00
35 BLb,Bondage(c) 400.00
36 BLb,MB 300.00
37 BLb,Mb 350.00
38 BLb,MB,GE,Bondage(c) 400.00
39 BLb,GE 500.00
40 BLb,GE,BLb(c) 300.00
41 BLb,GE, L:Werewolf Hunter . 300.00
42 BLb,GE 300.00
43 BLb,GE 300.00
44 BLb,GE 300.00
45 BLb,GEl. 300.00
46 BLb,GE 300.00
47 BLb,JGr, Dr. Drew. 300.00
48 BLb,JGr, L:Glory Forces 300.00
49 BLb,JGr. 300.00
50 BLb,JGr,Bondage(c) 350.00
51 BLb,JGr. 300.00
52 BLb,JGr,Bondage(c) 350.00
53 BLb,JGr,Prisoners of
    Devil Pass 250.00
54 JGr,When The Wild
    Commanches Ride 250.00

Rangers Comics #33
© Fiction House

---

55 JGr,Massacre Guns at
Pawnee Pass 250.00
56 JGr, Gun Smuggler of
Apache Mesa 250.00
57 JGr,Redskins to the
Rescue 225.00
58 JGr,Brides of the
Buffalo Men 225.00
59 JGr,Plunder Portage 225.00
60 JGr, Buzzards of
Bushwack Trail 225.00
61 BWh(c)Devil Smoke at
Apache Basin 200.00
62 BWh(c)B:Cowboy Bob 200.00
63 BWh(c) 200.00
64 BWh(c)B:Suicide Smith 200.00
65 BWh(c):Wolves of the
Overland Trail,Bondage(c) .. 225.00
66 BWh(c) 200.00
67 BWh(c)B:Space Rangers 200.00
68 BWh(c);Cargo for Coje 200.00
69 BWh(c);Great Red Death Ray 200.00

REAL CLUE
CRIME STORIES
See: CLUE COMICS

REAL FUNNIES
Nedor Publishing Co.,
Jan., 1943
1 (fa) 400.00
2 and 3 (fa) .... @200.00

REAL HEROES COMICS
Parents' Magazine Institiute,
Sept., 1941
1 HcK,Franklin Roosevelt 450.00
2 J, Edgar Hoover 250.00
3 General Wavell 200.00
4 Chiang Kai Shek, Churchill ... 225.00
5 Stonewall Jackson 250.00
6 Lou Gehrig 300.00
7 Chennault and his
Flying Tigers 250.00
8 Admiral Nimitz 250.00
9 The Panda Man 200.00
10 Carl Akeley-Jungle
Adventurer 200.00
11 Wild Jack Howard 200.00
12 General Robert L
Eichelberger 200.00
13 HcK,Victory at Climback 200.00
14 Pete Gray 200.00
15 Alexander Mackenzie 200.00
16 Balto of Nome Oct '46 ...... 200.00

REAL LIFE STORY
OF FESS PARKER
Dell Publishing Co., 1955
1 .... 150.00

REAL LIFE COMICS
Visual Editions/Better/
Standard/Nedor, Sept., 1941
1 ASh(c),Lawrence of
Arabia,Uncle Sam(c) 1,200.00
2 ASh(c),Liberty(c) 450.00
3 Adolph Hitler(c) 2,000.00
4 ASh(c)Robert Fulton,
Charles DeGaulle, Old Glory. 300.00
5 ASh(c)Alexander the Great ... 300.00
6 ASh(c)John Paul Jones,CDR . 250.00
7 ASh(c)Thomas Jefferson 250.00
8 Leonardo Da Vinci 250.00
9 US Coast Guard Issue 250.00
10 Sir Hubert Wilkens 250.00
11 ASh(c),Odyssey on a Raft. ... 225.00
12 ASh(c),ImpossibleLeatherneck 225.00
13 ASh(c)The Eternal Yank 225.00

14 ASh(c),Sir Isaac Newton. 225.00
15 ASh(c),William Tell 225.00
16 ASh(c),Marco Polo 225.00
17 ASh(c),Albert Einstein 225.00
18 ASh(c),Ponce De Leon 225.00
19 ASh(c),The Fighting Seabees. 225.00
20 ASh(c),Joseph Pulitzer 225.00
21 ASh(c),Admiral Farragut 225.00
22 ASh(c),Thomas Paine 225.00
23 ASh(c),Pedro Menendez 225.00
24 ASh(c),Babe Ruth 350.00
25 ASh(c),CQ,Marcus Whitman. . 200.00
26 ASh(c),CQ,Benvenuto Cellini . 200.00
27 ASh(c),CQ,A-Bomb Story 300.00
28 ASh(c),CQ,Robert Blake 200.00
29 ASh(c),CQ,Daniel DeFoe,
A-Bomb 250.00
30 ASh(c),CQ,Baron Robert Clive 200.00
31 ASh(c),CQ,Anthony Wayne .. 200.00
32 ASh(c),CQ,Frank Sinatra ... 225.00
33 ASh(c),CQ,Frederick Douglas 175.00
34 ASh(c),CQ,P Revere,J.Stewart 200.00
35 ASh(c),CQ,Rudyard Kipling . 175.00
36 ASh(c),CQ,Story of the
Automobile. 175.00
37 ASh(c),CQ,Francis Manion,
Motion Picture, Bing Crosby . 175.00
38 ASh(c),CQ,Richard Henry
Dana 175.00
39 ASh(c),CQ,Samuel FB Morse. 175.00
40 FGu,CQ,ASh(c),Hans Christian
Anderson, Bob Feller 250.00
41 CQ,Abe Lincoln,Jimmy Foxx . 200.00
42 Joseph Conrad,Fred Allen ... 175.00
43 Louis Braille,O.W.Holmes 150.00
44 Citizens of Tomorrow 150.00
45 ASh(c),FrancoisVillon,
Olympics, Burl Ives 200.00
46 ASh(c),The Pony Express. ... 200.00
47 ASh(c),Montezuma, Gershwin 200.00
48 ASh(c) 200.00
49 ASh(c),Gene Bearden,
Baseball. 200.00
50 FF,ASh(c),Lewis & Clark. 500.00
51 GE,ASh(c),Sam Houston ... 350.00
52 GE,FF,ASh(c),JSe&BE
Leif Erickson 500.00
53 GT,JSe&BE,Henry Wells &
William Fargo 250.00
54 GT,Alexander Graham Bell. . . 250.00
55 ASh(c),JSe&BE,The James
Brothers. 250.00
56 JSe&BE. 250.00
57 JSe&BE. 250.00
58 JSe&BE,Jim Reaves. 300.00
59 FF,JSe&BE,Battle Orphan
Sept '52 .... 250.00

REAL SPORTS COMICS
See: ALL SPORTS COMICS

REAL WESTERN HERO
See: WOW COMICS

REAL WEST ROMANCES
Crestwoood Publishing Co./
Prize Publ., April–May, 1949
1 S&K,Ph(c) 350.00
2 Ph(c),Spanking 200.00
3 JSe,BE,Ph(c) 200.00
4 S&K,JSe,BE,Ph(c) 275.00
5 S&K,MMe,JSe,Audie
Murphy Ph(c) 250.00
6 S&K,JSe,BE,Ph(c) 150.00

RECORD BOOK OF
FAMOUS POLICE CASES
St. John Publishing Co., 1949
1 N#,JKu,MB(c) 500.00

RED ARROW
P.L. Publishing Co.,
May, 1951
1 Bondage(c) 350.00
2 .... 200.00
3 P(c) 200.00

RED BAND COMICS
Enwil Associates,
Nov., 1944
1 The Bogeyman 600.00
2 O:Bogeyman,same(c)as#1 . 400.00
3 A:Captain Wizard 350.00
4 May, '45,Repof#3,Same(c) ... 350.00

RED CIRCLE COMICS
Enwil Associates
(Rural Home Public),
Jan., 1945
1 B:Red Riot,The Prankster 600.00
2 LSt,A:The Judge 400.00
3 LSt(A&c). 300.00
4 LSt(a&c) covers of #4
stapled over other comics ... 300.00

TRAIL BLAZERS
Street & Smith Publ., Jan., 1942
1 Wright Brothers 500.00
2 Benjamin Franklin,Dodgers ... 400.00
3 Red Barber,Yankees 500.00
4 Famous War song 250.00
Becomes:

RED DRAGON COMICS
Jan., 1943
5 JaB(c),B&O:Red Rover:
B:Capt.Jack Commando
Rex King&Jet,Minute Man . 1,500.00
6 O:Red Dragon. 4,000.00
7 The Curse of the
Boneless Men. 3,300.00
8 China V:Japan 1,200.00
9 The Reducing Ray,Jan '44 . 1,200.00

(2nd Series) Nov., 1947
1 B:Red Dragon. 1,500.00
2 BP 1,000.00
3 BP,BP(c),I:Dr Neff 800.00
4 BP,BP(c) 1,200.00
5 MMe,BP,BP(c) 600.00
6 BP,BP(c) 600.00
7 MMe,BP,BP(c),May, 49 ..... 600.00

Red Dragon #4
© *Red Dragon Comics*

All comics prices listed are for *Near Mint* condition.

RED MASK
See: TIM HOLT

RED RABBIT
Dearfield/
J. Charles Lave Publ. Co.,
Jan., 1941
1 (fa) 200.00
2 .... 125.00
3 .... 100.00
4 .... 100.00
5 .... 100.00
6 thru 10 .... @100.00
11 thru 22 .... @75.00

RED RYDER COMICS
Hawley Publ./
Dell Publ. Co. 1940
1 .... 4,700.00
Becomes:

HI-SPOT COMICS
Hawley Publications, 1940
2 Alley Oop, Capt. Easy...... 1,700.00
Becomes:

RED RYDER COMICS
Hawley Publ./Dell
Publ. Co., 1941
3 Alley Oop, Capt. Easy...... 2,000.00
4 .... 900.00
5 .... 900.00
6 .... 900.00
7 .... 650.00
8 .... 650.00
9 .... 650.00
10 .... 650.00
11 thru 20 .... @500.00
21 thru 30 .... @400.00
31 thru 40 .... @300.00
41 thru 50 .... @250.00
51 thru 60 .... @200.00
61 thru 70 .... @200.00
71 thru 80 .... @200.00
80 thru 99 .... @100.00
100 .... 150.00
101 thru 151 .... @100.00
Giant #1 .... 100.00
Giant #2 .... 100.00

RED SEAL COMICS
See: SCOOP

REDSKIN
Youthful Magazines,
Sept., 1950
1 WJo,Redskin,Bondage(c) 350.00
2 Apache Dance of Death...... 125.00
3 WJo(c),Daniel Boone........ 100.00
4 WJo(c),Sitting Bull- Red Devil
  of the Black Hills 100.00
5 DW....................... 100.00
6 Geronimo- Terror of the
  Desert,Bondage........... 250.00
7 Firebrand of the Sioux....... 100.00
8 .... 100.00
9 .... 100.00
10 Dead Man's Magic 100.00
11 RP,DW................... 100.00
12 Quanah Parker,Bondage(c) .. 250.00
Becomes:

FAMOUS WESTERN BADMEN
Dec., 1952
13 Redskin- Last of the
  Comanches 150.00
14 .... 100.00
15 The Dalton Boys Apr '52..... 100.00

REG'LAR FELLERS
Visual Editions (Standard), 1947
5 .... 100.00
6 .... 100.00

REMEMBER PEARL HARBOR
Street & Smith Publ., 1942
1 N# JaB,Battle of the
  Pacific,Uncle Sam(c)....... 700.00

RETURN OF THE OUTLAW
Minoan Publishing Co.,
Feb., 1953
1 Billy The Kid 125.00
2 .... 100.00
3 thru 11 .... @75.00

REVEALING ROMANCES
A.A. Wyn
(Ace Magazines), Sept., 1949
1 .... 150.00
2 .... 125.00
3 thru 6 .... @100.00

REX ALLEN COMICS
Dell Publishing Co.,
Feb., 1951
(1) see Dell Four Color #316
2 Western, Ph(c) all 200.00
3 thru 10 .... @150.00
11 thru 23 .... @125.00
24 ATh 135.00
25 thru 31................. @125.00

REX DEXTER OF MARS
Fox Features Syndicate,
Autumn, 1940
1 DBr,DBr(c) Battle ofKooba .. 3,000.00

REX MORGAN, M.D.
Argo Publications, 1950
1 .... 150.00
2 .... 100.00

RIBTICKLER
Fox Features Syndicate, 1945
1 .... 225.00
2 .... 150.00

Ribtickler #1
© *Fox Features Syndicate*

3 Cosmo Cat............... 125.00
4 thru 6 .... @100.00
7 Cosmo Cat............... 100.00
8 thru 9 .... @100.00

RICKY
Visual Editions (Standard Comics), 1953
1 .... 75.00

THE RIDER
Four Star Comics
(Ajax-Farrell Publ.), 1957
1 Swift Arrow............... 150.00
2 thru 5 .... @100.00
Becomes:

FRONTIER TRAIL
Ajax-Farrell Publ., 1958
6 .... 100.00

RIN TIN TIN
Dell Publishing Co.,
Nov., 1952
(1) see Dell Four Color #434
(1) see Dell Four Color #476
(1) see Dell Four Color #523
4 thru 10 Ph(c) all .... @100.00
11 thru 20 .... @125.00

RIPLEY's BELIEVE IT OR NOT!
Harvey Publications, 1953–54
1 BP 150.00
2 Li'l Abner 125.00
3 .... 125.00
4 .... 125.00

RIVETS
Argo Publications, 1956
1 .... 100.00
2 .... 75.00
3 .... 75.00

ROBIN HOOD
Sussex Publ. Co (Magazine Enterprises), 1955
1 FBe 200.00
2 FBe 150.00
3 FBe 150.00
4 FBe 150.00
5 FBe 150.00
6 FBe,BP 150.00
Becomes:

ADVENTURES OF ROBIN HOOD
Magazine Enterprises, 1957
7 BP, Richard Green Ph(c).... 200.00
8 Richard Green Ph(c) 200.00

ROBIN HOOD AND HIS MERRY MEN
See: THIS MAGAZINE IS HAUNTED

ROBIN HOOD TALES
Quality Comics Group, 1956
1 MB...................... 450.00
2 MB...................... 400.00
3 MB...................... 400.00
4 MB...................... 400.00
5 MB...................... 400.00
6 MB...................... 400.00
See: DC Comics

ROCKET COMICS
Hillman Periodicals, March, 1940
1 O:Red Roberts;B:Rocket Riley,Phantom Ranger,Steel Shank,Buzzard Baynes,Lefty Larson,The Defender,Man with 1,000 Faces 4,500.00
2 . . . . 2,000.00
3 May, '40 E:All Features 2,500.00

ROCKET KELLY
Fox Features Syndicate, Autumn, 1945–Oct., Nov., 1946
N# 450.00
1 . . . . 350.00
2 A:The Puppeteer 325.00
3 thru 6 . . . . @300.00

ROCKETMAN
Ajax/Farrell Publications, June, 1952
1 Space Stories of the Future . . . 600.00

ROCKET SHIP X
Fox Features Syndicate, Sept., 1951
1 . . . . 1,000.00
2 N# Variant of Original 550.00

ROCKY LANE WESTERN
Fawcett/Charlton Comics, May, 1949
1 Ph(c)B:Rocky Lane,Slim Pickins 1,500.00
2 Ph(c) 600.00
3 Ph(c) 500.00
4 Ph(c)CCB,Rail Riders Rampage,F Capt Tootsie. . . . 500.00
5 Ph(c)The Missing Stagecoaches 450.00
6 Ph(c)Ghost Town Showdown . 300.00
7 Ph(c)The Border Revolt. 350.00
8 Ph(c)The Sunset Feud 350.00
9 Ph(c)Hermit of the Hills 350.00
10 Ph(c)Badman's Reward 300.00
11 Ph(c)Fool's Gold Fiasco 250.00
12 Ph(c),CCB,Coyote Breed F:Capt Tootsie,Giant 250.00
13 Ph(c),Giant 250.00
14 Ph(c) 200.00
15 Ph(c)B:Black Jacks Hitching Post,Giant 225.00
16 Ph(c),Giant 200.00
17 Ph(c),Giant 200.00
18 Ph(c) 225.00
19 Ph(c),Giant 235.00
20 Ph(c)The Rodeo Rustler E:Slim Pickens 235.00
21 Ph(c)B: Dee Dickens 200.00
22 Ph(c) 175.00
23 thru 30 . . . . @200.00
31 thru 40. . . . . @175.00
41 thru 55. . . . . @175.00
56 thru 87. . . . . @150.00

ROD CAMERON WESTERN
Fawcett Publications, Feb., 1950
1 Ph(c) 750.00
2 Ph(c) 350.00
3 Ph(c),Seven Cities of Cipiola . 300.00
4 Ph(c),Rip-Roaring Wild West . 250.00
5 Ph(c),Six Gun Sabotage 250.00
6 Ph(c),Medicine Bead Murders 250.00
7 Ph(c),Wagon Train Of Death . 250.00
8 Ph(c),Bayou Badman 250.00

9 Ph(c),Rustlers Ruse 250.00
10 Ph(c),White Buffalo Trail 250.00
11 Ph(c),Lead Poison 225.00
12 Ph(c). 225.00
13 Ph(c). 225.00
14 Ph(c). 225.00
15 Ph(c). 225.00
16 thru 19 Ph(c) . . . . @225.00
20 Phc(c),Great Army Hoax. 225.00

ROLY-POLY COMICS
Green Publishing Co., 1945
1 B:Red Rube&Steel Sterling . . 400.00
6 A:Blue Cycle 250.00
10 A:Red Rube 300.00
11 . . . . 250.00
12 Black Hood 250.00
13 . . . . 250.00
14 A:Black Hood, Decapitation . . 650.00
15 A:Steel Fist;1946. . . . . 450.00

ROMANCE AND CONFESSION STORIES
St. John Publishing Co., 1949
1 MB(c),MB. 700.00

ROMANTIC WESTERN
Fawcett Publications, Winter, 1949
1 Ph(c) 300.00
2 Ph(c),AW,AMc 325.00
3 Ph(c) 250.00

ROOKIE COP
Charlton, 1955
27 . . . . 125.00
28 . . . . 100.00
29 . . . . 100.00
30 . . . . 100.00
31 thru 33 . . . . @100.00

ROUNDUP
D.S. Publishing Co., July–Aug., 1948
1 HcK 250.00
2 Drug 175.00
3 . . . . 150.00
4 . . . . 150.00
5 Male Bondage 175.00

ROY CAMPANELLA, BASEBALL HERO
Fawcett Publications, 1950
N# Ph(c),Life Story of the Battling Dodgers Catcher . . 1,000.00

ROY ROGERS COMICS
Dell Publishing Co., 1948
1 photo (c) 1,600.00
2 . . . . 600.00
3 . . . . 400.00
4 . . . . 400.00
5 . . . . 400.00
6 thru 10 . . . . @300.00
11 thru 18 . . . . @250.00
19 Chuck Wagon Charlie. 225.00
20 Trigger. 225.00
21 thru 30. . . . . @225.00
31 thru 46. . . . . @300.00
47 thru 50. . . . . @125.00
51 thru 56. . . . . @110.00
57 Drug 125.00
58 Drug 135.00
59 thru 80. . . . . @125.00
81 thru 91. . . . . @100.00
Becomes:

Roy Rogers and Trigger #111
© Dell Publishing Co.

ROY ROGERS AND TRIGGER
Aug., 1955
92 . . . . 100.00
93 . . . . 100.00
94 . . . . 100.00
95 . . . . 100.00
96 thru 99 . . . . @100.00
100 Trigger Returns. 125.00
101 thru 118 . . . . @100.00
119 thru 125 ATn . . . . @150.00
126 thru 131 . . . . @120.00
132 Dale Evans 150.00
133 thru 144 RsM. . . . . @110.00
145 . . . . 150.00

ROY ROGER'S TRIGGER
Dell Publishing Co., May, 1951
(1) see Dell Four Color #329
2 Ph(c) 250.00
3 P(c) 100.00
4 P(c) 100.00
5 P(c) 100.00
6 thru 17 P(c) . . . . @100.00

RULAH, JUNGLE GODDESS
See: ZOOT COMICS

RUSTY, BOY DETECTIVE
Good Comics/Lev Gleason Publ., 1955
1 . . . . 125.00
2 . . . . 100.00
3 . . . . 100.00
4 . . . . 100.00
5 . . . . 100.00

SAARI, THE JUNGLE GODDESS
P.L. Publishing Co., Nov., 1951
1 The Bantu Blood Curse 700.00

SABU, ELEPHANT BOY
Fox Features Syndicate, June, 1950
1(30) WW,Ph(c) 350.00
2 JKa,Ph(c),Aug.'50 . . . . 250.00

HAPPY HOULIHANS
Fables Publications
(E.C. Comics), Autumn, 1947
1 O:Moon Girl 750.00
2 . . . . 450.00
Becomes:

SADDLE JUSTICE
Spring, 1948
3 HcK,JCr,AF 800.00
4 AF,JCr, Grl 700.00
5 AF,Grl 600.00
6 AF,Grl 600.00
7 AF,Grl 600.00
8 AF,Grl, ... 650.00
Becomes:

SADDLE ROMANCES
Nov., 1949
9 Grl(c),Grl 700.00
10 AF(c),WW,Grl 725.00
11 AF(c),Grl 700.00

SAD SACK COMICS
Harvey Publications,
Sept., 1949
1 I:Little Dot 1,700.00
2 Flying Fool 600.00
3 . . . . 400.00
4 . . . . 300.00
5 . . . . 300.00
6 thru 10 . . . . @250.00
11 thru 21 . . . . @175.00
22 Back in the Army Again,
    The Specialist 200.00
23 thru 50 . . . . @150.00
51 thru 100 . . . . @100.00

SAINT, THE
Avon Periodicals,
Aug., 1947
1 JKa,JKa(c),Bondage(c) 1,500.00
2 . . . . 800.00
3 Rolled Stocking Leg(c). 700.00
4 MB(c) Longerie 700.00
5 Spanking Panel 800.00
6 B:Miss Fury 800.00
7 WJo(c),Detective Cases(c) . . . 600.00
8 P(c),Detective Cases(c) 650.00
9 EK(c),The Notorious
    Murder Mob 650.00
10 WW,P(c),V:The Communist
    Menace 600.00
11 P(c),Wanted For Robbery 400.00
12 P(c),The Blowpipe Murders
    March, 1952 . . . . 400.00

SAM HILL PRIVATE EYE
Close-Up Publications, 1950
1 The Double Trouble Caper . . . 250.00
2 . . . . 150.00
3 . . . . 125.00
4 Negligee panels 200.00
5 . . . . 100.00
6 . . . . 100.00
7 . . . . 100.00

SAMSON
Fox Features Syndicate,
Autumn, 1940
1 BP,GT,A:Wing Turner 3,800.00
2 BP,A:Dr. Fung 1,400.00
3 JSh(c),A:Navy Jones 1,000.00
4 WE,B:Yarko 850.00
5 WE 750.00
6 WE,O:The Topper;Sept'41 . . . 750.00

Samson #2
© Fox Features

SAMSON
Ajax Farrell Publ
(Four Star), April, 1955
12 The Electric Curtain 400.00
13 Assignment Danger 350.00
14 The Red Raider;Aug'55 . . . . . 350.00

SANDS OF THE SOUTH PACIFIC
Toby Press, Jan., 1953
1 2-Fisted Romantic Adventure . 300.00

SANTA CLAUS FUNNIES
Dell Publishing Co., 1942
N# WK 800.00
2 WK 500.00

SANTA CLAUS PARADE
Approved Comics (Ziff-Davis)/
St. John Publ., 1951
N# 400.00
2 . . . . 300.00
3 . . . . 250.00

SANTA'S CHRISTMAS COMICS
Best Books (Standard
Comics), 1952
N# Dizzy Duck 250.00

SCIENCE COMICS
Fox Features Syndicate,
Feb., 1940
1 GT,LF(c),O&B:Electro,Perisphere
    Payne,The Eagle,Navy Jones;
    B:Marga,Cosmic Carson,
    Dr. Doom; Bondage(c) . . . 8,000.00
2 GT,LF(c) 4,500.00
3 GT,LF(c),Dynamo 3,500.00
4 JK,Cosmic Carson 3,500.00
5 Giant Comiscope Offer
    Eagle(c) 2,000.00
6 Dynamop(c) 2,000.00
7 Bondage(c),Dynamo 2,200.00
8 Sept., 1940 Eagle(c). 2,000.00

SCIENCE COMICS
Humor Publications,
Jan., 1946
1 RP(c),Story of the A-Bomb . . . 250.00
2 RP(c),How Museum Pieces
    Are Assembled 125.00

3 AF,RP(c),How Underwater
    Tunnels Are Made 175.00
4 RP(c),Behind the Scenes at
    A TV Broadcast 100.00
5 The Story of the World's
    Bridges; Sept., 1946 . . . . . . 100.00

SCIENCE COMICS
Ziff-Davis Publ. Co.,
May, 1946
N# Used For A Mail Order
    Test Market 600.00

SCIENCE COMICS
Export Publication Enterprises,
March, 1951
1 How to resurrect a dead rat . . . 150.00

SCOOP COMICS
Harry 'A' Chesler Jr.,
Nov., 1941
1 I&B:Rocketman&Rocketgirl;B:Dan
    Hastings;O&B:Master Key . 2,400.00
2 A:Rocketboy,Eye Injury 2,500.00
3 Partial rep. of #2 . . . . 1,100.00
4 thru 7 do not exist
8 1945 . . . . 700.00
Becomes:

SNAP
Harry 'A' Chesler Jr., 1944
N# Humorous 175.00
Becomes:

KOMIK PAGES
Harry 'A' Chesler Jr., 1944
1(10) JK,Duke of Darkness 400.00
Becomes:

BULLS-EYE
Harry 'A' Chesler Jr., 1944
11 Green Knight, Skull (c) 600.00
Becomes:

KAYO
Harry 'A' Chesler Jr., 1945
12 Green Knight. 250.00
Becomes:

CARNIVAL
Harry 'A' Chesler Jr., 1945
(13) Guardineer 225.00
Becomes:

Carnival N#
© Harry A Chesler

RED SEAL COMICS
Harry 'A' Chesler, Jr./Superior, Oct., 1945
14 GT,Bondage(c),Black Dwarf 1,200.00
15 GT,Torture 650.00
16 GT 1,000.00
17 GT,Lady Satan,Sky Chief 750.00
18 Lady Satan,Sky Chief 750.00
19 Lady Satan,Sky Chief 700.00
20 Lady Satan,Sky Chief 750.00
21 Lady Satan,Sky Chief 550.00
22 Rocketman 450.00

SCOOTER COMICS
Rucker Publications, 1946
1 . . . . 150.00

SCOTLAND YARD
Charlton Comics, 1955
1 . . . . 175.00
2 thru 4 . . . . @125.00

SCREAM COMICS
Humor Publ./Current Books (Ace Magazines), Autumn, 1944
1 . . . . 250.00
2 . . . . 150.00
3 thru 15 . . . . @125.00
16 I:Lily Belle 150.00
17 . . . . 125.00
18 Drug 225.00
19 . . . . 125.00
Becomes:

ANDY COMICS
June, 1948
20 Teenage 125.00
21 . . . . 125.00
Becomes:

ERNIE COMICS
Sept., 1948
22 Teenage 125.00
23 thru 25 . . . . @100.00
Becomes:

ALL LOVE ROMANCES
May, 1949
26 Ernie 125.00
27 LbC 200.00
28 thru 32 . . . . @100.00

(Capt. Silvers Log of...) SEA HOUND, THE
Avon Periodicals, 1945
N# The Esmerelda's Treasure . . 250.00
2 Adventures in Brazil 200.00
3 Louie the Llama 150.00
4 In Greed & Vengence;
  Jan-Feb, 1946 . . . . 150.00

SECRET MISSIONS
St. John Publishing Co., 1950
1 JKu 300.00

SECRET MYSTERIES
See: CRIME MYSTERIES

SELECT DETECTIVE
D.S. Publishing Co., Aug.–Sept., 1948
1 MB,Exciting New Mystery
  Cases 400.00
2 MB,AMc,Dead Men 250.00
3 Face in theFrame;Dec-Jan'48 . 200.00

SENSATIONAL POLICE CASES
Avon Periodicals, 1952
N# JKu,EK(c) 600.00
2 . . . . 200.00
3 . . . . 200.00
4 . . . . 200.00

SERGEANT PRESTON OF THE YUKON
Dell Publishing Co., Aug., 1951
(1 thru 4) see Dell Four Color #344; #373, 397, 419
5 P(c) 125.00
6 Bondage, P(c) 175.00
7 thru 11 P(c) 125.00
12 P(c) 125.00
13 P(c),O:Sergeant Preston . . . 150.00
14 thru 17 P(c) . . . . @125.00
18 Yukon King,P(c) 125.00
19 thru 29 Ph(c) . . . . @150.00

SEVEN SEAS COMICS
Universal Phoenix Features/ Leader Publ., April, 1946
1 MB,RWb(c),B:South Sea
  Girl, Captain Cutlass 1,400.00
2 MB,RWb(c) 1,200.00
3 MB,AF,MB(c) 1,100.00
4 MB,MB(c) 1,200.00
5 MB,MB(c),Hangman's
  Noose 1,100.00
6 MB,MB(c);1947 . . . . 1,000.00

SHADOW COMICS
Street & Smith Publ., March, 1940
1-1 P(c),B:Shadow,Doc Savage,
  Bill Barnes,Nick Carter,
  Frank Merriwell,Iron Munro 8,500.00
1-2 P(c),B: The Avenger 3,200.00
1-3 P(c),A: Norgill the
  Magician 2,400.00
1-4 P(c),B:The Three
  Musketeers 1,800.00
1-5 P(c),E: Doc Savage 1,800.00
1-6 A: Captain Fury 1,500.00
1-7 O&B: The Wasp 1,600.00
1-8 A:Doc Savage 1,500.00
1-9 A:Norgill the Magician 1,500.00
1-10 O:Iron Ghost;B:The Dead
  End Kids 1,500.00
1-11 O:Hooded Wasp 1,500.00
1-12 Crime Does Not pay 1,400.00
2-1 . . . . 1,400.00
2-2 Shadow Becomes Invisible 2,500.00
2-3 O&B:Supersnipe;
  F:Little Nemo 2,100.00
2-4 F:Little Nemo 1,200.00
2-5 V:The Ghost Faker 1,200.00
2-6 A:Blackstone the Magician 1,100.00
2-7 V:The White Dragon 1,100.00
2-8 A:Little Nemo 1,100.00
2-9 The Hand of Death 1,100.00
2-10 A:Reebo the WonderHorse 1,100.00
2-11 V:Devil Kyoti 1,100.00
2-12 V:Devil Kyoti 1,000.00
3-1 JaB(c),V:Devil Kyoti 1,000.00
3-2 Red Skeleton Life Story . . . 1,000.00
3-3 V:Monstrodamus 1,000.00
3-4 V:Monstrodamus 1,000.00
3-5 V:Monstrodamus 1,000.00
3-6 V:Devil's of the Deep 1,100.00
3-7 V: Monstrodamus 1,000.00
3-8 E: The Wasp 1,000.00
3-9 The Stolen Lighthouse 1,000.00
3-10 A:Doc Savage 1,000.00
3-11 P(c),V: Thade 1,000.00
3-12 V: Thade 1,000.00

Shadow Comics Vol. 3 #1
© Fiction House

4-1 Red Cross Appeal on (c) . . . 800.00
4-2 V:The Brain of Nippon 800.00
4-3 Little Men in Space 800.00
4-4 ...Mystifies Berlin 800.00
4-5 ...Brings Terror to Tokio . . . 800.00
4-6 V:The Tarantula 800.00
4-7 Crypt of the Seven Skulls . . . 850.00
4-8 V:the Indigo Mob 800.00
4-9 Ghost Guarded Treasure
  of the Haunted Glen 800.00
4-10 V:The Hydra 800.00
4-11 V:The Seven Sinners 800.00
4-12 Club Curio 1,000.00
5-1 A:Flatty Foote 1,000.00
5-2 Bells of Doom 1,000.00
5-3 The Circle of Death 1,000.00
5-4 The Empty Safe Riddle . . . 1,000.00
5-5 The Mighty Master Nomad . 1,200.00
5-6 ...Fights Piracy Among
  the Golden Isles 750.00
5-7 V:The Talon 750.00
5-8 V:The Talon 750.00
5-9 V:The Talon 750.00
5-10 V:The Crime Master 750.00
5-11 The Clutch of the Talon . . . 750.00
5-12 Most Dangerous Criminal . 750.00
6-1 Double Z 600.00
6-2 Riddle of Prof.Mentalo 600.00
6-3 V:Judge Lawless 600.00
6-4 V:Dr. Zenith 600.00
6-5 . . . . 600.00
6-6 ...Invades the
  Crucible of Death 600.00
6-7 Four Panel (c) 600.00
6-8 Crime Among the Aztecs . . . 600.00
6-9 I:Shadow Jr. 650.00
6-10 Devil's Passage 600.00
6-11 The Black Pagoda 600.00
6-12 BP,BP(c),Atomic Bomb
  Secrets Stolen 650.00
7-1 The Yellow Band 650.00
7-2 A:Shadow Jr. 650.00
7-3 BP,BP(c),Crime Under
  the Border 800.00
7-4 BP,BP(c),One Tree Island,
  Atomic Bomb 900.00
7-5 A:Shadow Jr. 650.00
7-6 BP,BP(c),The Sacred Sword
  of Sanjorojo 800.00
7-7 Crime K.O. 650.00
7-8 ...Raids Crime Harbor 650.00
7-9 BP,BP(c),Kilroy Was Here . . 800.00
7-10 BP,BP(c),The Riddle of
  the Flying Saucer 1,000.00
7-11 BP,BP(c),Crime
  Doesn't Pay 800.00

All comics prices listed are for *Near Mint* condition.

7-12 BP,BP(c)Back From
  the Grave 800.00
8-1 BP,BP(c),Curse of the Cat . . 800.00
8-2 BP,BP(c),Decay,Vermin &
  Murder in the Bayou 800.00
8-3 BP,BP(c),The Spider Boy . . . 800.00
8-4 BP,BP(c),Death Rises
  Out of the Sea 800.00
8-5 BP,BP(c),Jekyll-
  Hyde Murders 800.00
8-6 Secret of Valhalla Hall 800.00
8-7 BP,BP(c),Shadow in Danger 800.00
8-8 BP,BP(c),...Solves a
  Twenty Year Old Crime 800.00
8-9 BP,BP(c),3-D Effect(c) 800.00
8-10 BP,BP(c),Up&Down(c). 800.00
8-11 BP,BP(c). 800.00
8-12 BP,BP(c),Arabs,Boat(c) 800.00
9-1 Airport(c) 800.00
9-2 BP,BP(c),Flying Cannon(c) . . 800.00
9-3 BP,BP(c),Shadow's Shadow . 800.00
9-4 BP,BP(c) 800.00
9-5 Death in the Stars;Aug'49 . . . 800.00

SHARP COMICS
H.C. Blackerby,
Winter, 1945
1 O:Planetarian(c) 600.00
2 O:The Pioneer 500.00

Sheena Queen of the Jungle #1
© Fiction House

SHEENA, QUEEN OF
THE JUNGLE
Real Adventures
(Fiction House)
Spring, 1942–Winter, 1952
1 Blood Hunger 4,200.00
2 Black Orchid of Death 1,800.00
3 Harem Shackles 1,400.00
4 The Zebra Raiders 800.00
5 War of the Golden Apes 750.00
6 . . . . 700.00
7 They Claw By Night 700.00
8 The Congo Colossus 700.00
9 and 10 . . . . @550.00
11 Red Fangs of the Tree Tribe . 550.00
12 . . . . 450.00
13 Veldt o/t Voo Doo Lions 450.00
14 The Hoo Doo Beasts of
  Mozambique 450.00
15 . . . . 450.00
16 Black Ivory 450.00
17 Great Congo Treasure Trek . . 450.00
18 Doom of the Elephant Drum . . 450.00

SHERLOCK HOLMES
Charlton Comics, 1955
1 . . . . 575.00
2 . . . . 500.00

SHIELD-WIZARD
COMICS
MLJ Magazines,
Summer, 1940
1 IN,EA,O:Shield 9,000.00
2 IN,O:Shield;I:Roy 4,000.00
3 IN,Roy,Child Bondage(c) . . . 2,500.00
4 IN,Shield,Roy,Wizard 2,200.00
5 IN,B:Dusty-Boy Dectective,
  Child Bondage 2,200.00
6 B:Roy the Super Boy,Child
  Bondage 2,000.00
7 Shield(c),Roy Bondage(c) . . 2,200.00
8 IN,Bondage(c) 2,000.00
9 IN,Shield/Roy(c) 1,400.00
10 IN,Shield/Roy(c) 1,400.00
11 IN,Shield/Roy(c) 1,400.00
12 IN,Shield/Roy(c) 1,400.00
13 Bondage (c);Spring'44 . . . . . 1,500.00

SHIP AHOY
Spotlight Publishers,
Nov., 1944
1 LbC(c) 250.00

SHOCK DETECTIVE
CASE(S)
See: CRIMINALS ON
THE RUN

SHOCK ILLUSTRATED
E.C. Comics, 1955
1 Drugs 300.00
2 AW,GI,RC. 200.00
3 RC,Of Great Rarity 3,500.00

SHOCK SUSPENSTORIES
Tiny Tot Comics
(E.C. Comics),
Feb.–March, 1952
1 JDa,JKa,AF(c),ElectricChair . 2,000.00
2 WW,JDa,Grl,JKa,WW(c). . . . 1,500.00
3 WW,JDa,JKa,WW(c). 1,000.00
4 WW,JDa,JKa,WW(c). 1,000.00
5 WW,JDa,JKa,WW(c),
  Hanging 1,200.00
6 WW,AF,JKa,WW(c),
  Bondage(c) 1,300.00
7 JKa,WW,GE,AF(c),Face
  Melting 1,300.00
8 JKa,AF,AW,GE,WW,AF(c) . . . 900.00
9 JKa,AF,RC,WW,AF(c) 800.00
10 JKa,WW,RC,JKa(c),Drug . . . 800.00
11 JCr,JKa,WW,RC,JCr(c) 700.00
12 AF,JKa,WW,RC,AF(c)
  Drug(c) 800.00
13 JKa,WW,FF,JKa(c). 1,000.00
14 JKa,WW,BK,WW(c) 700.00
15 JKa,WW,RC,JDa(c)
  Strangulation 600.00
16 GE,RC,JKa,GE(c),Rape 600.00
17 GE,RC,JKa,GE(c). 400.00
18 GE,RC,JKa,GE(c);Jan'55 . . . 400.00

SHOCKING MYSTERY
CASES
See: THRILLING CRIME
CASES

SILVER STREAK
COMICS
Your Guide/New Friday/
Comic House/Newsbrook
Publications/Lev Gleason,
Dec., 1939
1 JCo(a&c),I&B:The Claw,Red
  Reeves Capt.Fearless;B:Mr.Mid-
  night,Wasp;A:Spiritman . . 20,000.00
2 JSm,JCo,JSm(c) 6,500.00
3 JaB(c),I&O:Silver Streak;
  B:Dickie Dean,Lance Hale,
  Ace Powers,Bill Wayne,
  Planet Patrol 5,500.00
4 JCo,JaB(c)B:Sky Wolf;
  N:Silver Streak,I:Lance
  Hale's Sidekick-Jackie 2,500.00
5 JCo(a&c),Dickie Dean
  V:The Raging Flood 3,000.00
6 JCo,JaB,JCo(a&c),O&I:Daredevil
  [Blue & Yellow Costume];
  R:The Claw 25,000.00
7 JCo,N: Daredevil 15,000.00
8 JCo(a&c) 5,500.00
9 JCo,BoW(c) 3,000.00
10 BoW,BoW(c) 2,500.00
11 DRi(c) I:Mercury 2,000.00
12 DRi(c). 1,500.00
13 JaB,JaB(c),O:Thun-Dohr . . . 1,500.00
14 JaB,JaB(c),A:Nazi
  Skull Men 1,500.00
15 JaB,DBr,JaB(c),
  B:Bingham Boys. 1,200.00
16 DBr,BoW(c),Hitler(c) 1,600.00
17 DBr,JaB(c),E:Daredevil 1,200.00
18 DBr,JaB(c),B:The Saint 1,100.00
19 DBr,EA 900.00
20 BW,BEv,EA 900.00
21 BW,BEv 900.00
Becomes:

CRIME DOES NOT PAY
June, 1942
22(23) CBi(c),The Mad Musician
  & Tunes of Doom 5,000.00
23 CBi(c),John Dillinger-One
  Man Underworld 2,500.00
24 CBi(c),The Mystery of the
  Indian Dick 2,200.00
25 CBi(c),Dutch Shultz-King
  of the Underworld. 1,000.00
26 CBi(c),Lucky Luciano-The
  Deadliest of Crime Rats . . . 1,100.00
27 CBi(c),Pretty Boy Floyd 1,100.00
28 CBi(c), ... 1,100.00
29 CBi(c),Two-Gun Crowley-The
  Bad Kid with the Itchy
  Trigger Finger 1,000.00
30 CBi(c),"Monk"Eastman
  V:Thompson's Mob. 1,000.00
31 CBi(c) The Million Dollar
  Bank Robbery 600.00
32 CBi(c),Seniorita of Sin 600.00
33 CBi(c),Meat Cleaver Murder 1,000.00
34 CBi(c),Elevator Shaft 600.00
35 CBi(c),Case o/t MissingToe . 600.00
36 CBi(c) 600.00
37 CBi(c) 600.00
38 CBi(c) 600.00
39 FGu,CBi(c) 600.00
40 FGu,CBi(c) 600.00
41 FGu,RP,CBi(c),The Cocksure
  Counterfeiter 450.00
42 FGu,RP,CBi(c), Electrocution . 600.00
43 FGu,RP,CBi(c) 300.00
44 FGu,CBi(c),The Most Shot
  At Gangster 300.00
45 FGu,CBi(c) 300.00
46 FGu,CBi(c),ChildKidnapping(c)300.00
47 FGu,CBi(c),ElectricChair. . . . 450.00
48 FGu,CBi(c) 250.00

GOLDEN AGE

49 FGu,CBi(c) 250.00
50 FGu,CBi(c) 250.00
51 FGu,GT,CBi(c),1st Monthly. . . 225.00
52 FGu,GT,CBi(c) 225.00
53 FGu,CBi(c) 225.00
54 FGu,CBi(c) 225.00
55 FGu,CBi(c) 225.00
56 FGu,GT,CBi(c) 225.00
57 FGu,CBi(c) 225.00
58 FGu,CBi(c) 225.00
59 FGu,Cbi(c) 225.00
60 FGu,CBi(c) 225.00
61 FGu,GT,CBi(c) 225.00
62 FGu,CBi(c),Bondage(c) 225.00
63 FGu,GT,CBi(c) 200.00
64 FGu,GT,CBi(c) 200.00
65 FGu,CBi(c) 200.00
66 FGu,GT,CBi(c) 200.00
67 FGu,GT,CBi(c) 200.00
68 FGu,CBi(c) 200.00
69 FGu,CBi(c) 200.00
70 FGu,CBi(c) 200.00
71 FGu,CBi(c) 175.00
72 FGu,CBi(c) 175.00
73 FGu,CBi(c) 175.00
74 FGu,CBi(c) 175.00
75 FGu,CBi(c) 175.00
76 FGu,CBi(c) 175.00
77 FGu,CBi(c),Electrified Safe. . . 200.00
78 FGu,CBi(c) 175.00
79 FGu. 175.00
80 FGu. 175.00
81 FGu. 175.00
82 FGu. 175.00
83 FGu. 175.00
84 FGu. 175.00
85 FGu. 175.00
86 FGu. 175.00
87 FGu,P(c),The Rock-A-Bye
   Baby Murder 175.00
88 FGu,P(c),Death Carries Torch 175.00
89 FGu,BF,BF P(c),The Escort
   Murder Case 175.00
90 FGu,BF P(c),The Alhambra
   Club Murders 175.00
91 FGu,AMc,BF P(c),Death
   Watches The Clock 175.00
92 BF,FGu,BF P(c) 175.00
93 BF,FGu,AMc,BF P(c) 175.00
94 BF,FGu,BF P(c) 175.00
95 FGu,AMc,BF P(c) 175.00
96 BF,FGu,BF P(c),The Case of
   the Movie Star's Double 175.00
97 FGu,BF P(c) 175.00
98 BF,FGu,BF P(c),Bondage(c). . 200.00
99 BF,FGu,BF P(c) 175.00

Crime Does Not Pay #89
© Lev Gleason

100 FGu,BF,AMc,P(c),The Case
   of the Jittery Patient 200.00
101 FGu,BF,AMc,P(c) 125.00
102 FGu,BF,AMc,BF P(c) 125.00
103 FGu,BF,AMc,BF P(c) 125.00
104 thru 110 FGu. . . . . @125.00
111 thru 120 . . . . @125.00
121 thru 140. . . . . @125.00
141 JKu 125.00
142 JKu,CBi(c). 125.00
143 JKu,Comic Code. 125.00
144 I Helped Capture "Fat Face"
   George Klinerz 125.00
145 RP,Double Barrelled Menace 125.00
146 BP,The Con & The Canary . . 125.00
147 JKu,BP,A Long Shoe On the
   Highway;July, 1955 . . . . 200.00

SINGLE SERIES
United Features Syndicate, 1938

1 Captain & The Kids 1,400.00
2 Bronco Bill 750.00
3 Ella Cinders 600.00
4 Li'l Abner 1,200.00
5 Fritzi Ritz 300.00
6 Jim Hardy 600.00
7 Frankie Doodle 450.00
8 Peter Pat 450.00
9 Strange As it Seems 450.00
10 Little Mary Mixup. 450.00
11 Mr. & Mrs. Beans 450.00
12 Joe Jinx. 400.00
13 Looy Dot Dope 400.00
14 Billy Make Believe. 400.00
15 How It Began 450.00
16 Illustrated Gags. 275.00
17 Danny Dingle 325.00
18 Li'l Abner. 900.00
19 Broncho Bill. 650.00
20 Tarzan 1,700.00
21 Ella Cinders 450.00
22 Iron Vic 450.00
23 Tailspin Tommy 550.00
24 Alice In Wonderland 600.00
25 Abbie an' Slats 500.00
26 Little Mary Mixup. 450.00
27 Jim Hardy 450.00
28 Ella Cinders & Abbie AN'
   Slats 1942 . . . . 450.00

SIX GUN HEROES
Fawcett Publications, 1950

1 Rocky Lane,Hopalong Cassidy 650.00
2 . . . . 350.00
3 . . . . 250.00
4 . . . . 250.00
5 Lash Larue. 250.00
6 . . . . 175.00
7 . . . . 175.00
8 . . . . 175.00
9 . . . . 175.00
10 . . . . 175.00
11 thru 23 . . . . @125.00

Charlton Comics, 1954

24 . . . . 250.00
25 . . . . 125.00
26 thru 50 . . . . @100.00
51 thru 70 . . . . @100.00

SKELETON HAND
American Comics Group, Sept.–Oct., 1952

1 . . . . 650.00
2 The Were-Serpent of Karnak. . 450.00
3 Waters of Doom 350.00
4 Black Dust 350.00
5 The Rise & Fall of the
   Bogey Man 350.00
6 July–Aug., 1953 . . . . 350.00

SKIPPY'S OWN BOOK OF COMICS
M.C. Gaines, 1934

N# 6,000.00

SKY BLAZERS
Hawley Publications, Sept., 1940

1 Flying Aces,Sky Pirates. 900.00
2 Nov., 1940 . . . . 600.00

SKYMAN
Columbia Comics Group, 1941

1 OW,OW(c),O:Skyman,Face . 1,900.00
2 OW,OW(c),Yankee Doodle . . . 900.00
3 OW,OW(c) 550.00
4 OW,OW(c),Statue of
   Liberty(c) 1948 . . . . 550.00

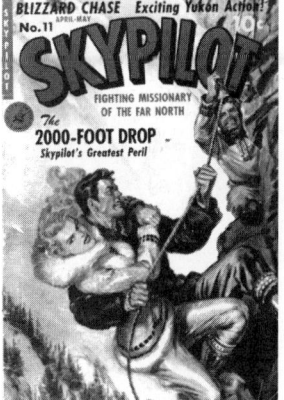

Sky Pilot #11
© Ziff-Davis Publishing

SKY PILOT
Ziff-Davis Publishing Co., 1950

10 NS, P(c),Lumber Pirates. 200.00
11 NS, P(c),The 2,00 Foot Drop;
   April–May, 1951. . . . . 175.00

SKY ROCKET
Home Guide Publ. (Harry 'A' Chesler), 1944

1 Alias the Dragon,Skyrocket . . . 500.00

SKY SHERIFF
D.S. Publishing, Summer, 1948

1 I:Breeze Lawson & the Prowl
   Plane Patrol 150.00

SLAM-BANG COMICS
Fawcett Publications, Jan., 1940

1 B:Diamond Jack,Mark Swift,
   Lee Granger,Jungle King . . 4,000.00
2 F:Jim Dolan Two-Fisted
   Crime Buster 1,800.00
3 A: Eric the Talking Lion 3,000.00
4 F: Hurricane Hansen-Sea
   Adventurer 1,500.00
5 . . . . 1,500.00
6 I: Zoro the Mystery Man;
   Bondage(c) 1,500.00
7 Bondage(c);Sept., 1940 . . . . 1,500.00

GOLDEN AGE

GOLDEN AGE *(vertical side tab)*

SLAPSTICK COMICS
Comic Magazine Distrib., Inc., 1945
N# Humorous Parody 350.00

SLASH-D DOUBLECROSS
St. John Publishing Co., 1950
N# 300.00

Slave Girl Comics #1
© Avon Periodicals

SLAVE GIRL COMICS
Avon Periodicals, Feb., 1949
1 EL 1,500.00
2 EL 1,200.00

SLICK CHICK COMICS
Leader Enterprises, Inc., 1947
1 Teen-Aged Humor 150.00
2 Teen-Aged Humor 100.00
3 1947 . . . . 100.00

SLUGGER
Lev Gleason Publications, 1956
1 CBi(c) 75.00

SMASH COMICS
Comics Magazine, Inc. (Quality Comics Group), Aug., 1939
1 WE,O&B:Hugh Hazard, Bozo the Robot,Black X, Invisible Justice: B:Wings Wendall, Chic Carter 6,000.00
2 WE,A:Lone Star Rider 2,000.00
3 WE,B:Captain Cook, John Law 1,100.00
4 WE,PGv,B:Flash Fulton 1,000.00
5 WE,PGv,Bozo Robot 1,000.00
6 WE,PGv,GFx,Black X(c) 1,000.00
7 WE,PGv,GFx,Wings Wendell(c) 900.00
8 WE,PGv,GFx,Bozo Robot 900.00
9 WE,PGv,GFx,Black X(c) 900.00
10 WE,PGv,GFx,Bozo Robot(c) . 900.00
11 WE,PGv,GFx,BP,Black X(c) . . 900.00
12 WE,PGv,GFx,BP,Bozo(c) 900.00
13 WE,PGv,GFx,AB,BP,B:Mango, Purple Trio,BlackX(c) 900.00
14 BP,LF,AB,PGv,I:The Ray . . . 4,800.00
15 BP,LF,AB,PGv,The Ram(c) . 2,000.00
16 BP,LF,AB,PGv,Bozo(c) 1,900.00
17 BP,LF,AB,PGv,JCo, The Ram(c) 1,900.00

18 BP,LF,AB,JCo,PGv, B&O:Midnight 2,500.00
19 BP,LF,AB,JCo,PGv,Bozo(c) . 2,400.00
20 BP,LF,AB,JCo,PGv, The Ram(c) 2,400.00
21 BP,LF,AB,JCo,PGv, ... 2,400.00
22 BP,LF,AB,JCo,PGv, B:The Jester 2,400.00
23 BP,AB,JCo,RC,PGv, The Ram(c) 1,300.00
24 BP,AB,JCo,RC,PGv,A:Sword, E:ChicCarter, N:WingsWendall 1,300.00
25 AB,JCo,RC,PGv,O:Wildfire . 1,300.00
26 AB,JCo,RC,PGv,Bozo(c) . . . 1,200.00
27 AB,JCo,RC,PGv, The Ram(c) 1,200.00
28 AB,JCo,RC,PGv, 1st Midnight (c) 1,200.00
29 AB,JCo,Rc,PGv,B; Midnight(c) 1,200.00
30 AB,JCo,PGv 1,200.00
31 AB,JCo,PGv 900.00
32 AB,JCo,PGv 900.00
33 AB,JCo,PGv,O:Marksman . . 1,000.00
34 AB,JCo,PGv 900.00
35 AB,JCo,RC,PGv 900.00
36 AB,JCo,RC,PGv, E:Midnight(c) 900.00
37 AB,JCo,RC,PGv,Doc Wacky Becomes Fastest Human on Earth 900.00
38 JCo,RC,PGv,B:YankeeEagle 1,500.00
39 PGv,B:Midnight(c) 900.00
40 PGv,E:Ray 900.00
41 PGv 800.00
42 PGv,B:Lady Luck 2,200.00
43 PGv,A:Lady Luck 900.00
44 PGv 700.00
45 PGv,E:Midnight(c) 700.00
46 RC,Twelve Hours to Live 700.00
47 Wanted Midnight, Dead or Alive 700.00
48 Midnight Meets the Menace from Mars 700.00
49 PGv,FGu,Mass of Muscle 700.00
50 I:Hyram the Hermit 700.00
51 A:Wild Bill Hiccup 500.00
52 PGv,FGu,Did Ancient Rome Fall, or was it Pushed? 500.00
53 Is ThereHonorAmongThieves. 400.00
54 A:Smear-Faced Schmaltz 450.00
55 Never Trouble Trouble until Trouble Troubles You 450.00
56 The Laughing Killer 450.00
57 A Dummy that Turns Into A Curse 450.00
58 . . . . 450.00
59 A Corpse that Comes Alive . . . 450.00
60 The Swooner & the Trush 450.00
61 . . . . 400.00
62 V:The Lorelet 400.00
63 PGv 450.00
64 PGv,In Search of King Zoris . . 450.00
65 PGv,V:Cyanide Cindy 450.00
66 Under Circle's Spell 450.00
67 A Living Clue 450.00
68 JCo,Atomic Dice 450.00
69 JCo,V:Sir Nuts 450.00
70 . . . . 450.00
71 . . . . 300.00
72 JCo,Angela,the Beautiful Bovine 300.00
73 . . . . 300.00
74 . . . . 300.00
75 The Revolution 300.00
76 Bowl Over Crime 300.00
77 Who is Lilli Dilli? 300.00
78 JCo,Win Over Crime 300.00
79 V:The Men From Mars 300.00
80 JCo,V:Big Hearted Bosco 300.00
81 V:Willie the Kid 300.00

82 V:Woodland Boy 300.00
83 JCo,Quizmaster 300.00
84 A Date With Father Time 300.00
85 JCo,A Singing Swindle 300.00
Becomes:

LADY LUCK
Comics Magazine (Quality Comics), 1949
86 (1) 1,500.00
87 thru 90 . . . . @1,000.00

SMASH HITS SPORTS COMICS
Essankay Publications, Jan., 1949
1 LbC,LbC(c) 400.00

SMILEY BURNETTE WESTERN
Fawcett Publications, March, 1950
1 Ph(c),B:Red Eagle 650.00
2 Ph(c) 500.00
3 Ph(c) 500.00
4 Ph(c) 500.00

SMILIN' JACK
Dell Publishing Co., 1948
1 . . . . 200.00
2 thru 8 . . . . @100.00

SMITTY
Dell Publishing Co., 1948
1 . . . . 150.00
2 . . . . 125.00
3 thru 7 . . . . @100.00

SNAP
See: SCOOP COMICS

SNAPPY COMICS
Cima Publications, (Prize), 1945
1 A:Animale 450.00

SNIFFY THE PUP
Animated Cartoons (Standard Comics), Nov., 1949
5 FF,Funny Animal 125.00
6 thru 9 Funny Animal . . . . . @100.00
10 thru 17 Funny Animal . . . . . @100.00
18 Sept., 1953 . . . . 100.00

SOLDIER AND MARINE COMICS
Charlton Comics, 1954
11 . . . . 125.00
12 thru 15 . . . . @100.00
Vol 2 #9 . . . . 100.00

SOLDIER COMICS
Fawcett Publications, Jan., 1952
1 Fighting Yanks on Flaming Battlefronts 200.00
2 Blazing Battles Exploding with Combat 150.00
3 . . . . 125.00
4 A Blow for Freedom 125.00
5 Only The Dead Are Free 125.00
6 Blood & Guts 125.00
7 The Phantom Sub 125.00
8 More Plasma! 135.00
9 Red Artillery 125.00
10 . . . . 125.00
11 Sept., 1953 . . . . 125.00

SOLDIERS OF FORTUNE
Creston Publications (American Comics Group), Feb.–March, 1952
1 OW(c),B:Ace Carter,
  Crossbones, Lance Larson . 300.00
2 OW(c) 175.00
3 OW(c) 125.00
4 . . . . 125.00
5 OW(c) 125.00
6 OW(c),OW,Bondage(c) 200.00
7 . . . . 125.00
8 OW thru 10. . . . . @125.00
11 OW,Format Change to War . . 100.00
12 . . . . 100.00
13 OW,Feb.–March, 1953 . . . . . . 100.00

Son of Sinbad #1
© *St John Publishing*

SON OF SINBAD
St. John Publishing Co., Feb., 1950
1 JKu,JKu(c),The Curse of the
  Caliph's Dancer 600.00

SPACE ACTION
Junior Books (Ace Magazines), June, 1952–Oct., 1952
1 Invaders from a Lost Galaxy 1,200.00
2 The Silicon Monster from
  Galaxy X 900.00
3 Attack on Ishtar 900.00

SPACE ADVENTURES
Capitol Stories/ Charlton Comics, July, 1952
1 AFa&LM(c) 800.00
2 . . . . 400.00
3 DG(c) 300.00
4 DG(c) 300.00
5 StC(c) 300.00
6 StC(c),Two Worlds 250.00
7 DG(c),Transformation 275.00
8 DG(c),All For Love 250.00
9 DG(c) 250.00
10 SD,SD(c). 800.00
11 SD,JoS 850.00
12 SD(c) 1,000.00
13 A:Blue Beetle 250.00
14 A:Blue Beetle 250.00
15 Ph(c) of Rocky Jones 250.00
16 BKa,A:Rocky Jones 300.00
17 A:Rocky Jones 225.00

18 A:Rocky Jones 225.00
19 . . . . 200.00
20 First Trip to the Moon 350.00
21 War at Sea 200.00
22 Does Not Exist
23 SD,Space Trip to the Moon. . . 300.00
24 . . . . 250.00
25 Brontosaurus. 250.00
26 SD,Flying Saucers 300.00
27 SD,Flying Saucers 300.00
28 Moon Trap. 200.00
29 Captive From Space 200.00
30 Peril in the Sky 200.00
31 SD,SD(c),Enchanted Planet . . 250.00
32 SD,SD(c),Last Ship
  from Earth 250.00
33 Galactic Scourge,
  I&O:Captain Atom 750.00
34 SD,SD(c),A:Captain Atom. . . . 275.00
35 thru 40 SD,SD(c),
  A:Captain Atom . . . . @275.00

SPACE BUSTERS
Ziff-Davis Publishing Co., Spring, 1952
1 BK,NS(c),Ph(c),Charge of
  the Battle Women 1,200.00
2 EK,BK,MA,NS(c),
  Bondage(c),Ph(c) 900.00
3 Autumn, 1952 . . . . 750.00

SPACE COMICS
See: FUNNY TUNES

SPACE DETECTIVE
Avon Periodicals, July, 1951
1 WW,WW(c),Opium Smugglers
  of Venus 1,700.00
2 WW,WW(c),Batwomen of
  Mercury 1,300.00
3 EK(c),SeaNymphs ofNeptune 600.00
4 EK,Flame Women of Vulcan,
  Bondage(c) 650.00

SPACE MOUSE
Avon Periodicals, April, 1953
1 Funny Animal 150.00
2 Funny Animal. 125.00
3 thru 5 Funny Animal . . . . . . @100.00

SPACE PATROL
Approved Comics (Ziff-Davis), Summer, 1952
1 BK,NS,Ph(c), The Lady of
  Diamonds 1,400.00
2 BK,NS,Ph(c),Slave King of
  Pluto,Oct.–Nov., 1952 . . . . 1,000.00

SPACE THRILLERS
Avon Periodicals, 1954
N# Contents May Vary. 1,800.00

SPACE WESTERN COMICS
See: YELLOWJACKET COMICS

SPARKLE COMICS
United Features Syndicate, 1948
1 Nancy, Li'l Abner 250.00
2 . . . . 150.00
3 . . . . 125.00
4 . . . . 125.00
5 . . . . 125.00

6 . . . . 125.00
7 . . . . 125.00
8 thru 10 . . . . @125.00
11 thru 20 . . . . @100.00
21 thru 32 . . . . @100.00
33 Peanuts. 125.00

SPARKLER COMICS
United Features Syndicate, July, 1940
1 Jim Handy 600.00
2 Frankie Doodle,Aug., 1940 . . . 400.00

SPARKLER COMICS
United Features Syndicate, July, 1941
1 BHg,O:Sparkman;B:Tarzan,Captain
  & the Kids,Ella Cinders,Danny
  Dingle,Dynamite Dunn, Nancy,
  Abbie an' Slats, Frankie
  Doodle,Broncho Bill 4,000.00
2 BHg, The Case of Poisoned
  Fruit 1,500.00
3 BHg 1,200.00
4 BHg,Case of Sparkman &
  the Firefly 1,200.00
5 BHg,Sparkman,Natch 1,000.00
6 BHg,Case of the Bronze
  Bees 1,000.00
7 BHg,Case of the Green
  Raiders 1,000.00
8 BHg,V:River Fiddler 1,000.00
9 BHg,N:Sparkman 1,000.00
10 BHg,B:Hap Hopper,
  Sparkman's ID revealed . . . 1,000.00
11 BHg,V:Japanese 700.00
12 BHg,Another N:Sparkman . . . 700.00
13 BHg,Hap Hopper Rides
  For Freedom 700.00
14 BHg,BHg(c),Tarzan
  V:Yellow Killer. 1,000.00
15 BHg 600.00
16 BHg,Sparkman V:Japanese . . 600.00
17 BHg,Nancy(c) 600.00
18 BHg,Sparkman in Crete 600.00
19 BHg,I&B:Race Riley,
  Commandos 600.00
20 BHg,Nancy(c) 600.00
21 BHg,Tarzan(c). 750.00
22 BHg,Nancy(c) 500.00
23 BHg,Capt&Kids(c). 500.00
24 BHg,Nancy(c) 500.00
25 BHg,BHg(c),Tarzan(c). 750.00
26 BHg,Capt&Kids(c). 500.00

Sparkler Comics #44
© *United Features*

GOLDEN AGE

27 BHg,Nancy(c)	500.00
28 BHg,BHg(c),Tarzan(c)	750.00
29 BHg,Capt&Kids(c)	500.00
30 BHg,Nancy(c)	500.00
31 BHg,BHg(c),Tarzan(c)	750.00
32 BHg,Capt&Kids(c)	300.00
33 BHg,Nancy(c)	300.00
34 BHg,BHg(c),Tarzan(c)	750.00
35 BHg,Capt&Kids(c)	300.00
36 BHg,Nancy(c)	300.00
37 BHg,BHg(c),Tarzan(c)	750.00
38 BHg,Capt&Kids(c)	350.00
39 BHg,BHg(c),Tarzan(c)	800.00
40 BHg,Nancy(c)	350.00
41 BHg,Capt&Kids(c)	200.00
42 BHg,BHg,Tarzan(c)	500.00
43 BHg,Nancy(c)	200.00
44 BHg,Tarzan(c)	500.00
45 BHg,Capt&Kids(c)	200.00
46 BHg,Nancy(c)	200.00
47 BHg,Tarzan(c)	500.00
48 BHg,Nancy(c)	200.00
49 BHg,Capt&Kids(c)	200.00
50 BHg,BHg(c),Tarzan(c)	500.00
51 BHg,Capt&Kids(c)	200.00
52 BHg,Nancy(c)	200.00
53 BHg,BHg(c),Tarzan(c)	500.00
54 BHg,Capt&Kids(c)	200.00
55 BHg,Nancy(c)	200.00
56 BHg,Capt&Kids(c)	200.00
57 BHg,F:Li'l Abner	200.00
58 BHg,A:Fearless Fosdick	350.00
59 BHg,B:Li'l Abner	350.00
60 BHg,Nancy(c)	200.00
61 BHg,Capt&Kids(c)	200.00
62 BHg,Li'L Abner(c)	200.00
63 BHg,Capt&Kids(c)	200.00
64 BHg,Valentines (c)	200.00
65 BHg,Nancy(c)	200.00
66 BHg,Capt&Kids(c)	200.00
67 BHg,Nancy(c)	200.00
68 BHg	200.00
69 BHg,B:Nancy (c)	200.00
70 BHg	200.00
71 thru 80 BHg	@150.00
81 BHg,E:Nancy(c)	150.00
82 BHg	150.00
83 BHg,Tarzan(c)	200.00
84 BHg	150.00
85 BHg,E:Li'l Abner	150.00
86 BHg	150.00
87 BHg,Nancy(c)	150.00
88 thru 96 BHg	@150.00
97 BHg,O:Lady Ruggles	350.00
98 BHg	100.00

99 BHg,Nancy(c)	100.00
100 BHg,Nancy(c)	125.00
101 thru 107 BHg	@100.00
108 & 109 BHg,ATh	150.00
110 BHg	100.00
111 BHg	100.00
112 BHg	100.00
113 BHg,ATh	125.00
114 thru 120 BHg	@100.00
Becomes:	

NANCY AND SLUGGO
St. John/Dell Publ. 1955

121	150.00
122 thru 130	@125.00
131 thru 145	@100.00

SPARKLING STARS
Holyoke Publishing Co., June, 1944

1 B:Hell's Angels,Ali Baba,FBI, Boxie Weaver,Petey & Pop	300.00
2 Speed Spaulding	250.00
3 FBI	150.00
4 thru 12	@150.00
13 O&I:Jungo, The Man-Beast	175.00
14	150.00
15	150.00
16	150.00
17 thru 19	@150.00
20 I:Fangs the Wolfboy	150.00
21 thru 28	@150.00
29 Bondage(c)	300.00
30 thru 32	@100.00
33 March, 1948	100.00

SPARKMAN
Frances M. McQueeny, 1944

1 O:Sparkman	450.00

SPARKY WATTS
Columbia Comics Group, 1942

1 A:Skyman,Hitler(c)	1,200.00
2	500.00
3	350.00
4 O:Skyman	350.00
5 A:Skyman	300.00
6	200.00
7	200.00
8	250.00
9	200.00
10 1949	200.00

[STEVE SAUNDERS] SPECIAL AGENT
Parents Magazine/ Commended Comics, Dec., 1947

1 J. Edgar Hoover, Ph(c)	200.00
2	150.00
3 thru 7	@125.00
8 Sept., 1949	125.00

SPECIAL COMICS
See: LAUGH COMICS

SPECIAL EDITION COMICS
Fawcett Publications, Aug., 1940

1 CCB,CCB(c),F:Captain Marvel	18,000.00

A SPECTACULAR FEATURE MAGAZINE
Fox Features Syndicate, 1950

1 (11) Samson and Delilah	350.00

Becomes:

SPECTACULAR FEATURES MAGAZINE
Fox Features Syndicate, 1950

2 (12) Iwo Jima	360.00
3 True Crime Cases	275.00

SPECTACULAR STORIES MAGAZINE
Hero Books (Fox Features Syndicate), 1950

3 Actual Crime Cases	500.00
4 Sherlock Holmes	325.00

SPEED COMICS
Brookwood/Speed Publ. Harvey Publications, Oct., 1939

1 BP,B&O:Shock Gibson,B:Spike Marlin,Biff Bannon	6,000.00
2 BP,B:Shock Gibson(c)	1,700.00
3 BP,GT	1,200.00
4 BP	1,000.00
5 BP,DBr	1,000.00
6 BP,GT	800.00
7 GT,JKu,Bondage, B:Mars Mason	800.00
8 JKu	850.00
9 JKu	850.00
10 JKu,E:Shock Gibson(c)	850.00
11 JKu,E:Mars Mason	850.00
12 B:The Wasp	900.00
13 I:Captain Freedom;B:Girls Commandos,Pat Parker	900.00
14 AAv,Pocket sized-100pgs	1,200.00
15 AAv,Pocket size	1,200.00
16 JKu,AAv,Pocket size	1,200.00
17 O:Black Cat	1,300.00
18 B:Capt.Freedom,Bondage(c)	1,100.00
19 S&K	1,000.00
20 S&K	1,000.00
21 JKu(c),Hitler & Tojo	1,200.00
22 JKu(c)	1,000.00
23 JKu(c),O:Girl Commandos	1,000.00
24 Hitler,Tojo & Mussilini(c)	1,100.00
25	1,000.00
26 GT,Flag (c),Black Cat	1,000.00
27 GT,Black Cat	1,000.00
28 E:Capt Freedom	1,000.00
29 Case o/t Black Marketeers	1,000.00
30 POW Death Chambers	1,000.00
31 ASh(c),Nazi Thrashing(c)	1,200.00
32 ASh(c)	1,100.00

Sparkler Comics #119
© United Features Syndicate

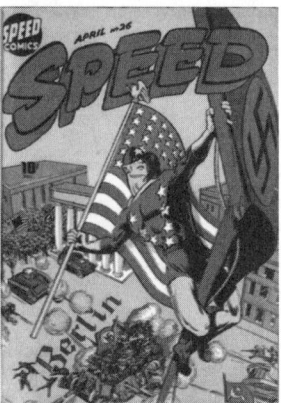

Speed Comics #26
© Harvey Publications

33 ASh(c) 1,100.00
34 ASh(c) 1,100.00
35 ASh(c),BlackCat'sDeathTrap 1,150.00
36 ASh(c) 1,100.00
37 RP(c) 1,100.00
38 RP(c),War Bond Plea with Iwo
   Jima flag allusion(c) 1,100.00
39 RP(c),B:Capt Freedom(c) . . 1,200.00
40 RP(c) 1,200.00
41 RP(c) 1,200.00
42 JKu,RP(c). 1,200.00
43 JKu,AAv,E:Capt Freedom(c) 1,250.00
44 BP,JKu,Four Kids on a raft,
   Jan.–Feb., 1947 . . . . 1,300.00

SPEED SMITH
THE HOT ROD KING
Ziff-Davis Publishing Co.,
Spring, 1952
1 INS,Ph(c),A:Roscoe
   the Rascal 300.00

SPIRIT, THE
Will Eisner
(Weekly Coverless
Comic Book), June, 1940
WE,O:SPirit 1,400.00
6/9/40 WE 700.00
6/16/40 WE,Black Queen . . . 400.00
6/23/40 WE,Mr Mystic 250.00
6/30/40 WE 250.00
7/7/40 WE,Black Queen 250.00
7/14/40 WE 200.00
7/21/40 WE 200.00
7/28/40 WE 200.00
8/4/40 WE 200.00
7/7/40-11/24/40,WE 165.00
11/10/40 WE,Black Queen . . 150.00
12/1/40 WE,Ellen
   Spanking(c) 225.00
12/8/40-12/29/40 . . . . 125.00
1941 WE Each 125.00
   3/16 WE I:Silk Satin 200.00
   6/15 WE I Twilight 125.00
   6/22 WE Hitler 125.00
1942 WE Each. 100.00
   2-1 Duchess 125.00
   2-15 . . . . 100.00
   2-23 . . . . 150.00
1943 WE Each,LF,WE scripts . . . 100.00
1944 JCo,LF 100.00
1945 LF Each. 100.00
1946 WE Each 100.00
   1/13 WE,O:The Spirit. 125.00
   1/20 WE,Satin 125.00
   3/17 WE,I:Nylon 125.00
   4/21 WE,I:Mr.Carrion. 150.00
   7/7 WE,I:Dulcet Tone&Skinny 125.00
   10/6 WE,I:F:Gell 100.00
1947 WE Each. 100.00
   7/13.,WE,Hansel &Gretel . . . 125.00
   7/20,WE,A:Bomb. 125.00
   9/28,WE,Flying Saucers 100.00
   10/5,WE, Cinderella 125.00
   12/7,WE,I:Power Puff 125.00
1948 WE Each 125.00
   1/11,WE,Sparrow Fallon 125.00
   1/25,WE,I:Last A Net 125.00
   3/14,WE,A:Kretuama. 125.00
   4/4,WE,A:Wildrice 125.00
   7/25,The Thing 100.00
   8/22,Poe Tale,Horror 125.00
   9/18, A:Lorelei 100.00
   11/7,WE,A:Plaster of Paris . . 100.00
1949 WE Each 100.00
   1/23 WE,I:Thorne 100.00
   8/21 WE,I:Monica Veto 100.00
   9/25 WE,A;Ice 100.00
   12/4 WE,I:Flaxen. 100.00
1950 WE Each 100.00
   1/8 WE,I:Sand Saref 150.00

THE STAR-LEDGER

Spirit Insert 3-26-50
© *Will Eisner*

2/10, Horror Issue 100.00
1951 WE(Last WE 8/12/51) . . @100.00
   Non-Eisners . . . . @25.00
1952 Non-Eisners . . . . @25.00
   7/27 WW,Denny Colt. 500.00
   8/3 WW,Moon 500.00
   8/10 WW.Moon 500.00
   8/17 WW,WE,Heart 400.00
   8/24 WW,Rescue. 400.00
   8/31 WW,Last Man 400.00
   9/7 WW,Man Moon 550.00
   9/14 WE. 150.00
   9/21 WE Space 350.00
   9/28 WE Moon. 400.00
   10/5 WE Last Story 250.00

SPIRIT, THE
Quality Comics Group/
Vital Publ., 1944
N# Wanted Dead or Alive! . . . 1,400.00
N# ...in Crime Doesn't Pay,LF(c) 700.00
N# ...In Murder Runs Wild . . . 600.00
4 ...Flirts with Death 500.00
5 ...Wanted Dead or Alive. 400.00
6 ...Gives You Triple Value 350.00
7 ...Rocks the Underworld 350.00
8 ...Cracks Down on Crime,LF(c) 350.00
9 ...Throws Fear Into the
   Heart of Crime 350.00
10 ...Stalks Crime,RC(c) 350.00
11 ...America's Greatest
   Crime Buster 325.00
12 WE(c),....The Famous Outlaw
   Who Smashes Crime 450.00
13 WE(c),...and Ebony Cleans Out
   the Underworld;Bondage(c) . 450.00
14 WE(c) 450.00
15 WE(c),Bank Robber at Large . 450.00
16 WE(c),The Case of the
   Uncanny Cat 450.00
17 WE(c),The Organ Grinding
   Bank Robber 550.00
18 WE,WE(c),'The Bucket
   of Blood 550.00
19 WE,WE(c),'The Man Who
   Murdered the Spirit' 550.00
20 WE,WE(c),'The Vortex' 550.00
21 WE,WE(c),'P'Gell of Paris' . . 550.00
22 WE(c),TheOctopus,Aug.1950 . 900.00

SPIRIT, THE
Fiction House Magazines,
1952
1 Curse of Claymore Castle . . . 600.00
2 WE,WE(c),Who Says Crime
   Doesn't Pay 550.00

3 WE/JGr(c),League of Lions . . 425.00
4 WE,WE&JGr(c),Last Prowl of
   Mr. Mephisto;Bondage (c) . 450.00
5 WE,WE(c),Ph(c)1954 . . . . 500.00

SPIRITMAN
Will Eisner, 1944
1 3 Spirit Sections from
   1944 Bound Together 300.00
2 LF, 2 Spirit Sections
   from 1944 Bound Together . . 250.00

SPITFIRE COMICS
Harvey Publ., Aug., 1941
1 MKd(c),100-pgs.,Pocket-size 1,200.00
2 100-pgs.,Pocket-size,
   Oct., 1941 . . . . 1,100.00

SPITFIRE
Malverne Herald/
Elliot Publ. Co., 1944
132 & 133. . . . . @350.00

SPOOK COMICS
Baily Publications, 1946
1 A:Mr. Lucifer 400.00

SPOOK DETECTIVE CASES
And: SPOOK
SUSPENSE MYSTERY
See: CRIMINALS ON
THE RUN

SPOOKY
Harvey Publications,
Nov., 1955
1 Funny Apparition 900.00
2 same 500.00
3 . . . . 400.00
4 . . . . 400.00
5 . . . . 400.00
6 thru 10 same . . . . @300.00
11 thru 20 same . . . . @200.00
21 thru 30 same . . . . @100.00
31 thru 40 same . . . . @100.00
41 thru 70 same . . . . @75.00
71 thru 90 same . . . . @60.00

SPOOKY MYSTERIES
Your Guide Publishing Co.,
1946
1 Rib-Tickling Horror 275.00

SPORT COMICS
See: TRUE SPORT
PICTURE STORIES

SPORTS STARS
Sport Stars, Inc. (Parents'
Magazine), 1946
1 Johnny Weissmuller. 600.00
2 Baseball Greats 350.00
3 . . . . 300.00
4 . . . . 300.00

SPORTS THRILLS
See: DICK COLE

SPOTLIGHT COMICS
Harry 'A' Chesler Jr.
Publications,
Nov., 1944
1 GT,GT(c),B:Veiled Avenger,
   Black Dwarf,Barry Kuda . . 1,300.00
2 . . . . 850.00
3 1945,Eye Injury 900.00

GOLDEN AGE

GOLDEN AGE (sidebar)

SPUNKY
Standard Comics,
April, 1949
1 FF,Adventures of a Junior
   Cowboy 125.00
2 FF 100.00
3 . . . . 75.00
4 . . . . 75.00
5 . . . . 75.00
6 . . . . 75.00
7 Nov., 1951 . . . . 75.00

SPY AND
COUNTERSPY
Best Syndicated Features
(American Comics Group),
Aug.–Sept., 1949
1 I&O:Jonathan Kent 400.00
2 . . . . 250.00
Becomes:

SPY-HUNTERS
Dec., 1949–Jan., 1950
3 Jonathan Kent 350.00
4 J.Kent. 200.00
5 J.Kent. 200.00
6 J.Kent. 200.00
7 OW(c),J.Kent. 200.00
8 OW(c),J.Kent. 200.00
9 OW(c),J.Kent. 200.00
10 OW(c),J.Kent. 200.00
11 . . . . 125.00
12 OW(c),MD. 125.00
13 and 14. . . . . @125.00
15 OW(c) 125.00
16 AW 200.00
17 . . . . 100.00
18 War (c) 100.00
19 and 20. . . . . @100.00
21 B:War Content 100.00
22 . . . . 100.00
23 Torture. 300.00
24 'BlackmailBrigade',July,1953 . 100.00

SPY SMASHER
Fawcett Publications,
Autumn, 1941
1 B;Spy Smasher 6,000.00
2 MRa(c) 2,600.00
3 Bondage (c) 2,000.00
4 1st ISb art 1,800.00
5 MRa,Mt. Rushmore(c) 1,800.00

Spy Smasher #1
© Fawcett Publications

6 MRa(a&c),V:The Sharks
   of Steel 1,500.00
7 MRa 1,500.00
8 AB 1,200.00
9 AB,Hitler,Tojo, Mussolini(c). . 1,600.00
10 AB,Did Spy Smasher
   Kill Hitler? 1,500.00
11 AB,Feb., 1943 . . . . 1,200.00

STAMP COMICS
Youthful Magazines/Stamp
Comics, Inc.,
Oct., 1951
1 HcK,Birth of Liberty 350.00
2 HcK,RP,Battle of White Plains 200.00
3 HcK,DW,RP,Iwo Jima 175.00
4 HcK,DW,RP 175.00
5 HcK,Von Hindenberg disaster . 200.00
6 HcK,The Immortal Chaplains. . 175.00
7 HcK,RKr,RP,B&O:Railroad . . . 250.00
Becomes:

THRILLING ADVENTURES
IN STAMPS
Jan., 1953
8 HcK, 100 Pgs.. . . . . 1,000.00

STAR COMICS
Comic Magazines/Ultem
Publ./Chesler
Centaur Publications,
Feb., 1937
1 B:Dan Hastings. 3,500.00
2 . . . . 1,500.00
3 African Blacks (c) 2,000.00
4 WMc(c),A:Little Nemo. 1,300.00
5 WMc(c),A:Little Nemo 1,200.00
6 CBi(c),FGu 1,200.00
7 FGu 1,100.00
8 BoW,BoW(c),FGu,A:Little
   Nemo,Horror 1,100.00
9 FGu,CBi(c) 1,100.00
10 FGu,CBi(c),BoW,A:Impyk . 1,400.00
11 FGu,BoW,JCo 1,100.00
12 FGu,BoW,B:Riders of the
   Golden West 900.00
13 FGu,BoW 900.00
14 FGu,GFx(c). 900.00
15 CBu,B:The Last Pirate 900.00
16 CBu,B:Phantom Rider 1,000.00
2-1 CBu,B:Phantom Rider(c) . 1,000.00
2-2 CBu,A:Diana Deane 800.00
2-3 GFx(c),CBu,Hollywood 750.00
2-4 CBu 750.00
2-5 CBu 750.00
2-6 CBu,E:Phantom Rider 750.00
2-7 CBu,Jungle Queen,
   Aug., 1939 . . . . 750.00

STARLET O'HARA IN
HOLLYWOOD
Standard Comics,
Dec., 1948
1 The Terrific Tee-Age Comic . . . 350.00
2 Her Romantic Adventures in
   Movie land 200.00
3 and 4, Sept., 1949 . . . . . . @150.00

STAR RANGER
Comics Magazines/Ultem/
Centaur Publ.,
Feb., 1937
1 FGu,I:Western Comic 3,500.00
2 . . . . 1,500.00
3 FGu 1,300.00
4 . . . . 1,300.00
5 . . . . 1,300.00
6 FGu 1,200.00
7 FGu 900.00

8 GFx,FGu,PGv,BoW 900.00
9 GFx,FGu,PGv,BoW 900.00
10 JCo,GFx,FGu,PGv,BoW . . . 1,500.00
11 . . . . 1,000.00
12 JCo(a&c),FGu,PGv 1,000.00
Becomes:

COWBOY COMICS
July, 1938
13 FGu,PGv 1,000.00
14 FGu,PGv. 900.00
Becomes:

STAR RANGER
FUNNIES
Oct., 1938
15 WE,PGv 1,400.00
2-1(16) JCo(a&c) 1,100.00
2-2(17) PGv,JCo,A:Night Hawk 1,000.00
2-3(18) JCo,FGu 900.00
2-4(19) A:Kit Carson 900.00
2-5(20) Oct., 1939 . . . . 900.00

STARS AND STRIPES
COMICS
Comic Corp of America
(Centaur Publications),
May, 1941
2 PGv,PGv(c),'Called to Colors',
   The Shark,The Voice 3,500.00
3 PGv,PGv(c),O:Dr.Synthe . . . 1,900.00
4 PGv,PGv(c),I:The Stars
   & Stripes 1,600.00
5 . . . . 1,200.00
6(5), Dec., 1941 . . . . 1,200.00

STAR STUDDED
Cambridge House, 1945
N# 25 cents (c) price;128 pgs.;
   32 F:stories 500.00
N# The Cadet,Hoot Gibson,
   Blue Beetle 400.00

STARTLING COMICS
Better Publ./Nedor Publ.,
June, 1940
1 WE,LF,B&O:Captain Future,
   Mystico, Wonder Man;
   B:Masked Rider 5,000.00
2 Captain Future(c) 2,000.00
3 same. 1,500.00
4 same. 1,400.00
5 same 1,300.00
6 same 1,300.00
7 same 1,300.00
8 ASh(c),Captain Future 1,300.00
9 Bondage(c) 1,300.00
10 O:Fighting Yank 7,000.00
11 Fighting Yank(c) 2,000.00
12 Hitler,Mussolini,Tojo (c) . . . 1,800.00
13 JBi 1,500.00
14 JBi 1,500.00
15 Fighting Yank (c) 1,500.00
16 Bondage(c),O:Four
   Comrades. 1,500.00
17 Fighting Yank (c),
   E:Masked Rider 1,100.00
18 JBi,B&O:Pyroman 2,000.00
19 Pyroman(c) 1,000.00
20 Pyroman(c),B:Oracle 1,000.00
21 HcK,ASh(c)bondage(c)
   O:Ape 1,200.00
22 HcK,ASh(c),Fighting Yank(c) 1,000.00
23 HcK,BEv,ASh(c),Pyroman(c) 1,000.00
24 HcK,BEv,ASh(c),Fighting
   Yank(c) 1,000.00
25 HcK,BEv,ASh(c),Pyroman(c) 1,000.00
26 BEv,ASh(c),Fighting Yank(c) 1,000.00
27 BEv,ASh(c),Pyroman(c). . . . 1,000.00
28 BEv,ASh(c),Fighting Yank(c) 1,000.00

29 BEv,ASh(c),Pyroman(c).... 1,000.00
30 ASh(c),Fighting Yank(c).... 1,000.00
31 ASh(c),Pyroman(c)........ 1,000.00
32 ASh(c),Fighting Yank(c).... 1,000.00
33 ASh(c),Pyroman(c)........ 1,000.00
34 ASh(c),Fighting Yank(c),
　　O:Scarab 1,200.00
35 ASh(c),Pyroman(c)........ 1,000.00
36 ASh(c),Fighting Yank(c) 800.00
37 ASh(c),Bondage (c) 800.00
38 ASh(c),Bondage(c)........ 1,000.00
39 ASh(c),Pyroman(c)........ 1,000.00
40 ASh(c),E:Captain Future ... 1,000.00
41 ASh(c),Pyroman(c)........ 1,000.00
42 ASh(c),Fighting Yank(c).... 1,000.00
43 ASh(c),Pyroman(c),
　　E:Pyroman 1,000.00
44 Grl(c),Lance Lewis(c) 1,200.00
45 Grl(c),I:Tygra 1,200.00
46 Grl,Grl(c),Bondage(c) 1,200.00
47 ASh(c),Bondage(c)........ 2,000.00
48 ASh(c),Lance Lewis(c)..... 1,000.00
49 ASh(c),Bondage(c),
　　E:Fighting Yank 7,500.00
50 ASh(c),Lance Lewis(c),
　　Sea Eagle.............. 1,100.00
51 ASh(c),Sea Eagle 1,100.00
52 ASh(c) 1,100.00
53 ASh(c),Sept., 1948....... 1,100.00

STARTLING TERROR TALES
Star Publications,
May, 1952
10 WW,LbC(c),The Story Starts 1,200.00
11 LbC(c),The Ghost Spider
　　of Death 2,500.00
12 LbC(c),White Hand Horror ... 500.00
13 JyD,LbC(c),Love From
　　a Gorgor 550.00
14 LbC(c),Trapped by the
　　Color of Blood 500.00
4 LbC(c),Crime at the Carnival . 400.00
5 LbC(c),The Gruesome
　　Demon of Terror 400.00
6 LbC(c),Footprints of Death ... 400.00
7 LbC(c),The Case of the
　　Strange Murder 400.00
8 RP,LbC(c),Phantom Brigade .. 400.00
9 LbC(c),The Forbidden Tomb . 400.00
10 LbC(c),The Horrible Entity ... 500.00
11 RP,LbC(c),The Law Will
　　Win, July, 1954 .... 400.00

STEVE CANYON COMICS
Harvey Publications,
Feb., 1948–Dec., 1948
1 MC,BP,O:Steve Canyon...... 275.00
2 MC,BP 175.00
3 MC,BP,Canyon's Crew 150.00
4 MC,BP,Chase of Death 150.00
5 MC,BP,A:Happy Easter 150.00
6 MC,BP,A:Madame Lynx..... 165.00

STEVE ROPER
Famous Funnies,
April, 1948
1 Reprints newspaper strips ... 150.00
2 .... 75.00
3 .... 60.00
4 .... 60.00
5 Dec., 1948 .... 60.00

STORY OF HARRY S. TRUMAN, THE
Democratic National Committee, 1948
N# Giveaway-The Life of Our
　　33rd President 200.00

STRAIGHT ARROW
Magazine Enterprises,
Feb.–March, 1950
1 OW,B:Straight Arrow & his
　　Horse Fury 1,000.00
2 BP,B&O:Red Hawk 400.00
3 BP,FF(c) 600.00
4 BP,Cave(c)................ 350.00
5 BP,StraightArrow'sGreatLeap . 350.00
6 BP 300.00
7 BP,The Railroad Invades
　　Comanche Country 300.00
8 BP 300.00
9 BP 300.00
10 BP 300.00
11 BP,The Valley of Time...... 350.00
12 thru 19 BP .... @350.00
20 BP,Straight Arrow's
　　Great War Shield......... 300.00
21 BP,O:Fury 350.00
22 BP,FF(c) 375.00
23 BP 200.00
24 BP,The Dragons of Doom.... 250.00
25 BP, Secret Cave 200.00
26 BP,Red Hawk vs. Vikings 200.00
27 BP 150.00
28 BP,Red Hawk 150.00
29 thru 35 BP .... @150.00
36 BP Red Hawk, Drug 100.00
37 BP 100.00
38 BP 100.00
39 BP,The Canyon Beasts...... 125.00
40 BP,Secret of the
　　Spanish Specters......... 125.00
41 BP 100.00
42 BP 100.00
43 BP,I:Blaze 125.00
44 BP 100.00
45 thru 53 BP .... @100.00
54 BP,March, 1956 .... 100.00

STRANGE CONFESSIONS
Approved Publications (Ziff-Davis),
Spring, 1952
1 EK,Ph(c) 800.00
2 Ph(c) 500.00
3 EK,Ph(c),Girls Reformatory ... 500.00
4 Ph(c),Girls Reformatory...... 500.00

STRANGE FANTASY
Farrell Publications/ Ajax Comics,
Aug., 1952
(2)1 Jungle Princess......... 750.00
2 Drug & Horror 600.00
3 The Dancing Ghost 550.00
4 Demon in the Dungeon,
　　A:Rocketman............ 550.00
5 Visiting Corpse 400.00
6 .... 400.00
7 A:Madam Satan 500.00
8 A:Black Cat 400.00
9 S&K,SD, Black Cat 475.00
10 .... 400.00
11 Fearful Things Can Happen
　　in a Lonely Place......... 450.00
12 The Undying Fiend 400.00
13 Terror in the Attic,
　　Bondage(c) 500.00
14 Monster in the Building,
　　Oct.–Nov., 1954.......... 400.00

STRANGE JOURNEY
America's Best, 1957
1 .... 300.00
2 Flying Saucer............. 200.00
3 .... 175.00
4 .... 175.00

STRANGE MYSTERIES
Superior Publ./Dynamic Publ.,
1951
1 LKa,Horror 1,100.00
2 .... 600.00
3 thru 5 .... @500.00
6 .... 400.00
7 .... 400.00
8 .... 400.00
9 Bondage,3-D type 500.00
10 .... 400.00
11 thru 18 .... @300.00
19 MB 350.00
20 reprint #1, new (c)........ 300.00
21 reprint 300.00

UNKNOWN WORLD
Fawcett Publications,
June, 1952
1 NS(c),Ph(c),Will You Venture
　　to Meet the Unknown 700.00
Becomes:

Steve Canyon Comics #1
© Harvey Comics

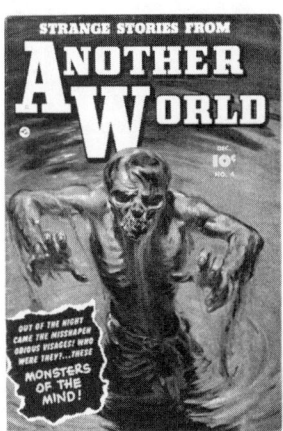

Strange Stories From Another World #4
© Fawcett Publications

STRANGE STORIES FROM ANOTHER WORLD

Aug., 1952

2 NS(c),Ph(c),Will You?
 Dare You 800.00
3 NS(c),Ph(c),The Dark Mirror . . 600.00
4 NS(c),Ph(c),Monsters of
 the Mind 600.00
5 NS(c),Ph(c),Dance of the
 Doomed, Feb., 1953 . . . . . . 600.00

STRANGE SUSPENSE STORIES

Fawcett Publications, June, 1952

1 BP,MSy,MBi 1,500.00
2 MBi,GE 900.00
3 MBi,GE(c) 700.00
4 BP 700.00
5 MBi(c),Voodoo(c) 700.00
6 BEv 400.00
7 BEv 400.00
8 AW 400.00
9 . . . . 400.00
10 . . . . 500.00
11 thru 13 . . . . @300.00
14 . . . . 350.00
15 AW,BEv(c). 350.00

Charlton Comics

16 . . . . 350.00
17 . . . . 300.00
18 SD,SD(c). 500.00
19 SD,SD(c). 700.00
20 SD,SD(c). 500.00
21 . . . . 250.00
22 SD(c). 450.00
Becomes:

THIS IS SUSPENSE!

Feb., 1955

23 WW 400.00
24 . . . . 150.00
25 . . . . 100.00
26 . . . . 100.00
Becomes:

STRANGE SUSPENSE STORIES

Oct., 1955

27 . . . . 200.00
28 . . . . 175.00
29 . . . . 175.00
30 . . . . 175.00
31 SD(c). 300.00
32 SD 300.00
33 SD 300.00
34 SD,SD(c). 650.00
35 SD 300.00
36 SD,SD(c). 300.00
37 SD 325.00
38 . . . . 300.00
39 SD 350.00
40 SD 300.00
41 SD 300.00
42 thru 44 . . . . @125.00
45 SD 250.00
46 . . . . 125.00
47 SD 250.00
48 SD 250.00
49 . . . . 125.00
50 SD 250.00
51 SD 150.00
52 SD 150.00
53 SD 150.00
54 thru 60 . . . . @125.00
61 thru 74 . . . . @100.00
75 Capt. Atom 250.00
76 Capt. Atom 100.00

77 Capt. Atom 100.00

STRANGE SUSPENSE STORIES

See: LAWBREAKERS

STRANGE TERRORS

St. John Publishing Co., June, 1952

1 The Ghost of Castle
 Karloff, Bondage(c) 900.00
2 UnshackledFlight intoNowhere 600.00
3 JKu,Ph(c),The Ghost Who
 Ruled Crazy Heights 750.00
4 JKu,Ph(c),Terror from
 the Tombs 900.00
5 JKu,Ph(c),No Escaping
 the Pool of Death 750.00
6 LC,PMo,Bondage(c),Giant. . . . 900.00
7 JKu,JKu(c),Cat's Death,Giant 1,000.00

STRANGE WORLD OF YOUR DREAMS

Prize Group, Aug., 1952

1 S&K(c),What Do They Mean–
 Messages Rec'd in Sleep . 1,000.00
2 MMe,S&K(c),Why did I Dream
 That I Was Being Married
 to a Man without a Face? . . . 800.00
3 S&K(c) 750.00
4 MMe,S&K(c),The Story of
 a Man Who Dreamed a Murder
 that Happened 600.00

STRANGE WORLDS

Avon Periodicals, Nov., 1950

1 JKu,Spider God of Akka . . . 2,000.00
2 WW,Dara of the Vikings . . . 1,800.00
3 AW&FF,EK(c),WW,JO. 3,500.00
4 JO,WW,WW(c),The
 Enchanted Dagger 2,000.00
5 WW,WW(c),JO,Bondage(c);
 Sirens of Space 1,500.00
6 EK,WW(c),JO,SC,
 Maid o/t Mist 1,000.00
7 EK, Sabotage on
 Space Station 1 . . . . 700.00
8 JKu,EK,The Metal Murderer . . 700.00
9 The Radium Monsters 700.00
18 JKu 600.00

Stuntman Comics #1
© Harvey Comics

19 Astounding Super
 Science Fantasies 600.00
20 WW(c),Fighting War Stories . . 200.00
21 EK(c). 150.00
22 EK(c),Sept.–Oct., 1955 . . . . . 150.00

STRICTLY PRIVATE

Eastern Color Printing, July, 1942

1 You're in theArmyNow-Humor . 300.00
2 F:Peter Plink, 1942 . . . . 300.00

STUNTMAN COMICS

Harvey Publications, April–May, 1946

1 S&K,O:Stuntman 1,900.00
2 S&K,New Champ of Split-
 Second Action 1,100.00
3 S&K,Digest sized,Mail Order
 Only, B&W interior,
 Oct.–Nov., 1946 . . . . 1,300.00

SUGAR BOWL COMICS

Famous Funnies, May, 1948

1 ATh,ATh(c),The Newest in
 Teen Age! 175.00
2 . . . . 100.00
3 ATh 125.00
4 . . . . 75.00
5 Jan., 1949 . . . . 75.00

SUN FUN KOMIKS

Sun Publications, 1939

1 F:Spineless Sam the
 Sweetheart 900.00

SUNNY, AMERICA'S SWEETHEART

Fox Features Syndicate, Dec., 1947

11 AF,AF(c) 1,800.00
12 AF,AF(c). 1,400.00
13 AF,AF(c). 1,400.00
14 AF,AF(c). 1,400.00

SUNSET CARSON

Charlton Comics, Feb., 1951–Aug., 1951

1 Painted, Ph(c);Wyoming
 Mail 1,200.00
2 Kit Carson-Pioneer 900.00
3 . . . . 700.00
4 Panhandle Trouble. 700.00

SUPER BOOK OF COMICS

Western Publishing Co., 1943

N# Dick Tracy 500.00
1 Dick Tracy, Smuggling 500.00
1a Smilin' Jack 250.00
2 Smitty,Magic Morro 250.00
3 Capt. Midnight 500.00
3a Moon Mullins 200.00
4 Red Ryder,Magic Morro. 300.00
4a Smitty. 200.00
5 Don Winslow,Magic Morro. . . . 300.00
5a DonWinslow,StratosphereJim 300.00
5a Terry & the Pirates 350.00
6 Don Winslow 300.00
6a King of the Royal Mounties . . 350.00
7 Little Orphan Annie 250.00
7a Dick Tracy 500.00
8 Dick Tracy 400.00
8a Dan Dunn. 200.00
9 Terry & the Pirates. 400.00
10 Red Ryder, Magic Morro. 200.00

SUPER-BOOK OF COMICS

Western Publishing Co., 1944

1 Dick Tracy (Omar)	300.00
1 Dick Tracy (Hancock)	200.00
2 Bugs Bunny (Omar)	200.00
2 Bugs Bunny (Hancock)	200.00
3 Terry & the Pirates (Omar)	250.00
3 Terry & the Pirates (Hancock)	250.00
4 Andy Panda (Omar)	100.00
4 Andy Panda (Hancock)	100.00
5 Smokey Stover (Omar)	100.00
5 Smokey Stover (Hancock)	100.00
6 Porky Pig (Omar)	200.00
6 Porky Pig (Hancock)	175.00
7 Smilin' Jack (Omar)	100.00
7 Smilin' Jack (Hancock)	100.00
8 Oswald the Rabbit (Omar)	100.00
8 Oswald the Rabbit (Hancock)	75.00
9 Alley Oop (Omar)	200.00
9 Alley Oop (Hancock)	175.00
10 Elmer Fudd (Omar)	100.00
10 Elmer Fudd (Hancock)	75.00
11 Little Orphan Annie (Omar)	100.00
11 Little Orphan Annie (Hancock)	100.00
12 Woody Woodpecker (Omar)	125.00
12 WoodyWoodpecker(Hancock)	100.00
13 Dick Tracy (Omar)	200.00
13 Dick Tracy (Hancock)	175.00
14 Bugs Bunny (Omar)	200.00
14 Bugs Bunny (Hancock)	150.00
15 Andy Panda (Omar)	100.00
15 Andy Panda (Hancock)	75.00
16 Terry & the Pirates (Omar)	200.00
16 Terry & the Pirates (Hancock)	175.00
17 Smokey Stover (Omar)	100.00
17 Smokey Stover (Hancock)	75.00
18 Porky Pig (Omar)	150.00
18 Smokey Stover (Hancock)	75.00
19 Smilin' Jack (Omar)	75.00
N# Smilin' Jack (Hancock)	50.00
20 Oswald the Rabbit (Omar)	50.00
N# Oswald the Rabbit (Hancock)	50.00
21 Gasoline Alley (Omar)	50.00
N# Gasoline Alley (Hancock)	50.00
22 Elmer Fudd (Omar)	75.00
N# Elmer Fudd (Hancock)	60.00
23 Little Orphan Annie (Omar)	75.00
N# Little Orphan Annie (Hancock)	60.00
24 Woody Woodpecker (Omar)	50.00
N# WoodyWoodpecker(Hancock)	50.00
25 Dick Tracy (Omar)	100.00
N# Dick Tracy (Hancock)	75.00
26 Bugs Bunny (Omar)	60.00
N# Bugs Bunny (Hancock)	50.00
27 Andy Panda (Omar)	50.00
27 Andy Panda (Hancock)	40.00
28 Terry & the Pirates (Omar)	125.00
28 Terry & the Pirates (Hancock)	100.00
29 Smokey Stover (Omar)	50.00
29 Smokey Stover (Hancock)	50.00
30 Porky Pig (Omar)	60.00
30 Porky Pig (Hancock)	50.00
N# Bugs Bunny (Hancock)	50.00

SUPER CIRCUS

Cross Publishing Co., Jan., 1951

1 Partial Ph(c)	200.00
2	125.00
3	100.00
4	100.00
5 1951	100.00

SUPER COMICS

Dell Publishing Co., May, 1938

1 Dick Tracy,Terry and the Pirates,Smilin'Jack,Smokey Stover,Orphan Annie,etc.	3,600.00

Super Comics #10
© Dell Publishing

2	1,400.00
3	1,200.00
4	1,100.00
5 Gumps(c)	1,000.00
6	750.00
7 Smokey Stover(c)	750.00
8 Dick Tracy(c)	750.00
9	750.00
10 Dick Tracy(c)	750.00
11	650.00
12	650.00
13	650.00
14	650.00
15	650.00
16 Terry & the Pirates	600.00
17 Dick Tracy(c)	600.00
18	600.00
19	600.00
20 Smilin'Jack(c)	625.00
21 B:Magic Morro	500.00
22 Magic Morro(c)	550.00
23 all star(c)	500.00
24 Dick Tracy(c)	550.00
25 Magic Morro(c)	500.00
26	500.00
27 Magic Morro(c)	500.00
28 Jim Ellis(c)	550.00
29 Smilin'Jack(c)	500.00
30 inc.The Sea Hawk	550.00
31 Dick Tracy(c)	500.00
32 Smilin' Jack(c)	525.00
33 Jim Ellis(c)	500.00
34 Magic Morro(c)	500.00
35 thru 40 Dick Tracy(c)	@500.00
41 B:Lightning Jim	350.00
42 thru 50 Dick Tracy(c)	@350.00
51 thru 54 Dick Tracy(c)	@250.00
55	250.00
56	250.00
57 Dick Tracy(c)	250.00
58 Smitty(c)	250.00
59	250.00
60 Dick Tracy(c)	275.00
61	235.00
62 Flag(c)	235.00
63 Dick Tracy(c)	235.00
64 Smitty(c)	225.00
65 Dick Tracy(c)	235.00
66 Dick Tracy(c)	235.00
67 Christmas(c)	235.00
68 Dick Tracy(c)	235.00
69 Dick Tracy(c)	235.00
70 Dick Tracy(c)	235.00
71 Dick Tracy(c)	200.00
72 Dick Tracy(c)	200.00
73 Smitty(c)	200.00

74 War Bond(c)	200.00
75 Dick Tracy(c)	200.00
76 Dick Tracy(c)	200.00
77 Dick Tracy(c)	200.00
78 Smitty(c)	150.00
79 Dick Tracy(c)	150.00
80 Smitty(c)	150.00
81 Dick Tracy(c)	150.00
82 Dick Tracy(c)	150.00
83 Smitty(c)	135.00
84 Dick Tracy(c)	150.00
85 Smitty(c)	135.00
86 All on cover	150.00
87 All on cover	150.00
88 Dick Tracy(c)	150.00
89 Smitty(c)	135.00
90 Dick Tracy(c)	150.00
91 Smitty(c)	135.00
92 Dick Tracy(c)	150.00
93 Dick Tracy(c)	150.00
94 Dick Tracy(c)	150.00
95 thru 99	@135.00
100	150.00
101 thru 115	@150.00
116 Smokey Stover(c)	100.00
117 Gasoline Alley(c)	100.00
118 Smokey Stover(c)	100.00
119 Terry and the Pirates(c)	110.00
120	100.00
121	100.00

SUPER-DOOPER COMICS

Able Manufacturing Co., 1946

1 A:Gangbuster	300.00
2	200.00
3 & 4	@150.00
5 A:Captain Freedom,Shock Gibson	150.00
6 & 7 same	@150.00
8 A:Shock Gibson, 1946	150.00

SUPER DUCK COMICS

MLJ Magazines/Close-Up (Archie Publ.), Autumn, 1944

1 O:Super Duck, Hitler	850.00
2	350.00
3 I:Mr. Monster	250.00
4 & 5	@225.00
6 thru 10	@200.00
11 thru 20	@150.00
21 thru 40	@125.00
41 thru 60	@100.00
61 thru 94	@75.00

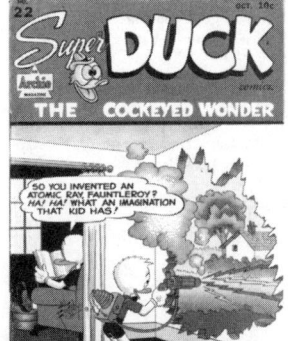

Super Duck #22
© Archie Comics

SUPER FUNNIES
Superior Comics Publishers, March, 1954
1 Dopey Duck 500.00
2 Out of the Booby-Hatch 200.00
Becomes:

SUPER WESTERN FUNNIES
1954
3 F:Phantom Ranger 100.00
4 F:Phantom Ranger,Sept., 1954 100.00

SUPERIOR STORIES
Nesbit Publishing Co., 1955
1 Wells-The Invisible Man 300.00
2 Ingrahams-Pirate of the Gulf . . 125.00
3 Clark-Wreck of Grosvenor 125.00
4 O'Henry-Texas Rangers 125.00

SUPER MAGICIAN COMICS
Street & Smith Publ., May, 1941
1 B:The MysteriousBlackstone 1,000.00
2 V:Wild Tribes of Africa 600.00
3 V:Oriental Wizard 600.00
4 V:Quetzal Wizard,O:Transo . . . 500.00
5 A:The Moylan Sisters 500.00
6 JaB,JaB(c),The Eddie
  Cantor story 500.00
7 In the House of Skulls 525.00
8 A:Abbott & Costello 550.00
9 V:Duneen the Man-Ape 525.00
10 V:Pirates o/t Sargasso Sea. . . 525.00
11 JaB(c),V:Fire Wizards 525.00
12 V:Baal 525.00
2-1 A:The Shadow 550.00
2-2 Temple of the 10,000 Idols . . 300.00
2-3 Optical Illusion on (c)-
  turn Jap into Monkey 300.00
2-4 V:Cannibal Killers 300.00
2-5 V:The Pygmies of Lemuriai . 300.00
2-6 V:Pirates & Indians 300.00
2-7 Can Blackstone Catch the
  Cannonball? 300.00
2-8 V:Marabout,B:Red Dragon . . 300.00
2-9 . . . . 300.00
2-10 Pearl Dives Swallowed By
  Sea Demons 300.00
2-11 Blackstone Invades
  Pelican Islands 300.00
2-12 V:Bubbles of Death 300.00
3-1 . . . . 350.00
3-2 Bondage(c),Midsummers
  Eve 300.00
3-3 The Enchanted Garden 300.00
3-4 Fabulous Aztec Treasure . . . 300.00
3-5 A:Buffalo Bill 300.00
3-6 Magic Tricks to Mystify 300.00
3-7 V:Guy Fawkes 300.00
3-8 V:Hindu Spook Maker 300.00
3-9 . . . . 300.00
3-10 V:The Water Wizards 300.00
3-11 V:The Green Goliath 300.00
3-12 Lady in White 300.00
4-1 Cannibal of Crime 225.00
4-2 The Devil's Castle 225.00
4-3 V:Demons of Golden River . . 225.00
4-4 V:Dr. Zero 225.00
4-5 Bondage(c) 225.00
4-6 V:A Terror Gang 225.00
4-7 . . . . 225.00
4-8 Mystery of the
  Disappearing Horse 225.00
4-9 A Floating Light? 225.00
4-10 Levitation 225.00
4-11 Lost, Strange Land
  of Shangri 225.00
4-12 I:Nigel Elliman 225.00

5-1 V:Voodoo Wizards of the
  Everglades,Bondage (c) 225.00
5-2 Treasure of the Florida
  Keys; Bondage (c) 225.00
5-3 Elliman Battles Triple Crime . 225.00
5-4 Can A Human Being Really
  Become Invisible 225.00
5-5 Mystery of the Twin Pools . . 225.00
5-6 A:Houdini 225.00
5-7 F:Red Dragon 500.00
5-8 F:Red Dragon,
  Feb.–March, 1947 . . . . 500.00

SUPERMOUSE
Standard Comics/Pines, Dec., 1948
1 FF,(fa) 400.00
2 FF,(fa) 200.00
3 FF,(fa) 150.00
4 FF,(fa) 150.00
5 FF,(fa) 150.00
6 FF,(fa) 150.00
7 thru 10 (fa) . . . . @125.00
11 thru 20 (fa) . . . . @125.00
21 thru 44 (fa) . . . . @100.00
45 (fa),Autumn, 1958 . . . . 100.00

SUPER-MYSTERY COMICS
Periodical House (Ace Magazines), July, 1940
1 B:Magno,Vulcan,Q-13,Flint
  of the Mountes 5,500.00
2 Bondage (c) 1,700.00
3 JaB,B:Black Spider 1,300.00
4 O:Davy;A:Captain Gallant . . 900.00
5 JaB,JM(c),I&B:The Clown . . 900.00
6 JM,JM(c),V:The Clown 750.00
2-1 JM,JM(c),O:Buckskin,
  Bondage(c) 800.00
2-2 JM,JM(c),V:The Clown 750.00
2-3 JM,JM(c),V:The Clown 750.00
2-4 JM,JM(c),V:The Nazis 750.00
2-5 JM,JM(c),Bondage(c) 750.00
2-6 JM,JM(c),Bondage(c),
  'Foreign Correspondent' 750.00
3-1 B:Black Ace 750.00
3-2 A:Mr, Risk, Bondage(c) 750.00
3-3 HK,HK(c),I:Lancer;B:Dr.
  Nemesis, The Sword 850.00
3-4 HK 1,400.00
3-5 HK,LbC,A:Mr. Risk 750.00
3-6 HK,LbC,A:Paul Revere Jr. . 750.00
4-1 HK,LbC,A:Twin Must Die . . 700.00

4-2 A:Mr. Risk 450.00
4-3 Mango out to Kill Davey! . . . 450.00
4-4 Danger Laughs at Mr. Risk . . 450.00
4-5 A:Mr. Risk 450.00
4-6 RP,A:Mr. Risk 450.00
5-1 RP 450.00
5-2 RP,RP(c),The Riddle of the
  Swamp-Land Spirit 450.00
5-3 RP,RP(c),The Case of the
  Whispering Death 450.00
5-4 RP,RP(c) 450.00
5-5 RP,Harry the Hack 450.00
5-6 . . . . 450.00
6-1 . . . . 350.00
6-2 RP,A:Mr. Risk 350.00
6-3 Bondage (c) 375.00
6-4 E:Mango;A:Mr. Risk 350.00
6-5 Bondage(c) 375.00
6-6 A:Mr. Risk 350.00
7-1 . . . . 350.00
7-2 KBa(c) 350.00
7-3 Bondage(c) 375.00
7-4 . . . . 350.00
7-5 . . . . 350.00
7-6 . . . . 350.00
8-1 The Riddle of the Rowboat . . 300.00
8-2 Death Meets a Train 300.00
8-3 The Man Who Couldn't Die . 300.00
8-4 RP(c) 300.00
8-5 GT,MMe,Staged for Murder . 300.00
8-6 Unlucky Seven,July, 1949 . . 300.00

ARMY AND NAVY COMICS
Street & Smith Publ., May, 1941
1 Hawaii is Calling You,Capt.
  Fury,Nick Carter. 800.00
2 Private Rock V;Hitler 500.00
3 The Fighting Fourth 500.00
4 The Fighting Irish 500.00
5 I:Super Snipe 800.00
Becomes:

SUPERSNIPE COMICS
Oct., 1942
6 A "Comic" With A Sense
  of Humor 1,700.00
7 A:Wacky, Rex King 800.00
8 Axis Powers & Satan(c),
  Hitler(c). 1,400.00
9 Hitler Voodoo Doll (c) 1,500.00
10 Lighting (c) 800.00
11 A:Little Nemo 800.00
12 Football(c). 800.00
2-1 B:Huck Finn 1,200.00
2-2 Battles Shark 650.00
2-3 Battles Dinosaur 500.00
2-4 Baseball(c). 500.00
2-5 Battles Dinosaur 500.00
2-6 A:Pochontas. 500.00
2-7 A:Wing Woo Woo 500.00
2-8 A:Huck Finn 500.00
2-9 Dotty Loves Trouble. 500.00
2-10 Assists Farm Labor
  Shortage 500.00
2-11 Dotty & the Jelly Beans . . . 500.00
2-12 Statue of Liberty. 500.00
3-1 Ice Skating(c). 450.00
3-2 V:Pirates(c) 450.00
3-3 Baseball(c). 450.00
3-4 Jungle(c) 450.00
3-5 Learn Piglatin. 450.00
3-6 Football Hero. 450.00
3-7 Saves Girl From Grisley 450.00
3-8 Rides a Wild Horse 450.00
3-9 Powers Santa's Sleigh. 450.00
3-10 Plays Basketball 450.00
3-11 Is A Baseball Pitcher 450.00
3-12 Flies with the Birds 450.00
4-1 Catches A Whale 300.00
4-2 Track & Field Athlete 300.00

Supermouse #1
© *Standard Comics*

4-3 Think Machine(c) 300.00
4-4 Alpine Skiier 300.00
4-5 Becomes a Boxer 300.00
4-6 Race Car Driver 300.00
4-7 Bomber(c) 300.00
4-8 Baseball Star 300.00
4-9 Football Hero 300.00
4-10 Christmas(c) 300.00
4-11 Artic Adventure 300.00
4-12 The Ghost Remover 300.00
5-1 Aug.–Sept., 1949 . . . . 300.00

Super Spy #1
© Centaur Publications

SUPER SPY
**Centaur Publications,
Oct.–Nov., 1940**
1 O:Sparkler 1,500.00
2 A:Night Hawk, Drew Ghost, Tim
   Blain, S.S. Swanson the Inner
   Circle, Duke Collins, Gentlemen
   of Misfortune 900.00

SUPER WESTERN COMICS
Youthful Magazines, Aug., 1950
1 BP,BP,(c),B:Buffalo Bill,Wyatt
   Earp,CalamityJane,SamSlade 200.00
2 . . . . 100.00
3 . . . . 100.00
4 March, 1951 . . . . 100.00

SUPER WESTERN FUNNIES
See: SUPER FUNNIES

SUPERWORLD COMICS
**Komos Publications
(Hugo Gernsback), April, 1940**
1 FP,FP(c),B:MilitaryPowers,BuzzAllen
   Smarty Artie, Alibi Alige . . 13,000.00
2 FP,FP(c),A:Mario 7,500.00
3 FP,FP(c),V:Vest Wearing
   Giant Grasshoppers 6,000.00

SURE-FIRE COMICS
See: LIGHTNING COMICS

SURPRISE ADVENTURES
See: TORMENTED

SUSPENSE COMICS
**Et Es Go Mag. Inc.
(Continental Magazines),
Dec., 1945**
1 LbC, Bondage(c),B:Grey
   Mask 7,000.00
2 DRi,I:The Mask 4,500.00
3 LbC,ASh(c),Bondage(c) . . . 35,000.00
4 LbC,LbC(c),Bondage(c) 3,500.00
5 LbC,LbC(c) 3,500.00
6 LbC,LbC(c),The End of
   the Road 3,500.00
7 LbC,LbC(c) 2,700.00
8 LbC,LbC(c) 6,700.00
9 LbC,LbC(c) 2,700.00
10 RP,LbC,LbC(c) 2,700.00
11 RP,LbC,EL,LbC(c),Satan(c) . 5,500.00
12 LbC,LbC(c),Dec., 1946 . . . . 2,500.00

SUSPENSE DETECTIVE
**Fawcett Publications,
June, 1952**
1 GE,MBi,MBi(c),Death Poised
   to Strike 700.00
2 GE,MSy 400.00
3 A Furtive Footstep 350.00
4 MBi,MSy,Bondage(c),A Blood
   Chilling Scream 350.00
5 MSy,MSy(c),MBi,A Hair-Trigger
   from Death, March, 1953 . . . 350.00

SUZIE COMICS
See: TOP-NOTCH COMICS

SWEENEY
**Standard Comics,
June, 1949**
4 Buzz Sawyer's Pal 125.00
5 Sept., 1949 . . . . 100.00

SWEET SIXTEEN
**Parents' Magazine Group,
Aug.–Sept., 1946**
1 Van Johnson story 300.00
2 Alan Ladd story 200.00
3 Rip Taylor 150.00
4 Elizabeth Taylor ph(c) 300.00
5 Gregory Peck story (c) 150.00
6 Dick Haymes(c) 150.00
7 Ronald Reagan(c) & story 300.00
8 Shirley Jones(c) 125.00
9 William Holden(c) 125.00
10 James Stewart(c) 150.00
11 . . . . 125.00
12 Bob Cummings(c) 125.00
13 Robert Mitchum(c) 150.00

SWIFT ARROW
**Farrell Publications (Ajax),
Feb.–March, 1954**
1 Lone Rider's Redskin Brother 250.00
2 . . . . 125.00
3 thru 4 . . . . @100.00
5 Oct.–Nov., 1954 . . . . 100.00
(2nd Series) April, 1957
1 . . . . 100.00
2 B:Lone Rider 100.00
3 Sept., 1957 . . . . 100.00

TAFFY
**Orbit Publications/Rural Home/
Taffy Publications,
March–April, 1945**
1 LbC(c),(fa),Bondage(c) 900.00
2 LbC(c),(fa) 450.00
3 (fa) 200.00
4 (fa) 200.00
5 LbC(c),A:Van Johnson 250.00

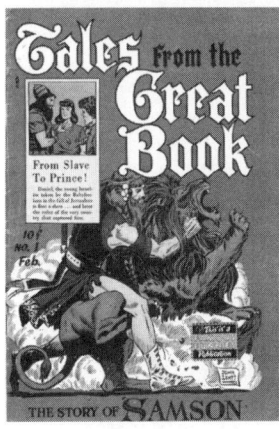

Tales From the Great Book #1
© Famous Funnies

6 A:Perry Como 150.00
7 A:Dave Clark 150.00
8 A:Glen Ford 150.00
9 A:Lon McCallister 150.00
10 A:John Hodiak 150.00
11 A:Mickey Rooney 165.00
12 Feb., 1948 . . . . 150.00

TAILSPIN
**Spotlight Publications,
Nov., 1944**
N# LbC(c),A:Firebird 400.00

TALES FROM THE CRYPT
See: CRIME PATROL

TALES FROM THE GREAT BOOK
Famous Funnies, 1955
1 Samson 125.00
2 Joshua 100.00
3 Joash the Boy King 100.00
4 David 100.00

TALES OF HORROR
**Toby Press/Minoan Publ. Corp,
June, 1952–Oct., 1954**
1 Demons of the Underworld . . . 600.00
2 What was the Thing in
   the Pool?,Torture 450.00
3 The Big Snake 300.00
4 The Curse of King Kala! 300.00
5 Hand of Fate 300.00
6 The Fiend of Flame 300.00
7 Beast From The Deep 300.00
8 The Snake that Held A
   City Captive 300.00
9 It Came From the Bottom
   of the World 350.00
10 The Serpent Strikes 300.00
11 Death Flower? 350.00
12 Guaranteed to Make Your
   Hair Stand on End,Torture . . . 350.00
13 Ghost with a Torch 350.00

TALES OF JACE PEARSON
See: JACE PEARSON

TALES OF TERROR
Toby Press, 1952
1 Just A Bunch of Hokey
   Hogwash 350.00

TALES OF TERROR ANNUAL
E.C. Comics, 1951
N# AF 9,000.00
2 AF 4,000.00
3 . . . . 3,000.00

TALLY-HO COMICS
Baily Publishing Co., 1944
N# FF,A:Snowman 700.00

Target Comics #5
© Novelty Press

TARGET COMICS
**Funnnies Inc./Novelty Publ./
Premium Group/Curtis
Circulation Co./Star
Publications, Feb., 1940**
1 BEv,JCo,CBu,JSm;B,O&I:Manowar,
White Streak,Bull's-Eye;B:City
Editor,High Grass Twins,T-Men,
Rip Rory,Fantastic Feature
Films, Calling 2-R 10,000.00
2 BEv,JSm,JCo,CBu,White
Streak(c) 5,000.00
3 BEv,JSm,JCo,CBu 2,800.00
4 JSm,JCo 2,800.00
5 CBu,BW,O:White Streak . 8,000.00
6 CBu,BW,White Streak(c) . 3,500.00
7 CBu,BW,BW(c),V:Planetoid
Stories,Space Hawk(c) . . . 10,000.00
8 CBu,BW,White Shark(c) . . 2,800.00
9 CBu,BW,White Shark(c) . . . 2,500.00
10 CBu,BW,JK(c),The
Target(c) 3,700.00
11 BW,The Target(c) 3,000.00
12 BW,same 2,800.00
2-1 BW,CBu 2,200.00
2-2 BW,BoW(c) 2,000.00
2-3 BW,BoW(c),The Target(c). . 1,500.00
2-4 BW,B:Cadet 1,500.00
2-5 BW,BoW(c),The Target(c). . 1,500.00
2-6 BW,The Target(c) 1,200.00
2-7 BW,The Cadet(c) 1,200.00
2-8 BW,same 1,200.00
2-9 BW,The Target(c) 1,200.00
2-10 BW,same 1,800.00
2-11 BW,The Cadet(c) 1,200.00
2-12 BW,same 1,200.00
3-1 BW,same 1,200.00
3-2 BW 1,200.00
3-3 BW,The Target(c) 1,200.00
3-4 BW,The Cadet(c) 1,200.00
3-5 BW 1,200.00
3-6 BW,War Bonds(c) 1,800.00

3-7 BW 1,200.00
3-8 BW,War Bonds(c) 1,800.00
3-9 BW 1,200.00
3-10 BW 1,200.00
3-11 . . . . 400.00
3-12 . . . . 400.00
4-1 JJo(c) 200.00
4-2 ERy(c) 200.00
4-3 AVi 200.00
4-4 . . . . 200.00
4-5 API(c),Statue of Liberty(c) . . . 200.00
4-6 BW 200.00
4-7 AVi 200.00
4-8,Christmas(c) 200.00
4-9 . . . . 200.00
4-10 . . . . 200.00
4-11 . . . . 200.00
4-12 . . . . 200.00
5-1 . . . . 175.00
5-2 The Target 150.00
5-3 Savings Checkers(c) 150.00
5-4 War Bonds Ph(c) 150.00
5-5 thru 5-12 . . . . @150.00
6-1 The Target(c) 150.00
6-2 . . . . 150.00
6-3 Red Cross(c) 150.00
6-4 . . . . 150.00
6-5 Savings Bonds(c) 150.00
6-6 The Target(c) 200.00
6-7 The Cadet(c) 200.00
6-8 AFa 200.00
6-9 The Target(c) 200.00
6-10 . . . . 200.00
6-11 . . . . 200.00
6-12 . . . . 200.00
7-1 . . . . 200.00
7-2 Bondage(c) 200.00
7-3 The Target(c) 150.00
7-4 DRi,The Cadet(c). 150.00
7-5 . . . . 150.00
7-6 DRi(c). 150.00
7-7 The Cadet(c) 150.00
7-8 DRi(c). 150.00
7-9 The Cadet(c) 150.00
7-10 DRi,DRi(c) 150.00
7-11 . . . . 150.00
7-12 JH(c) 150.00
8-1 . . . . 125.00
8-2 DRi,DRi(c),BK 125.00
8-3 DRi,The Cadet(c) 125.00
8-4 DRi,DRi(c) 125.00
8-5 DRi,The Cadet(c). 125.00
8-6 DRi,DRi(c) 125.00
8-7 BK,DRi,DRi(c) 125.00
8-8 DRi,The Cadet(c). 125.00
8-9 DRi,The Cadet(c) 125.00
8-10 DRi,KBa,LbC(c) 600.00
8-11 DRi,The Cadet 125.00
8-12 DRi,The Cadet. 125.00
9-1 DRi,LbC(c). 550.00
9-2 DRi. 125.00
9-3 DRi,Bondage(c),The Cadet(c) 200.00
9-4 DRi,LbC(c). 550.00
9-5 DRi,Baseball(c) 150.00
9-6 DRi,LbC(c). 550.00
9-7 DRi. 150.00
9-8 DRi,LbC(c). 550.00
9-9 DRi,Football(c). 150.00
9-10 DRi,LbC(c). 550.00
9-11,The Cadet 150.00
9-12 LbC(c),Gems(c). 550.00
10-1,The Cadet 150.00
10-2 LbC(c) 550.00
10-3 LbC(c) 550.00
Becomes:

TARGET WESTERN ROMANCES
**Star Publications,
Oct.–Nov., 1949**
106 LbC(c),The Beauty Scar 500.00

107 LbC(c),The Brand Upon His
Heart 450.00

TARZAN
**Dell Publishing Co.,
Jan.–Feb., 1948**
1 V:White Savages of Vari. . . . 2,500.00
2 Captives of Thunder Valley. . 1,000.00
3 Dwarfs of Didona 700.00
4 The Lone Hunter 700.00
5 The Men of Greed 700.00
6 Outlaws of Pal-ul-Don 600.00
7 Valley of the Monsters 600.00
8 The White Pygmies 600.00
9 The Men of A-Lur. 600.00
10 Treasure of the Bolgani 600.00
11 The Sable Lion 500.00
12 The Price of Peace 500.00
13 B:Lex Barker photo(c). 450.00
14 Lex Barker ph(c). 450.00
15 Lex Barker ph(c). 450.00
16 Lex Barker ph(c). 400.00
17 Lex Barker ph(c). 400.00
18 Lex Barker ph(c). 400.00
19 Lex Barker ph(c). 400.00
20 Lex Barker ph(c). 400.00
21 thru 24 Lex Barker ph(c). . . @350.00
25 Brothers of the Spear 375.00
26 thru 54 E:L.Barker ph(c) . . . @300.00
55 thru 70. . . . . @250.00
71 thru 79. . . . . @200.00
80 thru 90 B:ScottGordonPh(c) @150.00
91 thru 99. . . . . @125.00
100 . . . . 150.00
101 thru 110 E:S.GordonPh(c). @150.00
111 thru 120 . . . . @125.00
121 thru 131. . . . . @100.00

TEENA
Standard Comics, 1949
20 . . . . 100.00
21 . . . . 100.00
22 . . . . 100.00

TEEN-AGE ROMANCES
**St. John Publishing Co.,
Jan., 1949**
1 MB(c),MB. 700.00
2 MB(c),MB. 450.00
3 MB(c),MB. 450.00
4 Ph(c) 350.00
5 MB,Ph(c) 350.00
6 MB,Ph(c) 350.00
7 MB,Ph(c) 350.00
8 MB,Ph(c) 350.00

Teen-Age Romances #38
© St. John Publishing Col

9 MB,MB(c),JKu 400.00
10 thru 27 MB,MB(c),JKu . . . . @350.00
28 . . . . 100.00
29 . . . . 100.00
30 . . . . 100.00
31 thru 34 MB(c) . . . . @125.00
35 thru 42 MB(c),MB . . . . @125.00
43 MB(c),MB,Comics Code 200.00
44 MB(c),MB 150.00
45 MB(c),MB 200.00

TEEN-AGE TEMPTATIONS
St. John Publishing Co.,
Oct., 1952
1 MB(c),MB 800.00
2 MB(c),MB 300.00
3 MB(c),MB 400.00
4 MB(c),MB 400.00
5 MB(c),MB 400.00
6 MB(c),MB 400.00
7 MB(c),MB 400.00
8 MB(c),MB,Drug 450.00
9 MB(c),MB 400.00
Becomes:
GOING STEADY
Dec., 1954
10 MB(c),MB 275.00
11 MB(c),MB 150.00
12 MB(c),MB 150.00
13 MB(c),MB 200.00
14 MB(c),MB 250.00

TEENIE WEENIES, THE
Ziff-Davis Publishing Co.,
1951
10 . . . . 250.00
11 . . . . 250.00

TEEN LIFE
See: YOUNG LIFE

TEGRA, JUNGLE EMPRESS
See: ZEGRA, JUNGLE
EMPRESS

TELEVISION COMICS
Animated Cartoons
(Standard Comics), Feb., 1950
5 Humorous Format,I:Willie Nilly 150.00
6 . . . . 100.00
7 . . . . 100.00
8 May, 1950 . . . . 100.00

TELEVISION PUPPET
SHOW
Avon Periodicals, 1950
1 F:Sparky Smith,Spotty,
  Cheeta, Speedy 250.00
2 Nov., 1950 . . . . 150.00

TELL IT TO
THE MARINES
Toby Press, March, 1952
1 I:Spike & Pat 275.00
2 A:Madame Cobra 150.00
3 Spike & Bat on a
  Commando Raid! 125.00
4 Veil Dancing(c) 125.00
5 . . . . 125.00
6 To Paris 100.00
7 Ph(c),The Chinese Bugle 100.00
8 Ph(c),V:Communists in
  South Korea 100.00
9 Ph(c) 100.00
10 . . . . 100.00
11 . . . . 100.00
12 . . . . 100.00

13 John Wayne Ph(c) 200.00
14 Ph(c) 100.00
15 Ph(c),July, 1955 . . . . 100.00

TERRIFIC COMICS
See: HORRIFIC

TERRIFIC COMICS
Et Es Go Mag. Inc./
Continental Magazines,
Jan., 1944
1 LbC,DRi(c),F:Kid
  Terrific Drug 5,500.00
2 LcC,ASh(c),B:Boomerang,
  'Comics' McCormic 3,500.00
3 LbC,LbC(c) 3,500.00
4 LbC,RP(c) 7,000.00
5 LbC,BF,ASh(c),Bondage(c) 10,000.00
6 LbC,LbC(c),BF,Nov.,1944 . . 3,200.00

TERRIFYING TALES
Star Publications,
Jan., 1953
11 LbC,LbC(c),'TyrantsofTerror'. . 800.00
12 LbC,LbC(c),'Bondage(c),
  'Jungle Mystery'. 700.00
13 LbC(c),Bondage(c),'The
  Death-Fire,Devil Head(c). . . . 800.00
14 LbC(c),Bondage(c),'The
  Weird Idol' 650.00
15 LbC(c),'The Grim Secret',
  April, 1954 . . . . 650.00
Becomes:
JUNGLE THRILLS
Star Publications, Feb., 1952
16 LbC(c),'Kingdom of Unseen
  Terror' 750.00
Becomes:
TERRORS OF
THE JUNGLE
Star Publications, May, 1952
17 LbC(c),Bondage(c) 750.00
18 LbC(c),Strange Monsters 500.00
19 JyD,LbC(c),Bondage(c),The
  Golden Ghost Gorilla. 450.00
20 JyD,LbC(c),The Creeping
  Scourge 450.00
21 LbC(c),Evil Eyes of Death! . . . 500.00
4 JyD,LbC(c),Morass of Death . 500.00
5 JyD,LbC(c),Bondage(c),
  Savage Train 500.00
6 JyD,LbC(c),Revolt of the
  Jungle Monsters 500.00
7 JyD,LbC(c) 500.00
8 JyD,LbC(c),Death's Grim
  Reflection 500.00
9 JyD,LbC(c),Doom to
  Evil-Doers 500.00
10 JyD,LbC(c),Black Magic,
  Sept., 1954 . . . . 500.00

TERROR ILLUSTRATED
E.C. Comics,
Nov.–Dec., 1955
1 JCr,GE,Grl,JO,RC(c) 300.00
2 Spring, 1956 . . . . 200.00

BOY EXPLORERS
Harvey Comics, 1946
1 S&K(c),S&K,The Cadet 1,500.00
2 S&K(c),S&K 2,000.00
Becomes:
TERRY AND THE PIRATES
Harvey Comics, April, 1947
3 S&K,MC(c),MC,Terry and
  Dragon Lady 550.00
4 S&K,MC(c),MC 300.00

Terrors of the Jungle #9
© Star Comics

5 S&K,MC(c),MC,BP,
  Chop-Chop(c) 175.00
6 S&K,.MC(c),MC 175.00
7 S&K,MC(c),MC,BP 175.00
8 S&K,MC(c),MC,BP 175.00
9 S&K,MC(c),MC,BP 175.00
10 S&K,MC(c),MC,BP 175.00
11 S&K,MC(c),MC,BP,
  A:Man in Black 150.00
12 S&K,MC(c),MC,BP 150.00
13 S&K,MC(c),MC,Belly Dancers 150.00
14 thru 20 S&K,MC(c),MC . . . . @125.00
21 thru 26 S&K,MC(c),MC . . . . @110.00
27 Charlton Comics 100.00
28. . . . . 100.00
Becomes:
LONG JOHN SILVER
AND THE PIRATES
Charlton Comics, 1956–57
30 . . . . 125.00
31 . . . . 125.00
32 . . . . 125.00

TERRY-BEARS COMICS
St. John Publishing Co.,
June, 1952
1 . . . . 125.00
2 & 3 . . . . @100.00

TERRY-TOONS COMICS
Select, Timely, Marvel,
St. Johns, 1942
1 Paul Terry (fa). 3,000.00
2 . . . . 1,000.00
3 thru 6 . . . . @700.00
7 Hitler,Hirohito,Mussolini(c) 750.00
8 thru 20 . . . . @500.00
21 thru 37. . . . . @300.00
38 I&(c):Mighty Mouse 2,400.00
39 Mighty Mouse 700.00
40 thru 49 All Mighty Mouse . . @300.00
50 I:Heckle & Jeckle 600.00
51 thru 60. . . . . @200.00
61 thru 70. . . . . @150.00
71 thru 86. . . . . @150.00
Becomes:
PAUL TERRY'S COMICS
St. John Publishing Co.
85a Mighty Mouse, etc. 150.00
86a 100.00
87 thru 100 . . . . @100.00
101 thru 125 . . . . @100.00

GOLDEN AGE

Becomes:

ADVENTURES OF MIGHTY MOUSE

St. John Publ. Co., 1955
126 thru 128 . . . . @150.00

Pines, 1956
129 thru 143 . . . . @150.00

Dell Publ. Co., 1959
144 thru 155 . . . . @125.00

TEXAN, THE

St. John Publishing Co., Aug., 1948
1 GT,F:Buckskin Belle,The Gay
   Buckaroo,Mustang Jack 250.00
2 GT 125.00
3 BLb(c) 100.00
4 MB,MB(c) 275.00
5 MB,MB(c),Mystery Rustlers
   of the Rio Grande 275.00
6 MB(c),Death Valley
   Double-Cross 150.00
7 MB,MB(c),Comanche Justice
   Strikes at Midnight 250.00
8 MB,MB(c),Scalp Hunters
   Hide their Tracks 250.00
9 MB(c),Ghost Terror of
   the Blackfeet 250.00
10 MB,MB(c),Treason Rides
   the Warpath 125.00
11 MB,MB(c),Hawk Knife 300.00
12 MB. 350.00
13 MB,Doublecross at Devil'sDen 300.00
14 MB,Ambush at Buffalo Trail . . 300.00
15 MB,Twirling Blades Tame
   Treachery 300.00
Becomes:

FIGHTIN' TEXAN

Sept., 1952
16 GT,Wanted Dead or Alive . . . 125.00
17 LC,LC(c);Killers Trail,
   Dec., 1952 . . . . 100.00

TEX FARRELL

D.S. Publishing Co., March–April, 1948
1 Pride of the Wild West 225.00

TEX GRANGER

See: CALLING ALL BOYS

TEX RITTER WESTERN

Fawcett Publications/ Charlton Comics, Oct., 1950–May, 1959
1 Ph(c),B:Tex Ritter, his Horse
   White Flash, his dog Fury, and
   his mom Nancy. 1,000.00
2 Ph(c),Vanishing Varmints 450.00
3 Ph(c),Blazing Six-Guns 350.00
4 Ph(c),The Jaws of Terror 325.00
5 Ph(c),Bullet Trail 325.00
6 Ph(c),Killer Bait 250.00
7 Ph(c),Gunsmoke Revenge . . . 225.00
8 Ph(c),Lawless Furnace Valley 225.00
9 Ph(c),The Spider's Web 225.00
10 Ph(c),The Ghost Town 225.00
11 Ph(c),Saddle Conquest. 225.00
12 Ph(c),Prairie Inferno 175.00
13 Ph(c). 175.00
14 Ph(c). 175.00
15 Ph(c). 175.00
16 thru 19 Ph(c). . . . . @175.00
20 Ph(c),Stagecoach To Danger . 175.00
21 Ph(c), ... 200.00
22 Panic at Diamond B 150.00
23 A:Young Falcon. 125.00
24 Ph(c),Young Falcon. 125.00

25 A:Young Falcon 125.00
26 thru 38. . . . . @100.00
39 AW,AW(c) 100.00

Thing #16
© *Charlton Comics*

40 thru 46. . . . . @100.00

THING!, THE

Song Hits/Capitol Stories/ Charlton Comics, Feb., 1952
1 Horror 2,000.00
2 Crazy King(c) 1,500.00
3 Green skinned creature 1,500.00
4 AFa(c),I Was A Zombie 1,100.00
5 LM(c),Severed Head(c) 1,100.00
6 . . . . 1,100.00
7 Fingernail to Eye(c) 1,200.00
8 . . . . 1,500.00
9 Severe cruelty. 1,100.00
10 Devil(c) 900.00
11 SC,Cleaver, eye injury 1,100.00
12 SD,SD(c),Neck Blood
   Sucking. 1,100.00
13 SD,SD(c) 1,100.00
14 SD,SD(c) torture 1,100.00
15 SD,SD(c) 1,100.00
16 Eye Torture 600.00
17 BP,SD(c) 1,100.00
Becomes:

BLUE BEETLE

Feb., 1955
18 America's Fastest Moving
   Crusader Against Crime 300.00
19 JKa,Lightning Fast 300.00
20 JKa 350.00
21 The Invincible 250.00
Becomes:

MR. MUSCLES

March, 1956
22 World's Most Perfect Man. . . . 150.00
23 Aug., 1956. . . . . 100.00

THIS IS SUSPENSE

See: LAWBREAKERS

THIS IS SUSPENSE!

See: STRANGE SUSPENSE STORIES

THIS IS WAR

Standard Comics, July, 1952
5 ATh,Show Them How To Die . 200.00

6 ATh,Make Him A Soldier 125.00
7 One Man For Himself 100.00
8 Miracle on Massacre Hill 100.00
9 ATh,May, 1953 . . . . 125.00

THIS MAGAZINE IS HAUNTED

Fawcett Publications Oct., 1951
1 MBi,F:Doctor Death 1,000.00
2 GE 700.00
3 MBi,Quest of the Vampire . . . 500.00
4 BP,The Blind, The Doomed
   and the Dead 500.00
5 BP,GE,The Slithering Horror
   of Skontong Swamp! 650.00
6 Secret of the Walking Dead. . . 350.00
7 The Man Who Saw Too Much . 350.00
8 The House in the Web. 350.00
9 The Witch of Tarlo 350.00
10 I Am Dr Death,
   Severed Head(c). 600.00
11 BP,Touch of Death 350.00
12 BP. 350.00
13 BP,Severed Head(c). 600.00
14 BP,Horrors of the Damned . . . 350.00

Charlton Comics, 1954
15 DG(c) 300.00
16 SD(c). 550.00
17 SD,SD(c). 700.00
18 SD,SD(c). 600.00
19 SD(c). 550.00
20 SMz(c) 300.00
21 SD(c). 500.00
Becomes:

DANGER AND ADVENTURE

Feb., 1955
22 The Viking King,F:Ibis the
   Invincible 150.00
23 F:Nyoka the Jungle Girl
   Comics Code. 125.00
24 DG&AA(c). 100.00
25 thru 27 . . . . @100.00
Becomes:

ROBIN HOOD AND HIS MERRY MEN

April, 1956
28 . . . . 150.00
29 thru 37. . . . . @100.00
38 SD,Aug., 1958 . . . . 150.00

THIS MAGAZINE IS HAUNTED

See: CHARLIE CHAN

3-D ANIMAL FUN

Premier Magazines, 1953
1 Ziggy Pig, Silly Seal,etc. 500.00

CAPTAIN 3-D

Harvey Publ, 1953
1 . . . . 150.00

CHERRIOS 3D CLASSICS

Walt Disney Productions, 1954
1 . . . . 150.00

3-D CIRCUS

Fiction House, 1953
1 . . . . 500.00

3-D DARING ADVENTURES

St. John Publ, 1953
1 . . . . 400.00

GOLDEN AGE

3-Dell #1 Rootie Kazootie
© *Dell Publications*

3-D-ELL
Dell Publishing Co., 1953
1 Rootie Kazootie 500.00
3 Flunkey Louise 450.00

3-D DOLLY
Harvey Publ, 1953
1 Richie Rich 1,000.00

3-D EC CLASSICS
E.C. Comics 1954
1 . . . . 1,200.00
2 Tales from the Crypt of Terror 1,200.00

3-D FELIX THE CAT
Toby Press, 1953
N# 350.00

3-D FIRST CHRISTMAS
Fiction House, 1953
1 . . . . 250.00

3-D FUNNY MOVIES
Comic Media, 1953
1 Bugsey Bear 500.00

FUNNY 3-D
Harvey Publ., 1953
1 . . . . 350.00

3-D HAWK, THE
St. John Publ, 1953
1 MB,Western 400.00

3-D HOUSE OF TERROR
St. John Publ., 1953
1 . . . . 600.00

3-D I LOVE LUCY
1 Lucy, Desi, Ricky Jr. Ph(c) 600.00

3-D INDIAN WARRIORS
Star Publications, 1953
1 . . . . 250.00

(3-D Features Presents)
JET PUP
Dimensions Publ., 1953
1 . . . . 500.00

3-D JUNGLE THRILLS
Star Publications, 1953
1 . . . . 350.00

3-D KATY KEENE
Archie Publications, 1953
1 . . . . 500.00

3-D LITTLE EVA
St. John Publ, 1953
1 . . . . 350.00
2 . . . . 350.00

3-D LOVE
Steriographic Publications, 1953
1 . . . . 500.00

(Three Dimension Comics)
MIGHTY MOUSE
St. John Publ, 1953
1 . . . . 350.00
2 . . . . 350.00
3 . . . . 350.00

3-D NOODNICK
Comic Media, 1953
1 . . . . 350.00

3-D ROMANCE
Steriographic Publ., 1954
1 . . . . 500.00

(Harvey 3-D Hits)
SAD SACK
Harvey Publications, 1954
1 . . . . 400.00

3-D SHEENA,
JUNGLE QUEEN
Fiction House, 1953
1 . . . . 1,000.00

3-D SPACE KAT-ETS
Power Publishing, 1953
1 . . . . 350.00

3-D SUPER ANIMALS
Star Publications, 1953
1 Pidgy and the Magic Glasses . 350.00

3-D SUPER FUNNIES
Superior Comics Publ., 1953
1 Dopey Duck 350.00

3-D THREE STOOGES
St. John Publ., 1953
1 . . . . 700.00
2 . . . . 650.00

3-D TRUE 3D
Harvey Publ., 1953
1 . . . . 400.00
2 . . . . 350.00

3-D WESTERN FIGHTERS
Star Publications, 1953
1 . . . . 350.00

3-D Felix the Cat N#
© *Toby*

THREE RING COMICS
Spotlight Publishers, March, 1945
1 Funny Animal 200.00

THREE STOOGES
Jubilee Publ., Feb., 1949
1 JKu,Infinity(c) 1,700.00
2 JKu,On the Set of the
'The Gorilla Girl' 1,200.00
St. John Publishing Co.
1:JKu,'Hell Bent for
Treasure,' Sept., 1953 . . . . 1,200.00
2 JKu 900.00
3 JKu,3D 900.00
4 JKu,Medical Mayhem 800.00
5 JKu,Shempador-Matador
Supreme 800.00
6 JKu, ... 800.00
7 JKu,Ocotber, 1954 . . . . 800.00

THRILLING COMICS
**Better Publ./Nedor/
Standard Comics, Feb., 1940**
1 B&O:Doc Strange,B:Nickie
Norton 5,000.00
2 B:Rio Kid,Woman in Red
Pinocchio 2,500.00
3 B:Lone Eagle,The Ghost . . . 2,000.00
4 Dr Strange(c) 1,400.00
5 Bondage(c) 1,500.00
6 Dr Strange(c) 1,400.00
7 Dr Strange(c) 1,500.00
8 V:Pirates 1,500.00
9 ASh,Bondage(c) 1,500.00
10 V:Nazis 1,600.00
11 ASh(c),V:Nazis 1,300.00
12 ASh(c) 1,300.00
13 ASh(c),Bondage(c) 1,400.00
14 ASh(c) 1,000.00
15 ASh(c),V:Nazis 1,000.00
16 Bondage(c) 1,400.00
17 Dr Strange(c) 1,000.00
18 Dr Strange(c) 1,400.00
19 I&O:American Crusader 1,200.00
20 Bondage(c) 1,300.00
21 American Crusader(c) 1,000.00
22 Bondage(c) 1,200.00
23 American Crusader 1,000.00
24 I:Mike in Doc Strange 1,000.00

GOLDEN AGE

25 DR Strange(c)	1,000.00
26 Dr Strange(c)	1,000.00
27 Bondage(c)	1,200.00
28 Bondage(c)	1,200.00
29 E:Rio Kid;Bondage(c)	1,200.00
30 Bondage(c)	1,200.00
31 Dr Strange(c)	800.00
32 Dr Strange(c)	800.00
33 Dr Strange(c)	800.00
34 Dr Strange(c)	800.00
35 Dr Strange.	800.00
36 ASh(c),B:Commando	900.00
37 BO,ASh(c).	800.00
38 ASh(c).	800.00
39 ASh(c),E:American Crusader .	800.00
40 ASh(c).	800.00
41 ASh(c),F:American Crusader,	
Hitler.	1,800.00
42 ASh(c).	700.00
43 ASh(c).	700.00
44 ASh(c),Hitler(c).	1,400.00
45 EK,ASh(c).	600.00
46 ASh(c).	600.00
47 ASh(c).	600.00
48 EK,ASh(c).	600.00
49 ASh(c).	600.00
50 ASh(c).	600.00
51 ASh(c).	600.00
52 ASh(c),E:Th Ghost;	
Peto-Bondage(c).	900.00
53 ASh(c),B:Phantom Detective .	700.00
54 ASh(c),Bondage(c).	900.00
55 ASh(c),E:Lone Eagle	700.00
56 ASh(c),B:Princess Pantha	700.00
57 ASh(c).	600.00
58 ASh(c).	600.00
59 ASh(c).	600.00
60 ASh(c).	600.00
61 ASh(c),Grl,A:Lone Eagle	600.00
62 ASh(c).	600.00
63 ASh(c),GT.	600.00
64 ASh(c).	600.00
65 ASh(c),E:Commando Cubs,	
Phantom Detective	600.00
66 ASh(c).	600.00
67 FF,ASh(c).	650.00
68 FF,ASh(c).	650.00
69 FF,ASh(c).	650.00
70 FF,ASh(c).	650.00
71 FF,ASh(c).	650.00
72 FF,ASh(c),Sea Eagle	650.00
73 FF,ASh(c).	650.00
74 ASh(c),E:Princess Pantha;	
B:Buck Ranger	500.00
75 B:Western Front	250.00

Thrilling Crime Cases #49
© Star Publications

76 Western.	250.00
77 ASh(c).	250.00
78 Bondage(c).	350.00
79 BK.	250.00
80 JSe,BE,April, 1951 .	250.00

THRILLING CRIME CASES

**Star Publications,
June–July, 1950**

41 LbC(c),The Unknowns	400.00
42 LbC(c),The Gunmaster	325.00
43 LbC,LbC(c),The Chameleon.	350.00
44 LbC(c),Sugar Bowl Murder	350.00
45 LbC(c),Maze of Murder.	350.00
46 LbC,LbC(c),Modern	
Communications	325.00
47 LbC(c),The Careless Killer .	325.00
48 LbC(c),Road Black	325.00
49 LbC(c),The Poisoner.	650.00

Becomes:

SHOCKING MYSTERY CASES

Sept., 1952–Oct., 1954

50 JyD,LbC(c),Dead Man's	
Revenge	650.00
51 JyD,LbC(c),A Murderer's	
Reward	450.00
52 LbC(c),The Carnival Killer.	450.00
53 LbC(c),The Long Shot of Evil .	450.00
54 LbC(c),Double-Cross of Death	450.00
55 LbC(c),Return from Death	450.00
56 LbC(c),The Chase	500.00
57 LbC(c),Thrilling Cases	400.00
58 LbC(c),Killer at Large	400.00
59 LbC(c),Relentless Huntdown.	400.00
60 LbC(c),Lesson of the Law.	400.00

THRILLING TRUE STORY OF THE BASEBALL GIANTS

Fawcett Publications, 1952

N# Partial Ph(c),Famous Giants	
of the Past, Willie Mays	1,200.00
2 Yankees Ph(c),Joe DiMaggio,	
Yogi Berra,Mickey Mantle,	
Casey Stengel	1,000.00

THRILLS OF TOMORROW
See: TOMB OF TERROR

TICK TOCK TALES

**Magazine Enterprises,
Jan., 1946**

1 (fa) Koko & Kola	250.00
2 (fa) Calender	200.00
3 thru 10 (fa)	@150.00
11 thru 18 (fa)	@125.00
19 (fa),Flag(c)	125.00
20 thru 22 (fa)	@125.00
23 (fa),Mugsy Mouse	125.00
24 thru 33 (fa)	@125.00
34 (fa), 1951	125.00

TIM HOLT

**Magazine Enterprises,
Jan.–Feb., 1949**

1 thru 3 see: *A-1 Comics* #14, #17, #19	
4 FBe,Ph(c)	1,200.00
5 FBe,Ph(c).	700.00
6 FBe,Ph(c),I:Calico Kid	600.00
7 FBe,Ph(c),Man-Killer Mustang	500.00
8 FBe,Ph(c)	500.00
9 FBe,DAy(c),TerribleTenderfoot	500.00
10 FBe,DAy(c),The Devil Horse .	500.00
11 FBe,DAy(c),O&I:Ghost Rider .	750.00

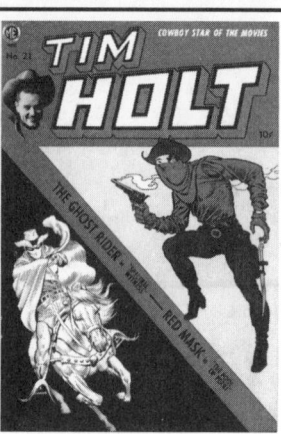

Tim Holt #21
© Magazine Enterprises

12 FBe,DAy(c),Battle at	
Bullock Gap.	250.00
13 FBe,DAy(c),Ph(c).	250.00
14 FBe,DAy(c),Ph(c),The	
Honest Bandits	250.00
15 FBe,DAy,Ph(c)	250.00
16 FBe,DAy,Ph(c)	250.00
17 FBe,DAy,Ph(c)	750.00
18 FBe,DAy,Ph(c)	300.00
19 FBe,DAy,They Dig By Night	175.00
20 FBe,DAy,O:Red Mask.	300.00
21 FBe,DAy,FF(c)	600.00
22 FBe,DAy	175.00
23 FF,FBe,DAy.	500.00
24 FBe,DAy,FBe(c)	175.00
25 FBe,DAy,FBe(c)	350.00
26 FBe,DAy,FBe(c)	175.00
27 FBe,DAy,FBe(c),V:Straw Man.	175.00
28 FBe,DAy,FBe(c),Ph(c)	175.00
29 FBe,DAy,FBe,Ph(c),	175.00
30 FBe,DAy,FBe(c),Lady Doom	
& The Death Wheel.	200.00
31 FBe,DAy,FBe(c)	200.00
32 FBe,DAy,FBe(c)	200.00
33 FBe,DAy,FBe(c)	200.00
34 FBe,DAy,FBe(c)	250.00
35 FBe,DAy,FBe(c)	250.00
36 FBe,DAy,FBe(c),Drugs	350.00
37 FBe,DAy,FBe(c)	250.00
38 FBe,DAy,FBe(c)	250.00
39 FBe,DAy,FBe(c),3D Effect	200.00
40 FBe,DAy,FBe(c)	200.00
41 FBe,DAy,FBe(c)	200.00

Becomes:

RED MASK

June–July, 1954

42 FBe,DAy,FBe(c),3D	300.00
43 FBe,DAy,FBe(c),3D	250.00
44 FBe,DAy,FBe(c),Death at	
Split Mesa,3D	250.00
45 FBe,DAy,FBe(c),V:False Red	
Mask	250.00
46 FBe,DAy,FBe(c)	250.00
47 FBe,DAy,FBe(c)	250.00
48 FBe,DAy,FBe(c),Comics Code	250.00
49 FBe,DAy,FBe(c)	250.00
50 FBe,DAy	250.00
51 FBe,DAy,The Magic of 'The	
Presto Kid'.	250.00
52 FBe,DAy,O:Presto Kid	275.00
53 FBe,DAy	200.00
54 FBe,DAy,Sept., 1957	275.00

TIM McCOY
See: ZOO FUNNIES

TIM TYLER COWBOY

Standard Comics, Nov., 1948

11	150.00
12	100.00
13 The Doll Told the Secret	100.00
14 Danger at Devil's Acres	100.00
15 Secret Treasure	100.00
16	100.00
17	100.00
18 1950	100.00

TINY TOTS COMICS

Dell Publishing Co., 1943

1 WK,fairy tales	700.00

TINY TOTS COMICS

E.C. Comics, March, 1946

N# Your First Comic Book	
B:Burton Geller(c) and art	600.00
2	300.00
3 Celebrate the 4th	275.00
4 Go Back to School	300.00
5 Celebrate the Winter	275.00
6 Do Their Spring Gardening	275.00
7 On a Thrilling Ride	275.00
8 On a Summer Vacation	275.00
9 On a Plane Ride	275.00
10 Merry X-Mas Tiny Tots	
E:Burton Geller(c)and art	275.00

TIP TOP COMICS

United Features, St. John, Dell, 1936

1 HF,Li'l Abner	12,000.00
2 HF	3,000.00
3 HF,Tarzan(c)	2,500.00
4 HF,Li'l Abner(c)	1,500.00
5 HF,Capt&Kids(c)	1,200.00
6 HF	1,100.00
7 HF	1,100.00
8 HF,Li'l Abner(c)	1,100.00
9 HF,Tarzan(c)	1,400.00
10 HF,Li'l Abner(c)	1,000.00
11 HF,Tarzan(c)	1,000.00
12 HF,Li'l Abner	800.00
13 HF,Tarzan(c)	1,000.00
14 HF,Li'l Abner(c)	800.00
15 HF,Capt&kids(c)	800.00
16 HF,Tarzan(c)	1,000.00
17 HF,Li'L Abner(c)	800.00
18 HF,Tarzan(c)	1,000.00
19 HF,Football(c)	800.00
20 HF,Capt&Kids(c)	800.00
21 HF,Tarzan(c)	850.00
22 HF,Li'i Abner(c)	550.00
23 HF,Capt&Kids(c)	550.00
24 HF,Tarzan(c)	850.00
25 HF,Capt&Kids(c)	550.00
26 HF,Li'L Abner(c)	550.00
27 HF,Tarzan(c)	850.00
28 HF,Li'l Abner(c)	550.00
29 HF,Capt&Kids(c)	550.00
30 HF,Tarzan(c)	850.00
31 HF,Capt&Kids(c)	550.00
32 HF,Tarzan(c)	850.00
33 HF,Tarzan(c)	850.00
34 HF,Capt&Kids(c)	850.00
35 HF	500.00
36 HF,HK,Tarzan(c)	850.00
37 HF,Tarzan	850.00
38 HF	500.00
39 HF,Tarzan	700.00
40 HF	500.00
41 Tarzan(c)	800.00
42	450.00
43 Tarzan(c)	550.00
44 HF	450.00
45 HF,Tarzan(c)	550.00
46 HF	450.00

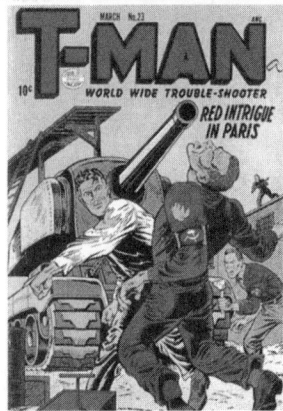

T-Man #21
© Quality Comics Group

47 HF,Tarzan(c)	550.00
48 HF	450.00
49 HF	450.00
50 HF,Tarzan(c)	550.00
51	400.00
52 Tarzan(c)	550.00
53	400.00
54 O:Minorman	550.00
55	350.00
56	350.00
57 BHg	450.00
58	300.00
59 BHg	450.00
60	300.00
61 and 62 BHg	@450.00
63 thru 90	@200.00
91 thru 99	@150.00
100	175.00
101 thru 150	@125.00
151 thru 188	@100.00
189 thru 225	@75.00

TIP TOPPER COMICS

United Features Syndicate, 1949

1 Abbie & Slats, Li'l Abner, etc.	200.00
2	150.00
3	125.00
4	125.00
5 Fearless Fosdick	125.00
6 Fearless Fosdick	125.00
7	100.00
8	100.00
9	100.00
10	100.00
11 thru 16	@100.00
17 Peanuts (c)	150.00
18 thru 24	@100.00
25 Peanuts	110.00
26 Peanuts	110.00

T-MAN

Comics Magazines (Quality Comics Group), Sept., 1951

1 JCo,Pete Trask-the Treasury Man	600.00
2 RC(c),The Girl with Death in Her Hands	300.00
3 RC(a&c),Death Trap in Iran	300.00
4 RC(a&c),Panama Peril	300.00
5 RC(a&c),Violence in Venice	300.00
6 RC(c),The Man Who Could Be Hitler	300.00

7 RC(c),Mr. Murder & The Black Hand	275.00
8 RC(c),Red Ticket to Hell	275.00
9 RC(c),Trial By Terror	275.00
10 RC	275.00
11 The Voice of Russia	175.00
12 Terror in Tokyo	175.00
13 Mind Assassins	175.00
14 Trouble in Bavaria, Hitler	200.00
15 The Traitor,Bondage(c)	175.00
16 Hunt For a Hatchetman	175.00
17 Red Triggerman	175.00
18 Death Rides the Rails	175.00
19 Death Ambush	175.00
20 The Fantastic H-Bomb Plot	200.00
21 The Return of Mussolini	150.00
22 Propaganda for Doom	165.00
23 Red Intrigue in Parid,H-Bomb	150.00
24 Red Sabotage	150.00
25 RC,The Ingenious Red Trap	150.00
26	125.00
27	125.00
29 thru 33	@125.00
34 Hitler (c)	150.00
35 thru 37	@125.00
38 Dec., 1956	125.00

TNT COMICS

Charles Publishing Co., Feb., 1946

1 FBI story,YellowJacket	450.00

TOM AND JERRY

DELL GIANT EDITIONS Dell Publishing Co., 1952–58

Back to School	300.00
Picnic Time	250.00
Summer Fun 1	350.00
Summer Fun 2	200.00
Winter Carnival 1	500.00
Winter Carnival 2	350.00
Winter Fun 3	200.00
Winter Fun 4	175.00
Winter Fun 5	150.00
Winter Fun 6	150.00
Winter Fun 7	150.00

TOM AND JERRY

See: OUR GANG COMICS

TOMB OF TERROR

Harvey Publications, June, 1952

1 BP,The Thing From the Center of the Earth	750.00
2 RP,The Quagmire Beast	500.00
3 BP,RP,Caravan of the Doomed, Bondage(c)	500.00
4 RP,I'm Going to Kill You, Torture	400.00
5 RP	400.00
6 RP,Return From the Grave	400.00
7 RP,Shadow of Death	400.00
8 HN,The Hive	400.00
9 BP,HN,The Tunnel	400.00
10 BP,HN,The Trial	400.00
11 BP,HN,The Closet	400.00
12 BP,HN,Tale of Cain	450.00
13 BP,What Was Out There	500.00
14 BP,SC,End Result	700.00
15 BP,HN,Break-up, Exploding Head	1,400.00
16 BP,Going,Going,Gone	600.00

Becomes:

THRILLS OF TOMORROW

Oct., 1954

17 RP,BP,The World of Mr. Chatt.	250.00

GOLDEN AGE

18 RP,BP,The Dead Awaken 200.00
19 S&K,S&K(c),A:Stuntman. 500.00
20 S&K,S&K(c),A:Stuntman. 500.00

TOM CAT See:BO

TOM CORBETT
SPACE CADET
Dell Publishing Co.,
Jan., 1952
See also Dell Four Color
4 based on TV show. 200.00
5 . . . . 150.00
6 . . . . 100.00
7 . . . . 100.00
8 . . . . 100.00
9 . . . . 100.00
10 and 11 . . . . @100.00

TOM CORBETT
SPACE CADET
Prize Publications,
May–June, 1955
1 Robot(c). 450.00
2 . . . . 350.00
3 Sept.–Oct., 1955 . . . . 350.00

TOM MIX COMICS
Ralston-Purina Co.,
Sept., 1940
1 O:Tom Mix. 4,500.00
2 . . . . 1,500.00
3 . . . . 900.00
4 thru 9 . . . . @750.00
Becomes:

TOM MIX
COMMANDOS COMICS
Nov., 1942
10 . . . . 750.00
11 Invisible Invaders 750.00
12 Terrible Talons Of Tokyo . . . 750.00

TOM MIX WESTERN
Fawcett Publications,
Jan., 1948
1 Ph(c),Two-Fisted
  Adventures 1,500.00
2 Ph(c),Hair-Triggered Action . . 600.00
3 Ph(c),Double Barreled Action . 500.00
4 Ph(c),Cowpunching 500.00
5 Ph(c),Two Gun Action 500.00
6 CCB,Most Famous Cowboy . . 350.00
7 CCB,A Tattoo of Thrills 300.00
8 EK,Ph(c),Gallant Guns 325.00
9 CCB,Song o/t Deadly Spurs . . 325.00
10 CCB,Crack Shot Western. . . . 325.00
11 CCB,EK(C),Triple Revenge . . 325.00
12 King of the Cowboys. 250.00
13 Ph(c),Leather Burns 250.00
14 Ph(c),Brand of Death 250.00
15 Ph(c),Masked Treachery. . . . 250.00
16 Ph(c),Death Spurting Guns. . . 250.00
17 Ph(c),Trail of Doom. 250.00
18 Ph(c),Reign of Terror 225.00
19 Hand Colored Ph(c) 250.00
20 Ph(c),CCB,F:Capt Tootsie. . . . 225.00
21 Ph(c) 225.00
22 Ph(c),The Human Beast. 225.00
23 Ph(c),Return of the Past. 225.00
24 Hand Colored Ph(c),
  The Lawless City. 225.00
25 Hand Colored Ph(c),
  The Signed Death Warrant . . 225.00
26 Hand Colored Ph(c),
  Dangerous Escape 225.00
27 Hand Colored Ph(c),
  Hero Without Glory 225.00
28 Ph(c),The Storm Kings 225.00

29 Hand Colored Ph(c),The
  Case of the Rustling Rose . . 225.00
30 Ph(c),Disappearance
  in the Hills 225.00
31 Ph(c) 175.00
32 Hand Colored Ph(c),
  Mystery of Tremble Mountain 175.00
33 . . . . 175.00
34 . . . . 175.00
35 Partial Ph(c),The Hanging
  at Hollow Creek. 175.00
36 Ph(c) 175.00
37 Ph(c) 175.00
38 Ph(c),36 pages 150.00
39 Ph(c) 175.00
40 Ph(c) 175.00
41 Ph(c) 175.00
42 Ph(c) 175.00
43 Ph(c) 150.00
44 Ph(c) 150.00
45 Partial Ph(c),The Secret
  Letter 150.00
46 Ph(c) 150.00
47 Ph(c) 150.00
48 Ph(c) 150.00
49 Partial Ph(c),Blind Date
  With Death. 150.00
50 Ph(c) 150.00
51 Ph(c) 150.00
52 Ph(c) 150.00
53 Ph(c) 150.00
54 Ph(c) 150.00
55 Ph(c) 150.00
56 Partial Ph(c),Deadly Spurs . . . 150.00
57 Ph(c)5 . . . . 150.00
58 Ph(c) 150.00
59 Ph(c) 150.00
60 Ph(c) 150.00
61 Partial Ph(c),Lost in the
  Night,May, 1953. . . . . 175.00

TOMMY OF THE
BIG TOP
King Features/
Standard Comics, 1948
10 Thrilling Circus Adventures. . . 150.00
11 . . . . 100.00
12 March, 1949 . . . . 100.00

TOM-TOM THE
JUNGLE BOY
Magazine Enterprises, 1946
1 (fa) 200.00
2 (fa) 150.00
3 Winter 1947,(fa),X-mas issue . 125.00
1 . . . . 100.00

TONTO
See: LONE RANGER'S
COMPANION TONTO

TONY TRENT
See: FACE, THE

TOP FLIGHT COMICS
Four Star/St. John Publ. Co.,
July, 1949
1 . . . . 125.00
1 Hector the Inspector 100.00

TOPIX COMICS
Topix/Catechetical Guild, 1942
1 Catholic 350.00
2 . . . . 250.00
3 . . . . 250.00
4 . . . . 200.00
5 . . . . 200.00
6 . . . . 200.00
7 . . . . 200.00

8 . . . . 200.00
Volume 2, any, except #5 . . . . . 200.00
5 Pope Pius XII. 250.00
Volume 3, any 200.00
Volume 4, any 175.00
Volume 5, any, except #12 . . . . . 150.00
12 Life of Christ 175.00
Volume 6, any 125.00
Volume 7, any 100.00
Volume 8, any #4 . . . . 150.00
4 Dagwood Splits Atom. 150.00
Volume 9, any, except #12 . . . . . 100.00
12 Christmas issue 100.00
Volume 10, any 100.00

TOP LOVE STORIES
Star Publications,
May, 1951
3 LbC(c) 300.00
4 LbC(c) 250.00
5 LbC(c) 250.00
6 LbC(c),WW 350.00
7 LbC(c) 250.00
8 LbC(c), WW Story 275.00
9 LbC(c) 250.00
10 thru 16 LbC(c) . . . . @250.00
17 LbC(c),WW 275.00
18 LbC(c). 250.00
19 LbC(c),JyD 250.00

TOP-NOTCH COMICS
MLJ Magazines,
Dec., 1939
1 JaB,JCo,B&O:The Wizard,
  B:Kandak,Swift of the Secret
  Service,The Westpointer,
  Mystic, Air Patrol,Scott
  Rand, Manhunter 12,000.00
2 JaB,JCo,B:Dick Storm,
  E:Mystic, B:Stacy Knight . . 5,000.00
3 JaB,JCo,EA(c),E:Swift of the
  Secret Service,Scott Rand 3,000.00
4 JCo,EA(c),MMe,O&I:Streak,
  Chandler 2,700.00
5 Ea(c),MMe,O&I:Galahad,
  B:Shanghai Sheridan 2,800.00
6 Ea(c),MMe,A:The Shield . . . 2,500.00
7 Ea(c),MMe,N:The Wizard . . 3,000.00
8 E:Dick Sorm,B&O:Roy The1
  Super Boy,The Firefly 2,500.00
9 O&I:Black Hood,
  B:Fran Frazier 10,000.00
10 A:Black Hood 3,000.00
11 . . . . 2,000.00
12 . . . . 2,000.00

Top-Notch #4
© MLJ Magazines

13	2,000.00
14 Bondage(c)	2,000.00
15 MMe	2,000.00
16	1,800.00
17 Bondage(c)	2,000.00
18	1,800.00
19 Bondage(c)	2,000.00
20	1,800.00
21	1,500.00
22	1,500.00
23 Bondage(c)	1,700.00
24 Black Hood Smashes Murder Ring	1,500.00
25 E:Bob Phantom	1,500.00
26	1,500.00
27 E:The Firefly	1,500.00
28 B:Suzie,Pokey Okay, Gag Oriented	1,500.00
29 E:Kandak	1,500.00
30	1,500.00
31	700.00
32	700.00
33 BWo,B:Dotty&Ditto	700.00
34 BWo	700.00
35 BWo	700.00
36 BWo	700.00
37 thru 40 BWo	@700.00
41	700.00
42 BWo	700.00
43	700.00
44 EW:Black Hood,I:Suzie	700.00
45 Suzie(c)	800.00

Becomes:

LAUGH COMIX
Summer, 1944

46 Suzie & Wilbur	400.00
47 Suzie & Wilbur	300.00
48 Suzie & Wilbur	300.00

Becomes:

SUZIE COMICS
Spring, 1945

49 B:Ginger	400.00
50 AFy(c)	300.00
51 AFy(c)	300.00
52 AFy(c)	300.00
53 AFy(c)	300.00
54 AFy(c)	350.00
55 AFy(c)	350.00
56 BWo,B;Katie Keene	200.00
57 thru 70 BWo	@200.00
71 thru 79 BWo	@150.00
80 thru 99 BWo	@150.00
100 Aug., 1954, BWo	150.00

Tor #1
© St John Publishing

TOPS
Tops Mag. Inc.
(Lev Gleason), July, 1949

1 RC&BLb,GT,DBa,CBi(c),I'll Buy That Girl,Our Explosive Children	2,000.00
2 FGu,BF,CBi(c),RC&BLb	1,800.00

TOPS COMICS
Consolidated Book Publishers, 1944

2000 Don on the Farm	300.00
2001 The Jack of Spades V:The Hawkman	200.00
2002 Rip Raiders	150.00
2003 Red Birch	100.00

TOP SECRET
Hillman Publications, Jan., 1952

1 The Tricks of the Secret Agent Revealed	300.00

TOP SECRETS
Street & Smith Publ., Nov., 1947

1 BP,BP(c),Of the Men Who Guard the U.S. Mail	450.00
2 BP,BP(c),True Story of Jim the Penman	350.00
3 BP, BP(c),Crime Solved by Mental Telepathy	300.00
4 Highway Pirates	300.00
5 BP,BP(c),Can Music Kill	300.00
6 BP,BP(c),The Clue of the Forgotten Film	300.00
7 BP,BP(c),Train For Sale	450.00
8 BP,BP(c)	300.00
9 BP,BP(c)	300.00
10 BP,BP(c),July–Aug., 1949.	350.00

TOPS IN ADVENTURE
Approved Comics (Ziff-Davis), Autumn, 1952

1 BP,Crusaders From Mars	700.00

TOP SPOT COMICS
Top Spot Publishing Co., 1945

1 The Duke Of Darkness	450.00

TOPSY-TURVY
R.B. Leffingwell Publ., April, 1945

1 I:Cookie	200.00

TOR
St. John Publishing Co., Sept., 1953

1 JKu,JKu(c),O;Tor,One Million Years Ago	150.00
2 JKu,JKu(c),3-D Issue	100.00
3 JKu,JKu(c),ATh,historic Life	125.00
4 JKu,JKu(c),ATh	125.00
5 JKu,JKu(c),ATh,Oct., 1954	125.00

TORCHY
Quality Comics Group, Nov., 1949

1 GFx,BWa(c),The Blonde Bombshell	2,500.00
2 GFx(a&c),Beauty at Its Best.	1,100.00
3 GFx,GFx(c),You Can't Beat Nature	1,100.00
4 GFx,GFx(c),The Girl to Keep Your Eye On	1,400.00

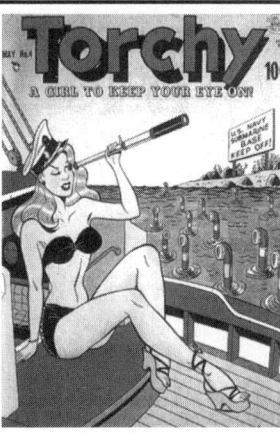

Torchy #4
© Quality Comics

5 BWa,GFx,BWa(c),At the Masquerade Party	1,700.00
6 Sept., 1950,BWa,GFx, BWa(c),The Libido Driven Boy Scout	1,700.00

TORMENTED, THE
Sterling Comics, July, 1954

1 Buried Alive	400.00
2 Sept., 1954,The Devils Circus	350.00

Becomes:

SURPRISE ADVENTURES
Sterling Comics, 1955

3 MSy	200.00
4	150.00
5 MSy	200.00

TOYLAND COMICS
Fiction House Magazines, Jan., 1947

1 Wizard of the Moon	400.00
2 Buddy Bruin & Stu Rabbit	250.00
3 GT,The Candy Maker	275.00
4 July, 1947	250.00

TOY TOWN COMICS
Toytown Publ./Orbit Publ., Feb., 1945

1 LbC,LbC(c)(fa)	650.00
2 LbC,(fa)	350.00
3 LbC,LbC(c),(fa)	300.00
4 thru 7 LbC,(fa) May, 1947	@300.00

TRAIL BLAZERS
See: RED DRAGON COMICS

TRAPPED
Harvey Publications, 1951

N#	150.00

TRAPPED!
Periodical Magazines (Ace Magazines), 1954

1	125.00
2 and 3	@60.00

TREASURE CHEST
George A Pflaum Publ., Inc., 1946

1	400.00
2 thru 4	@200.00

5 Dr Styx 225.00
6 . . . . 200.00
Vol 2, 1 thru 20 . . . . @150.00
Vol 3, 1 thru 5 (1947–48) . . . . . @150.00
Vol 3, #6 Verne,Voyage to Moon, 135.00
Vol 3, 7 thru 20 . . . . @110.00
Vol 4, 1 thru 20 (1948–49) . . . . @135.00
Vol 5, 1 thru 20 (1949–50) . . . . @125.00
Vol 6, 1 thru 20 (1950–51) . . . . @125.00
Vol 7, 1 thru 20 (1951–52) . . . . @125.00
Vol 8, 1 thru 20 (1952–53) . . . . @125.00
Vol 9, 1 thru 20 (1953–54) . . . . @100.00
Vol 10, 1 thru 10 (1954–55) . . . @100.00
Vol 10, #11 BP 100.00
Vol 10, 12 thru 20 . . . . @100.00
Vol 11, 1 thru 20 (1955–56) . . . @100.00
Vol 12, 1 thru 20 (1956–57) . . . @100.00
Vol 13, 1 thru 20 (1957–58) . . . . @75.00
Vol 14, 1 thru 20 (1958–59) . . . . @75.00
Vol 15, 1 thru 20 (1959–60) . . . . @75.00
Vol 16, 1 thru 20 (1960–61) . . . . @75.00
Vol 17, 1 thru 20 (1962–63)
   odd #s . . . . @75.00
   even #s "Godless Communism"
   2 RC 350.00
   4 and 6 . . . . @275.00
   8 thru 14 Stalin, WWII . . . . @300.00
   14 thru 20 Kruschev . . . . . @275.00

TREASURE COMICS
Prize Comics Group, 1943
1 S&K,Reprints of Prize Comics
   #7 through #11 . . . . 4,000.00

TREASURE COMICS
**American Boys Comics
(Prize Publications),
June–July, 1945**
1 HcK,B:PaulBunyan,MarcoPolo 700.00
2 HcK(a&c),B:Arabian Knight,
   Gorilla King,Dr.Styx 400.00
3 HcK 300.00
4 HcK 300.00
5 HcK,JK, Marco Polo 400.00
6 BK,HcK(a&c) 300.00
7 FF,HcK(a&c),Capt.Kidd, Jr. . . . 600.00
8 HcK,FF 600.00
9 HcK,DBa 300.00
10 JK,DBa,JK(c) 500.00
11 BK,HcK,DBa,The Weird
   Adventures of Mr. Bottle 350.00
12 DBa,DBa(c),Autumn, 1947 . . . 300.00

TREASURY OF COMICS
St. John Publishing Co., 1947
1 RvB,RvB(c),Abbie an' Slats . . 150.00
2 Jim Hardy 125.00
3 Bill Bimlin 125.00
4 RvB,RvB(c),Abbie an' Slats . . 125.00
5 Jim Hardy,Jan., 1948 . . . . 100.00

TREASURY OF COMICS
St. John Publishing Co., 1948
1 Abbott & Costello,
   Little Audrey 250.00
2 . . . . 125.00
3 thru 5 . . . . @110.00

TRIPLE THREAT
**Gerona Publications,
Winter, 1945**
1 F:King O'Leary,The Duke of
   Darkness,Beau Brummell . . 500.00

TRUE ANIMAL
PICTURE STORIES
True Comics Press, 1947
1 & 2 . . . . @125.00

TRUE AVIATION
PICTURE STORIES
**Parents' Institute/P.M.I.,
Aug., 1942**
1 How Jimmy Doolittle
   Bombed Tokyo 250.00
2 Knight of the Air Mail 200.00
3 The Amazing One-Man
   Air Force 150.00
4 Joe Foss America's No. 1
   Air Force 150.00
5 Bombs over Germany 150.00
6 Flight Lt. Richard
   Hillary R.A.F. 150.00
7 "Fatty" Chow China's
   Sky Champ 150.00
8 Blitz over Burma 150.00
9 Off the Beam 150.00
10 "Pappy" Boyington 150.00
11 Ph(c) 150.00
12 . . . . 150.00
13 Ph(c),Flying Facts 150.00
14 . . . . 150.00
15 True Aviation Adventures . . . 150.00
Becomes:

AVIATION AND MODEL
BUILDING
Dec., 1946
16 . . . . 125.00
17 Feb., 1947 . . . . 150.00

TRUE COMICS
**True Comics/
Parents' Magazine Press,
April, 1941–Aug., 1950**
1 My Greatest Adventure-by
   Lowell Thomas, Churchill . . . 450.00
2 BEv,The Story of the
   Red Cross 200.00
3 Baseball Hall of Fame 225.00
4 Danger in the Artic 150.00
5 Father Duffy-the Fighting
   Chaplain, Joe Louis 165.00
6 The Capture of Aquinaldo 200.00
7 JKa,Wilderness Adventures of
   George Washington 165.00
8 U.S. Army Wings 125.00
9 A Pig that Made History 125.00
10 Adrift on an Ice Pan 125.00
11 Gen. Douglas MacArthur 110.00
12 Mackenzie-King of Cananda . . 110.00
13 The Real Robinson Crusoe . . . 110.00
14 Australia war base of
   the South Pacific 110.00
15 The Story of West Point 125.00
16 How Jimmy Doolittle
   Bombed Tokyo 120.00
17 The Ghost of Captain Blig,
   B.Feller 125.00
18 Battling Bill of the
   Merchant Marine 135.00
19 Secret Message Codes 110.00
20 The Story of India 100.00
21 Timoshenko the Blitz Buster . . 110.00
22 Gen, Bernard L. Montgomery . 100.00
23 The Story of Steel 100.00
24 Gen. Henri Giraud-Master
   of Escape 100.00
25 Medicine's Miracle Men 100.00
26 Hero of the Bismarck Sea 100.00
27 Leathernecks have Landed . . . 110.00
28 The Story of Radar 100.00
29 The Fighting Seabees 100.00
30 Dr. Norman Bethune-Blood
   Bank Founder 100.00
31 Our Good Neighbor Bolivia,
   Red Grange 110.00
32 Men against the Desert 125.00
33 Gen.Clark and his Fighting 5th 150.00

34 Angel of the Battlefield 125.00
35 Carlson's Marine Raiders 125.00
36 Canada's Sub-Busters 125.00
37 Commander of the Crocodile
   Fleet 125.00
38 Oregon Trailblazer 125.00
39 Saved by Sub, FBI 125.00
40 Sea Furies 125.00
41 Cavalcade of England 100.00
42 Gen. Jaques Le Clerc-Hero
   of Paris 100.00
43 Unsinkable Ship 100.00
44 El Senor Goofy, Truman 100.00
45 Tokyo Express 100.00
46 The Magnificent Runt 100.00
47 Atoms Unleashed,
   Atomic Bomb 175.00
48 Pirate Patriot 100.00
49 Smoking Fists 100.00
50 Lumber Pirates 100.00
51 Exercise Musk-Ox 100.00
52 King of the Buckaneers 100.00
53 Baseline Booby 100.00
54 Santa Fe Sailor 100.00
55 Sea Going Santa 100.00
56 End of a Terror 100.00
57 Newfangled Machines 100.00
58 Leonardo da Vinci-500 years
   too Soon, Houdini 100.00
59 Pursuit Pirates, Bob Hope . . . 100.00
60 Emmett Kelly-The World's
   Funniest Clown 100.00
61 Peter Le Grand-
   Bold Buckaneer 100.00
62 Sutter's Gold 100.00
63 Outboard Outcome 100.00
64 Man-Eater at Large 100.00
65 The Story of Scotland Yard . . . 100.00
66 Easy Guide to Football
   Formations, Will Rogers 100.00
67 The Changing Zebra 100.00
68 Admiral Byrd 100.00
69 FBI Special Agent Steve
   Saunders, Jack Benny 100.00
70 The Case of the Seven
   Hunted Men 100.00
71 Story of Joe DiMaggio 150.00
72 FBI,Jackie Robinson 125.00
73 The 26 Mile Dash-Story of
   the Marathon, Walt Disney . . 100.00
74 A Famous Coach's Special
   Football Tips, Amos & Andy . 100.00
75 King of Reporters 100.00
76 Story of a Buried Treasure . . . 100.00
77 France's Greatest Detective . . 100.00
78 Cagliostro-Master Rogue 100.00
79 Ralph Bunche-Hero of Peace . 100.00

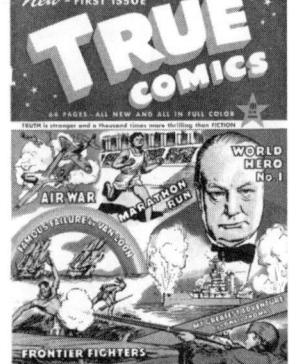

True Comics #1
© Parents' Magazine Press

80 Rocket Trip to the Moon 250.00
81 Red Grange 250.00
82 Marie Celeste Ship of
   Mystery 175.00
83 Bullfighter from Brooklyn. 175.00
84 King of the Buccaneers 175.00

TRUE CONFIDENCES
Fawcett Publications,
Autumn, 1949
1 . . . . 250.00
2 and 3 . . . . @125.00
4 DP 125.00

TRUE CRIME COMICS
Magazine Village, Inc.,
May, 1947
2 JCo(c),James Kent-Crook,
   Murderer,Escaped Convict;
   Drug 2,500.00
3 JCo(a&c),Benny Dickson-
   Killer;Drug 1,800.00
4 JCo(a&c),Little Jake-
   Big Shot 1,600.00
5 JCo(c),The Rat & the Blond
   Gun Moll;Drug 1,000.00
6 Joseph Metley-Swindler,
   Jailbird, Killer 800.00
2-1(7) ATh,WW,Ph(c),Phil
   Coppolla,Sept., 1949 . . . . 1,400.00

TRUE LOVE PICTORIAL
St. John Publishing Co., 1952
1 Ph(c) 300.00
2 MB 350.00
3 MB(c),MB,JKu 600.00
4 MB(c),MB,JKu 600.00
5 MB(c),MB,JKu 600.00
6 MB(c) 350.00
7 MB(c) 350.00
8 MB(c) 300.00
9 MB(c) 300.00
10 MB(c),MB 300.00
11 MB(c),MB 300.00

TRUE MOVIE AND TELEVISION
Toby Press, Aug., 1950
1 Liz Taylor, Ph(c) 900.00
2 FF,Ph(c),John Wayne,
   L.Taylor 600.00
3 June Allyson,Ph(c) 500.00
4 Jane Powell,Ph(c),Jan.,1951 . . 300.00

SPORT COMICS
Street & Smith Publ., Oct., 1940
1 F:Lou Gehrig 850.00
2 F:Gene Tunney 400.00
3 F:Phil Rizzuto 450.00
4 F:Frank Leahy 350.00
Becomes:

TRUE SPORT PICTURE STORIES
Street & Smith Publ.,
Feb., 1942–July-Aug., 1949
5 Joe DiMaggio 500.00
6 Billy Confidence 300.00
7 Mel Ott. 325.00
8 Lou Ambers 300.00
9 Pete Reiser 300.00
10 Frankie Sinkwich. 300.00
11 Marty Serfo 300.00
12 JaB(c),Jack Dempsey. 325.00
2-1 JaB(c),Willie Pep 300.00
2-2 JaB(c) 300.00
2-3 JaB(c),Carl Hubbell 325.00
2-4 Advs. in Football & Battle . . . 325.00
2-5 Don Hutson 300.00

2-6 Dixie Walker. 325.00
2-7 Stan Musial 350.00
2-8 Famous Ring Champions
   of All Time 325.00
2-9 List of War Year Rookies . . . 350.00
2-10 Connie Mack 325.00
2-11 Winning Basketball Plays . . 300.00
2-12 Eddie Gottleib 300.00
3-1 Bill Conn 300.00
3-2 Philadelphia Athletics 300.00
3-3 Leo Durocher 325.00
3-4 Rudy Dusek 275.00
3-5 Ernie Pyle 275.00
3-6 Bowling with Ned Day 275.00
3-7 Return of the Mighty (Home
   from War);Joe DiMaggio(c) . . 350.00
3-8 Conn V:Louis 325.00
3-9 Reuben Shark 275.00
3-10 BP,BP(c),Don "Dopey"
   Dillock 275.00
3-11 BP,BP(c),Death
   Scores a Touchdown 275.00
3-12 Red Sox V:Senators 275.00
4-1 Spring Training in
   Full Spring 275.00
4-2 BP,BP(c),How to Pitch 'Em
   Where They Can't Hit 'Em . . 275.00
4-3 BP,BP(c),1947 Super Stars . 250.00
4-4 BP,BP(c),Get Ready for
   the Olympics 235.00
4-5 BP,BP,(c),Hugh Casey 225.00
4-6 BP,BP(c),Phantom Phil
   Hergesheimer 225.00
4-7 BP,BP(c),How to Bowl Better 225.00
4-8 Tips on the Big Fight 235.00
4-9 BP,BP(c),Bill McCahan . . . 225.00
4-10 BP,BP(c),Great Football
   Plays 225.00
4-11 BP,BP(c),Football. 225.00
4-12 BP,BP(c),Basketball. 225.00
5-1 Satchel Paige 250.00
5-2 History of Boxing 225.00

TRUE-TO-LIFE ROMANCES
Star Publications,
Nov.–Dec., 1949
3 LbC(c),GlennFord/JanetLeigh . 350.00
4 LbC(c) 250.00
5 LbC(c) 250.00
6 LbC(c) 250.00
7 LbC(c) 250.00
8 LbC(c) 250.00
9 LbC(c) 250.00
10 LbC(c) 250.00
11 LbC(c) 250.00
12 LbC(c) 250.00
13 LbC(c),JyD 250.00
14 LbC(c),JyD 250.00
15 LbC(c),WW,JyD 275.00
16 LbC(c),WW,JyD 275.00
17 LbC(c),JyD 250.00
18 LbC(c),JyD 250.00
19 LbC(c),JyD 250.00
20 LbC(c),JyD 250.00
21 LbC(c),JyD 250.00
22 and 23 LbC(c) . . . . @250.00

TRUE WAR EXPERIENCES
Harvey Publications, 1952
1 . . . . 150.00
2 thru 4 . . . . @100.00

TUBBY
See: MARGE'S TUBBY

TUFFY
Best Books, Inc.
(Standard Comics) 1949
5 . . . . 125.00

6 true 9 . . . . @100.00

TUROK, SON OF STONE
Dell Publishing Co.,
Dec., 1954
(1) see Dell Four Color #596
(2) see Dell Four Color #656
3 Cavemen 450.00
4 & 5 . . . . @300.00
6 & 7 . . . . @250.00
8 Dinosaur, Lost Valley 300.00
9 thru 16 . . . . @225.00
17 Prehistoric Pigmies 250.00
18 thru 29. . . . . @150.00

TV SCREEN CARTOONS
(see REAL SCREEN COMICS)

TV TEENS
Charlton Comics, 1954
1 Ozzie & Babs. 125.00
2 . . . . 100.00
3 . . . . 100.00
4 . . . . 100.00
5 . . . . 100.00
6 Don Winslow 100.00
7 B:Mopsy. 100.00
8 thru 13 . . . . @100.00

TWEETY AND SYLVESTER
Dell Publishing Co.,
June, 1952
(1) see Dell Four Color #406
(2) see Dell Four Color #489
(3) see Dell Four Color #524
4 thru 20 . . . . @125.00
21 thru 37. . . . . @100.00

Twinkle #1
© Spotlight

TWINKLE COMICS
Spotlight Publications,
May, 1945
1 Humor Format 350.00

TWO-BIT WACKY WOODPECKER
Toby Press, 1952
1 . . . . 150.00
2 . . . . 120.00
3 . . . . 120.00

All comics prices listed are for *Near Mint* condition.   **CVA 2009 • Page 485**

TWO-FISTED TALES
**Fables Publications
(E.C. Comics),
Nov.–Dec., 1950–March, 1955**

18 JCr,WW,JSe,HK(a&c)	1,700.00
19 JCr,WW,JSe,HK(a&c)	1,400.00
20 JDa,WW,JSe,HK(a&c)	800.00
21 JDa,WW,JSe,HK(a&c)	750.00
22 JDa,WW,JSe,HK(a&c)	750.00
23 JDa,WW,JSe,HK(a&c)	600.00
24 JDa,WW,JSe,HK(a&c)	500.00
25 JDa,WW,JSe,HK(a&c)	500.00
26 JDa,JSe,HK(c),Action at the Changing Reservoir	350.00
27 JDa,JSe,HK(c)	350.00
28 JDa,JSe,HK(c)	350.00
29 JDa,JSe,HK(c)	400.00
30 JSe,JDa(a&c)	400.00
31 JDa,JSe,HK(c),Civil War Story	350.00
32 JDa,JKu,WW(c)	350.00
33 JDa,JKu,WW(c),A-Bomb	400.00
34 JDa,JDa(a&c)	350.00
35 JSe,JDa(a&c),Civil War Story	350.00
36 JDa,JSe(a&c),A Difference of Opinion	400.00
37 JSe(a&c),Bugles & Battle Cries	400.00
38 JSe(a&c)	400.00
39 JSe(a&c)	400.00
40 JDa,JSe,GE(a&c)	400.00
41 JSe,GE,JDa(c)	400.00
Ann. 1952 (#1)	1,600.00
Ann. 1953 (#2) JDa(c)	1,300.00

UNCLE CHARLIE'S FABLES
**Lev Gleason Publications,
Jan., 1952**

1 CBi(c),Ph(c)	200.00
2 BF,CBi(c),Ph(c)	125.00
3 CBi(c),Ph(c)	135.00
4 CBi(c),Ph(c)	135.00
5 CBi,Ph(c),Sept., 1952	135.00

UNCLE JOE'S FUNNIES
Centaur Publications, 1938

1 BEv,Puzzles & Comics	900.00

UNCLE MILTY
**Victoria Publications
(True Cross Comic), 1950**

1 Milton Berle	800.00
2	500.00
3	400.00
4	375.00

UNCLE SAM
See: BLACKHAWK

UNCLE SCROOGE
**Dell Publishing Co.,
March, 1952**

(1) see Dell Four Color #386	
(2) see Dell Four Color #456	
(3) see Dell Four Color #495	
4 Gladstone Album #11	1,000.00
5 Gladstone Special	800.00
6	700.00
7 CB, Seven Cities of Cibola	650.00
8 thru 10	@500.00
11 thru 23	@400.00
24 Christmas issue	400.00
25 thru 30	@300.00
31 thru 39	@250.00

UNDERWORLD
**D.S. Publishing Co.,
Feb.–March, 1948**

1 SMo(c),Violence	750.00
2 SMo(c),Electrocution	600.00
3 AMc,AMc(c),The Ancient Club	550.00
4 Grl,The Beer Baron Murder	500.00
5 Grl,The Postal Clue	350.00
6 The Polka Dot Gang	300.00
7 Mono-The Master	300.00
8 The Double Tenth	300.00
9 Thrilling Stories of the Fight against Crime,June, 1953	300.00

UNDERWORLD CRIME
**Fawcett Publications,
June, 1952**

1 The Crime Army	500.00
2 Jailbreak	350.00
3 Microscope Murder	300.00
4 Death on the Docks	300.00
5 River of Blood	300.00
6 The Sky Pirates	300.00
7 Bondage & Torture(c)	650.00
8 and 9 June, 1953	@300.00

UNITED COMICS
See: FRITZI RITZ

UNITED STATES FIGHTING AIR FORCE
**Superior Comics, Ltd.,
Sept., 1952**

1 Coward's Courage	150.00
2 Clouds that Killed	125.00
3 Operation Decoy	100.00
4 thru 28	@100.00
29 Oct., 1959	100.00

UNITED STATES MARINES
**Wm. H. Wise/Magazine Ent/
Toby Press, 1943–52**

N# MBi,MBi(c),Hellcat out of Heaven	300.00
2 MBi,Drama of Wake Island, Tojo	700.00
3 A Leatherneck Flame Thrower, Tojo	600.00
4 MBi	150.00
5 BP	100.00
6 BP	100.00
7 BP	100.00
8 thru 11	@100.00

UNKEPT PROMISE
Legion of Truth, 1949

1 Anti:Alcoholic Drinking	150.00

UNKNOWN WORLDS
See: STRANGE STORIES FROM ANOTHER WORLD

UNSEEN, THE
**Visual Editions
(Standard Comics), 1952**

5 ATh,The Hungry Lodger	600.00
6 JKa,MSy,Bayou Vengeance	400.00
7 JKz,MSy,Time is the Killer	400.00
8 JKz,MSy,The Vengeance Vat	300.00
9 JKz,MSy,Your Grave is Ready	450.00
10 JKz,MSy	400.00
11 JKz,MSy	300.00
12 ATh,GT,Till Death Do Us Part	400.00
13	300.00
14	300.00

15 ATh,The Curse of the Undead!, July, 1954	400.00

UNTAMED LOVE
**Comic Magazines
(Quality Comics Group),
Jan., 1950**

1 BWa(c),PGv	350.00
2 Ph(c)	250.00
3 PGv, Ph(c)	250.00
4 Ph(c)	250.00
5 PGv, Ph(c)	250.00

USA IS READY
Dell Publishing Co., 1941

1 Propaganda WWII	600.00

U.S. JONES
**Fox Features Syndicate,
Nov., 1941**

1 Death Over the Airways	1,900.00
2 Nazi (c),Jan., 1942	1,400.00

U.S. MARINES IN ACTION!
**Avon Periodicals,
Aug.–Dec., 1952**

1 On Land,Sea & in the Air	125.00
2 The Killer Patrol	100.00
3 EK(c),Death Ridge	100.00

*US Paratroops #4
© Avon.*

U.S. PARATROOPS
Avon Periodicals, 1951

1 WW	200.00
2 EK	125.00
3	100.00
4 thru 6 EK	@125.00

U.S. TANK COMMANDOS
**Avon Periodicals,
June, 1952**

1 EK(c),Fighting Daredevils of the USA	150.00
2 EK(c)	100.00
3 EK,EK(c),Robot Armanda	100.00
4 EK,EK(c),March, 1953	100.00

VALOR
E.C. Comics, March, 1955

1 AW,AT,WW,WW(c),Grl,BK	700.00
2 AW(c),AW,WWGrl,BK	500.00

GOLDEN AGE

3 AW,RC,BK,JOc(c) 400.00
4 WW(c),RC,Grl,BK,JO 400.00
5 WW(c),WW,AW,GE,Grl,BK . . . 350.00

VARIETY COMICS
Rural Home Publ./
Croyden Publ. Co., 1944
1 MvS,MvS(c),O:Capt, Valiant . . 300.00
2 MvS,MvS(c) 250.00
3 MvS,MvS(c) 200.00
4 . . . . 150.00
5 1946 . . . . 150.00

VAULT OF HORROR
See: WAR AGAINST CRIME

V...COMICS
Fox Features Syndicate,
Jan., 1942
1 V:V-Man, Nazi(c) 2,000.00
2 The Horror of the
    Dungeons, March, 1942 . . 1,400.00

VERI BEST
SURE FIRE COMICS
Holyoke Publishing Co., 1945
1 Capt Aero, Miss Victory, Red
    Cross, Devil Dogs 600.00

VERI BEST
SURE SHOT COMICS
Holyoke Publishing Co., 1945
1 reprint Holyoke One-Shots . . . 500.00

VIC FLINT
St. John Publishing Co.,
Aug., 1948
1 ...Crime Buster 200.00
2 . . . . 175.00
3 . . . . 150.00
4 . . . . 150.00
5 April, 1949 . . . . 150.00

VIC FLINT
Argo Publ., 1956
1 . . . . 100.00
2 . . . . 100.00

VIC JORDAN
Civil Service Publications,
April, 1945
1 Escape From a Nazi Prison . . 150.00

VIC TORRY AND HIS
FLYING SAUCER
Fawcett Publications, 1950
1 Ph(c),Revealed at Last 1,000.00

VICTORY COMICS
Hillman Periodicals,
Aug., 1941
1 RFv,REv(c),F:The Conqueror 5,000.00
2 BEv,BEv(c) 1,900.00
3 The Conqueror(c) 1,350.00
4 Dec., 1941 . . . . 1,300.00

VIC VERITY MAGAZINE
Vic Verity Publications,
1945
1 CCB,CCB(c),B:Vic Verity,Hot-
    Shot Galvan, Tom Travis . . . 300.00
2 CCB,CCB(c),Annual Classic
    Dance Recital 175.00
3 CCB 150.00

4 CCB,I:Boomer Young;The
    Bee-U-TiFul Weekend 150.00
5 CCB,Championship Baseball
    Game 150.00
6 CCB,High School Hero 150.00
7 CCB,CCB(c),F:Rocket Rex . . 150.00

VOODOO
Four Star Publ./Farrell/
Ajax Comics, May, 1952
1 MB,South Sea Girl 900.00
2 MB 700.00
3 Face Stabbing 550.00
4 MB,Rendezvous 550.00
5 Ghoul For A Day,Nazi 450.00
6 The Weird Dead,
    Severed Head 475.00
7 Goodbye World 450.00
8 MB, Revenge 550.00
9 Will this thing Never Stew? . . . 450.00
10 Land of Shadows & Screams . 450.00
11 Human Harvest 400.00
12 The Wazen Taper 400.00
13 Bondage(c),Caskets to
    Fit Everybody 450.00
14 Death Judges the
    Beauty Contest, Zombies . . . 400.00
15 Loose their Heads, Opium . . . 400.00
16 Fog Was Her Shroud 375.00
17 Apes Laughter,Electric Chair . 400.00
18 Astounding Fantasy 375.00
19 MB,Bondage(c);
    Destination Congo. 550.00
Ann.#1 100-pg. 2,000.00
Becomes:

VOODA
April, 1955
20 MB,MB(c),Echoes of
    an A-Bomb. 600.00
21 MB,MB(c),Trek of Danger. . . . 500.00
22 MB,MB(c),The Sun Blew
    Away, Aug., 1955. . . . . 500.00

WALT DISNEY'S
COMICS & STORIES
Dell Publishing Co.
N# 1943 dpt.store giveway 750.00
N# 1945 X-mas giveaway. 350.00

WALT DISNEY'S
COMICS & STORIES
Dell Publishing Co.,
Oct., 1940
1 (1940)FGu,Donald Duck &
    Mickey Mouse 35,000.00
2 . . . . 14,000.00
3 . . . . 5,000.00
4 1st Huey, Dewey & Louie
    Christmas(c) 3,500.00
4a Promo issue 5,500.00
5 Goofy(c) 2,700.00
6 . . . . 2,500.00
7 . . . . 2,500.00
8 Clarabelle Cow(c) 2,500.00
9 . . . . 2,500.00
10 . . . . 2,500.00
11 2nd Huey,Louie,Dewey(c) . . 2,500.00
12 . . . . 1,800.00
13 . . . . 1,700.00
14 . . . . 1,700.00
15 3 Little Kittens 1,600.00
16 3 Little Pigs 1,600.00
17 The Ugly Ducklings 1,600.00
18 . . . . 1,500.00
19 . . . . 1,500.00
20 . . . . 1,500.00
21 . . . . 1,500.00
22 . . . . 1,200.00
23 Flag 1,200.00

24 Flying Gauchito 1,100.00
25 . . . . 1,100.00
26 . . . . 1,100.00
27 Jose Carioca 1,100.00
28 . . . . 1,200.00
29 . . . . 1,100.00
30 . . . . 1,100.00
31 CB; Donald Duck 6,000.00
32 CB 3,000.00
33 CB 2,000.00
34 CB;WK; Gremlins. 1,600.00
35 CB;WK; Gremlins. 1,600.00
36 CB;WK; Gremlins 1,600.00
37 CB;WK; Gremlins 850.00
38 CB;WK; Gremlins 1,000.00
39 CB;WK; Gremlins, X-mas . . 1,000.00
40 CB;WK; Gremlins 1,000.00
41 CB;WK; Gremlins 900.00
42 CB 800.00
43 CB,Seven Dwarfs 800.00
44 CB 800.00
45 CB,Nazis in stories 800.00
46 CB,Nazis in stories 800.00
47 CB,Nazis in stories 800.00
48 CB,Nazis in stories 800.00
49 CB,Nazis in stories 800.00
50 CB,Nazis in stories 800.00
51 CB,Christmas 600.00
52 CB; Li'l Bad Wolf begins. 600.00
53 CB 600.00
54 CB 600.00
55 CB 600.00
56 CB 600.00
57 CB 600.00
58 CB,Flag 600.00
59 CB 600.00
60 CB 600.00
61 CB; Dumbo 500.00
62 CB 500.00
63 CB; Pinocchio 500.00
64 CB; Pinocchio, X-mas 500.00
65 CB; Pluto. 500.00
66 CB 500.00
67 CB 500.00
68 CB, Mickey Mouse 500.00
69 CB 500.00
70 CB 500.00
71 CB 400.00
72 CB 400.00
73 CB 400.00
74 CB 400.00
75 CB; Brer Rabbit. 400.00
76 CB; Brer Rabbit, X-mas 400.00
77 CB; Brer Rabbit. 400.00

Vic Jordan #1
© Civil Service Publ

All comics prices listed are for *Near Mint* condition.

78 CB	400.00
79 CB	400.00
80 CB	400.00
81 CB	400.00
82 CB;Bongo,Googy	400.00
83 CB;Bongo	400.00
84 CB;Bongo	400.00
85 CB	400.00
86 CB;Goofy & Agnes	400.00
87 CB;Goofy & Agnes	350.00
88 CB;Goofy & Agnes, I:Gladstone Gander	450.00
89 CB;Goofy&Agnes,Chip'n'Dale	350.00
90 CB;Goofy & Agnes	350.00
91 CB	300.00
92 CB	300.00
93 CB	300.00
94 CB	300.00
95 CB(c)	300.00
96 Little Toot	300.00
97 CB; Little Toot	300.00
98 CB; Uncle Scrooge	550.00
99 CB, Christmas(c)	300.00
100 CB	400.00
101 CB	300.00
102 CB	300.00
103 CB	275.00
104	275.00
105 CB	300.00
106 CB	300.00
107 CB, Donald super-powers	400.00
108	275.00
109	275.00
110 CB	300.00
111 CB	300.00
112 CB; drugs	400.00
113 CB	300.00
114 CB	300.00
115 WK(c)	300.00
116 Dumbo	150.00
117	150.00
118	150.00
119	150.00
120	150.00
121 Grandma Duck begins	150.00
122	150.00
123	200.00
124 CB,Christmas	250.00
125 CB;I:Junior Woodchucks	300.00
126 CB	250.00
127 CB	200.00
128 CB	200.00
129 CB	200.00
130 CB	200.00
131 CB	200.00
132 CB A:Grandma Duck	200.00
133 CB	200.00
134 I:The Beagle Boys	400.00
135 CB	200.00
136 CB	200.00
137 CB	200.00
138 CB,Scrooge & Money	300.00
139 CB	200.00
140 CB; I:Gyro Gearloose	400.00
141 CB	150.00
142 CB	150.00
143 CB; Little Hiawatha	150.00
144 CB; Little Hiawatha	150.00
145 CB; Little Hiawatha	150.00
146 CB; Little Hiawatha	150.00
147 CB; Little Hiawatha	150.00
148 CB; Little Hiawatha	150.00
149 CB; Little Hiawatha	150.00
150 CB; Little Hiawatha	150.00
151 CB; Little Hiawatha	150.00
152 thru 200 CB	@125.00
201 thru 203 CB	@100.00
204 CB, Chip 'n' Dale & Scamp.	100.00
205 thru 240 CB	@100.00
241 CB; Dumbo x-over	100.00
242 CB	100.00
243 CB	100.00

244 CB	100.00
245 CB	100.00
246 CB	100.00
247 thru 255 CB;Gyro Gearloose	@100.00
256 thru 263 CB;Ludwig Von Drake & Gearloose	@100.00

WALT DISNEY'S DELL GIANT EDITIONS
Dell Publishing Co.

1 CB,W.Disney'sXmas Parade('49)	1,300.00
2 CB,W.Disney'sXmas Parade('50)	1,000.00
3 W.Disney'sXmas Parade('51)	350.00
4 W.Disney'sXmas Parade('52)	300.00
5 W.Disney'sXmas Parade('53)	300.00
6 W.Disney'sXmas Parade('54)	300.00
7 W.Disney'sXmas Parade('55)	300.00
8 CB,W.Disney'sXmas Parade('56)	500.00
9 CB,W.Disney'sXmas Parade('57)	500.00
1 CB,W.Disney's Christmas in Disneyland (1957)	600.00
1 CB,W.Disney's Disneyland Birthday Party (1958)	600.00
1 W.Disney's Donald and Mickey in Disneyland (1958)	250.00
1 W.Disney's Donald Duck Beach Party (1954)	350.00
2 W.Disney's Donald Duck Beach Party (1955)	250.00
3 W.Disney's Donald Duck Beach Party (1956)	250.00
4 W.Disney's Donald Duck Beach Party (1957)	250.00
5 W.Disney's Donald Duck Beach Party (1958)	250.00
6 W.Disney's Donald Duck Beach Party (1959)	250.00
1 W.Disney's Donald Duck Fun Book (1954)	1,300.00
2 W.Disney's Donald Duck Fun Book (1954)	1,300.00
1 W.Disney's Donald Duck in Disneyland (1955)	350.00
1 W.Disney's Huey, Dewey and Louie (1958)	250.00
1 W.Disney's DavyCrockett('55)	400.00
1 W.Disney's Lady and the Tramp (1955)	650.00
1 CB,W.Disney's Mickey Mouse Almanac (1957)	600.00

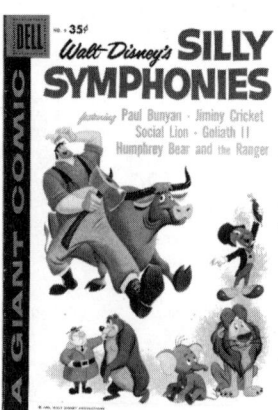

Walt Disney Dell Giant-Silly Symphonies #9 (Vol 10 No 6) © Walt Disney

1 W.Disney's Mickey Mouse Birthday Party (1953)	700.00
1 W.Disney's Mickey Mouse Club Parade (1955)	600.00
1 W.Disney's Mickey Mouse in Fantasyland (1957)	275.00
1 W.Disney's Mickey Mouse in Frontierland (1956)	300.00
1 W.Disney's Summer Fun('58)	300.00
2 CB,W.Disney'sSummer Fun('59)	300.00
1 W.Disney's Peter Pan Treasure Chest (1953)	2,400.00
1 Disney Silly Symphonies('52)	650.00
2 Disney Silly Symphonies('53)	550.00
3 Disney Silly Symphonies('54)	450.00
4 Disney Silly Symphonies('54)	450.00
5 Disney Silly Symphonies('55)	400.00
6 Disney Silly Symphonies('56)	400.00
7 Disney Silly Symphonies('57)	400.00
8 Disney Silly Symphonies('58)	400.00
9 Disney Silly Symphonies('59)	400.00
1 Disney SleepingBeauty('59)	600.00
1 CB,W.Disney's Uncle Scrooge Goes to Disneyland (1957)	600.00
1 W.Disney's Vacation in Disneyland (1958)	275.00
1 CB,Disney's Vacation Parade('50)	2,000.00
2 Disney'sVacation Parade('51)	600.00
3 Disney'sVacation Parade('52)	350.00
4 Disney'sVacation Parade('53)	350.00
5 Disney'sVacation Parade('54)	350.00
6 Disney's Picnic Party (1955)	300.00
7 Disney's Picnic Party (1956)	300.00
8 CB,Disney's Picnic Party (1957)	500.00

WALT DISNEY'S DELL JUNIOR TREASURY

1 W.Disney's Alice in Wonderland (1955)	250.00

WALT DISNEY PRESENTS
Dell Publishing Co., June–Aug., 1952

1 Ph(c), Four Color	200.00
2 Ph(c)	150.00
3 Ph(c)	150.00
4 Ph(c)	150.00
5 and 6 Ph(c)	@150.00

WAMBI JUNGLE BOY
Fiction House Magazines, Spring, 1942–Winter, 1952

1 HcK,HcK(c),Vengence of the Beasts	1,400.00
2 HcK,HcK(c),Lair of the Killer Rajah	750.00
3 HcK,HcK(c)	550.00
4 HcK,HcK(c),The Valley of the Whispering Drums	350.00
5 HcK,HcK(c),SwamplandSafari	300.00
6 Taming of the Tigress	275.00
7 Duel of the Congo Kings	275.00
8 AB(c),Friend of the Animals	275.00
9 Quest of the Devils Juju	275.00
10 Friend of the Animals	250.00
11	250.00
12 Curse of the Jungle Jewels	250.00
13 New Adventures of Wambi	175.00
14	175.00
15 The Leopard Legions	175.00
16	175.00
17 Beware Bwana!	175.00
18 Ogg the Great Bull Ape	175.00

GOLDEN AGE

WANTED COMICS
Toytown Comics/Orbit Publications, Sept.–Oct., 1947
9 Victor Everhart	350.00
10 Carlo Banone	200.00
11 Dwight Band	200.00
12 Ralph Roe	200.00
13 James Spencer;Drug	175.00
14 John "Jiggs" Sullivan;Drug	175.00
15 Harry Dunlap;Drug	125.00
16 Jack Parisi;Drug	135.00
17 Herber Ayers;Drug	135.00
18 Satan's Cigarettes;Drug	325.00
19 Jackson Stringer	125.00
20 George Morgan	125.00
21 BK,Paul Wilson	150.00
22 Strong violence	150.00
23 George Elmo Wells	125.00
24 BK,Bruce Cornett;Drug	150.00
25 Henry Anger	125.00
26 John Wormly	125.00
27 Death Always Knocks Twice	125.00
28 Paul H. Payton	125.00
29 Hangmans Holiday	125.00
30 George Lee	125.00
31 M Consolo	125.00
32 William Davis	125.00
33 The Web of Davis	125.00
34 Dead End	125.00
35 Glen Roy Wright	125.00
36 SSh,SSh(c),Bernard Lee Thomas	100.00
37 SSh,SSh(c),Joseph M. Moore	100.00
38 SSh,SSh(c)	100.00
39 The Horror Weed;Drug	250.00
40	100.00
41	100.00
42	100.00
43	100.00
44	100.00
45 Killers on the Loose;Drug	125.00
46 Charles Edward Crews	100.00
47	100.00
48 SSh,SSh(c)	100.00
49	100.00
50 JB(c),Make Way for Murder	150.00
51 JB(c),Dope Addict on a Holiday of Murder;Drug	135.00
52 The Cult of Killers; Classic Drug	135.00
53 April, 1953	100.00

WAR AGAINST CRIME
L.L. Publishing Co. (E.C. Comics), Spring, 1948
1 Grl, Stories from Police	1,200.00
2 Grl,Guilty of Murder	700.00
3 JCr(c)	700.00
4 AF,JCr(c)	600.00
5 JCr(c)	600.00
6 AF,JCr(c)	600.00
7 AF,JCr(c)	600.00
8 AF,JCr(c)	600.00
9 AF,JCr(c),The Kid	600.00
10 JCr(c),I:Vault Keeper	3,600.00
11 JCr(c)	2,200.00
Becomes:

VAULT OF HORROR, THE
April–May, 1950–Jan., 1955
12 AF,JCr(a&c),Wax Museum	8,500.00
13 AF,WW,JCr(c),Grl,Drug	2,400.00
14 AF,WW,JCr(c),Grl	2,000.00
15 AF,JCr(a&c),Grl,JKa	2,000.00
16 Grl,JKa,JCr(a&c)	1,500.00
17 JDa,Grl,JKa,JCr(a&c)	1,500.00
18 JDa,Grl,JKa,JCr(a&c)	1,400.00
19 JDa,Grl,JKa,JCr(a&c)	1,400.00
20 JDa,Grl,JKa,JCr(a&c)	1,200.00
21 JDa,Grl,JKa,JCr(a&c)	1,200.00
22 JDa,JKa,JCr(a&c)	1,200.00

War Against Crime #9
© EC Comics

23 JDa,Grl,JCr(a&c)	1,200.00
24 JDa,Grl,JO,JCr(a&c)	1,200.00
25 JDa,Grl,JKa,JCr(a&c)	1,200.00
26 JDa,Grl,JCr(a&c)	900.00
27 JDa,Grl,GE,JCr(a&c)	1,000.00
28 JDa,Grl,JCr(a&c)	1,000.00
29 JDa,Grl,JKa,JCr(a&c), Bradbury Adapt.	1,000.00
30 JDa,Grl,JCr(a&c)	1,000.00
31 JDa,Grl,JCr(a&c), Bradbury Adapt	800.00
32 JDa,Grl,JCr(a&c)	800.00
33 JDa,Grl,RC,JCr(c)	800.00
34 JDa,Grl,RC,JCr(a&c)	800.00
35 JDa,Grl,JCr(a&c),X-mas	800.00
36 JDa,Grl,BK,JCr(a&c),Drug	800.00
37 JDa,Grl,AW,JCr(a&c) Hanging	800.00
38 JDa,Grl,BK,JCr(a&c)	800.00
39 Grl,BK,RC,JCr(a&c) Bondage(c)	800.00
40 Grl,BK,JO,JCr(a&c)	900.00

WAR BATTLES
Harvey Publications, Feb., 1952
1 BP,Devils of the Deep	175.00
2 BP,A Present From Benny	125.00
3 BP	100.00
4	100.00
5	100.00
6 HN	100.00
7 BP	125.00
8	100.00
9 Dec., 1953	100.00

WAR BIRDS
Fiction House Magazines, 1952
1 Willie the Washout	225.00
2 Mystery MIGs of Kwanjamu	125.00
3 thru 6	@125.00
7 Winter, 1953,Across the Wild Yalu	125.00

WAR COMICS
Dell Publishing Co., May, 1940
1 AMc,Sky Hawk	900.00
2 O:Greg Gildam	500.00
3	350.00
4 O:Night Devils	400.00

WARFRONT
Fighting Forces Publ./ Harvey Publications
1 Korean War	200.00
2	150.00
3	125.00
4	125.00
5	125.00
6 thru 10	@125.00
11 thru 21	@100.00
22 HN	125.00
23 thru 33	@100.00
34 JK	100.00
35	100.00

WAR FURY
Comic Media/Harwell, 1952
1 DH,RP,hole in head	375.00
2 Violent	200.00
3 Violent	200.00
4 PMo,Violent	200.00

WAR HEROES
Dell Publishing Co., July–Sept., 1942
1 Gen. Douglas MacArthur (c)	400.00
2	300.00
3 Pro-Soviet	250.00
4 A:Gremlins	350.00
5	250.00
6	200.00
7	200.00
8 thru 11	@200.00

WAR HEROES
Ace Magazines, May, 1952
1 Always Comin'	150.00
2 LC,The Last Red Tank	125.00
3 You Got it	100.00
4 A Red Patrol	100.00
5 Hustle it Up	100.00
6 LC,Hang on Pal	125.00
7 LC	125.00
8 LC, April, 1953	125.00

WARPATH
Key Publications/ Stanmore, Nov., 1954
1 Red Men Raid	125.00
2 AH(c),Braves Battle	100.00
3 April, 1955	100.00

WARRIOR COMICS
H.C. Blackerby, 1944
1 Ironman wing Brady	400.00

WAR REPORT
Excellent Publ. (Ajax/Farrell Publ.), 1952
1	150.00
2 Burning bodies	250.00
3	125.00
4	125.00
5	125.00

WAR SHIPS
Dell Publishing Co., 1942
1 AMc	250.00

WAR STORIES
Dell Publishing Co., 1942
5 O:The Whistler	350.00
6 A:Night Devils	250.00
7 A:Night Devils	250.00
8 A:Night Devils	250.00

GOLDEN AGE

WARTIME ROMANCES
**St. John Publishing Co.,
July, 1951**

1 MB(c),MB	600.00
2 MB(c),MB	400.00
3 MB(c),MB	350.00
4 MB(c),MB	350.00
5 MB(c),MB	325.00
6 MB(c),MB	325.00
7 thru 8 MB(c),MB	@325.00
9 thru 12 MB(c),MB	@250.00
13 thru 15 MB(c)	@200.00
16 MB(c),MB	250.00
17 MB(c)	200.00
18 MB(c),MB	250.00

WAR VICTORY COMICS
**U.S. Treasury/War Victory/
Harvey Publ., Summer, 1942**

1 Savings Bond Promo with Top Syndicated Cartoonists, benefit USO	650.00

Becomes:

WAR VICTORY ADVENTURES
Summer, 1942

2 BP,2nd Front Comics	350.00
3 BP,F:Capt Cross of the Red Cross	300.00

WASHABLE JONES AND THE SHMOO
Toby Press Publ., 1953

1 Super Shmoo	275.00

WEB OF EVIL
**Comic Magazines, Inc.
(Quality Comics Group),
Nov., 1952**

1 Custodian of the Dead	1,000.00
2 JCo,Hangmans Horror	600.00
3 JCo	600.00
4 JCo(a&c),Monsters of the Mist	600.00
5 JCo(a&c),The Man who Died Twice,Electric Chair(c)	700.00
6 JCo(a&c),Orgy of Death	600.00
7 JCo(a&c),The Strangling Hands	600.00
8 JCo,Flaming Vengeance	550.00
9 JCo,The Monster in Flesh	550.00
10 JCo,Brain that Wouldn't Die	550.00
11 JCo,Buried Alive	550.00
12 Phantom Killer	350.00
13 Demon Inferno	350.00
14 RC(c),The Monster Genie	350.00
15 Crypts of Horror	350.00
16 Hamlet of Horror	350.00
17 Terror in Chinatown, Drug	375.00
18 Scared to Death,Acid Face	400.00
19 Demon of the Pit	350.00
20 Man Made Terror	350.00
21 Dec., 1954, Death's Ambush	350.00

WEB OF MYSTERY
**A.A. Wyn Publ.
(Ace Magazines), Feb., 1951**

1 MSy,Venom of the Vampires	800.00
2 MSy,Legacy of the Accursed	450.00
3 MSy,The Violin Curse	400.00
4 GC	400.00
5	400.00
6 LC	400.00
7 MSy	400.00
8 LC,LC(c),MSy,The Haunt of Death Lake	400.00
9 LC,LC(c)	400.00

10	400.00
11 MSy	400.00
12 LC	350.00
13 LC,LC(c)Surrealist	350.00
14 MSy	350.00
15	350.00
16	350.00
17 LC,LC(c)	350.00
18 LC	350.00
19 LC	350.00
20 LC, Beyond	350.00
21 MSy	350.00
22	350.00
23	350.00
24 LC	350.00
25 LC	350.00
26	350.00
27 LC, Beyond	350.00
28 RP,1st Comics Code issue	300.00
29 MSy,Sept., 1955	300.00

WEEKENDER, THE
**Rucker Publishing Co.,
Sept., 1945**

1-1 rep.(c), As Zip	250.00
1-2 thru 1-4	@275.00
2-1 rep.(c), As Dynamic	300.00
2-2 Jco,rep.(c), As Dynamic	275.00
2-3 WMc,Jan., 1946	275.00

WEIRD ADVENTURES
**P.L. Publishing,
May, 1951–Oct., 1951**

1 MB,Missing Diamonds	900.00
2 Puppet Peril	700.00
3 Blood Vengeance	600.00

Weird Adventures #1
© *PL Publishing*

WEIRD ADVENTURES
**Approved Comics
(Ziff-Davis),
July–Aug., 1951**

10 P(c),Seeker from Beyond	550.00

WEIRD CHILLS
**Key Publications,
July, 1954**

1 MBi(c),BW	1,300.00
2 Eye Torture(c)	1,600.00
3 Bondage(c),Nov., 1954	750.00

WEIRD COMICS
**Fox Features Syndicate,
April, 1940**

1 LF(c),Bondage(c),B:Birdman, Thor,Sorceress of Doom, BlastBennett,Typhon,Voodoo Man, Dr.Mortal	8,500.00
2 LF(c),Mummy(c)	3,500.00
3 JSm(c)	1,800.00
4 JSm(c)	1,800.00
5 Bondage(c),I:Dart,Ace; E:Thor	1,900.00
6 Dart & Ace(c)	1,500.00
7 Battle of Kooba	1,500.00
8 B:Panther Woman,Dynamo, The Eagle	1,500.00
9 V:Pirates	1,200.00
10 A:Navy Jones	1,200.00
11 Dart & Ace(c)	900.00
12 Dart & Ace(c)	900.00
13 Dart & Ace(c)	900.00
14 The Rage(c)	900.00
15 Dart & Ace (c)	900.00
16 Flag,The Encore(c)	900.00
17 O:Black Rider	850.00
18	850.00
19	850.00
20 Jan., 1941,I'm The Master of Life and Death	1,200.00

WEIRD FANTASY
**I.C. Publishing Co.
(E.C. Comics),
May–June, 1950**

13(1)AF,HK,JKa,WW,AF(c), Roger Harvey's Brain	3,500.00
14(2)AF,HK,JKa,WW,AF(c),Cosmic Ray Brain Explosion	2,000.00
15(3)AF,HK,JKa,WW,AF(c),Your Destination is the Moon	1,500.00
16(4)AF,HK,JKa,WW,AF(c)	1,500.00
17(5)AF,HK,JKa,WW,AF(c),Not Made by Human Hands	1,100.00
6 AF,HK,JKa,WW,AF(c),Robot	1,000.00
7 AF,JKa,WW,AF(c)	1,000.00
8 AF,JKa,WW,AF(c)	1,000.00
9 AF,Jka,WW,JO,AF(c)	1,000.00
10 AF,Jka,WW,JO,AF(c)	900.00
11 AF,Jka,WW,JO,AF(c)	1,000.00
12 AF,Jka,WW,JO,AF(c)	1,000.00
13 AF,WW,JKa,AF(c)	1,000.00
14 AF,JKa,WW,JO,AW&FF, AF(c)	900.00
15 AF,JKa,JO,AW&RKr,AF(c), Bondage(c)	1,000.00
16 AF,JKa,JO,AW&RKr,AF(c)	1,500.00
17 AF,JOP,JKa,AF(c),Bradbury	1,000.00
18 AF,JO,JKa,AF(c),Bradbury	1,000.00
19 JO,JKa,JO(c),Bradbury	1,000.00
20 JO,JKa,FF,AF(c)	1,000.00
21 JO,JKa,AW&FF(c)	1,200.00
22 JO,JKa,JO(c),Nov.,1953	700.00

With Weird Science, Becomes:

WEIRD SCIENCE FANTASY

WEIRD HORRORS
**St. John Publishing Co.,
June, 1952**

1 GT,Dungeon of the Doomed	900.00
2 Strangest Music Ever	500.00
3 PMo,Strange Fakir From the Orient, Drug	500.00
4 Murderers Knoll	400.00
5 Phantom Bowman	400.00
6 Monsters from Outer Space	800.00
7 LC,Deadly Double	800.00
8 JKu,JKu(c),Bloody Yesterday	600.00
9 JKu,JKu(c),Map Of Doom	600.00

Becomes:

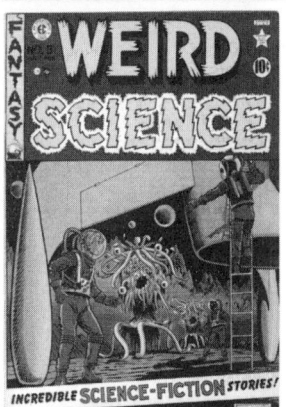

Weird Science #8
© *E.C. Comics*

NIGHTMARE
Dec., 1953
10 JKu(c),The Murderer's Mask . 800.00
11 BK,Ph(c),Fangs of Death 600.00
12 JKu(c),The Forgotten Mask .. 500.00
13 BP,Princess of the Sea..... 400.00
Becomes:

AMAZING GHOST STORIES
Oct., 1954
14 EK,MB(c),Pit & Pendulum.... 450.00
15 BP,Weird Thrillers 350.00
16 Feb., 1955, EK,JKu........ 400.00

WEIRD JUNGLE TALES
Star Publications, 1953
202 .... 150.00

WEIRD MYSTERIES
Gilmore Publications, Oct., 1952
1 BW(c) 1,500.00
2 BWi, Robot Woman 1,900.00
3 Severed Heads(c) 900.00
4 BW,Human headed ants(c) . 1,650.00
5 BW,Brains From Head(c) .. 1,800.00
6 Severed Head(c) 900.00
7 Used in "Seduction" 1,300.00
8 The One That Got Away 900.00
9 Epitaph,Cyclops, Violence.... 800.00
10 The Ruby 800.00
11 Voodoo Dolls............. 650.00
12 Sept., 1954.............. 650.00

WEIRD SCIENCE
E.C. Comics, 1950
1 AF(a&c),JKu,HK,WW 4,500.00
2 AF(a&c),JKu,HK,WW,Flying
   Saucers(c) 2,000.00
3 AF(a&c),JKu,HK 1,700.00
4 AF(a&c),JKu,HK 1,700.00
5 AF(a&c),JKu,HK,WW,
   Atomic Bomb(c) 1,500.00
6 AF(a&c),JKu,HK 1,500.00
7 AF(a&c),JKu,HK,Classic(c). 1,500.00
8 AF(a&c),JKu 1,500.00
9 WW(c),JKu,Classic(c)..... 1,600.00
10 WW(c),JKu,JO,Classic(c) . 1,500.00
11 AF,JKu,Space war......... 800.00
12 WW(c),JKu,JO,Classic(c) 800.00
13 WW(c),JKu,JO........... 800.00
14 WW(a&c),JO............. 900.00

15 WW(a&c),JO,Grl,AW,
   RKr,JKa 900.00
16 WW(a&c),JO,AW,RKr,JKa ... 800.00
17 WW(a&c),JO,AW,RKr,JKa ... 800.00
18 WW(a&c),JO,AW,RKr,
   JKa,Atomic Bomb 800.00
19 WW(a&c),JO,A
   FF,Horror(c)............. 900.00
20 WW(a&c),JO,AW,FF,JKa 900.00
21 WW(a&c),JO,AW,FF,JKa 900.00
22 WW(a&c),JO,AW,FF........ 900.00
Becomes:

WEIRD SCIENCE FANTASY
March, 1954
23 WW(a&c),AW,BK 1,000.00
24 WW,AW,BK,Classic(c) 1,000.00
25 WW,AW,BK,Classic(c) 1,100.00
26 AF(c),WW,RC,
   Flying Saucer(c) 800.00
27 WW(a&c),RC 800.00
28 AF(c),WW 900.00
29 AF(c),WW,Classic(c) 2,500.00
Becomes:

INCREDIBLE SCIENCE FANTASY
July–Aug., 1955
30 WW,JDa(c),BK,AW,RKr,JO .. 700.00
31 WW,JDa(c),BK,AW,RKr 750.00
32 JDa(c),BK,WW,JO 750.00
33 WW(c),BK,WW,JO 750.00

WEIRD TALES OF THE FUTURE
S.P.M. Publ./ Aragon Publications, March, 1952
1 RA 1,700.00
2 BW,BW(c), Jumpin Jupiter .. 2,500.00
3 BW,BW(c) 2,500.00
4 BW,BW(c) 2,000.00
5 BW,BW(c),Jumpin' Jupiter
   Lingerie(c) 2,500.00
6 Bondage(c) 1,100.00
7 BW,Devil(c)............. 2,000.00
8 July–Aug., 1953 .... 2,200.00

WEIRD TERROR
Allen Hardy Associates (Comic Media), Sept., 1952
1 RP,DH,DH(c),Dungeon of the
   Doomed;Hitler 900.00
2 HcK(c),PMo, Torture 700.00
3 PMo,DH,DH(c),Strong
   Violence............. 700.00
4 PMo,DH,DH(c),Severed Head. 700.00
5 PMo,DH,RP,DH(c),Hanging(c). 600.00
6 DH,RP,DH(c),Step into
   My Parlour, Severed Head .. 650.00
7 DH,PMo,DH(c),Blood o/t Bats. 650.00
8 DH,RP,DH(c),Step into
   My Parlour, Severed Head .. 625.00
9 DH,PMo,DH(c),The Fleabite .. 500.00
10 DH,BP,RP,DH(c) 500.00
11 DH,DH(c),Satan's Love Call .. 600.00
12 DH,DH(c),King Whitey 500.00
13 DH,DH(c),Wings of Death,
   Severed Head, Sept. 1954 .. 500.00

WEIRD THRILLERS
Approved Comics (Ziff-Davis), Sept.–Oct., 1951
1 Ph(c),Monsters & The Model 1,300.00
2 AW,P(c),The Last Man 1,000.00
3 AW,P(c),Princess o/t Sea . 1,300.00
4 AW,P(c),The Widows Lover... 900.00

5 BP,Oct., 1952,AW,P(c),
   Wings of Death 850.00

WESTERN ACTION THRILLERS
Dell Publishing Co., April, 1937
1 Buffalo Bill, Texas Kid...... 1,400.00

WESTERN ADVENTURES COMICS
A.A. Wyn, Inc. (Ace Magazines), Oct., 1948
N#(1)Injun Gun Bait 300.00
N#(2)Cross-Draw Kid 175.00
N#(3)Outlaw Mesa 175.00
4 Sheriff, Sal 125.00
5 .... 125.00
6 Rip Roaring Adventure 125.00
Becomes:

WESTERN LOVE TRAILS
Nov., 1949
7 .... 150.00
8 Maverick Love 125.00
9 March, 1950 .... 100.00

WESTERN BANDIT TRAILS
St. John Publishing Co., Jan., 1949
1 GT,MB(c), Blue Monk 375.00
2 GT,MB(c) 300.00
3 GT,MB,MB(c),Gingham Fury . 300.00

WESTERN CRIME BUSTERS
Trojan Magazines, Sept., 1950–April, 1952
1 Gunslingin' Galoots 500.00
2 K-Bar Kate 250.00
3 Wilma West 250.00
4 Bob Dale 250.00
5 Six-Gun Smith 250.00
6 WW 450.00
7 WW,Wells Fargo Robbery ... 450.00
8 .... 250.00
9 WW,Lariat Lucy 450.00
10 WW,Tex Gordon 500.00

Western Crime Busters #9
© *Trojan Magazines*

All comics prices listed are for *Near Mint* condition.

WESTERN CRIME CASES
See: OUTLAWS, THE

WESTERNER, THE
**Wanted Comics Group/
Toytown Publ.,
June, 1948**

14 F:Jack McCall	250.00
15 F:Bill Jamett	200.00
16 F:Tom McLowery	200.00
17 F:Black Bill Desmond	200.00
18 BK,F:Silver Dollar Dalton	250.00
19 MMe,F:Jess Meeton	150.00
20	150.00
21 BK,MMe	200.00
22 BK,MMe	200.00
23 BK,MMe	200.00
24 BK,MMe	200.00
25 O,I,B:Calamity Jane	200.00
26 BK,F:The Widowmaker	250.00
27 BK	250.00
28 thru 31	@100.00
32 E:Calamity Jane	100.00
33 A:Quest	100.00
34	100.00
35 SSh(c)	100.00
36	100.00
37 Lobo-Wolf Boy	100.00
38	100.00
39	100.00
40 SSh(c)	100.00
41 Dec., 1951	100.00

WESTERN FIGHTERS
**Hillman Periodicals,
April–May, 1948**

1 S&K(c)	500.00
2 BF(c)	200.00
3 BF(c)	150.00
4 BK,BF	175.00
5	125.00
6	125.00
7 BK	150.00
8	125.00
9	125.00
10 BK	150.00
11 AMC&FF	400.00
2-1 BK	150.00
2-2 BP	125.00
2-3 thru 2-12	@100.00
3-1 thru 3-11	@100.00
3-12 BK	125.00
4-1	100.00
4-2 BK	150.00
4-3 BK	150.00
4-4 BK	150.00
4-5 BK	150.00
4-6 BK	150.00
4-7 March–April, 1953	100.00

WESTERN FRONTIER
**P.L. Publishers
(Approved Comics),
May, 1951**

1 Flaming Vengeance	150.00
2	125.00
3 Death Rides the Iron Horse	75.00
4 thru 6	@75.00
7 1952	75.00

WESTERN HEARTS
**Standard Magazine, Inc.,
Dec., 1949**

1 JSe, Whip Wilson, Ph(c)	300.00
2 AW,FF, Palomino, Ph(c)	300.00
3 Rex Allen, Ph(c)	200.00
4 JSe,BE, Ph(c)	175.00
5 JSe,BE,Ray Milland, Ph(c)	175.00
6 JSe,BE,Irene Dunn, Ph(c)	175.00

7 JSe,BE,Jock Mahoney Ph(c)	175.00
8 Randolph Scott, Ph(c)	175.00
9 JSe,BE, Whip Wilson, Ph(c)	200.00
10 JSe,BE, Bill Williams,Ph(c)	175.00

WESTERN HERO
See: WOW COMICS

WESTERN KILLERS
Fox Features Syndicate, 1948

N# Lingerie	300.00
60 Violence	325.00
61 JCo,LSe	275.00
62	250.00
63	250.00
64	250.00

WESTERN LOVE
**Feature Publications
(Prize Comics Group),
July–Aug., 1949**

1 S&K, Randolph Scott	450.00
2 S&K, Whip Wilson	325.00
3 JSe,BE, Reno Brown	225.00
4 JSe,BE	225.00
5 JSe,BE, Dale Robertson	325.00

WESTERN PICTURE STORIES
**Comics Magazine Co.,
Feb., 1937–June, 1937**

1 WE,Treachery Trail, 1st Western	3,000.00
2 WE,Weapons of the West	1,600.00
3 WE,Dragon Pass	1,400.00
4 CavemanCowboy	1,400.00

WESTERN ROUGH RIDERS
**Stanmor Publ.
(Gilmore Magazines), 1954**

1	125.00
2	100.00
3	100.00
4	100.00

WESTERN THRILLERS
**Fox Features Syndicate,
Aug., 1948**

1 Velvet Rose	700.00
2	350.00
3 GT,RH(c)	250.00

Whack #3 © St John Publishing

4	275.00
5 Butch Cassidy	275.00
6 June, 1949	250.00

Becomes:

MY PAST CONFESSIONS
Aug., 1949

7	225.00
8	150.00
9	150.00
10	150.00
11 WW	300.00
12 Crimes Inc.	125.00

WESTERN TRUE CRIME
**Fox Features Syndicate,
Aug., 1948**

1 (#15) JKa, Zoot 14	450.00
2 (#16) JKa, Violence	350.00
3 JKa	325.00
4 JCr	325.00
5	250.00
6	250.00

Becomes:

MY CONFESSION
Aug., 1949–Feb., 1950

7 WW	400.00
8 WW,My Tarnished Reputation	350.00
9 I:Tormented Men	150.00
10 I Am Damaged Goods	150.00

WHACK
**St. John Publishing Co.,
Dec., 1953**

1 3-D	425.00
2 Steve Crevice,Flush Jordan V:Bing (Crosby)The Merciful	300.00
3 F:Little Awful Fannie	250.00

WHAM COMICS
**Centaur Publications,
Nov., 1940**

1 PG,The Sparkler & His Disappearing Suit	2,400.00
2 Dec., 1940,PG,PG(C), Men Turn into Icicles	1,600.00

WHIRLWIND COMICS
**Nita Publications,
June, 1940**

1 F:The Cyclone	3,300.00
2 A:Scoops Hanlon,Cyclone(c)	1,700.00
3 Sept., 1940,A:Magic Mandarin,Cyclone(c)	1,600.00

WHITE PRINCESS OF THE JUNGLE
Avon Periodicals, July, 1951

1 EK(c),Terror Fangs	900.00
2 EK,EK(c),Jungle Vengeance	600.00
3 EK,EK(c),The Blue Gorilla	500.00
4 Fangs of the Swamp Beast	450.00
5 EK,Coils of the Tree Snake Nov., 1952	450.00

WHITE RIDER AND SUPER HORSE
See: OUTLAWS, THE

WHIZ COMICS
**Fawcett Publications,
Feb., 1940**

1 O:Captain Marvel,B:Spy Smasher, Golden Arrow,Dan Dare, Scoop Smith, Ibis the Invincible, Sivana	125,000.00
2	12,000.00

3 Make way for
   Captain Marvel 7,000.00
4 Captain Marvel
   Crashes Through 6,000.00
5 Captain Marvel
   Scores Again! 5,000.00
6 Circus of Death 3,700.00
7 B:Dr Voodoo,Squadron
   of Death 3,700.00
8 Saved by Captain Marvel! . . 3,700.00
9 MRa,Captain Marvel
   on the Job. 3,700.00
10 Battles the Winged Death . . 3,700.00
11 Hurray for Captain Marvel . . 2,500.00
12 Captain Marvel rides
   the Engine of Doom 2,500.00
13 Worlds Most Powerful Man!. 2,500.00
14 Boomerangs the Torpedo . . 2,500.00
15 O:Sivana 2,400.00
16 Dr. Voodoo 2,300.00
17 Knocks out a Tank 2,300.00
18 V:Spy Smasher 2,300.00
19 Crushes the Tiger Shark . . . 1,900.00
20 V:Sivana 1,900.00
21 O:Lt. Marvels 2,000.00
22 Mayan Temple 1,300.00
23 GT,A:Dr. Voodoo 1,300.00
24 . . . . 1,300.00
25 O&I:Captain Marvel Jr., Stops
   the Turbine of Death. 12,000.00
26 . . . . 1,300.00
27 V:Death God of the
   Katonkas. 1,400.00
28 V:Mad Dervish of Ank-Har . . 1,400.00
29 Three Lt. Marvels (c), Pan
   American Olympics 1,400.00
30 CCB(c). 1,300.00
31 Douglass MacArthur
   & Spy Smasher(c) 1,100.00
32 Spy Smasher(c) 1,100.00
33 Spy Smasher(c) 1,400.00
34 Three Lt. Marvels (c) 750.00
35 Capt. Marvel and the
   Three Fates 1,000.00
36 Haunted Hallowe'en Hotel . . . 700.00
37 Return of the Trolls 700.00
38 Grand Steeplechase 700.00
39 A Nazi Utopia 700.00
40 A:Three Lt. Marvels, The
   Earth's 4 Corners 700.00
41 Captain Marvel 1,000 years
   from Now. 600.00
42 Returns in Time Chair. 600.00
43 V:Sinister Spies,
   Spy Smasher(c). 600.00

Whiz Comics #25
© Fawcett Publications

44 Life Story of Captain Marvel . . 650.00
45 Cures His Critics. 600.00
46. . . . . 600.00
47 Captain Marvel needs
   a Birthday 600.00
48 . . . . 600.00
49 Writes a Victory song 600.00
50 Captain Marvel's most
   embarrassing moment 600.00
51 Judges the Ugly-
   Beauty Contest 500.00
52 V:Sivana, Chooses
   His Birthday 500.00
53 Captain Marvel fights
   Billy Batson 500.00
54 Jack of all Trades 500.00
55 Family Tree 500.00
56 Tells what the Future Will Be . 500.00
57 A:Spy Smasher,Golden Arrow,
   Ibis. 500.00
58 . . . . 500.00
59 V:Sivana's Twin. 500.00
60 Missing Person's Machine . . . 500.00
61 Gets a first name 450.00
62 Plays in a Band. 450.00
63 Great Indian Rope Trick 450.00
64 Suspected of Murder 450.00
65 Lamp of Diogenes. 450.00
66 The Trial of Mr. Morris! 450.00
67 . . . . 450.00
68 Laugh Lotion, V:Sivana. 450.00
69 Mission to Mercury 650.00
70 Climbs the World's Mightiest
   Mountain 550.00
71 Strange Magician 500.00
72 V:The Man of the Future. 500.00
73 In Ogre Land. 500.00
74 Old Man River. 500.00
75 The City Olympics. 500.00
76 Spy Smasher becomes
   Crime Smasher 500.00
77 . . . . 500.00
78 Golden Arrow 500.00
79 . . . . 500.00
80 . . . . 500.00
81 . . . . 500.00
82 The Atomic Ship 500.00
83 Magic Locket. 500.00
84 . . . . 500.00
85 The Clock of San Lojardo 500.00
86 V:Sinister Sivanas. 500.00
87 The War on Olympia. 500.00
88 The Wonderful Magic Carpet . 500.00
89 Webs of Crime 500.00
90 . . . . 500.00
91 Infinity (c) 500.00
92 . . . . 500.00
93 Captain America become
   a Hobo?. 500.00
94 V:Sivana 500.00
95 Captain Marvel is grounded . . 500.00
96 The Battle Between Buildings. 500.00
97 Visits Mirage City 500.00
98 . . . . 500.00
99 V:Menace in the Mountains . . 500.00
100 Anniversary Issue 600.00
101 . . . . 500.00
102 A:Commando Yank 500.00
103 . . . . 500.00
104 Flag(c). 500.00
105 . . . . 500.00
106 A:Bulletman. 500.00
107 The Great Experiment 600.00
108 thru 114 . . . . @400.00
115 The Marine Invasion 400.00
116 . . . . 400.00
117 V:Sivana 400.00
118 thru 121 . . . . @400.00
122 V:Sivana 400.00
123 . . . . 400.00
124 . . . . 400.00
125 Olympic Games of the Gods 400.00

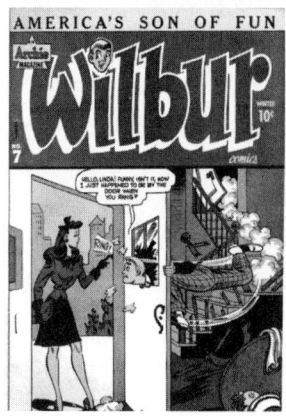
Wilbur Comics #7
© Archie Comics

126 . . . . 400.00
127 . . . . 400.00
128 . . . . 400.00
129 . . . . 350.00
130 . . . . 350.00
131 The Television Trap. 350.00
132 thru 142. . . . . @350.00
143 Mystery of the Flying Studio . 350.00
144 V:The Disaster Master 350.00
145 . . . . 350.00
146 . . . . 350.00
147 . . . . 350.00
148 . . . . 350.00
149 . . . . 350.00
150 V:Bug Bombs 450.00
151 . . . . 450.00
152 . . . . 450.00
153 V:The Death Horror 600.00
154 Horror Tale, I:Dr.Death 600.00
155 V:Legend Horror,Dr.Death . . 650.00

WHODUNIT?
D.S. Publishing Co.,
Aug.–Sept., 1948
1 MB,Weeping Widow 350.00
2 Diploma For Death 150.00
3 Dec.–Jan., 1949 . . . . 150.00

WHO IS NEXT?
Standard Comics,
Jan., 1953
5 ATh,RA,Don't Let Me Kill 300.00

WILBUR COMICS
MLJ Magazines
(Archie Publications),
Summer, 1944
1 F:Wilbur Wilkin-America's Song
   of Fun 800.00
2 . . . . 400.00
3 . . . . 300.00
4 . . . . 300.00
5 I:Katy Keene 1,500.00
6 F:Katy Keene. 350.00
7 F:Katy Keene. 350.00
8 F:Katy Keene. 350.00
9 F:Katy Keene. 350.00
10 F:Katy Keene 350.00
11 thru 20 F:Katy Keene . . . . @300.00
21 thru 30 F:Katy Keene . . . . @250.00
31 thru 40 F:Katy Keene . . . . @150.00
41 thru 56 F:Katy Keene . . . . @125.00
57 thru 89. . . . . @100.00
90 Oct., 1965. . . . . 100.00

GOLDEN AGE

WILD BILL ELLIOT

Dell Publishing Co.,
May, 1950

(1) see Dell Four Color #278
2 .... 150.00
3 thru 5 .... @100.00
6 thru 10 .... @100.00
(11-12) see Four Color #472, 520
13 thru 17 .... @100.00

WILD BILL HICKOK
AND JINGLES
See: YELLOWJACKET
COMICS

WILD BILL HICKOK

Avon Periodicals,
Sept.–Oct., 1949

1 Grl(c),Frontier Fighter 350.00
2 Ph(c),Gambler's Guns 150.00
3 Ph(c),Great Stage Robbery .. 100.00
4 Ph(c),Guerilla Gunmen 100.00
5 Ph(c),Return of the Renegade 100.00
6 EK,EK(c),Along the Apache
Trail 100.00
7 EK,EK(c)Outlaws of
Hell's Bend 100.00
8 Ph(c),The Border Outlaws ... 100.00
9 PH(c),Killers From Texas ... 100.00
10 Ph(c) 100.00
11 EK,EK(c),The Hell Riders 100.00
12 EK,EK(c),The Lost Gold Mine 100.00
13 EK,EK(c),Bloody Canyon
Massacre 125.00
14 .... 125.00
15 .... 100.00
16 JKa,Bad Men of Deadwood .. 100.00
17 JKa 100.00
18 JKa,Kit West 100.00
19 thru 23 .... @100.00
24 EK,EK(c) 100.00
25 EK,EK(c) 100.00
26 EK,EK(c) 100.00
27 EK,EK(c) 100.00
28 EK,EK(c),May–June, 1956 ... 100.00

WILD BOY OF
THE CONGO

Approved(Ziff-Davis)/
St. John Publ. Co.,
Feb.–March, 1951

10(1)NS,PH(c),Bondage(c),The
Gorilla God 400.00
11(2)NS,Ph(c),Star of the Jungle . 200.00
12(3)NS,Ph(c),Ice-Age Men..... 200.00
4 NS.Ph(c),Tyrant of the Jungle 250.00
5 NS,Ph(c),The White Robe
of Courage 150.00
6 NS,Ph(c) 150.00
7 MB,EK.Ph(c) 200.00
8 Ph(c),Man-Eater 150.00
9 Ph(c),Killer Leopard 150.00
10 .... 150.00
11 MB(c) 200.00
12 MB(c) 200.00
13 MB(c) 200.00
14 MB(c) 200.00
15 June, 1955 .... 150.00

WILD FRONTIER

Charlton Comics, 1955

1 Davy Crockett 125.00
2 same .... same
3 thru 7 same .... @100.00
7 O:Cheyenne Kid 100.00
Becomes:

CHEYENNE KID

WILL ROGERS WESTERN

Fox Features Syndicate, 1950

1 (5) 500.00
2 Ph(c) 400.00

WINGS COMICS

Wings Publ.
(Fiction House Magazines),
Sept., 1940

1 HcK,AB,GT,Ph(c),B:Skull Squad,
Clipper Kirk,Suicide Smith,
War Nurse,Phantom Falcons,
GreasemonkeyGriffin,Parachute
Patrol,Powder Burns 5,000.00
2 HcK,AB,GT,Bomber Patrol .. 2,000.00
3 HcK,AB,GT 1,500.00
4 HcK,AB,GT,B:Spitfire Ace ... 1,500.00
5 HcK,AB,GT,Torpedo Patrol . 1,500.00
6 HcK,AB,GT,Bombs for Berlin 1,000.00
7 HcK,AB 1,000.00
8 HcK,AB,The Wings of Doom 1,000.00
9 Sky-Wolf 900.00
10 The Upside Down 900.00
11 .... 800.00
12 Fury of the fire Boards 800.00
13 Coffin Slugs For The
Luftwaffe 800.00
14 Stuka Buster 800.00
15 Boomerang Blitz 800.00
16 O:Capt.Wings 900.00
17 Skyway to Death 700.00
18 Horsemen of the Sky 700.00
19 Nazi Spy Trap 700.00
20 The One Eyed Devil 700.00
21 Chute Troop Tornado 600.00
22 TNT for Tokyo 600.00
23 RP,Battling Eagles of Bataan . 600.00
24 RP,The Death of a Hero 600.00
25 RP,Suicide Squeeze 600.00
26 Tojo's Eagle Trap 600.00
27 BLb,Mile High Gauntlet..... 600.00
28 BLb,Tail Gun Tornado 600.00
29 BLb,Buzzards from Berlin ... 600.00
30 BLb,Monsters of the
Stratosphere 550.00
31 BLb,Sea Hawks away 550.00
32 BLb,Sky Mammoth 550.00
33 BLb,Roll Call of the Yankee
Eagles 550.00
34 BLb,So Sorry,Mr Tojo 550.00
35 BLb,RWb,Hell's Lightning 550.00
36 RWb,The Crash-Master 550.00
37 RWb,Sneak Blitz 550.00
38 RWb,Rescue Raid of the
Yank Eagle 550.00
39 RWb,Sky Hell/Pigboat Patrol . 550.00
40 RWb,Luftwaffe Gamble..... 550.00
41 RWb,.50 Caliber Justice 500.00
42 RWb,PanzerMeat forMosquito 500.00
43 RWb,Suicide Sentinels 500.00
44 RWb,Berlin Bombs Away ... 500.00
45 RWb,Hells Cargo 500.00
46 RWb,Sea-Hawk Patrol 500.00
47 RWb,Tojo's Tin Gibraltar.... 500.00
48 RWb 500.00
49 RWb,Rockets Away 500.00
50 RWb,Mission For a Madman . 500.00
51 RWb,Toll for a Typhoon 400.00
52 MB,Madam Marauder....... 400.00
53 MB,Robot Death Over
Manhattan 400.00
54 MB,Juggernauts of Death ... 400.00
55 MB..................... 400.00
56 MB,Sea Raiders Grave..... 400.00
57 MB,Yankee Warbirds over
Tokyo 400.00
58 MB..................... 400.00
59 MB,Prey of the Night Hawks.. 400.00
60 MB,E:Skull Squad,
Hell's Eyes 400.00
61 MB,Raiders o/t Purple Dawn . 350.00

Wings #60
© Fiction House Magazines

62 Twilight of the Wings 350.00
63 Hara Kiri Rides the Skyways . 350.00
64 Taps For Tokyo 350.00
65 AB,Warhawk for the Kill 350.00
66 AB,B:Ghost Patrol.......... 350.00
67 AB 350.00
68 AB,ClipperKirkBecomesPhantom
Falcon;O:Phantom Falcon... 350.00
69 AB,O:cont,Phantom Falcon .. 350.00
70 AB,N:Phantom Falcon;
O:Final Phantom Falcon 350.00
71 Ghost Patrol becomes
Ghost Squadron 350.00
72 V:Capt. Kamikaze.......... 350.00
73 Hell & Stormoviks 350.00
74 BLb(c),Loot is What She
Lived For 350.00
75 BLb(c),The Sky Hag 350.00
76 BLb(c),Temple of the Dead... 350.00
77 BLb(c),Sky Express to Hell... 350.00
78 BLb(c),Loot Queen of
Satan's Skyway 350.00
79 BLb(c),Buzzards of
Plunder Sky.............. 350.00
80 BLb(c),Port of Missing Pilots . 350.00
81 BLb(c),Sky Trail of the
Terror Tong 350.00
82 BLb(c),Bondage(c),Spider &
The Fly Guy.............. 400.00
83 BLb(c),GE,Deep Six For
Capt. Wings.............. 350.00
84 BLb(c),GE,Sky Sharks to
the Kill 350.00
85 BLb(c),GE............... 350.00
86 BLb(c),GE,Moon Raiders 350.00
87 BLb(c),GE............... 350.00
88 BLb(c),GE,Madmans Mission . 350.00
89 BLb(c),GE,Bondage(c),
Rockets Away 500.00
90 BLb(c),GE,Bondage(c),The
Radar Rocketeers 500.00
91 BLb(c),GT,Bondage(c),V-9 for
Vengeance............... 500.00
92 BLb(c),GE,Death's red Rocket 350.00
93 BLb(c),GE,Kidnap Cargo 600.00
94 BLb(c),GE,Bondage(c),Ace
of the A-Bomb Patrol....... 650.00
95 BLb(c),GE,The Ace of
the Assassins 350.00
96 BLb(c),GE............... 350.00
97 BLb(c),GE,The Sky Octopus . 350.00
98 BLb(c),GE,The Witch Queen
of Satan's Skyways 350.00
99 BLb(c),GE,The Spy Circus .. 350.00
100 BLb(c),GE,King o/t Congo . 400.00

    All comics prices listed are for *Near Mint* condition.

101 BLb(c),GE,Trator of
   the Cockpit 300.00
102 BLb(c),GE,Doves of Doom . . 300.00
103 BLb(c),GE 300.00
104 BLb(c),GE,Fireflies of Fury . . 300.00
105 BLb(c),GE 300.00
106 BLb(c),GE,Six Aces & A
   Firing Squad 300.00
107 BLb(c),GE,Operation Satan . 300.00
108 BLb(c),GE,The Phantom
   of Berlin 300.00
109 GE,Vultures of
   Vengeance Sky 300.00
110 GE,The Red Ray Vortex 300.00
111 GE,E:Jane Martin 250.00
112 The Flight of the
   Silver Saucers 250.00
113 Suicide Skyways 250.00
114 D-Day for Death Rays 250.00
115 Ace of Space 250.00
116 Jet Aces of Korea 250.00
117 Reap the Red Wind 250.00
118 Vengeance Flies Blind 250.00
119 The Whistling Death 250.00
120 Doomsday Mission 250.00
121 Ace of the Spyways 250.00
122 Last Kill Korea 250.00
123 The Cat & the Canaries . . . 250.00
124 Summer, 1954, Death
   Below Zero 250.00

WINNIE WINKLE
**Dell Publishing Co.,
1948**
1 . . . . 200.00
2 . . . . 150.00
3 thru 7 . . . . @150.00

WITCHCRAFT
**Avon Periodicals,
March–April, 1952**
1 SC,JKu,Heritage of Horror . . 1,100.00
2 SC,JKu,The Death Tattoo 800.00
3 EK,Better off Dead 600.00
4 Claws of the Cat,
   Boiling Humans 650.00
5 Ph(c),Where Zombies Walk . . 700.00
6 March, 1953 Mysteries of the
   Moaning Statue 800.00

WITCHES TALES
**Harvey Publications,
Jan., 1951**
1 RP,Bondage(c),Weird Yarns
   of Unseen Terror 900.00
2 RP,AAv,We Dare You 600.00
3 RP,Bondage(c)Forest of
   Skeletons 400.00
4 BP 400.00
5 BP,Bondage(c),Share
   My Coffin 450.00
6 BP,Bondage(c),Servants of
   the Tomb 400.00
7 BP,Screaming City 400.00
8 LEI(c),Bondage(c) 450.00
9 Fatal Steps 400.00
10 LEI,BP,I!!,Bondage 450.00
11 BP,Monster Maker 350.00
12 Bondage(c);The Web
   of the Spider 350.00
13 The Torture Jar 350.00
14 AAv,Transformation 350.00
15 Drooling Zombie 350.00
16 LEI,Revenge of a Witch 350.00
17 LEI,Dimension IV 350.00
18 LEI,HN,Bird of Prey 400.00
19 LEI,HN,The Pact 400.00
20 LEI,HN,Kiss & Tell 400.00
21 LEI,HN,The Invasion 400.00
22 LEI,HN,A Day of Panic 400.00
23 LEI,HN,The Wig Maker 400.00

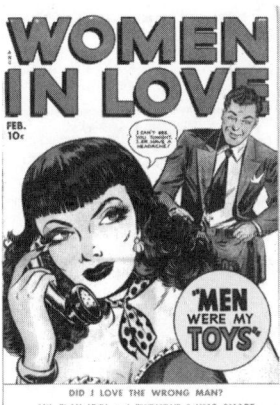

Winnie Winkle #1
© *Dell Publishing*

24 LEI,HN,The Undertaker 425.00
25 LEI,What Happens at 8:30 PM?
   Severed Heads(c) 500.00
26 LEI,Up There 350.00
27 LEI,The Thing That Grew . . . 350.00
28 AAv,Demon Flies 350.00
Becomes:

WITCHES WESTERN TALES
Feb., 1955
29 S&K(a&c),F:Davy Crockett . . . 350.00
30 S&K(a&c) 300.00
Becomes:

WESTERN TALES
Oct., 1955
31 S&K(a&c),F:Davy Crockett . . 250.00
32 S&K(a&c),F:Davy Crockett . . 250.00
33 S&K(a&c),July–Sept.,1956 . . 250.00

WITH THE MARINES ON THE BATTLEFRONTS OF THE WORLD
Toby Press, June, 1953
1 Flaming Soul, John
   Wayne, Ph(c) 400.00
2 Mar., 1954, Monty Hall, Ph(c) . 125.00

WITTY COMICS
**Irwin H. Rubin/Chicago Nite
Life News, 1945**
1 Pioneer, Jr. Patrol 400.00
2 1945 . . . . 200.00
3 thru 7 . . . . @150.00

WOMEN IN LOVE
**Fox Features Synd./
Hero Books/
Ziff-Davis, Aug., 1949**
1 . . . . 600.00
2 JKa,AF(c) 400.00
3 . . . . 250.00
4 WW 300.00

WOMEN OUTLAWS
**Fox Features Syndicate,
July, 1948**
1 Partial nudity 1,200.00
2 . . . . 900.00
3 . . . . 900.00
4 . . . . 700.00
5 . . . . 550.00

6 . . . . 550.00
7 . . . . 550.00
8 . . . . 550.00
N# Cody of the Pony Express . . . 400.00
Becomes:

MY LOVE MEMORIES
**Fox Features Syndicate,
Nov., 1949**
9 . . . . 250.00
10 . . . . 150.00
11 . . . . 175.00
12 WW 200.00

WONDERBOY
See: HORRIFIC

WONDER COMICS
**Great Publ./Nedor/
Better Publications,
May, 1944**
1 SSh(c),B:Grim Reaper,
   Spectro Hitler(c) 2,800.00
2 ASh(c),O:Grim Reaper,B:Super
   Sleuths,Grim Reaper(c) . . . 1,500.00
3 ASh(c),Grim Reaper(c) 1,300.00
4 ASh(c),Grim Reaper(c) 1,000.00
5 ASh(c),Grim Reaper(c) 1,000.00
6 ASh(c),Grim Reaper(c) 1,000.00
7 ASh(c),Grim Reaper(c) 1,000.00
8 ASh(c),E:Super Sleuths,
   Spectro 1,000.00
9 ASh(c),B:Wonderman 1,000.00
10 ASh(c),Wonderman(c) 850.00
11 Grl(c),B:Dick Devins 1,000.00
12 Grl(c),Bondage(c) 1,000.00
13 ASh(c),Bondage(c). 1,000.00
14 ASh(c),Bondage(c)
   E:Dick Devins 1,000.00
15 ASh(c),Bondage(c),B:Tara . . 1,300.00
16 ASh(c),A:Spectro,
   E:Grim Reaper 1,000.00
17 FF,ASh(c),A:Super Sleuth . . 1,400.00
18 ASh(c),B:Silver Knight 1,300.00
19 ASh(c),FF 1,300.00
20 FF,ASh(c),Oct., 1948 . . . . . 1,500.00

WONDER COMICS
**Fox Features Syndicate,
May, 1939**
1 BKa,WE,WE(c),B:Wonderman,
   DR.Kung,K-51 . . . . 28,000.00
2 WE,BKa,LF(c),B:Yarko the
   Great,A:Spark Stevens 9,000.00

Women in Love #4
© *Fox Features Syndicate*

Becomes:

WONDERWORLD COMICS

Fox Features Syndicate, July, 1939–Jan., 1942

3 WE,LF,BP,LF&WE,I:Flame .	14,000.00
4 WE,LF,BP,LF(c)	7,000.00
5 WE,LF,BP,GT,LF(c),Flame . .	3,500.00
6 WE,LF,BP,GT,LF(c),Flame . .	3,500.00
7 WE,LF,BP,GT,LF(c),Flame . .	5,500.00
8 WE,LF,BP,GT,LF(c),Flame . .	5,000.00
9 WE,LF,BP,GT,LF(c),Flame . .	3,500.00
10 WE,LF,BP,LF(c),Flame.	3,500.00
11 WE,LF,BP,LF(c),O:Flame. . .	3,500.00
12 BP,LF(c),Bondage(c),Flame.	2,500.00
13 LF(c),E:Dr Fung,Flame	2,500.00
14 JoS,Bondage(c),Flame	2,000.00
15 JoS&LF(c),Flame.	1,800.00
16 Flame(c).	1,500.00
17 Flame(c).	1,500.00
18 Flame(c).	1,500.00
19 Male Bondage(c),Flame . . .	1,600.00
20 Flame(c).	1,400.00
21 O:Black Club &Lion,Flame. .	1,300.00
22 Flame(c).	1,100.00
23 Flame(c).	1,000.00
24 Flame(c).	1,000.00
25 A:Dr Fung,Flame	1,000.00
26 Flame(c).	1,000.00
27 Flame(c).	1,000.00
28 Bondage(c)I&O:US Jones, B:Lu-nar,Flame.	1,500.00
29 Bondage(c),Flame	900.00
30 O:Flame(c),Flame	1,500.00
31 Bondage(c),Flame	900.00
32 Hitler(c),Flame	1,200.00
33 Male Bondage(c)	900.00

WONDERLAND COMICS

Feature Publications (Prize Comics Group), Summer, 1945

1 (fa),B:Alex in Wonderland	250.00
2	150.00
3 thru 8	@125.00
9 1947.	125.00

WONDERWORLD
See:WONDER COMICS

THE WORLD AROUND US

Gilberton Publications, 1958

1 GE,Dogs	125.00

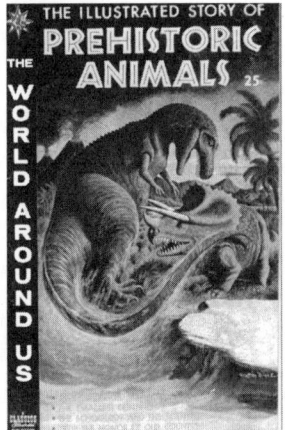

World Around Us #15
© Gilberton Publications

---

2 SC,Indians	125.00
3 LbC,Horses	125.00
4 LbC,Railroads	100.00
5 Grl,Space.	125.00
6 GE,The FBI	125.00
7 JO,Grl,Pirates	100.00
8 RC,GE,Grl,Flight	100.00
9 JO,Grl,EK,Army	100.00
10 EK,Navy	100.00
11 Marines	100.00
12 Grl,Coast Guard	100.00
13 JCo,Air Force	100.00
14 RC,GE,EK,The French Revolution	125.00
15 AW,GM,EK,Prehistoric Animals	135.00
16 EK,The Crusades	100.00
17 GE,RC,Festivals	100.00
18 AW,GE,RC,Great Scientists . .	100.00
19 RC,AW,GM,The Jungle.	125.00
20 RC,GE,AT,Communications . .	125.00
21 RC,GE,GM,American Presidents	125.00
22 GM,GE,Boating.	100.00
23 RC,GE,Great Explorers	100.00
24 GM,GE,Ghosts	125.00
25 GM,GE,Magic	125.00
26 The Civil War	150.00
27 RC,GE,CM,AT,High Adventure	100.00
28 RC,GE,GM,AT,LbC(c),Whaling	110.00
29 RC,GE,AT,GM,Vikings	125.00
30 RC,GE,JK,AT,Undersea Adventures	125.00
31 RC,GE,Grl,EK,JK,Hunting . . .	100.00
32 GM,JK,RC,GE,For Gold and Glory.	100.00
33 AT,GE,RC,Famous Teens . . .	110.00
34 RC,GE,Fishing	100.00
35 LcM,JK,GM,GE,Spies	110.00
36 JK,Fight For Life	100.00

WORLD FAMOUS HEROES MAGAZINE

Comic Corp. of America (Centaur) Oct., 1941

1 BLb,Paul Revere	1,700.00
2 BLb,Andrew Jackson,V: Dickinson, Lou Gehrig . . .	750.00
3 BLb,Juarez-Mexican patriot . .	700.00
4 BLb,Canadian Mounties	700.00

WORLD FAMOUS STORIES

Croyden Publ., 1945

1 Rip Van Winkle,Ali Baba	175.00

THE WORLD IS HIS PARISH

George A. Pflaum, 1953

N# Pope Pius XII	75.00

WORLD'S GREATEST STORIES

Jubilee Publications Jan., 1949

1 F:Alice in Wonderland	450.00
2 F:Pinocchio	400.00

WORLDS BEYOND

Fawcett Publications, 1951

1 BP,BBa.	700.00

Becomes:

WORLDS OF FEAR

Fawcett Publications, 1952

2 BP,SMo(c)	900.00
3 GE,SMo(c).	700.00
4 BP,MSy,SMo(c)	650.00
5 BP,MSy,SMo(c)	650.00

---

6 SMo(c).	650.00
7 SMo(c).	650.00
8 SMo(c).	650.00
9	650.00
10 no-eyed man, eyeballs(c) . .	1,500.00

WORLD WAR III

Ace Periodicals, March–May, 1953

1 Atomic Bomb (c)	1,400.00
2 The War That Will Never Happen	900.00

WOTALIFE COMICS
See: PHANTOM LADY

WOW COMICS

David McKay/Henle Publ., July, 1936–Nov., 1936

1 WE,DBr(c),Fu Manchu, Buck Jones.	5,000.00
2 WE,Little King	3,200.00
3 WE,WE(c), Popeye.	2,900.00
4 WE,BKa,AR,DBr(c),Popeye, Flash Gordon	3,500.00

Wow Comics #7
© Fawcett Publications

WOW COMICS

Fawcett Publications, Winter, 1940

N#(1)S&K,CCB(c),B&O:Mr Scarlett; B:Atom Blake,Jim Dolan,Rick O'Shay,Bondage(c)	27,000.00
2 B:Hunchback	5,000.00
3 V:Mummy Ray Gun	2,500.00
4 O:Pinky	2,600.00
5 F:Pinky the Whiz Kid	1,500.00
6 O:Phantom Eagle; B:Commando Yank	1,500.00
7 Spearhead of Invasion	1,000.00
8 All Three Heroes	1,000.00
9 A:Capt Marvel,Capt MarvelJr. Shazam,B:Mary Marvel . . .	2,500.00
10 The Sinister Secret of Hotel Hideaway	1,200.00
11	700.00
12 Rocketing adventures	700.00
13 Thrill Show	700.00
14 V:Mr Night	700.00
15 Shazam Girl of America	800.00
16 Ride to the Moon	800.00
17 V:Mary Batson,Alter Ego Goes Berserk	800.00
18 I:Uncle Marvel,Infinity(c) V is For Victory	800.00
19 A Whirlwind Fantasy	800.00

20 Mary Marvel's Magic Carpet. . 800.00
21 Word That Shook the World . . 450.00
22 Come on Boys-
  Everybody Sing 450.00
23 Trapped by the Terror of
  the Future 450.00
24 Mary Marvel 450.00
25 Mary Marvel Crushes Crime. . 450.00
26 Smashing Star-
  Studded Stories 350.00
27 War Stamp Plea(c) 350.00
28 Pinky 350.00
29 . . . . 350.00
30 In Mirror Land 350.00
31 Stars of Action 300.00
32 The Millinery Marauders 300.00
33 Mary Marvel(c) 300.00
34 A:Uncle Marvel 300.00
35 I:Freckles Marvel 400.00
36 Secret of the Buried City. . . . 300.00
37 7th War loan plea 300.00
38 Pictures That Came to Life. . . 300.00
39 The Perilous Packages. 300.00
40 The Quarrel of the Gnomes . . 300.00
41 Hazardous Adventures 275.00
42 . . . . 275.00
43 Curtain Time 275.00
44 Volcanic Adventure 275.00
45 Commando Yank 275.00
46 Commando Yank 275.00
47 Commando Yank 275.00
48 Commando Yank 275.00
49 Commando Yank 275.00
50 Mary Marvel/Commando Yank 275.00
51 Command Yank 250.00
52 . . . . 250.00
53 Murder in the Tall Timbers . . . 250.00
54 Flaming Adventure 250.00
55 Earthquake!. 250.00
56 Sacred Pearls of Comatesh . . 250.00
57 . . . . 250.00
58 E:Mary Marvel;The Curse
  of the Keys 250.00
59 B:Ozzie the Hilarious
  Teenager 250.00
60 thru 64 . . . . @250.00
65 A:Tom Mix 250.00
66 A:Tom Mix 250.00
67 A:Tom Mix 250.00
68 A:Tom Mix 250.00
69 A:Tom Mix,Baseball 250.00
Becomes:

REAL WESTERN HERO
Sept., 1948
70 It's Round-up Time 500.00
71 CCB,P(c),A Rip
  Roaring Rodeo 300.00
72 w/Gabby Hayes 300.00
73 thru 75 . . . . @300.00
Becomes:

WESTERN HERO
March, 1949
76 Partial Ph(c)&P(c) 400.00
77 Partial Ph(c)&P(c) 200.00
78 Partial Ph(c)&P(c) 200.00
79 Partial Ph(o)&P(c),
  Shadow of Death. 175.00
80 Partial Ph(c)&P(c) 200.00
81 CCB,Partial Ph(c)&P(c),
  F:Tootsie 200.00
82 Partial Ph(c)&P(c),
  A:Hopalong Cassidy 200.00
83 Partial Ph(c)&P(c) 200.00
84 Ph(c) 175.00
85 Ph(c) 175.00
86 Ph(c),The Case of the
  Extra Buddy, giant 175.00
87 Ph(c),The Strange Lands 175.00
88 Ph(c),A:Senor Diablo 175.00
89 Ph(c),The Hypnotist 175.00

90 Ph(c),The Menace of
  the Cougar, giant 150.00
91 Ph(c),Song of Death 150.00
92 Ph(c),The Fatal Hide-out,
  giant 150.00
93 Ph(c),Treachery at
  Triple T, giant 150.00
94 Ph(c),Bank Busters,giant 150.00
95 Ph(c),Rampaging River 150.00
96 Ph(c),Range Robbers,giant . . 150.00
97 Ph(c),Death on the
  Hook,giant 150.00
98 Ph(c),Web of Death,giant 150.00
99 Ph(c),The Hidden Evidence . . 150.00
100 Ph(c),A:Red Eagle,Giant . . . 150.00
101 Red Eagle, Ph(c) 150.00
102 thru 111 Ph(c) . . . . @150.00
112 Ph(c),March, 1952 . . . . 175.00

XMAS COMICS
Fawcett Publications, 1941
1 Whiz #21 . . . . 7,000.00
2 Capt. Marvel 2,500.00
7 Hoppy, Funny Animal 1,100.00
Second Series, 1949–52
4 Whiz, Capt. Marvel, Nyoka. . 1,100.00
5 . . . . 900.00
6 . . . . 900.00
7 Bill Boyd 900.00

X-VENTURE
Victory Magazines, 1947
1 Mystery Shadow, Atom
  Wizard 1,700.00
2 same 850.00

Yankee Comics #2
© Harry A Chesler Publications

YANKEE COMICS
Chesler Publications
(Harry A. Chesler),
Sept., 1941–March, 1942
1 F:Yankee Doodle Jones . . . 2,800.00
2 The Spirit of '41 . . . . 1,300.00
3 Yankee Doodle Jones 900.00
4 JCo,Yankee Doodle Jones . . . 900.00

YANKS IN BATTLE
Comic Magazine, Inc.
(Quality Comics Group), 1956
1 CCv 125.00
2 CCv 100.00
3 CCv 100.00
4 CCv 100.00

THE YARDBIRDS
Ziff-Davis Publishing Co., 1952
1 . . . . 125.00

YELLOWJACKET
COMICS
Levy Publ./Frank Comunale/
Charlton, Sept., 1944
1 O&B:Yellowjackets,B:Diana
  the Huntress 1,200.00
2 Rosita &The Filipino Kid 700.00
3 . . . . 650.00
4 Fall of the House of Usher. . . . 700.00
5 King of Beasts 700.00
6 . . . . 800.00
7 I:Diane Carter;The
  Lonely Guy 1,500.00
8 The Buzzing Bee Code 750.00
9 . . . . 700.00
10 Capt Grim V:The Salvage
  Pirates 750.00
Becomes:

JACK IN THE BOX
Charlton, Feb., 1946
11 Funny Animal,Yellow Jacket . . 300.00
12 Funny Animal 150.00
13 BW,Funny Animal 300.00
14 thru 16 Funny Animal . . . . . @150.00
Becomes:

COWBOY WESTERN
COMICS
Charlton, July, 1948
17 Annie Oakley,Jesse James. . . 275.00
18 JO,JO(c) 200.00
19 JO,JO(c),Legends of Paul
  Bunyan 200.00
20 JO(c),Jesse James 125.00
21 Annie Oakley VisitsDryGulch . 125.00
22 Story of the Texas Rangers . . 125.00
23 . . . . 125.00
24 Ph(c),F:James Craig 125.00
25 Ph(c),F:Sunset Carson 125.00
26 Ph(c) 150.00
27 Ph(c),Sunset Carson movie . . 900.00
28 Ph(c),Sunset Carson movie . 450.00
29 Ph(c),Sunset Carson movie . 450.00
30 Ph(c),Sunset Carson movie . 450.00
31 Ph(c) 100.00
32 thru 34 Ph(c) . . . . @100.00
35 thru 37 Sunset Carson . . . . @400.00
38 and 39 . . . . @100.00
Becomes:

SPACE WESTERN
COMICS
Charlton Comics, Oct., 1952
40 Spurs Jackson,V:The
  Saucer Men 1,000.00
41 StC(c),Space Vigilantes 700.00
42 StC(c),Atomic Bomb 800.00
43 StC(c),Battle of
  Spacemans Gulch 700.00
44 StC(c),The Madman of Mars . 700.00
45 StC(c),The Moon Bat,Hitler. . . 900.00
Becomes:

COWBOY WESTERN
COMICS
Oct., 1953
46 . . . . 300.00
Becomes:

COWBOY WESTERN
HEROES
Dec., 1953
47 . . . . 150.00
48 . . . . 150.00
Becomes:

GOLDEN AGE

COWBOY WESTERN
May–June, 1954
49 . . . . 125.00
50 F:Jesse James 125.00
51 thru 57 . . . . @100.00
58, Wild Bill Hickok, giant 125.00
59 thru 66 . . . . @100.00
67 AW&AT 150.00
Becomes:

WILD BILL HICKOK AND JINGLES
Aug., 1958
68 AW 125.00
69 AW 100.00
70 AW 100.00
71 . . . . 75.00
72 . . . . 75.00
73 . . . . 75.00
74 1960 . . . . 75.00

YOGI BERRA
Fawcett, 1957
1 Ph(c) 1,100.00

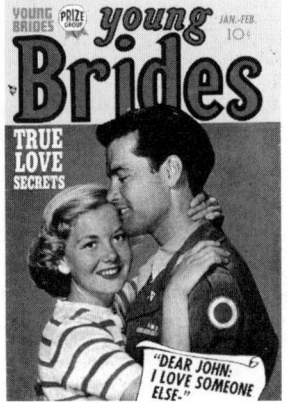

Young Brides #
© Prize Comics

YOUNG BRIDES
Feature Publications (Prize Comics), Sept.–Oct., 1952
1 S&K,Ph(c) 500.00
2 S&K,Ph(c) 250.00
3 S&K,Ph(c) 225.00
4 S&K 225.00
5 S&K 225.00
6 S&K 225.00
2-1 S&K 225.00
2-2 S&K 100.00
2-3 S&K 150.00
2-4 S&K 150.00
2-5 S&K 150.00
2-6 S&K 150.00
2-7 S&K 150.00
2-8 S&K 100.00
2-9 S&K 100.00
2-10 S&K 175.00
2-11 S&K 175.00
2-12 S&K 175.00
3-1 thru 4-1 . . . . @100.00
4-2 S&K 200.00
4-3 . . . . 100.00
4-4 S&K 175.00
4-5 . . . . 100.00

YOUNG EAGLE
Fawcett Publications/ Charlton Comics, Dec., 1950
1 Ph(c) 250.00
2 Ph(c),Mystery of Thunder
　Canyon 125.00
3 Ph(c),Death at Dawn 100.00
4 Ph(c) 100.00
5 Ph(c),The Golden Flood 100.00
6 Ph(c),The Nightmare Empire . . 100.00
7 Ph(c),Vigilante Vengeance . . . 100.00
8 Ph(c),The Rogues Rodeo 100.00
9 Ph(c),The Great Railroad
　Swindle 100.00
10 June, 1952, Ph(c),Thunder Rides
　the Trail,O:Thunder 100.00

YOUNG HEROES
Titan Publ. (American Comics Group), 1955
35 Frontier Scout 125.00
36 . . . . 125.00
37 . . . . 125.00

YOUNG KING COLE
Novelty Press/Premium Svcs. Co., Autumn, 1945
1-1 Detective Toni Gayle 500.00
1-2 . . . . 250.00
1-3 . . . . 200.00
1-4 . . . . 200.00
2-1 . . . . 150.00
2-2 . . . . 150.00
2-3 . . . . 150.00
2-4 . . . . 150.00
2-5 . . . . 150.00
2-6 . . . . 150.00
2-7 . . . . 150.00
3-1 . . . . 175.00
3-2 LbC 250.00
3-3 The Killer With The Hat 150.00
3-4 The Fierce Tiger 150.00
3-5 AMc 150.00
3-6 . . . . 175.00
3-7 LbC(c),Case of the
　Devil's Twin 300.00
3-8 . . . . 150.00
3-9 The Crime Fighting King 150.00
3-10 LbC(c) 250.00
3-11 LbC(c) 250.00
3-12 July, 1948,AMc(c) 150.00

YOUNG LIFE
New Age Publications, Summer, 1945
1 Partial Ph(c),Louis Prima 175.00
2 Partial Ph(c),Frank Sinatra . . . 200.00
Becomes:

TEEN LIFE
Winter, 1945
3 Partial Ph(c),Croon without
　Tricks,June Allyson(c) 150.00
4 Partial Ph(c),Atom Smasher
　Blueprints,Duke Ellington(c) . 125.00
5 Partial Ph(c), Build Your Own
　Pocket Radio, Jackie
　Robinson(c) 150.00

YOUNG LOVE
Feature Publ. (Prize Comics Group), Feb.–March, 1949
1 S&K,S&K(c) 700.00
2 S&K,Ph(c) 400.00
3 S&K,JSe,BE,Ph(c) 250.00
4 S&K,Ph(c) 175.00
5 S&K,Ph(c) 175.00
2-1 S&K,Ph(c) 250.00

2-2 Ph(c) 150.00
2-3 Ph(c) 150.00
2-4 Ph(c) 150.00
2-5 Ph(c) 150.00
2-6 S&K(c) 250.00
2-7 S&K(c),S&K 250.00
2-8 S&K 250.00
2-9 S&K(c),S&K 250.00
2-10 S&K(c),S&K 250.00
2-11 S&K(c),S&K 250.00
2-12 S&K(c),S&K 250.00
3-1 S&K(c),S&K 225.00
3-2 S&K(c),S&K 225.00
3-3 S&K(c),S&K 225.00
3-4 S&K(c),S&K 225.00
3-5 Ph(c) 175.00
3-6 BP,Ph(c) 175.00
3-7 Ph(c) 175.00
3-8 Ph(c) 175.00
3-9 MMe,Ph(c) 175.00
3-10 Ph(c) 175.00
3-11 Ph(c) 175.00
3-12 Ph(c) 175.00
4-1 S&K 175.00
4-2 Ph(c) 150.00
4-3 Ph(c) 150.00
4-4 Ph(c) 150.00
4-5 Ph(c) 150.00
4-5 Ph(c) 150.00
4-6 S&K,Ph(c) 150.00
4-7 thru 4-12 Ph(c) . . . . @125.00
5-1 thru 5-12 Ph(c) . . . . @125.00
6-1 thru 6-9 . . . . @75.00
6-10 thru 6-12 . . . . @75.00
7-1 thru 7-7 . . . . @75.00
7-8 thru 7-11 . . . . @75.00
7-12 thru 8-5 . . . . @75.00
8-6 thru 8-12 . . . . @75.00

YOUNG ROMANCE COMICS
Feature Publ./Headline/ Prize Publ., Sept.–Oct., 1947
1 S&K(c),S&K 800.00
2 S&K(c),S&K 500.00
3 S&K(c),S&K 400.00
4 S&K(c),S&K 400.00
5 S&K(c),S&K 400.00
6 S&K(c),S&K 400.00
2-1 S&K(c),S&K 350.00
2-2 S&K(c),S&K 350.00
2-3 S&K(c),S&K 350.00
2-4 S&K(c),S&K 350.00
2-5 S&K(c),S&K 350.00
2-6 S&K(c),S&K 350.00
3-1 thru 3-12 S&K(c),S&K . . . . @250.00
4-1 thru 4-12 S&K . . . . @250.00
5-1 ATh,S&K 250.00
5-2 . . . . 250.00
5-3 . . . . 225.00
5-4 thru 5-12 S&K . . . . @225.00
6-1 . . . . 100.00
6-2 . . . . 100.00
6-3 . . . . 100.00

YOUR UNITED STATES
Lloyd Jacquet Studios, 1946
1N# Teeming Nation of Nations . 350.00

ZAGO, JUNGLE PRINCE
Fox Features Syndicate, Sept., 1948
1 A:Blue Beetle 1,000.00
2 JKa 750.00
3 JKa 600.00
4 MB(c) 600.00
Becomes:

GOLDEN AGE

MY STORY
May, 1949
5 JKa,Too Young To Fall in Love 275.00
6 I Was A She-Wolf 125.00
7 I Lost My Reputation 125.00
8 My Words Condemned Me ... 125.00
9 WW,Wayward Bride 250.00
10 WW,March, 1950,Second Rate Girl 250.00
11 .... 125.00
12 Ph(c)................... 125.00

ZAZA THE MYSTIC
See: CHARLIE CHAN

TEGRA, JUNGLE EMPRESS
Fox Features Syndicate
Aug., 1948
1 Blue Bettle,Rocket Kelly 900.00
Becomes:

ZEGRA, JUNGLE EMPRESS
Oct., 1948
2 JKa 1,000.00
3 .... 750.00
4 .... 750.00
5 .... 750.00
Becomes:

MY LOVE LIFE
June, 1949–Aug., 1950
6 I Put A Price Tag On Love ... 200.00
7 An Old Man's Fancy 125.00
8 My Forbidden Affair 125.00
9 I Loved too Often 125.00
10 My Secret Torture 125.00
11 I Broke My Own Heart 125.00
12 I Was An Untamed Filly 125.00
13 I Can Never Marry You 100.00

ZIP COMICS
MLJ Magazines,
Feb., 1940–Summer, 1944
1 MMe,O&B:Kalathar,The Scarlet Avenger,Steel Sterling,B:Mr Satan,Nevada Jones,War Eagle Captain Valor 9,000.00
2 MMe,CBi(c)B:Steel Sterling(c) 3,700.00
3 MMe,CBi(a&c) 3,000.00
4 MMe,CBi(a&c) 2,400.00
5 MMe,CBi(a&c) 2,400.00
6 MMe,CBi(a&c) 2,200.00
7 MMe,CBi(a&c) 2,200.00
8 MMe,CBi(a&c),Bondage(c) . 2,200.00
9 CMMe,CBi(a&c),E:Kalathar, Mr Satan;Bondage(c) 2,300.00
10 MMe,CBi(a&c),B.Inferno .. 2,200.00
11 MMe,CBi(a&c).......... 1,700.00
12 MMe,CBi(a&c),Bondage(c) . 1,700.00
13 MMe,CBi(a&c),E:Inferno, Bondage(c),Woman in Electric Chair 2,000.00
14 MMe,CBi(a&c),Bondage(c) . 1,600.00
15 MMe,CBi(a&c),Bondage(c) . 2,000.00
16 MMe,CBi(a&c),Bondage(c) . 1,600.00
17 CBI(a&c),E:Scarlet Avenger Bondage(c)..... 2,000.00
18 IN(c),B:Wilbur.......... 2,000.00
19 IN(c),Steel Sterling(c).... 1,600.00
20 IN(c),O&I:Black Jack Hitler(c)................ 2,700.00
21 IN(c),V:Nazis 1,400.00
22 IN(c).................. 2,300.00
23 IN(c),Flying Fortress ... 1,500.00
24 IN(c),China Town Exploit ... 1,500.00
25 IN(c),E:Nevada Jones 1,500.00

26 IN(c),B:Black Witch, E:Capt Valor 1,500.00
27 IN(c),I:Web,V:Japanese 2,800.00
28 IN(C),O:Web,Bondage(c). ... 2,500.00
29 Steel Sterling & Web 1,200.00
30 V:Nazis................. 1,000.00
31 IN(c) 800.00
32 Nazi Skeleton, WWII 1,200.00
33 Bondage(c) 1,200.00
34 I:Applejack;Bondage(c)...... 900.00
35 E:Zambini 800.00
36 I:Senor Banana........... 800.00
37 .... 800.00
38 E:Web 800.00
39 O&B:Red Rube 800.00
40 Red Rube 700.00
41 .... 700.00
42 Red Rube 700.00
43 Steel Sterling(c). 700.00
44 Red Rube 700.00
45 E:Wilbur 700.00
46 Red Rube 700.00
47 Crooks Can't Win 750.00

ZIP-JET
St. John Publishing Co.,
Feb., 1953
1 Rocketman 1,200.00
2 April–May, 1953, Assassin of the Airlanes 750.00

ZIPPY THE CHIMP
Pines Comics, 1957
50 .... 75.00
51 .... 75.00

ZOO FUNNIES
Charlton Magazines, 1945
1 Funny Animals (1st Charlton) . 300.00
2 .... 200.00
3 .... 125.00
4 .... 125.00
5 .... 125.00
6 .... 100.00
7 .... 100.00
8 Diana the Huntress 100.00
9 .... 100.00
10 .... 100.00
11 thru 15 .... @100.00
Becomes:

TIM MCCOY
Charlton Comics, 1948
16 Western Movie Stories, John Wayne............ 700.00
17 Rocky Lane............. 500.00
18 Rod Cameron 500.00
19 Jessie James 500.00
20 Jimmy Wakley 500.00
21 Johnny Mack Brown 500.00
Becomes:

PICTORIAL LOVE STORIES
Charlton Comics, 1949
22 B:Me-Dan Cupld 250.00
23 .... 250.00
24 Fred Astaire 275.00
25 .... 250.00
26 .... 250.00

ZOO FUNNIES
Charlton Comics, 1953–55
1 Timothy the Ghost 150.00
2 Leo the Lyin' Lion......... 100.00
3 thru 7 .... @125.00
8 Nyoka.................. 150.00
9 Nyoka.................. 150.00
10 Nyoka 150.00
11 Nyoka 150.00

12 Nyoka 150.00
13 Nyoka 150.00

ZOOM COMICS
Carlton Publishing Co.,
Dec., 1945
N# O:Captain Milksop........ 600.00

Zoot Comics #16
© Fox Features

ZOOT COMICS
Fox Features Syndicate,
Spring, 1946
N#(1)(fa) 300.00
2 A:Jaguar(fa)................ 250.00
3 (fa) 150.00
4 (fa) 150.00
5 (fa) 125.00
6 (fa) 125.00
7 B:Rulah................ 1,500.00
8 JKa(c),Fangs of Stone 1,100.00
9 JKa(c),Fangs of Black Fury . 1,100.00
10 JKa(c),Inferno Land 1,100.00
11 JKa,The Purple Plague, Bondage(c)............. 1,200.00
12 JKa(c),The Thirsty Stone, Bondage(c) 800.00
13 Bloody Moon........... 750.00
14 Pearls of Pathos,Woman Carried off by Bird 1,000.00
15 Death Dancers 750.00
16 .... 750.00
Becomes:

RULAH, JUNGLE GODDESS
Aug., 1948
17 JKa(c),Wolf Doctor 1,500.00
18 JKa(c),Vampire Garden 1,100.00
19 JKa(c). 1,000.00
20 .... 1,000.00
21 JKa(c). 1,000.00
22 JKa(c). 1,000.00
23 .... 800.00
24 .... 800.00
25 .... 800.00
26 .... 800.00
27 .... 800.00
Becomes:

I LOVED
July, 1949–March, 1950
28 .... 150.00
29 thru 31................ @100.00
32 My Poison Love 100.00

DARK HORSE

ABE SAPIEN: DRUMS OF THE DEAD
Mar., 1998
1-shot Hellboy spin-off 3.00

ABE SAPIEN: THE DROWNING
Feb., 2008
1 (of 5) 3.00
2 thru 5 . . . . @3.00

ABYSS, THE
1989
1 MK,Movie Adaptation 2.50
2 MK, Movie Adaptation, pt.2 . . . . . 2.50

ACCIDENT MAN
(B&W) 1993
1 I:Accident Man. 2.50
2 thru 3 . . . . @2.50

ADVENTURES OF LUTHER ARKWRIGHT
DH/Valkyrie Press
(B&W) 1987–89
1 . . . . 2.50
2 thru 9 . . . . @2.50
(B&W) 1990
1 thru 9 Rep. . . . . @2.50

ADVENTURES OF THE MASK
1996
1 by Michael Eury & Marc
 Campos, TV cartoon adapt. . . 2.50
2 thru 12 TV cartoon adapt. . . . . @2.50
Ash can (1995) 3.00

AEON FLUX
Oct., 2005
1 (of 4) Timothy Green art 3.00
2 thru 4 . . . . @3.00

Adventures of the Mask #11
© Dark Horse Comics

AGE OF REPTILES
1993–94
1 DRd,Story on Dinosaurs 3.00
2 thru 4 DRd,Story on Dinosaurs @3.00

AGE OF REPTILES: THE HUNT
May, 1996
1 by Ricardo Delgado. 3.00
2 thru 5 . . . . @3.00

AGENTS OF LAW
Comics' Greatest World, 1995
1 KG, I:Law 2.50
2 A:Barb Wire 2.50
3 KG,DLw,The Judgment Gate. . . . 2.50
4 Open Golden City 2.50
5 Who is the Mystery figure 2.50
6 V:Predator 2.50

ALIEN RESURRECTION
Oct., 1997
1 (of 2) movie adaptation 2.50
2 DMc(c). 2.50

ALIENS
(B&W) 1988
1 Movie Sequel,R:Hicks,Newt . . . 22.00
1a 2nd printing 3.00
1b 3rd printing. 2.50
1c 4th printing. 2.50
2 Hicks raids Mental Hospital 9.00
2a 2nd printing 3.00
2a 3rd printing. 2.50
3 Realize Queen is on Earth 7.00
3a 2nd printing 3.00
4 Queen is freed, Newton on
 Aliens World 5.00
5 All out war on Aliens World 5.00
6 Hicks & Newt return to Earth. . . . 5.00

ALIENS (II)
[Mini-Series] 1989
1 DB,Hicks,Newt hijack ship. 5.00
1a 2nd Printing 3.00
2 DB,Crazed general trains aliens . 3.00
2a 2nd Printing 3.00
3 DB,HicksV:General Spears 3.00
3a 2nd Printing 2.50
4 DB,Heroes reclaim earth
 from aliens 3.00

ALIENS
1-shot Earth Angel, JBy (1994) 3.00
1-shot Glass Corridor, DvL (1998). . 3.00
1-shot Lovesick (1996) 3.00
1-shot Mondo Heat, I:Herk Mondo . 3.00
1-shot Mondo Pest (1995). 3.00
1-shot Pig, CDi,FH (1997) 3.00
1-shot Purge, IEd,PhH (1997). 3.00
1-shot Sacrifice, rep.Aliens UK
 (1993) 5.00
1-shot Salvation DGb,MMi,KN,
 F:Selkirk (1993). 5.00
1-shot Special (1997). 3.00
1-shot Stalker (1998) 3.00
1-shot Wraith (1998) 3.00
GN DNA War (2006) 7.00

ALIENS: ALCHEMY
Sept., 1997
1 thru 3 (of 3) JAr,RCo . . . . @3.00

ALIENS: APOCALYPSE — DESTROYING ANGELS
Jan., 1999
1 (of 4) MSh 3.00
2 thru 4 MSh . . . . @3.00

ALIENS: BERSERKER
1995
1 I:Crew of the Nemesis 3.00
2 thru 4 . . . . @3.00

ALIENS: COLONIAL MARINES
1993
1 I: Lt. Joseph Henry 4.00
2 I: Pvt. Carmen Vasquez. 3.00
3 thru 10 . . . . @3.00

ALIENS: EARTH WAR
1991
1 SK,JBo(c),Alien's War renewed. . 4.00
1a 2nd Printing 3.00
2 SK,JBo(c),To trap the Queen. . . . 4.00
3 SK,JBo(c) Stranded on
 Alien's planet 3.00
4 SK,JBo(c),Resolution,final 5.00

ALIENS: GENOCIDE
1991
1 Aliens vs. Aliens 3.50
2 Alien Homeworld 3.00
3 Search for Alien Queen 3.00
4 Conclusion, inc. poster 3.00

ALIENS: HAVOC
1997
1 and 2 (of 2) 'over 40 creators' . @3.00

ALIENS: HIVE
1992
1 KJo,I:Stanislaw Mayakovsky 4.00
2 KJo,A:Norbert 3.50
3 KJo,A:Julie,Gill. 3.25
4 KJo,A:Stan,Final 3.00

ALIENS: KIDNAPPED
Dec., 1997–Feb., 1998
1 thru 3 . . . . @3.00

ALIENS: LABYRINTH
1993
1 F:Captured Alien 3.00
2 thru 4 . . . . @3.00

ALIENS: MUSIC OF THE SPEARS
1994
1 I:Damon Eddington 3.00
2 thru 4TBd(c). . . . . @3.00

ALIENS: NEWT'S TALE
1992
1 How Newt Survived 5.50
2 JBo(c),Newt's point of view 5.50

ALIENS: ROGUE
1993
1 F:Mr.Kay 3.00
2 thru 4 V:Aliens . . . . @3.00

DARK HORSE

All comics prices listed are for *Near Mint* condition.

ALIENS: STRONGHOLD
1994
1 DoM,JP 3.00
2 thru 4 DoM,JP . . . . @3.00

ALIENS: SURVIVAL
Feb.–Apr., 1998
1 (of 3) TyH(c). 3.00
2 thru 3 . . . . @3.00

ALIENS/PREDATOR:
DEADLIEST OF
THE SPECIES
1993–95
1 B:CCI(s),JG,F:Caryn Delacroix . . 4.00
2 JG,V:Predator. 3.00
3 JG,F:Caryn Delacroix. 3.00
4 JG,V:Predator. 3.00
5 JG,Roadtrip 3.00
6 JG,in Space Station 3.00
7 thru 9 JG,EB. . . . . @3.00
10 CCI(s), Human Predators 3.00
11 CCI,EB,JBo(c),Delacroix vs.
　　DeMatier 3.00
12 Caryn's Fate 3.00

ALIENS VS. PREDATOR
1996
0 PN,KS,Rep.DHP#34-36,(B&W). . 7.00
1 Duel to the Death. 7.00
1a 2nd Printing 3.00
2 Dr. Revna missing 5.00
3 Predators attack Aliens 5.00
4 CW,F:Machiko & Predator. 5.00
GN Thrill of the Hunt (2004) 7.00
GN Civilized Beasts (2007) 7.00
Ann.#1 (1999) 5.00
1-shot Booty, rep. *Previews* 3.00

ALIENS VS. PREDATOR:
DUEL
1995
1 Trap, JS 3.00
2 War 3.00

ALIENS VS. PREDATOR:
ETERNAL
June, 1998
1 (of 4) IEd,GF(c) 3.00
2 thru 4 IEd,GF(c). . . . . @3.00

ALIENS VS. PREDATOR:
WAR
1995
0 Prelude to New Series. 3.00
1 RSd,MM,RCo(c) F:Machiko. 3.00
2 thru 4 . . . . @3.00

ALIENS VS. PREDATOR:
XENOGENESIS
Dec., 1999
1 (of 4) MvR 3.50
2 thru 4 MvR,trapped . . . . @3.50

ALIENS VS. PREDATOR
VS. THE TERMINATOR
Apr., 2000
1 (of 4) MSh,MvR 3.50
2 MSh,MvR,V:Terminator-Alien
　　hybrid. 3.50
3 MSh,MvR,on Predator ship 3.50
4 MSh,MvR,concl. 3.50

Aliens: Xenogenesis #2
© *Dark Horse Comics*

ALIENS: XENOGENESIS
Aug., 1999
1 DR 3.50
2 thru 4 . . . . @3.50

ALIEN 3
1992
1 thru 3 Movie Adaptation . . . . . . @3.00

AMAZING ADVENTURES
OF THE ESCAPIST, THE
Dec., 2003
1 Michael Chabon, 80-pg. 9.00
2 thru 8 . . . . @9.00

AMAZING SCREW-ON
HEAD, THE
May, 2002
1-shot MMi. 3.00

AMERICAN, THE
(B&W) 1987–89
1 CW,'Chinese Boxes,'D:Gleason . 5.00
2 CW,'Nightmares. 4.00
3 CW,Secrets of the American 4.00
4 CW,American vs.Kid America . . . 4.00
5 A:Kiki the Gorilla 4.00
6 Rashomon-like plot 3.50
7 Pornography business issue 3.50
8 Deals with violence issue 3.50
9 American Falls into a cult 3.50
Spec. (1990) 4.00

THE AMERICAN:
LOST IN AMERICA
1992
1 CMa, American joins a cult 2.50
2 CMa, V:'Feel-Good' cult. 2.50
3 CMa, 'Ape-Mask' cult. 2.50
4 CMa, Final issue 2.50
ColorSpec.#1 . . . . 3.00

AMERICAN SPLENDOR
1993–2000
1-shot Letterman by Harvey Pekar . 3.50
1-shot One Step Out of the
　　Nest (1994) 3.50
1-shot On the Job (1997). 3.50
1-shot Comics Con, JZe (1996). . . . 3.50

1-shot Music Comics (1997) 3.50
1-shot Odds & Ends (1997). 3.50
1-shot Transatlantic Comics (1998). 3.50
1-shot Terminal (1999). 3.50
1-shot Bedtime Stories (2000). 4.50
1-shot Portrait of The Artist
　　in his declining years (2001) . . . 4.00

AMERICAN SPLENDOR:
UNSUNG HERO
DH Maverick, Aug., 2002
1 (of 3) b&w 4.00
2 thru 3 . . . . @4.00

AMERICAN SPLENDOR:
WINDFALL
(B&W) 1995
1 Windfall Gained,pt.1 . . . . 4.25
2 Windfall Lost 4.25

ANCIENT JOE
DH Maverick, Oct., 2001
1 (of 3) B&W 3.00
2 . . . . 3.50
3 . . . . 3.50

ANGEL
1999–2001
1 Buffy spin-off 3.00
2 thru 9 . . . . @3.00
10 TSg 3.00
11 TSg 3.00
12 TSg,MMi(c) 3.00
13 TSg,demonic rats 3.00
14 TSg,Little Girl Lost 3.00
15 TSg,Past Lives,Buffy x-over 4.00
16 TSg,Past Lives,Buffy x-over 4.00
17 The Cordelia Special. 3.00
1–17a newsstand photo(c) . . . . . @4.00

ANGEL
2001–02
1 (of 4) 3.00
1a photo (c). 3.00
1b gold-foil (c). 13.00
1c gold-foil (c) signed 20.00
2 thru 4 . . . . @3.00
2a thru 4a photo (c) . . . . @3.00

ANIMAL CONFIDENTIAL
(B&W) 1992
1-shot parody. 2.50

APOCALYPSE NERD
(B&W) Feb., 2005
1 (of 6) Peter Bagge art 3.00
2 thru 6 . . . . @3.00

APPLESEED DATABOOK
(B&W–Manga) 1994
1 Flip Book, by Masamune Shirow. 5.00
1a 2nd printing 3.50
2 Flip Book 3.50

ARCHENEMIES
Apr., 2006
1 (of 4) by Drew Melbourne 3.00
2 thru 4 . . . . @3.00

ARMY OF DARKNESS
1992
1 . . . . 12.00
2 thru 3 . . . . @9.00

DARK HORSE

ATLAS
1994
1 BZ,I:Atlas 2.75
2 BZ,V:Sh'en Chui 2.75
3 BZ,V:Sh'en Chui 2.50
4 BZ, final issue 2.50

Babe #1
© Dark Horse Comics

BABE
Legend, 1994
1 JBy(a&s) 3.00
2 thru 4 JBy(a&s) . . . . @2.50

BABE 2
Legend, 1995
1 V:Shrewmanoid 2.50
2 A:Abe Sapien 2.50

BACCHUS
COLOR SPECIAL
1995
1 A:Thor 3.00
2 A:Abe Sapien 2.50

BADGER:
SHATTERED MIRROR
1994
1 R:Badger 3.00
2 thru 4 . . . . @3.00

BADGER: ZEN POP
FUNNY ANIMAL VERSION
1 MBn,R:Badger (1994) 3.00
2 Ham 3.00

BADLANDER, THE
Oct., 2007
1 (of 4) 3.00

BADLANDS
(B&W) 1991
1 I:Connie Bremen 3.50
2 Anne Peck, C.I.A. 3.00
3 Assassination Rumor 2.50
4 Connie heads South 2.50
5 November 22, 1963, Dallas 2.50
6 Kennedy Assination aftermath . . . 2.50

BAKERS MEET
JINGLE BELL, THE
Dec., 2006
1-shot PDi,KB 3.00

BARB WIRE
Comics' Greatest World, 1994
1 Foil(c),I:Deathcard 3.00
2 DLw,I:Hurricane Max 3.00
3 V:Mace Blitzkrieg 3.00
4 Ghost,pt.1 . . . . 3.00
5 Ghost,pt.2 . . . . 3.00
6 Hardhide, Ignition 3.00
7 A:Motorhead 3.00
8 V:Ignition 3.00
9 A:Mecha, V:Ignition 3.00
Movie Spec. (1996) 4.00

BARB WIRE:
ACE OF SPADES
1996
1 CW,TBd & DoM 3.00
2 thru 4 CW,TBd & DoM . . . . . . @3.00

BARRY WINDSOR-SMITH:
STORYTELLER
Oct., 1996
GNs 1 thru 9 9'x12½' . . . . @5.00

BASEBALL GREATS
1 Jimmy Piersall story 3.25
2 Bob Gibson 3.50
3 Harmon Killebrew 3.50

BASIL WOLVERTON'S
FANTASIC FABLES
(B&W) Oct., 1993
1 BW 2.50
2 BW 2.50

BATMAN/ALIENS
DH/DC, Mar., 1997
1 (of 2) RMz,BWr 5.00
2 conclusion 5.00

BATMAN/TARZAN: CLAWS
OF THE CATWOMAN
1999
1 (of 4) RMz,DvD(c),V:Dent,x-over . 3.00
2 thru 4 RMz,DvD(c) . . . . @3.00

BATTLE GODS:
WARRIORS OF
THE CHAAK
Apr., 2000
1 (of 9) by Francisco Ruiz
   Velasco 3.00
2 the Lucha Libre 3.00
3 F:Takan, El Charro 3.00
4 another tournament 3.00
5 The Chaak begins 3.00
6 Deathmatch: Takan vs. Chilbacan 3.00
7 sleeping god awakens 3.00
8 Hell breaks loose 3.00
9 concl. 3.00

BETTIE PAGE COMICS
1996–97
1-shot, some nudity (1996) 4.00
1-shot Bettie Page Comics: Spicy
   Adventure, by Jim Silke (1997) . 3.00
1 Queen of Hearts, movie adapt. . . 2.50

BETTIE PAGE:
QUEEN OF THE NILE
Dec., 1999
1 (of 3) low-budget time machine . . 3.00
2 and 3 concl. . . . . @3.00

BIG
1989
1 Movie Adaptation 3.00

BIG BLOWN BABY
(B&W) Aug., 1996
1 thru 4 by Bill Wray . . . . @3.00

BIG GUY AND
RUSTY THE ROBOT BOY
1995
1 and 2 V:Monster . . . . @5.00

BILLI 99
(B&W) 1991
1 'Pray for us Sinners' 4.50
2 'Trespasses' 4.00
3 'Daily Bread' 4.00
4 . . . . 4.00

BILLY THE KID'S
OLD-TIMEY ODDITIES
April, 2005
1 (of 4) KHt 3.00
2 thru 4 KHt . . . . @3.00

BLACKBURNE
COVENANT, THE
Apr., 2003
1 (of 4) FaN 3.00
2 thru 4 . . . . @3.00

BLACK CROSS
(B&W) 1987
1-shot special CW 3.00

BLACK CROSS:
DIRTY WORK
Apr., 1997
1-shot by Chris Warner 3.00

BLACK PEARL, THE
Sept., 1996
1 thru 5 by Mark Hamill . . . . @3.00

BLADE OF THE
IMMORTAL
(B&W–Manga) July, 1996
1 by Hiroaki Samura 10.00
2 thru 4 Criminal Conquest
   pt. 2 thru pt.4 . . . . @6.00
5 & 6 Genius (10-1996) . . . . @6.00
7 & 8 Fanatic (1-1997) . . . . @6.00
9 thru 11 Call of the Worm,48-pg. @6.00
12 thru 18 Dreamsong (7-1997) . . @4.00
19 & 20 Rin's Bane, 48-pg. . . . . . @4.50
21 thru 25 On Silent Wings . . . . . @4.00
26 On Silent Wings (1998) 48-pg. . . 4.50
27 thru 28 On Silent Wings . . . . . @4.00
29 thru 33 Dark Shadows (1999) . @4.00
34 Food (1999)48-pg. 4.50
35 thru 42 Hear of Darkness . . . . @4.00
43 thru 57 The Gathering (2000) . @4.00
58 thru 61, Secrets pt.1 thru pt.4 . @3.50
62 Stigmata 3.50
63 Husk 3.50
64 Skin,pt.1 . . . . 3.50

DARK HORSE

Blade of the Immortal #33
© Dark Horse Comics

65 Skin,pt.2	3.50
66 thru 72 Beasta pt.1 – pt. 7	@3.50
73 thru 78 Fall Frost pt.1– pt. 6	@3.50
79 The Wind and the Heron	3.50
80 Petals on the Wind	3.50
81 Shadows	3.50
82 Mourning Shadows	3.50
83 Path of Shadows	3.50
84 Thorns	3.50
85 Mirror of the Soul,pt.1(2003)	3.00
86 Mirror of the Soul,pt.2	3.00
87 Mirror of the Soul,pt.3	3.00
88 Light and Shadow	3.00
89 Crossroads	3.00
90 thru 95 Last Blood,pt.1–5	@3.00
95 Confession (2004)	3.00
96 thru 98 Twilight,pt.1–3 (2005)	@3.00
99 thru 103 Trickster,pt.1–4	@3.00
104 Forsaken (2005)	3.00
105 Duet	3.00
106 Cauldron	4.00
107 thru 111 Shortcut,pt.1–5	@3.00
112 thru 117 On the Perfection of Anatomy (2006)	@3.00
118 thru 121Sparrow Net, pt.1–4	@3.00
122 thru 126 Barefoot, pt.1–5	@3.00
127 Life in Death (2007)	3.00
128 thru 131 Badger Hole, pt.1–4	@3.00

BLAIR WHICH?
Dec., 1999
1-shot SA, Scary as heck 3.50

BLANCHE GOES TO HOLLYWOOD
(B&W) 1993
1 Turn of the Century N.Y. 3.00

BLANCHE GOES TO NEW YORK
(B&W) 1992
1 Turn of the Century Hollywood . . 3.00

BLAST CORPS
Sept., 1998
1-shot F:demolition experts 2.50

BLOOD WORLD
March 2003
1 and 2 (of 3) . . . . @3.00

BLUE LILY
1993
1 . . . . 4.00
2 thru 3 . . . . @4.00

BMWFILMS.COM —THE HIRE
July, 2004
1 (of 6) MWg,Scandal 3.00
2 MWg,Precious Cargo 3.00
3 MWg,Hijacked 3.00
4 MWg,Tycoon 3.00

BODY BAGS
Aug., 1996
1 thru 4 . . . . @3.00

BOOK OF NIGHT
(B&W) 1987
1 CV 2.50
2 thru 3 CV . . . . @2.50

BORIS THE BEAR
(B&W) 1986
1 V:Funny Animals 3.00
1a 2nd printing 2.50
2 V:Robots 2.50
3 V:Super Heroes 2.50
4 thru 7 . . . . @2.50
8 LargeSize 2.50
9 thru 12 . . . . @2.50
See: B & W Pub. section
Color Classics 1987
1 thru 7 . . . . @2.50

B.P.R.D.
2003
1-Shot Dark Waters, GyD 3.00
1-Shot Night Train, ScK 3.00
1-Shot The Soul of Venice,MMi . . . 3.00
1-Shot There's Something Under My Bed, AdP 3.00
June, 2008
1-shot War on Frogs, MMi(s) 3.00
1-shot The Ectoplasmic Man 3.00

B.P.R.D.: A PLAGUE OF FROGS
Mar., 2004
1 A Plague of Frogs 3.00
2 thru 5 A Plague of Frogs . . . . . @3.00

B.P.R.D.: THE BLACK FLAME
Aug., 2005
1 MMi,GyD 3.00
2 thru 6 MMi,GyD . . . . @3.00

B.P.R.D.: THE DEAD
2004–05
1 GyD,JAr,MMi 3.00
2 thru 5 . . . . @3.00

B.P.R.D.: GARDEN OF SOULS
Mar., 2007
1 (of 5) MMi,GyD,JAr 3.00
2 thru 5 . . . . @3.00

B.P.R.D.: KILLING GROUND
Aug., 2007
1 thru 5 (of 5) MMi,GyD,JAr . . . . @3.00

B.P.R.D.: 1946
Jan., 2008
1 (of 5) MMi(s) 3.00
2 thru 5 . . . . @3.00

B.P.R.D.: THE UNIVERSE MACHINE
April., 2006
1 MMi,GyD 3.00
2 thru 5 MMi,GyD . . . . @3.00

B.P.R.D.: THE WARNING
July, 2008
1 (of 5) MMi(s) 3.00
2 thru 5 . . . . @3.00

BRAVE
Mar., 1997
1 by Cully Hamner & Jason Martin . 3.00

BUBBLE GUM CRISIS: GRAND MAL
(Manga) 1994
1 thru 3 . . . . @2.75
4 final issue 2.50

BUFFY THE VAMPIRE SLAYER
Sept., 1998
1 JoB,AAd(c) Wu-Tang Fang 9.00
1a 2nd printing 4.00
1b gold foil logo 9.00
2 JoB, Halloween 6.00
3 JoB, Cold Turkey 6.00
4 White Christmas 6.00
5 Happy New Year 6.00
6 New Kid on the Block,pt.1 . . . . . 6.00
7 JoB, New Kid on the Block,pt.2 . . 6.00
8 The Final Cut 6.00
9 Hey, Good Looking,pt.1 . . . . 6.00
10 Hey, Good Looking,pt.2 . . . . . . 6.00
11 A Boy Named Sue 6.00
12 A Nice Girl Like You 6.00
12a gold foil (c) 13.00
13 F:Cordelia Chase 5.00
14 Bad Blood,pt.5 . . . . 5.00
15 Bad Blood,pt.6 . . . . 5.00
16 Food Chain 5.00
17 Bad Blood,pt.7 . . . . 4.00
18 Mardi Gras 3.00

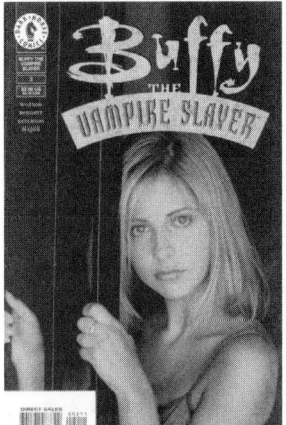

Buffy The Vampire Slayer #2
© Dark Horse Comics

DARK HORSE

DARK HORSE

19 Bad Blood, concl. 3.00	
20 Angel heads to L.A. 3.00	
21 Blood of Carthage,pt.1 . . . . 3.00	
22 Blood of Carthage,pt.2 . . . . 3.00	
23 Blood of Carthage,pt.3 . . . . 3.00	
24 Blood of Carthage,pt.4 . . . . 3.00	
25 Blood of Carthage,concl. 3.00	
26 Heart of the Slayer,pt.1 . . . . . . 3.00	
27 Heart of the Slayer,pt.2 . . . . . . 3.00	
28 revenge. 3.00	
29 Past Lives,pt.2,Angel x-over. . . . 5.00	
30 Past Lives,pt.4,Angel x-over. . . . 5.00	
31 Lost and Found. 5.00	
32 hobo ghost. 3.00	
33 Demonic Entomology 3.00	
34 Bug hunt, concl. 3.00	
35 False Memories,pt.1 . . . . 3.00	
36 False Memories,pt.2 . . . . 3.00	
37 False Memories,pt.3 . . . . 3.00	
38 False Memories,pt.4 . . . . 3.00	
39 Night of a Thousand Vampires . . 3.00	
40 JmP,Ugly Little Monsters,pt.1 . . 3.00	
41 JmP,Ugly Little Monsters,pt.2 . . 3.00	
42 JmP,Ugly Little Monsters,pt.3 . . 3.00	
43 JmP,Death of Buffy,pt.1. . . . . . . 3.00	
44 JmP,Death of Buffy,pt.2. . . . . . . 3.00	
45 JmP,Death of Buffy,pt.3. . . . . . . 3.00	
46 JmP,Withdrawal 3.00	
47 Hellmouth to Mouth,pt.1 . . . . . . 3.00	
48 Hellmouth to Mouth,pt.2 . . . . . . 3.00	
49 Hellmouth to Mouth,pt.3 . . . . . . 3.00	
50 Hellmouth to Mouth,pt.4 . . . . . . 3.50	
51 SLo,FaN,Viva Las Buffy,pt.1. . . 5.00	
52 SLo,Viva Las Buffy, pt.2 . . . . . . 5.00	
53 SLo,Viva Las Buffy, pt.3 . . . . . . 5.00	
54 SLo,Viva Las Buffy, pt.4 . . . . . . 5.00	
55 Dawn and Hoopy the Bear 5.00	
56 Slayer, Interrupted,pt.1 . . . . . . 5.00	
57 Slayer, Interrupted,pt.2 . . . . . . 5.00	
58 Slayer, Interrupted,pt.3 . . . . . . 5.00	
59 Slayer, Interrupted,pt.4 . . . . . . 5.00	
60 FaN,A Stake to the Heart,pt.1. . 5.00	
61 FaN,A Stake to the Heart,pt.2. . 5.00	
62 FaN,A Stake to the Heart,pt.3. . 5.00	
63 FaN,A Stake to the Heart,pt.4. . 5.00	
2a–63a newsstand photo(c). . . . . @3.00	
Ann. 1999, 64-pg. 5.00	
Spec. 1-shot Spike and Dru. 8.00	
Spec. 1-shot Giles 5.00	
Spec. 1-shot Giles, photo(c) . . . 8.00	
Spec. 1-shot Jonathan 3.00	
Spec. 1-shotA photo (c). 3.00	
Spec. 1-shot Lovers' Walk 3.00	
Spec. 1-shot-A photo (c) 3.00	
Spec. 1-shot Spike & Dru—The	
Queen of Hearts, photo (c) 3.00	
Spec. 1-shot Spike & Dru—All'sFair 3.00	
Spec. 1-shot Spike & Dru, ph(c) 3.00	
Spec. 1-shot Willow & Tara 4.00	
Spec. 1-shotA photo(c) 4.00	
Spec. 1-shotB foil photo(c) . . . 10.00	
Spec. 1-shotC foil photo(c) sgn 20.00	
Spec. 1-shotD red foil 17.00	
Spec.1-shot Lost & Found, FaN . . 3.00	
Spec.1-shotA photo (c) 3.00	
Spec.1-shot Buffy the Vampire	
Slayer/Angel: Reunion (2002). . 3.00	
Spec.1-shotA photo (c) 3.00	
Spec.1-shot Tales of the Slayers	
Broken Bottle of Djinn (2002) . 3.50	
Spec.1-shotA photo (c) 3.50	
Spec. 1-shot Chaos Bleeds (2003) . 3.00	
Spec. Chaos Bleeds, photo(c). . 3.00	
Spec. 1/2 Wizard Mag. (1999). . . . 10.00	
GN Ring of Fire, photo(c) 10.00	

**BUFFY
THE VAMPIRE SLAYER**
Mar., 2007

1 JoW, sequel to TV series. 8.00
1a later printings . . . . @5.00

2 JoW,Terrorist Threat 4.00	
2a later printings . . . . @3.00	
3 JoW,F:Willow. 6.00	
4 JoW,F:Willow 4.00	
5 JoW, The Chain 4.00	
5a&b variant (c)s. . . . . @4.00	
6 F:Faith 4.00	
7 Faith's Out to Kill a Slayer. 4.00	
8 JoW(s) 3.00	
9 JoW(s),Slayers battle to death . . 3.00	
10 JoW(s),Buffy & Willow vs.Demon 3.00	
11 JoW(s),A Beautiful Sunset 3.00	
12 Wolves at the Gate, pt.1 . . . . . . 3.00	
13 Wolves at the Gate, pt.2 . . . . . . 3.00	
14 Wolves at the Gate, pt.3 . . . . . . 3.00	
15 Wolves at the Gate, concl. 3.00	
16 Time of Your Life. 3.00	
17 Time of Your Life. 3.00	
18 Time of Your Life, JoW(s) 3.00	
19 Time of Your Life, JoW(s) 3.00	
20 Buffy/Fray, JLb 3.00	
8a thru 20a variant (c)s . . . . @5.00	

Buffy the Vampire Slayer: Angel #1
© Dark Horse Comics

**BUFFY
THE VAMPIRE SLAYER:
ANGEL**
May, 1999

1 thru 3 (of 3) . . . . @3.00
1a thru 3a newsstand, photo(c) . @3.00

**BUFFY
THE VAMPIRE SLAYER:
HAUNTED**
Dec., 2001

1 (of 4) deceased enemy's ghost . . 3.00
2 thru 4 . . . . @3.00
1a thru 4a photo (c) . . . . @3.00

**BUFFY
THE VAMPIRE SLAYER:
THE ORIGIN**
Feb., 1999

1 (of 3) DIB,JoB 3.00
2 & 3 . . . . @3.00
2a & 3a newsstand, photo(c) . . . @3.00

**BUFFY THE VAMPIRE
SLAYER: OZ**
July, 2001

1 (of 3) 3.00
1a photo(c) 3.00
1b gold foil photo (c). 13.00
1c gold foil photo(c) signed. . . . 25.00
1d fiery red foil photo(c) 17.00
2 . . . . 3.00
2a photo(c) 3.00
3 . . . . 3.00
3a photo(c) 3.00

**BUFFY THE VAMPIRE
SLAYER: WILLOW AND
TARA — WILDERNESS**
July, 2002

1 (of 2) 3.00
1a photo (c). 3.00
2 (of 2) 3.00
2a photo (c). 3.00

BY BIZARRE HANDS
(B&W) 1994

1 JLd(s). 2.50
2 JLd(s). 2.50
3 JLd(s). 2.50

**CANNON GOD
EXAXXION**
Manga, Nov., 2001

1 Stage 1, part 1 (of 8) 3.00
2 thru 8 Stage One,pt.2 thru pt.8 @3.00
9 Stage Two,pt.1 . . . . 3.00
10 Stage Two,pt.2 . . . . 3.50
11 Stage Two,pt.3 . . . . 3.50
13 thru 15. . . . . @3.50
16 thru 20 . . . . @3.00

CARAVAN KIDD
(B&W–Manga) 1992

1 thru 10 by Johji Manabe . . . . @2.50

[2nd Series] 1993

1 thru 10 F:Miam. . . . . @2.50
Holiday Spec. 2.50
Valentine's Day Spec. 2.50

[3rd Series] 1994

1 thru 8 . . . . @2.50
Christmas Special 2.50

**CATALYST: AGENTS
OF CHANGE**
Comics' Greatest World, 1994

1 JPn(c),V:US Army 2.50
2 JPn(c),I:Grenade 2.50
3 JPn(c),Rebel vs. Titan 2.50
4 JPn(c),Titan vs. Grace 2.50
5 JPn(c),V:Ape 2.50
6 and 7 . . . . @2.50

CHEVAL NOIR
(B&W) 1989

1 DSt(c). 4.00
2 thru 9 . . . . @3.50
10 80 pg. 4.50
11 80 pg. 4.50
12 MM(c) 4.50
13 thru 15. . . . . @4.50
16 thru 19 with 2-card strip 4.50
20 Great Power o/t Chninkel 4.50
21 Great Power o/t Chninkel 4.50
22 Great Power o/t Chninkel,concl. . 4.50
23 inc.'Rork','Forever War' concl. . . 4.50
24 In Dreams,pt.1 . . . . 4.50
25 In Dreams,pt.2 . . . . 4.50

26 In Dreams,pt.3 . . . . 4.50
27 I:The Man From Ciguri (Airtight
    Garage sequel) Dreams,pt.4 . . . 3.50
28 Ciguri cont. 3.50
29 Ciguri cont. 3.50
30 Ciguri,cont. 3.50
31 Angriest Dog in the World. 3.50
32 thru 40 . . . . @3.50
41 F:Demon. 3.50
42 F:Demon 3.50
43 F:Demon 3.50
44 F:Demon 3.50
45 thru 47 . . . . @3.50
48 SwM(c) 3.50
49 F:Rork 3.50
50 F:Rork. 3.50

CHOSEN
Dec., 2003
1 (of 3) MMr,PrG. 4.00
2 . . . . 3.00
3 . . . . 3.00

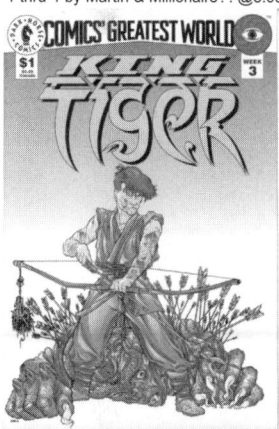

Chronowar #8
© Dark Horse Comics

CHRONOWAR
(B&W) Aug., 1996
1 (of 9) by Kazumasa Takayama . . 3.00
2 thru 9 . . . . @3.00

CITY OF OTHERS
Feb., 2007
1 (of 4) BWr 3.00
2 thru 4 . . . . @3.00

CLASSIC STAR WARS
1992
1 AW,newspaper strip reps. 6.00
2 thru 7 AW,newspaper reps. . . . @4.00
8 AW,newspaper reps. w/card 4.00
9 AW,newspaper reps. 4.00
10 AW,newspaper reps. 4.00
11 thru 19 AW,newspaper reps. . . @4.00
20 AW,newspaper strip reps., with
    trading card, final issue 4.00

CLASSIC STAR WARS:
A NEW HOPE
1994
1 AAd(c), rep. 4.25
2 AH(c), rep. 4.00

CLASSIC STAR WARS:
DEVILWORLDS
Aug., 1996
1 (of 2) by Alan Moore 3.00
2 . . . . 3.00

CLASSIC STAR WARS:
EARLY ADVENTURES
Aug., 1994–Apr., 1995
1 MiA(c), Gambler's World 3.00
2 RHo&MGr(c),Blackhole 3.00
3 EiS(c),Rebels of Vorzyd-5 . . . . . 3.00
3 bagged with trading card DH2 . . 5.00
4 RHo(c),Tatooine. 3.00
5 RHo(c),A:Lady Tarkin. 3.00
6 Weather Dominator 3.00
7 RHo(c),V:Darth Vader 3.00
8 KPI(c),X-Wing Secrets. 3.00
9 KPI(c),A:Boba Fett. 3.00

CLASSIC STAR WARS:
EMPIRE STRIKES BACK
1994
1 and 2 Movie Adaptation . . . . . . @4.00

CLASSIC STAR WARS:
HAN SOLO
AT STAR'S END
Mar., 1997
1 thru 3 by Alfredo Alcala . . . . . . @3.00

CLASSIC STAR WARS:
A LONG TIME AGO
(B&W) Mar., 1999
1 thru 6 rep. Marvel comics . . . . @6.00

CLASSIC STAR WARS:
RETURN OF THE JEDI
1994
1 Movie Adaptation 4.00
2 Movie Adaptation 3.50

CLASSIC STAR WARS:
VANDELHELM MISSION
1995
1-shot F:Han Solo, Lando 4.00

CLEANERS, THE
Nov., 2008
1 (of 4) 3.00

CLONEZONE
(B&W) 1989
Spec #1 . . . . 2.50

CLOWNS, THE
(PAGLIACCI)
Apr., 1998
1-shot B&W, CR. 3.00

COLORS IN BLACK
Comics From Spike, 1995
1 B.Passion Play. 3.00
2 Images 3.00
3 Back on the Bus 3.00
4 final issue. 3.00

COLUMBUS
(B&W) 1992
1-shot 2.50

COMIC BOOK
1 thru 4 9'x12' John Kricfalusi. . . @6.00

COMICS & STORIES
1996
1 thru 4 by Martin & Millionaire . . @3.00

Comics' Greatest World: King Tiger
© Dark Horse Comics

COMICS' GREATEST
WORLD
1993
(Arcadia)
1 B:MRi(s),FM(c),B:LW,B:O:Vortex,
    F:X,I:Seekers. 3.00
1a B&W proof ed. (1,500 made). . . 8.00
1b Hologram(c), with cards. 7.00
2 JoP,I:Pit Bulls. 2.50
3 AH,I:Ghost 5.00
4 I:Monster 2.50
(Golden City)
1 B:BKs(s),JOy(c),I:Rebel,
    Amaz.Grace,V:WarMaker 2.50
1a Gold Ed. 5.00
2 I:Mecha 2.50
3 WS(c),I:Titan 2.50
4 E:BKs(s),GP(c),JD,I:Catalyst. . . . 2.50
(Steel Harbor)
1 B:CW(s),PG,I:Barb Wire,
    V:Ignition 4.00
2 MMi(c),TNa,I:Machine 2.50
3 CW(a&s),I:Wolf Gang 2.50
4 E:CW(s),VGi,I:Motorhead 2.50
(Vortex)
1 B:RSd(s),LW,DoM,I:Division 13. . 2.50
2 I:Hero Zero. 2.50
3 PC,I:King Tiger 2.50
4 B:RSd(s),E:MRi(s)BMc,E:LW,
    F:O:Vortex,C:Vortex 2.50
Sourcebook 10.00

CONAN
Feb., 2004
1 KBk,CNr,JLi(c) from R.E.Howard 9.00
1a JSC(c) 2nd printing 5.00
1b CNr(c) 3rd printing 3.00
2 Frost Giant's Daughter 4.00
3 Asgard 3.00
4 Hyperborea 3.00
5 Breaks out of slavery. 3.00
6 Rebel 3.00
7 Rebellion 3.00
8 Born on the Battlefield 3.00

9 KBk,CNr. 3.00
10 KBk,CNr,Death in the Temple . . . 3.00
11 KBk,CNr,God the the Bowl 3.00
12 KBk,CNr,The Widowmaker. 3.00
13 KBk,CNr,V:Thoth-Amon 3.00
14 KBk,CNr,V:Thoth-Amon 3.00
15 KBk,Wolves in the Woods 3.00
16 KBk,Horror on Uskuth Hill. 3.00
17 KBk,CNr,The City of Thieves . . . 3.00
18 KBk,CNr,Siren-Song of Death . . 3.00
19 KBk,CNr,Thing in the Temple . . . 3.00
20 KBk,CNr,Tower of the Elephant . 3.00
21 KBk,CNr,Tower of the Elephant . 3.00
22 KBk,CNr,Tower of the Elephant . 3.00
23 KBk, The War of the Dead 3.00
24 KBk,CNr,The Hall of the Dead . . 3.00
24a nude variant 25.00
25 KBk,CNr,The Hand of the Mighty 3.00
26 KBk, TT,Seeds of Empire 3.00
27 KBk, TT,two stories 3.00
28 KBk, A night in Aquilonia. 3.00
29 MMi,CNr,The Hall of the Dead . . 3.00
30 MMi,CNr,The Hall of the Dead . . 3.00
31 MMi,CNr,The Hall of the Dead . . 3.00
32 KBk,Born on the Battlefield. 3.00
33 TT,CNr, pt.1, 40-pg. 3.00
34 TT,CNr, pt.2. . . . . 3.00
35 TT 3.00
36 TT Crom curse Picts & Prophets 3.00
37 TT,CNr,Honor Among Thieves . . 3.00
38 TT,CNr,Cursed and betrayed . . . 3.00
39 TT,CNr,Janissa Widowmaker . . . 3.00
40 TT,CNr,2 Wizards & a Funeral . . 3.00
41 TT,CNr,Rogues in the House . . . 3.00
42 TT,CNr,Rogues in the House . . . 3.00
43 TT,CNr,The Pits of Refuge 3.00
44 TT,CNr,The Pits of Refuge 3.00
45 KBk, Born on the Battlefield 3.00
46 Battle of Venarium 3.00
47 TT 3.00
48 TT(s),The Hand of Nergal. 3.00
49 TT(s),The Hand of Nergal. 3.00
50 TT(s),The Hand of Nergal, 56-pg 5.00
Spec. #1 Daughters of Midora 5.00
0 Spec. KBk,CNr,Conan the Legend
  prologue (2003). 2.50

CONAN AND THE BOOK OF THOTH
March., 2006
1 (of 4) KBk,KJo,48-pg. 5.00
2 thru 5 KBk,KJo,48-pg. . . . . . . @5.00

CONAN AND THE DEMONS OF KHITAI
Oct., 2005
1 (of 4) 3.00
2 . . . . 3.00
3 contains nude ad 8.00
3a 2nd printing 3.50
4 . . . . 3.00

CONAN AND THE JEWELS OF GWAHLUR
April, 2005
1 thru 3 CR . . . . @3.00

CONAN AND THE MIDNIGHT GOD
Jan., 2006
1 thru 5 (of 5) . . . . @3.00

CONAN AND THE SONGS OF THE DEAD
July., 2006
1 (of 4) JLd(s),TT 3.00
2 thru 5 . . . . @3.00

CONAN THE CIMMERIAN
June, 2008
0 TT(s) 2.50
1 TT(s) 3.00
1a variant JKu (c) 3.00
2 thru 5 TT(s),RCo . . . . @3.00

CONCRETE
(B&W) 1987
1 PC,R:Concrete, A Stone among
  Stones 9.00
1a 2nd printing 3.00
2 PC,'Transatlantic Swim'. 6.00
3 PC 5.00
4 PC 4.00
5 PC,'An Armchair Stuffed with
  Dynamite'. 4.00
6 PC,Concrete works on farm 4.00
7 PC,Concrete grows horns 4.00
8 PC,Climbs Mount Everest 4.00
9 PC,Mount Everest,pt.2. . . . . 4.00
10 PC,last Issue. 4.00
Spec. #1 Concrete ColorSpec.,PC
  (1989) 4.00
Spec. Concrete Celebrates Earth Day
  PC,Moebius (1990) 2.50
Spec. 1 A New Life, B&W rep.,
  O: Concrete (1989) 3.50
Spec. Concrete: Land & Sea,
  rep. #1 & #2 (1989) 3.25
Spec. Concrete: Odd Jobs,
  rep. #5 & #6 (1990) 3.50

CONCRETE: ECLECTICA
1993
1 PC,The Ugly Boy 3.25
2 PC 3.25

CONCRETE: FRAGILE CREATURE
1991
1 PC,Rulers o/t Omniverse,pt.1 . . . 4.00
2 PC,Rulers o/t Omniverse,pt.2 . . . 3.00
3 PC,Rulers o/t Omniverse,pt.3 . . . 3.00
4 PC,Rulers o/t Omniverse,pt.3 . . . 3.00

CONCRETE: THE HUMAN DILEMMA
(B&W) Dec., 2004
1 thru 6 (of 6) PC . . . . @3.50

Concrete: Killer Smile #1
© Dark Horse Comics

CONCRETE: KILLER SMILE
DH Legend, 1994
1 PC 3.50
2 thru 4 PC . . . . @3.00

CONCRETE: STRANGE ARMOR
Dec., 1997–Apr., 1998
1 (of 5) 3.00
2 thru 5 . . . . @3.00

CONCRETE: THINK LIKE A MOUNTAIN
(B&W) 1996
1 thru 6 PC,GfD(c) . . . . @3.00

CORMAC MAC ART
July, 1989
1 Robert E. Howard adapt. 3.00
2 thru 4 . . . . @3.00

CORNY'S FETISH
April 1998
GN by Renee French, 64-pg.. . . . . . 5.00

COUTOO
(B&W) 1994
1 Lt. Joe Kraft 3.50

CREEPY
(B&W) 1992
1 KD,TS,GC,SL,Horror 4.00
2 TS,CI,DC,Demonic Baby 4.00
3 JM,TS,JG,V:Killer Clown 4.00
4 TS,Final issue 4.00

CREATURE FROM THE BLACK LAGOON
1 Movie Adaptation 5.00

CRIMINAL MACABRE
May, 2003
1 (of 5) F:Cal McDonald 4.00
2 thru 5 . . . . @3.00
1a & 2a 2nd printings . . . . @3.00
1-shot Feet of Clay (2006). 3.00

CRIMINAL MACABRE: CEL BLOCK 666
July, 2008
1 (of 4) 3.00
2 thru 4 . . . . @3.00

CRIMINAL MACABRE: MY DEMON BABY
Sept., 2007
1 (of 4) 3.00
2 thru 4 . . . . @3.00

CRIMINAL MACABRE: TWO RED EYES
Dec., 2006
1 (of 4) 3.00
2 thru 4 . . . . @3.00

CRITICAL ERROR
1992
1 rep.Classic JBy story 2.75

CROMWELL STONE
(B&W) 1992
1-shot 3.50

[ANDREW VACHSS']
CROSS
1995
0 GfD(c),I:Cross,Rhino,Princess. . . 2.50
1 thru 7 . . . . @3.00

CRUSH
DH Rocket Comics, Oct., 2003
1 . . . . 3.00
2 thru 4 . . . . @3.00

Cud Comics #5
© Dark Horse Comics

CUD COMICS
(B&W) 1996
1 thru 8 by Terry LaBan . . . . @3.00

THE CURSE OF DRACULA
July, 1998
1 (of 3) MWn,GC 3.00
2 thru 3 . . . . @3.00

DAMN NATION
Feb., 2005
1 thru 3 . . . . @3.00

DANCE OF
LIFEY DEATH, THE
(B&W) 1994
1-shot ECa 4.00

DANGER UNLIMITED
DH Legend, 1994
1 JBy(a&s),KD,I:Danger Unlimited,
  B:BU:Torch of Liberty 2.50
2 JBy(a&s),KD,O:DangerUnlimited. 2.50
3 JBy(a&s),KD,O:Torch of Liberty. . 2.50
4 JBy(a&s),KD,Final Issue 2.50

DARE DETECTIVES, THE
Oct., 2004
GN Vol. 1 The Snowpea Plot. 6.00
GN Vol. 2 The Royal Treatment. . . . 7.00

DARK HORSE CLASSICS
(B&W) 1992
1 Last of the Mohicans 4.50
2 20,000 Leagues Under the Sea . 4.50

DARK HORSE CLASSICS:
ALIENS VS. PREDATOR
Feb., 1997
1 thru 6 Rep. . . . . @3.00

DARK HORSE CLASSICS:
GODZILLA,
KING OF THE MONSTERS
July, 1998
1 RSd,SBi,now color. 3.00
2 rep. from 1995 . . . . 3.00
3 rep. from 1995 . . . . 3.00
4 rep. Godzilla #2, from 1995. . . . . 3.00
5 & 6 . . . . @3.00

DARK HORSE CLASSICS:
PREDATOR:
JUNGLE TALES
1-shot Rep. 3.00

DARK HORSE CLASSICS:
STAR WARS—
DARK EMPIRE
1997
1 rep. by Tom Veitch,CK,DvD(c). . . 3.00
2 thru 6 rep., DvD(c) . . . . @3.00

DARK HORSE CLASSICS:
TERROR OF GODZILLA
Aug., 1998
1 by Kazuhisa Iwata, AAd(c). 3.00
2 & 3 . . . . @3.00
4 rep. of 1988 B&W 3.00
5 & 6 AAd(c) . . . . @3.00

DARK HORSE COMICS
1992
1 RL,CW,F:Predator,Robocop,
  I:Renegade,Time Cop,(double
  gatefold cover). 4.00
2 RL,CW,F:Predator,Robocop,
  Renegade,Time Cop 3.00
3 CW,F:Robocop,Time Cop,Aliens,
  Indiana Jones 3.00
4 F:Predator,Aliens,Ind.Jones. 3.00
5 F:Predator,E:Aliens 3.00
6 F:Robocop,Predator, E:Indiana
  Jones 3.00
7 F:Robocop,Predator,B:StarWars . 6.00
8 B&I:X,Robocop 8.00
9 F:Robocop,E:Star Wars 4.00
10 E:X,B:Godzilla,Predator,
  James Bond 3.50
11 F:Godzilla,Predator,James
  Bond,B:Aliens 2.75
12 F:Predator. 2.75
13 F:Predator,B:Thing 2.75
14 MiB(s),B:The Mark 2.75
15 MiB(s),E:The Mark,B:Aliens 2.75
16 B:Predator,E:Thing,Aliens. 2.75
17 B:Aliens,Star Wars:Droids. 2.75
18 E:Predator. 2.75
19 RL(c),B:X,E:Star Wars:Droids,
  Aliens. 2.75
20 B:Predator. 2.75
21 F:Mecha 2.75
22 B:Aliens, E:Mecha 2.75
23 B:The Machine 2.75
24 The Machine. 2.75
25 Final issue. 2.75

Dark Horse Comics #6
© Dark Horse Comics

DARK HORSE
DOWNUNDER
(B&W) 1994
1 F:Australian Writers 2.50
2 Australian Writers. 2.50
3 Australian Writers, finale 2.50

DARK HORSE
MAVERICK
Ann.2000 48-pg. B&W 5.00
Ann.2001 48-pg. B&W 5.00

DARK HORSE MONSTERS
Feb., 1997
1-shot 3.00

DARK HORSE
PRESENTS
(B&W) 1986
1 PC,I:Concrete 13.00
1a 2nd printing 3.00
2 PC,Concrete 6.00
3 Boris theBear,Concrete 5.00
4 PC,Concrete 5.00
5 PC,Concrete 5.00
6 PC,Concrete 5.00
7 I:MONQ 5.00
8 PC,Concrete 5.00
9 RSd 5.00
10 PC,Concrete, I:Masque 12.00
11 Masque 6.00
12 PC,Concrete, Masque 7.00
13 Masque 5.00
14 PC,Concrete, Masque 7.00
15 Masque 5.00
16 PC,Concrete, Masque 7.00
17 F:Roachmill. 5.00
18 PC,Concrete, Mask. 7.00
19 Masque 5.00
20 double,Flaming Carrot 9.00
21 Masque 5.00
22 I:Duckman. 5.00
23 WiS,Filipino Massacre 5.00
24 PC,I:Aliens 15.00
25 thru 31. . . . . @3.00
32 A:Concrete 5.00
33 F:Mr. Monster 3.00
34 Aliens 4.00
35 Predator 4.00
36 Aliens vs.Predator 5.00
36a painted cover 8.00

All comics prices listed are for *Near Mint* condition.

DARK HORSE

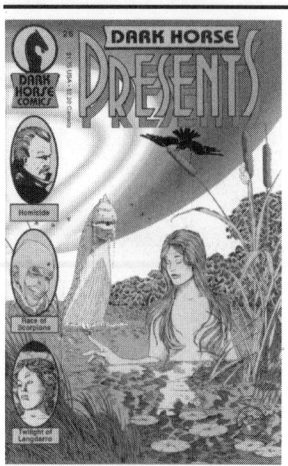

Dark Horse Presents #26
© Dark Horse Comics

37 The Heartbreakers 3.00
38 A:Concrete 4.00
39 Trekker 3.00
40 I:The Aerialist 3.00
41 Argosy. 3.00
42 Aliens 5.00
43 Aliens 4.00
44 Crash 3.00
45 Predator 3.00
46 Predator 4.00
47 Monkers 3.00
48 with 2-card strip 3.00
49 with 2-card strip 3.00
50 inc.'Heartbreakers', with
    2-card strip 4.00
51 FM(c),inc.'Sin City' 9.00
52 FM,inc. 'Sin City' 7.00
53 FM,inc. 'Sin City' 7.00
54 FM,Sin City;JBy Preview of
    Next Men,pt.1 . . . . 8.00
55 FM,Sin City;JBy Preview of
    Next Men (JBy),pt.2. . . . . 7.00
56 FM,Sin City,JBy,Next MenPt.3
    Aliens Genocide(prologue) 7.00
57 FM,SinCity;JBy Next Men,pt.4 . . 7.00
58 FM,Sin City,Alien Fire 7.00
59 FM,Sin City,Alien Fire 7.00
60 FM,Sin City 7.00
61 FM,Sin City 7.00
62 FM,E:Sin City 7.00
63 Moe,Marie Dakar 3.00
64 MWg,R:The Aerialist 3.00
65 B:Accidental Death 3.00
66 PC,inc.Dr.Giggles 3.00
67 B:Predator story (lead in to
    'Race War'),double size 4.50
68 F:Predator,Swimming Lessons
    (Nestrobber tie-in) 3.00
69 F:Predator. 3.00
70 F:Alec 3.00
71 F:Madwoman 3.00
72 F:Eudaemon 3.00
73 F:Eudaemon 3.00
74 F:Eudaemon 3.00
75 F:Chairman 3.00
76 F:Hermes Vs.the Eye,Ball Kid . . 2.50
77 F:Hermes Vs.the Eye,Ball Kid . . 2.50
78 F:Hermes Vs.the Eye,Ball Kid . . 2.50
79 B:Shadow Empires Slaves 2.50
80 AAd,I:Monkey Man & O'Brien . . 5.00
81 B:Buoy 3.00
82 B:Just Folks 3.00
83 Last Impression 3.00

84 MBn,F:Nexus,E:Hermes Vs. the
    Eye Ball Kid 3.00
85 Winner Circle, Eighth Woman . . 3.00
86 Eighth Woman 3.00
87 F:Concrete 4.00
88 Hellboy 3.00
89 Hellboy 4.00
90 Hellboy 3.00
91 Blackheart, Baden 3.00
92 Too Much Coffee Man 6.00
93 Cud, Blackheart,Coffee Man. . . . 8.00
94 A:Eyeball Kid,Coffee Man 6.00
95 Too Much Coffee Man 7.00
96 Kabuli Kid 3.00
97 F:Kabuki Kid 3.00
98 Pot Full of Noodles 3.00
99 Anthology title 3.00
100–#1 Lance Blastoff 4.50
100–#2 Hellboy 3.50
100–#3 Concrete 3.50
100–#4 Black Cross. 3.00
100–#5 Pan Fried Girl 3.00
101 BW,F:Aliens 3.00
102 F:Mr. Painter 3.00
103 F:The Pink Tornado 3.00
104 F:The Pink Tornado 3.00
105 F:The Pink Tornado 3.00
106 F:Godzilla 3.00
107 F:Rusty Razorclam 3.00
108 The Ninth Gland 3.00
109 The One Trick Ripoff. 3.00
110 F:Egg. 3.00
111 Ninth Gland 3.00
112 three stories, concl.. . . . . 3.00
113 Trypto the Acid Dog 3.00
114 F:Star Slammers/Lance Blastoff 3.00
115 flip-book Dr. Spin/The Creep. . . 3.00
116 Fat Dog Mendoza 3.00
117 F:Aliens 3.00
118 Monkeyman O'Brien 3.00
119 Trout 3.00
120 'One Last Job'. 3.00
121 F: Imago 3.00
122 'Lords of Misrule'. 3.00
123 F: Jack Zero 3.00
124 F:Predator. 3.00
125 F:Nocturnals 3.00
126 flip book, 48-pg. 4.50
127 F:The Nocturnals 3.00
128 F:Dan & Larry 3.00
129 F:Hammer. 3.00
130 F:Wanted Man 3.00
131 F:Girl Crazy. 3.00
132 flip book 3.00
133 F:Tarzan 3.00
134 F:The Dirty Pair. 3.00
135 F:The Fall, concl. 4.00
136 The Ark 3.00
137 Predator 3.00
138 F:Terminators 3.00
139 F:Roachmill. 3.00
140 F:Aliens 3.00
141 F:Buffy the Vampire Slayer. . . . 4.00
142 F:Lovecraftian tales. 3.00
143 F:Tarzan tales 3.00
144 F:Vortex. 3.00
145 F:Burglar Girls. 3.00
146 F:Aliens vs. Predator 3.00
147 F:Ragnok 3.00
148 The Nevermen 3.00
149 Wunderkind. 3.00
150 F:Buffy, 48-pg.. . . . . 5.00
151 F:Hellboy. 3.00
152 It! The Beast from Twenty
    Billion Years Beyond Earth 3.00
153 Helm of Harxis 3.00
154 Iron Reich 3000, flip-book. 3.00
155 Angel, flip-book 3.00
156 Witch's Son, flip-book 3.00
157 F:Witch's Son, final issue 15.00
Ann. 1997 F:Body Bags. 5.00
Ann. 1998 F:Hellboy 14.00

Ann. 1999 DHP, JR. 5.00
Ann. 2000 Girls Rule, 64-pg. 5.00
Fifth Anniv. Special DGi,PC,
    SBi,CW,MW,FM,Sin City,
    Aliens,Give Me Liberty 25.00
Milestone Ed.#1,rep.DHP#1 . . . . . . 2.50
Spec. Dark Horse 20 Years 2.50

DARK HORSE PRESENTS: ALIENS

1 Rep. 5.00
1a Platinum Edition. 8.00

DARKNESS FALLS: THE TOOTH FAIRY— THE TRAGIC LIFE OF MATILDA DIXON
Jan., 2003

1-shot CAd. 3.00

DEADFACE: DOING ISLANDS WITH BACCHUS
(B&W) 1991

1 rep. Bacchus apps. 3.00
2 rep. inc.'Book-Keeper of Atlantis . 3.00
3 rep. and new material 3.00

DEADFACE: EARTH, WATER, AIR & FIRE
(B&W) 1992

1 Bacchus & Simpson in Sicily 2.50
2 A:Don Skylla 2.50
3 Mafia/Kabeirol-War prep. 2.50
4 Last issue. 2.50

DEAD IN THE WEST
(B&W) 1993

1 TT,Joe Landsdale adapt. 5.00
2 TT,adapt. 5.00
Spec. #1 TT(c) 4.00

DEADLANDER, THE
2007

1 thru 4 . . . . @3.00

DEADLINE
(B&W) 1992

1 thru 8 . . . . @4.00

DEADLINE USA
(B&W) 1991

1 rep. Deadline UK,Inc. Tank Girl
    Johnny Nemo 5.00
2 inc. Tank Girl,Johnny Nemo. 5.00
3 . . . . 5.00

DEAD OR ALIVE— A CYBERPUNK WESTERN
Apr., 1998

1 (of 4) by Tatjana and Alberto
    Ponticelli 2.50
2 thru 4 . . . . @2.50

DEAD TO RIGHTS
Oct., 2002

1-shot 64-pg. 6.00

DECADE OF DARK HORSE, A
1996

1 (of 4) inc. Star Wars, Nexus,
    Ghost. 3.00
2 thru 4 . . . . @3.00

Decade of Dark Hourse #4
© Dark Horse Comics

[RANDY BOWEN'S] DECAPITATOR
June, 1998
1 (of 4) GEr,DoM 3.00
2 GEr 3.00
3 MMi,KJo,AAI 3.00
4 MMi, conclusion. 3.00

DEVIL CHEF
1994
1 I:Devil Chef 2.50

DEVIL'S FOOTPRINTS
March 2003
1 thru 4 . . . . @3.00

DIABLO: TALES OF SANCTUARY
Nov., 2001
1-shot 64-pg. 6.00

DIGIMON
June, 2000, Bi-weekly
1 thru 6 . . . . @3.00
7 thru 12 ND(c) 3.00

DIRTY PAIR
(B&W–Manga) 1999
1-shot Start the Violence, AWa(c) . . 3.00
1-shot Start the Violence, JPn(c) . . . 3.00

DIRTY PAIR: FATAL BUT NOT SERIOUS
(Manga) 1995
1 R:Kei,Yuri. 3.00
2 V:Kevin Sleet,Yuri 3.00
3 Anti Yuri 3.00
4 V:Terrorists. 3.00
5 conclusion 3.00

DIRTY PAIR: RUN FROM THE FUTURE
Jan., 2000
1 (of 4) AWa(c) 3.00
1a AH(c) 3.00
2 AWa(c) 3.00
2a BSf(c) 3.00
3 AWa(c) 3.00

3a Bruce Timm(c) 3.00
4 AWa(c) 3.00
4a HuR(c) 3.00

DIRTY PAIR: SIM HELL
(B&W–Manga) 1993
1 thru 4 by Adam Warren . . . . . . @3.25

DIRTY PAIR: SIM HELL: REMASTERED
May, 2001
1 thru 4 (of 4) full color, AWa . . . @3.00

DISNEY'S MONSTERS INC.
2001
1-shot movie adapt. 5.00

DISNEY'S TARZAN
June, 1999
1 and 2 Animated movie adapt. . . @3.00

DIVISION 13
Sept., 1994
1 & 2 . . . . @2.50
3 A:Payback 2.50
4 Carnal Genesis 2.50

DOC SAVAGE: CURSE OF THE FIRE GOD
1 R:Man of Bronze 3.00
2 Exploding Plane. 3.00
3 & 4 . . . . @3.00

DR. GIGGLES
1992
1 Horror movie adapt. 2.50
2 Movie adapt.contd. 2.50

DR. ROBOT
Apr., 2000
1-shot, by Bernie E. Mireault 3.00

DOMINION: CONFLICT 1 — NO MORE NOISE
(B&W–Manga) 1996
1 thru 6 by Masamune Shirow . . @3.00

DOMINION SPECIAL: PHANTOM OF THE AUDIENCE
(B&W–Manga)
1-shot by Masamune Shirow 2.50

DOMU: A CHILD'S DREAMS
(B&W–Manga)
1 Psychic Warfare 6.00
2 Murders Continue 6.00
3 Psychic war conclusion 6.00

DRACULA
1 Movie Adaptation 5.00

DRAGON PRINCE
June, 2005
1 (of 5) RMz,JJ 3.00

DRAKUUN
(B&W) Feb., 1997
Rise of the Dragon Princess
1 thru 6 (of 6) by Johji Manabe . . @3.00

Drakuun #13
© Dark Horse Comics

The Revenge of Gustav (Aug., 1997)
7 (1 of 6) by Johji Manabe 3.00
8 thru 12 pt.2 thru pt.6 . . . . @3.00
Shadow of the Warlock (Feb., 1998)
13 (1 of 6) by Johji Manabe. 3.00
14 thru 18 pt.2 thru pt.6 . . . . @3.00
The Hidden War (Sept., 1998)
19 (1 of 6) by Johji Manabe. 3.00
20 thru 24 pt.2 thru pt.6 . . . . . . @3.00
Flames of Empire (1999)
25 Flames of Empire (1 of 6). 3.00

DRAWING ON YOUR NIGHTMARES
Oct., 2003
1-shot Halloween 2003 Special 1 . . 4.00
1-shot Halloween Special 2 . . . . . . 10.00

DROOPY
Oct., 1995
1 Dr. Droopenstein 2.50
2 Turkey For Dinner 2.50
3 Santa's Little Helpers. 2.50

DUCKMAN
1990
1 by Everette Peck 2.50

DWIGHT T. ALBATROSS'S THE GOON NOIR
(B&W) Sept., 2006
1 thru 3 . . . . @3.00

DYLAN DOG
(B&W) Bonelli Mar., 1999
1 (of 6) by Tiziano Di Sclavi & Angelo
Stano, MMi(c), 96-pg. 5.00
2 thru 6 . . . . @5.00

EDGAR RICE BURROUGHS' RETURN OF TARZAN
Apr., 1997
1 adapted by Thomas Yeates
& John Totleben. 3.00
2 thru 3 . . . . @3.00

EDGAR RICE BURROUGHS' TARZAN
1996
Mugambi
1 Betrayed by 3 man-beasts...... 3.00
2 'Tarzan's Jungle Fury' 3.00
3 'Tarzan's Jungle Fury' 3.00
4 vs. the Tara virus 3.00
5 Cure to the Tara virus 3.00
6 .... 3.00
Tarzan and the Legion of Hate
7 pt.1......................... 3.00
8 pt.2......................... 3.00
9 pt.3......................... 3.00
10 pt.4, concl................... 3.00
Le Monstre, June, 1997
11 pt.1 .... 3.00
12 pt.2 Bernie Wrightson(c)...... 3.00
Modern Prometheus, Aug., 1997
13 pt.1 MK(c) in New York........ 3.00
14 pt.2 MK(c)................... 3.00
Tooth and Nail, Oct., 1997
15 pt.1 MSh(c)................. 3.00
16 pt.2 .... 3.00
Tarzan vs. the Moon Men
17 TT,AW,TY 3.00
18 TT,AW,TY 3.00
19 TT,AW,TY 3.00
20 TT,AW,TY 3.00
Primeval
21 thru 24 MGr............... @3.00
1-shot A Tale of Mugambi (1995)... 3.00

Edgar Rice Burroughs' Carson of Venus #2 © Dark Horse Comics

EDGAR RICE BURROUGHS' TARZAN: CARSON OF VENUS
May, 1998
1 (of 4) by Darko Macan and
　Igor Kordey, F:Carson Napier .. 3.00
2 thru 4 novels adapt. .... @3.00

EDGAR RICE BURROUGHS' TARZAN: THE LOST ADVENTURE
1995
1 Lost Manuscript 3.00
2 V:Gorgo the Buffalo 3.00
3 V:Bandits 3.00
4 V:Bandits 3.00

EDGAR RICE BURROUGHS' TARZAN: THE RIVERS OF BLOOD
Nov., 1999
1 .... 3.00
2 thru 8 .... @3.00

EDGAR RICE BURROUGHS' TARZAN— THE SAVAGE HEART
Apr., 1999
1 (of 4) MGr Jane is dead........ 3.00
2 thru 4 .... @3.00

EGON
Jan.–Feb., 1998
1 and 2 .... @3.00

EIGHTH WONDER, THE
Nov., 1997
1-shot by P. Janes & K. Plunkett ... 3.00

ELRIC: STORMBRINGER
DH/Topps, 1996
1 by Michael Moorcock & CR..... 3.00
2 thru 7 (of 7) .... @3.00

EL ZOMBO
April 2004
1 (of 3) 3.00
2 and 3 .... @3.00

EMILY THE STRANGE
(B&W) Aug., 2007
1 The Death Issue 3.50
2 The Fake Issue 3.50
3 .... 3.50
4 The Alone Issue............. 3.50

END LEAGUE, THE
Dec., 2007
1 .... 4.00
2 thru 8 .... @3.00

ENEMY
1994
1 MZ(c),StG(s),I:Enemy 2.75
2 MZ(c),StG(s),F:Heller......... 2.75
3 MZ(c),StG(s),A:Heller 2.50
4 .... 2.50
5 final issue................. 3.00

ESCAPISTS, THE
July, 2006
1 .... 3.00
2 thru 6 .... @3.00

EUDAEMON, THE
1993
1 Nel,I:New Eudaemon......... 3.00
2 Nel,V:Mordare 2.75
3 Nel,V:Mordare 2.75

EVIL DEAD
Jan., 2008
1 (of 4) 3.00
2 thru 4 .... 3.00

EVIL DEAD III: ARMY OF DARKNESS
1 JBo,Movie adaptation 4.00
2 JBo,Movie adaptation 3.50
3 JBo,Movie adaptation 3.00

EXQUISITE CORPSE
1990
1-shot Green 3.00
1-shot Red................... 3.00
1-shot Yellow 3.00

EYEBALL KID
(B&W) 1992
1 I:Eyeball Kid............... 2.50
2 V:Stygian Leech............. 2.50
3 V:Telchines Brothers,last iss..... 2.50

FAFHRD AND THE GRAY MOUSER
Jan., 2007
1-shot HC,MMi 3.00

FAT DOG MENDOZA
(B&W) 1992
1 I&O:Fat Dog Mendoza........ 2.50

FEAR AGENT
2007
20 Hatchet Job, pt.4 .... 3.00
21 Hatchet Job, pt. 5 .... 3.00
22 I Against I, pt.1 .... 3.00
23 I Against I, pt.2 .... 3.00
24 I Against I, pt.3 .... 3.00
25 I Against I, pt.4 .... 3.00
26 I Against I, pt.5 .... 3.00
27 I Against I, pt.6 .... 3.00

FEAR AGENT: HATCHED JOB
Nov., 2007
1 (of 4) 3.00
2 thru 3 .... @3.00

FEAR AGENT: THE LAST GOODBYE
June., 2007
1 .... 3.00
2 thru 4.................... @3.00

FEEDERS
Oct., 1999
1-shot MiA, prequel to Eyes
　to Heaven 3.00

FIERCE
June, 2004
1 .... 3.00
2 thru 4 .... @3.00

F5 ORIGIN
1-shot, rep.................. 3.00

FLAMING CARROT
(B&W) 2001
Previous issues: see B&W section
18 Uncle Billy's mail-order bride ... 4.00
18a Ash-Can-Limited 4.00
19 Hills Like White Elephants 4.00
20 Secret ice cream cult 4.00
21 Space Aliens 3.00
22 V:Space Aliens 3.00
23 Blipio appears............. 3.00
24 48-page 10th anniv. spec...... 4.00
25 F:TMNT,Mysterymen,with
　2-card strip 3.00
26 A:TMNT................... 3.00
27 TM(c),A:TMNT conclusion 3.00
28 Injured bumblebee 3.00
29 Man in the Moon,Iron City 3.00
30 V:Man in the Moon 3.00

31 A:Fat Fury 3.00
Ann. 1 by Bob Burden 5.00

FLAXEN
1992
1 Based on Model,w/poster 3.00

FLOATERS
(B&W) 1993–94
1 thru 6 From Spike Lee . . . . @2.50

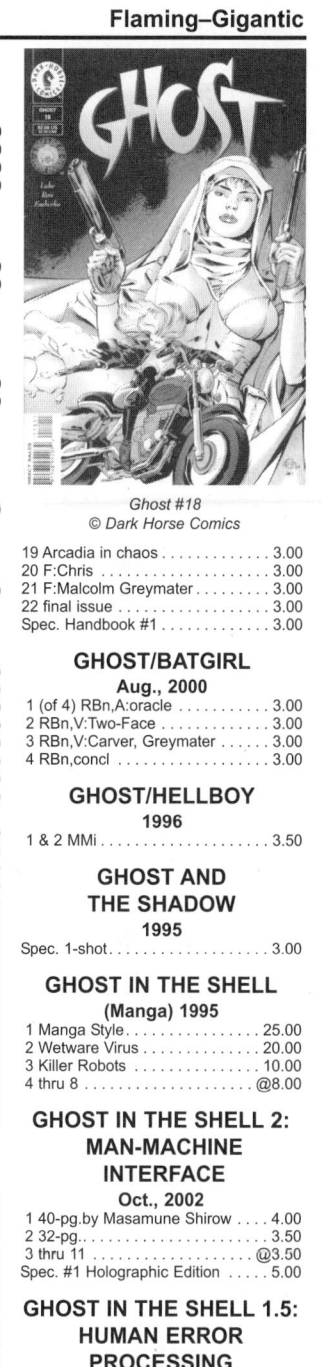

Foot Soldiers #3
© Dark Horse Comics

FOOT SOLDIERS, THE
1996
1 thru 4 by Jim Krueger 3.00
See also Image Comics

FORT: PROPHET OF THE UNEXPLAINED
June, 2002
1 (of 4) F:Charles Fort 3.00
2 thru 4 . . . . @3.00

FRANKENSTEIN
1 Movie Adaptation 4.00

FRAY
2001
1 . . . . 10.00
1a 2nd printing 3.00
2 thru 4 . . . . @8.00
5 thru 8 . . . . @5.00

FREAKS' AMOUR
1992
1 . . . . 4.00
2 . . . . 4.00
3 . . . . 4.00

FREAKSHOW
1 JBo,DMc,KB, 'Wanda the Worm
Woman,' 'Lillie'. 10.00

FREAKS OF THE HEARTLAND
Jan., 2004
1 (of 6) horror 3.00
2 thru 6 . . . . @3.00

FUSED: THINK LIKE A MACHINE
Dec., 2003
1 Robotic Cy-Bot. 3.00
2 . . . . 3.00
3 . . . . 3.00
4 . . . . 3.00

GALACTIC
DH Rocket Comics Aug., 2003
1 . . . . 3.00
2 & 3 . . . . @3.00

GAMERA
Aug., 1996
1 (of 4) by Dave Chipps &
Mozart Couto. 3.00
2 thru 4 . . . . @3.00

GARY GIANNI'S MONSTERMEN
Aug., 1999
1-shot 3.00

GHOST
Comics' Greatest World
Spec. AH(c) 4.00

GHOST
1995–98
1 by Eric Luke, R:Ghost 7.00
2 AH,MfM,Arcadia Nocturne,pt.2 . . 4.00
3 Arcadia Nocturn,pt.3 . . . . 4.00
4 . . . . 3.00
5 V:Predator 3.00
6 . . . . 3.00
7 Hell Night 3.00
8 thru 21 . . . . @3.00
22 The key is forever beyond
your reach 3.00
23 I: The Goblins 3.00
24 X is dead. 3.00
25 double size 4.00
26 Fairytale version 3.50
27 . . . . 3.50
28 CW(c),Painful Music,pt.1 . . . . . 3.50
29 CW(c),Painful Music,pt.2 . . . . . 3.50
30 CW(c),Painful Music,pt.3 . . . . . 3.50
31 CW(c),Painful Music,pt.4 . . . . . 3.50
32 A Pathless Land 3.50
33 Jade Cathedral,pt.1 . . . . 3.50
34 Jade Cathedral,pt.2 . . . . 3.50
35 Jade Cathedral,pt.3 . . . . 3.50
36 Jade Cathedral,pt.4 . . . . 3.50
Spec.#2 Immortal Coil 4.50
Spec.#3 Scary Monsters 4.50

GHOST
1998–2000
1 CW,O:Ghost. 3.00
2 CW,V:Dr.Trouvaille. 3.00
3 CW,V:Silhouette. 3.00
4 CW,The Devil Incido,O:pt.1 . . . . 3.00
5 CW,Stare at the Sun,O:pt.2 . . . . 3.00
6 CW,Stare at the Sun,O:pt.3 . . . . 3.00
7 CW,Shifter,pt.1,F:King Tiger . . . 3.00
8 CW,Shifter,pt.2. . . . . 3.00
9 CW,Shifter,pt.3. . . . . 3.00
10 CW,Shifter,pt.4 . . . . 3.00
11 CW,back in Arcadia. 3.00
12 Red Shadows,pt.1 (of 4). 3.00
13 Red Shadows,pt.2 . . . . 3.00
14 Red Shadows,pt.3 . . . . 3.00
15 Red Shadows,pt.4 . . . . 3.00
16 When the Devil Daydreams,pt.1 . 3.00
17 When the Devil Daydreams,pt.2 . 3.00
18 rogue agent. 3.00

Ghost #18
© Dark Horse Comics

19 Arcadia in chaos 3.00
20 F:Chris 3.00
21 F:Malcolm Greymater 3.00
22 final issue 3.00
Spec. Handbook #1 . . . . 3.00

GHOST/BATGIRL
Aug., 2000
1 (of 4) RBn,A:oracle 3.00
2 RBn,V:Two-Face 3.00
3 RBn,V:Carver, Greymater 3.00
4 RBn,concl 3.00

GHOST/HELLBOY
1996
1 & 2 MMi 3.50

GHOST AND THE SHADOW
1995
Spec. 1-shot. 3.00

GHOST IN THE SHELL
(Manga) 1995
1 Manga Style. 25.00
2 Wetware Virus 20.00
3 Killer Robots 10.00
4 thru 8 . . . . @8.00

GHOST IN THE SHELL 2: MAN-MACHINE INTERFACE
Oct., 2002
1 40-pg.by Masamune Shirow 4.00
2 32-pg.. 3.50
3 thru 11 . . . . @3.50
Spec. #1 Holographic Edition 5.00

GHOST IN THE SHELL 1.5: HUMAN ERROR PROCESSING
(B&W) Oct., 2006
1 by Shirow Masamune 3.00
2 thru 8 . . . . @3.00

GIGANTIC
Nov., 2008
1 (of 5) 3.50

All comics prices listed are for *Near Mint* condition.

DARK HORSE

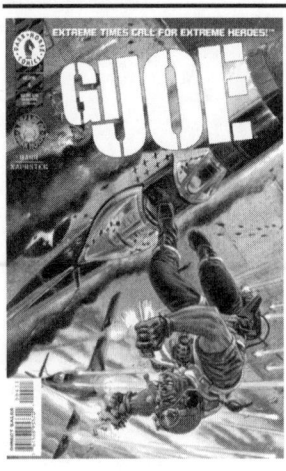

G.I. Joe #4
© Dark Horse Comics

G.I. JOE
1995
1 by Mike Barr & Tatsuya Ishida . . . 3.00	
2 thru 4 . . . . @3.00	

Vol. 2 1996
1 . . . . 3.00	
2 thru 4 . . . . @3.00	

GIRL CRAZY
(B&W) May, 1996
1 GHe 3.00	
2 and 3 GHe . . . . @3.00	

GIVE ME LIBERTY
1990
1 FM/DGb, Homes & Gardens 6.00	
2 FM/DGb 5.00	
3 and 4 FM/DGb . . . . @5.00	

GO BOY 7: HUMAN
ACTION MACHINE
DH Rocket Comics, July, 2003
1 TPe 3.00	
2 thru 8 . . . . @3.00	

GODZILLA
(B&W) 1988
1 Japanese Manga 5.00	
2 thru 6 . . . . @4.00	
Spec #1 . . . . 3.00	

GODZILLA
COLOR SPECIAL
1992
1 AAd,R:Godzilla,V:Gekido-Jin 3.50	
1a rep (1998) 3.00	
Spec.1 Godzilla vs. Barkley MBn(s),	
JBt,DvD (1993) 3.50	

GODZILLA
1995
0 RSd,The King of Monsters	
is back! 6.00	
1 R:Godzill 4.00	
2 V:Cybersaur. 4.00	
3 I:Bagorah the Bat Creature 4.00	
4 V:Bagorah,Cybersaur 4.00	
5 V:U.S. Army 4.00	
6 thru 14 . . . . @4.00	

15 'Thunder Downunder' 4.00	
16 'Thunder in the Past'. 4.00	
Spec.1 Godzilla vs. Hero Zero	
Tatsuya Ishida (1995) 2.50	

GOON, THE
June, 2003
1 . . . . 6.00	
2 . . . . 5.00	
3 thru 9 . . . . @4.00	
10 thru 30 . . . . @3.00	

GREEN LANTERN
VS. ALIENS
Aug., 2000
1 RMz,RL,F:Hal Jordan, x-over . . . 3.00	
2 (of 4) RMz,RL,F:Kyle Rayner . . . 3.00	
3 RMz,RL, without ring 3.00	
4 RMz,RL, V:Alien Queen. 3.00	

GRENDEL
Spec.1 Grendel Cycle, Grendel	
History (1995) 6.00	
Spec.1 Devil Quest (1995). 5.00	

GRENDEL:
BEHOLD THE DEVIL
(B&W&R) July, 2007
0 MWg 16-pgs. 2.50	
1 (of 8) MWg. 3.50	
2 thru 8 MWg 3.50	

GRENDEL: BLACK,
WHITE, AND RED
(B&W&R) Nov., 1998
1 (of 4) MWa, 48-pg. 5.00	
2 thru 4 MWa, 48-pg. . . . . @4.00	

GRENDEL CLASSICS
1995
1 Rep.#18–#19 Comico series 4.00	
2 Rep. 4.00	

GRENDEL: DEVIL BY
THE DEED
1993
1 MWg,RRa 4.00	
1 representation (1997) 4.00	

GRENDEL: DEVIL CHILD
June, 1999
1 and 2 MWg 3.00	

GRENDEL:
THE DEVIL INSIDE
DH Maverick, Sept., 2001
1 (of 3) MWg. 3.00	
2 . . . . 3.00	
3 concl. 3.00	

GRENDEL:
DEVIL'S LEGACY
Aug., 1996
1 by Matt Wagner 3.00	
2 thru 3 . . . . @3.00	

DH/Maverick, Mar., 2000
1 (of 12) MWg, rep. from 1986 . . . . 3.00	
2 thru 6 MWg . . . . @3.00	
7 MWg,V:Tujiro XIV 3.00	
8 MWg,back to N.Y. 3.00	
9 MWg,F:Dominic Riley 3.00	
10 MWg 3.00	
11 MWg 3.00	
12 MWg, concl. 3.00	

GRENDEL: DEVIL'S REIGN
May, 2004
1 (of 7) MWg. 3.50	
2 thru 7 . . . . @3.50	

GRENDEL:
GOD AND THE DEVIL
Jan., 2003
0 MWg,TSe. 3.50	
1 MWg (of 10). 3.50	
2 thru 9 MWg . . . . @3.50	
10 MWg, concl., 48-pg. 5.00	

GRENDEL:
RED, WHITE, & BLACK
DH Maverick, Sept., 2002
1 (of 4) 48-pg. B&W 5.00	
2 MWg,KJo,DIB 5.00	
3 . . . . 5.00	
4 MWg 5.00	

GRENDEL TALES:
DEVIL'S APPRENTICE
Sept., 1997
1 (of 3) 3.00	
2 thru 3 . . . . @3.00	

GRENDEL TALES:
DEVILS AND DEATHS
1994
1 . . . . 3.00	
2 . . . . 3.00	

GRENDEL TALES:
DEVIL'S CHOICES
1995
1 F:Goran 3.00	
2 thru 4 . . . . @3.00	

GRENDEL TALES:
FOUR DEVILS, ONE HELL
1 MWg(c),F:Four Grendels. 3.50	
2 MWg(c),F:Four Grendels. 3.50	
3 MWg(c),F:Four Grendels. 3.50	
4 MWg(c),F:Four Grendels. 3.50	
5 MWg(c),F:Four Grendels. 3.50	
6 MWg(c),last issue 3.25	

Grendel Tales, The Devil' in Our Midst
#2 © Dark Horse Comics

GRENDEL TALES: HOMECOMING
1994
1 Babylon Crash 3.00
2 Babylon Crash,pt. 2 . . . . 3.00
3 Too Dead To Die 3.00

GRENDEL TALES: THE DEVIL IN OUR MIDST
1994
1 MWg(c) 3.50
2 MWg(c) 3.25
3 thru 5 . . . . @3.00

GRENDEL TALES: THE DEVIL MAY CARE
1995
1 thru 6 mini-series 3.00

GRENDEL TALES: THE DEVIL'S HAMMER
1994
1 MWg(a&s),I:Petrus Christus 3.50
2 MWg(a&s),A:P.Christus 3.25
3 MWg(a&s),last issue 3.25

GRENDEL: WAR CHILD
1992
1 MWg 4.00
2 thru 9 MWg 3.00
10 MWg, final issue, dbl.size 4.00

GRIFTER AND THE MASK
Sept., 1996
1 by Seagle, Lima & Pimentel 2.50
2 . . . . 2.50

GROO: HELL ON EARTH
Sept., 2007
1 (of 4) SA 3.00
2 thru 4 SA . . . . @3.00
Spec. Groo 25th Anniv. Special 6.00

GUFF
Apr., 1998
1-shot by Sergio Aragones, flip
  book, with Meanie Babies
  card, B&W 2.50

GUNSMITH CATS
(B&W–Manga) 1995
1 I:Rally & Mini May 3.00
2 Revolver Freak 3.00
3 . . . . 3.00
4 V:Bonnie and Clyde 3.00
5 V:Bonnie and Clyde 3.00
6 Hostage Situation 3.00
7 thru 10 (10 part series) 3.00

GUNSMITH CATS: BAD TRIP
(B&W) June, 1998
1 (of 6) by Kenichi Sonoda 3.00
2 thru 6 . . . . @3.00

GUNSMITH CATS: BEAN BANDIT
(B&W) June, 1998
1 (of 9) by Kenichi Sonoda 3.00
2 thru 9 . . . . @3.00

GUNSMITH CATS: GOLDIE VS. MISTY
(B&W) Nov., 1997
1 (of 7) by Kenichi Sonoda 3.00
2 thru 7 . . . . @3.00

GUNSMITH CATS: KIDNAPPED
Nov., 1999
1 (of 10) by Kenichi Sonoda 3.00
2 thru 10 . . . . @3.00

GUNSMITH CATS: MISTER V
(B&W) Oct., 2000
1 (of 11) by Kenichi Sonoda 3.50
2 thru 11 . . . . @3.50
Spec. 3.00

GUNSMITH CATS: SHADES OF GRAY
(B&W) May, 1997
1 (of 5) by Kenichi Sonoda 3.00
2 thru 5 (of 5) . . . . @3.00

GUNSMITH CATS: THE RETURN OF GRAY
(B&W) Aug., 1996
1 thru 7 by Kenichi Sonoda . . . . @3.00

HAMMER OF GOD: BUTCH
1994
1 thru 3 MBn . . . . @2.50

HAMMER OF GOD: PENTATHLON
1994
1 MiB(s),NV 2.50

THE HAMMER: UNCLE ALEX
Aug., 1998
1-shot KJo 3.00

HAPPY BIRTHDAY MARTHA WASHINGTON
1995
1 Frank Miller 3.00

HARD BOILED
1990
1 GfD 7.00
2 and 3 . . . . @6.00

HARD LOOKS
(B&W) 1992
1 thru 10 AVs Adaptations . . . . . . @2.50
Book One 15.00

HARLAN ELLISON'S DREAM CORRIDOR
1995
1 Various stories 3.00
2 Various stories 3.00
3 JBy, I Have No Mouth and I
  Must Scream & other stories . . . 3.00
4 thru 6 . . . . @3.00
Spec.#1 Various stories 5.00
Spec. Quarterly, vol. 1 . . . . 6.00

Spec. Quarterly, vol. 2 . . . . 6.00

HAUNTED MAN, THE
Mar., 2000
1 (of 3) GJ,MBg 3.00
2 GJ,MBg 3.00
3 . . . . 3.00

HEARTBREAKERS
1996
1 . . . . 3.00
2 thru 4 . . . . @3.00

HEART OF EMPIRE: THE LEGACY OF LUTHER ARKWRIGHT
Apr., 1999
1 (of 9) BT 3.00
2 thru 5 . . . . @3.00
6 plot against royal family 3.50
7 countdown to cataclysm 3.50
8 . . . . 3.50
9 conclusion 3.00

HELL
DH Rocket Comics, July, 2003
1 BAu 3.00
2 thru 4 BAu . . . . @3.00

HELLBOY
Christmas Special (1997) MMi,
  48-pg 5.00
Spec. The Corpse and the
  Iron Shoes (1996) 4.00
Spec. The Wolves of St. August . . . 4.00
Hellboy Junior Halloween Special . . 4.00
Hellboy Junior Lurid Easter Special . 4.00
1-shot The Corpse 2.50
GN Animated Vol.1 Black
  Wedding Dress 7.00
GN Animated Vol. 2 Judgment Bell . 7.00
GN Animated Vol. 3 Menagerie 7.00

HELLBOY: ALMOST COLOSSUS
DH Legend, 1997
1 (of 2) MMi, sequel to *Wake the
  Devil* 4.00
2 (of 2) 4.00

Hellboy Almost Colosus #2
© *Dark Horse Comics*

HELLBOY: BOX FULL OF EVIL
Aug., 1999
1 (of 2) MMi 4.00
2 MMi, conclusion 4.00

HELLBOY: CONQUEROR WORM
May, 2001
1 (of 4) MMi 4.00
2 thru 4 . . . . @4.00

HELLBOY: THE CROOKED MAN
July, 2008
1 (of 3) RCo 4.00
2 thru 3 . . . . @4.00
1-shot In the Chapel of Moloch 4.00

HELLBOY: DARKNESS CALLS
Apr., 2007
1 (of 6) MMi . . . . @4.00
2 thru 6 . . . . @4.00

HELLBOY: THE ISLAND
June, 2005
1 and 2 MMi . . . . @4.00

HELLBOY: MAKOMA
Feb., 2006
1 MMi,RCo 4.00
2 MMi,RCo 4.00

HELLBOY: SEEDS OF DESTRUCTION
DH Legend, 1994
1 JBy,MMi,AAd,V:Vampire Frog,
 BU:Monkeyman & O'Brien 5.00
2 MMi(c),JBy,AAd,BU:Monkeyman
 & O'Brien 4.00
3 MMi(c),JBy,AAd,BU:Monkeyman
 & O'Brien 4.00
4 MMi(c),JBy,AAd,BU:Monkeyman
 & O'Brien 4.00

Hellboy: Wake the Devil #1
© Dark Horse Comics

HELLBOY: THE THIRD WISH
July, 2002
1 and 2 (of 2) MMi . . . . @4.00

HELLBOY: WAKE THE DEVIL
DH Legend, 1996
1 thru 5 (of 5) MMi . . . . @4.00

HELLBOY: WEIRD TALES
Feb., 2003
1 FaN 4.00
2 thru 8 . . . . @4.00

HELLBOY JR.
October 1999
1 and 2 (of 2) MMi . . . . @4.00

HELLGATE: LONDON
Oct., 2006
0 IEd 3.00
1 (of 4) IEd 3.00
2 thru 3 IEd . . . . @3.00

HELLHOUNDS
(B&W) 1994
1 I:Hellhounds 3.00
2 and 3 . . . . @3.00
Becomes:

HELLHOUNDS: PANZER CORPS
3 thru 6 . . . . @3.00

HELM, THE
Jan., 2008
1 thru 4 . . . . @3.50

HERBIE
1992
1 JBy,reps.& new material 3.00
2 Reps.& new material 2.50

HERETIC, THE
Nov., 1996
1 (of 4) by Rich DiLeonardo, Joe
 Phillips & Dexter Vines 3.00
2 thru 4 . . . . @3.00

HERMES VS. THE EYEBALL KID
1994
1 thru 3 Symphony of Blood 3.00

HERO ZERO
1994
1 First and last issue 2.50

HIEROGLYPH
Nov., 1999
1 RdD,F:Francisco Chavez 3.00
2 thru 4 RdD . . . . @3.00

HOMICIDE
(B&W) 1990
Spec. JAr,DoM 2.50

THE HORROR OF COLLIER COUNTY
Oct., 1999
1 (of 5) Halloween special 3.00
2 thru 5 concl. . . . . @3.00

HYPERSONIC
Nov., 1997
1 (of 4) DAn,GEr 3.00
2 thru 4 . . . . @3.00

INCREDIBLES, THE
Nov., 2004
1 thru 4 . . . . @3.00

INDIANA JONES AND THE ARMS OF GOLD
1994
1 In South America 4.00
2 In South America 4.00
3 V:Incan Gods 4.00
4 . . . . 4.00

INDIANA JONES AND THE FATE OF ATLANTIS
1991
1 DBa,Search for S.Hapgood with
 2-card strip 5.00
1a 2nd printing 3.00
2 DBa,Lost Dialogue of Plato with
 2-card strip 4.00
3 Map Room of Atlantis 4.00
4 Atlantis, Last issue 4.00

INDIANA JONES AND THE GOLDEN FLEECE
1994
1 thru 2 SnW . . . . @5.00

INDIANA JONES AND THE IRON PHOENIX
1994
1 . . . . 4.00
2 V:Nazis 4.00
3 A:Nadia Kirov 4.00
4 V:Undead 4.00

INDIANA JONES AND THE KINGDOM OF THE CRYSTAL SKULL
May, 2008
1 (of 2) Movie adapt. 6.00
2 . . . . 6.00

Indiana Jones and the Fate of Atlantis
#1 © Dark Horse Comics

DARK HORSE

INDIANA JONES AND THE SARGASSO PIRATES
1995
1 thru 4 . . . . @5.00

INDIANA JONES AND THE SHRINE OF THE SEA DEVIL
199
1 . . . . 4.00

INDIANA JONES AND THE SPEAR OF DESTINY
1995
1 I:Spear T/Pierced Christ 5.00
2 DSp, with Henry Jones 5.00
3 Search for the Shaft. 5.00
4 concl. 5.00

INDIANA JONES: THUNDER IN THE ORIENT
1993
1 DBa(a&s),in Tripoli. 4.00
2 DBa(a&s),Muzzad Ram. 4.00
3 DBa(a&s),V:Sgt.Itaki 4.00
4 DBa(a&s),In Hindu Kush 4.00
5 DBa(a&s),V:Japanese Army 4.00
6 DBa(a&s),last issue 4.00

INDIANA JONES AND THE TOMB OF THE GODS
June, 2008
1 thru 4 . . . . @4.00

INSANE
(B&W) 1988
1 and 2 . . . . @3.00

INSTANT PIANO
(B&W) 1994
1 Offbeat humor 4.00
2 . . . . 4.00
3 Various stories 4.00
4 Devil Puppet 4.00

INVINCIBLE ED:
2003
1 The Beating of Ed 3.50
2 I'm Too Sexy 4.00
3 Lance Lundgrin Unleashes 3.00
4 The End 3.00

IRONHAND OF ALMURIC
(B&W) 1991
1 Robert E. Howard adaption 2.50
2 A:Cairn,V:Yagas. 2.50
3 V:Yasmeena,The Hive Queen . . . 2.50
4 Conclusion 2.50

JAMES BOND 007: QUASIMODO GAMBIT
1995
1 I:Maximillion Quasimodo 4.00
2 V:Fanatical Soldiers 4.00
3 V:Steel 4.00

JAMES BOND 007: SERPENT'S TOOTH
1992
1 PG,DgM,V:Indigo 5.50

2 PG,DgM,V:Indigo 5.00
3 PG,DgM 5.25

JAMES BOND 007: SHATTERED HELIX
1994
1 V:Cerberus. 3.00
2 V:Cerberus. 3.00

JAMES BOND 007: A SILENT ARMAGEDDON
1993
1 V:Troy. 3.25
2 & 3 V:Omega . . . . @3.25

JINGLE BELLE
Nov., 2004
1 . . . . 3.00
2 thru 4 . . . . @3.00
1-shot-The Fight Before Christmas . 3.00

JOHN BOLTON'S STRANGE WINK
Mar., 1998
1 (of 3) 3.00
2 thru 3 . . . . @3.00

JOHNNY DYNAMITE
1994
1 . . . . 3.00
2 thru 4 . . . . @3.00

JOKER/MASK
May, 2000
1 (of 4) Batman x-over 3.00
2 Joker becomes Joker/Mask. 3.00
3 A:Harley Quinn, Poison Ivy 3.00
4 three nuclear bombs, concl. 3.00

JONNY DEMON
1994
1 SL(c),KBk,NV. 2.75
2 SL(c),KBk,NV. 2.75
3 SL(c),KBk,NV, final issue. 2.50

JOSS WHEDON'S FRAY
June, 2001
1 (of 8) 3.00
1a gold foil (c). 10.00
1b gold foil (c) signed 25.00
2 thru 8 . . . . @3.00
1 thru 6 2nd printings . . . . @3.00

JUDGE DREDD VS. ALIENS: INCUBUS
Mar., 2003
1 (of 4) 3.00
2 thru 4 . . . . @3.00

JUNIOR CARROT PATROL
(B&W) 1989
1 and 2 . . . . @3.00

KARAS
Nov., 2004
1-shot 3.00

KELLEY JONES' THE HAMMER
Sept., 1997
1 (of 4) KJo, horror series. 3.00
2 thru 4 KJo, ... @3.00

KELLEY JONES' THE HAMMER: THE OUTSIDER
Feb., 1999
1 (of 3) KJo 3.00
2 and 3 . . . . @3.00

KELLEY JONES' THE HAMMER: UNCLE ALEX
1998
1-shot 3.00

KINGS OF THE NIGHT
1990
1 Robert E. Howard adapt. 2.50
2 end Mini-Series 2.50

King Tiger/Motorhead #1
© *Dark Horse Comics*

KING TIGER/MOTORHEAD
1996
1 (of 2) by D.G. Chichester, Karl
  Waller & Eric Shanower 3.00
2 . . . . 3.00

KISS
July, 2002
1 JoC 4.00
2 thru 4 JoC . . . . @3.00
5 . . . . 3.00
6 . . . . 3.00
7 thru 10 SLo . . . . @3.00
11 . . . . 3.00
12 . . . . 3.00
13 MRn 3.00
1a thru 13a photo (c) . . . . @3.00

KONG
Oct., 2005
1 Movie adapt. (2005). 4.00
2 thru 3 . . . . @4.00

KULL
Nov., 2008
1 (of 6) The Shadow Kingdom 3.00

DARK HORSE

LAND OF NOD
(B&W) July, 1997
1 (of 4) by Jay Stephens 3.00
2 thru 4 . . . . @3.00

LAST TRAIN
TO DEADSVILLE
2004
1 (of 4) F:Cal McDonald 3.00
2 thru 4 . . . . @3.00

THE LEGEND OF
MOTHER SARAH
(B&W–Manga) 1995
1 I:Mother Sarah 4.00
2 Sarah and Tsutsu 4.00
3 Firing Squad 4.00
4 F:Toki 4.00
5 Yunnel Town 4.00
6 Kill or Be Killed 4.00
7 Firing Squad 4.00
8 Conclusion 4.00

THE LEGEND OF
MOTHER SARAH:
CITY OF THE ANGELS
(B&W–Manga) Oct., 1996
1 (of 9) by Katsuhiro Otomo and
　Takumi Nagayasu, 48-pg. 4.25
1 rep. (1997) 4.25
2 thru 4 . . . . 4.25
2 thru 4 rep. (1997) 4.25
5 Tsue a victim 4.25
6 Mother Teres questioned 4.25
7 put in front trenches 4.25
8 Teres suicide run 4.25
9 concl., 32-pg. 3.25

THE LEGEND OF
MOTHER SARAH:
CITY OF THE CHILDREN
(B&W–Manga) 1996
1 thru 4 (7 part mini-series) . . . . . @4.25
5 thru 7 . . . . @4.00

LITTLE LULU
(B&W) May, 2005
1 My Dinner with Lulu 10.00

Legend of Mother Sarah, City of the Angels #9 © Dark Horse Comics

2 Sunday Afternoon 10.00
3 In The Doghouse 10.00
4 Lulu Goes Shopping 10.00
5 Lulu Takes a Trip 10.00
6 Letters to Santa 10.00
7 Lulu's Umbrella Service 10.00
8 Late for School 10.00
9 Luck Lulu 10.00
10 All Dressed Up 10.00
11 April Fools 10.00
12 Leave it to Lulu 10.00
13 Too Much Fun 10.00
17 The Valentine 10.00

LIVING WITH THE DEAD
Oct., 2007
1 (of 3) RCo(c) 3.00
2 RCo(c) 3.00
3 RCo(c) 3.00

LOBSTER JOHNSON:
THE IRON PROMETHEUS
Sept., 2007
1 (of 5) MMi 3.00
2　thru 5 . . . . @3.00

LONE
DH Rocket Comics, Sept., 2003
thru 6 . . . . @3.00

LONE GUNMEN, THE
June, 2001
1-shot 3.00
1-shot photo(c) 3.00
1-shot photo (c) lim ed. 7.00
1-shot photo (c) lim ed. signed . . . 20.00

LONE WOLF 2100
May, 2002
1 (of 4) War Spore 4.00
2 thru 4 War Spore . . . . @3.00
5 thru 11 . . . . @3.00
1-shot The Red File 3.00

LORDS OF MISRULE
(B&W) Jan., 1997
1 by DAn, PSj 3.00
2 thru 6 . . . . @3.00

LOST IN SPACE
Apr., 1998
1 (of 3) sequel to film 3.00
2 thru 3 GEr(c) . . . . @3.00

LOVE ME TENDERLOIN
Jan., 2004
1-shot F:Cal McDonald 3.00

LUX AND ALBY
SIGN ON AND SAVE
THE UNIVERSE
(B&W) 1993
1 . . . . 3.00
2 thru 9 . . . . @3.00

THE MACHINE
Comics Greatest World, 1994
1 (a) The Barb Wire spin 2.50
2 V:Salvage 2.50
3 Freak Show 2.50
4 I:Skion 2.50

MADMAN
DH Legend, 1994
1 MiA(s) 8.00

2 MiA(s) 6.00
3 MiA(s) 5.00
4 MiA(s),Muscleman 5.00
5 MiA(s),I:The Blast 4.00
6 MiA(s),A:Big Guy, Big Brain-
　o-rama,pt.1 . . . . 12.00
7 MiA(s),FM,A:Big Guy, Big Brain-
　o-rama,pt.2 . . . . 6.00
8 MiA(s) 4.00
9 Micro Madman 4.00
10 . . . . 4.00
11 . . . . 4.00
Apr., 1999
12 MiA 3.00
13 MiA 3.00
14 MiA 3.00
15 MiA 3.00
16 MiA 3.00
G-Men From Hell (Aug., 2000)
17 Pt.1 MiA 3.00
18 Pt.2 MiA, Is Frank Einstein
　dead? 3.00
19 Pt.3 MiA 3.00
20 Pt.4 MiA, V:Mr.Monstadt 3.00

MADMAN/THE JAM
July, 1998
1and 2 MiA . . . . @3.00

Magic the Gathering #1
© Dark Horse Comics

MAGIC: THE GATHERING
Mar., 1998
1 (of 4) MGr,Initiation 3.00
2 MGr, Legacy 3.00
3 MGr, Crucible 3.00
4 MGr, Destiny 3.00

MAGNUS/NEXUS
DH/Valiant
1 and 2 MBn(s), SR . . . . @3.25

MANGA DARKCHYLDE
Feb., 2005
1 thru 3 . . . . @3.00

MAN WITH
THE SCREAMING BRAIN
2005
1 (of 4) 3.00
2 thru 4 . . . . @3.00
1a thru 4a Variant(c) . . . . @3.00

MARK, THE
1987–89
1 LSn, ... 3.00
2 & 3 LSn . . . . @3.00
4 thru 6 . . . . @3.00

[Second Series] 1993
1 MiB(s),in America,V:Archon. 3.00
2 MiB(s),V:Archon. 3.00
3 MiB(s),V:Archon,A:Pierce 3.00
4 MiB(s),last issue 3.00

MARSHALL LAW
GN Super Babylon, KON (1992) . . . 5.00
1-shot Marshall Law: Cape Fear . . . 3.00

MARSHALL LAW:
SECRET TRIBUNAL
1993
1 KON. 3.00
2 KON. 3.00

MARTHA WASHINGTON
DIES
July., 2007
1-shot 3.50

MARTHA WASHINGTON
GOES TO WAR
DH Legend, 1994
1 FM(s),DGb, V:Fat Boys Corp. . . . 3.25
2 FM(s),DGb, V:Fat Boys Corp. . . . 3.25
3 FM(s),DGb, V:Fat Boys Corp. . . . 3.25
4 FM(s),DGb, V:Fat Boys Corp. . . . 3.25
5 FM(s),DBb, final issue 3.25

MARTHA WASHINGTON
SAVES THE WORLD
Dec., 1997
1 (of 3) FM,DGb 3.25
2 thru 3 . . . . @3.25

MARTHA WASHINGTON
STRANDED IN SPACE
1995
1 . . . . 3.25

MARTIN MYSTRY
(B&W) DH/Bonelli, Mar., 1999
1 by Alfredo Castelli & Giancarlo
  Alessandrini, DGb(c) 92-pg. . . . 5.00
2 thru 6 . . . . @5.00

MASAKAZU KATSURA'S
SHADOW LADY
(B&W–Manga) Oct., 1998
Dangerous Love
1 (of 7) Masakazu Katsura 2.50
2 thru 7 . . . . @2.50
The Eyes of a Stranger, May, 1999
8 thru 12, pt.1–pt.5 . . . . @2.50
The Awakening
13 thru 19, pt.1–pt.7. . . . . @2.50
Sudden Death
20 thru 24, pt.1–pt.5. . . . . @2.50
Spec.48-pg. final issue. 4.00

MASK, THE
1991
0 'Who's Laughing Now' (B&W) . . . 6.00
1 I:Lt.Kellaway Mask 5.00
2 V:Rapaz & Walter 5.00
3 O:Mask 5.00
4 final issue. 5.00

MASK, THE
1994
1 Movie Adaptation 3.00
2 Movie Adaptation 2.50

MASK , THE
[Mini-series] 1995
The Mask Strikes Back (1995)
1 Mask Strikes Back,pt.1 . . . . 2.50
2 Mask Strikes Back,pt.2 . . . . 2.50
3 Mask Strikes Back,pt.3 . . . . 2.50
4 DoM,Mask Strikes Back,pt.4 . . . 2.50
5 Mask Strikes Back,pt.5 . . . . 2.50
The Hunt for Green October (1995)
6 Pt.1 . . . . 2.50
7 Pt.2 Kellaway vs. Ray Tuttle 2.50
8 Pt.3 F:Emily Tuttle 2.50
9 Pt.4 final issue 2.50
World Tour (1995)
10 thru 13 Pt.1–Pt 4 . . . . @2.50
Southern Discomfort (1996)
14 Pt.1 Mardi Gras time. 2.50
15 Pt.2 . . . . 2.50
16 Pt.3 . . . . 2.50
17 Pt.4 . . . . 2.50

MASK/MARSHALL LAW
Feb., 1998
1 (of 2) by Pat Mills and Kevin
  O'Neill 3.00
2 concl. 3.00

MASK RETURNS, THE
1992
1 inc.cut-out Mask. 5.00
2 Mask's crime spree 4.00
3 . . . . 4.00
4 . . . . 4.00

MASK: TOYS IN
THE ATTIC
Aug., 1998
1 (of 4) 3.00
2 thru 4 . . . . @3.00

MASK, THE:
VIRTUAL SURREALITY
1997
1-shot F: MMi,SA 3.00

MAXIMUM OVERLOAD
1 Masque (Mask) 12.00
2 thru 4 Mask . . . . @8.00

MAXIMUM OVERLOAD
1 . . . . 4.00
2 thru 5. . . . . @4.00

MAYHEM
1989
1 F:The Mask, The Mark 5.00
2 thru 4 . . . . @4.00

MECHA
Comics Greatest World, 1995
1 color. 3.00
2 color. 3.00
3 thru 6 B&W. . . . . @3.00
Spec.(#1) CW(c),color. 3.00

MEDAL OF HONOR
1994
1 Ace of Aces 2.50
2 . . . . 2.50
3 Andrew's Raid 2.50
4 Frank Miller(c) 2.50

5 final issue. 2.50
Spec. #1 JKu (1994) 2.50

MEZZ GALACTIC
TOUR 2494
1994
1 MBn,MV. 2.50

MICHAEL CHABON
PRESENTS THE
AMAZING ADVENTURES
OF THE ESCAPIST
Dec., 2003
1 Michael Chabon, 80-pg. 9.00
2 thru 9 . . . . @9.00

MIKE MIGNOLA'S
B.P.R.D.: HOLLOW EARTH
Jan., 2002
1 (of 3) 3.00
2 . . . . 3.00
3 . . . . 3.00
1-shot Something Under My Bed . . 3.00
1-shot The Soul of Venice 3.00
1-shot Dark Waters 3.00
1-shot Night Train 3.00

MILKMAN MURDERS, THE
July, 2004
1 JoC,SvP. 3.00
2 thru 4 JoC,SvP. . . . . @3.00

MR. MONSTER
(B&W) 1988
1 . . . . 4.00
2 . . . . 3.00
3 Alan Moore story 3.00
4 . . . . 3.00
5 I:Monster Boy. 3.00
6 . . . . 3.00
7 . . . . 3.00
8 V:Vampires (giant size) 5.00

MONKEYMAN & O'BRIEN
DH Legend, 1996
1 by Arthur Adams 3.00
2 and 3 . . . . @3.00
Spec. 3.00

Monkeyman and Obrien #2
© Dark Horse Comics

All comics prices listed are for *Near Mint* condition.

MONSTERS, INC.
Oct., 2001
1-shot 56-pg., Disney-Pixar 5.00

MORPHOS
THE SHAPE CHANGER
July, 1996
1-shot BHg. 5.00

MOTORHEAD
Comics Greatest World, 1995
1 V:Predator 2.50
2 Laughing Wolf Carnival 2.50
3 V:Jackboot 2.50
4 thru 6 . . . . @2.50
Spec.#1 JLe(c),V:Mace Blitzkrieg
  (1994) 4.00

MY NAME IS BRUCE
Dec., 2007
1-shot 3.00
1-shot My Name is Bruce (11-2008) 3.50

[BOB BURDEN'S ORIGINAL] MYSTERYMEN
July, 1999
1 . . . . 3.00
2 The Amazing Disc Man 3.00
3 F:Screwball 3.00
4 All Villain Comics #1 . . . . 3.50

MYSTERY MEN
July, 1999
1 (of 2) Movie adapt. 3.00
2 movie adaptation, concl. 3.00

MYST: THE BOOK OF THE BLACK SHIPS
Aug., 1997
1 (of 4) from CD-Rom game. 3.00
2 thru 4 . . . . @3.00

NAIL, THE
June, 2004
1 (of 4) 3.00
2 thru 4 . . . . @3.00

Nathan Never #1
© Dark Horse Comics

NATHAN NEVER
(B&W) DH/Bonelli, Mar., 1999
1 (of 6) by Michele Medda & Nicola
  Mari, AAd(c) 102-pg. 5.00
2 . . . . 5.00
3 . . . . 5.00
4 . . . . 5.00
5 . . . . 5.00
6 . . . . 5.00

NEVERMEN, THE
May, 2000
1 (of 4) GyD, V:Clockwork 3.00
2 GyD,V:Honshu. 3.00
3 GyD,V:Clockwork. 3.00
4 GyD,V:League of Crows 3.00

NEVERMEN, THE: STREETS OF BLOOD
Jan., 2003
1 thru 3 (of 3) GyD . . . . @3.00

NEW FRONTIER
(B&W) 1992
1 From series in Heavy Metal. 2.75
2 Who Killed Ruby Fields? 2.75
3 Conclusion. 2.75

NEW TWO FISTED TALES: VOL II
1993
1 War stories. 5.00

[JOHN BYRNE'S] NEXT MEN
1992
0 Rep Next Men from Dark Horse
  Presents 5.00
1 JBy,'Breakout'inc.trading card
  certificate 5.00
1a 2nd Printing Blue 3.00
2 JBy,World View 4.00
3 JBy,A:Sathanis. 4.00
4 JBy,A:Sathanis. 4.00
5 JBy,A:Sathanis. 4.00
6 JBy,O:Senator Hilltop,
  Sathanis,Project Next Men 3.50
7 JBy,I:M-4,Next Men Powers
  explained 3.50
8 JBy,I:Omega Project,A:M-4 . . . . 3.00
9 JBy,A:Omega Project,A:M-4 . . . 3.00
10 JBy,V:OmegaProject,A:M-4 . . . 3.00
11 JBy,V:OmegaProject,A:M-4. . . . 3.00
12 JBy,V:Dr.Jorgenson. 3.00
13 JBy,Nathan vs Jack 3.00
14 JBy,I:Speedboy 3.00
15 JBy,in New York 3.00
16 JBy,Jasmine's Pregnant 3.00
17 FM(c),JBy,Arrested 3.00
18 JBy,On Trial 3.00
Next Men: Faith (1993)
19 Faith, pt.1 JBy(a&s),V:Dr.
  Trogg, Blue Dahila. 3.25
20 Faith, pt.2 JBy,(a&s),F:Jack . . . 3.00
21 Faith,pt.3 MMi(c),JBy(a&s),
  I:Hellboy. 35.00
22 Faith,pt.4 JBy(a&s),Last issue . . 3.00
Next Men: Power (1994)
23 Power,pt.1, JBy(a&s) 2.75
24 Power,pt.2, JBy(a&s) 2.75
25 Power,pt.3, JBy(a&s) 2.75
26 Power,pt.4, JBY(a&s) concl. 2.50
Next Men: Lies (1994)
27 Lies,pt.1,JBy 2.50
28 Lies,pt.2,JBy 2.50
29 Lies,pt.3,JBy 2.50
30 Lies,pt.4, JBy 2.50

Next Men #11
© Dark Horse Comics

NEXUS: ALIEN JUSTICE
1992
1 . . . . 4.25
2 . . . . 4.25
3 . . . . 4.00

NEXUS: EXECUTIONER'S SONG
1996
1 (of 4) by Mike Baron, Steve
  Rude & Gary Martin 3.00
2 thru 4 . . . . @3.00

NEXUS: GOD CON
Apr., 1997
1 (of 2) 3.00
2 . . . . 3.00

NEXUS: THE LIBERATOR
1992
1 'Waking Dreams' 3.00
2 Civil War,D:Gigo 3.00
3 Civil War contd. 3.00
4 Last issue. 3.00

NEXUS MEETS MADMAN
1996
1-shot. 3.00

NEXUS: NIGHTMARE IN BLUE
(B&W) July, 1997
1 (of 4) MBn,SR,GyM 3.00
2 thru 4 . . . . @3.00

NEXUS: THE ORIGIN
1995
1 SR,O:Nexus. 5.00

NEXUS: OUT OF THE VORTEX
1 R:Nexus. 3.00
2 Zolot & Nexus Together. 3.00
3 O:Vortex. 3.00

NEXUS:
THE WAGES OF SIN
1995
1 The Client 3.00
2 V:Munson 3.00
3 SR(c&a) Murders in New Eden . . 3.00
4 . . . . 3.00

NIGHT BEFORE
CHRISTMASK
1 Rick Geary 10.00

NINA'S NEW AND
IMPROVED ALL-TIME
GREATEST
1994
1 Anthology: Nina Paley 2.50

NINTH GLAND, THE
(B&W) Mar., 1997
1-shot by Renee French 4.00

NOCTURNALS:
WITCHING HOUR
May, 1998
1-shot by Dan Brereton 5.00

NOSFERATU
(B&W) 1991
1 The Last Vampire. 4.00
2 . . . . 3.00

OH MY GODDESS!
(B&W–Manga) 1994
1 by Kosuke Fujishima. 5.00
2 & 3 . . . . @4.00
4 thru 6 . . . . @3.00

Part II, 1995
1 F:Keiichi. 4.00
2   thru 9. . . . . @3.00

Part III, 1996
1 Wishes are Granted. 3.00
2 Love Potion Number 9. . . . . 3.00
3 thru 5 . . . . @3.00
6 thru 11 Terrible Master Urd,
    pt.1 thru pt.6 . . . . @3.00

Part IV, 1996–97
1 Robot Wars 3.00
2 The Trials of Morisato,pt.1 . . . . . 3.00
3 The Trials of Morisato,pt.2 . . . . . 3.00
4 The Trials of Morisato,pt.3 . . . . . 3.00
5 The Queen of Vengeance 3.00
6 Mara Strikes Back,pt.1,48-pg. . . 4.00
7 Mara Strikes Back,pt.2. . . . . 3.00
8 Mara Strikes Back,pt.3. . . . . 3.00

Part V, 1997–98
1 The Forgotten Promise 3.00
2 The Lunch Box of Love 3.00
3 Meet Me by the Seashore, 48-pg.4.00
4 You're So Bad, 48-pg. 4.00
5 Ninja Master,pt.1 . . . . 3.00
6 Ninja Master,pt.2, 48-pg. 4.00
7 Miss Keiichi,pt.1, 48-pg. 4.00
7 & 8 Miss Keiichi,pt.2 . . . . 3.00
9 It's Lonely at the Top 3.50
10 Fallen Angel, 48-pg. 4.00
11 Play the Game, 48-pg. 4.00
12 Sorrow, Fear Not. 4.00

Part VI, 1998–99
1 Devil in Miss Urd,pt.1, 40-pg. . . . 3.50
2 Devil in Miss Urd,pt.2. . . . . 3.00
3 Devil in Miss Urd,pt.3. . . . . 3.00
4 Devil in Miss Urd,pt.4. . . . . 3.00
5 Devil in Miss Urd,pt.5. . . . . 3.00

Oh My Goddess Part VII #3
© *Dark Horse Comics*

6 SuperUrd 3.00

Part VII, 1999
1 (of 8)The Fourth Goddess,pt.1 . . 3.00
2 The Fourth Goddess,pt.2. . . . . . 3.00
3 The Fourth Goddess,pt.3. . . . . . 3.00
4 The Fourth Goddess,pt.4,40-pg. . 3.50
5 The Fourth Goddess,pt.5,40-pg. . 3.50

Part VIII, 1999
1 (of 2) Childhood's End,
    by Kosuke Fujishima 3.50
2 Childhood's End,pt.2 . . . . 3.50
3 The Queen and the Goddess . . . 3.50
4 Hail to the Chief,pt.1 . . . . 3.50
5 Hail to the Chief,pt.2 . . . . 3.50
6 Hail to the Chief,pt.3 . . . . 3.50

Part IX, 2000
1 Pretty in Scarlet 3.00
2 The Goddess's Apprentice. 3.00
3 Queen Sayoko,pt.1 . . . . 3.00
4 Queen Sayoko,pt.2 . . . . 3.50
5 Queen Sayoko,pt.3 (of 5) 3.00
6 Queen Sayoko,pt.4 . . . . 3.00
7 Queen Sayoko,pt.5 . . . . 3.50

PART X, Feb., 2001
1 The Secret of Speed 3.50
2 The Secret of Speed,concl. 3.00
3 one-shot. 3.50
4 Hand in Hand,pt.1 . . . . 3.00
5 Hand in Hand,pt.2 . . . . 3.50

PART XI, Aug., 2001
1 Banpei in Love,pt.1 (of 2) 3.50
2 Banpei in Love,pt.2 . . . . 3.50
3 Mystery Child,pt.1 (of 8) 3.00
4 Mystery Child,pt.2 . . . . 3.00
5 Mystery Child,pt.3 . . . . 3.00
6 Mystery Child,pt.4 . . . . 3.00
7 Mystery Child,pt.5 . . . . 3.50
8 Mystery Child,pt.6 . . . . 3.50
9 Mystery Child,pt.7 . . . . 3.00
10 Mystery Child,pt.8, 48-pg.. . . . . 4.00

PART XII, July, 2002
1 (of 3) Learning to Love,pt.1 . . . . 3.50
2 Learning to Love,pt.2. . . . . 3.50
3 Learning to Love,pt.3. . . . . 3.50

Continuing series (Oct., 2002)
91 Traveler,pt.1 (of 5). 3.00
92 Traveler,pt.2. . . . . 3.00
93 Traveler, pt.3. . . . . 3.00
94 Traveler, pt.4. . . . . 3.00
95 Traveler, pt.5. . . . . 3.50
96 The Phantom Racer, pt.1 . . . . . . 3.00

97 The Phantom Racer, pt.2 . . . . . . 3.00
98 The Phantom Racer, pt.3 . . . . . . 3.00
99 The Phantom Racer, pt.4 . . . . . . 3.00
100 Dr. Moreau, pt.1 . . . . 3.00
101 Dr. Moreau, pt.2 . . . . 3.00
102 Dr. Moreau, pt.3 . . . . 3.00
103 Dr. Moreau, pt.4 . . . . 3.00
104 Dr. Moreau, pt.5 . . . . 3.50
105 Sora Unchained,pt.1 . . . . 3.00
106 thru 110 Sora,pt.2–pt.6   . . . @3.00
111 and 112 Sora Unchained,
    pt.7–pt.8, 48-pg. . . . . . . @4.00

OKTANE
1995
1 R:Oktane 2.50
2 V:God Zero 2.50
3 V:God Zero 2.50
4 conclusion 2.50

ONE BAD RAT
1 BT 3.00
2 thru 4 . . . . @3.00

ORION
(B&W–Manga) 1993
1 SF by Masamune Shirow 2.50
2 F:Yamata Empire 3.00
3 thru 6 . . . . @3.00

OTIS GOES HOLLYWOOD
(B&W) Apr., 1997
1 (of 2) by Bob Fingerman 3.00
2 . . . . 3.00

OUTER ORBIT
Dec., 2006
1 (of 4) 3.00
2 thru 4 . . . . @3.00

OUT FOR BLOOD
(B&W) 1999
1 (of 4) GEr,F:Dan Sanger 3.00
2 The Wings; The Claws 3.00
3 . . . . 3.00
4 concl. 3.00

OUTLANDERS
(B&W–Manga) 1988
1 . . . . 4.00
2 . . . . 3.00
3 thru 7 . . . . @3.00
8 thru 20 . . . . @3.00
21 Operation Phoenix 3.00
22 thru 24 . . . . @3.00
25 thru 29 with 2-card strip . . . . . @3.00
30 . . . . 2.75
31 Tetsua dying 2.75
32 D:The Emperor 2.75
33 Story finale 2.75
#0 The Key of Graciale 2.75

OUTLANDERS:
EPILOGUE
(B&W) 1994
1 . . . . 2.75

OUTLAW 7
Aug., 2001
1 thru 4 . . . . @3.00

OUT OF THE VORTEX
Comics' Greatest World, 1993
1 B:JOs(s),V:Seekers 2.50
2 MMi(c),DaW,A:Seekers 2.50
3 WS(c),E:JOs(s),DaW,A:Seeker,
    C:Hero Zero. 2.50

All comics prices listed are for *Near Mint* condition.

Out of the Vortex #1
© Dark Horse Comics

4 DaW,A:Catalyst 2.50
5 V:Destroyers,A:Grace 2.50
6 V:Destroyers,A:Hero Zero 2.50
7 AAd(c),DaW,V:Destroyers,
   A:Mecha 2.50
8 DaW,A:Motorhead 2.50
9 DaW,V:Motorhead 2.50
10 MZ(c), A:Division 13 . . . . 2.50
11 V:Reaver Swarm 2.50
12 Final issue 2.50

PENNY ARCADE
Dec., 2005
1 25-cent issue 1.00

PERHAPANAUTS, THE
Nov., 2005
1 (of 4) TDz 3.00
2 thru 4 . . . . @3.00

PERHAPANAUTS:
SECOND CHANCES
Oct., 2005
1 thru 4 (of 4) TDz . . . . @3.00

PIGEONS FROM HELL
Apr., 2008
1 thru 4 (of 4) by Joe Lansdale . . @3.00

PI: THE BOOK OF ANTS
Artisan Entertainment, 1998
1-shot, movie adapt. 3.00

PLANET OF THE APES:
THE HUMAN WAR
June, 2001
1 (of 3) IEd,with trading card 3.00
1a photo (c) 3.00
2 IEd,JSC 3.00
2a photo (c) 3.00
3 IEd,JSC 3.00
3a photo (c) 3.00

PLANET OF THE APES
Sept., 2001
1 IEd,MWg 3.00
1b gold foil photo(c) 9.00
1c gold foil photo(c) signed 25.00
2 IEd 3.00

3 IEd 3.00
4 DAn,IEd,Bloodlines,pt.1 (of 3) . . . 3.00
5 DAn,IEd,Bloodlines,pt.2 . . . . 3.00
6 DAn,IEd,Bloodlines,pt.3 . . . . 3.00
1a thru 6a photo(c) . . . . @3.00

PLANET OF THE APES
(MOVIE)
1-shot Movie adaptation 7.00
1-shotA Movie adapt, foil (c) 9.00
1-shotB Movie, foil(c) signed 25.00

PRAIRIE MOON
AND OTHER STORIES
(B&W) 1992
1-shot 2.50

PREDATOR
1989
1 CW,Mini Series 6.00
1a 2ndPrinting 3.00
2 CW 5.00
3 CW 4.00
4 CW 3.00
1 thru 4 later printings . . . . @3.00

PREDATOR
1-shot Predator: Invaders from the
   Fourth Dimension (1994) 4.00
1-shot Predator Jungle Tales,
   Rite of Passage (1995) 3.00
1-shot Predator: Strange Roux
   (1995) 3.00
1-shot Predator: Captive (1998) . . . 3.00
GN Predator Flesh and Blood 7.00

PREDATOR:
BAD BLOOD
1993
1 CW,I:John Pulnick 3.00
2 CW,V:Predator 3.00
3 CW,V:Predator,C.I.A. 3.00
4 Last issue 3.00

PREDATOR: BIG GAME
1991
1 Corp.Nakai Meets Predator 3.50
2 Army Base Destroyed, with
   2-card strip 3.50
3 Corp.Nakai Arrested, with
   2-card strip 3.50
4 Nakai vs. Predator 3.50

PREDATOR: BLOODY
SANDS OF TIME
1992
1 DBa,CW,Predator in WWI 3.50
2 DBa,CW, WWII cont'd. 3.25

PREDATOR: COLD WAR
1991
1 Predator in Siberia 3.50
2 U.S. Elite Squad in Siberia 3.25
3 U.S. vs. USSR commandos 3.25
4 U.S. vs. USSR in Siberia 3.00

PREDATOR:
DARK RIVER
1996
1 thru 4 by Verheiden,RoR,RM . . @3.00

PREDATOR:
HELL & HOT WATER
1997
1 thru 3 MSh, GC & GWt . . . . . . @3.00

PREDATOR:
HELL COME A WALKIN'
Feb., 1998
1 (of 2) by Nancy Collins,
   Dean Ormston 3.00
2 concl. 3.00

PREDATOR:
HOMEWORLD
Mar., 1999
1 (of 4) 3.00
2 thru 4 . . . . @3.00

PREDATOR: KINDRED
1996
1 . . . . 3.00
2 thru 4 . . . . @3.00

PREDATOR: NEMESIS
Dec., 1997
1 and 2 (of 2) TTg(c) . . . . @3.00

PREDATOR: PRIMAL
1997
1 (of 2) Kevin J. Anderson(s),
   ScK,Low 3.00
2 (of 2) 3.00

PREDATOR: RACE WAR
1993
0 F:Serial Killer 3.00
1 V:Serial Killer 3.00
2 D:Serial Killer 3.00
3 in Prison 3.00
4 Last Issue 3.00

PREDATOR 2
1991
1 DBy, Movie Adapt,pt1 . . . . 3.50
2 MBr, Movie Adapt.,pt2 with
   2-card strip 3.00

PREDATOR VS.
JUDGE DREDD
Sept., 1997
1 (of 3) by John Wagner and
   Enrique Alcatena 3.00
2 thru 3 . . . . @3.00

Predator: Vs. Judge Dredd #2
© Dark Horse Comics

DARK HORSE

PREDATOR VS. MAGNUS ROBOT FIGHTER
Valiant/Dark Horse 1992
1 LW,A:Tekla	3.00
1a Platinum Ed.	5.00
1b Gold Ed.	3.00
2 LW,Magnus Vs. Predator, with 2-card strip	3.00

PREDATOR: XENOGENESIS
Aug., 1999
1 (of 4)	3.00
2 IEd	3.00
3 IEd	3.00
4	3.00

PRIMAL
Oct., 1992
1 Contd.from Primal:from the Cradle to the Grave	3.00
2 A:TJ Cyrus	2.50
GN Primal From the Cradle to the Grave	10.00

PROPELLER MAN
1993
1 I:Propeller Man	3.00
2 O:Propeller Man,w/2 card strip	3.00
3 V:Manipulator	3.00
4 V:State Police,w/2 card strip	3.00
5 V:Manipulator	3.00
6 V:Thing, w/2 card strip	3.00
7	3.00
8 Last issue,w/2 card strip	3.00

PUBO
DH Maverick, Nov., 2002
1 (of 3) by Leland Purvis, B&W	3.50
2 thru 3	@3.50

PUMPKINHEAD: THE RITES OF EXORCISM
1992
1 Based on the movie	2.50
2 thru 4	@2.50

RACE OF SCORPIONS
(B&W) 1990
Book 1 short stories	5.00
Book 2	5.00

RACE OF SCORPIONS
(B&W) 1991
1 A:Argos,Dito,Alma,Ka	2.50
2 thru 4	@2.50

RACK & PAIN
1994
1 GCa(c),I:Rack,Pain	3.00
2 GCa(c),V:Web	3.00
3 GCa(c),V:Web	3.00
4 GCa(c),Final Issue	3.00

RASCALS IN PARADISE
1994
1 I:Spicy Sanders	4.00
2	4.00
3 last issue	4.00

REAL ADVENTURES OF JONNY QUEST, THE
Sept., 1996
1	3.00

2	3.00
3	3.00
4 thru 12	@3.00

REBEL SWORD
(B&W–Manga) 1994
1 by Yoshikazu Yashiko	2.50
2	2.50
3	2.50
4 V:Ruken	2.50
5 Choice of Jiro	2.50
6 R:Ruken	2.50

REDBLADE
1993
1 V:Demons	3.00
2 V:Tull	3.00
3 Last Issue	3.00

RED ROCKET 7
Aug., 1997
1 (of 7) MiA	4.00
2 thru 7	@4.00

REID FLEMING/ FLAMING CARROT
(B&W) Jan., 2003
1-Shot Reid Fleming/Flaming Carrot	4.00

RETURN OF THE GREMLINS
Oct., 2006
1 (of 3) MRi	3.00
2 thru 3 MRi	@3.00
Mar., 2008
1 (of 3)	3.00
2 thru 3	@3.00

REVEAL
Oct., 2002
1 64-pg.	7.00

REVELATIONS
Aug., 2005
1 (of 6) PJe,HuR	3.00
2 thru 6	@3.00

REX MUNDI
Aug., 2006
1	3.00
2 thru 8	@3.00
9 thru 12 GyD	@3.00
13 thru 14	@3.00

RING OF ROSES
(B&W) 1991
1 Alternate world,1991	2.50
2 Plague in London	2.50
3 Plague cont.A:Secret Brotherhood of the Rosy Cross	2.50
4 Conclusion	2.50

RING OF THE NIEBELUNG, THE:
DH Maverick, 2000
RHINEGOLD, Feb., 2000
1 (of 4) CR	3.00
2 CR	3.00
3 CR	3.00
4 CR, concl.	3.00
VALKYRIE Aug., 2000
1 (of 3) CR	3.00
2 CR	3.00
3 CR, concl.	3.00

SIEGFRIED, Dec., 2000
1 (of 3) CR	3.00
2 CR	3.00
3 CR, concl.	3.00
GOTTERDAMMERUNG June, 2001
1 (of 4) CR	3.00
2	3.00
3	3.00
4 finale, 64-pg.	6.00

RIO AT BAY
1992
1 F:Doug Wildey art	3.00
2 F:Doug Wildey art	3.00

R.I.P.D.
Nov., 1999
1 (of 4) F:Rest in Peace Dept.	3.00
2 thru 4	@3.00

RIPLEY'S BELIEVE IT OR NOT
June, 2002
1 (of 4) Into Thin Air	3.00
2 Grim Reaping	3.00
3 Human Wonders	3.00
4 Strange Invaders	3.00

ROACHMILL
(B&W) 1988
1	3.50
2 thru 8	@3.50
9 and 10	@3.00

ROBERT E. HOWARD'S CONAN: FRAZETTA COVER SERIES
Dec., 2007
1 (of 8) Frost Giant's Daughter	3.50
2 The God in the Bowl	6.00

ROBOCOP: MORTAL COILS
1993
1 V:Gangs	2.75
2 V:Gangs	2.75
3 V:Coffin,V:Gangs	2.75
4	2.75

GRANT • GNAZZO • PATTERSON

Robocop: Mortal Coils #2
© Dark Horse Comics

All comics prices listed are for *Near Mint* condition.

ROBOCOP VERSUS TERMINATOR
1992
1 FM(s),WS,w/Robocop cut-out . . . 3.50
2 FM(s),WS,w/Terminator cut-out . . 3.00
3 FM(s),WS,w/cut-out 3.00
4 FM(s),WS,Conclusion 3.00

ROBOCOP: PRIME SUSPECT
1992
1 Robocop framed 2.75
2 thru 4 V:ZED-309s . . . . @2.50

ROBOCOP: ROULETTE
1993
1 V:ED-309s 2.75
2 I:Philo Drut 2.75
3 V:Stealthbot 2.75
4 last issue 2.75

ROBOCOP 3
1993
1 B:StG(s),Movie Adapt 2.75
2 V:Aliens,OCP 2.75
3 HNg,ANi(i) 2.75

Rocketeer Adventure Magazine #3
© Dark Horse Comics

ROCKETEER ADVENTURE MAGAZINE
1988–95
1 and 2 . . . . @4.00
3 . . . . 3.00

ROCKSTAR GAMES' ONI
Feb., 2001
1 video-game tie-in 3.00
1a gold foil (c) 7.00
2 . . . . 3.00
3 concl. 3.00

THE SAFEST PLACE IN THE WORLD
1995
SC, SD 2.50

SAMURAI: HEAVEN AND EARTH
Dec., 2004
1 (of 5) 3.00
2 thru 5 . . . . @3.00
Vol. 2
1 (of 5) RMz 3.00
2 thru 5 RMz,LRs . . . . @3.00

SCARLET TRACES: THE GREAT GAME
July, 2006
1 IEd 3.00
2 thru 4 . . . . @3.00

SCATTERBRAIN
June, 1998
1 (of 4) MMi 3.00
2 thru 4 . . . . @3.00

SCREAM, THE
Nov., 2007
1 (of 4) PDd(s) 3.00
2 thru 4 PDd(s) . . . . @3.00

SCREWBALL SQUIRREL
July, 1995
1 . . . . 2.75
2 thru 3 . . . . @2.75

SCORPION KING, THE
Mar., 2002
1 (of 2) movie adapt. 3.00
1a photo (c). 3.00
2 (of 2) movie adapt. 3.00
2a photo (c). 3.00

SECRET, THE
Feb., 2007
1 (of 4) 3.00
2 thru 4 . . . . @3.00

SECRET OF THE SALAMANDER
(B&W)
1 Jacquestardi, rep 3.00

SERENITY
July, 2005
1 movie adapt. 8.00
2 thru 3 . . . . @8.00
1a&b thru 3a&b variant(c). . . . . @15.00

SERGIO ARAGONES ACTIONS SPEAK
Jan., 2001
1 (of 6) 3.00
2 thru 6 . . . . @3.00

SERGIO ARAGONES' BOOGEYMAN
(B&W) June, 1998
1 (of 4) 3.00
2 thru 4 . . . . @3.00

SERGIO ARAGONES' DAY OF THE DEAD
Oct., 1998
1-shot 3.00

SERGIO ARAGONES' GROO
Jan.–Apr., 1998
1 (of 4) 3.00
2 thru 4 . . . . @3.00

SERGIO ARAGONES' GROO & RUFFERTO
Dec., 1998
1 thru 4 . . . . @3.00

SERGIO ARAGONES' GROO: DEATH AND TAXES
DH Maverick, Dec., 2002
1 thru 4 . . . . @3.00

SERGIO ARAGONES' GROO: MIGHTIER THAN THE SWORD
Jan., 2000
1 (of 4) SA 3.00
2 SA,V:Pipil Khan 3.00
3 SA,V:Relmihio 3.00
4 SA,concl. 3.00

SERGIO ARAGONES' LOUDER THAN WORDS
(B&W) July–Dec., 1997
1 (of 6) SA 3.00
2 thru 6 . . . . @3.00

SERGIO STOMPS STAR WARS
2000
1-shot SA, parody 3.00

SEX WARRIOR
1993
1 I:Dakini. 2.50
2 V:Steroids. 2.50

SHADOW, THE
1994
1 MK 3.00
2 MK 3.00

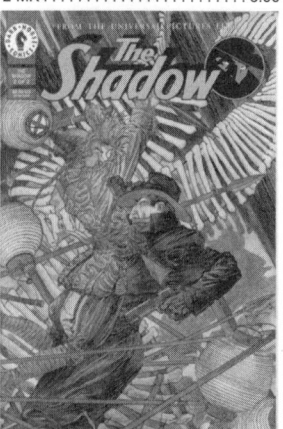

The Shadow #2
#1 © Dark Horse Comics

THE SHADOW AND DOC SAVAGE
1995
1 . . . . 3.50
2 The Shrieking Skeletons 3.50

THE SHADOW: HELL'S HEAT WAVE
1995
1 Racial War 3.00
2 MK,V:Ghost 3.00
3 Final issue 3.00

THE SHADOW: IN THE COILS OF LEVIATHAN
1993
1 MK,V:Monster 3.25
2 MK 3.25
3 MK,w/ GfD poster 3.25
4 MK,Final issue 3.25

THE SHADOW AND THE MYSTERIOUS 3
1994
1 Three stories 3.00

SHADOW EMPIRES: FAITH CONQURES
1994
1 CsM 3.00
2 thru 4 CsM . . . . @3.00

SHI: JUN-NEN
July 2004
1 BiT 3.00
2 thru 4 . . . . @3.00

SHINOBI
Nov., 2002
Spec.1-shot The Rise of Hotsuma . . 3.00

SHREK
Apr., 2003
1 (of 3) 3.00
2 and 3 . . . . @3.00

SILKE
Jan., 2001
1 TnD,F:Sandra Silke 3.00
1a variant(c) 3.00
2 TnD 3.00
3 TnD, The Hunt is on 3.00
4 TnD 3.00
4a variant(c) 3.00

SIN CITY:
DH-Legend
GN A Small Killing 14.00
GN Family Values (1997). 10.00
1-shot The Babe Wore Red (1994) . 6.00
1-shot The Babe Wore Red and
    other stories (1996) nudity 3.00
1-shot Lost Lonely, and Lethal, FM
    two-color 7.00
1-shot Sex and Violence, FM 6.00
1-shot Silent Night, FM (1995). 5.00

SIN CITY: A DAME TO KILL FOR
DH-Legend (B&W) 1993
1 FM(a&s),I:Dwight,Ava 6.00
2 FM(a&s),A:Ava 6.00
3 FM(a&s),D:Ava's Husband 6.00

1a thru 3a 2nd printings . . . . @3.00
4 thru 6 FM(a&s) . . . . @5.00

SIN CITY: HELL AND BACK
July 1999
1 (of 9) FM 6.00
2 . . . . 5.00
3 . . . . 5.00
4 Five Foot Two, Eyes of Blue 5.00
5 . . . . 5.00
6 quest for Esther 5.00
7 & 8 . . . . @5.00
9 56-pg.. . . . . 5.00

SIN CITY: JUST ANOTHER SATURDAY NIGHT
DH/Wizard
1/2 (Wizard, 24-pg.) 7.00
1/2 rep., Dark Horse, new (c) 3.00

SIN CITY: THAT YELLOW BASTARD
(B&W) 1996
1 F.Miller 6.00
2 thru 6 . . . . @5.00

SIN CITY: THE BIG FAT KILL
DH Legend, 1994
1 FM 5.00
2 FM 5.00
3 FM, Dump the Stiffs 5.00
4 FM, Town Without Pity 5.00
5 FM, final issue 5.00

SOCK MONKEY
(B&W) Sept., 1998
1 by Tony Millionaire 3.00
2 F:Uncle Gabby 3.00
VOLUME 2
1 and 2 . . . . @3.00
DH Maverick, Sept., 2002
Spec. #1 (of 2) 3.00
Spec. #2 . . . . 3.00
VOLUME 4, 2003
1 and 2 . . . . @3.00

SOCK MONKEY: THE INCHES INCIDENT
(B&W) Sept., 2006
1 (of 4) by Tony Millionaire 3.00
2 thru 4 . . . . @3.00

SOLO
1996
1 and 2 . . . . @2.50

SOLOMON KANE
Sept., 2008
1 (of 5) 3.00
1a variant JKu(c) 3.00
2 thru 3 Castle of the Devil . . . . . @3.00

SPACE CIRCUS
DH Maverick, July, 2000
1 (of 4) SA 3.00
2 thru 4 SA . . . . @3.00

SPACEHAWK
(B&W) 1989
1 BW reps. 3.50
2 thru 5 BW . . . . @3.50

SPACE PINCHY
Dec., 2005
1-shot Pleased Ta Meetya 3.00
1-shot Audrey's Super Power Pinch 3.00
1-shot The Laboratory of Love 3.00
1-shot Surrounded by Robots 3.00
1-shot The Pinch of the Illegal Brain
    Intrusion. 4.00

SPACE USAGI
[Vol. 3] 1996
1 thru 3 Stan Sakai . . . . @3.00

SPEAK OF THE DEVIL
July., 2007
1 (of 6) GHe 3.00
2 thru 6 GHe . . . . @3.00

SPECIES
1995
1 Alien Human Hybrid. 3.00
2 thru 4 SIL . . . . @3.00

SPECIES: HUMAN RACE
1996
1 PhH 3.00
2 . . . . 3.00
3 SBi 3.00
4 . . . . 3.00

Spirit of Wonder #5
© Dark Horse Comics

SPIRIT OF WONDER
(B&W) 1996
1 thru 5 by Kenji Tsuruia . . . . @3.00

SPYBOY
Oct., 1999
1 PDd,F:Alex Fleming. 3.00
2 PDd 3.00
3 PDd,F:Bombshell. 3.00
4 PDd,F:Judge and Jury. 3.00
5 PDd,V:Judge and Jury. 3.00
6 PDd,V:Barbie Q 3.00
7 PDd,V:Madam Imadam 3.00
8 PDd,V:Madam Imadam 3.00
9 PDd,V:Madam Imadam
    & Barbie Q. 3.00
10 PDd,death-defying action 3.00
11 PDd,V:Slackjaw. 3.00
12 PDd,V:Slackjaw. 3.00
13 PDd 3.00

DARK HORSE

All comics prices listed are for *Near Mint* condition.

14 PDd,F:SpyGirl	3.00
15 PDd	3.00
15a variant TnD (c)	3.00
16 PDd	3.00
17 PDd	3.00
Spec. 1-shot 48-pg.	5.00
Spec. Motorola Spec. (2000)	2.50

SPYBOY: FINAL EXAM
May, 2004

1 PDd	3.00
2 thru 4	@3.00

SPYBOY 13: THE M.A.N.G.A. AFFAIR
Apr., 2003

1 (of 3) PDd(s)	3.00
2 and 3	@3.00

SPYBOY/YOUNG JUSTICE
Feb., 2002

1 PDd, x-over	3.00
2 and 3	@3.00

STAN SHAW'S BEAUTY & THE BEAST
1 Based on the book.	5.00

STAR KID
1998

1-shot	3.00

STARSHIP TROOPERS
Sept., 1997

1 (of 2) movie adaptation	3.00
2 movie adaptation, concl.	3.00

STARSHIP TROOPERS: BRUTE CREATIONS
1997

1-shot RbC.	3.00

STARSHIP TROOPERS: DOMINANT SPECIES
Aug., 1998

1 (of 4)	3.00
2 JoB,RyE	3.00
3 & 4	@3.00

Starship Troopers #3
© Dark Horse Comics

STARSHIP TROOPERS: INSECT TOUCH
1997

1 by Warren Ellis & Paolo Parente	3.00
2 and 3 (of 3)	@3.00

STAR SLAMMERS
1996

Spec. 1	3.00

STARSTRUCK: THE EXPANDING UNIVERSE
(B&W) 1990

1 Book 1, with cards	3.00
2 Book 2, with 2-card strip	3.00
3 Book 3, with cards	3.00
4 Book 4, with cards	3.00

STAR WARS
Dec., 1998

1 F:Ki-Adi-Mundi	6.00
2 F:Ki-Adi-Mundi	5.00
3 F:Ki-Adi-Mundi	5.00
4 F:Sylvn	5.00
5 V:Ephant Mon	6.00
6 V:Jabba the Hutt	6.00
7 Outlander	5.00
8 Outlander, A:Jabba the Hutt	5.00
9 A:Tusken Raiders	5.00
10 TT,RL,F:Ki-Adi-Mundi	5.00
11 TT,RL,F:Aurra Sing	4.00
12 TT,Outlander,pt.6	4.00
13 TT,TL,A'Sharad Hett	4.00
14 TT,TL,on Malastare	4.00
15 TT,TL,Podracing	4.00
16 TT,TL,V:Lannik terrorists	4.00
17 TT,TL,V:Red Iaro terrorists	4.00
18 TT,TL,Smugglers Moon	4.00
19 JOs,JD,Twilight,pt.1	5.00
20 JOs,JD,Twilight,pt.2	5.00
21 JOs,JD,Twilight,pt.3	5.00
22 JOs,JD,Twilight,pt.4	5.00
23 Infinity's End,pt.1	5.00
24 Infinity's End,pt.2	5.00
25 Infinity's End,pt.3	5.00
26 Infinity's End,pt.4	5.00
27 Star Crash one-shot	3.00
28 Hunt for Aurra Sing,pt.1	3.00
29 Hunt for Aurra Sing,pt.2	3.00
30 Hunt for Aurra Sing,pt.3	3.00
31 Hunt for Aurra Sing,pt.4	3.00
32 Darkness,pt.1, JOs,JD	3.00
33 Darkness,pt.2, JOs,JD	3.00
34 Darkness,pt.3, JOs,JD	3.00
35 Darkness,pt.4, JOs,JD	3.00
36 Stark Hyperspace War,pt.1	3.00
37 Stark Hyperspace War,pt.2	3.00
38 Stark Hyperspace War,pt.3	3.00
39 Stark Hyperspace War,pt.4	3.00
40 The Devaronian Version,pt.1	3.00
41 The Devaronian Version,pt.2	3.00
42 Rite of Passage,pt.1	3.00
43 Rite of Passage,pt.2	3.00
44 Rite of Passage,pt.3	3.00
45 Rite of Passage,pt.4	3.00
becomes:	

STAR WARS: REPUBLIC
Oct., 2002

46 Republic,pt.1	3.00
47 Republic,pt.2	3.00
48 Republic,pt.3	3.00
49 Republic,pt.5	3.00
50 Republic,pt.6, 64-page	6.00
51 Republic,pt.7	3.00
52 Republic,pt.8	3.00
53 Blast Radius	3.00
54 Jedi Fugitive	3.00
55 Battle of Jabiim,pt.1	3.00

56 Battle of Jabiim,pt.2	3.00
57 Battle of Jabiim,pt.3	3.00
58 Battle of Jabiim,pt.4	3.00
59 Enemy Lines	3.00
60 Origin of Asajj Ventress	3.00
61 Bail Organa	3.00
62 On Hostile Ground	3.00
63 Quinlan Vos, Assassin	3.00
64 A Jedi's Tale	3.00
65 Mace Windu Unleashed,pt.1	3.00
66 Mace Windu Unleashed,pt.2	3.00
67 Great Power, Great Restraint	3.00
68 Born to Fight	3.00
69 Dreadnaughts of Rendili,pt.1	3.00
70 Dreadnaughts of Rendili,pt.2	3.00
71	3.00
72 Aayla Undercover	3.00
73 In the House of the Enemy	3.00
74 Same War, New Clones	3.00
75 Siege of Saleucami	3.00
76 Darkness, Light and Fire	3.00
77 Final Test of Quinlan Vos	3.00
78 Darth Vader, Right-hand Man	3.00
79 Into the Unknown	3.00
80 Jedi...Fugitive	3.00
81 The Hidden Enemy,pt.1	3.00
82 The Hidden Enemy,pt.2	3.00
83 The Hidden Enemy,pt.3	3.00
0 Spec. American Entertainment	10.00

STAR WARS: A NEW HOPE— SPECIAL EDITION
Jan.–Apr., 1997

1 EB, AW	6.00
2 thru 4	@5.00
Spec. Edition boxed set	30.00

STAR WARS: BOBA FETT—
1-shot Bounty on Bar-Kooda, (1995) 48-pg.	5.00
1-shot When the Fat Lady Swings.	7.00
1-shot Murder Most Foul (1997)	7.00
1-shot Twin Engins of Destruction	6.00
1-shot Agent of Doom, CK (2000)	6.00
1-shot Overkill (2006)	5.00

STAR WARS: BOBA FETT— ENEMY OF THE EMPIRE
Jan., 1999

1 (of 4) V:Dark Lord of the Sith	3.00
2 thru 4 IG	@3.00

STAR WARS: BOUNTY HUNTERS
Aug., 1999

1-shot Aurra Sing, TT	3.00
1-shot Kir Kanos, MRi,RSd	3.00
1-shot Scoundrel's Wages, F:Dengar, 4-LOM & Bossk	3.00

STAR WARS: CHEWBACCA
Jan., 2000

1 (of 4) various tales	4.00
1 gold foil (c)	9.00
2 thru 4	@3.50

STAR WARS: CLONE WARS
Sept., 2008

1 (of 6)	3.00
2 thru	@3.00

DARK HORSE

Star Wars: Crimson Empire, Council of Blood #5 © Dark Horse Comics

STAR WARS: CRIMSON EMPIRE
Dec., 1997–May, 1998
1 PG,CR,DvD(c) 9.00
3 PG,CR,DvD(c) 8.00
3 thru 5 PG,CR,DvD(c) . . . . @5.00

VOL II: COUNCIL OF BLOOD
1998
1 MRi,RSd,PG,DvD(c) 4.00
2 thru 6 RSd,PG,DvD(c) . . . . @3.00

STAR WARS: DARK EMPIRE
Dec., 1991
1 CK,Destiny of a Jedi 9.00
1a 2nd Printing 5.00
1b Gold Ed. 9.00
2 CK,Destroyer of worlds, very
   low print run 9.00
2a 2nd Printing 5.00
2b Gold Ed. 9.00
3 CK,V:The Emperor 5.00
3a 2nd printing 4.00
3b Gold Ed. 9.00
4 CK,V:The Emperor 5.00
4a Gold Ed. 9.00
5 CK,V:The Emperor 5.00
5a Gold Ed. 9.00
6 CK,V:Emperor,last issue 5.00
6a Gold Ed. 8.00
Gold editions, foil logo set 35.00
Platinum editions, embossed set. . 80.00

STAR WARS DARK EMPIRE II
1994
I 2nd chapter 10.00
2 F:Boba Fett 8.00
3 V:Darksiders 5.00
4 Luke Vs. Darksiders 5.00
5 Creatures. 5.00
6 CK,DvD(c), save the twins. 5.00
Platinum editions, set. 50.00

STAR WARS: DARK FORCE RISING
May–Oct., 1997
1 thru 6 (of 6) MBn,TyD,KN . . . . @5.00

STAR WARS: DARK TIMES
Oct., 2006
1 The Path to Nowhere. 5.00
2 thru 5 Path to Nowhere . . . . . . @4.00
6 Parallels, pt.1 . . . . 4.00
7 thru 10 Parallels, pt.2–pt.4. . . . @4.00
11 Vector, pt.5 x-over. 4.00
12 Vector, pt.6 . . . . 4.00

STAR WARS: DARTH MAUL
Sept., 2000
1 (of 4) RMz,JD,Struzan(c). 3.00
1 photo (c). 5.00
2 Struzan(c),V:Black Sun 3.00
3 RMz,JD,Struzan(c). 3.00
4 RMz,JD,Struzan(c). 3.00
2 thru 4 photo(c) . . . . @3.00

STAR WARS: DROIDS
April–Sept., 1994
1 F:C-3PO,R2-D2 . . . . 5.00
2 V:Thieves 3.00
3 on the Hosk moon 3.00
4 . . . . 3.00
5 A meeting 3.00
6 final issue. 3.00
Spec.#1 I:Olag Greck. 3.00

[2nd Series] Apr., 1995
1 Deputized Droids 3.00
2 Marooned on Nar Shaddaa 3.00
3 C-3PO to the Rescue 3.00
4 . . . . 3.00
5 Caretaker virus 3.00
6 Revolution 3.00
7 & 8 . . . . @3.00

STAR WARS: EMPIRE
Sept., 2002
1 Betrayal,pt.1. . . . . 3.50
2 Betrayal,pt.2. . . . . 3.50
3 Betrayal,pt.3. . . . . 3.50
4 Betrayal,pt.4. . . . . 3.00
5 National Public Radio adapt. 3.00
6 Surrender or Die 3.00
7 Sacrifice! 3.00
8 Darklighter,pt.1. . . . . 3.00
9 Darklighter,pt.2. . . . . 3.00
10 Yavin Base,pt.1. . . . . 3.00
11 Yavin Base,pt.2 . . . . 3.00
12 Darklighter,pt.3 . . . . 3.00
13 What Sin Loyalty?. 3.00
14 The Savage Heart. 3.00
15 Darklighter,pt.4 . . . . 3.00
16 To the Last Man,pt.1 . . . . 3.00
17 To the Last Man,pt.2 . . . . 3.00
18 To the Last Man,pt.3 . . . . 3.00
19 To the Last Man,pt.3 . . . . 3.00
20 Rebel base 3.00
21 Rebel base,pt.2. . . . . 3.00
22 F:Deena Shan 3.00
23 F:BoShek 3.00
24 Idiot's Array,pt.1 . . . . 3.00
25 Idiot's Array,pt.2 . . . . 3.00
26 Luke Skywalker Target 3.00
27 Promoted to General 3.00
28 Ghost Ship 3.00
29 In the Shadows of Their Fathers 3.00
30 Rebel vs. Rebel 3.00
31 The Price of Power 3.00
32 Ambush on Jabiim 3.00
33 Trapped on Jabiim 3.00
34 The Fate of a Planet. 3.00
35 Never Lie to Vader 3.00
36 thru 40 Wrong Side of the
   War, pt.1–pt.5. . . . . @3.00

STAR WARS: EMPIRE'S END
Oct.–Nov., 1995
1 R:Emperor Palpatine 3.50
2 conclusion 3.50

STAR WARS: EPISODE I THE PHANTOM MENACE
Apr., 1999
1 RdM,AW. 4.00
1a newsstand edition, photo (c) . . . 3.00
2 RdM,AW. 3.00
2a newsstand edition, photo (c) . . . 3.00
3 RdM,AW. 3.00
3a newsstand edition, photo (c) . . . 3.00
4 RdM,AW. 3.00
4a newsstand edition, photo (c) . . . 3.00
GN Phantom Menace RdM,AW. . . 13.00
Spec. Anakin Skywalker. 3.00
Spec. Anakin Skywalker, newsstand 3.00
Spec. Obi-Wan Kenobi. 3.00
Spec. Obi-Wan Kenobi, newsstand . 3.00
Spec. Queen Amidala 3.00
Spec. Qui-Gon Jinn 3.00

STAR WARS EPISODE II— ATTACK OF THE CLONES
Apr., 2002
1 (of 4) 48-pg. 4.00
2 thru 4 48-pg. . . . . @4.00
1A thru 4A photo (c) . . . . @4.00

STAR WARS: EPISODE III– REVENGE OF THE SITH
Mar., 2005
1 . . . . 4.00
2 thru 4 . . . . @4.00

STAR WARS: GENERAL GRIEVOUS
Mar., 2005
1 thru 4 . . . . @3.00

STAR WARS HANDBOOK
July, 1998
1 X-Wing Rogue Squadron. 4.00
2 Crimson Empire. 4.00
Dark Empire 4.00

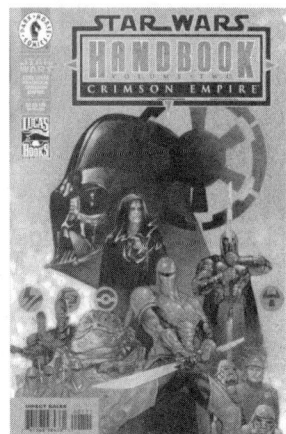

Star Wars: Handbook #2 © Dark Horse Comics

Star Wars: Heir to the Empire #4
© *Dark Horse Comics*

STAR WARS: HEIR TO THE EMPIRE
Oct., 1995–Apr., 1996
1 I:Grand Admiral Thrawn. 4.00
2 thru 6 . . . . @3.50

STAR WARS: INFINITIES — A NEW HOPE
May, 2001
1 (of 4) CW,TyH,Luke's attack fails,
　Death Star survives 3.00
1a gold foil photo (c). 9.00
2 CW,TyH 3.00
3 CW,TyH 3.00
4 CW,TyH, concl. 3.00

STAR WARS: INFINITIES — THE EMPIRE STRIKES BACK
July, 2002
1 thru 4 . . . . @3.00

STAR WARS: INFINITIES — RETURN OF THE JEDI
Nov., 2003
1 thru 4 . . . . @3.00

STAR WARS: JABBA THE HUTT—
1995–1996
1-shot The Garr Suppoon Hit 3.00
1-shot Hunger of Princess Nampi . . 3.00
1-shot The Dynasty Trap 3.00
1-shot Betrayal. 3.00
1-shot The Jabba Tape 3.00

STAR WARS: JANGO FETT
Dec., 2001
GN 64-pg..,RMz. 6.00

STAR WARS: JANGO FETT—OPEN SEASONS
Apr., 2002
1 (of 4) 3.00
2 thru 4 . . . . @3.00

STAR WARS: JEDI
Feb., 2003
Spec. Mace Windu, JOs,JD,48-pg. . 5.00
Spec. Shaak Ti, JOs,JD, 48-pg. . . . 5.00
Spec. Aayla Secura, JOs,JD,48-pg. 5.00
Spec. Dooku,JOs,JD,48-pg. 5.00
Spec. Yoda, 48-pg. 5.00

STAR WARS: JEDI ACADEMY LEVIATHAN
Oct., 1998
1 (of 4) by Kevin J. Anderson 3.00
2 thru 4 . . . . @3.00

STAR WARS: JEDI COUNCIL — ACTS OF WAR
June, 2000
1 (of 4) RSd, V:Yinchorri. 4.00
1b gold foil (c). 9.00
2 thru 4 RSd . . . . @4.00

STAR WARS: JEDI QUEST
Sept., 2001
1 . . . . 3.00
1a ruby red foil 9.00
1b ruby red foil, signed 25.00
2 thru 4 . . . . @3.00

STAR WARS: JEDI VS. SITH
Apr., 2001
1 (of 6) 3.00
1a gold foil, lim.e. 9.00
2 V:Darth Bane 3.00
3 thru 6 . . . . @3.00

STAR WARS: KNIGHTS OF THE OLD REPUBLIC
Jan., 2006
1 A Jedi Betrayed 8.00
2 F:Zayne Carrick 4.00
3 Ambush 4.00
4 The Noose Tightens 4.00
5 A Destroyer of Worlds 4.00
6 Commencement 3.00
7 Jedi vs. Mandalorians 3.00
8 Jedi vs. Mandalorians 3.00
9 Jedi vs. Mandalorians 3.00
10 . . . . 3.00
11 . . . . 3.00
12 . . . . 3.00
13 . . . . 3.00
14 . . . . 3.00
15 Days of Fear. 3.00
16 Nights of Anger 3.00
17 Nights of Anger 3.00
18 Nights of Anger 3.00
19 Daze of Hate. 3.00
20 Daze of Hate. 3.00
21 Daze of Hate. 3.00
22 Knights of Suffering 3.00
23 Knights of Suffering, pt.2 . . . . . 3.00
24 Knights of Suffering, pt.3 . . . . . 3.00
25 Vector, pt.1 . . . . 3.00
26 Vector, pt.2 . . . . 3.00
27 Vector, pt.3 . . . . 3.00
28 Vector, pt.4 . . . . 3.00
29 Exalted, pt.1 . . . . 3.00
30 Exalted, pt.1 . . . . 3.00
31 Turnabout 3.00
32 Vindication, pt.1 . . . . 3.00
33 Vindication, pt.2 . . . . 3.00
34 Vindication, pt.3 . . . . 3.00
35 Vindication, pt.4 . . . . 3.00
Spec. Knights/Rebellion flip-book . . 2.50
Spec. Handbook 3.00

STAR WARS: THE LAST COMMAND
Nov., 1997–July, 1998
1 thru 6 MBn . . . . @3.50

STAR WARS LEGACY
June, 2006
0 The Future of Star Wars 4.00
1 The Sith born anew 8.00
2 The Future in Question 6.00
3 A Princess in Peril 5.00
4 thru 8 . . . . @5.00
9 Trust Issues, pt.1 . . . . 3.00
10 Trust Issues,pt.2 . . . . 3.00
11 The Ghosts of Ossus 3.00
12 The Ghosts of Ossus 3.00
13 Ready to Die. 3.00
14 Dragon, pt. 1. . . . . 3.00
15 Dragon, pt. 2. . . . . 3.00
16 Dragon, pt. 3. . . . . 3.00
17 Dragon, pt. 4. . . . . 3.00
18 Claws of the Dragon, pt.5. . . . . 3.00
19 Claws of the Dragon, pt.6. . . . . 3.00
20 Space battle v. Sith Empire,pt.1 . 3.00
21 Space battle v. Sith Empire,pt.2 . 3.00
22 Fury of the Sith 3.00
23 Rav vs. Cade Skywalker. 3.00
24 F:Cade Skywalker. 3.00
25 Secret Jedi Temple, pt.1 . . . . . . 3.00
26 Secret Jedi Temple, pt.2 . . . . . . 3.00
27 . . . . 3.00
28 Vector, pt.9 . . . . 3.00
29 Vector, pt.10 . . . . 3.00
30 Vector, pt.11 . . . . 3.00
Spec. #0 1/2 revised 3.00

STAR WARS: MARA JADE— BY THE EMPEROR'S HAND
Aug., 1998
1 (of 6) by Timothy Zahn 5.00
2 thru 6 . . . . @4.00

STAR WARS: OBSESSION
Nov., 2004
1 (of 5) 5.00
2 thru 5 . . . . @5.00

STAR WARS: THE PROTOCOL OFFENSIVE
Sept., 1997
1-shot written by Anthony Daniels . . 5.00

STAR WARS: PURGE
Dec., 2005
1-shot Last Stand of the Jedi. 12.00

STAR WARS: QUI-GON & OBI-WAN—LAST STAND ON ORD MANTELL
Jan., 2001
1 . . . . 3.00
1a variant TnD (c). 3.00
1c gold foil (c). 9.00
2 . . . . 3.00
3 . . . . 3.00
1a thru 3a photo(c) . . . . @3.00

DARK HORSE

Star Wars: Mara Jade #3
© Dark Horse Comics

STAR WARS: QUI-GON & OBI-WAN—THE AURORIENT EXPRESS
Feb., 2002
1 (of 2) 3.00
2 . . . . 3.00

STAR WARS: REBELLION
Apr., 2006
1 F:Janek Sunber 3.00
2 thru 5 My Brother, My Enemy . @3.00
6 The Ahakista Gambit 3.00
7 thru 10 The Ahakista Gambit . . @3.00
11 Small Victories, pt.1 . . . . 3.00
12 Small Victories, pt.2 . . . . 3.00
13 Small Victories, pt.3 . . . . 3.00
14 Small Victories, pt.4 . . . . 3.00
15 Vector, pt.7 x-over 3.00
16 thru 19 . . . . @3.00

STAR WARS: RETURN OF TAG & BINK
March, 2006
1 & 2 . . . . @4.00

STAR WARS: THE RETURN OF THE JEDI
(B&W—Manga) June, 1999
1 (of 4) Shin-ichi Hiromoto,
96-pg.. 9.00
2 thru 4 . . . . @9.00

STAR WARS: RIVER OF CHAOS
May–Nov., 1995
1 LSi,JBr,Emperor sends spies . . . 4.00
2 Imperial in Allies Clothing 4.00
3 . . . . 4.00
4 F:Ranulf 4.00

STAR WARS: SHADOWS OF THE EMPIRE
May, 1996
1 (of 6) by John Wagner, Kilian
Plunkett & P. Craig Russell 4.00
2 thru 6 . . . . @4.00

STAR WARS: SHADOWS OF THE EMPIRE — EVOLUTION
Feb.–June, 1998
1 thru 5 . . . . @4.00

STAR WARS: SHADOW STALKER
Nov., 1997
1-shot from Star Wars Galaxy Mag. 4.00

STAR WARS: SPLINTER OF THE MIND'S EYE
Dec., 1995–June, 1996
1 thru 4 A.D.Foster novel adapt.. @4.00

STAR WARS: STARFIGHTER— CROSSBONES
Jan., 2002
1 (of 3) F:Nym, pirate captain 4.00
2 thru 3 from video game . . . . . . @4.00

STAR WARS: TAG & BINK ARE DEAD
Oct., 2001
1 (of 2) 5.00
2 . . . . 4.00
1-shot Revenge of the Clone
Menace 3.00

STAR WARS TALES
Sept., 1999
1 various authors, 64-pg. 10.00
2 thru 4, 64-pg. . . . . @8.00
5 F:Lando's Commandos 7.00
6 thru 9 . . . . @6.00
10 thru 24 . . . . @6.00
5a thru 24a photo(c) . . . . @10.00

STAR WARS: TALES FROM MOS EISLEY
1-shot, from Star Wars Galaxy
Mag. #2–#4 . . . . 4.00

STAR WARS: TALES OF THE JEDI
Oct., 1993
1 RV,I:Ulic Qel-Droma 6.00
2 RV,A:Ulic Qel-Droma 5.00
3 RV,D:Andur 5.00
4 RV,A:Jabba the Hut 4.00
5 RV,last issue 4.00

STAR WARS: TALES OF THE JEDI: DARK LORDS OF THE SITH
Oct., 1994–Mar., 1995
1 Bagged with card 3.50
2 . . . . 3.50
3 Krath Attack 3.50
4 F:Exar Kun 3.50
5 V:TehKrath 3.50
6 Final battle 3.50

STAR WARS: TALES OF THE JEDI: THE FREEDON NADD UPRISING
Aug.–Sept., 1997
1 . . . . 12.00

2 . . . . 10.00

STAR WARS: TALES OF THE JEDI: THE SITH WAR
Aug., 1995–Jan., 1996
1 F:Exar Kun 3.50
2 F:Ulic Oel-Droma 3.50
3 F:Exar Kun 3.50
4 thru 6 (6 part mini-series) . . . . @3.50

STAR WARS: TALES OF THE JEDI—THE FALL OF THE SITH EMPIRE
June–Oct., 1997
1 (of 5) 5.00
2 thru 5 . . . . @5.00

STAR WARS: TALES OF THE JEDI—THE GOLDEN AGE OF THE SITH
Oct., 1996–Feb., 1997
0 . . . . 3.00
1 thru 5 . . . . @4.00

STAR WARS: TALES OF THE JEDI— REDEMPTION
July, 1998
1 (of 5) by Kevin J. Anderson 10.00
2 thru 5 F:Ulic Qel-Droma . . . . . . @8.00

STAR WARS: UNDERWORLD—THE YAVIN VASSILIKA
Dec., 2000
1 (of 5) F:Han Solo 4.00
2 thru 5 . . . . @4.00
1a thru 5a photo (c) . . . . @4.00

STAR WARS: UNION
Nov., 1999
1 (of 4) by Stackpole 4.00
1a gold foil (c) 9.00
2 the wedding approaches 4.00
3 almost there 4.00
4 wedding day 4.00

*Star Wars: Tales of the Jedi
Redemption #3* © Dark Horse Comics

Star Wars: Vader's Quest #4
© Dark Horse Comics

STAR WARS: VADER'S QUEST
Feb., 1999
1 (of 4) DGb,AMK 4.00
2 thru 4 . . . . @4.00

STAR WARS: A VALENTINE STORY
Feb., 2003
1-shot PC 4.00

STAR WARS: X-WING— ROGUE LEADER
Sept., 2005
1 thru 3 . . . . @4.00

STAR WARS: X-WING ROGUE SQUADRON
July, 1995
The Rebel Opposition
1 F:Wedge Antilles 5.00
2 . . . . 4.00
3 F:Tycho Clehu 4.00
4 F:Tycho Clehu 4.00
½ Wizard limited exclusive 6.00
The Phantom Affair
5 thru 8 . . . . @4.00
Battleground Tatooine
9 thru 12 . . . . @4.00
The Warrior Princess
13 thru 16 . . . . @4.00
Requiem for a Rogue
17 thru 20 . . . . @4.00
In the Empire's Service
21 thru 24 . . . . @4.00
Making of Baron Fell
25 . . . . 5.00
Family Ties
26 thru 27 . . . . @4.00
Masquerade
28 thru 31 . . . . @4.00
Mandatory Retirement
32 thru 35 . . . . @4.00

STAR WARS: ZAM WESELL
Feb., 2002
GN RMz, 64-pg. 6.00

STEVE RUDE'S THE MOTH
Mar., 2004
1 thru 4 . . . . @3.00
Spec. Double sized 5.00

SUBHUMAN
Nov., 1998
1 (of 4) MSh 3.00
2 thru 4 MSh . . . . @3.00

SUPER MANGA BLAST
(B&W) Mar., 2000
1 128-pg. 5.00
2 thru 6 128-pg. . . . . @5.00
7 F:Oh My Goddess 5.00
8 F:Oh My Goddess 5.00
9 F:3x3 Eyes 5.00
10 F:Seraphic Feather 5.00
11 F:Oh My Goddess 5.00
12 F:Oh My Goddess 5.00
13 F:Club 9 . . . . 5.00
14 F:Club 9 . . . . 5.00
15 F:Club 9, 50-pg. 6.00
16 F:3x3 Eyes 6.00
17 F:Club 9 . . . . 6.00
18 F:Club 9 . . . . 6.00
19 Seraphic Feather 6.00
20 What's Michael? 6.00
21 F:Club 9 . . . . 6.00
22 Club 9, 3x3 Eyes 6.00
23 Club 9, What's Michael? 6.00
24 F:Seraphic Feather 6.00
25 F:Appleseed 6.00
26 F:Shadow Star 6.00
27 F:What's Michael? 6.00
28 thru 59 . . . . @6.00

SUPERMAN/MADMAN HULLABALOO
June–Aug., 1997
1 (of 3) MiA 3.00
2 and 3 (of 3) . . . . @3.00

SUPERMAN/TARZAN: SONS OF THE JUNGLE
Oct., 2001
1 (of 3) CDi,HuR 3.00
2 CDi,HuR. 3.00
3 CDi,HuR(c) 3.00

SUPERMAN VS. ALIENS
DC/Dark Horse, 1995
1 DJu,KN 6.00
2 V:Queen Alien 5.00
3 . . . . 5.00

SUPERMAN VS. ALIENS II
May, 2002
1 (of 4) CDi,JBg,KN, x-over 3.00
2 CDi,JBg,KN 3.00
3 CDi,JBg,KN 3.00
4 CDi,JBg,KN 3.00

SUPERMAN VS. THE TERMINATOR: DEATH TO THE FUTURE
Dec., 1999
1 (of 4) AIG,StP,x-over. 3.00
2 AIG,StP,into the future 3.00
3 AIG,StP,A:Supergirl 3.00
4 AIG,StP,concl. 3.00

SYN
Rocket Comics Aug., 2003
1 thru 5 KG . . . . @3.00

TALE OF ONE BAD RAT
1994
1 BT 3.00
2 thru 4 . . . . @3.00

TALES OF ORDINARY MADNESS
(B&W) 1992
1 JBo(c),Paranoid 3.00
2 JBo(c),Mood 2.50
3 JBo(c),A Little Bit of Neurosis . . . 2.50
4 . . . . 2.50

TALES OF THE FEAR AGENTS: TWELVE STEPS IN ONE
Oct., 2007
1-shot 3.00

TALES OF THE VAMPIRES
Dec., 2003
1 Josh Whedon. 7.00
2 thru 4 . . . . @7.00
5 . . . . 5.00

TALES TO OFFEND
July, 1997
1-shot by Frank Miller 3.00

TANK GIRL
(B&W) 1991
1 Rep. from U.K.Deadline Mag.
  with 2-card strip 4.50
2 V:Indiana Potato Jones 4.00
3 On the Run 4.00
4 . . . . 4.00
[2nd Series] 1993
1 . . . . 3.50
2 thru 4 . . . . @3.00

TARZAN/JOHN CARTER: WARLORDS OF MARS
1996
1 (of 4) E.R.Burroughs adapt. 3.00
2 thru 4 . . . . @3.00

TARZAN VS. PREDATOR AT THE EARTH'S CORE
1996
1 Tarzan vs. Predator 3.00
2 V:Predator 3.00
3 Tarzan on the Hunt 3.00
4 . . . . 3.00

TENTH, THE: NIGHTWALKER
Apr., 2002
1 (of 4) TnD 3.00
2 thru 4 . . . . @3.00
1a thru 4a variant (c). . . . . @3.00

TENTH, THE: RESURRECTED
Apr., 2001
1 TnD 3.00
1a variant(c) 7.00
1b variant(c) signed 15.00
2 TnD 3.00
3 TnD 3.00
4 TnD 3.00
3a and 4a variant (c)s . . . . @3.00

DARK HORSE

TERMINAL POINT
(B&W) 1993
1 . . . . 2.50
2 and 3 . . . . @2.50

TERMINATOR
1990
1 CW,Tempest 4.00
2 CW,Tempest 3.00
3 CW. 3.00
4 CW, conclusion 3.00

TERMINATOR
1-shot MW,3-D const(c2,
  pop-up inside (1991) 5.00
Spec. AIG,GyD,GeD(1998) 3.00

The Terminator #2
© Dark Horse Comics

TERMINATOR, THE
Sept., 1998
1 AIG,StP 3.00
2 F:Sarah Connor 3.00
3 F:Killerman. 3.00
4 F:D-800L & D-810X 3.00

TERMINATOR, THE:
THE DARK YEARS
Sept., 1999
1 (of 4) AIG,MvR 3.00
2 AIG,MvR,BWi,F:Jon Norden. 3.00
3 . . . . 3.00
4 AIG,MvR,concl.. . . . . 3.00

TERMINATOR:
END GAME
1992
1 JG,Final *Terminator* series. 3.00
2 JG,Cont.last Term.story 3.00
3 JG, Concl. 3.00

TERMINATOR:
ENEMY WITHIN
1991
1 cont. from Sec.Objectives 4.00
2 C890.L.threat contd. 3.00
3 Secrets of Cyberdyne 3.00
4 Conclusion. 3.00

TERMINATOR:
HUNTERS & KILLERS
1992
1 thru 3 V:Russians. . . . . @3.00

TERMINATOR:
SECONDARY
OBJECTIVES
1991
1 cont. 1st DH mini-series 4.00
2 PG,A:New Female Terminator . . . 3.00
3 PG,Terminators in L.A.&Mexico. . 3.00
4 PG,Terminator vs Terminator 3.00

TERRITORY, THE
Jan., 1999
1 (of 4) JaD,DvL,F:Ishmael. 3.00
2 thru 4 . . . . @3.00

TEX AVERY'S DROOPY
1 Dr. Droopenstein 2.50
2 and 3 . . . . @2.50

TEX AVERY'S
SCREWBALL SQUIRREL
1 I:Screwball Squirrel 2.50
2 Cleaning House 2.50
3 School of Hard Rocks 2.50

THING, THE
1991
1 JHi, Movie adaptation 4.00
2 JHi, Movie adaptation 3.50

THING FROM
ANOTHER WORLD:
CLIMATE OF FEAR
1994
1 Argentinian Military Base
  (Bahiathetis) 3.00
2 Thing on Base 3.00
3 Thing/takeover. 3.00
4 Conclusion. 3.00

THING FROM
ANOTHER WORLD:
ETERNAL VOWS
1993
1 PG,I:Sgt. Rowan 3.00
2 PG 3.00
3 PG,in New Zealand 3.00
4 PG,Last issue. 3.00

THIRTEEN O'CLOCK
(B&W)
1 Mr.Murmer,from Deadline USA . . 3.00

THE 13th SON
Oct., 2005
1 KJo, Worse Thing Waiting 3.00
2 thru 4 KJo. . . . . @3.00

3 X 3 EYES:
CURSE OF THE GESU
(B&W–Manga) 1995
1 I:Pai,Yakumo 3.00
2 thru 5 . . . . @3.00

300
May, 1998
1 (of 5) FM & Lynn Varley. 20.00
2 FM 18.00

3 FM 18.00
4 FM 15.00
5 FM . . . . @12.00

TIME COP
1994
1 Movie Adaptation 2.75
2 Movie Adaptation 2.50

TITAN
1994
Spec.#1 BS(c),I:Inhibitors 4.25

TITAN A.E.
May, 2000
1 (of 3) film prequel,pt.1 . . . . 3.00
2 thru 3 prequel,pt.2–pt.3 . . . . . . @3.00

Tongue Lash #2
© Dark Horse Comics

TONGUE*LASH
Aug., 1996
1 by Randy and Jean-Marc
  Lofficier & Dave Taylor 3.00
2 . . . . 3.00
[VOL. II] 1999
1 (of 2) 3.00
2 . . . . 3.00

TONY MILLIONAIRE'S
SOCK MONKEY
VOL. 3
1 & 2. . . . . @3.00

TOO MUCH COFFEE MAN
(B&W) July, 1997
1-shot by Shannon Wheeler 3.00

TORCH OF LIBERTY
1995
Spec. 2.50

TREKKER
(B&W) 1987
1 thru 4 . . . . @3.00
5 thru 7 . . . . @3.00
8 O:Trekker. 3.00
9 . . . . 3.00
Spec.#1 Sins of the Fathers 3.00

DARK HORSE

TRIPLE X
(B&W) 1994

1	4.00
2 V:Dr. Zemph	4.00
3	4.00
4 V:Rhine Lords	4.00
5 I:Klaar	4.00
6 Klaar captured	5.00
7 Revolution Consequences	5.00

Two Faces of Tomorrow #8
© Dark Horse Comics

TWO FACES OF TOMORROW, THE
(B&W–Manga) Aug., 1997

1 (of 13) from James P. Hogan novel, by Yukinobu Hoshino	3.00
2 thru 4	@3.00
5 thru 13	@4.00

TWO FISTED TALES

Spec. WW,WiS	5.00

2112

GN JBy,A:Next Men	2.50
2nd Printing	5.00

ULTRAMAN TIGA
Aug., 2003

1 thru 10 (of 10)	@4.00

UMBRELLA ACADEMY: APOCALYPSE SUITE
Sept., 2007

1 (of 6)	7.00
2	5.00
3 thru 5	4.00
6	3.00

UMBRELLA ACADEMY: DALLAS
Nov., 2008

1(of 6)	3.00
1a variant JLe (c)	3.00

[ANDREW VACHSS'] UNDERGROUND
(B&W) 1993

1 AVs(s)	4.25
2 thru 5 AVs(s)	@4.00

UNIVERSAL MONSTERS
1991

1 AAd,Creature From The Black Lagoon	5.50
1 Dracula	5.50
1 Frankenstein	5.50
1 The Mummy	5.50

URBAN LEGENDS
(B&W) 1993

1-shot	3.00

USAGI YOJIMBO
(B&W) 1996

1 by Stan Sakai	7.00
2 thru 9	@4.00
10 with Sergio Aragones	6.00
11 'The Lord of Owls'	6.00
12 'Vampire Cat of the Geishu'	3.00
13 thru 22 'Grasscutter,',pt.1 thru pt. #10	@3.00
23 My Father's Sword	3.00
24 The Demon Flute	3.00
25 Momo-Usagi-Taro	3.00
26 The Hairpin Murders,pt.1	3.00
27 The Hairpin Murders,pt.2	3.00
28 Courtesan conspiracy,pt.1	3.00
29 Courtesan conspiracy,pt.2	3.00
30 Inspector Ishida mystery	3.00
31 The Haunted Inn of Moon Shadow Hill	3.00
32 Two stories	3.00
33	3.00
34 Demon Mask,pt.1	3.00
35 Demon Mask,pt.2	3.00
36 Demon Mask,pt.3	3.00
37 F:Sasuke the Demon Queller	3.00
38 Priest Sanshobo's temple	3.00
39 Grasscutter II,pt.1	3.00
40 V:Captain Quark	3.00
41 V:Neko Ninja	3.00
42 Grasscutter II,pt.4	3.00
43 Grasscutter II	3.00
44 Grasscutter II	3.00
45 Grasscutter II	3.00
46 wraparound(c),pt.1	3.00
47 wraparound(c),pt.2	3.00
48	3.00
49 Three seasons	3.00
50 Usagi dead?	3.00
51 The Shrouded Moon	3.00
52 Kitsune's youth	3.00
53 hunt for four ronin	3.00
54 Lone Goat and Kid	3.00
55 Lord Yoshikawa is dying	3.00
56 Katsuichi vs. Nakamura Joji	3.00
57 Crows,pt.1, renegade ronin	3.00
58 Crows,pt.2	3.00
59 Crows,pt.3	3.00
60 duel at Kitanoji	3.00
61 F:Chizu	3.00
62 Cursed woods	3.00
63 SS, return of Kitsune	3.00
64 SS, Tomago	3.00
65 SS	3.00
66 SS,giant monsters,pt.1	3.00
67 SS,giant monsters,pt.2	3.00
68 SS,giant monsters,pt.3	3.00
69 SS,Fathers and Sons,pt.1	3.00
70 SS,Fathers and Sons,pt.2	3.00
71 to 99 SS	@3.00
100 SS	3.50
101 thru 115 SS	@3.00

USAGI YOJIMBO
1996

1 SS,color spec	4.00
2 SS,color spec	3.00
3 SS,color spec	3.00
4 thru 6	@3.00

USAGI YOJIMBO COLOR SPECIAL: GREEN PERSIMMON

1-shot by Stan Sakai	3.00

VAMPIRELLA
(B&W) 1992

1 'The Lion and the Lizard'Pt.1	4.50
2 'The Lion and the Lizard'Pt.2	4.00
3 'The Lion and the Lizard'Pt.3	4.00
4 'The Lion and the Lizard'Pt.3	4.00
Spec. Vampirella's Summer Night	4.00

VAN HELSING
May, 2004

1-shot Movie tie-in	3.00

VENUS WARS
(B&W–Manga) 1991

1 Aphrodia V:Ishtar, with 2-card strip	3.00
2 I: Ken Seno	2.50
3 Aphrodia V:Ishtar	2.50
4 Seno Joins Hound Corps	2.50
5 SenoV:Octopus Supertanks	2.50
6 Chaos in Aphrodia	2.50
7 All Out Ground War	2.50
8 Ishtar V:Aphrodia contd	2.50
9 Ishtar V:Aphrodia contd	2.50
10 Supertanks of Ishtar Advance	2.50
11 Aphrodia Captured	2.50
12 A:Miranda,48-pg	2.75
13 Hound Brigade-Suicide Assault	2.50
14 V:Army	2.50
15	2.50

VENUS WARS II
1992

1 V:Security Police	2.75
2 Political Unrest	2.50
3 Conspiracy	2.50
4 A:Lupica	2.50
5 Love Hotel	2.50
6 Terran Consulate	2.50
7 Doublecross	2.50
8 D:Lupisa	3.00
9 A:Matthew	3.00
10 A:Mad Scientist	3.00
11 thru 15 V:Troopers	@3.00

VERSION
(B&W–Manga) 1993

1.1 by Hisashi Sakaguchi	2.50
1.2 thru 1.8	@2.50

VERSION II
(B&W–Manga) 1993

2.1 by Hisashi Sakaguchi	2.50
2.2 thru 2.7	@2.50

VIRUS
1993

1 MP(c),F:The Wan Xuan & the crew of the Electra	3.00
2 MP(c),V:Captian Powell	3.00
3 MP(c),V:Virus	3.00
4 MP(c),Last issue	3.00

VORTEX, THE

1	2.50

WACKY SQUIRREL
(B&W) 1987

1 thru 4	@2.75
Spec. Halloween Adventure	2.75
Spec. Summer Fun	2.75

WALTER:
CAMPAIGN OF TERROR
1996
1 thru 4 . . . . @2.50

Warrior of Waverly Street #1
© Dark Horse Comics

WARRIOR OF
WAVERLY STREET, THE
Nov., 1996
1 (of 2) by M.Coto & J. Stokes 3.00
2 . . . . 3.00
1-shot Broodstorm 3.00

WARWORLD!
(B&W) 1989
1 . . . . 3.00

WHITE LIKE SHE
(B&W) 1994
1 thru 4 by Bob Fingerman . . . . . @3.00

WHO WANTS TO BE
A SUPERHERO?
Oct., 2006
1 Feedback 3.50
Spec. Feedback (July 2007) 3.50

WILL TO POWER
Comics' Greatest World, 1994
1 BS, A:X 2.50
2 BS, A:X,Monster 2.50
3 BS, A:X 2.50
4 BS, In Steel Harbor 2.50
5 V:Wolfgang 2.50
6 V:Motorhead 2.50
7 JOy(c),V:Amazing Grace 2.50
8 V:Catalyst. 2.50
9 Titan, Grace 2.50
10 Vortex alien, Grace 2.50
11 Vortex alien, King Titan 2.50
12 Vortex alien. 2.50

WITCHBLADE/ALIENS/
DARKNESS/PREDATOR:
MINDHUNTER
Dec., 2000
1 thru 3 . . . . @3.00
2a variant TnD (c). 3.00

WIZARD OF
FOURTH STREET
(B&W) 1987
1 . . . . 3.00
2 thru 4 . . . . @2.50

WOLF & RED
1995
1 Looney Tunes 2.50
2 Watchdog Wolf. 2.50
3 Red Hot Riding Hood. 2.50

WORLD BELOW, THE
Mar., 1999
1 thru 4 PC . . . . @2.50

WORLD BELOW II, THE
Dec., 1999
1 (of 4) PC 3.00
2 thru 4 PC,Deeper and Stranger. . 3.00

X
Comics' Greatest World, 1994
1 B:StG(s),DoM,JP,I:X-Killer 3.00
2 DoM,JP,V:X-Killer. 2.50
3 DoM,JP,A:Pit Bulls 2.50
4 DoM,JP 2.50
5 DoM,JP,V:Chaos Riders 2.50
6 Cyberassassins 2.50
7 Alamout 2.50
8 A:Ghost 2.50
9 War for Arcadia 2.50
10 War for Arcadia. 2.50
11 I:Coffin, War 2.50
12 V:Coffin, A:Monster. 2.50
13 D:X 2.50
14 conclusion to War 2.50
15 JS,SiG,war survivors 2.50
16 V:Headhunter 2.50
17 . . . . 2.50
18 V:Predator. 2.50
19 V:Challenge 2.50
20 thru 25. . . . . @2.50
Spec. #1 One Shot to the Head. . . . 2.50

XENA:
WARRIOR PRINCESS
Aug., 1999
1 . . . . 3.00
2 thru 9 . . . . @3.00
10 IEd,MD2,wayward viking 3.00
11 IEd,MD2,V:Lamia 3.00
12 IEd,MD2,Darkness Falls,concl.. . 3.00
13 IEd,MD2,F:Legion 3.00
14 conclusion. 3.00
1 to 14 newsstand photo(c) . . . . . @3.00

YOUNG CYNICS CLUB
(B&W) 1993
1 by Glenn Wong 2.50

THE YOUNG INDIANA
JONES CHRONICLES
1992
1 DBa,FS,TV Movie Adapt 3.25
2 DBa,TV Movie Adapt 2.75
3 DBa,GM. 2.75
4 DBa,GM. 2.75
5 DBa,GM. 2.75
6 BBa,GM,WW1,French Army 2.75
7 The Congo. 2.75
8 Africa,A:A.Schweitzer 2.50
9 Vienna,Sophie-daughter of Arch-
　Duke Ferdinand. 2.50
10 In Vienna continued 2.50
11 Far East 2.50

12 Fever Issue 2.50

YOU'RE UNDER ARREST!
(B&W–Manga) 1995–96
1 by Kosuke Fujishima 3.00
2 thru 8 . . . . @3.00

ZERO KILLER
July., 2007
1 (of 6) 3.00
2 thru 4 . . . . @3.00

ZOMBIEWORLD:
1-shot Eat Your Heart Out, KJo 3.00
1-shot Home for the Holidays 3.00

ZOMBIEWORLD:
CHAMPION
OF THE WORMS
Sept., 1997
1 (of 3) MMi 3.00
2 and 3 . . . . @3.00
Spec. Home for the Holidays. 3.00

ZOMBIEWORLD:
DEAD END
Jan., 1998
1 (of 2) by Stephen Blue. 3.00
2 . . . . 3.00

ZOMBIEWORLD:
THE TREE OF DEATH
May, 1999
1 (of 4) by P. Mills & J.Deadstock. . 3.00
2 thru 4 . . . . @3.00

ZOMBIEWORLD:
WINTER'S DREGS
May, 1998
1 (of 4) by Fingerman & Edwards. . 3.00
2 thru 4 . . . . @3.00

ZONE, THE
(B&W) 1990
1-shot 3.00

Zombie World: Three of Death #3
© Dark Horse Comics

All comics prices listed are for *Near Mint* condition.

IMAGE

AARON STRIPS
(B&W) Apr., 1997
1 thru 4 rep. from Sunday comic
 strips, by Aaron Warner . . . . . @3.00

ACTION PLANET
(B&W) Sept., 1997
Prev. Action Planet Comics
3 . . . . 4.00

ADRENALYNN
Aug., 1999
1 F:Sabina Nikoli. 2.50
2 TnD,V:Russian monster androids 2.50
3 TnD,V:last 2 Monster-cyborgs . . . 2.50
4 TnD,the real Sabina 2.50

ADVENTURES OF AARON
(B&W) March, 1997
by Aaron Warner
1 'Baby-sitter Gone Bad'. 3.00
2 'Thunder Thighs of the
 Terrordome' 3.00
3 'Baby-sitter Gone Bad,' concl. . . . 3.00
100 Super Special 3.00
Christmas Spectacular #1 . . . . 3.00

ADVENTURES OF BARRY WEEN, BOY GENIUS, THE
(B&W) March, 1999
1 (of 3) by Judd Winick 3.00
2 Growing Pains 3.00
3 School 3.00

ADVENTURES OF SPAWN
Jan., 2007
1 Director's Cut. 6.00
2 The Awakening War, pt.2 . . . . . . 6.00

ADVENTURE STRIP DIGEST
(B&W) April, 1998
1 by Randy Reynaldo 3.00
2 F:Rob Hanes, detective 3.00

AFTER THE CAPE
(B&W) Mar., 2007
1 (of 3) 3.00
2 Secret Life 3.00
3 Somewhere Below Rock Bottom. 3.00

AFTER THE CAPE II
(B&W) Nov., 2007
1 Seasons in Change 3.00
2 Knockin on Heaven's Door 3.00
3 Til Death Do Us Part 3.00

AGENTS, THE
(B&W) April, 2003
1 thru 6 BDn . . . . @3.00

AGE OF BRONZE
(B&W) Nov., 1998
1 EiS,The Trojan War 3.00
2 EiS,Death of Paris 3.00
3 EiS,F:Herakles, Hektor 3.00
4 EiS,I:Helen. 3.00

5 EiS,Achilles disguised 3.00
6 EiS,Helen gone 3.50
7 EiS,Odysseus mad? 3.50
8 EiS,Achilles missing. 3.50
9 EiS,Will war start? 3.50
10 EiS,Sacrifice,pt.1. . . . . 3.50
11 EiS,Sacrifice,pt.2. . . . . 3.50
12 EiS,You're not the Trojans? . . . 3.50
13 thru 18 EiS,Sacrifice,pt.4–pt.9 @3.50
19 EiS,Sacrifice,pt.10. . . . . 3.50
20 Betrayal, pt.1. . . . . 3.50
21 Betrayal, pt 2. . . . . 3.50
22 Betrayal, pt.3. . . . . 3.50
23 Betrayal, pt.4. . . . . 3.50
24 thru 26 Betrayal, pt.5–7. . . . . @3.50
27 . . . . 3.50
Spec.1-shot Behind the Scenes . . 3.50
Spec.#1 EiS, House of Horror 3.00
Spec.#2 . . . . 3.00

AGE OF HEROES, THE
(B&W) Halloween, 1996
1 JHI & JRy. 3.00
2 JHI & JRy. 3.00
3 JHI & JRy,Luko,Trickster &
 Aerwyn try to steal treasure . . . 3.00
4 JHI & JRy,Drake, the blind
 swordsman returns 3.00
5 JHI & JRy,O:Conor One-Arm. . . . 3.00
Spec. #1 rep. #1 & #2 . . . . 5.00
Spec. #2 rep. #3 & #4 . . . . 7.00

AGE OF HEROES: WEX
(B&W) Aug., 1998
1 by JHI,Vurtex. 3.00

AGENCY, THE
Top Cow, July, 2001
1 (of 6) PJe. 4.00
1a variant(c) 4.00
1b variant MS(c). 4.00
2 PJe. 2.50
3 PJe. 2.50
4 PJe,A Virtual Secret. 3.00
5 PJe,Virtual 3.00
6 PJe,concl. 48-pg. 5.00

Allegra #1
© Wildstorm

ALETHIA
May, 2008
1 (of 3) 3.50
2 thru 3 . . . . @3.50

ALIEN PIG FARM 3000
Apr., 2007
1 (of 4) WiS(c) 3.00
2 MaS(c) 3.00
3 WiS(c) 3.00
4 MaS(c) 3.00

ALLEGRA
WildStorm, 1996
1 ScC,SSe 2.50
2 thru 4 . . . . @2.50

ALLEY CAT
July, 1999
1 BNa,MHw,F:Alley Baggett 2.50
1a variant painted cover (1:4). . . . 3.50
2 BNa,MHw,women murdered 2.50
3 photo(c) 2.50
3a variant JJu cover (1:4). 2.50
4 into darkness 2.50
5 The Martyr,pt.1. . . . . 3.00
6 The Martyr,pt.2. . . . . 3.00
7 The Martyr,pt.3. . . . . 2.50
Wizard World Spec.#1 . . . . 2.50
Lingerie Edition 5.00

ALLIANCE, THE
Shadowline, 1995
1 JV,I:The Alliance, A Call
 to Arms 2.50
2 JV,Team comes together 'Like
 Pieces of a Puzzle' 2.50
3 I:Slash C 2.50
4 . . . . 2.50
1a thru 4a variant covers . . . . . @2.50

ALLIES, THE
Extreme, 1995
1 mini-series 2.50
2 thru 4 . . . . @2.50

ALTERATION
Feb., 2004
1 . . . . 3.00
1a variant (c) AAd. 3.00
2 thru 4 . . . . @3.00
2a thru 4a variant (c)s. . . . . @3.00

ALTERED IMAGE
April, 1998
1 JV,The Day Reality Went Wild. . . 2.50
2 JV,F:Everybody smooshed 2.50
3 JV,Middle Age Crisis, concl. 2.50

AMANDA AND GUNN
(B&W) April, 1997
1 JeR, Montana 2036 . . . . 3.00
2 (of 4) JeR. 3.00
3 (of 4) JeR. 3.00
4 (of 4) JeR, conclusion 3.00

AMAZING JOY BUZZARDS, THE
(B&W) Dec., 2004
1 I was a Teenage Monster 3.00

2 The Island of Maru. 3.00	
3 ...Go Hollywood 3.00	
4 ...Go Hollywood,pt.2 . . . . 3.00	
5 Ready...Set...Ignition 3.00	
6 Here Come the Spiders, pt.2 . . . . 3.00	
7 Go, El Campeon, Go, pt.1 . . . . . 3.00	

Vol. 2, 2005
1 Here Come the Spiders, pt.1 . . . . 3.00
2 thru 5 . . . . @3.00

ANGELA
TMP, 1994–95
1 NGa(s),GCa,A:Spawn 15.00
2 NGa(s),GCa,Angela's trial 14.00
3 NGa(s),GCa,In Hell 12.00
Spec. Pirate Spawn(c) 32.00
Spec. Pirate Angela(c) (1995) 30.00

ANGELA/GLORY: RAGE OF ANGELS
TMP/Extreme, 1996
1 x-over begins 5.00

ANT
1 . . . . 3.00
2 . . . . 3.00
3 A:Spawn 3.00
4 . . . . 3.00
5 thru 9 Moving On . . . . @3.00
10 thru 12 1992, Part Three 3.00
13 . . . . 3.00

APHRODITE IX
Top Cow, Aug., 2000
1 by David Finch. 4.00
1a variant JBz(c). 4.00
1a signed 15.00
1b variant Michale Turner(c). 4.00
1c variant MS(c) 4.00
2 amnesia 3.50
3 conspiracy 3.50
0 with pin-up & poster. 3.00
4 Who is she? 48-pg. 5.50
Spec.1 Convention spec., signed . 20.00
Preview ed., signed 5.00

ARCANUM
Top Cow, March, 1997
[Mini-series]
1 BPe, from Medieval
 Spawn/Witchblade. 3.00
1a variant MS(s) (1:4). 2.50
2 BPe, Chi in Asylum 2.50
3 BPe, Ming Chang captive in
 Atlantis. 2.50
4 BPe,'The End?' 2.50
5 BPe,Royale's secret journal 2.50
6 BPe,Safe Haven? 2.50
7 BPe,Egypt 2.50

ARCHIBALD SAVES
Nov., 2007
1-Shot Christmas 3.00
1-Shot Easter (2008) 3.50

AREA 52
Jan., 2001
1 . . . . 3.00
2 The Gloves are off 3.00
3 Out of the Frying Pan and
 into the Fire 3.00
4 Beginning of the End 3.00

ARIA
Avalon, Nov., 1998
1 by Brian Holguin & Jay Anacleto . 6.00
1a variant cover 8.00

2 A:Mad Gwynnion 3.00	
3 English Countryside. 3.00	
4 V:Dark One 3.00	
4a glow-in-the-dark(c). 10.00	
5 London, 1966. . . . . 3.00	
6 Subterranean Homesick Blues . . 3.00	
7 Mad Gods and Irish Men 3.00	

Preview ed. F:Kildare. 3.00
Spec.#1 Blanc & Noir, sketchbook. . 3.00
Spec.#1 alternate cover 7.00
Spec.#2 Blanc & Noir. 3.00
Sketchbook by Jay Anacleto 6.00
Coll.Ed.#1, rep.#1–#2 . . . . 6.00

ARIA/ANGELA: HEAVENLY CREATURES
Feb., 2000
1 (of 2) x-over 5.00
1a variant JQ(c) (1:4) 3.00
1b variant J.G. Jones(c) (1:4) 4.00
1c variant Jay Anacleto(c) (1:4) . . . 3.00
1 B&W 3.00
2 x-over concl. 3.00
2a variant(c) 4.00
Museum edition 125.00

ARIA: THE SOUL MARKET
March, 2001
1 Legend continues 4.00
1a Museum edition 125.00
2 F:Robin Goodfellow 3.00
3 A Dark Rider Approaches 3.00
4 Auction of imprisoned souls. 3.00
5 What price a soul? 3.00
6 Mortality 3.00
GN A Midwinter's Dream,40-pg. . . . 5.00

ARIA: A SUMMER SPELL
March, 2002
1 (of 2) London, summer 1967 . . . . 3.00
2 Kildare is in love 3.00

ARIA: THE USES OF ENCHANTMENT
Feb., 2003
1 thru 4 . . . . @3.00

ARKAGA
Sept., 1997
1 by Arnie Tang Jorgensen 3.00
2 Desire for revenge 3.00

ARMOR X
Mar., 2005
1 ASm 3.00
2 ASm 3.00
3 ASm 3.00
4 ASm, The End 3.00

ARMORY WARS, THE
June, 2007
1 . . . . 10.00
1a variant (c) 10.00
2 . . . . 25.00
3 thru 4 . . . . @5.00
5 . . . . 3.00

ARMORY WARS II, THE
June, 2008
1 (of 5) 2nd State Turbine Blade. . . 3.00
2 thru 5 2nd State Turbine Blade @3.00

ASCENSION
Top Cow, Sept., 1997
1 by David Finch,F:Angels 4.00
2 Andromeda fights alone 3.00

Ascension #3
© Top Cow

3 reunited with Lucien. 3.00
4 . . . . 3.00
5 Gregorieff and Dayak Army 3.00
6 Voivodul returns, concl. 3.00
7 Andy's problems worsen 2.50
8 revenge on Dayaks & Mineans . . 2.50
9 Andy exiled 2.50
10 A:D. Gavin Taylor 2.50
11 A:D. Gavin Taylor 2.50
12 A:turning point. 2.50
13 A:Grigorieff, Petra 2.50
14 V:Marcus,A:Andromeda 2.50
15 Rowena's secrets 2.50
16 Petra joins Lucien 2.50
17 a schism 2.50
18 V:new entity 2.50
19 to Petra's Minean home 2.50
20 Resurrection,pt.1. . . . . 2.50
21 Resurrection,pt.2. . . . . 2.50
22 trapped 3.00
23 Andromeda's new outfit 3.00
Coll.Ed.#1, rep.#1–#2 . . . . 5.00
Coll.Ed.#2 . . . . 5.00

ASTOUNDING SPACE THRILLS
April, 2000
1 Ken Kelly(c),Cydonian Contant . . 3.00
2 The Criminal Code. 3.00
3 Gordo:Earthling Prime,
 flip-book 3.00
4 The Craving of Consumorr,
 flip-book. 3.00
5 Attack of the Macrobes 3.00

ASTOUNDING WOLF-MAN
July, 2007
1 . . . . 3.00
1a director's cut 4.00
2 thru 3 . . . . @3.50
4 thru 12 . . . . @3.00

ASTRO
April, 2006
1 . . . . 7.00

ATHEIST, THE
(B&W) Feb., 2005
1 PhH,Incarnate 3.50
2 PhH,Incarnate,pt.2: The Tumor . . 3.50
3 PhH,Incarnate,pt.3: Desperate
 Measures. 3.50
4 PhH,Incarnate, pt.4: Sacrifice . . . 3.50

IMAGE

ATHENA INC.
2002
1-shot Agents Roster,48-pg. 6.00
The Beginning, 48-pg. 6.00
1 reoffered 3.00
2 Gwen has a stalker 3.00
2a variant(c) 3.00
3 Gwen hearing voices 3.00
3a variant(c) 3.00
4 Revelations 3.00
4a variant(c) 3.00
5 The Belly of the Beast 3.00
6 All Hell Breaks Loose. 3.00
5a– a variant (c) . . . . @3.00

ATOMIC TOYBOX
April, 1999
Odyssey Line
1 AaL,F:Ken Logan. 3.00
2 AaL,The Aliens are comming. . . . 3.00

AUTOMATION
Flypaper, 1998
1 Robots sent to Mars, and back . . 3.00
2 One goes mad. 3.00
3 Sherzad vs. Konak 3.00

AVIGON
(B&W) Oct., 2000
Spec. 56-pg. 6.00
GN 6.00
GN Gods and Demons (2005). . . . 20.00

THE AWAKENING
(B&W) Oct., 1997
1 (of 4) by Stephen Blue 3.00
2 thru 4 . . . . @3.00

BACKLASH
WildStorm, 1994–97
1 Taboo, 2 diff. covers 4.00
1a variant edition, 2 covers. 3.00
2 Savage Dragon 2.50
3 V:Savage Dragon 2.50
4 SRf,A:Wetworks. 2.50
5 SRf,A:Dane 2.50
6 BBh,SRf,A:Wetworks. 2.50
7 BBh,SRf,V:Bounty Hunters 2.50
8 RMz,BBh,BWS(c),WildStorm
   Rising,pt.8,w/2 cards 2.50

Backlash #26
© Wildstorm

8a Newsstand ed. 2.50
9 F:Taboo,Dingo,V:Chasers 2.50
10 I:Crimson. 2.50
11 R:Bloodmoon 2.50
12 R:Taboo,Crimson's Costume . . . 3.00
13 Taboo to the Rescue 2.50
14 A:Deathblow 2.50
15 F:Cyberjack. 2.50
16 F:Cole,Marc 2.50
17 F:Marc,Kink. 2.50
18 . . . . 2.50
19 Fire From Heaven,pt.2 . . . . 2.50
20 SRf,BBh,Fire From
   Heaven,pt.10 . . . . 2.50
21 SRf,BBh 2.50
22 SRf,BBh 2.50
23 SRf,BBh 2.50
24 SRf,BBh,return of Dingo 2.50
25 SRf,BBh,56-pg. special 4.00
26 SRf,BBh,IR:Gramalkin 2.50
27 SRf,BBh 2.50
28 SRf,BBh,Backlash leads PSI
   team to Europe 2.50
29 SRf,BBh,Haroth raises the
   remnants of Atlantis. 2.50
30 SRf,BBh,Backlash confronts
   Kherubim lords 2.50
31 SRf,BBh,team returns to PSI . . . 2.50
32 SRf,BBh,earth-shattering
   final issue 2.50

BACKLASH/SPIDER-MAN
WildStorm/Marvel, 1996
1 x-over,pt.1 . . . . 2.50
1a variant cover 3.00
2 x-over,pt.2 . . . . 2.50

BACK TO BROOKLYN
Sept., 2008
1 thru 3 GEn . . . . @3.00
1a variant (c). 3.00

BADGER
(B&W) May, 1997
1 MBn,'Betelgeuse'. 3.00
2 MBn,'Beefalo don't like fences' . . 3.00
3 MBn,'Loose Eel'. 3.00
4 MBn,'Hot House' 3.00
5 MBn,Octopi in the hot tub 3.00
6 MBn,Prime Minister of
   Klactoveedesteen 3.00
7 MBn,Crime Comics 3.00
8 MBn,Root. 3.00
9 MBn 3.00
10 MBn,Tuesday Ruby 3.00
11 MBn,Watch the Skies 3.00
12 MBn,The Lady Cobras 3.00
13 MBn,Horse Police 3.00
14 MBn,Badger Sells Out 3.00

BAD IDEAS
Apr., 2004
1 and 2 (of 2) 48-pg. . . . . @6.00

BAD PLANET
Dec., 2005
1 (of 6) 3.00
1 new printing 3.00
2 Alien Death Spiders 3.00
3 Super-Terror 3D. 3.50
4 . . . . 3.00
5 The Convict's Story 3.00
6 . . . . 3.00

BADROCK
Extreme, 1995
1a RLd(p),TM(c),A:Dragon 2.50
1b SPa(ic),A:Savage Dragon 2.50
1c DF(ic) 2.50

2 RLd,ErS(s),V:Girth,A:Savage
   Dragon, flip-book-Grifter/
   Badrock #2 . . . . 2.50
3 RLd,ErS,V:The Overlord 2.50
Ann.#1 I:Gunner, 48-pg. 3.00
Super-Spec. #1 A:Grifter & The
   Dragon. 2.50

BADROCK
AND COMPANY
Extreme, 1994–95
1 KG(s) 2.50
1a San Diego Comic Con ed. 3.00
2 RLd(c),Fuji 2.50
3 Overtkill,'Overt Operations' 2.50
4 TBm,MBm,TNu,A:Velocity 2.50
5 A:Grifter 2.50
6 Finale,A:ShadowHawk. 2.50

BALLISTIC
Top Cow, 1995
1 F:Wetworks 3.00
2 F:Wetworks,Jesters
   Transformation 3.00
3 F:Wetworks,final issue. 3.00

BALLISTIC ACTION
Top Cow, 1996
1 MSi(c), pin-ups. 3.00

BALLISTIC IMAGERY
Top Cow, 1996
1 F:Hellcop,Heavy Space,
   Cyberforce,anthology 3.00

BALLISTIC/WOLVERINE
Top Cow/Marvel, 1996
1 Devil's Reign,pt.4,x-over 4.00

BANISHED KNIGHTS
Dec., 2001
1 vampire civil war 3.00
1A variant(c) 3.00
1B holofoil(c). 5.00
2 F:Greyson & Belmiro 3.00

BASTARD SAMURAI
April, 2002
1 (of 3) 3.00
2 thru 3 F:Toshi. . . . . @3.00

Battle Chasers #1
© Cliffhanger

BATTLE CHASERS
Cliffhanger, April, 1998
1 JMd, fantasy, team-up 9.00
1a Chromium ed. (5,000 made) . . 35.00
2 JMd,F:Gully 5.00
3 JMd,new ally 4.00
4 JMd,Red Monika 4.00
4a,b,c JMd variant covers . . . . . . @3.00
5 JMd,V:Lord August,with 8-pg.
   Planetary #0 . . . . 3.00
6 JMd 3.00
6a variant AWa(c) 4.00

WildStorm/DC, Nov., 2000
7 JMd(c)(1:2) 3.00
7a variant JSC(c) (1:4) 4.00
7b variant HuR(c) (1:4) 7.00
8 JMd,V:Harvester 3.00
Prelude #1, JMd, 16-pg. 10.00

BATTLE HYMN
Dec., 2004
1 thru 5 . . . . @3.00

BATTLE OF THE PLANETS
Top Cow, July, 2002
1 AxR 3.00
1a-c variant(c)s . . . . @3.00
1d convention(c) 3.00
1e holofoil edition 6.00
2 AxR,attack on earth begins 3.00
3 AxR,The Firey Phoenix 3.00
4 Zoltar 3.00
5 Spectra connected to suicides. . . 3.00
6 Under A Blood Red Sky,pt.1 . . . 3.00
7 Under A Blood Red Sky,pt.2 . . . 3.00
8 Under A Blood Red Sky,pt.3 . . . 3.00
9 Under A Blood Red Sky,pt.4 . . . 3.00
10 Aftermath. 3.00
11 Second Encounters. 3.00
12 concl., 48-pg. 5.00
1-shot flip-book Thundercats 5.00
1-shot Mark 5.00
1-shot Battle Book 5.00
1-shot Hell, 48-pg. 5.00
2 animation (c) 5.00
1/2 reprint. 3.00

BATTLE OF THE
PLANETS:
COUP DE GRAS
Top Cow, June, 2005
1 (of 2) 3.00

BATTLE OF THE
PLANETS: MANGA
Top Cow, Oct., 2003
1 . . . . 3.00
2 . . . . 3.00
3 finale 3.00

BATTLE OF THE
PLANETS: PRINCESS
Top Cow, 2004
1 (of 6) 3.00
2 thru 6 Princess, pt.2–pt.6 . . . . . @3.00

BATTLE OF THE
PLANETS: WITCHBLADE
Top Cow, Jan., 2003
1 48-pg. 7.00

BATTLE POPE
June, 2005
1 . . . . 3.00
2 The Zombie Twins 3.00

3 . . . . 3.00
4 . . . . 3.00
5 . . . . 3.00
6 . . . . 3.00
7 Hellcorp in Shambles. 3.00
8 V:Brenda 3.00
9 New Home. 3.00
10 Celebrity Status. 3.00
11 48-pg. 5.00
12 . . . . 3.50
13 . . . . 3.00
14 Vs. God, conclusion 3.50

BATTLESTONE
Extreme, 1994
1 RLd,ErS,MMy,AV 2.50
1a variant cover 3.00
2 RLd,ErS,MMy,AV,I&D:Roarke,
   finale 2.50

BEDLAM
July, 2006
1-shot 48-page. 5.00

BEETLEBORGS
Extreme, Nov., 1996
1 from TV show 2.50

BERZERKERS
Extreme, 1995
1 F:Greylore,Hatchet,Psi-Storm,
   Cross,Wildmane,Youngblood#2 2.50
2 Into the Darkness 2.50
3 Slay Ride 2.50
4 final issue. 2.50

BEYOND AVALON
Jan., 2005
1 Wanderlust, pt.1 . . . . 3.00
2 Wanderlust, pt.2 . . . . 3.50
3 . . . . 3.50

BIG BANG COMICS
Big Bang Studios, 1996
(B&W) Prev.: Caliber
1 F:Mighty Man. 2.50
2 Silver Age Shadowhawk 2.50
3 . . . . 2.50
4 . . . . 3.00
5 Top Secret Origins. 3.00
6 Round Table of America and
   Knights of Justice meet, orig.
   mini-series #3 (color). 3.00
7 . . . . 3.00
8 F:Mister U.S. 3.00
9 I:Peter Chefren 3.00
10 F:Galahad 3.00
11 Faulty Towers is destroying
   Midway City 3.00
12 F:The Savage Dragon 3.00
13 by Jeff Weigel, 40-pg.spec. . . . 3.00
14 RB,A:The Savage Dragon 3.00
15 SBi(c),F:Dr. Weird. 3.00
16 F:Thunder Girl. 3.00
17 . . . . 3.00
18 Savage Dragon on Trial 3.00
19 O:Beacon,Hummingbird 3.00
20 F:Knight Watchman,Blitz. 3.00
21 F:Shadow Lady. 3.00
22 The Bird-Man of Midway City . . 3.00
23 Riddle of the Sphinx, sequel. . . 3.00
24 History of Big Bang,Vol.1 . . . . . 4.00
25 Anniv. iss. 4.00
26 Murder by Microphone, concl. . 3.00
27 History of Big Bang,Vol.2 . . . . . 4.00
28 Knight of the Living Dead,pt.1 . 4.00
29 Knight of the Living Dead,pt.2 . 4.00
30 F:Knight Watchman 4.00

Big Bang #22
© Big Bang Studios

31 F:Knight-Sprite 4.00
32 F:Pink Flamingo 4.00
33 Peril of Parallel Planets 4.00
34 To Save the Gods. 4.00
35 Big Bang vs. 1963 . . . . 4.00
Giant Sz. Ann.#1 Ultiman. 5.00
Summer Spec.b&w, 48-pg. (2003). . 5.00
1-shot Round Table of America 3.00

BIG BANG PRESENTS:
ULTIMAN FAMILY
Mar., 2005
1-shot F:The Ultimate Ape. 3.50

BIG BRUISERS
WildStorm, 1996
1 F:Maul,Impact,Badrock 3.50

BIG HAIR PRODUCTIONS
(B&W) Feb., 2000
1 by Andy Suriano,F:Astro-Bug . . . 3.50
2 . . . . 3.50

BLACK AND WHITE
Hack Studios, 1996
1 ATi,New heroes,'Beginnings' 2.50
2 ATi(p),apparent death 2.50
3 V:Chang. 2.50
Ashcan 5.00

BLACK ANVIL
Top Cow, 1996
1 & 2 . . . . 2.50

BLACK FLAG
Extreme, 1994
1 B&W Preview. 3.00

BLACK FOREST, THE
Mar., 2004
GN 10.00
GN Book 2 The Castle of Shadows. 7.00

BLACKLIGHT
June, 2005
1 JV 3.00
2 . . . . 3.00
3 Light From A Dead Star. 3.00
4 Suffer not a corpse to live, x-over 3.00

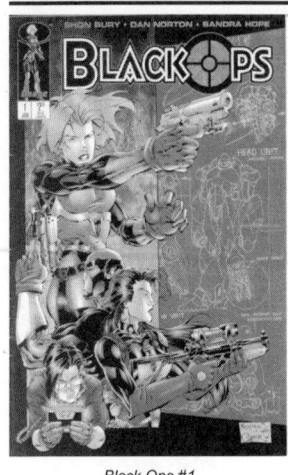

Black Ops #1
© WildStorm

BLACK MIST
(B&W) Feb., 2007
1 (of 4) 4.00
2 . . . . 4.00
3 . . . . 4.00
4 . . . . 5.00

BLACK OPS
WildStorm, 1996
1 thru 5 . . . . @2.50

BLACK TIDE
Nov., 2001
1 . . . . 3.00
1a variant(c) 3.00
1b variant(c) 3.00
2 Balance of Power 3.50
3 One Man's Enemy 3.50
4 Deception, Secrets and Lies 3.50

BLAIR WITCH: DARK TESTAMENTS
Oct., 2000
Spec. IEd,CAd 3.00

BLINDSIDE
Extreme, Aug., 1996
1 MMy & AV, F:Nucgaek Jeno 2.50
2 MMy & AV, Origin continues 2.50

BLISS ALLEY
(B&W) July, 1997
1 BML 3.00
2 BML,F:Wizard Walker 3.00
3 BML,Inky-Dinks 3.00

BLOKHEDZ
Nov., 2003
1 (of 4) 3.00
2 . . . . 3.00
Street Legends, 2004
3 thru 4 . . . . 3.00

BLOODHUNTER
Extreme, Nov., 1996
1 RV, Cabbot Stone rises from the
    slab 3.00

BLOOD LEGACY
Top Cow, April, 2000
1 MHw,The Story of Ryan 2.50
1a variant Keu Cha(c) 2.50
1b variant Mike Turner(c) 2.50
2 thru 4 MHw, F:Dr. Ryerson . . . @2.50
1-shot The Young Ones (2003) 4.00

BLOOD NATION
Platinum, Feb., 2007
1 (of 4) 3.00
2 thru 4 . . . . @3.00

BLOODPOOL
Exteme, 1995
1 I:Seoul,Rubbe,Wylder,
    'Discharged' 2.50
1a variant cover 2.50
2 The Hills Are Alive 2.50
3 Walk Like an Egyptian 2.50
4 final issue 2.50
[Regular Series] 1996
1 thru 3 JDy . . . . @2.50

BLOODSTREAM
Jan., 2004
1 (of 4) 3.00
2 of 4 . . . . @3.00

BLOODSTRIKE
Extreme, 1993
1 A:Brigade,Rub the Blood(c)
    Blood Brother prelude,x-over . . 3.50
2 I:Lethal,V:Brigade,BloodBrothers,
    pt.2,B:BU:Knight 3.00
3 B:ErS(s),ATi(c),V:Coldsnap,Blood
    Brothers,pt.4,'Turning Point' . . . 3.00
4 ErS(s) 3.00
5 KG,I:Noble,A:Supreme 3.00
6 KG(s),CAx,C&J:Chapel,'Inside
    Project:Born Again' 3.00
7 KG,RHe,A:Badrock,'Changing
    of the Guard' 3.00
8 RHe,A:Spawn,Sleeping & Waking 3.00
9 RHe,Extreme Prejudice,pt.3,
    I:Extreme Warrior,ATh,BU: Black
    & White 3.00
10 Extreme Prejudice,pt.7,
    V:Brigade, B:BU:Knight 3.00
25 I:Cabbot Bloodstrike 3.00
11 ErS(s),ATi(c),V:Coldsnap 3.00

Bloodstrike #2
© Image/Extreme

12 ErS(s) 3.00
13 KG,A:Supreme,'BetterOffDead' . . 3.00
14 KG(s),CAx,C&J:Chapel 3.00
15 KG,RHe,A:Badrock,War Games,
    pt.1,Extreme Sacrifice begins . . 3.00
16 KG,RHe,War Games,pt.3,Extreme
    Sacrifice ignites 3.00
17 KIA,V:The Horde 3.00
18 ExtremeSacrifice,pt.3,x-over 3.00
19 V:The Horde 3.00
20 R:Deadlock New Order 3.00
21 KA,V:Epiphany New Order 3.00
22 V:The Horde, last issue 3.00
25 see above, after #10
Ashcan 3.00

BLOODSTRIKE: ASSASSIN
Extreme, 1995
0 R:Battlestone 3.00
1 Debut new series 3.00
1a alternate cover 3.00
2 V:M.D.K. Assassins 3.00
3 V:Persuasion 3.00

BLOODWULF
Extreme, 1995
1 RLd,R:Bloodwulf 2.50
1b Run OJ Run 2.50
1c Alternate cover 2.50
1d Alternate cover 2.50
2 A:Hot Blood 2.50
3 Slippery When Wet 2.50
4 Darkness Gnaws at my Soul,
    final issue 2.50
Summer Spec.#1 V:Supreme
    Freeferall (1995) 2.50

BLUE
Aug., 1999
1 Android teenager 2.50
2 by Greg Aronowitz 2.50
3 rescue mission 2.50

BLUNTMAN AND CHRONIC
Aug., 2001
GN MiA 15.00

BODY BAGS
Nov., 2008
1-shot JPn 6.00

BODY BAGS: FATHER'S DAY
July, 2005
1 JPn,48-page 6.00
2 JPn,48-page 6.00
1-shot Three The Hard Way 6.00
1-shot One Shot (2006) 6.00

BODYCOUNT
March, 1996
1 KEa,SBs 2.50
2 thru 4 KEa,SBs . . . . @2.50

BOHOS
Flypaper (B&W) 1998
1 by Maggie Whorf & B.Penaranda 3.00
2 F:teenage bohemians 3.00
3 concl. 3.00

BOMB QUEEN
Feb., 2006
1 thru 4 . . . . @3.50
1-shot Bomb Queen vs. Blacklight . 3.50

BOMB QUEEN II
Oct., 2006
1 Queen of Hearts, pt.1 . . . . 3.50
2 thru 3 Queen of Hearts,pt.2–pt.3. 3.50

BOMB QUEEN III
Mar., 2007
1 (0f 4) JV, The Good, The Bad
   and the Lovely 3.50
1a variant incentive JLi (c) 3.50
2 thru 4 . . . . @3.50

BOMB QUEEN IV
Aug, 2007
1 (of 4) Suicide Bomber 3.50
2 thru 4 . . . . @3.50

BOMB QUEEN V
Shadowline, May, 2008
1 (of 6) Divine Comedy, pt.1 . . . . . 3.50
2 Divine Comedy, pt.2 . . . . 3.50
3 Divine Comedy, pt.3 . . . . 3.50
4 Divine Comedy, pt.4 . . . . 3.50
5 Divine Comedy, pt.5 . . . . 3.50
6 Divine Comedy, pt.6 . . . . 3.50

BONDS
Aug., 2007
1 (of 3) Allegro 4.00
2 Adagio 4.00
3 Finale 4.00

BONE
(B&W) Dec., 1995
[Prev.: Cartoon Books]
21 thru 25 . . . . @4.00
26 The Turning 4.00
27 end of Dragonslayer storyline . . 4.00
Bone Sourcebook 1.00
reprints with new covers
#1 thru #9 . . . . @3.00
10 rep. 'Great Cow Race' 3.00
Cartoon Books
11 Aftermath of the Great Cow
   Race 3.00
12 . . . . 3.00
13 Thar she blows 3.00
14 . . . . 3.00
15 Double or nothing 3.00
16 hiding from the Rat Creatures . . 3.00
17 with 5 new pages 3.00
18 Betrayed 3.00
19 'Three cheers for Dragon-slayer
   Phoney Bone' 3.00
20 Phoney Bone vs. Lucius 3.00

BONE REST
July, 2005
1 . . . . 3.00
2 Oplficium Dei, pt.1 . . . . 3.00
3 Opificium Dei,pt.2 . . . . 3.00
4 Opificium Dei, concl. 3.00
5 Second Coming, pt.1 . . . . 3.00
6 Second Coming, pt.2 . . . . 3.00
7 Second Coming, pt.3 . . . . 3.00
8 Second Coming, pt.4 . . . . 3.00

BOOF
TMP, 1994
1 . . . . 2.50
2 Meathook 2.50
3 Joyride 2.50
4 thru 6 . . . . @2.50

BOOF AND THE BRUISE CREW
TMP, 1994
1 . . . . 2.50
2 thru 5 . . . . @2.50
6 I:Mortar,O:Bruise Crew 2.50

BOOK OF SHADOWS
April, 2006
1 (of 2) 3.50
2 . . . . 3.50

BRASS
WildStorm, 1996
1 Rib,AWa,Folio Edition 3.50
2 Rib,AWa 2.50
3 Rib,AWa,concl. 2.50

BRAWL
(B&W) Oct, 2007
1 thru 3 . . . . @3.00

BRIGADE
Extreme, 1993
[1st Series]
1 RLd(s),MMy,I:Brigade,Genocide . 3.50
1a Gold ed. 7.00
2 RLd(s),V:Genocide,w/coupon#4 . 4.00
2a w/o coupon 2.25
2b Gold ed. 4.00
3 I:Birds of Prey,V:Genocide 2.50
4 CyP,Youngblood#5 flip 2.50
[2nd Series]
0 RLd(s),ATi(c),JMs,NRd,I:Warcry,
   A:Emp,V:Youngblood 2.50
1 I:Boone,Hacker,V:Bloodstrike,
   Blood Brothers,pt.1 . . . . 2.75
1a Gold ed. 3.00
2 C:Coldsnap,Blood Brothers,pt.3 . 3.00
3 ErS(s),GP(c),MMy,NRd(i),I:Roman
   V:Bloodstrike,Blood Brothers,
   pt.5 . . . . 2.50
4 Rip(s),MMy,RHe,Changes,
   BU:Lethal. 2.50
5 Rip(s),MMy,It's A VeryDeepSea . 2.50
6 Rip(s),MMy,I:Coral,Warlok,
   BU:Hackers Tale 2.50
7 Rip(s),MMy,V:Warlok 2.50
8 ErS(s),MMy,Extreme Prejudice,
   pt.2,BU:Black & White,pt.5 . . . . 2.50

Brigade #9
© Image/Extreme

9 ErS(s),MMy,Extreme Prejudice
   pt.6,ATh,BU:Black & White 2.50
25 ErS(s),MMy,D:Kayo,Coldsnap,
   Thermal 2.50
26 Images of Tomorrow 2.50
10 Extreme Prejudice 2.50
11 WildC.A.T.S. 2.50
12 Battlestone 2.50
13 Thermal 2.50
14 Teamate deaths 2.50
15 MWm,R:Roman Birds of Prey . . 2.50
16 ExtremeSacrifice,pt.4,x-over. . . 2.50
17 MWn,I:New Team 2.50
18 I:The Shape New Order 2.50
19 MWn,F:Troll,Glory 2.50
20 MWn,alien cult saga,concl. 2.50
21 F:ShadowHawk 2.50
22 Supreme Apocalypse,pt.4 . . . . . 2.50
23 . . . . 2.50
24 . . . . 2.50
25 & 26 see above
27 Extreme Babewatch 2.50
Sourcebook 3.00

BRIT
July, 2003
1-shot b&w, 48-pg. 5.00
1-shot Brit: Cold Death 5.00
1-shot Red,White,Black & Blue 5.00
Jan., 2007
1 . . . . 3.00
2 thru 6 . . . . @3.00
7 F:Invincible. 3.00
8 Invasion 3.00
9 Team up of the century 3.00
10 Brawl to end them all 3.00
11 V:The Emperor 3.00
12 . . . . 3.00

BROKEN TRINITY
Top Cow, July, 2008
1 RMz 3.00
1a variant (c) 3.00
1a San Diego variant 10.00
2 thru 3 RMz(s),PHh . . . . @3.00
2a thru 3a variant (c) . . . . @3.00
Spec. Broken Trinity:The Darkness . 3.00
Spec. a variant (c) 3.00
1-shot Broken Trinity: Angelus 3.00
1-shot a variant (c) 3.00
1-shot Witchblade 3.00
1-shot a variant (c) 3.00

BUGBOY
(B&W) June 1998
1-shot, by Mark Lewis, 48-pg. 4.00

BULLETPROOF MONK
Flypaper, Nov., 1998
1 in San Francisco 3.00
2 N.Y. Chinatown 3.00
3 conclusion 3.00
1-shot Tales of the B P M 3.00

BURGLAR BILL
(B&W) Nov., 2004
1 (of 6) by Paul Grist 3.00
2 thru 6 . . . . @3.00

BUTCHER KNIGHT
Top Cow, July, 2000
1 DT,F:Luther Washington 2.50
1a variant(c) MS (1:3) 2.50
1b variant(c) DT (1:3) 2.50
2 DT 2.50
3 DT,Blood & Gore 2.50
4 DT,concl. 3.00

CAPES
Sept., 2003
1 thru 3 . . . . @3.00

CARVERS
Flypaper, Oct., 1998
1 F:five snowboarders 3.00
2 J:Crazy Jack 3.00
3 V:Evil Yeti. 3.00

CASANOVA
June, 2006
1 . . . . 2.50
2 thru 6 . . . . @2.50
7 thru 14 . . . . @2.00

CASEFILES:
SAM AND TWITCH
May, 2003
1 Have You Seen Me?,pt.1. . . . . . . 3.00
2 thru 6 Have You Seen
  Me?, pt.2 thru pt.6 . . . . @3.00
7 Skeletons,pt.1 . . . . 3.00
8 Skeletons,pt.2 . . . . 3.00
9 Skeletons,pt.3 . . . . 3.00
10 Skeletons,pt.4 . . . . 3.00
11 Skeletons,pt.5 . . . . 3.00
12 Skeletons,pt.6 . . . . 3.00
13 Cops and Robbers 2.50
14 Ancient Chinese Secret,pt.1 . . . 2.50
15 Ancient Chinese Secret,pt.2 . . . 2.50
16 Ancient Chinese Secret,pt.3 . . . 2.50
17 Ancient Chinese Secret,pt.4 . . . 2.50
18 Ancient Chinese Secret,pt.5 . . . 2.50
19 Ancient Chinese Secret,pt.6 . . . 2.50
20 Fathers and Daughters, pt.1. . . . 2.50
21 Fathers and Daughters, pt.2. . . . 2.50
22 Fathers and Daughters, pt.3. . . . 2.50
23 . . . . 3.00
24 . . . . 3.00
25 Fathers and Daughters 3.00

CASUAL HEROES
Motown, 1996
1 . . . . 2.50
2 thru 6 . . . . @2.50

CELESTINE
Extreme, 1996
1 and 2 . . . . @2.50

Celestine #2
© Image/Extreme

CEMETERY BLUES
Jan., 2008
1 (of 3) Haunting of Hernesburg. . . 3.00
2 Haunting of Hernesburg, pt.2 . . . 3.00
3 Haunting of Hernesburg, pt.3 . . . 3.00

CHANNEL ZERO
(B&W) 1998
1 by Brian Wood 3.00
2 . . . . 3.00
3 gone global 3.00
4 Filter. 3.00
5 Brink of Millennium crash 3.00
6 Sound system 3.00

CHAPEL
Extreme, 1995
1 BWn,F:Chapel 3.50
2 V:Colonel Black 3.00
2a variant cover 2.50
[Regular Series]
1 BWn,F:Chapel 2.50
1a variant cover 2.50
2 V:Giger. 2.50
3 V:Giger. 2.50
4 Extreme Babewatch. 2.50
5 Hell on Earth,pt.1. . . . . 2.50
6 Hell on Earth,pt.2. . . . . 2.50
7 Shadowhunt x-over,pt.2 . . . . 2.50

CHARLATAN BALL
June, 2008
1 JoC(s) 2.50
2 thru 6 JoC(s) . . . . @2.50

CHASSIS
Nov., 1999
1 F:Chassis McBain 3.00
2 . . . . 3.00
2a variant Matt Busch(c). 3.00
3 Gizmotech Industries 3.00
4 . . . . 3.00
4a Collector's variant(c) 4.00
5 Slic's One Shot, flip-cover 3.00

CHEMIST, THE
July, 2007
1 . . . . 3.50
2 . . . . 3.50

CHILDHOOD'S END
(B&W) Oct., 1997
1 (of 5) JCf,community playground. 3.00

THE C.H.I.X.
THAT TIME FORGOT
Studiosaurus, Aug., 1998
1 F:Good Girl 3.00

CHOLLY AND FLYTRAP
Nov., 2004
1 (of 4) by Arthur Suydam 5.00
2 Center City. 5.00
3 . . . . 5.00
4 . . . . 5.00
Spec. Date With The Devil, 48-pg. . 6.00

CIRCLE, THE
Nov., 2008
1 Goliath Trap, pt.1 . . . . 3.00
2 thru 5 Goliath Trap,pt.2 – pt.5 . @3.00

CITY OF HEROES
Top Cow, May, 2005
1 Hard Crash, pt.1 . . . . 3.00

2 Hard Crash, pt.2 . . . . 3.00
3 Hard Crash, pt.3 . . . . 3.00
4 Smoke and Mirrors,pt.1 . . . . 3.00
5 Smoke and Mirrors,pt.2 . . . . 3.00
6 Smoke and Mirrors,pt.3 . . . . 3.00
7 DJu 3.00
8 DJu 3.00
9 DJu 3.00
10 thru 16 . . . . @3.00
17 . . . . 3.00
18 Ladies Night 3.00
19 Portals. 3.00
20 Threat from the Rikti,final issue . 3.00

CITY OF SILENCE
May, 2000
1 (of 3) WEI,GEr,F:Silencers 2.50
1a variant GEr,3-D(c)(1:4) 2.50
2 WEI,GEr. 2.50
3 WEI,GEr. 2.50

CLOCK MAKER, THE
Jan., 2003
1 (of 12) 2.50
2 thru 7 . . . . @2.50
5 to 7 (of 12) cancelled
Spec. Act One (#1ñ#4) 5.00
Spec. Act Two (#5ñ#7). 5.00
Spec. Act Three 5.00

CLOUDFALL
Nov., 2003
1-shot b&w 48-pg. 5.00
1-shot Cloudfall: Loose Ends. 5.00

CODE BLUE
(B&W) April, 1998
1 by Jimmie Robinson 3.00
2 F.I.T.E. creates havoc 3.00

CODENAME:
STYKE FORCE
Top Cow, 1994
1A MS(s),BPe,JRu(i). 3.50
1B Gold Embossed Cover 6.00
1C Blue Embossed Cover 9.00
2 MS(s),BPe,JRu(i). 2.50
3 MS(s),BPe,JRu(i). 2.50
4 MS(s),BPe,JRu(i). 2.50
5 MS(s),BPe,JRu(i). 2.50
6 MS(s),BPe,JRu(i). 2.50
7 MS(s),BPe,JRu(i). 2.50
8A Cyblade poster (Tucci) 4.00
8B Shi poster (Silvestri) 4.00
8C Tempest poster (Tan) 2.50
9 New Teamate. 2.50
10 SvG, B:New Adventure 2.50
11 F:Bloodbow 2.50
12 F:Stryker 2.50
13 SvG(s),F:Strkyer 2.50
14 New Jobs 2.50
Spec.#0 O:Stryke Force. 2.50

COMBAT
Jan., 1996
1 and 2 . . . . @2.50

COMMON FOE
May, 2005
1 (of 5) KG 3.50
2 thru 5 KG . . . . @3.50

COMMON GROUNDS
Top Cow, Jan., 2004
1 (of 6) DJu. 4.00
2 DJu,SK. 3.50
3 thru 6 DJu,SK. . . . . @3.00

COMPASS
Aug., 2007
1 thru 4 . . . . @3.00

CONSUMED
Platinum, July, 2007
1 thru 4 (of 4) JLi(c) . . . . @3.00

Cosmic Ray #2
© Image

COSMIC RAY
June, 1999
1 by Stephen Blue 3.00
1a alternate cover (1:2) 3.00
2 F:Raymond Mann 3.00
3 F:Star Marshalls. 3.00

COW, THE
Top Cow, April, 2000
.1 Spring edition. 3.00
2 Summer edition 3.00
3 Spring edition 2001 . . . . 3.00

CRAWL SPACE: XXXOMBIES
Oct, 2007
1 thru 4 . . . . @3.00

CREATURE FROM THE DEPTHS
July, 2007
1-shot 4.00

CREECH, THE
TMP, Oct., 1997
1 GCa,DaM,F:Chirs Rafferty. 2.50
2 GCa,DaM,F:Dennis Dross. 2.50

[GREG CAPULLO'S ORIGINAL] CREECH
TMP, Aug., 2001
1 A Vision of Death 2.50
2 Awakenings 2.50
3 The Resurrection 2.50

CREECH, THE: OUT FOR BLOOD
July, 2001
1 GCa,Out for Blood, Book 1 . . . . 5.00

---

2 GCa,48-pg. 5.00
3 GCa,Killing Machine perfected . . 5.00

CREED: UTOPIATE
Jan., 2002
1 (of 4) TKn. 3.50
2 TKn,disorder in dreamworld 3.00
3 TKn,fantasy vs. reality 3.00
4 TKn,Death of Creed. 3.00

CREEPS
Oct., 2001
1 (of 4) TMd 3.50
2 TMd,I:Gurgle,Chitter 3.00
3 TMd,Genesys Corporation. 3.00
4 TMd,through their eyes 3.00

CRIMSON
Cliffhanger, May, 1998
1 BAu,HuR,F:Alex Elder, vampire
  'Dawn to Dusk' 5.00
1a variant AWa(c) 7.00
1b Chromium Edition 12.00
2 BAu,HuR,V:Jelly-Bats,
  'Unlife Story' 3.00
2a variant AAd(c) 6.00
3 BAu,HuR,V:Rose,Payment
  in Blood 4.00
4 BAu,HuR,F:Red Hood,Children
  of Judas,pt.1 . . . . 3.50
5 BAu,HuR,A:Red Hood,Children
  of Judas,pt.2 . . . . 3.50
6 BAu,HuR,A:Red Hood,Children
  of Judas,pt.3 . . . . 3.50
7 BAu,HuR,Christmas day 3.00
½ Dynamic Forces exclusive 4.00
WildStorm/DC, 1999
8 thru 23 BAu,HuR . . . . @2.50
24 BAu,HuR, final issue. 3.50
Spec.#1 Scarlet X: Blood on the
  Moon, BAu,HuR,one-shot 4.00
Spec. Crimson Sourcebook #1 . . . 3.00

CRIMSON PLAGUE
June, 2000
1 GP,64-pg. 3.00
2 GP,Sole Survivor 2.50
3 GP,Blood trail 2.50
4 GP,Plague hits home 2.50

CROSS BRONX, THE
Sept., 2006
1 thru 4 . . . . @3.00
1a & 2a variant (c) . . . . @3.00

CROW, THE
TMP, Feb., 1999
1 JMu,F:Eric Draven. 3.00
1a variant TP cover (1:4) 3.00
2 JMu,hunt for killers 3.00
3 JMu,justice for killers 3.00
4 JMu,Line Between Devil's Teeth . 3.00
5 JMu,Skin of an Angel,pt.1 . . . . . 3.00
6 JMu,Skin of an Angel,pt.2 . . . . . 3.00
7 JMu,Touch of Evil,pt.1 . . . . 3.00
8 JMu,Touch of Evil,pt.2 . . . . 3.00
9 JMu,Wings and Black Feathers. . 3.00
Crow Mag.#1, 56-pg. rep. 5.00
Crow Mag.#2 . . . . 5.00
Crow Mag.#3 . . . . 5.00

CRUSH, THE
Motown Jan., 1996
1 Mini-series 3.00
2 Let Me Light Your Fire 3.00
3 Million Dollar Smile 3.00
4 . . . . 3.00
5 The Hip Hop Slide 3.00

CRYPT
Extreme, 1995
1 A:Prophet 2.50
1a variant cover 2.50
2 A:Prophet 2.50

CRYPTICS, THE
June, 2006
1 . . . . 3.50
2 To Heck and Back 3.50
3 . . . . 2.50

C-23 #2
© WildStorm

[JIM LEE'S] C-23
WildStorm, April, 1998
1 BCi,JMi,F:Corben Helix 2.50
2 JMi,TC(c),V:Angelans 2.50
3 JMi,TC(c),with game card 2.50
4 JMi,Corbin, banished. 2.50
5 JMi,RCo(c),Queen Mother. 2.50
5a variant JLe(c) (1:4) 3.00
6 JMi,RCo(c),V:Hyper Shock
  Troopers 2.50
7 JMi,RCo(c),Hail to the Queen . . 2.50
8 JMi,RCo(c),Long Live the King . . 2.50

CURSED
Top Cow, Sept., 2003
1 (of 4) It is Coming 3.00
2 The Walking Dead 3.00
3 The Nature of Curses 3.00
4 It is a Gift. 3.00

CURSE OF THE SPAWN
TMP, Sept., 1996
1 DT,DaM,F:Daniel Lianso 6.00
1a B&W variant. 16.00
2 DT,DaM,Dark Future,pt.2:
  Blood Lust 5.00
3 DT,DaM,Dark Future,pt.3:
  Corpse Candles. 5.00
4 DT,DaM 4.00
5 DT,DaM,Sam & Twitch search
  for Gretchen Culver. 3.00
6 DT,DaM,Sam & Twitch pursue
  Suture 3.00
7 DT,DaM,Suture is captured 3.00
8 DT,DaM,Suture escapes police
  custody 3.00
9 DT,DaM,Angela's secret origin . . 5.00

---

10 DT,DaM,Angela, Spawn Slayer. . 3.50	13 EcS,MS,O:Cyberdata 2.50
11 DT,DaM,Angela's story, concl. . . 3.50	14 EcS,MSI,V:T.I.M.M.I.E. 2.50
12 DT,DaM,Jessica Priest, movie	15 New Cyberdata Threat 2.50
photo(c). 3.50	16 O:Ripclaw 2.50
13 DT,DaM 'Heart of Darkness'. . . . 3.50	17 Regrouping 2.50
14 DT,DaM,Jessica, concl. 3.50	18 thru 24 . . . . @2.50
15 DT,DaM,Tempt an Angel,pt.1 . . 3.50	25 . . . . 4.00
16 DT,DaM,Tempt an Angel,pt.2 . . 3.50	26 KWo 2.50
17 DT,DaM. 3.50	27 F:Ash. 2.50
18 DT,DaM,F:Tony Twist 3.50	27a variant JQ&JP(c) (1:4) 4.00
19 DT,Curse & Tony Twist 3.50	28 A:Gabriel 2.50
20 DT,DaM,Monsters & Mythology . 3.50	29 . . . . 2.50
21 DT,DaM,Zeus Must Die. 3.50	30 ScL,'Devil's Reign' tie-in 2.50
22 DT,F:Ryan Hatchett 3.50	31 The team in conflict 2.50
23 DT,TM,R:Overtkill 3.50	32 Cyblade leads rejuvenated team 2.50
24 DT,TM,Pandemic 3.50	33 KWo, Cheleene in midst of
25 DT,TM,'Heart of Hell'. 2.50	civil war 2.50
26 DT,TM,V:The Crocodile. 2.50	34 KWo,Royal Blood,pt.3. . . . . 2.50
27 DT,TM,F:Marc Simmons 2.50	35 BTn,Royal Blood, concl. 2.50
28 DT,TM,V:Suture 2.50	Ashcan 1 (San Diego) 4.00
29 DT,TM,A:Jonathan Edward	Ashcan 1 (signed) 6.00
Custer 2.50	Sourcebook 1. . . . . 2.50
	Sourcebook 2 I:W.Zero 2.50

CYBERFORCE
Top Cow, 1992–93
[Limited Series]

0 WS,O:Cyber Force 2.50	Ann.#1 O:Velocity 2.50
1 MS,I:Cyberforce,w/coupon#3 . . . 5.00	Ann.#2 . . . . 3.00
1a w/o coupon 3.00	**Top Cow, March, 2006**
2 MS,V:C.O.P.S. 3.50	0 MS 3.00
3 MS 2.50	1 (of 2) RMz 3.00
4 MS,V:C.O.P.S,BU:Codename	2 . . . . 3.00
Styke Force. 2.50	2a variant b&w (c). 3.00

[Regular Series] 1993

1 EcS(s),MS,SW. 2.50	3 . . . . 3.00
1B Gold Foil Logo. 6.00	3a variant b&w (c). 3.00
2 EcS(s),MS,SW,Killer Instinct	4 . . . . 3.00
#2,A:Warblade. 2.50	5 . . . . 3.00
2B Silver Embossed Cover. 6.00	5a variant (c). 3.00
3 EcS(s),MS,SW,Killer Instinct #4,	6 Who will die 3.00
A:WildC.A.T.S. 2.50	6a variant (c). 3.00
3B Gold Embossed Cover 6.00	1-Shot Cyberforce/X-Men (2006). . . 4.00
4 EcS(s),MS,Ballistic 2.50	
5 EcS(s),MS 2.50	## CYBERFORCE/ CODE-
6 EcS(s),MS,Ballistic's Past 2.50	## NAME STRYKEFORCE:
7 S.H.O.C.s. 2.50	## OPPOSING FORCES
8 . . . . 2.50	### Sept., 1995
9 A:Huntsman 2.50	1 V:Dangerous Threat. 2.50
10 A:Huntsman 2.50	2 Team vs. Team. 2.50
10a Alternate Cover 4.00	
10b Silver Seal Oz-Con 500c 9.00	## CYBERFORCE ORIGINS
11 . . . . 2.50	### Top Cow, 1995
12 T.I.M.M.I.E. goes wild 2.50	1 O:Cyblade 2.50
	1B Gold Seal 1000c 6.00
	2 O:Stryker 2.50
	3 O:Impact 2.50
	4 Misery 3.00

CYBERFORCE UNIVERSE
SOURCEBOOK
Top Cow, 1994–95

1 . . . . 2.50	
2 MS,BTn 2.50	

CYBERNARY
WildStorm, 1995–96
1 thru 5 (of 5) mini-series . . . . . . @2.50

CYBERPUNX
Extreme, 1996

1 and 2 . . . . @3.00	
3 RLe & Ching Lau,F:Drake 3.00	

CYBLADE
Top Cow, Oct., 2008

1 and 2 . . . . @3.00	
1a variant (c) 3.00	

CYBLADE/SHI
Top Cow,1995
1 The Battle for Independents 3.00

Cyblade/Shi #1
© Top Cow

CY-GOR
TMP, July, 1999

1 RV,I:Fatima,Frankie & Zevon. . . . 2.50	
2 RV,Fire in the Mind,pt.2 . . . . 2.50	
3 RV,Needles and Pins 2.50	
4 RV, Exquisite Corpse. 2.50	
5 RV 2.50	
6 RV, the Terraplane 2.50	
7 RV,Young Doctor Acula 2.50	

DAMNED
Homage, June, 1997

1 (of 4) StG, MZ & DRo. 2.50	
2 StG, MZ & DRo,F:Mick Thorne . . 2.50	
3 StG, MZ & DRo 2.50	
4 StG, MZ & DRo 2.50	

DANGER GIRL
WildStorm/Cliffhanger 1998

1 JSC,AGo,'Dangerously Yours,'	
40-pg. 8.00	
1a chromium edition, 40-pg. 42.00	
1b Tour Edition 15.00	
2 I:Johnny Barracuda,'Dangerous	
Liaisons'. 5.00	
3 in Switzerland 4.00	
3a variant AH(c) 5.00	
3b variant TC(c) 5.00	
4 I:Major Maxim 3.00	
5 JSC,AGo 2.50	
5a variant JMd(c) 9.00	

WildStorm/DC, 1999

6 JSC,SW 2.50	
6a variant JMd(c) 5.00	
6b variant HuR(c) 4.00	
7 JSC,SW,concl.,48-pg. 6.00	

DARING ESCAPES
TMP, 1998

1 ANi,F:Harry Houdini 3.00	
2 ANi,search for Mystical Heart . . . 2.50	
3 A:Kimiel 2.50	
4 conclusion 2.50	

DARK ANGEL:
PHOENIX RESURRECTION
May, 2000

1 by Kia Asamiya, color manga . . . 3.00	
2 thru 4 . . . . @3.00	
1a thru 3a variant(c) . . . . @3.00	

Cyberforce #28
© Top Cow

DARKCHYLDE
See: Maximum, 1996
1 Image reoffer 5.00
1C flip-book-Glory/Angel,Angels in
   Hell,pt.1, San Diego Con. 4.00
1D remastered, RLd(c) 6.00
2 Image reoffer 5.00
2a variant cover 3.00
2b remastered, with poster 2.50
3 Image reoffer 3.50
3a remastered, with poster 2.50
Image, 1997
4 RQu,Ariel & Kauldron's past 5.00
5 RQu,No one here gets out alive . 4.00
Homage, 1998
0 RQu,Ariel's back, Ariel's past. . . 2.50

DARKCHYLDE/GLORY
Extreme
1-shot, four variant covers, by
   RLd, RQu, JDy & PtL 3.00

DARKCHYLDE:
THE DIARY
May, 1997
1-shot, RQu et al,diary excerpts . . . 5.00

DARKCHYLDE:
THE LEGACY
WildStorm, 1998
1 RQu,F:Ariel 2.50
2 RQu 2.50
WildStorm/DC, 1999
3 RQu,A:Silencer 2.50
4 RQu,Carnival of Fools 2.50
4a RQu,AAd(c), variant (c) 2.50
Summer Swimsuit Spectacular #1 . 4.00
Spec.Dreams of the Darkchylde #0 . 2.50

DARKCHYLDE/
WITCHBLADE
Top Cow, July, 2000
1 RQu,Nightmare City. 2.50

DARK CROSSINGS
Top Cow, May, 2000
Spec. #1 Dark Cloud Rising. 6.00
Spec. #2 Dark Cloud Overhead . . . 6.00

DARKER IMAGE
1993
1 BML,BCi(s),RLd,SK,JLe,I:Blood
   Wulf,Deathblow,Maxx 4.00
1a Gold logo(c) 8.00
1b White(c) 6.00
Ashcan 1 . . . . 4.00

DARK IVORY
Mar., 2008
1 (of 4) A Kiss in the Dreamhouse . 3.00
2 Spellbound. 3.00
3 Fall From Grace. 3.00
4 The Last Beat of My Heart 3.00

DARKMINDS
1998
1 PtL,cyberpunk,detective 8.00
2 Neon Dragon 5.00
2a variant cover 2.50
3 PtL,A:Neon Dragons 2.50
4 PtL,Paradox killer. 2.50
5 PtL,Unlikely friends, enemies . . . 3.00
6 PtL,Aurora Industries. 3.00
7 PtL,V:Mamuro Hayabusa. 3.00

8 Conclusion,1st story arc 2.50
½ PtL,Cyborg dreams. 2.50
VOL. II Feb., 2000
1 JMd(c) one year later. 2.50
1a variant PtL(c) 2.50
1b variant Omar Dogan(c) 2.50
2 Changing Faces. 2.50
2a variant PtL(c) 2.50
2b variant Michael Turner(c). 2.50
2c variant(c) 2.50
3 PtL(c),F:Reiko Tetsunori 2.50
3a variant Omar Dogan(c) 2.50
3b variant JQ(c) 2.50
4 PtL,cyborg attack. 2.50
5 PtL,The Prize. 2.50
6 PtL,9mm Answers 2.50
7 PtL,The Hunger 2.50
8 PtL,Born Again. 2.50
9 PtL,A Million and One 2.50
10 PtL,concl. 2.50
#0 The Bullet 2.50
#0a variant(c). 2.50

DARKMINDS:
MACROPOLIS
Jan., 2002
1 (of 8) PtL 3.00
1a variant(c) 3.00
2 F:Tiny 3.00
2a variant PtL(c) 3.00

DARKNESS, THE
Top Cow, 1996
0 Preview edition,B&W 15.00
½ 15.00
½ variant cover. 22.00
1/2 rep.+new story (2001),MS 3.00
1 GEn,MS,Coming of Age 20.00
1a Dark cover 10.00
1b Platinum cover. 25.00
2 GEn,MS 7.00
3 GEn,MS,Jackie pursued by
   many foes. 6.00
4 GEn,MS,Jackie explores
   Darkness power 6.00
5 GEn,MS,New York gangs on
   verge of all-out war 5.00
6 GEn,MS,F:JackieEstacado,concl. 4.00
7 MS 4.00
7a variant(c) 9.00
8 JBz,retribution 3.00
8a MS(c)(1:4) 7.00
9 Family Ties,pt.2,x-over 5.00
10 Family Ties,pt.3,x-over 6.00
11 GEn,MS,Hearts of Darkness . . . 3.50
11a Chromium(c) 19.00
11b variant(c). 5.00
12 GEn,Hearts of Darkness. 3.00
13 GEn,Hearts of Darkness 3.00
14 GEn,JBz,Hearts of Darkness . . 3.00
15 JBz,Spear of Destiny,pt.1 . . . . . 3.00
16 JBz,Spear of Destiny,pt.2 . . . . . 3.00
17 JBz,Spear of Destiny,pt.3 . . . . . 3.00
18 JBz,aftermath 3.00
19 JBz,No Mercy,pt.1. . . . . 3.00
20 JBz,No Mercy,pt.2. . . . . 2.50
21 JBz,Wynnwood 2.50
22 JBz,Where is Jenny? 2.50
23 JBz,SLo,new characters 2.50
24 JBz,SLo,road trip to Vegas 2.50
25 JBz,SLo,48-pg. 3.50
26 JBz,SLo,A:Joey Scarpaggio . . . 2.50
27 SLo,FBI continues assault 2.50
28 Darkness/Witchblade,pt.4,x-over 2.50
29 SLo,High Noon,pt.1 . . . . 2.50
30 SLo,High Noon,pt.2 . . . . 2.50
31 SLo,High Noon,pt.3 . . . . 2.50
32 SLo,Dark Days Ahead 2.50
33 SLo,Capris Castagliano,pt.1 . . . 2.50
34 SLo,Capris Castagliano,pt.2 . . . 2.50

The Darkness #1
© *Image Top Cow*

35 SLo,tour of his life. 2.50
36 SLo,Ripclaw,pt.3 . . . . 2.50
37 SLo,F:Robert Bearclaw. 2.50
38 SLo,V:Conquistador. 2.50
39 SLo,Jackie & Capris combine. . . 2.50
40 DK,Darkness falls? 2.50
40a variant MS(c) 2.50
various foil (c). . . . . @9.00
Coll.Ed.#1,rep. #1–#2 . . . . 5.00
Coll.Ed.#2,rep. #3–#4, 56-pg. 5.00
Coll.Ed.#3,rep.#5–#6, 56-pg. 5.00
Coll.Ed.#3, with slipcase. 10.00
Coll.Ed.#4,rep. #7–#8 . . . . 5.00
Coll.Ed.#1,deluxe,rep.#1–#6 . . . . 15.00
Coll.Ed.#5,rep.#11–#12 . . . . 6.00
Coll.Ed.#6,rep.#13–#14 . . . . 6.00
Spec. Infinity, SLo 3.50
Darkness/Witchblade,pt.3 x-over . 4.00
Spec.#1, Dark Ages 5.00
Spec. Vol. 2 #1 raw (no color) 3.00
1-shot Darkness/Hulk. 3.00

DARKNESS
Top Cow, Nov., 2002
1 PJe,DK. 3.00
1a holofoil(c) 6.00
2 DK 3.00
2 Megacon edition 6.00
3 DK 3.00
4 Under Cover of Darkness 3.00
5 You Lose Some 3.00
6 As the World Turns 3.00
7 PJe,F:Ernie Palanco 3.00
7a alternate (c) 3.00
8 PJe,Law by Jackie Estacado. . . . 3.00
9 PJe,Search for Blue Goldfish . . . 3.00
10 RMz,Hong Kong 3.00
11 RMz,Dragons and darklings . . . 3.00
12 RMz,Army of accoccinc 3.00
13 RMz,Mystical Dragons 3.00
14 Streets Run Red,pt.1 . . . . 3.00
15 Streets Run Red,pt.2 . . . . 3.00
16 Streets Run Red,pt.3 . . . . 3.00
17 Hell House, pt.1 . . . . 3.00
18 Hell House, pt.2 . . . . 3.00
19 Hell House, pt.3 . . . . 3.00
20 Hell House, pt.4 . . . . 3.00
21 The Reckoning 3.00
22 All in the Family ,pt.1 . . . . 3.00
23 All in the Family ,pt.2 . . . . 3.00
24 All in the Family, pt.3. . . . . 3.00
1-shot Wanted Dead (2004) 3.00
1-shot Black Sails (2005). 3.00

E3 variant (c) reprint 3.00
Spec. Darkness/Batman, SLo,MS,
  x-over (1999) 6.00
1-shot Darkness/Vampirella (2005) . 3.00
1-shot Darkness/Wolverine (2006) . 3.00

DARKNESS, THE:
Top Cow, Dec., 2006
Level 0 . . . . 3.00
Level 1 . . . . 3.00
Level 1a thru b variant (c)s . . . . . @3.00
Level 1c variant incentive (c) 3.00
Level 2 . . . . 3.00
Level 2a thru b variant (c)s . . . . . @3.00
Level 3 . . . . 3.00
Level 3a variant (c) 3.00
Level 4 . . . . 3.00
Level 4a variant (c) 3.00
Level 5 . . . . 3.00
Level 5a variant (c) 3.00

DARKNESS, THE
Top Cow, Dec., 2007
1 PhH(s),MS(c) 3.00
1a variant DK (c) 3.00
1b variant (c) 3.00
1c gold foil variant (c) 10.00
2 thru 9 PhH(s) . . . . @3.00
2a thru 9a variant (c)s . . . . @3.00
Spec. First Look, preview 2.50
Spec. Butcher (2008) 4.00
Spec. #4 Wizard World variant . . . 10.00

DARKNESS, THE/PITT
Top Cow, Dec., 2006
Spec. First Look 3.00
Spec. First Look Wizard World . . . 10.00

DARKNESS, THE/
SUPERMAN
DC/Top Cow, Dec., 2004
1 (of 2) RMz(s) 3.00
2 RMz(s) 3.00

DARKNESS AND
TOMB RAIDER
Top Cow, Mar., 2005
1-shot JaL,BTn. 3.00
1-shotA B&W cover 3.00

DARKNESS VS. MR. HYDE
Top Cow, Aug., 2005
1-shot Monster War #4 x-over 3.00
1-shotA variant (c) 3.00

DARK REALM
Oct., 2000
1 by Taeson Chang. 3.00
2 S.F.P.D. in chaos 3.00
3 flip-book 3.00
4 Prophecy is fulfilled 3.00

DARK SECTOR
Top Cow, Dec., 2008
0 BSz 3.00

DART
1996
1 thru 3 Jozef Szekeres . . . . @3.00

DAVID AND GOLIATH
Sept., 2003
1 . . . . 3.00
2 . . . . 3.00
3 . . . . 3.00

DAWN: THREE TIERS
June, 2003
1 thru 4 JLi . . . . @3.00
5 Hell Hath No Fury 3.00
6 . . . . 3.00

DEAD AHEAD
Sept., 2008
1 (of 3) Water Water Everywhere . . 4.00
2 Bait on the Wire 4.00

DEADLANDS
July, 1999
GN 1-shot role-play tie-in. 7.00

Deadly Duo
© Highbrow

DEADLY DUO, THE
Highbrow, 1994–95
1 A:Kill-Cat 2.50
2 A:Pitt, O:Kid Avenger 2.50
3 A:Roman, O:Kill-Cat. 2.50
[Second Series] 1995
1 A:Spawn. 2.50
2 A:Savage Dragon. 2.50
3 A:Grunge, Gen13. . . . . 2.50
4 Movie Mayhem 2.50

DEAD SPACE
Mar., 2008
1 (of 6) 3.00
2 thru 6 . . . . @3.00

DEADWORLD
(B&W) Mar., 2005
1 . . . . 3.50
2 thru 6 . . . . @3.50
7 Slaughterhouse, pt.1 . . . . 4.00
8 Slaughterhouse, pt.2 . . . . 4.00

DEATHBLOW
WildStorm, 1993–96
1 JLe,MN,I:Cybernary 3.00
2 JLe,BU:Cybernary 2.50
3 JLe(a&s),BU:Cybernary 3.00
4 JLe(s),TSe,BU:Cybernary 2.50
5 JLe(s),TSe,BU:Cybernary 2.50
5a different cover 5.00
6 Black Angel 2.50
7 . . . . 2.50
8 Black Angel 2.50

9 The Four Horsemen 2.50
10 Michael Cray, Sister Mary. 2.50
11 A:Four Horsemen 2.50
12 Final Battle 2.50
13 New Story Arc. 2.50
14 A:Johnny Savoy 2.50
15 F:Michael Cray 2.50
16 TvS,BWS(c),WildStorm
  Rising,pt.6,w/2 cards 2.50
16a Newsstand ed. 2.50
17 V:Gammorran Hunter Killers. . . . 2.50
18 F:Cybernary 2.50
19 F:Cybernary 2.50
20 A:Gen 13. . . . . 2.50
21 Brothers in Arms,pt.2,A:Gen13. . 3.50
22 Brothers in Arms,pt.3 . . . . 2.50
23 Brothers in Arms,pt.4 . . . . 2.50
24 Brothers in Arms,pt.5 . . . . 3.00
25 Brothers in Arms,pt.6 . . . . 2.50
26 Fire From Heaven prelude 2.50
27 Fire From Heaven,pt.8 . . . . 3.00
28 Fire From Heaven,finale,pt.3 . . . 2.50
29 last issue 2.50
0 JLe (1996) 3.00
Ashcan 1 . . . . 4.00

DEATHBLOW/WOLVERINE
WildStorm, Sept., 1996
1 RiB, AWs,x-over, set In San
  Francisco's Chinatown 2.50
2 RiB, AWs,concl 2.50

DEATH GRUB
May, 2008
1-shot 3.00

DEATH, JR.
Apr., 2005
1 (of 3) 5.00
2 . . . . 5.00
3 . . . . 5.00
Series 2, July, 2006
1 48-pg.. 5.00
2 48-pg.. 5.00
3 48-pg.. 5.00

DEATHMATE X-OVER
See: COLOR PUB.

DECEPTION, THE
(B&W) Flypaper, Jan., 1999
1 (of 3) F:Jordan Risk, magician . . 3.00
2 Framed for murder. 3.00
3 V:South American Drug Cartel . . 3.00

DEEP SLEEPER
Aug., 2004
1 & 2 See B&W section
3 The Vacant. 3.00
4 conclusion 3.00
Omnibus rep.#1 & #2. . . . . 6.00

DEFCON 4
WildStorm, 1996
1 mini-series 2.50
2 . . . . 2.50
3 . . . . 2.50
4 . . . . 2.50

DEFIANCE
Feb., 2002
1 The Messenger,pt.1 . . . . 3.00
2 thru 4 The Messenger,pt.2–pt.4 @3.00
5 thru 8 The Scabbard,pt.1–pt.4 . @3.00

Defcon 4 #4
© *Image/Wildstorm*

DEITY: REQUIEM
Feb., 2005
1-shot 56-pages 7.00

DEITY: REVELATIONS
June, 1999
1 F:Jamie 3.00
2 F:Joe Tripoli 3.00
3 A legend reborn 3.00
3a variant cover (1:10) 3.00

DEMONSLAYER
Nov., 1999
1 MMy 3.00
2 Jaclyn begins her quest. 3.00
3 MMy, Michael & the Demon 3.00
Shadow Edition,pt.1 B&W 5.00

VOL II
1 MMy,Into Hell,pt.1 . . . . 3.00
1a variant(c) (1:4) 3.00
2 MMy 3.00
3 MMy, enter Ebon 3.00

DERRING RISK
June, 1999
1 Fantasy Adventure. 2.50
1a AWa variant(c) 2.50

DESPERADO
Dec., 2005
1-shot Primer 2.50
1-shot Second Chances, 64-pg. . . . 5.00

DESPERADOES
Homage, Sept., 1997
1 by JMi & John Cassaday 7.00
2 V:Leander Peik 3.00
2a 2nd printing 2.50
3 V:Leander Peik 3.00
4 V:Leander Peik, concl. 3.00
5 V:Gideon Brood,pt.1. . . . . 3.00

DESPERATE TIMES
(B&W) June, 1998
1 by Chris Eliopoulos 3.00
2 Strip joint 3.00
3 EL(c) 3.00
4 Christmas special 3.00
5 EL(c), sideways 3.00
6 . . . . 3.00

Jan., 2004
0 . . . . 3.00
1 . . . . 3.00

DETONATOR, THE
Nov., 2004
1 Big Bang Theory, pt.1, MBn. 2.50
2 thru 4 . . . . @2.50
5 final issue 3.00

DEVASTATOR
(B&W) April, 1998
1 JHI and Greg Horn. 3.00
2 book 1,pt.2. . . . . 3.00
3 concl. to book 1 . . . . 3.00

DEVIL'S DUE STUDIOS
Mar., 2003
1-shot 2003 Preview 2.50

DISCIPLES, THE
April, 2001
1 The new magic 3.00
2 Recruit Her or Kill Her 3.00
3 Viva Las Vegas 3.00
4 The Apples of Sodom 3.00

A DISTANT SOIL
(B&W) Highbrow, Aug., 1993
Prev: Aria Comics
15 CDo,Ascension,pt.3 . . . . 3.00
16 CDo,A:Bast, Avatar. 3.00
17 CDo,D'mer & Bast conflict 3.00
18 CDo,'Ascension' finale 3.00
19 CDo,'Spires of Heaven,'pt.1 . . . 3.00
20 CDo,Lord Merai's suicide
   weakens Hierachy 3.00
21 CDo,'Exile for D'mer?' 3.00
22 CDo,Avatar's secrets,32-pg. . . . 3.00
23 CDo,three stories 3.00
24 CDo,malfunctioning spacesuit . . 3.00
25 CDo,NGa,Troll Bridge,48-pg. . . . 4.00
26 CDo,B.U.:Red-Cloak by
   E.Kushner 3.00
27 CDo,B.U.:Liaden tale 3.00
28 CDo,B.U.:Liaden tale, concl.. . . 3.00
29 CDo,B.U.:Delia Sherman story . . 3.00
30 . . . . 4.00
31 Sometimes the good guys lose . 4.00
32 F:Prince D'mer 4.00
33 Rebellion's final stand. 4.00
34 CDo, 64-pg. 5.00
35 CDo, 32-pg. 4.00
36 CDo. 4.00
37 CDo. 4.00
38 CDo, 40-pg. 4.50
Images of A Distant Soil. 3.00

DIVINE RIGHT:
THE ADVENTURES OF
MAX FARADAY
WildStorm, Sept., 1997
1 JLe,SW,Blaze of Glory 7.00
1a variant cover 7.50
1b variant, signed 30.00
1c Voyager pollybaged pack. 6.00
1d Spanish edition 5.00
2 JLe,SW,Disco Inferno 5.00
2a variant(c) 5.00
3 JLe,SW,F:Christie Blaze,Enemies
   of the State 4.00
4 JLe,SW,F:Lynch,The Love
   Connection 2.50
4a variant(c) 4.00
5 JLe,SW,V:Dominique Faust,Party
   Crashers 3.00

Divine Right #6
© *WildStorm*

6 JLe,SW,Truth or Consequences,
   Susanna Chaste located 3.00
7 JLe,SW,Into the Hollow Realm . . 3.00
8 JLe,SW,Tobru,V:Acheron. 3.00
8a variant SW(c). 3.00
Preview edition, JLe(c) (1997). 5.00
Coll.Ed.#1 . . . . 6.00
Coll.Ed.#2 . . . . 6.00

WildStorm/DC, 1999
9 JLe,SWi,Final Stand in
   Hollow Realm 3.00
10 JLe,SWi. 3.00
11 JLe,SWi,Divine Intervention 3.00
12 JLe,SWi,Divine Intervention 3.00
Coll.Ed.#3, rep.#5 & #6 . . . . 6.00

DOLL AND CREATURE
March, 2006
1 (of 4) 3.50
2 thru 4 . . . . @3.00

DOLLZ
April, 2001
1 RGr,TSg. 3.00
1a-1c variant(c)s 3.00
2 RGr 3.00
3 RGr 3.00

DOMINION
Jan., 2003
1 KG 3.00
2 thru 5 KG . . . . @3.00

DOOM'S IV
Extreme, 1994
1 RL(s),MPa, I:Doom's IV 2.50
1a variant(c),left side of art. 2.50
1b variant(c),right side of art 2.50
2 Rld(s),MPa,MECH-MAX 2.50
2a variant (c). 2.50
3 Dr. Lychee, Brick 2.50
4 Dr. Lychee, Syber-idol 2.50
Sourcebook 2.50

DOUBLE IMAGE
Feb., 2001
1 The Bod, flip-book, Codeflesh . . . 3.00
2 The Bod/Codeflesh 3.00
3 The Bod/Codeflesh 3.00
4 The Bod/Codeflesh 3.00
5 Trust in Me/Codeflesh 3.00

IMAGE

DOWN
Top Cow, Nov., 2005
1 (of 4) WEI,TyH 3.00
2 thru 4 . . . . @3.00

DRACULA VS. ZORRO
(B&W) Sept., 1998
1 DMG,RM 3.00
2 DMG,RM, conclusion 3.00

DRAGON, THE
March, 1995
1 rep. of Savage Dragon 2.50
2 thru 5 rep. of Savage Dragon . @2.50

THE DRAGON:
BLOOD AND GUTS
Highbrow, 1995
1 I:Grip 2.50
2 JPn,KIS 2.50
3 JPn,KIS 2.50

DRAGON PRINCE
Top Cow, Sept., 2008
1 RMz(s) 3.00
2 thru 3 RMz(s) . . . . @3.00
1a thru 3a variant (c)s . . . . @3.00
1b Balt. Comic Con variant 10.00

DRAIN
Nov., 2006
1 Decades. 3.00
2 Bleed With Me 3.00
3 In a Flash 3.00
4 Sole Survivor Guilt. 3.00
5 Crescendo 3.00
6 . . . . 3.00

DRAWING FROM LIFE
(B&W) May, 2007
1 JV 3.50
2 JV 3.50

DUNCAN'S KINGDOM
(B&W) Oct., 1999
1 by Gene Yang & Derek Kirk 3.00
2 . . . . 3.00

DUST
July, 2007
1 (of 2) 4.00
1a variant (c) 4.00
2 . . . . 4.00
2a variant (c) 4.00

DUSTY STAR
(B&W) April, 1997
0 sci-fi,western,adventure. 3.00
1 thru 3 . . . . @3.00

DUSTY STAR
Aug., 2005
1 . . . . 3.50
2 . . . . 3.50

DV8
WildStorm, 1996
1 WEI(s),HuR,'Lust for Life' 4.00
1a JLe(c). 5.00
1b Kevin Nowlan(c). 4.00
2 WEI(s),HuR,Gen-active serial
  killers,'Some Weird Sin'. 3.00
3 WEI(s), Neighborhood Threat . . . 3.00
4 WEI(s),HuR,Miss Drugstore. 3.00
5 Ivana sends DV8 to Japan 2.50

DV8 #5
© *WildStorm*

6 idle hands are the devil's tools . . 2.50
7 WEI(s),'Shades' 2.50
8 HuR,Sublime, Evo & Frostbite
  abandoned,'Three'. 2.50
9 MHs,'Evolution' 2.50
10 MHs,'In Service to Nothing' 2.50
11 MHs,F:Copycat,'Facets' 2.50
12 MHs,F:Freestyle,V:Sen.Killory . . 2.50
13 MHs,'The Sad Tales of
  Senator Killory' 2.50
14 MHs,TR,New Horizon,TR(c),
  'Barely Legal'. 5.00
14a TC(c) 2.50
14b Voyager bagged pack 3.50
15 MHs,F:Ivana Baiul,'Settling
  Accounts'. 2.50
16 MHs,V:Dominique Faust
  'Intersection' 2.50
17 MHs,Gen-Passive 2.50
18 MHs,Team 7,A:Grifter,'Same as
  It Ever Was'. 2.50
19 MHs,First Mision,pt.1,'Larger
  Concerns' 2.50
20 MHs,First Mision,pt.2,'Lounging
  in the Ammo Dump' 2.50
21 MHs,First Mision,pt.3,V:Anthrax . 2.50
22 MHs,V:Copycat,'Choices' 2.50
22a variant(c) JMd(1:4) 2.50
23 MHs,F:Threshold,'Gone to
  Ground' 2.50
24 MHs,F:Sublime,'Slip Stream,'
  prologue. 2.50
25 MHs,Slipstream,pt.1 . . . . 2.50
DV8 Rave,preview (1996) 3.00
Ann.#1 'Head Trips' (1998) 3.00
WildStorm/DC, 1999
26 MHs,TVs 2.50
27 MHs,TVs,V:Gen-Actives 2.50
28 MHs,TVs,F:Evo. 2.50
29 MHs,TVs 2.50
30 MHs,TVs,Things Fall Apart,pt.1 . 2.50
31 MHs,TVs,Things Fall Apart,pt.2 . 2.50
32 MHs,TVs,Things Fall Apart,pt.3 . 2.50
Ann.'99 Slipstream 3.50
#0 40-pg. 3.00

DV8 VS. BLACK OPS
WildStorm, Oct., 1997
1 Techromis Design,pt.1 . . . . 3.00
2 Techromis Design,pt.2 . . . . 3.00
3 Techromis Design,pt.3 . . . . 3.00

DYNAMO 5
Mar., 2007
1 F:Captain Dynamo. 3.00
2 thru 3 . . . . @3.50
4 . . . . 3.00
5 thru 7 . . . . @3.50
8 thru 12 . . . . @3.50
13 thru 19 . . . . @3.50
Ann. #1 . . . . 6.00

ECHO
March, 2000
1 A Broken World 2.50
1a variant(c) 2.50
2 Sacrifices 2.50
2a variant PtL(c) 2.50
3 Deadly new echo. 2.50
3a variant PtL(c) 2.50
4 PtL,Desperate Times 2.50
5 PtL,Welcoming Party 2.50
6 Conspiracy Theory. 2.50
6a variant PtL(c) 2.50
7 Anarchy,pt.1 . . . . 2.50
8 A Life Worth Living. 3.00
#0 Thick as Thieves 2.50
#0a variant(c). 2.50
#1 Holochrome edition 7.00

86 VOLTZ: DEAD GIRL
(B&W) Mar., 2005
1-shot 56-page. 6.00

ELECTROPOLIS
May, 2001
1 DMt, Infernal Machine,pt.1 . . . . . 3.00
2 DMt, Infernal Machine,pt.2 . . . . . 3.00
3 DMt, Heavy Meddle 3.00
4 DMt, Infernal Machine,pt.4 . . . . . 3.00

ELEKTRA/CYBLADE
Top Cow/Marvel, 1997
1-shot 'Devil's Reign,'pt.7
  (of 8) x-over. 3.00

ELEPHANTMEN
July., 2006
0 Unnatural Selection 3.00
1 See the Elephant. 3.00
2 Behemoth & Leviathan, flip-book. 3.00
3 Hip Flask 3.00
4 Hazardous Materials, Wounded
  Animals, flip-cover. 3.00
5 Exodus. 3.00
5a variant (c) 3.00
6 Abandoned by God 3.00
7 Captain Stoneheart 3.00
7a variant (c) 3.00
8 Moxa Cautery 3.00
9 Local Hippo 3.00
10 Unicorn 3.00
11 Man of Peace 3.00
12 Invasion Squid Force flip-cover . 3.00
13 Spore Wars 3.00
14 Fungicide 3.00
15 Human Remains 3.00
16 Dark Heart flip-cover. 3.00
17 The Monster is loose 3.00
17a variant (c) 3.00
18 Bad Girl. 3.00
18a variant (c) 3.00
Spec. The Pilot. 3.00

ELEPHANTMEN:
WAR TOYS
(B&W) Aug., 2007
1 (of 3) 3.00
2 thru 3 . . . . @3.00
1a thru 3a variant (c)s . . . . @3.00

EMISSARY
May, 2006

1 Revelations 1:4	3.50
2 Revelations 2:4	3.50
3 Revelations 3:4	3.50
4 Revelations 4:4	3.50
5 Revelations 2:1	3.50
6 Revelations 2.2	3.50
7 Revelations 2:3	3.50
8 Revelations 3:3	3.50

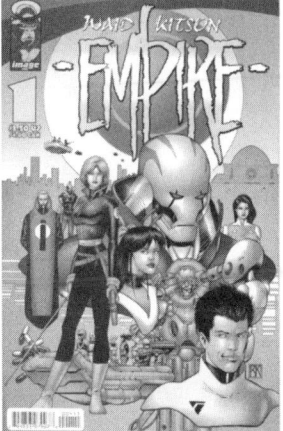

Empire #1
© Image

EMPIRE
May, 2000

1 MWa,BKi,F:Golgoth	5.00
2 MWa,BKi,F:Xanna	4.00
3 MWa,BKi,F:Lohkyn	4.00
4 MWa,BKi,Nature vs. nurture	4.00

ESPERS
April, 1997
(B&W) Vol. 3

1 JHI,A:Brian Marx,V:Architects	3.00
1a 2nd printing	3.00
2 JHI	3.00
3 JHI,Black Magic	3.00
4 JHI,Black Magic, concl.	3.00
5 JHI,two stories	3.00
6 JHI,F:Simon Ashley,Alan Black	3.00
7 JHI,Feel the Rapture	3.00
8 JHI, trip to Hong Kong	3.00
9 JHI,V:Architects	3.00

E.V.E. PROTOMECHA
Top Cow, Feb., 2000

1	3.00
1a variant JMd(c)	3.00
1b variant David Finch(c)	3.00
2 Gunner Unleashed.	3.00
2a variant Michael Turner(c)	3.00
2b variant SPa(c)	3.00
3 thru 6	@3.00

[ADVENTURES OF]
EVIL AND MALICE
June, 1999

1 by Jimmie Robinson	3.50
2 F:Max 2000	3.50
3 V:Cold Heart & Le'Chef	3.50
4 final showdown	3.50

EVO
Top Cow

1 MS,Endgame,pt.3 x-over	3.00

EXPATRIATE, THE
Feb., 2004

1	3.00
2 thru 7	@3.00

EXPOSURE
July, 1999

1 F:Shawna & Lisa	2.50
2 Mirrors to the Soul	2.50
3	2.50
2a & 3a alternate photo(c) (1:2)	@2.50
4 Spark-Spangled See-Through Girl	2.50
4a alternate photo(c) (1:2)	2.50
Prelude 16-pg	7.00
Prelude holo-foil	15.00

EXTREME ANTHOLOGY

1	2.50

EXTREME
CHRISTMAS SPECIAL

Various artists, new work	3.00

EXTREME DESTROYER
Extreme, 1996

1 prologue, x-over,bagged with card	2.50
2 epilogue, x-over	2.50

EXTREME HERO

1	3.00

EXTREME PREJUDICE
Extreme, Nov., 1994

0 Prelude to X-over	3.00

EXTREME SACRIFICE
Extreme, Jan., 1995

Prelude,x-over,pt.1, A:Everyone with trading card	2.50
Epiloque, x-over,pt.8, conclusion with trading card	2.50

EXTREME 3000

Prelude	2.50

EXTREME TOUR BOOK

Tour Book 1992	3.00
Tour Book 1994	25.00

EXTREMELY
YOUNGBLOOD
Extreme, Sept 1997

1 TBm&MBm(s)	3.50

EXTREME ZERO

0 RLd,CYp,ATi(i),I:Cybrid, Law & Order, Riok, Code 9, Lancers, Black Flag	3.00
0a Variant cover	3.00

FACELESS, THE
Aug., 2005

GN	7.00

FACTION PARADOX
Aug., 2003

1 War in Heaven	3.00
2	3.00

FALLING MAN
(B&W) Dec., 1997

1 (of 3) BMC,PhH	3.00
2 Floyd vs. Duncan	3.00
3	3.00

Fathom #13
© Top Cow

FATHOM
Top Cow, 1998

1 by Michael Turner,F:Aspen	7.00
2 war beneath the waves	5.00
3 Life changed forever	4.00
4 Connection to water	4.00
5 Aspen's connection to water	4.00
6 Admiral's plans revealed	4.00
7 Finale,pt.1	4.00
8 Finale,pt.2	5.00
9 Finale, conclusion, end	5.00
9a green foil (c)	16.00
10 Fathom returns	3.00
11 Fathom returns,pt.2	3.00
12 Tomb Raider & Witchblade x-over,pt.1	3.00
12a variant(c)	5.00
13 x-over,pt.2	3.00
13a variant(c)	5.00
14 Aspen & Vana, concl.	3.00
14a variant(c)	5.00
15 Killian's Blue Sun	2.50
15a variant(c)	5.00
16 Admiral's subterfuge discovered.	2.50
#0 rep. new Mike Turner(c)	2.50
1/2	4.00
Spec. Swimsuit ed.	
Fathom 2000 swimsuit calendar	4.00
Fathom 2000 smimsuit Spec.	4.00

FATHOM: KILLIAN'S TIDE
Top Cow, March, 2001

1 (of 4)	5.00
1a variant(c)	4.00
2 thru 4	@3.00

FEAR AGENT
Oct., 2005

1	3.00
2	3.00
3	3.00
4	3.00
5	3.00
6 Reignition, conc.	3.00
7 Homecoming	3.00

IMAGE

---

8 . . . . 3.00	
9 . . . . 3.00	
10 . . . . 3.00	
11 . . . . 3.00	

FEAR EFFECT
Top Cow, March, 2000
1-shot MHw, video game tie-in 5.00
Spec. 1 Fear Effect Retro Helix 3.00

FEARLESS
Nov., 2007
1 . . . . 3.00
2 thru 4 . . . . @3.00

FEATHER
Aug., 2003
1 thru 4 . . . . @3.00
5 48-pg. 6.00

FELL
Sept., 2005
1 WEI 15.00
2 WEI 12.00
3 WEI 5.00
4 thru 8 WEI . . . . @5.00
9 thru 10 WEI . . . . @4.00

FELON
Top Cow, Oct., 2001
1 (of 4) 3.00
2 . . . . 3.00
3 concl. 3.00
4 I:Elizabeth Freeh 3.00

FELT: TRUE TALES OF UNDERGROUND HIP HOP
(B&W) May, 2005
1-shot 3.00

FERRO CITY
(B&W) Aug., 2005
1 . . . . 3.00
2 thru 4 . . . . @3.00

F5
April, 2000
1 TnD,48-pg. 3.00
2 TnD,life or death 2.50
3 TnD 2.50
4 TnD, betrayed 2.50
Preview Book, TnD,24-pg. 2.50

FIREBIRDS
Nov., 2004
1-shot by Jay Faeber 6.00

FIREBREATHER
Jan 2003
1 (of 4) PhH(s) 3.00
2 thru 4 PhH(s) . . . . @3.00
1-shot Firebreather: The Iron
    Saint, PhH (2004) 6.00
May, 2008
1 PHh(s) 3.00
2 thru 7 PHh(s) . . . . @3.00

FIRE FROM HEAVEN
WildStorm, 1996
1 x-over,Chapter 1 . . . . 3.50
2 x-over,Finale 2 . . . . 2.50

FIRST BORN
Top Cow, June, 2007
Spec. First Look 2.00

Fire From Heaven #1
© *Wildstorm*

1 (of 3) RMz, MS(c) 3.00
1a variant (c) 3.00
2 RMz,MS(c). 3.00
2a variant (c) 3.00
3 RMz 3.00
3a variant (c) 3.00

FIRST BORN: AFTERMATH
Top Cow, Mar., 2008
One-Shot RMz(s) 4.00
Spec. Comics Con variant 10.00

FIRSTMAN
April, 1997
1 ASm,LukeHenry becomesApollo . 2.50

FLAK RIOT
June, 2005
1 (of 4) 3.00
2 . . . . 3.00
3 . . . . 3.00
4 . . . . 3.00

FLAMING CARROT
(B&W) Dec., 2004
1 by Bob Burden, Crouching Carrot,
    Hidden Hot Wing 3.00
2 . . . . 3.50
3 . . . . 3.50
4 . . . . 3.50
Spec. 3.50

FOOT SOLDIERS, THE
(B&W) Sept., 1997
Prev.: Dark Horse
1 by Jim Krueger, Graveyard of
    Forgotten Heroes 3.00
2 Tragedy o/t Travesty Tapestry . . . 3.00
3 Arch enemies,pt.3 . . . . 3.00
4 'It's a Wicked World Afterall' 3.00
5 Loose Ends 3.00

FOREVER AMBER
(B&W) July, 1999
1 by Don Hudson 3.00
1a variant cover (1:2) 3.00
2 Lady fights back. 3.00
3 Amber sent to jail. 2.50
4 Amber's revenge, concl. 3.00

FORSAKEN
Aug., 2004
1 Light of Other Days,pt.1 . . . . 3.00
2 Light of Other Days,pt.2. . . . . . . 3.00
3 Light of Other Days,pt.3. . . . . . . 3.00
4 The Light of Other Days,pt.4 . . . . 3.00
5 The Light of Other Days,pt.5 . . . . 3.00
6 The Light of Other Days,pt.6 . . . . 3.00

FOUR EYES
Sept., 2008
1 . . . . 3.50
1a variant (c) 3.50
2 thru 3 . . . . @3.50

FRANKENSTEIN MOBSTER
Oct., 2003
0 . . . . 3.00
0a variant (c). 3.00
1 MkW,Friday the 13th 3.00
2 MkW. 3.00
3 MkW,mystic control 3.00
4 MkW. 3.00
5 MkW,Blood debt. 3.00
6 Escape from police 3.00
7 Made Man, concl. 3.00
1a thru 7a variant (c). . . . . @3.00

FRANK FRAZETTA'S CREATURES
July, 2008
1 . . . . 4.00
1a variant (c) 4.00

FRANK FRAZETTA'S DARK KINGDOM
Apr., 2008
Part One 4.00
Part One variant (c) 4.00

FRANK FRAZETTA'S DEATH DEALER
Apr., 2007
1 (of 6) FF(c),Shadows of Mirahan 8.00
1a & b variant (c)s . . . . @8.00
2 . . . . 7.00
2a & b variant (c)s. . . . . @7.00
3 . . . . 4.00
3a & b variant (c)s. . . . . @4.00
4 . . . . 4.00
4a & b variant (c)s. . . . . @4.00
5 . . . . 4.00
5a & b variant (c)s. . . . . @4.00
6 . . . . 4.00
6a & b variant (c)s. . . . . @4.00
1 B&W spec. 3.00

FRANK FRAZETTA'S DRACULA MEETS THE WOLFMAN
Aug, 2008
1-shot 4.00
1-shot a variant (c)s . . . . @4.00

FRANK FRAZETTA'S SWAMP DEMON
May, 2008
1-shot 4.00
1-shot a variant (c) 4.00

FREAK FORCE
Highbrow, 1993–95
1 EL(s),KG 3.00

2 EL(s),KG 3.00
3 EL(s),KG 3.00
4 EL(s),KG,A:Vanguard. 3.00
5 EL(s),KG 3.00
6 EL(s),KG 3.00
7 EL(s),KG 3.00
8 EL(s),space ants 3.00
9 EL(s),Cyberforce 3.00
10 EL(s),Savage Dragon 3.00
11 EL(s),Invasion,pt.1 . . . . 3.00
12 EL(s),Invasion,pt.2 . . . . 3.00
13 EL(s),Invasion,pt.3 . . . . 3.00
14 EL(s),Team Defeated 3.00
15 EL(s),F:Barbaric 3.00
16 KG,EL(s),V:Chelsea Nirvana. . . . 3.00
17 EL,KG,major plots converge 3.00
18 Final Issue 3.00

[Series Two] March, 1997
1 EL,Star joins team,V:The
   Frightening Force 3.00
2 EL,Dart quits team 3.00
3 EL,'Lo there shall come..an
   ending'. 3.00

FREEDOM FORCE
Jan., 2005
1 (of 6) Founding Fathers 3.00
2 Casualty of War 3.00
3 Double Trouble 3.00
4 Mechanical Mayhem 3.00
5 Forbidden Fruit 3.00
6 Out of Time 3.00

FRESHMEN, THE
Top Cow, 2005
1 thru 3 Intro to Superpowers 101
   pt. 1 thru pt. 3 . . . . @3.00
4 What Time is it in Budapest. 3.00
5 Deepest Level of Truth 3.00
6 Finals 3.00
Spec. Yearbook (2005) 3.00
1-shot Freshmen Yearbook 3.00
Vol. 2
2 Fundamentals of Fear 3.00
2a variant incentive (c) 3.00
3 Fundamentals of Fear 3.00
3a variant (c)s . . . . @3.00
4 Fundamentals of Fear 3.00
5 Fundamentals of Fear 4.00
5a variant (c). 4.00
6 Fundamentals of Fear 4.00
6a variant (c) 4.00

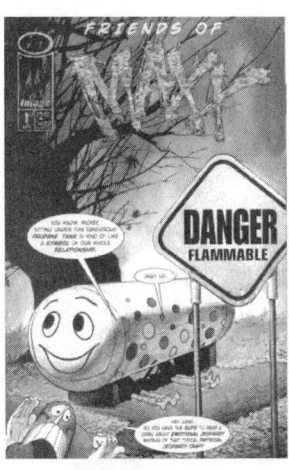

Friends of Max #22
© Image/I Before E

1 Fundamentals of Fear 3.00
Spec. Summer Vacation Special . . . 5.00

FRIENDS OF MAXX
I Before E, April, 1996
1 thru 3 WML&SK . . . . @3.00

FUSED!
March, 2002
1 Canned Heat,pt.1 (of 4). 3.00
1a variant(c) 3.00
2 Canned Heat,pt.2. . . . . 3.00
3 Canned Heat,pt.3. . . . . 3.00
4 Canned Heat,pt.4. . . . . 3.00

GALAXY-SIZE ASTOUNDING SPACE THIRLLS
March, 2001
1 Galaxy Size Showdown, 48-pg.
   flip-book. 5.00

GAMORRA SWIMSUIT SPECIAL
WildStorm, 1996
Spec.#1 . . . . 2.50

GAZILLION
Nov., 1998
1 HSm, Mars vs. Xof. 2.50
1a variant cover (1:4) 2.50

GEAR STATION, THE
March, 2000
1 DaF,Dominion of Souls 6.00
1a variant AxR(c) 2.50
1b variant PtL(c). 2.50
1c variant Michael Turner(c). 2.50
2 DaF,23rd Gear 2.50
2a variant AAd(c) 2.50
3 DaF,Who is Fable 2.50
4 DaF,first showdown 2.50
5 DaF,Gear Station Prime. 2.50
6 DaF 2.50

GEEKSVILLE
(B&W) Mar., 2000
#0 by R.Koslowski & G.Sassaman . 3.00
1 Breaking into the Biz,pt.1. . . . . . . 3.00
2 Breaking into the Biz,pt.2. . . . . . . 3.00
3 Back to the Con 3.00
4 Breaking into the Biz 3.00
5 Dark Sky 3.00
6 End of 3 Geeks 3.00

GEMINAR
(B&W) June, 2000
1 . . . . 5.00
2 F:Captain Champion 5.00

GEMINI
May, 2008
1 (of 5) 3.50
2 thru 5 . . . . @3.50

GEN¹³
WildStorm, 1994
0 Individual Hero Stories. 4.00
1 JLe(s),BCi(s),I:Fairchild,Grunge,
   Freefall,Burnout. 12.00
1a 2nd printing 4.00
2 JLe(s),BCi(s) 9.00
3 JLe(s),BCi(s),A:Pitt,'Payback' . . 7.00
4 JLe(s),BCi(s),'Free for All' 6.00
5 Final issue 5.00

5a WP variant cover. 8.00
[Regular Series] 1995
1a BCi(s),V:Mercenaries. 5.00
1b Common Cover 2 . . . . 5.00
1c Heavy Metal Gen. 8.00
1d Pulp Fiction Parody 9.00
1e Gen 13 Bunch 8.00
1f Lin-Gen-re. 9.00
1g Lil Gen 13 . . . . 8.00
1h Friendly Neighbor Grunge 8.00
1i Gen 13 Madison Ave 9.00
1j Gen-Et Jackson 8.00
1k Gen Dress Up cover 8.00
1l Verti-Gen. 8.00
1m Do It Yourself Cover 8.00
2 BCi,BWS(c),WildStorm Rising,
   pt.4, w/2 cards. 3.00
2a newstand ed. 2.50
3 BCi,'Magical Mystery Tour' 3.00
4 BCi,'Tourist Trap' 3.00
5 BCi,I:New Member,Family Feud . 3.00
6 BCi,JLe,I:The Deviants,
   'Roman Holiday' 3.00
7 BCi,JLe,European Vacation,pt.2
   'Veni, Vidi, Vici' 3.00
8 BCi,'Bewitched,Bothered
   and Bewildered'. 3.00
9 . . . . 3.00
10 Fire From Heaven,pt.3 . . . . 3.00
11 Fire From Heaven,pt.9 . . . . 3.00
12 F:Caitlin,her dad 3.00
13 A, B & C, each . . . . @3.00
14 'Higher Learning'. 2.50
15 Fraternity and Sorority rush 2.50
16. . . . . 2.50
17 BCi,JSC,AGo,battle royale in
   Tower of Luv,'Toy Soldiers' 2.50
18 BCi,JSC,AGo,V:Keepers,
   'Hello & Good-Byes' 2.50
19 BCi,JSC,AGo,Lynch & kids flee
   to Antarctica,'Bon Voyage'. 2.50
20 BCi,JSC,AGo,'To Boldly Go' . . . 2.50
21 BCi,JSC,AGo,V:D'Rahn,'Lost
   in Space' 2.50
22 BCi,civil war,'Homecoming'. 2.50
23 BCi,21st century 2.50
24 BCi,V:D'Rahn,'Judgment Day' . . 2.50
25 BCi,Homecoming,JsC(c). 3.50
25a TC(c),'Where Angels Fear
   to Tread' 3.50
25b Voyager bagged pack 3.50
26 JAr,GFr,CaS,When Worlds
   Collide 2.50
27 JAr,GFr,CaS,'Search & Seizure' . 2.50
28 JAr,GFr,CaS,'Remote Control' . . 2.50

Gen¹³ #12
© WildStorm

All comics prices listed are for *Near Mint* condition.

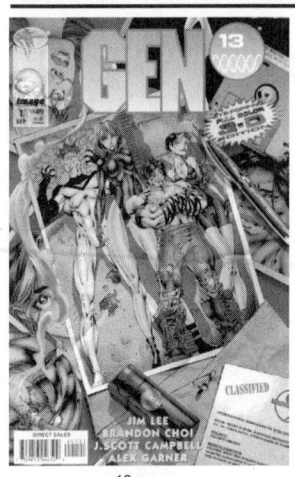

Gen13 3-D Special
© WildStorm

29 JAr,GFr,CaS,I:Tindalos,
'A Firm Grip on Reality' 2.50
30 JAr,GFr,CaS,'Stranger Than
Fiction' 2.50
31 JAr,GFr,CaS,Roxy's Big Score,
'Paradigm Shift' 2.50
32 JAr,GFr,CaS,'Red Skies at
Morning' 2.50
33 JAr,GFr,CaS,aftermaths, 'Burning
the Candle at Both Ends',
with 8-page Planetary #0 . . . . . 4.00
34 JAr,GFr,CaS,AAd,A:Roxy
& Sarah,'Overture' 2.50
35 JAr,GFr,CaS,John Lynch resigns,
'But You Can't Hide' 2.50
36 JAr,GFr,CaS,F:John Lynch,
'That Was Then' 2.50
College Yearbook 1997, Superheroes
at Large 2.50
Ann. #1 WEI,SDi'London'sBrilliant' . 3.00
1-Shot Gen13:Unreal World (1996) . 3.00
Gen13 3-D Special (1997) 5.00
3-D Spec. #1, (1997) 5.00
3-D Spec. #1, variant cover 5.00
3-D Spec. #1, (1998) 5.00

WildStorm/DC, 1999

37 JAr,GFr,CaS,Reaper 2.50
38 JAr,GFr,CaS,BU:Grunge 2.50
38a variant cover 2.50
39 JAr,GFr,CaS,Genocide 2.50
40 JAr,GFr,CaS,V:Reaper 2.50
41 JAr,GFr,CaS 2.50
42 JoC(s),KM,pro wrestlers 2.50
43 AWa(s&c),F:Fairchild 2.50
44 AWa(s&c),A:Mr.Magestic 2.50
45 SLo,EBe,JSb,fashion show 2.50
46 SLo,EBe,JSb,MightyJoeGrunge . 2.50
47 SLo,EBe,JSb 2.50
48 SLo,EBe,JSb 2.50
49 SLo,EBe,JSb 2.50
50 SLo,EBe,JSb,48-pg 4.00
50a variant JLe,SW(c) (1:4) 4.00
51 SLo,breather 2.50
52 SLo,F:Caitlin Fairchild 2.50
53 F:all Villains issue 2.50
54 SLo,EBe,SWi,F:Fairchild 2.50
55 EBe,Return to Pod 9,pt.2 . . . . . 2.50
56 EBe,Fairchild,pt.3 . . . . 2.50
57 BRa,EBe,Tokyo in danger 2.50
58 BRa,EBe,mini-monster
massacre 2.50
59 BRa,EBe,V:Gaijin13 . . . . 2.50
60 AWa,Behind the Power 2.50
61 AWa,Goin' back to Cali 2.50

62 AWa,fast food 2.50
63 AWa,EBe,sailboat outing 2.50
64 AWa,Superhuman Like You,pt.1 . 2.50
65 AWa,Superhuman Like You,pt.2 . 2.50
66 AWa,8 guest artists 2.50
67 AWa,EBe,ColdAir on MyBehind . 2.50
68 AWa,Slave to Love,pt.1 . . . . 2.50
69 AWa,Slave to Love,pt.2 . . . . 2.50
70 AWa,F:Sara Rainmaker 2.50
71 AWa,Think Like A Gun,pt.1 . . . . . 2.50
72 AWa,Think Like A Gun,pt.2 . . . . . 2.50
73 AWa,Think Like A Gun,pt.3 . . . . . 2.50
74 AWa,Think Like A Gun,pt.4 . . . . . 2.50
75 AWa,How the Story Ends,pt.1 . . . 2.50
76 AWa,How the Story Ends,pt.2 . . . 2.50
77 AWa,Story Ends,pt.3, 40-pg 3.50
Annual'99 JAr(s) 3.50
Ann. 2000 #1, Devil's
Night x-over,pt.1 . . . . 3.50
Spec. Wired 2.50
Spec.#1 3-D AAd 5.00
Spec.#1a variant(c) 5.00
Spec. Carny Folk 3.50
Spec. 1-shot Going West 2.50
GN Grunge Saves the World 6.00
GN Bootleg: Grunge— The Movie. 10.00
GN Medicine Song, 48-pg. 6.00
GN Gen13/Fantastic Four 6.00
GN Science Friction, 48-pg 6.00
GN London,New York,Hell 7.00
GN A Christmas Caper (2002) 6.00

GEN[13] BOOTLEG
WildStorm, Nov., 1996
1 MFm&AD,lost in the 'Linquist
Fault,'pt.1 . . . . 3.00
1a signed 15.00
2 'Linquist Fault,'pt.2 . . . . 3.50
3 Gen13 Fairy Tale 3.50
4 WS&LSi,F:Valaria,'Little Girl
Lost' 3.50
5 F:Fairchild,'Timesick,'pt.1 . . . . . . 3.50
6 F:Fairchild,'Timesick,'pt.2 . . . . . . 3.50
7 'Renaissance Ruckus' 3.50
8 AWa,'Grunge's Movie,'pt.1 . . . . . . 4.00
9 AWa,'Grunge's Movie,'pt.2 . . . . . . 4.00
10 AWa,'Grunge's Movie,'pt.3 . . . . . 4.00
11 AaL,WS,Chupacabra,pt.1 . . . . . . 2.50
12 AaL,WS,Chupacabra,pt.2 . . . . . . 2.50
13 F:Grunge,'The Trickster' 2.50
14 JMi,JoP,GL,bad neighbors 2.50
15 KNo,V:Trance,'Hanging,'pt.1 . . . . 2.50
16 KNo,V:Trance,'Hanging,'pt.2 . . . . 2.50
17 'Virgil Chu's Reality 2.50
18 MFm,'A Day at the Beach' 2.50
19 BKs,JhB,Satyr 2.50
20 CAd,F:John Lynch,'Numbskulls' . 2.50
Ann.#1 WEI,SDi, to NYC 3.00

GEN[13]: INTERACTIVE
WildStorm, Oct., 1997
1 vote via Internet 4.00
2 & 3 MHs,vote via Internet . . . . @3.00

GEN[13]/ GENERATION X
WildStorm, July, 1997
1 BCi&AAd,'Generation Gap' 3.00
1a variant JSC(c) 3.00
3-D edition, with glasses 5.00
3-Da variant cover, with glasses . . . 5.00

GEN[13]: MAGICAL DRAMA QUEEN ROXY
WildStorm, Oct., 1998
1 (of 3) AWa,Mall of Doom 4.00
2 AWa,V:Caitlin 4.00
3 AWa,dream sequence concl 4.00

Gen[13]/The Maxx #1
© WildStorm

GEN[13]/THE MAXX
WildStorm, 1995
Spec.#1 BML,x-over 4.00

GEN[13]/MONKEY MAN & O'BRIEN
WildStorm, June, 1998
1 (of 2) AAd 3.00
1a chromium edition 4.50
2 AAd,alternate universe, concl 3.00
2a variant AAd(c) 2.50

GEN[13]: ORDINARY HEROES
WildStorm, 1996
1 & 2 . . . . @3.00

GEN[12]
WildStorm, Feb., 1998
1 BCi,Team 7 tie-in,'The Legacy' . . 3.00
2 BCi,F:Morgan of I.O. 3.00
3 BCi,Dominique Faust 3.00
4 BCi,F:Miles Craven 3.00
5 BCi,Team 7 re-unites 3.00

GHOSTING
Platinum, Aug., 2007
1 (of 4) 3.00
2 . . . . 3.00

GHOST SPY
May, 2004
1 (of 6) 3.00
2 thru 5 . . . . @3.00

GIFT, THE
2004
8 Sacrifice 3.00
9 Corrupt 3.00
10 Unleashed 3.00
11 Betrayal 3.00
12 Death 3.00
13 The Dragon 3.00
14 O:Ancient One 3.00
1a director's cut 4.00

G.I. JOE
Sept., 2001
1 JSC(c) Reinstated,pt.1	15.00
1a 2nd printing	6.00
2 Reinstated,pt.2	6.00
3 JSC(c),Reinstated,pt.3	5.00
4 JSC(c),Reinstated,pt.4	5.00
5 F:Duke	3.50
6 Reckonings,pt.1	3.00
7 Storm Shadow	3.00
8 Destro & Cobra Commander	3.00
9 Snake-eyes vs. Storm Shadow	3.00
10 Dreadnoks	3.00
11 Mob rule in Chicago	3.00
12 JBz(c),V:Android Trooper	3.00
13 JBz(c),V:Firefly	3.00
14 Cobra Suburbs Return	3.00
15 Reunion	3.00
16 missing child	3.00
17 kidnap Flint & Baroness	3.00
18 search for Flint & Baroness	3.00
19	3.00
20 Storm Shadow	3.00
21 Snake-Eyes	4.00
22 Return of Serpentor,pt.1	4.00
21a & 22a variant (c)s	@9.00
23 Return of Serpentor,pt.2	3.00
24 Return of Serpentor,pt.3	3.00
25	3.00
24a thru 25a variant (c)s	@3.00
Spec. M.I.A., rep. #1 & #2	5.00

Devil's Due 2004
26 thru 30	@3.00
31	8.00
32	3.00
33	7.00
33 2nd printing	8.00
34 thru 41	@3.00
42 D:Lady Jaye	5.00

G.I. JOE: BATTLE FILES
April, 2002
1 (of 3) G.I. Joe, 48-pg.	6.00
2 F:Cobra	6.00
3 F:Vehicles and Tech	6.00

G.I. JOE FRONTLINE
Oct., 2002
1 LHa(s),DJu,BL,DvD(c)	3.00
2 DJu,BL,DvD(c) V:Destro	3.00
3 DJu,BL,DvD(c) V:Destro	3.00
4 DJu,BL,Silent Castle	3.00
5 thru 8 Icebound	@3.00
9 Kansas City	3.00
10	3.00
11 Chuckles	3.00
12 Chuckles	3.00
13 Chuckles	3.00
14 Chuckles	3.00
15 F:Stalker	3.00
16 Night Creepers	3.00
17 PJe,F:Beachhead	3.00
18	3.00
18a variant (c)	3.00
16a–17a variant (c)	@3.00

G.I. JOE VS. TRANSFORMERS
June, 2003
1	4.00
1a 2nd printing	3.00
2 thru 6	@3.00
1a–6a variant (c)	@5.00

GIRLS
May, 2005
1	6.00
1a 2nd & 3rd printings	@3.00

2	4.00
3 thru 24	3.00

GLISTER
Aug., 2007
1 Glister Butterworth and the Haunted Teapot, 64-pgs.	6.00
2 House Hunting	6.00
3 Glister and the Faerie Host	6.00

GLORY
Extreme, 1995
0 JDy	2.50
1 JDy,F:Glory	4.00
1a variant cover	4.00
2 JDy,V:Demon Father	3.00
3 JDy,A:Rumble & Vandal	2.50
4 Vandal vs. Demon Horde	2.50
4a JDy variant cover	3.00
5 Supreme Apocalypse,pt.3, F:Vandal	2.50
6 Drug Problem	2.50
7 F:Superpatriot	2.50
8 Extreme Babewatch	2.50
9 Extreme Destroyer,pt.5, x-over, bagged with card	2.50
10	2.50
11	2.50
12 JDy, EBe & JSb	3.50
13 JDy, EBe & JSb	2.50
14 JDy, EBe & JSb	2.50
15 JDy, EBe & JSb, Out for vengeance	2.50

continued: see Color Comics section

GLORY/ANGELA ANGELS IN HELL
Extreme, 1996
1	4.00

GLORY/AVENGELYNE
Extreme, 1996
1 V:B'lial,I:Faith	4.00
1a no chrome(c)	3.00

GLORY/AVENGELYNE: THE GODYSSEY
Extreme
1 RLd & JDy	3.00
1a photo(c)	4.00

GLORY/CELESTINE: DARK ANGEL
Extreme, Sept., 1996
1 (of 3) JDy,PtL,sequel to Rage of Angels, A:Maximage	2.50
2 JDy,PtL,'Doomsday+1'	2.50
3 JDy,PtL, conclusion	2.50

GLORY & FRIENDS
Extreme, 1995
Bikini Fest #1	2.50
Bikini Fest #2	2.50
LIngerie Special #1 (1995)	3.00
Christmas Special #1 (1995)	2.50

G-MAN
Dec., 2004
1 Learning to Fly	6.00

GODLAND
June, 2005
1 Cosmic Wheels in Motion	3.00
2 Every Breath You Take	3.00
3 The seismic Shift	3.00
4 The Torture Never Stops	3.00

Glory & Friends Bikini Fest #1
© Extreme

5 Combat Rock	3.00
6	3.00
7 Acid Raindrops	3.00
8 The Origin of the Universe	3.00
9 Funky Buster Round	3.00
10 The March of Ides	3.00
11 Never Say Janus	3.00
12 High Noon, Tea Time, 32-pg.	3.00
13	3.00
13a variant (c)	3.00
14	3.00
15 O Sister Where Art Thou	3.00
16 Strange But True	0.60
17 The Infinity Protocols	3.00
18 Dance Hall Crash Hall	3.00
19 High Head Stung	3.00
20 Viv Las Vulgar	3.00
21 JoC(s)	3.00
22 JoC(s) Detonate Reality Saga	3.00
23 JoC(s) World's Apart	3.00
24 JoC(s),Twelve-Finger Squeeze	3.00
25 JoC(s),The Mother Cutter	3.00
26 JoC(s),Trip Through the Wires	3.00
27 JoC(s),Kill the Wabbit	3.00
28 JoC(s),The Horror	3.00

GO GIRL!
Aug., 2000
1 TrR,F:Lindsay Goldman	3.50
2 TrR,wonderful life?	3.50
3 TrR,The Teacher from Hell	3.50
4 TrR,Vacation at dude ranch	3.50
5 TrR,origin of powers	3.50

GOLLY
Aug., 2008
1 PhH	3.00
2 thru 3 PhH	@3.00

GRAVESLINGER
Oct, 2007
1 (of 4)	3.00
2 thru 4	@3.50

GRAY AREA, THE
June, 2004
1 (of 3) JR2,KJ,48-pg.	6.00
2 JR2,KJ,32-pg.	4.00
3 JRw,KJ,48-pg.	6.00

IMAGE

GREASE MONKEY
March, 1998
1 TEI 3.00
2 TEI 3.00
3 TEI, The Calling; Rewards. 3.00

GRIFTER
WildStorm, 1995–96
1 BWS(c), WildStorm
　Rising,pt.5,w/2 cards 2.50
1a Newsstand ed. 2.50
2 V:Diabolik,pt.1 . . . . 3.00
3 V:Diabolik,pt.2 . . . . 3.00
4 R:Forgotten Hero. 3.00
5 Rampage of a Fallen Hero 3.00
6 V:Poerhouse 3.00
7 City of Angels,pt.1 . . . . 3.00
8 City of Angels,pt.2 . . . . 3.00
9 City of Angels,pt.3 . . . . 3.00
10 City of Angels,pt.4. . . . . 3.00

GRIFTER/BADROCK
Extreme, 1995
1 To Save Badrock's Mom 3.00
1a Variant cover 2.50
2 flip-book-Badrock #2 . . . . 3.00
3 double-size 3.50

GRIFTER-ONE SHOT
WildStorm, 1995
1 SS,DN 5.00

Grifter #8
© Image/WildStorm

GRIFTER
WildStorm, 1996
1 StG. 4.00
2 StG,V:Joe the Dead 3.00
3 StG,captured by MadJackPower . 3.00
4 StG,vs. Condition Red 3.00
5 StG,Grifter meets his dad,
　F:Molly Ingram. 3.00
6 StG,A:Santini 3.00
7 StG,MtB,I:Charlatan 3.00
8 StG,MtB,Zealot
　disappears,V:Soldier 3.00
9 StG,Zealot captured?, secret
　history of Quiet Men 3.00
10 StG,Grifter & Soldier go to
　rescue Zealot. 3.00
11 StG, renegade former agent 3.00
12 StG,'Who is Tanager?'. 3.00

13 StG,F:Condition Red,'Family
　Feud' 3.00
14 StG,V:Joe the Dead 3.00

GRIFTER/SHI
WildStorm, 1996
1 BCi,JLe,TC 3.00
2 BCi,JLe,TC 3.00

GROO
1994–95
1 SA 3.50
2 A:Arba, Dakarba 3.50
3 The Generals Hat 3.50
4 A Drink of Water. 3.50
5 SA,A Simple Invasion 3.50
6 SA,A Little Invention 3.50
7 The Plight of the Drazils 3.50
8 . . . . 3.50
9 I:Arfetto 3.50
10 The Sinkes 3.50
11 The Gamblers 3.50
12 . . . . 3.50

GROUNDED
July, 2005
1 (of 6) 3.00
2 thru 5 . . . . @3.00
6 32-pg.. 3.50

GRRL SCOUTS
Feb., 2003
1 (of 4) Work Sucks, b&w. 3.00
2 thru 4 . . . . @3.00

GUARDIAN ANGEL
May, 2002
1 (of 4) AWs,F:ChristianAngelos. . . 3.00
2 AWs,no place like home 3.00
3 AWs,Our onlyhope. 3.00
4 concl. 3.00

GUERILLAS
(B&W) Aug., 2008
1 (of 9) 4.00
2 . . . . 4.00

GUNCANDY
(B&W) July, 2005
1 (of 2) BSf 6.00
2 BSt 6.00

GUTSVILLE
May, 2007
1 (of 6) 3.00
2 thru 6 . . . . @3.00

GUTWRENCHER
Shadowline, Feb., 2008
1 (of 3) 3.50
2 thru 3 . . . . @3.50

HAMMER OF THE GODS:
HAMMER HITS CHINA
Feb., 2003
1 thru 3 . . . . @3.00

HAWAIIAN DICK
Dec., 2002
1 thru 3 Hawaii in 1953. . . . . . . @3.00

HAWAIIAN DICK
Nov., 2007
1 Screaming Black Thunder, pt.1 . . 3.00
2 Screaming Black Thunder, pt.2 . . 3.00

3 Screaming Black Thunder, pt.3 . . 3.00
4 Screaming Black Thunder, pt.4 . . 3.00
5 Screaming Black Thunder, pt.5 . . 3.00
6 Jazz Interlude 3.00

HAWAIIAN DICK:
THE LAST RESORT
Aug., 2004
1 (of 4) 3.00
2 & 3 . . . . @3.00
4 concl. 3.00

HAWKSHAWS
March, 2000
1 by Dietrich Smith 3.00
1a variant movie poster(c) 3.00
2 and 3 . . . . @3.00

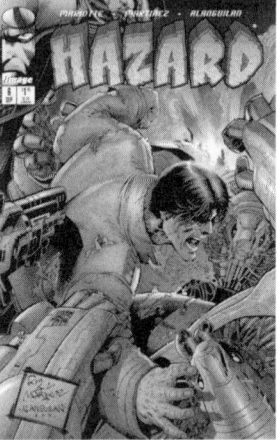

Hazard #6
© Image/WildStorm

HAZARD
WildStorm, 1996
1 JMi,RMr. 3.00
2 JMi,RMr 3.00
3 JMi,RMr 3.00
4 JMi,RMr 3.00
5 JMi,RMr,Hazard finds Dr. D'Oro . 3.00
6 JMi,RMr. 3.00
7 JMi,RMr,Hazard meets Prism . . . 3.00

HEADHUNTERS
(B&W) April, 1997
1 ChM,V:Army of Wrath 3.00
2 ChM,V:undead militia. 3.00
3 ChM,'Slaughterground' 3.00

HEARTBREAKERS
Superdigest, July 1998
1 B&W and color 104-pg. 10.00

HEAVEN'S DEVILS
Sept., 2003
1 (of 4) 3.00
2 thru 4 . . . . @3.00

HECTOR PLASM:
TOTENTANZ
Nov., 2008
1-shot 6.00

HEDGE KNIGHT, THE
Aug., 2003
1 (of 6) MsM	5.00
1a variant (c)	12.00
2	5.00
2a cardstock(c)	10.00
3	4.00
3a holofoil (c)	6.00

See also Color Comics section

HEIRS OF ETERNITY
Apr., 2003
1 (of 5)	3.00
2	3.00
3	3.00
4	3.00
5	3.00

HELLCOP
Avalon, Oct., 1998
1 JoC,F:Virgil Hilts	2.50
2 JoC,It's a small underwold after all	2.50
3 JoC,new circles of Hell	2.50
4 JoC,secrets of Hell revealed	2.50
5 JoC,Hell & High Water	2.50
5a variant cover	3.00

HELLHOLE
Top Cow, May, 1999
1 SLo,AdP,F:Michael Cabrini	2.50
2 SLo,AdP,The Devil's Candy	2.50
3 SLo,AdP,power brokers	2.50

HELLHOUNDS
Aug., 2003
1 Hadean Gates	3.00
2 thru 5	@3.00
6 EL(c),F:Savage Dragon	3.00
1a and 2a variant (c)	@3.00
5a variant (c)	3.00

HELLSHOCK
1994
1 I:Hellshock	3.50
2 Powers & Origin	3.50
3 New foe	3.50
4	3.50

HELLSHOCK
Jan., 1997
1 JaL,Something wrong with Daniel, 48-pg	3.00
2 JaL,Daniel learns to control powers	2.50
3 JaL,Daniel free of madness	2.50
4 JaL,Daniel searches for his mother, Jonakand plans escape from Hell	2.50
5 JaL,Jonakand and fallen angels tear hell apart	2.50
6 JaL,'The Milk of Paradise'	2.50
7 JaL,'A Mother's Story', double size	4.00
8 JaL,House of Torture	2.50

HELLSPAWN
TMP, July, 2000
1 The Clown,pt.1	4.00
2 The Clown,pt.2	3.00
3 Hate Me	3.00
4 Hate You	3.00
5 Selling Fear	3.00
6 Angels	5.00
7 The Group	2.50
8 The Suicide Gate	2.50
9 Chains	2.50
10 Clash	2.50

11 Conflicts of Interest	2.50
12 Monsters and Miracles	2.50
13 Heaven & Hell	2.50
14 Light of Day	2.50
15 Blinded	2.50
16 Hellworld,pt.4	2.50
17 The Killing Hand,pt.1	2.50
18 The Killing Hand,pt.2	2.50
19 The Killing Hand,pt.3	2.50
20 The Collection	2.50
21 The Collection,pt.2	2.50
22 Love Lost,pt.1	3.00
23 Love Lost,pt.2	2.50
24 In the Grip of Shadows	2.50
25 Remember Me?	2.50

HERO BY NIGHT
Platinum, Mar., 2007
1 thru 4	@3.00

HERO CAMP
May, 2005
1 (of 4)	3.00
2 I Still Haven't Found What I'm Looking For, pt.1	3.00
3	3.00
4 Parents Day	3.00

HIDING IN TIME
July, 2007
1 (of 4)	3.50
2 thru 3	@3.50

HOLY TERROR, THE
Aug., 2002
1 (of 4) PhH	3.00
2 thru 3 PhH	@3.00

HOMAGE STUDIOS
April, 1993
Swimsuit Spec.#1 JLe,WPo, MS	2.50

HONG ON THE RANGE
Matinee Entertainment/ Flypaper, Dec., 1997
1 (of 3) by William Wu & Jeff Lafferty	2.50
2 in Washout	2.50
3 Duke Goslin	2.50

HUMAN KIND
Top Cow, Aug., 2004
1 TnD,F:Alia Sparrow	3.00
2 TnD	3.00
3 TnD,Roads to New Rome,pt.3	3.00
4 All Roads Lead to (New) Rome	3.00
5 All Roads Lead to (New) Rome	3.00

HUNTER-KILLER
Top Cow, 2005
0 MWa,MS, B&W, 16-pg	1.00
1 MWa,MS	3.00
2 MWa,MS	3.00
2a variant JLi	3.00
3 MWa,MS	3.00
4 thru 6 MWa,MS	@3.00
7	3.00
8	3.00
9	3.00
9a variant (c)	3.00
10	3.00
11 The Deadly Game Continues	3.00
11a variant b&w (c), rare	4.00
12 The End of Morningstar?	3.00
Script-book 40-pg	5.00
1-shot Hunter-Killer Dossier	3.00

HYPERKINETIC
July, 2008
1 (of 4)	3.50
2 thru 4	@3.50
1a thru 4a variant (c)s	3.50

HYSTERIA: ONE MAN GANG
(B&W) March, 2006
1	3.00
2	3.00
3 All car chase issue	3.00
4	3.50

I HATE GALAXY GIRL
Shadowline, Nov., 2008
1 (of 3) Pretty, Vacant	3.50

I KILL GIANTS
(B&W) July, 2008
1 thru 5 (of 7)	@3.00

IMAGE COMICS
Dec., 2005
Spec. Holiday Spec. (2005)	10.00

Image Introduces Dog Soldiers
© Image

IMAGE INTRODUCES:
Oct., 2001
1 Primate	3.00
1b variant AGo(c)	3.00
(2) Legend of Isis	3.00
(3) The Believer	3.00
(4) Cryptopia	3.00
(5) Dog Soldiers	3.00

IMAGE MONSTER PILE UP
Aug., 2008
1	2.00

IMAGE TWO-IN-ONE
(B&W) Mar., 2001
1 EL,48-pg. F:Herculian & Duncan	3.00

IMAGE ZERO
1993
0 I:Troll,Deathtrap,Pin-ups,rep. Savage Dragon #4,O:Stryker, F:ShadowHawk	9.00

IMAGES OF SHADOWHAWK
1993–94
1 KG,V:Trencher 2.50
2 thru 3 V:Trencher 2.50

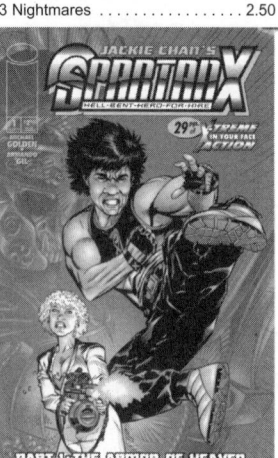

Imaginaries #2
© Image

IMAGINARIES, THE
Mar., 2005
1 (of 4) 3.00
2 thru 4 . . . . @3.00
2a variant (c). 3.00

IMMORTAL TWO
May, 1997
(B&W) Half-Tone
1 MsM,F:Gaijin & Gabrielle 2.50
2 MsM 2.50
3 MsM 2.50
4 MsM,V:Okami Red 2.50
5 MsM,new drug epidemic 2.50
6 MsM,First Order, cont. 2.50
7 MsM,vs. impossible odds 2.50
7 MsM,flip photo cover 2.50

IMPALER
Oct., 2006
1 thru 5 . . . . @3.00

INDUSTRY OF WAR
(B&W) Nov., 2005
1-shot 8.00

INFERNO: HELLBOUND
Top Cow, Nov., 2001
1 MS,DT,Hell loose on Earth 2.50
1a-1f variant(c) . . . . @2.00
2 thru 4 MS . . . . @2.75
#0 MS 16-pg., signed. 20.00

INFINITE HORIZON
Dec., 2007
1 (of 6) 3.00
2 Red Sky at Morning 3.00
3 thru 6 . . . . @3.00

IN HER DARKEST HOUR
Aug., 2007
1-shot 3.50

INNOCENTS, THE
Top Cow, July, 2006
1 . . . . 3.00
GN 10.00

INTIMIDATORS, THE
Dec., 2005
1 . . . . 3.50
2 . . . . 3.50
3 Who is Atrocity 3.50
4 Crash and Byrn 3.50
5 Prison Break 3.50
6 Last Best Hope 3.50
7 Blame Canada 3.50

INTRIGUE
Aug., 1999
1 F:Kirk Best 2.50
1a variant cover (1:4) 2.50
2 on the run from the law 2.50
3 V:NYPD SWAT team 2.50
3a variant HuR cover (1:4) 2.50
4 . . . . 2.50
5 . . . . 3.00
5a variant Mike Wieringo(c) 3.00

INVINCIBLE
Jan., 2003
1 O:Mark Grayson 15.00
2 . . . . 25.00
3 quality time. 15.00
4 human bombs 15.00
5 It Came From Outer Space 15.00
6 . . . . 12.00
7 Guardians of the Globe 12.00
8 shperhero funeral. 12.00
9 Perfect Strangers,pt.1 . . . . 12.00
10 Perfect Strangers,pt.2 . . . . . . 12.00
11 Perfect Strangers,pt.3 . . . . . . 25.00
12 Perfect Strangers,pt.4 . . . . 7.00
13 Perfect Strangers,epilogue 7.00
14 Alien invaders return 7.00
15 Aquaria 5.00
16 Immortal is back 3.50
17 High school graduation 3.50
18 Space flight to Mars 3.50
19 . . . . 3.50
20 Return of the Robot Zombie . . . 3.50
21 Return to Midnight City 3.50
22 Mark and Amber at college . . . 3.50
23 . . . . 3.50
24 Worst beating yet 3.50
25 A Different World, pt.1 . . . . 5.00
26 A Different World, pt.2 . . . . 3.00
27 A Different World, pt.3 . . . . 3.00
28 A Different World, pt.4 . . . . 3.00
29 . . . . 3.00
30 A Different World 3.00
31 Mark & Amber to Africa 3.00
32 Life with Amber and Eva. 3.00
33 Angstrom Levy 3.00
34 Angstrom Levy 3.00
35 . . . . 3.00
36 Re-animen Strike 3.00
37 . . . . 3.00
38 . . . . 3.00
39 . . . . 3.00
40 . . . . 3.00
41 . . . . 3.00
42 . . . . 2.00
43 Space Fight. 3.00
44 . . . . 3.00
45 In deep space. 3.00
46 . . . . 3.00
47 . . . . 3.00
48 Doc Seismic 3.00
49 Reanimen are back. 3.00
50 48-pgs. 5.00
51 JLe(c),New Costume 3.00
52 V:Kid Omni-Man 3.00

53 V:Titan 3.00
54 Fightmaster & Drop Kick 3.00
55 Omni-Man 3.00
56 . . . . 3.00
57 A:Astounding Wolf-Man x-over . . 3.00
58 Invincible & Atom Eve 3.00
Spec. #0 . . . . 2.50
Spec. Official Handbook of the
    Invincible Universe, Vol. 1 . . . . . 5.00
Spec. Script Book 4.00
Spec. Invincible Universe Primer #1 6.00

INVINCIBLE PRESENTS ATOM EVE
Dec., 2007
1(of 2) 3.00
2 . . . . 3.00

IRON GHOST
Apr., 2005
1 thru 6 CDi(s). . . . . @3.00

IRON WINGS
March, 2000
1 Legends of Iron Wings 2.50
1a variant Andy Park(c) 2.50
2 V:Amaxius 2.50
3 Nightmares 2.50

Jackie Chan's Spartan X #1
© Image

JACKIE CHAN'S SPARTAN X
(B&W) March, 1998
1 MGo,RM,Hell-Bent Hero for Hire. 3.00
2 MGo,to Russia 3.00
3 MGo,V:Kenshi 3.00
4 MGo,RM, in Istanbul 3.00
5 MGo,RM, Mind of God 3.00
5a MGo,RM, photo cover 3.00
6 MGo,RM, The Armor of Heaven . 3.00
6a MGo,RM, photo cover 3.00

JACK STAFF
Feb., 2003
1 Britain's Greatest hero 3.00
2 thru 7 . . . . @3.00
8 thru 21 . . . . @3.50
King-Size Spec. #1Weird World
    of Jack Staff. 6.00
Spec. #1 (2008) 3.50

JADE WARRIORS
Aug., 1999
1 MD2,Destruction of Japan 2.50
2 MD2,V:Ramthar 2.50
3 MD2,Blood of the Children 2.50
1a thru 3a photo(c) . . . . @2.50
3b movie poster style(c) 2.50

JINGLE BELLE
Top Cow, Nov., 2008
1-shot Santa vs. Frankenstein 3.00
1-shot variant (c) 3.00

JINN
Jan., 2000
1 F:Karen Lane 3.00
2 and 3 . . . . @3.00
1a thru 2a variant cover . . . . @3.00

JINX
(B&W) June, 1997
1 by Brian Michael Bendis 3.00
1a 2nd printing 3.00
2 F:Jinx, female bounty hunter 3.00
3 thru 5 . . . . @4.00
Spec.#1 Buried Treasure 4.00
Spec.#1 True Crime Confessions . . 4.00

JINX: TORSO
(B&W) Aug., 1998
1 by Brian Michael Bendis, 48-pg. . 4.00
2 search continues 4.00
3 Torso Killer 4.00
4 breaking the law 4.00
5 48-pg. 5.00
6 conclusion, 48-pg. 5.00
Spec. #@%!! short stories 4.00

JOHNNY DELGADO
IS DEAD
Spacedog, Sept., 2007
1 (of 2) 40-pgs. 4.00
2 . . . . 4.00

JOURNEYMAN
Aug., 1999
1 by Brandon McKinney 3.00
2 enemies become allies 3.00
3 V:Dragon King 3.00

J.U.D.G.E.
March, 2000
1 by Greg Horn,F:Victoria Grace . . 3.00
1a variant cover 3.00
2 V:John Lawson 3.00
3 Secret Rage,pt.3 . . . . 3.00

JUNKBOTZ ROTOGIN
Feb., 2003
1 . . . . 2.50

KABUKI
Sept., 1997
1 DMk,O:Kabuki 7.00
1a variant JSo(c). 7.00
2 DMk,O:Kabuki, pg.2 . . . . 5.00
3 DMk,surprise visitor 5.00
4 DMk,Akemi, romance 7.00
5 DMk,action. 4.00
6 DMk 3.00
7 DMk 3.00
7a DMk variant cover (1:2) 3.00
8 DMk 3.00
9 DMk, finale. 3.00
GN Reflections #1, 48-pg. 5.00
GN Reflections #1 signed 8.00

GN Reflections #2 art & stories 5.00
GN Reflections,Vol.3 . . . . 5.00
GN Reflections,Vol.4 . . . . 5.00
Spec. 1-shot The Ghost Play 3.00
Spec. #2 Images, rep. #2 & #3 . . . . 6.00
Kabuki 1/2 Wizard Mail-in 3.00
Kabuki 1/2 signed 6.00

KABUKI AGENTS
(B&W) Aug., 1999
1 DMk,F:Scarab 4.00
1a JQ(c), DMk signed 7.00
2 DMk,F:Scarab, Tiger Lily 3.00
3 DMk,F:Scarab, Tiger Lily 3.00
4 DMk,F:Scarab, Tiger Lily 3.00
5 thru 8 DMk . . . . @3.00
Artbook. 5.00
Kabuki Agents: Scarab #1 signed . . 6.00

KABUKI: THE ALCHEMY
Jan., 2004
1 (of 6) DMk 3.00
2 DMk 3.00

KABUKI CLASSICS
Feb., 1999
1 Fear the Reaper, rep. 9.00
2 Dance of Death 3.00
3 Circle of Blood, act 1, 48-pg. . . . 6.00
4 Circle of Blood, act 2 . . . . 4.00
5 Circle of Blood, act 3 . . . . 3.00
6 Circle of Blood, act 4 . . . . 3.00
7 Circle of Blood, act 5 . . . . 3.00
8 Circle of Blood, conclusion 3.00
9 Masks of the Noh, Act 1 . . . . 3.00
10 Masks of the Noh, Act 2 . . . . . . 3.00
11 Masks of the Noh, Act 3 . . . . . . 3.00
12 Masks of the Noh, concl. 3.00
Kabuki Classics #1 signed 7.00

KARZA
Feb., 2003
1 thru 4 Micronauts spin-off . . . . @3.00

KICK DRUM COMIX
Sept., 2008
1 (of 2) 6.00
2 . . . . 6.00

KID SUPREME
Supreme 1996–97
1 & 2 . . . . 2.50
3 DaF,ErS 2.50
4 DaF,ErS,Party time 2.50
5 DaF,ErS,'Birds of a Feather' 2.50
6 DaF,ErS,I: Sensational Spinner . . 2.50
7 DaF,ErS,Everything falls apart. . . 2.50

KID TERRIFIC
(B&W) Nov., 1998
1 A:Snedak & Manny Stellar 3.00

KILL ALL PARENTS
June, 2008
1 . . . . 4.00

KILLER INSTINCT
TOUR BOOK
1 All Homage Artist,I:Crusade 5.00
1a signed 20.00

KILLING GIRL
Aug., 2007
1 (of 5) 3.00
2 thru 5 . . . . @3.00

KILLRAZOR SPECIAL
Aug., 1995
1 O:Killrazor 2.50

KIN
Top Cow, Feb., 2000
1 GFr,Neanderthal 3.00
2 GFr,F:McLoon 3.00
3 GFr,Alaska revenge 3.00
4 GFr. 3.00
5 GFr,Born Free 3.00
6 GFr,40-pg.,The End? 4.00
6a variant AAd(c) 4.00
1st 6 as set, signed GFr. 25.00

KINDRED
WildStorm, 1994
1 JLe,BCi(s),BBh,I:Knidred 5.00
2 JLe,BCi(s),BBh,V:Kindred 3.50
3 JLe,BCi(s),BBh,V:Kindred 3.00
3a WPo(c),Alternate(c) 6.00
4 JLe,BCi(s),BBh,V:Kindred 3.00

'KINI
Flypaper, Feb., 1999
1 KK,BKs,F:Kim Walters 2.50

KISS:
THE PSYCHO CIRCUS
TMP, July, 1997
1 SvG,AMe 8.00
2 AMe, unearthly origins 6.00
3 AMe, Judgment o/t Elementals . . 5.00
4 AMe,Smoke and Mirrors,pt.1 . . . . 4.00
5 AMe,Smoke and Mirrors,pt.2 . . . . 4.00
6 AMe,Smoke and Mirrors, concl. . . 4.00
7 AMe,Creatures of the Night 3.00
8 AMe,Forever 3.00
9 AMe,Four Sides to Every Story . . 3.00
10 AMe,Destroyer,pt.1 . . . . 3.00
11 AMe,Destroyer,pt.2 . . . . 3.00
12 AMe,Destroyer,pt.3 (of 4) 3.00
13 AMe, Destroyer,pt.4 . . . . 3.00
14 AMe, in Feudal Japan 3.00
15 AMe, in Feudal Japan, choices. . 2.50
16 AMe, Ticket for Terror 2.50
17 AMe, World Without Heroes,pt.2 2.50
18 AMe, Sunburst Finish 2.50
19 Fate of the Psycho Circus 2.50
20 Mr. Makebelieve 2.50
21 Don't Talk to Strangers 2.50

Kiss Psycho Circus #5
© *Image/TMP*

IMAGE

22 Twin sisters 2.50
23 Tribunal of souls 2.50
24 Cat's Eye 2.50
25 . . . . 2.50
26 Nightingale's Song,pt.1. . . . . 2.50
27 Nightingale's Song,pt.2. . . . . 2.50
28 Perdition Blues 2.50
29 Shadow of the Moon,pt.1 . . . . . . 2.50
30 Shadow of the Moon,pt.2 . . . . . . 2.50
31 Sins of Omission. 2.50
32 Gallery of God's Mistakes. 2.50
33 Gallery of God's Mistakes,pt.2 . . 2.50
34 Far Corners of Night. 2.50

KISS 4K
Platinum, May, 2007
1 . . . . 4.00
1a Destroyer edition oversize 50.00
2 thru 5 . . . . @3.00
Spec. Kissmas Special, CDi(s) 5.00

KNIGHTMARE
Extreme, 1995
0 O:Knightmare. 2.50
1 I:Knightmare MMy 2.50
2 I:Caine 2.50
3 RLd,AV,The New Order,
     F:Detective Murtaugh 2.50
4 RLd,AV,MMy,I:Thrillkill 2.50
5 V:Thrillkill 2.50
6 Extreme Babewatch. 2.50
7 . . . . 2.50
8 I:Acid 2.50

KNIGHTS OF
THE JAGUAR
Top Cow, Jan., 2004
Spec. super limited 2.50

KNIGHTSTRIKE
Extreme, 1996
1 Extreme Destroyer,pt.6
     x-over, bagged with card 2.50

KNIGHT WATCHMAN
(B&W) May, 1998
1 by Gary Carlson & Chris Ecker . . 3.00
2 thru 4 Graveyard Shift,pt.2–pt.3 @3.00

KORE
Apr., 2003
1 . . . . 3.00
1a variant (c). 3.00
2 thru 5 . . . . @3.00

KURT BUSIEK'S
ASTRO CITY
Juke Box, 1995–96
1 I:Samaritan,'In Dreams'. 12.00
1a 2nd printing 2.50
2 I:Silver Agent,V:Shirak
     the Devourer 10.00
3 F:Jack in the Box. 10.00
4 I:Hanged Man,Safeguards. 11.00
5 I:Crackerjack 12.00
6 O:Samaritan,F:Winged Victory . 14.00

[Vol. 2] Homage, 1996
½ F:Hanged Man (1996) 5.00
1 KBk(s),BA,Welcome to
     Astro City. 9.00
1a Trunk(c). 8.00
1b 2nd printing 2.50
2 KBk(s),BA,O:First Family,
     F:Astra, Everyday Life. 7.00
2b 2nd printing 2.50
3 KBk(s),BA,Adventures in
     Other Worlds 7.00

Kurt Busiek's Astro City, Vol. 2 #10
© Image/Homage

4 KBk,BA,Teenager seeks to
     become teen sidekick,pt.1 (of 6) 6.00
5 Learning the Game 5.00
6 V: creatures of Shadow Hill 5.00
7 Aliens invade Astro City. 4.00
8 The aliens are out there 4.00
9 Honor Guard vs. Aliens finale . . . 4.00
10 meet the junkman. 4.00
11 Serpent's Teeth 4.00
12 F:Jack-In-The-Box 3.00
13 F:Looney Leo 3.00
14 F:Steeljack 3.00
15 F:supervillains 3.00
3-D #1 . . . . 5.00

Homage/DC, 1999
16 KBk(s), El Hombre 3.00
17 KBk(s), Mock Turtle 3.00
18 KBk(s), F:Steeljack 3.00
19 KBk(s), F:Steeljack 3.00
20 KBk(s). 3.00
21 KBk(s),F:Crackerjack 3.00
22 KBk(s),F:Samaritan. 3.00
Spec.1/2 KBk(s). 3.00

LABMAN
1996
1 I:Labman 4.00
1a variant cover 4.00
2 & 3 . . . . @4.00

LADY PENDRAGON
Nov., 1998
1 MHw,Destiny's Embrace 2.50
1a remastered, new cover 2.50
1b Dynamic Forces variant cover. . 7.00
1c JeL(c) glow-in-the-dark 20.00
1d Tour Edition 5.00
2 MHw,Destiny's Embrace,pt.2. . . . 3.00
3 MHw,Destiny's Embrace,pt.3. . . . 3.00
3a variant cover (1:4) 2.50
0 MHw, Secrets & Origins. 2.50
0a Eurosketch cover. 9.00
Preview (Wizard, Chicago Comicon) 5.00

LADY PENDRAGON:
DRAGON BLADE
April, 1999
1 MHw,Merlin trains Jennifer 2.50
1a variant cover (1:4) 2.50
1b Chrome Edition 5.00
2 MHw,F:Morgana 2.50
2a variant cover (1:4) 2.50

3 MHw,B.U.I:Alley Cat 3.00
4 MHw,Morgana returns 2.50
5 MHw,Spear of Destiny 2.50
6 MHw,Jennifer Drake resigns . . . 2.50
7 MHw,Future Prophecy,pt.1 . . . . . 4.00
8 MHw,Future Prophecy,pt.2 . . . . . 2.50
9 MHw,Future Prophecy,pt.3 . . . . . 2.50
10 MHw,Messianic Lineage,pt.1 . . 2.50
11 MHw,Messianic Lineage,pt.2 . . 2.50
12 MHw,Messianic Lineage,pt.3 . . 2.50
1a Glow-in-the-dark JaL(c). 2.50
Gallery Ed.#1 . . . . 3.00
Gallery Ed.#1a photo(c). 3.00

LADY PENDRAGON:
MORE THAN MORTAL
May, 1999
1 MHw,Pendragon vs. Protector. . . 2.50
1a variant cover (1:4) 7.00
1b Gold foil(c) 7.00

LADY SUPREME
Extreme, 1996
1 TMr. 2.50
2 TMr,Die & Let Die,pt.2 . . . . 2.50
3 TMr,V:Manassa 2.50
4 TMr,'Lady Supreme goes
     undercover' 2.50

LAST CHRISTMAS, THE
May, 2006
1 Twas the Fight Before Christmas 3.00
2 thru 5 . . . . @3.00

LAST SHOT
Aug., 2001
1 Foodclash,pt.1. . . . . 3.00
2 Metal in his Heart. 3.00
3 Six String Noose 3.00
4 Angel of Death 3.00

LAST SHOT:
FIRST DRAW
May, 2001
1 First Draw Revolver. 3.00

LAST STRAW MAN, THE
Feb., 2004
1 (of 3) 4.00
2 40-pg. 4.00

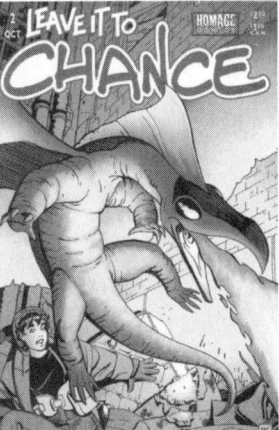

Leave It To Chance #2
© Image/Homage

LAZARUS
Oct, 2007
1 (of 3) 3.50
2 thru 3 . . . . @3.50

LEAVE IT TO CHANCE
Homage, 1996–98
1 JeR,PS,I:Chance Falconer 5.00
2 JeR,PS,Dragons are a Girl's
   Best Friend 5.00
Homage
3 JeR,PS,Chance and St. George
   race against time 5.00
4 JeR,PS 3.00
5 JeR,PS,'Trick or Threat' 3.00
6 JeR,PS,Return of Cap'n Hitch . . . 3.00
7 JeR,PS,'And Not a Drop to Drink 3.00
8 JeR,PS,Phantom of the Mall 3.00
9 JeR,PS,Midnite Monster
   Madness 3.00
10 JeR,PS,'Destroy All Monsters' . . 3.00
11 JeR,PS,Dead Men Can't Skate . 3.00
12 JeR,PS,visits her friend Dash . . . 3.00
13 JeR,PS,Reunion,48-pg. 5.00

LEGACY
May, 2003
1 thru 4 . . . . @3.00
4a variant (c) 3.00

LEGACY OF KAIN:
DEFIANCE
Jan., 2004
1-shot 3.00
1-shotA variant (c) 3.00

LEGEND OF ISIS
Feb., 2002
1 Origin of Isis 3.00

LEGEND OF SUPREME
Dec., 1994
1 KG(s),JJ,DPs,Revelations,pt.1 . . 2.50
2 Revelations,pt.2 . . . . 2.50
3 Conclusion 2.50

LETHAL
1996
1 & 2 . . . . @2.50

LEX TALIONIS:
A JUNGLE TALE
Jan., 2004
1-shot 48-pg. 6.00

LIBERTY COMICS
July, 2008
1-shot CBLDF Benefit 4.00
1-shot a variant (c) 4.00

LIBERTY MEADOWS
July, 2002
27 comic book convention 4.00
28 Ralph's Genetic Breakthrough . . 4.00
29 Brandy's Christmas Surprise . . . 4.00
30 Long Cold Winter,pt.1 . . . . 4.00
31 Long Cold Winter,pt.2 . . . . 4.00
32 The Cow is Back 3.50
33 Mad Cow, pt.2 . . . . 3.50
34 thru 37 . . . . @3.00
1-shot Sourcebook, 48-pg. 5.00

LIONS, TIGERS & BEARS
Jan., 2005
1 (of 4) Fear and Pride, pt.1 . . . . . 3.00

2 Fear and Pride, pt.2 . . . . 3.00
3 Fear and Pride, pt.3 . . . . 3.00
4 Fear and Pride, pt. 4 . . . . 3.00
Vol. 2
1 (of 4) Betrayal, pt.1 . . . . 3.00
2 thru 4 Betrayal, pt.2 thru pt.4 . . @3.00

LITTLE RED HOT:
BOUND
July, 2001
1 (of 3) by Dawn Brown 3.00
2 . . . . 3.00
3 . . . . 3.00

LITTLE RED HOT:
CHANE OF FOOLS
(B&W) Feb., 1999
1 (of 3) by Dawn Brown, F:Chane . 3.00
2 stranded in desert 3.00
3 Heaven vs. Hell 3.00

LOADED BIBLE
April, 2006
1-shot Jesus vs. Vampires 5.00
1-shot #2 Blood of Christ 5.00
1-shot #3 Communion, 48-pg. 5.00

LOOKING GLASS WARS:
HATTER M
Dec., 2005
1 (of 4) 4.00
2 . . . . 4.00
3 . . . . 3.50
4 . . . . 4.00

LOST ONES, THE
March, 2000
1 by Ken Penders 3.00
2 . . . . 3.00

LOVEBUNNY
& MR. HELL
Feb., 2003
1-shot 3.00
1-shot Savage Love 3.00

LOW ORBIT
Nov., 2006
1 64-pg. 7.00

Lynch #1
© *Image/Wildstorm*

LUCHA LIBRE
Sept., 2007
1 F:Luchadoritos, 48-pgs. 6.00
2 thru 3 . . . . @6.00
4 thru 6 . . . . @7.00

LULLABY:
WISDOM SEEKER
Feb., 2005
1 (of 4) 3.00
2 thru 4 . . . . @3.00

LYNCH
WildStorm, June, 1997
1 TVs,'Terror in the Jungle' 2.50

MACE GRIFFIN:
BOUNTY HUNTER
Top Cow, Apr., 2003
1-shot 3.00

MADAME MIRAGE
Top Cow, Apr., 2007
Spec. First Look 2.00
1 PDi(s) 3.00
1a variant (c) 5.00
2 thru 6 . . . . @3.00

MADMAN
ATOMIC COMICS
Apr., 2007
1 MiA 3.00
2 MiA 3.00
3 MiA, Swiped From Dimension X . 3.00
4 thru 6 . . . . @3.00
7 thru 10 MiA . . . . @3.00
11 thru 14 MiA . . . . @3.50

MAGDALENA
Top Cow, March, 2000
1 JBz,Darkness spin-off 4.00
1a variant MS(c) 4.00
1b variant Michael Turner(c) 4.00
2 JBz,secret revealed 2.50
3 JBz,Blood Divine,pt.3 . . . . 2.50
Preview, Magdalena/Blood
   Legacy, 22 pg.(2000) 3.00
1/2 Magdalena/Angelus, The Light
   and the Glory 3.00

MAGDALENA
Top Cow, July, 2003
1 (of 4) 3.00
2 thru 4 . . . . @3.00
1a and 2a variant (c) . . . . @3.00
Spec. Con. Preview 2.50

MAGDALENA/DAREDEVIL
Top Cow, Feb., 2008
1-shot x-over 4.00

MAGDALENA/
VAMPIRELLA
Top Cow, June, 2003
1-shot 3.00
1-shotA variant (c) 1:4 . . . . 3.00
1-shot (2004) 3.00
1-shot-A variant (c) (2004) 3.00

MAGDELENA VS.
DRACULA
Top Cow, Apr., 2005
1 (of 4) Monster War x-over 3.00

Mage #13
© *Image*

MAGE:
THE HERO DEFINED
1997

1 MWg,F:Kevin Matchstick	5.00
2 MWg,Kirby Hero, V:harpies	4.00
3 MWg,Isis, Gretch	3.00
4 MWg,Isis, drug	3.00
5 MWg,into Canada	3.00
6 MWg,V:Dragonslayer	2.50
7 MWg	2.50
8 MWg,V:Red Caps	2.50
9 MWg,Sibling Trio	2.50
10 MWg,enchanted by a succubus	2.50
11 MWg,Joe Phat, missing	2.50
12 MWg,Pale Incanter's Lair	2.50
13 MWg,What color is magic	2.50
14 MWg,Man Mountain of????	2.50
15 MWg, 48-pg. concl.	6.00
Spec. 3-D #1 (1998)	5.00

MAN AGAINST TIME
Motown 1996

1 'Every Hero'	2.50
2	2.50
3 'Pro Patria Mori'	2.50

MANIC
Feb., 2004

1-shot	3.00

MARS ATTACKS
1996

1 KG,BSz(of 4)	2.50
2 thru 4	@2.50

MASK OF ZORRO, THE
July, 1998

1 (of 4) DMG,RoW,RM,MGo(c),	3.00
2 DMG,RoW,RM,MGo(c)	3.00
3 DMG,RoW,MGo(c)	3.00
4 DMG,RoW,MGo concl.	3.00
4a photo cover	3.00

MASTERS OF
THE UNIVERSE
2002

1 He-Man returns	3.00
1b variant JSC(c)	3.00
1b variant EN(c)	3.00
2 thru 4	@3.00

2a–4a variant (c)	@3.00

Volume II

1	3.00
2 thru 8	@3.00
1a–2a variant (c)	@3.00
3a–4a holofoil (c)	@6.00
1-shot Icons of Evil: Beast Man	5.00

MAXIMAGE
Extreme, 1995–96

1 RLe(c)	2.50
2 Extreme Destroyer,pt.2, x-over, bagged with card	2.50
3	2.50
4 A:Angela,Glory	2.50
5 thru 8	@2.50
9 BML, Sex Slaves of Bomba Island	2.50
10 BML, The King of Emotion is back	2.50

MAXX, THE
1993

1/2 SK,from Wizard	10.00
1 SK,I:The Maxx	5.00
1a glow in the dark(c)	12.00
2 SK,V:Mr.Gone	4.00
3 SK,V:Mr.Gone	4.00
4 SK	4.00
5 SK	3.00
6 SK	3.00
7 SK,A:Pitt	3.50
8 SK,V:Pitt.	3.50
9 SK	3.00
10 SK	3.00
11 SK	2.50
12 SK	2.50
13 Maxx Wanders in Dreams	2.50
14 R:Julie	4.00
15 Julia's Pregnant	4.00
16 SK,Is Maxx in Danger?	4.00
17 SK,Gardener Maxx	4.00
18 SK,'Beware The Hooley'	2.50
19 SK,V:Hooley,'Last Fairy Tale'	3.50
20 SK,Questions are answered	2.50
21 AM(s),SK.	3.00
22 SK,'Other Peoples' Crap'	2.50
23 SK,'Having to Believe'	2.50
24 SK	2.50
25 SK,'Lost and Found'	2.50
26 SK	2.50
27 V:Iago the Killer Slug	2.50
28 Sara and Norberg look for Julie	2.50

Maxx #24
© *Image*

---

29 Sara and Gone defeat Iago the Slug	2.50
30 Lil' Sara faces her fears	2.50
31 F:The Library girl	2.50
32 F:The Library girl,pt.2	2.50
33 Sara's back	2.50
34 Mark and Julia	2.50
35 who knows?	2.50
36 bumfuzzled	2.50
37 Megan's story concl	2.50
38 Mark,Julie,Larry,pt.1 (of 4)	2.50
Spec. Friends of Maxx,F:Dude Japan	3.00
The Maxx 3-D #1	5.00

MECH DESTROYER
March, 2001

1 (of 4) Battle for Earth	3.00
2 Face of the Enemy	3.00
3 rescue the captives	3.00
4 V:The Crimson Death	3.00

MEDIEVAL SPAWN/
WITCHBLADE
May, 1996

1 thru 3	@5.00

MEGADRAGON & TIGER
March, 1999

1 by Tony Wong, from Hong Kong	3.00
2 F:Red Tiger	3.00
3 V:Single-Minded Arhat	3.00
4 V:Fiery Lord	3.00
5 F:Gigi	3.00

MEGAHURTZ
(B&W) Aug., 1997

1 JPi,I:Megahurtz	3.00
2 JPi,visit to Wonderland	3.00
3 JPi,V:N-Filtraitors	3.00
4 JPi,Liberaiders	3.00

MEGATON MAN:
BOMBSHELL
July, 1999

1 DSs,V:Unleash.	3.00

MEGATON MAN:
HARDCOPY
Fiasco (B&W) Feb., 1999

1 by Don Simpson	3.00
2 with 6 new pages	3.00

MELTDOWN
Dec., 2006

1 (of 2) F:The Flare, 48-pgs.	6.00
2	6.00

MESSENGER, THE
July, 2000

1-shot JOy, 48-pg.	6.00

MICE TEMPLAR, THE
Sept., 2007

1 56-pgs.	4.00
2 thru 6	@3.00

MICRONAUTS
June, 2002

1	3.00
2 thru 5	@3.00
6 Star Chamber,pt.1	3.00
7 Star Chamber,pt.2	3.00
8 thru 11 Invasion Earth,pt.1–4	@3.00
Spec. 2002 Con Special	3.00

MIDNIGHT NATION
Top Cow, Sept., 2000
1 MSz	5.00
1a variant GrF(c)	9.00
2 MSz,GrF, on the run	4.00
3 MSz,GrF, To Hell and inbetween	4.00
4 MSz,GrF, V:Walkers	4.00
5 MSz,GrF, Find your soul	4.00
6 MSz,GrF, Halfway	4.00
7 MSz,GrF, Change has begun	4.00
8 MSz,GrF, Road gets worse	4.00
9 MSz,GrF, New York, New York	4.00
10 MSz,GrF, Soul's price	4.00
11 MSz,GrF, Still the Road to Hell	4.00
12 MSz,GrF, The End of the Road	4.00

MIKE CAREY'S ONE-SIDED BARGAINS
(B&W) Dec., 2006
1-shot 64-pgs.	6.00

MIKE GRELL'S MAGGIE THE CAT
Jan., 1996
1 (of 4) Master Piece,pt.1	2.50
2 Master Piece,pt.2	2.50

MINISTRY OF SPACE
April, 2001
1 (of 3) WEl,CWn,World War II.	3.00
2 WEl,CWn	3.00
3 WEl,CWn,concl.	3.00
Omnibus #1 & #2	5.00
3	3.00

MISERY SPECIAL
Dec., 1995
1 Cyberforce Origins	3.00

MISPLACED
May, 2003
1 thru 3	@3.00
1a variant (c)s	3.00

MISTER UNIVERSE
Jan., 2008
1-shot	3.50

MONSTER FIGHTERS, INC.
April, 1999
1 Who you gonna call	3.00
2 Wake the dead.	3.00
1-shot The Black Book.	3.50

MONSTER FIGHTERS INC.: THE GHOSTS OF CHRISTMAS
Dec., 1999
1 The Fright Before Christmas	4.00

MONSTERMAN
(B&W) Sept., 1997
1 MM,from Action Planet	3.00
2 MM,Inhuman monsters	3.00
3 MM,King of Monsters.	3.00
4 MM, conclusion	3.00

MORA
Feb., 2005
1 All Beasts will Show Their Teeth	3.00
2 In the Gloaming	3.00
3 Dying Among the Shadows	3.00
4 Conslusion, pt.1	3.00

MORE THAN MORTAL/ LADY PENDRAGON
June, 1999
1 MHw,x-over	2.50
Prev. Edition 16-pg., B&W	5.00

MORE THAN MORTAL: OTHERWORLDS
Liar Comics, July, 1999
1 F:Derdre & Morand	3.00
1a variant cover (1:2)	5.00
2 in Otherworld	3.00
2a variant cover (1:2)	4.00
3 Lady in white	3.00
3a variant Derdre cover (1:2)	3.00
4 Woman in white, concl.	3.00
5 Famine,pt.1	3.00
6 Famine,pt.2	3.00
7 Famine,pt.3	3.00
Art Gallery #1.	3.50

MR. MONSTER VS. GORZILLA
(2 color) July, 1998
1-shot, MGi	3.00

MR. MONSTER'S GAL FRIDAY: KELLY
(B&W) Jan., 2000
1 MGi	3.50
2 MGi	3.50
3 MGi,AMo(s)	3.50

MR. RIGHT
Aug., 2001
1 TDF,RF,flip-book	3.00
2 TDF,RF,F:General Public	3.00

MOTH
July, 2003
1-shot 48-pg.	6.00

M-REX
Nov., 1999
1 by Joe Kelly & Duncan Rouleau	3.00
2 thru 5	@3.00
4a and 5a variant cover	@3.00
#1 Limited Tour Edition	5.00
Preview, B&W, 16-pg	5.00

MS. FORTUNE
(B&W) 1998
1 by Chris Marrinan	3.00
2 Carnage in the Caribbean	3.00
3 Doom at the Dawn of Time	3.00

M-THEORY
Shadowline, Sept., 2008
1 The Fear	3.50
2 Fearful Symmetry	3.50
3 The Master Plan	3.50

MUTANT EARTH
May, 2002
1 (of 4) F:Trakk	3.00
2 F:Zeithian warlord, Gallowz	3.00
3 thru 4	@3.00
1a thru 4a variant (c).	@3.00

MYTHSTALKERS
Mar., 2003
1 thru 4 The Labyrinth,pt.1–4	@3.00
5 London Nights	3.00
6 London Nights,pt.2.	3.00

7 Gangs of London	3.00
8 London Nights	3.00

NAMELESS, THE
(B&W) May, 1997
1 PhH,I:The Nameless, protector of Mexico City's lost children	3.00
2 thru 5	@3.00

NASH
July, 1999
1 MMy, by & starring Kevin Nash	2.50
1a variant cover (1:2)	3.00
2 MMy, the end of Nash?	2.50
2a variant cover (1:2)	2.50
#1 Photo-Split edition	3.00
Preview edition MMy,F:Kevin Nash	2.50
Preview ed.A variant cover (1:2)	2.50

Necromancer #1 (Wizard World cover)
© Top Cow

NECROMANCER, THE
Top Cow, Aug., 2005
1 Something in the way, pt.1	3.00
1a & 1b variant(c)s	@3.00
2 Something in the way, pt.2	3.00
3 Something in the way, pt. 3	3.00
4 thru 6	@3.00
1 Pilot Season.	3.00

NEGATIVE BURN
(B&W) May, 2006
1 64-pg.	6.00
2 thru 11	@6.00

NEON CYBER
July, 1999
1 F:Neon Dragons	2.50
1a variant cover (1:2)	2.50
1b glow-in-the-dark edition	7.00
2 gang alliance	2.50
2a variant cover (1:2)	2.50
3 Neon a suspect	2.50
4 who framed Neon?	2.50
5 thru 8	@2.50

NEWFORCE
Extreme, 1996
1 Extreme Destroyer,pt.8 x-over, bagged with card	2.50
2 thru 3	@2.50
4 Team disbands.	2.50

NEWMAN
Extreme, 1996
1 Extreme Destroyer,pt.3
x-over, bagged with card 2.50
2 . . . . 2.50
3 . . . . 2.50
4 Shadowhunt x-over,pt.5. . . . . . . 2.50

NEWMEN
Extreme, 1994
1 JMs 3.00
2 JMs,I:Girth 2.50
3 JMs,V:Girth,I:Ikonna 2.50
4 JMs,A:Ripclaw 2.50
5 JMs,Ripclaw,V:Ikonn 2.50
6 JMs 2.50
7 JMs 2.50
8 JMs,Team Youngblood. 2.50
9 ErS(s),JMs,Kodiak Kidnapped. . . 2.50
10 ExtremeSacrifice,pt.5,x-over. . . . 2.50
11 F:Reign 2.50
12 R:Elemental 2.50
13 ErS,I:Bootleg. 2.50
14 ErS,Dominion's Secret 2.50
15 I:Time Guild. 2.50
16 . . . . 2.50
16a variant cover 3.00
17 R:Girth. 2.50
18 F:Byrd 2.50
19 I:Bordda Khan,Shepherd 2.50
20 Extreme Babewatch 2.50
21 ErS,CSp,(1 of 5) 2.50
22 ErS,CSp, Who Needs the
Newmen? 2.50
23 ErS,CSp,Who are the Newmen? 2.50

NEW SHADOWHAWK, THE
June, 1995
1 KBk,I:New ShadowHawk. 3.00
2 KBk,V:Mutants 3.00
3 KBk,I:Trophy 3.00
4 KBk,V:Blowfish. 3.00
5 KBk, ... 3.00
6 KBk, ... 3.00
7 KBk, ... 3.00

NEW WORLD ORDER
Jan., 2008
1 Dawn of a New Day. 3.50
2 Global Warning 3.50
3 Tragety & Hope 3.50

NEXT ISSUE PROJECT
Dec., 2007
Fanastic Comics #24, 64-pg. 6.00

NIGHT CLUB, THE
Apr., 2005
1 (of 4) MBn 3.00
2 Junkyard Apocalypse. 3.00
3 Helluva Party 3.00
4 . . . . 3.00

NIGHTLY NEWS, THE
Nov., 2006
1 (of 6) 3.00
2 The Voice. 3.00
3 We Don't Need No Education . . . 3.00
4 Cults in Our Midst 3.00
5 True Believers 3.00
6 Revenge 3.00

NINE RINGS OF
WU-TANG, THE
Nov., 1999
1 by Brian Haberlin. 4.00
2 thru 5 . . . . @3.00

4a variant cover 3.00
#1 limited tour edition. 5.00
Preview, B&W, 16-pg. 5.00

NINE RINGS OF WU-TANG, THE: FATIMA'S REVENGE
May, 2000
1 by Brian Haberlin. 3.00

1963
April, 1993
1 Mystery Incorporated, AnM(s),
RV,DGb 2.50
1a Gold ed. 3.00
1b Bronze ed. 3.00
2 No One Escapes...The Fury,
RV,SBi,DGb,JV,I:The Fury. 2.50
3 Tales of the Uncanny,
RV,SBi,I:U.S.A. 2.50
4 Tales From Beyond
JV,SBi,I:N-Man, Johnny Beyond 2.50
5 Horus, Lord of Light,
JV,SBi,I:Horus 2.50
6 Tomorrow Syndicate,
JV,SBi,C:Shaft 2.50
Ashcan #1 . . . . 3.00
Ashcan #2 . . . . 2.50
Ashcan #4 . . . . 2.00

NINE VOLT
Top Cow, 1997
1 ACh 3.00
1a Variant(c) 4.00
2 ACh 3.00
3 ACh,V:crazed junkie terrorists . . . 2.50
4 ACh,V:Rev. Cyril Gibson 2.50

NOBLE CAUSES
Sept., 2001
1-shot First Impressions 3.00
1 two stories 5.00
2 . . . . 5.00
2a variant RGr(c) 5.00
3 three's a crowd 7.00
3a variant Ccs(c). 10.00
4 In Sickness and in Health,pt.4 . . . 3.00
4a variant(c) 3.00
1-shot Extended Family, 80-pg. . . . 5.00
July, 2004
1 . . . . 3.50
1a & 2a variant(c) . . . . @3.50
2 thru 4 . . . . @3.50
5 A:Invincible. 3.50
6 F:Liz Donnelly 3.50
7 A Day in the Life 3.50
8 V:Venture 3.50
9 F:Celeste 3.50
10 Wrong body 3.50
11 . . . . 3.50
12 Birth of Zephyr's Child 3.50
13 F:Blackthornes 3.50
14 . . . . 3.50
15 . . . . 3.50
16 thru 24. . . . . @3.50
25 48-pg. 5.00
25a variant (c) 5.00
26 thru 31. . . . . @3.50
32 Five Years have passed 3.50
33 F:Frost. 3.50
34 F:Frost. 3.50
35 V:Crucible 3.50
36 thru 40. . . . . @3.50

NOBLE CAUSES: DISTANT RELATIVES
July, 2003
1 thru 4 . . . . @3.00

NOBLE CAUSES: FAMILY SECRETS
Oct., 2002
1 (of 4) F:Liz Donnelly-Noble 3.50
2 spin control 3.00
3 guest stars galore 3.00
4 . . . . 3.00
1a– 3a variant(c). . . . . @3.00

NOCTURNALS: CARNIVAL OF BEASTS
July, 2008
1-shot 7.00

NO HONOR
Top Cow, Feb., 2001
1 (of 4) F:Tanne Yojimbo. 4.00
2 . . . . 4.00

No Honor #1
© Top Cow

3 . . . . 2.50
4 concl. 2.50
Prev. 16-pg. B&W 5.00

NO HONOR: MAKYO
Top Cow, Nov., 2001
1 . . . . 4.00

NORMALMAN
July, 2004
1-shot 20th Anniv. 3.00

NORMAL MAN/ MEGATON MAN SPECIAL
1 . . . . 2.50

NYC MECH
Apr., 2004
1 thru 6 . . . . @3.00

NYC MECH: BETA LOVE
May, 2005
1 and 2 . . . . @3.50
3 thru 6 . . . . @3.00

OBERGEIST: RAGNAROK HIGHWAY
Top Cow/Minotaur 2001
1 TyH 3.00

IMAGE

Obergeist: Ragnarok Highway
© Top Cow/Minotaur

2 TyH 3.00
3 TyH 3.00
4 TyH 3.00
5 TyH,Ambushed 3.00
6 TyH,His memory, Abyss's flame . 3.00

OBERGEIST: THE EMPTY LOCKET
Top Cow/Minotaur, 2002
1 TyH 3.00

OBJECTIVE FIVE
July, 2000
1 biological weapons 3.00
2 F:Lark, Alexis & DJ 3.00
3 Airborne Virus 3.00
4 Reunion 3.00
5 Hidden Enemies 3.00
6 in China 3.00
7 Origins 3.00

OCCULT CRIMES TASKFORCE
July, 2006
1 . . . . 3.00
2 thru 4 . . . . @3.00

OPERATION KNIGHTSTRIKE
May, 1995
1 RHe,A:Chapel,Bravo,Battlestone 2.50
2 In Afganistan 2.50
3 final issue 2.50

ORIGINAL ADVENTURES OF CHOLLY & FLYTRAP
Apr., 2005
1 (of 2) A Little Love, A Little Hate . 3.50
2 The Rites of Spring 3.50
Jan., 2006
1 (of 2) 48-pg 6.00
2 The Rights of Spring, 48-pg. 6.00

OTHERS, THE
March, 1995
0 JV(s),From ShadowHawk 2.50
1 JV(s)V:Mongrel 2.50
2 JV,Mongrel takes weapons 2.50

3 War 2.50
4 O:Clone 2.50

OVERKILL
Top Cow, Oct., 2000
1 PJe,x-over,A:Aliens,Predator 6.00
2 PJe,x-over,A:Aliens,Predator 6.00

OVERMAN
Dec., 2007
1 (of 5) 3.50
2 thru 5 . . . . @3.50

OXIDO
Sept., 2003
1 (of 6) LHa(s) 3.00
2 LHa(s) 3.00

PACT
1994
1 JV(s),WMc,I:Pact, C:Youngblood 2.50
2 JV(s),V:Youngblood 2.50
3 JV(s),V:Atrocity 2.50

PACT, THE
Mar., 2005
1 (of 4) Father's Day, JV 3.00
2 . . . . 3.00
3 . . . . 3.00
4 . . . . 3.00

PARADE (WITH FIREWORKS)
Sept., 2007
1 (of 2) 3.50
2 . . . . 3.50

PARADIGM
Sept., 2002
1 F:Chris Howells, 48-pg. b&w . . . 3.50
2 40-pg. b&w 3.50
3 40-pg. b&w 3.50
4 40-pg 3.50
5 . . . . 3.00
6 All About the Community 3.00
7 40-pg 3.00
8 Swirly Things 3.00
9 Real Swirly Things 3.00
10 . . . . 3.00
11 40-pg 3.50
12 40-pg 3.50

PARLIAMENT OF JUSTICE, THE
Mar., 2003
1-shot b&w, 56-pg 6.00

PARTS UNKNOWN: KILLING ATTRACTION
(B&W) April, 2000
1 Sci-Fi/UFO adventure 3.00

PARTS UNKNOWN: HOSTILE TAKEOVER
(B&W) June, 2000
1 by Beau Smith & Brad Gorby . . . 3.00
2 . . . . 3.00
3 & 4 . . . . @3.00

PATIENT ZERO
Mar., 2004
1 (of 4) Eternity's Past,pt.1 . . . . 3.00
2 thru 4 Eternity's Past,pt.2ñ4 . . @3.00

PAUL JENKINS' SIDEKICK
June, 2006
1 . . . . 3.50
2 thru 5 . . . . @4.00
Spec. Super Summer Spectacular . . 3.50
Spec. Super Summer Spect. #2 . . . 3.50

PAX ROMANA
Nov., 2007
1 Create the Future, Destroy
    the Past 3.50
2 I, Constantine 3.50
3 Nicaea and On 3.50
4 The Great Society 3.50

PERHAPANAUTS
Apr., 2008
1 Triangle, pt. 1 . . . . 3.50
2 Triangle, pt. 2 . . . . 3.50
3 Triangle, pt. 3 . . . . 3.50
4 Triangle, pt. 4 . . . . 3.50
5 Triangle, pt. 5 . . . . 3.50
6 Halloween Scare-Fest 3.50
Ann. #1 . . . . 3.50
Ann. #1a variant (c) 3.50

PHANTOM FORCE
Dec., 1993
1 RLd,JK,w/card 2.75
2 JK,V:Darkfire 2.50
See also Color Comics section

Phantom Guard #3
© Wildstorm

PHANTOM GUARD
WildStorm, Oct., 1997
1 by Sean Ruffner, Ryan Benjamin 3.00
1a variant cover 3.00
1b Voyager bagged pack 3.50
2 Martian wasteland 3.00
3 Lowell Zerium Mines 3.00
4 'Target Locked' 3.00
5 V:Vanox, ... 3.00
6 Countdown to Armageddon 3.00

PHANTOM JACK
Mar., 2004
1 Roach Motel 3.00
2 Back to Baghdad 3.00
3 Among the Enemy 3.00
4 Madison Blue, Who Are You 3.00
5 Sins of Saddam Hussein 3.00

IMAGE

PHONOGRAM
(B&W) Aug., 2006
1 Public Image	3.50
2 Can't Imagine World Without Me.	3.50
3 Faster.	3.50
4	3.50
5 Kissing With Dry Lips.	3.50
6 Live Forever.	3.50

PIECES FOR MOM:
A TALE OF THE UNDEAD
Jan., 2007
1-shot Zombie story	4.00

PIGTALE
(B&W) Jan., 2005
1 Private Eye: Boston Booth.	3.00
2 The Smell of Taxx	3.00
3 Dark Neon Rain`	3.00
4 Salty Pork & Bacon Tarts.	3.00

PILOT SEASON
Top Cow, 2007
1-shot Ripclaw (Aug. 2007)	3.00
1-shot Cyblade (Sept. 2007)	3.00
1-shot Velocity (Sept. 2007).	3.00
1-shot The Angelus (Oct. 2007).	3.00
1-shot Aphrodite IX (Nov. 2007)	3.00

Top Cow, 2008
1-shot Twilight Guardian (5-2008)	4.00
1-shot Lady Pendragon (5-2008)	4.00
1-shot Alibi (6-2008).	4.00
1-shot Genius (6-2008)	4.00
1-shot The Core (7-2008)	4.00
1-shot Urban Myths (7-2008).	4.00

PIRATES OF
CONEY ISLAND, THE
Oct., 2006
1	3.00
1a variant (c).	3.00
2	3.00
3	3.50
3a variant (c)	3.50
4 thru 8	@3.00
4a thru 8a variant (c)s	@3.00

PITT
Top Cow, 1993–95
1 DK,I:Pitt,Timmy	4.00

Pitt #2
© Top Cow

2 DK,V:Quagg.	3.00
3 DK,V:Zoyvod	4.00
4 DK,V:Zoyvod	3.00
5 DK	2.50
6 DK	2.50
7 DK	2.50
8 Ransom	2.50
9 DK,Artic Adventures.	2.50
Ashcan 1	3.00

PORTENT, THE
Feb., 2006
1 Condemnation	3.00
2 A Road of My Own.	3.00
3	3.00
4 Nezabudka.	3.00

POWER OF THE MARK
1 I:Ted Miller.	2.50
2 V:The Fuse	2.50
3 TMB(s), The Mark	2.50
4 TMB,Mark's secrets revealed	2.50

POWER RANGERS ZEO
Extreme, Sept., 1997
1 thru 3 TBm&MBm(s),TNu,NRd	@2.50

POWER RANGERS ZEO
YOUNGBLOOD
Extreme, Oct., 1997
1 RLd,TBm,MBm	3.00
2 RLd,TBm,MBm	3.00

POWERS
April, 2000
1 Who killed Retro Girl,pt.1.	15.00
2 Who killed Retro Girl,pt.2.	20.00
3 Who killed Retro Girl,pt.3.	15.00
4	12.00
5 A murder solved.	10.00
6	10.00
7 WEI, Ride Along.	7.00
8 Role Play,pt.1.	7.00
9 Role Play,pt.2.	7.00
10 Role Play,pt.3	7.00
11	5.00
12 Groupies	5.00
13 Groupies,pt.2	5.00
14 Groupies,pt.3	5.00
15 Supergroup,pt.1	5.00
16 Supergroup	5.00
17 incl. Bastard Samurai prequel	5.00
18 superhero wanted for murder	5.00
19 supergroup shocking concl.	5.00
20 supergroup explosive concl.	5.00
21 Anarchy,pt.1	3.50
22 Anarchy,pt.2	3.50
23 Anarchy,pt.3	3.50
24 Anarchy,pt.4	3.50
25 The Sellouts,pt.1.	3.50
26 The Sellouts,pt.2.	3.50
27 The Sellouts,pt.3.	3.00
28 The Sellouts,pt.4.	3.00
29 The Sellouts,pt.5.	3.00
30 The Sellouts,pt.6.	3.00
31 Forever,pt.1.	3.00
32 Forever,pt.2.	3.00
33 Forever,pt.3.	3.00
34 Forever,pt.4.	3.00
35 Forever,pt.5.	3.00
36 Forever,pt.6.	3.00
37 Forever,pt.7.	3.00
Spec.-1 Coloring & Activity Book	3.00
1/2 Wizard story + new	3.00
Scriptbook 344-pg.	20.00

VOLUME 2 (2004)
1 Legends,pt.1	3.00
2 Legends,pt.2	3.00
3 Legends,pt.3	3.00

PRETTY BABY MACHINE
May, 2008
1 (of 3) Three infamous mobsters	3.50
2 thru 3	@3.50

PRO
Aug., 2008
1-shot GEn new printing	8.00

PROOF
Oct, 2007
1	3.00
2 thru 4	@3.00
5 Mother's Day	3.00
6 Company of Men, pt.1	3.00
7 Company of Men, pt.2	3.00
8 Company of Men, pt.3.	3.00
9 A Perfect Gentleman	3.00
10 Thunderbirds are Go, pt.1	3.00
11 Thunderbirds are Go, pt.2.	3.00
12 Thunderbirds are Go, pt.3	3.00
13 A:Savage Dragon	3.50
14	3.50

PROPHET
Extreme, 1993–95
0 San Diego Comic-Con ed.	4.00
1 RLd(s)DPs,O:Prophet,I:Mary McCormick.	3.00
1a Gold ed.	4.00
2 RLd(s),DPs,C:Bloodstrike	2.50
3 RLd(s),DPs, V:Bloodstrike, I:Judas.	2.50
4 RLd(s),DPs,I:Omen,A:Judas	2.50
4a SPa(c),Limited ed.	3.00
5 SPa,Supreme Apocalypse,pt.2	3.00
6 SPa	2.50
7 SPa War Games,pt.1.	2.50
8 SPa War Games,pt.2.	2.50
9 SPa,Extreme Sacrifice Prelude	2.50
10 ExtremeSacrifice,pt.7,x-over.	2.50
Sourcebook	3.00
Ashcan #1	3.00
Ashcan #2	3.00

[Second Series] 1995
1 SPI, New Series.	3.50
2 SPI, New Direction.	2.50
2a variant cover	2.50
3 True Nature	2.50
4 The Dying Factor.	2.50
5	2.50
6	2.50

Prophet #2
© Image/Extreme

IMAGE

7 CDi,SPa 2.50
8 & 9 . . . . @2.50
Ann.#1 Supreme Apocalypse 2.50
Spec.#1 Babewatch special (1995) . 2.50

PROPHET/CHAPEL: SUPER SOLDIERS
May, 1996

1 . . . . 2.50
1A variant(c) b&w 2.50
2 . . . . 2.50

PSCYTHE
Sept., 2004

1 thru 2 (of 2) MT . . . . @4.00

PUFFED
July, 2003

1 thru 3 (of 3) . . . . @3.00

PVP
Mar., 2003

1 Player vs. Player 3.00
2 Lord of the Schwing 3.00
3 Lost and Found 3.00
4 V:Devilfish 3.00
5 Max Powers 3.00
6 Skull the Troll 3.00
7 Chilling events 3.00
8 Brent Sienna Dies 3.00
9 Skull in local Zoo 3.00
10 Skull hyper-intelligent 3.00
11 F:Savage Dragon 3.00
12 Halloween party 3.00
13 Christmas issue 3.00
14 A:Invincible 3.00
15 Geeks Gone Wild 3.00
16 thru 22 . . . . @3.00
23 Caffeine Rage 3.00
24 thru 29 . . . . @3.00
30 Time Tunnel 3.00
31 Incorrigable PVP 3.00
32 Together They Fight Crive 3.00
33 Girls Night Out 3.00
34 Double Date 3.00
35 Kill Pussycat Kill 3.50
36 Sci-fi Con 3.50
37 thru 43 . . . . @3.50
Spec #0 16-page, B&W 2.50
Spec. Replay #1, rep.#1 & #2 . . . . 5.00
10the Anniv. Spec. 5.00

Q-UNIT: REVENGE
Oct., 1999

1 KIA,BNa 3.00
1a variant cover (1:2) 3.00
2 KIA,BNa 3.00
2a variant cover (1:2) 3.00

RADISKULL AND DEVIL DOLL
Dec., 2002

1-shot b&w 2.50
1-shot Radiskull Hate Love 3.00

RADIX
Dec., 2001

1 mysterious new force 3.00
2 F:Val Fiores 3.00
3 . . . . 3.00
4 mysterious object 3.00

RAGMOP
(B&W)

Vol.2 #1 by Rob Walton 3.00
Vol.2 #2 . . . . 3.00

RANDY O'DONNEL IS THE MAN
May, 2001

1 TDF,RLm,flip-book 3.00
2 TDF,RLm,The Chosen 3.00
3 TDF,RLm,Terror of the
   Warrior Toads 3.00
4 TDF,Merciless are the Malok 3.00

REALM OF THE CLAW
Oct., 2003

1 (of 6) 3.00
2 . . . . 3.00
1a thru 2a variant (c)s . . . . @3.00

RED MASS FOR MARS, A
June, 2008

1 (of 4) Eternity 3.50
2 Liberty 3.50
3 Equality 3.50
4 Fraternity 3.50

RED STAR, THE
June, 2000

1 by Christian Gossett 8.00
2 Project: Antares 6.00
3 Fall of the Red Fleet 4.00
4 Marcus' mystic revelation 4.00
5 A worker's Tale 4.00
6 War torn Nokgorka 3.00
7 Nokgorka,pt.2 . . . . 3.00
8 Nokgorka,pt.3 . . . . 3.00
9 Marcus Antares is alive 3.00
9a variant(c) 3.00
Spec.#1 3-D Transformation 3.00

REGULATORS
June, 1995

1 F:Blackjack,'Touch of Scandal' . . 2.50
2 F:Vortex 2.50
3 F:Arson 2.50
4 F:Scandal 2.50

REPLACEMENT GOD AND OTHER STORIES, THE
(B&W) May, 1997

1 Knute vs. King Ursus 3.00
2 by Zander Cannon 3.00
3 thru 5 . . . . @3.00

Regulators #1
© Image

REPO
June, 2007

1 thru 5 . . . . @3.50

RESIDENT EVIL
WIldstorm March, 1998

1 comic/game magazine 56-pg. . . . 7.00
2 thru 4 comic/game mag. 56-pg. @5.50

RETRO ROCKET
March, 2006

1 thru 4 . . . . @3.00

RETURN OF SHADOWHAWK, THE
Sept., 2004

1-shot JV 3.00

REVENANT
Shadowline, Mar., 2008

1 thru 3 . . . . @3.50

REX MUNDI
Aug., 2002

0 . . . . 4.00
1 Unexpected visitor 3.50
2 Puzzle in the Painting 3.50
3 The Archbiship and the Pimp . . . 3.50
4 Shadows Beneath the City 3.00
5 Shadows Beneath the City 3.00
6 Secrets Revealed 3.00
7 Father of Wisdom 3.00
8 Suspicion grows 3.00
9 National library 3.00
10 Holy Grail 3.00
11 Treasure of the Temple 3.00
12 The Swan Knight 3.00
13 The Lost Kings 3.00
14 City of the Dead 3.00
15 Most Beloved 3.00
16 Path to Empire 3.00
17 Vine of David 3.00
18 Europe at War 3.00

RIDE, THE
June, 2004

1 and 2 Wheels of Change . . . . . @3.00
1a thru 2a signed . . . . @15.00
1-shot 2 for the Road, Shotgun;
   Big Plans (2004) 3.00
1-shot Foreign Parts,CDi & RMz(s) . 3.00
1-shot Halloween Special (2007) . . 3.50
1-shot The Ride: Savannah (2007) . 5.00

RIDE, THE: CHAIN REACTION
(B&W) July, 2006

1 and 2 (of 4) BSz . . . . @3.00

RIDE, THE: DIE, VALKYRIE
(B&W) June, 2007

1 thru 3 (of 3) BSf . . . . @3.00

RIPCLAW
Top Cow, 1995

1/2 Prelude to Series (Wizard) 3.00
1/2a Con versions 7.00
1 A:Killjoy, I:Shadowblade 3.00
2 Cyblade, Heatwave 3.00
3 EcS,BPe,AV,Alliance S.H.O.C.s . . 3.00
4 conclusion 3.00
Spec.#1 I:Ripclaw's Brother 3.00

[1st Regular Series]

1 thru 5 . . . . @2.50

IMAGE

RIPTIDE
1995
1 O:Riptide 2.50
2 O:Riptide 2.50

RISING STARS
Top Cow, March, 1999
1 A celestial event. 5.00
1a, b, & c variant covers 8.00
2 life & death of Peter Dawson. . . . 8.00
3 new special 8.00
4 . . . . 8.00
5 To the netherworld. 8.00
6 Things Fall Apart,pt.1. . . . . 8.00
7 Things Fall Apart,pt.2. . . . . 8.00
8 Things Fall Apart,pt.3. . . . . 5.00
9 Act Two,pt.1 . . . . 5.00
10 years later. 3.50
11 Specials out of control. 3.00
12 War for Chicago 3.00
12a Monstermart edition 10.00
12b Monstermart gold foil 17.00
12c Monstermart holofoil 25.00
13 Brothers 3.00
14 Patriot vs. Matthew Bright. 3.00
15 The Secret 3.00
16 finale 3.00
17 campaign to change the world . . 3.00
18 will they change the world 3.00
19 MSz,government vs. Specials . . 3.00
20 MSz. 3.00
21 MSz. 3.00
22 Phoenix in Ascension,pt.1. . . . . 3.00
23 BA,Phoenix in Ascension,pt.2. . 3.00
24 BA,Phoenix in Ascension,pt.3. . 4.00
1/2 rep. 3.00
#0 rep. from Wizard 2.50
Preview MSz, 16-pg., B&W 5.00
Prelude. 3.00

RISING STARS: BRIGHT
Top Cow, Feb., 2003
1 (of 3) 3.00
2 Authority. 3.00
3 Civilian Casualties 3.00

RISING STARS: UNTOUCHABLE
Top Cow, Sept., 2003
1 Story of Laurel Darkhaven. 3.00

RISING STARS: UNTOUCHABLE
Top Cow, March, 2006
1 (of 5) 3.00
2 thru 5 . . . . @3.00

RISING STARS: VOICES OF THE DEAD
Top Cow, Apr., 2005
1 (of 6) 3.00
2 thru 6 . . . . @3.00

ROBERTS, THE
Shadowline, Aug., 2008
1 (of 2) Robert Kenneth Sprunger . 6.00
2 Robert Joseph Steib 6.00

ROB ZOMBIE'S SPOOK SHOW
2004
Int. Omnibus #1 48-pg. 5.00
Int. Omnibus #2 48-pg. 5.00
12 International 3.00

ROCKETO JOURNEY TO THE HIDDEN SEA
Feb., 2006
7 Reunions 3.00
8 Histories. 3.00
9 Histories. 3.00
10 Histories 4.00
11 Illumination 4.00
12 . . . . 4.00

ROCK 'N' ROLL
(B&W) Nov., 2005
1-shot 3.50

ROMP
Dec., 2003
1-shot AdP 6.00

ROTOGIN: JUNKBOTZ
Apr., 2003
1 (of 8) 3.00
2 thru 4 . . . . @3.00
1a variant(c) 3.00

RTA Personality Crisis #1
© Image

RTA: PERSONALITY CRISIS
Aug., 2005
1-shot 3.50

RUMBLE GIRLS
(B&W) April, 2000
1 (of 8) Silky Warrior Tansie 3.50
2 . . . . 3.50
3 Sugar and Wax 3.50
4 Sapphire Bullets. 3.50
5 It's Not Romantic 3.50
6 Boy, Girl, Boy Girl 3.50
7 The Life of My Time, concl. 4.00

RUMBLE IN LA RAMBLA
May, 2006
1 (of 3) 3.00
2 You Snooze, You Lose. 3.00
3 Penthouse Massacre. 3.00

RUN!
Dec., 2003
1-shot MMr. 3.00

RUNES OF RAGNAN
Oct. 2006
1 thru 4 Flames of Muspell . . . . . @3.50

RUSSIAN SUNSET
Nov., 2006
1 and 2 (of 5) RMz . . . . @4.00

SAFFIRE
April, 2000
1 MtB,SRf,F:Melanie,Lyssa,
  Priscilla 3.00
1a variant JMd(c) 3.00
1b Mat Broome blue foil(c) 9.00
1c Joe Mac blue foil(c) 11.00
2 MtB,SRf,V:The Kraken 3.00
2a randy green(c) 9.00
2b signed & number 9.00
3 MtB,SRf,Hades Gate 3.00

SAINT ANGEL
2000
Preview 3.00
1 KIA,BNa,40-pg.,flip-book 4.00
1a variant(c) 4.00
2 KIA,BNa,40-pg.,flip-book 4.00
3 KIA,BNa,40-pg.,flip-book 4.00
4 KIA,BNa,40-pg.,flip-book 4.00

SAM & TWITCH
TMP, Aug., 1999
1 AMe,Spawn tie-in. 2.75
2 AMe,The Udaku,pt.2 . . . . 2.50
3 AMe,The Udaku,pt.3 . . . . 2.50
4 AMe,The Udaku,pt.4 . . . . 2.50
5 AMe,The Udaku,pt.5 . . . . 2.50
6 AMe,The Udaku,pt.6 . . . . 2.50
7 AMe,The Udaku,pt.7 . . . . 2.50
8 AMe,The Udaku,pt.8 . . . . 2.50
9 One Really Bad Day 2.50
10 Witch Hunter,pt.1 . . . . 2.50
11 Witch Hunter,pt.2 . . . . 2.50
12 Witch Hunter,pt.3 . . . . 2.50
13 Witch Hunter,pt.4 . . . . 2.50
14 Dumb Laws and Egg 2.50
15 Bounty Hunter Wars,pt.1 . . . . . 2.50
16 Bounty Hunter Wars,pt.2 . . . . . 2.50
17 Bounty Hunter Wars,pt.3 . . . . . 2.50
18 Bounty Hunter Wars,pt.4 . . . . . 2.50
19 Bounty Hunter Wars,pt.5 . . . . . 2.50
20 Jon Doe Affair,pt.1 . . . . 2.50
21 Jon Doe Affair,pt.2 . . . . 2.50
22 Jon Doe Affair,pt.3 . . . . 2.50
23 Jon Doe Affair,pt.4 . . . . 2.50
24 Jon Doe Affair,pt.5 . . . . 2.50
25 Jon Doe Affair,pt.6 . . . . 2.50
26 Jon Doe Affair,pt.7 . . . . 2.50
27 Death Row Confessions 2.50

SAMMY: TOURIST TRAP
Feb., 2003
1 thru 4 . . . . @3.00

SAM NOIR: RONIN HOLIDAY
(B&W) Feb., 2007
1 Life's a beach and then you die . 3.00
2 Rhino what you did last summer . 3.00
3 Wake Up and Smell the Coffin . . 3.00

SAM NOIR: SAMURAI DETECTIVE
(B&W) Sept., 2006
1 Payback is a Niche 3.00
2 Blood Thirst, Ask Question Later. 3.00
3 . . . . 3.00
Spec. #1 rep. #1–#3 . . . . 8.00

SAM STORIES: LEGS
Dec., 1999
1-shot SK, 24-pg 2.50

SAVAGE
Shadowline, Oct., 2008
1 (of 4) 3.50
2 . . . . 3.50

Savage Dragon #28
© Erik Larsen

SAVAGE DRAGON
Highbrow, July, 1992
1 EL,I:Savage Dragon 3.00
2 EL,I:Superpatriot 3.50
3 EL,V:Bedrock,with coupon#6. . . . 3.00
3a EL,w/o coupon 3.00
Spec. Savage Dragon Versus Savage
    Megaton Man #1 EL,DSm. 3.00
Gold ed. 12.00

[2nd Series] June, 1993
1 EL,I:Freaks 4.00
2 EL,V:Teen.Mutant Ninja Turtles,
    Flip book Vanguard #0 . . . . 3.00
3 EL,A:Freaks 3.00
4 EL,A:Freaks 3.00
5 EL,Might Man flip book 3.00
6 EL,A:Freaks 3.00
7 EL,Overlord 3.00
8 EL,V:Cutthroat,Hellrazor 3.00
9 EL 3.00
10 EL 3.00
11 EL,A:Overlord 3.00
12 EL, Enter She-Dragon 3.00
13 EL,Mighty Man,Star,I:Widow
    (appeared after issue #20) 3.00
13a Larsen version of 13 . . . . 3.00
14 Possessed,pt.1 . . . . 3.00
15 Possessed,pt.2 . . . . 3.00
16 Possessed,pt.3,V:Maoc 3.00
17 V:Dragonslayer 3.50
18 R:The Fiend 3.00
19 V:The Fiend 3.00
20 Rematch with Overlord 3.00
21 V:Overlord 3.00
22 A:Teenage Mutant Turtles 3.00
23 Rapture vs. SheDragon 3.00
24 Gang War,pt.1 . . . . 3.00
25 Gang War,pt.2 double size 4.00
26 thru 29 . . . . @3.00
30 EL,'Overlord Reborn' 3.00
31 'The Dragon is trapped in Hell' . . 3.00
32 Kill-Cat vs. Justice 3.00

33 fatherhood. 3.00
34 F:Hellboy,pt.1 . . . . 4.00
35 F:Hellboy,pt.2 . . . . 4.00
36 Dragon & Star try to rescue
    Peter Klaptin 3.00
37 mutants struggle in ruins of
    Chicago 3.00
38 Dragon vs. Cyberface. 3.00
39 Dragon vs. Dung. 3.00
40 'G-Man'. 3.00
41 Wedding issue 3.00
42 V:Darklord 3.00
43 Stranded on another world 3.00
44 in flying saucer 3.00
45 . . . . 3.00
46 She-Dragon vs. Vicious Circle . . 3.00
47 A knight and a mummy 3.00
48 Unfinished Business,pt.1 . . . . . . 3.00
49 Unfinished Business,pt.2 . . . . . . 3.00
50 Unfinished Business,pt.3,
    some reps., 96-pg. 6.00
51 F:She-Dragon 3.00
52 F:She-Dragon,V:Hercules. 3.00
53 EL,F:She Dragon 3.00
54 EL,V:imposter Dragon. 3.00
55 EL,Dragon & She-Dragon. 3.00
56 EL,Rita Medermade kidnapped . 3.00
57 EL,V:Overlord 3.00
58 EL,Dragon's Resurrection. 3.00
59 EL,return of Savage Dragon. . . . 3.00
60 EL,R:Devastator 3.00
61 EL,R:Rapture 3.00
62 EL,Savage Dragon married 3.00
63 EL,Dragon's honeymoon 3.00
64 EL,Overlord's secrets 3.00
65 EL,Possessed. 3.00
66 EL,Dragon shrunk. 3.00
67 EL,A:SuperPatriot 3.00
68 EL,V:PowerHouse. 3.00
69 EL 3.00
70 EL, Hell on Earth 3.00
71 EL,End of the World,prequel . . . 3.00
72 EL,End of the World,prequel . . . 3.50
73 EL,End of the World,pt.1 . . . . . . 3.50
74 EL,End of the World,pt.2 . . . . . . 3.50
75 EL,End of the World,pt.3 . . . . . . 5.00
76 EL,Hell on Earth begins 3.50
77 EL,Wildstar Returns 3.50
77a Variant JOy(c). 3.50
78 EL,Mind-slaves of the
    Brain-Child. 3.50
79 EL,Girl Trouble 3.50
80 EL,Lurkers beneath Lake Fear. . 3.50
81 EL,The Land Down Under 3.50
82 EL,The Bug Riders 3.50
83 EL,F:Madman 3.50
84 EL,F:Madman 3.50
85 EL,Peril in Pittsburgh 3.50
86 EL,Mighty Man returns 3.50
87 EL,Havoc in the Hidden City. . . . 3.50
88 EL,To Challenge the Gods 3.50
89 EL,Panic in Detroit 3.50
90 EL,Return to Chicago 3.50
91 EL,Rapture returns 3.50
92 EL,Reclaim the Earth,pt.1. . . . . . 3.50
93 EL,Reclaim the Earth,pt.2. . . . . . 3.50
94 EL,V:CyberFace 3.50
95 EL,V:Sebastian Khan,concl. 3.50
96 EL,V:The Creator 3.50
97 EL,F:She-Dragon 3.50
98 EL,return home 3.50
99 EL,Evil Twins 3.50
100 EL, Torn Between Two
    Worlds, 100-pg. 10.00
101 EL,F:son of Dragon. 3.00
102 EL,V:Afterbirth. 3.00
103 EL,Dragon & son 3.00
104 EL,secrets. 3.00
105 EL,F:The Candyman. 3.00
106 EL,Dragon as Santa 3.00
107 EL,flipcover Major Damage . . . 4.00
108 EL,Flying Shoes Incident 3.00

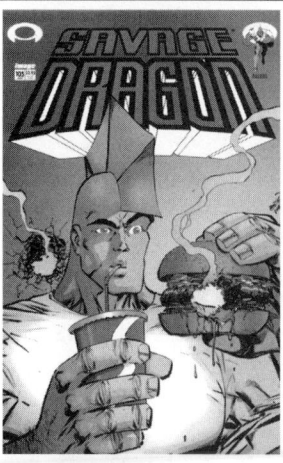

Savage Dragon #105
© Erik Larsen

109 EL,Danger in Dimension X . . . 3.00
110 EL,Lost in Dimension X 3.00
111 EL,Mako the man-shark 3.00
112 EL,V:Octopus & OpenFace. . . . 3.00
113 EL,Vicious Circle 3.00
114 EL,Cutthroat 3.00
115 EL,concl.,80-pg. 7.00
116 I:Negate. 3.00
117 EL,Powerless 3.00
118 EL,R:Arachnid 3.00
119 EL,Running Man,pt.1 . . . . 3.00
120 EL, The Running Man,pt.2 . . . 3.00
121 EL, The Running Man,pt.3 . . . 3.00
122 EL, Weapons of Mass
    Destruction, pt.1 . . . . 3.00
123 EL Regenerative Powers 3.00
124 EL, Dismal Dregs of Defeat . . . 3.00
125 EL, The Fly, 64-pg. 5.00
126 EL, Glum Lord. 3.00
127 EL, A World Against Him. 3.00
128 EL, Wanted 3.00
129 EL, ... 3.00
130 EL, V: Solar Man & Universo . . 3.00
131 EL Vengeance. 3.00
132 Rock City Diner, 80-pgs 7.00
133 A desperate search. 3.00
134 World Tour, pt.1. . . . . 3.00
135 Enter: Prism 3.00
136 EL, Prism Attacks 3.00
137 EL,A:Madman 3.00
138 EL,Adam Archer 3.00
139 EL,Enter: Invincible. 3.00
140 EL,Heroes unite 3.00
141 EL,Heroes unite 3.00
142 EL,Fall From Grace 3.50
Spec #0 O:Savage Dragon (2006) . 2.50
Spec. 1-shot Savage Dragon
    Companion,64-pg. 3.00
Spec. 1-shot Savage Dragon/
    Hellboy, collected ed. 6.00

SAVAGE DRAGON
DESTROYER DUCK
Nov., 1996
1 SvG,ChM,EL 4.00

SAVAGE DRAGON:
GOD WAR
2004
1 (of 4) 3.00
2 thru 4 . . . . @3.00

IMAGE

SAVAGE DRAGON, THE: RED HORIZON
Comics Feb., 1997
1 MsM 3.00
2 MsM,Dragon in the ER,A:Freak
   Force 3.00
3 (of 3) MsM,Freak Force beaten . . 3.00

SAVAGE DRAGON: MARSHAL LAW
(B&W) July, 1997
1 (of 2) PMs,KON,F:Marshal Law . . 3.00
2 PMs,KON, concl. 3.00

SAVAGE DRAGON: SEX & VIOLENCE
July, 1997
1 (of 2) TBm,MBm 3.00
2 TBm,MBm, AH, concl. 3.00

Savant Garde #6
© Wildstorm

SAVANT GARDE
WildStorm, March, 1997
1 'A team without a rule book' 2.50
2 Between killer & killer cat 2.50
3 V: strange Tapestry 2.50
4 'Any super-villain can take
   over the world' 2.50
5 'The Final Showdown' 2.50
6 BKs,Guilty until proven innocent . 2.50
7 BKs,death of John Colt 2.50
Fan Edition #1, with Fan #22 . . . . . 3.00
Fan Edition #2, with Fan #23 . . . . . 3.00
Fan Edition #3, with Fan #24 . . . . . 3.00

SCREAMLAND
Mar., 2008
1 (of 5) 3.00
2 thru 5 . . . . @3.00

SCUD, THE DISPOSABLE ASSASSIN
21 Over-Used Muse, pt.1 . . . . 3.50
22 Over-Used Muse, pt.2 . . . . 3.50
23 Over-Used Muse, pt.3 . . . . 3.50
24 Over-Used Muse, pt.4 . . . . 3.50

SEA OF RED
Mar., 2005
1 Terror on the High Seas 5.00
2 . . . . 3.50

---

3 . . . . 3.00
4 . . . . 3.00
5 Origin issue 3.00
6 . . . . 3.00
7 . . . . 3.00
8 . . . . 3.00
9 Estimated Casualties,pt.1 . . . . . . 3.00
10 Estimated Casualties, pt.2 . . . . 3.00
11 World in ruins 3.00
12 Golem from Mesopotamia 3.00
13 Conclusion 3.50

SEASON OF THE WITCH
Oct., 2005
0 B&W, 24-page 2.50
1 (of 4) Spring 3.50
2 Summer 3.50
3 Autumn 3.50
4 Winter 3.50

SECTION ZERO
June, 2000
1 KK,TG,UFO's etc. 2.50
2 KK,TG,Sargasso sea 2.50
3 KK,TG,Curse of Sargasso 2.50
4 KK,TG,Ground Zero revealed . . . 2.50
5 KK,TG,Sargasso vs. Crust 3.00
6 KK,TG,Fire and Rain 3.00

SEVENTH SHRINE, THE
Jan., 2005
1 (of 2) 56-pg. Robert Silverberg(s) 6.00
2 . . . . 6.00

'76
(B&W) Jan., 2008
1 (of 8) 3.00
2 thru 8 . . . . @3.00

SHADOWHAWK
Shadowline, Aug., 1992
1 JV,I:ShadowHawk,Black Foil(c),
   Pin-up, with coupon#1 . . . . 4.00
1a w/o coupon 3.00
2 JV,V:Arsenal,A:Spawn, I:Infiniti . 3.00
3 JV,V:Arsenal,w/glow-in-the-
   dark(c) 3.50
4 V:Savage Dragon 2.50
Ashcan #1 . . . . 2.50
Ashcan #2 . . . . 2.50
Ashcan #3 . . . . 2.50
Ashcan #4 . . . . 2.50

[2nd Series] 1993
1 JV,Die Cut(c) 2.50
1a Gold ed. 3.00
2 JV,ShadowHawk I.D. 2.50
2a Gold ed. 2.50
3 Poster(c),JV,w/Ash Can 2.50

[3rd Series] 1993
0 Zero issue 2.50
1 JV,CWf,V:Vortex,Hardedge,
   Red Foil(c) 2.50
1a Gold ed. 3.00
1b signed 6.00
2 JV,CWf,MA,I:Deadline,
   BU&I:US Male 2.50
3 JV(a&s),ShadowHawk has AIDS,
   V:Hardedge,Blackjak 2.50
4 JV(a&s),V:Hardedge 2.50
Note: #5 to #11 not used; #12 below
   is the next issue, the 12th overall.
12 Monster Within,pt.1 . . . . 2.50
13 Monster Within,pt.2 . . . . 2.50
14 Monster Within,pt.3 . . . . 2.50
15 Monster Within,pt.4 . . . . 2.50
16 Monster Within,pt.5 . . . . 2.50
17 Monster Within,pt.6 . . . . 2.50
18 JV,D:ShadowHawk 2.50
Spec.#1 . . . . 3.50

Gallery#1 . . . . 2.50

SHADOWHAWK
2005
1 JV(s) 3.00
2 Zapped 3.00
3 JV(s),V:Nocturn 3.00
4 . . . . 3.00
5 Dead Man Walking, x-over 3.00
6 Suffer not a corpse to live 3.00
7 My World On Fire, pt.1 . . . . 3.00
8 My World On Fire, pt.2 . . . . 3.00
9 Rise, pt.1 . . . . 3.50
10 Rise, pt.2 . . . . 3.50
11 Rise, pt.3 . . . . 3.50
12 Rise, pt.4 . . . . 3.50
13 Past Lives 3.50
14 On the Rebound, pt.1 . . . . 3.50
15 On the Rebound, pt.2 . . . . 3.50
1-shot Great Responsibility 2.00

SHADOWHAWK/ VAMPIRELLA
Feb., 1995
Book 2 V:Kaul 5.00
Book #1: see Vampi/ShadowHawk

SHADOWHUNT SPECIAL
Extreme, 1996
1 Shadowhunt x-over,pt.1 . . . . 2.50

SHADOWS
Feb., 2003
1 . . . . 3.00
2 . . . . 3.00
3 . . . . 3.00
4 b&w 3.00
5 b&w 3.00

SHAMAN'S TEARS
Creative Fire, 1993–96
0 MGr 2.50
1 MGr,I:Shaman,B:Origin 3.00
1a Siver Prism ed. 5.00
2 MGr,Poster(c) 2.50
3 MGr,V:Bar Sinister 2.50
4 MGr,V:Bar Sinister,E:Origin 2.50
5 MGr,R:Jon Sable 2.50
6 MGr,V:Jon Sable 2.50
7 MGr,V:Rabids 2.50
8 MGr,A:Sable 2.50
9 MGr,Becoming of Broadarrow . . . 2.50
10 Becoming of Broadarrow,pt.2 . . 2.50
11 Becoming of Broadarrow,pt.3 . . 2.50
12 Becoming of Broadarrow,pt.4 . . 2.50
13 The Offspring,pt.1 . . . . 2.50

SHANGRI-LA
Jan., 2004
GN 8.00

SHARK-MAN
Jan., 2008
1 . . . . 3.50
2 . . . . 3.50
3 . . . . 3.00

SHARKY
1998
1 by Dave Elliott & Alex Horley . . . 2.50
1a variant cover (5,000 made) 3.00
2 coma over 2.50
2a variant cover 3.00
3 R:Blazin' Glory 2.50
3a variant SBi(c) 2.50
4 tons of guest stars, concl. 2.50
4a variant DAy(c) 2.50

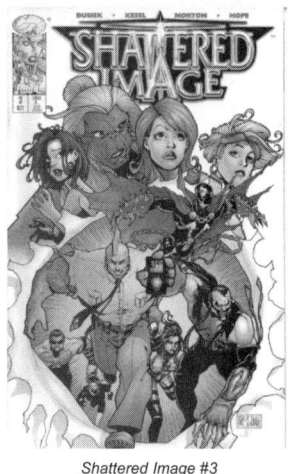

Shattered Image #3
© Image/Wildstorm

SHATTERED IMAGE
WildStorm, 1996
1 KBk,TnD,crossover 2.50
2 KBk 2.50
3 KBk 2.50
4 KBk,TnD,concl. 2.50

SHE-DRAGON
Feb., 2005
1-shot EL(s) 48-pg. 6.00

SHIDIMA
Jan., 2001
1 PtL, A Warlands saga 3.00
1a variant(c) 3.00
1b stormkote(c). 8.00
2 PtL 3.00
2a variant(c) 3.00
2b variant(c) 3.00
3 PtL 3.00
3a variant(c) 3.00
3b variant(c) 3.00
4 . . . . 3.00
5 . . . . 3.00
6 . . . . 3.00
0 24-pg. 2.50
0 variant(c) 2.50

SHIP OF FOOLS
(B&W) Sept., 1997
0 Bryan J.L. Glass, Michael
　Avon Oeming. 3.00
1 Death & Taxes,pt.1 . . . . 3.00
2 Death & Taxes,pt.2 . . . . 3.00
3 Death & Taxes,pt.3 . . . . 3.00
4 Death & Taxes,pt.4 . . . . 3.00

SHOCKROCKETS
April, 2000
1 (of 6) KBk,SI 2.50
2 KBk,SI,Command Decision 2.50
3 KBk,SI,The Triangle Trade 2.50
4 KBk,SI,Rocket Science 2.50
5 KBk,SI,sneak attack. 2.50
6 KBk,SI,Final Battle,flip-book 2.50

SHUT UP & DIE
(B&W) 1998
1 JHI and Kevin Stokes 3.00
2 JHI,Angry White Man. 3.00
3 JHI,Wife abducted 3.00

4 JHI 3.00
5 JHI,A:Earl Jackson. 3.00

SIEGE
WildStorm, 1997
1 JPe,AV,Nothing you believe
　is real. 2.50
2 JPe,AV,Omega goes to Hawaii
　for funeral 2.50
3 JPe,AV,Zontarian Crab Ships vs.
　Drop Ship 2.50
4 JPe,AV,Rescue of Omega Squad 2.50

SIGMA
WildStorm, 1996
1 BCi,Fire From Heaven prelude . . 2.50
2 BCi,Fire From Heaven,pt.6 . . . . . 2.50
3 BCi,Fire From Heaven,pt.14 . . . . 2.50

SILENCERS, THE
July, 2005
1 . . . . 3.00
2 . . . . 3.00

SILENT SCREAMERS
Oct., 2000
1 Nosferatu, 40-pg. 5.00

SIREN
(B&W) May, 1998
1 by J. Torres & Tim Levins 3.00
2 F:Zara Rush, private eye. 3.00
3 cpmc;isopm 3.00

'68
Jan., 2007
1-shot 4.00
1-shot-a variant (c) 4.00

SKINNERS
TMP, July, 2000
1 MtB,JMd. 3.00
1a variant PtL(c). 3.00
1b variant Andy Park(c) 3.00
1c variant MtB(c) 2-D 3.00
1d limited ed. Broom(c) 8.00
1e limited ed., signed 9.00
2 MtB,SRf. 3.00
2a variant JBz(c). 3.00

SMALL GODS
June, 2004
1 Killing Grin,pt.1 . . . . 3.00
2 Killing Grin,pt.2 . . . . 3.00
3 Killing Grin,pt.3 . . . . 3.00
4 Killing Grin,pt.4 . . . . 3.00
5 Dead Man's Hand,pt.1 . . . . 3.00
6 Dead Man's Hand, pt.2 . . . . 3.00
7 Dead Man's Hand, pt.3 . . . . 3.00
8 Dead Man's Hand, pt.4 . . . . 3.00
9 Dead Man's Hand, concl. 3.00
10 Nightingale, pt.1 . . . . 3.00
11 Nightingale, pt. 2. . . . . 3.00
12 Nightingale, pt. 3. . . . . 3.00
Spec. #1 Two Time 3.00
Vol. 2
1 (of 2) Innocence. 3.00

SOLAR LORD
March, 1999
1 by Khoo Fuk Lung 2.50
2 Nickson is Solar Lord. 2.50
3 V:5 enemies. 2.50
4 V:5 enemies. 2.50
5 V:The Emperor of Darkness . . . 2.50
6 O:Nickson 2.50
7 concl., book one 2.50

SOMETHING WICKED
Oct., 2003
1 (of 4) b&w 3.00
2 thru 4 Among the Living . . . . . . @3.00

SORROW
(B&W) Aug., 2007
1 (of 4) 3.00
2 thru 3 . . . . @3.00

SOUL OF A SAMURAI
Apr., 2003
1 (of 4) b&w, 48-pg. 4.00
2 . . . . 4.00
3 48-pg 6.00
4 48-pg. 6.00

SOUL REAVER:
LEGACY OF KAIN
Top Cow, June, 2000
1-shot MHw,video game tie-in 2.50

SOUL SAGA
Top Cow, 2000
1 SPa,F:Aries, Soulblade 5.00
1a variant(c) JMd (1:4) 5.00
1b variant Michael Turner(c) (1:4) . 5.00
2 SPa,death in the family 3.50
2a variant David Finch(c) 3.50
2b variant Pat Lee(c) 3.50
3 SPa, Khan Hordes. 2.50
4 SPa, Dominion vs. Khan 2.50
5 SPa, F:Ares 2.50
Coll.Ed.Vol.1 . . . . 6.00

SOULWIND
(B&W) March, 1997
1 quest for Soulwind begins 3.00
2 Nick becomes 'Captain Crash' . . 3.00
3 Captain Crash & Poke pursue
　Soulwind info. 3.00
4 concl. of story arc 3.00
5 The Day I Tried to Live,pt.1 . . . . 3.00
6 The Day I Tried to Live,pt.2 . . . . 3.00
7 The Day I Tried to Live,pt.3 . . . . 3.00
8 The Day I Tried to Live,pt.4 . . . . 3.00

SPARTAN:
WARRIOR SPIRIT
July, 1995
1 thru 4 . . . . @3.00

SPARTAN X
(B&W) Sept., 1998
1 MGo,RM,'Plague Train' 3.00
2 MGo,RM,'Plague Train,'pt.2 . . . . 3.00
3 MGo,RM,'Plague Train,'pt.3 . . . . 3.00

SPAWN
TMP, May, 1992
1 TM,I:Spawn,w/GP,DK pinups . . . 9.00
1a black & white 25.00
2 TM,V:The Violator 9.00
3 TM,V:The Violator 9.00
4 TM,V:The Violator,+coupon #2 . . 7.00
4a w/o coupon 3.00
5 TM,O:Billy Kincaid 6.00
6 TM,I:Overt-Kill 5.00
7 TM,V:Overt-Kill. 5.00
8 TM,AMo(s),F:Billy Kincaid 5.00
9 NGa(s),TM,I:Angela. 6.00
10 DS(s),TM,A:Cerebus. 5.00
11 FM(s),TM, Home Story 4.00
12 TM,Chapel killed Spawn 4.00
13 TM,A:Youngblood 4.00
14 TM,A:The Violator. 5.00

IMAGE

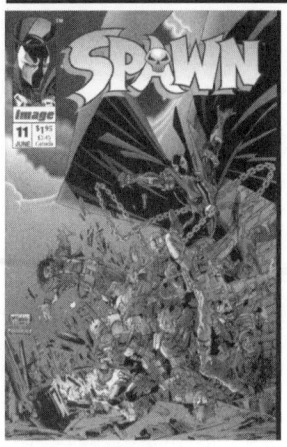

Spawn #11
© Todd McFarlane

15 TM, Myths II 4.00
16 GCa,I:Anti-Spawn 5.00
17 GCa,V:Anti-Spawn 5.00
18 GCa,ATi,D:Anti-Spawn 9.00
19 & 20 see after #25
21 TM,The Hunt,pt.1 . . . . 9.00
22 TM,The Hunt,pt.2 . . . . 4.00
23 TM,The Hunt,pt.3 . . . . 3.00
24 TM,The Hunt,pt.4 . . . . 3.00
25 Image X Book,MS,BTn 5.00
19 I:Houdini 5.00
20 J:Houdini 6.00
26 TM 4.00
27 I:The Curse 4.00
28 Faces Wanda 4.00
29 Returns From Angela 4.00
30 A:KKK 4.00
31 R:Redeemer 4.00
32 TM,GCa,New Costume 4.00
33 R:Violator 4.00
34 V:Violator 4.00
35 F:Sam & Twitch 4.00
36 Talks to Wanda 4.00
37 I:The Freak 4.00
38 . . . . 4.00
39 . . . . 4.00
40 V:Curse 4.00
41 V:Curse 4.00
42 thru 49 . . . . @4.00
50 48-pg 3.00
51 . . . . 3.00
52 . . . . 3.00
53 A:Malebolgia 3.00
54 return to New York, alliance
   with Terry Fitzgerald 3.00
55 plans to defeat Jason Wynn 3.00
56 efforts to defeat Jason Wynn . . . 3.00
57 . . . . 3.00
58 sequel to Spawn #29 . . . . 3.00
59 . . . . 3.00
60 battle between Spawn and
   Clown cont. 3.00
61 battle with Clown concl. 3.00
62 Spawn is Al Simmons for 1 day . 3.00
63 Operation: Wynn fall,pt.1 . . . . . . 3.00
64 Wynn falls, bagged with toy
   catalog 3.00
65 recap issue 2.50
66 TM,GCa,lives of alley bums 2.50
67 TM,GCa,Sam and Twitch 2.50
68 TM,GCa,R:Freak 2.50
69 TM,GCa,F:Freak 2.50
70 TM,GCa 2.50
71 TM,GCa,Cold Blooded Truth . . . 2.50
72 TM,GCa,Haunting of the Heap . . 2.50

73 TM,GCa,R:The Heap 2.50
74 TM,GCa,pathway to misery 2.50
75 TM,GCa,Deadly Revelations . . . 2.50
76 TM,GCa,Granny Blake 2.50
77 TM,GCa,confronts 2.50
78 TM,GCa,DaM,'Sins of Excess' . . 2.50
79 TM,GCa,DaM,Killer in N.Y. 2.50
80 TM,GCa,DaM,F:Sam & Twitch . . 2.50
81 TM,GCa,DaM,Sins are reborn . . 2.50
82 TM,GCa,DaM,sea of self-doubt . 2.50
83 TM,GCa,V:Jason Wynn 2.50
84 TM,GCa,DaM,Helle's Belles . . . 2.50
85 TM,GCa,DaM,Legend of
   Hellspawn 2.50
86 TM,GCa,DaM,V:Al Simmons . . . 2.50
87 TM,GCa,DaM,Al Simmons fate . 2.50
88 TM,GCa,DaM,Seasons of
   change 2.50
89 TM,GCa,DaM,secrets revealed . 2.50
90 TM,GCa,DaM,three stories 2.50
91 TM,GCa,DaM,Black Cat
   Bones,pt.1 . . . . 2.50
92 TM,GCa,DaM,Black Cat
   Bones,pt.2 . . . . 2.50
93 TM,GCa,DaM,Devil's Banquet . . 2.50
94 TM,GCa,DaM,Children's Hour . . 2.50
95 TM,GCa,DaM,Cracks in the
   Foundation 2.50
96 TM,GCa,DaM,Rules of
   Engagement 2.50
97 TM,GCa,DaM,Heaven's Folly . . . 2.50
98 TM,GCa,DaM,The Trouble
   with Angels 2.50
99 TM,GCa,DaM,Edge of Darkness 2.50
100A TM,GCa,DaM,TM(c)She dies . 9.00
100B TM,GCa,DaM,FM(c) 5.00
100C TM,GCa,DaM,GCa(c) 6.00
100D TM,GCa,DaM,AshleyWood(c) 5.00
100E TM,GCa,DaM,MMi(c) 5.00
100F TM,GCa,DaM,AxR(c) 5.00
101 TM,AMe,DaM,The Speed
   of Night 9.00
102 TM,AMe,DaM,Remains 2.50
103 TM,AMe,DaM,A Town Called
   Malice 2.50
104 TM,Retribution Overdrive,pt.1 . 2.50
105 TM,Retribution Overdrive,pt.2 . 2.50
106 TM,The Kingdom,pt.1 . . . . 2.50
107 TM,The Kingdom,pt.2 . . . . 2.50
108 TM,The Kingdom,pt.3 . . . . 2.50
109 TM,Hour of Cleansing
   Approaches 2.50
110 TM,The Kingdom,pt.4 . . . . 2.50
111 TM,The Kingdom,pt.5 . . . . 2.50
112 TM,The Kingdom,pt.6 . . . . 2.50
113 TM,The Kingdom,pt.7 . . . . 2.50
114 TM,The Bridge,pt.1 . . . . 2.50
115 TM,The Bridge,pt.2 . . . . 2.50
116 TM,Consequences 2.50
117 TM,A Season in Hell 2.50
118 TM,A Season in Hell,pt.2 . . . . . 2.50
119 TM,A Season in Hell,pt.3 . . . . . 2.50
120 TM,A Season in Hell,pt.4 . . . . . 2.50
121 TM,The Devil His Due 2.50
122 TM,Salvation Road 2.50
123 TM,Freedom in Nothingness . . 2.50
124 TM,Through These Eyes 2.50
125 TM,Wake Up Dreaming,pt.1 . . . 2.50
126 TM,Wake Up Dreaming,pt.2 . . . 2.50
127 TM Loose Threads,pt.1 . . . . . . 2.50
128 TM,Loose Threads,pt.2 . . . . . . 2.50
129 TM,Loose Threads,pt.3 . . . . . . 2.50
130 TM,Loose Threads,pt.4 . . . . . . 3.00
131 TM,God is a Bullet,pt.1 . . . . . . 3.00
132 TM,God is a Bullet,pt.2 . . . . . . 2.50
133 TM,God is a Bullet,pt.3 . . . . . . 2.50
134 TM,God is a Bullet,pt.4 . . . . . . 2.50
135 TM,Mad Shadows,pt.1 . . . . 2.50
136 TM,Mad Shadows,pt.2 . . . . 2.50
137 TM,Mad Shadows,pt.3 . . . . 2.50
138 TM,Mad Shadows,pt.4 . . . . 2.50
139 TM,Asunder,pt.1 . . . . 2.50

140 TM,Asunder,pt.2 . . . . 2.50
138 TM,A Thousand Clowns,pt.5 . . . 2.50
139 TM,Hellbound,pt.1 . . . . 2.50
140 TM(s),Hellbound,pt.2 . . . . 2.50
141 TM(s),Hellbound,pt.3 . . . . 2.50
142 TM(s),Devil to Pay, pt.1 . . . . . . 2.50
143 TM(s),Devil to Pay, pt.2 . . . . . . 2.50
144 TM(s),Devil to Pay, pt.3 . . . . . . 2.50
145 TM(s),Destination Anywhere . . . 2.50
146 TM(s),Destination Anywhere . . . 2.50
147 TM(s),Howl 2.50
148 TM(s),Random Patterns, pt.1 . . 2.50
149 TM(s),Random Patterns, pt.2 . . 2.50
150 TM(s),TM(c), 48-page 5.00
150a thru 150c variant(c)s 25.00
151 Beginning of the End 10.00
152 Another Spawn? 3.00
153 . . . . 3.00
154 . . . . 3.00
155 Angel Zera 3.00
156 . . . . 3.00
157 . . . . 3.00
158 The Rapture 3.00
159 Spawn bares his heart 3.00
160 V:The Disciple 3.00
161 Armageddon 3.00
162 Beyond Good and Evil 3.00
163 Reconstruction 3.00
164 New Beginnings 3.00
165 The Lodgers 3.00
166 The Return of the Clown 3.00
167 V:The Clown 3.00
168 The Crucible of the Clown 3.00
169 Hellhouse, pt. 1 . . . . 3.00
170 Hellhouse, pt. 2 . . . . 3.00
171 Poor Nyx 3.00
172 A Tale of Three Brothers 3.00
173 A Tale of Three Brothers 3.00
174 Gunslinger Spawn 3.00
175 Showdown with Gunslinger . . . 3.00
176 Monster in the Bumble 3.00
177 Monster in the Bumble, concl. . . 3.00
178 F:Sam & Twitch 3.00
179 Spawn vs. Himself 3.00
180 War is Hell, France 3.00
181 Inner Demon 3.00
182 The End of Spawn 3.00
183 Mammon's Plans 3.00
184 End of an Era 3.00
185 TM,WPo 3.00
186 TM,WPo 3.00
Ann.#1 Blood & Shadows, 64-pg. . . 5.00
GN Spawn Movie adapt. 5.00
GN Spawn: Blood and Salvation . . . 5.00
Fan Edition #1, with Fan #16 . . . . . . 5.00
Fan Edition #1a variant cover 4.00
Fan Edition #1b gold logo,retailer . . 5.00
Fan Edition #2, with Fan #17 . . . . . . 5.00
Fan Edition #2a variant cover 4.00
Fan Edition #2b gold logo,retailer . . 5.00
Fan Edition #2c platinum Foil logo . 5.00
Fan Edition #2, with Fan #18 . . . . . . 3.00
Fan Edition #2a variant cover 4.00
Fan Edition #3b gold logo,retailer . . 5.00
1-shot Spawn: Simony, 64-pg. 8.00
1-shot Spawn: Godslayer, 64-pg. . . . 7.00
Spec. Spawn 1 in 3-D 6.00

SPAWN: ARCHITECTS OF FEAR
Sept., 2007
1 56-pgs 7.00

SPAWN/BATMAN
Image/DC 1994
1 FM(s),TM 5.00

SPAWN BLOOD FEUD
June, 1995
1 V:Vampires 4.00

IMAGE

2	4.00
3 Hunted as a Vampire	4.00
4 V:Heartless John	4.00

SPAWN BIBLE
TMP, Aug., 1996

1 TM,GCa	15.00
2 Book of the Dead, 56-pg.	15.00

Spawn: The Dark Ages #13
© Todd McFarlane

SPAWN: THE DARK AGES
TMP, March, 1999

1 GF,LSh, from 12th century	2.50
1a variant TM(c) (1:4)	7.00
2 LSh,A:Black Knight	2.50
3 LSh,A:Black Knight	2.50
4 LSh,Lord Covenant	2.50
5 LSh,Lord Covenant	2.50
6 LSh,Sister Immaculata	2.50
7 LSh,Cogliostro	2.50
8 LSh,Acts of Contrition	2.50
9 LSh	2.50
10 LSh,F:Lord Covenant	2.50
11 LSh,Ghost on the Hill	2.50
12 LSh,The Faithful	2.50
13 LSh,Blood and Glory	2.50
14 LSh,The Innocent	2.50
15 LSh,New Beginnings	2.50
16 CWf,Heart of the HellSpawn	2.50
17 CWf,The Circle and the Worm	2.50
18 CWf,Crucified	2.50
19 CWf,Like Any Other Man	2.50
20 Voices in the Dark	2.50
21 Sins of the Hellspawn	2.50
22 The Seedling	2.50
23 The Beast	2.50
24 Bleed, Pagan, Bleed	2.50
25 The Plague of Man	2.50
26 Lesion	2.50
27 Bubonic Nights	2.50
28 Stonehaven,pt.1	2.50
29 Stonehaven,pt.2	2.50
30 The Beast of the Wood	2.50
31 Home to Roost	2.50

SPAWN GODSLAYER
May, 2007

1 thru 4 The Winter King, pt.1–4. @3.00	
5 Dromo's Tale	3.00
6 Return to Endra-La	3.00
7 Dire Things, pt.1	2.00
8 Dire Things, pt.2	3.00
9 Dire Things, pt. 3	3.00

SPAWN THE IMPALER
TMP Oct., 1996

1 (of 3) MGr, fully painted	4.00
2 thru 3 MGr	@4.00

SPAWN: THE UNDEAD
TMP, May, 1999

1 PJe,DT,CWf,F:Spawn	2.50
2 PJe,DT,CWf,F:Travis Ward	2.50
3 PJe,DT,CWf,Heaven vs. Hell	2.50
4 PJe,DT,CWf,suicide cult	2.50
5 PJe,DT,CWf,The Wind That Shakes the Barley	2.50
6 PJe,DT,CWf	2.50
7 PJe,DT,CWf,Up the Down Stairs	2.50
8 PJe,DT,CWf,One Lunch to Live.	2.50
9 PJe,DT,CWf,Waiting	2.50
10 PJe,DT,CWf,How to Win Friends and Influence People.	2.50
11 PJe,DT,CWf,Heaven and Hell and In Between	2.50

SPAWN/WILDC.A.T.S
Jan., 1996

1 AMo(s),Devilday, pt.1, x-over.	3.50
2 AMo(s),Devilday, pt.2	3.50
3 AMo(s),Devilday, pt.3	3.50
4 AMo(s),Devilday, pt.4	3.50

SPECIAL FORCES
Aug., 2007

1 (of 6) KB	3.00
2 thru 4	@3.00

SPIRIT OF THE TAO
Top Cow, May, 1998

1 BTn,F:Lance & Jasmine	2.50
2 BTn,mission to destroy base	2.50
3 BTn,V:Jaikap Clan	2.50
4 BTn,F:Jasmine & Lance	2.50
5 BTn, Antidote to virus	2.50
6 BTn, Tao grows stronger	2.50
7 BTn, V:Menicus	2.50
8 BTn, A:Messiah	2.50
9 BTn, The Dragon is Loose	2.50
10 BTn, Jasmine out of control	2.50
11 BTn, Dragon ash race	2.50
12 BTn, F:Disciple	2.50
13 BTn, friend or foe	2.50
14 BTn, must one die?	2.50
15 BTn,conclusion, 48-pg.	4.00

SPLITTING IMAGE
March, 1993

1 DsM,A:Marginal Seven	2.50
2 DsM,A:Marginal Seven	2.50

STAR
June, 1995

1 F:Star from Savage Dragon	2.50
2 Buried Alive	2.50
3 A:Savage Dragon,Rapture.	2.50
4 A:Savage Dragon,Rapture.	2.50

STARCHILD: MYTHOPOLIS
(B&W) 1997

0 JOn, 'Prologue'	3.00
1 JOn, 'Pinehead'	3.00
2 JOn, 'Pinehead,'pt.2	3.00
3 JOn, 'Pinehead,'pt.3	3.00
4 JOn, 'Fisher King,'pt.1	3.00
5 JOn, 'Fisher King,'pt.2	3.00

STARDUST KID, THE
May, 2005

1 (of 4) JMD,MP	3.50

2 JMD,MP, The Woman	3.50
3 JMD	3.50
4 JMD	3.50

STARFALL
Top Cow

Preview	3.00
Preview San Diego Comic Con	5.00

STAY PUFFED
Jan., 2004

1-shot	3.00
1-shot B variant (c)	3.00

STEVE NILES' STRANGE CASES
Aug., 2007

1 The Gathering	3.00
2 The Abattor	2.50
3	2.50

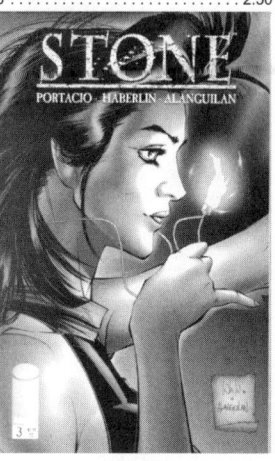

Stone #3
© Image/Avalon

STONE
Avalon Sept., 1998

2 WPo,V:Rook	2.50
3 WPo,A:Bann	2.50
4 WPo, conclusion	2.50

[VOL. II] Aug., 1999

1 WPo	2.50
1a Chromium Edition	7.00
2 WPo, search for murderer	2.50
2 Stonechrome edition	15.00
3 WPo,Blood from a Stone	2.50
4 WPo,A Rose by Any Other Name	2.50
5 Wpo, series resumes	3.00

STORMWATCH
WildStorm, 1993

0 JSc(c),O:StormWatch, V:Terrorists,w/card	2.50
1 JLe(c&s),ScC,TvS(i), I:StormWatch	2.50
1a Gold ed.	4.00
2 JLe(c&s),ScC,TvS(i),I:Cannon, Winter,Fahrenheit,Regent	2.50
3 JLe(c&s),ScC,TvS(i),V:Regent, I:Backlash	3.00
4 V:Daemonites	2.50
5 SRf(s),BBh,V:Daemonites	2.50
6 BCi,ScC,TC,A:Mercs	2.50
7 BCi,ScC,TC,A:Mercs	2.50

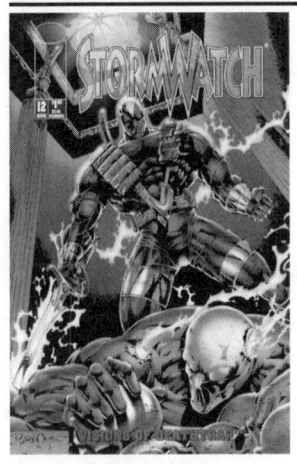

StormWatch #12
© Wildstorm

8 BCi,ScC,TC,A:Mercs 2.50
9 BCi,I:Defile. 2.50
10 V:Talos 2.50
10a variant(c). 5.00
11 RMz(s),the end? 2.50
12 RMz(s),V:Hellstrike,'Visions
 of Deathtrap' 2.50
13 V:M.A.D.-1 . . . . 2.50
14 Despot. 2.50
15 Batallion, Flashpoint 2.50
16 V:Defile. 2.50
17 D:Batallion. 2.50
18 R:Argos. 2.50
19 R:M.A.D.-1,L:Winter 2.50
20 F:Cannon,Winter,Bendix. 2.50
21 V:Wildcats 2.50
22 RMz,BWS(c),WildStorm
 Rising,pt.9,w/2 cards 2.50
22a Newsstand ed. 2.50
23 RMz(s),R:Despot,Warguard 2.50
24 V:Despot 2.50
25 SSe,ScC,BCi,A:Spartan 2.75
25a 2nd printing 2.50
26 V:Despot 2.50
27 V:Despot,Rebuilding,'And in
 the End' 2.50
28 F:Blademaster,Swift,Flint,
 Comanche,New Adventures . . . 2.50
29 I:Prism,Reorganization 2.50
30 V:Heaven's Fist. 2.50
31 V:Middle Eastern Terrorists. 2.50
32 . . . . 2.50
33 inc. Winters Journey 2.50
34 . . . . 2.50
35 Fire From Heaven,pt.5 . . . . 2.50
36 Fire From Heaven,pt.12 . . . . 2.50
37 Double size,F:Weatherman One,
 I:Rose Tatoo 8.00
38 WEI(s). 5.00
39 WEI(s). 5.00
40 WEI(s),virus. 5.00
41 WEI(s). 5.00
42 WEI(s),Weatherman discovers a
 conspiracy 5.00
43 WEI(s). 5.00
44 WEI(s),history of Jenny Sparks. . 5.00
45 WEI(s),Battalion visits
 his family 5.00
46 WEI(s),secrets and more
 secrets, prologue 5.00
47 WEI(s), JLe, SW, dangerous
 experiment gone awry 5.00
48 WEI(s),'Change or Die'pt.1 . . . . . 5.00
49 WEI(s),'Change or Die'pt.2 . . . . . 5.00

50 WEI(s),'Change or Die' concl.
 large size 8.00
Sourcebok JLe(s),DT 2.75
Spec.#1 RMz(s),DT 4.25
Spec.#2 F:Fleshpoint 2.50
Ashcan 1 . . . . 3.00

STORMWATCH
WildStorm, Oct., 1997
1 WEI,bacterial horror,'Strange
 Weather,'pt.1,'Hard Rain'. 5.00
1a Variant cover 5.00
1b Voyager bagged pack 5.00
2 WEI,Stormwatch Black team,
 'Strange Weather,'pt.2 . . . . 5.00
3 WEI,Black team,'Strange
 Weather,'pt.3,'A Storm Coming'. 5.00
4 WEI,A Finer World,pt.1 . . . . 5.00
5 WEI,A Finer World,pt.2 . . . . 5.00
6 WEI,A Finer World,pt.3 . . . . 5.00
7 WEI,Bleed,pt.1 . . . . 5.00
8 WEI,Bleed,pt.2 . . . . 5.00
9 WEI,Bleed,pt.3 . . . . 5.00
10 WEI,'No Reason'. 10.00
11 WEI,BHi,PNe,F:Jackson King,
 'No Direction Home' 10.00

STRANGE CASES
4 Big Demon on Campus 2.50

STRANGE EMBRACE
May, 2007
1 thru 8 . . . . @3.00

STRANGE GIRL
June, 2005
1 . . . . 3.00
1a variant MK(c) 3.00
2 thru 7 . . . . @3.00
8 Life after God, concl. 3.00
9 The End of the Road 3.00
10 Strange Girl returns 3.00
11 Detour to Hell 3.00
12 . . . . 3.00
13 . . . . 3.00
14 . . . . 3.50
15 . . . . 3.50
16 Golden Lights, pt.1 . . . . 3.50
17 Golden Lights, pt.2 . . . . 3.50
18 . . . . 3.00

STRANGERS
Mar., 2003
1 (of 6) 3.00
2 In the Inwards of the Night 3.00
3 Caresses such as Snakes Give . 3.00
4 The Livid Daylights 3.00
5 Icy till the Evening 3.00
6 Icy till the Evening 3.00
2a–6a variant (c). 3.00

STRANGERS IN
PARADISE VOL. 3
Homage,1996–97
1 TMr. 5.00
2 TMr. 4.00
3 TMr,David & Katchoo fight 3.50
4 TMr,Katchoo makes startling
 discovery 3.50
5 TMr,Francine's college days 3.50
6 TMr,Katchoo searches for David . 3.50
7 TMr. 3.50
8 TMr,demons of the past 3.50

STREET FIGHTER
Sept., 2003
1 Round One! Fight!. 5.00
2 . . . . 4.00

3 . . . . 4.00
4 Brothers 3.00
4a variant (c). 3.00
5 M.Bison 3.00
5a variant (c). 3.00
5b Power Cel Acetate (c) 5.00
6 The Beginning 3.00
6a variant (c). 4.00
6b Power Foil (c) 4.00
1a–3a variant (c). . . . . @5.00

STRIKEBACK!
WildStorm, 1996
1 rep & new art 2.50
2 thru 5 . . . . @2.50

STRONGARM
(B&W) Feb., 2007
1 thru 5 . . . . @3.00

STRYKEFORCE
Apr., 2004
1 thru 5 . . . . @3.00

STUPID COMICS
Sept., 2002
1-shot by Jim Mahfood,b&w 3.00
1-shot #2 . . . . 3.00
3 . . . . 3.00

SUBURBAN GLAMOUR
Sept., 2007
1 thru 4 . . . . @3.50

SUPER-PATRIOT
July, 1993
1 N:Super-Patriot 2.50
2 KN(i),O:Super-Patriot. 2.50
3 A:Youngblood. 2.50
4 . . . . 2.50

SUPER-PATRIOT:
LIBERTY AND JUSTICE
June, 1995
1 R:Covenant 2.50
2 Tokyo 2.50
3 Tokyo gets Trashed 2.50
4 Final issue 2.50

SUPERPATRIOT:
AMERICA'S FIGHTING
FORCE
July, 2002
1 (of 4) F:Johnny Armstrong 3.00
2 patriotic pandemonium 3.00
3 High Anxiety. 3.00
4 The Final Battle, concl. 3.00

SUPERPATRIOT:
WAR ON TERROR
July, 2004
1 (of 4) 3.00
2 thru 4 . . . . @3.00

SUPERSTAR:
AS SEEN ON TV
Jan., 2001
Spec. KBk,SI,48-pg. 6.00

SUPREME
Supreme, 1992
0 O:Supreme 2.50
1 B:RLd(s&i),BrM, V:Youngblood . . 3.00
1a Gold ed. 5.00

IMAGE

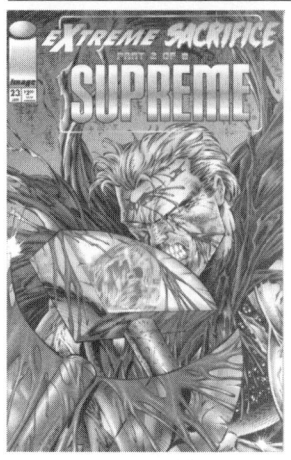

Supreme #23
© *Image/Supreme*

2 BrM,I:Heavy Mettle,Grizlock 3.00
3 BrM,I:Khrome. 3.00
4 BrM 3.00
5 BrM(a&s),Clv(i),I:Thor,V:Chrome. 2.50
6 BrM,Clv(i),I:Starguard,
  A:Thor,V:Chrome. 3.00
7 Rip,ErS(s),SwM,A:Starguard,
  A:Thor 3.00
8 Rip(s),SwM,V:Thor. 3.00
9 Rip&KtH(s),BrM,Clv(i), V:Thor. . . 3.00
10 KrH(s),BrM,JRu(i), BU:I:Black
  & White 3.00
11 Extreme Prejudice,pt.4,
  I:Newmen 3.00
12 SPa(c),RLd(s),SwM 4.00
25 SPa(c),RLd(s),SwM,V:Simple
  Simon,Images of Tomorrow. . . . 6.00
13 B:Supreme Madness 3.00
14 Supreme Madness,pt.2. . . . . . . 3.00
15 RLd(s)A:Spawn 3.00
16 V:StormWatch 3.00
17 Supreme Madness,pt.5. . . . . . . 3.00
18 E:Supreme Madness 3.00
19 V:The Underworld 3.00
20 V:The Unterworld 3.00
21 God Wars 3.00
22 RLd,CNn,God Wars, V:Thor . . . 3.00
23 ExtremeSacrifice,pt.2,x-over. . . . 3.00
24 Identity Questions 3.00
#25, see above, after #12
26 F:Kid Supreme 3.00
27 Rising Son,I:Cortex. 3.00
28 Supreme Apocalypse:Prelude . . 3.00
29 Supreme Apocalypse,pt.1 . . . . . 3.00
30 Supreme Apocalypse,pt.5 . . . . . 3.00
31 V:Equinox 3.00
32 V:Cortex 3.00
33 Extreme Babewatch 3.00
34 She-Supreme 3.00
35 Extreme Destroyer,pt.7
  x-over, bagged with card 3.00
36 . . . . 3.00
37 . . . . 3.00
38 . . . . 3.00
39 AMo. 3.00
40 AMo. 3.00
41 AMo. 5.00
42 AMo,'Secret Origins' 5.00
43 AMo,'Secrets of the Citadel
  Supreme' 3.00
44 See Color Comics section
Ann.#1 TMB,CAd,KG,I:Vergessen . . 3.00
Ashcan #1 . . . . 3.00
Ashcan #2 . . . . 2.00

SUPREME: GLORY DAYS
Oct., 1994
1 Supreme in WWI 3.00
2 (of 2) BNa&KIA(s),DdW,GyM,
  A:Superpatriot 3.00

SWORD, THE
Oct, 2007
1 thru 13 Luna brothers . . . . @3.00

SWORD OF DAMOCLES
WildStorm, 1996
1 prelude to Fire From Heaven
  x-over. 2.50
2 Fire From Heaven,Finale,pt.2 . . . 2.50

SWORD OF DRACULA
Oct., 2003
1 . . . . 3.00
2 The Elders,pt.2 . . . . 3.00
3 The Elders,pt.3 . . . . 3.00
4 The Elders,pt.4 . . . . 3.00
5 The Elders,pt.5 . . . . 3.00
6 Concl. 3.00

SYLVIA FAUST
Aug., 2004
1 (of 4) 3.00
2 . . . . 3.00
3 Fade. 3.00

TALES FROM
THE BULLY PULPIT
Aug., 2004
1-shot 64-pg. 7.00

TALES OF
THE DARKNESS
Top Cow, April, 1998
1 WPo,F:Jackie Estacado. 3.00
2 WPo,concl. first story. 3.00
3 Dungeon, Fire, and Sword,pt.1 . . 3.00
4 Dungeon, Fire & Sword 3.00
5 in Dark Ages 3.00
6 futuristic story. 3.00
1/2 . . . . 3.00

TALES OF TELLOS:
MAIDEN VOYAGE
March, 2001
1 48-pg.. 4.00

TALES OF TELLOS
Oct., 2004
1 (of 3) F:Dyn Jessa 3.50
2 thru 3 TDz . . . . @3.50

TALES OF
THE WITCHBLADE
Top Cow, 1996
1 TnD,F:Anne Bonney 9.00
1a TnD, variant cover (1:4). 12.00
1a signed, variant 20.00
2 TnD,F:Annabella 6.00
3 WEl,BTn,future 6.00
4 WEl,BTn,future,pt.2 . . . . 5.00
5 RiB,past 5.00
6 RGr, time of Celts 3.00
7 in Ancient Egypt. 3.00
7a variant cover (1:4) 8.00
8 ancient Egypt,pt.2 . . . . 3.00
9 ancient Egypt,pt.3 . . . . 3.00
Coll.Ed.#1, rep. #1–#2. . . . . 5.00
Coll.Ed.#2, rep.#3–#4 . . . . 6.00

TASK FORCE 1
July., 2006
1 . . . . 3.50
2 thru 4 . . . . @3.50

TEAM 1: STORMWATCH
June, 1995
1 I:First StormWatch Team 2.50
2 V:Helspont,D:Think Tank 2.50

TEAM 1: WILDC.A.T.S
July, 1995
1 I:First Wildcats Team 2.50
2 B:Cabal 2.50

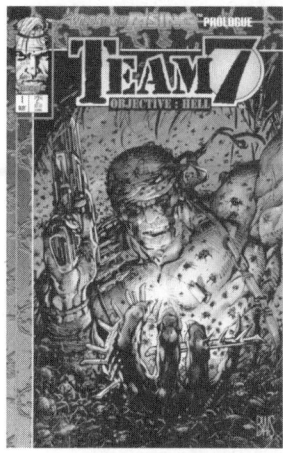

Team 7 Objective Hell #1
© *Image*

TEAM 7
WildStorm, 1994–95
1 New team. 4.00
2 New powers. 2.50
3 Members go insane 2.50
4 final issue,V:A Nuke 2.50
Ashcan 2.50

TEAM 7
OBJECTIVE: HELL
May, 1995
1 CDi,CW,BWS(c),WildStorm
  Rising,Prologue,w/2 cards. 3.00
1a Newsstand ed. 2.50
2 Cambodia 2.50

TEAM 7:
DEAD REACONING
Jan., 1996
1 CDi. 3.00
2 thru 4 CDi. . . . . @2.50

TEAM YOUNGBLOOD
Extreme, 1993
1 B:ErS(s),ATi(c),CYp,NRD(i),
  I:Masada,Dutch,V:Giger 2.50
2 ATi(c),CYp,NRd(i),V:Giger 2.50
3 RLd(s),CYp,NRd(i),C:Spawn,
  V:Giger 2.50
4 ErS(s). 2.50
5 ErS(s),CNn,I:Lynx 2.50
6 ErS(s),N:Psi-Fire,
  BU:Black&White 2.50

Team Youngblood #9
© Image/Extreme

7 ErS(s),CYp,ATh,Extreme
   Prejudice,pt.1,I:Quantum,
   BU:Black & White 2.50
8 ErS(s),CYp,ATh,Extreme Pre-
   judice,pt.5, V:Quantum,
   BU:Black & White 2.50
9 RLd 2.50
10 ErS(s),CYp,ATh. 2.50
11 RLd,ErS,Cyp 2.50
12 RLd,ErS,Cyp 2.50
13 ErS,Cyp. 2.50
14 RLd,ErS,Cya. 2.50
15 New Blood 2.50
16 RLd,ErS,TNu,I:New Sentinel,
   A:Bloodpool 2.50
17 ExtremeSacrifice,pt.6,x-over. . . 2.50
18 MS, membership drive 2.50
19 R:Brahma 2.50
20 Contact,pt.1 1000 yr Badrock . . 2.50
21 Contact,pt.2. . . . . 2.50
22 Shadowhunt x-over,pt.4 . . . . . . 2.50

TECH JACKET
2002
1 Origin issue 3.50
2 thru 8 . . . . @3.00

TEENAGE MUTANT
NINJA TURTLES
(B&W) Highbrow,
June, 1996
1 . . . . 4.00
2 . . . . 3.00
3 . . . . 3.00
4 Donatello resurrected 3.00
5 FFo,Warlord Komodo uses
   Splinter as guinea pig 3.00
6 FFo 3.00
7 FFo,Raphael joins Foot Clan?. . . 3.00
8 FFo,Michelangelo tries to rescue
   Casey Jones' daughter 3.00
9 Enter: the Knight Watchman 3.00
10 'Enter: The Dragon'. 3.00
11 V:DeathWatch,A:Vanguard 3.00
12 F:Raph, Foot Gang warfare 3.00
13 Shredder is back! 3.00
14 Shredder vs. Splinter 3.00
15 F:Donatello 3.00
16 reunited with Splinter 3.00
17 F:Leonardo 3.00
18 UFO Sightings 3.00
19 F:Leatherhead. 3.00

20 F:Triceraton. 3.00
21 A:Pimiko 3.00
22 F:Lady Shredder. 3.00
23 F:Lady Shredder. 3.00

TEKKEN FOREVER
Dec., 2001
1 (of 4) from Tekken 4 video game. 3.00
1a variant(c) 3.00
2 Iron Fist tournament 3.00

TELLOS
May, 1999
1 TDz, The Joining, part 1 . . . . 3.00
2 TDz, The Joining, part 2 . . . . 2.50
3 TDz, The Joining, part 3 . . . . 2.50
4 TDz,Hawke & Rikk. 2.50
4a variant JaL cover (1:4) 2.50
4b variant AAd cover (1:4) 2.50
4c variant RGr cover (1:4) 2.50
5 TDz,all-out battle 2.50
6 TDz,Aftermath 2.50
7 TDz,Darkness & Light 2.50
8 TDz,Tellos Joins Gorilla 2.50
8a variant Kia Asamiya(c). 2.50
8b variant HuR(c) 2.50
9 TDz,Jarek vs. Malesur. 2.50
10 TDz, concl. 3.00

TENTH, THE
Jan.,, 1997
1 BSt,TnD,Last stand against
   Hell on Earth 6.00
2 BSt,TnD,invasion of Darklon
   Corp. begins 5.00
3 BSt,TnD,Tenth & Espy team-up. . 4.00
4 BSt,TmD.confrontation with
   possible Armageddon 4.00
[Regular Series] Aug., 1997
1 TnD,BSt,V:Blackspell. 5.00
2 TnD,BSt,V:Blackspell. 4.00
3 TnD,BSt,Gozza,Eve. 4.00
4 TnD,BSt,teleported to Japan . . . 4.00
5 TnD,BSt 3.50
6 TnD,BSt,CollateralDamage,pt.1. . 3.50
7 TnD,BSt,CollateralDamage,pt.2. . 4.00
8 TnD,BSt,Dark Wind At
   Your Back 3.00
9 TnD,BSt,F:Adrenalynn 3.00
10 TnD,pt.1 (of 3). 3.00
10a variant TnD(c). 3.00
11 TnD,Victor retains Tenth 3.00
11a variant cover 3.00

Tenth, Darkk Dawn © Image

12 TnD,Black reign begins. 3.00
13 TnD,V:Rhazes Darkk 3.00
14 TnD,V:Rhazes Darkk 3.00
Coll.Ed.Vol.1 rep. #1–#2 . . . . 5.00
Spec.Configuration#1, sourcebook . 2.50
1-shot The Tenth: Darkk Dawn,
   48-page O:The Tenth (2005). . . 5.00

TENTH, THE:
BLACK EMBRACE
Feb., 1999
1 TnD,SLo, V:Gozza. 4.00
1a variant cover (1:2) 9.00
2 TnD,SLo, F:Esperanza 2.50
3 TnD,SLo, F:Adrenalynn 2.50
4 TnD,SLo, conclusion 2.50

TENTH, THE:
EVIL'S CHILD
Sept., 1999
1 TnD, F:Gozza 3.00
1a variant cover (1:3) 3.00
1b variant cover (1:3) 3.00
2 TnD, F:Twisted 3 . . . . 2.50
3 TnD 2.50
4 TnD, someone dies 2.50
Spec.Ed.#1, rep.#0 & #1/2. . . . . . 3.00

10TH MUSE, THE
Nov., 2000
1 MWn,KeL. 3.50
1a variant(c) 3.50
2 MWn,KeL,flip-book 3.50
2a variant(c) 3.50
2b photo(c) 3.50
3 MWn, critically wounded 3.50
3a variant(c) 3.50
3b photo(c) 3.50
4 MWn,Who is Medusa? 3.50
5 MWn,The Savage World 3.50
6 MWn,RCz,A:Serra 3.50
6 photo(c) 3.50
7 MWn,RCz,Maxwell Gideon 3.50
7a photo(c) 3.50
8 MWn,Assault on Olympus 3.50
8a photo(c) 3.50
9 MWn,San Francisco battle 3.50
9a photo(c) 3.50
10 MWn,RCr,I:The Odyssey 3.50
10a variant(c). 3.50
10b variant CBa(c). 3.50
11 RCr,The Endgame 3.50

TEXAS STRANGERS
Mar., 2007
1 Training Day, pt.1. . . . . 3.00
2 Training Day, pt. 2 . . . . 3.00
3 The Lone Stranger, pt.1. . . . . 3.00
4 The Lone Stranger, pt.2. . . . . 3.00

13 CHAMBERS
Sept., 2008
1-shot 6.00
1-shot a variant (c). 6.00

TIMESEEKERS
Aug., 2003
1 . . . . 3.00

TINCAN MAN
Jan., 2000
1 F:Alex Darkstar 3.00
1a variant GfD(c) (1:4) 3.00
2 no mercy 3.00
3 . . . . 3.00
Preview Book, 24-pg 3.00

IMAGE

TOMB RAIDER
Top Cow, Nov., 1999
1 DJu,JSb		5.00
2 DJu,JSb,quest for Medusa Mask.		3.00
3 DJu,JSb,secret of Medusa Mask.		3.00
4 DJu,JSb,Medusa Mask found		3.00
5 DJu,JSb,Ancient Futures		3.00
6 DJu,JSb,Death Dance		3.00
7 DJu,JSb,Dead Center,pt.1(of4)		3.00
8 DJu,JSb,Dead Center,pt.2		3.00
9 DJu,JSb,Death by Midnight		3.00
9a variant(c)		7.00
10 DJu,JSb,Eye of Creation		3.00
11 DJu,BTn		3.00
12 DJu,BTn		3.00
13 DJu,JSb,Honduras,pt.1		3.00
14 DJu,JSb,Honduras,pt.2		3.00
15 DJu,JSb,Without Limit		3.00
16 DJu,JSb,Pieces of Zero,pt.1		3.00
17 DJu,JSb,Pieces of Zero,pt.2		3.00
18 DJu,JSb,Pieces of Zero,pt.3		3.00
19 DJu,Pieces of Eight,pt.1		3.00
20 DJu,Pieces of Zero,pt.4		3.00
21 Hunt for Black Mandala		3.00
22 The Trap,pt.2		3.00
23 Path of the Tiger,pt.3		3.00
24 Isle of Hydra		3.00
25 Endgame,pt.1		3.00
26 Abyss,pt.1		3.00
27 Abyss,pt.2		3.00
28 Abyss,pt.3, Tempting Fate		3.00
29 V:Lord Vymes		3.00
30 Strange Flesh, 48-pg.		5.00
31 Conquista		3.00
32 Angel of Darkness,pt.1		3.00
33 Angel of Darkness,pt.2		3.00
34 Angel of Darkness,pt.3		3.00
35 Black Legion,pt.1		3.00
36 Black Legion,pt.2		3.00
37 Black Legion,pt.3		3.00
38 Bloodstone,pt.1		3.00
39 Bloodstone,pt.2		3.00
40 Risen		3.00
41 Spirit Walker,pt.1		3.00
42 Spirit Walker,pt.2		3.00
43 Tower of Souls,pt.1		3.00
44 Tower of Souls,pt.2		3.00
45 Inner Demons		3.00
46 Gathering Storm,pt.1		3.00
47 Gathering Storm,pt.2		3.00
48 Gathering Storm, pt.3		3.00
48a variant (c)		3.00
49 Vendetta		3.00
50 Alpha/Omega, 40-pg.		4.00
Spec. Gallery		3.00
Preview, B&W 16-pg.		2.50
0 Lara goes fishing		2.50
1/2 DJu, new(c).		3.00
Spec. Tomb Raider vs. Darkness		3.00
1-shot The Greatest Pleasure of All, Prelude, DJu,JJu (2002)		5.00
1-shot Takeover		3.00
1-shot Epiphany		5.00
1-shot Arabian Nights		3.00
1-Shot The Greatest Treasure of All, DJu(s),JJu, 48-page		7.00
Spec. Covery Gallery (2006)		3.00

TOMB RAIDER: JOURNEYS
Top Cow, Dec., 2001
1 (of 12) more Lara Croft		3.00
1A variant AH(c)		3.00
2 washed ashore in El Dorado		3.00
3 Sodom and Gomorrah		3.00
4 Deja vu.		3.00
5 Who's in your yearbook?		3.00
6		3.00
7 Maori Dream-Spear		3.00
8 way to the Underworld		3.00

9 Akio		3.00
10		3.00
11		3.00
12 Settling Old Scores		3.00

TOMB RAIDER VS. THE WOLF-MEN
Top Cow, May, 2005
2 (of 4) Monster War x-over		3.00

TOMB RAIDER/ WITCHBLADE
Top Cow, June, 2000
1/2 rep.		3.00

TOMB RAIDER/ WITCHBLADE REVISITED
Top Cow, Dec., 1998
1 Video game tie-in		3.00

TOMB RAIDER/ WITCHBLADE/ MAGDALENA/ VAMPIRELLA
Top Cow, Aug., 2005
1-shot Special		3.00
1-shot Special variant (c)s		@3.00

TOM JUDGE: END OF DAYS
Top Cow, Dec., 2002
1 PJe,40-pg.		4.00

TOOTH & CLAW
Aug., 1999
1 Reborn to rage.		3.00
2 MPa		3.00
3 MPa,Retribution,concl.		3.00

TOP COW
Top Cow, Feb., 1995–2006
Spec. Top Cow preview book		2.50
Spec. Freshmen, Necromance V.I.C.E. previews		2.50
Spec. Secrets: Winter Lingerie Special (1996)		3.00
Top Cow Bible		10.00
Top Cow/Ballistic Swimsuit Spec.#1 MS(c) (1995)		4.00
Top Cow's California Christmas Spectacular Spec. Pin-ups		3.00

TOP COW CLASSICS
Top Cow, 2000
Witchblade #1 B&W		3.00
The Darkness #1 B&W		3.00
Ascension #1		3.00
Fathom #1		3.00
Rising Stars #1 B&W		3.00
Cyberforce #1 B&W		3.00
Tomb Raider #1 B&W		3.00
Aphrodite IX #1, B&W		3.00
Midnight Nation #1, B&W		3.00
Witchblade #25, B&W		3.00
Magdalena #1 JBz,b&w		3.00
Tomb Raider/Wtchblace #1		3.00
Battle of the Planets #1		3.00
1-shot Book of Revelations (2003)		4.00

TOP COW/MARVEL: UNHOLY UNION
Top Cow, June, 2007
1-shot 40-pgs.		4.00

A TOUCH OF SILVER
(B&W) Jan., 1997
1 JV,'Birthday'		3.00
2 JV,'Dance'		3.00
3 JV,'Bullies'		3.00
4 JV,'Separation'		3.00
5 JV,inc. Tomorrow Syndicate vs. Round Table of America, 12-pg. color section		3.00
6 JV 'Choices' Aug., 1963.		3.00

TRAKK: MONSTER HUNTER
Sept., 2003
1 (of 6)		3.00
1a variant (c).		3.00
2		3.00
2a variant (c).		3.00
2b variant SBs(c)		3.00
3		3.00
3a variant SBS(c)		3.00

TRANSHUMAN
Mar., 2008
1 (of 4) Discovery		3.50
2 IPO.		3.50
3 Business Is War.		3.50
4 Marketing		3.50

TREKKER
May, 1999
1 RoR, in New Gelaph		3.00

Trencher #2
© *Image*

TRENCHER
May, 1993
1 KG,I:Trencher.		2.50
2 KG		2.50
3 KG,V:Supreme		2.50
4 KG,V:Elvis		2.50

TRIBE
March, 1993
1 TJn(s),LSn,I:The Tribe		2.50
1a Ivory(White) Editon		3.00
2		2.50
Ashcan 1		3.00

TRIPPER, THE
May., 2007
1-shot Movie Adapt. 48-pg.		6.00

TROLL
Extreme, Dec., 1993
1 RLd(s),JMs,I:Evangeliste, V:Katellan
Command 2.50
2 . . . . 2.50
Halloween Spec.#1 . . . . 2.50
X-Mas Stocking Stuffer #1 . . . . 3.00

TROLL: ONCE A HERO
Aug., 1994
1 Troll in WWII 2.50

Troubleman #2
© Image/Motown

TROUBLEMAN
Motown June, 1996
1 Charles Drost. 2.50
2 . . . . 2.50

TRUE STORY,
SWEAR TO GOD
(B&W) Sept., 2006
1 If This be Payday. 3.00
2 . . . . 3.00
3 Dog Day Afternoon 3.00
4 Flame On. 3.00
5 The Big Apple 3.00
6 The Little Things 3.50
8 . . . . 3.00
9 . . . . 3.00
10 Rules of Engagement. 3.50
11 Countdown 3.50

TRUTH, JUSTIN AND
THE AMERICAN WAY
March., 2006
1 (of 5) 3.00
2 . . . . 3.00
3 . . . . 3.00
4 The Wedding is Off 3.00
5 Crashing the Party. 3.00

TSUNAMI GIRL
Flypaper Jan., 1999
1 F:Michelle Vincent. 3.00
2 Sorayama(c), A:Alan Poe 3.00
3 Sorayama(c), Surreal conspiracy 3.00

TUG & BUSTER
(B&W) June, 1998
1 MaH, humor, F:Stinkfinger. 3.00

'21'
Top Cow, Feb., 1996
1 LWn,MDa. 2.50
2 LWn,MDa. 2.50
3 LWn,MDa. 2.50
4 LWn,MDa,'Time Bomb,'pt.1 . . . . 2.50
5 LWn,MDa,'Time Bomb,'pt.2 . . . . 2.50
6 LWn,MDa,'Time Bomb,'pt.3
 'Detonation' 2.50

TWO-BITS
Jan., 2005
1 Lullaby/Imaginaries flip-book 2.50

ULTRA
Aug., 2004
1 Seven Days, pt.1 . . . . 3.00
2 Seven Days, pt.2 . . . . 3.00
3 Seven Days, pt.3 . . . . 3.00
4 Seven Days, pt.4 . . . . 3.00
5 Seven Days, pt.5 . . . . 3.00
6 Seven Days, pt.6 . . . . 3.00
7 Seven Days, pt.7 . . . . 3.00
8 Seven Days, concl. 3.00

UMBRA
(B&W) June, 2006
1 (of 3) 52-pg. 6.00
2 . . . . 6.00
3 . . . . 6.00

UNBOUND
(B&W) Jan., 1998
1 by Joe Pruett & Michael Peters. . 3.00
2 . . . . 3.00
3 F:Marta & Erik 3.00

UNION
WildStorm, Feb., 1995
0 O:Union 2.50
0a WPo(c). 5.00
1 MT,I:Union,A:StormWatch 2.75
2 MT 2.75
3 MT 2.75
4 MT,Good Intentions 2.75

Regular Series 1995
1 R:Union, Crusade 2.50
2 V:Crusade & Mnemo 2.50
3 A:Savage Dragon. 2.50
4 JRo,BWS(c), WildStorm
 Rising,pt.3,w/2 cards 2.50
4a Newsstand ed. 2.50
5 V:Necros 2.50
6 V:Necros 2.50
7 Jill's Surprise 2.50
8 Regal Vengeance,pt.1 . . . . 2.50
9 Regal Vengeance,pt.2 . . . . 2.50
10 Regal Vengeance,pt.3 . . . . 2.50
1-shot Final Vengeance, MHs,
 V:Regent (1997) 2.50

UNION
WildStorm, 1996
1 MHs,RBn,'Knight of Faith' 2.50
2 MHs,RBn 2.50
3 MHs,RBn 2.50

UNIQUE
Platinum, Mar., 2007
1 thru 3 (of 3) 48-pgs. . . . . @3.00

UNIVERSE
Top Cow, Aug., 2001
1 PJe,The Triad of Powers 2.50
1 variant foil(c) 12.00
2 PJe,Pilgrimage into the Inferno . . 2.50
3 PJe,Judge finds Hell 2.50

4 PJe,plan for mankind's fate 2.50
5 PJe,express train to hell 2.50
6 PJe,family held hostage 2.50
7 PJe,successor to the devil. 2.50
8 PJe, Stairway to Heaven,48-pg. . 5.00

UNRAVEL
Apr., 2007
1 (of 4) Living in the Details 3.50
2 thru 3 . . . . @3.50

URBAN MONSTERS
Feb., 2008
1 Road Trip From Hell 3.50
2 Werewolves, Chupacabras &
 Monsters 3.50
3 Lights, Camera, Zombies 3.50

VAGABOND
Aug., 2000
1 RBn,SRf,F:Sharon Armstrong . . . 3.00
1a variant(c) 3.00
1b deluxe 9.00
1c signed. 11.00
1d ruby red foil(c) 11.50
2 RBn,SRf. 3.00

VAGRANT STORY
Top Cow, Sept., 2000
1 video game tie-in 3.00

VAMPIRE'S CHRISTMAS
GN JLi 48-pg.. . . . . 6.00

VANGUARD
Highbrow, 1993–94
1 EL(s),BU:I:Vanguard 3.00
2 EL(s),Roxann. 3.00
3 AMe 3.00
4 AMe 3.00
5 AMe,V:Aliens 3.00
6 V:Bank Robber 3.00
Spec. B&W 48-pg. 6.00

VANGUARD:
STRANGE VISITORS
(B&W) 1996
1 (of 4) SEa,BAn,A:Amok,'Strange
 Visitors' 3.00
2 thru 4 SEa,BAn . . . . @3.00

Vanguard: Strange Visitors #1
© Image

VELOCITY
Top Cow, 1995–95

1 V:Morphing Opponent	3.00
2 V:Charnel	3.00
3 thru 4	@3.00

VENTURE
Jan., 2003

1	3.00
2 thru 4	@3.00

V.I.C.E.
Top Cow, Oct., 2005

1	3.00
1a variant (c)s	@3.00
2	3.00
3	3.00
4	3.00
5	3.00

VICTORY
May, 2003

1 thru 4	@3.00
1a–4a variant (c)	@3.00

Vol. 2 Aug., 2004

1 (of 4)	3.00
2 thru 4	@3.00
2a–4a variant(c)s	@3.00

VIOLATOR
TMP, 1994

1 AMo(s),BS,I:Admonisher	5.00
2 AMo(s),BS	4.00
3 AMo(s),BS,last issue	4.00

VIOLATOR/BADROCK
Extreme, 1995

1 AMo(s),RLe(c),A:Celestine,'Rocks and Hard Places,'pt.1	2.50
2 AMo(s),RLe(c),V:Celestine,'Mondo Inferno'.	2.50
3 RLe(c),F: Mr. McAllister,'Where Angels Fear to Tread'	2.50
4 RLe(c),'Badrock's Bogus Journey,' final issue	2.50

VIOLENT MESSIAHS
June, 2000

1 F:Rankor Island	5.00
1a variant AMe(c) (1:4)	6.00
2	5.00
2a variant(c)	6.00
3 V:Citizen Pain	4.00
4 V:Jeremiah Parker	3.00
5 flip-book	3.00
6 Tonight The Door Opens	3.00
7 In the Final Stretch	3.00
8 North End Mansion	3.00
Spec. Genesis, 56-pg.	5.00

VIOLENT MESSIAHS: LAMENTING PAIN
Sept., 2002

1 (of 4) F:Lt. Cheri Major	3.00
2 thru 4	@3.00
1a–4a variant (c)	@3.00

VIX
June, 2008

1 (of 3) Just A Girl	3.50
2 A Sort of Fairytale	3.50
3 Good Enough	3.50

VOGUE
Extreme, 1995–96

1 F:Vogue,I:Redbloods	2.50

2	2.50
3 conclusion	2.50

VOLTRON: DEFENDER OF THE UNIVERSE
May, 2003

0	3.00
1 Revelations,pt.1	3.00
1a variant (c)s	3.00
2 thru 5 Revelations,pt.2–pt.5	@3.00

Voodoo #4
© *WildStorm*

VOODOO
WildStorm, Nov., 1997

1 AMo(s),WildStorm universe	2.50
2 AMo(s),in old New Orleans	2.50
3 AMo(s),Samedi	2.50
4 AMo(s), Christian Charles	2.50

WAHOO MORRIS
(B&W) Mar., 2000

1 Rock & Roll fantasy	3.00
2	3.00

WALKING DEAD
Oct., 2003

1	20.00
2 City of the Damned	15.00
3 Protection	10.00
4 Guns	8.00
5 Zombies	6.00
6 Grave Situations	6.00
7 Snowbound	5.00
8 Search for shelter	4.00
9 Zombie hell-hole	4.00
10 Safer shelter	4.00
11 All Good Things	4.00
12 Petty squabbles	4.00
13 CAd	4.00
14	3.00
15	3.00
16 CAd	3.00
17 CAd	3.00
18 CAd	3.00
19 CAd	3.00
20 CAd, Alone	3.00
21 CAd, Calm Before the Storm?	3.00
22 CAd	3.00
23 CAd	3.00
24 CAd	3.00
25	3.00
26	3.00

27	3.00
28	3.00
29 Zombie Attack	3.00
30 Near Death	3.00
31 New chapter begins	3.00
32 Surrounded	3.00
33	3.00
34	3.00
35	3.00
36 Marriage proposal	3.00
37 Ninth month begins	3.00
38 Preparation for War	3.00
39 Birth	3.00
40 Beginning	3.00
41 Death surrounds them	3.00
42 The Time Has Come	3.00
43 thru 49	@3.00
50 CAd	3.00
50a variant (1:100) EL (c)	3.00
51 thru 57	@3.00
Script Book #1	4.00
Spec. Walking Dead #1 (2008)	4.00

WANTED
Top Cow, Dec., 2003

1 (of 6) MMr	7.00
1a variant (c)s	7.00
1b Death Row edition	4.00
2 thru 5	@4.00
#1 Death Row edition,32-pg.	4.00
#2 Death Row edition,32-pg.	4.00
#3 Death Row edition,32-pg.	3.00
#4 Death Row edition,32-pg.	3.00
Spec. Wanted Dossier	3.00

WARBLADE: ENDANGERED SPECIES
WildStorm, 1995

1 I:Pillar	3.00
2 V:Ripclaw	2.50
3 I:Skinner	2.50
4 final issue	2.50

WARD OF THE STATE
May, 2007

1 (of 3)	3.50
2 thru 3	@3.50

WAR HEROES
June, 2008

1 (of 6) TyH	3.00
2 TyH, Boot Camp	3.00
3 TyH, Project Olympus	3.00
4 TyH	3.00

WARLANDS
Aug., 1999

1 by Pat Lee	2.50
1a, b & c variant covers	2.50
1d Armore Chrome edition	9.00
2 help from the Elves?	2.50
2a variant cover (1:2)	2.50
3 the Dataran invasion	2.50
3a variant cover (1:2)	2.50
4	2.50
5 trapped between enemies	2.50
6 enemies clash	3.00
7 the Dataran Horde	2.50
8	2.50
9 final battle begins	2.50
10 flip-book	3.00
11	2.50
12 concl.	2.50
Spec. Three stories	6.00
Chronicles Vol.1, rep.#1–#3.	8.00
Chronicles Vol.2, rep.#4–#6.	8.00

All comics prices listed are for *Near Mint* condition.

WARLANDS: AGE OF ICE
July, 2001
1 Awakening	3.00
2 flip-book	3.00
3 thru 5	@3.00
1a and 2a variant covers	@3.00
Spec. #0 (2002)	3.00
Spec. #1/2 (2002)	3.00

WATERLOO SUNSET
(B&W) July, 2004
1 (of 4) B&W,56-pg.	7.00
2 Moving in High Places	7.00
3 Pilgrim Tale & Dog Parties	7.00
4 Within the Hollow Crown & Pragma	7.00

WEAPON, THE
Platinum, June, 2007
1 (of 4)	3.00
2 thru 4	@3.00

WEAPON ZERO
Top Cow, 1995
T-Minus-4 WS	8.00
T-Minus-3 Alien Invasion	5.00
T-Minus-2 Formation of a Team	5.00
T-Minus-1 Alien Invasion	5.00
0 Whole Team Together	4.00
1	5.00
2	3.50
3	3.50
4 thru 9 WS,JBz	@3.00
10 WS,ScL,'Devil's Reign' tie-in	3.00
11 WS,JBz,Weapon Zero & Lilith return to T'srii moonbase	3.00
12 WS,JBz, What's wrong with Jamie	3.00
13 WS,JBz,problems with Jamie	3.00
14 JBz,T'Srrii have returned	3.00
15 JBz,T'Srrii,concl.,48-pg.	3.50
Weapon Zero/Silver Surfer Spec. x-over (1997)	3.00

WEASEL GUY: ROADTRIP
(B&W) Aug., 1999
1 by Steve Buccellato	3.00
1a variant cover (1:4)	3.00
2 Peril in Pennsylvania	3.00
2a variant cover (1:4)	3.00
3 Don't Mess With Texas	3.00
3a variant cover (1:4)	3.00
4 48-pg, guest stars	5.00
4a variant KIA(c) (1:4).	5.00

WETWORKS
WildStorm, 1994
1 WPo,Rebirth	4.00
2 WPo,BCi,Brakken,Blood Queen	3.00
3 WPo,BCi,V:Vampire	3.00
4 WPo,BCi,Dozer	2.50
5 WPo,BCi,Pilgrim's Turn	2.50
6 WPo,BCi,Civil War	2.50
7 WPo,BCi,F:Pilgrim	2.50
8 WPo,SW,BWS(c), WildStorm Rising,pt.7,w/2 cards	2.50
8a Newsstand ed.	2.50
9 F:Jester,Pilgrim Dozer	2.50
10 R:Dozer to Action	2.50
11 Blood Queen Vs. Dane	2.50
12 V:Vampire Nation	2.50
13 WPo(c)	2.50
14	2.50
15	2.50
16 Fire From Heaven,pt.4	2.50
17 FTa,Fire From Heaven,pt.11	2.50
18 FTa	2.50

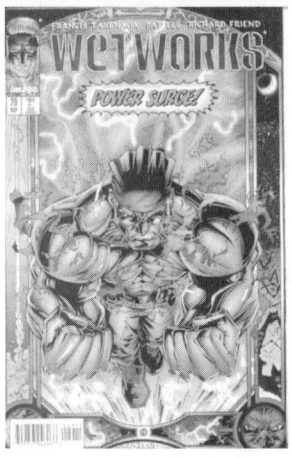

Wetworks #29
© *Wildstorm*

19 FTa	2.50
20 FTa	2.50
21 FTa	2.50
22 FTa,Dave vs.Bloodqueen concl.	2.50
23 FTa,Flattop & Crossbones, V:Lady Feign	2.50
24 FTa	2.50
25 FTa,Can Pilgrim withstand the beast that lurks within her, double size	4.50
26 team parts ways with Armand Waering	2.50
27 V:Craven, no rest for the weary	2.50
28 Vampire tracked in Pacific Northwest,A:Johnny Savoy	2.50
29 V:Soulbender,'Power Surge'	2.50
30 'Secret of the Siynn'	2.50
31 'Ashes to Ashes'	2.50
32 StG,PtL, V:Drakkar,'Sacrements of Damnation,'pt.1	2.50
32a Voyager pack, bagged with Phantom Guard preview	3.50
33 StG,PtL,Sacraments,pt.2	2.50
34 StG,PtL,Sacraments,pt.3	2.50
35 StG,PtL,Sacraments,pt.4	2.50
36 StG,'Maximum Security'	2.50
37 StG,V:St.Crispin,'Diversionary Tactics,'pt.1	2.50
38 StG,'DiversionaryTactics,'pt.2	2.50
39 StG,'Symbiote Seizure'	2.50
40 StG,'Drawn Swords'	2.50
41 StG,V:Stormwatch,'Drawn Swords,' conclusion	2.50
42 StG,'Flash Back,'pt.1	2.50
43 StG,'Flash Back,'conclusion	2.50
3-D Spec.#1 (1998)	5.00
Sourcebook #1 (1994)	2.50
Hero Ashcan	2.50
Promo Ashcans #1,#2,#3	@3.00

WETWORKS/VAMPIRELLA
WildStorm, 1997
1 JMi & GK, x-over	3.00

WHIZ KIDS
Apr., 2003
1-shot b&w, 48-pg.	5.00

WICKED, THE
Dec., 1999
1 RMr,FTa,supernatural thriller	3.00
1a variant Jay Anacleto(c)(1:4)	3.00
2 thru 7	@3.00

3a & 4a variant covers	@3.00
Special Medusa's Tale	4.00

WILDC.A.T.S
WildStorm, 1992
1 B:BCi(s),JLe, SW(i), I:Wild-C.A.T.S.	6.00
1a Gold ed.	9.00
1b Gold and Signed	9.00
2 JLe,SW(i),V:Master Gnome, I:Wetworks, Prism foil(c), with coupon #5	5.00
2a w/o coupon	2.50
3 RLd(c),JLe,SW(i), V:Youngblood	3.50
4 E:BCi(s),JLe,LSn,SW(i),w/card, A:Youngblood,BU:Tribe	3.50
4a w/red card	5.00
5 BCi(s),JLe,SW,I:Misery	3.00
6 BCi(s),JLe,SW,Killer Instinct, A:Misery,C:Ripclaw	3.00
7 BCi(s),JLe,SW, A:Cyberforce.	3.00
8 BCi(s),JLe,SW	4.00
9 BCi(s),JLe,SW	3.50
10 CCi(s),JLe,SW,I:Huntsman	3.00
11 CCi(s),JLe,SW,V:Triad, A:Huntsman	3.00
11a WPo(c)	5.00
12 JLe,CCi,A:Huntsman	3.00
13 JLe,CCi,A:Huntsman	3.00
14 X book	3.00
15 F:Black Razors	3.00
16 Black Razors	3.00
17 A:StormWatch	3.00
18 R:Hightower	3.00
19 V:Hightower	3.00
20 TC,JeR,BWS(c),WildStorm Rising,pt.2,w/2 cards	3.00
20a Newsstand ed.	3.00
21 Into Space Back Home	3.50
22 Space Adventures	3.50
23 F:Mr. Majestic's Team	3.50
24 O:Maul	3.50
25 double sized	5.00
26 AMo	3.50
27 AMo	3.50
28 AMo	3.50
29 AMo,Fire From Heaven,pt.7	3.50
30 AMo,BKs,Fire From Heaven,pt.13	3.50
31 AMo,BKs, 'Cats & Dogs'	3.50
32 AMo,BKs,'Catharsis'	3.50
33 AMo,BKs,'Belling the Cat'	3.50
34 AMo,MtB,New York seconds away from nuclear disaster	3.50
35 AMo,MtB,BKs,V:Crusade	3.00
36 AMo,MtB,BKs,V:Crusade, A:Union,pt.2	3.00
37 BCi,JPe,MtB,WildC.A.T.s team divided	3.00
38 BCi,JPe,MtB,Puritans debut	3.00
39 BCi,JPe,MtB,'C.A.T. Fight'	3.00
40 BCi,JPe,MtB,MtB(c),'Fight of Flight'	3.50
40a variant cover by TC	5.00
41 BCi,JPe,MtB,backwards in time	3.00
42 BCi,JPe,MTb,in WWI	3.00
43 BCi,JPe,MTb,in ancient China	3.00
44 BCi,JPe,MTb,'Paradise Lost'	3.00
45 BCi,JPe,MTb,'Circus Maximus'	3.00
46 BCi,JPe,MTb,escape from Rome	3.00
47 BCi,JPe,MTb,time trip concl.	3.00
47a variant JMd(c)	3.00
48 BCi,JPe,trapped in mothership	3.00
49 BCi,JPe,return to present	3.00
50 BCi, JPe,AMo,new costumes,40-pg.(June, 1998)	4.00
Ann.#1 JRo,LSn (1998)	3.00
Spec.#1 SrG(s),TC,SW,I:Destine, Pin-ups	3.50
Spec.#2	3.00
3-D #1 rep. #1 (1997)	5.00

IMAGE

3-Da variant cover 5.00
Volume 2: See COLOR

WILDC.A.T.S ADVENTURES
WildStorm, 1994
1 From animated TV series 3.00
2 Helspont,Troika 3.00
3 Caught in war 3.00
4 V:The President. 3.00
5 I:Lonely 3.00
6 I:Majestics 3.00
7 . . . . 3.00
8 Betrayed 3.00
9 V:Black Razors 3.00
10 F:Voodoo. 3.00
Sourcebook (JS(c). 3.00

WILDC.A.T.S/ALIENS
WildStorm, 1998
1-shot WEI,CSp,KN 6.00
1-shotA, variant GK&KN(c)(1:4) . . . 9.00

WILDC.A.T.S TRILOGY
June, 1993
1 BCi(s),JaL,V:Artemis 2.50
2 BCi(s),JaL,V:Artemis 2.50
3 BCi(s),JaL,V:Artemis 2.50

WILDC.A.T.S/X-MEN
WildStorm, Feb., 1997
1 (of 4) SLo,TC, giant Marvel/
Image x-over 5.00
1a alternate cover by JLe 5.00
2 & 4 see Marvel

WILDC.A.T.S/X-MEN
WildStorm/Marvel, 1997
Golden Age #1,SLo,TC 5.00
Golden Age #1a variant JLe(c) 5.00
3-D Golden Age #1, with glasses . . 5.00
3-D Golden Age #1, variant cover . . 5.00
Silver Age #1 SLo, JLe & SW,
x- over 4.50
Silver Age #1a NA&SW(c). 4.50
Silver Age #1b signed 20.00
Silver Age #1c signed, deluxe 30.00
3-D Silver Age #1, with glasses. . . . 6.50
3-D Silver Age #1, NA(c) variant . . . 6.50
Modern Age #1, JRo,AHu,MFm,
V:Hellfire Club 4.50

WildC.A.T.s #40
© WildStorm

Modern Age #1a variant cover. 4.50
3-D Modern Age #1, with glasses . . 5.00
3-D Modern Age #1, variant cover. . 5.00

WILDCORE
WildStorm, 1997–98
1 BBh,SRf,BBh(c), V:Drahn 2.50
1a variant TC(c) 2.50
1b Voyager bagged pack 3.00
2 BBh,SRf,Brawl joins. 2.50
3 BBh,SRf,V:D'rahn 2.50
4 BBh,SRf,A:Majestic 2.50
5 BBh,SRf,Tapestry 2.50
6 BBh,SRf,Zealot missing. 2.50
7 BBh,SRf,caught in fantasy world . 2.50
8 RBn,SRf,V:Tapestry 2.50
9 RBn,SRf,Zealot's soul restored . . 2.50
10 RBn,SRf,Trans-dimensional
trauma 2.50
GN Backlash & Taboo's African
Vacation. 6.00

WILDGUARD: CASTING CALL
Sept., 2003
1 (of 6) TNu 3.00
2 thru 6 TNu . . . . @3.00
1a–6a variant (c)s . . . . @3.00

WILDGUARD: FIRE POWER
Dec., 2004
1 . . . . 3.50

WILDGUARD: FOOL'S GOLD
July, 2005
1 (of 2) 3.50
2 . . . . 3.50

WILDGUARD: INSIDER
May, 2008
1 (of 3) 3.50
2 thru 3 . . . . @3.50

WILDSTAR: SKY ZERO
March, 1993
1 JOy,AG,I:WildStar. 2.50
1a Gold ed. 5.00
2 JOy,AG. 2.50
3 JOy,AG,V:Savage Dragon,
D:WildStar 2.50
4 JOy,AG,Last Issue,Pin-ups 2.50
[Regular Series] Sept., 1995
1 R:WildStar 2.50
2 V:Mighty Man. 2.50
3 . . . . 2.50
Ashcan. 2.50

WILDSTORM!
WildStorm, Aug., 1995
1 F:Spartan,Black Razors 2.50
2 F:Deathblow. 2.50
3 F:Taboo,Spartan 2.50
4 F:Nautika,Sunburst 2.50
Winter Wonderfest Spec.#1 . . . . . . 3.50
Spec.#1 Chamber of Horrors(1995) 3.50
Spec. Swimsuit Special '97 . . . . . . 2.50
Spec. Ultimate Sports Official
Program. 2.50
Sketchbook 3.00
Spec. Halloween '97 . . . . 2.50
GN Thunderbook #1 . . . . 7.00
GN Summer Spec., 48-pg. (DC) . . . 6.00

WILDSTORM ARCHIVES GENESIS
WildStorm, June, 1998
1 The #1 Collection, 238 pg 7.00

WILDSTORM RISING
WildStorm, May, 1995
1 JeR,BWS(c&a) WildStorm Rising,
pt.1:Tricked by Defile,w/2 cards 2.50
1a Newsstand ed. 2.50
2 RMz,BBo,BWS(c) WildStorm
Rising,pt.10,w/2 cards 2.50
2a Newsstand ed. 2.50
WildStorm Sourcebook #1 . . . . 2.50

WILDSTORM SPOTLIGHT
WildStorm, Feb., 1997
1 AMo,F:Majestic, at the end of
time 2.50
2 StG,RMr,Loner returns 2.50
3 StG,RMr,Secret past of original
Loner 2.50
4 F:Hellstrike,Stormwatch 2.50

Wildstorm Ultimage Sports, Official
Program © WildStorm

WILDSTORM ULTIMATE SPORTS
WildStorm, 1997
Official Program #1 . . . . 2.50

WILDSTORM UNIVERSE '97
WildStorm, Nov., 1997
Sourcebook #1 thru #3. . . . . @2.50

WINGS OF ANANSI
Aug., 2005
GN 7.00

WITCHBLADE
Top Cow, 1995–96
1 I:Witchblade 35.00
1A Special retailer edition 35.00
1B Wizard Ace edition,acetate(c) . . 20.00
2 . . . . 18.00
2 encore edition 7.00
3 . . . . 12.00
4 . . . . 9.00
5 . . . . 8.00

IMAGE

6 thru 8 . . . . @6.00
9 . . . . 7.00
9A variant cover 9.00
10 I:Darkness (Jackie Estacado). . . 7.00
10a variant Darkness cover (1:4) . 10.00
11 . . . . 6.00
12 Connection between Lisa,
    Microwave Murderer and
    Kenneth Irons 6.00
Witchblade 1/2 mail-in offer
    from Fan #8 . . . . 4.00

Top Cow, 1997

13 Dannette Boucher's secret past . 6.00
14 Sara searches for Microwave
    Murderer 5.00
15 'There is a war brewing...'. 4.00
16 'Will Witchblade come between
    Sarah and Jake?' 4.00
17 New York City in shambles. 4.00
18 Family Ties,pt.1,x-over 3.00
18a variant(c). 7.00
19 Family Ties,pt.4,x-over 4.00
20 Chief Siry, Ian Nottingham 3.00
21 another big surprise 3.00
22 F:Sara. 3.00
22a special. 9.00
23 F:Ian Nottingham 3.00
24 JPn,Sara learns truth 3.00
25 Save Jake's Life, 32 pg 3.50
26 'Grey'. 3.00
27 A:Kenneth Irons 3.00
27a variant cover, all villains 9.00
28 A:Jackie Estacado 3.00
29 A:Kenneth Irons 3.00
30 Siry & Irons. 3.00
31 How Sara's father died 3.00
32 answers and questions. 3.00
33 F:Eric. 3.00
34 F:Tommy Gallo 3.00
35 Sara gets who she wants 3.00
36 The Darkness,pt.1 x-over 3.00
37 V:wicked creatures 3.00
38 V:Demons of the Underworld . . . 3.00
39 V:Demons of the Underworld . . . 3.00
40 PJe,RV 3.00
41 PJe,RV,arsonist. 3.00
41a variant chrome (c). 5.00
42 PJe,pez dispensers 3.00
43 PJe,Impossible Murders 2.50
44 PJe,Impossible Murders 2.50
45 PJe 2.50
46 PJe 2.50
47 PJe 2.50
48 PJe 2.50
49 PJe,Firestarter is back 2.50
49a gold logo 7.00
50 PJe,48-pg.. . . . . 5.50
50a variant DK(c). 9.00
50b variant MS(c) 9.00
50c variant(c). 9.00
51 PJe,What is the Witchblade? . . . 2.50
52 PJe,The Inferno is Coming 2.50
53 PJe 2.50
54 Ian Nottingham resurrected . . . 2.50
55 Tora No Shi 4.00
55a Battle of the Planets(c) 12.00
55b Battle(c) signed. 12.00
56 Nottingham vs. Tora No Shi 2.50
57 Sonatine,pt.4 . . . . 2.50
58 Sara & Joe Siry. 2.50
59 Jackie Estacado is dead?. 2.50
60 Endgame,pt.2 x-over 3.00
61 Julie returns 3.00
61a sketch(c). 8.00
62 F:Magdalena. 3.00
63 F:Magdalena 3.00
64 F:Magdalena 3.00
65 F:Magdalena,concl.. . . . . 3.00
66 . . . . 3.00
67 Mother's Meat. 3.00
68 Road Trip,pt.1 . . . . 3.00
69 Road Trip,pt.2 . . . . 3.00

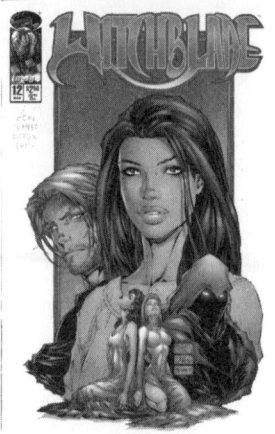

Witchblade #12
© *Top Cow*

70 return from trip 3.00
71 V:Shine 3.00
72 Level 42 . . . . 3.00
73 Level 42 . . . . 3.00
74 Death Pool 3.00
75 Death Pool, concl.,46-pg. 5.00
75a variant (c) 5.00
76 Death Pool follow-up. 3.00
77 F:Celestine 3.00
78 TnD(c). 3.00
79 TnD(c). 3.00
80 Witch Hunt,pt.1 . . . . 3.00
81 Witch Hunt,pt.2 . . . . 3.00
82 Witch Hunt,pt.3 . . . . 3.00
83 Witch Hunt,pt.4 . . . . 3.00
84 Witch Hunt,pt.5 . . . . 3.00
85 Witch Hunt,pt.6 . . . . 3.00
86 Warrior Spirit 3.00
87 Heart of the City 3.00
88 Partners 3.00
89 Fugitive,pt.1 . . . . 3.00
90 Fugitive,pt.2 . . . . 3.00
91 Fugitive,pt.3 . . . . 3.00
92 48-pg. 5.00
93 . . . . 3.00
94 Artifacts, pt.1 . . . . 10.00
95 Artifacts, pt.2 . . . . 12.00
96 . . . . 3.00
97 . . . . 3.00
97a variant (c) 3.00
98 . . . . 3.00
99 . . . . 3.00
100 . . . . 6.00
100 a thru c variant (c). . . . . @12.00
100d variant JLi incentive (c). 9.00
101 . . . . 3.00
102 . . . . 3.00
103 . . . . 3.00
103a variant b&w (c), rare 4.00
104 . . . . 3.00
105 Magdalena returns 3.00
105a variant (c) 3.00
106 In New Orleans, pt.1. . . . . 3.00
106a variant (c) 3.00
107 Trip home 3.00
108 New Bearer, Old Foe 3.00
109 Awakened 3.00
110 RMz(s),First Born x-over. 3.00
110a variant (c) 3.00
111 RMz(s),First Born x-over 3.00
112 RMz(s), First Born x-over 3.00
113 RMz(s), Who will be the bearer 3.00
113a variant (c) 3.00
114 RMz(c). 3.00

115 RMz(s) 3.00
116 RMz(s). 3.00
116a incentive variant (c) 3.00
117 thru 122 RMz(s) . . . . @3.00
114a thru 122a variant (c)s . . . . @3.00
1-shot Witchblade/Punisher. 4.00
Coll.Ed.Vol.#1 . . . . 5.00
Coll.Ed.Vol.#2 . . . . 5.00
Coll.Ed.Vol.#3 . . . . 5.00
Coll.Ed.Vol.#4, rep. #7 & #8 . . . . . 5.00
Coll.Ed.Vol.#5, rep. #9 & #10 . . . . 5.00
Coll.Ed.Vol.#6, rep. #11 & #12.. . . 5.00
Coll.Ed.Vol.#7, rep. #13 & #14 . . . 5.00
Coll.Ed.Vol.#8, rep. #15–#17 . . . . 7.00
Spec. Infinity SLo,AdP 3.50
Spec.#40 Preview book, B&W. . . . 5.00
Spec.#1 rep.movie photo cover . . . 2.50
Spec.Witchblade/Darkness,pt.2
    x-over, 48-pg. 4.00
Spec. Witchblade/Darkminds x-over 6.00
Gallery Edition #1 . . . . 3.00
Spec.1 Lady Death x-over 5.00
Spec. Tomb Raider 4.00
1/2 24-pg.. . . . . 3.00
1-shot Nottingham, 48-pg. 5.00
1-shot Witchblade Animated 3.00
GN Witchblade/Darkminds:
    The Return of Paradox 7.00
1-shot Witchblade/Wolverine 3.00
1-shot Witchblade: Blood Oath . . . 5.00
1-shot Witchblade and Tomb Raider,
    JaL,MT (2005) 3.00
1-shotA Witchblade and Tomb Raider,
    B&W cover (2005). 3.00
1-shot Art of Witchblade (2006). . . . 3.00
Spec. Bearers of the Blade (2006) . 3.00
Spec. Witchblade Tenth Anniv.
    Cover Gallery (2005) 3.00

WITCHBLADE: DESTINY'S CHILD

Top Cow, April, 2000

1 (of 3) O:Witchblade,pt.1 . . . . 3.00
2 O:Witchblade,pt.2 . . . . 3.00
3 O:Witchblade, concl. 3.00

WITCHBLADE/DEVI

Top Cow, Apr., 2008

1 RMz(s). 4.00
1a variant (c) 4.00

WITCHBLADE TAKERU MANGA

Top Cow, Feb., 2007

1 . . . . 3.00
2 . . . . 3.00
2a variant (c) 3.00
3 . . . . 3.00
4 . . . . 4.00
5 . . . . 4.00
6 . . . . 4.00
7 . . . . 4.00
8 . . . . 4.00
9 . . . . 4.00
5a thru 9a variant (c)s . . . . @4.00
10 thru 12 . . . . @4.00

WITCHBLADE/ THE DARKNESS

Top Cow

Spec. First Look. 1.00

WITCHBLADE VS. FRANKENSTEIN'S MONSTER

Top Cow, June, 2005

3 Monster War x-over 3.00

IMAGE

WITCHFINDER, THE
Liar, Oct., 1999
1 by R. Lugibihl & S. Scott 3.00
1a variant cover (1:2) 3.00
2 thru 3 . . . . @3.00

WOLVERINE/
WITCHBLADE
Top Cow, Jan., 1997
1-shot 'Devil's Reign'pt.5 (of 8) 4.00

WONDERLOST
(B&W) Dec., 2006
1 The Ups of the Downs,64-pgs. . . . 6.00
2 . . . . 6.00

WOOD BOY, THE
Mar., 2005
1 (of 2) Raymond Feist (s) 3.00
2 . . . . 3.00

WORLD CLASS COMICS
Aug., 2002
1-shot, 40-pg. b&w. 5.00

WYNONNA EARP
WildStorm, 1996–97
1 BSt,'Violent Territory' 2.50
2 BSt,The Law comes to San
   Diablo 2.50
3 BSt,desperate to stop Hemo
   from going nationwide 2.50
4 BSt,goes to New York,
   V:ancient evil 2.50
5 BSt,battle with Raduk—Eater
   of the Dead concl. 2.50

Youngblood#1
© Extreme

YOUNGBLOOD
Extreme, April, 1992
0 RLd,O:Youngblood,w/coupon#7 . 3.00
0a without coupon. 2.50
0b gold coupon 9.00
1 RLd,I:Youngblood (flipbook) 5.00
1a 2nd print.,gold border 2.50

1b RLd,Silent Edition 13.00
2 RLd,I:ShadowHawk 5.00
3 RLd,I:Supreme,Showdown 3.00
4 RLd,DK,A:Prophet,BU:Pitt 3.00
5 RLd,Flip book,w/Brigade #4 . . . . 2.50
6 RLd(a&s),J:Troll,Knight Sabre,
   2nd Die Hard, Proposal to Girl
   friend 3.50
7 Badrock, V:Overkill 2.50
8 Chapel, V:Spawn 2.50
9 . . . . 2.50
9a variant cover 5.00
10 Bravo, Badrock, Troll 2.50
Yr.Bk.#1 CYp,I:Tyrax,Kaman 2.75
Ashcan #1 . . . . 8.00
Ashcan #2 . . . . 4.00

[Volume 2] 1995
1 New Roster 2.50
2 The Program Continues 2.50
3 Extreme Babewatch. 2.50
4 Extreme Destroyer,pt.4
   x-over, bagged with card 2.50
5 . . . . 2.50
6 . . . . 2.50
7 Shadowhunt x-over,pt.3 . . . . 2.50
8 ErS,RCz. 2.50
9 ErS,RCz. 2.50
10 ErS,RCz 2.50
Spec. Baptism of Fire, F:Spawn . . . 2.50
See Color Pub. section

[Volume 3] Jan., 2008
1 JoC(s) 3.00
1a variant RLd(c) 3.00
2 thru 8 JoC(s) 3.00
2a thru 8a variant RLd(c)s . . . . . @3.00

YOUNGBLOOD
BATTLEZONE
April, 1993
1 BrM 2.50
2 . . . . 3.00

YOUNGBLOOD:
BLOODSPORT
Sept., 2008
1 RLd 3.00
1a Director's Cut, 32-pg.. . . . . 4.00

YOUNGBLOOD
STRIKEFILE
Extreme, 1993
1 JaL,RLd,I:Allies,A:Al Simmons
   (Spawn)I:Giger,Glory 3.00
1a Gold ed. 3.00
2 JaL,RLd,V:Super Patriot, Giger . . 3.00
2a Gold ed. 3.50
3 RLd,JaL,DaM(i), A:Super Partiot . 3.00
4 I:Overtkill 3.00
5 . . . . 3.00
6 and 7 flip books . . . . @3.00
8 Shaft 3.00
9 Knight Sabre 3.00
10 RLd,TNu,I:Bloodpool,Task,
   Psilence,Wylder,Rubble. 3.50
11 ExtremeSacrifice,pt.0,x-over
   O:Link Crypt 3.00
Ashcan. 3.00

YOUNGBLOOD/X-FORCE
Extreme/Marvel, 1996
1-shot Mojo visits Image x-over . . . 5.00
1-shot RLd variant cover 5.00

YOUNGBLOOD:
YEAR ONE
1 KBk(s),RLd, the early years. 2.50
2 KBk(s),RLd,V:Giger,Cybernet . . . 2.50

ZEALOT
WildStorm, 1995
1 O:Zealot. 2.50
2 In Japan. 2.50
3 V:Prometheus 2.50

ZERO G
Spacedog, Sept., 2008
1 (of 4) 3.00
2 thru 3 . . . . @3.00

ZERO GIRL
WildStorm/Homage, 2000
1 thru 4 . . . . @3.00

ZOMBIE KING
(B&W) Apr., 2005
1 . . . . 3.00

ZORRO MANTANZAS
Sept., 1999
1 (of 4) DMG & Mike Mayhew 3.00
2 DMG,V:Machete. 3.00

ZORRO'S LADY RAWHIDE:
OTHER PEOPLE'S BLOOD
(B&W) Feb., 1999
1 DMG,EM,JuB(c),cont. from Topps 3.00
2 DMG,EM,V:Scarlet Fever. 3.00
3 DMG,EM,V:Ansel Plague. 3.00
4 DMG,EM,V:Scarlet Fever. 3.00
5 DMG,EM,Whiplash. 3.00

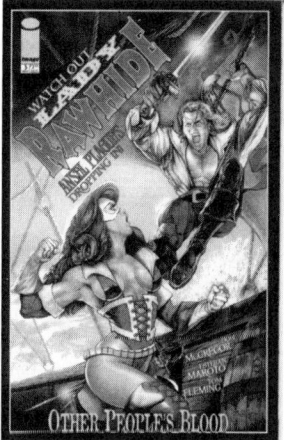

Zorro's Lady Rawhide:
Other People's Blood #3
© Image

COLOR COMICS

ABADAZAD
Crossgen Comics, 2003
1 . . . . 3.00
2 thru 6 . . . . @3.00

ABBOTT AND COSTELLO
Charlton Comics, 1968–71
1 . . . . 150.00
2 thru 9 . . . . @100.00
10 thru 21 . . . . @75.00
22 . . . . 60.00

ABC: A-Z
Wildstorm/DC, Sept., 2005
1-shot Tom Strong & Jack B. Quick . 4.00
1-shot Greyshirt & Cobweb 4.00
1-shot Terra Obscura & Splash
   Brannigan 4.00
1-shot Top 10 and Teams 4.00
1-shot Smax and First American . . . 4.00

ABIDING PERDITION
APC, 2005
1 . . . . 3.50
2 . . . . 3.50
1a thru 2a variant (c)s . . . . @3.50
1b SDCC edition 10.00
3 thru 4 . . . . @3.50
   Markosia, 2005
5 thru 6 . . . . @3.50
5a thru 6a variant (c) . . . . @3.50

ABYSS
Red 5 Comics, 2007
1 . . . . 3.00
2 thru 4 . . . . @3.00

ACES HIGH
Gemstone, 1999
1 (of 5) EC Comics reprint 3.00
2 GE,BK,JDa 3.00
3 GE,BK,WW,JDa 3.00
4 GE,BK,WW,JDa 3.00
5 GE,BK,WW,JDa 3.00

ACME NOVELTY LIBRARY
Fantagraphics, 1994–98
1 . . . . 6.00
2 thru 5 . . . . @6.00
6 thru 11 Jimmy Corrigan Meets
   His Dad, pt. 1 – pt. 6 (of 8) . . @4.50
12 Jimmy & Dad have lunch 5.00
13 Jimmy's Grandfather, 80-page . 11.00
14 F:Jimmy Corrigan 11.00
15 . . . . 10.00
1 thru 7, 2nd printings . . . . @4.00

ADAM-12
Gold Key, 1973–76
1 Photo(c), From TV show 100.00
2 thru 9 . . . . @50.00
10 . . . . 45.00

ADDAMS FAMILY
Gold Key, 1974–75
1 TV cartoon adapt. 175.00
2 . . . . 125.00
3 . . . . 100.00

ADLAI STEVENSON
Dell Publishing Co., 1966
1 Political Life Story 75.00

ADOLESCENT RADIOACTIVE BLACK BELT HAMSTERS
Dynamite Entertainment, 2008
1 thru 4 . . . . @3.50
1a thru 4a variant (c)s . . . . @3.50

ADRENALINE
A Wave Blue World, 2006
1 thru 4 . . . . @3.00

ADVENT RISING: ROCK THE PLANET
360ep Inc., 2005
1 . . . . 2.50
2 thru 5 . . . . @2.50

ADVENTURES OF BIO BOY, THE
Speakeasy Comics, 2005
1 . . . . 3.00
2 thru 5 . . . . @3.00

THE ADVENTURES OF PIPSQUEAK
Archie Publications Sept. 1959–July 1960
34 . . . . 75.00
35 thru 39 . . . . @50.00

ADVENTURES OF ROBIN HOOD
Gold Key, 1974–75
1 From Disney cartoon 50.00
2 thru 7 . . . . @25.00

ADVENTURES OF THE FLY
Archie Publications/ Radio Comics, 1959–65
1 JSm/JK,O:Fly,I:SpiderSpry
   A:Lancelot Strong/Shield . . 1,100.00
2 JSm/JK,DAy,AW 600.00
3 JDa, O:Fly 500.00
4 V:Dazzler NA panel 300.00
5 A:Spider Spry 200.00
6 V:Moon Men 200.00
7 A:Black Hood 225.00
8 A:Lancelot Strong/Shield 225.00
9 A:Lancelot Strong/Shield
   I:Cat Girl 200.00
10 A:Spider Spry 200.00
11 V:Rock Men 125.00
12 V:Brute Invaders 125.00
13 I:Kim Brand 125.00
14 I:Fly-Girl(Kim Brand) 150.00
15 A:Spider 125.00
16 A:Fly-Girl 125.00
17 A:Fly-Girl 125.00
18 A:Fly-Girl 125.00
19 A:Fly-Girl 125.00
20 O:Fly-Girl. 150.00
21 A:Fly-Girl 100.00
22 A:Fly-Girl 100.00
23 A:Fly-Girl,Jaguar 100.00
24 A:Fly-Girl 100.00
25 A:Fly-Girl 100.00
26 A:Fly-Girl,Black Hood 100.00
27 A:Fly-Girl,Black Hood 100.00

Adventures of the Fly #14
© Archie/Radio Comics

28 A:Black Hood 100.00
29 A:Fly-Girl,Black Hood 100.00
30 A:Fly-Girl,R:Comet 150.00
31 A:Black Hood, Shield, Comet . 150.00
Becomes:

FLYMAN

ADVENTURES OF THE JAGUAR
Archie Publications/ Radio Comics, 1961–63
1 I:Ralph Hardy/Jaguar. 500.00
2 10 cent cover. 200.00
3 Last 10 cent cover. 175.00
4 A:Cat-Girl 150.00
5 A:Cat-Girl 150.00
6 A:Cat-Girl 150.00
7 . . . . 125.00
8 . . . . 125.00
9 . . . . 125.00
10 . . . . 125.00
11 . . . . 125.00
12 A:Black Hood 125.00
13 A:Cat-Girl,A:Black Hood 125.00
14 A:Black Hood 125.00
15 V:Human Octopus,last issue . 125.00

ADVENTURES OF YOUNG DR. MASTERS
Archie Comics, 1964
1 . . . . 50.00
2 . . . . 25.00

ADVENTUROUS UNCLE SCROOGE McDUCK
Gladstone, 1997
1 . . . . 3.00
2 Don Rosa, A Little Something
   Special 3.00
3 The Black Widow. 3.00

AFTERBURN
Red 5 Comics, 2008
1 . . . . 3.00
2 thru 4 . . . . @3.00

AFTERMATH
Chaos! Comics, 2000
1 sequel to Armageddon 3.00
1 premium 8.00
Ashcan, Yellow 5.00
Ashcan, Blue 20.00

AGENT: AMERICA
Awesome Entertainment, 1997
1 RLe 2.50
2 RLe,JSb,JLb,F:Supreme,
    V:Smash 2.50

AGE OF INSECTS, THE: NOT HUMAN
Critical Mass, 2008
1 . . . . 6.00
2 thru 4 . . . . @6.00

AIDEN MCKAIN CHRONICLES: BATTLE FOR EARTH
Digital Webbing, 2005
1 . . . . 3.00
2 thru 3 . . . . @3.00

AIRBOY
Eclipse, 1986–89
1 TT/TY,D:Golden Age Airboy
    O:New Airboy 6.00
2 TT/TY,I:Marisa,R:SkyWolf 5.00
3 A:The Heap 5.00
4 A:Misery 5.00
5 DSt(c),R:Valkyrie 7.00
6 R:Iron Ace,I:Marlene 3.50
7 PG(c) 3.50
8 FH/TT(c) 3.50
9 thru 49 . . . . @3.00
50 AKu/NKu,double-size 4.00
Spec. Meets the Prowler 3.00
Spec. Mr. Monster 3.00
Spec. Vs Airmaidens 3.00

AIR FIGHTERS, SGT. STRIKE SPECIAL
Eclipse, 1988
1 A:Airboy,Valkyrie 3.00

AIRMAIDENS SPECIAL
Eclipse Comics, 1987
1 A:Valkyrie 3.00

AIR WAR STORIES
Dell Publishing Co., 1964
1 . . . . 75.00
2 . . . . 50.00
3 thru 8 . . . . @40.00

ALAN MOORE'S AWESOME ADVENTURES
Awesome Entertainment, 1999
1 AMo 2.50
1a alternate AxR cover 7.00
2 F:Young Guns 3.00
Spec. Awesome Univ. Handbook . . . 3.00
Spec.A alternate AxR cover 3.00

ALAN MOORE'S GLORY
Comic Cavalcade, 2001
0 Park (c) 3.50
0a variant(c)s . . . . @3.50
0e Lush Lands edition 6.00
0f Finch Prism Foil (c) 13.00
Avatar Press, 2001
Preview B&W 16-page 3.00

Preview signed gold (c) 9.00
1 (of 4) JLi(c) 3.50
1a variant(c)s . . . . @3.50
1g Finch Prism Foil (c) 13.00
1h Andy Park (c) 6.00
1i SSh(c) 6.00
1k Defender (c) 6.00
2 AMo,MMy, Finch (c) 3.50
2a variant(c)s . . . . @3.50
2e Glory Freedom (c) 6.00
2f Hall painted (c) 6.00

Alarming Adventures #1
© HarveyPublications

ALARMING ADVENTURES
Harvey Publications, 1962–63
1 AW,RC,JSe 150.00
2 AW,BP,RC,JSe 100.00
3 JSe 100.00

ALARMING TALES
Harvey Publications, 1957–58
1 JK,JK(c) 400.00
2 JK,JK(c) 250.00
3 JK 200.00
4 JK,BP 200.00
5 JK,AW 200.00
6 JK 200.00

ALBEDO, VOL. 3
Antarctic Press, 1994–95
Vol. 1 and II, See B&W
1 . . . . 3.00
2 thru 4 Various Artists . . . . @3.00

ALBION
Wildstorm/DC, June, 2005
1 (of 6) F:Old-time British heroes . . 3.00
2 . . . . 3.00
3 thru 6 . . . . @3.00

ALEISTER ARCANE
IDW Publishing, 2004
1 . . . . 4.00
2 . . . . 4.00
3 . . . . 4.00

ALIAS
Now Comics, 1990
1 BSz(c),Stranglehold 2.50
2 Stormfront 2.50
3 Firestorm 2.50
4 Blastpoint 2.50
5 Breakdown 2.50

ALIAS: AGENT BRISTOW
Arcade Comics, 2003
0 RLd 3.00
0a photo (c) 3.00
0b Dlx. Foil photo (c) 8.00
0c Chromium (c) 12.00
0d sgn art (c) 40.00
1 . . . . 3.00
1a photo (c) 3.00
1b Dlx. Foil photo (c) 6.00

ALICE IN WONDERLAND
Antarctic Press, 2006
1 (of 4) Rod Espinosa, Manga 3.50
2 thru 4 . . . . @3.50

ALIEN ARENA
Atomeka, 2002
1 (of 2) 3.00
2 . . . . 3.00
1a thru 2a variant (c) . . . . @3.00

ALIEN ENCOUNTERS
Eclipse Comics, 1985–87
1 . . . . 5.00
2 . . . . 4.00
3 I Shot the Last Martian 4.00
4 JBo(c) 4.00
5 RCo,Night of the Monkey 4.00
6 Now You See It,Freefall 4.00
7 . . . . 4.00
8 TY,Take One Capsule Every
    million Years,M.Monroe(c) 4.00
9 The Conquered 4.00
10 . . . . 4.00
11 TT,Old Soldiers 5.00
12 What A Relief,Eyes of
    the Sibyl 5.00
13 GN,The Light at the End 5.00
14 JRy,GN,TL,RT,Still born 5.00

ALIEN TERROR
Eclipse, 1986
3-D #1 Standard Procedure 3.00

ALIEN WORLDS
Pacific, 1982
1 AW,VM,NR 7.00
2 DSt 5.00
3 . . . . 4.00
4 DSt(i) 4.00
5 thru 7 . . . . 4.00
3-D #1 AAd,DSt 7.00
Eclipse, 1985
8 AW 2.50
9 . . . . 2.50

[CAPTAIN JOHNER AND] ALIENS, THE
Gold Key, 1967
1 Rep. Magnus Robot Fighter . . . 90.00

ALIUS REX
Alias Enterprises, 2006
1 . . . . 3.50

ALISTER THE SLAYER
Midnight Press, 1995
1 I:Alister The Slayer 2.50
2 V:Lady Hate 2.50
3 JQ&JP(c) V:Subterranean
    Vampire Bikers 2.50

ALL AMERICAN SPORTS
Charlton, 1967
1 . . . . 50.00

COLOR PUB.

ALL HALLOWS EVE
Innovation, 1991
1 . . . . 5.00

ALLEY OOP
Dell Publishing Co., 1962–63
1 . . . . 125.00
2 . . . . 100.00

ALLEY OOP ADVENTURES
Antarctic Press, 1998
1 . . . . 3.00
2 . . . . 3.00
3 I:Granny Green 3.00

ALLIES
Awesome Entertainment, 1999
1 RLe,AMo 2.50
1a alternate RLe cover 7.00

ALL NEW EXILES
Malibu Ultraverse, 1995–96
Infinity F:Juggernaut,Blaze 2.50
1 TKa,KeL,Beginning the Quest . . . 2.50
1a Computer painted cover (1:6) . . 2.50
1b signed edition 4.00
2 I:Hellblade, Phoenix flip issue . . 2.50
3 TKa,KeL,Phoenix Resurrection . . 2.50
4 thru 11 . . . . @2.50

ALPHA KORPS
Diversity Comics, 1996
1 I:Alpha Korps 3.00
2 The Price of Freedom, pt.2 . . . . . 2.50
3 The Price of Freedom, pt.3 . . . . . 2.50
1 thru 3 signed . . . . @5.00
4 The Price of Freedom, pt.4 . . . . . 2.50

ALTER EGO
First, 1986
1 RTs, Ron Harris 2.50
2 thru 4 . . . . @2.50
Heroic Publishing, 2005
GN 18.00

ALVIN (& THE CHIPMUNKS)
Dell Publishing Co., 1962–73
1 . . . . 175.00
2 . . . . 150.00
3 . . . . 125.00
4 thru 10 . . . . @125.00
11 thru 20 . . . . @100.00
21 thru 28 . . . . @100.00
1 Alvin for President & his pals in Merry Christmas with Clyde Crashcup & Leonardo . . 100.00

AMAZING CHAN & THE CHAN CLAN
Gold Key, 1973
1 . . . . 60.00
2 . . . . 40.00
3 and 4 . . . . @35.00

AMAZING HEROES SWIMSUIT ANNUALS
Fantagraphics, 1990–93
1990 Spec. A:Dawn 25.00
1990 2nd printing 15.00
1991 A: Dawn 20.00
1992 A: Dawn 20.00
1993 A: Dawn 20.00

AMAZON, THE
Comico, 1989
1 . . . . 2.50
2 . . . . 2.50
3 end mini-series 2.50

AMELIA RULES!
Renaissance Press, 2001
1 by Jimmy Gownley 3.00
2 thru 11 . . . . @3.00

AMELIA RULES!: SUPERHEROES
Renaissance Press, 2003
1 thru 6 (of 6) . . . . @3.00
7 thru 16 . . . . @3.00
17 48-pgs. 5.00
18 thru 20 . . . . @3.00
Spec. Super Summer Special 5.00

AMERICAN FLAGG
First, 1983–88
1 HC,I:American Flagg, Hard Times, pt.1 . . . . 5.00
2 HC,Hard Times,pt.2 . . . . 4.00
3 HC,Hard Times,pt.3 . . . . 4.00
4 HC,Southern Comfort,pt.1 . . . . . 4.00
5 thru 20 HC . . . . @4.00
21 HC thru 49. . . . . @3.50
50 HC,last issue. 3.50
Special #1 HC,I:Time2 . . . . 4.00
See Also: Howard Chaykin's American Flagg

AMERICAN FREAKSHOW
IDW Publishing, 2005
1 . . . . 4.00
2 thru 3 . . . . @4.00

Americomics #2 © AC Comics

AMERICOMICS
AC Comics, 1983
1 GP(c),O:Shade 5.00
2 . . . . 3.00
3 Blue Beetle 3.00
4 O:Dragonfly 3.00
5 and 6 . . . . @3.00
Spec.#1 Capt.Atom,BlueBeetle . . . 3.00

AMERICA'S BEST COMICS
WildStorm/DC, 2000
Spec.#1 64-page 7.00
America's Best Comics Sketchbook 6.00

AMERICAN WASTELAND: BLOOD AND DIESEL
Arcana Studio, 2007
1 . . . . 4.00
2 thru 3 . . . . @4.00

AMERICAN WAY, THE
Wildstorm/DC, Feb., 2006
1 (of 8) KSy,F:Civil Defense Corps. 3.00
2 KSy,A Hero Falls 3.00
3 KSy,I:New American 3.00
4 KSy,Battle with super-villain 3.00
5 KSy,V:Hellbent 3.00
6 KSy,Racial tensions 3.00
7 KSy,Super-hero civil war 3.00
8 KSy,finale 3.00

AMERICAN WOMAN
Antarctic Press, 1998
1 by Richard Stockton & Brian Denham 3.00
2 . . . . 3.00
2a deluxe 6.00

ANDROMEDA
Andromeda, 1995
1 I:Andromeda 2.50
2 Andromeda vs. Elite Force 2.50

ANGEL FIRE
Crusade Comics, 1997
1 BiT, from Shi #12, BiT(c) 3.00
1a with Roberto Flores cover 3.00
1b with photo cover 3.00
2 F:Shi 3.00
3 F:Shi, concl. 3.00

ANGEL: AFTER THE FALL
IDW, 2007
1a director's cut 6.00
2 thru 14 . . . . @4.00
2a thru 14a variant (c)s . . . . @4.00
9b limited foil edition 10.00

...AULD LANG SYNE
IDW Publishing, 2006
1 . . . . 4.00
1a variant (c) 4.00
2 thru 5 . . . . @4.00
2a thru 5a variant (c) . . . . @4.00

...MASKS
IDW Publishing, 2006
1-shot 48-pg. 7.50

...OLD FRIENDS
IDW Publishing, 2005
1 . . . . 4.00
2 thru 5 . . . . @4.00
2a thru 5a variant (c) . . . . @4.00

...THE CURSE
IDW Publishing, 2005
1 Buffy spin-off 7.00
1a variant (c)s . . . . @7.00
1b 2nd printing 4.00
2 . . . . 5.00
3 thru 5 . . . . @4.00
Spec. Cover Gallery 4.00

ANGEL SPOTLIGHT
IDW Publishing, 2006
Spec. Connor 4.00
Spec. Connor variant (c) 4.00
Spec. Illyria 4.00
Spec. Illyria variant (c) 4.00
Spec. Gunn 4.00
Spec. Gunn variant (c) 4.00

Spec. Wesley 4.00
Spec. Wesley variant (c) 4.00
Spec. Doyle 4.00
Spec. Doyle variant (c) 4.00

ANIMAL MYSTIC: WATER WARS
Sirius, 1996
1 (of 6) DOe 4.00
2 thru 6 DOe . . . . @3.00

ANNA MERCURY
Avatar Press, 2008
1 WEI 4.00
1a variant painted (c) 4.00
1b variant wraparound (c) 4.00
1c auxiliary edition 4.00
1d New York comicon edition 6.00
1e Wizard World Philly edition 6.00
1f Wizard World Chicago edition . . 6.00
2 thru 5 . . . . @4.00
2a thru 5a variant painted (c)s . . @4.00
2b thru 5b variant wraparound(c) @4.00
2c thru 3c auxiliary editions . . . . @4.00
2d Wizard World Philly edition . . . 6.00
2e Wizard World Chicago edition . . 6.00

ANNE RICE'S THE TALE OF THE BODY THIEF
Sicilian Dragon, 1999
1 (of 12) 3.00
2 F:Lestat 3.00
3 thru 7 . . . . @3.00

ANNIE OAKLEY AND TAGG
Gold Key, 1965
1 Ph(c), from TV show 90.00

ANT
Arcana Studios, 2004
1 . . . . 8.00
2 . . . . 5.00
3 thru 4 . . . . @3.50

ANT UNLEASHED
Big City, 2007
1 thru 6 . . . . @4.00
6a variant (c) 4.00

A1/BLOODMOON
Atomeka, 2004
Spec. Mister Monster-Worlds War2 . 7.00
Spec. Mister Monster #2 . . . . 7.00

ANYTHING GOES
Fantagraphics, 1986
1 GK,FlamingCarot,Savage 4.00
2 S:AnM,JK,JSt,SK 3.50
3 DS,NA(c),A:Cerebus 3.50
4 . . . . 3.50
5 A:TMNTurtles 5.00
6 . . . . 3.00

APE NATION
Adventure Comics, 1991
1 Aliens land on Planet of
   the Apes 3.00
2 General Ollo 3.00
3 V:Gen.Ollo,Danada 2.50
4 D:Danada 2.50

APOLLO SMILE
Eagle Wing, 1998
1 When the Levee Breaks 3.00
2 thru 3 . . . . @3.00

ARACHNAPHOBIA
Walt Disney, 1990
1 Movie Adapt. 6.00
1a Newsstand 3.00

ARAKNIS
Mushroom Comics, 1995–96
1 I:Araknis, Shades of Evil pt.1 . . . 3.50
2 Shades of Evil pt.2. . . . . 3.50
3 with pin-ups 2.50
4 . . . . 2.50
Mushroom Comics, 1996
0 Michael & Mario Ortiz 3.00
0 signed 4.00
1 . . . . 2.50
1 special edition 10.00
Mystic Comics
2 thru 6 . . . . @2.50

ARAKNIS: RETRIBUTION
Morning Star Productions, 1997
1 (of 4) by Michael & Mario Ortiz . . 2.50
1 signed 10.00
2 thru 4 . . . . @2.50

ARAKNIS: SHADES OF EVIL
Morning Star Productions
1 . . . . 2.50
2 thru 4 . . . . @2.50

ARCHAIC
Fenickx Productions, 2006
1 . . . . 3.00
2 thru 6 . . . . @3.00

ARCHANGELS: THE FALL
Cahaba Productions, 2005
1 . . . . 4.50
2 . . . . 4.50
3 . . . . 4.50

ARCHANGELS: THE SAGA
Eternal Studios, 1996
1 I:Cameron 2.50
2 V:Demons 2.50
3 and 4 . . . . @2.75
5 and 6 . . . . @2.50
7 . . . . 3.50
8 . . . . 4.50

ARCHARD'S AGENTS
Crossgen Comics, 2002
1 CDi(s) spin-off from Ruse 3.50

ARCHER & ARMSTRONG
Valiant, 1992
0 JiS(s),BWS,BL,I&O:Archer,
   I:Armstrong,The Sec 3.00
0 Gold Ed. 5 . . . . 4.00
1 FM(c),B:JiS(s),BWS,BL,Unity #3,
   A:Eternal Warrior 2.50
2 thru 26 . . . . @2.50

ARCHIE
Archie Publications, 1981
1 thru 300 see Golden Age
301 thru 325 . . . . @6.50
326 Cheryl Blossom 15.00
327 thru 335 . . . . @6.50
336 Michael Jackson 7.00
337 thru 400 . . . . @6.50
401 thru 429 . . . . @5.00
430 thru 529 . . . . @2.50
530 thru 591 . . . . @2.50
Archie's Christmas Stocking #4 . . . 2.50
Archie's Christmas Stocking #5 . . . 2.50
Archie's Christmas Stocking #6 . . . 2.75

Archie #215
© *Archie Publications*

Archie's Christmas Stocking #7 . . . . 3.00
Archie's Spring Break Spec.1 . . . . . 2.50
Archie's Spring Break Spec.2 . . . . . 2.50
Archie's Spring Break Spec.3 . . . . . 2.75
Archie's Spring Break Spec.4(1999) 2.75
Archie's Spring Break Spec.5(2000) 2.50
Archie's Vacation Spec.#4 . . . . 2.50
Archie's Vacation Spec.#5 . . . . 2.50
Archie's Vacation Spec.#6 . . . . 2.50
Archie's Vacation Spec.#7 . . . . 2.50
Archie's Vacation Spec.#8 . . . . 2.50

ARCHIE AND FRIENDS
Archie Publications, 1992
1 thru 10 . . . . @5.00
11 thru 14 . . . . @4.00
15 Babewatch 6.00
16 thru 19 . . . . @4.00
20 Archies Band 5.00
21 thru 48 . . . . @2.50
49 thru 56 Archie & Friends, Featuring
   Josie and the Pussy Cats . . . @2.50
57 thru 125 . . . . @2.50

ARCHIE AND ME
Archie Publications, 1964–87
1 . . . . 325.00
2 . . . . 200.00
3 . . . . 125.00
4 . . . . 100.00
5 . . . . 100.00
6 thru 10 . . . . @75.00
11 thru 20 . . . . @40.00
21 thru 26 . . . . @50.00
27 Superheroes Groovymas 50.00
28 thru 100 . . . . @20.00
101 thru 162 . . . . @15.00

ARCHIE AS PUREHEART THE POWERFUL
Archie Publications, 1966–67
1 superhero parody 200.00
2 . . . . 150.00
3 thru 6 Captain Pureheart . . . @125.00

ARCHIE AT RIVERDALE HIGH
Archie Publications, 1972
1 . . . . 100.00
2 . . . . 75.00
3 . . . . 50.00
4 . . . . 35.00

5	35.00
6 thru 10	@30.00
11 thru 30	@25.00
31 thru 46	@20.00
47 in drag	14.00
48 thru 88	@10.00
89 & 90 Cheryl Blossoms Band	@25.00
91	8.00
92 Cheryl Blossom	14.00
93 thru 95	@8.00
96 Cheryl Blossom	14.00
97 & 98	@8.00
99 Cheryl Blossom	14.00
100 thru 102	@7.00
103 Archie Dates Cheryl Blossom	14.00
104 thru 113	@8.00

ARCHIE COMICS DIGEST
Archie Comics Digest, 1973

1	175.00
2	75.00
3	60.00
4	60.00
5	60.00
6 thru 10	30.00
11 thru 32	@20.00
33 The Fly	25.00
34 thru 135	@6.00
136 Katy Keene	7.00
137 thru 204	@4.00
205 thru 230	@2.50

Archie Meets the Punisher #1
© Archie/Marvel

ARCHIE MEETS
THE PUNISHER
Archie/Marvel, 1994
1-shot crossover, same contents
as Punisher meets Archie 7.00

ARCHIE'S MADHOUSE
Archie Publications, 1959–69

1	500.00
2	300.00
3 thru 5	@200.00
6 thru 10	@150.00
11 thru 16	@100.00
17 thru 21	@75.00
22 I:Sabrina	500.00
23 thru 25 Sabrina	@200.00
26 thru 28	@100.00
29 thru 30	@50.00
31 thru 33 Sabrina	@100.00
34	50.00

35 B	70.00
36 Salem Cat & Sabrina	125.00
37 Sabrina	100.00
38 thru 66	50.00

ARCHIE'S PAL JUGHEAD
SEE: JUGHEAD

ARCHIE'S SUPERHERO
MAGAZINE
Archie Publications, 1979
1 JSm/SK,Rept.Double of Capt.
Strong #1,FLy,Black Hood ... 25.00
2 GM,NA/DG,AMc,I:'70's Black
Hood, Superhero rept ... 30.00

ARCHIE'S TV LAUGH-OUT
Archie Publications, 1969–86

1	200.00
2 giant	125.00
3 thru 6 giant	@60.00
7 Josie	150.00
8 thru 22	@75.00
23 thru 41	@40.00
42 thru 80	@30.00
81 thru 90	@35.00
91 Cheryl Blossom	40.00
92 thru 99	@25.00
100 Michael Jackson	40.00
101 thru 106	@25.00

ARCHIE 3000
Archie Publications, 1989–1991
1 thru 16 .... 2.50

ARCHIE'S WEIRD
MYSTERIES
Archie Comics, 1999
1 from animated series 4.00
2 Shriek 3.00
3 thru 25 .... @3.00
Becomes

ARCHIE'S MYSTERIES
Archie Comics, 2003
26 thru 34 .... @3.00

ARENA, THE
Alchemy, 1990
1 .... 2.50
1a signed, numbered, limited ... 3.00
2 .... 2.50

ARIANE & BLUEBEARD
Eclipse, 1988
Spec. CR 4.00

ARISTOKITTENS, THE
Gold Key, 1971–75

1 Disney	60.00
2	50.00
3	50.00
4	50.00
5 thru 9	@50.00

ARKANIUM
Dreamwave, 2002
1 triple gatefold cover 3.00
2 thru 6 .... @3.00

ARMAGEDDON
Chaos! Comics, 1999
1 (of 4) F:Lady Death, Evil Ernie .. 3.00
1a Premium edition 8.00
2 O:Chaos 3.00
3 .... 3.00
4 concl 3.00

ARMAGEDDON FACTOR
AC Comics, 1987
1 Sentinels of Justice 2.50
2 .... 2.50
3 (1990) 4.00

ARMOR
Continuity, 1985
1 TGr,NA,A:Silver Streak,
silver logo 5.00
1a 2nd printing,red logo 3.00
2 TGr,NA(c) 3.00
3 TGr,NA(c) 3.00
4 TGr,NA(c) 3.00
5 BS,NA(c) 3.00
6 TVE,NA(c) 3.00
7 NA(c) 3.00
8 FS,NA(c) 3.00
9 FS,NA&KN(c) 3.00
10 FS,NA&KN(c) 3.00
11 SDr(i),KN(c) 3.00
12 KN(c) 3.00
13 NA(c),direct sales 3.00
14 KN(c), newsstand 3.00
[2nd Series]
1 V:Hellbender,Trading Card .. 4.00
[3rd Series, Deathwatch 2000]
1 Deathwatch 2000 pt.3,w/card .. 4.00
2 Deathwatch 2000 pt.9,w/card .. 3.00
3 Deathwatch 2000 pt.15,w/card .. 3.00
4 .... 3.00
5 Rise of Magic 3.00
6 Rise of Magic 3.00

ARMORED TROOPER
VOTOMS
CPM Comics, 1996
1 TEI 3.00
2 thru 4 TEI .... @3.00

ARMORINES
Valiant, 1994
0 (from X-O #25),Card Stock (c),
Diamond Dealer Meeting 2.50
0a Gold Ed 3.00
1 JGz(s),JCf,B:White Death ... 2.50
2 thru 12 .... @2.50
Yearbook I:Linoff 3.00
Vol. 2
1 48-pg 4.00
2 .... 4.00
3 and 4 .... @2.50

ARMORQUEST GENESIS
Alias Enterprises, 2005
1 (of 6) 3.00
2 .... 3.00
3 .... 3.00
4 thru 5 .... @3.50

ARMY ATTACK
Charlton, 1964

1 SG	75.00
2 SG	60.00
3 SG	50.00
4	40.00

Vol. 2, 1965
38 thru 47 .... @40.00

ARMY OF DARKNESS
Dynamite Entertainment, 2005
1 Ash vs. Re-Animator 3.00
1a signed 15.00
1b thru 2b Broomstick foil ... 15.00
2 thru 4 .... @3.00
5 Old School 3.00
5a glow-in-the-dark (c) 15.00
5b variant glow-in-the-dark (c) ... 18.00
6 Old School 3.00

6b Glow-in-the-dark (c) 15.00
7 Old School 3.00
8 Ash vs. Dracula, pt.1 . . . . 3.00
9 Ash vs. Dracula, pt. 2 . . . . 3.00
10 . . . . 3.00
11 . . . . 3.00
12 . . . . 3.00
13 Death of Ashley J. Williams 3.00
6a thru 13a variant (c)s . . . . @3.00
Tales of Army of Darkness, Vol. 1 . . 6.00

...ASHES 2 ASHES
Devil's Due Publishing, 2004
1 . . . . 3.00
1a signed 18.00
1b director's cut 1-shot 5.00
2 thru 4 . . . . @3.00
Dynamite Entertainment, 2006
1b director's cut 5.00
1c director's cut foil (c) 18.00
1d photo (c) 7.00
2c variant glow-in-the-dark (c) . . 18.00

...FROM THE ASHES
Dynamite Entertainment, 2007
1 . . . . 3.50
2 thru 4 . . . . @3.50
5 . . . . 3.50
5a variant (c) 3.50
Becomes:

...LONG ROAD HOME
Dynamite Entertainment, 2008
6 thru 11 . . . . @3.50
6a thru 11a variant (c) . . . . @3.50
Becomes:

ARMY OF DARKNESS
Dynamite Entertainment, 2008
12 thru 16 . . . . @3.50
12a thru 16a variant (c)s . . . . @3.50

...SHOP TILL YOU
DROP (DEAD)
Devil's Due Publishing, 2004
1 . . . . 3.00
1a variant(c)s 3.00
2 thru 4 . . . . @3.00
Dynamite Entertainment, 2006
1 . . . . 3.00
1a variant glow-in-the-dark (c) . . 18.00
1d exclusive (c) 7.00
1e enhanced photo (c) 18.00
2 . . . . 3.00
2a variant Fiery red foil(c) 15.00
2b variant special foil (c) 18.00
2c variant glow-in-the-dark (c) . . 18.00
3 . . . . 3.00
3a variant Sabre foil (c) 15.00
3b variant glow-in-the-dark (c) . . 18.00
4 . . . . 3.00
4a variant glow-in-the-dark (c) . . . 9.00

ARMY OF DARKNESS/
XENA: WHY NOT?
Dynamite Entertainment, 2008
1 (of 4) 3.50
1a variant (c) 3.50
2 thru 4 . . . . @3.50

ARMY WAR HEROES
Charlton, 1963–70
1 . . . . 100.00
2 . . . . 40.00
3 thru 21 . . . . @30.00
22 GS,O&I:Iron Corporal 40.00
23 thru 38 . . . . @30.00

ARROW
Malibu, 1992
1 V:Dr.Sheldon,A:Man O'War 2.50

ARROWSMITH
Wildstorm/DC, 2003
1 (of 6) KBk(s),CPa 3.00
2 KBk(s),mystical aviator 3.00
3 KBk(s) thru 6 . . . . @3.00
Spec. Arrowsmith/Astro City 3.00

ARTESIA
Sirius, 1999
1 (of 6) by Mark Smylie 3.00
1a limited edition 10.00
2 thru 6 . . . . @3.00
Ann.#1 . . . . 3.50
Ann.#2 . . . . 4.00

ARTESIA AFIELD
Sirius, 2000
1 (of 6) by Mark Smylie 3.00
1a Limited Ed. 6.00
2 thru 6 . . . . @3.00
Annual #3 Artesia 5.00

ARTESIA AFIRE
Archaia Studios Press, 2003
1 (of 6) by Mark Smylie 4.00
2 . . . . 4.00
3 . . . . 4.00
4 . . . . 4.00
5 . . . . 4.00
6 . . . . 4.00

ARTESIA: BESIEGED
Archaia Studios, 2006
1 (of 6) The Calm Before 4.00
2 The Traitor King 4.00
3 As I Lay Dying 4.00

ASH
Event Comics, 1994
1 JQ,JP,Fire and Crossfire,pt.1 . . 10.00
1a David Finch/Batt(c) 3.00
1b omnichrome commemorative . 12.00
1c omnichrom signed & numbered 25.00
2 JQ,JP,Fire and Crossfire,pt.2 . . . 7.00
2a David Finch/Batt (c) 3.00
3 JQ,JP,Secret of Origin 4.50
4 I:Actor 3.00
5 I:New Character 3.00
6 V:Gabriel 3.00
0 Red Laser ed., Current Ash (c) . . 9.00
0 Red Laser ed., Future Ash (c) . . . 9.00

ASH:
CINDER AND SMOKE
Event Comics, 1997
1 MWa,BAu,HuR,JP 3.00
1a autographed virgin JQ cover . . 10.00
1b signed limited edition 12.00
2 HuR(c) 3.00
2 JQ(c) 3.00
3 (of 6) JQ&JP(c) 3.00
4 (of 6) JQ&JP(c) 3.00
5 (of 6) JQ&JP(c) 3.00
6 (of 6) JQ&JP(c) 3.00
3a thru 6a variant JP&HuR(c)s . . @3.00

ASH FILES, THE
Event Comics, 1997
1 JQ,JP 3.00
1 signed, limited 18.00

ASH: FIRE
AND CROSSFIRE
Event Comics, 1998
1 (of 5) JQ,JP 3.00
1a signed & numbered 20.00
2 . . . . 3.00

ASH: THE FIRE WITHIN
Event Comics, 1996
2 JQ,JP 3.00
3 JQ,JP, Ash Rooftop cover 3.00
3a JQ,JP, Ash Firefighter cover . . . 3.00

ASH/22 BRIDES
Event Comics, 1996
1 FaN,HuR,JP 3.00

ASPEN
Aspen 2003
1 Fathom 5.00
1a variant (c) 16.00
2 Fathom, Soulfire 3.50
2a San Diego 18.00
3 . . . . 3.00
3a Chicago 12.00
Aspen extended edition 9.00
Aspen Sketch Book 9.00
Aspen Swimsuit Special (2006) 9.00

Aspen Seasons Fall 2005 © Aspem

ASPEN SEASONS
Aspen, 2005
1 Spring 2005 . . . . 3.00
1 Fall 2005 . . . . 3.00
1 Summer 2006 . . . . 3.00

ASPEN SHOWCASE
Aspen, 2008
Grace #1 . . . . 3.00
Aspen Matthews #1 . . . . 3.00
Aspen Matthews #1a variant (c) . . . 3.00
Benoist #1 . . . . 3.00
Benoist #1a variant (c) 3.00

ASSASSIN
Archangel Studios, 2003
1 (of 4) 3.00
1a variant (c) 3.00
2 . . . . 3.00

ASSASSINAUTS
Narwain Publishing, 2006
1 . . . . 3.50

ASSASSIN SCHOOL
APC, 2003
1 . . . . 3.50
2 thru 5 . . . . @3.50
S.O.S.(Super one-shot) 6.00

All comics prices listed are for *Near Mint* condition.

Vol. 2 (2004)

0	3.00
1	3.50
2 thru 8	@3.50
8a limited sketch (c) (1:10)	3.50

ASTER
Entity Comics, 1995

0 O:Aster the Celestial Knight	4.50
1 I:Celestial Knight	5.00
1b 2nd printing	3.00
2	3.50
3 V:Tolmek	3.25
3a Variant cover	7.00
4 Final Issue	3.00

ASTER THE LAST CELESTIAL KNIGHT
Entity Comics, 1995

1 R:Aster Chromium Cover	3.00
1a Clear Chromium Edition	4.00
1b Holo Chrome Edition	5.00
2 World Defender	3.00

ASTRO BOY
Gold Key, 1965

1 I:Astro Boy	1,000.00

ASTRO BOY
Now, 1989
Prev. Original Astro Boy

18	3.00
19	3.00
20	3.00

ASTRO CITY
Wildstorm/DC, 2004

Astro City Spec. (2004)	4.00
Spec. A Visitor's Guide (2004)	6.00

...THE DARK AGE
Wildstorm/DC, June, 2005

1 (of 16) KBk(s), BA,AxR(c)	3.00
2 KBk(s),BA,AxR(c)	3.00
3 KBk(s),BA,AxR(c)	3.00
4 KBk(s),BA,AxR(c)	3.00

Book 2, Oct., 2006

1 KBu,BA, Eyes of a Killer	3.00
2 KBu,BA	3.00
3 KBu,BA	3.00
4 KBu,BA, Gangwar erupts	3.00
Spec. #2 Beautie	4.00

ASTRO CITY: LOCAL HEROES
Homage/DC, 2003

1 (of 5) KBk,BA	3.00
2 thru 5 KBk,BA	@3.00

ASTRO CITY: SAMARITAN
Wildstorm/DC, June, 2006

Spec. KBk, BA, 48-pg.	4.00

ASYLUM
Pendragon, 1995

1 thru 3	@3.00

ASYLUM
Maximum Press, 1995

1 Warchild, Beanworld, Avengelyne, Battlestar Galactica	3.00
2 I:Deathkiss	3.00
3	3.00
4 RLd,A:Cybrid	3.00
5 I:Black Seed	3.00
6 R:Steve Austin & Jaime Sommers	3.00

Asylum #3
© Maximum Press

7 RLe,F:Bloodwulf	3.00
8 RLd	3.00
9 RLd	3.00
10	3.00
11	3.00
12 MMy,F:Blindside	3.00
13	3.00

ATHENA VOLTAIRE: FLIGHT OF THE FALCON
Speakeasy Comics, 2006

1	3.00
2 thru 5	@3.00

ATHENA VOLTAIRE: FLIGHT OF THE FLACON
Ape Entertainment, 2006

1 Ape edition, 48-pg.	4.50
2	3.00
3	4.50
4	3.00

ATHENA VOLTAIRE: THE LEGEND OF MU-KING
Ape Entertainment, 2007

1 (of 4)	3.50
2 thru 4	@3.50

ATLANTIS RISING
Platinum Studios 2007

1 (of 5)	3.00
2 thru 3	@3.00
4 thru 5	@4.00

ATLAS
Avatar Press, 2002

1 Gossett (c)	3.50
1b thru 1e variant (c)s	@3.50
2 Brooks (c)	3.50
2b variant (c)	3.50

ATOM ANT
Gold Key, 1966

1	550.00

ATOM-AGE COMBAT
Fago Magazines, 1959

2 Nuclear Sub,A-Bomb	325.00
3 Space Missile	225.00

ATOMIC RABBIT
Charlton Comics, 1955–58

1	350.00
2	150.00
3 thru 10	@100.00
11	150.00

Becomes:

ATOMIC BUNNY
Charlton Comics, 1958

12	150.00
13 thru 18	@100.00
19 Dec., 1959	100.00

ATOMIC MOUSE
Charlton 1984, 1985

1	15.00
10 thru 12	@12.00

ATOMIC ROBO
Red 5 Comics, 2007

1 (of 6)	3.00
2 thru 6	@3.00

ATOMIC ROBO: THE DOGS OF WAR
Red 5 Comics, 2008

1 (of 5)	3.00
2 thru 4	@3.00

ATOMICS, THE
AAA Pop Comics, 1999

1 by Mike Allred	3.00
2 Zapman	3.00
3 Mutant Street Beatniks	3.00
4 refugees from the Innerverse	3.00
5 The Light	3.00
6 The Physical	3.00
7 I:The Skunk	3.00
8 F:The Laser	3.00
9 taken hostage	3.00
10	3.00
11 Heroes divided	3.00
12 with poster	3.50
13 World of Savage Dragon	3.50
14 World of Savage Dragon,pt.4	3.50
15 World of Savage Dragon,pt.5	3.50
16 World of Savage Dragon,pt.6	3.50
King Size Giant	10.00
King-Size Spec. Lessons in Light Lava & Lasers	9.00
King-Size Spec. Jigsaw	10.00
King-Size Vol. 3	9.00
King-Size Vol. 4, 80-page	9.00

ATOMIKA
Speakeasy Comics, 2005

1	3.00
1a signed	20.00
2 thru 6	@3.00
7 thru 9 God is Red	@3.00

ATOMIK ANGELS
Crusade Entertainment, 1996

1 BiT	3.00
1 variant cover (1:25)	5.00
2 BiT	3.00
3 BiT	3.00
4 BiT, conclusion	3.00

ATOMIK MIKE
Alias Enterprises, 2006

1	3.50
2 thru 4	@3.50

ATOMIK MIKE
Desperado Pub., 2007

1 thru 4	@4.00

ATTACK
Charlton Comics, 1958–59
54 100 pages	125.00
55 thru 60	@100.00

ATTACK
Charlton, 1962–64
#n	75.00
2 Jump Into Danger	50.00
3 SG, The Infiltrators	50.00

ATTACK
Charlton, 1971–75
1	35.00
2	20.00
3 thru 5	@12.00
6 thru 15	@10.00
Charlton, 1979
16 thru 20	@7.00
21 thru 48	7.00

ATTACK AT SEA
Charlton, 1968
1	30.00

ATTACK OF THE KILLER TOMATOES, THE
Viper Comics 2008
1 thru 2 (of 3)	@3.25

AUGIE DOGGIE
Gold Key, 1963
1 Hanna-Barbera character	350.00

AUTHORITY, THE
WildStorm/DC, 1999
1 WEl(s),BHi,PNe	12.00
2 WEl(s),BHi,PNe,V:Kaizen Gamorra	10.00
3 WEl(s),BHi,PNe,destruction	10.00
4 WEl(s),BHi,PNe,save L.A.	10.00
5 WEl(s),BHi,PNe,Swiftships,pt.1	10.00
6 WEl(s),BHi,PNe	7.00
7 WEl(s),BHi,PNe	7.00
8 WEl(s),BHi,PNe	7.00
9 WEl(s),BHi,PNe,OuterDark,pt.1	7.00
10 WEl(s),BHi,PNe,OuterDark,pt.2	7.00
11 WEl(s),BHi,PNe,OuterDark,pt.3	7.00
12 WEl(s),BHi,PNe,OuterDark,pt.4	7.00
13 MMr(s),TvS,Nativity,pt.1	11.00
14 MMr(s),TvS,Nativity,pt.2	6.00
15 MMr(s),TvS,Nativity,pt.3	6.00
16 MMr(s),TvS,Nativity,pt.4	6.00
17 MMr(s),TvS,Earth Inferno,pt.1	6.00
18 MMr(s),TvS,Earth Inferno,pt.2	6.00
19 MMr(s),TvS,Earth Inferno,pt.3	6.00
20 MMr(s),TvS,Earth Inferno,pt.4	6.00
21 JMC,All Tomorrow's Parties	6.00
22 MMr(s),TvS,Brave New World	6.00
23 TPe(s),Brave-World,pt.2	6.00
24 TPe(s),BU:Establishment,40-pg	3.50
25 TPe(s),Re-Space	3.50
26 TPe(s),F:Old Authority	3.50
27 MMr(s),New World Order,pt.2	3.50
28 MMr(s),AAd,F:Seth	3.50
29 New World Order,pt.4	3.50
Ann. 2000 #1, Devil's Night x-over, pt.2	5.00
GN The Authority: Kev (2002)	5.00
GN Scorched Earth	5.00
Volume 2
1 DT,F:Jack Hawksmoor, etc.	4.00
2 thru 13 DT	@3.00
14 WPo,Jack Hawksmore origin	3.00
Spec. #0, 40-pg.	3.00
X-Mas Spec. The Authority/Lobo x-over, 48-pg. (2003)	5.00
Spec. Authority/Lobo Spring Break Massacre, SBs, 48-page	5.00

The Authority #13 © Wildstorm

AUTHORITY, THE
Wildstorm/DC, Oct., 2006
1 GMo	3.00
1a variant (c)	3.00
2 GMo	3.00
Wildstorm/DC, Aug., 2008
1 World's End	3.00
2 The Carrier under siege	3.00
3 Midnighter vs. Army of the Mad	3.00
4 Rendlesham viral outbreak	3.00

...MAGNIFICENT KEVIN
Wildstorm, Sept., 2005
1 (of 5) GEn,F:Kev Hawkins	3.00
2 thru 5	@3.00

...MORE KEV
Wildstorm/DC, 2004
1 (of 4) GEn(s),GF	3.00
2 thru 4 GEn(s),GF	@3.00

...PRIME
Wildstorm/DC, Oct., 2007
1 DaR,Stormwatch vs. Authority	3.00
2 DaR,Stormwatch vs. Authority	3.00
3 DaR,Midnighter	3.00
4 DaR,Apollo and Midnighter	3.00
5 DaR,Apollo and Midnighter	3.00
6 DaR, new monster	3.00

...REVOLUTION
Wildstorm/DC, 2004
1	3.00
2	3.00
3 America in Revolution	3.00
4 War in Washington	3.00
5 Nation's capitol in rubble	3.00
6 thru 12 concl.	@3.00

AUTOMATIC KAFKA
Wildstorm/DC, 2002
1 JoC, Eye of the Storm	3.00
2 JoC,NPS agents	3.00
3 JoC,TV game show host	3.00
4 JoC	3.00
5 JoC	3.00
6 JoC	3.00
7 JoC,who is Galaxia	3.00
8 thru 9 JoC	@3.00

AVENGEBLADE
Maximum Press, 1996
1 RLe	3.00
2 RLe	3.00

AVENGELYNE
Maximum Press, 1995
1 RLd,I:Avengelyne Dir ed.	12.00
1a Newstand Edition	5.00
1b Holochrome Edition	15.00
1 gold edition	10.00
2 V:B'Lial	4.00
3 I:Magogi	4.00
3 variant cover, pin-up	5.00
Regular Series, 1996
0 RLd,O:Avengelyne	5.00
1 RLd,BNa,F:Devlin	4.00
1 variant photo cover	4.00
2 I:Darkchylde	10.00
2a variant photo cover	12.00
3	3.50
4 A:Cybrid	3.50
5 A:Cybrid,	3.50
6 RLd,F:Divinity	3.50
7 RLd,F:Divinity	3.50
8 RLd,	3.50
9 RLd,	3.50
10 BNa,The Possession, pt.1	3.50
11 BNa,The Possession, pt.2	3.50
12 BNa,The Possession, pt.3	3.50
13 BNa,The Possession, pt.4	3.50
14 A:Bloodwulf	3.50
15 A:Glory, Prophet	3.50
Swimsuit Edition	3.50
Swimsuit book, American Entertainment exclusive	7.50

AVENGELYNE
Awesome Entertainment, 1999
Prelude	3.00
1 RLe,RNa	3.00
1a, b & c variant covers	3.00
2 RLe,	3.00
3	3.50
Spec. Swimsuit, 1999	3.50
Spec.#1-shot Demonslayer (2000)	3.00
Spec.#1a Demonslayer variant (c)	3.00
Spec.#1b Demonslayer variant (c)	3.00
Spec.#1c Demonslayer variant (c).	3.00

...ARMAGEDDON
Maximum Press, 1996–97
1 (of 3) RLd	3.00
2 RLd,	3.00
3 BNa,ScC, finale	3.00

...BAD BLOOD
Avatar, 2000
1 Matt Haley (c)	3.50
1a thru 1b variant(c)s	@3.50
1c prism foil (c) previews excl.	13.00
1d Al Rio velvet (c)	20.00
1e leather (c)	25.00
1f platinum (c)	8.00
1g Ruby Red ed.	20.00
2	3.50
2a variant(c)s	@3.50
Prelude Rick Lyon (c)	5.00
Prelude Al Rio (c)	5.00
Prelude Bikini (c)	6.00
Prelude prism foil(c) 16-page	13.00
Prelude variant SSh(c),	6.00

...BIBLE: REVELATIONS
Maximum Press
one-shot RLd,	3.50

...DARK DEPTHS
Avatar Press, 2001
1 (of 2) Rio(c)	3.50
1a MMy(c)	3.50
1b Martin (c)	3.50
1c blue velvet (c)	25.00
1d prism foil exclusive (c)	13.00
1e Heavenly Body edition	6.00
1f Royal Blue (c)	75.00
2 (of 2) Rio(c)	3.50

2a MMy(c)............... 3.50
2b Lyon (c)............... 3.50
2c Blue leather (c)........... 25.00
1/2 Rio (c) 16-page........... 5.00
1/2 Lloyd painted (c)........... 5.00
1/2 Frillion (c)............. 5.00
1/2 Midnight Prayer (c)........ 6.00
1/2 Prism foil exclusive (c)...... 13.00

...DEADLY SINS
Maximum Press, 1996
1 RLd (c)................. 3.00
1 photo (c)............... 3.00
2 RLd(c)................. 3.00

...DRAGON REALM
Avatar Press, 2001
1/2 Rio (c)............... 5.00
1/2 Carrie Hall (c)........... 5.00
1/2 Lloyd (c)............. 5.00
1/2 Martin (c)............. 5.00
1/2 Dying Breath ed......... 6.00
1/2 Prism foil ed........... 13.00
1 (of 2) Rio (c)............ 3.50
1a thru 1b variant(c)s....... @3.50
1c red leather (c)........... 25.00
1d bondage (c)............ 6.00
1e prism foil (c)........... 13.00
1f venomous edition........ 6.00
1g venomous emerald foil..... 14.00
1h Fearless edition......... 5.00
2 Rio(c)................ 3.50
2a thru 2b variant(c)s....... @3.50
2c Shaw (c).............. 3.50
2d Ron Adrian (c).......... 6.00

...GLORY
Maximum Press, 1995
1 V:B'Lial................ 4.00
1a variant cover........... 5.00
Swimsuit Spec. #1.......... 3.00

.../GLORY: THE GODYSSEY
Maximum Press, 1996
1 RLd,BNa............... 3.00
2 thru 5 RLd.............. @3.00

.../PANDORA
Avatar, 2000
Spec. x-over.............. 3.50
Spec.Preview exclusive....... 3.50
Spec.Preview Bikini ed........ 6.00
Spec.McDaniel (c).......... 6.00
Spec.Previews exlusive Prism ed.. 13.00
Spec.Red Velvet............ 25.00
Spec.Ruby Red edition....... 20.00
Spec.Royal Blue........... 75.00

Avengelyne/Power #2
© Maximum Press

.../POWER
Maximum Press, 1995–96
1 RLd,V:Hollywood.......... 3.00
1 variant cover............ 3.50
2 RLd(c)................ 3.00
3..................... 3.00
3a photo (c).............. 3.00

.../PROPHET
Maximum Press, 1996
1 RLd,BNa,MD2............ 3.00
Awesome Entertainment, 2000
Rage of Furies #1 RLe(c)....... 3.00
  #1a IaC(c)............. 3.00
  #1b Grant(c)........... 3.00
  #1c Walker Bros.(c)....... 3.00
  #1d Wizard world ed....... 5.00
  #1e Wizard world, signed.... 10.00

...REVELATION
Avatar, 2000
1 Rio (c)................ 3.50
1a Haley (c).............. 3.50
1b Wraparound (c).......... 3.50
1c leather (c)............. 20.00
1d Matt Martin (c).......... 6.00
1e royal blue (c)........... 60.00
Previews prism foil (c)....... 13.00
Prelude Lyon (c)........... 6.00
Prelude platinum signed...... 11.00

...SERAPHACIDE
Avatar Press, 2001
1/2 Lyon (c).............. 5.00
1/2 Variant (c)s............ @5.00
1/2 Bound edition........... 6.00
1/2 Pax Romana (c)......... 6.00
1/2 Ron Adrian (c).......... 6.00
1 (of 2) Rio (c)............ 3.50
1a thru 1c variant (c)s....... @3.50
1d White Velvet (c)......... 20.00
1e Adam & Eve edition....... 6.00
1f Hard Woman (c).......... 6.00
1g Bikini (c).............. 6.00

.../SHI
Avatar Press, 2001
1/2 RLd (c) 16-page......... 4.00
1/2 variant(c)s............ @4.00
1/2d Victory (c)........... 6.00
1/2e Sean Shaw, Cross cover.... 6.00
1 Finch (c) x-over.......... 3.50
1a variant(c)s............ @3.50
1e Red Leather (c)......... 20.00
1f Prism foil (c).......... 13.00
1h Waller (c)............. 6.00
1i Face off cover.......... 6.00
1j ruby red edition.......... 25.00

.../SUPREMA
Awesome Entertainment, 2000
Rage of Furies #1 (2000)........ 4.00
  1a Wizard world ed......... 5.00
  1b signed.............. 10.00

.../WARRIOR NUN AREALA
Maximum Press, 1997
Spec................... 3.00
Awesome Entertainment, 1997
Spec. #2 The Nazarene Affair..... 3.00

AVENGERS, THE
Gold Key, 1968
1.................. 500.00

AWAKENING, THE
Archaia Studios, 2007
1 (of 10)................ 3.50
2.................... 3.50
3 thru 5................ @3.50

AWESOME
Awesome Entertainment, 1997
Holiday Spec. #1........... 2.50
Holiday Spec.'99........... 5.00
Spring '99 Tourbook......... 5.00

AXA
Eclipse, 1987
1 The Adopted............. 4.00
2 The Donor.............. 3.50

AXEL PRESSBUTTON
Eclipse, 1984
1 BB(c),Origin............. 3.00
2 SD,Wanted for Mass Murder.... 3.00
3 AD,Wanted for Mass Murder.... 3.00
4 TA,.................. 3.00
5 AD,Slave of the Narco-Pollen... 2.50
6 TA,Days in Downtown Delta Five 2.50

AXIS ALPHA
Axis Comics, 1994
1 LSn,I:BEASTIES,Dethgrip,
  Shelter,W.............. 3.00

AYA
Studio G, 2003
1..................... 3.00
2 thru 4................ @3.00

AYA
AK Entertainment, 2006
1 Clone Order, pt.1.......... 3.00
2 Clone Order: Resurrection..... 3.00
3 Clone Order: A Pharaoh Reborn. 3.00
4 One Bullet............. 3.00
5 Zero Tolerance, pt. 2........ 3.00
6 Zero Tolerance........... 3.00
7 thru 9................ @3.00

AZTEC ACE
Eclipse, 1984
1 NR(i),I:AztecAce........... 3.50
2 NR(i)................. 3.50
3 thru 9 NR(i)............ @3.00
10 NR(i)................ 3.00
11.................... 3.50
12 thru 15............... @2.50

BABES OF BROADWAY
Broadway, 1996
1..................... 3.00

BABY HUEY
Harvey, 1991
1..................... 7.00
2..................... 3.00
3 thru 9................ @3.00

...THE BABY GIANT
Harvey Publications, 1956–80
1.................. 900.00
2.................. 400.00
3 Anti-Pep Pills........... 300.00
4.................. 200.00
5.................. 200.00
6 thru 10.............. @150.00
11 thru 20............. @100.00
21 thru 40............. @75.00
41 thru 60............. @50.00
61 thru 79............. @40.00
80.................. 40.00
81 thru 95 giant size....... @50.00
96 Giant size............ 40.00
97 Giant size............ 40.00
98.................. 30.00
99.................. 15.00
100.................. 5.00
101.................. 5.00

...AND PAPA
Harvey Publications, 1962–68
1	350.00
2	250.00
3	200.00
4	200.00
5	200.00
6 thru 10	@150.00
11 thru 20	@100.00
21 thru 33	@75.00

...DUCKLAND
Harvey Publications, 1962–66
1	250.00
2 thru 5	@100.00
6 thru 10	@75.00
11 thru 20	@50.00
21 thru 33	@40.00

BABY SNOOTS
Gold Key, 1970
1 F:Uptite Mouse	40.00
2	20.00
3 thru 10	@20.00
11 thru 22	@12.00

BACHELOR FATHER
Dell Publishing Co., 1962
1	150.00
2	125.00

BACK TO THE FUTURE
Harvey, 1991
1 Chicago 1927	3.00
2 Cretaceous Period	3.00
3 World War I	3.00
4 Doc Retires	3.00

BAD COMPANY
Quality, 1988
1	3.00
2 thru 19	@3.00

BAD EGGS
Acclaim, 1996
1 thru 4 BL,DP,That Dirty Yellow Mustard	@3.00

BADGER
Capital, 1983
1 JBt,I:Badger,Ham,Daisy Yak,Yeti.	5.00
2 JBt,I:Riley,A:YakYeti	4.00
3 JBt,O:Badger,Ham	4.00
4 JBt,A'Ham	4.00

First, 1984–91
5 thru 16 BR	@3.00
17 JBt,I:Lamont	3.50
18 thru 39	@3.00
40 thru 49 RLm,	@3.50
50 RLm,TRoof off SuckerII	5.00
51 RLm,V:Demon	3.00
52 thru 54 TV	@4.00
55 thru 70	@3.00
Graphic Nov.BR,I:Mazis Sykes,D:Hodag	10.00
Badger Bedlam	5.00

...GOES BERSERK
First, 1989
1 I:Larry,Jessie	4.00
2 MZ,V:Larry,Jessie	3.50
3 JBt/MZ,V:Larry,Jessie	3.00
4 JBt/MZ,V:Larry,Jessie	3.00

...SAVES THE WORLD
IDW, 2007
1	4.00
2 thru 5	@4.00

BAD GIRLS OF BLACKOUT
Blackout Comics, 1995
0	3.50
1 I:Ms. Cyanide, Ice	3.50
Ann.#1 Hari Kari, Lady Vampre	3.50
Ann.#1 Commemorative ed.	10.00

BAD KITTY
Chaos! Comics, 2001
1 BnP	3.00
1a premium edition	9.00
2	3.00
3	3.00
Ashcan	6.00
Script #1	5.00
Script #1 premium	20.00

...MISCHIEF NIGHT
Chaos! Comics, 2001
1	3.00
1a premium edition	13.00
1b super premium edition	20.00

...RELOADED
Chaos! Comics, 2001
1	3.00
1a premium ed.	9.00
2 F:Chastity	3.00
3	3.00
4	4.00
2a thru 4a variant (c).	@7.50

BAD MOON RISING
Avatar Press, 2006
1	4.00
1a variant (c)s	@4.00

BADROCK/WOLVERINE
Awesome Entertainment, 1997
Spec. #1 JV,CYp,V:Sauron,48pg	5.00

BAKER STREET
Caliber, 1989
1	3.00
2 thru 10	@3.00

BALLAD OF HALO JONES
Quality, 1987
1 IG Alan Moore story	2.50
1a IG rep.	2.50
2 thru 12	@2.50

BALLAD OF SLEEPING BEAUTY, THE
Beckett Comics, 2004
1	2.50
2 thru 4	@2.50
5 thru 8	@2.50

BALOO & LITTLE BRITCHES
Gold Key, 1968
1 From Disney's Jungle Book	50.00

BAMBI
Gold Key, 1963
1 From Disney movie	100.00

BAMM-BAMM & PEBBLES FLINTSTONE
Gold Key, 1964
1	200.00

BANANA SPLITS, THE
Gold Key, 1969
1 From Hanna-Barbera	200.00
2	150.00
3 thru 8	@150.00

BANZAI GIRL
Sirius Entertainment, 2002
Preview book, lim. ed.	5.00
1 (of 4) by Jinky Coronado	3.00
2 thru 4	@3.00
2a thru 4a lim.,signed,ph(c)	@12.00
3	3.00
4	3.00
Ann. #1.	3.50
Fabulous Foto Book.	4.00

BANZAI GIRLS
Arcana Studio, 2007
1	4.00
2 thru 4	@4.00

Barbarians #1
© Atlas

BARBARIANS, THE
Atlas, 1975
1 O: Andrax,F:Iron Jaw	50.00

BARBAROSSA AND THE LOST CORSAIRS
Kandora Publishing, 2005
1	3.50
2 thru 5	@3.50

BARBIE & KEN
Dell Publishing Co. 1962
1	800.00
2	650.00
3	650.00
4	650.00
5	675.00

BARBIE TWINS ADVENTURES, THE
Topps, 1995
1 I:Shane, Sia	3.00

BARBI TWINS ADVENTURES
Studio Chikara, 1998
Color Spec. The Roswell Incident	4.00

BARNEY AND BETTY RUBBLE
Charlton Comics, 1973–76
1	60.00
2 thru 5	@30.00
6 thru 10	@25.00
11 thru 23	@20.00

BARNEY GOOGLE AND SNUFFY SMITH
Gold Key, 1964
1	65.00

Charlton, 1970
1	35.00
2	20.00
3 thru 6	@20.00

BARRY M. GOLDWATER
Dell Publishing Co., 1965
1	75.00

BAR SINISTER
Acclaim Windjammer, 1995
1 From Shaman's Tears	2.50
2 V:SWAT Team	2.50
3 F: Animus Prime	2.50
4 MGe,RHo,V:Jabbersnatch	2.50

BARTHOLOMEW OF THE SCISSORS
Bluewater Prod., 2008
1 (of 4)	4.00
2 thru 3	@4.00

BART-MAN
Bongo, 1993
1 Foil(c),I:Bart-Man	4.00
2 I:Penalizer	2.50
3 When Bongos Collide,pt.3, with card	2.50
4 Crime-Time,pt.1	2.50
5 Bad Guys Strike Back	2.50

BART SIMPSON COMICS
Bongo Comics, 2000
1	3.00
2 thru 9	@3.00
10 thru 26	@3.00
27 thru 39	@3.00

BART SIMPSONS TREEHOUSE OF HORROR
Bongo Comics, 1995
1 Bart People	3.00
2 thru 4	@3.00
5 48-pg.	3.50
6 and 7 64-page	@3.50
8	@3.50
9 thru 13	@5.00
1-shot Treehouse of Terror	2.50

BASEBALL
Kitchen Sink, 1991
1 WE (c) reprint of 1949 orig.	4.00
2 Ray Gotto (c), w/4 BB cards	3.00

BAT, THE
Adventure
1 R:The Bat,inspiration for Batman says Bob Kane	3.00

BATMAN/DANGER GIRL
Wildstorm/DC, Dec. 2004
1-shot x-over, 48-page	5.00

BAT MASTERSON
Dell, 1960
1	225.00
2	125.00
3 thru 8	@125.00

BATTLEBOOKS
Battlebooks Inc., 1999
all BTi(c)
Bubba-Busters Battlebook	5.00
Captain America Battlebook Blue print, signed edition	9.00
Colossus Battlebook	4.00
Daredevil Battlebook BTi(c)	4.00
Daredevil Battlebook JQ&JP(c)	4.00
Darkchylde A Battlebook	4.00
Darkchylde B Battlebook	4.00
The Darkness Battlebook	4.00
Dr. Doom Battlebook	4.00
Elektra Battlebook	4.00
Blue print, signed edition	12.00
Elektra Battlebook, revised	4.00
Gambit Battlebook	4.00
Green Goblin Battlebook	4.00
Iron Man Battlebook Blue print, signed edition	12.00
The Incredible Hulk Battlebook	4.00
Blue print, signed edition	12.00
Magneto Battlebook	4.00
President Clinton Battlebook	5.00
Rogue Battlebook	4.00
Blue print, signed edition	12.00
Sabretooth Battlebook	4.00
Shi: The Spirit of Benkei Battlebook	4.00
Blue print, signed edition	9.00
Spider-Man Battlebook Blue print, signed edition	12.00
Storm Battlebook	4.00
The Thing Battlebook	4.00
Tomoe: Fan's of Fury Battlebook	4.00
Vampirella Hell on Earth Battlebook	4.00
White Queen Battlebook	4.00
Witchblade Battlebook	4.00
Wolverine Battlebook	4.00
Wolverine with Bone Claws Battlebook Blue print, signed edition	13.00

BATTLEFIELD ACTION
Charlton, 1960–66
16 thru 30 See Golden Age	
31 thru 62	@25.00

Charlton, 1980–84
63 thru 89	@7.00

Battle of the Planets #7
© Whitman

BATTLE OF THE PLANETS
Gold Key, 1979
1 TV Cartoon	50.00
2 thru 5	@35.00

Whitman, 1980
6	20.00
7 thru 10	@20.00

BATTLER BRITTON
Wildstorm/DC, July 2006
1 GEn,CWi	3.00
2 thru 5 GEn,CWi	@3.00

BATTLESTAR GALACTICA
Maximum Press, 1995
1 Finds Earth	5.00
2 Council of Twelve	4.00
3 R:Adama	4.00
4 Pyramid Secrets	4.00
Spec. Ed. Painted Book (1997)	3.00
Battlestar Galactica: The Compendium #1 rep. from Asylum	3.00

BATTLESTAR GALACTICA
Realm Press, 1997
1 by Chris Scalf	4.00
1a variant cover	3.00
2 Law of Volhad	3.00
3 Prison of Souls, pt.1	3.00
3a alternate cover	3.00
4 Prison of Souls, pt.2	3.00
5	3.00
6 A Path of Darkness, pt.1	3.00
7 A Path of Darkness, pt.2	3.00
7a photo (c).	3.00
7b signed and numbered	6.00
8 Centurion Prime	3.00
Spec.#1 20 Yahren Reunion	5.00
Spec.#1 No Memory of Earth	3.00
Spec.#1 CenturionPrime,Scott(c)	3.00
Spec.#1 CenturionPrime,Parsons(c)	3.00
Spec.#2 Centurion Prime	3.00
Spec. 1999 Tourbook	3.00
Spec. 1999 Tourbook con. ed.	7.00
Spec. 1999 Tourbook sign.	30.00
Spec. Gallery #1	4.00
Tech Journal: The Galactica	4.00
Tech Journal: Ships of Fleet	4.00
Spec.No Man's Land	4.00
Spec.No Man's Land, deluxe	5.00
Cylon Dawn Spec. (2000)	4.00
Cylon Dawn Spec. deluxe	5.00
Darkest Night Spec. (2000)	4.00
Darkest Night Spec. variant (c)	5.00
Dire Prophecy Spec. (2000)	4.00
Dire Prophecy Spec. deluxe	5.00
Eve of Destruction Prelude(1999)	4.00
Spec.#1 Triad Triumph (2000)	4.00
Spec.#1a Triad Triumph,deluxe	5.00

BATTLESTAR GALACTICA
Dynamite Entertainment, 2006
0	1.00
1	3.00
1a photo foil	20.00
2 thru 12	@3.00
1a thru 12a variant (c)s	@3.00
2b thru 5b variant Cylon foil (c)s	@20.00

...APOLLO'S JOURNEY
Maximum Press, 1996
1 story by Richard Hatch	3.00
2	2.50
3	2.50

...CYLON APOCALYPSE
Dynamite Entertainment, 2007
1	3.50

1a variant (c)s . . . . @3.50
2 thru 4 . . . . @3.50
2a thru 4a variant (c)s. . . . . . . @3.50

...THE ENEMY WITHIN
Maximum Press, 1996
1 . . . . 3.00
2 thru 3 . . . . @2.50

...GHOSTS
Dynamite Entertainment, 2007
1 (of 4) 3.50
2 thru 3 . . . . @3.50

...JOURNEY'S END
Maximum Press, 1996
1 (of 4) RLd. 3.00
2 RLd 3.00
3 RLd, the end of Galactica? 3.00
4 RLd, conclusion 3.00

...ORIGINS
Dynamite Entertainment, 2007
2 thru 11 . . . . @3.50
2a thru 11a variant (c)s . . . . @3.50

...PEGASUS
Dynamite Entertainment, 2007
1-shot 5.00

Battlestar Galactica: Search For Sanctuary #1 © Realm Press

...SEARCH FOR SANCTUARY
Realm Press, 1998
1 (of 4) 3.00
2 Path of Darkness. 3.00
3 tensions grow. 3.00
4 . . . . 3.00

...STARBUCK
Maximum Press, 1997
1 (of 3) RLd. 3.00
2 RLd 3.00
3 RLd, the end of Galactica? 3.00

...ZAREK
Dynamite Entertainment, 2006
1 . . . . 3.50
1a photo foil (c) 5.00
2 thru 4 . . . . @3.50
2a thru 4a variant (c)s. . . . . @3.50

BATTLESTAR GALACTICA

SEASON THREE
Real Press, 1999
1 . . . . 3.00

1a alternate JaL(c) 5.00
1b Cylon Attack (c) 5.00
1c Cylon Attack (c) signed 30.00
2 . . . . 3.00
2a alternate cover. 5.00
2b pencil sketch cover 5.00
2c convention edition 5.00
3 Fire in the Sky 3.00
3a alternate cover. 5.00
3b convention edition 5.00
4 Scott (c) 3.00
5 Busch (c) 3.00
6 . . . . 3.00
7 . . . . 3.00
8 . . . . 3.00
4a thru 6a variant(c) . . . . @3.00
7a & 8a deluxe . . . . @5.00
Spec. 80-page Juggernaut. 9.00
Tour Book Sketch ed.. . . . . 25.00

...SEASON ZERO
Dynamite Entertainment, 2007
1 . . . . 3.00
1a variant (c) 3.00
2 thru 5 . . . . @3.00
2a thru 5a variant (c)s. . . . . @3.00
6 thru 12 . . . . @3.00
6a thru 12a variant (c)s . . . . @3.00

BATTLETECH
Blackthorne, 1987
1 . . . . 3.00
2 thru 6 . . . . @3.00
(Changed to Black & White)
1 3-D. 3.00
2 3-D. 3.00

BATTLETECH: FALLOUT
Malibu, Dec. 1994–Mar. 1995
0 Battletech. 3.00
1 3 tales, Based on FASA game. . . 3.00
1a gold foil limited edition 3.50
1b limited holographic editon 5.00
2 V:Clan Jade Falcon 3.00
3 R:Lea 3.00
4 Conclusion 3.00

BAY CITY JIVE
WildStorm/DC, 2001
1 (of 3) F:Sugah Rollins 3.00
1a variant (c) (1:4) 3.00
2 1976 streets of San Francisco. . . 3.00
3 Hell on Earth, concl. 3.00

BEAGLE BOYS, THE
Gold Key, 1964–79
1 . . . . 75.00
2 thru 5 . . . . @50.00
6 thru 10 . . . . @40.00
11 thru 20 . . . . @30.00
21 thru 47 . . . . @25.00

BEAGLE BOYS VERSUS UNCLE SCROOGE, THE
Gold Key, 1979
1 Case of the Missing Nuggets . . 20.00
2 There's Cash in the Trash 10.00
3 The Armored Car Caper 10.00
4 The Great Gift Grab 10.00
5 The Buccaneer's Map 10.00
6 The Foot Brake Fiasco 10.00
7 Vacation With Pay 10.00
8 Danger at Fifty Fathoms 10.00
9 The Bewitched Buck Baggers . . 10.00
10 The Frame-Up 10.00
11 Freebies Can be Costly 10.00
12 Number One Dollar. 10.00

BEANIE THE MEANIE
Fago Publications, 1958
1 . . . . 50.00
2 thru 3 . . . . @50.00

BEANY AND CECIL
Dell, 1962
1 . . . . 250.00
2 thru 5 . . . . @200.00

B.E.A.S.T.I.E.S.
Axis Comics, 1994
1 JS(a&s),I:Beasties 2.50

THE BEATLES, LIFE STORY
Dell Publishing Co., 1964
1 . . . . 1,000.00

BEAUTIFUL KILLER
Black Bull Entertainment, 2001
1 JP(s) 5.00
1a variant (c). 4.00
2 JP(s) 4.00
3 JP(s) 4.00
Preview Edition, limited 5.00

BEAUTY, THE
Beckett Comics, 2004
1 . . . . 2.50
2 thru 4 . . . . @2.50
5 thru 8 . . . . @2.50

BEAUTY AND THE BEAST
Innovation, 1993
1 From TV series 3.00
1a Deluxe 4.00
2 thru 7 . . . . @3.00

BEAUTY AND THE BEAST PORTRAIT OF LOVE
First, 1989–90
1 WP,TV tie in 9.00
2 . . . . 8.00
Book II:Night of Beauty 6.00

BEAUTY AND THE BEAST
Walt Disney, 1992
Movie adapt.(Prestige). 5.00
Movie adapt.(newsstand). 3.00
mini-series
1 Bewitched 3.00
2 Elsewhere 3.00
3 A:Catherine 3.00

BEDLAM!
Eclipse, 1985
1 SBi,RV,reprint horror 3.00
2 SBi,RV,reprint horror 3.00

BEEP BEEP
Dell, 1960
4 . . . . 85.00
5 . . . . 50.00
6 thru 14 . . . . @35.00

BEEP BEEP THE ROAD RUNNER
Gold Key, 1966
1 . . . . 50.00
2 thru 5 . . . . @35.00
6 thru 9 . . . . @25.00
10 thru 88 . . . . @15.00
Whitman, 1980
89 . . . . 10.00
90 thru 105. . . . . @25.00

COLOR PUB.

All comics prices listed are for *Near Mint* condition.

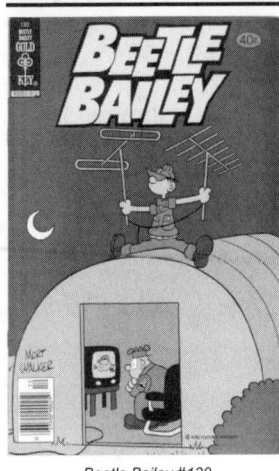

Beetle Bailey #130
© *Gold Key*

BEETLE BAILEY
Dell, 1956–62
5	75.00
6 thru 9	@50.00
10 thru 38	@35.00

Gold Key, 1962–66
39 thru 53	@30.00

King, 1966–67
54 thru 65	@25.00

Charlton, 1969–76
67	25.00
68 thru 119	@22.00

Gold Key, 1978
120	7.00
121 thru 131	@7.00

Whitman, 1980
132	7.00

BEETLE BAILEY
Harvey, 1992
1 F:Mort Walker's B.Bailey	4.00
2 Beetle builds a bridge	3.00
3 thru 12	@3.00

BEETLEJUICE
Harvey, 1991
1 EC,This is your lice	3.00
Holiday Special #1	3.00

BEN CASEY
**Dell Publishing Co.,
June-July, 1962**
1 Ph(c)	125.00
2 Ph(c)	100.00
3 Ph(c)	75.00
4 Drug, Ph(c)	100.00
5 Ph(c)	75.00
6 thru 10 Ph(c)	@75.00

BEOWULF
Speakeasy Comics, 2005
1	3.00
2 thru 6	@3.00
7 Altered States	3.00
8 Altered States	3.00
9 Mortal Coil, pt.1	3.00
10 Mortal Coil. pt.2	3.00
11 Epochs, pt.1	3.00
12 Epochs	3.00

Antarctic Press, 2006
1 (of 3)	3.50
2	3.50

3	3.50

IDW Publishing, 2007
1	4.00
2 thru 4	@4.00

BERNI WRIGHTSON MASTER OF THE MACABRE
Pacific, 1983
1 BWr	6.00
2 BWr	4.00
3 BWr	3.50
4 BWr	3.50

Eclipse, 1984
5 BWr	3.50

BEST CELLARS
Out of the Cellers, 1995
1 Eric Powells (1)	35.00

BEST OF BUGS BUNNY
Gold Key, 1966–68
1 Both Giants	100.00
2	75.00

BEST OF DENNIS THE MENACE, THE
**Hallden/Fawcett Publ.,
Summer, 1959–Spring, 1961**
1	150.00
2	100.00
3 thru 5	@100.00

BEST OF DONALD DUCK & UNCLE SCROOGE
Gold Key, 1964–67
1	175.00
2	125.00

BEST OF DONALD DUCK
Gold Key, 1965
1	150.00

BETTI COZMO
Antarctic Press, 1999
1 (of 3)	3.00
2	3.00
3 Raygun For Hire	3.00

BETTY
Archie Publications, 1992
1	@6.00
2 thru 39	@4.00
40 thru 60	@4.00
61 thru 80	@3.00
81 thru 100	@3.00
101 thru 142	@3.00
143 thru 177	@2.50

BETTY AND ME
Archie Publications, 1965–92
1	175.00
2	100.00
3 O:Superteen	110.00
4 thru 8 Superteen	@75.00
9 & 10	60.00
11 thru 21	@50.00
22 Archie Band	50.00
23 thru 37	@40.00
38 Sabrina	60.00
39 Josie & Sabrina	50.00
40 Archie & Betty in Cabin	35.00
41	35.00
42 Betty Vamp	35.00
43 thru 55	@30.00
56 thru 200	@15.00

BETTY AND VERONICA
Archie Publications, 1987
1	10.00
2 thru 10	@6.00
11 thru 50	@5.00
51 thru 104	@4.00
105 thru 119	@3.00
120 thru 141	@5.00
142 thru 160	@3.00
161 thru 181	@3.00
182 thru 203	@3.00
204 thru 231	@2.50
Summer Fun Special #5	3.00
Summer Fun Special #6	3.00
Summer Fun Special #7	3.00

BETTY & VERONICA SPECTACULAR
Archie Publications, 1992
1 thru 25	@3.00
26 thru 40	@3.00
41 thru 57	@3.00
58 thru 68	@3.00
69 thru 86	@2.25

BEVERLY HILLBILLYS
**Dell Publishing Co.,
April-June, 1963**
1 Ph(c)	300.00
2 Ph(c)	175.00
3 Ph(c)	150.00
4 Ph(c)	100.00
5 thru 9 Ph(c)	@150.00
10	100.00
11 thru 14 Ph(c)	@150.00
15 thru 21 Ph(c)	@100.00

BEWITCHED
**Dell Publishing Co.,
April-June, 1965**
1 Ph(c)	300.00
2	200.00
3 thru 13 Ph(c)	@125.00
14	100.00

BEYOND THE GRAVE
Charlton Comics, 1975–76
1 SD,TS(c),P(c)	60.00
2 thru 6	@35.00

Charlton Comics, 1983–84
7 thru 17	@30.00

BEYOND WONDERLAND
Zenescope Entertainment, 2008
0	1.00
1	3.00
2 thru 4	@3.00

BIG BADZ
Platinum Studios, 2008
1 (of 4)	4.00
2 thru 4	@4.00

BIG BANG
Caliber Press, 1994
0 Whole Timeline inc.	3.00
1 thru 3	@2.50
4 25 years after #3	2.50

BIGFOOT
IDW Publishing, 2005
1 thru 4	@4.00

BIG VALLEY, THE
Dell Publishing Co., 1966
1 Ph(c)	100.00
2 thru 6	@75.00

BILL BLACK'S
FUN COMICS
AC Comics
1 Cpt.Paragon,B&W 3.00
2 and 3 B&W. . . . . @2.50
4 Color 2.50

BILL
THE GALACTIC HERO
Topps, 1994
1 . . . . 5.00
2 thru 3 Harry Harrison adapt. . . @5.00

BILLY THE KID
Charlton Publ. Co., 1957–83
1 thru 8: MASKED RAIDER
(see Golden Age section)
9 DG(c),The Watergod 125.00
10 Rancho Malo. 100.00
11 O:Ghost Train 125.00
12 . . . . 100.00
13 AW,AT 125.00
14 No Limit Game 100.00
15 AW,O:Billy the Kid 125.00
16 AW, The Fastest Gun 125.00
17 Home Town Hero 100.00
18 The Scared Squatter. 100.00
19 The Underdog. 100.00
20 JSe,3-Aces 125.00
21 JSe, The Kid's Last Meal 125.00
22 JSe, The Crisis 125.00
23 JSe, The Guilty Gunslinger. . . 125.00
24 JSe, Caught with the Cash . . . 125.00
25 JSe, Geronimo's Revenge . . . 125.00
26 JSe, Gambler's Greed 125.00
27 Winner's Luck 75.00
28 The Big Man 75.00
29 The Fall Guy 75.00
30 Masked Rider 100.00
31 thru 40. . . . . @75.00
41 thru 60. . . . . @35.00
61 thru 65. . . . . @30.00
66 Boundy Hunter 35.00
67 thru 87 . . . . @20.00
88 thru 153. . . . . @10.00

BIN4RY
APC, 2004
1 . . . . 3.50
2 thru 4 . . . . @3.50
5 The Virus,pt.1 . . . . 3.50
6 . . . . 3.50
7 . . . . 3.50
0a variant (c). 3.00

BIONEERS
Mirage/Next, 1994
1 New Heroes. 2.75
2 . . . . 2.75
3 All-out War. 2.75

BIONIC COMMANDO
Devil's Due, 2008
0 . . . . 1.00
1 (of 4) 3.50
1a variant Capcom (c) 3.50

BIONIC WOMAN, THE
Charlton, 1977
1 Oct, 1977, TV show adapt. . . . 30.00
2 thru 5 . . . . @20.00

BIONIX
Maximum Press, 1996
1 (of 3) RLd,F:Steve Austin &
  Jaime Sommers 3.00
2 RLd,. 3.00

BIZARRE 3-D ZONE
Blackthorne, 1986
1 . . . . 3.00

BLACKBALL COMICS
Blackball Comics, 1994
1 KG,A:Trencher 3.25

BLACKBEARD LEGACY
Bluewater Prod., 2007
1 . . . . 4.00
1a thru 4a variant (c)s . . . . @4.00
2 thru 4 . . . . @4.00
Spec. #0 . . . . 4.00

[ORIGINAL] BLACK CAT
Recollections, 1988
1 thru 2 Reprints . . . . @3.00
3 thru 8 *see B&W Section*
9 thru 10 rep.. . . . . @3.00

Black Diamond #2
© AC Comics

BLACK DIAMOND
AC Comics, 1983
1 Colt B..U. story 4.00
2 thru 5 PG(c) . . . . @3.00

BLACK DIAMOND
AIT Planetlar, 2007
1 . . . . 3.00
2 thru 6 . . . . @3.00

BLACK ENCHANTRESS
Heroic Publishing, 2004
1 . . . . 3.00
2 thru 3 . . . . @3.00

BLACK FLAG
Maximum Press, 1995
1 Dan Fraga 3.00
2 I:New Character. 3.00
3 V:Network, I:Glitz. 3.00
4 V:Glitz, Network. 3.00
5 I:Jammers 3.00
6 I:Alphabots. 3.00

BLACK FURY
Charlton Comics, 1955
1 . . . . 100.00
2 . . . . 75.00
3 thru 15 . . . . @75.00
16 thru 18 SD. . . . . @100.00

19 and 20 . . . . @60.00
21 thru 56 . . . . @60.00
57 March-April, 1966 . . . . 50.00

BLACK HARVEST
Devil's Due Publishing, 2005
1 (of 6) by Josh Howard 3.25
2 thru 6 . . . . @3.25

BLACK HOLE, THE
Whitman, 1980
1 & 2 movie adaptation . . . . @3.00
3 & 4 new stories . . . . @3.00

BLACK HOOD
Archie/Red Circle, 1983
1 ATh,GM,DW. 4.00
2 ATh,DSp,A:Fox 3.00
3 ATh,GM 3.00

BLACK JACK
Charlton Comics, 1957–59
20 . . . . 100.00
21 . . . . 75.00
22 . . . . 100.00
23 AW,AT 100.00
24 thru 26 SD . . . . @110.00
27 . . . . 75.00
28 SD 110.00
29 & 30. . . . . @75.00

BLACKJACK:
BLOOD & HONOR
Dark Angel, 1997
1 by Alex Simmons,JoB, 1930s
  Adventure, Hildebrandts(c) 3.00
2 KeL, ... 3.00
3 Tim Cheng disappears. 3.00
4 . . . . 3.00

BLACK PHANTOM
AC Comics, 1989
1 F:Red Mask 3.00
2 thru 3 F:Red Mask . . . . @3.00

BLACK PLAGUE
Boom! Studios, 2006
1-shot 4.00
1-shot Previews exclusive (c) 7.00

BLACK RAVEN
Mad Monkey Press, 1996
1 Blueprints pt.1 . . . . 3.00
2 Blueprints pt.2 . . . . 3.00
3 V:Temple Assassins. 3.00
4 Blueprints pt.4 . . . . 3.00
GN#1 Blueprints. 7.00
GN#2 Blueprints. 5.00

BLACK SEPTEMBER
Malibu Ultraverse, 1995
Infinity End of Black September . . . 3.00

BLACK SUMMER
Avatar Press, 2007
0 (of 7) 2.50
0a variant wraparound (c) 2.50
1 . . . . 3.00
2 thru 4 . . . . @3.00
1a thru 4a wraparound (c) . . . . . @3.00
2b thru 6b Auxiliary editions . . . . @3.00
5 thru 7 . . . . @3.00
5a thru 7a wraparound (c)s . . . . @3.00
7b variant Zombies (c) . . . . @3.00
7c End of an Era (c) 6.00
Spec. Alpha edition 3.00
Spec. Alpha edition wraparound(c) . 3.00

COLOR PUB.

BLACK SUN
WildStorm/DC, 2002
Eye of the Storm
1 (of 6) TvS,F:Maggie Sun 3.00
2 thru 6 TvS . . . . @3.00

BLACK TERROR
Eclipse, 1989–90
1 . . . . 4.00
2 . . . . 4.00
3 . . . . 5.00

BLACK TERROR
Dynamite Entertainment, 2008
1 . . . . 3.50
2 . . . . 3.50

BLACK TIDE
Avatar Press, 2002
1A Park (c) 3.50
2 Miller (c). 3.50
3 Miller (c). 3.50
1a thru 3a variant (c)s. . . . . . . @3.50
Angel Gate Press
4 thru 8 . . . . @3.50
4a thru 8a variant (c) 3.50
9 thru 12 . . . . @3.00
9a thru 11a variant (c)s. . . . . . . @3.00
GN Vol. 1 Enter the Game. 8.00

BLACK TIGER: LEGACY OF FURY
Beyond Time Comics, 2004
1 (of 4) 3.00
2 thru 4 . . . . @3.00

BLACKBEARD LEGACY
Alias Enterprises, 2006
1 . . . . 3.50
2 thru 4 . . . . @3.50

BLACKPOOL
Phenomenon Comics, 2005
1 . . . . 3.00
2 thru 3 . . . . @3.00

BLACK WEB
Inks Comics
1 . . . . 2.75
2 thru 3 V:Seeker . . . . @2.75

Blast-Off #1
© Harvey Publications

BLADE OF KUMORI, THE
Devil's Due Publishing, 2004
1 RMz, Aftermath 3.00
1a variant (c). 3.00
2 thru 6 RMz, Aftermath . . . . . . @3.00

BLADE OF THE WARRIOR: KSHATRIYA
Virgin Comics 2008
1 . . . . 3.00
1a variant (c) 3.00
2 thru 4 . . . . @3.00

BLAST-OFF
Harvey Publications, 1965
1 JK,AW 100.00

BLAZIN' BRANDY
Scrap Pictures, 2007
0 12-pg.. 1.00
1 . . . . 3.00
2 thru 5 . . . . @3.00

BLAZING COMBAT
Warren Publishing Co., 1965–66
1 FF(c) 450.00
2 FF(c) 150.00
3 FF(c) 125.00
4 FF(c) 150.00

BLAZING SIX-GUNS
Skywald Comics, 1971
1 F: Red Mask, Sundance Kid . . . 35.00
2 Jesse James 25.00

BLONDIE AND DAGWOOD FAMILY
Harvey, 1963
1 . . . . 75.00
2 . . . . 50.00
3 . . . . 50.00
4 . . . . 50.00

BLONDIE COMICS
Harvey, 1963–65
142 thru 163 see golden age. . . @35.00
King, 1966–67
164 thru 175 . . . . @35.00
Becomes:

BLONDIE
Charlton, 1969–76
177 . . . . 15.00
178 thru 222. . . . . @10.00

BLOOD & ROSES
Sky Comics, 1993
1 I:Blood,Rose 3.00

BLOOD & ROSES: IN THE DARK
Afterburn, 2008
1 . . . . 3.00
1a variant sketch (c) 7.00
1-shot The Art of Blood & Roses . . . 3.00

BLOODBATH
Samson Comics
1 I:Alien,V:Starguile. 3.00

BLOOD BOWL: KILLER CONTRACT
Boom! Studios, 2008
1 . . . . 4.00
1a variant (c) 4.00

2 thru 5 . . . . @4.00
2a thru 5a variant (c)s . . . . @4.00

BLOODCHILDE
Millennium, 1994
0 O:Bloodchilde 3.00
1 Neil Gaiman, Vampires 3.00
1 signed (lim. to 500) 5.00
2 Neil Gaiman, Vampires 3.00
3 Neil Gaiman, Vampires 3.00
4 . . . . 3.00
5 Talk Show Host 3.00

BLOODFIRE
Lightning Comics, 1993
0 O:Bloodfire. 3.00
1 JZy(s),JJn, red foil 5.00
1a Platinum foil Ed. 5.00
1b B&W Promo Ed. Silver ink. . . . 4.00
1c B&W Promo Ed. Gold ink 6.00
2 JZy(s),JJn,O:Bloodfire 4.00
3 JZy(s),JJn,I:Dreadwolf,
   Judgement Day,Overthrow 3.00
4 JZy(s),JJn,A:Dreadwolf,. 3.00
5 JZy(s),JJn,I:Bloodstorm, w/card . 3.00
6 SZ(s),TLw,V:Storman. 3.00
7 SZ(s),TLw,A:Pres.Clinton 3.00
8 SZ(s),TLw,O:Prodigal 3.00
9 SZ(s),TLw,I:Prodigal
   (in Costume). 3.00
10 SZ(s),TLw,B:Rampage,
   I:Thorpe. 3.00
11 . . . . 3.00
12 . . . . 3.00

BLOODFIRE/HELLINA
Lightning Comics, 1995
1 V:Slaughterhouse 3.00

BLOODLORE
Brave New Worlds
1 Dreamweavers. 2.50
2 A Blow to the Crown 2.50

BLOODRAYNE
Digital Webbing, 2004
1-shot Skies Afire (2004) 10.00
1-shot Seeds of Sin (2005) 10.00
1-shot Lycan Rex (2005) 4.00
1-shot variant (c) 5.00
1-shot Dark Soul (2005). 4.00
1-shot Dark Soul variant (c) 5.00
1-shot Raw Convention Spec. 6.00
1-shot Twin Blades 8.00

...AUTOMATON
Digital Webbing, 2007
1 . . . . 4.00
1a variant (c) 4.00

...PLAGUE OF DREAMS
Digital Webbing, 2006
1 (of 3) 4.00
1a variant (c) 4.00
2 . . . . 4.00
3 . . . . 4.00
3a variant (c) 4.00

...PRIME CUTS
Digital Webbing, 2008
1 . . . . 4.00
2 . . . . 4.00
1a thru 2a variant (c)s . . . . @4.00

...RAW III
Digital Webbing, 2008
1 . . . . 4.00

...RED BLOOD RUN
Digital Webbing, 2007
1 (of 3) 4.00

1a variant (c) 4.00
2 thru 3 . . . . @4.00
2a thru 3a variant (c) . . . . @4.00

...TIBETAN HEIGHTS
Digital Webbing, 2007
1 . . . . 4.00
1a variant (c) 4.00

...TOKYO ROGUE
Digital Webbing, 2008
1 . . . . 4.00
1a variant (c) 4.00
2 thru 3 . . . . @4.00
2a thru 3a variant (c)s . . . . @4.00

BLOODSCENT
Comico, 1988
1 GC 3.00

BLOODSHOT
Valiant, 1992
0 KVH(a&s),DG(i),Chromium (c),
 O:Bloodshot,A:Eternal Warrior . 4.00
0a Gold Ed.,w/Diamond `Fall Fling'
 logo 10.00
I BWS(c),B:KVH(s),DP,BWi, V:Mafia,
 I:Carboni,1st Chromium(c) 4.00
2 thru 6 DP . . . . @2.50
7 thru 17 DP,JDx . . . . @2.50
18 thru 39 . . . . @2.50
40 thru 49 . . . . @10.00
50 . . . . 8.00
51 . . . . 12.00
Yearbook #1 KVH,briefcase bomb. . 4.25
Yearbook 1995 Villagers 3.00
Spec.GN Last Stand 10.00

Series Two
Acclaim, 1997
1 LKa(s),SaV, Behold, a Pale
 Horseman 2.50
1a variant cover 3.00
2 thru 16 LKa(s),SaV . . . . @2.50

BLOOD SWORD
Jademan, 1988
1 . . . . 3.00
2 thru 5 . . . . @3.00
6 thru 9 . . . . @3.00
10 thru 45 . . . . @3.00
46 V:Cannibal 3.00
47 thru 53 . . . . @3.00

BLOOD SWORD DYNASTY
Jademan, 1989
1 . . . . 3.00
2 thru 6 . . . . @2.75
7 thru 18 MB . . . . @2.75
19 thru 40 . . . . @2.75

BLUE BEETLE
Charlton Comics, 1964
(1st Silver Age Series)
1 O:Dan Garrett/BlueBeetle 150.00
2 . . . . 125.00
3 V:Mr.Thunderbolt 150.00
4 V:Praying Mantis Man 125.00
5 V:Red Knight 125.00
(2nd S.A. Series), 1965
Previously: UNUSUAL TALES
50 V:Scorpion 125.00
51 V:Mentor 125.00
52 V:Magno 125.00
53 V:Praying Mantis Man. 125.00
54 V:Eye of Horus 125.00
Becomes:

GHOSTLY TALES
(3rd S.A. Series), 1967
1 SD,I:Question 150.00

2 SD,O:TedKord,D:DanGarrett . . . 75.00
3 SD,I:Madmen,A:Question 40.00
4 SD,A:Question 40.00
5 SD,VicSage(Question) app.
 in Blue Beetle Story 40.00

BLUE PHANTOM, THE
Dell Publishing Co., 1962
1 . . . . 75.00

BLUE RIBBON
Archie/Red Circle, 1983
1 JK,AV,O:Fly rep. 7.00
2 TVe,Mr.Justice 6.00
3 EB/TD,O:Steel Sterling 6.00
4 . . . . 6.00
5 S&K,Shield rep. 6.00
6 DAy/TD,Fox 6.00
7 TD,Fox 6.00
8 NA,GM,Blackhood 7.00
9 thru 11 . . . . @6.00
12 SD,ThunderAgents 6.00
13 Thunderbunny 6.00
14 Web & Jaguar 6.00

BLUFF
Narwain Publishing, 2006
1 (of 3) 4.00
2 thru 3 . . . . @3.50

Bold Adventure #1
© Pacific

BOLD ADVENTURE
Pacific, 1987
1 & 2 . . . . @3.00
3 JSe. 3.00

BOLT & STARFORCE SIX
AC Comics, 1984
1 . . . . 3.00
Bolt Special #1 . . . . 3.00

BOMBABY:
THE SCREEN GODDESS
Amaze Ink/Slave Labor
Graphics, 2003
1 (of 4) 3.50
2 . . . . 3.50
3 and 4 . . . . @4.00

BOMBAST
Topps, 1993
1 V:Savage Dragon,Trading Card . 3.25

BONANZA
Dell Publishing Co., 1960
1 . . . . 350.00
2 . . . . 250.00
3 thru 10 . . . . @200.00
11 thru 20 . . . . @150.00
21 thru 37 . . . . @150.00
Gold Key, 1962
1 Ph(c), from TV series 350.00
2 . . . . 175.00
3 thru 9 . . . . @150.00
10 thru 37 . . . . @100.00

BOND OF
SAINT MARCEL, THE
Archaia Studios, 2008
1 . . . . 3.00

BORIS KARLOFF
TALES OF MYSTERY
Gold Key, 1963–80
1 (Thriller) 175.00
2 (Thriller) , ... 125.00
3 thru 8 . . . . @75.00
9 WW 100.00
10 JO 75.00
11 AW,JO 85.00
12 AT,AMc,JO 75.00
13 & 14 . . . . @50.00
15 RC,GE 50.00
16 thru 20 . . . . @50.00
21 JJ,Screaming Skull 100.00
22 thru 50 . . . . @40.00
51 thru 74 . . . . @30.00
75 thru 97 . . . . @25.00

BOYS, THE
Wildstorm/DC, Aug., 2006
1 GEn,DaR,Watchers of the Supers 3.00
2 GEn,DaR 3.00
3 GEn 3.00
4 GEn, DaR 3.00
5 GEn 3.00
6 GEn, DaR 3.00
7 GEn,DaR 3.00
8 GEn,DaR, Tek Knight 3.00
9 GEn,DaR, Tek Knight 3.00
10 GEn,DaR, ... 3.00
D.E.
11 thru 12 . . . . @3.00
13 thru 24 . . . . @3.00
24a variant (c) 3.00

BOY WHO MADE SILENCE
AAM Markosia, 2008
1 . . . . 4.00
2 thru 6 . . . . @3.50

BOZO
Innovation
1 1950's reprint stories 7.00

BOZO THE CLOWN
Blackthorne
1 thru2 3-D . . . . @3.00

BRADY BUNCH, THE
Dell Publishing Co., 1970
1 . . . . 250.00
2 . . . . 200.00

BRAIN BOY
Dell Publishing Co.,
April-June, 1962
1 . . . . 250.00
2 . . . . 200.00
3 thru 6 . . . . @175.00

COLOR PUB.

BRAM STOKER'S
BURIAL OF THE RATS
Roger Corman's Comics, 1995
1 .... 2.50
2 thru 3 film adaptation .... @2.50

BRASS
WildStorm/DC, 2000
1 (of 6) JAr,RiB 2.50
2 JAr,RiB 2.50
3 JAr,RiB 2.50
4 JAr,RiB 2.50
5 JAr,RiB,war is over 2.50
6 JAr,RiB,concl. 2.50

BRATH
Crossgen Comics, 2003
Prequel CDi(s) 3.00
1 CDi(s) 3.50
2 thru 10 CDi(s) .... @3.00
11 thru 17 .... @3.00

BREAKDOWN
Devil's Due Publishing, 2004
1 CDi 3.00
1a variant (c) 3.00
2 thru 6 CDi,Aftermath .... @3.00

BREAK-THRU
Malibu Ultraverse, 1993–94
1 GJ(s),GP,AV(i),A:All Ultraverse
   Heroes 2.75
1a Foil Edition 7.50
2 GJ(s),GP,AV(i),A:All Ultraverse
   Heroes 2.75

BREATHE
Markosia, 2007
1 (of 4) 3.00
2 thru 4 .... @3.00
1a thru 4a variant (c) .... @3.00

'BREED
Malibu Bravura
[Limited Series] 1994
1 JSn(a&s),Black (c),I:Stoner 3.00
2 JSn(a&s),I:Rachel 3.00
3 JSn(a&s),V:Rachel 3.00
4 JSn(a&s),I:Stoner's Mom 3.00
5 JSn(a&s),V:Rachel 3.00
6 JSn(a&s),final issue 3.00

'BREED II
Malibu Bravura
[Limited Series] 1994–95
1 JSn,The Book of Revelation 3.00
1a gold foil edition 4.00
2 JSn,A:Rachel 3.00
3 JSn,V:Actual Demon 3.00
4 JSn,Language of Demons 3.00
5 JSn,R:Rachael 3.00
6 JSn,final issue 3.00

BREEDING GROUND
Samson Comics
1 I:Mazit, Zero 2.50

BRENDA LEE STORY, THE
Dell Publishing Co., 1962
1 .... 150.00

BRENDA STARR
REPORTER
Dell Publishing Co., 1963
1 .... 300.00

Brenda Starr Reporter #1
© Dell Publishing

BRIAN BOLLAND'S
BLACK BOOK
Eclipse, 1985
1 BB 3.00

BRIAN PULIDO'S
BELLADONNA
Avatar Press, 2004
Preview 2.00
Preview variant (c)s 3.00
Convention Specials 3.00
1 .... 4.00
2 thru 5 .... @4.00
1a-b thru 5a-b variant (c)s .... @4.00
1c Lioness (c) 6.00
1d Serpent (c) 6.00
1e Animal protectors (c) 6.00
1f Prism foil (c) 13.00
2c Cloud Burst (c) 6.00
2d Ferocious (c) 6.00
2e Pure Rage (c) 6.00
3c premium (c) 10.00
3d Back from Dead (c) 6.00
3e Leader of Pack (c) 6.00
4c premium (c) 10.00
4d Warrior Spirit (c) 6.00
4e Moonlight (c) 6.00
5c premium (c) 10.00
5d Raw Power (c) 6.00
5e Art Nouveau (c) 6.00

BRIAN PULIDO'S
MEDIEVAL LADY DEATH
Avatar Press, 2005
1 .... 4.00
1a wraparound (c) 4.00
1b premium (c) 10.00
1c Fear Her Wrath (c) 6.00
1d portrait edition 6.00
2 thru 8 .... @4.00
2b thru 8b variant (c)s .... @6.00
2a thru 8a wraparound (c)s ..... @4.00
2c thru 8c premium (c)s ...... @10.00

BRIDES IN LOVE
Charlton Comics, 1956–65
1 .... 150.00
2 .... 125.00
3 thru 10 .... @75.00
11 thru 30 .... @75.00
31 thru 44 .... @60.00
45 .... 50.00

BRIGADE
Awesome Entertainment
Vol II, 2000
1 A:Badrock 3.00

BRODIE'S LAW
Markosia, 2006
Prev. Black & White
7 thru 10 .... @3.50

BROTHERS IN ARMS
Dynamite Entertainment, 2008
1 .... 4.00
1a variant (c) 4.00
2 thru 4 .... @4.00

BROTHERS
OF THE SPEAR
Gold Key, 1972
1 .... 75.00
2 .... 30.00
3 thru 9 .... @25.00
10 thru 17 .... @20.00
Whitman, 1982
18 .... 20.00

BROTHERS:
THE FALL OF LUCIFER
Markosia, 2006
1 (of 10) 3.50
1a variant (c)s .... @3.50
2 thru 5 .... @3.50

BRUCE LEE
Malibu, 1994
1 MBn(s), Stories of B.Lee 3.00
2 thru 6 .... @3.00

BRUTE, THE
Atlas, Feb.–July, 1975
1 .... 25.00
2 thru 3 .... @25.00

BUBBA
Silent Devil Productions, 2006
Super Sci-Fi Special 3.00

BUCKAROO BANZAI
Moonstone, 2008
Big-Size #1 .... 4.75
Big-Size #1A variant (c) 8.00

BUCKAROO BANZAI:
THE PREQUEL
Moonstone, 2008
1 and 2 (of 2) .... @4.00

BUCK ROGERS
Gold Key, 1964
1 P(c) 175.00
2 AMc,FBe,P(c),movie adapt 25.00
3 AMc,FBe,P(c),movie adapt 25.00
4 FBe,P(c) 25.00
5 AMc,P(c) 20.00
6 AMc,P(c) 20.00
Whitman
7 thru 9 AMc,P(c) .... @30.00
10 and 11 AMc,P(c) .... @20.00
12 and 13 P(c) .... @15.00
14 thru 16 .... @10.00

BUCK ROGERS IN
THE 25TH CENTURY
Gold Key, 1979
2 from TV Series 20.00

3 thru 7 . . . . @25.00
8 . . . . 30.00
9 . . . . 30.00
10 not published
11 thru 16 . . . . @15.00

BUCK ROGERS
TSR, 1990–91
1 O:Buck Rogers 3.00
2 thru 3 O:Buck Rogers . . . . @3.00
4 thru 6 Black Barney . . . . @3.00
7 thru 10 The Martian Wars . . . . @3.00

BUCKY O'HARE
Continuity, 1991
1 MGo. 2.75
2 thru 5 . . . . @2.50

BUDD'S BEAUTIES & BEASTS
Basement Comics, 2005
1-shot. 5.00
2 (b&w) (2006) 3.25

BUFFALO BILL JR.
Gold Key, 1965
1 . . . . 75.00

BUGS BUNNY
Dell, 1952
28 thru 85. . . . . @100.00
Gold Key, 1962
86 . . . . 100.00
87 thru 218. . . . . @50.00
Spec. Winter Fun (1967) 75.00
Whitman, 1980
219 thru 245. . . . . @20.00

BUGS BUNNY AND PORKY PIG
Gold Key, 1965
1 . . . . 150.00

BULLWINKLE
Dell, 1962
1 . . . . 300.00
Gold Key, 1962
1 Bullwinkle & Rocky 300.00
2 . . . . 200.00
3 thru 5 . . . . @150.00
6 and 7, rep. . . . . @150.00

Bullwinkle #16 © Gold Key

8 thru 11 . . . . 150.00
12 rep. 75.00
13 and 14 . . . . @85.00
15 thru 19 . . . . @75.00
20 thru 24, rep. . . . . @35.00
25 . . . . 50.00
Charlton Comics, 1970
1 . . . . 125.00
Becomes:

BULLWINKLE AND ROCKY
Charlton Comics, 1970–71
2 thru 7 . . . . @75.00

BULLWINKLE & ROCKY
Blackthorne, 1987
3-D 25.00

BULLWINKLE FOR PRESIDENT
Blackthorne, 1987
1 3-D Special 3.00

BURKE'S LAW
Dell Publishing Co., 1964
1 from TV Show 100.00
2 . . . . 75.00
3 . . . . 75.00

BUTTERNUT SQUASH
Speakeasy Comics, 2005
1 . . . . 4.00
2 . . . . 4.00

BUTCH CASSIDY
Skywald Comics, 1971
1 . . . . 30.00
2 & 3 . . . . @20.00

BUZZBOY: SIDEKICKS RULE
Sky Dog Press, 2006
1 . . . . 3.00
2 thru 3 . . . . @3.00

CABBOT: BLOODHUNTER
Maximum Press, 1997
1 . . . . 3.00
2 thru 4 RV . . . . @2.50

CADILLACS & DINOSAURS
Kitchen Sink, 1992
1 Rep. from Xenozoic Tales in 3-D. 6.00
Topps, 1994
BLOOD & BONES
1 thru 3 rep. Xenozoic Tales,
    all covers . . . . @3.00
MAN-EATER
1 thru 3, all covers 3.00
THE WILD ONES
1 thru 3, all covers 3.00

CAGES
Tundra, 1990
1 DMc 14.00
2 DMc 11.00
3 thru 4 DMc . . . . @7.50
5 thru 7 DMc 5.00

CAIN
Harris, 1993
1 B:DQ(s),I:Cain,Frenzy 5.00
2 BSz(c),HBk,V:Mortatira 3.25

CAIN'S HUNDRED
Dell Publishing Co., May-July, 1962
1 . . . . 45.00
2 . . . . 30.00

CALIBER
Radical Comics, 2008
1 (of 5) 1.00
1a variant (c) 1.00
1b variant (c) 1.00
2 thru 5 . . . . @3.00
2a thru 5a variant (c)s . . . . @3.00

CALIFORNIA RAISINS
Blackthorne, 1987
1 thru 4 3-D . . . . @2.50
5 3-D,O:Calif.Raisins 2.50
6 thru 8 3-D . . . . @2.50

CALVIN & THE COLONEL
Dell Publishing Co., April-June, 1962
1 . . . . 150.00
2 . . . . 100.00

CANNON BUSTERS
Devil's Due/UDON, 2004
1 . . . . 3.00
2 The Necklace. 3.00

CANNON HAWKE
Aspen, 2005
Prelude 2.50
1 . . . . 3.00
1a signed 25.00
thru 5 . . . . @3.00

CAPCOM SUMMER SPECIAL
Devil's Due, 2004
1 . . . . 12.00

CAP'N QUICK & FOOZLE
Eclipse, 1984–85
1 thru 3 . . . . @3.00

CAPT. ELECTRON
Brick Computers Inc., 1986
1 . . . . 2.50
2 . . . . 2.50

CAPTAIN ACTION
Moonstone, 2008
0 . . . . 2.00
0a variant (c) 2.00
1 . . . . 4.00
2 . . . . 4.00
1a thru 2a variant (c)s . . . . @4.00
1-shot First Mission, Last Day 4.00

CAPTAIN ATOM: ARMAGEDDON
Wildstorm/DC, Oct., 2005
1 AxR(c) 3.00
1a variant JLe(c). 3.00
2 . . . . 3.00
3 Void's Death. 3.00
4 V:Wildcats 3.00
5 A:The Authority 3.00
6 F:Engineer 3.00
7 Looks into the future 3.00
8 V:Authority 3.00
9 Finale. 3.50

CAPTAIN ATOM
See: STRANGE
SUSPENSE STORIES

CAPTAIN CANUCK
Comely Comix, 1975–81
1 I:Blue Fox	25.00
2 I:Red Coat	20.00
3 I:Heather	20.00
4 thru 14	15.00
Summer Spec. #1	15.00

...LEGACY
Comely/Semple Comics, 2006
1	3.00
1a special edition	8.00
2	4.00

...UNHOLY WAR
Comely Comix, 2004
1 thru 3	@2.50
4	4.00

CAPTAIN GLORY
Topps, 1993
1 A:Bombast,Night Glider, Trading Card	3.25

CAPTAIN GRAVITY
Penny Farthing Press, 1998
1 by S.Vrattos & K. Martin	12.00
2 No one escapes Law of Gravity	7.00
3	5.00
4	3.00
Spec. One True Hero	3.00

...THE POWER OF THE VRIL
Pennyfarthing Press, 2005
1 thru 6	@3.00

CAPTAIN HARLOCK: FALL OF THE EMPIRE
Eternity, 1992
1 R:Captain Harlock	2.50
2 V:Tadashi	2.50
3 Bomb on the Arcadia	2.50
4 Final issue	2.50

CAPTAIN JOHNER & THE ALIENS
Valiant, 1995
1 Rep. Magnus Robot Fighter #1–7 (Gold Key 1963–64)	3.00

Captain Johner & The Aliens
© Valiant

CAPTAIN MARVEL
M. F. Enterprises, 1966
1	75.00
2	50.00
3 Fights The Bat	40.00
4	40.00
5 Captain Marvel Presents the Terrible Five	40.00

CAPTAIN NAUTICUS
Entity, 1994
1 V:Fathom	3.00
2 V:Fathom's Henchman	3.00
3 Surf's Up	3.00

CAPTAIN NICE
Gold Key, 1967
1 Ph(c)	125.00

CAPTAIN PARAGON
Americomics, 1983
1 thru 4	@3.00

CAPTAIN POWER
Continuity, 1988
1a NA,TVtie-in(direct sale)	3.00
1b NA,TVtie-in(newsstand)	3.00
2 NA	3.00

CAPTAIN STERN
Kitchen Sink Press, 1993–94
1 BWr,R:Captain Stern	5.25
2 BWr,Running Out of Time	5.00
3 thru 5 BWr,Running Out of Time	@4.00

CAPTAIN THUNDER AND BLUE BOLT
Hero Graphics, 1987
1 I:Capt.Thunder & Paul Fremont.	2.50
2 Paul becomes Blue Bolt	2.50
3 O:Capt.Thunder	2.50
4 V:Iguana Boys	2.50
5 V:Ian Shriver, in Scotland	2.50
6 V:Krakatoa	2.50
7 V:Krakatoa	2.50
8 A:Sparkplug (from League of Champions)	2.50
9 A:Sparkplug	2.50
10 A:Sparkplug	2.50

CAPTAIN VENTURE & THE LAND BENEATH THE SEA
Gold Key, 1968
1	75.00
2	60.00

CAPTAIN VICTORY AND THE GALACTIC RANGERS
Pacific, 1982
1 JK	3.00
2 JK	3.00
3 JK,BU:NA,I:Ms.Mystic	3.00
4 JK	3.00
5 JK	3.00
6 thru 13 JK	@3.00
Spec.#1 JK	3.00

CAR 54, WHERE ARE YOU?
Dell Publishing Co., March-May, 1962
1 Ph(c)	150.00
2 thru 7 Ph(c)	@100.00

CARCA JOU RENAISSANCE
1 and 2	@3.00

CARNOSAUR CARNAGE
Atomeka, 1993
GN	5.00

CAROLINE KENNEDY
Charlton Comics, 1961
1	150.00

CASEY BLUE: BEYOND TOMORROW
Wildstorm/DC, May, 2008
1 (of 6)	3.00
2 thru 6	@3.00

CASEY JONES & RAPHAEL
Mirage, 1994
1 Family War	2.75
2 Johnny Woo Woo	2.75
3 V:Johnny Woo Woo	2.75
4 9mm Raphael	2.75

CASPER & FRIENDS
Harvey, 1991
1 thru 4	@3.00
5 short stories, cont	3.00

CASPER AND SPOOKY
Harvey, 1972
1	35.00
2 thru 7	@20.00

CASPER AND THE GHOSTLY TRIO
Harvey, 1972
1	35.00
2 thru 7	@20.00

Harvey, 1990
8	6.00
9 thru 10	@6.00

CASPER & WENDY
Harvey, 1972–73
1 52-pg. giant	40.00
2 thru 5	@20.00
6 thru 8	@20.00

CASPER ENCHANTED TALES
Harvey, 1992
1 short stories	3.00

CASPER THE FRIENDLY GHOST
Blackthorne, 1988
1 3-D	3.00

CASPER GHOSTLAND
Harvey, 1992
1 short stories	3.00

CASPER'S GHOSTLAND
Harvey Publications, Winter, 1958-59
1 giant	450.00
2	250.00
3 thru 10	@150.00
11 thru 20	@100.00
21 thru 40	@75.00
41 thru 61	@60.00

62 thru 77	@50.00
78 thru 97	@40.00
98 Dec., 1979	40.00

CASPER THE FRIENDLY GHOST
Harvey, 1990–91
Prev: The Friendly Ghost Casper

254 thru 260	@3.00

[Second Series], 1991–94

1 thru 14	@3.00
15 thru 28	@3.00

CASPER SPACE SHIP
Harvey, 1972

1	40.00
2 thru 5	@25.00

Becomes:

CASPER IN SPACE
Harvey, 1973

6	20.00
7 thru 8	@20.00

CASPER STRANGE GHOST STORIES
Harvey, 1974

1	40.00
2	20.00
3 thru 15	@20.00

CASPER T.V. SHOWTIME
Harvey, 1980

1	20.00
2 thru 5	@10.00

CASTLEVANIA: THE BELMONT LEGACY
IDW Publishing, 2005

1	4.00
2 thru 5	@4.00

CAST
Nautilus Comics, 2005

1	3.00
2 thru 4	@3.00

CATSEYE
Awesome/Hyperwerks, 1999

0 KIA,BNa,O:Catseye	3.00

CAULDRON
Real Comics, 1995

1 Movie Style Comic	3.00
1a Variat cover	3.00

CAVE KIDS
Gold Key, 1963

1	125.00
2	75.00
3 thru 5	@75.00
6	60.00
7 A:Pebbles & Bamm Bamm	65.00
8 thru 10	@50.00
11 thru 16	@50.00

CAVEWOMAN
Avatar, 1999

Color Spec.	3.50
Color Spec. Fauna (c)	3.50
Color Spec. prism foil (c)	13.00
Color Spec. Royal Blue	75.00

CENTURY
Awesome Entertainment, 2000

1 RLe	3.00

1a Millennium edition	5.00
2	3.00
2a Millennium edition	5.00
2b signed	13.00
3	3.00

CHAINS OF CHAOS
Harris, 1994

1 Vampirella, Rook	5.00
2 V:Chaoschild	3.25
3 Final issue	3.25

CHALLENGER DEEP
Boom! Studios, 2008

1 (of 4)	4.00
2 thru 4	@4.00

CHAMPIONS
Eclipse, 1986–87

1 I:Flare,League of Champions Foxbat, Dr.Arcane	10.00
2 I:Dark Malice	10.00
3 I:Lady Arcane	8.00
4 O:Dark Malice	10.00
5 O:Flare	6.00
6 D:Giant Demonmaster	6.00

[New Series]
Hero Graphics, 1987–88

1 EL,I:Madame Synn,Galloping Galooper	5.00
2 I:Fat Man, Black Enchantress	2.50
3 I:Sparkplug&Icicle,O:Flare	2.50
4 I:Exo-Skeleton Man	2.50
5 A:Foxbat	2.50
6 I:Mechanon, C:Foxbat	2.50
7 A:Mechanon,J:Sparkplug,Icicle	2.50
8 O:Foxbat	2.50
9 Flare #0 (Flare preview)	2.50
10 Olympus Saga #1	2.50
11 Olympus Saga #2	2.50
12 Olympus Saga #3	2.50
Ann.#1 O:Giant & DarkMalice	2.75
Ann.#2	4.00

CHAMPIONS CLASSIC
Hero Graphics, 1993

1 GP(c),Rep.1st champions series	2.50

CHAOS! BIBLE
Chaos! Comics, 1995

1 Character Profiles	3.50

Chmpions Classic #2 @ Hero Graphics

CHAOS! CHRONICLES– THE HISTORY OF A COSMOS
Chaos! Comics, 1999

Spec.	3.50
Spec. signed premium	15.00

CHAOS EFFECT
Valiant, 1994

Alpha DJ(c), BCh, JOy, A:All Valiant Characters	2.50
Alpha Red (c)	50.00
Omega DJ(c), BCh, JOy, A:All Valiant Characters	2.50
Omega Gold(c)	3.50
Epilogue pt.1	3.00
Epilogue pt.2	3.00

CHAOS! GALLERY
Chaos! Comics, 1997

1	3.00

CHAOS! NIGHTMARE THEATER
Chaos! Comics, 1997

1 (of 4) BWr(c)	2.50
2 BWr(c)	2.50
3 BWr(c)	2.50
4 BWr(c)	2.50

CHAOS QUARTERLY
Harris Comics, 1995

1 F:Lady Death	5.00
1a Premium Edition	11.00
1b Signed,limited edition	20.00

CHAPEL
Awesome Entertainment, 1997

1 BNa, from Spawn,Youngblood	3.00

CHARLEMAGNE
Defiant, 1994

1 JiS(s),From Hero	3.00
2 JiS(s),I:Charles Smith	2.75
3 JiS(s),A:War Dancer	2.75
4 DGC(s),V:Dark Powers	2.75
5 Schism prequel	2.75
6 V:Wardancer	2.75
7 R:To Vietnam	2.75

CHARLIE CHAN
Dell Publishing Co., 1965

1	100.00
2	75.00

CHARLTON ACTION: FEATURING STATIC
Charlton, 1985

1	8.00
2	5.00

CHARLTON BULLSEYE
Charlton, 1981–82

1 Blue Beetle, I:Rocket Rabbit	3.50
2 Capt. Catnip; Nell the Horse	2.50
3 Grundar	2.50
4 Vanguards	2.50
5 Warhund	2.50
6 Thunder-bunny	2.50
7 Captain Atom	2.50
8 weird stories	2.50
9	2.50
10	2.50
Spec. #1	2.00
Spec. #2 Atomic Mouse	2.00

All comics prices listed are for *Near Mint* condition.

CHARLTON BULLSEYE SPECIAL
Charlton, 1986
1 . . . . 9.00
2 . . . . 7.00

CHARLTON CLASSICS
Charlton, 1980
1 . . . . 7.00
2 . . . . 5.00
3 thru 9 . . . . @5.00

CHARLTON CLASSICS LIBRARY
Charlton, 1973
1 . . . . 25.00

CHARLTON PREMIERE
Charlton, 1967
1 . . . . 30.00
2 thru 5 . . . . @30.00

CHARLTON SPORT LIBRARY
Charlton, 1970
1 Professional Football 50.00

CHASE, THE
APC, 2004
1 (of 10) 3.50
2 . . . . 3.50
3 . . . . 3.50
4 . . . . 3.50

CHASSIS
Millennium/Expand, 1995
1 I:Chassis McBain, Aero Run 3.00
1 2nd printing 3.00
1 chrome cover 10.00
2 . . . . 3.00
2a with racing card 5.00
2b Amanda Conner cover 3.00
2c Amanda Conner cover, signed . 10.00
2d foil cover, signed 8.00
[Vol. 2] Hurricane Comics, 1998
0 by Joshua Dysart & Wm.O'Neill . 3.00
0a variant cover 3.00
1 . . . . 3.00
2 . . . . 3.00
3 . . . . 3.00

CHASTITY
Chaos! Comics, 2000
1/2 . . . . 3.00
1/2a premium ed., tattoo (c) 9.00
1/2b chromium edition 14.00
1 premium edition 9.00
Spec. #1 Reign of Terror (2000) . . . 3.00
Spec. #1 Reign of Terror, premium . 9.00
Spec. #1 Love Bites (2001) 3.00
Spec. #1 Love Bites, premium ed. . 9.00
Ashcan Love Bites (2001) 6.00

...CRAZYTOWN
Chaos! Comics, 2002
Ashcan b&w 6.00
1 (of 3) 3.00
1a premium edition 9.00
1b foil edition 15.00
2 thru 3 . . . . @3.00
2a and 3a variant (c) . . . . @7.50

...HEARTBREAKER
Chaos! Comics, 2002
1 . . . . 3.00
1a premium edition 9.00
1b super premium edition 15.00

...LUST FOR LIFE
Chaos! Comics, 1999
1 (of 4) PNu 3.00
1a alternate cover 7.00
1b alternate cover, signed 20.00
1c premium edition 10.00
2 V:Hemlock 3.00
3 . . . . 3.00

...RE-IMAGINED
Chaos! Comics, 2002
1 Gothic tale 3.00
1a premium edition 10.00
1b super premium edition 20.00
Ashcan re-imagined b&w 6.00

...ROCKED
Chaos! Comics, 1998
1 (of 4) PNu 3.00
1a & 1b variant covers 3.00
2 V:Jade 3.00
3 V:Jade 3.00
4 conclusion 3.00
Chastity/Cremator Preview
  Book, B&W 5.00

...SHATTERED
Chaos! Comics, 2001
1 BnP,LKa 3.00
1a premium edition 9.00
2 . . . . 3.00
3 . . . . 3.00
Ashcan 6.00

...THEATRE OF PAIN
Chaos! Comics, 1997
1 (of 3) BnP, ... 6.00
1a premium edition 12.00
2 . . . . 3.00
3 . . . . 3.00
3a premium edition 15.00

CHECKMATE
Gold Key, 1962
1 Ph(c) 100.00
2 Ph(c) 75.00

CHERYL BLOSSOM
Archie Comics, 1996
1 . . . . 2.50
2 thru 10 . . . . @2.50
11 thru 37 . . . . @2.50

...GOES HOLLYWOOD
Archie Comics, 1996
1 (of 3) by Dan Parent &
  Bill Golliher 3.50
2 and 3 . . . . @3.50

CHEYENNE KID
Charlton, 1957
1 thru 7: WILD FRONTIER
(see Golden Age section)
8 DG(c), Stolen Empire 100.00
9 Ragin Bear's Revenge 75.00
10 AW,AT,SD(c),Custer's Last
  Stand 125.00
11 Giant size, Geronimo 100.00
12 AW,AT 100.00
13 AW,AT 100.00
14 AW 100.00
15 . . . . 100.00
16 . . . . 75.00
17 Peacemaker Colt 75.00
18 The Crumbling Idol 75.00
19 Their Last Battle 75.00
20 JSe, The Victim 75.00
21 JSe, The Blue-Eyed Braves . . 100.00
22 JSe, Rustlers Bait 100.00
23 The Gunless Wonder 60.00
24 JSe, The Indian Fighters 75.00
25 JSe, Fury of the Gods 75.00

Cheyenne Kid #10 © *Charlton*

26 JSe, Fat of the Land 75.00
27 Bad Medicine 60.00
28 The Alamo 60.00
29 Cheaters' Row 60.00
30 JSe, A Short Injun War 75.00
31 thru 98 . . . . @20.00
99 Nov., 1973 . . . . 20.00

CHICKASAW ADVENTURES
Layne Morgan Media, 2005
1 . . . . 3.00
2 The Battle of Akia 3.00
3 Tears at Fort Coffee 3.00
4 The Making of a Storyteller 3.00

CHI-CHIAN
Sirius, 1997
1 (of 6) by Voltaire 3.00
2 thru 6 . . . . @3.00

CHILD'S PLAY 2
Innovation
1 Movie Adapt Pt 1 . . . . 2.50
2 thru 3 Adapt Pt 2–3 . . . . @2.50

CHILD'S PLAY 3
Innovation
1 Movie Adapt Pt 1 . . . . 2.50
2 Movie Adapt Pt.2 . . . . 2.50

CHILD'S PLAY: THE SERIES
Innovation
1 Chucky's Back 2.50
2 Straight Jacket Blues 2.50
3 M.A.R.K.E.D. 2.50
4 Chucky in Toys 4 You 2.50
5 Chucky in Hollywood 2.50

CHILDREN OF FIRE
Fantagor, 1987
1 thru 3 RCo . . . . @4.00

CHILLING ADVENTURES IN SORCERY AS TOLD BY SABRINA
Archie, 1972–74
1 . . . . 65.00
2 . . . . 40.00
3 thru 5 . . . . @30.00

CHIMERA
Crossgen Comics, 2003
1 RMz,BPe 3.00
2 thru 4 . . . . @3.00

CHIP 'N DALE
Dell Publishing, 1955–66
4 . . . . 125.00
5 thru 10 . . . . @100.00
11 thru 30 . . . . @100.00
Gold Key, 1967
1 reprints 75.00
2 thru 10 . . . . @30.00
11 thru 20 . . . . @20.00
21 thru 83 . . . . @15.00
Whitman, 1980
65 . . . . 12.00
66 thru 69 . . . . @12.00
70 thru 83 . . . . @7.00

CHIP 'N DALE
RESCUE RANGERS
Walt Disney, 1990
1 Rescue Rangers to the Rescue . 4.00
2   pt.2. . . . . 3.50
3 thru 7 . . . . @3.00
8 thru 18 . . . . @2.75

CHOO CHOO CHARLIE
Gold Key, 1969
1 . . . . 150.00

CHOSEN, THE
Click Comics, 1995
1 I:The Chosen 2.50
2 I:Herman Cortez 2.50

CHRISTIAN
Maximum Press, 1996
1 and 2 (of 3) RLd . . . . @3.00

CHROMA-TICK
SPECIAL EDITION
New England Press, 1992
1 Rep.Tick#1,new stories 4.00
2 Rep.Tick#2,new stories 5.00
3 thru 8 Reps.& new stories . . . . @3.50

CHROME
Hot Comics, 1986
1 Machine Man 3.50
2 thru 4 . . . . @3.00

CHROME WARRIORS
IN A '59 CHEVY
Black Out Comics, 1998
0 . . . . 3.00
1 Rob Roman & Tommy Castillo . . 3.00

CHROMIUM MAN, THE
Triumphant Comics, 1994
0 Blue Logo 6.00
0 Regular 2.50
1 I:Chromium Man,Mr.Death 3.50
2 I:Prince Vandal 3.00
3 thru 15 . . . . @2.50

...VIOLENT PAST
Triumphant Comics
1 thru 4 JnR(s) . . . . @2.50

CHRONICLES OF CORUM
First, 1987–88
1 Michael Moorcock adapt 3.00
2 . . . . 2.50
3 thru 12 . . . . @2.50

Chronicles of Chorum #3
© First

CHRONICLES OF
DR. HERBERT WEST, THE
Zenescope Entertainment, 2008
1 thru 3 (of 6) . . . . @3.00

CHRONO MECHANICS
Alias Enterprises, 2005
GN ATi 7.00
Precious Metal Coll.–Platinum 3.50
Precious Metal Collection–Gold #2 . 3.50
Precious Metal Collection–Gold #3 . 3.50
Precious Metal Coll.–Bronze #4 . . . 3.50

CHTULHU TALES
Boom! Studios, 2006
1 . . . . 7.00

CHUCK
Wildstorm/DC, June, 2008
1 From TV series 3.00
2 thru 6 . . . . @3.00

CHUCKY
Devil's Due, 2007
1 . . . . 3.50
1a variant (c) 3.50
2 thru 5 . . . . @3.50
2a thru 5a variant (c)s . . . . @3.50
Vol. 2, Devil's Due, 2008
1 (of 4) 3.50
1a variant (c) 3.50

CICERO'S CAT
Dell Publishing Co., 1959
1 . . . . 100.00
2 . . . . 75.00

CICI
Spilled Milk, 2002
1 (of 4) 3.00
2 thru 4 . . . . @2.50
1a Variant (c) 2.50

CIMMARON STRIP
Dell Publishing Co., 1968
1 . . . . 75.00

CISCO KID, THE
Moonstone, 2004
1 (of 3) 3.00

2 . . . . 3.00
3 . . . . 3.00

...GUNFIRE & BRIMSTONE
Moonstone Books, 2005
1 . . . . 3.00
2 . . . . 3.00
3 . . . . 3.00

...VS. WYATT EARP
Moonstone, 2008
1 . . . . 4.00

CITY KNIGHTS, THE
Windjammer 1995
1 I: Michael Walker 2.50
2 thru 4 . . . . @2.50

CITY OF DUST
Radical Comics, 2008
1 . . . . 4.00
1a variant (c)s . . . . @4.00
2 . . . . 3.00
3a variant (c)s . . . . @3.00

CITY OF HEROES
Blue King Studios, 2004
1 . . . . 3.00
2 thru 12 . . . . @3.00

CITY OF TOMORROW
Wildstorm/DC, Apr., 2005
1 (of 6) HC 3.00
2 HC 3.00
3 thru 6 HC . . . . @3.00

CITY KNIGHTS, THE
Windjammer, 1995
1 I:Michael Walker 2.50
2 I:Herald 2.50
3 V:Herald 2.50
4 V:Herald 2.50

CITY PERILOUS
Broadway Comics
1 GI,Remember the Future,pt.1 . . . 3.00
2 GI,Remember the Future,pt.2 . . . 3.00
Becomes:
KNIGHTS ON BROADWAY
3 thru 5 GI . . . . @3.00

CLASH
Moonstone, 2007
1 (of 5) 3.50
2 thru 4 . . . . @3.50

CLASSIC BATTLESTAR
GALACTICA
D.E. (Dynamite Ent.) 2006
1 . . . . 3.50
1a Classic Cylon foil (c) . . . .
2 thru 3 . . . . @3.00
2a thru 3a variant (c) 3.50
4 . . . . 3.50
4a variant (c) 3.50
5 . . . . 3.50
5a variant (c) 3.50

CLASSICS ILLUSTRATED
See Also: CLASSICS
ILLUSTRATED SECTION

CLASSICS ILLUSTRATED
First, 1990
1 GW,The Raven 5.00
2 RG,Great Expectations 5.00
3 KB,Thru the Looking Glass 5.00
4 BSz,Moby Dick 5.00

COLOR PUB.

5 SG,TM,KE, Hamlet. 5.00
6 PCr,JT, Scarlet Letter. 5.00
7 DSp,Count of Monte Cristo 5.00
8 Dr.Jekyll & Mr.Hyde 5.00
9 MP,Tom Sawyer. 5.00
10 Call of the Wild 5.00
11 Rip Van Winkle 5.00
12 Dr. Moreau 5.00
13 Wuthering Heights 5.00
14 Fall of House of Usher 5.00
15 Gift of the Magi 5.00
16 A: Christmas Carol 5.00
17 Treasure Island. 5.00
18 The Devils Dictionary 5.00
19 The Secret Agent 5.00
20 The Invisible Man 5.00
21 Cyrano de Bergerac 5.00
22 The Jungle Book. 5.00
23 Swiss Family Robinson. 5.00
24 Rime of Ancient Mariner 5.00
25 Ivanhoe 5.00
26 Aesop's Fables 5.00
27 The Jungle 5.00

CLASSICS ILLUSTRATED
Acclaim 1997–98
A Christmas Carol 5.00
A Connecticut Yankee in
  King Arthur's Court 5.00
All Quiet on the Western Front . . . 5.00
A Midsummer's Night Dream. 5.00
Around the World in 80 Days. 5.00
A Tale of Two Cities 5.00
The Call of the Wild 5.00
Captains Courageous 5.00
The Count of Monte Cristo 5.00
Crime and Punishment 5.00
Dr. Jekyll and Mr. Hyde 6.00
Don Quixote. 5.00
Frankenstein 6.00
From the Earth to the Moon. 5.00
Great Expectations 5.00
Gullivers Travels 5.00
Hamlet 5.00
The House of the Seven Gables . . . 5.00
Huckleberry Finn 5.00
The Hunchback of Notre Dame. . . . 5.00
The Illiad 5.00
The Invisible Man. 6.00
Jane Eyre. 5.00
Journey to the Center of the Earth . 5.00
Kidnapped 5.00
The Last of the Mohicans 5.00
Les Miserables. 5.00
Lord Jim. 5.00

Classics Illustrated: Gulliver's Travels
© Acclaim

Macbeth 5.00
The Master of Ballantrae 5.00
Moby Dick 5.00
Mysterious Island 5.00
The Odyssey 5.00
Oliver Twist 5.00
The Prince and the Pauper 5.00
The Red Badge of Courage. 5.00
Robinson Crusoe. 5.00
Romeo & Juliet 5.00
Silas Mariner 5.00
Tom Sawyer. 5.00
Wuthering Heights 5.00

CLASSICS ILLUSTRATED
2007
1 The Three Musketeers. 10.00
4 The Last of the Mohicans 10.00
5 Moby Dick 10.00
170 The Aeneid 10.00
6 A Tale of Two Cities 10.00
16 Gulliver's Travels 10.00
19 Huckleberry Finn. 10.00
26 Frankenstein. 10.00
42 Swiss Family Robinson. 10.00
47 Twenty Thousand Leagues
    Under the Sea 10.00
60 Black Beauty 10.00
64 Treasure Island. 10.00
91 Call of the Wild 10.00
133 The Time Machine 10.00
134 Romeo and Juliet 10.00
138 Journey to the Center
    of the Earth 10.00
The Roughrider 10.00

CLASSICS ILLUSTRATED
JUNIOR
Classics Illustrated
Junior, 2003–2005
501 Show White & Seven Dwarfs . . 4.00
502 The Ugly Duckling. 4.00
503 Cinderella 4.00
504 The Pied Piper 4.00
505 Sleeping Beauty 6.00
506 Three Little Pigs 6.00
507 Jack and the Beanstalk 6.00
508 Goldilocks & the Three Bears. . 6.00
509 Beauty and the Beast 6.00
510 Little Red Riding Hood 6.00
512 Rumplestiltskin 4.00
513 Pinocchio 6.00
514 Steadfast Tin Soldier. 4.00
515 Johnny Appleseed 4.00
519 Paul Bunyan 4.00
520 Thumbelina 4.00
530 The Golden Bird 4.00
535 The Wizard of Oz 4.00
536 The Chimney Sweep 4.00
539 The Enchanted Fish 4.00
540 Tinder Box. 4.00
546 The Elves and the Shoemaker . 4.00
548 Magic Pitcher 6.00
563 The Wishing Well 4.00
564 Salt Mountain 4.00
565 THe Silly Princess. 4.00
570 Pearl Princess. 4.00
571 How Fire Came to the Indians . 4.00

CLASSWAR
Com.X, 2001
1 . . . . 3.00
2 thru 3 . . . . @3.00
4 thru 6 . . . . @3.50
1 Metal edition 40.00

CLAUS
Draco, 1997
1 by Bowden & Guichardon 3.00
2 thru 4 . . . . @3.25

CLAW
THE UNCONQUERED
Wildstorm/DC, 2006
1 CDi, ASm 3.00
2 thru 6 CDi, ASm. . . . . @3.00

CLIVE BARKER'S
TAPPING THE VEIN
Eclipse, 1989–92
1 . . . . 9.00
2 thru 5 . . . . @8.50

CLIVE BARKER'S THE
GREAT AND SECRET
SHOW
IDW Publishing, 2006
1 . . . . 4.00
1a variant (c) 4.00
2 thru 3 . . . . @4.00
4 Primal Scenes 4.00
5 The Devils Inside 4.00
6 Slaves and Lovers 4.00
7 . . . . 4.00
8 thru 12 . . . . @4.00

CLIVE BARKER'S THE
THIEF OF ALWAYS
IDW Publishing, 2005
1 . . . . 7.50
2 thru 3 . . . . @7.50

CLOCKWORK GIRL
Arcana Studio, 2007
0 . . . . 2.50
1 (of 4) 2.50
2 . . . . 2.50
3 thru 4 . . . . @2.00

CLOSE SHAVES
OF PAULINE PERIL
Gold Key, 1970
1 . . . . 50.00
2 thru 4 . . . . @30.00

CLYDE CRASHCUP
Dell Publishing Co., 1963
1 . . . . 250.00
2 . . . . 200.00
3 thru 5 . . . . @175.00

COBALT BLUE
Innovation, 1989
Spec.#1 . . . . 3.00
Spec.#2 . . . . 3.00
1 and 2 . . . . @3.00

COBALT:
WARRIOR ANGEL
Mindchyld Comics, 2005
0 . . . . 4.00
1 . . . . 4.00
2 . . . . 4.00

CODE
Guardian Line, 2006
1 . . . . 3.00
2 thru 5 . . . . @3.00

CODENAME:
BLACK DEATH
Triumph Media, 2006
1 thru 4 . . . . @3.00

CODENAME: DANGER
Lodestone, 1985
1 RB/BMc,I:Makor. 3.50
2 KB,I:Capt.Energy 3.00
3 PS/RB 3.00
4 PG 3.00

CODE NAME: DOUBLE IMPACT
High Impact, 1997
1 RCI. 3.00
1 variant cover 9.00
1 signed holofoil cover 12.00

CODENAME: FIREARM
Malibu Ultraverse, 1995
0 I:New Firearm 3.00
1 F:Alec Swan. 3.00
2 Dual Identity. 3.00
3 F:Hitch and Lopez 3.00
4 F:Hitch and Lopez 3.00
5 Working Together. 3.00

CODENAME: STRIKEFORCE
Spectrum, 1984
1 . . . . 3.00

COLD HEAT
Picturebox, 2006
1 thru 6 . . . . @5.00

COLOSSAL SHOW, THE
Gold Key, 1969
1 . . . . 75.00

COLOUR OF MAGIC
Innovation
1 Terry Pratchet novel adapt. 3.00
2 The Sending of Eight. 3.00
3 Lure of the Worm. 3.00
4 final issue. 3.00

COLT .45
Dell Publishing Co., 1958
1 Ph(c) all 250.00
2 . . . . 225.00
3 . . . . 200.00
4 . . . . 200.00
5 . . . . 200.00
6 ATh. 225.00
7 thru 9 . . . . @200.00

COLT SPECIAL
AC Comics, 1985
1 thru 3 . . . . @3.00

COMBAT
Dell Publlshing Co., 1961
1 SG 100.00
2 SG 75.00
3 SG 75.00
4 JFK cover, Story 2-D 85.00
5 SG 75.00
6 SG 50.00
7 SG 50.00
8 SG 50.00
9 SG 50.00
10 SG. 50.00
11 thru 27 SG. . . . . @60.00
28 thru 40 SG. . . . . @50.00

COMET, THE
Archie/Red Circle, 1983
1 AN,CI,O:Comet 3.00
2 AN,CI,D:Hangman 3.00

COMIC ALBUM
Dell Publishing Co., March-May, 1958
1 Donald Duck 175.00
2 Bugs Bunny 125.00
3 Donald Duck 150.00
4 Tom & Jerry 100.00
5 Woody Woodpecker. 100.00
6 Bugs Bunny 100.00
7 Popeye. 110.00
8 Tom & Jerry 100.00
9 Woody Woodpecker. 100.00
10 Bugs Bunny 100.00
11 Popeye. 110.00
12 Tom & Jerry 75.00
13 Woody Woodpecker 75.00
14 Bugs Bunny 75.00
15 Popeye. 100.00
16 Flintstones. 125.00
17 Space Mouse 100.00
18 3 Stooges,Ph(c) 125.00

COMIX INTERNATIONAL
Warren Magazines, 1974
1 . . . . 150.00
2 WW,BW. 75.00
3 . . . . 40.00
4 RC 40.00
5 Spring, 1977 . . . . 40.00

CONCRETE JUNGLE: THE LEGEND OF THE BLACK LION
Acclaim, 1998
1 (of 6) CPr,JFy,F:Terry Smalls. . . . 2.50
2 CPr,JFy,Black Lion Order 2.50
3 CPr,JFy,The Man 2.50
4 CPr,JFy 2.50
5 CPr,JFy 2.50

CONNECT
Narwain Publishing, 2005
1 . . . . 4.00

CONSORTIUM OF JUSTICE
Chimaera Studios, 2008
1 . . . . 4.00
2 thru 3 . . . . @4.00

CONTAINMENT
IDW Publishing, 2005
1 . . . . 4.00
2 thru 5 . . . . @4.00

CONTRACT
A First Salvo, 2008
1 (of 3) 4.00
2 thru 3 . . . . @3.00
Spec. Solo Missions–Tsumi 3.00
Spec. Solo Missions–Jessie 3.00

CORBEN SPECIAL
Pacific, 1984
1 RCo 5.00

CORUM: THE BULL & THE SPEAR
First, 1989
1 thru 4 Michael Moorcock adapt.@2.50

COSMIC GUARD, THE
Devil's Due Publishing, 2004
1 JSn. 3.00
2 thru 6 JSn. . . . . @3.00

COUGAR, THE
Atlas, April–July, 1975
1 . . . . 25.00
2 O:Cougar 25.00

COUNTDOWN
WildStorm/DC, 2000
1 (of 8) JMi,AaL 2.50
2 thru 6 JMi,AaL . . . . @2.50
7 JMi,AaL,RyE,supercriminals 2.50
8 JMi,AAI,RyE,concl. 3.00

COUNTER-OPS
Antarctic Press, 2003
1 . . . . 4.00
2 thru 5 . . . . @4.00

COUNTER-STRIKE
Infinity Comics, 2000
1 (of 4) 2.50
1a premium chroma-foil (c). 10.00
2 thru 4 . . . . @2.50

COUP D'ETAT
Wildstorm/DC, 2004
1 (of 4) Sleeper, JLe 3.00
2 Stormwatch: Team Achilles 3.00
3 Wildcats Version 3.0 . . . . 3.00
4 The Authority, WPo 3.00
Spec. Afterword 3.00

COURTSHIP OF EDDIE'S FATHER
Dell Publishing Co., 1970
1 Ph(c) 100.00
2 Ph(c) 75.00

COVEN
Awesome Entertainment, 1997
1 IaC,JLb,JSb,V:The Pentad 7.00
1a variant covers 7.00
2 IaC,JLb,Who is Spellcaster? 5.00
3 IaC,JLb,V:The Pentad 5.00
4 IaC,JLb,Pentad, concl.. . . . . 4.00
5 IaC,JLb, ... 4.00
5 gold foil cover 8.00
6 IaC,JLb,Mardi Gras madness . . . 3.00
6 gold foil edition. 8.00
7 IaC,JLb,V:Babylon 2.50
8 IaC,JLb,F:Thor, the God
   of Thunder 2.50
9 IaC,JLb, ... 2.50

Coven #6
© aWESOME

All comics prices listed are for *Near Mint* condition.

Coll.Ed. #1, rep. #1–#2,
 new IaC(c). 5.00
Fan Appreciation #1, rep. #1,
 new cover 2.50
Coven/Menace S.D.Con
 preview book 5.00

VOL 2

1 IaC,JLb 2.50
1a, b & c variant covers 2.50
1d chrome edition 9.00
1e gold foil cover 8.00
2 IaC,JLb,V:Supreme 2.50
2a Lionheart (c). 8.00
2b signed 15.00
3 IaC,JLb, Long Flight Home 2.50
3 Ruby red edition 12.00
4 IaC,JLb 2.50
5 thru 7 . . . . @3.00
Coven Sourcebook #1 . . . . 3.00

COVEN 13

No Mercy Comics, 1997

1 by Rikki Rockett & Matt Busch . . 2.50
2 thru 4 . . . . @2.50

COVEN/RE:GEX

Awesome Entertainment, 1999

1 (of 2) RLe,JLb,IaC 2.50
1a alternate IaC cover 7.00
2 JLb, conclusion 2.50

COVEN: DARK ORIGINS

Awesome Entertainment, 1999

1 . . . . 2.50
1a & b variant covers 2.50

COVEN: DARK SISTER

Avatar Press, 2001

1/2 Rio (c). 4.00
1/2 Shaw (c) 4.00
1/2 Martin (c). 4.00
1/2 Raptor attack (c) 5.00
1/2 Previews Raptor prism foil (c) 13.00
1/2 Bad Vibes (c) 6.00
1 Park (c) 3.50
1a Rio (c) 3.50
1b Martin (c) 3.50
1c wraparound (c) 4.00
1d Blue leather (c) 20.00
1e Royal Blue edition, in case . . 65.00
1f Haunting Vision edition. 6.00
1g Prism foil edition 13.00
1h Embrace edition 6.00
1i Embrace edition, emerald (c) . . 14.00
2 Adrian (c) edition 6.00

COVEN: SPELLCASTER

Avatar Press, 2001

1/2 Bewitched edition 6.00
1/2 Bikini edition 6.00
1/2 Rio Royal Blue (c). 50.00
1 Finch (c). 3.50
1a Rio (c) 3.50
1b Martin (c) 3.50
1c Wraparound (c) 4.00
1d Leather. 20.00
1e Finch Ruby Red(c). 20.00
1f Rio prism foil (c) 11.00
1g Royal Blue edition 50.00
2 Rio (c) 3.50
2a Shaw (c). 3.50
2b Martin (c) 3.50
2c Lyon (c) 3.50
Spec. #1 Free Spirit edition 5.96

COVEN: TOOTH & NAIL

Avatar Press, 2001

1 Adrian (c). 3.50
1a Rio (c) 3.50
1b Waller (c) 3.50

1c MMy(c). 3.50
1d Wraparound (c) 3.50
1e leather (c). 20.00
1f Royal Blue (c). 50.00
1g Bikini Edition (c). 6.00
1h Bad Ladies (c) 6.00
1i Prism exclusive (c) 11.00
1j Fantom (c). 6.00
1k Training Day (c) 6.00
1/2 Woman Scorned (c) 6.00
1/2a Prism Foil edition 11.00
1/2b Fantom edition 6.00
1/2c Adrian (c) 16-pg. 4.00
1/2d Waller (c) 4.00
1/2e MMy(c) 4.00
1/2f Martin (c) 4.00

COVER GIRL

Boom! Studios, 2007

1 thru 5 . . . . @4.00

COWBOY IN AFRICA

Gold Key, 1968

1 Chuck Conners,Ph(c) 100.00

CRACKED

Major Magazines, 1958

1 AW 350.00
2 . . . . 200.00
3 thru 6 . . . . @200.00
7 thru 10 . . . . @150.00
11 thru 20 . . . . @125.00
21 thru 30 . . . . @75.00
31 thru 36 . . . . @60.00
37 Beatles 75.00
38 thru 45 . . . . @60.00
46 Beatles 65.00
47 thru 50. . . . . @60.00
51 Beatles 65.00
52 Mysters 65.00
53 thru 56 . . . . @60.00
57 Rolling Stones. 65.00
58 . . . . 60.00
59 Laurel & Hardy 65.00
60 & 61. . . . . @60.00
62 Beatles 65.00
63 thru 68 . . . . @60.00
69 Batman 65.00
70 Elvis 65.00
71 W.C. Fields 65.00
72 thru 99 . . . . @60.00
100 . . . . 75.00
101 thru 103 . . . . @35.00
104 Godfather 75.00
105 thru 114 . . . . @35.00
115 M.A.S.H. 45.00
116 thru 118 . . . . @35.00
119 Kung Fu 40.00
120 Six Million Dollar Man. 40.00
121 American Grafiti 40.00
122 thru 130. . . . . @23.00
131 Godfather 35.00
132 Baretta 35.00
133 Space:1999. . . . . 40.00
134 Fonz 35.00
135 Bionic Woman. 35.00
136 thru 145 . . . . @35.00
146 thru 148 Star Wars . . . . . . @50.00
149 Star Wars 45.00
150 thru 162 . . . . @30.00
163 Mork & Mindy, Alien 45.00
164 thru 174 . . . . @25.00
175 thru 200 . . . . @20.00
201 thru 300 . . . . @15.00
301 thru 348 . . . . @10.00

[THE INCREDIBLE] CRASH DUMMIES

Harvey, 1993

1 thru 3, from the toy series . . . . @2.50

CRAZYMAN

Continuity, 1992
[1st Series]

1 Embossed(c),NA/RT(i),
 O:Crazyman. 5.00
2 NA/BB(c) 2.50
3 DBa,V:Terrorists. 2.50
[2nd Series], 1993
1 Die Cut(c). 2.50
2 thru 3 . . . . 2.50
4 In Demon World. 2.50

CREATURE

Antarctic Press, 1997

1 (of 2) by D.Walker&J.Maranto . . 3.00
2 concl. 3.00

CREED/TEENAGE MUTANT NINJA TURTLES

Lightning Comics, 1996

1 . . . . 3.00
1 variant cover 3.00

Creed: Cranial Disorder #1
© *Lightning Comics*

CREED: CRANIAL DISORDER

Lightning Comics, 1996

1 (of 3) 3.00
1a variant cover, *Previews*
 exclusive 3.00
1b Platinum edition 8.00
1c Platinum edition, autographed 12.00
2 . . . . 3.00
2a variant cover 3.00

CREMATOR: HELL'S GUARDIAN

Chaos! Comics, 1998

1 (of 5) LJi. 3.00
2 . . . . 3.00
3 V:Asteroth 3.00
4 thru 5 . . . . @3.00

CRIME MACHINE

Skywald Publications, 1971

1 JK. 90.00
2 AT. 50.00

CRIME PATROL

Gemstone, 2000

1 rep.. . . . . 2.50

2 rep. Fall 1948. . . . . 2.50
3 rep. Winter 1948 . . . . 2.50
4 rep. Feb. 1949 . . . . 2.50
5 rep. 2.50
6 rep. 2.50
7 rep. 2.50
8 rep. Oct. 1949 . . . . 2.50
9 rep. Dec. 1949 . . . . 2.50
10 rep. Feb. 1950 issue 2.50

CRIME SUSPENSE STORIES
Russ Cochran, 1992
1 Rep. C.S.S. #1 (1950). 3.00
2 thru 7 Rep. C.S.S. . . . . @3.00
8 thru 15 Rep. . . . . @3.00
Gemstone, 1996
16 thru 27 EC comics reprint . . . . @3.00

CRIMSON NUN
Antarctic Press, 1997
1 (of 4) 3.00
2 . . . . 3.00
3 . . . . 3.00
4 concl 3.00

CRIMSON PLAGUE
Event Comics, 1997
1 GP,F:DiNA: Simmons 3.00
2 GP, ... 3.00

CROSSED
Avatar Press, 2008
0 GEn 1.00
0a variant wraparound (c) 1.00
1 . . . . 4.00
1a variant wraparound (c) 4.00
2 . . . . 4.00
2a variant wraparound (c) 4.00

CROSSFIRE
Eclipse, 1984–86
1 DSp 3.00
2 thru 11 DSp . . . . @2.50
12 DSp,DSt(c),M.Monroe(c) & story 2.50
13 DSp 2.50
14 DSp 2.50
15 DSp,O:Crossfire 2.50
16 DSp,The Comedy Place 2.50
17 DSp,Comedy Place, Pt.2 . . . . . 2.50
See B&W

CROSSFIRE & RAINBOW
Eclipse, 1986
1 DSp,V:Marx Brothers. 2.50
2 DSp,PG(c),V:Marx Brothers. 2.50
3 DSp,HC(c),A:Witness 2.50
4 DSp,DSt(c),This Isn't Elvis. 3.50

CROSSGEN CHRONICLES
Crossgen Comics, 2000
1 RMz, 48-pg. 4.50
2 RMz,GP. 4.00
2a 2nd printing 11.00
3 BKe,GP, 40-page 5.00
4 MWa,GP, 48-page 4.00
5 RMz,GP 4.00
6 thru 8 . . . . @4.00

CROSSOVERS, THE
CG Entertainment, 2003
1 (of 6) Cross Currents. 3.00
2 thru 11 . . . . @3.00

CROSSROADS
First, 1988
1 Sable,Whisper 4.00

2 Sable,Badger 4.00
3 JSon,JAl,Badger/Luther Ironheart 4.00
4 Grimjack/Judah Macabee 4.00
5 LM,Grimjack/Dreadstar/Nexus. . . 4.00

CROW, THE: CITY OF ANGELS
Kitchen Sink, 1996
1 thru 3 movie adaptation . . . . . . @3.00
1 thru 3 movie adaptation,
   photo covers . . . . @3.00

Crux #30
© Crossgen

CRUX
Crossgen Comics, 2001
1 MWa,SEp. 7.00
2 MWa,SEp. 5.00
3 thru 8 MWa,SEp. . . . . @3.00
9 thru 20 . . . . @3.00
21 thru 33 . . . . @3.00

CRYBABY
Event Comics, 1999
1 GrL,SLo 3.00
1a limited, signed 10.00

CRYING FREEMAN III
Viz, 1991
1 A:Dark Eyes,Oshu 6.00
2 A:Dark Eyes, V:Oshu. 5.25
3 Freeman vs. Oshu. 5.25
4 Freeman Defeated. 5.25
5 Freeman clones, A:Nitta 5.25
6 V:Nitta 5.25
7 . . . . 5.00
8 . . . . 5.00
9 . . . . 5.00

CRYING FREEMAN IV
Viz, 1992
1 B:The Pomegranate. 5.00
2 thru 7 . . . . @3.00
8 E:The Pomegranate. 3.00
[2nd Series]
1 The Festival. 2.50

CRYPTIC WRITINGS OF MEGADETH
Chaos! Comics, 1997
1 BnP 3.00
1a Tour Edition, leather. 20.00
1b Tour Edition, deluxe 30.00
2 BnP 3.00

3 BnP 3.00
4 BnP 3.00

CSI: CRIME SCENE INVESTIGATION
IDW Publishing, 2003
1 (of 5) 5.00
1a photo(c) 8.00
2 thru 3 . . . . @5.00
4 thru 5 . . . . @4.00
GN Thicker Than Blood 7.00
GN Miami–Smoking Gun. 7.00
GN Miami–Thou Shalt Not. 7.00
GN Miami–Blood/Money 7.00

...BAD RAP
IDW Publishing, 2003
1 (of 5) 4.00
2 . . . . 4.00
3 . . . . 4.00
5 . . . . 4.00

...DEMON HOUSE
IDW Publishing, 2004
1 (of 5) 4.00
2 thru 5 . . . . @4.00

...DOMINOS
IDW Publishing, 2004
1 . . . . 4.00
2 . . . . 4.00
3 . . . . 4.00
4 . . . . 4.00
5 . . . . 4.00

...DYING IN THE GUTTERS
IDW Publishing, 2006
1 . . . . 4.00
2 thru 5 . . . . @4.00

...MIAMI
IDW Publishing, 2003
GN Smoking Gun. 7.00
GN Thou Shalt Not 7.00
GN Blood/Money 7.00

...NY-BLOODY MURDER
IDW Publishing, 2005
1 . . . . 4.00
2 thru 5 . . . . @4.00

...SECRET IDENTITY
IDW Publishing, 2005
1 . . . . 4.00
2 thru 5 . . . . @4.00

CTHULHU TALES
Boom! Studios, 2008
1 . . . . 4.00
1a variant (c) 4.00
2 thru 9 . . . . @4.00
2a thru 9a variant (c)s . . . . @4.00

CURSED PIRATE GIRL
Archaia Studios, 2008
1 thru 3 . . . . @4.00

CURSE OF RUNE
Malibu Ultraverse, 1995
1A CU,Rune/Silver Surfer tie-in . . . 2.50
1B CU, alternate cover 2.50
2 COntrol of the Soul Gem 2.50
3 F:Marvel's Adam Warlock 2.50
4 N:Adam Warlock 2.50

CURSE OF THE BLOOD CLAN, THE
Dead Dog Comics, 2005
1 (of 3) by Mark Kidwell 5.00
1a variant (c) 5.00
2 thru 3 . . . . @5.00

CVO: AFRICAN BLOOD
IDW Publishing, 2006
1 thru 4 . . . . @4.00

CVO: COVERT VAMPIRIC OPERATIONS–ARTIFACT
IDW Publishing, 2003
1 thru 3 . . . . @4.00
GN 6.00
1-shot Human Touch (2004) 4.00
GN 6.00

CVO: HUMAN TOUCH
IDW Publishing, 2004
1-shot 4.00

CVO: ROGUE STATE
IDW Publishing, 2004
1 thru 5 . . . . @4.00

CYBER CITY
CPM Comics, 1995
Part One
1 I:Oedo City. 3.00
2 Sengoku. 3.00
Part Two
1 Based on Animated Movie. 3.00

CYBERCRUSH: ROBOTS IN REVOLT
Fleetway/Quality
1 inc.Robo-Hunter,Ro-Busters 2.50
2 and 3 . . . . @2.50
4 and 5 V:Terraneks . . . . @2.50

CYBERFROG
Harris, 1995
0 O:Cyberfrog 3.00
0 AAd(c), signed 18.00
0 Alternate AAd(c). 9.00
1 . . . . 2.50
2 thru 4 . . . . @3.00

...RESERVOIR FROG
Harris, 1996
1 Preview Ashcan, signed
    & numbered. 12.00
1 EL(c),V:the Swarm,
Mr. Skorpeone 3.00
2 . . . . 3.00

Cyberfrog #2
© Harris

CYBERHOOD
Entity Comics, 1995
1 R:Cyberhood 2.50
1a with PC Game 7.00

CYBERNARY 2.0
WildStorm/DC, 2001
1 (of 6) R:Yumiko Gamorra. 3.00
2 F:MechaMax 3.00
3 F:Toshiro 3.00
4 secret race of cyborgs 3.00
5 revolution or evolution 3.00
6 Kaizen Gamorra, concl. 3.00

CYBERPUNK
Innovation, 1989
1 . . . . 2.50
2 . . . . 2.50
Book 2,#1. . . . . 2.50
Book 2,#2. . . . . 2.50

CYBERPUNK: THE SERAPHIM FILES
Innovation, 1990
1 and 2 . . . . @2.50

CYBERPUNX
Maximum Press, 1997
1 MHw, ... 2.50

CYBERRAD
Continuity, 1991
1 NA layouts,I:Cyberran 3.00
2 NA I/o 2.50
3 NA I/o 2.50
4 NA I/o 2.50
5 NA I/o Glow in the Dark cov 5.00
6 NA I/o,Pullout poster 2.50
7 NA I/o,See-thru(c) 2.50
[2nd Series], 1992
1 Hologram cover 2.50
2 NA(c),The Disassembled Man. . . 2.50
[3rd Series]
1 Holo.(c),just say no 3.50
**[4th Series], 1993
Deathwatch 2000]**
1 Deathwatch 2000 pt.8,w/card . . . 2.50
2 Deathwatch 2000 pt. w/card 2.50

CYBRID
Maximum Press, 1995
1 F:Cybrid, I:The Clan 3.00

CYBRID
Maximum Press, 1997
0 RLd, 48pg 3.50
1 MsM,BNa. 3.00
2 MsM,BNa. 3.00

CYNDER
Immortelle Studios, 1996
1 thru 3: see B&W
Ann. #1 . . . . 3.00
Series II, 1997
1 A:Nira X 3.00

CYNDER/NIRA X
Immortelle Studios, 1996
1 x-over. 3.00
1 variant cover 3.00
1 gold edition 10.00

DAEMONSTORM
Caliber, 1997
1 TM(c),JMt. 4.00
1 signed 4.00

DAEMONSTORM: DEADWORLD
Caliber
one-shot 4.00

DAEMONSTORM: OZ
Caliber, 1997
1 . . . . 4.00

DAFFY DUCK
Gold Key, 1962
1 . . . . 75.00
2 thru 10 . . . . @75.00
11 thru 40 . . . . @40.00
41 thru 75 . . . . @25.00
76 thru 97 . . . . @15.00
Whitman, 1980
128 thru 131 . . . . @15.00
134 thru 145. . . . . @15.00

DAGAR THE INVINCIBLE
Gold Key, 1972–82
1 O:Daggar;I:Villians Olstellon
    & Scorpio. 50.00
2 . . . . 35.00
3 I:Graylon 25.00
4 . . . . 25.00
5 . . . . 25.00
6 1st Dark Gods story 20.00
7 thru 10 . . . . @20.00
11 thru 19 . . . . @15.00

DAI KAMIKAZE
Now, 1987–88
1 Speed Racer 7.00
1a 2nd printing 2.50
2 thru 12 . . . . @2.50

D'AIRAIN ADVENTURE
IDW Publishing, 2007
1 . . . . 5.00
2 . . . . 5.00
2a variant (c). 5.00
3 thru 4 . . . . @4.00
3a thru 4a variant (c) 4.00

DAISY AND DONALD
Gold Key, 1973
1 . . . . 50.00
2 thru 5 . . . . @25.00
6 . . . . 20.00
7 thru 10 . . . . @15.00
11 thru 41 . . . . @12.00
Whitman, 1980
42 thru 46 . . . . @16.00
47 . . . . 80.00
48 thru 59 . . . . @22.00

DAKTARI
Dell Publishing Co., 1967
1 Ph(c) 60.00
2 Ph(c) 40.00
3 Ph(c) 40.00
4 Ph(c) 40.00

DALGODA
Fantagraphics, 1984–86
1 . . . . 3.50
2 KN,I:Grinwood'Daughter 3.00
3 KN 2.50
4 thru 8 . . . . @2.50

DALKIEL: THE PROPHECY
Verotik, 1998
1-shot, prequel to Satanika 4.00

DAMAGED, THE
A-10 Comics, 2006
1 and 2 .... @3.00
3 thru 5 .... @3.50

DAN DARE
Virgin Comics 2007
1 thru 6 .... @3.00
7 44-pg. 6.00

DANGER GIRL:
BACK IN BLACK
Wildstorm/DC, Nov., 2005
1 (of 4) 3.00
2 thru 4 .... @3.00

DANGER GIRL:
BODY SHOTS
Wildstorm/DC, Apr., 2007
1 thru 4 .... @3.00

DANGER GIRL:
KAMIKAZE
WildStorm/DC, 2000
1 (of 2) 3.00
1a variant(c) 3.00
2 concl. 3.00
GN Viva Las Danger 5.00
Spec. Danger Girl 3-D 5.00
Spec. Hawaiian Punch 5.00

DANGER RANGER
Checker Comics, 1998
1 I:Kirby Jackson, BSz(c) 2.50
2 .... 2.50

DANGER'S DOZEN, THE
A First Salvo, 2007
1 thru 2 .... @3.50
3 64-pg. 7.00
1-shot Interlude 3.00

DANIEL BOONE
Gold Key, 1965–69
1 .... 150.00
2 thru 5 .... @125.00
6 thru 14 .... @100.00
15 .... 75.00

DARE
Fantagraphics, 1991
1 and 2 F:Dan Dare .... @2.75
3 and 4 F:Dan Dare .... @2.50

DARE THE IMPOSSIBLE
Fleetway/Quality
1 DGb,rep.Dan Dare from 2000AD 2.50
2 thru 14 DGb .... @2.50

DARK, THE
Continuum, 1990
1 LSn(c),MBr,V:Futura 4.00
2 LSn,Shot by Futura 3.00
3 MBr,Dark has amnesia 3.00
4 GT(c),MBr,O:The Dark. 3.00
Convention Book 1992 MBr,GP,
  MFm,MMi,VS,LSn,TV 5.00
Convention Book 1993 MBr,PC,
  ECh,BS,BWi,GP(c),Foil(c), ... 4.00
[2nd Series], 1994
1 Dark Regains Memory 3.00
1a Signed, Foil Cover 2.75
1 BS(c),Red Foil(c), ... 3.00
1a BS(c),newstand ed. 3.00
1b BS(c),Blue foil 3.00
2 War on Crime 2.75

3 Geoffery Stockton 2.50
3 BS(c),Foil(c), ... 3.00
4 I:First Monster 2.50
4 GP(c),Foil(c),w/cards 3.00
5 thru 9 .... @2.50

DARK CHYLDE
Maximum Press, 1996
1 RQu 9.00
1a Am.Entertainment edition..... 12.00
1b variant cover 9.00
2 RQu 7.00
2 Variant cover 6.00
3 RQu 4.00
3 Variant cover 5.00
4 RQu 5.00
5 RQu,No One Here Gets Out
  Alive 5.00
Spec. Dark Chylde/Avengelyne RLd,
  RQu,I:Witch Tower 3.00
Spec. Dark Chylde/Glory RQu, ... 3.00
Darkchylde Entertainment, 2001
0 remastered, RQu (2001) 3.00
Last Issue special (2002) 4.00
Last issue exclusive variant(c).. 4.00

DARKCHYLDE
REDEMPTION
Darkchylde Entertainment, 2001
1 RQu 3.00
2 thru 3 .... @3.00

DARK DAYS
IDW Publishing, 2003
1 (of 6) 4.50
2 thru 6 .... @4.25

DARK DOMINION
Defiant, 1993–94
1 SD,I:Michael Alexander 3.25
2 LWn(s),SLi(i), ... 2.75
3 LWn(s),SLi(i), ... 2.75
4 LWn(s),B:Hoxhunt 3.00
5 thru 7 LWn(s) .... @2.75
8 thru 12 LWn(s) .... @2.50

DARKEST HORROR OF
MORELLA, THE
Verotik, 2006
1 .... 4.00
1 fan club (c) 9.00

Dark Dominion #3
© *Defiant*

DARK 48
Digital Webbing, 2008
1 .... 4.00
2 .... 4.00

DARKHAM VALE
APC, 2003
1 (of 10) by Jack Lawrence 3.50
2 thru 9 .... @3.50
10 finale 4.00
Spec. #0 .... 3.00

DARKHAM VALE: THE
DRACOU IMPERATIVE
APC, 2004
1 .... 3.50
2 .... 3.50
3 .... 3.50
4 .... 3.50

DARKHAM VALE:
UPRISING
APC, 2005
1 (of 10) 3.50
2 thru 3 .... @3.50

DARKLON THE MYSTIC
Pacific, 1983
1 JSn 2.50

DARKMAN
Dynamite Entertainment, 2007
1 .... 3.50
2 thru 3 .... @3.00
2a thru 3a variant (c)s .... @3.00

DARKMAN VS. ARMY OF
DARKNESS
D.E. (Dynamite Ent.) 2006
1 (of 4) Kbk,RSt,JFy 3.50
2 .... 3.50
1a thru 2a variant (c)s .... @3.50
3 thru 4 .... @3.50
3a thru 4a variant (c)s .... @3.50

DARKMINDS:
MACROPOLIS
Dreamwave, 2002
1 .... 3.00
2 thru 4 .... @3.00
3a variant Pat Lee (c) 3.00
Vol. 2
1 thru 4 .... @3.00
PocketBook Vol. 1 .... 8.00

DARK MISTS
APC, 2005
1 (of 4) 3.50
Markosia, 2005
3 .... 3.50
4 .... 3.50

DARKNESS VS. EVA
Dynamite Entertainment, 2008
1 (of 4) 3.50
2 thru 4 .... @3.50
1a thru 2a variant (c)s .... @3.50

DARK ONE'S THIRD EYE
Sirius, 1996
one-shot Vol. 1 DOe 5.00
Vol. 2 DOe 5.00

DARK SHADOWS
Gold Key, 1969
1 W/Poster,Ph(c)............ 600.00
2 Ph(c) 250.00
3 W/Poster,Ph(c)............ 350.00
4 thru 7,Ph(c) ....@150.00
8 thru 10 .... 100.00
11 thru 20 ....@750.00
21 thru 35................. @65.00

DARK SHADOWS
Innovation, 1992
1 Based on 1990's TV series 3.50
2 O:Victoria Winters 2.50
3 Barnabus Imprisoned......... 2.50
4 V: Redmond Swann........... 2.75
[2nd Series]
1 A:Nathan 2.75
2 thru 4 .... 2.75
Dark Shadows:Resurrected..... 16.00

DARK SIDE
Maximum Press, 1997
1 RLd,RQu 3.00

DARKSHRINE
Antarctic Press, 1999
1 by Shelby Robertson 3.00
1a deluxe 6.00
2 16-page 2.50

DARKSTALKERS
Devil's Due/UDON, 2004
1 .... 3.00
2 thru 6 ....@3.00
5 power foil (c) 4.00
6 evil foil (c) 4.00

DARKSTORM
Alias Enterprises, 2006
0 .... 3.50

DARKWING DUCK
Walt Disney, 1991
1 I:Darkwing Duck............. 3.00
2 V:Taurus Bulba 3.00
3 Fowl Play................. 3.00
4 End o/t beginning,final issue 3.00

DARQUE PASSAGES
Acclaim, 1997
1 (of 4) sequal to Master Darque .. 2.50
1 signed edition................ 4.00
2 .... 2.50
3 A:Pere Jean, Voodoo King..... 2.50
4 conclusion 2.50

DAVID:
THE SHEPHERD'S SONG
Alias Enterprises, 2005
1 (of 3) 3.00
2 thru 3 ....@3.00

DAVY CROCKETT KING
OF THE WILD FRONTIER
Gold Key, 1963
1 .... 275.00
Gold Key, 1969
1 .... 80.00

DAWN
Sirius, 1995–97
1 JLi,R:Dawn 10.00
1a white trash edition 20.00
1b black light edition.......... 15.00
1c look sharp edition.......... 30.00

Dawn #1
© Sirius

2 JLi, Trip to Hell............. 7.00
2 variant cover 12.00
3 JLi 6.00
3 limited edition.............. 18.00
4 JLi,The Gauntlet 5.00
4a variant cover 10.00
5 JLi,Everybody Dies 4.00
5a variant cover 10.00
6 (of 6) JLi................. 4.00
6a variant cover 9.00
10th Anniv. Spec. 3.00
10th Anniv. Spec, sgn,num....... 5.00

DAWN: PIN-UP GODDESS
Linsner.com, 2001
Spec...................... 3.00
Spec. Limited, signed.......... 12.00

DAWN: THE RETURN
OF THE GODDESS
Sirius, 1999
1 (of 4) JLi.................. 3.00
1a limited, signed 20.00
2 A:Marinen................. 3.00
3 thru 4 ....@3.00
2a thru 4a deluxe ....@20.00

DAY OF THE DEAD:
THE RISING OF BUB
Dead Dog Comics, 2006
1 (of 3) 5.00
2 thru 3 ....@5.00

DAZEY'S DIARY
Dell Publishing Co., 1962
1 .... 75.00

D-DAY
Charlton, 1963
1 .... 50.00
2 thru 6 ....@30.00

DEAD @ 17
Viper Comics, 2003
1 (of 4) 20.00
2 .... 15.00
3 thru 4 ....@10.00
Rough Cut #1................. 12.00
Rough Cut #2 .... 5.00
Rough Cut #3 .... 5.00
Vol. 2 (2006)
1 .... 3.25
2 thru 3 ....@3.25

...BLOOD OF SAINTS
Viper Comics, 2004
1 (of 4) 10.00
2 thru 4 ....@4.00

...PROTECTORATE
Viper Comics, 2005
1 (of 3) 3.00
Vol. 2 (2006)
1 .... 3.25
2 thru 7 ....@3.25

...REVOLUTION
Viper Comics, 2004
1 (of 4) 3.00
2 thru 4 ....@3.00

DEAD BOYS:
DEATH'S EMBRACE
London Night, 1996
1 EHr...................... 3.00
1 platinum edition............. 6.00

DEAD CLOWN
Malibu, 1996
1 I:Force America 2.50
2 I:Sadistic Six 2.50
3 TMs(s),last issue 2.50

DEADFORCE
Antarctic Press, 1999
1 (of 3) by Roy Burdine 3.00
2 .... 3.00
3 .... 3.00

DEAD KING
Chaos! Comics, 1997
1 (of 4) Burnt, pt.1, F:Homicide ... 3.00
2 Burnt, pt.2 .... 3.00
3 Burnt, pt.3 .... 3.00
4 Burnt, pt.4, concl........... 3.00

DEAD, THE:
KINGDOM OF FLIES
Berserker, 2008
1 .... 4.00
2 .... 4.00

DEAD MEN TELL
NO TALES
Arcana Studio, 2005
1 (of 4) 4.00
2 thru 4 ....@4.00

DEAD, SHE SAID
IDW, 2008
1 BWr 4.00
2 thru 3 ....@4.00

DEADSIDE
Acclaim, 1998
1 (of 4) PJe, ... 2.50
2 thru 4 ....@2.50

DEADWORLD:
SLAUGHTERHOUSE
Desperado Pub., 2008
1 .... 4.00
2 .... 4.00

DEAL WITH THE DEVIL
Alias Enterprises, 2005
1 (of 5) 2.50
2 thru 5 ....@3.00

DEAN KOONTZ'S FRANKENSTEIN: PRODIGAL SON
Dabel Brothers Prod., 2008
1 (of 5) 3.00
2 thru 5 . . . . @3.00

DEAR NANCY PARKER
Gold Key, 1963
1 P(c) 60.00
2 P(c) 40.00

DEATH AND THE MAN WHO WOULD NOT DIE
Silent Devil, 2007
1 (of 4) 3.00
2 . . . . 3.00

DEATHBLOW
Wildstorm/DC, Oct., 2006
1 . . . . 3.00
1a variant (c). 3.00
2 . . . . 3.00
3 . . . . 3.00
3a variant BSf (c) (1:10). 3.00
4 . . . . 3.00
4a variant BB (c). 3.00
5 V: U.S. government 3.00
6 . . . . 3.00
7 World's Deadliest Man. 3.00
8 I.O. & Pentagon vs. T.H.E.M. . . . 3.00
9 It ends here, final issue 3.00

DEATHBLOW: BY BLOWS
WildStorm/DC, 1999
1 (of 3) AMo,JBa 3.00
2 AMo,JBa 3.00

DEATH COMES TO DILLINGER
Silent Devil Productions, 2006
1 (of 2) 3.00
2 . . . . 3.00

DEATHDEALER
Verotika, 1995
1 FF(c), I:Deathdealer. 15.00
2 thru 4 FF(c) . . . . @12.00

DEATHMASK
Future Comics, 2003
1 DvM,DG,BL 3.00
2 thru 9 . . . . @3.00

DEATHMATE
Valiant/Image, 1993
Preview (Advanced Comics) 2.50
Preview (Previews) 2.50
Preview (Comic Defense Fund). . . . 4.00
Prologue BL,JLe,RLd,Solar meets
Void 3.25
Prologue Gold 4.00
Blue SCh, HSn, F:Solar, Magnus,
Battlestone, Livewire, Stronghold,
Impact, Striker, Harbinger, Brigade,
Supreme 3.00
Blue Gold Ed. 4.00
Yellow BCh,MLe,DP,F:Armstrong,
H.A.R.D.C.A.T.S.,Ninjak,Zealot,
Shadowman,Grifter,Ivar. 3.00
Yellow Gold Ed. 4.00
Black JLe,MS,F:Warblade,Ripclaw,
Turok,X-O Manowar 4.00
Black Gold Ed. 6.00
Red RLd,JMs, ... 4.00

Red Gold Ed. 3.00
Epilogue. 2.50
Epilogue Gold 3.00

DEATH OF HARI KARI
Blackout Comics, 1997
0 . . . . 3.00
0 super Sexy Kari Cover. 10.00
0 3-D super Sexy Kari Cover 15.00

DEATH OF LADY VAMPRE
Blackout Comics, 1995
1 V:Baraclaw. 3.00
1 Commemorative Issue. 10.00

DEATHRACE 2020
Cosmic Comics, 1995
1 Pat Mills, Tony Skinner 2.50
2 V:Spyda, Sawmill Jones 2.50
3 O:Frankenstein 2.50
4 Deathrace cont. 2.50
5 F:Death Racers, D:Alcoholic 2.50
6 V:Indestructiman 2.50
7 Smallville Mall 2.50

DEATH RATTLE
Kitchen Sink, 1985–88
1 . . . . 4.00
2 thru 7 . . . . @4.00
8 I:Xenozoic Tales. 9.00
9 thru 18 . . . . @3.00

DECOY
Pennyfarthing Press, 1999
1 (of 4) 2.75
2 thru 4 . . . . @2.75

DECOY: STORM OF THE CENTURY
Pennyfarthing Press, 2002
1 (of 4) 3.00
2 thru 4 . . . . @3.00

DEEPAK CHOPRA'S BEYOND
Virgin Comics 2008
1 (of 5) 3.00
2 thru 4 . . . . @3.00

DEEPAK CHOPRA'S BUDDHA: A STORY OF ENLIGHTENMENT
Virgin Comics 2008
1 . . . . 4.00
2 thru 6 . . . . @3.00

DEE SNIDER'S STRANGELAND: SEVEN SINS
Fangoria Comics, 2007
1 (of 4) 4.00
2 thru 4 . . . . @4.00

DEFENDERS, THE
Dell Publishing Co., 1962
1 . . . . 75.00
2 . . . . 50.00

DEFEX
Devil's Due Publishing, 2004
1 Aftermath 3.00
1a variant (c). 3.00
2 thru 6 Aftermath . . . . @3.00

Defex #1
© *Devil's Due Publishing*

DEFIANT: ORIGIN OF A UNIVERSE
Defiant, 1993
1 Giveaway 2.50

DEITY
Hyperwerks, 1997
0 . . . . 3.00
1 KIA 5.00
1a Director's Cut. 3.00
2 thru 6 KIA . . . . @3.00
Vol. II Awesome/Hyperworks, 1998
1 KIA,BNa, F:Jamie 3.00
1a Limited edition 8.00
1b Silver Foil edition 13.00
1c Gold Edition 20.00
2 KIA,BNa, A:Diamond Diaz 3.00
3 KIA,BNa, The Soul Crusher. 3.00
4 KIA,BNa, A:Ogden 3.00
5 KLa,BNa,V:Ma'Shiva 3.00

DEITY II: CATSEYE
Hyperwerks, 1998
1 KIA,BNa,F:Digby 3.00
2 KIA,BNa,A:II. 3.00
3 KIA,BNa,F:Catseye 3.00
4 KIA,BNa,conclusion 3.00

DELIVERER
Zion Comics
1 thru 3 . . . . @2.50
4 F:Cabriel 2.50
5 V:Division 2.50

DEMON-HUNTER
Atlas, 1975
1 The Harvester of Eyes. 25.00

DEMONIQUE
London Night, 1996
0 Manga 3.00
1 thru 2 EHr . . . . @3.00

DEMONSLAYER
Avatar Press, 2001
0 16-page, signed. 6.00

...FUTURE SHOCK
Avatar Press, 2002
1/2 Eradicate Edition 6.00

...PATH OF TIME
Avatar, 2002
1 MMy	3.50
1a Medieval (c)	3.50
1b Ninja (c)	3.50
1c Western (c)	3.50
1d Matt Martin (c)	3.50
1e Serenity (c)	6.00
1f bondage (c)	6.00
1g Prism foil (c)	13.00
1/2	4.00
1/2 Pirate (c)	4.00
1/2 Cave Girl (c)	4.00
1/2 Bikini (c)	4.00
1/2 Martin (c)	4.00

...PROPHECY
Avatar Press, 2001
1 MMy	3.50
1a Celtic (c)	3.50
1b Hell on Wheels (c)	3.50
1c Leather (c)	20.00
1d lace edition	6.00
1e Bad Omens (c)	6.00
1f Mouth of Evil edition	6.00
1g Prism foil (c)	13.00

...RAVE
Avatar Press, 2001
Spec.	3.50
Spec. Bad Schoolgirl (c)	3.50
Spec. Silent Moment (c)	3.50
Rave in Style (c)	6.00
Rave Previews prism foil (c)	13.00

...REBIRTH
Awesome Entertainment, 2000
1	3.00

...VENGEANCE
Avatar Press, 2001
1 (of 2) MMy (c)	3.50
1a Park (c)	3.50
1b Wraparound (c)	4.00
1c Red Velvet (c)	20.00
1d prism foil (c)	13.00
1e fire (c)	6.00
1f ice (c)	6.00
1g Royal Blue edition	75.00
2 MMy, concl.	3.50
2a Bikini (c)	3.50
2b Jungle Girl (c)	3.50
2c Ruins edition	6.00

DEMON'S REGRET
Digital Webbing, 2008
1 thru 3	@4.00

DEMONWARS: EYE FOR AN EYE
Crossgen Comics, 2003
1 thru 5	@3.00

DEMONWARS: THE DEMON AWAKENS
Devil's Due, 2007
1	5.00
1a cardstock (c)	9.00
2 thru 3	@5.50
2a thru 3a cardstock (c)	@9.50

DEMONWARS: TRIAL BY FIRE
Crossgen Comics, 2002
2 thru 5	@3.00

DEN
Fantagor, 1988
1 thru 10 RCo	@2.50

DEN SAGA
Tundra/Fantagor, 1992–94
1 RCo,O:Den begins	5.00
2 thru 4 RCo	@5.00

DENNIS THE MENACE
Fawcett, 1960-61
Fun Book #1	75.00
And his Pal Joey #1	50.00
And his Dog Ruff #1	50.00
Television Special #1	60.00
Triple Feature #1	60.00
Television Special #2	35.00

...AND HIS FRIENDS
[VARIOUS SUBTITLES]
Fawcett, 1969–1980
1 thru 10 rep.	@35.00
11 thru 20 rep.	@20.00
21 thru 46 rep.	@15.00

...GIANTS
[VARIOUS SUBTITLES]
Fawcett, 1955–69
N# Vacation Special	250.00
N# Christmas	200.00
2	150.00
3	150.00
4	150.00
5	150.00
6 thru 10	@150.00
11 thru 20	@100.00
21 thru 30	@75.00
31 thru 75	@60.00
Becomes:	

...BONUS MAGAZINE
[VARIOUS SUBTITLES]
Fawcett, 1970–79
76 thru 100	@20.00
101 thru 120	@15.00
121 thru 185	@10.00
186 thru 196 Big Bonus Series	@8.00
Becomes:	

DENNIS THE MENACE
Fawcett, 1979–80
#16 Fun Fest	5.00
#17 Fun Fest	5.00
#10 Big Bonus Series	5.00
#11 Big Bonus Series	5.00

DEPUTY DAWG
Gold Key, 1965
1	225.00

Dennis the Menace #174
© Fawcett

DER VANDALE
Innervision, 1998
1 (of 3)	2.50
2 (of 3)	2.50
3 (of 3)	2.50
3 variant cover	2.50

DESERT STORM JOURNAL
Apple Comics, 1991
1 Hussein on (c)	2.75
1a Schwartzkopf on (c)	2.75
2 thru 8	@2.75

DESOLATION JONES
Wildstorm/DC, May, 2005
1 WEI(s),JWi	3.00
2 WEI(s),JWi	3.00
3 WEI(s),JWi	3.00
4 WEI(s),JWi	3.00
5 WEI(s),JWi	3.00
6 WEI(s),JWi	3.00
7 WEI(s), To Be In England	3.00
8 WEI(s)	3.00
9 WEI(s) Sex, Lies, & Murder	3.00

DESPERADOES: BANNERS OF GOLD
IDW Publishing, 2004
1 thru 5	@4.00

DESPERADOES: BUFFALO DREAMS
IDW Publishing, 2007
1	4.00
2 thru 4	@4.00

DESTROYER DUCK
Eclipse, 1982–84
1 JK,AA,SA,I:Groo	12.00
2 JK,AA,Starling	5.00
3 thru 7 JK	@5.00

DESTRUCTOR, THE
Atlas, 1975
1 thru 4 WW,SD	@25.00

DETECTIVES, INC.
Eclipse, 1985
1 MR,rep.GraphicNovel	3.00
2 MR	2.50
[2nd Series]	
1 GC,A Terror of Dying Dreams	2.50
2 GC	2.50
3 GC,Cut to the Bone	2.50

DETONATOR
Chaos! Comics, 1994–95
1 I:Detonator	3.00
2 V:Messiah & Mindbender	3.00

DEVI
Virgin Comics, 2006
1 by Siddharth Kotian	3.50
2 thru 5	@3.25
6 thru 16	@3.00
17 thru 22	@3.00
Spec. Devi/Witchblade	3.00
Spec. Devi/Witchblace variant (c)	3.00

DEVIL KIDS STARRING HOT STUFF
Harvey Publications, 1962–81
1	500.00
2	200.00
3 thru 10	@150.00

11 thru 20	@100.00
21 thru 30	@75.00
31 thru 40	@60.00
41 thru 50 68 pgs.	@50.00
51 thru 55 62 pgs.	@40.00
56 thru 70	@35.00
71 thru 100	@25.00
101 thru 107	@20.00

DEVILMAN
Verotika, 1995

1 Go Nagi	3.00
1a San Diego Con Gatefold edition	5.00
2 F:Devilman	3.00
3 Through History	3.00
4 French Revolution	3.00
5 Custer's Last Stand	3.00

DEVIL MAY CRY
Dreamwave, 2004

1 thru 4	@4.00
1a thru 4a variant (c)s	@4.00

DEVIL'S KEEPER
Alias Enterprises, 2005

1	1.00
2 thru 4	@3.00
2a variant (c)	3.00

DEVLIN
Maximum Press, 1996

1 A:Avengelyne,3-part mini-series	2.50
2 (of 3) RLd,BNa,A:Avengelyne	2.50

DIARY OF NIGHT
Bloodfire, 2007

1 thru 4	@3.00

DICK TRACY
Blackthorne, 1986

1 3-D	3.00

DICK TRACY:
BIG CITY BLUES

1 Mini Series	4.00
2 Mini Series	6.00
3 Mini Series	6.00

DIGITAL GRAFFITI
APC, 2003

1 thru 4	@3.50

DINO ISLAND
Mirage, 1993

1 and 2	@2.75

DINOSAUR REX
Upshot/Fantagraphics, 1987

1 thru 3 by Jan Strand & Henry Mayo	@3.00

DINOSAURS
Walt Disney

1 Citizen Robbie(From TV)	3.00

DINOSAURS ATTACK
Eclipse, 1991

1 HT,Based on Topps cards	3.50
2 and 3 HT,Based on cards	@3.50

DINOSAURS FOR HIRE
[1st Series] see: B&W
[2nd Series] Malibu, 1993–94

1 B:TMs,BNa,A:Reese,Archie, Lorenzo	3.00
2 thru 12	@2.50

DINO WARS:
EXTINCTION FILES
Antarctic Press, 2007

1	3.50

DINOWARS: JURASSIC
WAR OF THE WORLDS
Antarctic Press 2006

1 (of 4)	3.50
2 thru 4	@3.50

DISNEY ADVENTURES
Walt Disney

1	3.00
2	3.00
3 thru 13	@3.00
14 thru 28	@3.00

DISNEY COLOSSAL
COMICS COLLECTION
Walt Disney

1 inc.DuckTales, Chip'n'Dale	3.00
2 thru 9	@3.00

DISNEY COMICS IN 3-D
Walt Disney, 1992

1 F:Donald & Uncle Scrooge	3.00

DISNEY COMICS SPEC:
DONALD & SCROOGE

1 inc."Return to Xanadu"	9.00

DISNEY JUNIOR
Disney Press, 2006

GN #1 Finding Nemo	5.00
GN #2 Lilo & Stitch	5.00
GN #3 Disney's Tall Tails	5.00
GN #4 Kid Gravity	5.00

DISNEYLAND
BIRTHDAY PARTY
Gladstone, 1985

1 CB	15.00

DIVER DAN
Dell Publishing Co.,
Feb.-April, 1962

1	100.00
2	90.00

DIVINE INTERVENTION
WildStorm/DC, 1999

1	3.00
Wildcats, pt.2, JLe,SLo,RiB	3.00
Gen13, pt.3, JLe,SLo,RiB	3.00

DNA HACKER
CHRONICLES
Bloodfire, 2008

1 (of 6)	3.00
2 thru 3	@3.00

DNAGENTS
Eclipse, 1983–85

1 O:DNAgents	4.00
2	3.00
3 thru 8	@2.50
9 DSp	2.50
10 thru 25	@2.50

See also: NEW DNAGENTS

DOC FRANKENSTEIN
Burlyman Entertainment, 2004

1	7.00

DNAgents #20 © Eolipse

1a 2nd printing	4.00
2	5.00
3 thru 6	@3.50
3a thru 6a sketch (c)	@3.50

DOC SAVAGE
Gold Key, 1966

1	175.00

DOC SAVAGE
Millennium

1 V:Russians	2.50

DOC SAVAGE,
THE MAN OF BRONZE
Millennium, 1992

1 Monarch of Armageddon,pt.1	3.00
2 Monarch of Armageddon,pt.2	3.00
3 Monarch of Armageddon,pt.3	3.00
4 Monarch of Armageddon,pt.4	3.00

...DEVIL'S THOUGHTS
Millennium, 1992

1 V:Hanoi Shan	2.50
2 V:Hanoi Shan	2.50
3 Final issue	2.50

...DOOM DYNASTY
Millennium, 1991

1 and 2	@2.50

...MANUAL OF BRONZE
Millennium, 1992

1 Fact File	2.50

...REPEL
Millennium, 1992

1 DvD(c)	2.50

DOCTOR BOOGIE
Media Arts, 1987

1 and 2	@2.50

DOCTOR CHAOS
Triumphant Comics, 1993

1 JnR(s),I:Doctor Chaos	2.50
2 JnR(s),	2.50
3 JnR(s),The Coming of the Cry,pt.1,I:Cry	2.50
4 JnR(s),The Coming of the Cry,pt.2,b:Ky'Li	2.50
5 JnR(s),E:Coming of the Cry,pt.3,V:Cry	2.50
6 Recovery	2.50

7 w/coupon	2.50
8 w/coupon	2.50
9 V:Mirth	2.50
10 Co. X #3	2.50
11 Co. X #4	2.50
12 A:Charlotte	2.50

DR. JJ
Narwain Publishing, 2006
1 The Devil's Psychologist 4.00

DR. KILDARE
Dell Publishing Co., April-June, 1962

1	150.00
2 thru 9	@100.00

Doctor Solar Man of the Atom #20
© Gold Key

DOCTOR SOLAR MAN OF THE ATOM
Gold Key, 1962

1 BF,I:Dr. Solar	400.00
2 BF,I:Prof.Harbinger	150.00
3 BF,The Hidden Hands	125.00
4 BF,The Deadly Sea	125.00
5 BF,I:Dr.Solar in costume	150.00
6 FBe,I:Nuro	100.00
7 FBe,Vanishing Oceans	100.00
8 FBe,Thought Controller	100.00
9 FBe,Transivac The Energy Consuming Computer	100.00
10 FBe,The Sun Giant	100.00
11 FBe,V:Nuro	75.00
12 FBe,The Mystery of the Vanishing Silver	75.00
13 FBe,Meteor from 100 Mill.BC	75.00
14 FBe,Solar's Midas Touch	75.00
15 FBe O:Dr.Solar	100.00
16 FBe,V:Nuro	75.00
17 FBe,The Fatal Foe	75.00
18 FBe,The Mind Master	75.00
19 FBe,SolarV:Solar	75.00
20 AMc,Atomic Nightmares	75.00
21 AMc,Challenge from Outer Space	50.00
22 AMc,Nuro,I:King Cybernoid	50.00
23 AMc,A:King Cybernoid	50.00
24 EC,The Deadly Trio	50.00
25 EC,The Lost Dimension	50.00
26 EC,When Dimensions Collide.	50.00
27 (1969) The Ladder to Mars	50.00
28 (1981),1-pg AMc,The Dome of Mystery	40.00
29 DSp,FBe,Magnus	40.00
30 DSp,FBe,Magnus	40.00

COLOR PUB.

DR. TOMORROW
Acclaim, 1997

1 (of 12) BL,Bart Simms finds Angel Computer	2.50
2 thru 12 BL	@2.50

DOCTOR WHO
IDW, 2008

1	4.00
2 thru 6	@4.00

DOCTOR WHO CLASSICS
IDW, 2008

1	4.00
2 thru 10	@4.00

DOCTOR WHO: THE FORGOTTEN
IDW, 2008

1	4.00
2 thru 4	@4.00

DOGS OF WAR
Defiant, 1994

1 F:Shooter,Ironhead	2.75
2	2.50
3 Mouse Deserts	2.50
4 Schism Prequel	2.50
5 X-over	2.50
6 Aftermath	2.50

DOKTOR SLEEPLESS
Avatar Press, 2007

1	4.00
2 thru 5	@4.00
1a thru 5a wraparound (c)	@4.00
2b Auxiliary edition	4.00
3b Auxiliary edition	4.00
4b Auxiliary edition	3.00
6 thru 12	@4.00
6a thru 12a wraparound (c)s	@4.00
1b Wizard World Chicago edition	6.00
1c Wizard World Philly edition	6.00
6b Mad Scientist edition	6.00
8b Sing edition	6.00
9b Cheers (c)	4.00

DOKTOR SLEEPLESS MANUAL
Avatar Press, 2008

1	4.00
1a variant wraparound (c)	4.00
1b auxiliary edition	4.00

DOLLMAN
Eternity, 1991

1 Movie adapt. sequel	2.50
2 V:Sprug & Braindead Gang	2.50
3 Toni Costa Kidnapped	2.50
4	2.50

DOMINION
Boom! Studios, 2007

1	4.00
2 thru 5	@4.00

DONALD DUCK
Dell/Gold Key, 1962

85 thru 97	75.00
98 rep. #46 CB	75.00
99	65.00
100	75.00
101 thru 111	@50.00
112 I:Moby Duck	60.00
113 thru 133	@50.00
134 CB rep	50.00
135 CB rep	50.00

136 thru 156	@40.00
157 CB rep	40.00
158 thru 163	@40.00
164 CB rep	40.00
165 thru 216	@30.00

Whitman, 1980

217	30.00
218	30.00
219 CB rep	30.00
220 and 221	@50.00
222 scarce	300.00
223 thru 224	@75.00
225 thru 240	@30.00
241 thru 245	@35.00

Gladstone

246 CB,Gilded Man	25.00
247 CB	20.00
248 CB,Forbidden Valley	20.00
249 CB	20.00
250 CB,Pirate Gold	20.00
251 CB,Donald's Best Xmas	15.00
252 CB,Trail o/t Unicorn	8.00
253 CB	8.00
254 CB, in old Calif	9.00
255 CB	8.00
256 CB,Volcano Valley	8.00
257 CB,Forest Fire	8.00
258 thru 266 CB	@8.00
267 thru 277 CB	@8.00
278 CB	9.00
279 CB	9.00
280 thru 298 CB rep	@6.00
299 Life Guard Daze	5.00
300 Donald's 300th Triumph' 48pg	6.00
301 The Gold Finder	5.00
302 Monkey Business	5.00
303 The Cantankerous Cat	5.00
304 Donald Duck Rants about Ants	5.00
305 Mockingbird Ridge	5.00
306 Worst Class Mail	5.00
307 Going to Sea	5.00
308 Worst Class Mail	5.00

DONALD DUCK ADVENTURES
Gladstone, 1987

1 CB,Jungle Hi-Jinks	8.00
2 CB,Dangerous Disquise	6.00
3 CB,Lost in the Andes	6.00
4 CB,Frozen Gold	6.00
5 CB,Rosa	6.00
6 CB	3.00
7 CB	3.00
8 CB,Rosa	6.00
9 CB	3.00
10 CB	3.00
11 CB	3.00
12 CB,Rosa,Giant-size	6.00
13 CB,Rosa(c)	3.50
14 CB	3.00
15 CB	3.00
16 CB	3.00
17 CB	3.00
18 CB,No Such Varmint	3.00
19 CB	4.00
20 CB,Giant-size (1990)	4.00
21 CB,Rosa(c) (1993)	4.00
22 CB,The Pixilated Parrot	4.00
23 thru 30	@4.00
31 thru 40	@3.00
41 Bruce McDuck	3.00
42 The Saga of Sourdough Sam	3.00
43 The Lost Charts of Columbus	3.00
44 The Kitchy-Kaw Diamond	3.00
45 The Red Duck	3.00
46	3.00
47 CB,Trick or Treat	3.00
48 The Saphead Factor	3.00

Walt Disney, 1990

1 Don Rosa, The Money Pit	6.00
2 CB	3.00

All comics prices listed are for *Near Mint* condition.

3	3.00
4 CB	3.00
5	3.00
6	3.00
7	3.00
8	3.00
9 CB	3.00
10 Run-Down Runner	3.00
11 Whats for Lunch-Supper	3.00
12 Head of Rama Putra	3.00
13 JustAHumble,BumblingDuck	3.00
14 CB,Day Gladstone's Luck Ran Out	4.00
15 A Tuft Luck Tale	3.00
16 Magica's Missin'Magic	3.00
17 CB,Secret of Atlantis	4.00
18 Crocodile Donald	3.00
19 Not So Silent Service	3.00
20 Ghost of Kamikaze Ridge	3.00
21 CB,The Golden Christmas Tree	4.00
22 The Master Landscapist	5.00
23 The Lost Peg Leg Mine	3.00
24 On Stolen Time	4.00
25 Sense of Humor	3.00
26 CB,Race to the South Seas	4.00
27 CB,Nap in Nature	4.00
28 Olympic Tryout	3.00
29 CB,rep.March of Comics#20	4.00
30 A:The Vikings	3.00
31 The Sobbing Serpent of Loch McDuck	3.00
32 It Was No Occident	3.00
33 Crazy Christmas on Bear Mountain	3.00
34 Sup.Snooper Strikes Again	4.00
35 thru 38 CB rep	@4.00

DONALD DUCK ALBUM
Dell Publishing Co., May-July, 1959
1 CB(c)	150.00
2	100.00

DONALD DUCK AND FRIENDS
Gemstone Publishing, 2003
308 thru 333	@3.00
334 thru 347	@3.00
348	3.50

DONATELLO
Mirage, 1986
1 Teenage Mutant Ninja Turles	10.00

DON BLUTH'S DRAGON'S LAIR
Crossgen Comics, 2003
1 (of 6) Singe's Revenge	3.00
2 thru 3	@3.00

DON BLUTH'S SPACE ACE
Crossgen Comics, 2003
1 (of 6) Defender of the Universe	3.00
2 thru 3	@3.00

DONE TO DEATH
Markosia, 2006
1	3.50
2 thru 5	@3.50

DONNA MIA
Dark Fantasy Prod., 1995
1 I:Donna Mia	4.00
1a Deluxe Edition	5.00
1b signed & numbered (100 copies)	9.00
2	3.00

Doomsday+1 #6
© *Charlton*

DOOMSDAY + 1
Charlton, 1975–79
1 JBy,JBy(c)	35.00
2 JBy(c),P(c)	30.00
3 JBy,JBy(c),P(c)	25.00
4 JBy,JBy(c),P(c),I:Lok	25.00
5 and 6 JBy,JBy(c),P(c)	@25.00
7 thru 12 JBy,JBy(c),rep	@15.00

DOOMSDAY SQUAD
Fantagraphics, 1986
1 rep. JBy	3.00
2 rep. JBy	3.00
3 rep. SS,A:Usagi Yojimbo	3.00
4 thru 7, rep. JBy	@3.00

DOROTHY
Illusive Arts Entertain., 2005
1	5.00
1a 2nd printing	5.00
2 thru 4	@5.00
5 thru 8	@5.00

DOUBLE DARE ADVENTURES
Harvey Publications, 1966
1 I:B-man,Glowing Gladiator, Magicmaster	125.00
2 AW/RC rep. A:B-Man,Glowing Gladiator, Magicmaster	75.00

DOUBLE IMPACT
High Impact Studios, 1995–96
1 RCI,I:China & Jazz, chrome(c)	7.00
1 holographic rainbow (c) with certificate	12.00
1 rainbow (c), no certificate	9.00
1 chromium variant (c)	8.00
2 RCI,V:Castillo	3.00
2a signed, with certificate	4.00
3 China on cover	5.00
3a Jazzler on cover	3.00
3b Nikki on cover	3.00
3c Blondage	6.00
4 F:Mordred, The Rattler	3.00
4a Phoenix variant (c)	6.00
5 RCI	3.00
6 Buttshots	4.00
6a Jazz (c)	3.00
6a signed	6.00
7 I:Nikki Blade	3.00
8	3.00

8a variant (c)	4.00
Gold edition, Lingerie special	3.00
Volume 2, 1996–97	
0 RCI	3.00
1 RCI	3.00
1a deluxe edition	4.00
1b prism foil (c)	5.00
1c gold foil (c)	5.00
2 RCI	3.00
3	3.00
3a special edition RCI(c)	8.00

...ALIVE
ABC Studios, 1999
1 RCI,F:China & Jazz	3.00
1a deluxe	7.00

.../HELLINA
High Impact, 1996
1-shot RCI	3.00

.../LETHAL STRYKE: DOUBLE STRIKE
High Impact/London Night, 1996
1-shot RCI	3.00

...SUICIDE RUN
High Impact, 1997
1 RCI	3.00
1 gold edition	10.00
1 platinum edition	20.00
2	3.00
2a Suicide Cover	10.00

...2069
ABC Studios, 1999
1 RCI,Independent Day	3.00
1a premium edition	5.00
1b Sexy China ed.	5.00

DOUBLE LIFE OF PRIVATE STRONG
Archie Publications, 1959
1 JSm/JK,I:Lancelot Strong/ Shield, The Fly	1,000.00
2 JSm/JK,GT A:Fly	750.00

DRACULA
Dell, 1962
2	60.00
3 thru 5	@40.00
6 thru 8	@25.00

DRACULA
Dell Publishing Co., 1966
1 see: Movie Classics	
2 O:New Dracula (super-powers)	75.00
3 Rain of Terror	50.00
4 The Origin of Fleeta	50.00
5 not published	
6 rep. #2 (1972)	45.00
7 rep. #3 (1972)	35.00
8 rep. #4 (1973)	35.00

[BRAM STOKER'S] DRACULA
Topps, 1992
1 MMi,Movie adaptation (trading cards in each issue)	5.00
1a Red Foil Logo	9.00
1b 2nd Print	3.00
2 MMi,Movie adapt.contd	4.00
3 MMi,Movie adapt.contd	4.00
4 MMi,Movie adapt.concludes	4.00

DRACULA CHRONICLES
Topps
1 True Story of Dracula	2.50
2 RTs,rep. Vlad #2	2.50
3 RTs,rep. Vlad #3	2.50

COLOR PUB.

DRACULA'S REVENGE
IDW Publishing, 2004
1 . . . . 4.00
2 . . . . 4.00

DRACULA VS CAPONE
Silent Devil Productions, 2006
1 (of 3) 3.00

DRACULA VS KING ARTHUR
Silent Devil Productions, 2005
1 thru 3 . . . . @3.00
4 . . . . 5.00

DRACULA VS ZORRO
Topps, 1993
1 DMg(s),TY,Black(c), ... 3.25
2 DMg(s),TY,w/Zorro #0 . . . . 3.00

DRACULA: VLAD THE IMPALER
Topps, 1993
1 EM,I:Vlad Dracua, w/cards 3.25
1a Red Foil 10.00
2 EM, w/cards 3.25
3 EM,w/cards 3.00

DRAFTED
Devil's Due, 2007
1 . . . . 3.50
2 . . . . 3.50
3 thru 12 . . . . @3.50

DRAGON CROSS
Big City Comics, 2007
1 . . . . 3.25
2 thru 9 . . . . @3.25
7a variant (c) 3.25

DRAGONFLIGHT
Eclipse, 1991
1 Anne McCaffrey adapt. 5.00
2 novel adapt 5.00
3 novel adapt 5.00

DRAGONFLY
AC Comics, 1985
1 . . . . 3.50
2 thru 8 . . . . @2.50

DRAGONLANCE: CHRONICLES
Devil's Due Publishing, 2005
Vol. 1 Dragons of Autumn Twilight
1 (of 8) 3.00
1B signed edition 9.00
2 thru 3 . . . . @3.00
2a thru 3a collector's edition . . . @6.00
4 thru 8 . . . . @3.00
4a thru 8a collector's edition . . . . @6.00
Spec. rep. #1 & #2 . . . . 6.00
Vol. II Dragons of Winter Night
1 (of 4) 5.00
1a cardstock (c) 8.00
2 thru 4 . . . . @5.00
2a thru 4a cardstock (c) . . . . . . @9.00
Vol. III Dragons of Spring Dawning
1 . . . . 3.50
1a variant prestige (c) . . . . @5.50
2 thru 9 . . . . @3.50
2a thru 9a variant prestige (c) . @5.50
10 thru 12 . . . . @3.50
10a thru 12a variant prestige (c) . @5.50

DRAGONLANCE: THE LEGEND OF HUMA
Devil's Due Publishing, 2004
1 . . . . 3.00
1a variant (c) 3.00
2 thru 6 . . . . @3.00

DRAGONLANCE LEGENDS: TIME OF THE TWINS
Devil's Due, 2008
1 (of 3) 5.50
1a variant prestige (c) 9.50
2 thru 3 . . . . @5.50
2a thru 3a variant prestige (c)s . @9.50

DRAGONLANCE LEGENDS: WAR OF THE TWINS
Devil's Due, 2008
1 (of 3) 5.50
1a variant (c) 5.50

DRAGONPRO
Antarctic Press, 2006
0 . . . . 3.50

DRAGONRING
Aircel, 1987–88, Vol. 2
1 . . . . 3.50
2 O:Dragonring 2.50
3 thru 15 . . . . @2.50
See also: B&W

DRAGON'S LAIR
Arcana Studio, 2006
1 . . . . 5.00
2 . . . . 3.00
3 thru 4 . . . . @4.00

DRAG-STRIP HOTRODDERS
Charlton 1963
1 . . . . 125.00
2 thru 5 . . . . @75.00
6 thru 16 . . . . @60.00
Becomes:

WORLD OF WHEELS
Charlton, 1967
17 thru 21 . . . . @40.00
22 thru 32 . . . . @35.00

DRAKKON WARS, THE
Realm Press, 1997
0 by Richard Hatch & Chris Scalf . . 3.00
1 . . . . 3.00

DREADNOUGHT: INVASION SIX
Talcmedia Press, 2008
1 thru 4 . . . . @4.00

DREADSTAR
First, 1986–91
27 JSn,from Epic,traitor 3.00
28 thru 49 . . . . @3.00
50 JSn,AMe,Pawns 4.25
51 thru 64 . . . . @4.00

DREADSTAR
Malibu Bravura, 1994–95
1 JSn(c),PDd(s),EC,I:New Dreadstar (Kalla),w/stamp 2.75

Dreadstar #6 © Malibu

2 JSn(c),PDd(s),EC,w/stamp 2.50
3 JSn(c),PDd(s),EC,w/stamp 2.75
4 PDd,EC,Kalla's origin,w/stamp . . 2.50
5 PDd,F:Vanth,w/stamp 2.50
6 PDd,w/stamp 2.50

DREAMER, THE
IDW, 2008
1 . . . . 4.00
1a variant (c) 4.00

DREAMLAND CHRONICLES, THE
Astonish Comics, 2003
1 . . . . 3.50
2 . . . . 3.50
Alias Enterprises, 2005
2 and 3 (of 4) . . . . @4.50

DREAMLAND CHRONICLES, THE
IDW, 2008
1 . . . . 4.00
1a variant (c) 4.00
2 thru 5 . . . . @4.00
3a thru 5a variant (c)s . . . . @4.00

DREAMS OF THE DARKCHYLDE
Darkchylde Entertainment, 2000
1 RQu,BPe 3.00
2 thru 6 . . . . @3.00
4a Fear 2001 edition 6.00

DREDD RULES
Fleetway/Quality, 1991–93
1 SBs(c),JBy,Prev.unpubl. in USA . 5.00
2 inc.Eldster Ninja Mud Wrestling Vigilantes 3.50
3 inc.That Sweet Stuff 3.50
4 Our Man in Hondo City 3.50
5 thru 17 . . . . @3.25
18 F:Jonny Cool 3.00
19 V:Hunter's Club 3.00
20 . . . . 4.00

DRIFT MARLO
Dell Publishing Co., May–July, 1962
1 . . . . 90.00
2 . . . . 70.00

DRUNKEN FIST
Jademan, 1988
1 . . . . 3.25
2 . . . . 2.50
3 thru 9 . . . . @2.50
10 thru 53 . . . . @2.50

DUCKMAN
Topps, 1994
1 USA Cartoon 2.50
2 XXX Files 2.50
3 I:King Chicken 2.50
4 V:Toys 2.50
5 F:Cornfed 2.50
6 Star Trek Parody 2.50
7 rep. 1990 B&W 1st app., now
  in color 2.50

...THE MOB FROG SAGA
Topps, 1994
1 I:Mob Frog 2.50
2 D:Mob Frog 2.50
3 In the Name of the Duck 2.50

DUCK TALES
Gladstone, 1990
1 CB(r)I:LaunchpadMcQuck 7.00
2 CB(r) 4.00
3 . . . . 4.00
4 CB(r) 4.00
5 thru 11 . . . . @4.00
12 & 13 . . . . @5.00

Duck Tales #4
© Walt Disney

DUCK TALES
Walt Disney, 1990
1 Scrooge's Quest:The Ice Demon 4.00
2 thru 19 . . . . @3.00

DUDLEY DO-RIGHT
Charlton Comics, 1970–71
1 From TV series 150.00
2 thru 7 . . . . @125.00

DUEL MASTERS
Dreamwave, 2003
1 . . . . 3.00
1a variant (c)s . . . . @3.00
2 thru 8 . . . . @3.00
Pocket Edition Vol. 2 . . . . 11.00

DUMMY'S GUIDE
TO DANGER, A
Viper Comics, 2006
1 (of 4) 3.25
2 thru 4 . . . . @3.25

...LOST AT SEA
Viper Comics 2008
1 . . . . 3.25
2 thru 4 . . . . @3.25

DUNC & LOO
Dell Publishing Co., 1961
1 . . . . 150.00
2 . . . . 125.00
3 thru 8 . . . . @75.00

DUNGEONS & DRAGONS:
THE LOST CITY
Twenty First Century, 1999
1 (of 6) game tie-in 5.00
2 thru 6 . . . . @5.00

...AMBER CASTLE
Twenty First Century, 2000
1 (of 6) game tie-in 5.00

...TEMPEST'S GATE
Kenzer & Company, 2001
1 (of 4) Born of Fire 3.00
2 Forged in Tears 3.00
3 Tempered in Fellowship 3.00
4 Sheathed in Justice 3.00

...WHERE SHADOWS FALL
Kenzer & Company, 2003
1 (of 5) 3.50
2 thru 5 . . . . @3.50

DUO STARS
IDW, 2008
1 . . . . 4.00
2 . . . . 4.00

DUST TO DUST
Moonstone, 2008
1Jesse James vs. Machine
  Gun Kelley 4.00

DWIGHT D. EISENHOWER
Dell Publishing Co., 1969
1 . . . . 75.00

DYNAMO
Tower Comics, 1966
1 WW,MSy,RC,SD,I:Andor 150.00
2 WW,DA,GT,MSy,Weed solo
  story A:Iron Maiden 100.00
3 WW,GT,Weed solo story,
  A:Iron Maiden 100.00
4 WW,DA,A:Iron Maiden 100.00

DYNAMO JOE
First, 1986–87
1 . . . . 3.00
2 . . . . 2.50
3 thru 14 . . . . @2.50
Spec.#1 . . . . 2.50

EARTH 4
Continuity, 1993
1 Deathwatch 2000 Pt.6,w/card . . . 2.50
2 Deathwatch 2000 Pt.11,w/card . . 2.50
3 V:Hellbenders, w/card 2.50
[2nd Series]
1 WMc 2.50
2 thru 3 . . . . @2.50

EAST MEETS WEST
Innovation
1 . . . . 2.50
2 thru 3 . . . . @2.50

EBERRON:
EYE OF THE WOLF
Devil's Due Publishing, 2006
1-shot 5.00
1-shot-a cardstock (c) 9.00

ECHO OF FUTUREPAST
Continuity, 1984–85
1 NA,MGo,I:Bucky O'Hare,
  Frankenstein 4.00
2 NA,MGo,A:Bucky O'Hare, Dracula,
Werewolf 3.50
3 NA,MGo,A:Bucky 3.50
4 NA,MGo,A:Bucky 3.50
5 NA,MGo,A:Drawla&Bucky 3.50
6 Ath,B:Torpedo 3.50
7 ATh 3.50
8 Ath 3.25
9 Ath,Last issue 3.25

ECHOES OF THE DAMNED
Devil's Due, 2008
1 (of 3) 3.50

ECLIPSE
GRAPHIC NOVELS
Eclipse
1 Axa 7.00
2 MR,I Am Coyote 7.00
3 DSt,Rocketeer 9.00
3a hard cover 25.00
4 Silver Heels 9.00
4a hard cover 25.00
5 Sisterhood of Steel 9.00
6 Zorro in Old Calif. 8.00

ECLIPSE MONTHLY
Eclipse, 1983–84
1 SD,DW,I:Static&Rio 2.50
2 GC,DW 2.50
3 thru 10 DW . . . . @2.50

ED BURNS'
DOCK WALLOPER
Virgin Comics 2007
2 thru 5 . . . . @3.00

EDGAR RICE
BURROUGHS'
A PRINCESS OF MARS
IDW Publishing, 2006
1 . . . . 4.00

EDGE
Malibu Bravura, 1994–95
1 GK,I:Edge 2.50
2 GK,STg,Gold Stamp 2.50
3 GK,The Ultimates 2.50
4 GK,V:Mr. Ultimate 2.50

EDGE OF CHAOS
Pacific, 1983
1 GM 2.50
2 GM 2.50
3 GM 2.50

EIGHT LEGGED FREAKS
WildStorm/DC, 2002
Spec. movie adapt. 64-pg 7.00

87th PRECINCT
Dell Publishing Co.,
April–June, 1962
1 BK 200.00
2 . . . . 175.00

EL ARSENAL
Arcana Studio, 2005
1 (of 3) 3.00
2 thru 3 . . . . @3.00

EL CAZADOR
Crossgen Comics, 2003
1 CDi,SEp 3.00
2 thru 3 CDi,SEp . . . . @3.00
4 thru 8 . . . . @3.00
Spec. #1 Bloody Ballad of
  Blackjack Tom 3.00

ELEMENTALS
Comico, 1984–88
1 BWg,I:Destroyers. 5.00
2 BWg. 3.50
3 BWg. 3.50
4 thru 12 BWg. . . . . @3.00
13 thru 22 . . . . @3.00
23 thru 29. . . . . @3.00
Spec.#1 . . . . 3.00
Spec.#2 . . . . 3.00
[Second Series], 1989–94
1 . . . . 3.00
2 thru 4 . . . . @3.00
5 thru 28 . . . . @3.00
Spec.#1 Lingerie special 3.00
GN The Natural Order, rep. 10.00
GN Death & Resurrection 13.00
[Third Series], 1995
1 R:Elementals, polybagged with
  Chrysalis promo card 3.00
2 R:Original Monolith, polybagged
  with Chrysalis promo card. 3.00
3A Destroy the Shadowspear 3.00
3B variant cover 3.00
4 Memoirs,pt.1 . . . . 3.00
5 Memoirs,pt.2 . . . . 3.00
GN Ghost of a Chance 6.00
Spec. Babes, photo multimedia
  bikini special 4.00
Spec. Hot Bikini Valentine 4.00
Spec. All New Summer Special 5.00
Spec.#1 Lingerie Metalite 4.00

...HOW THE WAR WAS ONE
Comico, 1996
1 . . . . 3.00
2 . . . . 3.00
3 . . . . 3.00
4 . . . . 3.00

...THE VAMPIRE'S REVENGE
Comico, 1996–97
1 thru 4 . . . . @3.00

...VS. THE CHARNEL PRIESTS
Comico, 1996
Spec. 1 (of 2) 3.00
2 . . . . 3.00

ELFLORD
Aircel, 1986–88
Volume 1: *See B&W*
Volume II
1 . . . . 3.50
2 . . . . 3.00
3 thru 20 . . . . @3.00
21 double size 5.00
22 thru 24. . . . . @3.00
Spec.#1 . . . . 3.00
25 thru 32, see B&W

ELFQUEST:
BLOOD OF TEN CHIEFS
Warp Graphics, 1993–95
1 WP. 3.00
2 WP. 3.00
3 WP,B:Swift Spear pt. 1. . . . . 3.00
4 WP,B:Swift Spear pt. 2. . . . . 3.00
5 thru 20 . . . . @3.00

Elfquest Hidden Years #9 1/2
© Warp Graphics

...HIDDEN YEARS
Warp Graphics, 1992
1 WP 3.00
2 WP, w/coupon promo. 3.00
3 WP, w/coupon promo.Cont.sty.
  previewed in Harbinger#11 . . . . 3.50
4 WP,w/coupon 3.00
5 WP,O:Skywise 3.00
6 WP,F:Timmain 3.00
7 F:Timmain 3.00
8 Daughter's Day 3.00
9 WP(s),Enemy Face 3.00
9 1/2 WP,JBy,Holiday Spec. 3.50
10 thru 14 WP . . . . @3.00
15 WP Wolfrider Tribe Splits 3.50
16 thru 18 WP 3.00
19 thru 24. . . . . @3.00
25 B&W Wolfrider's Death 3.00
26 thru 29 B&W finale . . . . @3.00

...JINK
Warp Graphics, 1994–96
1 Future 3.50
2 thru 7 . . . . @3.00
8 B&W V:Black Snakes 3.00
9 thru 12 . . . . 3.00

...NEW BLOOD
Warp Graphics, 1992–96
1 JBy,artists try Elfquest 5.00
2 Barry Blair story 3.50
3 thru 5 . . . . @3.00
6 thru 31 . . . . @3.00
32 B&W Sorrow's End 3.00
33 thru 35 B&W 3.00
Summer Spec.1993 . . . . 4.25

...THE REBELS
Warp Graphics, 1994–96
1 Aliens, set several hundred
  years in future 3.00
2 thru 8 . . . . @3.00
9 B&W Brother vs. Brother 3.00
10 thru 12 . . . . @3.00

...SHARDS
Warp Graphics, 1994–96
1 Division 3.50
2 thru 5 . . . . @3.00
6 thru 11 . . . . @3.00
12 B&W F:High One Timmain 3.00
13 thru 16 B&W finale . . . . @3.00

...WAVE DANCERS
Warp Graphics, 1993–96
1 Foil enhanced 3.50
2 thru 6 . . . . @3.00
Spec. #1. . . . . 3.00

ELIMINATOR
COLOR SPECIAL
Eternity, 1991
1 DDo(c) set in the future 3.00

ELIMINATOR
Malibu Ultraverse, 1995
0 Man,DJa,MZ,Zothros tries to re-
  open passage to the Godwheel 3.00
1 MZ,Man,DRo, The Search for the
  Missing Infinity Gems,I:Siren. . . 3.00
1a Black Cover ed. 4.00
2 MZ 2.50
3 MZ, Infinity Gem tie-in,finale 2.50

ELK'S RUN
Hoarse and Buggy Prod., 2005
1 . . . . 3.00
2 thru 3 . . . . @3.00
Speakeasy Comics, 2005
4 thru 7 . . . . @3.00

ELRIC
Pacific, 1983–84
1 CR,MGi,Michael Moorcock adapt 4.00
2 CR,MGi,Elric of Melnibone 3.00
3 thru 6 CR,MGi . . . . @3.00

...(ONE LIFE)
Topps, 1996
0 NGa,CPR, One Life, based on
  Michael Moorcock character . . . 3.00

...THE BANE OF
THE BLACK SWORD
First, 1988–89
1 Michael Moorcock adapt. 3.00
2 . . . . 3.00
3 thru 6 . . . . @3.00

...SAILOR ON
THE SEAS OF FATE
First, 1985–86
1 Michael Moorcock adapt. 4.00
2 thru 7 . . . . @3.00

...THE VANISHING TOWER
First, 1987–88
1 Michael Moorcock adapt. 3.00
2 thru 6 . . . . @3.00

...THE WEIRD OF
THE WHITE WOLF
First, 1986–87
1 Michael Moorcock adapt. 3.00
2 thru 5 . . . . @3.00
Graphic Novel CR 7.00

ELSINORE
Alias Enterprises, 2005
1 (of 9) 2.50
2 thru 7 . . . . @3.00
Elsinore Case Files #1: Arrivals. . . . 3.00
Devil's Due Publishing, 2006
4 . . . . 4.00
5 thru 9 . . . . @3.25

ELVEN
Malibu Ultraverse, 1994
0 Rep.,A:Prime, double size 3.00
Mini-Series 1994–95
1 A:Prime, Primevil 2.50
2 AaL,R:Maxi-Man 2.50
3 AaL,V:Duey, Primevil 2.50
4 AaL,F:Primevil 2.50

E-MAN
Charlton Comics, 1973–75
1 JSon,O:E-Man 35.00
2 SD 20.00
3 . . . . 20.00
4 SD 20.00
5 SD,Miss Liberty Belle 20.00
6 JBy,Rog 2000 . . . . 20.00
7 JBy,Rog 2000 . . . . 20.00
8 J:Nova 25.00
9 JBy,Rog 2000 . . . . 20.00
10 JBy,Rog 2000 . . . . 20.00

E-MAN
First, 1983
1 JSon,O:E-Man & Nova, A:Rog
  2000, 1 pg. JBy 3.00
2 JSon,I:F-Men (X-Men satire) 1-
  page Mike Mist 2.50
3 thru 25 JSon. . . . . @2.50
Spec. #1 . . . . 2.75

E-MAN
Comico, 1989–90
1 JSon. 2.75
2 and 3 JSon. . . . . @2.50

E-MAN
Alpha Productions, 1993
1 JSon. 2.75

E-MAN
Digital Webbing, 2008
1-shot Dolly 7.00
1-shot The Idol 4.00

E-MAN: RECHARGED
Digital Webbing, 2006
1-shot 4.00

EMERGENCY
Charlton Comics, 1976
1 JSon(c),JBy 45.00
2 JSon. 25.00
3 Thru 4 . . . . 25.00

ENCHANTED: THE AWAKENING
Sirius, 1998
1 by Robert Chang 3.00
2 . . . . 3.00
3 conclusion 3.00

END OF STORY: MITRABHED
Virgin Comics, 2007
1 . . . . 3.00
2 . . . . 3.00
3 Panchatantra 3.00

ENGINE
Shadow Planet, 2002
1 by Tim Tyler 3.50
1a signed sketch edition 10.00
2 thru 3 . . . . @3.00

ENGINEER, THE
Archaia Studios, 2007
1 thru 3 . . . . @4.00

ENIGMA CIPHER, THE
Boom! Studios, 2006
1 (of 5) 4.00
2 . . . . 4.00

ENIGMAS, THE
Digital Webbing, 2006
1-shot 6.00

ENSIGN O'TOOLE
Dell Publishing Co., 1962
1 . . . . 50.00
2 . . . . 40.00

EPILOGUE
IDW, 2008
1 . . . . 4.00
2 thru 3 . . . . @4.00
2a thru 3a variant (c) . . . . @4.00

EPSILON WAVE, THE
Independent, 1985
1 Darkest Before Dawn 3.00
2 Tango in Texas City 2.50
3 One More Step Toward Darkness 2.50
4 Afterlife 2.50
Elite Comics, 1986
5 thru 10 . . . . @2.50

ESC.(ESCAPE)
Comico, 1996
1 SPr. 3.00
2 thru 4 SPr. . . . . @3.00

ESC: NO EXIT
Comico, 1997
1 . . . . 3.00
1 medallion edition 10.00
2 . . . . 3.00

ESCAPE OF THE LIVING DEAD
Avatar Press, 2005
1 . . . . 4.00
1a Wraparound (c) 4.00
1b Variant(c)s . . . . @4.00
2 thru 5 . . . . @4.00
2a thru 5a wraparound (c)s . . . . . @4.00
2b thru 5b variant (c)s . . . . @4.00
Ann. #1 . . . . 5.00
Ann. #1a variant (c)s 5.00

...AIRBORNE
Avatar Press, 2006
1 . . . . , . 4.00
2 thru 3 . . . . @4.00
1a thru 2a wraparound (c) 4.00
1b thru 3b variant (c)s . . . . @4.00

...FEARBOOK
Avatar Press, 2006
1 . . . . 4.00
1a wraparound (c) 4.00
1b variant (c)s . . . . @4.00

ESPERS
Eclipse, 1986
1 I:ESPers. 3.00
2 JBo(c),V:Terrorists 3.00
3 V:Terrorists. 3.00
4 Beirut 3.00
5 The Liquidators 3.00
6 V:Benito Giovanetti 3.00

ESPIONAGE
Dell Publishing Co., May-July, 1964
1 . . . . 75.00
2 . . . . 50.00

ESTABLISHMENT, THE
WildStorm/DC, 2001
1 IEd,CAd,F:Charlie Arrows 2.50
2 IEd,CAd 2.50
3 IEd,CAd 2.50
4 IEd,CAd 2.50
5 IEd,CAd 2.50
6 IEd,CAd 2.50
7 IEd,CAd 2.50
8 IEd,CAd, in Russia 2.50
9 IEd,CAd, demon-god embryos . . 2.50
10 IEd,CAd, Charlie Arrows. 2.50
11 IEd,CAd, DeadSpace 2.50
12 IEd,CAd, Moonbase Straker. . . . 2.50
13 IEd,CAd, final issue 2.50

ESTANCIA
Hammock Entertainment, 2006
1 (of 17) 3.50
2 . . . . 3.50
3 thru 7 . . . . @3.50

ETERNAL WARRIOR
Valiant, 1992
1 FM(c),JDx,Unity #2,O:Eternal
  Warrior,Armstrong 4.00
1a Gold Ed. 12.00
1b Gold Foil Logo 20.00
2 thru 10 . . . . @3.00
11 thru 49 . . . . @3.50
50 . . . . 9.00
Yearbook #1 . . . . 4.25
Yearbook #2 . . . . 4.00
Wings of Justice WWI 2.50
Quarterly
Time and Treachery 4.00
Digital Alchemy 4.00
Spec. Blackworks AHo, ... 4.00

ETERNAL WARRIORS
Acclaim, 1997
Quarterly
Archer & Armstrong AHo 4.00
Mog AHo 4.00
The Immortal Enemy AHo 4.00

Eternal Warriors Blackworks #1
© Valiant

ETERNITY SMITH
Renegade, 1986
1 thru 5 . . . . @3.50
[Vol. 2] Hero, 1987
1 thru 9 . . . . @2.50
Heroic Publishing
1 Man Vs. Machine. 2.50
2 Man Vs. Machine. 2.50

EVA THE IMP
Red Top Comic/Decker, 1957
1 . . . . 50.00
2 . . . . 50.00

EVANGELINE
Comico, 1984
1 Guns of Mars. 4.00
2 . . . . 3.00
Lodestone, 1986
1 . . . . 2.50
2 . . . . 2.50
First, 1988
1 . . . . 3.00
2 thru 9 . . . . @2.50
10 thru 12 . . . . @2.00

EVERQUEST
WildStorm/DC, 2001
GN The Ruins of Kunark, JLe 6.00
GN Transformation. 6.00

EVERYBODY'S DEAD
IDW, 2008
1 . . . . 4.00
2 thru 5 . . . . @4.00

EVERYTHING'S ARCHIE
Archie Publications, 1969
1 Giant 125.00
2 Giant 75.00
3 thru 5 Giant . . . . @50.00
6 thru 10 Giant . . . . @35.00
11 thru 20 . . . . @25.00
21 thru 40 . . . . @15.00
41 thru 134 . . . . @10.00

EVE: VAMPIRE DIVA
Arcana Studio, 2007
1 (of 4) 4.00
2 thru 4 . . . . @4.00

EVIL ERNIE
(THE SERIES)
Chaos! Comics, 1998
1 V:Purgatori. 3.00
2 Search for Chastity, A:Savior. . . . 3.00
3 V:Purgatori. 3.00
4 return to New Jersey 3.00
5 two beings 3.00
6 heart of America 3.00
7 Unholy Nights 3.00
8 Trauma,pt.1 . . . . 3.00
9 Trauma,pt.2 . . . . 3.00
10 Trauma,pt.3. . . . . 3.00
...DEPRAVED
Chaos! Comics, 1999
1 (of 3) 4.00
1a premium edition 9.00
2 . . . . 3.00
3 . . . . 3.00
...DESTROYER
Chaos! Comics, 1997
Prev.#1 . . . . 3.00
1 (of 9) BnP 3.00
2 BnP 3.00
3 to Atlanta 3.00
4 siege of Atlanta 3.00

Evil Ernie: Destroyer #6
© *Chaos! Comics*

5 . . . . 3.00
6 Nuclear launch codes 3.00
7 Nuclear attack 3.00
8 Nuclear attack continues 3.00
9 New forms of living dead, concl. . . 3.00
...IN SANTA FE
Devil's Due Publishing, 2005
1 . . . . 3.00
2 thru 4 . . . . @3.00
...REVENGE
Chaos! Comics, 1994–95
1 SHu,BnP,A:LadyDeath,glow(c) . . 7.00
1a limited, glow-in-the-dark (c) . . 15.00
1a Commemorative edition. 12.00
2 SHu,BnP,Loses Smiley 6.00
3 SHu,BnP,V:Dr. Price 5.00
4 SHu,BnP,Final Issue 5.00
...STRAIGHT TO HELL
Chaos! Comics, 1995–96
1 Rampage in Hell, coffin(c) 4.00
1 limited, chromium edition. 15.00
2 Cremator 4.00
3 . . . . 4.00
3a Chastity (c). 18.00
4 and 5 . . . . @4.00
Ashcan 2.50
Spec. 20.00
...THE RESURRECTION
Chaos! Comics, 1993–94
1 R:Evil Ernie 15.00
1a gold edition 35.00
2 Enhanced cover 11.00
3 Massive Mayhem Lady Death
   poster. 11.00
4 final issue, extra pages 11.00
Ashcan Resurrection (2001) 20.00
...VS. THE MOVIE MONSTERS
Chaos! Comics
1 one-shot 3.00
1 omega edition 5.00
1 premium edition, signed 15.00
...VS. THE SUPER-HEROES
Chaos! Comics, 1995
1 one-shot 3.50
1a foil (c). 30.00
1b limited 10.00
Spec. #2 by Hart Fisher
   & Steve Butler 3.00
Spec. #2, Premium edition 10.00

...WAR OF THE DEAD
Chaos! Comics, 1999
1 (of 3) 3.00
1a premium. 10.00
2 . . . . 3.00
3 concl. 3.00

EVIL ERNIE'S
BADDEST BATTLES
Chaos! Comics, 1996
1-shot, imaginary battles. 3.00

EXALTED
Udon Entertainment, 2005
1 . . . . 3.50
1 Power foil (c) 12.50
2 thru 4 . . . . @3.50
5 40-page 5.00
2a thru 5a Power foil (c)s . . . . @12.50

EXECUTIONER
Innovation, 1993
1 Don Pendleton(s),F:Mack Bolan . 4.00
1a Collector's Gold Ed. 3.00
1b Tyvek cover 4.00
2 War against Mafia 2.75
3 War against Mafia,pt.3. . . . . 2.75

EXEMPLARS
1 and 2 . . . . @2.50

EXILES
Malibu Ultraverse, 1993
1 TMs(s),PaP,I:Exiles 4.00
1a w/out card 2.50
1b Gold hologram ed. 10.00
1c Ultra-limited 12.00
2 V:Kort. 3.00
3 BWS,Mastodon,BU:Rune 4.00
4 V:Kort. 3.00

EX MACHINA
Wildstorm/DC, 2004
1 F:Mitchell Hundred,40-pg. 3.00
2 thru 5 State of Emergency . . . @3.00
6 thru 10 Tag. . . . . @3.00
11 V:Fortune Tellers 3.00
12 thru 14 Fact vs. Fiction . . . . . @3.00
15 thru 16 Off the Grid . . . . . . @3.00
17 thru 20 . . . . @3.00
21 thru 24 Smoke, Smoke . . . . . @3.00
25 Bradbury, Chief of Security. . . . 3.00
26 thru 29 Power Down . . . . . . @3.00
30 thru 33 Ex Cathedra . . . . . . @3.00
34 The Great Machine. 3.00
35 F:Mitchell Hundred 3.00
36 F:Mitchell Hundred 3.00
37 F:Trouble. 3.00
38 F:Trouble. 3.00
39 Dirty Tricks 3.00
Spec. #1 Inside the Machine 3.00
Spec. Masquerade Special (2007). . 3.50
Spec. #1 Mayor Hundred's past. . . . 3.00
Spec. #2 Life and Death 3.00

EX-MUTANTS
Malibu, Nov. 1992–Apr. 1994
1 I&O:Ex-Mutants 2.50
2 thru 18 . . . . @2.50

EXO-SQUAD
Topps, 1994
[Mini-Series]
0 . . . . 2.50
1 From Animated Series 2.50
2 F:Nara Burns 2.50
3 V:Neo-Sapiens. 2.50

EXPLORERS
Explorer Press, 1995
1 I:Explorers 3.00
2 The Cellar 3.00

EXPOSURE SPECIAL
Avatar Press, 2000
1 . . . . 3.50
1a photo(c) 3.50

EXPOSURE: SECOND COMING
Avatar Press, 2000
1 (of 2) Angel (c) 40-page 5.00

EXTINCTIONERS
Vision Comics, 1998
1 by Shawntae Howard &
   Malcolm Earle 4.00
2 . . . . 4.00

EXTINCTION EVENT
Wildstorm/DC, 2003
1 (of 5) BBh,humans vs. dinos 2.50
2 thru 5 BBh . . . . @2.50

EXTRA
Gemstone, 1999
1 (of 5) 2.50
2 thru 4 . . . . @2.50
5 final issue 2.50

EXTREMES VIOLET
Blackout Comics, 1995
0 I:Violet 3.00
Becomes:

EXTREMES OF VIOLET
Blackout Comics, 1995
1 V:Drug Lords 3.00
2 A:Matt Chaney 3.00

EYE OF THE STORM
Rival Productions
1 I:Killian, Recon, Finesse, Stray . . 3.00
2 Conspiracy 3.00
3 3-D Comic Background 3.00
4 F:Recon 3.00
5 Sinclair & Rott 3.00
Ann. 48-pg. 5.00

EZRA
Arcana Studio, 2004
1 . . . . 3.00
2 thru 3 . . . . @3.00
4 . . . . 3.00

...EVOKED EMOTIONS
Arcana Studio, 2006
1 (of 3) 4.00
2 thru 3 . . . . @4.00

FADE FROM GRACE
Beckett Comics, 2004
1 . . . . 2.50
2 thru 5 . . . . @2.50

FALLEN ANGEL
IDW Publishing, 2005
2 PDd 4.00
3 thru 11 PDd . . . . @4.00
12 thru 32 . . . . @4.00

FALL OF CTHULHU, THE
Boom! Studios, 2007
0 . . . . 4.00
0a variant (c) 4.00

---

1 . . . . 4.00
1a 4.00
2 thru 9 . . . . @4.00
2a thru 9a variant (c) . . . . @4.00
10 thru 14 . . . . @4.00
10a thru 14a variant (c)s . . . . . @4.00
Cover Gallery 4.00
Cover Gallery variant (c) 4.00

...GODWAR
Boom! Studios, 2008
1 . . . . 4.00
1a variant (c)s 4.00
2 thru 4 . . . . @4.00
2a thru 4a variant (c)s . . . . @4.00

...APOCALYPSE
Boom! Studios, 2008
1 . . . . 4.00
1a variant (c)s 4.00

FAMILY AFFAIR
Gold Key, 1970
1 W/Poster,Ph(c). 100.00
2 . . . . 50.00
3 Ph(c) 50.00
4 Ph(c) 50.00

FAMILY GUY
Devil's Due Publishing, 2006
1 100 Ways to Kill Lots 6.00
2 Family Comes First 6.00
3 Books Don't Taste Very Good . . . 6.00
4 48-pgs. 6.00

FAMOUS INDIAN TRIBES
Dell Publishing Co., 1962
1 . . . . 27.00
2 . . . . 15.00

FANTASTIC VOYAGE
Gold Key, 1969
1 . . . . 90.00
2 . . . . 65.00

FANTASTIC VOYAGES OF SINBAD, THE
Gold Key, 1965
1 Ph(c) 125.00
2 June, 1967 . . . . 100.00

FANTASY FEATURES
AC Comics, 1987
1 . . . . 3.00
2 . . . . 3.00

FARO KORBIT
APC, 2003
1 (of 4) 3.50
2 thru 4 . . . . @3.50

FARSCAPE
Boom! Studios, 2008
1 From TV series 4.00
1a variant (c) 4.00
1b variant photo (c) 4.00

FARSCAPE: WAR TORN
WildStorm/DC, 2001
1 (of 2) MWm, F:John Crichton . . . 5.00
2 MWm,48-page 5.00

FAT ALBERT
Gold Key, 1974–79
1 . . . . 50.00
2 . . . . 35.00
3 thru 10 . . . . @35.00
11 thru 29 . . . . @30.00

FATALE
Broadway, 1995
1 thru 6 JJo, Inherit the
   Earth, pt.5 . . . . @3.00
7 Fatale now Queen of the World. . 3.00
8 Crown of Thorns, pt.2 . . . . 3.00
9 Crown of Thorns, pt.3 . . . . 3.00

FATE'S FIVE
Innervision, 1998
1 (of 4) 2.50
1 variant cover 2.50
2 (of 4) 2.50
3 (of 4) 2.50

FATHOM
Comico, 1987
1 thru 3 From Elementals . . . . . @2.50
[2nd Series], 1993
1 thru 3 . . . . @2.50
Aspen, 2005
0 . . . . 5.00
1 . . . . 4.00
1a signed 30.00
2 thru 4 . . . . @4.00
5 thru 11 . . . . @4.00
1-shot Fathom Beginnings 2.50
Vol. 3, Aspen MLT, 2008
0 . . . . 2.50
1 . . . . 3.00
1a variant (c)s . . . . @3.00
2 thru 3 . . . . @3.00
2a thru 3a variant (c)s . . . . @3.00

...DAWN OF WAR
Aspen, 2003
0 . . . . 2.50
1 . . . . 3.00
2 . . . . 3.00
3 . . . . 3.00
Spec. Cannon Hawke #1 . . . . 3.00

...KIANI
Aspen MLT, 2006
0 . . . . 2.50
1 . . . . 3.00
2 thru 4 . . . . @3.00

...KILLIAN'S VESSEL
Aspen MLT, 2007
1 . . . . 3.00
1a variant (c) 3.00

Fathom Dawn of War #1
© Aspen

COLOR PUB.

FATMAN, THE HUMAN FLYING SAUCER
Lightning Comics, 1967
1 CCB,O:Fatman & Tin Man . . . 100.00
2 CCB 75.00
3 CCB,(Scarce). 80.00

FAUST: BOOK OF M
Avatar Press, 1999
1 (of 3) DQ,TV 4.00
1a (of 3) prism foil (c) 11.00
1b signed, leather cover 18.00
1c Royal Blue edition 60.00
2 . . . . 4.00
3 . . . . 4.00

FEARBOOK
Eclipse
1 SBi,RV,A Dead Ringer 2.50

FEAR THE DEAD
Boom! Studios, 2006
GN A Zombie Survivor's Journal . . . 6.00

FELIX THE CAT
Harvey, 1991
1 thru 4 . . . . @4.00
5 thru 7 . . . . @3.00

FELIX THE CAT: THE MOVIE
Felix Comics, 1998
1-shot, issued a mere 10 years
   after movie. 4.00

FELIX'S NEPHEWS INKY & DINKY
Harvey Publications, 1957
1 . . . . 125.00
2 thru 7 . . . . @75.00

FEM 5
Entity, 1995
1 thru 4 five-part series . . . . @3.00
1 signed & numbered 13.00

FEMFORCE
AC Comics, 1985
1 O:Femforce 10.00
2 A:Captain Paragon. 5.00
3 Skin Game. 5.00
4 Skin Game. 5.00
5 Back in the Past. 5.00
6 EL,Back in the Past. 5.00
7 HB,O:Captain Paragon 5.00
8 V:Shade 5.00
9 V:Dr.Rivits 5.00
10 V:Dr.Rivits 5.00
11 D:Haunted Horsemen 4.00
12 V:Dr.Rivits 4.00
13 V:She-Cat 4.00
14 V:Alizarin Crimson 4.00
15 V:Alizarin Crimson 4.00
16 thru 56 See Black & White Pub.
57 V:Goat God. 3.00
58 I:New Sentinels. 3.00
59 I:Paragon 3.00
60 V:Sentinels 3.00
61 F:Tara 3.00
62 V:Valkyra 3.00
63 I:Rayda 3.00
64 thru 67. . . . . @3.00
68 Spellbound 3.00
69 She-Cat Possessed 3.00
70 Island Out of Time 3.00
71 Darkfire Returns 3.00
72 w/Sentinels of Justice. 4.00

72a no extras. 3.00
73 w/Compact Comic. 4.00
73a Regular edition 3.00
74 Daughter of Darkness. 4.00
74a Regular edition 3.00
75 Gorby Poster. 5.00
75a Regular edition 3.00
76 Daughters pt. 3, polybagged
   with Compact Comic 4.00
76a no bag or comic 3.00
77 V:Sea Monster 3.00
78 V:Gorgana, bagged with comic. . 5.00
78a no bag or comic 3.00
79 V:Iron Jaw, polybagged
   with Index 5.00
79a no bag or index. 3.00
80 polybagged with Index 6.00
80a F:Mr. Brimstone, Rad 3.00
81 polybagged with Index 6.00
81a Valentines Day Spec. 3.00
82 polybagged with Index 6.00
82a F:Ms. Victory. 3.00
83 F:Paragon 3.00
84 The Death of Joan Wayne
   polybagged with index #4B 6.00
84a no bag or index. 3.00
85 Synn vs. Narett, polybagged
   with card 5.00
85a no bag or card 3.00
86 polybagged with index #5. . . . . 5.00
86a unbagged, no suplements . . . 3.00
87 Pandemonium in Paradise,
   polybagged with plate 9.00
87a unbagged, no plate. 3.00
88 F:Garganta, polybagged with
   index #6. . . . . 6.00
89 polybagged with index 6.00
90 polybagged with index 6.00
91 polybagged with index 6.00
92 polybagged with index 6.00
88a thru 92a unbagged, no index @3.00
93 on see Black & White Pub.
Spec.#1 . . . . 2.50
Untold Origin Spec #1 . . . . 5.00

FEMFORCE: UP-CLOSE
AC Comics, 1992–95
1 F:Stardust 4.00
2 F:Stardust 4.00
3 . . . . 4.00
4 . . . . 4.00
5 thru 8 with Sticker . . . . @4.00
5a thru 8a Regular Edition . . . . . @3.00
9 thru 11 . . . . @3.00

Femforce Up-Close #10
© AC Comics

FEMME NOIR: THE DARK CITY DIARIES
Ape Entertainment, 2008
1 . . . . 4.00
1a variant (c) 4.00
2 thru 4 . . . . @4.00
2a thru 4a variant (c)s . . . . @4.00

FERRET
Malibu, 1992
1 (From Protectors),DZ,V:Purple
   Dragon Tong,A:Iron Skull 2.50
[Regular Series] 1992–93
1 . . . . 2.50
2 thru 11 . . . . @2.50

FERRYMAN, THE
Wildstorm/DC, Oct., 2008
1 . . . . 3.50
2 thru 3 . . . . @3.50

FICTION CLEMENS
Ape Entertainment, 2008
1 (of 3) 52-pg. 6.00
2 thru 3 . . . . @6.00

FIGHT THE ENEMY
Tower Comics, 1966
1 BV,Lucky 7. . . . . 60.00
2 AMc 40.00
3 WW,AMc 40.00

FIGHTIN' ARMY
Charlton 1956–84
16 . . . . 40.00
17 thru 19 . . . . @50.00
20 SD 90.00
21 thru 23 . . . . @50.00
24 Giant 75.00
25 thru 50 . . . . @35.00
51 thru 74 . . . . @30.00
75 Lonely War 40.00
76 thru 88 . . . . @22.00
89 thru 92 SD . . . . @25.00
93 thru 99 . . . . @20.00
100 . . . . 25.00
101 thru 145 . . . . @20.00
146 thru 165 . . . . @10.00
166 thru 172. . . . . @10.00

FIGHTIN' FIVE
Charlton 1964
28 . . . . 100.00
29 thru 39. . . . . @50.00
40 . . . . 100.00
41 . . . . 75.00
Charlton 1981
42. . . . . 6.00
43 thru 497. . . . . @6.00

FIGHTING AMERICAN
Harvey, 1966
1 SK,Rep Fighting American
   from 1950's 150.00

FIGHTING AMERICAN
Awesome Entertainment
1 . . . . 7.00
1a variant (c). 4.00
1b Platinum (c) 12.00
2 . . . . 4.00
Coll.Ed.#1 rep.#1–#2 . . . . 5.00
Spec.#1 Fighting American: Cold War
   RLe,JLb. 2.50

...DOGS OF WAR
Awesome Entertainment, 1998
1 JSn,SPa,F:John Flagg. 2.50

1a Tour Edition, RLe cover 5.00
1b Tour Edition, signed 12.00
2 JSn,SPa,other super-soldiers . . . 2.50
2a variant cover 2.50
3 A:Crimson Dragon 2.50
4 Who is No Name? 2.50
Spec.'98 Con preview,b&w,16-page 5.00

...RULES OF THE GAME
Awesome Entertainment, 1997
1 JLb 3.00
2 JLb 2.50
3 JLb, Baby Buzz Bomber 2.50

FIGHTIN' MARINES
Charlton 1955
14 . . . . 250.00
15 MB(c) 125.00
16 . . . . 50.00
17 MB 175.00
18 thru 24 . . . . @50.00
25 Giant 100.00
26 Giant, 100-pgs. 165.00
27 thru 77 . . . . @40.00
78 Shot Gun Baker 30.00
79 thru 81 . . . . @30.00
82 Giant 75.00
83 thru 100 . . . . @25.00
101 thru 140 . . . . @20.00
141 thru 170 . . . . @8.00
171 thru 176 scarce 10.00

FIGHTIN' NAVY
Charlton 1956
74 . . . . 90.00
75 thru 81 . . . . @50.00
82 giant 75.00
83 giant 100-pgs. 100.00
84 thru 100 . . . . @40.00
101 UFO 45.00
102 thru 125 . . . . @25.00
Charlton 1983
126 thru 133 . . . . 25.00

FINAL DESTINATION: SPRING BREAK
Zenescope Entertainment, 2006
1 (of 5) 4.00
2 thru 5 . . . . @4.00

FINAL GIRL
Antarctic Press, 2007
1 . . . . 4.00
2 thru 5 . . . . @3.50

FIRE AND BRIMSTONE
Antarctic Press, 2008
1 (of 3) 4.00
2 thru 3 . . . . @4.00

FIREARM
Malibu Ultraverse, 1993–95
0 w/video,I:Duet 3.00
1 I:Firearm,Alec Swan 2.50
1 silver foil, limited edition. 4.00
2 BWS,A:Hardcase,BU:Rune 2.75
3 thru 10 . . . . @2.50
11 Ultraverse Premier #5,BU:Prime. 3.50
12 thru 18 . . . . @2.50

FIREBLAST: ADVENTURES IN THE 30TH CENTURY
Masterpiece Comics, 2006
1-shot 3.00

FIRST, THE
Crossgen Comics, 2000
1 BKs,BS 6.00

2 thru 13 BKs,BS . . . . @5.00
14 thru 25 . . . . @3.00
26 thru 36 . . . . @3.00
37 Atwaal returns 3.00

FIRST ADVENTURES
First, 1985
1 thru 5 . . . . @2.50

FIRST GRAPHIC NOVELS
First 1984
1 JBi,Beowolf 8.00
1a 2nd Printing 7.00
2 TT,Time Beavers 10.00
3 HC,American Flag Hard Times . 12.00
4 Nexus,SR. 10.00
5 Elric,CR 20.00
6 Enchanted Apples of Oz 6.00
7 Secret Island of Oz 10.00
8 HC,Time 2 . . . . 28.00
9 TMNT. 20.00
10 TMNT II. 18.00
11 Sailor on the Sea 15.00
12 HC,American Flagg 15.00
13 Ice King 10.00
14 TMNT III 14.00
15 Hex Breaker 10.00
16 Forgotten Forest 11.00
17 Mazinger 11.00
18 TMNT IV 13.00
19 O;Nexus 10.00
20 American Flagg 16.00

FIRST WAVE: HEART OF A KILLER
Andromeda Entertainment, 2000
1 by Dan Parsons, TV tie-in 3.00
1a photo (c). 3.00
2 . . . . 4.00
2a photo (c). 4.00
2b signed 10.00
2c sketch edition 20.00

FIRST WAVE: IN THE BEGINNING
Andromeda Entertainment, 2001
1 . . . . 3.00
1a photo (c). 3.00

FIRST WAVE: JORDAN RADCLIFFE
Andromeda Entertainment, 2001
1 painted (c) 3.00
1a photo (c). 3.00
1b limited foil (c) 10.00

FISH POLICE
Comico, 1987
Vol 2 #6 thru #15 rep. . . . . @2.50
Vol 2 #16 rep. 3.00
Vol 2 #17 rep.,AuA. 3.00
1 Color Special (July 1987) 3.50

FIST OF JUSTICE
Digital Webbing, 2007
1 . . . . 4.00
2 thru 3 . . . . @4.00
1a variant (c) 4.00

FLAMEHEAD
JNCO Comics, 1998
1 I:Flamehead. 2.50
2 thru 5 . . . . @2.50

Flare #9
© Hero Graphics

FLARE
Hero Graphics
1 I:Darkon&Prof.Pomegranite. 4.00
2 Blonde Bombshell,A:Galooper. . . 3.00
3 I:Sky Marshall 3.00
Ann.#1 . . . . 4.50
[2nd Series]
1 A:Galloping Galooper. 3.00
2 A:Lady Arcane 3.00
3 I:Britannia. 3.00
4 A:Indigo 2.50
5 R:Eternity Smith,O:Die Kriegerin . 4.00
6 I:Tigress 3.50
7 V:The Enemies 4.00
8 Morrigan Wars#4,A:Icicle Dragon 3.50
9 Morrigan Wars Pt.7 (B&W) 3.50

FLARE
Heroic Publishing, 2004
1 . . . . 3.00
2 . . . . 3.00
3 thru 9 . . . . @3.00
30 . . . . 3.00
31 thru 32 . . . . @3.00
33 thru 35 . . . . @3.25
36 thru 37 . . . . @3.00

FLARE ADVENTURES
Hero Graphics, 1992
1 rep. 3.00
2 flipbook w/Champions Classics . . 3.00
3 flipbook w/Champions Classics . . 3.00
Becomes: B&W

FLARE ADVENTURES
Heroic Publishing, 2005
1 The League of Champions 3.00
15 . . . . 3.00
16 thru 18 . . . . @3.25
19 . . . . 4.50
19a variant (c) 4.50

FLASH GORDON
Gold Key, 1965
1 . . . . 125.00

FLASH GORDON
King, 1966–69
1 AW,DH,A:Mandrake 150.00
1a Comp. Army giveaway. 125.00
2 FBe,A:Mandrake,R:Ming 100.00

All comics prices listed are for *Near Mint* condition.   **CVA 2009 • Page 619**

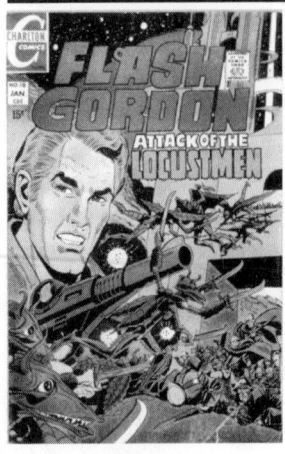

Flash Gordon #18
© Charlton

3 RE,"Lost in the Land of
The Lizardmen" 110.00
4 AW,B:Secret Agent X-9 . . . . . . 120.00
5 AW 120.00
6 RC,On the Lost Continent
of Mongo 110.00
7 MR, rep. In the Human Forest . 110.00
8 RC,JAp 110.00
9 AR,rep 120.00
10 AR,rep 120.00
11 RC 100.00

Charlton, 1969–70

12 RC 75.00
13 JJ 75.00
14 . . . . 60.00
15 . . . . 60.00
16 . . . . 60.00
17 Brick Bradford story 60.00
18 MK,Attack of the Locust Men . . 60.00

Gold Key, 1975

19 Flash returns to Mongo 15.00
20 thru 30 . . . . @10.00
31 thru 37 AW movie adapt . . . . @10.00

FLASH GORDON
Ardden Entertainment, 2008
1 . . . . 4.00
1a variant (c) 4.00
2 thru 3 . . . . @4.00
2a thru 3a variant (c)s . . . . @4.00

FLESH AND BONES
UpShot, 1986
1 Moore 3.00
2 thru 4 Moore . . . . @3.00

FLINTSTONES
Harvey
1 . . . . 3.00
2 Romeo and Juliet 3.00

FLINTSTONES
Archie, 1995
1 thru 10 . . . . @3.50
2 thru 14 . . . . @3.00
15 Frankenstone's Monster 3.00
20 An Heir-Raising Tale 3.00
21 King Fred The Last 3.00
22 Something Gruesome This
Way Comes 3.00

FLINTSTONES, THE
Dell Publishing Co., 1961
#1 *see Dell Giant*
2 . . . . 200.00
3 thru 6 . . . . @150.00

Gold Key, 1962
7 . . . . 150.00
8 A:Mr.& Mrs J. Evil Scientists . . 125.00
9 A:Mr.& Mrs.J. Evil Scientists . . 125.00
10 A:Mr.&Mrs.J. Evil Scientists . . 125.00
11 I:Pebbles 150.00
12 The Too-Old Cowhand 100.00
13 thru 15 . . . . @100.00
16 I:Bamm-Bamm 135.00
17 thru 20 . . . . @100.00
21 thru 23 . . . . @70.00
24 I:Gruesomes 100.00
25 thru 29 . . . . @100.00
30 Dude Ranch Roundup 100.00
31 Christmas(c) 100.00
32 . . . . 65.00
33 A:Dracula & Frankenstein 70.00
34 I:The Great Gazoo 125.00
35 . . . . 65.00
36 The Man Called Flintstone . . . 65.00
37 thru 60 . . . . @65.00

FLINTSTONES, THE
Charlton Comics, 1970
1 . . . . 150.00
2 . . . . 90.00
3 thru 7 . . . . @60.00
8 Summer Vacation 100.00
9 . . . . 60.00
10 . . . . 60.00
11 thru 20 . . . . @50.00
21 thru 50 . . . . @50.00

FLINTSTONES IN 3-D
Blackthorne
1 . . . . 3.00
2 . . . . 3.00
3 thru 5 . . . . @3.00

FLIPPER
Gold Key, 1966
1 Ph(c) from TV series 125.00
2 and 3 Ph(c) . . . . @100.00

FLOOD RELIEF
Malibu Ultraverse, 1994
GN Ultraverse Heroes 5.00

FLY, THE
Archie/Red Circle, 1983
1 JSn,A:Mr.Justice 6.00
2 thru 9 RB,SD . . . . @5.00

FLYING SAUCERS
Dell, 1967
1 . . . . 75.00
2 thru 5 . . . . @50.00

FLYMAN
Archie Publications
{Prev: Adventures of the Fly}
31 I:Shield (Bill Higgins), A:Comet,
Black Hood 100.00
32 I:Mighty Crusaders 85.00
33 A:Mighty Crusaders, R:Hangman
Wizard 85.00
34 MSy,A:Black Hood,Shield,Comet
Shield back-up story begins . . 75.00
35 O:Black Hood 75.00
36 O:Web,A:Hangman in Shield
strip 75.00
37 A:Shield 75.00
38 A:Web 60.00
39 A:Steel Sterling 60.00

FOOTSOLDIERS
Maximum Press, 1996
1 KJo,PhH, ... 3.00

FOOZLE
Eclipse, 1985
1 . . . . 2.50
2 . . . . 2.50
3 . . . . 2.50

FORBIDDEN PLANET
Innovation, 1992
1 thru 4 Movie Adapt . . . . @2.50
GN rep.#1–#4 (1997) 9.00

FORCE OF THE BUDDHA'S PALM
Jademan, 1988–93
1 . . . . 3.00
2 thru 10 . . . . @2.50
11 thru 24 . . . . @2.50
25 thru 43 . . . . @2.50
44 D:White Crane 3.00
45 thru 55 . . . . @2.50

4-D MONKEY
Dr. Leung's, 1988–90
1 thru 11 . . . . @2.50

FOREVER WAR, THE
NBM
GN Vol. 1 Joe Haldeman adapt. . . . 9.00
GN Vol. 2 Joe Haldeman adapt. . . . 9.00
GN Vol. 3 Joe Haldeman adapt. . . . 9.00

FORGOTTEN REALMS: THE DARK ELF TRILOGY
Devil's Due Publishing, 2005
Book I: Homeland
1 (of 3) 5.00
1b convention special 9.00
2 thru 3 . . . . @5.00
2a thru 3a collector's edition . . . . @8.00
The Legend of Drizzt,
Book II: Exile
1 (of 3) 5.00
1a collector's edition 8.00
2 . . . . 5.00
2a collector's edition 8.00
3 . . . . 5.00
3a collector's edition 8.00
Book III Sojourn
1 (of 3) 5.00
1a variant (c) 8.00
2 thru 3 . . . . @5.00
2a thru 3a variant (c)s . . . . @9.00
Book IV The Crystal Shard
1 (of 3) 5.00
1a Card stock variant (c) 8.00
2 . . . . 5.00
2a Card stock variant (c) 8.00
3 . . . . 5.00
3a prestige (c) 9.00
Book V Streams of Silver
1a prestige (c) 9.50
2 thru 3 . . . . @5.50
2a thru 3a prestige (c) . . . . @9.50
The Halfling's Gem, 2007
1 . . . . 5.50
1a prestige (c) 9.50
3 . . . . 5.50
3a prestige (c) 9.50

...THE LEGACY
Devil's Due, 2008
1 (of 3) 5.50
2 thru 3 . . . . @5.50
1a thru 3a prestige (c)s . . . . @9.50

All comics prices listed are for *Near Mint* condition.

COLOR PUB.

...STARLESS NIGHT
Devil's Due, 2008 (Vol. 8)
1 (of 3)	5.50
2	5.50
1a thru 2a prestige (c)s	@9.50

FOUNDATION
Boom! Studios, 2007
1	4.00
2 thru 5	@4.00

FOURTH HORSEMEN, THE
Fangoria Comics, 2007
1 (of 4)	4.00
2 thru 4	@4.00

FOXFIRE
Malibu Ultraverse, 1996
1 From Phoenix Resurrection	2.50
2 Fate of Mastodon revealed	2.50
3	2.50
4	2.50

FRANK
Nemesis, 1994
1 thru 4 DGc(s),GgP	@3.00
1a thru 4a variant(c)	@3.00

FRANK FRAZETTA FANTASY ILLUSTRATED
Frank Frazetta, 1998
1	6.00
1a variant cover	8.00
3 thru 9	@6.00
3 Neil Gaiman signed & numb.	25.00
3 Daniel signed & numbered	20.00

FRANK FRAZETTA DEATH DEALER
Verotik, 1997
1 thru 4 by Glenn Danzig	@7.00

FRANK MILLER'S ROBOCOP
Avatar Press/Pulsar Press, 2003
1	3.50
1b robosteel (c)	15.00
2 thru 9	@3.50
1a thru 5a wraparound (c)	@4.00
6a thru 9a wraparound (c)	@3.50
2b Civic Duty edition	4.00
4b thru 8b special edition (c)s	@6.00

Pulsar Press, 2006
9 Savior (c)	6.00
Spec. Killing Machine	6.00
Spec. Killing Machine variant (c)	3.00
Spec. Killing Machine no escape variant(c)	6.00

FRANKENSTEIN
Dell Publishing Co., 1964
1	125.00
2	75.00
3 and 4	@60.00

FRANKENSTEIN
Caliber
Novel Adaptation	3.00

FRANKENSTEIN
Topps, 1994
1 thru 4	@3.00

FRANKENSTEIN
Malibu
1 thru 3 movie promo	@2.50

FRANKENSTEIN DRACULA WAR
Topps, 1995
1 Frank Vs. Drac.	3.00
2 F:Saint Germaine.	3.00
3 Frank Vs. Drac.	3.00

FRANKENSTEIN JR.
Gold Key, 1967
1	200.00

FREDDY
Dell Publishing Co., 1963
1	50.00
2 and 3	@40.00

FREDDY'S DEAD: THE FINAL NIGHTMARE
Innovation
1 and 2 Movie adaption	@3.00
GN Movie Adapt.	7.00
3-D Special.	2.50

FREDDY VS. JASON VS. ASH
Wildstorm/DC, Nov., 2007
1 (of 6)	3.00
1a & 1b variant (c)s	3.00
2 thru 6	@3.00

FRED PERRY'S S-GUILD
Antarctic Press, 2006
1	3.50

FREEDOM FORMULA
Radical Comics, 2008
1 (of 5)	3.00
1a variant (c)	3.00
2 thru 4	@3.00
2a thru 4a variant (c)s	@3.00

FREE FALL
Narwain Publishing, 2005
1 thru 5	@4.00

FREEMIND
Future Comics, 2003
5 and 6	@3.50
7 thru 13	@3.00

Freex #4
© *Malibu*

FREEX
Malibu Ultraverse, 1993–95
1 I:Freex w/Ultraverse card	3.00
1a Ultra-Limited	4.00
1b Full Hologram (c)	5.00
2 L:Valerie,I:Rush	3.00
3 A:Rush	3.00
4 GJ(s),DdW,BWS,BU:Rune	2.75
5 thru 18	@2.50
Giant Size#1 A:Prime.	2.50

FRIDAY FOSTER
Dell Publishing Co., 1972
1	45.00

FRIDAY THE 13th
Avatar Press, 2005
Spec. #1	4.00
Spec. #1 variant (c)s	4.00
Spec. #1 variant special (c)s	@6.00
Spec. #1 glow (c)	15.00
Spec. #1 Blood Red Con (c)	5.00
Spec. #1 Prism foil (c)	13.00
Spec. Fearbook #1	4.00
Spec. Fearbook #1 variant (c)s	@4.00
Spec. Fearbook #1 leather (c)	20.00

Wildstorm/DC, Dec., 2006
1	3.00
1a variant (c)	3.00
2	3.00
3 Secret of Crystal Lake	3.00
4 Camp Crystal Lake	3.00
5 Forest at Crystal Lake	3.00
6 Curse of Camp Crystal	3.00

...ABUSER AND THE ABUSED
Wildstorm/DC, April, 2008
1-shot	3.50

...BAD LAND
Wildstorm/DC, Jan., 2008
1(of 2) RMz(s), O:Jason	3.00
2 RMz(s),finale	3.00

...BLOODBATH
Avatar Press, 2005
1	4.00
2 thru 3	@4.00
1a thru 3a wraparound (c)s	@4.00
1b thru 3b variant (c)s	@4.00
2c thru 3c Die-dut (c)s	@10.00
1d thru 3d Special (c)s	@6.00
1e Leather (c)	20.00

...HOW I SPENT MY SUMMER VACATION
Wildstorm/DC, Sept, 2007
1	3.00
2 Horror continues	3.00

...JASON VS. JASON X
Avatar Press, 2006
1 (of 2) by Mike WOlfer	4.00
1a wraparound (c)	4.00
1b variant (c)s	@4.00
1c Nano steel (c)	15.00
1d Blood red convention (c)	5.00
1e Face Off (c)	6.00
2	4.00
2a wraparound (c)	4.00
2b variant (c)s	@4.00
2c Nano steel (c)	15.00
2d Blood red convention (c)	5.00

FRIDAY THE 13TH: PAMELA'S TALE
Wildstorm/DC, July, 2007
1 Jason's Mother	3.00
2 finale	3.00

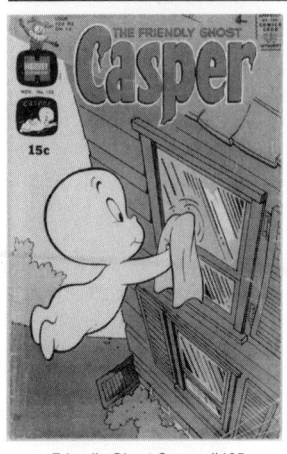

Friendly Ghost Casper #135
© Harvey Publications

FRIENDLY GHOST
CASPER, THE
Harvey Publications, 1958

1	750.00
2	500.00
3 thru 10	@400.00
11 thru 20	@250.00
21 thru 30	@100.00
31 thru 50	@75.00
51 thru 100	@60.00
101 thru 159	@50.00
160 thru 163 52 pgs.	@35.00
164 thru 253	@20.00

Becomes:

CASPER
THE FRIENDLY GHOST

FRIGHT NIGHT
Now, 1988–90

1 thru 22	@2.50

FRIGHT NIGHT 3-D
Now, 1992

1 Dracula,w/3-D Glasses	3.00
2	3.00

FRIGHT NIGHT II
Now

Movie Adaptation	4.00

FRINGE
Wildstorm/DC, Aug., 2008

1 From TV series	3.00
2 thru 4	@3.00

FROGMEN, THE
Dell Publishing Co., 1962

1 GE,Ph(c)	150.00
2 GE,FF	100.00
3 GE,FF	100.00
4	75.00
5 ATh.	85.00
6 thru 11	@65.00

FROM HEAVEN TO HELL
Dead Dog Comics, 2005

1	5.00
2	5.00

FRONTLINE COMBAT
EC Comics, 1995

1 thru 4 rep.	@3.00

Gemstone, 1996

5 thru 13 rep.	@3.00
14 WW(c)	3.00
15	3.00

F-TROOP
Dell Publishing Co., 1966

1 Ph(c)	175.00
2 thru 7 Ph(c)	@100.00

FULL CIRKLE
Full Circle Publications, 2004

1 (of 3) SBs.	4.00
1a variant (c).	3.50
1b signed, either cover	@10.00
1c 2nd printing	3.50
2	3.50
2a variant (c).	3.50
2b 2nd printing	3.50
3	4.00
3a variant (c)	4.00
1b and 3b Classic silver foil (c).	@8.00
Preview book 16-pg.	3.00
Preview book, signed.	5.00

Full Circle, 2007
Vol. 2

2	4.00

FULL MOON CRAZE
Masterpiece Comics, 2007

1 (of 6)	3.00
2	3.00
3 thru 4	@4.00

FUN-IN
Gold Key, 1970–74

1	125.00
2	75.00
3 thru 6	@75.00
7 thru 15	@60.00

FUNKY PHANTOM
Gold Key, 1972–75

1	100.00
2 thru 13	@35.00

FURIOUS FIST OF THE
DRUNKEN MONKEY:
ORIGIN OF THE SPECIES
Sllent Devil Productions, 2006

1 (of 3)	3.00
2 thru 3	@3.00

FURRY NINJA HIGH
SCHOOL STRIKES BACK
Shanda Fantasy Arts, 2003

1 (of 2)	5.00
2	5.00

FUSED
Boom! Studios, 2005

1-shot	7.00

FUTURAMA COMICS
Bongo Comics, 2000

1 thru 6	@3.50
7 thru 10	@3.00
11 thru 21	@3.00
22 thru 40	@3.00
Spec. Futurama/Simpsons: Infinity Secret Crossover Crisis, pt.1	2.50
Spec. Futurama/Simpsons Crossover Crisis, pt.2	2.50

FUTURIANS
Lodestone, 1985

1 DC,I:Dr.Zeus	2.50
2 DC,I:MsMercury	2.50
3 DC	2.50
Eternity Graphic Novel, DC, Rep. +new material	10.00

FX
IDW, 2008

1 JBy.	4.00
2 thru 6	@4.00

GALACTICA:
THE NEW MILLENNIUM
Realm Press, 1999

1 Battlestar Galactica	3.00
1 convention edition	5.00
1a signed	12.00
2 Busch (c)	3.00
2a Scalf (c)	3.00
2b convention edition	5.00
3	3.00
3a	3.00
4	3.00
4a deluxe	5.00
Spec. Fangs of the Beast	4.00
Spec. Fangs of the Beast,deluxe.	5.00
Tour Book, Conv. Ed., signed	15.00
Spec.Search for Sanctuary	4.00

GALAXY QUEST:
GLOBAL WARNING
IDW, 2008

1	4.00
2 thru 4	@4.00
2a thru 4a variant (c)s	@4.00

GALL FORCE:
ETERNAL STORY
CPM, 1995

1 F:Solnoids	3.00
2 V:Paranoid	3.00
3	3.00
4 Implant Secrets	3.00

GALLANT MEN, THE
Gold Key, 1963

1 RsM	50.00

GALLEGHER
BOY REPORTER
Gold Key, 1965

1	50.00

GALVESTON
Boom! Studios, 2008

1	4.00
1a variant (c)	4.00
2 thru 3	@4.00
2a thru 3a variant (c)s	@4.00

GAMEKEEPER
Virgin Comics, 2008
Series 2

1	3.00
1a variant (c)	3.00
2 thru 7	@3.00

GARGOYLES
Amaze Ink/SLG, 2006

1	7.00
2 thru 3	@4.00
4 thru 5	@3.50
6 thru 12	@4.00

GARRISON'S GORRILLAS
Dell Publishing Co., 1968
1 Ph(c) 75.00
2 thru 5 Ph(c) . . . . @50.00

GARTH ENNIS'
BATTLEFIELDS:
THE NIGHT WITCHES
Dynamite Entertainment, 2008
1 thru 2 . . . . @3.00

...CHRONICLES OF
WORMWOOD
Avatar Press, 2007
1 . . . . 4.00
1a variant wraparound (c) 4.00
2 thru 6 . . . . @4.00
2a thru 6a variant wraparound (c)@4.00

...STREETS OF GLORY
Avatar Press, 2007
Prev. 2.50

Garth Ennis' 303 #1
© Avatar Press

...303
Avatar Press, 2004
1 (of 6) 4.00
1a wraparound (c). 4.00
1b gold foil (c). 7.00
2 thru 6 . . . . @4.00
2a thru 6a wraparound (c). . . . . @4.00

GASP!
American Comics Group
March, 1967
1 . . . . 75.00
2 thru 4, Aug. 1967 . . . . @50.00

GATE CRASHER
RING OF FIRE
Black Bull Entertainment, 2000
1 (of 4) MWa,JP,ACo,JP 2.50
1a variant (c) 5.00
2 MWa,JP,ACo,JP. 2.50
3 MWa,JP,ACo,JP. 2.50
4 MWa,JP,ACo,ACo(c) 2.50
2a thru 3a variant JJu(c)s . . . . @2.50

GATE CRASHER
Black Bull Entertainment, 2000
1 MWa,JP,ACo,F:Alex Wagner. . . . 2.50

1a variant Wizard World (c) 5.00
2 MWa,JP,ACo,Blue Tonya, Otmar. 2.50
3 MWa,JP,ACo,F:Hazard 2.50
4 MWa,JP,ACo,ACo(c) 2.50
5 MWa,JP,ACo,AAd(c) 2.50
6 MWa,JP,ACo 2.50
2a thru 6a variant (c)s . . . . @2.50

GATE OF THE EAST WIND
Praxis Comics, 2008
1 (of 7) 4.00
2 thru 3 . . . . @4.00

GATESVILLE COMPANY
Speakeasy Comics, 2005
1 . . . . 3.00
2 & 3 . . . . @3.00

GEARHEAD
Arcana Studio, 2007
1 thru 4 . . . . @4.00

GEARS OF WAR
Wildstorm/DC, Oct., 2008
1 . . . . 4.00
1a variant (c) (1:10) 4.00
2 . . . . 4.00

GEARZ
Bluewater Prod., 2008
1 thru 4 . . . . @4.00
2a thru 4a variant (c)s . . . . @4.00

G.E.I.
Cyberosia Publishing, 2004
1 thru 3 . . . . @3.50

GEN-ACTIVE
WildStorm/DC, 2000
1 V:DV8,48-pg.quarterly 4.00
2 several stories 4.00
2a variant JPn (c) 4.00
3 BSz,JLe(c). 4.00
3a variant Lee Bermejo (c). 4.00
4 R:Wildcore 4.00
4a variant (c). 4.00
5 F:Sublime. 4.00
5a variant (c) (1:2) 4.00
6 Freakville 4.00

GENE FUSION
Beckett Entertainment, 2003
1 Monsters on Parade,pt.1 . . . . . . 3.00
2 Monsters on Parade,pt.2 . . . . . . 3.00
3 Monsters on Parade,pt.3 . . . . . . 3.00
4 Battle under the Big Tent 3.00

GENE RODDENBERRY'S
LOST UNIVERSE
Teckno-Comics, 1994
0 I:Sensua. 2.50
1 Gene Roddenberry's 2.50
2 Grange Discovered 2.50
3 Secrets Revealed 2.50
4 F:Penultra 2.50
5 I:New Alien Race 2.50
6 Two Doctor Granges 2.50
7 F:Alaa Chi Tskare 2.50

...XANDER IN LOST UNIVERSE
Teckno-Comics, 1995
1 V:Black Ghost 3.00
2 V:Walker. 3.00
3 V:Lady Sensua 3.00
4 thru 7 . . . . @3.00
8 F:Lady Sensua. 3.00
[Mini-Series], 1995
1 RoR,F:L.Nimoy's Primortals 3.00

GENE SIMMONS
DOMINATRIX
IDW, 2007
1 . . . . 4.00
2 thru 6 . . . . @4.00

GENE SIMMONS'
HOUSE OF HORRORS
Arcade/Simmons Comics
Group, 2006
1 . . . . 3.00
1a variant (c). 3.00

GENE SIMMONS'
JAZAN WILD
Arcade/Simmons Comics
Group, 2006
1 . . . . 3.00
1a variant (c)s . . . . @3.00
Spec House of Horrors, Halloween
    Edition #1, 90-pg. 6.00

GENE SIMMONS ZIPPER
IDW Publishing, 2007
1 thru 6 . . . . @4.00

GENESIS
Malibu, 1993
0 GP,w/Pog,F:Widowmaker,
    A:Arrow 3.50
0a Gold Ed.. . . . . 5.00

GENESIS FIVE
Guardian Line, 2006
1 thru 5 . . . . @3.00

GENSAGA:
ANCIENT WARRIOR
Entity Comics, 1995
1 I:Gensaga 2.50
1a with Computer Games. 2.50
2 V:Dinosaurs 2.50
3 V:Lord Abyss 2.50

GEN13
WildStorm/DC, 2002
1 CCI,Dylon & Ethan York. 3.00
2 CCI,Herod strikes. 3.00
3 CCI,Herod strikes. 3.00
4 CCI,Hamza 3.00
5 CCI,V:Preston Kills 3.00
6 CCI,V:Purple Haze. 3.00
7 CCI,V:The Chrome 3.00
8 CCI,V:The Chrome 3.00
9 CCI,the alter or the morgue. . . . 3.00
10 CCI,October Surprise,pt.4. . . . . 3.00
11 CCI,Two Caitlins 3.00
12 CCI,G-Nome 3.00
13 CCI,G-Nome 3.00
14 CCI,F:Caitlin 3.00
15 CCI,V:The Clique 3.00
16 CCI,finale 3.00
See also Image Comics section

GEN13
MOVIE ADAPTATION
WildStorm/DC, 2001
1 JMi, animated movie adapt.. . . . . 2.50

GEN13
Wildstorm/DC, Oct., 2006
1 . . . . 3.00
1a variant (c). 3.00
2 . . . . 3.00

COLOR PUB.

2a variant (c)	3.00
3 On the Run	3.00
3a variant AWa (c)	3.00
4 Caught by a Psycho	3.00
4a variant (c) (1:10)	3.00
5 V:Heaven Zeleven	3.00
6 V:Heaven Zeleven	3.00
7 V:Flesh-eating dinosaurs	3.00
8	3.00
9 Tranquility	3.00
10 Tranquility	3.00
11 The Liberty Snots	3.00
12 Authori-teens	3.00
13 F:Megan	3.00
14 New York City adventure	3.00
15 New York City adventure	3.00
16 F:Caitlin	3.00
17 15 Minutes Project	3.00
18 Team tension	3.00
19 Rally around Caitlin	3.00
20 15 Minutes Project	3.00
21 World's End	3.00
22 New York apocalypse	3.00
23 New World Order	3.00
24 Post-Apocalyptic Mall	3.00

GEN13: ARMAGEDDON
Wildstorm/DC, Nov., 2007

1 F:Caitlin	3.00

GENTLE BEN
Dell Publishing Co., 1968

1 Ph(c)	60.00
2	40.00
3 thru 5	@35.00

GEOMANCER
Valiant, 1994

1 RgM, I:Geomancer	3.00
2 thru 8	@2.50

GEORGE A ROMERO'S

DAWN OF THE DEAD
IDW Publishing, 2004

1	4.00
1a variant photo (c)	4.00
2 thru 3	@4.00

...NIGHT OF THE LIVING DEAD
Avatar Press, 2007

Spec. Just A Girl	3.00
Spec. Just A Girl variant (c)s	@3.00
Spec. Hunger	3.00
Spec. Hunger variant (c)s	@3.00
Spec. Hunger San Diego comic con	6.00

...NIGHT OF THE LIVING DEAD:
THE BEGINNING
Avatar Press, 2006

1	4.00
1a variant (c)s	@4.00
1b variant Splatter (c)	7.00
1c Leather (c)	20.00
2	4.00
2a variant (c)s	@4.00
2b variant splatter (c)	7.00

GEORGE OF THE JUNGLE
Gold Key, 1969

1 From animated TV show	250.00
2	200.00

GEORGE R. R. MARTIN'S
WILD CARDS:
THE HARD CALL
Dabel Brothers Prod., 2008

1 (of 6)	3.00
2 thru 6	@3.00

COLOR PUB.

GE ROUGE
Verotik, 1997

1 by Glenn Danzig & Calvin Irving	3.00
1 fan club cover (2000)	5.00
2 and 3	@3.00
Biz:GE Rouge #? SBs	3.00

GET SMART
Dell Publishing Co., 1966

1 Ph(c) all	200.00
2 SD	175.00
3 SD	150.00
4 thru 8	@125.00

[FILMATION'S]
GHOSTBUSTERS
First, 1987

1	3.00
2 thru 4	@3.00

GHOST BUSTERS II
Now, 1989

1 thru 3 Mini-series	@3.00

GHOSTBUSTERS
88MPH Studios, 2004

1	3.00
1a variant (c)	3.50
2 thru 3	@3.25

88MPH Studios, 2005

1	4.00

GHOSTBUSTERS: LEGION
88MPH Studios, 2004

1 (of 4)	5.00
1a 2nd printing	3.00
2 thru 4	@3.00
1a thru 4a variant (c)s	@3.50

GHOSTBUSTERS:
THE OTHER SIDE
IDW, 2008

1	4.00
2	4.00

GHOSTING
Platinum Studios, 2007

1 (of 5)	3.00
2 thru 5	@3.00

GHOSTLY TALES
Charlton, 1966
Previously: Blue Beetle

55 I&O Dr. Graves	125.00
56 thru 70	@75.00
71 thru 100	@60.00
101 thru 169	@50.00

GHOST MANOR
Charlton, 1968

1	65.00
2 thru 19	@30.00
Becomes:	

GHOSTLY HAUNTS
Charlton, 1971

20	20.00
21 thru 58	@15.00

GHOST MANOR
Charlton, 1971

1	60.00
2 thru 29	@30.00
30 thru 77	@20.00

Ghost Manor #71
© Charlton

GHOST STORIES
Dell Publishing Co., 1962

1	125.00
2	60.00
3 thru 10	@55.00
11	65.00
12 thru 19	@50.00
20	65.00
21 thru 33	@50.00
34 rep	50.00
35 rep	65.00
36 & 37 rep	@50.00

GHOST WHISPERER:
THE HAUNTED
IDW, 2008

1	4.00
2 thru 5	@4.00
2a variant (c)	4.00

GIANT COMICS
Charlton Comics Summer, 1957

1 A:Atomic Mouse,Hoppy	250.00
2 A:Atomic Mouse	200.00
3	200.00

GIDGET
Dell Publishing Co., 1966

1 Ph(c),Sally Field	175.00
2 Ph(c),Sally Field	125.00

GIFT, THE
First, 1990

Holiday Special	6.00

GIFT, THE
Overcast Comics, 2003

1	6.00
2	4.00
3 thru 5	@3.50
6 thru 7	@3.00

GIGANTOR
Antarctic Press, 2000

1 (of 12) BDn	2.50
2 V:Red Reich	2.50
3	2.50
4 Doppleganger,pt.1	2.50
5 Doppleganger,pt.2	2.50
6 Doppleganger,pt.3	2.50
7 Rulers of the Sea	2.50

8 . . . . 2.50
9 Sting of the Spider 3.00
10 Sting of the Spider, pt.2 . . . . 3.00
11 Badge of Danger, pt.1 . . . . 3.00
12 Badge of Danger, pt.2, concl. . . . 3.00

G.I. JOE 3-D
Blackthorne, 1987
1 . . . . 3.00
2 thru 5 . . . . @2.50
Ann. #1 . . . . 2.50

G.I. JOE
Devil's Due Publishing, 2004
(Prev. Pub. by Image)
26 thru 35 . . . . @3.00
36 thru 41 Union of the Snake . . . @3.00
42 double size, 48-page 4.50
43 double size 4.50
31 Collector's club edition 10.00
Digest #1 G.I. Joe Arashikage
    Showdown 11.00

...AMERICA'S ELITE
Devil's Due Publishing, 2005
0 . . . . 2.50
0 2nd printing, new cover 3.00
1 . . . . 4.00
1a signed 15.00
2 thru 4 . . . . @4.00
5 thru 6 48-pg. . . . . @5.00
7 thru 17 . . . . @4.00
18 thru 19 . . . . @4.00
20 . . . . 4.00
21 thru 24 Sins of the Mother . . . @4.00
25 World War III 7.00
26 thru 29 World War III, pt.2–pt.5 @5.00
30 WWIII, pt.6 48-pg. 5.50
31 thru 35 WWIII, pt.7 thru pt.11 . @4.00
36 WWIII, pt.12 48-pg. 5.50
13a cardstock (c) 6.00
1-shot Data Desk Handbook 3.00
1-shot Hunt for Cobra Commander . 2.50

...DECLASSIFIED
Devil's Due Publishing, 2006
1 (of 3) 5.00
1a variant cardstock (c) 9.00
2 thru 3 . . . . @5.00
2a thru 3a variant cardstock (c) . @9.00

...DREADNOKS: DECLASSIFIED
Devil's Due Publishing, 2006
1 (of 3) 5.00
1a cardstock (c) 9.00
2 (of 3) 5.00
2a cardstock (c) 9.00
3 . . . . 5.50
3a cardstock (c) 9.50

...G.I. JOE REBORN
Devil's Due Publishing, 2004
Spec #1 . . . . 5.00

...MASTER & APPRENTICE
Devil's Due Publishing, 2004
1 . . . . 3.00
1 Philly con. exclusive 9.00
2 thru 4 . . . . @3.00
Vol. II
1 thru 4 . . . . @3.00

...A NEW BEGINNING
IDW, 2008
0 . . . . 1.00

...RELOADED
Devil's Due Publishing, 2004
1 CDi 3.00
2 thru 14 . . . . @3.00
1-shot Cobra Reborn 5.00

G.I. Joe: Sigma 6 #1
© Devil's Due

...SCARLETT DECLASIFIED
Devil's Due Publishing, 2006
1-shot 5.00

...SIGMA 6
Devil's Due Publishing, 2005
1 thru 6 . . . . @3.00
Digest, 144-pg. 11.00

...SPECIAL MISSIONS
Devil's Due Publishing, 2006
1-shot Manhattan 5.00
1-shot Toyko 5.00
1-shot Antarctica 5.00
1-shot Brazil 5.50
1-shot The Enemy 5.50

...STORM SHADOW
Devil's Due, 2007
1 . . . . 3.50
2 thru 7 . . . . @3.50

...TRANSFORMERS
Devil's Due Publishing, 2004
Vol. II
1 . . . . 5.00
1a variant (c) 5.00
2 thru 4 . . . . @3.00
2a thru 4a variant (c) . . . . @3.00

...VS. COBRA
Fun Publications, 2008
1-shot Fall Special 5.00

...VS TRANSFORMERS: THE ART OF WAR
Devil's Due Publishing, 2006
1 (of 5 . . . . 3.00
1a variant (c)s . . . . @3.00
2 thru 5 . . . . @3.00
2a thru 5a variant (c) . . . . @3.00

...VS. TRANSFORMERS IV: BLACK HORIZON
Devil's Due, 2007
1 (of 2) 3.00
1a variant (c) 3.00
2 . . . . 5.50
2a variant (c) 5.50

GIL THORP
Dell Publishing Co., 1963
1 . . . . 75.00

GIMOLES
Alias Enterprises, 2005
1 (of 4) 2.50
2 thru 4 . . . . @3.00

GINGER FOX
Comico, 1988
1 thru 4 . . . . @2.50

GIN-RYU
Believe In Yourself, 1995
1 F:Japanese Sword 2.75
2 Identity Revealed 2.75
3 . . . . 2.75
4 Manhunt For Gin-Ryu 2.75

G.I. R.A.M.B.O.T.
Wonder Color, 1987
1 thru 3 . . . . @2.50

GIRL FROM U.N.C.L.E.
Gold Key, 1967
1 The Fatal Accidents Affair 150.00
2 The Kid Commandos Caper . . 100.00
3 The Captain Kidd Affair 100.00
4 One-Way Tourist Affair 100.00
5 The Harem-Scarem Affair 100.00

GIRL GENIUS
Studio Foglio, 2001
0 Secret Blueprints Preview B&W . 2.50
1 by Phil & Kaja Foglio 3.00
2 and 3 . . . . @3.00
4 40-page 4.00
5 . . . . 3.00
6 40-page (cancelled?) 4.00
7 40-page 4.00

GLOBAL FREQUENCY
WildStorm/DC, 2002
1 (of 12) WEI 3.00
2 WEI,SDi 3.00
3 WEI,LSh 3.00
4 WEI,RMr 3.00
5 WEI,JMu 3.00
6 WEI, ... 3.00
7 WEI,Detonation 3.00
8 WEI,Miranda Zero disappears . . . 3.00
9 WEI,Cathedral Lung. 3.00
10 WEI,Supenviolence 3.00
11 WEI,Aleph 3.00
12 WEI,concl. 3.00

...GLOOM, THE
APC, 2005
1 . . . . 3.50
2 thru 6 . . . . @3.50

GLOOM, THE
Markosia, 2005
3 thru 5 . . . . @3.50

GLORY
Maximum Press, 1996
1 15 see Image
16 JDy 2.50
17 JDy 2.50
18 JDy 2.50
19 JDy,A:Demeter, Silverfall 2.50
20 JDy,A:Silverfall 2.50
21 JDy 2.50
22 JDy 2.50
23 A:Prophet 2.50
Awesome Entertainment, 1999
0 AMo 2.50
0a & b alternate covers. 2.50
0c Timeless Beauty MMy(c) 6.00
1 AMo & ATi 3.50
2 AMo & ATi 3.00

GLORY/CELESTINE: DARK ANGEL
Maximum Press, 1996
1 & 2 See: Image
3 (of 3) JDy 2.50

GLORY/LIONHEART: RAGE OF FURIES
Awesome Entertainment, 2000
1 . . . . 3.00

GOAT, THE: H.A.E.D.U.S.
Acclaim, 1998
Spec. CPr,KG,F:Vincent Van Goat . . 4.00

GOBLIN CHRONICLES
Ape Entertainment, 2008
1 . . . . 3.50
1a variant (c) 3.50
2 thru 3 . . . . @3.50
2a thru 3a variant (c)s . . . . @3.50

GOBLIN LORD, THE
Goblin Studios, 1996
1 (of 6) sci-fi/fantasy 2.50
2 signed & numbered 10.00
3 . . . . 2.50
3a signed & numbered 10.00
4 thru 6 . . . . @2.50

GODFATHER CHRONICLES, THE
Boom! Studios, 2008
1 . . . . 4.00
2 thru 3 . . . . @4.00

GODS FOR HIRE
Hot Comics, 1986
1 . . . . 2.50
2 thru 7 . . . . @2.50

GODWHEEL
Malibu Ultraverse, 1995
0 R:Argus to Godwheel 2.50
1 I:Primevil 2.50
2 Hardcase new costume 2.50
3 F:Lord Pumpkin 2.50

GODYSSEY
Maximum 1996
1 . . . . 3.50

GO-GO
Charlton Comics, 1966
1 Miss Bikini Luv 125.00
2 Beatles 150.00
3 Blooperman 60.00
4 . . . . 60.00
5 . . . . 60.00
6 JAp,Petula Clark, Ph(c) 75.00
7 Beach Boys 65.00
8 JAp,Monkees, Ph(c) 75.00
9 Ph(c),Oct., 1967 . . . . 50.00

GO-GO GORILLA & THE JUNGLE CREW
Ape Entertainment, 2005
Supper Spec. 3.00
Winter Fun Spec. 3.50

GOLD DIGGER
Vol 2, Antarctic Press, 1999
1 by Fred Perry, F:Gina Diggers . . . 2.50
2 . . . . 2.50
3 by Fred Perry 2.50

Gold Digger #68
© Antarctic Press

4 tinted glass is magical 2.50
5 . . . . 2.50
6 ancient cauldrons 2.50
7 Halls of the Extremely Dead 2.50
8 Gone Fishing 2.50
9 Fauntleroy..a God? 2.50
10 Arms Master of Jade 2.50
11 Arms Master of Jade 2.50
12 Arms Master of Jade 3.00
13 Tournament of Arms 3.00
14 Tournament of Arms 3.00
15 . . . . 3.00
16 thru 26 . . . . @3.00
27 thru 37 . . . . @3.00
38 thru 42 . . . . @3.50
43 thru 57 . . . . @3.00
50a variant (c) 3.00
58 thru 68 . . . . @3.00
69 thru 74 . . . . @3.00
75 Heroes (c) 3.00
75a Villains (c) 3.00
76 thru 90 . . . . @3.00
91 thru 101 . . . . @3.00
Ann. 2003 B&W 5.00
Ann. 2004 B&W 5.00
Ann. 2005 B&W 4.50
Ann. 15th Special 5.00
Ann., 2006 Special 4.50
Anniv. Spec. #2 (2007) 5.00
Ann. 2008 . . . . 4.50
Swimsuit Spec. #1 . . . . 4.50
Spec. Swimsuit 2001 . . . . 4.50
Spec. Swimsuit 2002 . . . . 4.50
Spec. Swimsuit 2003 . . . . 4.50
Spec. Swimsuit 2004 . . . . 4.50
Spec. Swimsuit Spec. 2005 . . . . . 4.50
Spec. Swimsuit Spec. 2006 . . . . . 4.50
Spec. Swimsuit Spec. 2007 . . . . . 4.50
End of Summer Swimsuit (2002) . . 4.50
End of Summer Swimsuit (2003) . . 4.50
End of Summer Swimsuit (2004) . . 4.50
End of Summer Swimsuit (2005) . . 4.50
End of Summer Swimsuit (2006) . . 4.50
End of Summer Swimsuit (2007) . . 4.50
End of Summer Swimsuit 2008 . . . 4.50
Spec. Halloween Spec. #1 . . . . . . 3.00
Spec. Halloween Special, 2006 . . . 3.00
Spec. Halloween 2008 (B&W) 3.00
Spec. Christmas 2007 (B&W) 3.50
Spec. Peebo Tales (2007) 3.50
Spec. Peebo Tales #2 (2007) 3.50
Spec. Peebo Tales #3 (2008) 3.50
Spec. Peebo Tales #4 (2008) 3.50
Spec. Gold Digger Adventures #1
  O:Pink Avenger 3.00

Spec. Gold Digger color remix #1 . . 3.00
Spec. Gold Digger color remix #2 . . 3.00
Spec. Gold Digger color remix #3 . . 3.00
Spec. Gold Digger color remix #4 . . 3.00
Spec. Gold Digger Tangent #1 . . . . 3.00
Spec. Gold Digger Tangent #2 . . . . 3.00
Dreadwing's Mymior Spec. (2008) . . 3.00

GOLD DIGGER BETA
Antarctic Press, 1998
Spec. 0 by Ben Dunn, Special
  Origin Issue, 24pg 2.50
1A bu Fred Perry, John Pound (c) . 3.00
1B Jeff Henderson (c) 3.00
2 and 3 . . . . @3.00

GOLD DIGGER SOURCEBOOK
Antarctic Press, 2007
1 . . . . 4.00
2 thru 22 . . . . @4.00

GOLD DIGGER: TIFFANY & CHARLOTTE
Antarctic Press, 2008
1 . . . . 3.50
2 thru 4 . . . . @3.50

GOLDEN COMICS DIGEST
Gold Key, 1969–76
1 Tom & Jerry,Woody Woodpecker,
  Bugs Bunny 75.00
2 Hanna-Barbera,TV Fun
  Favorites 100.00
3 Tom & Jerry, Woody
  Woodpecker 50.00
4 Tarzan 50.00
5 Tom & Jerry, Woody Woodpecker,
  Bugs Bunny 30.00
6 Bugs Bunny 30.00
7 Hanna-Barbera,TV Fun
  Favorites 75.00
8 Tom & Jerry, Woody Woodpecker,
  Bugs Bunny 25.00
9 Tarzan 60.00
10 Bugs Bunny 25.00
11 Hanna-Barbera,TV Fun
  Favorites 75.00
12 Tom & Jerry,Bugs Bunny 25.00
13 Tom & Jerry 25.00
14 Bugs Bunny,Fun Packed
  Funnies 25.00
15 Tom & Jerry, Woody
  Woodpecker, Bugs Bunny 25.00
16 Woody Woodpecker 25.00
17 Bugs Bunny 25.00
18 Tom & Jerry 25.00
19 Little Lulu 45.00
20 Woody Woodpecker 25.00
21 Bugs Bunny Showtime 25.00
22 Tom & Jerry Winter Wingding . . 25.00
23 Little Lulu & Tubby Fun Fling . . 40.00
24 Woody Woodpecker Fun
  Festival 22.00
25 Tom & Jerry 22.00
26 Bugs Bunny Halloween Hulla-
  Boo-Loo,Dr. Spektor article . . . 22.00
27 Little Lulu & Tubby in Hawaii . . 45.00
28 Tom & Jerry 22.00
29 Little Lulu & Tubby 45.00
30 Bugs Bunny Vacation Funnies . 22.00
31 Turk, Son of Stone 50.00
32 Woody Woodpecker
  SummerFun 22.00
33 Little Lulu & Tubby Halloween
  Fun 45.00
34 Bugs Bunny Winter Funnies . . . 22.00
35 Tom & Jerry Snowtime Funtime 22.00

All comics prices listed are for *Near Mint* condition.

36 Little Lulu & Her Friends 45.00
37 WoodyWoodpecker County Fair 22.00
38 The Pink Panther 25.00
39 Bugs Bunny Summer Fun 22.00
40 Little Lulu 45.00
41 Tom & Jerry Winter Carnival . . . 22.00
42 Bugs Bunny 22.00
43 Little Lulu in Paris 45.00
44 Woody Woodpecker Family Fun
   Festival 22.00
45 The Pink Panther 25.00
46 Little Lulu & Tubby 45.00
47 Bugs Bunny 22.00
48 The Lone Ranger 22.00

GOLDEN PICTURE
STORY BOOK
Racine Press (Western), 1961
1 Huckleberry Hound 350.00
2 Yogi Bear 350.00
3 Babes In Toy Land 500.00
4 Walt Disney 450.00

GOLDEN PLATES, THE
AAA Pop Comics, 2004
1 (of 12) 8.00
1a 2nd printing 8.00
2 thru 4 . . . . @8.00

GOMER PYLE
Gold Key, 1966
1 Ph(c) from TV show 150.00
2 and 3 . . . . @100.00

GOOD AND EVIL
No Greater Joy, 2008
1 The Beginning 3.00
2 Abraham 3.00
3 Moses 3.00
4 Exodus 3.00

GOOD GUYS
Defiant, 1993
1 JiS(s),I:Good Guys 3.75
2 JiS(s),V:Mulchmorg 3.25
3 V:Chasm 2.75
4 Seduction of the Innocent 3.25
5 I:Truc 3.00
6 A:Charlemagne 2.75
7 JiS(s),V:Scourge 2.50
8 thru 11 . . . . @2.50

GOOFY ADVENTURES
Walt Disney, 1990
1 Balboa de Goofy 3.00
2 . . . . 3.00
3 thru 17 . . . . @3.00

GOON
Albatross 2002
1 . . . . 60.00
2 . . . . 30.00
3 thru 5 b&w . . . . @25.00
Spec. Color special 7.00

GOOP, THE
JNCO Comics, 1998
1 . . . . 2.50
2 thru 4 . . . . @2.50

GORGO
Charlton Comics, 1961–65
1 SD,from Movie 450.00
2 SD(c&a),Return of Gorgo 250.00
3 SD(c&a) 200.00
4 SD(c) 150.00
5 The Day Manhattan Died 150.00
6 thru 11 . . . . @150.00

12 Monster's Rendezvous 125.00
13 thru 15 . . . . @125.00
16 SD,Menace from the Deep . . . 125.00
17 thru 23 . . . . @100.00

GORGO'S REVENGE
Charlton Comics, 1962
1 From movie 100.00
Becomes:

THE RETURN OF GORGO
Charlton Comics, 1963
2 SD(c&a),Creature from
   Corpus III 75.00
3 Hidden Witness 75.00

GORILLA GORILLA
Disney Press, 2006
GN Vol. 1 . . . . 5.00

G.O.T.H.
Verotik, 1995
1 . . . . 3.00
2 . . . . 3.00
3 . . . . 3.00

THE GOTHIC SCROLLS,
DRAYVEN
Davdez Arts, 1997
1 16pg. 2.50
1a limited edition, new cover 3.00
2 and 3 . . . . @2.50
4 V:Lucifer 2.50
GN 13.00

GRANT MORRISON'S
DOCTOR WHO
IDW, 2008
1 . . . . 4.00
2 . . . . 4.00

GRATEFUL DEAD
COMIX
Kitchen Sink, 1993
1 TT,inc.DireWolf(large format) 5.50
2 TT,inc.Jack Straw 5.00
3 TT,inc. Sugaree 5.00
4 TT,inc. Sugaree 5.00
5 TT,Uncle John's Band 5.00
6 TT,Eagle Mall #1 . . . . 5.00

Greatful Dead Comix #2
© Kitchen Sink

GRAVE DOUG
FRESHLEY, THE
Archaia Studios, 2008
1 (of 5) 4.00
2 . . . . 4.00

GRAVEL
Avatar Press, 2008
0 WEI(s) 2.00
0a wraparound (c) 2.00
0b auxiliary edition 2.00
0c convention edition 2.00
1 . . . . 4.00
2 thru 8 . . . . @4.00
1a thru 8a wraparound (c)s . . . . @4.00
1b thru 3b auxiliary editions . . . . @4.00
1c Wizard World LA edition 6.00

GRAVESTONE
Malibu, July 1993–Feb. 1994
1 D:Gravestone,V:Wisecrack 2.50
1a Newstand Ed. 2.50
2 A:Eternal Man, V:Night Plague . . 2.50
2a Newstand Ed. 2.50
3 Genesis Tie in,w/skycap 2.50
4 thru 9 . . . . @2.50

GREASE MONKEY
Kitchen Sink, 1997
1 by Tim Elred 3.50
2 by Tim Elred 3.50

GREAT AMERICAN
WESTERN
AC Comics, 1987
1 Santee, Dark Rider, Missourian . . 2.50
2 F:The Durango Kid 3.00
3 . . . . 3.00
4 F:Lash LaRue 3.50
5 Sunset Carson 5.00
6 King of the Bull Whip 6.00

GREATEST
AMERICAN HERO
Arcana Studio, 2008
1 (of 6) TV series adaptation 3.50

GREEN HORNET, THE
Gold Key, 1967
1 Bruce Lee,Ph(c) 400.00
2 Ph(c) 300.00
3 Ph(c) 250.00

GREEN HORNET
Now, 1989
1 O:40's Green Hornet 7.00
1a 2nd Printing 4.00
2 O:60's Green Hornet 5.00
3 thru 5 . . . . @4.00
6 . . . . 3.00
7 BSz(c),I:New Kato 3.00
8 thru 12 . . . . @3.50
13 V:Ecoterrorists 3.50
14 V:Ecoterrorists 3.50
Spec.#1 . . . . 2.50
Spec.#2 . . . . 2.50
[2nd Series], 1991
1 V:Johnny Dollar Pt.1 . . . . 2.50
2 V:Johnny Dollar Pt.2 . . . . 2.50
3 V:Johnny Dollar Pt.3 . . . . 2.50
4 V:Ex-Con/Politician 2.50
5 V:Ex-Con/Politician 2.50
6 Arkansas Vigilante 2.50
7 thru 9 The Beast . . . . @2.50
10 Green Hornet-prey 2.50
11 F:Crimson Wasp 2.50

12 Crimson Wasp/Johnny Dollar
   Pt.1,polybagged w/Button 4.00
13 TD(i),Wasp/Dollar Pt.2 . . . . 2.50
14 TD(i),Wasp/Dollar Pt.3 . . . . 2.50
15 TD(i),Secondsight 2.50
16 A:Commissioner Hamilton 2.50
17 V:Gunslinger 2.50
18 V:Sister-Hood 2.50
19 V:Jewel Thief 2.50
20 F:Paul's Friend 2.50
21 V:Brick Arcade 2.50
22 V:Animal Testers, with
   Hologravure card. 4.00
23 with Hologravure card. 4.00
24 thru 25 Karate Wars . . . . @2.50
26 B:City under Siege 2.50
27 with Hologravure card. 2.50
28 V:Gangs 2.50
29 V:Gangs 2.50
30 thru 37. . . . . @2.50
38 R:Mei Li. 2.50
39 Crimson Wasp 4.50
40 . . . . 4.50
41 . . . . 2.50
42 Baby Killer. 2.50
43 Wedding Disasters 2.50
44 F:Amy Hamilton 2.50
45 Plane Hijacking. 2.50
46 Airport Terrorists 2.50
Ann.#1 The Blue & the Green 2.50
1993 Ann 3.00

...DARK TOMORROW
Now, 1993
1 thru 3 Hornet Vs Kato . . . . @3.00

...SOLITARY SENTINAL
Now, 1992
1 Strike Force 3.00
2 thru 3 . . . . @3.00

GREENHAVEN
Aircel, 1988
1 thru 3 BaB,See Elford #18–20 @3.00

GREEN PLANET
Charlton, 1962
1 DG 125.00

GRENDEL
Comico, 1986–91
1 MW 8.00
1a 2nd printing 2.50
2 MW 5.00
3 thru 6 MW . . . . @4.00
7 MW 4.00
8 thru 12 MW . . . . @4.00
13 KSy(c) MW 3.50
14 KSy(c) MW 3.00
15 KSy(c) MW 3.00
16 MW,Mage 6.00
17 thru 19 MW,Mage . . . . @5.00
20 thru 32 MW . . . . @3.00
33 MW,giant-size 3.50
34 thru 36 MW . . . . @3.00
37 MW 6.00
38 MW 9.00
39 MW,D:Grendel 10.00
40 MW,D:Orion Assante 30.00

GREYLORE
Sirius, 1985–86
1 thru 5 . . . . @2.50

GREYSHIRT:
INDIGO SUNSET
WildStorm/DC, 2001
America's Best Comics
1 (of 6) RV 3.50
2 RV 3.50

---

3 RV 3.50
4 RV, Star of Indigo. 3.50
5 RV, Fanman 3.50
6 RV, Black Jack Hawkins 3.50

GRIFTER & MIDNIGHTER
Wildstorm/DC, Mar., 2007
1 (of 6) CDi 3.00
2 thru 6 CDi. . . . . @3.00

GRIM GHOST, THE
Atlas, 1975
1 . . . . 20.00
2 . . . . 20.00
3 . . . . 20.00

Grimjack #66
© *First*

GRIMJACK
First, 1984–91
1 TT Teenage suicide story. 3.00
2 thru 20 TT A:Munden's Bar . . . @2.50
21 thru 25. . . . . @2.50
26 1st color TMNTurtles. 10.00
27 thru 50. . . . . @2.50
51 thru 81. . . . . @2.50

...CASEFILE
First, 1990
1 thru 5 rep. . . . . @2.50

GRIMJACK: KILLER
INSTINCT
IDW Publishing, 2005
1 JOs,TT 4.00
2 thru 6 . . . . @4.00

GRIMM FAIRY TALES
Zenescope Entertainment, 2005
1 Little Red Riding Hood. 20.00
2 Cinderella. 50.00
3 Hansel & Gretel 60.00
4 Rumpelstilskin 15.00
5 Sleeping Beauty. 6.00
6 The Robber Bridegroom 5.00
7 Snow White 6.00
8 Jack and the Bean Stalk 6.00
9 Goldilocks 6.00
10 The Frog King. 6.00
11 Bluebeard 6.00
12 Pied Piper 6.00
13 Beauty and the Beast, pt.1 . . . 6.00
14 thru 16 . . . . @8.00
17 thru 19 . . . . @4.00
22 thru 32 . . . . @3.00

---

33 x-over 1001 Arabian Nights 3.00
Ann. #1 . . . . 6.00
Ann. 2008 . . . . 6.00
Spec. Beauty and the Beast 5.00
Giant-Size #1 . . . . 6.00

...RETURN TO WONDERLAND
Zenescope Entertainment, 2007
0 . . . . 3.00
1 (of 7) 9.00
2 . . . . 10.00
3 . . . . 6.00
4 thru 6 . . . . @4.00

...THE PIPER
Zenescope Entertainment, 2008
1 (of 4) 3.00
2 thru 4 . . . . @3.00

GRIMM'S GHOST
STORIES
Gold Key/Whitman, 1972–82
1 . . . . 40.00
2 . . . . 25.00
3 . . . . 25.00
4 . . . . 25.00
5 AW 30.00
6 . . . . 15.00
7 . . . . 15.00
8 AW 20.00
9 . . . . 15.00
10 . . . . 15.00
11 thru 16 . . . . @12.00
17 RC. 15.00
18 thru 60. . . . . @10.00

GRIMOIRE, THE
Speakeasy Comics, 2005
1 . . . . 3.00
2 thru 6 . . . . @3.00
7 thru 12 . . . . @3.00

GROO THE WANDERER
Pacific, 1982–84
1 SA,I:Sage,Taranto 25.00
2 SA,A:Sage 15.00
3 SA,C:Taranto 15.00
4 SA,C:Sage. 15.00
5 SA,I:Ahax 15.00
6 SA,I:Gratic 18.00
7 SA,I:Chakaal 18.00
8 SA,A:Chakaal 18.00
Eclipse
Spec.#1 SA,O:Groo,rep Destroyer
   Duck #1 . . . . 23.00

GROUP LARUE, THE
Innovation, 1989
1 MBn 2.50
2 . . . . 2.50
3 . . . . 2.50

GRUMPY OLD MONSTERS
IDW Publishing, 2003
1 (of 4) 2.50
2 thru 4 . . . . @4.00

GRUNLAND
Narwain Publishing, 2006
GN 6.00

GRUNTS
Arcana Studio, 2006
1 (of 3) 4.00
2 thru 3 . . . . @4.00

GUARDIAN HEROES
Alias Enterprises, 2006
1-shot 3.50

GUILLOTIN
ABC, 1997
1 JQ(c)	3.00
1a RCI(c)	6.00
1b gold cover, polybagged with trading card	10.00
2	3.00
2a Serpent (c)	6.00
2b Cold Series (c)	6.00

GULLIVER'S TRAVELS
Dell Publishing Co., 1965
1	100.00
2 and 3	@75.00

GUMBY
Comico, 1987
1 AAd,Summer Fun Special	5.00
2 AAd,Winter Fun Special	3.50

GUMBY IN 3-D
Blackthorne
Spec.#1	4.00
2 thru 7	@3.00

GUMBY
Wildcard Production, 2006
1	4.00
2 thru 4	@4.00

GUN FU: THE LOST CITY
Axiom, 2003
1	3.50
1a variant (c)	6.00
2 thru 4	@3.50
2a thru 4a variant (c)s	@3.50
Preview signed edition	3.00

GUNSMOKE
Gold Key, 1969
1 Ph(c), from TV series	125.00
2 thru 6	@100.00

GUY RITCHIE'S GAMEKEEPER
Virgin Comics, 2007
1	3.00
2 thru 5	@3.00
1a variant (c)	3.00

HACK/SLASH
Devil's Due Publishing, 2004
1	5.00
1-shot Girls Gone Dead	5.00
1-shot variant(c)	5.00
1-shot Comic Book Carnage	5.00
1-shot Final Revenge of Evil Ernie	5.00
1-shot Trailers	3.25
1-shot Slice Hard preview special	1.00
1-shot Slice Hard	5.00
1-shot Slice Hard variant (c)	5.00
1-shot Hack/Slash vs. Chucky	5.50
1-shot Hack/Slash vs. Chucky variant (c)	@5.50

Devil's Due, 2007
1	3.50
1a variant (c)	3.50
2 thru 6	@3.50
2a thru 6a variant (c)	@3.50
7 thru 18	@3.50
7a thru 18 variant (c)s	@3.50
Ann. Suicide Girls	5.50
Ann. Suicide Girls variant (c)	5.50

...LAND OF LOST TOYS
Devil's Due Publishing, 2005
1 (of 3)	3.25
2 thru 3	@3.25

HALL OF FAME
J.C. Productions, 1983
1 WW,GK,ThunderAgents	2.50
2 WW,GK,ThunderAgents	2.50
3 WW,Thunder Agents	2.50

HALLOWEEN
Chaos! Comics, 2000
1 premium glow-in-the-dark (c)	13.00
1 chromium edition	16.00

HALLOWEEN
Devil's Due, 2008
30th Anniv. Special	5.50
30th Anniv. Spec. variant prestige	9.50

...THE FIRST DEATH OF LAURIE STRODE
Devil's Due, 2008
1 (of 3)	3.50
2 thru 3	@3.50
1a thru 3a variant (c)s	@3.50

...NIGHTDANCE
Devil's Due, 2008
1 (of 4)	3.50
2	3.50
1a thru 4a variant (c)s	@3.50
1b thru 4b variant Master (c)s	@5.50
1c thru 2c second printing	@3.50

HALLOWEEN II: THE BLACKEST EYE
Chaos! Comics, 2001
Spec.	3.00
Spec. premium	10.00

HALLOWEEN III: THE DEVIL'S EYES
Chaos! Comics, 2001
Spec.	3.00
Spec. variant (c)	3.00
Spec. Previews exclusive	3.00

HALLOWEEN HORROR
Eclipse, 1987
1	3.00

HALO: AN ANGEL'S STORY
Sirius, 1996
1 by Chris Knowles	3.00
2	3.00
3	3.00

HAMMER KID
Alias Enterprises, 2006
1-shot	3.50

HAMMER OF GOD
First, 1990
1 thru 4	@2.50
Deluxe #1 Sword of Justice Bk#1	5.00
Deluxe #2 Sword of Justice Bk#2	5.00

HAMSTER VICE
Blackthorne, 1985–87
1 thru 10	@2.50
3-D #1	2.50

HAND OF FATE
Eclipse, 1988
1 I:Artemis Fate	2.50
2 F:Artemis & Alexis	2.50
3 Mystery & Suspense	2.50

Hammer of God, Sword of Justice #2
© First

HANDS OF THE DRAGON
Atlas, 1975
1	18.00

HANNA-BARBERA ALL-STARS
Archie, 1995
1 thru 5	@3.00

HANNA-BARBERA BAND WAGON
Gold Key, 1962–63
1	250.00
2	160.00
3	135.00

HANNA-BARBERA PARADE
Charlton Comics, 1971–72
1	150.00
2 thru 10	@75.00

HANNA-BARBERA PRESENTS
Archie, 1995
1 thru 15	@3.00

HANNA-BARBERA SUPER TV HEROES
Gold Key, 1968
1 B:Birdman,Herculiods,Moby Dick, Young Samson & Goliath	350.00
2	250.00
3 thru 7 Oct. 1969	@225.00

HARBINGER
Valiant, 1992
0 DL,O:Sting,V:Harada, from TPB (Blue Bird Ed.)	35.00
0 from coupons	4.00
1 DL,JDx,I:Sting,Torque, Zeppelin,Flamingo,Kris	20.00
2 DL,JDx,V:Harbinger Foundation, I:Dr.Heyward	10.00
3 DL,JDx,I:Ax,Rexo, V:Spider Aliens	10.00
4 DL,JDx,V:Ax,I:Fort, Spikeman,Dog,Bazooka	10.00
5 DL,JDx,I:Puff,Thumper, A:Solar,V:Harada	10.00

6 DL,D:Torque,A:Solar,
V:Harada,Eggbreakers 8.00
1a thru 6a w/o coupon . . . . @2.00
7 DL,Torque's Funeral 8.00
8 thru 40 . . . . @2.50
41 V:Harbinger. 8.00

HARBINGER FILES:
HARADA
Valiant, 1994
1 BL,DC,O:Harada 2.75
2 Harada's ultimate weapon 2.50

HARDCASE
Malibu Ultraverse, 1993–95
1 I:Hardcase,D:The Squad 3.00
1a Ultra-Limited, silver foil 4.00
1b Full Hologram (c). 6.00
1c Platinum edition 3.50
2 w/Ultraverse card. 3.00
3 Hard decisions. 2.75
4 A:Strangers 2.75
5 BWS,V:Hardwire,BU:Rune 2.75
6 thru 15 . . . . @2.50
16 NIM-E 3.50
17 thru 24 . . . . @2.50
25 Mundiquest,concl. 3.00
26 Time Gem Disaster 3.00

H.A.R.D. CORPS
Valiant, 1992
1 JLe(c),DL,BL,V:Harbinger
Foundation,I:Flatline,D:Maniac . 2.50
1a Gold Ed. 2.50
2 thru 30 . . . . @2.50

HARDY BOYS, THE
Gold Key, 1970
1 . . . . 100.00
2 thru 4 . . . . @60.00

HARDY BOYS
NBM Books, 2004
1 The Ocean of Osyria, pt.1 . . . . . . 3.00
2 The Ocean of Osyria, pt.2 . . . . . . 3.00
3 The Ocean of Osyria, pt.3 . . . . . . 3.00
4 Identity Theft, pt.1 . . . . 3.00
5 Identity Theft, pt.2 . . . . 3.00
GN Vol. 1 The Ocean of Osyria 8.00
GN Vol. 2 Identity Theft 8.00
GN Vol. 3: Madhouse. 8.00
Papercutz, 2005
GN Vol. 4 Malled 8.00
GN Vol. 5 Sea You, Sea Me 8.00
GN Vol. 6 Hyde & Shriek 8.00
GN Vol. 7 Opposite Numbers 8.00

HARI KARI
Blackout Comics, 1995
0 I:Hari Kari. 3.00
1 . . . . 3.00
1a commemorative, variant(c) . . . 10.00
Specials & 1-shots
1 The Beginning, O:Kari (1996) . . . 3.00
1a The Beginning, commemorative,
signed 10.00
1 Bloodshed (1996) 3.00
1a Bloodshed, deluxe, variant(c) . 10.00
1 Live & Untamed! (1996) 3.00
1 Rebirth (1996) 3.00
0 The Silence of Evil (1996) 3.00
0 The Silence of Evil, limited,
foil stamped 13.00
? The Diary of Kari Sun (1997). . . . 3.00
? The Diary of Kari Sun, deluxe . . 10.00
0 Life or Death (1997) 3.00
0a Life or Death, super sexy
parody edition 13.00
1 Passion & Death (1997) 3.00

Hari Kari The Silence of Evil #0
© Blackout Comics

1 Passion & Death, photo(c). 10.00
1 Possessed by Evil (1997) 3.00
1 Resurrection (1997). 3.00

HARLEM
GLOBETROTTERS
Gold Key, 1972
1 . . . . 75.00
2 thru 12, Jan. 1975 . . . . @50.00

HARRIERS
Entity, 1995
1 I:Macedon Arsenal, Cardinal 3.00
1a with Video Game 7.00
2 and 3 V:Kr'llyn . . . . @2.50

HARSH REALM
Harris, 1994
1 thru 6 JHi(s), ... @3.00

HARVEY HITS
Harvey Publications, 1957–67
1 The Phantom 500.00
2 Rags Rabbit 100.00
3 Richie Rich 3,000.00
4 Little Dot's Uncles 350.00
5 Stevie Mazie's Boy Friend . . . 100.00
6 JK(c),BP,The Phantom 400.00
7 Wendy the Witch 700.00
8 Sad Sack's Army Life 200.00
9 Richie Rich's Golden Deeds 1,100.00
10 Little Lotta 300.00
11 Little Audrey Summer Fun . . . 250.00
12 The Phantom 400.00
13 Little Dot's Uncles. 300.00
14 Herman & Katnip 100.00
15 The Phantom 400.00
16 Wendy the Witch. 800.00
17 Sad Sack's Army Life 200.00
18 Buzzy & the Crow 100.00
19 Little Audrey 200.00
20 Casper & Spooky 200.00
21 Wendy the Witch. 400.00
22 Sad Sack's Army Life 150.00
23 Wendy the Witch. 400.00
24 Little Dot's Uncles 250.00
25 Herman & Katnip 100.00
26 The Phantom 350.00
27 Wendy the Good Little Witch . 500.00
28 Sad Sack's Army Life 150.00
29 Harvey-Toon 150.00
30 Wendy the Witch 400.00

31 Herman & Katnip 100.00
32 Sad Sack's Army Life 150.00
33 Wendy the Witch 300.00
34 Harvey-Toon 100.00
35 Funday Funnies 100.00
36 The Phantom 300.00
37 Casper & Nightmare 200.00
38 Harvey-Toon 150.00
39 Sad Sack's Army Life 150.00
40 Funday Funnies 100.00
41 Herman & Katnip 100.00
42 Harvey-Toon 100.00
43 Sad Sack's Army Life 150.00
44 The Phantom 300.00
45 Casper & Nightmare 150.00
46 Harvey-Toon 100.00
47 Sad Sack's Army Life 100.00
48 The Phantom 300.00
49 Stumbo the Giant 250.00
50 Harvey-Toon 100.00
51 Sad Sack's Army Life 50.00
52 Casper & Nightmare 90.00
53 Harvey-Toons 40.00
54 Stumbo the Giant 100.00
55 Sad Sack's Army Life 40.00
56 Casper & Nightmare 75.00
57 Stumbo the Giant 100.00
58 Sad Sack's Army Life 40.00
59 Casper & Nightmare 75.00
60 Stumbo the Giant 100.00
61 Sad Sack's Army Life 40.00
62 Casper & Nightmare 75.00
63 Stumbo the Giant 90.00
64 Sad Sack's Army Life 40.00
65 Casper & Nightmare 60.00
66 Stumbo the Giant 75.00
67 Sad Sack's Army Life 40.00
68 Casper & Nightmare 60.00
69 Stumbo the Giant 75.00
70 Sad Sack's Army Life 40.00
71 Casper & Nightmare 60.00
72 Stumbo the Giant 75.00
73 Little Sad Sack 40.00
74 Sad Sack's Muttsy 40.00
75 Casper & Nightmare 55.00
76 Little Sad Sack 40.00
77 Sad Sack's Muttsy 40.00
78 Stumbo the Giant 75.00
79 Little Sad Sack 40.00
80 Sad Sack's Muttsy 40.00
81 Little Sad Sack 40.00
82 Sad Sack's Muttsy 40.00
83 Little Sad Sack 40.00
84 Sad Sack's Muttsy 35.00
85 Gabby Gob 35.00
86 G.I. Juniors 30.00
87 Sad Sack's Muttsy 35.00
88 Stumbo the Giant 65.00
89 Sad Sack's Muttsy 35.00
90 Gabby Goo 30.00
91 G.I. Juniors 30.00
92 Sad Sack's Muttsy 35.00
93 Sadie Sack 30.00
94 Gabby Goo 30.00
95 G.I. Juniors 30.00
96 Sad Sack's Muttsy 35.00
97 Gabby Goo 30.00
98 G.I. Juniors 30.00
99 Sad Sack's Muttsy 35.00
100 Gabby Goo 30.00
101 G.I. Juniors 25.00
102 Sad Sack's Muttsy 30.00
103 Gabby Goo 25.00
104 G.I. Juniors 25.00
105 Sad Sack's Muttsy 30.00
106 Gabby Goo 25.00
107 G.I. Juniors 25.00
108 Sad Sack's Muttsy 30.00
109 Gabby Goo 25.00
110 G.I. Juniors 25.00
111 Sad Sack's Muttsy 30.00
112 G.I. Juniors 25.00

All comics prices listed are for *Near Mint* condition.

113 Sad Sack's Muttsy. 30.00
114 G.I. Juniors 25.00
115 Sad Sack's Muttsy. 30.00
116 G.I. Juniors 25.00
117 Sad Sack's Muttsy. 30.00
118 G.I. Juniors 25.00
119 Sad Sack's Muttsy. 30.00
120 G.I. Juniors 25.00
121 Sad Sack's Muttsy 30.00
122 G.I. Juniors 25.00

HATE
Fantagraphics, 1990
1 thru 15, see B&W
16 thru 29. . . . . @3.00
30 48pg. 4.00
Ann.#1 48-page (2000) 4.00
Ann.#2 (2001) 4.00
Ann.#3 (2002) 4.00
Ann.#4 (2003) 5.00
Ann.#5 (2004) 5.00
Ann.#6 (2006) 5.00
Ann.#7 (2007) 5.00

HAUNTED
Charlton, 1971–84
1 . . . . 65.00
2 . . . . 30.00
3 thru 5 . . . . @30.00
6 thru 10 . . . . @25.00
11 thru 20 . . . . @20.00
21 thru 50. . . . . @15.00
51 thru 75. . . . . @10.00

HAUNTED, THE
Chaos! Comics, 2001
1 (of 4) PDd 3.00
1a variant Nat Jones (c) 3.00
1b premium ed. 10.00
2 PDd 3.00
2a variant Molenaar (c). 7.50
3 PDd 3.00
3a variant (c). 7.50
4 . . . . 3.00
4a variant (c). 7.50
Ashcan, b&w 6.00

HAUNTED, THE:
GRAY MATTERS
Chaos! Comics, 2002
1 . . . . 3.00
1a premium edition 10.00

HAUNTED LOVE
Charlton, 1973–75
1 . . . . 75.00
2 . . . . 30.00
3 thru 5 . . . . @30.00
6 thru 11 . . . . @25.00

HAUNT OF FEAR
Gladstone, 1991
1 EC Rep. H of F #17,WS#28 . . . . 3.00
2 EC Rep. H of F #5,WS #29. . . . 3.00

HAUNT OF FEAR
Russ Cochran, 1991
1 EC Rep. H of F #15. . . . . 3.00
2 thru 5 EC Rep. H of F . . . . @3.00
Second Series, 1992
1 EC Rep. H of F #14,WS#13 . . . . 2.50
2 EC Rep. H of F #18,WF#14 . . . . 2.50
3 EC Rep. H of F #19,WF#18 . . . . 2.50
4 EC Rep. H of F #16,WF#15 . . . . 2.50
5 EC Rep. H of F #5,WF#22 . . . . 2.50
6 EC Rep. H of F 2.50
7 EC Rep. H of F 2.50
8 thru 15 Rep. . . . . @2.50

Gemstone
16 thru 28 EC comics reprint . . . . @2.50

HAVE GUN, WILL TRAVEL
Dell Publishing Co., 1958
1 Richard Boone Ph(c) all. 250.00
2 . . . . 200.00
3 . . . . 200.00
4 thru 14 . . . . @150.00

HAWKMOON
COUNT BRASS
First
1 Michael Moorcock adapt. 2.50
2 thru 4 . . . . @2.50

...JEWEL IN THE SKULL
First, 1986
1 Michael Moorcock adapt. 3.00
2 thru 4 . . . . @2.50

...MAD GOD'S AMULET
First, 1987
1 Michael Moorcock adapt. 2.50
2 thru 4 . . . . @2.50

...SWORD OF THE DAWN
First, 1987
1 Michael Moorcock adapt. 2.50
2 thru 4 . . . . @2.50

...THE RUNESTAFF
First, 1988
1 Michael Moorcock adapt. 2.50
2 thru 4 . . . . @2.50

HEADLOCKED:
THE TRYOUT
AAM Markosia, 2008
1 (of 3) 3.50
2 . . . . 3.50

HEAVY METAL
MONSTERS
3-D-Zone, 1992
1 w/3-D glasses 4.00

HECTOR HEATHCOTE
Gold Key, 1964
1 . . . . 150.00

HEDG
Papyrus Media, 2002
1 by Patrick Sherman 3.00
1 signed 3.00
2 thru 4 . . . . @3.00

HEDGE KNIGHT, THE
Devil's Due Publishing, 2004
Previously published by Image
1 to 3 Collected edition, BV&JuB(c) 9.00
4 thru 6 . . . . @3.00
4a thru 6a variant (c)s . . . . @6.00

HELDEN
Caption Comics, 2001
1 (of 6) by Ralf Paul 3.00
2 thru 5 . . . . @3.00
6 concl. 52-pg. 4.00

HELIOS:
IN WITH THE NEW
Speakeasy Comics, 2005
1 & 2 (of 4) . . . . @3.00
Dakuwaka Productions, 2006
3 48-pg. 5.00

HELIOS:
UNDER THE GUN
Dakuwaka Productions, 2006
1 . . . . 3.00
2 thru 4 . . . . @3.00

HELLINA/
DOUBLE IMPACT
Lightning, 1996
1-shot JCy(c) 3.00
1-shot variant (c). 3.00

HELLINA:
HEART OF THORNS
Lightning Comics, 1996
1 . . . . 3.00
1 autographed edition 10.00
2 . . . . 3.00
2 variant cover 3.00
2 platinum edition 6.00

HELLINA: HELLBORN
Lightning, 1997
1 . . . . 3.00
1 autographed edition 10.00

Hellina, Nira X #1
© Lightning Comics

HELLINA/NIRA X:
ANGEL OF DEATH
Lightning, 1996
1A cover A. 3.00
1B cover B 3.00
1C Platinum cover 9.00
1D signed 9.00

HELLINA/NIRA X:
CYBERANGEL
Lightning, 1996
1 autographed edition 10.00

HELIOS
Dakuwaka Productions, 2004
1 . . . . 3.00
2 thru 4 . . . . @3.00

HELL, MICHIGAN
FC9 Publishing, 2005
1 thru 4 . . . . @3.00

COLOR PUB.

COLOR PUB.

HERBIE
American Comics Group
April-May, 1964
1	350.00
2 thru 4	@150.00
5 A:Beatles,Dean Martin, Frank	
Sinatra	200.00
6	125.00
7	125.00
8 O:Fat Fury	150.00
9	125.00
10	125.00
11 thru 13	@100.00
14 A:Nemesis,Magic Man	100.00
15 thru 22	@100.00
23 Feb., 1967	100.00

HERCULES
Charlton Comics, 1967
1	75.00
2 thru 7	@40.00
8 scarce	50.00
9 thru 13 Sept. 1969	@40.00

HERCULES
Radical Comics, 2008
1 (of 5)	1.00
1a variant (c)	1.00
2 thru 5	@3.00
2a thru 5a variant (c)s	@3.00

HERCULES: THE
LEGENDARY JOURNEYS
Topps, 1996
1 & 2	@3.00
3 RTs,JBt,SeM,The Shaper,pt.1	5.00
3a Xena Ph(c)	15.00
4 RTs,JBt,SeM,The Shaper,pt.2	5.00
5 RTs,JBt,SeM,The Shaper,pt.3	5.00

HERE COMES
THE BIG PEOPLE
Event Comics, 1997
1 ACo&JP(c)	3.00
1b JfD(c)	3.00
1c JQ&JP alternate (c)	10.00
1d JQ&JP alternate (c) signed	30.00

HERESY
Ape Entertainment, 2008
1 (of 4)	3.00
1a variant (c)	3.00
2 thru 3	@3.00

Hero Alliance #11 © Innovation

HERO ALLIANCE
Wonder Color Comics, 1987
1	2.50
Innovation, 1989–91
1 RLm,BS(c),R:HeroAlliance	6.00
2 RLm,BS(c),Victor vs.Rage	5.00
3 RLm,A:Stargrazers	4.00
4 BS(c),Fearful Symmetry	3.00
5 RLm(c)	2.50
6 BS(c),RLm pin-up	3.25
7 V:Magnetron	2.50
8 I:Vector	2.50
9 BS(c),V:Apostate	2.50
10 Living Legends, A:Sentry	2.50
11 Obligations, F:Kris Dunlop	2.50
12 Legacy, I:Bombshell	2.50
13 V:Bombshell	2.50
14 Kris Solo Story	2.50
15 JLA Parody Issue	2.50
16 V:Sepulchre	2.50
17 O:Victor,I&D:Misty	2.50
Annual #1 PS,BS,RLm	3.00
Spec.#1 Hero Alliance update	2.50
Spec.Hero Alliance & Justice Machine:	
Identity Crises	2.50

...THE END OF THE
GOLDEN AGE
Pied Piper, 1986
1 Bart Sears/Ron Lim	20.00
1a signed	25.00
1b 2nd printing	2.50
2	12.00
3	3.00
Graphic Novel	10.00
Innovation, 1989
1 RLm	5.00
1A 2nd printing	2.50
2 RLm	4.00
3 RLm	3.00

...QUARTERLY
Innovation, 1991
1 Hero Alliance stories	2.75
2 inc. Girl Happy	2.75
3 inc. Child Engagement	2.75
4	2.75

HERO AT LARGE
Speakeasy Comics, 2005
1	3.00
2	3.00
3 thru 4	@3.00

HERO BY NIGHT
Platinum Studios, 2007
1	4.00
1a variant (c)	4.00
2 thru 5	@4.00

HERO SQUARED
Atomeka, 2004
Spec. #1 X-tra Sized, KG,JMD	4.00
Spec. #1 X-tra Sized, Previews	4.00
Boom! Studios, 2005
1 (of 3) KG,JMD	4.00
1a Pull My Finger (c)	4.00
2 thru 3	@4.00
4	4.00
5 thru 7 ongoing series	@4.00
Spec. #1 Brainless Sitcom (c)	7.00

HI-ADVENTURE HEROES
Gold Key, 1969
1	75.00
2	65.00

HIGH CHAPPARAL
Gold Key, 1968
1	100.00

HIGHLANDER: THERE
CAN BE ONLY ONE
D.E. (Dynamite Ent.) 2006
0	2.50
1	3.00
1a variant (c)s	@3.00
1b variant Immortal gold foil (c)	20.00
2	3.00
2a variant (c)s	@3.00
3 thru 12	@3.00
3a thru 12a variant (c)s	@3.00

HIGHLANDER: THE WAY
OF THE SWORD
Dynamite Entertainment, 2007
2 thru 4	@3.50
4a variant (c)	3.50

HIGH ROADS
WildStorm/DC, 2002
1 (of 6),SLo(s),F:Nick Highroad	3.00
2 SLo(s),Paris	3.00
3 SLo(s),Nic Highroad	3.00
4 SLo(s),Iron Cross Brotherhood	3.00
5 SLo(s),Sloan,Bombridge	3.00
6 SLo(s),concl.	3.00

HIGH ROLLERS
Boom! Studios, 2008
1 (of 4)	4.00
2 thru 4	@4.00

HIGH SCHOOL
CONFIDENTIAL DIARY
Charlton Comics, 1960
1	75.00
2 thru 11	@50.00
Becomes:	

CONFIDENTIAL DIARY
12	60.00
13 thru 17 March, 1963	@50.00

HIGH VOLTAGE
Blackout, 1996
0	3.00

HIGHWAYMEN, THE
Wildstorm/DC, June, 2007
1 (of 5)	3.00
2	3.00
3 BSf(c)	3.00
4 BSf(c)	3.00
5 BSf(c),finale	3.00

HI-SCHOOL ROMANCE
DATE BOOK
Harvey Publications, 1962
1 BP	90.00
2	60.00
3 March, 1963	65.00

HIS NAME IS ROG...
ROG 2000
A Plus Comics
1	2.50

HOBBIT, THE
Eclipse
1	8.00
1a 2ndPrinting	6.00
2	7.00
2a 2ndPrinting	5.00
3	6.00

All comics prices listed are for *Near Mint* condition.

HOGAN'S HEROES
Dell Publishing Co., 1966
1 Ph(c)	150.00
2 Ph(c)	125.00
3 JD,Ph(c)	125.00
4 thru 8 Ph(c)	@100.00
8 and 9	@100.00

HOLLYWOOD NOIR
Narwain Publishing, 2006
GN Vol. 1	6.00

HONEY WEST
Gold Key, 1966
1	200.00

HONEYMOONERS
Lodestone, 1986
1	4.00
5 Mag.	3.00

[2nd Series] Triad, 1987
1 They Know What They Like	5.00
2 The Life You Save	4.00
3 X-mas special,inc.Art Carney interview	4.00
4 In the Pink	4.00
5 Bang, Zoom, To the Moon	4.00
6 Everyone Needs a Hero inc. Will Eisner interview	4.00
7	4.00
8	4.00
9 Jack Davis(c)	5.00
10 thru 13	@4.00

HONG KONG
Blackout Comics, 1996
0 A:Hari Kari	3.00
0 limited commemorative edition	10.00

HOPE FALLS
AAM Markosia, 2007
1 thru 5	@3.50
4a variant (c)	4.50

HORRORWOOD
Ape Entertainment, 2006
1 thru 4	@3.50

HORSEMEN
Griot Enterprises, 2002
1 (of 3)	3.00
2 thru 3	@3.00
3.5	3.00

HOT ROD RACERS
Charlton Comics, 1964
1	150.00
2 thru 5	@100.00
6 thru 15 July, 1967	@75.00

HOTSPUR
Eclipse, 1987
1 RT(i),I:Josef Quist	3.00
2 RT(i),Amulet of Kothique Stolen	3.00
3 RT(i),Curse of the SexGoddess	3.00

HOT STUFF, THE LITTLE DEVIL
Harvey Publications, 1957
1	800.00
2 1st Stumbo the Giant	400.00
3 thru 5	@250.00
6 thru 10	@200.00
11 thru 20	@175.00
21 thru 40	@150.00
41 thru 60	@100.00
61 thru 100	@75.00

101 thru 105	@40.00
106 thru 112 52 pg Giants	@50.00
113 thru 139	@20.00
140 thru 177	@15.00

HOT STUFF SIZZLERS
Harvey Publications, 1960
1 F:Hot Stuff	350.00
2	150.00
3	125.00
4	125.00
5	125.00
6 thru 10	@100.00
11 thru 15	@90.00
16 thru 20	@85.00
21 thru 30	@60.00
31 thru 44	@50.00
45 E:68 pgs	50.00
46 thru 50	@40.00
51 thru 59	@30.00

HOUSE AT THE EDGE OF NOWHERE
Bloodfire, 2007
1 (of 4)	3.00
2 thru 4	@3.00

Howard Chaykin's American Flagg #3
© First

HOWARD CHAYKIN'S AMERICAN FLAGG!
First, 1988
1 thru 9	@3.00
10 thru 12	@3.00

H.P.LOVECRAFT'S CTHULHU
Millennium, 1991
1 I:Miskatonic Project,V:Mi-Go	3.00
2 Arkham, trading cards	3.00
3	2.50

H.R. PUFNSTUF
Gold Key, 1970
1	350.00
2 & 3	@175.00
4 thru 8	@150.00

HUCK & YOGI JAMBOREE
Dell Publishing Co., March, 1961
1	175.00

HUCKLEBERRY HOUND
Charlton, 1970
1	100.00
2 thru 7	@75.00
8 Jan., 1972	80.00

HUCKLEBERRY HOUND
Dell Publishing Co., May-July, 1959
1	200.00
2	150.00
3 thru 7	@150.00
8 thru 10	@125.00
11 thru 17	@100.00

Gold Key, 1962
18 Chuckleberry Tales	150.00
19 Chuckleberry Tales	125.00
20 Chuckleberry Tales	100.00
21 thru 30	@75.00
31 thru 43	@60.00

HUEY, DEWEY & LOUIE JUNIOR WOODCHUCKS
Gold Key, 1966
1	100.00
2 thru 5	@60.00
6 thru 17	@50.00
18	40.00
19 thru 25	@50.00
26 thru 30	@40.00
31 thru 57	@40.00
58	35.00
59	35.00
60 thru 80	@30.00
81 1984	30.00

HUNGER, THE
Speakeasy Comics, 2005
1	3.00
2 thru 5	@3.00
6 thru 8	@3.00

HUNK
Charlton, 1961
1	60.00
2 thru 11	@30.00

HUNTER, THE
Dare, 2007
1	6.00
2 thru 3	@6.00

HUNTER'S MOON
Boom! Studios, 2007
1	4.00
1a variant (c)	4.00
2 thru 5	@4.00

HYBRID
Studio 407, 2008
1 (of 4)	2.75
2 thru 3	@3.50

HYBRID BASTARDS
Archaia Studios, 2007
2 thru 3	@3.50

HYBRIDS
Continuity, 1993
0 Deathwatch 2000 prologue	5.00
1 Deathwatch 2000 pt.4,w/card	3.00
2 Deathwatch 2000 pt.13,w/card	3.00
3 Deathwatch 2000 w/card	3.00
4 A:Valeria	3.00
5 O:Valeria	3.00

[2nd Series], 1994
1 Rise of Magic	3.00

COLOR PUB.

HYBRIDS: ORIGIN
Continuity, 1993
1 thru 5 . . . . @3.00

HYDE-25
Harris, 1995
1 New Drug. 3.00

HYPER-ACTIVES, THE
Alias Enterprises, 2005
0 . . . . 1.00
1 thru 4 . . . . @3.50

I SPY
Gold Key, 1966
1 Bill Cosby Ph(c). 400.00
2 Ph(c) 300.00
3 thru 4 AMc,Ph(c) . . . . @200.00
5 thru 6 Ph(c) Sept.1968. . . . @200.00

I-Bots #7
© *Big Comics*

I-BOTS
Big Comics, 1996
1 F:Lady Justice 2.50
2 thru 4 . . . . @2.50
5 thru 6 StG(s),PB. . . . . @2.50
7 PB,Rebirth,pt.1, triptych (c) 2.50
8 PB,Rebirth,pt.2, triptych (c) 2.50
9 PB,Rebirth,pt.3, Original I-Bots
    return, triptych (c) 2.50

ICICLE
Hero Graphics
1 A:Flare,Lady Arcane,
    V:Eraserhead. 5.00

IDAHO
Dell, 1963
1 . . . . 35.00
2 thru 8 . . . . 20.00

I DREAM OF JEANNIE
Dell Publishing Co., 1965
1 Ph(c),B.Eden 300.00
2 Ph(c),B.Eden 200.00

IGOR
IDW, 2008
1 Movie prequel 4.00
2 thru 4 . . . . @4.00
1 Movie Adaptation 4.00
2 thru 4 . . . . @4.00

I'M DICKENS –
HE'S FENSTER
Dell Publishing Co.,
May-July, 1963
1 Ph(c) 100.00
2 Ph(c) 80.00

IMP
Slave Labor, 1994
1 . . . . 2.50

IMPACT
Gemstone, 1999
1 EC Comic reprint 3.00
2 thru 5 . . . . @3.00
Annual #1 rep. #1–#5 . . . . 13.50

IMPOSSIBLE TALES
After Hours, 2006
1 and 2 (of 2) . . . . @4.00

INANNA'S TEARS
Archaia Stodios, 2007
1 (of 5) 4.00
2 thru 5 . . . . @4.00

INCAL
Humanoids Publishing, 2001
1 thru 13 . . . . 3.00

INCURSION
Platinum Studios, 2007
2 thru 4 . . . . @4.00

INDIA AUTHENTIC
Virgin Comics, 2007
1 Ganesha 3.00
2 Kaali. 3.00
3 Indra, King of the Gods 3.00
4 Uma 3.00
5 Shiva 3.00
6 Vishnu – The Narasimha Avatar . 3.00
7 Yama – The Lord of Death 3.00
8 Garuda. 3.00
9 Kartikkeya 3.00
10 Parashuram 3.00
11 Hanuman 3.00
12 Andhaka 3.00
13 Lakshmi. 3.00
14 Saraswati 3.00
15 Krishna 3.00
16 The Saffron Princess 3.00

INFANTRY
Devil's Due Publishing, 2004
1 Aftermath, JoC 3.00
1a variant (c). 3.00
2 thru 6 . . . . @3.00

INFINITEENS
FC9 Publishing, 2005
1 . . . . 3.00
1a variant (c) 3.00
2 thru 4 . . . . @3.00
Moonstone Books, 2006
1 . . . . 3.50
2 . . . . 3.00
3 thru 4 . . . . @3.50

INMATES:
PRISONERS OF SOCIETY
Delta Comics, 1997
1 (of 4) 3.00
2 thru 4 . . . . @3.00

INNER CIRCLE
Mushroom Comics, 1995
1.1 I:Point Blank 2.50
1.2 V:Deathcom 2.50
1.3 V:Deathcom 2.50
1.4 V:Deathcom 2.50

INNOCENTS
Radical Comics, 1995
1 I:Innocent. 2.50

INNOVATORS
Dark Moon, 1995
1 I:Innovator, LeoShan 2.50
2 O:Mr. Void 2.50
3 I:Quill 2.50

INSANE CLOWN POSSE
Chaos Comics, 1999
1 . . . . 3.00
1 premium edition 9.00
1 Jeckel Brothers premium ed. . . . 9.00
3 Raze the Desertz of Glass 9.00
3a variant (c). 9.00
Spec. The Amazing Jeckel Brothers 3.00

...DARK CARNIVAL
Chaos! Comics, 2002
1 . . . . 3.00
1a premium edition 9.00

...MR. JOHNSON'S HEAD
Chaos Comics, 2002
Ashcan 6.00
1 (of 2) 3.00
1a premium edition 9.00

...THE PENDULUM
Chaos! Comics, 2000
1 polybagged with CD single 6.00
1a variant (c). 9.00
2 polybagged 6.00
3 polybagged 6.00
4 polybagged 6.00
5 Road Rage, polybagged 6.00
6 . . . . 6.00
7 Pendulum's Promise 6.00
8 Sport hunting, with CD-ROM . . . 6.00
9 Glimpse of Crystal Death. 6.00
10 . . . . 6.00
11 with CD-ROM 6.00
12 . . . . 6.00
Spec. #1 Hallowicket 3.00

INSANE JANE
Bluewater Prod., 2008
1 . . . . 4.00
1a Bluewater puzzle (c) 4.00
2 thru 4 . . . . @4.00
1a thru 4a variant (c)s. . . . . @4.00

INSPECTOR, THE
Gold Key, 1974
1 BU:Pink Panther 45.00
2 BU:Pink Panther 30.00
3 thru 5 . . . . @25.00
6 . . . . 20.00
Becomes:

INSPECTOR AND THE
PINK PANTHER, THE
7 thru 19 . . . . @20.00

INTERVIEW WITH
A VAMPIRE
Innovation, 1991
1 based on novel,preq.to Vampire
    Chronicles 3.50
2 thru 11 . . . . @3.00

IN THE BLOOD
Boom! Studios, 2005
1 (of 4) 4.00
1a Previews exclusive (c) 7.00
2 . . . . 4.00
3 . . . . 4.00

INTIMATE
Charlton Comics, 1957
1 thru 3 . . . . @75.00
Becomes:

TEEN-AGE LOVE
4 . . . . 60.00
5 thru 9 . . . . @40.00
10 thru 35. . . . . @40.00
36 thru 96. . . . . @40.00

INTIMATES, THE
Wildstorm/DC, Nov., 2004
1 JoC(s),JLe 3.00
2 JoC(s),JLe 3.00
3 JoC(s),JLe,Blaster Pill Marathon . 3.00
4 JoC(s),JLe,School Dance 3.00
5 JoC(s),JLe,Hivejournal 3.00
6 JoC(s),JLe(c)F:Secret of Sykes. . 3.00
7 JoC(s),Last day of school year . . 3.00
8 JoC(s),Summer vacation 3.00
9 JoC(s),Summer vacation 3.00
10 JoC(s),Vacation's end. 3.00
11 JoC(s),Back to School 3.00
12 JoC(s),Kids revolt 3.00

INTRUDER
TSR, 1990–91
1 thru 4 . . . . @3.00
5 thru 8 The Next Dimension . . . @3.00

INVADERS FROM HOME
Piranha Press, 1990
1 thru 6 . . . . @2.50

INVADERS, THE
Gold Key, 1967
1 Ph(c),DSp 200.00
2 Ph(c),DSp 150.00
3 Ph(c),DSp 150.00
4 Ph(c),DSp 150.00

INVINCIBLE FOUR OF KUNG FU & NINJA
Dr. Leungs
1 . . . . 3.00
2 thru 4 . . . . @2.50
5 thru 11 . . . . @2.50

IO
Invictus Studios, 1994
1 I:IO. 2.75
2 . . . . 2.75
3 V:Major Damage 2.75

IRON AND THE MAIDEN
Aspen MLT, 2007
1 . . . . 4.00
2 thru 4 . . . . @4.00
1a thru 4a variant (c)s. . . . . @4.00

IRON HORSE
Dell Publishing Co., March, 1967
1 . . . . 50.00
2 . . . . 50.00

IRONJAW
Atlas, Jan.–July, 1975
1 NA(c),MSy 20.00

Ironjaw #4
© Atlas

2 NA(c) 15.00
3 . . . . 15.00
4 O:IronJaw 15.00

IRON AND THE MAIDEN
Aspen MLT, 2007
0 . . . . 2.50

...BRUTES, BIMS AND THE CITY
Aspen MLT, 2008
1 . . . . 3.00

IRON MARSHAL
Jademan, 1990
1 . . . . 2.50
2 thru 10 . . . . @2.50
11 thru 32 . . . . @2.50

ISAAC ASIMOV'S I-BOTS
Tekno-Comix, 1995
1 I:I-Bots 2.50
2 O:I-Bots 2.50
3 V:Black OP 2.50

IT'S ABOUT TIME
Gold Key, 1967
1 Ph(c) 75.00

ITCHY & SCRATCHY
Bongo Comics, 1993
1 DaC(s), ... 4.00
2 DaC(s), ... 3.50
3 . . . . 3.50

IVANHOE
Dell Publishing Co., 1963
1 . . . . 60.00

I WAS KIDNAPPED BY LESBIAN PIRATES FROM OUTER SPACE
Platinum Studios, 2008
1 (of 6) 1.00
2 thru 6 . . . . @4.00

JACK HUNTER
Blackthorne, 1988
1 . . . . 2.50
2 thru 3 . . . . @2.50

JACKIE CHAN ADVENTURES
Tokyopop Press, 2003
GN Vol. 1 (of 3) Cine-Manga 8.00
GN Vol. 2 . . . . 8.00
GN Vol. 3 . . . . 8.00

JACKIE CHAN'S SPARTAN X
Topps, 1997
1 The Armor of Heaven, pt.1 . . . . . 3.00
2 The Armor of Heaven, pt.2 . . . . . 3.00
3 (of 6) 3.00

JADE
Chaos! Comics, 2001
1 . . . . 3.00
1a premium edition 9.00
2 . . . . 3.00
3 . . . . 3.00
4 . . . . 3.00
4a variant 7.50
Preview book 2.50
Preview book, premium 6.00
Ashcan Jade #1 . . . . 6.00

JADE FIRE
Kandora Publishing, 2005
1 . . . . 3.50
2 thru 4 . . . . @3.50

JADE: REDEMPTION
Chaos! Comics, 2001
1 (of 4) 3.00
1 premium edition 9.00
2 thru 4 . . . . @3.00
2a thru 4a variant (c). . . . . @6.00
Ashcan 5.00

JADEMAN COLLECTION
Jademan, 1989
1 . . . . 4.00
2 . . . . 3.00
3 thru 5 . . . . @2.50

JADEMAN KUNG FU SPECIAL
Jademan, 1988
1 I:Oriental Heroes, Blood
  Sword, Drunken Fist 5.00

JADE WARRIORS: SLAVE OF THE DRAGON
Avatar Press, 2000
1 (of 3) MD2, 40-page 3.50
1a photo (c). 3.50
1b wraparound (c). 3.50
2 MD2 . . . . 3.50
2a photo (c). 3.50

JAGUAR GOD
Verotika, 1995
1 Frazetta, I:Jaguar God. 3.00
2 V:Yi-Cha. 3.00
3 V:Yi-Cha. 3.00
4 V:Yi-Cha. 3.00
5 AOI 3.00
6 LSh,AOI. 3.00
7 LSh,AOI. 3.00
8 AOI. 3.00
Spec.#1 Return to X'ibala,RCo . . . 5.00
Spec. Jaguar God Illustrations. . . . 4.00
Spec. fan club edition 10.00

COLOR PUB.

JALILA
Studio G, 2003
1 . . . . 3.00
2 thru 4 . . . . @3.00
AK Entertainment, 2006
1 Overwhelmed, pt.1 . . . . 3.00
2 First Mission. 3.00
3 Overwhelmed. 3.00
4 Overwhelmed, pt. 2 . . . . 3.00
5 Overwhelmed, pt. 3 . . . . 3.00
6 War Crimes 3.00
7 thru 9 . . . . @3.00

JAMES BOND 007
Eclipse, 1991
1 MGr,PerfectBound 5.50
2 MGr 5.00
3 MGr,end series 5.00
GN Licence to Kill, MGr I/o 8.00

JAMES BOND: GOLDENEYE
Topps, 1995
1 Movie adaptation 3.00
2 thru 3 Movie adaptation . . . . . @3.00

JASON & THE ARGONAUTS: KINGDOM OF HADES
Bluewater Productions, 2007
2 (of 4) 3.50
3 thru 4 . . . . @3.50
3a thru 4a variant (c)s . . . . @3.50
5 . . . . 4.00

JASON GOES TO HELL
Topps, 1993
1 Movie adapt.,w/3 cards 3.25
2 thru 3 Movie adapt.,w/3 cards . @3.25

JASON VS. LEATHERFACE
Topps, 1995
1 Jason Meets Leatherface 15.00
2 SBi(c) Leatherface's family 15.00
3 SBi(c),conclusion 12.00

JASON X
Avatar Press, 2005
Spec. #1 . . . . 4.00
Spec. #1a Wraparound (c). 4.00
Spec. #1b Variant(c)s . . . . @4.00
Spec. #1c Blood red convention (c) . 5.00
Spec. #1d Extreme Force (c) 6.00
Spec. #1e Headless (c) 6.00
Spec. #1f Victim (c) 6.00

JAVA
Committed Comics, 2004
1 thru 3 . . . . @3.00

JAVERTS
Firstlight, 1994
1 thru 5 Pieces of an Icon . . . . . . @3.00

JAZAN WILD'S CARNIVAL OF SOULS
Markosia, 2005
1 thru 3 (of 3) . . . . @3.50
1a thru 3a variant (c)s . . . . @3.50

JAZAN WILD'S FUNHOUSE OF HORRORS
Carnival Comics, 2008
1 The House of Horrors 3.00

JENNA
Narwain Publishing, 2005
1 . . . . 4.00
2 . . . . 4.00
2a limited ed. with CD. 8.00
3 . . . . 4.00
1-shot Panic in New York. 3.00

JENNA JAMESON'S SHADOW HUNTER
Virgin Comics 2007
0 25
1 thru 3 . . . . @3.00
2a thru 3a variant (c)s . . . . @3.00

JENNA MEETS 100 GIRLS
Narwain Publishing, 2006
1 (of 2) x-over 3.50

JENNY SPARKS: THE SECRET HISTORY OF THE AUTHORITY
WildStorm/DC, 2000
1 (of 5) MMr,JMC 8.00
1a variant (c) (1:4) 4.00
2 MMr,JMC 3.00
3 MMr,JMC,O:Jack Hawksmoor . . . 3.00
4 MMr,JMC 3.00
5 MMr,JMC,conclusion 3.00

JEREMIAH HARM
Boom! Studios, 2005
1 KG,AIG. 4.00
1a convention (c) 7.00
2 thru 5 . . . . @4.00

JET
WildStorm/DC, 2000
1 (of 4) DAn,ALa,F:Jodi Slayton . . . 2.50
2 DAn,ALa,Midnight to Midnight . . . 2.50
3 DAn,ALa,V:Timewaster 2.50
4 DAn,ALa,concl. 2.50

JET DREAM
Gold Key, 1968
1 . . . . 60.00

JETSONS, THE
Gold Key, 1963
1 . . . . 500.00

The Jetsons #33
© *Gold Key*

2 . . . . 300.00
3 thru 10 . . . . @200.00
11 thru 20 . . . . @150.00
21 thru 36 Oct. 1970 . . . . @125.00
Charlton Comics, 1970
1 from Hanna-Barbera TV show . 150.00
2 . . . . 100.00
3 thru 10 . . . . @75.00
11 thru 20 Dec. 1973 . . . . @60.00
Harvey Comics, 1991–92
1 thru 5 . . . . @3.00
Archie, 1995
1 . . . . 3.00
2 thru 17 . . . . @3.00

JEZEBELLE
WildStorm/DC, 2001
1 (of 6) F:Harper Harrison 2.50
1a variant(c) (1:2) 2.50
2 BRa(s) 2.50
3 BRa(s) F:Harper Harrison 2.50
4 BRa(s),Seance&Sensibility,pt.1 . 2.50
5 BRa(s),Seance&Sensibility,pt.2 . 2.50
6 BRa(s),concl. 2.50

JEZEBEL JADE
Comico, 1988
1 AKu,A:Race Bannon 3.00
2 AKu 3.00
3 AKu 3.00

JFH: JUSTICE FOR HIRE
Creative Talent Comm., 2007
1 (of 12) with DVD 4.00
2 thru 4 . . . . @4.00
1a thru 4a variant (c)s . . . . @4.00

JIGSAW
Harvey Publications, 1966
1 . . . . 50.00
2 . . . . 40.00

JIMBO
Bongo Comics, 1995
1 R:Jimbo 3.00
2 thru 4 . . . . @3.00

JIM BUTCHER'S THE DRESDEN FILES: WELCOME TO THE JUNGLE
Dabel Brothers Prod., 2008
1 (of 4) 4.00
2 thru 4 . . . . @4.00

JIM BUTCHER'S THE DRESDEN FILES: STORM FRONT
Dabel Brothers Prod., 2008
1 (of 4) 4.00
2 . . . . 4.00

JIM REAPER
Silent Devil Productions, 2006
1 Week One 4.00

JINDAI
Zenescope Entertainment, 2005
1 . . . . 3.00
2 thru 8 . . . . @3.00

JOE & MAX
Guardian Line, 2006
1 . . . . 3.00
2 thru 5 . . . . @3.00

J. N. WILLIAMSON'S MASQUES
Innovation, 1992
1 TV,From horror anthology 5.00
2 Olivia(c) inc.Better Than One . . . 5.00

JOHN BOLTON, HALLS OF HORROR
Eclipse, 1985
1 JBo. 3.00
2 JBo. 3.00

JOHN CARTER OF MARS
Gold Key, 1964
1 . . . . 150.00
2 . . . . 100.00
3 . . . . 100.00

JOHN DOE
Boom! Studios, 2006
Preview book 2.50

JOHN F. KENNEDY LIFE STORY
(WITH 2 REPRINTS)
Dell Publishing Co., 1964
1 . . . . 100.00
2 . . . . 75.00
3 . . . . 75.00

JOHN JAKES MULLKON EMPIRE
Tekno Comix, 1995
1 I:Mulkons 2.50
2 O:Mulkons 2.50
3 D:Company Man 2.50
4 Disposal Problems. 2.50
5 F:Granny 2.50
6 Where's Karma 2.50

JOHN LAW
Eclipse, 1983
1 WE. 2.50

JOHNNY JASON TEEN REPORTER
Dell Publishing Co., 1962
1 . . . . 50.00
2 . . . . 40.00

JOHNNY NEMO
Eclipse, 1985–86
1 I:Johnny Nemo. 2.50
2 . . . . 2.50
3 F:Sindy Shade 2.50

JOHN STEELE SECRET AGENT
Gold Key, 1964
1 . . . . 150.00

JOHN WOO'S SEVEN BROTHERS
Virgin Comics, 2006
1 . . . . 3.00
1a variant (c) 3.00
2 thru 8 . . . . @3.00
3a thru 8a variant (c) . . . . @3.00
Spec. Extended #1 & #2 . . . . 7.00

JONNY QUEST
Gold Key, 1964
1 TV show. 700.00

Johnny Quest #1
© Comico

JONNY QUEST
Comico, 1986
1 DW,SR,A:Dr.Zin 6.00
2 WP/JSon,O:RaceBannon 4.00
3 DSt(c). 4.00
4 TY/AW,DSt(i) 3.50
5 DSt(c)A:JezebelJade 3.00
6 AKu 3.00
7 . . . . 3.00
8 KSy 3.00
9 MA 3.00
10 King Richard III 3.00
11 JSon,BSz(c) 3.00
12 DSp. 3.00
12 DSp 3.00
13 CI 3.00
14 thru 31 . . . . @3.00
Spec.#1 . . . . 3.00
Spec.#2 . . . . 3.00

...CLASSICS
Comico, 1987
1 DW. 3.00
2 DW,O:Hadji 3.00
3 DW. 3.00

JON SABLE
First, 1983
1 MGr,A:President 4.50
2 MGr,Alcohol Issue 3.50
3 thru 6 MGr,O:Jon Sable . . . . . . @3.00
7 thru 24 MGr . . . . @2.50
25 thru 29 MGr,Shatter . . . . @3.00
30 thru 56 MGr. . . . . @2.50

JON SABLE, FREELANCE: BLOODTRAIL
IDW Publishing, 2005
1 MGr 4.00
2 thru 6 . . . . @4.00

JONAS: TALES OF AN IRONSTAR
Codedeco Inc., 2004
1 . . . . 4.00
2 thru 6 . . . . @4.00

JOSIE
Archie Publications, 1963
1 . . . . 300.00
2 . . . . 150.00
3 . . . . 100.00
4 . . . . 100.00

5 . . . . 100.00
6 thru 10. . . . . @75.00
11 thru 20 . . . . @50.00
21 thru 30 . . . . @40.00
31 thru 40. . . . . @35.00
41 thru 54 . . . . @35.00
55 thru 74 . . . . @25.00
75 thru 105 . . . . @25.00
106 Oct., 1962 . . . . 25.00

JOVA'S HARVEST
Arcana Studio, 2005
1 (of 3) 5.00
2 . . . . 5.00
3 . . . . 3.50

JUDGE COLT
Gold Key, 1969
1 . . . . 50.00
2 . . . . 35.00
3 . . . . 35.00
4 Sept., 1970 . . . . 35.00

JUDGE DREDD
Eagle, 1983
1 BB,I:Judge Death(in USA). 9.00
2 BB(c&a),The Oxygen Board 7.00
3 BB(c),Judge Dredd Lives. 6.00
4 BB(c),V:Perps 6.00
5 thru 10 BB(c),V:Perps . . . . . . @5.00
11 BB(c). 4.00
12 BB(c). 4.00
13 BB(c), The Day the Law
   Died, pt.5. . . . . 4.00
14 BB(c),Dredd vs. Dredd 4.00
15 thru 21 BB(c). . . . . @4.00
22 thru 27 BB(c),V:Perps . . . . . . @3.00
28 A:Judge Anderson,V:Megaman . 4.00
29 A:Monty, the guinea pig 3.00
30 V:Perps 3.00
31 Destiny's Angel, Pt. 1 . . . . 3.00
32 Destiny's Angel, Pt. 2 . . . . 3.00
33 V:League of Fatties. 3.00
34 V:Executioner 3.00

JUDGE DREDD
Quality Press, 1986
1 Cry of the Werewolf Pt.1 . . . . . . 6.00
2 Cry of the Werewolf Pt.2 . . . . . . 5.00
3 Anti-smoking 4.00
4 Wreckers 4.00
5 Highwayman 4.00
6 thru 9 . . . . @3.00
10 thru 44. . . . . @3.00
45 thru 61. . . . . @2.50
Becomes:

...CLASSICS
62 thru 75. . . . . @2.50
76 Diary of a Mad Citizen 3.00
77 . . . . 3.00
Judge Dredd Special #1 . . . . 2.50

...AMERICA
Fleetway
1 I:America 3.50

...JUDGE CHILD QUEST
Eagle, 1984
1 thru 3 . . . . @3.00
4 BB(c) 3.00
5 . . . . 3.00

...CRIME FILE
Eagle, 1984
1 Ron Smith, The Perp Runners . . 2.50
2 thru 6 . . . . @2.50
Quality (Prestige format), 1989
1 A:Rogue Trooper 6.50
2 IG,V:Fatties, Energy Vampires &
   Super Fleas. 6.00

COLOR PUB.

3 Battles foes from dead A:Judge
  Anderson 6.00

...EARLY CASES
Eagle, 1986
1 Robot Wars, Pt.1 . . . . 4.00
2 Robot Wars, Pt.2 . . . . 3.00
3 V:Perps 3.00
4 IG, Judge Giant 3.00
5 V:Perps 3.00
6 V:Judge killing car Elvis. 3.00

...HARDCASE PAPERS
Fleetway/Quality
1 V:The Tarantula 7.50
2 Junkies & Psychos 6.50
3 Crime Call Vid. Show. 6.50
4 Real Coffee,A:Johnny Alpha 6.50

...THE MEGAZINE
Fleetway/Quality, 1991
1 Midnite's Children Pt.1
  A:Chopper, Young Death. 5.50
2 Midnite's Children Pt.2. . . . . 5.00
3 . . . . 5.00
23 thru 34 . . . . @4.00
35 thru 43 . . . . @5.50
44 thru 45 . . . . @7.00
Egmont Fleetway Limited
46 thru 75 . . . . @7.00

JUDGMENT DAY
Lightning Comics, 1993
1 B:JZy(s),KIK,V:Razorr,Rift,
  Nightmare, red prism(c). 5.00
1a Gold Prism(c). 5.00
1b Purple Prism(c) 7.00
1c Misprint,Red Prism(c), Bloodfire
  Credits inside. 8.00
1d Misprint,Gold Prism(c), Bloodfire
  Credits inside. 8.00
1e Misprint,Green Prism(c),
  Bloodfire Credits inside 8.00
1f B&W promo ed. Gold ink 5.00
1g B&W promo ed. platinum ed. . . 7.00
2 TLw,I:War Party,BU:Perg,
  w/Perg card 4.00
3 ErP,O:X-Treme. 3.25
4 ErP,In Hell 3.25
5 TLw,In Hell 3.25
6 TLw,I:Red Front,O:Salurio 3.25
7 O:Safeguard 3.25
8 thru 10 . . . . @3.00

JUDGMENT DAY
Maximum Press, 1997
Alpha AMo(s) 2.50
Alpha variant cover 2.50
Omega AMo(s). 2.50
Omega variant cover 2.50
Final Judgment AMo(s) 2.50
Final Judgment variant cover. 2.50

JUDO GIRL
Alias Enterprises, 2005
1 (of 4) 3.00
2 thru 4 . . . . @3.00
2a thru 4a variant (c)s. . . . . @3.00
Vol. 2
1 (of 4) 3.50
1a variant (c) 3.50
2 thru 4 . . . . @3.50

JUDOMASTER
Charlton Comics, 1966
(Special War Series #4)
  I:Judomaster 60.00
89 FMc,War stories begin 50.00
89 (90) FMc,A:Thunderbolt 40.00
91 FMc,DG,A:Sarge Steel 40.00
92 FMc,DG,A:Sarge Steel 40.00

---

93 FMc,DG,I:Tiger 40.00
94 FMc,DG,A:Sarge Steel 40.00
95 FMc,DG,A:Sarge Steel 40.00
96 FMc,DG,A:Sarge Steel 40.00
97 FMc,A:Sarge Steel 40.00
98 FMc,A:Sarge Steel 40.00

Jughead #173
© *Archie Publications*

JUGHEAD
Archie Publications
1965–1987
127 thru 130 . . . . @50.00
131 thru 150 . . . . @40.00
151 thru 160 . . . . @25.00
161 thru 200 . . . . @20.00
201 thru 250 . . . . @15.00
251 thru 300 . . . . @12.00
301 thru 352 . . . . @10.00

JUGHEAD
Archie Publications
[2nd Series], 1987
1 thru 45 . . . . @6.00
Becomes:

ARCHIE'S PAL JUGHEAD
June, 1993
46 thru 50 . . . . @3.50
51 thru 70 . . . . @2.50
71 thru 99 . . . . @2.50
100 A Storm Over Uniforms, x-over
  (Betty #57, Archie #467) 2.50
101 thru 122 . . . . @2.50
123 thru 161 . . . . @2.50
162 thru 192 . . . . @2.50

JUGHEAD AS
CAPTAIN HERO
Archie Publications, 1966
1 . . . . 100.00
2 . . . . 65.00
3 thru 7 . . . . @50.00

JUGHEAD'S FANTASY
Archie Publications, 1960
1 Sir Jugalot 300.00
2 Peter Goon 200.00
3 Superjughead 175.00

JUGHEAD'S FOLLY
Archie Publications, 1957
1 Jughead like Elvis 675.00

JUGHEAD'S JOKES
Archie Publications, 1967
1 . . . . 125.00
2 . . . . 75.00
3 thru 5 . . . . @40.00
6 thru 10 . . . . @35.00
11 thru 30 . . . . @25.00
31 thru 77 . . . . @10.00
78 Sept., 1982 . . . . 10.00

JUGHEAD WITH
ARCHIE DIGEST
Archie Publications,
March, 1974
1 . . . . 100.00
2 . . . . 60.00
3 thru 10 . . . . @50.00
11 thru 91 . . . . @20.00
92 thru 129 . . . . @15.00
130 thru 138 . . . . @10.00
139 thru 144 . . . . @10.00
145 thru 155 . . . . @7.00
156 thru 171 . . . . @5.00
172 thru 179 . . . . @5.00

JUMPER JUMPSCARS
Onipress, 2007
1 (of 4) 4.00
2 thru 4 . . . . @4.00

JUNCTION 17
Antarctic Press, 2003
1 color manga 3.50
2 thru 4 . . . . @3.00

JUNGLE ADVENTURES
Skywald, March–June, 1971
1 F:Zangar,Jo-Jo,Blue Gorilla 40.00
2 F:Sheena, Jo-Jo,Zangar 35.00
3 F:Zangar,Jo-Jo,White Princess . 35.00

JUNCTION 17
Antarctic Press, 2003
1 . . . . 3.50
2 thru 4 . . . . @3.00

JUNGLE BOOK
Gold Key, 1964
1 . . . . 75.00

JUNGLE COMICS
Blackthorne, 1988
1 DSt(c). 3.00
2 . . . . 3.00
3 . . . . 3.00
See B&W

JUNGLE GIRL
Dynamite Entertainment, 2008
4 thru 5 . . . . @3.00
4a thru 5a variant (c) . . . . @3.50
SEASON 2
Dynamite Entertainment, 2008
1 . . . . @3.50
1a variant (c) 3.50

JUNGLE JIM
Charlton, 1969–70
22 . . . . 60.00
23 . . . . 40.00
24 . . . . 40.00
25 . . . . 40.00
26 . . . . 40.00
27 . . . . 50.00
28 . . . . 50.00

JUNGLE TALES OF TARZAN
Charlton Comics, 1964
1 . . . . 100.00
2 . . . . 75.00
3 . . . . 75.00
4 July, 1965 . . . . 75.00

JUNGLE TWINS, THE
Gold Key, 1972
1 F:Tono and Kono 30.00
2 thru 5 . . . . @15.00
6 thru 17 . . . . @10.00

JUNGLE WAR STORIES
Dell Publishing Co., 1962
1 P(c) all 75.00
2 thru 11 . . . . @50.00
Becomes:

GUERRILLA WAR
12 thru 14 . . . . @50.00

JUNIOR WOODCHUCKS
Walt Disney, 1991
1 CB,Bubbleweight Champ. 3.00
2 CB,Swamp of no Return 3.00
3 Rescue Run-Around 3.00
4 Cave Caper 3.00

JURASSIC PARK
Topps, 1993
1 Movie Adapt.,w/card 5.00
1a Newsstand Ed. 4.00
2 Movie Adapt.,w/card 3.25
3 Movie Adapt.,w/card 3.25
4 Movie Adapt.,w/card 3.25
2a thru 4a Newsstand Ed. . . . . . @2.75
Ann.#1 Death Lizards 4.00

...ADVENTURES
Topps, 1994
1 thru 10 reprints titles . . . . @3.00

...RAPTOR
Topps, 1993
1 SE w/Zorro #0 ashcan & cards . . . 3.25
2 w/3 cards 3.00

...RAPTORS ATTACK
Topps, 1994
1 SEt(s), ... 2.75
2 thru 4 SEt(s), ... @2.75

...RAPTOR HIJACK
Topps
1 SEt(s), ... 2.50
2 thru 4 SEt(s), ... @2.50

...THE LOST WORLD
Topps, 1997
1 (of 4) movie adapt 3.00
2 thru 4 . . . . @3.00

JUST A PILGRIM
Black Bull Entertainment, 2001
1 GEn,MT(c). 6.00
1a variant (c). 12.00
2 GEn,GF(r) 4.00
3 GEn,KN(c), Bloody Baskets 4.00
4 GEn,BSz(c) Firestarter 4.00
5 GEn,JMC(c). 4.00
Preview Ed. 8.00

...GARDEN OF EDEN
Black Bull Entertainment, 2002
1 GEn,JJu(c). 7.00
1a variant GF (c). 4.00
2 thru 4 GEn,CE . . . . @4.00
Preview ed. limited. 7.00

JUSTICE CITY CHRONICLES
Ape Entertainment, 2005
1 (of 2) 3.50
2 . . . . 3.50

Justice Machine #3
© Noble Comics

JUSTICE MACHINE
Noble Comics, 1981–85
1 JBy(c) Mag size,B&W 30.00
2 MGu,Mag size,B&W 16.00
3 MGu,Mag size,B&W 10.00
4 MGu,Bluecobalt 8.00
5 MGu 7.00
Texas Comics
Ann.#1:BWG,I:Elementals,
  A: Thunder Agents. 5.00

JUSTICE MACHINE
[Featuring the Elementals]
Comico, 1986
1 . . . . 2.50
2 . . . . 2.50
3 . . . . 2.50
4 . . . . 2.50

JUSTICE MACHINE
Comico, 1987–89
1 MGu 2.50
2 MGu. 2.50
3 thru 14 MGu . . . . @2.50
15 thru 27 MGu . . . . @2.50
28 MGu 2.50
29 MGu,IW 2.50
Ann.#1 . . . . 2.50
SummerSpectacular 1 . . . . 2.75
MINI SERIES, 1990
1 thru 4 F:Elementals . . . . @2.50
Innovation, 1990
1 . . . . 2.50
2 thru 4 The Ragnarok Portfolio . @2.50
5 thru 7 Demon trilogy . . . . . . @2.50

JUSTICE MACHINE: CHIMERA CONSPIRACY
Millennium
1 AH,R&N:Justice Machine,
  wraparound cover 2.50

JUST MARRIED
Charlton Comics, 1958
1 . . . . 125.00
2 . . . . 75.00
3 thru 10 . . . . @50.00

11 thru 30 . . . . @35.00
31 thru 113 . . . . @25.00
114 Dec., 1976. . . . . 15.00

KABOOM
Awesome Entertainment, 1997
1 JLb,JMs, ... 5.00
1a variant (c)s 6.00
2 JLb,JMs, ... 3.00
3 JLb,JMs, ... 4.00
4 JLb,JMs,Kaboom the
  Barbarian,pt.1 (of 3) 2.50
5 JLb,JMs,Barbarian,pt.2 . . . . . . 2.50
6 JLb,JMs,Barbarian,pt.3 . . . . . . 2.50
VOL II
1 (of 3) 2.50
2 JLe,JLb,F:Kyra. 2.50
3 JLe,JLb, conclusion 2.50
Collected #1 & #2 . . . . 6.00

KABUKI
Caliber Press, 1994–96
1 Color Gallery,32 paintings(1995) . 7.00
1-shot Color Special, inc.
  pin-up gallery (1996) 3.00
1-shot Fear the Reaper (1994) 7.00

KABUKI: SKIN DEEP
Caliber, 1996
1 DMk 4.00
2 DMk(c) 3.50
2 AxR(c) 6.00
3 Origin issue 3.50
4 . . . . 3.50

KADE
Arcana Studios, 2003
1 . . . . 3.00
2 thru 5 . . . . @3.00

KADE: SHIVA'S SUN
Arcana Studio, 2007
0 . . . . 2.50
1 . . . . 4.00
2 thru 4 . . . . 4.00

KADE: SUN OF PERDITION
Arcana Studio, 2006
1 (of 4) 4.00
2 thru 4 . . . . @4.00

KAMIKAZE: 1946
Antarctic Press, 2000
1 Pickadon 3.00
2 Operation Olympic. 3.00
3 Queens of the Seas. 3.00
4 Operation Coronet. 3.00
5 Kaitens. 3.00
6 Fortress Japan. 3.00

KAMIKAZE
Wildstorm/DC, 2003
1 (of 5) extreme sport 3.00
2 thru 6 . . . . @3.00

KARMA INCORPORATED
Viper Comics, 2005
1 . . . . 3.00
2 . . . . 3.00
3 . . . . 3.00

KARNEY
IDW Publishing, 2005
1 . . . . 4.00
2 thru 4 . . . . @4.00

KATO OF THE GREEN HORNET
Now, 1991
1 BA,1st Kato solo story	2.50
2 BA,Kato in China contd.	2.50
3 Kato in China contd	2.50
4 Final Issue	2.50

KATO II
Now, 1992
1 VM,JSh,A:Karthage	2.50
2 VM,JSh,V:Karthage	2.50
3 VM,JSh,V:Karthage	2.50

KATY KEENE FASHION BOOK MAGAZINE
Archie Publications, 1955
1 Woggon(a&c)	800.00
2	500.00
3 thru 10 not published	
11 thru 18	@350.00
19	300.00
20	300.00
21	300.00
22	300.00
23 Winter 1958-59	300.00

KATY KEENE PINUP PARADE
Archie Publications, 1955
1	750.00
2	400.00
3	350.00
4	350.00
5	350.00
6	300.00
7	300.00
8	300.00
9	300.00
10 Woggon art	300.00
11 Story on comics	350.00
12	300.00
13	300.00
14	300.00
15 Sept., 1961	700.00

KEE-FU FIGHTERS
Roxbox Entertainment, 2006
1	3.25
2	3.25

KELLY GREEN
Eclipse
1 SDr,O:Kelly Green	2.50
2 SDr,One,Two,Three	2.50
3 SDr,Million Dollar Hit	2.50
4 SDr,Rare	4.00

KEN LASHLEY'S LEGENDS
DHJ Comics, 2002
1 (of 6) by Ken Lashley	3.00
1a variant (c)	3.00
1b previews exclusive	5.00
2	3.00

KEEP, THE
IDW Publishing, 2005
1 F.Paul Wilson (s)	4.00
2 thru 5	@4.00

KID DEATH & FLUFFY
Event Comics, 1997
Spec.#1 Halloween Spec. John Cebollero(c)	3.00
Spec.#1a Halloween Spec. JQ(c)	3.00

KID MONTANA
Charlton Comics, 1957
Previously: DAVY CROCKETT
see Golden Age
9	100.00
10	85.00
11	75.00
12	75.00
13 AW	75.00
14 thru 20	@75.00
21 thru 35	@60.00
36 thru 49	@60.00
50 March, 1965	60.00

Killer Instict #3
© Acclaim

KILLER INSTINCT
Acclaim
1 thru 3	@2.50
Spec. Brothers by Art Holcomb	2.50

KILLERS, THE
Atlas, 2008
1 (of 4)	3.00
2	3.00

KILLER 7
Devil's Due Publishing, 2006
1	3.00
1a variant cardstock (c)	6.00
2 thru 4	@3.00
2a thru 4a variant cardstock (c)	@6.00

KILLERS, THE: WAR'S END
Speakeasy Comics, 2006
1 (of 5)	3.00
2 thru 3	@3.00

KILLER STUNTS, INC.
Alias Enterprises, 2005
1 (of 4)	2.50
2 thru 4	@3.00

KILLER TALES
Eclipse, 1985
1 Tim Truman	3.00

KILLER, THE
Archaia Studios, 2006
1 (of 10)	4.00
2 thru 9	@4.00

KILLING PICKMAN
Archaia Studios, 2007
1 (of 6)	3.50
2	3.50
3 thru 4	@3.50

KILLZONE
Dreamwave, 2004
1	3.00
2	3.00
3	3.00

KINDRED II
WildStorm/DC, 2002
1 (of 4) BBh	2.50
2 BBh	2.50
3 BBh,Backlash & Grifter	2.50
4 BBh,concl.	2.50

KING LEONARDO AND HIS SHORT SUBJECTS
Dell Publishing Co., 1961–62
1	200.00
2 thru 4	@150.00

KING LOUIE & MOWGLI
Gold Key, 1968
1	60.00

KING OF DIAMONDS
Dell Publishing Co., 1962
1 Ph(c)	75.00

KING OF FIGHTERS: MAXIMUM IMPACT
Dr. Masters Publications, 2005
3 thru 6	3.00
7 thru 8	@3.00

KING OF FIGHTERS, THE: NESTS SAGA
HK Comics, 2006
1	3.00
1a variant (c)s	@3.00

KISS KISS BANG BANG
Crossgen, 2004
1	3.00
2 thru 7	@3.00

KIT KARTER
Dell Publishing Co., 1962
1	50.00

KNIGHTHAWK
Windjammer, 1995
1 NA(c&a),I:Knighthawk the Protector,V:Nemo	2.75
2 NA(c&a),Birth of Nemo	2.50
3 NA,V:Nemo	2.50
4 NA,V:Nemo	2.50
5 I:Cannon, Brick	2.50
6 V:Cannon, Brick	2.50

KNIGHTS OF THE ROUND TABLE
Dell Publishing Co.,1963-64
1 P(c)	60.00

KNUCKLES
Archie Comics, 1997
1	2.50
2 thru 31	@2.50
32 thru 33	@2.50

KOLCHAK TALES: NIGHT STALKER OF THE LIVING DEAD
Moonstone, 2008
1 (of 3) 4.00
2 thru 3 . . . . @4.00

KOLCHAK: TALES OF THE NIGHT STALKER
Moonstone, 2003
1 . . . . 3.50
2 thru 7 . . . . @3.50
GN Devil in the Details 7.00
1-shot Black & White & Red
  All Over 5.00
Ann. #1. . . . . 6.50
Ann. #1A variant sketch (c) 9.00

KOLCHAK TALES: THE FRANKENSTEIN AGENDA
Moonstone, 2007
1 (of 3) 3.50
2 thru 3 . . . . @3.50

KONA
Dell Publishing Co., 1962
1 P(c) all,SG 150.00
2 SG 75.00
3 SG 75.00
4 SG,B:Anak 75.00
5 thru 10 SG . . . . @75.00
11 thru 21 SG . . . . @50.00

KONGA
Charlton Comics, 1960–65
1 SD,DG(c), movie adapt. 450.00
2 DG(c) 200.00
3 SD 150.00
4 SD 150.00
5 SD 150.00
6 thru 15 SD . . . . @100.00
16 thru 23 . . . . @75.00

KONGA'S REVENGE
Charlton Comics
2 Summer, 1962 . . . . 100.00
3 SD,Fall, 1964 . . . . 50.00
1 Dec., 1968 . . . . 35.00

KONG: KING OF SKULL ISLAND
Markosia, 2007
0 . . . . 2.00
1 (of 5) 4.00
1a variant (c) 4.50
2 thru 5 . . . . @4.00
4a thru 5a variant (c)s . . . . @4.50

KOOKIE
Dell Publishing Co., 1962
1 . . . . 150.00
2 . . . . 125.00

KORAK, SON OF TARZAN
Gold Key, 1964
1 . . . . 150.00
2 thru 11 . . . . @75.00
12 thru 21 . . . . @50.00
22 thru 30 . . . . @40.00
31 thru 40 . . . . @35.00
41 thru 44 . . . . @25.00
45 Jan., 1972 . . . . 25.00
Continued by DC

KORG: 70,000 B.C.
Charlton, 1975
1 . . . . 20.00
2 thru 9 . . . . @15.00

KRAZY KAT
Gold Key, 1964
1 . . . . 60.00

KROFFT SUPERSHOW
Gold Key, 1978
1 . . . . 40.00
2 thru 6 . . . . @25.00

KRUSTY COMICS
Bongo Comics, 1995
1 Rise and Fall of Krustyland 2.50
2 Rise and Fall of Krustyland 2.50
3 Rise and Fall of Krustyland 2.50

KULL IN 3-D
Blackthorne
1 . . . . 2.50
2 . . . . 2.50
3 . . . . 2.50

LAD: A DOG
Dell Publishing Co., 1961
1 . . . . 75.00
2 . . . . 60.00

LADY ARCANE
Hero Graphics, 1992
1 A: Flare,BU:O:Giant 5.00
2 thru 4 . . . . @3.00

LADY DEATH
Chaos! Comics, 1994
1 BnP, A:Evil Ernie 15.00
1a signed gold foil. 20.00
2 BnP 15.00
3 BnP 10.00
Specials & 1-shots
1 Swimsuit Edition 10.00
1a Velvet Edition 18.00
1 rep. with 8-page pin-up gallery . . 3.00
1 Lady Death in Lingerie,
  various artists 5.00
1 Lady Death & the Women of
  Chaos! Gallery, pin-ups (1996) . 2.50
1-shot Dragon Wars (1998) 3.00

Lady Death: Swim Suit Special #1
© Chaos! Comics

1-shotA Dragon Wars, Premium Ed,
  Sketchbook cover 15.00
1-shot Retribution (1998) 3.00
1-shotA Retribution (1998) variant
  cover 3.00
1-shotB Retribution, premium ed. . 10.00
Chaos! Comics, 1998
? signed, limited 12.00
1 . . . . 3.00
1a signed, limited 9.00
2 R:Lady Demon. 3.00
3 V:Levithia 3.00
4 V:Pagan 3.00
5 The Harrowing, pt.1 . . . . 3.00
6 V:Uriel 3.00
7 V:Moloch 3.00
8 time to sieze Hell 3.00
9 world scythe of the covenant. . . 3.00
10 Goddess War,pt.2 x-over 3.00
11 V:Cremator 3.00
12 Unholy Nights 3.00
13 MD2,DQ,Inferno, pt.1 . . . . . . 3.00
13a signed 15.00
14 MD2,DQ,Inferno, pt.2 . . . . . . 3.00
15 MD2,DQ,Inferno, pt.3 . . . . . . 3.00
15a variant cover 6.00
16 MD2,DQ,Inferno, pt.4 . . . . . . 3.00
Swimsuit Spec.#1, signed 15.00
Chaos! Comics, 1999
1/2 Tribute Book 12.00
0 ashcan, yellow 9.00
0 ashcan, yellow, signed. 18.00
0 ashcan, blue 20.00
1 (of 12) by Steve Hughes 3.00
1a signed 12.00
1b deluxe Steve Hughes (c) 13.00
Spec. Swimsuit 2001 #1 . . . . 3.00
Spec. Swimsuit 2001 #1 premium . 10.00
Vol. 1 Lady Death's Black Book . . 9.00
Vol. 1 Black Book,premium ed. . . 12.00
Halloween Special Ashcan. 6.00
Halloween Spec. Ashcan, premium 3.00
Halloween Spec. #1 . . . . 3.00
Halloween Spec. #1a premium ed. 10.00
Halloween Spec. #1b
  super-premium edition. 20.00
Halloween Spec. 1c foil edition . . 20.00

...ALIVE
Chaos! Comics, 2001
1 (of 4) 3.00
1a premium edition 10.00
2 thru 4 . . . . @3.00
4a variant Scott Lewis (c) 7.50
Ashcan 6.00

.../BAD KITTY
Chaos! Comics, 2001
1 . . . . 3.00
1a premium ed. 9.00
2 . . . . 3.00

...BEDLAM
Chaos! Comics, 2002
1 BAu 3.00
1a premium edition 9.00

...BLACKLANDS
Avatar Press, 2006
1/2 . . . . 3.00
1/2 wraparound (c). 3.00
1/2 variant (c)s . . . . @3.00
1/2 premium. 10.00
1 . . . . 4.00
1a wraparound (c) 4.00
1b variant (c)s . . . . @4.00
1c premium (c) 10.00
2 . . . . 4.00
2b variant premium (c) 10.00
3 . . . . 4.00
4 . . . . 4.00
2a thru 4a variant (c)s. . . . . @4.00

.../CHASTITY
Chaos! Comics, 2001
1 x-over........................ 3.00
1a premium edition............. 10.00

.../CHASTITY/
BAD KITTY: UNITED
Chaos! Comics, 2002
1............................. 3.00
1a premium edition............. 10.00

.../THE CROW
Chaos! Comics, 2002
1............................. 3.00
1a premium edition............. 10.00
1b super premium edition....... 20.00
Script #1..................... 5.00
Script #1 premium edition...... 20.00
Ashcan........................ 6.00
Ashcan, premium edition........ 20.00
Preview book b&w.............. 2.00
Preview book, premium edition... 6.00

...THE CRUCIBLE
Chaos! Comics, 1996
1 (of 6) BnP,SHu,............. 3.50
1 leather limited edition....... 15.00
2 BnP,SHu,................... 3.50
3 BnP,SHu,................... 3.50
4 BnP,SHu,................... 3.50
5 BnP,SHu,................... 3.50
6 BnP,SHu,V:Genocide,concl.... 3.00
GN Collected ed. Vol. 1........ 6.00
GN Collected ed. Vol. 2........ 6.00
GN Collected ed. Vol. 3........ 6.00
Spec. Script.................. 5.00

...DARK ALLIANCE
Chaos! Comics, 2002
Ashcan b&w................... 6.00
Ashcan premium edition........ 15.00
1 (of 5) F:everybody.......... 3.00
1a premium edition............ 10.00
2 thru 5..................... @3.00
2a thru 5a Alternate cover (c)... @7.50

...DARK MILLENNIUM
Chaos! Comics, 2000
1 (of 3)..................... 3.00
1a premium edition............ 7.00
1a signed, limited............ 9.00
2............................ 3.00
3............................ 3.00
Preview Book B&W............. 5.00

...DEATH BECOMES HER
Chaos! Comics, 1997
0 follows the *Crucible*, leads to
Wicked Ways............... 3.00

.../EVIL ERNIE
Chaos! Comics, 2002
Ashcan....................... 6.00
Ashcan premium edition........ 15.00
1 BnP, sequel to Dark Alliance.... 3.50
1a premium edition............ 9.00
1b super premium edition....... 15.00
1c foil edition............... 15.00

...THE GAUNTLET
Chaos! Comics, 2002
Ashcan b&w................... 6.00
1 (of 4)..................... 3.00
1a premium edition............ 9.00
1b foil edition............... 15.00
2............................ 3.00
2a Variant JSC (c)............ 7.50

...THE GODDESS RETURNS
Chaos! Chomics, 2002
1 (of 2) JOs................. 3.00
1a premium edition............ 9.00
2............................ 3.00
2a variant (c)............... 7.50

...HEARTBREAKER
Chaos! Comics, 2002
1............................ 3.00
1a premium edition............ 9.00
1b super premium edition....... 15.00
1c foil (c).................. 15.00
1d MegaCon foil edition........ 20.00

.../JADE
Chaos! Comics, 2002
1............................ 3.00
1 premium edition............. 9.00

...JUDGMENT WAR
Chaos! Comics, 1999
Prelude....................... 3.00
1 (of 3)..................... 3.00
1a premium.................. 9.00
2............................ 3.00
3 Hell is vanquished, concl.... 3.00
Preview Book B&W............. 5.00

...LAST RITES
Chaos! Comics, 2001
1 (of 4) RCl(c).............. 3.00
1 premium ed. RCl(c).......... 12.00
2............................ 3.00
2 variant DkG(c)............. 7.50
3............................ 3.00
3a variant (c)............... 7.50
4............................ 3.00
4a variant (c)............... 7.50

...LOST SOULS
Avatar Press, 2005
0............................ 3.00
0a variant (c)s.............. @3.00
0b premium (c)............... 9.00
1 (of 2)..................... 3.00
1a wraparound (c)............ 3.00
1b variant (c)s.............. @3.00
1c premium (c)............... 9.00
2............................ 3.00
2a wraparound (c)............ 3.00
2b variant (c)s.............. @3.00
2c premium (c)............... 9.00

...LOVE BITES
Chaos! Comics, 2001
1............................ 3.00
1 premium edition............. 9.00
Ashcan....................... 6.00

...MASTERWORKS SPECIAL
Avatar Press, 2007
1-shot....................... 5.00
1-shot variant (c)s........... @5.00

.../ MEDIEVAL WITCHBLADE
Chaos! Comics, 2001
1 BAu,x-over................. 3.50
1a variant MS (c) (1:4)....... 3.50
1b premium edition............ 9.00
1c super premium............. 15.00
Preview book................. 2.00
Preview book, premium ed....... 6.00
Ashcan 12-page, B&W.......... 6.00

...MISCHIEF NIGHT
Chaos! Comics, 2001
1............................ 3.00
1a premium edition............ 11.00
1b super premium edition....... 15.00

...PIRATE QUEEN
Avatar Press
Spec. 40-pgs................. 5.00
Spec. variant (c)s........... @5.00

...RE-IMAGINED
Chaos! Comics, 2002
1 Spanish Inquisition.......... 3.00
1a premium edition............ 9.00
1b super premium edition....... 15.00

Ashcan Re-imagined (b&w)....... 6.00

...RIVER OF FEAR
Chaos! Comics, 2001
1............................ 3.00
1a premium ed................ 9.00

...SACRILEGE
Avatar Press, 2007
0 (of 2)..................... 3.00
0a variant (c)s.............. @3.00
1............................ 4.00
1a variant (c)s.............. @4.00
2............................ 4.00
2a variant (c)s.............. @4.00

.../SHI
Avatar Press, 2006
Preview...................... 2.50
Preview variant (c).......... 3.00
Preview variant Premium (c).... 9.00
0............................ 3.00
0a variant (c)s.............. @3.00
1............................ 4.00
1a variant (c)s.............. @4.00
2............................ 4.00
2a variant (c)s.............. @4.00

...THE MOURNING
Chaos! Comics, 2002
Ashcan....................... 6.00
1 (of 2)..................... 3.00
1a premium edition............ 9.00
2............................ 3.00
2a variant (c)............... 7.50

Lady Death: The Odyssey#3
© Chaos! Comics

...THE ODYSSEY
Chaos! Comics, 1996
Sneak Peek Preview............ 2.00
1 embossed cover............. 5.00
1 SHu(c) premium edition....... 12.00
2............................ 3.00
3............................ 3.00
4............................ 3.00
4a variant cover............. 12.00
Micro Premium Preview Book.... 12.00

...THE RAPTURE
Chaos! Comics, 1999
1 (of 4) BnP,V:Father Orbec.... 3.00
1a dynamic forces cover....... 7.00
1b dynamic forces, signed..... 12.00
1c premium edition........... 9.00
2 Heaven vs. Hell............ 3.00
3 V:Asteroth................. 3.00

4 BnP	3.00
Preview Book B&W	5.00
Collected ed. Vol. 1	6.00
Collected ed. Vol. 2	6.00

...THE WICKED
Avatar Press, 2005

½	3.00
½a variant (c)	@3.00
½b premium (c)	9.00
1	4.00
1a Wraparound (c)	4.00
1b Variant(c)s	@4.00
1c Premium (c)	9.00

...TRIBULATION
Chaos! Comics, 2000

1	3.00
1a premium edition, tattoo (c)	9.00
1b chromium (c)	13.00
1c chrome (c) signed	18.00
2	3.00
3	3.00
4 concl.	3.00
Ashcan B&W	6.66

...VAMPIRELLA:
DARK HEARTS
Chaos!/Harris, 1999

Spec. x-over, 40-page	3.50
Spec. Premium Edition	9.00

...VS. PANDORA
Avatar Press, 2007

1	3.00
1a variat (c)s	3.00
1 Super sexy cover	6.00

...VS. PURGATORI
Chaos! Comics, 2000

1 gold foil	30.00
1 premium ed.	9.00

...VS. VAMPIRELLA II
Chaos!/Harris, 2000

1 x-over	3.50
1a premium ed.	9.00
1b Gold foil ed.	25.00
1c Blue foil ed.	45.00

...WARRIOR TEMPTRESS
Avatar Press

Spec.	4.00
Spec. variant (c)s	@4.00

LADY DEATH
Crossgen Code 6 Comics, 2003

1	3.00
2 thru 12 A Medieval Tale	@3.00
GN Vol. 1 A Medieval Tale	10.00
Season Two, 2004	
1 Spell Storm	3.00
2 thru 6 The Wild Hunt	@3.00

LADY DEATH
Avatar, 2004

1 10th Anniv. Edition	4.00
1a painted (c)	4.00
1b premium (c)	10.00
1c variant (c)s	@6.00
1d 10th Anniv. Prism foil (c)	13.00
Spec. Swimsuit 2005	4.00
Spec. Swimsuit 2005 variant(c)s	@6.00
Spec. Swimsuit 2005 premium (c)	10.00
Spec. Swimsuit 2005 Prism foil (c)	13.00
2007 Swimsuit Spec. 16-pgs.	3.00
2007 Swimsuit Spec. Variant (c)s	@3.00
2007 Swimsuit golden (c)	6.00
2007 Swimsuit moonlight (c)	6.00
2007 Swimsuit serpents (c)	6.00
Spec. Leather & Lace 2005	
Various (c)s	@6.00
Spec. Bikini, 2005	4.00

Spec. Bikini, 2005 variant (c)s	@4.00
Spec. Bikini, 2005 variant (c)s	@6.00
Ann. #1	5.00
Ann. #1a variant (c)s	@5.00
Ann. #1b premium (c)	10.00
Spec. 2006 Fetishes	4.00
Spec. 2006 Fetishes variant (c)s	@4.00
Spec. 2006 Fetishes prem. (c)s	@6.00
1-shot Dark Horizons	3.00
1-shot Dark Horizons variant (c)s	@3.00
1-shot Dark Horizons premium (c)	10.00

LADY DEATH II: BETWEEN
HEAVEN & HELL
Chaos! Comics, 1995

1 V:Purgatori	5.00
1a Limited Edition 5,000c	25.00
1b premium velvet cover, signed	30.00
2 Lives As Hope	4.00
3 V:Purgatori	4.00
4 final issue	4.00

LADY DEMON
Chaos! Comics, 2000

1 (of 3)	3.00
1a premium ed.	9.00
2	3.00
3 concl.	3.00
Preview book B&W	5.00

LADY PENDRAGON
Maximum Press, 1996

1 mini-series	2.50
2	2.50
3 (of 3) MD2	2.50

LADY RAWHIDE
Topps, 1995

1 All New Solo series	5.00
2 It Can't Happen Here,pt.2	3.50
3	3.00
4	3.00
5 conclusion	3.00
Spec.#1 Rep. Zorro #2-#3	6.50
Topps, 1996, Mini-Series	
1 DMG	4.00
1a DMG,signed, numbered	9.00
2 DMG	3.00
3 DMG	3.00
4 DMG, EM, Intimate Wounds	3.00
5 DMG, EM	3.00
6 DMG	3.00
7 DMG	3.00

Lancelot Link Secret Chimp #6
© Gold Key

...OTHER PEOPLE'S BLOOD
Topps, 1996
Mini-Series

1 DMG,EM,A Slice of Breast	3.00

LADY VAMPRE
Blackout, 1995

0 B&W	3.50
1	3.00

LAI WAN,
DREAM WALKER
Moonstone Books, 2005

1	3.00
2	3.50

LANCELOT LINK,
SECRET CHIMP
Gold Key, 1971

1	100.00
2 thru 8	@60.00

LANCELOT STRONG,
THE SHIELD
Red Circle, 1983

1 A:Steel Sterling	3.50
2 A:Steel Sterling	2.50
3 AN/EB,D:Lancelot Strong	2.50

LANCER
Gold Key, 1969

1 TV Adapt	60.00
2 thru 3	@40.00

LAND OF THE DEAD
IDW Publishing, 2005

2 thru 5	@4.00
4a thru 5a photo (c)	@4.00

LAND OF THE GIANTS
Gold Key, 1968

1 TV Adapt	125.00
2 thru 5	@75.00

LANDSALE & TRUMAN'S
DEAD FOLKS
Avatar Press, 2003

1	3.50
1a wraparound (c)	4.00
2 thru 3	@3.50
2a thru 3a wraparound (c)	@4.00

LARAMIE
Dell, 1962

1	125.00

LAREDO
Gold Key, 1966

1 TV Adapt	50.00

LARS OF MARS
Eclipse, 1987

1 3-D MA	3.00

LASER ERASER &
PRESSBUTTON
Eclipse, 1985–87

1 GL,R:Laser Eraser	2.50
2 GL	2.50
3 GL,CK,Tsultrine'	2.50
4 MC,Death	2.50
5 MC,JRy,Gates of Hell	2.50
6 Corsairs of Illunium	2.50
3-D#1 MC,GL(c),Triple Cross	2.50

COLOR PUB.

LASH LARUE WESTERN
AC Comics
1	3.50
Annual	3.00

LAST BASTION, THE
Speakeasy Comics, 2006
1 (of 6)	3.00
2	3.00

LAST OF THE VIKING HEROES
Genesis West, 1987
1 JK	4.00
2 JK	3.50
3	3.50
4	3.50
5A sexy cover	4.00
5B mild cover	3.50
6	3.50
7 AA(c)	3.50
8	3.50
9 Great Battle of Nidhogger	3.50
10 Death Among the Heroes	3.50
Summer Spec.#1 FF,JK	3.50
Summer Spec.#2	3.00
Summer Spec.#3,A:TMNT	2.50

LAST REIGN: KINGS OF WAR
Boom! Studios, 2008
1 thru 2	@4.00
1a thru 2a variant (c)	@4.00

Lauth #26
© Archie Publications

LAUGH
Archie, 1987–91
1	6.00
2 thru 10	@5.00
11 thru 29	@3.00

LAUREL AND HARDY
Dell Publishing Co., 1962
1	125.00
2	75.00
3	75.00
4	75.00

LAUREL & HARDY
Gold Key, 1967
1	100.00
2 Oct., 1967	75.00

LAURELL K. HAMILTON'S ANITA BLAKE, VAMPIRE HUNTER
Dabel Brothers Productions, 2006
1	3.00
1a variant (c)s	@6.00
2 Guilty Pleasures	3.00
2a variant (c)s	@6.00
3	3.00
3a variant (c)s	@6.00

LAWMAN
Dell Publishing Co., 1959
1 Ph(c) all	250.00
2	150.00
3 ATh	135.00
4	100.00
5 thru 7	@100.00
8 thru 11	@100.00

LAW AND ORDER
Maximum Press, 1995
1 MMy,D:Law,I:New Law, Order	2.50
2 V:Max Spur	2.50
3 V:Law's Murderer	2.50

LAW OF DREDD
Quality
1 V:Perps	5.00
2 BB,Lunar Olympics	4.00
3 BB,V:Judge Death	3.00
4 thru 7	@3.00
Fleetway
8 Blockmania	3.00
9 BB,DGi,Framed for murders	3.00
10 thru 32	@2.50
33 League of Fatties,final issue	3.00

LAZARUS: IMMORTAL COILS
AAM Markosia, 2008
1 (of 5)	4.00
2 thru 3	@3.50

LAZARUS: THE MANY REINCARNATIONS
Lodestone Publishing, 2000
1 by Zak Hennessey	3.00
2	3.00
4 thru 7	@3.00

LEADING MAN
Oni Press, 2006
1 (of 5)	3.50
2 thru 5	@3.50

LEAGUE OF CHAMPIONS
Hero Graphics, 1990
{Cont. from Champions #12}
1 Olympus Saga #4	3.00
2 Olympus Saga #5,O:Malice	3.00
3 Olympus Saga ends	3.00

LEAGUE OF EXTRA-ORDINARY GENTLEMEN
WildStorm/DC, 1999
America's Best Comics
1 (of 6) AMo(s),KON	3.00
2 thru 6 AMo(s),KON	@3.00
GN Collected Edition	6.00
Vol. II (July, 2002)
1 AMo(s),KON	3.50
2 AMo(s),KON,Martian marauders	3.50
3 AMo(s),KON,traitor	3.50
4 AMo(s),KON,	3.50
5 AMo(s),KON, one dies	3.50
6 AMo(s),KON,finale	3.50

LEFT ON MISSION
Boom! Studios, 2007
1	4.00
2 thru 5	@4.00

LEGACY
Majestic, 1993
0 platinum	9.00
1 I:Legacy	2.50
2	2.50

LEGACY
Antarctic Press, 1999
1 by Fred Perry	3.00
2 thru 5	@3.00

LEGEND
Wildstorm/DC, Feb., 2005
1 (of 4) HC,RH, 48-page	6.00
2 HC,RH	6.00
3 HC,RH, Vietnam war	6.00
4 HC,RH,concl.	6.00

LEGEND OF CUSTER, THE
Dell Publishing Co., 1968
1 Ph(c)	50.00

LEGEND OF ISIS, THE
Alias Enterprises, 2005
1 (of 4)	3.00
2 thru 6	@3.00
7	3.00
8	3.00
9	3.50
10 God War x-over	3.50
11 Rise of Darkness	3.50
12 Rise of Darkness, pt.2	3.50
13 Rise of Darkness, pt.3	3.50
11 thru 12	@3.50

LEGEND OF ISIS
Bluewater Productions, 2007
1	3.50
2 thru 4	@3.50
4a variant (c)	3.50

LEGEND OF THE ELFLORD
Davdez Arts, 1998
1 by Barry Blair & Colin Chan	3.00
2	2.50
3	3.00
4	3.00
GN Vol. 1 112-page	12.00

LEGEND OF THE SAGE
Chaos! Comics, 2001
1 (of 4) F:Victoria Noble	3.00
1a premium edition	9.00
2	3.00
2a variant (c)	7.50
3	3.00
3a variant (c)	7.50
4	3.00
4a variant (c)	7.50
Preview Book	2.00
Preview Book, premium edition	6.00

LEGENDS OF JESSE JAMES, THE
Gold Key, 1966
1	50.00

All comics prices listed are for *Near Mint* condition.

LEGENDS OF LUXURA
Comic Cavalcade, 1998
Commemorative #1 by Kirk Lindo . . 6.00
Commemorative #1a deluxe 15.00

LEGENDS OF NASCAR
Vortex, 1990
1 HT,Bill Eliott ($1.50 cover Price)
  15,000 copies 10.00
1a ($2.00 cover price) 45,000
  copies 5.00
1b 3rd pr., 80,000 copies 4.00
2 Richard Petty 4.00
3 Ken Schroder. 3.50
4 Bob Alison 3.00
5 Bill Elliott 3.00
6 Jr. Johnson 3.00
7 Sterling Marlin 3.00
8 Benny Parsons 3.00
9 Rusty Wallace 3.00
10 thru 14 . . . . @3.00

LEGENDS OF THE STARGRAZERS
Innovation, 1989
1 thru 5 . . . . @2.50

LEGION OF THE SUPERNATURAL
IDW, 2008
1 . . . . 4.00
2 . . . . 4.00

LEONARD NIMOY'S PRIMORTALS
Teckno-Comics, 1994
1 I:Primortals. 5.50
2 Zeerus Reveals Himself 4.00
3 thru 15 . . . . @2.50
Big Entertainment, 1996
0 SEa,MKb 2.50
1 thru 7 . . . . @2.50

LEONARDO
Mirage, 1986
1 TMNT Character. 5.00

LEOPARD
Millennium
1 I:Leopard 3.00
1a Gold Cover. 4.00
2 O:Leopard,V:Razor's Edge 3.00

LETHAL INSTINCT
Alias Enterprises, 2005
1 (of 6) 2.50
2 thru 5 . . . . @3.00
6 . . . . 3.50

LETHAL STRYKE
London Night Studios, 1995
1 F:Stryke 3.00
1a commemorative (1999) 6.00
2 O:Stryke. 3.00
Ann. #1 FHr 3.00
Ann. #1 platinum edition 10.00

LETHAL STRIKE/ DOUBLE IMPACT: LETHAL IMPACT
London Night, 1996
1 by Jude Millien 3.00
1 limited 5.00

LEXIAN CHRONICLES, THE: FULL CIRCLE
APC, 2005
1 . . . . 3.50
1a signed 15.00
1b red foil (c). 9.00
2 thru 5 . . . . @3.50
5a variant (c) 3.50
Markosia, 2005
6 thru 12 . . . . @3.50
7a thru 10a variant (c)s . . . . . . @3.50
11 . . . . 3.50
12 Full Circle 3.50
12a Commemorative sgn ed.. . . . . 7.00

LIBERALITY FOR ALL
ACC Studios, 2005
1 (of 8) 3.00
2 . . . . 3.00
3 . . . . 3.00
3a variant (c) 3.00
4 . . . . 3.00
4a variant (c) 3.00

LIBERTY COMICS
Heroic Purlishing, 2007
1 thru 3 . . . . @4.50

LIBERTY GIRL
Heroic Publishing, 2006
1 . . . . 3.25
2 . . . . 3.25
3 thru 4 . . . . @3.00

LIBERTY PROJECT, THE
Eclipse, 1987–88
1 I:Liberty Project 2.50
2 . . . . 2.50
3 V:Silver City Wranglers 2.50
4 . . . . 2.50
5 . . . . 2.50
6 F:Cimarron,Misery and Gin 2.50
7 I:Menace 2.50
8 V:Savage 2.50

LIDSVILLE
Gold Key, 1972
1 . . . . 100.00
2 . . . . 75.00
3 and 4 . . . . @75.00
5 Oct., 1973 . . . . 75.00

LIEUTENANT, THE
Dell Publishing Co., April-June, 1962
1 Ph(c) 65.00

LIFE WITH ARCHIE
Archie Publications, 1958
1 . . . . 500.00
2 . . . . 250.00
3 . . . . 175.00
4 . . . . 175.00
5 . . . . 175.00
6 . . . . 125.00
7 . . . . 125.00
8 . . . . 125.00
9 . . . . 125.00
10 . . . . 125.00
11 thru 20 . . . . @100.00
21 thru 30. . . . . @75.00
31 thru 40. . . . . @65.00
41 . . . . 60.00
42 B:Pureheart. 125.00
43 . . . . 75.00
44 . . . . 75.00
45 R.I.V.E.R.D.A.L.E.. . . . . 125.00
46 O:Pureheart 100.00

Life With Archie #42
© Archie Publications

47 thru 59. . . . . @65.00
60 thru 100. . . . . @60.00
101 thru 200. . . . . @25.00
201 thru 285. . . . . @15.00

LIGHT FANTASTIC, THE
Innovation, 1992
1 Terry Pratchett adapt. 2.50
2 Adaptation continues 2.50
3 Adaptation continues 2.50
4 Adapt.conclusion 2.50

LIGHTNING COMICS PRESENTS
Lightning Comics, 1994
1 B&W Promo Ed. 3.50
1a B&W Promo Ed. Platinum 3.50
1b B&W Promo Ed. Gold 3.50

L'IL HELLIONS: DAY AT THE ZOO
SIlent Devil Productions, 2006
1 . . . . 4.00

LILLITH: DEMON PRINCESS
Antarctic Press, 1996
1 (of 3) from Warrior Nun Areala . . 3.00
1a Commemorative Edition (1999). 6.00
2 and 3 . . . . @3.00

LILO & STITCH
Disney Press, 2006
GN Vol. 1 . . . . 5.00

LIMBO CITY
Dreamwave, 2002
1 BAu,BBh 3.00
2 thru 3 . . . . @3.00

LINCOLN-16
Skarwood Productions, 1997
1 GI. 3.00
2 GI. 3.00
3 GI. 3.00

LINDA LARK
Dell Publishing Co., 1961
1 . . . . 50.00
2 thru 8 . . . . @35.00

All comics prices listed are for *Near Mint* condition.

LINUS, THE LIONHEARTED
Gold Key, 1965
1 . . . . 150.00

LIONHEART
Awesome Entertainment, 1999
1 IaC,JLb, from *The Coven* 3.00
1 Wizard World exclusive 5.50
2 IaC,JLb 3.00
2a variant cover 3.00
2b variant IaC cover 7.00
3 concl 3.00

LIPPY THE LION AND HARDY HAR HAR
Gold Key, 1963
1 . . . . 175.00

LISA COMICS
Bongo Comics, 1995
1 F:Lisa Simpson 3.00

LITTLE AMBROSE
Archie Publications, 1958
1 . . . . 175.00

LITTLE ARCHIE
Archie Publications, 1956
1 . . . . 1,200.00
2 . . . . 500.00
3 . . . . 300.00
4 . . . . 300.00
5 . . . . 300.00
6 thru 10 . . . . @250.00
11 thru 20 . . . . @200.00
21 thru 30 . . . . @150.00
31 thru 40 . . . . @100.00
41 thru 60 . . . . @100.00
61 thru 80 . . . . @75.00
81 thru 100 . . . . @30.00
101 thru 180 . . . . @15.00

LITTLE ARCHIE MYSTERY
Archie Publications, 1963
1 . . . . 225.00
2 Oct., 1963 . . . . 150.00

LITTLE AUDREY & MELVIN
Harvey Publications, 1962
1 . . . . 225.00
2 thru 5 . . . . @100.00
6 thru 10 . . . . @75.00
11 thru 20 . . . . @65.00
21 thru 40 . . . . @30.00
41 thru 50 . . . . @30.00
51 thru 53 52 pgs Giant size . . . @30.00
54 thru 60 . . . . @35.00
61 Dec., 1973 . . . . 30.00

LITTLE AUDREY TV FUNTIME
Harvey Publications, 1962
1 A:Richie Rich 200.00
2 same 150.00
3 same 100.00
4 . . . . 100.00
5 . . . . 100.00
6 thru 10 . . . . @75.00
11 thru 20 . . . . @50.00
21 thru 32 . . . . @35.00
33 Oct., 1971 . . . . 35.00

LITTLE DOT DOTLAND
Harvey Publications, 1962
1 . . . . 200.00
2 . . . . 150.00
3 . . . . 100.00
4 . . . . 100.00
5 . . . . 100.00
6 thru 10 . . . . @75.00
11 thru 20 . . . . @60.00
21 thru 50 . . . . @50.00
51 thru 60 . . . . @40.00
61 Dec., 1973 . . . . 40.00

LITTLE DOT'S UNCLES & AUNTS
Harvey Enterprises, 1961
1 . . . . 300.00
2 . . . . 200.00
3 . . . . 200.00
4 thru 5 . . . . @150.00
6 thru 10 . . . . @125.00
11 thru 20 . . . . @100.00
21 thru 40 . . . . @75.00
41 thru 51 . . . . @50.00
52 April, 1974 . . . . 50.00

LITTLE LOTTA
Harvey Publications, 1955
1 B:Richie Rich and Little Lotta . 700.00
2 . . . . 350.00
3 . . . . 300.00
4 . . . . 275.00
5 . . . . 300.00
6 thru 10 . . . . @250.00
11 thru 20 . . . . @150.00
21 thru 40 . . . . @100.00
41 thru 60 . . . . @100.00
61 thru 80 . . . . @75.00
81 thru 99 . . . . @75.00
100 thru 103 52 pgs . . . . @75.00
104 thru 120 . . . . @40.00
121 May, 1976 . . . . 40.00

LITTLE LOTTA FOODLAND
Harvey Publications, 1963
1 68 pgs 300.00
2 . . . . 200.00
3 . . . . 150.00
4 . . . . 200.00
5 . . . . 200.00
6 thru 10 . . . . @200.00
11 thru 20 . . . . @100.00
21 thru 26 . . . . @75.00
27 . . . . 50.00
28 . . . . 25.00
29 Oct., 1972 . . . . 50.00

LITTLE MERMAID
Walt Disney, 1992
1 based on movie 3.00
2 Serpent Teen 3.00
3 Guppy Love 3.00
4 . . . . 3.00

LITTLE MONSTERS, THE
Gold Key, 1964
1 . . . . 125.00
2 . . . . 75.00
3 thru 10 . . . . @50.00
11 thru 20 . . . . @35.00
21 thru 43 . . . . @35.00
44 Feb., 1978 . . . . 35.00

LITTLE MONSTERS
Now, 1990
1 thru 6 . . . . @2.50

Little Sad Sack #1
© Harvey Publications

LITTLE SAD SACK
Harvey Publications, 1964
1 Richie Rich(c) 100.00
2 . . . . 75.00
3 . . . . 75.00
4 . . . . 75.00
5 . . . . 75.00
6 thru 19 Nov. 1967 . . . . @75.00

LITTLE STOOGES, THE
Gold Key, 1972
1 . . . . 75.00
2 . . . . 50.00
3 . . . . 45.00
4 . . . . 45.00
5 thru 7 March, 1974 . . . . @45.00

LIVING CORPSE, THE
Zenescope Entertainment, 2007
0 . . . . 1.50
1/2 . . . . 0.25
1 . . . . 3.00
2 thru 6 . . . . @3.00

LIVING IN INFAMY
Ludovico Technique, 2005
1 (of 4) 3.00
2 thru 4 . . . . @3.00

LIZ
Narwain Publishing, 2006
1 . . . . 4.00

LLOYD LLEWELLYN
Fantagraphics, 1987
Spec. #1 . . . . 2.50

LOBO
Dell Publishing Co., 1965
1 . . . . 60.00
2 . . . . 50.00

LOCKE
Blackthorne
1 PO.Jones 2.50
2 TD 2.50
3 thru 5 . . . . @2.50

LOCKE & KEY
IDW, 2008
1 . . . . 4.00
2 thru 6 . . . . @4.00

LONE RANGER, THE
Gold Key, 1964
1 . . . . 125.00
2 . . . . 75.00
3 . . . . 60.00
4 . . . . 60.00
5 . . . . 60.00
6 thru 10 . . . . @50.00
11 thru 18 . . . . @50.00
19 thru 27 . . . . @40.00
28 March, 1977 . . . . 40.00

LONE RANGER, THE
D.E. (Dynamite Ent.) 2006
1 . . . . 4.00
1a silver foil (c) 15.00
1b director's cut 5.00
2 . . . . 4.00
3 . . . . 3.00
4 thru 11 . . . . @3.00
12 thru 15 . . . . @3.50
13 authentix edition 5.00

LONE RANGER AND TONTO, THE
Topps, 1994
1 JLd,TT,RM,The Last Battle 2.50
2 JLd,TT,RM 2.50
3 JLd,TT,RM, O:Lone Ranger. 2.50
4 JLd,TT,RM, It Crawls 2.50

LONG COUNT, THE
Archaia Studios, 2007
1 (of 6) 3.50
2 thru 3 . . . . @3.50

LOOKING FOR GROUP
Blind Ferrett, 2007
1 . . . . 3.00
2 thru 5 . . . . @3.00

LOONEY TUNES
Dell, 1955
166 . . . . 75.00
167 thru 246 . . . . @75.00

LOONEY TUNES AND MERRIE MELODIES
Dell, 1950
108 . . . . 80.00
109 thru 153 . . . . @80.00
Becomes:

LOONEY TUNES AND MERRIE MELODIES COMICS
Dell, 1954
154 . . . . 75.00
155 thru 165 . . . . @75.00
Becomes:

LOONEY TUNES
Dell, 1955
166 . . . . 75.00
167 thru 246 . . . . , . . . @76.00

LOONEY TUNES
Gold Key, 1975
1 reprints 50.00
2 thru 10 . . . . @30.00
11 thru 30 . . . . @15.00
Whitman, 1980
31 . . . . 15.00
32 thru 47 . . . . @15.00

LORD PUMPKIN
Malibu, Oct. 1994
0 Sludge 2.50

LORE
IDW Publishing, 2003
1 . . . . 6.00
2 . . . . 4.00
3 . . . . 4.00
4 . . . . 4.00

LOST BOOKS OF EVE, THE
Viper Comics, 2006
1 . . . . 3.25
2 thru 4 . . . . @3.25

LOST BOYS, THE: REIGN OF FROGS
Wildstorm/DC, May, 2008
1 thru 4 . . . . @3.50

LOST HEROES
Davdez Arts, 1998
0 by Rob Prior, lost SF heroes 3.00
1 thru 5 . . . . @3.00
6 . . . . 3.00
GN 5/6 56-page 8.00

LOST IN SPACE
Innovation, 1991
{based on TV series}
1 O:Jupiter II Project. 3.50
2 Cavern of IdyllicSummersLost. . . 3.00
2a Special Edition 3.00
3 Do Not Go Gently into that Good
   Night,Bill Mumy script 3.00
4 People are Strange 3.00
5 The Perils of Penelope 3.00
6 thru 12 . . . . @3.00
Project Krell 3.00
Ann.#1 (1991) 3.00
Ann.#2 (1992) 3.00
1Spec.#1 & #2 rep. Seduction of
   the Innocent. . . . . @3.00
GN Strangers among Strangers . . . 6.00
1-shot Project Robinson, follows
   story in issue #12 (1993). 2.50
Becomes:

LOST IN SPACE: VOYAGE TO THE BOTTOM OF THE SOUL
Innovation, 1993–94
13 thru 18 . . . . @3.00

LOST PLANET
Eclipse, 1987–88
1 BHa,I:Tyler FLynn 2.50
2 BHa,R:Amelia Earhart 2.50
3 BHa 2.50
4 BHa,Devil's Eye. 2.50
5 BHa,A:Amelia Earhart 2.50
6 . . . . 2.50

LOVE AND CAPES
Maerkle Press, 2008
1 . . . . 4.00
2 thru 8 . . . . @4.00

LOVECRAFT
Adventure Comics
1 The Lurking Fear adapt. 3.00
2 Beyond the Wall of Sleep 3.00
3 The Tomb. 3.00
4 The Alchemist 3.00

LOVE DIARY
Charlton Comics, 1958
1 . . . . 150.00
2 . . . . 125.00
3 thru 10 . . . . @100.00
11 thru 15 . . . . @100.00
16 thru 20 . . . . @100.00
21 thru 40 . . . . @75.00
41 thru 101 . . . . @20.00
102 Dec., 1976 . . . . 20.00

LUCIFER'S HAMMER
Innovation, 1993–94
1 thru 6 Larry Niven & Jerry
   Pournelle novel adaptation . . @2.50

Lucifer's Hammer#2
© *Innovation*

LUCY SHOW, THE
Gold Key, 1963
1 Ph(c) 300.00
2 Ph(c) 250.00
3 thru 5 . . . . 200.00

LUDWIG VON DRAKE
Dell Publishing Co., 1961
1 . . . . 125.00
2 thru 4 . . . . @75.00

LUFTWAFFE 1946
Antarctic Press, 1998
1 color special, by Ted Namura . . . 3.00

LUGER
Eclipse, 1986–87
1 TY,I:Luger,mini-series 2.50
2 TY 2.50
3 TY,BHa,V:Sharks 2.50

LULLABY
Alias Enterprises, 2005
Vol. 2
1 . . . . 3.00
2 . . . . 3.00
3 . . . . 3.00
3a convention foil (c) signed. 15.00
4 . . . . 3.50
5 . . . . 3.50
5a variant (c) 5.00

...ONCE UPON A TIME
Alias Enterprises, 2006
GN Vol. 1 Pied Piper of Hamelin . . . 6.00

LUNATIC FRINGE
Innovation, 1989
1 . . . . 2.50
2 . . . . 2.50

LURKERS
IDW Publishing, 2004
1 . . . . 4.00
2 thru 4 . . . . @4.00

LUXURA
Comic Cavalcade, 1998
Commemorative #1 by Kirk Lindo . . 6.00
Commemorative #1a deluxe 15.00

LUXURA COLLECTION
Brainstorm
Commemorative edition, red foil
   cover, 48pg. 10.00

LYNCH MOB
Chaos! Comics, 1994
1 GCa(c), I:Mother Mayhem. 3.00
2 Lynch Mob Loses. 2.50
3 1994 Time Trip. 2.50
3a Gold cover 3.00
4 Mother Mayhem at UN 2.50

LYNDON B. JOHNSON
Dell Publishing Co.,
March, 1965
1 Ph(c) 50.00

M
Eclipse, 1990–91
1 thru 4 JMu . . . . @5.50

MACK BOLAN,
THE EXECUTIONER:
THE DEVIL'S TOOLS
IDW, 2008
1 . . . . 4.00
2 thru 5 . . . . @4.00

MACROSS
Comico
1 . . . . 35.00
Becomes:

ROBOTECH, THE
MACROSS SAGA

MAD FOLLIES
E.C. Comics, 1963
(N#). 450.00
2 1964. . . . . 350.00
3 1965. . . . . 250.00
4 1966. . . . . 275.00
5 1967. . . . . 200.00
6 1968. . . . . 175.00
7 1969. . . . . 175.00

MAD HOUSE
Red Circle, 1974–82
95 thru 97 Horror stories . . . . . . @22.00
98 thru 130 Humor stories . . . . . @15.00
Annual #8 thru #11 . . . . @18.00

MADMAN
Tundra, 1992
1 . . . . 15.00
2 . . . . 12.00
3 . . . . 7.00
Oni Press, 2003
King-Size Super Special 7.00

MADMAN ADVENTURES
Tundra, 1992
1 R & N:Madman 15.00
2 . . . . 9.00
3 . . . . 8.00

MADMAN PICTURE
EXHIBITION
AAA Pop Comics, 2002
1 (of 4) 4.00
2 thru 4 . . . . 4.00

MADRAVEN
HALLOWEEN SPECIAL
Hamilton Comics, 1995
1 Song of the Silkies. 3.00

MAD SPECIAL
E.C. Publications, Inc., 1970
1 . . . . 200.00
2 . . . . 125.00
3 . . . . 100.00
4 thru 8 . . . . @100.00
9 thru 13 . . . . @75.00
14 . . . . 60.00
15 . . . . 60.00
16 . . . . 50.00
17 . . . . 50.00
18 . . . . 50.00
19 thru 21 . . . . @50.00
22 thru 31 . . . . @35.00
32 . . . . 35.00
33 thru 58 . . . . @20.00

Mage #3
© Comico

MAGE
Comico, 1984–86
1 MWg,I:Kevin Matchstick 10.00
2 MWg,I:Edsel 9.00
3 MWg,V:Umbra Sprite 6.00
4 MWg,V:Umbra Sprite 6.00
5 MWg,I:Sean (Spook) 6.00
6 MWg,Grendel begins 15.00
7 MWg,Grendel. 9.00
8 MWg,Grendel. 6.00
9 MWg,Grendel. 6.00
10 MWg,Grendel,Styx 6.00
11 MWg,Grendel,Styx 6.00
12 MWg,D:Sean,Grendel. 6.00
13 MWg,D:Edsel,Grendel 5.00
14 MWg,Grendel,O:Kevin 5.00
15 MWg,D:Umbra Sprite 11.00

MAGE KNIGHT:
STOLEN DESTINY
IDW Publishing, 2002
1 (of 5) by TDz & D.Cabrera. 3.50
2 thru 5 . . . . @3.50

MAGIC FLUTE
Eclipse, 1989
1 CR 5.00

MAGIC THE GATHERING:
Acclaim
GN Serra Angel + card 6.00
GN Legend of the Fallen Angel +
   card 6.00
GN Dakkon Blackblade + card 6.00

...ANTIQUITIES WAR
Acclaim Armada, 1995
1 Based on the Antiquities Set 2.75
2 F:Urza, Mishra 2.50
3 I:Tawnos, Ashod. 2.50
4 The War Begins 2.50

...ARABIAN KNIGHTS
Acclaim Armada, 1995
1 Based on Rare Card set 2.75
2 V:Queen Nailah 2.50

...CONVOCATIONS
Acclaim Armada, 1995
1 Gallery of Art from Game. 2.50

...FALLEN EMPIRES
Acclaim Armada, 1995
1 with pack of cards 2.75
2 F:Tymolin 2.50

...HOMELANDS
Acclaim Armada, 1995
1 I:Feroz, Serra. 6.00

...ICE AGE
Acclaim Armada, 1995
1 Dominaia, from card game 3.00
2 Ice Age Adventures 2.50
3 CV(c) Planeswalker battles 2.50
4 final issue. 2.50

...SHADOW MAGE, THE
Acclaim Armada, 1995
1 I:Jared 3.00
2 F:Hurloon the Minotaur 2.75
3 VMk(c&a),V:Juggernaut. 2.50
4 Final issue 2.50

...URZA-MISHRA WAR, THE
Acclaim Armada
1 & 2 with Ice Age II card 6.00

...WAYFARER
Acclaim Armada, 1995
1 R:Jared 2.75
2 I:New Land. 2.50
3 R:Liana, Ravidel 2.50
4 I:Golthonor. 2.50
5 Final Issue 2.50

...THE LEGENDS OF:
THE ELDER DRAGONS
1 & 2 . . . . @2.50
JEDIT OJANEN
1 & 2 . . . . @2.50
SHANDALAR
1 & 2 . . . . @2.50

MAGILLA GORILLA
Gold Key, 1964
1 . . . . 175.00
2 thru 10 Dec. 1968 . . . . @125.00

MAGILLA GORILLA
Charlton Comics, 1970
1 .... 100.00
2 thru 5 .... @60.00

MAGIQUE
WildStorm/DC, 2000
Ann. 2000 #1, Devil's
  Night x-over, pt.4 .... 3.50

MAGNUS:
ROBOT FIGHTER
Gold Key, 1963
1 RM,I:Magnus,Teeja,A-1,
  I&B:Capt.Johner&aliens 500.00
2 RM,I:Sen.Zeremiah Clane.... 250.00
3 RM,I:Xyrkol 250.00
4 RM,I:Mekamn,Elzy........ 150.00
5 RM,The Immortal One...... 150.00
6 RM,I:Talpa 125.00
7 RM,I:Malev-6,ViXyrkol.... 175.00
8 RM,I:Outsiders(Chet, Horio,
  Toun, Malf). 140.00
9 RM, I:Madmot........... 140.00
10 RM,Mysterious Octo-Rob 140.00
11 RM,I:Danae,Neo-Animals 125.00
12 RM,The Volcano Makers 125.00
13 RM,I:Dr Lazlo Noel 130.00
14 RM,The Monster Robs 125.00
15 RM,I:Mogul Radur. 125.00
16 RM,I:Gophs. 125.00
17 RM,I:Zypex 125.00
18 RM,I:V'ril Trent 125.00
19 RM,Fear Unlimited 125.00
20 RM,I:Bunda the Great. 125.00
21 RM, Space Spectre........ 125.00
22 Rep. #1 .... 100.00
23 DSp,Mission Disaster 100.00
24 Pied Piper of North Am 100.00
25 The Micro Giants 100.00
26 The Venomous Vaper 100.00
27 Panic in Pacifica 100.00
28 Threats from the Depths ... 100.00
29 thru 46 rep. .... @40.00

MAGNUS:
ROBOT FIGHTER
Valiant, 1991
0 PCu,BL,Emancipator,w/ BWS
  card 9.00
0a PCu,BL,w/o card 3.00
1 ANi,BL,B:Steel Nation 9.00
2 ANi,BL,Steel Nation #2 .... 7.00
3 ANi,BL,Steel Nation #3 .... 7.00
4 ANi,BL,E:Steel Nation 7.00
5 DL,BL(i),I:Rai(#1),V:Slagger
  Flipbook format 7.00
6 DL,A:Solar,V:Grandmother
  A:Rai(#2)................... 6.00
7 DL,EC,V:Rai(#3) 6.00
8 DL,A:Rai(#4),Solar,X-O
  Armor.E·Flipbooks 3.50
1a thru 8a w/o coupon .... @2.00
9 EC,V:Xyrkol,E-7 .... 3.50
10 V:Xyrkol. 3.50
11 V:Xyrkol. 3.50
12 I:Turok,V:Dr. Noel,
  I:Asylum,40pgs 15.00
13 thru 20 .... @2.50
21 JaB,R:Malevalents, Grandmother.................... 3.00
21a Gold Ed. 4.00
22 JaB,D:Felina,V:Malevalents,
  Grandmother 2.50
23 thru 24 V:Malevolents ..... @2.50
25 N:Magnus,R:1-A,silver-foil(c) ... 3.00
26 thru 63................. @2.50
64 Ultimatum, F:Destroyer..... 12.00
Yearbook #1................. 4.00

MAGNUS
(ROBOT FIGHTER)
Acclaim, 1997
1 Magnus back from the future.... 3.00
2 thru 7 .... @2.50
8 thru 18 TPe .... @2.50

MAJESTIC
Wildstorm/DC, Jan., 2005
1 DAn&ALa(s),A:Superman 3.00
1a variant (c).................. 3.00
2 DAn&ALa(s),Earth life abducted . 3.00
3 DAn&ALa(s),Earth life abducted . 3.00
4 DAn&ALa(s),Earth life abducted . 3.00
5 DAn&ALa(s),Demon Night..... 3.00
6 DAn&ALa(s),V:old friend 3.00
7 DAn&ALa(s),Daemonites...... 3.00
8 DAn&ALa(s),present day...... 3.00
9 DAn&ALa(s),A:Zealot 3.00
10 DAn&ALa(s),Kherubim secrets.. 3.00
11 DAn&ALa(s) 3.00
12 DAn&ALa(s) 3.00
13 DAn&ALa(s),A:Zealot 3.00
14 DAn,ALa(s),V:Javen......... 3.00
15 DAn,ALa(s),Imperitor V. Shapers 3.00
16 DAn,ALa(s),Duel of his life 3.00
17 DAn,ALa(s), final issue 3.00

MAJOR DAMAGE
Invictus Studios, 1994
1 I:Major Damage.............. 2.50
2 V:Godkin 2.50
3 First Contact Conclusion 2.50

MAN CALLED A-X
Malibu Bravura, 1994–95
[Limited Series]
0 1st Puzzle piece 3.00
1 MWn,SwM 3.00
1a Gold foil Edition 4.00
2 MWn,SwM,VLElectobot........ 3.00
3 MWn,SwM,Mercy Island 3.00
4 MWn,SwM,One Who Came
  Before 3.00
5 MWn,SwM,Climax 3.00

MAN CALLED KEV, A
Wildstorm/DC, July, 2006
1 (of 5) GEn(s) 3.00
2 thru 5 GEn(s) .... @3.00

MANDRAKE
THE MAGICIAN
King Comics, 1966
1 .... 100.00
2 .... 75.00
3 .... 75.00
4 A:Girl Phantom............. 75.00
5 Cape Cod Caper 75.00
6 .... 75.00
7 O:Lothar.................. 75.00
8 .... 75.00
9 A:Brick Bradford............ 75.00
10 A:Rip Kirby 90.00

MAN FROM U.N.C.L.E.
Gold Key, 1965
1 The Explosive Affair........ 400.00
2 The Forthur Cookie Affair 200.00
3 The Deadly Devices Affair 100.00
4 The Rip Van Solo Affair 100.00
5 Ten Little Uncles Affair 100.00
6 The Three Blind Mice Affair ... 100.00
7 The Pixelated Puzzle Affair
  I:Jet Dream (back-up begins) 110.00
8 The Floating People Affair 100.00
9 Spirit of St.Louis Affair 100.00
10 The Trojan Horse Affair..... 100.00

11 Three-Story Giant Affair 100.00
12 Dead Man's Diary Affair 100.00
13 The Flying Clowns Affair..... 100.00
14 Great Brain Drain Affair 100.00
15 The Animal Agents Affair.... 100.00
16 Instant Disaster Affair 100.00
17 The Deadly Visions Affair ... 100.00
18 The Alien Affair 100.00
19 Knight in Shining
  Armor Affair 100.00
20 Deep Freeze Affair 100.00
21 rep. #10 .... 75.00
22 rep. #7.................. 75.00

MAN FROM U.N.C.L.E.
Entertainment, 1987
1 thru 11 .... @3.00

Man From U.N.C.L.E. #2
© Millennium

MAN FROM U.N.C.L.E.
Millennium, 1993
1 The Birds of Prey Affair,pt.1.... 3.00
2 The Birds of Prey Affair,pt.2.... 3.00

MANGA SHI, 2000
Crusade Entertainment, 1997
1 (of 3) BiT, Final Jihad, flip-book
  Shi: Heaven and Earth 3.00
2 BiT, flip-book Tomoe:
  Unforgettable Fire preview 3.00
3 BiT, conclusion............. 3.00

MANIFEST ETERNITY
Wildstorm/DC, June, 2006
1 SLo 3.00
2 thru 6 SLo .... @3.00

MAN IN BLACK
Harvey Publications, 1957
1 BP 250.00
2 thru 3 BP .... @175.00
4 BP, March, 1958 .... 175.00

MANIK
Millennium/Expand, 1995
1 I:Macedon, Arsenal,Cardinal 3.00

MANKIND
Chaos! Comics, 1999
1-shot StG.................... 3.00
1-shotA photo cover 3.00
1-shotB variant cover 7.00
1-shotC variant cover, signed.... 50.00

All comics prices listed are for *Near Mint* condition.

MAN OF THE ATOM
Valiant Heroes Special Project
Acclaim, 1997
Spec. 4.00

MAN OF WAR
Eclipse, 1987–88
1 thru 3 . . . . @2.50

Man of War #6
© Malibu

MAN OF WAR
Malibu, 1993–94
1 thru 3 V:Lift 2.50
1a thru 5a Newsstand Ed. 2.50
4 w/poster. 2.50
5 V:Killinger. 2.50
6 KM,Genesis Crossover 2.50
7 DJu,Genesis Crossover. 2.50
8 TMs(s),A:Rocket Ranger 2.50
9 thru 12 . . . . @2.50

MANTECH
ROBOT WARRIORS
Archie Publications 1984–85
1 thru 4 . . . . @5.00

MANTRA
Malibu Ultraverse, 1993–95
1 AV,I:Mantra,w/Ultraverse card . . . 3.00
1a Full Hologram (c). 9.00
1b Silver foil (c). 5.00
2 AV,V:Warstrike 3.00
3 AV,V:Kismet Deadly 3.00
4 BWS,Mantra's marriage,
   BU:Rune story 2.50
5 thru 9 . . . . @2.50
10 NBy(c),DaR,B:Archmage Quest,
   Flip/UltraversePremiere #2 . . . . 3.00
11 thru 24 . . . . @2.50
Giant Sized#1 GP(c),I:Topaz 2.50
Ashcan #1 . . . . 2.50
Malibu Ultraverse, 1995–96
Infinity N:Mantra. 2.50
1 Mantra in all Female Body. 2.50
1a Computer Painted Cover. 2.50
2 Phoenix flip issue. 2.50
3 thru 7 . . . . @2.50

...SPEAR OF DESTINY
Malibu Ultraverse, 1995
1 Search for Artifact 2.50
2 MiB,Eden vs. Aladdin. 2.50

MAN WITH NO NAME, THE
Dynamite Entertainment, 2008
1 The Good, the Bad & the Uglier . 3.50
1a variant zombie (c) 3.50
2 thru 7 . . . . @3.50

MANY ADVENTURES OF
MIRANDA MERCURY
Archaia Studios Press, 2008
295 Now available in this dimension 4.00
296 . . . . 3.50
297 . . . . 3.50

MANY GHOSTS OF
DOCTOR GRAVES, THE
Charlton 1967
1 . . . . 90.00
2 thru 10 . . . . @40.00
11 thru 18 . . . . @30.00
19 thru 36 . . . . @25.00
37 thru 72 . . . . @15.00
Becomes:

DR. GRAVES
Charlton 1985
73 thru 75 . . . . @10.00

MANY WORLDS OF
TESLA STRONG, THE
Wildstorm/DC, 2003
1 through the dimensions 6.00

MARK KIDWELL'S
RECLUSE
Fangoria Comics, 2007
1 thru 3 . . . . @4.00

MARCO POLO
Charlton, 1962
nn 175.00

MARGE'S LITTLE LULU
Gold Key, 1962
See Dell series
165 thru 166 giant . . . . @200.00
167 thru 169 . . . . @50.00
170 thru 207 . . . . @30.00
Becomes:

LITTLE LULU
Gold Key, 1972
207 thru 220 . . . . @20.00
221 thru 257 . . . . @10.00

MARINE WAR HEROES
Charlton, 1964
1 . . . . 50.00
2 thru 18 . . . . @25.00

MARINES ATTACK
Charlton, 1964
1 . . . . 50.00
2 thru 9 . . . . @25.00

MARK OF CHARON
Grossgen Comics, 2003
1 thru 5 JoB. . . . . @3.00

MARK RAND'S
SKY TECHNOLOGIES INC.
Red Mercenary, 1995
1 I:Jae,Elliot,Firnn 3.00

MARKSMAN, THE
Hero Graphics, 1988
1 O:Marksman,Pt.#1 . . . . 2.50
2 O:Marksman,Pt.#2 . . . . 2.50
3 O:Marksman ends.I:Basilisk 2.50
4 A:Flare 2.50
5 I:Radar,Sonar. 2.50
Ann. #1, A:Champions. 2.50

MARRIED... WITH
CHILDREN
Now, 1990
1 . . . . 4.00
1a 2nd printing 2.50
2 Ph(c) 3.00
3 Kelly Ph(c) 3.00
4 thru 7 Ph(c) . . . . @2.50
[2nd Series], 1991
1 Peg-Host of Radio Show 2.50
2 The Bundy Invention 2.50
3 Psychodad,(photo cover). 2.50
4 Mother-In-Law,(photo cover) . . . 2.50
5 Bundy the Crusader. 2.50
6 Bundy J: The Order of the
   Mighty Warthog 2.50
7 Kelly the VJ 2.50
Spec. Ph(c) (1992). 2.50
Spec. Bud Bundy, Fanboy in
   Paradise 3.00
3-D Spec.(1993). 2.50
1-shot Buck's Tale (1994) 2.50
Annual 1994 . . . . 3.50

...DYSFUNCTIONAL FAMILY
Now
1 I:The Bundies. 2.50
2 TV Appearance 2.50
3 Morally Pure Bundys 2.50

...FLASHBACK SPECIAL
Now, 1993
1 Peg and Al's first date 2.50
2 and 3 . . . . @2.50

...KELLY BUNDY SPECIAL
Now, 1992
1 with poster. 2.50
2 and 3 with poster . . . . @2.50

...KELLY GOES TO KOLLEGE
Now, 1994
1 thru 3 . . . . @2.50

...LOTTO FEVER
Now, 1994
1 thru 3 . . . . @2.50

...QUANTUM QUARTET
Now, 1993
1 thru 4 Fantastic Four parody . . @2.50
Fall 1994 Spec., flip book 2.50

...2099
Mirage, 1993
1 thru 3 Cable Parody . . . . @2.50

MARS
First, 1984
1 thru 12 . . . . @2.50

MARS ATTACKS
Topps, 1994
1 KG(s). 5.00
2 thru 6 KG(s) . . . . @4.00
[Series 2], 1995
1 Counterstrike 3.50
2 thru 5 Counterstrike . . . . @3.00
6 Rescue of Janice Brown,pt.1 . . . 3.00
7 Rescue of Janice Brown,pt.2 . . . 3.00
8 . . . . 3.00
Spec. Baseball 3.00

...HIGH SCHOOL
Topps, 1997
Spec. #1 (of 2) BSz(c) 3.00
Spec. #2 . . . . 3.00

...THE SAVAGE DRAGON
Topps, 1996
1 thru 4 . . . . @3.00

MARSHAL
Dabel Brothers Prod., 2006
1 thru 4 . . . . @4.00

MARVEL/ULTRAVERSE BATTLEZONES
Malibu Ultraverse, 1996
1 DPs(c),The Battle of the Heroes . 4.00

MASKED MAN
Eclipse, 1985–88
1 . . . . 3.00
2 thru 10 . . . . @2.50

MASKS: TOO HOT FOR TV
Wildstorm/DC, 2003
3pec. 5.00

MASTER DARQUE
Acclaim, 1997
Spec. F:Brixton Sound, 48pg. 4.00

MASTERS OF HORROR
IDW Publishing, 2005
1 . . . . 4.00
1a variant (c) 4.00
2 thru 4 . . . . @4.00

MASTERS OF THE UNIVERSE
Crossgen Comics, 2003
Spec. The Power of Fear 3.00
1 Rise of the Snake Men 3.00
Encyclopedia, Vol. 1 . . . . 3.00
MVCreations, 2004
Vol. 3
1 . . . . 3.00
2 thru 6 . . . . @3.00
1a Quadruple Gatefold 9.00
Season One Encyclopedia #4 . . . . . 3.00
Season One Encyclopedia #5 . . . . . 3.50

...ICONS OF EVIL
Crossgen Comics, 2003
Spec. Tri-Klops 3.00
1 Mer-Man 5.00
1 Trapjaw 5.00

MASTERWORK SERIES
Seagate DC, 1983
1 FFrep.DC,Shining Knight 4.00
2 FFrep.DC,Shining Knight 4.00
3 BWr,Horror DC rep. 4.00

MATADOR
Wildstorm/DC, May, 2005
1 (of 6) BSf,F:Lt. Isabel Cardona . . 3.00
2 thru 6 BSf . . . . @3.00

MATT BUSCH'S DARIA JONTAK
Realm Press, 2000
1 sexy sci-fi 4.00
1a deluxe 5.00
2 . . . . 4.00
2a deluxe 5.00
Companion Book 3.00

Companion Book, deluxe 4.00
Andromeda Entertainment/ PlanetMatt, 2001
Spec. Where Angels Fear to Tread . 4.00
Spec. deluxe 5.00

MAVERICK
Dell Publishing Co., 1958
1 Ph(c) Garner photos 500.00
2 Ph(c) 250.00
3 Ph(c) 250.00
4 Ph(c) 250.00
5 Ph(c) 250.00
6 thru 14 Ph(c) last Garner . . . @200.00
15 thru 19 Ph(c) R. Moore . . . . @175.00

MAVERICK MARSHALL
Charlton Comics, 1958
1 . . . . 100.00
2 thru 6 . . . . @75.00
7 May, 1960 . . . . 75.00

MAVERICKS
Dagger, 1994
1 PuD,RkL, I:Mavericks 0.00
2 PuD,RkL 3.00
3 thru 5 . . . . @3.00

MAXIMORTAL
King Hell/Tundra, 1992
1 RV,A:True-Man 4.50
2 Crack in the New World 4.25
3 RV,Secret of the Manhattan
   Project revealed 4.25
4 . . . . 4.25
5 A:True Man 3.25
6 A:El Guano 3.25

MAXIMUM FORCE
Atomeka, 2002
Spec. #1 SBs, ... 3.00

Maya #1
© *Gold Key*

MAYA
Dell, 1967
1 . . . . 35.00
Gold Key, 1968
1 . . . . 50.00

MAZE AGENCY
Comico, 1988–91
1 O:Maze Agency 3.00
2 thru 6 . . . . @2.50

7 . . . . 2.75
8 thru 11 . . . . @2.50
12 . . . . 2.50
13 thru 15 . . . . @2.50
16 thru 23 . . . . @2.50
Spec. #1 . . . . 2.75

MAZE AGENCY, THE
IDW Publishing, 2005
1 MiB 4.00
2 thru 4 . . . . @4.00

McHALE'S NAVY
Dell Publishing Co. May-July, 1963
1 Ph(c) from TV show 150.00
2 Ph(c) 100.00
3 Ph(c) 100.00

McKEEVER & THE COLONEL
Dell Publishing Co., 1963
1 Ph(c) 125.00
? Ph(c) 90.00
3 Ph(c) 90.00

M.D.
Gemstone, 1999
1 (of 5) New Direction 3.00
2 thru 4 . . . . @3.00
Annual #1 . . . . 13.50

M.D. GEIST
CPM, 1995
1 Cartoon Adaptation 3.00
2 J:Army 3.00
3 V:Final Terminator 3.00

M.D. GEIST: GROUND ZERO
CPM, 1996
1 thru 3 . . . . @3.00

MECHANICS
Fantagraphics, 1985
1 HB,rep.Love & Rockets 3.00
2 HB,rep.Love & Rockets 2.50
3 HB,rep.Love & Rockets 2.50

MEDIEVAL LADY DEATH
Avatar Press, 2006
Sourcebook 4.00
Sourcebook, wraparound (c) 4.00
Sourcebook, premium (c) 9.00

...BELLADONNA
Avatar Press, 2005
½ 3.00
½ variant (c)s . . . . @3.00
1 . . . . 4.00
1a variant (c)s . . . . @4.00
1b Special (c)s . . . . @6.00

...WAR OF THE WINDS
Avatar Press, 2006
1 (of 8) 4.00
1a wraparound (c) 4.00
1b variant premium (c) 9.00
1c Special (c)s 6.00
2 thru 5 . . . . @4.00
2a thru 4a wraparound (c)s . . . . @4.00
2b thru 4b premium (c)s . . . . . . @9.00
5a variant (c)s . . . . @4.00
5b variant premium (c) 9.00
6 . . . . 4.00
6a variant (c)s . . . . @4.00

COLOR PUB.

MEDIA STARR
Innovation, 1989
1 thru 3 . . . . @2.50

MEGACITY 909
Devil's Due/Studio ICE, 2004
1 thru 8 . . . . @3.00
1a thru 6a variant (c). . . . . @3.00

MEGA DRAGON & TIGER
Comicsone.com, 2002
GN #3 thru #6 . . . . @14.00
GN #7. . . . . 15.00

MEGALITH
Continuity, 1990
1 MT 6.00
2 MT 4.00
3 MT, Painted issue 3.00
4 NA,TVE 3.00
5 NA,TVE 3.00
6 MN 3.00
7 MN 3.00
8 . . . . 3.00
9 SDr(i) 3.00
10 . . . . 3.00
[2nd Series], 1993
Deathwatch, 2000
0 Deathwatch 2000 prologue 5.00
1 Deathwatch 2000 Pt.5,w/card . . . 3.00
2 Deathwatch 2000 Pt.10,w/card. . . 3.00
3 pt.16,Indestructible(c),w/card. . . . 3.00
4 & 5 Rise of Magic. . . . . @3.00
6 & 7 . . . . @3.00

MEGAMAN
Dreamwave, 2003
1 . . . . 3.00
1a holofoil (c) 6.00
2 thru 4 . . . . @3.00
Pocket edition. 11.00

MEGAS, THE
Virgin Comics, 2008
1 . . . . 3.00
2 thru 4 . . . . @3.00

MEGATON
Entity Comics, 1993
Holiday Spec. w/card 3.00

MEGATON EXPLOSION
1 RLd,AMe,I:Youngblood preview 25.00

MEGATON MAN
Kitchen Sink, 1984
1 Don Simpson art,I:MegatonMan . 6.00
1a rep. B&W 3.00
2 . . . . 4.00
3 and 4 . . . . @3.00
5 . . . . 3.00
6 Border Worlds 3.00
7 Border Worlds 3.00
8 Border Worlds 3.00
9 Border Worlds 3.00
10 final issue, 1986 . . . . 3.00

MEK
DC/Homage, 2002
2 WEI 3.00
3 WEI, concl. 3.00

MELTING POT
Kitchen Sink, 1993
1 . . . . 4.00
2 and 3 . . . . @3.00
4 . . . . 3.50

Men From Earth #1
© *Future Fun*

MELVIN MONSTER
Dell Publishing Co.1965
1 . . . . 175.00
2 thru 10 . . . . @150.00

MEN FROM EARTH
Future Fun, 1991
1 based on Matt Mason toy 6.50

MENACE
Awesome Entertainment, 1998
1 by Jada Pinkett & Don Fraga . . . 2.50
1a signed 15.00
2 . . . . 2.50
3 . . . . 2.50

MENDY AND THE GOLEM
The Golem Network, 2003
1 The Key 3.00
2 Blackout 3.00
3 . . . . 3.00
4 Meltdown 3.00
5 Beyond Control 3.00

MERCHANTS OF DEATH
Eclipse, 1988
1 King's Castle, The Hero 3.50
2 King's Castle,Soldiers of Fortune 3.50
3 Ransom, Soldier of Fortune. 3.50
4 ATh(c),Ransom, Men o/t Legion . 3.50
5 Ransom,New York City Blues . . . 3.50

MERCY SPARX
Devil's Due, 2008
0 . . . . 1.00
1 . . . . 3.50
1a variant (c) 3.50
2 . . . . 3.50
2a variant (c) 3.50

MERIDIAN
Crossgen Comics, 2000
1 BKs 4.50
2 BKs 4.50
3 BKs 4.00
4 BKs 4.00
5 BKs 4.00
6 thru 11 BKs . . . . @3.50
12 thru 44 BKs . . . . @3.00

MERLIN REALM
Blackthorne, 1985
1 3-D 2.50

METABARONS
Humanoids Publishing, 2000
1 . . . . 3.00
2 thru 9 . . . . @3.00
10 thru 17 . . . . @3.00

META DOCS
Antarctic Press, 2005
1-shot Type A. 3.00
1-shot Code Black 3.50

META 4
First 1990
1 IG. 4.50
2 IG. 2.50
3 IG/JSon,final monthly. 2.50

METAL GEAR SOLID
IDW 2004
1 Video Game tie-in 15.00
1a retail edition 6.00
2 thru 12 . . . . @4.00

METAL GEAR SOLID: SONS OF LIBERTY
IDW Publishing, 2005
0 . . . . 4.00
1 . . . . 4.00
1a variant (c). 4.00
2 thru 9 . . . . @4.00
2a thru 9a variant (c). . . . . @4.00
9 thru 12 . . . . @4.00
9a thru 12a variant (c)s . . . . @4.00

METAL LOCUS: HARD DRIVE
Speakeasy Comics, 2006
1 (of 4) 3.00
2 . . . . 3.00
3 . . . . 3.00

METALLIX
Future Comics, 2003
0 Tag-Team Super-Hero 3.50
1 . . . . 3.50
2 . . . . 3.50
3 thru 5 . . . . @3.50
6 thru 12 . . . . @3.00

METAL MILITIA
Entity Comics, 1995
1 I:Metal Militia 2.50
1a with Video Game 7.00
2 ICO 2.50
3 F:Detective Calahan 2.50
Ashcan 2.50

METAMORPHOSIS
Narwain Publishing, 2006
1 (of 3) 4.00

METAPHYSIQUE
Malibu Bravura, 1995
1 NBy,I:Metaphysique. 3.00
1a Gold foil edition 4.00
2 NBy,Mandelbrot malfunctions . . . 3.00
3 I:Harridas. 3.00
4 D:Maj.Character,B:Superious . . . 3.00
5 V:Astral Kid 3.00
6 Apocalyptic Armageddon, finale . 3.00
Ashcan NBy,B&W 2.50

MICHAELANGELO
Mirage
1 TMNT Character. 15.00

MICHAEL LENT'S PREY: ORIGIN OF THE SPECIES
Dabel Brothers Productions, 2006

1	3.00
2 thru 4	@3.00

MICHAEL TURNER'S FATHOM
D.E. (Dynamite Ent.) 2006

Prelude #1	3.00
Prelude #1 variant (c)s	@3.00

MICKEY & DONALD
Gladstone, 1988

1 1449 Firestone	8.00
2	4.00
3 Man of Tomorrow	3.00
4 thru 15	@3.00
16 giant-size	3.00
17	3.00
18	4.00

Becomes:

DONALD AND MICKEY

19 thru 26	@3.00

MICKEY MANTLE COMICS
Magnum, 1991

1 JSt,Rise to Big Leagues	4.00

MICKEY MOUSE
Dell

85 thru 156	@35.00
157 thru 158	@25.00
159 thru 179	@15.00
180 thru 204	@10.00

Gold Key 1962

Mickey Mouse Album (1963)	40.00
Mickey Mouse Club (1964)	45.00
Mickey Mouse Surprise Party (1979)	45.00

Whitman, 1980

205 thru 207	@40.00
208 Scarce	125.00
209 thru 218	@20.00

MICKEY MOUSE
Gladstone, 1986

219 FG,Seven Ghosts	20.00
220 FG,Seven Ghosts	10.00
221 FG,Seven Ghosts	10.00
222 FG,Editor in Grief	5.00
223 FG,Editor in Grief	4.00
224 FG,Crazy Crime Wave	4.00
225 FG,Crazy Crime Wave	4.00
226 FG,Captive Castaways	4.00
227 FG,Captive Castaways	4.00
228 FG,Captive Castaways	4.00
229 FG,Bat Bandit	4.00
230 FG,Bat Bandit	3.00
231 FG,Bobo the Elephant	3.00
232 FG,Bobo the Elephant	3.00
233 FG,Pirate Submarine	3.00
234 FG,Pirate Submarine	3.00
235 FG,Photo Racer	3.00
236 FG,Photo Racer	3.00
237 FG,Race for Riches	3.00
238 FG,Race for Riches	3.00
239 FG,Race for Riches	3.00
240 FG,March of Comics	3.00
241 FG	4.00
242 FG	3.00
243 FG	3.00
244 FG,60th Anniv	5.00
245 FG,Giant Ants	4.00
246 FG	3.00
247 FG	3.00
248 FG	3.00

249 FG	5.00
250 FG	3.00
251 FG	3.00
252 FG	3.00
253 FG	3.00
254 FG	3.00

Mickey Mouse #1
© Walt Disney

255 and 256 FG	@4.00

MICKEY MOUSE
Walt Disney, 1990

1 The Phantom Gondolier	4.00
2	3.50
3 thru 19	@3.00

MICKEY MOUSE AND FRIENDS
Gemstone Publishing, 2003

257 thru 270	@3.25
271 thru 296	@3.00
297	3.50
1-shot Mickey Mouse meets Blotman (2005)	6.00

MICKEY MOUSE MEETS BLOTMAN
Gemstone Publishing, 2005

1-shot	6.00
1-shot Blotman Returns (2006)	6.00

MICKEY'S TWICE UPON A CHRISTMAS
Gemstone Publishing, 2004

Spec. video adapt.	4.00

MICKEY SPILLANE'S MIKE DANGER
Tekno Comix, 1995

1 I:Mike Danger	3.00
2 thru 11	@2.50

Big Entertainment, 1996

1 thru 10	@2.50

MICROBOTS, THE
Gold Key, 1971

1	30.00

MICRONAUTS
Devil's Due Publishing, 2004

1 thru 4	@3.00

MIDKNIGHT
Red 5 Comics, 2007

1 thru 2	@3.00

MIDNIGHTER
Wildstorm/DC, Nov., 2006

1 GEn,CSp,KIS	3.00
1a & b variant (c)s	@3.00
2 GEn,CSp,KIS	3.00
2a variant AAd (c)	3.00
3 GEn,CSp,KIS	3.00
3a variant JPe (c) (1:10)	3.00
4 GEn,CSp,KIS,To Kill Hitler	3.00
4a variant GF (c) (1:10)	3.00
5 GEn,CSp,KIS,Killing Machine	3.00
6 GEn,GF,KIS,Feudal Japan.	3.00
7 DaR,KIS	3.00
8 JPL,Hawksmoor challenge	3.00
9 JP,BSf,Space station virus	3.00
10 KG,CSp,KIS,	3.00
11 A sultry siren	3.00
12 Back in New York	3.00
13 V:Anthem	3.00
14 Superhero fascists	3.00
15 V:Anthem	3.00
16 Assassin8	3.00
17 V:Assassin8	3.00
18 F:Assassin8	3.00
19 V:Assassin 8	3.00
20 final issue	3.00

...ARMAGEDDON
Wildstorm/DC, Oct., 2007

1 London destroyed by Carrier	3.00

MIDNIGHT EYE: GOKU PRIVATE INVESTIGATOR
Viz

1 A.D. 2014: Tokyo city	5.25
2 V:Hakuryu,A:Yoko	5.00
3 A:Ryoko,Search for Ryu	5.00
4 Goku vs. Ryu	5.00
5 Leilah Abducted	5.00
6 Lisa's I.D. discovered	5.00

MIDNIGHT KISS
APC, 2005

1 thru 3	@3.50

Markosia, 2005

4 & 5	@3.50
5a variant (c)	3.50

MIDNIGHT TALES
Charlton, 1972

1	25.00
2 thru 18	@15.00

MIGHTY COMICS
Archie, 1966
{Prev: Flyman}

40 A:Web	60.00
41 A:Shield, Black Hood	50.00
42 A:Black Hood	50.00
43 A:Shield, Black Hood,Web	50.00
44 A:Black Hood, Steel Sterling Shield.	50.00
45 Shield-Black Hood team-up O:Web	50.00
46 A:Steel Sterling, Black Hood, Web.	50.00
47 A:Black Hood & Mr.Justice	50.00
48 A:Shield & Hangman.	50.00
49 Steel Sterling-Black Hood team-up, A:Fox	50.00

[ALL NEW ADVENTURES OF] THE MIGHTY CRUSADERS
Archie/Red Circle, 1965
[1st Series]
1 O:Shield (Joe Higgins & Bill
  Higgins) 125.00
2 MSy,O:Comet 75.00
3 O:Fly-Man 65.00
4 A:Fireball,Jaguar,Web,Fox,
  Blackjack Hangman & more
  Golden Age Archie Heroes ... 70.00
5 I:Ultra-Men&TerrificThree..... 65.00
6 V:Maestro,A:Steel Sterling 65.00
7 O:Fly-Girl,A:Steel Sterling 65.00
[2nd Series], 1983
1 RB,R:Joe Higgins & Lancelot
  Strong as the SHIELD, Mighty
  Crusaders, A:Mr.Midnight 7.00
2 RB,V:Brain Emperor & Eterno .. 5.00
3 RB,I:Darkling 5.00
4 DAy,TD 4.00
5 .... 4.00
6 DAy,TD,Shield 4.00
7 .... 4.00
8 .... 4.00
9 Trial of the Shield 4.00
10 .... 4.00
11 DAy,D:Gold Age Black Hood, I:
  Riot Squad, series based on
  toy lines 5.00
12 DAy,I:She-Fox 5.00
13 Last issue 5.00

MIGHTY HERCULES, THE
Gold Key, 1963
1 .... 275.00
2 .... 250.00

Mighty Magnor #2
© Malibu

MIGHTY MAGNOR, THE
Malibu, 1993
1 SA 2.50
2 thru 6 SA .... @2.50

MIGHTY MORPHIN POWER RANGERS
Hamilton, 1994–95
1 From TV Series 2.75
2 Switcheroo 2.50
3 .... 2.50
4 F:White Ranger 2.50
5 F:Pink Ranger 2.50

6 V:Garganturon 2.50
[Series 2], 1995
1 Unstoppable Force 2.50
2 V:Mechanical Octopus 2.50
3 .... 2.50
4 Lost Ranger 2.50
[Series 3], 1995
1 O:Green Ranger 2.50
2 O:Green Ranger 2.50
3 I:New Megazords 2.50

MIGHTY MOUSE
Dell, 1966
166 .... 45.00
167 thru 172 .... 45.00

ADVENTURES OF MIGHTY MOUSE
Gold Key, 1962
1 .... 50.00
Becomes:

MIGHTY MOUSE
Gold Key, 1964
161 thru 165 .... @75.00
Also continued as:

ADVENTURES OF MIGHTY MOUSE
Gold Key, 1979
166 thru 172 .... @10.00

MIGHTY MOUSE
Spotlight, 1987
1 FMc,PC(c) 3.00
2 FMc,CS(c) 3.00
1 Holiday Special 3.00

MIGHTY MUTANIMALS
Archie Publications, 1991
[Mini-Series]
1 Cont.from TMNT Adventures#19,
  A:Raphael, Man Ray, Leather-
  head, Mondo Gecko,Deadman,
  Wingnut & Screwloose 2.50
2 V:Mr.Null,Malinga,Soul and Bean
  and the Malignoid Army 2.50
3 Alien Invasion help off, Raphael
  returns to Earth 2.50
Spec.#1 rep. all #1-3 +SBi pin-ups . 3.00

MIGHTY MUTANIMALS
Archie, 1992
1 Quest for Jagwar's Mother 2.50
2 V:Snake Eyes 2.50
3 .... 2.50
4 Days of Future Past 2.50
5 Into the Sun 2.50
6 V:Null & 4 Horsemen Pt#2 ..... 2.50
7 Jaws of Doom 2.50

MIGHTY SAMSON
Gold Key, 1964–82
1 O:Mighty Samson 160.00
2 .... 125.00
3 .... 125.00
4 .... 125.00
5 .... 125.00
6 thru 10 .... @80.00
11 thru 20 .... @75.00
21 thru 32 .... @50.00

MIKE GRELL'S SABLE
First, 1990
1 thru 8 rep. .... @2.50
9 .... 2.50
10 Triptych 2.50

MIKE SHAYNE PRIVATE EYE
Dell Publishing Co., 1961-62
1 .... 75.00
2 .... 50.00
3 .... 50.00

MILLENNIUM INDEX
Independent Comics, 1988
1 .... 2.50
2 .... 2.50

MILLIE THE LOVABLE MONSTER
Dell, 1962
1 .... 75.00
2 .... 65.00
3 .... 50.00
4 thru 6 .... @25.00

MILTON THE MONSTER & FEARLESS FLY
Gold Key, 1966
1 .... 175.00

MIRACLE BRIGADE, THE
Counteractive Comics, 2006
1 .... 3.00

MIRACLEMAN
Eclipse, 1985–94
1 R:Miracleman 15.00
2 AD,Moore,V:Kid Miracleman ... 10.00
3 AD,Moore,V:Big Ben 10.00
4 AD,Moore,R:Dr.Gargunza 10.00
5 AD,Moore,O:Miracleman 10.00
6 Moore,V:Miracledog, D:Evelyn
  Cream 10.00
7 Moore,D:Dr.Gargunza 15.00
8 Moore 9.00
9 RV,Moore,Birth of Miraclebaby . 13.00
10 JRy,RV,Moore 10.00
11 JTo,Moore,Book III,
  I:Miraclewoman 25.00
12 thru 14 Moore .... @25.00
15 Moore 120.00
16 Moore 35.00
17 Golden Age 15.00
18 .... 12.00
19 thru 22 .... @14.00
23 Silver Age 30.00
24 BWS(c),NGa(s) 36.00
25 .... 9.00
26 thru 28 .... @4.00
3-D Special #1 .... 5.00

MIRACLEMAN APOCRYPHA
Eclipse, 1991–92
1 inc. Rascal Prince 8.00
2 Miracleman, Family Stories 8.00
3 .... 8.00

MIRACLEMAN FAMILY
Eclipse, 1988
1 British Rep.,A:Kid Miracleman.. 12.00
2 Alan Moore (s) 12.00

MIRACLE SQUAD, THE
Upshot/Fantagraphics, 1986
1 Hollywood 30's 2.50
2 thru 4 .... @2.50

MIRROR'S EDGE
Wildstorm/DC, Nov., 2008
1 (of 6) Video game tie-in 4.00

MISADVENTURES OF CLARK & JEFFERSON
Ape Entertainment, 2007
1 . . . . 3.50
2 thru 4 (of 4) . . . . @3.50

MISCELLANEOUS ADVENTURES OF STYKMAN, THE
A.K.A. Comics, 2007
1 . . . . 3.00
2 thru 5 . . . . @3.00

MISCHIEF NIGHT
Avatar Press, 2006
1 . . . . 4.00
1a wraparound (c). 4.00
1b variant (c)s . . . . @4.00
1c variant Splatter (c) 7.00
1d variant Ruby Red Foil Con. (c) . 5.00
1e variant Damned Duo (c) 4.00

MISERERE
Dark Planet Productions, 2004
1 The Sheathed Sword. 6.50
2 . . . . 5.00

MISERERE
Narwain Publishing, 2006
1 (of 3) 3.50
2 thru 3 . . . . @3.50

MISERICORDIA
Archaia Studios, 2007
1 (of 11). 4.00
2 thru 3 . . . . @4.00

MISS FURY
Adventure Comics, 1991
1 O:Cat Suit 3.00
2 Miss Fury impersonator. 3.00
3 A:Three Miss Fury's. 3.00
4 conclusion 3.00

MISSION IMPOSSIBLE
Dell Publishing Co., 1967
1 Ph(c) 150.00
2 Ph(c) 125.00
3 Ph(c) 100.00
4 Ph(c) 100.00
5 Ph(c) 100.00

MISSIONS IN TIBET
Dimension Comics, 1995
1 I:New Series 2.50
2 F:Orlando,Ting,Alex. 2.50
3 Two Worlds Collide 2.50
4 V:Sada. 2.50

MISS PEACH
(& SPECIAL ISSUES)
Dell Publishing Co., 1963
1 . . . . 150.00

MISPLACED
Devil's Due Publishing, 2004
3 and 4 . . . . @3.00
1-shot Misplaced@17 . . . . 5.00

MR. AND MRS. J. EVIL SCIENTIST
Gold Key, 1963
1 . . . . 150.00
2 thru 4 . . . . @100.00

MISTER ED, THE TALKING HORSE
Gold Key, 1962
1 From TV show 150.00
2 thru 6 . . . . @90.00

MR. MAGOO
Dell, 1963
3 . . . . 125.00
4 thru 5 . . . . @125.00

MR. MAJESTIC
WildStorm/DC, 1999
1 JoC,A:Desmond. 2.50
1a variant cover 3.00
2 JoC,time gone berserk 2.50
3 JoC,F:Maxine Manchester. 2.50
4 JoC,F:Junior Majestic 2.50
5 JoC 2.50
6 JoC,F:Desmond. 2.50
7 JoC,Universal Law,pt.1 . . . . 2.50
8 JoC,Universal Law,pt.2 . . . . 2.50
9 JoC,Universal Law,pt.3 . . . . 2.50

MR. MONSTER
Eclipse, 1985–87
1 I:Mr. Monster 7.00
2 DSt(c). 5.00
3 V:Dr. NoZone 3.50
4 Trapped in Dimension X 3.00
5 V:Flesh-eating Amoebo 3.00
6 KG,SD,reprints 3.00
7 . . . . 3.00
8 V:Monster in the Atomic Telling
  Machine. 3.00
9 V:Giant Clams 3.00
10 R:Dr.No Zone, 3-D 3.00

MR. MONSTER ATTACKS
Tundra, 1992
1 DGb,SK,short stories. 4.25
2 SK,short stories cont. 4.25
3 DGb,last issue 4.25

MR. MONSTER SUPERDUPER SPECIAL
Eclipse, 1986–87
1 . . . . 3.00
2 . . . . 3.00
3 . . . . 3.00
4 . . . . 3.00
5 . . . . 3.00
6 . . . . 4.00
3-D Spec. Hi-Octane Horror,JKu,
  Touch of Death reprint. 5.00
Triple Treat. 4.00

MR. MONSTER TRUE CRIME
Eclipse, 1986
1 . . . . 3.00
2 . . . . 3.00
3-D Spec. #1 . . . . 3.00

MR. MUSCLES
Charlton Comics, 1956
22 . . . . 100.00
23 . . . . 75.00

MR. MYSTIC
Eclipse
1 . . . . 2.50
2 thru 3 . . . . @2.50

MR. T
APC, 2005
1 . . . . 3.50
1a foil (c). 6.00
1b foil (c), signed 12.00
1c sketch edition. 40.00
1d Comix Shop (c) 7.00
2 . . . . 3.50
3 . . . . 3.50
4 . . . . 3.50
5 . . . . 3.50

MR. T AND THE T FORCE
Now, 1993
1 NA,R:Mr.T,V:Street Gangs. 2.50
1a Gold Ed.. . . . . 9.00
2 NA,V:Demons 2.50
3 NBy,w/card. 2.50
4 NBy,In Urban America 2.50
5 thru 10, with card . . . . @2.50

Mister X #2
© Vortex

MISTER X
Vortex, 1984
1 HB 7.00
2 HB 5.00
3 HB 3.50
4 HB 3.00
5 thru 10 . . . . @3.00
11 thru 13 . . . . @3.00
14 . . . . 3.00

MOBY DUCK
Gold Key, 1967–70
1 Walt Disney 50.00
2 thru 6 . . . . @25.00
7 thru 11 . . . . @20.00
Gold Key, 1973
12 thru 30 . . . . @15.00

MODERN MAN
Narwain Publishing, 2006
1 and 2 (of 4) . . . . @4.00

MODNIKS, THE
Gold Key, 1967
1 . . . . 50.00
2 . . . . 30.00

MOD SQUAD
Dell Publishing Co., 1969–71
1 . . . . 125.00
2 thru 8 . . . . @75.00

MOD WHEELS
Gold Key, 1971–76
1 . . . . 75.00
2 thru 18 . . . . @50.00
19 . . . . 40.00

MONARCHY
WildStorm/DC, 2001
1 JMC,V:Young Authoritans 2.50
2 JMC,F:Union 2.50
3 JMC,Vox Populi,pt.1 . . . . 2.50
4 JMC,Vox Populi,pt.2 . . . . 2.50
5 JMC,Boy Who Talked to Spiders . 2.50
6 JMC,Making the Metropolitan . . . 2.50
7 JMC,Making the Metropolitan . . . 2.50
8 JMC,Making the Metropolitan . . . 2.50
9 JMC,Metropolitan epilog 2.50
10 JMC,V:Chimera. 2.50
11 JMC,V:Higher Power. 2.50
12 JMC,final issue 2.50

MONKEE'S, THE
Dell Publishing Co., 1967
1 Ph(c) 200.00
2 Ph(c) 150.00
3 Ph(c) 150.00
4 Ph(c) 150.00
5 . . . . 125.00
6 Ph(c) 125.00
7 Ph(c) 125.00
8 and 9 . . . . @120.00
10 Ph(c) 125.00
11 thru 17 . . . . @100.00

MONOLITH
Comico, 1991
1 From Elementals 2.50
2 Seven Levels of Hell 2.50
3 Fugue and Variation 2.50
4 Fugue and Variation 2.50

MONROE'S, THE
Dell Publishing Co., 1967
1 Ph(c) 50.00

MONSTER CLUB
Autumn Press, 2003
1 . . . . 3.50
2 thru 11 . . . . @3.50
12 40-pg. 3.50
Vol. 2
0 . . . . 3.00
1 thru 6 . . . . @3.50
Preview ed. 3.00

MONSTER HUNTERS
Charlton, 1975–79
1 TS,The Boar's Head Beast 40.00
2 TS,Fish Fry; The Kukulkaton . . . 30.00
3 TS,The Dictator 20.00
4 TS,Hidden Paradise. 20.00
5 TS,The Last Monster Hunter . . . 20.00
6 SD,MZ,The Beast or the Burden 25.00
7 MZ,TS,Blood Oath. 20.00
8 TS,SD,Wormholes. 25.00
9 MZ,Hour of the Werewolf. 15.00
10 SD,The Conglomerate 25.00
11 The Montego Frame 15.00
12 Snake Charmer. 15.00
13 SD,JSon,A Little Witchcraft. . . . 20.00
14 SD,Giant from the Unknown. . . 40.00
15 SD,reps. 20.00
16 TS,The Kilgore Monster 15.00
17 TS,reps from issue #3. . . . . . . 15.00
18 SD,Incident at Soulbridge. 20.00
Modern, 1977
1 & 2 rep issues 1 and 2 . . . . . . @3.00

MONSTER MASSACRE
Atomeka
1 SBs, DBr,DGb 8.50
1a Black Edition 35.00

MONSTER MAYHEM SERIES
Dead Dog Comics, 2005
1 Frankenstein 6.00
1a variant (c) 6.00
1 Creature. 6.00
1a variant (c) 6.00

MONSTERPOCOLYPSE
Desperado Pub., 2008
1 . . . . 4.00
2 thru 3 . . . . @4.00

MONSTER WORLD
WildStorm/DC, 2001
1 (of 4) SLo. 3.00
2 SLo, 5 young heroes 3.00
3 SLo, ... 3.00
4 SLo,concl. 3.00

MONTE COOK'S PTOLUS
Dabel Brothers Prod., 2006
1 (of 6) 3.00
2 thru 5 . . . . @3.00

MORBID ANGEL
London Night, 1996
? Angel's Tear, signed. 10.00
1 Commemorative (1999). 10.00

MORBID ANGEL: PENANCE
London Night, 1996
Revised Color Spec., double size . . 4.00

More Than Mortal #5
© Liar Comics

MORE THAN MORTAL
Liar Comics, 1997
1 . . . . 3.00
1a 2nd printing 3.00
1b convention, sign, num 9.00
2 Derdre vs. the Host 3.00
2a variant painted cover 6.00
3 MS(c) 3.00
4 thru 6 . . . . @3.00

...SAGAS
Liar Comics, 1998
1 by Sharon Scott & Romano
   Molenaar 3.00
1a variant Tim Vigil(c). 3.00
1b variant JLi(c) 9.00
2 thru 3 . . . . @3.00

...TRUTHS AND LEGENDS
Liar Comics, 1998
1 by Sharon Scott, Steve Firchow,
   Mark Prudeaux, O:Witchfinder . 4.00
1a signed 9.00
2 thru 5 . . . . @3.00
5a variant cover (1:4) 3.00
6 . . . . 3.00

MORLOCK 2001
Atlas, Feb.–July, 1975
1 thru 2 O:Morlock . . . . @15.00
3 SD,BW,F:Midnight Men 20.00

MORRIGAN
Sirius, 1997
1 by Lorenzo Bartoli & Saverio
   Tenuta 3.00
2 and 3 . . . . @3.00
GN rep. #1–#3 . . . . 10.00

MORTAL KOMBAT
Malibu, 1994
0 Four stories 3.00
1 Based on the Video Game 3.00
1a Foil Ed 4.00
1b with new material. 3.00
2 . . . . 3.00
3 . . . . 3.00
4 . . . . 3.00
5 I:Mortal Kombat II 3.00
6 Climax 3.00
Spec. #1 Tournament edition 4.00
Spec. #2 Tournament edition II . . . 4.00
Spec #1 Baraka, V:Scorpion 3.00

...BATTLEWAVE
Malibu, 1995
1 New series. 3.00
2 Action, Action, Action 3.00
3 The Gathering 3.00
4 F:Goro 3.00
5 F:Scorpion 3.00
6 final issue. 3.00

...GORO, PRINCE OF PAIN
Malibu, 1994
1 Goro. 3.00
1a Platinum Edition. 6.25
2 Goro, V:Kombatant 3.00
3 Goro, V:God of Pain 3.00

...KITANA & MILEENA
Malibu, 1995
1 Secrets of Outworld 3.00

...KUNG LAO
Malibu, 1995
1 one-shot Battlewave tie-in 3.00

...RAYDEN AND KANO
Malibu, 1995
1 J:Rayden Kano 3.00
1a Deluxe Edition 5.00
2 A:Reptile 3.00
3 Kano, conclusion 3.00

...U.S. SPECIAL FORCES
Malibu, 1995
1 V:Black Dragon 3.50
2 V:Black Dragon 3.00

COLOR PUB.

MORTAL KOMBAT: DECEPTION
Atomeka, 2005
0	4.00
0a chrome	10.00

MOSTLY WANTED
WildStorm/DC, 2000
1 (of 4) SLo,F:Sister Crenn.	2.50
2 SLo(s),F:Andi Mooncrest	2.50
3 SLo(s),	2.50
4 SLo(s),conclusion	2.50

MOUSE GUARD
Archaia Studio Press, 2006
1 Belly of the Beast.	22.00
1a 2nd printing	8.00
2 Shadows Within.	15.00
2a 2nd printing	5.00
3 Rise of the Axe.	11.00
3 (2nd printing)	4.00
4 The Dark Ghost.	8.00
5 Midnight's Dawn	7.00

...WINTER 1152
Archaia Studios Press
1 thru 6	@4.00

MOVIE CLASSIC
Dell, 1961–69
Around the World Under the Sea	50.00
Battle of the Bulge	50.00
Bon Voyage	50.00
The Cat	45.00
The Castilian	45.00
Cheyenne Autumn	90.00
Circus World	175.00
The Creature	150.00
Countdown	50.00
David Ladd's Life Story	125.00
Die, Monster, Die	90.00
The Dirty Dozen	75.00
Dr. Who and the Daleks	200.00
Dracula	125.00
El Dorado	225.00
Ensign Pulver	50.00
Frankenstein	125.00
Frankenstein, 2nd printing	50.00
The Great Race	75.00
The Hallelujah Trail	75.00
Hatari	125.00
The Horizontal Leiutenant	45.00
The Incredible Mr. Limpet	75.00
Jack the Giant Killer	135.00
Jason and the Argonauts	150.00
Lancelot and Guinevere	80.00
Lawrence of Arabia	100.00
Lion of Sparta	55.00
Mad Monster Party	150.00
The Masque of the Red Death	100.00
Maya	60.00
The Magic Sword	85.00
McHale's Navy	75.00
Merrill's Marauders	50.00
The Mouse on the Moon	50.00
The Mummy	150.00
The Music Man	80.00
The Naked Prey	90.00
The Night of the Grizzly	60.00
Operation Crossbow	50.00
Operation Bikini	50.00
The Prince and the Pauper	55.00
The Raven	100.00
Ring of Bright Water	60.00
The Runaway	50.00
Santa Claus Conquers the Martians	150.00
Ski Party	75.00
Smoky	75.00
Six Black Horses	50.00

Tales of Terror	100.00
Three Stooges Meet Hercules	165.00
Tomb of Ligeia	90.00
Twice Told Tales	100.00
Treasure Island	60.00
Two on a Guillotine	60.00
The Valley of Gwangi	150.00
War Gods of the Deep	50.00
The War Wagon	150.00
The Wolf Man	140.00
Who's Minding the Mint	50.00
Zulu	125.00

MOVIE COMICS
Gold Key/Whitman, 1962–70
Alice in Wonderland	60.00
Aristocats	150.00
Bambi 1	100.00
Bambi 2	75.00
Beneath the Planet of the Apes	150.00
Big Red	60.00
Blackbeard's Ghost	60.00
Buck Rogers Giant Movie Edition	75.00
Bullwhip Griffin	60.00
Captain Sinbad	125.00
Chitty, Chitty Bang Bang	150.00
Cinderella	75.00
Darby O'Gill & the Little People	80.00
Dumbo	75.00
Emil & the Detectives	50.00
Escapade in Florence	150.00
Fall of the Roman Empire	60.00
Fantastic Voyage	100.00
55 Days at Peking	60.00
Fighting Prince of Donegal	60.00
First Men of the Moon	75.00
Gay Purr-ee	100.00
Gnome Mobile	60.00
Goodbye, Mr. Chips	60.00
Happiest Millionaire	60.00
Hey There, It's Yogi Bear	125.00
Horse Without a Head	50.00
How the West Was Won	125.00
In Search of the Castaways	125.00
Jungle Book, The	150.00
Kidnapped	60.00
King Kong	75.00
King Kong N#.	125.00
Lady and the Tramp	60.00
Lady and the Tramp 1	100.00
Lady and the Tramp 2	50.00
Legend of Lobo, The	50.00
Lt. Robin Crusoe	50.00
Lion, The	50.00
Lord Jim	50.00
Love Bug, The	60.00

Movie Comics: King Kong
© Gold Key

Mary Poppins	100.00
Mary Poppins 1	125.00
McLintock	225.00
Merlin Jones as the Monkey's Uncle	125.00
Miracle of the White Stallions	50.00
Misadventures of Merlin Jones	125.00
Moon-Spinners, The	135.00
Mutiny on the Bounty	60.00
Nikki, Wild Dog of the North	50.00
Old Yeller	60.00
One Hundred & One Dalmatians	75.00
Peter Pan 1	75.00
Peter Pan 2	50.00
P.T. 109	75.00
Rio Conchos	60.00
Robin Hood	50.00
Shaggy Dog & the Absent-Minded Professor	60.00
Sleeping Beauty	135.00
Snow White & the Seven Dwarfs	60.00
Son of Flubber	60.00
Summer Magic	135.00
Swiss Family Robinson	60.00
Sword in the Stone	135.00
That Darn Cat	135.00
Those Magnificent Men in Their Flying Machines	60.00
Three Stooges in Orbit	200.00
Tiger Walks, A	75.00
Toby Tyler	60.00
Treasure Island	60.00
20,000 Leagues Under the Sea	60.00
Wonderful Adventures of Pinocchio	75.00
Wonderful World of Brothers Grimm	60.00
X, the Man with the X-Ray Eyes	135.00
Yellow Submarine w/poster	450.00

MS. MYSTIC
Pacific
1 NA,Origin	7.00
2 NA,Origin,I:Urth 4	6.00
Continuity, 1988
1 NA,Origin rep.	3.00
2 NA,Origin,I:Urth 4 rep	3.00
3 NA,New material	3.00
4 TSh	3.00
5 DT	3.00
6 and 7	@3.00
8 CH/Sdr,B:Love Story	3.00
9 DB	3.00
9a Newsstand(c)	3.00
[3rd Series], 1993
1 O:Ms.Mystic	2.50
2 A:Hybrid	2.50
3 thru 4	@2.50
[4th Series, Deathwatch 2000]
1 Deathwatch 2000 pt.8,w/card	2.50
2 Deathwatch 2000 w/card	2.50
3 Indestructible cover, w/card	2.50

MS. TREE'S THRILLING DETECTIVE ADVENTURES
Eclipse, 1983
1 Millor pin up	5.00
2	4.00
3	4.00
Becomes:

MS. TREE
Eclipse, 1983
4 thru 6	@4.00
7	4.00
8	8.00
9	4.00
Aardvark–Vanaheim, 1984
10	4.00
Renegade
1 3-D	4.00

MS. VICTORY GOLDEN ANNIVERSARY
AC Comics
1 Ms.Victory celebration 5.00

MS. VICTORY SPECIAL
AC Comics, 1985
1 . . . . 2.50

MU
Devil's Due/Studio ICE, 2004
1 . . . . 3.00
1a variant (c). 3.00
2 thru 4 . . . . @3.00
2a thru 4a variant (c). . . . . @3.00

MUMMY MOVIE PREQUEL: THE RISE & FALL OF XANGO'S AX
IDW Publishing, 2008
1 . . . . 4.00
1a variant (c) 4.00
2 thru 4 . . . . @4.00

Mummy, Or Ramses the Damned #11
© Millennium

MUMMY, OR RAMSES THE DAMNED, THE
Millennium, 1992
1 Anne Rice Adapt. 5.00
2 JM,Mummy in Mayfair 3.75
3 JM 3.25
4 JM, To Egypt 3.00
5 JM,The Mummy's Hand. 2.50
6 JM,20th Century Egypt 2.50
7 JM,More Ramses Past Revealed 2.50
8 JM,Hunt for Cleopatra 2.50
9 JM,Cleopatra's Wrath contd. . . . 2.50
10 JM,Subterranian World 2.50
11 JM 2.50

MUMMY, THE: VALLEY OF THE GODS
Chaos! Comics, 2001
1 (of 3) MWn,MtB, movie tie-in 3.00
1a variant (c). 3.00
1b premium. 9.00
2 . . . . 3.00
2a Scorpion King photo (c). 3.00
3 . . . . 3.00

3a Imhotep phoco (c) 3.00
Ashcan. 6.00

MUNDEN'S BAR ANNUAL
First, 1988
1 BB,JOy,JSn,SR 3.00

MUNSTERS, THE
Gold Key, 1965–68
1 . . . . 350.00
2 . . . . 200.00
3 thru 5 . . . . @175.00
6 thru 16 . . . . @150.00

MUPPET BABIES
Harvey, 1993
1 Return of Muppet Babies. 2.50

MURCIELAGA/SHE-BAT
Studio G, 2001
1 by D.Gross & R.Lopez. 3.00
2 thru 4 . . . . @3.00

MUSH MOUSE AND PUNKIN PUSS
Gold Key, 1965
1 Hanna-Barbera 150.00

MUTANT CHRONICLES— GOLGOTHA
Valiant
1 thru 4 + game trading card . . . @3.00

MUTATION
Speakeasy Comics, 2005
1 . . . . 3.00
2 thru 5 . . . . @3.00

MUTATION
Markosia, 2006
1 . . . . 3.50
1a variant (c) 3.50
2 thru 4 . . . . @3.50

MY FAVORITE MARTIAN
Gold Key, 1964–66
1 . . . . 275.00
2 . . . . 150.00
3 . . . . 125.00
4 . . . . 125.00
5 . . . . 125.00
6 thru 9 . . . . @125.00

MY LITTLE MARGIE
Charlton Comics, 1954–65
1 Ph(c) 500.00
2 Ph(c) 250.00
3 thru 8 . . . . @150.00
9 . . . . 135.00
10 . . . . 125.00
11 thru 19 . . . . @100.00
20 Giant Size 175.00
21 thru 35 . . . . @100.00
36 thru 53 . . . . @100.00
54 Beatles (c). 300.00

MY LITTLE MARGIE'S BOY FRIEND
Charlton Comics, 1955–58
1 . . . . 200.00
2 . . . . 150.00
3 thru 11 . . . . @100.00

MYSTERIES OF UNEXPLORED WORLDS/ SON OF VULCAN
Charlton Comics, 1956
1 . . . . 500.00
2 . . . . 275.00
3 SD,SD(c) 400.00
4 SD,Forbidden Room 450.00
5 SD,SD(c) 450.00
6 SD 450.00
7 SD, giant 500.00
8 SD 425.00
9 SD 425.00
10 SD,SD(c). 425.00
11 SD,SD(c). 425.00
12 SD,Charm Bracelet. 300.00
13 thru 18 . . . . @150.00
19 SD(c). 300.00
20 . . . . 150.00
21 thru 24 SD. . . . . @300.00
25 . . . . 100.00
26 SD. 300.00
27 thru 30 . . . . @100.00
31 thru 45 . . . . @80.00
46 I:Son ofVulcan,Dr.Kong(1965) 100.00
47 V:King Midas. 80.00
48 V:Captain Tuska 80.00
Becomes:

SON OF VULCAN
49 DC redesigns costume 75.00
50 V:Dr.Kong 75.00

MYSTERIOUS SUSPENSE
Charlton, 1968
1 SD,F:Question 125.00

MYSTERY COMICS DIGEST
Gold Key, 1972–75
1 WW,Riley's Believe It Or Not. . . 60.00
2 WW,Boris Karloff 60.00
3 RC,GEv,Twilight Zone 60.00
4 Ripley's Believe It or Not 50.00
5 Boris Karloff 50.00
6 Twilight Zone 50.00
7 Believe It Or Not 50.00
8 RC,AW,Boris Karloff. 50.00
9 Twilight Zone 50.00
10 thru 13. . . . . @50.00
14 1st Xorkon. 50.00
15 thru 20 . . . . @50.00
21 thru 26 . . . . @40.00

MYSTIC
Crosgen Comics, 2000
1 RMz,BPe 6.00
2 RMz,BPe 5.00
3 RMz,BPe 4.00
4 RMz,BPe 3.25
5 RMz,BPe 3.25
6 thru 10 . . . . @3.25
11 . . . . 4.00
12 thru 43 . . . . @3.00

MYSTIC EDGE
Antarctic Press, 1998
1 F:Risa & Symattra. 3.00

NANCY & SLUGGO
Dell Publishing Co., 1957
146 B:Peanuts 150.00
147 Peanuts. 125.00
148 Peanuts. 125.00
149 Peanuts. 125.00
150 thru 161 . . . . @125.00
162 thru 165. . . . . @200.00
166 thru 176 A:OONA . . . . . . @200.00
177 thru 187 . . . . @125.00

NARCOPOLIS
Avatar Press, 2008
1	4.00
2 thru 4	4.00
1a thru 4a variant wraparound (c)	@4.00

NARWAIN PREVIEW
Narwain Publishing, 2005
Spec.	2.50
Spec. variant (c).	2.50

NASCAR HEROES
Nascar Comics, 2007
1	4.00
2	4.00
4 Nascar Villains Special	4.00
5 Mystery of Drive Z	4.00

NATIONAL VELVET
Dell Publishing Co., 1961
1 Ph(c)	150.00
2 Ph(c)	75.00

NEAT STUFF
Fantagraphics, 1986
1	4.50
2	3.00
3 thru 7	@2.50

NECESSARY EVIL
Desperado Publishing, 2007
1	4.00
2	4.00
3 thru 8	@4.00

NECROMANTRA/ LORD PUMPKIN
Malibu Ultraverse, 1995
1 A:Loki (from Marvel)	3.00
2 MiB,V:Godwheel, flipbook	3.00
3 O:Lord Pumpkin	3.00
4 Infinity Gem tie-in.	3.00
4a variant cover	3.50

NECRONOMICON
Boom! Studios, 2008
1 (of 4)	4.00
2 thru 4	@4.00

NECROPOLIS THE JUDGE DEATH INVASION
Fleetway, 1991
1 SBs(c),CE,A:Dark Judges/ Sisters Of Death	3.00
2 thru 9	@3.00

NECROSCOPE
Malibu, 1992
1 Novel adapt., holo(c)	3.25
1a 2nd printing	3.00
2 thru 4 Adapt. cont.	@3.00

Book II, Oct. 1994
1	3.00
2 thru 5	3.00

NECROWAR
Dreamwave, 2003
1 thru 4	@3.00

NEGATION
Crossgen Comics, 2001
1 MWa,PaP,F:Obregon Kaine.	3.00
2 MWa,PaP,Kaine's master-plan	3.00
3 MWa,PaP,F:Captain Fluxor	3.00
4 thru 12 PaP	@3.00

13 thru 27	@3.00
Spec. #1 Negation: Lawbringer	3.00
Prequel MWa,PaP	3.00

NEGATION WAR
Crossgen Comics, 2004
1	3.00
2 thru 6	@3.00

NEGATIVE EXPOSURE
Humanoids Publishing, 2001
1 by Enrico Mirini	3.00
2	3.00
3 thru 4	@3.00

NEIL GAIMAN'S

LADY JUSTICE
Tekno Comix (1995)
1 I:Lady Justice.	2.50
1a	6.00
2 V:Blood Pirate	2.50
3 V:Blood Pirate	2.50
4 New Story Arc	2.50
5 Street Gang War	2.50
6 Street Gang War	2.50
7 thru 11	@2.50

Big Entertainment, April, 1996
1 thru 4	@2.50
5 DIB(s).	2.50
6 DIB(s),Woman About Town, pt.1	2.50
7 DIB(s),Woman About Town, pt.2	2.50
8 DIB(s),Woman About Town, pt.3	2.50

...MR. HERO THE NEWMATIC MAN
Tekno-Comics, 1994
1 I:Mr. Hero, Tecknophage	2.50
2 A:Tecknophage	2.50
3 I:Adam Kaine.	2.50
4 I:New Body	2.50
5 Earthquake	2.50
6 I:New Character.	2.50
7 I:Deadbolt, Bloodboil	2.50
8 V:Avatar	2.50
9 in London.	2.50
10 V:Demon.	2.50
11 V:Monster	2.50
12 The Great Goward	2.50
13 thru 17	@2.50

...PHAGE
Tekno-Comics, 1996
1	2.50

...PHAGE: SHADOW DEATH
Big Entertainment, 1996
1 thru 4	@2.50
5 O:Orlando Holmes,A:Lady Messalina	2.50
6 conclusion	2.50

...TECKNOPHAGE
Teckno-Comics, 1995
1 I:Kalighoul, Tom Vietch	2.50
1a Steel Edition.	4.00
2 F:Mayor of New Yorick.	2.50
3 Phange Building.	2.50
4 Horde eevils.	2.50
5 Middle Management	2.50
6 Escape from Phange.	2.50
7 Mecca	2.50

...WHEEL OF WORLDS
Teckno-Comics, 1995
0 Deluxe Edition w/Posters.	3.00
0a I:Lady Justice.	2.50
1	3.25

NEMESIS THE WARLOCK
Eagle, 1984
1 thru 8	@2.50

NEO DAWN
Committed Comics, 2004
1 thru 3	@3.00

Neotopia #1
© Antarctic

NEOTOPIA
Antarctic Press, 2003
1 Princess for a Day	4.00
2 Philios to the Rescue.	4.00
3 thru 5	@4.00

Vol. 2
1 (of 6)	3.00
2	3.00
3	4.00
4 thru 5	@3.00

Vol. 3
1 thru 5	@3.00

Vol. 4
1	3.00
2 thru 5	@3.00

NEOZOIC
Red 5 Comics, 2007
1	3.00
2 thru 7	@3.00

NEPTUNE
Narwain Publishing, 2006
1-shot 48-pg. JP	6.00

NEUTRAL WORLD
APC, 2003
1 thru 4	@3.50

NEUTRO
Dell, 1967
1	75.00

NEW ADVENTURES OF FELIX THE CAT
Felix Comics, Inc., 1992
1 New stories	2.50
2 The Magic Paint Brush	2.50

NEW ADVENTURES OF PHANTOM BLOT, THE
Gold Key, 1964
1 Disney	100.00
2	80.00
3 thru 7	@50.00

All comics prices listed are for *Near Mint* condition.

NEW ADVENTURES OF PINOCCHIO
Dell Publishing Co., 1962
1 . . . . 150.00
2 and 3 . . . . @125.00

NEW ADVENTURES OF SPEED RACER
Now, 1993
0 Premiere, 3-D cover 2.50
1 thru 11 . . . . @2.50

NEW AMERICA
Eclipse, 1987–88
1 A:Scout 2.50
2 A:Scout 2.50
3 A:Roman Catholic Pope 2.50
4 A:Scout 2.50

NEW DNAGENTS, THE
Eclipse, 1985–87
1 R:DNAgents 2.50
2 thru 17 . . . . @2.50
3-D #1 . . . . 2.50

NEW DYNAMIX, THE
Wildstorm/DC, March, 2008
1 (of 5) 3.00
1a variant JLe (c) (1:10) 3.00
2 thru 5 . . . . @3.00
2 thru 5 variant (c)s (1:10) . . . @3.00

NEW JUSTICE MACHINE
Innovation, 1989
1 and 2 . . . . @2.50
2 . . . . 2.50

NEW KABOOM
Awesome Entertainment, 1999
1 RLe,JLb 2.50

NEW LINE CINEMA'S TALES OF HORROR
Wildstorm/DC, Sept., 2007
1 . . . . 3.00

NEWMEN
Maximum Press, 1997
1–22 see Image
23 ErS,CSp,AG,Anthem, pt.3 . . . . . . 2.50
24 ErS,CSp,AG,Anthem, pt.4 . . . . . . 2.50
25 ErS,CSp,AG,Anthem, pt.5 . . . . . . 2.50

NEW ORLEANS SAINTS
1 Playoff season(football team) . . . 6.00

NEWSTRALIA
Innovation, 1989
1 and 2 . . . . @2.50
3 . . . . 2.50

NEW TERRYTOONS
Dell Publishing Co., 1960–61
1 . . . . 100.00
2 thru 8 . . . . @60.00
Gold Key, 1962
1 F:Heckle & Jeckle 150.00
2 . . . . 125.00
3 thru 10 . . . . @50.00
11 thru 20 . . . . @40.00
21 thru 30 . . . . @25.00
31 thru 40 . . . . @20.00
41 thru 54 . . . . @15.00

NEW WAVE, THE
Eclipse, 1986–87
1 Error Pages 2.50
1a Correction 2.50
2 . . . . 2.50
3 Space Station Called Hell 2.50
4 Birth of Megabyte 2.50
5 PG(c),O:Avalon 2.50
6 O:Megabyte 2.50
7 Avalon disappears 2.50
8 V:Heap,V:Druids 2.50
9 . . . . 2.50
10 V:Heap Team 2.50
11 . . . . 2.50
12 . . . . 2.50
13 V:Volunteers 2.50
14 1/3 issue 2.50

NEW WAVE vs. THE VOLUNTEERS
Eclipse, 1987
1 3-D,V:Volunteers 2.50
2 3-D,V:Volunteers 2.50

NEXT MAN
Comico, 1985
1 I&O:Next Man 2.50
2 thru 5 . . . . @2.50

NEXT NEXUS
First, 1989
1 SR 2.50
2 SR 2.50
3 SR 2.50
4 SR 2.50

NEXUS
Capital, 1983
1 SR,I:Judah Maccabee 5.00
2 SR,Origin,V:Bellows. 4.00
3 SR,Sundra Captive 4.00
4 SR,V:Ziggurat 4.00
5 SR,I'm Bored! 4.00
6 SR,A:Badger,TrialogueTrilogy#1 . 4.00
First, 1985
7 SR,A:Badger,TrialogueTrilogy#2 . 4.00
8 SR,A:Badger,TrialogueTrilogy#3 . 3.00
9 thru 49 . . . . @2.50
50 SF,double size,A:Badger Pt.6
  Crossroads tie-in 3.50
51 thru 80 . . . . @2.50

Nexus #2
© Capital

NEXUS
Rude Dude Prod.
99 Space Opera, Act. 1 . . . . 3.00
100 Space Opera, Act 2, 48-pgs. . . . 6.00
101 Space Opera, Act. 3 . . . . 3.00
102 Space Opera, Act. 4 . . . . 3.00
1-shot Nexus' Greatest Hits (2007) . 2.00
1-shot Nexus: The Origin 4.00

NEXUS LEGENDS
First, 1989
1 thru 23 . . . . @2.50

N-GUARD
AAM Markosia, 2008
1 . . . . 3.50
2 thru 4 . . . . @3.50

NICKI SHADOW
Relentless Comics, 1997
1 by Eric Burnham & Ted Naifeh . . 2.50
2 Killing Zone, pt.2 . . . . 2.50
3 Killing Zone, pt.3 . . . . 2.50
4 Killing Zone, concl. 2.50

NIGHT & FOG
Studio 407, 2008
1 and 2 (of 4) . . . . @2.75
3 . . . . 3.50

NIGHT GLIDER
Topps, 1993
1 V:Bombast,C:Captain Glory,
  Trading Card 3.25

NIGHTHUNTER
Empire Comics, 2001
1 (of 12) 3.75
2 thru 4 . . . . @3.75

NIGHTJAR
Avatar Press, 2004
1 (of 4) 3.50
2 thru 4 . . . . @3.50
1a and 4a wraparound (c)s . . . . . @3.50

...HOLLOW BONES
Avatar Press, 2004
1 . . . . 4.00
1a wraparound (c). 4.00

NIGHT MAN, THE
Malibu Ultraverse, 1993–95
1 I:Night Man,Deathmask 2.75
1a Silver foil (c). 4.00
2 thru 15 . . . . @2.50
16 I:Bloodfly 3.50
17 thru 23 . . . . @2.50
Ann.#1 V:Pilgrim, 64pg. 4.00
Malibu Ultraverse, 1995
Infinity Night Man vs. Night Man . . . 2.50
1 Discovers New powers 2.50
1a Computer Painted Cover 2.50
2 thru 4 . . . . @2.50

NIGHT MAN/GAMBIT
Malibu, 1996
1 . . . . 2.50
2 . . . . 2.50
3 . . . . 2.50

NIGHTMARE
Innovation, 1989
1 AN 2.50

NIGHTMARE AND CASPER
Harvey Publications, 1963
1 . . . . 125.00
2 . . . . 75.00
3 thru 5 . . . . @75.00
Becomes:

CASPER AND NIGHTMARE
6 B:68 pgs. 100.00
7 . . . . 75.00
8 . . . . 75.00
9 . . . . 75.00
10 . . . . 75.00
11 thru 20 . . . . @50.00
21 thru 30 . . . . @30.00
31 . . . . 30.00
32 E:68 pgs 30.00
33 thru 45 . . . . @25.00
46 Aug., 1974 . . . . 25.00

NIGHTMARE ON ELM STREET
Blackthorne, 1991
1 thru 3 3-D . . . . @2.50

NIGHTMARE ON ELM STREET, A
Avatar Press, 2005
Spec. #1 . . . . 4.00
Spec. #1 variant (c)s 4.00
Spec. #1 glow (c) 15.00
Spec. #1 Blood Red Con (c) 5.00
Spec. #1 Painted (c) 6.00
Spec. #1 Carcass (c) 6.00
Spec. Fearbook #1 . . . . 4.00
Spec. Fearbook #1 variant (c)s . . @4.00

...PARANOID
Avatar Press, 2005
1 thru 3 . . . . @4.00
1a thru 3a wraparound (c)s . . . . @4.00
1b thru 3b variant (c)s . . . . @4.00
1c Special (c)s . . . . @6.00
1d leather (c) 15.00
2c Die-cut (c) 9.00

NIGHTMARE ON ELM STREET, A
Wildstorm/DC, Oct., 2006
1 CDi 3.00
1a variant (c) 3.00
2 CDi 3.00
3 CDi 3.00
4 CDi 3.00
5 CDi, Aztec secrets 3.00
6 CDi, Aztec Manuscript 3.00
7 CDi, Freddy vs. demon 3.00
8 CDi, Fast food and Freddy 3.00

NIGHTMARES ON ELM STREET
Innovation, 1991
1 Yours Truly, Freddy Krueger Pt.1 3.00
2 Yours Truly ,Freddy Krueger Pt.2 2.50
3 Loose Ends Pt.1,Return to
     Springwood 2.50
4 Loose Ends Pt 2 . . . . 2.50
5 . . . . 2.50
6 . . . . 2.50

NIGHTMARES
Eclipse, 1985
1 . . . . 2.50
2 . . . . 2.50

NIGHT MARY
IDW Publishing, 2005
1 . . . . 4.00
2 . . . . 4.00
3 thru 5 . . . . @4.00

NIGHT MUSIC
Eclipse, 1984–88
1 . . . . 2.50
2 . . . . 2.50
3 CR, Jungle Bear 3.00
4 Pelias & Melisande 2.50
5 Pelias 2.50
6 same as Salome #1
7 same as Red Dog #1
Graphic Novel 8.00

NIGHT OF THE LIVING DEAD
Dead Dog Comics, 2004
1 Barbara's Zombie Chronicles . . . 5.00
1a gold foil (c) 5.00
2 Barbara's Zombie Chronicles . . . 5.00
3 . . . . 5.00

NIGHT OF THE LIVING DEAD
Avatar Press, 2008
Ann. #1 40th anniversary, 40-pg. . . . 5.00
Ann. #1 variant (c)s . . . . @5.00
Ann. #1 L.A. convention edition 5.00
Ann. #1 Vows (c) 6.00
Ann. #1 Wizard World Philly edition 6.00
Ann. #1 San Diego con edition 6.00

NIGHT OF THE LIVING DEAD: BACK FROM THE GRAVE
Avatar Press, 2006
1-shot 3.00
1-shot variant (c)s . . . . @3.00
1-shot Splatter (c) 6.00
1-shot Head shot (c) 6.00
1-shot Haunting (c) 6.00
1-shot Necro-foil (c) 20.00
1-shot Sketch (c) 30.00

NIGHTSHADE
No Mercy Comics, 1997
1 by Mark Williams 2.50
2 . . . . 2.50
3 . . . . 2.50

NIGHTS INTO DREAMS
Archie Comics, 1997
1 based on Sega game 2.50
2 . . . . 2.50
3 thru 6 . . . . @2.50

NIGHT TRIBES
WildStorm/DC, 1999
1-shot Night Tribes unite 5.00

NIGHTVEIL
AC Comics, 1984
1 . . . . 3.50
2 . . . . 2.50
3 thru 7 . . . . @2.50
Spec.#1 . . . . 2.50

9 LIVES OF FELIX
Harvey, 1991
1 . . . . 2.50
2 . . . . 2.50
3 . . . . 2.50
4 . . . . 2.50

NINJA BOY
WildStorm/DC, 2001
1 Ancient Japan, 40-pg. 3.50
2 . . . . 3.00
3 . . . . 3.00
4 . . . . 3.00
5 . . . . 3.00
6 Bishamon, God of War 3.00

NINJA HIGH SCHOOL
Eternity, 1992
1 Reps.orig.N.H.S.in color 2.50
2 thru 13 reprints . . . . @2.50

NINJA HIGH SCHOOL
Antarctic Press, 2000
1 thru 74 see B&W
75 . . . . 3.00
76 Quagmire gang 3.00
77 . . . . 3.00
78 World Domination Tour 3.00
79 Dog Supreme 3.00
80 Jeremy Feeple is back 3.00
81 F:Diamond Diane 3.00
82 F:Quagmire Koalas 3.00
83 Time passes 3.00
84 Past, Present, Future 3.00
85 Time has past 3.00
86 Queen of the Conglomerate 3.00
87 Invaded by the Shallrams 3.00
88 Battle Chef battle 3.00
89 Sammie's secret 3.00
90 Earth's champion 3.00
91 The Toughest Contest 3.00
92 Round 2 . . . . 3.00
93 Round 3 . . . . 3.00
94 F:Red Ninja,V:Lendo Rivalsan . 3.00
95 Ichi in a new place 3.00
96 Dash the Impede 3.00
97 F:Asrial, Jeremy 3.00
98 Asrial found 3.00
99 F:Lendo Rivalson dies 3.00
100 F:Asrial, Jeremy, & Ichi
     BDn(c) 48-pg. 5.00
100a Fred Perry (c) 5.00
100b Robert Dejesus (c) 5.00
100c Rod Espinosa (c) 5.00
101 thru 110 . . . . @3.50
111 . . . . 3.50
112 . . . . 3.50
113 . . . . 3.50
114 . . . . 3.50
115 thru 140 . . . . @3.00

Ninja High School #93
© Antarctic Press

141 . . . . 2.50
142 thru 144 . . . . @3.00
Yearbook 2001 . . . . 4.00
Yearbook 2002 . . . . 4.00
Yearbook 2003 . . . . 5.00
Yearbook 2004 . . . . 5.00
Yearbook, 2005 . . . . 5.00
Yearbook, 2006 . . . . 4.50
Spec. Swimsuit special 2002 . . . . . . 4.50
Spec. Prom Formula (2004) B&W . . 6.00
Class Reunion Spec. (2007) 5.00

...VERSION 2
Antarctic Press, 1999
1 by Ben Dunn 6.00
2 . . . . 5.00
3 . . . . 4.00
4 . . . . 3.00
5 thru 8 . . . . @2.50
9 Yumei strikes back 2.50
10 . . . . 2.50
11 Time & space distorted 2.50
12 When Worlds Colide, last issue . 2.50

...FEATURING SPEED RACER
Eternity, 1993
1B 3.00
2B 3.00

NINJA SCROLL
Wildstorm/DC, Sept., 2006
1 Anime 3.00
1a variant JLe (c) 3.00
2 . . . . 3.00
3a, variant JLe (c). 3.00
3 . . . . 3.00
4 thru 12 . . . . @3.00

NINJAK
Valiant, 1994
0: O:Ninjak, Pt. 1 . . . . 2.50
00: O:Ninjak, Pt.2 . . . . 2.50
1 B:MMo(s),JQ,JP,Chromium(c),
   I:Dr.Silk,Webnet 3.00
1a Gold Ed 4.00
2 thru 28 . . . . @2.50
Yearbook #1, Dr. Silk 4.00
Acclaim, 1996
1 KBk(s), Denny Meechum
   becomes Ninjak 2.50
2 thru 12 KBk(s) . . . . @2.50

99, THE
Teshkeel Media, 2007
1 . . . . 3.00
2 . . . . 3.00
3 thru 7 . . . . @3.00
Ann. 2008 . . . . 4.00

N.I.O.
Acclaim, 1998
1 (of 4) by Shon Bury & JPi 2.50
2 thru 4 . . . . @2.50

NIRA X: ANIME
Entity Comics, 1997
1 BMs 3.00
1a deluxe, foil cover 3.50
2 BMs 3.00
2a deluxe, foil cover 3.50
Swimsuit #0 . . . . 2.75
Swimsuit #0 Manga (c) 2.75

NIRA X: CYBERANGEL
Entity, 1994
1 From pages of Zen 3.00
1a 2nd printing 2.75
2 V:Parradox. 2.50
3 In Hydro-Dams 2.50

Nira X: Cyberangel #3
© Entity

4 final issue 2.50
4a with computer game 7.00
Ashcan 2.50
[Series 2], 1995
1 R:Nira X 4.00
1a Clear Chromium Edition 7.00
1b Holo-Chrome edition 9.00
2 Alien Invasion. 2.50
3 Mecha New York 2.50
4 Final Issue 2.50
[Series 3], 1996
0 . . . . 2.75
0a signed & numbered 7.00
1 . . . . 2.50
1a gold edition, signed & numb. . . . 5.00
2 . . . . 2.50
3 . . . . 3.00

NIRA X/CYNDER: ENDANGERED SPECIES
Entity Comics, 1996
1 . . . . 3.00
1a gold ink enhanced, bagged . . . 11.00

NITROGEN: PROPHET
Arcade Comics, 2006
1 . . . . 4.00
1a variant (c)s . . . . @4.00

NJPW: THE RISE OF THE TIGER
Narwain Publishing, 2006
1 (of 5) 4.00
2 . . . . 4.00

NOCTURNALS
Malibu Bravura, 1995
1 DIB,I:Nocturnals. 3.00
1a Glow-in-the-Dark 4.00
2 DIB,I:Komodo, Mister Fane 3.00
3 DIB,F:Raccoon. 3.00
4 DIB,I:The Old Wolf. 3.00
5 Discovered by Police 3.00
6 DIB 3.00

NOCTURNALS: THE DARK FOREVER
Oni Press, 2001
1 by Dan Brereton 3.00
2 . . . . 3.00
3 . . . . 3.00

NO HERO
Avatar Press, 2008
0 16-pg. 1.00
0a variant wraparound (c) 1.00
0b auxiliary edition 1.00
0c San Diegao Comic con edition . 2.00
1 . . . . 4.00
1a variant wraparound (c) 4.00
2 thru 3 . . . . @4.00
2a thru 3a variant wrap(c)s . . . . . @4.00
Spec. Sketchbook B&W. 4.00

NOMAN
Tower Comics, 1966
1 GK,OW,WW,AW 150.00
2 OW,WW,A:Dynamo 100.00

NORTH WIND
Boom! Studios, 2007
1 . . . . 4.00
2 thru 5 . . . . @4.00

NO TIME FOR SERGEANTS
Dell Publishing Co., 1958
1 Ph(c) 175.00
2 Ph(c) 100.00
3 Ph(c) 100.00

NOVA HUNTER
Ryal Comics
1 thru 3 . . . . @2.50
4 Climax 2.50
5 Death and Betrayal 2.50

NUKLA
Dell, 1965
1 . . . . 75.00
2 thru 4 . . . . @50.00

NUMBER OF THE BEAST
Wildstorm/DC, April, 2008
1 (of 6) The Paladins 3.00
2 thru 8 . . . . @3.00
1a thru 2a variant (c)s (1:10) . . . @3.00

NURSES, THE
Gold Key, April, 1963
1 . . . . 75.00
2 . . . . 60.00
3 . . . . 60.00

NYOKA, JUNGLE GIRL
Charlton Comics, 1955–57
14 . . . . 150.00
15 thru 22 . . . . @125.00

NYOKA, THE JUNGLE GIRL
AC Comics, 1988
1 and 2 Further Adventures of
   Nyoka, the Jungle Girl . . . . . . @2.50

OBLIVION
Comico, 1995
1 R:The Elementals 2.50
2 I:Thunderboy, Lilith 2.50
3 I:Fen, Ferril 2.50
4 War 3.00
5 The Unholy Trilogy. 3.00

OCCULT FILES OF DR. SPEKTOR
Gold Key, April, 1973
1 I:Lakot 75.00

2 thru 5	@30.00
6 thru 10	@30.00
11 I:Spertor as Werewolf	30.00
12 and 13	@25.00
14 A:Dr. Solar	50.00
15 thru 24	@20.00

Whitman

25 rep	20.00

OCEAN
Wildstorm/DC, 2004

1 (of 6) WEI(s),CSp,KIS	3.00
2 WEI,CSp,KIS	3.00
3 WEI,CSp,KIS	3.00
4 WEI,CSp,KIS	3.00
5 WEI,CSp,KIS	3.00
6 WEI,CSp,KIS,48-pg., concl.	4.00

ODD SQUAD, THE
Devil's Due, 2008

1	3.50
1a variant (c)	3.50
2 thru 3	@3.50
2a thru 3a variant (c)s	@3.50

ODYSSEY, THE
Avatar/TidalWave Studios, 2002

1A RCz (c)	3.50
1B MMy (c)	3.50
1C Parajullo (c)	3.50
1D Murphy (c)	3.50

ODYSSEY, THE: ABSOLUTE POWER
Alias Enterprises, 2006

1-shot	5.00

OF BITTER SOULS
Speakeasy Comics, 2005

1	3.00
2 thru 3	@3.00
4 thru 6	@3.00

Vol. 2, Markosia, 2006

1	3.50
1a variant (c)s	@3.50
2 and 3	@3.50
3a variant (c)	3.50
4	3.50
4a limited variant (c)	6.00

O.G. WHIZ
Gold Key, 1971–79

1	100.00
2	60.00
3 thru 6	@50.00
7 thru 11	@40.00

OKKO: CYCLE OF EARTH
Archaia Studios, 2008

1 (of 4)	@4.00
2	4.00

OKKO: CYCLE OF WATER
Archaia Studios, 2006

1 (of 4)	4.00
2 thru 4	@4.00

OINK: BLOOD AND CIRCUS
Kitchen Sink, 1997

1 (of 4) by John Mueller	5.00
2 thru 4	@5.00

OLYMPUS HEIGHTS
IDW Publishing, 2004

1	4.00
2 thru 5	@4.00

O'MALLEY AND THE ALLEY CATS
Gold Key, 1971–74

1	45.00
2 thru 9	@40.00

OMEGA CHASE
Th3rd World Studios, 2007

1	3.50
2 thru 4	@3.50

OMEGA ONE
Big City, 2007

1 thru 4	@3.25

OMEGA ONE: ROGUE
Big City, 2008

1	3.25
2	3.25

OMEGA 7
Omega 7

1 V:Exterminator X	4.00
? by Alonzo L. Washington	4.00
0	3.00

OMEGA SAGA, THE
Southpaw Publishing, 1998

0 by Mike Gerardo & Chris Navetta	3.00
1 Episode One, pt.1	3.00
2 Episode One, pt.2	3.00

Axess Comics

3 by Mike Gerardo, Heroes (c)	3.00
3b Villains (c)	3.00

OMEN, THE
Chaos! Comics, 1998

Preview Book, BnP	2.50
1 by PNu & Justiniano	3.00
2 thru 5	@3.00
1-shot The Omen Vexed	3.00

ON A PALE HORSE
Innovation

1 Piers Anthony adapt	5.00
2 Magician,I:Kronos	5.00
3	5.00
4 VV,	5.00
5	5.00
6	5.00

On A Pale Horse #5
© Innovation

ONE-ARM SWORDSMAN
Dr. Leung's

1	3.00
2	3.00
3	2.75
4 thru 11	@2.50

100 GIRLS
Arcana Studio, 2004

1 thru 7	@3.00
1a 2nd printing	3.00

100 GIRLS/JENNA
Arcana Studio, 2006

1 (of 2)	4.00

1001 ARABIAN NIGHTS: THE ADVENTURES OF SINBAD
Zenescope Entertainment, 2008

0	1.00
1 thru 6	@3.00
7 x-over Grimm Fairy Tales	3.00
3a variant (c)	3.00

OPERATION: STORMBREAKER
Acclaim Special Event, 1997

Spec. F:Teutonic Knight	4.00

OPPOSITE FORCES
Alias Enterprises, 2005

Vol. 2

1 (of 4)	2.00
2	3.00
3	3.00
4	3.00

ORBIT
Eclipse, 1990

1 DSt(c)	4.00
2	4.00
3	5.00

ORIENTAL HEROES
Jademan, 1988–92

1 by Tony Wong & MBn	2.50
2	2.50
3 thru 13	@2.50
14 thru 40	@2.50
41 thru 44	2.00
45 thru 53	@2.50

ORIGINAL ASTRO BOY
Now, 1987

1 KSy	3.00
2 thru 17 KSy	@3.00

ORIGINAL CAPTAIN JOHNAR AND THE ALIENS
Valiant, 1995

1 Reprint from Magnus	3.00
2 Russ Manning rep.	3.00

ORIGINAL DICK TRACY
Gladestone, 1990

1 rep.V:Mrs.Pruneface	2.50
2 rep.V:Influence	2.50
3 rep.V:TheMole	2.50
4 rep.V:ItchyOliver	2.50
5 rep.V:Shoulders	2.50

COLOR PUB.

ORIGINAL DR. SOLAR MAN OF THE ATOM
Valiant, 1995
1 Reprint 3.00
2 Reprints 3.00
3 Reprints 3.00

ORIGINAL E-MAN
First, 1985
{rep. Charlton stories}
1 JSon,O:E-Man & Nova 2.50
2 JSon,V:Battery,SamuelBoar 2.50
3 JSon,City in the Sand 2.50
4 JSon,A:Brain from Sirius 2.50
5 JSon,V:T.V. Man 2.50
6 JSon,I:Teddy Q 2.50
7 JSon,Vamfire 2.50

ORIGINAL MAGNUS ROBOT FIGHTER
Valiant, 1995
1 Reprint 3.00
2 Russ Manning Art 3.00
3 Russ Manning 3.00

ORIGINAL SHIELD
Archie, 1984
1 DAy/TD,O:Shield 2.50
2 DAy,O:Dusty 2.50
3 DAy 2.50
4 DAy 2.50

ORIGINAL TUROK, SON OF STONE
Valiant, 1995
1 Reprint 3.00
2 Alberto Gioletti art 3.00
3 Alberto Gioletti 3.00
4 Reprints 3.00

ORIGIN OF THE DEFIANT UNIVERSE
Defiant, 1994
1 O:Defiant Characters 2.50

ORIGINS
Malibu Ultraverse,
1 O:Ultraverse Heroes 2.50

ORION THE HUNTER
Alias Enterprises, 2006
1 (of 4) 3.00
2 . . . . 3.00
3 . . . . 3.50
4 . . . . @3.50
Bluewater Prod., 2008
Giant #148-pg. 7.00

ORSON SCOTT CARD'S WYRMS
Dabel Brothers Prod., 2006
1 . . . . 3.00
1a variant (c) 6.00
2 thru 5 . . . . @3.00
2a thru 5a variant (c)s . . . . @6.00

OUTBREED 999
Blackout Comics, 1994
1 thru 4 . . . . @3.00
5 Search For Daige 3.00

OUTCAST SPECIAL
Valiant, 1995
1 R:The Outcast. 2.50

Outbreed #3
© Blackout Comics

OUTER LIMITS, THE
Dell Publishing Co., 1964
1 P(c) 250.00
2 thru 5 P(c) . . . . @125.00
6 thru 10 P(c) . . . . @100.00
11 thru 18 P(c) . . . . @75.00

OUTER SPACE
Charlton, 1968
1 . . . . 80.00

OUTLAW SCORN: 3030AD
Arcana Studio, 2006
1 (of 6) 4.00
2 . . . . 4.00
2a sketch (c) 15.00
3 thru 4 . . . . @3.00

OUTLAWS OF THE WEST
Charlton Comics, 1957–70
1 thru 10: CODY OF THE PONY
EXPRESS (see Golden Age section)
11 . . . . 100.00
12 . . . . 75.00
13 . . . . 75.00
14 Giant size 125.00
15 . . . . 75.00
16 . . . . 75.00
17 . . . . 75.00
18 SD 135.00
19 . . . . 60.00
20 thru 40 . . . . @60.00
41 thru 50 . . . . @40.00
51 thru 70 . . . . @25.00
71 thru 81 . . . . @20.00
Charlton, 1979
82 . . . . 150.00
83 thru 88 . . . . @100.00

OUT OF THIS WORLD
Charlton Comics, 1956–59
1 . . . . 400.00
2 . . . . 200.00
3 SD 500.00
4 SD 500.00
5 SD 500.00
6 SD 500.00
7 SD,SD(c) 550.00
8 SD 450.00
9 SD 350.00
10 SD,Perfect Forcaster 350.00

11 SD 400.00
12 SD 350.00
13 thru 15 . . . . @200.00
16 . . . . 400.00

OUTPOSTS
Blackthorne, 1997
1 thru 6 . . . . @2.50

OUT THERE
WildStorm/DC, 2001
1 HuR, Cliffhanger 2.50
2 HuR, ... 2.50
3 HuR 2.50
4 HuR 2.50
5 HuR 2.50
6 HuR 2.50
7 HuR,Road to El Dorado,pt.1 . . . 2.50
8 HuR,Road to El Dorado,pt.2 . . . 2.50
9 HuR,Road to El Dorado,pt.3 . . . 2.50
10 HuR,Road to El Dorado,pt.4 . . . 3.00
11 HuR,Road to El Dorado,pt.5 . . . 3.00
12 HuR,Road to El Dorado,pt.6 . . . 3.00
13 HuR,The War in Hell,pt.1 . . . . . 3.00
14 HuR,The War in Hell,pt.2 . . . . . 3.00
15 HuR,Draedalus's Domain 3.00
16 HuR,Dreadrealm 3.00
17 HuR,all-silent issue 3.00
18 HuR,V:Draedalus 3.00

OWL, THE
Gold Key, April, 1967
1 . . . . 125.00
2 April, 1968 . . . . 90.00

OZ/WONDERLAND CHRONICLES, THE
Buymetoys.com, 2005
0 . . . . 3.00
Preview (B&W). 3.00
1 JJu (c) 3.50
1a variant (c) 3.50
2 . . . . 3.50
2a variant (c) 3.50
3 . . . . 3.50
3a variant (c) 3.50
Spec. Jack & Cat 3.50
Spec. Jack & Cat Tales #1 . . . . . . 4.00
Spec. Jack & Cat Tales #1variant(c) 4.00

PACIFIC PRESENTS
Pacific, 1992
1 DSt,Rocketeer,(3rd App.). 12.00
2 DSt,Rocketeer,(4th App.) 9.00
3 SD,I:Vanity 2.50
4 and 5 . . . . @2.50

P.A.C.
Artifacts Inc., 1993
1 I:P.A.C. 2.50

PAINKILLER JANE
Event Comics, 1997
1 JQ(c) 3.00
1 RL(c) 3.00
1 Red foil logo, signed 20.00
2 JQ&JP(c) 3.00
2 JP&RL(c) 3.00
3 JQ&JP(c) 3.00
3a JP&RL(c) 3.00
4 JQ&JP(c) A Too Bright Place
   For Dying 3.00
4a RL&JP(c) 3.00
5 JQ&JP(c) Purgatory
   Station—Next Stop Hell 3.00
5a RL&JP(c) 3.00
6 RL&JP(c) Blood Harvest 3.00
6a BSz&JP(c) 3.00

7 Jane in the Jungle,
  pt.1,BiT&JP(c) 3.00
7a RL&JP(c) 3.00
Spec.#0 O:Painkiller Jane,48-pg. . . 4.00
Spec.#0A signed 25.00
Spec. Painkiller Jane/Hellboy
  Ancient Laughter (1998) 3.00
Spec. Painkiller Jane/Hellboy,
  signed 18.00
Spec. Painkiller Jane/The Darkness,
  signed, limited edition, JQ(c). . 25.00
D.E. (Dynamite Ent.) 2006
0 . . . . 2.50
0a variant (c) 2.50
1 JP 3.50
1a variant AH(c) 3.50
1b variant Blood Red foil (c). 15.00
1c variant wraparound (c) 9.00
2 JP. 3.50
2a variant b&w (c) 12.00
3 JP. 3.50
3a variant (c)s . . . . @3.50
5 . . . . 3.50
5a variant (c)s 3.50

...DARKCHYLDE
Event Comics, 1998
1 BAu,RQu 3.00
1a signed & numbered 25.00
1b Omnichrome edition. 12.00
1c Omnichrome, signed 25.00
1d Dynamic Forces cover 7.00

...VS. THE DARKNESS:
STRIPPER
Event Comics, 1997
1 GEn,JP,x-over, Amanda Connor
  cover 3.00
1a Greg & Tim Hildebrandt 3.00
1b MS(c) 3.00
1c JQ(c) 3.00

PAKKINS' LAND
Alias Enterprises, 2005
Vol. 2
1 . . . . 3.00
2 thru 8 . . . . @3.00

PANDEMONIUM:
DELIVERANCE
Chaos! Comics, 1998
1-shot by Jesse Leon McCann &
  Jack Jadson 3.00

PANIC
Gemstone, 1997
1 thru 12 EC Comics reprint . . . . @2.50

PANTERA
Rock-it Comix, 1994
1 . . . . 4.00
1a Gold Ed.. . . . . 20.00

PANTHA
Harris Comics, 1997
1 (of 2) MT 3.50
1 Marilyn Monroe MT alt.cov. 10.00
2 MT alternate (c) 10.00
2 photo (c). 10.00

PARA
Pennyfarthing Press, 2004
1 . . . . 3.00
2 thru 6 . . . . @3.00

PARADISE
Twenty First Century, 2000
1 thru 7 . . . . @3.00

Paradox #3
© Arcana Studio

PARADOX
Arcana Studio, 2005
1 (of 4) 3.00
2 . . . . 3.00
3 . . . . 3.00

PARAGON
DARK APOCALYPSE
AC, 1993
1 thru 4, Fem Force crossover . . @3.00

PARANOIA
Adventure Comics, 1991
1 (based on video game) Clone1 . . 3.25
2 King-R-Thr-2 . . . . 3.00
3 R:Happy Jack,V:N3F 3.00
4 V:The Computer 3.00
5 V:The Computer 3.00
6 V:Lance-R-Lot,last issue 3.00

PARIAH
Revolution Comics, 2006
1 . . . . 3.00
2 thru 4 . . . . @3.00
4a variant (c) 3.00

PARTRIDGE FAMILY, THE
Charlton Comics, 1971–73
1 . . . . 125.00
2 thru 4 . . . . @60.00
5 Summer Special 125.00
6 thru 21 . . . . @50.00

PASSOVER
Maximum Press, 1996
1 (of 2) BNa 3.00
2 BNa,A:Avengelyne. 3.00

PATH, THE
Crossgen Comics, 2002
1 RMz,BS 5.00
2 thru 4 RMz,BS . . . . @3.00
9 thru 23 . . . . @3.00
Prequel 48-pg. 5.00

PATHWAYS TO
FANTASY
Pacific, 1984
1 BS,JJ art 3.00

PATRICIA BRIGGS'
MERCY THOMPSON:
HOMECOMING
Dabel Brothers Prod., 2008
1 (of 4) 4.00

PATRIOTS, THE
WildStorm/DC, 1999
1 BCi&JPe(s) 2.50
2 BCi&JPe(s) 2.50
3 thru 7 BCi&JPe(s) . . . . @2.50
8 BCi&JPe(s),V:Stealthers 2.50
9 BCi&JPe(s) 2.50
10 JPe(s),final issue 2.50

PAT SAVAGE:
WOMAN OF BRONZE
Millennium, 1992
1 F:Doc Savage's cousin 2.50

PEACEKEEPER
Future Comics, 2003
1 . . . . 3.00
2 thru 5 . . . . @3.00

PEACEMAKER
Charlton, 1967
1 A:Fightin' 5 . . . . 5.00
2 A:Fightin' 5 . . . . 3.00
3 A:Fightin' 5 . . . . 3.00
4 O:Peacemaker,A:Fightin' 5 . . . . 4.00
5 A:Fightin' 5 . . . . 2.50

PEANUTS
Dell Publishing Co., 1958
1 . . . . 300.00
2 . . . . 300.00
3 . . . . 250.00
4 . . . . 200.00
5 thru 13 . . . . @175.00
Gold Key, 1963
1 . . . . 225.00
2 thru 4 . . . . @175.00

PEARL HARBOR
Antarctic Press, 2001
1 by Ted Nomura, Movie tie-in 4.00
2 movie tie-in, concl. 4.00
Spec. 60th Anniv. spec., 64-pg. . . . 13.00
Spec. 60th Anniv., Japanese (c) . . 13.00

PEBBLES &
BAMM-BAMM
Charlton Comics, 1972–76
1 . . . . 100.00
2 thru 10 . . . . @50.00
11 thru 36 . . . . @45.00

PEBBLES FLINTSTONE
Gold Key, 1963
1 A Chip off the old block 175.00

PENNY AND AGGIE
Alias Enterprises, 2005
1 . . . . 3.00
2 . . . . 3.00
3 . . . . 3.00
4 . . . . 3.00

PERFECT DARK:
JANUS' TEARS
Prima Publishing, 2006
1 . . . . 3.50
2 thru 3 . . . . @3.50
4 thru 6 . . . . @3.50

COLOR PUB.

PERFECT DARK ZERO
Prima Publishing, 2006
1 (of 6) 3.50

PERG
Lightning Comics, 1993
1 Glow in the dark(c),JS(c),
  B:JZy(s),KIK,I:Perg 3.75
1a Platinum Ed. 5.00
1b Gold Ed. 7.00
1 gold edition, glow-in-the-dark
  flip cover 25.00
2 KIK,O:Perg. 3.25
2a Platinum Ed. 5.00
3 Flip Book (c). 3.25
3a Platinum Ed. 5.00
4 TLw,I:Hellina 9.00
4a Platinum Ed 5.00
5 A:Hellina. 3.25
6 PIA,A:Hellina 3.25
7 .... 3.00
8 V:Police 3.00

PERRY MASON
MYSTERY MAGAZINE
Dell Publishing Co., 1964
1 .... 150.00
2 Ray Burr Ph(c). 100.00

PETER PAN: RETURN
TO NEVERNEVER LAND
Adventure
1 Peter in Mass. 2.50
2 V:Tiger Lily. 2.50

PETER POTAMUS
Gold Key, 1965
1 .... 175.00

PETTICOAT JUNCTION
Dell Publishing Co., 1964
1 Ph(c) 150.00
2 Ph(c) 100.00
3 Ph(c) 100.00
4 .... 100.00
5 Ph(c) 100.00

PHANTOM, THE
Gold Key, 1962
1 RsM 300.00
2 B:King, Queen & Jack 200.00
3 .... 150.00
4 .... 150.00
5 .... 150.00
6 .... 150.00
7 The Super Apes. 150.00
8 .... 150.00
9 .... 150.00
10 The Sleeping Giant. 150.00
11 E:King,Queen and Jack 125.00
12 B:Track Hunter 125.00
13 .... 125.00
14 The Historian 125.00
15 .... 125.00
16 .... 125.00
17 Samaris. 125.00
King Comics, 1966
18 The Treasure of the Skull
  Cave;BU:Flash Gordon 100.00
19 The Astronaut & the Pirates ... 75.00
20 A:GirlPhantom,E:FlashGordon . 75.00
21 BU:Mandrake 75.00
22 Secret of Magic Mountain. ... 75.00
23 .... 75.00
24 A:Girl Phantom 75.00
25 .... 60.00
26 .... 60.00
27 .... 60.00

The Phantom #22
© *King Comics*

28 .... 60.00
29 *never published*
Charlton Comics, 1969–77
30 .... 50.00
31 JAp,Phantom of Shang-Ri-La . . 50.00
32 JAp,The Pharaoh Phantom ... 50.00
33 The Jungle People 50.00
34 thru 39. .... @45.00
40 The Ritual 45.00
41 thru 43 .... @35.00
44 To Right A Wrong 35.00
45 .... 35.00
46 I:Piranha 30.00
47 thru 72. .... @30.00
73 .... 25.00
74 .... 30.00

PHANTOM
Wolf Publishing, 1992
1 Drug Runners 2.50
2 Mystery Child of the Sea 2.50
3 inc.feature pages on
  Phantom/Merchandise. 2.50
4 TV Jungle Crime Buster 2.50
5 Castle Vacula-Transylvania 2.50
6 The Old West. 2.50
7 Sercet of Colussus 2.75
8 Temple of the Sun God 2.75

PHANTOM, THE
Moonstone, 2002
1 CDi. 3.50
2 thru 8 .... @3.50
9 thru 13 .... @3.50
14 thru 20 .... @3.50
12a Limited ed. (c). 4.50
17a thru 19a limited ed ...... @4.50
21 thru 24 .... @3.50
25 48-pg. 6.00
26 .... 4.00
26a variant (c) 4.00
Ann. #1 .... 6.50
Ann. #1 Limited Ed. 9.00
Ann. #2 .... 6.00
Ann. #2A variant Noir (c) 9.00

PHANTOM BOLT, THE
Gold Key, 1964–66
1 A:Mr X 125.00
2 Super Goof 100.00
3 thru 7 .... @75.00

PHANTOM FORCE
Genesis West, 1994
Previously: Image
0 JK/JLe(c). 3.00
3 thru 10 .... @3.00

PHANTOM JACK: THE
NOWHERE MAN AGENDA
Speakeasy Comics, 2006
1 .... 3.00
2 thru 3 .... @3.00

PHAZE
Eclipse, 1988
1 BSz(c),Takes place in future 2.50
2 PG(c),V:The Pentagon. 2.50
3 Schwieger Vs. Mammoth. 2.50

PHOENIX
Atlas, 1975
1 thru 4 .... @20.00

PHOENIX RESURRECTION
Malibu Ultraverse, 1995–96
0 Intro to Phoenix Resurrection ... 2.50
Genesis, A:X-Men 4.00
Revelations, A:X-Men 4.00
Aftermath, A:X-Men 4.00

PIERCE
Imperium Comics, 2006
1 .... 3.00
2 thru 4 .... @3.00

PINK PANTHER, THE
Gold Key, April 1971
1 .... 100.00
2 thru 10 .... @75.00
11 thru 30 .... @50.00
31 thru 74. .... @30.00
75 thru 80 .... @50.00
81 thru 87. .... @35.00

PIRACY
Gemstone, 1998
1 EC comics reprint 2.50
2 thru 7 EC comics reprints .... @2.50

PIRATE CORP.
Eternity
1 thru 5 .... @2.50

PIRATES VS. NINJAS II:
UP THE ANTE
Antarctic Press, 2007
1 .... 3.50
1a variant (c) 3.50
2 thru 8 .... @3.50

PIRATE TALES
Boom! Studios, 2006
1 .... 7.00

P.I.'S, THE
First, 1985
1 JSon,Ms.Tree,M Mauser 2.50
2 JSon,Ms.Tree,M Mauser 2.50
3 JSon,Ms.Tree,M Mauser 2.50

PISTOLFIST
Bluewater Prod., 2008
1 (of 4) 3.50
2 thru 4 .... @4.00

PISTOLFIST: REVOLUTIONARY WARRIOR
Alias Enterprises, 2006
1 (of 4)	3.50
2	3.50
3 thru 4	@3.50

PITT
Full Bleed Studios, 1996
1 thru 9, see Image
10 thru 14 DK	@2.50
14a variant cover	7.00
15 DK	2.50
16 DK, Ugly Americans, pt.1	2.50
17 DK, Ugly Americans, pt.2	2.50
18 DK, Ugly Americans, pt.3, concl.	2.50
19 by Brian Dawson	3.00
20 DK, Urgral Thul	2.50
Spec. In the Blood	2.50

PITT CREW
Full Bleed Studios, 1998
1 Monster	2.50
2 F:Rai-Kee	2.50
3 Tyrants	2.50
4 The Slayer	2.50
5	2.50

PITT: BIOGENESIS
Full Bleed Studios, 2000
1 (of 3) DK	2.50
2 DK	2.50

PIXIE AND DIXIE AND MR. JENKS
Gold Key, 1963
1	100.00

PLAGUE OF THE LIVING DEAD
Avatar Press, 2007
Spec. #1 40-pgs.	5.00
Spec. #1 variant (c)s	5.00
1	2.50
1a variant (c)s	@3.00
2 thru 6	@2.50
2a thru 6a variant (c)s	@3.00

PLANETARY
WildStorm/DC, 1999
1 WEI	9.00
2 thru 12 WEI	@5.00
13 WEI,secret history of Elijah Snow	4.00
14 WEI,The Four vs. Planetary	4.00
15 WEI,in Australia	4.00
16 WEI	4.00
17 WEI Elijah Snow's past	3.00
18 WEI,The Gun Club	3.00
19 WEI,Mystery in Space	3.00
20 WEI,Mystery in Space,pt.2	3.00
21 WEI	3.00
22 WEI(s),Torture of William Leather	3.00
23 WEI(s),F.The Drummer	3.00
24 WEI(s),Dark Secrets	3.00
25 WEI(s),A Trap for the Four	3.00
26 WEI(s)	3.00

PLAN 9 FROM OUTER SPACE
Malibu
GNv Movie Adapt.	5.00

PLANETARY BRIGADE
Boom! Studios, 2006
1	3.00
2	3.00

PLANETARY BRIGADE: ORIGINS
Boom! Studios, 2006
1 Old School (c)	4.00
1a New School (c)	4.00
2	4.00
3	4.00

PLANET COMICS
Blackthorne, 1988
1 DSt(c)	3.00
2	3.00
3	3.00
4	3.00

Planet of Vampires #2
© Atlas Comics

PLANET OF VAMPIRES
Atlas, Feb.–July, 1975
1 NA(c),1st PB	25.00
2 NA(c)	25.00
3 RH	25.00

POGROM
Devil's Due, 2008
1 (of 7) 48-pg.	5.50
2 thru 4	@3.50

POGZ N SLAMMER
Blackout Comics, 1995
1 I:Pogz N Slammer	2.50
2 Contact Other Schools	2.50

POINT BLANK
WildStorm/DC, 2002
Eye of the Storm
1 (of 5) CWi, super-hero noir	3.00
2 CWi	3.00
3 CWi,F:Jack Hawksmoor	3.00
4 CWi	3.00
5 CWi,concl.	3.00

POISON ELVES
Sirius Entertainment, 1998
Color Special #1 by Drew Hayes	3.00
Color Spec.#1 limited	10.00

POIZON
London Night Studios, 1995
0	3.00
0 signed gothchik edition	9.00
? O:Poizon	3.00
?a Commemorative (1999)	6.00
1 and 2 EHr.	@3.00
1a signed	7.00

POIZON: CADILLACS AND GREEN TOMATOES
London Night, 1997
2 thru 3	@3.00
6 deluxe	5.00

POIZON: DEMON HUNTER
London Night, 1998
1	3.00
1 Green Death edition	12.00

POIZON: LOST CHILD
London Night Studios, 1996
0	3.00
1 mini series	3.00
1 signed	9.00
1 Green Death edition	12.00
2 thru 3	@3.00

POKEMAN TALES:
Viz Communications, 1999
1 thru 16 boardbooks	@5.00
Gift Set Vol. 1	20.00
Gift Set Vol. 2	20.00
Movie Spec.	5.00

POKEMAN THE MOVIE 2000: REVELATION LUGIA
Viz Communications, 2000
1	4.00
2 & 3	@4.00
Spec. Pikachu's Rescue Adventure	4.00
Art of Pokeman The Movie 2000	10.00

POKEMAN: THE FIRST MOVIE
Viz Communications, 1999
1 (of 4) Mewtwo Strikes Back	4.00
2	4.00
3	4.00
4 conclusion	4.00
Spec. Pikachu's Vacation	4.00
Art of Pokeman: First Movie	9.00

POPEYE
Gold Key, 1962
1-65 See Golden Age Section
66	125.00
67	100.00
68 thru 80	@75.00

King Comics, 1966
81 thru 92	@60.00

Charlton, 1969
94 thru 99	@60.00
100	75.00
101 thru 138	@35.00

Gold Key, 1978
139 thru 143	@25.00
144 50th Aniv. Spec.	30.00
155	@25.00

Whitman, 1980
156 thru 157	@25.00
158 thru 159	@35.00
162 thru 168	@25.00
169 thru 171	@30.00

POPEYE
Harvey Comics, 1993–94
1 thru 7 . . . . @2.50
Summer Spec.#1 . . . . 2.50

POPEYE SPECIAL
Ocean, 1987–88
1 & 2 . . . . @2.50

Porky Pig #98
© Walt Disney

PORKY PIG
Gold Key, 1965
1 . . . . 75.00
2 thru 10 . . . . @40.00
11 thru 30 . . . . @25.00
31 thru 55 . . . . @20.00
56 thru 70 . . . . @15.00
71 thru 93 . . . . @10.00
Whitman, 1979
94 thru 96 . . . . @12.00
97 scarce 50.00
98 thru 109 . . . . @12.00

POSSESSED, THE
Wildstorm/DC July, 2003
1 (of 6) LSh,demons 3.00
2 thru 5 LSh,demon-infested. . . . @3.00
6 LSh,concl. 3.00

POTTER'S FIELD
Boom! Studios, 2007
1 (of 3) 4.00
2 thru 3 . . . . @4.00

POWER & GLORY
Malibu Bravura, 1994
1A HC(a&s),I:American
  Powerhouse. 3.00
1B alternate cover. 3.00
1c Blue Foil (c) 5.00
1d w/seirgraph 5.00
1e Newsstand 3.00
2 HC(a&s), O:American
  Powerhouse. 2.75
3 HC(a&s). 2.50
4 HC(a&s). 2.50
Winter Special 3.00

POWER AND THE GLORY, THE
Narwain Publishing, 2005
1 . . . . 7.50

POWER FACTOR
Wonder Color Comics, 1986
1 . . . . 4.00
2 thru 3 . . . . @3.00

POWER FACTOR
Innovation, 1990
1 thru 4 . . . . @2.50

POWERKNIGHTS
Amara, 1995
P I:Powerknights 2.50

POWERMARK
Quest Ministries International, 2004
1 The Mission 3.00
2 Wake of Leviathan 3.00
3 Under Fire 3.00
4 Betrayal 3.00
5 Face Off. 3.00
6 They All Fall Down 3.00
7 High & Mighty 3.00

POWER OF PRIME
Malibu Ultraverse, 1995
1 O:Prime Powers,Godwheel tie-in 2.50
2 V:Doc Gross, Godwheel tie-in . . 2.50
3 F:Prime Phade. 2.50
4 F:Elven,Turbocharge 2.50

POWER OF THE VALKYRIE
Arcana Studio, 2006
1 . . . . 4.00
2 . . . . 4.00

POWER RANGERS ZEO/YOUNGBLOOD
Maximum Press, 1997
1 TNu,NRd 3.00

POWERS THAT BE
Broadway Comics
Preview Editions, 1995
1 thru 3 B&W. . . . . @2.50
Regular Series, 1995
1 JiS,I:Fatale, Star Seed. 3.00
2 . . . . 3.00
3 . . . . 3.00
4 . . . . 3.00
5 It's the End of the World As We
  Know It,pt.1 . . . . 3.00
6 End/World As We Know It,pt.2 . . 3.00
Becomes:

STAR SEED
7 End/World As We Know It,pt.3 . . 3.00
8 End/World As We Know It,pt.4 . . 3.00
9 End/World As We Know It,pt.5 . . 3.00
10 End/World As We Know It,pt.6. . 3.00
11 End/World As We Know It,pt.7. . 3.00

PRESIDENTIAL MATERIAL
IDW, 2008
Barack Obama 4.00
John McCain 4.00
Flipbook 8.00

PRIEST
Maximum Press, 1996
1 RLd, F:Michael O'Bannon 3.00
2 RLd,BNa, ... 3.00
3 RLd 3.00

PRIMAL RAGE
Sirius, 1996
1 TAr,from video game 3.00
1 foil cover, limited edition 3.00
2 TAr,DOe(c). 3.00

PRIME
Malibu Ultraverse, 1993–95
1 B:GJ(s),I:Prime 4.00
1a Ultra-Limited 5.00
1b Full Hologram (c). 5.00
2 V:Organism 8, with Ultraverse
  card 3.00
3 NBy,I:Prototype 3.00
4 NBy,V:Prototype. 3.00
5 NBy,BWS,I:Maxi-Man, BU:Rune . 3.00
6 NBy,A:Pres. Clinton 2.75
7 thru 11 . . . . @2.50
12 NBy,(Ultraverse Premiere#3)
  I:Planet Class 3.50
13 NBy,V:Kutt,Planet Class 3.00
14 thru 26 . . . . @2.50
Ashcan (first) 7.00
Ashcan #1 BV(c),B&W. 2.00
Ann.#1 R:Doc Gross 4.00

PRIME
Malibu Ultraverse, 1995–96
Infinty I:Spider-Prime 3.00
1 Spider-Prime vs. Lizard 2.50
1a Computer painted cover 2.50
2 thru 8 . . . . @2.00
9 and 10 . . . . @2.00
11 thru 15 . . . . @2.50

PRIME/CAPTAIN AMERICA
Malibu Ultraverse, 1996
1 GJ,NBy 4.00

PRIME VS. HULK
Malibu, 1995
0 . . . . 9.00
0a signed premium edition 12.00

PRIMER
Comico, 1982–84
1 . . . . 15.00
2 I:Grendel 95.00
3 . . . . 9.00
4 C:Maxx. 9.00
5 I:Maxx 50.00
6 I:Evangelyne 18.00
[Volume 2], 1996
1 F:Lady Bathory 3.00

PRIMORDIA
Archaia Studios, 2007
1 . . . . 4.00
2 . . . . 4.00
3 . . . . 4.00

PRIMUS
Charlton Comics, 1972
1 . . . . 25.00
2 thru 5 . . . . @15.00
6 thru 7 . . . . @12.00

PRINCE OF HEROES
Antarctic Press, 2008
1 (of 3) by Rod Espinosa 3.50
2 thru 3 . . . . @3.50

PRINCESS SALLY
Archie Comics, 1995
1 Sonic tie-in. 3.00
2 . . . . 3.00
3 . . . . 3.00

All comics prices listed are for *Near Mint* condition.

PRINCE VANDAL
Triumphant
1 JnR(s),	2.50
2 JnR(s),	2.50
3 JnR(s),ShG,I:Claire,V:Nicket, Vandal goes to Boviden.	2.50
4 JnR(s),ShG,Game's End	2.50
5 JnR(s),ShG,The Sickness, the rat appears	2.50
6 JnR(s),ShG,B:Gothic	2.50

PRIORITY: WHITE HEAT
AC Comics, 1986
1 thru 2 miniseries.	@2.50

PRISTEEN 16
IDW, 2008
1	4.00
2	4.00

PROFESSIONAL: GOGOL 13
Viz
1	5.00
2	5.00
3	5.00

PROFESSOR COFFIN
Charlton, 1985
19 From Midnight Tales	10.00
20 thru 21	@10.00

PROFESSOR OM
Innovation, 1990
1 I:Rock Warrior	2.50
2 Samurai Drama	2.50

PROGRAMME, THE
Wildstorm/DC, July, 2007
1 (of 12) PrM(s)	3.00
1a variant (c) (1:10)	3.00
2 thru 4 PrM(s)	@3.00
5 PrM(s)	3.00
6 PrM(s)	3.00
7 PrM(s), Russian Dolls	3.00
8 PrM(s), Soviet super-humans	3.00
9 PrM(s), Race War in the South	3.00
10 PrM(s), Race War	3.00
11 PrM(s), Max a superman	3.00
12 PrM(s),conclusion	3.00

PROJECT A-KO 0
Antarctic Press, 1994
0 digest size	5.00

Malibu, 1994
1 thru 4 Based on anime movie	@3.00

PROJECT A-KO 2
CPM, 1995
1 Space Saga	3.00
2 Space Saga	3.00
3 Queen Margarita	3.00

PROJECT A-KO: VERSUS THE UNIVERSE
CPM, 1995
1 Based on Animation	3.00
2 strange magician	3.00
3	3.00
4 (of 5) TEI	3.00

PROJECT EON
Speakeasy Comics, 2005
1 (of 2)	6.00

Mar kosia, 2006
1	5.00
2 thru 3	@3.50

PROJECT: KALKI
Virgin Comics 2008
1 (of 4)	3.00
2 thru 4	@3.00

PROJECT SUPERPOWERS
Dynamite Entertainment, 2007
0 AxR	1.00
0 variant AxR(c)	1.00
1 (of 7)	3.50
1a variant (c)	3.50
2 thru 7	@3.50
2a thru 5a variant (c)	@3.50
Vol. 2
Prelude	1.00

PROMETHEA
WildStorm/DC, 1999
America's Best Comics
1 AMo(s),F:Sophie Bangs,40-pg.	3.50
2 AMo(s),Judgment of Solomon	3.00
3 AMo(s),Misty Magic Land	3.00
4 AMo(s),CV,JWi.	3.00
5 AMo(s),JWi,F:WW1	3.00
6 AMo(s),JWi,F:Grace Brannagh	3.00
7 AMo(s),JWi,F:Sophie Bangs	3.00
8 AMo(s),JWi,V:Goetic demons	3.00
9 AMo(s),JWi,The Temple.	3.00
10 AMo(s),JWi,Sex, Stars and Serpents	3.00
11 AMo(s),JWi,giant monster	3.00
12 AMo(s),JWi,flip-book	3.00
13 AMo(s),JWi,	3.00
14 AMo(s),JWi, Lunar Realm.	3.00
15 AMo(s),JWi,	3.00
16 AMo(s),JWi,Five Swell Guys.	3.00
17 AMo(s),JWi,Stacia vs. Hell	3.00
18 AMo(s),JWi,double demonic	3.00
19 AMo(s),JWi,Tree of Life	3.00
20 AMo(s),JWi,edge of existence	3.00
21 AMo(s),JWi,Binah	3.00
22 AMo(s),JWi,Jack Foust	3.00
23 AMo(s),JWi,40-pg.	3.50
24 AMo(s),JWi	3.00
25 AMo(s),JWi,A Higher Court.	3.00
26 AMo(s),JWi,Later	3.00
27 AMo(s),JWi,Tom Strong	3.00
28 AMo(s),JWi,Jack Faust	3.00
29 AMo(s),JWi	3.00
30 AMo(s),JWi,Painted Doll	3.00
31 AMo(s),JWi	3.00
32 AMo(s),JWi, final issue	4.00
32a variant edition, on posters, plus signed book	50.00

PROPHECY
Immortelle Studios, 1998
1 by Hawk, Lovalle, & Wong, F:Cynder & War Dragon	3.00
2	3.00

PROPHECY OF THE SOUL SORCERER
Arcane Comics, 1999
1 (of 4) by Eric Dean Seaton	3.00
2	3.00
3	3.00
4	3.00
5	3.00
6 Nighthawk vs. Morbid	3.00
3a thru 6a variant (c)s	@3.00
7	3.00

PROPHET II
Awesome Entertainment, 1999
1	3.00
1a holochrome wraparound (c).	12.00

PROPHET: LEGACY
Awesome Entertainment, 1999
1 RLe	3.00
2	3.00
2a variant (c).	3.00
3	3.00

PROPHET/CABLE
Maximum, 1997
1 (of 2) RLd x-over	3.50
2 RLd x-over,A:Domino, Kirby, Blaquesmith.	3.50

PROPHET OF DREAMS
Broken Tree Publications, 2002
1 (of 6) by Lawler & Vasquez	3.50
2 thru 6	@3.00

Protectors #12
© Malibu

PROTECTORS
Malibu, 1992–94
1 I:Protectors, inc. JBi poster (direct)	3.00
1a thru 12a Newsstand	@2.50
2 thru 20	@2.50
Protectors Handbook	2.50

PROTOTYPE
Malibu Ultraverse, 1993–95
1 V:Ultra-Tech,w/card	2.50
1a Ultra-lim. silver foil(c)	5.00
1b Hologram	6.00
2 thru 18	@2.50
G-Size, Hostile Takeover	2.50
Spec.#0 LeS,JQ/JP(c)	2.50

PROTOTYPE: TURF WAR
Malibu Ultraverse,
1 LeS,V:Techuza.	2.50
2 LeS,F:Ranger,Arena	2.50
3	2.50

PROWLER
Eclipse, 1987
1 I:Prowler.	2.50
2 GN,A:Original Prowler	2.50
3 GN	2.50
4 GN	2.50
5 GN, adaption of Vampire Bat.	2.50
6 w/flexi-disk record	2.50

COLOR PUB.

PROWLER IN 'WHITE ZOMBIE', THE
Eclipse, 1988
1 . . . . 2.50

PRUDENCE & CAUTION
Defiant, 1994
1 CCl(s) 4.00
2 thru 5 CCl(s) . . . . @2.50
1a Spanish Version 3.25
2a thru 5a Spanish Version . . . . . @2.50

PSI-LORDS: REIGN OF THE STARWATCHERS
Valiant, 1994
1 MLe,DG,Chromium(c),Valiant
  Vision,V:Spider Aliens 3.00
2 MLe,DG,V:Spider Aliens 2.50
3 MLe,DG,Chaos Effect-Epsilon#2,
  A:Solar 2.50
becomes:

PSI-LORDS
4 V:Ravenrok 2.50
5 V:Ravenrok 2.50
6 . . . . 2.50
7 Micro-Invasion 2.50
8 A:Solar the Destroyer 2.50
9 Frozen Harbingers 2.50
10 F:Ravenrok 2.50

PSYCHO
Innovation
1 Hitchcock movie adapt 2.50
2 & 3 continued . . . . @2.50

PSYCHOANALYSIS
Gemstone, 1999
1 (of 4) 2.50
2 thru 3 . . . . @2.50

PSYCHOBLAST
First, 1987
1 thru 9 . . . . @2.50

PUBLIC ENEMY
American Mule Ent., 2006
0 . . . . 3.00
1 . . . . 4.00
2 thru 5 . . . . @3.00

PUDGY PIG
Charlton Comics, 1958
1 . . . . 100.00
2 . . . . 75.00

PUNCTURE
Com.X, 2001
1 (of 12) by R. Uttley & B.Oliver . . . 3.00
2 thru 4 . . . . @3.00
3 thru 6 . . . . @4.00

PUNX
Windjammer, 1995
1 KG,I:Punx 2.50
2 KG,A:Harbinger 2.50
3 KG,F:P.M.S 2.50
4 KG,final issue 2.50
Spec.#1 . . . . 2.50

PUPPET MASTER
Eternity
1 Movie Adapt.Andre Toulon 2.50
2 Puppets Protecting Diary 2.50
3 R:Andre Toulon 2.50
4 . . . . 2.50

PUPPET MASTER: CHILDREN OF THE PUPPET MASTER
Eternity
1 Killer Puppets on the loose 2.50
2 concl. 2.50

Purgatori #1
© Chaos! Comics

PURGATORI
Chaos! Comics, 1998
1 DQ from slave to Goddess? 3.00
2 Goddess War,pt.1, x-over 3.00
3 Goddess War, epilog 3.00
4 Unholy Nights 3.00
5 V:Karmilla 3.00
6 . . . . 3.00
7 V:Dracula 3.00
1-shot prelude 3.00
1-shot signed, limited + print 15.00
Coll. Vol.1 thru Vol. 4 . . . . @6.00

Chaos! Comics, 2000
1/2 . . . . 3.00
1/2 premium edition, tattoo(c) 9.00
1/2 chromium (c) 12.00
1/2 chromium signed 15.00
1/2 Ashcan 7.00
0 . . . . 3.00
0 premium edition 9.00
0 Ashcan 7.00

...DARKEST HOUR
Chaos! Comics, 2001
1 . . . . 3.00
1a premium ed. RCl(c) 9.00
2 . . . . 3.00
2a variant (c) 7.50

...THE DRACULA GAMBIT
Chaos! Comics, 1997
1 DQ & Brian LeBlanc 3.00
1a signed 15.00
1b premium 9.00
Sketchbook, b&w 3.50

...EMPIRE
Chaos! Comics, 2000
1 (of 3) 3.00
1a premium 9.00
1b Comic Legal Defense
  Fund ed. 9.00
2 thru 3 . . . . @3.00
Preview Book B&W 5.00

...GODDESS RISING
Chaos! Comics, 1999
1 (of 4) MD2 . . . . 3.00
1a premium edition 9.00
2 thru 4 . . . . @3.00
Preview Book B&W 5.00

...GOD HUNTER
Chaos! Comics, 2002
Ashcan b&w 6.00
1 (of 2) 3.00
1a premium edition 9.00
2 . . . . 3.00
2a variant Rio & Broeker (c) 7.50

...GOD KILLER
Chaos! Comics, 2002
1 (of 2) 3.00
1a premium edition 9.00
2 . . . . 3.00
2a variant (c) 7.50

...HEARTBREAKER
Chaos! Comics, 2002
1 . . . . 3.00
1a premium edition 9.00
1b super premium edition 20.00
1c MegaCon foil edition 25.00

...LOVE BITES
Chaos! Comics, 2001
1 . . . . 3.00
1 premium edition 9.00
Ashcan 6.00

...MISCHIEF NIGHT
Chaos! Comics, 2001
1 . . . . 3.00
1a premium edition 12.00
1b super premium edition 15.00

...THE HUNTED
Chaos! Comics, 2001
1 . . . . 3.00
1a premium edition 9.00
2 . . . . 3.00
2a variant (c) 7.50
Ashcan 6.00

...RAVENOUS
Chaos! Comics, 2002
Ashcan b&w 6.00
1 (of 2) 3.00
1a premium edition 9.00

...RE-IMAGINED
Chaos! Comics, 2002
1 Salem witch trials 3.00
1a premium edition 9.00
1b super premium edition 15.00
Ashcan Purgatori re-imagined . . . 6.00

...SANCTIFIED
Chaos! Comics, 2002
1 BnP 3.00
1 premium edition 9.00

...TRICK OR TREAT
Chaos! Comics, 2002
1 . . . . 3.00
1a premium edition 9.00
1b super premium edition 20.00

...THE VAMPIRES MYTH
Chaos! Comics, 1996
1 (of 3) 4.00
1-shot limited chromium edition . . 15.00
2 BnP,JBa 3.00
3 BnP,JBa, final issue 3.00

...VS. CHASTITY
Chaos! Comics, 2000
1 Alpha ending 3.00
1a Omega ending 3.00
1b deluxe 10.00

...VS. LADY DEATH
Chaos! Comics, 2000
1 .... 3.00
1a premium edition 9.00
Ashcan B&W 7.00

...VS. VAMPIRELLA
Chaos! Comics, 2000
1 .... 3.00
1 premium 9.00

PURGATORI
Devil's Due Publishing, 2005
1 .... 3.00
2 .... 3.00
3 thru 6 .... @3.00

PUSH
Wildstorm/DC, Nov., 2008
1 (of 6) Movie tie-in 3.50
2 .... 3.50

QUANTUM & WOODY
Acclaim, 1997
1 CPr(s),MBr Woodrow Van
    Chelton & Eric Henderson
    become unlikely superheros ... 4.00
1a Variant (c) 5.00
2 CPr(s),MBr,World's worst
    superhero team 3.00
3 CPr(s),MBr,Woody buys a goat .. 3.00
4 CPr(s),MBr. 3.00
5 thru 10 CPr(s) .... @2.75
11 thru 17 CPr(s) .... @2.50
18 thru 27 .... @2.50

QUANTUM LEAP
Innovation, 1991
{based on TV series}
1 1968 Memphis 3.50
1a Special Edition 2.50
2 Ohio 1962,Freedom of
    the Press 3.00
3 1958, The $50,000 Quest 3.00
4 Small Miracles 2.50
5 .... 2.50
6 .... 2.50
7 Golf Pro,School Bus Driver 2.50
8 1958,Bank Robber 2.50
9 NY 1969,Gay Rights 2.50
10 1960s' Stand-up Comic 2.50
11 1959,Dr.(LSD experiments) 2.50
12 .... 2.50
Acclaim, 1997
1 BML(s),Into the Void, pt.1 ..... 2.50
2 BML(s),Into the Void, pt.2 ..... 2.50
3 BML(s),Into the Void, pt.3 ..... 2.50
Spec. The Leaper Before 4.00

QUEEN OF THE DAMNED
Innovation, 1991
1 Anne Rice Adapt.On the Road
    to the Vampire Lestat 3.50
2 Adapt. continued 2.50
3 The Devils Minion 2.50
4 thru 8 Adapt.continued ...... @2.50

QUICK-DRAW MCGRAW
Dell, 1960
2 .... 125.00
3 .... 125.00
4 Snaggle Pus 150.00
5 .... 125.00
6 .... 125.00
7 thru 11 .... @100.00
Gold Key, 1962
12 .... 140.00
13 .... 140.00

---

14 .... 75.00
15 .... 75.00
Charlton Comics, 1970–72
1 TV Animated Cartoon 100.00
2 .... 75.00
3 .... 75.00
4 thru 8 .... @75.00

Q-UNIT
Harris
1 I:Q-Unit,w/card 3.25

RACE AGAINST TIME
Dark Ange., 1997
1 and 2 .... @2.50

RACE FOR THE MOON
Harvey Publications, 1958
1 BP 250.00
2 JK,AW,JK/AW(c) 400.00
3 JK,AW,JK/AW(c) 500.00

RACER-X
Premiere
Spec.#1 .... 5.00
Now, 1988
thru 11 .... @2.50
[2nd Series], 1989
1 thru 10 .... @2.50

RACER X
WildStorm/DC, 2000
1 (of 3) Rex Racer's secrets 2.50
1a variant (c) (1:4) 2.50
2 racing thrills 2.50
3 conclusion 3.00

RACK & PAIN: KILLERS
Chaos! Comics, 1996
1 (of 4) JaL(c) 3.00
2 BnP,LJi,JaL(c) 3.00
3 (of 4) BnP,LJi 3.00
4 BnP,LJi, final issue 3.00

RADICAL DREAMER
Blackball, 1994
0 .... 2.50
1 thru 5 V:Jorge Futran .... @2.50

RADIOACTIVE MAN
Bongo, 1993
1 I:Radioactive Man 4.00
1 80pg offered again 3.25
88 V:Lava Man 2.50
212 V:Hypno Head 2.50
412 V:Dr. Crab, with trading card .. 2.50
679 with trading card 2.50
1000 Final issue 2.50
Bongo Comics, 2000
100 .... 2.50
136 .... 2.50
222 .... 2.50
4 .... 2.50
575 new Radioactive Man born ... 2.50
106 new Radioactive Man insane .. 2.50
7 .... 2.50
8 Official Movie Adaptation 3.00
199 .... 3.00
Spec. Movie Adaptation 3.00

RAGGEDY ANN AND ANDY
Dell, 1964
1 .... 75.00
2 thru 4 .... @50.00
Gold Key, 1971
1 .... 50.00
2 thru 6 .... @35.00

Rai #27
© Valiant

RAI
Valiant, 1991
0 DL,O:Bloodshot,I:2nd Rai,D:X-O,
    Archer,Shadowman,F:all Valiant
    heroes,bridges Valiant Universe
    1992-4001 .... 7.00
1 V:Grandmother 9.00
2 V:Icespike 12.00
3 V:Humanists,Makiko 32.00
4 V:Makiko,rarest Valiant 20.00
5 Rai leaves earth, C:Eternal
    Warrior 10.00
6 FM(c),Unity#7,V:Pierce 6.00
7 WS(c),Unity#15,V:Pierce,
    D:Rai,A:Magnus 6.00
8 Epilogue of Unity in 4001 ...... 6.00
Becomes:

RAI AND THE FUTURE FORCE
Valiant, 1993
9 F:Rai,E.Warrior of 4001,Tekla,
    X-O Commander,Spylocke ... 5.00
9a Gold Ed. 15.00
10 thru 26 .... @3.00
Becomes:

RAI
Valiant, 1994
27 thru 33 .... @3.00

RAISE THE DEAD
D.E. (Dynamite Ent.) 2007
1 .... 3.50
1a variant (c) 3.50
2 thru 4 .... @3.50
2a thru 4a variant (c) .... @3.50

RAKAN
Studio G, 2003
1 .... 3.00
2 Den of Thieves 3.00
3 and 4 .... @3.00

RAKAN
AK Entertainment, 2006
1 Sabretooth 3.00
2 Chessmaster 3.00
3 The Sword of Majido 3.00
4 The Devil's Axe 3.00
5 Den of Thieves, pt.1 .... 3.00
6 Den of Thieves, pt. 2 .... 3.00
7 thru 9 .... @3.00

All comics prices listed are for *Near Mint* condition.

RALPH SNART ADVENTURES
Now
[Volumes 1 & 2]
see B&W
9 and 10, color 2.50
[Volume 3], 1988
1 . . . . 4.00
2 thru 10 . . . . @3.00
11 thru 21 . . . . @2.50
22 thru 26 . . . . @2.50
[Volume 4], 1992
1 thru 3, with 1 of 2 trading cards . . 2.50
[Volume 5], 1993
1 thru 5, with 1 of 2 trading cards . . 2.50
3-D Spec.#1 with 3-D glasses and
   12 trading cards. 3.50

RAMAYAN REBORN
Virgin Comics, 2006
1 . . . . 3.00
2 thru 3 . . . . @3.00

RAMAYAN 3392 A.D.
Virgin Comics
4 thru 7 . . . . @3.00

RAMAYANI 3392 A.D. RELOADED
Virgin Comics, 2007
1 . . . . 3.00
2 thru 5 . . . . @3.00
6 thru 10 . . . . @3.00
Spec. Guidebook 3.00

RANDOM ENCOUNTER
Viper Comics
1 thru 4 . . . . @3.00

RANDOM 5
Amara Inc., 1995
1 I:Random 5 . . . . 2.50

RANGO
Dell Publishing Co., 1967
1 Tim Conway Ph(c) . . . 60.00

RANMA 1/2
Viz, 1992
1 I:Ranma 50.00
2 I:Upperclassmen Kuno 30.00
3 F:Upperclassmen Kuno 25.00
4 Confusion. 5.00
5 A:Ryoga 5.00
6 Ryoga plots revenge 9.00
7 Conclusion 5.00
[Part 2], 1992
1 . . . . 8.00
2 . . . . 5.00
3 thru 7 . . . . @4.00
8 . . . . 5.00
9 . . . . 6.00
10 and 11 . . . . @3.00
continued, see B&W Pub.

RAPHAEL
Mirage, 1987
1 TMNTurtle characters 8.00

RARE BREED
Dark Moon Productions, 1995
1 V:Anarchy 2.50
2 V:Anarchy 2.50

RASH
Narwain Publishing, 2005
1 . . . . 4.00
2 . . . . 4.00

RAT BASTARD
Crucial Comics, 1997
1 by The Huja Brothers 2.50
2 thru 6 . . . . @2.50

RAT PATROL, THE
Dell Publishing Co., 1967
1 Ph(c) 125.00
2 . . . . 100.00
3 thru 6 Ph(c) . . . . @75.00

Raven #3
© Renaissance Comics

RAVEN
Renaissance Comics, 1993
1 I:Raven 2.50
2 V:Macallister 2.50
3 . . . . 2.50
4 . . . . 2.50
5 . . . . 2.50
6 V:Nightmare Creatures 2.75

RAVEN HOUSE
Crossgen Comics, 2004
1 . . . . 3.00
2 . . . . 3.00

RAVENING
Avatar, 1998
1/2 Busch (c) F:Ravyn & Glyph . . . 3.00
1/2a Meadows(c) 3.00
1/2d Sketched Edition. 30.00
1/2e Blood Red Foil, signed 9.00

RAVENS AND RAINBOWS
Pacific, 1983
1 . . . . 2.50

RAVER
Malibu, 1993
1 Prism cover 3.00
1a Newsstand 2.50
2 . . . . 2.50
3 Walter Koenig(s) 2.50
4 . . . . 2.00
5 . . . . 2.00

RAWHIDE
Dell, 1962
1 . . . . 250.00
Gold Key, 1963
1 From TV series 250.00
2 . . . . 225.00

RAY BRADBURY CHRONICLES
Byron Press
1 short stories 10.00
2 short stories 10.00
3 short stories 10.00

RAY BRADBURY COMICS
Topps, 1993–94
1 thru 5 with Trading Card . . . . @3.25
Spec.#1 The Illustrated Man 3.00
Spec. Trilogy of Terror 2.50
Spec. The Martian Chronicles 3.00

RAY HARRYHAUSEN PRESENTS:
BACK TO MYSTERIOUS ISLAND
Bluewater Prod., 2008
1 . . . . 4.00
2 thru 4 . . . . @4.00
3a variant (c) 4.00
...ELEMENTALS
Bluewater Prod., 2008
1 (of 4) 4.00
2 thru 3 . . . . @4.00
...FLYING SAUCERS VS. THE EARTH
Bluewater Prod., 2008
1 (of 4) 4.00
1a variant (c) 4.00
2 thru 4 . . . . 4.00
4a variant (c) 4.00
...SINBAD, ROGUE OF MARS
Bluewater Prod., 2007
1 . . . . 3.50
2 thru 3 . . . . @3.50
1a thru 3a variant (c)s . . . . @3.50
1b limited ed. 7.00
4 . . . . 3.50
5 . . . . 4.00
...20 MILLION MILES MORE
Bluewater Prod. 2007
1 . . . . 3.50
2 thru 4 . . . . @3.50
...WRATH OF THE TITANS
Bluewater Prod. 2007
1 . . . . 3.50
2 thru 4 . . . . @3.50

RAYMOND E. FEIST'S MAGICIAN: APPRENTICE
Dabel Brothers Prod., 2006
1 (of 6) 3.00
1a variant Don Maitz (c) 6.00
2 thru 6 . . . . @3.00
2a thru 6a variant (c)s . . . . @6.00

RAZOR
London Night Studios, 1992
0 . . . . 9.00
0a 2nd printing (Fathom 1992) . . . 4.00
0b reprint (1995) 3.00
1 I:Stryke (Fathom 1992) 8.00
1a second printing 3.00
2 J.O'Barr (c) 9.00

2a limited ed., red & blue	15.00
2b platinum ed.	16.00
3 Jim Balent (c)	7.00
3a with poster	12.00
4	4.00
4a with poster	9.00
5	7.00
5a platinum ed.	12.00
6	5.00
7	4.00
8 thru 10	@3.00
11 & 12 B&W, Rituals,pt.1&2	@3.00
1/2 (1995).	5.00
Ann.#1 I:Shi (1993)	25.00
Ann.#2 O:Razor B&W (1994)	35.00

Becomes:

RAZOR UNCUT
See: B&W Section

RAZOR
Volume 2
London Knight, 1996

1 DQ,	3.00
1a holochrome edition	5.00
2 DQ	3.00
2a holochrome edition	4.00
3 thru 7	@3.00
Razor Analog Burn.	2.50

...AND SHI SPECIAL
London Night Studios, 1994

1 Rep. Razor Ann.#1 + new art	5.00
1a platinum version.	9.00

...ARCHIVES
London Night, 1997

1 & 2 see B&W
3 rep. Razor #10–12.	7.00

...BURN
London Night Studios, 1994

1 V:Styke.	3.00
1a signed	5.00
2 Searching for Styke	3.00
2a Platinum.	7.00
3 Stryke's War.	3.00
4 D:Razor, bagged	3.00
5 Epilogue.	3.00

...CRY NO MORE
London Night Studios, 1995

1-shot	3.00
1a variant	4.00
1b Commemorative (1999).	6.00

...HEX & VIOLENCE
EH! Productions, 2000

0 EHr.	3.00

.../MORBID ANGEL:
SOUL SEARCH
London Night, 1996

1 (of 3)	3.00
1 platinum edition	5.00
1 Chromium edition.	7.00
2	3.00
3	3.00

.../POISON/AREALA WARRIOR
NUN: LITTLE BAD ANGELS
London Night, 1999

Spec. x-over Raxor cover	4.00
Spec.A Poison cover	4.00
Spec.B Areala cover	4.00

...THE RAVENING
Avatar

1	3.50
1a Previews cover	3.50
1b Bondage cover.	6.00

...THE SUFFERING
London Night Studios, 1994

1	4.00
1a Director's cut	3.00
1b signed, limited	9.00
2	3.00
2a Director's cut	2.50
3 final chapter	3.00

Razor Torture #6
© London Night Studios

...TORTURE
London Night Studios, 1995

0 Razor back from dead	4.00
0a signed edition.	7.00
1	3.00
1a Commemorative (1999).	6.00
2	3.00
3 EHr.	3.00
4	3.00
5& 6 alt. cover, signed	@4.00
7	3.00

...SWIMSUIT SPECIAL
London Night Studios, 1995

1 pin-ups	3.00
1a platinum version.	7.00
1b commemorative edition	4.00

.../WARRIOR NUN
AREALA: DARK MENACE
London Night, 1999

Spec. x-over	4.00
Spec.A x-over, variant cover	4.00

.../WARRIOR NUN AREALA:
FAITH
London Night, 1996

1 by Jude Millien	3.00
1a variant cover	4.00

RAZOR'S EDGE,
THE: REDBIRD
Wildstorm/DC, March, 2005

1 (of 5) JPn.	3.00
2 JPn.	3.00
3 JPn.	3.00

RAZOR'S EDGE,
THE: WARBLADE
Wildstorm/DC, 2004

1 SBs	3.00
2 SBs	3.00
3 SBs	3.00
4 thru 5 SBs	@3.00

REAL GHOSTBUSTERS
Now, 1988

1 KSy(c)	4.50
2 thru 7	@2.50
8 thru 24	@2.50

[2nd Series], 1991

1 Halloween Special	2.50
Ann. 3-D w/glasses & pinups.	3.00

[Super Information
Hijinks:]
REALITY CHECK!
Sirius, 1996

1 by Tavisha Wolfgarth	3.00
2 Surfing the Internet	3.00
3 E is for Europa.	3.00
4 thru 8	@3.00
9 Nonesuch Nonsense, pt.1	3.00
10 Nonesuch Nonsense, pt.2	3.00
11 Nonesuch Nonsense, pt.3	3.00
12 Nonesuch Nonsense, pt.4	3.00

REAL WAR STORIES
Eclipse, 1987–91

1 BB	3.00
1a 2nd printing	2.50
2	5.00

RE-ANIMATOR
Adventure Comics, 1991

1 movie adaption	3.00
2 movie adaption	3.00

RE-ANIMATOR
Adventure

1 Prequel to Orig movie	2.50

...DAWN OF
THE RE-ANIMATOR
Adventure, 1992

1 Prequel to movie	2.50
2	2.50
3	2.50
4 V:Erich Metler	2.50

...TALES OF HERBERT WEST
Adventure Comics

1 H.P.Lovecraft stories	5.00

RED
DC Wildstorm July, 2003
America's Best Comics

1 (of 3) WEI,CHm	3.00
2 WEI,CHm	3.00
3 WEI,CHm.	3.00

REDBALL 6
Atomic Pop Art, 2007

1	3.00
2	3.00
3	3.50

RED DOG
Eclipse, 1988

1 CR,Mowgli Jungle Book story	2.50

RED DRAGON
Comico, 1995

1 SBs,I:Red Dragon	2.50
2 How Soon is Nau?	3.00

REDEEMER, THE
Black Library, 2002

1	3.50
2 thru 4	@3.50

COLOR PUB.

REDEEMERS
Antarctic Press, 1997
1 (of 5) by Herb Mallette
  & Patrick Blain 3.00
2 . . . . 3.00

RED MENACE
Wildstorm/DC, Nov., 2006
1 (of 6) JOy,AV 3.00
1a variant (c). 3.00
2 JOy,AV 3.00
2a variant MK (c) 3.00
3 JOy,AV 3.00
4 JOy,AV, Under house arrest 3.00
5 JOy,AV,Imprisoned on Alcatraz . . 3.00
6 JOy,AV,finale 3.00

RED PROPHET: TALES OF ALVIN MAKER
Dabel Brothers Prod., 2006
1 (of 6) 3.00
1a variant (c) 6.00
2 thru 3 . . . . @3.00
2a thru 3a variant (c)s . . . . @6.00

RED SONJA in 3-D
Blackthorne
1 thru 3 . . . . @2.50

RED SONJA
Cross Plains Comics, 1999
1 Death in Scarlet,pt.1 . . . . 3.00
1a photo (c). 3.00
2 Death in Scarlet,pt.2 . . . . 3.00
3 Death in Scarlet,pt.3 . . . . 3.00

RED SONJA
D.E. (Dynamite Entertain.), 2005
0 . . . . 5.00
1 . . . . 5.00
1a thru 1e variant (c)s . . . . @5.00
2 thru 7 . . . . @4.00
8 Arrowsmith 4.00
9 Arrowsmith 4.00
10 Arrowsmith 4.00
11 Arrowsmith 4.00
12 Return of Kulan
  Gath, pt. 1, JLe(c) 4.00
13 Return of Kulan Gath, pt. 2. . . 3.00
14 Return of Kulan Gath, pt. 3. . . 3.00
15 Return of Kulan Gath, pt. 4. . . 3.00
16 Return of Kulan Gath, pt. 5. . . 3.00
17 Return of Kulan Gath 3.00
18 thru 29 . . . . @3.00
2a thru 17a variant (c)s . . . . . . @5.00
18 thru 29a variant (c)s . . . . . . @3.00
30 thru 40. . . . . @3.00
30a thru 40a variant (c)s . . . . . @3.00
Ann. #1 (2006). 3.50
Giant Size #1. . . . . 5.00
Giant Size #1a variant (c) 5.00
Giant Size #2 . . . . 5.00
1-shot Red Sonja Goes East. 5.00
1-shot Red Sonja Goes East
  power foil (c) 15.00
1-shot One More Day 5.00
1-shot Monster Isle 5.00
1-shot Monster Isle variant (c) . . . 5.00
1-shot Red Sonja/Claw 5.00
Spec. Vacant Shell 5.00
Spec. Vacant Shell variant (c) 5.00

RED SONJA/CLAW THE UNCONQUERED: DEVIL'S HANDS
Wildstorm/DC, March, 2006
1 (of 4) ASm 3.00
1a variant JLe (c) 3.00

2 ASm 3.00
2a variant JLe (c) 3.00
3 ASm, Imprisoned 3.00
3a variant JLe (c) 3.00
4 ASm,Claw embraces evil. 3.00
4a variant JLe(c). 3.00

RED SONJA VS. THULSA DOOM
D.E. (Dynamite Ent.) 2001
1 (of 4) 3.50
2 . . . . 3.50
3 . . . . 3.50
4 . . . . 3.50
1a thru 3a variant (c) . . . . @3.50
1b thru 2b Fiery red Foil editions . 20.00

RED STAR, THE
Archangel Studios, 2002
Vol. 2
2 . . . . 3.00
3 . . . . 3.00
4 . . . . 3.00
5 . . . . 3.00
6 . . . . 3.00
Annual #1 foil (c) signed 10.00
Spec. Red Star: Sword of Lies. . . . 4.50

REESE'S PIECES
Eclipse, 1985
1 reprint from Web of Horror 2.50
2 reprint from Web of Horror 2.50

Re:Gex #0
© *Awesome Entertainment*

RE: GEX
Awesome Entertainment, 1998
0 RLe, ... 2.50
0a Red Foil variant 4.00
1 RLe,JLb 2.50
1a Platinum cover 7.00
1b Red Foil cover 10.00
1c Variant RL cover 4.00
1d prime 3.00
1e prime millennium ed. 5.00
2 RLe,JLb 2.50
2a prime 3.00
2b Millennium edition 5.00
3 RLe,A:The Coven,V:Youngblood . 2.50
Con Spec. '98 . . . . 5.00
Orlando Megacon ashcan 9.00
Orlando Megacon ashcan, signed . 20.00

REGGIE
Archie Publications, 1963–65
15 thru 18. . . . . @75.00
Becomes:

REGGIE AND ME
Archie Publications, 1966–80
19 . . . . 60.00
20 thru 23. . . . . @50.00
24 thru 40. . . . . @35.00
41 thru 50. . . . . @25.00
51 thru 99. . . . . @20.00
100 . . . . 25.00
101 thru 126. . . . . @15.00

REGGIE'S WISE GUY JOKES
Archie Publications, April, 1968
1 . . . . 75.00
2 . . . . 40.00
3 . . . . 40.00
4 . . . . 40.00
5 thru 15 Giants . . . . @40.00
16 thru 28 Giants . . . . @35.00
29 thru 40. . . . . @25.00
41 thru 60. . . . . @20.00
11 thru 59. . . . . @15.00
60 Jan., 1982. . . . . 15.00

RELOAD
DC Homage, 2003
1 (of 3) WEI,JP 3.00
2 WEI,JP 3.00
3 WEI,JP, concl. 3.00

REMAINS
IDW Publishing, 2004
1 thru 5 . . . . @4.00

REPTILICUS
Charlton Comics, 1961
1 . . . . 400.00
2 . . . . 250.00
Becomes:

REPTISAURUS
1962
3 . . . . 150.00
4 thru 7 . . . . @125.00
8 Summer, 1963 . . . . 125.00

RESIDENT EVIL: FIRE & ICE
WildStorm/DC, 2000
1 (of 4) from videogame 2.50
2 . . . . 2.50
3 . . . . 2.50
4 concl. 2.50

RESISTANCE, THE
WildStorm/DC, 2002
1 JP(s),techno sci-fi 3.00
2 JP(s) 3.00
3 JP(s) 3.00
4 JP(s) 3.00
5 JP(s),V:Sampizi 3.00
6 JP(s),V:Sampizi & GCC. 3.00
7 JP(s),F:Version Mary 3.00
8 JP(s),F:Version Mary 3.00

REST
Devil's Due, 2008
0 . . . . 1.00
1 . . . . 3.50
1a variant (c) 3.50
2 . . . . 3.50
2a variant photo (c) 3.50

RET ROMANNE
Bluewater Prod., 2008
1 (of 4) 4.00
1a variant (c)s . . . . @4.00
2 thru 3 . . . . @4.00
2a thru 3a variant (c)s . . . . @4.00

RETURN OF GORGO, THE
Charlton, 1963
2 thru 3 . . . . 125.00

RETURN OF KONGA, THE
Charlton Comics, 1962
N# 125.00

RETURN OF MEGATON MAN
Kitchen Sink, 1988
1 Don Simpson art (1988) 2.50
2 Don Simpson art 2.50
3 Don Simpson art 2.50

RETURN OF THE SUPER PIMPS
Dial "C" for Comics, 2007
1 (of 6) 2.00
2 thru 4 . . . . @3.00
6 . . . . 3.00

RETURN TO JURASSIC PARK
Topps, 1995
1 R:Jurassic Park 3.00
2 V:Blosyn Team, Army. 3.00
3 The Hunted 3.00
4 Army 3.00
5 Heirs to the Thunder,pt.1 . . . . . . 3.00
6 Heirs to the Thunder,pt.2 . . . . . . 3.00
7 Inquiring Minds,pt.1 . . . . 3.00
8 Photo Finish, concl. 3.00
9 Jurassic Jam issue 3.00

REVENGE OF THE PROWLER
Eclipse, 1988
1 GN,R:Prowler. 2.50
2 GN,A:Fighting Devil Dogs with
 Flexi-Disk. 2.50
3 GN,A:Devil Dogs 2.50
4 GN,V:Pirahna. 2.50

REVENGERS
Continuity, 1985
1 NA,O:Megalith,I:Crazyman 4.00
2 NA,Megalith meets Armor & Silver
Streak,Origin Revengers#1 . . . . . . 2.50
3 NA/NR,Origin Revengers #2 . . . . 2.50
4 NA,Origin Revengers #3 . . . . 2.50
5 NA,Origin Revengers #4 . . . . 2.50
6 I:Hybrids. 3.00
Spec. #1 F:Hybrids 5.00

REVERE
Alias Enterprises, 2006
1 (of 4) 3.50
2 . . . . 3.50
3 . . . . 3.50
4 . . . . 3.50

REVOLUTION ON THE PLANET OF THE APES
MR Comics, 2005
1 (of 6) 4.00
2 thru 6 . . . . @4.00

RIBIT
Comico
thru 4 FT,Mini-series . . . . @3.00

Richie Rich #176
© Harvey Publications

RICHIE RICH
Harvey Publications, 1960–91
1 Inc.Casper,Little Dot 5,000.00
2 Inc. Little Dot, Little Lotta . . . 1,600.00
3 Inc. Little Dot, Little Lotta . . . 1,000.00
4 Inc. Little Dot, Little Lotta . . . 1,000.00
5 . . . . 1,000.00
6 . . . . 600.00
7 . . . . 600.00
8 Christmas(c) 600.00
9 . . . . 600.00
10 . . . . 600.00
11 thru 20 . . . . @500.00
21 thru 41 . . . . @500.00
42 Flying Saucer 500.00
43 thru 55 . . . . @250.00
56 Super Richie 150.00
57 . . . . 100.00
58 . . . . 100.00
59 Buck 125.00
60 thru 80 . . . . @100.00
81 thru 99 . . . . @50.00
100 Irona-Robot Maid 60.00
101 thru 111 . . . . @40.00
112 thru 116 52 pg Giants . . . . @50.00
117 thru 120 . . . . @40.00
121 thru 136 . . . . @30.00
137 Mr. Cheepers 30.00
138 thru 160 . . . . @20.00
161 thru 180 . . . . @15.00
181 thru 236 . . . . @12.00
237 Money Monster 12.00
238 thru 254 . . . . @7.00

RICHIE RICH
Harvey, 1991
1 thru 15 . . . . @3.00
16 thru 28 . . . . @3.00

...AND CADBURY
Harvey, 1977
1 . . . . 25.00
2 thru 10 . . . . @15.00
11 thru 29 . . . . @10.00

...& CASPER
Harvey, 1974
1 . . . . 50.00
2 thru 5 . . . . @30.00
6 thru 10 . . . . @20.00

11 thru 25 . . . . @15.00
26 thru 45 . . . . @10.00

...AND DOLLAR THE DOG
Harvey, 1977
1 . . . . 25.00
2 thru 10 . . . . @15.00
11 thru 24 . . . . @10.00

...AND GLORIA
Harvey, 1977
1 . . . . 25.00
2 thru 10 . . . . @15.00
11 thru 25 . . . . @10.00

...AND HIS GIRLFRIENDS
Harvey, 1979
1 . . . . 20.00
2 thru 10 . . . . @15.00
11 thru 16 . . . . @10.00

...AND HIS MEAN COUSIN REGGIE
Harvey, 1979
1 . . . . 20.00
2 thru 3 . . . . @15.00

...BANK BOOKS
Harvey, 1972–82
1 . . . . 75.00
2 Money Monster 55.00
3 thru 5 . . . . @50.00
6 thru 10 . . . . @35.00
11 thru 20 . . . . @25.00
21 thru 30 . . . . @15.00
31 thru 40 . . . . @10.00
41 thru 59 . . . . @8.00

...BILLIONS
Harvey, 1974–82
1 . . . . 50.00
2 thru 5 . . . . @30.00
6 thru 10 . . . . @25.00
11 thru 20 . . . . @15.00
21 thru 30 . . . . @10.00
31 thru 48 . . . . @8.00

...CASH
Harvey, 1974
1 . . . . 50.00
2 thru 10 . . . . @25.00
11 thru 20 . . . . @15.00
21 thru 47 . . . . @10.00

...DIAMONDS
Harvey, 1972–82
1 . . . . 75.00
2 thru 5 . . . . @35.00
6 thru 10 . . . . @30.00
11 thru 20 . . . . @25.00
21 thru 30 . . . . @12.00
31 thru 59 . . . . @10.00

...DOLLARS & CENTS
Harvey Publications, 1963–82
1 . . . . 400.00
2 . . . . 200.00
3 thru 5 . . . . @150.00
6 thru 10 . . . . @100.00
11 thru 24 . . . . @70.00
25 Nurse Jenny 75.00
26 thru 30 . . . . @60.00
31 thru 43 . . . . @50.00
44 thru 60 . . . . @40.00
61 thru 70 . . . . @30.00
71 thru 99 . . . . @20.00
100 Anniversary 25.00
102 thru 109 . . . . @20.00

...FORTUNES
Harvey, 1971–82
1 . . . . 75.00
2 thru 5 . . . . @50.00
6 thru 10 . . . . @40.00

11 Orion	25.00
12 thru 20	@20.00
21 thru 30	@10.00
31 thru 63	@8.00

...GEMS
Harvey, 1974–82

1	50.00
2 thru 5	@30.00
6 thru 10	@25.00
11 thru 20	@20.00
21 thru 30	@10.00
31 thru 35	@8.00
36 Orion	10.00
37	8.00
38 Stone-Age Riches	10.00
39 thru 43	@8.00

...GOLD AND SILVER
Harvey, 1975–82

1	50.00
2	30.00
3	30.00
4	30.00
5	30.00
6 thru 10	@25.00
11 thru 20	@20.00
21 thru 30	@10.00
31 thru 33	@8.00
34 Stone-Age Riches	10.00
35 thru 42	@8.00

...INVENTIONS
Harvey, 1977

1	25.00
2 thru 10	@15.00
11 thru 26	@12.00

...JACKPOTS
Harvey, 1974–82

1	75.00
2 thru 5	@50.00
6 thru 15	@30.00
16 Super Richie	32.00
17 thru 20	@25.00
21 thru 30	@12.00
31 thru 58	@10.00

...MILLIONS
Harvey Publications, 1961–82

1	400.00
2	250.00
3 thru 10	@150.00
11 thru 20	@100.00
21 thru 30	@75.00
31 Orion, giant	50.00

Richie Rich Profits #14
© *Harvey*

32 thru 60	@45.00
61 thru 67	@35.00
68 Super Richie	35.00
69 thru 74	@25.00
75 thru 94	@20.00
95 thru 113	@15.00

...MONEY WORLD
Harvey, 1972–82

1 Mayda Monny	85.00
2 Super Richie	60.00
3 thru 5	@50.00
6 thru 10	@35.00
11 thru 20	@18.00
21 thru 30	@10.00
31 thru 59	@8.00

...PROFITS
Harvey, 1974–82

1	60.00
2 thru 5	@30.00
6 thru 10	@25.00
11 thru 20	@20.00
21 thru 30	@10.00
31 thru 47	@8.00

...RICHES
Harvey, 1972–82

1 Money Monster	90.00
2 thru 5	@50.00
6 thru 10	@30.00
11 thru 16	@20.00
17 Super Richie	22.00
18 thru 30	@15.00
31 thru 59	@10.00

...SUCCESS STORIES
Harvey Publications, 1964–82

1	500.00
2 thru 5	@250.00
6 thru 10	@125.00
11 thru 26	@100.00
27 Penny Van Dough	75.00
28 thru 43	@65.00
44 Super Richie	35.00
45 thru 55	@35.00
56 thru 66	@30.00
67 thru 105	@20.00

...VAULT OF MYSTERY
Harvey, 1974–82

1	50.00
2 thru 5	@30.00
6 thru 10	@15.00
11 thru 20	@10.00
21 thru 30	@10.00
31 thru 47	@10.00

...ZILLIONZ
Harvey, 1976–82

1	35.00
2 thru 5	@20.00
6 thru 10	@15.00
11 thru 20	@10.00
21 thru 33	@8.00

RIFLEMAN, THE
Dell Publishing Co., 1959

1 Chuck Connors Ph(c) all	500.00
2 Ph(c)	300.00
3 ATh,Ph(c)	275.00
4 Ph(c)	250.00
5 Ph(c)	250.00
6 ATh	275.00
7 thru 10 Ph(c)	225.00
11 thru 12	200.00

Gold Key, 1962

13 thru 20	@150.00

RIN TIN TIN AND RUSTY
Dell, 1957

21	75.00
22 thru 38	@75.00

Gold Key, 1963

1	100.00

RIOT
Riot Media, 2005

1	3.00
2	3.00

RIOT GEAR
Triumphant, 1993

1 JnR(s),I:Riot Gear	2.50
2 JnR(s),I:Rabin	2.50
3 JnR(s),I:Surzar	2.50
4 JnR(s),D:Captain Tich	2.50
5 JnR(s),reactions	2.50
6 JnR(s),Tich avenged	2.50
7 JnR(s),Information Age	2.50
8 JnR(s),	2.50

RIOT GEAR: VIOLENT PAST
Triumphant, 1994

1	2.50
2	2.50

R.I.P.
TSR, 1990–91

1 thru 4	@3.00
5 thru 8 Brasher, Avenger of the Dead	@3.00

RIPFIRE
Malibu, 1995

0 Prequel to Ripfire Series	2.50

RIPLEY'S BELIEVE IT OR NOT!
Gold Key, 1965–80

1	150.00
2 thru 3	@125.00
4 Ph(c),AMc	75.00
5 GE,JJ	60.00
6 AMc	60.00
7	50.00
8	60.00
9	50.00
10 GE	60.00
11	40.00
12	40.00
13	40.00
14	40.00
15 GE	45.00
16 thru 20	@40.00
21 thru 30	@25.00
31 thru 38	@22.00
39 RC	22.00
40 thru 50	@20.00
51 thru 94	@15.00

RISE OF THE SNAKEMEN
Crossgen Comics 2003

1	3.00
2 thru 3	@3.00

RISK
Maximum Press, 1995

1 V:Furious	2.50

ROAD TO HELL
IDW Publishing, 2006

1	4.00
2 thru 3	@4.00

ROB
Awesome Entertainment, 1999

1 RLe	2.50

ROBERT JORDAN'S NEW SPRING
Red Eagle Publishing, 2005
1 . . . . 4.00
2 thru 4 . . . . @4.00
5 thru 8 CDi. . . . . @4.00

ROBERT E. HOWARD'S
Cross Plains Comics, 1999
GN Marchers of Valhalla 7.00
GN Wolfshead 7.00
GN Worms of the Earth 10.00

ROBIN HOOD
Dell, 1963
1 . . . . 40.00

ROBIN HOOD
Eclipse, 1991
1 TT,Historically accurate series. . . 2.75
2 and 3 TT. . . . . @2.75

ROBINSON CRUSOE
Dell, 1964
1 . . . . 30.00

ROBOCOP: WAR PARTY
Avatar Press, 2005
1 . . . . 4.00
1a variant (c)s . . . . @4.00
1b Matt Martin (c) 6.00
1c ED-209 photo (c) 6.00
2 . . . . 4.00
2a wraparound (c). 4.00
3 . . . . 4.00
3a wraparound (c). 4.00
2b thru 3b variant (c). . . . . @4.00

ROBOCOP: WILD CHILD
Avatar Press, 2005
1 16-page 3.00
1a photo (c). 3.00
1b variant (c). 3.00
1c wraparound (c). 3.00
1d Heaven Above (c) 6.00
1e Detroit's Finest (c) 6.00

ROBO DOJO
WildStorm/DC, 2002
1 (of 6) MWn, 40-pg.. . . . . 3.50
2 MWn,. 3.00
3 MWn,. 3.00
4 MWn,Techno Council. 3.00
5 MWn,Robojin revolt 3.00
6 MWn,traitor revealed, concl. . . . 3.00

ROBO HUNTER
Eagle
1 . . . . 2.50
2 thru 5 . . . . @2.50

ROBOTECH
Antarctic Press, 1997
1 by Fred Perry & BDn 3.00
2 . . . . 3.00
3 . . . . 3.00
4 Rolling Thunder, pt.1 . . . . 3.00
5 Rolling Thunder, pt.2 . . . . 3.00
6 Rolling Thunder, pt.3 . . . . 3.00
7 Rolling Thunder, pt.4 . . . . 3.00
8 Variants, pt.1 . . . . 3.00
9 Variants, pt.2 . . . . 3.00
10 Variants, pt.3 . . . . 3.00
11 Variants, pt.4 . . . . 3.00
GN Megastorm by Fred Perry
    & Ben Dunn 8.00
Spec.1-shot Robotech: Final Fire . . 3.00

Spec.1-shot Robotech: Class
    Reunion 3.00

ROBOTECH
Wildstorm/DC, 2002
0 JLe 2.50
1 (of 6) JLe 3.00
2 thru 5 . . . . @3.00
6 SeP, concl. 3.00
Spec. Robotech Sourcebook 3.00

ROBOTECH: GENESIS THE LEGEND OF ZOR
Eternity
1 O:Robotech w/cards 3.00
1a Limited Edition,extra pages
    with cards #1 & #2. . . . . 6.00
2 thru 6, each with cards. . . . . . @2.50

ROBOTECH IN 3-D
Comico, 1985
1 . . . . 2.50

ROBOTECH: INVASION
Wildstorm/DC, 2004
thru 5 . . . . @3.00

ROBOTECH: LOVE AND WAR
Wildstorm/DC July, 2003
1 (of 6) Max and Miriya. 3.00
2 flight school 3.00
3 Max and Miriya meet. 3.00
4 Max and Miriya fight 3.00
5 Dixon dead. 3.00
6 conclusion 3.00

Robotech The Macross Saga #4
© Comico

ROBOTECH, THE MACROSS SAGA
Comico, 1985–89
(formerly Macross)
2 . . . . 5.00
3 . . . . 4.00
4 . . . . 3.50
5 . . . . 3.50
6 J:Rick Hunter 3.50
7 V:Zentraedi 3.00
8 A:Rick Hunter. 3.00
9 V:Zentraedi 3.00
10 Blind Game. 3.00
11 V:Zentraedi. 3.00

12 V:Zentraedi 3.00
13 V:Zentraedi 3.00
14 Gloval's Reports 3.00
15 V:Zentraedi 3.00
16 V:Zentraedi 3.00
17 V:Zentraedi 3.00
18 D:Roy Fokker 3.00
19 V:Khyron 3.00
20 V:Zentraedi 3.00
21 A New Dawn 3.00
22 V:Zentraedi 3.00
23 Reckless 3.00
24 HB,V:Zentraedi 3.00
25 Wedding Bells. 3.00
26 The Messenger. 3.00
27 Force of Arms 3.00
28 Reconstruction Blues 3.00
29 Robotech Masters. 3.00
30 Viva Miriya 3.00
31 Khyron's Revenge 3.00
32 Broken Heart. 3.00
33 A Rainy Night 3.00
34 Private Time 3.00
35 Season's Greetings 3.00
36 last issue. 3.00
Graphic Novel #1 . . . . 6.00

ROBOTECH MASTERS
Comico, 1985–88
1 . . . . 4.00
2 . . . . 3.00
3 Space Station Liberty. 3.00
4 V:Bioroids. 2.50
5 V:Flagship 2.50
6 Prelude to Battle 2.50
7 The Trap 2.50
8 F:Dana Sterling 2.50
9 Star Dust 2.50
10 V:Zor 2.50
11 A:De Ja Vu 2.50
12 2OR. 2.50
13 . . . . 2.50
14 Clone Chamber,V:Zor 2.50
15 Love Song. 2.50
16 V:General Emerson 2.50
17 Mind Games 2.50
18 Dana in Wonderland 2.50
19 . . . . 2.50
20 A:Zor,Musica. 2.50
21 Final Nightmare 2.50
22 The Invid Connection 2.50
23 Catastrophe, final issue 2.50

ROBOTECH: THE NEW GENERATION
Comico, 1985–88
1 . . . . 4.00
2 The Lost City 3.00
3 V:Yellow Dancer. 3.00
4 A:Yellow Dancer. 3.00
5 SK(i),A:Yellow Dancer 3.00
6 F:Rook Bartley. 3.00
7 Paper Hero 3.00
8 . . . . 3.00
9 KSy,The Genesis Pit 3.00
10 V:The Invid 3.00
11 F:Scott Bernard. 3.00
12 V:The Invid 3.00
13 V:The Invid 3.00
14 Annie's Wedding 3.00
15 Seperate Ways 3.00
16 Metamorphosis 3.00
17 Midnight Sun. 3.00
18 . . . . 3.00
19 . . . . 3.00
20 Birthday Blues. 3.00
21 Hired Gun 3.00
22 The Big Apple 3.00
23 Robotech Wars 3.00
24 Robotech Wars 3.00
25 V:Invid, last issue 3.00

ROBOTECH: PRELUDE TO THE SHADOW CHRONICLES
Wildstorm/DC, Oct., 2005
1 (of 5) JWp,JWt.............. 3.50
2 thru 5 .... @3.50

ROBOTECH SPECIAL DANA'S STORY
Eclipse
1 .... 5.00

ROBOTECH II: THE SENTINELS
Eternity
Swimsuit Spec.#1 .... 3.00

ROBOTIKA
Archaia Studio Press, 2006
1 .... 4.00
2 .... 4.00
3 .... 4.00
4 .... 4.00

ROBOTIKA: FOR A FEW RUBLES MORE
Archaia Studios, 2007
1 (of 4) 3.50
2 .... 3.50
3 .... 4.00

ROB ZOMBIE'S SPOOKSHOW INTERNATIONAL
Crossgen Comics, 2003
1 (of 5) 3.50
2 .... 3.00
3 .... 3.00
MVCreations (2004)
4 thru 10 .... @3.00

ROCK 'N' ROLL
Revolutionary, 1990
Prev: Black & White
15 Poison.................. 6.00
16 Van Halen............... 5.00
17 Madonna................ 6.00
18 AliceCooper.............. 5.00
19 Public Enemy, 2 Live Crew..... 5.00
20 Queensryche.............. 5.00
21 Prince 5.00
22 AC/DC................. 5.00
23 Living Color.............. 5.00
24 Anthrax 5.00
25 Z.Z.Top................ 5.00
26 Doors 5.00
27 Doors 5.00
28 Ozzy Osbourne............ 6.00
29 The Cure................ 5.00
30 .... 5.00
31 Vanilla Ice 5.00
32 Frank Zappa.............. 5.00
33 Guns n' Roses 5.00
34 The Black Crowes........... 5.00
35 R.E.M.................. 5.00
36 Michael Jackson........... 5.00
37 Ice T.................. 5.00
38 Rod Stewart 5.00
39 New Kids on the Block 5.00
40 N.W.A./Ice Cube........... 5.00
41 Paula Abdul.............. 5.00
42 Metallica II............... 5.00
43 Guns 'N' Roses 5.00
44 Scorpions 5.00
45 Greatful Dead............. 5.00

46 Grateful Dead 5.00
47 Grateful Dead 5.00
48 (now b/w),Queen 5.00
49 Rush 5.00
50 Bob Dylan Pt.1 .... 5.00
51 Bob Dylan Pt.2 .... 5.00
52 Bob Dylan Pt.3 .... 5.00
53 Bruce Springsteen 5.00
54 U2 Pt.1 .... 5.00
55 U2 Pt.2 .... 5.00
56 David Bowie 5.00
57 thru 58 .... @4.00
59 Eric Clampton 5.00
60 thru 63 .... @4.00
64 San Francisco............. 4.00
65 Pink Floyd 4.00

ROCK 'N' ROLL HIGH SCHOOL
Cosmic Comics, 1995
1 Sequel to the movie.......... 2.50

ROCKETEER
Walt Disney, 1991
1 DSt(c)RH,MovieAdaptation 7.00
Newsstand Version 3.25

ROCKETEER ADVENTURE MAGAZINE
Comico, 1988
1 DSt,MK,Rocketeer(6thApp.) ... 10.00
2 DSt,MK,Rocketeer(7thApp.) 8.00

Rocketeer Special #1
© Eclipse

ROCKETEER SPECIAL
Eclipse, 1984
1 DSt, Rocketeer(5th App.)...... 15.00

ROCKET MAN: KING OF THE ROCKET MEN
Innovation, 1991
1 thru 4 Adapts movie series ... @2.50

ROCKETO
Speakeasy Comics, 2005
1 .... 9.00
2 thru 3 .... @8.00
4 thru 6 .... @5.00

ROCKET RANGER
Adventure Comics, 1991
1 (of 12) from computer game 3.00

ROCKY AND HIS FIENDISH FRIENDS
Gold Key, 1962
1 .... 350.00
2 .... 250.00
3 .... 250.00
4 .... 200.00
5 .... 200.00

ROCKY HORROR PICTURE SHOW
Calibre/Tome, 1990
1 .... 6.00
1a 2nd printing 3.25
2 .... 3.50
3 The Conclusion 3.25
Rocky Horror Collection reps..... 5.00

ROG 2000
Pacific, 1982
1 One-Shot, JBy 2.50

ROGER RABBIT
Walt Disney, 1990
1 I:Rick Flint, The Trouble
  with Toons 5.50
2 .... 3.50
3 .... 3.00
4 .... 3.00
5 .... 3.00
6 thru 9 .... @3.00
10 Tuned-in-toons 3.00
11 Who Framed Rick Flint....... 3.00
12 Somebunny to Love 3.00
13 Honey,I Stink with Kids 3.00
14 Who Fired Jessica Rabbit...... 3.00
15 The Great Toon Detective...... 3.00
16 See you later Aviator 3.00
17 Flying Saucers over Toontown .. 3.00
18 I Have Seen the Future 3.00

ROGER RABBIT'S TOONTOWN
Walt Disney, 1991
1 Baby Herman,Jessica stories ... 2.50
2 Pre-Hysterical Roger 2.50
3 Lumberjack of tomorrow 2.50
4 The Longest Daze 2.50

ROGUES
Dark Planet Productions, 2004
1 .... 3.00
2 thru 5 .... @3.00
6 .... 5.50

ROGUE ANGEL: TELLER OF TALL TALES
IDW, 2008
1 .... 4.00
2 thru 5 .... @4.00

ROGUE TROOPER
Fleetway/Quality, 1986
1 thru 5 .... @2.50
6 thru 21 .... @2.50
22/23 .... 2.50
24 .... 2.50
25/26 .... 2.50
27 thru 43 .... @2.50

ROGUE TROOPER: THE FINAL WARRIOR
Fleetway
1 RS,Golden Rebellion,pt 1 ...... 3.00
2 thru 3 .... @3.00
4 Saharan Ice-Belt War 3.00

ROKKIN
Wildstorm/DC, July, 2006
1 . . . . 3.00
2 thru 6 . . . . @3.00

ROLAND:
DAYS OF WRATH
Terra Major, 1999
1 (of 4) 3.00
2 thru 4 . . . . @3.00

ROMAN HOLIDAYS, THE
Gold Key, 1973
1 . . . . 75.00
2 thru 4 . . . . @50.00

ROOK, THE
Harris Comics, 1995
0 O:Rook. 3.00
1 N:Rook. 3.00
2 I:Coffin 3.00
3 The Spider Obsidian 3.00

ROOM 222
Dell Publishing Co., 1070
1 . . . . 100.00
2 . . . . 75.00
3 Drug. 75.00
4 Ph(c) 60.00

ROSE
Cartoon Books, 2000
1 (of 3) 48-pg. 6.00
2 JSi,CV,48-pg. 6.00
3 JSi,CV,48-pg., concl. 6.00

ROSWELL
Bongo Comics, 1996
1 by Bill Morrison,The Story
   of the Century 3.00
2 The Untold Story 3.00
3 The Untold Story, concl. 3.00
4 V:Mutato. 3.00
5 . . . . 3.00
6 time-traveling comic collector . . . 3.00

ROUTE 666
Crossgen Comics, 2002
1 . . . . 3.00
2 thru 5 . . . . @3.00
6 thru 24 . . . . @3.00

ROY ROGERS
AND TRIGGER
Gold Key, 1967
1 . . . . 275.00

ROY ROGERS
WESTERN CLASSICS
AC Comics, 1989
1 . . . . 3.00
2 . . . . 3.00
3 . . . . 3.00
4 . . . . 4.00

ROY THOMAS' ANGHEM
Heroic Publishing, 2006
1 . . . . 3.25
2 thru 3 . . . . @3.25

RUFF AND READY
Dell Publishing Co., 1958
1 . . . . 300.00
2 . . . . 200.00
3 . . . . 200.00
4 thru 12 . . . . @125.00

RUGRATS
COMIC ADVENTURES
New England Comics, 1999
VOL. 1
1 thru 10 . . . . @3.00
VOL. 2
1 thru 10 . . . . @3.00
VOL. 3
1 . . . . 3.00
2 thru 9 . . . . @3.00

RUN, BUDDY, RUN
Gold Key, 1967
1 . . . . 60.00

Rune #5
© *Malibu*

RUNE
Malibu Ultraverse, 1994–95
0 BWS(a&s) 4.00
1 BWS(a&s),from Ultraverse 2.50
1a Foil cover 4.00
2 CU(s),BWS,V:Aladdin 2.50
3 DaR,BWS,(Ultraverse Premiere
   #1), Flip book. 3.75
4 thru 9 . . . . @2.50
G-Size #1 . . . . 2.50

RUNE
Malibu Ultraverse, 1995–96
Infinity V:Annihilus 2.50
1 A:Adam Warlock 2.50
1a Computer painted cover 2.50
2 thru 6 . . . . @2.50

RUNE:
HEARTS OF DARKNESS
Malibu Ultraverse, 1996
1 DgM(s),KHt,TBd, flip book. 2.50
2 DgM,KHt,TBd, flip book. 2.50
3 DgM,KI lt,TBd, flip book. 2.50

RUNE/SILVER SURFER
Ultravrse 1995
1 BWS(c),A:Adam Warlock. 6.00
1a Lim. edition (5,000 made) 8.00
1b Standard ed.newsprint. 3.00

RUNES OF RAGNAN
Silent Devil Productions, 2005
1 . . . . 3.00
2 thru 4 . . . . @3.00

RUNNERS:
THE BIG SNOW JOB
Archaia Studios, 2008
1 (of 5) 4.00
2 . . . . 3.50

RUSE
Crossgen Comics, 2001
1 MWa. 8.00
2 MWa. 3.50
3 thru 14 . . . . @3.00
15 thru 27 . . . . @3.00
Spec. Archard's Agents,
   Deadly Dare (2004). 3.00

RUST
Now, 1987
1 . . . . 4.00
2 . . . . 3.00
3 . . . . 2.50
4 . . . . 2.50
5 thru 11 . . . . @2.50
12 I:Terminator. 9.00
13 thru 15 . . . . @2.50
[Volume 2], 1989
1 thru 10 . . . . @2.50

RUST
Malibu
1 O:Rust 3.00
2 V:Marion Labs 3.00
3 I:Ashe Sapphire,5th Anniv. 3.00
4 I:Rustmobile. 3.00

RUULE: GANGLORDS
OF CHINATOWN
Beckett Entertainment, 2003
1 . . . . 6.00
2 thru 3 . . . . @6.00
4 thru 5 . . . . @3.00

RUULE: KISS & TELL
Beckett Entertainment, 2004
1 . . . . 3.00
2 thru 5 . . . . @3.00
6 thru 8 . . . . @2.50

SABLE
First, 1988–90
1 AIDS story 2.50
2 thru 28 . . . . @2.50

SABRE
Eclipse, 1982–85
1 PG 2.50
2 PG 3.00
3 thru 14 . . . . @2.50

SABRINA, THE
TEENAGE WITCH
Archie Publications, 1971–83
1 . . . . 300.00
2 Archie. 150.00
3 Archie. 125.00
4 . . . . 100.00
5 . . . . 100.00
6 thru 10 . . . . @100.00
11 thru 30 . . . . @75.00
31 thru 40 . . . . @40.00
41 thru 76 . . . . @25.00
77 . . . . 30.00

SABRINA
THE TEENAGE WITCH
Archie Comics, 1996
one-shot photo cover. 7.00

COLOR PUB.

1 photo cover 5.00
2 Trouble in Time 5.00
3 photo cover 5.00
4 photo cover 5.00
5 Driver's License 5.00
6 Treasure Troubles 5.00
7 The Sculpture Switch. 5.00
8 The Cable Girl, photo (c) 5.00
9 Farewell Feline 5.00
10 No Brain, No Pain. 5.00
11 thru 17 . . . . @3.00
18 thru 33 photo (c) . . . . @3.00
[Volume 2], 2000
1 thru 3 from animated series . . . @2.50
4 thru 13 . . . . @2.50
14 thru 62 . . . . @2.50
63 thru 98 . . . . @2.25
Halloween Spooktacular #1 . . . . . . 2.50
Halloween Spooktacular #2 . . . . . . 2.50
Holiday Spectacular #3 . . . . 2.50
GN The Magic Revisited 7.50

SADHU, THE:
WHEEL OF DESTINY
Virgin Comics, 2008
1 (of 5) 3.00
2 thru 4 . . . . @3.00

SAD SACK
AND THE SARGE
Harvey Publications, 1957–82
1 . . . . 300.00
2 . . . . 150.00
3 . . . . 100.00
4 . . . . 100.00
5 . . . . 100.00
6 thru 10 . . . . @100.00
11 thru 20 . . . . @75.00
21 thru 40 . . . . @50.00
41 thru 50 . . . . @35.00
51 thru 90 . . . . @25.00
91 thru 96 52 pg Giants . . . . @15.00
97 thru 155 . . . . @15.00

SAD SACK'S ARMY LIFE
Harvey Publications, 1963–76
1 . . . . 150.00
2 thru 10 . . . . @75.00
11 thru 20 . . . . @50.00
21 thru 30 . . . . @40.00
31 thru 50 . . . . @30.00
51 thru 61 . . . . @25.00

SAD SACK'S
FUNNY FRIENDS
Harvey Publications, 1955–69
1 . . . . 250.00
2 thru 10 . . . . @100.00
11 thru 20 . . . . @75.00
21 thru 30 . . . . @50.00
31 thru 40 . . . . @35.00
41 thru 75 . . . . @30.00

SAD SACK
LAUGH SPECIAL
Harvey Publications, 1958
1 . . . . 160.00
2 . . . . 120.00
3 thru 20 . . . . @100.00

SAD SACK in 3-D
Blackthorne
1 and 2 . . . . @2.50

SAD SACK SACK WORLD
Harvey, 1964
1 . . . . 100.00

2 thru 20 . . . . @50.00
21 thru 31 . . . . @30.00
32 thru 46 . . . . @15.00

Sad Sack U.S.A. #2
© Harvey

SAD SACK USA
Harvey, 1972
1 . . . . 30.00
2 thru 7 . . . . @20.00

SADHU
Virgin Comics, 2006
1 thru 5 . . . . @3.00

SAFETY-BELT MAN
ALL HELL
Sirius, 1996
1 . . . . 3.00
2 . . . . 3.00
3 . . . . 3.00
4 Linsner back (c) 4.00
5 . . . . 3.00

SAGA OF
THE METABARONS
Humanoids Publishing, 1999
1 (of 16) Sci-fi 3.00
2 thru 9 . . . . @3.00

SAINT LEGEND
Comicsone.com, 2002
GN #3 thru #6 . . . . @14.00
GN #7 thru GN #10 . . . . @15.00

SALEM
Boom! Studios, 2008
1 . . . . 4.00
1a variant (c) 4.00
2 thru 4 . . . . @4.00

SALVADOR
Boom! Studios, 2007
1 . . . . 4.00
2 thru 4 . . . . @4.00

SAM AND MAX, FREE-
LANCE POLICE SPECIAL
Comico, 1987–89
1 . . . . 3.00

SAM SLADE
ROBOHUNTER
Quality, 1986–89
1 . . . . 2.50
2 thru 10 . . . . @2.50
11 thru 21 . . . . @2.50
22/23 . . . . 2.50
24 . . . . 2.50
25/26 . . . . 2.50
27 thru 33 . . . . @2.50

SAMSONS
Samsons Comics, 1995
1/2 Various Artists 2.50

SAMUREE
Windjammer, 1995
1 I:Samuree 2.50
2 V: The Dragon 2.50
3 V: The Dragon 2.50

SAMURAI
Eclipse
1 . . . . 2.50
2 . . . . 2.50
3 thru 5 . . . . @2.50

SAMURAI GUARD
Colburn Comics, 2000
1 by Kirk C. Abrigo 2.50
2 . . . . 2.50
3 thru 6 . . . . @3.00

SAMUREE
Continuity, 1987
1 NA,A:Revengers 2.50
2 A:Revengers 2.50
3 NA,A:Revengers 2.50
4 A:Revengers 2.50
5 BSz(c),A:Revengers 2.50
6 A:Revengers 2.50
7 . . . . 2.50
8 Drug story 2.50
9 Drug story 2.50
[2nd Series], 1993
1 thru 3 Rise of Magic. . . . . @2.50

SANDSCAPE
Dreamwave, 2003
1 . . . . 3.00
2 thru 4 . . . . @3.00

SANTANA
Rock-it Comix, 1994
1 TT(c&s),TY. 4.00

SARGE STEEL/
SECRET AGENT
Charlton, 1964–66
1 DG,I:SargeSteel & IvanChung . . 75.00
2 DG,I:Werner Von Hess 50.00
3 DG,V:Smiling Skull. 50.00
4 DG,V:Lynx 50.00
5 FMc,V:Ivan Chung 50.00
6 FMc,A:Judomaster. 60.00
7 DG 50.00
8 V:Talon. 50.00
Becomes:

SECRET AGENT
9 DG,A:The Lynx. 75.00
10 DG,JAp,A:Tiffany Sinn 50.00

SATANIKA
Verotik, 1995
0 . . . . 3.00
1 New ongoing series. 4.00
2 Femininity 3.50

3 thru 5 . . . . @3.00
6 thru 10 . . . . @3.00
10a Wingbird variant cover 5.00
11 SBi,final issue 4.00
11a Jason Blood variant (c) 10.00
11b Superfest 99 limited 15.00
1-shot Satanika X (adult) 5.00
1-shot Satanika vs.Shilene 10.00

SATANIKA TALES
Verotik, 2005
2 . . . . 4.00
2a variant (c). 5.00
2b Limited fan (c) 10.00

SATAN'S SIX
Topps, 1993
1 F:Satan's Six,w/3 cards 3.25
2 V:Kalazarr,w/3 cards 3.00
3 w/3 cards 3.00
4 w/3 cards 3.00

SAURIANS:
UNNATURAL SELECTION
Crossgen Comics, 2002
1 (of 2) 3.00
2 . . . . 3.00

SAVAGE BROTHERS
Boom! Studios, 2006
1 (of 3) 3.50
2 thru 3 . . . . @3.50

SAVAGE COMBAT TALES
Atlas, Feb.–July, 1975
1 F:Sgt Strykers Death Squad . . . 20.00
2 ATh,A:Warhawk 30.00
3 final issue. 15.00

SAVAGE DRAGON/
TEENAGE MUTANT
NINJA TURLTES
CROSSOVER
Mirage, 1993
1 EL(s). 3.00

SAVAGE RED SONJA
QUEEN OF THE
FROZEN WASTES
D.E. (Dynamite Ent.) 2006
1 (of 4) 3.50
1a foil (c) 4.00
2 thru 4 . . . . @3.50
2 thru 4a variant (c)s . . . . @3.50

SAVAGE TALES
D.E. (Dynamite Ent.) 2007
1 . . . . 5.00
1a variant (c)s . . . . @5.00
2 . . . . 5.00
3 . . . . 5.00
4 . . . . 5.00
5 . . . . 5.00
6 thru 10 . . . . @5.00
7a variant (c) 5.00

SAVAGE WORLD
Kandora Publishing, 2005
1 . . . . 3.50
2 . . . . 3.50
3 . . . . 3.50

SAVED BY THE BELL
Harvey, 1992
1 based on TV series 2.50

2 thru 5 . . . . @2.50

SAWED-OFF MOJO
Speakeasy Comics, 2006
1 (of 6) 3.00
2 thru 3 . . . . @3.00

SCAMP
Dell, 1958
5 . . . . 75.00
6 thru 16 . . . . @60.00

SCAMP
Gold Key, 1967
1 Disney 60.00
2 thru 10 . . . . @25.00
11 thru 20 . . . . @20.00
21 thru 45. . . . . @10.00

SCARFACE:
DEVIL IN DISGUISE
IDW, 2007
1 . . . . 4.00
2 thru 4 . . . . @4.00

SCARFACE:
SCARRED FOR LIFE
IDW Publishing, 2006
1 . . . . 4.00
2 thru 5 . . . . @4.00
1a thru 5a variant (c)s . . . . @4.00

SCARLET CRUSH
Awesome Entertainment, 1998
1 by John Stinsman 2.50
2 . . . . 2.50
3 Icaria's decision 2.50
4 Nirasawa arrives 2.50

SCARLETT'S CURSE
Praxis Comics, 2007
0-1 combo 4.00
2 thru 6 . . . . @3.00

SCARLET VERONICA
Ape Entertainment, 2008
1 (of 4) 3.00
2 . . . . 3.50

SCARY TALES
Charlton, 1975
1 JSon. 50.00

Scary Tales #26
© Charlton

2 . . . . 25.00
3 SD,P(c) 25.00
4 TS,SD,JSon,P(c) 40.00
5 SD 40.00
6 . . . . 25.00
7 SD 30.00
8 SD 30.00
9 TS 40.00
10 . . . . 25.00
11 SD 30.00
12 SD 25.00
13 . . . . 20.00
14 SD. 25.00
15 SD 25.00
16 SD 25.00
17 . . . . 20.00
18 BP 25.00
19 SD 25.00
20 JSon 18.00
21 SD 25.00
22 . . . . 15.00
23 thru 28 . . . . @14.00
30 thru 37 . . . . @12.00
38 Mr. Jigsaw 15.00
39 SD 20.00
40 thru 46 . . . . @15.00

SCATTERBRAIN
APC, 2005
1 . . . . 3.50
2 thru 4 . . . . @3.50

SCATTERBRAIN
Markosia, 2006
1 . . . . 3.50
1a variant (c)s . . . . @3.50
2 thru 4 . . . . @3.50
3a variant (c) 3.50

SCAVENGERS
Quality, 1988–89
1 thru 7 . . . . @2.50
8 thru 14 . . . . @2.50

SCAVENGERS
Triumphant Comics, 1993–94
0 Fso(c),JnR(s), ... 2.50
0a `Free Copy' 2.50
0b Red Logo 2.50
1 JnR(s),I:Scavengers,Ximos,
    C:Doctor Chaos. 2.50
1a 2nd Printing 2.50
2 JnR(s), ... 2.50
3 JnR(s),I:Lurok 2.50
4 JnR(s), ... 2.50
5 Fso(c),JnR(s),D:Jack Hanal. . . . 2.50
6 JnR(s), ... 2.50
7 JnR(s),I:Zion 2.50
8 JnR(s),Nativity 2.50
9 JnR(s),The Challenge 2.50
10 JnR(s),Snowblind 2.50

SCHISM
Defiant
1 thru 4 Defiant's x-over. . . . . . . @3.25

SCION
Crossgen Comics, 2000
1 RMz 5.00
2 RMz 5.00
3 RMz 4.50
4 . . . . 3.00
5 . . . . 3.00
6 . . . . 4.00
7 thru 18 . . . . @3.00
19 thru 30 RMz . . . . @3.00
31 thru 44 RMz . . . . @3.00

COLOR PUB.

SCI-TECH
WildStorm/DC, 1999
1 (of 4) BCi,Ebe,. 2.50
2 BCi,EBe,. 2.50
3 BCi,EBe 2.50
4 BCi,EBe,concl. 2.50

SCOOBY DOO
Gold Key, 1970–75
1 . . . . 250.00
2 . . . . 175.00
3 . . . . 150.00
4 . . . . 150.00
5 . . . . 150.00
6 thru 20 . . . . @100.00
21 thru 30 . . . . @75.00

SCOOBY DOO
Charlton Comics, 1975–76
1 . . . . 150.00
2 thru 5 . . . . @75.00
6 thru 11 . . . . @60.00

SCOOBY-DOO
Harvey, 1992
1 . . . . 7.00
2 thru 3 . . . . @6.00

SCOOBY DOO
Archie, 1995
1 . . . . 6.00
2 thru 10 . . . . @5.00
11 thru 21 . . . . @4.00

SCOOBY DOO MYSTERY COMICS
Gold Key, 1973
17 thru 30 . . . . @55.00

SCORCHED EARTH
Tundra, 1991
1 Earth 2025,I:Dr.EliotGodwin 3.50
2 Hunt for Eliot 3.00
3 Mystical Transformation 3.00

SCORPION, THE
Atlas, 1975
1 HC, bondage cover 30.00
2 HC,BWi,MK 25.00
3 . . . . 20.00

SCORPION CORP.
Dagger, 1993
1 PuD,JRI,CH, ... 2.75
2 PuD,JRI,CH,V:Victor Kyner 2.75
3 PuD,BIH,V:Victor Kyner 2.75

SCORPIO ROSE
Eclipse, 1983
1 MR/TP,I:Dr.Orient. 2.50
2 MR/TP 2.50

SCOUT
Eclipse, 1985–87
1 TT,I:Scout,Fash.In Action. 6.00
2 TT,V:Buffalo Monster 3.00
3 thru 18 TT . . . . @2.50
19 TT,w/Record,V:Lex Lucifer 3.00
20 thru 24 TT . . . . @2.50

SCOUT: WAR SHAMAN
Eclipse, 1988–89
1 TT,R:Scout (now a father) 2.50
2 thru 16 TT . . . . @2.50

SCREAM QUEEN
Boom! Studios, 2008
1 . . . . 4.00
1a variant (c) 4.00
2 thru 5 . . . . @4.00

SEADRAGON
Elite, 1986–87
1 . . . . 3.00
1a 2nd printing 2.50
2 thru 8 . . . . @2.50

SEA HUNT
Dell Publishing Co., 1958
1 L.BridgesPh(c) all 275.00
2 . . . . 200.00
3 ATh. 225.00
4 RsM 200.00
5 RsM 200.00
6 RsM 200.00
7 . . . . 150.00
8 RsM 200.00
9 RsM 200.00
10 RsM. 200.00
11 RsM. 200.00
12 . . . . 200.00
13 RsM. 200.00

SEAQUEST
Nemesis, 1994
1 HC(c),DGC,KP,AA,Based on
TV Show 2.50

SEASON OF THE REAPER, THE: WINTER
Speakeasy Comics, 2005
1 (of 3) 3.00
2 thru 3 . . . . @3.00

SEBASTIAN
Walt Disney
1 From Little Mermaid. 2.50
2 While da Crab's Away 2.50

SECOND LIFE OF DR. MIRAGE, THE
Valiant, 1993
1 B:BL(s),BCh,V:Mast.Darque 2.50
1a Gold Ed. 3.00
2 thru 19 . . . . @2.50

Second Life of Dr. Mirage #9
© *Valiant*

SECOND STAGE TURBINE BLADE
Eve Ink 2004
1 . . . . 60.00
1a Diamond 40.00
2 . . . . 25.00

SECRET AGENT
Gold Key, 1966
1 . . . . 250.00
2 . . . . 200.00

SECRET CITY SAGA
Topps, 1993
0 JK. 3.25
0 Gold Ed. 15.00
0 Red 10.00
1 thru 4 with 3 cards . . . . @3.25

SECRET HISTORY, THE
Archaia Studios, 2007
1 (of 7) 6.00
2 thru 7 . . . . @6.00

SECRET HISTORY OF THE AUTHORITY: JACK HAWKSMOOR
Wildstorm/DC, March, 2008
1 (of 6) F:Hawksmoor 3.00
2 thru 6 . . . . @3.00

SECRET SKULL
IDW Publishing, 2004
1 . . . . 4.00
2 thru 4 . . . . @4.00

SECRETS OF THE VALIANT UNIVERSE
Valiant, 1994
1 from Wizard 2.50
2 BH,Chaos Effect-Beta#4,A:Master
Darque,Dr.Mirage,Max St.James,
Dr. Eclipse 2.50

SECRET SQUIRREL
Gold Key, 1966
1 . . . . 225.00

SECRET WEAPONS
Valiant, 1993
1 JSP(a&s),BWi(i),I:Dr.Eclipse,
A:Master Darque,A:Geoff,
Livewire,Stronghold,Solar,X-O,
Bloodshot,Shadowman 2.75
1a Gold Ed. 4.00
2 thru 23 . . . . @2.50

SECRET WEAPONS: PLAYING WITH FIRE
Valiant
1 & 2 . . . . @2.50

SEDUCTION OF THE INNOCENT
Eclipse, 1985–86
1 ATh,Hanged by the Neck, reps. . . 3.00
2 . . . . 3.00
3 ATh,The Crushed Gardenia 3.00
4 ATh,NC,World's Apart 3.00
5 ATh,The Phantom Ship 3.00
6 ATh,RA,Hands of Don Jose 3.00
3-D #1 DSt(c) 5.00
3-D #2 ATh,MB,BWr,Man Who Was
Always on Time 5.00

COLOR PUB.

SEEKER
Sky Comics, 1995
1 JMt(s),I:Seeker 2.50

SENSEI
First, 1989
1 Mini-Series. 2.75
2 . . . . 2.75
3 . . . . 2.75
4 . . . . 2.75

SENTINELS OF JUSTICE
AC Comics, 1990
1 Capt.Paragon. 2.50
2 . . . . 2.50
3 EL art 2.50
4 EL art 2.50
5 . . . . 2.50
6 . . . . 2.50
7 . . . . 2.50

SENTRY: SPECIAL
Innovation, 1991
1 . . . . 2.75

SERAPHIM
Innovation, 1990
1 and 2 . . . . @2.50

SERINA
Antarctic, 1996
1 . . . . 3.00

SERPENTINA
Lightning, 1997
1 . . . . 3.00
1a variant cover 3.00

SE7EN
Zenescope Entertainment, 2006
1 (of 7) Gluttony 4.00
2 Greed. 4.00
3 Sloth 4.00
4 Lust 4.00
5 Pride 4.00
6 Envy. 4.00
7 Wrath 4.00

SEVEN BROTHERS
Virgin Comics 2007
Series 2
1 . . . . 3.00
2 . . . . 3.00
3 . . . . 3.00
4 . . . . 3.00

SEVEN SISTERS
Zephyr Comics, 1997
1 by Curley, Cruickshank & Garcia. 3.00
2 thru 4 . . . . @3.00

SEVENTH SHRINE, THE
Devil's Due Publishing, 2004
1 (of 2) R.Silverberg adapt. 6.00
2 . . . . 6.00

77 SUNSET STRIP
Dell Publishing Co., 1960
1 Ph(c) 150.00
2 Ph(c),RsM 150.00

77 SUNSET STRIP
Gold Key, 1962
1 from TV series, Ph(c). 150.00
2 . . . . 150.00

SHADE SPECIAL
AC Comics, 1984
1 . . . . 2.50

SHADOW, THE
Archie Comics, 1964–65
1 . . . . 150.00
2 . . . . 100.00
3 . . . . 100.00
4 . . . . 100.00
5 . . . . 100.00
6 and 8 . . . . @75.00

SHADOWFLAME
Arcana Studio, 2007
1 (of 4) 4.00
2 thru 4 . . . . @4.00

SHADOW MAN
Valiant, 1992
0 BH,TmR,Chromium (c),O:Maxim
  St.James,Shadowman. 4.00
0a Newstand ed. 5.00
0b Gold Ed. 15.00
1 DL,JRu,I&O.Shadowman. 9.00
2 DL,V:Serial Killer 5.00
3 V:Emil Sosa 5.00
4 DL,FM(c),Unity#6,A:Solar 5.00
5 DL,WS(c),Unity#14, A:Archer &
  Armstrong 5.00
6 SD,L:Lilora 3.00
7 DL,V:Creature 3.00
8 JDx(i),I:Master Darque. 3.50
9 JDx(i),V:Darque's Minions 3.50
10 BH,I:Sandria 3.00
11 BH,N:Shadowman. 3.00
12 BH,V:Master Darque. 3.00
13 BH,V:Rev.Shadow Man 3.00
14 BH,JDx,V:Bikers 3.00
15 BH,JDx,V:JB,Fake Shadow
  Man,C:Turok 3.00
16 BH,JDx,I:Dr.Mirage, Carmen . . 3.50
17 BH,JDx,A:Archer & Armstrong . . 3.00
18 BH,JDx,A:Archer & Armstrong . . 3.00
19 BH,A:Aerosmith 6.00
20 BH,A:Master Darque,
  V:Shadowman's Father 3.00
21 BH,I:Maxim St.James (1895
  Shadowman) 3.00
22 V:Master Darque. 3.00
23 BH(a&s),A:Doctor Mirage,
  V:Master Darque 3.00
24 BH(a&s),V:H.A.T.E. 3.00
25 RgM,w/Valiant Era card 3.00
26 w/Valiant Era card. 3.50
27 BH,V:Drug Lord. 3.00
28 BH,A:Master Darque. 3.00
29 Chaos Effect-Beta#1,V:Master
  Darque. 3.00
30 R:Rotwak 3.00
31 thru 33 . . . . @3.00
34 Voodoo in Carribean. 3.00
35 A:Ishmael 3.00
36 F:Ishmael 3.00
37 A:X-O, V:Blister. 3.00
38 V:Ishmael, Blister 3.00
39 RH,TmR,Explores Powers 3.00
40 BH,TmR,I,Vampire! 3.00
41 A:Steve Massarsky 3.00
42 . . . . 3.00
43 V:Smilin Jack 8.00

SHADOWMAN
Acclaim, 1996
1 GEn(s),Deadside, pt.1 . . . . 7.00
2 GEn(s),Deadside, pt.2 . . . . 4.00
3 GEn(s),Deadside, pt.3 . . . . 4.00
4 GEn(s),Deadside, pt.4 . . . . 4.00
5 thru 19 JaD,CAd . . . . @4.00
20 Deadside vortes 7.00

Shadowman Vol. 2 #9
© Acclaim

VOLUME 3 (1999)
1 DAn,ALa,48-page 12.00
2 . . . . 12.00
3 Flip-book 12.00
4 Flip-book 15.00
5 . . . . 15.00
6 . . . . 30.00
7 final issue 30.00

SHADOWMANCER
Markosia, 2005
1 . . . . 3.50
1a variant (c)s. . . . . @3.50
2 thru 10 . . . . @3.50
2a thru 10a variant (c) . . . . @3.50

SHADOW OF THE TORTURER, THE
Innovation, 1991
1 thru 6 Gene Wolfe adapt. . . . . @2.50

SHADOWPLAY
IDW Publishing, 2005
1 . . . . 4.00
2 . . . . 4.00
3 . . . . 4.00
4 . . . . 4.00
1a thru 4a variant (c). . . . . @4.00

SHADOW REAVERS
Black Bull Entertainment, 2001
1 Nel,KM(c). 5.00
1a variant TDr(c). 9.00
2 Nel,GF(c) 3.00
3 Nel 3.00
2a thru 3a variant TDr(c)s . . . . . @5.00
4 Nel 3.00
4a variant limited master edition. . . 5.00
5 Nel 3.00
5a variant limited master edition. . . 5.00
Preview Edition 3.00
Preview Edition, limited 5.00

SHADOW STATE
Preview Editions
1 and 2 B&W . . . . @2.50
Broadway, 1995
1 thru 4 F:BloodS.C.R.E.A.M. . . @2.50
5 JiS, Image Isn't Everything,
  concl. 2.50
6 Anger of Lovers, pt.1 . . . . 2.50
7 Anger of Lovers, pt.2 . . . . 3.00

COLOR PUB.

SHAIANA
Entity, 1995
1 R:Shaiana from Aster	3.75
1a clear chromium	8.00
1b Holochrome	9.00
2 Guardians of Earth	2.50

SHAOLIN
Black Tiger Press
1 I:Tiger	3.00
2 I:Crane	3.00

SHAOLIN COWBOY
Burlyman Entertainment, 2004
1	3.50
2 thru 5	@3.50
6	3.50
7	3.50
3a thru 7a variant (c)s	@3.50

SHARK-MAN
Thrill House, 2006
1	4.00

SHATTER
First, 1985–88
1	3.00
2	2.50
3	2.50
4 thru 14	@2.50
Spec. #1 Computer Comic	5.00
#1a 2nd Printing	2.00

SHAUN OF THE DEAD
IDW Publishing, 2005
1	4.00
2 thru 4	@4.00

SHAUN THE SHEEP
Titan Publishing, 2007
1	5.00
2 thru 10	@5.00

SHE-DEVILS ON WHEELS
Aircel
1 V:Man-Eaters	3.00
2 V:Man-Eaters	3.00
3 V:Man-Eaters	3.00

SHEENA
Devil's Due, 2007
Preview Spec.	2.50
Priview Spec. variant (c)	2.50
1	3.50
1a variant (c)s	@3.50
2 thru 7	@3.50
2a & b thru 7 a & b variant (c)s	@3.50

SHEENA: QUEEN OF THE JUNGLE
London Night
0 by Gabriel Cain & Wilson	3.00
0a Zebra Edition	5.00
0b Leopard Edition	5.00
0c Alligator Edition	5.00

...BOUND
London Night, 1998
1 (of 4) by Everette Hartsoe & Art Wetherell	3.00
1 ministry ed.	5.00
1 Leather retro edition	12.00

...DARK RISING
Devil's Due, 2008
1	3.50

1a variant (c)	@3.50
2 thru 3	@3.50
2a thru 3a variant (c)s	@3.50

SHERIFF OF TOMBSTONE
Charlton Comics, 1958–61
1 AW,JSe	150.00
2	100.00
3 thru 10	@100.00
11 thru 17	@75.00

SHERLOCK HOLMES & KOLCHAK, THE NIGHT STALKER: CRY OF THUNDER
Moonstone, 2008
1 (of 3)	4.00
1a variant (c)	4.00
2	4.00
2a variant (c)	5.00
2b variant sketch (c)	7.00

SHIELD, THE: SPOTLIGHT
IDW Publishing, 2004
1	4.00
2 thru 5	@4.00

Shi The Way of the Warrior #4
© Crusade Comics

SHI (THE WAY OF THE WARRIOR)
Crusade Comics, 1994–97
1 BiT,HMo,I:Shi	9.00
2 BiT	5.00
2a BiT, reissue, new cover	3.00
3 BiT	5.00
4 BiT	4.00
5 V:Arashi	3.00
5a variant cover	6.00
6 V:Tomoe	3.00
7 V:Nara Warriors	3.00
8 New costume	3.00
9 thru 11	@3.00
12 Way of the Warrior, concl, flip-book Way of the Warrior Angel Fire.	3.00
Spec. #1 Shi/Cyblade,Battle of the Independents (1995)	4.00
Spec.#1a Shi/Cyblade,variant(c)	6.00
Ashcan #1, sign & num. (2000)	10.00
Spec. #1 10th Anniv. Edition (2004).	3.00

Crusade Entertainment, 2004
1 10th Anniv. Edition (2004)	3.00
1 10th Anniv. Graphite ed.	20.00

...THE SERIES
Crusade Entertainment, 1997
1 sequel to Shi: Heaven and Earth, F:Tomoe.	3.50
2 Unforgettable Fire, concl.	3.00
3 A Rock and a Hard Place, pt.1	3.00
4 A Rock and a Hard Place, pt.2	3.00
5 A Rock and a Hard Place, pt.3	3.00
6	3.00
7 Photographer's lucky picture	3.00
8 V:Gemini Dawn twins	3.00
9 Bad Blood, pt.1	3.00
9a variant BTi(c)	3.00
9b variant Ahn (c)	3.00
9c variant Kevin Lau (c)	3.00
10 Bad Blood, pt.2	3.00
10a variant BTi(c)	3.00
10b variant Ahn (c)	3.00
10c variant Kevin Lau (c)	3.00
11 Bad Blood, pt.3	3.00
12 The Dark Crusade, pt.1 (of 8).	3.00
13 The Dark Crusade, pt.2 (of 8).	3.00
14 The Dark Crusade, pt.3 (of 8).	3.00
15 The Dark Crusade, pt.4 (of 8).	3.00
16 The Dark Crusade, pt.5 (of 8).	3.00
1-shot The Essential Dark Crusade.	3.00
1-shot Shi:Five Year Celebration	5.00
1-shotA,B,C,&D variant covers	5.00
#0 & Wolverine/Shi flip book	3.00
Spec. Shi/Vampirella,x-over(1997).	3.00
Spec. Shi: Nightstalkers, VMk, F:T.C.B. (1997)	3.50
Spec. Shi: Masquerade (1997)	3.50
Spec. Shi: Art of War Tour Book Wizard Chicago con (1998).	6.00
G.I. Preview Edition (2001)	5.00
Spec. Through the Ashes (2001).	3.00

...AKAI
Crusade Entertainment, 2001
1 BTi, I:RAF Victoria Cross.	3.00
1 antiques edition	25.00
Ashcan, signed & numbered	9.00

...BLACK WHITE & RED
Crusade Entertainment, 1998
1 Night of the Rat, pt.1	3.00
2 Night of the Rat, pt.2	3.00
Coll. Ed. rep. #1–#2	7.00

...EAST WIND RAIN
Crusade Entertainment, 1997
1 BiT,MSo, fully painted	3.50
2 BiT, concl.	3.50

...HEAVEN AND EARTH
Crusade Entertainment, 1997
1 (of 3) BiT	3.00
1 variant cover	3.00
2 BiT	3.00
3 BiT	3.00
4 BiT	3.00

...HOT TARGET
Crusade Entertainment, 2003
1	3.00

...PANDORA'S BOX
Avatar Press, 2003
Preview Edition 16-pg. B&W	6.00
Preview BiT(c)	2.00
Preview prism foil (c)	11.00
1/2 prism foil (c)	11.00
1/2 royal blue (c)	60.00
1 BiT(c)	3.50
1a variant (c)s	@3.50
1b prism foil (c)	11.00
1 royal blue edition	60.00

...POISONED PARADISE
Avatar, 2002
Preview 16-pg., b&w 2.00
Preview, Ron Adrian (c) 6.00
Preview, prism foil edition 11.00
1 (of 2) BiT,Karl Waller,Martin(c). . . 3.50
1a BiT(c) 3.50
1b Waller (c) 3.50
1c Wraparound exclusive (c) 3.50
1d Angel of Death (c) 6.00
1e Angel of Death ruby foil (c) 9.00
1f prism (c) 11.00
2 BiT(c). 3.50
2a-2c variant(c)s . . . . @3.50
1/2 Blossom (c) 6.00
1/2 variant (c)s . . . . @4.00
1/2 Royal Blue foil 75.00

...REKISHI
Crusade Entertainment, 1997
1 (of 2) BiT 3.00
2 BiT, conclusion. 3.00
Coll.Ed. Shi:Reshiki, sourcebook,
    MS(c). 5.00

...VS 10TH MUSE
Bluewater Productions, 2007
1-shot x-over 3.50

...VS. TOMOE
Crusade, April, 1996
Spec. #1 BiT, double size 4.00
GN Unforgettable Fire, rep. 7.00

...SENRYAKU
Crusade, 1995
1 BiT,R:Shi 3.00
1a variant cover 5.00
1 (of 3) 2nd edition 2.50
2 BiT,Arts of Warfare. 3.00
2 2nd edition 2.50
3 BiT 3.00
3 2nd edition 2.50

...YEAR OF THE DRAGON
Crusade Entertainment, 2000
1 (of 3) BiT 3.00
1a variant (c). 3.00
1b signed & numbered 9.00
1c true colors ed. BiT 6.00
1d true colors ed. ruby red 20.00
2 Ana Tears (c) BiT 3.00
2a Death Incarnate (c) BiT 3.00
3 BTi, concl. 3.00
Ashcan, signed & numbered 9.00
Coll. Ed. Black,White,Red 7.00
GN #1 & #2 Black,White,Red 6.00
Poster Book 3.00

SHOCK SUSPENSE
STORIES
Russ Cochran Press, 1992
1 reps.horror stories 2.50
2 inc.Kickback. 2.50
3 thru 4 . . . . @2.50
5 thru 7 reps.horror stories . . . . @2.50
8 reps.horror stories 2.50
Gemstone
18 EC comics reprint 2.50

SHOCK THE MONKEY
Millennium/Expand, 1995
1 Shock therapy 3.00

SHON C. BURY'S NOX
Narwain Publishing, 2006
2 . . . . 4.00

SHOTGUN MARY
Antarctic Press, 1995
1 I:Shotgun Mary 3.00

1a with CD Soundtrack. 9.00
1b Red Foil cover 8.00
2 . . . . 3.00
Spec. Shooting Gallery 3.00
Spec. Deviltown 3.00
Spec. Deviltown, commem. (1999) . 6.00

SHOTGUN MARY
Antarctic Press, 1998
1 by Herb Mallette & Kelsey
    Shannon 3.00
2 Early Days, pt.2 . . . . 3.00
3 Early Days, pt.3 . . . . 3.00

...BLOOD LORE
Antarctic Press, 1997
1 (of 4) by Herb Mallette
    & Neil Googe. 3.00
2 . . . . 3.00
3 . . . . 3.00
4 concl. 3.00

...SON OF THE BEAST,
DAUGHTER OF LIGHT
Antarctic Press, 1997
1 . . . . 3.00

SHOTGUN WEDDING
Speakeasy Comics, 2005
1 . . . . 3.00
2 . . . . 3.00

Shrugged #1
© Aspin MLT

SHRUGGED
Aspen MLT., 2006
Spec. Beginnings 3.00
0 . . . . 7.00
1 . . . . 5.00
2 thru 5 . . . . @3.00
6 thru 8 . . . . @3.00

SICK
Charlton, 1976
109 . . . . 20.00
110 thru 134. . . . . 20.00
Annual #1. . . . . 40.00
Annual #2. . . . . 40.00

SIEGEL & SHUSTER
Eclipse, 1984–85
1 . . . . 2.50
2 . . . . 2.50

SIGIL
Crossgen Comics, 2000
1 BKs 5.00
2 BKs 3.25
3 thru 5 BKs . . . . @3.50
6 thru 12 BKs . . . . @3.25
13 thru 18 MWa,SEa . . . . @3.00
19 thru 30 SEa . . . . @3.00
31 thru 43 CDi(s) . . . . @3.00

SILENCERS, THE
Moonstone, 2003
1 . . . . 3.50
2 . . . . 3.50
3 . . . . 3.00
4 . . . . 3.00
1-shot Bitter Fruit, Bumper Edition . 5.00

SILENT DRAGON
Wildstorm/DC, July, 2005
1 (of 6) 3.00
2 thru 6 . . . . @3.00

SILENT GHOST
Speakeasy Comics, 2005
1 . . . . 3.00
2 . . . . 3.00
Markosia, 2006
1 . . . . 3.50
2 . . . . 3.50
3 thru 4 . . . . @3.50
4a variant (c) 3.50

SILENT HILL
IDW Publishing, 2005
1 Paint it Black 7.50
GN Among the Damned. 7.50
GN The Grinning Man 7.50

...DEAD/ALIVE
IDW Publishing, 2005
1 . . . . 4.00
1a 4.00
2 thru 5 . . . . @4.00
2a thru 5a variant (c) 4.00

...DYING INSIDE
IDW Publishing, 2004
1 . . . . 5.00
2 thru 5 . . . . @4.50

...SINNER'S REWARD
IDW, 2008
1 thru 4 . . . . @4.00

SILENT MOBIUS
Viz, 1991–92
1 Katsumi 5.75
2 Katsumi vs. Spirit. 5.25
3 Katsumi trapped within entity. . . . 5.00
4 Nami vs. Dragon 5.00
5 Kiddy vs. Wire 5.00
6 Search for Wire 5.00

SILENT MOBIUS II
Viz, 1991
1 AMP Officers vs. Entities cont . . . 5.00
2 Entities in Amp H.Q. 5.00
3 V:Entity. 5.00
4 The Esper Weapon 5.00
5 Last issue. 5.00

SILENT MOBIUS III
Viz, 1992
1 F:Lebia/computer network 2.75
2 Lebia/computer link cont. 2.75
3 Lebia in danger 2.75
4 Return to Consciousness 2.75
5 Conclusion 2.75

All comics prices listed are for *Near Mint* condition.

Silken Ghost #1
© Crossgen Comics

SILKEN GHOST, THE
Crossgen Comics, 2003
1 (of 5) CDi 3.00
2 thru 5 . . . . @3.00
Vol. 1 Silken Ghost Traveler 10.00

SILVERBACK
Comico, 1989–90
1 thru 3 . . . . @2.50

SILVER CROSS
Antarctic Press, 1997
1 (of 3) by Ben Dunn 3.00
2 . . . . 3.00

SILVERHEELS
Pacific, 1983–84
1 and 3 . . . . @2.50

SILVER STAR
Pacific, 1983–84
1 thru 6 JK . . . . @2.50

SILVER STAR
Topps, 1993
1 w/Cards 3.00

SILVER STORM
Silverline, 1998
1 . . . . 2.50
2 . . . . 2.50
3 . . . . @2.50

SIMPSONS COMICS
Bongo Comics, 1993
1 Colossal Homer 12.00
2 A:Sideshow Bob 7.00
3 F:Bart 7.00
4 F:Bart 6.00
5 A:Itchy & Scratchy 5.00
6 F:Lisa 5.00
7 Circus in Town 5.00
8 Mr. Burns Voyage 5.00
9 Autobiographies 5.00
10 Tales of the Kwik-E-Mart 5.00
11 Ned Flanders Public Enemy 4.00
12 In the Blodome 4.00
13 F:Bart & Millhouse 4.00
14 Homer owns beer company 4.00
15 Waltons parody 4.00
16 thru 49 . . . . @4.00
50 80-pg. 6.00

51 thru 99 . . . . @3.00
100 SA,100-pg. 7.00
101 thru 111 . . . . @3.00
112 thru 148 . . . . 3.00
Spec. Simpsons Classics #1
  thru #14 . . . . @4.00
Simpsons Winter Wingding #1
  thru #3 . . . . @5.00
Simpsons Super Spectacular #1 . . 5.00
Simpsons Super Spectacular #2
  thru #6 . . . . @3.00
Spec. Summer Shindig #1 . . . . 5.00
Simpsons Treasure Trove #1 & #2 @4.00

SIMPSONS COMICS & STORIES
Welsh Publishing, 1993
1 with poster 4.00
1a without poster 2.50
Bongo Comics, 1998
1 F:Bartman, Itchy & Scratchy 3.00

SIMPSONS/FUTURAMA CROSSOVER CRISIS
Bongo Comics, 2005
Part II
1 (of 2) 3.00
2 . . . . 3.00

SINBAD JR
Dell, 1965
1 . . . . 60.00
2 thru 3 . . . . @45.00

SINGULARITY SEVEN
IDW Publishing, 2004
1 . . . . 4.00
2 thru 4 . . . . @4.00

SINS OF THE FALLEN: THE NIGHTSTALKER
Zenescope Entertainment, 2005
1 . . . . 3.00
2 thru 5 . . . . @3.00

SINTHIA
Lightning, 1997
1A by Joseph Adam, Daughter
  of Lucifer 3.00
1B 3.00
1c Platinum Edition 9.00
1d Autographed Edition 9.00
2 Sisters of Darkness 3.00
2a variant cover 3.00
3 Wagner(c) 3.00
3a variant Abrams cover 3.00
3b deluxe variant cover 9.00
4 Wagner(c) 3.00
4a variant John Cleary cover 3.00

SIR APROPOS OF NOTHING
IDW, 2008
1 PDd(s) 4.00
1a variant (c) 4.00

SIRE, THE
After-Shock Comics, 2006
1 (of 3) 3.00
2 . . . . 3.00
3 Revelations 3.50

SIREN
Malibu Ultraverse, 1995
Infinity V:War Machine 2.50
1 V:War Machine 2.50
1a Computer painted cover 2.50

2 Phoenix flip issue 2.50
3 Phoenix Resurrection 2.50
Spec. #1 O:Siren 2.50

SISTERHOOD, THE
Archaia Studios, 2008
1 (of 3) 3.50
2 thru 3 . . . . @3.50

SISTERS OF MERCY
Maximum, 1995–96
1 . . . . 2.50
1a variant(c) 2.50
2 . . . . 2.50
3 . . . . 2.50
No Mercy Comics
4 . . . . 2.50
5 . . . . 2.50

... PARADISE LOST
London Night, 1997
1 by Ricki Rockett & Mark Williams 2.50
2 . . . . 2.50
3 . . . . 2.50
4 . . . . 2.50

...WHEN RAZORS CRY CRIMSON TEARS
No Mercy Comics, 1996
1 . . . . 2.50

SIX-GUN HEROES
Charlton, 1960
7 . . . . 175.00
8 thru 10 . . . . @175.00

SIX-GUN SAMURAI
Alias Enterprises, 2005
1 . . . . 2.50
2 . . . . 3.00
3 . . . . 3.00
4 thru 6 . . . . @3.00

SIX MILLION DOLLAR MAN, THE
Charlton, 1976
1 JSon,Lee Majors Ph(c) 35.00
2 NA(c),JSon,Ph(c) 20.00
3 Ph(c) HC,NA 22.00
4 thru 9 Ph(c) . . . . @20.00

666: MARK OF THE BEAST
Fleetway/Quality, 1986
1 I:Fludd, BU:Wolfie Smith 2.50
2 thru 18 . . . . @2.50

SIX STRING SAMURAI
Awesome Entertainment, 1998
1 RLe 3.00

SKATEMAN
Pacific, 1983
1 NA 2.50

SKYE RUNNER
Wildstorm/DC, April, 2006
1 . . . . 3.00
1a variant JLe (c) 3.00
2 thru 5 . . . . @3.00
6 finale 3.00

SKY SHARKS
Antarctic Press, 2007
1 (of 5) 3.50
2 thru 5 . . . . @3.50

SKY WOLF
Eclipse, 1988
1 V:Baron Von Tundra 2.50
2 TL,V:Baron Von Tundra 2.50
3 TL,cont. in Airboy #41 . . . . 2.50

SLAINE THE BERSERKER
Quality, 1987–89
1 thru 14 . . . . @2.50
15/16 . . . . 2.50
17 . . . . 2.50
18/19 . . . . 2.50
20 . . . . 2.50
Becomes:

SLAINE THE KING
Quality, 1989
21 thru 26 . . . . @2.50

SLAINE
Fleetway
1 thru 4 SBs,From 2000 AD . . . . @5.00

SLAINE THE HORNED GOD
Egmont Fleetway, 1998
1 (of 3) Pat Millagan & SBs, 68pg.. 7.00
2 (of 3) Pat Millagan & SBs, 68pg.. 7.00
3 68-pg., conclusion 7.00

SLAUGHTER
APC, 2003
1 . . . . 3.50
2 and 3 . . . . @3.50

SLEEPER
Wildstorm/DC, 2003
1 SeP,F:Holden Carver. 3.00
2 SeP 3.00
3 SeP,O:Miss Misery. 3.00
4 SeP,behind the curtain. 3.00
5 SeP,F:Holden Carver. 3.00
6 SeP,Holden's past 3.00
7 SeP,things get worse. 3.00
8 SeP,Doppelganger. 3.00
9 SeP,secret records. 3.00
10 thru 12 SeP . . . . @3.00
Season Two (2004)
1 (of 12) SeP 3.00
2 thru 5 SeP . . . . @3.00
6 SeP 3.00
7 SeP 3.00
8 SeP,All-girl spy extravaganza . . . 3.00
9 SeP 3.00
10 SeP 3.00
11 SeP 3.00
12 SeP. 3.00

SLIDERS
Valiant, 1996
1 & 2 . . . . @2.50

SLIDERS: DARKEST HOUR
Acclaim, 1996
1 DGC,DG. 2.50
2 DGC,DG. 2.50
3 DGC,DG, Concl.. . . . . 2.50
Spec. RgM, Montezuma IV rules the
world 4.00
Spec. #2 Secrets 4.00

SLIDERS: ULTIMATUM
Valiant, 1996
1 & 2 . . . . @2.50

Sliders Darkest Hour #2
© Acclaim

SLIMER
Now, 1989
1 thru 15 . . . . @2.50
Becomes:

SLIMER & REAL GHOSTBUSTERS
16 thru 18. . . . . @2.50

SLUDGE
Malibu Ultraverse, 1993–94
1 BWS,I:Sludge,BU:I:Rune. 2.75
1a Ultra-Limited 5.00
2 thru 13 AaL . . . . @2.50
Red X-Mas 2.50

SMAX
Wildstorm/DC, 2003
1 (of 5) AMo,F:Jeff Smax 3.00
2 AMo,O:Smax 3.00
3 AMo,funeral 3.00
4 . . . . 3.00
5 AMo,V:Morningbright 3.00

SMILEY
Chaos! Comics, 1998
1 the Psychotic Button 3.00
Spec. Smiley Anti-Holiday Spec. . . 3.00
Spec. Smiley Psychotic Button's
Spring Break Road Trip. 3.00
Spec. Whacky Wrestling Spec. 3.00

SMOKE
What's Next Entertainment, 2000
1 (of 12) by Ty Rawls 3.00
2 . . . . 3.25
3 . . . . 3.25
4 . . . . 3.00
5 . . . . 3.25

SMOKE
IDW Publishing, 2005
1 Good Boys Grow Up 7.50
2 The Judas 7.50
3 The Men on the Chessboard. . . . 7.50

SMOKE AND MIRROR
Speakeasy Comics, 2005
1 . . . . 3.00
2 . . . . 3.00
3 thru 6 . . . . @3.00

SMOKE & MIRROR
Markosia, 2006
Vol. 2
1 . . . . 3.50
1a variant (c)s . . . . @3.50
2 thru 4 . . . . @3.50
2a thru 3a variant (c)s . . . . @3.50

SMOKEY BEAR
Gold Key, 1970
1 . . . . 45.00
2 thru 6 . . . . @25.00
3 thru 13 . . . . @15.00

SNAGGLEPUSS
Gold Key, 1962–63
1 . . . . 150.00
2 . . . . 125.00
3 . . . . 125.00
4 . . . . 125.00

SNAKED
IDW, 2007
1 thru 3 . . . . @4.00

SNAKE EYES DECLASSIFIED
Devil's Due Publishing, 2005
1 . . . . 3.00
2 thru 3 . . . . @3.00
4 thru 6 . . . . @3.00

SNAKE PLISSKEN CHRONICLES
Crossgen Comics, 2003
1 thru 3 . . . . @3.00

SNAKES ON A PLANE
Wildstorm/DC, Sept., 2006
1 CDo, movie adapt., ph(c). 3.00
2 CDo, movie adapt., ph(c). 3.00
1a & 2a, variant (c)s . . . . @3.00

SNAKEWOMAN
Virgin Comics, 2006
0 . . . . 2.50
1 . . . . 4.00
2 thru 5 . . . . @3.50
6 thru 10 . . . . @3.00

...CURSE OF THE 68
Virgin Comics, 2008
1 . . . . 3.00
2 thru 4 . . . . @3.00

...TALE OF THE SNAKE CHARMER
Virgin Comics, 2007
1 thru 6 . . . . @3.00

SNAK POSSE
HCom, 1994
1 thru 2 . . . . @2.50

SNOOPER AND BLABBER DETECTIVES
Gold Key, 1962–63
1 . . . . 150.00
2 . . . . 125.00
3 . . . . 125.00

SNOW WHITE & THE SEVEN DWARFS
Gold Key, 1963
1 . . . . 10.00

COLOR PUB.

SNOW WHITE & SEVEN DWARFS GOLDEN ANNIVERSARY
Gladstone, 1987
1 w/poster & stickers 24.00

SNOWYBROOK INN
Counteractive Comics, 2006
1 . . . . 3.00

SOAP OPERA LOVE
Charlton, 1983
1 . . . . 40.00
2 thru 3 . . . . @40.00

Soap Opera Romances #1
© Charlton

SOAP OPERA ROMANCES
Charlton, 1982–83
1 . . . . 40.00
2 thru 5 . . . . @30.00

SO DARK THE ROSE
CFD, 1995
1 Fully Painted 3.00

SOJOURN
Dreamer Comics, 1998
1 by Jim Somerville, Stranger
   & Stranger, pt.1 . . . . 3.00
2 Stranger & Stranger, pt.2 . . . . . . 3.00
3 Malice in Wonderland 3.00
4 A Game of Conscience, pt.1 . . . . 3.00
5 A Game of Conscience, pt.2 . . . . 2.50
6 A Game of Conscience, pt.3 . . . . 3.25
7 A Game of Conscience, pt.4 . . . . 3.25
8 The Hunt 3.25
9 The Hunt, pt.2 . . . . 3.25
10 The Hunt, Bloodied 3.25

SOJOURN
Crossgen Comics, 2001
1 RMz 7.00
2 thru 5 RMz . . . . @5.00
6 thru 17 RMz 3.00
18 thru 24 . . . . @3.00
25 IEd 2.50
26 thru 37 . . . . @3.00
Collected Ed. #1 . . . . 4.00
Prequel RMz 3.00

SOJOURN/LADY DEATH
Crossgen Comics, 2004
1 (of 2) 3.00
2 . . . . 3.00

SOLAR: HELL ON EARTH
Acclaim, 1997
1 (of 4) CPr,DCw,Seleski twins
   have power of God 2.50
2 CPr,Goat Month prelude 2.50
3 CPr,RT,V:Jimmy Six. 2.50
4 CPr, ... 2.50

SOLAR: MAN OF THE ATOM
Valiant, 1991
1 BWS,DP,BL,B:2nd Death B:Alpha
   & Omega 8.00
2 BWS,DP,BL,V:Dr Solar 7.00
3 BWS,DP,BL,V:Harada I:Harbinger
   Foundation. 8.00
4 BWS,DP,BL,E:2nd Death V:Dr
   Solar 6.00
5 BWS,EC,V:Alien Armada 6.00
6 BWS,DP,SDr, V:Alien Armada X-
   O Armor 6.00
7 BWS,DP,SDr, V:Alien Armada X-
   O Armor 6.00
8 BWS,V:Dragon of Bangkok 6.00
9 BWS,DP,SDr, V:Erica's Baby. . . . 7.00
10 BWS,DP,SDr,JDx,I:Eternal
   Warrior,E:Alpha&Omega 15.00
10a 2nd printing. 7.00
11 SDr,A:Eternal Warrior, Prequel
   to Unity #0 . . . . 3.00
12 SDr,FM(c),Unity#9,O:Pierce,
   Albert 2.50
13 DP,SDr,WS(c),Unity #17,
   V:Pierce. 2.50
14 DP,SDr,I:Bender (becomes
   Dr.Eclipse). 3.00
15 SD,V:Bender 3.00
16 thru 57. . . . . @2.50
58 I:Atman, The Inquisitor 5.00
59 and 60 KG. . . . . @6.00

SOLITAIRE
Malibu Ultraverse, 1993–94
1 black baged edition with playing
   card: Ace of Clubs, Diamonds,
   Hearts or Spades. 2.75
1d Newsstand edition,no card 2.50
2 thru 12 . . . . @2.50

SOLLITARIA
Praxis Comics, 2007
1 . . . . 4.00
2 thru 4 . . . . @3.00

SOLOMON KANE
Blackthorne
1 3-D Special 2.50
2 3-D Special 2.50
1 thru 4 . . . . @2.50

SOLUS
Crossgen Comics, 2003
1 BKs,GP,RM,48-pg. 3.00
2 thru 10 . . . . @3.00

SOLUTION
Malibu Ultraverse, 1993–95
0 DaR,O:Solution 4.00
1 DaR,I:Solution 2.50
1a foil cover 4.00
2 thru 17 . . . . @2.50

SOME NEW KIND OF SLAUGHTER
Archaia Studios, 2007
1 (of 4) 4.00
2 thru 4 . . . . @4.00

SOMERSET HOLMES
Pacific, 1983–84
1 BA,AW,I:Cliff Hanger &
   Somerset Holmes 2.50
2 thru 4 BA,AW . . . . @2.50
Eclipse, 1984
5 BA,AW 2.50
6 BA 2.50

SONIC THE HEDGEHOG
Archie Publications 1993
Mini-series
1 . . . . 25.00
2 . . . . 20.00
3 . . . . 20.00

SONIC THE HEDGEHOG
Archie Publications, 1993
1 A:Mobius,V:Robotnik 35.00
2 . . . . 25.00
3 thru 6 . . . . @15.00
7 thru 10 . . . . @15.00
11 thru 30 . . . . @15.00
31 thru 39 . . . . @7.00
40 thru 54 . . . . @7.00
55 thru 77 . . . . @7.00
78 thru 99 . . . . @20.00
100 . . . . 4.00
101 thru 116 . . . . @4.00
117 thru 142 . . . . @4.00
143 thru 194 . . . . @4.00
GN Sonic Firsts, rep.#0, #1/4
   ashcan,#3,#4,#13 . . . . 5.00
Sonic Live Spec.#1 . . . . 2.50

SONIC QUEST: THE DEATH EGG SAGA
Archie Comics, 1997
1 (of 3) by Mike Gallagher & MaG,
   cont. from Sonic the Hedgehog
   #41. . . . . 2.50
2 and 3 . . . . @2.50

SONIC THE HEDGEHOG PRESENTS KNUCKLES CHASTIC
Archie Comics, 1995
1 I:New Heroes 2.50
Sonic Versus Knuckles Battle Royal
   Spec.#1 . . . . 2.50

SONIC THE HEDGEHOG PRESENTS TAILS
Archie Comics, 1995
1 F:Tails 2.50
2 F:Tails 2.50

SONIC'S FRIENDLY NEMESIS: KNUCKLES
Archie Comics, 1996
1 . . . . 2.50

SONIC SUPER SPECIAL
Archie Comics, 1997
1 Brave New World. 2.50
3 Sonic Firsts 2.50
4 The Return of the King 2.50
5 Sonic Kids 2.50
6 Expanded Sonic #50, 48pg 2.50

COLOR PUB.

7 F:Shadowhawk, The Maxx,
Savage Dragon 2.50
8 four stories, 48-pg. 2.50
9 R:Sonic Kids 2.50
10 Some Enchantra Evening. 2.50
11 . . . . 2.50
12 48-pg. 2.50
13 thru 15 . . . . @2.50

SONIC X
Archie Comics, 2005
1 (of 4) 2.50
2 See Sonic; Sea Battle 2.50
3 thru 39 . . . . @2.50

SOULCATCHER
Moonstone, 2004
1 (of 2) 3.50
2 . . . . 3.50

SOULFIRE
Aspen Entertainment, 2003
0 The Day the Magic Died 10.00
1 . . . . 8.00
1a previews exclusive (c) 7.00
1b signed 25.00
2 . . . . 10.00
3 . . . . 10.00
4 . . . . 10.00
4a thru 4c variant (c). . . . . @9.00
5 . . . . 5.00
6 . . . . 5.00
7 . . . . 4.00
8 . . . . 3.00
9 . . . . 3.00
10 . . . . 4.00
Coll. Ed. #1 . . . . 7.00
Volume 2
0 . . . . 2.50

...CHAOS REIGN
Aspen MLT, 2006
Spec. Beginnings. 5.00
0 . . . . 5.00
1 thru 3 . . . . @3.00

...DYING OF THE LIGHT
Aspen, 2005
0 . . . . 5.00
0a signed 20.00
1 . . . . 5.00
1a signed edition. 35.00
2 . . . . 4.00
3 . . . . 5.00
4 . . . . 4.00
5 . . . . 4.00

...NEW WORLD ORDER
Aspen MLT, 2007
0 . . . . 3.00
1 . . . . 3.00
1a variant (c) 3.00
2 . . . . 3.00

...SHADOW MAGIC
Aspen MLT, 2008
0 . . . . 2.50
0a variant (c) 2.50

SOULMAN
Quantum Comics, 1998
1 . . . . 3.00
2 . . . . 3.00
3 16-pg. 3.00
4 16-pg. 3.00
5 24-pg. 3.00

SOUPY SALES
COMIC BOOK
Archie Publications, 1965
1 . . . . 150.00

SPACE ADVENTURES
Charlton, 1967–79, Volume 3
1 (#60) O&I:Paul Mann & The
Saucers From the Future . . . 100.00
2 thru 8 (1968–69) . . . . @75.00
9 thru 13 (1978–79) . . . . @30.00

SPACE:
ABOVE AND BEYOND
Topps, 1995
1 thru 3 TV pilot adaptation. . . . . @3.00

...THE GAUNTLET
Topps, 1996
1 . . . . 3.00
2 (of 2) 3.00

SPACE ADVENTURES
Charlton, 1958
23 From Nyoka 300.00
24 thru 27 . . . . @250.00
28 thru 32 . . . . @100.00
33 SD, Capt. Atom 700.00
34 thru 40 Capt. Atom . . . . @300.00
41 thru 59 . . . . @50.00

SPACE ARK
AC Comics, 1985–87
1 . . . . 3.00
2 . . . . 2.50

SPACE FAMILY
ROBINSON
Gold Key, 1962–69
1 DSp 500.00
2 . . . . 250.00
3 . . . . 175.00
4 . . . . 175.00
5 . . . . 175.00
6 B:Captain Venture 150.00
7 . . . . 150.00
8 . . . . 150.00
9 . . . . 150.00
10 . . . . 150.00
11 thru 20 . . . . @100.00
21 thru 36 . . . . @75.00

SPACE GHOST
Gold Key, 1967
1 . . . . 600.00

SPACE GHOST
Comico, 1987
1 SR,V:Robot Master 10.00

SPACE GIANTS, THE
Pyramid Comics, 1997
0 . . . . 2.50
0a deluxe 2.50
1 . . . . 2.50
3 by Jeff Newman. 2.50

SPACE MAN
Dell Publishing Co., 1962–72
1 . . . . 125.00
2 . . . . 75.00
3 . . . . 75.00
4 thru 10 . . . . @50.00

SPACE: 1999
Charlton, 1975–76
1 . . . . 30.00
2 JSon,Survival. 25.00
3 JBy,Bring Them Back Alive 20.00
4 JBy. 20.00
5 JBy. 20.00
6 JBy. 20.00

7 . . . . 20.00
8 B&W. 20.00

SPACE: 1999
A Plus Comics
1 GM,JBy 2.50

SPACE USAGI
Mirage, 1993
1 thru 3 From TMNT . . . . @2.75

Space War #3
© Charlton

SPACE WAR
Charlton Comics, 1959
1 . . . . 250.00
2 . . . . 150.00
3 . . . . 125.00
4 SD,SD(c) 250.00
5 SD,SD(c) 250.00
6 SD 250.00
7 . . . . 100.00
8 SD,SD(c) 250.00
9 . . . . 100.00
10 SD,SD(c). 250.00
11 . . . . 100.00
12 thru 15. . . . . @100.00
16 thru 27. . . . . @100.00
Becomes:

FIGHTIN' FIVE
28 SD,SD(c). 100.00
29 SD,SD(c). 100.00
30 SD,SD(c). 125.00
31 SD,SD(c). 125.00
32 . . . . 35.00
33 SD,SD(c). 125.00
34 Sd,SD(c). 125.00

SPACE WAR
Charlton, 1978
28 . . . . 15.00
29 thru 34. . . . . 10.00

SPARKS
Catastrophic Comics, 2008
1 . . . . 3.00
2 thru 6 . . . . @3.00

SPECIAL EDUCATION
National Press Comics, 2006
1 thru 4 . . . . @3.00

COLOR PUB.

SPECIAL WAR SERIES
Charlton, 1965
1 D-Day. 50.00
2 The Company of the Dead 30.00
3 War and Attack 25.00
4 Judo Master. 75.00
Becomes:

ATTACK!
Charlton, 1966
3 SG, Green Inferno of Viet Nam . 30.00
4 SG, Frozen Rendezvous 30.00
Becomes:

ATTACK AT SEA
Charlton, 1968
5 Channel Tag. 30.00

SPECIES
Avatar Press/Pulsar Press, 2005
Spec. #1 . . . . 4.00
Spec. #1a Wraparound (c). 4.00
Spec. #1b Variant(c)s . . . . @4.00

SPECTER 7
Antarctic Press, 2002
1 (of 3) by Craig Babiar 5.00
2 and 3 . . . . @5.00

SPECWAR
Peter Four Productions, 2002
1 . . . . 3.25
2 thru 5 . . . . @3.25
6 thru 8 . . . . @3.25

Speed Buggy #7
© Charlton

SPEED BUGGY
Charlton, 1975
1 . . . . 30.00
2 thru 9 . . . . @25.00

SPEED DEMONS
Charlton, 1957
5 . . . . 50.00
6 thru 10 . . . . @50.00
Becomes:

SUBMARINE ATTACK
Charlton, 1958
11 . . . . 50.00
12 thru 30 . . . . @40.00
31 thru 54 . . . . @30.00

SPEED RACER
Now, 1987–90
1 . . . . 3.50
1a 2nd printing 2.50
2 thru 33 . . . . @2.50
34 thru 38 . . . . @2.50
Spec. #1 . . . . 2.50
#1 2nd printing 2.00
Spec. #2 . . . . 3.50
Classics, Vol #2 . . . . 4.00
Classics, Vol #3 . . . . 4.00
[2nd Series]
1 R:Speed Racer 2.50
2 . . . . 2.50
3 V:Giant Crab 2.50
4 . . . . 2.50
5 Racer-X 2.50
6 . . . . 2.50
7 . . . . 2.50

SPEED RACER
WildStorm/DC, 1999
1 Demon on Wheels. 2.50
2 . . . . 2.50
3 concl. 2.50

SPEED RACER: CHRONICLES OF THE RACER
IDW, 2008
1 . . . . 4.00
2 thru 4 . . . . @4.00
1a thru 4a variant (c)s . . . . @4.00

SPEED RACER: THE NEXT GENERATION: BIRTHRIGHT
IDW, 2008
1 . . . . 4.00
1a variant (c) 4.00

SPELLBINDERS
Quality, 1986–88
1 Nemesis the Warlock. 2.50
2 thru 12 Nemesis the Warlock. . @2.50

SPELLGAME
Speakeasy Comics, 2005
2 . . . . 3.00
3 . . . . 3.00
4 thru 7 . . . . @3.00

S.P.I.C.E.
Awesome Entertainment, 1998
1 RLe,JLb,F:Kaboom 2.50

SPIDER
Eclipse, 1991
1 TT,Blood Dance 7.00
2 TT,Blood Mark 6.00
3 TT,The Spider Unmasked 5.50

SPIDER: REIGN OF THE VAMPIRE KING
Eclipse, 1992
1 TT,I:Legion of Vermin. 5.25
2 thru 4 TT . . . . @2.50

SPIDER-MAN/BADROCK
Maximum Press, 1997
1 (of 2) DJu,MMy x-over 3.00
2 DJu,DaF x-over 3.00

SPIKE
IDW Publishing, 2005
1-shot Spike: Old Times,
  Buffy spin-off 7.50
1-shotA variant (c) 7.50
1-shot Old Wounds 7.50
1-shot Lost & Found 7.50
1-shot Lost & Found, variant (c) . . . 7.50

...AFTER THE FALL
IDW, 2008
1 . . . . 4.00
1a variant (c) 4.00
2 thru 4 . . . . @4.00
2a thru 4a variant (c)s . . . . @4.00

...ASYLUM
IDW Publishing, 2006
1 . . . . 4.00
1a variant (c). 4.00
2 thru 5 . . . . @4.00
2a thru 5a variant (c) . . . . @4.00

...SHADOW PUPPETS
IDW, 2007
1 thru 4 . . . . @4.00
1a thru 4a variant (c) . . . . @4.00

...VS. DRACULA
IDW Publishing, 2006
1 PDd 4.00
1a variant (c)s 4.00
2 thru 5 . . . . @4.00
2a thru 5a variant (c) . . . . @4.00

SPINE-TINGLING TALES
Gold Key, 1975
1 . . . . 20.00
2 thru 4 . . . . @12.00

SPIRAL PATH
Eclipse, 1986
1 V:Tairngir 2.50
2 V:King Artuk 2.50

SPIRIT, THE
Harvey, 1966
1 WE,O:Spirit 150.00
2 WE,O:The Octopus 100.00

SPIRIT, THE
Kitchen Sink, 1983–92
1 WE(c) (1983) 5.25
2 WE(c). 4.25
3 WE(c) (1984) 4.00
4 WE(c) 4.00
5 thru 7 WE(c) . . . . @3.00
8 thru 11 WE(c) (1985) . . . . @3.00
See: B&W Pub. section

SPIRIT, THE: THE NEW ADVENTURES
Kitchen Sink, 1997
1 AMo,DGb 4.00
2 Eisner/Stout cover 3.50
2a Eisner/Schultz cover 3.50
3 AMo,Last Night I Dreamed of
  Dr. Cobra 3.50
4 Dr. Broca von Bitelbaum 3.50
5 Cursed Beauty. 3.50
6 Swami Vashti Bubu 3.50
7 Central City 3.50
8 by Joe Lansdale 3.50
9 . . . . 3.50
10 CAd,BRa. 3.50

SPIRIT OF THE AMAZON
NW Studios, 2002
1 . . . . 3.00
2 thru 7 . . . . @3.00

SPOOKS
Devil's Due, 2008
1 (of 4) 3.50
2 thru 4 . . . . @3.50
1a thru 4a variant prestige (c)s . @5.50

SPOOKS: OMEGA TEAM
Devil's Due, 2008
0 . . . . 1.00
1 . . . . 3.50
1a variant (c) 3.50
2 thru 3 . . . . @3.50
2a thru 3a variant (c)s . . . . @3.50

SPOOKY HAUNTED HOUSE
Harvey Publications, 1972–75
1 . . . . 50.00
2 . . . . 40.00
3 thru 5 . . . . @40.00
6 thru 10 . . . . @30.00
11 thru 15 . . . . @25.00

SPOOKY SPOOKTOWN
Harvey Publications, 1960–70
1 B:Casper,Spooky,68 pgs 300.00
2 . . . . 175.00
3 . . . . 150.00
4 . . . . 150.00
5 . . . . 150.00
6 thru 10 . . . . @100.00
11 thru 20 . . . . @75.00
21 thru 30 . . . . @75.00
31 thru 39 E:68 pgs . . . . @60.00
40 thru 45 . . . . @40.00
46 thru 66 . . . . @30.00

SPOONER
Astonish Comics, 2004
1 . . . . 3.00
2 thru 4 . . . . @3.00

SPRINGHEELED JACK
Full Circle Publications, 2006
1 new printing 4.00
2 new printing 4.00
3 new printing 4.00

SPYMAN
Harvey, 1966
1 GT,JSo,1st prof work,
  I:Spyman 150.00
2 DAy,JSo,V:Cyclops 100.00
3 . . . . 75.00

SQUAD, THE
Malibu
0-A Hardcase's old team 2.50
0-B 2.50
0-C L.A.Riots 2.50

SQUALOR
First, 1989
1 . . . . 2.75
2 . . . . 2.75
3 . . . . 2.75

STAINLESS STEEL RAT
Eagle, 1986
1 Harry Harrison adapt. 2.50
2 thru 6 . . . . @2.50

STAR BLAZERS
Comico, 1989
1 . . . . 3.00
2 . . . . 3.00
3 . . . . 3.00

4 . . . . 3.00
[2nd Series]
1 . . . . 3.00
2 . . . . 3.00
3 thru 5 . . . . @3.00

STARBLAZERS
Argo Press, 1995
0 Battleship Yamato 3.00
1 F:Dereck Wildstar 3.00
2 After the Comet War 3.00
3 . . . . 3.00
4 TEI 3.00
5 thru 12 . . . . @3.00

STARDUST KID
Boom! Studios, 2006
4 . . . . 3.50
5 . . . . 3.50

STARFORCE SIX SPECIAL
AC Comics, 1984
1 . . . . 2.50

Stargate #3
© Entity

STARGATE
Entity Comics, 1996
1 . . . . 3.00
2 . . . . 3.00
3 . . . . 3.00
4 . . . . 3.00
4a deluxe limited edition 3.50

STARGATE ATLANTIS: WRAITHFALL
Avatar Press/Pulsar Press, 2006
1 . . . . 4.00
1a variant (c)s . . . . @4.00
1b variant photo (c)s . . . . @4.00
2 . . . . 4.00
2a variant (c)s . . . . @4.00
2b variant photo (c)s . . . . @4.00
3 . . . . 4.00
3a variant (c)s . . . . @4.00

STARGATE: DOOMSDAY WORLD
Entity Comics, 1996
1 new crew explores 2nd StarGate 3.00
1 prism-foil edition. 3.50

2 . . . . 3.00
3 . . . . 3.00
3 deluxe 3.50

STARGATE SG–1
Avatar, 2003
Convention Spec. 3.00
Convention Spec. Photo (c) 4.00
Spec. First Prime Edition 6.00
Convention Spec. 2004 . . . . 3.00
Convention Spec. 2004, ph(c) . . . 4.00
2005 Convention Special 3.00
2005 Convention Special
  variant (c)s . . . . @3.00
2006 Convention Special 3.00
2006 Convention Special
  variant (c)s . . . . @3.00
2007 Special 3.00
2007 Special variant (c)s . . . . . . @3.00
Spec. 2007 Special photo (c). . . . 10.00

...ARIS BOCH
Avatar, 2004
1 . . . . 3.00
1a photo (c). 3.00
1b wraparound (c). 3.00

...DANIEL'S SONG
Avatar Press/Pulsar Press, 2005
1 . . . . 3.00
1a photo(c) 3.00
1b wraparaound (c). 3.00

...FALL OF ROME
Avatar, 2004
Prequel. 3.00
Prequel wraparound (c). 3.00
Prequel photo(c) 3.00
1 . . . . 4.00
2 thru 3 . . . . @4.00
1a thru 3a photo (c)s. . . . . @4.00
1b thru 3b wraparound (c)s. . . . . @4.00

...P.O.W.
Avatar, 2004
1 . . . . 3.50
1b photo (c). 3.50
2 . . . . 3.50
2b photo (c). 3.50
3 . . . . 3.50
1a thru 3a wraparound (c)s . . . . @3.50
3b photo (c). 3.50

...RA REBORN
Avatar Press/Pulsar Press, 2005
Prequel 3.00
Prequel variant (c)s . . . . @3.00
Prequel Carter painted (c) 6.00

...RED DAWN
Avatar Press/Pulsar Press, 2006
Spec., 2006 convention (c) 6.00

STARGODS
Antarctic Press, 1998
1 by Zachary, Clark & Beaty 3.00
1a deluxe 6.00
2 The Golden Bow 3.00
2a deluxe, with poster. 6.00
Spec. Stargods Visions 3.00

STARK RAVEN
Hardline Studios, 2000
1 The Screaming Rain,pt.1 . . . . . . 3.00
2 The Screaming Rain,pt.2 . . . . . . 3.00
3 . . . . 3.00
Endless Horizons, 2000
4 . . . . 3.00
5 . . . . 3.00
6 Ken Kelly (c) 3.00
7 . . . . 3.00
8 . . . . 3.00

COLOR PUB.

STARKWEATHER
Arcana Studio, 2004
1 . . . . 3.00
2 thru 5 . . . . @3.00

STARKWEATHER: IMMORTAL
Archaia Studios, 2007
0 . . . . 5.00
1 (of 4) 4.00
2 . . . . 4.00
3 thru 4 . . . . @4.00

STAR MASTERS
AC Comics, 1994
1 . . . . 2.50

STAR REACH CLASSICS
Eclipse, 1984
1 JSn,NA(r) 2.50
2 AN 2.50
3 HC 2.50
4 FB(r) 2.50
5 . . . . 2.50
6 . . . . 2.50

STAR SEED
See: POWERS THAT BE

STARSHIP TROOPERS
Markosia, 2006
0 Previews exclusive 3.00
0a signed edition. 9.00
0 . . . . 5.00
1 Alamo Bay 3.50
1a variant (c)s . . . . @3.50
1b director's cut 3.50
2 thru 4 Alamo Bay, pt. 2–pt. 4 . . @3.50
2a thru 4a variant (c)s . . . . @3.50
5 thru 10 . . . . @3.50

...DAMAGED JUSTICE
Markosia, 2006
1 . . . . 3.00
1a variant (c)s . . . . @3.00
1b variant sketch (c) signed 9.00
1c director's cut 3.50
2 thru 4 . . . . @3.50
2a thru 4a variant (c) . . . . @3.50

...DEAD MAN'S HAND
Markosia, 2006
1 (of 4) 4.00
1a variant (c)s . . . . @4.00
1b Ltd. Sketch (c) signed 9.00
1c Re-marked Previews exclusive 35.00
2 thru 4 . . . . @3.50
2a thru 4a variant (c)s . . . . @3.50
2b thru 4b signed Previews
  exclusives . . . . @9.00

STAR SLAMMERS
Malibu Bravura, 1994
1 WS(a&s) 2.75
2 WS(a&s),F:Meredith 2.75
3 WS(a&s) 2.50
4 WS(a&s) 2.50
5 WS,Rojas Choice. 2.50

STARSLAYER
Pacific, 1982–83
1 MGr,O:Starslayer 4.00
2 MGr,DSt,I:Rocketeer 9.00
3 DSt,MGr,A:Rocketeer(2ndApp.). . 6.00
4 MGr,Baraka Kuhr 2.50
5 MGr,SA,A:Groo 7.00
6 MGr.conclusion story 2.50
First, 1983–85
7 MGr layouts 2.50

8 MGr layouts, MG 2.50
9 MGr layouts, MG 2.50
10 TT,MG,I:Grimjack 4.00
11 thru 34 . . . . @2.50
Graphic Novel 10.00

STARSLAYER DIRECTORS CUT
Windjammer, 1995
1 R:Starslayer, Mike Grell 2.50
2 I:New Star Slayer 2.50
3 Jolly Rodger. 2.50
4 V:Battle Droids 2.50
5 I:Baraka Kuhi 2.50
6 V:Valkyrie. 2.50
7 MGr(c&a),Can Torin destroy? . . . 2.50
8 MGr(c&a),JAI, Can Torin live with
  his deeds?,final issue 2.50

Star Trek #4
© Gold Key

STAR TREK
Gold Key, 1967–79
1 Planet of No Return 1,500.00
2 Devil's Isle of Space 1,000.00
3 Invasion of City Builders 500.00
4 Peril of Planet Quick Change . 500.00
5 Ghost Planet 500.00
6 When Planets Collide 300.00
7 Voodoo Planet 300.00
8 Youth Trap 250.00
9 Legacy of Lazarus 250.00
10 Sceptre of the Sun 200.00
11 Brain Shockers 200.00
12 Flight of the Buccaneer. 150.00
13 Dark Traveler 150.00
14 Enterprise Mutiny 150.00
15 Museum a/t End of Time. . . . 150.00
16 Day of the Inquisitors 150.00
17 Cosmic Cavemen 150.00
18 The Hijacked Planet 150.00
19 The Haunted Asteroid 150.00
20 A World Gone Mad 150.00
21 The Mummies of Heitus VII . . 125.00
22 Siege in Superspace. 125.00
23 Child's Play 125.00
24 The Trial of Capt. Kirk 125.00
25 Dwarf Planet 125.00
26 The Perfect Dream 125.00
27 Ice Journey 125.00
28 The Mimicking Menace 125.00
29 rep. Star Trek #1 . . . . 125.00
30 Death of a Star 100.00
31 The Final Truth. 100.00
32 The Animal People 100.00
33 The Choice 100.00

34 The Psychocrystals. 100.00
35 rep. Star Trek #4 . . . . 100.00
36 A Bomb in Time 100.00
37 rep. Star Trek #5 . . . . 75.00
38 One of our Captains
  is Missing. 75.00
39 Prophet of Peace 75.00
40 AMc,Furlough to Fury, A:
  Barbara McCoy 75.00
41 AMc,The Evictors 75.00
42 World Against Time. 75.00
43 World Beneath the Waves 75.00
44 Prince Traitor 75.00
45 rep. Star Trek #7 . . . . 75.00
46 Mr. Oracle 75.00
47 AMc,This Tree Bears Bitter
  Fruit 75.00
48 AMc,Murder on Enterprise 75.00
49 AMc,A Warp in Space 75.00
50 AMc,The Planet of No Life 75.00
51 AMc,DestinationAnnihilation6 . . 60.00
52 AMc,And A Child Shall
  Lead Them 60.00
53 AMc,What Fools..Mortals Be . . 60.00
54 AMc,Sport of Knaves 60.00
55 AMc,A World Against Itself 60.00
56 AMc,No Time Like The Past,
  A:Guardian of Forever. 60.00
57 AMc,Spore of the Devil 60.00
58 AMc,Brain Damaged Planet . . . 60.00
59 AMc,To Err is Vulcan. 60.00
60 AMc,The Empire Man 60.00
61 AMc,Operation Con Game 60.00

STAR TREK:
ALL OF ME
WildStorm/DC, 2000
1-shot AaL,RyE 6.00

...DIVIDED WE FALL
WildStorm/DC, 2001
1 (of 4) TNG & DS9 x-over 3.00
2 thru 4 . . . . @3.00

...ENTER THE WOLVES
WildStorm/DC, 2001
1-shot, 48-pg. 6.00

STAR TREK: DEEP SPACE NINE
Malibu, 1993
1 Direct ed. 3.25
1a Photo(c). 3.00
1b Gold foil 5.00
2 w/skycap 3.50
3 thru 9 . . . . @2.75
10 Descendants 2.50
11 A Short Fuse 2.75
12 Baby on Board 2.50
13 Problems with Odo 2.75
14 on Bejor 2.75
15 mythologic dilemma 2.75
16 thru 32 . . . . @2.50
Ann.#1 Looking Glass 4.00
Spec. #1 Collision Course 3.50
Spec. #0 Terok Nor 3.00

CELEBRITY SERIES: ...BLOOD AND HONOR
Malibu, 1995
1 Mark Lenard(s) 3.00
2 Rules of Diplomacy 3.00

...LIGHTSTORM
Malibu, 1994
1 Direct ed. 3.50
1a Silver foil 8.00

...HEARTS AND MINDS
Malibu, 1994
1 . . . . 3.00

2 . . . . 2.50
3 Into the Abyss,X-over preview. . . 2.50
4 final issue 2.50

...THE MAQUIS
Malibu, 1995
1 Federation Renegades 2.50
1a Newsstand, photo(c) 2.50
2 Garack 2.50
3 F:Quark, Bashir 2.50

...THE NEXT GENERATION
Malibu, 1994
1 Prophet & Losses, pt.2 . . . . 2.50
2 Prophet & Losses, pt.4 . . . . 2.50

STAR TREK:
DEEP SPACE NINE
N-VECTOR
WildStorm/DC, 2000
1 (of 4),F:Kira 2.50
2 sabotage 2.50
3 N-Vector viroid 2.50
4 F:Quark,concl. 2.50

STAR TREK:

ALIENS SPOTLIGHT
IDW Publishing 2007
Gorn spec. 4.00
Gorn spec. variant (c) 4.00
Vulcans spec. 4.00
Vulcans spec. variant (c) 4.00
Andorians spec. 4.00
Andorians spec. variant (c) 4.00
Orions spec. 4.00
Orions spec. variant (c) 4.00
Borg spec. 4.00
Borg spec. variant (c) 4.00
Romulans spec. 4.00
Romulans spec. variant (c) 4.00

...ASSIGNMENT EARTH
IDW, 2008
1 JBy 4.00
2 thru 5 JBy . . . . @4.00

...KLINGONS:
BLOOD WILL TELL
IDW Publishing, 2007
1 . . . . 4.00
2 thru 5 . . . . @4.00
1a thru 5a variant (c). . . . . @4.00
1b Klingon-Language variant 5.00

...MIRROR IMAGES
IDW, 2008
1 . . . . 4.00
1a variant (c) 4.00
2 thru 5 . . . . @4.00

...NEW FRONTIER
IDW Publishing, 2008
1 . . . . 4.00
2 thru 5 . . . . @4.00

...ROMULANS:
THE HOLLOW CROWN
IDW, 2008
1 . . . . 4.00
2 . . . . 4.00

STAR TREK:
THE NEXT GENERATION:

INTELLIGENCE GATHERING
IDW Publishing, 2008
1 . . . . 4.00
2 thru 5 . . . . @4.00
1a thru 4a variant (c)s . . . . @4.00

...THE KILLING SHADOWS
WildStorm/DC, 2000
1 (of 4) V:Bodai Shin, assassin . . 2.50
2 thru 4 V:Bodai Shin . . . . @2.50

...THE LAST GENERATION
IDW, 2008
1 . . . . 4.00

...PERCHANCE TO DREAM
WildStorm/DC, 1999
1 (of 4) 2.50
2 thru 4 . . . . @2.50

...THE SPACE BETWEEN
IDW Publishing, 2007
1 . . . . 4.00
2 thru 6 . . . . @4.00
1a thru 6a variant (c). . . . . @4.00

STAR TREK: VOYAGER
WildStorm/DC, 2000
Spec. Elite Force 6.00
Spec. Avalon Rising 6.00

STAR TREK: VOYAGER
Malibu
A V:Maquis 2.75
Aa Newsstand, photo(c) 2.50
B conclusion. 2.75
Ba Newsstand, photo(c) 2.50

STAR TREK: VOYAGER —
PLANET KILLER
WildStorm/DC, 2001
1 (of 3) F:Kirk,Janeway. 3.00
2 Doomsday Machine 3.00
3 concl. 3.00

STAR TREK: YEAR FOUR
IDW Publishing, 2007
1 . . . . 4.00
2 thru 5 . . . . @4.00
6 . . . . 4.00
1a thru 6a variant (c)s. . . . . @4.00
Spec. IDW Focus On Star Trek 3.00

...THE ENTERPRISE
EXPERIMENT
IDW Publishing, 2008
1 thru 5 . . . . @4.00

STAR WARS IN 3-D
Blackthorne, 1987
1 thru 7 . . . . @4.00

STARWATCHERS
Valiant
1 MLe,DG,Chromium(c),Valiant
    Vision, ... 3.50

S.T.A.T.
Majestic, 1993
1 FdS(s),PhH,I:S.T.A.T. 2.50

STATIC-X
Chaos! Comics, 2002
1 by BnP, with CD-Rom 6.00
1a photo (c) with CD-Rom 6.00
1b collector's edition 15.00
Vol. 2
1 with CD-Rom 6.00
1a collector's edition 15.00

STATION
Boom! Studios, 2008
1 (of 5) 4.00
2 thru 4 . . . . @4.00

STEALTH SQUAD
Petra Comics, 1993
1 I:Stealth Squad 2.50

STEAMPUNK
WildStorm/DC Cliffhanger, 2000
1 CBa 2.50
1 chromium edition . . . .
2 CBa,V:Absinthe 2.50
3 CBa,F:Cole Blaquesmith 2.50
4 CBa,CBa(c) 2.50
4a variant JSC (c) (1:4) 2.50
4b variant JMd (c) (1:4) 2.50
4c variant HuR (c) (1:4) 2.50
5 CBa,V:Abbey Monsters 2.50
6 Mechanica Sundown,pt.1 . . . . . . 2.50
7 Mechanica Sundown,pt.2 . . . . . . 2.50
8 Mechanica Sundown,pt.3 . . . . . . 2.50
9 Mambutu X, pt.1 . . . . 2.50
10 Mambutu X, pt.2 . . . . 2.50
11 CBa, Stonehenge secret 2.50
12 CBa, 40-pg. final issue 3.50

STEED & MRS. PEEL
Eclipse, 1990
1 IG,The Golden Game 5.00
2 IG,The Golden Game. 5.00
3 IG,The Golden Game. 5.00

STEEL CITY HAWK
Narwain Publishing, 2006
1 (of 4) 4.00
2 . . . . 4.00

STEEL CLAW
Quality, 1986
1 H:Ken Bulmer 4.00
2 . . . . 4.00
3 . . . . 4.00
4 . . . . 4.00

Steel Sterling #6
© Archie Publications

STEEL STERLING
Archie Publications, 1984
(formerly LANCELOT STRONG)
4 EB 4.00
5 EB 4.00
6 EB 4.00
7 EB 4.00

COLOR PUB.

STEVE CANYON 3-D
Kitchen Sink, 1986
Milton Caniff & Peter Poplaski(c),
w/glasses (1985) 6.00

STEPHEN COLBERT'S TEK JANSEN
Oni Press, 2008
1 . . . . 4.00
2 thru 5 . . . . @4.00

STEVE ZODIAC & THE FIREBALL XL-5
Gold Key, 1964
1 . . . . 150.00

STING OF THE GREEN HORNET
Now, 1992
1 Polybagged w/trading card 2.75
2 inc.Full color poster 2.75
3 inc.Full color poster 2.75

STONE COLD STEVE AUSTIN
Chaos! Comics, 1999
1 (of 4) Whoop Ass personified . . . 3.00
1b Premium 9.00
2 . . . . 3.00
3 . . . . 3.00
4 . . . . 3.00
1a thru 4a photo (c) . . . . @3.00

STORMBRINGERS
Stormbringer Studios, 2007
1 . . . . 5.00
2 . . . . 3.00
3 . . . . 3.00

STORMING PARADISE
Wildstorm/DC, July 2008
1 (of 6) World War II 3.00
2 thru 5 . . . . @3.00

STORMQUEST
Caliber, 1994
1 I:Stormquest 2.50
2 Time Stone 2.50
3 BU:Seeker 2.50
4 F:Shalimar 2.50
5 Reunion 2.50
6 V:Samuroids 2.50

STORMWATCH: PHD
Wildstorm/DC, Nov., 2006
1 DoM 3.00
1 a & b variant (c)s . . . . @3.00
2 DoM, The Walking Ghost 3.00
2a variant (c) 3.00
3 DoM, in Las Vegas 3.00
3a variant (c) (1:10) 3.00
4 DoM,Ladies night out 3.00
4a variant (c) (1:10) 3.00
5 DoM,Secrets revealed 3.00
6 DoM,Jackson King's secrets . . . 3.00
7 DoM,Assault on Precinct 18 . . . . 3.00
8 ASm,F:StormWatch Prime 3.00
9 ASm,Dying cast member 3.00
10 ASm,Slaughterhouse Smith . . . 3.00
11 ASm,The real Assassin 3.00
12 ASm,The Walking Ghost 3.00
13 World's End 3.00
14 Satellite existence 3.00
15 F:The Establishment 3.00
16 Soviet-era WMD 3.00

STORMWATCH PHD: ARMAGEDDON
Wildstorm/DC, Dec., 2007
1 F:John Doran 3.00

STORMWATCH: TEAM ACHILLES
WildStorm/DC, 2002
Eye of the Storm
1 WPo,SW,new team 3.00
2 WPo,SW,extremists vs. U.N. 3.00
3 WPo,SW,military action 3.00
4 WPo,SW,hunt for Ivana Baiul . . . 3.00
5 WPo,F:The Authority 3.00
6 WPo,F:The Authority 3.00
7 MT,V:Ivana Baiul 3.00
8 F:Jukko Hamalainen 3.00
9 WPo,V:super-human 3.00
10 WPo 3.00
11 WPo 3.00
12 WPo,funeral 3.00
13 BSz,The Suiciders 3.00
14 WPo,Citizen Soldier 3.00
15 The Suiciders 3.00
16 V:Citizen Soldier 3.00
17 V:Citizen Soldier 3.00
18 O:Citizen Soldier 3.00
19 Citizen Soldier,concl. 3.00
20 . . . . 3.00
21 . . . . 3.00
22 Hallibastard 3.00
23 Baron Chaos 3.00
24 Project Entry Universe 3.00

STRANDED, THE
Virgin Comics, 2007
1 . . . . 3.00
2 thru 5 . . . . @3.00

STRANGE DAYS
Eclipse, 1984–85
1 . . . . 4.00
2 thru 3 . . . . @3.00
3 . . . . 3.00

STRANGERS, THE
Malibu Ultraverse, 1993–95
1 I:Strangers 3.00
1a Ultra-Limited 4.00
1b Full Hologram (c) 5.00
2 A:J.D.Hunt,w/Ultraverse card . . . 3.00
3 I:TNTNT 2.50
4 thru 12 . . . . @2.50
13 (Ultraverse Premiere#4) 3.50
14 thru 26 . . . . @2.50
Ann.#1 Death 4.00
Ashcan 1 (signed) 8.00
Ashcan 1 (unsigned) 8.00

STRANGE SUSPENSE STORIES
Charlton, 1967
1 . . . . 45.00
2 thru 9 . . . . @35.00

STRANGE SUSPENSE STORIES/ CAPTAIN ATOM
Charlton Comics, 1965
75 SD,O:CaptainAtom,1960Rep.. 250.00
76 SD, Capt.Atom,1960Rep. 150.00
77 SD, Capt.Atom,1960Rep. 150.00
Becomes:

CAPTAIN ATOM
Charlton Comics, 1965–67
78 SD, new stories begin 150.00

Captain Atom #84
© *Charlton*

79 SD,I:Dr.Spectro 100.00
80 SD 100.00
81 SD,V:Dr.Spectro 100.00
82 SD,I:Nightshade,Ghost 100.00
83 SD,I:Ted Kord/Blue Beetle 75.00
84 SD,N:Captain Atom. 75.00
85 SD,A:Blue Beetle,I:Punch &
Jewelee 75.00
86 SD,A:Ghost, Blue Beetle 75.00
87 SD,JAp,A:Nightshade 75.00
88 SD/FMc,JAp,A:Nightshade 75.00
89 SD/FMc,JAp,A:Nightshade,
Ghost, last issue Dec.,1967 . . 75.00

STRAW MEN
Zenescope Entertainment, 2008
1 . . . . 3.00
2 thru 5 . . . . @3.00

STREET FIGHTER
Ocean, 1986–87
1 thru 3 . . . . @3.00

STREET FIGHTER
Malibu, 1993
1 based on Video Game 3.00
2 thru 3 Based on Video Game . @3.00

STREET FIGHTER
Devil's Due/UDON, 2004
7 . . . . 4.50
7a variant (c). 4.50
8 thru 14 . . . . 3.00
8a thru 14a variant (c)s . . . . @3.00

STREET FIGHTER REMIX
Udon Entertainment, 2008
0 . . . . 4.00

STREET FIGHTER II
Udon Entertainment, 2005
0 . . . . 2.00
6 . . . . 3.00
6a variant (c) 3.00

...TURBO
Udon Entertainment, 2008
1 . . . . 4.00
1a variant (c) 4.00
2 . . . . 4.00
2a variant (c) 4.00

STREET FIGHTER LEGENDS: SAKURA
Udon Entertainment, 2006
1 . . . . 4.00
1a variant (c) 4.00
2 thru 4 . . . . @4.00
2 thru 4a variant (c) . . . . @4.00

STREET SHARKS
Archie Comics, 1995
1 & 2 Based on Cartoons . . . . . @2.50

STREETS OF GLORY
Avatar Press, 2007
1 . . . . 4.00
1a wraparound (c) 4.00
1b thru 2b auxiliary editions . . . . @4.00
3 thru 6 . . . . @4.00
3a thru 6a wraparound (c)s . . . . @4.00

STRIKE!
Eclipse, 1988
1 TL,RT,I&O:New Strike 2.50
2 TL,RT 2.50
3 TL,RT 2.50
4 TL,RT,V:Renegade CIA Agents . . 2.50
5 TL,RT,V:Alien Bugs 2.50
6 TL,RT,Legacy of the Lost 2.50
Spec. #1 Strike vs. Sgt.
    Strike TL,RT,The Man 2.50

STRIKEBACK
Malibu Bravura, 1994–95
1 . . . . 3.00
2 . . . . 3.00
3 V:Doberman 3.00
4 V:Dragonryder Island 3.00
Spec.#1 KM,JRu,V:Dragon 3.50

STRIKEFORCE AMERICA
Comico, 1995
1 ScC,SK(c),I:StrikeforceAmerica . . 2.50
2 V:Superior-prisoner 3.00
3 Breakout, pt.2 . . . . 3.00
[Volume 2], 1995
1 ScC,polybagged with Chrysalis
    promo card 3.00

STRONTIUM DOG
[Mini Series]
Eagle, 1985
1 . . . . 3.00
2 thru 4 . . . . @3.00
[Regular Series]
Quality, 1988
Story line continued from 2000 A.D.
7 thru 14 . . . . @2.50
15/16 . . . . 2.50
17 . . . . 2.50
18/19 . . . . 2.50
20 thru 29 . . . . @2.50
Spec.#1 . . . . 2.50
[2nd Series], 1997
1 thru 6 . . . . @2.50

STRYKE
London Night Studios, 1995
0 I:Stryke 5.00
1 . . . . 4.00

STUMBO TINYTOWN
Harvey Publications, 1963–66
1 . . . . 300.00
2 . . . . 150.00
3 . . . . 125.00
4 thru 5 . . . . @125.00
6 thru 13 . . . . @100.00

STUPID HEROES
Next, 1994
1 PeL(s),w/ 2 card-strip 2.75
2 . . . . 2.75
3 F:Cinder 2.75

SUBSPECIES
Eternity, 1991
1 Movie Adaptation 3.00
2 Movie Adaptation 2.50
3 Movie Adaptation 2.50
4 Movie Adaptation 2.50

SULLENGRAY
Ape Entertainment, 2005
1 (of 4) 3.50
2 thru 4 . . . . @3.50

SUNDOWN
Arcana Studio, 2005
1 (of 3) 3.00
2 thru 3 . . . . @3.00

SUN GLASSES AFTER DARK
Verotik, 1995
1 . . . . 3.00
2 and 3 . . . . @3.00
4 thru 6 . . . . @4.00
6 fan club cover 5.00
? prequel, San Diego Con ed. 3.00

SUN-RUNNERS
Pacific, 1984
1 . . . . 2.50
2 . . . . 2.50
3 . . . . 2.50
Eclipse, 1984–86
4 thru 7 . . . . @2.50
Summer Special #1 . . . . 2.50

SUNSET CARSON
AC Comics
1 Based on Cowboy Star 5.00

SUPER
Aberrant Press, 2007
1 (of 6) 3.00
2 thru 4 . . . . @3.00

SUPERBABES: FEMFORCE
AC Comics
1 Various Artists 5.00

SUPER BAD JAMES DYNOMITE
IDW Publishing, 2005
1 (s) by Wayans brothers 4.00
2 . . . . 4.00
3 . . . . 4.00
4 . . . . 4.00
5 . . . . 4.00

SUPERCAR
Gold Key, 1962–63
1 . . . . 450.00
2 . . . . 200.00
3 . . . . 200.00
4 . . . . 225.00

SUPERCOPS
Now, 1990
1 thru 4 . . . . @2.50

Super Car #2
© Gold Key

SUPER CRAZY TNT BLAST
Speakeasy Comics, 2005
1 . . . . 3.00
2 . . . . 3.00
3 thru 5 . . . . @3.00

SUPER FXXXXXS
Top Shelf Productions, 2005
1 by James Kochalka 7.00
2 . . . . 5.00
3 . . . . 5.00
4 . . . . 5.00

SUPER GOOF
Gold Key, 1965–82
1 . . . . 75.00
2 thru 10 . . . . @50.00
11 thru 20 . . . . @35.00
21 thru 30 . . . . @30.00
31 thru 74 . . . . @25.00

SUPERHEROES
Dell, 1967
1 . . . . 60.00
2 thru 4 . . . . @35.00

SUPER HEROES VERSUS SUPERVILLIANS
Archie Publications, 1966
1 A:Flyman,Black Hood,The Web,
    The Shield 100.00

SUPERHUMAN SAMURAI SYBER SQUAD
Hamilton Comics, 1995
0 Based on TV Show 3.00

SUPER MARIO BROS.
Valiant, 1991
1 thru 6 . . . . @2.50
Spec. #1 . . . . 2.50

SUPERMARKET
IDW Publishing, 2006
1 . . . . 4.00
2 . . . . 4.00
3 . . . . 4.00
4 . . . . 4.00

SUPERNATURAL FREAK MACHINE
IDW Publishing, 2005
1 A Cal McDonald Mystery 4.00
1a signed 15.00
2 thru 5 . . . . @4.00

SUPERNATURAL: ORIGINS
Wildstorm/DC, May, 2007
1 PHe, from TV show 3.00
2 . . . . 3.00
3 Harvelle's Roadhouse Bar 3.00
4 South Dakota priest 3.00
5 American Southwest 3.00
6 His greatest Test 3.00

SUPERNATURAL: RISING SON
Wildstorm/DC, April, 2008
1 (of 6) 3.00
1a variant (c) (1:10) 3.00
2 thru 6 . . . . @3.00

SUPERNAUT
Anarchy, 1997
1 (of 3) 3.00
1 gold logo 6.00
2 by Rob Hand, Hand of Doom . . . 3.00
2a gold logo 6.00

SUPER REAL
Super Real Graphics, 2005
1 by Jason Martin 3.25
2 . . . . 3.25
2a variant (c) 3.25
3 . . . . 3.50
3a variant (c) 3.50
4 . . . . 3.50

SUPER TEEN*TOPIA
Alias Enterprises, 2006
0 . . . . 2.50
1 . . . . 3.50
2 thru 4 . . . . @3.50

SUPREME
Maximum Press, 1997
#1–#43 see Image
44 AMo, JoB, A:Glory 3.00

Supreme #51
© Awesome Entertainment

45 AMo, JoB, A:Glory 3.00
46 AMo,Suprema 3.00
47 AMo 3.00
48 AMo 2.50
49 AMo 2.50
50 double size 4.00
51 . . . . 3.50
52A AMo, Book 1 . . . . 3.50
52B AMo, Book 2, continuation . . . 3.50
53 AMo,CSp,AG,V:Omniman 3.00
54 AMo,CSp,AG,Ballad of Judy
    Jordan 3.00
55 AMo,CSp,AG,Silence At
    Gettysburg 3.00
56 AMo,CSp,AG,Reflections,pt.1 . . 3.00
57 AMo,CSp,AG,Reflections,pt.2 . . 3.00
58 AMo,CSp,AG,A World of
    His Own 3.00
59 AMo,CSp,AG,Professor Night of
    the Prism World 3.00
60 AMo,CSp,AG,F:Radar in Puppy
    Love 3.00
61 AMo,CSp,AG,Meet Mr. Meteor . . 3.00

SUPREME: THE RETURN
Awesome Entertainment, 1999
1 AMo,CSp,AG 3.00
1a variant AxR cover 7.00
2 AMo,JSn, ... 3.00
3 thru 8 . . . . @3.00

SUPREMA/SUPREME SACRIFICE
Arcade Comics, 2006
Flipbook 4.00

SURF 'N' WHEELS
Charlton, 1969
1 . . . . 45.00
2 thru 6 . . . . @30.00

SURGE
Eclipse, 1984
1 A:DNAgents 3.00
2 A:DNAgents 3.00
3 A:DNAgents 3.00
4 A:DNAgents 3.00

SURROGATES
Top Shelf Productions, 2005
1 (of 5) 3.00
2 . . . . 3.00
3 thru 5 . . . . @3.00

SURVIVORS
Spectrum, 1984
1 Mag. size, (B&W) 5.00
2 A Hunter's Rage 3.50
3 The Old One 2.50
4 Face-Off 2.50

SUSPIRA: THE GREAT WORKING
Chaos! Comics, 1997
1 (of 4) PNa 3.00
2 PNa 3.00
3 PNa 3.00
4 PNa 3.00

SWORD OF DRACULA/ VAMPIRELLA:EXTENDED AND DANGEROUS
Digital Webbing, 2007
1-shot 4.00
1-shot variant (c) 4.00

SWORD OF RED SONJA, THE: DOOM OF THE GODS
D.E. (Dynamite Ent.) 2007
1 . . . . 3.50
3 thru 4 . . . . 3.50
3a thru 4a variant (c)s . . . . @3.50

SWORD OF VALOR
A Plus Comics
1 . . . . 2.50
2 . . . . 2.50
3 . . . . 2.50
4 . . . . 2.50

SWORDS OF TEXAS
Eclipse, 1987
1 FH,New America 2.50
2 FH,V:Baja Badlands 2.50
3 FH,TY(c),V:Dogs of Danger 2.50
4 FH,V:Samurai Master 2.50

SYMBIOTES, THE
Drive Comics, 2004
1 (of 8) 3.00
2 thru 5 . . . . @3.00

SYMBOLS OF JUSTICE
High Impact Studios, 1995
1 I:Granger,Justice,Rayven 3.00
2 V:Devil's Brigade 3.00

SYPHONS
Now, 1988
1 . . . . 2.50
2 thru 7 . . . . @2.50

SYPHONS: COUNTDOWN
Now, 1994
1 F:Brigade 3.00
2 Led By Cross 3.00
3 Blown Cover 3.00
1995 Ann. Doomsday Device 3.00

SYPHONS: THE STARGATE STRATAGEM
Now, 1994
1 . . . . 3.00
2 . . . . 3.00
3 . . . . 3.00

TAD WILLIAMS BURNING MAN
Alias Enterprises, 2005
1 (of 3) 3.00
2 thru 3 . . . . @3.00

TAG
Boom! Studios, 2006
1 (of 3) KG 4.00
2 . . . . 4.00
3 . . . . 4.00

TAG: CURSED
Boom! Studios, 2007
1 . . . . 4.00
2 thru 5 . . . . @4.00
2a variant (c) 4.00

TALENT
Boom! Studios, 2006
1 . . . . 4.00
1a 2nd printing 4.00
2 . . . . 3.00
3 . . . . 4.00
4 . . . . 4.00

TALES CALCULATED TO DRIVE YOU BATS
Archie Publications, 1961–62
1	250.00
2	150.00
3	100.00
4	100.00
5	100.00
6	100.00

TALES FROM THE CRYPT
Gladstone, 1990–91
1 E.C.rep.AW/FF,GS	5.00
2 rep.	4.00
3 rep.	3.50
4 rep.	3.00
5 rep.TFTC #45	3.00
6 rep.TFTC #42	3.00

TALES FROM THE CRYPT
Russ Cochran Publ, 1992
1 rep. TFTC #31,CSS#12	3.00
2 rep. TFTC #34,CSS#15	3.00
3 rep. TFTC, CSS	3.00
4 rep. TFTC #43,CSS#18	3.00
5 rep. TFTC,CSS#23	3.00

[2nd Series]
1 rep.horror stories	3.00
2 inc.The Maestro's Hand	3.00
3 thru 6	@3.00
7 thru 8	@3.00

Gemstone, 1996
16 thru 30 EC comics reprint	@3.00

TALES FROM THE CRYPT
Papercutz, 2007
1	4.00
2 thru 3	@4.00
4 thru 9	@4.00

TALES FROM WONDERLAND
Zenescope Entertainment, 2008
Spec The Queen of Hearts	4.00
Spec. The Mad Hatter	4.00
Spec. Alice	4.00

TALES OF ALVIN MAKER: RED PROPHET
Dabel Brothers Prod., 2006
1	3.00
1a	6.00
2 thru 6	@3.00
2a thru 6a variant (c)	@6.00

TALES OF BLOODY MARY
Bloody Mary Comics, 2005
1 (of 8)	3.00
2 thru 4	@3.00
5 thru 8	@3.00

TALES OF EVIL
Atlas Comics, 1975
1 Werewolf	25.00
2 Bog Beast	20.00
3 Man-Monster	20.00

TALES OF MIDNIGHT
Beyond Starlight, 2006
Vol. 2
1	3.00
2 thru 3	@3.00

TALES OF PENANCE: TRIAL OF THE CENTURY
Arcana Studio, 2008
1 (of 4)	4.00
2 thru 4	@4.00

TALES OF TERROR
Eclipse, 1985–87
1	3.00
2 Claustrophobia'	3.00
3 GM,Eyes in the Darkness	3.00
4 TT,TY,JBo(c),The Slasher	3.00
5 Back Forty,Shoe Button Eyes	3.00
6 Good Neighbors	3.00
7 SBi,JBo,SK(i),Video	3.00
8 HB,Revenant,Food for Thought	3.00
9	3.00
10	3.00
11 TT,JBo(c),Black Cullen	3.00
12 JBo,FH,Last of the Vampires	3.00
13	3.00

TALES OF THE CHAMPIONS
Heroic Publishing, 2005
1	3.00
2	3.00
3 F:Tigress	3.00
4	3.25

TALES OF THE GREEN BERET
Dell Publishing Co., 1967
1 SG	60.00
2 thru 5	@50.00

Tales of the Green Hornet #3
© Now

TALES OF THE GREEN HORNET
Now, 1990
1 NA(c),O:Green Hornet Pt.1	3.00
2 O:Green Hornet Pt.2	2.50
3 Gun Metal Green	2.50
4 Targets	2.50

TALES OF THE MYSTERIOUS TRAVELER
Charlton Comics, 1956
1 DG	700.00
2 SD	600.00

3 SD,SD(c)	500.00
4 SD,SD(c)	600.00
5 SD,SD(c)	600.00
6 SD,SD(c)	600.00
7 SD	550.00
8 SD	550.00
9 SD	550.00
10 SD,SD(c)	575.00
11 SD,SD(c)	575.00
12	300.00
13	325.00
14 (1985)	25.00
15 (1985)	20.00

TALES OF THE REALM
Crossgen Comics, 2003
1 (of 6)	3.00
2	3.00

TALES OF THE SUN RUNNERS
Sirius Comics, 1986
1	2.50
2 and 3	@2.50

TALESPIN
Walt Disney, 1991
(Reg.-Series)
1 Sky-Raker, Pt.1	2.50
2 Sky-Raker, Pt.2	2.50
3 Idiots Abroad	2.50
4 Contractual Desperation	2.50
5 The Oldman & the Sea Duck	2.50
6 F'reeze a Jolly Good Fellow	2.50

TALESPIN
Walt Disney, 1991
[Mini-Series]
1 Take-off Pt.1	3.00
2 Take-off Pt 2	3.00
3 Take-off Pt 3,Khan Job	3.00
4 Take-off pt 4	3.00

TALEWEAVER
WildStorm/DC, 2001
1 (of 6) 40-pg.	3.50
2	3.00
2a variant (c)	3.00
3 thru 6	@3.00

TALISMEN
Atlantis Studios, 2005
1 (of 4)	3.00
2 thru 4	@3.00

TALL TALES OF VISHNU SHARMA, THE: PANCHATANTRA
Virgin Comics, 2007
1	3.00
2 thru 5	@3.00

TANK GIRL: THE GIFTING
IDW Publishing, 2007
1	4.00
2 thru 4	@4.00
1a thru 4a variant (c)	4.00

TANK GIRL: VISIONS OF BOOGA
IDW, 2008
1	4.00
2 thru 4	@4.00

TAOLAND
Severe Reality Productions
4 1st full color issue		6.00
5 48pg.		6.00

TAOLAND ADVENTURES
Antarctic Press, 1999
1 by Jeff Amano		3.00
2		3.00

TARGET AIRBOY
Eclipse, 1988
1 SK,A:Clint		2.50

Targitt #2
© Atlas

TARGITT
Atlas, 1975
1 thru 3		@20.00

TAROT WITCH OF THE BLACK ROSE
Broadsword Comics, 2000
1 JBa(c)		3.00
2		3.00
3		3.00
4		3.00
5 JBa		3.00
6 Goulish Intentions		3.00
7 Return of the Dark Witch,pt.1		3.00
8 Return of the Dark Witch,pt.2		3.00
9 Return of the Dark Witch,pt.3		3.00
2a thru 16a signed		@10.00
1b, 4b, 6b, 8b, 9b, 10b deluxe		@20.00
7b double-deluxe edition		25.00
10 Quest for the Black Rose Sword		3.00
11 Black Rose Sword,pt.2		3.00
12		3.00
13		3.00
13b previews exlusive (c)		15.00
14		3.00
15		3.00
16		3.00
17 Cold Spell		3.00
18 Diary of a Witch		3.00
19 Mists of Darkness, pt.1		3.00
20 Mists of Darkness, pt.2		3.00
21 Mists of Darkness, pt.3		3.00
22 Mists of Darkness, pt.4		3.00
23 Ghouls Gone Wild		3.00
24 Ghouls Gone Wild,pt.2		3.00
25 thru 34		@3.00
35 thru 47		@3.00
48 thru 53		@3.00

19a photo (c)		10.00
19b exclusive previews (c)		10.00
30b signed		10.00
31b variant (c)		3.00
31c with photo		15.00
31d signed		10.00
32b signed		10.00
37b photo (c)		15.00
48a thru 53a variant (c)s		3.00
11b thru 40b Deluxe		@20.00

TARZAN, LORD OF THE JUNGLE
Gold Key, 1965
1		150.00

TARZAN OF THE APES
Gold Key, 1962–72
prev. Dell (see Golden Age)
132		100.00
133		80.00
134		80.00
135		90.00
136		80.00
137		80.00
138		80.00
139 I:Korak.		90.00
140 thru 154		@80.00
155 O:Tarzan		100.00
156 thru 161		@60.00
162 TV photo (c)		80.00
163		60.00
164		60.00
165 TV photo (c)		80.00
166		60.00
167		60.00
168 TV photo (c)		80.00
169 A:Leopard Girl		60.00
170		60.00
171 TV photo (c)		100.00
172 thru 177		@50.00
178 O:Tarzan, rep. #155		50.00
179 thru 191		@50.00
192 Tarzan and the Foreign Legion adaptation		50.00
193 thru 199		@50.00
200		60.00
201 thru 205		@50.00
206 last issue		50.00
Continued by DC; see also Marvel

TARZAN: THE BECKONING
Malibu, 1992
1 TY,I:The Spider Man		2.75
2 TY,Going back to Africa		2.50
3 thru 6		2.50

TARZAN THE WARRIOR
Malibu, 1992
1 SBs(c),O:Tarzan		3.50
2 & 3		@2.75
4 Wom'cha's Ship		2.75
5		2.75

TARZAN: LOVE, LIES, AND THE LOST CITY
Malibu, 1992
1 MWg&WS(s),Short Stories		4.00
2 The lost city of Opar		2.50
3 Final issue		2.50

TASMANIAN DEVIL & HIS TASTY FRIENDS
Gold Key, 1962
1		300.00

TASTEE-FREEZ COMICS
Harvey Comics, 1957
1 Little Dot		400.00
2 Rags Rabbit		75.00
3 Casper		100.00
4 Sad Sack		75.00
5 Mazie		75.00
6 Dick Tracy		100.00

T-BIRD AND THROTTLE
Viper Comics 2008
0		3.25
1		3.25
2 thru 3		@3.25

TEAM ANARCHY
Anarchy, 1993
1 I:Team Anarchy		2.75
2 thru 3		2.75
4 PuD,MaS,I:Primal		2.75

TEAM YANKEE
First, 1989
1 Harold Coyle novel adapt.		2.50
2 thru 6		@2.50

TEAM ZERO
Wildstorm/DC, Dec., 2006
1 CDi(s),DoM,World War II		3.00
2 Deathblow gathers his team		3.00
3 CDi(s),DoM,Peenemunde		3.00
4 CDi(s),DoM,V: Red Army		3.00
5 CDi(s),DoM,V: Red Army		3.00
6 CDi(s),DoM, conclusion		3.00

TEEN-AGE CONFIDENTIAL CONFESSIONS
Charlton Comics, 1960–64
1		75.00
2 thru 5		@50.00
6 thru 10		@40.00
11 thru 22		@30.00

TEENAGE HOTRODDERS
Charlton Comics, April, 1963
1		100.00
2 thru 5		@60.00
6 thru 10		@50.00
11 thru 23		@50.00
24		50.00
Becomes:

TOP ELIMINATOR
25 thru 29		@50.00
Becomes:

DRAG 'N' WHEELS
30		100.00
31 thru 39		60.00
40 thru 50 Scot Jackson		50.00
51 thru 59 May, 1973		40.00

TEENAGE MUTANT NINJA TURTLES
First
1		6.00
2		4.50

TEENAGE MUTANT NINJA TURTLES
Archie, 1988
(From T.V. Series)
1 O:TMNT,April O'Neil,Shredder Krang		6.00
2 V:Shredder,O:Bebop & Rocksteady		4.00
3 V:Shredder & Krang		3.00

TEENAGE MUTANT NINJA TURTLES
Mirage, 1993
1 A:Casey Jones.............. 3.00
2 JmL(a&s)................. 3.00
3 thru 13 ....@2.75

TEENAGE MUTANT NINJA TURTLES ADVENTURES
Archie, 1988 [2nd Series]
1 Shredder,Bebop,Rocksteady
   return to earth 5.00
2 I:Baxter Stockman 3.00
3 Three Fragments #1 .... 3.00
4 thru 9 ....@2.50
10 thru 25 ....@2.50
26 thru 40...................@2.50
41 thru 70...................@2.50
1990 Movie adapt(direct)........ 5.50
1990 Movie adapt(newsstand)..... 2.50
1991 TMNT meet Archie 2.50
1991 Movie Adapt II............. 2.50
Spec.#2 Ghost of 13 Mile Island ... 2.50
Spec.#3 Night of the Monsterex ... 2.50
TMNT Mutant Universe Sourcebook 2.00

TEENAGE MUTANT NINJA TURTLES ANIMATED
Dreamwave, 2003
1 .... 3.00
2 thru 9 ....@3.00

TEENAGE MUTANT NINJA TURTLES/ FLAMING CARROT
Mirage/Dark Horse, 1993
1 JmL 3.00
2 JmL 3.00
3 JmL 3.00
4 JmL 3.00

TMNT PRESENTS:
Archie, 1993

...APRIL O'NEIL
1 A:Chien Khan,Vid Vicious 2.50
2 V:White Ninja,A:V.Vicious 2.50
3 V:Vhien Khan,concl........... 2.50
Spec. April O'Neil, May East Saga . 2.50

...DONATELLO AND LEATHERHEAD
1 .... 2.50
2 .... 2.50

...MERDUDE VS. RAY FILLET
1 .... 2.50
2 .... 2.50
3 .... 2.50

TMNT:
THE MALTESE TURTLE
Mirage
Spec. F:Raphael Detective 3.00

...YEAR OF THE TURTLE
Archie Comics, 1995
1 All New Era 2.50

[JACK KIRBY'S] TEENAGENTS
[Mini-Series] Topps, 1993
1 WS,AH,w/3 cards............ 3.00
2 NV,w/3 cards 3.00
3 NV,w/3 cards 3.00

---

4 NV,w/3 leftover? cards........ 3.00

TEEN CONFESSIONS
Charlton Comics, 1959–76
1 .... 150.00
2 .... 125.00
3 .... 100.00
4 .... 100.00
5 .... 100.00
6 .... 100.00
7 .... 100.00
8 .... 100.00
9 .... 100.00
10 thru 30.................@100.00
31 Beatles cover 225.00
32 .... 25.00
33 .... 25.00
34 .... 25.00
35 .... 25.00
36 .... 25.00
37 Beatles cover,Fan Club story . 250.00
38 thru 97.................@20.00

TEEN SECRET DIARY
Charlton Comics, 1959–61
1 .... 100.00
2 .... 75.00
3 .... 75.00
4 .... 75.00
5 .... 75.00
6 thru 11 ....@75.00

TEKKEN 2
Knightstone, 1997
1 (of 4) Tekken Saga, pt.3 .... 3.00
2 .... 3.00
2a photo cover 3.00
3 .... 3.00
3a photo cover 3.00

Tekken Saga #1
© Knightstone

TEKKEN SAGA
Knightstone, 1997
1 .... 4.00
2 .... 3.00
3 .... 3.00
4 Paul vs. Kazuya............. 3.00
5 Paul a prisoner 3.00
Nightstone Unlimited & Tekken ?... 3.00

TEMPEST
Big City Comics, 2007
1 .... 3.25
2 thru 9 ....@3.25

7a variant (c) 3.25
Spec. Tainted Alpha x-over 3.25
Spec. Tainted Charlie x-over 3.25

TEMPLAR CHRONICLES, THE: THE HERETIC
Markosia, 2007
1 .... 3.50
2 thru 4 ....@3.50
2a thru 4a sketch (c) ....@6.00

10
Boom! Studios 2005
1-shot 7.00

TENSE SUSPENSE
Fago Publications, 1958–59
1 .... 150.00
2 .... 100.00

10TH MUSE
Avatar/Tidal Wave Studios, 2002
1A MWn,RCz, Andy Park (c) 3.50
1D ODa(c)................... 3.50
1C RCz(c).................... 3.50
1D Mark Brooks (c)............ 3.50
1E Valdez (c) 3.50
2 RCz(c).................... 3.50
2a Caldwell (c) 3.50
2b Rousseau (c).............. 3.50
2 RCz(c).................... 3.50
2a Green (c) 3.50
2b Grant (c)................. 3.50
Angel Gate, 2003
1-shot Book of Lights 3.00
Alias Enterprises, 2005
Volume 2
1 .... 3.00
1a foil (c)................... 5.00
1b signed, foil (c) 25.00
2 thru 9 ....@3.00
2a thru 9a variant (c)s........@3.00
2b foil, photo (c) 5.00
5a variant (c) signed 15.00
10 .... 3.50
10a variant (c) 3.50
11 God War x-over............ 3.50
12 God War x-over, pt.5......... 3.50
13 Who killed Wonder Boy? 3.50
14 .... 3.50
15 thru 17.................@3.50
Bluewater Productions, 2007
1-shot giant 6.00

10th MUSE/EZRA
Arcana Studios, 2006
1 .... 4.00
1a variant signed photo (c) 15.00

TERMINATOR, THE
Now, 1988–89
1 .... 9.00
2 .... 7.00
3 .... 7.00
4 thru 11 ....@5.00
12 I:JohnConnor($1.75,cov,dbl.sz) . 5.00
13 thru 17.................@5.00
Spec. #1................... 5.00

...ALL MY FUTURES PAST
Now, 1990
1 Painted Art................. 4.00
2 Painted Art................. 4.00

...THE BURNING EARTH
Now, 1990
1 .... 12.00
2 .... 10.00
3 thru 5 ....@9.00

TERMINATOR 2: CYBERNETIC DAWN
Malibu, 1995–96
1 thru 4 . . . . @3.00
0 flip-book/T2 Nuclear Twilight 3.00

TERMINATOR 2: INFINITY
D.E. (Dynamite Ent.) 2007
1 . . . . 4.00
1a variant (c)s . . . . @4.00
2 thru 5 . . . . @4.00
6 thru 7 JP. 3.50
6a thru 7a variant (c)s . . . . @3.50

TERMINATOR 2: NUCLEAR TWILIGHT
Malibu, 1995–96
1 thru 4 . . . . @3.00
0 flip-book, see above

TERMINATOR 3
Beckett Entertainment, 2003
1 Before the Rise 6.00
2 Before the Rise 6.00
3 Eyes of the Rise 6.00
4 Eyes of the Rise 6.00
5 Fragmented 6.00
6 Fragmented 6.00

TERRAFORMERS
Wonder Comics, 1987
1 . . . . 3.00
2 . . . . 3.00
3 . . . . 3.00
4 . . . . 3.00

TERRANAUTS
Fantasy General, 1986
1 . . . . 3.00
2 . . . . 3.00

TERRA OBSCURA
Wildstorm/DC June, 2003
America's Best Comics
1 (of 6) AMo(s) 3.00
2 AMo(s),F:Grant Halford 3.00
3 thru 5 AMo(s) . . . . @3.00
6 AMo(s),concl.,40-pg. 4.00
Vol. 2, 2004
1 AMo(s) 3.00
2 AMo(s) 3.00
3 . . . . 3.00
4 AMo(s),KIS. 3.00
5 AMo(s),KIS. 3.00
6 AMo(s),KIS, Showdown in space. 3.00

TERRITORY 51
Lawdog Comics, 2004
1 . . . . 3.00
1 convention edition, signed 11.00
2 . . . . 4.00

TEXAS CHAINSAW MASSACRE
Avatar Press, 2005
Spec. #1 . . . . 4.00
Spec. #1 variant (c)s 4.00
Spec. #1 glow (c). 12.00
Spec. #1 Bloodbath (c) 6.00
Spec. #1 Blood Red Con (c) 5.00
Spec. #1 painted (c). 6.00
Spec. #1 Lurking (c) 6.00
Spec. #1 Prism foil (c) 11.00
Spec. Fearbook #1 . . . . 4.00
Spec. Fearbook #1 variant (c)s . . @4.00
Spec. Fearbook #1 leather (c) . . . 20.00

TEXAS CHAINSAW MASSACRE: THE GRIND
Avatar Press, 2005
1 . . . . 4.00
1a Wraparound (c) 4.00
1b Variant(c)s . . . . @4.00
1c leather (c). 15.00
1d Red foil convention (c). 5.00
2 . . . . 4.00
2a Wraparound (c) 4.00
2b Variant(c)s . . . . @4.00
2c Die-cut (c) 9.00
3a Wraparound (c) 4.00
3b variant (c)s. 4.00
3c Die-cut (c) 10.00

TEXAS CHAINSAW MASSACRE
Wildstorm/DC, Nov., 2006
1 DAn,ALa 3.00
1a varaint (c). 3.00
2 DAn,ALa 3.00
3 DAn,ALa 3.00
4 DAn,ALa 3.00
5 DAn,ALa 3.00
6 DAn,ALa, Who lives?. 3.00
Spec. Cut 3.00

...ABOUT A BOY
Wildstorm/DC, July, 2007
1 DAn,ALa,O:Leatherface. 3.00

...BY HIMSELF
Wildstorm/DC, Aug., 2007
1 DAn,ALa,Hewitt Clan. 3.00

...RAISING CAIN
Wildstorm/DC, May, 2008
1 (of 3) 3.50
2 thru 3 . . . . @3.50

Texas Rangers in Action #47
© Charlton

TEXAS RANGERS IN ACTION
Charlton Comics, 1956–70
5 . . . . 150.00
6 and 7 . . . . @100.00
8 SD 200.00
9 and 10 . . . . @100.00
11 AW 175.00
12 . . . . 100.00
13 AW 150.00
14 thru 20 . . . . @100.00
21 thru 30. . . . . @60.00
31 thru 59. . . . . @50.00

60 B:Riley's Rangers 60.00
61 thru 79. . . . . @30.00

THAT WILKIN BOY
Archie Publications, 1969
1 . . . . 70.00
2 thru 10 . . . . @50.00
11 thru 20 . . . . @30.00
21 thru 26 E:Giant size . . . . . . @25.00
27 thru 52. . . . . @25.00

THESPIAN
Dark Moon, 1995
1 I:Thespian 2.50
2 V:Lemming. 2.50
3 Lord of Manhattan 2.50

THIRD WORLD WAR
Fleetway, 1990–91
1 HamburgerLady. 2.50
2 . . . . 2.50
3 The Killing Yields 2.50
4 thru 6 . . . . @2.50

13: ASSASSIN
TSR, 1990–91
1 thru 4 from game . . . . @3.00
5 thru 8 The Search for
   Maggie Darr. . . . . @3.00

30 DAYS OF NIGHT
IDW Publishing, 2002
1 by S.Niles & B.Templesmith . . . 60.00
1a 2nd printing 7.00
2 . . . . 40.00
3 . . . . 20.00
Spec. Bloodsucker Tales (2004) . . . 4.00
Annual 2004. . . . . 5.00
Annual 2005 . . . . 7.50

30 DAYS OF NIGHT:
BEYOND BARROW
IDW Publishing, 2007
1 . . . . 4.00
2 thru 3 . . . . @4.00

...BLOODSUCKER TALES
IDW Publishing, 2004
1 . . . . 4.00
2 thru 10 . . . . @4.00

...DEAD SPACE
IDW Publishing 2005
1 . . . . 4.00
2 . . . . 4.00
3 . . . . 4.00

...EBEN AND STELLA
IDW Publishing, 2007
1 . . . . 4.00
2 thru 4 . . . . @4.00

...RED SNOW
IDW Publishing
1 . . . . 4.00
2 thur 3 . . . . 4.00

...RETURN TO BARROW
IDW Publishing, 2004
1 . . . . 4.00
2 thru 6 . . . . @4.00

...SPREADING THE DISEASE
IDW Publishing, 2006
1 . . . . 4.00
2 thru 5 . . . . @4.00
1a thru 5a variant (c)s . . . . @4.00

THOSE ANNOYING POST BROTHERS
Vortex, 1985
1 . . . . 3.00
2 thru 5 . . . . @2.50
6 thru 18 . . . . @2.50
See also B&W listings

3-D ZONE PRESENTS
Renegade, 1987–89
1 Dr. Jekyll and Mr. Hyde 2.50
2 Weird Tales of Basil Wolverton . . 2.50
3 thru 10 . . . . @2.50
11 3-D Danse Macabre 2.50
12 3-D Presidents 2.50
13 Flash Gordon 2.50
14 Tyranostar 2.50
15 3-Dementia 2.50
16 Space Vixens 2.50
17 thru 20 . . . . 2.50

3 LITTLE KITTENS
Broadsword Comics, 2002
1 JBa, Purrr-fect weapons 3.00
2 Puss N Bullets 3.00
3 Purrr-Fect Weapons 3.00
1a thru 3a deluxe . . . . @15.00
1b thru 3b signed . . . . @9.00

THREE STOOGES
Dell Publishing Co., 1959
6 Ph(c),B:Prof. Putter 300.00
7 Ph(c) 300.00
8 Ph(c) 300.00
9 Ph(c) 300.00
Gold Key, 1962
10 Ph(c) 250.00
11 Ph(c) 250.00
12 Ph(c) 250.00
13 Ph(c) 250.00
14 Ph(c) 250.00
15 Ph(c) Go Around the World . . 250.00
16 Ph(c),E:Prof. Putter 200.00
17 Ph(c),B:Little Monsters 200.00
18 Ph(c) 200.00
19 Ph(c) 200.00
20 Ph(c) 200.00
21 Ph(c) 200.00
22 Ph(c),Movie Scenes 200.00
23 thru 30 Ph(c) . . . . @175.00
31 thru 50 Ph(c) . . . . @150.00
51 . . . . 150.00
52 thru 55 Ph(c) . . . . @150.00

THREE STOOGES 3-D
Eclipse, 1991
1 thru 3 reprints from 1953 . . . . . @2.50
4 reprints from 1953 . . . . 3.50

THRESHOLD
Narwain Publishing, 2006
1 (of 5) 4.00

THRILL-O-RAMA
Harvey Publications, 1965–66
1 A:Man in Black(Fate),DW,AW . 100.00
2 AW,A:Pirana,I:Clawfang,
  The Barbarian 75.00
3 A:Pirana, Fate 60.00

THRUD THE BARBARIAN
Thrud Comics, 2006
1 . . . . 3.00
2 Phalanx of frosty foes 4.00
3 thru 5 . . . . @4.00

Thunder Agents #10
© Tower

THUNDER AGENTS
Tower, 1965–69
1 WW,RC,GK,MSy,GT,I:Thunder
  Agents,IronMaiden,Warlord . . 350.00
2 WW,MSy,D:Egghead 200.00
3 WW,DA,MSy,V:Warlords 150.00
4 WW,MSy,RC,I:Lightning 150.00
5 WW,RC,GK,MSy 150.00
6 WW,SD,MSy,I:Warp Wizard . . 125.00
7 WW,MSy,SD,D:Menthor 125.00
8 WW,MSy,GT,DA,I:Raven 125.00
9 OW,WW,MSy,A:Andor 125.00
10 WW,MSy,OW,A:Andor 125.00
11 WW,DA,MSy 100.00
12 SD,WW,MSy 100.00
13 WW,OW,A:Undersea Agent . . 100.00
14 SD,WW,GK,N:Raven,A:Andor 100.00
15 WW,OW,GT,A:Andor. 90.00
16 SD,GK,A:Andor. 90.00
17 WW,OW,GT 90.00
18 SD,OW,RC 75.00
19 GT,I:Ghost. 75.00
20 WW,RC,MSy,all reprints 75.00

T.H.U.N.D.E.R. AGENTS
J.C. Productions, 1983
1 MA,Centerfold 5.00
2 I:Vulcan 5.00

T.H.U.N.D.E.R. AGENTS
Maximum, 1995
1 . . . . 3.00
2 . . . . 3.00

THUNDERBIRD
Atlantis Studios, 2005
1 . . . . 3.00
2 . . . . 3.00

THUNDERBOLT
Charlton Comics, 1966–67
1 PAM,O:Thunderbolt 75.00
Prev: Son of Vulcan
51 PAM,V:Evila 50.00
52 PAM,V:Gore the Monster 35.00
53 PAM,V:The Tong 35.00
54 PAM,I:Sentinels. 35.00
55 PAM,V:Sentinels. 35.00
56 PAM,A:Sentinels 35.00
57 A:Sentinels 35.00
58 PAM,A:Sentinels 35.00
59 PAM,A:Sentinels. 35.00
60 PAM,JAp,I:Prankster. 40.00

THUNDERBOLT JAXON
Wildstorm/DC, Feb., 2006
1 (of 5) DGb,JHi 3.00
2 thru 5 DGb,JHi . . . . @3.00

THUNDERCATS
WildStorm/DC, 2002
0 JSC, preview issue 5.00
1a (of 5) King Lion-O 5.00
1b variant AAd (c). 3.50
2a V:Mumm-ra 3.00
2b variant JLe(c). 3.00
3 F:Lion-O. 3.00
3a variant JMd(c) 3.00
4 F:New Thundera 3.00
5 concl. 3.00
GN Thundercats/Battle
  of the Planets 5.00
Sourcebook 3.00

...DOGS OF WAR
Wildstorm/DC June, 2003
1 (of 5) 10 years in future 3.00
2 New Thundera 3.00
3 BBh,AV 3.00
4 BBh,AV 3.00
5 BBh,AV 3.00

...ENEMY'S PRIDE
Wildstorm/DC June, 2004
1 Cat vs. Cat. 3.00
2 . . . . 3.00
3 . . . . 3.00
4 . . . . 3.00
5 . . . . 3.00

...HAMMERHAND'S REVENGE
Wildstorm/DC, 2003
1 (of 5) 3.00
2 F:Lion-O. 3.00
3 . . . . 3.00
4 (two covers). 3.00
5 (two covers). 3.00
Spec. Superman/Thundercats 6.00

...ORIGINS
Wildstorm/DC, 2003
Spec. Heroes & Villains,pt.1 . . . . . 3.50
Spec. Villains & Heroes,pt.1 . . . . . 3.50

...THE RETURN
Wildstorm/DC, 2003
1 (of 5) EBe,F:Lion-O 3.00
2 EBe,V:Mumm-Ra 3.00
3 EBe 3.00
4 EBe,Wilykat 3.00
5 EBe, concl.. . . . . 3.00

TICK, THE
New England Comics, 2001
1 all new, all color 4.00
1a variant (c), ... 4.00
2 thru 5 . . . . @4.00
6 return of Proto-Tick 4.00
Spec. Big Halloween 2000. . . . . . . 3.50
Spec. Big Halloween 2001. . . . . . . 4.00
Spec. Introducing the Tick (2002) . . 4.00
Spec. Circus Maximus Update 4.00
Spec. Comic Con Extravaganza . . . 4.00
Spec. 20th Anniv. Special. 6.00

...& ARTIE
New England Comics, 2002
1 . . . . 3.50
2 BEd(c) 3.50

...BIG XMAS TRILOGY
New England Comics, 2002
1 . . . . 4.00
2 . . . . 4.00
3 . . . . 4.00

...DAYS OF DRAMA
New England Comics, 2005
1	5.00
2	4.00
3 thru 6	@4.00

...INCREDIBLE INTERNET COMIC
New England Comics, 2001
1	4.00

TIGER AND CRANE
Bluewater Prod., 2008
1 (of 4)	4.00
2 thru 4	@4.00

Tiger Girl #1
© Gold Key

TIGER GIRL
Gold Key, 1968
1	50.00

TIGER-MAN
Atlas, 1975
1 thru 3	@15.00

TIGERS OF TERRA
Antarctic Press, 2000
Vol. 3
1 (of 4) War Against the Sun	3.00
2 Night of the Amazons	3.00
3	3.00
4 Planet of War	3.00
Spec.	4.00

TIME TUNNEL, THE
Gold Key, 1967
1 from TV show	150.00
2	100.00

TIME TWISTERS
Quality, 1987–89
1 AMo(s),AD,DGb	2.50
2 AMo(s),DGb,Wheels of Fury	2.50
3 AMo(s),The Wages of Sin	2.50
4 AMo(s),Bad Timing	2.50
5 PrM(s),The Collector	2.50
6 AMo(s),AIG	2.50
7 AMo(s),Twist Ending	2.50
8 thru 21	@2.50

TIMEWALKER
Valiant, 1994
0 BH,DP,O:3 Immortals	3.00

---

1 DP, BH	2.50
2 thru 15	@2.50
Yearbook F:Harada	3.00

TIPPY'S FRIENDS GO-GO & ANIMAL
Tower Comics, 1966–69
1	150.00
2	75.00
3	75.00
4	75.00
5 thru 7	@75.00
8 Beatles on cover & back	150.00
9 thru 15	@75.00

TIPPY TEEN
Tower Comics, 1965–70
1	200.00
2 thru 27	@100.00

TITANIUM RAIN
Archaia Studios, 2008
1 (of 12)	3.00

TOHUBOHU
New Breed Comics, 1999
1	3.25
2 thru 5	@3.00
6 A Serpent in the Garden	3.25

TOKA
Dell, 1964
1 Jungle King	70.00
2 thru 10	@30.00

TOKYO STORM WARNING
Wildstorm/DC June, 2003
1 (of 3) giant robots	3.00
2 thru 3 WEI	@3.00

TOM AND JERRY
Gold Key, 1962–75
213 thru 214 giants	@125.00
215 thru 240	@40.00
241 thru 291	@25.00
Tom & Jerry Summer Fun (1967)	75.00
Giant #1 Tom & Jerry, the Mouse from T.R.A.P.	75.00

Gold Key, 1977–80
292 thru 300	@20.00
301 thru 327	@15.00

Whitman, 1980
328 thru 341 scarce	@45.00
342 thru 344	@25.00

TOM & JERRY
Harvey, 1991–94
1	2.50
2 thru 18	@2.50

TOM MIX WESTERN
AC Comics, 1988
1	3.00

TOMMI-GUNN
London Night, 1997
0	3.00
1 signed	12.00
1a, chromium, elite edition	15.00
2 thru 3	@3.00

TOMMI-GUNN: KILLER'S LUST
London Night, 1997
1	3.00
1 Japanese Chromium edition	10.00
2	3.00

TOMOE
Crusade Entertainment, 1996
0 BiT,	3.00
1 BiT,Fan Appreciation Edition	3.00
2	3.00

TOMOE/WITCHBLADE: FIRE SERMON
Crusade Entertainment, 1996
1	5.00
1a Gold foil	9.00

TOMOE: UNFORGETTABLE FIRE
Crusade Entertainment, 1997
1 (of 3)	3.00

TOMORROW STORIES
WildStorm/DC, 1999
America's Best Comics
1 AMo,AxR(c) anthology	4.00
1a AxR(c),variant cover	3.50
2 AMo(s),KN,RV,JBa.	3.00
3 AMo(s),KN,RV,JBa.	3.00
4 AMo(s),KN,RV,JBa.	3.00
5 AMo(s),KN,RV,JBa.	3.00
6 AMo(s),RV,JBa.	3.00
7 AMo(s),RV,JBa.	3.00
8 AMo(s),RV,JBa.	3.00
9 AMo(s),RV,JBa.	3.00
10 AMo(s),RV,JBa,Jack B. Quick.	3.00
11 AMo(s),RV,JBa,AAd,F:Cobweb.	3.00
12 AMo(s),RV,JBa, x-over	3.00
Spec. #1 AMo(s) 64-page	7.00
Spec. #2 AMo(s)	7.00

TOM STRONG
WildStorm/DC, 1999
America's Best Comics
1 AMo(s),CSp,40-pg.	4.00
2 AMo(s),CSp,Millennium City	3.00
3 AMo(s),CSp,Millennium City	3.00
4 AMo,CSp,AAd,Berlin in WW2	3.00
5 AMo,JOy,CSp,Memories of Pangea	3.00
6 AMo,CSp,DGb, Dead Man's Hand	3.00
7 AMo,CSp,GFr.	3.00
8 AMo,CSp,Lost Mesa	3.00
9 AMo,CSp,.	3.00
10 AMo,CSp,F:Warren Strong	3.00
11 AMo,CSp,F:Tom Strange.	3.00
12 AMo,CSp,F:Tom Strange,pt.2	3.00
13 AMo,CSp,Warren Strong.	3.00
14 AMo,CSp,Space Family Strong.	3.00
15 AMo,CSp,Val Var Garm	3.00
16 AMo(s),CSp,KIS,Modular Man	3.00
17 AMo(s),CSp,KIS,Weird Rider	3.00
18 AMo(s),CSp,KIS,Weird Rider	3.00
19 AMo(s),CSp,KIS	3.00
20 AMo(s),CSp,KIS,JOy,pt.1	3.00
21 AMo(s),CSp,KIS,JOy,pt.2	3.00
22 AMo(s),CSp,KIS,JOy,pt.3	3.00
23 CSp,KIS,rescue mission	3.00
24 CSp,KIS,	3.00
25 JPL,F:Strongmen of America	3.00
26 MSh(s),PFe.	3.00
27 SwM	3.00
28	3.00
29 DFg	3.00
30 DFg,Terrible Life of Tom Strong	3.00
31 JOy, Michael Moorcock(s)	3.00
32 JOy, Michael Moorcock(s)	3.00
33 JOy, F:Pneuman	3.00
34 JP,PG, central China	3.00
35 CSp,KIS, Snow Queen sequel	3.00
36 AMo,CSp,KIS,End of World	3.00

TOM STRONG'S TERRIFIC TALES
WildStorm/DC, 2001
America's Best Comics
1 AMo,AAd 3.50
2 AMo,AAd 3.00
3 AMo,AAd,JOy 3.00
4 AMo(s),AAd,Jonni Future. 3.00
5 AMo(s),SA,AAd(c) 3.00
6 AMo(s),JOy,AAd 3.00
7 AMo(s),AAd 3.00
8 AMo(s),AAd, young Tom 3.00
9 AMo(s),three stories. 3.00
10 AMo(s),three stories 3.00
11 AMo(s), ... 3.00
12 AMo(s),AAd, final issue. 3.00

TOM SULLIVAN'S BOOKS OF THE DEAD
Dead Dog Comics, 2005
1 Devilhead. 5.00
1a variant (c) 5.00
2 . . . . 5.00
3 . . . . 5.00
4 . . . . 5.00

TOM TERRIFIC!
Pines Comics
Summer, 1957
1 . . . . 300.00
2 . . . . 250.00
3 thru 5 . . . . @250.00
6 Fall, 1958. . . . . 250.00

TONY LOCO
Illusive Arts, 2006
1 . . . . 3.50
2 thru 3 . . . . @3.50

TOP CAT
Dell, 1961
1 . . . . 275.00
2 thru 3 . . . . @135.00
Gold Key, 1962
4 . . . . 125.00
5 . . . . 125.00
6 thru 10 . . . . @100.00
11 thru 20 . . . . @75.00
21 thru 31 . . . . @50.00

TOP CAT
Charlton Comics, 1970–73
1 . . . . 125.00
2 thru 10 . . . . @75.00
11 thru 20 . . . . @50.00

TOP TEN
WildStorm/DC, 1999
America's Best Comics
1 AMo(s),GeH,40-pg. 3.50
2 AMo(s),GeH. 3.00
3 thru 9 AMo(s),GeH. . . . . @3.00
10 AMo(s),GeH,killer revealed. . . . 3.00
11 AMo(s),GeH,aftermath 3.00
12 AMo(s),GeH,season finale 3.00

TOP TEN: BEYOND THE FARTHEST PRECINCT
Wildstorm/DC, Aug., 2005
1 (of 5) JOy. 3.00
2 thru 5 JOy. . . . . @3.00

TOP TEN SEASON TWO
Wildstorm/DC, Oct., 2008
1 . . . . 3.00
2 . . . . 3.00

TOP THAT! PUZZLE ADVENTURES
Top That! Publishing, 2005
1 Halfpipe Heroes 4.00
2 Freaky Fredas Ghost. 4.00
3 Chinese Mystery 4.00
4 Aztec Madness 4.00
5 Shadow on the Wall. 4.00
6 Celtic Double Cross. 4.00

TOR IN 3-D
Eclipse, 1986
1 JKu. 3.00
1a B&W limited 100 sign 5.00
2 JKu. 3.00

TORMENTRESS: MISTRESS OF HELL
Blackout Comics, 1977
0 . . . . 3.00

TOTAL ECLIPSE
Eclipse, 1988–89
1 BHa,BSz(c),A:Airboy,Skywolf . . . 4.00
2 BHa,BSz(c),A:New Wave, Liberty Project 4.00
3 BHa,BSz(c),A:Scout,Ms.Tree . . . 4.00
4 BHa,BSz(c),A:Miracleman, Prowler 4.00
5 BHa,BSz(c),A:Miracleman, Aztec Ace 4.00

TOTAL ECLIPSE, THE SERAPHIM OBJECTIVE
Eclipse, 1988
1 tie-in Total Eclipse #2 . . . . 2.50

Total War #2
© Gold Key

TOTAL WAR
Gold Key, 1965
1 WW 150.00
2 WW 125.00
Becomes:

M.A.R.S. PATROL
3 WW 125.00
4 . . . . 100.00
5 . . . . 100.00
6 thru 10 . . . . @100.00

TOTEM
Big City Comics, 2007
1 . . . . 3.25
2 thru 9 . . . . @3.25

7a variant (c) 3.25
Spec. Tainted Bravo x-over 3.25
Spec. Tainted Delta x-over. 3.25

TOY BOX
Alias Enterprises, 2006
0 . . . . 3.50

TOY BOY
Continuity, 1986–91
1 NA.I&O:Toy Boy,A:Megalith 3.00
2 TVE 3.00
3 TVE 3.00
4 TVE 3.00
5 TVE 3.00
6 TVE 3.00
7 MG 3.00

TRAGG AND THE SKY GODS
Gold Key, 1975
1 . . . . 20.00
2 thru 8 . . . . @15.00

TRAILOR PARK OF TERROR
Imperium Comics, 2006
Vol. 2
1 . . . . 4.00
1 variant(c) 4.00
2 . . . . 4.00
3 . . . . 4.00
4 . . . . 4.00
5 . . . . 3.00
6 thru 8 . . . . @4.00
9 thru 10 . . . . @4.00
Spec. Halloween Special 4.00
Spec. Halloween Special #2 . . . . . 4.00

TRANQUILITY
Wildstorm/DC, Dec., 2006
1 . . . . 3.00
1a variant JSC (c) 3.00
2 . . . . 3.00
2a variant (c) (1:10) 3.00
3 Mr. Articulate's murder. 3.00
3a variant (c) (1:10) 3.00
Becomes:

WELCOME TO TRANQUILITY
Wildstorm/DC, Mar., 2007
4 . . . . 3.00
4a variant (c) 3.00
5 Battle to the death 3.00
6 Who killed Mr. Articulate? 3.00
7 F:Sheriff Lindo 3.00
8 Three tales. 3.00
9 Paradox Box 3.00
10 Secrets revealed. 3.00
11 Plague of the undead 3.00
12 V:Astral Man 3.00

TRANQUILITY: ARMAGEDDON
Wildstorm/DC, Nov., 2007
1 F:Maximum Man 3.00

TRANSFORMERS
1 Robotics. 2.50
2 . . . . 2.50
3 . . . . 2.50

TRANSFORMERS: ...ARMADA
Dreamwave, 2002
1 . . . . 4.00

2	3.00
3 thru 17	@3.00
18 thru 32 Energon	@3.00
Spec. Summer Special #1	5.00

Transformers Generation One #4
© Dreamwave

2005 Annual	6.00
Energon Official Guidebook #1	5.00

...BEAST WARS
Dreamwave, 2005

1	3.00
2	3.00

...GENERATION ONE
Dreamwave, 2002

1	7.00
1a exclusive holofoil (c)	20.00
2 thru 6	@5.00
5a thru 6a variant (c)	@4.00
7 thru 10	@4.00
0	3.50
Preview book, exclusive (c)	4.00

Vol. 2

1 (of 6)	3.50
1a chrome edition	6.00
2 thru 14	@3.00
GN More than meets the Eye, guide	5.25
GN More than meets the Eye #3	5.25
2004 Datatracks	2.50

.../G.I. JOE
Dreamwave, 2003

1	3.00
1a holofoil (c)	6.00
2 thru 6	@3.00
1-shot Divided Front	3.00

.../G.I. JOE: DIVIDED FRONT
Dreamwave, 2004

1	3.00
2 thru 6	@3.00

...MICROMASTERS
Dreamwave, 2004

1 (of 4)	3.00
2 thru 3	@3.00

...MORE THAN
MEETS THE EYE
Dreamwave, 2003

1 (of 8)	5.25
2 thru 7	@5.25
8 final issue	6.00

Vol. 2 Transformers Armada

1 thru 3 More than Meets the Eye	@5.00

...THE WAR WITHIN
Dreamwave, 2002

1	3.00
2 thru 6	@3.00

Vol. 2 The Dark Ages

1	3.00
2	3.00
3 thru 6	@3.00

Vol. 3 The Age of Wrath

1	3.00
2 thru 6	@3.00

TRANSFORMERS
IDW Publishing, 2005

0	2.00
1 Infiltration	3.00
1a variant (c)s	@3.00
2 thru 6 Infiltration	3.00
2a thru 6a variant (c)s	@3.00
Spec. Animated movie adaptation	4.00
Spec. Anim. movie adapt. variant (c)	4.00
Cover Gallery	6.00

...EVOLUTIONS:
HEARTS OF STEEL
IDW Publishing, 2006

1 CDi	3.00
1a variant (c)	3.00
2 thru 4 CDi	@3.00
2a thru 4a variant (c)	@3.00

...GENERATIONS
IDW Publishing, 2006

1	2.50
1a variant (c)	2.50
2	2.50
2a variant (c)	2.50
3 thru 9	@2.50
3a thru 9a variant (c)	@2.50
10 thru 12	@3.00
10a thru 12a variant (c)	@3.00

...SPOTLIGHT
IDW Publishing, 2006

1-shot Hot Rod	4.00
1-shot Hot Rod variant (c)	4.00
1-shot Nightbeat	4.00
1-shot Nightbeat variant (c)	4.00
1-shot Shockwave	4.00
1-shot Shockwave variant (c)	4.00
Spec. Kup	4.00
Spec. Galvatron	4.00
Spec. Optimus Prime	4.00
Spec. Six Shot	4.00
Spec. Ultra Magnus	4.00
Spec. Ramjet	4.00
Spec. Soundwave	4.00
Specials variant (c)s	@4.00
Spec. Blaster	4.00
Spec. Arcee	4.00
Spec. Arcee variant (c)	4.00
Spec Grimlock	4.00
Spec Grimlock variant (c)	4.00
Spec. Mirage	4.00
Spec. Cyclonus	4.00
Spec. Cyclonus variant (c)	4.00
Spec. Wheelie	4.00
Spec. Wheelie variant (c)	4.00
Spec. Hardhead	4.00
Spec. Hardhead variant (c)	4.00
Spec. Doubledealer	4.00
Spec. Doubledealer variant (c)	4.00
Spec. Spotlight	4.00
Spec. Spotlight variant (c)	4.00
Spec. Blurr	4.00
Spec. Blurr variant (c)	4.00
Optimus Prime 3-D	6.00

...TARGET: 2006
IDW Publishing, 2007

1	4.00
2 thru 5	@4.00

1a thru 5a variant (c)	@4.00

...ANIMATED: THE ARRIVAL
IDW, 2008

1	4.00
1a variant (c)	4.00
2 thru 4	@4.00
2a thru 4a variant (c)s	@4.00

TRANSFORMERS, THE:

...ALL HAIL MEGATRON
IDW, 2008

1	4.00
1a variant (c)	4.00
2 thru 5	@4.00
2a thru 5a variant (c)s	@4.00

...BEAST WARS
IDW Publishing, 2006

1	3.00
1a variant (c)	3.00
2	3.00
3	3.00
4	3.00
2a thru 4a variant (c)	3.00
Sourcebook #3	4.00
Sourcebook #4	7.50

...BEAST WARS:
THE ASCENDING
IDW, 2007

1	4.00
2	4.00
1a thru 2a variant (c)	@4.00
3	4.00
4	4.00
Spec. Sourcebook #1	7.00

...DEVASTATION
IDW, 2007

1	4.00
2	4.00
3	4.00
4 thru 6	@4.00
6a variant (c)s	@4.00

...ESCALATION
IDW Publishing, 2006

1	4.00
1a variant b&w (c)	4.00
2 thru 6	@4.00
2a thru 6a variant (c)s	@4.00

...FOCUS ON DECEPTICONS
IDW, 2008

Spec.	3.00

...MEGATRON ORIGIN
IDW Publishing, 2007

1	4.00
2 thru 4	@4.00
1a thru 4a variant (c)	@4.00

...ANIMATED MOVIE
IDW, 2006

3 Movie Adaptation	4.00
4	4.00

...MOVIE ADAPTATION
IDW, 2007

1	4.00
2 thru 4	@4.00

...MOVIE PREQUEL
IDW, 2007

2 thru 4	@4.00
2a thru 4a variant (c)	@4.00

...MOVIE PREQUEL:
SAGA OF THE ALLSPARK
IDW, 2008

1	4.00
1a variant (c)	4.00

COLOR PUB.

2 thru 4 . . . . @4.00
2a thru 4a variant (c)s . . . . @4.00

...MOVIE SEQUEL:
THE REIGN OF STARSCREAM
IDW, 2008

1 . . . . 4.00
1a variant (c) 4.00
2 thru 5 . . . . @4.00
2a thru 5a variant (c)s . . . . @4.00
Spec. Movie Prequel 4.00
Spec. Movie Prequel variant (c) . . . 4.00

...STORMBRINGER
IDW Publishing, 2006

1 . . . . 3.00
1a variant (c) 3.00
2 . . . . 3.00
3 . . . . 3.00
4 . . . . 3.00
2a thru 4a variant (c) . . . . @3.00

TRANSFORMERS, THE:
BEST OF UK:

DINOBOTS
IDW, 2007

1 . . . . 4.00
2 . . . . 4.00
3 . . . . 4.00
4 thru 6 . . . . @4.00

...SPACE PIRATES
IDW, 2008

1 . . . . 4.00
2 thru 5 . . . . @4.00

...TIME WARS
IDW, 2008

1 . . . . 4.00
2 thru 4 . . . . 4.00

TRANSFORMERS:
TIMELINES
Fun Publications, 2006

1-shot Beast Wars 5.00
1-shot Summer Special (2007) 5.00
3 Featuring Nightbeat 4.00
1-shot Summer Special 5.00
1-shot Fall Special 5.00

TRANSFORMERS in 3-D
Blackthorne

1 thru 5 . . . . @2.50

TRAVEL OF JAMIE
McPHEETERS, THE
Gold Key, 1963

1 Kurt Russell 60.00

TRAVELLER
Maximum Press, 1996

1 (of 3) RLd,MHw, ... 3.00

TRIAL BY FIRE
Crossgen Comics, 2002

1 (of 5) 3.00

TRIBE
Axis Comics, 1993–94

1 see Image Comics section
2 TJn(s),LSn,V:Alex 2.50
3 TJn(s),LSn, ... 2.50
Good Comics, 1996
0 TJn,LSn 3.00
1 TJn,LSn,Choice and
  Responsibility 3.00
2 TJn,LSn,Choice and
  Responsibility 3.00

TRIBULATION FORCE
Tyndale House, 2002

GN Vol. #1 . . . . 6.00
GN Vol. #2 thru Vol. 5 . . . . @6.00

TRICK 'R TREAT
Wildstorm/DC, Oct., 2007

1 . . . . 3.00
2 thru 4 . . . . @3.00

TRINITY ANGELS
Acclaim, 1997

1 KM,DPs, Maria, Gianna &
  Theresa Barbella become Trinity
  Angels 2.50
2 thru 12 KM . . . . @2.50

TROLL LORDS
Comico, 1989–90

Spec. #1 . . . . 2.50
1 . . . . 2.50
2 thru 4 . . . . @2.50

TRON
Amaze Ink

3 thru 6 . . . . @4.00

TRON: DEREZZED
88MPH Studios, 2004

1 (of 4) 3.00
2 thru 3 . . . . @3.00
1a thru 3a variant (c)s . . . . @3.50

TRON: THE GHOST
IN THE MACHINE
Amaze Ink/SLG, 2006

1 . . . . 3.50
2 . . . . 3.50

TROUBLEMAKERS
Acclaim, 1996

1 FaN(s) 2.50
2 thru 19 FaN(s) . . . . @2.50

TROUBLE WITH GIRLS
Comico, 1987–88

1 . . . . 3.00
2 thru 4 . . . . @2.50

TRUE LOVE
Eclipse, 1986

1 ATh,NC,DSt(c),reprints. 3.00
2 ATh,NC,BA(c),reprints 3.00

TRUE ROMANCE
Pyramid Comics, 1997

1 . . . . 2.50
1a deluxe 3.00
2 thru 4 . . . . @2.50

TUFF GHOSTS
STARRING SPOOKY
Harvey Publications, 1962–72

1 . . . . 250.00
2 thru 5 . . . . @150.00
6 thru 10 . . . . @100.00
11 thru 20 . . . . @75.00
21 thru 30 . . . . @50.00
31 thru 39 . . . . @40.00
40 thru 42 52 pg. Giants . . . . . . @45.00
43 . . . . 45.00

TURISTAS: THE OTHER
SIDE OF PARADISE
IDW Publishing, 2006

Book 1 . . . . 4.00

TUROK
Acclaim, 1998

1 FaN 3-D cover 2.50
2 FaN,A:Armorines 2.50
3 FaN,Lazarus Concordance 2.50
4 FaN, real President? 2.50

Turok Dinosaur Hunter #20
© Valiant

TUROK: CHILD OF BLOOD
Acclaim, 1997

1-shot FaN, 48pg 4.00

TUROK:
COMIC BOOK MAGAZINE
Acclaim, 1998

Seeds of Evil 5.00
Adon's Curse 5.00
Turok/Shadowman 5.00

TUROK:
DINOSAUR HUNTER
Valiant, 1993

1 BS,Chromium(c),O:Turok
  retold,V:Monark 3.00
1a Gold Ed. 4.00
2 thru 13 . . . . @2.75
14 V:Dino-Pirate 2.50
15 RgM,V:Dino-Pirate 2.50
16 Chaos Effect-Beta#3, V:Evil
  Shaman 2.75
17 thru 47 . . . . @2.50
Yearbook #1 MBn(s),DC, N&V:Mon
  Ark 4.25
Yearbook 1995 MGr,The Hunted . . 3.00
Spec. Tales of the Lost Land 4.00

TUROK QUARTERLY—
REDPATH
Acclaim, 1997

March 1997, FaN(s),Spring Break
  in the Lost Land 4.00
June 1997, FaN(s), Killer loose in
  Oklahoma City 4.00

TUROK/SHADOWMAN
Acclaim, 1999
1-shot 4.00

TUROK 3:
SHADOW OF OBLIVION
Acclaim, 2000
Spec. 48-page 5.00

TUROK/SHAMAN'S TEARS
Valiant, 1995
1 MGr,Ghost Dance Pt. 1 . . . . 2.50
2 MGr,JAl,White Buffalo
   kidnapped,V:Bar Sinister 2.50
3 V:Supremeists/Circle Sea 2.50

TUROK: SON OF STONE
Gold Key, 1962
1 thru 29 see Golden Age
30 . . . . 150.00
31 Drug 165.00
32 thru 40. . . . . @125.00
41 thru 50. . . . . @100.00
51 thru 60. . . . . @75.00
61 thru 75. . . . . @65.00
76 thru 91. . . . . @50.00
Whitman
92 thru 130. . . . . @50.00
Giant #1 . . . . 200.00

TUROK: THE HUNTED
Valiant, 1996
1 & 2 . . . . 2.50

Turok/Timewalker #1
© Acclaim

TUROK/TIMEWALKER
Acclaim, 1997
1 of 2 FaN(s),Seventh Sabbath . . . 2.50
2 of 2 FaN(s),Seventh Sabbath . . . 2.50

TURTLE SOUP
Millennium, 1991
1 Book 1, short stories 2.50
2 thru 4 . . . . @2.50

TV CASPER &
COMPANY
Harvey Publications, 1963–74
1 B:68 pg. Giants 250.00
2 . . . . 150.00
3 . . . . 150.00
4 . . . . 150.00

---

5 . . . . 150.00
6 . . . . 100.00
7 . . . . 100.00
8 . . . . 100.00
9 . . . . 100.00
10 . . . . 100.00
11 thru 20 . . . . @75.00
21 thru 31 E:68 pg. Giants. . . . . @50.00
32 thru 46 . . . . @40.00

TWEETY AND
SYLVESTER
Gold Key, 1963–84
1 . . . . 75.00
2 thru 10 . . . . @60.00
11 thru 30 . . . . @40.00
31 thru 121 . . . . @15.00
Whitman, 1980
103 thru 104 . . . . @15.00
105 thru 107 scarce . . . . @40.00
108 thru 121 . . . . @25.00

12 O'Clock High
Dell, 1965
1 . . . . 100.00
2 . . . . 75.00

24: NIGHTFALL
IDW Publishing, 2006
1 . . . . 3.00
1a variant (c) 3.00
2 . . . . 4.00
3 . . . . 4.00
4 thru 5 . . . . @4.00
2a thru 5a variant (c) . . . . @4.00

24: COLD WARRIORS
IDW, 2008
1-shot 48-pg. 7.50

21 DOWN
WildStorm/DC, 2002
1 JP,JJu(c),F:Preston Kills 3.00
2 JP,JJu(c),Herod 3.00
3 JP,JJu(c),Bear Mountain 3.00
4 JP,JJu(c) 3.00
5 JP,JJu(c) 3.00
6 JP,JJu(c),The Conduit 3.00
7 JP,JJu(c),secret of Herod 3.00
8 JP,Roadside Attractions,pt.1 . . . 3.00
9 JP,Roadside Attractions,pt.2 . . . 3.00
10 JP,Roadside Attractions,pt.3 . . . 3.00
11 JP,Roadside Attractions,pt.4 . . . 3.00
12 JP,Roadside Attractions,concl. . . 3.00

22 BRIDES
Event, 1996
1 . . . . 3.00
2 . . . . 3.00
2a variant (c). 4.00
3 . . . . 3.00
3a variant (c). 4.00
4 . . . . 3.00

TWILIGHT AVENGER
Elite, 1986
1 thru 4 . . . . @2.50

TWILIGHT EXPERIMENT
Wildstorm/DC, Feb., 2005
1 (of 6) JP(s) 3.00
2 JP(s) 3.00
3 JP(s) 3.00
4 JP(s) 3.00
5 JP(s) 3.00
6 JP(s) 3.00

TWILIGHT MAN
First, 1989
1 Mini-Series. 2.75
2 Mini-Series. 2.75
3 Mini-Series. 2.75
4 Mini-Series. 2.75

TWILIGHT MEN
Markosia, 2006
1 . . . . 3.50
2 thru 4 . . . . @3.50

TWILIGHT X-TRA
Antarctic Press, 1999
1 (of 3) by Joe Wright 2.50
2 . . . . 2.50
3 conclusion 2.50

TWILIGHT X: WAR
Antarctic Press, 2005
1 (of 7) by Joe Wight, Manga 3.00
2 thru 7 . . . . @3.00

TWILIGHT ZONE
Dell, 1961
1 . . . . 150.00
2 . . . . 150.00

TWILIGHT ZONE, THE
Gold Key, 1962
See also: Four Color #1173 & #1288
1 RC,FF,GE,P(c) all 250.00
2 . . . . 150.00
3 ATh,MSy 125.00
4 ATh. 125.00
5 . . . . 110.00
6 . . . . 110.00
7 . . . . 110.00
8 . . . . 110.00
9 ATh. 125.00
10 . . . . 100.00
11 . . . . 100.00
12 AW 100.00
13 AW,RC,FBe,AMc. 100.00
14 RC,JO,RC,AT 100.00
15 RC,JO 100.00
16 . . . . 75.00
17 . . . . 75.00
18 . . . . 75.00
19 JO 75.00
20 . . . . 70.00
21 RC 70.00
22 JO 70.00
23 JO 70.00
24 . . . . 60.00
25 GE,RC,ATh 60.00
26 RC,GE. 60.00
27 GE. 60.00
28 thru 31 . . . . @50.00
32 GE. 55.00
33 thru 38 . . . . @50.00
39 WMc 50.00
40 . . . . 35.00
41 . . . . 35.00
42 . . . . 35.00
43 RC. 40.00
44 thru 49 . . . . @35.00
50 FBe,WS. 35.00
51 AW 40.00
52 thru 56 . . . . @30.00
57 FBe 30.00
58 . . . . 30.00
59 FBe,AMc. 35.00
60 thru 70 . . . . @25.00
71 rep. 20.00
72 . . . . 25.00
73 rep. 20.00
74 . . . . 25.00
75 . . . . 25.00
76 . . . . 25.00

77 FBe 30.00
78 FBe,AMc,The Missing Mirage. 230.00
79 rep 20.00
80 FBe,AMc 30.00
81 . . . . 30.00
82 AMc 35.00
83 FBe,WS 35.00
84 FBe,AMc 35.00
85 . . . . 30.00
86 rep 25.00
87 thru 91 . . . . @30.00

TWILIGHT ZONE
Now, 1990
1 NA,BSz(c) 8.00
1a 2nd printing Prestige +Harlan
   Ellison story 6.00
[Volume 2]
#1 The Big Dry (direct) 3.00
#1a Newsstand 2.50
2 Blind Alley 2.50
3 Extraterrestrial 2.50
4 The Mysterious Biker 2.50
5 Queen of the Void 2.50
6 Insecticide 2.50
7 The Outcasts,Ghost Horse . . . 2.50
8 Colonists on Alcor 2.50
9 Dirty Lyle's House of Fun
   (3-D Holo) 3.00
10 Stairway to Heaven,Key
   to Paradise 2.50
11 TD(i),Partial Recall 2.50
3-D Spec 2.50
Ann. #1 . . . . 2.75
[Volume 3]
1 thru 2 . . . . @2.50

TWIN BLADES:
KILLING WORDS
Alias Enterprises, 2006
1 . . . . 3.50
1a variant (c) 3.50
2 . . . . 3.50
3 . . . . 3.50

TWISTED TALES
Pacific, 1982–84
1 RCo. Infected 5.00
2 thru 8 . . . . @4.00
Eclipse
9 . . . . 4.00
10 GM,BWr 5.50

TWISTED TALES OF
BRUCE JONES
Eclipse, 1982–84
1 . . . . 3.00
2 . . . . 3.00
3 . . . . 3.00
4 . . . . 3.00

TWO FISTED TALES
Russ Cochran, 1992
1 JSe,HK,WW,JCr,reps 2.50
2 Reps inc.War Story 2.50
3 rep 2.50
4 thru 6 rep . . . . @2.50
7 thru 8 rep . . . . @2.50
Gemstone
17 thru 24 EC comics reprints . . . @2.50

TWO GUNS
Boom! Studios, 2007
1 (of 4) 4.00
2 thru 3 . . . . @4.00
2a thru 3a variant (c) . . . . @4.00
4 . . . . 4.00
5 . . . . 4.00

TWO-STEP
Wildstorm/DC Oct. 2003
1 (of 3) WEl(s),ACo,JP 3.00
2 WEl(s),ACo,JP 3.00
3 WEl(s),ACo,JP,concl 3.00

2000 A.D. #5
© Eagle

2000 A.D. MONTHLY
Eagle, 1985
1 A:JudgeDredd 4.00
2 A:JudgeDredd 3.00
3 A:JudgeDredd 2.50
4 A:JudgeDredd 2.50
5 . . . . 2.50
6 . . . . 2.50
[2nd Series]
1 thru 4 . . . . @2.50
Quality
5 thru 27 . . . . @2.50
28/29 . . . . 2.50
30 . . . . 2.50
31/32 . . . . 2.50
33 thru 37 . . . . @2.50
Becomes:

2000 A.D. SHOWCASE
38 thru 54 . . . . @2.50
Rebellion, 2003
1 . . . . 2.50
2 . . . . 2.50
3 . . . . 2.50

2 TO THE CHEST
Dark Planet Productions, 2004
1 thru 5 . . . . @3.00

TZU THE REAPER
Murim Studios, 1997
1 by Gary Cohn & C.S. Chun 3.00
2 . . . . 3.00
3 . . . . 3.00
4 . . . . 3.00
5 . . . . 3.00

TZU: SPIRITS OF DEATH
Murim Studios, 1997
1 . . . . 3.00

UFO FLYING SAUCERS
Gold Key, 1968
1 . . . . 75.00
2 . . . . 50.00
3 thru 13 . . . . @35.00

Becomes:

UFO & OUTER SPACE
Gold Key, 1978
14 thru 25 . . . . @20.00

ULTIMATE SPORTS
FORCE PRESENTS:
Ultimate Sports Entertainment
2004
1 Hardwood Heroes 4.00
1 The Guardians 4.00
1 The Zone 4.00
1 Air and Space 4.00

ULTRAFORCE
Malibu Ultraverse, 1994–95
1 Prime, Prototype 2.50
2 thru 10 . . . . @2.50
Spec.#0 . . . . 2.50
[2nd Series], 1995–96
Infinity Fant. Ultraforce Four 2.50
1 George Perez cover 2.50
1a Computer painted cover 2.50
2 thru 15 . . . . @2.50

...AVENGERS
Malibu Ultraverse, Aug. 1995
1 GP 4.00

...SPIDER-MAN
Malibu Ultraverse, 1996
1 . . . . 4.00

ULTRAMAN
Nemesis, 1994
1 EC,O:Ultraman 2.50
2 . . . . 2.50
3 . . . . 2.50
4 V:Blue Ultraman 2.50

ULTRAMAN
Harvey, 1993
1 . . . . 5.00
2 . . . . 5.00
3 . . . . 5.00

ULTRAMAN
Harvey/Ultracomics, 1993
1 with 1 of 3 cards 2.50
2 with 1 of 3 cards & virgin cover . . 2.50
3 with 1 of 3 cards & virgin cover . . 2.50

ULTRAVERSE
DOUBLE FEATURE
Malibu Ultraverse, 1995
1 F:Prime, Solitaire 4.00

...FUTURE SHOCK
Malibu Ultraverse, 1996
1 one-shot,MPc,alternate futures . . 2.50

...ORIGINS
Malibu Ultraverse, 1994
1 O:Ultraverse Heroes 2.60
1a Silver foil cover 12.50

...UNLIMITED
Malibu Ultraverse, 1996
1 F:Warlock 2.50
2 LWn,KWe, A:All-New Exiles,
   V:Maxis 2.50

...YEAR ZERO: THE DEATH
OF THE SQUAD
Malibu Ultraverse, 1995
0-A Hardcase's old team 2.50
0-B 2.50
0-C L.A. Riots 2.50
1 JHI,A:Squad, Mantra 3.00

COLOR PUB.

2 JHI,DaR(c) prequel to Prime#1 . .	3.00
3 Cont. Year Zero Story	3.00
4 I:NM-E	3.00

...YEAR ONE
Malibu Ultraverse, 1995

1 Handbook, double size	5.00
2 Prime	2.50

...YEAR TWO
Malibu Ultraverse, 1996

1 Marvel/Ultraverse/Info	5.00

Uncle Scrooge #62
© Walt Disney

UNCLE SCROOGE
Dell/Gold Key, 1962

40 CB,X-Mas	250.00
41	225.00
42	225.00
43 CB	225.00
44 CB	225.00
45 CB	225.00
46 Lost Beneath the Sea	225.00
47 CB	225.00
48 CB	225.00
49 CB,Loony Lunar Gold Rush . .	225.00
50 CB,Rug Riders in the Sky. . . .	225.00
51 CB,How Green Was my	
Lettuce	200.00
52 CB,Great Wig Mystery	200.00
53 CB,Interplanetary Postman. . .	200.00
54 CB,Billion-Dollar Safari!	200.00
55 CB,McDuck of Arabia	200.00
56 CB,Mystery of the Ghost	
Town Railroad	200.00
57 CB,Swamp of No Return	200.00
58 CB,Giant Robot Robbers	200.00
59 CB,North of the Yukon	200.00
60 CB,Phantom of Notre Duck . .	175.00
61 CB,So Far and No Safari	175.00
62 CB,Queen of the Wild	
Dog Pack.	175.00
63 CB,House of Haunts!	175.00
64 CB,Treasure of Marco Polo! . .	250.00
65 CB,Micro-Ducks from	
OuterSpace	175.00
66 CB,Heedless Horseman	175.00
67 CB rep.	175.00
68 CB,Hall of the Mermaid	
Queen!.	175.00
69 CB,Cattle King!	175.00
70 CB,The Doom Diamond!.	175.00
71 CB	175.00
72 CB rep.	175.00
73 CB rep.	175.00
74 thru 110 . . . . @125.00
111 thru 148 . . . . @60.00
149.	35.00

150 thru 168. . . . . @35.00
169 thru 173. . . . . @35.00

Whitman, 1980

174 thru 176. . . . . @35.00
177 and 178. . . . . @40.00
179 Rare 800.00
180 thru 182. . . . . @60.00
183 thru 195. . . . . @25.00
196 and 197. . . . . @30.00
1981 thru 209. . . . . @35.00

Gladstone, 1986

210 CB,Beagle Boys	20.00
211 CB,Prize of Pizzaro.	18.00
212 CB,city-golden roofs	18.00
213 CB,city-golden roofs	18.00
214 CB	18.00
215 CB, a cold bargain	18.00
216 CB	18.00
217 CB,7 cities of Cibola	18.00
218 CB	18.00
219 Don Rosa,Son of Sun	30.00
220 CB,Don Rosa	10.00
221 CB,A:BeagleBoys	4.00
222 CB,Mysterious Island	4.00
223 CB	4.00
224 CB,Rosa,Cash Flow	7.00
225 CB	4.00
226 CB,Rosa	5.00
227 CB,Rosa	5.00
228 CB	4.00
229 CB	4.00
230 CB	5.00
231 CB,Rosa(c)	4.00
232 CB	4.00
233 CB	4.00
234 CB	4.00
235 Rosa	7.00
236 CB	4.00
237 CB	4.00
238 CB	4.00
239 CB	4.00
240 CB	4.00
241 CB,giant	7.00
242 CB,giant	7.00

Walt Disney, 1990

243 CB,Pie in the Sky	4.00
244	3.50
245	3.50
246	3.50
247	3.50
248	3.50
249	3.50
250 CB	5.00
251	3.00
252 No Room For Human Error . . .	3.00
253 Fab.Philosophers Stone	3.00
254 The Filling Station	3.00
255 The Flying Dutchman	3.00
256 CB,Status Seeker	3.00
257 Coffee,Louie or Me	3.00
258 CB,Swamp of no return	3.00
259 The only way to Go.	3.00
260 The Waves Above, The	
Gold Below	3.00
261 Rosa,Return to Zanadu, Pt.1 .	6.00
262 Rosa,Return to Zanadu, Pt.2 .	6.00
263 Rosa,Treasure Under Glass . .	6.00
264 Snobs Club	3.00
265 CB,Ten Cent Valentine	3.00
266 The Money Ocean,Pt.1	3.00
267 The Money Ocean,Pt 2.	3.00
268 CB,Rosa,Island in the Sky . . .	3.00
269 The Flowers	3.00
270 V:Magica DeSpell	3.00
271 The Secret o/t Stone	3.00
272 Canute The Brute's Battle Axe .	3.00
273 CB,Uncle Scrooge-Ghost	3.25
274 CB,Hall of the Mermaid Queen.	3.25
275 CB,Rosa,Christmas Cheers,inc.	
D.Rosa centerspread	3.25
276 Rosa, thru 277 . . . . @7.00
278 thru 280. . . . . @3.00

Gladstone, 1993

281 Rosa	7.00
282 thru 284. . . . . @3.00
285 Rosa, Life & Times	11.00
286 thru 293 Rosa, Life & Times . @6.00
294 thru 299. . . . . @3.00
300 Rosa & Barks	5.00
301 Statuesque Spendthrifts	3.00
302.	3.00
303 Rocks to Riches	3.00
304 My Private Eye	3.00
305 Vigilante of Pizen Bluff	3.00
306.	3.00
307 Temper Temper.	3.00
308 Revenge of the Witch	3.00
Prestige format, 64pg.	
309 Whadalottajargon	8.00
310 The Sign of the Triple	
Distelfink	8.00
311 The Last Lord of Eldorado . . .	8.00
312 The Hands of Zeus.	8.00
313 The Fantastic River Race	8.00
314	8.00
315 The Flying Scot, pt.1	8.00
316 The Flying Scot, pt.2	8.00
317 Pawns of the Lamp Garou . . .	8.00
318 Cowboy Captain of Cutty Sark .	8.00
319 The Horse Radish Story	8.00
320 The Mysterious Stone Ray . . .	8.00
321 The Giant Robot Robbers	8.00
322 Secret of the Lost	
Dutchman's Mine.	8.00

UNCLE SCROOGE
Gemstone Publishing, 2003

319 thru 347. . . . . @7.00
348 thru 361. . . . . @7.00
362 thru 366. . . . . @7.50
367 thru 372. . . . . @8.00
373 thru 384. . . . . @8.00

UNCLE SCROOGE
ADVENTURES
Gladstone, 1987

1 CB,McDuck of Arabia	9.00
2 translated from Danish	5.00
3 translated from Danish	5.00
4 CB	5.00
5 Rosa	5.00
6 CB	3.50
7 CB	3.00
8 CB	3.00
9 Rosa	3.50
10 CB.	3.00
11 CB.	3.00
12 CB.	3.00
13 CB.	3.00
14 Rosa	3.50
15 CB.	3.00
16 CB.	3.00
17 CB.	3.00
18 CB.	3.00
19 CB,Rosa(c).	3.50
20 CB,giant	6.00
21 CB,giant	6.00
22 Rosa(c)	6.00
23 CB,giant	4.00
24 thru 26. . . . . @2.50
27 Rosa,O:Jr. Woodchuck	4.00
28 giant	4.00
29	2.50
30 giant	5.00
31 thru 32. . . . . @3.00
33 Barks.	5.00
34 thru 40. . . . . @3.00
41	2.50
42 The Dragon's Amulet	2.50
43 Queen of the Wild Dog Pack . . .	2.50
44	2.50
45 Secret of the Duckburg Triangle .	2.50
46 The Tides Turn	2.50

COLOR PUB.

47 The Menehune Mystery 2.50
48 The Tenth Avatar. 2.50
49 Dead-Eye Duck. 2.50
50 CB,The Secret of Atlantis 3.00
51 . . . . 2.50
52 The Black Diamond 2.50
53 Secret of the Incas 2.50
54 Secret of the Incas, pt.2 . . . . . . 2.50

UNCLE SCROOGE ADVENTURES
Gladstone, 1997–98
Don Rosa Specials
Spec.#1 (of 4). 11.00
Spec.#2 thru #4 . . . . @10.00
Van Horn Specials
Spec.#1 . . . . 10.00
Spec.#2 . . . . 10.00
Spec.#3 . . . . 10.00
Spec.#4 . . . . 10.00

UNCLE SCROOGE ADVENTURES IN COLOR
Gladstone, 1987–98
Carl Barks reprints
1 thru 32 . . . . @10.00
33 thru 35. . . . . @11.00
36 32pg. 9.00
37 thru 53. . . . . @10.00
54 Hall of the Mermaid Queen. . . . 10.00
55 The Doom Diamond 10.00
56 two adventures 10.00

UNCLE SCROOGE & DONALD DUCK
Gold Key, 1965
1 rep.. . . . . 150.00

UNCLE SCROOGE AND DONALD DUCK
Gladstone, 1997
1 . . . . 2.50
2 Christmas stories. 2.50
3 Back to Long Ago 2.50

UNCLE SCROOGE AND MONEY
Gold Key, 1967
1 . . . . 135.00

UNCLE SCROOGE GOES TO DISNEYLAND
Gladstone, 1985
1 CB,etc. 100pp 13.00

UNDEAD, THE
Chaos! Comics Black Label,, 2001
Ashcan 6.00
Ashcan, premium edition 15.00
1 zombie wasteland 5.00
1a previews exclusive (c) 5.00
1b signed edition. 12.00
1c premium edition 9.00
1d super-premium edition. 15.00
1e foil (c). 15.00

UNDERDOG
Charlton, 1970
1 Planet Zot 150.00
2 Simon Sez/The Molemen 100.00
3 Whisler's Father. 100.00
4 The Witch of Pycoon 100.00
5 The Snowmen 100.00
6 The Big Shrink 100.00

7 The Marbleheads. 100.00
8 The Phoney Booths 100.00
9 Tin Man Alley 100.00
10 Be My Valentine (Jan., 1972) . 100.00

Underdog #9
© Gold Key

UNDERDOG
Gold Key, 1975
1 The Big Boom 125.00
2 The Sock Singer Caper 75.00
3 The Ice Cream Scream 75.00
4 . . . . 75.00
5 . . . . 75.00
6 Head in a Cloud. 75.00
7 The Cosmic Canine 75.00
8 . . . . 75.00
9 . . . . 75.00
10 Bouble Trouble Gum. 75.00
11 The Private Life of
  Shoeshine Boy 50.00
12 The Deadly Fist of Fingers 50.00
13 . . . . 50.00
14 Shrink Shrank Shrunk. 50.00
15 Polluter Palooka 50.00
16 The Soda Jerk 50.00
17 Flee For Your Life 50.00
18 Rain Rain Go Away...Okay . . . 50.00
19 Journey To the Center of
  the Earth 50.00
20 The Six Million Dollar Dog 50.00
21 Smell of Success 55.00
22 Antlers Away 55.00
23 Wedding Bells In Outer Space
  (Feb.,1979) 55.00

UNDERDOG
Whitman, 1975
1 . . . . 100.00
2 thru 10 . . . . @50.00
11 thru 23 . . . . @40.00

UNDERDOG
Spotlight, 1987
1 FMc,PC(c),The Eredicator. 5.00
2 FMc,CS(c), Prisoner of Love/
  The Return of Fearo 5.00

UNDERDOG
Harvey, 1993
1 . . . . 5.00
2 thru 5 . . . . @4.00

UNDERDOG IN 3-D
Blackthorne
1 Wanted Dead or Alive 2.50

UNDERLORDS
Eidolon Entertainment, 2005
1 . . . . 2.95
2 thru 4 . . . . @2.95

UNDERSEA AGENT
Tower, 1966–97
1 F:Davy Jones,UnderseaAgent. 150.00
2 thru 4 . . . . @125.00
5 O&I:Merman 125.00
6 GK,WW(c) 125.00

UNDERTAKER
Chaos! Comics, 1999
Preview BSt, WWF character 2.50
Preview, photo (c). 2.50
1 Prophecy of the Dead 3.00
1a photo cover 3.00
2 V:Embalmer & Paul Bearer 3.00
3 O:Undertaker 3.00
4 Kane 3.00
5 Jezebel 3.00
6 thru 12 . . . . @3.00
2a thru 12a photo covers . . . . . . @3.00
Halloween Spec. 3.00
Halloween Spec. photo(c) 3.00

UNDERWORLD: RED IN TOOTH AND CLAW
IDW Publishing, 2004
1 . . . . 4.00
2 thru 3 . . . . @4.00

UNDERWORLD: RISE OF THE LYCANS
IDW, 2008
1 . . . . 4.00
2 . . . . 4.00
2a variant (c) 4.00

UNEARTHLY SPECTACULARS
Harvey, 1965
1 DW,AT,I:Tiger Boy 100.00
2 WW,AW,GK,I:Earthman,Miracles,
  Inc. A:Clawfang,TigerBoy 75.00
3 RC,AW,JO,A:Miracles,Inc. 65.00

U.N. FORCE
Gauntlet Comics, 1995
0 BDC(s). 3.00
1 B:BDC(s),I:U.N.Force 3.00
2 O:Indigo 3.00
3 . . . . 3.00
4 A:Predator. 3.00
5 B:Critical Mass. 3.00

U.N. FORCE FILES
Gauntlet Comics
1 KP(c),F:Hunter Seeker, Lotus . . . 3.00

UNHUMAN
Narwain Publishing, 2006
1 BAu,TMd 4.00

UNION OF JUSTICE
Quantum Comics, 1998
1 by David Watkins & Steve Kurth . 3.00
2 . . . . 3.00
3 A:Golden Age Union 3.00

UNIQUE
Platinum Studios, 2007
1 (of 3) 3.00
2 . . . . 3.00
3 . . . . 3.00

UNITED FREE WORLDS
Devil's Due, 2008
1 . . . . 3.50
2 thru 3 . . . . @3.50

UNITED FREE WORLDS
Fantasy Prone, 2008
1 (of 6) 3.00
2 . . . . 3.00

UNITY
Valiant, 1992
0 BWS,BL,Chapter#1,A:All Valiant
  Heroes,V:Erica Pierce 4.00
0a Red ed.,w/red logo 65.00
1 BWS,BL,Chapter#18,A:All Valiant
  Heroes,D:Erica Pierce 4.00

UNITY 2000
Acclaim, 1999
1 (of 6) 7.00
2 . . . . 12.00
3 . . . . 25.00

UNIT ZERO: MARQUIS FILES
Marquis Models, 2004
1 . . . . 4.00
2 thru 5 . . . . 4.00

UNIVERSAL SOLDIER
Now, 1992
1 Based on Movie,Holo.(c) 2.75
2 Luc & Ronnie on the run
  from UniSols 2.50
2a Photo cover 2.50
3 Photo(c) 2.50

UNKNOWN WORLDS OF FRANK BRUNNER
Eclipse, 1985
1 and 2 FB . . . . @4.00

UNTAMED LOVE
Fantagraphics, 1987
1 FF 3.00

UNTOLD TALES OF
Chaos! Comics, 2000
Purgatori #1 . . . . 3.00
Purgatori #1 premium ed. 13.00
Chastity #1 . . . . 3.00
Chastity premium #1 . . . . 13.00
Lady Death #1 . . . . 3.00
Lady Death #1 premium 13.00
Lady Death #1 chromium ed. 16.00

UNUSUAL TALES
Charlton Comics, 1955–65
1 . . . . 500.00
2 . . . . 300.00
3 thru 5 . . . . @200.00
6 SD,SD(c) 400.00
7 SD,SD(c) 450.00
8 SD,SD(c) 450.00
9 SD,SD(c) 500.00
10 SD,SD(c). 550.00
11 SD 500.00
12 SD 400.00
13 . . . . 200.00

14 SD 350.00
15 SD,SD(c) 425.00
16 thru 20 . . . . @150.00
21 . . . . 100.00
22 SD 125.00
23 . . . . 100.00
24 . . . . 100.00
25 thru 27 SD . . . . @225.00
28 . . . . 100.00
29 SD 225.00
30 thru 49 . . . . @85.00

URTH 4
Continuity, 1990
1 TVE,NA(c) 2.50
2 thru 3 TVE,NA . . . . @2.50
4 NA,Last issue. 2.50

Usagi Yojimbo #10
© Mirage

USAGI YOJIMBO
Mirage, 1993
1 A:TMNT 6.00
2 thru 16 . . . . @5.00
17 . . . . 8.00

U.S. AIR FORCE COMICS
Charlton, 1958
1 . . . . 100.00
2 . . . . 50.00
3 thru 20 . . . . @40.00
21 thru 37 . . . . @30.00

U.S. MARINES
Charlton, 1964
1 . . . . 45.00

U. T. F., THE
Speakeasy Comics, 2006
1 (of 3) 3.00
2 . . . . 3.00

U. T. F.: UNDEAD TASK FORCE
Ape Entertainment, 2006
1 . . . . 3.00
3 . . . . 3.00

VALERIA, THE SHE BAT
Continuity, 1993
1 NA,I:Valeria 9.00
2 thru 4 . . . . [Not Released]

5 Rise of Magic. 2.50
Windjammer, 1995
1 (of 2) NA,Valeria & 'Rilla 2.50
2 (of 2) NA,BSz, final issue 2.50

VALHALLA
Antarctic Press, 1999
1 BDn set in 1939. . . . . 3.00

VALIANT VISION STARTER KIT
Valiant, 1993
1 w/3-D Glasses 3.00
2 F:Starwatchers 3.00

VALKYRIE
Eclipse, 1988
1 PG,I:Steelfox,C:Airboy, Sky Wolf . 3.00
2 PG,O:New Black Angel 2.50
3 PG 2.50
[2nd Series]
1 BA,V:Eurasian Slavers 2.50
2 BA,V:Cowgirl 2.50
3 BA,V:Cowgirl 2.50

VALKYRIES
Alias Enterprises, 2006
1 . . . . 3.50
2 . . . . 3.50

VALLEY OF THE DINOSAURS
Charlton, 1975
1 Hanna-Barbera TV adapt. 30.00
2 thru 11 . . . . @20.00

VALOR
Gemstone, 1998
1 EC comics reprint 2.50
2 . . . . 2.50
3 AW, The Cloak of Command 2.50
4 WW(c) 2.50
5 final issue. 3.50

VAMPEROTICA
Brainstorm, 1996
1–16 see B&W
17 . . . . 3.00
17a signed 5.00
17 Holochrome cover. 30.00
18 Blood of the Damned (color). . . . 3.00
18a signed 5.00
19 Hunter's Blood 3.00
19a deluxe 3.00
20 Vampire Quest 3.00
21 hunting & feeding 3.00
22 . . . . 3.00

VAMPEROTICA LINGERIE
Comic Cavalcade, 1998
Commemorative #1 by Kirk Lindo . . 6.00
Commemorative #1a deluxe 15.00

VAMPI
Harris Comics, 2000
1/2 24-pg. 9.00
1/2 variant edition 18.00
1 Switchblade Kiss,pt.1. . . . . 3.00
1c signed & numbered 15.00
1d gold foil 25.00
1e convention special, B&W. 10.00
1g limited holochrome edition 20.00
1g royal blue edition 40.00
1h Platinum edition 15.00
1i limited edition 9.00
2 Switchblade Kiss,pt.2. . . . . 8.00
1b thru 2b limited chrome (c) . . @12.00
2c limited holochrome edition 20.00

COLOR PUB.

Vampi #3
© *Harris Comics*

3 Switchblade Kiss,pt.3. . . . . 5.00
4 Dark Angel Rising,pt.1 . . . . 3.00
5 Dark Angel Rising,pt.2. . . . . . . 3.00
6 Dark Angel Rising,pt.3. . . . . . . 3.50
7 Underworld, pt.1 (of 3). 3.00
8 Underworld, pt.2 . . . . 3.00
9 Underworld, pt.3 . . . . 3.00
1a thru 9a deluxe . . . . @9.00
Ashcan Vampi Dark Angel Rising
    platinum leather limited B&W . 15.00
Ashcan Vampi Underworld preview. 6.00
Ashcan Tainted Love 6.00
Vampi #1 preview 3.00
Anarchy Studios, 2001
10 . . . . 3.00
10b convention ed. 9.00
10c convention ed., signed 15.00
11 . . . . 3.00
12 . . . . 3.00
12b holo-fx chrome ed. 12.00
12c gold-fx chrome 20.00
13 . . . . 3.00
14 framed, I:Xenocyde. 3.00
15 V:Xenocyde. 3.00
16 saved by Xenocide 3.00
17 Ultimatrix, pt.2. . . . . 3.00
18 Ultimatrix, pt.3. . . . . 3.00
19 Serpent's Kiss, pt.1. . . . . 3.00
20 Serpent's Kiss, pt.2. . . . . 3.00
21 Serpent's Kiss, pt.3. . . . . 3.00
22 Serpent's Kiss, pt.4. . . . . 3.00
23 Fallout, pt.1 . . . . 3.00
24 Fallout, pt.2 . . . . 3.00
25 . . . . 3.00
10a thru 16a deluxe . . . . @9.00
14a thru 25a limited . . . . @9.00
Sketchbook platinum leather 15.00
Ashcan Vampi:End Game 6.00
Ashcan Vampi #19–#21 . . . . 6.00
Ashcan Ultimatrix Leather Gold. . . 15.00
Ashcan Vampi: Anarchy in the USA
    giant-sized, limited (2001) 6.00

VAMPI (DIGITAL)
Harris Comics, 2001
1 digital art 3.00
1a limited ed. 9.00
Preview edition, digital 3.00
Ashcan, Underworld gold leather. . 15.00

VAMPI VICIOUS
Anarchy Studios, 2003
Prototype Convention edition. 9.00
1 . . . . 3.00

1a variant (c). 3.00
1 royal blue edition 40.00
1 gold foil edition. 30.00
2 . . . . 3.00
3 . . . . 3.00
2a thru 3a variant (c) 3.00

...CIRCLE
Anarchy Studios, 2004
Ashcan Vicious Circle 6.00
1 . . . . 3.00
2 thru 3 . . . . @3.00
1a thru 3a variant (c) . . . . @9.00

...GEMINI EFFECT
Anarchy Studios, 2005
1 . . . . 3.00
1a limited 9.00
2 . . . . 3.00
2a limited 9.00

...RAMPAGE
Anarchy Studios, 2004
1 . . . . 3.00
1a limited 9.00
2 . . . . 3.00
2a limited 9.00

VAMPI VS. XIN
Anarchy Studios, 2004
1 & 2 . . . . @3.00
1a thru 2a limited . . . . @9.00

VAMPIRE LESTAT
Innovation, 1990–91
1 Anne Rice Adapt. 15.00
1a 2nd printing 4.00
1b 3rd printing. 2.50
2 . . . . 5.00
2a 2nd printing 4.00
2b 3rd printing. 2.50
3 . . . . 5.00
3a 2nd printing 2.50
4 . . . . 5.00
4a 2nd printing 2.50
5 . . . . 5.00
6 . . . . 5.00
7 . . . . 5.00
8 . . . . 5.00
9 scarce 8.00
9a 2nd Printing 3.00
10 . . . . 5.00
11 Those Who Must Be Kept. 4.00
12 conclusion. 4.00
Vampire Companion #1 . . . . 4.00
Vampire Companion #2 (preview
    Interview With The Vampire . . . 3.00
Vampire Companion #3 . . . . 3.00
GN rep.#1–#12 (Innovation) 25.00
GN rep.#1–#12 (Ballantine) 25.00

VAMPIRELLA
Warren Publishing Co.,
1969–83
1 NA,FF(c),I:Vampirella 850.00
2 B:Amazonia 300.00
3 Very scarce 750.00
4 . . . . 250.00
5 FF(c) 265.00
6 . . . . 250.00
7 FF(c) 275.00
8 B:horror 225.00
9 BWS,BV(c),WW 225.00
10 No Vampirella,WW 100.00
11 TS,FF(c)O&I Pendragon. 200.00
12 WW 200.00
13 . . . . 175.00
14 . . . . 175.00
15 . . . . 175.00
16 . . . . 175.00
17 B:Tomb of the Gods 175.00

18 . . . . 175.00
19 WW,1973 Annual 150.00
20 thru 25 . . . . @125.00
26 . . . . 100.00
27 1974 Annual 120.00
28 thru 30 . . . . @100.00
31 FF(c) 120.00
32 thru 36 . . . . @75.00
37 1975 Annual 80.00
38 . . . . 75.00
39 . . . . 75.00
40 . . . . 75.00
41 thru 45 . . . . @50.00
46 O:Vampirella 65.00
47 thru 99 . . . . @50.00
100 Double Size 125.00
101 thru 110 . . . . @75.00
111 Giant Edition 100.00
112 . . . . 75.00
Ann. #1 WW. 450.00
Special #1 . . . . 300.00
Harris, 1998
113 Low distribution 500.00

VAMPIRELLA
Harris, 1992
0 Dracula Wars 5.00
0a Blue version 18.00
1 V:Forces of Chaos, w/coupon for
    DSt poster 15.00
1a 2nd printing 5.00
2 AH(c) 14.00
3 A:Dracula 7.00
4 A:Dracula 6.00
5 . . . . 6.00
Spec. #1 Vampirella/Shadowhawk:
    Creatures of the Night (1995) . . 5.50
Harris Comics, 1996
0 gold foil signed & numbered . . . 18.00
1 Commemorative Edition 3.00
1a Commemorative Edition,
    sgn & num. 9.00
25th Anniv. Spec., FF(c). 6.00
25th Anniv. Spec., lim. 7.00
Spec. Death of Vampirella,
    memorial, chromium cover . . . 15.00
Spec. 1-shot Vampirella/Cain,
    flipbook, 72-pg. (1996) 7.00
Spec. Vampirella Pin-up (1995) . . . 3.50

VAMPIRELLA
(MONTHLY)
Harris Comics, 1998–2000
1 Ascending Evil, pt.1 . . . . 3.00
1a ultra-violent cover 3.00
1b JaL(c). 9.00
2 Ascending Evil, pt.2 . . . . 3.00
2a JaL(c). 9.00
3 Ascending Evil, pt.3 . . . . 3.00
3a JaL(c). 9.00
4 Holy War, pt.1 . . . . 3.00
4a Crimson ed., Joe Linsner (c) . . 3.00
5 Holy War, pt.2 . . . . 3.00
6 Holy War, pt.3 . . . . 3.00
7 Queen's Gambit, pt.1 . . . . 3.00
7a chromium Edition 9.00
8 Queen's Gambit, pt.2 . . . . 3.00
9 Queen's Gambit, pt.3, concl. . . . 3.00
10 Hell on Earth, pt.1, V:Nyx 3.00
10a variant JaL cover 9.00
11 Hell on Earth, pt.2. . . . . 3.00
12 Hell on Earth, pt.3,
    New costume. 3.00
12a variant cover, new costume . . 3.00
12b chromium cover 9.00
13 World's End,pt.1 . . . . 3.00
13b Pantha cover. 3.00
14 World's End,pt.2 . . . . 3.00
15 World's End,pt.3 . . . . 3.00
13a thru 15a variant (c)s . . . . . . @3.00
16 Pantha #1 . . . . 3.00

17 Pantha #2 . . . . 3.00
16b limited photo ed. 9.00
16a thru 17a Phantha photo(c)s . @3.00
18 Rebirth, pt.1,JaL(c) 3.00
19 Rebirth, pt.2, ... 3.00
20 Rebirth, pt.3 . . . . 3.00
21 Dangerous Games,pt.1 . . . . 3.00
21c Millennium ed. 15.00
22 Dangerous Games,pt.2 . . . . 3.00
22a Dorian (c) 9.00
16c thru 22c Julie Strain (c)s . . . . @9.00
23 Vampirella/Lady Death:
    The Revenge, pt.1 . . . . 3.00
23a limited ed. 9.00
21b thru 23b limited chrome ed. @15.00
24 Death Valley, Vampirella (c) . . . 3.00
24a Pantha (c) 9.00
25 Death Valley, vol.2 . . . . 3.00
25a alternate (c) 3.00
25b Monte Moore (c) 15.00
26 The End #1 . . . . 3.00
26a alternate (c) 9.00
26b platinum ed. 20.00
Ashcan, Ascending Evil, b&w, 16pg. 2.50
Ashcan, Ascending Evil, b&w,
    signed, limited 25.00
Ashcan, Queen's Gambit,B&W 6.00
Ashcan, Queen's Gambit,signed . . 25.00
Ashcan World's End, B&W,16pg. . . 6.00
Ashcan Rebirth preview,B&W,16-pg 6.00
Vampirella/Lady Death Limited
    Preview Ashcan, B&W. 6.00
Vampirella, Queen's Gambit #1
    special edition, alternate (c) . . . 9.00
    Chromium Edition 10.00
Spec.#0 A:Lady Death,B.U.:Pantha. 3.00
Spec.#0a Pantha(c). 3.00
Spec.#0b Vampirella(c) 9.00
Spec.#0c Vampirella(c), signed . . 30.00
Spec.#0d Pantha(c) 9.00
Spec. Vampirella/Dracula: The
    Centennial, A:Pantha,16pg. . . . 2.00
Spec. Vampirella/Dracula: The
    Centennial, 48pg. (1997). 5.00
Spec.#1 Dangerous Games,
    holochrome (2001) 15.00
Ann.Ed.#2 Rebirth 10.00
Ann.Ed.#3 Rebirth,Bruce Timm(c). 10.00
Julie Strain Special. 4.00
Julie Strain Special variant(c) . . . 10.00
Julie Strain Spec. chrome (c) 15.00
Julie Strain Spec. holochrome(c). . 25.00

VAMPIRELLA
Harris Comics, 2001
0 Gold edition 15.00
1 Nowheresville, Mayhew (c) 3.00
1a JSC (c). 3.00
1b Anacleto (c) 3.00
1c JaL (c) 3.00
1d commemorative ed. B&W, FF(c) 9.00
1e Chicago convention edition 9.00
1f Chicago convention, limited . . . 15.00
1g photo edition, limited 9.00
1h gold edition 25.00
1i holographic chrome (c) 12.00
1j royal blue edition. 50.00
1k gold-fx chrome (c) 20.00
1l Ascending evil gold (c) 15.00
2 thru 4 . . . . @3.00
4c holo FX chrome (c) 12.00
4d gold-fx chrome 30.00
2a thru 22a limited . . . . @9.00
2b thru 22b photo (c) . . . . @9.00
5 thru 22 . . . . @3.00
7c thru 10c limited Pantha
    MT(c) . . . . @9.00
7d Pantha holo fx MC(c). 15.00
Ashcan #1 giant-size 6.00
Ashcan #4–#6 giant-size, 16-pg. . . 6.00
Preview #7–#9 16-pg. 3.00
Ashcan #7–#9 giant-size,16-pg. . . 6.00

Ashcan #11–#13 . . . . 6.00
1-shot Vampirella Genesis (2001) . . 3.00
1-shot Vampirella Genesis,
    variant 9.00
Spec. Model Search. 10.00
Spec. Halloween 2004 . . . . 5.00

VAMPIRELLA:
BLOOD LUST
Harris, 1997
1 (of 2) JeR & JJu. 5.00
2 JJu(c). 5.00
Book 1, JJu(c) Virgin edition 11.00
Book 2, JJu(c) Virgin edition 11.00

...CLASSIC
Harris Comics, 1995
1 Dark Angel 3.50
2 V:Demogorgon. 3.25
3 V:Were Beast. 3.25
4 R:Papa Voodoo 3.25
5 . . . . 3.00

...CROSSOVERS
Harris, 1996–98
1-shot Vampirella vs.
    Eudaemon (1996) 9.00
1-shot StG,SSh,Vampirella/
    Wetworks, image x-over (1997) 3.00
1-shotA Vamp/Wetworks,
    SS&KN(c) 9.00
1-shot Vampirella/Shi (1997) 3.00
1-shotA Vamp/Shi, Chromium ed. . 7.00
1-shotA Vamp/Shi, penciled(c). . . . 9.00
Ashcan #1, Vamp/Shi, 16pg 3.00
1-shot Vampirella/Painkiller
    Jane, foil JQ(c) (1998). 3.50
1-shotA Vampirella/Painkiller
    Jane, alternate RL&JP(c) 9.00
1 Crossover art gallery 3.00
1a Art gallery, chromium ed. 9.00
1b Art gallery, holochrome(c) 20.00

Vengeance Death and Destruction #1
© Harris

...DEATH AND DESTRUCTION
Harris
1 limited preview ashcan 4.00
1a The Dying of the Light 3.00
1b signed & numbered 3.00
1c satin edition 20.00
1d Lim. Ed., Mark Beachum (c) . . . 9.00
2 The Nature of the Beast 3.00
3 TSg,ACo,JP,JJu(c),Mistress
    Nyx kills Vampi 3.00

.../LADY DEATH
Harris/Chaos!, 1999
1 x-over. 3.50
1a Valentine ed. 9.00
1b signed and numbered 15.00
1c gold edition. 25.00
1d penciled edition 9.00
Spec.#1 TheEnd,chrome(c)(2000). 12.00
Spec.#1a The End,holochrome(c) . 20.00
Spec.#1 Revenge, chrome(c)
    (2000) 12.00
Spec.#1a Revenge,holochrome(c) 20.00

...LIVES
Harris, 1996–97
1 Linen Edition 7.00
1a Censored Photo cover edition . . 8.00
2 Vengeance edition 3.00
2a alternate edition, AH(c) 9.00
3 WEI(s),ACo,JP,Graveyard edition,
    JSC(c) 3.00
2b thru 3b Model photo edition . . @3.00

...OF DRAKULON
Harris Comics, 1996
1 V:assassin 3.00
1a alternate MiB(c) 9.00
2 Dracula returns 3.00
3 thru 5 . . . . @3.00

...QUARTERLY
Anarchy Studios/Harris Comics
Spec. Summer 2007 . . . . 5.00
Spec. Summer 2007 variant (c) . . . 5.00
Spec. Winter 2008 . . . . 5.00
Spec. Winter 2008 variant (c) 5.00
Spec. Spring 2008 . . . . 5.00
Spec. Spring 2008 variant (c) 5.00
Spec. Summer 2008 . . . . 5.00
Spec. Summer 2008 variant (c) . . . 5.00
Spec. Halloween 2008 . . . . 3.50

...SAD WINGS OF DESTINY
Harris, 1996
1 DQ(s),JJu(c) 4.00
1 signed & numbered (#1,500). . . . 5.00
Gold Emblem Seal Edition. 4.00

...STRIKES
Harris Comics, 1995
1 The Prize,pt.1 . . . . 3.00
1a limited, signed & numbered. . . . 9.00
1b full moon background 3.50
2 V:Dante Corp.,A:Passion 3.00
3 V:subway stalker 3.00
4 IEd,RN, Soul Food. 3.00
5 DQ,RN,F:Eudaemon 3.00
5 signed & numbered, (200). 9.00
6 . . . . 3.00
6 signed, alternate cover 9.00
6 signed & numbered 11.00
7 silver special flip book 3.00
Ann. #1 new cover. 9.00

...VS. HEMORRHAGE
Harris, 1997
1 IEd,MIB 3.50
1 signed & numbered 10.00
1 Linen edition, signed & numb. . . 20.00
1 MIB alternate cover 9.00
2 IEd,MIB 3.50
3 (of 3) IEd,MIB. 3.50

...VS. PANTHA
Harris, 1997
Showcase #1 preview 2.00
1 MMr,MT, MT(c) Vampirella vs.
    Pantha 3.50
1 MMr,MT, MT(c) Pantha vs.
    Vampirella 3.50
1a MMr,MT, MT(c). 9.00

COLOR PUB.

.../WITCHBLADE
Harris Comics, 2003

1	3.00
1a variant (c)	9.00
Spec. Union of the Damned	3.00
Spec. Variant (c)	9.00

Anarchy Studios/Harris Comics
Ashcan San Diego Comic Con
B&W, 16-page ... 5.00

.../WITCHBLADE: FEAST
Anarchy Studios/Harris Comics, 2005

1	3.00
1a & 1b variant (c)s	@9.00

VAMPIRE THE MASQUERADE
Moonstone, 2001

1-shot Toreador	6.00
1-shot Nosferatu (2002)	7.00
1-shot Beckett	7.00
1-shot Ventrue	7.00
1-shot Calebros	6.00
1-shot Giovanni	5.50
1-shot Assamite	5.50
1-shot Lasombra	5.50
1-shot Isabel	5.00
1-shot Lucita	5.00

VAMPRESS LUXURA, THE
Brainstorm, 1996

1	3.00
1a gold edition	9.00
2	3.00
2a gold foil	9.00

VANDALA
Chaos! Comics, 2000

1	3.00
1 premium	10.00

VANDALA II
Chaos! Comics, 2001

1 PDa,EBe	3.00
1a premium ed. Matt Hughes (c)	9.00

VANGUARD ILLUSTRATED
Pacific, 1983

1	3.00
2 DSt(c)	3.00
3 thru 5 SR	@3.00
6 GI	3.00
7 GE,I:Mr.Monster	6.00

VARICK: CHRONICLES OF THE DARK PRINCE
Q Comics, 1999

1 by Nick Marcari & Major Fareed	2.50
2 32-pg	2.50
3 thru 6	@2.50

VARUK
Counteractive Comics, 2006

1	3.00

VAULT OF HORROR
Gladstone, 1990–91

1 Rep.GS,WW	5.00
2 Rep.VoH #27 & HoF #18	3.00
3 Rep.VoH #13 & HoF #22	3.00
4 Rep.VoH #23 & HoF #13	3.00
5 Rep.VoH #19 & HoF #5	3.00
6 Rep.VoH #32 & WF #6	3.00
7 Rep.VoH #26 & WS #7	3.00

VAULT OF HORROR
Russ Cochran Publ., 1991–92

1 Rep.VoH #28 & WS #18	4.00
2 Rep.VoH #33 & WS #20	3.00
3 Rep.VoH #26 & WS #7	3.00
4 Rep.VoH #35 & WS #15	3.00
4 Rep.VoH #18 & WS #11	3.00
5 Rep.VoH #18 & WS #11	3.00

2nd Series

1 thru 7 Rep.VoH	@3.00
8	3.00

Gemstone

17 thru 29 EC comics reprints	@3.00

VECTOR
Now, 1986

1	3.00
2 thru 5	@3.00

VEGAS KNIGHTS
Pioneer, 1989

1	2.50
2	2.50
3	2.50

Vengeance of Vampirella #11
© Harris

VENGEANCE OF VAMPIRELLA
Harris, 1994

1 Hemmorhage	6.00
1a Gold Edition	9.00
1 gold edition, signed, numbered	12.00
2 Dervish	3.00
3 On the Hunt	3.00
4 Teenage Vampires	3.00
5 Teenage Vampires	3.00
6	3.00
7	3.00
8 bagged w/card	3.00
9	3.00
10 Bad Jack Rising	3.00
11 Pits of Hell, w/card	3.00
12 V:Passion	3.00
13 V:Passion	3.00
14 Prelude to the Walk,pt.2	3.00
15 The Mystery Walk,pt.1	3.25
16 The Mystery Walk,pt.2	3.25
17 The Mystery Walk,pt.3	3.25
18 The Mystery Walk,pt.4	3.00
19 The Mystery Walk,pt.5	3.00
20 Mystery Walk epilog	3.00
14a thru 19a Buzz	@5.00
21 thru 24	@3.00
25 The End	3.00

25 variant cover, signed & numbered	8.00
25 signed & numbered (2,500)	8.00
25 gold edition, signed & numb.	15.00
25 alternate cover, signed by Jae Lee & numbered (#1,500)	12.00
Mini-comic gold foil, signed	15.00

VENTURE
AC Comics, 1986

1	3.00
2 thru 4	@3.00

VERONICA
Archie Publications, April, 1989

1	@7.00
2 thru 10	@5.00
11 thru 38	@4.00
39 Love Show Dolon	6.00
40 thru 50	@4.00
51 thru 71	@3.50
72 thru 93	@3.00
94 thru 97	@2.50
98 thru 120	@2.50
121 thru 133	@2.50
134 thru 156	@2.50
157 thru 191	@2.50

VEROTIKA
Verotika, 1995

1 thru 3 Jae Lee, Frazetta	@3.00
4 thru 9	@3.00
1-shot Rogues Gallery of Villians (1998)	4.00

VEROTIK ILLUSTRATED
Verotik, 1997

1 48pg	7.00
2	7.00
3	7.00
3a alternate cover	7.00
3 variant cover	9.00

VEROTIK WORLD
Verotik, 2004

2	4.00
3	4.00
2a variant (c)	9.00
2b Parody (c)	5.00
3a variant (c)	9.00
3b Shrunken Head (c)	9.00

VESPER
Acetylene Comics, 2001

Preview B&W	3.00
1 Girls Night Out	2.50
1a JOb (c)	2.50
2	2.50
2a variant Wizardworld 2001(c)	5.00
3 The Word for the Day	2.50
3a variant HbK(c)	2.50
4	2.50
5 Soul Harvest	2.50
6	2.50
6a variant (c)	2.50
7 Return of Gruel	3.00

VICKI
Atlas, 1975

1 Rep	75.00
2 thru 4	@40.00

VICTORIAN
Penny Farthing Press, 1999

1	3.00
2 thru 5	@3.00
6 thru 13	@3.00
14 thru 24	@3.00
25 74-pg.	6.00

VICTORIA'S SECRET SERVICE
Alias Enterprises, 2005

0	2.00
1	3.00
2 thru 5	@3.50
3	3.50

VILLAINS
Viper Comics, 2006

1 (of 4)	3.25
2	3.25
3	3.25
4	3.25

VILLAINS & VIGILANTES
Eclipse, 1986–87

1 A:Crusaders,Shadowman	3.00
2 A:Condor	3.00
3 V:Crushers	3.00
4 V:Crushers	3.00

VINCENT PRICE PRESENTS
Bluewater Prod., 2008

1 (of 4)	4.00
2 thru 3	@4.00

VINTAGE MAGNUS ROBOT FIGHTER
Valiant, 1992

1 rep. Gold Key Magnus #22 (which is #1)	5.00
2 rep. Gold Key Magnus #3	4.50
3 rep. Gold Key Magnus #13	3.50
4 rep. Gold Key Magnus #15	3.50

VIOLET ROSE
Bluewater Prod., 2008

1	3.50
1a variant (c)	3.50
2	4.00
2a variant (c)	4.00

VIP
TV Comics, 2000

1 (of 3)	3.00
2 thru 3	@3.00
1a thru 3a photo (c)	@3.00
Preview Edition	6.00

Virtex #0
© Octomica Entertainment

VIRGINIAN, THE
Gold Key, 1963

1	100.00

VIRTEX
Oktomica Entertainment, 1998

0 16-pg.	2.50
1 V:Ripnun	2.50
2 V:Ripnun	2.50
3 alternate endings	2.50
4 Night of the Ninjella,pt.1	2.50
5 Night of the Ninjella,pt.2	3.00
6 All My Sins Remembered	3.00

VIRTUA FIGHTER
Malibu, 1995

1 New Video Game Comic	3.00

VISITOR
Valiant, 1994

1 New Series	2.50
2 thru 13	@2.50

VISITOR VS. VALIANT
Valiant, 1994

1 V:Solar	3.00
2	3.00

VOLTRON
Solson, 1985

1 TV tie-in	4.00
2	4.00
3	4.00

VOLTRON: A LEGEND FORGED
Devil's Due, 2008

1 (of 5)	3.50
1a variant (c)s	@3.50
2 thru 4	@3.50
2a thru 4a variant (c)s	@3.50
4b variant foil (c)	10.00

VOLTRON: DEFENDER OF THE UNIVERSE
Devil's Due/UDON, 2004
Vol 2

1	3.00
2 thru 12	@3.00

VOODOO CHILD
Virgin Comics, 2007

1	3.00
2 thru 6	@3.00

VORTEX
Vortex, 1982–88

1 Peter Hsu art	9.00
2 Mister X on cover	6.00
3 thru 4	@4.00
5 thru 8	@3.00
9 thru 13	@2.50

VORTEX
Comico, 1991

1 SBt,from Elementals	2.50
2 SBt,	2.50

VORTEX: THE SECOND COMING
Entity, 1996

1 (of 6)	3.00
1a variant cover	3.00
2	3.00

VOYAGES OF SHE-BUCCANEER, THE
Great Big Comics, 2008

1 (of 3)	4.00
2 thru 3	@4.00

VOYAGE TO THE BOTTOM OF THE SEA
Gold Key, 1964–70

1	200.00
2 thru 5	@125.00
6 thru 14	@75.00
15 and 16 reprints	@50.00

VOYAGE TO THE DEEP
Dell Publishing Co., 1962

1 P(c)	125.00
2 P(c)	75.00
3 P(c)	75.00
4 P(c)	75.00

VSS: NEMESIS RISING
Bluewater, 2007

1	3.50
2 thru 5	@3.50

WACKY ADVENTURES OF CRACKY
Gold Key, 1972–75

1	30.00
2 thru 11	@25.00
12	20.00

WACKY WITCH
Gold Key, 1971–75

1	75.00
2	30.00
3 thru 20	@25.00
21	20.00

WAGON TRAIN
Dell, 1960

4	100.00
5 ATh	125.00
6 thru 13	100.00

WAGON TRAIN
Gold Key, 1964

1	125.00
2	100.00
3	100.00
4	100.00

WAKE THE DEAD
IDW Publishing, 2003

1 (of 5)	4.00
2	4.00
3 thru 5	@4.00

WALK-IN
Virgin Comics, 2006

1	3.00
2 thru 6	@3.00

WALLACE & GROMIT
Titan Publishing 2002

GN Catch of the Day	9.00
GN The Whippet Vanishes	9.00
GN The Bootiful Game	9.00
11	6.00
13 thru 16	@6.00
GN A Pier too Far	9.00
Yearbook 2007	10.00

WALLY
Gold Key, 1962–63
1	60.00
2 thru 4	@50.00

WALLY WOOD'S
THUNDER AGENTS
Delux, 1984–86
1 GP,KG,DC,SD,I:New Menth	6.00
2 GP,KG,DC,SD,The Raven	5.00
3 KG,DC,SD	5.00
4 GP,KG,RB,DA	5.00
5 JOy,KG,A:CodenamDangr	5.00

WALT DISNEY
ANNUALS
Walt Disney's Autumn Adventure	4.00
Walt Disney's Holiday Parade #1	3.50
Walt Disney's Spring Fever	3.50
Walt Disney's Summer Fun	3.50
Walt Disney's Holiday Parade #2	3.50

WALT DISNEY PRESENTS
Dell, 1959
2	125.00
3 thru 6	@75.00

WALT DISNEY'S
AUTUMN ADVENTURE
Disney, 1990
1 Rep. CB	4.00

WALT DISNEY'S
CHRISTMAS PARADE
Gold Key, 1967
1	75.00
2 thru 9	@75.00

WALT DISNEY'S
CHRISTMAS PARADE
Gemstone Publishing, 2003
1	9.00

WALT DISNEY'S
COMICS AND STORIES
Dell/Gold Key, 1962
264 CB,Von Drake & Gearloose	75.00
265 CB,Von Drake & Gearloose	75.00
266 CB,Von Drake & Gearloose	75.00
267 CB,Von Drake & Gearloose	75.00
268 CB,Von Drake & Gearloose	75.00
269 CB,Von Drake & Gearloose	75.00
270 CB,Von Drake & Gearloose	75.00
271 CB,Von Drake & Gearloose	75.00
272 CB,Von Drake & Gearloose	75.00
273 CB,Von Drake & Gearloose	75.00
274 CB,Von Drake & Gearloose	75.00
275 CB	70.00
276 CB	70.00
277 CB	70.00
278 CB	70.00
279 CB	70.00
280 CB	70.00
281 CB	70.00
282 CB	70.00
283 CB	70.00
284	40.00
285	40.00
286 CB	50.00
287	40.00
288 CB	50.00
289 CB	50.00
290	40.00
291 CB	50.00
292 CB	50.00

293 CB; Grandma Duck's Farm Friends	50.00
294 CB	50.00
295	40.00
296	40.00
297 CB; Gyro Gearloose	50.00
298 CB; Daisy Duck's Dairy	50.00
299 CB rep.	50.00
300 CB rep.	50.00
301 CB rep.	50.00
302 CB rep.	50.00
303 CB rep.	50.00
304 CB rep.	50.00
305 CB rep. Gyro Gearloose	50.00
306 CB rep.	50.00
307 CB rep.	50.00
308 CB rep.	50.00
309 CB	50.00
310 CB	50.00
311 CB	50.00
312 CB	50.00
313 thru 327	@30.00
328 CB rep.	40.00
329	30.00
330	30.00
331	30.00
332	30.00
333	30.00
334	30.00
335 CB rep.	40.00
336	30.00
337	30.00
338	30.00
339	30.00
340	30.00
341	30.00
342 thru 350 CB rep.	@30.00
351 thru 361 CB rep. with poster	@60.00
351a thru 361a. without poster	@30.00
361 thru 400 CB rep.	@50.00
401 thru 409 CB rep.	@30.00
410 CB rep. Annette Funichello	30.00
411 thru 429 CB rep.	@30.00
430	20.00
431 CB rep.	25.00
432 CB rep.	25.00
433	20.00
434 CB rep.	25.00
435 CB rep.	25.00
436 CB rep.	25.00
437	20.00
438	20.00
439 CB rep.	22.00
440 CB rep.	22.00
441	20.00

Walt Disney's Comics and Stories #446
© Walt Disney

442 CB rep.	22.00
443 CB rep.	22.00
444	20.00
445	20.00
446 thru 465 CB rep.	@22.00
466	22.00
467 thru 473 CB rep.	@22.00

Whitman, 1980
474 thru 478 CB rep.	@20.00
479 CB	75.00
480 CB Rare	175.00
481 thru 484	@75.00
485 thru 505	@25.00
506	20.00
507 CB rep.	22.00
508 CB rep.	22.00
509 CB rep.	22.00
510 CB rep.	22.00

Gladstone, 1986
511 translation of Dutch	32.00
512 translation of Dutch	25.00
513 translation of Dutch	25.00
514 translation of Dutch	11.00
515 translation of Dutch	11.00
516 translation of Dutch	11.00
517 translation of Dutch	6.00
518 translation of Dutch	6.00
519 CB,Donald Duck	6.00
520 translation of Dutch, Rosa	11.00
521 Walt Kelly	6.00
522 CB,WK,nephews	6.00
523 Rosa,Donald Duck	15.00
524 Rosa,Donald Duck	15.00
525 translation of Dutch	15.00
526 Rosa,Donald Duck	10.00
527 CB	6.00
528 Rosa,Donald Duck	15.00
529 CB	6.00
530 Rosa,Donald Duck	7.00
531 WK(c),Rosa,CB	7.00
532 CB	6.00
533 CB	6.00
534 CB	6.00
535 CB	6.00
536 CB	6.00
537 CB	6.00
538 CB	6.00
539 CB	6.00
540 CB new art	6.00
541 double-size,WK(c)	6.00
542 CB	7.00
543 CB,WK(c)	6.00
544 CB,WK(c)	6.00
545 CB	6.00
546 CB,WK,giant	7.00
547 CB,WK,Rosa,giant	15.00

Walt Disney, 1990
548 CB,WK,Home is the Hero	10.00
549 CB,	5.00
550 CB,prev.unpub.story!	8.00
551	5.00
552	5.00
553	5.00
554	5.00
555	5.00
556	5.00
557	5.00
558 Donald's Fix-it Shop	5.00
559 Bugs	5.00
560 CB,April Fools Story	5.00
561 CB,Donald the Flipist	5.00
562 CB,3DirtyLittleDucks	5.00
563 CB,Donald Camping	5.00
564 CB,Dirk the Dinosaur	5.00
565 CB,DonaldDuck,TruantOfficer.	5.00
566 CB,Will O' the Wisp	5.00
567 CB,Turkey Shoot.	5.00
568 CB,AChristmas Eve Story	5.00
569 CB, New Years Resolutions	5.00
570 CB,Donald the Mailman +Poster	5.00
571 CB,Atom Bomb	8.00

572 CB,April Fools 5.00
573 TV Quiz Show 5.00
574 Pinnochio,64pgs 6.00
575 Olympic Torch Bearer, Li'l
 Bad Wolf,64 pgs. 6.00
576 giant 6.00
577 A:Truant Officers,64 pgs. 6.00
578 CB,Old Quacky Manor 5.00
579 CB,Turkey Hunt 5.00
580 CB,The Wise Little Red Hen,
 64 pg.-Sunday page format 5.50
581 CB,Duck Lake 5.50
582 giant 5.50
583 giant 5.50
584 . . . . 5.00
585 CB, giant 5.50

Gladstone, 1993

586 . . . . 5.00
587 thru 599 . . . . @5.00
600 CB 6.00
601 thru 605 prestige format . . . . @7.00
606 Winging It 7.00
607 Number 401 . . . . 7.00
608 Sleepless in Duckburg 7.00
609 . . . . 7.00
610 Treasures Untold 7.00
611 Romance at a Glance 7.00
612 The Sod Couple 7.00
613 Another Fine Mess 7.00
614 Airheads 7.00
615 Backyard Battlers 7.00
616 . . . . 7.00
617 Tree's A Crowd 7.00
618 A Dolt from the Blue 7.00
619 Queen of the Ant Farm 7.00
620 Caught in the Cold Rush 7.00
621 Room and Bored. 7.00
622 . . . . 7.00
623 All Quacked Up. 7.00
624 Their Loaded Forebear 7.00
625 Mummery's the Word 7.00
626 A Real Gone Guy 7.00
627 To Bee or Not to Bee 7.00
628 Officer for a Day 7.00
629 The Ghost Train 7.00
630 two Donald Duck stories 7.00
631 Music Hath Charms 7.00
632 A Day in a Duck's Life 7.00
633 All Donald issue 7.00
634 The Runaway Train 7.00
635 Volcano Valley 7.00
636 Mission to Codfish Cove 7.00
637 Pizen Springs Dude Ranch 7.00

WALT DISNEY'S
COMICS AND STORIES
Gemstone Publishing, 2003

634 thru 650 . . . . @7.00
651 thru 662 . . . . @7.00
663 thru 676 . . . . @7.00
677 thru 681 . . . . @7.50
682 thru 687 . . . . @8.00
688 thru 699 . . . . @8.00
Spec. Walt Disney's Vacation
 Parade 9.00
Spec. Vacation Parade #2 . . . . . . 9.00
Spec. Vacation Parade #3 . . . . . . 9.00
Spec. Vacation Parade #5 . . . . . . 10.00
Spec. Christmas Parade 9.00
Spec. Christmas Parade #1 . . . . . 9.00
Spec. Christmas Parade #2 . . . . . 9.00
Spec. Christmas Parade #3 . . . . . 9.00
Spec. Christmas Parade #4 . . . . . 7.00
Spec. Christmas Parade #5 . . . . . 9.50

WALT DISNEY
COMICS DIGEST
Gold Key, 1968–76
[All done by Carl Barks]

1 Rep,Uncle Scrooge 125.00

2 CB,ATh 75.00
3 CB,ATh 75.00
4 CB,ATh 75.00
5 CB,Daisy Duck 125.00
6 thru 13 CB,ATh . . . . @60.00
14 ATh 35.00
15 ATh 35.00
16 ATh,rep.Donald Duck #26 . . . . . 60.00
17 CB,ATh 45.00
18 CB,ATh 45.00
19 CB,ATh 45.00
20 CB,ATh 45.00
21 CB,ATh 35.00
22 CB,ATh 35.00
23 CB,ATh 35.00
24 CB,ATh,Zorro 35.00
25 thru 31 CB,ATh . . . . @35.00
32 ATh 30.00
33 ATh 35.00
34 ATh,rep.Four Color #318 . . . . . 35.00
35 ATh 35.00
36 ATh 35.00
37 ATh 35.00
38 ATh,rep.Disneyland#1 . . . . 35.00
39 ATh 35.00
40 ATh,FG 30.00
41 ATh 25.00
42 CB 30.00
43 CB 30.00
44 Rep. Four Color #29 & others . 75.00
45 . . . . 25.00
46 CB 25.00
47 . . . . 25.00
48 . . . . 25.00
49 . . . . 25.00
50 CB 25.00
51 rep.Four Color #71 . . . . 35.00
52 CB 25.00
53 . . . . 25.00
54 . . . . 25.00
55 . . . . 25.00
56 CB,rep. Uncle Scrooge #32 . . . 30.00
57 CB 25.00

WALT DISNEY'S
GALLAGHER, BOY
REPORTER
Gold Key, 1965

1 . . . . 75.00

WALT DISNEY
SHOWCASE
Gold Key, 1970–80

1 Boatniks (photo cover) 40.00
2 Moby Duck 30.00
3 Bongo & Lumpjaw 25.00
4 Pluto 25.00
5 $1,000,000 Duck (photo cover) . 30.00
6 Bedknobs & Broomsticks 25.00
7 Pluto 25.00
8 Daisy & Donald 25.00
9 101 Dalmatians rep. 35.00
10 Napoleon & Samantha 30.00
11 Moby Duck rep. 20.00
12 Dumbo rep. 25.00
13 Pluto rep. 25.00
14 World's Greatest Athlete 30.00
15 3 Little Pigs rep. 25.00
16 Aristocats rep. 30.00
17 Mary Poppins rep. 30.00
18 Gyro Gearloose rep. 40.00
19 That Darn Cat rep. 35.00
20 Pluto rep. 25.00
21 Li'l Bad Wolf & 3 Little Pigs . . . 20.00
22 Unbirthday Party rep. 30.00
23 Pluto rep. 25.00
24 Herbie Rides Again rep. 25.00
25 Old Yeller rep. 25.00
26 Lt. Robin Crusoe USN rep. 25.00
27 Island at the Top of the World . . 30.00

28 Brer Rabbit, Bucky Bug rep. . . . 25.00
29 Escape to Witch Mountain 30.00
30 Magica De Spell rep. 45.00
31 Bambi rep. 25.00
32 Spin & Marty rep. 25.00
33 Pluto rep. 20.00
34 Paul Revere's Ride rep. 20.00
35 Goofy rep. 20.00
36 Peter Pan rep. 20.00
37 Tinker Bell & Jiminy Cricket rep. 20.00
38 Mickey & the Sleuth, Pt. 1 . . . . 20.00
39 Mickey & the Sleuth, Pt. 2 . . . . 20.00
40 The Rescuers 20.00
41 Herbie Goes to Monte Carlo . . . 20.00
42 Mickey & the Sleuth 20.00
43 Pete's Dragon 25.00
44 Return From Witch Mountain
 & In Search of the Castaways . 25.00
45 The Jungle Book rep. 25.00
46 The Cat From Outer Space 20.00
47 Mickey Mouse Surprise Party . . 20.00
48 The Wonderful Adventures of
 Pinocchio 20.00
49 North Avenue Irregulars; Zorro . 20.00
50 Bedknobs & Broomsticks rep. . 20.00
51 101 Dalmatians 20.00
52 Unidentified Flying Oddball 20.00
53 The Scarecrow 20.00
54 The Black Hole 20.00

WALT DISNEY'S
THE SCARECROW
Gold Key, 1965

1 and 2 . . . . @75.00

WALT DISNEY'S
THE SCARECROW OF
ROMNEY MARSH
Gold Key, 1964

1 . . . . 75.00

WALTER LANTZ
WOODY WOODPECKER
Dell, 1952

72 . . . . 40.00
Gold Key, 1962
73 thru 75 . . . . @75.00
76 thru 120 . . . . @25.00
121 thru 186 . . . . @15.00
Spec. Summer Fun (1966) 30.00
Whitman, 1980
188 thru 189 . . . . @15.00
190 thru 191 scarce . . . . @40.00
193 thru 201 . . . . @25.00

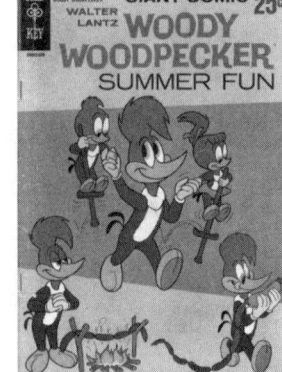

Walter Lantz Woody Woodpecker
Summer Fun #1 © Gold Key

WALT KELLY'S CHRISTMAS CLASSICS
Eclipse, 1987
1 .... 5.00

WALT KELLY'S SPRINGTIME TALES
Eclipse, 1988
1 .... 5.00

WAR
Charlton, 1975
1 .... 25.00
2 thru 10 .... @15.00
11 thru 48 .... @8.00

WAR AGAINST CRIME
Gemstone, 2000
1 rep.. .... 2.50
2 rep. Summer 1942........... 2.50
3 rep. Fall 1948................ 2.50
4 rep. Winter 1948 .... 2.50
5 rep. Feb. 1949............... 2.50
6 rep. June 1949............... 2.50
7 rep.. .... 2.50
8 rep. Aug. 1949............... 2.50
9 rep. Oct. 1949 .... 2.50
10 rep. Dec. 1949 issue........ 2.50
11 rep. Feb. 1950 issue 2.50

WAR AND ATTACK
Charlton, 1964
1 WW 75.00

WAR AT SEA
Charlton, 1957
22 .... 50.00
23 thru 30 .... @40.00
31 thru 42................... @30.00

WARCAT SPECIAL
Entity Press, 1995
1 I:Warcat 3.00

WARCHILD
Maximum Press, 1995
1 I:Sword, Stone 3.50
2 I:Morganna Lefay............ 3.00
3 V: The Black Knight.......... 2.50
4 Rescue Merlyn............... 2.50
[2nd Series]
1 .... 2.50

WAR DANCER
Defiant, 1994
1 B:JiS(s),I:Ahrq Tsolmec........ 2.75
2 I:Massakur................. 2.75
3 V:Massakur................. 2.75
4 JiS(s),A:Nudge.............. 3.25

WARFRONT
Harvey, 1965
36 .... 75.00
37 thru 39.............. @75.00

WARGOD
Chimaera Studios, 2008
1 .... 4.00
2 thru 3 .... @4.00

WARHAMMER:
CROWN OF DESTRUCTION
Boom! Studios, 2008
1 .... 4.00
1a variant (c) 4.00

2 thru 3 .... @4.00
2a thru 3a variant (c)s .... @4.00

...CONDEMNED BY FIRE
Boom! Studios, 2008
1 .... 4.00
1a variant (c) 4.00
2 thru 4 .... @4.00
2a thru 4a variant (c)s .... @4.00

...FORGE OF WAR
Boom! Studios, 2007
1 .... 3.00
1a variant (c) 3.00
2 thru 5 .... @3.00
2a thru 5a variant (c) .... @3.00

WARHAMMER 40K
Boom! Studios, 2006
0 .... 3.00
0a previews variant (c) 3.00
1 .... 3.00
1a previews exclusive........... 3.00
2 thru 5 .... @3.00
3a theu 5a variant (c) .... @3.00

...DAMNATION CRUSADE
Boom! Studios
2 .... 3.00
2a variant Previews exclusive (c) . 3.00
6 .... 3.00
3a variant (c) 3.00

...BLOOD AND THUNDER
Boom! Studios, 2007
1 .... 4.00
1a variant (c) 4.00
2 thu 3 .... @4.00
2a thru 3a variant (c) .... @4.00
4 .... 4.00
4a variant (c) 4.00

...DEFENDERS OF ULTRAMAR
Boom! Studios, 2008
1 .... 4.00
1a variant (c) 4.00

...EXTERMINATUS
Boom! Studios, 2008
1 (of 5) 4.00
1a variant (c) 4.00
2 thru 5 .... @4.00
2a thru 5a variant (c)s .... @4.00

...FIRE AND HONOR
Boom! Studios, 2008
1 (of 4) 4.00
1a variant (c) 4.00
2 thru 4 .... @4.00
2a thru 4a variant (c)s......... @4.00

...INQUISITOR
Boom! Studios, 2007
1 (of 5) 3.00
1a variant (c) 3.00

WARHAWKS
TSR, 1990–91
1 thru 6 from game .... @3.00
7 thru 10 The Battle of Britain ... @3.00

WARHAWKS 2050
TSR
1 Pt.1 .... 3.00

WAR HEROES
Charlton Comics, 1963–67
1 .... 75.00
2 J.F.Kennedy................. 60.00
3 thru 10 .... @35.00
11 thru 26 .... @30.00
27 Devils Brigade............. 45.00

WARLASH
CFD, 1995
1 Project Hardfire 3.00

WARLANDS: MALAGEN'S CAMPAIGN
Dreamwave, 2005
1 .... 3.00
2 thru 3 .... @3.00
Pocketbook Vol. 1 .... 10.00

WARMASTER
1 and 2 .... @4.00

WAR OF THE UNDEAD
IDW Publishing, 2007
1 .... 4.00
2 thru 3 .... @4.00

WAR OF THE WORLDS: SECOND WAVE
Boom! Studios, 2006
1 .... 3.00
2 thru 6 .... @3.00

Warp #3
© First

WARP
First, 1983
1 FB,JSon,I:Lord Cumulus & Prince
  Chaos, play adapt pt.1 .... 4.00
2 thru 10 .... @3.00
11 thru 19 .... @2.50
Spec. #1 HC,O:Chaos 2.50
Spec. #2 MS/MG,V:Ylem 2.50
Spec. #3 .... 2.50

WARREN ELLIS' BLACK GAS
Avatar Press, 2006
1 .... 4.00
1a wraparound (c) 4.00
1b variant (c)s................ @4.00
2 .... 4.00
2a wraparound (c) 4.00
2b variant (c)s................ @4.00
2c Auxiliary edition 4.00
3 .... 4.00
3a wraparound (c) 4.00
3b variant (c)s................ @4.00
Spec. #1 thru #3 Auxiliary ed. .... @4.00

All comics prices listed are for *Near Mint* condition.

Vol. 2

1	4.00
1a wraparound (c)	4.00
1b variant (c)s	@4.00
1c Blood red concention (c)	5.00
2	4.00
2a wraparound (c)	4.00
2b variant (c)s	@4.00
3	4.00
3a variant (c)s	@4.00

WARREN ELLIS' WOLFSKIN
Avatar Press, 2006

1	4.00
1a wraparound (c)	4.00
1b variant (c)s	@4.00
1c Blood Red convention (c)	5.00
1d Variant Bloodlust (c)	6.00
1e auxiliary ed.	4.00
2	4.00
2a wraparound (c)	4.00
2b variant (c)s	@4.00
3	4.00
3a wraparound (c)	4.00
3b variant (c)s	@4.00

WARRIOR BUGS, THE
Artcoda Productions, 2002

1	3.00
2	3.00
3	3.00
4	3.00
5	3.00

WARRIOR NUN AREALA
Antarctic Press, 1995

1 V:Lilith	4.00
1a limited edition.	8.00
2 V:Lilith	3.00
3 V:Hellmaster	3.00
3 silver edition.	12.00
BOOK II: RITUALS, 1996	
1 Land of Rising Sun	3.00
1 Red edition.	9.00
1 signed	9.00
2 I:Cheetah	3.00
3 Iraq, 1989.	3.00
4	3.00
5 Rituals,pt.5.	3.00
6	3.00
Spec. Warrior Nun Portraits	4.00

Warrior Nun Areala, Vol. 3 #2
© Antarctic

Spec. Warrior Nun Portraits Commemorative Edition (1999).	6.00
BOOK III, 1997	
1 The Hammer & the Holocaust	3.00
2 Hammer & the Holocaust,pt.2	3.00
3 Hammer & the Holocaust,pt.3	3.00
4 Holy Man, Holy Terror,pt.1	3.00
5 Holy Man, Holy Terror,pt.2	3.00
6 by Barry Lyga & Ben Dunn	3.00
Spec. Warrior Nun Areala/Glory by Ben Dunn	3.00
Spec. poster edition	6.00
Spec. Warrior Nun Areala vs. Razor, BDn,JWf x-over	4.00
Spec.Warrior Nun Areala vs. Razor commemorative (1999).	6.00
Spec.Warrior Nun Areala/Avengelyne comm. edition (1999).	6.00
VOL 3	
1 F:Sister Shannon Masters	2.50
2	2.50
3	2.50
4 Antichrist arrives	2.50
5	2.50
6 Crimson Nun	2.50
7 V:Ruprecht Marsh	2.50
8 V:Mr.Zhu	2.50
9 in the Vatican	2.50
10 V:Nebelhexa	2.50
11 A:Demoness Lillith	2.50
12 F:Lillith.	3.50
13 V:Julius Salvius.	3.00
14 Rebirth, pt.2	3.00
15 Rebirth, pt.3	3.00
16 Rebirth, pt.4	3.00
17 Seven Deadly Sins, pt.1	3.00
18 Seven Deadly Sins, pt.2	3.00
19 Seven Deadly Sins, pt.3	3.00
Ann.2000 b&W.	4.00

WARRIOR NUN AREALA: SCORPIO ROSE
Antarctic Press, 1996

1 SEt & BDn	3.00
1a commemorative (1999)	6.00
2 thru 4 (of 4)	@3.00

WARRIOR NUN DEI: AFTERTIME
Antarctic Press, 1997

1 (of 3) by Patrick Thornton	3.00
1 Commemorative edition (1999).	6.00
2	3.00
3	3.00

WARRIOR NUN: FRENZY
Antarctic Press, 1998

1 (of 2) by Miki Horvatic & Esad T. Ribic	3.00
2	3.00

WARRIOR NUN LAZARUS
Antarctic Press, 2006

0	3.50

WARRIOR NUN: NO JUSTICE
Antarctic Press, 2002

1 F:Areala,V:The Judge	4.00

WARRIOR NUN: RESURRECTION
Antarctic Press, 1998

1 by Ben Dunn	3.00
1a deluxe	6.00
2 quest for lost God Armor	3.00

3	3.00

WARRIORS OF PLASM
Defiant, 1993–95

1 JiS(s),DL,A:Lorca.	3.25
2 JiS(s),DL,Sedition Agenda.	3.25
3 JiS(s),DL,Sedition Agenda.	3.25
4 JiS(s),DL,Sedition Agenda.	3.25
5 JiS(s),B:The Demons of Darkedge.	2.75
6 JiS(s),The Demons of Darkedge,pt.2	2.75
7 JiS(s),DL,	2.75
8 JiS(s),DL,40-pg.	3.00
9 JiS(s),LWn(s),DL,40-pg.	3.00
10 DL	2.50
GN Home for the Holidays.	6.00

WARRIOR'S WAY
Bench Press Studios, 1998

1	3.00
2 thru 7	@3.00

WARSTRIKE
Malibu Ultraverse, 1994–95

1 HNg,TA,in South America	2.50
2 HNg,TA,Gatefold(c)	2.50
3 in Brazil	2.50
4 HNg,TA,V:Blind Faith.	2.50
5	2.50
6 Rafferty	2.50
7 Origin	2.50

WARSTRIKE: PRELUDE TO GODWHEEL
Malibu Ultraverse, 1994

1 Blind Faith/Lord Pumpkin	2.50

WART AND THE WIZARD
Gold Key, 1964

1	75.00

WAR WINGS
Charlton, 1968

1	30.00

WATCH, THE: CASUS BELLI
Phosphorescent Comics, 2004

1	3.25
2 thru 3	@3.25

WATERDOGS
Roaring Studio, 2002

1 (of 3)	3.00
2 thru 3	@3.00

WATERWORLD
Acclaim, 1997

1 of 4 V:Leviathan.	2.50
2 of 4 Children of Leviathan	2.50
3 of 4 KoK.	2.50
4 of 4 KoK Children of Leviathan	2.50

WAVE WARRIORS
Astroboys

1	2.50
2	2.50

WAYFARERS
Eternity

1	2.50
2	2.50

COLOR PUB.

WAY OF THE RAT
Crossgen Comics, 2002
1 CDi 4.00
2 thru 4 . . . . @3.00
5 thru 7 CDi. . . . . @3.00
8 thru 24 CDi. . . . . @3.00

WEASEL GUY WITCHBLADE
Hyperwerks, 1998
1-shot by Steve Succellato 3.00
1a variant Jeff Matsuda(c) 5.00
1b variant Karl Altstoeter(c) 8.00

WEB OF HORROR
Major Magazines, 1969
1 JJ(c),Ph(c),BWr 150.00
2 JJ(c),Ph(c),BWr 125.00
3 BWr,April, 1970 . . . . 125.00

WEAPON, THE
Platinum Studios, 2007
1 (of 4) 4.00
2 thru 4 . . . . @3.00

WEDDING OF POPEYE AND OLIVE, THE
Ocean Comics, 1999
1 PDa,. 2.75
1a signed, numbered 14.00
Spec. Sketch edition 40.00

WEIRD FANTASY
Russ Cochran, 1992
1 Reps 3.50
2 Reps.inc.The Black Arts. 3.00
3 thru 4 rep. . . . . @3.00
5 thru 7 rep. 3.00
8 . . . . 3.00
Gemstone
9 thru 22 EC comics reprint . . . . @3.00

WEIRD SCIENCE
Gladstone, 1990–91
1 Rep. #22 + Fantasy #1 . . . . 4.00
2 Rep. #16 + Fantasy #17 . . . . . . 3.50
3 Rep. #9 + Fantasy #14 . . . . 3.50
4 Rep. #27 + Fantasy #11 . . . . . . 3.00
Russ Cochran/Gemstone, 1992
1 thru 21 EC comics reprint . . . . @3.00

WEIRD SCIENCE–FANTASY
Russ Cochran/Gemstone, 1992
1 Rep. W.S.F. #23 (1954). 3.50
2 Rep. Flying Saucer Invasion 3.00
3 Rep.. . . . . 3.00
4 thru 6 Rep. . . . . @3.00
7 rep #29. . . . . 3.00
8 . . . . 3.00

WEIRD SUSPENSE
Atlas, Feb.–July, 1975
1 thru 3 F:Tarantula. . . . . @25.00

WEIRD TALES ILLUSTRATED
Millennium, 1992
1 KJo,JBo,PCr,short stories 5.00

WELCOME TO HOXFORD
IDW, 2008
1 . . . . 4.00
1a variant (c) 4.00
2 thru 4 . . . . @4.00
2a thru 4a variant (c)s . . . . @4.00

WENDIGO
Arcana Studio, 2008
1 (of 4) 4.00
2 . . . . 2.00

WENDY, THE GOOD LITTLE WITCH
Harvey Publications, 1960–76
1 . . . . 450.00
2 . . . . 225.00
3 thru 10 . . . . @150.00
11 thru 20 . . . . @100.00
21 thru 30 . . . . @75.00
31 thru 50 . . . . @50.00
51 thru 64 . . . . @30.00
65 O:Wendy 50.00
66 thru 69 . . . . @25.00
70 thru 74 giants . . . . @30.00

Wendy Witch World #43
© Harvey Publications

75 thru 97 . . . . @8.00

WENDY WITCH WORLD
Harvey Publications, 1961–74
1 . . . . 300.00
2 thru 5 . . . . @150.00
6 thru 10 . . . . @100.00
11 thru 20 . . . . @75.00
21 thru 30 . . . . @60.00
31 thru 39 . . . . @50.00
40 thru 50 . . . . @40.00
51 thru 53 . . . . @30.00

WENDY AND THE NEW KIDS ON THE BLOCK
Harvey, 1991
1 . . . . 3.00
2 thru 3 . . . . @3.00

WEREWOLF
Dell, 1966
1 . . . . 50.00
2 thru 3 . . . . @30.00

WEREWOLVES: CALL OF THE WILD
Moonstone Books, 2006
1 . . . . 3.00
2 . . . . 3.50
3 . . . . 3.50

WESTERN ACTION
Atlas, 1975
1 F:Kid Cody,Comanche Kid 25.00

WESTWYND
Westwynd, 1995
1 I:Sable,Shiva,Outcast,Tojo. 2.50

WETWORKS: ARMAGEDDON
Wildstorm/DC, Nov., 2007
1 F:Dane. 3.00

WETWORKS: WORLDSTORM
Wildstorm/DC, Sept., 2006
1 WPo. 3.00
1a variant (c). 3.00
1b variant WPo (c) 3.00
2 WPo. 3.00
3 WPo. 3.00
4 WPo. 3.00
4a variant (c). 3.00
5 WPo,Blood Box 3.00
6 WPo,Night Tribes. 3.00
7 WPo,PrG 3.00
8 WPo,PrG 3.00
9 DaR,V:Vampires 3.00
10 JMD(s),Can a cyborg die? 3.00
11 JMD(s),Mother One 3.00
12 JMD(s),Red's story 3.00
13 JMD(s),WPo(c),Team reunited . . 3.00
14 JMD(s),WPo(c),V:Vampires . . . 3.00
15 JMD(s),WPo(c),v:Night Tribes . . 3.00

WHAT WERE THEY THINKING?
Boom! Studios, 2005
1-shot Keith Giffen remix 4.00
1-shot Some People Never Learn . . 4.00
1-shot Monster Mash-Up 4.00
Go West Young Man 4.00
Some People Never Learn 4.00
Monster Mash-up. 4.00

WHEELIE AND THE CHOPPER BUNCH
Charlton, 1975
1 . . . . 40.00
2 thru 7 . . . . @30.00

WHERE'S HUDDLES
Gold Key, 1971
1 Hanna-Barbera 45.00
2 . . . . 30.00
3 . . . . 30.00

WHISPER
Capital, 1983–84
1 MG(c). 8.00
2 . . . . 6.00
First
1 . . . . 2.50
2 thru 10 . . . . @2.50
11 thru 19 . . . . @2.50
20 O:Whisper. 2.50
21 thru 26. . . . . @2.50
27 Ghost Dance #2 . . . . 2.50
28 Ghost Dance #3 . . . . 2.50
29 thru 37. . . . . @2.50
Spec. #1. 4.00

WHISPER
Boom! Studios, 2006
1 . . . . 4.00

WHITE FANG
Walt Disney, 1990
1 Movie Adapt. 6.00

WHITE PICKET FENCES
Ape Entertainment, 2007
1 (of 3) 3.50
2 thru 3 . . . . @3.50

WHITE TRASH
Tundra
1 I:Elvis & Dean 4.00
2 Trip to Las Vegas contd. 4.00
3 V:Purple Heart Brigade 4.00

WHODUNNIT
Eclipse, 1986–87
1 DSp,A:Jay Endicott 3.00
2 DSp,Who Slew Kangaroo? . . . 3.00
3 DSp,Who Offed Henry Croft . . . 3.00

WIDOW MADE IN BRITAIN
N Studio
1 I:Widow 2.75
2 F:Widow. 2.75
3 Rampage 2.75
4 In Jail. 2.75

WIDOW METAL GYPSIES
London Night Studios, 1995
1 I:Emma Drew. 3.00
2 Father Love 3.00
3 Final issue 3.00

WILD ANIMALS
Pacific, 1982
1 . . . . 3.00

WILD BOYS
Masterpiece Comics, 2007
1 . . . . 3.00
2 thru 4 . . . . @3.00

WILDCATS
WildStorm/DC, 1999
Previously from Image
VOLUME 2
1 SLo,TC, ... 2.50
1a variant cover 2.50
1b variant cover 2.50
1c variant cover 2.50
1d variant cover 2.50
1e variant cover 2.50
2 SLo,TC. 2.50
3 SLo,TC,F:Grifter 2.50
4 SLo,TC, ... 2.50
5 SLo,BHi,PNe,. 2.50
6 SLo, ... 2.50
7 SLo,R:Pike. 2.50
8 JoC(s),SeP,TC(c). 2.50
8a variant JLe&SW(c) (1:4) 2.50
9 JoC(s),SeP,TC(c),Las Vegas. . . . 2.50
10 JoC(s),SeP,TC(c),Las Vegas . . 2.50
11 JoC(s),SeP,TC(c),R:Ladytron . . 2.50
12 JoC(s),SeP,TC(c),go west 2.50
13 JoC(s),SeP,F:Void. 2.50
14 JoC(s),SeP,Serial Boxes,pt.1 . . 2.50
15 JoC(s),SeP,Serial Boxes,pt.2 . . 2.50
16 JoC,SeP,Serial Boxes,pt.3 . . . . 2.50
17 JoC,SeP,Serial Boxes,pt.4 . . . . 2.50
18 JoC,SeP,Serial Boxes,pt.5 . . . . 2.50
19 JoC,SeP,Serial Boxes,pt.6 . . . . 2.50
20 JoC,SDi,F:Grifter, Maul. 2.50
21 JoC,SDi,F:Grifter, Maul, pt.2. . . 2.50
22 JoC,SeP,R:Grifter 2.50
23 JoC,SeP,F:Grifter 2.50
23a variant WPo(c) (1:4) 2.50
24 JoC,SeP,F:Voodoo 2.50

25 JoC,SeP, 40-pg. 3.50
26 JoC,SeP, control of Halo. 2.50
27 JoC,SeP,Grifter vs. Zealot 2.50
28, JoC,SeP,Voodoo,final issue . . 2.50
Spec. WildC.A.Ts: Mosaic. 4.00
Ann. 2000 #1, Devil's
   Night x-over, pt.3 . . . . 3.50
GN Ladytron. 6.00

WILDCATS
Wildstorm/DC, July, 2008
1 World's End 3.00
2 World's End 3.00
3 The Nevada garden. 3.00
4 Rumble in Nevada. 3.00
5 Spartan in Post-Apocalyptic Earth 3.00

...ARMAGEDDON
Wildstorm/DC, Dec., 2007
1 F:Nemesis 3.00

...NEMESIS
Wildstorm/DC, Sept., 2005
1 (of 9) Zealot and Coda sisters. . . 3.00
2 . . . . 3.00
3 thru 9 . . . . @3.00

... VERSION 3.0
Wildcats/DC, 2002
Eye of the Storm
1 JoC,old and new team members. 3.00
2 JoC,Jack Marlowe,Halo corp. . . . 3.00
3 JoC 3.00
4 JoC, ... 3.00
5 JoC 3.00
6 JoC 3.00
7 JoC,I:Beef Boys. 3.00
8 JoC,BU:The Authority,pt.3 . . . . . 3.00
9 JoC,new Grifter 3.00
10 JoC,new Grifter. 3.00
11 JoC,Lights Out in Garfield. 3.00
12 JoC,Jack Marlowe 3.00
13 JoC,Mister Wax. 3.00
14 JoC,Halo Corp. 3.00
15 JoC,Car of tomorrow. 3.00
16 JoC,new assassin. 3.00
17 JoC,SeP 3.00
18 JoC 3.00
19 JoC(s) 3.00
20 JoC(s),new team. 3.00
21 JoC(s),Grifter's team. 3.00
22 JoC(s),Coda War One 3.00
23 JoC(s),Coda War One 3.00
24 JoC(s),final issue 3.00

...WORLDSTORM
Wildstorm/DC, Sept., 2006
1 GMo,JLe,SWi. 3.00
1a variant TM,JLe (c) 3.00
1b variant JLe (c) 3.00
2 GMo,JLe,SW 3.00
2a variant EL (c) 3.00

WILDFIRE
Zion Comics
1 thru 3 V:Mr. Reeves . . . . @2.50
4 Lord D'Rune. 2.50

WILD GIRL
Wildstorm/DC, Nov., 2004
1 (of 6) SwM 3.00
2 SwM 3.00
3 SwM. 3.00
4 SwM 3.00
5 SwM,JWi 3.00
6 SwM,JWi 3.00

WILDSIDERZ
Wildstorm/DC, Aug., 2005
0 JSC 2.00
1 (of 5) JSC, 40-page 3.50

Wildgirl #5
© Wildstorm/DC

2 JSC 3.50
3 JSC 3.50

WILDSTORM
Wildstorm/DC, 2005
Spec. Winter special 5.00

WILDSTORM FINE ARTS SPOTLIGHT
Wildstorm/DC, Dec., 2006
1-shot Jim Lee 3.50
1-shot J. Scott Campbell 3.50
1-shot On the Authority 3.50
1-shot Gen13 . . . . 3.50
1-shot Wildcats 3.50

WILD TIMES
WildStorm/DC, 1999
Deathblow 2.50
DV8 . . . . 2.50
Gen13 . . . . 2.50
Grifter. 2.50
Wetworks 2.50

WILD WEST
Charlton, 1966
58 From Black Fury 25.00

WILD WEST C.O.W.- BOYS OF MOO MESA
Archie, 1992–93
1 Based on TV cartoon. 2.50
2 Cody kidnapped. 2.50
3 Law of the Year Parade,
   last issue 2.50
(Regular series)
1 Valley o/t Thunder Lizard. 2.50
2 Plains, Trains & Dirty Deals. 2.50

WILD WESTERN ACTION
Skywald, 1971
1 . . . . 35.00
2 . . . . 35.00
3 . . . . 35.00

WILD WILD WEST
Gold Key, 1966–69
1 TV show tie-in 300.00
2 . . . . 250.00
3 thru 7 . . . . @200.00

WILD WILD WEST
Millennium, 1990–91
1 . . . . 3.00
2 thru 4 . . . . @3.00

WILL EISNER'S
3-D CLASSICS
Kitchen Sink, 1985
WE art, w/glasses (1985). 3.00

WILLOW CREEK
Zenescope Entertainment, 2008
0 . . . . 0.75
1 (of 5) 3.00
2 thru 5 . . . . @3.00

WILL TRIUMPH
FIGHTS ALONE
Devil's Due, 2008
1 (of 3) 3.50

WIN A PRIZE COMICS
Charlton Comics, 1955
1 S&K,Edgar Allen Poe adapt.. 1,100.00
2 S&K 800.00
Becomes:

TIMMY THE TIMID GHOST
Charlton Comics, 1957
3 . . . . 150.00
4 . . . . 125.00
5 . . . . 125.00
6 thru 10 . . . . @100.00
11 giant 125.00
12 giant 125.00
13 thru 19 . . . . @100.00
20 thru 25 . . . . @100.00
26 thru 44 . . . . @25.00
45 1966 . . . . 25.00

WINGMAN
Arcana Studio, 2008
1 (of 3) 4.00

WINNIE-THE-POOH
Gold Key, 1977
1 . . . . 35.00
2 thru 5 . . . . @20.00
6 thru 17 . . . . @15.00
Whitman, 1980
18 thru 19 . . . . @20.00
20 thru 21 scarce . . . . @40.00
22 very scarce 50.00
23 thru 33 . . . . @20.00

WINTER MEN, THE
Wildstorm/DC, Aug., 2005
1 (of 8) JPL, U.S.S.R. soldiers 3.00
2 thru 5 . . . . @3.00

WINTERWORLD
Eclipse, 1987–88
1 JZ,I:Scully, Wynn 3.00
2 JZ,V:Slave Farmers 3.00
3 JZ,V:Slave Farmers 3.00

WISP
Oktomica Entertainment, 1999
1 All Along the Watchtower,pt.1 . . . 2.50
2 All Along the Watchtower,pt.2 . . . 2.50
3 All Along the Watchtower,pt.3 . . . 3.00
4 The Acheron Protocol 3.00

W.I.T.C.H.
Hyperion Books, 2005
GN Vol. 1 . . . . 5.00
GN Vol. 2 . . . . 5.00

GN Vol. 3 . . . . 5.00
GN Vol. 4 . . . . 5.00
GN Vol. 5 Legends Revealed 5.00
GN Vol. 6 Forces of Change 5.00

WITCHBLADE:
SHADES OF GRAY
D.E. (Dynamite Ent.) 2007
1 (of 4) 3.50
2 thru 4 . . . . @3.50
1a thru 4a variant (c)s . . . . @3.50

WITCHGIRLS, INC.
Heroic Publishing Inc., 2005
1 . . . . 4.00
2 . . . . 3.00
3 thru 4 . . . . @3.25
5 . . . . 4.50
5a variant (c) 4.50

WITCHING HOUR, THE
Millennium/Comico, 1992
1 Anne Rice adaptation 2.50
2 thru 5 . . . . @2.50

WITCHMAN
Avatar Press, 2006
1 . . . . 4.00
1a wraparound (c) 4.00
1b variant (c)s . . . . @4.00

WOLF
Moonstone, 2008
1 Twilight Crusade 4.00

WOLFMAN
Dell, 1964
1 . . . . 140.00

WOLFSKIN
Avatar Press, 2008
Ann. #1 40-pg. 5.00
Ann. #1a variant (c) 5.00
Ann. #1b variant wraparound (c) . . 5.00
Ann. #1c variant barbaric (c) 6.00

WONDERLAND
Amaze Ink/Slave Labor
Graphics, 2006
1 . . . . 3.50
2 thru 4 . . . . @3.50
5 . . . . 4.00
6 . . . . 4.00

WOOD BOY, THE
Devil's Due Publishing, 2004
1 (of 2) 3.00
2 . . . . 3.00

WOODSY OWL
Gold Key, 1973
1 . . . . 25.00
2 thru 10 . . . . @15.00

WOODY WOODPECKER
AND FRIENDS
Harvey, 1991
1 . . . . 3.00
2 thru 4 . . . . @3.00

WOODY WOODPECKER
Harvey, 1991–93
1 thru 5 . . . . @2.50

WORLD OF ADVENTURE
Gold Key, 1963
1 . . . . 50.00
2 . . . . 30.00
3 . . . . 30.00

WORLD OF ARCHIE
Archie, 1992
1 thru 22 . . . . @2.50

WORLD OF WARCRAFT
Wildstorm/DC, Nov., 2007
1 Based on videogame 3.00
1a variant JLe (c) 3.00
2 thru 13 . . . . @3.00
2a thru 8a variant JLe(c) . . . . @3.00

WORLD OF WARCRAFT:
ASHBRINGER
Wildstorm/DC, Sept., 2008
1 . . . . 4.00
2 thru 3 . . . . 4.00

World of Wood #2
© Eclipse

WORLD OF WOOD
Eclipse, 1986–87
1 WW 4.00
2 WW,DSt(i) 4.00
3 WW 4.00
4 WW 4.00

WORLDS OF
DUNGEONS & DRAGONS
Devil's Due, 2008
1 (of 8) 48-pg 5.50
2 thru 8 . . . . @5.50
1a thru 7a variant prestige (c)s . @0.50
8a variant (c) 5.50

WORLDSTORM
Wildstorm/DC, Oct., 2006
1-shot Preview 3.00
2 . . . . 3.00

WORLDSTORM:
REVELATIONS
Wildstorm/DC, Jan., 2008
1 (of 6) Wildstorm Armageddon . . . 3.00
2 thru 6 . . . . @3.00

All comics prices listed are for *Near Mint* condition.

WORLD WAR STORIES
Dell, 1965

1 . . . . 60.00
2 thru 3 . . . . @40.00

WORLD WAR II: 1946
Antarctic Press, 1999

1 by Ted Nomura 4.00
2 Born to Die. 4.00
3 Battle for Moscow 4.00
4 Flying Tigers 4.00
5 . . . . 4.00
6 The Hunley vs. the Potsdam 4.00
7 The Yamato 4.00
8 Tuskegee Airmen. 4.00
9 Firestorm 4.00
10 Destination: Space 4.00
11 Night Witches 4.00
12 Korea 4.00
Ann. 2000 b&w 4.00

WORLD-WATCH
Wild & Wolly Press, 2004

1 . . . . 12.00
2 . . . . 8.00
3 . . . . 5.00

WORMWOOD: GENGLEMAN CORPSE
IDW Publishing, 2006

1 . . . . 4.00
2 thru 7 . . . . @4.00

WORMWOOD: CALAMARI RISING
IDW, 2007

1 thru 4 . . . . @4.00

WRAITHBORN
Wildstorm/DC, Sept., 2005

1 (of 6) JBz 3.00
2 JBz. 3.00

WRATH
Malibu Ultraverse, 1994–95

1 B:MiB(s),DvA,JmP,C:Mantra 2.50
1a Silver foil 3.00
2 DvA,JmP,V:Hellion 2.50
3 DvA,JmP,V:Radicals, I:Slayer 2.50
4 DvA,JmP,V:Freex. 2.50
5 DvA,JmP,V:Freex. 2.50
6 DvA,JmP 2.50
7 DvA,JmP,I:Pierce,Ogre, Doc
   Virtual 2.50
8 . . . . 2.50
9 A:Prime 2.50
G-Size #1. . . . . 2.50

WRAITHBORN
Wildstorm/DC, Sept., 2005

3 thru 6 JBz. . . . . @3.00

WULF THE BARBARIAN
Atlas, 1975

1 O:Wulf 15.00
2 NA,I:Berithe The Swordsman . . 12.00
3 & 4 . . . . @8.00

WWF BATTLEMANIA
Valiant

1 WWF Action 2.50
2 thru 5 . . . . @2.50

WYATT EARP
Dell Publishing Co., 1957

1 RsM 200.00

2 RsM 150.00
3 RsM 135.00
4 . . . . 100.00
5 Ph(c) 100.00
6 . . . . 100.00
7 . . . . 100.00
8 . . . . 100.00
9 . . . . 100.00
10 . . . . 100.00
11 . . . . 90.00
12 RsM. 90.00
13 AT 90.00

WYATT EARP VS. THE CISCO KID
Moonstone, 2008

1 . . . . 4.00

WYATT EARP FRONTIER MARSHAL
Charlton, 1956

12 From Range Busters. 100.00
13 thru 19 . . . . @60.00
20 AW 100.00
21 thru 30 . . . . @40.00
31 thru 60 . . . . @25.00
61 thru 72 . . . . @15.00

Wynonna Earp: Home on the Strange #2 © IDW Publishing

WYNONNA EARP: HOME ON THE STRANGE
IDW Publishing, 2003

1 . . . . 4.00
2 thru 3 . . . . @4.00
1a thru 2a variant (c)s . . . . @4.00

XANADU
Eclipse, 1988

1 . . . . 2.50

XENYA
Sanctuary Press, 1994

1 Hildebrandt Brothers 4.00
2 . . . . 3.25
3 . . . . 3.25
4 conclusion, Homecoming. 3.00

XENA VS. ARMY OF DARKNESS: WHAT, AGAIN?
Dynamite Entertainment, 2008

1 . . . . 3.50
2 . . . . 3.50

1a thru 2a variant (c) . . . . @3.50

XENA, WARRIOR PRINCESS
D.E. (Dynamite Ent.) 2006

1 . . . . 3.50
1a variant (c)s . . . . @3.50
1a photo foil (c) 15.00
2 Pantheon Pandemonium 3.50
3 Stalk Like an Egyptian 3.50
4 Contest of Pantheons 3.50
5 thru 8 . . . . @3.50
2a thru 4a variant (c)s. . . . . @3.50
5a thru 8a variant (c)s. . . . . @3.50
Ann. #1 Strange Visitor 5.00
Ann. #1 variant (c)s . . . . @5.00

XENA: WARRIOR PRINCESS
Topps, 1997

1 RTs,Revenge of the Gorgons,
   pt.1 . . . . 5.00
1a photo (c). 8.00
2 (of 2) rescue of Gabrielle 4.00
[VOL 2]
0 AaL Temple of the Dragon God . . 3.00
1 (of 3) Joxer, Warrior Prince, pt.1 . 5.00
1a deluxe 8.00
2 Joxer, Warrior Prince, pt.2 . . . . . 4.00
2a photo (c). 4.00

...BLOOD LINES
Topps, 1997

1 (of 3) ALo. 3.00
1a photo (c). 3.00
2 (of 3) ALo. 3.00
2a photo (c). 3.00

...CALLISTO
Topps, 1997

1 (of 3) RTs, ... 3.00
1a photo (c). 3.00
2 (of 3) RTs, ... 3.00
2a photo (c). 3.00
3 (of 3) RTs, ... 3.00
3a photo (c). 3.00

...ORPHEUS
Topps, 1998

1 (of 3) 3.00
2 thru 3 (of 3) . . . . @3.00
1a thru 3a photo (c)s. . . . . @3.00

...THE ORIGINAL OLYMPICS
Topps, 1998

1 (of 3) 3.00
1a photo cover 3.00
2 F:Hercules 3.00
2a photo cover 3.00
3 . . . . 3.00
3a photo cover 3.00

...THE WEDDING OF XENA & HERCULES
Topps, 1998

1-shot. 3.00
1-shot photo (c) 3.00

...THE WRATH OF HERA
Topps, 1998

1 (of 2) 3.00
1a photo cover edition 3.00
2 conclusion 3.00
2a photo cover edition 3.00

...XENA AND THE DRAGON'S TEETH
Topps, 1997

1 (of 3) RTs, ... 3.00
1a photo (c). 3.00
2 (of 3) RTs, ... 3.00
2a photo (c). 3.00

3 (of 3) RTs, ... 3.00
3a photo (c). 3.00

XENOTECH
Mirage, 1993–94
1 I:Xenotech 2.75
2 . . . . 2.75
3 w/2 card strip 2.75

X-FILES
Topps, 1994–97
1 From Fox TV Series 35.00
1a Newstand 25.00
2 Aliens Killing Witnesses 20.00
3 The Return. 18.00
4 Firebird,pt.1 . . . . 12.00
5 Firebird,pt.2 . . . . 9.00
6 Firebird,pt.3 . . . . 8.00
7 Trepanning Opera 7.00
8 Silent Cities of the Mind,pt.1 . . . 6.00
9 Silent Cities of the Mind,pt.2 . . . 5.00
10 Feeling of Unreality,pt.1 . . . . . . 5.00
11 Feeling of Unreality,pt.2 . . . . . . 5.00
12 Feeling of Unreality,pt.3 . . . . . . 5.00
13 A Boy and His Saucer. 5.00
14 . . . . 4.00
15 Homo of the Drave 4.00
16 Home of the Brave,pt.2. . . . . . . 3.50
17 DgM,CAd 3.50
18 thru 21 . . . . @3.50
22 JRz,CAd,The Kanishibari 3.00
23 JRz,CAd,Donor. 3.00
24 JRz,Silver Lining. 3.00
25 JRz,CAd,Remote Control,pt.1 . . 3.00
26 JRz,CAd,Remote Control,pt.2 . . 3.00
27 JRz,CAd,Remote Control,pt.3 . . 3.00
28 JRz,Be Prepared, pt.1,
   V:Windigo 3.00
29 JRz,Be Prepared, pt.2 . . . . 3.00
30 JRz,Surrounded, pt.1 . . . . 3.00
31 JRz,Surrounded, pt.2 (of 2) 3.00
32 . . . . 3.00
33 widows on San Francisco. 3.00
33 variant photo (c) 3.00
34 Project HAARP. 3.00
35 Near Death Experience. 3.00
36 Near Death Experience, pt.2 . . . 3.00
37 JRz,The Face of Extinction. . . . 3.00
38 JRz,. 3.00
39 JRz, Widow's Peak. 3.00
40 Devil's Advocate 3.00
40a photo cover 3.00
41 Severed. 3.00
41a photo cover 3.00
Ann.#1 Hollow Eve 5.00
Ann.#2 E.L.F.S. 4.50
Spec.#1 Rep. #1-#3. . . . . 6.00
Spec.#2 Rep. #4-#6 Firebird 5.00
Spec.#3 Rep. #7-#9. . . . . 5.00
Spec.#4 Rep. 5.00
GN Afterflight 6.00
GN Official Movie Adapt. (1998) . . 6.00

X-FILES, THE
Wildstorm/DC, Nov., 2008
1 (of 6) 3.50
1a variant (c) (1:10) 3.50
Spec. #0 . . . . 3.00
Spec. #0a variant (c) (1:10) 3.00

X-FILES DIGEST
Topps, 1995
1 All New Series, 96pg. 4.00
2 and 3 . . . . 4.00

X-FILES, THE:
GROUND ZERO
Topps, 1997
1 (of 4) based on novel 3.00
2 thru 4 . . . . @3.00

X-FILES, THE:
SEASON ONE
Topps, 1997
1 RTs,JVF(c) Deep Throat 5.00
Deep Throat, variant (c). 7.50
2 RTs,JVF(c) Squeeze 4.00
Squeeze, RTs, JVF(c) 5.00
3 RTs,SSc,Conduit 4.00
Conduit, RTs 5.00
4 RTs,The Jersey Devil. 4.00
5 RTs,Shadows. 4.00
Shadows JVF(c). 5.00
6 Fire. 4.00
Fire. 5.00
7 RTs,JVF,Ice 4.00
Ice 5.00
8 RTs,Space 4.00
Space JVF(c) 5.00
Spec. Pilot Episode RTs,JVF
   new JVF(c) 5.00
Beyond the Sea JVF(c) 5.00

XIMOS: VIOLENT PAST
Triumphant, 1994
1 JnR(s) 2.50
2 JnR(s) 2.50

XIN
Anarchy Studios, 2002
Alpha Preview edition 2.50
Alpha Preview, collector's ed. 9.00
Ashcan limited edition 6.00
Ashcan gold foil leather 12.00
1 Legend of the Monkey King. 3.00
1a variant JMd(c) 3.00
1b Royal blue edition 20.00
1c gold foil edition. 20.00
1d holo foil fx edition. 9.00
2 thru 3 . . . . @3.00
2a thru 3a variant limited (c) . . . . @9.00

XIN: JOURNEY OF
THE MONKEY KING
Anarchy Studios, 2003
1 . . . . 3.00
1a variant (c). 3.00
2 thru 3 . . . . @3.00
2a thru 3a variant (c) 3.00
1b thru 3b limited edition. . . . . . . @9.00

X ISLE
Boom! Studios, 2006
1 (of 5) 3.00
2 thru 5 . . . . @3.00

X-O MANOWAR
Valiant, 1992
0 JQ,O:Aric,1st Full Chromium(c). . 5.00
0a Gold Ed. 30.00
1 BL,BWS,I:Aric,Ken. 9.00
2 BL(i),V:Lydia,Wolf-Class Armor . . 6.00
3 I:X-Caliber,A:Solar 6.00
4 MM,A:Harbinger,C:Shadowman
   (Jack Boniface) 7.00
5 thru 13 . . . . @3.00
14 BS,A:Turok,I:Randy Cartier 3.50
15 BS,A:Turok 2.50
15a Red Ed. 7.00
16 thru 24. . . . . @2.50
25 JCf,JGz,PaK,I:Armories,
   BU:Armories#0 . . . . 3.00
26 JGz(s),RLv,F:Ken 2.50
27 JGz,RLe,A:Turok,Geomancer,
   Stronghold,Livewire 2.50
28 JGz,RLe,D:X-O,V:Spider
   Aliens,w/Valiant Era card. 2.75
29 thru 67. . . . . @2.50
68 last issue. 12.00

X-O Manowar, Vol. 2 #8
© Acclaim

Series Two, Acclaim, 1997
1 Rand Banion v. R.A.G.E. 3.00
2 thru 20 . . . . @3.00

XOMBIE
Devil's Due, 2007
1 . . . . 3.50
1a variant (c) 3.50
2 thru 6 . . . . @3.50
2a thru 6a variant (c) . . . . @3.50

XIII
Alias Enterprises, 2005
1 Day of the Black Sun. 2.50
2 thru 5 . . . . @3.00
6 . . . . 3.00

YAKKY DOODLE
& CHOPPER
Gold Key, 1962
1 . . . . 150.00

YANG
Charlton, 1973–76
1 . . . . 25.00
2 thru 13 . . . . @12.00
Charlton, 1985
14 . . . . 7.00
15 thru 17. . . . . @5.00

YEAH!
Homage/DC, 1999
1 GHe 3.00

YENNY
Alias Enterprises, 2005
1 . . . . 2.50
1a variant (c) 3.00
2 thru 4. . . . . @3.00
5 thru 10 . . . . @3.50

YIN FEI
Leung's Publications, 1988–90
5 . . . . 3.00
6 thru 11 . . . . @3.00

YOGI BEAR
Dell, 1962
#1 thru #6, See Dell Four Color
7 thru 9 . . . . 125.00

COLOR PUB.

Gold Key, 1962

10	150.00
11 Jellystone Follies	135.00
12	100.00
13 Surprise Party	135.00
14 thru 19	@100.00
20 thru 29	@50.00
30 thru 42	@45.00

YOGI BEAR
Charlton Comics, 1970–76

1	75.00
2 thru 10	@50.00
11 thru 35	40.00

YOGI BEAR
Harvey, 1992

1	4.00
2 thru 6	@3.00

YOGI BEAR
Archie Comics, 1997

1	2.50

Yosemite Sam #69
© Whitman

YOSEMITE SAM
Gold Key/Whitman, 1970–84

1	75.00
2 thru 10	@35.00
11 thru 40	@25.00
41 thru 81	@20.00

YOU'LL HAVE THAT
Viper Comics, 2006

1-shot	3.25

YOUNGBLOOD
Maximum Press/Extreme
Volume 2, 1996

Vol. 1 & Vol. 2 #1–#10, see Image

11 RLd,RCz,	2.50
12 Rle, V:Lord Dredd,A:New Man,double size	3.50
13 RLd,RCz,F:Die-Hard	2.50
14 RLd,RCz,	2.50
Super Spec.#1 ErS,CSp,AG	3.00

YOUNGBLOOD
Awesome Entertainment, 1998

1 AMo,SSr	2.50
1a variant covers, 7 different	@2.50
1b foil logo	6.00
1c plus custom illustration	60.00

2 AMo,SSr,Baptism of Fire	2.50
3 AMo,SSr,V:Professor Night	2.50
4 AMo,SSr,Young Guns	2.50
5 AMo,SSr,Young Guns	2.50
1-shot, Youngblood/X-Force x-over,48pg. (1998)	5.00

...BLOODSPORT
Arcade Comics, 2002

1 MMr,RLd, RLd(c)	5.00
1a variant Quietly (c)	6.00
1b variant Park (c)	4.00
1c Foil ed.	9.00
1d Foil ed., signed	15.00
1e convention sketch ed.	40.00
1f San Diego con lim. ed.	9.00
1g San Diego con lim. signed	15.00
1h ltd (c)	15.00
2 MMr,RLd, RLd(c)	3.00
2a variant Quietly (c)	3.00
2b variant Park (c)	3.00
2c Foil ed.	9.00
2d Foil ed., signed	15.00
Spec. Imperial #1 Dossier	4.00
Spec. Imperial #1 Max edition	9.00
Spec. Imperial #1 signed	9.00

...CLASSICS
Image/Extreme, 1996

1 RLd,ErS,series rewritten & redrawn, new cover	2.50
2 RLd,ErS	2.50
3 RLd,ErS	2.50

...GENESIS
Awesome Entertainment, 2000

1	4.00
1a signature edition	9.00

Arcade Comics, 2004

2	4.00
2a RLd(c)	9.00

...IMPERIAL
Arcade Comics, 2004

0	4.00
0a max edition	9.00
1 (of 12) Mmy,RLd(c)	3.00
1a max edition	12.00
1b premium, signed edition	18.00
2 Rld,MMy	3.00
2a max edition	12.00
2b Authentic sign ed.	18.00

YOUNG DOCTORS, THE
Charlton, 1963

1	50.00
2 thru 6	@30.00

YOUNG LAWYERS, THE
Dell, 1971

1	40.00
2	30.00

YOUNG REBELS, THE
Dell, 1971

1	30.00

ZAK RAVEN, ESQ.
Avatar/Tidalwave Studios, 2002

1A Cha (c)	3.50
1B Arlem (c)	3.50
1C Miller (c)	3.50
1D Murphy (c)	3.50

ZANE GREY'S STORIES
OF THE WEST
Dell, 1955

27 thru 39	@75.00

Gold Key, 1964

1	50.00

ZEIN
AK Entertainment, 2006

1 Enter the Scarab	3.00
2 Origins	3.00
3 The Rise of Anubis	3.00
4 Year of the Beast	3.00
5 Judgment Day	3.00
7 thru 9	@3.00

ZEIN GHOSTS
OF HELIOPOLIS
Studio G, 2003

1	3.00
2 thru 4	@3.00

ZEN
Zen Comics, 2003

0	3.00
1	3.00
2 thru 4	@3.00

ZENDRA
Pennyfarthing Press, 2001
Volume 2

1 (of 6) Windmills of the World	3.00
2 All the Flesh Inherits	3.00
3 thru 5	@3.00
6	3.00

ZEN INTERGALACTIC
NINJA
Archie, 1992

1 Rumble in the Rain Forest prequel, inc.poster	3.00
2 Rumble in Rain Forest #1	3.00
3 Rumble in Rain Forest #2	3.00

Entity Comics, 1994

0 Chromium (c),JaL(c)	4.00
1 Joe Orbeta	3.00
1a Platinum Edition	20.00
2 Deluxe Edition w/card	5.00
3 V:Rawhead	3.00
4 thru 7	@3.25
GN A Fire Upon The Earth	13.00

[2nd Series]

1 Joe Orbeta	5.00
2	5.00
3 thru 5	@2.50

Zen Comics, 1998

Commemorative Ed. #1	6.00

Studio Chikara, 1999

1	4.00
1 variant (c)	10.00
2	4.00
3	4.00

Devil's Due, 2008

1	1.00

ZEN/NIRA X:
HELLSPACE
Zen Comics

1	3.00

ZEN: NOVELLA
Eternity Comics

1 thru 8	@3.00

ZEN SPECIALS
Eternity

Spring#1 V:Lord Contaminous	2.50
April Fools#1 parody issue	2.50
Color Spec.#0	3.50

ZEN: WARRIOR
Eternity Comics, 1994

1 vicious video game	3.00

ZENDRA
Pennyfarthing Press, 2001
1 (of 6) 3.00
2 thru 6 . . . . @3.00

ZENITH PHASE I
Fleetway
1 thru 3 . . . . @2.50

ZENITH PHASE II
Fleetway
1 thru 2 . . . . @2.50

ZERO GIRL: FULL CIRCLE
DC/Homage, 2002
2 SK 3.00
3 SK 3.00
4 SK 3.00
5 SK, concl.. . . . . 3.00

ZERO PATROL
Continuity, 1984–90
1 EM,NA,O&I:Megalith 4.00
2 EM,NA 4.00
3 EM,NA,I:Shaman 3.00
4 EM,NA 3.00
5 EM 3.00
6 thru 8 EM . . . . @3.00

ZERO TOLERANCE
First, 1990–91
1 TV 3.50
2 TV 3.00
3 TV 3.00
4 TV 3.00

ZMD: ZOMBIES OF MASS DESTRUCTION
Red 5 Comics, 2008
1 (of 6) 3.25
2 thru 3 . . . . @3.25

ZODY, THE MOD ROB
Gold Key, 1970
1 . . . . 40.00

ZOMBIE-PROOF
Moonstone 2007
1 . . . . 3.50
2 . . . . 3.50
3 . . . . 3.50

ZOMBIE TALES
Boom! Studios, 2008
1 . . . . 4.00
1a variant (c) 4.00
2 thru 8 . . . . @4.00
2a thru 8a variant (c). . . . . @4.00
Spec. The War at Home 4.00
Spec.A The War at Home var.(c) . 4.00

ZOMBIE-SAMA
Crusade Entertainment, 2007
1 . . . . 5.00
1-shot 48-pg, ... 7.00

ZOMBIES!
IDW Publishing, 2006
1 . . . . 4.00
2 thru 4 . . . . @4.00
3a thru 4a variant (c)s . . . . @4.00

...ECLIPSE OF THE UNDEAD
IDW Publishing, 2006
1 . . . . 4.00
2 thru 4 . . . . @4.00

...FEAST
IDW Publishing, 2006
1 . . . . 4.00
2 . . . . 4.00
3 . . . . 4.00
4 . . . . 4.00
5 . . . . 4.00

...HUNTERS
IDW, 2008
1 . . . . 4.00
1a variant (c) 4.00
2 . . . . 4.00

...VS. ROBOTS
IDW Publishing, 2006
1 . . . . 4.00
2 . . . . 4.00

...VS. ROBOTS VS. AMAZONS
IDW 2007
1 . . . . 4.00
2 . . . . 4.00
3 . . . . 4.00

ZOMBIE TALES: THE DEAD
Boom! Studios, 2006
1 . . . . 7.00

ZOOM SUIT
Superverse Productions, 2006
1 (of 4) 3.00
2 thru 4 . . . . @3.00
1a thru 4a variant (c)s . . . . @3.00
1b thru 4b variant sketch (c)s . . @9.00
1 Suspended Animation Edition . . . 3.00
2 Fantasticreal.com edition 9.00

ZOONIVERSE
Eclipse, 1986–87
1 I:Kren Patrol,wrap-around(c) 3.00
2 . . . . 3.00
3 . . . . 3.00
4 V:Wedge City 3.00
5 Spak vs. Agent Ty-rote. 3.00
6 last issue 3.00

ZORRO
Dell Publ. Co., 1959–61
1 thru 8, see Dell 4-Color
8 . . . . 200.00
9 . . . . 225.00
10 . . . . 200.00
11 . . . . 200.00
12 ATh 225.00
13 . . . . 150.00
14 . . . . 150.00
15 . . . . 150.00

ZORRO
Gold Key, 1966–68
1 ATh,Rep. 150.00
2 Rep. 100.00
3 Rep. 100.00
4 Rep. 100.00
5 Rep. 100.00
6 Rep. 100.00
7 Rep. 100.00
8 Rep. 100.00
9 Rep. 100.00

Zorro #15 © Dell Publishing

ZORRO
Topps, Nov., 1993
0 BSf(c),DMG(s), came bagged
with Jurassic Park Raptor #1 and
Teenagents #4 . . . . 4.00
1 DMG(s),V:Machete 3.00
2 DMG(s) 5.00
3 DMG(s) I:Lady Rawhide 10.00
4 MGr(c),DMG(s),V:Moonstalker . . 3.00
5 MGr,DMG(s),V:Moonstalker. . . . 3.00
6 A:Lady Rawhide. 8.00
7 A:Lady Rawhide. 7.00
8 MGr(c),DMG(s) 3.00
9 A:Lady Rawhide. 4.00
10 A:Lady Rawhide. 4.50
11 A:Lady Rawhide. 8.00

ZORRO
Papercutz, 2005
1 Scars 3.00
2 Scars 3.00
3 Scars 3.00
4 Drownings 2.00
5 Drownings 3.00
6 Drownings 3.00
7 thru 10 . . . . @3.00
GN Vol. 1 Scars 8.00
GN Vol. 2 Drownings 8.00
GN Vol. 3 Vultures 8.00

ZORRO
Dynamite Entertainment, 2008
1 MWg 3.50
1a variant (c)s . . . . @3.50
2 thru 9 . . . . @3.50

ZOT!
Eclipse, 1984–85
1 by Scott McCloud 7.00
2 . . . . 4.00
3 Art and Soul. 4.00
4 Assault on Castle Dekko 3.00
5 Sirius Business 3.00
6 It's always darkest 3.00
7 Common Ground 3.00
8 Through the Door 3.00
9 Gorilla Warfare. 3.00
10 T.K.O. The Final Round 3.00
10a B&W 6.00
10b 2nd printing 3.00
Original Zot! Book 1 . . . . 10.00
(Changed to B & W)

All comics prices listed are for *Near Mint* condition.

B&W COMICS

A1
Atomeka Press, 1989–92
1 BWS,A:Flaming Carrot,Mr.X.... 10.00
2 BWS,JHw,ECa.............. 10.00
3 BBo(c),ECa 10.00
4 SBs(c),JHw 6.00
5 WiS(c),NGa(s),KJo 7.00
6A JHw,F:Tank Girl 5.00

AARDWOLF
Aardwolf, 1994
1 DC,GM(c)................... 3.00
1a Certificate ed. signed....... 12.00
2 World Toughest Milkman 3.00
3 R.Block(s),O:Aardwolf 3.00

AARON STRIPS
Amazing Aaron Prod., 1999
1 thru 4, see Image
5 thru 9 .... @3.00
10 48-pg. 4.00

A.B.C. WARRIORS
Fleetway/Quality, 1990
1 .... 2.50
2 thru 8 .... @2.50

ABSOLUTE ZERO
Antarctic Press, 1995
1 .... 3.00
2 Rooftop,Athena 3.00
3 Stan Sakai 3.50
4 3-D Man and Kirby............ 3.00
5 Super Powers 3.00
6 Super Powers 3.00

AC ANNUAL
AC Comics, 1990
1 F:She-Cat; Tara; Nyoka....... 4.00
2 F:Yankee Girl; Ms.Victory 5.00
3 Vault of Heroes; Jet Girl 3.50
4 F:Sentinels of Justice 4.00

ACE COMICS PRESENTS
Ace, 1987
1 thru 7 .... @3.00

ACE McCOY
ACG Comics, 1999
1 thru 4 FF .... @3.00

ACE OF DIAMONDS
Lone Star Press, 2000
0 .... 3.00
1 .... 4.00
2 .... 3.00
3 .... 3.00

ACES
Eclipse, 1988
1 thru 5, mag. size .... @3.00

ACG'S AMAZING COMICS
ACG Comics, 2000
1 thru 5 F:Dragon Lady........ @3.00

ACHILLES STORM
Brainstorm, 1997
1 by Sandra Chang............ 3.00

...DARK SECRET
Brainstorm, 1997
1 by Sandra Chang............. 3.00
2 .... 3.00
2a luxury edition 5.00

ACME
Fandom House, 1985–89
1 thru 9 .... @3.00

ACOLYTE CHRONICLES
Azure Press, 1995
1 I:Korath 3.00
2 V:Korath................... 3.00

A COP CALLED TRACY
ACG Comics, 1998
1 by Chester Gould............. 3.00
2 thru 9 .... @3.00
9a deluxe 3.00
10 thru 18.................. @3.00
19 thru 24 giant-size,64-pg.... @6.00
Ann.#1 .... 3.00

ACTION GIRL COMICS
Slave Labor Graphics, 1994
1 thru 7 .... @3.00
1 thru 7, later printings .... @2.75
8 thru 12 .... @3.00
13 Halloween issue 3.00
14 F:Elizabeth Lavin 3.00
15 .... 3.00
16 GoGo Gang,pt.1 .... 2.75
17 GoGo Gang,pt.2 .... 2.75
18 Blue Monday............... 3.00
19 Halloween 3.00

ADAM AND EVE A.D.
Bam, 1985–87
1 thru 10 .... @3.00

ADDAM OMEGA
Antarctic Press, 1997
1 (of 4) by Bill Hughes 3.00
2 thru 4 .... @3.00

ADOLESCENT RADIOACTIVE BLACK-BELT HAMSTERS
Eclipse, 1986
1 I:Bruce,Chuck,Jackie,Clint...... 3.00
1a 2nd printing 2.50
2 thru 9 .... @2.50
3 I:Bad Gerbil 2.50
[2nd Series] Parody Press
1 thru 2.................. @2.50

ADVENTURERS
Aircel/Adventure, 1986
0 Origin Issue 3.00
1 with Skeleton 7.00
1a Revised cover 5.00
1b 2nd printing 3.00
2 thru 9 .... @3.00

...BOOK II
Adventure Publ., 1987
0 O:Man Gods 3.00
1 .... 3.00
2 thru 9 .... @3.00

Adventurers Book Three #1
© Adventure Publications

...BOOK III
Adventure Publ., 1989
1A Lim.(c)Ian McCaig 2.50
1B Reg.(c)Mitch Foust 2.50
2 thru 6 .... @2.50

ADVENTURES INTO THE UNKNOWN
A Plus Comics, 1990
1 AW,WW, rep. classic horror..... 3.00
2 thru 3 AW .... @3.00
Halloween Spec. reps. Charlton &
   American Comics GroupHorror. 2.50
ACG Comics, 1997
1 FF,AW, Charlton comics reprint.. 3.00

ADVENTURES OF BARRY WEEN BOY GENIUS
Oni Press, 2000
1 (of 6) by Judd Winick.......... 3.00
2 thru 6 Monkey Tales,pt.2 thru 6 @3.00

ADVENTURES OF CHRISSY CLAWS, THE
Heroic, 1991
1 thru 2 .... @3.25

ADVENTURES OF CHUK THE BARBARIC
White Wolf, 1987
1 thru 2 .... @3.00

ADVENTURES OF HERCULES
ACG Comics, 1998
1 by Sam Glanzman............ 3.00
ACG Comics, 2002
1 reprint of 2 Charlton comics 6.00
1a deluxe 16.00
2 64-page 6.00

ADVENTURES OF LIBERAL MAN, THE
Political Comics, 1996
1 by Marcus Pierce & Pete Garcia . 3.00
2 V:Right Wing talk show hosts . . . 3.00
3 Contract with America,'pt.2 . . 3.00
4 Terminate with Extreme
   Prejudice,'pt.2 . . . . 3.00
5 Extreme Prejudice,pt.3 . . . . 3.00
6 . . . . 3.00
7 1996 Election issue 3.00
9 . . . . 3.00
10 The Last Boy Scouts,pt.2 . . . . . 3.00

ADVENTURES OF LUTHER ARKWRIGHT
Valkyrie Press, 1987–89
1 thru 9 . . . . @3.00
See Also: Dark Horse section

ADVENTURES OF THE AEROBIC DUO
Lost Cause Productions
1 thru 3 . . . . @2.50
4 Gopher Quest 2.50
5 V:Stupid Guy 2.50

ADVENTURES OF THEOWN
Pyramid, 1986
1 thru 3, Limited series . . . . . . @3.00

AESOP'S FABLES
Fantagraphics, 1991
1 Selection of Fables 2.50
2 Selection of Fables 2.50
3 inc. Boy who cried wolf 2.50

AETOS
Hall of Heroes, 1997
1 by Dan Parsons 2.50
1 variant cover 4.00
2 . . . . 2.50

AETOS THE EAGLE
Ground Zero, 1997
1 (of 3) by Dan Parsons 3.00
2 . . . . 3.00
3 concl. 3.00

AETOS 2: CHILDREN OF THE GRAVES
Orphan Underground, 1995
1 A:Nightmare 2.50

AGENT UNKNOWN
Renegade, 1987
1 thru 3 . . . . @3.00

AGE OF HEROES, THE
Halloween Comics, 1996
1 JHI 3.50
1A signed 7.00
2 JHI 3.50
2A signed 7.00

AGONY ACRES
AA2 Entertainment, 1995
1 thru 3 . . . . @2.50
4 and 5 . . . . @3.00

AIRFIGHTERS CLASSICS
Eclipse, 1987
1 O:Airboy,rep.Air Fighters#2 . . . . 4.00
2 rep.Old Airboy appearances 4.00
3 thru 6 . . . . @4.00

AIRWAVES
Caliber, 1990
1 Radio Security 2.50
2 A:Paisley,Ganja 2.50
3 Formation of Rebel Alliance. 2.50
4 Big Annie,pt. 1 . . . . 2.50
5 Big Annie,pt 2 . . . . 2.50

AKIKO
Sirius, 1996–2004
1 MCi, Akiko on the Planet Smoo. . 6.00
2 MCi,Captife of SKy Pirates 4.00
3 thru 17 MCi . . . . @3.00
18 MCi,Alia Rellapor, concl. 3.00
19 MCi,The Story Tree,pt.1 . . . . 3.00
20 MCi,F:Mr. Beeba. 3.00
21 MCi,On the Road 3.00
22 MCi,On the Transport Ship 3.00
23 thru 24 MCi,Follow me . . . . . @3.00
25 MCi,Done in One, 32pg. 3.00
26 thru 31 MCi,Bornstone's Elixir. @3.00
32 thru 34 MCi,On Planet Earth. . @3.00
35 thru 39 Moonshopping . . . . . @3.00
39 Big Bag of This and That 3.00
40 thru 47 Battle of Boach's Keep @3.00
48 thru 49 Akiko on Planet Earth . @3.00
50 MCi,44-pg. 3.50
51 MCi,Quality Assortment 3.00
52 MCi 3.00
1-shot Akiko on the Planet Smoo . . 4.00
1-shot Akiko on the Planet Smoo,
   signed & numbered, color 6.00

ALAN MOORE'S:

HYPOTHETICAL LIZARD
Avatar Press, 2004
Preview 2.50
Preview, wraparound (c) 3.00
Preview, convention (c) 6.00
1 (of 4) 4.00
1a wraparound (c). 4.00
1b Tarot (c) 4.00
2 thru 4 . . . . @3.50
2a thru 4a wraparound (c). . . . . @3.50
2b thru 4b Tarot (c) . . . . @4.00

...THE COURTYARD
Avatar Press, 2003
1 . . . . 3.50
2 . . . . 3.50
1a thru 2a wraparound (c). . . . . @4.00

...YUGGOTH CULTURES
Avatar Press, 2003
1 thru 3 . . . . @3.50
1 thru 3a wraparound (c) 4.00
Necrocomicon ashcan, 16-pg. 5.00

ALBEDO
Thoughts & Images, 1985 89
0 white cover, yellow drawing table
   Blade Runner 250.00
0a white(c) 100.00
0b blue(c),1st ptg 75.00
0c blue(c),2nd ptg. 35.00
0d blue(c),3rd ptg 20.00
0e Photo(c),4th ptg.,inc. extra
   pages. 15.00
1 SS,I:Nilson Groundthumper,
   dull red cover. 100.00
1a bright red cover 50.00
2 SS,I:Usagi Yojimbo 500.00
3 SS,Erma, Usagi 35.00

4 SS,Usagi 40.00
5 Nelson Groundthumper 10.00
6 Erma, High Orbit 6.00
7 thru 14 . . . . @6.00

[Vol. II] Antarctic Press, 1991–93
1 New Erma Story. 3.00
2 E.D.F. HQ. 3.00
3 Birth of Erma's Child 3.00
4 Non action issue 3.00
5 The Outworlds 3.00
6 War preparations 3.00
7 Ekosiak in Anarchy 3.00
8 EDF High Command 3.00
Spec. Color 3.00

Vol. III
1 . . . . 3.50

Vol 5 Anthropomorphics
Shanda Fantasy Arts, 2004
1 . . . . 5.00
3 Menace From Space 5.00

ALBERT
Narwain Publishing, 2006
1 (of 4) 3.00
2 thru 4 . . . . @3.00

ALICE IN THE LOST LAND
Radio Comix, 2000
1 (of 4) by Shuzilow Ha 3.00
2 thru 4 . . . . @3.00

Alien Fire #1
© Kitchen Sink Press

ALIEN FIRE
Kitchen Sink Press, 1987
1 Eric Vincent art 3.50
2 Eric Vincent art 3.00
3 Eric Vincent art 3.00

ALIEN NATION:

...A BREED APART
Adventure Comics, 1990
1 Friar Kaddish 3.00
2 Friar Kaddish 2.50
3 The `Vampires' Busted 2.50
4 Final Issue 2.50

...THE FIRSTCOMERS
Adventure Comics, 1991
1 New Mini-series. 2.50
2 Assassin. 2.50
3 Search for Saucer 2.50
4 Final Issue 2.50

Alien Nation, The Spartans #2
© Adventure Comics

...THE PUBLIC ENEMY
Adventure Comics, 1991
1 'Before the Fall'. 2.50
2 Earth & Wehlnistrata 2.50
3 Killer on the Loose. 2.50

...THE SKIN TRADE
Adventure Comics, 1991
1 'Case of the Missing Milksop' . . . 2.50
2 'To Live And Die in L.A'. 2.50
3 A:Dr. Jekyll. 2.50
4 D.Methoraphan Exposed. 2.50

...THE SPARTANS
Adventure Comics, 1990
1 JT/DPo,Yellow wrap. 4.00
1a JT/DPo,Green wrap. 4.00
1b JT/DPo,Pink wrap 4.00
1c JT/DPo,blue wrap 4.00
1d LTD collectors edition 7.00
2 JT,A:Ruth Lawrence. 2.50
3 JT/SM,Spartians 2.50
4 JT/SM,conclusion 2.50

ALISON DARE, LITTLE MISS ADVENTURES
Oni Press, 2001
1 (of 3) 3.00
Vol. 2
1 (of 2) Heart of the Maiden 3.00
2 Heart of the Maiden. 3.00
1-shot 48-pg. (2000) 4.50

ALLY
Ally Winsor Productions, 1995
1 I&O: Ally. 3.00
2 and 3'. . . . . @3.00

ALONG THE CANADIAN
Obion Comics, 2004
1 thru 6 . . . . @3.00

ALTERNATE HEROES
Prelude Graphics, 1986
1 and 2 . . . . @3.00

AMAZING COMICS PREMIERES
Amazing, 1987
1 thru 9 . . . . @3.00

AMAZON WOMAN
Fantaco, 1994
1 . . . . 3.00
2 . . . . 3.00
VOL. 2 (1996)
1 thru 4 . . . . @3.00
Christmas Spec. 5.00
Beach Party 6.00
Amazing Colossal Amazon
   Woman #1. . . . . 8.00
Amazing Colossal Amazon Album. 13.00
Jungle Annual #1. . . . . 6.00
Jungle Album. 10.00
Spec. Invaders of Terror (1996). . . . 6.00
1-shot Attack of the Amazon Girls,
   cont. nudity. 5.00

AMERICAN SPLENDOR
Harvey Bekar, 1976–90
1 thru 15 . . . . @3.25
Tundra, 1991
16 . . . . 4.00

AMERICAN WOMAN
Antarctic Press, 1998
1 by B.Denham & R.Stockton. 3.00

AMERICA'S GREATEST COMICS
AC Comics, 2002
1 F:Phantom Lady, golden-age rep. 7.00
2 F:Mysta on the Moon. 7.00
3 F:Spy Smasher 7.00
4 F:Yarko, Master Magician 7.00
5 F: Captain Science 7.00
6 thru 16 . . . . @7.00

ANATOMIC BOMBS
Brainstorm, 1998
1 Angelissa, by Mike James. 3.00
1a Bad Tabitha, by Mike James . . . 3.00
1b Bad Tabitha, photo cover edition 4.00

ANGEL GIRL
Angel Entertainment, 1997
0 by David Campiti & Al Rio 3.00
1 by D.Campiti & R.Fraga. 3.00
1 deluxe 6.00
Spec. #1 Angels Illustrated Swimsuit
   Special. 5.00
1-shot Against All Evil 3.00
1-shot Before the Wings 3.00
1-shot Demonworld, by Ellis Bell &
   Mark Kuettner 3.00
1-shot Doomsday, by Ellis Bell &
   Mark Kuettner 3.00

ANGEL GIRL: HEAVEN SENT
Angel Entertainment, 1997
0 by David Campiti & Al Rio 3.00
1 . . . . 3.00

ANGEL HEAT: THE NINTH ORDER
Amazing Comics, 1997
1 . . . . 3.00
2 "Book of Revelations" 3.00
1a signed 3.00
3 Helcio the Redeemer. 3.00

ANGEL OF DEATH
Innovation, 1991
1 thru 4 . . . . @2.25

ANGEL SCRIPTBOOK
IDW Publishing, 2006
1 City Of 4.00
1a variant (c) 4.00
2 A Hole in the World 4.00
3 Spin the Bottle 4.00
4 Waiting in the Wings 4.00
5 Five by Five. 4.00
6 Sanctuary 4.00
7 Smile Time. 4.00
2a thru 7a variant (cs) . . . . @4.00

ANGELS 750
Antarctic Press, 2004
1 (of 9) 3.00
2 thru 5 . . . . @3.00

ANGRY YOUTH COMIX
Fantagraphics Books, 2000
1 by Johnny Ryan. 3.00
2 thru 5 . . . . 3.00
6 thru 9 . . . . @3.50
10 48-page. 5.00
11 thru 14 . . . . @3.50

ANIMAL MYSTIC
Cry For Dawn/Sirus, 1993–95
1 DOe. 25.00
1a variant, signed. 35.00
1b 2nd printing, new (c) 7.00
2 I:Klor. 25.00
2a 2nd printing, new (c) 6.00
3 . . . . 12.00
3a 2nd printing 5.00
4 last issue 4.00
4a special 15.00

ANIMAL MYSTIC: KLOR
Sirius, 1999
1 thru 3 DOe. . . . . @3.00

ANTARES CIRCLE
Antarctic Press, 1990
1 . . . . 2.50
2 . . . . 2.50

ANUBIS
Unicorn Books
1 I:Anubis 2.50
2 F:Anubis. 2.50
3 . . . . 2.50
Didactic Chocolate Press
3 by Scott Berwanger 2.75
4 thru 6 . . . . @2.75
Adventure Comics
7 'Sandy's Plight' 2.75
8 . . . . 3.00

A-OK
Antarctic Press, 1993
1 Ninja H.S. spin-off series. 2.50
2 F:Paul,Moniko,James. 2.50
3 Confrontation 2.50
4 . . . . 2.50

APATHY KAT
Entity, 1995
1 . . . . 2.75
1 signed, numbered 10.00
1a & 2a 2nd printings . . . . @2.75
2 thru 4 . . . . @2.75

APE CITY
Adventure Comics, 1990
1 Monkey Business. 3.00
2 thru 4 . . . . @2.50

APOCALYPSE PLAN, THE
Narwain Publishing, 2006
1 (of 3) 3.50
2 . . . . 3.00

APPARITION, THE
Caliber, 1995
1 thru 4 . . . . @3.00
5 `Black Clouds' 3.00

APPLESEED
Eclipse, 1988
1 MSh,rep. Japanese comic 8.00
2 MSh,arrival in Olympus City 6.00
3 MSh,Olympus City politics 5.00
4 MSh,V:Director 5.00
5 MSh,Deunan vs. Chiffon 5.00
Book Two, 1989
1 MSh,AAd(c),Olympus City 4.00
2 MSh,AAd(c),Hitomi vs.EswatUnit 4.00
3 MSh,AAd(c),Deunan vs.Gaia. . . . 4.00
4 MSh,AAd(c),V:Robot Spiders 4.00
5 MSh,AAd(c),Hitome vs.Gaia 4.00
Book Three, 1989
1 MSh,Brigreos vs.Biodroid 5.00
2 MSh,V:Cuban Navy 4.00
3 MSh,`Benandanti' 4.00
4 MSh,V:Renegade biodroid 4.00
5 MSh 4.00
Book Four, 1990
1 MSh,V:Munma Terrorists 3.50
2 MSh,V:Drug-crazed Munma 3.50
3 Msh,V:Munma Drug Addicts 3.50
4 MSh,Deunan vs. Pani 3.50

ARAMIS
Comics Interview, 1988
1 mini-series 2.50
2 & 3 . . . . @2.50

AREA 88
Eclipse, 1987
1 I:Shin Kazama 3.00
1a 2nd printing 2.50
2 Dangerous Mission 2.50
2a 2nd printing 2.50
3 O:Shin,Paris '78. . . . . 2.50
4 thru 36 . . . . @2.50
Viz Communications, 1988
37 thru 42 . . . . @2.50

AREALA, ANGEL OF WAR
Antarctic Press, 1998
1 F:Warrior Nun Areala, color 3.00
2 color. 3.00
3 b&w 3.00
4 b&w, conclusion. 3.00

ARGONAUTS
Eternity
1 . . . . 3.00
2 thru 5 . . . . @2.50

ARISTOCRATIC X-TRA-TERRESTRIAL TIME-TRAVELING THIEVES
Fictioneer Books, 1987
1 V:IRS 2.50
2 V:Realty. 2.50
3 V:MDM. 2.50
4 thru 12 . . . . @2.50

ARIZONA: A SIMPLE HORROR
London Night/EH Prod., 1998
1 (of 3) by J. Kennedy & J. Beck . . 3.50
2 double sized. 3.00
3 . . . . 3.00
1-shot Wild at Heart, signed alt.(c) . 9.00

A.R.M.
Adventure Comics, 1990
1 Larry Niven adapt, pt.1 . . . . 2.50
2 Death by Ecstasy, pt.2 . . . . 2.50
3 Death by Ecstasy, pt.3 . . . . 2.50

ARMAGEDDON PATROL
Alchemy Texts, 1999
Spec. The Shot 3.00
1 (of 2) Cherries 3.00
2 Cherries 3.00
Spec. Maiden America (2002) 3.00
Spec. Fatal Mistakes 3.00
Spec. Life and Death 3.50
Spec. First Mission #1 . . . . 3.50
Spec. First Mission #2 . . . . 3.50
Spec. First Mission #3 . . . . 3.50

ARMED & DANGEROUS
Valiant, 1995
1 thru 4 . . . . @3.00
Spec.#1 . . . . 3.00

Armed & Dangerous #3
© *Armada/Acclaim*

ARMED & DANGEROUS
Acclaim (Armada), 1996
1 BH,Hell's Slaughterhouse, pt.1 . . 3.00
2 BH,Hell's Slaughterhouse, pt.2 . . 3.00
3 BH,Hell's Slaughterhouse, pt.3 . . 3.00
4 BH,Hell's Slaughterhouse, pt.4 . . 3.00
[Vol. 2] Acclaim, 1996
1 BH,When Irish Eyes are
   Dying, pt.1 . . . . 3.00
2 BH,When Irish Eyes, pt.2 . . . . . . 3.00
3 BH,When Irish Eyes, pt.3 . . . . . . 3.00
4 BH,When Irish Eyes, pt.4 . . . . . . 3.00

ARROW SPOTLIGHT
Arrow Comics, 1998–99
Adventures of Simone & Ajax 3.00
Allison Chains 3.00
Descendants of Toshin. 3.00
Max Velocity, by Jack Snider 3.00
Red Vengeance, by Chris Kemple. . 3.00

Talonback. 3.00

ARSENIC LULLABY
A Silent Comics, 1999
Spec. May '99 . . . . 2.50
Spec. July '99. . . . . 2.50
Spec. Sept.'99 . . . . 2.50
Spec. Jan. 2000. . . . . 2.50
8 thru 15 . . . . @2.50
Sept. 2001 . . . . 2.65
Nov. 2001. 2.65
Christmas 2001 . . . . 2.65
Spec. Christmas Special 2.50
Spec. Halloween Special 2.75
Volume 2, 2002
1 by Douglas Paszkiewicz 3.00
2 . . . . 3.00
3 . . . . 3.00
4 . . . . 3.00
AAA Milwaukee Publishing
Lost issue, signed (2002). 4.00
15 thru 16 . . . . @3.00
17 . . . . 3.00
Arsenic Lullaby Pub., 2005
18 thru 20 . . . . @3.00

ASHES
Caliber, 1990–91
1 thru 6 . . . . @2.50

ASHLEY DUST
Knight Press, 1995
1 thru 3 . . . . @2.50
4 V:Allister Crowley. 2.50
5 Metaphysical Adventure. 2.50

A SORT OF HOMECOMING
Alternative Comics 2003
1 (of 3) 3.50
2 and 3 . . . . @3.50

ASRIAL VS. CHEETAH
Antarctic Press, 1995–96
1 & 2 Ninja High School Gold
   Digger x-over. . . . . @3.00

ASSASSINATE HITLER!
New England Comics, 2001
1 (of 3) by Ron Ledwell 3.75
2 thru 3 . . . . @3.75

ASSASSINETTE
Pocket Change Comics, 1994
1 thru 4 . . . . @2.50
5 V:Nemesis 2.50
6 The Second Coming,pt.2. . . . . . . 2.50
7 The Second Coming,pt.3 . . . . 2.50
8 V:Crazy Actor. 2.50
9 . . . . 2.50
10 final issue. 2.50
Spec. Assassinette Returns 2.50
Spec. Assassinette Violated 2.50
Deluxe Assassinette Violated 4.25

ASSASSINETTE: HARDCORE 1995
Pocket Change Comics
1 By Shadow Slasher Team 2.50
2 V:Bolero 2.50

AS TOLD BY...
NDP Comics, 2004
1 Rapunzel 3.00
2 Sleeping Beauty. 3.00
3 Goldilocks 3.00

ASSEMBLY
Antarctic Press, 2003
1 (of 4) 3.00
2 thru 4 . . . . @3.50

ASTOUNDING
SPACE THRILLS
Day One Comics, 1998
1 by Steve Conley, The Codex
   Reckoning,pt.1. . . . . 3.00
2 Bros. Hildebrandt (c) 3.00
3 Aspects of Iron 3.00
4 The Robot Murders 3.00
5 Gordo returns. 3.00

...BLOOP
Day One Comics, 2004
1 . . . . 3.00
2 . . . . 3.00

ASTRA
CPM Manga, 2001
1 . . . . 3.00
1a variant JBa (c) 3.00
1b variant JBa(c) signed. 30.00
2 thru 5 . . . . @3.00
6 thru 8 . . . . @3.00

ASTRONAUTS
IN TROUBLE:
LIVE FROM THE MOON
Gun Dog Comics, 1999
1 (of 5) 3.00
2 thru 5 . . . . @3.00
AIT Comics, 1999
Spec.#1 Cool Ed's 3.00
Spec.#1 CAd, One Shot, One Beer. 8.00

ASTRONAUTS IN
TROUBLE: SPACE:, 1959
AIT/Planetlar, 2000
1 (of 3) by Larry Young, CAd 3.00
2 thru 3 . . . . @3.00

ATHENA
A.M. Works, 1995
1 thru 14 by Dean Hsieh . . . . @3.00
Antarctic Press, 1996
0 . . . . 4.00

ATOMIC CITY TALES
Kitchen Sink, 1996
1 by Jay Stephens 3.50
2 thru 4 . . . . @3.50

ATOMIC COMICS
1 . . . . 2.75
Becomes:

MARK I

ATOMIC MAN
Blackthorne, 1986
1 . . . . 3.00
2 & 3 . . . . @2.50

ATOMIC MOUSE
A Plus Comics, 1990
1 A:Atomic Bunny 2.50

A TRAVELLER'S TALE
Antarctic Press
1 I:Goshin the Traveller 2.50
2 . . . . 2.50

AUGUST
Arrow Comics, 1998
1 . . . . 3.00
2 thru 4 . . . . @3.00

AUTUMN
Caliber Press, 1995
1 I:James Turell 3.00

AUTUMN
Amaze Ink/SLG, 2004
1 . . . . 3.00
2 thru 5 . . . . @3.00

AVALON
Harrier, 1987
1 . . . . 2.50
2 thru 3 . . . . @2.50

AVANT GUARD
Day 1 Comics, 1994
1 thru 4 F:Feedback . . . . @2.50

AVATARS
Avatar Press, 1998
1 (of 2) by Gregory & Holaso 4.00
2 F:Pandora & Atlas 3.50

AV IN 3D
Aardvark–Vanaheim, 1984
1 Color,A:Flaming Carrot 6.00

AVELON
Drawbridge Studios, 1998
1 The Scrolls of Dyom, pt. 1 . . . . . . 3.00
2 The Scrolls of Dyom, pt. 2 . . . . . . 3.00
3 The Scrolls of Dyom, pt. 3 . . . . . . 3.00
4 The Scrolls of Dyom, pt. 4 . . . . . . 3.00
5 Way of the Wylden, 112-page . . . 6.00

AVELON
Kenzer & Company, 1998
1 . . . . 3.00
2 thru 11 Legacy of Thrain . . . . . @3.00
11 & 12 Heir to Legend . . . . @3.00

AVENUE X
Innovation, 1992
1 Based on NY radio drama 2.50

Avenue X #1
© Innovation

Purple Spiral
3 signed & numbered 3.00

AWAKENING COMICS
Awakening Comics, 1997
1 by Steve Peters 3.50
2 . . . . 3.50
3 thru 4 . . . . @3.00
Awakening Comics, 1999
1 by Steve Peters 3.50
Spec. Millennium Bug Fever 3.00

AWAKENINGS
Eighth Day Entertainment, 2004
1 (of 6) 3.00
2 thru 5 . . . . @3.00

AXED FILES, THE
Entity Comics, 1995
1 X-Files Parody 2.50
1 3rd printing, parody 2.75

B-MOVIE PRESENTS
B-Movie Comics, 1986
1 Captain Daring. 2.50
2 The World of X-Ray 2.50
3 Tasma, Queen of the Jungle 2.50
4 Matrix the Accellerator 2.50

B.A.B.E. FORCE
Comics Conspiracy, 2002
1 . . . . 3.00
2 thru 3 . . . . @3.00
Basement Comics, 2003
4 . . . . 3.00
4a special ed. 8.95

B.A.B.E. FORCE:
BACK TO SCHOOL
Forcewerks Productions, 2004
1 . . . . 2.50
2 . . . . 2.50

B.A.B.E. FORCE:
JURASSIC TRAILER PARK
Forcewerks Productions, 2004
1 . . . . 2.50
2 . . . . 2.50

BABY ANGEL X
Brainstorm, 1996
1 . . . . 3.00
2 . . . . 3.00
3 gold edition 5.00
3a signed edition. 9.00

BABY ANGEL X:
SCORCHED EARTH
Brainstorm, 1997
1 by Scott Harrison 3.00
2 . . . . 3.00

BABYLON CRUSH
Boneyard Press, 1995
1 I:Babylon Crush 3.00
2 V:A Gang 3.00
3 V:Mafiaso Brothers 3.00
4 & 5 . . . . @3.00

CFD
6 & 7 . . . . @4.00
Boneyard, 1998
1-shot Buddha, F:Lesbian dominatrix
   vigilante 5.00
Spec. Babylon Bondage Christmas . 3.00

Spec. Girlfriends. 3.00
Spec. The Last Shepherd 3.00

BAD APPLES
High Impact, 1997
1 . . . . 3.00
1 Bad Candies cover 9.00
2 . . . . 3.00
2 deluxe 12.00
3 by Billy Patton 3.00
Vol. 2, ABC Studios, 1999
1 RCI. 3.00
1a deluxe variant 8.00
2 . . . . 3.00
Vol 3
1 by Greg Narvasa 3.00
1a gold manga 9.00

BAD APPLES:
HIGH EXPECTATIONS
ABC Studios, 1999
1 . . . . 3.00
1a Beach Fun (c) 8.00
2 . . . . 3.00
2a deluxe 8.00

BAKER STREET
(Prev. color)
Caliber, 1989
3 . . . . 3.25
4 . . . . 2.50
5 & 6 Children of the Night . . . . . @2.50
7 thru 10 Children of the Night . . @2.50
Spec. Graphitti #1 Elementary,
My Dear. 2.50

BALANCE OF POWER
MU Press, 1990–91
1 thru 4 . . . . @2.50

BALLAD OF UTOPIA
Black Daze, 2000
1 by B.Buchanan & M.Hoffman . . . 3.00
2 thru 5 . . . . @3.00
Antimatter/Hoffman Int., 2003
7 thru 8 . . . . @3.00

BANANA SUNDAY
Oni Press Inc., 2005
1 (of 4) 3.00
2 thru 4 . . . . @3.00

BANDY MAN, THE
Caliber, 1996
1 SPr,CAd. 3.00
2 SPr,CAd,JIT 3.00
3 SPr,CAd,JIT, conclusion. 3.00

BAOH
Viz, 1990
1 thru 8 . . . . @3.00

BARABBAS
Slave Labor, 1986
1 . . . . 4.50
2 thru 4 . . . . @2.50

BARBARIANS
ACG Comics
1 by Jeff Jones, Mike Kaluta,
Wayne Howard 3.00
2 WW 3.00

BARBARIC TALES
Pyramid, 1986
1 . . . . 3.00
2 and 3 . . . . @2.25

BARBAROUS
I:Ron, 1998
1 by Ron Riley, 'Tween A Roch
and a Hard Place, pt.1 . . . . 2.75
2 'Tween A Roch and a Hard
Place, pt.2 (of 2) 2.75
3 The Fifth Kind, pt.1 (of 2). 2.75
4 The Fifth Kind, pt.2 . . . . 2.75

BASEBALL SUPERSTARS
Revolutionary, 1991–93
1 Nolan Ryan 2.50
2 Bo Jackson 2.50
3 Ken Griffey Jr. 2.50
4 Pete Rose 2.50
5 Rickey Henderson 2.50
6 Jose Canseco 2.50
7 Cal Ripkin Jr. 2.50
8 Carlton Fisk 2.50
9 George Brett 2.50
10 Darryl Strawberry 2.50
11 Frank Thomas 2.50
12 Ryne Sandberg (color) 2.75
13 Kirby Puckett (color) 2.75
14 Roberto & Sandy Alomar (color). 2.75
15 Roger Clemens (color) 2.75
16 Mark McGuire 3.00
17 Avery & Glavin 3.00
18 Dennis Eckersley 3.00
19 Dave Winfield 3.00
20 Jim Abbott. 3.00

BASTARD!!
Viz Communications, 2001
1 thru 2 Wizard . . . . @4.00
3 thru 5 Ninja. . . . . @4.00
6 thru 8 Fighter . . . . @4.00
9 thru 10 Vampire . . . . @4.00
11 thru 15 Empress . . . . @4.00

BATTLE ANGEL ALITA
Viz Communications, 1992
1 I:Daisuka,Alita 8.00
2 Alita becomes warrior 6.00
3 A:Daiuke,V:Cyborg. 4.00
4 Alita/Cyborg,A:Makaku 4.00
5 The Bounty Hunters' Bar 4.00

Battle Angel Alita Part Eight #5
© Viz Communications

6 Confrontation 4.00
7 Underground Sewers,A:Fang . . . 3.00
8 & 9 . . . . @2.75
Part Two, 1993
1 V:Zapan 3.00
2 V:Zapan 3.00
3 F:Ido. 2.75
4 thru 7 V:Zapan . . . . @2.75
Part Three, 1993
1 thru 5 . . . . @2.75
6 . . . . 5.00
7 thru 13 . . . . @2.75
Part Four, 1994
1 . . . . 2.75
2 thru 7 . . . . @2.75
Part Five, 1995
1 thru 6 . . . . @2.75
7 . . . . 3.00
Part Six, 1995–96
1 . . . . 3.00
2 thru 8 YuK . . . . @3.00
Part Seven, 1996
1 thru 8 YuK . . . . @3.00
Part Eight, 1997
1 thru 9 YuK . . . . @3.00

BATTLE ANGEL ALITA:
LAST ORDER
Viz Communicatons, 2002
1 by Yukito Kishiro 3.00
2 thru 6 . . . . @3.00

BATTLE ARMOR
Eternity, 1988
1 thru 4 . . . . @2.50

BATTLE BEASTS
Blackthorne, 1988
1 thru 4 . . . . @2.50

BATTLE GIRLZ
Antarctic Press, 2002
1 by Rod Espinosa 3.00
2 thru 6 . . . . @3.00

BATTLEGROUND EARTH
Best Comics, 1996
1 . . . . 2.50
2 . . . . 2.50
3 'Destiny Quest: The Vengeance'
concl. 2.50
4 V:Conjura. 2.50
5 'The Pit of Black Death'. 2.50

BATTLE POPE
Funk-O-Tron, 2000
1 . . . . 3.00
2 thru 4 . . . . @3.00
Spec.#1 Shorts. 5.00
Spec.#2 Shorts. 5.00
Spec.#3 Shorts. 5.00
Spec.#1 Christmas Popetacular . . 5.00

...MAYHEM
Funk-O-Tron, 2001
1 thru 2 . . . . @3.00

...SAINT MICHAEL
Funk-O-Tron, 2001
1 thru 3 . . . . @3.00

...WRATH OF GOD
Funk-O-Tron, 2002
1 (of 3) by R.Kirkman & T.Moore . . 3.50
2 thru 3 . . . . @3.50

BATTLESTAR
BLACK & WHITE
Realm Press, 2000
1-shot Battlestar Galactica 3.00

BATTLETECH
Blackthorne, 1987
(Prev. Color)
7 thru 12 . . . . @2.50
Ann.#1 . . . . 4.50

BATTRON
NEC
1 thru 2 WWII story . . . . @2.75

BEAR
Amaze Ink/SLG, 2003
1 by Jamie Smart 3.00
2 thru 10 . . . . @3.00

BEAST WARRIOR
OF SHAOLIN
Pied Piper, 1987
1 thru 5 . . . . @2.50

THE BEATLES
EXPERIENCE
Revolutionary, 1991–92
1 Beatles 1960's 3.00
2 Beatles 1964-1966 . . . . 2.50
3 . . . . 2.50
4 Abbey Road, Let it be 2.50
5 The Solo Years 2.50
6 Paul McCartney & Wings 2.50
7 The Murder of John Lennon 2.50
8 final issue 2.50

BECK AND CAUL
Gauntlet, 1994
1 I:Beck and Caul 3.00
2 thru 6 . . . . @3.00
Ann.#1 A Single Step 3.50

BELLE STAR:
QUEEN OF BANDITS
Moonstone, 2005
1 and 2 . . . . @3.00

BENZINE
Antarctic Press, 2000
1 manga, by Ben Dunn 5.00
2 thru 7 . . . . @5.00

BERLIN
Drawn & Quarterly, 1999
1 by Jason Lutes 3.00
2 thru 8 . . . . @3.00
9 thru 10 . . . . @3.50
11 thru 16 . . . . @4.00

BERZERKER
Gauntlet (Caliber), 1993
1 thru 6 . . . . @3.00

BEST OF THE WEST
AC Comics, 1998
1 F:Durango Kid 5.00
2 F:The Haunted Horseman 5.00
3 F:The Haunted Horseman 5.00
4 thru 32 . . . . @6.00
33 thru 67 . . . . @7.00
68 . . . . 9.00
69 . . . . 10.00

BETHANY THE VAMPFIRE
Brainstorm, 1997
0 O:Bethany 3.00
1 by Holly Galightly 3.00
1a luxury edition 5.00
2 & 3 . . . . @3.00

BETTIE PAGE
THE '50s RAGE
Illustration Studio, 2001
1 revised edition, Steve Woron 3.25
2 all pin-up layout 3.25
2 tame cover 3.25
Ann.#1 revised 3.25

BEYOND MARS
Blackthorne, 1989
1 thru 5 . . . . @2.50

BIG BANG PRESENTS
Big Bang Comics, 2006
1 Protoplasm 3.00
2 Super Frankenstein 3.00
3 . . . . 4.00
4 Protoplasman 4.00
5 Tennrex 4.00
6 Agents of Badge, 64-pgs. 8.00

BIGGER
Free Lunch Comics, 1998
Spec.#1 . . . . 3.50
1 (of 4) The Devil's Concubine 3.00
2 thru 4 Devil's Concubine,pt.2–4 @3.00

BIG NUMBERS
Mad Love
1 BSz,AMo(s) 6.00
2 BSz,AMo(s) 5.50

BILL THE BULL:
BURNT CAIN
Boneyard, 1992
1 I:Bill the Bull 3.00
2 & 3 For Hire . . . . @3.00

...ONE SHOT, ONE
BOURBON, ONE BEER
Boneyard, 1994
1 . . . . 3.00
2 . . . . 3.00

Bill the Bull: Burnt Cain
© Boneyard

BILLY DOGMA
Millennium, 1997
1 by Dean Haspiel 3.00
1a signed print edition 5.00
2 . . . . 3.00
3 . . . . 3.00
4 They Found A Sawed-Off in
 My Afro 3.00

BILLY NGUYEN
PRIVATE EYE
Caliber, 1990
1 . . . . 2.50
1a 2nd printing 2.50
2 thru 6 . . . . @2.50

BIO-BOOSTER
ARMOR GUYVER
Viz Communications
Part One, 1993
1 by Yoshiki Takaya 4.00
2 thru 12 . . . . @3.00
Part Two, 1994–95
1 F:Sho 2.75
2 thru 7 . . . . @2.75
Part Three, 1995
1 Sho Unconscious 2.75
2 thru 7 . . . . @2.75
Part Four, 1995–96
1 thru 7 . . . . @3.00
Part Five, 1996
1 thru 7 . . . . @3.00
Part Six, 1996–97
1 thru 6 by Yoshiki Takaya . . . . . . @3.00

BIZARRE HEROES
Kitchen Sink, 1990
1 DSs, parody 2.50
Fiasco Comics
1 DSs, reprint 3.00

BLACK BELT CLUB
Blue Sky Press 2006
1 Seven Wheels of Power 5.00
2 Night of the Mountain of Fear . . . 5.00

[Original] BLACK CAT
Recollections, 1991
4 rep 2.50
5 A:Ted Parrish 2.50
6 50th Anniv. Issue 2.50
7 rep 2.50

BLACK COAT:
CALL TO ARMS
Speakeasy Comics, 2006
1 (of 4) 3.00
2 thru 3 . . . . @3.00
Ape Entertainment, 2006
4 . . . . 3.00

BLACK COAT, THE:
OR GIVE ME DEATH
Ape Entertainment, 2007
1 (of 4) 3.50
2 thru 4 . . . . @3.50

BLACK-EYED SUSAN
Mad Yak Press, 2004
1 . . . . 3.50
2 thru 4 . . . . @3.00

BLACK HEART IRREGULARS, THE
Blue King Studios, 2005
1 .... 3.00
2 thru 5 .... @3.00

BLACK HOLE
Kitchen Sink, 1995
1 by Charles Burns 3.50
1 new printing 4.50
2 .... 3.50
3 .... 3.50
3 2nd printing 4.50

Fantagraphics Books, 2000
5 by Charles Burns 4.00
6 thru 10 .... @4.50
11 thru 12 .... @5.00

BLACK KISS
Vortex, 1988
1 HC,Adult 7.00
1a 2nd printing 4.00
1b 3rd printing 2.50
2 HC 6.00
2a 2nd printing 3.00
3 HC 5.00
4 HC 4.00
5 & 6 HC .... @2.50
7 thru 12 HC .... @2.50

BLACKMASK
Eastern Comics, 1988
1 thru 6 .... @2.50

BLACK MIST
Caliber Core, 1998
1 by James Pruett & Mike Perkins,
  Blood of Kali,pt.1 .... 3.00
1a variant MV(c) 3.00
1b variant Jordan Raskin(c) 3.00
1c variant GyD(c) 3.00
1d premium edition, signed 10.00
2 thru 5 Blood of Kali,pt.2–pt.5 .. @3.00
Spec. Dawn of Armageddon, Blood
  of Kali,pt.6 & pt.7, 48-pg...... 4.00

BLACK SCORPION
Special Studio, 1991
1 Knight of Justice 2.75
2 A Game for Old Men 2.75
3 Blackmailer's Auction........ 2.75

BLACKTHORNE 3 in 1
Blackthorne, 1987
1 & 2 .... @2.50

BLACK ZEPPELIN
Renegade, 1985
1 GD 3.00
2 thru 6 GD .... @2.50

BLADE OF SHURIKEN
Eternity, 1987
1 thru 8 .... @2.50

BLAIR WITCH PROJECT
Oni Press, 1999
Spec. Movie adapt. 3.00

BLAIR WITCH CHRONICLES
Oni Press, 2000
1 (of 4) by Jen Van Meter
  & Guy Davis 3.00
2 thru 4 .... @3.00

BLONDE AVENGER
Blonde Avenger Comics, 1998
25 flip-book, Full Metal Corset..... 4.00
27 Full Metal Corset,pt.2 .... 4.00
Spec. Short Blonde Girl with
  the Two Big Boobs 4.00

BLONDE AVENGER: DANGEROUS CONCLUSIONS
Brainstorm, 1997
1 V:Victor Von Fuchs 3.00
1a photo deluxe cover 4.00
2 .... 3.00
2a photo deluxe cover 4.00

BLOOD & ROSES ADVENTURES
Knight Press, 1995
1 F:Time Agents 3.00
2 F:Time Agents 3.00
3 Search for Time Agents 3.00
4 Time Adventures 3.00

BLOOD 'N' GUTS
Aircel, 1990
1 thru 3 .... @2.50

BLOODBROTHERS
Eternity, 1988
1 thru 4 .... @2.50

BLOOD IS THE HARVEST
Eclipse, 1992
1 I:Nikita,Milo 4.50
2 V:M'Raud D:Nikita? 2.50
3 Milo captured 2.50
4 F:Nikita/Milo............... 2.50

BLOOD JUNKIES
Eternity, 1991
1 Vampires on Capitol Hill 2.50
2 final issue................. 2.50

BLOOD OF DRACULA
Apple, 1987–90
1 .... 3.00
2 thru 7 .... @3.00

Blood of Dracula #18
© Apple

BLOOD OF THE INNOCENT
Warp Graphics, 1986
1 .... 3.00
2 thru 4 .... @3.00

BLOOD ORANGE
Fantagraphics Books, 2004
1 .... 6.00
2 thru 4 .... @6.00

BLOODSHED
Damage, 1993
1 Little Brother 3.00
1a Commemorative issue........ 4.00
1b Encore edition, gold foil(c).... 3.50
2 Little Brother 3.00
3 O:Bloodshed 3.00
3 'The Wastelands,' cont. 3.50
4 The City 3.50
5 the end is near.............. 3.50
6 .... 3.50
7 Lies, concl................. 3.50
'M' 3.50
'M' deluxe 5.00
Spec. Lunatics Fringe 3.50
Spec. Lies Epilogue, final issue.... 3.50
Spec. Chris Mass #1 .... 3.50
Spec. Requiem 3.50

BLOODTHIRSTY PIRATE TALES
Black Swan Press, 1995
1 .... 2.50
2 .... 2.50
3 .... 2.50
4 'Blockade of Charleston Harbor'. 2.50
5 'The Queen Anne's Revenge' ... 2.50
6 Blackhand's Party 2.50
7 Battle of Ocracoke Inlet....... 3.00
8 final issue................. 3.00

BLOODWING
Eternity, 1988
1 .... 2.50
2 thru 5 .... @2.50

BLOODY SCHOOL
Curtis Comics, 2002 (Manga)
1 by S.Yang & K. Yoo 3.00
2 thru 5 .... @3.00

BLUDGEON
Aardwolf, 1997
1 by JPi & David Chylsetk 3.00
2 'Alise in Wonderland'.......... 3.00
3 'Seeing Red' 3.00

BLUE BULLETEER
AC Comics, 1989
1 .... 2.50

BLUE MONDAY: ABSOLUTE BEGINNERS
Oni Press, 2000
1 (of 4) 3.00
2 thru 4 .... @3.00
Spec. Nobody's Fool 3.00
Spec. Lovecats (2002).......... 3.00
Spec. Dead Man's Party (2002).... 3.00

8 thru 14 .... @3.00
15 with Record & Mask 4.00
16 .... 5.00
17 thru 20 .... @4.50

All comics prices listed are for *Near Mint* condition.

...THE KIDS ARE ALRIGHT
Oni Press, 2000
1 by Chynna Clugston-Major 3.00
2 . . . . 3.00
3 concl. 3.00

...PAINTED MOON
Oni Press, 2004
1 (of 4) 3.00
2 thru 4 . . . . @3.00

BOGIE MAN: CHINATOON
Atomeka
1 I:Francis Claine 3.00
2 F:Bogie Man 3.00
3 thru 4 F:Bogie Man 3.00

BOGIE MAN: MANHATTEN PROJECT
Apocalypse
1-shot D.Quale Assassination Plot . 4.00

BONAFIDE
Bonafide Productions
1 F:Doxie 'th Mutt 3.50
2 F:Doxie 'th Mutt 3.50
3 F:Doxie 'th Mutt 3.50

Bone #13
© Cartoon Books

BONE
Cartoon Books, 1991
1 by Jeff Smith,I:Bone 95.00
1a 2nd printing 10.00
1b 3rd Printing 8.00
2 JSi,I:Thorn 40.00
2a 2nd printing 7.00
3 JSi 30.00
3a 2nd printing 5.00
4 JSi 18.00
5 JSi 15.00
6 JSi 15.00
7 JSi 12.00
8 JSi,The Great Cow Race,pt.1 . . . 9.00
9 JSi,The Great Cow Race,pt.2 . . . 8.00
1c thru 9a later printings . . . . . . @3.00
10 JSi,The Great Cow Race,pt.3 . . . 8.00
11 JSi 4.00
12 JSi 4.00
13 JSi 8.00
14 thru 20 JSi, ... @4.00
21 thru 27, *see Image*
21 thru 27 reprints . . . . @3.00

28 JSi,`Rockjaw: Master of the
    Eastern Border' 3.00
29 JSi. 3.00
30 JSi. 3.00
31 JSi. 3.00
32 JSi,Bartleby the Rat Creature Cub
    saga, concl. 3.00
33 JSi,Phoney's fate 3.00
34 JSi,Kingdok Slayer 3.00
35 JSi,Return of Gran'ma Ben. 3.00
36 JSi,Return of Rockjaw 3.00
37 JSi,Extravaganza Issue 3.00
38 JSi,48-pg. 5.00
39 JSi,Ghost Circles 3.00
40 JSi,wrap-around cover 3.00
41 JSi,Deep in enemy territory . . . 3.00
42 JSi, ... 3.00
43 JSi,sacred wall 3.00
44 JSi,rooftop eatery 3.00
45 JSi,Inner Circle of Power 3.00
46 JSi,Rat Creature Army 3.00
47 JSi,Making money 3.00
48 JSi,Surrender or Die 3.00
49 JSi,The usurper Tarsil 3.00
50 JSi,War, Rat Creatures 3.00
51 JSi,Casualties 3.00
52 thru 53. . . . . @3.00
54 This Mortal Coil 3.00
55 Final issue. 3.00
Spec.10th Anniv. Ed.with PVC fig. . . 6.00

BONEYARD
NBM Books, 2001
1 by Richard Moore 3.00
2 thru 4 . . . . @3.00
5 thru 19 . . . . @3.00
20 thru 26 . . . . @3.00
Spec. Swimsuit Issue. 3.00

BOOK, THE
DreamSmith Studios, 1998
1 epic fantasy 72pg. 3.50
2 . . . . 3.50
3 thru 7 . . . . @4.00
Ashcan Preview, 24-pg. 5.00
Ashcan Preview, GP(c) 9.00
Handbook, 32-pg. 2.25

BOOK OF BALLADS AND SAGAS
Green Man Press, 1995
1 False Knight in the Road 3.00
2 thru 4 . . . . 3.00
5 . . . . 3.50

BOOK OF THE TAROT
Caliber Tome Press, 1998
1 History/Development o/t Tarot . . . 4.00
1a 64pg. 5.00
1b signed 5.00

BOOKS OF LORE
Peregrine
Spec.#1 fantasy anthology. 3.00
Spec.#2 . . . . 3.00
Spec.#3 . . . . 3.00
1-shot Shattered Lives 3.00

BOOKS OF LORE: THE KAYNIN GAMBIT
Peregrine, 1998
0 by K. Tucker & D. Napoliello 3.00
1 (of 4) 3.00
1a Xavier (c) 3.00
2 thru 4 . . . . @3.00

BOOKS OF LORE: THE SHAPE OF EVIL
Peregrine Entertainment, 1999
1 (of 2) 3.00
2 . . . . 3.00

BOOKS OF LORE: THE STORYTELLER
Peregrine Entertainment, 2000
1 (of 3) by K.Tucker & P.Xavier . . . 3.00
2 & 3 . . . . @3.00

BOOKS WITH PICTURES
Very Dynamic Comics, 2007
1 . . . . 3.00
2 thru 6 . . . . @3.00

BOONDOGGLE
Knight Press, 1995
1 Waffle War 3.00
2 thru 3 Waffle War . . . . @3.00

BOONDOGGLE
Caliber Tapestry, 1997
Spec. 3.00
Spec., signed 3.00
1 thru 4 . . . . @3.00

BORDER WORLDS
Kitchen Sink, 1986
1 adult. 3.00
2 thru 7 . . . . @3.00
Spec.#1 Border Worlds: Marooned . 3.00

BORIS' ADVENTURE MAGAZINE
Nicotat, 1988
1 & 2 . . . . @2.50
3 thru 6 . . . . @3.00

BORIS THE BEAR
Nikotat, 1987
1–12: *See Dark Horse section*
13 thru 29 . . . . @2.50
30 thru 34 . . . . @2.50

BORN TO KILL
Aircel, 1991
1 thru 3 . . . . @2.50

BOSTON BOMBERS
Caliber
1 . . . . 2.50
2 . . . . 2.50
Spec.#1 . . . . 4.00
Note: other issues are flip-books with:
Oz #17; The Searchers #5; Raven
Chronicles #12; & LegendLore #6

BOUNTY
Caliber, 1991
1 `Bounty,''Navarro,'pt.1 . . . . 2.50
2 & 3`Bounty,''Navarro,'pt.2–pt3 @2.50

BOUNTY KILLER
Americanime Productions 2006
1 . . . . 3.50
1a variant (c) 3.50
2 . . . . 3.50
3 . . . . 4.00
1 Manga 4.00
2 thru 4 . . . . @4.00

BOX OFFICE POISON
Antarctic Press, 1996
1 by Alex Robinson.	8.00
2	6.00
3 thru 5	@4.00
6 thru 10	@3.00
11 thru 21	@3.00
Big Super Spec.#1	5.00

BRADLEYS, THE
Fantagraphics, 1999
1 (of 6) by Peter Bagge	3.00
2 thru 6	@3.00

BRAT PACK
King Hell Publications, 1990
1	6.00
1a 2nd printing	3.00
2 thru 5	@4.00
Brat Pack Collection	13.00

BRATPACK/MAXIMORTAL
King Hell, 1996
Super Spec.#1 RV	3.00
Super Spec.#2 RV	3.00

BREAKFAST
AFTER NOON
Oni Press, 2000
1 (of 6) by Andi Watson	3.00
2 thru 6	@3.00

BREAKNECK BLVD.
Slave Labor Graphics, 1995–96
1 thru 3 Jhonen Vasques art. . . .	@3.00
4 by Timothy Markin	3.00
5 & 6	@3.00

BRENDA STARR,
ACE REPORTER
ACG Comics, 1998
1 by Dale Messick, Charlton rep. . .	3.00
2	3.00
Spec.#1 Pin-ups,rep. from 40s and 50s (1998)	3.00

BRIAN PULIDO'S
GYPSY
Avatar Press, 2004
Preview	2.50
Preview variant (c)s	3.00
Preview Starlight (c).	6.00
Preview Holy Grail (c)	6.00
1	3.50
1a variant (c)s	@3.50
1b premium (c)	10.00
1c defensive (c)	6.00

...KILLER GNOMES
Avatar Press, 2004
1	3.50
1a wraparound (c).	3.50

...LADY DEATH:
ABANDON ALL HOPE
Avatar Press, 2004
1/2 Spec. 16-page	3.00
1/2 Spec. variant (c)s	3.00
1/2 Spec. Premium (c)	9.00
1/2 Spec. Vengeance edition	6.00
1/2 Spec. Empress (c)	6.00
1 (of 4)	4.00
2	4.00
3	4.00
4	4.00
1a thru 4a variant (c).	@4.00

1b thru 4b premium (c)	@10.00

...LADY DEATH: DEAD RISING
Avatar Press, 2004
Spec. 16-page	2.50
Spec.A Medieval (c).	6.00
Spec.B Classic (c)	6.00
Spec C Leather (c).	25.00
Spec. D Sketch (c)	30.00
Spec. prism (c).	13.00

...UNHOLY
Avatar Press, 2004
Preview	2.00
Preview variant (c)s	3.00
1 (of 3)	3.50
2	3.50
3	3.50
1a thru 3a variant (c).	@3.50
1b thru 3b wraparound (c).	@3.50
1c thru 3c premium (c)	@10.00
Preview Rock & Roll (c).	6.00

...WAR ANGEL
Avatar Press, 2005
1	3.50
1a variant (c)s	3.50
1b premium (c)	9.00
1c Fiery Reaper edition	6.00
1d Hells Belle (c)	6.00
2	3.50
2a variant (c)s	@3.50
2b premium (c)	9.00
3	3.50
3a variant (c)s	@3.50
3b premium (c)	9.00

...WAR ANGEL:
BOOK OF DEATH
Avatar Press, 2004
Spec.	2.50
Spec. variant(c)s	@3.00
Spec. Attitude ed.	6.00
Spec. Feral (c)	6.00
Spec. Bad Omen (c)	6.00
1 thru 3	@3.50
1a thru 3a variant (c)s	@3.50
1b thru 3b premium (c)	@9.00

BRILLIANT BOY
Circus Comics, 1997
1	3.00
2 Drake,pt.1 (of 5).	3.00
3 Drake,pt.2	2.50
4 Drake,pt.3	2.50
5 Drake,pt.4	2.50
6 Drake,pt.5	2.50
7 & 8 The Great Thunder,pt.1–2 .	@2.50

BRODIE'S LAW
Studio G, 2004
1 (of 6)	3.00
2 thru 6	@3.00

BROID
Eternity, 1990
1 thru 4	@2.50

BROKEN HALO: IS
THERE NOTHING SACRED
Broken Halos Comics, 1998
1 by Donald J. Vigil & Tim Vigil. . .	3.00
2	3.00
3	3.00
Ashcan, limited ed. 16-pg.	7.00

BROKEN HEROES
Sirius, 1998
1 by Fillbach Bros.	2.50

2 The Neon Graveyard	2.50
3 Rocket Man	2.50
4 thru 12 final issue	@2.50

BRONX
Eternity, 1991
1 A.Saichann Short Stories.	2.50
2 & 3	@2.50

Aircel
Reprint	3.00

BRU-HED
Schism Comics, 1994
1 Blockhead	3.00
1a 2nd printing	2.75
2 Blockhead	3.00
Vol. 1 Bru-Hed's Bunnies, Baddies & Buddies (1998).	2.50
Vol. 1 Bru-Hed's Guide to Gettin' Girls Now	2.50
Vol. 2 Bru-Hed's Guide	2.50

BRUTAL PLANET
Neko Press, 2002
1 by Matt Kimball & Dark One . . .	3.00
2	3.00
1a mini-print edition	5.00
3	3.00
4	3.00

BUBBA THE REDNECK
WEREWOLF
Brass Ball Comics 2003
1	3.00
2 thru 3	@3.00
4 thru 7	@3.00

Buce-N-Gar #2
© RAK

BUCE-N-GAR
RAK, 1996
1	2.50
2 thru 3	@2.50

BUCKAROO BANZAI
Moonstone Books, 2005
Preview	1.00
1 Return of the Screw.	3.50
1a variant (c)	3.50
1b Special edition (c)	4.50
2 thru 3	@3.50
2a thru 3a variant (c)s	@3.50
2b Dorman Special Ed (c)	4.50
3b Nestler Special Ed (c)	4.50

BUCK GODOT: ZAP GUN FOR HIRE
Palliard Press, 1993
1 I:Buck Godot 3.00
2 thru 6 . . . . @3.00
Studio Foglio, 1997
7 by Phil Foglio & Barb Kaalberg . . 3.00
8 finale 3.50

BUFFALO WINGS
Antarctic Press, 1993
1 . . . . 2.50
2 . . . . 2.50

BUG
Planet X Productions, 1997
1 . . . . 2.50
2 . . . . 2.50

B.U.G.G.S
Acetylene Comics, 2001
1 . . . . 2.50
1a variant San Diego Con (c) 3.00
2 thru 5 . . . . @2.50
3a variant (c) 2.50

BUGTOWN
Aeon, 2004
1 (of 6) MHo 3.00
2 thru 6 . . . . @3.00

BULLET CROW
Eclipse, 1987
1 & 2 Fowl of Fortune . . . . @2.50

BULWARK
Millennium, 1995
1 I:Bulwark 3.00
2 O:Bulwark 3.00

BUREAU OF MANA INVESTIGATION
Radio Comix, 2002
1 by C.Hanson & E.Garcia 3.00
2 thru 5 . . . . @3.00

BURGLAR BILL
Dancing Elephant Press, 2003
1 (of 6) by Paul Grist 3.00
2 thru 5 . . . . @3.00

BURNING BLUE, THE
Crusade Entertainment, 2001
1 BTi 3.00
1a computer gen (c) 3.00

BUSHIDO
Eternity, 1988
1 thru 6 . . . . @2.50

BUSHIDO
Americanime Productions 2006
1 Manga 3.50
2 thru 3 . . . . @4.00

BUZZARD
Cat Head Comics, 1990–95
1 thru 9 . . . . @3.00
10 thru 20 . . . . 3.50

BUZZBOY
Sky Dog Press, 1998
1 (of 4) by J. Gallagher & T. Ogline 3.00

---

2 by J. Gallagher & Steve Hauk . . . 3.00
3 . . . . 3.00
4 conclusion 3.00

CADILLACS AND DINOSAURS
Kitchen Sink, 1992
3-D comic 4.00

CALIBER CORE
Caliber, 1998
0 48pg 3.00
1 Gestalt cover 3.00
1a Rain People cover 3.00
1b Spiral cover 3.00
2 F:Al-Haquat 3.00

CALIBER DOUBLE FEATURE
Caliber, 2000
1 48-pg 4.00
2 . . . . 4.00
3 . . . . 4.00

CALIBER FOCUS
Caliber, 2000
1 48-pg 4.00
2 thru 4 . . . . @4.00

CALIBER PRESENTS
Caliber, 1989
1 TV,I:Crow 70.00
2 Deadworld 10.00
3 Realm 4.00
4 Baker Street 4.00
5 TV,Heart of Darkness, Fugitive . . 3.50
6 TV,Heart of Darkness, Fugitive . . 3.50
7 TV,Heart of Darkness,
   Dragonfeast 3.50
8 TV,Cuda,Fugitive 3.50
9 Baker Street,Sting Inc 3.50
10 Fugitive, The Edge 3.50
11 Ashes,Random Thoughts 3.50
12 Fugitive,Random Thoughts 3.50
13 Random Thoughts,Synergist . . . 3.50
14 Random Thoughts,Fugitive 3.50
15 Fringe, F:The Crow 4.00
16 Fugitive, The Verdict 3.50
17 Deadworld, The Verdict 3.50
18 Orlak,The Verdict 3.50
19 Taken Under,Go-Man 3.50
20 The Verdict,Go-Man 3.50
21 The Verdict,Go-Man 3.50
22 The Verdict,Go-Man 3.50
23 Go-Man,Heat Seeker 3.50
24 Heat Seeker,MacktheKnife 3.50
Christmas Spec. A:Crow,Deadworld
   Realm,Baker Street 10.00
Summer Spec. inc. the Silencers,
   Swords of Shar-Pei (preludes) . 4.00
1-Shot 3.00
1-shot Hybrid 3.00

CALIBER SPOTLIGHT
Caliber, 1995
1 F:Kabuki,Oz 3.00

CALIBRATIONS
Caliber, 1996
1 WEI,MCy,`Atmospherics,'pt.1 . . 3.00
2 WEI,MCy,`Atmospherics,'pt.2 . . 3.00
3 WEI,MCy,`Atmospherics,'pt.3 . . 3.00
4 WEI,MCy,`Atmospherics,'pt.4 . . 3.00
5 WEI,MCy,`Atmospherics,' concl. . 3.00

CALIFORNIA GIRLS
Eclipse, 1987
1 . . . . 2.50
2 thru 8 . . . . @2.50

CALL ME PRINCESS
CPM Manga, 1999
1 by Tomoko Taniguchi 3.00
1a variant cover 3.00
2 thru 6 . . . . @3.00

CAMELOT ETERNAL
Caliber, 1990
1 . . . . 3.00
2 . . . . 2.50
3 . . . . 2.50
4 Launcelot & Guinevere 2.50
5 Mordred Escapes 2.50
6 MorganLeFay returns from dead . 2.50
7 Revenge of Morgan 2.50
8 Launcelot flees Camelot 2.50

CANDYAPPLEBLACK
Good Intentions Paving, 2004
1 . . . . 3.50
2 thru 7 . . . . @3.50

Canton Kid #1
© Millennium

CANTON KID
Millennium, 1997
1 . . . . 2.50
Blam Comics, 2005
1 (of 4) 3.50
2 thru 4 . . . . @3.50

CAPTAIN CANUCK REBORN
Semple Comics, 1993–96
0 thru 3 by Richard Comely . . . . @2.50

CAPT. CONFEDERACY
Steel Dragon, 1985–88
1 adult 6.00
2 thru 4 . . . . @2.50
4a 2.50
5 thru 12 . . . . @2.50

CAPT. ELECTRON
Brick Computers Inc., 1986
1 . . . . 2.50
2 . . . . 2.50

CAPTAIN HARLOCK
Eternity, 1989
1 BDn.	3.00
1a 2nd printing	2.50
2 thru 3	@2.50
4 thru 13	@2.25
Christmas special.	2.50
Spec.#1 The Machine People	2.50

CAPTAIN HARLOCK DEATHSHADOW RISING
Eternity, 1991
1	2.75
2	2.50
3	2.50
4 Harlock/Nevich Truce.	2.50
5 Reunited with Arcadia Crew	2.50
6	3.00

CAPTAIN HARLOCK: FALL OF THE EMPIRE
Eternity, 1992
1	2.50
2 thru 4	@2.50

[ADVENTURES OF] CAPTAIN JACK
Fantagraphics, 1986
1	4.00
2 thru 12	@2.50

CAPTAIN KOALA
Koala Comics, 1997
1	3.00
2 thru 7	@2.50

CAPTAIN STERNN: RUNNING OUT OF TIME
Kitchen Sink, 1993
1 BWr(c) (1993)	6.00
2 BWr(c)	6.00
3 BWr(c) (1994)	6.00
4 BWr(c)	6.00

CAPTAIN THUNDER AND BLUE BOLT
Hero Graphics, 1987
1 New stories	3.50
2 Hard Targets	3.50

CARDCAPTOR SAKURA
Mixx Entertainment, 1999
1	3.00
2 thru 6 by Clamp	@3.00

Tokyopop.Com, 2000
7 thru 34	@3.00

CARTOON HISTORY OF THE UNIVERSE
Rip Off Press, 1987
1 Gonick art	2.50
2 Sticks & Stones	2.50
3 River Realms.	2.50
4 Old Testament.	2.50
5 Brains & Bronze.	2.50
6 These Athenians.	2.50
7 All about Athens.	2.50
8 and 9	@2.50

CASES OF SHERLOCK HOLMES
Renegade, 1986
1 thru 19	@2.50

CASTLE WAITING
Olio, 1997
1 by Linda Medley	10.00
1a 2nd printing	3.00
2	5.00
2a 2nd printing	3.00
3 Labors of Love.	3.00
4 birth of Lady Jain's baby	3.00
5	3.00
6 City Mouse, Country Mouse,pt.1	3.00
7 City Mouse, Country Mouse,pt.2	3.00
Spec. The Curse of Brambly Hedge (1996)	3.00
Spec. Curse of Brambly Hedge, revised 1998, 96-pg.	9.00

Vol. 2, 2000
1 by Linda Medley	3.00
2 Solicitine,pt.1	3.00
3 thru 7	@3.00
#13 (Vol. 2, #6)	3.00
#14 (Vol. 2, #7)	3.00
#15 thru #16	@3.00

Fantagraphics, 2006 [Vol. 2]
1 64-pg.	6.00
2	5.00
3 thru 12	@4.00

CAT & MOUSE
Aircel, 1989–92
1	4.00
2	3.00
3 thru 8	@2.50
9 Cat Reveals Identity	2.50
10 Tooth & Nail	2.50
11 Tooth & Nail.	2.50
12 Tooth & Nail, Demon.	2.50
13 `Good Times, Bad Times'.	2.50
14 Mouse Alone.	2.50
15 Champion ID revealed	2.50
16 Jerry Critically Ill	2.50
17 Kunoichi vs. Tooth.	2.50
18 Search for Organ Donor	2.50
Graphic Novel	10.00

CAT CLAW
Eternity, 1990
1 O:Cat Claw	2.75
1a 2nd printing	2.50
2 thru 9	@2.50

CATFIGHT
Lightning Comics, 1996
1 V:Prince Nightmare	4.00

Catfight, Dream Into Action #1
© Lightning Comics

1a Gold Edition	6.00
Spec.#1 Dream Warrior, V:The Slasher	2.75
Spec.#1 Dream intoAction,A:Creed.	3.00
Spec.#1a signed and numbered	8.00
Spec.#1 Escape From Limbo	2.75
Spec.#1a variant cover (1996).	2.75
Spec.#1b platinum cover	6.00
Spec.#1d variant nude cover.	8.00
Spec.#1 Sweet Revenge (1997)	3.00
Spec.#1a variant cover	3.00

CAT-MAN RETRO COMIC
AC Comics, 1997
0 by Bill Black & Mark Heike	6.00
1 thru 3	@6.00
Ashcan #1 I:Catman & Kitten	6.00

CAVEWOMAN
Basement/Caliber, 1994–95
1	70.00
1a by Budd Root 2nd printing	4.00
1b 3rd printing, new cover	3.00
2	40.00
2a 2nd printing	3.00
2 3rd printing, new cover	3.00
3 and 4	@35.00
5 Cavewoman vs. Klyde, Round Two	25.00
6	25.00

Basement Comics 2002
1-shot Movie special edition	9.00
1-shot movie oscar-gold edition	10.00
1-shot Summer Spec. My Kylde has Fleas (2004)	3.50
1-shot Prehistoric Pin-ups #4.	3.50
Spec. Meriem's Gallery #4.	3.25
Spec. Meriem's Gallery #4 spec.ed.	9.00
1-shot flip book Cavewoman Jungle Tales #3/ Blonde Medusa #1	3.75
1-shot Jungle Jam	3.50
1-shot Jungle Jam special ed.	7.00
Spec. Quest for Klyde (2008)	3.50

CAVEWOMAN INTERVENTION
Basement Comics, 2000
1 by Devon Massey	3.00
2	3.00
1a thru 2a variant (c)s.	@8.00
1b thru 2b foil (c) editions	@9.00
Spec. Klyde & Meriem 1-shot	3.00
Spec. Klyde & Meriem, KDM(c).	9.00
Spec. Klyde & Meriem green foil	9.00
Spec. Klyde & Meriem, Beauty, Blizzard & the Beast	8.00
Spec. Beauty, Blizzard, gold foil	9.00
Spec. Prehistoric Pin-ups	4.50
Spec. Prehistoric Pin-ups gold foil	9.00
Spec. Prehistoric Pin-ups, Book 2	4.50
Spec. Prehistoric Pin-ups 2,lim.	8.00
Spec. Prehistoric Pin-ups 2, gold foil	9.00
Spec. Prehistoric Pin-ups 3	4.50
Spec. Prehistoric Pin-Ups 3 Spec.	9.00
Cavewoman Cover Gallery, 48-pg.	4.50
Cavewoman Cover Gallery spec.	9.00
1-shot He Said, She Said	3.50
1-shot He Said, She Said special	9.00
1-shot Cavewoman The Movie	3.25

CAVEWOMAN: JUNGLE TALES
Basement Comics, 2000
1 by Budd Root	3.00
1a Frank Cho (c).	9.00
2	3.00
2a spec. edition.	8.00

CAVEWOMAN: MERIEM'S GALLERY
Basement Comics, 2001
1	3.50
2 pin-up book	3.50
3	3.00
4	3.25
1a thru 4a special ed.s	@9.00

CAVEWOMAN: MISSING LINK
Basement Comics, 1997
1 (of 4)	3.00
2 thru 4	@3.00

CAVEWOMAN: ODYSSEY
Caliber, 1999
1 (of 5)	3.00
2 thru 4	@3.00

Basement Comics, 2000
1a front row seat (c) by Budd Root	8.00
1b foil (c).	9.00
2a variant (c).	6.00
2b jungle green foil (c)	9.00
1-shot spec.	3.00
1-shot spec. variant (c)	8.00
1-shot spec. foil (c)	9.00

CAVEWOMAN: PANGAEAN SEA
Basement Comics, 1999
0 Origin issue	3.00
0 variant AAd (c).	8.00
0 special Root (c).	9.00
0 green foil (c).	9.00
0 alternate gold foil (c)	9.00
1 by Bud Root.	5.00
2	3.00
3 thru 8	@3.25
9	3.50
10	3.25
11	3.50
1a thru 9a special edition (c).	@8.00
1b thru 5b foil (c) editions	@9.00
6b thru 7b foil (c) editions	@8.00
Spec. #1 Prehistoric Pin-ups	4.50
Prologue	3.00

CAVEWOMAN: RAIN
Caliber, 1996
1 by Budd Root.	7.00
2	5.00
1a thru 2a 2nd printings	@3.00
3	4.00
4	4.00
5	3.50
3a thru 5a 2nd editions, new (c)s	@3.00
6 thru 8	@3.00

CAVEWOMEN: RAPTOR
Basement Comics, 2002
1 (of 2)	3.25
2	3.25
1a thru 2a special editions	@8.00
1b thru 2b Foil (c) editions	@9.00

CAVEWOMAN: RELOADED
Basement Comics, 2005
1 thru 5	@4.00
2a thru 3a special edition	@7.00

CECIL KUNKLE
Darkline Comics, 1987
1	2.50

CELESTIAL MECHANICS
Innovation, 1990
1 thru 3	@2.50

CELESTIAL ZONE
Asiapac Books, 2000
1 by Wee Tian Beng	9.00
2 thru 8	@9.00
9 152-pg.	9.00
11 Fantasy on Moonlit Lotus	9.00
12 THe Battle of Maling	9.00
13 Assault on Mt. Dream-Cloud.	10.00
14 An Onerous Battle.	10.00
15 Capturing Mt. Dream-Cloud	10.00
16 Chi Xue & Xuan Hua injured	10.00

TCZ Studio, 2002
17 thru 25 152-pg.	@10.00

Vol. 2
1	10.00
2 thru 16	@9.50

CEMENT SHOOZ
Horse Feathers, 1991
1 with color pin-up	2.50

CEMETARIANS, THE
Amaze Ink/SLG, 2006
1	3.00
2 thru 6	@3.00

Cerebus #15
© *Aardvark-Vanaheim*

CEREBUS
Aardvark–Vanaheim, 1977
0	3.00
0a Gold Ed.	10.00
1 B:DS(s&a),I:Cerebus	500.00
1a Counterfeit	10.00
2 DS,V:Succubus	110.00
3 DS,I:Red Sophia	125.00
4 DS,I:Elrod	75.00
5 DS,A:The Pigs	60.00
6 DS,I:Jaka	60.00
7 DS,R:Elrod.	45.00
8 DS,A:Conniptins	45.00
9 DS,I&V:K'cor	45.00
10 DS,R:Red Sophia	45.00
11 DS,I:The Cockroach	30.00
12 DS,R:Elrod	30.00
13 DS,I:Necross.	25.00
14 DS,V:Shadow Crawler	25.00
15 DS,V: Shadow Crawler	25.00
16 DS, at the Masque	20.00
17 DS, 'Champion'	20.00
18 DS,Fluroc	20.00
19 DS,I:Perce & Greet-a	20.00
20 DS,Mind Game.	20.00
21 DS,A:CaptCockroach,rare	40.00
22 DS,D:Elrod	20.00
23 thru 29 DS	@10.00
30 DS,Debts.	15.00
31 DS,Chasing Cootie	15.00
32 DS.	8.00
33 DS,Friction	5.00
34 thru 50 DS.	@6.00
51 DS,(scarce).	12.00
52 DS.	5.00
53 DS,C:Wolveroach	7.00
54 DS,I:Wolveroach	9.00
55 DS,A:Wolveroach	8.00
56 DS,A:Wolveroach	8.00
57 DS	5.00
58 DS	5.00
59 DS,Memories,pt.V.	5.00
60 DS,more vignettes	5.00
61 DS,A:Flaming Carrot.	6.00
62 DS,A:Flaming Carrot.	6.00
63 thru 66 DS.	@5.00
67 thru 70 DS.	@5.00
71 thru 81 DS.	@4.00
82 thru 100 DS.	@3.50
101 thru 125 DS.	@3.00
126 thru 130 DS.	@2.50
131 thru 146 DS.	@4.00
147 Neil Gaiman, DS.	6.00
148 thru 150 DS.	@3.00
151 DS,B:Mothers & Daughters, Book 1: Flight,pt.1	4.00
152 thru 155 DS,Flight,pt.2–pt.5	@4.00
151a thru 53a 2nd printings	@4.00
156 thru 160 DS,Flight,pt.6–pt.10	@3.00
161 DS,Flight,pt.11, Bone story	15.00
162 DS,E:M&D,Bk.1:Flight pt.12	3.00
163 DS, Book 2: Women,pt.1	2.75
164 thru 174 Women,pt.2–12.	@3.00
175 thru 186 Reads,pt.1–12	@3.00
187 DS, Book 4:Minds,pt.1	3.00
188 thru 199 Minds,pt.2–13	@3.00
200	3.50
201 thru 219 Guys,pt.1 to pt.19.	@3.00
220 thru 231 Rick'sStory,pt.1–12	@3.00
232 thru 265 GoingHome,pt.1–34	@2.50
266 thru 296 LatterDays,pt.1– pt.31	@2.50
297 Latter Days, pt.32	2.50
298 Latter Days, pt.33	2.50
299 Latter Days, pt.34	2.50
300 Latter Days, pt.35, finale.	2.50
Spec.#1 Cerebus Companion	3.50
Spec. Following Cerebus #1	4.00
Spec. Following Cerebus #2	4.00
Spec. Following Cerebus #3	4.00
Spec. Following Cerebus #4	4.00
Spec. Following Cerebus #5	4.00
Spec. Following Cerebus #6 thru #10	@4.00
Spec. #1 Cerebus Jam MA,BHa,TA, WE,A:Spirit (1985).	9.00

Reprints:
1A thru 28A DS rep	@2.50

CEREBUS CHURCH & STATE
Aardvark–Vanaheim, 1991
1 DS rep #51	2.50
2 thru 30 DS rep #52-#80	@2.50

CEREBUS HIGH SOCIETY
Aardvark–Vanaheim, 1990
1 thru 14 DS (biweekly)	@2.50
15 thru 24 DS rep.	@2.50
25 DS rep. #50, final	2.50

CHAINSAW VIGILANTE
New England Press
1 Tick Spinoff 3.25
2 & 3 . . . . @2.75

CHANGE COMMANDER GOKU II
Antarctic Press, 1996
1 (of 4) by Ippongi Bang 3.00
2 thru 3 . . . . @3.00

Charlie Chan #4
© Eternity

CHARLIE CHAN
Eternity, 1989
1 thru 6 . . . . @2.50

CHARM SCHOOL
Amaze Ink/SLG, 2000
1 by Elizabeth Watasin 3.00
2 . . . . 3.00
4 Vampire Dragster Dean 3.00
5 Vampire Dragster Dean 3.00
6 fight to the death 3.00
7 thru 9 . . . . 3.00
10 . . . . 10.00

CHASER PLATOON
Aircel, 1990–91
1 Interstellar War 2.50
2 Ambush 2.50
3 New Weapon 2.50
4 Saringer Battle Robot 2.50
5 Behind Enemy Lines 2.50
6 Operation Youthtest 2.50

CHERUBS: PARADISE LOST
Desperado Publishing, 2007
1 (of 4) 4.00
2 thru 4 . . . . @4.00

CHESTY SANCHEZ
Antarctic Press, 1995
1 & 2 . . . . @3.00
Giant Size Spec. #1 (1999) 6.00

CHIBI-POP MANGA
Chibi-Pop (1998)
2 thru 6 64-pg. . . . . @4.00

VOL 2
1 72-pg. 4.00
2 thru 6 . . . . @4.00

CHICANOS
IDW Publishing, 2005
1 . . . . 4.00
2 thru 9 . . . . @4.00

CHILDREN OF THE GRAVE
Shooting Star Comics, 2005
1 (of 4) 3.00
2 thru 4 . . . . @3.00

CHINA & JAZZ
ABC Comics, 1999
1 RCI 3.00

VOL. 2
1 (of 3) RCI 3.00
2 RCI 3.00
Spec. Raising Hell 5.00

...CODE NAME DOUBLE IMPACT
High Impact, 1996
1 and 2 . . . . @3.00

...TRIGGER HAPPY
ABC Comics, 1998
1 (of 4) by Clayton Henry 3.00
1a Jazz Bikini cover 4.00
1b China Bikini cover 4.00
1c gold variant cover 6.00
2 . . . . 3.00
2a Playtoy edition 6.00
2b Mercenary edition 6.00
2c Gold edition 6.00
Spec. Trigger Happy Special 3.00
Spec.A manga cover 8.00
Spec. China & Jazz 3.00

...SUPERSTARS
ABC Studios, 1999
1 (of 3) 3.00
Spec. China Platinum 3.00

CHIRALITY
CPM Manga Comics, 1997
6 by Satoshi Urushihara, SS(c) . . . 3.00
7 final battle for Shiori's life 3.00
8 thru 18 . . . . @3.00
Spec. Gallery, pin-up book 4.00

CHIRALITY: TO THE PROMISED LAND
CPM Comics, 1997
1 by Satoshi Urushihara 3.00
2 thru 4 . . . . @3.00

CHISUJI
Antarctic Press, 2005
1 (of 6) 3.00
2 thru 3 . . . . @3.00

CIRCLE WEAVE, THE
Indigo Bean Productions, 1995
1 Apprentice to a God 2.50
2 Apprentice to a God,pt.2 . . . . 2.50
3 Apprentice to a God,pt.3 . . . . 2.50
4 Apprentice to a God,pt.4 . . . . 2.50
5 Apprentice to a God,pt.5 . . . . 2.50

CLAN APIS
Active Synapse, 1998
1 (of 5) by Jay Hosler, F:Bees 3.00
2 F:Nyuki, Zambur 3.00
3 . . . . 3.00

4 . . . . 3.00
5 conclusion 3.00

CLERKS: THE COMIC BOOK
Oni Press, 1998
1 KSm & Jim Mahfood 12.00
1a 2nd printing 4.00
Spec. The Lost Scene 5.00
Holiday Special 5.00

CLIFFHANGER COMICS
AC Comics, 1990
1 Masked Marvel, rep. 2.50
2 Don Winslow, rep. 2.50
1A & 2A . . . . @3.00

COBB: OFF THE LEASH
IDW Publishing, 2006
1 . . . . 4.00
2 thru 3 . . . . @4.00

COBRA
Viz, 1990–91
1 thru 6 . . . . @3.00
7 . . . . 3.25
8 V:SnowHawks 3.25
9 Zados 3.25
10 thru 12 . . . . @3.25

COCOPIAZO
Amaze Ink/SLG, 2004
1 . . . . 3.00
2 thru 6 . . . . @3.00

COFFIN
Oni Press, 2000
1 . . . . 3.00
2 thru 4 . . . . @3.00

COLD BLOODED CHAMELEON COMMANDOS
Blackthorne, 1986
1 thru 7 . . . . @2.50

COLD EDEN
Legacy, 1995
1 Last City on Earth 2.50
2 V:Mutant Hunting Pack 2.50
3 D6 Tower 2.50

COLE BLACK
Rocky Hartberg, 1980
1 Newspaper strip format 15.00
2 thru 4 . . . . @10.00
5 . . . . 12.00

Vol. 2, 1985
1 . . . . 3.50
2 & 3 . . . . @2.50

COLT
K-Z Comics
1 . . . . 4.00
2 pin-up by Laird 6.00
2 pin-up by Henbeck 2.50
3 thru 5 . . . . @2.50

COMIC BOOK HEAVEN
Amaze Ink/SLG, 2001

Vol. 2
1 . . . . 2.50
2 thru 9 . . . . @2.50
10 48-pg. 3.50

COMICS EXPRESS
Eclipse, 1989
1 thru 4 . . . . @3.00
5 thru 11 . . . . @4.00

COMING OF APHRODITE
Hero Graphics
1 Aphrodite/modern day 4.00

COMMAND REVIEW
Thoughts & Images, 1986
1 rep. Albedo #1-4 . . . . 6.00
2 rep. Albedo #5-8 . . . . 4.00
3 rep. Albedo #9-13 . . . . 4.00

CONQUEROR
Harrier, 1984–86
1 . . . . 3.50
2 thru 4 . . . . @2.50
5 thru 9 . . . . @2.50

CONSPIRACY COMICS
Revolutionary, 1991
1 Marilyn Monroe 2.50
2 Who Killed JFK 2.50
3 Who Killed RFK 2.50

CONSTRUCT
Caliber New Worlds, 1996
1 (of 6) PJe,LDu, sci-fi,48pg 4.00
2 PJe,LDu 3.00
3 PJe,LDu 3.00
4 PJe,LDu 3.00
5 PJe,LDu 3.00
6 PJe,LDu, conclusion 3.00

CORPORATE NINJA
Amaze Ink/SLG, 2005
1 . . . . 3.00
2 thru 3 . . . . @3.00

CORRECTOR YUI
Tokyopop Press, 2001
1 48-pg. 3.00
2 . . . . 3.00
3 . . . . 3.00
4 . . . . 3.00

CORTO MALTESE: BALLAD OF THE SALT SEA
NBM, 1997
1 by Hugo Pratt 3.00
1 a 2nd printing 3.00
2 by Hugo Pratt 3.00
3 Escondida 3.00
4 . . . . 3.00
5 . . . . 3.00
6 . . . . 3.00
7 final issue 3.00

COSMIC HEROES
Eternity, 1988
1 Buck Rogers rep. 2.50
2 thru 6 Buck Rogers rep. . . . . . . @2.50
7 thru 9 Buck Rogers rep. . . . . . . @2.50
10 . . . . 3.50
11 . . . . 4.00

COUNTER PARTS
Tundra, 1993
1 thru 3 . . . . @3.00

Cosmic Heroes #7
© *Eternity*

COURTNEY CRUMRIN:

AND THE NIGHT THINGS
Oni Press, 2002
1 (of 4) by Ted Naifeh 3.00
2 thru 4 . . . . @3.00

...IN THE TWILIGHT KINGDOM
Oni Press, 2003
1 (of 4) 3.00
2 thru 4 . . . . @3.00

...THE COVEN OF MYSTICS
Oni Press, 2003
1 (of 4) by Ted Naifeh 3.00
2 thru 4 . . . . @3.00

...& THE PRINCE OF NOWHERE
Oni Press, 2007
1-shot 6.00

COVENTRY
Fantagraphics, 1996
1 BWg, `The Frogs of God' 4.00
2 BWg, `Thirteen Dead Guys
   Named Bob' 4.00
3 BWg 4.00
4 . . . . 4.00

COWBOY BEBOP
Tokyopop Press, 2002
1 (of 4) by Yukata Nanten 3.00
2 thru 4 . . . . @3.00
Spec. Complete Anime Guide #1. . 13.00
Spec. Complete Anime
   Guide #2–#6 . . . . @13.00

CRAY BABY ADVENTURES, THE
Electric Milk, 1997
1 by Art Baltazar 3.00
TV Comics, 1997
1 2nd printing 3.00
2 thru 5 . . . . @3.00
Advent.Spec.San Diego Con
   lim. ed. 5.00

...WRATH OF THE PEDDIDLERS
TV Comics, 1998
1 (of 3) by Art Baltazar 3.00
2 . . . . 3.00

3 concl. 3.00

CREATURES OF THE ID
Caliper, 1990
1 F. Einstein(a) 30.00

CREED
Hall of Heroes, 1994
1 TKn,I:Mark Farley 18.00
1A Wizard Ace edition rep. 15.00
2 TKn,Camping 20.00

CREED
Lightning Comics, 1995
1-shot TKn retelling of #1&#2 . . . . 2.75
See also: Color

CREED/TEENAGE MUTANT NINJA TURTLES
Lightning Comics, 1996
1 TKn(c) 3.00
2 TKn(c) 3.00
1 Gold Collector's Edition 6.00
1 Platinum Edition. 10.00

CREED: CRANIAL DISORDER
Lightning Comics, 1996
1 . . . . 4.00
1A Previews variant cover 3.00
1B Platinum Edition 6.00
1C signed platinum edition 8.00
2 . . . . 3.00
2b variant cover 3.00
3 . . . . 3.00
3b variant cover 3.00
3c limited edition 10.00

CREED: THE GOOD SHIP & THE NEW JOURNEY HOME
Lightning Comics, 1998
1 . . . . 3.00
1a variant cover 3.00
1b limited edition. 10.00

CREED: MECHANICAL EVOLUTION
Gearbox Press, 2000
1 (of 2) 3.00
1a variant (c). 3.00
1b signed 10.00
2 . . . . 3.00

CREED: USE YOUR DELUSION
Avatar Press, 1998
1 (of 2) by Trent Kaniuga 3.00
1 white leather 30.00
2 . . . . 3.00
2 deluxe 5.00
GN rep. #1–#2 . . . . 4.00

CRIMEBUSTER
ACG Comics, 2000
1 (of 3) F:Dick Tracy 3.00
2 & 3 . . . . @3.00

CRIME CLASSICS
Eternity, 1988
1 thru 11 rep. Shadow comic
   strip . . . . @2.50
12 . . . . 2.50

CRIMSON DREAMS
Crimson
1 thru 11 . . . . @2.50

CRITTERS
Fantagraphics Books, 1986–90
1 SS,Usagi Yojimbo,Cutey 7.00
2 Captain Jack,Birthright. 6.00
3 SS,Usagi Yojimbo,Gnuff 5.00
4 Gnuff,Birthright. 5.00
5 Birthright 5.00
6 SS,Usagi Yojimbo,Birthright. . . . 5.00
7 SS,Usagi Yojimbo,Jack Bunny . . 5.00
8 SK,Animal Graffiti,Lizards 5.00
9 Animal Graffiti 5.00
10 SS,Usagi Yojimbo 5.00
11 SS,Usagi Yojimbo, ... 3.00
12 Birthright II 2.50
13 Birthright II,Gnuff. 2.50
14 SS,Usagi Yojimbo,BirthrightII . . 3.00
15 Birthright II,CareBears 2.50
16 SS,Groundthumper,Gnuff 2.50
17 Birthright II,Lionheart. 2.50
18 Dragon's 2.50
19 Gnuff,Dragon's 2.50
20 Gnuff 2.50
21 Gnuff. 2.50
22 Watchdogs,Gnuff 2.50
23 Flexi-Disc,X-Mas Issue 4.00
24 Angst,Lizards,Gnuff. 2.50
25 Lionheart,SBi,Gnuff. 2.50
26 Angst,Gnuff. 2.50
27 SS,Ground Thumper. 2.50
28 Blue Beagle,Lionheart 2.50
29 Lionheart,Gnuff 2.50
30 Radical Dog,Gnuff 2.50
31 SBi,Gnuffs,Lizards 2.50
32 Lizards,Big Sneeze. 2.50
33 Gnuff,Angst,Big Sneeze. 2.50
34 Blue Beagle vs. Robohop. 2.50
35 Lionheart,Fission Chicken 2.50
36 Blue Beagle,Fission Chicken . . . 2.50
37 Fission Chicken 2.50
38 SS,double size,Usagi Yojimbo . 4.00
39 Fission Chicken 2.50
40 Gnuff 2.50
41 Duck'Bill Platypus 2.50
42 Glass Onion 2.50
43 Lionheart. 2.50
44 Watchdogs 2.50
45 Ambrose the Frog 2.50
46 Lionheart 2.50
47 Birthright 2.50
48 Birthright 2.50
49 Birthright 2.50
50 SS,Neil the Horse, UsagiYojimbo 5.00
Spec.1 Albedo,rep+new 10pgStory . 2.50

CROSSFIRE
Eclipse, 1987
Prev. Color
18 thru 26 DSp. . . . . @2.50

CROW, THE
Caliber, 1989
1 . . . . 55.00
1a 2nd Printing 6.00
1b 3rd Printing 5.00
2 . . . . 35.00
2a 2nd Printing 4.00
2b 3rd Printing 4.00
3 . . . . 25.00
3a 2nd Printing 4.00
4 . . . . 25.00

Tundra, 1992
1 reps. Crow #1, #2 . . . . 15.00
2 . . . . 8.00
3 . . . . 10.00

CROW, THE: DEAD TIME
Kitchen Sink, 1996
1 . . . . 5.00
2 . . . . 4.00
3 . . . . 3.00

CROW, THE: DEMON IN DISGUISE
Kitchen Sink, 1997
1 (of 4) by John J. Miller &
Dean Ormston 3.00
2 . . . . 3.00
3 . . . . 3.00

The Crow: FLesh and Blood #3
© Kitchen Sink

CROW, THE: FLESH AND BLOOD
Kitchen Sink, 1996
1 thru 3 . . . . @3.00

CROW, THE: WAKING NIGHTMARES
Kitchen Sink, 1997
1 PhH 3.00
2 thru 4 PhH . . . . @3.00

CROW, THE: WILD JUSTICE, 1996
Kitchen Sink
1 thru 3 CAd . . . . @3.00

CROW/RAZOR: KILL THE PAIN
London Night, 1998
1 (of 3) JOb,EHr, ... 3.00
1b EHr & Jerry Beck, Director's
Cut, 40pg. 5.00
2 . . . . 3.00
3 . . . . 3.00
4 . . . . 3.00
1a thru 4a Ministry of Night (c) . . @5.00
Spec. Finale 3.00
Spec. Finale, Ministry (c) 5.00
0 . . . . 3.00
0a Ministry (c). 5.00
1-shotA Tour Book, cover A 5.00
1-shotB Tour Book, cover B 5.00
1-shotC Tour Book, cover C 5.00
1-shotD Tour Book, ministry edition. 5.00

Spec. Nocturnal Masque 48-pg. . . . 6.00
EH! Productions, 1999
Spec. The Lost Chapter 5.00
Spec. The Lost Chapter,
Elite Fan Ed. 6.00

CROW OF THE BEAR CLAN
Blackthorne, 1986
1 . . . . 2.50
2 thru 6 . . . . @2.50

CRUSADERS
Guild, 1982
1 Southern Knights, Mag. size . . . 10.00

CRUSHER JOE
Ironcat, 1999
1 by Haruka Takachiho 3.00
2 thru 6 . . . . @3.00

CRY FOR DAWN
Cry For Dawn, 1989–90
1 . . . . 95.00
1a 2nd Printing 35.00
1b 3rd Printing 22.00
2 . . . . 55.00
2a 2nd Printing 18.00
3 . . . . 38.00
4 . . . . 18.00
5 . . . . 18.00
6 . . . . 18.00
7 Corporate Ladder,Rock A
Bye Baby 12.00
8 Decay,This is the Enemy 12.00
9 . . . . 12.00
1-shot Subtle Violents,F:Ryder . . 3.00

CRYING FREEMAN
Viz, 1989
1 . . . . 4.00
2 . . . . 3.50
3 thru 5 . . . . @3.50
6 thru 8 . . . . @3.00

CRYING FREEMAN II
Viz, 1990–91
1 . . . . 4.00
2 . . . . 3.50
3 . . . . 3.50
4 thru 6 . . . . @3.00
7 V:Bugnug 3.00
8 Emu & The Samurai Sword 3.00
9 Final Issue 3.00

CRYING FREEMAN III
Viz, 1991
1 thru 10 . . . . @4.00

CRYING FREEMAN IV
Viz, 1992
1 thru 3 . . . . @4.00
4 thru 8 . . . . @2.75

CRY FREEMAN V
Viz, 1993
1 Return to Japan 4.00
2 A:Tateoka-assassin 4.00
3 . . . . 4.00
4 A:Bagwana. 4.00
5 V:Tsunaike 4.00
6 V:Aido Family. 4.00
7 V:Tsunaike 4.00
GN:Taste of Revenge 15.00

CRYPT OF DAWN
Sirius, 1996
```
1 JLi(c) . . . . . . . . . . . . . . . . . . . . . 6.00
1 variant cover . . . . . . . . . . . . . . . 9.00
2 JLi(c) . . . . . . . . . . . . . . . . . . . . . 4.00
3 . . . . . . . . . . . . . . . . . . . . . . . . . 3.00
4 JLi(c) . . . . . . . . . . . . . . . . . . . . . 3.00
5 JLi(c) . . . . . . . . . . . . . . . . . . . . . 3.00
6 Vanguard of Comics . . . . . . . . . 3.00
```

CRYPTOZOO CREW
NBM Books, 2005
```
1 . . . . . . . . . . . . . . . . . . . . . . . . . 3.00
2 The Improbable Snowman . . . . . 3.00
Spec. Mothman con edition . . . . . . 3.00
```

CRYSTAL BREEZE
High Impact, 1996
```
1 thru 3 . . . . . . . . . . . . . . . . . @3.00
Spec.#1 Crystal Breeze Unleashed . 3.00
Spec.#1 Crystal Breeze Revenge . . 3.00
Spec.#1a gold edition cover . . . . . 10.00
```

CSI: DYING IN
THE GUTTERS
IDW Publishing, 2006
```
1 . . . . . . . . . . . . . . . . . . . . . . . . . 4.00
2 thru 3 . . . . . . . . . . . . . . . . . @4.00
```

CUBE
Class Enterpriese, 1998
```
1 by Patrick Fillion . . . . . . . . . . . . 3.00
2 . . . . . . . . . . . . . . . . . . . . . . . . . 3.00
3 . . . . . . . . . . . . . . . . . . . . . . . . . 3.00
4 . . . . . . . . . . . . . . . . . . . . . . . . . 3.00
5 . . . . . . . . . . . . . . . . . . . . . . . . . 3.00
```

CUDA
Rebel Studios
```
1 I:Cuda,Zora,V:Shanga Bai . . . . . . 2.50
CUDA B.C. (Rebel Studios) signed 13.00
```
Avatar Press, 1998
```
1 (of 4) by Tim & Joe Vigil . . . 3.50
2 . . . . . . . . . . . . . . . . . . . . . . . . . 3.50
3 . . . . . . . . . . . . . . . . . . . . . . . . . 3.50
4 . . . . . . . . . . . . . . . . . . . . . . . . . 3.50
1 thru 4 gore (c)s . . . . . . . . . . @6.00
0 80-pg. . . . . . . . . . . . . . . . . . . . . 8.00
0a Gore (c) . . . . . . . . . . . . . . . . . . 9.00
```

CUTEY BUNNY
Army Surplus Comix, 1982
```
1 . . . . . . . . . . . . . . . . . . . . . . . . . 7.00
2 . . . . . . . . . . . . . . . . . . . . . . . . . 4.00
3 . . . . . . . . . . . . . . . . . . . . . . . . . 4.00
4 . . . . . . . . . . . . . . . . . . . . . . . . . 4.00
```
Eclipse, 1985
```
5 X-Men, Batman parody . . . . . . . 3.00
```

CUTIE HONEY
Ironcat, 1997
```
1 crime fighting android . . . . . . . . 3.00
2 . . . . . . . . . . . . . . . . . . . . . . . . . 3.00
3 Wonderful Mask. . . . . . . . . . . . . 3.00
4 thru 6 . . . . . . . . . . . . . . . . . @3.00
```
VOL 2, 1998
CUTIE HONEY '90
```
1 Sorayama cover. . . . . . . . . . . . . 3.00
2 thru 6 . . . . . . . . . . . . . . . . . @3.00
```

CYBER 7
Eclipse, 1989
```
1 by Shuho Itahashi . . . . . . . . . . . 2.50
2 thru 7 . . . . . . . . . . . . . . . . . @2.50
```

Cyber 7, Book 2 #7
© Rockland

Book 2: Rockland, 1990
```
1 . . . . . . . . . . . . . . . . . . . . . . . . . 2.50
2 . . . . . . . . . . . . . . . . . . . . . . . . . 2.50
3 thru 7 . . . . . . . . . . . . . . . . . @2.50
8 thru 10 . . . . . . . . . . . . . . . . @2.50
```

CYBERFROG
Hall of Heroes, 1994
```
1 I:Cyberfrog. . . . . . . . . . . . . . . . . 5.00
1a 2nd printing . . . . . . . . . . . . . . 2.50
2 V:Ben Riley . . . . . . . . . . . . . . . . 4.00
2a 2nd printing . . . . . . . . . . . . . . 2.50
```

CYBERFROG
Harris, 1997
```
1 3rd Anniv. Special . . . . . . . . . . . 3.00
1a Walt Simonson(c) . . . . . . . . . . 6.00
1b signed & numbered . . . . . . . . 9.00
2 . . . . . . . . . . . . . . . . . . . . . . . . . 3.50
2a variant cover . . . . . . . . . . . . . 4.00
3 . . . . . . . . . . . . . . . . . . . . . . . . . 3.50
4 . . . . . . . . . . . . . . . . . . . . . . . . . 3.50
4a signed . . . . . . . . . . . . . . . . . . . 9.00
Ashcan Cyberfrog: Amphibionix. . . 6.00
Spec. Cyberfrog Amphibionix(2001) 3.00
```

CYBERFROG VS CREED
Harris, 1997
```
1 . . . . . . . . . . . . . . . . . . . . . . . . . 3.50
1 Creed vs. Cyberfrog, alternate
    edition . . . . . . . . . . . . . . . . . . . 9.00
```

CYBERZONE
Jet Black Grafiks, 1994
```
1 thru 8 Never-never Land . . . . . @2.50
```

CYCLONE BILL
AND THE TALL TALES
Moonstone Books, 2004
```
1 . . . . . . . . . . . . . . . . . . . . . . . . . 3.00
2 . . . . . . . . . . . . . . . . . . . . . . . . . 3.00
3 . . . . . . . . . . . . . . . . . . . . . . . . . 3.00
```

CYCLOPS
Blackthorne
```
1 Mini-series . . . . . . . . . . . . . . . . . 2.50
2 . . . . . . . . . . . . . . . . . . . . . . . . . 2.50
3 . . . . . . . . . . . . . . . . . . . . . . . . . 2.50
```

CYCOPS
Comics Interview, 1988
```
1 Mini-series, BSz. . . . . . . . . . . . . 2.50
2 . . . . . . . . . . . . . . . . . . . . . . . . . 2.50
3 . . . . . . . . . . . . . . . . . . . . . . . . . 2.50
```

CYNDER
Immortelle Studios, 1995
```
1 I:Cynder. . . . . . . . . . . . . . . . . . . 5.00
2 . . . . . . . . . . . . . . . . . . . . . . . . . 3.00
3 conclusion . . . . . . . . . . . . . . . . . 2.50
```
Second Series, 1996
```
1 thru 3 . . . . . . . . . . . . . . . . . . . . 3.00
```

CYNDER/HELLINA
Immortelle Studios, 1996
```
Spec. 1 x-over . . . . . . . . . . . . . . . 3.00
```

DAEMONIFUGE:
THE SCREAMING CAGE
Black Library, 2002
```
1 by Kev Walker . . . . . . . . . . . . . . 2.50
2 and 3 . . . . . . . . . . . . . . . . . @2.50
```

DAIKAZU
Ground Zero
```
1 . . . . . . . . . . . . . . . . . . . . . . . . . 5.00
2 . . . . . . . . . . . . . . . . . . . . . . . . . 3.00
3 . . . . . . . . . . . . . . . . . . . . . . . . . 3.00
1a thru 3a 2nd Printings . . . . . . @2.50
4 thru 8 . . . . . . . . . . . . . . . . . @2.50
```

DAISY KUTTER
Viper Comics, 2004
```
1 . . . . . . . . . . . . . . . . . . . . . . . . . 4.00
2 thru 4 . . . . . . . . . . . . . . . . . @4.00
```

DA'KOTA
Millennium, 1997
```
1 by Pavlet & Petersen . . . . . . . . . 3.00
1 signed . . . . . . . . . . . . . . . . . . . . 5.00
1 foil edition. . . . . . . . . . . . . . . . . 9.00
2 . . . . . . . . . . . . . . . . . . . . . . . . . 3.00
2 foil edition. . . . . . . . . . . . . . . . . 5.00
3 . . . . . . . . . . . . . . . . . . . . . . . . . 3.00
3a variant cover . . . . . . . . . . . . . 3.00
3b foil deluxe edition. . . . . . . . . . 7.00
Spec.#1 Orig.Art Edition . . . . . . . 10.00
```

DAMNED, THE
Oni Press, 2006
```
1 . . . . . . . . . . . . . . . . . . . . . . . . . 3.50
2 thru 5 . . . . . . . . . . . . . . . . . @3.50
```

DAMPYR
IDW Publishing, 2005
```
GN #1 Devil's Son . . . . . . . . . . . . 8.00
GN #2 Night Tribe . . . . . . . . . . . . 8.00
GN #3 Sand Specters . . . . . . . . . . 8.00
GN #4 Nocturne in Red . . . . . . . . 8.00
GN #5 Under the Stone Bridge . . . 8.00
GN #6 Lamiah . . . . . . . . . . . . . . . 8.00
GN #7 From the Darkness. . . . . . . 8.00
GN #8 Coast of Skeletons. . . . . . . 8.00
GN #9 Forbidden Zone . . . . . . . . . 8.00
GN #10 House of Blood. . . . . . . . . 8.00
```

DANGEROUS TIMES
Evolution, 1989
```
1 MK . . . . . . . . . . . . . . . . . . . . . . 2.50
2 MA(c). . . . . . . . . . . . . . . . . . . . . 2.50
2a 2nd printing . . . . . . . . . . . . . . 2.50
3 MR(c). . . . . . . . . . . . . . . . . . . . . 2.50
3a 2nd printing . . . . . . . . . . . . . . 2.50
4 thru 6 GP(c) . . . . . . . . . . . . . @2.50
```

DAN TURNER HOLLYWOOD DETECTIVE
Eternity, 1991
1 `Darkstar of Death` 2.50
Spec.#1 Dan Turner, Homicide
  Hunch, Dan Turner Framed . . . 2.50
Spec.#1 Dan Turner, The Star
  Chamber, Death of Folly
  Hempstead 2.50

DARK ANGEL
Boneyard, 1991
1 by Hart Fisher 2.50
2 . . . . 2.50

DARK ANGEL
Boneyard, 1997
1 by H.Fisher & J.Helkowski. 2.50
2 . . . . 2.50
3 by Hart Fisher & John Cassaday. 2.50
4 The Quiet Demon 2.50
Spec.#1 Dark Angel/Bill the Bull,
  48-pg. (1998). 5.00
Spec. 1999. . . . . 5.00
GN Last Decade Dead Century. . 16.00
GN deluxe 20.00

DARK ANGEL
CPM Manga, 1999
1 by Kia Asamiya 3.00
2 thru 9 . . . . @3.00
10 thru 31 . . . . @3.00

DARK ASSASSIN
Silverwolf, 1987
1 thru 3 . . . . @2.50
Vol. 2
1 thru 5 . . . . @2.50

DARK FANTASIES
Dark Fantasy, 1994–97
0 Donna Mia foil (c) 8.00
0 Destiny Angel foil (c) 7.50
1 Jli (c) 8.00
1a test print Jli (c). 9.00
1 2nd printing 4.00
1 signed & numbered 8.00
2 Kevin J. Taylor Girl (c) 4.00
2a foil stamped 3.00
3 JOb Crow (c) 4.00

Dark Fantasies #6
© Dark Fantasy

3a foil stamped 3.50
4 . . . . 4.00
4a foil stamped 3.50
5 . . . . 4.00
5a foil stamped 3.50
6 Angel Destiny. 4.00
6a foil stamped 3.50
7 . . . . 4.00
7a foil stamped 3.50
8 . . . . 4.00
8 Blue cover 3.50
8 Red cover 3.50
8 deluxe foil-enhanced 4.00
9 Destiny Angel (c) 3.50
9a Destiny Angel, red foil (c) 4.00
9b Horror (c) 3.50
9c Horror, red foil (c). 4.00
10 . . . . 3.50
10a red foil (c) 4.00
Spec.#1 Summers Eve Pin-up. . . 3.00
Spec.#1 foil-stamped 3.50

DARK FRINGE
Brainstorm, 1996
1 . . . . 3.00

DARK FRINGE: SPIRITS OF THE DEAD
Brainstorm, 1997
1 by Eman Torre & John Kisse . . . 3.00
2 concl. 3.00

DARK ISLAND
Davdez Arts, 1998
1 by Barry Blair & Colin Chan. . . . 2.50
2 thru 4 . . . . @2.50

DARKLIGHT: PRELUDE
Sirius, 2000
1 (of 3) by Teri Sue Wood. 3.00
2 . . . . 3.00
3 concl 3.00

DARK LORD
RAK
1 thru 3 . . . . @2.50

DARK MANGA
London Night
1 Featuring Demonique 5.00

DARK MUSE
Dark Muse Productions
1 with mini-comic 3.50
1a with mini-comic 5.00
2 . . . . 4.00
3 F:Coffin Joe 4.00

DARK OZ
Arrow Comics, 1997
1 (of 5) by Griffith, Kerr & Bryan. . . 2.75
2 thru 5 . . . . @2.75
Spec. Bill Bryan's Oz Collection . . 3.00

DARK PERIL
Quantum Comics, 1998
1 . . . . 3.00
2 thru 4 . . . . @3.00

DARK REGIONS
White Wolf, 1987
1 . . . . 2.50
2 . . . . 2.50
3 Scarce 3.00
4 and 5 . . . . @2.50

DARK VISIONS
Pyramid, 1987
1 I:Wasteland Man 2.50
2 thru 4 . . . . @2.50

DARK WOLF
Eternity, 1988
1 and 2 . . . . @2.50
Volume 2
1 thru 14 . . . . @2.50
Ann. #1. 2.50

DARQUE RAZOR
London Night, 1996
? by Dan Membeila & Albert Holaso,
  Dark Birth 2.50
? necro-embossed edition 10.00
1 thru 3 . . . . @3.00

DAYS OF DARKNESS
Apple, 1992
1 From Pearl Harbor
  to Midway. 2.75
2 Pearl Harbor Attack,cont 2.75
3 Japanese Juggernaut 2.75
4 Bataan Peninsula. 2.75
GN 15.00

DEADBEATS
Claypool Comics, 1993
1 thru 13 . . . . @2.50
14 thru 25. . . . . @2.50
26 thru 50. . . . . @2.50
51 thru 82. . . . . @2.50

DEAD EYES OPEN
Amaze Ink/SLG, 2005
1 . . . . 3.00
2 thru 6 . . . . @3.00

DEAD SONJA: SHE-ZOMBIE WITH A SWORD
Blatant Comics, 2006
1 spoof 4.00
1a Zombie Bloodbath (c) 4.00
1b Dead Sexy (c) 10.00

DEADTIME STORIES
New Comics, 1987
1 AAd,WS 2.50

DEADWORLD
Arrow, 1986
1 Arrow Pyb 5.00
2 . . . . 4.00
3 V:King Zombie 3.50
4 V:King Zombie 3.50
5 Team Rests 3.50
6 V:King Zombie 3.50
7 F:KZ & Deake, Graphic(c). 3.50
8 V:Living Corpse, Graphic(c) . . . 2.50
9 V:Sadistic Punks, Graphic(c). . . 2.50
10 V:King Zombie, Graphic(c) 2.50
7a thru 10a Tame cover . . . . @2.50
11 V:King Zombie, Graphic(c) 3.00
12 I:Percy, Graphic(c) 3.00
13 V:King Zombie, Graphic(c) 3.00
14 V:Voodoo Cult,Graphic(c) 3.00
15 Zombie stories,Graphic(c) 3.00
11a thru 15a Tame cover . . . . . . @2.50
16 V:`Civilized' Community 2.50
17 V:King Zombie 2.50
18 V:King Zombie 2.50
19 V:Grakken. 2.50
20 V:King Zombie 2.50

21 Dead Killer	2.50
22 L:Dan & Joey	2.50
23 V:King Zombie	2.50
24	2.50
25 (R:Vince Locke)	2.50
26	2.50

Caliber

1 thru 11	@3.00
12 thru 15 Death Call	@3.00
Spec. Deadworld Archives, rep.	2.50
Spec. Bits & Pieces, rep.	
Caliber Presents #2&#8	2.50
Spec. To Kill A King,R:Deadkiller	3.00

DEADWORLD: FROZEN OVER
Desperado, 2006

1 (of 4)	4.00
2 thru 4	@4.00

DEATH ANGEL
Lightning, 1997

1 by J. Cleary & Anderson	3.00
1 variant cover	3.00
1 limited edition A	9.00
1 limited edition B	9.00

DEATH RATTLE
Kitchen Sink, 1995
(Prev. Color)

1 thru 3	@3.50
4	3.00
5	2.50
6 Steve Bissette(c)	2.50
7 Ed Gein	2.50
8 I:Xenozoic Tales	9.00
9 BW,rep.	2.50
10 AW,rep.	2.50
11 thru 15	@2.50
16 BW,Spacehawk	2.50
17 Rand Holmes(c)	2.50
18 FMc	2.50

DEATHWORLD
Adventure Comics, 1990

1 Harry Harrison adapt.	2.50
2 thru 4	@2.50

BOOK II, 1991

1 Harry Harrison adapt.	2.50
2 thru 4	@2.50

BOOK III, 1991

1 H.Harrison adapt.,colonization.	2.50
2 Attack on the Lowlands	2.50
3 Attack on the Lowlands contd.	2.50
4 last issue	2.50

DEE VEE
Dee Vee, 1997

1 ECa, F:Alex	3.00
2 ECa	3.00
3 ECa	3.00
4 thru 14	@3.00
Spec. #1 Life is Cheap.	3.00
Spec., 2001, 64-page.	5.00

DEEP SLEEPER
Oni Press, 2004

1 (of 4)	3.50
2 thru 4	@3.50

DEFENSELESS DEAD
Adventure Comics, 1991

1 Larry Niven adapt. A:Gil	2.50
2 A:Organlegger	2.50
3 A:Organlegger	2.50

DELETE
Digital Noixe, 2004

1	3.00
2 thru 5	@3.00

DELTA TENN
Entertainment, 1987

1 thru 11	@2.50

DEMO
AIT/Planet Lar, 2003

1 (of 12)	4.00
2 thru 12	@3.00

DEMON BABY
SQP/666 Comics, 1997

1 by Rich Larson, seq. to Hell	
on Heels	3.00
2 & 3	@3.00
1a thru 3a deluxe	@9.00

DEMON BITCH
Forbidden, 1997–98

1-shot	3.00
Spec.#1 Demon Bitch vs.	
Angel Girl.	3.00
Spec.#1 Demon Bitch: Devilspawn, by	
Angela Benoit & Nirut Chaswan	3.00
Spec.#1 Demon Bitch: Hellslave,	
Free on Earth cover	3.00
Spec.#1 Demon Bitch: Tales of	
the Damned	3.00

DEMONGATE
Sirius, 1996–97

1 thru 12 by Bao Lin Hum &	
Colin Chan	@2.50

DEMON GUN
Crusade Entertainment, 1996

1 thru 3 GCh,KtH	@3.00

DEMON HUNTER
Aircel, 1989

1 thru 4	@2.50

DEMON HUNTER
Davdez Arts, 1998

1 by Barry Blair & Colin Chan	2.50
2 F:Hunter Gordon	2.50
3	2.50

DEMONIQUE
London Night, 1997

? by SKy Owens, A:Anvil	3.00
1 by Membeila & Owens.	3.00
2 F:Viper	3.00
3 Mayhem	3.00
4 Final issue	3.00

DEMONIQUE: ANGEL OF NIGHT
London Night, 1997

1 (of 3) by Skylar Owens	3.00
2	3.00
3 final issue	3.00

DEMONSLAYER: LORDS OF NIGHT
Avatar Press, 2003

1/2 Fire Edition.	6.00
1/2 Ice Edition	6.00
1/2 Attitude Edition.	6.00
Preview	2.50
Preview variant (c)s	6.00

1	3.50
1a variant (c)s	3.50
1b wraparound (c).	4.00

DEMON WARRIOR
Eastern, 1987

1 thru 14	@2.50

DEMONWARS: THE DEMON SPIRIT
Devil's Due, 2008

1 (of 3) 48-pg.	5.50
1a variant prestige (c)	9.50
2 thru 3	@5.50
2a thru 3a variant prestige (c)s	@9.50

DENIZENS OF DEEP CITY
Jabberwocky, 1988

1 thru 8	@2.50

DERRECK WAYNE JACKSON'S STRAPPED
Gothic Images, 1994

1 Confrontational Factor	2.50
2 thru 6	@2.50

Descending Angels #1
© *Millennium*

DESCENDING ANGELS
Millennium, 1995

1 I:3 Angels	2.50
2 F:Jim Johnson	3.00
3 F:Jim Johnson	3.00

DESERT PEACH
Thoughts & Images, 1988

1 thru 4	@2.50

DESTINY ANGEL
Dark Fantasy, 1996

1 (of 3)	4.00
1 2nd printing	4.00
1a deluxe	4.50
2 `Sunless Garden'.	3.50
2a foil cover	4.00
2b photo cover	4.00

DESTROY
Eclipse, 1986
1 Large Size 5.00
2 Small Size,3-D 5.00

DETECTIVE, THE
Caliber, 1998
1 by Gerard Goffaux 3.00
2 . . . . 3.00
3 Clutches of the Past 3.00

DEVIL JACK
Doom Theatre, 1995
1 I:Devil Jack 3.00
1a Directors Cut 3.00
2 V:Belegosi 3.00
3 . . . . 3.00

DEVIL'S PANTIES, THE
Silent Devil Productions, 2006
1 by Jennie Breeden 5.00
2 thru 14 . . . . @5.00

DIABOLIK
Scorpion Productions, 1999
VOL. 1
1 Terror Aboard The Karima 6.00
2 Fight Against Time 6.00
3 Crumbs for the Scum 6.00
4 Family with no morals 6.00
5 & 6 . . . . @6.00
VOL. 2
1 Target: Diabolik 6.00
2 One Crazy Love 6.00
3 . . . . 6.00
4 Interrupted Game 6.00

DICK DANGER
Olsen Comics, 1998
1 by W.W. Olsen 3.00
2 F:Red Olga 3.00
3 The Angel Murder 3.00
4 Is Hitler Still Alive? 3.00
5 Nikita, The Cat Girl 3.00

DICKS
Caliber, 1997
1 (of 4),GEn,JMC, ... 3.00
2 thru 4 GEn,JMC . . . . @3.00

DICK TRACY CRIMEBUSTER
ACG Comics, 1998
1 by M.A.Collins & D.Locher 3.00
2 thru 9 . . . . @3.00

DICK TRACY DETECTIVE
ACG Comics, 1999
1 (of 4) by Chester Gould 3.00
2 thru 4 . . . . @3.00

DICK TRACY
Blackthorne, 1984 89
1 thru 12 . . . . @6.50
13 thru 25 . . . . @7.50
Becomes:

DICK TRACY MONTHLY/WEEKLY
Blackthorne, 1988
1 thru 25 monthly . . . . @3.00
26 thru 108 weekly . . . . @4.00
Unprinted Stories #3 . . . . 3.00
1 3-D Special 3.00
Spec. #1 . . . . 3.00

Spec. #2 . . . . 3.00
Spec. #3 . . . . 3.00

DICK TRACY: THE EARLY YEARS
Blackthorne, 1987
1 thru 3, 78-pg. . . . . @7.50
4 thru 6 . . . . @3.50
7 and 8 . . . . @4.00

DICK TRACY UNPRINTED STORIES
Blackthorne, 1987
1 thru 4 . . . . @3.00

DICTATORS
Antarctic Press, 2004
Hitler #1 (of 4) 3.00
Hitler #2 thru #4 . . . . @3.00
Saddam Hussein #1 . . . . 4.00
Saddam Hussein #2 . . . . 4.00

DIGITAL DRAGON
Peregrine Entertainment, 1999
1 by Bryan Heyboer 3.00
2 thru 4 . . . . @3.00

DIGITAL WEBBING PRESENTS
Digital Webbing 2001
1 thru 5 . . . . 3.00
6 thru 18 . . . . @3.00
19 thru 25 . . . . @3.50
26 . . . . 6.00
27 thru 31 . . . . @4.00

DIM-WITTED DARRYL
Slave Labor Graphics, 1998
1 by Michael Bresnahan 3.00
2 thru 5 . . . . @3.00

DINOSAURS FOR HIRE
Eternity, 1988
1 . . . . 3.00
1a Rep. 2.50
2 thru 9 . . . . @2.50
Fall Classic #1 . . . . 2.50
GN Guns 'N' Lizards 10.00
Malibu, 1993
#1 3-D special 3.50

DIRTY PAIR
Eclipse, 1988
1 . . . . 8.00
2 . . . . 7.00
3 . . . . 6.00
4 end mini-series 6.00
Vol. 2, 1989
1 thru 5 . . . . @5.00
Vol. 3, 1990
1 thru 5 . . . . @5.00

DISCIPLES
Caliber Core, 1998
1 Climate of fear 3.00
2 . . . . 3.00

A DISTANT SOIL
Warp Graphics, 1983
1 A:Panda Khan 9.00
2 . . . . 5.00
3 . . . . 4.00
4 . . . . 3.00
5 thru 9 . . . . @3.00

Dirty Pair Vol. 2 #2
© Eclipse

Aria Press, 1991
1 F:Seasons of Spring 6.00
1a-2nd to 4th printing 2.50
2 Seasons of Spring,pt.2 . . . . 5.00
3 thru 8 . . . . @3.00
9 thru 11 Knights of the Angel . . . @3.00
12 thru 14 . . . . @3.00
GN Knights of the Angel, deluxe . . 16.00
GN Immigrant Song rep.#1–#3 . . . . 7.00
See Image Comics

DITKO'S WORLD: STATIC
Renegade, 1986
1 . . . . 2.50
2 thru 3 SD . . . . @2.50

DOCTOR
Ironcat, 1997
1 (of 5) by Bang Ippongi 3.00
2 . . . . 3.00
4 . . . . 3.00
5 Pay Back in the City of
　Santa La Paz 3.00
6 final issue 3.00

DR. BLINK: SUPERHERO SHRINK
Dork Storm Press, 2004
0 . . . . 3.00
1 . . . . 3.00
2 thru 3 . . . . @3.50

DR. GORPON
Eternity, 1991
1 I:Dr.Gorpon,V:Demon 2.50
2 A:Doofus,V:ChocolateBunny . . . 2.50
3 D:Dr.Gorpon 2.50

DR. RADIUM
Silverline
1 . . . . 3.00
2 thru 4 . . . . @2.50

DR. RADIUM: MAN OF SCIENCE
Slave Labor, 1992
1 And Baby makes 2, BU: Dr.
　Radiums' Grim Future 2.50

DOCTOR WEIRD
Caliber Press, 1994
1 V:Charnogg 2.50
2 V:Charnogg 2.50

DR. WONDER
Old Town Publishing, 1996
1 thur 5 . . . . @3.00

DODEKAIN
Antarctic Press, 1994
1 and 2 by Masayuki Fujihara . . . @3.00
3 Rampage Vs. Zogerians 3.00
4 V:Zogerians 3.00
5 F:Takuma 3.00
6 Dan vs. Takuma 2.75
7 V:Okizon 2.75
8 V:Okizon 3.00

DOGAROO
Blackthorne, 1988
1 . . . . 2.50

DOGS O'WAR, THE
Crusade Entertainment, 1996–97
1 (of 3) 3.00
2 thru 3 . . . . @3.00

DOGWITCH
Sirius Entertainment 2002
1 . . . . 3.50
1a signature plate edition 10.00
2 thru 17 . . . . @3.00
18 Finale special 3.50
18a Signature plate edition 12.00

DOLLS
Sirius, 1998
1-shot science fiction 3.00

Dominion #1
© *Eclipse*

DOMINION
Eclipse Manga, 1990
1 by Masamune Shirow 3.00
2 thru 6 . . . . @2.50

DOMINO CHANCE
Chance, 1982
1 1,000 printed 10.00
1a 2nd printing 3.50
2 thru 6 . . . . @3.00

---

7 I:Gizmo 7.00
8 A:Gizmo 11.00
9 . . . . 2.50

[2nd Series]
1 . . . . 3.00
2 and 3 . . . . @2.50

DONATELLO
Mirage, 1986
1-shot A:TMNTurtles 12.00

DONNA MIA
Avatar Press, 1997
0 by Tevlin Utz 3.00
0b leather cover 15.00
0c signed 8.00
1 . . . . 4.00
1a signed 8.00
1b Royal Blue edition 40.00
2 . . . . 4.00
2a deluxe 4.50
3 (of 3) 3.00
3a deluxe 8.00
Giant Size #1 . . . . 3.00
Giant Size #1 leather cover 15.00
Giant Size #1 signed 8.00
Giant Size #2 . . . . 4.00
Giant Size #2 Deluxe 10.00
Spec. Infinity 3.00
Spec.#1 Pin-up (1997) 3.00

DON SIMPSON'S BIZARRE HEROES
Fiasco Comics, 1990
0 thru 7 . . . . 3.00
8 V:Darkcease 3.00
9 R:Yan Man 3.00
10 F:Mainstreamers 3.00
11 Search for Megaton Man 3.00
12 . . . . 3.00
13 House of Megaton Man 3.00
14 Cec Vs. Dark Cease 3.00

DOOMED
IDW Publishing, 2005
1 . . . . 7.00
1a variant (c) 7.00
2 thru 3 . . . . @8.00
2a thru 3a variant (c) . . . . @8.00
4 . . . . 10.00
4a variant (c) 10.00

DOOMSDAY + 1
ACG Comics, 1998
1 by JBn rep. Charlton 3.00
2 A Faceless Foe 3.00
3 . . . . 3.00
4 The Hidden Enemy 3.00
5 Rule of Fear 3.00
6 . . . . 3.00
7 NA(c), final issue 3.00

DORK
Amaze Ink/SLG, 1993–2001
1 EDo 3.00
2 EDo 3.00
3 EDo 3.00
1 thru 3 2nd printings . . . . @3.00
4 thru 7 . . . . @3.00
8 . . . . 3.50
9 thru 11 . . . . @3.00

DORK TOWER
Corsair Publishing, 1998
1 by John Kovalic 3.00
2 thru 8 . . . . @3.50

Dork Storm, 2000
9 Angry Young Fan 3.00
10 Road Rules 3.00
11 World of Dorkness 3.00
12 . . . . 3.00
13 . . . . 3.00
14 Gilly, Warrior Princess 3.00
15 . . . . 3.00
16 Trader of the Last Orc 3.00
17 Halloween in Mud Bay 3.00
17 At the Big Con 3.00
18 Understanding Games 3.00
19 Junk Food Issue 3.00
20 Featuring Gilly 3.00
21 20th Century Boy 3.00
22 Daily Carson 3.00
23 Dork Tower Frag 3.00
24 . . . . 3.00
25 . . . . 4.00
26 thru 32 . . . . @3.00
33 thru 35 . . . . @3.50
Spec. Lord of the Rings 3.00
Swimsuit Special #1 . . . . 3.00
Best of Dork Tower #1 . . . . 2.25
1-shot Wizkids Special 3.00

DOUBLE IMPACT
High Impact Studios, 1995–96
1 I: China & Jazz 3.00
1a Chromium (c) variant, signed . . 6.00
1b Rainbow (c) w/certificate 12.00
1c Rainbow (c) w/o certificate 9.00
2 Castilo's Crime 3.00
2b silver version 9.00
2c signed, w/certificate 5.00
3 . . . . 5.00
3a Bondage (c) 12.00
4 . . . . 5.00
4a Phoenix (c) 12.00
5 . . . . 5.00
6 China cover 3.00
6a Jazz cover 3.00
6b signed China or Jazz(c) 12.00
6c bondage(c) 9.00
7 & 8 . . . . @3.00
8a variant (c) 8.00

2nd Series, 1996–97
0 . . . . 3.00
1 . . . . 3.00
1a chromium (c) 4.00
1b Chromium variant edition 12.00
1c Christmas (c) 9.00
2 . . . . 3.00
2a Sweedish Erotica(c) 9.00
Spec.#1 Double Impact/Lethal Strike:
   Double Strike, x-over 3.00
Spec.#1 Double Impact/Nikki Blade:
   Hard Core x-over (1997) 3.00
   Platinum variant RCl(c) 9.00
   Gold Metal variant RCl(c) . . . 15.00
Spec.#1 Raising Hell, RCl,RkB 3.00

ABC Comics, 1998
1 encore 3.00
1a encore, Chicago cover 6.00
1b encore, San Diego nude cover . 6.00
Spec. Double Impact/Luxura (1998) 3.00
Spec. Vampeurotica edition 6.00
Bikini Spec. 3.00
Christmas Spec. 3.00
Christmas Spec., gold foil 9.00
Coll.#1 . . . . 3.00
Coll.#1a x-mas 8.00
Spring Spec.#1 . . . . 3.00
Spring Spec.#1a manga cover 8.00
Summer Bikini Spec. 1999 . . . . . . 3.00
Gallery Collection #1 . . . . 5.00
Lingerie Special 3.00

DOUBLE IMPACT:

ALIVE

ABC Comics, 1999

1 (of 3) Double Impact Alive 2000 . 3.00
1a Double Impact Alive 2000,
    gold foil ed. 8.00
1b Red Leather. 12.00
2 RCI. 3.00
2a Manga cover 8.00
2c silver embossed foil 9.00

...ASSASSINS FOR HIRE

High Impact, 1997

1 RCI,RkB 3.00
2 . . . . 3.00

ABC Comics, 1998

1 . . . . 3.00

...FROM THE ASHES

ABC Comics, 1998

1 (of 2) RCI 3.00
2 RCI. 3.00
2A variant cover A. 6.00
2B variant cover B 6.00

...HOT SHOTS

ABC Studios, 1999

1 RCI. 3.00
2 . . . . 3.00

...MERCS

ABC Comics, 1999

1 (of 3) RCI 3.00
1a deluxe 8.00
2 RCI. 3.00
2a deluxe 9.00

...ONE STEP BEYOND

ABC Comics, 1998

1 (of 2) RCI 3.00
1a Leather cover. 15.00

...RAW

ABC Comics, 1997

1 (of 3) RCI, adult 3.00
1b Star photo (c). 9.00
1A Wraparound cover A 6.00
1B Wraparound cover B 6.00
2 thru 3 . . . . @3.00
3A Variant cover A 6.00

VOL. 2

1 (of 3) adult material 3.00

...RAZOR

ABC Studios, 1999

1 (of 3) 3.25
1b Previews exclusive 8.00
1c Manga alt.(c) 8.00
2 . . . . 3.25

...SUICIDE RUN

ABC Comics, 1998

1 (of 2) RCI 3.00
1b Leather cover. 12.00
2 adult material 3.00
Collected edition 3.00
Collected, gold foil 9.00

...2069

ABC Comics, 1999

1 Virgin Encore Edition 3.00
1a Deluxe Erotica edition 8.00
Christmas Spec. 3.00
Christmas Spec. Previews (c) 8.00

...X

ABC Comics, 2000

1 . . . . 6.00
1a alternate (c) 6.00
2 . . . . 6.00
2 deluxe, vinyl (c) 15.00

Intro 15.00

DRACULA IN HELL

Apple, 1992

1 O:Dracula. 2.50
2 O:Dracula contd. 2.50

DRACULA: SUICIDE CLUB

Adventure, 1992

1 I:Suicide Club in UK. 2.50
2 Dracula/Suicide Club cont. 2.50
3 Club raid,A:Insp.Harrison. 2.50
4 Vision of Miss Fortune 2.50

DRACULA'S COZY COFFIN

Draculina Publishing, 1995

1 thru 4 Halloween issue . . . . . . @3.00

DRAGON ARMS

Antarctic Press 2002

1 48-pg. 5.00
2 thru 6 . . . . @3.50
1-shot Stand Alone Special 3.00

DRAGON ARMS: CHAOS BLADE

Antarctic Press, 2004

1 . . . . 3.00
2 thru 6 . . . . @3.00

DRAGONBALL

Viz Communications, 1998

1 (of 12) by Akira Toriyama. 8.00
2 thru 4 . . . . @5.00
5 thru 12 . . . . @3.00

PART TWO, 1999

1 (of 15) by Akira Toriyama. 5.00
2 thru 4 . . . . @4.00
5 thru 15 . . . . @3.00

PART THREE, 2000

1 (of 14) by Akira Toriyama 3.00
2 thru 5 . . . . @3.00
8 thru 14 . . . . @3.00

PART FOUR, 2001

1 thru 4 (of 10) . . . . @3.00
5 thru 10 . . . . @3.00

PART FIVE, 2002

1 (of 7) 3.00
2 thru 6 . . . . @3.00
7 . . . . 3.00

Part 6

1 . . . . 3.50
2 . . . . 3.50

DRAGONBALL Z

Viz Communications, 1998

1 (of 9) by Akira Toriyama. 11.00
2 thru 9 . . . . @5.00

PART TWO (1998)

1 (of 14) by Akira Toriyama. 4.00
2 thru 9 . . . . @3.50
10 thru 14 . . . . @3.50

PART THREE (1999)

1 (of 10) by Akira Toriyama. 3.50
2 thru 10 . . . . @3.00

PART 4 (2000)

1 thru 13 (of 15) . . . . @3.00

PART 5 (2001)

1 (of 12) 3.00
2 thru 10 . . . . @3.00

DRAGONFORCE

Aircel, 1988

1 DK 6.00
2 thru 7 DK . . . . @4.00
8 thru 12 . . . . @4.00
13. . . . . 2.50
Vol. 1 thru Vol. 5 Dragonforce
    Chronicles, rep. . . . . @3.00

DRAGON KNIGHTS

Tokyopop Press, 2001

1 by Mineko Ohkami. 3.00
2 thru 6 . . . . @3.00

DRAGON QUEST

Silverwolf, 1986

1 TV 10.00
2 TV 6.00
3 TV 5.00

DRAGONRING

[1st Series]

1 B.Blair,rare 110.00

Aircel, 1986

1 . . . . 3.50
2 . . . . 2.50
3 thru 6 . . . . @2.50

Dragonrok Saga #3
© Hanthercraft

DRAGONROK SAGA

Hanthercraft

1 . . . . 2.50
2 thru 12 . . . . @2.50

DRAGON WARS

Ironcat, 1998

1 by Ryukihei 3.00
2 thru 11 . . . . @3.00

DREAD OF NIGHT

Hamilton, 1991

1 Horror story collection 4.00
2 Json, inc.'Genocide' 4.00

DREAM ANGEL AND ANGEL GIRL

Angel Entertainment, 1998

1 . . . . 3.00

All comics prices listed are for *Near Mint* condition.

DREAM ANGEL:
THE QUANTUM DREAMER
Angel Entertainment, 1997
1 by Mort Castle & Adriana Melo . . 3.00
2 . . . . 3.00

DREAM ANGEL:
WORLD WITHOUT END
Angel Entertainment, 1998
1 Dream world cover 3.00

DREAMERY
Eclipse, 1986
1 . . . . 2.50
2 thru 13 . . . . @2.50

DREAMGIRL
Angel Entertainment, 1996
0 by David Campitti & Al Rio 3.00
1 . . . . 3.00
1 deluxe 6.00
1 Manga cover 5.00

DREAMLANDS
Caliber New Worlds, 1996
1 . . . . 3.00
2 flip book with Boston Bombers #33.00

DREAMTIME
Blind Rat, 1995
1 Young Deserter 3.00
2 Gypsy Trouble 2.50

DREAMWALKER
Caliber Tapestry, 1997
1 . . . . 3.00
2 thru 4 . . . . @3.00
5 by Jenni Gregory, 2nd story arc. . 3.00
6 2nd story arc, concl. 3.00

...CAROUSEL
Avatar, 1998
0 . . . . 3.00
1 by Jenni Gregory 3.00
2 conclusion 3.00

...SUMMER RAIN
Avatar, 1999
1 by Jenni Gregory 3.00

...AUTUMN LEAVES
Avatar, 1999
1 by Jenni Gregory 3.00
2 conclusion 3.00

DREAMWOLVES
Dramenon Studios, 1994
1 . . . . 3.00
2 . . . . 3.00
3 F:Desiree 3.00
4 and 5 V:Venefica . . . . @3.00
6 R:Carnifax 3.00
7 . . . . 3.00
8 F:Wendy Bascum 3.00

DROWNERS, THE
New Flame Publishing, 2004
1 (of 4) 3.00
2 thru 4 . . . . @3.00

DUEL
Antarctic Press, 2005
0 . . . . 3.00
1 (of 4) Rise of the Blackhawk . . . 3.00
2 Jet War in the South Atlantic 3.50
3 Germany 1945 . . . . 3.00

Duel #0
© Antarctic Press

DUNGEON
NBM Books 2002
1 by L. Trondheim & J. Star 3.00
2 thru 8 . . . . @3.00

DUNGEON:
THE EARLY YEARS
NBM Books, 2004
1 thru 2 . . . . @3.00

DUNGEONEERS
Silverwolf, 1986
1 thru 8 . . . . @2.50

DUNGEONS & DRAGONS:
BLACK & WHITE
Kenzer & Company, 2002
1 (of 8) by J.Limke & R.Pereira . . . 3.00
2 thru 6 . . . . @3.00

DUNGEONS & DRAGONS
IN SHADOW OF DRAGONS
Kenzer & Company, 2001
1 (of 8) The Last of My Father 3.00
2 thru 8 . . . . @3.00

DWELLING, THE
Chaos! Comics/Black Label
Graphics, 2002
Ashcan 6.00
1 BnP 5.00
1a premium edition 9.00
1b super premium edition 15.00
1c signed edition 12.00
Spec. #1 script edition 5.00
Spec. #1 premium script edition . . 20.00

EAGLE
Crystal, 1986
1 . . . . 3.00
1a signed & limited 5.00
2 thru 5 . . . . @2.75
6 thru 17 . . . . @2.50
Apple, 1988
18 thru 26 . . . . @2.50

EAGLE
Viz Communications, 2000
1 (of 14) The Candidate,112-pg. . . . 7.00
2 Scandal 7.00
3 The Vice-President 7.00
4 New Hampshire 7.00
5 On the Battlefield 7.00
6 King of New York 7.00
7 Pandora's Box 7.00
8 The Debate 7.00
9 Passion 7.00
10 Gone to Texas. 7.00
11 Super Tuesday 7.00
12 Suspicion 7.00
13 Illegitimate child 7.00
14 Confession 7.00
15 The Nomination 7.00
16 The General 7.00
17 Coming Home 7.00
18 Frame Up 7.00
19 Fires in the Plain 7.00
20 Someone You Can Trust. 7.00
21 End of the Trail 7.00
22 Father & Son. 7.00

EAGLE: DARK MIRROR
Comic Zone
1 A:Eagle, inc reps 2.75
2 In Japan, V:Lord Kagami 2.75
3 . . . . 3.00
4 . . . . 3.00

EAGLES DARE
Aager Comics, 1994
1 thru 4 . . . . 2.50
5 V:Dragon 2.50

EARTH WAR
Newcomers Publishing, 1995
1 and 2 from Newcomers Illus. 3.00

EASY WAY
IDW Publishing, 2005
1 . . . . 4.00
2 thru 4 . . . . @4.00

EAT-MAN
Viz Communications, 1997
1 (of 6) by Akihito Yoshitami 3.00
2 thru 6 . . . . @3.00
PART TWO, 1998
1 (of 5) by Akihito Yoshitami 3.00
2 (of 5) 3.50
3 thru 5 . . . . @3.25

EB'NN THE RAVEN
Now
1 . . . . 5.00
2 . . . . 3.00
3 thru 9 . . . . @2.50

EBONIX-FILES, THE
Blatant Comics, 1998
1A TV parody, cover A 4.00
1B TV parody, cover B 4.00

ECHO
Abstract Studio, 2008
1TMo 3.50
2 thru 8 . . . . @3.50

ED THE HAPPY CLOWN
Drawn & Quarterly, 2005
1 (of 9) 3.00
2 thru 3 . . . . @3.00
4 thru 9 . . . . @3.00

EDDIE CAMPELL'S BACCHUS
Eddie Campell Comics, 1995
1 V:Telchines. 7.00
1 2nd printing 3.00
2 thru 10 V:Telchines 4.00
11 thru 26 ECa. . . . . @3.00
27 thru 37 ECa. . . . . @3.00
38 thru 60. . . . . @3.00

EDDY CURRENT
Mad Dog, 1987
1 thru 12 . . . . @2.50

EDGAR ALLAN POE
Eternity, 1988
1 Black Cat 2.50
2 Pit & Pendulum 2.50
3 Masque of the Red Death 2.50
4 Murder in the Rue Morgue 2.50
5 Tell Tale Heart 2.50

EIGHTBALL
Fantagraphics, 1989
1 . . . . 11.00
2 . . . . 8.00
3 . . . . 7.00
4 . . . . 6.00
1a thru 4a later printings . . . . . . @3.00
5 thru 8 . . . . @6.00
9 thru 10 . . . . @4.00
11 A:Ghost World 4.00
12 F:Ghost World. 4.00
13 thru 19. . . . . @4.00
20 . . . . 5.00
21 48-pg. 5.00
22 . . . . 7.00
23 . . . . 7.00

ELFLORD
Aircel, 1986
1 I:Hawk 5.00
1a 2nd printing 3.50
2 . . . . 3.00
2a 2nd printing 2.50
3 V:Doran 3.00
4 V:Doran 3.00
5 V:Doran 2.50
6 V:Nendo 2.50
Compilation Book. 5.00
(Vol 2), #1 to #24, see Color
25 thru 31 . . . . @2.50
32 . . . . 2.50

ELFLORD: RETURN OF THE KING
Nightwynd, 1992
1 . . . . 2.50
2 thru 4 . . . . @2.50

ELFLORD: SUMMER MAGIC
Nightwynd, 1993
1 thru 4 . . . . @2.50

ELFLORD
Warp Graphics, 1997
1 (of 4) by Barry Blair & Colin Chan 3.00
2 thru 4 . . . . @3.00

ELFLORD: ALL THE LONELY PLACES
Warp Graphics, 1997
1 (of 4)Barry Blair & Colin Chan . . . 3.00
Becomes:

HAWK AND WINDBLADE: ALL THE LONELY PLACES
2 (of 2) 3.00

ELFLORD CHRONICLES
Aircel, 1990
1 (of 12) thru 8 rep B.Blair . . . . . @2.50

ELFLORD CUTS LOOSE
Warp Graphics, 1997
1 by Barry Blair and Colin Chan . . . 3.00
2 F:Hawk Erik-san 3.00
3 . . . . 3.00
4 all out attack 3.00
5 north to safety 3.00
6 homeward 3.00
7 back to Greenhaven 3.00
8 Greenhaven Siege. 3.00
9 Felines, Nothing More Than
Felines. 3.00

ELFLORD: HAWK
China Winds, 1998
1-shot by Barry Blair and
Colin Chan. 3.50

ELFQUEST
Warp Graphics, 1979–85
1 WP. 30.00
1a WP,2nd printing 9.00
1b WP,3rd printing 5.00
1c WP,4th printing (1989) 4.00
2 WP 16.00
3 WP 12.00
4 WP 12.00
5 WP 12.00
6 WP 12.00
2a thru 6a WP,2nd printing . . . . . @4.00
7 WP 10.00
8 WP 10.00
9 WP 10.00
2a thru 9a WP,later printings . . . . @3.00
10 thru 15 . . . . @6.00
16 WP,I:DistantSoil 8.00
17 thru 21 WP . . . . @5.00
Warp Graphics, 1996
4 thru 14 ed. RPi. . . . . @5.00
15 . . . . 5.50
16 What if Cutter never
became chief. 5.50

Elfquest #2
© Warp Graphics

17 F:Fire-Eye 5.50
18 Dreamtime, concl. 5.50
19 Wolfrider begins 5.50
20 . . . . 5.50
21 20th anniv. 5.50
22 F:Wolfrider 5.00
23 F:WaveDancers 5.00
24 F:Wolfrider 5.00
25 F:Wolfrider 5.00
26 Wild Hunt 5.00
27 . . . . 5.00
28 F:Ember & Teir 5.00
29 three new stories 5.00
30 new stories 5.00
31 new stories 5.00
32 Wild Hunt,pt.1, 24-pg. 3.50
33 Wild Hunt,pt.2 . . . . 3.50
34 Wild Hunt,pt.3 . . . . 3.50
35 Wild Hunt,pt.4 . . . . 3.50
Spec.#1 Worldpool,pt.1 (1997) . . . 3.50
Spec.#2 Worldpool,pt.2 (1997) . . . 3.50
Spec. Metamorphosis, WP,
RPi (1996) 3.00
Spec. Elfquest: Wolfrider 3.00
Summer Spec. 2001 Recognition . 3.00
Summer Spec. 2001 Wolfshadow . . 4.00

...KAHVI
Warp Graphics, 1995
1 thru 6 I:Kahvi . . . . @2.50

...KINGS OF THE BROKEN WHEEL
Warp Graphics, 1990–92
1 thru 9 WP . . . . @2.50

...SEIGE AT BLUE MOUNTAIN
Warp Graphics/Apple 1987–88
1 WP,JSo 7.00
1a 2nd printing 3.00
2 WP 6.00
2a 2nd printing 3.00
3 WP 5.00
3a 2nd printing 2.50
4 thru 8 WP . . . . @5.00

...TWO SPEAR
Warp Graphics, 1995
1 thru 3 (of 5) Two-Spears past . @2.50

...WORLDPOOL
Warp Graphics, 1997
Spec.#1& 2 (of 2) . . . . @3.00

ELFTREK
Dimension, 1986
1 Elfquest's Star Trek parody 2.50
2 . . . . 2.50

ELF WARRIOR
Adventure, 1987
1 . . . . 3.00
2 thru 5 . . . . @2.50

EL HAZARD: THE MAGNIFICENT WORLD
Viz Communications, 2000
1 by Hidetomo Tsubura. 3.00
2 thru 5 . . . . @3.00
Part 2, 2001
1 . . . . 3.00
2 thru 5 . . . . @3.00
Part 3, 2001
1 (of 6) 3.00
2 thru 6 . . . . @3.00

ELVIRA, MISTRESS OF THE DARK
Claypool Comics, 1993
1	6.00
2 thru 35	@4.00
36 thru 74 photo covers	@3.50
75 Mistress of the Jungle,pt.1	3.50
76 Mistress of the Jungle,pt.2	3.50
77 Rome on the Range	3.50
78 thru 90 photo covers	@3.50
91 thru 103	@3.00
104 thru 127	@3.00
128 thru 138	@2.50
139 thru 150	@2.50
151 thru 166	@2.50

EMBRACE: HUNGER OF THE FLESH
London Night, 1997
1 DQ,last of the original vampire race	3.00
1a DQ,deluxe	6.00
1b signed by Kevin West	12.00
2 DQ	3.00
2a DQ,deluxe	6.00
3 by Dan Membiela & Kevin West, concl.	3.00

EMERALDAS
Eternity, 1990
1 thru 4	@2.50

EMMA DAVENPORT
Lohann Hill Press, 1995
1 I:Emma Davenport	2.75
2	2.75
3 O:Hammerin Jim	2.75
4 Cookie Woofer War	2.75

EMO BOY
Amaze Ink/SLG, 2005
1	3.00
2 thru 11	@3.00

EMPIRE
Eternity, 1988
1 thru 4	@2.50

EMPIRE LANES
Northern Lights, 1986–87
1	2.50
2 thru 4	@2.50

EMPTY ZONE
Sirius, 1998
1 by Jason Alexander	3.00
1a limited edition	5.00
2 thru 4	2.50

VOL. 2 TRANSMISSIONS, 1999
1 by Jason Alexander	3.00
2 thru 7	@3.00
8 History Lessions,pt.1	3.00

EMPTY ZONE: CONVERSATIONS WITH THE DEAD
Sirius Entertainment, 2002
1 (of 5) by Jason Alexander	3.00
2 thru 3	@3.00

ENCHANTED
Sirius, 1997
1 (of 3) by Robert Chang	3.00
2 and 3	@3.00

Enchanted Valley #1
© *Blackthorne*

ENCHANTED VALLEY
Blackthorne, 1987
1	2.50
2	2.50

ENCHANTER
Eclipse, 1987
1	2.50
2 thru 3	@2.50

ENNIS AND MCCREA'S BIGGER DICKS
Avatar Press, 2002
1 (of 4) GEn,JMC,F:Dougie & Ivor	5.00
1a Guaranteed to Offend cover	5.00
2 thru 4	@5.00
2a thru 4a offensive (c)	@5.00

ENNIS AND MCCREA'S DICKS 2
Avatar Press, 2002
1 (of 4)	3.50
2 thru 4	@3.50
1a thru 4a offensive (c)	@4.00
X-Mas Spec. #1	3.50
X-Man Spec. #1 offensive (c)	4.00

ENTROPY TALES
Entropy
1	2.50
2 Domino Chance	2.50
3 thru 5	@2.50

EPSILON WAVE
Elite
1	3.00
2 thru 5	@2.50

EQUINE THE UNCIVILIZED
GraphXpress
1	4.00
2	2.50
3 thru 6	@2.50

EQUINOX CHRONICLES
Innovation, 1991
1 I:Team Equinox, Black Avatar	2.50
2 Black Avatar Plans US conquest	2.50

ERADICATORS
Greater Mercury, 1990–91
1 RLm (1st Work)	5.00
1a 2nd printing	2.50
2	2.50
3 Vigil	2.50
4 thru 8	@2.50

ERIC PRESTON IS THE FLAME
B-Movie Comics, 1987
1 Son of G.A.Flame	2.50

ESCAPE TO THE STARS
Visionary
1	2.50
2 thru 7	@2.50

[2nd Series]
1	2.50
2	2.50

ESCAPE VELOCITY
Escape Velocity Press, 1986
1 and 2	@2.50

ESMERALDAS
Eternity
1	2.50
2 thru 4	2.50

ESP
Curtis Comics, 2002 (Manga)
1 by Jihoon Park & Takyoung Lee	3.00
2 thru 5	@3.00

Vol. 2
1	3.00

ESPERS
Halloween Comics, 1996
1 JHl, R:ESPers	3.00
1 JHl,signed	3.00
2 JHl,signed	3.00
3 JHl,	3.00
3 JHl,signed	3.00
4 thru 6 JHl, conclusion	@3.00

Volume 2
1 `Undertow'	3.00
2	3.00

EVENFALL
Amaze Ink/SLG, 2003
3	3.00
4	3.00
5	3.00
6 thru 8	@3.00

EVERETTE HARTSOE'S RAZOR
EH! Productions, 2000
1	3.50
1a Ruby Foil	5.00
2	4.00

EVIL ERNIE
Eternity, 1991–92
1 SHu,BnP,I&O:Evil Ernie, Lady Death	65.00
1a Spec. 1992 reprint, 16 extra pages	24.00
2 Death & Revival of Ernie, A:Lady Death, 1st (c)	25.00
3 Psycho Plague, A:Lady Death	22.00
4 A:Lady Death	20.00
5 A:Lady Death	20.00

EVIL ERNIE
Chaos! Comics
1 thru 5 reprints . . . . @3.00
Spec. Youth Gone Wild, die-cut
   cover, Director's cut. 5.00

Chaos! Comics, 1996
1 thru 5 encore presentation 3.00
TPB Revenge 13.00
Preview Book Depraved 5.00
Pieces of Me Script 5.00

...THE HORROR
Chaos! Comics, 2002
Ashcan b&w. 6.00
1 BnP 4.50
1a premium edition 10.00
1b signed edition. 15.00
1c super-premium edition 20.00
Spec. Script edition 5.00
Spec. Script Edition, premium 20.00

...MANHATTAN DEATH TRIP
Chaos! Comics, 2002
1 BnP 3.50
1a premium edition 10.00
1b super-premium edition 20.00
Spec. #1 script 5.00
Spec. #1 script, premium edition . . 20.00

...RETURNS
Chaos! Comics, 2001
1 BnP 4.00
1a premium edition 9.00
1b super-premium edition 15.00
1c signed ed. 11.00
Ashcan 6.00
Script #1 . . . . 5.00
Script #1 premium edition 15.00

EVIL EYE
Fantagraphics, 1998
1 by Richard Sala 3.00
2 Glass Scorpion,pt.2 . . . . 3.00
3 thru 7 . . . . @3.00
8 thru 11 . . . . @3.50
12 . . . . 4.00

EXIT
Caliber, 1995
1 I:New series 3.00
2 thru 4 'The Traitors,'pt.2–pt.4 . . . 3.00
Epilogue 3.00

EX LIBRIS
Amaze Ink/SLG, 2005
1 by James Turner 3.00
2 thru 6 . . . . @3.00

EX-MUTANTS
Amazing Comics, 1986
1 AC/RLm 5.00
1a 2nd printing 2.50
2 and 3 . . . . @3.00
4 and 5 . . . . @2.50
Ann. #1 . . . . 2.50
Pin-Up Spec. #1 . . . . 2.50

Pied Piper Comics
6 thru 8 . . . . @2.50

EX-MUTANTS:
THE SHATTERED
EARTH CHRONICLES
Eternity, 1988
1 thru 3 . . . . @2.50
4 & 5 RLd(c) . . . . @2.75
6 thru 14 . . . . @2.50
Winter Special #1 . . . . 2.50

Ex-Mutants #7
© Pied Piper Comics

EXPERTS, THE
Near Mint Press, 2006
1 . . . . 3.00
2 . . . . 3.00
3 . . . . 3.50

EXPLORERS
Caliber Tapestry, 1997
1 . . . . 3.00
2 . . . . 3.00
3 'Nahuatl' 3.00
4 'The Sky is Falling' 3.00

EXTINCTIONERS
Shanda Fantasy Arts
VOL 2, 1999
1 thru 9 . . . . @3.00
10 thru 15 48-pg. . . . . @5.00
Spec. #2 Tales of the Endangered. . 5.00
Spec. #3 Tales of the Endangered. . 5.00

EYE OF MONGOMBO
Fantagraphics Books, 1990–91
1 . . . . 3.00
2 thru 7 . . . . @2.50

FADE FROM BLUE
Second to Some Studios 2002
1 by Murphy & Dalrymple 2.50
1a second printing 2.50
2 thru 9 . . . . @2.50
10 concl. 48-pg. 5.00

FAITH
Lightning Comics, 1997
1 (of 2) 3.00
1a variant cover 3.00
1b Limited, cover A 9.00
1c Limited, cover B 9.00
1d signed & numbered 9.00
1 encore edition 3.00
1a encore, cover B 3.00
1b deluxe encore edition, cover A . 9.00
1c deluxe encore edition, cover B . 9.00

FAMILY BONES
King Tractor, 2006
1 (of 10) 3.50
2 thru 4 . . . . @3.50
5 . . . . 2.75

FANG: TESTAMENT
Sirius, 1997
1 by Kevin J. Taylor 2.50
2 thru 4 . . . . @2.50

FANGS OF THE WIDOW
London Night Studios, 1995
1 O:The Widow 3.00
1a platinum edition 5.00
2 Body Count 3.00
3 Emma Revealed 3.00
4 and 5 . . . . @3.00

Ground Zero, 1995
7 thru 9 'Metal Gypsies,'pt.#1–#3 @3.00
10 thru 13 rep. Widow: Bound by
   Blood #1–#4 + additional
   material 3.50
14 'Search and Destroy'pt.1 . . . . . . 3.00
15 'Search and Destroy'pt.2 . . . . . . 3.00
Ann. #1 Search and Destroy 6.00

FANTASCI
Warp Graphics-Apple, 1986
1 . . . . 2.50
2 and 3 . . . . @2.50
4 . . . . 4.00
5 thru 8 . . . . @2.50
9 'Apple Turnover' 2.50

FANTASTIC FABLES
Silver Wolf, 1987
1 and 2 . . . . @2.50

FANTASTIC PANIC
Antarctic, 1993–94
1 thru 8 Ganbear . . . . @2.75

Vol. 2, 1995
1 thru 4 . . . . @2.75
4 thru 9 . . . . @3.00
10 concl. 3.50

FANTASTIC STORIES
Basement Comics, 2001
1 F:Grakoom, the Forgotten God . . 3.00
1a special edition 9.00
2 Lost Women of the Moon 3.00
2a special edition 9.00
3 . . . . 3.00
3a special edition 9.00

FANTASY QUARTERLY
Independent, 1976
1 1978 1st Elfquest 65.00

FART WARS:
SPECIAL EDITION
Entity Comics, 1997
1 Star Wars trilogy parody,A:Nira X 2.75
1a Empire Attacks Back cover 2.75
1b Return of the One-Eye cover. . . 2.75

FAR WEST
Antarctic Press, 1998
1 (of 4) by Richard Moore 3.00
2 thru 4 . . . . @3.00

VOL. 2
1 (of 4) 3.00
2 . . . . 2.50

FATALIS
Caliber Core, 1998
1 by Mark Chadbourn
   & Vince Danks. 3.00
1a signed & numbered 7.00
2 . . . . 3.00

FAT NINJA
Silver Wolf Comics, 1985–86
1 .... 2.50
2 Vigil 2.50
3 thru 8 .... @2.50

FAUST
Northstar, 1985
1 Vigil 25.00
1a Vigil,2nd Printing 4.00
1b Vigil,3rd Printing. 3.00
1c Tour Edition 25.00
2 Vigil 13.00
2a Vigil,2nd Printing 3.00
2b Vigil,3rd Printing. 2.50
3 Vigil 10.00
3a Vigil,2nd Printing 2.50
4 Vigil 5.00
5 Vigil 5.00
6 Vigil 5.00

Rebel Studios
7 Vigil 5.00
8 TV 3.50
9 TV,Love of the Damned. 3.50
10 E:DQ(s),TV,Love o/t Damned ... 3.50

VOL. II
1 TV,Love of the Damned. 2.50

FAUST/777: THE WRATH
Avatar Press, 1998
0 by David Quinn & Tim Vigil,
  Darkness in Collision x-over ... 3.00
0a wrap 4.00
0b leather cover 15.00
0c Royal Blue edition 50.00
0d Platinum edition 12.00
1 (of 4) 3.50
2 Darkness in Collision,pt.3 ...... 3.50
3 .... 3.50
4 .... 3.50
Faust Hornbook 5.00

FAUST:
SINGHA'S TALONS
Avatar, 2000
1/2 .... 3.50
1/2 wraparound (c). 4.00
1/2 Beachum (c) 6.00
1/2 prism foil. 11.00
1/2 royal blue edition 60.00
1/2 Blood Curse 5.00
1 (of 4) 4.00
1a wraparound (c). 4.50
1c red foil leather 25.00
1d prism foil 13.00
1 commemorative 6.00
2 thru 4 .... @4.00
2a thru 4a previews exclusive. .. @4.50
Preview Book 6.00

FELIX THE CAT
Felix Comics, 1997
1 inc. Felix's Cafe 2.50
2 Crusin' for a Brusin' 2.50
3 Ah Choo 2.50
4 inc. Spaced Out. 2.50
5 Holiday/Winter issue 2.50
6 The Felix Force 2.50
7 A Rash of Trash. 2.50
8 Halloween 2.50
Cat-A-Strophic Wrestling Spec.#1 . 2.50
Felix Summer Splash #1 .... 2.50

FELIX THE CAT
TRUE CRIME STORIES
Felix Comics, 2000
1 .... 2.50

Spec.#1 Blockbuster movie
  bonanza. 2.50
Spec. Felix Jurassic Jamboree ... 2.50
Spec. Felix Magic Bag of Tricks ... 2.50
Spec. Felix Laff-A-Palooza 2.50
1-shot Felix's Totally Wacky News. . 2.50
1-shot Halloween Spectacular #13 . 2.50
1-shot House of 1000 Ha Ha's 2.50
1-shot Felix the Cat's TV
  Extravaganza (2002) 2.50
1-shot Buy This Comic. 2.50
1-shot Amazing Colossal
  Felix the Cat 2.50
1-shot Silly Stories #1 .... 2.50

FEM FANTASTIQUE
AC Comics, 1988
1 .... 2.50

Femforce #21
© AC Comics

FEMFORCE
AC Comics, 1987
1 thru 15 See Color
16 thru 43. .... @3.00
44 V:Lady Luger,F:Garganta 5.00
45 thru 56. .... @3.00
57 thru 92 See Color
93 thru 99 .... @3.00
93a thru 99a deluxe .... @6.00
100 Anniv. issue, with poster 8.00
100A signed, with poster 11.00
100B no poster, not signed 4.00
101 thru 103 Yesterday Syndrome@5.00
104 thru 106 Return From the
  Ashes. .... @5.00
107 Darkgods: Rampage,pt.1 ..... 5.00
108 Darkgods: Rampage,pt.2 ..... 5.00
109 Darkgods: Rampage,pt.3 ..... 6.00
110 thru 117 .... @6.00
118 44-pg. 7.00
118a spec. edition, 60-pg. 9.00
119 The Missing Mask 7.00
120 Superbabes,pt.1 .... 7.00
121 Superbabes,pt.2 .... 7.00
121a Femme Noir (c). 10.00
122 Superbabes,pt.3 .... 7.00
122a spec. editions, variant(c). ... @9.00
123 thru 146 .... @7.00
Spec.#1 FemForce Timelines,
  O:Femforce (1995) 3.00
Spec.#1 FemForce:Frightbook,
  Horror tales by Briefer,
  Ayers, Powell. 3.00
Spec.#2 (2001) 6.00
Spec.#1 Femforce:Uncut (2001) .. 10.00

Untold Origin of FemForce 5.00
Secret Files of Femforce, deluxe. . . 5.00
Pulp Fiction Portfolio #2. .... 18.00
Spec. #1 Femforce vs. The Claw. . 7.00
Spec. #1 Rampaging She-Cat. 7.00
1-shot Claws of the She-Cat 5.00
Features #1: Giantess 7.00

FEMFORCE SPECIAL
AC Comics, 1999
1 Femforce Special: Rayda–
  The Cyberian Connection ... 3.00
1a Variant cover 3.00
1b Variant cover, signed 9.00
2 .... 3.00
3 conclusion 4.00

FEVER, THE
Dark Vision Publishing, 1995
1 O:The Fever. 2.50
2 Fever's Father 2.50
3 thru 5 .... @2.50

FIFTIES TERROR
Eternity, 1988
1 thru 6 .... @2.50

FIGHTING YANK
AC Comics, 2001
1 by Hack Koilby. 6.00
2 .... 6.00
3 Cave Girl 6.00
4 .... 6.00
5 Three Chambers of Horror 6.00

FINDER
Lightspeed Comics, 1996
1 thru 5 by Carla Speed McNeil . @3.00
6 thru 19 .... @3.00
20 thru 38. .... @3.00

FINDER FOOTNOTES
Lightspeed Press
1 thru 4 .... @6.00

FIRE TEAM
Aircel, 1990
1 thru 3 by Don Lomax .... @2.50
4 V:Vietnamese Gangs 2.50
5 Cam in Vietnam 2.50
6 .... 2.50

FISH POLICE
Fishwrap Productions, 1985
1 1st printing 7.00
1a 2nd printing 3.00
Becomes:

INSPECTOR GILL
OF THE FISH POLICE
2 .... 5.00
3 thru 11 .... @4.00
[Vol 2] Comico Publ., 1987
5 thru 12 .... @3.50
13 thru 17 **see Color issues**
Apple Publ.
18 thru 24. .... @2.50

FISH SHTICKS
Apple, 1991
1 and 2 Fish Police .... @2.75
3 and 4 .... @2.50

FIST OF GOD
Eternity, 1988
1 thru 4 .... @2.50

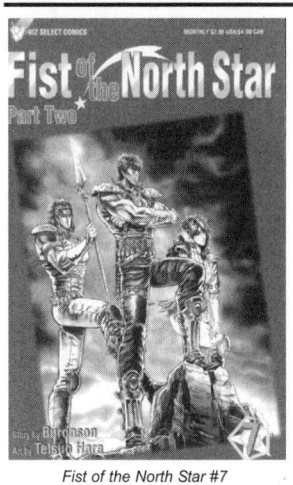

Fist of the North Star #7
© Viz Select

FIST OF THE NORTH STAR
Viz Select, 1996
1 thru 3 . . . . @3.25
4 . . . . 2.50
5 . . . . 3.25
6 thru 7 . . . . @3.00
Part Three
1 thru 5 by Buronson
  & Tetsuo Hara . . . . @3.00
Part Four, 1996
1 thru 7 . . . . @3.00

FLAG FIGHTERS
Ironcat, 1997
1 by Masaomi Kanzaki 3.00
2 Student Flagger,pt.1 . . . . 3.00
3 Student Flagger,pt.2 . . . . 3.00
4 Student Flagger,pt.3 . . . . 3.00
5 . . . . 3.00
6 Death Window 3.00
7 F:Murasame 3.00

FLAMING CARROT
Aardvark–Vanaheim, 1984
1 1981 Killian Barracks. 50.00
1a 1984. . . . . 25.00
2 . . . . 20.00
3 . . . . 17.00
4 thru 6 . . . . @12.00
Renegade
7 . . . . 10.00
8 . . . . 9.00
9 & 10 . . . . @8.00
11 & 12. . . . . @6.00
13 thru 15. . . . . @5.00
15a variant without cover price 8.00
16 and 17. . . . . @5.00
See: Dark Horse

FLARE
Hero Graphics, 1990
1 thru 7 See Color
8 thru 14 . . . . 3.00

FLARE FIRST EDITION
Hero Graphics, 1993
1 Flare as teenager 5.00
2 . . . . 4.00
3 thru 11 . . . . @3.50

FLARE VS. TIGRESS
Hero Graphics
1 and 2 . . . . @3.50

FORBIDDEN KINGDOM
Eastern Comics, 1987
1 thru 11 . . . . @2.50

FORBIDDEN VAMPIRE TALES
Forbidden, 1997
0 . . . . 3.00
1 sexy vampire 3.00
2 thru 7 . . . . @3.00
Spec.#1 Vault of Innocents 3.00

FORBIDDEN WORLDS
ACG, 1996
1 SD,JAp,rep. 2.50

FORCE SEVEN
Lone Star Press, 1999
1 . . . . 3.00
2 thru 7 . . . . @3.00

FORCE 10
Crow Comics, 1995
0 Ash Can Preview 2.50
1 I:Force 10. . . . . 2.50
2 Children of the Revolution,pt#2 . . 2.50
3 Against all Odds. 2.50

FORETERNITY
Antarctic Press, 1997
1 by Rod Espinoza 3.00
2 and 3 . . . . @3.00

FOREVER WARRIORS
Aardwolf, 1996
1 (of 3) RTs,RB 3.00
2 RTs,RB. 3.00
3 RTs,RB, concl. 3.00

FOREVER WARRIORS
CFD, 1997
1 RB,RTs. 3.00
2 RB,RTs,KN. 3.00
3 RB,RTs, finale 3.00

FORGIVE ME FATHER
High Impact, 2004
1 . . . . 3.00
2 . . . . 3.00
1a thru 2a variant (c)s. . . . . @6.00
Bulletproof Comics
3 . . . . 3.00

FORTY WINKS
Oddjobs Limited, 1997
1 (of 4) by Sneed & Peters 3.00
2 Everything Right is Wrong Again . 3.00
3 Where Your Eyes Don't Co 3.00
4 There Might be Giants 3.00
Peregrine Entertainment, 1998
Christmas Spec. 3.00
TV Party Spec. 3.00
Spec.#1 Buzzboy (2000) 3.00

FORTY WINKS: MR. HORRIBLE
Peregrine Entertainment, 2000
1 . . . . 3.00
2 . . . . 3.00

FORTY WINKS: THE FABLED PIRATE QUEEN OF THE SOUTH CHINA SEA
Peregrine Entertainment, 1999
1 by Vincent Sneed & Martinez . . . 3.00
2 . . . . 3.00
3 . . . . 3.00

FOX COMICS
1 Spec. 3.00
25 . . . . 3.00
26 . . . . 3.50

FRAGILE PROPHET
Lost in the Dark Press, 2005
1 . . . . 3.00
2 . . . . 3.00
3 . . . . 3.00

FRANK
Fantagraphics
1 JWo 3.00
2 JWo 4.00
3 . . . . 4.00
4 . . . . 4.00

FRANKENSTEIN
Eternity
1 . . . . 2.50
2 . . . . 2.50
3 . . . . 2.50

FRANK THE UNICORN
Fish Warp
1 thru 7 . . . . @2.50

FREAK-OUT ON INFANT EARTHS
Blackthorne, 1987
1 Don Chin 2.50
2 Don Chin 2.50

FREAKS
Monster Comics
1 Movie adapt. 2.50
2 Movie adapt.cont. 2.50
3 thru 4 Movie adapt. . . . . @2.50

FREAKSHOW
Atomic Diner, 2004
1 . . . . 3.00
2 thru 12 . . . . @3.00

FRED THE POSSESSED FLOWER
Happy Predator, 1998
1 The Plant Behind the Scenes . . . 3.00
2 . . . . 3.00
3 Interview with a Demon 3.00
4 The People vs. Hell 3.00
5 . . . . 3.00
6 The Origin of Fred 3.00

FRENCH ICE
Renegade Press, 1987
1 thru 15 . . . . @2.50

FRIENDS
Renegade, 1987
1 thru 5 . . . . @2.50

FRIGHT
Eternity
1 .... 2.50
2 thru 13 .... @2.50

FRINGE
Caliber
1 .... 2.50
2 thru 7 .... @2.50

FROM BEYOND
Studio Insidio
1 Short stories-horror 2.50
2 inc.Clara Mutilares............ 2.50
3 inc.The Experiment 2.50
4 inc.Positive Feedback 2.50

FROM HELL
Tundra, 1991
1 .... 20.00
1a 2nd printing 10.00
2 .... 10.00
[Vol. Three] Kitchen Sink
1 AMo,ECa 10.00
2 AMo,ECa 7.00
2a 2nd printing 6.00
3 .... 7.00
3a 2nd printing 6.00
4 .... 7.00
4 new printing 5.00
5 .... 7.00
5 new printing 5.00
6 .... 7.00
7 .... 7.00
8 .... 7.00
8 AMo,ECa,new printing 5.00
9 AMo,ECa 7.00
9 new printing 5.00
10 AMo,ECa 7.00
10 new printing 5.00
Spec. Dance of the Gull Catchers . . 5.00

FROM THE DARKNESS
Adventure Comics, 1990
1 JBa......................... 20.00
2 .... 25.00
3 and 4 .... @9.00

FROM THE DARKNESS II
BLOOD VOWS
Cry For Dawn
1 R:Ray Thorn,Desnoires 9.00
2 V:Desnoires 8.00
3 .... 8.00

FROM THE VOID
1 1st B.Blair,1982 .... 60.00

FROST:
THE DYING BREED
Caliber
1 thru 3 Vietnam Flashbacks ... @3.00

F–III BANDIT
Antarctic Press, 1995
1 F:Akira, Yoohoo 3.00
2 F:Yukio..................... 3.00
3 F:Were-Women 3.00
4 .... 3.00
5 Romeo & Juliet story 3.00
6 thru 8 .... @3.00

FUGITOID
Mirage
1-shot TMNT Tie-in............ 8.00

Fugatoid 1-shot
© Mirage

FULL METAL FICTION
London Night, 1997
1 EHr 4.00
1a Nun with a Gun edition 9.00
1b dark room edition cover....... 4.00
2 .... 4.00
2a signed 9.00
3 'Hellborne' concl............. 4.00
4 thru 8 .... @4.00

FURIES
Carbon-Based, 1996
1 thru 6 .... @2.75

FURRLOUGH
Antarctic Press, 1991
1 Funny Animal Military stories.... 3.00
2 thru 10 .... @2.50
11 thru 20 .... @2.75
21 thru 33 .... @2.75
34 .... 3.00
35 48pg 4.00
36 thru 40 .... @3.00
41 thru 51 .... @3.00
Best of Furlough, Vol.1 .... 5.00
Best of Furlough, Vol.2 .... 5.00
Radio Comix, 1997
52 thru 75.................. @3.00
76 thru 99 .... @3.00
100 80-pg. 6.00
101 .... 3.00
102 thru 139................. @3.00
140 thru 177................. @3.50
178 thru 187................. @4.00
Furrlough's Finest Vol. 1 .... 6.00
Furrlough's Finest Vol. 2 .... 6.00
Furrlough Presents Sex Kitten #1 .. 5.00

FURRY NINJA
HIGH SCHOOL
Shanda Fantasy Arts, 2002
1 (of 2) x-over (self) parody 5.00
2 x-over, concl................. 5.00

FURY
Aircel
1 thru 3 .... @2.50

FURY OF HELLINA, THE
Lightning Comics, 1995
1 V:Luciver 3.50
1a limited & signed 8.00
1b platinum 8.00

FUSION
Eclipse, 1987
1 .... 2.50
2 thru 17 .... @2.50

FUTABA-KUN CHANGE
Ironcat, 1998
1 by Hiroshi Aro 3.00
2 thru 6 .... @3.00
VOL. 2
1 .... 3.00
2 thru 6 .... @3.00
VOL. 3, 1999
1 .... 3.00
2 thru 6 .... @3.00
VOL. 4, 2000
1 .... 3.00
2 thru 6 .... @3.00
VOL. 5, 2000
1 by Hiroshi Aro 3.00
2 thru 6 .... @3.00
VOL. 6, 2001
1 .... 3.00
2 thru 6 .... @3.00
VOL. 7, 2001
1 .... 3.00
2 thru 6 .... @3.00
VOL. 8
1 thru 6 .... @3.00

FUTURAMA
Slave Labor, 1989
1 thru 4 .... @2.50

FUTURETECH
Mushroom Comics, 1995
1 Automotive Hi-Tech 3.50
2 Cyber Trucks 3.50

GAIJIN
Caliber, 1990
1-shot, 64pg.................. 3.50
1 thru 3 .... @2.50

GALAXION
Helikon, 1997
1 by Tara Jenkins, science fiction. . 2.75
2 .... 2.75
3 .... 2.75
4 Choices 2.75
5 .... 2.75
6 Communication 2.75
7 Song of Hiawatha 2.75
8 Persuasion.................. 2.75
9 Deal with the Devil.......... 2.75
10 .... 2.75
11 .... 2.75
Spec. #1, 16pg. 2.00
GN Vol 1 .... 16.00
Spec. Flip Book Galaxion
   & Amy Unbound 2.75

GARGOYLES: BAD GUYS
Amaze Ink/SLG, 2007
1 .... 3.50
2 thru 6 .... @3.50

GATEKEEPER
GK Publishing, 1987
1 .... 2.50
2 and 3 .... @3.00

GATES OF THE NIGHT
Jademan
1 thru 4 .... @3.50

GEAR
Fireman Press, 1998
1 (of 6) by Douglas TenNaple 3.00
2 thru 6 . . . . @3.00

GEISHA
Oni Press, 1998
1 (of 4) by Andi Watson 3.00
2 thru 4 . . . . @3.00

GENERIC COMIC BOOK
Comics Conspiracy, 2001
1 thru 4 . . . . @2.50
5 . . . . 2.50
5a Hyper Fanboy variant edition. . . 6.00
6 thru 13 . . . . @2.50

GENOCYBER
Viz, 1993
1 I:Genocyber 2.75
2 thru 5 . . . . @2.75

GEOBREEDERS
CPM Manga, 1999
1 by Akhiro Ito 3.00
2 thru 10 . . . . @3.00
11 thru 36 . . . . @3.00

GHOSTS OF DRACULA
Eternity
1 A:Dracula & Houdini 2.50
2 A:Sherlock Holmes 2.50
3 A:Houdini 2.50
4 Count Dracula's Castle 2.50
5 Houdini, Van Helsing, Dracula
   team-up 2.50

GI GOVERNMENT ISSUED
Paranoid Press, 1994
1 thru 7 F:Mac, Jack . . . . @2.50

GIANT SHANDA ANIMAL
Shanda Fantasy Arts, 1998
1 . . . . 5.00
2 . . . . 5.00
3 . . . . 5.00
4 . . . . 4.50
5 thru 12 . . . . @5.00

GIDEON HAWK
Big Shot Comics, 1995
1 I:Gideon Hawk, Max 9471 . . . . . . 2.50
2 The Jewel of Shamboli,pt.2 . . . . . 2.50
3 The Jewel of Shamboli,pt.3 . . . . . 2.50
2 The Jewel of Shamboli,pt.4 . . . . . 2.50
3 The Jewel of Shamboli,pt.5 . . . . . 2.50

GIGANTOR
Antarctic Press, 2000
1 (of 12) by Ben Dunn 3.00
2 thru 8 . . . . @3.00

GIRL GENIUS
Studio Foglio, 2001
1 thru 5 . . . . @3.00
Airship Entertainment, 2002
6 thru 10 . . . . @4.00
11 thru 14 . . . . @4.00

GIRLS OF NINJA
HIGH SCHOOL, 1997
Antarctic Press
Spec. 4.00
Spec. 1998 cover A 3.00
Spec. 1998 cover B 3.00

Spec. 1999 . . . . 3.00

GIZMO
Mirage, 1987
1 . . . . 5.50
2 . . . . 3.00
3 thru 7 . . . . @2.50

GIZMO & THE FUGITOID
Mirage, 1989
1 and 2 . . . . @2.50

GLAMOURPUSS
Aardvark Vanaheim, 2008
1 by Dave Sim 3.00
2 variant fashion (c) 3.00
3 thru 4 . . . . @3.00

GLOOM COOKIE
Slave Labor Graphics, 1999
1 by Serena Valentino
   & Ted Naifeh 3.00
2 thru 5 . . . . @3.00
6 Sebastian's Search 3.00
7 thru 9 . . . . @3.00
10 thru 29 . . . . @3.00
Color Spec. A Monster's Christmas . 4.00

GOBBLEDYGOOK
Mirage, 1986
1 1st series, Rare 1,100.00
2 1st series, Rare 550.00
1 TMNT series reprint 6.00

GOJIN
Antarctic Press, 1995
1 F:Terran Defense Force 3.00
2 F:Terran Defense Force 3.00
3 V:Alien Monster 3.00
4 Aliens Bone 3.00
5 thru 8 . . . . @3.00

GOLD DIGGER
Antarctic Press, 1992
[Limited Series]
1 Geena & Cheetah in Peru 8.00
2 Adventures contd 6.00
3 Adventures contd 6.00
4 Adventures contd 5.00
[Volume 2], 1993
1 by Fred Perry 10.00
2 Fred Perry 8.00
3 Fred Perry 8.00
4 Fred Perry 6.00
5 misnumbered as #0 . . . . 5.00
6 thru 8 by Fred Perry . . . . @4.00
9 and 10 by Fred Perry . . . . @3.50
11 thru 27 by Fred Perry . . . . . . @3.00
28 and 29 by Fred Perry . . . . . . @3.00
30 thru 39 . . . . @3.00
40 Wedding day 3.00
41 Gold Digger Beta 3.00
42 . . . . 3.00
43 Beta Phase phenomenon 3.00
44 Beta tool 3.00
45 F:Priestess Tanya 3.00
46 Agent M 3.00
47 Old Dirty Bastard 3.00
48 . . . . 3.00
49 The Library of Time 3.00
50 . . . . 3.00
50a deluxe 6.00
Ann. 1995, 48-pg. 4.00
Ann. 1996 . . . . 4.00
Ann. 1997 . . . . 4.00
Ann. 1998 . . . . 4.00
Ann. 2000 b&w 4.00
Ann. 2001 . . . . 4.00

Gold Digger #36
© Antarctic Press

Ann. 2002 B&W 4.00
Best of Gold Digger Ann. Vol. 1 . . . . 3.00
Mangazine Spec. #1 . . . . 3.00

GOLD DIGGER/
NINJA HIGH SCHOOL
Antarctic Press, 1998
Spec. Asrial vs. Cheetah Compilation,
   x-over rep. 5.00
Spec. Science Fair Compilation,
   x-over rep. 5.00

GOLD DIGGER:
EDGE GUARD
Radio Comix, 2000
1 (of 4) by John Barrett 3.00
2 thru 6 . . . . @3.00
7 finale 3.00

GOLD DIGGER: THRONE
OF SHADOWS
Antarctic Press, 2006
1 Manga 3.00
2 thru 4 . . . . @3.00

GOLDEN AGE GREATS
AC Comics, 1995
Vol.#1 thru #6 40s and 50s . . . . @10.00
Vol. 7 Best of the West 10.00
Vol. 8 F:Phantom Lady, Miss
   Victory 10.00
Vol. 9 Fabulous Femmes of Fiction
   House 10.00
Vol. 11 Roy Rogers & The Silver
   Screen Cowboys 12.00
Vol. 12 Thrilling Science Fiction . . . 10.00
Vol. 13 . . . . 10.00
Vol. 14 The Comic Book Jungle . . 12.00

GOLDEN-AGE
MEN OF MYSTERY
AC Comics, 1996
5 . . . . 7.00
7 . . . . 6.00
8 . . . . 6.00
9 . . . . 6.00
10 Masked comic book
   heroes, 52 pg. 7.00
11 rep. Cat-Man comics 7.00
12 Espionage, WE 7.00

13 F:Daredevil vs. The Claw 7.00
14 F:Commando Yank 7.00
15 F:Captain 3-D 7.00
16 F:Mr. Scarlet, Airboy 7.00
Becomes:

MEN OF MYSTERY
AC Comics, 1999
17 F:Stuntman 7.00
18 . . . . 7.00
19 Space edition 7.00
19a spec. ed. 68-pg. 9.00
20 F:Phantom Lady 7.00
21 Fawcett superheroes 7.00
22 Manhunter. 7.00
23 Skyman 7.00
24 Captain Flash 7.00
25 . . . . 7.00
26 Emerald. 7.00
27 The Fog Robbers 7.00
28 F:Black Terror,Miss Masque 7.00
29 The Lynx, Wildfire 7.00
30 War Years 7.00
31 Speed and Space 7.00
32 Phantom Lady. 7.00
33 Red white and blue. 7.00
34 Halloween Issue 7.00
35 F:Spy Smasher. 7.00
36 F:Captain Flash 7.00
37 F:Cat-Man and Kitten 7.00
38 Spy Smasher vs. Iron Mask 7.00
39 Spy Smasher, Airboy 7.00
40 The Black Terror 7.00
41 Bulletman 7.00
42 Blue Bolt 7.00
43 The Flame 7.00
44 Cat-Man and Bulletman 7.00
45 thru 69 . . . . @7.00
70 thru 76 . . . . @10.00
Coll. Ed. #7 . . . . 20.00
Digest Spec. #1 . . . . 16.00
Spotlight Spec. #1 . . . . 15.00
Ann. #1 Spy Smasher Special 8.00

GOLDEN WARRIOR
Industrial Design, 1997
1 by Eric Bansen & RB 3.00
2 thru 3 . . . . @3.00

GOLDEN WARRIOR ICZER ONE
Antarctic, 1994
1 thru 5 . . . . @3.00

GO-MAN
Caliber
1 . . . . 2.50
2 thru 4 . . . . @2.50
Graphic Novel `N` 10.00

GOOD GIRLS
Fantagraphics, 1987
1 adult. 2.50
2 thru 4 . . . . @2.50

GOON, THE
Avatar Press, 1999
1 by Eric Powell 40.00
2 . . . . 20.00
3 . . . . 20.00

GORE SHRIEK
Fantaco, 1986
1 . . . . 2.50
2 and 3 . . . . @2.50
4 +Mars Attacks 3.00
5 . . . . 3.00
6 . . . . 3.50
Vol 2 #1 . . . . 2.50

GORI LORI
Chanting Monks 2006
1 . . . . 2.50
2 thru 3 . . . . @2.50

GOTHESS: DARK ECSTASY
SCC Entertainment, 1997
1 (of 3) 3.00
2 . . . . 3.00
3 . . . . 3.00

GRACKLE, THE
Acclaim, 1996
1 MBn,PG,Double Cross, pt.1 . . . . . 3.00
2 MBn,PG,Double Cross, pt.2 . . . . . 3.00
3 MBn,PG,Double Cross, pt.3 . . . . . 3.00
4 MBn,PG,Double Cross, pt.4 . . . . . 3.00

GRAPHIC STORY MONTHLY
Fantagraphics
1 thru 7 . . . . @3.00

GRAPHIQUE MUSIQUE
Slave Labor, 1989–90
1 . . . . 35.00
2 . . . . 30.00
3 . . . . 25.00

Gravediggers #4 #4
© Acclaim

GRAVEDIGGERS
Acclaim, 1996
1 (of 4) 3.00
2 thru 4 . . . . @3.00

GRAVE TALES
Hamilton, 1991
1 JSon,GM, mag. size 8.00
2 JSon,GM,short stories 6.00
3 JSon,GM, inc.`Stake Out` 6.00

GREAT DETECTIVE STARRING SHERLOCK HOLMES
ACG Comics, 1999
1 by Otto Lagoni 3.00
2 thru 5 . . . . @3.00

GREEN BERETS
ACG, 2000
1 JKu. 3.00
2 thru 7 JKu, Robin Moore . . . . . @3.00

GREENLEAF IN EXILE
Cat's Paw Comics, 1998
1 by Doug Anderson 3.00
2 thru 7 . . . . @3.00

GREMLIN TROUBLE
Anti-Ballistic Pixelation, 1995
1 & 2 Airstrike on Gremlin Home @3.00
1 new printing . . . . @3.00
3 thru 5 . . . . @3.00
6 `Fun with Electricity'. 3.00
7 `Cypher in Fairyland' 3.00
8 . . . . 3.00
9 F:Candy Tsai 3.00
10 The Tuberians are coming 3.00
11 V:X-the-Unmentionable. 3.00
12 preemptive strike on Site X. 3.00
13 Gremlin-Goblin war. 3.00
14 . . . . 3.00
15 Battle of 5 Armies 3.00
16 . . . . 3.00
17 kidnapped to Fairyland 3.00
18 . . . . 3.00
19 The Sky Stone 3.00
20 Ring Fortress 3.00
21 A-Girls 3.00
22 Gremlin Guild 3.00
23 escape from Mordovania 3.00
24 thru 30 . . . . @3.00
Spec. #1 Super Special 3.00
Super Special Final (2004) 3.25

GRENDEL
Comico, 1983
1 MW,O:Hunter Rose, rare 165.00
2 MW,O:Argent, rare. 125.00
3 MW,rare. 125.00

GRENUORD
Fantagraphics Books, 2005
1 (of 6) 5.00
2 . . . . 5.00
3 . . . . 5.00

GREY
Viz Select, 1989
Book 1 . . . . 5.00
Book 2 scarce 5.50
Book 3 . . . . 3.00
Book 4 . . . . 3.00
Book 5 . . . . 3.00
Book 6 thru Book 9 . . . . @2.50

GREYMATTER
Alaffinity Studios, 1993
1 thru 14 by Marcus Harwell . . . @3.00

GRIFFIN, THE
Slave Labor, 1988
1 . . . . 2.50
1a 2nd printing 2.50
2 thru 4 . . . . @2.50
5 . . . . 2.50
Amaze Ink, 1997
1 by DVa & Phil Allora 3.00
2 by DVa & Paul Way 3.00

GRIPS
Silver Wolf, 1986
1 Vigil 12.00
2 Vigil 9.00
3 Vigil 8.00

4 Vigil 7.00
Vol 1 #1 rep 2.50
Volume 2
1 . . . . 2.50
2 . . . . 2.50
3 thru 8 . . . . @2.50
9 thru 12 . . . . @2.50

GROUND ZERO
Eternity
1 Science Fiction mini-series 2.50
2 Alien Invasion Aftermath 2.50

GRRL SCOUTS
Oni Press, 1999
1 (of 4) by Jim Mahfood 3.00
2 thru 4 . . . . @3.00
Amazing Aaron, 1999
1 Aaron Warner. 3.00
2 . . . . 3.00

Guerrilla Groundhog #1
© Eclipse

GUERRILLA GROUNDHOG
Eclipse, 1987
1 . . . . 2.50
2 . . . . 2.50

GUILLOTINE
Silver Wolf, 1987
1 thru 2 . . . . @2.50

GUN CRISIS
Ironcat, 1998
1 (of 3) by Masoami Kanzaki 3.00
2 & 3 . . . . @3.00

GUNDAM WING
Mixx Entertainment, 2000
1 . . . . 5.00
2 thru 4 . . . . @4.00
Tokyopop.Com, 2000
5 thru 12 . . . . @3.00
...BATTLEFIELD OF PACIFISTS
Tokyopop Press, 2001
1 48-pg. 3.00
2 thru 5 . . . . @3.00
...ENDLESS WALTZ
Tokyopop Press, 2002
1 (of 5) 3.00
2 thru 4 . . . . @3.00

...G-UNIT
Tokyopop Press, 2002
1 (of 12) 3.00
2 . . . . 3.00
...THE LAST OUTPOST
Tokyopop Press, 2002
1 (of 12) 3.00
2 thru 4 . . . . @3.00
...THE ORIGIN
Viz Communications, 2002
GN #1 by Yoshikazu Yasuhiko. 8.00
GN #2 thru #12 . . . . @8.00

GUNFIGHTERS IN HELL: ORIGINAL SIN
Broken Halos, 2001
1 . . . . 4.00
1a variant (c). 6.00
1 limited edition 16-pg. 7.00
2 24-pg. 4.00
2a cardstock (c) 4.50
2b limited edition. 6.00

GUN FURY
Aircel, 1989
1 thru 10 . . . . @2.50

GUN FURY RETURNS
Aircel, 1990
1 . . . . 3.00
2 . . . . 3.00
3 V:The Yes Men 2.50
4 . . . . 2.50

GUNNER
Gun Dog Comics, 1999
1 . . . . 3.00
2 thru 7 by Eric Yonge. . . . . @3.00

GUNS OF SHAR-PEI
Caliber
1 The Good,the Bad & the Deadly . 3.00
2 & 3 . . . . @3.00

GUTWALLOW
Numbskull Press, 1998
1 by Dan Berger 3.00
2 thru 7 The Gingerbread Man . . @3.00
Digital Webbing 2002
1 (of 3) 3.00
2 Fury of the Furry 3.00
3 concl. 3.00

GUNWITCH, THE: OUTSKIRTS OF DOOM
Oni Press, 2001
1 by DIB 3.00
2 thru 3 . . . . @3.00

GYPSY
Avatar Press, 2005
1 . . . . 3.50
1a Wraparound (c) 3.50
1b Variant(c)s . . . . @3.50
1c Die-cut (c) 10.00
2 . . . . 4.00
2a wraparound (c). 4.00
2b Variant(c)s . . . . @4.00
2c premium (c) 10.00

GYRE
Abaculus, 1997
1 by Martin Shipp & Marc Laming . 3.00
2 . . . . 3.00

3 Soul Keeper, pt. 3.00
4 thru 6 . . . . @3.00
Spec. Edition 56-pg. 4.50

HALL OF HEROES
Hall of Heroes, 1993
1 I:Dead Bolt. 10.00
2 and 3 . . . . @4.50
Ashcan, 8-pg. 6.00
Halloween Horror Special 2.50
Halloween Horror Special '98 . . . . 2.50

HALL OF HEROES PRESENTS
Hall of Heroes, 1996–97
0 by Doug Brammer & Matt Roach,
   'Slingers' by Matt Martin 2.50
1 . . . . 2.50
1a signed & numbered 4.00
2 'The Last Days'. 2.50
3 'The Power of the Golem'. 2.50
4 F:Turaxx the Trobbit. 2.50
5 . . . . 2.50

HALLOWIENERS
Mirage
1 . . . . 2.50
2 . . . . 2.50

HAMMER GIRL
Brainstorm, 1996
1 dinosaur, sci-fi adventure. 3.00
2 . . . . 3.00
2a deluxe 5.00

HAMSTER VICE
Blackthorne, 1986
1 . . . . 3.50
2 . . . . 2.50
3 thru 11 . . . . @2.50
Eternity, 1989
1 and 2 . . . . @2.50

HANGED MAN
Caliber, 1998
1 (of 2) by AIG & Arthur Ranson. . . 3.00
2 (of 2) 3.00

HARD BOILED COMICS
Goodbum Studios 2006
1 . . . . 3.00
2 thru 4 . . . . @3.00

HARD ROCK COMICS
Revolutionary, 1992
1 Metallica-The Early Years 6.00
2 Motley Crew. 4.00
3 Jane's Addiction. 3.50
4 Nirvana 4.00
5 Kiss 9.00
5a 2nd printing 5.00
6 Def Leppard II 3.00
7 Red Hot Chili Peppers. 3.00
8 Pearl Jam. 3.00
9 Queen II. 3.00
10 Birth of Punk. 3.00
11 Pantera 3.00
12 Hendrix 3.00
13 Dead Kennedys 3.00
14 Van Halen II 2.50
15 Megadeath 2.50
16 Joan Jett 2.50
17 Not printed
18 Queensryche. 2.50
19 Tesla 2.50
20 The Sweet. 2.50

HARI KARI
Blackout, 1995
1	3.00
1a platinum	8.00
1-shot Possessed by Evil(1997)	3.00
1-shot Hari Kari Goes Hollywood	
(1997)	3.00
Deluxe	15.00
Spec #1 Sexy Summer Rampage,	
gallery issue (1997)	3.00
Deluxe, super sexy cover	10.00
1-shot Cry of Darkness (1998)	3.00
Variant photo ultra sexy ed.	10.00
1-shot The Last Stand (1998)	3.00
Ultra sexy edition	10.00
Deluxe	15.00

HARI KARI MANGA
Blackout Comics, 1998
Spec. 0 Sex, Thugs & Rock 'n' Roll	3.00
1-shot Manga Adventures (1997)	3.00
1-shot Deadly Exposure, by Rob	
Roman & Nigel Tully	3.00
Deluxe	15.00
1-shot Deadtime Stories, by Rob	
Roman & Nigel Tully	3.00
Deluxe edition	15.00
1-shot Manga To Die For	3.00
Deluxe	15.00
1-shot Running From Poison	3.00

HARPY:
PRIZE OF THE OVERLORD
Ground Zero, 1996
1 (of 6)	3.00
2 thru 6	@3.00
1-shot Harpy Preview, prequel.	3.00

Peregrine, 1998
Spec. Harpy Pin-up Book	3.00

HARTE OF DARKNESS
Eternity, 1991
1 I:Dennis Harte,Vampire	
private-eye	2.50
2 V:Satan's Blitz St.Gang	2.50
3 Jack Grissom/Vampire	2.50
4 V:Jack Grissom, conc.	2.50

HARVEST KING
Caliber, 1998
1 by Joe Casey & Mike	
Macropoulos	3.00
2	3.00
3	3.00

HARVY FLIP BOOK
Blackthorne
1 thru 3	@2.50

HATE
Fantagraphics, 1990
1	15.00
2	10.00
3	9.00
4	8.00
5	8.00
6	8.00
7	7.00
8 thru 10	@6.00
11 and 12	@5.00
1a to 12a reprints	@2.50
13 thru 15	@4.00
Hate Jamboree, 64-pg.	4.00
See Color	

Hate #2
© Fantagraphics

HAVOC, INC.
Radio Comix, 1998
1 by Mark Barnard & Terrie Smith	3.00
2 thru 9	@3.00
10	3.50

HEAVEN SENT
Antarctic Press, 2004
1 BDn	3.00
2 thru 5	@3.00
6 thru 11	@3.00
Stand Alone Special (2005)	3.00

HELLEN KILLER
Arcana Studio, 2008
1 (of 4)	4.00
2 thru 4	@3.00

HELLGIRL
Knight Press, 1995
1 I:Jazzmine Grayce	3.00
1-shot Demonseed II, Bob Hickey &	
Bill Nichols (1997)	3.00
1-shot Demonsong, Bob Hickey &	
Bill Nichols (1997)	3.00
1-shot Purgatory (1997)	3.00

HELLINA
Lightning Comics, 1994
1-shot I&O:Hellina	5.00
Commemorative	10.00
1996 rep. gold	5.00
Spec. Hellina: Genesis with poster	
(1996)	3.00
Platinum edition	4.00
Spec. Hellina: In the Flesh (1997)	
two diff. mild covers	@3.00
Spec. Hellina: Naked Desire (1997)	3.00
Cover B	3.00
Signed,	3.00
Spec. Hellina: Taking Back the Night	
(1995) V:Michael Naynar	3.00
Spec. Hellina: Wicket Ways (1995)	
A:Perg	2.75
Encore editions	3.00
Encore variant (c)	3.00
Spec. Hellina: X-Mas in Hell (1996)	
two different covers	@3.00
Platinum edition	5.00
Spec. Hellina: The Relic	3.00
Variant cover	3.00

Spec. 1997 Pin-up	3.50
1997 Pin-up, cover B.	3.50
X-Over Hellina/Catfight (1995)	
V:Prince of Sommia	2.75
Gold	4.00
Encore edition, mild covers,	
2 different	@3.00
X-Over Hellina/Cynder (1997) covA	3.00
Cover B	3.00
Spec Hellina #1 Skybolt Toyz	
lim. ed. (1997)	2.50

...HEART OF THORNS
Lightning Comics, 1996
1 (of 2)	3.00
1b autographed	5.00
2	2.75
2a variant cover	2.75
2b platinum edition	6.00

...HELL'S ANGEL
Lightning Comics, 1996
1	2.75
1a platinum edition	8.00
1a platinum edition, signed	9.00
1c nude platinum edition	12.00
2	2.75
2a platinum edition	8.00
1 encore edition, cover A	3.00
1a encore edition, cover B	3.00
1b deluxe encore edition, cover A	5.00
1c deluxe encore edition, cover B	5.00

...KISS OF DEATH
Lightning Comics, 1995
1-shot A:Perg	4.00
1-shot gold edition	9.00
1-shot Encore editions	3.00

Lightning, 1997
1A	3.00
1B variant cover	3.00
1 encore, signed & numbered	5.00

HELLINA
Avatar Press, 2003
0	3.50
0a variant (c).	3.50
0b wraparound (c).	4.00
0c Hard Ruler Edition	6.00
0d Prism foil edition	13.00

...SEDUCTION
Avatar Press, 2003
1/2 Carnage Edition	6.00
1/2 Statuesque Edition	6.00
Preview	2.50
Preview variant (c)	6.00
Preview Bad Girl edition	6.00
1	3.50
1a wraparound (c).	4.00

...VS PANDORA
Avatar Press, 2003
0 16-pg.	2.50
0a variant (c)s	@4.00
1 (of 3)	3.50
2 thru 3	@3.50
1a thru 3a variant (c)s	@3.50
Preview	2.50
Preview variant (c)	6.00
Preview Hellina's Army variant (c).	6.00

HELSING
Caliber Core, 1998
1W by Gary Reed & Low,	
Wozniak(c).	3.00
1L Loudon (c)	3.00
1 variant cover	8.00
1 premium, signed	9.00
2	3.00
3	3.00

4 Secrets and Lies 3.00
Spec. Dawn of Armageddon, Secrets
    & Lies, concl. 48-pg. 4.00

HELTER SKELTER
Rog Heavy Industries, 1996
1 . . . . 3.00
2 . . . . 3.00

Antarctic Press, 1997
0 by Mike Harris & Duc Tran 3.00
1 (of 4) 3.00
2 thru 6 . . . . @3.00

Hepcats #0
© Antarctic Press

HEPCATS
Double Diamond, 1989
1 . . . . 15.00
2 . . . . 12.00
3 Snow Blind. 12.00
4 thru 9 . . . . @9.00
10 thru 13 . . . . @3.50
14 Chapter 12 . . . . 3.00
15 Snowblind Chp. 13 . . . . 3.00

Antarctic Press, 1996
0 . . . . 3.00
1 by Martin Wagner 3.00
2 `Trial by Intimacy'. 3.00
3 Snowblind,pt.1 . . . . 3.00
4 Snowblind,pt.2 . . . . 3.00
5 Snowblind,pt.3 . . . . 3.00
6 Snowblind,pt.4 . . . . 3.00
7 Snowblind,pt.5 Intrusion 3.00
8 Snowblind,pt.6 Super Heroes . . . 3.00
9 Snowblind,pt.7 Kevin & Kathryn . 3.00
10 Snowblind,pt.8 Exorcism,
    Prelude 3.00
11 Snowblind,pt.10 Exorcism(a) . . . 3.00
12 Snowblind,pt.10 Exorcism(b) . . . 3.00

HERCULES
A Plus Comics
1 Herculos Saga. 2.50

HERCULES
Blatant Comics, 1997
1 TV parody (c). 3.00
1a Movie parody (c) 3.00
1b 3-D Rendered (c). 3.00

HERCULES PROJECT
Monster Comics, 1991
1 Origin issue,V:Mutants 2.50

HEROBEAR AND THE KID
Astonish Comics, 2000
1 . . . . 12.00
1a 2nd printing 3.50
2 . . . . 10.00
2a 2nd printing 3.50
3 . . . . 3.50
4 . . . . 3.50
5 Belief 3.50

HEROBEAR AND THE KID: SAVING TIME
Astonish Comics, 2004
1 (of 3) partial color. 3.50

HEROES
Blackbird, 1987
1 . . . . 5.00
2 . . . . 3.00
3 . . . . 2.50
4 comic size 2.50
5 thru 7 . . . . @2.50

HEROES ANONYMOUS
Bongo Comics, 2003
1 (of 6) 3.00
2 thru 6 . . . . @3.00

HEROES INCORPORATED
Double Edge Publishing
1 I:Heroes, Inc. 3.00
2 Betrayal 3.00

HEROIC TALES
Lone Star Press, 1997
1 by Robb Phipps & Bill Williams . . 2.50
2 Steel of a Soldier's Heart,pt.2 . . . 2.50
3 Steel of a Soldier's Heart,pt.3 . . . 2.50
4 . . . . 2.50
5 . . . . 2.50
6 The Belles of Freedom, prequel . 2.50
7 The Children of Atlas,pt.1 . . . . . . 2.50
8 by B.Williams & J.Parker, I:Atlas . 2.50

HEROINES, INC.
Avatar
1 thru 5 . . . . @2.50

HERO SANDWICH
Slave Labor, 1987
1 thru 4 . . . . @2.50
5 thru 8 . . . . @2.50
9 . . . . 2.50
GN 8.00

HEY MISTER
Insomnia Comics, 1997
1 . . . . 2.50
2 . . . . 2.50

Top Shelf
3 by Pete Sickman-Garner 3.00
4 . . . . 3.00
Spec. Behind the Green Door 3.00
Spec. The Trouble With Jesus. 3.00
Spec. Eyes on the Prize 3.00
Spec. Dial "M" for Mister 3.50

HICKEE
Alternative Comics 2003
Vol. 2
1 . . . . 5.00
2 . . . . 5.00
Vol. 3
1 . . . . 3.00
2 . . . . 3.00

HIGH CALIBER
Caliber, 1997
1 64pg. 4.00
1 signed edition. 4.00
2 64pg. 4.00
3 48pg. 4.00
4 . . . . 4.00

HIGH SCHOOL AGENT
Sun Comics, 1992
1 I:Kohsuke Kanamori 2.50
2 Treasure Hunt at North Pole 2.50
3 and 4 . . . . @2.50

HIGH SOCIETY
Aardvark–Vanaheim
1 DS,Cerebus 25.00

HIGHWAY 13
Amaze Ink/SLG, 2000
1 thru 11 by Les McClaine . . . . . @3.00

HILLY ROSE'S SPACE ADVENTURES
Astro Comics, 1995
1 confronts Steeltrap. 6.00
1 2nd & 3rd pr. by B.C. Boyer 3.00
2 . . . . 5.00
2 2nd & 3rd printing 3.00
3 . . . . 3.50
3 2nd printing 3.00
4 thru 9 . . . . @3.00

HIT THE BEACH
Antarctic, 1993
1 . . . . 3.00
1a deluxe edition. 5.00
2 & 3 . . . . @3.00
Spec. funny animal 3.00
Spec. 32 pg 3.00
Spec. deluxe 4.00
Spec. deluxe poster edition 5.00
Spec. 48-pg., 1999. . . . . 4.00
Spec. (#7) 48-pg., 2000. . . . . 4.00
Ann. 2001. . . . . 4.00
Ann. 2002. . . . . 4.00
1-shot Hit the Beach 2003 . . . . 5.00
1-shot Hit the Beach 2004 . . . . 5.00
1-shot Hit the Beach 2005 . . . . 5.00
1-shot Hit the Beach 2006 . . . . 6.00
Spec. 2007. . . . . 6.00

HITOMI AND HER GIRL COMMANDOS
Antarctic Press, 1992
1 Shadowhunter,from Ninja HS . . . 2.50
2 Synaptic Transducer 2.50
3 Shadowhunter in S.America 2.50
4 V:Mr.Akuma,last issue 2.50
[Series II]
1 . . . . 2.75
2 thru 10 . . . . @2.75

HOAX
Mental Note Press, 2005
1 . . . . 3.00
2 thru 3 . . . . @3.00
Fantagraphics Books 2006
4 . . . . 4.00

HOLLIDAY
Saddle Tramp Press 2002
1 F: Doc Holliday 2.50
2 thru 3 . . . . @2.50
4 thru 7 . . . . @3.00

B & W PUB.

HOLLYWOOD'S GOLDEN ERA, 1930S
A-List Comics, 1999
1 (of 3) 3.00
2 . . . . 3.00
3 . . . . 3.00

HOLO BROTHERS, THE
Monster Comics, 1991
1 thru 10 . . . . @2.50
Fantagraphics
Spec.#1 . . . . 2.50

HOLY KNIGHT
Pocket Change Comics
1 thru 3 . . . . @2.50
4 V:His Past 2.50
5 V:Souljoiner 2.50
6 V:Demon Priest 2.50
7 Silent Scream,pt.2 . . . . 2.50
8 'Dragon Quest,'pt.1 . . . . 2.50
9 'Dragon Quest,'pt.2 . . . . 2.50
10 'Dragon Quest,'pt.3 . . . . 2.50
11 'Dragon Quest,'pt.4 . . . . 2.50

HONK
Fantagraphics, 1986
1 Don Martin 2.75
2 . . . . 2.75
3 . . . . 2.75

HONOR AMONG THIEVES
Gateway Graphics, 1987
1 and 2 . . . . @2.50

HONOR BRIGADE
Spinner Rack Comics, 2007
1 . . . . 3.00
2 thru 6 . . . . @3.00

HONOR OF THE DAMNED
Americanime Productions, 2005
1 Manga by Nevin Arnold 3.50
2 . . . . 3.50
3 . . . . 3.50
4 . . . . 4.00

HOON
Eenieweenie Comics, 1995
1 I:Hoon 2.50
2 Calazone Disaster 2.50
3 Reality Check 2.50
4 thru 8 . . . . @2.50

HOON, THE
Caliber Tapestry, 1996
1 . . . . 3.00
2 & 3 . . . . @3.00

HOPELESS SAVAGES
Oni Press, 2001
1 . . . . 3.00
2 thru 4 . . . . @3.00

HOPELESS SAVAGES: GROUND ZERO
Oni Press, 2002
1 (of 4) 3.00
2 thru 4 . . . . @3.00

HOROBI
Viz, 1990
1 . . . . 4.00
2 thru 8 . . . . @3.75

Hopeless Savages #1
© Oni Press

Book 2, 1990–91
1 by Yoshihisa Tagami 3.50
2 D:Okado,Shoko Kidnapped 4.25
3 Madoka Attacks Zen 4.25
4 D:Abbess Mitsuko 4.25
5 Catharsis! 4.25
6 Shuichi Vs. Zen 4.25
7 Shuichi vs. Zen, conc. 4.25

HORROR IN THE DARK
Fantagor
1 RCo,Inc.Blood Birth 2.50
2 RCo,Inc.Bath of Blood 2.50
3 RCo 2.50
4 RCo,Inc.Tales of the
    Black Diamond 2.50

H.P. LOVECRAFT'S THE CALL OF CTHULHU AND OTHERS
Cross Plains Comics, 1999
1-shot RTs,EM 6.00

H.P. LOVECRAFT'S THE DREAM-QUEST OF UNKNOWN KADATH
Mock Man Press, 1997
1 (of 5) by Jason Thompson 3.00
1 2nd printing 3.00
2 thru 5 . . . . @3.00

H.P. LOVECRAFT'S THE RETURN OF CTHULHU
Cross Plains Comics, 2000
1-shot RTs & EM 6.00

HSU AND CHAN
Amaze Ink/SLG, 2003
1 thru 5 . . . . @3.00
6 thru 7 . . . . @3.00

HUGO
Fantagraphics, 1985
1 . . . . 4.00
2 thru 4 . . . . @2.50

HUMAN GARGOYLES
Eternity, 1988
Book one 2.50
Book two 2.50
Book three 2.50
Book four 2.50

HUNT AND THE HUNTED, THE
Newcomers Publishing
1 I:Aramis Thiron 3.00
2 V:Werewolves 3.00
3 Rio De Janero 3.00
4 F:Aramis Thiron 3.00

HURRICANE GIRLS
Antarctic Press, 1995
1 & 2 Tale of Dinon . . . . @3.50
3 thru 7 seven part series . . . . . @3.00

HUZZAH
1 I:Albedo's Erma Felna 50.00

HY-BREED
Division Publishing
1 thru 3 F:Cen Intel . . . . @2.50
4 thru 9 . . . . @2.50

HYPER DOLLS
Ironcat Manga, 1998
1 by Shinpei Itoh, F:Miyu & Maika . 3.00
2 thru 6 . . . . @3.00
VOL 2
1 . . . . 3.00
2 thru 6 . . . . @3.00
VOL 3
1 . . . . 3.00
2 thru 6 . . . . @3.00
VOL 4, 2000
1 . . . . 3.00
2 thru 6 . . . . @3.00
VOL 5, 2000
1 . . . . 3.00
2 thru 6 . . . . @3.00

I.F.S. ZONE
1 thru 6 . . . . @2.50

I AM LEGEND
Eclipse, 1991
1 Novel adapt. aka Omega Man . . . 6.00
2 thru 3 68-pg. . . . . @6.00

ICARUS
Aircel, 1987
1 thru 9 . . . . @2.50

ICON DEVIL
Spider
1 by Neil Hanson 2.50
2 . . . . 2.50
2nd Series
1 thru 5 . . . . @2.50

I DREAM OF JEANNIE
Airwave Comics, 2002
1 JJu(c) 3.00
1 special edition 6.00
2 . . . . 3.00
2a variant photo (c) 3.00
3 . . . . 3.00
Preview Book #1 . . . . 7.00
Spec. Trick-or-Treats Annual #1 . . . 3.50
Spec.#1 Wishbook (2001) 3.00
Spec.#1 Wishbook, photo (c) 3.00
Spec. Spring Spectacular 3.50
Spec. Spring Spectacular, photo(c) . 3.50

I HUNT MONSTERS
Antarctic Press 2004
1 . . . . 3.00
2 thru 9 . . . . @3.00

Vol. 2
1 by Rod Espinosa 3.00
2 thru 9 . . . . @3.00
Spec. Tales From Sleepy Hollow . . . 3.00

ILIAD
Amaze Ink, 1997
1 by Darren Brady & Alex Ogle . . . 3.00
2 thru 7 . . . . @3.00

ILIAD II
MicMac
1 . . . . 3.00
1a 2nd cover variation 3.00
2 . . . . 2.50
3 . . . . 2.50
4 . . . . 2.50

ILLUMINATUS
Rip Off, 1990
1 . . . . 2.50
2 . . . . 2.50
3 . . . . 2.50

INDUSTRIACIDE
Broken Tree Publications, 2002
1 (of 6) by Sean Dietrich 3.00
2 thru 6 . . . . @3.00

INFERNO
Caliber Press, 1995
1 I:City of Inferno 3.00
2 Search for Identity 3.00
3 V:Malateste 3.00
4 by MCy and Michael Gaydos . . . 3.00
5 . . . . 3.00

INTERZONE
Brainstorm Comics
1 w/4 cards 2.50
2 w/4 cards 2.50

INTO THE STORM
Curtis Comics, 2002
Vol. 1 Manga
1 by Jihoon Park & Takyoung Lee . 3.00
2 thru 4 . . . . @3.00
Vol. 2
1 . . . . 3.00

INU YASHA
Viz Communications, 1997
1 thru 5 (of 10) by Rumiko
Takahashi. . . . . @3.00
PART TWO:
A FEUDAL FAIRY TALE
Viz Communications, 1998
1 (of 9) by Rumiko Takahashi . . . 3.00
2 thru 7 . . . . @3.00
8 thru 15 (of 15) . . . . @3.25
PART THREE, 1999
1 (of 7) thru 7 . . . . @3.25
PART FOUR, 1999
1 (of 7) by Rumiko Takahashi. . . . @3.25
2 thru 7 . . . . @3.25
PART FIVE, 2000
1 (of 11) by Rumiko Takahashi 3.00
2 thru 11 . . . . @3.00
PART SIX, 2001
1 (of 15) 3.00
2 thru 7 . . . . @3.00
8 thru 15 . . . . @3.00
PART SEVEN, 2002
1 (of 8) by Rumiko Takahashi. 3.00

2 thru 7 . . . . @3.00

INVADERS FROM MARS
Eternity, 1990
1 . . . . 2.50
2 . . . . 2.50
3 . . . . 2.50
BOOK II, 1991
1 Sequel to '50's SF classic 2.50
2 Pact of Tsukus/Humans. 2.50
3 Last issue. 2.50

INVASION '55
Apple, 1990
1 . . . . 2.50
2 . . . . 2.50
3 . . . . 2.50

INVISIBLE PEOPLE
Kitchen Sink
1 WE,I:Peacus Pleatnik 3.00
2 WE,The Power. 3.00
3 WE,Final issue. 3.00

ISLAND
Tokyopop Press, 2001
1 48-pg.. 3.00
2 thru 4 . . . . @3.00
2nd Series, 2002
1 thru 7 . . . . @3.00

IT'S SCIENCE
WITH DR. RADIUM
Slave Labor, 1986
1 . . . . 2.50
2 thru 9 . . . . @2.50
Spec #1 . . . . 3.00

JACKAROO, THE
Eternity, 1990
1 GCh 2.50
2 & 3GCh . . . . @2.50

JACK HUNTER
Blackthorne, 1987
1 . . . . 3.50
2 thru 3 . . . . @3.50

JACK STAFF
Dancing Elephant Press, 2000
1 by Paul Grist 3.00
2 thru 4 . . . . @3.00
5 . . . . 3.00
6 . . . . 3.00
7 . . . . 3.00
8 56-pg.. 4.50
9 thru 12 . . . . @3.00

JACK THE LANTERN
Castle Rain Entertainment 2002
0a signed and numbered 8.00
1 thru 3 . . . . @3.00
4 The quest. 3.00
5 The quest. 3.50
1-shot 1942 . . . . 4.00

...GHOSTS
Castle Rain Entertainment, 2006
1 . . . . 2.50
2 thru 3 . . . . 4.00
Preview (2008) 2.00

JACK THE RIPPER
Eternity
1 thru 4 . . . . @2.50

JAM, THE
Slave Labor, 1989
1 . . . . 3.00
2 thru 5 . . . . @3.00
Dark Horse, 1993
6 thru 8 . . . . 3.00
Caliber, 1995
9 . . . . 3.00
9 signed edition. 3.00
10 It's a Kafka Thing 3.00
11 thru 14 . . . . @3.00
15 `The Kinetic',pt.3. . . . . 3.00

JANE'S WORLD
Girl Twirl, 2003
1 by Paige Braddock 3.00
2 thru 12 . . . . @3.00
13 thru 20 56-pg. . . . . @6.00
21 thru 24 . . . . @5.00

Jason and the Argonauts #4
© Caliber

JASON AND THE
ARGONAUTS
Caliber
1 . . . . 2.50
2 thru 5 . . . . @2.50

JAY & SILENT BOB
Oni Press, 1998
1 (of 4) by Kevin Smith & Duncan
Fregedo 5.00
1a Ph(c) 7.00
1b 2nd printing 3.00
2 thru 4 . . . . @4.00

JAZZ
High Impact, 1996
1 . . . . 3.00
1 Gold variant edition RCI(c) 9.00
2 . . . . 3.00
2a deluxe edition. 9.00
3 . . . . 3.00
3a variant (c). 9.00

JAZZ THE SERIES
ABC Comics, 1999
1 RCI(c). 3.00
1a DOe(c). 3.00
2 . . . . 3.00

All comics prices listed are for *Near Mint* condition.

JAZZ: SOLITAIRE
ABC Comics, 1998
1 (of 4) by Jose Varese 3.00
1a photo cover 6.00
2 ....3.00
2a Variant Exotika (c) 6.00
2b Variant Naughty (c) 6.00
3 ....3.00
Collected Ed. 5.00

JAZZ: SUPERSTAR
ABC Comics, 1998
1 (of 3) by Jose Varese 3.00
1a JQ cover 6.00

JAZZ AGE CHRONICLES
Caliber, 1990
1 thru 6 ....@2.50
7 ....2.50

JCP FEATURES
J.C. Productions, 1982
1 1st MT;S&K,NA/DG rep.
A:T.H.U.N.D.E.R.Agents,
TheFly, Black Hood Mag.Size . 11.00

JENNA AND NINJA HIGH
Narwain Publishing, 2006
1 (of 3) Ninja High School x-over . . 3.50
2 BDn 3.50
3 ....3.50

JENNY FINN
Oni Press, 1999
1 (of 4) by MMi & Troy Nixey 3.00
2 MMi 3.00
3 MMi 3.00
4 MMi, concl..................4.00

JEREMIAH
Fantagraphics, 1982–83
GN #1.......................35.00
GN #2.......................32.00

JEREMIAH:
BIRDS OF PREY
Adventure Comics, 1991
1 I: Jeremiah,A:Kurdy 4.00
2 conclusion 4.00

Jeremiah The Heirs #1
© Adventure Comics

...EYES LIKE BURNING COALS
Adventure Comics, 1991
1 & 2 fourth series.............@4.00

...A FISTFUL OF SAND
Adventure Comics
1 A:Captain Kenney 4.00
2 conclusion 4.00

...THE HEIRS
Adventure Comics, 1991
1 Nathanial Bancroft estate 4.00
2 conclusion 4.00

JERRY IGERS
FAMOUS FEATURES
Blackthorne
1 ....3.00
2 thru 4 ....@2.50
Pacific
5 thru 8 ....@2.50

JETCAT CLUBHOUSE
Oni Press, 2001
1 by Jay Stephens 3.25
2 thru 5 ....@3.25

JIM
Fantagraphics, 1987–90
1 ....15.00
2 ....12.00
3 and 4 ....@8.00
Second Series, 1994
1 ....4.00
1a 2nd printing 3.00
2 ....3.50
2a 2nd printing 3.00
3 thru 5 ....@3.00

JINGLE BELLE
Oni Press, 1999
1 (of 2) by PDi................3.00
2 PDi.......................3.00
All-Star Holiday Hullabaloo 5.00
1-shot Jingle Belle Jubilee.......3.00
1-shot The Mighty Elves 3.00
1-shot Winter Wingding 3.00

J. O'BARR's THE CROW
Kitchen Sink, 1998
0 F:Eric Draven, 48-pg. 3.50
1 ....3.50
2 Demon in Disguise 3.50

JOE PSYCHO
& MOO FROG
Goblin Studios, 1996
1 Fanatics Edition..............2.50
1 Fanatics signed and numbered
Edition 9.00
2 ....2.50
2 signed & numbered 9.00
3 ....2.50
4 ....2.50
4B San Diego Con cover 5.00
5 ....2.50
Spec. Psychosis Abnormalis 2.50

JOE R. LANSDALE's
BY BIZARRE HANDS
Avatar Press, 2004
1 ....3.50
2 thru 6 ....3.50
1a thru 6a wraparound (c)s.....@3.50
4 thru 6 connecting covers .....@6.00

JOE R. LANSDALE'S
THE DRIVE-IN
Avatar Press, 2003
1 (of 4) 3.50
2 thru 4 ....@3.50
1a thru 4a wraparound (c)......@4.00
Vol. 2, 2006
1 (of 4) 3.50
2 thru 4 ....@3.50
1a thru 4a wraparound (c)......@3.50

JOHNNY ATOMIC
Eternity
1 I:Johnny A.Tomick 2.50
2 Project X-contingency plan 2.50
3 ....2.50

JOHNNY COMET
ACG Comics, 1999
1 ....3.00
2 ....3.00
3 thru 5 FF, rep. ....@3.00

JOHNNY HIRO
Adhouse Books, 2007
1 ....3.00
2 thru 3 ....3.00

JOHNNY RAYGUN
Jetpack Press, 2003
1 ....3.00
2 thru 6 ....@3.00
Spec. Quarterly #1.............3.00

JOHNNY
THE HOMICIDAL MANIAC
Slave Labor, 1996
1 by Jhonen Vasquez..........28.00
1 3rd printing 15.00
1 signed, limited 15.00
2 ....12.00
2 3rd printing 12.00
3 ....10.00
3 3rd printing 6.00
4 ....5.00
4 2nd & 3rd printing 3.00
5 ....4.00
5 2nd printing 3.00
6 ....3.00
7 ....3.00

JOURNEY
Aardvark–Vanaheim, 1983
1 ....7.00
2 ....6.00
3 ....5.00
4 thru 7 ....@3.00
8 thru 14 ....@2.50
Fantagraphics, 1985
15 thru 28..................@2.50

JR. JACKALOPE
1 orange cover,1981............8.00
1a Yellow cover,1981 ....10.00
2 ....8.00

JULIE'S JOURNEY/
GRAVITY
Paper Live Studios, 1998
1 by David Keye 2.50
2 thru 6 ....@2.50

JUNGLE COMICS
Blackthorne, 1988
4 thru 6 ....@2.50

JUNGLE COMICS
A-List Comics, 1997
1 reprint of golden age	3.00
2 thru 6	@3.00

JUNGLE FANTASY
Avatar Press, 2002
Preview	2.50
Preview, Fauna (c)	2.50
Preview, Wild (c)	6.00
1	3.50
1b wraparound (c)	4.00
2	3.50
3	3.50
3b Back to the Hunt Edition	6.00
4	3.50
4b volcanic edition	6.00
5	3.50
1a thru 5a variant (c)s	@3.50
1/2 Winged Death Edition	6.00
Ann. #1	5.00
Ann. #1a variant (c)s	@5.00

JUNGLE GIRLS
AC Comics, 1989–93
1 incGold.Age reps.	3.00
2 Tara, Nyoka, Cave Girl	3.00
3 Greed,A:Tara	3.00
4 CaveGirl	3.00
5 Camilla	3.00
6 TigerGirl	3.00
7 CaveGirl	3.00
8 Sheena Queen o/t Jungle	3.00
9 Wild Girl,Tiger Girl,Sheena	3.00
10 F:Tara,Cave Girl,Nyoka	3.00
11 F:Sheena,Tiger Girl,Nyoka	3.00
12 F:Sheena,Camilla,Tig.Girl	3.00
13 F:Tara, Tiger Girl	3.00
14 Wildside	3.00
15 Wildside	3.00
16 Wildside	3.00

JUNIOR
Fantagraphics, 2000
1 (of 5) by Peter Bogge	3.00
2 thru 5	@3.00

JUPITER
Sandberg Publishing, 1999
1 by Jason Sandberg	3.00
2 thru 10	@3.00

JURASSIC JANE
London Night, 1997
1 by Sky Owens, F:Tira, elf princess of Atlantis	3.00
2 Sky Owens	3.00
3 Sky Owens	3.00
4 EHr, Sky Owens	3.00
5 by Preston Owens	3.00
6 by Sky Owens	3.00
7 by Sky Owens	3.00
Coll. Ed.	5.00

JUSTY
Viz Communications, 1988
1 thru 9	@2.50

KABUKI:
CIRCLE OF BLOOD
Caliber Press, 1995
1 R:Kabuki	6.00
2 Kabuki Goes Rogue	5.00
3 V:Noh Agents	5.00
4 V:Noh Agents	3.50
5 V:Kai	3.00
6	3.00

Kabuki: Masks of the Noh #4
© Caliber

...DANCE OF DEATH
London Night Studios, 1995
1 1st Full series	8.00

...MASKS OF THE NOH
Caliber, 1996
1A JQ(c)	3.00
1B Mays/Mack(c)	3.00
1C Buzz(c)	3.00
2	3.00
3 DMk	3.00
4 epilog	3.00

KAFKA
Renegade, 1987
1 thru 6	@2.50
The Execution Spec.	2.50

KAMUI
Eclipse, 1987
1 Sanpei Shirato Art	4.00
1a 2nd printing	2.50
2 Mystery of Hanbie	3.00
2a 2nd printing	2.50
3 V:Ichijiro	2.50
3a 2nd printing	2.50
4 thru 15	@2.50
16 thru 37	@2.50

KANE
Dancing Elephant, 1993
1 by Paul Grist	5.00
2 thru 13	@4.00
14 thru 22	@3.50
23 thru 33	@3.00

KAOS MOON
Caliber, 1996
1 by DdB	3.50
1a 2nd edition	3.00
2	3.50
2a 2nd edition, new cover	3.00
3	5.00
4 Anubian Nights, Chapter 2	5.00
GN Full Circle, rep #1–#2	6.00

KAPTAIN KEEN AND KOMPANY
Vortex, 1986
1	2.50
2 and 7	@2.50

KATHARSIS
Americanime Corp. 2006
1 Manga	3.50
2 thru 3	@3.50

KATMANDU
Antarctic Press, 1993
1 thru 3	@2.75
4 & 5 Woman of Honor	2.75
6 F:Laska	2.75

Med Systems
7 and 8	@2.50

Vision Comics, 1996
9 `When Warriors Die,'pt.3(of 3)	2.50
10 `The Curse of the Blood,'pt.1	2.50
11 `The Curse of the Blood,'pt.2	2.50
12 `The Curse of the Blood,' concl	3.00
13 `The Search For Magic,'pt.1	3.00

Shanda Fantasy Arts
14 `The Search For Magic,'pt.2	3.00
15 `The Search For Magic,'pt.3	3.00
16 `Ceremonies,'pt.1 (of 3)	3.00
17 `Ceremonies,'pt.2	3.00
18 `Ceremonies,'pt.3	3.00
19 `Peace Keeper,'pt.1	3.00
20 `Peace Keeper,'pt.2	3.00
21 `Peace Keeper,'pt.3	3.00
22	3.00
23 and 24	@3.00
25 thru 36 48-pg.	@5.00
Ann. #1 48-pg.	5.00
Ann. #2	5.00
Ann. #3	5.00
Ann. #4	5.00
Ann. #5	5.00
Ann. #6	5.00
Spec. Katmandu	5.00

KEIF LLAMA
Fantagraphics
1 thru 6	@3.00

KEIF LLAMA: GAS WAR
Oni Press, 1999
1 by Matt Howarth	3.00

KEIF LLAMA: XENOTECH
Aeon, 2005
1 (of 6) by Matt Howarth	3.00
2 thru 6	@3.00

KELLEY BELLE, POLICE DETECTIVE
Newcomers Publishing
1 Debut issue	3.00
2 Case of the Jeweled Scarab	3.00
3 Case o/t Jeweled Scarab,pt.2	3.00

KICKASS GIRL: SKELETONS IN THE CLOSET
Neko Press 2003
1	3.00
1a variant (c)	3.00
1b mini-print edition	5.00
2 thru 4	@3.00

KID CANNIBAL
Eternity, 1991
1 I:Kid Cannibal	2.50
2 Hunt for Kid Cannibal	2.50
3 A:Janice	2.50
4 final issue	2.50

KIKU SAN
Aircel, 1988
1 thru 6 . . . . @2.50

KILLBOX
Antarctic Press, 2002
1 . . . . 5.00
2 thru 3 . . . . @5.00

KILLING STROKE
Eternity, 1991
1 British horror tales 2.50
2 inc.`Blood calls to Blood' 2.50
3 and 4 . . . . @2.50

KILROY
Caliber Core, 1998
1C by Joe Pruett & Feliciano
  Zecchin, John Cassaday(c). . . . 3.00
1P JoP (c) 3.00
1a premium edition 9.00
2 . . . . 3.00
3 . . . . 3.00
4 O:Kilroy 3.00
Spec. Dawn of Armageddon,
  x-over, 48-pg. 4.00
Spec.#1 The Origin 5.00
Spec.#2 The Origin,pt.2 . . . . 5.00

KILROY IS HERE
Caliber Press, 1995
1 Kilroy Rescues Infant. 3.00
2 Reflections,pt.2 . . . . 3.00
3 Reflections,pt.3 . . . . 3.00
4 Lincoln Memorial 3.00
5 thru 8 . . . . @3.00
9 and 10 . . . . @3.00
11 WEI,RPc,`Screen' 3.00
12 Khymer Rouge 3.00
Spec. Kilroy: Daemonstorm (1997) . 3.00

KIMBER, PRINCE OF FEYLONS
Castle Graphics 1991
1 . . . . 3.50
Antarctic Press, 1992
1 I:Kimber 2.50
2 V:Lord Tyrex. 2.50

KINDERGOTH
Bloodfire, 2004
1 . . . . 3.00
2 thru 4 . . . . @3.00

KINGDOM OF THE WICKED
Caliber, 1996
1 IEd 3.00
2 thru 4 IEd . . . . @3.00

KING KONG
Monster Comics, 1991
1 . . . . 2.50
2 thru 6 . . . . @2.50

KINGS IN DISGUISE
Kitchen Sink, 1988
1 thru 5 . . . . @2.50
6 end Mini-series 2.50

KING ZOMBIE
Caliber, 1998
1L by Tom Sniegoski & Jacen
  Burroughs, VcL(c) 3.00
1M Meadows (c). 3.00

2 . . . . 3.00
3 . . . . 3.00

KIRBY KING OF THE SERIALS
Blackthorne, 1989
1 . . . . 2.50
2 thru 4 . . . . @2.50

Kissing Chaos #4
© Oni Press

KISSING CHAOS
Oni Press, 2001
1 (of 8) by Arthur Dela Cruz 2.50
2 16-pg. 2.50
3 16-pg. 2.50
4 . . . . 3.00
5 16-pg. 2.50
6 16-pg. 2.50
7 16-pg. 2.50
8 24-pg. 2.50

KISSING CHAOS: NONSTOP BEAUTY
Oni Press, 2002
1 (of 4) by Arthur Dela Cruz 3.00
2 . . . . 3.00
3 thru 4 . . . . @3.00
1-shot 1000 Words 3.00
1-shot Nine Lives. 3.00
1-shot Sweet Nothings. 3.50

KITZ 'N' KATZ
Phantasy
1 . . . . 3.50
Eclipse
2 . . . . 2.50
3 . . . . 2.50
4 and 5 . . . . @2.50

KNEWTS OF THE ROUND TABLE
Pan Entertainment, 1998
1 . . . . 2.50
2 thru 6 . . . . @2.50

KNIGHTMARE
Antarctic Press, 1994
1 . . . . 2.75
2 . . . . 2.75
3 Wedding Knight,pt.1 . . . . 2.75

4 Wedding Knight,pt.2 . . . . 2.75
5 F:Dream Shadow. 2.75
6 V:Razorblast 2.75

KNIGHT MASTERS
1 thru 7 . . . . @2.50

KNIGHTS OF THE DINNER TABLE
Alderac Group, 1994
1 . . . . 40.00
2 . . . . 25.00
3 . . . . 15.00
Kenzer & Company, 1997
4 Have Dice Will Travel 12.00
5 Master of the Game. 12.00
6 on the high seas 9.00
7 Lord of Steam 9.00
8 A:magic cow. 5.00
9 To Dice for Sister Sara 5.00
16 thru 18 . . . . @5.00
19 thru 49. . . . . @3.00
50 double-size 5.00
51 thru 69 . . . . @3.00
70 thru 99 . . . . @4.00
100 giant 136-pg. 8.00
101 thru 108 . . . . @4.00
109 thru 145 . . . . @5.00
Spec. Black Hands Gaming Society 3.00
Spec. Origins 2003 . . . . 3.00
Spec #2 Black Hands Gaming. . . . 3.00
Spec. Origins 2004 . . . . 3.00
Spec. Last Man Standing. 3.50

...EVERKNIGHTS
Kenzer & Company, 2002
1 . . . . 3.00
2 thru 14 . . . . @3.00
Spec. Vs. King Arthur (2004) 3.00

...HACKMASTERS
Kenzer & Company, 2000
1 . . . . 3.00
2 thru 8 . . . . @3.00
9 and 11 . . . . @3.00
11 . . . . 3.00
Becomes:

...HACKMASTERS OF EVERKNIGHT
11 thru 15 . . . . @3.00

...ILLUSTRATED
Kenzer & Company, 2000
1 . . . . 3.00
2 thru 8 . . . . @3.00
9 thru 41 . . . . @3.00
Travelers Special #1 . . . . 3.00

...MINI-SERIES
Kenzer & Company, 2003
1 (of 3) 3.00
2 thru 3 . . . . @3.00
1a thru 3a variant (c). . . . . @3.00

KNIGHTS OF THE DINNER TABLE/FAANS
Six-Handed Press, 1999
X-over Spec. 3.00

KNIGHT WATCHMAN
Caliber Press, 1994
1 Graveyard Shift,pt. 1 . . . . 3.00
2 Graveyard Shift,pt. 2 . . . . 3.00

KODOCHA: SANA'S STAGE
Tokyopop Press, 2002
1 (of 5) by Miho Obana. 3.00

2 . . . . 3.00
3 thru 5 . . . . @3.00

KOMODO & THE DEFIANTS
Victory
1 . . . . 2.50
2 thru 6 . . . . @2.50

KONI WAVES
Arcana Studio, 2006
1 (of 3) 3.00
2 thru 3 . . . . @3.00

KORVUS
Human Monster Press, 1997
1 by Mick Fernette 3.00
2 . . . . 3.00
Arrow Comics, 1998
3 . . . . 3.00
VOL 2
1 & 2 . . . . @3.00

KUNG FU WARRIORS
(Prev. ROBOWARRIORS)
CFW
12 . . . . 2.50
13 thru 19 . . . . @2.50

KUNOICHI
Lightning Comics, 1996
1 2 diff. mild covers 3.00
1 platinum edition 6.00
1 autographed edition 9.00

KYRA
Elsewhere, 1989
1 thru 5 by Robin Ator . . . . @2.50

L33T: COMICS FOR GAMERS
Keenspot Entertainment, 2002
1 . . . . 5.00
2 thru 4 . . . . @5.00
5 24-pg. 3.00
6 thru 11 . . . . @5.00

LABOR FORCE
Blackthorne, 1986
1 thru 4 . . . . @2.50
5 thru 8 . . . . @2.50

LA COSA NOSTROID
Fireman Press, 1997
1 by Don Harmon & Rob Schrab . . 3.00
2 by Don Harmon & Edvis 3.00
3 . . . . 3.00
4 . . . . 3.00
5 . . . . 3.00
6 x-over madness 3.00
7 . . . . 3.00
8 . . . . 3.00
9 . . . . 3.00
10 final issue of Volume 1 . . . . 3.00

LACUNAE
CFD Productions, 1995
1 thru 4 F:Monkey Boys 2.50
5 thru 10 . . . . @2.50
11 HMo 2.50
12 HMo 2.50

LADIES OF LONDON NIGHT
London Night, 1997
Fall Special 5.00
Winter Special 5.00
    Winter Wonderland Edition 7.00
Spring 98 Special 5.00
Spotlight: Devon Michaels 4.00

Lady Arcane #3
© Heroic Publishing

LADY ARCANE
Heroic Publishing, 1992
1 color 4.00
2 thru 4 . . . . @3.50

LADY DEATH:
DEATH GODDESS
Chaos! Comics
Spec. 16-page 2.50
Spec. variant (c) 6.00
Spec. premium (c) 10.00

...INFERNAL SINS
Avatar Press, 2006
1-shot 2.50
1-shot wraparound (c) 3.00
1-shot variant (c)s . . . . @3.00
1-shot premium (c) 10.00
0 blood red foil convention (c) . . . 5.00
0 Repos (c) 6.00

...QUEEN OF THE DEAD
Avatar Press, 2007
1-shot 3.00
1-shot variant (c)s . . . . @3.00

LADY VAMPRE
Blackout Comics, 1996
0 (1995) 2.75
1 flip-book 3.00
0 Immortal No More (1998) 3.00
Spec.#1 In the Flesh (1996) 3.00
Spec.#1a photo sexy cover 10.00

...RETURNS
Blackout Comics, 1998
1 by Rob Roman & Kirk Manley . . . 3.00
1a Deluxe edition 15.00

LAFFIN GAS
Blackthorne, 1986
1 thru 12 . . . . @2.50

LAND, THE
Caliber, 1999
1 by Donald Marquez 3.00
2 . . . . 3.00
3 . . . . 3.00
4 conclusion 3.00

LANDER
Mermaid Producions
1 Power of the Dollar,pt.1 . . . . 2.50
2 Power of the Dollar,pt.2 . . . . 2.50
3 Power of the Dollar,pt.3 . . . . 2.50
Vol. 2
1 `By Whose Authority,'pt.1 . . . . . . 2.75
2 `By Whose Authority,'pt.2 . . . . . . 2.75

LAND OF OZ
Arrow Comics, 1998
1 by Gary Bishop & Bill Bryan 3.00
2 thru 6 . . . . @3.00

LAND OF OZ, THE
Antarctic Press, 2008
1 (of 8) Manga 3.00
1a wraparound variant (c) 4.00
2 thru 4 . . . . @3.00

LAST DITCH
Edge Press
1 CCa(s),THa, ... 2.50

LAST GENERATION
Black Tie Studios, 1987
1 . . . . 5.00
2 . . . . 4.00
3 thru 5 . . . . @2.50
Book One Rep. 7.00

LAST MINUTE
Aces & Eights Publ., 2004
1 . . . . 3.00
2 thru 6 . . . . 6.00

LAST SIN OF MARK GRIM, THE
Silent Devil Productions, 2006
1 (of 4) 3.00
2 thru 3 . . . . @3.00
Shanda Fantasy Arts, 2006
4 . . . . 3.00

LATEX ALICE
Basement Comics, 2003
0 . . . . 3.00
0a special edition 8.00
1 Blonde Ambition 3.00
1a Blonde Ambition, special 9.00
Spec. Papercuts 3.00
Spec. #1 Paper Cuts 9.00
Bikini Bash Gallery #1 spec. 9.00

LAZARUS CHRONICLES
Basement Comics 2006
1 . . . . 3.50
1 special edition 2.50
2 . . . . 3.25

LEAGUE OF CHAMPIONS
Hero Comics, 1990
(cont. from Innovation L.of C. #3)
1 GP,F:Sparkplug,Icestar 3.50
2 GP(i),F:Marksman,Flare,Icicle . . . 3.50
3 . . . . 3.50
4 F:Sparkplug,League 3.50
5 Morrigan Wars,pt.#1 . . . . 3.50

6 Morrigan Wars,pt.#3 . . . . 3.50
7 Morrigan Wars,pt.#6 . . . . 3.50
8 Morrigan Wars Conclusion 3.50
9 A:Gargoyle 3.50
10 A:Rose 3.50
11 thru 12 . . . . 4.00
13 V:Malice 4.00
14 V:Olympians 4.00
15 V:Olympians 3.00

LE FEMME VAMPRIQUE
Brainstorm, 1997
1 . . . . 3.50

LEGENDLORE
Caliber New Worlds
1 JMt signed 3.00
3 JMt 3.00
4 JMt 3.00
5 JMt 3.00
6 flip book w/Boston Bombers #4 . 3.00
7 JMt 3.00
8 JMt 3.00

...REALM WARS
Caliber New Worlds
1 by Joe Martin & Philip Xavier,
  Fawn cover by Xavier 3.00
1a Falla cover by Boller 3.00
1b signed 3.00
2 thru 4 . . . . @3.00

...WRATH OF THE DRAGON
Caliber Fantasy, 1998
1 by JMt & Philip Xavier 3.00
1 variant Philip Xavier(c). 3.00
2 . . . . 3.00
3 . . . . 3.00
4 . . . . 3.00
5 Prisoner set free 3.00
Spec. Handbook 4.00
1-shot Legendlore: Slave of Fate
  by JMt & Philip Xavier 3.00
1-shot The Wind Spirits, 48-pg. . . . 4.00
Giant Size Spec. 48-pg. 4.00

LEGEND OF LEMNEAR
CPM Manga, 1997
1 . . . . 3.00
2 thru 18 . . . . @3.00

LEGENDS FROM DARKWOOD
Antarctic Press, 2003
1 . . . . 3.50
2 thru 3 . . . . @3.50
4 . . . . 3.00
Summer Fun Spec. 3.00
Special 3.00

LEGENDS OF CAMELOT
Caliber Fantasy, 1999
Excalibur 3.00
Quest For Honor 3.00
Merlin 3.00
The Enchanted Lady 3.00
Sir Balin & The Dolorous Stroke . . . 3.00

LEGENDS OF LUXURA
Brainstorm, 1996
1 platinum edition 5.00
2 gold edition 5.00
3 . . . . 3.00

LEGION ANTHOLOGY
Limelight, 1997
1 four stories 3.00
2 . . . . 3.00

3 F:Binary Angel 3.00
4 . . . . 3.00
5 Binary Angel. 3.00

LEGION X-I
Greater Mercury
1 McKinney 5.00
2 McKinney,rare 15.00
Volume 2, 1989
1 thru 4 . . . . @2.50

LEGION X-2
Vol 2 #1 . . . . 2.50
Vol 2 #2 . . . . 2.50
Vol 2 #3 . . . . 2.50
Vol 2 #4 . . . . 2.50

LENORE
Slave Labor, 1998
1 by Roman Dirge. 3.00
2 thru 12 . . . . @3.00

LENSMAN
Eternity, 1990
1 E.E.`Doc' Smith adapt. 2.50
2 . . . . 2.50
3 . . . . 2.50
4 . . . . 2.50
5 On Radelix. 2.50
6 . . . . 2.50
Collectors Spec #1, 56 pgs. 4.00

...GALACTIC PATROL
Eternity, 1990
1 thru 7 E.E. `Doc' Smith adapt. . @2.50

...WAR OF THE GALAXIES
Eternity, 1990
1 thru 7 . . . . @2.50

LEONARDO
Mirage, 1986
1-shot TMNTurtles 13.00

LETHAL LADIES OF BRAINSTORM
Brainstorm, 1997
1 F:Luxura, Vampfire, etc.. . . . . . . 3.00
1 luxury edition 5.00

LETHARGIC LAD ADVENTURES
Crusade Entertainment, 1997
1 by Greg Hyland 3.00
2 . . . . 3.00
Becomes:

LETHARGIC LAD
TV Comics, 1997
3 by Greg Hyland 3.00
4 . . . . 3.00
5 . . . . 3.00
TPB Big Book of Lethargic Lad . . . 16.00
Lethargic Comics
6 by Greg Hyland 3.00
7 thru 14 . . . . @3.00
Dork Storm Press, 2002
Ann. #1 Jumbo-sized. 4.00
Ann. #2 Jumbo-sized. 4.00
Ann. #3 Jumbo-sized 4.00

LEVEL X
Caliber, 1997
1 . . . . 3.00
2 32pg. 3.00
3 48pg. 4.00

...THE NEXT REALITY
Caliber, 1997
1 (of 2) by Dan Harbison & Randy
  Buccini, 64pg. 4.00
2 48pg. 4.00

LIBBY ELLIS
Eternity, 1988
1 . . . . 2.50
2 thru 4 . . . . @2.50

LIBERATOR
Eternity
1 . . . . 2.50
2 thru 6 . . . . @2.50

LIBERTY FROM HELL
Radio Comix, 2003
1 . . . . 3.00
2 thru 6 . . . . 3.00

Liberty Meadows #26
© Insight Studios

LIBERTY MEADOWS
Insight Studios, 1999
1 by Frank Cho 25.00
2 . . . . 15.00
3 . . . . 10.00
4 thru 6 . . . . @10.00
7 thru 10 . . . . @7.00
11 thru 20 . . . . @6.00
21 thru 23 . . . . @5.00
24 Virtual Reality Adventure 5.00
25 Pool Party 5.00
26 Fossil Dinosaurs 5.00
Spec. Wedding Album 10.00

L.I.F.E. BRIGADE
Blue Comet
1 A:Dr. Death 2.50
1a 2nd printing 2.50
2 . . . . 2.50

LIFE OF A FETUS
Slave Labor, 1999
1 by Andy Ristaino 3.00
2 thru 7 . . . . @3.00

LIFEQUEST
Caliber, 1997
1 by Matt Vanderpol 3.00
2 thru 6 . . . . @3.00

LITTLE GLOOMY
Amaze Ink/SLG, 1999
1 by Landry Walker & Eric Jones . . 3.00
2 thru 6 . . . . @3.00
Halloween Spec. 3.50

LITTLE GLOOMY'S SUPER SCARY MONSTER SHOW
Amaze Ink/SLG, 2005
1 . . . . 3.00
2 . . . . 3.00
3 . . . . 3.00

LITTLE SCROWLIE
Amaze Ink/SLG, 2003
4 thru 7 . . . . @3.00
8 thru 15 . . . . @3.00

LITTLE STAR
Oni Press, 2005
1 . . . . 3.00
2 thru 6 . . . . @3.00

LITTLE WHITE MOUSE
Caliber, 1998
1 by Paul Sizer 3.00
2 Fever Dreams 3.00
3 Filthy Jake 3.00
4 . . . . 3.00

...ENTROPY DREAMING
Blue Line Pro Comics, 2001
1 by Paul Sizer 3.00
2 Nuts and Bolts 3.00
3 thru 4 . . . . @3.00

...OPEN SPACE
Blue Line Pro Comics, 2002
1 (of 4) by Paul Sizer 3.00
2 thru 4 . . . . @3.00

LIVINGSTONE MOUNTAIN
Adventure Comics, 1991
1 I:Scat,Dragon Rax 2.50
2 Scat & Rax Create Monsters. . . . 2.50
3 Rax rescue attempt 2.50
4 Final issue 2.50

LLOYD LLEWELLYN
Fantagraphics, 1986
1 Mag Size 4.00
2 thru 6 Mag Size . . . . @2.50
7 Regular Size 2.50

LOCAL
Oni Press, 2005
1 (of 12) 3.00
1a 2nd printing 3.00
2 Polaroid Boyfriend 3.00
3 Thories and Defenses 3.00
4 The Two Brothers 3.00
5 Last Lonely Days at the
    Oxford Theater 3.00
6 Megan and Gloria, Apartment 5A 3.00
7 Smash the State 3.00
8 Food as Subotitute. 3.00
9 Wish You Were Here 3.00
10 The Process 3.00
11 thru 12 . . . . @3.00

LODOSS WAR:
CHRONICLES OF THE HEROIC KNIGHT
CPM Manga, 2000
1 by Ryo Mizuno & M. Natsumoto . 3.00
2 thru 19 . . . . @3.00

...DEELIT'S TALE
CPM Manga, 2001
1 by R. Mizuno & S. Yoneyama . . . 3.00
1a signed & numbered 15.00
2 thru 4 . . . . @3.00
5 thru 8 . . . . @3.00

...THE GREY WITCH
CPM Manga, 1998
1 by Ryo Mizuno & Yoshihiko Ochi. 3.00
2 by Ryo Mizuno & Akikiro Yamada 3.00
3 thru 10 . . . . @3.00
11 thru 22 . . . . @3.00

...THE LADY OF PHARIS
CPM Manga, 1999
1 by Ryo Mizuno & Akihiro Yamada 3.00
2 thru 7 . . . . @3.00

LOGAN'S RUN
Adventure Comics, 1990
1 thru 6 Novel adapt. . . . . @2.50

LOGAN'S WORLD
Adventure Comics, 1991
1 Seq. to Logan's Run 2.50
2 thru 6 . . . . @2.50

LONER
Fleetway
1 Pt.1 (of 7) 2.50
2 thru 6 Pt.2 thru Pt.6 . . . . @2.50

LONE WOLF & CUB
First, 1987–91
1 FM(c) 8.00
1a 2nd printing 2.50
1b 3rd printing 2.50
2 . . . . 4.00
2a 2nd printing 2.50
3 . . . . 4.00
4 thru 10 . . . . @4.00
11 thru 36 . . . . @3.00
37 and 38 . . . . @4.00
39 120-pg. 6.00
40 . . . . 3.25
41 MP(c), 60-pg. 4.00
42 thru 45 MP(c) . . . . @3.25

LOOKERS
Avatar Press, 1997
1 . . . . 3.00
1 deluxe 5.00
1 signed 12.00
2 . . . . 3.00
2 Deluxe cover 8.00
Spec. #1 . . . . 3.00
Spec. #1 signed 8.00
Spec. Allure of the Serpent (1999) . 3.50
Spec. Slaves of Anubis (1998). . . . 3.50

LORD OF THE DEAD
Conquest
1 R.E.Howard adapt. 3.00

LORI LOVECRAFT
Caliber, 1997
1 MV, 48pg 4.00
1a signed 4.00
1-shot The Dark Lady (1997) 3.00
1-shot Repression (1998). 3.00
Spec. The Big Comeback (1998). . . 3.00

AV Publications, 2000
1 by P.Ventrella & M.Vosburg 3.00
2 into the past 3.00

Lookers #1
© *Avatar Press*

LOST, THE
Caliber, 1996
1 . . . . 3.00
1a special ed. 7.00
1b signed 3.00
2 thru 4 . . . . @3.00

LOST CONTINENT
Eclipse, 1990
1 thru 5, Manga. . . . . @3.50

LOST SQUAD
Devil's Due Publishing, 2005
1 thru 6 . . . . @3.00

LOST STORIES
Creative Frontiers, 1998
1 . . . . 3.00
2 . . . . 3.00
3 . . . . 3.00
4 The Big Horn Bruhaha. 3.00
5 Strike Force O'Shea,pt.1 . . . . . . 3.00
6 Strike Force O'Shea,pt.2 . . . . . . 3.00
7 Gnome for a Day 3.00
8 A Vampire Too Far 3.00
9 The Undertroll Saga,pt.1 . . . . . . 3.00

LOST WORLD, THE
Millennium, 1996
1 & 2 Arthur Conan Doyle adapt. @3.00

LOTHAR
Powerhouse Graphics
1 I:Lothar,Galactic Bounty Hunter. . 2.50
2 I:Nightcap. 2.50

LOUIS RIEL
Drawn & Quarterly, 1999
1 (of 10) by Chester Brown 3.00
2 thru 5 . . . . @3.00
6 thru 10 . . . . @3.00

LOVE AND ROCKETS
Fantagraphics Books, 1982–96
1 HB,B&W cover, adult 30.00
1a HB,Color cover 20.00
1b 2nd printing 4.00
2 HB 10.00
3 HB 6.00
4 HB 6.00

5 HB 6.00
6 HB 5.00
7 HB 6.00
8 HB 6.00
9 HB 5.00
10 HB. 5.00
11 thru 21 HB . . . . @3.00
22 thru 39 HB . . . . @3.00
40 thru 50 . . . . @3.00
Bonanza rep. 3.00

Vol. 2, 2001

1 GHe,JHr, ... 4.00
1a 2nd printing 4.00
2 thru 9 . . . . @4.00
10 . . . . 6.00
11 thru 19 . . . . @4.50
20 . . . . 7.00

LOVE FIGHTS
Oni Press, 2003
1 . . . . 3.00
2 thru 4 . . . . @3.00
5 . . . . 6.00
6 thru 12 . . . . @3.00

LOVE HINA
Tokyopop Press, 2002
1 (of 4) by Ken Akamatsu 3.00
2 thru 4 . . . . @3.00

LOVE IN TIGHTS
Amaze Ink, 1998
1 . . . . 3.00
Spec. Valentine's Day Special 3.00
Spec. Spring Fling 3.00
Anniv. #1 . . . . 3.00
6 & 7 . . . . @3.00

LOVELY PRUDENCE
Millennium, 1997
1 by Maze 3.00
2 . . . . 3.00
3 Nightmares of Breeding 3.00
#M 24-pg.. . . . . 2.50
#M 24-pg., signed 3.00
Spec. Swimsuit Special 3.00
Christmas Misery Spec.#1 . . . . 3.00

LOVE THE WAY YOU LOVE
Oni Press 2006
1 . . . . 6.00
2 . . . . 6.00
3 thru 6 . . . . @6.00

LUBA
Fantagraphics, 1998
1 by Gilbert Hernandez 3.00
2 thru 5 . . . . @3.00
6 thru 10 . . . . @3.50

LUBA'S COMICS & STORIES
Fantagraphics, 2000
1 by Gilbert Hernandez. 3.00
2 GHe 3.50
3 GHe, Ofelia 3.50
4 GHe, The Light of Venus 3.50
5 GHe, Lovers and Hector 3.50
6 GHe 3.50
7 GHe, Fritz After Dark 3.50

LUFTWAFFE 1946
[Mini-Series]
Antarctic Press, 1996
1 . . . . 5.00
2 thru 4 . . . . @4.00

Luftwaffe Vol. 2 #5
© *Antarctic Press*

Antarctic Press, 1997
1 by Ted Namura & BDn. 3.00
2 Luftsturm,pt.2 . . . . 3.00
3 Luftsturm,pt.3 . . . . 3.00
4 Luftsturm,pt.4 . . . . 3.00
5 new weapons 3.00
6 Projekt Saucer,pt.1 . . . . 3.00
7 Projekt Saucer,pt.2 . . . . 3.00
8 Projekt Saucer,pt.3 . . . . 3.00
9 Projekt Saucer,pt.4 . . . . 3.00
10 Projekt Saucer,pt.5 . . . . 3.00
11 Projekt Saucer, epilogue 3.00
12 Richthofen's Flying Circus,pt.1 . . 3.00
13 Richthofen's Flying Circus,pt.2 . . 3.00
14 Jagdeschwader,pt.2 . . . . 3.00
15 Jagdeschwader,pt.3 . . . . 3.00
16 Jagdeschwader,pt.4 . . . . 3.00
17 Jagdeschwader,pt.5 . . . . 3.00
18 Schweinfurt 3.00
Tech Manual Vol. 1 . . . . 4.00
Tech Manual Vol. 2 . . . . 4.00
Tech Manual Vol. 3 Rocket Fighters 4.00
Tech Manual Vol. 4 Amerika
   Bombers 4.00
Tech Manual Vol. 5 Wonder
   Weapons 4.00
Tech. Manual Vol. 6 . . . . 6.00
Spec.#1 Triebflugel 3.00
Spec.#1 World War II: 1946. . . . . . 4.00
Ann. #1 prototype artwork 3.00

New Volume (2002)
1 Tigers of the Luftwaffe 6.00
2 thru 18 . . . . @6.00

Volume 5
1 . . . . 6.00
2 thru 3 . . . . @6.00
Annual #2. . . . . 5.00
Annual #2. . . . . 5.00
TPB Technical Manual 22.00
TPB Vol. 1 Sourcebook 6.00

LUM*URUSEI YATSURA
Viz Communications
1 Art by Rumiko Takahashi 3.00
2 . . . . 3.00
3 . . . . 3.00
4 . . . . 3.00
5 . . . . 3.25
6 thru 8 . . . . @3.00

LUNAR DONUT
Cosmic Lunchbox Comics, 1996
1 by Parham & Tucker 3.00

2 thru 4 . . . . @3.00
Lunar Donut
5 . . . . 3.00
6 Powdered Sugar 3.00

LURID
IDW Publishing, 2002
1 by Paul Lee & Adam Huntley. . . . 3.00
2 . . . . 3.00
3 . . . . 3.00

LUST FOR LIFE
Slave Labor, 1997
1 by Jeff LeVine 3.00
2 . . . . 3.00
3 . . . . 3.00
4 . . . . 3.00

LUXURA
Brainstorm, 1996
Convention Book 2 . . . . 3.00
Ann.#1 48pg (1998) 4.00
Pin-up mag. Luxura: The Good, The
   Bad and the Beautiful (1999) . . 4.00
Spec.1 Luxura & Vampfire, x-over
   by Fauve (1997) 3.00
Luxura Leather, Platinum edition . . . 5.00
Luxura Leather, Signed edition 8.00

LUXURA/BABY ANGEL X
Brainstorm, 1996
Spec. x-over. 3.00
Spec. deluxe 5.00
Luxury edition. 8.00
Deluxe luxury edition 12.00

LUXURA/WIDOW: BLOOD LUST
Brainstorm
Omega x-over pt.2 concl.. . . . . 3.00
Omega Fusion cover 5.00
Luxury edition. 8.00
Deluxe luxury edition 12.00
See: Widow/Luxura for pt.1

LYNX: AN ELFLORD TALE
Peregrin, 1999
1 by Barry Blair 3.00
2 by Barry Blair & Colin Chan. 3.00
3 & 4 . . . . @3.00

M.A.C.H. 1
Fleetway
1 I:John Probe-Secret Agent 2.50
2 thru 9 . . . . @2.50

MACKENZIE QUEEN
Matrix, 1985
1 . . . . 3.75
2 thru 5 . . . . @3.75

MACROSS II
Viz Comics, 1992
1 Macross Saga sequel 2.75
2 A:Ishtar. 2.75
3 F:Reporter Hibiki,Ishtar 2.75
4 V:Feff,The Marduk 2.75
5 . . . . 2.75
6 . . . . 2.75
7 Sylvie Confesses. 2.75
8 F:Ishtar. 2.75
9 V:Marduk Fleet 2.75
10 . . . . 2.75

...THE MICRON CONSPIRACY
Viz, 1994
1 Manga 2.75

MAD DOGS
Eclipse, 1992
1 I:Mad Dogs(Cops) 2.50
2 V:Chinatown Hood 2.50
3 . . . . 2.50

MAD RACCOONS
MU Press, 1991
1 thru 7 by Cathy Hill, Angst of
  an Artist . . . . @3.00

MAELSTROM
Aircel, 1987
1 thru 13 . . . . @2.50

MAGGOTS
Hamilton, 1991
1 JSon, mag size 4.00
2 JSon, mag size 4.00
3 GM/JSon,inc.`Some Kinda
  Beautiful' 4.00

MAGICAL MATES
Antarctic Press, 1995
1 & 2 Manga, by Mio Odaqi , , , , @3.00
0 thru 8 (of 8) . . . . @3.00

MAGICAL POKEMON JOURNEY
Viz Communications, 2000
1 How Do You Do, Pikachu 5.00
2 Cooking with Jigglypuff 5.00
3 Pokemon Holiday. 5.00
4 Fun at the Beach 5.00
PART 2, 2000
1 thru 4 . . . . @5.00
PART 3, 2000
1 thru 4 . . . . @5.00
PART 4, 2001
1 thru 4 Love Potion Pursuit . . . . @5.00
PART 5, 2001
1 thru 4 . . . . @5.00
PART 6, 2001
1 (of 4) 5.00
2 thru 4 . . . . @5.00
PART 7, 2002
1 . . . . 5.00
2 thru 4 . . . . @5.00

MAGIC PRIEST
Antarctic Press, 1998
1 (of 3) by B.Lyga & N.Googe 3.00
2 . . . . 3.00

MAGIC WHISTLE
Alternative Press, Vol 2
1 by Sam Henderson 3.00
2 thru 8 . . . . @3.00
9 96-pg. 9.00
10 . . . . 9.00

MAGUS
Caliber Core, 1998
1L by Gary Reed & Craig Brasfield,
  VcL(c) 3.00
1D GyD(c). 3.00
1 premium edition, signed 9.00
2 Magus secrets 3.00
3 Lilith & Beezlebub 3.00
1-shot Magus: The Forever King . . . 3.00
Spec. Dawn of Armageddon,
  x-over, 48-pg. 3.00

MAI, THE PSYCHIC GIRL
Eclipse, 1987
1 I:Mai,Alliance of 13 Sages 3.75
1a 2nd printing 2.50
2 V:Wisdom Alliance. 2.50
2a 2nd printing 2.50
3 V:Kaieda,I:Ojii-San. 2.50
4 . . . . 2.50
5 thru 19 . . . . @2.50
20 thru 28 . . . . @2.50

MAID ATTACK
White Lightning Prod., 2003
1 (of 4) 4.00
2 thru 4 . . . . @4.00

MAINTENANCE
Onipress, 2006
1 . . . . 3.50
2 thru 10 . . . . 3.50

MAISON IKKOKU
Viz Comics, 1993
1 thru 7 Manga 3.00
[Part Two]
1 thru 6 . . . . 3.00
[Part Three]
1 thru 6 . . . . 3.00
[Part Four]
1 thru 6 F:Kyoko 3.00
7 thru 10 . . . . @3.00
[Part Six], 1996
1 thru 11 by Rumiko Takahashi. . @3.50
[Part Seven], 1997
1 thru 8 by Rumiko Takahashi . . @3.25
9 thru 13 . . . . @3.50
[Part Eight], 1998
1 (of 8) 3.25
2 . . . . 3.50
3 thru 8 . . . . @3.25
[Part Nine], 1999
1 (of 10) 3.25
2 thru 10 . . . . @3.25

MANDRAKE
1 . . . . 4.00
2 . . . . 4.00
3 . . . . 4.00
Ultimate Mandrake. 15.00

MANDRAKE MONTHLY
1 . . . . 4.00
2 . . . . 4.00
3 . . . . 5.00
4 . . . . 5.00
5 . . . . 5.00
6 . . . . 7.00
Special #1 . . . . 7.00

MAN-EATING COW
New England Comics, 1992
1 Spin-off from the Tick. 3.25
2 O:Mr.Krinkles,A:Lt.Valentine 2.75
3 Final issue 2.75
Bonanza #1, 128pg (1996) 5.00
Bonanza #2, 100pg. 5.00

MAN FROM U.N.C.L.E.
Entertainment Publ., 1987
1 `Number One with a Bullet Affair. 3.50
2 `Number One with a Bullet Affair. 3.00
3 `The E-I-E-I-O Affair' 3.00
4 `The E-I-E-I-O Affair,' concl. 3.00
5 `The Wasp Affair' 3.00
6 `Lost City of THRUSH Affair' 3.00
7 `The Wildwater Affair' 3.00

Mackenzie Queen #3
© Matrix

8 `The Wilder West Affair' 3.00
9 `The Canhadian Lightning Affair'. 3.00
10 `The Turncoat Affair'. 3.00
11 `Craters of the Moon Affair'. 3.00

MANGA EX
Antarctic Press, 2001
1 . . . . 7.00
2 thru 6 . . . . @7.00

MANGAPHILE
Radio Comix, 1999
1 . . . . 3.00
2 thru 5 . . . . @3.00
6 thru 11 . . . . @3.00
12 48-pg. 4.00
13 48-pg. 4.00
14 thru 21 48-pg. . . . . @4.00
22 thru 25. . . . . @5.00

MANGA VIZION
Viz Communications
Vol. 1, 1995
1 thru 10 Ogre Slayer . . . . @5.00
Vol. 2, 1996
1 thru 12 . . . . @5.00
Vol. 3, 1997
1 thru 8 . . . . @5.00
Vol. 4
1 thru 8 . . . . @5.00

MANGAZINE
Antarctic Press, 1985
1 newsprint cover 12.00
1a reprint. 3.00
2 . . . . 9.00
3 . . . . 8.00
4 . . . . 8.00
5 . . . . 8.00
New Series
1 . . . . 3.00
2 . . . . 3.00
3 thru 13 . . . . @2.50
14 New Format 3.00
15 thru 44. . . . . @3.00
VOL. 3, 1999
1 thru 15 . . . . @9.00
16 thru 27 140+-pg. . . . . @9.00
28 thru 39 . . . . @9.00
40 thru 70 . . . . @10.00

B & W PUB.

MANIMAL
Renegade, 1986
1 EC,rep.................. 2.50

MAN OF RUST
Blackthorne, 1986
1 Cover A 2.50
1 Cover B 2.50

MANSLAUGHTER
Brainstorm, 1996
1 .... 3.00
1a gold foil edition............ 5.00

MARCANE
Eclipse
1 Book 1,JMu 6.00

MARK I
(Prev.: Atomic Comics)
2 .... 2.50

MARK MILLAR'S THE UNFUNNIES
Avatar, 2003
1 .... 3.50
2 thru 3 .... @3.50
1a Platinum (c) 6.00
1a thru 3a offensive (c)....... @3.50

MARMALADE BOY
Tokyopop Press, 2001
1 (of 5) by Wataru Yoshizumi 3.00
2 thru 5 .... 3.00

MARQUIS, THE
Caliber, 1997
1 GyD 3.00
1 spec. double gatefold cover.... 6.00
2 Marquis cover by Vincent Locke . 3.00
2a Marquis view of world GyD(c) . 3.00
3 .... 3.00
Spec. The Marquis, Gallery of
  Hell, GyD 4.00
Spec. The Marquis: Les Preludes,
  GyD prelude edition (1996).... 3.00
Spec.A Les Preludes, signed...... 3.00

MARQUIS, THE: A SIN OF ONE
Oni Press, 2003
1 GyD 3.00

MARQUIS, THE: DANSE MACABRE
Oni Press, 2000
1 (of 5) by Guy Davis 3.00
2 thru 5 .... @3.00

MARTIAN SUCCESSOR NADESICO
CPM Manga, 1999
1 by Kia Asamiya 3.00
2 .... 3.00
3 .... 3.00
4 thru 15 .... @3.00
16 thru 26 .... @3.00

MASKED WARRIOR X
Antarctic Press, 1996
1 (of 6) by Masayuki Fujihara..... 3.50
2 .... 3.00
3 The Girls of Olympus,' pt.2 .... 3.00
4 `Protect the Silver Fortress'.... 3.00

MASQUERADE
Eclipse
1 .... 2.50
2 thru 3 .... @2.50

MATAAK
K-Blamm, 1995
1 I:Mataak 2.50
2 Spirit of Peace 2.50

MATT CHAMPION
Metro
1 EC 2.50
2 EC 2.50

MAVIS
Exhibit A, 1998
1 BLs, F:Wolff & Byrd's secretary . 3.00
2 .... 3.00
5 (2008) 3.50

MAX HAMM FAIRY TALE DETECTIVE
Nite Owl Comix 2002
1 by Frank Cammuso 5.00
Vol. 2
1 (of 3) 5.00
2 thru 3 .... @5.00

MAXION
CPM, 1999
1 by Takeshi Takebayashi........ 3.00
2 thru 26 .... @3.00

MAX OF THE REGULATORS
Atlantic
1 .... 4.00
2 thru 4 .... @3.50

MAXWELL MOUSE FOLLIES
Renegade, 1986
1 Large format (1981)........... 4.00
1a Comic Size(1986) 3.00
2 thru 6 .... @2.50

MAYHEM
1 Mask(c) 9.00
2 thru 6 .... @8.00

MAZE AGENCY
Caliber, 1997
1 The Death of Justice Girl
  reprint series 3.00
1a signed 3.00
2 and 3 .... @3.00
2a and 3a variant AH(c)s ...... @3.00

MEASLES
Fantagraphics, 1998
1 by Gilbert Hernandez.......... 3.00
2 thru 8 .... @3.00

MEAT CAKE
Fantagraphics, 1995
1 thru 4 .... @2.50
5 thru 8 .... @3.00
9 thru 16 .... @4.00

MECHANOIDS
Caliber, 1991
1 .... 2.50
2 thru 5 .... @3.50

Measles #1
© Fantagraphics

MEDABOTS
Viz Communications, 2002
Part 1
1 (of 4) by Rin Horuma 2.75
2 thru 4 .... @2.75
Part 2
1 (of 4) New Challenges......... 2.75
2 thru 4 .... @2.75
Part 3
1 (of 4) 2.75
2 thru 4 .... @2.75
Part 4
1 by Horumarin 2.75
2 thru 4 .... 2.75

MEGATON
Megaton, 1983
1 JG(c),EL(1stProWork),GD,MG,
  A:Ultragirl,Vanguard 14.00
2 EL,JG(pin-up),A:Vanguard..... 11.00
3 MG,AMe,JG,EL,I:Savage
  Dragon.................. 18.00
4 AMe,EL,2nd A:Savage Dragon
  (inc.EL profile) 9.00
5 AMe,RLd(inside front cover) 5.00
6 AMe,JG(inside back cover),
  EL(Back cover) 5.00
7 AMe 5.00
8 RLd,I:Youngblood(Preview).... 18.00

MEGATON MAN MEETS THE UNCATEGORIZABLE X-THEMS
Jabberwocky, 1989
1 .... 2.50

MEGATON MAN VS. FORBIDDEN FRANKENSTEIN
Fiasco Comics, 1996
1 by Don Simpson & Anton Drek .. 3.00

MEMORY MAN
Emergency Stop Press, 1995
1 thru 2 Some of the Space Man .. 3.00

MEN IN BLACK
Aircel, 1991
1 by Lowell Cunningham & Sandy
  Carruthers, basis of Movie . . . 40.00
2 . . . . 22.00
3 F:Jay, Arbiter Doran 22.00
[Book II], 1991
1 . . . . 25.00
2 thru 3 . . . . @12.00

MEN IN BLACK:
THE ROBORG INCIDENT
Castle
1 thru 3 . . . . @3.00

MEN'S ALTERED WARS
CHRONICLES
Antarctic Press, 2001
Ann. #1 Magazine 6.00
Ann. #2 . . . . 6.00
Antarctic Press, 2003
1 . . . . 5.00
2 thru 3 . . . . @5.00

MERCEDES
Angus Publishing, 1995
8 thru 15 by Mike Friedland
  & Grant Fuhst . . . . @3.00
VOL. 4
1 thru 4 . . . . @3.00
VOL. 5, 1997
1 . . . . 3.00
2 . . . . 3.00
3 . . . . 3.00
Spec. Senseless Acts of
  Beauty (1998) 3.00

MERCHANTS OF DEATH
Eclipse, 1988
1 . . . . 2.50
2 thru 5 . . . . @2.50

MERCY
Avatar Press, 1997
0 O:Mercy 3.00
0b leather cover 25.00
1 (of 2) by Bill Maus 3.00
1 leather cover 22.00
1 signed 10.00

MERLIN
Adventure Comics, 1990
1 BMC,Merlin's Visions 2.50
2 V:Warlord Carados 2.50
3 . . . . 2.50
4 Ninevah 2.50
5 D:Hagus 2.50
6 Final Issue 2.50
[2nd Series]
1 Journey of Rhiannon & Tryon . . . 2.50
2 Conclusion 2.50

MERMAID'S GAZE
Viz Comics, 1995
1 thru 3 V:Shingo 2.75
4 final issue 2.75

METACOPS
Monster Comics, 1991
1 and 2 . . . . @2.50

METAL GUARDIAN FAUST
Viz Communications, 1997
1 by Tetsuo Ueyama . . . . @3.00

2 thru 8 . . . . @3.00

METAL HURLANT
Humanoids Publishing, 2002
1 . . . . 4.00
2 thru 3 . . . . @4.00
4 thru 9 . . . . @4.00

METROPOLIS
Caliber, 1997
0 movie adaptation, series
  prequel,48pg 4.00
1 The Last Fredersen, pt.1 . . . . . . 3.00
2 The Last Fredersen, pt.2 . . . . . . 3.00
3 The Last Fredersen, pt.3 . . . . . . 3.00

METAPHYSIQUE
Eclipse
1 NB,Short Stories 2.50
2 NB,Short Stories 2.50

MIAMI MICE
Rip Off Press, 1986
1 1st printing 3.00
1a 2nd printing 2.50
3 . . . . 2.50
4 Record,A:TMNT 3.00

MICHELANGELO
Mirage, 1986
1 TMNT 17.00
1a 2nd Printing 4.50

MICHELANGELO:
THE THIRD KIND
Mirage, 2008
1 (of 4) 3.25
2 thru 3 . . . . @3.25

Micra #1
© SFictioneer

MICRA
Fictioneer, 1986
1 . . . . 4.00
2 . . . . 3.00
3 . . . . 3.00
4 thru 8 . . . . @2.50

MIDDLEMAN, THE
Viper Comics, 2005
1 . . . . 3.00
2 thru 4 . . . . @3.00

Vol. 2, 2006
1 . . . . 2.50
2 thru 4 . . . . @3.00

MIDNIGHT
Blackthorne
1 thru 4 . . . . @2.50

MIDNIGHT MOVER
Oni Press, 2003
1 (of 4) 3.00
2 thru 4 . . . . @3.00

MIDNIGHT PANTHER
CPM Comics, 1997
1 Manga, translated 3.00
2 . . . . 3.00
3 . . . . 3.00
4 . . . . 3.00
5 . . . . 3.00
6 Den of Scoundrels 3.00
7 The Sleeping Town 3.00
8 to Reincarnation City 3.00
9 O:Midnight Panthers 3.00
10 . . . . 3.00
11 . . . . 3.00
12 . . . . 3.00
Spec. Breaking Up is Hard to Do . . . 3.00

...FEUDAL FANTASY
CPM Manga, 1998
1 by Yu Asagiri 3.00
2 thru 5 . . . . @3.00

...SCHOOL DAZE
CPM Comics, 1998
1 (of 5) by Yu Asagiri 3.00
2 thru 5 . . . . @3.00

MIDNIGHT SUN
Amaze Ink/SLG, 2006
1 (of 5) 3.00
2 thru 3 . . . . @3.00

MIDNITE SKULKER
Target, 1986
1 thru 7 . . . . @2.50

MIGHTY GUY
C&T, 1987
1 . . . . 2.50
2 thru 6 . . . . @2.50
Summer Fun Spec #1 . . . . 2.50

MIGHTY MITES
Eternity, 1986
1 I:X-Mites 2.50
2 & 3 . . . . @2.50

MIGHTY MOUSE
ADVENTURE MAGAZINE
Spotlight, 1987
1 . . . . 5.00

MIGHTY TINY
Antarctic
1 . . . . 2.50
2 thru 4 . . . . @2.50
5 . . . . 2.50
Mouse Marines Collection rep. 7.50

MIKE HOFFMAN: ISLAND
OF THE TIKI GODDESS
Basement, 2007
Spec. 3.00

MIKE HOFFMAN'S LOST WORLDS OF FANTASY AND SCI-FI
Antimater/Hoffman Int., 2003
```
1 .......................... 3.00
2 thru 10 ................. @3.00
1a thru 10a special edition ..... @9.00
```

MIKE HOFFMAN'S MONSTERS AND MAIDENS
Antimater/Hoffman International, 2003
```
1 .......................... 3.50
2 .......................... 3.00
```

MIKE HOFFMAN'S TIGRESS
Black Daze, 2000
```
1 by Mike Hoffman ............ 3.00
```
Antimater/Hoffman Int., 2003
```
Spec. Cover Gallery Spec........ 9.00
```

MILK & CHEESE
Slave Labor, 1991–97
```
1 EDo, Milk Products gone bad .. 45.00
1a 2nd thru 7th printing......... 4.00
2 .......................... 27.00
2a 2nd thru 4th printing......... 4.00
3 .......................... 20.00
3a 2nd thru 4th printing......... 4.00
4 .......................... 12.00
4a 2nd & 3rd printing ........... 4.00
5 .......................... 12.00
5a 2nd & 3rd printing ........... 4.00
6 ........................... 7.00
6a 2nd printing ................. 3.00
7 ........................... 6.00
Other #1 ...................... 2.75
Third #1 ...................... 2.75
Fourth #1 ..................... 2.75
First #2....................... 2.75
Six Six Six #1................. 2.75
Six Six Six 2nd printing, EDo... 2.75
Latest Thing................... 3.00
```

MILLENNIUM 2.5: THE BUCK ROGERS SAGA
ACG Comics, 2000
```
1 by Dick Calkin .............. 3.00
2 thru 4 ................... @3.00
```

MILTON CANIFF'S TERRY & THE PIRATES
ACG Comics, 1999
```
1 by Milton Caniff ............ 3.00
2 .......................... 3.00
3 .......................... 3.00
4 .......................... 3.00
```

MINESHAFT
Fantagraphics Books, 2005
```
1 .......................... 5.00
16 .......................... 5.00
17 .......................... 6.00
18 thru 20.................. @7.00
```

MINIMUM WAGE
Fantagraphics, 1995
```
Vol. 1, new printing........... 11.00
```
Vol. 2, 1995
```
1 thru 4 ................... @3.00
5 by Bob Fingerman .......... 3.00
6 .......................... 3.00
```

```
7 .......................... 3.00
8 .......................... 3.00
9 Artsy Fartsy ............... 3.00
10.......................... 3.00
```

MIRACLE GIRLS
Tokyopop Press, 2000
```
1 .......................... 3.00
2 thru 23 .................. @3.00
```

MIRACLE SQUAD BLOOD & DUST
Apple, 1989
```
1 thru 3 .................. @2.50
```

MISPLACED
Devil's Due Publishing, 2004
```
1 by Joshua Blaylock .......... 3.00
2 .......................... 3.00
3 .......................... 3.00
```

MISTER BLANK
Amaze Ink, 1997
```
0 by Chris Hicks .............. 2.50
0a 2nd printing ............... 2.50
1 F:Sam Smith ............... 3.00
2 thru 14 .................. @3.00
```

MISTER X
Vortex, Vol 2, 1989–90
```
1 thru 11 .................. @2.50
```

MOBILE POLICE PATLABOR
Viz Communications, 1997
```
1 (of 12) by Masami Yuki ........ 3.00
```
PART TWO, 1998
```
1 by Masami Yuki ............. 3.00
2 thru 6 ................... @3.00
```

MOBILE SUIT GUNDAM 0079
Viz Communications, 1999
```
1 (of 8) by Kazhisa Kondo ....... 3.00
2 thru 7 ................... @3.00
```
PART TWO, 1999
```
1 (of 5) .................... 3.00
2 thru 5 ................... @3.00
```

MOBILE SUIT GUNDAM WING: BLIND TARGET
Viz Communications, 2001
```
1 thru 4 ................... @3.00
```

MOBILE SUIT GUNDAM WING: EPISODE ZERO
Viz Communications, 2001
```
1 thru 8 ................... @3.00
```

MOBILE SUIT GUNDAM WING: GROUND ZERO
Viz Communications, 2000
```
1 (of 4) by Reku Fuyynagi ....... 3.00
2 thru 4 ................... @3.00
```

MOEBIUS COMICS
Caliber, 1996
```
1 Moe ...................... 3.00
2 Moe ...................... 3.00
3 Moe ...................... 3.00
4 Moe,MP ................... 3.00
5 Moe,SL ................... 3.00
6 Moe ...................... 3.00
```

MONNGA
Daikaiyu Enterprises, 1995
```
1 & 2 Titanic Omega........... 4.00
```

MONOGRAPHS
Coppervale, 1997
```
1 by James Owen.............. 3.00
2 Bob Phantom............... 3.00
3 Sidekick Wanted—Benefits
   Available ................ 3.00
4 thru 6 ................... 3.00
```

MONSTER BOY
Slave Labor, 1997
```
1 by Bob Supina .............. 3.00
2 thru 4 ................... @3.00
```

Monster Possee #3
© *Malibu Adventure*

MONSTER POSSE
Malibu Adventure, 1992
```
1 I:Monster Posse............. 2.50
2 I:P.O.N.E,Wack Mack Dwac's
   sister,D-Vicious ............. 2.50
3 .......................... 2.50
```

MONSTERS ATTACK
Globe
```
1 GM,JSe ................... 2.50
2 GC ...................... 2.50
3 ATh,GC .................. 2.50
```

MONSTERS FROM OUTER SPACE
Adventure, 1992
```
1 .......................... 2.50
2 thru 3 ................... @2.50
```

MONSTER HIGH
Sirius Entertainment, 2001
```
1 (of 3) by Aaron Bordner........ 3.00
2 .......................... 3.00
3 .......................... 3.00
```

MOONSTONE MONSTERS
Moonstone Books, 1999
```
1-shot Werewolves ............. 3.00
1-shot Mummies ............... 3.00
1-shot Sea Creatures........... 3.00
1-shot Vampire Vixens........... 3.00
1-shot Ghosts................. 3.00
1-shot Witches................ 3.00
```

1-shot Demons. 3.00
1-shot Zombies 3.00

MOONSTONE NOIR
Moonstone 2002
GN Boston Blackie. 5.50
GN The Hat Squad 5.50
GN Jack Hagee, Private Eye. 5.50
GN The Mysterious Traveler 5.50
GN The Lone Wolf, Vol. #1 . . . . . . 5.00
GN Johnny Dollar 5.00
GN Mysterious Traveler Returns . . . 5.00
GN Bulldog Drummond 5.00

MORBID ANGEL:
DESPERATE ANGELS
London Night, 1998
0 EHr, & Jude Millien 3.00
0A Powell(c) 5.00
0B Powell(c) 5.00

...PENANCE
London Night Studios, 1995
1 I:Brandon Watts. 4.00

...TO HELL AND BACK
London Night, 1996
1 (of 3) EHr. 4.00
2 and 3 . . . . @3.00

MORE THAN MORTAL: A LEGEND REBORN
Avatar Press, 2006
Spec. 2.50
Spec. Wraparound (c) 3.00
Spec. variant (c) 3.00
Spec. Premium (c) 10.00
Spec. Ruby Red Con Foil (c) 5.00
Spec. Heroic (c) 6.00

MORNING GLORY
Radio Comix, 1998
1 by Loran Gayton & Michael Vega 3.00
2 thru 6 . . . . @3.00

MORTAL COIL
Mermaid
1 thru 3 . . . . @2.50
4 F:Red-Line,Gift 2.50
5 Pin-Up Issue 2.50

MORTOL COILS
Red Eye Press, 2003
1 . . . . 2.50
2 . . . . 3.50
3 . . . . 2.50

MORTAR MAN
Marshall Comics, 1993
1 I:Mortar Man 2.50
2 thru 3 . . . . @2.50

MOSAIC
Oktober Black Press
1 F:Halo,Daeva. 2.50
2 "Gun Metal Gray". 2.50
3 . . . . 2.50
4 Elf(c) 2.50
5 Wisps. 2.50

MOSAIC
Sirius, 1999
1 by Kyle Hotz 3.00
2 thru 5 conclusion . . . . @3.00

MR. BEAT ADVENTURES
Moordam Comics, 1997
1 . . . . 3.00
1 deluxe 5.00
Spec. House of Burning Jazz Love . 3.00
Spec. deluxe 5.00
Two-Fisted Atomic Action
  Super Spec. 3.00
Two-Fisted Atomic Action
  Super Spec., deluxe 10.00
Two-Fisted Atomic Action
  Super Spec., mega deluxe . . . 20.00
Spec. Mr. Beat: Superstar 3.00
Spec. Mr. Beat: Superstar, deluxe . 10.00
Ann.#1 Babes and Bongos 3.00

MR. FIXITT
Apple, 1989
1 and 2 . . . . @2.50

MR. KEEN: TRACER OF LOST PERSONS
Moonstone, 2003
1 (of 3) 3.00
2 thru 3 . . . . @3.00

MR. MOTO
Moonstone, 2003
1 (of 3) Welcome Back, Mr. Moto . . 3.00
2 thru 3 . . . . @3.00

MR. MYSTIC
Eclipse
1 Will Eisner 2.50

MR. NIGHTMARE'S WONDERFUL WORLD
Moonstone, 1995
1 thru 3 Dreams So Real,
  pt.1–pt.3. . . . . @3.00

MS. TREE
Aardvark–Vanaheim, 1984
1-10 see Other Pub. (color)
11 thru 18 . . . . @2.50
Renegade, 1985
19 thru 49. . . . . @2.50
50 . . . . 4.50
1 3-D Classic 3.00

Ms. Tree #34
© Renegade

MULTIPLE WARHEADS
Onipress, 2007
1 . . . . 6.00
2 . . . . 3.00

MUMMY, THE
Monster Comics
1 A:Dr.Clarke,Prof.Belmore. 2.50
2 Mummy's Curse. 2.50
3 A:Carloph. 2.50
4 V:Carloph, conc. 2.50

MUMMY'S CURSE
Aircel, 1990
1 thru 4 B.Blair . . . . @2.50

MUNSTERS, THE
TV Comics, 1998
1 photo (c). 3.00
1a variant (c). 8.00
2 Beverly Owen(c) 3.00
2 Pat Priest (c) 3.00
2 Pat Priest (c) signed 15.00
3 . . . . 3.00
3a Celebrity autograph edition . . . 19.00
4 . . . . 3.00
4a variant photo (c) 3.00
4b variant (c) celebrity autograph
  edition 19.00
5 Herman photo (c). 3.00
5 Grandpa photo (c) 3.00
Spec. Comic Con edition 10.00
Celebrity Autograph Edition: Butch
  Patrick 23.00
Spec.#1 Herman/Grandpa (c) 3.00
Spec.#1a Grandpa (c) 3.00
Halloween Spec. Munsters 1313 . . . 3.00
Golden Age Adventure Spec.A(c) . . 3.00
Golden Age Adventure Spec.B(c) . . 3.00

MUNSTERS CLASSICS
TV Comics
0 The Fregosi Emerald. 3.00
0 variant (c). 8.00

MURCIELAGA: SHE-BAT
Hero Graphics, 1993
1 Daerick Gross reps. 2.50
2 Reps. contd 3.00

MURDER
Renegade, 1986
1 SD 2.50
2 CI(c) 2.50
3 SD 2.50
[2nd series]
1 . . . . 2.50

MURDER CAN BE FUN
Slave Labor, 1996
1 thru 6 . . . . @3.00
2 2nd printing 3.00
7 . . . . 3.00
8 . . . . 3.00
9 Seedy Side of Sex 3.00
10 We Love Sports 3.00
11 . . . . 3.00
12 Amusement Park Terror 3.00

MURDER ME DEAD
El Capitan Books, 2000
1 (of 8) by David Lapham. 3.00
2 . . . . 3.00
3 thru 8 . . . . @3.00
9 64-pg.. 5.00

MUTANT, TEXAS: TALES OF SHERIFF IDA RED
Oni Press, 2002
1 (of 4) by Paul Dini & J. Bone 3.00
2 thru 4 . . . . @3.00

MUTANT ZONE
Aircel, 1991
1 Future story 2.50
2 F.B.I. Drone Exterminators 2.50
3 conclusion 2.50

MY INNER BIMBO
Oni Press, 2006
1 (of 5) 3.00
2 thru 4 . . . . @3.00
8 thru 10 . . . . @3.50

MYRIAD
Approbation Comics, 2005
1 (of 6) 3.00
2 thru 6 . . . . @3.00

MYSTERY MAN
Slave Labor Graphics, 1988
1 thru 5 . . . . @2.50

MYTH ADVENTURES
Warp Graphics, 1984
1 Mag size 2.50
2 thru 4 . . . . @2.50
5 Comic size 2.50
6 thru 11 . . . . @2.50
12 . . . . 2.50

MYTH CONCEPTIONS
Apple, 1987
1 . . . . 2.50
2 thru 8 . . . . @2.50

MYTHOGRAPHY
Bardic Press, 1966
1 F:Poison Elves 6.00
2 fantasy stories 6.00
3 fantasy stories, inc. Elfquest 6.00
4 . . . . 5.00
5 72-pg. 5.00
6 F:Anubis Squadron 72pg. 5.00
7 80-pg. 5.00
8 72-pg. 5.00

Mythos #1
© Wonder Comix

MYTHOS
Wonder Comix, 1987
1 . . . . 2.50
2 . . . . 2.50

NANTUCKET BROWN ROASTERS
House of Usher, 2003
1 (of 2) 2.50
2 . . . . 2.00
GN Second Law of
   Thermodynamics 7.50
1-shot The Lady of Shadows 2.50
GN The Third Twin 5.00

NAT TURNER
Kyle Baker Publishing, 2005
1 . . . . 3.00
2 . . . . 3.00
3 . . . . 3.00
4 . . . . 3.00

NATURE OF THE BEAST
Caliber
1 `The Beast' 3.00
2 . . . . 3.00
3 . . . . 3.00

NAUGHTY BITS
Fantagraphics, 1991–2004
1 by Roberta Gregory 5.00
2 thru 10 F:Bitchy Bitch . . . . @4.00
11 thru 20 . . . . @3.50
21 I:Bitchy Butch 3.00
22 Adult-erated 3.00
23 O:Bitchy Butch 3.00
24 thru 39 . . . . @3.00
40 . . . . 3.50

NAUSICAA OF THE VALLEY OF WIND
Viz Select, 1988
Book One 4.50
Book Two 5.50
Book Three 4.00
Book Four 3.00
Book Five 2.50
Book Six 3.00
Book Seven 3.00

[Part 2] 1989
#1 thru #4 . . . . @3.00

[Part 3] 1993
#1 thru #3 . . . . @3.00

NAUTILUS
Shanda Fantasy Arts, 1999
1 (of 6) by Mike Curtis &
   Louis Frank 3.00
2 thru 6 . . . . @3.00

NAZRAT
Imperial, 1986
1 . . . . 2.50
2 thru 6 . . . . @2.50

NECROSCOPE
Caliber, 1997
1 Brian Lumley adapt. 3.00
1 signed 3.00
2 thru 4 . . . . @3.00

NEGATIVE BURN
Caliber, 1993
1 I:Matrix 7, Flaming Carrot 5.00
2 . . . . 3.50

3 Bone preview 12.00
4 thru 12 various stories . . . . . . @4.00
13 Strangers in Paradise 11.00
14 thru 18 various stories . . . . . . @4.00
19 Flaming Carrot 5.00
20 In the Park 4.00
21 Trollords 4.00
22 Father the Dryad 4.00
23 I:The Creep 4.00
24 The Factor 4.00
25 The Factor 4.00
26 Very Vicki 4.00
27 Nancy Kate 4.00
28 Favorite Song 4.00
29 thru 33 . . . . @4.00
34 Kaos Moon 6.00
35 thru 38 . . . . @4.00
39 `Iron Empires,' pt. 4 . . . . 4.00
40 `Suzi Romaine' 4.00
41 `Iron Empires,' cont. 4.00
42 . . . . 4.00
43 `Iron Empires,' concl. 4.00
44 `Skeleton Key' 4.00
45 `Divine Winds' 4.00
46 `A Bullet For Me' 4.00
47 . . . . 4.00
48 special 80-pg. issue 5.00
49 special 80-pg. issue 5.00
50 96-pg., final issue 7.00

NEIL THE HORSE
Aardvark–Vanaheim, 1983
1 Art:Arn Sara, satire 5.00
1a 2nd printing 2.50
2 . . . . 3.00
3 . . . . 4.00
4 . . . . 3.00
5 Video Warriors 2.50
6 Video Warriors 2.50
7 Video Warriors 2.50
8 Outer Space 2.50
9 Canine the Barbarian 2.50
10 Canine the Barbarian 2.50

Renegade, 1985
11 Fred Astair 2.50
12 . . . . 2.50
13 . . . . 2.50
14 Special 3.00
15 . . . . 2.50

NEMESIS THE WARLOCK
Fleetway, 1989
1 thru 16 . . . . @2.50

NEON GENESIS EVANGELION
Viz Communication, 1997
1 (of 6) by Gainax & Yoshiyuki
   Sadamoto 3.25
1 special collectors edition 3.00
2 thru 6 . . . . @3.00
2 thru 6 special collectors ed. . . . @3.00

BOOK TWO, 1998
1 (of 5) by Yoshiyuki Sadamoto . . . 3.00
1 special collectors edition 3.00
2 thru 5 . . . . @3.00
2 thru 5 special collectors ed. . . . @3.00

BOOK THREE, 1998
1 thru 6 by Yoshiyuki Sadamoto . @3.00
1a thru 6a Collectors edition . . . . @3.00

BOOK FOUR, 1999
1 thru 7 by Yoshiyuki Sadamoto . @3.00
1a thru 7a special collectors ed. . @3.00

BOOK FIVE, 2000
1 . . . . 3.00
1a collectors ed. 3.00
2 thru 7 . . . . @3.00
2a thru 7a deluxe . . . . @3.00

BOOK SIX, 2001
1 thru 4 . . . . @3.50
1a thru 4a coll. ed. . . . . @3.50
BOOK SEVEN
1 (of 7) 3.50
2 thru 5 . . . . @3.00
6 . . . . 3.50
2a thru 5a collector's edition . . . . @3.00
6a collector's edition . . . . @3.50

NERVOUS REX
Blackthorne, 1985
1 . . . . 3.00
1a 2nd printing 2.50
2 . . . . 3.00
3 . . . . 3.00
4 . . . . 2.50
5 thru 10 . . . . @2.50
GraphicNovel 3.50

NEW ADVENTURES OF TERRY & THE PIRATES
ACG Comics, 1998
1 by Bros. Hildebrandt 3.00
2 thru 7 . . . . @3.00

NEWCOMERS ILLUSTRATED
Newcomers Publishing
1 thru 5 various artists. . . . . @3.00
6 Science Fiction 3.00
7 thru 8 . . . . @3.00
9 Shocking Machines 3.00
10 . . . . 3.00
11 Hitman. 3.00
12 final issue 3.00

NEW FRONTIERS
Evolution
1 A:Action Master, Green Ghost. . . 2.50
2 . . . . 2.50

NEW HORIZONS
Shanda Fantasy Arts, 1997
1 . . . . 5.00
2 thru 5 . . . . @4.50
6 thru 15 . . . . @5.00

NEW HUMANS
Pied Piper, 1987
1 and 2 . . . . @2.50

NEW HUMANS
Eternity, 1987
1 . . . . 2.50
2 thru 15 . . . . @2.50
Ann. #1. . . . . 3.00

NEW HUMANS
1 Shattered Earth Chronicles 2.50

NEW LOVE
Fantagraphics, 1996
1 GHe, Love & Rockets tie in 3.00
2 thru 3 GHe . . . . @3.00
4 thru 6 GHe . . . . @3.00

NEW REALITY
1 thru 6 . . . . @2.50

NEWSTRALIA
Innovation, 1989
(Prev. Color)
4 . . . . 2.50
5 . . . . 2.50

NEW TALES OF OLD PALOMAR
Fantagraphics Books 2006
1 GHe 8.00
2 . . . . 8.00
3 . . . . 8.00

New Triumph #3
© Matrix Graphics

NEW TRIUMPH
Matrix Graphics, 1985
1 F:Northguard 3.00
1a 2nd printing 2.50
2 thru 4 . . . . @2.50

NEW VAMPIRE MIYU
Ironcat, 1997
1 by Narumi Kakinouchi 3.00
2 thru 6 . . . . @3.00
7 The Past Lies Beyond a Door,
   finale 3.00
VOL. 2, 1998
1 by Narumi Kakinouchi 3.00
2 thru 6 . . . . @3.00
VOL. 3, 1998
1 . . . . 3.00
2 thru 7 . . . . @3.00
VOL. 4, 1999
1 by Narumi Kakinouchi 3.00
2 thru 6 . . . . @3.00
VOL. 5
1 thru 7 . . . . @3.00

NEW WORLD ORDER
Blazer Studios, 1993
1 . . . . 2.50
2 thru 8 . . . . @2.50

NEW YORK CITY OUTLAWS
Outlaw
1 thru 5 . . . . @2.50

NEW YORK, YEAR ZERO
Eclipse, 1988
1 thru 4 . . . . @2.50

NEXT EXIT
Amaze Ink, SLG, 2004
1 by Christy Kijewski. 3.00
2 thru 11 . . . . @3.00

NEXUS
Capital, 1981
1 SR,I:Nexus,large size 18.00
2 SR,Mag size 12.00
3 SR,Mag size 10.00

NIGHT CRY
CFD Productions, 1995
1 Evil Ernie & Razor story 8.00
1 signed 9.00
2 . . . . 6.00
3 . . . . 5.00
4 . . . . 4.00
4a platinum (c) 6.00
5 . . . . 4.00
6 . . . . 2.75
6a signed 8.00

NIGHT LIFE
Caliber
1 thru 7 . . . . @2.50

NIGHTMARES & FAIRY TALES
Amaze Ink/SLG, 2002
1 . . . . 3.00
2 thru 5 . . . . @3.00
6 thru 14 . . . . @3.00
15 thru 20. . . . . @3.00
21 thru 23 . . . . @3.50

NIGHT MASTER
Silver Wolf, 1987
1 Vigil 5.50
2 Vigil 2.50
3 . . . . 2.50

NIGHT OF THE LIVING DEAD
Fantaco
0 prelude 2.50
1 based on cult classic movie. 5.00
2 Movie adapt,continued. 5.00
3 Movie adapt,conclusion 5.00
5 . . . . 6.00

NIGHT'S CHILDREN
Fantaco
1 . . . . 3.50
2 thru 4 . . . . @3.50

NIGHT'S CHILDREN
Millennium, 1995
1 The Ripper, Klaus Wulfe 4.00
Spec. High Noon (1996) 3.00
Spec. The Churchyard (1997) 3.25

...THE VAMPIRE
Millennium, 1995
1 F:Klaus Wulfe 3.00
2 F:Klaus Wulfe 3.00

NIGHT STREETS
Arrow, 1986
1 . . . . 2.50
2 thru 4 . . . . @2.50

NIGHTVISION
London Night, 1996
1 DQ,KHt, All About Eve 3.00
1 signed 13.00
1a erotica edition 10.00
Rebel Studios, 1997
3 Love Bleeding Pictures 2.50
4 Winter 3.00

NIGHT WARRIORS: DARKSTALKERS' REVENGE

Viz Communications, 1998
1 (of 6) by Run Ishida 3.00
2 . . . . 3.25
3 thru 6 . . . . @3.00

NIGHTWOLF: THE PRICE

Devil's Due Publishing, 2006
0 . . . . 1.00
1 thru 3 . . . . @3.00
4 . . . . 3.50
5 . . . . 3.00

NIGHT ZERO

Fleetway
1 thru 4 . . . . @2.50

NIKKI BLADE

High Impact, 1997
0 . . . . 3.00
0a deluxe adult cover 10.00
0b gold edition variant cover 15.00
Spec.#0 Nikki Blade: Forever Nikki
  (1997) MIB(c). 3.00
  Deluxe RCI(c) 10.00

ABC Comics, 1998
Spec. Nikki Blade: Blades of Death
  (1998) by RCI & Clayton Henry. 3.00
  Puzzle variant A cover. 6.00
  Puzzle variant B cover 6.00
  Puzzle variant C cover 6.00
Spec. Nikki Blade: Revenge 3.00

NIMROD, THE

Fantagraphics, 1998
1 by Lewis Trondheim 3.00
2 thru 4 . . . . @3.00
5 . . . . 4.00
6 . . . . 3.50
7 . . . . 4.00

NINJA

Eternity
1 . . . . 3.00
2 thru 13 . . . . @2.50

NINJA ELITE

Adventure, 1987
1 . . . . 2.50
2 thru 8 . . . . @2.50

NINJA FUNNIES

Eternity
1 . . . . 2.50
2 thru 5 . . . . @2.50

NINJA HIGH SCHOOL

Antarctic, 1987
1 . . . . 15.00
2 thru 4 . . . . @11.00

Eternity, 1988
5 thru 22 . . . . @4.00
23 Zardon Assassin 3.00
24 . . . . 3.00
25 Return of the Zetramen 3.00
26 Stanley the Demon 3.00
27 Return of the Zetramen 3.00
28 Threat of the super computer . . . 3.00
29 V:Super Computer 3.00
30 I:Akaru. 3.00
31 Jeremy V:Akaru 3.00
32 thru 34 V:Giant Monsters Pt.1
  thru Pt. 3 . . . . @3.00
35 thru 43 . . . . @3.00

44 Combat Cheerleaders. 2.75
45 Cheerleader Competition 2.75
46 Monsters From Space. 2.75
47 . . . . 2.75
48 F:Jeremy Feeple. 2.75
49 thru 51 . . . . @3.00
52 thru 57 Time Warp, pt.4–pt.8 . @3.00
58 Zardon ambassador, BU:BDn. . . 3.00
59 Akaru overwhelmed 3.00
60 to the Himalayas. 3.00
61 ancient Himalayan temple 3.00
62 Hillbilly girl. 3.00
63 F:Tetsuo Rivalsan 3.00
64 Jeremy Feeple: Saboteur? 3.00
65 Quagmire Trial of the Century . . 3.00
66 . . . . 3.00
67 F:Eolata. 3.00
68 F:Akaru & Asrial 3.00
69 Guri-Guri Island 3.00
70 Mad Bomber in Space 2.50
71 traitor in secret police 3.00
72 . . . . 2.50
73 . . . . 2.50
74 Girl Scouts 2.50
Special #1 . . . . 3.00
Special #2 . . . . 3.00
Special #3 . . . . 3.00
Special #3 1/2 . . . . 3.00
Ann. 1989. 3.00
Ann.#3 . . . . 4.00
Yearbook 1994. . . . . 4.00
Yearbook 1995. . . . . 4.00
Yearbook 1996. . . . . 4.00
Yearbook 1997, cover A. 4.00
Yearbook 1997, cover B 4.00
Yearbook 1998, cover A. 3.00
Yearbook 1998, cover B 3.00
Spec. Girls of Ninja High School
  (1997) 4.00
Spec. Girls of Ninja High School
  1998 cover A 3.00
  1998 cover B 3.00
Spec. 1999 . . . . 3.00
Spotlight #4 Rod Espinosa 3.00
Summer Spec.#1 . . . . 3.00

Antarctic Press, 2000
145 thru 166 . . . . @3.00
Swimsuit Spec. 2000 . . . . 4.50
Swimsuit Spec. 2001 . . . . 4.50
Yearbook 2007. . . . . 4.50
Yearbook 2008 . . . . 4.50

NINJA HIGH SCHOOL GIRLS

Antarctic Press
0 . . . . 2.75
1 and 2 rep. . . . . @2.75
3 thru 5 rep. . . . . @4.00
Yearbook 4.00

NINJA HIGH SCHOOL PERFECT MEMORY

Antarctic Press, 1993
1 thru 2, 96pg . . . . @5.00

NINJA HIGH SCHOOL SMALL BODIES

Antarctic Press
1 "Monopolize" 2.50
2 Omegadon Cannon 2.75
3 Omegadon Cannon 2.75
3a deluxe 4.50
4 Omegadon Cannon 2.75
5 Wrong Order 2.75
6 Chicken Rage 3.00
7 . . . . 3.00

Nira X: Exodus #1
© Avatar

NIRA X:

CYBERANGEL

Entity Comics, 1996
1 . . . . 5.00
1a deluxe 8.00
2 BMs 4.00
3 and 4 BMs . . . . @3.00
4a with PC Game 8.00
Ann.#1 BMs flip-cover 2.75

2nd Mini Series, 1995
1 . . . . 4.00
1a 2nd printing 2.50
2 thru 4 . . . . @2.50

3rd Mini Series, 1995–96
1 . . . . 2.50
1a Gold(c) 5.00
2 . . . . 2.50
3 . . . . 3.00

Regular Series
1 . . . . 2.75
1a with game 7.00
2 thru 4 . . . . @2.75
4a with game 7.00
Spec. Nira X:Headwave, encore
  special toy edition 2.50
  Encore special toy edition,
  signed & numbered. 13.00
Spec. Nira X:Memoirs (1997) BMs . 2.75
  Deluxe 3.50

...EXODUS

Avatar, 1997
0 (of 2) BMs 3.00
0a Leather cover. 15.00
0b signed 9.00
1 (of 2) 3.00
1a leather cover 15.00
1b signed 9.00
2 . . . . 3.00
Spec. Shoot First 3.00
Spec. Summer Splash 5.00

...HISTORY

Avatar Press, 1999
1 (of 2) by Bill Maus 3.50
2 . . . . 3.50

...SOUL SKURGE

Entity, 1996
1 (of 3) BMs, A:Vortex. 2.75
2 BMs, ... 2.75
3 . . . . 2.75

NIRA X/HELLINA:
HEAVEN & HELL
Entity Comics
1 San Diego Con edition, BMs 5.00
1a foil 3.00

NITRO-GEN
Arcade Comics, 2005
Preview, limited 7.00
1 .... 4.00
1a signed ed. 10.00
1b resketch ed. 25.00

NOBODY
Oni Press, 1998
1 (of 4) 3.00
2 thru 4 .... @3.00

NODWICK
Henchman Publishing, 2000
1 by Aaron Williams 3.00
2 & 3 .... @3.00

Dork Storm, 2000
1 by Aaron Williams 3.00
2 thru 5 .... @3.00
6 thru 11 .... @3.00
12 thru 30 .... @3.00
31 thru 35 .... 3.00
36 .... 3.00

NO GUTS, NO GLORY
Fantaco
1-shot, K.Eastman's 1st solo
   work since TMNT 3.00

NOMADS OF ANTIQUITY
1 thru 6 .... @2.50

NO NEED FOR TENCHI
Viz Comics
PART ONE
1 thru 7 (of 7) .... @3.00
PART TWO, 1996
1 thru 7 by Hitoshi Okuda ...... @3.00
PART THREE, 1997
1 (of 6) by Hitoshi Okuda 3.00
2 .... 3.00
3 thru 6 .... @3.00
PART FOUR, 1997
1 (of 6) by Hitoshi Okuda 3.00
2 thru 6 .... @3.00
PART FIVE, 1998
1 (of 6) 3.00
2 thru 6 .... @3.00
PART SIX, 1998
1 (of 6) 3.00
2 thru 6 .... @3.00
PART SEVEN, 1999
1 (of 6) 3.00
2 thru 6 .... @3.00
PART EIGHT, 1999
1 (of 5) by Hitoshi Okuda 3.25
2 thru 5 .... @3.00
PART NINE
1 (of 6) by Hitoshi Okuda 3.00
2 thru 6 .... @3.00
PART TEN, 2000
1 (of 7) 3.00
2 thru 7 .... @3.00
PART ELEVEN, 2001
1 .... 3.50
2 thru 4 .... @3.50

No Need For Tenchi Vol. 12 #4
© *Viz Comics*
PART TWELVE, 2001
1 thru 4 (of 6) .... @3.50
5 thru 6 .... @3.00

NORM, THE
The Norm Comics, 2003
1 .... 5.00
2 thru 8 .... @5.00
9 thru 11 .... @3.00
1-shot The 12 Steps to Marriage ... 5.00

NORMAL MAN
Aardvark–Vanaheim, 1984
1 .... 4.00
2 thru 9 .... @3.00
Renegade
10 thru 19 .... @2.50

NOSFERATU:
PLAGUE OF TERROR
Millennium
1 I:Orlock 2.50
2 19th Century India,A:Sir W.
   Longsword 2.50
3 WWI/WWII to Viet Nam 2.50
4 O:Orlock,V:Longsword,conc..... 2.50

NOTHING BETTER
Dementian Comics, 2005
1 by Tyler Page 3.00
2 thru 4 .... @3.00

NOVA GIRLS
MN Design, 1998
1 The Immortality Quest, pt.1 ..... 2.50
1a JJu (c) 3.00
1b photo (c) 4.00
1 variant Starship Discover #0(c) .. 4.00
1 variant Phazer #0 cover....... 4.00
2 The Immortality Quest, pt.2 ..... 2.50
2a deluxe 3.00
3 The Immortality Quest, pt.3 ..... 2.50
3a deluxe 3.00
Space 34–24–34 Gold Seal 10th
   Anniv. Edition............... 75.00

NOWHERE
Drawn & Quarterly Oct., 1996
1 by Debbie Drechsler 3.75
2 thru 5 .... @3.75

NOWHERESVILLE
Caliber, 1996
1 thru 3 by MRc .... @3.00
Spec. The History of Cool 3.00

NUCLEAR WAR
New England Comics, 2000
1 by Ron Ledwell 3.50
2 thru 4 .... @3.50

NYOKA
THE JUNGLE GIRL
AC Comics
3 thru 5 .... @2.50

OAK
Fat Cat March, 1997
1 by M.F. Mangione & Al Diaz 2.75
2 thru 6 .... @2.75

OCTOBRIANA
Revolution Comics
0 16pg. 2.00
1 `The Octobriana Files,'pt.1 ..... 3.00
2 `The Octobriana Files,'pt.2 ..... 3.00
3 `The Octobriana Files,'pt.3 ..... 3.00
4 `The Octobriana Files,'pt.4 ..... 3.00
5 `The Octobriana Files,'pt.5 ..... 3.00

Alchemy Texts, 2001
Spec. 30th Anniv. Spec.......... 3.00

ODDBALLZ
NBM Books, 2002
1 by Trondheim & Larcenet 3.00
2 thru 4 .... @3.00
5 thru 8 .... @3.00

ODDBALLZ:
VENETIAN BLIND
NBM Books, 2003
1 .... 3.00
2 .... 3.00

ODD JOB
Amaze Ink/SLG, 2000
1 by Ian Smith & Tyson Smith 3.00
2 thru 8 .... @3.00

OFFERINGS
Cry For Dawn
1 Sword & Sorcery stories 7.00
2 and 3 .... @6.00

OFFICIAL BUZ SAWYER
Pioneer, 1988
1 .... 2.50
2 thru 6 .... @2.50

OFFICIAL
JOHNNY HAZARD
Pioneer, 1988
1 thru 3 .... @2.50
4 .... 2.50
5 .... 2.50

OFFICIAL JUNGLE JIM
Pioneer, 1988
1 thru 5 AR,rep. .... @2.50
6 AR,rep. 2.50
7 thru 10 AR,rep. .... @2.50
11 thru 20 AR,rep. .... @2.50
Ann.#1 .... 2.50
Giant Size 4.00

OFFICIAL MANDRAKE
Pioneer, 1988
1 thru 5	@2.50
6 thru 10	@2.50
11	3.00
12	2.50
13 thru 17	@2.50
Ann. #1	4.00
King Size #1	4.00
Giant Size #1	4.00

OFFICIAL MODESTY BLAISE
Pioneer, 1988
1 thru 4	@2.50
5	2.50
6 thru 14	@2.50
Ann. #1	4.00
King Size #1	4.00

OFFICIAL PRINCE VALIANT
Pioneer, 1988
1 Hal Foster,rep.	2.50
2 thru 10	@2.50
11 thru 24	@2.50
Ann. #1	4.00
King Size #1	4.00

OFFICIAL RIP KIRBY
Pioneer, 1988
1 thru 3 AR	@2.50
4 AR	2.50
5 and 6 AR	@2.50

OFFICIAL SECRET AGENT
Pioneer, 1988
1 thru 5 AW rep	@2.50
6 AW	2.50
7 thru 9 AW	@2.50

OF MIND AND SOUL
Rage Comics, 1997
0	3.00
1	2.50
2	2.50
3	2.50
Spec. Standing on a Beach	2.50
Spec. Soul'd Out`	3.00
Spec. A Day in Hell	3.00
Spec. 1-shot	2.50

OHM'S LAW
Imperial Comics
1 thru 2	@2.50
3 V:Men in Black	2.50
4 A:Damonstriek	2.50
5 F:Tryst	2.50

OH MY GOTH!
Sirius/Dog Star, 1998
1 by Voltaire	3.00
2 thru 4	@3.00

...HUMANS SUCK!
Sirius Entertainment, 2000
1 (of 3)	3.00
1 deluxe	5.00
2 and 3	@3.00

OJO
Oni Press, 2004
1 (of 5)	3.00
2 thru 5	@3.00

OKTOBERFEST
Now & Then
1 (1976) Dave Sim	20.00

OMEGA
North Star
1 1st pr by Rebel,rare	50.00
1a Vigil(Yellow Cov.)	15.00
2	2.50

OMEGA ELITE
Blackthorne
1	2.50
2	2.50

Omen #2
© North Star

OMEN
North Star, 1987
1	8.00
1a 2nd printing	2.50
2 thru 4	@3.50

OMICRON
Pyramid, 1987
1 and 2	@2.50
3	2.50

OMNI MEN
Blackthorne, 1989
1 & 2	@2.50

ONE-POUND GOSPEL
Viz Communications, 1996
1	3.50
2	3.50
3 & 4	@3.00

ROUND TWO, 1997
1	3.00
2 thru 8 by Rumiko Takahashi	@3.00

PART 7
1 (of 13) by Rumiko Takahashi	3.00

1000 DEATHS OF BARON VON DONUT
Arsenic Lullaby Publishing 2005
1	3.00
2	3.00
3	3.00

ONI DOUBLE FEATURE
Oni Press, 1997
1 F:Jay & Silent Bob	10.00
1a 2nd printing	3.00
2 F:Car Crash on the 405	3.50
3 F:Troy Nixey	3.50
4 F:A River in Egypt	3.50
5 F:Fan Girl From Hell	4.00
6 inc. NGa Only the End of the World, pt.1	3.00
7 inc. NGa Only the End of the World, pt.2	3.00
8 inc. NGa Only the End of the World, pt.3	3.00
9 thru 10	@3.00
11 Usagi Yojimbo	3.50
12 Bluntman & Chronic	7.00
13	3.00

ONIGAMI
Antarctic Press, 1998
1 (of 3) by Michael Lacombe, sequel to Winter Jade storyline from Warrior Nun: Black and White	3.00
2 thru 3	@3.00

OPEN SEASON
Renegade, 1987
1	2.50
2 thru 7	@2.50

OPPOSITE FORCES
Funny Pages Press, 2002
1 by Tom Bancroft	3.00
1a Convention Exclusive (c)	3.00
2 thru 4	@3.00

OPTIC NERVE
Adrian Tomine, 1990
1 thru 5, mini-comic	10.00
6	7.00
7	5.00
8	3.00
9	4.00

OPTIC NERVE
Drawn & Quarterly, 1995
1 Summer Job	9.00
1a 2nd printing	6.00
2 thru 4	@5.00
5 thru 11	@4.00

ORACLE PRESENTS
Oracle, 1986
1 thru 4	@2.50

ORBIT
Eclipse, 1990
1 thru 3	@5.00

OR ELSE
Drawn & Quarterly, 2004
1	3.50
2 thru 3	@4.00
4	6.00
5	5.00

ORIGINAL TOM CORBETT
Eternity, 1990
1 thru 10 rep. newspaper strips	@3.00

OUTLAW OVERDRIVE
Blue Comet Press
1 Red Edition I:Deathrow	3.00
1a Black Edition	3.00
1b Blue Edition	3.00

OZ
Imperial Comics, 1996
1 Land of Oz Gone Mad	8.00
2 Land of Oz Gone Mad	7.00
3 Land of Oz Gone Mad	6.00
4 Tin Woodsmen	6.00
5 F:Pumkinhead	6.00
6 Emerald City	6.00
7 V:Bane Wolves	4.00
8 V:Nome Hordes	4.00
9 Freedom Fighters Vs. Heroes	4.00
10 thru 15	@4.00
16	3.50
Spec.#1	6.00
Spec. Scarecrow #1	3.00
Spec. Lion #1	3.00
Spec. Tin Man #1	3.00
Spec. Freedom Fighters #1	3.00

Caliber `New Worlds'
17 by Ralph Griffith, Stuart Kerr & Tim Holtrop	3.50
18 thru 20	@3.00
21 `Witches War' pt.1 (of 5)	3.00
22	3.00

OZ: ROMANCE IN RAGS
Caliber, 1996
1 thru 3 Bill Bryan	@3.00

OZ SQUAD
Patchwork Press, 1992
1	4.00
2 thru 8	@3.00

OZ: STRAW AND SORCERY
Caliber `New Worlds', 1997
1 thru 3	@3.00

PAKKINS' LAND
Caliber Tapestry, 1996
1	6.00
1a signed edition	3.00
1a second edition, new cover	3.00
2	4.00
2a second edition, new cover	3.00
3	4.00
3 2nd edition, new cover	3.00
4 thru 6	@3.00
GN Book One: Paul's Adventure	10.00

...FORGOTTEN DREAMS
Caliber, 1998
1 by Gary & Rhoda Shipman	3.00
2 thru 5	@3.00

...QUEST FOR KINGS
Caliber, 1997
1G by Gary & Rhoda Shipman, Shipman(c)	3.00
1J by Gary & Rhoda Shipman, JSi(c)	3.00
2	3.00
3 Rahsha's city	3.00
4	3.00
5	3.00

PALANTINE
Gryphon Rampant, 1995
1 thru 5 V:Master of Basilisk	2.50

PALEO TALES: LATE CRETACEOUS
Zeromayo Studios, 2001
1 thru 6	3.00
Empty Sky, 2003
7	3.00

8	3.00

PALOOKA-VILLE
Drawn & Quarterly
1 third printing	3.00
1 10th Anniv. Ed.	3.75
10 by Seth	3.75
11 Clyde Fans, pt.2	3.75
12 Clyde Fans, pt.3	3.75
13 Clyde Fans	3.75
14 thru 15	@3.75
16 thru 18	@4.75
19	5.00

PANDA KHAN
1 thru 4	@2.50

PANDEMONIUM
Curtis Comics, 2002
Vol. 1 Manga
1 by Jaeongtae Lee	3.00
2 thru 5	@3.00
Vol. 2
1	3.00

PANDORA
Brainstorm, 1996
1 (of 2)	3.00

Pandora/Razor #1
© Avatar

PANDORA
Avatar Press, 1997
0	3.00
1 signed	10.00
2 (of 2)	3.00
2 deluxe	9.00
X-over Pandora/Ranzor:Devil Inside (1998) signed	10.00
Haley (c)	5.00
X-over Pandora/Razor (1999)	3.50
Leather cover, signed	12.00
Expanded Edition	5.00
X-over Pandora/Shotgun Mary: Demon Nation (1998)	3.00
Deluxe	5.00
Leather	15.00
Royal Blue edition	40.00
X-over Pandora/Widow (1997)	4.00
Leather cover	15.00
Spec. Arachnophobia	3.50
Spec. Pandora Special (1997)	3.00
Leather cover	15.00
Avatar convention (c) ed.	15.00

Spec. Pandora Pin-up (1997)	3.00
Signed	15.00
Spec. Nudes (1997)	3.50
GN Love and War (2003)	6.00

PANDORA'S CHEST
Avatar Press, 1999
1 (of 3)	2.75

PANDORA:
DEMONOGRAPHY
Avatar Press, 1997
1	3.00
2 (of 3)	3.00
3 (of 3)	3.00

...DEVILS ADVOCATE
Avatar Press, 1999
1 (of 3)	3.50
1a Previews exclusive foil (c)	11.00
2	3.50
3	3.50

...PANDEMONIUM
Avatar Press, 1997
1 Pandora goes to Hell	3.00
1 leather cover	25.00
1 signed	10.00
2 (of 3)	3.00

PANTHEON
Lone Star Press, 1998
1 (of 12)	3.00
2 Welcome to the Machine	3.00
3 V:Death Boy	3.00
4 F:Tangeroa	3.00
5 Under Pressure	3.00
6 All-villain issue	3.00
7 thru 9	@3.00
10 thru 12	@3.00
13	5.00
Spec. Ancient History (1999)	3.50

PANZER: 1946
Antarctic Press, 2004
1	6.00
2	6.00
3	6.00
4	6.00
5	6.00

PAPER CUTS
1 E Starzer-1982	12.00
2 and 3	@2.50

PARIS
Amaze Ink/SLG, 2005
1	3.00
2 thru 4	@3.00

PARTICLE DREAMS
Fantagraphics, 1986
1	3.00
2 thru 6	@2.50

PARTNERS IN PANDEMONIUM
Caliber
1 Hell on Earth	2.50
2 Sheldon & Murphy are mortal	2.50
3 A:Abra Cadaver	2.50

PARTS UNKNOWN
Eclipse, 1992
1 I:Spurr, V:Aliens	2.50
2 Aliens on Earth cont.	2.50

B & W PUB.

All comics prices listed are for *Near Mint* condition.

Parts Unknown: Dark Intentions #3
© Knight Press

PARTS UNKNOWN:
DARK INTENTIONS
Knight Press, 1995

0	3.00
1 I:Prelude to limited Series	3.00
2 thru 3 V:Luggnar	@3.00
4	3.00
1-shot, Handbook, The Roswell Agenda	3.00
Super-Ann. #1	4.00

PATRICK THE WOLF BOY
Blindwolf Studios, 2000

1 by Art Baltazar & Franco	3.00
Halloween Special	3.00
Next Halloween Special	3.00
Valentine's Day Special	3.00
Christmas Spec.	3.00
Mother's Day Special	3.00
Summer Spec.	3.00
Superhero Spec.(2002)	3.00
Sci-Fi Special (2002)	3.00
Another Halloween Special (2002)	3.00
Spec. This Year's Halloween Spec.	3.00
Spec. Grimm Reaper Super Spec.	3.00
Spec. Wedding Special	3.00
Spec. After School Special	3.00
Spec. Rock-n-Roll spec.	3.00
Spec. Father's Day spec.	3.00
Spec. Happy Birthday	3.00

PATTY CAKE
Caliber Tapestry, 1996

1 by Scott Roberts	3.00
2 thru 4	@3.00
Christmas special	4.00

PATTY-CAKE & FRIENDS
Slave Labor, 1997

1 by Scott Roberts	3.00
2 thru 15	@3.00
Halloween Spec.	4.00

VOL. 2, 2000

1 by Scott Roberts, 48-pg.	5.00
2 thru 15	@5.00

PAULA PERIL
Atlantis Studios 2006

1	3.00
2 Case of the Haunted Museum.	3.00
3	3.00

PAUL THE SAMURAI
New England Comics, 1991

1 thru 3	@2.75
Bonanza #2 100pg.	5.00
GN Collected	9.00

PENDULUM
Adventure, 1993

1 Big Hand,Little Hand	2.50
2 The Immortality Formula	2.50
3	2.50

PENNY CENTURY
Fantagraphics, 1997

1 by Jaime Hernandez	3.00
2 thru 7	@3.00

PENTACLE:
THE SIGN OF THE FIVE
Eternity, 1991

1	2.50
2 Det.Sandler,H.Smitts	2.50
3 Det.Sandler becomes New Warlock	2.50
4 5 warlocks Vs. Kaji	2.50

PETE THE P.O.'D
POSTAL WORKER
Sharkbait Press, 1998

1 by Marcus Pierce & Pete Garcia, Route 666	3.00
2 prison mail	3.00
3 To Aliens with Love	3.00
4 Special Delivery to Conad the Alien	3.00
5 England Vacation	3.00
6 Benedict Postman	3.00
7 Postman on Elm Street	3.00
8 Postman on Elm Street	3.00
9 Pete Meets Jerry Ringer	3.00
10 Y2K Express	3.00
11 Postal Wars	3.00
12	3.00
X-mas Spec.#1	3.50
Spec. War Journal	3.00

PHANTOM

1 thru 3	@6.00
4 and 5	@7.00

PHANTOM OF FEAR CITY
Claypool, 1994–95

1 thru 12	2.50

PHANTOM OF
THE OPERA
Eternity

1	2.50

PHASE ONE
Victory, 1986

1	3.00
2	2.50
3 thru 5	@2.50

PHIGMENTS
Amazing, 1987

1	5.00
2	2.50
3	2.50

PINEAPPLE ARMY
Viz Communications, 1988

1 thru 10	@2.50

PINK FLOYD EXPERIENCE
Revolutionary, 1991

1 based on rock group	2.50
2 Dark Side of the Moon.	2.50
3 Dark Side of the Moon, Wish you were here	2.50
4 The Wall	2.50
5 A Momentary lapse of reason	2.50

PIRATE CLUB
Amaze Ink/SLG, 2004

1	3.00
2 thru 4	@3.00
5 thru 7	@3.00
8 thru 10	@3.00

PIRATE CORPS!
Eternity, 1987

6 and 7	@2.50
Spec. #1	2.50

PIRATES VS. NINJAS
Antarctic Press, 2007

1 (of 3)	3.50
2 thru 4	@3.50
1-shot Global Harming	3.50
1-shot For President	3.50
Ann. 2008	3.50

PIRANHA! IS LOOSE
Special Studio

1 Drug Runners,F:Piranha	3.00
2 Expedition into Terror.	3.00

PIXY JUNKET
Viz, 1993

1 thru 6	@2.75

P.J. WARLOCK
Eclipse, 1986

1 thru 3	@2.50

PLANET COMICS
Blackthorne, 1988
(Prev. Color)

4 and 5	@2.50

PLANET COMICS
A-List Comics, 1997

1 by L.Hampton & R.Leonardo	2.50
2 rep. from 1940	3.00
3	3.00
4 thru 6	@3.00

PLANET COMICS
ACG Comics, 2000

1 WW, rep.	7.00
2 64-pg.	6.00

PLANET OF THE APES
Adventure Comics, 1990

1 WD,collect.ed.	6.00
1 2 covers	4.00
1a 2nd printing	2.50
1b 3rd printing	2.50
2	3.00
3	3.00
4	3.00
5 D:Alexander?	3.00
6 Welcome to Ape City	3.00
7	3.00
8 Christmas Story	2.75
9 Swamp Ape Village	2.75
10 Swamp Apes in Forbidden City	2.75
11 Ape War continues	2.75
12 W:Alexander & Coure	2.75

13 Planet of Apes/Alien Nation/ Ape City x-over 2.75	
14 Countdown to Zero Pt.1 . . . . 2.75	
15 Countdown to Zero Pt.2 . . . . 2.75	
16 Countdown to Zero Pt.3 . . . . 2.75	
17 Countdown to Zero Pt.4 . . . . 2.75	
18 Ape City (after Ape Nation mini-series 2.75	
19 1991 `Conquest..' tie-in. 2.75	
20 Return of the Ape Riders 2.75	
21 The Terror Beneath,Pt.1 . . . . 2.75	
22 The Terror Beneath,Pt.2 . . . . 2.75	
23 The Terror Beneath,Pt.3 . . . . 2.75	
Ann #1,`Day on Planet o/t Apes' . . 3.50	
Lim.Ed. #1 . . . . 5.00	

...BLOOD OF THE APES
Adventure Comics, 1991

1 A:Tonus the Butcher 3.00
2 Valia/Taylorite Connection 2.75
3 Ape Army in Phis 2.75
4 . . . . 2.75

...FORBIDDEN ZONE
Adventure

1 Battle for the Planet of the Apes
  & Planet of the Apes tie-in. 2.75
2 A:`Julius 2.75

...SINS OF THE FATHER
Adventure Comics, 1992

1 Conquest Tie-in 2.75

...URCHAKS' FOLLY
Adventure Comics, 1991

1 . . . . 3.00
2 thru 4 . . . . @2.75

PLANET 29
Caliber

1 A Future Snarl Tale 2.50
2 A:Biff,Squakman 2.50

PLAN 9 FROM OUTER SPACE
Eternity, 1991

1 . . . . 2.50
2 and 3 . . . . @2.50

PLASTIC LITTLE
CPM Comics, 1997

1 (of 5) Manga, by Satoshi
  Urushihara R:Captain Tita 3.00
2 F:Joshua Balboa 3.00
3 . . . . 3.00
4 . . . . 3.00
5 concl. 3.00

PLASTRON CAFE
Mirage, 1992

1 RV,inc.North by Downeast. 2.50
2 thru 4 . . . . @2.50

POE
Cheese Comics, 1996

1 by Jason Asala, reoffer 3.00
2 . . . . 3.00
3 `The System of Doctor Tarr and
  Professor Fether'. 3.00
4 thru 6 . . . . @3.00

Sirius/Dog Star
VOL 2, 1997

1 by Jason Asala 3.00
2 House of Usher, pt.1 (of 4) 3.00
3 House of Usher, pt.2 . . . . 3.00
4 House of Usher, pt.3 . . . . 3.00
5 House of Usher, pt.4 . . . . 3.00
6 . . . . 3.00
7 . . . . 3.00

---

8 Small Town 3.00
9 Small Town, pt.2 . . . . 3.00
10 Small Town, pt.3 . . . . 3.00
11 Gold & Lead, pt.1 . . . . 3.00
12 Gold and Lead, pt.2 . . . . 3.00
13 F:Pluto the cat. 3.00
14 A:Mad Meg Mayflower 3.00
15 Airship 3.00
16 path of next demon 3.00
17 22 one-page stories 3.00
18 Airship 3.00
19 thru 24 Balloon Hoax . . . . @3.00

POINT BLANK
Acme/Eclipse, 1989

1 . . . . 3.00
2 thru 5 . . . . @3.00

POISON ELVES
Mulehide Graphics, 1993–95
Previously: I, Lusipher

8 DHa(c&a) 12.00
9 DHa 10.00
10 DHa 10.00
11 DHa, comic size 10.00
12 DI la 10.00
13 DHa 13.00
14 and 15 DHa . . . . @13.00
15a 2nd printing 6.00
16 and 17 DHa . . . . @7.00
17a 2nd printing 6.00
18 DHa 7.00
19 DHa 7.00
20 DHa 7.00

2nd Series, Sirius, 1995–2007

1 F:Lusipher 5.00
2 V:Assassins Guild 4.00
3 Sanctuary, pt.3 . . . . 4.00
4 Sanctuary, pt.4 . . . . 4.00
5 Sanctuary, pt.5 . . . . 4.00
6 I:Lester Gran 4.00
7 thru 24 . . . . @4.00
25 DHa 3.00
26 DHa 3.00
27 DHa 3.00
28 DHa,F:Lusiphur 3.00
29 DHa 3.00
30 DHa,F:Vido 3.00
31 DHa 3.00
32 DHa, Cassandra is dead 3.00
33 DHa, temporary truce 3.00
34 DHa, Lusiphur's feminine side . . 3.00

Poison Elves #11
© Sirius

---

35 DHa, Purple Marauder reappears 3.00	
36 DHa, Lusiphur tracked down . . . 3.00	
37 DHa, questionable help 3.00	
38 DHa. 3.00	
39 DHa. 3.00	
40 DHa, Sanctuary, concl. 3.00	
41 DHa, on to Amrahly'nn 3.00	
42 DHa, Just in Town for the Night,pt.1 . . . . 3.00	
43 DHa, Town for the Night, pt.2 . . 3.00	
44 DHa, Town for the Night, pt.3 . . 3.00	
45 DHa, Petunia 3.00	
46 DHa, High Price of Unemployment 2.50	
47 The Fairy and the Imp 2.50	
48 South for the Winter,pt.1 . . . . . . 2.50	
49 South for the Winter,pt.2 . . . . . . 2.50	
50 South for the Winter,pt.3 . . . . . . 3.00	
51 South for the Winter,pt.4 . . . . . . 3.00	
52 South for the Winter,pt.5 . . . . . . 3.00	
53 South for the Winter,pt.6 . . . . . . 3.00	
54 South for the Winter,pt.7 . . . . . . 3.00	
55 thru 60. . . . . @3.00	
61 by The Fillbach Brothers. 3.00	
62 thru 68 . . . . @3.00	
09 thru 82. . . . . @3.00	
Spec. Poison Elves Companion. . . . 3.50	
Sketchbook 3.00	
Sketchbook, limited 13.00	

POISON ELVES:
DOMINION
Sirius Entertainment, 2005

1 . . . . 3.50
1a limited, sign, numbered 12.00
2 . . . . 3.50
3 thru 6 . . . . @3.50

...HYENA
Sirius Entertainment, 2004

1 (of 4) 3.00
2 thru 4 . . . . @3.00

...LOST TALES
Sirius Entertainment, 2006

1 . . . . 3.00
2 thru 12 . . . . @3.00

...LUSIPHER & LIRILITH
Sirius Entertainment, 2001

1 (of 4) by Drew Hayes 3.00
1a limited ed. 9.00
2 . . . . 3.00
2a delux 9.00
3 . . . . 3.00
3a limited 6.50
4 . . . . 3.00
4a limited 6.50

...PARINTACHIN
Sirius Entertainment, 2001

1 (of 3) 3.00
2 . . . . 3.00
3 . . . . 3.00

...VENTURES
Sirius Entertainment, 2005

1 Cassandra 3.50
2 Lynn 3.50
3 Purple Marauder 3.50
4 Jace 3.50
5 Fleece 3.50
6 Chowmba 3.50

POIZON: DEMON HUNTER
London Night, 1998

1 . . . . 3.00
2 . . . . 3.00
3 . . . . 3.00
4 double sized finale. 3.00

All comics prices listed are for *Near Mint* condition.

POKEMON ADVENTURES
Viz Communications, 1999
1 (of 5) Mysterious Mew 6.00
2 Wanted: Pikachu 6.00
3 The Snorlax Stop 6.00
4 . . . . 6.00
5 The Ghastly Ghosts 6.00

PART TWO, 2000
1 (of 6) Team Rocket Returns 3.00
2 The Hunt for Eevee 3.00
3 The Nidoking Safari 3.00
4 Mission: Magmar 3.00
5 The Dangerous Dragonite 3.00
6 The Mythical Moltres 3.00

PART THREE, 2000
1 . . . . 3.00
2 thru 7 . . . . @3.00

PART FOUR, 2001
Spec. 5.00

PART FIVE, 2001
1 . . . . 5.00
2 thru 5 . . . . @5.00

PART SIX
1 (of 4) 5.00
2 thru 4 . . . . @5.00

PART SEVEN
1 (of 5) 5.00
2 thru 5 . . . . @5.00

POKEMON:

ELECTRIC
PIKACHU BOOGALOO
Viz Communications, 1999
1 (of 4) by Toshihiro Ono, 48-pg. . . 3.50
2 . . . . 3.00
3 . . . . 3.00
4 finale 3.00

...ELECTRIC TALE
OF PIKACHU
Viz Communications, 1998
1 (of 4) by Toshihiro Ono 10.00
1a 2nd printing 4.00
2 . . . . 7.00
2a 2nd printing 4.00
3 . . . . 4.00
4 . . . . 4.00
GN The Electric Tale of Pikachu . . 13.00

...PIKACHU SHOCKS BACK
Viz Communications, 1999
1 (of 4) by Toshihiro Ono 3.25
2 thru 4 . . . . @3.25

...SURF'S UP PIKACHU
Viz Communications, 1999
1 (of 4) 3.00
2 thru 3 . . . . @3.00
4 . . . . 3.50

POKEMON TALES
Viz Communications, 2001
Prev. Color
17 Mewtwos Watching You 5.00
18 Magnemites Mission 5.00
19 Don't Laugh Charizard 5.00
20 Onix Underground 5.00
Gold and Silver Board Books
Vol. 1 Chikorita 5.50
Vol. 2 Cyndaquil 5.50
Vol. 3 Totodile 5.50
Vol. 4 Muddy Pichi 5.50
Vol. 5 Wobuffet Watches Clouds . . . 5.50
Vol. 6 Swinub's Nose 5.50
Vol. 7 Wake Up Lugia 5.50
Vol. 8 Look Out Hondour 5.50
Vol. 9 Corsola's Brave New World . . 5.50

POLLY AND THE PIRATES
Oni Press, 2005
1 by Ted Naifeh 3.00
2 . . . . 3.00
3 thru 6 . . . . @3.00

POOT
Fantagraphics, 1997
1 by Walt Holcombe 3.00
2 Swollen Holler, pt.2 . . . . 3.00
3 sex issue 3.00
4 final issue, 40-pg. 4.00

POPCORN
Discovery, 1993
1 . . . . 4.00

POP PARODY
Studio Chikara, 1999
Big Fat Sci-Fi Spec.:Stawars 3.00
Pokymon–World Domination 3.00
Dixxi Chix vs. Spice Galz 3.00
The Blair Snitch Project 4.00

PORTIA PRINZ
OF THE GLAMAZONS
Eclipse, 1986
1 thru 6 . . . . @2.50

POST BROTHERS
Rip Off Press
15 thru 18 . . . . @2.50
19 and 20 . . . . @2.50

POWER COMICS
Power Comics, 1977
1 Smart-Early Aardvark 15.00
1a 2nd printing 7.00
2 I:Cobalt Blue 10.00
3 and 4 . . . . @8.00
5 . . . . 8.00

POWER COMICS
Eclipse, 1988
1 BB,DGb,Powerbolt. 2.50
2 BB,DGb 2.50
3 BB,DGb 2.50

PPV
Antarctic Press, 2002
1 by Tom Root & Jerzy Drozd 3.00
2 thru 3 . . . . @3.00

PRETEEN DIRTY GENE
KUNG FU KANGAROOS
Blackthorne, 1986
1 and 2 . . . . @2.50

PREY
Monster Comics
1 I:Prey,A:Andrina 2.50
2 V:Andrina 2.50
3 conclusion 2.50

PRIMITIVES
Spartive Studios, 1995
1 thru 3 On the Moon . . . . @2.50

PRIME CUTS
Fantagraphics
1 adult 3.50
2 thru 6 . . . . @3.50
7 thru 12 . . . . @4.00

Primer #3
© Comico

PRIMER
Comico, 1982
1 . . . . 10.00
2 MW,I:Grendel 100.00
3 . . . . 9.00
4 . . . . 8.00
5 SK(1st work),I:Maxx 30.00
6 IN,Evangeline 14.00

PRIME SLIME TALES
Mirage, 1986
1 . . . . 5.00
2 . . . . 2.50
3 thru 6 . . . . @2.50

PRINCE VALIANT
1 thru 4 . . . . @5.00
Spec #1 . . . . 7.00

PRINCE VALIANT
MONTHLY
Pioneer
1 thru 6 . . . . @4.00
6 . . . . 5.00
7 . . . . 5.00
8 . . . . 5.00
9 . . . . 7.00

PRINCESS PRINCE
CPM Manga, 2000
1 . . . . 3.00
1a Leah Hernandez (c) 3.00
2 thru 14 . . . . @3.00
15 . . . . 3.00
16 . . . . 3.00

PRIVATE BEACH
Amaze Ink/SLG, 2001
1 by David Hahn 3.00
2 . . . . 3.00
3 . . . . 3.00
4 . . . . 3.00
5 thru 8 . . . . @3.00

PRIVATE EYES
Eternity, 1988
1 Saint rep. 2.50
2 . . . . 2.50
3 . . . . 2.50
4 . . . . 2.50
5 . . . . 2.50

PROJECT ARMS
Viz Communications, 2002
1 by Ryoji Minagawa 3.25
2 thru 6 .... @3.25

Protheus #2
© Caliber

PROTHEUS
Caliber, 1986
1 .... 2.50
2 .... 2.50

PS238
Dork Storm Press, 2002
1 .... 3.00
2 thru 5 .... @3.00
6 thru 14 .... @3.00
15 thru 19 .... @3.00
20 thru 36 .... @3.00

PSI–JUDGE ANDERSON
Fleetway, 1989
1 thru 15 .... @2.50

PULP FICTION
A-List Comics, 1997
1 thru 2 rep. of golden age ..... @2.50
3 thru 7 .... @3.00
Spec. Art of Pulp Fiction 3.00

PUMA BLUES
Aardvark–Vanaheim, 1986
1 10,000 printed 4.00
1a 2nd printing 2.50
2 .... 3.00
3 thru 19 .... @2.50
20 Special 2.50
Mirage
21 thru 24 .... @2.50
25 .... 2.50
26 thru 28 .... @2.50

PURITY
Dakuwaka Productions 2006
1 .... 3.00
2 thru 4 .... @3.00

PVP
Dork Storm Press, 2001
1 by Scott Kurtz 3.00
2 .... 3.00

3 .... 3.00
4 thru 8 .... @3.00
Collected ed. #1 Hat Trick 3.00

QUACK!
Star Reach, 1976
1 Duckaneer 11.00
1a 2nd printing 4.00
2 Newton the Rabbit Wonder 8.00
3 Dave Sim, The Beavers 8.00
4 Dave Sim 8.00
5 Dave Sim 8.00
6 .... 8.00

QUAGMIRE USA
Antarctic Press, 2004
1 .... 3.00
2 thru 6 .... @3.00

QUANTUM MECHANICS
Avatar, 1999
1 (of 2) by Barry Gregory &
Jacen Burrows 3.50
1a wraparound cover 4.00
2 conclusion 3.50
2a wraparound cover 4.00

QUANTUM: ROCK OF AGES
Dreamchilde Press, 2003
1 (of 12) 3.00
2 thru 4 .... @3.00

QUEEN & COUNTRY
Oni Press, 2001
1 by Greg Rucka & Steve Rolston 12.00
2 .... 10.00
3 thru 5 .... @5.00
6 thru 24 .... @3.00
25 .... 6.00
26 thru 28 .... @3.00
29 thru 32 .... @3.00

QUEEN & COUNTRY: DECLASSIFIED
Oni Press, 2002
1 (of 3) 3.00
2 thru 3 .... @3.00
Vol. 2
1 .... 3.00
2 thru 3 .... @3.00
Vol. 3
1 (of 3) 3.00
2 .... 3.00

QUEST FOR DREAMS LOST
Literacy Vol. of Chicago, 1987
1-shot inc. TMNTurtles 2.50

QUEST PRESENTS
Quest, 1983
1 JD 2.50
2 JD 2.50
3 JD 2.50

QUICKEN FORBIDDEN
Cryptic Press, 1998
1 .... 3.00
2 .... 3.00
3 .... 3.00
4 .... 3.00
5 .... 3.00
6 Trial Separation, pt.1 .... 3.00
7 Trial Separation, pt.2 .... 3.00

8 Trial Separation, concl. 3.00
9 Anxiety Disorder, pt.1 .... 3.00
10 Anxiety Disorder, pt.2 .... 3.00
11 thru 13 .... @3.00

RABID MONKEY
D.B.I. Comics, 1997
1 thru 4 by Joel Steudler ...... @2.50
5 thru 7 .... @2.50
8 thru 13 .... @2.50
#1–#5 Autographed pack 12.00
Dreamriders Workshop, 1998
Vol. 2
1 .... 3.00

RADICAL DREAMER
Mark's Giant Economy Sized Comics, 1995–96
1 thru 3 F:Max Wrighter ...... @3.00
4 is Max the Devil? 3.00
VOL 2, 1998
1 (of 6) by Mark Wheatley, sci-fi ... 3.00

RAGMOP
Planet Lucy Press, 1995
See Image also
1 by Rob Walton, 3rd. printing 3.00
2 thru 8 reoffer .... @2.75
8 thru 10 .... @2.75
VOL 2, 1997
3 by Rob Walton 3.00
4 O-ring saga, pt. 2 (of 3) 3.00

RAGNAROK
Tokyopop Press, 2002
1 (of 4) by Myung Jin Lee 3.00
2 thru 4 .... @3.00

RAGNAROK GUY
Sun Comics, 1992
1 I:Ragnarok Guy, Honey 2.50
2 The Melder Foundation 2.50
3 Guy/Honey mission contd... .... 2.50
4 I:Big Gossage 2.50

RAIJIN COMICS
Gutsoon! Entertainment, 2002
1 manga 5.00
2 thru 36 .... @5.00
37 thru 44 .... @6.00
45 .... 9.00
46 .... 6.00

RAIKA
Sun Comics
1 thru 12 .... @2.50

RAISING HELL
ABC Comics, 1997
1 .... 3.00
1a gold series, 2 extra pages 3.00
2 RCI,F:China & Jazz 3.00
3 conclusion, A:Wild Things 3.00
3 Baby Cheeks edition 9.00
3 Baby Cheeks Gold Edition..... 12.00

RALPH SNART
Now, 1986
1 .... 5.00
2 .... 4.00
3 .... 4.00
[Volume 2] 1986
1 .... 3.00
2 thru 8 .... @2.50
Trade Paperback 3.00

RAMBO
Blackthorne, 1988
1 thru 5 . . . . @2.50

RAMBO III
Blackthorne
1 . . . . 2.50

RAMM
Megaton Comics, 1987
1 and 2 . . . . @2.50

RANMA 1/2
Viz, 1993
Parts 1 & 2, see color
PART 3, 1993–94
1 thru 13 . . . . @3.00
PART 4, 1995
1 thru 11 . . . . @3.00
PART 5, 1996
1 thru 9 . . . . @3.00
10 thru 12. . . . . @3.00
PART 6, 1996
1 thru 8 (of 14) . . . . @3.00
9 thru 14 . . . . @3.00
PART 7, 1998
1 (of 14) 3.00
2 thru 14 . . . . @3.00
PART 8, 1999
1 (of 13) thru 5 . . . . @3.00
6 thru 13 . . . . @3.00
PART 9, 2000
1 (of 11) 3.00
2 thru 11 . . . . @3.00
PART 10, 2001
1 (of 11). 3.00
2 thru 8 . . . . @3.00
9 thru 11 . . . . @3.00
PART 11, 2002
1 (of 11) 3.00
2 thru 11 . . . . 3.00
Part 12 (March, 2003)
1 . . . . 3.00

RAPHAEL
Mirage, 1985
1 TMNT. 17.50
1a 2nd printing 7.50

RAPTUS
High Impact
1 . . . . 3.00
1 2nd printing, new cover 3.00
2 . . . . 3.00
3 . . . . 3.00

RAPTUS:
DEAD OF NIGHT
High Impact
1 . . . . 3.00
2 thru 3 . . . . @3.00

RAT FINK
World of Fandom
1 . . . . 2.50
2 . . . . 2.50
3 . . . . 2.50

RAVAGER
Kosmic Comic, 1997
0 Ashcan. 2.50
1 The First Coming. 4.00
2 . . . . 4.00

3 . . . . 4.00
4 by Kirk Patrick & Babak
　Homayoun 4.00
5 . . . . 4.00
6 by Kirk Patrick & Romel Cruz . . . 4.00

RAVEN
Ariel Press, 2003
1 . . . . 2.50
2 thru 6 . . . . @2.50
7 thru 10 . . . . @2.50

RAVEN CHRONICLES
Caliber Press, 1995
1 . . . . 3.00
1a Special Edition 6.00
2 Landing Zone. 3.00
3 The Rain People 3.00
4 The Healer. 3.00
5 thru 9 . . . . @3.00
Caliber `New Worlds'
10 by Scott Andrews, Laurence
　Campbell & Tim Perkins 3.00
11 `The Ghost of Alonzo Mann' . . . 3.00
12 `The Compensators' flip book
　with Boston Bombers #1 . . . . . . 3.00
13 48pg, bagged with back issue . . 4.00
14 . . . . 3.00
15 . . . . 3.00
16 inc. Black Mist. 3.00
Spec. Heart of the Dragon 3.00
GN 192pg rep. 17.00

The Ravening #0
© Avatar

RAVENING, THE
Avatar Press, 1997
0 Trevlin Utz (c) 4.00
0 Matt Martin (c) 4.00
0 Matt Haley (c) 4.00
0 leather cover 20.00
0 signed 12.00
1 . . . . 3.00
1 leather cover 20.00
1 Avatar con cover edition 12.00
2 (of 2) 3.00
Spec. Secrets of the Ravening 2.75

RAW CITY
Dramenon Studios
1 I:Dya,Gino 3.00
2 V:Crucifier 3.00
3 The Siren's Past 3.00

RAZOR
London Night, 1992
6 signed 20.00
10 signed 15.00
GN Let Us Prey, rep. of Razor/Wild
　Child, 80pg. 5.00
X-over Razor/Embrace: The
　Spawning (1997) 3.00
　Carmen Electra photo (c) 3.00
　Carmen Electra photo
　embossed (c), signed 19.00
Spec. Razor: Switchblade
　Symphony, Tour Book, limited
　black leather 15.00

...UNCUT
London Night Studios, 1995
Prev. RAZOR (Ind. Color)
13 . . . . 3.00
14 V:Child Killer. 3.00
15 Questions About Father 3.00
16 Nicole's Life,pt.1 . . . . 3.00
17 Nicole's Life,pt.2 . . . . 3.00
18 . . . . 3.00
19 thru 21 Kiss from a Rose . . . . @3.00
22 thru 24 . . . . @3.00
25 mild cover I:Knyfe 3.00
25b signed 13.00
26 . . . . 3.00
27 thru 28 A:Sade, pt.1–2 . . . . @3.00
29 . . . . 3.00
30 . . . . 3.00
31 `Strength by Numbers' 3.00
32 double sized 3.50
33 `Let Us Prey,' pt.2 . . . . 3.00
34 `Let Us Prey,' pt.4 (of 4) 3.00
35 Let the battle begin. 3.00
36 all-out war for Queen City. 3.00
37 `After the Fall' pt.1 . . . . 3.00
38 `After the Fall,' pt.2 . . . . 3.00
39 `Money For Hire'. 3.00
40 thru 43 `Father's Bane,' pt.1–4 @3.00
44 Razor finds abandoned child . . . 3.00
45 thru 49 American Tragedy. . . . @3.00
45a commemmorative edition, EHr . 5.00
50 back in Asylum, Tony Daniel (c) . 3.00
50a Michael Bair (c). 5.00
50b Stephen Sandoval (c). 5.00
50c Blood Red Velvet EHr (c) 25.00
Spec. Deep Cuts (1997) 5th Anniv.
　rep. #6,#13–#15, 80 pg 5.00
EH! Productions, 1999
51 . . . . 3.00

...ANALOG BURN
London Night Studios, 1999
1 by Lee Duhig 2.50
2 . . . . 2.50

...ARCHIVES
London Night, 1997
1 EHr, rep #1–#4 . . . . 5.00
1a signed 12.00
2 thru 4 EHr, reps . . . . @5.00

...THE DARKEST NIGHT
London Night, 1998
1 . . . . 5.00
1a white velvet 20.00
2 velvet edition 10.00
EH! Productions, 1999
1 . . . . 5.00
1a Velvet Edition, signed 25.00
2 . . . . 5.00
3 . . . . 5.00
3a Fan ed.. . . . . 6.00

...GOTHIC
London Night, 1998
1 (of 4) by EHr and Scott Wilson . . 3.00
1 leather 12.00

2 EHr 3.00
2a Graphic/violent cover 6.00
2b Gothic/leather cover 15.00

EH! Productions
3 . . . . 3.00
3a Elite Fan ed. 5.00
4 . . . . 3.00
4a Elite Fan ed. 5.00
Spec. Gotherotica 5.00

...TORTURE
London Night, 1995
0 chromium signed 4.00
1 platinum signed 3.00

RAZOR:

THE FURIES
Avatar, 2000
1 48-pg. 5.00
1a Previews Exclusive 5.00

...TILL I BLEED DAYLIGHT
Avatar, 2000
1 (of 2) Tim Vigil (c) 3.50
1a wraparound (c). 4.00
1b Vampire Razor (c) 5.00
1c adult (c) 6.00
1d prism foil 13.00
1e expanded edition 5.00
2 . . . . 3.50
2a wraparound (c). 4.00
2b adult (c) 6.00
2c expanded edition, 56-pg. 5.00

...BLEEDING HEART
Avatar Press, 2001
1 Fillion (c) 3.50
1a Martin (c) 3.50
1b Wraparound (c) 5.00
1c Adult (c) 6.00
1d Worship (c) 6.00

RAZOR/DARK ANGEL:
THE FINAL NAIL
Boneyard/London Night
1 X-over (Boneyard Press) 4.00
2 X-over concl.(London Night) 3.00

RAZORGUTS
Monster Comics, 1992
1 thru 4 . . . . 2.50

RAZOR'S EDGE
London Night, 1999
0 Razor/Stryke (c) 5.00
0b Night Vixen (c) 5.00
1 . . . . 5.00
1a Arizona (c) 5.00
2 Razorblaze (c) 5.00
2a Battle Girl (c) 6.00
2b Nightvixen (c). 5.00
3 . . . . 5.00
3a Nightvixen (c). 5.00
4 . . . . 5.00
4a (c) 5.00
5 . . . . 5.00
5a Stryke (c) 5.00

EH! Productions, 1999
6 48-pg. 5.00
7 thru 9 . . . . @5.00

REACTOMAN
B-Movie Comics
1 . . . . 2.50
1a signed,numbered 2.75
2 thru 4 . . . . @2.50
collection 5.00

REAGAN'S RAIDERS
Solson
1 thru 6 . . . . @2.50

REALM
Arrow, 1986
1 Fantasy 6.00
2 . . . . 4.00
3 . . . . 3.00
4 TV,Deadworld 21.00
5 I:L.Kazan 2.50
6 thru 13 . . . . @2.50

Caliber Press, 1990
14 thru 18 . . . . @2.50
19 . . . . 2.50

REAL STUFF
Fantagraphic, 1990
1 . . . . 2.50
2 . . . . 2.50
3 thru 12 . . . . 2.50

REAPER
Newcomers Publishing
1 V:The Chinde 3.00
2 . . . . 3.00
3 conclusion 3.00

REBELLION
Daikaiyu Enterprises, 1995
1 I:Rebellion 2.50

RED DIARY
Caliber, 1998
1 (of 4) F:Marilyn, JFK, Hoover,
   CIA. 4.00
1a deluxe 7.00
2 . . . . 4.00
3 (of 4) 4.00
1 signed) 4.00
4 . . . . 4.00

RED FOX
Harrier, 1986
1 scarce 6.00
1a 2nd printing 2.50
2 rare 5.00
3 . . . . 3.00
4 I:White Fox. 3.00
5 I:Red Snail 3.00
6 . . . . 2.50
7 Wbolton 2.50
8 . . . . 2.50
9 Demoslurth 2.50

REFLECTIONS
Fantagraphics Books 2006
1 . . . . 8.00
2 thru 3 . . . . @8.00

RE:GEX: BLACK & WHITE
Awesome Entertainment, 1999
1 RLe,JLb 3.00

REHD
Antarctic Press, 2003
0 . . . . 2.50
1 thru 3 . . . . @3.00

REID FLEMING, WORLD'S
TOUGHEST MILKMAN
Blackbird-Eclipse, 1986
1 David Boswell,I:Reid Fleming . . . 5.00
1a 2nd printing 3.00
1b 3rd–5th printing . . . . @2.50

Reid Fleming, Vol, 2 #3
© Blackbird/Eclipse

Volume 2, 1986
#1 Rogues to Riches Pt.1 . . . . . . 5.00
#2 Rogues to Riches Pt.2 (1987) . . 3.00
#2a Later printings 2.50
#3 Rogues to Riches Pt.3 (1988) . . 3.00
#3a Later printings 2.50
#4 Rogues to Riches Pt.4 (1989) . . 3.00
#5 Rogues to Riches Pt.5 (1990) . . 2.50

Deep-Sea Comics, 1987
3 `Rogue to Riches,' pt.2,4th pr . . . 3.00
4 `Rogue to Riches,' pt.3,3rd pr . . . 3.00
5 `Rogue to Riches,' pt.4,2nd pr . . . 3.00
6 `Rogue to Riches,' pt.5,2nd pr . . . 3.00
7 `Another Dawn,'Pt.1 . . . . 3.00
8 `Another Dawn,'Pt.2 . . . . 3.00
9 `Another Dawn,'Pt.3 . . . . 3.00
Spec#1 Origins (1998) 3.00

RENEGADES OF JUSTICE
Blue Masque
1 I:Monarch,Bloodshadow 2.50
2 Madfire 2.50
3 Television Chronicles 2.50
4 R:Karen Styles 2.50

RENFIELD
Caliber, 1994
1 thru 3 . . . . @3.00
GN Conclusion of series 9.00

REPLACEMENT GOD
Amaze Ink, 1995
1 Child in The Land of Man 6.00
1a 2nd & 3rd printing 3.00
2 Eye of Knute 4.00
3 & 4 `Bravery' . . . . @3.50
5 thru 7 . . . . @3.00
8 Fairie, book one, concl. 3.00

REPLACEMENT GOD
& OTHER STORIES
Handicraft Guild, 1998
Previously published by Image
6 by Zander Cannon, 80pg. 7.00

RESURRECTION
Oni Press, 2007
1 . . . . 3.50
Retro Mix #1 . . . . 3.00
2 thru 6 . . . . @3.50
Ann. #1 40-pg. (2008) 3.50

RETALIATOR
Eclipse
1 I&O:Retaliator 2.50
2 O:Retaliator cont. 2.50
3 thru 5 . . . . @2.50

Retief #2
© *Adventure*

RETIEF
Adventure, 1987–88
1 thru 6 Keith Laumer adapt. . . . @2.50
[Vol. 2], 1989–90
1 thru 6 . . . . @2.50
Spec.#1 Retief:Garbage Invasion . . 2.50
Spec.#1 Retief:The Giant Killer,
　V:Giant Dinosaur (1991) 2.50
Spec.#1 Grime & Punishment,
　Planet Slunch (1991). 2.50
...OF THE CDT
Adventure, 1990
1 Keith Laumer Novel Adapt. 2.50
2 thru 6 . . . . @2.50
...AND THE WARLORDS
Adventure Comics
1 Keith Laumer Novel Adapt. 2.50
2 Haterakans 2.50
3 Retief Arrested for Treason 2.50
4 Final Battle (last issue) 2.50
...DIPLOMATIC IMMUNITY
Adventure Comics, 1991
1 Groaci Invasion. 2.50
2 Groaci story cont. 2.50
RETRO-DEAD
Blazer Unlimited, 1995
1 Dimensional Rift. 3.00
2 by Dan Reed 3.00
RETROGRADE
Eternity
1 thru 4 . . . . @2.50
RETURN OF
HAPPY THE CLOWN
Caliber Press
1 & 2 V:Oni 3.00

RETURN OF LUM URUSEI* YATSURA, THE
Viz Comics, 1994
1 thru 6 . . . . @3.00
PART TWO, 1995
1 thru 13 . . . . @3.00
PART THREE, 1996
1 thru 11 by Rumiko Takahashi. . @3.00
PART FOUR, 1997
1 thru 11 by Rumiko Takahashi. . @3.00
RETURN OF THE SKYMAN
Ace Comics, 1987
1 SD 2.50
REVOLVER
Renegade, 1985
1 SD 2.50
2 thru 12 . . . . @2.50
Ann. #1. 2.50
REVOLVING DOORS
Blackthorne, 1986
1 . . . . 2.50
2 & 3 . . . . @2.50
Graphic Novel 4.00
REX LIBRIS
Amaze Ink/SLG, 2005
1 . . . . 3.00
2 thru 8 . . . . @3.00
8 thru 13 . . . . @3.50
RHEINTOCHTER
Antarctic Press, 1998
1 by Y.Paquette & M.Lacombe 3.00
2 (of 2) concl. 3.00
RHUDIPRRT PRINCE OF FUR
MU Press, 1990–91
1 thru 6 . . . . @2.50
7 thru 12 . . . . @3.00
RICHARD MATHESON'S HELL HOUSE
IDW Publishing, 2004
1 48-pgs. 6.50
2 thru 4 . . . . @6.50
RICH JOHNSTON'S HOLED UP
Avatar Press, 2004
1 . . . . 3.50
2 thru 3 . . . . @3.50
1a thru 3a homeland
　security (c)s . . . . @3.50
RICK RAYGUN
1 . . . . 2.50
2 thru 8 . . . . @2.50
RIO KID
Eternity
1 I:Rio Kid 2.50
2 V:Blow Torch Killer. 2.50
3 . . . . 2.50
RIOT
Viz, 1995
1 F:Riot,Axel 2.75
2 & 3 . . . . 2.75
4 final issue 2.75

RIOT ACT TWO
Viz Comics, 1996
1 thru 7 . . . . @3.00
RIP IN TIME
Fantagor, 1986
1 RCo,Limited series 3.00
2 thru 5 RCo . . . . @2.50
RIVAL SCHOOLS
Udon Entertainment, 2006
1 . . . . 5.00
2 . . . . 5.00
3 . . . . 5.00
1a thru 3a variant (c) . . . . @5.00
1b Power cell (c) 12.50
ROACHMILL
Blackthorne, 1986
1 . . . . 5.00
2 . . . . 3.00
3 and 4. . . . . @3.00
See: Dark Horse
ROBERT E. HOWARD'S
Cross Plains Comics, 1999
1-shot Horror, 64-pg. 6.00
1-shot Black Stone. 4.00
ROB HANES ADVENTURES
WCG Comics, 2000
1 by Randy Renoldo 2.50
2 thru 3 . . . . @2.50
4 . . . . 2.75
5 thru 8 . . . . @3.00
ROBIN HOOD
Eternity, 1989
1 thru 4 . . . . @2.50
ROBO DEFENSE TEAM MECHA RIDER
Castle Comics
1 I:RDT Mecha Rider 3.00
2 Identity of Outlaw. 3.00
ROBOTECH
Eternity
1-shot Untold Stories 2.50
Academy Comics, 1995–96
0 Robotech Information 2.50
Spec. Robotech: Macross Tempest
　F:Roy Fokker, Tempest (1995) . 3.00
Spec. Robotech: Mech Angel,
　I:Mech Angel (1995) 3.00
Spec. Robotech: The Misfits, from
　Southern Cross transferred to
　Africa 3.00
Spec. #1 & #2 Robotech The Movie,
　Benny R. Powell & Chi . . . . . @3.00
Spec. Robotech Romance. 3.00
Spec. Robotech: Sentinels Star Runners
　Carpenter's Journey (1996) . . . 3.00
GN The Threadbard Heart. 10.00
Antarctic Press, 1998
Ann. #1. 3.00
Spec.#1 Robotech: Escape (1998) . 3.00
...ACADEMY BLUES
Academy Comics
0 Classroom Blues 3.50
1 F:Lisa. 3.00
2 Bomb at the Academy 3.00
3 Roy's Drinking Buddy 3.00

...AFTERMATH
Academy Comics
1 thru 10 R:Bruce Lewis	@3.00
11 Zentradi Traitor	3.00
12 and 13	@3.00

...CLONE
Academy Comics
1 Dialect of Duality	3.00
2 V:Monte Yarrow	3.00
3 Ressurection	3.00
4 Ressurection	3.00
5 F:Bibi Ava	3.00

...COVERT OPS
Antarctic Press, 1998
1 (of 2) by Greg Lane	3.00
2	3.00

...INVID WAR
Eternity, 1993
1 No Man's Land	2.50
2 V:Defoliators	2.50
3 V:The Invid,Reflex Point	2.50
4 V:The Invid	2.50
5 Moonbase Aluce II	2.50
6 Moonbase-Zentraedi plot	2.50
7 Zentraedi plot contd.	2.50
8 A:Lancer	2.50
9 A:Johnathan Wolfe	2.50
10	2.50
11 F:Rand	2.50
12 thru 15	2.50

...INVID WAR AFTERMATH
Eternity
1 thru 6 F:Rand	2.75

...MORDECAI
Academy Comics
1	3.00
2 Annie meets her clone	3.00

...RETURN TO MACROSS
Eternity, 1993
1 thru 12	@2.50

Academy Comics
13 thru 17 Roy Fokker	@2.75
18 F:The Faithful	2.75
19 F:Lisa	2.75
20 F:Lisa	2.75
21 V:Killer Robot	3.00
22 War of the Believers	3.00
23 War of the Believers,pt.2	3.00
24 War of the Believers,pt.3	3.00
25 War of the Believers,pt.4	3.00
26 thru 30	@3.00
31 What is the Federalist Plan?	3.00
32 thru 34	@3.00
35 Typhoon threatens Macross Island	3.00
36	3.00
37 round up of Federalist Agents.	3.00

...SENTINELS: RUBICON
Antarctic Press, 1998
1 (of 7)	3.00
2 Shadows of the Past	3.00

...VERMILION
Antarctic Press, 1997
1 (of 4) by Duc Tran	3.00
2 Why did Hiro die?	3.00
3	3.00
4	3.00

...WARRIORS
Academy Comics, 1995
1 F:Breetai	3.00
2 F:Mirya	3.00
3 F:Mirya	3.00
GN The Terror Maker	10.00

...WINGS OF GIBRALTAR
Antarctic Press, 1998
1 (of 2) by Lee Duhig	3.00
2	3.00

ROBOTECH II
THE SENTINELS
Eternity, 1988
1	3.00
2 & 3	@2.50
1a thru 3a 2nd printings	@2.50
4 thru 16	@2.50

Book 2, 1990
1 thru 12	@2.50
13 thru 20	@2.50
Wedding Special #1 (1989)	2.50
Wedding Special #2	2.50
Robotech II Handbook	2.50

Book Three
1 thru 8 V:Invid	2.50

Book Four
Academy Comics, 1995
1 by Jason Waltrip	3.00
2 thru 4 F:Tesla	@2.75
5 JWp,JWt,interior of Haydon IV	3.00
6 thru 8	@3.00
9 JWp,JWt,Breetai, Wolf & Vince return to Tirol	3.00
10 JWp,JWt,Ark Angel attacked by The Black Death Destroyers	3.00
11 JWp,JWt,Tirol, Wolff, Vince & Breetai on trial for treason	3.00
12 JWp,JWt,Dr. Lang exposes General Edwards' evil designs	3.00
13 F:Tesla	2.75
14 V:Invid	2.75
15	2.75
16	2.75
17 V:Invid Mechas	2.75
18 F:"HIN"	3.00
19 V:Invid	3.00
20 Final Aplp. Invid Regiss	3.00
21 Predator and Prey	3.00
22 A Clockwork Planet	3.00
Halloween Special JWp,JWt,	3.00

...CYBERPIRATES
Eternity, 1991
1 The Hard Wired Coffin	2.50
2 thru 4	@2.50

Robotech II The Sentinels,
Cyberpirates #1 © Eternity

...THE MALCONTENT PRISING
Eternity
1 thru 12	@2.50

ROBO WARRIORS
CFW
1 thru 11	@2.50
Becomes:

KUNG FU WARRIORS

ROCK 'N' ROLL COMICS
Revolutionary, 1989
1 Guns & Roses	10.00
1a 2nd printing	3.50
1b 3rd printing	3.00
1c 4th-7th printing	3.00
2 Metalica	11.00
2a 2nd printing	3.00
2b 3rd-5th printing	3.00
3 Bon Jovi	9.00
4 Motley Crue	5.00
5 Def Leppard	5.00
6 Rolling Stones	8.00
6a 2nd-4th printing	3.00
7 The Who	5.00
7a 2nd-3rd printing	3.00
9 Kiss	15.00
9a 2nd-3rd Printing	5.00
10 Warrant/Whitesnake	6.00
10a 2nd Printing	5.00
11 Aerosmith	5.00
12 New Kids on Block	5.00
12a 2nd Printing	2.50
13 LedZeppelin	6.00
14 Sex Pistols	5.00
See Independent Color	

ROCKET RANGERS
Adventure, 1992
1	3.00
2	3.00
3	3.00

ROCKIN' ROLLIN'
MINER ANTS
Fate Comics, 1992
1 As seen in TMNT #40	2.50
1a Gold Variant copy	7.50
2 Elephant Hunting, A:Scorn, Blister	2.50
3 V:Scorn, Inc.,K.Eastman Ant pin-up	2.50
4 Animal Experiments,V:Loboto	2.50

ROOTER
Custom Comics of America, 1996–97
1 Sweatin' Bullets	3.00
2 Big Bad Beaver	3.00
3 The Big Izzy	3.00
4 Da Voodoo Blues	3.00
5	3.00
6 Blues Power	3.00
Ann. #1, 120pg.	15.00

VOL 2, 1998
1 by Kelly Campbell	3.00
2	3.00
3 Hot Rocks Mojo	3.00

ROSE
Hero Graphics, 1993
1 From The Champions	3.50
2 A:Huntsman	3.50
3 thru 5	@3.00

ROSE 'N' GUNN
Bishop Press, 1995
1 Deadly Duo	5.00
2 V:Marilyn Monroe	3.00
3 Presidential Affairs	3.00
4 Without Each Other	3.00
5 V:Red	3.00
6 & 7	@3.00
Creator's Choice Rep. #1	3.00
Creator's Choice Rep. #2	3.00
Creator's Choice Rep. #3	3.00

ROSE AND GUNN
London Night, 1996
1	3.00
1b signed	9.00
2	3.00
3	3.00

...RECKONING
London Night
1 (of 2)	3.00

ROVERS
Eternity
1 thru 7	@2.50

RUBES REVIVED
Fish Warp
1 thru 3	@2.50

RUK BUD WEBSTER
Fish Warp
1	2.50
2 thru 3	@2.50

RUMBLE PAK
Eigomanga, 2004
1	5.00
2 thru 5	@5.00

Devil's Due Publishing 2005
1 Manga	6.00
2 thru 3	@6.00

RUNNERS: BAD GOODS
Serve Man Press, 2003
1	3.00
2 thru 5	@3.00

SADE
Bishop Press, 1995
0 B:Adventures of Sade	3.00
1	3.00
1a variant	6.00
2	3.00

SADE SPECIAL
Bishop Press
1 V:Razor	5.00
1a signed	7.00

SADE
London Night, 1996
1	3.00
2 thru 5	@3.00

SADE/ROSE AND GUNN
London Night, 1996
1 Confederate Mist	3.00

SADE: TESTAMENTS OF PAIN
London Night, 1997
1 (of 2)	3.00

SAGA OF THE MAN-ELF
Trident, 1989
1 thru 5	@2.50

SAGE
Fantaco, 1995
1 O:Sage	5.00

Sailor Moon #8
© Mixx Entertainment

SAILOR MOON
Mixx Entertainment, 1998
1 by Naoko Tekeuchi	20.00
2 thru 5	@12.00
6 thru 11	@5.00
12 thru 20	@5.00
Scout Guide: Sailor Mars: Fire	13.00
Scout Guide: Sailor Venus: Love..	13.00
Scout Guide: Sailor Jupiter: Thunder	13.00
Novel A Scout is Born	5.00
Novel The Power of Love	5.00
Novel 3: Mercury Rising	5.00

Tokyopop.Com, 2000
21 thru 25	@3.00
26 thru 35	@3.00

SAINT GERMAINE
Caliber `Core', 1997
0 O:St. Germaine	4.00
1 VcL, two immortals, St. Germain cover	3.00
1 Lilith cover	3.00
2 VcL	3.00
3 VcL	3.00
3a signed	3.00
4 VcL	3.00
5 The Kilroy Mandate, VcL(c)	3.00
5a Meyer (c)	3.00
6 Kilroy Mandate	3.00
8 Ghost Dance	3.00
8 The Man in the Iron Mask	3.00
10 The Tragedy of Falstaff	3.00
11 by Gary Reed & James Lyle	3.00
GN Shadows Fall, rep. #1–#4	15.00
Spec. Casanova's Lament, 48-pg..	4.00
Spec. Restoration, VcL	4.00

...PRIOR ECHOES
Caliber `Core', 1998
1 (of 4) by Gary Reed	3.00
2	3.00
3	3.00

SAINT TAIL
Tokyopop Press, 2000
1	3.00
2 thru 13	@3.00
14 thru 16	@3.00
17 thru 20	@3.00

SAMURAI (1st series)
1	50.00
2	25.00
3	25.00
4	25.00
5	25.00

SAMURAI
Aircel, 1985
1 rare	6.00
1a 2nd printing	3.00
1b 3rd printing	2.50
2	5.00
2a 2nd printing	2.50
3	3.00
4	3.00
5 thru 12	@2.50
13 DK (1st art)	4.00
14 thru 16 DK	@4.00
17 thru 23	@2.50

[3rd series], 1988
#1 thru 3	@2.50
#4 thru 7	@2.50
Compilation Book	5.00

SAMURAI
Warp Graphics, 1997
1 by Barry Blair & Colin Chan	3.00
2	3.00
3	3.00
4	3.00

SAMURAI FUNNIES
Solson
1 thru 3	@2.50

SAMURAI PENGUIN
Solson, 1986
1	3.00
2 I:Dr.Radium	2.50
3	2.50
4	2.50
5 FC	2.50
6 color	2.50
7	2.50
8	2.50
9	2.50

SAMURAI 7
Gauntlet Comics
1 I: Samurai 7	2.50

SAMURAI, SON OF DEATH
Eclipse
1	4.00
1a 2nd printing	4.00

SANCTUARY
Viz Communications, 1993
1 World of Yakuza	5.00
2 thru 4	@5.00
5 thru 9	@5.00

[Part Two], 1994
1 thru 9	@5.00

[Part Three], 1994–95
1 thru 8	@3.50

[Part Four], 1995–96
1 thru 7	@3.50

[Part Five], 1996
7 thru 13 by Sho Fumimura &
  Ryoichi Ikegami . . . . @3.50

SANCTUARY
Fantagraphics Books 2006
1 (of 6) 4.00
2 thru 3 . . . . @4.00

SAPPHIRE
Ariel Press, 1996
1 by Vince Danks 3.00
6 thru 9 . . . . @3.00

SAVAGE HENRY
Vortex, 1987
1 . . . . 2.50
2 thru 13 . . . . @2.50

Rip Off Press, 1991
14 thru 15 . . . . @2.50
16 thru 24 . . . . @2.50

SAVAGE HENRY: POWERCHORDS
Aeon, 2004
1 (of 3) 3.00
2 and 3 . . . . @3.00
Spec. Puppet Trap 3.00

SAVAGE PLANET
Basement Comics, 2002
1 by Dan Parson & Kevin Rasel . . . 3.00
1a special edition 8.95
2 . . . . 3.00
2a special edition 8.95
3 . . . . 3.25
3a special edition 8.95

Basement Comics, 2007
1-shot Secrets of the Empire 3.50

SCARLET IN GASLIGHT
Eternity, 1988
1 A:SherlockHolmes 4.00
2 . . . . 3.00
3 & 4 . . . . @2.50

SCARLET SCORPION/ DARKSIDE
AC Comics, 1995
1 & 2 Flipbooks 3.50

SCARLET THUNDER
Amaze Ink, 1995
1 . . . . 2.50
2 thru 3 . . . . @2.50

SCARY GODMOTHER
Sirius Entertainment, 2001
1 by Jill Thompson 3.00
2 thru 6 concl. . . . . @3.00

SCARY GODMOTHER: BLOODY VALENTINE
Sirius Entertainment, 1998
1 . . . . 4.00
1a signed and numbered 9.00
Holiday Spooktactular 3.00

SCARY GODMOTHER: WILD ABOUT HARRY
Sirius Entertainment, 2000
1 (of 3) by Jill Thompson 3.00
2 . . . . 3.00

3 concl. 3.00

SCIENCE FAIR
Antarctic Press, 2005
1 (of 8) 3.00
2 thru 4 . . . . @3.00

SCIMIDAR
Eternity
1 . . . . 4.00
1a 2nd Printing 2.50
2 and 3 . . . . @3.00
4 HotCover 3.50
4A MildCover 3.00

SCOOTER GIRL
Oni Press, 2003
1 (of 6) 3.00
2 thru 6 . . . . @3.00

SCORN
SCC Entertainment, 1996
Lingerie Spec. 3.00
Lingerie Spec. deluxe 10.00
Super Spec.#1 rep. Deadly
  Rebellion, Headwave, Fabric
  of the Mind. 5.00
X-over Scorn/Ardy: Alien Influence
  (1997) by Rob Potchak & Timothy
  Johnson 4.00
  Bill Maus (c). 4.00
  Deluxe gold 10.00
X-over Scorn/Dracula: The Vampire's
  Blood (1997) 4.00
  Dracula cover 4.00
  Scorn cover 4.00
Spec.#1A Scorn; Dead or Alive
  (1997) Mike Morales(c) 4.00
  Andrea Seri(c) 4.00
Spec.# Scorn:Deadly Rebellion . . . 4.00
  Birthday Suit cover 10.00
  Celebrity photo cover 10.00
Spec.#1 Scorb: Fractured (1997)
  Fear cover 4.00
  Rage cover 4.00
Spec: Scorn: Heatwave (1997) by
  Chris Crosby & Mike Morales . . 4.00
Spec. Scorn: Hostage 4.00
Spec. Scorn: Naked Truth (1997) . . 4.00

SCRATCH
Outside, 1986
1 . . . . 3.00
2 thru 4 . . . . @2.50

SCREAMING ANGELS
Antarctic Press, 2004
1 (of 3) 3.50
2 thru 3 . . . . @3.50

SCREWTOOTH
Amaze Ink/SLG2006
1 by Black Olive 3.00
2 . . . . 3.00
3 . . . . 3.00

SCUD: DISPOSABLE ASSASSIN
Fireman Press, 1994
1 I:Scud. 20.00
1a 3rd printing. 10.00
2 . . . . 10.00
3 . . . . 10.00
4 thru 6 F:Scud . . . . @10.00
7 Lupine Thoughts 8.00
8 Scud Looks for His Arm 8.00
9 Scud Looks for His Arm 8.00

Scud: Disposable Assassin #1
© FiremanPress

10 thru 16 by Rob Schrab . . . . . @8.00
17 thru 19 . . . . @8.00
20 Horse series, concl. 8.00

SCUD: TALES FROM THE VENDING MACHINE
Fireman Press, 1998
1 . . . . 5.00
2 thru 5 . . . . @5.00

SEAMONSTERS & SUPERHEROES
Amaze Ink/SLG, 2003
1 . . . . 3.00
2 thru 8 . . . . @3.00

SEARCHERS
Caliber 'New Worlds', 1996
1A Red cover, signed 3.00
1B Blue cover, signed 3.00
3 . . . . 3.00
4 . . . . 3.00
5 flip book with Boston Bombers . . 3.00

SEARCHERS: APOSTLE OF MERCY
Caliber, 1997
1 (of 2) 4.00
2 . . . . 4.00

Vol 2?
1 . . . . 3.00
2 . . . . 3.00
3 (of 3) 48pg 4.00

SECRET FILES
Angel Entertainment, 1996
0 gold edition 6.00
0 commemorative edition 3.00
1 . . . . 3.00
1 spooky silver foil edition. 5.00
2 . . . . 3.00
2 deluxe 5.00
Spec. Secret Files vs. Vampire Girls:
  The Vampire Effece (1997) . . . 3.00
Pin-up Book Secret Files: Erotic
  Experiments (1997) 3.00
Spec.#1 Secret Files: F.B.I.
  Conspiracy (1997)F:Sabrina
  & Susanna Sorenson 3.00

SECRET FILES:
THE STRANGE CASE
Angel Entertainment, 1996
0 by David Campitti & Al Rio	3.00
1 by David Campitti & Al Rio	3.00

SECRET MESSAGES
NBM Books, 2001
1 Abductions, pt.1	3.00
2 Abductions, pt.2	3.00
3 Abductions, pt.3	3.00
4 Abductions, pt.4	3.00
5 Abductions, pt.5	3.00

SECTION 8
Noir Press, 1995
1 Anthology series	2.50
2 thru 6	@2.50
7 'Retribution,' pt.1	2.50
8 'Retribution,' pt.2	2.50
9	2.50
10 'Chance'	2.50

SEEKER
Caliber `Core', 1998
1M by Gary Reed & Chris Massarotto, Meadows(c)	3.00
1W David Williams(c)	3.00
1a variant Greg Louden (c).	3.00
1 premium, signed	10.00
2	3.00
3	3.00
4	3.00
5 Gestalt vs. LeAnn Heywood	3.00
Spec. Dawn of Armageddon, x-over, 48-pg.	4.00

SEMI-AUTO ANGEL:
SECOND HEAVEN
Alias Enterprises, 2006
1 (of 6)	3.50
2	3.50

SENTINEL
Harrier, 1986
1	2.50
2 thru 4	@2.50

SERENITY ROSE
Amaze Ink/SLG, 2003
1	3.00
2 thru 6	@3.00

7 GUYS OF JUSTICE, THE
False Idol Studios, 2000
1 Jerque Imperitive,pt.1	2.50
2 Jerque Imperitive,pt.2	2.50
3 Jerque Imperitive,pt.3	2.50
4 thru 11	@2.50
12 thru 16	@2.50

777: THE WRATH
Avatar Press, 1998
1 (of 3) by David Quinn & Tim Vigil	3.00
1a wraparound cover	3.50
1c leather cover	6.00
1d royal blue foil logo	60.00
1e signed	15.00
1f foil platinum edition	17.00
2	3.00
3 concl.	3.00

SEVENTH SYSTEM, THE
Sirius Entertainment, 1997
1 (of 6) by Roel	3.00
2 thru 6	@3.00

SFA SPOTLIGHT
Shanda Fantasy Arts, 1999
4 Tales of the Morphing Period	4.50
5 Zebra, by Carl Gafford	4.50
6 Women in Fur 1999	5.00
7 Tales From Supermegatopia	5.00
8 Women in Fur 2000	5.00
9 Knight & Mouse	5.00
10 Atomic Mouse	5.00
11 Plush Beauties	5.00
12 Courageous Man Adventures	5.00
13 Women in Fur 2001	5.00
14 Fission Chicken	5.00
15 Women in Fur 2002	5.00
16 Star Quack	5.00

SHADES OF BLUE
AMP Comics, 2001
1	2.50
2 thru 4	@2.50
5 Silence, pt.3	2.50
6 F:Heidi, Marcus	2.50
7 Winter, pt.1	3.00
8 Winter, pt.2	3.00
9 Winter, pt.3	3.00
10	3.00

Digital Webbing, 2003
1 thru 5	@3.00

SHADES OF GRAY
COMICS AND STORIES
Caliber Tapestry, 1996
1	3.00
2	3.00
3	3.00
4	3.00
Super Summer Spec. rep.	4.00

SHADOW CROSS
Darkside Comics, 1995
1 I:Shadow Cross	5.00
2 thru 7	@2.50

SHADOWGEAR
Antarctic Press, 1999
1 by Locke	3.00
2	3.00
3 conclusion	3.00

SHADOWALKER
Aircel
1 thru 4	@2.50

SHADOW SLASHER
Pocket Change Comics, 1994
1 I:Shadow Slasher	2.50
2 V:Riplash	2.50
3 F:Matt Baker	2.50
4 Evolution	2.50
5 F:Riplash	2.50
6 Next Victim	2.50
7 What Can Kill Him	2.50
8	2.50
9 final issue	2.50

SHANDA [THE PANDA]
Mu, 1992
1	2.50

Antarctic Press, 1993
1 thru 11	@2.75
12 thru 14	@3.00

Med Systems
15 and 16	@2.50

Vision Comics, 1996
17 by Mike Curtis & Michelle Light	2.50
18 'Rocky Horror Picture Show'	2.50
19 'Shine on Me, Cajun Moon'	2.50
20 falling in love	2.50
22 Bright Eyes	3.00

Shanda Fantasy, 1999
23 Sweet Young Things	3.00
24 graduation night	3.00
25 48-pg.	5.00
26 thru 30	@3.00
31 thru 33	@3.00
34 48-pg.	5.00
35 thru 47	@5.00

SHANGHAIED
Eternity
1 & 2	@2.50
3 & 4	@2.50

SHARDS
Acension Comics, 1994
1 I:Silver, Raptor, RIpple	2.50
2 F:Anomoly	2.50

Shattered Earth #8
© *Eternity*

SHATTERED EARTH
Eternity, 1988–89
1	2.50
2 thru 9	@2.50

SHATTERPOINT
Eternity, 1990
1 thru 4 Broid miniseries	@2.50

SHEBA
Vol. 2, Sirius Dogstar, 1997
1 by Walter S. Crane IV	2.50
2 thru 4	@2.50

Sick Mind Press
5 thru 7	@3.00

Vol 3, Shanda Fantasy Arts, 2001
1 by Walter Crane IV	5.00
2 thru 4	@5.00

SHE-CAT
AC Comics, 1989
1 thru 4	@2.50

SHE-DEVILS ON WHEELS
Aircel, 1992
1 thru 3 by Bill Marimon	3.00

SHERLOCK HOLMES
Eternity, 1988
1 thru 22 . . . . @2.50

SHERLOCK HOLMES
Caliber/Tome Press, 1997
1-shot Dr. Jekyll and Mr. Holmes by
Steve Jones & Seppo Makinen . 3.00
1-shot Return of the Devil 4.00
1-shot Return of the Devil, signed . . 4.00

SHERLOCK HOLMES CASEBOOK
Eternity
1 and 2 . . . . @2.50

SHERLOCK HOLMES: CHRONICLES OF CRIME AND MYSTERY
Northstar
1 `The Speckled Band' 2.50

SHERLOCK HOLMES; HOUND OF THE BASKERVILLES
Caliber/Tome Press, 1997
1 (of 3) by Martin Powell & PO 3.00

SHERLOCK HOLMES: MARK OF THE BEAST
Caliber/Tome Press, 1997
1 (of 3) by Martin Powell
& Seppo Makinen 3.00
2 . . . . 3.00
GN 13.00

SHERLOCK HOLMES MYSTERIES
Moonstone, 1997
1-shot by Joe Gentile & Richard
Gulick. 3.00
1-shot Sherlock Holmes and the
Clown Prince of London (2001). 3.00

SHERLOCK HOLMES OF THE '30's
Eternity
1 thru 7 strip rep. . . . . @3.00

SHERLOCK HOLMES READER
Caliber `Tome Press', 1998
1 Curse of the Beast. 4.00
2 The Loch Ness Horror 4.00
3 The Loch Ness Horror 4.00
4 The Loch Ness Horror 4.00
5 . . . . 4.00

SHERLOCK HOLMES: RETURN OF THE DEVIL
Adventure, 1992
1 V:Moriarty. 2.50
2 V:Moriarty. 2.50

SHERLOCK JUNIOR
Eternity
1 Rep.NewspaperStrips 2.50
2 Rep.NewspaperStrips 2.50
3 Rep.NewspaperStrips 2.50

SHI
Crusade, 1999
0 rough cut edition 5.00
0 ashcan, signed. 9.00
Spec.#1 Black,White & Red. 3.00
Spec. San Diego (Con) Art of War
Tour Book 1998 . . . . 9.00
Spec. Lim. Ed. Shi/Daredevil
Banzai 14.00
Spec.#1 Kaidan, macabre 3.00
Spec.#1 Kaidan, signed & numb. . 20.00
Spec. Shi/First Wave, Voices
of the Dead x-over (2001) 3.00
Spec. Shi/FirstWave,variant BiT(c) . 3.00
Spec. Shi/FirstWave,signed 10.00
Spec. First Wave/Shi, Voices of
the Dead, pt.2 x-over (2001) . . . 3.00
Spec. FirstWave/Shi,variant BiT(c) . 3.00
Coll. Ed. Heaven & Earth,
Yin & Yang,96-pg. 6.00
Year of the Dragon preview book . 3.00
Year of the Dragon tour book 5.00
Year of the Dragon tour Wizard . . . 5.00
Year of the Dragon tour San Diego . 5.00
Umadoshi Tour Book, 2002 . . . . . 5.00
Umadoshi, Tour Book, sketch (c) . . 5.00
Umadoshi, Tour Book, Pittsburgh . 5.00
Tour Book, Art of War, remarked . . 20.00
Tour Bok Year of the Dragon,
remarked 20.00
Tour Book, Year of the Serpent
remarked 20.00

Avatar Press, 2005/ Avatar Fan Club
Shi: Poisoned Paradise preview . . . 6.00
Shi: Pandora's Box preview. 6.00

SHI: THE ILLUSTRATED WARRIOR
Crusade Entertainment, 2002
1 (of 7) BiT 3.00
2 BiT thru 7 . . . . @3.00

SHI: SEMPO
Avatar, 2003
1/2 Prism Foil Edition. 10.00
1/2 Royal Blue Edition 60.00
1/2 Prism Foil (c) 10.00
Preview edition. 2.50
Preview variant (c). 6.00
Preview wraparound (c). 6.00
Preview prism foil (c) 13.00
1 . . . . 3.50
1a variant (c). 3.50
2 . . . . 3.50
2a variant (c). 3.50
2b wraparound (c). 4.00

SHIP OF FOOLS
Caliber, 1996
1 signed edition. 3.00
2 `Dante's Compass' 3.00
3 The Great Escape begins 3.00
4 MiA. 3.00
5 MiA. 3.00
Spec. #1, Bon Voyage, Go to Hell,
Mama Hades 4.00
continued: See Image Comics

SHOCK THE MONKEY
Millennium
1 & 2 Entering the Psychotic Mind . 4.00

SHONEN JUMP
Viz Communications, 2002
1 thru 8 . . . . @5.00

Vol. 2
1 thru 12 . . . . @5.00
Vol. 3
1 thru 10 . . . . @5.00
35 thru 49 . . . . @5.00

SHOUJO
Antarctic Press, 2003
1 thru 4 . . . . @6.00

SHRED
CFW
1 thru 10 . . . . @2.50

SHRIEK
Fantaco
1 . . . . 5.00
2 . . . . 5.00
3 . . . . 8.00

Shuriken #6
© Victory

SHURIKEN
Victory, 1986
1 Reggi Byers 5.00
1a 2nd printing 2.50
2 . . . . 3.00
3 thru 13 . . . . @2.50
Graphic Nov. Reggie Byers 8.00

Eternity, 1991
1 Shuriken vs. Slate 2.50
2 Neutralizer, Meguomo 2.50
3 R:Slate. 2.50
4 Morgan's Bodyguard Serrate. . . . 2.50
5 Slate as Shuriken & Megumo . . . 2.50
6 Hunt for Bionauts, final issue. . . . 2.50

...COLD STEEL
Eternity, 1989
1 thru 6 . . . . @2.50

SHURIKEN TEAM-UP
ETernity, 1989
1 thru 3 . . . . @2.50

SILBUSTER
Antarctic Press, 1994
1 thru 10 . . . . @3.50
11 I:Kizuki Sister 3.50
12 thru 14 . . . . @3.50
15 . . . . 4.00
16 thru 19 . . . . @3.50

B & W PUB.

SILENT INVASION
Renegade, 1986
1 .... 4.00
2 thru 12, final issue .... @3.00
Combined Ed. #1 & #2 .... 17.00

SILENT INVASION
Caliber
4 Red Shadows, pt.1 .... 3.00
5 Red Shadows, pt.2 .... 3.00

SILENT INVASION: ABDUCTIONS
Caliber, 1998
1 by Larry Hancock & Michael
Cherkos 3.00

SILENT MOBIUS
Viz Communications
Part 1 thru Part 4: See Color
Part 5 INTO THE LABYRINTH, 1999
1 (of 6) by Kia Asamiya 3.00
2 thru 4 .... @3.00
5 & 6 .... @3.25
Part 6 KARMA, 1999
1 (of 7) by Kia Asamiya 3.25
2 thru 7 .... @3.25
Part 7 CATASTROPHE, 2000
1 (of 6) by Kia Asamiya 3.00
2 thru 6 .... @3.00
Part 8 LOVE & CHAOS, 2000
1 thru 7 .... 3.00
Part 9 ADVENTURERS, 2001
1 thru 6 (of 6) .... @3.00
Part 10 TURNABOUT, 2002
1 (of 6) by Kia Asamiya 3.00
2 thru 6 .... @3.00
Part 11 BLOOD, 2002
1 (of 5) by Kia Asamiya 3.00
2 thru 5 .... @3.00
Part 12 HELL, 2003
1 thru 3 .... @3.00

SILENT RAPTURE
Brainstorm, 1996
1 Jacob Grimm vs. Six Devils
of Twilight................ 3.00
1a Vicious variant edition 5.00
Avatar Press, 1997
2 by Jude Millien.............. 3.00
2a deluxe (c)................. 9.00

SILLY DADDY
Joe Chiappetta, 1995
1 .... 3.50
2 thru 5 .... 3.00
6 thru 18 .... @2.75

SILVER STORM
Aircel, 1990
1 thru 4 .... @2.50

SINBAD
Adventure, 1989
1 thru 4 .... @2.50

SINBAD: HOUSE OF GOD
Adventure Comics, 1991
1 Caliph's Wife Kidnapped 2.50
2 Magical Genie 2.50
3 Escape From Madhi 2.50
4 A:Genie 2.50

Silver Storm #4
© *Aircel*

SINNAMON
Catfish Comics, 1995
1 remastered.................. 2.75
1a remastered deluxe.............. 3.75
6 thru 8 .... @2.75
Mythic Comics
9 'Ashes to Ashes—The Pyre-Anna
Saga,' pt.2................ 2.75
10 'Twas Beauty Bashed
The Beast'............... 2.75
11........................ 2.75
12 M.G.Delaney (c) 2.75
12 Poliwko (c) 2.75
Archives #1 .... 2.75

SISTER ARMAGEDDON
Dramenon Studios
1 & 2 Nun with a Gun .... @2.50
3 Mother Superior.............. 2.50
4 V:Apoligon 3.00

SKELETON KEY
Amaze Ink, 1995
1 1 I:Skeleton Key 4.00
1 2nd printing 3.00
2 F:Tansin 3.00
3 V:Japanese Burglar 3.00
4 V:Closet Monster 3.00
5 thru 10 .... @3.00
11........................ 3.00
12........................ 3.00
14 by Andi Watson............. 3.00
15 'The Celestial Calendar' 3.00
16 thru 30................. @3.00
Spec...................... 5.00
Spec.Skeleton Key/Sugar Kat 3.00
VOL 2
1 (of 4) 3.00
2 .... 3.00
3 .... 3.00
4 conclusion 3.00

SKULL MAN
Tokyopop Press, 2000
1 (of 5) 3.00
2 thru 5 .... @3.00

SKUNK, THE
Entity Comics, 1997
#Uno 2.75
5 BMs 2.75

6 BMs 2.75
Collection #1 rep. #1–#3 .... 5.00
Collection #1a signed & numbered 10.00
Collection #2 rep. #4–#6 .... 5.00

SKUNK/FOODANG
FOODANG/SKUNK
Entity Comics
Spec. 1 BMs, BMs(c)........... 2.75
Spec. 1a BMs, Mike Duggan(c).... 2.75

SKYNN & BONES: DEADLY ANGELS
Brainstorm, 1996
1 .... 3.00

SKYNN & BONES: FLESH FOR FANTASY
Brainstorm, 1997
1 erotic missions............... 3.00
2 erotic missions.............. 3.00
Spec. #1 Dare to Bare 3.00

SLACKER COMICS
Slave Labor, 1994
1 thru 15 by Doug Slack .... @3.00
16 .... 3.00
17 .... 3.00
18 .... 3.00
19 .... 3.00

SLAUGHTERHOUSE
Caliber
1 Bizarre medical Operations 3.00
2 House of Death 3.00
3 House of Death 3.00
4 Dead Killer vs. Mosaic........ 3.00

SLAUGHTERMAN
Comico, 1983
1 .... 2.50
2 .... 2.50

SLAYERS
CPM Manga, 1998
1 by Hajime Kanzaka & Rui
Araizumi.................. 3.00
2 thru 6 .... @3.00
Spec. #1 F:Lina Inverse......... 3.00
Spec. #2 thru #6............. @3.00

SLAYERS: SUPER–EXPLOSIVE DEMON STORY
CPM Manga, 2001
1 by H. Kanzaka & S. Yoshinaka .. 3.00
2 thru 6 .... @3.00

SMILE
Tokyopop Press, 2000
Vol. 3
1 magazine 3.00
2 thru 12 magazine........... @5.00
Vol. 4
1 magazine 5.00
2 thru 4 .... @5.00
5 thru 6 .... @6.00
7 .... 5.00

SMITH BROWN JONES
Kiwi Studios, 1997
1 thru 5 .... @3.00

All comics prices listed are for *Near Mint* condition.

B & W PUB.

SMITH BROWN JONES: ALIEN ACCOUNTANT
Slave Labor, 1998
1 by Jon Hastings 3.00
2 . . . . 3.00
3 . . . . 3.00
4 . . . . 3.00
Spec.#1 Halloween Special 3.00
Spec. Convention Mayhem 6.00

SNOWMAN
Hall of Heroes, 1996
1 . . . . 12.00
1a variant (c) 15.00
1 3rd printing 2.75
1 San Diego Con. ed. 5.00
2 . . . . 8.00
2a 2nd printing 2.75
2b variant (c) 9.00
3 . . . . 6.00
3a variant (c) 7.00

Snowman #0
© *Avatar*

SNOWMAN
Avatar Press, 1997
0 by Matt Martin, O:Snowman 3.00
0a Frozen Fear extra-bloody 5.00
0b Leather cover 20.00
0c signed 9.00
Spec.#1 Snowman 1944 . . . . 4.00
Spec.#1 Snowman 1944, deluxe . . . 5.00
Spec.#1 Snowman 1944, signed . . . 9.00
1-shot Flurries, Glynn (c) 5.00
1-shotA Flurries, Snowman (c) 5.00

...DEAD & DYING
Avatar Press, 1997
1 (of 3) by Matt Martin 3.00
1 deluxe 5.00
1 signed 9.00
2 . . . . 3.00
2 deluxe 5.00
3 by Matt Martin 3.00
3 Frozen Fear 5.00
3 White Velvet 25.00

...HORROR SHOW
Avatar Press, 1998
1 by Matt Martin 3.00
1a Frozen Fear (c) 5.00
1b Leather cover 20.00
1 deluxe 5.00

SNOWMAN: 1994
Entity, 1996
1 flip cover #0, by Matt Martin,
  O:Snowman. 3.00
1 signed, numbered 7.00
3 . . . . 2.75
3 deluxe, variant, foil cover 3.50
4 . . . . 2.75
4 deluxe, variant, foil cover 3.50

SNOWMAN2
Avatar Press, 1997
1 (of 2) Snowman vs. Snowman . . 3.00
1a Face-off cover 5.00
1b Leather cover 20.00
1c Royal Blue edition 35.00
2 concl. 3.00
2a Sudden Death variant cover . . . 5.00

SOLD OUT
Fantaco, 1986
1 & 2 . . . . @2.50

SOLO EX-MUTANTS
Eternity
1 thru 6 . . . . @2.50

SOMETHING DIFFERENT
Wooga Central, 1991
1 Tears of God 2.50
2 1601 . . . . 2.50

SONAMBULO: SLEEP OF THE JUST
Ninth Circle Studios, 1999
1 (of 3) by Rafael Navarro 3.00
2 . . . . 3.00
3 (of 3) 3.00
Spec. Strange Tales (2000) 4.00
Spec. Ghost of a Chance (2002) . . . 5.00
Spec. Mexican Stand-off (2004) 3.00

SONG OF THE SIRENS
Millennium
Earth 3.00
Earth, signed print edition 7.00
Fire 3.00
Fire, signed print edition 9.00
Wind 3.00
Wind collectors edition 5.00
Wind with trading card 5.00
Secrets, Lies, & Videotape Pin-Up
  Special 3.00
Secrets, Lies, & Videotape Pin-Up
  Special, foil logo 6.00
Secrets, Lies, & Videotape Pin-Up
  Special, deluxe 10.00

SOUL
Samson Comics
1 . . . . 2.50
2 thru 3 F:Sabbeth . . . . @2.50

SOULFIRE
Aircel
1 mini-series 2.50
2 . . . . 2.50
3 . . . . 2.50

SOULSEARCHERS AND CO.
Claypool, 1993–2007
1 thru 10 Peter David(s) . . . . @5.00
11 thru 20 . . . . @3.00
21 thru 24 . . . . @3.00
25 ACo&SL(c) 2.50

26 O:Soulsearchers, pt.1 . . . . 2.50
27 O:Soulsearchers, pt.2 . . . . 2.50
28 O:Soulsearchers, pt.3 . . . . 2.50
29 O:Soulsearchers, pt.4 . . . . 2.50
30 thru 74 . . . . @2.50
75 thru 82 . . . . @2.50

SOUTHERN KNIGHTS
Guild, 1983
1 See Crusaders
2 . . . . 7.00
3 and 4 . . . . @5.00
5 thru 7 . . . . @4.00
Fictioneer, 1985
8 thru 11 . . . . @3.00
12 thru 33 . . . . @3.00
34 . . . . 3.00
35 The Morrigan Wars Pt.#2 . . . . . 3.50
36 Morrigan Wars Pt.#5 . . . . 3.50
37 Hell in a Handbasket 3.00
Ann. #1 . . . . 2.50
DreadHalloweenSpec #1 . . . . 2.50
Primer #1 . . . . 2.50

SOUTHERN SQUADRON
Aircel, 1990
1 . . . . 2.50
2 thru 4 . . . . @2.50
Eternity
1 I:SQUAD 2.50
2 . . . . 2.50
3 . . . . 2.50
4 . . . . 2.50

SOUTHERN SQUADRON FREEDOM OF INFO. ACT.
Aircel, 1992
1 F.F.#1 Parody/Tribute cov 2.50
2 A:Waitangi Rangers 2.50
3 . . . . 2.50

SPACE ARK
Apple, 1986
1 & 2 see color
3 . . . . 2.50
4 . . . . 2.50
5 . . . . 2.50

SPACE BEAVER
Ten-Buck Comics, 1986
1 . . . . 2.50
2 . . . . 2.50
3 O&I:Stinger 2.50
4 A:Stinger 2.50
5 . . . . 2.50
6 O:Rodent 2.50
7 thru 12 . . . . @2.50

SPACED
Anthony Smith Publ., 1988
1 I:Zip; 800 printed 30.00
2 . . . . 20.00
3 I:Dark Teddy 15.00
4 . . . . 15.00
5 and 6 . . . . @5.00
7 and 8 . . . . @2.50
Eclipse
9 . . . . 2.50
10 . . . . 2.50
11 thru 13 . . . . @2.50

SPACE PATROL
Adventure, 1992
1 . . . . 2.50
2 . . . . 2.50
3 . . . . 2.50

All comics prices listed are for *Near Mint* condition.

SPACE USAGI

Mirage Studios, 1992
1 Stan Sakai,Future Usagi 3.00
2 Stan Sakai.Future Usagi 3.00
3 Stan Sakai.Future Usagi 3.00

SPACE WOLF

Antarctic Press
1 From Albedo,by Dan Flahive 2.50

SPANDEX TIGHTS

Lost Cause Prod.
Vol. 1, 1994
1 thru 6 . . . . @2.50

Vol. 2, 1997
1 . . . . 2.50
2 prelude to Space Opera. 3.00
6 . . . . 3.00
Spec. Vs. Mighty Awful Sour
  Rangers, signed 3.00

SPANDEX TIGHTS
PRESENTS:

SPACE OPERA

Lost Cause Productions, 1997
Part 1 by Bryan J.L. Glass & Bob
  Dix, parody 3.00
Part 1, signed, Star Wars parody. . . 3.00
Part 2 ‘Star Bored,’ pt.2 . . . . 3.00
Part 3 . . . . 3.00

...THE GIRLS OF ‘95

Lost Cause Productions
1 The Good, Bad and Deadly,
  signed (1997) 4.00

...WIN A DREAM DATE
WITH SPANDEX-GIRL

Lost Cause Productions
1 (of 3) (1998). 3.00
2 . . . . 3.00
3 . . . . 3.00

SPANDEX TIGHTS:
THE LOST ISSUES

Lost Cause Productions
1 (of 4) 3.00
2 . . . . 3.00
3 . . . . 3.00
4 concl. 3.00

SPANK THE MONKEY

Arrow Comics, 1999
1 by Randy Zimmerman 3.00
2 thru 6 . . . . @3.00
Skip Month Spec.#1. . . . . 3.00

SPANK THE MONKEY ON
THE COMIC MARKET

Arrow Comics, 2000
1 (of 3) by Randy Zimmerman 3.25
2 and 3 . . . . @3.25

SPARROW

Millennium, 1995
1 I:Sparrow 3.00
2 . . . . 3.00
3 Valley of Fire 2.50

SPEED RACER CLASSICS

Now, 1998
1 . . . . 3.00
1a 2nd Printing 2.50

SPENCER SPOOK

A.C.E. Comics
1 thru 8 . . . . @2.50

SPICY TALES

Eternity, 1998
1 thru 20 . . . . @2.50
Special #2 . . . . 2.50

The Spirit #82
© Kitchen Sink

SPIRIT, THE

Kitchen Sink, 1986
Note: #1 to #11 are in color
12 thru 86 WE,rep (1986–92) . . . @3.00
GN The Spirit Casebook 17.00
TPB Vol.2 All About P’Gell 19.00
GN The Spirit Jam, 50 artists in
  48-pg. (1998) 6.00

SPIRIT, THE:
THE ORIGIN YEARS

Kitchen Sink, 1997
1 F:The Origin of the Spirit 3.00
2 F:The Black Queen’s Army 3.00
3 F:Palyachi,The Killer Clown. . . . 3.00
4 F:The Return of the Orang 3.00
5 WE 3.00
6 WE,Kiss of Death 3.00
7 F:The Kidnapping of Ebony 3.00
8 F:Christmas Spirit of 1940 . . . . . 3.00
9 WE 3.00
10 F:The Substitute Spirits. 3.00

SPIRITS

Mindwalker, 1995
1 thru 3 Silver City 3.00
4 Caleb Escapes Zeus 3.00

SPITTIN’ IMAGE

Eclipse, 1992
1 Marvel & Image parody 2.50

SQUEE

Slave Labor, 1997
1 by Jhonen Vasquez 5.00
1a 2nd printing 3.00
2 thru 4 . . . . @3.00

STAIN

Fathom Press, 1998
1 Byler (c) 3.00

1b limited edition. 8.00
2 . . . . 3.00
3 . . . . 3.00
4 . . . . 3.00
1a thru 4a Vigil (c). . . . . @3.00
5 King cover 3.00
5a Ang cover. 3.00
6 . . . . 3.00
7 . . . . 3.00

STAINLESS STEEL
ARMIDILLO

Antarctic Press, 1995
1 I:Saisni, Tania Badan 3.00
2 V:Mirage. 3.00
3 V:Mirage. 3.00
4 Spirit of Gaia 3.00
5 V:Giant. 3.00
6 finale 3.00

STARCHILD

Taliesin Press, 1992–97
0 . . . . 12.00
1 . . . . 18.00
1a 2nd printing 4.00
2 . . . . 15.00
2a 2nd printing 4.00
3 . . . . 8.00
4 . . . . 6.00
5 thru 13 . . . . @5.00
14 . . . . 3.00

Coppervale
TPB Coll. Ed. Awakenings, rep.
  #1–#12. . . . . 5.00
Essential Starchild, Book 3 . . . . . . 7.00
Essential Starchild, Book 4 . . . . . . 7.00
Essential Starchild, Book 5 . . . . . . 7.00

STARCHILD:
CROSSROADS

Coppervale, 1995
1 . . . . 3.00
2 thru 4, reoffer, by James Owen @3.00
Conoisseurs Edition. 100.00

STARGATE: ATLANTIS

Avatar/Pulsar Press, 2005
Preview 2.50
Preview photo (c). 3.00
Preview painted (c) 3.00
Preview Ready to Serve (c). 6.00
Preview Weir painted (c) 6.00
Preview Chicago Gold Seal (c) . . . 5.00
Preview Look to the Future (c) . . . 6.00
Preview Royal blue foil (c) 75.00
Preview Royal Prism (c) 13.00

STARGATE:
THE NEW ADVENTURES
COLLECTION

Entity, 1997
1 rep. Underworld; One Nation
  Under Ra 6.00
1a photo cover 5.00

STARGATE:

ONE NATION UNDER RA

Entity, 1997
1 . . . . 3.00
1a deluxe 3.50

...REBELLION

Entity, 1997
1 (of 3) from novel, sequel to movi 3.00
1 deluxe 3.50
2 . . . . 3.00

B & W PUB.

2 deluxe 3.50	
3 (of 3) 3.00	
3 foil cover 3.50	
GN rep. 80-pg. 8.00	
GN photo (c) 8.00	

...UNDERWORLD
Entity, 1997

1 . . . . 3.00	
1a deluxe 3.50	

STAR HAWKS
ACG Comics, 2000

1 by Ron Goulart & Gil Kane 3.00	
2 . . . . 3.00	
3 . . . . 3.00	

STARK: FUTURE
Aircel, 1986

1 . . . . 2.50	
2 thru 5 . . . . @2.50	
6 thru 14 . . . . @2.50	

STARLIGHT AGENCY
Antarctic Press, 1991

1 I:Starlight Agency 2.50	
2 Anderson Kidnapped 2.50	
3 . . . . 2.50	

STAR RANGERS
Adventure, 1987

1 thru 3 . . . . @3.00	
4 . . . . 2.50	

BOOK II

1 . . . . 2.50	
2 . . . . 2.50	

STAR REACH
Taliesin Press, 1974

1 HC,I:CodyStarbuck 15.00	
2 DG,JSn,NA(c) 6.00	
3 FB 6.00	
4 HC,HC(c) 6.00	
5 JSon,HC(c) 6.00	
6 GD,Elric 6.00	
7 DS 6.00	
8 CR,KSy 6.00	
9 KSy 6.00	
10 KSy 6.00	
11 GD. 6.00	
12 MN,SL 10.00	
13 SL,KSy 10.00	
14 . . . . 10.00	
15 . . . . 10.00	
16 thru 18 . . . . @9.00	

STAR WESTERN
ACG Comics, 2000

1 . . . . 6.00	
2 John Wayne. 6.00	
3 Clint Eastwood. 6.00	
4 Clayton Moore 6.00	
5 F:Tonto. 6.00	
6 F:Fess Parker 6.00	
7 F:Masked Riders of the Plains . . 6.00	
8 James Arness-Matt Dillon(c) 6.00	
9 Sam Elliott photo (c) 6.00	
10 Chuck "Rifleman" Connors 6.00	
11 John Hart 6.00	
12 Davy Crockett, Daniel Boone . . . 6.00	
13 Gabby Hayes 6.00	

STEALTH FORCE
Malibu, 1987

1 thru 7 . . . . @2.50	

Eternity, 1988

8 . . . . 2.50	

STEALTH SQUAD
Petra Comics, 1993

0 O:Stealth Squad 2.50	
1 I:Stealth Squad 2.50	
2 I:New Member 2.50	

Volume II

1 F:Solar Blade. 2.50	
2 American Ranger Vs.Jericho. . . . 2.50	

STEELE DESTINES
Nightscapes

1 & 2 I:One Eyed Stranger 3.00	
3 Kidnapped by Aliens 3.00	

STEVE CANYON
Kitchen Sink

1 thru 14 by Doug Allen . . . . @5.00	
3-D Spec. #1 (1986) 6.00	

STEVE DITKO'S STRANGE
AVENGING TALES
Fantagraphics, 1997

1 SD 3.00	
2 SD 3.00	

STEVE GRANT'S
MORTAL SOULS
Avatar Press, 2002

1 . . . . 3.50	
2 . . . . 3.50	
3 . . . . 3.50	
1a thru 3a wraparound (c)s. . . . . @4.00	

STEVE GRANT'S
MY FLESH IS COOL
Avatar Press, 2003

1 . . . . 3.50	
2 . . . . 3.50	
3 . . . . 3.50	
1a thru 3a wraparound (c)s. . . . . @3.50	

STEVEN
Kitchen Sink

1 . . . . 4.00	
1a 2ndPrinting. 3.00	
2 . . . . 4.00	
3 . . . . 3.00	
4 and 5 . . . . @3.50	

STICKBOY
Revolutionary

1 . . . . 2.50	
2 thru 5 . . . . @2.50	

STIG'S INFERNO
Vortex, 1985

1 . . . . 5.00	
2 . . . . 3.50	
3 . . . . 3.00	
4 . . . . 3.00	
5 . . . . 2.50	

Eclipse

6 . . . . 2.50	
7 . . . . 2.50	

STINZ
Fantagraphics, 1989

1 . . . . 4.00	
2 . . . . 4.00	
3 . . . . 4.00	
4 . . . . 4.00	

[2nd series]
Brave New Words, 1990

1 thru 3 . . . . 2.50	

STITCH
Slave Labor, 1999

1 (of 4) by Tom Kovac 3.00	
2 thru 4 . . . . @3.00	

STORMBRINGER
Taliesin Press

1 thru 3 . . . . @2.50	

STORMWATCHER
Eclipse, 1989

1 thru 4 . . . . @2.50	

STRANGEHAVEN
Abiogenesis Press, 1995

1 Surrealistic Comic 3.00	
2 Secret Brotherhood 3.00	
3 thru 10 by Gary S. Millidge . . . @3.00	
11 thru 18 . . . . @3.00	

STRANGE HEROES
Lone Star Press, 2000

1 . . . . 3.00	
2 thru 7 . . . . @3.00	

Strange Sports Stories #1
© Adventure

STRANGE SPORTS
STORIES
Adventure, 1992

1 w/2 card strip 2.50	
2 The Pick-Up Game,w/cards. 2.50	
3 Spinning Wheels,w/cards 2.50	
4 thru 6 w/cards . . . . @2.50	

STRANGE WEATHER
LATELY
Metaphrog, 1997

1 . . . . 3.50	
2 thru 4 . . . . @3.50	
5 thru 10 . . . . @3.00	

STRANGERS IN
PARADISE
Antarctic Press, 1993–94

1 by Terry Moore,I:Katchoo 65.00	
1a 2nd printing 10.00	
1b 3rd printing. 5.00	
2 . . . . 45.00	
3 . . . . 35.00	

B & W PUB.

Strangers in Paradise #10
© Abstract Studio

Abstract Studio, 1994

1 TMr, Gold Logo edition	15.00
1a 2nd printing	6.00
2 and 3, Gold Logo edition	@9.00
4	6.00
5 R:Mrs. Parker.	6.00
6	5.00
7 Darcey Uses Francine	5.00
8 thru 13 TMr	@4.00

VOL. 2

1 TMr, Gold Logo edition, I Dream of You.	3.00
2 thru 13 gold logo	@3.00

VOL III, 1997

1 thru 8 See Image	
9 TMr,Detective Walsh returns	4.00
10	4.00
11	3.00
12	3.00
13 High School, pt.1 (of 3).	3.00
14 High School, pt.2	9.00
15 High School, pt.3	3.00
16A Francine/Katchoo Princess Warrior (c)	22.00
16B Tambi Princess Warrior (c).	25.00
17	3.00
18 Francine & Datchoo	3.00
19 Lifesize nude of Francine	3.00
20 Night at the Opera	3.00
21 All not well in paradise	3.00
22 The Big Rift.	3.00
23 Katchoo moves out.	3.00
24 steamy affairs	3.00
25 All Beach, All the Time	3.00
26	3.00
27 at odds with the Big Six	3.00
28 thru 35.	@3.00
36 Katchoo vs. Veronica	3.00
37 return to Tennessee	3.00
38 from rags to ritches.	3.00
39 Good news and bad news	3.00
40 Engaged to right brother?.	3.00
41 Expelled from college	3.00
42 Slumber Party.	3.00
43 Tropic Of Desire	3.00
44 Marooned	3.00
45 Francine and Katchoo.	3.00
46 Molly & Poo, Borderline Lover	3.00
47 Francine pregnant.	3.00
48 Casey's Story	3.00
49 Molly & Poo.	3.00
50 Celebrate #50	3.00
51	3.00
52 Francine & Katchoo	3.00

53 My Maiden Voyage	3.00
54 Girl Trouble, pt.1	3.00
55 Girl Trouble, pt.2	3.00
56 Girl Trouble, pt.3	3.00
57 Blue Bird of Happiness	3.00
58 thru 77.	@3.00
78 thru 90	@3.00
90a & 90b variant (c)s	@3.00
Spec. Sourcebook	3.00
Spec. #93268 Songs & Lyrics	2.75

STRANGELOVE
Entity Comics, 1995

1 I:Strangelove	2.50
2 V:Hyper Bullies	2.50
3 I:Bogie	2.50

STRANGEWAYS
Speakeasy Comics, 2005

1	2.50
2 thru 4	@2.50

STRANGE WORLDS
Eternity

1	4.00
2 thru 4	@4.00

STRATA
Renegade, 1986

1	3.00
2	2.50
3	2.50
4 thru 6	@2.50

STRAW MEN
All American, 1989

1 thru 5	@2.50
6 thru 8	@2.50

STRAY BULLETS
El Capitan, 1995

1	11.00
1a 2nd & 3rd printing	4.00
2	7.00
2a 2nd printing	3.50
3	6.00
4	6.00
5 Dysfunctional Family	4.00
6 F:Amy Racecar	4.00
7 Virginias Freedom	4.00
8 DL,`Lucky to Have Her'	3.00
9 DL,`26 Guys Named Nick'.	3.00
10 DL,`Here Comes the Circus'.	3.00
11 DL,`How to Cheer Up Your Best Friend'	3.00
12 DL, People Will be Hurt	3.00
13 DL `Selling Candy'	3.00
14 DL,The Killers arrive,48pg	3.50
15 Sex and Violence	3.00
16	3.00
17 While Ricky Fish Was Sleeping	3.00
18 Sex and Violence, pt.2	3.00
19 Young and sexy	3.00
20 Motel	3.00
21	3.00
22 40-pg.	3.50
23 thru 30	@3.50
31 thru 34	@3.50
35 thru 40	@3.50
41	3.50

STREET ANGEL
Amaze Ink/SLG, 2004

1	3.00
2 thru 5	@3.00

STREET FIGHTER
Ocean Comics, 1986

1	2.50
2 thru 4 limited series	@2.50

STREET FIGHTER II
Udon Entertainment, 2005

0 Manga	2.50
1	4.00
2 thru 5	@3.00
2a thru 6a variant (c)s	@3.00
1b thru 6b power foil (c)s	@12.50

STREET HEROES 2005
Eternity, 1989

1	2.50
2 thru 3	@2.50

STREET MUSIC
Fantagraphics

1	2.75
2	2.75
3	3.00
4	3.00
5	2.50
6	4.00

STREET POET RAY
Fantagraphics, 1989

1	2.50
2	2.50
3	3.00
4	3.00

STREET WOLF
Blackthorne, 1986

1 limited series	2.50
2	2.50
3	2.50
Graphic Novel	7.00

STRIKER: SECRET OF THE BERSERKER
Viz Communications

1 & 2 V:The Berserker	@2.75
3 F:Yu and Maia	2.75

STRIKER: THE ARMORED WARRIOR
Viz Communications, 1992

1 Overture.	2.75
2 V:Child Esper.	2.75
3 Professor taken hostage	2.75

STRONGHOLD
Devil's Due Publishing, 2006

1 (of 3) PhH	5.00
2 thru 3	@5.00

STUDENTS OF THE UNUSUAL
3 Boys Productions, 2004

1	3.00
2	3.00
3 thru 6	@3.50

STUPID, STUPID RAT TAILS:THE ADVENTURES OF BIG JOHNSON BONE
Cartoon Books, 1999

1 I:Big Johnson Bone,FrontierHero	3.00
2	3.00

STYGMATA
Entity, 1994
0	3.00
1 V:The Rodent	3.00
2 thru 3	@3.00
Yearbook #1 (1995)	3.00

SUBCULTURE
Ape Entertainment, 2007
1 (of 4)	3.50
2 thru 4	@3.50

SUBTLE VIOLENTS
CFD Productions, 1991
1 Linsner (c&a)	10.00
1a San Diego Con	40.00

SUDDEN GRAVITY
Caliber, 1998
1 by Greg Ruth	3.00
2	3.00
3	3.00
4	3.00
5 story arc concl.	3.00
Spec. Panopticon, 64-page	5.00

SUGAR BUZZ
Slave Labor, 1998
1 by I.Carney & W. Phoenix	3.00
2	3.00
3	3.00
4	3.00
5	3.00
6 F:Ultra Spacers	3.00
7 I:Precious & Percival	3.00
8 thru 10	@3.00

SUGAR RAY FINHEAD
Wolf Press, 1992
1 I&O Sugar Ray Finhead	2.50
2 I:Bessie & Big-Foot Benny the Pit Bull Man	3.00
3 thru 7 Mardi Gras	@3.00
9 & 10	@3.00

SULTRY TEENAGE SUPER-FOXES
Solson, 1987
1 thru 4 RB,Woj	@2.50

SUPER HERO HAPPY HOUR
Geekpunk, 2003
1	3.00
2 thru 5	@3.00

SUPERMODELS IN THE RAINFOREST
Sirius, 1998
1 (of 3)	3.00
2 and 3	@3.00

SURVIVALIST CHRONICLES
Survival Art
1	6.50
2	6.50
3 I:Bessie & Big Foot Benny	2.25

SURROGATE SAVIOR
Hot Brazer Comic Pub.
1 I:Ralph	2.50
2 Baggage	2.50

SWAN
Little Idylls, 1995
1 thru 3 Ghost of Lord Kaaren	@3.00
4 V:Slake	3.00

SWEET CHILDE BATTLE BOOK
Advantage Graphics, 1995
1 I:Tasha Radcliffe	2.50

SWEET CHILDE: LOST CONFESSIONS
Anarchy Bridgeworks, 1997
1 F:Tasha Radcliffe	3.00

SWEET LUCY
Brainstorm Comics
1 with 4 cards	2.50
2	2.50

SWERVE
Amaze Ink, 1995
1 thru 3 by Kyle Hunter	@2.50

SWIFTSURE
Harrier Comics, 1985
1	2.50
2	2.50
3 thru 8	@2.50
9	9.00
9a 2nd printing	2.50
10	2.50
11	2.50

SWITCH B.L.A.Z.E. MANGA
London Night, 1999
0	3.50
? Con special	5.00
? Con special, Japanese (c)	6.00
1	3.50
1a Elite fan ed.	6.00
1b Anime cell ed.	20.00

SWORD OF VALOR
A Plus Comics
1 JAp,rep.Thane of Bagarth	2.50
2 JAp/MK rep	2.50
3 & 4	@2.50

SWORDS AND SCIENCE
Pyramid
1 thru 3	@2.50

SWORDS OF CEREBUS
Aardvark–Vanaheim
1 rep. Cerebus 1-4	15.00
1a reprint editions	10.00
2 rep. Cerebus 5-8	12.00
2a reprint editions	8.00
3 rep. Cerebus 9-12	12.00
3a reprint editions	8.00
4 rep. Cerebus 13-16	12.00
4a reprint editions	8.00
5 rep. Cerebus 17-20	12.00
5a reprint editions	8.00
6 rep. Cerebus 21-25	12.00
6a reprint editions	8.00

SWORDS OF SHAR-PAI
Caliber, 1991
1 Mutant Ninja Dog	2.50
2 Shar-Pei	2.50
3 Final issue	2.50

Swords of Cerebus
© Aardvark–Vanaheim

SWORDS OF VALORS: ROBIN HOOD
A Plus Comics
1 rep. of Charlton comics	2.50
2 thru 4	@2.50

SYSTEM SEVEN
Arrow, 1987
1	2.50
2 thru 4	@2.50

TALES FROM THE ANIVERSE
Arrow
1 7,400 printed	9.00
2	4.00
3 10,000 printed	2.50
4	2.50

[2nd series]
Massive Comics Group
1	2.50
2 thru 3	@2.50

TALES FROM THE BOG
Aberation Press, 1995
1 thru 4 by Marcus Lusk	@3.00
1a thru 4a Director's cut	@4.00
5 thru 7	@4.00
8	3.00

TALES FROM THE EDGE
Vanguard, 1993
5 thru 10	@3.00
5a thru 10a signed	@6.00
11 F:Sacred Monkeys	3.00
12 spec.F:Steranko	4.00
12a signed, limited	15.00
13 F:Steranko	3.00
14	3.00
15 Sienkiewicz special	4.00
Spec. Nightstand Chillers Benefit Edition	5.00
Spec. Nightstand Chillers, signed	10.00
Spec. Sienkiewicz Special	10.00

TALES FROM THE HEART
Entropy, 1988–94
1	2.50
2 thru 7	@2.50

B & W PUB.

TALES OF LEONARDO
Mirage Studios, 2006
1 (of 4) Blind Sight 3.25
2 thru 4 Blind Sight . . . . @3.25

TALES OF RAPHAEL: BAD MOON RISING
Mirage Studios, 2007
1 (of 4) 3.25
2 thru 4 . . . . @3.25

TALES OF THE BEANWORLD
Eclipse, 1985
1 . . . . 10.00
2 . . . . 4.00
3 . . . . 2.50
4 I:Beanish 2.50
5 thru 20 . . . . @2.50
21 . . . . 3.00

TALES OF THE FEHNRIK
Antarctic Press, 1995
1 I:Lady Zeista 3.00

TALES OF THE JACKALOPE
Blackthorne, 1986
1 . . . . 4.00
2 . . . . 3.00
3 and 4 . . . . @2.50
5 thru 9 . . . . @2.50

TALES OF THE NINJA WARRIORS
CFW
1 thru 14 . . . . @2.50
15 thru 19 . . . . @2.50

TALES OF THE PLAGUE
Eclipse
1 RCo 4.00

TALES OF THE SUNRUNNERS
Sirius, 1986
Vol. 2
1 thru 3 . . . . @2.50
Christmas Spec. 2.50

TALES OF THE TEENAGE MUTANT NINJA TURTLES
Mirage, 1987
1 . . . . 8.00
1B 2nd printing 3.00
2 . . . . 8.00
3 . . . . 5.00
4 . . . . 5.00
5 . . . . 5.00
6 thru 9 . . . . @4.00
Mirage Studios, 2004
1 . . . . 3.00
2 thru 9 . . . . @3.00
10 thru 16 . . . . @3.25
17 thru 29 . . . . @3.25
30 thru 52 . . . . @3.25

TALES TOO TERRIBLE TO TELL
New England Comics, 1991
1 . . . . 3.50
2 thru 6 Pre-code horror stories . @3.50

TALL TAILS
Vision Comics, 1998
1 Earth Shaking 3.00
1a Anime Blast cover 3.00
1b Spell Warrior cover 3.00
1c signed 5.00
2 Fire Quest, Pt.1 . . . . 3.00
3 Fire Quest, Pt.2 . . . . 3.00
4 Pain and Compromises,pt.1 . . . 3.00
5 . . . . 3.00
6 Trail Blazing, pt.1 . . . . 3.00
7 Trail Blazing, pt.2 . . . . 3.00
8 When It Almost Happened. 3.00
GN Vol. 1 . . . . 9.00

TANTALIZING STORIES
Tundra, 1992
1 F:Frank & Montgomery Wart 2.50
2 Frank & Mont.stories cont.. . . . . 2.50

TAOLAND
Sunitek
1 V:The Crocodile Warlord 2.50
2 & 3 I:New Enemy . . . . @3.25

TEAM NIPPON
Aircel
1 . . . . 2.50
2 thru 7 by Barry Blair . . . . @2.50

Teenage Mutant Ninja Turtles #2
© Mirage Studios

TEENAGE MUTANT NINJA TURTLES*
Mirage Studios, 1981
***Counterfeits Exist - Beware**
1 I:Turtles 275.00
1a 2nd printing 25.00
1b 3rd printing. 20.00
1c 4th printing 12.00
1d 5th printing. 4.00
2 . . . . 75.00
2a 2nd printing 12.00
2b 3rd printing. 4.00
3 . . . . 55.00
3a 2nd printing 3.50
3b Special printing,rare. 50.00
4 . . . . 40.00
4a 2nd printing 3.50
5 A:Fugitoid. 20.00
5a 2nd printing 3.50
6 A:Fugitoid. 15.00
6a 2nd printing 2.50
7 A:Fugitoid. 8.00

7a 2nd printing 2.50
8 A:Cerebus 9.00
9 . . . . 8.00
10 V:Shredder 8.00
11 A:Casey Jones 6.00
12 thru 18 . . . . @6.00
19 Return to NY. 4.00
20 Return to NY. 4.00
21 Return to NY,D:Shredder 4.00
22 thru 32 . . . . @4.00
33 color, Corben 3.50
34 Toytle Anxiety 3.50
35 Souls Withering. 3.50
36 Souls Wake. 3.50
37 Twilight of the Rings 3.50
38 Spaced Out Pt.1, A:President
    Bush 3.50
39 Spaced Out Pt.2 . . . . 3.50
40 Spaced Out concl.,I:Rockin'
    Rollin' Miner Ants (B.U. story) . . 2.50
41 Turtle Dreams issue 2.50
42 Juliets Revenge 2.50
43 Halls of Lost Legends 2.50
44 V:Ninjas. 2.50
45 A:Leatherhead. 2.50
46 V:Samurai Dinosaur 2.50
47 Space Usagi 2.50
48 Shades of Grey Part 1 . . . . 2.50
49 Shades of Grey Part 2 . . . . 2.50
50 Eastman/Laird,new direction,
    inc.TM,EL,WS pin-ups. 3.00
51 City at War #2 . . . . 2.50
52 City at War #3 . . . . 2.50
53 City at War #4 . . . . 2.50
54 City at War #5 . . . . 2.50
55 thru 65 . . . . @2.50
1990 Movie adaptation 6.50
Spec. The Haunted Pizza 2.50
Volume 2
1 . . . . 2.75
2 thru 8 . . . . @2.75
9 V:Baxter Bot. 2.75
10 Mr. Braunze 2.75
11 F:Raphael 2.75
12 V:DARPA. 2.75
13 J:Triceraton 2.75
Vol. 4, 2001
1 PLa & Jim Lawson. 3.00
2 thru 24 PLa . . . . @3.00
24 thru 30 . . . . @3.00

...THE MOVIE PREQUEL
Mirage Studios, 2007
1 Raphael 3.25
2 Michelangelo 3.25
3 DOnatello. 3.25
4 April 3.25
5 Leonardo 3.25

...THE MOVIE ADAPTATION
Mirage Studios, 2007
1-shot 5.00

...TRAINING MANUAL
1 . . . . 5.00
2 thru 5 . . . . @3.00

TEMPEST COMICS PRESENTS
Academy Comics
1 I:Steeple, Nemesis. 2.50

TEMPORARY
Origin Comics, 2005
1 Cubes and Ladders 4.00
2 The Real Me 4.00
3 The Real Me 3.00
4 A Dirt Nap 3.00
5 Twilight. 3.00

10TH MUSE/ DEMONSLAYER
Avatar Press, 2002
Preview, 16-pg. 2.25
1 MMy(c). 3.50
1a Matt Martin (c) 3.50
1b SSh(c) 3.50
1c Karl Waller (c) 3.50
1d wraparound (c). 3.50
1e Red Leather (c) 20.00
1f prism foil edition 11.00
1g Aftermath (c) 6.00
1h Art Nouveau (c) 6.00
1/2 MMy bikini (c) 6.00
1/2 Conflict edition 6.00
1/2 Catfight (c) 6.00

TERROR ON THE PLANET OF THE APES
Adventure Comics, 1991
1 MP,collectors edition 2.50
2 MP, the Forbidden Zone 2.50
3 . . . . 2.50

TERRY AND THE PIRATES
ACG Comics, 1998
1 by Georges Wunder, Charlton
   reprint 3.00
2 . . . . 3.00
3 . . . . 3.00

TERRY & THE PIRATES
Tony Raiola, 2001
Feature Comics #6, 1938 reprint . . . 8.00
Feature Comics #2 1937 reprint . . . 8.00
Feature Comics #28 1938 reprint . . 8.00
Raven Evermore 1941 reprint 8.00

TERRY MOORE'S PARADISE, TOO
Abstract Studio, 2000
1 . . . . 3.00
2 . . . . 3.00
3 . . . . 3.00
4 . . . . 3.00
5 thru 14 . . . . @3.00

TEX BENSON
Metro Comics
1 thru 4 . . . . @2.50

39 SCREAMS
Thunder Baas
1 thru 6 . . . . @2.50

THEY WERE 11
Viz
1 Galactic University. 2.75
2 The Accident 2.75
3 Virus. 2.75
4 V:Virus 2.75

THIEVES AND KINGS
I Box, 1994–97
1 F:Ruebel The Intrepid 7.00
1a 2nd printing 2.50
2 . . . . 6.00
2a 2nd printing 2.50
3 . . . . 5.00
3a 2nd printing 2.50
4 . . . . 4.00
5 . . . . 4.00
6 V:Shadow Lady 4.00
7 V:Shadow Lady 3.00
8 thru 18 by Mark Oakley . . . . . . @3.00
19 thru 24 . . . . @2.50

25 thru 36. . . . . @2.50
37 thru 39. . . . . @2.50
40 thru 47 . . . . @3.00
48 thru 49 . . . . @3.50

THIRD DEGREE
NBM Books, 2002
1 by Cris Rowley & Justin Norman. 3.00
2 thru 4 . . . . @3.00

THIRTEEN STEPS
Desperado Pub., 2007
1 . . . . 4.00
2 thru 5 . . . . @4.00

THORR SUERD OR SWORD OF THOR
Vincent
1 . . . . 3.00
1a 2nd printing 2.50
2 . . . . 2.50
3 . . . . 2.50

THOSE ANNOYING POST BROS.
1 thru 18 see Color
Becomes:
POST BROTHERS
Rip Off, 1991–94
19 thru 38 . . . . @2.50
Becomes:
THOSE ANNOYING POST BROS.
Vortex, 1994
39 thru 45 . . . . @2.50
46 thru 56. . . . . @3.00
57 Russ working on chaos wave. . . 3.00
58 Fearsome chaos wave 3.00
59 Recondite Silicates 3.00
60 . . . . 3.00
61 Assassinate JFK's ghost. 3.00
62 Post Digestion 64pg. 6.00
63 . . . . 6.00
GN Distrub the Neighbors 10.00
Ann. #3 Before the Flood, 56pg. . . 5.00

THREAT
Fantagraphics, 1985
1 . . . . 5.00
2 . . . . 3.00
3 and 4 . . . . @2.50
5 thru 10 . . . . @2.50

3 X 3 EYES
Innovation
1 Labyrinth of the Demons
  Eye,Pt.1. . . . . 2.50
2 Demons Eye, Pt.2 . . . . 2.50
3 Demons Eye, Pt.3 . . . . 2.50
4 Demons Eye, Pt.4 . . . . 2.50
5 Demons Eye, concl. 2.50

THREE GEEKS, THE
3 Finger Prints, 1997
1 by Rich Koslowski, Going
  to the Con, pt.1 . . . . 8.00
2 Going to the Con, pt.2 . . . . 6.00
3 Going to the Con, pt.3 (of 3) 3.00
4 . . . . 4.00
5 five more geeks 2.50
6 F:Allen 2.50
7 . . . . 2.50
8 48-pg. 4.00
9 24-pg. 2.50
10 Happy Birthday Allen 2.50
10a variant cover 3.50

11 Happy Birthday Allen, pt.2 . . . . . 2.50

THREE ROCKETEERS
Eclipse
1 JK,AW,rep. 2.50
2 JK,AW,rep. 2.50

THREE STRIKES
Oni Press, 2003
1 (of 5) 3.00
2 thru 5 . . . . @3.00

Threshold #2
© Avatar

THRESHOLD
Sleeping Giant, 1996
1 . . . . 2.50
2 . . . . 2.50

[2nd Series], 1997
1 . . . . 2.50
2 . . . . 2.50
3 . . . . 2.50

Avatar Press, 1998
1 Snowman cover. 4.50
1a Tales of the Cyberangels cover . 4.50
1b Furies cover. 4.50
1c Fuzzie Dice cover 4.50
2 Snowman cover. 5.00
3 Ravening (c) 5.00
4 Donna Mia (c) 5.00
5 Black Reign (c) 5.00
6 Luna cover 5.00
7 Darkness in Collision,
  Cavewoman(c) 5.00
8 Vigil/Cuda (c) 5.00
9 August (c). 5.00
2a thru 9a variant (c)s. . . . . @5.00
10 Calico (c). 5.00
11 Scythe (c) 5.00
12 Snowman (c). 5.00
13 Snowman (c). 5.00
14 Kaos Moon (c) 5.00
15 Luna (c). 5.00
16 Scythe (c) 5.00
17 Cimmerian (c) 5.00
18 Nightvision (c) 5.00
19 Pandora (c). 5.00
20 Kaos Moon (c) 5.00
21 Jungle Girl (c) 5.00
22 . . . . 5.00
23 Ravening (c) 5.00
24 Faust: Singha's Talons 5.00
25 thru 30 Dark Blue (c). . . . . . . @5.00
10a thru 30a variant (c)s . . . . . . @5.00
31 Luna (c). 5.00

32 Ravening (c) 5.00
33 thru 38 Pandora (c) . . . . @5.00
39 Razor (c) 5.00
40 Lookers (c) 5.00
41 thru 43 Razor (c) . . . . @5.00
45 Demonslayer (c) 5.00
46 Demonslayer (c) 5.00
47 Pandora (c) 5.00
31a thru 47a variant (c)s . . . . . . @5.00
48 Pandora (c) 5.00
49 Pandora (c) 5.00
48a thru 49a connecting (c) 6.00
50 64-pg. 9.00
50 connecting (c)s 9.00
50a variant (c)s . . . . @9.00
51 . . . . 5.00
51b Pandora Western edition 6.00
52 . . . . 5.00
51a and 52a variant (c)s . . . . . . @5.00
53 . . . . 5.00
53a wraparound (c) 5.00
53b Talented Twosome (c) 6.00
54 . . . . 5.00
54a variant (c) 5.00
54b School Days (c) 6.00
Pin-Ups Mythic Sirens (2007) 5.00
Pin-Ups Mythic Sirensvariant (c)s @5.00

THRESHOLD OF REALITY
Maintech, 1986
1 5,000 printed 2.50
2 thru 4 . . . . @2.50

THUNDERBIRD
Newcomers Publishing
1 & 2 2 Stories . . . . @3.00
3 . . . . 3.00
4 I:Mercer 3.00
5 R:Raven 3.00
6 & 7 . . . . @3.00
8 final issue 3.50
Ann.#1 The Great Escape 3.50

THUNDER BUNNY
Mirage, 1985
1 O:Thunder Bunny 2.50
2 VO:Dr.Fog 2.50
3 I:GoldenMan 2.50
4 V:Keeper 2.50
5 I:Moon Mess 2.50
6 V:Mr.Endall. 2.50
7 VI:Dr.Fog 2.50
8 . . . . 2.50
9 VS:Gen. Agents 2.50
10 thru 12. . . . . @2.50

THUNDER MACE
Rak, 1986
1 Proto type-blue & red very
    rare:1,000 printed 15.00
1a four color cover 3.00
2 thru 5 . . . . @2.50
6 . . . . 2.50
7 . . . . 2.50
Graphic Novel, rep.1-4. . . . . 5.00

TICK
New England Comics, 1988
1 BEd 45.00
1a 2nd printing 10.00
1b 3rd printing. 8.00
1c 4th printing. 5.00
2 BEd 50.00
2a 2nd printing 10.00
2b 3rd printing. 4.00
2c 4th printing. 2.50
3 BEd 10.00
3a 2nd printing 3.00
4 BEd 8.00
4a 2nd printing 3.00

Tick #9
© New England Comics

5 BEd 8.00
6 BEd 7.00
7 BEd,A:Chairface Chippendale. . . 7.00
8 BEd 6.00
8a Spec.No Logo edition 12.00
9 BEd,A:Chainsaw Vigilante,
    Red Eye. 5.00
10 BEd. 5.00
11 thru 12 BEd. . . . . @4.00
9 thru 12, new printings . . . . . . @3.00
Spec. Ed. #1, I:Tick 25.00
Spec. Ed. #2, 2nd App. Tick 20.00
Spec. #1 Reprise edition 6.00
The Tick Big Yule Log Special 1998 3.50
The Tick Big Yule Log Special 1999 3.50
Tick's Big Yule Log Special 2001 . . . 3.50
Big Giant Summer Special #1, The
    Sidekicks are Revolting 3.50
Big Summer Annual #1 . . . . 3.50
Tick's Big Red-N-Green X-mas 4.00
TPB Tick Bonanza #3 . . . . 5.00
TPB Tick Bonanza #4 . . . . 5.00
Spec.#1 Back to School. 3.50
Big Halloween Special #1 . . . . 3.50
Massive Summer Double Spectacle
    Photo-Cover set of 2 . . . . 8.00
13 Pseudo-Tick, not by Edlund . . . 3.50
Big Year 2000 Spectacle 3.50
Big Romantic Adventure #1, 2nd ed. 3.50
Big Tax Time Terror #1. . . . . 3.50
Big Mother's Day Spec. #1 . . . . . . 3.50
Big Halloween Special 2000 . . . . . 3.50
Big Father's Day Special 3.50
Big Cruise Ship Vacation Spec.#1 . 3.50
Massive Summer Double Spec.#1 . 3.50
Massive Summer Double Spec.#2 . 3.50

TICK AND ARTHUR, THE
New England Comics, 1999
1 by Sean Wang & Mike Baker . . . 3.50
2 Return of the Thorn,pt.2 . . . . 3.50
3 Return of the Thorn,pt.3 . . . . 3.50
4 Tick & Arthur meet Flea & Doyle . 3.50
5 Flea & Doyle superheroes? 3.50
6 Chainsaw Vigilantes 3.50
TPB Bonanza #1 rep. #1–#3 . . . . . 5.50
TPB Bonanza #2 rep. #4–#6 . . . . . 5.50

TICK, THE:
BIG BLUE DESTINY
New England Comics, 1997
1 by Eli Stone, Keen edition 3.00
1 Wicked Keen edition 5.00
2A cover A. 3.00

3B cover B 3.00
3 . . . . 3.50
4 . . . . 3.50
5 The Chrysalis Crisis. 3.50

...CIRCUS MAXIMUS
New England Comics, 2000
1 (of 4) by Sean Wang 3.50
2 . . . . 3.50
3 . . . . 3.50
4 concl. 3.50
Spec.#1 Circus Maximus
    Redux (2001). 3.50

...GIANT CIRCUS
OF THE MIGHTY
New England Press, 1992
1 A-O. 3.00
2 P-Z. 3.00
3 . . . . 3.00

...GOLDEN AGE
New England Comics, 2002
1 Entertaining cover 5.00
1a Classic cover 5.00
2 extremely creepy cover 5.00
2a Ferociously heroic cover 5.00
3 Bleeding Heart (c) 5.00
3a Criminally Maniacal (c) 5.00

...HEROES OF THE CITY
New England Comics, 1999
1 three stories. 3.50
2 . . . . 3.50
3 . . . . 3.50
4 . . . . 3.50
5 . . . . 3.50
6 . . . . 3.50
TPB Bonanza #1 rep. #1–#3 . . . . . 5.50
TPB Bonanza #2 rep. #4–#6 . . . . . 5.50

...KARMA TORNADO
New England Press, 1993
1 . . . . 4.00
1 2nd printing 3.00
2 . . . . 3.50
2 2nd printing 3.00
3 thru 9 . . . . @3.50
3 thru 9 2nd printings . . . . @3.00
TPB #1 second edition. 14.00
TPB Bonanza Edition, Vol.2. . . . . . 5.00
TPB Bonanza Edition, Vol.3. . . . . . 5.00

...THE: LUNY BIN
New England Comics, 1998
1 (of 3) by Eli Stone, Back to
    the Luny Bin 3.50
2 To the Rescue 3.50
3 Six Eyes in Tears. 3.50
Preview Special, 32pg 2.50
TPB Luny Bin Trilogy 120-pg. 5.00

TICK'S BACK, THE
New England Comics, 1997
0 by Eli Stone, V:Toy DeForce 3.00

TIGERS OF
THE LUFTWAFTE
Antarctic Press, 2001
1 48-pg. 6.00
2 48-pg. 6.00
3 48-pg. 6.00
4 Wild Angels, 48-pg. 6.00
5 Black Devil, 48-pg. 6.00
6 Black Devil, pt.2. . . . . 6.00
7 April Fools phoney issue 6.00
8 Fighter General 6.00
9 Adolf Galland 6.00
10 final issue 6.00

TIGERS OF TERRA
Mind-Visions, 1992
1 6,000 printed	4.50
1a Signed & Num.	14.00
2	2.50
2a Signed & Num.	11.00
5 thru 7	@3.50
8 thru 10	@3.75

Antarctic, 1993
11 and 12	@4.00

[Vol. 2], 1993
0 thru 14	@2.75
15 Totenkopf Police,pt.2.	2.75
16 Battleship Arizona,pt.3	2.75
17 thru 22.	@3.00
23 'Trouble with Tigers' pt.3	3.00
24 48pg 10th Anniv.	4.00
25 'Battle for Terra' pt.1	3.00

TIGER-X
Eternity, 1988
Special #1	2.50
Spec. #1a 2nd printing	2.50
1 thru 3	@2.50

Book II, 1989
1 thru 4	@2.50

TIGRESS
Hero Graphics, 1992
1 Tigress vs. Flare	4.00
2	3.00
3 A:Lady Arcane	3.00
4 inc. B.U. Mudpie	4.00
5	4.00
6	4.00

TIGRESS
Basement Comics, 1998
1 by Budd Root and Mike Hoffman	3.00
2 concl.	3.00
1-shot Mike Hoffman special	9.00
1-shot green foil edition	12.50
1-shot gold foil edition	12.50

TIGRESS TALES
Amryl Entertainment, 2001
1 by Mike Hoffman	3.00
2 Slave Planet.	3.00

Basement Comics, 2001
1a spec. edition.	9.00
2 Special Edition.	9.00
2 Blue foil (c).	10.00
3a Special ed.	9.00
3b special edition, purple foil	10.00
4	3.00
4a Special ed.	9.00
4b special edition, gold foil	10.00
5	3.00
5a Special ed.	9.00
Pin-Up book (2001)	3.50
Pin-Up Book, special edition	9.00

TIGRESS: THE HIDDEN LANDS
Basement Comics, 2002
1 by Mike Hoffman	3.50

TIME DRIFTERS
Innovation, 1990
1	2.50
2	2.50
3	2.50

TIME GATES
Double Edge
1 SF series,The Egg #1	2.50

2 The Egg #2	2.50
3 Spirit of the Dragon #1.	2.50
4 Spirit of the Dragon #2.	2.50
4a Var.cover	2.50

Time Jump War #2
© Apple

TIME JUMP WAR
Apple
1 thru 3	@2.50

TIME MACHINE
Eternity, 1990
1 thru 3 H.G. Wells adapt.	@2.50

TIME TRAVELER AI
CPM Manga, 1999
1 by Ai Ijima & Takeshi Takebayashi	3.00
2 thru 13	@3.00
14 thru 21.	@3.00

TIME WARRIORS
Fantasy General, 1986
1 rep.Alpha Track #1	2.50
1a Bi-Weekly.	2.50
2	2.50
3	2.50

TIM VIGIL'S WEBWITCH
Avatar Press, 2002
Preview, 16-pg.	2.25
Preview, Temptress (c)	6.00
Preview, Serenity (c)	6.00
Preview, prism foil exclusive(c)	13.00
Preview Cave of Evil edition	6.00
1 (of 3) Finch(c)	3.50
2 Vigil(c)	3.50
3 Adrian (c)	3.50
1a thru 3a variant(c)	@3.50
1b thru 3b wraparound (c)s.	@4.00
Webwitch Companion	5.00
Webwitch Companion Waller (c)	5.00
Webwitch Companion Martin (c)	5.00

TO BE ANNOUNCED
Strawberry Jam, 1986
1 thru 6	@2.50

TOMB TALES
Cryptic Entertainment, 1997
1	3.00
2	3.00

3	3.00
4 A Rare Gem.	3.00
5	3.00
6 The Flame Game.	3.00
7 Invasion of the Shoddy Snatchers	3.00

TOM CORBETT SPACE CADET
Eternity, 1990
1	2.50
2	2.50
3	2.50
4	2.50

TOM CORBETT II
Eternity, 1990
1	2.50
2	2.50
3	2.50
4	2.50

TOMMI GUNN: KILLERS LUST
London Night, 1997
1	3.00
1 photo cover	6.00
Ann. #1.	3.00

TOM MIX HOLIDAY ALBUM
Amazing Comics
1	3.50

TOM MIX WESTERN
AC Comics, 1988
1	2.50
2	2.50

TOMMY & THE MONSTERS
New Comics
1 thru 3	@2.50

TOMMY ROCKET AND THE GOOBER PATROL
Top Hat Comics April, 1997
1	2.50
2	2.50
3	2.50
4	3.00
5	2.50
6 conclusion	2.50

TOMORROW MAN
Antarctic, 1993
1 R:Tommrow Man	3.00
Spcc.#1 48-pg.	4.00

TOMORROW MAN
Antarctic Press, 2000
1 Requiem for Nepton,pt.1	5.00
2 Requiem for Nepton,pt.2	3.00
3 Requiem for Nepton,pt.3	3.00

TONY DIGEROLAMO'S JERSEY DEVIL
South Jersey Rebellion
1 by Tony DiGerolamo	3.00
2	3.00
3	2.50
4	3.00
5 Robin Hood of the Pines,pt.1	2.50
6 Robin Hood of the Pines,pt.2	3.00

B & W PUB.

TONY DIGEROLAMO'S
THE TRAVELERS
Kenzer & Company, 2000
1 thru 3	@2.50
7	3.00
8 Vlad Tepes in Romania	3.00
9 Arcimedes & Time Machine	3.00
10 Strange storm	3.00
11 Wrath of the Imprechaun	3.00
12 thru 20	@3.00

Wingnut Comics, 2003
21 thru 25	@3.00

TONY DIGEROLAMO'S
THE FIX
South Jersey Rebellion, 2001
1 thru 4	@2.50

TOO MUCH COFFEE MAN
Adhesive Comics, 1994
1 F:Too Much Coffee Man	14.00
1a 2nd printing	4.00
2 Wheeler (s&a)	8.00
3 Wheeler (s&a)	6.00
4 In love	6.00
5 thru 7	@4.00
8 thru 10	@3.00
Mag. #11 64-pg.	5.00
Mag. #12	5.00
Mag. #13 thru #22	@5.00

TOO MUCH HOPELESS
SAVAGES
Oni Press, 2003
1 (of 4)	3.00
2 thru 3	@3.00

TORG
Adventure
1 Based on Role Playing Game	2.50
2 thru 3 Based on Game	@2.50

TOR JOHNSON:
HOLLYWOOD STAR
Monster Comics
1 Biographical story	2.50

TORRID AFFAIRS
Eternity, 1988
1	2.50
2	2.50
3 thru 5, 60-pg.	@3.00

TOTALLY ALIEN
Trigon
1	12.00
2	9.00
3	8.00

TOUCH OF DEATH
Brain Scan Studios, 2003
0	2.50
1 thru 3	@2.50

TOUGH GUYS AND
WILD WOMEN
Eternity, 1989
1 thru 2	@2.50

TOUPYDOOPS
Lobrau Productions 2006
1 by Kevin McShane	3.50
2 thru 7	@3.50

TOZZER 2
Ablaze Media, 2004
1 (of 5)	3.00
2 thru 5	@3.00

TRACKER
Blackthorne, 1988
1	2.50
2 thru 4	@2.50

TRAILER PARK
OF TERROR
Imperium Comics, 2003
1	3.00
2 thru 8	@3.00
5a variant (c)	3.00
Spec. Halloween Special	4.00
Spec. Halloween Special #2	4.00

TRANSFORMERS, THE
IDW, 2007
1 Movie Prequel	4.00

TRANSIT
Vortex, 1987
1	2.50
2 thru 6	@2.50

TRICKSTER
KING MONKEY
Eastern
1 thru 5	@2.50

TRIDENT
Trident, 1989
1 thru 7	@3.50
8	4.50

TRIUMVERATE
Mermaid Productions
1 I:Trimverate	2.50
2 & 3 Team captured	@2.50
4 V:Ord,Ael	2.50

TROLLORDS
Tru Studios, 1986
1 1st printing	5.00
1a 2nd printing	2.50

Trollords #1 (2nd printing)
© Tru Studios

2	3.00
3	2.50
4 thru 15	@2.50
#1 special	2.50

TROLLORDS
Apple Comics, 1989–90
1 thru 6	@2.50

TROLLORDS
Caliber Tapestry, 1996
1 and 2	@3.00

TROLLORDS:
DEATH & KISSES
Apple Comics, 1989
1	2.50
2 thru 5	@2.50

TROUBLE EXPRESS
Radio Comix, 1998
1 by Will Allison	3.00
2 thru 4	@3.00

TROUBLE SHOOTERS
Nightwolf, 1995
1 I:Trouble Shooters	2.50
2 V:Ifrit,Djin,Ghul	2.50
3 V:Morgath	2.50

TROUBLE WITH GIRLS
Eternity, 1989–91
1	3.00
2 thru 14	@2.50
15 thru 21	@2.50
22 Lester's Origin	2.50
Ann. #1	3.00
Graphic Novel	8.00
Graphic Novel #2	8.00
Xmas special 'World of Girls'	3.00

NEW SERIES
1 thru 4 see color
5 thru 11	@2.50

TROUBLE WITH TIGERS
Antarctic Press, 1992
1 Ninja High School/Tigers x-over	2.50
2	2.50

TRUE STORY,
SWEAR TO GOD
Clib's Boy Comics, 2001
5 thru 6	@3.00
7 thru 15	@3.00
16 thru 17	@3.00

TRUFAN ADVENTURES
THEATRE
Paragraphics, 1986
1	7.00
2 3-D issue	5.00

TUPELO
Amaze Ink/SLG, 2003
1 thru 4	@3.00

TURTLE SOUP
Mirage, 1985
1 A:TMNTurtles	6.00

TURTLES TEACH KARATE
Solson
1	4.00
2	3.50

TV WESTERN
AC Comics, 2001
1 F:Jock Mahoney, Range Rider . . 6.00
Becomes:

WESTERN MOVIE HERO
AC Comics, 2001
2 F:Monte Hale 6.00
3 F:John Wayne 6.00
4 F:Rex Allen 7.00

TWILIGHT AVENGER
Eternity, 1988
1 thru 18 . . . . @2.50

Miracle Studios
Spec. Twilight Avenger Super
   Summer Special 2.75

TWILIGHT-X: INTERLUDE
Antarctic Press, 1992
1 . . . . 2.50
2 thru 3 by Joseph Wright . . . . . . @2.50
Vol. 2, 1993
1 thru 5 . . . . @2.50

TWILIGHT-X QUARTERLY
Antarctic Press, 1994
1 thru 3 by Joseph Wright . . . . . @3.00
4 Celebration 3.00

TWILIGHT X: STORM
Antarctic Press, 2003
1 . . . . 3.50
2 thru 6 . . . . @3.50
7 thru 8 . . . . @3.00

TWIST
Kitchen Sink, 1988
1 . . . . 2.50
2 and 3 . . . . @2.50

TWISTED TANTRUMS OF THE PURPLE SNIT
Blackthorne, 1986
1 . . . . 2.50
2 . . . . 2.50

2008 PRESIDENTIAL CANDIDATES
Antarctic Press, 2008
1-shot McCain 4.00
1-shot Obama 4.00

2001 NIGHTS
Viz, 1990–91
1 by Yukinobu Hoshino 5.00
2 . . . . 4.00
3 thru 5 . . . . @3.75
6 thru 10 . . . . @4.25

ULTIMATE STRIKE
London Night, 1996
1 . . . . 2.50
1 holochrome edition 12.00
2 . . . . 2.50
3 thru 5 . . . . @2.50
6 sequel to Strike #0 . . . . 2.50
7 by Kevin Hill, 'Strike: Year
   One' concl. 2.50
8 Year One, ... 2.50
9 Year One, cont. 2.50
10 thru 12 . . . . @2.50

ULTRA KLUTZ
Onward Comics, 1986
1 . . . . 2.50
2 thru 30 . . . . @2.50
31 . . . . 3.00

UNCANNY MAN-FROG
Mad Dog
1 and 2 . . . . @2.50

UNCENSORED MOUSE
Eternity, 1989
1 Mickey Mouse 10.00
2 Mickey Mouse 11.00

UNFORGIVEN, THE
Trinity Comics Ministries
Mission of Tranquility
1 thru 6 V:Dormian Grath . . . . . @2.50
7 I:Faith 2.50

UNICORN ISLE
Genesis West, 1986
1 . . . . 2.50
2 thru 3 . . . . @2.50
Apple, 1987
4 thru 6 . . . . @2.50

UNLEASHED
Caliber Press
1 F:Carson Davis 3.00
2 V:North Harbor Crime 3.00

UNSUPERVISED EXISTENCE
Fantagraphics
1 . . . . 2.50
2 and 3 . . . . @2.50

UNTOLD TALES OF EVIL ERNIE
Chaos! Comics, 2000
Pieces of Me #1 . . . . 3.50
Black Death premium #1 . . . . 13.00
Evil Ernie:chromium #1 . . . . 16.00
Relentless 1 BnP (2002) 5.00
Relentless 1a premium ed. 10.00
Relentless 1b Super premium ed. . . 20.00
Relentless 1c signed ed. 15.00
Relentless, Script 5.00
Relentless Script, premium ed. . . . 20.00

UNTOUCHABLES
1 . . . . 2.50
2 thru 20 . . . . @2.50

UNTOUCHABLES
Caliber, 1997
1K by Joe Pruett & John Kissee,
   MK(c) 3.00
1S Showman (c) 3.00
2 . . . . 3.00
3 MK (c) 3.00
4 MK (c) 3.00
Spec. High Society Killer (1998) . . . 4.00

UPTIGHT
Fantagraphics Books 2006
1 thru 3 . . . . @2.50

URSA MINORS
Amaze Ink/SLG, 2006
1 . . . . 3.00
2 thru 4 . . . . @3.00

Usagi Yojimbo #29
© Fantagraphics

USAGI YOJIMBO
Fantagraphics, 1987
1 SS 10.00
1a 2nd printing 5.00
2 SS,Samurai 8.00
3 SS,Samurai,A:Croakers 6.00
4 SS 5.00
5 SS 5.00
6 SS 5.00
7 SS 5.00
8 SS,A Mother's Love 5.00
8a 2nd printing 3.00
9 SS 5.00
10 SS,A:Turtles 5.00
10a 2nd printing 3.00
11 thru 18 SS . . . . @4.00
19 SS,Frost & Fire,A:Nelson
   Groundthumper 4.00
20 thru 21 SS . . . . @4.00
22 SS,A:Panda Khan 4.00
23 SS,V:Ninja Bats 4.00
24 SS 4.00
25 SS,A:Lionheart 4.00
26 SS,Gambling 4.00
27 SS 4.00
28 thru 31 SS,Circles pt.1–4 . . @4.00
32 . . . . 4.00
33 SS,Ritual Murder 4.00
34 thru 37 . . . . 4.00
Spec.#1 SS,SummerSpec, C:Groo 45.00
Radio Comix
Vol. 1 The Art of Usagi Yojimbo . . . 4.00

UTOPIATES, THE
Bloodfire Studios 2006
1 (of 4) 3.00
2 thru 4 . . . . @3.00

VAGABOND
Viz Communications, 2001
1 (of 8) by Takehiko Inoue 5.00
2 thru 16 . . . . @5.00

VAISTRON
Amaze Ink/SLG, 2005
1 thru 5 . . . . @3.00

VALENTINE
Red Eye Press, 1997
1 by Dan Cooney 3.00
2 thru 6 Cinderella Undercover . . @3.00

B & W PUB.

7 thru 8 Red Rain . . . . @3.50
9 Gun for Hire. 3.50
10 . . . . 3.00
11 thru 13. . . . . @3.50
1-shot Valentine (2005) 3.00

VALENTINO
Renegade, 1985

1 . . . . 2.50
2 and 3 . . . . @2.50

Vamperotica Ann. #1
© Brainstorm Comics

VAMPEROTICA
Brainstorm Comics, 1994

1 I:Luxura 8.00
1a 2nd & 3rd printing 3.00
2 . . . . 6.00
2 2nd printing 3.00
3 . . . . 4.00
4 I:Blood Hunter 4.00
5 Deadshot 4.00
6 Deadshot 4.00
7 Baptism 4.00
8 Pains,Peepers 4.00
9 thru 11 . . . . @4.00
12 thru 16 . . . . @3.00
17 thru 22 see: color
20 signed 5.00
23 . . . . 3.00
23 encore edition 3.00
24 . . . . 3.00
25 . . . . 3.00
26 . . . . 3.00
27 . . . . 3.00
28 A:China & Jazz 3.00
29 mild cover 3.00
30 Legends of Luxura x-over, concl. 3.00
31 V:Red Militia 3.00
32 . . . . 3.00
33 by Kirk Lindo 3.00
34 V:Pontius Vanthor 3.00
34a luxury edition. 5.00
35 . . . . 3.00
36 I:Countess Vladimira. 3.00
36a photo cover edition 4.00
37 . . . . 3.00
37a statue cover 3.00
38 . . . . 3.00
39 Death From Above, pt.1 . . . . . . 3.00
40 Death From Above, pt.2 . . . . . . 3.00
41 . . . . 3.00
42 Hostile Seduction 3.00
43 Harvest 3.00
44 F:Luxura 3.00

45 The Kindred Kill 3.00
45b photo cover 4.00
46 Murder Most Foul 3.00
47 Camelot. 3.00
48 Reflections Over Blood 3.00
49 Love's Story 3.00
50 final issue, 48-pg. 5.00
50b commemorative edition, Julie
    Strain photo (c) 7.00
50c commem. signed. 10.00
Commemorative Edition. 3.00
Lingerie Special #1 . . . . 3.00
Spec. Lingerie, encore edition 3.00
Spec. Lingerie, deluxe 4.00
Spec. Swimsuit, encore edition . . . 3.00
Gallery #1. . . . . 5.00
Gallery #2. . . . . 5.00
Bondage Spec. #1 . . . . 3.00
Bondage Spec. #1, manga 4.00
Ann. #1 Encore 3.00
Spec.#2 Dare to Bare 3.00
Spec.#4 Encore Edition, new(c) . . . 3.00
Spec.#5 Encore Edition 3.00
Spec.#1 Vamperotica Presents:
    Countess Vladimira (1998) 3.00
Vamperotica Collector Vol. 1 . . . . . 4.00
Pin-Up #1 (2000) 3.00
Spec. Blood of Japan. 3.00
1-shot Blond Goddess (2003) 3.00
1-shot Dark Fantasy 3.00
1-shot Bondage Gallery 3.00
Spec. #1 Voluptuous Vamps (2004) 3.00
GN Blood of the Impaler 8.00
GN Deadly Vixens 8.00
GN Drop Dead Dangerous 8.00
GN Vamperotica Maximum
    Excitement (2001) 8.00
GN Vamperotica Slave to
    Love (2000) 8.00
GN Dark Ages, series rep.. . . . . . . 8.00

VAMPEROTICA:
BLOND GODDESS
Vamperotica, 2003

1-shot Blond Goddess 3.00
1-shot Dark Fantasy 3.00
1-shot Bondage Gallery 3.00

...DARK FICTION
Vamperotica Ent., 2001

1 F:Vampress Luxura 3.00
1a adult (c) 4.00
1b premium edition 5.00
2 . . . . 3.00
3 . . . . 3.00
4 . . . . 3.00

...DIVIDE & CONQUER
Brainstorm, 1999

1 V:The Juicious Edicts 3.00
1b Commemorative #1 . . . . 5.00
1c Commemorative #1 deluxe 7.00
2 conclusion 3.00

...ILLUSTRATED
Brainstorm

1 F:Vampress Luxura 3.00
1b premium ed.. . . . . 5.00
1c premium signed 6.00
2 . . . . 3.00
3 . . . . 3.00
4 . . . . 3.00
5 . . . . 3.00
6 . . . . 3.00

...LUST FOR LUXURA
Vamperotica, 2002

1 by Kirk Lindo 3.00
1a premium edition 5.00
2 . . . . 3.00
3 . . . . 3.00

1c Sketch cover edition 4.00
3a photo(c) 5.00

...MANGA
Brainstorm, 1998

1 . . . . 3.00
2 . . . . 3.00

...TALES
Brainstorm, 1998

1 . . . . 3.00
2 thru 5 . . . . @3.00

...TALES FROM THE
BLOODVAULT
Vamperotica Ent., 2000

Mag. #1 . . . . 5.00
Mag. #1b premium ed.. . . . . 7.00

...VOLUPTUOUS VAMPS
Vamperotica, 2004

1 . . . . 3.00

...WHEN DARKNESS FALLS
Vamperotica Ent., 2002

1 . . . . 3.00
1b premium edition 5.00
2 . . . . 3.00
3 . . . . 3.00

VAMPEROTICA'S
PIN-UP ILLUSTRATED
Vamperotica, 2004

1 . . . . 5.00
2 thru 3 . . . . @5.00

VAMPFIRE
Brainstorm, 1996

1 . . . . 3.00
1b commemorative photo cover . . 10.00
2 . . . . 3.00
2b signed 5.00
2d Remastered 3.00
2e signed 10.00
2f deluxe with litho 20.00
3 remastered. 4.00
3a signed 10.00
3b deluxe 20.00
Pin-Up Spec. 3.00
Pin-Up Spec. deluxe 4.00
Tour Book #1 . . . . 3.00

...EROTIC ECHO
Brainstorm, 1997

1 by Fauve 3.00
1b photo cover 3.00
2 . . . . 3.00
2b photo cover 3.00

...NECROMANTIQUE
Brainstorm, 1997

1 by Holly Golightly. 3.00
1b luxury edition, virgin cover. 5.00
1c luxury edition, signed 15.00
1d regular, signed 8.00
2 by Fauve 3.00

VAMPIRE BITES
Brainstorm, 1995

1 . . . . 3.00
2 . . . . 3.00

VAMPIRE CONFESSIONS
Brainstorm, 1998

1 . . . . 3.00

VAMPIRE DAHLIA, THE
Ironcat, 2001

1 (of 6) by Narumi Kakinouchi 3.00
2 thru 6 . . . . @3.00

VAMPIRE GIRLS:

CALIFORNIA 1969

Angel Entertainment, 1996

1 blood red foil deluxe edition. 6.00
2 . . . . 3.00
2 deluxe 6.00

...NEW YORK 1979

Angel Entertainment, 1996

0 . . . . 3.00
0 gold edition 8.00
1 . . . . 3.00

...BUBBLEGUM & BLOOD

Angel Entertainment, 1996

1 . . . . 3.00
1 deluxe edition. 6.00
2 . . . . 3.00
2 deluxe edition. 6.00

...EROTIQUE

Angel Entertainment, 1996

1 . . . . 3.00
2 . . . . 3.00
3 . . . . 3.00
4 . . . . 3.00
5 . . . . 3.00
6 . . . . 3.00
7 Bloodsucker cover 3.00
Spec. Gravedigger (1996) by
    Alexandra Scott & Bill Wylie . . . 3.00
Spec. Paris 1968 (1997) by
    Alexandra Scott & Dean Burnett 3.00
Spec. Titanic 1912 (1998) by
    Alexandra Scott & Dean Burnett 3.00

...EROTIQUE: GRAVEDIGGER

Angel Entertainment, 1996

1 by Alexandra Scott & Bill Wylie . . 3.00

...VS. ANGEL GIRL

Angel Entertainment, 1997

1 . . . . 3.00

VAMPIRELLA

Harris

1 DC,SL,Summer Nights,48pg. . . . 4.00
Pantha Ashcan, 16-pg. 6.00
Dangerous Games Preview Ashcan 6.00
Hell on Earth, Leather Ashcan. . . . 15.00
Hell on Earth, Leather Ashcan,
    signed 30.00
30th Ann. Spec. Julie
    Strain photo (c) 10.00
Painkiller Jane preview Ashcan 6.00
Spec.#1 Vampirella vs. Hemorrhage,
    Limited Preview Ashcan 5.00
Vampirella/Lady Death Ashcan
    16-pg., Rematch 6.00
Vampirella/Lady Death Ashcan
    16-pg., Finale 6.00
Vampirella/Lady Death Ashcan
    16-pg., Revenge, platinum . . . 20.00
Vampirella 2999 A.D.
    Manga Ashcan. 8.00
Vampirella 2999 A.D. Manga
    Ashcan, leather edition 15.00
Vampirella 3000 A.D.
    Manga Ashcan. 8.00
Vampirella 3000 A.D.Manga
    Ashcan, leather edition 15.00

VAMPIRELLA

Harris Comics, 2002

#1 magazine reprint from 1969. . . 30.00
#1 royal blue foil (c) 60.00
#1 platinum foil (c) 20.00

VAMPIRELLA

Anarchy/Harris Comics, 2004

Spec. Vol. 1 Black & White
    Collection 5.00
Spec. Halloween Special #1 . . . . . 10.00
Spec. Halloween Special #1 JJu
    virgin (c). 19.00
Spec. 2006 Halloween Special 3.00
Spec. 2006 Halloween limited
    B&W (c)s . . . . @20.00
Spec. Intimate Visions 4.00
Spec. Intimate Visions Joe Jusko 14.00
Spec. Intimate Visions #1 virgin (c) 15.00
Spec. #1 Quarterly Spring 2007. . . . 5.00
Spec. #1 variant (c) 5.00

Vampirella Silver Anniversary #2
(Good Girl cover) © Harris

VAMPIRELLA

Silver Anniversary Collection

Harris, 1996

0 Vampirella of Darkulon, EM 3.00
1 good girl edition 2.50
1a bad girl edition 2.50
2 good girl edition 2.50
2a bad girl edition 2.50
3 good girl edition 2.50
3a bad girl edition. 2.50
4 Silkie(c) 2.50
4a MBc(c) 2.50

VAMPIRELLA COMICS MAGAZINE

Harris Comics, 2003

1 . . . . 4.00
1a photo (c). 10.00
1b Frankenstein Mobster (c). 10.00
1c JP(c). 10.00
2 thru 9 . . . . @4.00
2a thru 9a photo (c)s. . . . . @10.00

VAMPIRELLA:

MORNING IN AMERICA

Harris/Dark Horse, 1991–92

Book 1 thru 4 . . . . @7.00
Book 2 thru 4 . . . . @5.00

...NOVELLA

Anarchy/Harris Comics, 2004

1 Deadly Sins 4.00
1a limited 10.00

...RETRO

Harris, 1998

1 (of 3) rep. Warren stories. 2.50
2 (of 3) rep. Warren stories. 2.50
3 (of 3) rep. Warren stories. 2.50

...LEGENDARY TALES

Harris Comics, 2000

1 . . . . 3.00
1a deluxe 10.00
1b Julie Strain photo (c) 10.00
2 . . . . 3.00
2a variant (c). 10.00
2b Julie Strain photo (c) 10.00

...REVELATIONS

Anarchy/Harris Comics, 2005

Prototype ed. 5.00
0 16-page 9.00
0a variant JJu virgin (c) 9.00
1 . . . . 3.00
1a variant (c). 3.00
1b & c variant virgin (c)s 12.00
2 . . . . 3.00
2a variant (c) 3.00
2b & c variant virgin (c)s. 12.00
3 . . . . 3.00
3a variant (c) 3.00
3b & c variant virgin (c)s 9.00

Book 2

1 prototype edition 5.00
1 prototype limited edition 15.00

VAMPIRE MIYU

Antarctica Press, 1996

1 I:Vampire Princess Miyu 3.00
2 thru 5 . . . . @4.00
6 48pg. 5.00

VAMPIRE PRINCESS MIYU

Ironcat, 2000

1 by Narumi Kakinouchi 3.00
2 thru 4 . . . . @3.00

VAMPIRE PRINCESS YUI

Ironcat, 2000

Vol. 1

1 . . . . 3.00
2 thru 6 . . . . @3.00

Vol. 2

1 . . . . 3.00
2 thru 6 . . . . @3.00

VAMPIRE YUI

Ironcat, 2000

Vol. 3

1 . . . . 3.00
2 thru 4 . . . . @3.00
5 thru 6 . . . . @3.00

Vol. 4 (2002)

1 thru 7 . . . . @3.00

Vol. 5

1 . . . . 3.00
2 thru 7 . . . . @3.00

VAMPIRE'S TATTOO

London Night, 1997

1 (of 2) by Art Wetherell 3.00
2 . . . . 3.00
3 . . . . 3.00

VAMPIRE VERSES, THE

CFD Productions, 1995

1 thru 3 . . . . @3.00

VAMPIRE ZONE, THE
Brainstorm, 1998
1 .... 3.00

Vampyres #3
© Eternity

VAMPYRES
Eternity, 1988
1 thru 4 .... @2.50

VENGEANCE OF DREADWOLF
Lightning Comics
1 O:Dreadwolf................ 2.75

VENGEANCE OF THE AZTECS
Caliber, 1993
1 .... 2.50
2 .... 2.50

VERDICT
Eternity, 1988
1 thru 4 .... @2.50

VEROTIKA
Verotika, 1995–97
1 Magical Times 10.00
2 .... 7.00
3 .... 5.00
4 thru 6 .... @4.00
7 thru 15 .... @3.00

VERY VICKY
Meet Danny Ocean, 1993
1 .... 3.50
1a 2nd printing 3.00
2 thru 8 .... @2.50
Spec. Calling All Hillbillies 2.50

VIC & BLOOD
Renegade, 1987
1 and 2 RCo,Ellison .... @2.50

VICKY VALENTINE
Renegade, 1985
1 thru 4 .... @2.50

VICTIM
Silver Wolf, 1987
1 & 2 .... @2.50

VICTIMS
Eternity, 1988
1 thru 5 .... @2.50

VIDEO
Lost in the Dark Press, 2004
1 .... 3.00
2 thru 4 .... @3.00
5 thru 6 .... @3.00

VIDEO CLASSICS
Eternity
1 Mighty Mouse 3.50
2 Mighty Mouse 3.50

VIETNAM JOURNAL
Apple Comics, 1987
1 .... 5.00
1a 2nd printing 3.00
2 .... 3.00
3 thru 5 .... @3.00
6 thru 13 .... @3.00
14 thru 16 .... @3.00

VIGIL
Duality Press, 1997
Baby Steps.................... 3.00
Dirt, by A.Laudermilk & M.Iverson . 3.00
Slash and Burn, Bloodline story . 3.00
The Vegas Shuffle, Bloodline story . 3.00
Desertion 3.00
Outreach 3.00
Penetration................... 3.00
Daddy's Little Girl, final issue 3.00

VIGIL: DESERT FOXES
Millennium, 1995
1 & 2 F:Grace Kimble .... @4.00

VIGIL: ERUPTION
Millennium, 1996
1 (of 2) vampire hunters 4.00
2 (of 2) 4.00

VIGIL: FALL FROM GRACE
Innovation, 1992
1 `State of Grace' 2.75
2 The Graceland Hunt 2.50

VIGIL: SCATTER SHOTS
Duality Press, 1997
1 by A.Laudermilk & M.Iverson.... 4.00
2 .... 4.00

VIRGIN: SLUMBER
Entity, 1997
1 BMs 2.75
1 deluxe 3.50

VIRGIN: SURROUNDED
Entity, 1997
1 BMs 2.75
1 deluxe 3.50

VIRGIN: TILL DEATH DO US PART
Entity, 1997
1 BMs 2.75
1 deluxe 3.50

VISIONS
Vision Publication, 1979–83
1 I:Flaming Carrot............ 60.00
2 Flaming Carrot............. 35.00
3 Flaming Carrot............. 20.00
4 Flaming Carrot............. 25.00

VISUAL ASSAULT OMNIBUS
Visual Assault Comics, 1995
1 thru 4 O:Dimensioner........ @3.00

VIXEN
Meteor Comics
1 & 2 Battle of the Vixens ...... @3.00

VORTEX
Hall of Heroes, 1993
1 .... 12.00
1a commemorative 5.00
2 .... 8.00
3 thru 5 .... @3.50
6 V:The Reverend............. 3.00

VORTEX SPECIAL: CYBERSIN
Avatar Press, 1997
1 by Matt Martin & Bil Maus 3.00
1b velvet cover 12.00
1c signed 8.00
1d Snowman spec. (c) 5.00

VORTEX: DR. KILBOURN
Entity, 1997
1 by Matt Martin 3.00
1a deluxe 3.50

VORTEX: INTO THE DARK
Entity, 1997
1 .... 3.00
1 deluxe 3.50

VOX
Apple, 1989
1 JBy(c)..................... 2.50
2 thru 5 .... @2.50

WABBIT WAMPAGE
Amazing Comics, 1987
1 .... 2.50

WAFFEN SS
New England Comics, 2000
1 by Ron Ledwell 3.50
2 thru 7 .... @3.50

WAITING PLACE, THE
Slave Labor, 1997
5 thru 6 .... @3.00

Vol. 2, 2000
1 .... 3.00
2 .... 3.00
3 A Sporting Chance........... 3.00
4 I Care..................... 3.00
5 The Road Home 3.00
6 thru 7 .... @3.00
8 Under a Frozen Sky.......... 3.00
9 thru 11 Intrusions, pt.1–3 .... @3.00

WALKING DEAD
Aircel
1 .... 2.50
2 thru 4 .... @2.50
Zombie Spec. 1 .... 2.50

WALK THROUGH OCTOBER
Caliber
1 I:Mr. Balloon	3.00
2	3.00
3 All Hallow's Eve	3.00

WALT THE WILDCAT
Motion Comics, 1995
1 I:Walt the Wildcat	2.50

WANDERING STAR
Pen & Ink, 1993
1 I:Casandra Andrews	10.00
1a 2nd & 3rd printing	3.00
2	7.00
3	5.00
4	4.00
5	4.00
6 thru 11	@3.00

Sirius, 1995–97
12 thru 20 TWo	@2.50
21 TWo, final issue	2.50

WANDERLUST
Antarctic Press, 2000
1 (of 3) by Bryant Shiu	2.50
2	2.50
3 conclusion	2.50

WARCAT
Alliance Comics
1 thru 7 A:Ebonia	@2.50

WARD: A BULLET SERIES
Liar Comics
1 Foresight,pt.1	2.50
2 Foresight,pt.2	2.50
3 Foresight,pt.3	2.50

WARLOCK 5
Aircel, 1986
1	6.00
2	5.00
3	6.00
4	5.00
5	5.00
6 thru 11	@4.00
12	3.50
13	3.50
14 thru 16	@3.00
17	3.00
18	3.00
19 thru 22	@3.00
Book 2 #1 thru #7	@3.00

WARLOCK 5
Sirius, 1997
1 (of 4) by Barry Blair & Colin Chan	2.50
2	2.50
3	2.50
4 finale	2.50

WARLOCKS
Aircel, 1988
1 thru 3	@2.50
4 thru 12	@2.50
Spec #1 Rep.	2.50

WARMAGEDDON ILLUSTRATED
Digital Webbing, 2005
1	6.00
2	6.00

WAR OF THE WORLDS
Eternity
1 TV tie-in	2.50
2	2.50
3 thru 6	@2.50

War of the Worlds #1
© Caliber

WAR OF THE WORLDS, THE
Caliber 'New Worlds', 1996
1 from H.G. Wells	3.00
1a signed	3.00
2 war for Kansas City	3.00
3 Haven & The Hellweed	3.00
4	3.00
5	3.00

WAR OF THE WORLDS: THE MEMPHIS FRONT
Arrow Comics, 1998
1 (of 5) by Randy Zimmerman & Richard Gulick	3.00
2 thru 5	@3.00
Spec.#1 signed & numbered	3.00

WARREN ELLIS'
Avatar Press, 2004–05
1-shot Angel Stomp Future	3.50
1-shot Frank Ironwine	3.50
1-shot Quit City	3.50
1-shot Simon Spector	3.50

...APPARAT
Avatar Press, 2004
Preview	2.50

...ATMOSPHERICS
Avatar Press, 2002
GN	6.00

...BAD WORLD
Avatar Press, 2001
1 (of 3)	3.50
2	3.50
3	3.50
1a thru 3a wraparound (c).	@4.00

...SCARS
Avatar Press, 2002
1 (of 6)	3.50
2 thru 6	@3.50
1a–6a wraparound (c).	4.00

...STRANGE KISS
Avatar Press, 1999
1	3.00
1a	4.00
1b signed	25.00
2	2.50
2a wraparound (c).	4.00
3	3.00
3a wraparound (c).	4.00

...STRANGER KISSES
Avatar Press, 2000
1 (of 3)	3.00
1a leather signed	20.00
2	3.00
3	3.00
1a thru 3a wraparound (c).	@4.00

WARREN ELLIS' STRANGE KILLINGS
Avatar Press, 2002
1 (of 3) WEI	3.50
1a wraparound (c).	4.00
2	3.50
2a wraparound (c).	4.00
3	3.50
3a wraparound (c).	3.50

...THE BODY ORCHARD
Avatar Press, 2002
1 (of 6) WEI.	3.50
2 thru 6 WEI	@3.50
1a thru 6a wraparound (c).	@4.00

...NECROMANCER
Avatar Press, 2004
1	3.50
2 thru 6	@3.50
1a thru 6a wraparound (c)s.	@3.50

...STRONG MEDICINE
Avatar Press, 2003
1	3.50
2 thru 3	@3.50
1a thru 3a wraparound (c).	@4.00

WARRIOR NUN AREALA:
BOOKS OF PERIL
Antarctic Press, 2001
1 (of 4)	3.00
2 The Book of Sharate	3.00
3 Book of Xitan	3.00
4 Devil's Deal	3.00
5 Scepter of the Crescent Moon.	3.00
6 Scepter of the Crescent Moon.	3.00
7 Scepter of the Crescent Moon.	3.00
8 The Good Son, pt.1	3.00
9 The Good Son, pt.2	3.00
10 The Good Son, pt.3	3.00
11 Dissension, pt.1	3.00
12 Dissension, pt.2	3.00
13 Dissension, pt.3	3.00
14 Curse of Looming Plague,pt.1	3.50
15 Curse of Looming Plague,pt.2	3.50
16 Curse of Looming Plague,pt.3	3.50
17 Soul Reaper	3.50
18 Soul Reaper, pt.2	3.50
19 Soul Reaper, pt.3	3.50
20 thru 22	@3.50
Spec. Swimsuit Special (2002)	4.00

...DANGEROUS GAME
Antarctic Press, 2001
1 (of 3)	3.00
2 thru 3	@3.00

...GHOSTS OF THE PAST
Antarctic Press, 2001
1 (of 4)	3.00
2 thru 4	@3.00

...THE MANGA
Antarctic Press, 2000
1-shot 3.00

WARRIOR NUN AREALA/RAZOR: DARK PROPHECY
London Night, 1999
1 16-pg. 2.50
2 16-pg. 2.50
Antarctic Press
3 . . . . 2.50
4 . . . . 2.50

WARRIOR NUN: BLACK AND WHITE
Antarctic Press, 1997
1 . . . . 3.00
2 . . . . 3.00
3 . . . . 3.00
4 Winter Jade, pt.1 F:Ninja Nun . . . 3.00
5 Winter Jade, pt.2 . . . . 3.00
6 Winter Jade, pt.3 . . . . 3.00
7 . . . . 3.00
8 . . . . 3.00
9 Return of the Redeemers 3.00
10 Return of Lillith 3.00
11 The Redeemers, cont. 3.00
12 The Redeemers, cont. 3.00
13 I:Sister Trinity 3.00
14 Redeemers saga again. 3.00
15 F:Sister Trinity. 3.00
16 F:Sister Trinity. 3.00
17 Showdown 3.00
18 Reaction 3.00
19 Carnivale. 3.00
20 Twilight Earth 3.00
21 Lost Souls of Blue
    Mountain 2.50
Spec. Warrior Nun Areala/Razor:
    Revenge 3.00
Spec.A Revenge, deluxe 6.00

WARRIOR NUN BRIGANTIA
Antarctic Press, 2000
1 V:Fata Morgana 3.00
2 Sister Anna 3.00
3 . . . . 3.00

WARRIORS
1 . . . . 2.50
2 thru 7 . . . . @2.25

WARZONE
Entity, 1995
1 I:Bella & Supra. 3.00
2 F:Bladeback, Alloy, Granite 3.00
3 F:Bladeback. 3.00

WASTELAND
Oni Press, 2006
1 . . . . 15.00
2 . . . . 11.00
3 . . . . 8.00
4 . . . . 8.00
5 thru 13 . . . . @5.00
14 thru 22 . . . . @3.50

WEAPONS FILE
Antarctic Press, 2005
1 photo reference 5.00
2 photo reference 5.00
3 Manga 5.00

WEASEL
Fantagraphics, 1999
1 by Dave Cooper, 48-page 5.00
2 . . . . 5.00
3 . . . . 5.00
5 . . . . 5.00
6 . . . . 13.00
6a signed 19.95

WEATHER WOMAN
CPM Manga, 2000
1 signed & limited 15.00
4 thru 8 . . . . @3.00

WEBWITCH
Avatar Press, 1997
0 by Raff Ienco 3.00
1 (of 2) signed. 9.00
1 (of 2) 3.00
2 (of 2) 3.00
Boxed Set, all rare editions 35.00

WEBWITCH: PRELUDE TO WAR
Avatar Press, 1998
1 by Raff Jenco 3.00
1b Leather cover. 25.00

WEBWITCH: WAR
Avatar Press, 1998
1 (of 2) by Bill Maus 3.00
1b Leather cover. 25.00
2 conclusion 3.00

WEIRDFALL
Antarctic Press, 1995
1 I:Weirdfall. 2.75
2 O:Weirdfall 2.75
3 . . . . 2.75

WEIRD SPACE
ACG Comics, 2000
1 rep. collection. 3.00
2 pre-code sci-fi, BW 3.00
3 . . . . 3.00
4 . . . . 3.00
5 . . . . 3.00

WEIRDSVILLE
Blindwolf Studios, 1997
1 . . . . 3.50
1 2nd printing 3.00
2 . . . . 3.50
2 2nd printing 3.00
3 . . . . 3.50
3 2nd printing 3.00
4 . . . . 3.50
5 . . . . 3.00
6 The Usual Weirdoes, concl. 3.00
7 . . . . 3.00
8 An American Werewolf in
    Weirdsville, pt.1 (of 2) 3.00
9 An American Werewolf in
    Weirdsville, pt.2 . . . . 3.00
10 . . . . 3.00

WEIRDSVILLE/CRYBABY: HEY YOU TWO
Blindwolf Studios, 1999
1 . . . . 3.00

WEREWOLF
Blackthorne, 1988–89
1 TV tie-in 2.50
2 thru 7 . . . . @2.50

Werewolf #2
© Blackthorne

WESTERN TALES OF TERROR
Hoarse and Buggy Prod., 2004
1 . . . . 3.50
2 thru 5 . . . . @3.50

WHAT IS THE FACE?
A.C.E. Comics, 1986
1 SD/FMc,I:New Face. 2.50
2 SD/FMc 2.50
3 SD 2.50

WHISPERS & SHADOWS
Oasis
1 8 1/2 x 11. . . . . 2.50
1a Regular size. 2.50
2 8 1/2 x 11. . . . . 2.50
3 8 1/2 x 11. . . . . 2.50
4 thru 9 . . . . @2.50

WHITE DEVIL
Eternity, 1991
1 thru 6 adult. . . . . @2.50

WHITE ORCHID, THE
Atlantis
1 (of 6) 3.00
2 . . . . 3.00
3 . . . . 3.00
4 . . . . 3.50
5 `Death Trap,' pt.1 . . . . 3.00
6 The Price of Vengeance 3.50

WHITEOUT
Oni Press, 1998
1 (of 4) by Greg Rucka &
    Steve Leiber 3.00
2 . . . . 3.00
3 . . . . 3.00
4 conclusion 3.00

WHITEOUT: MELT
Oni Press, 1999
1 (of 4) by Greg Rucka
    & Steve Lieber 3.00
2 . . . . 3.00
3 . . . . 3.00
4 concl. 3.00

B & W PUB.

WHITE RAVEN
Visionary Publications
1 Government Intrigue	3.00
2	3.00
3 Mystery Man Gets Wheels	3.00
4 Facility	3.00
5 V:Douglas	3.00
6	3.00
7	3.00

WHITLEY STRIEBER'S BEYOND COMMUNION
Caliber, 1997
1 UFO Odyssey	3.00
1 signed	3.00
1 special edition, signed by Strieber	7.00
1a 2nd printing	3.00
2	3.00
3	3.00
4	3.00

WICKED
Millennium, 1994
1 thru 4	@2.50

WICKED: THE RECKONING
Millennium
1 R:Wicked	3.00
2 F:Rachel Blackstone	3.00

WIDOW
Ground Zero, 1996
Cinegraphic Spec.#1: Daughter of Darkness	4.00

WIDOW/LUXURA: BLOOD LUST
Ground Zero, 1996
Alpha x-over, pt.1	3.50
see Luxura/Widow for pt. 2

WIDOW: BOUND BY BLOOD
Ground Zero, 1996
1 thru 5 by Mike Wolfer	@3.50

WIDOW: PROGENY
Ground Zero, 1997
1 by Mike Wolfer & Karl Moline	3.00
2 (of 3)	3.00
3 concl.	3.00

WIDOW
Avatar Press, 1997
0 by Mike Wolfer	4.00
0b Black leather cover	25.00
0 signed	10.00

WIDOW: THE ORIGIN
Avatar Press, 1997
1 (of 3) by Mike Wolfer	4.00
1a leather cover	25.00
2 (of 3)	3.00

WILD, THE
1	2.50
2 thru 7	@2.50

WILDFLOWER
Sirius/Dog Star, 1998
1 by Billy Martinez	2.50
2 thru 6	@2.50

WILDFLOWER:
DARK EUPHORIA
Neko Press, 2004
1	3.00
2	3.00
1a thru 2a variant (c)s	@4.00

...THE LOST YESTERDAYS
Neko Press, 2003
1	3.00

...TRIBAL SCREAMS
Neko Press, 2002
1 Martinez (c)	3.00
1a Dark One (c)	5.00
2 thru 4	@3.00
Spec. Wildflower Y2K, 16-pg.	10.00

...TWO TALES
Neko Press, 2003
1-shot signed & numbered	3.00

WILD FRONTIER
Shanda Fantasy Arts, 2000
1 (of 2)	3.00
2 concl.	3.00
3	3.00

WILD KNIGHTS
Eternity, 1988
1	2.50
2 thru 10	@2.50
Shattered Earth Chron. #1	2.50

WILDLIFE
Antarctic, 1993
1	2.75
2 thru 12	@2.75

WILD THINGZ
ABC Comics, 1998
0 RCI & Armando Huerta	3.00
0a painted cover	6.00
0b Fan edition	6.00
0c Summer edition	6.00
1 (of 2) RCI	3.00
1a virgin cover	3.00
1b gold cover	6.00
1c Platinum cover	6.00

WILLOW
Angel Entertainment, 1996
0 commemorative edition	3.00
1	3.00
1 black magic foil edition	6.00
2	3.00
2 gold edition	8.00

WIND BLADE
1 Elford 1st Blair	40.00

WINGS
A-List Comics, 1997
1 rep. of golden age	2.50
2 thru 5	@3.00

WITCH
Amaze Ink/SLG, 2001
1 by Lorna Miller	3.00
2 thru 4	@3.00

WIZARD OF TIME
David House, 1986
1	2.50
1a 2nd printing(blue)	2.50
2 and 3	@2.50

Wizards of the Last Resort #1
© Blackthorne

WIZARDS OF THE LAST RESORT
Blackthorne, 1987
1	2.50

WOLFF & BYRD, COUNSELORS OF THE MACABRE
Exhibit A, 1994
1	6.00
1a new printing	3.00
2 thru 4	@3.50
5 thru 11	@2.50
12 thru 16 BLs	@2.50
17 thru 23	@2.50
Spec.#1 Greatest Writs (1997) BLs	3.00
Spec. #1 Secretary Mavis (1998)	3.00
Spec. #2 Secretary Mavis (1999)	3.00
Becomes:	

SUPERNATURAL LAW
Exhibit A Press, 2000
24	2.50
25 The end of 1999	2.50
26 Black Market Souls	2.50
27 Creatures of the Night, with lawyers	2.50
28 While the City Doesn't Sleep	2.50
29 thru 31	@2.50
32	3.00
33 thru 35	@2.50
36 thru 40	@3.00
45	3.50
Spec. #101 10th anniversary	3.50
1-shot First Amendment	3.50
Spec. Wolf & Byrd #1 new printing	3.00
Spec. #1 With a Silver Bullet	3.50
Spec. #1 At the Box Office	3.50
Spec. Wolff & Byrd The Movie	3.50

WORDSMITH
Renegade, 1985
1	3.00
2 thru 6	@2.50
7 thru 12	@2.50

Series 2, Caliber, 1996
1 thru 6	@3.00

WORLD HARDBALL LEAGUE
Titus Press, 1994
1 F:Big Bat 3.00
2 F:Big Bat 3.00
3 Mount Evrest 3.00
4 Juan Hernandez 3.00

WORLD OF WOOD
Eclipse, 1986
1 thru 4 see color
5 Flying Saucers 2.50

WORLDS OF H.P. LOVECRAFT
Caliber Tome Press, 1997
1-shot The Alchemist 3.00
1-shot The Tomb 3.00
1-shot The Lurking Fear 3.00
1-shot Beyond the Walls of Sleep . 3.00

WORLD WAR 2
New England Comics, 2001
3 Eastern Front, pt.2 . . . . 3.50
4 Falaise Pocket 3.50
5 D-Day 3.50
6 Tarawa 3.50
7 Afrika Korps 3.50
8 Midway 3.50

WORLD WAR 2: STALINGRAD
New England Comics, 2000
1 by Ron Ledwell 3.50
2 . . . . 3.50

WORLDWATCH
Austen Comics, 2004
1 thru 7 . . . . @3.00

WRETCH, THE
Caliber, 1996
1 PhH 3.00
2 PhH 3.00

Amaze Ink, 1997
3 PhH 3.00
4 PhH 3.00
5 PhH & Jim Woodyard 3.00
6 PhH & Bruce McCorkindale 3.00
7 PhH 3.00

WULF & BATSY
Viper Comics, 2008
1 thru 4 . . . . @3.25

WU WEI
Animus, 1995
1 'Debaser' 2.50
2 Blind Whisper 2.50
3 . . . . 2.50
4 . . . . 2.50
5 'Testament' pt.5 . . . . 2.50
6 by Oscar Stern 2.50
7 Explicador 3.00
8 Dead Skin 3.00
9 Apotheosis or Bang You're Dead. 3.00

WW2
New England Comics, 2003
1-shot Snipers 4.00
1-shot War in the Air 4.00
1-shot Mercenaries 4.00
1-shot U-Boats 4.00
1-shot Hitler's Special Forces 4.00
1-shot Last Ditch Stand at Berlin . . . 4.00

1-shot Hitler's Paratroopers
  The Assult on Crete 4.00
1-shot Tobruk 4.00
1-shot Rommel 4.00
1-shot Waffen Storm Troops 4.00
1-shot Flying Tigers 4.00

WW2: PRESENTS KAMAKAZI
New England Comics, 2007
1 . . . . 4.00

WYATT EARP: DODGE CITY
Moonstone, 2005
1 CDi 3.00
2 thru 3 CDi . . . . @3.00

WYRD: THE RELUCTANT WARRIOR
Amaze Ink, 1999
1 (of 6) JSn 3.00
2 . . . . 3.00
3 Telemarketing Horrors 3.00
4 Maxi-Man 3.00
5 thru 6 . . . . @3.00

XANADU
Thoughts & Images, 1988
1 thru 5 . . . . @2.50

Xenon #2
© Eclipse

XENON
Eclipse, 1987
1 . . . . 3.00
2 thru 23 . . . . @2.50

XENO'S ARROW
Cup O' Tea Studios, 1999
1 by Greg Beettam 2.50
2 thru 10 . . . . @2.50

Radio Comix, 2001
Book 2
1 (of 6) 3.00
2 thru 5 . . . . @3.00

XENOZOIC TALES
Kitchen Sink, 1986
1 by Mark Schultz 9.00
1a Reprint 2.50

2 . . . . 5.00
2a Reprint 2.50
3 . . . . 6.00
4 . . . . 5.00
5 thru 13 . . . . @5.00
14 MSh 5.00

X-FLIES BUG HUNT
Twist and Shout, 1997
1 Vampires 3.00
2 Monsters 3.00
3 Aliens 3.00
4 The Truth 3.00
Conspiracy 3.00
Spec. #1 Flies in Black 3.00

XIOLA
Zion Comics
1 thru 3 F:Kantasia . . . . @2.50
4 Visitor 2.50

XMEN
1 Parody 2.50

X-1999
Viz Communications
1 I:Kamir Shiro 2.75
2 thru 5 F:Princess Hitane . . . . . @2.75
6 Battle for X-1999 . . . . 2.75

X-THIEVES
1 . . . . 3.00
2 . . . . 2.50
3 . . . . 2.50

YAHOO
Fantagraphics, 1988
1 thru 4 . . . . @2.50

YAKUZA
Eternity, 1987
1 thru 5 . . . . @2.50

YAWN
Parody Press
1 Spawn parody 2.50
Enigma
1 Spawn parody rep.? 2.75

YELLOW CABALLERO
Viz Communications, 2001
1 thru 4 Pikachu's New Partner . @3.00

YETS
Airwave Comics, 2003
1 . . . . 3.50
2 . . . . 3.50
3 . . . . 3.50

YOU & ME
Ironcat, 2002
Volume 1
1 . . . . 3.00
2 thru 6 . . . . @3.00
Volume 2
1 . . . . 3.00

YOUNG DRACULA: PRAYER OF THE VAMPIRE
Boneyard Press, 1997
1 (of 5) sequel to Young Dracula:
  Diary of a Vampire 3.00
2 Empire of Madness, pt.2 . . . . . . 3.00

3 Children of Madness 3.00
4 Madness Prime 3.00
5 V:Cartiphilus. 4.00

YOUNG MASTERS
New Comics, 1987
1 thru 10 . . . . @2.50

YUGGOTH CREATURES
Avatar Press, 2004
1 . . . . 4.00
2 thru 3 . . . . @4.00
1a thru 3a wraparound (c). . . . . . @4.00
1b thru 3b connecting (c) 6.00

Z
Keystone Graphics, 1994
1 . . . . 2.75
2 House of Windsor-YakonaraI. . . . 2.75
3 House of Windsor-YakonaraII . . . 2.75

ZACHERLEY'S MIDNIGHT TERRORS
Chanting Monks Press, 2004
1 . . . . 4.00
2 . . . . 4.00
3 . . . . 4.00
4 . . . . 4.00

ZED
Gagne International, 2001
1 by Michel Gagne 3.00
2 . . . . 3.00
3 . . . . 3.50
4 . . . . 3.00
5 Resurrection 3.00
6 In the Shadow of Maxuss 3.00
7 thru 8 . . . . @3.50

ZELL THE SWORDDANCER
Thoughts & Images, 1986
1 Steve Gallacci 5.50
2 and 3 . . . . @2.50

ZEN BOUNTY HUNTER
SSSComics.Com, 2005
1 . . . . 3.00
2 thru 3 . . . . @3.00

ZEN ILLUSTRATED NOVELLA
Entity
1 thru 4 R:Bruce Lewis . . . . @3.00
5 Immortal Combat. 3.00
6 Bubble Economy 3.00
7 Zen City 3.00
8 V:Assassins 3.00

ZEN, INTER-GALACTIC NINJA
Zen, 1987
1 . . . . 15.00
2 . . . . 9.00
3 thru 9 . . . . @6.00
X-mas Spec #1,V:Black Hole Bob . . 3.00
[2nd Series]
1 `Down to Earth' 3.00
2 RA, A:Jeremy Baker 3.00
2a polybagged, limited 5.00
3 thru 5 . . . . @3.00
[3rd Series]
0 . . . . 3.00
1 thru 3 A:Niro. . . . . @3.00

Sourcebook #1. . . . . 3.50

ZEN: THE NEW ADVENTURES
Zen Comics, 1997
1 SSt & Joel Orbeta 2.50
2 . . . . 3.00
3 . . . . 3.00
4 . . . . 3.00

ZEN INTERGALACTIC NINJA: STARQUEST
Entity
1 thru 6 V:Nolan the Destroyer . . @3.00
7 V:Dimensional 3.00
8 thru 9 I:New Team . . . . @3.00
10 In Deep Space 3.00
11 Dimensional Terrorists. 3.00

ZEN INTERGALACTIC NINJA VS. MICHEAL JACK-ZEN
Entity
1 Cameos Galore 3.00

ZENISMS WIT AND WISDOMS
Entity
1 R:Bruce Lewis 3.00

ZEN: MISTRESS OF CHAOS
1 . . . . 3.00

ZENITH: PHASE II
Fleetway
1 GMo(s),SY,Rep.2000 AD 2.50

ZERO ZERO
Fantagraphics, 1995
1 thru 7 . . . . @5.00
8 . . . . 6.00
9 thru 15 . . . . @5.00
16 . . . . 6.00
17 thru 22 . . . . @5.00
23 F:`Tired'. 5.00
24 F:Smilin' Ed. 4.00
25 . . . . 4.00
26 final issue, 56-pg. 5.00
27 really final 64-pg. 5.00

ZETRAMAN
Antarctic, 1991
1 thru 3 . . . . @2.50
[Vol. 2], 1992
1 and 2 . . . . @2.75

ZETRAMAN: REVIVAL
Antarctic Press, 1993
1 thru 3 . . . . @2.75

ZILLION
Eternity, 1993
1 . . . . 2.50
2 thru 4 . . . . @2.50

ZOLASTRAYA AND THE BARD
Twilight Twins, 1987
1 thru 5 . . . . @2.50

TOM MASON & HARRISON FONG

Zillion #2
© Eternity

ZOMBIE COMMANDOS FROM HELL
Boneyard Press, 2002
1 . . . . 3.00
1a soundtrack edition 6.00
2 thru 3 . . . . @3.00
2a thru 3a soundtrack edition . . . @6.00
4 . . . . 3.00

ZOMBIE-SAMA
Narwain Publishing, 2006
1-shot BTi 5.00
1-shot variant (c) 5.00
1-shot special ed. 13.00

ZOMBIE HIGHWAY
Digital Webbing, 2004
1 . . . . 4.00
2 thru 3 . . . . @4.00

ZOMBIE WAR: EARTH MUST BE DESTROYED
Fantaco, 1993
1 thru 3 Kevin Eastman . . . . @4.00

ZONE CONTINUUM
Caliber
1 Master of the Waves 3.00
2 . . . . 3.00

ZOOT!
Fantagraphics, 1993
1 thru 5 . . . . @2.50

ZOT!
Eclipse, 1987
(#1-#10 Soo: Color)
11 New Series 3.00
12 thru 15. . . . . @3.00
16 A:De-Evolutionaries 3.00
17 thru 36. . . . . @3.00

ZU
Mu Press, 1995
1 thru 11 . . . . @3.00
12 `The Monkey Tales'. 3.00
13 thru 14. . . . . @3.00
15 `Curse of the Re-Possessed' . . . 3.00
16 thru 20. . . . . @3.00

Classics Illustrated

001-THE THREE MUSKETEERS
By Alexandre Dumas
10/41 (—) MKd(a&c),
Original,10¢ (c) Price 8,000.00
05/43 (10) MKd(a&c),
No(c)Price; rep 500.00
11/43 (15) MKd(a&c),Long
Island Independent Ed; 325.00
6/44 (18/20) MKd(a&c),
Sunrise Times Edition;rep . . . 225.00
7/44 (21) MKd(a&c),Richmond
Courier Edition;rep 200.00
6/46 (28) MKd(a&c);rep 150.00
4/47 (36) MKd(a&c),
New ClLogo;rep 75.00
6/49 (60) MKd(a&c),CI Logo;rep . . 50.00
10/49 (64) MKd(a&c),CI Logo;rep . 50.00
12/50 (78) MKd(a&c),15¢(c)
Price; CI Logo;rep 30.00
03/52 (93) MKd(a&c),
CI Logo;rep 30.00
11/53 (114) CI Logo;rep 25.00
09/56 (134) MKd(a&c),New
P(c),CI Logo,64 pgs;rep 30.00
03/58 (143) MKd(a&c),P(c),
CI Logo,64 pgs;rep 25.00
05/59 (150) GE&RC New Art,
P(c),ClLogo;rep 30.00
03/61 (149) GE&RC,P(c),
CI Logo;rep 18.00
62-63 (167) GE&RC,P(c),
CI Logo;rep 18.00
04/64 (167) GE&RC,P(c),
CI Logo;rep 18.00
01/65 (167) GE&RC,P(c),
CI Logo;rep 18.00
03/66 (167) GE&RC,P(c),
CI Logo;rep 18.00
11/67 (166) GE&RC,P(c),
CI Logo;rep 18.00
Sp/69 (166) GE&RC,P(c),25¢(c)
Price,ClLogo, Rigid(c);rep 18.00
Sp/71 (169) GE&RC,P(c),
CI Logo,Rigid(c);rep 18.00

002-IVANHOE
By Sir Walter Scott
1941 (—) EA,MKd(c),Original . 3,500.00
05/43 (1) EA,MKd(c),word "Presents"
Removed From(c);rep 400.00
11/43 (15) EA,MKd(c),Long Island
Independent Edition;rep 250.00
6/44 (18/20) EA,MKd(c),Sunrise
Times Edition;rep 200.00
07/44 (21) EA,MKd(c),Richmond
Courrier Edition;rep 175.00
06/46 (28) EA,MKd(c),rep 150.00
07/47 (36) EA,MKd(c),New
CI Logo; rep 100.00
06/49 (60) EA,MKd(c),CI Logo;rep 50.00
10/49 (64) EA,MKd(c),CI Logo;rep 40.00
12/50 (78) EA,MKd(c),15¢(c)
Price; CI Logo;rep 30.00
11/51 (89) EA,MKd(c),CI Logo;rep 25.00
04/53 (106) EA,MKd(c),CI
Logo;rep 20.00
07/54 (121) EA,MKd(c),CI
Logo;rep 30.00

CI #1-The Three Musketeers
© *Gilberton Publications*

01/57 (136) NN New Art,New
P(c),CI Logo;rep 30.00
01/58 (142) NN,P(c),CI Logo;rep . . 18.00
11/59 (153) NN,P(c),CI Logo;rep . . 18.00
03/61 (149) NN,P(c),CI Logo;rep . . 18.00
62/63 (167) NN,P(c),CI Logo;rep . . 15.00
05/64 (167) NN,P(c),CI Logo;rep . . 15.00
01/65 (167) NN,P(c),CI Logo;rep . . 15.00
03/66 (167) NN,P(c),CI Logo;rep . . 15.00
09/67 (166) NN,P(c),CI Logo;rep . . 15.00
1968 (166) NN,P(c),CI Logo;rep . . 15.00
Wr/69 (169) NN,P(c),CI
Logo Rigid(c);rep 15.00
Wr/71 (169) NN,P(c),CI
Logo,Rigid(c);rep 15.00

003-THE COUNT OF MONTE CRISTO
By Alexandre Dumas
03/42 (—) ASm(a&c),Orig 2,200.00
05/43 (10) ASm(a&c);rep 400.00
11/43 (15) ASm(a&c),Long Island
Independent Edition;rep 250.00
06/44 (18/20) ASm(a&c),
Sunrise Times Edition;rep . . . 225.00
06/44 (20) ASm(a&c),Sunrise
Times Edition;rep 200.00
07/44 (21) ASm(a&c),Richmond
Courier Edition;rep 175.00
06/46 (28) ASm(a&c);rep 150.00
04/47 (36) ASm(a&c),New
CI Logo; rep 100.00
06/49 (60) ASm(a&c),CI
Logo;rep 60.00
08/49 (62) ASm(a&c),CI
Logo;rep 75.00
05/50 (71) ASm(a&c),CI
Logo;rep 50.00
09/51 (87) ASm(a&c),15¢(c)
Price, CI Logo;rep 30.00
11/53 (113) ASm(a&c),
CI Logo; rep 25.00
11/56 (—) LC New Art,New
P(c), CI Logo;rep 25.00
03/58 (135) LC,P(c),CI Logo;rep . . 30.00
11/59 (153) LC,P(c),CI Logo;rep . . 18.00
03/61 (161) LC,P(c),CI Logo;rep . . 18.00
62/63 (167) LC,P(c),CI Logo;rep . . 15.00
07/64 (167) LC,P(c),CI Logo;rep . . 15.00
07/65 (167) LC,P(c),CI Logo;rep . . 15.00
07/66 (167) LC,P(c),CI Logo;rep . . 15.00
1968 (166) LC,P(c),25¢(c)
Price, CI Logo;rep 15.00
Wn/69 (169) LC,P(c),CI Logo,
Rigid(c);rep 15.00

004-THE LAST OF THE MOHICANS
By James Fenimore Cooper
08/42 (—) RR(a&c),Original . . 2,000.00
06/43 (12) RR(a&c),Price
Balloon Deleted;rep 400.00
11/43 (15) RR(a&c),Long Island
Independent Edition;rep 250.00
06/44 (20) RR(a&c),Long Island
Independent Edition;rep 225.00
07/44 (21) RR(a&c),Queens
Home News Edition;rep 200.00
06/46 (28) RR(a&c),rep 150.00
04/47 (36) RR(a&c),New
CI Logo; rep 100.00
06/49 (60) RR(a&c),CI Logo;rep . . 50.00
10/49 (64) RR(a&c),CI Logo;rep . . 35.00
12/50 (78) RR(a&c),15¢(c)
Price,CI Logo rep 35.00
11/51 (89) RR(a&c),CI Logo;rep . . 30.00
03/54 (117) RR(a&c),CI Logo;rep . 28.00
11/56 (135) RR,New P(c),
CI Logo; rep 28.00
11/57 (141) RR,P(c),CI Logo;rep . . 30.00
05/59 (150) JSe&StA New Art;
P(c), CI Logo;rep 35.00
03/61 (161) JSe&StA,P(c),CI
Logo; rep 15.00
62/63 (167) JSe&StA,P(c),CI
Logo; rep 15.00
06/64 (167) JSe&StA,P(c),CI
Logo; rep 15.00
08/65 (167) JSe&StA,P(c),CI
Logo; rep 15.00
08/66 (167) JSe&StA,P(c),CI
Logo; rep 15.00
1967 (166) JSe&StA,P(c),25¢(c)
Price, CI Logo;rep 15.00
Sp/69 (169) JSe&StA,P(c),CI
Logo, Rigid(c);rep 15.00

005-MOBY DICK
By Herman Melville
09/42 (—) LZ(a&c),Original . . 2,300.00
05/43 (10) LZ(a&c),Conray Products
Edition, No(c)Price;rep 450.00
11/43 (15) LZ(a&c),Long Island
Independent Edition;rep 300.00
06/44 (18/20) LZ(a&c),Sunrise
Times Edition;rep 250.00
07/44 (20) LZ(a&c),Sunrise
Times Edition;rep 225.00
07/44 (21) LZ(a&c),Sunrise
Times Edition;rep 200.00
06/46 (28) LZ(a&c);rep 150.00
04/47 (36) LZ(a&c),New CI
Logo;rep 100.00
06/49 (60) LZ(a&c),CI Logo;rep . . 50.00
08/49 (62) LZ(a&c),CI Logo;rep . . . 55.00
05/50 (71) LZ(a&c),CI Logo;rep . . . 40.00
09/51 (87) LZ(a&c),15¢(c)
Price, CI Logo;rep 30.00
04/54 (118) LZ(a&c),CI Logo;rep . . 25.00
03/56 (131) NN New Art,New
P(c), CI Logo;rep 35.00
05/57 (138) NN,P(c),CI Logo;rep . . 18.00

CI #13-Dr Jekyll & Mr Hyde
© Gilberton Publications

01/59 **(148)** NN,P(c),CI Logo;rep . . 18.00
09/60 **(158)** NN,P(c),CI Logo;rep . . 18.00
62/63 **(167)** NN,P(c),CI Logo;rep . . 18.00
06/64 **(167)** NN,P(c),CI Logo;rep . . 18.00
07/65 **(167)** NN,P(c),CI Logo;rep . . 18.00
03/66 **(167)** NN,P(c),CI Logo;rep . . 18.00
09/67 **(166)** NN,P(c),CI Logo;rep . . 18.00
Wn/69 **(166)** NN,P(c),25¢(c) Price,
CI Logo, Rigid(c);rep 25.00
Wn/71 **(169)** NN,P(c),CI Logo;rep . 20.00

006-A TALE OF TWO CITIES
By Charles Dickens
11/42 **(——)** StM(a&c),Original . . 2,000.00
09/43 **(14)** StM(a&c),No(c)
Price; rep 400.00
03/44 **(18)** StM(a&c),Long Island
Independent Edition;rep 275.00
06/44 **(20)** StM(a&c),Sunrise
Times Edition;rep 235.00
06/46 **(28)** StM(a&c);rep 150.00
09/48 **(51)** StM(a&c),New CI
Logo; rep 75.00
10/49 **(64)** StM(a&c),CI
Logo;rep 40.00
12/50 **(78)** StM(a&c),15¢(c)
Price, CI Logo; rep 30.00
11/51 **(89)** StM(a&c),CI Logo;rep . . 30.00
03/54 **(117)** StM(a&c),CI
Logo;rep 25.00
05/56 **(132)** JO New Art,New
P(c), CI Logo;rep 35.00
09/57 **(140)** JO,P(c),CI Logo;rep . . 15.00
11/57 **(147)** JO,P(c),CI Logo;rep . . 15.00
09/59 **(152)** JO,P(c),CI Logo;rep . 250.00
11/59 **(153)** JO,P(c),CI Logo;rep . . 18.00
03/61 **(149)** JO,P(c),CI Logo;rep . . 18.00
62/63 **(167)** JO,P(c),CI Logo;rep . . 15.00
06/64 **(167)** JO,P(c),CI Logo;rep . . 15.00
08/65 **(167)** JO,P(c),CI Logo;rep . . 15.00
05/67 **(166)** JO,P(c),CI Logo;rep . . 15.00
Fl/68 **(166)** JO,NN New P(c),
25¢(c)Price,CI Logo;rep 25.00
Sr/70 **(169)** JO,NN P(c),CI
Logo, Rigid(c);rep 20.00

007-ROBIN HOOD
By Howard Pyle
12/42 **(——)** LZ(a&c),Original . . . 1,400.00
06/43 **(12)** LZ(a&c),P.D.C.
on(c) Deleted;rep 350.00
03/44 **(18)** LZ(a&c),Long Island
Independent Edition;rep 225.00

06/44 **(20)** LZ(a&c),Nassau
Bulletin Edition;rep 250.00
10/44 **(22)** LZ(a&c),Queens
City Times Edition;rep 225.00
06/46 **(28)** LZ(a&c),rep 150.00
09/48 **(51)** LZ(a&c),New CI
Logo;rep 75.00
06/49 **(60)** LZ(a&c),CI Logo;rep . . 35.00
10/49 **(64)** LZ(a&c),CI Logo;rep . . 32.00
12/50 **(78)** LZ(a&c),CI Logo;rep . . 32.00
07/52 **(97)** LZ(a&c),CI Logo;rep . . 35.00
03/53 **(106)** LZ(a&c),CI Logo;rep. . 30.00
07/54 **(121)** LZ(a&c),CI Logo;rep. . 30.00
11/55 **(129)** LZ,New P(c),
CI Logo;rep 35.00
01/57 **(136)** JkS New Art,P(c);rep . 30.00
03/58 **(143)** JkS,P(c),CI Logo;rep . 18.00
11/59 **(153)** JkS,P(c),CI Logo;rep . 15.00
10/61 **(164)** JkS,P(c),CI Logo;rep . 15.00
62/63 **(167)** JkS,P(c),CI Logo;rep . 15.00
06/64 **(167)** JkS,P(c),CI Logo;rep . 20.00
05/65 **(167)** JkS,P(c),CI Logo;rep . 15.00
07/66 **(167)** JkS,P(c),CI Logo;rep . 15.00
12/67 **(166)** JkS,P(c),CI Logo;rep . 20.00
Sr/69 **(169)** JkS,P(c),CI
Logo, Rigid(c);rep 15.00

008-ARABIAN KNIGHTS
By Antoine Galland
03/43 **(——)** LCh(a&c),Original . . 2,200.00
09/43 **(14)** LCh(a&c);rep 750.00
01/44 **(17)** LCh(a&c),Long Island
Independent Edition;rep 750.00
06/44 **(20)** LCh(a&c),Nassau
Bulletin Edition,64 pgs;rep . . . 600.00
06/46 **(28)** LCh(a&c),rep 400.00
09/48 **(51)** LCh(a&c),New CI
Logo; rep 400.00
10/49 **(64)** LCh(a&c),CI
Logo;rep 300.00
12/50 **(78)** LCh(a&c),CI
Logo;rep 250.00
10/61 **(164)** ChB New Art,P(c),
CI Logo;rep 225.00

009-LES MISERABLES
By Victor Hugo
03/43 **(——)** RLv(a&c),Original . . 1,500.00
09/43 **(14)** RLv(a&c);rep 400.00
03/44 **(18)** RLv(a&c),Nassau
Bulletin Edition;rep 275.00
06/44 **(20)** RLv(a&c),Richmond
Courier Edition;rep 250.00
06/46 **(28)** RLv(a&c);rep 200.00
09/48 **(51)** RLv(a&c),New CI
Logo; rep 100.00
05/50 **(71)** RLv(a&c),CI
Logo;rep 75.00
09/51 **(87)** RLv(a&c),CI Logo,
15¢(c)Price;rep 60.00
03/61 **(161)** NN New Art,GMc
New P(c), CI Logo;rep. 60.00
09/63 **(167)** NN,GMc P(c),CI
Logo; rep 35.00
12/65 **(167)** NN,GMc P(c),CI
Logo; rep 35.00
1968 **(166)** NN,GMc P(c),25¢(c)
Price, CI Logo;rep 35.00

010-ROBINSON CRUSOE
By Daniel Defoe
04/43 **(——)** StM(a&c),Original . . 1,400.00
09/43 **(14)** StM(a&c);rep 400.00
03/44 **(18)** StM(a&c),Nassau Bulletin
Ed.,'Bill of Rights'Pge.64;rep. 300.00
06/44 **(20)** StM(a&c),Queens
Home News Edition;rep. 250.00
??/45 **(23)** StM(a&c);rep 150.00
06/46 **(28)** StM(a&c);rep 150.00
09/48 **(51)** StM(a&c),New CI
Logo; rep 75.00

10/49 **(64)** StM(a&c),CI Logo;rep . . 50.00
12/50 **(78)** StM(a&c),15¢(c)
Price, CI Logo;rep 35.00
07/52 **(97)** StM(a&c),CI Logo;rep. . 32.00
12/53 **(114)** StM(a&c),CI
Logo;rep 30.00
01/56 **(130)** StM,New P(c),CI
Logo; rep 32.00
09/57 **(140)** SmC New Art,P(c),
CI Logo;rep 32.00
11/59 **(153)** SmC,P(c),CI Logo;rep 16.00
10/61 **(164)** SmC,P(c),CI Logo;rep 16.00
62/63 **(167)** SmC,P(c),CI Logo;rep 18.00
07/64 **(167)** SmC,P(c),CI Logo;rep 20.00
05/65 **(167)** SmC,P(c),CI Logo;rep 16.00
06/66 **(167)** SmC,P(c),CI Logo;rep 18.00
Fl/68 **(166)** SmC,P(c),CI Logo,
25¢(c)Price;rep 18.00
1968 **(166)** SmC,P(c),CI Logo,No
Twin Circle Ad;rep 16.00
Sr/70 **(169)** SmC,P(c),CI Logo,
Rigid(c);rep 16.00

011-DON QUIXOTE
By Miguel de Cervantes Saavedra
05/43 **(——)** LZ(a&c),Original . . . 1,300.00
03/44 **(18)** LZ(a&c),Nassau
Bulletin Edition;rep 350.00
07/44 **(21)** LZ(a&c),Queens
Home News Edition;rep. 250.00
06/46 **(28)** LZ(a&c);rep 150.00
08/53 **(110)** LZ,TO New P(c),New
CI Logo;rep 50.00
05/60 **(156)** LZ,TO P(c),Pages
Reduced to 48,CI Logo;rep . . . 30.00
1962 **(165)** LZ,TO P(c),CI Logo;rep 20.00
01/64 **(167)** LZ,TO P(c),CI
Logo;rep 20.00
11/65 **(167)** LZ,TO P(c),CI
Logo;rep 20.00
1968 **(166)** LZ,TO P(c),CI Logo,
25¢(c)Price;rep 40.00

CI #18-The Hunchback of Notre Dame
© Gilberton Publications

012-RIP VAN WINKLE & THE HEADLESS HORSEMAN
By Washington Irving
06/43 **(——)** RLv(a&c),Original. 1,300.00
11/43 **(15)** RLv(a&c),Long Island
Independent Edition;rep 350.00
06/44 **(20)** RLv(a&c),Long Island
Independent Edition;rep 250.00

Classics Illus.

10/44 **(22)** RLv(a&c),Queens
City Times Edition;rep 225.00
06/46 **(28)** RLv(a&c);rep 150.00
06/49 **(60)** RLv(a&c),New Cl
Logo;rep 75.00
08/49 **(62)** RLv(a&c),Cl
Logo;rep 45.00
05/50 **(71)** RLv(a&c),Cl
Logo;rep 35.00
11/51 **(89)** RLv(a&c),15¢(c)
Price, Cl Logo;rep 30.00
04/54 **(118)** RLv(a&c),Cl
Logo;rep 32.00
05/56 **(132)** RLv,New P(c),
Cl Logo; rep 35.00
05/59 **(150)** NN New Art;P(c),
Cl Logo; rep 35.00
09/60 **(158)** NN,P(c),Cl Logo;rep. 20.00
62/63 **(167)** NN,P(c),Cl Logo;rep. 20.00
12/63 **(167)** NN,P(c),Cl Logo;rep. 20.00
04/65 **(167)** NN,P(c),Cl Logo;rep. 22.00
04/66 **(167)** NN,P(c),Cl Logo;rep. 20.00
1969 **(166)** NN,P(c),Cl Logo,
25¢(c)Price,Rigid;rep. 26.00
Sr/70 **(169)** NN,P(c),Cl Logo,
Rigid(c);rep 25.00

013-DR. JEKYLL
AND MR. HYDE
By Robert Louis Stevenson

08/43 **(—)** AdH(a&c),Original . . 2,000.00
11/43 **(15)** AdH(a&c),Long Island
Independent Edition;rep 500.00
06/44 **(20)** AdH(a&c),Long Island
Independent Edition;rep 300.00
06/46 **(28)** AdH(a&c),No(c)
Price; rep 225.00
06/49 **(60)** AdH,HcK New(c),New Cl
Logo,Pgs.reduced to 48;rep . . 75.00
08/49 **(62)** AdH,HcK(c),Cl
Logo;rep 45.00
05/50 **(71)** AdH,HcK(c),Cl
Logo;rep 40.00
09/51 **(87)** AdH,HcK(c),Erroneous
Return of Original Date,
Cl Logo;rep 40.00
10/53 **(112)** LC New Art,New
P(c), Cl Logo;rep 40.00
11/59 **(153)** LC,P(c),Cl Logo;rep . . 20.00
03/61 **(161)** LC,P(c),Cl Logo;rep . . 20.00
62/63 **(167)** LC,P(c),Cl Logo;rep . . 20.00
08/64 **(167)** LC,P(c),Cl Logo;rep . . 20.00
11/65 **(167)** LC,P(c),Cl Logo;rep . . 20.00
1968 **(166)** LC,P(c),Cl Logo,
25¢(c)Price;rep 22.00
Wr/69 **(169)** LC,P(c),Cl Logo,
Rigid(c);rep 20.00

014-WESTWARD HO!
By Charles Kingsley

09/43 **(—)** ASm(a&c),Orig.. . . . 3,000.00
11/43 **(15)** ASm(a&c),Long Island
Independent Edition;rep 900.00
07/44 **(21)** ASm(a&c);rep 650.00
06/46 **(28)** ASm(a&c),No(c)
Price; rep 600.00
11/48 **(53)** ASm(a&c),Pages reduced
to 48, New Cl Logo;rep 450.00

015-UNCLE TOM'S CABIN
By Harriet Beecher Stowe

11/43 **(—)** RLv(a&c),Original . . 1,200.00
11/43 **(15)** RLv(a&c),Blank
Price Circle, Long Island
Independent Ed.;rep 350.00
07/44 **(21)** RLv(a&c),Nassau
Bulletin Edition;rep 250.00
06/46 **(28)** RLv(a&c),No(c)
Price; rep. 200.00

CC #11 (Gilberton 1943)
© Gilberton Publications

11/48 **(53)** RLv(a&c),Pages Reduced
to 48, New Cl Logo;rep 75.00
05/50 **(71)** RLv(a&c),Cl Logo;rep. . 45.00
11/51 **(89)** RLv(a&c),15¢(c)
Price, Cl Logo;rep 45.00
03/54 **(117)** RLv,New P(c),Cl
Logo, Lettering Changes;rep. . 32.00
09/55 **(128)** RLv,P(c),"Picture
Progress"Promotion,Cl
Logo;rep 22.00
03/57 **(137)** RLv,P(c),Cl Logo;rep . 15.00
09/58 **(146)** RLv,P(c),Cl Logo;rep . 15.00
01/60 **(154)** RLv,P(c),Cl Logo;rep . 15.00
03/61 **(161)** RLv,P(c),Cl Logo;rep . 17.00
62/63 **(167)** RLv,P(c),Cl Logo;rep . 15.00
06/64 **(167)** RLv,P(c),Cl Logo;rep . 15.00
05/65 **(167)** RLv,P(c),Cl Logo;rep . 15.00
05/67 **(166)** RLv,P(c),Cl Logo;rep . 15.00
Wr/69 **(166)** RLv,P(c),Cl
Logo, Rigid(c);rep 26.00
Sr/70 **(169)** RLv,P(c),Cl
Logo, Rigid(c);rep 25.00

016-GULLIVER'S TRAVELS
By Johnathan Swift

12/43 **(—)** LCh(a&c),Original. 1,200.00
06/44 **(18/20)** LCh(a&c),Queen's
Home News Edition,No(c)Price;
rep 300.00
10/44 **(22)** LCh(a&c),Queen's
Home News Editon;rep 225.00
06/46 **(28)** LCh(a&c);rep 150.00
06/49 **(60)** LCh(a&c),Pgs. Reduced
To 48, New Cl Logo;rep 75.00
08/49 **(62)** LCh(a&c),Cl Logo;rep . 45.00
10/49 **(64)** LCh(a&c),Cl Logo;rep . 45.00
12/50 **(78)** LCh(a&c),15¢(c)
Price, Cl Logo;rep 35.00
11/51 **(89)** LCh(a&c),Cl Logo;rep. . 30.00
03/60 **(155)** LCh,New P(c),Cl
Logo; rep 35.00
1962 **(165)** LCh,P(c),Cl Logo;rep . 20.00
05/64 **(167)** LCh,P(c),Cl Logo;rep . 20.00
11/65 **(167)** LCh,P(c),Cl Logo;rep . 20.00
1968 **(166)** LCh,P(c),Cl Logo,
25¢(c)Price;rep 20.00
Wr/69 **(169)** LCh,P(c),Cl
Logo, Rigid(c);rep 20.00

017-THE DEERSLAYER
By James Fenimore Cooper

01/44 **(—)** LZ(a&c),Original . . 1,000.00
03/44 **(18)** LZ(a&c),No(c)Price;
rep 350.00

10/44 **(22)** LZ(a&c),Queen's
City Times Edition;rep 200.00
06/46 **(28)** LZ(a&c);rep 150.00
06/49 **(60)** LZ(a&c),Pgs. Reduced
to 48,New Cl Logo;rep 75.00
10/49 **(64)** LZ(a&c),Cl Logo;rep. . . 35.00
07/51 **(85)** LZ(a&c),15¢(c)
Price, Cl Logo;rep 30.00
04/54 **(118)** LZ(a&c),Cl Logo;rep . . 28.00
05/56 **(132)** LZ(a&c),Cl Logo;rep. . 25.00
11/66 **(167)** LZ(a&c),Cl Logo;rep. . 25.00
1968 **(166)** LZ,StA New P(c),Cl
Logo, 25¢(c)Price;rep 35.00
Sg/71 **(169)** LZ,StA P(c),Cl Logo,
Rigid(c), Letters From Parents
and Educators;rep 25.00

018-THE HUNCHBACK
OF NOTRE DAME
By Victor Hugo

03/44 **(—)** ASm(a&c),Original
Gilberton Edition 1,400.00
03/44 **(—)** ASm(a&c),Original
Island Publications Edition . 1,200.00
06/44 **(18/20)** ASm(a&c),Queens
Home News Edition;rep. 350.00
10/44 **(22)** ASm(a&c),Queens
City Times Edition;rep 250.00
06/46 **(28)** ASm(a&c);rep. 225.00
06/49 **(60)** ASm,HcK New(c)8 Pgs.
Deleted, New Cl Logo;rep. . . . 75.00
08/49 **(62)** ASm,HcK(c),Cl
Logo;rep 40.00
12/50 **(78)** ASm,HcK(c),15¢(c)
Price; Cl Logo;rep 35.00
11/51 **(89)** ASm,HcK(c),Cl
Logo;rep 32.00
04/54 **(118)** ASm,HcK(c),Cl
Logo;rep 35.00
09/57 **(140)** ASm,New P(c),Cl
Logo; rep 32.00
09/58 **(146)** ASm,P(c),Cl Logo;rep 32.00
09/60 **(158)** GE&RC New Art,GMc
New P(c),Cl Logo;rep 20.00
1962 **(165)** GE&RC,GMc P(c),Cl
Logo; rep 20.00
09/63 **(167)** GE&RC,GMc P(c),Cl
Logo; rep 20.00
10/64 **(167)** GE&RC,GMc P(c),Cl
Logo; rep 20.00
04/66 **(167)** GE&RC,GMc P(c),Cl
Logo; rep 20.00
1968 **(166)** GE&RC,GMc P(c),Cl
Logo, 25¢(c)Price;rep 20.00
Sr/70 **(169)** GE&RC,GMc P(c),Cl
Logo, Rigid(c);rep 20.00

019-HUCKLEBERRY FINN
By Mark Twain

04/44 **(—)** LZ(a&c),Original
Gilberton Edition 800.00
04/44 **(—)** LZ(a&c),Original Island
Publications Company Ed. . . 850.00
03/44 **(18)** LZ(a&c),Nassau
Bulletin Editon;rep 350.00
10/44 **(22)** LZ(a&c),Queens City
Times Edition;rep 250.00
06/46 **(28)** LZ(a&c);rep 200.00
06/49 **(60)** LZ(a&c),New Cl Logo,
Pgs.Reduced to 48;rep 75.00
08/49 **(62)** LZ(a&c),Cl Logo;rep. . . 40.00
12/50 **(78)** LZ(a&c),Cl Logo;rep. . . 35.00
11/51 **(89)** LZ(a&c),Cl Logo;rep. . . 30.00
03/54 **(117)** LZ(a&c),Cl Logo;rep . . 30.00
03/56 **(131)** FrG New Art,New
P(c), Cl Logo; rep 30.00
09/57 **(140)** FrG,P(c),Cl Logo;rep . 20.00
05/59 **(150)** FrG,P(c),Cl Logo;rep . 20.00
09/60 **(158)** FrG,P(c),Cl Logo;rep . 20.00
1962 **(165)** FrG,P(c),Cl Logo;rep . . 20.00
62/63 **(167)** FrG,P(c),Cl Logo;rep . 20.00

06/64 **(167)** FrG,P(c),Cl Logo;rep . 20.00
06/65 **(167)** FrG,P(c),Cl Logo;rep . 20.00
10/65 **(167)** FrG,P(c),Cl Logo;rep . 20.00
09/67 **(166)** FrG,P(c),Cl Logo;rep . 20.00
Wr/69 **(166)** FrG,P(c),Cl Logo,
25¢(c)Price, Rigid(c);rep 20.00
Sr/70 **(169)** FrG,P(c),Cl Logo,
Rigid(c);rep 20.00

020-THE CORSICAN BROTHERS
By Alexandre Dumas
06/44 **(—)** ASm(a&c),Original
Gilberton Edition 700.00
06/44 **(—)** ASm(a&c),Original
Courier Edition. 550.00
06/44 **(—)** ASm(a&c),Original Long
Island Independent Edition . . 550.00
10/44 **(22)** ASm(a&c),Queens
City Times Edition;rep 275.00
06/46 **(28)** ASm(a&c);rep 250.00
06/49 **(60)** ASm(a&c),No(c)Price,
New Cl Logo,Pgs. Reduced
to 48;rep 225.00
08/49 **(62)** ASm(a&c),Cl
Logo;rep 175.00
12/50 **(78)** ASm(a&c),15¢(c)
Price, Cl Logo;rep 165.00
07/52 **(97)** ASm(a&c),Cl
Logo;rep 150.00

CC #19, Huckleberry Finn
© Gilberton Publications

021-FAMOUS MYSTERIES
By Sir Arthur Conan Doyle Guy de Maupassant & Edgar Allan Poe
07/44 **(—)** AdH,LZ,ASm(a&c),
Original Gilberton Edition . . 1,400.00
07/44 **(—)** AdH,LZ,ASm(a&c),
Original Island Publications
Edition; No Date or Indicia 1,500.00
07/44 **(—)** AdH,LZ,ASm(a&c),
Original Richmond Courier
Edition. 1,300.00
10/44 **(22)** AdH,LZ,ASm(a&c),
Nassau Bulletin Edition;rep . . 500.00
09/46 **(30)** AdH,LZ,ASm(a&c);
rep 350.00
08/49 **(62)** AdH,LZ,ASm(a&c),
New Cl Logo;rep 300.00
04/50 **(70)** AdH,LZ,ASm(a&c),
Cl Logo;rep 275.00
07/51 **(85)** AdH,LZ,ASm(a&c),
15¢(c) Price,Cl Logo;rep 250.00
12/53 **(114)** ASm,AdH,LZ,New
P(c), Cl Logo;rep 250.00

022-THE PATHFINDER
By James Fenimore Cooper
10/44 **(—)** LZ(a&c),Original
Gilberton Edition 650.00
10/44 **(—)** LZ(a&c),Original
Island Publications Edition; . . 550.00
10/44 **(—)** LZ(a&c),Original
Queens County Times Edition 550.00
09/46 **(30)** LZ(a&c),No(c)
Price;rep 200.00
06/49 **(60)** LZ(a&c),New Cl Logo,
Pgs.Reduced To 48;rep 50.00
08/49 **(62)** LZ(a&c),Cl Logo;rep . . . 45.00
04/50 **(70)** LZ(a&c),Cl Logo;rep . . . 35.00
07/51 **(85)** LZ(a&c),15¢(c)
Price, Cl Logo;rep 32.00
04/54 **(118)** LZ(a&c),Cl Logo;rep . . 30.00
05/56 **(132)** LZ(a&c),Cl Logo;rep . . 30.00
09/58 **(146)** LZ(a&c),Cl Logo;rep . . 35.00
11/63 **(167)** LZ,NN New P(c),Cl
Logo; rep 30.00
12/65 **(167)** LZ,NN P(c),Cl
Logo;rep 30.00
08/67 **(166)** LZ,NN P(c),Cl
Logo;rep 30.00

023-OLIVER TWIST
By Charles Dickens (First Classic produced by the Iger shop)
07/45 **(—)** AdH(a&c),Original . . . 700.00
09/46 **(30)** AdH(a&c),Price
Circle is Blank;rep 450.00
06/49 **(60)** AdH(a&c),Pgs. Reduced
To 48, New Cl Logo;rep 50.00
08/49 **(62)** AdH(a&c),Cl
Logo;rep 45.00
05/50 **(71)** AdH(a&c),Cl
Logo;rep 35.00
07/51 **(85)** AdH(a&c),15¢(c)
Price Cl Logo;rep 32.00
04/52 **(94)** AdH(a&c),Cl
Logo;rep 32.00
04/54 **(118)** AdH(a&c),Cl
Logo;rep 30.00
01/57 **(136)** AdH,New P(c),Cl
Logo; rep 30.00
05/59 **(150)** AdH,P(c),Cl Logo;rep . 25.00
1961 **(164)** AdH,P(c),Cl Logo;rep . 25.00
10/61 **(164)** GE&RC New Art,P(c),
Cl Logo;rep 35.00
62/63 **(167)** GE&RC,P(c),Cl
Logo;rep 15.00
08/64 **(167)** GE&RC,P(c),Cl
Logo;rep 15.00
12/65 **(167)** GE&RC,P(c),
Cl Logo;rep 15.00
1968 **(166)** GE&RC,P(c),Cl
Logo, 25¢(c)Price;rep 15.00
Wr/69 **(169)** GE&RC,P(c),Cl
Logo, Rigid(c);rep 15.00

024-A CONNECTICUT YANKEE IN KING ARTHUR'S COURT
By Mark Twain
09/45 **(—)** JH(a&c),Original 550.00
09/46 **(30)** JH(a&c),Price Circle
Blank;rep 200.00
06/49 **(60)** JH(a&c),8 Pages
Deleted,New Cl Logo;rep 50.00
08/49 **(62)** JH(a&c),Cl Logo;rep . . . 45.00
05/50 **(71)** JH(a&c),Cl Logo;rep . . . 35.00
09/51 **(87)** JH(a&c),15¢(c) Price
Cl Logo;rep 30.00
07/54 **(121)** JH(a&c),Cl Logo;rep . . 30.00
09/57 **(140)** JkS New Art,New
P(c),Cl Logo; rep 35.00
11/59 **(153)** JkS,P(c),Cl Logo;rep . 18.00

1961 **(164)** JkS,P(c),Cl Logo;rep. . 15.00
62/63 **(167)** JkS,P(c),Cl Logo;rep . 15.00
07/64 **(167)** JkS,P(c),Cl Logo;rep . 15.00
06/66 **(167)** JkS,P(c),Cl Logo;rep . 15.00
1968 **(166)** JkS,P(c),Cl logo,
25¢(c)Price;rep 15.00
Sg/71 **(169)** JkS,P(c),Cl Logo,
Rigid(c);rep 15.00

025-TWO YEARS BEFORE THE MAST
By Richard Henry Dana Jr.
10/45 **(—)** RWb,DvH,Original; . . 600.00
09/46 **(30)** RWb,DvH,Price Circle
Blank;rep 200.00
06/49 **(60)** RWb,DvH,8 Pages
Deleted,New Cl Logo;rep 50.00
08/49 **(62)** RWb,DvH,Cl Logo;rep . 45.00
05/50 **(71)** RWb,DvH,Cl Logo;rep . 35.00
07/51 **(85)** RWb,DvH,15¢(c) Price
Cl Logo;rep 30.00
12/53 **(114)** RWb,DvH,Cl Logo;rep 28.00
05/60 **(156)** RWb,DvH,New P(c),
Cl Logo, 3 Pgs. Replaced
By Fillers;rep 32.00
12/63 **(167)** RWb,DvH,P(c),Cl
Logo; rep 15.00
12/65 **(167)** RWb,DvH,P(c),Cl
Logo; rep 15.00
09/67 **(166)** RWb,DvH,P(c),Cl
Logo; rep 15.00
Wr/69 **(169)** RWb,DvH,P(c),25¢(c)
Price, Cl Logo,Rigid(c);rep . . . 15.00

026-FRANKENSTEIN
By Mary Wollstonecraft Shelley
12/45 **(—)** RWb&ABr(a&c),
Original 1,500.00
09/46 **(30)** RWb&ABr(a&c),
Price Circle Blank;rep 400.00
06/49 **(60)** RWb&ABr(a&c),
New Cl Logo;rep 175.00
08/49 **(62)** RWb&ABr(a&c),
Cl Logo;rep 165.00
05/50 **(71)** RWb&ABr(a&c),
Cl Logo;rep 75.00
04/51 **(82)** RWb&ABr(a&c),
15¢(c) Price,Cl Logo;rep 65.00
03/54 **(117)** RWb&ABr(a&c),
Cl Logo;rep 30.00
09/58 **(146)** RWb&ABr,NS
New P(c), Cl Logo; rep 35.00
11/59 **(153)** RWb&ABr,NS
P(c),Cl Logo; rep 50.00
01/61 **(160)** RWb&ABr,NS
P(c),Cl Logo; rep 16.00
165 **(1962)** RWb&ABr,NS P(c),
Cl Logo; rep 16.00
62/63 **(167)** RWb&ABr,NS P(c),
Cl Logo; rep 15.00
06/64 **(167)** RWb&ABr,NS P(c),
Cl logo; rep 15.00
06/65 **(167)** RWb&ABr,NS P(c),
Cl Logo; rep 15.00
10/65 **(167)** RWb&ABr,NS P(c),
Cl Logo; rep 15.00
09/67 **(166)** RWb&ABr,NS P(c),
Cl Logo; rep. 15.00
Fl/69 **(169)** RWb&ABr,NS P(c),25¢(c)
Price,Cl Logo,Rigid(c);rep . . . 15.00
Sg/71 **(169)** RWb&ABr,NS P(c),
Cl Logo, Rigid(c);rep 15.00

027-THE ADVENTURES MARCO POLO
By Marco Polo & Donn Byrne
04/46 **(—)** HFl(a&c);Original. . . 550.00
09/46 **(30)** HFl(a&c);rep 200.00

Classics Illus.

04/50 **(70)** HFI(a&c),8 Pages Deleted,
No(c) Price,New CI Logo;rep . 45.00
09/51 **(87)** HFI(a&c),15¢(c)
Price,CI Logo;rep 30.00
03/54 **(117)** HFI(a&c),CILogo;rep. . 25.00
01/60 **(154)** HFI,New P(c),CI
Logo;rep 25.00
1962 **(165)** HFI,P(c),CI Logo;rep . . 15.00
04/64 **(167)** HFI,P(c),CI Logo;rep . . 15.00
06/66 **(167)** HFI,P(c),CI Logo;rep . . 15.00
Sg/69 **(169)** HFI,P(c),CI Logo,
25¢(c)Price,Rigid(c);rep. 15.00

028-MICHAEL STROGOFF
By Jules Verne
06/46 **(——)** AdH(a&c),Original . . . 550.00
09/48 **(51)** AdH(a&c),8 Pages
Deleted,New CI Logo;rep . . . 200.00
01/54 **(115)** AdH,New P(c),CI
Logo; rep 45.00
03/60 **(155)** AdH,P(c),CI Logo;rep. . 20.00
11/63 **(167)** AdH,P(c),CI Logo;rep. . 20.00
07/66 **(167)** AdH,P(c),CI Logo;rep. . 20.00
Sr/69 **(169)**AdH,NN,NewP(c),25¢(c)
Price, CI Logo,Rigid(c);rep . . . 30.00

029-THE PRINCE
AND THE PAUPER
By Mark Twain
07/46 **(——)** AdH(a&c),Original . . . 850.00
06/49 **(60)** AdH,New HcK(c),New CI
Logo,8 Pages Deleted;rep. . . 100.00
08/49 **(62)** AdH,HcK(c),CILogo;rep 50.00
05/50 **(71)** AdH,HcK(c),CILogo;rep 35.00
03/52 **(93)** AdH,HcK(c),CILogo;rep 32.00
12/53 **(114)** AdH,HcK(c),CI
Logo;rep 30.00
09/55 **(128)** AdH,New P(c),CI
Logo; rep 30.00
05/57 **(138)** AdH,P(c),CI Logo;rep. . 18.00
05/59 **(150)** AdH,P(c),CI Logo;rep. . 18.00
1961 **(164)** AdH,P(c),CI Logo;rep . . 18.00
62/63 **(167)** AdH,P(c),CI Logo;rep. . 18.00
07/64 **(167)** AdH,P(c),CI Logo;rep. . 18.00
11/65 **(167)** AdH,P(c),CI Logo;rep. . 18.00
1968 **(166)** AdH,P(c),CI Logo,
25¢(c)Price;rep 18.00
Sr/70 **(169)** AdH,P(c),CI Logo,
Rigid(c);rep 18.00

030-THE MOONSTONE
By William Wilkie Collins
09/46 **(——)** DRi(a&c),Original 550.00
06/49 **(60)** DRi(a&c),8 Pages
Deleted,New CI Logo;rep . . . 100.00
04/50 **(70)** DRi(a&c),CI Logo;rep. . 65.00
03/60 **(155)** DRi,LbC New P(c),
CI Logo;rep 90.00
1962 **(165)** DRi,LbC P(c),CI Logo;
rep 35.00
01/64 **(167)** DRi,LbC P(c),CI Logo;
rep 28.00
09/65 **(167)** DRi,LbC P(c),CI Logo;
rep 20.00
1968 **(166)** DRi,LbC P(c),CI Logo,
25¢(c)Price;rep 18.00

031-THE BLACK ARROW
By Robert Louis Stevenson
10/46 **(——)** AdH(a&c),Original . . . 500.00
09/48 **(51)** AdH(a&c),8 Pages
Deleted,New CI Logo;rep 75.00
10/49 **(64)** AdH(a&c),CI
Logo;rep 35.00
09/51 **(87)** AdH(a&c),15¢(c)
Price;CI Logo;rep 30.00
06/53 **(108)** AdH(a&c),CI
Logo;rep 28.00
03/55 **(125)** AdH(a&c),CI
Logo;rep 27.00

03/56 **(131)** AdH,New P(c),CI
Logo; rep 22.00
09/57 **(140)** AdH,P(c),CI Logo;rep. . 20.00
01/59 **(148)** AdH,P(c),CI Logo;rep. . 20.00
03/61 **(161)** AdH,P(c),CI Logo;rep. . 20.00
62/63 **(167)** AdH,P(c),CI Logo;rep. . 20.00
07/64 **(167)** AdH,P(c),CI logo;rep . 20.00
11/65 **(167)** AdH,P(c),CI Logo;rep. . 20.00
1968 **(166)** AdH,P(c),CI Logo,
25¢(c)Price;rep 20.00

032-LORNA DOONE
By Richard Doddridge
Blackmore
12/46 **(——)** MB(a&c),Original 550.00
10/49 **(53/64)** MB(a&c),8 Pages
Deleted,New CI Logo;rep . . . 150.00
07/51 **(85)** MB(a&c),15¢(c)
Price, CI Logo;rep 65.00
04/54 **(118)** MB(a&c),CI Logo;rep . 35.00
05/57 **(138)** MB,New P(c); Old(c)
Becomes New Splash Pge.,CI
Logo;rep 35.00
05/59 **(150)** MB,P(c),CI Logo;rep. . 20.00
1962 **(165)** MB,P(c),CI Logo;rep . . 20.00
01/64 **(167)** MB,P(c),CI Logo;rep. . 22.00
11/65 **(167)** MB,P(c),CI Logo;rep. . 22.00
1968 **(166)** MB,New P(c),
CI Logo;rep 35.00

033-THE ADVENTURES
OF SHERLOCK HOLMES
By Sir Arthur Conan Doyle
01/47 **(——)** LZ,HcK(c),Original . 1,800.00
11/48 **(53)** LZ,HcK(c),"A Study in Scarlet"
Deleted,New CI Logo 700.00
05/50 **(71)** LZ,HcK(c),CI Logo;rep 500.00
11/51 **(89)** LZ,HcK(c),15¢(c)
Price,CI Logo;rep 400.00

034-MYSTERIOUS ISLAND
By Jules Verne
Last Classic Comic
02/47 **(——)** RWb&DvH,Original . . 600.00
06/49 **(60)** RWb&DvH,8 Pages
Deleted,New CI Logo;rep 65.00
08/49 **(62)** RWb&DvH,CI Logo;rep 45.00
05/50 **(71)** RWb&DvH,CI Logo;rep 65.00
12/50 **(78)** RWb&DvH,15¢(c) Price,
CI Logo;rep 35.00
02/52 **(92)** RWb&DvH,CI Logo;rep 35.00
03/54 **(117)** RWb&DvH,CI Logo;
rep 35.00

CI #33, Sherlock Holmes
© Gilberton Publications

09/57 **(140)** RWb&DvH,New P(c),
CI Logo;rep 35.00
05/60 **(156)** RWb&DvH,P(c),CI
Logo;rep 20.00
10/63 **(167)** RWb&DvH,P(c),CI
Logo;rep 20.00
05/64 **(167)** RWb&DvH,P(c),CI
Logo;rep 20.00
06/66 **(167)** RWb&DvH,P(c),CI
logo;rep 20.00
1968 **(166)** RWb&DvH,P(c),CI Logo,
25¢(c)Price;rep 20.00

CLASSICS ILLUSTRATED
Gilberton 1947-60s

035-LAST DAYS
OF POMPEII
By Lord Edward Bulwer Lytton
First Classics Illustrated
03/47 **(——)** HcK(a&c),Original . . . 600.00
03/61 **(161)** JK,New P(c),
15¢(c)Price;rep 65.00
01/64 **(167)** JK,P(c);rep 30.00
07/66 **(167)** JK,P(c);rep 30.00
Sg/70 **(169)** JK,P(c),25¢(c)
Price, Rigid(c);rep 30.00

036-TYPEE
By Herman Melville
04/47 **(——)** EzW(a&c),Original . . . 350.00
10/49 **(64)** EzW(a&c),No(c)price,
8 pages deleted;rep. 90.00
03/60 **(155)** EzW,GMc New
P(c);rep 35.00
09/63 **(167)** EzW,GMc P(c);rep . . 25.00
07/65 **(167)** EzW,GMc P(c);rep . . 25.00
Sr/69 **(169)** EzW,GMc P(c),25¢(c)
Price, Rigid(c);rep 25.00

037-THE PIONEERS
By James Fenimore Cooper
05/47 **(37)** RP(a&c),Original 350.00
08/49 **(62)** RP(a&c),8 Pages
Deleted;rep 45.00
04/50 **(70)** RP(a&c);rep 35.00
02/52 **(92)** RP(a&c),15¢(c)price;
rep 35.00
04/54 **(118)** RP(a&c);rep 30.00
03/56 **(131)** RP(a&c);rep 30.00
05/56 **(132)** RP(a&c);rep 30.00
11/59 **(153)** RP(a&c);rep 25.00
05/64 **(167)** RP(a&c);rep 25.00
06/66 **(167)** RP(a&c);rep 25.00
1968 **(166)** RP,TO New P(c),
25¢(c)Price;rep 35.00

038-ADVENTURES
OF CELLINI
By Benvenuto Cellini
06/47 **(——)** AgF(a&c),Original . . . 450.00
1961 **(164)** NN New Art,New P(c);
rep 35.00
12/63 **(167)** NN,P(c);rep 25.00
07/66 **(167)** NN,P(c);rep 25.00
Sg/70 **(169)** NN,P(c),25¢(c)
Price, Rigid(c);rep 28.00

039-JANE EYRE
By Charlotte Bronte
07/47 **(——)** HyG(a&c),Original . . . 450.00
06/49 **(60)** HyG(a&c),No(c)Price,
8 pages deleted;rep. 50.00
08/49 **(62)** HyG(a&c);rep 45.00
05/50 **(71)** HyG(a&c);rep 35.00
02/52 **(92)** HyG(a&c),15¢(c)
Price; rep 32.00
04/54 **(118)** HyG(a&c);rep 32.00

01/58 **(142)** HyG,New P(c);rep. . . . 32.00
01/60 **(154)** HyG,P(c);rep. 32.00
1962 **(165)** HjK New Art,P(c);rep . . 32.00
12/63 **(167)** HjK,P(c);rep 32.00
04/65 **(167)** HjK,P(c);rep 32.00
08/66 **(167)** HjK,P(c);rep 32.00
1968 **(166)** HjK,NN New P(c);rep . 75.00

040-MYSTERIES

**(The Pit & the Pendulum,
The Adventures of Hans Pfall,
Fall of the House of Usher)
By Edgar Allan Poe**
08/47 **(——)** AgF,HyG,HcK(a&c),
Original 1,000.00
08/49 **(62)** AgF,HyG,HcK(a&c),
8 Pages deleted;rep 350.00
09/50 **(75)** AgF,HyG,
HcK(a&c);rep. 300.00
02/52 **(92)** AgF,HyG,HcK(a&c)
15¢(c) Price;rep. 250.00

041-TWENTY YEARS AFTER

By Alexandre Dumas
09/47 **(——)** RBu(a&c),Original . . . 600.00
08/49 **(62)** RBu,HcK New(c),No(c)
Price, 8 Pages Deleted;rep . . . 65.00
12/50 **(78)** RBu,HcK(c),15¢(c)
Price;rep 45.00
05/60 **(156)** RBu,DgR New P(c);
rep 35.00
12/63 **(167)** RBu,DgR P(c);rep . . . 50.00
11/66 **(167)** RBu,DgR P(c);rep. . . . 50.00
Sg/70 **(169)** RBu,DgR P(c),25¢(c)
Price, Rigid(c);rep 50.00

042-SWISS FAMILY ROBINSON

By Johann Wyss
10/47 **(42)** HcK(a&c),Original. . . . 300.00
08/49 **(62)** HcK(a&c),No(c)price,
8 Pages Deleted,Not Every Issue
Has 'Gift Box' Ad;rep 75.00
09/50 **(75)** HcK(a&c);rep 35.00
03/52 **(93)** HcK(a&c);rep 32.00
03/54 **(117)** HcK(a&c);rep 30.00
03/56 **(131)** HcK,New P(c);rep. . . . 28.00
03/57 **(137)** HcK,P(c);rep 28.00
11/57 **(141)** HcK,P(c);rep 28.00
09/59 **(152)** NN New art,P(c);rep. . 28.00
09/60 **(158)** NN,P(c);rep 25.00
12/63 **(165)** NN,P(c);rep 30.00
12/63 **(167)** NN,P(c);rep 15.00
04/65 **(167)** NN,P(c);rep 15.00
05/66 **(167)** NN,P(c);rep. 15.00
11/67 **(166)** NN,P(c);rep. 15.00
Sg/69 **(169)** NN,P(c);rep 15.00

043-GREAT EXPECTATIONS

By Charles Dickens
11/47 **(——)** HcK(a&c),Original . . 1,400.00
08/49 **(62)** HcK(a&c),No(c)Price,
8 pages deleted;rep. 900.00

044-MYSTERIES OF PARIS

By Eugene Sue
12/47 **(44)** HcK(a&c),Original . . 1,000.00
08/47 **(62)** HcK(a&c),No(c)Price,
8 Pages Deleted,Not Every Issue
Has 'Gift Box' Ad;rep 400.00
12/50 **(78)** HcK(a&c),15¢(c)
Price; rep 350.00

045-TOM BROWN'S SCHOOL DAYS

By Thomas Hughes
01/48 **(44)** HFI(a&c),Original,
1st 48 Pge. Issue 250.00
10/49 **(64)** HFI(a&c),No(c)
Price;rep 60.00
03/61 **(161)** JTg New Art,GMc
New P(c);rep 30.00
02/64 **(167)** JTg,GMc P(c);rep . . . 20.00
08/66 **(167)** JTg,GMc P(c);rep . . . 20.00
1968 **(166)** JTg,GMc P(c),
25¢(c)Price;rep. 20.00

046-KIDNAPPED

By Robert Louis Stevenson
04/48 **(47)** RWb(a&c),Original . . . 250.00
08/49 **(62)** RWb(a&c),Red Circle
Either Blank or With 10¢;rep . 100.00
12/50 **(78)** RWb(a&c),15¢(c)
Price; rep 35.00
09/51 **(87)** RWb(a&c);rep. 32.00
04/54 **(118)** RWb(a&c);rep 30.00
03/56 **(131)** RWb,New P(c);rep . . . 30.00
09/57 **(140)** RWb,P(c);rep. 18.00
05/59 **(150)** RWb,P(c);rep. 18.00
05/60 **(156)** RWb,P(c);rep. 18.00
1961 **(164)** RWb,P(c),Reduced Pge.
Width;rep 18.00
62/63 **(167)** RWb,P(c);rep. 18.00
03/64 **(167)** RWb,P(c);rep. 18.00
06/65 **(167)** RWb,P(c);rep. 18.00
12/65 **(167)** RWb,P(c);rep. 18.00
09/67 **(167)** RWb,P(c);rep 18.00
Wr/69 **(166)** RWb,P(c),25¢(c)
Price, Rigid(c);rep 18.00
Sr/70 **(169)** RWb,P(c),Rigid(c);rep. 18.00

047-TWENTY THOUSAND LEAGUES UNDER THE SEA

By Jules Verne
05/58 **(47)** HcK(a&c),Original. . . . 250.00
10/49 **(64)** HcK(a&c),No(c)
Price; rep. 45.00
12/50 **(78)** HcK(a&c),15¢(c)
Price; rep. 35.00
04/52 **(94)** HcK(a&c);rep 35.00
04/54 **(118)** HcK(a&c);rep 30.00
09/55 **(128)** HcK,New P(c);rep . . . 30.00
07/56 **(133)** HcK,P(c);rep. 25.00
09/57 **(140)** HcK,P(c);rep. 18.00
01/59 **(148)** HcK,P(c);rep. 18.00
05/60 **(156)** HcK,P(c);rep. 18.00
62/63 **(165)** HcK,P(c);rep. 18.00
05/48 **(167)** HcK,P(c);rep. 18.00
03/64 **(167)** HcK,P(c);rep. 18.00
08/65 **(167)** HcK,P(c);rep. 18.00
10/66 **(167)** HcK,P(c);rep. 18.00
1968 **(166)** HcK,NN New P(c),
25¢(c)Price;rep 25.00
Sg/70 **(169)** HcK,NN New P(c),
Rigid(c);rep 25.00

048-DAVID COPPERFIELD

By Charles Dickens
06/48 **(47)** HcK(a&c),Original. . . . 250.00
10/49 **(64)** HcK(a&c),Price Circle
Replaced By Image of Boy
Reading;rep 45.00
09/51 **(87)** HcK(a&c),15¢(c)
Price; rep. 35.00
07/54 **(121)** HcK,New P(c);rep. . . . 30.00
10/56 **(130)** HcK,P(c);rep. 18.00
09/57 **(140)** HcK,P(c);rep. 18.00
01/59 **(148)** HcK,P(c);rep. 18.00
05/60 **(156)** HcK,P(c);rep 18.00

62/63 **(167)** HcK,P(c);rep. 18.00
04/64 **(167)** HcK,P(c);rep. 18.00
06/65 **(167)** HcK,P(c);rep. 18.00
05/67 **(166)** HcK,P(c);rep. 18.00
R/67 **(166)** HcK,P(c);rep. 25.00
Sg/69 **(166)** HcK,P(c),25¢(c)
Price, Rigid(c);rep 18.00
Wr/69 **(169)** HcK,P(c),Rigid(c);rep. 18.00

*CI #47, 20,000 Leagues under the Sea
© Gilberton Publications*

049-ALICE IN WONDERLAND

By Lewis Carroll
07/48 **(47)** AB(a&c),Original 275.00
10/49 **(64)** AB(a&c),No(c)Price;
rep 75.00
07/51 **(85)** AB(a&c),15¢(c)Price;
rep 50.00
03/60 **(155)** AB,New P(c);rep. 50.00
1962 **(165)** AB,P(c);rep. 35.00
03/64 **(167)** AB,P(c);rep 30.00
06/66 **(167)** AB,P(c);rep 30.00
Fl/68 **(166)** AB,TO New P(c),25¢(c)
Price, New Soft(c);rep 50.00
Fl/68 **(166)** AB,P(c),Both Soft &
Rigid(c)s;rep. 100.00

050-ADVENTURES OF TOM SAWYER

By Mark Twain
08/48 **(51)** ARu(a&c),Original. . . . 250.00
09/48 **(51)** ARu(a&c),Original. . . . 300.00
10/49 **(64)** ARu(a&c),No(c)
Price; rep. 35.00
12/50 **(78)** ARu(a&c),15¢(c)
Price; rep. 30.00
04/52 **(94)** ARu(a&c);rep 30.00
12/53 **(114)** ARu(a&c);rep 30.00
03/54 **(117)** ARu(a&c);rep 25.00
05/56 **(132)** ARu(a&c);rep 25.00
09/57 **(140)** ARu,New P(c);rep. . . . 22.00
05/59 **(150)** ARu,P(c);rep. 25.00
10/61 **(166)** New Art,P(c);rep. 15.00
62/63 **(167)** P(c);rep. 15.00
01/65 **(167)** P(c);rep. 15.00
05/66 **(167)** P(c);rep. 15.00
12/67 **(166)** P(c);rep. 15.00
Fl/69 **(169)** P(c),25¢(c) Price,
Rigid(c);rep 15.00
Wr/71 **(169)** P(c);rep. 15.00

Classics Illus.

All comics prices listed are for *Near Mint* condition.

051-THE SPY
By James Fenimore Cooper
09/48 **(51)** AdH(a&c),Original,
Maroon(c) 250.00
09/48 **(51)** AdH(a&c),Original,
Violet(c) 225.00
11/51 **(89)** AdH(a&c),15¢(c)
Price; rep 35.00
07/54 **(121)** AdH(a&c),rep 30.00
07/57 **(139)** AdH,New P(c);rep. . . . 30.00
05/60 **(156)** AdH,P(c);rep. 18.00
11/63 **(167)** AdH,P(c);rep. 18.00
07/66 **(167)** AdH,P(c);rep. 18.00
Wr/69 **(166)** AdH,P(c),25¢(c)Price,
Both Soft & Rigid(c)s;rep. 35.00

052-THE HOUSE OF SEVEN GABLES
By Nathaniel Hawthorne
10/48 **(53)** HyG(a&c),Original . . . 250.00
11/51 **(89)** HyG(a&c),15¢(c)
Price; rep 35.00
07/54 **(121)** HyG(a&c);rep 30.00
01/58 **(142)** GWb New Art,New
P(c); rep. 35.00
05/60 **(156)** GWb,P(c);rep 18.00
1962 **(165)** GWb,P(c);rep 18.00
05/64 **(167)** GWb,P(c);rep 18.00
03/66 **(167)** GWb,P(c);rep 18.00
1968 **(166)** GWb,P(c),25¢(c)
Price; rep 18.00
Sg/70 **(169)** GWb,P(c),Rigid(c);rep 18.00

053-A CHRISTMAS CAROL
By Charles Dickens
11/48 **(53)** HcK(a&c),Original. . . . 300.00

054-MAN IN THE IRON MASK
By Alexandre Dumas
12/48 **(55)** AgF,HcK(c),Original . . 250.00
03/52 **(93)** AgF,HcK(c),15¢(c)
Price; rep 45.00
09/53 **(111)** AgF,HcK(c);rep 60.00
01/58 **(142)** KBa New Art,New
P(c); rep. 35.00
01/60 **(154)** KBa,P(c);rep. 18.00
1962 **(165)** KBa,P(c);rep 18.00
05/64 **(167)** KBa,P(c);rep. 18.00
04/66 **(167)** KBa,P(c);rep. 18.00
Wr/69 **(166)** KBa,P(c),25¢(c)
Price, Rigid(c);rep 18.00

055-SILAS MARINER
By George Eliot
01/49 **(55)** AdH,HcK(c),Original . . 250.00
09/50 **(75)** AdH,HcK(c),Price Circle
Blank,'Coming next'Ad(not
usually in reps.);rep. 45.00
07/52 **(97)** AdH,HcK(c);rep 32.00
07/54 **(121)** AdH,New P(c);rep. . . . 30.00
01/56 **(130)** AdH,P(c);rep. 18.00
09/57 **(140)** AdH,P(c);rep. 18.00
01/60 **(154)** AdH,P(c);rep. 18.00
1962 **(165)** AdH,P(c);rep 18.00
05/64 **(167)** AdH,P(c);rep. 18.00
06/65 **(167)** AdH,P(c);rep. 18.00
05/67 **(166)** AdH,P(c);rep. 18.00
Wr/69 **(166)** AdH,P(c),25¢(c) Price,
Rigid(c);rep,Soft & Stiff 35.00

056-THE TOILERS OF THE SEA
By Victor Hugo
02/49 **(55)** AgF(a&c),Original. . . . 350.00

01/62 **(165)** AT New Art,New
P(c); rep. 60.00
03/64 **(167)** AT,P(c);rep. 35.00
10/66 **(167)** AT,P(c);rep. 35.00

057-THE SONG OF HIAWATHA
By Henry Wadsworth Longfellow
03/49 **(55)** AB(a&c),Original. . . . 200.00
09/50 **(75)** AB(a&c),No(c)price,'
Coming Next'Ad(not usually
found in reps.);rep 50.00
04/52 **(94)** AB(a&c),15¢(c)
Price;rep 35.00
04/54 **(118)** AB(a&c),rep 32.00
09/56 **(134)** AB,New P(c);rep 30.00
07/57 **(139)** AB,P(c);rep. 18.00
01/60 **(154)** AB,P(c);rep. 18.00
62/63 **(167)** AB,P(c),Erroneosly
Has Original Date;rep 18.00
09/64 **(167)** AB,P(c);rep. 18.00
10/65 **(167)** AB,P(c);rep. 18.00
Fl/68 **(166)** AB,P(c),25¢(c)Price;
rep. 18.00

058-THE PRAIRIE
By James Fenimore Cooper
04/49 **(60)** RP(a&c),Original 200.00
08/49 **(62)** RP(a&c);rep 75.00
12/50 **(78)** RP(a&c),15¢(c) Price
In Double Circle;rep. 35.00
12/53 **(114)** RP(a&c);rep 30.00
03/56 **(131)** RP(a&c);rep 30.00
05/56 **(132)** RP(a&c);rep 30.00
09/58 **(146)** RP,New P(c);rep. 30.00
03/60 **(155)** RP,P(c);rep 20.00
05/64 **(167)** RP,P(c);rep. 18.00
04/66 **(167)** RP,P(c);rep. 18.00
Sr/69 **(169)** RP,P(c),25¢(c)
Price; Rigid(c);rep 18.00

059-WUTHERING HEIGHTS
By Emily Bronte
05/49 **(60)** HcK(a&c),Original. . . . 225.00
07/51 **(85)** HcK(a&c),15¢(c)
Price; rep 50.00
05/60 **(156)** HcK,GB New P(c);rep 35.00
01/64 **(167)** HcK,GB P(c);rep. 25.00
10/66 **(167)** HcK,GB P(c);rep. 25.00
Sr/69 **(169)** HcK,GBP(c),25¢(c)
Price, Rigid(c);rep 22.00

060-BLACK BEAUTY
By Anna Sewell
06/49 **(62)** AgF(a&c),Original 200.00
08/49 **(62)** AgF(a&c);rep 250.00
07/51 **(85)** AgF(a&c),15¢(c) Price;
rep. 40.00
09/60 **(158)** LbC&NN&StA New
Art, LbC New P(c);rep. 35.00
02/64 **(167)** LbC&NN&StA,LbC
P(c); rep. 30.00
03/66 **(167)** LbC&NN&StA,LbC
P(c); rep. 30.00
03/66 **(167)** LbC&NN&StA,LbC
P(c), 'Open Book'Blank;rep. . . . 30.00
1968 **(166)** LbC&NN&StA,AIM New
P(c) 25¢(c) Price;rep. 75.00

061-THE WOMAN IN WHITE
By William Wilke Collins
07/49 **(62)** AB(a&c),Original,
Maroon & Violet(c)s. 250.00
05/60 **(156)** AB,DgR New P(c);rep 40.00
01/64 **(167)** AB,DgR P(c);rep. 30.00
1968 **(166)** AB,DgR P(c),
25¢(c)Price;rep 30.00

CI #58 The Prairie
© Gilberton Publications

062-WESTERN STORIES
(The Luck of Roaring Camp & The Outcasts of Poker Flat)
By Bret Harte
08/49 **(62)** HcK(a&c),Original. . . . 200.00
11/51 **(89)** HcK(a&c),15¢(c)
Price; rep 40.00
07/54 **(121)** HcK(a&c),rep 32.00
03/57 **(137)** HcK,New P(c);rep. . . . 30.00
09/59 **(152)** HcK,P(c);rep. 20.00
10/63 **(167)** HcK,P(c);rep. 20.00
06/64 **(167)** HcK,P(c);rep. 18.00
11/66 **(167)** HcK,P(c);rep. 18.00
1968 **(166)** HcK,TO New P(c),
25¢ Price;rep. 30.00

063-THE MAN WITHOUT A COUNTRY
By Edward Everett Hale
09/49 **(62)** HcK(a&c),Original. . . . 200.00
12/50 **(78)** HcK(a&c),15¢(c)Price
In Double Circles;rep. 40.00
05/60 **(156)** HcK,GMc New P(c);
rep. 35.00
01/62 **(165)** AT New Art,GMc P(c),
Added Text Pages;rep 32.00
03/64 **(167)** AT,GMc P(c);rep. 18.00
08/66 **(167)** AT,GMc P(c);rep. 18.00
Sr/69 **(169)** AT,GMc P(c),25¢(c)
Price, Rigid(c);rep 18.00

064-TREASURE ISLAND
By Robert Louis Stevenson
10/49 **(62)** AB(a&c),Original. 250.00
04/51 **(82)** AB(a&c),15¢(c)
Price;rep 40.00
03/54 **(117)** AB(a&c);rep 32.00
03/56 **(131)** AB,New P(c);rep. 30.00
05/57 **(138)** AB,P(c);rep. 18.00
09/58 **(146)** AB,P(c);rep. 18.00
09/60 **(158)** AB,P(c);rep. 18.00
1962 **(165)** AB,P(c);rep 18.00
62/63 **(167)** AB,P(c);rep. 18.00
06/64 **(167)** AB,P(c);rep. 18.00
12/65 **(167)** AB,P(c);rep. 18.00
10/67 **(166)** AB,P(c);rep. 22.00
10/67 **(166)** AB,P(c),GRIT Ad
Stapled In Book;rep. 100.00
Sg/69 **(169)** AB,P(c),25¢(c)
Price, Rigid(c);rep 18.00

Classics Illus.

065-BENJAMIN FRANKLIN
By Benjamin Franklin
11/49 **(64)** AB,RtH,GS(Iger Shop),
  HcK(c),Original 200.00
03/56 **(131)** AB,RtH,GS(Iger Shop),
  New P(c) ;rep 35.00
01/60 **(154)** AB,RtH,GS(Iger Shop),
  P(c);rep 20.00
02/64 **(167)** AB,RtH,GS(Iger Shop),
  P(c);rep 18.00
04/66 **(167)** AB,RtH,GS(Iger Shop),
  P(c);rep 18.00
Fl/69 **(169)** AB,RtH,GS(Iger Shop),
  P(c), 25¢(c)Price,Rigid(c);rep . 20.00

066-THE CLOISTER AND THE HEARTH
By Charles Reade
12/49 **(67)** HcK(a&c),Original. . . . 400.00

067-THE SCOTTISH CHIEFS
By Jane Porter
01/50 **(67)** AB(a&c),Original. 200.00
07/51 **(85)** AB(a&c),15¢(c)
  Price;rep 40.00
04/54 **(118)** AB,New P(c);rep 32.00
01/57 **(136)** AB,New P(c);rep. 32.00
01/60 **(154)** AB,P(c);rep. 20.00
11/63 **(167)** AB,P(c);rep. 25.00
08/65 **(167)** AB,P(c);rep. 20.00

068-JULIUS CEASAR
By William Shakespeare
02/50 **(70)** HcK(a&c),Original. . . . 200.00
07/51 **(85)** HcK(a&c),15¢(c)
  Price; rep 40.00
06/53 **(108)** HcK(a&c);rep 32.00
05/60 **(156)** HcK,LbC New P(c);rep35.00
1962 **(165)** GE&RC New Art,
  LbC P(c);rep 35.00
02/64 **(167)** GE&RC,LbC P(c);rep . 18.00
10/65 **(167)** GE&RC,LbC P(c),Tarzan
  Books Inside(c);rep 25.00
1967 **(166)** GE&RC,LbC P(c);rep . 18.00
Wr/69 **(169)** GE&RC,LbC P(c),
  Rigid(c);rep 18.00

069-AROUND THE WORLD IN 80 DAYS
By Jules Verne
03/50 **(70)** HcK(a&c),Original. . . . 200.00
09/51 **(87)** HcK(a&c),15¢(c)
  Price; 45.00
03/55 **(125)** HcK(a&c);rep 32.00
01/57 **(136)** HcK,New P(c);rep. . . . 32.00
09/58 **(146)** HcK,P(c);rep. 20.00
09/59 **(152)** HcK,P(c);rep. 20.00
1961 **(164)** HcK,P(c);rep. 20.00
62/63 **(167)** HcK,P(c);rcp. 18.00
07/64 **(167)** HcK,P(c);rep. 18.00
11/65 **(167)** HcK,P(c);rep. 18.00
07/67 **(166)** HcK,P(c);rep. 18.00
Sg/69 **(169)** HcK,P(c),25¢(c)
  Price, Rigid(c);rep 18.00

070-THE PILOT
By James Fenimore Cooper
04/50 **(71)** AB(a&c),Original. 175.00
10/50 **(75)** AB(a&c),15¢(c)
  Price;rep 45.00
02/52 **(92)** AB(a&c);rep 32.00
03/55 **(125)** AB(a&c);rep 35.00
05/60 **(156)** AB,GMc New P(c);rep 30.00
02/64 **(167)** AB,GMc P(c);rep 30.00
05/66 **(167)** AB,GMc P(c);rep 28.00

071-THE MAN WHO LAUGHS
By Victor Hugo
05/50 **(71)** AB(a&c),Original. . . . 250.00
01/62 **(165)** NN,NN New P(c);rep 125.00
04/64 **(167)** NN,NN P(c);rep 100.00

072-THE OREGON TRAIL
By Francis Parkman
06/50 **(73)** HcK(a&c),Original. . . . 150.00
11/51 **(89)** HcK(a&c),15¢(c)
  Price; rep. 40.00
07/54 **(121)** HcK(a&c);rep 32.00
03/56 **(131)** HcK,New P(c);rep. . . . 30.00
09/57 **(140)** HcK,P(c);rep. 20.00
05/59 **(150)** HcK,P(c);rep. 18.00
01/61 **(164)** HcK,P(c);rep. 18.00
62/63 **(167)** HcK,P(c);rep. 18.00
08/64 **(167)** HcK,P(c);rep. 18.00
10/65 **(167)** HcK,P(c);rep. 18.00
1968 **(166)** HcK,P(c),25¢(c)Price;
  rep 18.00

073-THE BLACK TULIP
By Alexandre Dumas
07/50 **(75)** AB(a&c),Original. . . . 550.00

074-MR. MIDSHIPMAN EASY
By Captain Frederick Marryat
08/50 **(75)** BbL,Original 500.00

075-THE LADY OF THE LAKE
By Sir Walter Scott
09/50 **(75)** HcK(a&c),Original. . . . 150.00
07/51 **(85)** HcK(a&c),15¢(c)
  Price; rep. 40.00
04/54 **(118)** HcK(a&c);rep 35.00
07/57 **(139)** HcK,New P(c);rep. . . . 35.00
01/60 **(154)** HcK,P(c);rep. 18.00
1962 **(165)** HcK,P(c);rep. 18.00
04/64 **(167)** HcK,P(c);rep. 18.00
05/66 **(167)** HcK,P(c);rep. 18.00
Sg/69 **(169)** HcK,P(c),25¢(c)
  Price, Rigid(c);rep 18.00

076-THE PRISONER OF ZENDA
By Anthony Hope Hawkins
10/50 **(75)** HcK(a&c),Original. . . . 150.00
07/51 **(85)** HcK(a&c),15¢(c) Price;
  rep 40.00
09/53 **(111)** HcK(a&c),rep 35.00
09/55 **(128)** HcK,New P(c);rep. . . . 35.00
09/59 **(152)** HcK,P(c);rep. 20.00
1962 **(165)** HcK,P(c);rep 18.00
04/64 **(167)** HcK,P(c);rep. 18.00
09/66 **(167)** HcK,P(c);rep. 18.00
Fl/69 **(169)** HcK,P(c),25¢(c) Price,
  Rigid(c);rep 18.00

077-THE ILLIAD
By Homer
11/50 **(78)** AB(a&c),Original. 175.00
09/51 **(87)** AB(a&c),15¢(c)
  Price;rep 40.00
07/54 **(121)** AB(a&c);rep 35.00
07/57 **(139)** AB,New P(c);rep. 35.00
05/59 **(150)** AB,P(c);rep. 20.00
1962 **(165)** AB,P(c);rep. 18.00
10/63 **(167)** AB,P(c);rep. 18.00
07/64 **(167)** AB,P(c);rep. 18.00
05/66 **(167)** AB,P(c);rep. 18.00
1968 **(166)** AB,P(c),25¢(c)
  Price;rep 18.00

078-JOAN OF ARC
By Frederick Shiller
12/50 **(78)** HcK(a&c),Original. . . . 150.00
09/51 **(87)** HcK(a&c),15¢(c)
  Price; rep. 40.00
11/53 **(113)** HcK(a&c);rep 35.00
09/55 **(128)** HcK,New P(c);rep. . . . 35.00
09/57 **(140)** HcK,P(c);rep. 20.00
05/59 **(150)** HcK,P(c);rep. 20.00
11/60 **(159)** HcK,P(c);rep. 18.00
62/63 **(167)** HcK,P(c);rep. 18.00
12/63 **(167)** HcK,P(c);rep. 18.00
06/65 **(167)** HcK,P(c);rep. 18.00
06/67 **(166)** HcK,P(c);rep. 18.00
Wr/69 **(166)** HcK,TO New P(c),
  25¢(c)Price, Rigid(c);rep 35.00

079-CYRANO DE BERGERAC
By Edmond Rostand
01/51 **(78)** AB(a&c),Original,Movie
  Promo Inside Front(c) 175.00
07/51 **(85)** AB(a&c),15¢(c)
  Price;rep 40.00
04/54 **(118)** AB(a&c);rep 35.00
07/56 **(133)** AB,New P(c);rep. 35.00
05/60 **(156)** AB,P(c);rep. 30.00
08/64 **(167)** AB,P(c);rep. 30.00

080-WHITE FANG
By Jack London
(Last Line Drawn (c)
02/51 **(79)** AB(a&c),Original. 175.00
09/51 **(87)** AB(a&c);rep 40.00
03/55 **(125)** AB(a&c);rep 35.00
05/56 **(132)** AB,New P(c);rep. 35.00
09/57 **(140)** AB,P(c);rep. 20.00
11/59 **(153)** AB,P(c);rep. 20.00
62/63 **(167)** AB,P(c);rep. 18.00
09/64 **(167)** AB,P(c);rep. 18.00
07/65 **(167)** AB,P(c);rep. 18.00
06/67 **(166)** AB,P(c);rep. 18.00
Fl/69 **(169)** AB,P(c),25¢(c)
  Price, Rigid(c);rep 18.00

081-THE ODYSSEY
By Homer
(P(c)s From Now on)
03/51 **(82)** HyG,AB P(c),Original . 175.00
08/64 **(167)** HyG,AB P(c);rep. 30.00
10/66 **(167)** HyG,AB P(c);rep. 30.00
Sg/69 **(169)** HyG,TyT New P(c),
  Rigid(c);rep 35.00

CI #75, Around the World in 80 Days

All comics prices listed are for *Near Mint* condition.

082-THE MASTER OF BALLANTRAE

By Robert Louis Stevenson
04/51 **(82)** LDr,AB P(c),Original . . 150.00
08/64 **(167)** LDr,AB P(c);rep 30.00
Fl/68 **(166)** LDr,Syk New P(c),
Rigid(c);rep 35.00

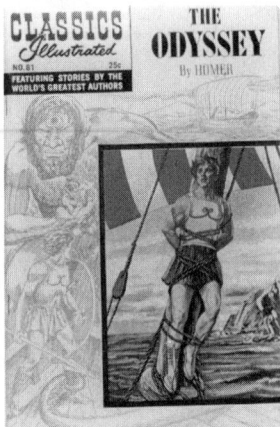

CI #96, The Odyssey
© Gilberton Publications

083-THE JUNGLE BOOK

By Rudyard Kipling
05/51 **(85)** WmB&AB,AB P(c),
Original 150.00
08/53 **(110)** WmB&AB,AB P(c);rep 20.00
03/55 **(125)** WmB&AB,AB P(c);rep 20.00
05/56 **(134)** WmB&AB,AB P(c);rep 20.00
01/58 **(142)** WmB&AB,AB P(c);rep 20.00
05/59 **(150)** WmB&AB,AB P(c);rep 18.00
11/60 **(159)** WmB&AB,AB P(c);rep 18.00
62/63 **(163)** WmB&AB,AB P(c);rep 18.00
03/65 **(167)** WmB&AB,AB P(c);rep 18.00
11/65 **(167)** WmB&AB,AB P(c);rep 18.00
05/66 **(167)** WmB&AB,AB P(c);rep 18.00
1968 **(166)** NN Art,NN New P(c),
Rigid(c);rep 35.00

084-THE GOLD BUG & OTHER STORIES

(Inc. The Telltale Heart & The Cask of Amontillado)
By Edgar Allan Poe
06/51 **(85)** AB,RP,JLv,AB P(c),
Original 200.00
07/64 **(167)** AB,RP,JLv,AB
P(c);rep 125.00

085-THE SEA WOLF

By Jack London
08/51 **(85)** AB,AB P(c),Original . . 150.00
07/54 **(121)** AB,AB P(c);rep 20.00
05/56 **(132)** AB,AB P(c);rep 20.00
11/57 **(141)** AB,AB P(c);rep 20.00
03/61 **(161)** AB,AB P(c);rep 18.00
02/64 **(167)** AB,AB P(c);rep 18.00
11/65 **(167)** AB,AB P(c);rep 18.00
Fl/69 **(169)** AB,AB P(c),25¢(c)
Price,Rigid(c);rep 18.00

086-UNDER TWO FLAGS

By Oiuda
08/51 **(87)** MDb,AB P(c),Original. 125.00
03/54 **(117)** MDb,AB P(c);rep 25.00

07/57 **(139)** MDb,AB P(c);rep 20.00
09/60 **(158)** MDb,AB P(c);rep 20.00
02/64 **(167)** MDb,AB P(c);rep 18.00
08/66 **(167)** MDb,AB P(c);rep 18.00
Sr/69 **(169)** MDb,AB P(c),25¢(c)
Price, Rigid(c);rep 18.00

087-A MIDSUMMER NIGHTS DREAM

By William Shakespeare
09/51 **(87)** AB,AB P(c),Original . . 125.00
03/61 **(161)** AB,AB P(c);rep 20.00
04/64 **(167)** AB,AB P(c);rep 18.00
05/66 **(167)** AB,AB P(c);rep 18.00
Sr/69 **(169)** AB,AB P(c),25¢(c)
Price; rep 18.00

088-MEN OF IRON

By Howard Pyle
10/51 **(89)** HD,LDr,GS,Original . . 125.00
01/60 **(154)** HD,LDr,GS,P(c);rep . . 20.00
01/64 **(167)** HD,LDr,GS,P(c);rep . . 18.00
1968 **(166)** HD,LDr,GS,P(c),
25¢(c)Price;rep 18.00

089-CRIME AND PUNISHMENT

By Fedor Dostoevsky
11/51 **(89)** RP,AB P(c),Original . . 125.00
09/59 **(152)** RP,AB P(c);rep 25.00
04/64 **(167)** RP,AB P(c);rep 18.00
05/66 **(167)** RP,AB P(c);rep 18.00
Fl/69 **(169)** RP,AB P(c),25¢(c)
Price, Rigid(c);rep 18.00

090-GREEN MANSIONS

By William Henry Hudson
12/51 **(89)** AB,AB P(c),Original . . 125.00
01/59 **(148)** AB,New LbC P(c);rep . 30.00
1962 **(165)** AB,LbC P(c);rep 18.00
04/64 **(167)** AB,LbC P(c);rep 18.00
09/66 **(167)** AB,LbC P(c);rep 18.00
Sr/69 **(169)** AB,LbC P(c),25¢(c)
Price, Rigid(c);rep 18.00

091-THE CALL OF THE WILD

By Jack London
01/52 **(92)** MDb,P(c),Original 125.00
10/53 **(112)** MDb,P(c);rep 20.00
03/55 **(125)** MDb,P(c),'PictureProgress'
Onn. Back(c);rep 20.00
09/56 **(134)** MDb,P(c);rep 20.00
03/58 **(143)** MDb,P(c);rep 18.00
1962 **(165)** MDb,P(c);rep 18.00
1962 **(167)** MDb,P(c);rep 18.00
04/65 **(167)** MDb,P(c);rep 18.00
03/66 **(167)** MDb,P(c);rep 18.00
03/66 **(167)** MDb,P(c),Record
Edition;rep 18.00
11/67 **(166)** MDb,P(c);rep 18.00
Sg/70 **(169)** MDb,P(c),25¢(c)
Price, Rigid(c);rep 18.00

092-THE COURTSHIP OF MILES STANDISH

By Henry Wadsworth Longfellow
02/52 **(92)** AB,AB P(c),Original . . 100.00
1962 **(165)** AB,AB P(c);rep 20.00
03/64 **(167)** AB,AB P(c);rep 20.00
05/67 **(166)** AB,AB P(c);rep 20.00
Wr/69 **(169)** AB,AB P(c),25¢(c)
Price, Rigid(c);rep 20.00

093-PUDD'NHEAD WILSON

By Mark Twain
03/52 **(94)** HcK,HcK P(c),Original 125.00
1962 **(165)** HcK,GMc New P(c);rep 25.00
03/64 **(167)** HcK,GMc P(c);rep . . . 20.00
1968 **(166)** HcK,GMc P(c),25¢(c)
Price, Soft(c);rep 20.00

094-DAVID BALFOUR

By Robert Louis Stevenson
04/52 **(94)** RP,P(c),Original 125.00
05/64 **(167)** RP,P(c);rep 25.00
1968 **(166)** RP,P(c),25¢(c)Price;rep 25.00

095-ALL QUIET ON THE WESTERN FRONT

By Erich Maria Remarque
05/52 **(96)** MDb,P(c),Original. . . . 200.00
05/52 **(99)** MDb,P(c),Original. 85.00
10/64 **(167)** MDb,P(c);rep 35.00
11/66 **(167)** MDb,P(c);rep 35.00

096-DANIEL BOONE

By John Bakeless
06/52 **(97)** AB,P(c),Original 100.00
03/54 **(117)** AB,P(c);rep 20.00
09/55 **(128)** AB,P(c);rep 20.00
05/56 **(132)** AB,P(c);rep 20.00
——— **(134)** AB,P(c),'Story of
Jesus'on Back(c);rep 20.00
09/60 **(158)** AB,P(c);rep 20.00
01/64 **(167)** AB,P(c);rep 18.00
05/65 **(167)** AB,P(c);rep 18.00
11/66 **(167)** AB,P(c);rep 18.00
Wr/69 **(166)** AB,P(c),25¢(c)
Price, Rigid(c);rep 25.00

097-KING SOLOMON'S MINES

By H. Rider Haggard
07/52 **(96)** HcK,P(c),Original 100.00
04/54 **(118)** HcK,P(c);rep 20.00
03/56 **(131)** HcK,P(c);rep 20.00
09/51 **(141)** HcK,P(c);rep 20.00
09/60 **(158)** HcK,P(c);rep 18.00
02/64 **(167)** HcK,P(c);rep 18.00
09/65 **(167)** HcK,P(c);rep 18.00
Sr/69 **(169)** HcK,P(c),25¢(c)
Price; Rigid(c);rep 20.00

098-THE RED BADGE OF COURAGE

By Stephen Crane
08/52 **(98)** MDb,GS,P(c),Original. 100.00
04/54 **(118)** MDb,GS,P(c);rep 20.00
05/56 **(132)** MDb,GS,P(c);rep 20.00
01/58 **(142)** MDb,GS,P(c);rep 20.00
09/59 **(152)** MDb,GS,P(c);rep 20.00
03/61 **(161)** MDb,GS,P(c);rep 20.00
62/63 **(167)** MDb,GS,P(c),Erronously
Has Original Date;rep 20.00
09/64 **(167)** MDb,GS,P(c);rep 20.00
10/65 **(167)** MDb,GS,P(c);rep 20.00
1968 **(166)** MDb,GS,P(c),25¢(c)
Price, Rigid(c);rep 30.00

099-HAMLET

By William Shakespeare
09/52 **(98)** AB,P(c),Original 125.00
07/54 **(121)** AB,P(c);rep 20.00
11/57 **(141)** AB,P(c);rep 20.00
09/60 **(158)** AB,P(c);rep 18.00
62/63 **(167)** AB,P(c),Erronously
Has Original Date;rep 18.00
07/65 **(167)** AB,P(c);rep 18.00

04/67 **(166)** AB,P(c);rep 18.00
Sg/69 **(169)** AB,EdM New P(c),
   25¢(c)Price, Rigid(c);rep 30.00

100-MUTINY ON
THE BOUNTY
By Charrles Nordhoff
10/52 **(100)** MsW,HcK P(c),Orig. . 100.00
03/54 **(117)** MsW,HcK P(c);rep . . . 20.00
05/56 **(132)** MsW,HcK P(c);rep . . . 20.00
01/58 **(142)** MsW,HcK P(c);rep . . . 20.00
03/60 **(155)** MsW,HcK P(c);rep . . . 18.00
62/63 **(167)** MsW,HcK P(c),Erroneously
   Has Original Date;rep 18.00
05/64 **(167)** MsW,HcK P(c);rep . . . 18.00
03/66 **(167)** MsW,HcK P(c),N#
   or Price;rep 20.00
Sg/70 **(169)** MsW,HcK P(c),
   Rigid(c); rep. 18.00

101-WILLIAM TELL
By Frederick Schiller
11/52 **(101)** MDb,HcK P(c),Orig. . 100.00
04/54 **(118)** MDb,HcK P(c);rep . . . 20.00
11/57 **(141)** MDb,HcK P(c);rep . . . 20.00
09/60 **(158)** MDb,HcK P(c);rep . . . 18.00
62/63 **(167)** MDb,HcK P(c),Erroneously
   Has Original Date;rep 18.00
11/64 **(167)** MDb,HcK P(c);rep . . . 18.00
04/67 **(166)** MDb,HcK P(c);rep . . . 18.00
Wr/69 **(169)** MDb,HcK P(c)25¢(c)
   Price, Rigid(c);rep 18.00

102-THE WHITE
COMPANY
By Sir Arthur Conan Doyle
12/52 **(101)** AB,P(c),Original 150.00
1962 **(165)** AB,P(c);rep 40.00
04/64 **(167)** AB,P(c);rep. 40.00

103-MEN AGAINST
THE SEA
By Charles Nordhoff
01/53 **(104)** RP,HcK P(c),Original 125.00
12/53 **(114)** RP,HcK P(c);rep 30.00
03/56 **(131)** RP,New P(c);rep. 35.00
03/59 **(149)** RP,P(c);rep. 30.00
·09/60 **(158)** RP,P(c);rep. 30.00
03/64 **(167)** RP,P(c);rep. 25.00

104-BRING 'EM BACK
ALIVE
**By Frank Buck & Edward
Anthony**
02/53 **(105)** HcK,HcK P(c)Original100.00
04/54 **(118)** HcK,HcK P(c);rep 20.00
07/56 **(133)** HcK,HcK P(c);rep 20.00
05/59 **(150)** HcK,HcK P(c);rep 18.00
09/60 **(158)** HcK,HcK P(c);rep 18.00
10/63 **(167)** HcK,HcK P(c);rep 18.00
09/65 **(167)** HcK,HcK P(c);rep 18.00
Wr/69 **(169)** HcK,HcK P(c),25¢(c)
   Price, Rigid(c);rep 18.00

105-FROM THE EARTH
TO THE MOON
By Jules Verne
03/53 **(106)** AB,P(c),Original 100.00
04/54 **(118)** AB,P(c);rep 20.00
03/56 **(132)** AB,P(c);rep. 20.00
11/57 **(141)** AB,P(c);rep. 20.00
09/58 **(146)** AB,P(c);rep 20.00
05/60 **(156)** AB,P(c);rep. 20.00
62/63 **(167)** AB,P(c),Erroneously
   Has Original Date;rep 18.00
05/64 **(167)** AB,P(c);rep. 18.00

05/65 **(167)** AB,P(c);rep 18.00
10/67 **(166)** AB,P(c);rep 18.00
Sr/69 **(169)** AB,P(c),25¢(c)
   Price, Rigid(c);rep 18.00
Sg/71 **(169)** AB,P(c);rep. 18.00

106-BUFFALO BILL
By William F. Cody
04/53 **(107)** MDb,P(c),Original. . . 100.00
04/54 **(118)** MDb,P(c);rep 20.00
03/56 **(132)** MDb,P(c);rep 20.00
01/58 **(142)** MDb,P(c);rep 20.00
03/61 **(161)** MDb,P(c);rep 18.00
03/64 **(167)** MDb,P(c);rep 18.00
07/67 **(166)** MDb,P(c);rep 18.00
Fl/69 **(169)** MDb,P(c),Rigid(c);rep . 18.00

107-KING OF THE
KHYBER RIFLES
By Talbot Mundy
05/53 **(108)** SMz,P(c),Original . . . 100.00
04/54 **(118)** SMz,P(c);rep. 20.00
09/58 **(146)** SMz,P(c);rep 20.00
09/60 **(158)** SMz,P(c);rep. 18.00
62/63 **(167)** SMz,P(c),Erroneously
   Has Original Date;rep 18.00
62/63 **(167)** SMz,P(c);rep 18.00
10/66 **(167)** SMz,P(c);rep 18.00

108-KNIGHTS OF THE
ROUND TABLE
By Howard Pyle?
06/53 **(108)** AB,P(c),Original 125.00
06/53 **(109)** AB,P(c),Original 70.00
03/54 **(117)** AB,P(c);rep 20.00
11/59 **(153)** AB,P(c);rep. 18.00
1962 **(165)** AB,P(c);rep. 18.00
04/64 **(167)** AB,P(c);rep. 18.00
04/67 **(166)** AB,P(c);rep. 18.00

109-PITCAIRN'S ISLAND
By Charles Nordhoff
07/53 **(110)** RP,P(c),Original 125.00
1962 **(165)** RP,P(c);rep 20.00
03/64 **(167)** RP,P(c);rep. 20.00
06/67 **(166)** RP,P(c);rep. 20.00

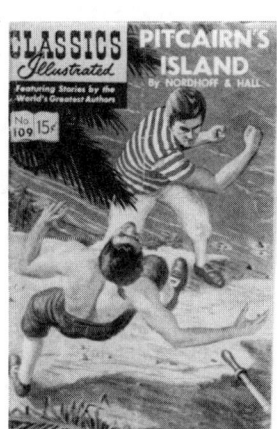

Cl #105, Pitcairns Island
© Gilberton Publications

110-A STUDY IN
SCARLET
By Sir Arthur Conan Doyle
08/53 **(111)** SMz,P(c),Original . . . 200.00
1962 **(165)** SMz,P(c);rep 150.00

111-THE TALISMAN
By Sir Walter Scott
09/53 **(112)** HcK,HcK P(c),Orig.. . 125.00
1962 **(165)** HcK,HcK P(c);rep 20.00
05/64 **(167)** HcK,HcK P(c);rep. . . . 20.00
Fl/68 **(166)** HcK,HcK P(c),
   25¢(c)Price;rep 20.00

112-ADVENTURES OF
KIT CARSON
By John S. C. Abbott
10/53 **(113)** RP,P(c),Original 125.00
11/55 **(129)** RP,P(c);rep 20.00
11/57 **(141)** RP,P(c);rep 20.00
09/59 **(152)** RP,P(c);rep. 18.00
03/61 **(161)** RP,P(c);rep. 18.00
62/63 **(167)** RP,P(c);rep. 18.00
02/65 **(167)** RP,P(c);rep. 18.00
05/66 **(167)** RP,P(c);rep. 18.00
Wr/69 **(166)** RP,EdM New P(c),
   25¢(c)Price, Rigid(c);rep 25.00

113-THE FORTY-FIVE
GUARDSMEN
By Alexandre Dumas
11/53 **(114)** MDb,P(c),Original . . . 150.00
07/67 **(166)** MDb,P(c);rep 50.00

114-THE RED ROVER
By James Fenimore Cooper
12/53 **(115)** PrC,JP P(c),Original . 150.00
07/67 **(166)** PrC,JP P(c);rep 50.00

115-HOW I FOUND
LIVINGSTONE
By Sir Henry Stanley
01/54 **(116)** SF&ST,P(c),Original . 200.00
01/67 **(167)** SF&ST,P(c);rep 60.00

116-THE BOTTLE IMP
By Robert Louis Stevenson
02/54 **(117)** LC,P(c),Original 200.00
01/67 **(167)** LC,P(c);rep. 60.00

117-CAPTAINS
COURAGEOUS
By Rudyard Kipling
03/54 **(118)** PrC,P(c),Original . . . 200.00
02/67 **(167)** PrC,P(c);rep 32.00
Fl/69 **(169)** PrC,P(c),25¢(c)
   Price, Rigid(c);rep 30.00

118-ROB ROY
By Sir Walter Scott
04/54 **(119)** RP,WIP,P(c),Original . 200.00
02/67 **(167)** RP,WIP,P(c);rep 60.00

119-SOLDERS OF
FORTUNE
By Richard Harding Davis
05/54 **(120)** KS,P(c),Original 150.00
03/67 **(166)** KS,P(c);rep. 32.00
Sg/70 **(169)** KS,P(c),25¢(c)
   Price, Rigid(c);rep 30.00

120-THE HURRICANE
By Charles Nordhoff
1954 **(121)** LC,LC P(c),Original . . 150.00
03/67 **(166)** LC,LC P(c);rep 45.00

121-WILD BILL HICKOK
Author Unknown
07/54 **(122)** MI,ST,P(c),Original . . 110.00
05/56 **(132)** MI,ST,P(c);rep 20.00
11/57 **(141)** MI,ST,P(c);rep 20.00
01/60 **(154)** MI,ST,P(c);rep 20.00
62/63 **(167)** MI,ST,P(c);rep 18.00
08/64 **(167)** MI,ST,P(c);rep 18.00
04/67 **(166)** MI,ST,P(c);rep 18.00
Wr/69 **(169)** MI,ST,P(c),Rigid
(c);rep 18.00

122-THE MUTINEERS
By Charles Boardman Hawes
09/54 **(123)** PrC,P(c),Original . . . 125.00
01/57 **(136)** PrC,P(c);rep 20.00
09/58 **(146)** PrC,P(c);rep 20.00
09/60 **(158)** PrC,P(c);rep 18.00
11/63 **(167)** PrC,P(c);rep 18.00
03/65 **(167)** PrC,P(c);rep 18.00
08/67 **(166)** PrC,P(c);rep 18.00

123-FANG AND CLAW
By Frank Buck
11/54 **(124)** LnS,P(c),Original . . . 125.00
07/56 **(133)** LnS,P(c);rep 20.00
03/58 **(143)** LnS,P(c);rep 20.00
01/60 **(154)** LnS,P(c);rep 18.00
62/63 **(167)** LnS,P(c),Erroneously
Has Original Date;rep 18.00
09/65 **(167)** LnS,P(c);rep 18.00

124-THE WAR OF THE WORLDS
By H. G. Wells
01/55 **(125)** LC,LC P(c),Original . 200.00
03/56 **(131)** LC,LC P(c);rep 20.00
11/57 **(141)** LC,LC P(c);rep 20.00
01/59 **(148)** LC,LC P(c);rep 20.00
05/60 **(156)** LC,LC P(c);rep 25.00
1962 **(165)** LC,LC P(c);rep 20.00
62/63 **(167)** LC,LC P(c);rep 20.00
11/64 **(167)** LC,LC P(c);rep 20.00
11/65 **(167)** LC,LC P(c);rep 20.00
1968 **(166)** LC,LC P(c),25¢(c)
Price; rep 20.00
Sr/70 **(169)** LC,LC P(c),Rigid
(c);rep 20.00

125-THE OX BOW INCIDENT
By Walter Van Tilberg Clark
03/55 **(—)** NN,P(c),Original 125.00
03/58 **(143)** NN,P(c);rep 20.00
09/59 **(152)** NN,P(c);rep 20.00
03/61 **(149)** NN,P(c);rep 20.00
62/63 **(167)** NN,P(c);rep 18.00
11/64 **(167)** NN,P(c);rep 18.00
04/67 **(166)** NN,P(c);rep 18.00
r/69 **(169)** NN,P(c),25¢(c)
Price, Rigid(c);rep 18.00

126-THE DOWNFALL
By Emile Zola
05/55 **(—)** LC,LC P(c),Original,'
Picture Progress'Replaces
Reorder List. 125.00
08/64 **(167)** LC,LC P(c);rep 30.00
1968 **(166)** LC,LC P(c),25¢(c)
Price;rep 30.00

127-THE KING OF THE MOUNTAINS
By Edmond About
07/55 **(128)** NN,P(c),Original 150.00
06/64 **(167)** NN,P(c);rep 22.00
Fl/68 **(166)** NN,P(c),25¢(c)
Price;rep 22.00

Cl #135, Waterloo
© Gilberton Publications

128-MACBETH
By William Shakespeare
09/55 **(128)** AB,P(c),Original 125.00
03/58 **(143)** AB,P(c);rep 20.00
09/60 **(158)** AB,P(c);rep 20.00
62/63 **(167)** AB,P(c);rep 18.00
06/64 **(167)** AB,P(c);rep 18.00
04/67 **(166)** AB,P(c);rep 18.00
1968 **(166)** AB,P(c),25¢(c)
Price;rep 18.00
Sg/70 **(169)** AB,P(c),Rigid(c);rep . . 18.00

129-DAVY CROCKETT
Author Unknown
11/55 **(129)** LC,P(c),Original 200.00
09/66 **(167)** LC,P(c);rep 125.00

130-CAESAR'S CONQUESTS
By Julius Caesar
01/56 **(130)** JO,P(c),Original 125.00
01/58 **(142)** JO,P(c);rep 20.00
09/59 **(152)** JO,P(c);rep 20.00
03/61 **(149)** JO,P(c);rep 20.00
62/63 **(167)** JO,P(c);rep 18.00
10/64 **(167)** JO,P(c);rep 18.00
04/66 **(167)** JO,P(c);rep 18.00

131-THE COVERED WAGON
By Emerson Hough
03/56 **(131)** NN,P(c),Original 125.00
03/58 **(143)** NN,P(c);rep 20.00
09/59 **(152)** NN,P(c);rep 20.00
09/60 **(158)** NN,P(c);rep 20.00
62/63 **(167)** NN,P(c);rep 18.00
11/64 **(167)** NN,P(c);rep 18.00
04/66 **(167)** NN,P(c);rep 18.00
Wr/69 **(169)** NN,P(c),25¢(c)
Price, Rigid(c);rep 18.00

132-THE DARK FRIGATE
By Charles Boardman Hawes
05/56 **(132)** EW&RWb,P(c),Orig.. 125.00
05/59 **(150)** EW&RWb,P(c);rep . . . 20.00
01/64 **(167)** EW&RWb,P(c);rep . . . 20.00
05/67 **(166)** EW&RWb,P(c);rep . . . 20.00

133-THE TIME MACHINE
By H. G. Wells
07/56 **(133)** LC,P(c),Original 175.00
01/58 **(142)** LC,P(c);rep 20.00
09/59 **(152)** LC,P(c);rep 20.00
09/60 **(158)** LC,P(c);rep 20.00
62/63 **(167)** LC,P(c);rep 20.00
06/64 **(167)** LC,P(c);rep 25.00
03/66 **(167)** LC,P(c);rep 20.00
03/66 **(167)** LC,P(c),N# Or Price;
rep 20.00
12/67 **(166)** LC,P(c);rep 20.00
Wr/71 **(169)** LC,P(c),25¢(c)
Price, Rigid(c);rep 20.00

134-ROMEO AND JULIET
By William Shakespeare
09/56 **(134)** GE,P(c),Original 125.00
03/61 **(161)** GE,P(c);rep 20.00
09/63 **(167)** GE,P(c);rep 18.00
05/65 **(167)** GE,P(c);rep 18.00
06/67 **(166)** GE,P(c);rep 18.00
Wr/69 **(166)** GE,EdM New P(c),
25¢(c)Price, Rigid(c);rep 32.00

135-WATERLOO
By Emile Erckmann & Alexandre Chatrian
11/56 **(135)** Grl,AB P(c),Original . 125.00
11/59 **(153)** Grl,AB P(c);rep 20.00
62/63 **(167)** Grl,AB P(c);rep. 18.00
09/64 **(167)** Grl,AB P(c);rep. 18.00
1968 **(166)** Grl,AB P(c),25¢(c)
Price; rep 18.00

136-LORD JIM
By Joseph Conrad
01/57 **(136)** GE,P(c),Original 150.00
62/63 **(165)** GE,P(c);rep 18.00
03/64 **(167)** GE,P(c);rep 18.00
09/66 **(167)** GE,P(c);rep 18.00
Sr/69 **(169)** GE,P(c),25¢(c)
Price, Rigid(c);rep 18.00

137-THE LITTLE SAVAGE
By Captain Frederick Marryat
03/57 **(136)** GE,P(c),Original 125.00
01/59 **(148)** GE,P(c);rep 20.00
05/60 **(156)** GE,P(c);rep 20.00
62/63 **(167)** GE,P(c);rep 18.00
10/64 **(167)** GE,P(c);rep 18.00
08/67 **(166)** GE,P(c);rep 18.00
Sg/70 **(169)** GE,P(c),25¢(c)
Price, Rigid(c);rep 18.00

138-A JOURNEY TO THE CENTER OF THE EARTH
By Jules Verne
05/57 **(136)** NN,P(c),Original 175.00
09/58 **(146)** NN,P(c);rep 20.00
05/60 **(156)** NN,P(c);rep 20.00
09/60 **(158)** NN,P(c);rep 20.00
62/63 **(167)** NN,P(c);rep 18.00
06/64 **(167)** NN,P(c);rep 20.00
04/66 **(167)** NN,P(c);rep 18.00
1968 **(166)** NN,P(c),25¢(c)
Price;rep 18.00

139-IN THE REIGN OF TERROR
By George Alfred Henty
07/57 **(139)** GE,P(c),Original 125.00
01/60 **(154)** GE,P(c),rep 20.00
62/63 **(167)** GE,P(c),Erroneously
   Has Original Date;rep 18.00
07/64 **(167)** GE,P(c);rep 20.00
1968 **(166)** GE,P,P(c),25¢(c)
   Price;rep 18.00

140-ON JUNGLE TRAILS
By Frank Buck
09/57 **(140)** NN,P(c),Original 125.00
05/59 **(150)** NN,P(c);rep 20.00
01/61 **(160)** NN,P(c);rep 20.00
09/63 **(167)** NN,P(c);rep 18.00
09/65 **(167)** NN,P(c);rep 18.00

141-CASTLE DANGEROUS
By Sir Walter Scott
11/57 **(141)** StC,P(c),Original 150.00
09/59 **(152)** STC,P(c);rep 20.00
62/63 **(167)** StC,P(c);rep 18.00
07/67 **(166)** StC,P(c);rep 18.00

142-ABRAHAM LINCOLN
By Benjamin Thomas
01/58 **(142)** NN,P(c),Original 150.00
01/60 **(154)** NN,P(c);rep 20.00
09/60 **(158)** NN,P(c);rep 20.00
10/63 **(167)** NN,P(c);rep 18.00
07/65 **(167)** NN,P(c);rep 18.00
11/67 **(166)** NN,P(c);rep 18.00
Fl/69 **(169)** NN,P(c),25¢(c) Price,
   Rigid(c);rep 18.00

CI #156, Off on a Comet
© Gilberton Publications

143-KIM
By Rudyard Kipling
03/58 **(143)** JO,P(c)Original 125.00
62/63 **(165)** JO,P(c);rep 18.00
11/63 **(167)** JO,P(c);rep 18.00
08/65 **(167)** JO,P(c);rep 18.00
Wr/69 **(169)** JO,P(c),25¢(c) Price,
   Rigid(c);rep 18.00

144-THE FIRST MEN IN THE MOON
By H. G. Wells
05/58 **(143)** GWb,AW,AT,RKr,
   GMC P(c), Original 175.00
11/59 **(153)** GWb,AW,AT,RKr,
   GMC, P(c); rep 20.00
03/61 **(161)** GWb,AW,AT,RKr,
   GMC, P(c); rep 18.00
62/63 **(167)** GWb,AW,AT,RKr,
   GMC, P(c); rep 18.00
12/65 **(167)** GWb,AW,AT,RKr,
   GMC, P(c); rep 18.00
Fl/68 **(166)** GWb,AW,AT,RKr,GMC
   P(c),25¢(c) Price,Rigid(c);rep . 18.00
Wr/69 **(169)** GWb,AW,AT,RKr,GMC
   P(c), Rigid(c);rep 28.00

145-THE CRISIS
by Winston Churchill
07/58 **(143)** GE,P(c),Original 125.00
05/60 **(156)** GE,P(c);rep 20.00
10/63 **(167)** GE,P(c);rep 18.00
03/65 **(167)** GE,P(c);rep 18.00
1968 **(166)** GE,P(c),25¢(c)
   Price;rep 18.00

146-WITH FIRE AND SWORD
By Henryk Sienkiewicz
09/58 **(143)** GWb,P(c),Original . . 125.00
05/60 **(156)** GWb,P(c);rep 25.00
11/63 **(167)** GWb,P(c);rep 20.00
03/65 **(167)** GWb,P(c);rep 20.00

147-BEN-HUR
By Lew Wallace
11/58 **(147)** JO,P(c),Original 125.00
11/59 **(153)** JO,P(c);rep 65.00
09/60 **(158)** JO,P(c);rep 20.00
62/63 **(167)** JO,P(c),Has the
   Original Date;rep 20.00
—— **(167)** JO,P(c);rep 18.00
02/65 **(167)** JO,P(c);rep 18.00
09/66 **(167)** JO,P(c);rep 18.00
Fl/68 **(166)** JO,P(c),25¢(c)Price,
   Both Rigid & Soft (c)s;rep . . . 50.00

148-THE BUCKANEER
By Lyle Saxon
01/59 **(148)** GE&RJ,NS P(c),orig. 125.00
—— **(568)** GE&RJ,NS P(c),Juniors
   List Only;rep 20.00
62/63 **(167)** GE&RJ,NS P(c);rep . . 20.00
09/65 **(167)** GE&RJ,NS P(c);rep . . 20.00
Sr/69 **(169)** GE&RJ,NS P(c),25¢(c)
   Price, Rigid(c);rep 20.00

149-OFF ON A COMET
By Jules Verne
03/59 **(149)** GMc,P(c),Original . . . 125.00
03/60 **(155)** GMc,P(c);rep 20.00
03/61 **(149)** GMc,P(c);rep 20.00
12/63 **(167)** GMc,P(c);rep 18.00
02/65 **(167)** GMc,P(c);rep 18.00
10/66 **(167)** GMc,P(c);rep 18.00
Fl/68 **(166)** GMc,EdM New P(c),
   25¢(c)Price;rep 30.00

150-THE VIRGINIAN
By Owen Winster
05/59 **(150)** NN,DrG P(c),Original 175.00
1961 **(164)** NN,DrG P(c);rep 30.00
62/63 **(167)** NN,DrG P(c);rep. 35.00
12/65 **(167)** NN,DrG P(c);rep. 30.00

151-WON BY THE SWORD
By George Alfred Henty
07/59 **(150)** JTg,P(c),Original . . . 125.00
1961 **(164)** JTg,P(c);rep. 25.00
10/63 **(167)** JTg,P(c);rep 25.00
1963 **(167)** JTg,P(c);rep 25.00
07/67 **(166)** JTg,P(c);rep 25.00

152-WILD ANIMALS I HAVE KNOWN
By Ernest Thompson Seton
09/59 **(152)** LbC,LbC P(c),Orig. . . 150.00
03/61 **(149)** LbC,LbC P(c),P(c);rep 20.00
09/63 **(167)** LbC,LbC P(c);rep 18.00
08/65 **(167)** LbC,LbC P(c);rep 18.00
fl/69 **(169)** LbC,LbC P(c),25¢(c)
   Price, Rigid(c);rep 18.00

153-THE INVISIBLE MAN
By H. G. Wells
11/59 **(153)** NN,GB P(c),Original . 150.00
03/61 **(149)** NN,GB P(c);rep 20.00
62/63 **(167)** NN,GB P(c);rep 18.00
02/65 **(167)** NN,GB P(c);rep 18.00
09/66 **(167)** NN,GB P(c);rep 18.00
Wr/69 **(166)** NN,GB P(c),25¢(c)
   Price, Rigid(c);rep 18.00
Sg/71 **(169)** NN,GB P(c),Rigid(c),
   Words Spelling'Invisible Man'
   Are' Solid'Not'Invisible';rep . . . 18.00

154-THE CONSPIRACY OF PONTIAC
By Francis Parkman
01/60 **(154)** GMc,GMc P(c),
   Original 125.00
11/63 **(167)** GMc,GMc P(c);rep . . . 30.00
07/64 **(167)** GMc,GMc P(c);rep . . . 30.00
12/67 **(166)** GMc,GMc P(c);rep . . . 30.00

155-THE LION OF THE NORTH
By George Alfred Henty
03/60 **(154)** NN,GMc P(c),Orig. . . 125.00
01/64 **(167)** NN,GMc P(c);rep 25.00
1967 **(166)** NN,GMc P(c),25¢(c)
   Price; rep 20.00

156-THE CONQUEST OF MEXICO
By Bernal Diaz Del Castillo
05/60 **(156)** BPr,BPr P(c),Original 125.00
01/64 **(167)** BPr,BPr P(c);rep. 20.00
08/67 **(166)** BPr,BPr P(c);rep. 20.00
Sg/70 **(169)** BPr,BPr P(c),25¢(c)
   Price; Rigid(c);rep 18.00

157-LIVES OF THE HUNTED
By Ernest Thompson Seton
07/60 **(156)** NN,LbC P(c),Original 150.00
02/64 **(167)** NN,LbC P(c);rep. 28.00
10/67 **(166)** NN,LbC P(c);rep. 28.00

158-THE CONSPIRATORS
By Alexandre Dumas
09/60 **(156)** GMc,GMc P(c),
   Original 150.00
07/64 **(167)** GMc,GMc P(c);rep . . . 28.00
10/67 **(166)** GMc,GMc P(c);rep . . . 28.00

Classics Illus.

159-THE OCTOPUS
By Frank Norris
11/60 **(159)** GM&GE,LbC P(c),
Original 150.00
02/64 **(167)** GM&GE,LbC P(c);rep. 28.00
166 **(1967)** GM&GE,LbC P(c),25¢(c)
Price;rep 28.00

160-THE FOOD OF THE GODS
By H.G. Wells
01/61 **(159)** TyT,GMc P(c),Orig. . . 150.00
01/61 **(160)** TyT,GMc P(c),Original;
Same Except For the HRN# . . 60.00
01/64 **(167)** TyT,GMc P(c);rep 28.00
06/67 **(166)** TyT,GMc P(c);rep 28.00

161-CLEOPATRA
By H. Rider Haggard
03/61 **(161)** NN,Pch P(c),Original 125.00
01/64 **(167)** NN,Pch P(c);rep 30.00
08/67 **(166)** NN,Pch P(c);rep 30.00

162-ROBUR THE CONQUEROR
By Jules Verne
05/61 **(162)** GM&DPn,CJ P(c),
Original 125.00
07/64 **(167)** GM&DPn,CJ P(c);rep. 28.00
08/67 **(166)** GM&DPn,CJ P(c);rep. 28.00

163-MASTER OF THE WORLD
By Jules Verne
07/61 **(163)** GM,P(c),Original. . . . 125.00
01/65 **(167)** GM,P(c);rep 28.00
1968 **(166)** GM,P(c),25¢(c)
Price;rep 28.00

164-THE COSSACK CHIEF
By Nicolai Gogol
1961 **(164)** SyM,P(c),Original . . . 125.00
04/65 **(167)** SyM,P(c);rep 28.00
Fl/68 **(166)** SyM,P(c),25¢(c)
Price;rep 28.00

165-THE QUEEN'S NECKLACE
by Alexandre Dumas
01/62 **(164)** GM,P(c),Original. . . . 125.00

CI Jr. #169, Negro Americans
© Print Mint

04/65 **(167)** GM,P(c);rep 28.00
Fl/68 **(166)** GM,P(c),25¢(c)
Price;rep 28.00

166-TIGERS AND TRAITORS
By Jules Verne
05/62 **(165)** NN,P(c),Original 175.00
02/64 **(167)** NN,P(c);rep 40.00
11/66 **(167)** NN,P(c);rep 40.00

167-FAUST
By Johann Wolfgang von Goethe
08/62 **(165)** NN,NN P(c),Original . 250.00
02/64 **(167)** NN,NN P(c);rep 100.00
06/67 **(166)** NN,NN P(c);rep 100.00

168-IN FREEDOM'S CAUSE
By George Alfred Henty
Wr/69 **(169)** GE&RC,P(c),
Original, Rigid (c). 275.00

169-NEGRO AMERICANS THE EARLY YEARS
AUTHOR UNKNOWN
Sg/69 **(166)** NN,NN P(c),
Original, Rigid(c) 300.00
Sg/69 **(169)** NN,NN P(c),
Rigid; rep 125.00

CLASSICS ILLUSTRATED GIANTS
An Illustrated Library of Great
Adventure Stories -(reps. of
Issues 6,7,8,10) 2,200.00
An Illustrated Library of Exciting
Mystery Stories -(reps. of
Issues 30,21,40,13) 2,400.00
An Illustrated Library of Great
Indian Stories -(reps. of
Issues 4,17,22,37) 2,200.00

CLASSICS ILLUSTRATED JUNIOR
Oct., 1953–Spring., 1971
501-Snow White and the
Seven Dwarfs 150.00
502-The Ugly Duckling 100.00
503-Cinderella 75.00
504-The Pied Piper 75.00
505-The Sleeping Beauty 75.00
506-The Three Little Pigs 75.00
507-Jack and the Beanstalk 75.00
508-Goldilocks & the Three Bears. 75.00
509-Beauty and the Beast. 75.00
510-Little Red Riding Hood 75.00
511-Puss-N-Boots 75.00
512-Rumpelstiltskin 75.00
513-Pinocchio 75.00
514-The Steadfast Tin Soldier . . . 100.00
515-Johnny Appleseed 75.00
516-Aladdin and His Lamp 75.00
517-The Emperor's New Clothes . 75.00
518-The Golden Goose 75.00
519-Paul Bunyan 75.00
520-Thumbelina. 75.00
521-King of the Golden River 75.00
522-The Nightingale. 75.00
523-The Gallant Tailor 75.00
524-The Wild Swans 75.00
525-The Little Mermaid 75.00
526-The Frog Prince 75.00
527-The Golden-Haired Giant 75.00
528-The Penny Prince 75.00
529-The Magic Servants 75.00

530-The Golden Bird 75.00
531-Rapunzel 75.00
532-The Dancing Princesses. 75.00
533-The Magic Fountain 75.00
534-The Golden Touch 75.00
535-The Wizard of Oz 100.00
536-The Chimney Sweep 75.00
537-The Three Fairies 75.00
538-Silly Hans 75.00
539-The Enchanted Fish 75.00
540-The Tinder-Box 75.00
541-Snow White and Rose Red . . 75.00
542-The Donkey's Tail 75.00
543-The House in the Woods 75.00
544-The Golden Fleece. 75.00
545-The Glass Mountain 75.00
546-The Elves and the Shoemaker 75.00
547-The Wishing Table 75.00
548-The Magic Pitcher. 75.00
549-Simple Kate 75.00
550-The Singing Donkey 75.00
551-The Queen Bee 75.00
552-The Three Little Dwarfs 75.00
553-King Thrushbeard 75.00
554-The Enchanted Deer 75.00
555-The Three Golden Apples. . . . 75.00
556-The Elf Mound 75.00
557-Silly Willy. 75.00
558-The Magic Dish,LbC(c). 75.00
559-The Japanese Lantern,LbC(c) 90.00
560-The Doll Princess,LbC(c) 90.00
561-Hans Humdrum,LbC(c). 75.00
562-The Enchanted Pony,LbC(c) . 90.00
563-The Wishing Well,LbC(c) 75.00
564-The Salt Mountain,LbC(c). . . . 75.00
565-The Silly Princess,LbC(c). . . . 75.00
566-Clumsy Hans,LbC(c). 75.00
567-The Bearskin Soldier,LbC(c). . 75.00
568-The Happy Hedgehog,LbC(c). 75.00
569-The Three Giants 75.00
570-The Pearl Princess 75.00
571-How Fire Came to the Indians 75.00
572-The Drummer Boy 75.00
573-The Crystal Ball 75.00
574-Brightboots 75.00
575-The Fearless Prince 75.00
576-The Princess Who Saw
Everything 90.00
577-The Runaway Dumpling 100.00

CLASSICS ILLLUSTRATED SPECIAL ISSUE
Dec., 1955–July, 1962
N# United Nations 425.00
129-The Story of Jesus,Jesus on
mountain(c) 150.00
129a-Three Camels(c). 175.00
129b-Mountain(c),HRN to 161 . . 125.00
129c-Mountain(c) (1968) 100.00
132A-The Story of America 125.00
135A-The Ten Commandments . . 125.00
138A-Adventures in Science 125.00
138Aa-HRN to 149 . . . . 100.00
138Ab-rep.,12/61 . . . . 100.00
141A-GE,The Rough Rider 125.00
144A-RC,GE,Blazing the Trails . . 125.00
147A-RC,GE,Crossing the
Rockies 125.00
150A-Grl,Royal Canadian Police. 125.00
153A-GE,Men, Guns, & Cattle. . . 125.00
156A-GE,GM,The Atomic Age . . 125.00
159A-GE,GM,Rockets, Jets and
Missiles 125.00
162A-RC,GE,War Between
the States 200.00
165A-RC/GE,JK,Grl,To the Stars. 125.00
166A-RC/GE,JK,Grl,World War II 150.00
167A-RC/GE,JK,Prehistoric
World 150.00
167Aa-HRN to 167 . . . . 125.00

UNDERGROUND

ADVENTURES OF FAT FREDDY'S CAT, THE
Rip Off Press, Feb., 1977
1 . . . . 20.00
2 . . . . 12.00
3 . . . . 15.00
4 . . . . 10.00
5 & 6 . . . . @10.00

AMAZING DOPE TALES
Greg Shaw
1 Untrimmed black and white pages,
out of order;artist unknown . . 125.00
2 Trimmed and proper pages . . . 100.00

AMERICAN SPLENDOR
Harvey Pekar, May, 1976
1 B:Harvey Pekar Stories,
HP,RCr,GDu,GBu 30.00
2 HP,RCr,GDu,GBu 10.00
3 HP,RCr,GDu,GBu 10.00
4 HP,RCr,GDu,GBu 8.00
5 HP,RCr,GDu,GBu 8.00
6 HP,RCr,GDu,GBu,GSh 7.00
7 HP,GSh,GDu,GBu 5.00
8 HP,GSh,GDu,GBu 3.00
9 and 10 HP,GSh,GDu,GBu . . . . @3.00
11 . . . . 3.00
12 . . . . 4.50
13 thru 19 . . . . @4.00
20 E:Harvey Pekar Stories 4.00

ANTHOLOGY OF SLOW DEATH
Wingnut Press/Last Gasp
1 140 pgs, RCr,RCo, GiS, DSh,
Harlan Ellison VB,RTu 40.00

APEX TREASURY OF UNDERGROUND COMICS, THE
Links Books Inc., Oct., 1974
1 . . . . 40.00

APEX TREASURY OF UNDERGROUND COMICS –BEST OF BIJOU FUNNIES
Quick Fox, 1981
1 Paperback,comix,various artists 25.00

ARCADE THE COMICS REVUE
Print Mint Inc. Spring, 1975
1 ASp,BG,RCr,SRo,SCW 25.00
2 ASp,BG,RCr,SRo 15.00
3 ASp,BG,RCr,RW,SCW 10.00
4 ASp,BG,RCr,WBu,RW,SCW . . . 10.00
5 thru 7 ASp,BG,SRo,RW,SCW . @7.50

BABYFAT
Comix World/Clay Geerdes, 1978
1 B:8pg news parodies, one page
comix by various artists 4.50
2 thru 9 same . . . . @3.00
10 thru 26 same . . . . @2.00

BATTLE OF THE TITANS
University of Illinois SF Society, 1972
1 Sci-Fi;VB,JGa 50.00

BEST BUY COMICS
Last Gasp Eco-Funnies
1 Rep Whole Earth Review;RCr . . . 3.50
1-shot R. Crumb reprints (2004) . . . 2.50

BEST OF BIJOU FUNNIES, THE
Links Books Inc., 1975
1 164 pgs,paperback 260.00

BEST OF RIP-OFF PRESS
Rip Off Press Inc., 1973
1 132 pgs paperback,SCW,
RCr,SRo,RW 30.00
2 100 pgs,GS,FT 35.00
3 100 pgs,FS 15.00
4 132 pgs,GiS,DSh 16.00

BIG ASS
Rip Off Press, 1969–71
1 28 pgs,RCr 90.00
2 RCr 60.00

BIJOU FUNNIES
Bijou Publishing Empire, 1968
1 B:JLy,editor;RCr,GS SW 310.00
2 RCr,GS,SW 135.00
3 RCr,SWi,JsG 80.00
4 SWi,JsG 45.00
5 SWi,JsG 50.00
6 E:JLy,editor,SWi,RCr,JsG 40.00
7 and 8 . . . . @40.00

BINKY BROWN MEETS THE HOLY VIRGIN MARY
Last Gasp Eco-Funnies, March, 1972
N# Autobiography about Growing up
w/a Catholic Neurosis,JsG . . . 25.00

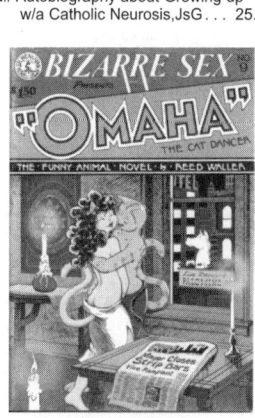

Bizarre Sex #9
© Kitchen Sink (1972)

2nd Printing:only text in
bottom left panel 12.00
TPB Sampler (2004) 16.95

BIZARRE SEX
Kitchen Sink Komix, May, 1972
1 B:DKi,editor,various artists 30.00
2 . . . . 25.00
3 . . . . 20.00
4 thru 6 . . . . @15.00
7 . . . . 10.00
8 . . . . 10.00
9 Omaha the Cat Dancer,RW 25.00
10 inc.Omaha the Cat Dancer,RW 20.00

BLACK LAUGHTER
Black Laughter Pub. Co, Nov,. 1972
1 James Dixon art 70.00

BLOOD FROM A STONE (GUIDE TO TAX REFORM)
New York Public Interest Research Group Inc., 1977
1 Tax reform proposals 15.00

BOBBY LONDON RETROSPECTIVE AND ART PORTFOLIO
Cartoonist Representatives
1 . . . . 20.00

BOBMAN AND TEDDY
Parrallax Comic Books Inc., 1966
1 RFK & Ted Kennedy's struggle to
control Democratic party 55.00

BODE'S CARTOON CONCERT
Dell, Sept., 1973
1 132 pgs; VB 27.50

BOGEYMAN COMICS
San Fransisco Comic Book Co., 1969
1 Horror,RHa 70.00
2 Horror,RHa 50.00
The Company & Sons
3 . . . . 35.00

BUFFALO RAG/THE DEAD CONCERT COMIX
Kenny Laramey, Dec., 1973
1 Alice in Wonderland parody 65.00

CAPTAIN GUTS
The Print Mint,1969
1 Super patriotV:Counter
culture 30.00
2 V:Black Panthers 20.00
3 V:Dope Smugglers 20.00

CAPTAIN STICKY
Captain Sticky, 1974–75
1 Super lawyer V:SocialInjustice . 20.00

Collected Cheech Wizard
© Co & Sons (1972)

CARTOON HISTORY OF THE UNIVERSE
Rip Off Press, Sept., 1978
1 Evolution of Everything;
　B:Larry Gonick 12.00
2 Sticks and Stones 8.00
3 River Realms-Sumer & Egypt . . 8.00
4 Part of the Old Testament 5.00
5 Brains and Bronze 5.00
6 Who are these Athenians 5.00

CASCADE COMIX MONTHLY
Everyman Studios, March, 1978
1 Interviews,articles about
　comix & comix artists 8.00
2 and 3 same . . . . @8.00
4 thru 11 . . . . @4.00
12 thru 23. . . . . @3.00

CHECKERED DEMON
Last Gasp, July, 1977
1 SCW 15.00
2 SCW 8.50
3 SCW 6.50

CHEECH WIZARD
Office of Student Publications, Syracuse U, 1967
n/n VB. 165.00

CHERRY POPTART
Last Gasp, 1982–85
1 by Larry Welz. 10.00
2 . . . . 7.00
Becomes:

CHERRY
3 . . . . 5.00
4 . . . . 5.00
5 . . . . 5.00
6 thru 13 . . . . @4.00
Kitchen Sink
14 . . . . 4.00
15. . . . . 4.00
TPB Cherry Collection #1 . . . . 15.00
TPB Cherry Collection #2 . . . . 15.00
TPB Cherry Collection #3 . . . . 13.00
Cherry's Jubilee #1 thru #4 . . . . . @3.00

CHICAGO MIRROR
Jay Lynch/Mirror Publishing Empire, Autumn, 1967
1 B:Bijou Funnies 50.00
2 same 40.00
3 same 125.00

COCAINE COMIX
Last Gas, Inc., 1976–82
1 . . . . 15.00
2 thru 4 . . . . @10.00
2005
1 . . . . 3.00
2 . . . . 3.00

COLLECTED CHEECH WIZARD, THE
Company & Sons, 1972
n/n VB. 65.00
Print Mint, 1976
n/n VB 15.00

COLLECTED TRASHMAN #1, THE
Fat City & The Red Mountain Tribe Productions
n/n SRo. 32.50

COMICS & COMIX
Oct., 1975
1 . . . . 15.00

COMIX BOOK
**Magazine Management Co.
Oct., 1974**
1 Compilation for newsstand
　distribution 20.00
2 and 3 . . . . @10.00
Kitchen Sink Enterprises
4 . . . . 20.00
5 . . . . 10.00

COMIX COLLECTOR, THE
Archival Press Inc., Dec., 1979
1 Fanzine 6.00
2 & 3 Fanzine . . . . @5.00

COMMIES FROM MARS
Kitchen Sink, March, 1973
1 TB 40.00
Last Gasp
2 thru 5 TB . . . . @15.00

COMPLETE FRITZ THE CAT
Belier Press 1978
n/n RCr,SRo,DSh. 70.00

CONSPIRACY CAPERS
The Conspiracy, 1969
1 Benefit Legal Defense of the
　Chicago-8 . . . . 110.00

DAN O'NEIL'S COMICS & STORIES
Company & Sons, Vol.1
1 B:Dan O'Neill. 50.00
2 & 3 . . . . @30.00
1971 Vol. 2
1 . . . . 6.50
2 and E:Dan O'Neill . . . . @4.50

DAS KAMPF
Vaughn Bode, May, 1963
N# 100 Loose pgs. 800.00
2nd Printing 52pgs.-produced by
　W.Bachner & Bagginer,1977 . . 25.00

DEADBONE EROTICA
Bantam Books Inc., April, 1971
n/n 132 pgs VB. 50.00

DEADCENTER CLEAVAGE
April, 1971
1 14 pgs 50.00

DEATH RATTLE
Kitchen Sink, June, 1972
1 RCo,TB 25.00
2 TB 20.00
3 TB 16.00

DESPAIR
The Print Mint, 1969
1 RCr 50.00

DIRTY DUCK BOOK, THE
Company & Sons, March, 1972
1 Bobby London 30.00

DISNEY RAPES THE 1st AMENDMENT
Dan O'Neil, 1974
1 Benefit Air Pirates V:Disney
　Law suit; Dan O'Neill 15.00

DR. ATOMIC
Last Gasp Eco-Funnies, Sept., 1972
1 B:Larry S. Todd 15.00
2 and 3 . . . . @12.00
4 . . . . 10.00
5 E:Larry S. Todd 8.00
6 . . . . 6.00

DR. ATOMIC'S MARIJUANA MULTIPLIER
Kistone Press, 1974
1 How to grow great pot 10.00

DOPE COMIX
Kitchen Sink, Feb., 1978
1 Drugs comix;various artists 10.00
2 same 8.00
3 & 4 LSD issue . . . . @6.00
5 Omaha the Cat Dancer, RW . . . 10.00

DOPIN DAN
Last Gasp Eco-Funnies, April, 1972
1 TR 15.00
2 and 3 TR . . . . @10.00
4 Todays Army,TR. 9.00

DORI STORIES
Last Gasp, 2004
TPB Dori Deda collection. 20.00

DRAWINGS BY S. CLAY WILSON
San Francisco Graphics
1 28 pgs 210.00

Underground

DYING DOLPHIN
The Print Mint ,1970
n/n 20.00

EBON
**San Francisco Comic
Book Company**
1 Comix version; RCr 30.00
1 Tabloid version. 20.00

EL PERFECTO COMICS
The Print Mint, 1973
N# Benefit Timothy Leary 30.00
2nd Printing-1975 . . . . 4.00

ETERNAL TRUTH
Sunday Funnies Comic Corp
1 Christian Comix 25.00

EVERMUCH WAVE
Atlantis Distributors
1 Nunzio the Narc; Adventures
of God 65.00

E.Z. WOLF'S
ASTRAL OUTHOUSE
Last Gasp, 2005
1-shot 3.00

FABULOUS FURRY
FREAK BROTHERS, THE
**COLLECTED ADVENTURES OF
Rip Off Press, #1 Feb., 1971**
1 GiS 100.00
**FURTHER ADVENTURES OF
Rip Off Press, #2**
1 GiS,DSh 65.00
**A YEAR PASSES LIKE
NOTHING WITH
Rip Off Press #3**
1 GiS. 25.00
**BROTHER CAN YOU
SPARE $.75 FOR
Rip Off Press #4**
1 GiS,DSh 20.00
**FABULOUS FURRY
FREAK BROTHERS, THE
Rip Off Press #5**
1 GiS,DSh 15.00
**SIX SNAPPY SOCKERS
FROM THE ARCHIVES OF
Rip Off Press #6**
1 GiS 10.00

FANTAGOR
1970
1 (Corben), fanzine 135.00
Last Gasp
1a 22.00
2 & 3 . . . . @25.00
4 . . . . 35.00

FEDS 'N' HEADS
Gilbert Shelton/Print Mint, 1968
N# I:Fabulous Furry Freak Bros.;
Has no 'Print Mint' Address
24 pgs. 425.00
2nd printing, 28 pgs. 60.00
3rd printing, May, 1969 . . . . 50.00
4th printing, Says 'Forth
Printing' 25.00

5th-12th printings . . . . @10.00
13th printing 7.00
14th printing 6.00

FELCH
Keith Green
1 RW,SCW,RCr. 45.00

FEVER PITCH
**Kitchen Sink Enterprises,
July, 1976**
1 RCo 25.00
Jabberwocky Graphix
2 250 signed & numbered 20.00
3 400 signed & numbered 18.00
4 . . . . 10.00

50'S FUNNIES
Kitchen Sink Enterprises, 1980
1 Larry Shell, editor,various
artists 10.00

*Fabulous Furry Freak Brothers #9
© Rip Off Press*

FLAMING CARROT
**Kilian Barracks Free Press,
1981**
1 Bob Budden,various artists 15.00

FLASH THEATRE
Oogle Productions, 1970
1 44 pgs 50.00

FLESHAPOIDS FROM
EARTH
Popular Culture, Dec., 1974
1 36 pgs 40.00

THE COMPLETE FOO!
Bijou Publishing, Sept., 1980
1 RCr, Charles Crumb, r:Crumb
brothers fanzines 50.00

FRITZ BUGS OUT
Ballentine Books, 1972
n/n RCr. 75.00

FRITZ THE CAT
Ballentine Books, 1969
n/n RCr. 135.00

FRITZ THE NO-GOOD
Ballentine Books, 1972
n/n RCr. 65.00

FRITZ: SECRET AGENT
FOR THE CIA
Ballentine Books, 1972
n/n RCr. 65.00

FUNNY AMINALS
**Apex Novelties/Don Donahue,
1972**
1 RCr 70.00

GAY COMIX
Kitchen Sink Sept., 1981
1 36 pgs 8.00
2 36 pgs 6.00

GEN OF HIROSHIMA
**Educomics/Leonard Rifas,
Jan., 1980**
1 Antiwar comix by Hiroshima
survivor Keiji Nakazawa 10.00
2 same 8.00

GHOST MOTHER COMICS
John "Mad" Peck, 1969
1 SCw,JsG 55.00

GIMMEABREAK COMIX
Rhuta Press, Feb., 1971
2 48 pgs, #0 & #1 were advertised,but
may not have been printed 135.00

GIRLS & BOYS
Lynda J. Barry, 1980
1 B:12 pgs with every other page
blank, all Barry art 12.00
2 thru 10 same . . . . @8.00
11 thru 20 same . . . . @6.00
20 thru 25 same . . . . @5.00

GOD NOSE
**Jack Jackson/
Rip Off Press, 1964**
N# 42 pgs. 150.00
2nd printing,Pinkish(c);44p 60.00
3rd printing,Blue Border(c) 30.00
4th printing,Red Border(c) 15.00

GOTHIC BLIMP
WORKS LTD.
**East Village Other/
Peter Leggieri, 1969**
1 VB,Editor,various artists. 225.00
2 same 145.00
3 KDe,editor 135.00
4 KDe,editor 130.00
5 thru 7 KDe,editor . . . . @125.00
8 various artists. 185.00

GREASER COMICS
Half-Ass Press, Sept., 1971
1 28 pgs, George DiCaprio 25.00
Rip Off Press, July, 1972
2 George DiCaprio 15.00

GRIM WIT
Last Gasp, 1972
1 RCo 40.00
2 RCo 30.00

All comics prices listed are for *Near Mint* condition.

HAROLD HEAD, THE COLLECTED ADVENTURES OF
Georgia Straight, 1972
1 .... 50.00
2 .... 20.00

HARRY CHESS THAT MAN FROM A.U.N.T.I.E.
The Uncensored Adventures, Trojan Book Service, 1966
N# 1st Comix By & For Gay
Community 165.00

HEAR THE SOUND OF MY FEET WALKING....
Glide Urban Center, 1969
1 Dan O'Neill, 128 pgs. 75.00

HISTORY OF UNDERGROUND COMIX
Straight Arrow Books, 1974
1 Book by Mark James Estren about
Underground Comix 50.00

HOMEGROWN FUNNIES
Kitchen Sink, 1971
1 RCr 65.00

HONKYTONK SUE, THE QUEEN OF COUNTRY SWING
Bob Boze Bell, 1979
1 BBB 17.00
2 & 3 BBB .... @12.00

IKE LIVES
Warm Neck Funnies, 1973
1 20 pgs, Mark Fisher 15.00

IMAGE OF THE BEAST
Last Gast, 1973
1 Phillip Jose Farmer adapt...... 16.00
1 rep. 1979 .... 10.00

INSECT FEAR
Last Gasp, 1970
1 SRo,GiS,RHa,JsG 90.00
Print Mint, 1970–72
2 .... 30.00
3 .... 20.00

IT AIN'T ME BABE
Last Gasp Eco-Funnies, 1970
n/n First all women comix
Womens Liberation theme ... 40.00

JAPANESE MONSTER
Carol Lay, July, 1979
1 8pgs, Carol Lay 10.00

JESUS LOVES YOU
Zondervan Books/Craig Yoe, 1972
1 Christian, RCr 35.00

Mr Natural #3
© Kitchen Sink (1998) 10th printing

THE NEW ADVENTURES OF JESUS
Rip Off Press, Nov., 1971
1 44 pgs, FSt 50.00

JIZ
Apex Novelty, 1969
1 36 pgs; RCr, SRo, VMo, SCW; hand
trimmed and unevenly stapled 65.00

JUNKWAFFEL
The Print Mint, 1971
1 VB 35.00
2 and 3 VB .... @30.00
4 VB,JJ 25.00

KANNED KORN KOMIX
Canned Heat Fan Club, 1969
1 20pgs.................... 25.00

KAPTAIN AMERIKA KOMIX
Brief Candle Comix, March 1970
1 anti U.S. involvement in Laos... 35.00

KING BEE
Apex/Don Donahue & Kerry Clark, 1969
1 RCr,SCW 150.00

KURTZMAN COMIX
Kitchen Sink, Sept., 1976
1 HK,RCr,GiS,DKi,WE 30.00

LAUGH IN THE DARK
Last Gasp
n/n KDe,RHa,SRo,SCW 20.00

LENNY OF LAVEDO
Sunbury Productions/Print Mint, 1965
N# Green(c);1st Joel Beck-a ... 600.00
2nd printing, Orange(c)....... 400.00
3rd printing, White(c) 200.00

THE MACHINES
Office of Student Publications Syracuse University, 1967
1 VB 150.00

THE MAN
Office of Student Publications Syracuse University, 1966
1 VB 175.00

MAGGOTZINE
Charles Schneider, May, 1981
1 Various Artists,conceptual
maggot stuff 10.00

MANTICORE
Joe Kubert School of Cartooning & Graphic Arts Inc., Autumn, 1976
1 Fanzine,various artists....... 10.00

MEAN BITCH THRILLS
The Print Mint, 1971
1 SRO.................... 15.00

MICKEY RAT
Los Angeles Comic Book Co., May, 1972
1 Robert Armstrong........... 35.00
2 same 35.00
3 same 15.00

MR. NATURAL
San Fransisco Comic Book Co., August, 1970
1 RCr 140.00
2 RCr 70.00
Kitchen Sink
3 RCr, (B&W) 35.00

MOM'S HOMEMADE COMICS
Kitchen Sink, June, 1969
1 DKi, RCr............... 140.00
The Print Mint
2 DKi.................... 40.00
Kitchen Sink Enterprises
3 DKi,RCr................. 30.00

MONDAY FUNNIES, THE
Monday Funnies, 1977
1 8pgs,various artists 8.00
2 16pgs,various artists 10.00
3 16pgs,various artists 8.00
4 16pgs,various artists 7.00

MONDAY FUNNIES, THE
Passtime Publ., July–Aug., 1980
1 thru 8 Marc L.Reed .... @8.00

MOONCHILD COMICS
Nicola Cuti, 1968
0 Nicola Cuti 35.00
2 Nicola Cuti................. 35.00
3 Nicola Cuti................. 35.00

MOONDOG
The Print Mint, March, 1970
1 All George Metzer 25.00
2 same 18.00
3 and 4 same .... @12.00

All comics prices listed are for *Near Mint* condition.

Mens Adventure Comix #6
© Penthouse (1996)

MORE ADVENTURES OF FAT FREDDY'S CAT
Rip Off Press, Jan., 1981
1 GiS. 14.00

MOTOR CITY COMICS
Rip Off Press, April, 1969
1 RCr 180.00
2 RCr 140.00

MOUSE LIBERATION FRONT
COMMUNIQUE #2, August, 1979
1 SRo, SCW, VMo,DKi; Disney's sues
Dan O'Neil's Air Pirates. 15.00

NARD 'N' PAT, JAYZEY LYNCH'S
Cartoonists Cooperative Press, March, 1974
1 Jay Lynch. 18.00
2 Jay Lynch. 12.00
Kitchen Sink Press, 1972
3 . . . . 17.00

NEVERWHERE
Ariel Inc., Feb., 1978
1 RCo 25.00

NICKEL LIBRARY
Gary Arlington
1 1 pg heavy stock colored
paper, Reed Crandall 5.00
2 Kim Deitch 2.50
3 Harrison Cady 2.50
4 Frank Frazetta 4.00
5 Will Eisner 4.00
6 Justin Green 2.50
7 C.C. Beck 4.00
8 Wally Wood 4.00
9 Winsor McCay 2.50
10 Jim Osborne 2.50
11 Don Towsley 2.50
12 Frank Frazetta 4.00
13 Will Eisner. 4.00
14 Bill Griffith 2.50
15 George Herriman 2.50
16 Cliff Sterrett 2.50
17 George Herriman 2.50
18 Rory Hayes & Simon Deitch. . . . 2.50

19 Disney Studios 2.50
20 Alex Toth 2.50
21 Will Eisner. 2.50
22 Jack Davis 3.00
23 Alex Toth 2.50
24 Michele Brand 2.50
25 Roger Brand 2.50
26 Arnold Roth 2.50
27 Murphy Anderson 2.50
28 Wally Wood 3.00
29 Jack Kirby 4.00
30 Harvey Kurtzman 3.00
31 Jay Kinney 2.50
32 Bill Plimpton 2.50
33 . . . . 2.50
34 Charles Dallas 2.50
35 thru 39. . . . . @2.50
40 Bill Edwards 2.50
41 Larry S. Todd 2.50
42 Charles Dallas 2.50
43 Jim Osborne 2.50
43 1/2 Larry S. Todd 2.50
44 Jack Jackson 2.50
45 Rick Griffin 2.50
46 Justin Green 2.50
47 and 48 Larry S. Todd. . . . . . . @2.50
49 Charles Dallas 2.50
50 Robert Crumb 4.00
51 Wally Wood 4.00
52 Charles Dallas 4.00
53 and 54 Larry S. Todd. . . . . . . @2.50
55 Charles Dallas 2.50
56 Jim Chase 2.50
57 Charles Dallas 2.50
58 Larry S. Todd 2.50
59 Dave Geiser 2.50
60 Charles Dallas 2.50

NO DUCKS
Last Gasp, 1977–79
1 . . . . 15.00
2 . . . . 12.00
2005
2 . . . . 2.95

ODD WORLD OF RICHARD CORBEN
Warren Publishing, 1977
1 84pgs paperback 20.00

O.K. COMICS
Kitchen Sink, June, 1972
1 and 2 Bruce Walthers . . . . . . @15.00

O.K. COMICS
O.K. Comic Company, 1972
1 Tabloid with comix, articles,
reviews, nudie cuties photos. . 30.00
2 thru 18 . . . . @20.00

OMAHA THE CAT DANCER
Steel Dragon Press, 1984
1 RW,F:Omaha, Shelly, Chuck . . . 15.00
Kitchen Sink, 1986
1 RW. 10.00
2 RW 8.00
3 thru 5 . . . . @7.00
6 thru 10 . . . . @6.00
11 thru 20 . . . . @5.00
Spec.#0, 25th Anniv. Classic 15.00
Images of Omaha, RW benefit 8.00
Images No. 2 . . . . 7.00
TPB Collected Omaha #1, rep. . . . 15.00
TPB Collected Omaha #2, rep. . . . 13.00
TPB Collected Omaha #3, rep. . . . 13.00
TPB Collected Omaha #4, rep. . . . 13.00
TPB Collected Omaha #5, rep. . . . 13.00

1 . . . . 6.00
2 . . . . 6.00

ORACLE COMIX
Thru Black Holes Comix Productions, Oct., 1980
1 and 2 Michael Roden . . . . @6.00

PENGUINS IN BONDAGE
Sorcerer Studio/ Wayne Gibson, July, 1981
1 8pgs,Wayne Gibson 5.00

PHANTOM LADY
Randy Crawford, June, 1978
1 Sex funnies 6.00

PHUCKED UP FUNNIES
Suny Binghamton, 1969
1 ASp;insert bound in yearbook . 425.00

PINK FLOYD, THE
October, 1974
1 sold at concerts 35.00

PLASTIC MAN
Randy Crawford, May, 1977
1 Sex funnies,RandyCrawford . . . 12.00

PORK
Co-op Press, May, 1974
1 SCW 15.00

PORTFOLIO OF UNDERGROUND ART
Schanes & Schanes, 1980
1 SRo,SCW,VMo,RW and many others
13 loose sheets in folder, 32pg
book, 1200 signed & numb. . . 90.00

POWERMAN AND POWER MOWER SAFETY
Frank Burgmeir, Co. Outdoor Power Equipment
1 VB; educational comic about power
mower safety 200.00

San Francisco Comics #3
© Crumb

PROMETHIAN ENTERPRISES
Promethian Enterprises
Memorial Day, 1969
1 B:Jim Vadeboncuor editor 80.00
2 same 60.00
3 thru 5 .... @25.00

PURE ART QUARTERLY
John A. Adams, July, 1976
1 16pgs, All John A.Adams...... 12.00
2 thru 5 same .... @12.00
6 thru 10 same .... @10.00
11 thru 14 same .... @8.00

PURE TRANCE
Last Gasp, 2005
GN 20.00

QUAGMIRE COMICS
Kitchen Sink, Summer, 1970
1 DKi,Peter Poplaski 15.00

RAW
Raw Books, 1980
1 36pgs,10pgs insert 325.00
2 36pgs,20pgs insert 185.00
3 52pgs,16pgs insert 155.00
4 44pgs,32pgs insert,Flexi
  disk record 125.00

R. CRUMB'S COMICS AND STORIES
Rip Off Press, 1969
1 RCr 135.00

Slow Death #5
© Last Gasp

RAWARARAWAR
Rip Off Press, 1969
1 GSh...................... 70.00

RED SONJA & CONAN "HOT AND DRY"
Randy Crawford, May, 1977
1 Sex funnies,Randy Crawford... 10.00

REID FLEMING WORLD'S TOUGHEST MILKMAN
David E. Boswell, Dec., 1980
1 .... 7.00

RIP OFF COMIX
Rip Off Press, April, 1977
1 GiS,FSt,JsG,DSh 20.00
2 thru 5 GiS,FSt .... @12.00
6 thru 10 .... @6.00

ROWLF
Rip Off Press, July, 1971
1 RCo 55.00

RUBBER DUCK TALES
The Print Mint, March, 1971
1 Michael J Becker 22.00
2 Michael J Becker 17.00

SACRED & PROFANE
Last Gasp, Inc., 2005
1-shot...................... 5.00

S. CLAY WILSON TWENTY DRAWINGS
Abington Book Shop Inc., 1967
N# (a),Cowboy(c) 550.00
  (b),Pirate(c) 500.00
  (c),Motorcyclist(c)........ 500.00
  (d),Demon(c) 500.00
  (e),Deluxe with all 4
  variations on same(c) with
  Gold Embossed Lettering . 700.00

SAN FRANCISCO COMIC BOOK
San Francisco Comic Book Co., Jan.-Feb., 1970
1 .... 125.00
2 .... 25.00
3 .... 20.00
4 .... 15.00
5 .... 15.00
6 .... 15.00

SAVAGE HUMOR
The Print Mint, 1973
1 .... 12.00

SAY WHAT?
Loring Park Shelter Community Cartooning Workshop, April, 1979
1 B:Charles T. Smith,editor,
  various artists 12.00
2 thru 6 same .... @10.00

SCARYGIRL
Last Gasp Inc., 2005
GN 15.00

SCHIZOPHRENIA, CHEECH WIZARD
Last Gasp Eco-Funnies, 1973
1 VB 30.00

SEX AND AFFECTION
C.P. Family Publishers, 1974
1 Sex Education for Children 10.00

SHORT ORDER COMIX
Head Press/Family Fun, 1973
1 50 cents,36pgs............. 12.00
2 75 cents,44pgs 8.00
Last Gasp, Inc., 2005
1-shot...................... 3.00

SKULL COMICS
Rip Off Press
1 Horror,RHa 50.00
Last Gasp, 1970
2 GiS,DSh,RCo 30.00
3 SRo,DSh,RCo 20.00
4 DSh,Lovecraft issue 20.00
5 SRo,RCo,Lovecraft issue 20.00
6 RCo,Herman Hesse 20.00

SLOW DEATH FUNNIES
Last Gasp, 1970–92
1 Ecological Awarness & Red
  Border on (c) 50.00
2nd-4th Printings White
  Border(c) 12.00
Becomes:

SLOW DEATH
2 Silver(c);1st edition' 34 pgs ... 100.00
2b Non Silver(c);Says 1st
  Edition, 34 pgs. 20.00
2nd Amorphia Ad on pg 34 ...... 8.00
3rd Yellow Skull on (c) 8.00
4th `Mind Candy For the Masses'
  Ad on pg. 34 .... 7.00
5th $1.00(c) price 5.00
3 thru 5 .... @12.00
6 thru 11 .... @6.00

SMILE
Kitchen Sink, Summer, 1970
1 Jim Mitchell 15.00
2 Jim Mitchell 12.00
3 Jim Mitchell 11.00

SNARF
Kitchen Sink, Feb., 1972
1 DKi,editor,various artists 27.00
2 thru 5 same .... @15.00
6 thru 9 same .... @6.50
1987–90
10 thru 15 .... @5.00

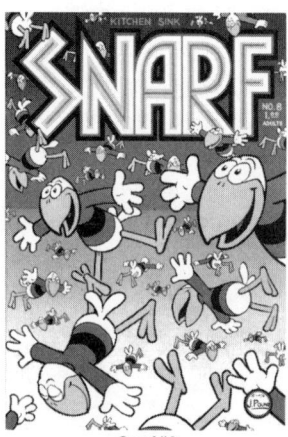
Snarf #8
© Kitchen Sink

All comics prices listed are for *Near Mint* condition.

SNATCH COMICS
Apex Novelties, 1968
1 RCr,SCW 325.00
2 RCr,SCW 175.00
3 RCr,SCW,RW. 90.00

SNATCH SAMPLER
Keith Green, 1979
n/n RCr,SCw,RW,RHa 35.00

SPACE INVADERS COMICS, DON CHIN'S
Comix World/Clay Geerdes, April, 1972
1 8pgs 10.00

SPASM!
Last Gasp Eco-Funnies, April, 1973
1 JJ 15.00

STONED PICTURE PARADE
San Francisco Comic Book Co., 1975
1 RCr,SRo,SCW,WE. 25.00

SUBVERT COMICS
Rip Off Press, Nov., 1970
1 SRo 25.00
2 SRo 20.00
3 SRo 15.00

TALES OF SEX & DEATH
Print Mint, 1971
1 JsG,KDe.RHa,SRo. 35.00
2 JsG,KDe.RHa,SRo. 20.00

THRILLING MURDER COMICS
San Francisco Comic Book Co., 1971
1 SCW,KDe,RCr,SRo,Jim
Arlington,editor 32.00

2 (TWO)
Keith Green, Feb., 1975
1 SCW 12.00

VAMPIRELLA
Randy Crawford, June, 1978
1 Sex Funnies. 8.00

VAUGHN BODE THE PORTFOLIO
Northern Comfort Com., 1976
1 VB,16pgs 135.00

VAUGHN BODE PORTFOLIO #1
Vaughn Bode Productions, 1978
1 VB,10 pgs 35.00

VAUGHN BODE'S CHEECH WIZARD, THE COLLECTED ADVENTURES OF THE CARTOON MESSIAH
Northern Comfort Com., 1976
1 VB,88pgs 60.00

VAUGHN BODE'S DEADBONE, THE FIRST TESTAMENT OF CHEECH WIZARD
Northern Comfort Com., 1975
1 VB 75.00

VIETNAM
N# 20pgs. Role of Blacks in
the War,TG Lewis 135.00

WEIRDO
Last Gasp Eco-Funnies, 1981–93
1 thru 3 RCr . . . . @12.00
4 thru 10 . . . . @7.50
11 thru 28 . . . . @5.00

WEIRDO, THE
Rodney Schroeter, Oct., 1977
1 B:Rodney Schroezer,1pg. 7.00
2 88pgs. 7.00
3 44pgs. 7.00

WIMMEN'S COMIX
Last Gasp Eco-Funnies, 1972–85
1 All women artists&comix 15.00
2 thru 3 same . . . . @12.00
4 thru 10 same . . . . @8.00

WONDER WART-HOG AND THE NURDS OF NOVEMBER
Rip Off Press, Sept., 1980
1 GiS 20.00

Zap-1
© Apex Novelties

WONDER WART-HOG, CAPTAIN CRUD & OTHER SUPER STUFF
Fawcett Publications, 1967
1 GiS,VB 25.00

YELLOW DOG
The Print Mint, May, 1968
1 4pgs,RCr 45.00
2 and 3 8pgs,RCr . . . . @30.00
4 8pgs,RCr,SCW 30.00
5 8pgs,RCr,SCW,KDe 30.00
6 thru 12 . . . . @25.00
13/14 52pgs RCr,Jay Lynch. 12.00
15 Don Scheneker,editor 65.00
16. . . . . 55.00
17 thru 24 . . . . @15.00

YOUNG AND LUSTLESS
San Francisco Comic Book Co., 1972
1 BG 20.00

YOUNG LUST
Company & Sons, Oct., 1970
1 BG,ASp 30.00
Print Mint
2 BG 15.00
3 BG,JsG,RCr,ASp 15.00
4 KDe,BG,SRo 12.00
Last Gasp
5 BG,SRo 9.00
6 SRo,KDe 8.00
7 and 8 . . . . @5.00

YOW
Last Gasp, April, 1978
1 BG 7.00
2 BG 6.00
Becomes:

ZIPPY
3 BG 6.50

ZAP COMIX
Apex Novelties, Oct., 1967
0 RCr 400.00
1 RCr 375.00
2 RCr,SCW 150.00
3 RCr,SCW,VMo,SRo 60.00
4 VMo,RW,RCr,SCW.SRo,GiS . . . 60.00
5 RW,GiS,RCr,SCW,SRo 50.00
6 RW,GiS,RCr,SCW,SRo 30.00
7 RW,GiS,RCr,SCW,SRo 20.00
8 RW,GiS,RCr,SCW,SRo 15.00
9 RW,GiS,RCr,SCW,SRo 20.00
Last Gasp
10 thru 14 . . . . @10.00

ZIPPY: NATION OF PINHEADS
Last Gasp, Inc., 2005
GN 6.00

ZIPPY: YOW!
Last Gasp, Inc., 2004
1-shot from comic strip 2.50
3 . . . . 3.50

1—9

10 699
100 Bullets 130
100 Girls 663
100 Girls/Jenna 663
100 Greatest Marvels 297
100 Pages of Comics 450
100% 130
1000 Deaths of Baron von
    Donut 778
1001 Arabian Nights: the
    Adventures of Sinbad 663
101 Ways to End the Clone
    Saga 297
10th Muse 699
10th Muse/Demonslayer 799
10th Muse/Ezra 699
10th Muse the 570
12 O'clock High 706
13: Assassin 700
13 Chambers 570
1963 558
'76 564
'68 565
2 (Two) 831
2 to the Chest 707
2-Gun Kid 210
2000 A.D. Monthly 707
2001: a Space Odyssey 339
2001 Nights 803
2010 339
2020 Visions 179
2099 A.D. 339
2099 Apocalypse 339
2099 Genesis 339
2099: Manifest Destiny 339
2099 Special: the World
    of Doom 339
2099 Unlimited 339
2099: World of Tomorrow 339
'21' 572
21 down 706
2112 530
22 Brides 706
24: Cold Warriors 706
24: Nightfall 706
(3-D Features Presents)
    Jet Pup 479
3 Little Kittens 701
3 X 3 Eyes 799
3 X 3 Eyes: Curse of the Gesu . 529
3-D Adventures of Superman
    . . . . . 177, 335, 478, 479, 701
30 Days of Night 700
30 Days of Night: 701
300 529
39 Screams 799
13th Son, the 529
4-D Monkey 620
411 245
4most 415
5 Cent Comics 406
50's Funnies 827
52 79
52 Aftermath: the Four Horsemen 79
666: Mark of the Beast 686
7 Guys of Justice the 790
77 Sunset Strip 683
777: the Wrath 790
80 Page Giants 77
86 Voltz: Dead Girl 544
87th Precinct 614
9 Lives of Felix 661
99 the 662

A A A A

A Christmas Carol 818
A Connecticut Yankee in King
    Arthur's Court 815
A Cop Called Tracy 726
A Date with Judy 66
A Date with Millie 229
A Date with Patsy 229
A Distant Soil 543, 745
A Feature Presentation 404
A Journey to the Center of
    the Earth 822
A Man Called Ax 119
A Midsummer Nights Dream . . . 820
A Moon, a Girl . . Romance . . . 447
A Sort of Homecoming 729
A Spectacular Feature
    Magazine 468

A Study in Scarlet 821
A Tale of Two Cities 813
A Touch of Silver 571
A Traveller's Tale 730
A. Bizarro 25
A.B.C. Warriors 726
A.R.M. 729
A-Next 202, 204, 368, 728
A1 726
A1/Bloodmoon 581
Aardwolf 726
Aaron Strips 532, 726
Abadazad 578
Abbie An' Slats 368
Abbott and Costello 368, 578
Abc: A-Z 578
Abe Sapien: Drums of the Dead 500
Abe Sapien: the Drowning 500
Abiding Perdition 578
Abraham Lincoln 823
Abraham Stone 193
Absolute Zero 726
Abyss 578
Abyss the 500
Ac Annual 726
Accelerate 25
Accident Man 500
Ace Comics 368
Ace Comics Presents 726
Ace McCoy 726
Ace of Diamonds 726
Aces 726
Aces High 369, 578
Acg's Amazing Comics 726
Achilles Storm 726
Acme 726
Acme Novelty Library 578
Acolyte Chronicles 726
Action 25
Action Girl Comics 726
Action Philosophers 726
Action Planet 532
Actual Confessions 271
Actual Romances 193
Adam and Eve A.D. 726
Adam: Legend of the Blue
    Marvel 193
Adam Strange 30
Adam-12 578
Addam Omega 726
Addams Family 578
Adlai Stevenson 578
Adolescent Radioactive Black
    Belt Hamsters 578, 726
Adrenaline 578
Adrenalynn 532
Advanced Dungeons & Dragons . 30
Advent Rising: Rock the Planet 578
Adventure Comics 30, 33
Adventure into Fear 245
Adventure into Mystery 193
Adventure Is My Career 369
Adventure Strip Digest 532
Adventurers 726
Adventurers Book I 726
Adventurers Book III 726
Adventures 369
Adventures in 3-D 369
Adventures in the DC Universe . . 33
Adventures in Wonderland 369
Adventures into Darkness 369
Adventures into Terror 264
Adventures into the Unknown . . 726
Adventures into the Unknown! . . 369
Adventures into Weird Worlds . . 193
Adventures Marco Polo, the . . . 815
Adventures of Aaron 532
Adventures of Alice 369
Adventures of Alan Ladd, the . . 33
Adventures of Barry Ween Boy
    Genius 532, 726
Adventures of Big Boy, the . . 193
Adventures of Bio Boy the . . . 578
Adventures of Bob Hope, the . . 33
Adventures of Captain America . 193
[Adventures Of] Captain Jack . . 737
Adventures of Cellini 816
Adventures of Chrissy
    Claws the 726
Adventures of Chuk the
    Barbaric 726

Adventures of Cyclops &
    Phoenix 193
Adventures of Dean Martin
    and Jerry Lewis 33
[Adventures Of] Evil and Malice 545
Adventures of Fat Freddy's
    Cat, the 825
Adventures of Ford Fairlane . . 33
Adventures of Hercules 726
Adventures of Homer Cobb . . . 369
Adventures of Homer Ghost . . 193
Adventures of Kit Carson 821
Adventures of Liberal Man 727
Adventures of Little Orphan
    Annie Comics 369
Adventures of Luther
    Arkwright 500, 727
Adventures of Mighty
    Mouse 369, 478, 654
Adventures of Ozzie and Harriet . 33
Adventures of Pinky Lee 193
Adventures of Pipsqueak, the . . 578
Adventures of Rex the
    Wonder Dog 33
Adventures of Robin Hood 460, 578
Adventures of Sherlock
    Holmes, the 816
Adventures of Spawn 532
Adventures of Spider-Man 193
Adventures of Superboy 158
Adventures of Superman 163
Adventures of Superman 162
Adventures of the Aerobic Duo . 727
Adventures of the Fly 578
Adventures of the Jaguar 578
Adventures of the Mask 500
Adventures of the Outsiders . . 48
Adventures of the X-Men 193
Adventures of Theown 727
Adventures of Tom Sawyer . . . 817
Adventures of Young
    Dr. Masters 578
Adventures on the Planet
    of the Apes 193
Adventurous Uncle Scrooge
    McDuck 578
Aeon Flux 500
Aesop's Fables 727
Aetos 727
Aetos 2: Children of the Graves 727
Aetos the Eagle 727
After the Cape 532
After the Cape II 532
Afterburn 578
Aftermath 578
Age of Bronze 532
Age of Heroes the 532, 727
Age of Heroes: Wex 532
Age of Insects The: Not Human 579
Age of Reptiles 500
Age of Reptiles: the Hunt 500
Age of the Sentry the 193
Agency the 532
Agent: America 579
Agent Unknown 727
Agent X 193
Agents of Atlas 193
Agents of Law 500
Agents the 532
Aggie Mack 370
Agony Acres 727
Aiden McKain Chronicles:
    Battle for Earth 579
Air 34
Air Ace 370
Air Fighters Comics 370
Air Fighters Sgt. Strike Special . 579
Air War Stories 579
Airboy 579
Airboy Comics 370
Airfighters Classics 727
Airmaidens Special 579
Airwaves 727
Akiko 727
Akira 193
Al Capp's Dogpatch Comics . . 370
Al Capp's Shmoo 371
Al Capp's Wolf Gal 371
Alan Moore's Awesome
    Adventures 579
Alan Moore's Glory 579

Alan Moore's Hypothetical
    Lizard 727
Alan Moore's the Courtyard . . . 727
Alan Moore's Yuggoth Cultures . 727
Alarming Adventures 579
Alarming Tales 579
Albedo 579, 727
Albert 727
Albion 579
Aleister Arcane 579
Alethia 532
Alf 194
Alias 194, 579
Alias: Agent Bristow 579
Alice 371
Alice in the Lost Land 727
Alice in Wonderland 579, 817
Alien 3 501
Alien Arena 579
Alien Encounters 579
Alien Fire 727
Alien Legion 194
Alien Legion: on the Edge 194
Alien Legion: One Planet
    at a Time 194
Alien Legion: Tenants of Hell . . 194
Alien Nation: a Breed Apart . . . 727
Alien Nation: the Firstcomers . . 728
Alien Nation: the Public Enemy . 728
Alien Nation: the Skin Trade . . . 728
Alien Nation: the Spartans 728
Alien Pig Farm 3000 532
Alien Resurrection 500
Alien Terror 579
Alien Worlds 579
Aliens 500
Aliens (II) 500
Aliens: Alchemy 500
Aliens: Apocalypse Destroying
    Angels 500
Aliens: Berserker 500
Aliens: Colonial Marines 500
Aliens: Earth War 500
Aliens: Genocide 500
Aliens: Havoc 500
Aliens: Hive 500
Aliens: Kidnapped 500
Aliens: Labyrinth 500
Aliens: Music of the Spears . . . 500
Aliens: Newt's Tale 500
Aliens/Predator: Deadliest
    of the Species 501
Aliens: Rogue 500
Aliens: Stronghold 501
Aliens: Survival 501
Aliens Vs. Predator 501
Aliens Vs. Predator: Duel 501
Aliens Vs. Predator: Eternal . . 501
Aliens Vs. Predator Vs.
    The Terminator 501
Aliens Vs. Predator: War 501
Aliens Vs. Predator:
    Xenogenesis 501
Aliens: Xenogenesis 501
Alison Dare Little Miss
    Adventures 728
Alister the Slayer 579
Alius Rex 579
All American Sports 579
Alley Oop 371
All Funny Comics 35
All Good Comics 371
All Great 371
All Great Comics 393
All Hallows Eve 580
All Hero Comics 371
All Humor Comics 371
All Love Romances 463
[All New Adventures Of]
    the Mighty Crusaders 654
All New Exiles 580
All Picture All True Love Story . 371
All Quiet on the Western Front . 820
All Select Comics 194
All Sports Comics 371
All Star Batman and Robin
    the Boy Wonder 36
All Star Comics 36
All Star Squadron 36
All Star Superman 37
All Surprise 194
All Top Comics 371

All Winners Comics 194, 195
All Your Comics 371, 372
All-American Comics
. . . . 34-36, 183, 194, 371, 728
All-American Men of War 34
All-American Western 34
All-Teen Comics 195
All-True Crime 296
Allegra 532
Alley Cat 532
Alley Oop 371, 580
Alley Oop Adventures 580
Alliance the 532
Allies 580
Allies the 532
Allura and the Cyberangels . . . 728
Ally 728
Along the Canadian 728
Alpha Flight 196
Alpha Korps 580
Alter Ego 580
Alteration 532
Altered Image 532
Alternate Heroes 728
Alvin (& the Chipmunks) 580
Amanda and Gunn 532
Amazing Adult Fantasy 197
Amazing Adventure Funnies . . . 372
Amazing Adventures 196, 372
Amazing Adventures of
the Escapist the 501
Amazing Chan & the Chan Clan 580
Amazing Comics 196
Amazing Comics Premieres . . . 728
Amazing Detective Cases 196
Amazing Dope Tales 825
Amazing Fantasy 197
Amazing Fantasy 196
Amazing Ghost Stories 491
Amazing Heroes Swimsuit
Annuals 580
Amazing Joy Buzzards the 532
Amazing Mysteries 196
Amazing Mystery Funnies 372
Amazing Screw-On Head the . . 501
Amazing Spider-Man. 196, 201, 202
Amazing Willie Mays 372
Amazing X-Men the 202
Amazing-Man Comics 372
Amazon 192
Amazon the 580
Amazon Woman 728
Amazons Attack 37
Amber: the Guns of Avalon 37
Ambush Bug 37
Ambush Bug Year None 37
Amelia Rules! 580
Amelia Rules!: Superheroes . . . 580
America in Action 372
America VS. Justice Society 37
America's Best Comics 580
America's Best Comics 372
America's Biggest Comics Book 372
America's Funniest Comics 372
America's Greatest Comics 728
America's Greatest Comics 372
American Air Forces, the 372
American Century 37
American Dream 202
American Flagg 580
American Freak: a Tale of
the Un-Men 37
American Freakshow 580
American Graphics 372
American Library 372
American: Lost in America, the . 501
American Splendor
. . . . 37, 501, 728, 825
American Splendor: Season Two 37
American Splendor: Unsung
Hero 501
American Splendor: Windfall . . . 501
American the 501
American Virgin 37
American Wasteland: Blood
and Diesel 580
American Way the 580
American Woman 580, 728
Americomics 580
Amethyst 37
Amusing Stories 728
Anarky 37

Anatomic Bombs 728
Anchors Andrews 372
Ancient Joe 501
[Andrew Vachss'] Cross 507
[Andrew Vachss'] Underground . 530
Andromeda 580
Andy Comics 463
Andy Devine Western 372
Angel 372, 501
Angel & the Ape 38
Angel: 580
Angel and the Ape 38
Angel Fire 580
Angel Girl 728
Angel Girl: Heaven Sent 728
Angel Heat: the Ninth Order . . . 728
Angel of Death 728
Angel: Revelations 202
Angel Scriptbook 728
Angel Spotlight 580
Angela 533
Angela/Glory: Rage of Angels . 533
Angels 750 728
Angeltown 38
Angry Youth Comix 728
Anima 38
Animal Adventures 373
Animal Antics 38, 373
Animal Comics 373
Animal Confidential 501
Animal Fables 373
Animal Fair 373
Animal Mystic 728
Animal Mystic: Klor 728
Animal Mystic: Water Wars 581
Animal-Man 38
Animaniacs 38
Animated Comics 373
Animated Movie-Tunes 202
Anita Blake Vampire Hunter:
First Death 202
Anita Blake Vampire Hunter:
Guilty Pleasures 202
Anita Blake Vampire Hunter:
the Laughing Corpse 202
Anna Mercury 581
Anne Rice's the Tale of the
Body Thief 581
Annie Oakley 202
Annie Oakley & Tagg 373
Annie Oakley and Tagg 581
Annihilation 202
Ant 533, 581
Ant Unleashed 581
Ant-Man 202
Antares Circle 728
Anthology of Slow Death 825
Anthro 38
Anubis 728
Anything Goes 581
Apache 373
Apache Kid 203
Apache Skies 203
Apache Trail 373
Apathy Kat 728
Ape City 728
Ape Nation 581
Apex Treasury of Underground
Comics –Best of Bijou
Funnies 825
Apex Treasury of Underground
Comics, the 825
Aphrodite Ix 533
Apocalypse Nerd 501
Apocalypse Plan the 729
Apollo Smile 581
Apparition the 729
Appleseed 729
Appleseed Databook 501
Approved Comics 373
Aquaman 39
Aquaman: Sword of Atlantis . . . 40
Aquaman: Time & Tide 40
Arabian Knights 813
Arachnaphobia 581
Arak 40
Araknis 581
Araknis: Retribution 581
Araknis: Shades of Evil 581
Aramis 581
Arana: the Heart of the Spider . 203
Arcade the Comics Revue . . . 825

Arcana: the Books of Magic 40
Arcanum 533
Archaic 581
Archangels: the Fall 581
Archangels: the Saga 581
Archard's Agents 581
Archenemies 501
Archer & Armstrong 581
Archibald Saves 533
Archie 581
Archie 3000 582
Archie and Friends 581
Archie and Me 581
Archie as Pureheart
the Powerful 581
Archie at Riverdale High 581
Archie Comics 373
Archie Comics Digest 582
Archie Meets the Punisher 582
Archie's Giant Series Magazine 373
Archie's Girls Betty
and Veronica 373
Archie's Joke Book Magazine . 373
Archie's Madhouse 582
Archie's Mechanics 373
Archie's Pal, Jughead 373
Archie's Pals 'N' Gals 374
Archie's Rival Reggie 374
Archie's Superhero Magazine . 582
Archie's Tv Laugh-Out 582
Archie's Weird Mysteries 582
Area 52 533
Area 88 729
Areala Angel of War 729
Arena the 582
Argonauts 729
Aria 533
Aria: a Summer Spell 533
Aria/Angela: Heavenly
Creatures 533
Aria: the Soul Market 533
Aria: the Uses of Enchantment . 533
Ariane & Bluebeard 582
Arik Khan 729
Arion Lord of Atlantis 40
Arion the Immortal 40
Aristocratic X-Tra- Terrestrial
Time- Traveling Thieves . . 729
Aristokittens the 582
Arizona: a Simple Horror 729
Arizona Kid 203
Arkaga 533
Arkanium 582
Arkham Asylum: Living Hell 40
Armageddon 582
Armageddon 2001 40
Armageddon 2001 Armageddon:
the Alien Agenda 40
Armageddon Factor 582
Armageddon: Inferno 40
Armageddon Patrol 729
Armed & Dangerous 729
Armor 582
Armor X 533
Armored Trooper Votoms 582
Armorines 582
Armorquest Genesis 582
Armory Wars II the 533
Armory Wars the 533
Army @ Love 40
Army @ Love: the Art of War . . . 40
Army and Navy Comics 474
Army Attack 582
Army of Darkness 501, 582
Army of Darkness/Xena:
Why Not? 583
Army War Heroes 583
Around the World in 80 Days . . 819
Arrgh! 203
Arrow 583
Arrow Spotlight 729
Arrow, the 374
Arrowhead 203
Arrowsmith 583
Arsenal 40
Arsenic Lullaby 729
Artesia 583
Artesia Afield 583
Artesia Afire 583
Artesia: Besieged 583
As Told By 729
Ascension 533

Ash 583
Ash/22 Brides 583
Ash: Cinder and Smoke 583
Ash Files the 583
Ash: Fire and Crossfire 583
Ash: the Fire Within 583
Ashes 729
Ashley Dust 729
Aspen 583
Aspen Seasons 583
Aspen Showcase 583
Asrial Vs. Cheetah 729
Assassin 583
Assassin School 583
Assassinate Hitler! 729
Assassinauts 583
Assassinette 729
Assassinette: Hardcore 1995 . 729
Assassins 192
Assembly 730
Aster 584
Aster the Last Celestial Knight . 584
Astonishing 203
Astonishing Tales 203
Astonishing X-Men 203, 204
Astounding Space Thrills . 533, 730
Astounding Space Thrills: Bloop 730
Astounding Wolf-Man 533
Astra 730
Astro 533
Astro Boy 584
Astro City 584
Astro City: Local Heroes 584
Astro City: Samaritan 584
Astronauts in Trouble:
\Live from the Moon 730
Astronauts in Trouble:
Space: 1959 730
Asylum 584
Atari Force 40
Atheist the 533
Athena 730
Athena Inc 534
Athena Voltaire: Flight of
the Flacon 584
Athena Voltaire: the Legend
of Mu-King 584
Atlantis Chronicles 40
Atlantis Rising 584
Atlas 502, 584
Atom & Hawkman 41
Atom Ant 584
Atom the 40
Atom the Cat 381
Atom-Age Combat 374, 584
Atoman 374
Atomic Attack 374
Atomic Bomb 374
Atomic City Tales 730
Atomic Comics 374, 730
Atomic Man 730
Atomic Mouse 374, 584, 730
Atomic Overdrive 730
Atomic Rabbit 584
Atomic Robo 584
Atomic Robo: the Dogs of War . 584
Atomic Thunderbolt, the 374
Atomic Toybox 534
Atomic War! 374
Atomics the 584
Atomik Angels 584
Atomik Mike 584
Atomika 584
Attack 374, 585
Attack at Sea 585
Attack of the Killer Tomatoes . . 585
Attack of the Mutant Monsters . 730
Augie Doggie 585
August 730
Authentic Police Cases 374
Authority the 585
Automatic Kafka 585
Automation 534
Autumn 730
Av in 3d 730
Avalon 730
Avant Guard 730
Avatar 41
Avatars 730
Avelon 730
Avengeblade 585
Avengelyne 585, 586

Avengers................204
Avengers and Power Pack
  Assemble.............207
Avengers: Celestial Quest.....207
Avengers Classic..........207
Avengers: Earth's Mightiest
  Heroes...............207
Avengers: Earth's Mightiest
  Heroes II.............207
Avengers Fairy Tales........207
Avengers Forever..........207
Avengers Handbook........207
Avengers Icons: the Vision...207
Avengers Icons: Tigra......207
Avengers Infinity.........207
Avengers/Invaders........207
Avengers/JLA.............41
Avengers next............207
Avengers Spotlight.......208
Avengers the.............586
Avengers: the Initiative...208
Avengers: the Terminatrix
  Objective.............208
Avengers/Thunderbolts...208
Avengers: Timeslide......208
Avengers Two: Wonder Man
  & the Beast...........208
Avengers: United They Stand..208
Avengers Unleashed......208
Avengers West Coast.....208
Avenue X................730
Aviation and Model Building...484
Aviation Cadets..........374
Avigon..................534
Avon One-Shots.........374
Awakening, the..........534
Awakening Comics........730
Awakening the...........586
Awakenings.............730
Awesome...............586
Awesome Comics.........730
Awful Oscar.............297
Axa...................586
Axed Files the..........730
Axel Pressbutton........586
Axis Alpha.............586
Aya...................586
Azrael.................41
Azrael/Ash.............41
Azrael plus.............41
Aztec Ace.............586
Aztek: the Ultimate Man...42

B B B B
B.A.B.E. Force..........730
B.A.B.E. Force: Back to School 730
B.A.B.E. Force: Jurassic Trailer
  Park.................730
B.E.A.S.T.I.E.S..........589
B.P.R.D................503
B.P.R.D.: 1946..........503
B.P.R.D.: a Plague of Frogs...503
B.P.R.D.: Garden of Souls....503
B.P.R.D.: Killing Ground.....503
B.P.R.D.: the Black Flame....503
B.P.R.D.: the Dead........503
B.P.R.D.: the Universe Machine 503
B.P.R.D.: the Warning.....503
B.U.G.G.S..............736
B-Sides..............212, 730
Babe...............375, 502
Babe 2................502
Babe Ruth Sports Comics....375
Babes of Area 51........730
Babes of Broadway......586
Baby Angel X...........730
Baby Angel X: Scorched Earth.730
Baby Huey.............586
Baby Snoots............587
Babyfat...............825
Babylon 5.............42
Babylon 5: in Valen's Name...42
Babylon Crush..........730
Bacchus Color Special....502
Bachelor Father.........587
Back to Brooklyn.........534
Back to the Future.......587
Backlash..............534
Backlash/Spider-Man.....534
Bad Apples............731
Bad Apples: High Expectations.731
Bad Company...........587
Bad Eggs.............587

Bad Girls of Blackout......587
Bad Ideas.............534
Bad Kitty..............587
Bad Moon Rising........587
Bad Planet.............534
Badge of Justice........391
Badger.............534, 587
Badger: Shattered Mirror....502
Badger: Zen Pop Funny
  Animal Version........502
Badlander the..........502
Badlands..............502
Badrock...............534
Badrock and Company....534
Badrock/Wolverine......587
Baffling Mysteries.......375
Baker Street.......587, 731
Baker Street: Graphitti.....731
Bakers Meet Jingle Bell the...502
Balance of Power........731
Balder the Brave.........208
Ballad of Halo Jones.....587
Ballad of Sleeping Beauty the..587
Ballad of Utopia.........731
Ballistic..............534
Ballistic Action.........534
Ballistic Imagery........534
Ballistic/Wolverine......534
Baloo & Little Britches...587
Bambi................587
Bamm-Bamm & Pebbles
  Flintstone...........587
Banana Splits the.......587
Banana Sunday........731
Bandy Man the.........731
Bang-Up Comics........375
Banished Knights.......534
Banner...............208
Banner Comics........375
Banzai Girl............587
Banzai Girls...........587
Baoh.................731
Bar Sinister...........588
Barabbas.............731
Barb Wire.............502
Barb Wire: Ace of Spades...502
Barbarians............731
Barbarians the.........587
Barbaric Tales.........731
Barbarossa and the Lost
  Corsairs.............587
Barbarous............731
Barbi Twins Adventures....587
Barbie................208
Barbie & Ken..........587
Barbie Fashion.........209
Barbie Twins Adventures the..587
Barker, the............375
Barney and Betty Rubble...588
Barney Baxter..........375
Barney Google & Snuffy Smith.375
Barney Google and Snuffy Smith
  588
Barnyard Comics.......375
Barry M. Goldwater......588
Barry Windsor-Smith: Storyteller502
Bart Simpson Comics....588
Bart Simpsons Treehouse
  of Horror............588
Bart-Man.............588
Bartholomew of the Scissors..588
Baseball..............588
Baseball Comics........375
Baseball Greats.........502
Baseball Heros.........375
Baseball Superstars......731
Baseball Thrills.........375
Basil.................375
Basil Wolverton's Fantasic
  Fables..............502
Bastard Samurai........534
Bastard!!..............731
Bat Lash..............42
Bat Masterson..........588
Bat the...............588
Bat-Thing.............192
Batgirl................42
Batgirl Adventures.......42
Batgirl: Year One........42
Batman...............42
Batman & Superman:
  World's Finest........48

Batman Adventures........47
Batman Adventures: the
  Lost Years...........47
Batman/Aliens..........502
Batman/Aliens II.........47
Batman and Robin Adventures..48
Batman and the Mad Monk....52
Batman and the Monster Men...52
Batman and the Outsiders...47, 48
Batman: Bane of the Demon....48
Batman Beyond.........48
Batman Black & White.....48
Batman: Book of the Dead....48
Batman: Cacophony.......48
Batman/Catwoman: Trail of
  the Gun..............48
Batman Chronicles.......48
Batman: City of Light......49
Batman: Confidential.....49
Batman: Cyber Revolution...49
Batman/Danger Girl......588
Batman: Dark Detective....49
Batman: Dark Knight of the
  Round Table..........49
Batman: Dark Victory.....49
Batman: Death and the Maidens 49
Batman: Death Mask......49
Batman/Deathblow: after the Fire 49
Batman: Family.........49
Batman Family..........49
Batman: Gcpd..........49
Batman: Gordon of Gotham...49
Batman: Gordon's Law.....49
Batman: Gotham Adventures..49
Batman: Gotham after Midnight.50
Batman: Gotham County Line...50
(Batman:) Gotham Nights....50
Batman: Gotham Knights....50
Batman/Grendel........50
Batman: Harley & Ivy.....50
Batman: Haunted Gotham...50
Batman/Hellboy/Starman...51
Batman: Hollywood Knight....51
Batman: Huntress: Cry for Blood.51
Batman: It's Joker Time.....51
Batman: Jazz..........51
Batman: Jekyll & Hyde.....51
Batman: Journey into Knight....51
Batman/Judge Dredd:
  Die Laughing.........51
Batman: League of Batmen...51
Batman: Legends of the
  Dark Knight..........51
Batman/Lobo: Deadly Serious..52
Batman: Man-Bat........52
Batman: Nevermore......52
Batman: No Man's Land....52
Batman: Orpheus Rising....52
Batman: Outlaws.......52
Batman/Predator III: Blood Ties..53
Batman: Run Riddler Run....52
Batman: Secrets.........52
Batman: Shadow of the Bat....52
Batman Strikes the........53
Batman/Superman/Wonder
  Woman: Trinity........53
Batman: Sword of Azrael....53
Batman/Tarzan: Claws
  of the Catwoman.......502
Batman: Tenses.........53
Batman: the Ankh........48
Batman: the Cult.........49
Batman: the Dark Knight Returns 49
Batman: the Dark Knight
  Strikes Again.........49
Batman: the Doom That
  Came to Gotham.......49
Batman: the Long Halloween...52
Batman: Toyman.........53
Batman: Turning Points......53
Batman Vs. Predator.....53
Batman Vs. Predator II
  Bloodmatch..........53
Batman/Wildcat.........54
Batman: Year One Hundred....54
Battle................209
Battle Action...........209
Battle Angel Alita........731
Battle Angel Alita: Last Order...731
Battle Armor...........731
Battle Attack...........375
Battle Beasts..........731

Battle Brady............286
Battle Chasers.........535
Battle Classics..........54
Battle Cry.............375
Battle Fire............375
Battle Girlz............731
Battle Gods: Warriors of
  the Chaak...........502
Battle Hymn...........535
Battle of the Planets....535, 588
Battle of the Planets: Coup
  De Gras.............535
Battle of the Planets: Manga...535
Battle of the Planets: Princess.535
Battle of the Planets:
  Witchblade..........535
Battle of the Titans.......825
Battle Pope.........535, 731
Battle Pope Mayhem......731
Battle Pope Presents:
  Saint Michael.........731
Battle Report...........376
Battle Squadron........376
Battle Stories..........376
Battlebooks........209, 588
Battlefield.............209
Battlefield Action.....399, 588
Battlefront..........209, 375
Battleground..........209
Battleground Earth......731
Battler Britton..........588
Battlestar Black & White....732
Battlestar Galactica..209, 588, 589
Battlestone............535
Battletech..........589, 732
Battletech: Fallout.......589
Battron...............732
Bay City Jive..........589
Beagle Boys the........589
Beagle Boys Versus
  Uncle Scrooge the.....589
Beanie Meanie........589
Beany & Cecil.........376
Beany and Cecil........589
Bear.................732
Beast................209
Beast Boy.............54
Beast Warrior of Shaolin....732
Beatles Experience, the....732
Beatles Life Story, the.....589
Beautiful Killer.........589
Beauty and the Beast....209, 589
Beauty and the Beast
  Portrait of Love.......589
Beauty the............589
Beavis & Butt-Head......210
Beck and Caul.........732
Bedlam...............535
Bedlam!..............589
Bee 29, the Bombardier...376
Beep Beep............589
Beep Beep the Road Runner..589
Beetle Bailey..........590
Beetleborgs...........535
Beetlejuice............590
Before the Fantastic 4:.....210
Belle Star: Queen of Bandits..732
Ben Bowie & His Mountain Men 376
Ben Casey............590
Ben-Hur..............823
Benjamin Franklin......819
Benzine..............732
Beowolf..............54
Beowulf..............590
Berlin................732
Berni Wrightson Master
  of the Macabre........590
Berzerker.............732
Berzerkers............535
Best Buy Comics.......825
Best Cellars............590
Best Comics..........376
Best Love.............210
Best of Bijou Funnies, the....825
Best of Bugs Bunny......590
Best of Dennis the Menace the.590
Best of Donald Duck......590
Best of Donald Duck
  & Uncle Scrooge.......590
Best of Rip-Off Press......825
Best of the Brave & the Bold....54

Best of the West 732
Best Western 210
Bethany the Vampfire 732
Betti Cozmo. 590
Bettie Page Comics. 502
Bettie Page: Queen of the Nile . 502
Bettie Page the '50s Rage 732
Betty 590
Betty & Veronica Spectacular . . 590
Betty and Me. 590
Betty and Veronica 590
Beverly Hillbillys 590
Beware 210, 386
Beware Terror Tales 376
Beware the Creeper 54
Bewitched 590
Beyond Avalon 535
Beyond Mars 732
Beyond, the 376
Beyond the Grave 590
Beyond Wonderland 590
Beyond! 210
Bible Tales for Young Folk. . . . 210
Big 502
Big All-American Comic Book . . 54
Big Ass 825
Big Badz 590
Big Bang 590
Big Bang Comics. 535
Big Bang Presents 732
Big Bang Presents: Ultiman
   Family 535
Big Blown Baby. 502
Big Book of Fun Comics 54
Big Bruisers 535
Big Chief Wahoo 376
Big Guy and Rusty the Robot
   Boy. 502
Big Hair Productions 535
Big Hero Six 210
Big Numbers 732
Big Shot Comics 376
Big Top Comics, the 377
Big Town 54
Big Valley the 590
Big-3 377
Bigfoot 590
Bigger 732
Bijou Funnies 825
Bill Barnes 370
Bill Barnes, America's Air Ace . 370
Bill Battle, the One-Man Army. . 377
Bill Black's Fun Comics. 591
Bill Boyd Western 377
Bill Stern's Sports Book. 377
Bill the Bull: Burnt Cain 732
Bill the Bull: One Shot One
   Bourbon One Beer. 732
Bill the Galactic Hero. 591
Billi 99 502
Billy and Buggy Bear. 377
Billy Batson and the Magic of
   Shazam 54
Billy Buckskin Western 210
Billy Bunny 377
Billy Dogma 732
Billy Nguyen Private Eye. 732
Billy the Kid 591
Billy the Kid Adventure
   Magazine 377
Billy the Kid and Oscar 377
Billy the Kid's Old-Timey
   Oddities 502
Billy West. 377
Bin4ry 591
Bingo Comics 377
Binky Brown Meets the Holy
   Virgin Mary. 825
Bio-Booster Armor Guyver 732
Bioneers 591
Bionic Commando. 591
Bionic Woman the 591
Bionix. 591
Birds of Prey 54
Birds of Prey: 55
Birds of Prey: Manhunt 54
Birthday Boy the 732
Bishop 210
Bishop: the Last X-Man. 210
Bishop: Xavier's Security
   Enforcer. 210
Bite Club 55

Bite Club: Vampire Crime Unit . . 55
Bizarre 3-D Zone. 591
Bizarre Adventures 279
Bizarre Heroes 732
Bizarre Sex 825
Black Adam: the Dark Age 55
Black and White 535
Black Anvil 535
Black Arrow, the 816
Black Axe 210
Black Beauty 818
Black Belt Club 732
Black Canary 55
Black Canary/Oracle: Birds
   of Prey 55
Black Cat Comics 377
Black Cat Mystery 377
Black Cat Mystic 377
Black Cat Western 377
Black Coat: Call to Arms 732
Black Coat The: or Give Me
   Death 732
Black Cobra. 377
Black Condor. 55
Black Cross 502
Black Cross: Dirty Work 502
Black Diamond 591
Black Diamond Western 395
Black Enchantress 591
Black Flag 535, 591
Black Forest the 535
Black Fury 591
Black Goliath 210
Black Harvest 591
Black Heart Irregulars the 733
Black Hole 733
Black Hole the 591
Black Hood 56, 435, 591
Black Jack 591
Black Kiss 733
Black Knight, the 378
Black Knight the 210
Black Lamb the 56
Black Laughter 825
Black Lightning 56
Black Magic 378
Black Mask 56
Black Mist 536, 733
Black Ops 536
Black Orchid 57
Black Panther 210, 211
Black Pearl the 502
Black Phantom 591
Black Plague 591
Black Raven 591
Black Rider 195
Black Rider Rides Again 211
Black Scorpion 733
Black September 591
Black Summer 591
Black Sun 592
Black Terror. 379, 592
Black Tide 536, 592
Black Tiger: Legacy of Fury . . . 592
Black Tulip, the 819
Black Web 592
Black Widow 211
Black Widow 2. 211
Black Widow: Pale Little Spider 211
Black Zeppelin. 733
Black-Eyed Susan 732
Blackball Comics. 591
Blackbeard Legacy 591, 592
Blackburne Covenant the 502
Blackened 732
Blackhawk. 55, 378
Blackjack: Blood & Honor 591
Blacklight. 535
Blackmask. 733
Blackpool. 592
Blackstone, Master Magician
   Comics. 379
Blackstone the Magician 211
Blackstone, the Magician
   Detective 379
Blackthorne 3 in 1 733
Blackwulf 211
Blade 211
Blade of Kumori the 592
Blade of Shuriken 733
Blade of the Immortal 502
Blade of the Warrior: Kshatriya . 592

Blade Runner. 211
Blade the Vampire Hunter 211
Blade: Vampire Hunter 211
Blair Which? 503
Blair Witch Chronicles. 733
Blair Witch: Dark Testaments . . 536
Blair Witch Project. 733
Blanche Goes to Hollywood . . . 503
Blanche Goes to New York . . . 503
Blast Corps 503
Blast-Off 592
Blaze 211
Blaze Carson. 212
Blaze of Glory 212
Blaze the Wonder Collie 212
Blazin' Brandy 592
Blazing Combat. 592
Blazing Comics 379
Blazing Six-Guns. 592
Blazing West 379
Blazing Western 379
Blind Fear 733
Blindside 536
Blink. 212
Bliss Alley 536
Blokhedz 536
Blonde Avenger. 733
Blonde Avenger: Dangerous
   Conclusions 733
Blonde Phantom 194
Blondie and Dagwood Family . . 592
Blondie Comics 379, 592
Blood 212
Blood 'N' Guts 733
Blood & Glory 212
Blood & Roses 592
Blood & Roses Adventures . . . 733
Blood & Roses: in the Dark. . . 592
Blood & Shadows 57
Blood: a Tale 57
Blood and Water 57
Blood Bowl: Killer Contract . . . 592
Blood from a Stone (Guide to
   Tax Reform) 825
Blood Is the Harvest . . . 379, 733
Blood Junkies 733
Blood Legacy 536
Blood Nation 536
Blood of Dracula 733
Blood of the Demon 57
Blood of the Innocent 733
Blood Orange 733
Blood Sword 593
Blood Sword Dynasty 593
Blood Syndicate 57
Blood World. 503
Bloodbath 57, 592
Bloodbrothers 733
Bloodchilde 592
Bloodfire 592
Bloodfire/Hellina 592
Bloodhound 57
Bloodhunter 536
Bloodletting 733
Bloodlines 212
Bloodlore 592
Bloodpack 57
Bloodpool 536
Bloodrayne 592
Bloodscent. 592
Bloodseed 212
Bloodshed 733
Bloodshot 593
Bloodstone 212
Bloodstream 536
Bloodstrike. 536
Bloodstrike: Assassin 536
Bloodthirsty Pirate Tales 733
Bloodwing 733
Bloodwulf. 536
Bloody Mary 57
Bloody Mary: Lady Liberty. 57
Bloody School 733
Bludgeon 733
Blue 536
Blue Beetle 57, 478, 593
Blue Beetle, the 379
Blue Bolt 380
Blue Bulleteer 733
Blue Circle Comics 380
Blue Devil 58
Blue Lily. 503

Blue Monday: Absolute
   Beginners. 734
Blue Monday: Painted Moon. . . 734
Blue Monday: the Kids Are
   Alright. 734
Blue Phantom the 593
Blue Ribbon. 593
Blue Ribbon Comics 380
Bluff. 593
Bluntman and Chronic. 536
Bmwfilms.com the Hire 503
Bo 380
Bob & Betty & Santa's Wishing
   Well 381
[Bob Burden's Original]
   Mysterymen 518
Bob Colt 381
Bob Steele Western 381
Bob Swift 381
Bob the Galactic Bum 58
Bobby Benson's B-Bar-B Riders 381
Bobby Comics 381
Bobby London Retrospective
   and Art Portfolio. 825
Bobman and Teddy 825
Bode's Cartoon Concert 825
Body Bags. 503, 536
Body Bags: Father's Day 536
Body Doubles 58
Bodycount 536
Bogeyman Comics 825
Bogie Man: Chinatoon. 734
Bogie Man: Manhatten Project . 734
Bohos 536
Bold Adventure 593
Bold Stories. 381
Bolt & Starforce Six. 593
Bomb Queen 536
Bomb Queen II 537
Bomb Queen III 537
Bomb Queen Iv 537
Bomb Queen V 537
Bomba the Jungle Boy 58
Bombay: the Screen Goddess 593
Bombast 593
Bomber Comics 381
Bonafide 734
Bonanza 593
Bond of Saint Marcel the. 593
Bonds 537
Bone 537, 734
Bone Rest 537
Boneshaker 734
Boneyard 734
Boof 537
Boof and the Bruise Crew 537
Book of All Comics 381
Book of Ballads and Sagas. . . . 734
Book of Comics, the 381
Book of Fate the 58
Book of Lost Souls 212
Book of Night 503
Book of Shadows 537
Book of the Dead 212
Book of the Tarot. 734
Book the 734
Books of Doom 212
Books of Faerie the. 58
Books of Faerie The: Auberon's
   Tale 58
Books of Faerie The: Molly's
   Story 50
Books of Lore: the Kaynin
   Gambit. 734
Books of Lore: the Shape
   of Evil. 734
Books of Lore: the Storyteller . 734
Books of Magic 58
Books of Magick The: Life
   During Wartime 58
Books with Pictures. 734
Boondoggle 734
Booster Gold 58
Boots and Her Buddies 381
Border Patrol 381
Border Worlds 734
Boris Karloff Tales of Mystery . 593
Boris the Bear 503, 734
Boris' Adventure Magazine . . . 734
Born 212
Born to Kill 734

Boston Bombers 734
Bottle Imp, the 821
Bouncer, the 381
Bounty 734
Bounty Killer 734
Box Office Poison 735
Boy Comics 381
Boy Commandos 59
Boy Detective 382
Boy Explorers 477
Boy Who Made Silence 593
Boys the 593
Boys' Ranch 382
Bozo 593
Bozo the Clown 593
Bradleys the 735
Brady Bunch the 593
Brain Boy 593
Brain, the 382
Brainbanx 59
Bram Stoker's Burial of the Rats 594
[Bram Stoker's] Dracula 611
Brass 537, 594
Brat Pack 735
Brath 594
Bratpack/Maximortal 735
Brave 503
Brave and the Bold 59
Brave Old World 60
Brawl 537
Breach 60
Break the Chain 212
Break-Thru 594
Breakdown 594
Breakfast after Noon 735
Breakneck Blvd. 735
Breathe 594
Breathtaker 60
'Breed 594
'Breed II 594
Breeding Ground 594
Brenda Lee Story the 594
Brenda Starr 382
Brenda Starr Ace Reporter . . . 735
Brenda Starr Reporter 382, 594
Brian Bolland's Black Book 594
Brian Pulido's Belladonna 594
Brian Pulido's Gypsy 735
Brian Pulido's Killer Gnomes . . . 735
Brian Pulido's Lady Death:
　Abandon All Hope 735
Brian Pulido's Lady Death:
　Dead Rising 735
Brian Pulido's Medieval Lady
　Death 594
Brian Pulido's Unholy 735
Brian Pulido's War Angel 735
Brian Pulido's War Angel: Book
　of Death 735
Brick Bradford 382
Brides Diary 378
Brides in Love 594
Brigade 537, 594
Brilliant Boy 735
Bring 'Em Back Alive 821
Brit 537
Broadway Romances 382
Brodie's Law 594, 735
Broid 735
Broken Halo: Is There Nothing
　Sacred 735
Broken Heroes 735
Broken Trinity 537
Broncho Bill 382
Bronx 735
Brother Man 735
Brother Power the Geek 60
Brotherhood the 212
Brothers in Arms 594
Brothers of the Spear 594
Brothers: the Fall of Lucifer . . . 594
Bru-Hed 735
Bruce Gentry 382
Bruce Jones': Outer Edge 735
Bruce Jones': Razor's Edge . . . 735
Bruce Lee 594
Bruce Wayne: Agent of
　S.H.I.E.L.D. 192
Brutal Planet 735
Brute Force 212
Brute the 594
Bubba 594

Bubba the Redneck Werewolf . . 735
Bubble Gum Crisis: Grand Mal . 503
Buccaneers 433
Buce-N-Gar 735
Buck Duck 212
Buck Godot: Zap Gun for Hire . 736
Buck Jones 382
Buck Rogers 382, 594, 595
Buck Rogers in the 25th
　Century 594
Buckaneer, the 823
Buckaroo Banzai 212, 594, 735
Buckaroo Banzai: the Prequel . 594
Bucky O'Hare 595
Budd's Beauties & Beasts 595
Buddies in the U. S. Army 382
Buffalo Bill 382, 821
Buffalo Bill Jr. 595
Buffalo Bill Jr. 382
Buffalo Bill Picture Stories 382
Buffalo Rag/the Dead Concert
　Comix 825
Buffalo Wings 595
Buffy the Vampire Slayer . . 503, 504
Buffy the Vampire Slayer: Angel 504
Buffy the Vampire Slayer:
　Haunted 504
Buffy the Vampire Slayer: Oz . . 504
Buffy the Vampire Slayer:
　the Origin 504
Buffy the Vampire Slayer: Willow
　and Tara Wilderness 504
Bug 212, 736
Bug Movies 382
Bugboy 537
Bughouse 382
Bugs Bunny 382, 595
Bugs Bunny and Porky Pig . . . 595
Bugtown 736
Bullet Crow 736
Bullet Points 212
Bulletman 382
Bulletproof Monk 537
Bullets & Bracelets 192
Bulls-Eye 383, 462
Bullseye: Greatest Hits 212
Bullwinkle 595
Bullwinkle & Rocky 212, 595
Bullwinkle for President 595
Bulwark 736
Bureau of Mana Investigation . . 736
Burglar Bill 537, 736
Burke's Law 595
Burning Blue the 736
Bushido 736
Buster Bear 383
Buster Brown Comics 383
Buster Bunny 383
Buster Crabbe 383
Butch Cassidy 595
Butcher Knight 537
Butcher the 60
Butternut Squash 595
Buz Sawyer 383
Buzz 736
Buzzard 736
Buzzboy 736
Buzzboy: Sidekicks Rule 595
Buzzy 60
By Bizarre Hands 504

C C C C

C-M-O Comics 388
Cabbot: Bloodhunter 595
Cable 212, 213
Cable & Deadpool 213
Cable & X-Force 213
Cable Tv 213
Cadillacs & Dinosaurs 213, 595
Cadillacs and Dinosaurs 736
Caesar's Conquests 822
Cage 213
Cages 595
Cain 595
Cain's Hundred 595
Caliber 595
Caliber Core 736
Caliber Double Feature 736
Caliber Focus 736
Caliber Presents 736
Caliber Spotlight 736
Calibrations 736
California Girls 736

California Raisins 595
Caligari 2050 736
Call Me Princess 736
Call of Duty The: the Brother
　Hood 213
Call of Duty: the Precinct, the . . 213
Call of Duty: the Wagon, the . . . 213
Call of the Wild, the 820
Call the 213
Calling All Boys 383
Calling All Girls 383
Calling All Kids 383
Calvin & the Colonel 595
Camelot 3000 60
Camelot Eternal 736
Camera Comics 383
Camp Candy 213
Camp Comics 383
Campus Loves 384
Campus Romances 384
Candy 384
Candyappleblack 736
Cannon Busters 595
Cannon God Exaxxion 504
Cannon Hawke 595
Cannonball Comics 384
Canteen Kate 384
Canton Kid 736
Cap'n Quick & Foozle 595
Capcom Summer Special 595
Caper 60
Capes 538
Capt. Confederacy 736
Capt. Electron 595, 736
Capt. Savage & His Leatherneck
　Raiders 218
Captain 3-D 478
Captain Action 60, 595
Captain Aero Comics 384
Captain America 214, 217
Captain America & the Falcon . 217
Captain America Comics 213
Captain America: Dead Man
　Running 217
Captain America: Sentinel
　of Liberty 217
Captain America: the Chosen . . 217
Captain America: What Price
　Glory 217
Captain America: White 217
Captain Atom 60, 384
Captain Atom: Armageddon . . . 595
Captain Battle 384
Captain Battle, Jr. 384
Captain Britain and Mi13 217
Captain Canuck 596
Captain Canuck Reborn 736
Captain Carrot 61
Captain Carrot and the Final Ark . 61
Captain Courageous Comics . . 375
Captain Easy 384
Captain Fearless Comics 384
Captain Flash 384
Captain Fleet 384
Captain Flight Comics 384
Captain Gallant 384
Captain Glory 596
Captain Gravity 596
Captain Guts 825
Captain Harlock 737
Captain Harlock Deathshadow
　Rising 737
Captain Harlock: Fall of the
　Empire 596, 737
Captain Jet 384
Captain Johner & the Aliens . . . 596
[Captain Johner And] Aliens the 579
Captain Kidd 393
Captain Koala 737
Captain Marvel 218, 596
Captain Marvel Adventures 384
Captain Marvel Jr. 385
Captain Midnight 386
Captain Nauticus 596
Captain Nice 596
Captain Paragon 596
Captain Planet 218
Captain Power 596
Captain Rocket 386
Captain Science 386
Captain Stern 596

Captain Sternn: Running out
　of Time 737
Captain Steve Savage 386
Captain Sticky 825
Captain Storm 61
Captain Thunder and Blue
　Bolt 596, 737
Captain Tootsie & the Secret
　Legion 386
Captain Universe 219
Captain Venture & the Land
　Beneath the Sea 596
Captain Victory and the Galactic
　Rangers 596
Captain Video 386
Captain Wizard 386
Captains Courageous 821
Car 54 Where Are You? 596
Car Warriors 219
Caravan Kidd 504
Carca Jou Renaissance 596
Cardcaptor Sakura 737
Care Bears 219
Carnage 219
Carnival 462
Carnosaur Carnage 596
Caroline Kennedy 596
Cartoon History of the
　Universe 737, 826
Cartoon Kids 219
Carvers 538
Casanova 538
Cascade Comix Monthly 826
Casefiles: Sam and Twitch 538
Cases of Sherlock Holmes 737
Casey Blue: Beyond Tomorrow . 596
Casey Crime Photographer . . . 219
Casey Jones & Raphael 596
Casper & Friends 596
Casper & Wendy 596
Casper and Spooky 596
Casper and the Ghostly Trio . . . 596
Casper Enchanted Tales 596
Casper Ghostland 596
Casper Space Ship 597
Casper Strange Ghost Stories . 597
Casper T.V. Showtime 597
Casper, the Friendly Ghost . . . 386
Casper the Friendly Ghost 596, 597
Casper's Ghostland 596
Cast 597
Castle Dangerous 823
Castle Waiting 737
Castlevania: the Belmont
　Legacy 597
Casual Heroes 538
Cat & Mouse 737
Cat Claw 737
Cat the 219
Cat-Man Retro Comic 737
Catalyst: Agents of Change . . . 504
Catfight 737
Catholic Comics 386
Catman Comics 387
Catseye 597
Catwoman 61
Catwoman/Wildcat 62
Caught 219
Cauldron 597
Cavalier Comics 387
Cave Kids 597
Cavewoman 597, 737
Cavewoman Intervention 737
Cavewoman: Jungle Tales 737
Cavewoman: Meriem's Gallery . 738
Cavewoman: Missing Link 738
Cavewoman: Odyssey 738
Cavewoman: Pangaean Sea . . 738
Cavewoman: Rain 738
Cavewoman: Reloaded 738
Cavewoman: Raptor 738
Cecil Kunkle 738
Celestial Mechanics 738
Celestial Zone 738
Celestine 538
Cement Shooz 738
Cemetarians the 738
Cemetery Blues 538
Centurions 62
Century 597
Century: Distant Sons 219
Century of Comics 387

Cerebus. 738
Cerebus Church & State. 738
Cerebus High Society. 738
Cerebus Jam. 739
Cerebus Reprints. 739
Chain Gang War. 62
Chains of Chaos. 597
Chainsaw Vigilante. 739
Challenger Deep. 597
Challenger, the. 387
Challengers of the Fantastic. . . 192
Challengers of the Unknown. . . 62
Chamber of Chills. 219, 387
Chamber of Clues. 387
Chamber of Darkness. 219
Champ Comics. 387
Champion Comics. 387
Champion of Kitara: Dum
    Dum & Dragons. 739
Champions. 219, 597
Champions Classic. 597
Champions the 219
Change Commander Goku II. . 739
Channel Zero 538
Chaos Effect 597
Chaos Quarterly 597
Chaos! Bible 597
Chaos! Chronicles the History
    of a Cosmos 597
Chaos! Gallery 597
Chaos! Nightmare Theater . . . 597
Chapel. 538, 597
Charlatan Ball 538
Charlemagne. 597
Charlie Chan. . . . 387, 597, 739
Charlie McCarthy. 387
Charlton Action: Featuring Static597
Charlton Bullseye 597
Charlton Bullseye Special 598
Charlton Classics 598
Charlton Classics Library 598
Charlton Premiere 598
Charlton Sport Library 598
Charm School 739
Chase 63
Chase the 598
Chaser Platoon 739
Chassis 538, 598
Chastity. 598
Checkered Demon 826
Checkmate 63, 598
Cheech Wizard 826
Chemist the. 538
Cherrios 3d Classics 478
Cherry 826
Cherry Poptart. 826
Cherubs: Paradise Lost. 739
Cheryl Blossom. 598
Chesty Sanchez 739
Cheval Noir 504
Cheyenne 387
Cheyenne Kid 598
Chi-Chian 598
Chibi-Pop Manga 739
Chicago Mirror. 826
Chicanos 739
Chickasaw Adventures 598
Chief, the. 387
Child's Play 2 598
Child's Play 3 598
Child's Play: the Series 598
Childhood's End 538
Children of Fire 598
Children of the Grave 739
Children's Crusade 63
Chili 219
Chilling Adventures in Sorcery
    as Told by Sabrina. 598
Chilling Tales. 386
Chimera. 599
China & Jazz 739
China & Jazz Code Name
    Double Impact 739
China & Jazz: Superstars 739
China & Jazz: Trigger Happy . . 739
Chip 'N Dale 599
Chip 'N Dale Rescue Rangers . 599
Chirality. 739
Chirality: to the Promised Land. 739
Chiron 739
Chisuji 739
C.H.I.X. That Time Forgot, the . 538

Choice Comics 387
Cholly and Flytrap 538
Choo Choo Charlie 599
Chosen 505
Chosen the 599
Christian 599
Christmas Carnival 387
Christmas with the Super-Heroes 63
Chroma-Tick Special Edition. . . 599
Chrome 599
Chrome Warriors in a '59 Chevy 599
Chromium Man the 599
Chronicles of Corum 599
Chronicles of Dr. Herbert
    West the. 599
Chrono Mechanics 599
Chronos. 63
Chronowar. 505
Chtulhu Tales. 599
Chuck 599
Chuck Norris 219
Chuckle the Giggly Book of
    Comic Animals. 387
Chucky 599
Cicero's Cat. 599
Cici 599
Cimmaron Strip 599
Cinder & Ashe 63
Cindy Comics 268
Cinema Comics Herald 388
Cinnamon: El Ciclo 63
Circle the 538
Circle Weave the 739
Circus Comics 388
Circus of Fun Comics 388
Circus the Comic Riot 388
Cisco Kid Comics 388
Cisco Kid, the 388
Cisco Kid the 599
Citizen V 219
Citizen V & the V Battalion: the
    Everlasting. 219
City Knights the 599
City of Dust 599
City of Heroes 538, 599
City of Others 505
City of Silence 538
City of Tomorrow 599
City Perilous 599
Civil War 219
Civil War Chronicles 220
Civil War: Front Line 220
Civil War: House of M 220
Civil War: X-Men. 220
Civil War: Young Avengers &
    Runaways 220
Claire Voyant. 388
Clan Apis 739
Clande Inc. 739
Clandestine 220
Clash 64, 599
Classic Battlestar Galactica . . . 599
Classic Conan 223
Classic Punisher 303
Classic Star Wars 505
Classic Star Wars: a Long
    Time Ago 505
Classic Star Wars: a New Hope 505
Classic Star Wars: Devilworlds . 505
Classic Star Wars: Early
    Adventures. 505
Classic Star Wars: Empire
    Strikes Back. 505
Classic Star Wars: Han Solo
    at Star's End 505
Classic Star Wars: Return of
    the Jodi 505
Classic Star Wars: Vandelhelm
    Mission. 505
Classic X-Men. 364
Classics Illlustrated Special
    Issue 824
Classics Illustrated 599, 600
Classics Illustrated Giants. . . . 824
Classics Illustrated Junior . 600, 824
Classwar 600
Claus. 600
Claw the Unconquered 64, 600
Claws. 220
Clay Cody, Gunslinger 388
Clean Fun, Starring 'Shoogafoots
    Jones' 388

Cleaners the 505
Cleopatra. 824
Clerks: the Comic Book. 739
Cliffhanger Comics 739
Climax! 388
Clint the Hamster 739
Clive Barker's Book of the
    Damned 220
Clive Barker's Hellraiser 220
Clive Barker's Tapping the Vein 600
Clive Barker's the Great and
    Secret Show 600
Clive Barker's the Thief of
    Always 600
Cloak & Dagger. 220
Cloak and Dagger 388
Clock Maker the 538
Clockwork Girl 600
Cloister and the Hearth, the . . . 819
Clonezone 505
Close Shaves of Pauline Peril. . 600
Cloudfall 538
Clown Comics 388
Clowns the (Pagliacci). 505
Clue Comics 388
Clutching Hand, the. 388
Clyde Beatty 388
Clyde Crashcup. 600
Cobalt Blue 600
Cobalt: Warrior Angel 600
Cobb: off the Leash. 739
Cobra. 739
Cocaine Comics 826
Cocomalt Big Book of Comics . 388
Cocopiazo 739
Code 600
Code Blue 538
Code Name: Double Impact . . . 601
Code Name: Spitfire 323
Code of Honor. 220
Codename: Black Death 600
Codename: Danger. 601
Codename: Firearm 601
Codename: Genetix 220
Codename: Knockout 64
Codename: Strikeforce 601
Codename: Styke Force 538
Cody of the Pony Express 383, 388
Coffin 739
Cold Blooded Chameleon
    Commandos 739
Cold Eden 739
Cold Heat 601
Cole Black 739
Collected Cheech Wizard, the. . 826
Collected Trashman #1, the . . . 826
Colonel Kilgore 739
Colors in Black 505
Colossal Features Magazine. . . 388
Colossal Show the 601
Colossus 220
Colossus Comics. 388
Colossus: God's Country 220
Colour of Magic 601
Colt 739
Colt .45 601
Colt Special 601
Columbia Comics 388
Columbus 505
Combat 220, 538, 601
Combat Casey 345
Combat Kelly. 221
Combat Kelly and the Deadly
    Dozen 220
Combat Zone 221
Comedy Comics 221
Comet Man 221
Comet the 64, 601
Comic Album. 601
Comic Book. 505
Comic Book Heaven 739
Comic Books. 388
Comic Capers 221
Comic Cavalcade 64
Comic Comics 389
Comic Land. 389
Comic Pages. 417
Comics & Comix 826
Comics & Stories. 505
Comics Calendar, the 389
Comics Express 740
Comics for Kids. 221

Comics Magazine 417
Comics Novel 389
Comics on Parade. 389
Comics Revue. 389
Comics, the 389
Comics' Greatest World 505
Coming of Aphrodite 740
Comix Book. 221, 826
Comix Collector, the 826
Comix International 601
Comix Zone. 221
Command Review. 740
Commander Battle and the
    Atomic Submarine 389
Commando Adventures. 221
Commies from Mars 826
Common Foe 538
Common Grounds. 538
Compass 539
Complete Book of Comics and
    Funnies 389
Complete Book of True Crime
    Comics. 389
Complete Comics 197
Complete Fool, the 827
Complete Fritz the Cat 826
Complete Mystery 221
Conan 221, 223, 505
Conan and the Book of Thoth. . 506
Conan and the Demons of
    Khitai 506
Conan and the Jewels of
    Gwahlur 506
Conan and the Midnight God . . 506
Conan and the Songs of the
    Dead 506
Conan Classics 223
Conan: Death Covered in Gold. 221
Conan: River of Blood. 223
Conan/Rune 223
Conan the Adventurer 221
Conan the Barbarian 221
Conan the Barbarian Vs. The
    Lord of the Spiders 223
Conan the Cimmerian 506
Conan: the Flame and
    the Fiend 223
Conan: the King 223
Conan: the Return of Styrm . . . 223
Conan: the Savage 224
Conan: the Scarlet Sword 223
Conan: the Usurper 223
Concrete 506
Concrete: Eclectica 506
Concrete: Fragile Creature . . . 506
Concrete Jungle: the Legend
    of the Black Lion 601
Concrete: Killer Smile 506
Concrete: Strange Armor 506
Concrete: the Human Dilemma. 506
Concrete: Think like a Mountain 506
Condom-Man. 740
Coneheads 224
Confessions Illustrated 389
Congo Bill 64
Congorilla 64
Conjurors. 64
Connect. 601
Connor Hawke: Dragon's Blood. 64
Conqueror 740
Conqueror Comics 389
Conqueror of the Barren Earth . 64
Conquest. 389
Conquest of Mexico, the 823
Consortium of Justice 601
Conspiracy 224
Conspiracy Capers 826
Conspiracy Comics 740
Conspiracy of Pontiac, the . . . 823
Conspirators, the 823
Constellation Graphics 740
Construct. 740
Consumed 539
Contact Comics 389
Containment 601
Contest of Champions. 224
Contest of Champions II 224
Contract. 601
Coo Coo Comics 389
"Cookie". 389
Cool World. 64
Cops 64

Cops: the Job 224
Corben Special 601
Cormac Mac Art 506
Corny's Fetish 506
Corporate Ninja 740
Corrector Yui 740
Corsican Brothers, the 815
Corto Maltese: Ballad of the
   Salt Sea 740
Corum: the Bull & the Spear . . 601
Cosmic Boy 64
Cosmic Guard the 601
Cosmic Heroes 740
Cosmic Odyssey 64
Cosmic Powers 224
Cosmic Powers Unlimited . . . 224
Cosmic Ray 539
Cosmo Cat 389
Cosmo the Merry Martian . . . 390
Cossack Chief, the 824
Cougar the 601
Count Duckula 224
Count of Monte Cristo, the . . . 812
Countdown 64, 601
Countdown: Arena 65
Countdown Presents: 65
Countdown to Adventure 65
Countdown to Mystery 65
Counter Parts 740
Counter-Ops 601
Coup D'etat 601
Courage Comics 390
Courtney Crumrin & the Coven
   of Mystics 740
Courtney Crumrin & the Night
   Things 740
Courtney Crumrin and the Prince
   of Nowhere 740
Courtney Crumrin in the Twilight
   Kingdom 740
Courtship of Eddie's Father . . . 601
Courtship of Miles Standish, the 820
Coutoo 506
Coven 601
Coven 13 602
Coven: Dark Origins 602
Coven: Dark Sister 602
Coven/Re: Gex 602
Coven: Spellcaster 602
Coven: Tooth & Nail 602
Coventry 740
Cover Girl 602
Covered Wagon, the 822
Cow Puncher 390
Cow the 539
Cowboy Action 349
Cowboy Bebop 740
Cowboy Comics 470
Cowboy in Africa 602
Cowboy Romances 224
Cowboy Western 498
Cowboy Western Comics 497
Cowboy Western Heroes 497
Cowboys 'N' Injuns 390
Cowgirl Romances 229
Coyote 224
Crack Comics 390
Crack Western 390
Crackajack Funnies 390
Cracked 602
Crash Comics 390
Crash Dummies 602
Crawl Space: Xxxombies 539
Cray Baby Adventures the . . . 740
Cray Baby Adventures: Wrath
   of the Peddidlers 740
Crazy 224
Crazyman 602
Creature 602
Creature Commandos 65
Creature from the Black Lagoon 506
Creature from the Depths . . . 539
Creatures of the Id 740
Creatures on the Loose 337
Creech the 539
Creech The: out for Blood . . . 539
Creed 740
Creed: Cranial Disorder . . 602, 740
Creed: Mechanical Evolution . . 740
Creed/Teenage Mutant Ninja
   Turtles 602, 740

Creed: the Good Ship & the
   New Journey Home 740
Creed: Use Your Delusion 740
Creed: Utopiate 539
Creeper the 65
Creeps 539
Creepy 506
Cremator: Hell's Guardian . . . 602
Crew 224
Crime and Justice 390, 391
Crime and Punishment . . . 391, 820
Crime Bible: the Five Lessons
   of Blood 65
Crime Buster 740
Crime Can't Win 268
Crime Cases Comics 224
Crime Classics 740
Crime Clinic 391
Crime Detective Comics 391
Crime Detector 391
Crime Does Not Pay 464
Crime Exposed 225
Crime Files 391
Crime Illustrated 391
Crime Incorporated 391
Crime Machine 602
Crime must Lose! 225
Crime must Pay the Penalty . . 391
Crime must Stop 391
Crime Mysteries 391
Crime on the Waterfront 402
Crime Patrol 392, 602
Crime Reporter 392
Crime Smasher 392
Crime Smashers 392
Crime Suspense Stories 603
Crime Suspenstories 392
Crime-Fighting Detective 392
Crimebuster 740
Crimefighters 225
Crimes by Women 392
Criminal 225
Criminal Macabre 506
Criminal Macabre: Cel
   Block 666 506
Criminal Macabre: My Demon
   Baby 506
Criminal Macabre: Two
   Red Eyes 506
Criminals on the Run 392
Crimson 539
Crimson Avenger 65
Crimson Dreams 741
Crimson Nun 603
Crimson Plague 539, 603
Crisis Aftermath: the Battle
   for Bludhaven 65
Crisis Aftermath: the Spectre . . 65
Crisis on Infinite Earths 65
Crisis, the 823
Critical Error 506
Critical Mass 225
Critters 741
Cromwell Stone 507
Cross Bronx the 539
Crossed 603
Crossfire 603, 741
Crossfire & Rainbow 603
Crossgen Chronicles 603
Crossing Midnight 65
Crossovers the 603
Crossroads 603
Crow of the Bear Clan 741
Crow/Razor: Kill the Pain 741
Crow the 539, 741
Crow The: City of Angels 603
Crow The: Dead Time 741
Crow The: Demon in Disguise . 741
Crow The: Flesh and Blood . . . 741
Crow The: Waking Nightmares . 741
Crow The: Wild Justice 1996 . . 741
Crown Comics 393
Crucible 65
Cruel and Unusual 65
Crusader from Mars 393
Crusaders 66, 741
Crusades the 66
Crush 507
Crush the 539
Crusher Joe 741
Crux 603
Cry for Dawn 741

Cry Freeman V 741
Crybaby 603
Cryin' Lion, the 393
Crying Freeman 741
Crying Freeman II 741
Crying Freeman III 603, 741
Crying Freeman Iv 603, 741
Crypt 539
Crypt of Dawn 742
Crypt of Shadows 225
Crypt of Terror 392
Cryptic Writings of Megadeth . . 603
Cryptics the 539
Cryptozoo Crew 742
Crystal Breeze 742
Csi: Crime Scene Investigation . 603
Csi: Dying in the Gutters 742
Cthulhu Tales 603
Cube 742
Cud Comics 507
Cuda 742
Cupid 225
Curly Kayoe Comics 393
Curse of Dracula, the 507
Curse of Rune 603
Curse of the Blood Clan the . . 603
Curse of the Spawn 539
Cursed 539
Cursed Pirate Girl 603
Cutey Bunny 742
Cutie Honey 742
Cvo: African Blood 604
Cvo: Covert Vampiric
   Operations Artifact 604
Cvo: Human Touch 604
Cvo: Rogue State 604
Cy-Gor 540
Cyber 7 742
Cyber City 604
Cybercrush: Robots in Revolt . . 604
Cyberella 66
Cyberforce 540
Cyberforce/Code-Name
   Strykeforce: Opposing
   Forces 540
Cyberforce Origins 540
Cyberforce Universe
   Sourcebook 540
Cyberfrog 604, 742
Cyberfrog vs Creed 742
Cyberhood 604
Cybernary 540
Cybernary 2.0 604
Cyberpunk 604
Cyberpunk: the Seraphim Files . 604
Cyberpunx 540, 604
Cyberrad 604
Cyberspace 3000 225
Cyberzone 742
Cyblade 540
Cyblade/Shi 540
Cyborg 66
Cybrid 604
Cyclone Bill and the Tall Tales . 742
Cyclone Comics 393
Cyclops 225, 742
Cycops 742
Cygnus X-1 742
Cynder 604, 742
Cynder/Hellina 742
Cynder/Nira X 604
Cyrano De Bergerac 819

D D D D

D.P. 7 236
D'airain Adventure 604
D-Day 606
Da'kota 742
Daemonifuge: the Screaming
   Cage 742
Daemonstrom 604
Daemonstrom: Deadworld . . . 604
Daemonstrom: Oz 604
Daffy 393
Daffy Duck 393, 604
Daffy Tunes Comics 393
Dagar, Desert Hawk 393
Dagar the Invincible 604
Dagwood 393
Dai Kamikaze 604
Daikazu 742
Daily Bugle 225
Daisy and Donald 604

Daisy and Her Pups 393
Daisy Comics 393
Daisy Handbook 393
Daisy Kutter 742
Dakota North 225
Daktari 604
Dale Evans Comics 66
Dalgoda 604
Dalkiel: the Prophecy 604
Damage 66
Damage Control 225
Damaged the 605
Damn Nation 507
Damned 540
Damned the 742
Damonstreik 742
Dampyr 742
Dan Dare 605
Dan O'Neil's Comics & Stories . 826
Dan Turner Hollywood Detective 743
Dan'l Boone 394
Dance of Lifey Death the 507
Dances with Demons 225
Dandy Comics 393
Danger 393
Danger and Adventure 478
Danger Girl 540
Danger Girl: Back in Black . . . 605
Danger Girl: Body Shots 605
Danger Girl: Kamikaze 605
Danger Is Our Business 393
Danger Ranger 605
Danger Trail 66
Danger Unlimited 507
Danger's Dozen the 605
Dangerous Times 742
Daniel Boone 605, 820
Danny Blaze 394
Dare 605
Dare Detectives the 507
Dare the Impossible 605
Daredevil 225, 227
Daredevil: Battlin' Jack Murdock 228
Daredevil Comics 394
Daredevil: Father 228
Daredevil: Ninja 228
Daredevil: Redemption 228
Daredevil/Shi Shi/Daredevil . . . 228
Daredevil/Spider-Man 228
Daredevil: the Man
   Without Fear 228
Daredevil: the Target 228
Daredevil Vs. Punisher 228
Daredevil: Yellow 228
Daring Comics 229
Daring Escapes 540
Daring Love 394
Daring Mystery Comics 228
[Daring New Adventures Of]
   Supergirl 159
Dark 48 605
Dark Angel 253
Dark Angel 743
Dark Angel: Phoenix
   Resurrection 540
Dark Assassin 743
Dark Chylde 605
Dark City Angel 743
Dark Claw Adventures the 192
Dark Crossings 541
Dark Crystal 229
Dark Days 605
Dark Dominion 605
Dark Fantasies 743
Dark Frigate, the 822
Dark Fringe 743
Dark Fringe: Spirits of the Dead 743
Dark Guard 229
Dark Horse Classics 507
Dark Horse Classics: Aliens
   Vs. Predator 507
Dark Horse Classics: Godzilla
   King of the Monsters 507
Dark Horse Classics: Predator:
   Jungle Tales 507
Dark Horse Classics: Star Wars
   Dark Empire 507
Dark Horse Classics: Terror
   of Godzilla 507
Dark Horse Comics 507
Dark Horse Downunder 507
Dark Horse Maverick 507

Dark Horse Monsters 507
Dark Horse Presents. 507
Dark Horse Presents: Aliens. . . 508
Dark Island 743
Dark Ivory 541
Dark Lord 743
Dark Man. 229
Dark Manga. 743
Dark Mansion of Forbidden
  Love the. 66
Dark Mists 605
Dark Muse. 743
Dark Mysteries 394
Dark One's Third Eye 605
Dark Oz 743
Dark Peril 743
Dark Realm 542
Dark Regions 743
Dark Sector 542
Dark Shadows. 394, 606
Dark Side 606
Dark Star 743
Dark the. 605
Dark Tower: the Gunslinger
  Born 229
Dark Tower: the Long
  Road Home 229
Dark Tower: Treachery 229
Dark Visions 743
Dark Wolf. 743
Darkchylde 541
Darkchylde/Glory. 541
Darkchylde Redemption 605
Darkchylde: the Diary 541
Darkchylde: the Legacy. 541
Darkchylde/Witchblade 541
Darker Image 541
Darkest Horror of Morella the . . 605
Darkham Vale 605
Darkham Vale: the Dracou
  Imperative 605
Darkham Vale: Uprising 605
Darkhawk 229
Darkhold 229
Darklight: Prelude 743
Darklon the Mystic. 605
Darkman 229, 605
Darkman Vs. Army of Darkness 605
Darkminds 541
Darkminds: Macropolis . . . 541, 605
Darkness 541
Darkness and Tomb Raider. . . . 542
Darkness Falls: the Tooth Fairy
  the Tragic Life of Matilda
  Dixon 508
Darkness the 541, 542
Darkness The: 542
Darkness The/Pitt 542
Darkness The/Superman 542
Darkness Vs. Eva 605
Darkness Vs. Mr. Hyde 542
Darkseid Vs. Galactus the
  Hunger. 66
Darkshrine 606
Darkstalkers 606
Darkstars 66
Darkstorm 606
Darkwing Duck 606
Darque Passages 606
Darque Razor 743
Dart 542
Das Kampf 826
Date with Danger 394
Daughters of the Dragon. 229
David and Goliath 542
David Balfour. 820
David Copperfield 817
David: the Shepherd's Song . . 606
Davy Crockett 394, 822
Davy Crockett King of the
  Wild Frontier 606
Dawn 606
Dawn: Pin-Up Goddess. 606
Dawn: the Return of the
  Goddess 606
Dawn: Three Tiers. 542
Day of Judgment. 66
Day of the Dead: the Rising
  of Bub 606
Day of Vengeance. 66
Daydreamers. 230
Days of Darkness 743

Dazey's Diary 606
Dazzler 230
DC 100-Page Superspectacular . 67
DC Challenge 66
DC Comics Presents. . . . 66, 67
DC Countdown 67
DC First. 67
DC Graphic Novel 67
DC Infinite Halloween Special. . . 67
DC/Marvel: All Access. 67
DC Millennium Editions. 67
DC One Million 67
DC Replica Editions 67
DC Science Fiction Graphic
  Novel 67
DC Special 68
DC Special Series 68
DC Special: the Return of
  Donna Troy 68
DC Super-Stars. 68
DC: the New Frontier 67
DC Two Thousand. 68
DC Universe 68
DC Versus Marvel Marvel
  Versus DC 192
DC Vs. Marvel. 68
DC/Wildstorm: Dreamwar 68
Dead @ 17 606
Dead Ahead 542
Dead Boys: Death's Embrace. . 606
Dead Clown. 606
Dead Corps(e). 68
Dead End Crime Stories 394
Dead Eyes Open. 743
Dead in the West. 508
Dead King 606
Dead Men Tell No Tales 606
Dead of Night 230
Dead of Night Featuring
  Devil-Slayer 230
Dead of Night Featuring
  Man-Thing 230
Dead or Alive a Cyberpunk
  Western 508
Dead She Said 606
Dead Sonja: She-Zombie
  with a Sword 743
Dead Space 542
Dead The: Kingdom of Flies . . 606
Dead to Rights 508
Dead-Eye Western Comics. . . . 394
Deadbeats 743
Deadbone Erotica 826
Deadcenter Cleavage 826
Deadenders 68
Deadface: Doing Islands with
  Bacchus. 508
Deadface: Earth Water Air
  & Fire. 508
Deadforce 606
Deadkiller 743
Deadlander the 508
Deadlands 542
Deadliest Heroes of Kung Fu . . 230
Deadline 230, 508
Deadline Usa. 508
Deadly Duo the 542
Deadly Foes of Spider-Man . . 230
Deadly Hands of Kung Fu. . . . 230
Deadman. 68
Deadpool. 230, 231
Deadpool/Gli 231
Deadshot. 69
Deadside 606
Deadtime Stories. 743
Deadwood Gulch 394
Doadworld. 542, 743
Deadworld: Frozen over 744
Deadworld: Slaughterhouse . . . 606
Deal with the Devil 606
Dean Koontz's Frankenstein:
  Prodigal Son 607
Dear Beatrice Fairfax 394
Dear Heart. 438
Dear Nancy Parker 607
Death and the Man Who Would
  Not Die. 607
Death Angel. 744
Death Comes to Dillinger 607
Death Gallery 69
Death Grub 542
Death Hunt 744

Death Jr. 542
Death Metal. 231
Death Metal Vs. Genetix. 231
Death of Angel Girl 744
Death of Bloodfire 744
Death of Hari Kari 607
Death of Lady Vampre 607
Death of the New Gods. 69
Death Rattle 607, 744, 826
Death: the High Cost of Living . . 69
Death: the Time of Your Life . . . 69
Death's Head 231, 744
Death's Head II 231
Death's Head II/Die Cut 232
Death's Head II/Killpower:
  Battletide 232
Death-Wreck 232
Death3. 231
Deathblow 542, 607
Deathblow: by Blows. 607
Deathblow/Wolverine 542
Deathdealer. 607
Deathdreams of Dracula 744
Deathlok 231
Deathlok: Detour 231
Deathlok Special 231
Deathmark. 744
Deathmask 607
Deathmate. 607
Deathrace 2020. 607
Deathstroke: the Terminator . . . 69
Deathwish 69
Deathworld 744
Debbie Dean, Career Girl 395
Decade of Dark Horse a 508
Deception the 542
Decimation: House of M 232
Decoy 607
Decoy: Storm of the Century. . . 607
Dee Snider's Strangeland:
  Seven Sins 607
Dee Vee 744
Deep Sleeper 542, 744
Deep the 232
Deepak Chopra's Beyond 607
Deepak Chopra's Buddha: a
  Story of Enlightenment . . . 607
Deerslayer, the 814
Defcon 4 542
Defenders 232, 233
Defenders of Dynatron City. . . 233
Defenders of the Earth 233
Defenders the 607
Defenseless Dead. 744
Defex 607
Defiance 542
Defiant: 607
Deity 607
Deity II: Catseye 607
Deity: Requiem 543
Deity: Revelations 543
Delete 744
Deliverer 607
Dell Giant Comics 395
Dell Giant Editions. 395
Dell Junior Treasury 395
Della Vision 233
Delta Tenn 744
Demo. 744
Demolition Man 69
Demon. 69
Demon Baby 744
Demon Bitch 744
Demon Gun. 744
Demon Hunter. 744
Demon The: Driven out. 70
Demon Warrior 744
Demon's Regret 608
Demon's Tails 744
Demon-Hunter. 607
Demongate 744
Demonique 607, 744
Demonique: Angel of Night . . . 744
Demonslayer. 543, 607
Demonslayer: Lords of Night. . . 744
Demonwars: Eye for an Eye . . . 608
Demonwars: the Demon
  Awakens 608
Demonwars: Trial by Fire 608
Den 608
Den Saga 608

Denizens of Deep City 744
Dennis the Menace. . 233, 395, 608
Deputy Dawg. 608
Der Vandale. 608
Derreck Wayne Jackson's
  Strapped 744
Derring Risk. 543
Descending Angels 744
Desert Peach 744
Desert Storm Journal 608
Desolation Jones. 608
Despair 826
Desperado. 395, 543
Desperadoes. 543
Desperadoes: Banners of Gold. 608
Desperadoes: Buffalo Dreams . 608
Desperadoes: Quiet of the Grave 70
Desperate Times. 543
Destiny: a Chronicle of Deaths
  Foretold 70
Destiny Angel 744
Destroy 745
Destroyer Duck 608
Destroyer: Terror, the 233
Destroyer the 233
Destructor the 608
Detective Comics 70
Detective Dan, Secret Op, 48 . . 396
Detective Eye 396
Detective Picture Stories. 396
Detective the 745
Detectives Inc.. 608
Detention Comics 75
Detonator. 608
Detonator the 543
Devastator 543
Devi 608
Devil Chef 509
Devil Dinosaur. 233
Devil Dinosaur Spring Fling. . . 233
Devil Dogs. 396
Devil Jack 745
Devil Kids Starring Hot Stuff . . . 608
Devil May Cry 609
Devil's Due Studios 543
Devil's Footprints. 509
Devil's Keeper 609
Devil's Panties the. 745
Devil's Workshop. 745
Devil-Dog Dugan 233
Devilman 609
Devlin 609
Dexter Comics. 396
Dexter the Demon 286
Dexter's Laboratory. 75
Diablo: Tales of Sanctuary . . . 509
Diabolik 745
Diary of Night 609
Dick Cole. 396
Dick Danger 745
Dick Tracy 609, 745
Dick Tracy: Big City Blues. . . . 609
Dick Tracy Comics Monthly. . . 396
Dick Tracy Crimebuster. 745
Dick Tracy Detective 745
Dick Tracy Magazine. 745
Dick Tracy Monthly 396
Dick Tracy: the Early Years. . . 745
Dick Tracy Unprinted Stories. . . 745
Dick Wingate of the U. S. Navy 397
Dickie Dare 396
Dicks 745
Dictators 745
Die-Cut 233
Die-Cut Vs. G-Force 233
Digimon 509
Digital Dragon 745
Digital Graffiti. 609
Digital Webbing Presents 745
Digitek 233
Dim-Witted Darryl 745
Dime Comics. 397
Ding Dong 397
Dinky Duck 397
Dino Island 609
Dino Wars: Extinction Files . . . 609
Dinosaur Rex 609
Dinosaurs 609
Dinosaurs: a Celebration. 233
Dinosaurs Attack. 609
Dinosaurs for Hire 609, 745

Dinowars: Jurassic War of
  the Worlds 609
Dippy Duck 233
Dirty Duck Book, the 826
Dirty Pair 509, 745
Dirty Pair: Fatal but Not Serious 509
Dirty Pair: Run from the Future. 509
Dirty Pair: Sim Earth 745
Dirty Pair: Sim Hell 509
Dirty Pair: Sim Hell:
  Remastered 509
Disavowed. 75
Disciples 745
Disciples the 543
Disney Adventures 609
Disney Afternoon 233
Disney Colossal Comics
  Collection 609
Disney Comic Hits. 233
Disney Comics in 3-D 609
Disney Comics Spec: Donald
  & Scrooge 609
Disney Junior 609
Disney Presents 233
Disney Rapes the 1st
  Amendment 826
Disney's Monsters Inc. 509
Disney's Tarzan. 509
Disneyland Birthday Party. 609
District X 233
Ditko's World: Static 745
Diver Dan 609
Divine Intervention 609
Divine Right: the Adventures
  of Max Faraday 543
Division 13. 509
Dixie Dugan. 397
Dizzy Don Comics 397
Dizzy Duck 375
Dmz. 75
Dna Hacker Chronicles 609
Dnagents 609
Do You Believe in Nightmares . 399
Do-Do 398
Doc Carter V. D. Comics. 397
Doc Frankenstein 609
Doc Samson 234
Doc Savage 75, 234, 609
Doc Savage Comics 397
Doc Savage: Curse of the
  Fire God. 509
Doc Savage the Man of Bronze 609
Doc Weird's Thrill Book. 746
Doctor 745
Doctor Boogie 609
Doctor Chaos 609
Doctor Fate 75
Doctor Mid-Nite 75
Doctor Octopus: Negative
  Exposure 234
Doctor Solar Man of the Atom. . 610
Doctor Spectrum 234
Doctor Strange 235
Doctor Strange: the Oath 235
Doctor Strangefate 192
Doctor Weird 746
Doctor Who 235, 610
Doctor Who Classics. 610
Doctor Who: the Forgotten 610
Dodekain 746
Dodo and the Frog 85
Dogaroo. 746
Dogs O'War the. 746
Dogs of War 610
Dogwitch 746
Doktor Sleepless 610
Doktor Sleepless Manual 610
Doll and Creature 543
Doll Man 398
Dollman 610
Dolls 746
Dolly Dill 235
Dollz 543
Domination Factor. 235
Dominion 543, 610, 746
Dominion: Conflict 1 No More
  Noise 509
Dominion Special: Phantom
  of the Audience 509
Domino 235
Domino Chance 746
Domu: a Child's Dreams 509

Don Bluth's Dragon's Lair 611
Don Bluth's Space Ace 611
Don Fortune Magazine 398
Don Newcombe. 398
Don Quixote 813
Don Simpson's Bizarre Heroes. 746
Don Winslow of the Navy 398
Donald and Mickey Merry
  Christmas. 398
Donald Duck 398, 610
Donald Duck Adventures. 610
Donald Duck Album. 611
Donald Duck and Friends 611
Donald Duck Giveaways 398
Donatello 611, 746
Done to Death 611
Donna Mia 611, 746
Doom. 236
Doom 2099 235
Doom Force 75
Doom Patrol 124
Doom Patrol 75
Doom: the Emperor Returns . . . 236
Doom's Iv 543
Doomed. 746
Doomsday. 76
Doomsday + 1 . . . . 611, 746
Doomsday Squad 611
Doorway to Nightmare 76
Dope Comix 826
Dopey Duck Comics 236
Dopin Dan 826
Dori Stories 826
Dork. 746
Dork Tower 746
Dorothy 611
Dorothy Lamour 431
Double Action Comics 76
Double Comics 399
Double Dare Adventures 611
Double Dragon 236
Double Edge 236
Double Edge Double 746
Double Image 543
Double Impact 611, 746
Double Impact 2069 747
Double Impact Alive 747
Double Impact: Assassins for
  Hire 747
Double Impact: from the Ashes. 747
Double Impact: Hot Shots 747
Double Impact Mercs 747
Double Impact: One Step
  Beyond. 747
Double Impact Raw. 747
Double Impact/Razor. 747
Double Impact Suicide Run. . . . 747
Double Impact X 747
Double Life of Private Strong . . 611
Double Talk 399
Double Trouble 399
Double up 399
Down 544
Down with Crime 399
Downfall, the 822
Dr. Anthony King Hollywood
  Love Doctor 397
Dr. Atomic. 826
Dr. Atomic's Marijuana Multiplier 826
Dr. Blink: Superhero Shrink. . . . 745
Dr. Fate. 75
Dr. Giggles 509
Dr. Gorpon. 745
Dr. Jekyll and Mr. Hyde. 814
Dr. Jj 610
Dr. Kildare 610
Dr. Radium 745
Dr. Radium: Man of Science . . . 745
Dr. Robot 509
Dr. Strange 234
Dr. Strange Classics 235
Dr. Tomorrow 610
Dr. Wonder 746
Dr. Zero 235
Dracula 509, 611, 747
Dracula Chronicles 611
Dracula in Hell 747
Dracula Lives 236
Dracula: Lord of the Undead. . . 236
Dracula: Suicide Club 747
Dracula: the Lady in the Tomb . 747
Dracula: Vlad the Impaler 612

Dracula vs Capone 612
Dracula vs King Arthur 612
Dracula vs Zorro 612
Dracula Vs. Zorro 544
Dracula's Cozy Coffin 747
Dracula's Revenge 612
Draft the 236
Drafted. 612
Drag-Strip Hotrodders 612
Dragon Arms 747
Dragon Arms: Chaos Blade. . . . 747
Dragon: Blood and Guts, the . . 544
Dragon Cross 612
Dragon Knights 747
Dragon Lines 236
Dragon of the Valkyr 747
Dragon Prince 509, 544
Dragon Quest 747
Dragon Strike 236
Dragon the 544
Dragon Wars 747
Dragon Weekly 747
Dragon's Lair 612
Dragon's Teeth/Dragon's Claws 236
Dragonball. 747
Dragonball Z 747
Dragonflight 612
Dragonfly. 612
Dragonforce. 747
Dragonforce Chronicles. 747
Dragonlance 76
Dragonlance: Chronicles. 612
Dragonlance Legends: Time
  of the Twins 612
Dragonlance Legends: War
  of the Twins 612
Dragonlance: the Legend of
  Huma 612
Dragonmist 747
Dragonpro 612
Dragonring 612, 747
Dragonrok Saga 747
Dragonslayer. 236
Drain 544
Drakkon Wars the 612
Drakuun 509
Drawing from Life 544
Drawing on Your Nightmares . . 509
Drawings by S. Clay Wilson . . . 826
Drax the Destroyer 236
Dread of Night 747
Dreadlands 236
Dreadnought: Invasion Six 612
Dreadstar 236, 612
Dreadstar & Company. 236
Dream Angel and Angel Girl . . 747
Dream Angel: the Quantum
  Dreamer. 748
Dream Angel: World
  Without End 748
Dream Police. 236
Dreamer the 612
Dreamery. 748
Dreamgirl 748
Dreaming the. 76
Dreamland Chronicles the. 612
Dreamlands 748
Dreams of the Darkchylde. 612
Dreamtime. 748
Dreamwalker. 748
Dreamwalker: Autumn Leaves . 748
Dreamwalker: Carousel. 748
Dreamwalker: Summer Rain . . 748
Dreamwolves. 748
Dredd Rules 612
Drift Marlo 612
Drifters. 748
Droids 236
Droopy. 509
Drowners the 748
Druid 236
Drunken Fist 613
Drywall and Oswald Show the . 748
Duck Tales. 235
Duckman 509, 613
Dudley 399
Dudley Do-Right 613
Duel. 748
Duel Masters 613
Dumbo Weekly 399
Dummy's Guide to Danger a. . . 613
Dunc & Loo 613

Duncan's Kingdom 544
Dune 236
Dungeon 748
Dungeon: the Early Years 748
Dungeoneers. 748
Dungeons & Dragons: 613
Dungeons & Dragons: Black
  & White 748
Dungeons & Dragons in
  Shadow of Dragons. 748
Duo Stars 613
Durango Kid 399
Dust. 544
Dust to Dust 613
Dusty Star 544
Dv8 544
Dv8 Vs. Black Ops 544
Dwelling the. 748
Dwight D. Eisenhower. 613
Dwight T. Albatross's the
  Goon Noir 509
Dying Dolphin 827
Dylan Dog 509
Dynamic Classics 77
Dynamic Comics 399
Dynamite 399
Dynamo 613
Dynamo 5 544
Dynamo Joe 613
Dynomutt 236

E E E E
E. Z. Wolf's Astral Outhouse . . . 827
E.V.E. Protomecha 545
E-Man 615
Eagle. 399, 748
Eagle: Dark Mirror. 748
Eagle, the 399
Eagles Dare 748
Earth 4. 613
Earth Lore: Legend of Bek
  Larson 748
Earth Lore: Reign of
  Dragon Lord. 748
Earth War 748
Earth X 236
Earth: Year Zero 748
Earthworm Jim 236
East Meets West. 613
Easy Way 748
Eat Right to Work and Win . . . 399
Eat-Man. 748
Eb'nn the Raven 748
Eberron: Eye of the Wolf. 613
Ebon 827
Ebonix-Files the 748
Echo 544
Echo of Futurepast 613
Echoes of the Damned 613
Eclipse Graphic Novels 613
Eclipse Monthly 613
Eclipso. 77
Eclipso: the Darkness Within . . 77
Ectokid. 236
Ed Burns' Dock Walloper 613
Ed the Happy Clown 748
Eddie Campell's Bacchus 749
Eddie Stanky 399
Eddy Current 749
Eden's Trail 237
Edgar Allan Poe 749
Edgar Rice Burroughs' a
  Princess of Mars 613
Edgar Rice Burroughs'
  Return of Tarzan 509
Edgar Rice Burroughs'
  Tarzan 510
Edgar Rice Burroughs'
  Tarzan: Carson of Venus . . 510
Edgar Rice Burroughs'
  Tarzan: the Lost Adventure 510
Edgar Rice Burroughs'
  Tarzan: the Rivers of Blood 510
Edgar Rice Burroughs' Tarzan
  the Savage Heart. 510
Edge 613, 749
Edge of Chaos 613
Eerie 399
Eerie Adventures. 400
Egbert 400
Egon 510
Egypt 77
Eh! 400

Eight Legged Freaks 613
Eightball 749
Eighth Wonder the 510
El Arsenal 614
El Bombo Comics 400
El Cazador 614
El Diablo 77
El Hazard: the Magnificent
    World 749
El Perfecto Comics 827
El Zombo 510
Electric Undertow 237
Electric Warrior 77
Electropolis 544
Elektra 237
Elektra & Wolverine: the
    Redeemer 237
Elektra: Assassin 237
Elektra/Cyblade 544
Elektra: Glimpse & Echo 237
Elektra: Root of Evil 237
Elektra: Saga 237
Elektra: the Hand 237
Elektra/Witchblade 237
Elementals 614
Elephantmen 544
Elephantmen: War Toys 544
Elf Warrior 749
Elford 614, 749
Elford: All the Lonely Places . . 749
Elford Chronicles 749
Elford Cuts Loose 749
Elford: Hawk 749
Elford: Return of the King 749
Elford: Summer Magic 749
Elflore: the High Seas 749
Elfquest 77, 237, 749
Elfquest: 614
Elfquest: Kahvi 749
Elfquest: Kings of the Broken
    Wheel 749
Elfquest: Seige at Blue
    Mountain 749
Elfquest: the Discovery 77
Elfquest: Two Spear 749
Elfquest: Worldpool 749
Elftrek 749
Eliminator 614, 750
Eliminator Color Special 614
Elk's Run 614
Ella Cinders 400
Ellery Queen 400
Elongated Man 77
Elric 614
Elric: Stormbringer 510
Elric: the Making of a Sorcerer . . 77
Elsewhere Prince 237
Elseworld's Finest 77
Elsie the Cow 400
Elsinore 614
Elven 615
Elvira 77, 237, 750
Elvira Mistress of the Dark 750
Embrace: Hunger of the Flesh . 750
Emeraldas 615
Emergency 615
Emily the Strange 510
Emissary 545
Emma Davenport 750
Emma Frost 237
Emo Boy 750
Empire 77, 545, 750
Empire Lanes 750
Empty Zone 750
Empty Zone: Conversations
    with the Dead 750
Enchanted 750
Enchanted: the Awakening 615
Enchanted Valley 750
Enchanter 750
Enchanter: Apocalypse Wind
    Novella 750
Enchanting Love 400
End League the 510
End of Story: Mitrabhed 615
Ender's Game 237
Enemy 510
Enemy Ace: War in Heaven 77
Enforcers 750
Engine 615
Engineer the 615
Enginehead 77

Enigma 77
Enigma Cipher the 615
Enigmas the 615
Ennis and McCrea's Bigger
    Dicks 750
Ennis and McCrea's Dicks 2 . . 750
Ensign O'Toole 615
Entropy Tales 750
Epic 238
Epic Anthology 238
Epic Illustrated 238
Epic Lite 238
Epilogue 615
Epsilon Wave 750
Epsilon Wave the 615
Equine the Uncivilized 750
Equinox Chronicles 750
Eradicator 77
Eradicators 750
Eric Preston Is the Flame 750
Ernie Comics 463
Esc: No Exit 615
Esc.(Escape) 615
Escape from Fear 400
Escape of the Living Dead 615
Escape to the Stars 750
Escape Velocity 750
Escapists the 510
Esmeraldas 750
Esp 750
Espers 545, 615, 750
Espionage 615
Essential Vertigo: 77
Establishment the 615
Estancia 615
Eternal 238
Eternal Truth 827
Eternal Warrior 615
Eternal Warriors 615
Eternals 238
Eternals: Herod Factor 238
Eternity Smith 616
Eternity Triple Action 750
Etta Kett 400
Eudaemon the 510
Eva the Imp 616
Evangeline 616
Eve: Vampire Diva 616
Evenfall 750
Event Presents the
    Ash Universe 750
Everette Hartsoe's Razor 750
Evermuch Wave 827
Everquest 616
Everybody's Dead 616
Everyman 238
Everything Happens to Harvey . . 78
Everything's Archie 616
Evil Dead 510
Evil Dead III: Army of Darkness 510
Evil Ernie 616, 750, 751
Evil Ernie: Manhattan
    Death Trip 751
Evil Ernie Returns 751
Evil Ernie: the Horror 751
Evil Ernie's Baddest Battles . . . 616
Evil Eye 751
Evo 545
Ewoks 238
Ex Libris 751
Ex Machina 616
Ex-Mutants 616, 751
Exalted 616
Excalibur 238, 239
Excalibur: Sword of Power 239
Exciting Comics 400
Exciting Romances 401
Exciting War 401
Exciting X-Patrol 192
Executioner 616
Exemplars 616
Exiles 239, 616
Exit 751
Exo-Squad 616
Expatriate the 545
Experts the 751
Exploits of Daniel Boone 401
Explorer Joe 401
Explorers 617, 751
Exposed 401
Exposure 545
Exposure: Second Coming 617

Exposure Special 617
Exquisite Corpse 510
Exterminators the 78
Extinction Event 617
Extinctioners 617, 751
Extra 617
Extra Comics 401
Extra! 401
Extreme 3000 545
Extreme Anthology 545
Extreme Christmas Special . . . 545
Extreme Destroyer 545
Extreme Hero 545
Extreme Justice 78
Extreme Prejudice 545
Extreme Sacrifice 545
Extreme Tour Book 545
Extreme Zero 545
Extremely Silly 751
Extremely Youngblood 545
Extremes Violet 617
Extremist 78
Eye of Mongombo 751
Eye of the Storm 617
Eyeball Kid 510
Ezra 617

F F F F
F III Bandit 754
F-Troop 622
F5 546
F5 Origin 510
Fables 78
Fabulous Furry Freak Brothers . 827
Face, the 401
Faceless the 545
Faction Paradox 545
Factor X 239
Fade from Blue 751
Fade from Grace 617
Fafhrd and the Gray
    Mouser 240, 510
Fairy Tale Parade 401
Fairy Tales 401
Faith 751
Faithful 240
Faker 78
Falcon 240
Fall of Cthulhu the 617
Fallen Angel 78, 617
Fallen Angels 240
Fallen Son: the Death of
    Captain America 240
Falling Man 545
Family Affair 617
Family Bones 751
Family Dynamic 78
Family Funnies 401
Family Guy 617
Family Man 78
Famous Comics 401
Famous Crimes 401
Famous Fairy Tales 401
Famous Feature Stories 401
Famous Funnies 401
Famous Gang, Book of Comics 398
Famous Gangsters 402
Famous Indian Tribes 617
Famous Mysteries 815
Famous Stars 402
Famous Stories 402
Famous Western Badmen 460
Fanboy 78
Fang and Claw 822
Fang: Testament 751
Fangs of the Widow 751
Fantagor 827
Fantasci 751
Fantastic 386
Fantastic Adventures 751
Fantastic Comics 402
Fantastic Fables 751
Fantastic Fears 402
Fantastic Five 240
Fantastic Force 240
Fantastic Four 240
Fantastic Four: 1 2 3 4 244
Fantastic Four 2099 244
Fantastic Four: a Death in the . 244
Fantastic Four and Power Pack 244
Fantastic Four: Atlantis Rising . 244
Fantastic Four: First Family . . . 244

Fantastic Four: Foes 244
Fantastic Four: House of M 244
Fantastic Four/Iron Man: Big
    in Japan 244
Fantastic Four Roast 244
Fantastic Four: the End 244
Fantastic Four the World's
    Greatest Comic Magazine . 244
Fantastic Four: True Story 244
Fantastic Four Unlimited 244
Fantastic Four Unplugged 244
Fantastic Four: Unstable
    Molecules 244
Fantastic Four Vs. X-Men 244
Fantastic Four's Big Town 244
Fantastic Panic 751
Fantastic Stories 751
Fantastic Voyage 617
Fantastic Voyages of Sinbad . . 617
Fantastic World of Hanna-
    Barbera 244
Fantastic Worlds 402, 751
Fantasy Features 617
Fantasy Masterpieces . . . 244, 245
Fantasy Quarterly 751
Fantoman 372
Far West 751
Farewell to Weapons 245
Fargo Kid 432
Faro Korbit 617
Farscape 617
Farscape: War Torn 617
Fart Wars: Special Edition 751
Fast Fiction 402
Fastlane Illustrated 751
Fat Albert 617
Fat and Slat 403
Fat and Slat Joke Book 403
Fat Dog Mendoza 510
Fat Ninja 752
Fatale 617
Fatalis 751
Fate 78
Fate's Five 617
Fathom 545, 617
Fathom: Killian's Tide 545
Fatman the Human Flying
    Saucer 618
Fault Lines 79
Faust 752, 824
Faust/777: the Wrath 752
Faust: Book of M 618
Faust: Singha's Talons 752
Favorite Comics 403
Fawcett Funny Animals 403
Fawcett Miniatures 403
Fawcett Movie Comics 403
Fear 245
Fear Agent 510, 545
Fear Agent: Hatched Job 510
Fear Agent: the Last Goodbye . 510
Fear Effect 546
Fear the Dead 618
Fearbook 618
Fearless 546
Feather 546
Feature Books 403
Feature Comics 404
Feature Films 79
Feature Funnies 403
Federal Men Comics 404
Feds 'N' Heads 827
Feeders 510
Felch 827
Felix and His Friends 404
Felix the Cat 404, 618, 752
Felix tho Cat: tho Movie 618
Felix the Cat True Crime Stories 752
Felix's Nephews Inky & Dinky . 618
Fell 546
Felon 546
Felt: True Tales of Underground
    Hip Hop 546
Fem 5 618
Fem Fantastique 752
Femforce 618, 752
Femforce Special 752
Femforce: Up-Close 618
Femme Noir: the Dark City
    Diaries 618
Ferdinand the Bull 404
Ferret 618

Ferro City 546
Ferryman the. 618
Feud 245
Fever Pitch 827
Fever the 752
Fiction Clemens 618
Fierce 510
Fifties Terror 752
Fight Against Crime. 404
Fight Against the Guilty 405
Fight Comics 405
Fight for Tomorrow 79
Fight Man 245
Fight the Enemy 618
Fightin' Air Force 405
Fightin' Army 618
Fightin' Five 618
Fightin' Marines 619
Fightin' Navy 619
Fightin' Texan 478
Fighting American 79, 405, 618
Fighting Davy Crockett 434
Fighting Fronts! 405
Fighting Indians of the
   Wild West. 405
Fighting Leathernecks 405
Fighting Man, the 405
Fighting Undersea Commandos 405
Fighting War Stories 405
Fighting Yank. 405, 752
Film Funnies 245
[Filmation's Ghostbusters 624
Film Star Romances 406
Filth the 79
Final Crisis 79
Final Cycle 752
Final Destination: Spring Break. 619
Final Girl 619
Final Night the 80
Finder 752
Finder Footnotes 752
Fire and Brimstone 619
Fire from Heaven 546
Fire Team 752
Firearm 619
Firebirds 546
Fireblast: Adventures in the
   30th Century 619
Firebrand. 80
Firebreather. 546
Firehair Comics 406
Firestar 245
Firestorm 80
Firestorm, the Nuclear Man. 85
First Adventures 619
First Born. 546
First Born: Aftermath 546
First Graphic Novels 619
First Issue Special. 80
First Men in the Moon, the 823
First the 619
First Wave. 752
First Wave: Double Vision. . . . 752
First Wave: Genesis of
   a Genius 752
First Wave: Heart of a Killer . . . 619
First Wave: in the Beginning . . . 619
First Wave: Jordan Radcliffe . . . 619
Firstman 546
Fish Police 245, 619, 752
Fish Shticks 752
Fist of God. 752
Fist of Justice 619
Fist of the North Star. 753
Flag Fighters 753
Flak Riot 546
Flame, the 406
Flamehead 619
Flaming Carrot . 510, 546, 753, 827
Flaming Love. 406
Flaming Western Romances . . . 406
Flare 619, 753
Flare Adventures 619
Flare First Edition 753
Flare Vs. Tigress 753
Flash & Green Lantern: the
   Brave & the Bold 84
Flash Comics 80
Flash Gordon
     . . . . 84, 245, 406, 619, 620
Flash The: Fastest Man Alive . . 84
Flash Theatre 827

Flash Plus, the 84
Flashpoint 84
Flaxen 511
Flesh and Bones 620
Fleshapoids from Earth 827
Flinch. 84
Flintstone Kids. 245
Flintstones 245, 620
Flintstones and the Jetsons the . 84
Flintstones in 3-D 620
Flintstones the 620
Flip. 406
Flipper 620
Flippity & Flop 84
Floaters 511
Flood Relief 620
Fly Boy 406
Fly the 84, 620
Flyin' Jenny 406
Flying A's Range Rider, the. . . . 406
Flying Aces 406
Flying Cadet 406
Flying Hero Barbie 245
Flying Models 406
Flying Saucers 620
Flyman 620
Food of the Gods, the 824
Foodini. 406
Foofur 245
Foolkiller 245
Foolkiller: Short Time 245
Foolkiller: White Angels. 245
Foot Soldiers the 511, 546
Football Thrills 406
Footsoldiers. 620
Foozle 620
For Your Eyes Only 245
Forbidden Kingdom 753
Forbidden Love 406
Forbidden Planet. 620
Forbidden Tales of Dark Mansion 84
Forbidden Vampire Tales. 753
Forbidden Worlds 406, 753
Force 10 753
Force of the Buddha's Palm . . . 620
Force Seven 753
Force Works 245
Foreign Intrigues 399
Foremost Boys 415
Foreternity 753
Forever Amber 546
Forever Maelstrom 84
Forever People 84
Forever People the 84
Forever War the 620
Forever Warriors 753
Forgive Me Father. 753
Forgotten Realms 84
Forgotten Realms: the Dark
   Elf Trilogy 620
Formerly Known as the Justice
   League. 84
Forsaken 546
Fort: Prophet of the
   Unexplained. 511
Forty Winks 753
Forty Winks: Mr. Horrible. 753
Forty Winks: the Fabled Pirate
   Queen of the South China
   Sea 753
Forty-Five Guardsmen, the 821
Foundation 621
Four Color 407
Four Eyes 546
Four Favorites 414
Four Horsemen 84
Four Kunoichi: Enter the Sinja . 753
Four Star Battle Tales 84
Four Star Spectacular 84
Fourth Horsemen the 621
Fox and the Crow 84
Fox Comics 753
Foxfire 621
Foxhole 415
Foxy Fagan 415
Fraggle Rock. 245
Fragile Prophet 753
Francis Brother of the Universe 245
Frank 621, 753
Frank Buck 415
Frank Frazetta Death Dealer. . . 621

Frank Frazetta Fantasy
   Illustrated. 621
Frank Frazetta's Creatures 546
Frank Frazetta's Dark Kingdom 546
Frank Frazetta's Death Dealer . 546
Frank Frazetta's Dracula
   Meets the Wolfman 546
Frank Frazetta's Swamp Demon546
Frank Merriwell at Yale 415
Frank Miller's Robocop 621
Frank the Unicorn 753
Frankenstein 288
Frankenstein . . . 511, 621, 753, 815
Frankenstein Comics. 415
Frankenstein Dracula War. . . . 621
Frankenstein Jr.. 621
Frankenstein Mobster 546
Frankie 202
Frankie & Lana 202
Frankie Fuddle 202
Frankies Frightmares 753
Franklin Richards 245
Fray. 511
Freak Force. 546
Freak-Out on Infant Earths . . . 753
Freaks 753
Freaks of the Heartland. 511
Freaks' Amour 511
Freakshow 511, 753
Fred Hembeck. 246
Fred Perry's S-Guild 621
Fred the Possessed Flower . . . 753
Freddy 621
Freddy Vs. Jason Vs. Ash. . . . 621
Freddy's Dead: the Final
   Nightmare 621
Free Fall 621
Freedom Fighters 84
Freedom Force 547
Freedom Formula 621
Freedom Train 415
Freemind 621
Freex 621
French Ice 753
Freshmen the 547
Friday Foster 621
Friday the 13th 621
Friday the 13th: Pamela's Tale . 621
Friendly Ghost Casper the . . . 622
Friendly Neighbor- Hood
   Spider-Man 246
Friends 753
Friends of Maxx. 547
Fright 246, 754
Fright Night 622
Fright Night 3-D. 622
Fright Night II. 622
Fringe 622, 754
Frisky Animals 416
Frisky Animals on Parade 415
Frisky Fables. 415
Fritz Bugs out 827
Fritz: Secret Agent for the Cia. . 827
Fritz the Cat. 827
Fritz the No-Good 827
Fritzi Ritz. 416
Frogman Comics. 416
Frogmen the 622
From Beyond. 754
From Beyond the Unknown. . . . 85
From Heaven to Hell 622
From Hell. 754
From Here to Insanity 416
From the Darkness 754
From the Darkness II Blood
   Vows 754
From the Earth to the Moon . . . 821
From the Void 754
Front Page Comic Book 416
Frontier Fighter 394
Frontier Fighters 85
Frontier Romances 416
Frontier Scout Daniel Boone. . . 395
Frontier Trail 460
Frontier Western 246
Frontline Combat. 416, 622
Frost: the Dying Breed 754
Fugitives from Justice 416
Fugitoid 754
Full Cirkle 622
Full Metal Fiction 754
Full Moon Craze 622

Fun Comics 254
Fun-In 622
Funky Phantom. 622
Funland 416
Funland Comics 416
Funnies Annual, the 417
Funnies on Parade 417
Funnies, the (1st Series) 416
Funnies, the (2nd Series) 416
Funny 3-D 479
Funny Aminals. 827
Funny Book 417
Funny Films. 417
Funny Folks. 85
Funny Frolics. 246
Funny Funnies 417
Funny Pages 417
Funny Picture Stories 417
Funny Stocking Stuffer 85
Funny Stuff 85
Funny Tunes 246, 417
Funnyman 417
Furies 754
Furious Fist of the Drunken
   Monkey: Origin of the
   Species 622
Furrlough. 754
Furry Ninja High School 754
Furry Ninja High School
   Strikes Back. 622
Further Adventures of Cyclops
   and Phoenix. 246
[Further Adventures Of]
   Indiana Jones 259
Fury. 246, 754
Fury/Agent 13 246
Fury of Firestorm. 85
Fury of Hellina the. 754
Fury of S.H.I.E.L.D. 246
Fury: Peacemaker. 246
Fused 622
Fused: Think like a Machine . . . 511
Fused! 547
Fusion 754
Futaba-Kun Change 754
Futurama 754
Futurama Comics 622
Future Comics. 417
Future World Comics 417
Futuretech 754
Futurians 622, 754
Fx 622

G G G G

G.E.I. 623
G.I. Combat. 87, 418
G.I. in Battle 419
G.I. Jane 419
G.I. Joe 419, 512, 549, 625
G.I. Joe 3-D. 625
G.I. Joe: a Real American Hero 250
G.I. Joe and the Transformers . 250
G.I. Joe: Battle Files 549
G.I. Joe European Missions . . . 250
G.I. Joe Frontline. 549
G.I. Joe Special Missions 250
G.I. Joe Universe 250
G.I. Joe Vs. Transformers 549
G.I. R.A.M.B.O.T. 625
G.I. Tales 311
G.L.A. 250
G.O.T.H. 627
G-Force 549
Gabby Hayes Western 417
Gaijin. 754
Galactic 511
Galactic Guardians 246
Galactica: the New Millennium . 622
Galactus the Devourer 246
Galaxion 754
Galaxy Quest: Global Warning . 622
Galaxy-Size Astounding
   Space Thrills 547
Gall Force: Eternal Story. 622
Gallant Men the. 622
Gallegher Boy Reporter 622
Galveston 622
Gambit. 246
Gambit & Bishop: Sons of
   the Atom 247
Gambit and the X-Ternals 247
Gamekeeper 622
Gamera 511

Gammarauders 86
Gamorra Swimsuit Special 547
Gang Busters 86
Gang World 418
Gangsters and Gun Molls 418
Gangsters Can't Win 418
Gargoyle 247
Gargoyles 247, 622
Garrison's Gorrillas 623
Garth Ennis' 623
Gary Gianni's Monstermen 511
Gasoline Alley 418
Gasp! 623
Gate Crasher 623
Gate Crasher Ring of Fire 623
Gate of the East Wind 623
Gatekeeper 754
Gates of the Night 754
Gatesville Company 623
Gay Comics 247
Gay Comix 827
Gazillion 547
Ge Rouge 624
Gear 755
Gear Station the 547
Gearhead 623
Gears of War 623
Gearz 623
Geeksville 547
Geisha 755
Gem Comics 418
Geminar 547
Gemini 547
Gemini Blood 86
Gems of the Samurai 755
Gen of Hiroshima 827
Gen-Active 623
Gen12 548
Gen13 . . . . 547, 623
Gen13: Armageddon 624
Gen13 Bootleg 548
Gen13/Generation X 548
Gen13: Interactive 548
Gen13: Magical Drama Queen
    Roxy 548
Gen13/Monkey Man & O'Brien . 548
Gen13 Movie Adaptation 623
Gen13: Ordinary Heroes 548
Gen13/the Maxx 548
Gene Autry Comics 418
Gene Autry's Champion 418
Gene Dogs 247
Gene Fusion 623
Gene Roddenberry's 623
Gene Simmons Dominatrix 623
Gene Simmons Zipper 623
Gene Simmons' House of
    Horrors 623
Gene Simmons' Jazan Wild . . . 623
General Douglas Macarthur . . . 418
Generation Hex 192
Generation M 247
Generation next 247
Generation X 247
Generation X/Gen 13 248
Generation X: Underground . . . 248
Generic Comic 248
Generic Comic Book 755
Genesis 86, 623
Genesis Five 623
Genetix 248
Genext 248
Genocyber 755
Gensaga: Ancient Warrior 623
Gentle Ben 624
Geobreeders 755
Geomancer 624
George a Romero's 624
George of the Jungle 624
George Pal's Puppetoon's 418
George R. R. Martin's Wild
    Cards: the Hard Call . . . 624
Georgie Comics 248
Gerald McBoing-Boing and the
    Nearsighted Mr. Magoo . . . 418
Geriatric Gangrene Jujitsu
    Gerbils 755
Geronimo 418
Get Lost 418
Get Smart 624
Getalong Gang 248
Ghost 418, 511

Ghost and the Shadow 511
Ghost/Batgirl 511
Ghost Breakers 418
Ghost Busters II 624
Ghost/Hellboy 511
Ghost in the Shell 511
Ghost in the Shell 1.5: Human
    Error Processing 511
Ghost in the Shell 2: Man-
    Machine Interface 511
Ghost Manor 624
Ghost Mother Comics 827
Ghost Rider 248, 249
Ghost Rider 2099 250
Ghost Rider/Ballistic/Cyblade . 249
Ghost Rider/Blaze Spirits of
    Vengeance 249
Ghost Rider: Danny Ketch 249
Ghost Rider Finale 249
Ghost Rider: Highway to Hell . . 250
Ghost Rider: the Hammer Lane 249
Ghost Rider: Trail of Tears 250
Ghost Spy 548
Ghost Stories 624
Ghost Whisperer: the Haunted . 624
Ghostbusters 624
Ghostbusters: Legion 624
Ghostbusters: the Other Side . 624
Ghostdancing 86
Ghosting 548, 624
Ghostly Tales 624
Ghostly Weird Stories 380
Ghosts 86
Ghosts of Dracula 755
Gi Government Issued 755
Giant Boy Book of Comics 418
Giant Comics 624
Giant Comics Edition 418
Giant Shanda Animal 755
Giant-Size Chillers 250
Giant-Size Dracula 250
Giantkiller 87
Gideon Hawk 755
Gidget 624
Gift Comics 419
Gift the 548, 624
Gigantic 511
Gigantor 624, 755
Giggle Comics 419
Gil Thorp 625
Gilgamesh II 88
Gimmeabreak Comix 827
Gimoles 625
Gin-Ryu 625
Ginger 419
Ginger Fox 625
Girl Comics 250
Girl Crazy 512
Girl from U.N.C.L.E. 625
Girl Genius 625, 755
Girl Who Would Be Death the . . 88
Girls 549
Girls & Boys 827
Girls in Love 419
Girls of Ninja High School 1997 755
Girls' Life 250
Girls' Love Stories 88
Girls' Romances 88
Give Me Liberty 512
Gizmo 755
Gizmo & the Fugitoid 755
Gladiator/Supreme 250
Glister 549
Global Frequency 625
Gloom Cookie 755
Gloom the 625
Glory 549, 625
Glory & Friends 549
Glory/Angela Angels in Hell . . . 549
Glory/Avengelyne 549
Glory/Avengelyne: the
    Godyssey 549
Glory/Celestine: Dark
    Angel 549, 626
Glory/Lionheart: Rage of Furies 626
Glx-Mas 251
Gnatrat 755
Gnatrat: the Movie 755
Go Boy 7: Human Action
    Machine 512
Go Girl! 549
Go-Go 626, 756

Goat The: H.A.E.D.U.S. 626
Gobbledygook 755
Goblin Chronicles 626
Goblin Lord the 626
God Nose 827
Goddess 88
Godfather Chronicles the 626
Godland 549
Gods for Hire 626
Godwheel 626
Godyssey 626
Godzilla 251, 512
Godzilla Color Special 512
Going Steady 477
Gojin 755
Gold Bug & Other Stories, the . 820
Gold Digger 626, 755
Gold Digger Beta 626
Gold Digger: Edge Guard 755
Gold Digger/Ninja High School . 755
Gold Digger Sourcebook 626
Gold Digger: Throne
    of Shadows 755
Gold Digger: Tiffany & Charlotte 626
Gold Medal Comics 419
Golden Age 88
Golden Age Greats 755
Golden Arrow 419
Golden Comics Digest 626
Golden Lad 419
Golden Picture Story Book 627
Golden Plates the 627
Golden Warrior 756
Golden Warrior Iczer One 756
Golden West Love 419
Golden-Age Men of Mystery . . . 755
Goldwyn 3-D 756
Golly 549
Gomer Pyle 627
Good and Evil 627
Good Girl Comics 756
Good Girls 756
Good Guys 627
Goofy Adventures 627
Goofy Comics 419
Goon 627
Goon the 512, 756
Goop the 627
Gore Shriek 756
Gorgo 627
Gorgo's Revenge 627
Gori Lori 756
Gorilla Gorilla 627
Gotham Central 88
Gotham Girls 88
Gotham Underground 88
Gothess: Dark Ecstasy 756
Gothic Blimp Works Ltd. 827
Gothic Scrolls Drayven, the . . . 627
Grackle the 756
Grant Morrison's Doctor Who . . 627
Graphic Story Monthly 756
Graphique Musique 756
Grateful Dead Comix 627
Grave Dog Freshley the 627
Grave Tales 756
Gravediggers 756
Gravel 627
Graveslinger 549
Gravestone 627
Gravity 251
Gray Area the 549
Grease Monkey 550, 627
Greaser Comics 827
Great American Comics
    Presents–? The Secret
    Voice 420
Great American Western 627
Great Comics 420
Great Detective Starring
    Sherlock Holmes 756
Great Expectations 817
Greatest American Hero 627
Greatest Hits 88
Green Arrow 88
Green Arrow/Black Canary 90
Green Arrow Longbow Hunters . 90
Green Arrow: the Wonder Years . 90
Green Arrow: Year One 90
Green Berets 756
Green Giant Comics 420
Green Goblin 251

Green Hornet 627
Green Hornet Comics 420
Green Hornet the 627
Green Lama 420
Green Lantern 90, 92, 93
Green Lantern & Sentinel:
    Heart of Darkness 93
Green Lantern: Circle of Fire . . 93
Green Lantern Corps 91
Green Lantern Corps 93
Green Lantern Corps Quarterly . 93
Green Lantern Corps: Recharge . 93
Green Lantern: Dragon Lord . . 93
Green Lantern: Emerald Dawn . 93
Green Lantern: Evil's Might . . . 94
Green Lantern/Green Arrow . . . 94
Green Lantern: Mosaic 94
Green Lantern: Rebirth 94
Green Lantern: the New Corps . 94
Green Lantern Vs. Aliens 512
Green Mansions 820
Green Mask, the 420
Green Planet 628
Greenhaven 628
Greenleaf in Exile 756
[Greg Capullo's Original]
    Creech 539
Gregory 94
Gremlin Trouble 756
Grendel 512, 628, 756
Grendel: Behold the Devil 512
Grendel: Black White and Red . 512
Grendel Classics 512
Grendel: Devil by the Deed . . . 512
Grendel: Devil Child 512
Grendel: Devil's Legacy 512
Grendel: Devil's Reign 512
Grendel: God and the Devil . . . 512
Grendel: Red White & Black . . . 512
Grendel Tales: Devil's
    Apprentice 512
Grendel Tales: Devil's Choices . 512
Grendel Tales: Devils
    and Deaths 512
Grendel Tales: Four Devils
    One Hell 512
Grendel Tales: Homecoming . . 513
Grendel Tales: the Devil in
    Our midst 513
Grendel Tales: the Devil
    May Care 513
Grendel Tales: the Devil's
    Hammer 513
Grendel: the Devil Inside 512
Grendel: War Child 513
Grenuord 756
Grey 756
Greylore 628
Greymatter 756
Greyshirt: Indigo Sunset 628
Griffin 94
Griffin the 756
Grifter 550
Grifter & Midnighter 628
Grifter and the Mask 513
Grifter/Badrock 550
Grifter/Shi 550
Grifter-One Shot 550
Grim Ghost the 628
Grim Wit 827
Grimjack 628
Grimjack: Killer Instinct 628
Grimm Fairy Tales 628
Grimm's Ghost Stories 628
Grimoire the 628
Grip: the Strange World of Men . 94
Grips 756
Groo 550
Groo Chronicles 251
Groo: Hell on Earth 513
Groo the Wanderer 628
Groovy 251
Gross Point 94
Ground Zero 757
Grounded 550
Group Large the 628
Grrl Scouts 550, 757
Grumpy Old Monsters 628
Grunland 628
Grunts 628
Guardian Angel 550
Guardian Heroes 628

Guardian of Metropolis 94
Guardians 251
Guardians of Metropolis 94
Guardians of the Galaxy 251
Guerillas 550
Guerrilla Groundhog 757
Guff 513
Guillotin 629, 757
Guillotine 757
Gulliver's Travels 814
Gulliver's Travels 629
Gumby 629
Gumby in 3-D 629
Gumps, the 420
Gun Crisis 757
Gun Fu: the Lost City 629
Gun Fury 757
Gun Fury Returns 757
Gun Theory 252
Guncandy 550
Gundam: the Origin 757
Gundam Wing 757
Gundam Wing: Battlefield of
  Pacifists 757
Gundam Wing: Endless Waltz . 757
Gundam Wing: G-Unit. 757
Gundam Wing: the Last Outpost757
Gunfighter 403
Gunfighters in Hell: Original Sin 757
Gunfire. 94
Gunhawk 212
Gunhawks 252
Gunner 757
Gunrunner 252
Guns Against Gangsters 420
Guns of Shar-Pei. 757
Guns of the Dragon. 94
Gunslinger 331
Gunslingers 252
Gunsmith Cats 513
Gunsmith Cats: Bad Trip. 513
Gunsmith Cats: Bean Bandit. . . 513
Gunsmith Cats: Goldie
  Vs. Misty 513
Gunsmith Cats: Kidnapped . . . 513
Gunsmith Cats: Mister V 513
Gunsmith Cats: Shades of Gray 513
Gunsmith Cats: the Return
  of Gray. 513
Gunsmoke. 420, 629
Gunsmoke Trail. 420
Gunsmoke Western. 195
Gunwitch The: Outskirts
  of Doom 757
Gutsville. 550
Gutwallow 757
Gutwrencher 550
Guy Gardner 94
Guy Gardner: Collateral Damage 94
Guy Gardner: Reborn 94
Guy Ritchie's Gamekeeper . . . 629
Gypsy 757
Gyre. 757

H H H H

H.A.R.D. Corps 630
H.P. Lovecraft's the Call of
  Cthulhu and Others 760
H.P. Lovecraft's the Dream-
  Quest of Unknown Kadath 760
H.P. Lovecraft's the Return
  of Cthulhu 760
H.P. Lovecraft's Cthulhu . . . 633
H.R. Pufnstuf. 633
H-E-R-O 98
Ha Ha Comics 420
Hack/Slash 629
Hacker Files 94
Hades 757
Hall of Fame 629
Hall of Heroes 757
Hall of Heroes Presents 757
Halloween 629
Halloween Horror 629
Halloween II: the Blackest Eye . 629
Halloween III: the Devil's Eyes . 629
Hallowieners 757
Halo: an Angel's Story. 629
Halo Brothers 757
Halo: Uprising 252
Hamlet. 821
Hammer Girl 757
Hammer Kid 629

Hammer Locke 94
Hammer of God. 629
Hammer of God: Butch. 513
Hammer of God: Pentathlon . . . 513
Hammer of the Gods: Hammer
  Hits China 550
Hammer: Uncle Alex, the 513
Hamster Vice. 629, 757
Hand of Fate 421, 629
Hands of the Dragon. 629
Hanged Man 757
Hangman Comics 435
Hanna-Barbera All-Stars 629
Hap Hazard Comics 421
Happy Birthday Martha
  Washington 513
Happy Comics. 421
Happy Houlihans 462
Happy Rabbit 421
Harbinger. 629
Harbinger Files: Harada 630
Hard Boiled 513
Hard Boiled Comics 757
Hard Looks 513
Hard Rock Comics 757
Hard Time 94
Hard Time Season Two. 94
Hardcase. 630
Hardcore Station 94
Hardware. 95
Hardy Boys 630
Hardy Boys the 630
Hari Kari 630, 758
Hari Kari Manga 758
Harlan Ellison's Dream Corridor 513
Harlem Globetrotters 630
Harley Quinn 95
Harold Head, the Collected
  Adventures of 828
Harpy: Prize of the Overlord . . 758
Harriers 630
Harrowers 252
Harry Chess That Man from
  A. U. N. T. I. E. 828
Harsh Realm 630
Harte of Darkness 758
Harvest King 758
Harvey. 252
Harvey Comic Hits 421
Harvey Comics Library 421
Harvey Hits 630
Harvey Presents: Casper 252
(Harvey 3-D Hits) Sad Sack . . . 479
Harvy Flip Book. 758
Hate. 631, 758
Haunt of Fear 421, 631
Haunt of Horror: Lovecraft. . . . 252
Haunt of Horrors: Edgar Allan
  Poe 252
Haunted 631
Haunted Love 631
Haunted Man the. 513
Haunted the. 631
Haunted The: Gray Matters. . . . 631
Haunted Thrills 421
Have Gun Will Travel 631
Haven: the Broken City 95
Havoc Inc. 758
Havok & Wolverine 252
Hawallan Dick 550
Hawaiian Dick: the Last Resort 550
Hawk & Dove 95
Hawk, the 421
Hawkeye 252
Hawkeye: Earth's Mightiest
  Marksman 252
Hawkgirl. 96
Hawkman 95, 96
Hawkmoon 631
Hawkshaws 550
Hawkworld. 96
Hazard. 550
He Is Just a Rat 758
He-Man 422
Head the 758
Headhunters 550
Headline Comics. 421
Headlocked: the Tryout 631
Headmasters. 252
Hear the Sound of My Feet
  Walking. 828

Heart of Empire: the Legacy
  of Luther Arkwright. 513
Heartbreakers 513, 550
Heathcliff 252
Heathcliff's Funhouse 252
Heaven Sent 758
Heaven's Devils. 550
Heavy Hitters. 252
Heavy Liquid 96
Heavy Metal Monsters . . . 631, 758
Heckle and Jeckle. 422
Heckler the 96
Hector Heathcote 631
Hector Plasm: Totentanz 550
Hedg 631
Hedge Knight II: Sworn Sword . 252
Hedge Knight the 551, 631
Hedy Devine Comics. 252
Hedy Wolfe 252
Heirs of Eternity. 551
Helden 631
Helios 631
Helios: in with the New 631
Helios: under the Gun 631
Hell 513
Hell Michigan. 631
Hell's Angel 253
Hellblazer 96
Hellblazer Special: 98
Hellblazer/the Books of Magic. . 98
Hellboy 513
Hellboy: Almost Colossus 513
Hellboy: Box Full of Evil 514
Hellboy: Conqueror Worm. . . . 514
Hellboy: Darkness Calls 514
Hellboy Jr. 514
Hellboy: Makoma 514
Hellboy: Seeds of Destruction. . 514
Hellboy: the Crooked Man. . . . 514
Hellboy: the Island. 514
Hellboy: the Third Wish. 514
Hellboy: Wake the Devil 514
Hellboy: Weird Tales 514
Hellcat 252
Hellcop 551
Hellgate: London 514
Hellgirl 758
Hellhole 551
Hellhound 253
Hellhounds 514, 551
Hellina 758
Hellina/Double Impact. 631
Hellina: Heart of Thorns . . 631, 758
Hellina: Hell's Angel 758
Hellina: Hellborn 631
Hellina: Kiss of Death 758
Hellina/Nira X: Angel of Death . 631
Hellina/Nira X: Cyberangel . . . 631
Hellina: Seduction 758
Hellina vs Pandora 758
Hello Pal Comics. 422
Hellraiser III Hell on Earth . . . 253
Hellshock. 551
Hellspawn 551
Hellstorm Prince of Lies 253
Hellstorm: Son of Satan 253
Helm the 514
Helmet of Fate the 98
Helsing 758
Helter Skelter 759
Henry. 422
Henry Aldrich Comics 422
Hepcats 759
Herbie 514, 632
Hercules 253, 632, 759
Hercules and the Heart
  of Chaos 253
Hercules Prince of Power 253
Hercules Project 759
Hercules: the Legendary
  Journeys 632
Hercules Unbound 98
Here Comes the Big People . . . 632
Here's Howie Comics 98
Heresy. 632
Heretic the 514
Hermes Vs. The Eyeball Kid . . . 514
Hero. 253
Hero Alliance 632
Hero at Large 632
Hero by Night 551, 632
Hero Camp 551

Hero for Hire 253
Hero Hotline 98
Hero Sandwich 759
Hero Squared 632
Hero Zero 514
Herobear and the Kid 759
Herobear and the Kid:
  Saving Time. 759
Heroes. 98, 759
Heroes Against Hunger. 98
Heroes Anonymous. 759
Heroes for Hire 253
Heroes for Hope 253
Heroes from Wordsmith 759
Heroes Incorporated 759
Heroes of the Wild Frontier. . . . 375
Heroes Reborn: the Return. . . . 253
Heroic Comics. 422
Heroic Tales. 759
Heroines Inc. 759
Hex 98
Hey Mister 759
Hi Hi Puffy Amiyumi. 98
Hi-Ho Comics 423, 460, 632
Hickee 759
Hickory 423
Hiding in Time 551
Hieroglyph 514
High Caliber 759
High Chapparal 632
High Roads 632
High Rollers. 632
High School Agent. 759
High School Confidential Diary . 632
High Shining Brass 759
High Society 759
High Voltage 632
Highlander: the Way of the
  Sword. 632
Highlander: There Can Be
  Only One 632
Highway 13 759
Highwaymen the 632
Hillbilly Comics 423
Hilly Rose's Space Adventures . 759
His Name Is Rog... Rog 2000 . . 632
History of DC Universe 98
History of Underground Comix . 828
Hit Comics. 423
Hit the Beach. 759
Hitchhiker's Guide to the Galaxy. 98
Hitman. 98
Hitomi and Her Girl
  Commandos 759
Hoax 759
Hobbit the 632
Hogan's Heroes. 633
Hokum & Hex 253
Holiday Comics 253, 423
Holliday 759
Hollywood Comics. 423
Hollywood Confessions. 423
Hollywood Diary 423
Hollywood Film Stories 423
Hollywood Funny Folkes. 85
Hollywood Noir 633
Hollywood Secrets. 423
Hollywood Superstars 254
Hollywood's Golden Era 1930s. 760
Holo Brothers the 760
Holy Knight 760
Holy Terror the. 551
Holyoke One-Shot. 424
Homage Studios 551
Homegrown Funnies 828
Homer Hooper. 254
Homer the Happy Ghost 254
Homicide 514
Honey West. 633
Honeymoon 247
Honeymooners 633
Hong Kong 633
Hong on the Range. 551
Honk 760
Honkytonk Sue, the Queen
  of Country Swing 828
Honor among Thieves. 760
Honor Brigade 760
Honor of the Damned 760
Hood the 254
Hooded Horseman 379, 451
Hook 254

Hoon	760	Huntress the	103	Incredible Science Fiction	425	Invisible People	761
Hoon the	760	Hurricane Comics	425	Incredibles the	514	Invisible Scarlet O'Neil	426
Hooray Comics	424	Hurricane Girls	760	Incursion	634	Invisibles	104
Hoot Gibson Western	424	Hurricane, the	822	Independence Day	259	Io	635
Hopalong Cassidy	99, 424	Huzzah	760	India Authentic	634	Ion	104
Hope Falls	633	Hy-Breed	760	Indian Braves	375	Iron and the Maiden	635
Hopeless Savages	760	Hybrid	633	Indian Chief	425	Iron Fist	261
Hopeless Savages: Ground		Hybrid Bastards	633	Indian Fighter	425	Iron Fist/Wolverine	261
Zero	760	Hybrids	633	Indian Warriors	451	Iron Ghost	552
Hoppy the Marvel Bunny	424	Hybrids: Origin	634	Indiana Jones and the		Iron Horse	635
Horobi	760	Hyde-25	634	Arms of Gold	514	Iron Lantern	192
Horrific	424	Hyper Dolls	760	Indiana Jones and the		Iron Man	261, 263
Horror from the Tomb	448	Hyper Mystery Comics	425	Fate of Atlantis	514	Iron Man & Submariner	264
Horror in the Dark	760	Hyper-Actives the	634	Indiana Jones and the		Iron Man and Power Pack	264
Horror of Collier County, the	514	Hyperkind	256	Golden Fleece	514	Iron Man: Bad Blood	264
Horror Show	760	Hyperkind Unleashed	256	Indiana Jones and the		Iron Man/Captain America:
Horrorist	99	Hyperkinetic	551	Iron Phoenix	514	Casualties of War	264
Horrors the	254	Hypersonic	514	Indiana Jones and the		Iron Man: Director of
Horrorwood	633	Hysteria: One Man Gang	551	Kingdom of the		S.H.I.E.L.D.	264
Horse Feather Comics	424			Crystal Skull	514	Iron Man: Enter the Mandarin	264
Horsemen	633	**I I I I**		Indiana Jones and the		Iron Man: House of M	264
Hot Rod and Speedway Comics	424	I *Heart* Marvel	257	Last Crusade	260	Iron Man: Hypervelocity	264
Hot Rod Comics	424	I Am Legend	760	Indiana Jones and the		Iron Man: Inevitable	264
Hot Rod King	424	I Dream of Jeannie	634, 760	Sargasso Pirates	515	Iron Man: Legacy of Doom	264
Hot Rod Racers	633	I Hate Galaxy Girl	551	Indiana Jones and the		Iron Man: the Iron Age	264
Hot Rods and Racing Cars	424	I Hunt Monsters	760	Shrine of the Sea Devil	515	Iron Man: Viva Las Vegas	264
Hot Shots	254	I Kill Giants	551	Indiana Jones and the		Iron Marshal	635
Hot Stuff Sizzlers	633	I Love Lucy Comics	425	Spear of Destiny	515	Iron Vic	426
Hot Stuff the Little Devil	633	I Loved	499	Indiana Jones and the		Iron Wings	552
Hot Wheels	99	I Spy	634	Temple of Doom	260	Ironhand of Almuric	515
Hotspur	633	I Was Kidnapped by Lesbian		Indiana Jones and the		Ironjaw	635
Hourman	99	Pirates from Outer Space	635	Tomb of the Gods	515	Is this Tomorrow?	426
House at the Edge of Nowhere	633	I.F.S. Zone	760	Indiana Jones: Thunder		Isaac Asimov's I-Bots	635
House II	254	I'm Dickens He's Fenster	634	in the Orient	515	Isis	104
House of Frightenstein	760	I-Bots	634	Indians	425	Island	761
House of Horror	760	Ibis, the Invincible	425	Indians on the Warpath	425	Island of Dr. Moreau	264
House of M	254	Icandy	103	Industriacide	761	Ismet	761
House of M: Avengers	254	Icarus	760	Industrial Gothic	103	It Ain't Me Babe	828
House of Mystery	99	Iceman	256	Industry of War	552	It Really Happened	426
House of Secrets	101	Icicle	634	Infantry	634	It's a Duck's Life	264
House of Seven Gables, the	818	Icon	103	Inferior Five	103	It's about Time	635
How I Found Livingstone	821	Icon Devil	760	Inferno	103, 761	It's Fun to Stay Alive	426
How Stalin Hopes We Will		Idaho	634	Inferno: Hellbound	552	It's Gametime	104
Destroy America	425	Ideal	256	Infinite Crisis	103	It's Science with Dr. Radium	761
How to Shoot	425	Ideal Comics	256	Infinite Horizon	552	Itchy & Scratchy	635
Howard Chaykin's American		Identity Crisis	103	Infiniteens	634	Ivanhoe	635, 812
Flagg!	633	Identity Disk	257	Infinity Abyss	260	
Howard the Duck	254	Idol	257	Infinity Crusade	260	**J J J J**
Howdy Doody	424	If the Devil Would Talk	425	Infinity Gauntlet	260	J. N. Williamson's Masques	637
Howl	760	Igor	634	Infinity Inc	103	J. O'Barr's the Crow	762
Hsu and Chan	760	Ike Lives	828	Infinity War	260	J.U.D.G.E.	553
Huck & Yogi Jamboree	633	Iliad	761	Informer, the	425	J-2	265
Huckleberry Finn	814	Iliad II	761	Inhumanoids	260	Jace Pearson of the Texas
Huckleberry Hound	633	Illiad, the	819	Inhumans	260	Rangers	426
Huey Dewey & Louie Junior		Illuminator	760	Inmates: Prisoners of Society	634	Jack Armstrong	426
Woodchucks	633	Illuminatus	761	Inner Circle	634	Jack Cross	104
Hugga Bunch	254	Illustrated Stories of the Operas	425	Innocents	634	Jack Hunter	635, 761
Hugo	760	Image Comics	551	Innocents the	552	Jack in the Box	497
Hulk	255	Image Introduces:	551	Innovators	634	Jack Kirby's Fourth World	104
Hulk & Thing: Hard Knocks	255	Image Monster Pile up	551	Insane	515	Jack Kirby's Galactic Bounty
Hulk 2099	255	Image Two-In-One	551	Insane Clown Posse	634	Hunters	264
Hulk and Power Pack	255	Image Zero	552	Insane Jane	634	[Jack Kirby's] Teenagents	699
Hulk Chronicles: WWH	255	Images of Shadowhawk	552	Insect Fear	828	Jack of Fables	104
Hulk: Destruction	255	Imaginaries the	552	Inside Crime	426	Jack of Hearts	264
Hulk: Gray	255	Immortal Iron Fist	257	Inspector the	634	Jack of Nines	761
Hulk: Nightmerica	255	Immortal Two	552	Instant Piano	515	Jack Staff	552, 761
Hulk Smash	255	Immortalis	257	Interface	260	Jack the Giant Killer	426
Hulk the	254	Imp	634	International Comics	391	Jack the Lantern	761
Hulk: the Movie	255	Impact	425, 634	International Crime Patrol	392	Jack the Lantern: Ghosts	761
Hulk/Wolverine: 6 Hours	255	Impaler	552	Interview with a Vampire	634	Jack the Ripper	761
Human Defense Corps	102	Imperial Guard	257	Interzone	761	Jackaroo the	761
Human Fly	255	Impossible Man Summer		Intimate	635	Jackie Chan Adventures	635
Human Gargoyles	760	Vacation	257	Intimate Confessions	426	Jackie Chan's Spartan X	552, 635
Human Kind	551	Impossible Tales	634	Intimates the	635	Jackie Gleason	426
Human Race the	102	Impulse	103	Intimidators the	552	Jackie Gleason and the
Human Target	102	In Freedom's Cause	824	Into the Storm	761	Honeymooners	104
Human Target Special	102	In Her Darkest Hour	552	Intrigue	426, 552	Jackie Robinson	426
Human Torch	256	In the Blood	635	Intruder	635	Jackpot Comics	426
Human Torch Comics	256	In the Reign of Terror	823	Inu Yasha	761	Jade	635
Humbug	425	Inanna's Tears	634	Invaders	260	Jade Fire	635
Humdinger	425	Incal	634	Invaders from Home	635	Jade: Redemption	635
Humphrey Comics	425	Incal the	257	Invaders from Mars	761	Jade Warriors	553
Hunchback of Notre Dame, the	814	Incomplete Death's Head	257	Invaders the	635	Jade Warriors: Slave of the
Hunger the	633	Incredible Hercules	255	Invasion '55	761	Dragon	635
Hunk	633	Incredible Hulk	254	Invasion!	104	Jademan Collection	635
Hunt and the Hunted the	760	Incredible Hulk	257	Invincible	552	Jademan Kung Fu Special	635
Hunted	425	Incredible Hulk: Future		Invincible Ed:	515	Jaguar	104
Hunter the	633	Imperfect	259	Invincible Four of Kung Fu		Jaguar God	635
Hunter: the Age of Magic	103	Incredible Hulk/Pitt	259	& Ninja	635	Jalila	636
Hunter's Heart	103	Incredible Hulk Vs. Wolverine	259	Invincible Iron Man	260	Jam the	761
Hunter's Moon	633	Incredible Science Fantasy	491	Invincible Presents Atom Eve	552	Jamboree	426
Hunter-Killer	551			Invisible Man, the	823	James Bond 007	636

James Bond 007: a Silent
  Armageddon 515
James Bond 007: Quasimodo
  Gambit 515
James Bond 007: Serpent's
  Tooth 515
James Bond 007: Shattered
  Helix 515
James Bond: Goldeneye. 636
James Bond Jr. 264
James O'Barr Original Sins. . . . 761
James O'Barr Tasty Bites 761
Jane Arden 426
Jane Eyre 816
Jane's World 761
Jann of the Jungle. 266
Japanese Monster. 828
Jason & the Argonauts:
  Kingdom of Hades 636
Jason and the Argonauts 761
Jason Goes to Hell 636
Jason Vs. Leatherface 636
Jason X 636
Java. 636
Javerts. 636
Jay & Silent Bob 761
Jazan Wild's Carnival of Souls . 636
Jazan Wild's Funhouse of
  Horrors. 636
Jazz. 761
Jazz Age Chronicles 762
Jazz: Solitaire 762
Jazz: Superstar 762
Jazz the Series 761
Jcp Features 762
Jeanie Comics. 229
Jeep Comics 426
Jeff Jordan, U. S. Agent 426
Jemm Son of Saturn 104
Jenna. 636
Jenna and Ninja High 762
Jenna Jameson's Shadow
  Hunter 636
Jenna Meets 100 Girls 636
Jenny Finn 762
Jenny Sparks: the Secret
  History of the Authority . . . 636
Jeremiah 762
Jeremiah: a Fistful of Sand . . . 762
Jeremiah: Birds of Prey 762
Jeremiah: Eyes like Burning
  Coals 762
Jeremiah Harm 636
Jeremiah: the Heirs. 762
Jerry Drummer 427
Jerry Igers Famous Features . . 762
Jesse James 427
Jest 427
Jesus Loves You 828
Jet 636
Jet Aces. 427
Jet Dream 636
Jet Fighters 427
Jetcat Clubhouse 762
Jetsons the 636
Jetta of the 21st Century. 427
Jezebel Jade 636
Jezebelle 636
Jfh: Justice for Hire 636
Jiggs and Maggie 427
Jigsaw 636
Jihad 264
Jim. 762
Jim Bowie 393
Jim Butcher's the Dresden
  Files: Storm Front 636
Jim Butcher's the Dresden
  Files: Welcome to the
  Jungle 636
Jim Dandy 427
Jim Hardy 427
[Jim Lee's] C-23 539
Jim Ray's Aviation Sketch Book 427
Jim Reaper 636
Jimbo. 636
Jimmy Wakely 105
Jindai. 636
Jing Pals 427
Jingle Belle 515, 553, 762
Jingle Jangle Comics 427
Jinn 553
Jinx 553

Jinx: Torso 553
Jiz 828
JLA 105
JLA: 106
JLA/Avengers 264
JLA-Z. 106
JLX 192
JLX Unleashed 192
Jo-Jo Comics 428
Joan of Arc 819
Joe & Max 636
Joe College 427
Joe Louis. 427
Joe Palooka 427
Joe Psycho & Moo Frog 762
Joe R. Lansdale's by Bizarre
  Hands 762
Joe R. Lansdale's the Drive-In . 762
Joe Sinn 762
Joe Yank 428
John Bolton Halls of Horror. . . 637
John Bolton's Strange Wink . . 515
[John Byrne's] Next Men 518
John Carter of Mars 637
John Carter Warlord of Mars. . . 264
John Constantine Hellblazer
  Special: Papa Midnite 106
John Doe. 637
John F. Kennedy Life Story . . . 637
John Hix Scrapbook 428
John Jakes Mullkon Empire . . 637
John Law. 637
John Romita Jr 30th Anniversary
  Special. 264
John Steele Secret Agent 637
John Wayne Adventure Comics 428
John Woo's Seven Brothers . . 637
Johnny Atomic. 762
Johnny Comet. 762
Johnny Danger 428
Johnny Dark 762
Johnny Delgado Is Dead. 553
Johnny Dynamite 399, 515
Johnny Hazard 428
Johnny Hiro 762
Johnny Jason Teen Reporter . 637
Johnny Law, Sky Ranger 428
Johnny Mack Brown 428
Johnny Nemo 637
Johnny Raygun 762
Johnny the Homicidal Maniac . 762
Johnny Thunder 106
Joker Comics 264
Joker/Mask 515
Joker the 106
Joker The: Last Laugh 106
Joker's Asylum the 106
Jolly Jingles 426
Jon Juan 428
Jon Sable 637
Jon Sable Freelance: Bloodtrail 637
Jonah Hex 107
Jonas: Tales of an Ironstar . . . 637
Jonni Thunder 107
Jonny Demon 515
Jonny Double 107
Jonny Quest 637
Josie 637
Joss Whedon's Fray 515
Journey 762
Journey into Fear 428
Journey into Mystery. 265
Journey Into Mystery. 334
Journey Into Unknown Worlds . 195
Journeyman. 553
Jova's Harvest. 637
Jr. Jackalope 762
JSA 107
JSA: All-Stars 108
JSA Classified 108
JSA: Strange Adventures #3. . . 108
JSA: the Liberty Files 108
JSA: the Unholy Three 108
Jubilee. 265
Judge Colt 637
Judge Dredd 108, 637
Judge Dredd: Legends of
  the Law 108
Judge Dredd Vs. Aliens:
  Incubus 515
Judge Parker. 428
Judgment Day. 638

Judo Girl 638
Judo Joe 428
Judomaster 638
Judy Canova 371
Juggernaut 265
Juggernaut: the Eighth Day . . 265
Jughead. 638
Jughead as Captain Hero 638
Jughead with Archie Digest. . . 638
Jughead's Fantasy 638
Jughead's Folly 638
Jughead's Jokes 638
Juke Box 429
Julie's Journey/Gravity 762
Julius Ceasar 819
Jumbo Comics 429
Jumper Jumpscars 638
Junction 17 638
Jungle Action. 265, 266
Jungle Adventures. 638
Jungle Book 638
Jungle Book, the 820
Jungle Comics . 430, 638, 762, 763
Jungle Fantasy 763
Jungle Girl. 638
Jungle Girls 763
Jungle Jim. 431, 638
Jungle Jo. 431
Jungle Lil 431
Jungle Tales 266
Jungle Tales of Tarzan 639
Jungle Thrills 477
Jungle Twins the 639
Jungle War Stories 639
Junie Prom 432
Junior. 763
Junior Carrot Patrol 515
Junior Comics 432
Junior Funnies. 401
Junior Hopp Comics 432
Junior Miss 432
Junior Woodchucks 639
Junkbotz Rotogin 553
Junkwaffel 828
Jupiter. 763
Jurassic Jane 763
Jurassic Park. 639
Just a Pilgrim. 639
Just Married 639
Justice 108, 266, 763
Justice City Chronicles 639
Justice Comics 266
Justice: Four Balance 266
Justice Inc. 108
Justice League: a Midsummer's
  Nightmare 110
Justice League Adventures. . . . 108
Justice League America 109
Justice League Elite 108
Justice League Europe 109
Justice League International . . . 109
Justice League International . . . 110
Justice League of America . . . 110
Justice League Task Force 112
Justice League Unlimited 112
Justice League [International] . . 109
Justice League [International]
  Quarterly 110
Justice Leagues 112
Justice Machine 639
Justice Machine: Chimera
  Conspiracy. 639
Justice Riders 112
Justice Society of America 112
Justice Traps the Guilty. 432
Justy 763

K K K K

Ka'a'nga Comics 432
Ka-Zar 266
Kaboom. 639
Kabuki 266, 553, 639
Kabuki Agents 553
Kabuki: Circle of Blood 763
Kabuki Classics. 553
Kabuki: Dance of Death 763
Kabuki: Masks of the Noh 763
Kabuki: Skin Deep. 639
Kabuki: the Alchemy 553
Kade 639
Kade: Shiva's Sun 639
Kade: Sun of Perdition 639
Kafka. 763

Kamandi: at Earth's End 113
Kamandi the Last Boy on Earth 112
Kamikaze. 639
Kamikaze: 1946 639
Kamui 763
Kane 763
Kanned Korn Komix 828
Kansas Thunder 763
Kaos Moon 763
Kaptain Amerika Komix 828
Kaptain Keen and Kompany . . 763
Karas 515
Karate Kid 113
Karma Incorporated 639
Karney 639
Karza. 553
Kasco Comics 432
Katharsis 763
Kathy 266
Katmandu 763
Kato II 640
Kato of the Green Hornet 640
Katy Keene 432
Katy Keene Fashion Book
  Magazine 640
Katy Keene Pinup Parade. . . . 640
Katzenjammer Kids 432
Kayo 462
Kee-Fu Fighters 640
Keen Detective Funnies 432
Keen Komics 432
Keen Teens 432
Keep the 640
Keif Llama 763
Keif Llama: Gas War 763
Keif Llama: Xenotech 763
Kelley Belle Police Detective. . . 763
Kelley Jones' the Hammer 515
Kelley Jones' the Hammer:
  the Outsider 515
Kelley Jones' the Hammer:
  Uncle Alex 515
Kelly Green 640
Kellys, The. 268
Ken Lashley's Legends 640
Ken Maynard Western 433
Ken Shannon 433
Ken Stuart 433
Kent Blake of the Secret
  Service. 267
Kents the 113
Kerry Drake Detective Cases . . 433
Kewpies. 433
Key Comics 433
Key Ring Comics. 433
Kick Drum Comix 553
Kick-Ass 267
Kickass Girl: Skeletons in
  the Closet 763
Kickers Inc. 267
Kid & Play 267
Kid Cannibal 763
Kid Colt Outlaw 267
Kid Cowboy 433
Kid Death & Fluffy 640
Kid Eternity 113, 433
Kid from Dodge City 267
Kid from Texas 267
Kid Komics 267
Kid Montana 640
Kid Movie Comics 268
Kid Slade Gunfighter 286
Kid Supreme 553
Kid Terrific 553
Kid Zoo Comics. 433
Kiddie Karnival 433
Kidnapped 817
Kiku San 764
Kill All Parents 553
Kill Your Boyfriend 113
Killbox 764
Killer 7 640
Killer Instinct 640
Killer Instinct Tour Book. 553
Killer Stunts Inc. 640
Killer Tales 640
Killer the 640
Killers, the 433
Killers the 640
Killers The: War's End. 640
Killfrenzy 268
Killing Girl 553

Killing Pickman 640
Killing Stroke 764
Killpower: the Early Years 268
Killraven 268
Killrazor Special 553
Killzone 640
Kilroy 764
Kilroy Is Here 764
Kilroys, the 433
Kim 823
Kimber Prince of Feylons 764
Kin 553
Kindergoth 764
Kindred 553
Kindred II 640
Kinetic 113
King Arthur & the Knights
   of Justice 268
King Bee 828
King Comics 434
King Conan 223
King Kong 764
King Leonardo and His Short
   Subjects 640
King Louie & Mowgli 640
King of Diamonds 640
King of Fighters: Maximum
   Impact 640
King of Fighters The: Nests
   Saga 640
King of the Khyber Rifles 821
King of the Mountains, the 822
King of the Royal Mounted 434
King Solomon's Mines 820
King Tiger/Motorhead 515
King Zombie 764
Kingdom Come 113
Kingdom of the Wicked 764
Kingdom the 113
Kingpin 268
Kings in Disguise 764
Kings of the Night 515
'Kini 553
Kirby King of the Serials 764
Kiss 515
Kiss 4k 554
Kiss Kiss Bang Bang 640
Kiss: the Psycho Circus 553
Kissing Chaos 764
Kissing Chaos: Nonstop Beauty 764
Kissnation 268
Kit Carson 434
Kit Karter 640
Kitty Pryde & Wolverine 268
Kitty Pryde: Agent of
   S.H.I.E.L.D. 268
Kitz 'N' Katz 764
Klor 764
Klown Shock 764
Knewts of the Round Table 764
Knight Masters 764
Knight Watchman 554, 764
Knighthawk 640
Knightmare 554, 764
Knights of Pendragon 268
Knights of the Dinner Table . . . 764
Knights of the Dinner Table:
   Everknights 764
Knights of the Dinner Table/
   Faans 764
Knights of the Dinner Table:
   Hackmasters 764
Knights of the Dinner Table
   Illustrated 764
Knights of the Dinner Table
   Mini-Series 764
Knights of the Jaguar 554
Knights of the Round Table 640, 821
Knightstrike 554
Knuckles 640
Ko Komics 434
Kobalt 113
Kobra 113
Kodocha: Sana's Stage 764
Kolchak Tales: Night Stalker
   of the Living Dead 641
Kolchak: Tales of the Night
   Stalker 641
Kolchak Tales: the
   Frankenstein Agenda 641
Komic Kartoons 268
Komik Pages 462

Komodo & the Defiants 765
Kona 641
Kong 515
Kong: King of Skull Island 641
Kong the Untamed 113
Konga 641
Konga's Revenge 641
Koni Waves 765
Kookie 641
Korak Son of Tarzan 113, 641
Kore 554
Korg: 70 000 B.C. 641
Korvus 765
Krazy Kat 641
Krazy Kat Comics 434
Krazy Komics 268, 269
Krazy Krow 269
Krazy Life 453
Kree-Skrull War 269
Krofft Supershow 641
Krull 269
Krusty Comics 641
Krypto the Superdog 113
Krypton Chronicles 113
Kull 515
Kull and the Barbarians 269
Kull in 3-D 641
Kull the Conqueror 269
Kung Fu Warriors 765
Kunoichi 765
Kurt Busiek's Astro City 554
Kurtzman Comix 828
Kyra 765

L L L L

L.A.W. 113
L.E.G.I.O.N. '89-94 114
L.I.F.E. Brigade 766
L'il Hellions: Day at the Zoo . . . 645
L33t: Comics for Gamers 765
La Cosa Nostroid 765
Lab Rats 113
Labman 554
Labor Force 765
Labor Is a Partner 434
Labrynth 269
Lacunae 765
Lad: a Dog 641
Ladies of London Night 765
Lady Arcane 641, 765
Lady Death 641, 643
Lady Death: Death Goddess . . . 765
Lady Death II: Between
   Heaven & Hell 643
Lady Death: Infernal Sins 765
Lady Death: Queen of the Dead 765
Lady Demon 643
Lady Luck 466
Lady of the Lake, the 819
Lady Pendragon 554, 643
Lady Pendragon: Dragon Blade 554
Lady Pendragon: More than
   Mortal 554
Lady Rawhide 643
Lady Supreme 554
Lady Vampre 643, 765
Lady Vampre Returns 765
Laff-A-Lympics 269
Laffin Gas 765
Laffy-Daffy Comics 434
Lai Wan Dream Walker 643
Lana 269
Lance Barnes: Post Nuke Dick 269
Lance O'Casey 434
Lance Stanton Wayward
   Warrior 765
Lancelot Link Secret Chimp . . . 643
Lancelot Strong the Shield 643
Lancer 643
Land of Nod 516
Land of Oz 765
Land of the Dead 643
Land of the Giants 643
Land of the Lost 434
Land the 765
Lander 765
Landsale & Truman's Dead
   Folks 643
Laramie 643
Laredo 643
Large Feature Comics 434
Larry Doby, Baseball Hero 435

Lars of Mars 435, 643
Laser Eraser & Pressbutton . . . 643
Lash Larue Western 435, 644
Lassie 435
Last American 269
Last Avengers Story, the 269
Last Bastion the 644
Last Christmas the 554
Last Days of Pompell 816
Last Days of the Justice Society 113
Last Defenders the 269
Last Ditch 765
Last Fantastic Four Story the . . 269
Last Generation 765
Last Hero Standing 269
Last Minute 765
Last of the Mohicans, the 812
Last of the Viking Heroes 644
Last Planet Standing 269
Last Reign: Kings of War 644
Last Shot 554
Last Shot: First Draw 554
Last Sin of Mark Grim the 765
Last Starfighter the 269
Last Straw Man the 554
Last Train to Deadsville 516
Latest Comics 435
Latex Alice 765
Laugh 644
Laugh Comics 435
Laugh Comix 483
Laugh in the Dark 828
Laurel & Hardy 644
Laurel and Hardy 435, 644
Laurell K. Hamilton's Anita
   Blake Vampire Hunter 644
Law and Order 644
Law of Dredd 436
Law-Crime 436
Lawbreakers 435
Lawbreakers Always Lose 269
Lawbreakers Suspense Stories 436
Lawdog 269
Lawman 644
Lazarus 555
Lazarus Chronicles 765
Lazarus Five 114
Lazarus: Immortal Coils 644
Lazarus: the Many
   Reincarnations 644
Le Femme Vamprique 766
Leading Comics 114
Leading Man 644
League of Champions 644, 765
League of Extra- Ordinary
   Gentlemen 644
League of Justice 114
Leave it to Binky 114
Leave it to Chance 555
Left on Mission 644
Legacy 555, 644
Legacy of Kain: Defiance 555
Legend 644
Legend of Custer the 644
Legend of Isis 555, 644
Legend of Isis the 644
Legend of Lemnear 766
Legend of Mother Sarah, the . . 516
Legend of Mother Sarah:
   City of the Children, the . . 516
Legend of Supreme 555
Legend of the Eight Dragon
   Gods 766
Legend of the Elfford 644
Legend of the Hawkman 114
Legend of the Sage 644
Legend of the Shield 114
Legend of Wonder Woman 114
Legendlore 766
Legendlore: Realm Wars 766
Legendlore: Wrath of
   the Dragon 766
Legends 114
Legends from Darkwood 766
Legends of Camelot 766
Legends of Daniel Boone the . . 114
Legends of Jesse James the . . 644
Legends of Luxura 645, 766
Legends of Nascar 645
Legends of the Dark Claw 192
Legends of the DC Universe . . . 114

Legends of the Legion 114
Legends of the Stargrazers 645
Legends of the World Finest . . . 114
Legion Anthology 766
Legion Lost 115
Legion of Monsters 269
Legion of Night 269
Legion of Substitute Heroes . . . 115
Legion of Super-Heroes . . . 115-117
Legion of Super-Heroes 117
Legion of the Supernatural 645
Legion: Science Police 117
Legion the 115
Legion Worlds 117
Legion X-I 766
Legionnaires 115
Legionnaires Three 115
Lenny of Lavedo 828
Lenore 766
Lensman 766
Lensman: Galactic Patrol 766
Lensman: War of the Galaxies . 766
Leonard Nimoy's Primortals . . . 645
Leonardo 645, 766
Leopard 645
Les Miserables 813
Lethal 555
Lethal Foes of Spider-Man 269
Lethal Instinct 645
Lethal Ladies of Brainstorm . . . 766
Lethal Strike Archives 766
Lethal Strike/Double Impact:
   Lethal Impact 645
Lethal Strike: Shadow Viper . . . 766
Lethal Stryke 645
Lethargic Lad Adventures 766
Level X 766
Level X: the next Reality 766
Lex Luthor: Man of Steel 117
Lex Talionis: a Jungle Tale 555
Lexian Chronicles The: Full
   Circle 645
Li'l Abner 436
Li'l Genius 437
Li'l Ghost 437
Li'l Jinx 437
Li'l Kids 270
Li'l Menace 437
Li'l Pals 270
Li'l Pan 438
Libby Ellis 766
Liberality for All 645
Liberator 766
Liberty Comics 436, 555, 645
Liberty from Hell 766
Liberty Girl 645
Liberty Guards 436
Liberty Meadows 555, 766
Liberty Project the 645
Liberty Scouts 436
Lidsville 645
Lieutenant the 645
Life of a Fetus 766
Life of Captain Marvel 270
Life of Christ 270
Life of Pope John-Paul II 270
Life Story 436
Life the Universe and
   Everything 117
Life with Archie 645
Life with Snarky Parker 436
Life With Millie 229
Lifequest 766
Light and Darkness War 270
Light Brigade the 117
Light Fantastic the 645
Lightning Comics 436
Lightning Comics Presents 645
Lilith: Demon Princess 645
Lilo & Stitch 645
Limbo City 645
Limited Collectors Edition 117
Lincoln-16 645
Linda 436, 453
Linda Carter Student Nurse . . . 270
Linda Lark 645
Linus the Lionhearted 646
Lion King 270
Lion of the North, the 823
Lionheart 646
Lions Tigers & Bears 555

Lippy the Lion and Hardy
  Har Har 646
Lisa Comics 646
Little Al of the F. B. I. 437
Little Al of the Secret Service . . 437
Little Ambrose 646
Little Angel 437
Little Annie Rooney 437
Little Archie 646
Little Archie Mystery 646
Little Aspirin 270
Little Audrey 437
Little Audrey & Melvin 646
Little Audrey Tv Funtime 646
Little Beaver 437
Little Bit 437
Little Dot 437
Little Dot Dotland. 646
Little Dot's Uncles & Aunts . . . 646
Little Eva 437
Little Giant Comics 437
Little Giant Detective Funnies . . 437
Little Giant Movie Funnies . . . 437
Little Gloomy 767
Little Gloomy's Super Scary
  Monster Show 767
Little Groucho 437
Little Ike 437
Little Iodine 437
Little Jack Frost 437
Little Joe 437
Little Lana 269
Little Lenny 270
Little Lizzie 270
Little Lotta 646
Little Lotta Foodland 646
Little Lulu 516
Little Max Comics 437
Little Mermaid 646
Little Mermaid the 270
Little Miss Muffet 438
Little Miss Sunbeam Comics . . 438
Little Monsters 646
Little Monsters the 646
Little Orphan Annie 438
Little Red Hot: Bound 555
Little Red Hot: Chane of Fools . 555
Little Roquefort 438
Little Sad Sack 646
Little Savage, the 822
Little Scouts 438
Little Scrowlie 767
Little Star 767
Little Stooges the 646
Little White Mouse (The Series) 767
Little White Mouse: Entropy
  Dreaming 767
Little White Mouse:
  Open Space 767
Littlest Snowman 438
Lives of the Hunted 823
Livewires 270
Living Bible, the 438
Living Corpse the 646
Living in Infamy 646
Living with the Dead 516
Livingstone Mountain 767
Liz 270
Lloyd Llewellyn 646, 767
Loaded Bible 555
Lobo. 118, 646
Lobo the Duck 192
Lobocop 118
Lobster Johnson: the Iron
  Prometheus 516
Local 767
Locke 646
Locke & Key 647
Loco Vs. Pulverine 767
Lodoss War: Chronicles of
  the Heroic Knight 767
Lodoss War: Deelit's Tale . . . 767
Lodoss War: the Grey Witch . . 767
Lodoss War: the Lady of Pharis 767
Logan 270
Logan's Run 270, 767
Logan's World 767
Lois Lane 118
Loki 270
Lone 516
Lone Eagle 438
Lone Gunmen the 516

Lone Ranger 438
Lone Ranger and Tonto the . . . 647
Lone Ranger the 647
Lone Ranger's Companion
  Tonto, the 438
Lone Ranger's Famous
  Horse Hi-Yo Silver, the . . 438
Lone Rider 438
Lone Wolf & Cub 767
Lone Wolf 2100 516
Lonely Heart 438
Loner 767
Loners the 270
Long Bow 438
Long Count the 647
Long Hot Summer the 118
Long John Silver and
  the Pirates 477
Longshot 270
Lookers 767
Looking for Group 647
Looking Glass Wars: Hatter M . 555
Looney Tunes 119, 439, 647
Looney Tunes and Merrie
  Melodies 438, 647
Loose Cannons 270
Lord Jim 822
Lord of the Dead 767
Lord Pumpkin 647
Lords of Avalon: Knight of
  Darkness 270
Lords of Avalon: Sword of
  Darkness 270
Lords of Misrule 516
Lore 647
Lorelei 767
Lori Lovecraft 767
Lorna Doone 816
Lorna the Jungle Girl 270
Losers 119
Losers Special 119
Lost Books of Eve the 647
Lost Boys The: Reign of Frogs . 647
Lost Continent 767
Lost Heroes 647
Lost in Space 516, 647
Lost Ones the 555
Lost Planet 647
Lost Squad 767
Lost Stories 767
Lost the 767
Lost World the 767
Lost Worlds 439
Lothar 767
Louis Riel 767
Love Adventures 271
Love and Capes 647
Love and Rockets 767
Love Classics 271
Love Diary 647
Love Dramas 271
Love Fights 768
Love Hina 768
Love in Tights 768
Love Me Tenderloin 516
Love Romances 256
Love Secrets 271
Love Tales 271
Love the Way You Love 768
Love Trails 271
Lovebunny & Mr. Hell 555
Lovecraft 647
Loveland 271
Loveless 119
Lovely Prudence 768
Lovers 194
Low Orbit 555
Luba 768
Luba's Comics & Stories 768
Lucha Libre 555
Lucifer 119
Lucifer's Hammer 647
Lucky "7" Comics 439
Lucky Comics 439
Lucky Duck 439
Lucky Fights it Through 439
Lucky Star 439
Lucy Show the 647
Lucy, the Real Gone Gal 439
Ludwig von Drake 647
Luftwaffe 1946 . . . . 647, 768
Luger 647

Lullaby 647
Lullaby: Wisdom Seeker 555
Lum*urusei Yatsura 768
Lunar Donut 768
Lunatic Fringe 648
Lunatik 271
Lurid 768
Lurkers 648
Lust for Life 768
Lux and Alby Sign on and
  Save the Universe 516
Luxura 648, 768
Luxura/Baby Angel X. 768
Luxura Collection 648
Luxura/Widow: Blood Lust . . . 768
Lynch 555
Lynch Mob 648
Lyndon B. Johnson 648
Lynx: an Elfford Tale 768

M M M M

M 648
M.A.C.H. 1 768
M.D. 651
M.D. Geist 651
M.D. Geist: Ground Zero 651
M-Rex 557
Macbeth 822
Mace Griffin: Bounty Hunter . . 555
Machine, the 516
Machine Man 271
Machine Man 2020 271
Machine Teen 271
Machines, the 828
Mack Bolan the Executioner:
  the Devil's Tools. 648
Mackenzie Queen 768
Macross 648
Macross II 768
Macross II: the Micron
  Conspiracy 769
Mad 439
Mad about Millie 271
Mad Dog 271
Mad Dogs 769
Mad Follies 648
Mad Hatter, the 439
Mad House 648
Mad Raccoons 769
Mad Special 648
Madame Mirage 555
Madame Xanadu 119
Madballs 271
Made Men 271
Madhouse 439
Madman 516, 648
Madman Adventures 648
Madman Atomic Comics 555
Madman Picture Exhibition 648
Madman/the Jam 516
Madraven Halloween Special . . 648
Madrox 271
Maelstrom 769
Magdalena 555
Magdalena/Daredevil 555
Magdalena/Vampirella. 555
Magdelena Vs. Dracula. 555
Mage 648
Mage Knight: Stolen Destiny . . 648
Mage: the Hero Defined 556
Maggots 769
Maggotzine 828
Magic Comics 439
Magic Flute 648
Magic Priest 769
Magic: the Gathering 516
Magic the Gathering: 648
Magic Whistle 769
Magical Mates 769
Magical Pokemon Journey 769
Magik. 271
Magilla Gorilla 648, 649
Magique. 649
Magnetic Men Featuring
  Magneto 192
Magneto 271
Magneto & the Magnetic Men . . 192
Magneto: Dark Seduction 271
Magneto Rex 271
Magnus (Robot Fighter) 649
Magnus/Nexus 516
Magnus: Robot Fighter 649
Magus 769

Mai the Psychic Girl 769
Maid Attack 769
Maintenance 769
Maison Ikkoku 769
Majestic 119, 649
Major Bummer 119
Major Damage 649
Major Hoople Comics 440
Major Inapak the Space Ace . . 440
Major Victory Comics 440
Mammoth Comics 440
Man Against Time 556
Man Called A-X 649
Man Called Kev a 649
Man Comics 271
Man from Atlantis 272
Man from U.N.C.L.E. 649, 769
Man in Black 649
Man in the Iron Mask 818
Man O'Mars 440
Man of Rust 770
Man of Steel 120
Man of the Atom 650
Man of War 440, 650
Man, the 828
Man Who Laughs, the 819
Man with No Name the 650
Man with the Screaming Brain . 516
Man Without a Country, the . . . 818
Man-Bat. 119, 272, 769
Man-Bat Vs. Batman 119
Mandrake 272, 769
Mandrake Monthly. 769
Mandrake the Magician. 649
Manga Darkchylde 516
Manga ex 769
Manga Shi 2000 649
Manga Vizion. 769
Mangaphile 769
Magazine. 769
Manhunt! 440
Manhunter 119
Manic. 556
Manifest Eternity 649
Manik 649
Manimal. 770
Mankind. 649
Manslaughter. 770
Mantech Robot Warriors 650
Manticore. 828
Mantra 650
Mantus Files 770
Many Adventures of Miranda
  Mercury 650
Many Ghosts of Doctor
  Graves the 650
Many Loves of Dobie Gillis . . . 120
Many Worlds of Tesla
  Strong the 650
Marcane 770
March of Comics 440
Marco Polo 650
Marge's Little Lulu 441
Marge's Little Lulu 650
Marge's Tubby. 442
Margie Comics 221
Marine War Heroes 650
Marines at War 233
Marines Attack. 650
Marines in Action. 272
Marines in Battle 272
Mark Hazzard: Merc 272
Mark I 770
Mark Kidwell's Recluse 650
Mark Millar's the Unfunnies. . . 770
Mark of Charon 650
Mark Rand's Sky Technologies
  Inc. 650
Mark the 517
Mark Trail 442
Marksman the 650
Marmaduke Mouse 442
Marmalade Boy 770
Marquis the 770
Marquis The: a Sin of One . . . 770
Marquis The: Danse Macabre . 770
Married... with Children 770
Mars 650
Mars Attacks 650
Mars Attacks 556
Marshal 651
Marshall Law. 272, 517

Marshall Law: Secret Tribunal. . 517
Martha Washington Dies. 517
Martha Washington Goes
  to War 517
Martha Washington Saves
  the World 517
Martha Washington Stranded
  in Space. 517
Martian Manhunter 120
Martian Successor Nadesico . . 770
Martin Kane. 442
Martin Mystry. 517
Marvel 283
Marvel & DC Presents. 273
Marvel 1602 280
Marvel 1602: Fantastick Four . . 280
Marvel 1602: New World. 280
Marvel 1985 279
Marvel 65th Anniversary 280
Marvel Action Hour: Fantastic
  Four 272
Marvel Action Hour: Iron Man . . 272
Marvel Action Universe 272
Marvel Adventures 272
Marvel Adventures Fantastic
  Four 272
Marvel Adventures Hulk 272
Marvel Adventures Iron Man . . 272
Marvel Adventures Spider-Man . 273
Marvel Adventures Starring
  Daredevil 273
Marvel Adventures
  Super Heroes 273
Marvel Adventures
  the Avengers 273
Marvel Adventures the Thing . . 273
Marvel Adventures Two-In-One . 273
Marvel Age: Fantastic Four . . . 273
Marvel Age: Fantastic
  Four Tales 273
Marvel Age: Hulk. 273
Marvel Age Runaways 273
Marvel Age: Sentinel 273
Marvel Age: Spider-Man 273
Marvel Age Spider-Man Tales . . 273
Marvel Apes 273
Marvel Atlas. 273
Marvel Boy 203, 273
Marvel Chillers. 273
Marvel Christmas Special 273
Marvel Classics Comics 273
Marvel Collectors Item Classics 273
Marvel Comics. 273
Marvel Comics Presents . . 275, 276
Marvel Comics Super Special. . 276
Marvel Double Feature 276
Marvel Double-Shot. 276
Marvel Family, the. 442
Marvel Fanfare 276, 277
Marvel Feature 277
Marvel Frontier Comics Special 277
Marvel Graphic Novel 277
Marvel Halloween: the
  Supernaturals Tour Book . . 277
Marvel Heroes 277
Marvel: Heroes and
  Legends 1997 277
Marvel Holiday Special 277
Marvel Illustrated. 277
Marvel Kids 277
Marvel Knights 278
Marvel Knights 2009 278
Marvel Knights 4 278
Marvel Knights: Double-Shot . . 278
Marvel Knights Spider-Man. . . . 278
Marvel Knights Tour Book 278
Marvel Legacy. 278
Marvel Magic Handbook 278
Marvel Mangaverse. 278
Marvel Masterpieces Collection 278
Marvel Masterpieces II
  Collection. 278
Marvel Milestones 278
Marvel Mini-Books. 279
Marvel Monsters 279
Marvel Movie Premiere 279
Marvel Movie Showcase
  Featuring Star Wars 279
Marvel Movie Spotlight Featuring
  Raiders of the Lost Ark . . . 279
Marvel Mystery Comics. 274
Marvel Mystery Comics. 279

Marvel Nemesis: the Imperfects 279
Marvel No-Prize Book. 279
Marvel: Portraits of a Universe . 279
Marvel Poster Book. 279
Marvel Premiere 279
Marvel Presents 279
Marvel Preview 279, 280
Marvel Remix 280
Marvel Romance Redux 280
Marvel Saga 280
Marvel Select 280
Marvel Selects: Fantastic Four . 280
Marvel Selects: Spider-Man . . . 280
Marvel: Shadows & Light 280
Marvel Spectacular 280
Marvel Spotlight 280, 281
Marvel Spotlight: Civil War . . . 281
Marvel Spotlight on Captain
  America 281
Marvel Spotlight on Dr. Strange 281
Marvel Spotlight on
  Silver Surfer. 281
Marvel Super Action 281
Marvel Super Special 276
Marvel Super-Heroes 281
Marvel Superheroes 281
Marvel Superheroes Megazine . 281
Marvel Swimsuit 281
Marvel Tails 281
Marvel Tales 274
Marvel Tales 281, 282
Marvel Team-Up 282, 283
Marvel: the Lost Generation . . 278
Marvel Treasury of Oz. 283
Marvel Treasury Special 283
Marvel Triple Action. 283
Marvel Two-In-One 283, 284
Marvel/Ultraverse Battlezones . 651
Marvel Universe 284
Marvel Universe: Millennial
  Visions 284
Marvel Universe: Official
  Handbook to 284
Marvel Universe: the End 284
Marvel Valentine's Special . . . 284
Marvel Westerns 284
Marvel X-Men Collection. 284
Marvel Young Guns
  Sketch Book 284
Marvel Zombies. 284, 285
Marvel Zombies 2 285
Marvel Zombies 3 285
Marvel's Greatest Comics 273
Marvelous Adventures of
  Gus Beezer 285
Marvels 280
Marvels of Science 442
Marville 285
Marvin Mouse 285
Mary Jane 285
Mary Jane: Homecoming 285
Mary Marvel Comics 442
Masakazu Katsura's Shadow
  Lady. 517
Mask 120
Mask Comics. 443
Mask/Marshall Law 517
Mask of Zorro the 556
Mask Returns the 517
Mask the 517
Mask The: Virtual Surreality . . 517
Mask: Toys in the Attic 517
Masked Man 651
Masked Marvel 443
Masked Raider, the 443
Masked Ranger. 443
Masked Warrior X 770
Masks: Too Hot for Tv 651
Masquerade 770
Master Comics 443
Master Darque 651
Master of Ballantrae, the. 820
Master of Kung Fu: Bleeding
  Black 286
Master of Kung Fu Special
  Marvel Ed. 285
Master of the World. 824
Masters of Horror 651
Masters of Terror 286
Masters of the Universe
  . . . . 120, 286, 556, 651
Masterwork Series. 651

Mataak. 770
Matador 651
Matt Busch's Daria Jontak 651
Matt Champion 770
Matt Slade Gunfighter 286
Maverick 286, 651
Maverick Marshall 651
Mavericks 651
Mavis 770
Max Hamm Fairy Tale Detective 770
Max of the Regulators. 770
Maximage 556
Maximortal. 651
Maximum Force. 651
Maximum Overload 517
Maximum Security. 286
Maxion. 770
Maxwell Mouse Follies 770
Maxx the 556
Maya 651
Mayhem 517, 770
Maze Agency. 651, 770
Maze Agency the. 651
Mazie. 444
'Mazing Man 120
McHale's Navy 651
McKeever & the Colonel 651
MD. 444
Mean Bitch Thrills 828
Measles. 770
Meat Cake. 770
Mech Destroyer 556
Mecha 517
Mechanics 651
Mechanoids 770
Mecharider: the Regular Series 770
Medabots. 770
Medal of Honor 517
Medal of Honor Comics. 444
Media Starr 652
Medieval Lady Death 651
Medieval Spawn/Witchblade . . 556
Meet Corliss Archer. 444
Meet Merton 444
Meet Miss Bliss 286
Meet Miss Pepper 439
Meet the New Post Gazette
  Sunday Funnies. 444
Mega Dragon & Tiger 652
Mega Morphs 286
Megacity 909. 652
Megadragon & Tiger 556
Megahurtz 556
Megalith. 652
Megaman 652
Megas the 652
Megaton 652, 770
Megaton Explosion 652
Megaton Man 652
Megaton Man: Bombshell 556
Megaton Man: Hardcopy 556
Megaton Man Meets the
  Uncategorizable X-Thems . 770
Megaton Man Vs. Forbidden
  Frankenstein 770
Mek 652
Mekanix 286
Mel Allen Sports Comics 444
Melissa Moore: Bodyguard . . . 770
Meltdown. 556
Melting Pot 652
Melvin Monster 652
Melvin the Monster 286
Memories. 286
Memory Man 770
Men Against Crime 421
Men Against the Sea. 821
Men from Earth 652
Men in Action 286, 444
Men in Black 286, 771
Men in Black: Retribution 286
Men in Black: the Roborg
  Incident 771
Men of Courage 444
Men of Iron 820
Men of War 120
Men's Adventures 338
Men's Altered Wars Chronicles. 771
Menace 286, 652
Mendy and the Golem. 652
Mephisto Vs. Four Heroes . . . 286
Mercedes. 771

Merchants of Death. 652, 771
Mercy. 771
Mercy Sparx 652
Meridian. 652
Merlin. 771
Merlin Realm 652
Mermaid's Gaze 771
Merry Comics 444
Merry Mouse 444
Merry-Go-Round Comics 444
Messenger the 556
Meta 4 652
Meta Docs 652
Metabarons 652
Metacops. 771
Metal Gear Solid 652
Metal Gear Solid: Sons of
  Liberty 652
Metal Guardian Faust 771
Metal Hurlant 771
Metal Locus: Hard Drive 652
Metal Men 121
Metal Militia 652
Metallix 652
Metamorpho 121
Metamorpho Year One 121
Metamorphosis 652
Metaphysique 652, 771
Meteor Comics 444
Meteor Man 286
Metropol A.D. 286
Metropolis 771
Metropolis S.C.U. 121
Mezz Galactic Tour 2494. 517
Miami Mice 771
Mice Templar the. 556
Michael Chabon Presents the
  Amazing Adventures of
  the Escapist. 517
Michael Lent's Prey: Origin
  of the Species 653
Michael Moorcock's Multiverse . 121
Michael Strogoff 816
Michael Turner's Fathom. 653
Michaelangelo 652
Michelangelo 771
Mickey & Donald 653
Mickey Finn 444
Mickey Mantle Comics 653
Mickey Mouse. 445, 653
Mickey Mouse and Friends . . . 653
Mickey Mouse Magazine. . 444, 445
Mickey Mouse Meets Blotman . 653
Mickey Rat 828
Mickey Spillane's Mike Danger . 653
Mickey's Twice upon
  a Christmas 653
Micra 771
Microbots the. 653
Micronauts. 286, 556, 653
Middleman the. 771
Midget Comics 445
Midknight. 653
Midnight. 445, 771
Midnight Eye: Goku Private
  Investigator 653
Midnight Kiss. 653
Midnight Mass. 121
Midnight Mass: Here There Be
  Monsters 121
Midnight Men. 286
Midnight Mover 771
Midnight Nation 557
Midnight Panther. 771
Midnight Panther: Feudal
  Fantasy 771
Midnight Panther: School Daze. 771
Midnight Sons Unlimited 287
Midnight Sun 771
Midnight Tales 653
Midnighter 653
Midnite Skulker 771
Mighty Atom, the 453
Mighty Avengers 287
Mighty Bear. 254
Mighty Comics 653
Mighty Guy 771
Mighty Hercules the 654
Mighty Heroes 287
Mighty Magnor the 654
Mighty Marvel Western 287
Mighty Midget Comics 445

Mighty Mites 771
Mighty Morphin Power Rangers 654
Mighty Mouse 479
Mighty Mouse 287, 445, 654
Mighty Mouse Adventure
   Magazine 771
Mighty Mouse Adventure
   Stories 445
Mighty Mouse Adventures 369
Mighty Mutanimals 654
Mighty Samson 654
Mighty Tiny 771
Mike Barnett, Man Against
   Crime 445
Mike Carey's One-Sided
   Bargains 557
Mike Grell's Maggie the Cat . . . 557
Mike Grell's Sable 654
Mike Hoffman: Island of the
   Tiki Goddess 771
Mike Hoffman's Lost Worlds
   of Fantasy and Sci-Fi 772
Mike Hoffman's Monsters
   and Maidens 772
Mike Hoffman's Tigress 772
Mike Mignola's B.P.R.D.:
   Hollow Earth 517
Mike Shayne Private Eye 654
Military Comics 445
Milk & Cheese 772
Milkman Murders the. 517
Millennium 121
Millennium 2.5: the Buck
   Rogers Saga 772
Millennium Fever 121
Millennium Index 654
Millie the Lovable Monster 654
Millie the Model 287
Milt Gross Funnies 446
Milton Caniff's Terry & the
   Pirates 772
Milton the Monster & Fearless
   Fly 654
Mineshaft. 772
Minimum Wage 772
Ministry of Space. 557
Minute Man 446
Minx the. 121
Miracle Brigade the 654
Miracle Comics 446
Miracle Girls 772
Miracle Squad Blood & Dust . . 772
Miracle Squad the 654
Miracleman 654
Miracleman Apocrypha 654
Miracleman Family 654
Mirror's Edge 654
Misadventures of Clark &
   Jefferson 655
Miscellaneous Adventures
   of Stykman the. 655
Mischief Night 655
Miserere 655
Misericordia 655
Misery Special 557
Misplaced 557, 655, 772
Miss America Comics 287
Miss America Magazine 287
Miss Beverly Hills of Hollywood 122
Miss Cairo Jones. 446
Miss Fury. 655
Miss Fury Comics 287
Miss Liberty 436
Miss Melody Lane of Broadway 122
Miss Peach 655
Mission: Impossible. 287
Mission Impossible 655
Missions in Tibet 655
Mister Blank 772
Mister E. 122
Mister Ed the Talking Horse . . . 655
Mister Miracle 122
Mister Mystery. 446
Mister Risk 420
Mister Universe 446, 557
Mister X. 655, 772
Misty 287
Mites 772
Mitzi Comics 288
Mnemovore . . . .:. . . 122
Mobfire 122
Mobile Police Patlabor 772

Mobile Suit Gundam 0079 772
Mobile Suit Gundam Wing:
   Blind Target 772
Mobile Suit Gundam Wing:
   Episode Zero 772
Mobile Suit Gundam Wing:
   Ground Zero 772
Moby Dick 812
Moby Duck 655
Mod Squad 655
Mod Wheels 656
Modeling with Millie 229
Modern Comics. 446
Modern Love. 446
Modern Man 655
Modern Pulp 772
Modesty Blaise 122
Modniks the. 655
Moebius. 288
Moebius Comics 772
Moebius: Fusion 288
Mogobi Desert Rats 772
Molly Manton's Romances 288
Molly O'Day. 447
Mom's Homemade Comics 828
Moment of Silence 288
Monarchy. 656
Monday Funnies, the. 828
Monkee's the 656
Monkey and the Bear, the 288
Monkeyman & O'Brien 517
Monnga 772
Monographs 772
Monolith 656
Monolith the 122
Monroe's the 656
Monster 447
Monster Boy 772
Monster Club. 656
Monster Crime Comics 447
Monster Fighters Inc. 557
Monster Fighters Inc.: the
   Ghosts of Christmas 557
Monster High. 772
Monster Hunters 656
Monster Massacre. 656
Monster Mayhem Series 656
Monster Menace 288
Monster of Frankenstein 288
Monster Posse 772
Monster World. 656
Monsterman 557
Monsterpocolypse 656
Monsters Attack. 772
Monsters from Outer Space . . . 772
Monsters Inc. 518
Monsters on the Prowl 219
Monsters Unleashed 288
Monte Cook's Ptolus 656
Monte Hale Western 443
Monty Hall of the U. S. Marines 447
Moon Girl 447
Moon Girl and the Prince 447
Moon Girl Fights Crime 447
Moon Knight 288, 289
Moon Mullins. 447
Moonchild Comics 828
Moondog 828
Moonshadow. 123, 289
Moonstone Monsters. 772
Moonstone Noir. 773
Moonstone, the 816
Mopsy. 447
Mora 557
Morbid Angel. 656
Morbid Angel: Desperate Angels773
Morbid Angel: Penance . . 656, 773
Morbid Angel: to Hell and Back. 773
Morbius 289
Morbius Revisited 289
More Adventures of Fat
   Freddy's Cat 828
More Fun Comics 126
More than Mortal. 656
More than Mortal: a Legend
   Reborn 773
More than Mortal/Lady
   Pendragon 557
More than Mortal: Otherworlds . 557
Morlock 2001. 656
Morlocks 289
Morning Glory 773

Morphos the Shape Changer . . 518
Morrigan 656
Mort the Dead Teenager 289
Mortal Coil. 773
Mortal Kombat. 656
Mortal Kombat: Deception. 657
Mortar Man 773
Mortol Coils 773
Mosaic. 773
Mostly Wanted. 657
Moth 557
Mother Teresa 289
Motion Picture Comics 447
Motion Pictures Funnies Weekly 447
Motor City Comics. 829
Motor Mouth & Killpower. 289
Motorhead. 518
Mountain World. 773
Mouse Guard 657
Mouse Liberation Front 829
Movie Classic 657
Movie Comics 123, 447, 657
Movie Love 447
Movie Thrillers 447
Movie Tunes 202
Mr. and Mrs. J. Evil Scientist. . . 655
Mr. Anthony's Love Clinic 446
Mr. Beat Adventures 773
Mr. District Attorney. 122
Mr. Fixitt. 773
Mr. Keen: Tracer of
   Lost Persons 773
Mr. Magoo 655
Mr. Majestic. 655
Mr. Midshipman Easy 819
Mr. Monster 517, 655
Mr. Monster Attacks. 655
Mr. Monster Superduper Special655
Mr. Monster True Crime 655
Mr. Monster Vs. Gorzilla 557
Mr. Monster's Gal Friday: Kelly. 557
Mr. Moto 773
Mr. Muscles 478, 655
Mr. Mystic 655, 773
Mr. Natural. 828
Mr. Nightmare's Wonderful
   World 773
Mr. Right 557
Mr. T 655
Mr. T and the T Force 655
Ms. Christ 773
Ms. Fortune 557
Ms. Marvel 289
Ms. Mystic 657
Ms. Tree 773
Ms. Tree Quarterly 123
Ms. Tree's Thrilling Detective
   Adventures. 657
Ms. Victory Golden Anniversary 658
Ms. Victory Special 658
Mu 658
Mucha Lucha. 123
Muktuk Wolfsbreath: Hard-
   Boiled Shaman 123
Multiple Warheads. 773
Mummy Movie Prequel: the
   Rise & Fall of Xango's Ax . 658
Mummy or Ramses the
   Damned the. 658
Mummy the 773
Mummy The: Valley of the Gods 658
Mummy's Curse 773
Munden's Bar Annual 658
Munsters Classics 773
Munsters the 658, 773
Muppet Babies 289, 658
Muppets Take Manhattan 289
Murcielaga/She-Bat. 658
Murcielaga: She-Bat 773
Murder. 773
Murder Can Be Fun. 773
Murder, Incorporated. 447
Murder Me Dead 773
Murderous Gangsters 448
Mush Mouse and Punkin Puss . 658
Mutant 2099 290
Mutant Chronicles Golgotha . . . 658
Mutant Earth 557
Mutant Misadventures Of]
   Cloak & Dagger. 220
Mutant Texas: Tales of
   Sheriff Ida Red. 774

Mutant X 290
Mutant X: Future Shock 290
Mutant Zone 774
Mutants: Generation next 290
Mutants: the Amazing X-Men . . 290
Mutants: the Astonishing X-Men 290
Mutation. 658
Mutatis. 290
Muties 290
Mutineers, the 822
Mutiny 448
Mutiny on the Bounty 821
Mutopia X 290
Mutt and Jeff 123
My Confession 492
My Diary 290
My Experience 371
My Favorite Martian 658
My Friend Irma 290
My Girl Pearl 290
My Greatest Adventure 123
My Inner Bimbo 774
My Life. 444
My Little Margie. 658
My Little Margie's Boy Friend . . 658
My Love. 290
My Love Life 499
My Love Memories 495
My Love Secret. 453
My Name Is Bruce. 518
My Name Is Chaos 124
My Name Is Holocaust 124
My Own Romance. 290
My past Confessions. 492
My Romance 290
My Secret Life 448
My Secret Story. 393
My Story 499
Myriad 774
Mys-Tech Wars 290
Myst: the Book of the Black
   Ships 518
Mysteries. 817
Mysteries of Paris 817
Mysteries of Unexplored
   Worlds/Son of Vulcan 658
Mysteries Weird and Strange . . 448
Mysterious Adventures 448
Mysterious Island 816
Mysterious Stories. 448
Mysterious Suspense 658
Mysterious Traveler Comics . . . 448
Mystery Comics. 448
Mystery Comics Digest 658
Mystery in Space 124, 125
Mystery Man 774
Mystery Men 518
Mystery Men Comics. 448
Mystery Tales 290
Mystic 291, 658
Mystic Arcana 291
Mystic Comics 291
Mystic Edge. 658
Mystical Tales 291
Mystique 291
Myth Adventures 774
Myth Conceptions 774
Mythography 774
Mythos. 291, 774
Mythos: the Final Tour. 125
Mythstalkers 557

N N N N

N.I.O. 662
N-Guard. 660
Nail the 518
'Nam Magazine the 291
'Nam the 291
Nameless the 557
Names of Magic the 125
Namor. 291
Namor the Sub-Mariner. 292
Namora 291
Nancy & Sluggo 658
Nancy and Sluggo. 468
Nantucket Brown Roasters . . . 774
Napoleon and Uncle Elby 448
Narcopolis 659
Nard 'N' Pat, Jayzey Lynch's. . . 829
Narwain Preview 659
Nascar Heroes 659
Nash 557
Nat Turner 774

Nathan Never 518
Nathaniel Dusk 125
Nathaniel Dusk II 125
National Comics 125, 448
National Velvet 659
Nature Boy 394
Nature of the Beast 774
Naughty Bits 774
Nausicaa of the Valley of Wind . 774
Nautilus 774
Navy Action 292
Navy Combat 292
Navy Heroes 449
Navy Patrol 449
Navy Tales 292
Navy Task Force 449
Nazrat 774
Nazz the 125
Neat Stuff 659
Necessary Evil 659
Necromancer the 557
Necromantra/Lord Pumpkin . . . 659
Necronomicon 659
Necropolis the Judge Death
    Invasion 659
Necroscope 659, 774
Necrowar 659
Negation 659
Negation War 659
Negative Burn 557, 774
Negative Exposure 659
Negro Americans the Early
    Years 824
Negro Heroes 449
Negro Romance 449
[Neil Gaiman & Charles Vess']
    Stardust 149
Neil Gaiman's 659
Neil Gaiman's Neverwhere 125
Neil the Horse 774
Nellie the Nurse 292
Nemesis the Warlock 659, 774
Neo Dawn 659
Neon Cyber 557
Neon Genesis Evangelion 774
Neotopia 659
Neozoic 659
Neptune 659
Nervous Rex 775
Neutral World 659
Neutro 659
Nevada 125
Nevermen the 518
Nevermen The: Streets of Blood 518
Neverwhere 829
New Adventures of Charlie
    Chan 125
New Adventures of Cholly
    & Flytrap 292
New Adventures of Felix
    the Cat 659
New Adventures of Jesus, the . 828
New Adventures of Phantom
    Blot the 659
New Adventures of Pinocchio . 660
New Adventures of Speed
    Racer 660
[New Adventures Of] Superboy. 157
New Adventures of Terry
    & the Pirates 775
New America 660
New Avengers 292
New Avengers: Illuminati 293
New Avengers/Transformers . . . 293
New Book of Comics 125
New Comics 125
New Dnagents the 660
New Dynamix the 660
New Eradicators 775
New Eternals: Apocalypse Now 293
New Excalibur 293
New Exiles 293
New Frontier 518
New Frontiers 775
New Fun Comics 126
New Funnies 416
New Gods the 126
New Guardians 127
New Hero Comics 775
New Horizons 775
New Humans 775
New Invaders 260

New Justice Machine 660
New Kaboom 660
New Line Cinema's Tales of
    Horror 660
New Love 775
New Mangaverse 293
New Mutants 294
New Mutants the 293
New Orleans Saints 660
New Pulp Adventures Special . . 775
New Reality 775
New Romances 449
New Shadowhawk the 558
New T.H.U.N.D.E.R. Agents the 128
New Tales of Old Palomar 775
New Teen Titans 127
New Terrytoons 660
New Titans 127
New Triumph 775
New Two Fisted Tales: Vol II . . 518
New Universal 294
New Vampire Miyu 294
New Warriors 294
New Wave the 660
New Wave Vs. The Volunteers . 660
New World Disorder 775
New World Order 558, 775
New X-Men 294
New X-Men 361
New Year's Evil: 128
New York City Outlaws 775
New York World's Fair 128
New York Year Zero 775
Newcomers Illustrated 775
Newforce 557
Newman 558
Newman 558, 660
Newstralia 660, 775
Newuniversal: Shockfront 294
Next Exit 775
Next Man 660
Next Nexus 660
Next the 128
Nextwave 294
Nexus 660, 775
Nexus: Alien Justice 518
Nexus: Executioner's Song . . . 518
Nexus: God Con 518
Nexus Legends 660
Nexus Meets Madman 518
Nexus: Nightmare in Blue 518
Nexus: out of the Vortex 518
Nexus: the Liberator 518
Nexus: the Origin 518
Nexus: the Wages of Sin 519
Nfl Superpro 294
Nick Fury Agent of S.H.I.E.L.D. 294
Nick Fury Versus S.H.I.E.L.D. . . 295
Nick Fury's Howling
    Commandos 254, 295
Nickel Comics 449
Nickel Library 829
Nicki Shadow 660
Night 775
Night & Fog 660
Night Angel 775
Night Before Christmask 519
Night Club the 558
Night Cry 775
Night Force 128
Night Glider 660
Night Life 660
Night Man/Gambit 660
Night Man the 660
Night Mary 661
Night Master 775
Night Music 661
Night Nurse 295
Night of the Living Dead . 661, 775
Night of the Living Dead:
    Back from the Grave 661
Night Rider 295
Night Streets 775
Night Thrasher 295
Night Tribes 661
Night Warriors: Darkstalkers'
    Revenge 776
Night Zero 776
Night's Children 775
Night's Children: the Vampire . . 775
Nightbreed 295

Nightcat 295
Nightcrawler 295
Nightfall: the Black Chronicles . 128
Nighthawk 295
Nighthunter 660
Nightjar 660
Nightly News the 558
Nightmare 295, 449, 491, 660
Nightmare and Casper 661
Nightmare Circus 295
Nightmare on Elm Street . . 295, 661
Nightmare on Elm Street a 661
Nightmares 661
Nightmares & Fairy Tales 775
Nightmares on Elm Street 661
Nightmask 295
Nights into Dreams 661
Nightshade 661
Nightside 295
Nightstalkers 295
Nightveil 661
Nightvision 775
Nightwatch 295
Nightwing 128
Nightwing and Huntress 129
Nightwolf: the Price 776
Nikki Blade 776
Nimrod the 776
Nina's New and Improved
    All-Time Greatest 519
Nine Rings of Wu-Tang the . . . 558
Nine Volt 558
Ninja 776
Ninja Boy 661
Ninja Elite 776
Ninja Funnies 776
Ninja High School 661, 776
Ninja High School Girls 776
Ninja High School Perfect
    Memory 776
Ninja High School Small
    Bodies 519
Ninja Scroll 662
Ninjak 662
Ninth Gland the 519
Nira X: Anime 662
Nira X: Cyberangel 662, 776
Nira X/Cynder: Endangered
    Species 662
Nira X/Hellina: Heaven & Hell . . 776
Nira X: Exodus 776
Nira X: History 776
Nira X: Soul Skurge 776
Nitro-Gen 777
Nitrogen: Prophet 662
Njpw: the Rise of the Tiger . . . 662
No Ducks 829
No Escape 295
No Guts No Glory 777
No Hero 662
No Honor 558
No Honor: Makyo 558
No Need for Tenchi 777
No Time for Sergeants 662
Noble Causes 558
Noble Causes: Distant Relatives 558
Noble Causes: Family Secrets . 558
Nobody 777
Nocturnals 662
Nocturnals: Carnival of Beasts . 558
Nocturnals: the Dark Forever . . 662
Nocturnals: Witching Hour 519
Nocturne 295
Nodwick 777
Nomad 295
Nomads of Antiquity 777
Noman 662
Norm the 777
Normal Man 777
Normal Man/Megaton Man
    Special 558
Normalman 558
North Wind 662
Northlanders 129
Northstar 295
Northwest Mounties 449
Nosferatu 519
Nosferatu: Plague of Terror . . . 777
Not Brand Echh 295
Nothing Better 777
Nothing Can Stop the
    Juggernaut 296

Nova 296
Nova Girls 777
Nova Hunter 662
Nowhere 777
Nowheresville 777
Nth Man 296
Nuclear War 777
Nukla 662
Number of the Beast 662
Nurses the 662
Nuts! 449
Nutsy Squirrel 129
Nutty Comics 450
Nutty Life 453
NYC Mech 558
NYC Mech: Beta Love 558
Nyoka Jungle Girl 662
Nyoka the Jungle Girl 450, 662, 777
NYX 296
NYX: No Way Home 296

OOOO

O. K. Comics 829
O.G. Whiz 663
O'Malley and the Alley Cats . . . 663
Oak 777
Oaky Doaks 450
Obergeist: Ragnarok Highway . 558
Obergeist: the Empty Locket . . 559
Objective Five 559
Oblivion 662
Obnoxio the Clown 296
Occult Crimes Taskforce 559
Occult Files of Dr. Spektor 662
Ocean 663
Octobriana 777
Octopus, the 824
Odd Job 777
Odd Squad the 663
Odd World of Richard Corben . 829
Oddballz 777
Oddballz: Venetian Blind 777
Odyssey the 663
Odyssey, the 820
Odyssey The: Absolute Power . 663
Of Bitter Souls 663
Of Mind and Soul 778
Off on a Comet 823
Offcastes 296
Offerings 777
Official Buz Sawyer 777
Official Handbook of the
    Marvel Universe 296
Official How to Draw G.I. Joe . 777
Official How to Draw Robotech . 777
Official How to Draw
    Transformers 777
Official Johnny Hazard 777
Official Jungle Jim 777
Official Mandrake 778
Official Marvel Index: 296
Official Marvel Timeline 296
Official Modesty Blaise 778
Official Prince Valiant 778
Official Rip Kirby 778
Official Secret Agent 778
Official True Crime Cases 296
Oh My Goddess! 519
Oh My Goth: Humans Suck! . . . 778
Oh My Goth! 778
Ohm's Law 778
Oink: Blood and Circus 663
Ojo 778
OK Comics 450
Okay Comics 450
Okko: Cycle of Earth 663
Okko: Cycle of Water 663
Oklahoma Kid 450
Oktane 519
Oktoberfest 778
Oliver Twist 815
Olympians 296
Olympus Heights 663
Omac 129
Omac Project the 129
Omaha the Cat Dancer 829
Omega 778
Omega 7 663
Omega Chase 663
Omega Elite 778
Omega Flight 296
Omega Men 129

Omega Men the 130
Omega One. 663
Omega One: Rogue 663
Omega Saga the. 663
Omega: the Unknown 297
Omega the Unknown 297
Omen. 778
Omen the 663
Omicron. 778
Omni Men 778
On a Pale Horse 663
On Jungle Trails 823
On the Air 450
On the Spot. 450
One Bad Rat 519
One Shot Western. 778
One the 297
One-Arm Swordsman . . . 663, 778
Oni Double Feature. 778
Onigami 778
Onslaught 297
Onslaught Reborn 297
Onyx Overlord 297
Open Season 778
Open Space 297
Operation Knightstrike. 559
Operation Peril 450
Operation: Stormbreaker. . . . 663
Opposite Forces 663, 778
Optic Nerve 778
Or Else 778
Oracle Comix 829
Oracle Presents 778
Orbit 663, 778
Order the 297
Oregon Trail, the 819
Oriental Heroes 663
Origin. 297
Origin of the Defiant Universe . . 664
Original Adventures of Cholly
    & Flytrap 559
Original Astro Boy 663
[Original] Black Cat 591, 732
Original Captain Johnar
    and the Aliens 663
Original Dick Tracy 663
Original Dr. Solar Man
    of the Atom 664
Original E-Man. 664
Original Ghost Rider 297
Original Ghost Rider
    Rides Again 297
Original Magnus Robot Fighter. 664
Original Shield. 664
Original Tom Corbett 778
Original Turok Son of Stone . . 664
Origins. 664
Origins of Reid Fleming World's
    Toughest Milkman 778
Orion 130, 519
Orion the Hunter 664
Orlak: Flesh & Steel 778
Orlak Redux 778
Ororo: Before the Storm . . . 297
Orson Scott Card's Wyrms . . 664
Osborn Journals the 297
Oscar Comics 297
Other Side the 130
Others the 559
Otherworld. 130
Otis Goes Hollywood. 519
Our Army at War 130
Our Fighting Forces 132
Our Fighting Men in Action . . 450
Our Flag Comics 450
Our Gang Comics 450
Our Love 297
Our Love Story 297
Out for Blood. 519
Out of the Night. 451
Out of the Shadows 451
Out of the Vortex. 519
Out of this World 664
Out There 664
Outbreed 999 664
Outcast Special 664
Outcasts 134
Outer Limits the. 664
Outer Orbit 519
Outer Space 387, 664
Outlanders. 519
Outlanders: Epilogue. 519

Outlaw 7 519
Outlaw Fighters. 297
Outlaw Kid. 297
Outlaw Nation 134
Outlaw Overdrive 778
Outlaw Scorn: 3030ad. 664
Outlaws 134, 451
Outlaws of the West 664
Outlaws, the 451
Outposts 664
Outsiders: Five of a Kind. . . 134
Outsiders the. 134
Over the Edge and under
    a Buck 297
Overkill 559
Overman 559
Owl the 664
Ox Bow Incident, the. 822
Oxido 559
Oxydol-Dreft 451
Oz 779
Oz: Romance in Rags. 779
Oz Squad 779
Oz: Straw and Sorcery 779
Oz/Wonderland Chronicles the . 664
Ozark Ike. 451
Ozzie and Babs. 451

P P P P

P.A.C. 664
P.I.'s the 666
P.J. Warlock. 780
Pacific Presents 664
Pact. 559
Pact the 559
Pageant of Comics 451
Painkiller Jane. 664
Pakkins' Land 665, 779
Pakkins' Land: Forgotten
    Dreams 779
Pakkins' Land: Quest for Kings. 779
Palantine 779
Paleo Tales: Late Cretaceous . . 779
Palooka-Ville 779
Panda Khan 779
Pandemonium 779
Pandemonium: Deliverance . . 665
Pandora. 779
Pandora: Demonography . . . 779
Pandora Devils Advocate . . . 779
Pandora: Pandemonium 779
Pandora's Chest 779
Panhandle Pete and Jennifer . . 451
Panic. 451, 665
Pantera 665
Pantha 665
Pantheon 779
Panzer: 1946. 779
Paper Cuts 779
Para. 665
Parade (With Fireworks) . . . 559
Paradigm 559
Paradise 665
Paradise X. 298
Paradise X/Ragnarok 298
Paradise X: the Heralds 298
Paradox. 665
Paragon 298
Paragon Dark Apocalypse. . . 665
Parallax: Emerald Night 134
Paramount Animated Comics . . 451
Paranoia 665
Pariah 665
Paris 779
Parliament of Justice the. . . . 559
Parole Breakers 451
Particle Dreams. 779
Partners in Pandemonium. . . 779
Partridge Family the 665
Parts of a Hole 779
Parts Unknown 779
Parts Unknown: Dark Intentions 780
Parts Unknown: Hostile
    Takeover 559
Parts Unknown: Killing
    Attraction 559
Passover 665
Pat Boone 134
Pat Savage: Woman of Bronze. 665
Pat the Brat 452
Patches 452
Path the 665
Pathfinder, the 815

Pathways to Fantasy. 665
Patient Zero. 559
Patricia Briggs' Mercy Thompson:
    Homecoming 665
Patrick the Wolf Boy 780
Patriots the 665
Patsy & Hedy 298
Patsy & Her Pals. 298
Patsy Walker. 298
Patsy Walker: Hellcat 298
Patty Cake. 780
Patty Powers 233
Patty-Cake & Friends 780
Paul Jenkins' Sidekick. 559
Paul Terry's Comics 478
Paul the Samurai. 780
Paula Peril. 780
Pawnee Bill 452
Pax Romana 559
Pay-Off 452
Peacekeeper 665
Peacemaker 134, 665
Peanuts 665
Pearl Harbor 665
Pebbles & Bamm-Bamm. . . . 665
Pebbles Flintstone. 665
Pedro. 452
Penance: Relentless 298
Pendulum 780
Penguin Triumphant 135
Penguins in Bondage 829
Penny 452
Penny and Aggie 665
Penny Arcade 520
Penny Century 780
Pentacle: the Sign of the Five . . 780
Pep Comics 452
Perfect Crime, the 452
Perfect Dark: Janus' Tears . . . 665
Perfect Dark Zero 666
Perg. 666
Perhapanauts 559
Perhapanauts: Second
    Chances. 520
Perhapanauts the 520
Perry Mason Mystery Magazine 666
Pete the P.O.'d Postal Worker. . 780
Peter Cannon: Thunderbolt. . . 135
Peter Pan: Return to
    Neverland 666
Peter Panda 135
Peter Parker: Spider-Man . . . 299
Peter Parker, Spider-Man . . . 319
Peter Parker the Spectacular
    Spider-Man 298
Peter Paul's 4 in 1 Jumbo
    Comic Book 452
Peter Penny and His Magic
    Dollar 452
Peter Porkchops 135
Peter Porker 299
Peter Potamus 666
Peter Rabbit 452
Peter the Little Pest. 299
Petticoat Junction 666
Phantom 299, 666, 780
Phantom 2040. 299
Phantom Bolt the. 666
Phantom Force 559, 666
Phantom Guard 559
Phantom Jack 559
Phantom Jack: the Nowhere
    Man Agenda 666
Phantom Lady 453, 829
Phantom of Fear City 780
Phantom of the Opera. 780
Phantom Stranger 135
Phantom the 135, 666
Phantom Zone the. 135
Phase One 780
Phaze 666
Phigments 780
Phil Rizzuto 453
Phoenix 666
Phoenix (Untold Story) 299
Phoenix Resurrection 666
Phoney Pages 780
Phonogram 560
Phucked up Funnies 829
Pi: the Book of Ants. 520
Pictorial Love Stories 499
Picture Crimes. 453

Picture News. 453
Picture Parade 453
Picture Progress 453
Picture Scope Jungle
    Adventures 453
Picture Stories from American
    History 453
Picture Stories from Science. . . 453
Picture Stories from the Bible . . 135
Picture Stories from World
    History 453
Pieces for Mom: a Tale
    of the Undead 560
Pierce 666
Pigeons from Hell 520
Pigtale 560
Pilgrim's Progress 299
Pilot Season 560
Pilot, the 819
Pin-Up Pete 453
Pineapple Army 780
Pinhead 299
Pinhead and Foodini 453
Pinhead Vs. Marshall Law. . . . 300
Pink Floyd Experience 780
Pink Floyd, the 829
Pink Panther the 666
Pinky and the Brain. 135
Pinocchio & the Emperor
    of the Night 300
Pint-Sized X-Babies:
    Murderama 300
Pioneer Picture Stories 453
Pioneers, the. 816
Piracy 453, 666
Piranha! Is Loose 780
Pirate Club 780
Pirate Corp. 666
Pirate Corps! 780
Pirate Tales 666
Pirates Comics 453
Pirates of Coney Island the . . 560
Pirates of Dark Waters 300
Pirates Vs. Ninjas 780
Pirates Vs. Ninjas II:
    Up the Ante 666
Pistolfist. 666
Pistolfist: Revolutionary Warrior 667
Pitcairn's Island 821
Pitt 560, 667
Pitt: Biogenesis 667
Pitt Crew 667
Pitt the 300
Pixie and Dixie and Mr. Jenks. . 667
Pixies, the 453
Pixy Junket 780
Plague of the Living Dead. . . 667
Plan 9 from Outer Space . 667, 781
Planet 29. 781
Planet Comics 454, 667, 780
Planet of the Apes. . 300, 520, 780
Planet of the Apes (Movie) . . . 520
Planet of the Apes: Blood
    of the Apes. 781
Planet of the Apes: Forbidden
    Zone. 781
Planet of the Apes: Sins
    of the Father 781
Planet of the Apes: the Human
    War 520
Planet of the Apes
    Urchaks' Folly 781
Planet of Vampires 667
Planet Terry 300
Planet-X. 781
Planetary. 667
Planetary Brigade 667
Planetary Brigade: Origins . . 667
Plasmer. 300
Plastic Forks 300
Plastic Little. 781
Plastic Man 135, 454, 829
Plastron Cafe 781
Playful Little Audrey. 455
Plop! 135
Pocahontas 455
Pocket Comics 455
Poe 781
Pogo Possum 455
Pogrom 667
Pogz N Slammer. 667
Point Blank 667, 781

Poison Elves 667, 781
Poison Elves: Dominion 781
Poison Elves: Hyena. 781
Poison Elves: Lost Tales 781
Poison Elves: Lusipher & Linlith 781
Poison Elves: Parintachin 781
Poison Elves: Ventures 781
Poizon 667
Poizon: Cadillacs and Green
Tomatoes 667
Poizon: Demon Hunter . . . 667, 781
Poizon: Lost Child 667
Pokeman Tales: 667
Pokeman: the First Movie 667
Pokeman the Movie 2000:
Revelation Lugia 667
Pokemon Adventures 782
Pokemon: Electric Pikachu
Boogaloo 782
Pokemon: Pikachu
Shocks Back 782
Pokemon: Surf's up Pikachu. . . 782
Pokemon Tales 782
Pokemon: the Electric Tale
of Pikachu 782
Pokewomon: Gotta Shag
'Em All!. 782
Police Academy. 300
Police Action 300
Police Against Crime. 455
Police Badge 323
Police Badge #479 300
Police Comics 455
Police Line-Up. 456
Police Trap 456
Polly and the Pirates 782
Poot. 782
Pop Parody 782
Popcorn. 782
Popeye 456, 667, 668
Popeye Special 668
Popples 300
Popular Comics 456
Pork. 829
Porky Pig 368
Portent the. 560
Portfolio of Underground Art . . 829
Portia Prinz of the Glamazons . 782
Possessed the. 668
Post Brothers 782
Potter's Field 668
Powdered Toast-Man 300
Power & Glory. 668
Power and the Glory the 668
Power Comics 456, 782
Power Company the 136
Power Factor. 668
Power Line 300
Power Man 668
Power of Prime 668
Power of Shazam!. 136
Power of the Atom. 136
Power of the Mark. 136
Power of the Valkyrie 668
Power Pachyderms 301
Power Pack 301
Power Pack: Day One. 301
Power Pack: Peer Pressure . . . 301
Power Rangers Zeo 560
Power Rangers Zeo/
Youngblood 668
Power Rangers Zeo
Youngblood 560
Powerhouse Pepper Comics. . . 300
Powerknights. 668
Powerless 300
Powerman and Power Mower
Safety. 829
Powermark 668
Powerpuff Girls 136
Powers 301, 560
Powers That Be. 668
Ppv 782
Prairie Moon and Other Stories 520
Prairie, the 818
Preacher 136
Preacher Special: Saint
of Killers. 136
Predator. 520
Predator 2 520
Predator: Bad Blood 520
Predator: Big Game 520

Predator: Bloody Sands of Time 520
Predator: Cold War 520
Predator: Dark River 520
Predator: Hell & Hot Water . . . 520
Predator: Hell Come a Walkin' . 520
Predator: Homeworld 520
Predator: Kindred 520
Predator: Nemesis. 520
Predator: Primal 520
Predator: Race War. 520
Predator Vs. Judge Dredd. . . . 520
Predator Vs. Magnus
Robot Fighter. 521
Predator: Xenogenesis 521
Premiere 782
Presidential Material 668
Preteen Dirty Gene Kung
Fu Kangaroos 782
Pretty Baby Machine 560
Prey. 782
Prez. 136
Price the 782
Pride & Joy 136
Pride of the Yankees. 456
Priest. 668
Primal 521
Primal Force 136
Primal Rage 668
Prime. 668
Prime/Captain America 668
Prime Cuts 782
Prime Slime Tales 782
Prime Vs. Hulk 668
Primer 668, 782
Primitives 782
Primordia 668
Primus 668
Prince 137
Prince and the Pauper, the 816
Prince Namor the Sub-Mariner . 301
Prince of Heroes 668
Prince Valiant 301, 782
Prince Valiant Monthly. 782
Prince Vandal 669
Princess Natasha 137
Princess Prince 782
Princess Sally 668
Priority: White Heat 669
Prison Break 456
Prisoner of Zenda, the 819
Prisoner the. 137
Pristeen 16 669
Private Beach 782
Private Eye 301
Private Eyes 782
Prize Comics 456
Prize Comics Western. 457
Prize Mystery 457
Pro. 560
Professional: Gogol 13 669
Professor Coffin. 669
Professor Om 669
Professor Xavier and the X-Men 301
Programme the 669
Project A-Ko 0 669
Project Arms 783
Project Eon 669
Project: Kalki 669
Project Superpowers. 669
Promethea. 669
Promethian Enterprises. 829
Proof 560
Propeller Man 521
Prophecy 669
Prophecy of the Soul Sorcerer . 669
Prophet 560
Prophet/Cable. 669
Prophet/Chapel: Super Soldiers 561
Prophet II. 669
Prophet: Legacy 669
Prophet of Dreams 669
Proposition Player 137
Protectors 669
Protheus 783
Prototype 669
Prototype: Turf War 669
Prowler 669
Prowler in 'White Zombie' the . . 670
Prowler the 301
Prudence & Caution 670
PS238 783
Pscythe 561

Psi Force 302
Psi Judge Anderson 783
Psi-Lords: Reign of the
Starwatchers 670
Psyba-Rats the 137
Psycho. 670
Psycho the 137
Psychoanalysis 457, 670
Psychoblast. 670
Psychonauts 302
Psylocke & Angel: Crimson
Dawn 302
Public Defender in Action 456
Public Enemies 457
Public Enemy 670
Pubo 521
Pudd'nhead Wilson 820
Pudgy Pig 670
Puffed 561
Pulp Fantastic 137
Pulp Fiction 783
Pulse the 302
Puma Blues. 783
Pumpkinhead: the Rites of
Exorcism 521
Punch and Judy Comics 457
Punch Comics. 457
Puncture 670
Punisher 302, 303
Punisher 2099 304
Punisher Armory 303
Punisher/Captain America:
Blood and Glory. 303
Punisher Kills the Marvel
Universe. 303
Punisher Magazine 303
Punisher Meets Archie 303
Punisher Movie Comic 303
Punisher P.O.V. 304
Punisher Presents: Barracuda
Max 304
Punisher: the Movie 303
Punisher Vs. Bullseye 304
Punisher War Journal 304
Punisher War Zone 304
Punisher: Year One. 305
Punx 670
Puppet Comics 458
Puppet Master. 670
Puppet Master: Children
of the Puppet Master. 670
Pure Art Quarterly 830
Pure Trance. 830
Purgatori 670, 671
Purity 783
Purple Claw, the 458
Push 671
Pussycat 305
Puzzle Adventures 703
PVP 561, 783

Q Q Q Q
Q-Unit: Revenge 561, 671
Quack!. 783
Quagmire Comics 830
Quagmire Usa 783
Quantum & Woody 671
Quantum Leap 671
Quantum Mechanics 783
Quantum: Rock of Ages 783
Quasar. 305
Queen & Country 783
Queen & Country: Declassified. 783
Queen of the Damned. 671
Queen of the West, Dale Evans 458
Queen's Necklace, the 824
Quest. 305
Quest for Dreams Lost 783
Quest Presents 783
Question Quarterly 137
Question the 137
Questprobe 305
Quick Trigger Western 349
Quick-Draw McGraw 671
Quicken Forbidden 783
Quicksilver. 305

R R R R
R. Crumb's Comics and Stories 830
R.E.B.E.L.S. '94 '96 137
R.I.P. 676
R.I.P.D. 521
Rabid Monkey 783

Race Against Time 671
Race for the Moon 671
Race of Scorpions. 521
Racer X. 671
Racer-X. 671
Rack & Pain 521
Rack & Pain: Killers. 671
Racket Squad in Action 458
Radical Dreamer 671, 783
Radioactive Man 671
Radiskull and Devil Doll 561
Radix 561
Raggedy Ann and Andy . . 458, 671
Ragman 137
Ragman: Cry of the Dead 137
Ragmop. 561, 783
Ragnarok. 783
Ragnarok Guy 783
Rags Rabbit 458
Rai. 671
Raiders of the Lost Ark 305
Raijin Comics 783
Raika 783
Raise the Dead 671
Raising Hell 783
Rakan 671
Ralph Kiner Home Run King. . . 458
Ralph Snart 783
Ralph Snart Adventures 672
Ramar of the Jungle 458
Ramayan 3392 A.D. 672
Ramayan Reborn 672
Ramayani 3392 A.D. Reloaded. 672
Rambo. 784
Rambo III. 784
Ramm 784
Rampaging Hulk the 305
Random 5 672
Random Encounter 672
[Randy Bowen's] Decapitator . . 509
Randy O'Donnel Is the Man . . . 561
Range Busters 458
Range Romances 458
Rangeland Love 305
Rangers Comics 458
Rangers of Freedom 458
Rango 672
Ranma 1/2. . . . . 672, 784
Rann/Thanagar: Holy War. 137
Rann/Thanagar War the 137
Raphael. 672, 784
Raptus. 784
Raptus: Dead of Night. 784
Rare Breed 672
Rascals in Paradise 521
Rash 672
Rat Bastard 672
Rat Fink. 784
Rat Patrol the 672
Ravage 2099. 305
Ravager. 784
Raven 137, 672, 784
Raven Chronicles 784
Raven House 672
Ravening 672
Ravening the 784
Ravens and Rainbows 672
Raver. 672
Raw 830
Raw City 784
Raw Media Mags. 784
Rawararawar. 830
Rawhide 672
Rawhide Kid 306
Ray, the 137
Ray Bradbury Chronicles 672
Ray Bradbury Comics 672
Ray Harryhausen Presents. . . . 672
Raymond E. Feist's Magician:
Apprentice 672
Razor. 672, 673, 784
Razor Analog Burn 784
Razor: Archives 784
Razor: Bleeding Heart. 784
Razor/Dark Angel: the Final Nail 784
Razor: Gothic 784
Razor: the Darkest Night. 784
Razor: the Furies. 784
Razor: till I Bleed Daylight. . . . 785
Razor: Torture 785
Razor Uncut 785
Razor's Edge 785

Razor's Edge The: Redbird....	673
Razor's Edge The: Warblade ..	673
Razorguts	785
Razorline First Cut	306
Re: Gex	674
Re: Gex: Black & White	785
Re-Animator	673
Reactoman	785
Reagan's Raiders	785
Real Adventures of Jonny Quest the	521
Real Clue Crime Stories	388
Real Experiences	331
Real Fact Comics	137
Real Funnies	459
Real Ghostbusters	673
Real Heroes Comics	459
Real Life Comics	459
Real Life Story of Fess Parker	459
Real Love	421
Real Screen Comics	137
Real Sports Comics	371
Real Stuff	785
Real War Stories	673
Real West Romances	459
Real Western Hero	497
Realm	785
Realm of the Claw	561
Realworlds	137
Reaper	785
Rebel Sword	521
Rebellion	785
Record Book of Famous Police Cases	459
Red	673
Red & Stumpy	785
Red Arrow	459
Red Badge of Courage, the	820
Red Band Comics	459
Red Circle Comics	459
Red Diary	785
Red Dog	673
Red Dragon	673
Red Dragon Comics	459
Red Fox	785
Red Mask	480
Red Mass for Mars a	561
Red Menace	674
Red Prophet: Tales of Alvin Maker	674
Red Rabbit	460
Red Raven Comics	256
Red Rocket 7	521
Red Rover, the	821
Red Ryder Comics	460
Red Seal Comics	462
Red Sonja	306, 674
Red Sonja & Conan "Hot and Dry"	830
Red Sonja/Claw the Unconquered: Devil's Hands	674
Red Sonja in 3-D	674
Red Sonja Vs. Thulsa Doom	674
Red Star the	561, 674
Red Tornado	138
Red Warrior	306
Red Wolf	306
Redball 6	673
Redblade	521
Redeemer the	673
Redeemers	674
Redskin	460
Reese's Pieces	674
Reflections	785
Reg'lar Fellers	460
Reggie	674
Reggie's Wise Guy Jokes	674
Regulators	561
Rehd	785
Reid Fleming/Flaming Carrot	521
Reid Fleming World's Toughest Milkman	785, 830
Reign in Hell	138
Reign of the Zodiac	138
Reivers	785
Reload	674
Remains	674
Remarkable Worlds of Phineas B. Fuddle	138
Remember Pearl Harbor	460
Ren and Stimpy Show	306
Renegades of Justice	785
Renfield	785
Reno Browne	221
Repentance	785
Replacement God	785
Replacement God & Other Stories	785
Replacement God and Other Stories the	561
Repo	561
Reptilicus	674
Resident Evil	561
Resident Evil: Fire & Ice	674
Resistance the	674
Rest	674
Restaurant at the End of the Universe	138
Resurrection Man	138
Ret Romanne	675
Retaliator	786
Retief	786
Retief and the Warlords	786
Retief: Diplomatic Immunity	786
Retief of the Cdt	786
Retro Rocket	561
Retro-Dead	786
Retrograde	786
Return of Gorgo the	675
Return of Happy the Clown	786
Return of Konga the	675
Return of Lum Urusei* Yatsura the	786
Return of Megaton Man	675
Return of Shadowhawk the	561
Return of the Gremlins	521
Return of the Jedi	306
Return of the Outlaw	460
Return of the Skyman	786
Return of the Super Pimps	675
Return to Jurassic Park	675
Reveal	521
Revealing Romances	460
Revelations	521
Revenant	561
Revenge of the Prowler	675
Revengers	675
Revere	675
Revolution on the Planet of the Apes	675
Revolver	786
Revolving Doors	786
Rex Allen Comics	460
Rex Dexter of Mars	460
Rex Hart	211
Rex Morgan, M. D.	460
Rex Mundi	521, 561
Rheintochter	786
Rhudiprt Prince of Fur	786
Ribit	675
Ribtickler	460
Rich Johnston's Holed up	786
Richard Dragon	138
Richard Dragon Kung Fu Fighter	138
Richard Matheson's Hell House	786
Richie Rich	307, 675, 676
Rick Raygun	786
Ricky	460
Ride the	561
Ride The: Chain Reaction	561
Ride The: Die Valkyrie	561
Rider, the	460
Rifleman the	676
Rima the Jungle Girl	138
Rin Tin Tin	460
Rin Tin Tin and Rusty	676
Ring of Roses	521
Ring of the Niebelung The:	521
Ring the [Of the Nieblung]	138
Ringo Kid	307
Ringo Kid Western	307
Rio at Bay	521
Rio Kid	786
Riot	307, 676, 786
Riot Act Two	786
Riot Gear	676
Riot Gear: Violent past	676
Rip Hunter Time Master	138
Rip in Time	786
Rip off Comix	830
Rip Van Winkle & the Headless Horseman	813
Ripclaw	561
Ripfire	676
Ripley's Believe it or Not	521
Ripley's Believe it or Not!	460
Ripley's Believe it or Not!	676
Riptide	562
Rise of the Snakemen	676
Rising Stars	562
Rising Stars: Bright	562
Rising Stars: Untouchable	562
Rising Stars: Voices of the Dead	562
Risk	676
Rival Schools	786
Rivets	460
Roachmill	521, 786
Road to Hell	676
Rob	676
Rob Hanes Adventures	786
Rob Roy	821
Rob Zombie's Spook Show	562
Rob Zombie's Spookshow International	678
Robert E. Howard's	677, 786
Robert E. Howard's Conan: Frazetta Cover Series	521
Robert Jordan's New Spring	677
Roberts the	562
Robin	138
Robin 3000	139
Robin Hood	460, 677, 786, 813
Robin Hood and His Merry Men	478
Robin Hood Tales	139, 460
Robin plus	139
Robin: Year One	139
Robinson Crusoe	677, 813
Robo Defense Team Mecha Rider	786
Robo Dojo	677
Robo Hunter	677
Robo Warriors	787
Robocop	307
Robocop 3	522
Robocop II	307
Robocop: Mortal Coils	521
Robocop: Prime Suspect	522
Robocop: Roulette	522
Robocop Versus Terminator	522
Robocop: War Party	677
Robocop: Wild Child	677
Robotech	677, 786
Robotech: Academy Blues	786
Robotech: Aftermath	787
Robotech: Clone	787
Robotech: Covert Ops	787
Robotech Defenders	139
Robotech: Genesis the Legend of Zor	677
Robotech II: the Sentinels	678
Robotech II the Sentinels	787
Robotech II: the Sentinels: Cyberpirates	787
Robotech II: the Sentinels: the Malcontent Uprising	787
Robotech in 3-D	677
Robotech: Invasion	677
Robotech: Invid War	677
Robotech: Invid War Aftermath	787
Robotech: Love and War	677
Robotech: Masters	677
Robotech: Mordecai	787
Robotech: Prelude to the Shadow Chronicles	678
Robotech: Return to Macross	787
Robotech: Sentinels: Rubicon	787
Robotech Special Dana's Story	678
Robotech the Macross Saga	677
Robotech: the New Generation	676
Robotech: Vermilion	787
Robotech: Warriors	787
Robotech: Wings of Gibraltar	787
Robotika	678
Robotika: for a Few Rubles More	678
Robotix	307
Robur the Conqueror	824
Rock 'N' Roll	562, 678
Rock 'N' Roll Comics	678
Rock 'N' Roll High School	678
Rocket Comics	461
Rocket Kelly	461
Rocket Man: King of the Rocket Men	678
Rocket Raccoon	307
Rocket Ranger	678
Rocket Rangers	787
Rocket Ship X	461
Rocketeer	678
Rocketeer Adventure Magazine	522, 678
Rocketeer Special	678
Rocketman	461
Rocketo	678
Rocketo Journey to the Hidden Sea	562
Rockin' Rollin' Miner Ants	787
Rocko's Modern Life	307
Rockstar Games' Oni	522
Rocky and His Fiendish Friends	678
Rocky Horror Picture Show	678
Rocky Lane Western	461
Rod Cameron Western	461
Rog 2000	678
Rogan Gosh	139
Roger Rabbit	678
Roger Rabbit's Toontown	678
Rogue	307
Rogue Angel: Teller of Tall Tales	678
Rogue Trooper	678
Rogue Trooper: the Final Warrior	678
Rogues	678
Rokkin	679
Roland: Days of Wrath	679
Rolling Stones: the Sixties	787
Roly-Poly Comics	461
Rom	307
Roman Holidays the	679
Romance and Confession Stories	461
Romance Diary	307
Romance Tales	307
Romance Trail	139
Romances of Nurse Helen Grant, the	307
Romances of the West	307
Romantic Affairs	288
Romantic Western	461
Romeo and Juliet	822
Romeo Tubbs	448
Romp	562
Ronin	140
Rook the	679
Rookie Cop	461
Room 222	679
Rooter	787
Roots of the Swamp Thing	140
Rose	679, 787
Rose 'N' Gunn	788
Rose & Thorn	140
Rose and Gunn	788
Rose and Gunn: Reckoning	788
Roswell	679
Rotogin: Junkbotz	562
Roundup	461
Route 666	679
Rovers	788
Rowlf	830
Roy Campanella, Baseball Hero	461
Roy Roger's Trigger	461
Roy Rogers and Trigger	461, 679
Roy Rogers Comics	461
Roy Rogers Western Classics	679
Roy Thomas' Anghem	679
Royal Roy	307
Rta: Personality Crisis	562
Rubber Duck Tales	830
Rubes Revived	788
Rudolph the Red Nosed Reindeer	140
Ruff and Ready	679
Rugged Action	307
Rugrats Comic Adventures	679
Ruins	307
Ruk Bud Webster	788
Rulah, Jungle Goddess	499
Rumble Girls	562
Rumble in La Rambla	562
Rumble Pak	788
Run Buddy Run	679
Run!	562
Runaways	308
Rune	679
Rune: Hearts of Darkness	679
Rune/Silver Surfer	679

Runes of Ragnan 562, 679
Runners: Bad Goods. 788
Runners: the Big Snow Job . . 679
Ruse 679
Rush City. 140
Russian Sunset. 562
Rust 679
Rusty, Boy Detective 461
Rusty Comics 268
Ruule: Ganglords of Chinatown 679
Ruule: Kiss & Tell 679

S S S S

S. Clay Wilson Twenty
   Drawings 830
S.C.I.-Spy 142
S.P.I.C.E. 690
S.T.A.R. Corps 149
S.T.A.T. 693
Saari, the Jungle Goddess 461
[Saban's] Mighty Morphin
   Power Rangers 287
[Saban's] Mighty Morphin Power
   Rangers: Ninja Rangers/
   VR Troope 287
Sable 679
Sable & Fortune 308
Sabre 679
Sabretooth 308
Sabretooth & Mystique 308
Sabretooth Classics 308
Sabretooth: Mary Shelley
   Overdrive 308
Sabrina the Teenage Witch . . . 679
Sabu, Elephant Boy 461
Sachs & Violens 308
Sacred & Profane 830
Sad Sack and the Sarge 680
Sad Sack Comics 462
Sad Sack in 3-D 680
Sad Sack Laugh Special 680
Sad Sack Sack World 680
Sad Sack Usa 680
Sad Sack's Army Life 680
Sad Sack's Funny Friends . . . 680
Saddle Justice 462
Saddle Romances 462
Sade 788
Sade/Rose and Gunn 788
Sade Special 788
Sade: Testaments of Pain 788
Sadhu 680
Sadhu The: Wheel of Destiny . 680
Safest Place in the World, the. . 522
Safety-Belt Man All Hell. 680
Saffire 562
Saga of Crystar 308
Saga of Original Human Torch . 308
Saga of Ras Al Ghul 140
Saga of the Man-Elf 788
Saga of the Metabarons 680
(Saga of The) Sub-Mariner . . . 327
Saga of the Swamp Thing. 140
Sage 788
Sailor Moon 788
Saint 788
Saint Angel 562
Saint Germaine 788
Saint Germaine: Prior Echoes. . 788
Saint Legend 680
Saint Sinner. 308
Saint Tail 788
Saint, the 462
Salem 680
Salvador 680
Salvation Run 140
Sam & Max Go to the Moon . . . 308
Sam & Twitch 502
Sam and Max Free- Lance
   Police Special 680
Sam Hill Private Eye 462
Sam Noir: Ronin Holiday. 562
Sam Noir: Samurai Detective . . 562
Sam Slade Robohunter. 680
Sam Stories: Legs. 563
Sammy: Tourist Trap 562
Samson 462
Samsons 680
Samurai. 680, 788
Samurai (1st Series) 788
Samurai 7 788
Samurai Cat 308

Samurai Funnies 788
Samurai Guard 680
Samurai: Heaven and Earth . . . 522
Samurai Jack 140
Samurai: Legend. 308
Samurai Penguin. 788
Samurai Son of Death. 788
Samuree 680
San Francisco Comic Book. . . . 830
Sanctuary 788, 789
Sandman 140
Sandman Mystery Theatre . . . 141
Sandman Mystery Theatre:
   Sleep of Reason 141
Sandman Presents: 141
Sandman The: the Dream
   Hunters 141
Sands of the South Pacific . . . 462
Sandscape 680
Santa Claus Funnies 462
Santa Claus Parade 462
Santa Claws 789
Santa's Christmas Comics . . . 462
Santana 680
Sapphire 789
Sarge Steel/Secret Agent 680
Satan's Six 681
Satana 308
Satanika 680
Satanika Tales 681
Saurians: Unnatural Selection. . 681
Savage 563
Savage Brothers 681
Savage Combat Tales 681
Savage Dragon 563
Savage Dragon Destroyer Duck 563
Savage Dragon: God War 563
Savage Dragon: Marshal Law. . 564
Savage Dragon: Sex & Violence 564
Savage Dragon/Teenage
   Mutant Ninja Turltes
   Crossover 681
Savage Dragon The: Red
   Horizon 564
Savage Henry 789
Savage Henry: Powerchords . . 789
Savage Humor 830
Savage Planet. 789
Savage Planet: Secrets
   of the Empire 789
Savage Red Sonja Queen
   of the Frozen Wastes 681
Savage Sword of Conan 308
Savage Tales. 309, 681
Savage World 681
Savant Garde 564
Saved by the Bell 681
Sawed-Off Mojo. 681
Say What?. 830
Scalped 141
Scamp 681
Scarab 141
Scare Tactics. 141
Scarface: Devil in Disguise . . . 681
Scarface: Scarred for Life 681
Scarlet Crush 681
Scarlet in Gaslight. 789
Scarlet Scorpion/Darkside. . . . 789
Scarlet Spider 309
Scarlet Spider Unlimited 309
Scarlet Thunder. 789
Scarlet Traces: the Great Game 522
Scarlet Veronica 681
Scarlet Witch 309
Scarlett 142
Scarlett's Curse. 681
Scary Godmother 789
Scary Godmother: Bloody
   Valentine 789
Scary Godmother: Wild
   about Harry 789
Scary Tales 681
Scarygirl 830
Scatterbrain 522, 681
Scavengers 681
Schism. 681
Schizophrenia, Cheech Wizard. 830
Sci-Tech. 682
Science Comics 462
Science Fair 789
Scimidar 789
Scion 681

Scooby Doo. 682
Scooby Doo Mystery Comics . . 682
Scooby-Doo 142, 309, 682
Scoop Comics 462
Scooter Comics 462
Scooter Girl 789
Scorched Earth 682
Scorn 789
Scorpio Rose. 682
Scorpio Corp. 682
Scorpion King the 522
Scorpion the 682
Scotland Yard 462
Scottish Chiefs, the 819
Scout 682
Scout: War Shaman 682
Scratch 142, 789
Scream Comics 463
Scream Queen 682
Scream the 522
Screaming Angels 789
Screamland 564
Screwball Squirrel 522
Screwtooth 789
Scribbly 142
Scrimidar 789
Scud: Disposable Assassin . . . 789
Scud: Tales from the Vending
   Machine 789
Scud the Disposable Assassin . 564
Se7en 683
Sea Devils 142
Sea Hunt 682
Sea of Red 564
Sea Wolf, the. 820
Seadragon 682
Seamonsters & Superheroes . . 789
Seaquest. 682
Searchers 789
Searchers: Apostle of Mercy . . 789
Season of the Reaper The:
   Winter 682
Season of the Witch 564
Sebastian 682
Sebastian O 142
Second Life of Dr. Mirage the . 682
Second Stage Turbine Blade . . 682
Secret Agent 682
Secret City Saga 682
Secret Defenders 309
Secret Files 789
Secret Files & Origins 142
Secret Files: the Strange Case . 790
Secret Hearts 142
Secret History of the Authority:
   Jack Hawksmoor 682
Secret History the 682
Secret Invasion 310
Secret Invasion: Fantastic Four 310
Secret Invasion: Front Line . . . 310
Secret Invasion: Inhumans . . . 310
Secret Invasion: Runaways/
   Young Avengers. 310
Secret Invasion: Spider-Man:
   Brand New Day 310
Secret Invasion: Thor 310
Secret Invasion: X-Men. 310
Secret Messages 790
Secret Missions 463
Secret Mysteries 391
Secret of the Salamander 522
Secret Origins 142
Secret Origins of Super-Villains 142
Secret Six 142
Secret Skull 682
Secret Society of Super-Heroes 142
Secret Squirrel 682
Secret Story Romances 310
Secret the 522
Secret War 310
Secret Wars. 310
Secret Wars II 310
Secret Weapons 682
Secret Weapons: Playing
   with Fire. 682
Secrets of Haunted House . . . 142
Secrets of Sinister House 143
Secrets of the Legion of Super-
   Heroes. 143
Secrets of the Valiant Universe. 682
Sectaurs 310
Section 8 790

Section Zero 564
Seduction of the Innocent 682
Seeker. 683, 790
Seeker 3000 310
Seekers into the Mystery. 143
Select Detective 463
Semi-Auto Angel: Second
   Heaven 790
Semper Fi 310
Sensation Comics 143, 144
Sensation Mystery. 144
Sensational Police Cases 463
Sensational Spider-Man 310
Sensational Spider-Man 278
Sensei 683
Sentinel 310, 790
Sentinel Squad O*n*e 310
Sentinels of Justice 683
Sentry 310
Sentry: Special 683
Sentry the 311
Seraphim 683
Seraphin 790
Serenity 522
Serenity Rose 790
Sergeant Barney Barker 311
Sergeant Bilko. 144
Sergeant Bilko's Pvt. Doberman 144
Sergeant Preston of the Yukon . 463
Sergio Aragones Actions Speak 522
Sergio Aragones Massacres
   Marvel 311
Sergio Aragones' Boogeyman . 522
Sergio Aragones' Day of
   the Dead 522
Sergio Aragones' Groo 522
Sergio Aragones' Groo & Rufferto
   522
Sergio Aragones' Groo:
   Death and Taxes 522
Sergio Aragones' Groo:
   Mightier than the Sword . . 522
[Sergio Aragone's] Groo the
   Wanderer 251
Sergio Aragones' Louder than
   Words 522
Sergio Stomps Star Wars 522
Serina 683
Serpentina 683
Seven Block. 311
Seven Brothers 683
Seven Seas Comics 463
Seven Sisters 683
Seven Soldiers 144
Seven Soldiers: Frankenstein . 144
Seven Soldiers: Guardian 144
Seven Soldiers: Klarion the
   Witch Boy 144
Seven Soldiers: Mister Miracle . 144
Seven Soldiers: Shining Knight. 144
Seven Soldiers: the Bulleteer . 144
Seven Soldiers: Zatanna 144
Seventh Shrine the 564, 683
Seventh System the 790
Sex and Affection 830
Sex Warrior 522
Sf Short Stories. 790
Sfa Spotlight 790
Sgt. Fury & His Howling
   Commandos. 311
Sgt. Rock. 132
Sgt. Rock Special 144
Sgt. Rock: the Lost Battalion. . . 144
Sgt. Rock: the Prophecy 144
Sgt. Rock's Prize Battle Tales . 144
Shade 144
Shade Special 683
Shade the 144
Shade the Changing Man 144
Shades of Blue 790
Shades of Gray Comics and
   Stories 790
Shado Song of the Dragon . . . 145
Shadow and Doc Savage, the . 523
Shadow and the
   Mysterious 3, the 523
Shadow Cabinet 145
Shadow Comics 463
Shadow Cross. 790
Shadow Empires: Faith
   Conqures. 523
Shadow Man 683

Shadow of Batman 145
Shadow of the Batman 145
Shadow of the Torturer the 683
Shadow Reavers. 683
Shadow Slasher 790
Shadow State 683
Shadow Strikes!, the 146
Shadow the 145, 522, 683
Shadow War of Hawkman. 146
Shadow's Fall 145
Shadowalker 790
Shadowdragon 145
Shadowflame. 683
Shadowgear 790
Shadowhawk. 564
Shadowhawk/Vampirella 564
Shadow: Hell's Heat Wave, the. 523
Shadowhunt Special 564
Shadow: in the Coils of
  Leviathan, the 523
Shadowman 683
Shadowmancer 683
Shadowmasters. 311
Shadowpact. 145
Shadowplay. 683
Shadowriders. 311
Shadows 564
Shadows & Light 311
Shaiana 684
Shaman's Tears. 564
Shanda [The Panda] 790
Shang-Chi: Master of Kung Fu . 312
Shanghaied 790
Shangri-La. 564
Shanna the She Devil: Survival
  of the Fittest. 312
Shanna the She-Devil 312
Shaolin 684
Shaolin Cowboy 684
Shards. 790
Shark-Man. 564, 684
Sharky 565
Sharp Comics 464
Shatter. 684
Shattered Earth 790
Shattered Image 565
Shatterpoint. 790
Shaun of the Dead 684
Shaun the Sheep 684
Shazam/Superman: First
  Thunder 146
Shazam: the Monster Society
  of Evil. 146
Shazam the New Beginning . . . 146
Shazam! 146
Shazam! Family 146
She Hulk: Ceremony. 312
She-Hulk 312, 565, 684, 790
Sheba 790
Sheena 312, 684
Sheena: Queen of the Jungle . . 684
Sheena, Queen of the Jungle . . 464
Sheriff of Tombstone 684
Sherlock Holmes. . . . 146, 464, 791
Sherlock Holmes & Kolchak the
  Night Stalker: Cry of
  Thunder 684
Sherlock Holmes Casebook . . . 791
Sherlock Holmes: Chronicles of
  Crime and Mystery 791
Sherlock Holmes: Hound of the
  Baskervilles 791
Sherlock Holmes: Mark of
  the Beast 791
Sherlock Holmes Mysteries. . . . 791
Sherlock Holmes of the '30's . . 791
Sherlock Holmes Reader 791
Sherlock Holmes: Return of
  the Devil. 791
Sherlock Junior 791
Sherry the Showgirl. 312
Shi 791
Shi (The Way of the Warrior) . . 684
Shi: Jun-Nen 523
Shi: Sempo 791
Shi: the Illustrated Warrior. . . . 791
Shidima 565
Shield 312
Shield The: Spotlight 684
Shield-Wizard Comics 464
Shinobi 523
Ship Ahoy 464

Ship of Fools 565, 791
Shock Detective Cases. 392
Shock Illustrated 464
Shock Suspense Stories. 685
Shock Suspenstories 464
Shock the Monkey 685, 791
Shocking Mystery Cases. 480
Shockrockets. 565
Shogun Warriors 312
Shon C. Bury's Nox. 685
Shonen Jump 791
Short Order Comix 830
Shotgun Mary 685
Shotgun Wedding 685
Shoujo. 791
Showcase 146
Showcase '93 147
Showcase '94 147
Showcase '95 147
Showcase '96 147
Showgirls. 313
Shred. 791
Shrek. 523
Shriek 791
Shroud 313
Shrugged 685
Shuriken: Cold Steel 791
Shuriken Team-Up. 791
Shut up & Die 565
Sick 685
Siege 565
Siegel & Shuster 685, 791
Sigil 685
Sigma 565
Silas Mariner 818
Silbuster 791
Silencers the 565, 685
Silent Dragon 685
Silent Ghost. 685
Silent Hill 685
Silent Invasion. 792
Silent Invasion: Abductions . . . 792
Silent Mobius. 685, 792
Silent Mobius II 685
Silent Mobius III. 685
Silent Rapture 792
Silent Screamers 565
Silent War 313
Silke 523
Silken Ghost the 686
Silly Daddy 792
Silly Tunes 313
Silver Age 147
Silver Age DC Classics 147
Silver Cross. 686
Silver Sable 313
Silver Star 565
Silver Storm. 686, 792
Silver Streak Comics. 464
Silver Surfer 313, 314
Silver Surfer: in Thy Name . . . 314
Silver Surfer: Loftier
  than Mortals. 314
Silver Surfer: Requiem 314
Silver Surfer/Superman. 314
Silver Surfer Vs. Dracula. 314
Silver Surfer/Warlock:
  Resurrection 314
Silver Surfer/Weapon Zero 314
Silverback 686
Silverblade. 147
Silverhawks 313
Silverheels. 686
Silvers Log Of. . .) Sea
  Hound, the. 463
Simon Dark 147
Simon/Kirby Reader 792
Simpsons Comics 686
Simpsons Comics & Stories . . . 686
Simpsons/Futurama Crossover
  Crisis 686
Sin City: 523
Sin City: a Dame to Kill for . . . 523
Sin City: Hell and Back 523
Sin City: Just Another Saturday
  Night 523
Sin City: That Yellow Bastard . 523
Sin City: the Big Fat Kill 523
Sinbad. 792
Sinbad: House of God. 792
Sinbad Jr. 686

Single Series 465
Singularity Seven 686
Sinister House of Secret Love . 143
Sinnamon 792
Sins of the Fallen: the
  Nightstalker 686
Sins of Youth 147
Sinthia 686
Sir Apropos of Nothing 686
Sire the 686
Siren 565, 686
Sister Armageddon 792
Sisterhood of Steel 314
Sisterhood the. 686
Sisters of Mercy 686
Six from Sirius 314
Six from Sirius II 314
Six Gun Heroes. 465
Six Million Dollar Man the 686
Six String Samurai 686
Six-Gun Western. 314, 686
Skaar: Son of Hulk 314
Skateman 686
Skeleton Hand. 465
Skeleton Key 792
Skeleton Warriors 314
Skin 13 792
Skin Graft 147
Skinners 565
Skippy's Own Book of Comics . 465
Skrull Kill Crew 314
Skrulls 315
Skrulls Vs. Power Pack. 315
Skull and Bones 147
Skull Comics 830
Skull Man 792
Skull the Slayer 315
Skunk/Foodang 792
Skunk the 792
Sky Blazers 465
Sky Doll 315
Sky Pilot 465
Sky Rocket 465
Sky Sharks 686
Sky Sheriff 465
Sky Wolf 687
Skye Runner 686
Skyman 465
Skynn & Bones: Deadly Angels 792
Skynn & Bones: Flesh for
  Fantasy 792
Slack 792
Slacker Comics 792
Slaine 687
Slaine the Berserker 687
Slaine the Horned God 687
Slam-Bang Comics 465
Slapstick 315
Slapstick Comics 466
Slash Maraud 147
Slash-D Doublecross. 466
Slaughter. 687
Slaughterhouse 792
Slaughterman 792
Slave Girl Comics 466
Slayers 792
Slayers: Super Explosive
  Demon Story 792
Sledge Hammer 315
Sleeper 687
Sleepwalker. 315
Sleeze Brothers. 315
Slick Chick Comics 466
Sliders 687
Sliders: Darkest Hour 687
Sliders: Ultimatum. 687
Slimer 687
Slingers 315
Slow Death 830
Slow Death Funnies 830
Sludge 687
Slugger 466
Small Gods 565
Smallville. 147
Smash Comics 147, 466
Smash Hits Sports Comics 466
Smax. 147, 687
Smile 792, 830
Smiley 687
Smiley Burnette Western 466
Smilin' Jack 466
Smith Brown Jones 792

Smith Brown Jones: Alien
  Accountant. 793
Smitty 466
Smoke 687
Smoke & Mirror 687
Smoke and Mirror 687
Smokey Bear. 687
Smurfs. 315
Snagglepuss 687
Snak Posse 687
Snake Eyes Declassified. 687
Snake Plissken Chronicles 687
Snaked 687
Snakes on a Plane 687
Snakewoman. 687
Snap 462
Snappy Comics 466
Snarf 830
Snatch Comics 831
Snatch Sampler. 831
Sniffy the Pup 466
Snooper and Blabber
  Detectives 687
Snow White & Seven Dwarfs
  Golden Anniversary 688
Snow White & the Seven
  Dwarfs 687
Snowman 793
Snowman: 1994 793
Snowman: Dead & Dying 793
Snowman: Horror Show 793
Snowman2 793
Snowybrook Inn 688
So Dark the Rose 688
Soap Opera Love 688
Soap Opera Romances. 688
Sob: Special Operations Branch 793
Sock Monkey 523
Sock Monkey: the Inches
  Incident 523
Socketeer 793
Sojourn 688
Sojourn/Lady Death 688
Solar: Hell on Earth. 688
Solar Lord 565
Solar: Man of the Atom 688
Solarman 315
Sold out 793
Solders of Fortune. 822
Soldier and Marine Comics. . . . 466
Soldier Comics 466
Soldier X 315
Soldiers of Fortune 467
Solitaire 688
Sollitaria. 688
Solo 148, 315, 523
Solo Avengers 315
Solo Ex-Mutants 793
Solomon Kane 315, 523, 688
Solus 688
Solution 688
Some New Kind of Slaughter . . 688
Somerset Holmes 688
Something Different. 793
Something Wicked 565
Son of Ambush Bug 148
Son of M 316
Son of Satan 316
Son of Sinbad 467
Son of Vulcan 148
Sonambulo: Sleep of the Just. . 793
Song of Hiawatha, the. 818
Song of the Cid 793
Song of the Sirens 793
Sonic Disruptors 148
Sonic Quest: the Death Egg
  Saga 688
Sonic Super Special 688
Sonic the Hedgehog 688
Sonic the Hedgehog Presents
  Knuckles Chastic. 688
Sonic the Hedgehog Presents
  Tails 688
Sonic X 689
Sonic's Friendly Nemesis:
  Knuckles 688
Sorrow 565
Soul 793
Soul of a Samurai. 565
Soul Reaver: Legacy of Kain . . 565
Soul Saga 565
Soulcatcher 689

Soulfire 689, 793
Soulman 689
Soulsearchers and Co. 793
Soulwind 565
Soupy Sales Comic Book 689
Southern Knights. 793
Southern Squadron 793
Southern Squadron Freedom
  of Info Act. 793
Sovereign Seven 148
Soviet Super Soldiers 316
Space: 1999 689
Space: above and Beyond 689
Space Action 467
Space Adventures 467, 689
Space Ark 689, 793
Space Beaver 793
Space Busters 467
Space Circus 523
Space Comics 417
Space Detective 467
Space Family Robinson 689
Space Ghost 148, 689
Space Giants the. 689
Space Invaders Comics, Don
  Chin's. 831
Space Man 689
Space Mouse 467
Space Patrol 467, 793
Space Pinchy 523
Space Squadron 316
Space Thrillers 467
Space Usagi 523, 689, 794
Space War. 689
Space Western Comics. 497
Space Wolf 794
Space Worlds 316
Spaced 793
Spacehawk 523
Spaceknights 316
Spaceman. 316
Spandex Tights 794
Spandex Tights Presents:
  Space Opera 794
Spandex Tights Presents:
  the Girls of '95 794
Spandex Tights Presents:
  Win a Dream Date with
  Spandex-Girl 794
Spandex Tights: the Lost Issues 794
Spank the Monkey 794
Spank the Monkey on the
  Comic Market 794
Sparkle Comics 467
Sparkler Comics 467
Sparkling Stars 468
Sparkman 468
Sparkplug 794
Sparkplug Special 794
Sparks 689
Sparky Watts 468
Sparrow. 794
Spartan: Warrior Spirit. 565
Spartan X 565
Spasm! 831
Spawn 565
Spawn: Architects of Fear 566
Spawn/Batman 566
Spawn Bible 567
Spawn Blood Feud 566
Spawn Godslayer 567
Spawn: the Dark Ages 567
Spawn the Impaler 567
Spawn: the Undead. 567
Spawn/Wildc.A.T.S 567
Speak of the Devil. 523
Special Collector's Edition. . . . 316
Special Comics 435
Special Edition 148
Special Edition Comics 468
Special Education 689
Special Forces 567
Special Marvel Edition. 316
Special War Series 690
Species 523, 690
Species: Human Race 523
Spectacular Features Magazine 468
Spectacular Scarlet Spider . . . 316
Spectacular Spider-Man . . 316, 317
Spectacular Stories Magazine . 468
Specter 7. 690
Spectre the 148, 149

Specwar 690
Speed Buggy. 690
Speed Comics. 468
Speed Demon 192
Speed Demons 690
Speed Force 149
Speed Racer 690
Speed Racer: Chronicles
  of the Racer. 690
Speed Racer Classics. 794
Speed Racer: the next
  Generation: Birthright 690
Speed Smith the Hot Rod King. 469
Speedball 317
Spellbinders 317, 690
Spellbound 317
Spellgame 690
Spelljammer 149
Spencer Spook 794
Spicy Tales 794
Spider 690
Spider Kiss 794
Spider: Reign of the Vampire
  King 690
Spider-Boy 192, 318-323, 690
Spider-Man Vs. Dracula 322
Spider-Man Vs. Venom 322
Spider-Man Vs. Wolverine 322
Spidey and the Mini Marvels. . 323
Spidey Super Stories 323
Spike 690
Spine-Tingling Tales 690
Spineless Man. 794
Spiral Path. 690
Spirit of the Amazon 690
Spirit of the Tao 567
Spirit of Wonder 523
Spirit, the 149, 690, 794
Spirit the: the New Adventures 690
Spirit The: the Origin Years . . . 794
Spiritman 469
Spirits 794
Spitfire 469
Spitfire and the Troubleshooters 323
Spitfire Comics 469
Spittin' Image. 794
Splitting Image 567
Spoof. 323
Spook Comics 469
Spook Detective Cases. 392
Spook Suspense and Mystery . 393
Spooks 691
Spooks: Omega Team. 691
Spooky 469
Spooky Haunted House 691
Spooky Mysteries 469
Spooky Spooktown 691
Spooner. 691
Sport Comics. 485
Sport Stars 323
Sports Action 323
Sports Stars 469
Sports Thrills 396
Spotlight 323
Spotlight Comics 469
Springheeled Jack. 691
Spumco Comic Book. 323
Spunky 470
Spy and Counterspy 470
Spy Cases. 268
Spy Fighters 323
Spy Smasher. 470
Spy, the 818
Spy Thrillers 323
Spy-Hunters 470
Spyboy 523
Spyboy 13: the M.A.N.G.A. Affair
  524
Spyboy: Final Exam 524
Spyboy/Young Justice. 524
Spyke 323
Spyman 691
Squad the 691
Squadron Supreme 323
Squadron Supreme: Hyperion
  Vs. Nighthawk 323
Squalor 691
Squee 794
St. George. 308
Stain 794
Stainless Steel Armidillo 794

Stainless Steel Rat 691
Stalker 149
Stalkers 324
Stamps Comics 470
Stan Lee Meets. 324
Stan Shaw's Beauty &
  the Beast 524
Stand The: Captain Trips 324
Stanley & His Monster. 84
Stanley & His Monster. 149
Star 567
Star Blazers. 691
Star Bleech the Generation Gap 794
Star Comics. 470
Star Comics Magazine 324
Star Crossed 149
Star Hawks 795
Star Hunters 149
Star Kid 524
Star Master 324
Star Masters 692
Star Ranger 470
Star Ranger Funnies 470
Star Rangers 795
Star Reach 795
Star Reach Classics 692
Star Slammers 524, 692
Star Spangled Comics . . 150, 152
Star Spangled War Stories 151
Star Studded 470
Star Trek 152, 324, 692
Star Trek: 692, 693
Star Trek: Deep Space Nine 324,
  692
Star Trek: Deep Space Nine
  N-Vector. 693
Star Trek: Early Voyages 324
Star Trek: Starfleet Academy . . 324
Star Trek: the Modala Imperative
  152
Star Trek: the next Generation . 152
Star Trek: the next Generation 693
Star Trek: the next Generation
  Deep Space Nine 153
Star Trek: the next Generation
  III Wind. 153
Star Trek the next Generation
  Modala Imperative. 153
Star Trek: the next Generation
  Riker Special 324
Star Trek the next Generation
  Shadowheart 153
Star Trek: the next Generation/
  X-Men: Second Contact . . 324
Star Trek: the Untold Voyages . 324
Star Trek: Unlimited. 324
Star Trek: Voyager 324, 693
Star Trek: Voyager Planet Killer 693
Star Trek: Voyager: Splashdown 324
Star Trek/X-Men 324
Star Trek: Year Four 693
Star Wars 324, 524
Star Wars: a New Hope Special
  Edition 524
Star Wars: a Valentine Story . . 528
Star Wars: Boba Fett 524
Star Wars: Boba Fett Enemy
  of the Empire 524
Star Wars: Bounty Hunters . . . 524
Star Wars: Chewbacca 524
Star Wars: Clone Wars 524
Star Wars: Crimson Empire . . . 525
Star Wars: Dark Empire 525
Star Wars Dark Empire II 525
Star Wars: Dark Force Rising . . 525
Star Wars: Dark Times 525
Star Wars: Darth Maul. 525
Star Wars: Droids 525
Star Wars: Empire. 525
Star Wars: Empire's End. 525
Star Wars: Episode I the
  Phantom Menace 525
Star Wars Episode II Attack
  of the Clones 525
Star Wars: Episode III Revenge
  of the Sith 525
Star Wars: General Grievous . . 525
Star Wars Handbook. 526
Star Wars: Heir to the Empire. . 526
Star Wars in 3-D 693
Star Wars: Infinities a
  New Hope 526

Star Wars: Infinities Return
  of the Jedi 526
Star Wars: Infinities the Empire
  Strikes Back. 526
Star Wars: Jabba the Hutt . . . 526
Star Wars: Jango Fett 526
Star Wars: Jango Fett Open
  Seasons. 526
Star Wars: Jedi 526
Star Wars: Jedi Academy
  Leviathan 526
Star Wars: Jedi Council Acts
  of War 526
Star Wars: Jedi Quest. 526
Star Wars: Jedi Vs. Sith 526
Star Wars: Knights of the Old
  Republic. 526
Star Wars Legacy 526
Star Wars: Mara Jade by the
  Emperor's Hand. 526
Star Wars: Obsession. 526
Star Wars: Purge. 526
Star Wars: Qui-Gon & Obi-Wan
  Last Stand on Ord
  Mantell 526, 527
Star Wars: Rebellion 527
Star Wars: Return of Tag & Bink 527
Star Wars: River of Chaos . . . 527
Star Wars: Shadow Stalker. . . . 527
Star Wars: Shadows of the
  Empire 527
Star Wars: Shadows of the
  Empire Evolution 527
Star Wars: Splinter of the
  Mind's Eye 527
Star Wars: Starfighter
  Crossbones 527
Star Wars: Tag & Bink Are Dead 527
Star Wars Tales 527
Star Wars: Tales from Mos
  Eisley. 527
Star Wars: Tales of the Jedi . . 527
Star Wars: Tales of the Jedi:
  Dark Lords of the Sith 527
Star Wars: Tales of the Jedi
  Redemption 527
Star Wars: Tales of the Jedi
  the Golden Age of the Sith 527
Star Wars: Tales of the Jedi: the
  Freedon Nadd Uprising . . . 527
Star Wars: Tales of the Jedi:
  the Sith War. 527
Star Wars: Tales of the Jedi
  the Fall of the Sith Empire. 527
Star Wars: the Last Command . 526
Star Wars: the Protocol
  Offensive 526
Star Wars: the Return of
  the Jedi 527
Star Wars: Underworld the
  Yavin Vassilika 527
Star Wars: Union. 527
Star Wars: Vader's Quest 528
Star Wars: X-Wing Rogue
  Leader 528
Star Wars: Zam Wesell 528
Star Western 795
Star-Lord Special Edition 324
Starblast 324
Starblazers 691
Starbrand 324
Starchild 794
Starchild: Crossroads 794
Starchild: Mythopolis 567
Stardust Kid 691
Stardust Kid the. 567
Starfall 567
Starfire. 149
Starforce Six Special. 691
Stargate. 691
Stargate: Atlantis 794
Stargate Atlantis: Wraithfall . . . 691
Stargate: Doomsday World . . . 691
Stargate: One Nation under Ra 794
Stargate: Rebellion 794
Stargate Sg 1 691
Stargate: the New Adventures
  Collection 794
Stargate: Underworld 795
Stargods 691
Starjammers 324
Stark: Future 795

Stark Raven 691
Starkweather 692
Starkweather: Immortal 692
Starlet O'Hara in Hollywood . . . 470
Starlight Agency 795
Starlord 324
Starman 149
Starriors 324
Stars and S.T.R.I.P.E. 150
Stars and Stripes Comics 470
Starship Troopers 524, 692
Starship Troopers: Brute
   Creations 524
Starship Troopers: Dominant
   Species 524
Starship Troopers: Insect Touch 524
Starslayer 692
Starslayer Directors Cut 692
Starstruck 324
Starstruck: the Expanding
   Universe 524
Startling Comics 470
Startling Stories: the Incorrigible
   Hulk 324
Startling Stories: the Thing Night
   Falls on Yancy St. 324
Startling Terror Tales 471
Starwatchers 693
Static 153, 795
Static Shock!: Rebirth of the
   Cool 153
Static-X 693
Station 693
Stay Puffed 567
Stealth Force 795
Stealth Squad 693, 795
Steampunk 693
Steed & Mrs. Peel 693
Steel 153
Steel City Hawk 693
Steel Claw 693
Steel Sterling 693
Steel the Indestructible Man . . . 153
Steele Destines 795
Steelgrip Starkey 325
Steeltown Rockers 325
Stephen Colbert's Tek Jansen . . 694
Steve Canyon 795
Steve Canyon 3-D. 694
Steve Canyon Comics 471
Steve Ditko's Strange Avenging
   Tales 795
Steve Grant's Mortal Souls 795
Steve Grant's My Flesh Is Cool 795
Steve Niles' Strange Cases . . . 567
Steve Roper 471
Steve Rude's the Moth 528
Steve Zodiac & the Fireball XI-5 694
Steven 795
Stickboy 795
Stig's Inferno 795
Sting of the Green Hornet 694
Stinz 795
Stitch 795
Stoker's Dracula 325
Stone 567
Stone Cold Steve Austin 694
Stoned Picture Parade 831
Stories by Famous Authors
   Illustrated 403
Stories of Romance 325
Storm 325
Stormbreaker: the Saga of
   Beta Ray Bill 325
Stormbringer 795
Stormbringers 694
Storming Paradise 694
Stormquest 694
Stormwatch 567, 568
Stormwatch: Phd. 694
Stormwatch Phd: Armageddon . 694
Stormwatch: Team Achilles 694
Stormwatcher 795
Story of Harry S. Truman, the . . 471
Straight Arrow 471
Stranded the 694
Strange 325
Strange Adventures 153, 155
Strange Behavior 795
Strange Brew 795
Strange Cases 568
Strange Combat Tales 325

Strange Confessions 471
Strange Days 694
Strange Embrace 568
Strange Fantasy 471
Strange Girl 568
Strange Heroes 795
Strange Journey 471
Strange Mysteries 471
Strange Sports Stories . . . 155, 795
Strange Stories from Another
   World 472
Strange Stories of Suspense . . 307
Strange Suspense Stories
   . . . . 436, 472, 694
Strange Suspense Stories/
   Captain Atom 694
Strange Tales 325, 326
Strange Tales: Dark Corners. . . 326
Strange Tales of the Unusual . . 326
Strange Terrors 472
Strange Weather Lately 795
Strange World of Your Dreams . 472
Strange Worlds 326, 472, 796
Strangehaven 795
Strangelove 796
Strangers 568
Strangers in Paradise . . . 568, 795
Strangers the 694
Strangeways 796
Strata 796
Straw Men 694, 796
Strawberry Shortcake 326
Stray Bullets 796
Stray Toasters 326
Street Angel 796
Street Fighter 568, 694, 796
Street Fighter II 694, 796
Street Fighter Legends: Sakura 695
Street Fighter Remix 694
Street Heroes 2005 796
Street Music 796
Street Poet Ray 796
Street Sharks 695
Street Wolf 796
Streets 155
Streets of Glory 695
[Steve Saunders] Special Agent 468
Strictly Private 472
Strike! 695
Strikeback 695
Strikeback! 568
Strikeforce America 695
Strikeforce Morituri 326
Striker: Secret of the Berserker. 796
Striker: the Armored Warrior . . . 796
Strong Guy Reborn 327
Strongarm 568
Stronghold 796
Strontium Dog 695
Stryfe's Strike File 327
Stryke 695
Strykeforce 568
Students of the Unusual 796
Stumbo Tinytown 695
Stuntman Comics 472
Stupid Comics 568
Stupid Heroes 695
Stupid Stupid Rat Tails: the
   Adventures of Big
   Johnson Bone 796
Stygmata 797
Sub-Mariner 327, 328
Subculture 797
Subhuman 528
Subspecies 695
Subtle Violents 797
Suburban Glamour 568
Suburban Jersey Ninja
   She-Devils 328
Subvert Comics 831
Sudden Gravity 797
Sugar & Spike 155
Sugar Bowl Comics 472
Sugar Buzz 797
Sugar Ray Finhead 797
Suicide Squad 156
Suicide Squad: Raise the Flag . 156
Sullengray 695
Sultry Teenage Super-Foxes . . 797
Sun Fun Komiks 472
Sun Girl 328
Sun Glasses after Dark 695

Sun-Runners 695
Sundown 695
Sunfire & Big Hero 6 328
Sunny, America's Sweetheart . . 472
Sunset Carson 472, 695
Super 695
Super Bad James Dynomite . . 695
Super Book of Comics 472
Super Circus 473
Super Comics 473
Super Crazy Tnt Blast 695
Super DC Giant 158
Super Duck Comics 473
Super Friends 158, 159
Super Funnies 474
Super Fxxxxxs 695
Super Goof 695
Super Hero Happy Hour 797
Super Heroes Battle Super
   Gorilla 160
Super Heroes Versus
   Supervillians 695
Super Magician Comics 474
Super Manga Blast 528
Super Mario Bros. 695
Super Powers 171
Super Rabbit 328
Super Real 696
Super Soldier: Man of War . . . 192
Super Soldiers 328
Super Spy 475
Super Teen*topia 696
Super Western Comics 475
Super Western Funnies 474
Super-Team Family . . . .
   . 172, 192, 328, 473, 474, 568
Superbabes: Femforce 695
Superboy 156-158
Superboy & the Legion of
   Super-Heroes 157
Superboy & the Ravers 158
Superboy plus 158
Superboy/Risk Double-Shot . . 158
Superboy's Legion. 158
Supercar 695
Supercops 695
Supergirl 159
Supergirl and the Legion of
   Superheroes 117
Superheroes 695
Superhuman Samurai Syber
   Squad 695
[Super Information Hijinks:]
   Reality Check! 673
Superior Stories 474
Superman 160, 164
Superman (Miniature) 164
Superman & Batman: Generations
   an Imaginary Tale 167
Superman & Batman:
   Generations II 167
Superman & Batman:
   Generations III 167
Superman & Batman vs
   Aliens & Predators. 167
Superman & Batman vs
   Vampires and Werewolves 167
Superman & Batman: World's
   Funnest 167
Superman & Bugs Bunny 167
Superman Adventures 166
Superman and the Great
   Cleveland Fire 164
Superman/Batman 166
Superman: Birthright 167
Superman Confidential 167
Superman: Day of Doom. 167
Superman/Doomsday: Hunter/
   Prey 167
Superman Family 169
Superman for All Seasons 167
Superman/Gen13 167
Superman: Last Son of Earth . . 167
Superman/Madman Hullabaloo. 528
Superman: Metropolis 167
Superman: New Krypton
   Special 169
Superman Record Comic 164
Superman: Red Son 169
Superman Returns 169
Superman: Save the Planet . . . 171
Superman: Secret Identity. 169

Superman: Silver Banshee . . . 169
Superman Spectacular 164
Superman: Strength 171
Superman/Supergirl: Maelstrom 171
Superman/Tarzan: Sons of the
   Jungle 528
Superman: the Dark Side 167
Superman: the Doomsday Wars 167
Superman: the Man of Steel . . . 168
Superman: the Man
   of Tomorrow. 168
Superman the Secret Years . . . 171
Superman Vs. Aliens. 528
Superman Vs. Aliens II 528
Superman Vs. Amazing
   Spider-Man 171
Superman Vs. Predator. 171
Superman Vs. The Terminator:
   Death to the Future 528
Superman/Wonder Woman:
   Whom Gods Destroy 171
Superman Workbook. 164
Superman's Buddy 164
Superman's Christmas
   Adventure 164
Superman's Girl Friend Lois
   Lane. 169
Superman's Nemesis
   Lex Luthor 169
Superman's Pal Jimmy Olsen . . 170
Superman's Pal Jimmy Olsen
   Special 171
Superman-Tim Store Pamphlets 164
Supermarket 695
Supermen of America 171
Supermodels in the Rainforest . 797
Supermouse 474
Supernatural Freak Machine. . . 696
Supernatural: Origins 696
Supernatural: Rising Son 696
Supernatural Thrillers 328
Supernaturals 328
Supernaut 696
Superpatriot: America's Fighting
   Force 568
Superpatriot: War on Terror. . . 568
Supersnipe Comics 474
Superstar: as Seen on Tv 568
Superswine 797
Superworld Comics 475
Suprema/Supreme Sacrifice . . 696
Supreme 568, 696
Supreme: Glory Days 569
Supreme Power 328
Supreme Power: Hyperion 328
Supreme Power: Nighthawk . . . 328
Supreme: the Return. 696
Sure-Fire 436
Surf 'N' Wheels 696
Surge. 696
Surprise Adventures 483
Surrogate Savior 797
Surrogates. 696
Survivalist Chronicles 797
Survivors 696
Suspense 328
Suspense Comics 475
Suspense Detective 475
Suspira: the Great Working. . . . 696
Suzie Comics 483
Swamp Thing 172
Swan 797
Sweeney 475
Sweet Childe Battle Book 797
Sweet Childe: Lost Confessions 797
Sweet Lucy 797
Sweet Sixteen 475
Sweethearts 386
Swerve 797
Swift Arrow 475
Swiftsure 797
Swiss Family Robinson 817
Switch B.L.A.Z.E. Manga 797
Sword of Damocles 569
Sword of Dracula 569
Sword of Dracula/Vampirella:
   Extended and Dangerous . 696
Sword of Red Sonja The:
   Doom of the Gods 696
Sword of Sorcery. 173
Sword of the Atom. 173
Sword of Valor. 696, 797

Sword the 569
Swords and Science 797
Swords of Cerebus 797
Swords of Shar-Pai 797
Swords of Texas 696
Swords of the Swashbucklers . . 329
Swords of Valors: Robin Hood . 797
Sylvia Faust 569
Symbiotes the 696
Symbols of Justice 696
Syn 528
Syphons 696
Syphons: Countdown 696
Syphons: the Stargate
    Stratagem 696
System Seven 797

T T T T

T.H.U.N.D.E.R. Agents 701
T-Man 481, 698
Tad Williams Burning Man 696
Taffy 475
Tag 696
Tag: Cursed 696
Tailgunner Jo 173
Tailspin 475
Taken under Compendium . . . 797
Takion 173
Tale of One Bad Rat 528
Talent 696
Tales Calculated to Drive You
    Bats 697
Tales from the Aniverse 797
Tales from the Bog 797
Tales from the Bully Pulpit 569
Tales from the Crypt . . . 392, 697
Tales from the Edge 797
Tales from the Great Book 475
Tales from the Heart 797
Tales from Wonderland 697
Tales of Alvin Maker: Red
    Prophet 697
Tales of Asgard 329
Tales of Bloody Mary 697
Tales of Evil 697
Tales of G.I. Joe 329
Tales of Horror 475
Tales of Jace Pearson of the
    Texas Rangers 426
Tales of Justice 266
Tales of Leonardo 798
Tales of Midnight 697
Tales of Ordinary Madness 528
Tales of Penance: Trial of the
    Century 697
Tales of Raphael: Bad Moon
    Rising 798
Tales of Sex & Death 831
Tales of Suspense 329
Tales of Suspense: Captain
    America/Iron Man 329
Tales of Tellos 569
Tales of Tellos: Maiden Voyage . 569
Tales of Terror 475, 697
Tales of Terror Annual 476
Tales of the Age of Apocalypse . 329
Tales of the Age of Apocalypse:
    Sinister Bloodline 329
Tales of the Beanworld 798
Tales of the Champions 697
Tales of the Darkness 569
Tales of the Fear Agents:
    Twelve Steps in One 528
Tales of the Fehrnik 798
Tales of the Green Beret 697
Tales of the Green Hornet 697
Tales of the Green
    Lantern Corps 173
Tales of the Jackalope 798
Tales of the Legion of Super
    Heroes 173
Tales of the Marines 233
Tales of the Marvels:
    Blockbuster 329
Tales of the Marvels: Inner
    Demons 329
Tales of the Marvels: Wonder
    Years 329
Tales of the Mysterious Traveler 697
Tales of the New Teen Titans . . 173
Tales of the Ninja Warriors 798
Tales of the Plague 798

Tales of the Realm 697
Tales of the Sinestro Corps
    Presents 173
Tales of the Sun Runners 697
Tales of the Sunrunners 798
Tales of the Teen Titans 127
Tales of the Teenage Mutant
    Ninja Turtles 798
Tales of the Unexpected . . 173, 175
Tales of the Vampires 528
Tales of the Witchblade 569
Tales of the Zombie 329
Tales to Astonish 329, 330
Tales to Offend 528
Tales Too Terrible to Tell 798
Talespin 697
Taleweaver 697
Talisman, the 821
Talismen 697
Tall Tails 798
Tall Tales of Vishnu Sharma
    The: Panchatantra 697
Tally-Ho Comics 476
Tangent '98 175
Tangent Comics 175
Tangent Comics: Superman's
    Reign 175
Tangled Web 330
Tank Girl 175, 528
Tank Girl: Apocalypse 175
Tank Girl: the Gifting 697
Tank Girl: the Odyssey 175
Tank Girl: Visions of Booga 697
Tantalizing Stories 798
Taoland 698, 798
Taoland Adventures 698
Target Airboy 698
Target Comics 476
Target Western Romances 476
Targitt 698
Tarot Witch of the Black Rose . . 698
Tarzan 175, 330, 476
Tarzan Family 175
Tarzan/John Carter: Warlords
    of Mars 528
Tarzan Lord of the Jungle 698
Tarzan: Love Lies and the
    Lost City 698
Tarzan of the Apes 330, 698
Tarzan: the Beckoning 698
Tarzan the Warrior 698
Tarzan Vs. Predator at the
    Earth's Core 528
Task Force 1 569
Task Force Alpha 798
Taskmaster 330
Tasmanian Devil & His Tasty
    Friends 698
Tastee-Freez Comics 698
Tattered Banners 175
Team 1: Stormwatch 569
Team 1: Wildc.A.T.S 569
Team 7 569
Team 7: Dead Reaconing 569
Team 7 Objective: Hell 569
Team America 331
Team Anarchy 698
Team Helix 331
Team Nippon 798
Team Titans 175
Team X 2000 331
Team X/Team 7 331
Team Yankee 698
Team Youngblood 569
Team Zero 698
Tech Jacket 570
Technophilia 798
[Ted McKeever's] Metropol . . . 286
Teen Beat 175
Teen Comics 195
Teen Confessions 699
Teen Life 498
Teen Secret Diary 699
Teen Titans 175
Teen Titans East 176
Teen Titans Go! 176
Teen Titans Spotlight 176
Teen Titans: Year One 176
Teen-Age Romances 476, 477, 698
Teena 476
Teenage Hotrodders 698

Teenage Mutant Ninja
    Turtles 570, 698, 699
Teenage Mutant Ninja
    Turtles Adventures 699
Teenage Mutant Ninja
    Turtles Animated 699
Teenage Mutant Ninja
    Turtles/Flaming Carrot 699
Teenage Mutant Ninja Turtles:
    the Movie Adaptation 798
Teenage Mutant Ninja Turtles:
    the Movie Prequel 798
Teenage Mutant Ninja Turtles* . 798
Teenage Romance 290
Teenie Weenies, the 477
Tegra, Jungle Empress 499
Tekken 2 699
Tekken Forever 570
Tekken Saga 570
Television Comics 477
Television Puppet Show 477
Tell it to the Marines 477
Tellos 570
Tempest 176, 699
Tempest Comics Presents 798
Templar Chronicles The: the
    Heretic 699
Temporary 798
Tempus Fugitive 176
Tense Suspense 699
Tenth the 570
Tenth The: Black Embrace 570
Tenth The: Evil's Child 570
Tenth The: Nightwalker 528
Tenth The: Resurrected 528
Terminal City 176
Terminal City: Aerial Graffiti . . . 176
Terminal Point 529
Terminator 529
Terminator 2 331
Terminator 2: Cybernetic Dawn . 700
Terminator 2: Infinity 700
Terminator 2: Nuclear Twilight . . 700
Terminator 3 700
Terminator: End Game 529
Terminator: Enemy Within 529
Terminator: Hunters & Killers . . 529
Terminator the 529, 699
Terminator The: the Dark Years 529
Terra 177
Terra Obscura 700
Terraformers 700
Terranauts 700
Terrarists 331
Terrific Comics 424, 477
Terrifying Tales 477
Territory 51 700
Territory the 529
Terror Illustrated 477
Terror Inc 331
Terror on the Planet of the Apes 799
Terror Titans 177
Terrors of the Jungle 477
Terry & the Pirates 799
Terry and the Pirates 477, 799
Terry Moore's Paradise Too . . . 799
Terry-Bears Comics 477
Tessie the Typist 331
Testament 177
Tex Avery's Droopy 529
Tex Avery's Screwball Squirrel . 529
Tex Benson 799
Tex Dawson Gunslinger 331
Tex Farrell 478
Tex Granger 383
Tex Morgan 331
Tex Ritter Western 478
Tex Taylor 331
Texan, the 700
Texas Chainsaw Massacre 700
Texas Chainsaw Massacre: the
    Grind 700
Texas Kid 331
Texas Rangers in Action 700
Texas Strangers 570
Thanos 331
Thanos Quest 331, 332
That Wilkin Boy 700
Thespian 177
They Were 11 799
Thieves and Kings 799

Thing from Another World:
    Climate of Fear 529
Thing from Another World:
    Eternal Vows 529
Thing/She-Hulk 332
Thing the 332, 529
Thing The: Freakshow 332
Thing!, the 478
Third Degree 799
Third World War 700
Thirteen O'clock 529
Thirteen Steps 799
This Is Suspense 436
This Is Suspense! 472
This Is War 478
This Magazine Is Haunted 387, 478
Thor 334, 335
Thor: Blood Oath 335
Thor Corps 335
Thor: Godstorm 335
Thor: Son of Asgard 335
Thor the Mighty 332
Thor: Vikings 335
Thorion of the New Asgods 192
Thorr Suerd or Sword of Thor . . 799
Those Annoying Post Bros 799
Those Annoying Post Brothers . 701
Threat 799
Three Geeks the 799
Three Mouseketeers, the 177
Three Musketeers 335
Three Musketeers, the 812
Three Ring Comics 479
Three Rocketeers 799
Three Stooges 479, 701
Three Stooges 3-D 701
Three Strikes 799
Threshold 701, 799
Threshold of Reality 800
Thrill-O-Rama 701
Thriller 177
Thrilling Adventures in Stamps . 470
Thrilling Comics 177, 479
Thrilling Crime Cases 480
Thrilling Murder Comics 831
Thrilling True Story of the
    Baseball Giants 480
Thrillkiller 177
Thrillkillers '62 177
Thrills of Tomorrow 481
Thrud the Barbarian 701
Thunder Agents 701
Thunder Bunny 800
Thunder Mace 800
Thunderbird 701, 800
Thunderbolt 701
Thunderbolt Jaxon 701
Thunderbolts 335
Thunderbolts Presents:
    Zemo Born Better 336
Thundercats 336, 701
Thunderstrike 336
Tick 800
Tick and Arthur the 800
Tick Circus Maximus 800
Tick: Giant Circus of the Mighty 800
Tick: Karma Tornado 800
Tick the 701
Tick The: Big Blue Destiny 800
Tick The: Golden Age 800
Tick The: Heroes of the City . . . 800
Tick The: I uny Bin 800
Tick Tock Tales 480
Tick's Back the 800
Tiger and Crane 702
Tiger Girl 702
Tiger-Man 702, 801
Tigers and Traitors 824
Tigers of Terra 702, 801
Tigers of the Luftwaffe 800
Tigress 801
Tigress Tales 801
Tigress: the Hidden Lands 801
Tim Holt 480
Tim McCoy 499
Tim Tyler Cowboy 480
Tim Vigil's Webwitch 801
Timber Wolf 177
Time Breakers 177
Time Cop 529
Time Drifters 801
Time Gates 801

Time Jump War . . . 801
Time Machine . . . 801
Time Machine, the . . . 822
Time Masters . . . 177
Time Traveler Ai . . . 801
Time Tunnel the . . . 702
Time Twisters . . . 702
Time Warp . . . 177
Time Warriors . . . 801
Timely Presents: Human Torch Comics . . . 336
Timeseekers . . . 570
Timeslip Collection . . . 336
Timeslip: the Coming of the Avengers . . . 336
Timespirits . . . 336
Timestryke . . . 336
Timewalker . . . 702
Tincan Man . . . 570
Tiny Tessie . . . 331
Tiny Titans . . . 177
Tiny Tot Funnies . . . 401
Tiny Tots Comics . . . 480
Tip Top Comics . . . 481
Tip Topper Comics . . . 481
Tippy Teen . . . 702
Tippy's Friends Go-Go & Animal 702
Titan . . . 529
Titan A.E. . . . 529
Titaness . . . 801
Titanium Rain . . . 702
Titans . . . 177
Titans The/Legion of Super-Heroes: Universe Ablaze . . . 177
Titans The/Young Justice: Graduation Day . . . 177
Tmnt: . . . 699
Tmnt Presents: . . . 699
Tmnt Training Manual . . . 798
Tnt Comics . . . 481
To Be Announced . . . 801
Toe Tags Featuring George Romero . . . 177
Tohubohu . . . 702
Toilers of the Sea, the . . . 818
Toka . . . 702
Tokyo Storm Warning . . . 702
Tom & Jerry . . . 702
Tom and Jerry . . . 450, 481, 702
Tom Brown's School Days . . . 817
Tom Cat . . . 381
Tom Corbett II . . . 801
Tom Corbett Space Cadet . 482, 801
Tom Judge: End of Days . . . 571
Tom Mix Comics . . . 482
Tom Mix Commandos Comics . 482
Tom Mix Holiday Album . . . 801
Tom Mix Western . . . 482, 702, 801
Tom Strong . . . 702
Tom Strong's Terrific Tales . . . 703
Tom Sullivan's Books of the Dead . . . 703
Tom Terrific! . . . 703
Tom-Tom the Jungle Boy . . . 482
Tomahawk . . . 177
Tomb of Darkness . . . 210
Tomb of Dracula . . . 336, 337
Tomb of Terror . . . 481
Tomb Raider . . . 571
Tomb Raider: Journeys . . . 571
Tomb Raider/Witchblade . . . 571
Tomb Raider/Witchblade/ Magdalena/Vampirella . . . 571
Tomb Raider/Witchblade Revisited . . . 571
Tomb Tales . . . 801
Tommi Gunn: Killers Lust . . . 801
Tommi-Gunn . . . 702
Tommy & the Monsters . . . 801
Tommy of the Big Top . . . 482
Tommy Rocket and the Goober Patrol . . . 801
Tomoe . . . 702
Tomoe: Unforgettable Fire . . . 702
Tomoe/Witchblade: Fire Sermon 702
Tomorrow Knights . . . 337
Tomorrow Man . . . 801
Tomorrow Stories . . . 702
Tongue*lash . . . 529
Tony Digerolamo's Jersey Devil 801
Tony Digerolamo's the Fix . . . 802

Tony Digerolamo's the Travelers 802
Tony Loco . . . 703
Tony Millionaire's Sock Monkey 529
Tony Trent . . . 401
Too Much Coffee Man . . . 529, 802
Too Much Hopeless Savages . . 802
Tooth & Claw . . . 571
Top Cat . . . 703
Top Cow . . . 571
Top Cow Classics . . . 571
Top Cow/Marvel: Unholy Union. 571
Top Dog . . . 337
Top Flight Comics . . . 482
Top Love Stories . . . 482
Top Secret . . . 483
Top Secrets . . . 483
Top Spot Comics . . . 483
Top Ten . . . 703
Top Ten: Beyond the Farthest Precinct . . . 703
Top Ten Season Two . . . 703
Top-Notch Comics . . . 482
Topix Comics . . . 482
Tops . . . 483
Tops Comics . . . 483
Tops in Adventure . . . 483
Topsy-Turvy . . . 483
Tor . . . 178, 337, 483
Tor in 3-D . . . 703
Tor Johnson: Hollywood Star . . 802
Torch of Liberty . . . 529
Torchy . . . 483
Torg . . . 802
Tormented, the . . . 483
Tormentress: Mistress of Hell . 703
Torrid Affairs . . . 802
Total Eclipse . . . 703
Total Eclipse the Seraphim Objective . . . 703
Total Justice . . . 178
Total Recall . . . 178
Total War . . . 703
Totally Alien . . . 802
Totem . . . 703
Touch . . . 178
Touch of Death . . . 802
Tough Guys and Wild Women . 802
Tough Kid Squad Comics . . . 337
Toupydoops . . . 802
Tower of Shadows . . . 337
Toxic Avenger . . . 337
Toxic Crusaders . . . 337
Toxin . . . 337
Toy Box . . . 703
Toy Boy . . . 703
Toy Town Comics . . . 483
Toyland Comics . . . 483
Tozzer 2 . . . 802
Tracker . . . 802
Tragg and the Sky Gods . . . 703
Trail Blazers . . . 459
Trailer Park of Terror . . . 802
Trailor Park of Terror . . . 703
Trakk: Monster Hunter . . . 571
Tranquility . . . 703
Tranquility: Armageddon . . . 703
Transformers . . . 337, 703, 704
Transformers: . . . 703
Transformers Comics Magazine 338
Transformers in 3-D . . . 705
Transformers the Movie . . . 338
Transformers The: . . . 704
Transformers The: Best of Uk: . 705
Transformers The: Movie Prequel 802
Transformers: Timelines . . . 705
Transformers Universe . . . 338
Transhuman . . . 571
Transit . . . 802
Transmetropolitan . . . 178
Transmutation of Ike Garuda . . 338
Trapped . . . 483
Trapped! . . . 483
Travel of Jamie McPheeters the 705
Traveller . . . 705
Treasure Chest . . . 483
Treasure Comics . . . 484
Treasure Island . . . 818
Treasury of Comics . . . 484
Trekker . . . 529, 571
Trenchcoat Brigade . . . 179
Trencher . . . 571

Trial by Fire . . . 705
Trials of Shazam . . . 179
Tribe . . . 571, 705
Tribulation Force . . . 705
Trick 'R Treat . . . 705
Trickster King Monkey . . . 802
Trident . . . 802
Trigger . . . 179
Trinity . . . 179
Trinity Angels . . . 705
Triple Threat . . . 484
Triple X . . . 530
Tripper the . . . 571
Triumph . . . 179
Triumverate . . . 802
Troll . . . 572
Troll Lords . . . 705
Troll: Once a Hero . . . 572
Trollords . . . 802
Trollords: Death & Kisses . . . 802
Tron . . . 705
Tron: Derezzed . . . 705
Tron: the Ghost in the Machine . 705
Trouble . . . 338
Trouble Express . . . 802
Trouble Magnet . . . 179
Trouble Shooters . . . 802
Trouble with Girls . . . 705, 802
Trouble with Girls: Night of the Lizard . . . 338
Trouble with Tigers . . . 802
Troublemakers . . . 705
Troubleman . . . 572
True Adventures . . . 338
True Animal Picture Stories . . . 484
True Aviation Picture Stories . . 484
True Believers . . . 338
True Comics . . . 484
True Complete Mystery . . . 221
True Confidences . . . 485
True Crime . . . 802
True Crime Comics . . . 485
True Life Tales . . . 338
True Love . . . 705
True Love Pictorial . . . 485
True Movie and Television . . . 485
True Romance . . . 705
True Secrets . . . 338
True Sport Picture Stories . . . 485
True Story Swear to God . 572, 802
True War Experiences . . . 485
True Western . . . 338
True-To-Life Romances . . . 485
Trufan Adventures Theatre . . . 802
Truth Justin and the American Way . . . 572
Truth: Red White Black . . . 338
Try-Out Winner Book . . . 338
Tsunami Girl . . . 572
Tuff Ghosts Starring Spooky . . 705
Tuffy . . . 485
Tug & Buster . . . 572
Tupelo . . . 802
Turistas: the Other Side of Paradise . . . 705
Turok . . . 705
Turok 3: Shadow of Oblivion . . 706
Turok: Child of Blood . . . 705
Turok: Comic Book Magazine . . 705
Turok: Dinosaur Hunter . . . 705
Turok/Shadowman . . . 706
Turok/Shaman's Tears . . . 706
Turok: Son of Stone . . . 706
Turok, Son of Stone . . . 485
Turok: the Hunted . . . 706
Turok/Timewalker . . . 706
Turtle Soup . . . 706, 802
Turtles Teach Karate . . . 802
TV Casper & Company . . . 706
TV Screen Cartoons . . . 485
TV Stars . . . 338
TV Teens . . . 485
TV Western . . . 803
TV Screen Cartoons . . . 137
Tweety and Sylvester . . . 485, 706
Twelve the . . . 338
Twenty Thousand Leagues under the Sea . . . 817
Twenty Years after . . . 817
Twilight . . . 179
Twilight Avenger . . . 706, 803

Twilight Experiment . . . 706
Twilight Man . . . 706
Twilight Men . . . 706
Twilight X: Storm . . . 803
Twilight X: War . . . 706
Twilight X-Tra . . . 706
Twilight Zone . . . 706, 707
Twilight Zone the . . . 706
Twilight-X: Interlude . . . 803
Twin Blades: Killing Words . . . 707
Twinkle Comics . . . 485
Twist . . . 803
Twisted Tales . . . 707
Twisted Tales of Bruce Jones . . 707
Twisted Tantrums of the Purple Snit . . . 803
Two Faces of Tomorrow the . . . 530
Two Fisted Tales . . . 530, 707
Two Gun Western . . . 219
Two Guns . . . 707
Two Years Before the Mast . . . 815
Two-Face Year One . . . 179, 338, . . . 339, 485, 486, 572, 707
Two-Gun Western . . . 210
Typee . . . 816
Typhoid . . . 339
Tyranny Rex . . . 803
Tzu: Spirits of Death . . . 707
Tzu the Reaper . . . 707

U U U U
U.N. Force . . . 709
U.N. Force Files . . . 709
U.S. 1 . . . 343
U.S.A. Comics . . . 343
U.S. Agent . . . 343
U.S. Air Force Comics . . . 710
U.S. Jones . . . 486
U.S. Marines . . . 710
U.S. Marines in Action! . . . 486
U.S. Paratroops . . . 486
U.S. War Machine . . . 343
U.S. War Machine 2.0 . . . 343
U.S. Tank Commandos . . . 486
UFO Flying Saucers . . . 707
Ultimate Adventures (Of Hawk-Owl & Zippy) . . . 339
Ultimate Civil War Spider-Ham Crisis . . . 339
Ultimate Daredevil & Elektra . . 339
Ultimate Elektra . . . 339
Ultimate Extinction . . . 339
Ultimate Fantastic Four . . . 339
Ultimate Human . . . 340
Ultimate Iron Man . . . 340
Ultimate Iron Man II . . . 340
Ultimate Marvel . . . 340
Ultimate Marvel Magazine . . . 340
Ultimate Marvel Team-Up . . . 340
Ultimate Nightmare . . . 340
Ultimate Origins . . . 340
Ultimate Power . . . 340
Ultimate Secret . . . 340
Ultimate Six . . . 340
Ultimate Spider-Man . . . 340
Ultimate Sports Force Presents: . . . 707
Ultimate Strike . . . 803
Ultimate Tales . . . 341
Ultimate Vision . . . 341
Ultimate War . . . 341
Ultimate Wolverine Vs. Hulk . . 341
Ultimate X-Men . . . 341, 342
Ultimates 2 . . . 341
Ultimates 3 . . . 341
Ultimates Saga . . . 340, 341
Ultimates Secrets . . . 340
Ultimates the . . . 340
Ultimatum . . . 342
Ultra . . . 572
Ultra Klutz . . . 803
Ultra X-Men Collection . . . 342
Ultra X-Men III . . . 342
Ultraforce . . . 707
Ultraforce/Avengers . . . 342
Ultragirl . . . 342
Ultraman . . . 707
Ultraman Tiga . . . 530
Ultraverse . . . 707
Ultron . . . 342
Umbra . . . 572
Umbrella Academy: Apocalypse Suite . . . 530

Umbrella Academy: Dallas 530
Un-Men the 180
Unauthorized Bio of Lex Luthor 179
Unbound 572
Uncanny Man-Frog 803
Uncanny Origins 342
Uncanny Tales............. 342
Uncanny Tales from the Grave . 342
Uncanny X-Men 359
Uncensored Mouse.......... 803
Uncle Charlie's Fables 486
Uncle Joe's Funnies 486
Uncle Milty................ 486
Uncle Sam................ 179
Uncle Sam and the Freedom
    Fighters 179
Uncle Sam Quarterly........ 378
Uncle Scrooge......... 486, 708
Uncle Scrooge & Donald Duck . 709
Uncle Scrooge Adventures 708, 709
Uncle Scrooge Adventures
    in Color 709
Uncle Scrooge and Donald
    Duck............... 709
Uncle Scrooge and Money 709
Uncle Scrooge Goes to
    Disneyland 709
Uncle Tom's Cabin 814
Undead the 709
Under Two Flags 820
Underdog................ 709
Underdog in 3-D 709
Underlords............... 709
Undersea Agent 709
Undertaker............... 709
Underworld 179, 343, 486
Underworld Crime 486
Underworld: Red in Tooth
    and Claw 709
Underworld: Rise of the Lycans 709
Underworld Unleashed 179
Unearthly Spectaculars....... 709
Unexpected, The 174
Unforgiven the............. 803
Unhuman................ 709
Unicorn Isle 803
Union 572
Union Jack 343
Union of Justice........... 709
Unique............. 572, 710
Unit Zero: Marquis Files 710
United Comics 416
United Free Worlds 710
United States Fighting Air Force 486
United States Marines....... 486
Unity 710
Unity 2000 710
Universal Monsters 530
Universal Soldier........... 710
Universal War One 343
Universe 572
Universe X............... 343
Unkept Promise............ 486
Unknown Soldier 152
Unknown Soldier 180
Unknown World 471
Unknown Worlds of Frank
    Brunner 710
Unknown Worlds of Science
    Fiction 343
Unleashed 803
Unravel 572
Unsane 254
Unseen, the 486
Unsupervised Existence 803
Untamod 343
Untamed Love........ 486, 710
U. T. F. the.............. 710
U. T. F.: Undead Task Force ... 710
Untold Legend of Batman 180
Untold Legend of Captain
    Marvel the 343
Untold Tales of 710
Untold Tales of Evil Ernie ... 803
Untold Tales of Spider-Man... 343
Untold Tales of the New
    Universe.............. 343
Untouchables 803
Unusual Tales 710
Uptight................. 803
Urban Legends 530
Urban Monsters........... 572

Ursa Minors.............. 803
Urth 4 710
Usa Is Ready.............. 486
Usagi Yojimbo 530, 710, 803
Usagi Yojimbo Color Special:
    Green Persimmon 530
User................... 180
Utopiates the 803

V V V V
V 180
V for Vendetta 180
V. . . Comics 487
V.I.C.E. 573
Vagabond 572, 803
Vagrant Story............. 572
Vaistron 803
Valentine 803
Valentino 804
Valeria the She Bat 710
Valhalla 710
Valiant Vision Starter Kit 710
Valkyrie 343, 710
Valkyries 710
Valley of the Dinosaurs 710
Valor 180, 486, 710
Vamperotica 710, 804
Vamperotica: Blond Goddess . 804
Vamperotica: Dark Fiction 804
Vamperotica: Divide & Conquer 804
Vamperotica Illustrated 804
Vamperotica Lingerie........ 804
Vamperotica Lust for Luxura . 804
Vamperotica Manga 804
Vamperotica Tales.......... 804
Vamperotica: Tales from the
    Bloodvault 804
Vamperotica: Voluptuous Vamps804
Vamperotica: When Darkness
    Falls 804
Vamperotica's Pin-Up Illustrated 804
Vampfire 804
Vampfire: Erotic Echo 804
Vampfire: Necromantique 804
Vampi 710
Vampi (Digital) 711
Vampi Vicious 711
Vampi Vs. Xin 711
Vampire Bites 804
Vampire Confessions 804
Vampire Dahlia the 804
Vampire Girls: Bubblegum
    & Blood 805
Vampire Girls: California 1969 . 805
Vampire Girls Erotique 805
Vampire Girls Erotique:
    Gravedigger.......... 805
Vampire Girls: New York 1979 . 805
Vampire Girls Vs. Angel Girl .. 805
Vampire Lestat............ 711
Vampire Miyu............. 805
Vampire Princess Miyu 805
Vampire Princess Yui 805
Vampire Tales 343
Vampire the Masquerade 713
Vampire Verses the 805
Vampire Yui 805
Vampire Zone the 806
Vampire's Christmas 572
Vampire's Tattoo 805
Vampirella (Monthly)....... 711
Vampirella............... 712
Vampirella Comics Magazine . 805
Vampirella: Legendary Tales .. 805
Vampirella: Morning in America. 805
Vampirella Novella.......... 805
Vampirella Retro 805
Vampirella: Revelations...... 805
Vampornrella............. 806
Vampress Luxura the 713
Vampyres 806
Van Helsing.............. 530
Vandala 713
Vandala II 713
Vanguard 572
Vanguard Illustrated 713
Vanguard: Strange Visitors .. 572
Vapor Loch 806
Varick: Chronicles of the Dark
    Prince............... 713
Variety Comics 487

Varuk 713
Vaughn Bode Portfolio #1 ... 831
Vaughn Bode the Portfolio ... 831
Vaughn Bode's Cheech Wizard,
    the Collected Adventures
    of the Car............. 831
Vaughn Bode's Deadbone, the
    First Testament of Cheech
    Wizard 831
Vault of Evil 344
Vault of Horror 713
Vault of Horror, the 489
Vector 713
Vegas Knights 713
Velocity 573
Vengeance of Dreadwolf..... 806
Vengeance of the Aztecs 806
Vengeance of Vampirella 713
Venom.................. 344
Venom: along Came a Spider.. 344
Venom: Carnage Unleashed.. 344
Venom: Dark Origin........ 344
Venom: Finale 344
Venom: Funeral Pyre 344
Venom: Lethal Protector 344
Venom: License to Kill....... 344
Venom: Nights of Vengeance . 344
Venom: on Trial 344
Venom: Seed of Darkness ... 344
Venom: Separation Anxiety... 344
Venom: Sign of the Boss..... 344
Venom: Sinner Takes All 344
Venom: the Enemy Within.... 344
Venom: the Hunger 344
Venom: the Hunted 344
Venom: the Mace 344
Venom: the Madness 344
Venom: Tooth and Claw 344
Venom Vs. Carnage 344
Venture 573, 713
Venus 344
Venus Wars 530
Venus Wars II 530
Verdict 806
Veri Best Sure Fire Comics ... 487
Veri Best Sure Shot Comics .. 487
Vermillion 180
Veronica 713
Verotik Illustrated.......... 713
Verotik World............. 713
Verotika 713, 806
Version 530
Version II 530
Vertical................. 180
Vertigo Jam 180
Vertigo Pop!............. 180
Vertigo Preview 180
Vertigo Secret Files: Hellblazer. 180
Vertigo Verite:............ 180
Vertigo Visions:........... 180
Very Best of Marvel Comics .. 345
Very Vicky............... 806
Vesper 713
Vext 180
Vic & Blood 806
Vic Flint 487
Vic Jordan.............. 487
Vic Torry and His Flying Saucer 487
Vic Verity Magazine........ 487
Vicki................... 713
Vicky Valentine 806
Victim.................. 806
Victims................. 806
Victoria's Secret Service 714
Victorian 713
Victory.................. 573
Victory Comics 487
Video 806
Video Classics............ 806
Video Jack............... 345
Vietnam................. 831
Vietnam Journal 806
Vigil................... 806
Vigil: Desert Foxes 806
Vigil: Eruption 806
Vigil: Fall from Grace........ 806
Vigil: Scatter Shots 806
Vigilante................ 180
Vigilante: City Lights Prairie
    Justice 181
Villains.................. 714
Villains & Vigilantes........ 714

Villains United 181
Vimanarama!............. 181
Vincent Price Presents 714
Vinson Watson's Rage 806
Vinson Watson's Sweet Childe . 806
Vintage Magnus Robot Fighter . 714
Vinyl Underground the 181
Violator 573
Violator/Badrock 573
Violent Messiahs 573
Violent Messiahs: Lamenting
    Pain 573
Violet Rose 714
Vip 714
Viper 181
Virgin: Slumber 806
Virgin: Surrounded 806
Virgin: till Death Do Us Part .. 806
Virginian, the 823
Virginian the 714
Virtex 714
Virtua Fighter............. 714
Virus 530
Vision & Scarlet Witch....... 345
Vision the................ 345
Visionaries 345
Visions................. 806
Visitor 714
Visitor Vs. Valiant 714
Visual Assault Omnibus 806
Vix 573
Vixen 806
Vixen: Return of the Lion 181
Vogue 573
Void Indigo 345
Voltron.................. 714
Voltron: a Legend Forged 714
Voltron: Defender of the
    Universe 573, 714
Vooda 487
Voodoo 487, 573
Voodoo Child............. 714
Vortex 714, 806
Vortex: Dr. Kilbourn 806
Vortex: into the Dark 806
Vortex Special: Cybersin 806
Vortex the 530
Vortex: the Second Coming .. 714
Vox 806
Voyage to the Bottom
    of the Sea 714
Voyage to the Deep 714
Voyages of She-Buccaneer the 714
Vss: Nemesis Rising........ 714

W W W W
W.I.T.C.H. 721
Wabbit Wampage 806
Wacky Adventures of Cracky . 714
Wacky Duck.............. 236
Wacky Squirrel 530
Wacky Witch 714
Waffen Ss 806
Wagon Train 714
Wahoo Morris 573
Waiting Place the 806
Wake the Dead 714
Walk Through October 807
Walk-In 714
Walking Dead 573, 807
Wallace & Gromit 714
Wally 715
Wally the Wizard 345
Wally Wood's Thunder Agents . 715
Walt Disney Annuals 715
Walt Disney Comics Digest... 716
Walt Disney Presents .. 488, 715
Walt Disney Showcase 716
Walt Disney's Autumn
    Adventure 715
Walt Disney's Christmas Parade 715
Walt Disney's Comics & Stories 487
Walt Disney's Comics and
    Stories 715, 716
Walt Disney's Dell Giant
    Editions 488
Walt Disney's Dell Junior
    Treasury............. 488
(Walt Disney's) Donald Duck.. 398
Walt Disney's Gallagher
    Boy Reporter 716
(Walt Disney's) Mickey Mouse . 444

Walt Disney's the Scarecrow . . . 716
Walt Disney's the Scarecrow
 of Romney Marsh 716
Walt Kelly's Christmas Classics 717
Walt Kelly's Springtime Tales . . 717
Walt the Wildcat 807
Walter: Campaign of Terror 531
Walter Lantz Woody
 Woodpecker 716
Wambi Jungle Boy 488
Wanderers 181
Wandering Star 807
Wanderlust 807
Wanted 573
Wanted Comics 489
Wanted: the World's Most
 Dangerous Villians 181
War 717
War Action 345
War Adventures 345
War Against Crime 489, 717
War and Attack 717
War at Sea 717
War Battles 489
War Birds 489
War Combat 345
War Comics 345, 489
War Dancer 717
War Fury 489
War Heroes 489, 573, 717
War Is Hell 346
War Is Hell: the First Flight
 of the Phantom Eagle 346
War Machine 346
War Machine: Weapon of Shield263
War Man 347
War of the Gods 182
War of the Undead 717
War of the Worlds 807
War of the Worlds:
 Second Wave 717
War of the Worlds, the 822
War of the Worlds the 807
War of the Worlds: the
 Memphis Front 807
War Report 489
War Ships 489
War Stories 489
War Story 182
War That Time Forgot the 182
War the 345
War Victory Adventures 490
War Victory Comics 490
War Wings 718
Warblade: Endangered Species 573
Warcat 807
Warcat Special 717
Warchild 807
Ward: a Bullet Series 807
Ward of the State 573
Warfront 489, 717
Wargod 717
Warhammer 40k 717
Warhammer: 717
Warhawks 717
Warhawks 2050 717
Warheads 345
Warheads: Black Dawn 345
Warlands 573
Warlands: Age of Ice 574
Warlands: Malagen's Campaign 717
Warlash 717
Warlock 346
Warlock 5 807
Warlock and the Infinity Watch . 346
Warlock Chronicles 346
Warlocks 807
Warlord 181
Warlord the 182
Warmageddon Illustrated 807
Warmaster 717
Warp 717
Warpath 489
Warren Ellis' 807
Warren Ellis' Apparat 807
Warren Ellis' Atmospherics 807
Warren Ellis' Bad World 807
Warren Ellis' Black Gas 717
Warren Ellis' Scars 807
Warren Ellis' Strange Killings . . 807
Warren Ellis' Strange Killings:
 Necromancer 807

Warren Ellis' Strange Killings:
 Strong Medicine 807
Warren Ellis' Strange Killings:
 the Body Orchard 807
Warren Ellis' Strange Kiss 807
Warren Ellis' Stranger Kisses . . 807
Warren Ellis' Wolfskin 718
Warrior Bugs the 718
Warrior Comics 489
Warrior Nun Areala 718
Warrior Nun Areala:
 Books of Peril 807
Warrior Nun Areala:
 Dangerous Game 807
Warrior Nun Areala:
 Ghosts of the past 807
Warrior Nun Areala/
 Razor: Dark Prophecy 808
Warrior Nun Areala:
 Scorpio Rose 718
Warrior Nun Areala: the Manga. 808
Warrior Nun: Black and White. . 808
Warrior Nun Brigantia 808
Warrior Nun Dei: Aftertime 718
Warrior Nun: Frenzy 718
Warrior Nun Lazarus 718
Warrior Nun: No Justice 718
Warrior Nun: Resurrection 718
Warrior of Waverly Street the . . 531
Warrior's Way 718
Warriors 808
Warriors of Plasm 718
Warstrike 718
Warstrike: Prelude to Godwheel 718
Wart and the Wizard 718
Wartime Romances 490
Warworld! 531
Warzone 808
Washable Jones and
 the Shmoo 490
Wasteland 182, 808
Watch The: Casus Belli 718
Watchmen 182
Waterdogs 718
Waterloo 822
Waterloo Sunset 574
Waterworld 718
Wave Warriors 718
Way of the Rat 719
Wayfarers 718
Weapon the 574, 719
Weapon X 347
Weapon X: Days of Future Now 347
Weapon X: First Class 347
Weapon Zero 574
Weapons File 808
Weasel 808
Weasel Guy: Roadtrip 574
Weasel Guy Witchblade 719
Weather Woman 808
Weaveworld 347
Web of Evil 490
Web of Horror 719
Web of Mystery 490
Web of Scarlet Spider 347
Web of Spider-Man 347
Web the 182
Webspinners: Tales of
 Spider-Man 348
Webwitch 808
Webwitch: Prelude to War 808
Webwitch: War 808
Wedding of Popeye and
 Olive the 719
Weekender, the 490
Weird 182
Weird Adventures 490
Weird Chills 490
Weird Comics 490
Weird Fantasy 490, 719
Weird Horrors 490
Weird Jungle Tales 491
Weird Mysteries 491
Weird Science 491, 719
Weird Science Fantasy . . . 491, 719
Weird Secret Origins 182
Weird Space 808
Weird Suspense 719
Weird Tales Illustrated 719
Weird Tales of the Future 491
Weird Terror 491
Weird the 182

Weird Thrillers 491
Weird War Tales 182, 183
Weird Western Tales 183
Weird Wondertales 348
Weird Worlds 183
Weirdfall 808
Weirdo 831
Weirdo, the 831
Weirdsville 808
Weirdsville/Crybaby: Hey You
 Two 808
Welcome to Hoxford 719
Wendigo 719
Wendy and the New Kids on
 the Block 719
Wendy Parker Comics 348
Wendy the Good Little Witch . . . 719
Wendy Witch World 719
Werewolf 719, 808
Werewolf by Night 348
Werewolves: Call of the Wild . . 719
West Coast Avengers 348
Western Action 719
Western Action Thrillers 491
Western Adventures Comics . . . 491
Western Bandit Trails 491
Western Comics 183
Western Crime Busters 491
Western Crime Cases 451
Western Fighters 492
Western Frontier 492
Western Gunfighters 203
Western Gunfighters 349
Western Hearts 492
Western Hero 497
Western Kid 349
Western Killers 492
Western Life Romances 290
Western Love 492
Western Love Trails 491
Western Outlaws 349
Western Outlaws & Sheriffs . . . 210
Western Picture Stories 492
Western Rough Riders 492
Western Stories 818
Western Tales 495
Western Tales of Black Rider . . 195
Western Tales of Terror 808
Western Team-Up 349
Western Thrillers 349, 492
Western Trails 349
Western True Crime 492
Western Winners 195
Westerner, the 492
Westward Ho! 814
Westwynd 719
Wetworks 574
Wetworks: Armageddon 719
Wetworks/Vampirella 574
Wetworks: Worldstorm 719
Whack 492
Wham Comics 492
What If 350
What If? 349-351
What Is the Face? 808
What the -?! 351
What Were They Thinking? 719
Wheelie and the Chopper
 Bunch 719
Where Creatures Roam 351
Where Monsters Dwell 351
Where's Huddles 719
Whip Wilson 211
Whirlwind Comics 492
Whisper 719
Whispers & Shadows 808
White Company, the 821
White Devil 808
White Fang 720, 819
White like She 531
White Orchid the 808
White Picket Fences 720
White Princess of the Jungle . . 492
White Raven 809
White Rider and Super Horse . . 451
White Tiger 351
White Trash 720
Whiteout 808
Whiteout: Melt 808
Whitley Strieber's Beyond
 Communion 809
Whiz Comics 492

Whiz Kids 574
Who Is Next? 493
Who Wants to Be a Superhero? 531
Who's Who 183
Who's Who in Impact 184
Who's Who in Star Trek 184
Who's Who in the DC Universe 183
Who's Who in the Legion 184
Who's Who Update '87 184
Who's Who Update '88 184
Whodunit? 493
Whodunit 720
Wicked 809
Wicked the 574
Wicked: the Reckoning 809
Widow 809
Widow: Bound by Blood 809
Widow/Luxura: Blood Lust 809
Widow Made in Britain 720
Widow Metal Gypsies 720
Widow: Progeny 809
Widow: the Origin 809
Wilbur Comics 494
Wild 351
Wild Animals 720
Wild Animals I Have Known . . . 823
Wild Bill Elliot 494
Wild Bill Hickok 494, 822
Wild Bill Hickok and Jingles . . . 498
Wild Boy of the Congo 494
Wild Boys 720
Wild Cards 351
Wild Dog 184
Wild Frontier 494, 809
Wild Girl 720
Wild Knights 809
Wild the 809
Wild Thing 351
Wild Thingz 809
Wild Times 720
Wild West 351, 720
Wild West C.O.W.- Boys of
 Moo Mesa 720
Wild Western 351
Wild Western Action 720
Wild Wild West 184, 720, 721
Wildc.A.T.S 574
Wildc.A.T.S Adventures 575
Wildc.A.T.S/Aliens 575
Wildc.A.T.S Trilogy 575
Wildc.A.T.S/X-Men: the
 Dark Age 351, 575
Wildcats 720
Wildcore 575
Wildfire 720
Wildflower 809
Wildflower: Dark Euphoria 809
Wildflower: the Lost Yesterdays 809
Wildflower: Tribal Screams . . . 809
Wildflower: Two Tales 809
Wildguard: Casting Call 575
Wildguard: Fire Power 575
Wildguard: Fool's Gold 575
Wildguard: Insider 575
Wildlife 809
Wildman 809
Wildsiderz 720
Wildstar: Sky Zero 575
Wildstorm 720
Wildstorm Archives Genesis . . . 575
Wildstorm Fine Arts Spotlight . . 720
Wildstorm Rising 575
Wildstorm Spotlight 575
Wildstorm Ultimate Sports 575
Wildstorm Universe '97 575
Wildstorm! 575
Will Eisner's 3-D Classics 721
Will Rogers Western 494
Will to Power 531
Will Triumph Fights Alone 721
William Shatner's Tek World . . . 351
William Tell 821
Willie Comics 257
Willie the Wise-Guy 352
Willow 352, 809
Willow Creek 721
Wimmen's Comix 831
Win a Prize Comics 721
Wind Blade 809
Windraven 809
Windy & Willy 184
Wingman 721

Wings 809
Wings Comics 494
Wings of Anansi 575
Winnie Winkle 495
Winnie-The-Pooh 721
Winter Men the 721
Winter Soldier: Winter Kills . . . 352
Winterworld 721
Wisdom 352
Wise Son: the White Wolf 184
Wisp 721
Witch 809
Witchblade 575
Witchblade/Aliens/Darkness/
  Predator: Mindhunter. 531
Witchblade: Destiny's Child. . . 576
Witchblade/Devi 576
Witchblade: Shades of Gray . . . 576
Witchblade Takeru Manga. . . . 576
Witchblade/the Darkness 576
Witchblade Vs. Frankenstein's
  Monster 576
Witchcraft 184, 495
Witchcraft: La Terreur 184
Witches 352
Witches Tales 495
Witches Western Tales 495
Witchfinder the 577
Witchgirls Inc. 721
Witching Hour the 184, 721
Witching the 184
Witchman 721
With Fire and Sword 823
With the Marines on the
  Battlefronts of the World . . 495
Witness the 352
Witty Comics 495
Wizard of Fourth Street. 531
Wizard of Time 809
Wizards of the Last Resort . . . 809
Wolf 721
Wolf & Red 531
Wolf & Byrd Counselors of
  the Macabre. 809
Wolfman 721
Wolfpack 352
Wolfskin. 721
Wolverine 352, 353
Wolverine & Punisher:
  Damaging Evidence 353
Wolverine and Power Pack . . . 353
Wolverine/Captain America . . . 353
Wolverine: Days of Future past. 354
Wolverine: Doombringer 354
Wolverine/Doop. 354
Wolverine Encyclopedia 354
Wolverine: First Class 354
Wolverine/Gambit: Victims . . . 354
Wolverine/Hulk 354
Wolverine: Manifest Destiny . . . 354
Wolverine/Netsuke 354
Wolverine Origins 354
Wolverine/Punisher 354
Wolverine/Punisher: Revelation 354
Wolverine Saga 354
Wolverine: Snikt!. 354
Wolverine: Soultaker 354
Wolverine: the End 354
Wolverine/Witchblade 577
Wolverine: X-Isle 354
Woman in White, the. 818
Women in Love 495
Women Outlaws 495
Won by the Sword. 823
Wonder Comics 495
Wonder Duck. 354
Wonder Girl 184
Wonder Man 354
Wonder Wart-Hog and the
  Nurds of November 831
Wonder Woman 184, 187
Wonderboy 424
Wonderland. 721
Wonderland Comics 496
Wonderlost 577
Wonderman 354
Wonderworld Comics 496
Wood Boy the 577, 721
Woodsy Owl 721
Woody Woodpecker 721
Woody Woodpecker and
  Friends. 721

Wordsmith 809
World Around Us, the 496
World below II the 531
World below the 531
World Championship Wrestling. 355
World Class Comics 577
World Famous Heroes
  Magazine 496
World Famous Stories. 496
World Hardball League 810
World Is His Parish, the 496
World of Adventure 721
World of Archie 721
World of Fantasy 355
World of Krypton 187
World of Metropolis 187
World of Mystery 355
World of Smallville. 187
World of Suspense 355
World of Warcraft 721
World of Warcraft: Ashbringer . . 721
World of Wood 721, 810
World War 2 810
World War 2: Stalingrad 810
World War Hulk 355
World War Hulk: Aftermash:
  Damage Control 355
World War Hulk: Front Line. . . . 355
World War Hulk: Gamma Corps 355
World War Hulk: Warbound. . . . 355
World War Hulk: X-Men. 355
World War II: 1946 722
World War III 190, 496
World War Stories 722
World Without End 190
World-Watch 722
Worlds Beyond 496
Worlds Collide 188
Worlds of Dungeons & Dragons 721
Worlds of Fantasy 810
Worlds of Fear. 496
Worlds of H.P. Lovecraft 810
Worlds Unknown 355
Worldstorm 721
Worldstorm: Revelations 721
Worldwatch 810
Wormwood: Calamari Rising. . . 722
Wormwood: Gengleman Corpse 722
Wotalife 453
Wow Comics 496
Wraithborn 722
Wrath. 722
Wrath of the Spectre 190
Wretch the 810
Wu Wei 810
Wulf the Barbarian 722
Wuthering Heights. 818
WW2 810
WW2: Presents Kamakazi 722
WWF Battlemania 722
Wyatt Earp 355, 722
Wyatt Earp: Dodge City. 810
Wyatt Earp Frontier Marshal. . . 722
Wyatt Earp Vs. The Cisco Kid. . 722
Wynonna Earp. 577
Wynonna Earp: Home on the
  Strange 722
Wyrd: the Reluctant Warrior . . . 810
Wyrms 355

X X X X

X. 531
X Isle 723
X.S.E. 366
X-Babes Vs. Justice Babes. . . . 810
X-Men Vs. Avengers 366
X-Men Vs. The Brood 366
X-Men 361
X-Patrol 192, 355, 357, 358,
   . 361, 363-367, 497, 723, 810
Xanadu 722, 810
Xavier Institute Alumni
  Yearbook 355
Xena Vs. Army of Darkness:
  What Again? 722
Xena: Warrior Princess . . . 531, 722

Xena Warrior Princess 722
Xeno's Arrow. 810
Xenobrood. 190
Xenon 810
Xenotech 723
Xenozoic Tales 810
Xenya 722
Xero 190
XIII 723
Ximos: Violent past 723
Xin 723
Xin: Journey of the Monkey
  King 723
Xiola 810
Xmas Comics 497
Xmen. 810
Xombi 190
Xombie 723

Y Y Y Y

Y: the Last Man 190, 191
Yahoo 810
Yakky Doodle & Chopper 723
Yakuza. 810
Yang 723
Yankee Comics 497
Yanks in Battle 497
Yardbirds, the 497
Yawn 497
Yeah! 191, 723
Year One: Batman/Ra's Al Ghul 191
Year One: Batman/Scarecrow. . 191
Yellow Caballero 810
Yellow Claw. 367
Yellow Dog 831
Yellowjacket Comics 497
Yenny 723
Yets 810
Yin Fei 723
Yogi Bear. 367, 723, 724
Yogi Berra 498
Yosemite Sam 724
You & Me. 810
You'll Have That 724
You're under Arrest!. 531
Young All Stars 191
Young Allies Comics 367
Young and Lustless. 831
Young Avengers 367
Young Brides. 498
Young Cynics Club 531
Young Doctors the. 724
Young Dracula: Prayer of
  the Vampire 810
Young Eagle 498
Young Hearts. 367
Young Heroes 498
Young Heroes in Love. 191
Young Indiana Jones
  Chronicles, the. 531
Young Justice 191
Young Justice: Sins of Youth. . . 191
Young King Cole 498
Young Lawyers the 724
Young Liars 191
Young Life 498
Young Love 191, 498
Young Lust 831
Young Masters. 811
Young Men 224
Young Rebels the 724
Young Romance Comics. 498
Young X-Men. 367
Youngblood 577, 724
Youngblood Battlezone 577
Youngblood: Bloodsport 577
Youngblood Strikefile. 577
Youngblood/X-Force 577
Youngblood: Year One 577
Your United States 498
Yow 831
Yuggoth Creatures. 811
Yuppies from Hell 367

Z Z Z Z

Z 811
Zacherley's Midnight Terrors . . . 811
Zago, Jungle Prince 498
Zak Raven Esq.. 724
Zane Grey's Stories of the West 724
Zap Comix. 831
Zatanna 191
Zaza the Mystic 387

Zealot 577
Zed 811
Zegra, Jungle Empress. 499
Zein 724
Zein Ghosts of Heliopolis 724
Zell the Sworddancer 811
Zen 724
Zen Bounty Hunter 811
Zen Illustrated Novella. 811
Zen Inter- Galactic Ninja 811
Zen Intergalactic Ninja 724
Zen Intergalactic Ninja:
  Starquest 811
Zen Intergalactic Ninja Vs.
  Micheal Jack-Zen. 811
Zen: Mistress of Chaos 811
Zen/Nira X: Hellspace 724
Zen: Novella 724
Zen Specials 724
Zen: the New Adventures 811
Zen: Warrior 724
Zendra. 724, 725
Zenisms Wit and Wisdoms . . . 811
Zenith Phase I 725
Zenith: Phase II 811
Zenith Phase II 725
Zero G. 577
Zero Girl 191, 577
Zero Girl: Full Circle 725
Zero Hour: Crisis in Time 191
Zero Killer 531
Zero Patrol 725
Zero Tolerance 725
Zero Zero. 811
Zetraman 811
Zetraman: Revival 811
Ziggy Pig Silly Seal 367
Zillion 811
Zip Comics 499
Zip-Jet 499
Zippy 831
Zippy: Nation of Pinheads. . . . 831
Zippy the Chimp 499
Zippy: Yow! 831
ZMD: Zombies of Mass
  Destruction. 725
Zody the Mod Rob 725
Zolastraya and the Bard 811
Zombie 367
Zombie Commandos from Hell . 811
Zombie Highway 811
Zombie King 577
Zombie Tales 725
Zombie Tales: the Dead 725
Zombie The: Simon Garth. . . . 367
Zombie War: Earth must Be
  Destroyed. 811
Zombie-Proof. 725, 811
Zombies! 725
Zombieworld. 531
Zombieworld: Champion of the
  Worms 531
Zombieworld: Dead End 531
Zombieworld: the Tree of Death 531
Zombieworld: Winter's Dregs . . 531
Zone Continuum 811
Zone the 531
Zoo Funnies 499
Zoom Comics 499
Zoom Suit 725
Zooniverse. 725
Zoot Comics 499
Zoot! 811
Zorro 367, 725
Zorro Mantanzas 577
Zorro's Lady Rawhide: Other
  People's Blood. 577
Zot! 725, 811
Zu 811

CVA GRADING GUIDE

Grading comics is an objective art. This grading guide outlines the many conditions you should look for when purchasing comics, from the highest grade and top condition to the lowest collectible grade and condition. Your own comics will fall into one of these categories. A more complete description and our comments on comics grades can be found inside. We would like to point out, however, that no reader or advertiser is required to follow this or any other standard. All prices in Comics Values Annual are for comics in Near Mint condition. Happy collecting!

Mint: Perfect, pristine, devoid of any trace of wear or printing or handling flaws. Covers must be fully lustrous with sharply pointed corners. No color fading. Must be well centered. Many "rack" comics are not "Mint" even when new.

Near Mint: Almost perfect with virtually no wear. No significant printing flaws. Covers must be essentially lustrous with sharp corners. Spine is as tight as new. In older comics, minimal color fading is acceptable, as is slight aging of the paper. Most price guides, including CVA, quote prices in this grade.

Very Fine: Well preserved, still pleasing in appearance. Small signs of wear, most particularly around the staples. Most luster is readily visible. Corners may no longer be sharp, but are not rounded. Typical of a comic read only a few times and then properly stored.

Fine: Clean, presentable, with noticeable signs of wear. Some white may show through enamel around staples, and moderate rounding of corners. No tape or writing damage. Book still lies flat.

Very Good: A well worn reading copy with some minor damage such as creasing, small tears or cover flaking. Some discoloration may be evident, with obvious wear around the staples. Little luster remains, and some rolling of the spine may be seen when comic is laid flat on the table.

Good: A fully intact comic with very heavy wear. Tears, cover creases and flaking, and rolled spine will all be evident. No tape repairs present. Only very scarce or valuable issues are collected in this state.

The adjoining price table shows the prices for the other collectible grades which correspond to any "near mint" price given in this book.

Mint	Near Mint	Very Fine	Fine	Very Good
$6,000	$5,000	$3,500	$2,000	$1,000
4,800	4,000	2,800	1,600	800
3,600	3,000	2,100	1,200	600
2,400	2,000	1,400	800	400
1,800	1,500	1,050	600	300
1,200	1,000	700	400	200
1,080	900	630	360	180
960	800	560	320	160
900	750	525	300	150
840	700	490	280	140
780	650	455	260	130
720	600	420	240	120
660	550	385	220	110
600	500	350	200	100
570	475	332	190	95
540	450	315	180	90
510	425	297	170	85
480	400	280	160	80
450	375	262	150	75
420	350	245	140	70
390	325	227	130	65
360	300	210	120	60
330	275	192	110	55
300	250	175	100	50
270	225	157	90	45
240	200	140	80	40
210	175	122	70	35
180	150	105	60	30
150	125	87	50	25
120	100	70	40	20
114	95	66	38	19
108	90	63	36	18
102	85	59	32	17
96	80	56	32	16
90	75	52	30	15
84	70	49	28	14
78	65	45	26	13
72	60	42	24	12
66	55	38	22	11
60	50	35	2	10
54	45	31	18	9
48	40	28	16	8
42	35	24	14	7
36	30	21	12	6
30	25	17	10	5
24	20	14	8	4
22	18	12	7	4
21	17	11	7	4
18	15	10	6	3
17	14	9	5	3
16	13	9	5	3
15	12	8	5	2
14	11	7	4	2
12	10	7	4	2
11	9	6	4	2
10	8	5	3	1
9	7	5	3	1
7	6	4	3	1
6	5	4	2	1
5	4	3	2	0
4	3	2	1	0
3	2	2	0	0
2	1	0	0	0

More Comics Companions

2009 Comic Book Checklist & Price Guide, 1961-Present 15th Edition

by Maggie Thompson,
Brent Frankenhoff and Peter Bickford

From original super-hero artwork on the cover to the 125,000 comic book listings inside, this is the ultimate go-to guide for the comic community. Listings identify cover date, creator details, and near mint price.

Softcover • 7 x 10 • 840 pages
2,000 b&w photos
Item# Z2111 • $19.99

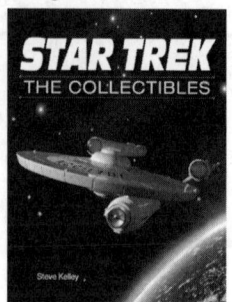

Star Trek: The Collectibles
by Steve Kelley

More than 40 years of Star Trek treasures appear in this photographically exciting new guide from noted Trekkie Steve Kelley, including action figures, games, posters, uniforms, and original scripts, all with collector pricing.

Softcover • 8-1/4 x 10-7/8 • 256 pages
1,000 color photos
Item# Z1921 • $24.99

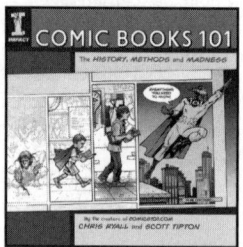

Comic Books 101
The History, Methods and Madness
Chris Ryall and Scott Tipton

Explore the humble beginnings of comic books thru their present-day status as the impetus for Hollywood blockbusters as you discover the history and legends of the industry, including Stan Lee, Clive Barker, Harlan Ellison and many more.

Softcover • 8 x 8 • 288 pages
Item# Z2757 • $22.99

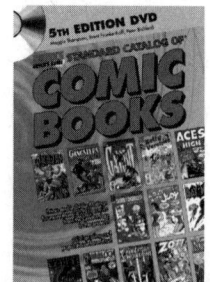

Comics Buyer's Guide Standard Catalog of Comic Books DVD 5th Edition
by Maggie Thompson and Brent Frankenhoff

This new edition of the ultimate comic book buyer's best guide is bigger and bolder than ever, and package on a single CD-ROM you can use with your Mac or PC. Packed with more than 180,000 comics, this all-encompassing resource features comics from all eras – Golden Age to the present, hundreds of series reviews and color photos of comic book covers.

Format: CD-ROM • **Item# Z3059 • $29.99**

Order directly from the publisher at www.krausebooks.com

Krause Publications, Offer **ACB9**
P.O. Box 5009
Iola, WI 54945-5009
www.krausebooks.com

Call **800-258-0929** 8 a.m. - 5 p.m. to order direct from the publisher, or visit booksellers nationwide or antiques and hobby shops.

Please reference offer **ACB9** with all direct-to-publisher orders